D0956811

THE CONCISE PLANETARY EPHEMERIS FOR 1950 to 2000 A.D. at NOON

Given at noon ephemeris time in the true longitude and true declination coordinates of date

THE HIERATIC PUBLISHING CO.
P.O. BOX 133 MEDFORD, MASSACHUSETTS 02155
UNITED STATES OF AMERICA, EARTH

International Standard Book Numbers: 0-915820-03-X Hard
0-915820-04-8 Soft

Manufactured in the United States of America.

Distributed exclusively in Continental Europe by *Wolf Metz Import,* Gessnerallee 42, 8011 Zürich, Switzerland.

Distributed exclusively in the British Isles by *L. N. Fowler & Co. Ltd.,* 1201 High Road, Chadwell Heath, Romford Essex RM6 4DH, England.

The indestructable stars are under the throne of His face.

(Egyptian Hymn to Osiris, ca. 1500 B.C.)

VIDIMUS ENIM STELLUM EJUS IN ORIENTE,
ET VENIMUS ADORARE EUM.

We saw His star as it rose and have come to do Him homage.

(Matthew 2:2-3)

τῶν τε πλείστων καὶ ὁλοσχερῶν συμπτωμάτων ἐναργῶς οὕτω
τὴν ἀπὸ τοῦ περιέχοντος αἰτίαν ἐμφανιζόντων.

It is clearly evident that most events of a widespread nature draw their causes from the enveloping heavens.

(Claudius Ptolemy's Tetrabiblos I.1, ca 130 A.D.)

ज्योतिर्गणे शास्त्रपथातिवृत्तो
यद्ब्रह्महत्यां मुनयोवदंति ॥

An error in the calculation of an ephemeris is as sinful as the murder of a Brahmin.

(Varāha Mihira's Brihat Jātaka, ca. 540 A.D.)

Sir, I have studied it, you have not!

(Sir Isaac Newton's reply to comet-discoverer Halley's questioning the basis of Astrology, ca. 1680)

INTRODUCTION

The Concise Planetary Ephemeris for 1950 to 2000 A.D. at Noon is an economical, durable, and compact listing of planetary longitudes and declinations. It responds to the needs of those who require a convenient, accurate, and sturdy volume at a reasonable price. It maintains the same rigorous, scientific accuracy as the more comprehensive volume, *The Complete Planetary Ephemeris for 1950 to 2000 A.D.,* which has been adopted internationally by astronomical and space laboratories of both government and university and is now a standard work. The present volume offers the same excellence to the wider community in a more compact and less expensive form.

Like man's venture into space it is the culmination of centuries of scientific endeavor and introduces a new clarity into the generation of planetary ephemerides. Its mode of calculation explicitly recognizes the fact that each planet flows in harmony with all the other heavenly bodies. At every instant of time each planet's movement is determined by its own momentum together with the sum of the forces of the other celestial orbs. This unifying gravitational theory, known since the time of Isaac Newton, was modelled mathematically to simultaneously generate the planetary positions.

This approach has powerful practical advantages over the traditional, approximate methods which treat each planet separately. Moreover, this unifying vision provides joy for the spirit together with deep philosophical and psychological clarity. It points the way back to the wisdom of the ancient belief in the Great Chain of Being.

The Authors

This work evolved from the studies of two scientists on the Apollo Project, which succeeded in putting a man on the moon in 1969. They bring with them a broad tradition of learning from the Ludwig Maximillian University in Munich, the Massachusetts Institute of Technology, and from the Imperial College of the University of London. Their professional background includes membership in the American Astronomical Society, the American Physical Society, the American Institute of Aeronautics and Astronautics, and the British Institute of Electrical Engineers.

They believe that science and astrology should enrich and sustain each other in the quest for a vision of the truth. Providing scientific ephemerides is one way that science can bring rigor and discipline to the task. Conversely, through the synthesis of man's interaction with the cosmos, astrology can add insights into events that are meaningless when taken in isolation.

Ephemeris Generation

With the advent of large, high speed digital computers it has become feasible to simultaneously integrate the planetary equations of motion (cf. KARL STUMPFF: *Himmelsmechanik,* Berlin 1965). Of the major ephemerides available only this volume and the *Complete Planetary Ephemeris* are generated using such a completely unifying approach. Even the *American Ephemeris and Nautical Almanac* of the United States government does not utilize this completely unified method. This approach clarifies and unites the equations and their solutions and, using reverse integration, provides a self check on the accuracy of the solution.

The integration was performed in a heliocentric, equatorial inertial system referred to the mean equinox and equator of 1950.0. The results are a best fit, in the least-squares sense, to planetary positions observed over many years. The astronomical constants used were those agreed upon at the Twelfth General Assembly of the International Astronomical Union at Hamburg in 1964. For publication the results were first referred to the mean equinox of date at Greenwich midnight using the precessional values of NEWCOMB (cf. M. H. ANDOYER: *Bulletin Astronomique* v. XXVIII). Subsequently they were expressed with respect to the true equinox of date using the nutational values of WOOLARD (cf. the *Astronomical Papers prepared for the use of the American Ephemeris and Nautical Almanac,* v. 15 part 1, 1953).

The calculations were performed on an IBM model 370/185 computer with a core memory of 2 million bytes using 16 significant decimal digits. The results were rounded to the nearest 0′.1 for publication using computer driven phototypesetting equipment. To the precision given the results represent the true geometric positions of the planets and will not need improvement as more precise observational data becomes available. For this reason this volume can be used with confidence as a standard work.

INTRODUCTION

The Concise Planetary Ephemeris for 1950 to 2000 A. D. at Noon (L'Ephéméride Planétaire Abrégée de 1950 à 2000 A. J. C. à midi) donne d'une façon économique, durable et concise la liste des longitudes et déclinaisons planétaires. Elle répond aux besoins des personnes ayant besoin d'un ouvrage pratique, précis et solide à un prix raisonnable. Celui-ci respecte la même exactitude rigoureuse et scientifique que le volume d'ensemble, *The Complete Planetary Ephemeris for 1950 to 2000 A.D.* (L'Ephéméride Planétaire Complète de 1950 à 2000 A. J. C.), qui a été adopté internationalement par les laboratoires d'astronomie et de l'espace aussi bien publics qu'universitaires et qui est maintenant un ouvrage standard. Ce présent volume offre la même perfection à une audience plus vaste sous une forme plus concise et à meilleur marché.

Tout comme l'aventure de l'homme dans l'espace, il représente l'apogée d'une entreprise scientifique de plusieurs siècles et introduit une clarté nouvelle dans la génération des éphémérides planétaires. Ses modes de calcul reflètent explicitement le fait que chaque planète se déplace en harmonie avec les autres corps célestes. A chaque instant la trajectoire de chaque planète est déterminée par la combinaison de sa propre quantité de mouvement et de la somme des forces dues aux autres astres. Cette théorie gravitationnelle unifiée, connue depuis l'époque d'Isaac Newton, a été simulée mathématiquement de façon à produire simultanément les positions planétaires. Cette approche possède des avantages pratiques puissants par rapport aux méthodes d'approximation traditionnelles qui traitent chaque planète séparément.

De plus, cette conception unifiée est une source de joie pour l'esprit ainsi que d'une profonde clarté philosophique et psychologique. Elle montre le chemin remontant à la sagesse de l'ancienne croyance en la Grande Chaîne de l'Existence.

Les Auteurs

Cet ouvrage est né des études de deux savants du projet Apollo qui réussit à poser un homme sur la lune en 1969. Ils apportent avec eux la longue tradition des enseignements venant de l'Université Ludwig Maximillian à Munich, du Massachusetts Institute of Technology et de l'Imperial College de l'Université de Londres. Leur expérience professionnelle est illustrée par leur appartenance à la Société Astronomique Américaine, la Société Physique Américaine, L'Institut Américain d'Aéronautique et d'Astronautique et L'Institut Britannique des Ingénieurs Electriciens.

Ils croient que la science et l'astrologie doivent s'enrichir et se soutenir mutuellement à la recherche d'une vision de la vérité. La réalisation d'éphémérides scientifiques est un des moyens par lesquels la science peut apporter rigueur et discipline à cette tâche. Réciproquement, par la synthèse de l'interaction de l'homme avec le cosmos, l'astrologie peut ajouter à la compréhension de phénomènes qui n'ont pas de sens pris isolément.

Obtention des Ephémérides

Grâce à l'avènement de calculateurs numériques de grande capacité et à vitesse de calcul élevée, il a été possible d'intégrer simultanément les équations planétaires de mouvement (cf. Karl Stumpff: *Himmelsmechanik,* Berlin 1965). Parmi les éphémérides importantes disponibles, seul ce volume et *The Complete Planetary Ephemeris* sont obtenus en utilisant cette approche totalement unifiée. Même *The American Ephemeris and Nautical Almanac* du gouvernement des Etats-Unis n'utilise pas cette méthode totalement unifiée. Cette approche clarifie et unifie les équations et leurs solutions et, utilisant une intégration inverse, fournit une vérification implicite de la précision de la solution.

L'intégration a été réalisée sur un système inertiel héliocentrique et équatorial prenant comme référence l'équinoxe moyenne et l'équateur de 1950.0. Les résultats représentent une correspondance optimale, au sens des moindres carrés, avec les positions planétaires observées au long de nombreuses années. Les constantes astronomiques utilisées sont celles qui furent convenues lors de la Vingtième Assemblée Générale de l'Union Astronomique Internationale à Hambourg en 1964. En vue de la publication les résultats furent d'abord rapportés à l'équinoxe moyenne de date à minuit Greenwich en utilisant les valeurs de précession de Newcomb (cf. M. H. Andoyer: *Bulletin Astronomique* v. XXVIII). Par la suite ils furent exprimés par rapport à la vraie valeur de l'équinoxe de date en utilisant les valeurs de nutation de Woolard (cf. les *Papers Prepared for the use of the American Ephemeris and Nautical Almanac*, v. 15, partie 1, 1953).

Les calculs furent réalisés sur un ordinateur IBM modèle 370/185 possédant une mémoire centrale de 2 millions de mots utilisant 16 décimales. Les résultats furent arrondis à 0',1 près en vue d'une publication par photo-impression commandée par ordinateur. A la précision donnée les résultats représentent les positions géométriques vraies des planètes et ne nécessiteront aucune amélioration au fur et à mesure que des données d'observation plus précises seront disponibles. Pour cette raison ce volume peut être utilisé avec confiance en tant qu'ouvrage standard.

INTRODUCCIÓN

The Concise Planetary Ephemeris for 1950 to 2000 A. D. at Noon (La Concisa Effemeride Planetaria dal 1950 al 2000 dopo Cristo a mezzogiorno) é un elenco delle longitudini e delle declinazioni planetarie a formato ridotto, di buona durata ed a buon prezzo.

Esso risponde al fabbisogno di coloro che desiderano possedere un volume pratico, solido ed a prezzo ragionevole. In esso si é mantenuta la medesima rigorosa precisione scientifica del volume più esteso, *The Complete Planetary Ephemeris for 1950 to 2000 A. D.* (La Completa Effemeride Planetaria dal 1950 al 2000 dopo Cristo), adottato su scala internazionale da laboratori astronomici e spaziali universitari nonché governamentali ed attualmente riconosciuto come un classico nel suo campo. Il presente volume offre gli stessi standard di eccellenza ad un pubblico più vasto, a formato ridotto ed a minor costo.

Come l'impresa umana nello spazio, esso rappresenta il culmine dello sforzo scientifico di secoli e getta una luce nuova sulla generazione delle effemeridi planetarie. Il metodo di calcolo sul quale é basato riconosce esplicitamente il fatto che ogni pianeta orbita in armonia con tutti gli altri corpi celesti. Ad ogni istante nel tempo, ciascun movimento del pianeta é determinato dall'impulso che gli é proprio assieme al totale delle forze delle altre sfere celestiali. Questa teoria gravitativa unificatrice, nota dall'epoca di Isacco Newton, é stata modellata matematicamente in modo da dare simultaneramente la posizione dei pianeti.

Questo modo di procedere presenta dei vantaggi enormi dal punto di vista pratico in confronto ai metodi approssimativi tradizionali, che trattano ciascun pianeta separatamente. Per di più, questa visione unificatrice rallegra lo spirito e serba, nel contempo, una profonda chiarezza filosofica e psicologica. Da essa viene indicata la via che riconduce alla saggezza dell'antica credenza nella Grande Catena dell'Essere.

Gli Autori

Questa opera proviene dagli studi di due scienziati che presero parte al Progetto Apollo, mediante il quale fu possibile mandare l'uomo sulla luna nel 1969. Con loro ci perviene la vasta tradizione culturale dell'Uniersità Ludwig Maximillian di Monaco di Baviera, l'Istituto di Tecnologia del Massachusetts ed il Collegio Imperiale di Londra. Il loro curriculum professionale include la partecipazione alla Società Americana di Astronomia, alla Società Americana di Fisica, all'Istituto Americano di Aereonautica ed Astronautica ed all'Istituto Britannico di Ingegneria Elettrica.

E' loro credenza che scienza ed astrologia dovrebbero arricchirsi e sostenersi a vicenda nella ricerca di una visione di verità. Uno dei modi in cui la scienza può aiutare a portare rigore e disciplina a questo compito, consiste nel fornire effemeridi scientifiche. Da parte sua, l'astrologia può meglio discernere, mediante la sintesi delle interazioni tra uomo e cosmo, tra eventi che sarebbero senza significato se fossero presi uno per uno.

La Generazione Dell'Effemeride

Con l'invenzione delle grosse calcolatrici numeriche ad alta velocità, é diventato possibile procedere all'integrazione simultanea delle equazioni di moto planetarie (Rif.: KARL STUMPFF, *Himmelsmechanik,* Berlino 1965). Tra le maggiori effemleridi che si trovano in circolazione, soltanto quelle indicate in questo volume e nella *Complete Planetary Ephemeris*, sono generate tramite un metodo così totalmente unificatore. Neppure l'American Ephemeris and Nautical Almanac del governo statunitense utilizza un metodo così totalmente unficatore. Questo modo di procedere elucida ed unisce le equazioni e le loro soluzioni e fornisce allo stesso tempo, mediante l'integrazione all'inverso, la prova della precisione della soluzione.

L'integrazione é stata compiuta in un sistema inerziale, eliocentrico ed equatoriale, basato sull'equinozio medio e sull'equatore del 1950.0. I risultati sono quelli che, col metodo dei quadrati-minimi, danno il miglior adattamento alle posizioni dei pianeti osservate per un periodo di molti anni. Le costanti astronomiche impiegate sono quelle concordate durante la Dodicesima Assemblea dell'Unione Astronomica Internazionale tenutasi ad Amburgo nel 1964. I risultati destinati a pubblicazione si riferivano in un primo tempo all'equinozio medio di data alla mezzanotte di Greenwich, facendo uso dei valori precessionali di NEWCOMB (Rif. M. H. ANDOYER: *Bulletin Astronomique*, v. XXVIII). In seguito, i risultati furono espressi per rapporto all'equinozio reale di data, facendo uso dei valori nutativi di WOOLARD (Rif. *Astronomical Papers prepared for the use of the American Ephemeris and Nautical Almanac*, v. 15, parte 1, 1953).

I calcoli sono stati eseguiti su di una calcolatrice IBM modello 370/185 con una memoria di 2 milioni di ''biti'', utilizzando 16 cifre decimali significative. Ai fini della pubblicazione, i risultati sono stati arrotondati allo 0',1 più vicino, per mezzo dell'apparato fototipografico guidato dalla calcolatrice. Dal punto di vista della precisione sopra-indicata, i risultati rappresentano le vere posizioni geometriche dei pianeti e non occorrerà apportare miglioramenti una volta in possesso di dati di osservazione più esatti. Per tale ragione questo volume può essere adottato con piena fiducia come un classico nel suo campo.

INTRODUZIONE

The Concise Planetary Ephemeris for 1950 to 2000 A.D. at Noon (El Breviario de Efemérides Planetarias de 1950 a 2000 a mediodía) ofrece en una edición económica, duradera y compacta, una recopilación de datos sobre longiutdes y declinaciones de planetas. Satisface las necesidades de aquéllos que exigen una edición rigurosa a un precio razonable. Mantiene la misma tónica de rigurosidad y precisión científica que el volumen *The Complete Planetary Ephemeris for 1950 to 2000 A.D.* (Tratado Completo de Efemérides Planetarias de 1950 a 2000) que ya ha sido adoptado universalmente por laboratorios de astronomía y de ciencias del espacio dependientes tanto de organismos gubernamentales como de Universidades y que puede ser considerado hoy como una obra clásica. El objeto de la presente edición es pues el de, de una manera mas econímica y compacta, hacer asequible la misma calidad de información, a un sector de público más amplio.

Por analogía con la aventura del hombre en el espacio el presente trabajo representa la culminación de siglos de labor científica con vistas a presentar de una manera clara la idea de efemérides planetarias. Su método de cálculo explícito parte del principio de que cada planeta se mueve en el espacio en armonía con el resto de los cuerpos celestes. El movemiento de cada planeta en un instante de tiempo determinado viene establecido por su propio momento y por la resultante de las fuerzas que los demás astros ejercen sobre él. Esta teoría gravitacional, conocida desde los tiempos de Isaac Newton, ha sido utilizada en el contexto de un modelo matemático que permite generar las posiciones de los planetas simultáneamente.

Este método presenta notables ventajas de tipo práctico sobre los métodos clásicos que utilizando procedimientos aproximados tratan a cada planeta como un ente aislado. Más aún, este enfoque unificador proporciona alegría al espíritu y madurez filosófica. Nos recuerda la antigua sabia creencia en la Gran Cadena del Ser.

Sobre los Autores

Este trabajo es fruto de las investigaciones de dos científicos del proyecto Apolo, que consiguió colocar con éxito un hombre en la superficie lunar en 1969. En ellos convergen tradiciones culturales de centros como la Universidad Ludwig Maximillian de Munich, el

Instituto Technológico de Massachusetts y el Colegio Imperial de la Universidad de Londres. Son miembros acreditados de la Sociedad Americana de Física, la Sociedad Americana de Astronomía, el Instituto Americano de Aeronáutica y Astronáutica y el Instituto Británico de Ingenieros Eléctricos.

Es creencia de los autores que ciencia y astrología deben enriquecerse y sustentarse mutuamente en la búsqueda de la verdad. Aportar datos sobre efemérides científicas es un modo en que la ciencia puede contribuir a hacer rigurosa y disciplinada esa tarea. Por otra parte es a través de la síntesis de la interacción del hombre con el cosmos que la astrología puede hacer aportaciones valiosas en el estudio de acontecimientos que si aislados no tendrían ningún sentido.

Generación de Efemérides

Con el advenimiento de computadores de alta velocidad digital ha resultado posible integrar simultáneamente el sistema de ecuaciones que describe el movimiento de los planetas (vease KARL STUMPFF: *Himmelsmechanik,* Berlín 1965). Solamente en este Breviario y en el ya citado *Complete Planetary Ephemeris,* se hace un estudio de estas efemérides utilizando el método unificador al que más arriba nos referíamos. Ni siquiera el *American Ephemeris and Nautical Almanac* utiliza un método tan completo como el nuestro. Nuestro procedimiento clasifica y unifica las ecuaciones y sus correspondientes soluciones y utilizando métodos integrales somete a pruebas de autoconsistencia a los resultados obtenidos.

La integración se realiza en un sistema inercial, heliocéntrico y ecuatorial, tomando como referencia la posición del equinoccio y del ecuador en 1950.0. Los resultados se derivan de un ajuste, por métodos de mínimos cuadrados, a las posiciones de los planetas observadas durante varios años. Las constantes astronómicas utilizadas fueron las adoptadas en la XII Reunión General de la Unión Internacional de Astronomía celebrada en Hamburgo en 1964. Los resultados publicados fueron en un principio referidos al equinoccio medio de medianoche en Greenwich utilizando como valores para la precesión los dados por NEWCOMB (vease M. H. ANDOYER: *Bulletin Astroomique,* vol. XXVIII) y posteriormente fueron expresados respecto al verdadero equinoccio utilizando los valores para la nutación calculados por WOOLARD (veanse los *Papers Prepared for the use of the American Ephemeris and Nautical Almanac,* Vol. 15, parte 1, 1953).

Los cálculos fueron realizados en una calculadora IBM modelo 370/185, con una memoria de dos millones de bites o registros y utilizando dieciséis cifras decimales significativas. Posteriormente fueron redondeados con una precisión de 0'.1 utilizando para su publicación final un equipo de fotoimpresión controlado por computador. Los resultados publicados representan, con la precisión señalada, la verdadera posición de los planetas y no necesitarán mejora alguna cuando se disponga de observaciones astronómicas más precisas. Esa es la razón por la que el presente volumen puede ser ya considerado como una referencia clásica.

ENLEITUNG

The Concise Planetary Ephemeris for 1950 to 2000 A.D. at Noon (Kurzer planetarischer Almanach für 1950 bis 2000 A.D. am Mittag) ist eine preiswerte, haltbare und bündige Zusammenstellung der Längen und Deklinationen der Planeten. Der Almanach ist für all die gedacht, die einen geeigneten, genauen und widerstandsfähigen Band zu einem günstigem Preis benötigen. Er weist dieselbe rigorose wissenschaftliche Genauigkeit wie das umfassendere Werk auf — *The Complete Planetary Ephemeris for 1950 to 2000 A. D.* (Vollständiger planetarischer Almanach für 1950 bis 2000 A. D.) — der international von astronomischen wie Weltraumlabors der Regierungen und Universitäten als maßgebendes Werk verwendet wird. Das vorliegende Buch stellt dieselbe hervorragende Leistung einer breiteren Leserschaft in kürzerer und billigerer Form zur Verfügung.

Ähnlich wie das Vordringen der Menschheit in den Weltraum stellt es den Höhepunkt von jahrhundertelanger wissenschaftlicher Untersuchung dar und gibt den planetarischen Almanachs eine bisher unbekannte Klarheit. Die Berechnungsmethode erkennt explizit an, daß jeder Planet sich harmonisch mit all den anderen Himmelskörpern bewegt. Zu jedem Zeitpunkt unterliegt die Bewegung jedes Planeten seinem eigenen Impuls wie auch die Summe der Kräfte, die von den anderen Himmelsbahnen herrühren. Diese, seit der Zeit Isaac Newtons, bekannte vereinigte Theorie der Schwerkraft wurde im mathematischen Modell nachvollzogen, um die Positionen der Planeten simultan zu bestimmen.

Dieser Lösungsweg hat beträchtliche praktische Vorteile gegenüber der üblichen Annäherungsmethode, in der jeder Planet einzeln betrachtet wird. Weiterhin erfreut diese vereinigte Theorie den Geist und zeigt die tiefe philosophische und psychologische Klarheit auf. Hier wird wieder auf den alten Glauben der Großen Kette des Seiens zurückverwiesen.

Die Verfasser

Dieses Werk entstand aus den Studien zweier Wissenschaftler des Apollo Projektes, das im Jahre 1969 zur ersten bemannten Landung auf dem Mond führte. Sie verkörpern eine lange Tradition der Forschung der Ludwig-Maximillian-Universität München, des Massachusetts Institute of Technology und des Imperial College der Universität London. Zu ihren beruflichen Qualifikationen gehört die Mitgliedschaft in der American Astronomical Society, American Physical Society, American Institute of Aeronautics and Astronautics sowie British Institute of Electrical Engineers.

Sie meinen, daß sich Wissenschaft und Astrologie auf der Suche nach der Wahrheit gegenseitig bereichern und stützen sollen. Ein wissenschaftlicher Almanach ist ein Weg, mit dem die Wissenschaft dieser Aufgabe Strenge und Disziplin geben kann. Und umgekehrt kann die Astrologie durch die Synthese der Wechselwirkung von Mensch und Kosmos Einsicht in Geschehen gewinnen, die — wenn einzeln betrachtet — bedeutungslos sind.

Der Almanach

Durch die großen digitalen Schnellrechner ist es jetzt möglich, die Bewegungsgleichungen der Planeten gleichzeitig zu integrieren (vgl. Karl Stumpff: *Himmelsmechanik,* Berlin, 1965). Unter all den Almanachs wird nur dieses Werk sowie der *Complete Planetary Ephemeris* mit dieser vollständig vereinigten Methoden erstellt. Selbst der *American Ephemeris and Nautical Almanac* der US-Regierung stüzt sich nicht auf diese vollständig vereinigte Methode. Dieser Weg vereinigt und verdeutlicht die Gleichungen und ihre Lösungen und ermöglicht durch umgekehrtes Integrieren eine Selbstprüfung der Lösungsgenauigkeit.

Die Integration wurde in einem heliozentrischen, äquatorialen Trägheitssystem durchgeführt, das als mittlerer Äquator und mittleres Äquinoktium von 1950.0 bezeichnet wird. Die Lösungen sind eine beste Passung — kleinste Fehlerquadrate — an die über lange Jahre beobachteten Planetenpositionen. Die hierbei verwendeten astronomischen Konstanten sind die Werte, die von der 12. Allgemeinversammlung der Internationalen Astronomischen Vereinigung 1964 in Hamburg festgelegt wurden. Für die Veröffentlichung wurden die Ergebnisse erst auf das jewegliche mittlere Äquinoktium — Greenwich Mitternacht — umgesetzt, wobei die Präzessionswerte von NEWCOMB verwendet wurden (vgl. M. H. ANDOYER: *Bulletin Astronomique* v. XXVIII). Danach wurden sie bezügliche des jeweiligen wahren Äquinoktiums ausgedrückt, wobei die Nutationswerte von WOOLARD verwendet wurden (vgl. *Astronomical Papers prepared for the use of the American Ephemeris and Nautical Almanac*, Bd. 15, Teil 1, 1953.).

Die Berechnungen wurden mit einer IBM 370/185 Rechenanlage von 2 M bytes auf 16 Dezimal-Stellen genau bestimmt. Die Ergebnisse wurden auf die nächste Zehntelstelle (0',1) gerundet und im rechnergestützen Lichtdruckerfahren gedruckt. Die Ergebnisse stellen — mit der angegebenen Präzision — die wahren geometrischen Positionen der Planeten dar und müssen nicht verbessert werden, wenn präzisere Beobachtungsdaten zur Verfügung stehen. Aus diesem Grunde kann man den Almanach mit Zuversicht als maßgebendes Werk verwenden.

JANUARY 1950

LONGITUDE at NOON

DAY	EPHEMERIS SIDEREAL TIME h m s	☉ ° ′	☊ ° ′	☽ ° ′	☿ ° ′	♀ ° ′	♂ ° ′	♃ ° ′	♄ ° ′	♅ ° ′	♆ ° ′	♇ ° ′
1 S	18 42 16.2	10♑31.2	12♈ 5.1	7♊32.4	29♑58.6	17♒ 9.2	2♎23.8	6♒37.5	19♍26.1	2♋39.4	17♎16.4	17♌47.1
2 M	18 46 12.8	11 32.3	12 1.9	19 59.3	0♒57.4	17 28.4	2 45.5	6 51.1	19R25.8	2R36.9	17 16.9	17R46.0
3 T	18 50 9.3	12 33.5	11 58.8	2♋42.1	1 49.8	17 45.7	3 6.9	7 4.7	19 25.4	2 34.3	17 17.5	17 44.9
4 W	18 54 5.9	13 34.6	11 55.6	15 40.8	2 35.1	18 0.8	3 28.0	7 18.3	19 24.8	2 31.8	17 18.0	17 43.8
5 T	18 58 2.4	14 35.7	11 52.4	28 54.3	3 12.3	18 13.8	3 48.7	7 32.0	19 24.2	2 29.3	17 18.4	17 42.7
6 F	19 1 59.0	15 36.9	11 49.2	12♌20.3	3 40.6	18 24.6	4 9.1	7 45.8	19 23.4	2 26.8	17 18.9	17 41.5
7 S	19 5 55.6	16 38.0	11 46.1	25 56.7	3 59.0	18 33.1	4 29.1	7 59.5	19 22.6	2 24.3	17 19.3	17 40.3
8 S	19 9 52.1	17 39.1	11 42.9	9♍41.2	4 6.8	18 39.2	4 48.7	8 13.3	19 21.6	2 21.8	17 19.6	17 39.1
9 M	19 13 48.7	18 40.3	11 39.7	23 32.2	4R 3.4	18 43.0	5 7.9	8 27.2	19 20.5	2 19.4	17 20.0	17 37.9
10 T	19 17 45.2	19 41.4	11 36.5	7♎28.7	3 48.2	18 44.4	5 26.7	8 41.0	19 19.3	2 16.9	17 20.2	17 36.7
11 W	19 21 41.8	20 42.6	11 33.4	21 30.3	3 21.2	18R43.3	5 45.2	8 55.0	19 18.0	2 14.5	17 20.5	17 35.4
12 T	19 25 38.4	21 43.7	11 30.2	5♏36.6	2 42.6	18 39.8	6 3.2	9 8.9	19 16.6	2 12.1	17 20.7	17 34.2
13 F	19 29 34.9	22 44.8	11 27.0	19 46.6	1 53.2	18 33.7	6 20.8	9 22.9	19 15.1	2 9.7	17 20.9	17 32.9
14 S	19 33 31.5	23 46.0	11 23.8	3♐58.8	0 54.0	18 25.2	6 38.0	9 36.9	19 13.5	2 7.4	17 21.1	17 31.6
15 S	19 37 28.0	24 47.1	11 20.7	18 10.1	29♑46.8	18 14.1	6 54.7	9 50.9	19 11.8	2 5.0	17 21.2	17 30.3
16 M	19 41 24.6	25 48.2	11 17.5	2♑16.5	28 33.6	18 0.6	7 10.9	10 5.0	19 10.0	2 2.7	17 21.3	17 29.0
17 T	19 45 21.1	26 49.3	11 14.3	16 13.3	27 16.6	17 44.6	7 26.8	10 19.1	19 8.0	2 0.4	17 21.3	17 27.7
18 W	19 49 17.7	27 50.5	11 11.1	29 55.9	25 58.3	17 26.2	7 42.1	10 33.2	19 6.0	1 58.2	17 21.4	17 26.3
19 T	19 53 14.3	28 51.6	11 8.0	13♒20.5	24 41.0	17 5.4	7 56.9	10 47.4	19 3.9	1 55.9	17R21.3	17 25.0
20 F	19 57 10.8	29 52.6	11 4.8	26 24.9	23 27.1	16 42.4	8 11.3	11 1.5	19 1.6	1 53.7	17 21.3	17 23.6
21 S	20 1 7.4	0♒53.7	11 1.6	9♓ 8.8	22 18.5	16 17.2	8 25.1	11 15.7	18 59.3	1 51.5	17 21.2	17 22.3
22 S	20 5 3.9	1 54.8	10 58.4	21 33.6	21 16.6	15 50.0	8 38.5	11 29.9	18 56.9	1 49.5	17 21.1	17 20.9
23 M	20 9 0.5	2 55.9	10 55.2	3♈42.2	20 22.6	15 20.8	8 51.4	11 44.2	18 54.4	1 47.3	17 21.0	17 19.5
24 T	20 12 57.1	3 56.9	10 52.1	15 38.8	19 37.3	14 49.9	9 3.6	11 58.4	18 51.8	1 45.3	17 20.8	17 18.2
25 W	20 16 53.6	4 57.9	10 48.9	27 28.4	19 0.9	14 17.4	9 15.4	12 12.6	18 49.1	1 43.2	17 20.6	17 16.8
26 T	20 20 50.2	5 58.9	10 45.7	9♉16.5	18 33.6	13 43.5	9 26.6	12 26.9	18 46.3	1 41.2	17 20.3	17 15.4
27 F	20 24 46.7	6 59.9	10 42.5	21 8.5	18 15.2	13 8.4	9 37.2	12 41.2	18 43.4	1 39.2	17 20.0	17 13.9
28 S	20 28 43.3	8 0.9	10 39.4	3♊ 9.8	18 5.4	12 32.4	9 47.3	12 55.5	18 40.5	1 37.3	17 19.7	17 12.5
29 S	20 32 39.8	9 1.8	10 36.2	15 24.9	18 3.7	11 55.8	9 56.8	13 9.7	18 37.4	1 35.4	17 19.4	17 11.1
30 M	20 36 36.4	10 2.7	10 33.0	27 57.8	18D 9.8	11 18.7	10 5.7	13 24.0	18 34.2	1 33.5	17 19.0	17 9.7
31 T	20 40 33.0	11 3.6	10 29.8	10♋50.6	18 22.9	10 41.4	10 14.0	13 38.3	18 31.0	1 31.7	17 18.6	17 8.3

DECLINATION at NOON

DAY	EPHEMERIS SIDEREAL TIME h m s	☉ ° ′	☊ ° ′	☽ ° ′	☿ ° ′	♀ ° ′	♂ ° ′	♃ ° ′	♄ ° ′	♅ ° ′	♆ ° ′	♇ ° ′
1 S	18 42 16.2	23S 1.9	4N46.7	25N37.8	21S16.3	15S 0.4	1N21.6	19S11.4	6N 1.9	23N41.4	5S18.8	23N18.0
4 W	18 54 5.9	22 45.3	4 43.0	27 28.6	20 5.2	14 9.6	0 59.1	19 1.2	6 3.1	23 41.6	5 19.3	23 19.7
7 S	19 5 55.6	22 24.8	4 39.3	16 14.0	18 59.8	13 22.1	0 38.0	18 50.7	6 4.8	23 41.8	5 19.6	23 21.4
10 T	19 17 45.2	22 0.2	4 35.6	2S40.5	18 9.2	12 38.5	0 18.2	18 40.1	6 6.8	23 41.9	5 19.8	23 23.1
13 F	19 29 34.9	21 31.8	4 31.8	20 43.4	17 40.6	11 59.7	0 0.0	18 29.2	6 9.1	23 42.1	5 19.9	23 24.8
16 M	19 41 24.6	20 59.6	4 28.1	28 23.6	17 36.2	11 26.7	0S16.5	18 18.1	6 11.9	23 42.2	5 19.9	23 26.5
19 T	19 53 14.3	20 23.8	4 24.4	20 51.1	17 51.3	11 0.0	0 31.4	18 6.7	6 15.0	23 42.3	5 19.7	23 28.2
22 S	20 5 3.9	19 44.5	4 20.7	4 48.2	18 18.1	10 40.3	0 44.4	17 55.2	6 18.4	23 42.4	5 19.5	23 29.9
25 W	20 16 53.6	19 1.9	4 16.9	12N 1.9	18 49.9	10 28.0	0 55.6	17 43.5	6 22.1	23 42.5	5 19.1	23 31.6
28 S	20 28 43.3	18 16.2	4 13.2	24 48.8	19 21.7	10 23.0	1 4.8	17 31.6	6 26.1	23 42.6	5 18.6	23 33.3
31 T	20 40 33.0	17 27.6	4 9.4	28 3.8	19 50.1	10 24.9	1 11.9	17 19.6	6 30.4	23 42.6	5 18.0	23 34.9

FEBRUARY 1950

LONGITUDE at NOON

DAY	EPHEMERIS SIDEREAL TIME h m s	☉ ° ′	☊ ° ′	☽ ° ′	☿ ° ′	♀ ° ′	♂ ° ′	♃ ° ′	♄ ° ′	♅ ° ′	♆ ° ′	♇ ° ′
1 W	20 44 29.5	12♒ 4.5	10♈26.7	24♋ 4.2	18♑42.6	10♒ 4.3	10♎21.6	13♒52.6	18♍27.7	1♋29.9	17♎18.1	17♌ 6.8
2 T	20 48 26.1	13 5.3	10 23.5	7♌37.4	19 8.4	9R27.5	10 28.7	14 6.9	18R24.3	1R28.1	17R17.6	17R 5.4
3 F	20 52 22.6	14 6.2	10 20.3	21 27.7	19 39.7	8 51.3	10 35.1	14 21.3	18 20.9	1 26.4	17 17.1	17 3.9
4 S	20 56 19.2	15 7.0	10 17.1	5♍30.9	20 16.1	8 16.0	10 40.9	14 35.6	18 17.3	1 24.7	17 16.6	17 2.5
5 S	21 0 15.7	16 7.8	10 13.9	19 42.5	20 57.1	7 41.8	10 46.0	14 49.9	18 13.7	1 23.1	17 16.0	17 1.1
6 M	21 4 12.3	17 8.6	10 10.8	3♎58.2	21 42.3	7 8.9	10 50.4	15 4.2	18 10.0	1 21.5	17 15.4	16 59.6
7 T	21 8 8.8	18 9.4	10 7.6	18 14.1	22 31.4	6 37.5	10 54.2	15 18.5	18 6.2	1 20.0	17 14.7	16 58.2
8 W	21 12 5.4	19 10.1	10 4.4	2♏27.5	23 24.1	6 7.9	10 57.3	15 32.8	18 2.4	1 18.5	17 14.1	16 56.7
9 T	21 16 2.0	20 10.9	10 1.2	16 36.5	24 20.0	5 40.2	10 59.6	15 47.1	17 58.5	1 17.0	17 13.3	16 55.3
10 F	21 19 58.5	21 11.6	9 58.1	0♐39.9	25 18.8	5 14.5	11 1.2	16 1.4	17 54.5	1 15.6	17 12.6	16 53.9
11 S	21 23 55.1	22 12.3	9 54.9	14 36.6	26 20.4	4 50.9	11 2.2	16 15.7	17 50.5	1 14.2	17 11.8	16 52.4
12 S	21 27 51.6	23 13.0	9 51.7	28 25.5	27 24.5	4 29.6	11 2.4	16 30.0	17 46.5	1 12.9	17 11.1	16 51.0
13 M	21 31 48.2	24 13.7	9 48.5	12♑ 5.3	28 30.9	4 10.7	11R 1.8	16 44.3	17 42.3	1 11.7	17 10.3	16 49.6
14 T	21 35 44.7	25 14.3	9 45.4	25 34.3	29 39.4	3 54.1	11 0.5	16 58.6	17 38.1	1 10.4	17 9.4	16 48.2
15 W	21 39 41.3	26 15.0	9 42.2	8♒50.6	0♒50.0	3 40.0	10 58.4	17 12.8	17 33.9	1 9.3	17 8.5	16 46.8
16 T	21 43 37.8	27 15.6	9 39.0	21 52.8	2 2.4	3 28.3	10 55.5	17 27.0	17 29.5	1 8.1	17 7.6	16 45.4
17 F	21 47 34.4	28 16.1	9 35.8	4♓39.8	3 16.5	3 19.1	10 51.9	17 41.2	17 25.2	1 7.0	17 6.7	16 43.9
18 S	21 51 31.0	29 16.7	9 32.6	17 11.6	4 32.4	3 12.4	10 47.5	17 55.4	17 20.8	1 6.0	17 5.7	16 42.5
19 S	21 55 27.5	0♓17.2	9 29.5	29 29.0	5 49.7	3 8.1	10 42.3	18 9.6	17 16.3	1 5.0	17 4.7	16 41.1
20 M	21 59 24.1	1 17.7	9 26.3	11♈33.9	7 8.6	3 6.3	10 36.3	18 23.8	17 11.8	1 4.1	17 3.7	16 39.7
21 T	22 3 20.6	2 18.2	9 23.1	23 29.2	8 28.9	3D 6.9	10 29.5	18 37.9	17 7.3	1 3.2	17 2.7	16 38.4
22 W	22 7 17.2	3 18.6	9 19.9	5♉18.8	9 50.5	3 9.9	10 22.0	18 52.0	17 2.8	1 2.4	17 1.6	16 37.0
23 T	22 11 13.7	4 19.0	9 16.8	17 7.0	11 13.4	3 15.1	10 13.7	19 6.1	16 58.2	1 1.6	17 0.5	16 35.6
24 F	22 15 10.3	5 19.4	9 13.6	28 58.8	12 37.6	3 22.7	10 4.6	19 20.2	16 53.5	1 0.9	16 59.4	16 34.3
25 S	22 19 6.8	6 19.7	9 10.4	10♊59.2	14 3.0	3 32.5	9 54.7	19 34.2	16 48.9	1 0.2	16 58.3	16 32.9
26 S	22 23 3.4	7 20.0	9 7.2	23 13.2	15 29.6	3 44.5	9 44.1	19 48.2	16 44.2	0 59.6	16 57.1	16 31.6
27 M	22 26 60.0	8 20.3	9 4.0	5♋45.4	16 57.3	3 58.6	9 32.7	20 2.2	16 39.5	0 59.0	16 55.9	16 30.3
28 T	22 30 56.5	9 20.5	9 0.9	18 39.4	18 26.2	4 14.7	9 20.5	20 16.2	16 34.8	0 58.5	16 54.7	16 28.9

DECLINATION at NOON

DAY	EPHEMERIS SIDEREAL TIME h m s	☉ ° ′	☊ ° ′	☽ ° ′	☿ ° ′	♀ ° ′	♂ ° ′	♃ ° ′	♄ ° ′	♅ ° ′	♆ ° ′	♇ ° ′
1 W	20 44 29.5	17S10.8	4N 8.2	26N 8.0	19S58.4	10S26.9	1S13.8	17S15.5	6N31.9	23N42.6	5S17.8	23N35.5
4 S	20 56 19.2	16 18.5	4 4.5	12 5.5	20 18.5	10 36.7	1 18.0	17 3.3	6 36.6	23 42.7	5 17.1	23 37.1
7 T	21 8 8.8	15 23.7	4 0.7	7S57.2	20 30.4	10 51.0	1 20.0	16 50.9	6 41.5	23 42.8	5 16.2	23 38.7
10 F	21 19 58.5	14 26.5	3 57.0	24 16.2	20 32.8	11 8.5	1 19.7	16 38.4	6 46.5	23 42.8	5 15.3	23 40.2
13 M	21 31 48.2	13 27.1	3 53.2	28 0.4	20 24.9	11 28.0	1 16.9	16 25.8	6 51.8	23 42.8	5 14.2	23 41.7
16 T	21 43 37.8	12 25.7	3 49.5	17 44.3	20 6.2	11 48.1	1 11.6	16 13.1	6 57.2	23 42.8	5 13.1	23 43.1
19 S	21 55 27.5	11 22.5	3 45.7	0 53.8	19 36.3	12 8.0	1 3.8	16 0.3	7 2.8	23 42.9	5 11.8	23 44.5
22 W	22 7 17.2	10 17.8	3 42.0	15N34.2	18 54.9	12 26.7	0 53.6	15 47.4	7 8.5	23 42.9	5 10.5	23 45.9
25 S	22 19 6.8	9 11.6	3 38.2	26 42.8	18 2.1	12 43.4	0 40.9	15 34.5	7 14.2	23 42.9	5 9.1	23 47.2
28 T	22 30 56.5	8 4.2	3 34.5	27 13.7	16 57.7	12 57.5	0 26.0	15 21.6	7 20.0	23 42.9	5 7.6	23 48.4

MARCH 1950

DAY	EPHEMERIS SIDEREAL TIME	☉	☊	☽	☿	♀	♂	♃	♄	♅	♆	♇
	h m s	° ′	° ′	° ′	° ′	° ′	° ′	° ′	° ′	° ′	° ′	° ′
LONGITUDE at NOON												
1 W	22 34 53.1	10♓20.7	8♈57.7	1♌57.5	19♒56.2	4♒32.9	9♎ 7.6	20♒30.1	16♍30.0	0♋58.0	16♎53.5	16♌27.6
2 T	22 38 49.6	11 20.9	8 54.5	15 40.0	21 27.4	4 52.9	8R54.0	20 44.0	16R25.3	0R57.6	16R52.2	16R26.4
3 F	22 42 46.2	12 21.1	8 51.3	29 45.2	22 59.7	5 14.9	8 39.7	20 57.8	16 20.5	0 57.2	16 50.9	16 25.1
4 S	22 46 42.7	13 21.2	8 48.2	14♍ 9.1	24 33.0	5 38.6	8 24.6	21 11.6	16 15.7	0 56.9	16 49.6	16 23.8
5 S	22 50 39.3	14 21.3	8 45.0	28 46.2	26 7.5	6 4.1	8 8.9	21 25.4	16 11.0	0 56.7	16 48.4	16 22.6
6 M	22 54 35.8	15 21.4	8 41.8	13♎29.6	27 43.1	6 31.3	7 52.5	21 39.2	16 6.2	0 56.5	16 47.0	16 21.4
7 T	22 58 32.4	16 21.4	8 38.6	28 12.6	29 19.8	7 0.1	7 35.4	21 52.9	16 1.4	0 56.4	16 45.7	16 20.2
8 W	23 2 28.9	17 21.4	8 35.4	12♏49.2	0♓57.6	7 30.4	7 17.7	22 6.5	15 56.6	0 56.3	16 44.3	16 19.0
9 T	23 6 25.5	18 21.3	8 32.3	27 14.6	2 36.5	8 2.3	6 59.4	22 20.1	15 51.8	0 56.2	16 42.9	16 17.8
10 F	23 10 22.0	19 21.3	8 29.1	11♐25.8	4 16.5	8 35.6	6 40.4	22 33.7	15 47.0	0D56.3	16 41.5	16 16.6
11 S	23 14 18.6	20 21.2	8 25.9	25 21.1	5 57.7	9 10.2	6 20.9	22 47.2	15 42.3	0 56.3	16 40.0	16 15.4
12 S	23 18 15.2	21 21.1	8 22.7	9♑ 0.0	7 40.1	9 46.2	6 0.9	23 0.7	15 37.5	0 56.4	16 38.6	16 14.3
13 M	23 22 11.7	22 20.9	8 19.6	22 22.9	9 23.6	10 23.5	5 40.4	23 14.2	15 32.8	0 56.6	16 37.1	16 13.2
14 T	23 26 8.3	23 20.8	8 16.4	5♒30.3	11 8.3	11 2.0	5 19.4	23 27.6	15 28.0	0 56.8	16 35.7	16 12.1
15 W	23 30 4.8	24 20.6	8 13.2	18 23.3	12 54.2	11 41.7	4 57.9	23 40.9	15 23.3	0 57.1	16 34.2	16 11.0
16 T	23 34 1.4	25 20.3	8 10.0	1♓ 2.9	14 41.3	12 22.5	4 36.1	23 54.2	15 18.6	0 57.5	16 32.7	16 9.9
17 F	23 37 57.9	26 20.1	8 6.8	13 30.1	16 29.6	13 4.3	4 13.9	24 7.4	15 13.9	0 57.8	16 31.1	16 8.9
18 S	23 41 54.5	27 19.8	8 3.7	25 46.1	18 19.1	13 47.2	3 51.4	24 20.6	15 9.3	0 58.3	16 29.6	16 7.8
19 S	23 45 51.0	28 19.4	8 0.5	7♈52.2	20 9.8	14 31.1	3 28.6	24 33.7	15 4.7	0 58.8	16 28.1	16 6.8
20 M	23 49 47.6	29 19.1	7 57.3	19 50.3	22 1.8	15 16.0	3 5.6	24 46.8	15 0.1	0 59.3	16 26.5	16 5.8
21 T	23 53 44.1	0♈18.7	7 54.1	1♉42.3	23 55.0	16 1.7	2 42.5	24 59.8	14 55.6	0 59.9	16 24.9	16 4.9
22 W	23 57 40.7	1 18.3	7 51.0	13 31.0	25 49.5	16 48.3	2 19.1	25 12.7	14 51.1	1 0.6	16 23.4	16 3.9
23 T	0 1 37.2	2 17.8	7 47.8	25 19.6	27 45.1	17 35.8	1 55.7	25 25.6	14 46.6	1 1.3	16 21.8	16 3.0
24 F	0 5 33.8	3 17.3	7 44.6	7♊11.7	29 41.9	18 24.0	1 32.3	25 38.4	14 42.2	1 2.1	16 20.2	16 2.1
25 S	0 9 30.4	4 16.7	7 41.4	19 11.5	1♈39.9	19 13.1	1 8.8	25 51.2	14 37.8	1 2.9	16 18.6	16 1.2
26 S	0 13 26.9	5 16.2	7 38.3	1♋23.5	3 39.0	20 2.9	0 45.5	26 3.9	14 33.5	1 3.8	16 17.0	16 0.4
27 M	0 17 23.5	6 15.6	7 35.1	13 52.0	5 39.1	20 53.4	0 22.2	26 16.5	14 29.2	1 4.7	16 15.4	15 59.6
28 T	0 21 20.0	7 14.9	7 31.9	26 41.3	7 40.1	21 44.6	29♍59.0	26 29.1	14 25.0	1 5.7	16 13.8	15 58.7
29 W	0 25 16.6	8 14.2	7 28.7	9♌54.8	9 42.0	22 36.4	29 36.0	26 41.6	14 20.8	1 6.7	16 12.2	15 57.9
30 T	0 29 13.1	9 13.5	7 25.5	23 34.6	11 44.6	23 28.9	29 13.3	26 54.0	14 16.7	1 7.8	16 10.5	15 57.2
31 F	0 33 9.7	10 12.7	7 22.4	7♍40.9	13 47.7	24 22.0	28 50.8	27 6.3	14 12.6	1 8.9	16 8.9	15 56.4
DECLINATION at NOON												
1 W	22 34 53.1	7S41.5	3N33.2	24N22.3	16S33.7	13S 1.6	0S20.5	15S17.3	7N22.0	23N42.9	5S 7.1	23N48.7
4 S	22 46 42.7	6 32.7	3 29.5	8 9.7	15 13.8	13 11.4	0 2.6	15 4.3	7 27.8	23 42.9	5 5.6	23 49.9
7 T	22 58 32.4	5 23.2	3 25.7	12S34.9	13 42.5	13 17.5	0N17.1	14 51.4	7 33.6	23 42.9	5 3.9	23 50.9
10 F	23 10 22.0	4 12.9	3 22.0	26 50.7	11 59.7	13 19.6	0 38.6	14 38.5	7 39.3	23 42.8	5 2.2	23 51.9
13 M	23 22 11.7	3 2.2	3 18.2	26 36.7	10 5.6	13 17.3	1 1.4	14 25.6	7 45.0	23 42.8	5 0.5	23 52.8
16 T	23 34 1.4	1 51.2	3 14.4	14 2.0	8 0.4	13 10.6	1 25.3	14 12.7	7 50.5	23 42.8	4 58.7	23 53.6
19 S	23 45 51.0	0 40.0	3 10.7	3N 9.8	5 44.4	12 59.4	1 49.8	13 60.0	7 56.0	23 42.8	4 56.9	23 54.3
22 W	23 57 40.7	0N31.1	3 6.9	18 52.8	3 18.2	12 43.7	2 14.4	13 47.3	8 1.2	23 42.8	4 55.0	23 54.9
25 S	0 9 30.4	1 42.1	3 3.2	28 1.2	0 42.8	12 23.3	2 38.6	13 34.7	8 6.3	23 42.7	4 53.1	23 55.5
28 T	0 21 20.0	2 52.7	2 59.4	25 43.8	2N 0.4	11 58.5	3 2.0	13 22.3	8 11.2	23 42.7	4 51.3	23 56.0
31 F	0 33 9.7	4 2.7	2 55.6	11 8.1	4 48.8	11 29.2	3 24.1	13 10.0	8 15.9	23 42.6	4 49.3	23 56.4

APRIL 1950

DAY	EPHEMERIS SIDEREAL TIME	☉	☊	☽	☿	♀	♂	♃	♄	♅	♆	♇
LONGITUDE at NOON												
1 S	0 37 6.2	11♈11.9	7♈19.2	22♍11.6	15♈51.2	25♒15.7	28♍28.6	27♒18.6	14♍ 8.6	1♋10.1	16♎ 7.2	15♌55.7
2 S	0 41 2.8	12 11.1	7 16.0	7♎ 1.7	17 54.9	26 10.0	28R 6.7	27 30.8	14R 4.7	1 11.3	16R 5.6	15R55.0
3 M	0 44 59.3	13 10.2	7 12.8	22 4.2	19 58.5	27 4.9	27 45.3	27 42.9	14 0.8	1 12.6	16 3.9	15 54.3
4 T	0 48 55.9	14 9.3	7 9.7	7♏10.4	22 1.7	28 0.3	27 24.2	27 54.9	13 57.0	1 13.9	16 2.3	15 53.7
5 W	0 52 52.4	15 8.3	7 6.5	22 11.2	24 4.2	28 56.1	27 3.6	28 6.8	13 53.2	1 15.3	16 0.6	15 53.1
6 T	0 56 49.0	16 7.3	7 3.3	6♐58.6	26 5.8	29 52.5	26 43.5	28 18.7	13 49.6	1 16.7	15 59.0	15 52.5
7 F	1 0 45.6	17 6.3	7 0.1	21 26.6	28 6.1	0♓49.4	26 23.9	28 30.5	13 46.0	1 18.2	15 57.3	15 51.9
8 S	1 4 42.1	18 5.3	6 56.9	5♑31.8	0♉ 4.6	1 46.8	26 4.8	28 42.2	13 42.4	1 19.7	15 55.7	15 51.4
9 S	1 8 38.7	19 4.2	6 53.8	19 12.9	2 1.1	2 44.6	25 46.3	28 53.8	13 39.0	1 21.3	15 54.0	15 50.8
10 M	1 12 35.2	20 3.1	6 50.6	2♒30.8	3 55.2	3 42.8	25 28.5	29 5.4	13 35.6	1 22.9	15 52.4	15 50.3
11 T	1 16 31.8	21 2.0	6 47.4	15 27.6	5 46.6	4 41.4	25 11.2	29 16.8	13 32.3	1 24.6	15 50.7	15 49.9
12 W	1 20 28.3	22 0.9	6 44.2	28 6.3	7 34.8	5 40.4	24 54.6	29 28.2	13 29.0	1 26.3	15 49.1	15 49.4
13 T	1 24 24.9	22 59.7	6 41.1	10♓29.9	9 19.6	6 39.8	24 38.7	29 39.4	13 25.9	1 28.1	15 47.5	15 49.0
14 F	1 28 21.4	23 58.5	6 37.9	22 41.5	11 0.7	7 39.6	24 23.4	29 50.6	13 22.8	1 29.9	15 45.8	15 48.6
15 S	1 32 18.0	24 57.2	6 34.7	4♈44.0	12 37.8	8 39.7	24 8.9	0♓ 1.7	13 19.8	1 31.7	15 44.2	15 48.3
16 S	1 36 14.5	25 56.0	6 31.5	16 39.9	14 10.8	9 40.3	23 55.2	0 12.7	13 17.0	1 33.7	15 42.6	15 48.0
17 M	1 40 11.1	26 54.7	6 28.3	28 31.3	15 39.2	10 41.0	23 42.1	0 23.6	13 14.2	1 35.6	15 41.0	15 47.7
18 T	1 44 7.7	27 53.4	6 25.2	10♉20.4	17 3.1	11 42.1	23 29.8	0 34.4	13 11.5	1 37.6	15 39.4	15 47.4
19 W	1 48 4.2	28 52.0	6 22.0	22 9.2	18 22.1	12 43.6	23 18.3	0 45.1	13 8.8	1 39.6	15 37.8	15 47.1
20 T	1 52 0.8	29 50.6	6 18.8	3♊60.0	19 36.2	13 45.3	23 7.6	0 55.6	13 6.3	1 41.7	15 36.2	15 46.9
21 F	1 55 57.3	0♉49.1	6 15.6	15 55.1	20 45.2	14 47.2	22 57.7	1 6.1	13 3.9	1 43.8	15 34.6	15 46.7
22 S	1 59 53.9	1 47.7	6 12.5	27 57.5	21 49.1	15 49.5	22 48.5	1 16.5	13 1.5	1 46.0	15 33.0	15 46.5
23 S	2 3 50.4	2 46.2	6 9.3	10♋10.4	22 47.6	16 52.0	22 40.2	1 26.7	12 59.2	1 48.2	15 31.5	15 46.4
24 M	2 7 47.0	3 44.6	6 6.1	22 37.4	23 40.9	17 54.8	22 32.6	1 36.9	12 57.1	1 50.4	15 29.9	15 46.3
25 T	2 11 43.5	4 43.0	6 2.9	5♌22.3	24 28.6	18 57.8	22 25.9	1 46.9	12 55.0	1 52.7	15 28.4	15 46.2
26 W	2 15 40.1	5 41.4	5 59.7	18 28.6	25 10.9	20 1.1	22 20.0	1 56.8	12 53.0	1 55.0	15 26.8	15 46.1
27 T	2 19 36.6	6 39.8	5 56.6	1♍59.6	25 47.7	21 4.6	22 14.8	2 6.6	12 51.2	1 57.4	15 25.3	15 46.1
28 F	2 23 33.2	7 38.1	5 53.4	15 57.1	26 18.8	22 8.3	22 10.4	2 16.3	12 49.4	1 59.8	15 23.8	15 46.1
29 S	2 27 29.8	8 36.4	5 50.2	0♎20.9	26 44.4	23 12.3	22 6.9	2 25.9	12 47.7	2 2.2	15 22.3	15 46.1
30 S	2 31 26.3	9 34.6	5 47.0	15 8.5	27 4.3	24 16.4	22 4.1	2 35.3	12 46.1	2 4.7	15 20.9	15D46.2
DECLINATION at NOON												
1 S	0 37 6.2	4N25.9	2N54.4	4N22.9	5N45.6	11S18.5	3N31.1	13S 5.9	8N17.3	23N42.6	4S48.7	23N56.5
4 T	0 48 55.9	5 35.0	2 50.6	16S23.6	8 35.2	10 43.4	3 51.0	12 53.9	8 21.7	23 42.6	4 46.8	23 56.7
7 F	1 0 45.6	6 43.3	2 46.8	28 14.6	11 19.9	10 4.1	4 8.7	12 42.0	8 25.7	23 42.5	4 44.9	23 56.9
10 M	1 12 35.2	7 50.5	2 43.1	24 15.9	13 53.7	9 20.8	4 24.1	12 30.4	8 29.5	23 42.5	4 42.9	23 57.0
13 T	1 24 24.9	8 56.6	2 39.3	9 51.2	16 11.2	8 33.7	4 37.0	12 18.9	8 33.0	23 42.4	4 41.1	23 57.0
16 S	1 36 14.5	10 1.3	2 35.5	7N19.8	18 8.0	7 43.1	4 47.1	12 7.7	8 36.1	23 42.3	4 39.2	23 56.9
19 W	1 48 4.2	11 4.6	2 31.7	21 53.1	19 41.8	6 49.1	4 54.5	11 56.8	8 38.9	23 42.2	4 37.4	23 56.8
22 S	1 59 53.9	12 6.1	2 28.0	28 35.9	20 51.6	5 52.0	4 58.9	11 46.2	8 41.4	23 42.1	4 35.6	23 56.5
25 T	2 11 43.5	13 5.9	2 24.2	23 24.2	21 37.3	4 52.2	5 0.5	11 35.9	8 43.5	23 42.0	4 33.8	23 56.2
28 F	2 23 33.2	14 3.8	2 20.4	7 17.3	21 59.3	3 49.8	4 59.4	11 26.0	8 45.3	23 41.9	4 32.1	23 55.8

MAY 1950

DAY	EPHEMERIS SIDEREAL TIME	☉	☊	☽	☿	♀	♂	♃	♄	♅	♆	♇
	h m s	° ′	° ′	° ′	° ′	° ′	° ′	° ′	° ′	° ′	° ′	° ′
						LONGITUDE at NOON						
1 M	2 35 22.9	10♉32.8	5♈43.9	0♏14.0	27♉18.7	25♓20.8	22♍ 2.1	2♓44.7	12♍44.7	2♋ 7.2	15♎19.4	15♌46.2
2 T	2 39 19.4	11 31.0	5 40.7	15 29.1	27 27.7	26 25.4	22R 0.8	2 53.9	12R43.3	2 9.7	15R17.9	15 46.3
3 W	2 43 16.0	12 29.2	5 37.5	0♐43.7	27 31.2	27 30.2	22 0.3	3 3.0	12 42.0	2 12.3	15 16.5	15 46.5
4 T	2 47 12.5	13 27.3	5 34.3	15 47.3	27R29.5	28 35.2	22D 0.6	3 11.9	12 40.8	2 14.9	15 15.1	15 46.6
5 F	2 51 9.1	14 25.4	5 31.2	0♑31.3	27 22.7	29 40.3	22 1.6	3 20.8	12 39.8	2 17.6	15 13.7	15 46.8
6 S	2 55 5.7	15 23.5	5 28.0	14 49.6	27 11.1	0♈45.7	22 3.3	3 29.5	12 38.8	2 20.3	15 12.3	15 47.0
7 S	2 59 2.2	16 21.6	5 24.8	28 39.5	26 55.0	1 51.3	22 5.8	3 38.1	12 38.0	2 23.0	15 11.0	15 47.3
8 M	3 2 58.8	17 19.6	5 21.6	12♒ 1.2	26 34.7	2 57.0	22 8.9	3 46.6	12 37.2	2 25.8	15 9.7	15 47.6
9 T	3 6 55.3	18 17.6	5 18.4	24 57.1	26 10.6	4 2.9	22 12.8	3 54.9	12 36.5	2 28.6	15 8.3	15 47.9
10 W	3 10 51.9	19 15.6	5 15.3	7♓30.9	25 43.2	5 8.9	22 17.4	4 3.1	12 36.0	2 31.4	15 7.0	15 48.2
11 T	3 14 48.4	20 13.6	5 12.1	19 47.2	25 13.0	6 15.1	22 22.7	4 11.1	12 35.5	2 34.3	15 5.7	15 48.6
12 F	3 18 45.0	21 11.5	5 8.9	1♈50.6	24 40.6	7 21.4	22 28.6	4 19.0	12 35.2	2 37.1	15 4.5	15 49.0
13 S	3 22 41.5	22 9.4	5 5.7	13 45.2	24 6.5	8 27.9	22 35.2	4 26.8	12 34.9	2 40.0	15 3.2	15 49.4
14 S	3 26 38.1	23 7.3	5 2.6	25 34.9	23 31.4	9 34.5	22 42.5	4 34.4	12 34.8	2 43.0	15 2.0	15 49.8
15 M	3 30 34.7	24 5.2	4 59.4	7♉22.8	22 55.8	10 41.3	22 50.4	4 41.9	12 34.8	2 46.0	15 0.8	15 50.3
16 T	3 34 31.2	25 3.1	4 56.2	19 11.5	22 20.5	11 48.2	22 59.0	4 49.3	12 34.8	2 49.0	14 59.6	15 50.8
17 W	3 38 27.8	26 0.9	4 53.0	1♊ 3.0	21 45.9	12 55.2	23 8.2	4 56.5	12D35.0	2 52.0	14 58.5	15 51.3
18 T	3 42 24.3	26 58.7	4 49.9	12 59.1	21 12.8	14 2.4	23 18.1	5 3.5	12 35.3	2 55.1	14 57.3	15 51.8
19 F	3 46 20.9	27 56.5	4 46.7	25 1.4	20 41.6	15 9.6	23 28.5	5 10.4	12 35.7	2 58.1	14 56.2	15 52.4
20 S	3 50 17.4	28 54.2	4 43.5	7♋11.4	20 12.9	16 17.0	23 39.5	5 17.1	12 36.1	3 1.2	14 55.1	15 53.0
21 S	3 54 14.0	29 52.0	4 40.3	19 31.1	19 47.0	17 24.5	23 51.2	5 23.7	12 36.7	3 4.4	14 54.1	15 53.6
22 M	3 58 10.6	0♊49.7	4 37.1	2♌ 2.7	19 24.4	18 32.1	24 3.4	5 30.2	12 37.4	3 7.5	14 53.0	15 54.3
23 T	4 2 7.1	1 47.4	4 34.0	14 48.8	19 5.5	19 39.8	24 16.2	5 36.4	12 38.2	3 10.7	14 52.0	15 55.0
24 W	4 6 3.7	2 45.0	4 30.8	27 52.4	18 50.4	20 47.6	24 29.5	5 42.5	12 39.1	3 13.9	14 51.0	15 55.7
25 T	4 10 0.2	3 42.6	4 27.6	11♍16.5	18 39.5	21 55.6	24 43.4	5 48.5	12 40.1	3 17.2	14 50.0	15 56.4
26 F	4 13 56.8	4 40.2	4 24.4	25 3.4	18 32.8	23 3.6	24 57.8	5 54.3	12 41.3	3 20.4	14 49.1	15 57.1
27 S	4 17 53.4	5 37.8	4 21.3	9♎14.4	18 30.5	24 11.7	25 12.7	5 59.9	12 42.5	3 23.7	14 48.2	15 57.9
28 S	4 21 49.9	6 35.4	4 18.1	23 48.7	18D32.7	25 20.0	25 28.2	6 5.5	12 43.8	3 27.0	14 47.4	15 58.8
29 M	4 25 46.5	7 33.0	4 14.9	8♏42.8	18 39.4	26 28.3	25 44.2	6 10.8	12 45.2	3 30.3	14 46.5	15 59.6
30 T	4 29 43.0	8 30.5	4 11.7	23 50.3	18 50.5	27 36.7	26 0.6	6 15.9	12 46.8	3 33.7	14 45.7	16 0.4
31 W	4 33 39.6	9 28.0	4 8.6	9♐ 1.9	19 6.1	28 45.2	26 17.5	6 20.9	12 48.4	3 37.0	14 44.9	16 1.3
						DECLINATION at NOON						
1 M	2 35 22.9	14N59.5	2N16.6	13S 28.4	21N58.1	2S 45.2	4N55.5	11S 16.3	8N46.7	23N41.8	4S 30.4	23N55.3
4 T	2 47 12.5	15 53.0	2 12.9	27 30.0	21 34.6	1 38.6	4 49.0	11 7.1	8 47.8	23 41.7	4 28.8	23 54.7
7 S	2 59 2.2	16 44.2	2 9.1	25 8.6	20 50.7	0 30.1	4 40.1	10 58.2	8 48.4	23 41.5	4 27.3	23 54.1
10 W	3 10 51.9	17 32.9	2 5.3	11 6.2	19 49.6	0N39.7	4 28.8	10 49.8	8 48.8	23 41.3	4 25.9	23 53.3
13 S	3 22 41.5	18 18.9	2 1.5	6N 0.6	18 36.6	1 50.6	4 15.3	10 41.8	8 48.7	23 41.2	4 24.5	23 52.5
16 T	3 34 31.2	19 2.2	1 57.7	20 52.1	17 19.3	3 2.4	3 59.6	10 34.3	8 48.3	23 41.0	4 23.2	23 51.7
19 F	3 46 20.9	19 42.5	1 54.0	28 21.3	16 6.0	4 14.7	3 41.8	10 27.2	8 47.5	23 40.8	4 21.9	23 50.7
22 M	3 58 10.6	20 19.9	1 50.2	24 10.0	15 4.2	5 27.2	3 22.1	10 20.7	8 46.4	23 40.6	4 20.8	23 49.7
25 T	4 10 0.2	20 54.1	1 46.4	9 17.4	14 19.4	6 39.6	3 0.6	10 14.6	8 44.8	23 40.3	4 19.8	23 48.6
28 S	4 21 49.9	21 25.1	1 42.6	10S 43.4	13 54.6	7 51.6	2 37.3	10 9.1	8 43.0	23 40.1	4 18.8	23 47.5
31 W	4 33 39.6	21 52.7	1 38.8	26 17.6	13 50.3	9 2.9	2 12.5	10 4.1	8 40.7	23 39.8	4 18.0	23 46.3

JUNE 1950

DAY	EPHEMERIS SIDEREAL TIME	☉	☊	☽	☿	♀	♂	♃	♄	♅	♆	♇
						LONGITUDE at NOON						
1 T	4 37 36.1	10♊25.4	4♈ 5.4	24♐ 7.3	19♉26.2	29♈53.8	26♍34.9	6♓25.7	12♍50.1	3♋40.4	14♎44.1	16♌ 2.2
2 F	4 41 32.7	11 22.9	4 2.2	8♑56.6	19 50.6	1♉ 2.4	26 52.7	6 30.3	12 51.9	3 43.8	14R43.4	16 3.2
3 S	4 45 29.3	12 20.3	3 59.0	23 22.0	20 19.3	2 11.2	27 11.0	6 34.8	12 53.8	3 47.2	14 42.6	16 4.1
4 S	4 49 25.8	13 17.8	3 55.9	7♒19.0	20 52.2	3 20.1	27 29.7	6 39.1	12 55.8	3 50.6	14 42.0	16 5.1
5 M	4 53 22.4	14 15.2	3 52.7	20 46.5	21 29.2	4 29.0	27 48.8	6 43.2	12 57.9	3 54.0	14 41.3	16 6.1
6 T	4 57 18.9	15 12.6	3 49.5	3♓46.0	22 10.2	5 38.1	28 8.4	6 47.1	13 0.2	3 57.5	14 40.7	16 7.1
7 W	5 1 15.5	16 10.0	3 46.3	16 21.2	22 55.2	6 47.2	28 28.4	6 50.9	13 2.5	4 0.9	14 40.1	16 8.1
8 T	5 5 12.1	17 7.4	3 43.1	28 37.0	23 44.0	7 56.4	28 48.8	6 54.5	13 4.9	4 4.4	14 39.5	16 9.2
9 F	5 9 8.6	18 4.8	3 40.0	10♈38.5	24 36.5	9 5.7	29 9.6	6 57.9	13 7.4	4 7.9	14 38.9	16 10.3
10 S	5 13 5.2	19 2.1	3 36.8	22 30.9	25 32.7	10 15.0	29 30.8	7 1.1	13 9.9	4 11.4	14 38.4	16 11.4
11 S	5 17 1.7	19 59.5	3 33.6	4♉19.1	26 32.5	11 24.4	29 52.4	7 4.1	13 12.6	4 14.9	14 38.0	16 12.5
12 M	5 20 58.3	20 56.9	3 30.4	16 7.1	27 35.8	12 33.9	0♎14.4	7 7.0	13 15.4	4 18.4	14 37.5	16 13.7
13 T	5 24 54.8	21 54.2	3 27.3	27 58.3	28 42.5	13 43.5	0 36.7	7 9.6	13 18.3	4 22.0	14 37.1	16 14.9
14 W	5 28 51.4	22 51.5	3 24.1	9♊55.2	29 52.7	14 53.2	0 59.4	7 12.1	13 21.3	4 25.5	14 36.7	16 16.1
15 T	5 32 48.0	23 48.9	3 20.9	21 59.7	1♊ 6.1	16 2.9	1 22.5	7 14.4	13 24.3	4 29.1	14 36.3	16 17.3
16 F	5 36 44.5	24 46.2	3 17.7	4♋12.9	2 22.9	17 12.6	1 46.0	7 16.5	13 27.5	4 32.6	14 36.0	16 18.5
17 S	5 40 41.1	25 43.5	3 14.6	16 35.6	3 42.9	18 22.5	2 9.7	7 18.4	13 30.7	4 36.2	14 35.7	16 19.8
18 S	5 44 37.6	26 40.8	3 11.4	29 8.5	5 6.2	19 32.4	2 33.9	7 20.2	13 34.1	4 39.8	14 35.5	16 21.1
19 M	5 48 34.2	27 38.1	3 8.2	11♌52.4	6 32.6	20 42.4	2 58.4	7 21.7	13 37.5	4 43.4	14 35.3	16 22.4
20 T	5 52 30.8	28 35.4	3 5.0	24 48.2	8 2.2	21 52.4	3 23.2	7 23.1	13 41.0	4 47.0	14 35.1	16 23.7
21 W	5 56 27.3	29 32.6	3 1.9	7♍57.7	9 34.9	23 2.5	3 48.3	7 24.2	13 44.6	4 50.6	14 34.9	16 25.1
22 T	6 0 23.9	0♋29.9	2 58.7	21 22.6	11 10.7	24 12.6	4 13.7	7 25.2	13 48.3	4 54.2	14 34.8	16 26.4
23 F	6 4 20.4	1 27.1	2 55.5	5♎ 4.8	12 49.6	25 22.8	4 39.5	7 25.9	13 52.1	4 57.8	14 34.7	16 27.8
24 S	6 8 17.0	2 24.3	2 52.3	19 5.6	14 31.5	26 33.0	5 5.5	7 26.5	13 55.9	5 1.4	14 34.6	16 29.2
25 S	6 12 13.6	3 21.5	2 49.2	3♏25.0	16 16.3	27 43.3	5 31.8	7 26.9	13 59.9	5 5.0	14 34.5	16 30.6
26 M	6 16 10.1	4 18.8	2 46.0	18 1.1	18 4.1	28 53.7	5 58.5	7 27.1	14 3.9	5 8.6	14 34.5	16 32.0
27 T	6 20 6.7	5 16.0	2 42.8	2♐49.6	19 54.7	0♊ 4.1	6 25.4	7 27.1	14 8.0	5 12.2	14D34.6	16 33.5
28 W	6 24 3.2	6 13.1	2 39.6	17 43.7	21 48.0	1 14.6	6 52.6	7R26.9	14 12.2	5 15.8	14 34.6	16 34.9
29 T	6 27 59.8	7 10.3	2 36.4	2♑35.0	23 43.9	2 25.2	7 20.0	7 26.5	14 16.4	5 19.4	14 34.7	16 36.4
30 F	6 31 56.3	8 7.5	2 33.3	17 14.5	25 42.2	3 35.8	7 47.8	7 25.9	14 20.8	5 23.0	14 34.8	16 37.9
						DECLINATION at NOON						
1 T	4 37 36.1	22N 1.2	1N37.6	28S 16.4	13N53.3	9N26.5	2N 3.9	10S 2.6	8N39.9	23N39.7	4S 17.7	23N45.9
4 S	4 49 25.8	22 24.2	1 33.8	22 34.4	14 14.5	10 36.4	1 37.1	9 58.4	8 37.3	23 39.5	4 17.0	23 44.7
7 W	5 1 15.5	22 43.8	1 30.0	6 51.4	14 52.1	11 45.0	1 8.9	9 54.8	8 34.3	23 39.2	4 16.4	23 43.3
10 S	5 13 5.2	22 59.7	1 26.2	10N12.5	15 43.4	12 51.8	0 39.5	9 51.8	8 30.9	23 38.9	4 15.9	23 42.0
13 T	5 24 54.8	23 12.1	1 22.4	23 39.3	16 45.5	13 56.5	0 8.8	9 49.4	8 27.3	23 38.5	4 15.5	23 40.6
16 F	5 36 44.5	23 20.7	1 18.7	28 22.8	17 55.2	14 58.9	0S 23.1	9 47.6	8 23.3	23 38.2	4 15.2	23 39.1
19 M	5 48 34.2	23 25.6	1 14.9	20 59.7	19 9.2	15 58.7	0 56.0	9 46.5	8 19.0	23 37.8	4 15.1	23 37.7
22 T	6 0 23.9	23 26.8	1 11.1	4 21.2	20 23.9	16 55.4	1 29.9	9 46.0	8 14.4	23 37.5	4 15.0	23 36.1
25 S	6 12 13.6	23 24.3	1 7.3	15S 3.6	21 35.0	17 48.8	2 4.8	9 46.2	8 9.5	23 37.1	4 15.0	23 34.6
28 W	6 24 3.2	23 18.1	1 3.5	27 42.1	22 37.5	18 38.5	2 40.4	9 47.0	8 4.4	23 36.7	4 15.2	23 33.0

JULY 1950

LONGITUDE at NOON

DAY	EPHEMERIS SIDEREAL TIME	☉	☊	☽	☿	♀	♂	♃	♄	♅	♆	♇
	h m s	° ′	° ′	° ′	° ′	° ′	° ′	° ′	° ′	° ′	° ′	° ′
1 S	6 35 52.9	9♋ 4.7	2♈30.1	1♒34.6	27♊42.9	4♊46.4	8♎15.8	7♓25.1	14♍25.2	5♋26.6	14♎35.0	16♌39.4
2 S	6 39 49.5	10 1.9	2 26.9	15 30.0	29 45.6	5 57.1	8 44.0	7R24.1	14 29.7	5 30.2	14 35.2	16 40.9
3 M	6 43 46.0	10 59.1	2 23.7	28 58.4	1♋50.1	7 7.9	9 12.5	7 23.0	14 34.3	5 33.8	14 35.4	16 42.5
4 T	6 47 42.6	11 56.2	2 20.6	12♓ 0.1	3 56.3	8 18.8	9 41.3	7 21.6	14 38.9	5 37.4	14 35.6	16 44.0
5 W	6 51 39.1	12 53.4	2 17.4	24 37.7	6 3.8	9 29.6	10 10.3	7 20.1	14 43.6	5 41.0	14 35.9	16 45.6
6 T	6 55 35.7	13 50.6	2 14.2	6♈55.6	8 12.4	10 40.6	10 39.5	7 18.3	14 48.4	5 44.6	14 36.2	16 47.2
7 F	6 59 32.3	14 47.8	2 11.0	18 58.6	10 21.6	11 51.6	11 9.0	7 16.4	14 53.3	5 48.1	14 36.6	16 48.8
8 S	7 3 28.8	15 45.0	2 7.9	0♉52.3	12 31.4	13 2.7	11 38.7	7 14.3	14 58.2	5 51.7	14 37.0	16 50.4
9 S	7 7 25.4	16 42.3	2 4.7	12 41.9	14 41.3	14 13.8	12 8.7	7 12.0	15 3.3	5 55.3	14 37.4	16 52.1
10 M	7 11 21.9	17 39.5	2 1.5	24 32.1	16 51.1	15 25.0	12 38.9	7 9.5	15 8.4	5 58.9	14 37.8	16 53.7
11 T	7 15 18.5	18 36.7	1 58.3	6♊27.1	19 0.5	16 36.3	13 9.3	7 6.8	15 13.5	6 2.4	14 38.3	16 55.4
12 W	7 19 15.1	19 34.0	1 55.2	18 30.3	21 9.3	17 47.5	13 40.0	7 3.9	15 18.8	6 5.9	14 38.8	16 57.0
13 T	7 23 11.6	20 31.2	1 52.0	0♋44.1	23 17.3	18 58.9	14 10.9	7 0.9	15 24.1	6 9.5	14 39.4	16 58.7
14 F	7 27 8.2	21 28.4	1 48.8	13 9.9	25 24.2	20 10.3	14 41.9	6 57.6	15 29.4	6 13.0	14 39.9	17 0.4
15 S	7 31 4.7	22 25.7	1 45.6	25 48.3	27 30.0	21 21.7	15 13.3	6 54.2	15 34.8	6 16.5	14 40.5	17 2.1
16 S	7 35 1.3	23 23.0	1 42.4	8♌39.0	29 34.4	22 33.2	15 44.8	6 50.6	15 40.3	6 20.0	14 41.2	17 3.8
17 M	7 38 57.8	24 20.2	1 39.3	21 41.7	1♌37.4	23 44.7	16 16.5	6 46.8	15 45.9	6 23.5	14 41.8	17 5.5
18 T	7 42 54.4	25 17.5	1 36.1	4♍55.8	3 38.9	24 56.3	16 48.4	6 42.8	15 51.5	6 26.9	14 42.5	17 7.2
19 W	7 46 51.0	26 14.7	1 32.9	18 21.0	5 38.8	26 7.9	17 20.6	6 38.7	15 57.2	6 30.4	14 43.3	17 9.0
20 T	7 50 47.5	27 12.0	1 29.7	1♎57.3	7 37.0	27 19.6	17 52.9	6 34.4	16 2.9	6 33.8	14 44.0	17 10.7
21 F	7 54 44.1	28 9.3	1 26.6	15 44.9	9 33.6	28 31.3	18 25.5	6 29.9	16 8.7	6 37.2	14 44.8	17 12.5
22 S	7 58 40.6	29 6.6	1 23.4	29 44.1	11 28.4	29 43.1	18 58.2	6 25.3	16 14.5	6 40.6	14 45.6	17 14.3
23 S	8 2 37.2	0♌ 3.9	1 20.2	13♏54.4	13 21.5	0♋54.9	19 31.1	6 20.5	16 20.4	6 44.0	14 46.5	17 16.0
24 M	8 6 33.7	1 1.2	1 17.0	28 14.5	15 12.9	2 6.8	20 4.2	6 15.5	16 26.4	6 47.4	14 47.3	17 17.8
25 T	8 10 30.3	1 58.5	1 13.9	12♐41.6	17 2.5	3 18.7	20 37.5	6 10.4	16 32.4	6 50.7	14 48.3	17 19.6
26 W	8 14 26.9	2 55.8	1 10.7	27 11.2	18 50.4	4 30.7	21 11.0	6 5.1	16 38.5	6 54.1	14 49.2	17 21.4
27 T	8 18 23.4	3 53.1	1 7.5	11♑37.8	20 36.5	5 42.7	21 44.6	5 59.7	16 44.6	6 57.4	14 50.2	17 23.2
28 F	8 22 20.0	4 50.4	1 4.3	25 55.1	22 21.0	6 54.7	22 18.4	5 54.1	16 50.8	7 0.7	14 51.2	17 25.0
29 S	8 26 16.5	5 47.7	1 1.2	9♒57.2	24 3.7	8 6.9	22 52.4	5 48.4	16 57.0	7 3.9	14 52.2	17 26.8
30 S	8 30 13.1	6 45.1	0 58.0	23 39.7	25 44.7	9 19.1	23 26.6	5 42.6	17 3.4	7 7.2	14 53.3	17 28.7
31 M	8 34 9.6	7 42.5	0 54.8	7♓ 0.1	27 24.0	10 31.3	24 0.9	5 36.6	17 9.7	7 10.5	14 54.4	17 30.5

DECLINATION at NOON

DAY	EPHEMERIS SIDEREAL TIME	☉	☊	☽	☿	♀	♂	♃	♄	♅	♆	♇
1 S	6 35 52.9	23N 8.2	0N59.7	24S 4.3	23N26.3	19N24.4	3S 16.9	9S 48.4	7N59.0	23N36.3	4S 15.5	23N31.4
4 T	6 47 42.6	22 54.7	0 55.9	8 38.6	23 56.2	20 6.1	3 54.0	9 50.5	7 53.3	23 35.8	4 15.9	23 29.8
7 F	6 59 32.3	22 37.6	0 52.1	8N49.3	24 3.1	20 43.4	4 31.8	9 53.3	7 47.4	23 35.4	4 16.4	23 28.2
10 M	7 11 21.9	22 17.0	0 48.3	22 48.6	23 45.2	21 15.9	5 10.1	9 56.6	7 41.2	23 35.0	4 17.0	23 26.5
13 T	7 23 11.6	21 52.9	0 44.6	28 28.3	23 3.0	21 43.5	5 49.0	10 0.6	7 34.8	23 34.5	4 17.7	23 24.9
16 S	7 35 1.3	21 25.4	0 40.8	21 56.2	21 59.2	22 5.8	6 28.3	10 5.2	7 28.2	23 34.1	4 18.6	23 23.2
19 W	7 46 51.0	20 54.6	0 37.0	5 34.7	20 37.4	22 22.9	7 8.0	10 10.4	7 21.3	23 33.6	4 19.5	23 21.5
22 S	7 58 40.6	20 20.7	0 33.2	13S 43.6	19 1.5	22 34.3	7 48.1	10 16.1	7 14.3	23 33.1	4 20.5	23 19.9
25 T	8 10 30.3	19 43.7	0 29.4	27 8.2	17 15.2	22 40.2	8 28.4	10 22.3	7 7.1	23 32.6	4 21.7	23 18.2
28 F	8 22 20.0	19 3.7	0 25.6	25 27.4	15 21.6	22 40.3	9 8.8	10 29.0	6 59.7	23 32.2	4 22.9	23 16.6
31 M	8 34 9.6	18 21.0	0 21.8	10 45.7	13 23.2	22 34.6	9 49.4	10 36.1	6 52.1	23 31.7	4 24.3	23 14.9

AUGUST 1950

LONGITUDE at NOON

DAY	EPHEMERIS SIDEREAL TIME	☉	☊	☽	☿	♀	♂	♃	♄	♅	♆	♇
1 T	8 38 6.2	8♌39.9	0♈51.6	19♓57.8	29♌ 1.6	11♋43.6	24♎35.4	5♓30.5	17♍16.1	7♋13.7	14♎55.5	17♌32.3
2 W	8 42 2.8	9 37.3	0 48.4	2♈34.4	0♍37.5	12 55.9	25 10.1	5R24.2	17 22.5	7 16.9	14 56.6	17 34.1
3 T	8 45 59.3	10 34.7	0 45.3	14 52.9	2 11.7	14 8.2	25 44.9	5 17.8	17 29.0	7 20.0	14 57.8	17 36.0
4 F	8 49 55.9	11 32.1	0 42.1	26 57.5	3 44.2	15 20.7	26 19.9	5 11.3	17 35.5	7 23.2	14 59.0	17 37.8
5 S	8 53 52.4	12 29.6	0 38.9	8♉52.8	5 15.0	16 33.1	26 55.0	5 4.7	17 42.0	7 26.3	15 0.2	17 39.6
6 S	8 57 49.0	13 27.0	0 35.7	20 44.1	6 44.0	17 45.7	27 30.3	4 58.0	17 48.6	7 29.4	15 1.5	17 41.5
7 M	9 1 45.5	14 24.5	0 32.6	2♊36.4	8 11.4	18 58.2	28 5.8	4 51.1	17 55.3	7 32.4	15 2.7	17 43.3
8 T	9 5 42.1	15 22.1	0 29.4	14 34.3	9 37.0	20 10.9	28 41.4	4 44.2	18 2.0	7 35.5	15 4.0	17 45.2
9 W	9 9 38.7	16 19.6	0 26.2	26 42.1	11 0.9	21 23.5	29 17.1	4 37.1	18 8.7	7 38.5	15 5.4	17 47.0
10 T	9 13 35.2	17 17.2	0 23.0	9♋ 2.9	12 22.9	22 36.3	29 53.1	4 30.0	18 15.5	7 41.4	15 6.7	17 48.8
11 F	9 17 31.8	18 14.7	0 19.9	21 39.2	13 43.2	23 49.0	0♏29.1	4 22.7	18 22.3	7 44.4	15 8.1	17 50.7
12 S	9 21 28.3	19 12.3	0 16.7	4♌31.9	15 1.5	25 1.9	1 5.4	4 15.4	18 29.1	7 47.3	15 9.5	17 52.5
13 S	9 25 24.9	20 10.0	0 13.5	17 41.1	16 17.9	26 14.7	1 41.8	4 8.0	18 36.0	7 50.2	15 11.0	17 54.4
14 M	9 29 21.4	21 7.6	0 10.3	1♍ 5.5	17 32.4	27 27.6	2 18.3	4 0.5	18 42.9	7 53.1	15 12.4	17 56.2
15 T	9 33 18.0	22 5.3	0 7.1	14 43.4	18 44.8	28 40.6	2 55.0	3 53.0	18 49.9	7 55.9	15 13.9	17 58.1
16 W	9 37 14.5	23 3.0	0 4.0	28 32.4	19 55.1	29 53.6	3 31.8	3 45.4	18 56.9	7 58.7	15 15.4	17 59.9
17 T	9 41 11.1	24 0.7	0 0.8	12♎30.1	21 3.2	1♌ 6.6	4 8.7	3 37.7	19 3.9	8 1.4	15 16.9	18 1.8
18 F	9 45 7.7	24 58.4	29♓57.6	26 34.3	22 9.0	2 19.7	4 45.8	3 30.0	19 10.9	8 4.2	15 18.5	18 3.6
19 S	9 49 4.2	25 56.1	29 54.4	10♏43.1	23 12.3	3 32.9	5 23.1	3 22.3	19 18.0	8 6.9	15 20.1	18 5.4
20 S	9 53 0.8	26 53.9	29 51.3	24 54.6	24 13.3	4 46.1	6 0.5	3 14.5	19 25.2	8 9.6	15 21.7	18 7.3
21 M	9 56 57.3	27 51.7	29 48.1	9♐ 6.7	25 11.5	5 59.3	6 38.0	3 6.7	19 32.3	8 12.2	15 23.4	18 9.1
22 T	10 0 53.9	28 49.5	29 44.9	23 17.5	26 7.0	7 12.6	7 15.7	2 58.8	19 39.4	8 14.8	15 25.0	18 11.0
23 W	10 4 50.4	29 47.3	29 41.7	7♑24.2	26 59.5	8 25.9	7 53.4	2 51.0	19 46.6	8 17.3	15 26.7	18 12.8
24 T	10 8 47.0	0♍45.2	29 38.5	21 24.0	27 48.9	9 39.2	8 31.3	2 43.1	19 53.8	8 19.9	15 28.4	18 14.6
25 F	10 12 43.5	1 43.0	29 35.4	5♒13.6	28 35.1	10 52.6	9 9.4	2 35.2	20 1.1	8 22.3	15 30.1	18 16.4
26 S	10 16 40.1	2 40.9	29 32.2	18 50.1	29 17.7	12 6.0	9 47.5	2 27.3	20 8.3	8 24.8	15 31.8	18 18.2
27 S	10 20 36.7	3 38.8	29 29.0	2♓11.1	29 56.6	13 19.5	10 25.8	2 19.4	20 15.6	8 27.2	15 33.6	18 20.0
28 M	10 24 33.2	4 36.7	29 25.8	15 15.1	0♎31.7	14 33.0	11 4.2	2 11.5	20 22.9	8 29.6	15 35.3	18 21.8
29 T	10 28 29.8	5 34.7	29 22.7	28 1.8	1 2.5	15 46.6	11 42.7	2 3.6	20 30.2	8 31.9	15 37.1	18 23.6
30 W	10 32 26.3	6 32.7	29 19.5	10♈31.8	1 28.9	17 0.2	12 21.4	1 55.7	20 37.6	8 34.2	15 39.0	18 25.3
31 T	10 36 22.9	7 30.7	29 16.3	22 47.1	1 50.5	18 13.8	13 0.2	1 47.9	20 44.9	8 36.4	15 40.8	18 27.1

DECLINATION at NOON

DAY	EPHEMERIS SIDEREAL TIME	☉	☊	☽	☿	♀	♂	♃	♄	♅	♆	♇
1 T	8 38 6.2	18N 6.1	0N20.5	4S 45.2	12N43.1	22N31.4	10S 3.0	10S 38.5	6N49.5	23N31.5	4S 24.7	23N14.4
4 F	8 49 55.9	17 19.8	0 16.8	12N36.9	10 41.8	22 18.0	10 43.5	10 46.2	6 41.8	23 31.1	4 26.2	23 12.7
7 M	9 1 45.5	16 30.9	0 13.0	25 11.8	8 40.4	21 58.8	11 24.1	10 54.2	6 33.9	23 30.6	4 27.8	23 11.1
10 T	9 13 35.2	15 39.6	0 9.2	28 12.0	6 40.6	21 33.8	12 4.5	11 2.4	6 25.8	23 30.1	4 29.4	23 9.6
13 S	9 25 24.9	14 46.1	0 5.4	18 46.6	4 43.9	21 3.3	12 44.8	11 10.9	6 17.6	23 29.7	4 31.2	23 8.0
16 W	9 37 14.5	13 50.4	0 1.6	0 35.7	2 51.9	20 27.2	13 24.8	11 19.6	6 9.3	23 29.2	4 33.0	23 6.5
19 S	9 49 4.2	12 52.7	0S 2.2	18S 21.4	1 6.3	19 45.9	14 4.5	11 28.4	6 0.9	23 28.8	4 34.9	23 5.0
22 T	10 0 53.9	11 53.2	0 6.0	28 27.5	0S 30.9	18 59.4	14 43.7	11 37.2	5 52.4	23 28.4	4 36.9	23 3.6
25 F	10 12 43.5	10 52.1	0 9.8	23 1.6	1 57.3	18 8.1	15 22.5	11 46.1	5 43.9	23 27.9	4 38.9	23 2.2
28 M	10 24 33.2	9 49.4	0 13.6	6 54.9	3 9.8	17 12.1	16 0.6	11 54.8	5 35.3	23 27.5	4 41.0	23 0.8
31 T	10 36 22.9	8 45.3	0 17.4	10N52.9	4 4.8	16 11.7	16 38.1	12 3.5	5 26.6	23 27.2	4 43.2	22 59.5

SEPTEMBER 1950

DAY	EPHEMERIS SIDEREAL TIME	☉	☊	☽	☿	♀	♂	♃	♄	♅	♆	♇
	h m s	° ′	° ′	° ′	° ′	° ′	° ′	° ′	° ′	° ′	° ′	° ′
LONGITUDE at NOON												
1 F	10 40 19.4	8♍28.7	29♓13.1	4♉50.7	2♎ 7.2	19♌27.5	13♏39.0	1♓40.1	20♍52.3	8♋38.6	15♎42.6	18♌28.9
2 S	10 44 16.0	9 26.8	29 10.0	16 46.3	2 18.6	20 41.2	14 18.1	1R32.3	20 59.7	8 40.8	15 44.5	18 30.6
3 S	10 48 12.5	10 24.9	29 6.8	28 38.1	2 24.5	21 55.0	14 57.2	1 24.6	21 7.1	8 42.9	15 46.4	18 32.3
4 M	10 52 9.1	11 23.0	29 3.6	10♊30.8	2 24.5	23 8.8	15 36.4	1 16.9	21 14.5	8 45.0	15 48.3	18 34.1
5 T	10 56 5.6	12 21.2	29 0.4	22 29.1	2R18.4	24 22.7	16 15.8	1 9.3	21 21.9	8 47.1	15 50.2	18 35.8
6 W	11 0 2.2	13 19.4	28 57.2	4♋37.7	2 6.1	25 36.6	16 55.3	1 1.7	21 29.3	8 49.1	15 52.2	18 37.5
7 T	11 3 58.7	14 17.6	28 54.1	17 0.7	1 47.4	26 50.6	17 34.9	0 54.2	21 36.8	8 51.0	15 54.1	18 39.2
8 F	11 7 55.3	15 15.9	28 50.9	29 41.5	1 22.2	28 4.6	18 14.6	0 46.7	21 44.2	8 52.9	15 56.1	18 40.9
9 S	11 11 51.9	16 14.2	28 47.7	12♌42.5	0 50.5	29 18.6	18 54.5	0 39.4	21 51.7	8 54.8	15 58.1	18 42.6
10 S	11 15 48.4	17 12.6	28 44.5	26 4.8	0 12.5	0♍32.7	19 34.5	0 32.1	21 59.2	8 56.7	16 0.1	18 44.3
11 M	11 19 45.0	18 11.0	28 41.4	9♍47.5	29♍28.6	1 46.8	20 14.5	0 24.9	22 6.7	8 58.4	16 2.1	18 45.9
12 T	11 23 41.5	19 9.4	28 38.2	23 48.4	28 39.1	3 0.9	20 54.7	0 17.8	22 14.2	9 0.2	16 4.2	18 47.6
13 W	11 27 38.1	20 7.8	28 35.0	8♎ 3.8	27 44.8	4 15.1	21 35.0	0 10.8	22 21.7	9 1.9	16 6.2	18 49.2
14 T	11 31 34.6	21 6.2	28 31.8	22 29.0	26 46.6	5 29.3	22 15.4	0 3.9	22 29.2	9 3.5	16 8.3	18 50.8
15 F	11 35 31.2	22 4.7	28 28.6	6♏58.6	25 45.6	6 43.6	22 55.9	29♒57.1	22 36.7	9 5.1	16 10.3	18 52.4
16 S	11 39 27.7	23 3.2	28 25.5	21 27.6	24 42.9	7 57.8	23 36.6	29 50.4	22 44.2	9 6.6	16 12.4	18 54.0
17 S	11 43 24.3	24 1.8	28 22.3	5♐51.6	23 40.0	9 12.1	24 17.3	29 43.9	22 51.7	9 8.1	16 14.5	18 55.6
18 M	11 47 20.8	25 0.4	28 19.1	20 7.0	22 38.4	10 26.5	24 58.1	29 37.4	22 59.2	9 9.6	16 16.6	18 57.1
19 T	11 51 17.4	25 59.0	28 15.9	4♑11.4	21 39.7	11 40.8	25 39.1	29 31.1	23 6.7	9 10.9	16 18.7	18 58.7
20 W	11 55 13.9	26 57.6	28 12.8	18 3.2	20 45.2	12 55.2	26 20.1	29 24.9	23 14.1	9 12.3	16 20.9	19 0.2
21 T	11 59 10.5	27 56.2	28 9.6	1♒41.5	19 56.5	14 9.7	27 1.3	29 18.9	23 21.6	9 13.6	16 23.0	19 1.7
22 F	12 3 7.1	28 54.9	28 6.4	15 6.1	19 14.9	15 24.1	27 42.5	29 13.0	23 29.1	9 14.8	16 25.1	19 3.2
23 S	12 7 3.6	29 53.6	28 3.2	28 16.9	18 41.3	16 38.6	28 23.9	29 7.2	23 36.5	9 16.0	16 27.3	19 4.7
24 S	12 11 0.2	0♎52.3	28 0.0	11♓13.9	18 16.7	17 53.1	29 5.3	29 1.6	23 44.0	9 17.2	16 29.5	19 6.1
25 M	12 14 56.7	1 51.1	27 56.9	23 57.5	18 1.7	19 7.7	29 46.8	28 56.1	23 51.5	9 18.3	16 31.6	19 7.6
26 T	12 18 53.3	2 49.9	27 53.7	6♈28.4	17 56.7	20 22.2	0♐28.5	28 50.8	23 58.9	9 19.3	16 33.8	19 9.0
27 W	12 22 49.8	3 48.8	27 50.5	18 47.5	18D 1.9	21 36.8	1 10.2	28 45.7	24 6.3	9 20.3	16 36.0	19 10.4
28 T	12 26 46.4	4 47.6	27 47.3	0♉56.0	18 17.1	22 51.5	1 52.0	28 40.7	24 13.7	9 21.3	16 38.2	19 11.8
29 F	12 30 42.9	5 46.5	27 44.2	12 56.1	18 42.2	24 6.1	2 33.9	28 35.9	24 21.1	9 22.2	16 40.4	19 13.2
30 S	12 34 39.5	6 45.5	27 41.0	24 50.2	19 16.7	25 20.8	3 15.9	28 31.2	24 28.5	9 23.0	16 42.6	19 14.5
DECLINATION at NOON												
1 F	10 40 19.4	8N23.6	0S18.7	16N 5.1	4S18.4	15N50.7	16S50.4	12S 6.3	5N23.7	23N27.0	4S43.9	22N59.1
4 M	10 52 9.1	7 17.9	0 22.4	26 59.2	4 42.5	14 44.9	17 26.9	12 14.8	5 14.9	23 26.7	4 46.2	22 57.8
7 T	11 3 58.7	6 11.0	0 26.2	27 19.0	4 37.2	13 35.3	18 2.6	12 22.9	5 6.2	23 26.4	4 48.5	22 56.7
10 S	11 15 48.4	5 3.2	0 30.0	15 28.9	3 57.9	12 22.2	18 37.3	12 30.8	4 57.4	23 26.1	4 50.8	22 55.5
13 W	11 27 38.1	3 54.7	0 33.8	4S 1.2	2 43.5	11 6.1	19 11.0	12 38.3	4 48.6	23 25.8	4 53.2	22 54.5
16 S	11 39 27.7	2 45.5	0 37.6	22 12.8	0 59.8	9 47.1	19 43.6	12 45.4	4 39.8	23 25.5	4 55.6	22 53.5
19 T	11 51 17.4	1 35.8	0 41.4	28 38.2	0N58.0	8 25.6	20 15.0	12 52.1	4 31.0	23 25.3	4 58.1	22 52.5
22 F	12 3 7.1	0 25.9	0 45.2	19 46.6	2 48.6	7 2.0	20 45.1	12 58.3	4 22.3	23 25.1	5 0.6	22 51.7
25 M	12 14 56.7	0S44.2	0 49.0	2 46.5	4 11.9	5 36.5	21 13.8	13 4.0	4 13.6	23 24.9	5 3.1	22 50.9
28 T	12 26 46.4	1 54.3	0 52.8	14N28.1	4 54.8	4 9.5	21 41.0	13 9.2	4 5.0	23 24.8	5 5.6	22 50.2

OCTOBER 1950

DAY	EPHEMERIS SIDEREAL TIME	☉	☊	☽	☿	♀	♂	♃	♄	♅	♆	♇
LONGITUDE at NOON												
1 S	12 38 36.0	7♎44.5	27♓37.8	6♊41.4	20♍ 0.3	26♍35.6	3♐58.1	28♒26.7	24♍35.9	9♋23.8	16♎44.8	19♌15.9
2 M	12 42 32.6	8 43.5	27 34.6	18 33.4	20 52.2	27 50.3	4 40.3	28R22.4	24 43.3	9 24.6	16 47.1	19 17.2
3 T	12 46 29.1	9 42.6	27 31.4	0♋30.3	21 51.7	29 5.1	5 22.6	28 18.3	24 50.6	9 25.3	16 49.3	19 18.5
4 W	12 50 25.7	10 41.7	27 28.3	12 36.5	22 58.2	0♎19.9	6 4.9	28 14.3	24 57.9	9 25.9	16 51.5	19 19.8
5 T	12 54 22.3	11 40.8	27 25.1	24 56.7	24 11.0	1 34.7	6 47.4	28 10.5	25 5.2	9 26.5	16 53.7	19 21.0
6 F	12 58 18.8	12 40.0	27 21.9	7♌35.2	25 29.3	2 49.5	7 30.0	28 6.9	25 12.5	9 27.0	16 55.9	19 22.3
7 S	13 2 15.4	13 39.2	27 18.7	20 35.6	26 52.3	4 4.4	8 12.7	28 3.5	25 19.8	9 27.5	16 58.2	19 23.5
8 S	13 6 11.9	14 38.4	27 15.6	4♍ 0.8	28 19.5	5 19.3	8 55.4	28 0.2	25 27.0	9 27.9	17 0.4	19 24.6
9 M	13 10 8.5	15 37.7	27 12.4	17 51.5	29 50.3	6 34.2	9 38.3	27 57.2	25 34.2	9 28.3	17 2.6	19 25.8
10 T	13 14 5.0	16 37.0	27 9.2	2♎ 6.5	1♎23.9	7 49.2	10 21.2	27 54.3	25 41.4	9 28.6	17 4.9	19 26.9
11 W	13 18 1.6	17 36.4	27 6.0	16 42.1	3 0.0	9 4.2	11 4.2	27 51.7	25 48.6	9 28.8	17 7.1	19 28.1
12 T	13 21 58.1	18 35.8	27 2.8	1♏32.3	4 38.1	10 19.1	11 47.3	27 49.2	25 55.7	9 29.0	17 9.4	19 29.2
13 F	13 25 54.7	19 35.2	26 59.7	16 29.1	6 17.7	11 34.1	12 30.5	27 46.9	26 2.8	9 29.2	17 11.6	19 30.2
14 S	13 29 51.2	20 34.6	26 56.5	1♐24.0	7 58.5	12 49.2	13 13.8	27 44.9	26 9.9	9 29.3	17 13.8	19 31.3
15 S	13 33 47.8	21 34.1	26 53.3	16 9.2	9 40.1	14 4.2	13 57.2	27 43.0	26 16.9	9 29.3	17 16.0	19 32.3
16 M	13 37 44.4	22 33.6	26 50.1	0♑38.5	11 22.5	15 19.2	14 40.6	27 41.3	26 23.9	9 29.3	17 18.3	19 33.3
17 T	13 41 40.9	23 33.2	26 47.0	14 48.2	13 5.2	16 34.3	15 24.2	27 39.9	26 30.9	9 29.3	17 20.5	19 34.3
18 W	13 45 37.5	24 32.7	26 43.8	28 36.6	14 48.2	17 49.4	16 7.8	27 38.6	26 37.8	9R29.1	17 22.7	19 35.2
19 T	13 49 34.0	25 32.3	26 40.6	12♒ 4.1	16 31.2	19 4.5	16 51.5	27 37.5	26 44.7	9 29.0	17 24.9	19 36.2
20 F	13 53 30.6	26 32.0	26 37.4	25 12.4	18 14.1	20 19.6	17 35.2	27 36.7	26 51.5	9 28.8	17 27.2	19 37.1
21 S	13 57 27.1	27 31.6	26 34.2	8♓ 3.7	19 56.9	21 34.7	18 19.1	27 36.0	26 58.4	9 28.5	17 29.4	19 37.9
22 S	14 1 23.7	28 31.4	26 31.1	20 40.7	21 39.5	22 49.9	19 3.0	27 35.6	27 5.2	9 28.2	17 31.6	19 38.8
23 M	14 5 20.2	29 31.1	26 27.9	3♈ 5.7	23 21.7	24 5.0	19 47.0	27 35.4	27 11.9	9 27.8	17 33.8	19 39.6
24 T	14 9 16.8	0♏30.8	26 24.7	15 20.8	25 3.6	25 20.2	20 31.1	27 35.3	27 18.6	9 27.4	17 36.0	19 40.4
25 W	14 13 13.3	1 30.6	26 21.5	27 27.8	26 45.0	26 35.3	21 15.2	27D35.5	27 25.3	9 26.9	17 38.2	19 41.2
26 T	14 17 9.9	2 30.4	26 18.4	9♉28.4	28 26.0	27 50.5	21 59.4	27 35.8	27 31.9	9 26.4	17 40.4	19 42.0
27 F	14 21 6.5	3 30.3	26 15.2	21 24.0	0♏ 6.6	29 5.7	22 43.7	27 36.4	27 38.4	9 25.8	17 42.5	19 42.7
28 S	14 25 3.0	4 30.1	26 12.0	3♊16.3	1 46.7	0♏20.9	23 28.1	27 37.1	27 45.0	9 25.1	17 44.7	19 43.4
29 S	14 28 59.6	5 30.1	26 8.8	15 7.4	3 26.3	1 36.1	24 12.5	27 38.1	27 51.4	9 24.4	17 46.9	19 44.0
30 M	14 32 56.1	6 30.0	26 5.7	26 59.6	5 5.4	2 51.4	24 57.0	27 39.2	27 57.9	9 23.7	17 49.0	19 44.7
31 T	14 36 52.7	7 30.0	26 2.5	8♋56.0	6 44.1	4 6.6	25 41.6	27 40.6	28 4.2	9 22.9	17 51.1	19 45.3
DECLINATION at NOON												
1 S	12 38 36.0	3S 4.4	0S56.6	26N15.9	4N53.3	2N41.2	22S 6.7	13S13.8	3N56.4	23N24.7	5S 8.2	22N49.5
4 W	12 50 25.7	4 14.1	1 0.4	27 56.2	4 10.8	1 12.1	22 30.8	13 17.8	3 47.9	23 24.6	5 10.7	22 49.0
7 S	13 2 15.4	5 23.4	1 4.2	17 41.5	2 54.8	0S17.6	22 53.1	13 21.2	3 39.5	23 24.6	5 13.3	22 48.5
10 T	13 14 5.0	6 32.0	1 7.9	1S 9.3	1 14.1	1 47.6	23 13.7	13 24.0	3 31.2	23 24.6	5 15.8	22 48.1
13 F	13 25 54.7	7 40.0	1 11.7	20 31.0	0S42.6	3 17.4	23 32.3	13 26.2	3 23.1	23 24.6	5 18.4	22 47.8
16 M	13 37 44.4	8 46.9	1 15.5	28 40.6	2 48.5	4 46.8	23 49.0	13 27.7	3 15.0	23 24.7	5 20.9	22 47.6
19 T	13 49 34.0	9 52.7	1 19.3	20 48.2	4 58.4	6 15.3	24 3.7	13 28.6	3 7.1	23 24.8	5 23.4	22 47.5
22 S	14 1 23.7	10 57.2	1 23.1	4 19.5	7 8.6	7 42.7	24 16.3	13 28.8	2 59.3	23 24.9	5 25.9	22 47.4
25 W	14 13 13.3	12 0.2	1 26.9	12N57.0	9 16.6	9 8.6	24 26.7	13 28.4	2 51.8	23 25.1	5 28.4	22 47.5
28 S	14 25 3.0	13 1.6	1 30.7	25 25.7	11 20.5	10 32.7	24 34.8	13 27.4	2 44.4	23 25.3	5 30.8	22 47.6
31 T	14 36 52.7	14 1.1	1 34.4	28 11.6	13 19.2	11 54.6	24 40.7	13 25.7	2 37.1	23 25.5	5 33.2	22 47.8

NOVEMBER 1950

DAY	EPHEMERIS SIDEREAL TIME	☉	☊	☽	☿	♀	♂	♃	♄	♅	♆	♇
	h m s	° ′	° ′	° ′	° ′	° ′	° ′	° ′	° ′	° ′	° ′	° ′
						LONGITUDE at NOON						
1 W	14 40 49.2	8♏30.0	25♓59.3	21♋ 0.3	8♏22.3	5♏21.9	26♐26.2	27♒42.2	28♍10.6	9♋22.0	17♎53.3	19♌45.9
2 T	14 44 45.8	9 30.0	25 56.1	3♌16.5	9 60.0	6 37.1	27 10.9	27 43.9	28 16.8	9R21.1	17 55.4	19 46.4
3 F	14 48 42.3	10 30.1	25 52.9	15 49.2	11 37.3	7 52.4	27 55.7	27 45.9	28 23.0	9 20.2	17 57.5	19 47.0
4 S	14 52 38.9	11 30.3	25 49.8	28 42.7	13 14.1	9 7.7	28 40.5	27 48.1	28 29.2	9 19.2	17 59.6	19 47.5
5 S	14 56 35.5	12 30.4	25 46.6	12♍ 1.2	14 50.5	10 23.0	29 25.4	27 50.4	28 35.3	9 18.1	18 1.7	19 47.9
6 M	15 0 32.0	13 30.6	25 43.4	25 47.4	16 26.5	11 38.3	0♑10.4	27 53.0	28 41.4	9 17.0	18 3.7	19 48.4
7 T	15 4 28.6	14 30.8	25 40.2	10♎ 2.0	18 2.1	12 53.7	0 55.5	27 55.7	28 47.4	9 15.9	18 5.8	19 48.8
8 W	15 8 25.1	15 31.1	25 37.1	24 43.1	19 37.4	14 9.0	1 40.6	27 58.7	28 53.3	9 14.7	18 7.8	19 49.2
9 T	15 12 21.7	16 31.4	25 33.9	9♏45.1	21 12.3	15 24.3	2 25.8	28 1.8	28 59.2	9 13.5	18 9.8	19 49.5
10 F	15 16 18.2	17 31.7	25 30.7	24 59.6	22 46.8	16 39.7	3 11.0	28 5.2	29 5.0	9 12.2	18 11.9	19 49.9
11 S	15 20 14.8	18 32.1	25 27.5	10♐15.8	24 21.0	17 55.0	3 56.3	28 8.7	29 10.7	9 10.8	18 13.8	19 50.2
12 S	15 24 11.4	19 32.5	25 24.4	25 22.7	25 55.0	19 10.5	4 41.7	28 12.5	29 16.5	9 9.5	18 15.9	19 50.5
13 M	15 28 7.9	20 32.9	25 21.2	10♑11.1	27 28.6	20 25.8	5 27.2	28 16.4	29 22.1	9 8.1	18 17.8	19 50.7
14 T	15 32 4.5	21 33.3	25 18.0	24 34.6	29 1.9	21 41.2	6 12.7	28 20.5	29 27.6	9 6.6	18 19.8	19 51.0
15 W	15 36 1.0	22 33.7	25 14.8	8♒30.5	0♐34.9	22 56.5	6 58.2	28 24.8	29 33.1	9 5.1	18 21.7	19 51.1
16 T	15 39 57.6	23 34.2	25 11.6	21 59.0	2 7.7	24 11.9	7 43.8	28 29.3	29 38.5	9 3.5	18 23.6	19 51.3
17 F	15 43 54.1	24 34.7	25 8.5	5♓ 2.5	3 40.2	25 27.3	8 29.4	28 34.0	29 43.9	9 1.9	18 25.5	19 51.4
18 S	15 47 50.7	25 35.2	25 5.3	17 44.9	5 12.5	26 42.7	9 15.2	28 38.8	29 49.1	9 0.3	18 27.4	19 51.5
19 S	15 51 47.3	26 35.7	25 2.1	0♈10.3	6 44.5	27 58.0	10 0.9	28 43.9	29 54.3	8 58.6	18 29.3	19 51.6
20 M	15 55 43.8	27 36.3	24 58.9	12 23.0	8 16.3	29 13.4	10 46.7	28 49.1	29 59.5	8 56.9	18 31.1	19 51.6
21 T	15 59 40.4	28 36.9	24 55.8	24 26.5	9 47.9	0♐28.8	11 32.6	28 54.5	0♎ 4.5	8 55.1	18 32.9	19 51.6
22 W	16 3 36.9	29 37.5	24 52.6	6♉24.1	11 19.3	1 44.2	12 18.5	29 0.0	0 9.5	8 53.3	18 34.7	19 51.6
23 T	16 7 33.5	0♐38.1	24 49.4	18 18.1	12 50.4	2 59.6	13 4.4	29 5.8	0 14.4	8 51.5	18 36.5	19 51.6
24 F	16 11 30.0	1 38.7	24 46.2	0♊10.4	14 21.3	4 15.0	13 50.4	29 11.7	0 19.2	8 49.6	18 38.2	19R51.5
25 S	16 15 26.6	2 39.4	24 43.1	12 2.5	15 51.9	5 30.3	14 36.5	29 17.8	0 24.0	8 47.7	18 40.0	19 51.4
26 S	16 19 23.2	3 40.1	24 39.9	23 55.8	17 22.2	6 45.7	15 22.6	29 24.0	0 28.6	8 45.7	18 41.7	19 51.3
27 M	16 23 19.7	4 40.8	24 36.7	5♋51.6	18 52.3	8 1.1	16 8.7	29 30.5	0 33.2	8 43.7	18 43.4	19 51.1
28 T	16 27 16.3	5 41.5	24 33.5	17 51.8	20 22.0	9 16.5	16 54.9	29 37.0	0 37.7	8 41.7	18 45.0	19 50.9
29 W	16 31 12.8	6 42.3	24 30.4	29 58.7	21 51.3	10 31.9	17 41.1	29 43.8	0 42.2	8 39.6	18 46.7	19 50.7
30 T	16 35 9.4	7 43.1	24 27.2	12♌15.5	23 20.3	11 47.3	18 27.4	29 50.7	0 46.5	8 37.5	18 48.3	19 50.5
						DECLINATION at NOON						
1 W	14 40 49.2	14S20.5	1S35.7	26N29.0	13S57.4	12S21.4	24S42.2	13S25.0	2N34.8	23N25.6	5S34.0	22N47.9
4 S	14 52 38.9	15 17.4	1 39.5	14 15.4	15 47.5	13 39.8	24 45.0	13 22.5	2 27.8	23 25.8	5 36.3	22 48.3
7 T	15 4 28.6	16 12.0	1 43.3	5S 0.3	17 30.4	14 55.2	24 45.4	13 19.4	2 21.1	23 26.1	5 38.6	22 48.7
10 F	15 16 18.2	17 4.1	1 47.1	23 12.8	19 5.3	16 7.2	24 43.4	13 15.6	2 14.6	23 26.5	5 40.8	22 49.3
13 M	15 28 7.9	17 53.7	1 50.8	28 0.4	20 31.8	17 15.4	24 38.9	13 11.2	2 8.4	23 26.8	5 43.0	22 49.9
16 T	15 39 57.6	18 40.4	1 54.6	16 56.5	21 49.2	18 19.5	24 32.1	13 6.3	2 2.4	23 27.2	5 45.1	22 50.6
19 S	15 51 47.3	19 24.1	1 58.4	0N21.1	22 56.9	19 19.1	24 22.7	13 0.7	1 56.7	23 27.6	5 47.1	22 51.3
22 W	16 3 36.9	20 4.7	2 2.2	16 43.2	23 54.3	20 13.9	24 11.0	12 54.6	1 51.3	23 28.0	5 49.1	22 52.2
25 S	16 15 26.6	20 41.9	2 6.0	27 4.5	24 40.7	21 3.6	23 56.7	12 48.0	1 46.2	23 28.5	5 51.0	22 53.2
28 T	16 27 16.3	21 15.7	2 9.7	26 51.5	25 15.6	21 47.9	23 40.1	12 40.8	1 41.3	23 28.9	5 52.8	22 54.2

DECEMBER 1950

DAY	EPHEMERIS SIDEREAL TIME	☉	☊	☽	☿	♀	♂	♃	♄	♅	♆	♇
						LONGITUDE at NOON						
1 F	16 39 6.0	8♐43.9	24♓24.0	24♌45.7	24♐48.7	13♐ 2.7	19♑13.7	29♒57.8	0♎50.8	8♋35.4	18♎49.9	19♌50.2
2 S	16 43 2.5	9 44.7	24 20.8	7♍33.4	26 16.7	14 18.2	20 0.1	0♓ 5.0	0 54.9	8R33.3	18 51.5	19R49.9
3 S	16 46 59.1	10 45.6	24 17.6	20 43.0	27 44.0	15 33.6	20 46.5	0 12.5	0 59.1	8 31.1	18 53.0	19 49.6
4 M	16 50 55.6	11 46.5	24 14.5	4♎17.9	29 10.6	16 49.0	21 33.0	0 20.0	1 3.1	8 28.9	18 54.6	19 49.2
5 T	16 54 52.2	12 47.4	24 11.3	18 20.8	0♑36.3	18 4.5	22 19.5	0 27.7	1 7.0	8 26.7	18 56.1	19 48.9
6 W	16 58 48.7	13 48.3	24 8.1	2♏51.6	2 1.1	19 19.9	23 6.0	0 35.6	1 10.8	8 24.4	18 57.5	19 48.4
7 T	17 2 45.3	14 49.2	24 4.9	17 47.0	3 24.7	20 35.3	23 52.6	0 43.6	1 14.5	8 22.1	18 59.0	19 48.0
8 F	17 6 41.9	15 50.2	24 1.8	3♐ 0.2	4 47.0	21 50.7	24 39.2	0 51.7	1 18.1	8 19.8	19 0.4	19 47.5
9 S	17 10 38.4	16 51.2	23 58.6	18 21.0	6 7.7	23 6.2	25 25.8	1 0.0	1 21.7	8 17.4	19 1.8	19 47.0
10 S	17 14 35.0	17 52.2	23 55.4	3♑37.6	7 26.6	24 21.6	26 12.5	1 8.5	1 25.1	8 15.1	19 3.1	19 46.5
11 M	17 18 31.5	18 53.2	23 52.2	18 38.8	8 43.4	25 37.0	26 59.2	1 17.1	1 28.5	8 12.7	19 4.5	19 46.0
12 T	17 22 28.1	19 54.2	23 49.1	3♒15.8	9 57.7	26 52.4	27 46.0	1 25.8	1 31.7	8 10.3	19 5.8	19 45.4
13 W	17 26 24.7	20 55.2	23 45.9	17 23.5	11 9.1	28 7.9	28 32.8	1 34.7	1 34.9	8 7.8	19 7.1	19 44.8
14 T	17 30 21.2	21 56.3	23 42.7	1♓ 0.8	12 17.1	29 23.3	29 19.6	1 43.7	1 38.0	8 5.4	19 8.3	19 44.2
15 F	17 34 17.8	22 57.3	23 39.5	14 9.4	13 21.3	0♑38.7	0♒ 6.4	1 52.9	1 40.9	8 2.9	19 9.5	19 43.5
16 S	17 38 14.3	23 58.4	23 36.4	26 53.1	14 21.1	1 54.1	0 53.3	2 2.2	1 43.8	8 0.5	19 10.7	19 42.8
17 S	17 42 10.9	24 59.4	23 33.2	9♈16.6	15 15.7	3 9.5	1 40.2	2 11.6	1 46.6	7 58.0	19 11.9	19 42.1
18 M	17 46 7.5	26 0.5	23 30.0	21 25.2	16 4.4	4 24.9	2 27.1	2 21.1	1 49.2	7 55.4	19 13.0	19 41.4
19 T	17 50 4.0	27 1.6	23 26.8	3♉23.8	16 46.5	5 40.3	3 14.0	2 30.8	1 51.8	7 52.9	19 14.1	19 40.6
20 W	17 54 0.6	28 2.6	23 23.6	15 16.6	17 21.0	6 55.7	4 1.0	2 40.6	1 54.3	7 50.4	19 15.2	19 39.8
21 T	17 57 57.1	29 3.7	23 20.5	27 7.3	17 47.1	8 11.1	4 48.0	2 50.5	1 56.6	7 47.8	19 16.2	19 39.0
22 F	18 1 53.7	0♑ 4.8	23 17.3	8♊58.7	18 3.9	9 26.4	5 35.0	3 0.6	1 58.9	7 45.3	19 17.2	19 38.2
23 S	18 5 50.2	1 5.9	23 14.1	20 52.7	18 10.5	10 41.8	6 22.0	3 10.8	2 1.0	7 42.7	19 18.2	19 37.4
24 S	18 9 46.8	2 7.0	23 10.9	2♋50.9	18R 6.2	11 57.2	7 9.1	3 21.1	2 3.1	7 40.2	19 19.2	19 36.5
25 M	18 13 43.4	3 8.2	23 7.8	14 54.3	17 50.3	13 12.6	7 56.1	3 31.5	2 5.1	7 37.6	19 20.1	19 35.6
26 T	18 17 39.9	4 9.3	23 4.6	27 3.9	17 22.6	14 27.9	8 43.2	3 42.0	2 6.9	7 35.0	19 21.0	19 34.7
27 W	18 21 36.5	5 10.4	23 1.4	9♌20.7	16 43.2	15 43.3	9 30.3	3 52.6	2 8.7	7 32.4	19 21.8	19 33.8
28 T	18 25 33.0	6 11.5	22 58.2	21 46.5	15 52.6	16 58.6	10 17.4	4 3.4	2 10.3	7 29.9	19 22.6	19 32.8
29 F	18 29 29.6	7 12.6	22 55.1	4♍23.4	14 51.8	18 14.0	11 4.6	4 14.2	2 11.8	7 27.3	19 23.4	19 31.8
30 S	18 33 26.2	8 13.8	22 51.9	17 14.1	13 42.4	19 29.3	11 51.7	4 25.2	2 13.3	7 24.7	19 24.1	19 30.8
31 S	18 37 22.7	9 14.9	22 48.7	0♎21.9	12 26.4	20 44.7	12 38.9	4 36.3	2 14.6	7 22.1	19 24.9	19 29.8
						DECLINATION at NOON						
1 F	16 39 6.0	21S46.0	2S13.5	15N40.5	25S38.2	22S26.4	23S21.0	12S33.0	1N36.8	23N29.4	5S54.5	22N55.3
4 M	16 50 55.6	22 12.4	2 17.3	2S27.3	25 48.3	22 58.9	22 59.6	12 24.7	1 32.6	23 29.8	5 56.1	22 56.5
7 T	17 2 45.3	22 35.0	2 21.1	20 58.9	25 45.4	23 25.2	22 35.8	12 16.0	1 28.7	23 30.3	5 57.7	22 57.7
10 S	17 14 35.0	22 53.7	2 24.8	28 19.9	25 29.6	23 45.1	22 9.8	12 6.7	1 25.2	23 30.8	5 59.1	22 59.1
13 W	17 26 24.7	23 8.2	2 28.6	18 28.4	25 1.5	23 58.4	21 41.5	11 57.0	1 22.1	23 31.3	6 0.4	23 0.4
16 S	17 38 14.3	23 18.7	2 32.4	0 59.3	24 22.6	24 5.1	21 11.0	11 46.7	1 19.3	23 31.8	6 1.7	23 1.9
19 T	17 50 4.0	23 24.9	2 36.2	15N40.1	23 35.6	24 5.1	20 38.5	11 36.1	1 16.9	23 32.3	6 2.8	23 3.4
22 F	18 1 53.7	23 26.9	2 39.9	26 35.0	22 44.8	23 58.4	20 3.8	11 25.0	1 14.8	23 32.8	6 3.8	23 4.9
25 M	18 13 43.4	23 24.7	2 43.7	27 12.1	21 55.3	23 44.9	19 27.3	11 13.5	1 13.1	23 33.3	6 4.7	23 6.5
28 T	18 25 33.0	23 18.2	2 47.5	16 39.0	21 12.0	23 24.9	18 48.8	11 1.5	1 11.8	23 33.7	6 5.5	23 8.1
31 S	18 37 22.7	23 7.5	2 51.2	0S49.8	20 38.1	22 58.4	18 8.5	10 49.2	1 10.9	23 34.2	6 6.2	23 9.8

JANUARY 1951

DAY	EPHEMERIS SIDEREAL TIME	☉	☊	☽	☿	♀	♂	♃	♄	♅	♆	♇
	h m s	° ′	° ′	° ′	° ′	° ′	° ′	° ′	° ′	° ′	° ′	° ′
LONGITUDE at NOON												
1 M	18 41 19.3	10♑16.1	22♓45.5	13♎49.7	11♑ 6.4	21♑60.0	13♒26.0	4♓47.4	2♎15.8	7♋19.5	19♎25.5	19♌28.7
2 T	18 45 15.8	11 17.3	22 42.4	27 40.3	9R44.8	23 15.3	14 13.2	4 58.7	2 16.9	7R16.9	19 26.2	19R27.7
3 W	18 49 12.4	12 18.4	22 39.2	11♏54.4	8 24.5	24 30.7	15 0.4	5 10.1	2 17.9	7 14.3	19 26.8	19 26.6
4 T	18 53 9.0	13 19.6	22 36.0	26 31.0	7 7.9	25 46.0	15 47.7	5 21.5	2 18.7	7 11.7	19 27.4	19 25.5
5 F	18 57 5.5	14 20.8	22 32.8	11♐25.5	5 57.1	27 1.3	16 34.9	5 33.1	2 19.5	7 9.2	19 27.9	19 24.4
6 S	19 1 2.1	15 21.9	22 29.7	26 30.7	4 54.0	28 16.6	17 22.1	5 44.8	2 20.2	7 6.6	19 28.5	19 23.2
7 S	19 4 58.6	16 23.1	22 26.5	11♑36.7	3 59.8	29 31.9	18 9.4	5 56.6	2 20.7	7 4.1	19 28.9	19 22.1
8 M	19 8 55.2	17 24.3	22 23.3	26 33.3	3 15.1	0♒47.2	18 56.6	6 8.4	2 21.2	7 1.5	19 29.4	19 20.9
9 T	19 12 51.7	18 25.5	22 20.1	11♒11.3	2 40.5	2 2.5	19 43.9	6 20.4	2 21.5	6 59.0	19 29.8	19 19.7
10 W	19 16 48.3	19 26.6	22 16.9	25 24.1	2 15.8	3 17.7	20 31.2	6 32.4	2 21.7	6 56.5	19 30.2	19 18.5
11 T	19 20 44.9	20 27.8	22 13.8	9♓ 8.7	2 0.8	4 33.0	21 18.5	6 44.5	2 21.8	6 53.9	19 30.5	19 17.2
12 F	19 24 41.4	21 28.9	22 10.6	22 24.8	1 55.1	5 48.2	22 5.7	6 56.7	2 21.8	6 51.5	19 30.8	19 16.0
13 S	19 28 38.0	22 30.1	22 7.4	5♈15.0	1D58.1	7 3.5	22 53.0	7 9.0	2R21.7	6 49.0	19 31.1	19 14.8
14 S	19 32 34.5	23 31.2	22 4.2	17 43.3	2 9.2	8 18.7	23 40.3	7 21.5	2 21.5	6 46.6	19 31.4	19 13.5
15 M	19 36 31.1	24 32.4	22 1.1	29 54.5	2 27.7	9 33.9	24 27.6	7 33.9	2 21.2	6 44.1	19 31.6	19 12.2
16 T	19 40 27.7	25 33.5	21 57.9	11♉54.0	2 53.0	10 49.1	25 14.9	7 46.4	2 20.8	6 41.7	19 31.8	19 11.0
17 W	19 44 24.2	26 34.6	21 54.7	23 46.8	3 24.4	12 4.3	26 2.2	7 59.1	2 20.2	6 39.3	19 31.9	19 9.6
18 T	19 48 20.8	27 35.6	21 51.5	5♊37.3	4 1.4	13 19.5	26 49.4	8 11.7	2 19.6	6 36.9	19 32.0	19 8.3
19 F	19 52 17.3	28 36.7	21 48.4	17 29.6	4 43.4	14 34.6	27 36.7	8 24.5	2 18.8	6 34.6	19 32.1	19 7.0
20 S	19 56 13.9	29 37.7	21 45.2	29 26.7	5 29.9	15 49.7	28 23.9	8 37.3	2 18.0	6 32.3	19 32.1	19 5.6
21 S	20 0 10.4	0♒38.8	21 42.0	11♋30.9	6 20.6	17 4.8	29 11.2	8 50.2	2 17.0	6 29.9	19 32.1	19 4.3
22 M	20 4 7.0	1 39.8	21 38.8	23 43.8	7 14.9	18 19.9	29 58.4	9 3.2	2 15.9	6 27.7	19 32.1	19 2.9
23 T	20 8 3.6	2 40.8	21 35.7	6♌ 6.2	8 12.5	19 35.0	0♓45.6	9 16.2	2 14.7	6 25.4	19R32.0	19 1.6
24 W	20 12 0.1	3 41.8	21 32.5	18 38.8	9 13.2	20 50.0	1 32.9	9 29.3	2 13.4	6 23.2	19 31.9	19 0.2
25 T	20 15 56.7	4 42.8	21 29.3	1♍21.9	10 16.6	22 5.1	2 20.1	9 42.5	2 12.0	6 21.0	19 31.7	18 58.8
26 F	20 19 53.2	5 43.8	21 26.1	14 16.1	11 22.4	23 20.1	3 7.3	9 55.7	2 10.5	6 18.8	19 31.6	18 57.4
27 S	20 23 49.8	6 44.8	21 22.9	27 22.2	12 30.6	24 35.1	3 54.5	10 9.0	2 8.9	6 16.7	19 31.4	18 56.0
28 S	20 27 46.3	7 45.7	21 19.8	10♎41.1	13 40.8	25 50.1	4 41.6	10 22.3	2 7.2	6 14.6	19 31.1	18 54.6
29 M	20 31 42.9	8 46.7	21 16.6	24 14.3	14 52.9	27 5.0	5 28.8	10 35.7	2 5.4	6 12.5	19 30.9	18 53.1
30 T	20 35 39.5	9 47.6	21 13.4	8♏ 2.7	16 6.7	28 20.0	6 16.0	10 49.2	2 3.5	6 10.5	19 30.5	18 51.7
31 W	20 39 36.0	10 48.5	21 10.2	22 6.6	17 22.2	29 34.9	7 3.1	11 2.7	2 1.5	6 8.4	19 30.2	18 50.3
DECLINATION at NOON												
1 M	18 41 19.3	23S 3.1	2S52.5	7S12.1	20S29.2	22S48.1	17S54.7	10S45.1	1N10.7	23N34.4	6S 6.4	23N10.4
4 T	18 53 9.0	22 46.9	2 56.3	23 49.1	20 10.8	22 13.3	17 12.2	10 32.3	1 10.3	23 34.8	6 7.0	23 12.1
7 S	19 4 58.6	22 26.6	3 0.0	27 39.0	20 6.0	21 32.4	16 28.0	10 19.1	1 10.3	23 35.2	6 7.4	23 13.8
10 W	19 16 48.3	22 2.3	3 3.8	15 6.9	20 14.8	20 45.7	15 42.3	10 5.6	1 10.7	23 35.7	6 7.7	23 15.6
13 S	19 28 38.0	21 34.2	3 7.6	3N15.4	20 34.1	19 53.6	14 55.2	9 51.7	1 11.5	23 36.1	6 7.9	23 17.3
16 T	19 40 27.7	21 2.3	3 11.3	19 11.4	20 59.0	18 56.3	14 6.7	9 37.6	1 12.6	23 36.4	6 7.9	23 19.1
19 F	19 52 17.3	20 26.8	3 15.1	27 55.4	21 25.0	17 54.1	13 17.1	9 23.1	1 14.2	23 36.8	6 7.9	23 20.8
22 M	20 4 7.0	19 47.8	3 18.8	25 32.8	21 48.3	16 47.4	12 26.3	9 8.4	1 16.1	23 37.2	6 7.7	23 22.6
25 T	20 15 56.7	19 5.5	3 22.6	12 30.4	22 6.0	15 36.5	11 34.4	8 53.5	1 18.4	23 37.5	6 7.4	23 24.4
28 S	20 27 46.3	18 20.1	3 26.3	5S56.4	22 16.2	14 21.8	10 41.6	8 38.2	1 21.0	23 37.8	6 7.0	23 26.1
31 W	20 39 36.0	17 31.7	3 30.1	22 44.0	22 17.4	13 3.6	9 48.0	8 22.8	1 24.0	23 38.1	6 6.5	23 27.8

FEBRUARY 1951

DAY	EPHEMERIS SIDEREAL TIME	☉	☊	☽	☿	♀	♂	♃	♄	♅	♆	♇
LONGITUDE at NOON												
1 T	20 43 32.6	11♒49.4	21♓ 7.1	6♐25.2	18♑39.1	0♓49.8	7♓50.3	11♓16.2	1♎59.4	6♋ 6.5	19♎29.8	18♌48.8
2 F	20 47 29.1	12 50.3	21 3.9	20 55.9	19 57.5	2 4.7	8 37.4	11 29.9	1R57.2	6R 4.5	19R29.4	18R47.4
3 S	20 51 25.7	13 51.2	21 0.7	5♑34.1	21 17.2	3 19.6	9 24.5	11 43.5	1 54.9	6 2.6	19 29.0	18 46.0
4 S	20 55 22.2	14 52.1	20 57.5	20 13.8	22 38.2	4 34.5	10 11.6	11 57.3	1 52.6	6 0.8	19 28.6	18 44.6
5 M	20 59 18.8	15 53.0	20 54.4	4♒47.7	24 0.3	5 49.3	10 58.7	12 11.1	1 50.1	5 59.0	19 28.1	18 43.1
6 T	21 3 15.4	16 53.8	20 51.2	19 9.0	25 23.5	7 4.1	11 45.8	12 24.9	1 47.5	5 57.2	19 27.5	18 41.7
7 W	21 7 11.9	17 54.6	20 48.0	3♓11.8	26 47.8	8 18.9	12 32.8	12 38.7	1 44.8	5 55.5	19 27.0	18 40.2
8 T	21 11 8.5	18 55.4	20 44.8	16 52.4	28 13.1	9 33.6	13 19.8	12 52.6	1 42.0	5 53.8	19 26.4	18 38.8
9 F	21 15 5.0	19 56.2	20 41.6	0♈ 9.2	29 39.4	10 48.3	14 6.8	13 6.6	1 39.2	5 52.1	19 25.7	18 37.3
10 S	21 19 1.6	20 56.9	20 38.5	13 2.9	1♒ 6.7	12 3.0	14 53.8	13 20.6	1 36.3	5 50.5	19 25.1	18 35.9
11 S	21 22 58.1	21 57.7	20 35.3	25 35.8	2 35.0	13 17.7	15 40.8	13 34.6	1 33.2	5 48.9	19 24.4	18 34.4
12 M	21 26 54.7	22 58.3	20 32.1	7♉51.5	4 4.1	14 32.3	16 27.7	13 48.7	1 30.1	5 47.4	19 23.7	18 33.0
13 T	21 30 51.2	23 59.0	20 28.9	19 54.5	5 34.2	15 46.9	17 14.6	14 2.7	1 26.9	5 45.9	19 22.9	18 31.5
14 W	21 34 47.8	24 59.6	20 25.8	1♊49.6	7 5.2	17 1.5	18 1.5	14 16.9	1 23.6	5 44.4	19 22.1	18 30.1
15 T	21 38 44.4	26 0.3	20 22.6	13 41.6	8 37.1	18 16.0	18 48.3	14 31.0	1 20.3	5 43.0	19 21.3	18 28.6
16 F	21 42 40.9	27 0.8	20 19.4	25 35.2	10 9.9	19 30.5	19 35.1	14 45.2	1 16.9	5 41.7	19 20.5	18 27.2
17 S	21 46 37.5	28 1.4	20 16.2	7♋34.5	11 43.6	20 45.0	20 21.9	14 59.4	1 13.4	5 40.4	19 19.6	18 25.8
18 S	21 50 34.0	29 1.9	20 13.1	19 43.1	13 18.2	21 59.4	21 8.7	15 13.7	1 9.8	5 39.1	19 18.7	18 24.3
19 M	21 54 30.6	0♓ 2.4	20 9.9	2♌ 3.6	14 53.7	23 13.8	21 55.4	15 27.9	1 6.1	5 37.9	19 17.8	18 22.9
20 T	21 58 27.1	1 2.9	20 6.7	14 38.0	16 30.2	24 28.2	22 42.2	15 42.2	1 2.4	5 36.7	19 16.8	18 21.5
21 W	22 2 23.7	2 3.3	20 3.5	27 27.0	18 7.5	25 42.5	23 28.8	15 56.6	0 58.6	5 35.6	19 15.9	18 20.1
22 T	22 6 20.2	3 3.7	20 0.3	10♍30.9	19 45.8	26 56.8	24 15.5	16 10.9	0 54.8	5 34.6	19 14.8	18 18.7
23 F	22 10 16.8	4 4.1	19 57.2	23 48.9	21 25.1	28 11.0	25 2.1	16 25.3	0 50.9	5 33.5	19 13.8	18 17.3
24 S	22 14 13.4	5 4.4	19 54.0	7♎20.0	23 5.3	29 25.2	25 48.7	16 39.7	0 46.9	5 32.6	19 12.8	18 15.9
25 S	22 18 9.9	6 4.8	19 50.8	21 2.6	24 46.5	0♈39.4	26 35.3	16 54.1	0 42.9	5 31.7	19 11.7	18 14.6
26 M	22 22 6.5	7 5.1	19 47.6	4♏55.0	26 28.7	1 53.6	27 21.8	17 8.5	0 38.8	5 30.8	19 10.6	18 13.3
27 T	22 26 3.0	8 5.4	19 44.5	18 55.8	28 11.9	3 7.6	28 8.3	17 23.0	0 34.7	5 30.0	19 9.5	18 11.9
28 W	22 29 59.6	9 5.7	19 41.3	3♐ 3.0	29 56.1	4 21.7	28 54.7	17 37.4	0 30.5	5 29.3	19 8.3	18 10.6
DECLINATION at NOON												
1 T	20 43 32.6	17S15.0	3S31.4	26S21.0	22S15.6	12S36.8	9S29.9	8S17.6	1N25.1	23N38.2	6S 6.3	23N28.4
4 S	20 55 22.2	16 22.8	3 35.1	26 19.4	22 3.3	11 14.5	8 35.3	8 1.8	1 28.5	23 38.4	6 5.7	23 30.0
7 W	21 7 11.9	15 28.2	3 38.9	11 40.8	21 40.1	9 49.5	7 40.0	7 45.8	1 32.3	23 38.7	6 4.9	23 31.7
10 S	21 19 1.6	14 31.1	3 42.6	7N 6.2	21 5.7	8 22.2	6 44.2	7 29.7	1 36.3	23 38.9	6 4.1	23 33.3
13 T	21 30 51.2	13 31.9	3 46.4	22 6.9	20 19.6	6 53.0	5 47.9	7 13.4	1 40.6	23 39.1	6 3.1	23 34.9
16 F	21 42 40.9	12 30.7	3 50.1	28 34.5	19 21.8	5 22.2	4 51.3	6 57.0	1 45.2	23 39.2	6 2.0	23 36.4
19 M	21 54 30.6	11 27.7	3 53.9	23 26.9	18 11.9	3 50.1	3 54.4	6 40.4	1 50.0	23 39.4	6 0.9	23 37.8
22 T	22 6 20.2	10 23.1	3 57.6	8 20.8	16 50.0	2 17.1	2 57.3	6 23.7	1 55.0	23 39.5	5 59.6	23 39.2
25 S	22 18 9.9	9 17.1	4 1.3	10S48.6	15 16.0	0 43.5	2 0.2	6 6.9	2 0.2	23 39.6	5 58.3	23 40.6
28 W	22 29 59.6	8 9.8	4 5.1	25 44.9	13 30.0	0N50.3	1 3.0	5 50.0	2 5.6	23 39.7	5 56.9	23 41.9

MARCH 1951

DAY	EPHEMERIS SIDEREAL TIME	☉	☊	☽	☿	♀	♂	♃	♄	♅	♆	♇
	h m s	° ′	° ′	° ′	° ′	° ′	° ′	° ′	° ′	° ′	° ′	° ′
LONGITUDE at NOON												
1 T	22 33 56.1	10♓ 5.9	19♓38.1	17♐14.8	1♓41.4	5♈35.7	29♓41.2	17♓51.9	0♎26.2	5♋28.5	19♎ 7.2	18♌ 9.2
2 F	22 37 52.7	11 6.1	19 34.9	1♑29.1	3 27.6	6 49.7	0♈27.5	18 6.4	0R21.9	5R27.9	19R 6.0	18R 7.9
3 S	22 41 49.2	12 6.3	19 31.7	15 43.0	5 15.0	8 3.6	1 13.9	18 20.9	0 17.6	5 27.3	19 4.7	18 6.6
4 S	22 45 45.8	13 6.5	19 28.6	29 53.5	7 3.4	9 17.5	2 0.2	18 35.4	0 13.2	5 26.7	19 3.5	18 5.3
5 M	22 49 42.3	14 6.6	19 25.4	13♒57.1	8 52.8	10 31.4	2 46.5	18 49.9	0 8.8	5 26.2	19 2.2	18 4.0
6 T	22 53 38.9	15 6.7	19 22.2	27 50.4	10 43.4	11 45.2	3 32.8	19 4.4	0 4.3	5 25.8	19 0.9	18 2.7
7 W	22 57 35.4	16 6.8	19 19.0	11♓30.2	12 35.0	12 58.9	4 19.0	19 19.0	29♍59.8	5 25.4	18 59.6	18 1.5
8 T	23 1 32.0	17 6.8	19 15.9	24 54.0	14 27.6	14 12.7	5 5.2	19 33.5	29 55.3	5 25.0	18 58.3	18 0.2
9 F	23 5 28.6	18 6.8	19 12.7	8♈ 0.3	16 21.3	15 26.3	5 51.3	19 48.0	29 50.7	5 24.7	18 56.9	17 59.0
10 S	23 9 25.1	19 6.8	19 9.5	20 48.8	18 16.0	16 40.0	6 37.4	20 2.6	29 46.1	5 24.5	18 55.6	17 57.8
11 S	23 13 21.7	20 6.7	19 6.3	3♉20.4	20 11.6	17 53.5	7 23.5	20 17.1	29 41.5	5 24.3	18 54.2	17 56.6
12 M	23 17 18.2	21 6.6	19 3.1	15 37.1	22 8.1	19 7.1	8 9.5	20 31.7	29 36.8	5 24.2	18 52.8	17 55.4
13 T	23 21 14.8	22 6.5	18 60.0	27 41.9	24 5.4	20 20.5	8 55.5	20 46.2	29 32.1	5 24.1	18 51.3	17 54.3
14 W	23 25 11.3	23 6.4	18 56.8	9♊38.6	26 3.5	21 33.9	9 41.4	21 0.7	29 27.5	5 24.1	18 49.9	17 53.1
15 T	23 29 7.9	24 6.1	18 53.6	21 31.5	28 2.2	22 47.3	10 27.3	21 15.3	29 22.8	5 24.1	18 48.5	17 52.0
16 F	23 33 4.4	25 5.9	18 50.4	3♋25.3	0♈ 1.4	24 0.6	11 13.2	21 29.8	29 18.1	5D24.2	18 47.0	17 50.9
17 S	23 37 1.0	26 5.6	18 47.3	15 24.7	2 0.9	25 13.9	11 59.0	21 44.3	29 13.3	5 24.3	18 45.5	17 49.8
18 S	23 40 57.5	27 5.4	18 44.1	27 34.1	4 0.5	26 27.1	12 44.8	21 58.9	29 8.7	5 24.6	18 44.0	17 48.8
19 M	23 44 54.1	28 5.0	18 40.9	9♌57.6	6 0.0	27 40.3	13 30.5	22 13.4	29 3.9	5 24.8	18 42.5	17 47.7
20 T	23 48 50.6	29 4.6	18 37.7	22 38.4	7 59.2	28 53.3	14 16.2	22 27.9	28 59.2	5 25.1	18 41.0	17 46.7
21 W	23 52 47.2	0♈ 4.2	18 34.5	5♍38.8	9 57.6	0♉ 6.4	15 1.9	22 42.3	28 54.5	5 25.5	18 39.5	17 45.7
22 T	23 56 43.8	1 3.7	18 31.4	18 59.6	11 55.1	1 19.3	15 47.4	22 56.8	28 49.7	5 25.9	18 37.9	17 44.7
23 F	0 0 40.3	2 3.3	18 28.2	2♎40.2	13 51.2	2 32.2	16 33.0	23 11.2	28 45.0	5 26.3	18 36.4	17 43.7
24 S	0 4 36.9	3 2.7	18 25.0	16 38.2	15 45.5	3 45.0	17 18.5	23 25.7	28 40.3	5 26.9	18 34.8	17 42.8
25 S	0 8 33.4	4 2.2	18 21.8	0♏49.9	17 37.7	4 57.8	18 3.9	23 40.1	28 35.6	5 27.4	18 33.2	17 41.8
26 M	0 12 30.0	5 1.6	18 18.7	15 10.7	19 27.3	6 10.5	18 49.3	23 54.5	28 30.9	5 28.1	18 31.6	17 40.9
27 T	0 16 26.5	6 0.9	18 15.5	29 35.5	21 14.0	7 23.2	19 34.7	24 8.9	28 26.2	5 28.7	18 30.0	17 40.0
28 W	0 20 23.1	7 0.3	18 12.3	13♐59.4	22 57.2	8 35.7	20 20.0	24 23.2	28 21.5	5 29.5	18 28.4	17 39.2
29 T	0 24 19.6	7 59.6	18 9.1	28 18.3	24 36.6	9 48.3	21 5.3	24 37.6	28 16.9	5 30.2	18 26.8	17 38.3
30 F	0 28 16.2	8 58.9	18 5.9	12♑29.1	26 11.8	11 0.7	21 50.5	24 51.9	28 12.3	5 31.1	18 25.2	17 37.5
31 S	0 32 12.7	9 58.2	18 2.8	26 30.0	27 42.3	12 13.1	22 35.7	25 6.2	28 7.7	5 32.0	18 23.6	17 36.7
DECLINATION at NOON												
1 T	22 33 56.1	7S47.1	4S 6.3	28S 5.0	12S51.9	1N21.6	0S44.0	5S44.4	2N 7.5	23N39.7	5S56.4	23N42.3
4 S	22 45 45.8	6 38.4	4 10.1	24 5.0	10 49.9	2 55.3	0N13.1	5 27.4	2 13.0	23 39.8	5 54.9	23 43.4
7 W	22 57 35.4	5 28.8	4 13.8	7 53.5	8 36.2	4 28.4	1 9.9	5 10.3	2 18.7	23 39.8	5 53.4	23 44.6
10 S	23 9 25.1	4 18.6	4 17.5	10N42.7	6 11.4	6 0.8	2 6.6	4 53.3	2 24.5	23 39.8	5 51.7	23 45.6
13 T	23 21 14.8	3 7.9	4 21.3	24 26.7	3 36.6	7 31.9	3 2.8	4 36.2	2 30.3	23 39.8	5 50.1	23 46.5
16 F	23 33 4.4	1 56.9	4 25.0	28 31.0	0 53.6	9 1.6	3 58.6	4 19.1	2 36.1	23 39.8	5 48.3	23 47.4
19 M	23 44 54.1	0 45.7	4 28.7	20 57.9	1N54.8	10 29.4	4 54.0	4 2.0	2 41.9	23 39.7	5 46.6	23 48.2
22 T	23 56 43.8	0N25.4	4 32.5	4 21.7	4 44.4	11 55.0	5 48.7	3 45.0	2 47.6	23 39.6	5 44.8	23 48.9
25 S	0 8 33.4	1 36.3	4 36.2	15S 3.3	7 29.5	13 18.1	6 42.8	3 28.0	2 53.3	23 39.6	5 42.9	23 49.5
28 W	0 20 23.1	2 46.9	4 39.9	27 40.9	10 3.7	14 38.4	7 36.1	3 11.1	2 58.9	23 39.4	5 41.0	23 50.0
31 S	0 32 12.7	3 57.0	4 43.7	24 56.9	12 20.8	15 55.6	8 28.7	2 54.2	3 4.4	23 39.3	5 39.2	23 50.5

APRIL 1951

DAY	EPHEMERIS SIDEREAL TIME	☉	☊	☽	☿	♀	♂	♃	♄	♅	♆	♇
	h m s	° ′	° ′	° ′	° ′	° ′	° ′	° ′	° ′	° ′	° ′	° ′
LONGITUDE at NOON												
1 S	0 36 9.3	10♈57.4	17♓59.6	10♒19.7	29♈ 8.0	13♉25.4	23♈20.8	25♓20.5	28♍ 3.1	5♋32.9	18♎21.9	17♌36.0
2 M	0 40 5.8	11 56.6	17 56.4	23 57.5	0♉28.4	14 37.7	24 5.9	25 34.7	27R58.6	5 33.9	18R20.3	17R35.2
3 T	0 44 2.4	12 55.8	17 53.2	7♓23.3	1 43.3	15 49.9	24 51.0	25 48.9	27 54.1	5 34.9	18 18.7	17 34.5
4 W	0 47 59.0	13 54.9	17 50.1	20 36.8	2 52.3	17 2.1	25 36.0	26 3.1	27 49.6	5 36.0	18 17.0	17 33.8
5 T	0 51 55.5	14 54.0	17 46.9	3♈37.7	3 55.4	18 14.1	26 20.9	26 17.3	27 45.2	5 37.2	18 15.4	17 33.1
6 F	0 55 52.1	15 53.1	17 43.7	16 25.9	4 52.3	19 26.1	27 5.9	26 31.4	27 40.8	5 38.4	18 13.7	17 32.5
7 S	0 59 48.6	16 52.1	17 40.5	29 1.4	5 42.9	20 38.0	27 50.7	26 45.5	27 36.5	5 39.6	18 12.1	17 31.8
8 S	1 3 45.2	17 51.2	17 37.3	11♉24.8	6 27.0	21 49.9	28 35.6	26 59.6	27 32.2	5 40.9	18 10.5	17 31.3
9 M	1 7 41.7	18 50.1	17 34.2	23 37.0	7 4.6	23 1.7	29 20.3	27 13.7	27 28.0	5 42.3	18 8.8	17 30.7
10 T	1 11 38.3	19 49.1	17 31.0	5♊39.8	7 35.5	24 13.4	0♉ 5.0	27 27.7	27 23.8	5 43.7	18 7.2	17 30.2
11 W	1 15 34.8	20 48.0	17 27.8	17 35.7	7 59.8	25 25.0	0 49.7	27 41.6	27 19.6	5 45.1	18 5.5	17 29.7
12 T	1 19 31.4	21 46.8	17 24.6	29 28.0	8 17.4	26 36.6	1 34.3	27 55.5	27 15.5	5 46.6	18 3.9	17 29.2
13 F	1 23 27.9	22 45.7	17 21.5	11♋20.7	8 28.5	27 48.0	2 18.9	28 9.4	27 11.5	5 48.2	18 2.2	17 28.7
14 S	1 27 24.5	23 44.4	17 18.3	23 18.3	8 33.2	28 59.4	3 3.4	28 23.2	27 7.5	5 49.8	18 0.6	17 28.3
15 S	1 31 21.1	24 43.2	17 15.1	5♌25.6	8R31.6	0♊10.7	3 47.8	28 37.0	27 3.6	5 51.4	17 58.9	17 27.8
16 M	1 35 17.6	25 41.9	17 11.9	17 47.3	8 23.9	1 21.9	4 32.2	28 50.8	26 59.7	5 53.1	17 57.3	17 27.5
17 T	1 39 14.2	26 40.6	17 8.8	0♍28.1	8 10.5	2 33.0	5 16.6	29 4.4	26 55.9	5 54.8	17 55.7	17 27.1
18 W	1 43 10.7	27 39.2	17 5.6	13 31.6	7 51.8	3 44.0	6 0.9	29 18.1	26 52.2	5 56.6	17 54.0	17 26.8
19 T	1 47 7.3	28 37.8	17 2.4	27 0.3	7 28.1	4 55.0	6 45.1	29 31.7	26 48.5	5 58.4	17 52.4	17 26.5
20 F	1 51 3.8	29 36.4	16 59.2	10♎54.6	6 60.0	6 5.8	7 29.3	29 45.3	26 44.9	6 0.3	17 50.8	17 26.2
21 S	1 55 0.4	0♉34.9	16 56.0	25 12.4	6 28.0	7 16.5	8 13.5	29 58.8	26 41.4	6 2.2	17 49.2	17 25.9
22 S	1 58 56.9	1 33.4	16 52.9	9♏49.1	5 52.9	8 27.2	8 57.6	0♈12.2	26 37.9	6 4.1	17 47.6	17 25.7
23 M	2 2 53.5	2 31.9	16 49.7	24 37.7	5 15.3	9 37.7	9 41.6	0 25.6	26 34.6	6 6.1	17 46.0	17 25.5
24 T	2 6 50.0	3 30.3	16 46.5	9♐30.0	4 35.9	10 48.2	10 25.6	0 39.0	26 31.3	6 8.2	17 44.5	17 25.3
25 W	2 10 46.6	4 28.7	16 43.3	24 17.6	3 55.4	11 58.5	11 9.5	0 52.2	26 28.0	6 10.3	17 42.9	17 25.2
26 T	2 14 43.2	5 27.1	16 40.2	8♑53.6	3 14.7	13 8.8	11 53.4	1 5.5	26 24.9	6 12.4	17 41.3	17 25.1
27 F	2 18 39.7	6 25.5	16 37.0	23 13.2	2 34.5	14 18.9	12 37.3	1 18.7	26 21.8	6 14.6	17 39.8	17 25.0
28 S	2 22 36.3	7 23.8	16 33.8	7♒13.8	1 55.4	15 29.0	13 21.1	1 31.8	26 18.8	6 16.8	17 38.2	17 24.9
29 S	2 26 32.8	8 22.2	16 30.6	20 55.2	1 18.2	16 39.0	14 4.9	1 44.9	26 16.0	6 19.1	17 36.8	17D25.0
30 M	2 30 29.4	9 20.5	16 27.4	4♓18.3	0 43.4	17 48.8	14 48.5	1 57.9	26 13.1	6 21.4	17 35.3	17 25.0
DECLINATION at NOON												
1 S	0 36 9.3	4N20.2	4S44.9	20S48.9	13N 1.6	16N20.6	8N46.1	2S48.6	3N 6.2	23N39.3	5S38.5	23N50.6
4 W	0 47 59.0	5 29.5	4 48.6	3 34.9	14 47.8	17 33.0	9 37.5	2 31.9	3 11.5	23 39.1	5 36.6	23 50.9
7 S	0 59 48.6	6 37.8	4 52.3	14N16.5	16 6.7	18 41.6	10 28.0	2 15.3	3 16.6	23 38.9	5 34.7	23 51.1
10 T	1 11 38.3	7 45.2	4 56.1	26 14.3	16 56.4	19 46.0	11 17.4	1 58.7	3 21.5	23 38.7	5 32.8	23 51.3
13 F	1 23 27.9	8 51.4	4 59.8	27 43.9	17 15.5	20 45.8	12 5.8	1 42.4	3 26.2	23 38.5	5 31.0	23 51.3
16 M	1 35 17.6	9 56.2	5 3.5	18 1.8	17 4.0	21 40.8	12 53.0	1 26.2	3 30.6	23 38.3	5 29.1	23 51.2
19 T	1 47 7.3	10 59.5	5 7.2	0 29.2	16 23.5	22 30.8	13 39.0	1 10.2	3 34.8	23 38.0	5 27.3	23 51.1
22 S	1 58 56.9	12 1.2	5 10.9	18S34.8	15 18.4	23 15.4	14 23.7	0 54.4	3 38.6	23 37.7	5 25.4	23 50.9
25 W	2 10 46.6	13 1.1	5 14.6	28 25.2	13 56.4	23 54.5	15 7.2	0 38.8	3 42.2	23 37.4	5 23.7	23 50.6
28 S	2 22 36.3	13 59.1	5 18.3	21 42.4	12 27.8	24 27.8	15 49.2	0 23.4	3 45.5	23 37.1	5 21.9	23 50.2

MAY 1951

DAY	EPHEMERIS SIDEREAL TIME	☉	☊	☾	☿	♀	♂	♃	♄	♅	♆	♇
	h m s	° ′	° ′	° ′	° ′	° ′	° ′	° ′	° ′	° ′	° ′	° ′
						LONGITUDE at NOON						
1 T	2 34 25.9	10♉18.7	16♓24.3	17♓25.1	0♉11.5	18♊58.6	15♉32.2	2♈10.8	26♍10.4	6♋23.7	17♎33.8	17♌25.0
2 W	2 38 22.5	11 16.9	16 21.1	0♈17.8	29♈43.0	20 8.2	16 15.8	2 23.7	26R 7.8	6 26.1	17R32.3	17 25.0
3 T	2 42 19.0	12 15.2	16 17.9	12 58.2	29 18.4	21 17.8	16 59.3	2 36.5	26 5.2	6 28.5	17 30.8	17 25.1
4 F	2 46 15.6	13 13.3	16 14.7	25 28.0	28 57.9	22 27.2	17 42.8	2 49.3	26 2.7	6 31.0	17 29.3	17 25.2
5 S	2 50 12.2	14 11.5	16 11.6	7♉48.4	28 41.7	23 36.5	18 26.3	3 1.9	26 0.3	6 33.4	17 27.9	17 25.4
6 S	2 54 8.7	15 9.6	16 8.4	20 0.3	28 30.1	24 45.7	19 9.7	3 14.5	25 58.1	6 36.0	17 26.5	17 25.5
7 M	2 58 5.3	16 7.7	16 5.2	2♊ 4.7	28 23.1	25 54.8	19 53.0	3 27.1	25 55.9	6 38.5	17 25.1	17 25.7
8 T	3 2 1.8	17 5.8	16 2.0	14 2.8	28 20.8	27 3.7	20 36.3	3 39.5	25 53.8	6 41.1	17 23.7	17 26.0
9 W	3 5 58.4	18 3.8	15 58.9	25 56.2	28D23.2	28 12.5	21 19.5	3 51.9	25 51.7	6 43.8	17 22.3	17 26.2
10 T	3 9 54.9	19 1.8	15 55.7	7♋47.3	28 30.3	29 21.2	22 2.7	4 4.2	25 49.8	6 46.5	17 21.0	17 26.5
11 F	3 13 51.5	19 59.8	15 52.5	19 38.9	28 42.0	0♋29.8	22 45.9	4 16.4	25 48.0	6 49.2	17 19.6	17 26.8
12 S	3 17 48.0	20 57.8	15 49.3	1♌34.9	28 58.2	1 38.2	23 28.9	4 28.6	25 46.3	6 51.9	17 18.3	17 27.1
13 S	3 21 44.6	21 55.7	15 46.1	13 39.7	29 18.9	2 46.5	24 12.0	4 40.6	25 44.7	6 54.7	17 17.0	17 27.5
14 M	3 25 41.2	22 53.6	15 43.0	25 58.1	29 43.9	3 54.7	24 54.9	4 52.6	25 43.2	6 57.5	17 15.7	17 27.9
15 T	3 29 37.7	23 51.4	15 39.8	8♍35.1	0♉13.2	5 2.7	25 37.9	5 4.5	25 41.7	7 0.3	17 14.5	17 28.3
16 W	3 33 34.3	24 49.3	15 36.6	21 35.5	0 46.5	6 10.5	26 20.7	5 16.3	25 40.4	7 3.2	17 13.3	17 28.7
17 T	3 37 30.8	25 47.1	15 33.4	5♎ 3.0	1 23.7	7 18.2	27 3.5	5 28.1	25 39.2	7 6.1	17 12.0	17 29.2
18 F	3 41 27.4	26 44.8	15 30.3	18 59.5	2 4.9	8 25.8	27 46.3	5 39.7	25 38.1	7 9.0	17 10.9	17 29.7
19 S	3 45 23.9	27 42.6	15 27.1	3♏24.4	2 49.7	9 33.1	28 29.0	5 51.3	25 37.0	7 12.0	17 9.7	17 30.2
20 S	3 49 20.5	28 40.4	15 23.9	18 13.6	3 38.1	10 40.4	29 11.7	6 2.8	25 36.1	7 15.0	17 8.6	17 30.8
21 M	3 53 17.1	29 38.1	15 20.7	3♐19.7	4 30.0	11 47.5	29 54.3	6 14.1	25 35.3	7 18.0	17 7.5	17 31.4
22 T	3 57 13.6	0♊35.7	15 17.6	18 32.6	5 25.2	12 54.3	0♊36.9	6 25.4	25 34.6	7 21.1	17 6.4	17 32.0
23 W	4 1 10.2	1 33.4	15 14.4	3♑41.6	6 23.7	14 1.0	1 19.4	6 36.6	25 34.0	7 24.1	17 5.3	17 32.7
24 T	4 5 6.7	2 31.0	15 11.2	18 36.8	7 25.4	15 7.6	2 1.8	6 47.7	25 33.5	7 27.2	17 4.2	17 33.3
25 F	4 9 3.3	3 28.7	15 8.0	3♒11.1	8 30.1	16 13.9	2 44.3	6 58.7	25 33.0	7 30.4	17 3.2	17 34.0
26 S	4 12 59.9	4 26.3	15 4.8	17 20.6	9 37.9	17 20.1	3 26.6	7 9.6	25 32.7	7 33.5	17 2.2	17 34.7
27 S	4 16 56.4	5 23.9	15 1.7	1♓ 4.6	10 48.6	18 26.1	4 8.9	7 20.4	25 32.5	7 36.7	17 1.2	17 35.5
28 M	4 20 53.0	6 21.4	14 58.5	14 24.5	12 2.1	19 31.9	4 51.2	7 31.1	25 32.4	7 39.9	17 0.3	17 36.2
29 T	4 24 49.5	7 19.0	14 55.3	27 23.4	13 18.5	20 37.5	5 33.4	7 41.7	25 32.4	7 43.1	16 59.4	17 37.0
30 W	4 28 46.1	8 16.5	14 52.1	10♈ 4.7	14 37.7	21 42.9	6 15.6	7 52.2	25D32.5	7 46.3	16 58.5	17 37.8
31 T	4 32 42.6	9 14.1	14 49.0	22 32.1	15 59.5	22 48.1	6 57.7	8 2.6	25 32.7	7 49.6	16 57.6	17 38.7
						DECLINATION at NOON						
1 T	2 34 25.9	14N55.1	5S 22.0	5S 0.6	11N 3.7	24N55.3	16N29.8	0S 8.3	3N48.4	23N36.7	5S 20.3	23N49.7
4 F	2 46 15.6	15 48.8	5 25.7	12N45.2	9 53.0	25 16.8	17 9.0	0N 6.6	3 51.0	23 36.4	5 18.6	23 49.1
7 M	2 58 5.3	16 40.2	5 29.4	25 22.0	9 1.9	25 32.1	17 46.6	0 21.2	3 53.3	23 36.0	5 17.1	23 48.5
10 T	3 9 54.9	17 29.1	5 33.1	27 56.1	8 32.9	25 41.3	18 22.6	0 35.6	3 55.2	23 35.6	5 15.6	23 47.7
13 S	3 21 44.6	18 15.3	5 36.8	19 22.2	8 26.4	25 44.3	18 57.0	0 49.6	3 56.7	23 35.1	5 14.1	23 46.9
16 W	3 33 34.3	18 58.8	5 40.5	2 55.4	8 41.1	25 41.2	19 29.8	1 3.3	3 57.9	23 34.7	5 12.8	23 46.1
19 S	3 45 23.9	19 39.4	5 44.2	16S 7.3	9 14.8	25 32.0	20 0.8	1 16.6	3 58.7	23 34.2	5 11.5	23 45.1
22 T	3 57 13.6	20 17.0	5 47.9	27 56.9	10 5.1	25 17.0	20 30.1	1 29.7	3 59.1	23 33.7	5 10.3	23 44.1
25 F	4 9 3.3	20 51.4	5 51.6	22 45.1	11 9.6	24 56.2	20 57.6	1 42.3	3 59.2	23 33.2	5 9.2	23 43.0
28 M	4 20 53.0	21 22.7	5 55.3	6 13.4	12 25.8	24 29.9	21 23.3	1 54.6	3 58.9	23 32.6	5 8.2	23 41.8
31 T	4 32 42.6	21 50.6	5 58.9	11N35.5	13 51.4	23 58.3	21 47.2	2 6.4	3 58.2	23 32.0	5 7.3	23 40.6

JUNE 1951

DAY	EPHEMERIS SIDEREAL TIME	☉	☊	☾	☿	♀	♂	♃	♄	♅	♆	♇
						LONGITUDE at NOON						
1 F	4 36 39.2	10♊11.6	14♓45.8	4♉48.5	17♉24.1	23♋53.1	7♊39.8	8♈12.9	25♍33.0	7♋52.9	16♎56.8	17♌39.5
2 S	4 40 35.8	11 9.1	14 42.6	16 56.7	18 51.3	24 57.9	8 21.8	8 23.0	25 33.4	7 56.2	16R55.9	17 40.4
3 S	4 44 32.3	12 6.6	14 39.4	28 58.5	20 21.2	26 2.4	9 3.8	8 33.1	25 33.9	7 59.5	16 55.1	17 41.3
4 M	4 48 28.9	13 4.1	14 36.3	10♊55.6	21 53.7	27 6.8	9 45.7	8 43.0	25 34.5	8 2.9	16 54.4	17 42.3
5 T	4 52 25.4	14 1.5	14 33.1	22 49.2	23 28.9	28 10.9	10 27.6	8 52.8	25 35.2	8 6.2	16 53.7	17 43.2
6 W	4 56 22.0	14 59.0	14 29.9	4♋40.7	25 6.6	29 14.7	11 9.4	9 2.5	25 36.0	8 9.6	16 53.0	17 44.2
7 T	5 0 18.6	15 56.4	14 26.7	16 31.8	26 46.9	0♌18.3	11 51.2	9 12.1	25 36.9	8 13.0	16 52.3	17 45.2
8 F	5 4 15.1	16 53.8	14 23.6	28 24.6	28 29.7	1 21.7	12 32.9	9 21.6	25 37.9	8 16.4	16 51.6	17 46.2
9 S	5 8 11.7	17 51.2	14 20.4	10♌21.9	0♊15.2	2 24.8	13 14.6	9 30.9	25 39.0	8 19.9	16 51.0	17 47.3
10 S	5 12 8.2	18 48.6	14 17.2	22 27.4	2 3.1	3 27.7	13 56.3	9 40.2	25 40.3	8 23.4	16 50.5	17 48.4
11 M	5 16 4.8	19 46.0	14 14.0	4♍45.0	3 53.6	4 30.2	14 37.9	9 49.3	25 41.6	8 26.8	16 49.9	17 49.5
12 T	5 20 1.3	20 43.3	14 10.8	17 19.6	5 46.5	5 32.5	15 19.4	9 58.3	25 43.1	8 30.3	16 49.4	17 50.7
13 W	5 23 57.9	21 40.7	14 7.7	0♎15.7	7 41.7	6 34.5	16 0.9	10 7.1	25 44.6	8 33.8	16 48.9	17 51.8
14 T	5 27 54.5	22 38.0	14 4.5	13 37.7	9 39.3	7 36.1	16 42.3	10 15.8	25 46.2	8 37.3	16 48.4	17 53.0
15 F	5 31 51.0	23 35.3	14 1.3	27 28.5	11 39.1	8 37.5	17 23.7	10 24.4	25 47.9	8 40.8	16 48.0	17 54.2
16 S	5 35 47.6	24 32.5	13 58.1	11♏48.6	13 41.0	9 38.5	18 5.0	10 32.8	25 49.7	8 44.4	16 47.6	17 55.4
17 S	5 39 44.1	25 29.8	13 55.0	26 35.6	15 44.9	10 39.2	18 46.3	10 41.2	25 51.6	8 47.9	16 47.2	17 56.6
18 M	5 43 40.7	26 27.1	13 51.8	11♐43.3	17 50.5	11 39.5	19 27.6	10 49.3	25 53.6	8 51.4	16 46.9	17 57.8
19 T	5 47 37.3	27 24.3	13 48.6	27 2.2	19 57.7	12 39.5	20 8.7	10 57.4	25 55.8	8 55.0	16 46.6	17 59.1
20 W	5 51 33.8	28 21.5	13 45.4	12♑20.8	22 6.3	13 39.1	20 49.9	11 5.3	25 58.0	8 58.6	16 46.3	18 0.4
21 T	5 55 30.4	29 18.8	13 42.3	27 28.0	24 16.0	14 38.3	21 31.0	11 13.0	26 0.2	9 2.1	16 46.1	18 1.7
22 F	5 59 26.9	0♋16.0	13 39.1	12♒14.8	26 26.5	15 37.2	22 12.0	11 20.7	26 2.6	9 5.7	16 45.8	18 3.1
23 S	6 3 23.5	1 13.2	13 35.9	26 35.4	28 37.6	16 35.6	22 53.1	11 28.1	26 5.1	9 9.3	16 45.7	18 4.4
24 S	6 7 20.1	2 10.4	13 32.7	10♓27.6	0♋49.0	17 33.7	23 34.0	11 35.5	26 7.7	9 12.9	16 45.5	18 5.8
25 M	6 11 16.6	3 7.6	13 29.6	23 52.3	3 0.4	18 31.3	24 14.9	11 42.7	26 10.4	9 16.5	16 45.4	18 7.2
26 T	6 15 13.2	4 4.9	13 26.4	6♈52.2	5 11.6	19 28.5	24 55.8	11 49.7	26 13.1	9 20.1	16 45.3	18 8.6
27 W	6 19 9.7	5 2.1	13 23.2	19 31.2	7 22.2	20 25.2	25 36.7	11 56.6	26 16.0	9 23.7	16 45.2	18 10.0
28 T	6 23 6.3	5 59.3	13 20.0	1♉53.7	9 32.1	21 21.5	26 17.5	12 3.3	26 18.9	9 27.3	16 45.2	18 11.4
29 F	6 27 2.8	6 56.5	13 16.9	14 3.7	11 41.0	22 17.3	26 58.2	12 9.9	26 22.0	9 31.0	16 45.2	18 12.9
30 S	6 30 59.4	7 53.7	13 13.7	26 5.0	13 48.7	23 12.6	27 38.9	12 16.3	26 25.1	9 34.6	16D45.3	18 14.4
						DECLINATION at NOON						
1 F	4 36 39.2	21N59.2	6S 0.2	16N43.3	14N21.6	23N46.6	21N54.7	2N10.3	3N57.9	23N31.8	5S 7.0	23N40.2
4 M	4 48 28.9	22 22.5	6 3.8	27 1.0	15 55.7	23 8.2	22 16.1	2 21.6	3 56.7	23 31.3	5 6.2	23 38.9
7 T	5 0 18.6	22 42.3	6 7.5	26 36.7	17 33.0	22 25.2	22 35.6	2 32.5	3 55.1	23 30.6	5 5.5	23 37.6
10 S	5 12 8.2	22 58.6	6 11.2	15 45.4	19 10.1	21 37.8	22 53.2	2 42.9	3 53.2	23 30.0	5 5.0	23 36.2
13 W	5 23 57.9	23 11.2	6 14.9	1S 25.8	20 43.0	20 46.4	23 8.9	2 52.8	3 50.9	23 29.3	5 4.5	23 34.7
16 S	5 35 47.6	23 20.1	6 18.5	19 27.0	22 7.0	19 51.2	23 22.6	3 2.3	3 48.3	23 28.7	5 4.1	23 33.2
19 T	5 47 37.3	23 25.3	6 22.2	28 16.9	23 16.8	18 52.8	23 34.5	3 11.2	3 45.3	23 28.0	5 3.9	23 31.7
22 F	5 59 26.9	23 26.9	6 25.9	19 34.9	24 7.2	17 51.4	23 44.3	3 19.7	3 42.0	23 27.2	5 3.7	23 30.2
25 M	6 11 16.6	23 24.7	6 29.5	1 31.2	24 34.1	16 47.4	23 52.3	3 27.6	3 38.4	23 26.5	5 3.7	23 28.6
28 T	6 23 6.3	23 18.8	6 33.2	15N44.5	24 35.9	15 41.1	23 58.3	3 34.9	3 34.4	23 25.8	5 3.8	23 26.9

JULY 1951

LONGITUDE at NOON

DAY	EPHEMERIS SIDEREAL TIME h m s	☉ ° ′	☊ ° ′	☽ ° ′	☿ ° ′	♀ ° ′	♂ ° ′	♃ ° ′	♄ ° ′	♅ ° ′	♆ ° ′	♇ ° ′
1 S	6 34 56.0	8♋51.0	13♓10.5	8♊ 0.8	15♋55.1	24♌ 7.4	28♊19.6	12♈22.6	26♍28.4	9♋38.2	16♎45.4	18♌15.9
2 M	6 38 52.5	9 48.2	13 7.3	19 53.4	18 0.0	25 1.7	29 0.2	12 28.7	26 31.7	9 41.9	16 45.5	18 17.4
3 T	6 42 49.1	10 45.4	13 4.1	1♋44.8	20 3.3	25 55.4	29 40.8	12 34.6	26 35.1	9 45.5	16 45.6	18 19.0
4 W	6 46 45.6	11 42.7	13 1.0	13 36.8	22 4.9	26 48.5	0♋21.3	12 40.4	26 38.6	9 49.1	16 45.8	18 20.5
5 T	6 50 42.2	12 39.9	12 57.8	25 30.9	24 4.7	27 41.1	1 1.8	12 46.0	26 42.1	9 52.7	16 46.0	18 22.1
6 F	6 54 38.8	13 37.1	12 54.6	7♌28.7	26 2.7	28 33.1	1 42.3	12 51.4	26 45.8	9 56.3	16 46.2	18 23.6
7 S	6 58 35.3	14 34.3	12 51.4	19 32.3	27 58.8	29 24.4	2 22.7	12 56.7	26 49.5	9 59.9	16 46.5	18 25.2
8 S	7 2 31.9	15 31.5	12 48.3	1♍44.1	29 53.0	0♍15.1	3 3.0	13 1.8	26 53.3	10 3.6	16 46.8	18 26.8
9 M	7 6 28.4	16 28.7	12 45.1	14 7.3	1♌45.2	1 5.1	3 43.3	13 6.7	26 57.2	10 7.2	16 47.1	18 28.4
10 T	7 10 25.0	17 26.0	12 41.9	26 45.2	3 35.6	1 54.3	4 23.6	13 11.5	27 1.2	10 10.8	16 47.5	18 30.1
11 W	7 14 21.6	18 23.2	12 38.7	9♎41.7	5 23.9	2 42.9	5 3.8	13 16.1	27 5.3	10 14.4	16 47.9	18 31.7
12 T	7 18 18.1	19 20.4	12 35.6	23 0.4	7 10.3	3 30.7	5 44.0	13 20.5	27 9.5	10 17.9	16 48.3	18 33.4
13 F	7 22 14.7	20 17.6	12 32.4	6♏44.1	8 54.8	4 17.6	6 24.1	13 24.7	27 13.7	10 21.5	16 48.8	18 35.0
14 S	7 26 11.2	21 14.8	12 29.2	20 53.9	10 37.3	5 3.8	7 4.2	13 28.8	27 18.0	10 25.1	16 49.3	18 36.7
15 S	7 30 7.8	22 12.0	12 26.0	5♐28.6	12 17.8	5 49.1	7 44.2	13 32.6	27 22.4	10 28.7	16 49.8	18 38.4
16 M	7 34 4.3	23 9.2	12 22.9	20 23.9	13 56.4	6 33.5	8 24.2	13 36.3	27 26.8	10 32.2	16 50.3	18 40.1
17 T	7 38 0.9	24 6.4	12 19.7	5♑32.3	15 33.1	7 17.0	9 4.2	13 39.8	27 31.4	10 35.8	16 50.9	18 41.8
18 W	7 41 57.5	25 3.7	12 16.5	20 44.3	17 7.8	7 59.5	9 44.1	13 43.2	27 36.0	10 39.3	16 51.5	18 43.5
19 T	7 45 54.0	26 0.9	12 13.3	5♒49.4	18 40.5	8 41.0	10 24.0	13 46.3	27 40.7	10 42.8	16 52.2	18 45.3
20 F	7 49 50.6	26 58.1	12 10.1	20 38.4	20 11.3	9 21.5	11 3.8	13 49.3	27 45.4	10 46.3	16 52.9	18 47.0
21 S	7 53 47.1	27 55.4	12 7.0	5♓ 4.3	21 40.0	10 0.9	11 43.6	13 52.1	27 50.2	10 49.8	16 53.6	18 48.8
22 S	7 57 43.7	28 52.7	12 3.8	19 3.3	23 6.9	10 39.2	12 23.4	13 54.7	27 55.2	10 53.4	16 54.4	18 50.6
23 M	8 1 40.2	29 49.9	12 0.6	2♈34.7	24 31.6	11 16.4	13 3.1	13 57.1	28 0.1	10 56.9	16 55.1	18 52.4
24 T	8 5 36.8	0♌47.2	11 57.4	15 40.0	25 54.3	11 52.3	13 42.8	13 59.3	28 5.2	11 0.3	16 55.9	18 54.1
25 W	8 9 33.4	1 44.5	11 54.3	28 22.4	27 14.9	12 27.0	14 22.5	14 1.3	28 10.3	11 3.8	16 56.8	18 55.9
26 T	8 13 29.9	2 41.8	11 51.1	10♉46.0	28 33.4	13 0.5	15 2.1	14 3.1	28 15.5	11 7.2	16 57.6	18 57.7
27 F	8 17 26.5	3 39.2	11 47.9	22 55.4	29 49.8	13 32.5	15 41.6	14 4.8	28 20.7	11 10.6	16 58.5	18 59.5
28 S	8 21 23.0	4 36.5	11 44.7	4♊54.8	1♍ 3.9	14 3.3	16 21.2	14 6.2	28 26.0	11 14.0	16 59.4	19 1.3
29 S	8 25 19.6	5 33.9	11 41.6	16 48.4	2 15.7	14 32.5	17 0.7	14 7.4	28 31.4	11 17.4	17 0.4	19 3.1
30 M	8 29 16.1	6 31.3	11 38.4	28 39.7	3 25.1	15 0.3	17 40.1	14 8.5	28 36.8	11 20.8	17 1.4	19 5.0
31 T	8 33 12.7	7 28.7	11 35.2	10♋31.6	4 32.1	15 26.6	18 19.5	14 9.3	28 42.3	11 24.1	17 2.4	19 6.8

DECLINATION at NOON

DAY	SIDEREAL TIME	☉	☊	☽	☿	♀	♂	♃	♄	♅	♆	♇
1 S	6 34 56.0	23N 9.2	6S 36.8	26N37.1	24N13.0	14N32.9	24N 2.4	3N41.7	3N30.1	23N25.0	5S 4.0	23N25.3
4 W	6 46 45.6	22 55.9	6 40.5	27 1.1	23 27.9	13 23.3	24 4.7	3 47.9	3 25.5	23 24.2	5 4.3	23 23.6
7 S	6 58 35.3	22 39.1	6 44.1	16 45.2	22 24.1	12 12.6	24 5.0	3 53.5	3 20.6	23 23.5	5 4.7	23 21.9
10 T	7 10 25.0	22 18.7	6 47.8	0 1.4	21 5.2	11 1.2	24 3.4	3 58.5	3 15.5	23 22.7	5 5.2	23 20.2
13 F	7 22 14.7	21 54.8	6 51.4	17S45.7	19 34.9	9 49.6	24 0.0	4 2.8	3 10.0	23 21.9	5 5.8	23 18.5
16 M	7 34 4.3	21 27.6	6 55.1	28 8.4	17 56.3	8 38.3	23 54.8	4 6.6	3 4.3	23 21.1	5 6.6	23 16.7
19 T	7 45 54.0	20 57.2	6 58.7	21 40.1	16 12.1	7 27.8	23 47.8	4 9.7	2 58.4	23 20.3	5 7.4	23 15.0
22 S	7 57 43.7	20 23.5	7 2.3	3 37.5	14 24.6	6 18.5	23 39.0	4 12.1	2 52.2	23 19.4	5 8.4	23 13.3
25 W	8 9 33.4	19 46.8	7 6.0	14N29.2	12 36.2	5 11.1	23 28.5	4 13.9	2 45.7	23 18.6	5 9.4	23 11.5
28 S	8 21 23.0	19 7.1	7 9.6	26 11.4	10 48.8	4 6.0	23 16.3	4 15.0	2 39.1	23 17.8	5 10.6	23 9.8
31 T	8 33 12.7	18 24.5	7 13.2	27 29.7	9 4.4	3 4.1	23 2.5	4 15.4	2 32.2	23 17.0	5 11.8	23 8.1

AUGUST 1951

LONGITUDE at NOON

DAY	SIDEREAL TIME	☉	☊	☽	☿	♀	♂	♃	♄	♅	♆	♇
1 W	8 37 9.3	8♌26.1	11♓32.0	22♋26.6	5♍36.6	15♍51.2	18♋58.9	14♈10.0	28♍47.9	11♋27.5	17♎ 3.4	19♌ 8.6
2 T	8 41 5.8	9 23.5	11 28.9	4♌26.7	6 38.4	16 14.2	19 38.2	14 10.4	28 53.5	11 30.8	17 4.5	19 10.5
3 F	8 45 2.4	10 20.9	11 25.7	16 33.6	7 37.5	16 35.4	20 17.5	14 10.7	28 59.2	11 34.0	17 5.6	19 12.3
4 S	8 48 58.9	11 18.4	11 22.5	28 48.7	8 33.7	16 54.9	20 56.8	14 10.7	29 4.9	11 37.3	17 6.7	19 14.2
5 S	8 52 55.5	12 15.9	11 19.3	11♍13.7	9 26.9	17 12.5	21 36.0	14R10.6	29 10.7	11 40.6	17 7.9	19 16.0
6 M	8 56 52.0	13 13.4	11 16.1	23 50.3	10 17.0	17 28.3	22 15.2	14 10.2	29 16.6	11 43.8	17 9.1	19 17.9
7 T	9 0 48.6	14 10.9	11 13.0	6♎40.3	11 3.8	17 42.0	22 54.3	14 9.7	29 22.5	11 47.0	17 10.3	19 19.7
8 W	9 4 45.2	15 8.4	11 9.8	19 45.9	11 47.2	17 53.8	23 33.4	14 8.9	29 28.5	11 50.1	17 11.5	19 21.6
9 T	9 8 41.7	16 5.9	11 6.6	3♏ 8.8	12 26.9	18 3.4	24 12.5	14 8.0	29 34.5	11 53.3	17 12.8	19 23.4
10 F	9 12 38.3	17 3.4	11 3.4	16 50.8	13 2.8	18 10.9	24 51.5	14 6.9	29 40.6	11 56.4	17 14.1	19 25.3
11 S	9 16 34.8	18 1.0	11 0.3	0♐52.3	13 34.6	18 16.2	25 30.4	14 5.5	29 46.7	11 59.5	17 15.4	19 27.2
12 S	9 20 31.4	18 58.6	10 57.1	15 12.5	14 2.2	18 19.3	26 9.4	14 4.0	29 52.9	12 2.6	17 16.8	19 29.1
13 M	9 24 27.9	19 56.2	10 53.9	29 48.6	14 25.4	18 20.0	26 48.3	14 2.3	29 59.1	12 5.7	17 18.2	19 30.9
14 T	9 28 24.5	20 53.8	10 50.7	14♑35.6	14 43.9	18R18.5	27 27.2	14 0.4	0♎ 5.4	12 8.7	17 19.5	19 32.8
15 W	9 32 21.0	21 51.4	10 47.5	29 26.9	14 57.4	18 14.5	28 6.0	13 58.3	0 11.7	12 11.7	17 21.0	19 34.7
16 T	9 36 17.6	22 49.0	10 44.4	14♒14.9	15 5.9	18 8.2	28 44.8	13 55.9	0 18.1	12 14.6	17 22.4	19 36.5
17 F	9 40 14.2	23 46.7	10 41.2	28 51.9	15 9.1	17 59.4	29 23.5	13 53.4	0 24.5	12 17.5	17 23.9	19 38.4
18 S	9 44 10.7	24 44.4	10 38.0	13♓11.6	15R 6.7	17 48.3	0♌ 2.3	13 50.7	0 31.0	12 20.4	17 25.4	19 40.2
19 S	9 48 7.3	25 42.1	10 34.8	27 9.2	14 58.8	17 34.8	0 40.9	13 47.9	0 37.5	12 23.3	17 26.9	19 42.1
20 M	9 52 3.8	26 39.8	10 31.7	10♈42.6	14 45.1	17 19.0	1 19.6	13 44.8	0 44.0	12 26.1	17 28.5	19 43.9
21 T	9 56 0.4	27 37.5	10 28.5	23 51.7	14 25.7	17 0.8	1 58.2	13 41.5	0 50.6	12 29.0	17 30.0	19 45.8
22 W	9 59 56.9	28 35.3	10 25.3	6♉38.2	14 0.6	16 40.4	2 36.8	13 38.1	0 57.2	12 31.7	17 31.6	19 47.6
23 T	10 3 53.5	29 33.1	10 22.1	19 5.2	13 29.9	16 17.8	3 15.3	13 34.4	1 3.9	12 34.5	17 33.2	19 49.5
24 F	10 7 50.0	0♍31.0	10 19.0	1♊16.7	12 53.7	15 53.1	3 53.8	13 30.6	1 10.6	12 37.2	17 34.9	19 51.3
25 S	10 11 46.6	1 28.8	10 15.8	13 17.1	12 12.6	15 26.4	4 32.3	13 26.6	1 17.3	12 39.8	17 36.5	19 53.2
26 S	10 15 43.2	2 26.7	10 12.6	25 11.0	11 27.0	14 57.9	5 10.7	13 22.4	1 24.1	12 42.5	17 38.2	19 55.0
27 M	10 19 39.7	3 24.7	10 9.4	7♋ 2.6	10 37.4	14 27.7	5 49.1	13 18.1	1 30.9	12 45.1	17 39.9	19 56.8
28 T	10 23 36.3	4 22.6	10 6.2	18 56.2	9 44.8	13 55.9	6 27.5	13 13.5	1 37.8	12 47.6	17 41.6	19 58.6
29 W	10 27 32.8	5 20.6	10 3.1	0♌55.0	8 50.0	13 22.7	7 5.8	13 8.8	1 44.7	12 50.2	17 43.4	20 0.5
30 T	10 31 29.4	6 18.6	9 59.9	13 2.2	7 53.9	12 48.3	7 44.1	13 3.9	1 51.6	12 52.7	17 45.1	20 2.3
31 F	10 35 25.9	7 16.7	9 56.7	25 20.1	6 57.9	12 12.9	8 22.4	12 58.9	1 58.6	12 55.1	17 46.9	20 4.1

DECLINATION at NOON

DAY	SIDEREAL TIME	☉	☊	☽	☿	♀	♂	♃	♄	♅	♆	♇
1 W	8 37 9.3	18N 9.7	7S 14.4	25N22.1	8N30.6	2N44.3	22N57.5	4N15.4	2N29.8	23N16.7	5S 12.3	23N 7.5
4 S	8 48 58.9	17 23.5	7 18.1	12 50.4	6 53.6	1 47.8	22 41.5	4 14.9	2 22.7	23 15.9	5 13.7	23 5.8
7 T	9 0 48.6	16 34.8	7 21.7	4S48.9	5 25.0	0 56.3	22 24.0	4 13.7	2 15.4	23 15.1	5 15.1	23 4.1
10 F	9 12 38.3	15 43.7	7 25.3	21 29.6	4 7.6	0 11.0	22 5.0	4 11.8	2 7.9	23 14.3	5 16.7	23 2.5
13 M	9 24 27.9	14 50.4	7 28.9	28 23.0	3 5.0	0S 27.1	21 44.5	4 9.3	2 0.2	23 13.6	5 18.4	23 0.8
16 T	9 36 17.6	13 54.9	7 32.5	18 44.3	2 21.0	0 56.8	21 22.6	4 6.1	1 52.3	23 12.8	5 20.1	22 59.3
19 S	9 48 7.3	12 57.5	7 36.2	0N18.6	2 0.0	1 17.0	20 59.3	4 2.2	1 44.4	23 12.1	5 21.9	22 57.7
22 W	9 59 56.9	11 58.2	7 39.8	17 54.0	2 6.3	1 26.8	20 34.7	3 57.7	1 36.3	23 11.3	5 23.8	22 56.2
25 S	10 11 46.6	10 57.1	7 43.4	27 37.6	2 42.5	1 25.7	20 8.9	3 52.6	1 28.1	23 10.6	5 25.8	22 54.7
28 T	10 23 36.3	9 54.5	7 47.0	26 10.2	3 47.5	1 13.6	19 41.8	3 46.9	1 19.7	23 10.0	5 27.8	22 53.3
31 F	10 35 25.9	8 50.5	7 50.6	14 19.8	5 14.6	0 51.0	19 13.6	3 40.6	1 11.3	23 9.3	5 29.9	22 51.9

SEPTEMBER 1951

DAY	EPHEMERIS SIDEREAL TIME	☉	☊	☽	☿	♀	♂	♃	♄	♅	♆	♇
	h m s	° ′	° ′	° ′	° ′	° ′	° ′	° ′	° ′	° ′	° ′	° ′
						LONGITUDE at NOON						
1 S	10 39 22.5	8♍14.7	9♓53.5	7♍50.1	6♍ 3.0	11♍36.7	9♌ 0.6	12♈53.7	2♎ 5.5	12♋57.5	17♎48.7	20♌ 5.8
2 S	10 43 19.0	9 12.9	9 50.4	20 33.5	5R10.5	11R 0.1	9 38.8	12R48.3	2 12.6	12 59.9	17 50.6	20 7.7
3 M	10 47 15.6	10 11.0	9 47.2	3♎30.6	4 21.5	10 23.1	10 17.0	12 42.8	2 19.7	13 2.3	17 52.5	20 9.5
4 T	10 51 12.1	11 9.1	9 44.0	16 41.5	3 37.3	9 46.0	10 55.1	12 37.1	2 26.7	13 4.6	17 54.3	20 11.2
5 W	10 55 8.7	12 7.3	9 40.8	0♏ 6.1	2 58.8	9 9.0	11 33.2	12 31.3	2 33.8	13 6.8	17 56.2	20 13.0
6 T	10 59 5.3	13 5.5	9 37.6	13 43.8	2 27.0	8 32.4	12 11.2	12 25.3	2 40.9	13 9.0	17 58.1	20 14.7
7 F	11 3 1.8	14 3.7	9 34.5	27 33.8	2 2.7	7 56.5	12 49.2	12 19.2	2 48.1	13 11.2	18 0.0	20 16.5
8 S	11 6 58.4	15 2.0	9 31.3	11♐35.2	1 46.6	7 21.4	13 27.1	12 12.9	2 55.3	13 13.4	18 1.9	20 18.2
9 S	11 10 54.9	16 0.3	9 28.1	25 46.3	1 39.1	6 47.4	14 5.1	12 6.5	3 2.4	13 15.4	18 3.9	20 19.9
10 M	11 14 51.5	16 58.6	9 24.9	10♑ 5.1	1D40.5	6 14.6	14 42.9	12 0.0	3 9.7	13 17.5	18 5.9	20 21.6
11 T	11 18 48.0	17 56.9	9 21.8	24 28.6	1 51.0	5 43.3	15 20.8	11 53.4	3 16.9	13 19.5	18 7.8	20 23.3
12 W	11 22 44.6	18 55.2	9 18.6	8♒53.2	2 10.6	5 13.7	15 58.6	11 46.6	3 24.1	13 21.4	18 9.8	20 25.0
13 T	11 26 41.1	19 53.6	9 15.4	23 14.5	2 39.2	4 45.8	16 36.4	11 39.7	3 31.4	13 23.4	18 11.8	20 26.7
14 F	11 30 37.7	20 52.0	9 12.2	7♓28.0	3 16.6	4 19.9	17 14.1	11 32.8	3 38.7	13 25.2	18 13.9	20 28.3
15 S	11 34 34.2	21 50.5	9 9.0	21 29.2	4 2.4	3 56.1	17 51.8	11 25.7	3 46.0	13 27.0	18 15.9	20 30.0
16 S	11 38 30.8	22 48.9	9 5.9	5♈14.4	4 56.2	3 34.4	18 29.5	11 18.5	3 53.3	13 28.8	18 17.9	20 31.6
17 M	11 42 27.3	23 47.4	9 2.7	18 40.8	5 57.5	3 15.0	19 7.1	11 11.2	4 0.6	13 30.5	18 20.0	20 33.2
18 T	11 46 23.9	24 46.0	8 59.5	1♉47.1	7 5.8	2 58.0	19 44.7	11 3.8	4 8.0	13 32.2	18 22.1	20 34.8
19 W	11 50 20.5	25 44.5	8 56.3	14 33.6	8 20.5	2 43.3	20 22.3	10 56.3	4 15.3	13 33.9	18 24.2	20 36.4
20 T	11 54 17.0	26 43.1	8 53.2	27 2.0	9 40.9	2 31.1	20 59.8	10 48.8	4 22.7	13 35.5	18 26.3	20 38.0
21 F	11 58 13.6	27 41.8	8 50.0	9♊15.0	11 6.5	2 21.3	21 37.3	10 41.1	4 30.1	13 37.0	18 28.4	20 39.5
22 S	12 2 10.1	28 40.5	8 46.8	21 16.4	12 36.5	2 13.9	22 14.8	10 33.4	4 37.4	13 38.5	18 30.5	20 41.1
23 S	12 6 6.7	29 39.2	8 43.6	3♋10.7	14 10.6	2 9.1	22 52.2	10 25.7	4 44.9	13 40.0	18 32.7	20 42.6
24 M	12 10 3.2	0♎38.0	8 40.4	15 2.5	15 47.9	2 6.6	23 29.6	10 17.9	4 52.3	13 41.4	18 34.8	20 44.1
25 T	12 13 59.8	1 36.8	8 37.3	26 56.5	17 27.9	2 6.5	24 7.0	10 10.0	4 59.7	13 42.7	18 37.0	20 45.6
26 W	12 17 56.3	2 35.6	8 34.1	8♌57.6	19 10.3	2D 8.7	24 44.3	10 2.1	5 7.1	13 44.0	18 39.1	20 47.1
27 T	12 21 52.9	3 34.5	8 30.9	21 9.7	20 54.4	2 13.3	25 21.6	9 54.1	5 14.5	13 45.3	18 41.3	20 48.6
28 F	12 25 49.4	4 33.4	8 27.7	3♍36.3	22 40.0	2 20.2	25 58.8	9 46.1	5 21.9	13 46.5	18 43.5	20 50.0
29 S	12 29 46.0	5 32.3	8 24.6	16 20.1	24 26.6	2 29.3	26 36.0	9 38.1	5 29.3	13 47.6	18 45.7	20 51.4
30 S	12 33 42.5	6 31.3	8 21.4	29 22.1	26 14.0	2 40.5	27 13.2	9 30.1	5 36.8	13 48.7	18 47.9	20 52.8
						DECLINATION at NOON						
1 S	10 39 22.5	8N28.9	7S51.8	8N48.4	5N46.6	0S41.2	19N 3.9	3N38.4	1N 8.5	23N 9.1	5S30.6	22N51.4
4 T	10 51 12.1	7 23.1	7 55.4	9S29.5	7 23.2	0 6.5	18 34.2	3 31.4	0 59.9	23 8.5	5 32.8	22 50.1
7 F	11 3 1.8	6 16.4	7 58.9	24 38.7	8 49.1	0N34.9	18 3.4	3 23.9	0 51.3	23 7.9	5 35.1	22 48.8
10 M	11 14 51.5	5 8.7	8 2.5	27 36.9	9 50.8	1 20.8	17 31.7	3 16.0	0 42.7	23 7.4	5 37.4	22 47.6
13 T	11 26 41.1	4 0.2	8 6.1	15 12.3	10 19.9	2 8.3	16 59.1	3 7.6	0 34.0	23 6.8	5 39.7	22 46.5
16 S	11 38 30.8	2 51.2	8 9.7	4N 9.5	10 12.7	2 55.1	16 25.6	2 59.0	0 25.3	23 6.4	5 42.1	22 45.4
19 W	11 50 20.5	1 41.6	8 13.3	20 45.2	9 29.9	3 39.0	15 51.2	2 50.0	0 16.5	23 5.9	5 44.5	22 44.4
22 S	12 2 10.1	0 31.7	8 16.9	28 17.9	8 15.5	4 18.5	15 16.0	2 40.8	0 7.8	23 5.5	5 46.9	22 43.5
25 T	12 13 59.8	0S38.5	8 20.4	24 16.8	6 35.8	4 52.2	14 40.1	2 31.5	0S 1.0	23 5.2	5 49.4	22 42.6
28 F	12 25 49.4	1 48.7	8 24.0	10 42.9	4 38.1	5 19.6	14 3.6	2 22.0	0 9.8	23 4.9	5 51.9	22 41.8

OCTOBER 1951

DAY	EPHEMERIS SIDEREAL TIME	☉	☊	☽	☿	♀	♂	♃	♄	♅	♆	♇
						LONGITUDE at NOON						
1 M	12 37 39.1	7♎30.3	8♓18.2	12♎42.5	28♍ 1.8	2♍53.8	27♌50.3	9♈22.0	5♎44.2	13♋49.8	18♎50.1	20♌54.2
2 T	12 41 35.6	8 29.3	8 15.0	26 19.7	29 49.9	3 9.2	28 27.4	9R13.9	5 51.6	13 50.8	18 52.3	20 55.6
3 W	12 45 32.2	9 28.4	8 11.8	10♏11.2	1♎37.9	3 26.6	29 4.4	9 5.8	5 59.0	13 51.7	18 54.5	20 56.9
4 T	12 49 28.8	10 27.5	8 8.7	24 13.5	3 25.9	3 45.9	29 41.4	8 57.8	6 6.4	13 52.6	18 56.7	20 58.2
5 F	12 53 25.3	11 26.6	8 5.5	8♐22.8	5 13.6	4 7.1	0♍18.4	8 49.7	6 13.8	13 53.4	18 58.9	20 59.5
6 S	12 57 21.9	12 25.8	8 2.3	22 35.4	7 0.9	4 30.1	0 55.3	8 41.7	6 21.2	13 54.2	19 1.1	21 0.8
7 S	13 1 18.4	13 25.0	7 59.1	6♑48.2	8 47.7	4 54.8	1 32.2	8 33.6	6 28.6	13 55.0	19 3.3	21 2.1
8 M	13 5 15.0	14 24.2	7 56.0	20 58.9	10 34.0	5 21.2	2 9.1	8 25.7	6 35.9	13 55.6	19 5.6	21 3.3
9 T	13 9 11.5	15 23.5	7 52.8	5♒ 5.4	12 19.7	5 49.3	2 45.9	8 17.7	6 43.3	13 56.3	19 7.8	21 4.5
10 W	13 13 8.1	16 22.8	7 49.6	19 6.5	14 4.8	6 18.9	3 22.6	8 9.8	6 50.7	13 56.8	19 10.0	21 5.7
11 T	13 17 4.6	17 22.1	7 46.4	3♓ 0.8	15 49.3	6 50.1	3 59.3	8 1.9	6 58.0	13 57.3	19 12.3	21 6.9
12 F	13 21 1.2	18 21.4	7 43.3	16 46.7	17 33.0	7 22.7	4 36.0	7 54.1	7 5.3	13 57.8	19 14.5	21 8.0
13 S	13 24 57.7	19 20.8	7 40.1	0♈22.5	19 16.1	7 56.8	5 12.6	7 46.3	7 12.6	13 58.2	19 16.7	21 9.2
14 S	13 28 54.3	20 20.2	7 36.9	13 46.6	20 58.5	8 32.3	5 49.3	7 38.7	7 20.0	13 58.6	19 19.0	21 10.3
15 M	13 32 50.9	21 19.7	7 33.7	26 56.9	22 40.2	9 9.0	6 25.8	7 31.1	7 27.2	13 58.9	19 21.3	21 11.4
16 T	13 36 47.4	22 19.1	7 30.5	9♉52.3	24 21.2	9 47.1	7 2.3	7 23.5	7 34.5	13 59.2	19 23.5	21 12.5
17 W	13 40 44.0	23 18.6	7 27.4	22 32.2	26 1.5	10 26.3	7 38.8	7 16.1	7 41.8	13 59.4	19 25.7	21 13.5
18 T	13 44 40.5	24 18.2	7 24.2	4♊57.0	27 41.2	11 6.8	8 15.2	7 8.7	7 49.0	13 59.5	19 27.9	21 14.5
19 F	13 48 37.1	25 17.8	7 21.0	17 8.3	29 20.2	11 48.4	8 51.6	7 1.4	7 56.2	13 59.6	19 30.2	21 15.5
20 S	13 52 33.6	26 17.4	7 17.8	29 8.8	0♏58.6	12 31.1	9 28.0	6 54.2	8 3.4	13 59.7	19 32.4	21 16.5
21 S	13 56 30.2	27 17.0	7 14.7	11♋ 2.0	2 36.3	13 14.9	10 4.3	6 47.1	8 10.5	13R59.6	19 34.6	21 17.4
22 M	14 0 26.7	28 16.7	7 11.5	22 52.5	4 13.5	13 59.7	10 40.6	6 40.2	8 17.6	13 59.6	19 36.8	21 18.3
23 T	14 4 23.3	29 16.5	7 8.3	4♌45.0	5 50.0	14 45.5	11 16.8	6 33.3	8 24.7	13 59.5	19 39.1	21 19.2
24 W	14 8 19.8	0♏16.2	7 5.1	16 44.9	7 26.0	15 32.3	11 53.0	6 26.6	8 31.8	13 59.3	19 41.3	21 20.0
25 T	14 12 16.4	1 16.0	7 1.9	28 57.3	9 1.5	16 19.9	12 29.1	6 19.9	8 38.9	13 59.0	19 43.5	21 20.9
26 F	14 16 13.0	2 15.9	6 58.8	11♍26.9	10 36.4	17 8.4	13 5.2	6 13.4	8 45.9	13 58.8	19 45.7	21 21.7
27 S	14 20 9.5	3 15.8	6 55.6	24 17.8	12 10.7	17 57.8	13 41.2	6 7.1	8 52.9	13 58.4	19 47.9	21 22.5
28 S	14 24 6.1	4 15.7	6 52.4	7♎32.3	13 44.6	18 48.0	14 17.2	6 0.9	8 59.9	13 58.0	19 50.0	21 23.2
29 M	14 28 2.6	5 15.6	6 49.2	21 11.0	15 18.0	19 38.9	14 53.2	5 54.8	9 6.8	13 57.6	19 52.2	21 23.9
30 T	14 31 59.2	6 15.6	6 46.1	5♏12.0	16 50.9	20 30.7	15 29.1	5 48.9	9 13.7	13 57.1	19 54.4	21 24.6
31 W	14 35 55.7	7 15.6	6 42.9	19 31.3	18 23.3	21 23.1	16 4.9	5 43.1	9 20.6	13 56.5	19 56.5	21 25.3
						DECLINATION at NOON						
1 M	12 37 39.1	2S58.7	8S27.6	7S38.4	2N28.8	5N40.2	13N26.4	2N12.4	0S18.5	23N 4.6	5S54.4	22N41.1
4 T	12 49 28.8	4 8.5	8 31.1	23 41.4	0 13.1	5 53.9	12 48.6	2 2.9	0 27.2	23 4.4	5 56.9	22 40.5
7 S	13 1 18.4	5 17.9	8 34.7	27 53.0	2S 5.0	6 0.7	12 10.3	1 53.5	0 35.8	23 4.3	5 59.4	22 40.0
10 W	13 13 8.1	6 26.6	8 38.2	16 48.8	4 22.5	6 0.7	11 31.5	1 44.3	0 44.4	23 4.1	6 2.0	22 39.5
13 S	13 24 57.7	7 34.5	8 41.8	1N51.0	6 37.5	5 54.1	10 52.3	1 35.2	0 52.9	23 4.1	6 4.5	22 39.1
16 T	13 36 47.4	8 41.5	8 45.3	19 1.7	8 48.7	5 41.0	10 12.7	1 26.5	1 1.3	23 4.1	6 7.0	22 38.8
19 F	13 48 37.1	9 47.4	8 48.9	27 52.6	10 54.8	5 21.9	9 32.8	1 18.1	1 9.6	23 4.1	6 9.5	22 38.7
22 M	14 0 26.7	10 52.0	8 52.4	25 8.0	12 55.2	4 57.0	8 52.6	1 10.1	1 17.8	23 4.2	6 12.0	22 38.6
25 T	14 12 16.4	11 55.1	8 56.0	12 38.8	14 49.1	4 26.6	8 12.2	1 2.5	1 25.9	23 4.3	6 14.4	22 38.6
28 S	14 24 6.1	12 56.7	8 59.5	5S16.1	16 36.1	3 51.1	7 31.5	0 55.5	1 33.8	23 4.5	6 16.9	22 38.7
31 W	14 35 55.7	13 56.4	9 3.0	22 14.1	18 15.4	3 11.0	6 50.7	0 48.9	1 41.6	23 4.7	6 19.3	22 38.8

NOVEMBER 1951

LONGITUDE at NOON

DAY	EPHEMERIS SIDEREAL TIME h m s	☉ ° ′	☊ ° ′	☽ ° ′	☿ ° ′	♀ ° ′	♂ ° ′	♃ ° ′	♄ ° ′	♅ ° ′	♆ ° ′	♇ ° ′
1 T	14 39 52.3	8♏15.7	6♓39.7	4♐ 2.7	19♏55.3	22♍16.2	16♍40.7	5♈37.5	9♎27.4	13♋55.9	19♎58.7	21♌26.0
2 F	14 43 48.8	9 15.7	6 36.5	18 39.2	21 26.8	23 10.0	17 16.4	5R32.0	9 34.2	13R55.3	20 0.8	21 26.6
3 S	14 47 45.4	10 15.8	6 33.3	3♑13.7	22 57.9	24 4.5	17 52.1	5 26.7	9 40.9	13 54.6	20 3.0	21 27.2
4 S	14 51 42.0	11 16.0	6 30.2	17 40.7	24 28.6	24 59.6	18 27.8	5 21.6	9 47.7	13 53.8	20 5.1	21 27.8
5 M	14 55 38.5	12 16.2	6 27.0	1♒56.1	25 58.7	25 55.3	19 3.4	5 16.6	9 54.3	13 53.0	20 7.2	21 28.3
6 T	14 59 35.1	13 16.3	6 23.8	15 58.2	27 28.5	26 51.6	19 38.9	5 11.9	10 1.0	13 52.2	20 9.3	21 28.8
7 W	15 3 31.6	14 16.5	6 20.6	29 46.6	28 57.8	27 48.4	20 14.4	5 7.3	10 7.5	13 51.3	20 11.4	21 29.3
8 T	15 7 28.2	15 16.8	6 17.5	13♓21.9	0♐26.6	28 45.8	20 49.8	5 2.8	10 14.1	13 50.3	20 13.5	21 29.7
9 F	15 11 24.7	16 17.0	6 14.3	26 44.9	1 54.9	29 43.7	21 25.2	4 58.6	10 20.6	13 49.3	20 15.5	21 30.2
10 S	15 15 21.3	17 17.3	6 11.1	9♈56.6	3 22.8	0♎42.1	22 0.5	4 54.5	10 27.0	13 48.2	20 17.6	21 30.5
11 S	15 19 17.8	18 17.6	6 7.9	22 57.4	4 50.1	1 41.0	22 35.7	4 50.6	10 33.4	13 47.1	20 19.6	21 30.9
12 M	15 23 14.4	19 17.9	6 4.8	5♉47.3	6 16.9	2 40.5	23 10.9	4 47.0	10 39.7	13 45.9	20 21.6	21 31.2
13 T	15 27 11.0	20 18.3	6 1.6	18 26.2	7 43.1	3 40.3	23 46.0	4 43.5	10 46.0	13 44.7	20 23.6	21 31.5
14 W	15 31 7.5	21 18.7	5 58.4	0♊53.8	9 8.6	4 40.7	24 21.1	4 40.2	10 52.3	13 43.5	20 25.6	21 31.8
15 T	15 35 4.1	22 19.1	5 55.2	13 10.2	10 33.5	5 41.5	24 56.1	4 37.0	10 58.5	13 42.2	20 27.6	21 32.1
16 F	15 39 0.6	23 19.5	5 52.0	25 16.2	11 57.6	6 42.7	25 31.1	4 34.1	11 4.6	13 40.8	20 29.5	21 32.3
17 S	15 42 57.2	24 20.0	5 48.9	7♋13.4	13 20.9	7 44.3	26 6.0	4 31.4	11 10.7	13 39.4	20 31.5	21 32.5
18 S	15 46 53.7	25 20.5	5 45.7	19 4.5	14 43.2	8 46.3	26 40.9	4 28.9	11 16.7	13 38.0	20 33.4	21 32.6
19 M	15 50 50.3	26 21.0	5 42.5	0♌52.9	16 4.5	9 48.7	27 15.7	4 26.6	11 22.7	13 36.5	20 35.3	21 32.8
20 T	15 54 46.9	27 21.6	5 39.3	12 43.0	17 24.7	10 51.5	27 50.4	4 24.5	11 28.6	13 35.0	20 37.2	21 32.9
21 W	15 58 43.4	28 22.1	5 36.2	24 39.8	18 43.5	11 54.7	28 25.1	4 22.6	11 34.5	13 33.4	20 39.1	21 32.9
22 T	16 2 40.0	29 22.8	5 33.0	6♍48.8	20 0.8	12 58.2	28 59.7	4 20.9	11 40.3	13 31.8	20 40.9	21 33.0
23 F	16 6 36.5	0♐23.4	5 29.8	19 15.5	21 16.4	14 2.0	29 34.2	4 19.4	11 46.0	13 30.1	20 42.7	21 33.0
24 S	16 10 33.1	1 24.1	5 26.6	2♎ 5.0	22 30.1	15 6.2	0♎ 8.7	4 18.1	11 51.7	13 28.4	20 44.5	21 33.0
25 S	16 14 29.7	2 24.8	5 23.5	15 21.2	23 41.7	16 10.7	0 43.1	4 17.0	11 57.3	13 26.8	20 46.4	21 33.0
26 M	16 18 26.2	3 25.5	5 20.3	29 6.1	24 50.7	17 15.5	1 17.4	4 16.2	12 2.9	13 25.0	20 48.1	21R32.9
27 T	16 22 22.8	4 26.3	5 17.1	13♏19.1	25 56.8	18 20.6	1 51.7	4 15.5	12 8.4	13 23.1	20 49.9	21 32.8
28 W	16 26 19.3	5 27.1	5 13.9	27 56.3	26 59.6	19 25.9	2 25.9	4 15.0	12 13.8	13 21.3	20 51.6	21 32.7
29 T	16 30 15.9	6 27.9	5 10.8	12♐50.7	27 58.7	20 31.6	2 60.0	4 14.8	12 19.1	13 19.4	20 53.3	21 32.5
30 F	16 34 12.4	7 28.7	5 7.6	27 53.0	28 53.5	21 37.5	3 34.0	4 14.8	12 24.4	13 17.5	20 55.0	21 32.3

DECLINATION at NOON

DAY	SIDEREAL TIME	☉	☊	☽	☿	♀	♂	♃	♄	♅	♆	♇
1 T	14 39 52.3	14S15.9	9S 4.2	25S55.3	18S46.7	2N56.6	6N37.1	0N46.9	1S44.2	23N 4.8	6S20.1	22N38.9
4 S	14 51 42.0	15 12.9	9 7.7	26 7.7	20 15.1	2 10.8	5 56.2	0 41.2	1 51.8	23 5.1	6 22.4	22 39.2
7 W	15 3 31.6	16 7.7	9 11.2	12 11.9	21 34.5	1 21.2	5 15.3	0 36.2	1 59.2	23 5.5	6 24.7	22 39.6
10 S	15 15 21.3	17 0.0	9 14.7	6N26.0	22 44.4	0 28.1	4 34.4	0 31.8	2 6.4	23 5.9	6 26.9	22 40.1
13 T	15 27 11.0	17 49.7	9 18.3	21 53.0	23 44.1	0S28.1	3 53.5	0 28.1	2 13.4	23 6.3	6 29.1	22 40.7
16 F	15 39 0.6	18 36.6	9 21.8	28 6.1	24 32.9	1 27.0	3 12.7	0 25.1	2 20.2	23 6.8	6 31.3	22 41.4
19 M	15 50 50.3	19 20.6	9 25.3	22 47.6	25 10.1	2 28.3	2 32.0	0 22.9	2 26.7	23 7.3	6 33.3	22 42.1
22 T	16 2 40.0	20 1.5	9 28.8	8 56.1	25 35.2	3 31.6	1 51.6	0 21.4	2 33.1	23 7.8	6 35.3	22 43.0
25 S	16 14 29.7	20 39.1	9 32.3	9S 0.2	25 47.6	4 36.5	1 11.3	0 20.6	2 39.2	23 8.4	6 37.3	22 43.9
28 W	16 26 19.3	21 13.2	9 35.8	24 32.2	25 47.0	5 42.5	0 31.3	0 20.6	2 45.0	23 9.0	6 39.1	22 44.9

DECEMBER 1951

LONGITUDE at NOON

DAY	SIDEREAL TIME	☉	☊	☽	☿	♀	♂	♃	♄	♅	♆	♇
1 S	16 38 9.0	8♐29.5	5♓ 4.4	12♑53.1	29♐43.5	22♎43.7	4♎ 8.0	4♈14.9	12♎29.6	13♋15.5	20♎56.6	21♌32.1
2 S	16 42 5.6	9 30.4	5 1.2	27 42.4	0♑27.9	23 50.1	4 41.9	4D15.3	12 34.7	13R13.5	20 58.3	21R31.9
3 M	16 46 2.1	10 31.2	4 58.0	12♒14.4	1 6.0	24 56.7	5 15.6	4 15.9	12 39.8	13 11.4	20 59.9	21 31.6
4 T	16 49 58.7	11 32.1	4 54.9	26 25.7	1 37.2	26 3.6	5 49.4	4 16.7	12 44.7	13 9.4	21 1.4	21 31.3
5 W	16 53 55.2	12 33.0	4 51.7	10♓15.5	2 0.4	27 10.7	6 23.0	4 17.7	12 49.6	13 7.3	21 3.0	21 30.9
6 T	16 57 51.8	13 33.9	4 48.5	23 45.1	2 14.9	28 18.0	6 56.5	4 19.0	12 54.5	13 5.1	21 4.5	21 30.6
7 F	17 1 48.4	14 34.8	4 45.3	6♈56.5	2 19.9	29 25.6	7 30.0	4 20.4	12 59.2	13 2.9	21 6.0	21 30.2
8 S	17 5 44.9	15 35.7	4 42.2	19 52.5	2R14.5	0♏33.3	8 3.4	4 22.0	13 3.9	13 0.7	21 7.5	21 29.8
9 S	17 9 41.5	16 36.7	4 39.0	2♉35.4	1 58.3	1 41.3	8 36.7	4 23.9	13 8.5	12 58.5	21 9.0	21 29.3
10 M	17 13 38.0	17 37.6	4 35.8	15 7.2	1 30.6	2 49.4	9 9.9	4 25.9	13 13.0	12 56.3	21 10.4	21 28.8
11 T	17 17 34.6	18 38.6	4 32.6	27 29.4	0 51.5	3 57.8	9 43.0	4 28.1	13 17.4	12 54.0	21 11.8	21 28.3
12 W	17 21 31.1	19 39.6	4 29.5	9♊42.9	0 1.3	5 6.3	10 16.0	4 30.6	13 21.8	12 51.7	21 13.2	21 27.8
13 T	17 25 27.7	20 40.6	4 26.3	21 48.7	29♐ 0.8	6 15.0	10 49.0	4 33.2	13 26.0	12 49.3	21 14.5	21 27.3
14 F	17 29 24.3	21 41.6	4 23.1	3♋47.6	27 51.3	7 23.9	11 21.8	4 36.1	13 30.2	12 47.0	21 15.8	21 26.7
15 S	17 33 20.8	22 42.6	4 19.9	15 40.7	26 34.9	8 33.0	11 54.6	4 39.1	13 34.3	12 44.6	21 17.1	21 26.1
16 S	17 37 17.4	23 43.7	4 16.8	27 30.0	25 13.9	9 42.2	12 27.3	4 42.4	13 38.3	12 42.3	21 18.4	21 25.5
17 M	17 41 13.9	24 44.7	4 13.6	9♌17.9	23 50.9	10 51.6	12 59.8	4 45.9	13 42.3	12 39.8	21 19.6	21 24.8
18 T	17 45 10.5	25 45.8	4 10.4	21 7.7	22 28.8	12 1.2	13 32.3	4 49.5	13 46.1	12 37.4	21 20.8	21 24.1
19 W	17 49 7.1	26 46.8	4 7.2	3♍ 3.5	21 10.3	13 10.9	14 4.7	4 53.3	13 49.8	12 34.9	21 22.0	21 23.4
20 T	17 53 3.6	27 47.9	4 4.1	15 10.1	19 57.9	14 20.8	14 36.9	4 57.3	13 53.5	12 32.5	21 23.2	21 22.7
21 F	17 57 0.2	28 49.0	4 0.9	27 32.8	18 53.5	15 30.8	15 9.1	5 1.5	13 57.1	12 30.0	21 24.3	21 21.9
22 S	18 0 56.7	29 50.1	3 57.7	10♎16.6	17 58.5	16 40.9	15 41.1	5 5.9	14 0.5	12 27.5	21 25.4	21 21.1
23 S	18 4 53.3	0♑51.2	3 54.5	23 26.3	17 13.8	17 51.2	16 13.1	5 10.5	14 3.9	12 24.9	21 26.4	21 20.3
24 M	18 8 49.9	1 52.4	3 51.3	7♏ 5.2	16 39.9	19 1.6	16 44.9	5 15.3	14 7.2	12 22.4	21 27.4	21 19.5
25 T	18 12 46.4	2 53.5	3 48.2	21 14.5	16 16.9	20 12.1	17 16.6	5 20.3	14 10.4	12 19.9	21 28.4	21 18.6
26 W	18 16 43.0	3 54.7	3 45.0	5♐52.0	16 4.3	21 22.8	17 48.2	5 25.4	14 13.5	12 17.3	21 29.4	21 17.8
27 T	18 20 39.5	4 55.8	3 41.8	20 52.3	16 1.6	22 33.6	18 19.7	5 30.7	14 16.5	12 14.7	21 30.3	21 16.9
28 F	18 24 36.1	5 57.0	3 38.6	6♑ 6.3	16D 8.3	23 44.4	18 51.0	5 36.3	14 19.4	12 12.2	21 31.2	21 15.9
29 S	18 28 32.6	6 58.2	3 35.5	21 23.2	16 23.5	24 55.4	19 22.3	5 41.9	14 22.2	12 9.6	21 32.0	21 15.0
30 S	18 32 29.2	7 59.4	3 32.3	6♒32.1	16 46.6	26 6.5	19 53.3	5 47.8	14 24.9	12 7.0	21 32.9	21 14.0
31 M	18 36 25.8	9 0.5	3 29.1	21 23.8	17 16.7	27 17.7	20 24.3	5 53.9	14 27.4	12 4.4	21 33.7	21 13.0

DECLINATION at NOON

DAY	SIDEREAL TIME	☉	☊	☽	☿	♀	♂	♃	♄	♅	♆	♇
1 S	16 38 9.0	21S43.7	9S39.3	26S45.0	25S33.4	6S49.3	0S 8.4	0N21.4	2S50.6	23N 9.7	6S40.9	22N46.0
4 T	16 49 58.7	22 10.5	9 42.7	13 22.9	25 7.2	7 56.5	0 47.7	0 22.9	2 55.9	23 10.3	6 42.5	22 47.2
7 F	17 1 48.4	22 33.4	9 46.2	5N14.4	24 29.3	9 3.7	1 26.6	0 25.2	3 0.9	23 11.0	6 44.1	22 48.4
10 M	17 13 38.0	22 52.3	9 49.7	20 54.2	23 40.5	10 10.5	2 5.0	0 28.2	3 5.6	23 11.7	6 45.6	22 49.8
13 T	17 25 27.7	23 7.2	9 53.2	27 56.6	22 42.2	11 16.6	2 43.1	0 31.9	3 10.0	23 12.5	6 47.0	22 51.2
16 S	17 37 17.4	23 17.9	9 56.6	23 32.4	21 38.6	12 21.6	3 20.6	0 36.4	3 14.1	23 13.2	6 48.3	22 52.6
19 W	17 49 7.1	23 24.5	10 0.1	10 21.8	20 39.8	13 25.1	3 57.5	0 41.5	3 17.8	23 13.9	6 49.5	22 54.1
22 S	18 0 56.7	23 26.9	10 3.6	6S55.4	19 59.0	14 26.6	4 33.9	0 47.3	3 21.3	23 14.7	6 50.6	22 55.7
25 T	18 12 46.4	23 25.0	10 7.0	22 52.7	19 43.3	15 25.9	5 9.6	0 53.7	3 24.3	23 15.4	6 51.6	22 57.3
28 F	18 24 36.1	23 18.8	10 10.5	27 31.4	19 51.3	16 22.5	5 44.7	1 0.8	3 27.1	23 16.2	6 52.5	22 58.9
31 M	18 36 25.8	23 8.5	10 13.9	15 15.4	20 16.2	17 16.0	6 19.0	1 8.5	3 29.4	23 16.9	6 53.2	23 0.7

JANUARY 1952

DAY	EPHEMERIS SIDEREAL TIME	☉	☊	☽	☿	♀	♂	♃	♄	♅	♆	♇
	h m s	° ′	° ′	° ′	° ′	° ′	° ′	° ′	° ′	° ′	° ′	° ′
						LONGITUDE at NOON						
1 T	18 40 22.3	10♑ 1.7	3♓25.9	5♓52.4	17♐53.2	28♏29.0	20♎55.1	6♈ 0.1	14♎29.9	12♋ 1.8	21♎34.4	21♌12.0
2 W	18 44 18.9	11 2.9	3 22.8	19 55.1	18 35.3	29 40.3	21 25.8	6 6.5	14 32.3	11R59.2	21 35.2	21R11.0
3 T	18 48 15.4	12 4.0	3 19.6	3♈31.9	19 22.5	0♐51.8	21 56.4	6 13.0	14 34.6	11 56.6	21 35.8	21 9.9
4 F	18 52 12.0	13 5.2	3 16.4	16 44.8	20 14.2	2 3.3	22 26.8	6 19.7	14 36.8	11 54.0	21 36.5	21 8.8
5 S	18 56 8.6	14 6.4	3 13.2	29 36.9	21 10.0	3 14.9	22 57.0	6 26.6	14 38.9	11 51.4	21 37.1	21 7.7
6 S	19 0 5.1	15 7.6	3 10.1	12♉11.8	22 9.4	4 26.7	23 27.2	6 33.7	14 41.0	11 48.9	21 37.8	21 6.7
7 M	19 4 1.7	16 8.7	3 6.9	24 32.9	23 11.9	5 38.5	23 57.2	6 40.9	14 42.8	11 46.3	21 38.3	21 5.5
8 T	19 7 58.2	17 9.8	3 3.7	6♊43.3	24 17.2	6 50.4	24 27.0	6 48.3	14 44.6	11 43.7	21 38.9	21 4.4
9 W	19 11 54.8	18 11.0	3 0.5	18 45.8	25 25.1	8 2.3	24 56.7	6 55.8	14 46.3	11 41.1	21 39.4	21 3.2
10 T	19 15 51.3	19 12.1	2 57.3	0♋42.4	26 35.2	9 14.3	25 26.2	7 3.5	14 47.9	11 38.5	21 39.8	21 2.0
11 F	19 19 47.9	20 13.2	2 54.2	12 35.0	27 47.4	10 26.4	25 55.6	7 11.4	14 49.3	11 36.0	21 40.2	21 0.8
12 S	19 23 44.5	21 14.3	2 51.0	24 25.2	29 1.5	11 38.6	26 24.8	7 19.4	14 50.7	11 33.4	21 40.6	20 59.6
13 S	19 27 41.0	22 15.4	2 47.8	6♌14.7	0♑17.2	12 50.8	26 53.8	7 27.5	14 51.9	11 30.9	21 41.0	20 58.4
14 M	19 31 37.6	23 16.5	2 44.6	18 5.4	1 34.4	14 3.1	27 22.7	7 35.8	14 53.1	11 28.3	21 41.3	20 57.1
15 T	19 35 34.1	24 17.6	2 41.5	29 59.6	2 53.0	15 15.5	27 51.4	7 44.2	14 54.1	11 25.8	21 41.6	20 55.9
16 W	19 39 30.7	25 18.7	2 38.3	12♍ 0.2	4 12.8	16 27.9	28 20.0	7 52.8	14 55.1	11 23.3	21 41.9	20 54.6
17 T	19 43 27.3	26 19.8	2 35.1	24 10.7	5 33.9	17 40.4	28 48.3	8 1.5	14 55.9	11 20.8	21 42.1	20 53.3
18 F	19 47 23.8	27 20.9	2 31.9	6♎34.8	6 56.0	18 53.0	29 16.5	8 10.3	14 56.6	11 18.4	21 42.3	20 52.0
19 S	19 51 20.4	28 22.0	2 28.8	19 16.9	8 19.1	20 5.6	29 44.5	8 19.3	14 57.2	11 15.9	21 42.4	20 50.7
20 S	19 55 16.9	29 23.0	2 25.6	2♏20.8	9 43.1	21 18.3	0♏12.3	8 28.5	14 57.7	11 13.5	21 42.5	20 49.3
21 M	19 59 13.5	0♒24.1	2 22.4	15 50.1	11 8.1	22 31.0	0 39.9	8 37.7	14 58.1	11 11.0	21 42.6	20 48.0
22 T	20 3 10.0	1 25.2	2 19.2	29 46.7	12 33.9	23 43.8	1 7.3	8 47.1	14 58.4	11 8.6	21 42.7	20 46.7
23 W	20 7 6.6	2 26.2	2 16.1	14♐10.3	14 0.5	24 56.6	1 34.4	8 56.6	14 58.6	11 6.3	21 42.7	20 45.3
24 T	20 11 3.2	3 27.3	2 12.9	28 58.0	15 27.9	26 9.5	2 1.4	9 6.3	14 58.7	11 3.9	21R42.6	20 43.9
25 F	20 14 59.7	4 28.3	2 9.7	14♑ 3.3	16 56.1	27 22.4	2 28.2	9 16.1	14R58.6	11 1.6	21 42.6	20 42.5
26 S	20 18 56.3	5 29.3	2 6.5	29 17.5	18 25.0	28 35.4	2 54.7	9 26.0	14 58.5	10 59.3	21 42.5	20 41.1
27 S	20 22 52.8	6 30.4	2 3.3	14♒30.3	19 54.6	29 48.4	3 21.1	9 36.1	14 58.3	10 57.0	21 42.4	20 39.8
28 M	20 26 49.4	7 31.4	2 0.2	29 31.7	21 25.0	1♑ 1.5	3 47.2	9 46.2	14 57.9	10 54.8	21 42.3	20 38.4
29 T	20 30 45.9	8 32.4	1 57.0	14♓13.5	22 56.0	2 14.5	4 13.0	9 56.5	14 57.4	10 52.6	21 42.1	20 37.0
30 W	20 34 42.5	9 33.3	1 53.8	28 30.5	24 27.7	3 27.6	4 38.6	10 6.9	14 56.9	10 50.4	21 41.8	20 35.5
31 T	20 38 39.1	10 34.3	1 50.6	12♈20.3	26 0.1	4 40.8	5 4.0	10 17.4	14 56.2	10 48.2	21 41.6	20 34.1
						DECLINATION at NOON						
1 T	18 40 22.3	23S 4.1	10S 15.1	9S 1.4	20S 27.0	17S 33.1	6S 30.3	1N 11.2	3S 30.1	23N 17.2	6S 53.4	23N 1.2
4 F	18 52 12.0	22 48.2	10 18.5	9N 56.1	21 2.9	18 22.0	7 3.7	1 19.8	3 32.0	23 17.9	6 54.1	23 3.0
7 M	19 4 1.7	22 28.3	10 22.0	23 50.9	21 40.3	19 7.0	7 36.2	1 28.9	3 33.6	23 18.6	6 54.6	23 4.7
10 T	19 15 51.3	22 4.3	10 25.4	27 55.7	22 15.1	19 47.9	8 8.0	1 38.5	3 34.7	23 19.3	6 55.0	23 6.5
13 S	19 27 41.0	21 36.5	10 28.8	20 49.1	22 44.2	20 24.3	8 38.9	1 48.6	3 35.5	23 20.0	6 55.2	23 8.3
16 W	19 39 30.7	21 4.9	10 32.3	6 7.9	23 5.8	20 55.9	9 8.9	1 59.3	3 35.9	23 20.6	6 55.4	23 10.1
19 S	19 51 20.4	20 29.7	10 35.7	11S 9.7	23 18.4	21 22.4	9 38.0	2 10.4	3 36.0	23 21.3	6 55.4	23 12.0
22 T	20 3 10.0	19 51.0	10 39.1	25 12.5	23 20.9	21 43.7	10 6.2	2 21.9	3 35.6	23 21.9	6 55.3	23 13.8
25 F	20 14 59.7	19 9.0	10 42.5	26 29.7	23 12.6	21 59.5	10 33.4	2 33.9	3 34.9	23 22.5	6 55.1	23 15.6
28 M	20 26 49.4	18 23.8	10 45.9	11 44.3	22 52.9	22 9.6	10 59.6	2 46.4	3 33.9	23 23.1	6 54.9	23 17.4
31 T	20 38 39.1	17 35.6	10 49.3	8N 6.1	22 21.4	22 14.1	11 24.7	2 59.2	3 32.4	23 23.6	6 54.4	23 19.2

FEBRUARY 1952

DAY	EPHEMERIS SIDEREAL TIME	☉	☊	☽	☿	♀	♂	♃	♄	♅	♆	♇
						LONGITUDE at NOON						
1 F	20 42 35.6	11♒35.2	1♓47.5	25♈42.9	27♑33.3	5♑53.9	5♏29.1	10♈28.0	14♎55.4	10♋46.1	21♎41.3	20♌32.7
2 S	20 46 32.2	12 36.1	1 44.3	8♉40.8	29 7.1	7 7.1	5 53.9	10 38.7	14R54.5	10R44.0	21R41.0	20R31.2
3 S	20 50 28.7	13 36.9	1 41.1	21 17.2	0♒41.6	8 20.4	6 18.5	10 49.6	14 53.5	10 41.9	21 40.6	20 29.8
4 M	20 54 25.3	14 37.8	1 37.9	3♊36.3	2 16.9	9 33.6	6 42.8	11 0.5	14 52.4	10 39.9	21 40.2	20 28.3
5 T	20 58 21.8	15 38.6	1 34.8	15 42.3	3 52.9	10 46.9	7 6.9	11 11.6	14 51.2	10 37.9	21 39.8	20 26.9
6 W	21 2 18.4	16 39.4	1 31.6	27 39.1	5 29.6	12 0.2	7 30.6	11 22.7	14 49.9	10 35.9	21 39.3	20 25.4
7 T	21 6 15.0	17 40.2	1 28.4	9♋30.5	7 7.1	13 13.6	7 54.1	11 34.0	14 48.4	10 34.0	21 38.8	20 24.0
8 F	21 10 11.5	18 40.9	1 25.2	21 19.6	8 45.4	14 26.9	8 17.4	11 45.3	14 46.9	10 32.1	21 38.3	20 22.5
9 S	21 14 8.1	19 41.7	1 22.0	3♌ 9.2	10 24.4	15 40.3	8 40.3	11 56.8	14 45.3	10 30.2	21 37.8	20 21.0
10 S	21 18 4.6	20 42.4	1 18.9	15 1.5	12 4.2	16 53.7	9 2.9	12 8.3	14 43.6	10 28.4	21 37.2	20 19.6
11 M	21 22 1.2	21 43.1	1 15.7	26 58.6	13 44.9	18 7.2	9 25.2	12 19.9	14 41.8	10 26.6	21 36.6	20 18.1
12 T	21 25 57.7	22 43.7	1 12.5	9♍ 2.4	15 26.4	19 20.6	9 47.2	12 31.7	14 39.9	10 24.9	21 35.9	20 16.7
13 W	21 29 54.3	23 44.4	1 9.3	21 14.8	17 8.7	20 34.1	10 8.9	12 43.5	14 37.9	10 23.2	21 35.2	20 15.2
14 T	21 33 50.8	24 45.0	1 6.2	3♎37.5	18 51.9	21 47.6	10 30.2	12 55.4	14 35.7	10 21.6	21 34.5	20 13.8
15 F	21 37 47.4	25 45.6	1 3.0	16 12.9	20 35.9	23 1.2	10 51.3	13 7.4	14 33.5	10 20.0	21 33.8	20 12.3
16 S	21 41 44.0	26 46.2	0 59.8	29 3.0	22 20.8	24 14.7	11 11.9	13 19.5	14 31.2	10 18.4	21 33.0	20 10.8
17 S	21 45 40.5	27 46.8	0 56.6	12♏10.2	24 6.7	25 28.4	11 32.3	13 31.7	14 28.9	10 16.9	21 32.3	20 9.4
18 M	21 49 37.1	28 47.3	0 53.5	25 36.5	25 53.4	26 42.0	11 52.3	13 43.9	14 26.4	10 15.4	21 31.5	20 8.0
19 T	21 53 33.6	29 47.8	0 50.3	9♐23.3	27 41.0	27 55.6	12 11.8	13 56.2	14 23.8	10 14.0	21 30.6	20 6.6
20 W	21 57 30.2	0♓48.3	0 47.1	23 30.9	29 29.4	29 9.3	12 31.1	14 8.6	14 21.2	10 12.6	21 29.7	20 5.1
21 T	22 1 26.7	1 48.8	0 43.9	7♑58.0	1♓18.8	0♒22.9	12 49.9	14 21.1	14 18.4	10 11.3	21 28.8	20 3.7
22 F	22 5 23.3	2 49.3	0 40.7	22 41.0	3 9.0	1 36.6	13 8.3	14 33.7	14 15.6	10 10.0	21 27.9	20 2.3
23 S	22 9 19.8	3 49.7	0 37.6	7♒34.7	5 0.1	2 50.3	13 26.3	14 46.3	14 12.7	10 8.7	21 26.9	20 0.9
24 S	22 13 16.4	4 50.1	0 34.4	22 31.8	6 51.9	4 4.0	13 43.9	14 59.0	14 9.6	10 7.5	21 25.9	19 59.5
25 M	22 17 12.9	5 50.5	0 31.2	7♓24.2	8 44.5	5 17.7	14 1.0	15 11.8	14 6.6	10 6.4	21 24.9	19 58.1
26 T	22 21 9.5	6 50.8	0 28.0	22 4.0	10 37.8	6 31.4	14 17.8	15 24.7	14 3.4	10 5.3	21 23.8	19 56.7
27 W	22 25 6.1	7 51.2	0 24.9	6♈24.6	12 31.7	7 45.2	14 34.0	15 37.6	14 0.1	10 4.2	21 22.8	19 55.3
28 T	22 29 2.6	8 51.4	0 21.7	20 21.5	14 26.0	8 58.9	14 49.8	15 50.6	13 56.8	10 3.2	21 21.7	19 53.9
29 F	22 32 59.2	9 51.7	0 18.5	3♉52.8	16 20.7	10 12.7	15 5.2	16 3.6	13 53.4	10 2.3	21 20.5	19 52.5
						DECLINATION at NOON						
1 F	20 42 35.6	17S 18.9	10S 50.5	13N 57.6	22S 8.2	22S 14.2	11S 32.9	3N 3.5	3S 31.9	23N 23.8	6S 54.3	23N 19.8
4 M	20 54 25.3	16 27.0	10 53.9	26 2.6	21 20.4	22 10.9	11 56.6	3 16.8	3 30.0	23 24.2	6 53.7	23 21.5
7 T	21 6 15.0	15 32.5	10 57.3	27 12.2	20 20.1	22 1.6	12 19.3	3 30.4	3 27.7	23 24.7	6 53.0	23 23.2
10 S	21 18 4.6	14 35.7	11 0.7	17 41.3	19 7.2	21 46.5	12 40.8	3 44.3	3 25.1	23 25.1	6 52.3	23 24.9
13 W	21 29 54.3	13 36.7	11 4.1	1 44.9	17 41.4	21 25.7	13 1.3	3 58.5	3 22.2	23 25.5	6 51.4	23 26.5
16 S	21 41 44.0	12 35.7	11 7.4	15S 21.5	16 2.7	20 59.1	13 20.6	4 12.9	3 19.0	23 25.9	6 50.4	23 28.1
19 T	21 53 33.6	11 32.8	11 10.8	27 2.2	14 11.3	20 26.9	13 38.8	4 27.6	3 15.4	23 26.2	6 49.4	23 29.6
22 F	22 5 23.3	10 28.3	11 14.2	24 45.0	12 7.2	19 49.4	13 55.7	4 42.5	3 11.6	23 26.5	6 48.2	23 31.1
25 M	22 17 12.9	9 22.3	11 17.6	8 12.6	9 51.2	19 6.6	14 11.4	4 57.6	3 7.5	23 26.7	6 47.0	23 32.5
28 T	22 29 2.6	8 15.1	11 20.9	11N 41.9	7 24.2	18 18.8	14 25.9	5 12.9	3 3.2	23 27.0	6 45.6	23 33.9

MARCH 1952

LONGITUDE at NOON

DAY	EPHEMERIS SIDEREAL TIME h m s	☉ ° ′	☊ ° ′	☽ ° ′	☿ ° ′	♀ ° ′	♂ ° ′	♃ ° ′	♄ ° ′	♅ ° ′	♆ ° ′	♇ ° ′
1 S	22 36 55.7	10♓51.9	0♓15.3	16♉58.5	18♓15.7	11♒26.4	15♏20.1	16♈16.7	13♎49.9	10♋ 1.4	21♎19.4	19♌51.2
2 S	22 40 52.3	11 52.1	0 12.1	29 40.9	20 10.6	12 40.2	15 34.5	16 29.9	13R46.4	10R 0.5	21R18.2	19R49.9
3 M	22 44 48.8	12 52.3	0 9.0	12♊ 3.4	22 5.4	13 54.0	15 48.4	16 43.1	13 42.7	9 59.7	21 17.0	19 48.5
4 T	22 48 45.4	13 52.4	0 5.8	24 10.4	23 59.7	15 7.7	16 1.8	16 56.4	13 39.1	9 58.9	21 15.8	19 47.2
5 W	22 52 41.9	14 52.5	0 2.6	6♋ 6.5	25 53.3	16 21.5	16 14.7	17 9.7	13 35.3	9 58.3	21 14.6	19 45.9
6 T	22 56 38.5	15 52.5	29♒59.4	17 56.5	27 45.9	17 35.3	16 27.0	17 23.1	13 31.5	9 57.6	21 13.3	19 44.6
7 F	23 0 35.0	16 52.5	29 56.3	29 44.9	29 37.0	18 49.1	16 38.9	17 36.6	13 27.6	9 57.0	21 12.0	19 43.3
8 S	23 4 31.6	17 52.5	29 53.1	11♌35.7	1♈26.3	20 2.9	16 50.2	17 50.1	13 23.7	9 56.5	21 10.7	19 42.1
9 S	23 8 28.2	18 52.5	29 49.9	23 32.4	3 13.3	21 16.7	17 1.0	18 3.7	13 19.7	9 56.0	21 9.5	19 40.9
10 M	23 12 24.7	19 52.4	29 46.7	5♍37.8	4 57.6	22 30.5	17 11.2	18 17.3	13 15.7	9 55.6	21 8.1	19 39.7
11 T	23 16 21.3	20 52.3	29 43.5	17 54.1	6 38.6	23 44.4	17 20.8	18 30.9	13 11.6	9 55.2	21 6.8	19 38.4
12 W	23 20 17.8	21 52.1	29 40.4	0♎22.7	8 15.9	24 58.2	17 29.8	18 44.6	13 7.4	9 54.9	21 5.4	19 37.2
13 T	23 24 14.4	22 51.9	29 37.2	13 4.5	9 49.0	26 12.0	17 38.2	18 58.3	13 3.2	9 54.6	21 4.0	19 36.1
14 F	23 28 10.9	23 51.7	29 34.0	25 59.9	11 17.3	27 25.8	17 46.1	19 12.1	12 59.0	9 54.4	21 2.6	19 34.9
15 S	23 32 7.5	24 51.5	29 30.8	9♏ 8.8	12 40.4	28 39.7	17 53.3	19 25.9	12 54.7	9 54.2	21 1.2	19 33.7
16 S	23 36 4.0	25 51.2	29 27.7	22 31.1	13 57.8	29 53.5	17 59.8	19 39.8	12 50.3	9 54.1	20 59.7	19 32.6
17 M	23 40 0.6	26 50.9	29 24.5	6♐ 6.5	15 9.0	1♓ 7.4	18 5.8	19 53.7	12 46.0	9 54.0	20 58.3	19 31.5
18 T	23 43 57.1	27 50.5	29 21.3	19 54.5	16 13.7	2 21.2	18 11.0	20 7.6	12 41.5	9 54.0	20 56.8	19 30.4
19 W	23 47 53.7	28 50.2	29 18.1	3♑54.7	17 11.5	3 35.1	18 15.6	20 21.6	12 37.1	9D54.1	20 55.3	19 29.3
20 T	23 51 50.2	29 49.8	29 14.9	18 6.1	18 2.1	4 48.9	18 19.5	20 35.6	12 32.6	9 54.2	20 53.8	19 28.3
21 F	23 55 46.8	0♈49.4	29 11.8	2♒26.9	18 45.3	6 2.8	18 22.7	20 49.6	12 28.1	9 54.3	20 52.3	19 27.2
22 S	23 59 43.3	1 48.9	29 8.6	16 54.5	19 20.8	7 16.7	18 25.3	21 3.7	12 23.6	9 54.5	20 50.7	19 26.2
23 S	0 3 39.9	2 48.4	29 5.4	1♓25.1	19 48.5	8 30.5	18 27.1	21 17.8	12 19.0	9 54.8	20 49.2	19 25.2
24 M	0 7 36.5	3 47.9	29 2.2	15 53.8	20 8.5	9 44.4	18 28.1	21 31.9	12 14.4	9 55.1	20 47.6	19 24.2
25 T	0 11 33.0	4 47.4	28 59.1	0♈15.2	20 20.6	10 58.3	18 28.5	21 46.1	12 9.8	9 55.5	20 46.1	19 23.3
26 W	0 15 29.6	5 46.8	28 55.9	14 23.6	20 25.0	12 12.1	18R28.1	22 0.3	12 5.2	9 55.9	20 44.5	19 22.3
27 T	0 19 26.1	6 46.2	28 52.7	28 14.3	20R21.8	13 26.0	18 26.9	22 14.5	12 0.5	9 56.4	20 42.9	19 21.4
28 F	0 23 22.7	7 45.5	28 49.5	11♉44.0	20 11.4	14 39.9	18 25.0	22 28.7	11 55.9	9 56.9	20 41.3	19 20.5
29 S	0 27 19.2	8 44.9	28 46.3	24 51.3	19 54.0	15 53.7	18 22.4	22 43.0	11 51.2	9 57.5	20 39.7	19 19.7
30 S	0 31 15.8	9 44.2	28 43.2	7♊36.5	19 30.3	17 7.6	18 19.0	22 57.3	11 46.6	9 58.2	20 38.2	19 18.9
31 M	0 35 12.3	10 43.4	28 40.0	20 1.9	19 0.8	18 21.5	18 14.8	23 11.6	11 41.9	9 58.9	20 36.5	19 18.1

DECLINATION at NOON

DAY	EPHEMERIS SIDEREAL TIME h m s	☉	☊	☽	☿	♀	♂	♃	♄	♅	♆	♇
1 S	22 36 55.7	7S29.7	11S23.2	21N49.9	5S41.0	17S44.4	14S34.9	5N23.2	3S 0.2	23N27.1	6S44.7	23N34.7
4 T	22 48 45.4	6 20.7	11 26.5	28 9.4	3 0.5	16 48.9	14 47.3	5 38.8	2 55.5	23 27.2	6 43.3	23 35.9
7 F	23 0 35.0	5 11.0	11 29.9	22 51.5	0 16.9	15 49.2	14 58.4	5 54.5	2 50.6	23 27.3	6 41.7	23 37.1
10 M	23 12 24.7	4 0.7	11 33.2	9 1.2	2N23.9	14 45.4	15 8.3	6 10.3	2 45.5	23 27.4	6 40.2	23 38.1
13 T	23 24 14.4	2 50.0	11 36.6	8S26.0	4 54.8	13 38.0	15 16.8	6 26.1	2 40.3	23 27.5	6 38.5	23 39.1
16 S	23 36 4.0	1 38.9	11 39.9	23 24.8	7 8.1	12 27.2	15 24.0	6 42.1	2 35.0	23 27.5	6 36.8	23 40.0
19 W	23 47 53.7	0 27.8	11 43.2	27 44.8	8 56.5	11 13.3	15 29.8	6 58.1	2 29.5	23 27.4	6 35.1	23 40.9
22 S	23 59 43.3	0N43.3	11 46.6	16 55.8	10 14.1	9 56.7	15 34.2	7 14.1	2 24.0	23 27.4	6 33.3	23 41.6
25 T	0 11 33.0	1 54.2	11 49.9	2N29.3	10 56.4	8 37.6	15 37.2	7 30.2	2 18.5	23 27.2	6 31.5	23 42.2
28 F	0 23 22.7	3 4.8	11 53.2	20 1.9	11 1.3	7 16.3	15 38.6	7 46.3	2 12.9	23 27.1	6 29.7	23 42.8
31 M	0 35 12.3	4 14.8	11 56.5	27 54.9	10 29.5	5 53.3	15 38.6	8 2.3	2 7.4	23 26.9	6 27.8	23 43.2

APRIL 1952

LONGITUDE at NOON

DAY	EPHEMERIS SIDEREAL TIME h m s	☉ ° ′	☊ ° ′	☽ ° ′	☿ ° ′	♀ ° ′	♂ ° ′	♃ ° ′	♄ ° ′	♅ ° ′	♆ ° ′	♇ ° ′
1 T	0 39 8.9	11♈42.6	28♒36.8	2♋11.0	18♈26.1	19♓35.3	18♏ 9.9	23♈25.9	11♎37.2	9♋59.6	20♎34.9	19♌17.3
2 W	0 43 5.4	12 41.8	28 33.6	14 8.3	17R47.0	20 49.2	18R 4.2	23 40.3	11R32.6	10 0.4	20R33.3	19R16.5
3 T	0 47 2.0	13 40.9	28 30.5	25 58.8	17 4.3	22 3.0	17 57.7	23 54.6	11 27.9	10 1.3	20 31.7	19 15.7
4 F	0 50 58.5	14 40.0	28 27.3	7♌47.6	16 19.1	23 16.8	17 50.5	24 9.0	11 23.2	10 2.2	20 30.0	19 15.0
5 S	0 54 55.1	15 39.0	28 24.1	19 39.9	15 32.1	24 30.6	17 42.5	24 23.4	11 18.6	10 3.1	20 28.4	19 14.3
6 S	0 58 51.7	16 38.1	28 20.9	1♍40.4	14 44.4	25 44.5	17 33.8	24 37.8	11 13.9	10 4.2	20 26.7	19 13.7
7 M	1 2 48.2	17 37.0	28 17.7	13 53.0	13 56.9	26 58.3	17 24.3	24 52.2	11 9.3	10 5.2	20 25.1	19 13.0
8 T	1 6 44.8	18 36.0	28 14.6	26 20.7	13 10.4	28 12.1	17 14.0	25 6.6	11 4.7	10 6.3	20 23.4	19 12.4
9 W	1 10 41.3	19 34.9	28 11.4	9♎ 5.6	12 25.9	29 25.9	17 3.0	25 21.0	11 0.0	10 7.5	20 21.8	19 11.8
10 T	1 14 37.9	20 33.7	28 8.2	22 8.0	11 44.0	0♈39.7	16 51.3	25 35.4	10 55.5	10 8.7	20 20.1	19 11.2
11 F	1 18 34.4	21 32.6	28 5.0	5♏27.4	11 5.4	1 53.5	16 38.8	25 49.9	10 50.9	10 10.0	20 18.5	19 10.7
12 S	1 22 31.0	22 31.4	28 1.9	19 1.7	10 30.7	3 7.3	16 25.6	26 4.3	10 46.4	10 11.3	20 16.8	19 10.1
13 S	1 26 27.5	23 30.1	27 58.7	2♐48.3	10 0.2	4 21.1	16 11.8	26 18.7	10 41.9	10 12.6	20 15.2	19 9.7
14 M	1 30 24.1	24 28.9	27 55.5	16 43.9	9 34.4	5 34.9	15 57.2	26 33.2	10 37.4	10 14.0	20 13.5	19 9.2
15 T	1 34 20.6	25 27.6	27 52.3	0♑45.8	9 13.5	6 48.7	15 41.9	26 47.6	10 32.9	10 15.5	20 11.9	19 8.7
16 W	1 38 17.2	26 26.3	27 49.2	14 51.4	8 57.7	8 2.5	15 26.0	27 2.1	10 28.5	10 17.0	20 10.3	19 8.3
17 T	1 42 13.7	27 24.9	27 46.0	28 58.9	8 47.0	9 16.3	15 9.5	27 16.5	10 24.2	10 18.6	20 8.6	19 7.9
18 F	1 46 10.3	28 23.6	27 42.8	13♒ 7.2	8 41.6	10 30.1	14 52.3	27 31.0	10 19.8	10 20.2	20 7.0	19 7.6
19 S	1 50 6.9	29 22.2	27 39.6	27 14.9	8 41.3	11 43.9	14 34.5	27 45.4	10 15.5	10 21.8	20 5.4	19 7.3
20 S	1 54 3.4	0♉20.8	27 36.4	11♓20.7	8D46.1	12 57.7	14 16.3	27 59.9	10 11.3	10 23.6	20 3.8	19 7.0
21 M	1 57 60.0	1 19.3	27 33.3	25 22.6	8 55.8	14 11.5	13 57.4	28 14.4	10 7.1	10 25.3	20 2.2	19 6.7
22 T	2 1 56.5	2 17.8	27 30.1	9♈17.9	9 10.4	15 25.3	13 38.0	28 28.8	10 2.9	10 27.1	20 0.6	19 6.5
23 W	2 5 53.1	3 16.3	27 26.9	23 3.4	9 29.7	16 39.0	13 18.2	28 43.2	9 58.8	10 28.9	19 59.0	19 6.2
24 T	2 9 49.6	4 14.8	27 23.7	6♉35.8	9 53.4	17 52.8	12 58.0	28 57.6	9 54.8	10 30.8	19 57.4	19 6.1
25 F	2 13 46.2	5 13.2	27 20.6	19 52.3	10 21.6	19 6.6	12 37.3	29 12.0	9 50.8	10 32.7	19 55.8	19 5.9
26 S	2 17 42.7	6 11.6	27 17.4	2♊51.1	10 53.9	20 20.3	12 16.3	29 26.4	9 46.8	10 34.7	19 54.2	19 5.8
27 S	2 21 39.3	7 10.0	27 14.2	15 31.5	11 30.2	21 34.1	11 55.0	29 40.8	9 42.9	10 36.7	19 52.7	19 5.6
28 M	2 25 35.9	8 8.3	27 11.0	27 54.6	12 10.4	22 47.8	11 33.5	29 55.2	9 39.1	10 38.8	19 51.1	19 5.6
29 T	2 29 32.4	9 6.6	27 7.8	10♋ 2.8	12 54.3	24 1.6	11 11.7	0♉ 9.5	9 35.3	10 40.9	19 49.6	19 5.5
30 W	2 33 29.0	10 4.9	27 4.7	21 59.8	13 41.7	25 15.3	10 49.7	0 23.9	9 31.6	10 43.0	19 48.1	19 5.5

DECLINATION at NOON

DAY	EPHEMERIS SIDEREAL TIME h m s	☉	☊	☽	☿	♀	♂	♃	♄	♅	♆	♇
1 T	0 39 8.9	4N37.9	11S57.6	27N48.0	10N11.4	5S25.3	15S38.2	8N 7.7	2S 5.5	23N26.9	6S27.2	23N43.4
4 F	0 50 58.5	5 46.9	12 0.9	20 11.9	8 59.2	4 0.3	15 36.2	8 23.7	2 0.0	23 26.6	6 25.4	23 43.7
7 M	1 2 48.2	6 55.0	12 4.2	5 10.7	7 29.1	2 34.4	15 32.6	8 39.7	1 54.6	23 26.4	6 23.5	23 43.9
10 T	1 14 37.9	8 2.0	12 7.5	12S23.5	5 54.7	1 7.6	15 27.6	8 55.5	1 49.3	23 26.1	6 21.6	23 44.1
13 S	1 26 27.5	9 7.8	12 10.8	25 42.7	4 28.5	0N19.6	15 21.0	9 11.4	1 44.0	23 25.7	6 19.7	23 44.1
16 W	1 38 17.2	10 12.3	12 14.1	26 8.6	3 19.6	1 47.0	15 13.0	9 27.1	1 39.0	23 25.4	6 17.9	23 44.1
19 S	1 50 6.9	11 15.2	12 17.4	12 33.7	2 32.7	3 14.2	15 3.5	9 42.7	1 34.1	23 24.9	6 16.1	23 43.9
22 T	2 1 56.5	12 16.5	12 20.7	6N43.4	2 9.2	4 40.9	14 52.8	9 58.2	1 29.4	23 24.5	6 14.3	23 43.7
25 F	2 13 46.2	13 16.0	12 23.9	22 30.8	2 8.5	6 6.8	14 41.0	10 13.6	1 24.9	23 24.0	6 12.5	23 43.4
28 M	2 25 35.9	14 13.5	12 27.2	27 47.8	2 28.8	7 31.6	14 28.4	10 28.8	1 20.7	23 23.5	6 10.8	23 43.0

MAY 1952

DAY	EPHEMERIS SIDEREAL TIME	☉	☊	☽	☿	♀	♂	♃	♄	♅	♆	♇
	h m s	° ′	° ′	° ′	° ′	° ′	° ′	° ′	° ′	° ′	° ′	° ′
	LONGITUDE at NOON											
1 T	2 37 25.5	11♉ 3.1	27♒ 1.5	3♌50.1	14♈32.4	26♈29.0	10♏27.6	0♉38.2	9♎28.0	10♋45.2	19♎46.5	19♌ 5.5
2 F	2 41 22.1	12 1.3	26 58.3	15 38.8	15 26.4	27 42.7	10R 5.5	0 52.5	9R 24.4	10 47.5	19R 45.0	19 5.5
3 S	2 45 18.6	12 59.5	26 55.1	27 31.5	16 23.6	28 56.4	9 43.3	1 6.8	9 20.9	10 49.7	19 43.5	19D 5.6
4 S	2 49 15.2	13 57.6	26 52.0	9♍33.6	17 23.7	0♉10.1	9 21.1	1 21.0	9 17.5	10 52.0	19 42.1	19 5.7
5 M	2 53 11.7	14 55.7	26 48.8	21 49.9	18 26.7	1 23.8	8 58.9	1 35.2	9 14.2	10 54.4	19 40.6	19 5.8
6 T	2 57 8.3	15 53.7	26 45.6	4♎24.7	19 32.6	2 37.5	8 36.9	1 49.4	9 10.9	10 56.8	19 39.2	19 5.9
7 W	3 1 4.9	16 51.8	26 42.4	17 20.9	20 41.1	3 51.2	8 15.0	2 3.6	9 7.7	10 59.2	19 37.7	19 6.1
8 T	3 5 1.4	17 49.8	26 39.3	0♏39.7	21 52.2	5 4.9	7 53.3	2 17.8	9 4.5	11 1.7	19 36.3	19 6.3
9 F	3 8 58.0	18 47.8	26 36.1	14 20.1	23 5.9	6 18.6	7 31.8	2 31.9	9 1.5	11 4.2	19 34.9	19 6.5
10 S	3 12 54.5	19 45.7	26 32.9	28 19.3	24 22.1	7 32.2	7 10.6	2 46.0	8 58.5	11 6.7	19 33.6	19 6.8
11 S	3 16 51.1	20 43.7	26 29.7	12♐32.7	25 40.7	8 45.9	6 49.7	3 0.1	8 55.7	11 9.3	19 32.2	19 7.1
12 M	3 20 47.6	21 41.6	26 26.5	26 54.3	27 1.7	9 59.6	6 29.1	3 14.2	8 52.9	11 12.0	19 30.9	19 7.4
13 T	3 24 44.2	22 39.5	26 23.4	11♑18.7	28 25.0	11 13.3	6 8.9	3 28.2	8 50.1	11 14.6	19 29.6	19 7.8
14 W	3 28 40.8	23 37.3	26 20.2	25 40.8	29 50.6	12 26.9	5 49.2	3 42.2	8 47.5	11 17.3	19 28.3	19 8.1
15 T	3 32 37.3	24 35.2	26 17.0	9♒57.2	1♉18.5	13 40.6	5 29.8	3 56.1	8 44.9	11 20.0	19 27.0	19 8.5
16 F	3 36 33.9	25 33.0	26 13.8	24 5.6	2 48.6	14 54.3	5 11.0	4 10.1	8 42.5	11 22.8	19 25.7	19 9.0
17 S	3 40 30.4	26 30.8	26 10.7	8♓ 5.2	4 21.0	16 7.9	4 52.7	4 23.9	8 40.1	11 25.5	19 24.5	19 9.4
18 S	3 44 27.0	27 28.6	26 7.5	21 55.6	5 55.6	17 21.6	4 35.0	4 37.8	8 37.8	11 28.4	19 23.3	19 9.9
19 M	3 48 23.5	28 26.3	26 4.3	5♈36.8	7 32.4	18 35.3	4 17.8	4 51.6	8 35.6	11 31.2	19 22.1	19 10.4
20 T	3 52 20.1	29 24.1	26 1.1	19 8.4	9 11.4	19 48.9	4 1.3	5 5.4	8 33.5	11 34.1	19 20.9	19 10.9
21 W	3 56 16.7	0♊21.8	25 58.0	2♉29.5	10 52.6	21 2.6	3 45.5	5 19.1	8 31.5	11 37.0	19 19.7	19 11.5
22 T	4 0 13.2	1 19.5	25 54.8	15 39.1	12 36.0	22 16.3	3 30.3	5 32.8	8 29.5	11 40.0	19 18.6	19 12.1
23 F	4 4 9.8	2 17.2	25 51.6	28 35.8	14 21.5	23 29.9	3 15.8	5 46.4	8 27.7	11 42.9	19 17.5	19 12.7
24 S	4 8 6.3	3 14.8	25 48.4	11♊18.7	16 9.3	24 43.6	3 2.0	6 0.0	8 26.0	11 45.9	19 16.4	19 13.3
25 S	4 12 2.9	4 12.5	25 45.2	23 47.5	17 59.3	25 57.3	2 49.0	6 13.6	8 24.3	11 49.0	19 15.3	19 14.0
26 M	4 15 59.4	5 10.1	25 42.1	6♋ 2.7	19 51.4	27 10.9	2 36.7	6 27.1	8 22.8	11 52.0	19 14.3	19 14.7
27 T	4 19 56.0	6 7.7	25 38.9	18 6.0	21 45.6	28 24.6	2 25.3	6 40.5	8 21.3	11 55.1	19 13.3	19 15.4
28 W	4 23 52.6	7 5.3	25 35.7	0♌ 0.1	23 42.0	29 38.2	2 14.6	6 54.0	8 20.0	11 58.2	19 12.3	19 16.2
29 T	4 27 49.1	8 2.8	25 32.5	11 48.7	25 40.4	0♊51.9	2 4.7	7 7.3	8 18.7	12 1.4	19 11.3	19 16.9
30 F	4 31 45.7	9 0.4	25 29.4	23 36.5	27 40.8	2 5.5	1 55.6	7 20.6	8 17.6	12 4.5	19 10.4	19 17.7
31 S	4 35 42.2	9 57.9	25 26.2	5♍28.4	29 43.2	3 19.2	1 47.4	7 33.9	8 16.5	12 7.7	19 9.5	19 18.6
	DECLINATION at NOON											
1 T	2 37 25.5	15N 8.9	12S 30.5	21N 16.8	3N 7.8	8N 54.9	14S 15.1	10N 43.9	1S 16.7	23N 23.0	6S 9.1	23N 42.5
4 S	2 49 15.2	16 2.0	12 33.7	7 0.2	4 3.5	10 16.4	14 1.5	10 58.7	1 13.0	23 22.4	6 7.5	23 41.9
7 W	3 1 4.9	16 52.8	12 37.0	10S 22.7	5 13.6	11 35.9	13 48.0	11 13.4	1 9.5	23 21.8	6 5.9	23 41.2
10 S	3 12 54.5	17 41.0	12 40.2	24 40.3	6 36.4	12 53.0	13 34.8	11 27.9	1 6.4	23 21.1	6 4.4	23 40.5
13 T	3 24 44.2	18 26.5	12 43.5	26 30.3	8 10.0	14 7.3	13 22.3	11 42.2	1 3.6	23 20.4	6 2.9	23 39.6
16 F	3 36 33.9	19 9.3	12 46.7	13 39.9	9 52.7	15 18.6	13 10.7	11 56.3	1 1.1	23 19.7	6 1.6	23 38.7
19 M	3 48 23.5	19 49.1	12 49.9	5N 10.4	11 42.7	16 26.5	13 0.4	12 10.2	0 59.0	23 19.0	6 0.3	23 37.7
22 T	4 0 13.2	20 26.0	12 53.2	21 14.6	13 37.8	17 30.7	12 51.7	12 23.8	0 57.2	23 18.2	5 59.1	23 36.7
25 S	4 12 2.9	20 59.6	12 56.4	27 41.6	15 35.7	18 30.8	12 44.7	12 37.2	0 55.7	23 17.4	5 57.9	23 35.6
28 W	4 23 52.6	21 30.0	12 59.6	22 12.9	17 33.4	19 26.6	12 39.8	12 50.3	0 54.6	23 16.6	5 56.9	23 34.4
31 S	4 35 42.2	21 57.1	13 2.8	8 36.7	19 27.0	20 17.7	12 37.0	13 3.1	0 53.9	23 15.7	5 55.9	23 33.1

JUNE 1952

DAY	EPHEMERIS SIDEREAL TIME	☉	☊	☽	☿	♀	♂	♃	♄	♅	♆	♇
	LONGITUDE at NOON											
1 S	4 39 38.8	10♊55.4	25♒23.0	17♍29.9	1♊47.4	4♊32.9	1♏40.0	7♉47.1	8♎15.6	12♋11.0	19♎ 8.6	19♌19.5
2 M	4 43 35.3	11 52.9	25 19.8	29 46.4	3 53.2	5 46.5	1R 33.3	8 0.2	8R 14.8	12 14.2	19R 7.8	19 20.3
3 T	4 47 31.9	12 50.3	25 16.7	12♎22.9	6 0.6	7 0.1	1 27.6	8 13.3	8 14.0	12 17.5	19 7.0	19 21.2
4 W	4 51 28.5	13 47.7	25 13.5	25 23.1	8 9.4	8 13.8	1 22.6	8 26.3	8 13.4	12 20.8	19 6.2	19 22.2
5 T	4 55 25.0	14 45.1	25 10.3	8♏49.5	10 19.3	9 27.4	1 18.5	8 39.3	8 12.8	12 24.1	19 5.4	19 23.1
6 F	4 59 21.6	15 42.5	25 7.1	22 42.1	12 30.1	10 41.0	1 15.1	8 52.2	8 12.3	12 27.4	19 4.7	19 24.1
7 S	5 3 18.1	16 39.9	25 4.0	6♐58.2	14 41.6	11 54.7	1 12.6	9 5.0	8 12.0	12 30.7	19 3.9	19 25.1
8 S	5 7 14.7	17 37.3	25 0.8	21 32.6	16 53.6	13 8.3	1 10.9	9 17.8	8 11.7	12 34.1	19 3.2	19 26.1
9 M	5 11 11.3	18 34.6	24 57.6	6♑18.1	19 5.6	14 22.0	1 10.0	9 30.5	8 11.6	12 37.4	19 2.6	19 27.1
10 T	5 15 7.8	19 31.9	24 54.4	21 6.7	21 17.6	15 35.6	1 9.9	9 43.2	8 11.5	12 40.8	19 2.0	19 28.2
11 W	5 19 4.4	20 29.3	24 51.2	5♒50.9	23 29.2	16 49.3	1D 10.6	9 55.8	8D 11.6	12 44.3	19 1.4	19 29.3
12 T	5 23 0.9	21 26.6	24 48.1	20 24.7	25 40.1	18 2.9	1 12.1	10 8.3	8 11.7	12 47.7	19 0.8	19 30.4
13 F	5 26 57.5	22 23.9	24 44.9	4♓44.2	27 50.1	19 16.6	1 14.4	10 20.7	8 12.0	12 51.1	19 0.3	19 31.5
14 S	5 30 54.0	23 21.2	24 41.7	18 47.5	29 58.9	20 30.3	1 17.4	10 33.1	8 12.3	12 54.6	18 59.7	19 32.7
15 S	5 34 50.6	24 18.5	24 38.5	2♈34.2	2♋ 6.5	21 43.9	1 21.2	10 45.4	8 12.8	12 58.1	18 59.3	19 33.9
16 M	5 38 47.2	25 15.8	24 35.4	16 5.1	4 12.5	22 57.6	1 25.8	10 57.6	8 13.3	13 1.6	18 58.8	19 35.1
17 T	5 42 43.7	26 13.1	24 32.2	29 21.0	6 16.8	24 11.3	1 31.1	11 9.8	8 14.0	13 5.1	18 58.4	19 36.3
18 W	5 46 40.3	27 10.3	24 29.0	12♉23.3	8 19.4	25 25.0	1 37.1	11 21.8	8 14.7	13 8.6	18 58.0	19 37.5
19 T	5 50 36.8	28 7.6	24 25.8	25 12.6	10 20.0	26 38.7	1 43.9	11 33.8	8 15.6	13 12.1	18 57.6	19 38.8
20 F	5 54 33.4	29 4.9	24 22.7	7♊49.8	12 18.6	27 52.4	1 51.4	11 45.8	8 16.5	13 15.7	18 57.3	19 40.1
21 S	5 58 30.0	0♋ 2.2	24 19.5	20 15.3	14 15.2	29 6.1	1 59.7	11 57.6	8 17.6	13 19.2	18 57.0	19 41.4
22 S	6 2 26.5	0 59.5	24 16.3	2♋30.0	16 9.8	0♋19.9	2 8.7	12 9.4	8 18.8	13 22.8	18 56.8	19 42.8
23 M	6 6 23.1	1 56.7	24 13.1	14 34.7	18 2.1	1 33.6	2 18.3	12 21.1	8 20.0	13 26.4	18 56.6	19 44.1
24 T	6 10 19.6	2 54.0	24 10.0	26 31.0	19 52.2	2 47.3	2 28.6	12 32.6	8 21.4	13 30.0	18 56.4	19 45.5
25 W	6 14 16.2	3 51.2	24 6.8	8♌21.0	21 40.2	4 1.0	2 39.6	12 44.1	8 22.8	13 33.6	18 56.2	19 46.9
26 T	6 18 12.8	4 48.4	24 3.6	20 7.7	23 26.0	5 14.8	2 51.3	12 55.5	8 24.4	13 37.2	18 56.1	19 48.3
27 F	6 22 9.3	5 45.7	24 0.4	1♍54.8	25 9.5	6 28.5	3 3.6	13 6.9	8 26.0	13 40.8	18 56.0	19 49.7
28 S	6 26 5.9	6 42.9	23 57.2	13 46.4	26 50.8	7 42.2	3 16.5	13 18.1	8 27.8	13 44.4	18 55.9	19 51.1
29 S	6 30 2.4	7 40.1	23 54.1	25 47.3	28 29.9	8 56.0	3 30.1	13 29.2	8 29.6	13 48.0	18 55.9	19 52.6
30 M	6 33 59.0	8 37.3	23 50.9	8♎ 2.6	0♌ 6.7	10 9.7	3 44.3	13 40.2	8 31.5	13 51.6	18 55.9	19 54.1
	DECLINATION at NOON											
1 S	4 39 38.8	22N 5.4	13S 3.9	3N 7.0	20N 3.1	20N 33.7	12S 36.6	13N 7.3	0S 53.8	23N 15.4	5S 55.7	23N 32.7
4 W	4 51 28.5	22 27.8	13 7.1	13S 56.1	21 43.7	21 18.2	12 36.8	13 19.8	0 53.5	23 14.5	5 54.8	23 31.3
7 S	5 3 18.1	22 46.7	13 10.3	26 19.7	23 8.2	21 57.3	12 39.2	13 32.0	0 53.6	23 13.6	5 54.1	23 29.9
10 T	5 15 7.8	23 2.1	13 13.4	24 28.8	24 11.9	22 31.0	12 43.8	13 43.9	0 54.1	23 12.6	5 53.5	23 28.5
13 F	5 26 57.5	23 13.7	13 16.6	8 50.8	24 51.3	22 58.8	12 50.6	13 55.4	0 55.0	23 11.6	5 53.0	23 27.0
16 M	5 38 47.2	23 21.8	13 19.8	10N 4.3	25 5.6	23 20.7	12 59.5	14 6.7	0 56.2	23 10.6	5 52.6	23 25.5
19 T	5 50 36.8	23 26.0	13 23.0	24 0.4	24 55.8	23 36.5	13 10.4	14 17.7	0 57.7	23 9.6	5 52.3	23 23.9
22 S	6 2 26.5	23 26.6	13 26.1	27 20.9	24 24.7	23 46.0	13 23.3	14 28.3	0 59.7	23 8.5	5 52.1	23 22.2
25 W	6 14 16.2	23 23.5	13 29.3	19 23.4	23 35.6	23 49.3	13 38.1	14 38.6	1 1.9	23 7.5	5 52.0	23 20.6
28 S	6 26 5.9	23 16.6	13 32.5	4 38.3	22 32.0	23 46.1	13 54.5	14 48.5	1 4.5	23 6.4	5 52.0	23 18.9

JULY 1952

DAY	EPHEMERIS SIDEREAL TIME	☉	☊	☽	☿	♀	♂	♃	♄	♅	♆	♇
	h m s	° ′	° ′	° ′	° ′	° ′	° ′	° ′	° ′	° ′	° ′	° ′
LONGITUDE at NOON												
1 T	6 37 55.5	9♋34.5	23♒47.7	20♎37.3	1♌41.3	11♋23.5	3♏59.1	13♉51.2	8♎33.6	13♋55.3	18♎55.9	19♌55.6
2 W	6 41 52.1	10 31.7	23 44.5	3♏35.7	3 13.7	12 37.2	4 14.5	14 2.0	8 35.7	13 58.9	18 55.9	19 57.1
3 T	6 45 48.7	11 28.9	23 41.4	17 1.0	4 43.7	13 51.0	4 30.5	14 12.7	8 37.9	14 2.5	18D56.0	19 58.6
4 F	6 49 45.2	12 26.0	23 38.2	0♐54.5	6 11.5	15 4.7	4 47.1	14 23.4	8 40.2	14 6.1	18 56.1	20 0.1
5 S	6 53 41.8	13 23.2	23 35.0	15 15.0	7 37.0	16 18.5	5 4.2	14 33.9	8 42.7	14 9.8	18 56.3	20 1.7
6 S	6 57 38.3	14 20.4	23 31.8	29 58.2	9 0.1	17 32.2	5 21.8	14 44.3	8 45.2	14 13.4	18 56.5	20 3.3
7 M	7 1 34.9	15 17.6	23 28.7	14♑57.3	10 20.8	18 46.0	5 40.0	14 54.7	8 47.7	14 17.0	18 56.7	20 4.8
8 T	7 5 31.5	16 14.7	23 25.5	0♒ 3.3	11 39.1	19 59.8	5 58.7	15 4.9	8 50.4	14 20.7	18 57.0	20 6.4
9 W	7 9 28.0	17 11.9	23 22.3	15 7.1	12 55.0	21 13.6	6 17.9	15 15.0	8 53.2	14 24.3	18 57.2	20 8.1
10 T	7 13 24.6	18 9.1	23 19.1	0♓ 0.3	14 8.3	22 27.3	6 37.6	15 25.0	8 56.1	14 27.9	18 57.5	20 9.7
11 F	7 17 21.1	19 6.3	23 16.0	14 36.5	15 19.0	23 41.1	6 57.8	15 34.9	8 59.0	14 31.6	18 57.9	20 11.3
12 S	7 21 17.7	20 3.5	23 12.8	28 51.8	16 27.1	24 54.9	7 18.5	15 44.7	9 2.1	14 35.2	18 58.3	20 13.0
13 S	7 25 14.2	21 0.8	23 9.6	12♈44.7	17 32.5	26 8.8	7 39.7	15 54.4	9 5.3	14 38.8	18 58.7	20 14.7
14 M	7 29 10.8	21 58.0	23 6.4	26 15.5	18 35.0	27 22.6	8 1.4	16 3.9	9 8.5	14 42.5	18 59.2	20 16.4
15 T	7 33 7.4	22 55.2	23 3.3	9♉25.6	19 34.7	28 36.5	8 23.5	16 13.3	9 11.8	14 46.1	18 59.6	20 18.1
16 W	7 37 3.9	23 52.4	23 0.1	22 17.4	20 31.3	29 50.3	8 46.0	16 22.7	9 15.2	14 49.7	19 0.1	20 19.8
17 T	7 41 0.5	24 49.7	22 56.9	4♊53.3	21 24.7	1♌ 4.1	9 9.0	16 31.8	9 18.7	14 53.3	19 0.7	20 21.5
18 F	7 44 57.0	25 47.0	22 53.7	17 15.8	22 15.0	2 18.0	9 32.4	16 40.9	9 22.2	14 56.9	19 1.3	20 23.3
19 S	7 48 53.6	26 44.2	22 50.5	29 27.1	23 1.8	3 31.9	9 56.3	16 49.8	9 25.9	15 0.4	19 1.9	20 25.0
20 S	7 52 50.2	27 41.5	22 47.4	11♋29.4	23 45.1	4 45.7	10 20.6	16 58.6	9 29.6	15 4.0	19 2.5	20 26.7
21 M	7 56 46.7	28 38.8	22 44.2	23 24.7	24 24.7	5 59.6	10 45.3	17 7.3	9 33.4	15 7.6	19 3.1	20 28.5
22 T	8 0 43.3	29 36.1	22 41.0	5♌14.8	25 0.5	7 13.5	11 10.4	17 15.9	9 37.3	15 11.1	19 3.8	20 30.3
23 W	8 4 39.8	0♌33.4	22 37.8	17 2.1	25 32.3	8 27.4	11 35.9	17 24.3	9 41.3	15 14.7	19 4.6	20 32.1
24 T	8 8 36.4	1 30.7	22 34.7	28 48.8	25 59.9	9 41.3	12 1.8	17 32.6	9 45.4	15 18.2	19 5.3	20 33.9
25 F	8 12 32.9	2 28.1	22 31.5	10♍37.7	26 23.1	10 55.2	12 28.1	17 40.7	9 49.5	15 21.7	19 6.1	20 35.7
26 S	8 16 29.5	3 25.4	22 28.3	22 32.0	26 41.9	12 9.1	12 54.8	17 48.7	9 53.7	15 25.2	19 6.9	20 37.5
27 S	8 20 26.1	4 22.8	22 25.1	4♎35.4	26 56.0	13 23.0	13 21.8	17 56.6	9 58.0	15 28.7	19 7.8	20 39.3
28 M	8 24 22.6	5 20.1	22 22.0	16 51.9	27 5.2	14 36.9	13 49.2	18 4.3	10 2.4	15 32.2	19 8.7	20 41.1
29 T	8 28 19.2	6 17.5	22 18.8	29 25.7	27 9.6	15 50.8	14 17.0	18 11.9	10 6.9	15 35.6	19 9.6	20 42.9
30 W	8 32 15.7	7 14.8	22 15.6	12♏20.7	27R 8.8	17 4.7	14 45.1	18 19.3	10 11.4	15 39.1	19 10.5	20 44.8
31 T	8 36 12.3	8 12.2	22 12.4	25 40.3	27 2.9	18 18.6	15 13.5	18 26.6	10 16.0	15 42.5	19 11.5	20 46.6
DECLINATION at NOON												
1 T	6 37 55.5	23N 6.1	13S 35.6	12S 8.0	21N17.3	23N36.7	14S 12.6	14N58.1	1S 7.5	23N 5.3	5S52.1	23N17.2
4 F	6 49 45.2	22 51.9	13 38.8	25 20.9	19 54.5	23 20.9	14 32.1	15 7.3	1 10.8	23 4.2	5 52.4	23 15.4
7 M	7 1 34.9	22 34.2	13 41.9	25 43.0	18 26.5	22 58.9	14 52.9	15 16.1	1 14.4	23 3.0	5 52.7	23 13.7
10 T	7 13 24.6	22 13.0	13 45.0	10 46.9	16 55.7	22 30.8	15 14.9	15 24.6	1 18.3	23 1.9	5 53.2	23 11.9
13 S	7 25 14.2	21 48.3	13 48.2	8N46.1	15 24.7	21 56.8	15 38.0	15 32.8	1 22.5	23 0.7	5 53.8	23 10.1
16 W	7 37 3.9	21 20.3	13 51.3	23 23.5	13 56.0	21 17.0	16 1.9	15 40.5	1 27.0	22 59.6	5 54.5	23 8.3
19 S	7 48 53.6	20 48.9	13 54.4	27 35.2	12 32.2	20 31.7	16 26.7	15 47.8	1 31.8	22 58.4	5 55.3	23 6.5
22 T	8 0 43.3	20 14.5	13 57.5	20 23.7	11 16.1	19 41.1	16 52.1	15 54.8	1 36.9	22 57.2	5 56.2	23 4.7
25 F	8 12 32.9	19 36.9	14 0.6	5 59.1	10 11.0	18 45.6	17 18.1	16 1.3	1 42.3	22 56.1	5 57.2	23 2.9
28 M	8 24 22.6	18 56.5	14 3.7	10S 38.2	9 20.2	17 45.3	17 44.6	16 7.4	1 47.9	22 54.9	5 58.3	23 1.1
31 T	8 36 12.3	18 13.2	14 6.8	24 17.8	8 47.4	16 40.6	18 11.3	16 13.2	1 53.7	22 53.8	5 59.5	22 59.3

AUGUST 1952

DAY	EPHEMERIS SIDEREAL TIME	☉	☊	☽	☿	♀	♂	♃	♄	♅	♆	♇
LONGITUDE at NOON												
1 F	8 40 8.8	9♌ 9.6	22♒ 9.2	9♐26.6	26♌51.8	19♌32.5	15♏42.3	18♉33.7	10♎20.7	15♋45.9	19♎12.5	20♌48.4
2 S	8 44 5.4	10 7.0	22 6.1	23 40.0	26R35.5	20 46.4	16 11.4	18 40.7	10 25.4	15 49.3	19 13.5	20 50.3
3 S	8 48 2.0	11 4.5	22 2.9	8♑18.0	26 14.1	22 0.3	16 40.9	18 47.6	10 30.3	15 52.8	19 14.6	20 52.2
4 M	8 51 58.5	12 1.9	21 59.7	23 15.7	25 47.8	23 14.3	17 10.6	18 54.3	10 35.2	15 56.1	19 15.7	20 54.1
5 T	8 55 55.1	12 59.3	21 56.5	8♒25.4	25 16.7	24 28.2	17 40.7	19 0.8	10 40.1	15 59.4	19 16.8	20 55.9
6 W	8 59 51.6	13 56.8	21 53.4	23 38.0	24 41.2	25 42.1	18 11.0	19 7.2	10 45.1	16 2.8	19 17.9	20 57.8
7 T	9 3 48.2	14 54.3	21 50.2	8♓43.8	24 1.8	26 56.0	18 41.6	19 13.4	10 50.2	16 6.1	19 19.1	20 59.7
8 F	9 7 44.7	15 51.8	21 47.0	23 34.5	23 19.0	28 9.9	19 12.6	19 19.5	10 55.4	16 9.3	19 20.3	21 1.5
9 S	9 11 41.3	16 49.3	21 43.8	8♈ 3.7	22 33.4	29 23.8	19 43.8	19 25.4	11 0.6	16 12.6	19 21.5	21 3.4
10 S	9 15 37.8	17 46.8	21 40.7	22 7.7	21 45.7	0♍37.8	20 15.3	19 31.1	11 5.9	16 15.8	19 22.8	21 5.3
11 M	9 19 34.4	18 44.4	21 37.5	5♉45.4	20 56.8	1 51.7	20 47.0	19 36.7	11 11.2	16 19.0	19 24.1	21 7.2
12 T	9 23 31.0	19 42.0	21 34.3	18 57.8	20 7.5	3 5.6	21 19.1	19 42.1	11 16.6	16 22.2	19 25.4	21 9.0
13 W	9 27 27.5	20 39.6	21 31.1	1♊47.3	19 18.8	4 19.5	21 51.4	19 47.3	11 22.1	16 25.4	19 26.7	21 10.9
14 T	9 31 24.1	21 37.2	21 27.9	14 17.5	18 31.6	5 33.5	22 23.9	19 52.4	11 27.6	16 28.5	19 28.1	21 12.8
15 F	9 35 20.6	22 34.9	21 24.8	26 31.9	17 47.0	6 47.4	22 56.8	19 57.3	11 33.2	16 31.6	19 29.4	21 14.7
16 S	9 39 17.2	23 32.6	21 21.6	8♋34.5	17 5.7	8 1.4	23 29.9	20 2.0	11 38.9	16 34.7	19 30.9	21 16.6
17 S	9 43 13.7	24 30.3	21 18.4	20 28.8	16 28.8	9 15.3	24 3.2	20 6.5	11 44.6	16 37.8	19 32.3	21 18.4
18 M	9 47 10.3	25 28.0	21 15.2	2♌18.0	15 57.0	10 29.3	24 36.8	20 10.9	11 50.4	16 40.8	19 33.8	21 20.3
19 T	9 51 6.8	26 25.8	21 12.1	14 5.0	15 30.9	11 43.2	25 10.7	20 15.1	11 56.2	16 43.8	19 35.2	21 22.2
20 W	9 55 3.4	27 23.5	21 8.9	25 52.5	15 11.3	12 57.1	25 44.7	20 19.1	12 2.1	16 46.8	19 36.8	21 24.1
21 T	9 58 60.0	28 21.4	21 5.7	7♍42.6	14 58.7	14 11.1	26 19.1	20 22.9	12 8.0	16 49.7	19 38.3	21 26.0
22 F	10 2 56.5	29 19.2	21 2.5	19 37.6	14 53.3	15 25.0	26 53.6	20 26.5	12 14.0	16 52.6	19 39.8	21 27.8
23 S	10 6 53.1	0♍17.0	20 59.3	1♎39.8	14D55.7	16 39.0	27 28.4	20 30.0	12 20.0	16 55.5	19 41.4	21 29.7
24 S	10 10 49.6	1 15.0	20 56.2	13 51.4	15 5.9	17 53.0	28 3.5	20 33.3	12 26.2	16 58.4	19 43.1	21 31.6
25 M	10 14 46.2	2 12.9	20 53.0	26 15.0	15 24.0	19 6.9	28 38.8	20 36.4	12 32.3	17 1.2	19 44.7	21 33.5
26 T	10 18 42.7	3 10.8	20 49.8	8♏53.2	15 50.1	20 20.8	29 14.2	20 39.2	12 38.5	17 4.0	19 46.4	21 35.3
27 W	10 22 39.3	4 8.7	20 46.6	21 48.8	16 24.1	21 34.8	29 49.9	20 41.9	12 44.8	17 6.7	19 48.0	21 37.2
28 T	10 26 35.8	5 6.7	20 43.5	5♐ 4.4	17 5.9	22 48.7	0♐25.8	20 44.5	12 51.0	17 9.4	19 49.7	21 39.0
29 F	10 30 32.4	6 4.7	20 40.3	18 42.1	17 55.3	24 2.6	1 1.9	20 46.8	12 57.4	17 12.1	19 51.4	21 40.8
30 S	10 34 28.9	7 2.7	20 37.1	2♑42.9	18 51.9	25 16.5	1 38.2	20 48.9	13 3.8	17 14.8	19 53.2	21 42.7
31 S	10 38 25.5	8 0.7	20 33.9	17 6.2	19 55.6	26 30.4	2 14.7	20 50.8	13 10.2	17 17.4	19 54.9	21 44.5
DECLINATION at NOON												
1 F	8 40 8.8	17N58.2	14S 7.8	26S50.6	8N41.0	16N18.1	18S 20.2	16N15.0	1S 55.7	22N53.4	5S59.9	22N58.7
4 M	8 51 58.5	17 11.4	14 10.9	23 54.9	8 37.2	15 8.0	18 47.2	16 20.2	2 1.9	22 52.2	6 1.2	22 56.9
7 T	9 3 48.2	16 22.2	14 14.0	6 50.6	8 57.2	13 54.2	19 14.1	16 24.9	2 8.3	22 51.1	6 2.6	22 55.2
10 S	9 15 37.8	15 30.5	14 17.1	12N54.0	9 39.7	12 37.1	19 40.9	16 29.2	2 14.9	22 50.0	6 4.1	22 53.5
13 W	9 27 27.5	14 36.6	14 20.1	25 37.7	10 40.0	11 17.0	20 7.4	16 33.1	2 21.6	22 48.9	6 5.7	22 51.8
16 S	9 39 17.2	13 40.6	14 23.2	26 46.7	11 49.9	9 54.1	20 33.6	16 36.5	2 28.6	22 47.8	6 7.4	22 50.1
19 T	9 51 6.8	12 42.6	14 26.3	17 16.2	12 59.8	8 28.9	20 59.4	16 39.5	2 35.8	22 46.7	6 9.2	22 48.5
22 F	10 2 56.5	11 42.9	14 29.3	1 48.9	14 0.2	7 1.6	21 24.5	16 42.1	2 43.1	22 45.7	6 11.0	22 46.9
25 M	10 14 46.2	10 41.4	14 32.4	14S 35.1	14 43.2	5 32.6	21 49.0	16 44.2	2 50.6	22 44.7	6 13.0	22 45.3
28 T	10 26 35.8	9 38.4	14 35.4	26 11.8	15 2.9	4 2.3	22 12.7	16 45.8	2 58.2	22 43.7	6 14.9	22 43.8
31 S	10 38 25.5	8 34.1	14 38.4	25 18.9	14 55.2	2 30.9	22 35.5	16 47.0	3 6.0	22 42.7	6 17.0	22 42.4

SEPTEMBER 1952

DAY	EPHEMERIS SIDEREAL TIME	☉	☊	☽	☿	♀	♂	♃	♄	♅	♆	♇
	h m s	° ′	° ′	° ′	° ′	° ′	° ′	° ′	° ′	° ′	° ′	° ′
						LONGITUDE at NOON						
1 M	10 42 22.1	8♍58.7	20♒30.8	1♒49.4	21♌ 5.8	27♍44.3	2♐51.4	20♉52.6	13♎16.6	17♋19.9	19♎56.7	21♌46.3
2 T	10 46 18.6	9 56.8	20 27.6	16 47.4	22 22.3	28 58.2	3 28.3	20 54.1	13 23.2	17 22.5	19 58.5	21 48.1
3 W	10 50 15.2	10 54.9	20 24.4	1♓53.2	23 44.5	0♎12.1	4 5.4	20 55.5	13 29.7	17 25.0	20 0.3	21 49.9
4 T	10 54 11.7	11 53.0	20 21.2	16 57.9	25 11.9	1 25.9	4 42.6	20 56.6	13 36.3	17 27.4	20 2.2	21 51.7
5 F	10 58 8.3	12 51.2	20 18.0	1♈52.5	26 44.1	2 39.8	5 20.1	20 57.6	13 42.9	17 29.8	20 4.0	21 53.5
6 S	11 2 4.8	13 49.4	20 14.9	16 29.1	28 20.4	3 53.7	5 57.7	20 58.3	13 49.6	17 32.2	20 5.9	21 55.3
7 S	11 6 1.4	14 47.6	20 11.7	0♉41.9	0♍ 0.5	5 7.5	6 35.5	20 58.9	13 56.3	17 34.6	20 7.8	21 57.0
8 M	11 9 57.9	15 45.9	20 8.5	14 27.7	1 43.6	6 21.4	7 13.4	20 59.2	14 3.0	17 36.9	20 9.7	21 58.8
9 T	11 13 54.5	16 44.1	20 5.3	27 46.0	3 29.5	7 35.2	7 51.6	20 59.4	14 9.8	17 39.1	20 11.6	22 0.5
10 W	11 17 51.0	17 42.5	20 2.2	10♊38.6	5 17.5	8 49.0	8 29.9	20R59.3	14 16.6	17 41.4	20 13.5	22 2.3
11 T	11 21 47.6	18 40.8	19 59.0	23 9.0	7 7.2	10 2.9	9 8.4	20 59.1	14 23.4	17 43.5	20 15.5	22 4.0
12 F	11 25 44.1	19 39.2	19 55.8	5♋21.4	8 58.3	11 16.7	9 47.0	20 58.6	14 30.3	17 45.7	20 17.5	22 5.7
13 S	11 29 40.7	20 37.6	19 52.6	17 20.6	10 50.3	12 30.5	10 25.8	20 58.0	14 37.2	17 47.8	20 19.5	22 7.4
14 S	11 33 37.2	21 36.1	19 49.4	29 11.5	12 43.0	13 44.4	11 4.9	20 57.2	14 44.2	17 49.9	20 21.5	22 9.1
15 M	11 37 33.8	22 34.6	19 46.3	10♌58.4	14 36.1	14 58.2	11 44.0	20 56.1	14 51.2	17 51.9	20 23.5	22 10.8
16 T	11 41 30.4	23 33.2	19 43.1	22 45.4	16 29.2	16 12.0	12 23.3	20 54.9	14 58.1	17 53.8	20 25.6	22 12.5
17 W	11 45 26.9	24 31.7	19 39.9	4♍35.9	18 22.2	17 25.8	13 2.7	20 53.4	15 5.2	17 55.8	20 27.6	22 14.1
18 T	11 49 23.5	25 30.3	19 36.7	16 32.7	20 15.0	18 39.6	13 42.4	20 51.7	15 12.2	17 57.6	20 29.7	22 15.7
19 F	11 53 20.0	26 29.0	19 33.6	28 38.0	22 7.3	19 53.4	14 22.1	20 49.9	15 19.3	17 59.5	20 31.7	22 17.3
20 S	11 57 16.6	27 27.6	19 30.4	10♎53.2	23 59.0	21 7.2	15 2.0	20 47.8	15 26.4	18 1.3	20 33.8	22 19.0
21 S	12 1 13.1	28 26.3	19 27.2	23 19.5	25 50.1	22 21.0	15 42.1	20 45.6	15 33.5	18 3.0	20 35.9	22 20.5
22 M	12 5 9.7	29 25.1	19 24.0	5♏57.8	27 40.5	23 34.7	16 22.3	20 43.1	15 40.6	18 4.7	20 38.0	22 22.1
23 T	12 9 6.2	0♎23.8	19 20.8	18 48.8	29 30.1	24 48.5	17 2.7	20 40.4	15 47.8	18 6.3	20 40.1	22 23.7
24 W	12 13 2.8	1 22.6	19 17.7	1♐53.5	1♎18.9	26 2.2	17 43.2	20 37.6	15 55.0	18 7.9	20 42.3	22 25.2
25 T	12 16 59.3	2 21.4	19 14.5	15 12.8	3 6.8	27 16.0	18 23.8	20 34.5	16 2.2	18 9.4	20 44.4	22 26.7
26 F	12 20 55.9	3 20.3	19 11.3	28 47.6	4 53.9	28 29.7	19 4.6	20 31.3	16 9.4	18 10.9	20 46.6	22 28.2
27 S	12 24 52.4	4 19.1	19 8.1	12♑38.8	6 40.0	29 43.4	19 45.5	20 27.9	16 16.6	18 12.4	20 48.7	22 29.7
28 S	12 28 49.0	5 18.0	19 5.0	26 46.6	8 25.3	0♏57.1	20 26.5	20 24.3	16 23.8	18 13.8	20 50.9	22 31.2
29 M	12 32 45.6	6 17.0	19 1.8	11♒10.0	10 9.6	2 10.7	21 7.6	20 20.4	16 31.1	18 15.1	20 53.1	22 32.6
30 T	12 36 42.1	7 15.9	18 58.6	25 46.7	11 53.1	3 24.4	21 48.9	20 16.5	16 38.4	18 16.4	20 55.2	22 34.1

DAY	EPHEMERIS SIDEREAL TIME	☉	☊	☽	☿	♀	♂	♃	♄	♅	♆	♇
						DECLINATION at NOON						
1 M	10 42 22.1	8N12.4	14S39.4	21S29.8	14N46.1	2N 0.2	22S42.8	16N47.3	3S 8.6	22N42.4	6S17.7	22N41.9
4 T	10 54 11.7	7 6.4	14 42.4	3 3.7	13 59.3	0 27.9	23 4.2	16 47.9	3 16.5	22 41.5	6 19.8	22 40.5
7 S	11 6 1.4	5 59.5	14 45.5	16N19.0	12 44.8	1S 4.7	23 24.4	16 48.0	3 24.5	22 40.7	6 22.0	22 39.2
10 W	11 17 51.0	4 51.6	14 48.5	26 56.8	11 6.5	2 37.3	23 43.2	16 47.6	3 32.6	22 39.9	6 24.2	22 37.9
13 S	11 29 40.7	3 42.9	14 51.5	25 13.8	9 9.8	4 9.6	24 0.8	16 46.8	3 40.7	22 39.1	6 26.5	22 36.7
16 T	11 41 30.4	2 33.6	14 54.5	13 48.8	7 0.3	5 41.3	24 16.8	16 45.5	3 49.0	22 38.4	6 28.9	22 35.6
19 F	11 53 20.0	1 23.9	14 57.5	2S21.2	4 43.1	7 11.9	24 31.3	16 43.8	3 57.3	22 37.7	6 31.2	22 34.5
22 M	12 5 9.7	0 13.9	15 0.5	18 13.2	2 22.0	8 41.2	24 44.1	16 41.6	4 5.6	22 37.1	6 33.6	22 33.5
25 T	12 16 59.3	0S56.3	15 3.4	27 18.1	0 0.0	10 8.9	24 55.2	16 38.9	4 14.0	22 36.6	6 36.1	22 32.6
28 S	12 28 49.0	2 6.4	15 6.4	22 51.9	2S20.8	11 34.6	25 4.4	16 35.9	4 22.4	22 36.1	6 38.5	22 31.8

OCTOBER 1952

DAY	EPHEMERIS SIDEREAL TIME	☉	☊	☽	☿	♀	♂	♃	♄	♅	♆	♇
						LONGITUDE at NOON						
1 W	12 40 38.7	8♎14.9	18♒55.4	10♓32.2	13♎35.7	4♏38.1	22♐30.3	20♉12.3	16♎45.6	18♋17.7	20♎57.4	22♌35.5
2 T	12 44 35.2	9 13.9	18 52.2	25 20.4	15 17.4	5 51.7	23 11.8	20R 7.9	16 52.9	18 18.9	20 59.6	22 36.9
3 F	12 48 31.8	10 13.0	18 49.1	10♈ 3.8	16 58.2	7 5.3	23 53.4	20 3.4	17 0.2	18 20.0	21 1.8	22 38.3
4 S	12 52 28.3	11 12.1	18 45.9	24 34.6	18 38.3	8 18.9	24 35.2	19 58.7	17 7.5	18 21.1	21 4.0	22 39.6
5 S	12 56 24.9	12 11.3	18 42.7	8♉46.3	20 17.5	9 32.6	25 17.1	19 53.9	17 14.9	18 22.2	21 6.3	22 41.0
6 M	13 0 21.4	13 10.4	18 39.5	22 34.0	21 55.9	10 46.1	25 59.1	19 48.8	17 22.2	18 23.2	21 8.5	22 42.3
7 T	13 4 18.0	14 9.6	18 36.4	5♊55.7	23 33.5	11 59.7	26 41.1	19 43.6	17 29.5	18 24.1	21 10.7	22 43.6
8 W	13 8 14.5	15 8.9	18 33.2	18 51.7	25 10.4	13 13.3	27 23.3	19 38.2	17 36.9	18 25.0	21 12.9	22 44.9
9 T	13 12 11.1	16 8.1	18 30.0	1♋24.5	26 46.5	14 26.8	28 5.6	19 32.7	17 44.2	18 25.9	21 15.2	22 46.1
10 F	13 16 7.6	17 7.4	18 26.8	13 38.1	28 21.8	15 40.3	28 48.0	19 27.0	17 51.5	18 26.6	21 17.4	22 47.4
11 S	13 20 4.2	18 6.8	18 23.6	25 37.5	29 56.4	16 53.9	29 30.6	19 21.2	17 58.9	18 27.4	21 19.6	22 48.6
12 S	13 24 0.8	19 6.2	18 20.5	7♌28.0	1♏30.4	18 7.4	0♑13.2	19 15.1	18 6.2	18 28.1	21 21.9	22 49.8
13 M	13 27 57.3	20 5.6	18 17.3	19 15.0	3 3.6	19 20.9	0 55.9	19 9.0	18 13.5	18 28.7	21 24.1	22 50.9
14 T	13 31 53.9	21 5.1	18 14.1	1♍ 3.5	4 36.2	20 34.4	1 38.7	19 2.7	18 20.9	18 29.3	21 26.3	22 52.1
15 W	13 35 50.4	22 4.6	18 10.9	12 58.1	6 8.1	21 47.8	2 21.7	18 56.3	18 28.2	18 29.8	21 28.6	22 53.2
16 T	13 39 47.0	23 4.1	18 7.8	25 2.4	7 39.3	23 1.3	3 4.7	18 49.7	18 35.5	18 30.2	21 30.8	22 54.3
17 F	13 43 43.5	24 3.7	18 4.6	7♎19.1	9 9.9	24 14.8	3 47.8	18 43.0	18 42.9	18 30.6	21 33.0	22 55.4
18 S	13 47 40.1	25 3.3	18 1.4	19 49.8	10 39.8	25 28.2	4 31.1	18 36.2	18 50.2	18 31.0	21 35.3	22 56.4
19 S	13 51 36.6	26 2.9	17 58.2	2♏35.0	12 9.1	26 41.6	5 14.4	18 29.2	18 57.5	18 31.3	21 37.5	22 57.4
20 M	13 55 33.2	27 2.6	17 55.0	15 34.3	13 37.7	27 55.0	5 57.8	18 22.1	19 4.8	18 31.5	21 39.7	22 58.4
21 T	13 59 29.7	28 2.3	17 51.9	28 46.6	15 5.6	29 8.4	6 41.3	18 15.0	19 12.1	18 31.7	21 42.0	22 59.4
22 W	14 3 26.3	29 2.1	17 48.7	12♐10.4	16 32.8	0♐21.8	7 24.9	18 7.7	19 19.4	18 31.9	21 44.2	23 0.3
23 T	14 7 22.8	0♏ 1.9	17 45.5	25 44.3	17 59.4	1 35.2	8 8.6	18 0.3	19 26.6	18 31.9	21 46.4	23 1.2
24 F	14 11 19.4	1 1.7	17 42.3	9♑27.5	19 25.2	2 48.5	8 52.4	17 52.8	19 33.9	18 32.0	21 48.6	23 2.1
25 S	14 15 16.0	2 1.5	17 39.2	23 19.3	20 50.3	4 1.8	9 36.3	17 45.3	19 41.1	18 32.0	21 50.8	23 3.0
26 S	14 19 12.5	3 1.4	17 36.0	7♒19.6	22 14.7	5 15.2	10 20.2	17 37.7	19 48.4	18R31.9	21 53.1	23 3.9
27 M	14 23 9.1	4 1.3	17 32.8	21 28.0	23 38.2	6 28.5	11 4.3	17 30.0	19 55.6	18 31.8	21 55.3	23 4.7
28 T	14 27 5.6	5 1.2	17 29.6	5♓43.4	25 0.8	7 41.7	11 48.3	17 22.2	20 2.8	18 31.6	21 57.5	23 5.5
29 W	14 31 2.2	6 1.1	17 26.4	20 4.1	26 22.5	8 55.0	12 32.5	17 14.3	20 9.9	18 31.4	21 59.7	23 6.3
30 T	14 34 58.7	7 1.1	17 23.3	4♈26.6	27 43.3	10 8.2	13 16.7	17 6.4	20 17.1	18 31.1	22 1.9	23 7.0
31 F	14 38 55.3	8 1.1	17 20.1	18 46.1	29 2.9	11 21.3	14 1.0	16 58.4	20 24.2	18 30.7	22 4.0	23 7.7

DAY	EPHEMERIS SIDEREAL TIME	☉	☊	☽	☿	♀	♂	♃	♄	♅	♆	♇
						DECLINATION at NOON						
1 W	12 40 38.7	3S16.4	15S 9.4	5S59.8	4S38.9	12S57.9	25S11.7	16N32.4	4S30.8	22N35.6	6S41.0	22N31.0
4 S	12 52 28.3	4 26.0	15 12.3	13N48.4	6 53.1	14 18.5	25 17.0	16 28.4	4 39.2	22 35.3	6 43.5	22 30.4
7 T	13 4 18.0	5 35.2	15 15.3	26 8.4	9 2.7	15 36.1	25 20.3	16 24.1	4 47.6	22 34.9	6 46.0	22 29.8
10 F	13 16 7.6	6 43.7	15 18.2	25 45.6	11 6.8	16 50.3	25 21.5	16 19.4	4 55.9	22 34.7	6 48.5	22 29.3
13 M	13 27 57.3	7 51.4	15 21.2	15 6.2	13 5.0	18 0.8	25 20.5	16 14.4	5 4.3	22 34.5	6 51.0	22 28.9
16 T	13 39 47.0	8 58.2	15 24.1	0S43.6	14 56.6	19 7.2	25 17.3	16 9.0	5 12.5	22 34.4	6 53.5	22 28.6
19 S	13 51 36.6	10 3.8	15 27.0	16 54.2	16 41.1	20 9.1	25 11.9	16 3.3	5 20.7	22 34.3	6 55.9	22 28.4
22 W	14 3 26.3	11 8.1	15 29.9	26 50.4	18 18.0	21 6.4	25 4.2	15 57.3	5 28.9	22 34.3	6 58.4	22 28.2
25 S	14 15 16.0	12 10.9	15 32.9	23 33.0	19 46.5	21 58.5	24 54.3	15 51.1	5 36.9	22 34.4	7 0.8	22 28.2
28 T	14 27 5.6	13 12.0	15 35.8	8 0.9	21 6.1	22 45.3	24 42.0	15 44.7	5 44.9	22 34.5	7 3.3	22 28.3
31 F	14 38 55.3	14 11.2	15 38.7	11N24.0	22 16.0	23 26.3	24 27.5	15 38.1	5 52.7	22 34.8	7 5.7	22 28.4

NOVEMBER 1952

DAY	EPHEMERIS SIDEREAL TIME	☉	☊	☾	☿	♀	♂	♃	♄	♅	♆	♇
	h m s	° ′	° ′	° ′	° ′	° ′	° ′	° ′	° ′	° ′	° ′	° ′
						LONGITUDE at NOON						
1 S	14 42 51.8	9♏ 1.1	17♒16.9	2♉57.1	0♐21.4	12♐34.5	14♑45.4	16♉50.4	20≏31.3	18♋30.3	22≏ 6.2	23♌ 8.4
2 S	14 46 48.4	10 1.1	17 13.7	16 54.1	1 38.7	13 47.6	15 29.9	16R42.4	20 38.4	18R29.9	22 8.3	23 9.0
3 M	14 50 45.0	11 1.2	17 10.6	0♊32.4	2 54.5	15 0.7	16 14.4	16 34.3	20 45.4	18 29.3	22 10.5	23 9.7
4 T	14 54 41.5	12 1.3	17 7.4	13 49.0	4 8.9	16 13.8	16 58.9	16 26.2	20 52.4	18 28.8	22 12.6	23 10.3
5 W	14 58 38.1	13 1.5	17 4.2	26 43.2	5 21.5	17 26.9	17 43.6	16 18.0	20 59.4	18 28.2	22 14.7	23 10.8
6 T	15 2 34.6	14 1.7	17 1.0	9♋15.9	6 32.3	18 39.9	18 28.3	16 9.9	21 6.4	18 27.5	22 16.9	23 11.4
7 F	15 6 31.2	15 1.9	16 57.9	21 30.3	7 41.0	19 52.9	19 13.0	16 1.7	21 13.3	18 26.8	22 19.0	23 11.9
8 S	15 10 27.7	16 2.1	16 54.7	3♌30.5	8 47.3	21 5.9	19 57.9	15 53.5	21 20.2	18 26.0	22 21.1	23 12.4
9 S	15 14 24.3	17 2.4	16 51.5	15 21.6	9 51.0	22 18.9	20 42.8	15 45.3	21 27.1	18 25.2	22 23.1	23 12.8
10 M	15 18 20.9	18 2.8	16 48.3	27 9.1	10 51.8	23 31.8	21 27.7	15 37.2	21 34.0	18 24.3	22 25.2	23 13.2
11 T	15 22 17.4	19 3.1	16 45.1	8♍58.7	11 49.3	24 44.7	22 12.7	15 29.0	21 40.8	18 23.4	22 27.3	23 13.6
12 W	15 26 14.0	20 3.5	16 42.0	20 55.7	12 43.0	25 57.6	22 57.8	15 20.9	21 47.5	18 22.4	22 29.3	23 14.0
13 T	15 30 10.5	21 3.9	16 38.8	3≏ 4.8	13 32.5	27 10.4	23 42.9	15 12.8	21 54.3	18 21.4	22 31.3	23 14.3
14 F	15 34 7.1	22 4.3	16 35.6	15 29.8	14 17.3	28 23.3	24 28.1	15 4.7	22 1.0	18 20.3	22 33.3	23 14.6
15 S	15 38 3.6	23 4.8	16 32.4	28 13.0	14 56.8	29 36.1	25 13.3	14 56.7	22 7.7	18 19.2	22 35.3	23 14.9
16 S	15 42 0.2	24 5.4	16 29.3	11♏15.5	15 30.5	0♑48.9	25 58.7	14 48.7	22 14.3	18 18.1	22 37.3	23 15.2
17 M	15 45 56.7	25 5.9	16 26.1	24 36.3	15 57.4	2 1.6	26 44.0	14 40.8	22 20.9	18 16.9	22 39.3	23 15.4
18 T	15 49 53.3	26 6.5	16 22.9	8♐13.3	16 16.9	3 14.3	27 29.4	14 32.9	22 27.4	18 15.6	22 41.3	23 15.6
19 W	15 53 49.9	27 7.0	16 19.7	22 3.0	16 28.4	4 27.0	28 14.8	14 25.1	22 33.9	18 14.3	22 43.2	23 15.8
20 T	15 57 46.4	28 7.6	16 16.6	6♑ 1.5	16 30.9	5 39.6	29 0.3	14 17.4	22 40.4	18 12.9	22 45.1	23 15.9
21 F	16 1 43.0	29 8.3	16 13.4	20 5.4	16R23.9	6 52.2	29 45.8	14 9.8	22 46.8	18 11.5	22 47.0	23 16.0
22 S	16 5 39.5	0♐ 8.9	16 10.2	4♒11.5	16 6.6	8 4.7	0♒31.4	14 2.2	22 53.1	18 10.0	22 48.9	23 16.1
23 S	16 9 36.1	1 9.6	16 7.0	18 18.0	15 38.8	9 17.2	1 17.0	13 54.7	22 59.5	18 8.5	22 50.7	23 16.2
24 M	16 13 32.7	2 10.3	16 3.9	2♓23.7	15 0.1	10 29.6	2 2.7	13 47.3	23 5.7	18 7.0	22 52.5	23 16.2
25 T	16 17 29.2	3 11.0	16 0.7	16 27.7	14 10.9	11 42.0	2 48.4	13 40.0	23 11.9	18 5.4	22 54.4	23 16.2
26 W	16 21 25.8	4 11.7	15 57.5	0♈29.4	13 11.6	12 54.4	3 34.1	13 32.9	23 18.1	18 3.8	22 56.2	23R16.1
27 T	16 25 22.3	5 12.4	15 54.3	14 27.4	12 3.6	14 6.7	4 19.9	13 25.8	23 24.2	18 2.1	22 57.9	23 16.0
28 F	16 29 18.9	6 13.2	15 51.1	28 19.6	10 48.4	15 18.9	5 5.7	13 18.9	23 30.2	18 0.4	22 59.7	23 15.9
29 S	16 33 15.4	7 13.9	15 48.0	12♉ 3.5	9 28.3	16 31.1	5 51.5	13 12.0	23 36.2	17 58.6	23 1.4	23 15.8
30 S	16 37 12.0	8 14.7	15 44.8	25 35.9	8 5.8	17 43.2	6 37.3	13 5.3	23 42.1	17 56.9	23 3.1	23 15.6

DAY	EPHEMERIS SIDEREAL TIME	☉	☊	☾	☿	♀	♂	♃	♄	♅	♆	♇
						DECLINATION at NOON						
1 S	14 42 51.8	14S30.4	15S39.6	17N 2.6	22S37.0	23S38.7	24S22.1	15N35.9	5S55.3	22N34.8	7S 6.4	22N28.5
4 T	14 54 41.5	15 26.9	15 42.5	26 55.4	23 32.5	24 11.8	24 4.5	15 29.2	6 3.0	22 35.1	7 8.8	22 28.8
7 F	15 6 31.2	16 21.0	15 45.4	23 52.5	24 16.1	24 38.7	23 44.7	15 22.4	6 10.5	22 35.5	7 11.1	22 29.2
10 M	15 18 20.9	17 12.7	15 48.3	11 37.3	24 46.7	24 59.2	23 22.6	15 15.7	6 17.9	22 35.9	7 13.3	22 29.7
13 T	15 30 10.5	18 1.8	15 51.1	4S33.8	25 3.0	25 13.2	22 58.3	15 9.0	6 25.2	22 36.4	7 15.5	22 30.2
16 S	15 42 0.2	18 48.0	15 54.0	19 56.9	25 3.1	25 20.5	22 31.8	15 2.4	6 32.3	22 36.9	7 17.6	22 30.9
19 W	15 53 49.9	19 31.3	15 56.9	27 14.7	24 44.9	25 21.1	22 3.2	14 55.9	6 39.2	22 37.5	7 19.7	22 31.7
22 S	16 5 39.5	20 11.3	15 59.7	20 10.3	24 5.6	25 14.9	21 32.4	14 49.6	6 45.9	22 38.2	7 21.7	22 32.5
25 T	16 17 29.2	20 48.0	16 2.6	2 56.0	23 2.3	25 2.2	20 59.7	14 43.6	6 52.4	22 38.9	7 23.6	22 33.5
28 F	16 29 18.9	21 21.2	16 5.4	15N23.3	21 36.8	24 42.9	20 25.0	14 37.8	6 58.7	22 39.6	7 25.5	22 34.5

DECEMBER 1952

DAY	EPHEMERIS SIDEREAL TIME	☉	☊	☾	☿	♀	♂	♃	♄	♅	♆	♇
						LONGITUDE at NOON						
1 M	16 41 8.6	9♐15.5	15♒41.6	8♊54.0	6♐43.6	18♑55.3	7♒23.2	12♉58.8	23≏48.0	17♋55.0	23≏ 4.8	23♌15.4
2 T	16 45 5.1	10 16.3	15 38.4	21 55.6	5R24.7	20 7.3	8 9.1	12R52.4	23 53.8	17R53.1	23 6.5	23R15.2
3 W	16 49 1.7	11 17.2	15 35.3	4♋39.7	4 11.4	21 19.3	8 55.0	12 46.1	23 59.6	17 51.2	23 8.1	23 15.0
4 T	16 52 58.2	12 18.1	15 32.1	17 6.6	3 6.1	22 31.1	9 41.0	12 39.9	24 5.3	17 49.3	23 9.7	23 14.7
5 F	16 56 54.8	13 18.9	15 28.9	29 18.1	2 10.3	23 42.9	10 27.0	12 33.9	24 10.9	17 47.3	23 11.3	23 14.4
6 S	17 0 51.3	14 19.8	15 25.7	11♌17.3	1 25.2	24 54.7	11 13.0	12 28.1	24 16.5	17 45.3	23 12.9	23 14.1
7 S	17 4 47.9	15 20.8	15 22.6	23 8.3	0 51.4	26 6.4	11 59.1	12 22.4	24 22.1	17 43.3	23 14.5	23 13.7
8 M	17 8 44.5	16 21.8	15 19.4	4♍55.8	0 29.0	27 18.0	12 45.1	12 16.9	24 27.5	17 41.2	23 16.0	23 13.4
9 T	17 12 41.0	17 22.7	15 16.2	16 45.2	0 17.8	28 29.6	13 31.2	12 11.6	24 32.9	17 39.1	23 17.5	23 12.9
10 W	17 16 37.6	18 23.7	15 13.0	28 41.9	0 17.1	29 41.0	14 17.3	12 6.4	24 38.2	17 36.9	23 18.9	23 12.5
11 T	17 20 34.1	19 24.7	15 9.9	10≏51.3	0D26.5	0♒52.4	15 3.4	12 1.3	24 43.4	17 34.8	23 20.4	23 12.0
12 F	17 24 30.7	20 25.7	15 6.7	23 18.0	0 44.9	2 3.7	15 49.5	11 56.5	24 48.6	17 32.5	23 21.8	23 11.5
13 S	17 28 27.3	21 26.8	15 3.5	6♏ 5.8	1 11.7	3 15.0	16 35.7	11 51.8	24 53.7	17 30.3	23 23.2	23 11.0
14 S	17 32 23.8	22 27.8	15 0.3	19 16.9	1 46.0	4 26.1	17 21.9	11 47.3	24 58.8	17 28.0	23 24.5	23 10.4
15 M	17 36 20.4	23 28.9	14 57.1	2♐51.4	2 26.9	5 37.2	18 8.1	11 43.0	25 3.7	17 25.7	23 25.9	23 9.8
16 T	17 40 16.9	24 30.0	14 54.0	16 47.5	3 13.7	6 48.2	18 54.3	11 38.9	25 8.6	17 23.4	23 27.2	23 9.2
17 W	17 44 13.5	25 31.1	14 50.8	1♑ 1.2	4 5.8	7 59.1	19 40.5	11 35.0	25 13.4	17 21.1	23 28.4	23 8.6
18 T	17 48 10.1	26 32.2	14 47.6	15 26.9	5 2.4	9 9.9	20 26.7	11 31.2	25 18.1	17 18.7	23 29.7	23 7.9
19 F	17 52 6.6	27 33.3	14 44.4	29 58.5	6 3.1	10 20.5	21 13.0	11 27.7	25 22.8	17 16.3	23 30.9	23 7.2
20 S	17 56 3.2	28 34.4	14 41.3	14♒30.0	7 7.4	11 31.1	21 59.2	11 24.3	25 27.4	17 13.9	23 32.1	23 6.5
21 S	17 59 59.7	29 35.5	14 38.1	28 56.5	8 14.7	12 41.6	22 45.5	11 21.2	25 31.8	17 11.5	23 33.2	23 5.8
22 M	18 3 56.3	0♑36.7	14 34.9	13♓14.6	9 24.8	13 52.0	23 31.7	11 18.2	25 36.3	17 9.0	23 34.3	23 5.0
23 T	18 7 52.8	1 37.8	14 31.7	27 22.2	10 37.3	15 2.2	24 18.0	11 15.5	25 40.6	17 6.5	23 35.4	23 4.2
24 W	18 11 49.4	2 38.9	14 28.6	11♈18.1	11 51.9	16 12.3	25 4.3	11 12.9	25 44.8	17 4.1	23 36.5	23 3.4
25 T	18 15 46.0	3 40.0	14 25.4	25 2.0	13 8.3	17 22.3	25 50.6	11 10.6	25 49.0	17 1.6	23 37.5	23 2.6
26 F	18 19 42.5	4 41.2	14 22.2	8♉33.7	14 26.4	18 32.2	26 36.8	11 8.5	25 53.1	16 59.0	23 38.5	23 1.7
27 S	18 23 39.1	5 42.3	14 19.0	21 53.1	15 46.0	19 41.9	27 23.1	11 6.5	25 57.1	16 56.5	23 39.5	23 0.8
28 S	18 27 35.6	6 43.5	14 15.9	4♊59.9	17 6.9	20 51.6	28 9.4	11 4.9	26 1.0	16 54.0	23 40.5	22 59.9
29 M	18 31 32.2	7 44.6	14 12.7	17 53.9	18 28.9	22 1.0	28 55.7	11 3.3	26 4.8	16 51.5	23 41.4	22 59.0
30 T	18 35 28.8	8 45.7	14 9.5	0♋34.7	19 51.9	23 10.3	29 42.0	11 2.0	26 8.6	16 48.9	23 42.3	22 58.1
31 W	18 39 25.3	9 46.9	14 6.3	13 2.6	21 15.9	24 19.4	0♓28.2	11 0.9	26 12.2	16 46.3	23 43.1	22 57.1

DAY	EPHEMERIS SIDEREAL TIME	☉	☊	☾	☿	♀	♂	♃	♄	♅	♆	♇
						DECLINATION at NOON						
1 M	16 41 8.6	21S50.7	16S 8.2	26N20.0	20S 0.9	24S17.2	19S48.5	14N32.5	7S 4.7	22N40.4	7S27.2	22N35.6
4 T	16 52 58.2	22 16.5	16 11.0	24 38.8	18 36.9	23 45.2	19 10.1	14 27.4	7 10.6	22 41.2	7 28.9	22 36.8
7 S	17 4 47.9	22 38.5	16 13.8	13 2.7	17 44.7	23 7.2	18 30.0	14 22.8	7 16.2	22 42.1	7 30.5	22 38.1
10 W	17 16 37.6	22 56.4	16 16.7	2S47.3	17 29.9	22 23.4	17 48.3	14 18.7	7 21.6	22 43.0	7 32.1	22 39.4
13 S	17 28 27.3	23 10.3	16 19.5	18 20.0	17 46.7	21 34.2	17 4.9	14 15.0	7 26.7	22 43.9	7 33.5	22 40.8
16 T	17 40 16.9	23 20.0	16 22.2	27 3.0	18 24.8	20 39.7	16 20.1	14 11.8	7 31.5	22 44.9	7 34.8	22 42.3
19 F	17 52 6.6	23 25.5	16 25.0	21 18.7	19 14.8	19 40.3	15 33.8	14 9.2	7 36.0	22 45.8	7 36.0	22 43.8
22 M	18 3 56.3	23 26.7	16 27.8	4 11.1	20 9.6	18 36.5	14 46.2	14 7.1	7 40.3	22 46.8	7 37.1	22 45.4
25 T	18 15 46.0	23 23.7	16 30.6	14N16.1	21 4.1	17 28.4	13 57.4	14 5.6	7 44.3	22 47.8	7 38.2	22 47.1
28 S	18 27 35.6	23 16.6	16 33.3	25 51.4	21 54.6	16 16.5	13 7.4	14 4.6	7 48.0	22 48.8	7 39.1	22 48.8
31 W	18 39 25.3	23 5.2	16 36.1	25 22.0	22 38.8	15 1.2	12 16.4	14 4.3	7 51.3	22 49.8	7 39.9	22 50.5

JANUARY 1953

LONGITUDE at NOON

DAY	EPHEMERIS SIDEREAL TIME	☉	☊	☽	☿	♀	♂	♃	♄	♅	♆	♇
	h m s	° ′	° ′	° ′	° ′	° ′	° ′	° ′	° ′	° ′	° ′	° ′
1 T	18 43 21.9	10♑48.0	14♒ 3.1	25♋18.2	22♐40.7	25♒28.4	1♓14.5	11♉ 0.0	26♎15.7	16♋43.7	23♎43.9	22♌56.1
2 F	18 47 18.4	11 49.1	13 60.0	7♌22.8	24 6.3	26 37.2	2 0.7	10R59.4	26 19.2	16R41.2	23 44.7	22R55.1
3 S	18 51 15.0	12 50.3	13 56.8	19 18.5	25 32.6	27 45.9	2 47.0	10 58.9	26 22.6	16 38.6	23 45.4	22 54.0
4 S	18 55 11.5	13 51.4	13 53.6	1♍ 8.2	26 59.6	28 54.4	3 33.2	10 58.6	26 25.9	16 36.0	23 46.1	22 53.0
5 M	18 59 8.1	14 52.6	13 50.4	12 55.4	28 27.2	0♓ 2.7	4 19.4	10 58.5	26 29.0	16 33.4	23 46.8	22 51.9
6 T	19 3 4.7	15 53.7	13 47.3	24 44.5	29 55.5	1 10.8	5 5.7	10D58.7	26 32.1	16 30.8	23 47.5	22 50.8
7 W	19 7 1.2	16 54.9	13 44.1	6♎40.2	1♑24.2	2 18.7	5 51.9	10 59.0	26 35.1	16 28.2	23 48.1	22 49.6
8 T	19 10 57.8	17 56.0	13 40.9	18 47.3	2 53.6	3 26.5	6 38.1	10 59.6	26 38.0	16 25.5	23 48.6	22 48.5
9 F	19 14 54.3	18 57.2	13 37.7	1♏10.9	4 23.4	4 34.0	7 24.3	11 0.4	26 40.8	16 22.9	23 49.2	22 47.3
10 S	19 18 50.9	19 58.3	13 34.6	13 55.3	5 53.8	5 41.3	8 10.4	11 1.3	26 43.5	16 20.3	23 49.7	22 46.2
11 S	19 22 47.5	20 59.5	13 31.4	27 4.2	7 24.6	6 48.5	8 56.6	11 2.5	26 46.1	16 17.7	23 50.2	22 45.0
12 M	19 26 44.0	22 0.6	13 28.2	10♐39.4	8 56.0	7 55.4	9 42.8	11 3.9	26 48.6	16 15.2	23 50.6	22 43.8
13 T	19 30 40.6	23 1.8	13 25.0	24 40.9	10 27.9	9 2.1	10 28.9	11 5.5	26 51.0	16 12.6	23 51.0	22 42.5
14 W	19 34 37.1	24 2.9	13 21.9	9♑ 5.9	12 0.2	10 8.6	11 15.0	11 7.3	26 53.3	16 10.0	23 51.4	22 41.3
15 T	19 38 33.7	25 4.0	13 18.7	23 49.5	13 33.1	11 14.8	12 1.2	11 9.3	26 55.6	16 7.4	23 51.7	22 40.0
16 F	19 42 30.2	26 5.2	13 15.5	8♒44.3	15 6.5	12 20.8	12 47.3	11 11.5	26 57.7	16 4.9	23 52.0	22 38.8
17 S	19 46 26.8	27 6.3	13 12.3	23 42.3	16 40.3	13 26.6	13 33.4	11 13.9	26 59.7	16 2.3	23 52.3	22 37.5
18 S	19 50 23.4	28 7.4	13 9.1	8♓35.3	18 14.8	14 32.1	14 19.5	11 16.6	27 1.6	15 59.8	23 52.6	22 36.2
19 M	19 54 19.9	29 8.5	13 6.0	23 16.3	19 49.7	15 37.3	15 5.5	11 19.4	27 3.4	15 57.3	23 52.8	22 34.9
20 T	19 58 16.5	0♒ 9.6	13 2.8	7♈40.5	21 25.2	16 42.3	15 51.6	11 22.4	27 5.1	15 54.8	23 52.9	22 33.6
21 W	20 2 13.0	1 10.6	12 59.6	21 45.1	23 1.2	17 46.9	16 37.6	11 25.6	27 6.7	15 52.3	23 53.1	22 32.2
22 T	20 6 9.6	2 11.7	12 56.4	5♉29.0	24 37.8	18 51.2	17 23.6	11 29.0	27 8.2	15 49.8	23 53.2	22 30.9
23 F	20 10 6.1	3 12.7	12 53.3	18 52.8	26 15.0	19 55.2	18 9.5	11 32.6	27 9.5	15 47.4	23 53.2	22 29.5
24 S	20 14 2.7	4 13.7	12 50.1	1♊58.1	27 52.8	20 58.9	18 55.5	11 36.4	27 10.8	15 44.9	23 53.2	22 28.2
25 S	20 17 59.3	5 14.7	12 46.9	14 46.7	29 31.2	22 2.3	19 41.4	11 40.3	27 12.0	15 42.5	23 53.2	22 26.8
26 M	20 21 55.8	6 15.7	12 43.7	27 20.8	1♒10.3	23 5.3	20 27.3	11 44.5	27 13.0	15 40.1	23 53.2	22 25.4
27 T	20 25 52.4	7 16.6	12 40.6	9♋42.6	2 49.9	24 7.9	21 13.1	11 48.8	27 14.0	15 37.8	23R53.1	22 24.0
28 W	20 29 48.9	8 17.6	12 37.4	21 54.0	4 30.3	25 10.2	21 58.9	11 53.4	27 14.9	15 35.4	23 53.0	22 22.6
29 T	20 33 45.5	9 18.5	12 34.2	3♌56.8	6 11.3	26 12.0	22 44.7	11 58.1	27 15.6	15 33.1	23 52.9	22 21.1
30 F	20 37 42.0	10 19.4	12 31.0	15 52.9	7 53.0	27 13.5	23 30.5	12 3.0	27 16.2	15 30.8	23 52.7	22 19.7
31 S	20 41 38.6	11 20.3	12 27.8	27 44.1	9 35.4	28 14.6	24 16.2	12 8.1	27 16.8	15 28.5	23 52.5	22 18.3

DECLINATION at NOON

DAY	EPHEMERIS SIDEREAL TIME	☉	☊	☽	☿	♀	♂	♃	♄	♅	♆	♇
1 T	18 43 21.9	23S 0.4	16S37.0	22N36.4	22S51.9	14S35.4	11S59.2	14N 4.3	7S52.4	22N50.1	7S40.1	22N51.1
4 S	18 55 11.5	22 43.5	16 39.8	9 30.4	23 25.0	13 16.1	11 7.0	14 4.7	7 55.3	22 51.1	7 40.8	22 52.9
7 W	19 7 1.2	22 22.6	16 42.5	6S33.4	23 48.5	11 54.1	10 13.9	14 5.7	7 57.9	22 52.1	7 41.3	22 54.7
10 S	19 18 50.9	21 57.6	16 45.2	21 1.8	24 1.5	10 29.9	9 20.1	14 7.3	8 0.2	22 53.1	7 41.7	22 56.5
13 T	19 30 40.6	21 28.8	16 48.0	27 14.2	24 3.2	9 3.8	8 25.6	14 9.4	8 2.2	22 54.0	7 42.1	22 58.4
16 F	19 42 30.2	20 56.3	16 50.7	18 24.3	23 53.0	7 36.1	7 30.5	14 12.1	8 3.8	22 55.0	7 42.3	23 0.3
19 M	19 54 19.9	20 20.2	16 53.4	0N30.6	23 30.6	6 7.2	6 34.9	14 15.4	8 5.1	22 55.9	7 42.4	23 2.1
22 T	20 6 9.6	19 40.6	16 56.1	18 17.8	22 55.5	4 37.4	5 39.0	14 19.2	8 6.1	22 56.8	7 42.3	23 4.0
25 S	20 17 59.3	18 57.8	16 58.8	27 1.1	22 7.5	3 7.3	4 42.7	14 23.5	8 6.7	22 57.6	7 42.2	23 5.9
28 W	20 29 48.9	18 11.8	17 1.5	23 29.8	21 6.2	1 37.0	3 46.2	14 28.3	8 6.9	22 58.5	7 41.9	23 7.7
31 S	20 41 38.6	17 23.0	17 4.2	10 56.5	19 51.4	0 6.9	2 49.6	14 33.5	8 6.9	22 59.3	7 41.6	23 9.6

FEBRUARY 1953

LONGITUDE at NOON

DAY	EPHEMERIS SIDEREAL TIME	☉	☊	☽	☿	♀	♂	♃	♄	♅	♆	♇
1 S	20 45 35.2	12♒21.2	12♒24.7	9♍32.7	11♒18.5	29♓15.2	25♓ 2.0	12♉13.3	27♎17.2	15♋26.3	23♎52.2	22♌16.8
2 M	20 49 31.7	13 22.0	12 21.5	21 21.0	13 2.3	0♈15.4	25 47.6	12 18.7	27 17.5	15R24.0	23R51.9	22R15.4
3 T	20 53 28.3	14 22.9	12 18.3	3♎12.1	14 46.8	1 15.2	26 33.3	12 24.3	27 17.7	15 21.9	23 51.6	22 14.0
4 W	20 57 24.8	15 23.7	12 15.1	15 9.2	16 32.0	2 14.5	27 18.9	12 30.1	27 17.9	15 19.7	23 51.3	22 12.5
5 T	21 1 21.4	16 24.5	12 12.0	27 16.1	18 17.9	3 13.3	28 4.5	12 36.1	27 17.9	15 17.6	23 50.9	22 11.0
6 F	21 5 17.9	17 25.3	12 8.8	9♏37.0	20 4.5	4 11.6	28 50.1	12 42.2	27R17.8	15 15.5	23 50.5	22 9.6
7 S	21 9 14.5	18 26.1	12 5.6	22 16.0	21 51.7	5 9.4	29 35.6	12 48.5	27 17.5	15 13.4	23 50.1	22 8.1
8 S	21 13 11.1	19 26.9	12 2.4	5♐17.2	23 39.6	6 6.7	0♈21.1	12 55.0	27 17.3	15 11.4	23 49.6	22 6.7
9 M	21 17 7.6	20 27.6	11 59.3	18 43.5	25 28.0	7 3.4	1 6.6	13 1.6	27 16.9	15 9.4	23 49.1	22 5.2
10 T	21 21 4.2	21 28.3	11 56.1	2♑36.9	27 16.9	7 59.6	1 52.1	13 8.3	27 16.3	15 7.5	23 48.6	22 3.8
11 W	21 25 0.7	22 29.0	11 52.9	16 57.0	29 6.2	8 55.2	2 37.5	13 15.3	27 15.7	15 5.5	23 48.0	22 2.3
12 T	21 28 57.3	23 29.7	11 49.7	1♒41.0	0♓55.9	9 50.1	3 22.8	13 22.4	27 15.0	15 3.7	23 47.4	22 0.8
13 F	21 32 53.8	24 30.4	11 46.5	16 43.2	2 45.8	10 44.5	4 8.2	13 29.6	27 14.1	15 1.8	23 46.8	21 59.3
14 S	21 36 50.4	25 31.0	11 43.4	1♓55.2	4 35.7	11 38.1	4 53.5	13 37.0	27 13.2	15 0.0	23 46.1	21 57.9
15 S	21 40 46.9	26 31.7	11 40.2	17 7.4	6 25.6	12 31.1	5 38.8	13 44.6	27 12.1	14 58.2	23 45.4	21 56.4
16 M	21 44 43.5	27 32.3	11 37.0	2♈10.1	8 15.1	13 23.4	6 24.0	13 52.3	27 11.0	14 56.5	23 44.7	21 54.9
17 T	21 48 40.0	28 32.8	11 33.8	16 54.9	10 4.0	14 15.0	7 9.2	14 0.1	27 9.7	14 54.8	23 43.9	21 53.5
18 W	21 52 36.6	29 33.4	11 30.7	1♉16.1	11 52.1	15 5.7	7 54.4	14 8.1	27 8.4	14 53.2	23 43.1	21 52.0
19 T	21 56 33.2	0♓33.9	11 27.5	15 10.8	13 39.1	15 55.7	8 39.5	14 16.3	27 6.9	14 51.6	23 42.3	21 50.6
20 F	22 0 29.7	1 34.3	11 24.3	28 38.7	15 24.5	16 44.9	9 24.6	14 24.6	27 5.4	14 50.0	23 41.5	21 49.1
21 S	22 4 26.3	2 34.8	11 21.1	11♊41.9	17 7.9	17 33.2	10 9.6	14 33.0	27 3.7	14 48.5	23 40.6	21 47.7
22 S	22 8 22.8	3 35.2	11 18.0	24 23.3	18 48.9	18 20.5	10 54.6	14 41.6	27 1.9	14 47.0	23 39.7	21 46.3
23 M	22 12 19.4	4 35.6	11 14.8	6♋47.0	20 27.0	19 7.0	11 39.6	14 50.3	27 0.1	14 45.6	23 38.8	21 44.8
24 T	22 16 15.9	5 35.9	11 11.6	18 56.9	22 1.6	19 52.5	12 24.5	14 59.1	26 58.2	14 44.2	23 37.8	21 43.4
25 W	22 20 12.5	6 36.2	11 8.4	0♌56.8	23 32.2	20 36.9	13 9.4	15 8.1	26 56.1	14 42.9	23 36.9	21 42.0
26 T	22 24 9.0	7 36.5	11 5.2	12 50.0	24 58.1	21 20.3	13 54.2	15 17.2	26 54.0	14 41.6	23 35.8	21 40.6
27 F	22 28 5.6	8 36.7	11 2.1	24 39.5	26 18.7	22 2.7	14 39.0	15 26.4	26 51.8	14 40.4	23 34.8	21 39.2
28 S	22 32 2.1	9 37.0	10 58.9	6♍27.9	27 33.5	22 43.8	15 23.7	15 35.7	26 49.4	14 39.2	23 33.8	21 37.8

DECLINATION at NOON

DAY	EPHEMERIS SIDEREAL TIME	☉	☊	☽	☿	♀	♂	♃	♄	♅	♆	♇
1 S	20 45 35.2	17S 6.0	17S 5.1	5N44.7	19S23.5	0N23.1	2S30.7	14N35.4	8S 6.8	22N59.5	7S41.4	23N10.2
4 W	20 57 24.8	16 13.5	17 7.7	10S18.8	17 50.7	1 52.4	1 34.0	14 41.3	8 6.2	23 0.3	7 40.9	23 12.0
7 S	21 9 14.5	15 18.5	17 10.4	23 22.7	16 4.5	3 20.7	0 37.4	14 47.6	8 5.4	23 1.0	7 40.3	23 13.7
10 T	21 21 4.2	14 21.0	17 13.1	26 48.7	14 5.3	4 47.7	0N19.1	14 54.3	8 4.2	23 1.6	7 39.6	23 15.4
13 F	21 32 53.8	13 21.4	17 15.7	15 26.9	11 54.1	6 13.0	1 15.5	15 1.4	8 2.7	23 2.2	7 38.8	23 17.1
16 M	21 44 43.5	12 19.9	17 18.4	4N33.9	9 32.6	7 36.3	2 11.5	15 8.9	8 0.8	23 2.8	7 37.9	23 18.8
19 T	21 56 33.2	11 16.6	17 21.0	21 25.3	7 3.8	8 57.2	3 7.2	15 16.7	7 58.7	23 3.3	7 36.9	23 20.3
22 S	22 8 22.8	10 11.7	17 23.6	27 14.2	4 32.4	10 15.3	4 2.5	15 24.8	7 56.2	23 3.8	7 35.8	23 21.9
25 W	22 20 12.5	9 5.5	17 26.2	20 58.1	2 5.3	11 30.1	4 57.2	15 33.2	7 53.5	23 4.2	7 34.6	23 23.3
28 S	22 32 2.1	7 58.0	17 28.8	7 8.8	0N 9.2	12 41.2	5 51.4	15 41.9	7 50.5	23 4.6	7 33.3	23 24.7

MARCH 1953

LONGITUDE at NOON

DAY	EPHEMERIS SIDEREAL TIME	☉	☊	☽	☿	♀	♂	♃	♄	♅	♆	♇
	h m s	° '	° '	° '	° '	° '	° '	° '	° '	° '	° '	° '
1 S	22 35 58.7	10♓37.2	10♒55.7	18♍17.2	28♓41.8	23♈23.9	16♈ 8.5	15♉45.2	26♎47.1	14♋38.1	23♎32.7	21♌36.5
2 M	22 39 55.3	11 37.4	10 52.5	0♎ 9.3	29 43.0	24 2.7	16 53.2	15 54.8	26R44.6	14R37.0	23R31.6	21R35.1
3 T	22 43 51.8	12 37.5	10 49.4	12 6.1	0♈36.7	24 40.2	17 37.8	16 4.5	26 42.0	14 36.0	23 30.5	21 33.7
4 W	22 47 48.4	13 37.6	10 46.2	24 9.6	1 22.3	25 16.4	18 22.4	16 14.4	26 39.3	14 35.0	23 29.3	21 32.4
5 T	22 51 44.9	14 37.7	10 43.0	6♏22.1	1 59.5	25 51.3	19 6.9	16 24.3	26 36.6	14 34.0	23 28.1	21 31.0
6 F	22 55 41.5	15 37.7	10 39.8	18 46.2	2 27.9	26 24.7	19 51.4	16 34.4	26 33.7	14 33.2	23 26.9	21 29.7
7 S	22 59 38.0	16 37.8	10 36.6	1♐24.9	2 47.3	26 56.6	20 35.8	16 44.5	26 30.8	14 32.3	23 25.7	21 28.4
8 S	23 3 34.6	17 37.8	10 33.5	14 21.5	2 57.7	27 27.1	21 20.2	16 54.8	26 27.8	14 31.5	23 24.5	21 27.1
9 M	23 7 31.1	18 37.7	10 30.3	27 38.9	2 59.1	27 55.9	22 4.6	17 5.2	26 24.7	14 30.8	23 23.2	21 25.8
10 T	23 11 27.7	19 37.7	10 27.1	11♑19.9	2R51.6	28 23.2	22 48.9	17 15.7	26 21.5	14 30.1	23 21.9	21 24.6
11 W	23 15 24.2	20 37.6	10 23.9	25 25.9	2 35.6	28 48.7	23 33.2	17 26.3	26 18.3	14 29.5	23 20.6	21 23.3
12 T	23 19 20.8	21 37.5	10 20.8	9♒56.4	2 11.5	29 12.5	24 17.5	17 37.0	26 14.9	14 28.9	23 19.3	21 22.1
13 F	23 23 17.3	22 37.3	10 17.6	24 48.2	1 40.0	29 34.4	25 1.7	17 47.8	26 11.6	14 28.3	23 17.9	21 20.8
14 S	23 27 13.9	23 37.2	10 14.4	9♓55.3	1 1.9	29 54.5	25 45.8	17 58.7	26 8.1	14 27.9	23 16.5	21 19.6
15 S	23 31 10.5	24 37.0	10 11.2	25 9.0	0 18.0	0♉12.7	26 29.9	18 9.7	26 4.6	14 27.4	23 15.2	21 18.4
16 M	23 35 7.0	25 36.7	10 8.0	10♈19.0	29♓29.6	0 28.8	27 14.0	18 20.9	26 0.9	14 27.1	23 13.7	21 17.3
17 T	23 39 3.6	26 36.5	10 4.9	25 15.2	28 37.6	0 42.9	27 58.0	18 32.1	25 57.3	14 26.8	23 12.3	21 16.1
18 W	23 43 0.1	27 36.1	10 1.7	9♉49.2	27 43.3	0 54.8	28 42.0	18 43.3	25 53.5	14 26.5	23 10.9	21 15.0
19 T	23 46 56.7	28 35.8	9 58.5	23 55.8	26 47.9	1 4.6	29 25.9	18 54.7	25 49.7	14 26.3	23 9.4	21 13.9
20 F	23 50 53.2	29 35.4	9 55.3	7♊32.9	25 52.6	1 12.0	0♉ 9.8	19 6.2	25 45.9	14 26.1	23 8.0	21 12.8
21 S	23 54 49.8	0♈35.0	9 52.2	20 41.4	24 58.6	1 17.2	0 53.7	19 17.8	25 42.0	14 26.0	23 6.5	21 11.7
22 S	23 58 46.3	1 34.6	9 49.0	3♋24.6	24 6.8	1 20.1	1 37.5	19 29.5	25 38.1	14 26.0	23 5.0	21 10.7
23 M	0 2 42.9	2 34.1	9 45.8	15 46.7	23 18.2	1 20.4	2 21.3	19 41.2	25 34.0	14 26.0	23 3.5	21 9.6
24 T	0 6 39.4	3 33.6	9 42.6	27 52.9	22 33.5	1R18.4	3 5.0	19 53.0	25 30.0	14D26.1	23 2.0	21 8.6
25 W	0 10 36.0	4 33.0	9 39.4	9♌48.1	21 53.4	1 13.8	3 48.6	20 4.9	25 25.8	14 26.2	23 0.5	21 7.6
26 T	0 14 32.5	5 32.4	9 36.3	21 37.1	21 18.4	1 6.8	4 32.2	20 16.8	25 21.7	14 26.4	22 58.9	21 6.6
27 F	0 18 29.1	6 31.7	9 33.1	3♍24.1	20 48.8	0 57.2	5 15.8	20 28.9	25 17.5	14 26.6	22 57.4	21 5.7
28 S	0 22 25.6	7 31.1	9 29.9	15 12.5	20 24.9	0 45.2	5 59.3	20 41.0	25 13.2	14 26.9	22 55.8	21 4.7
29 S	0 26 22.2	8 30.3	9 26.7	27 5.0	20 6.8	0 30.7	6 42.7	20 53.2	25 8.9	14 27.2	22 54.2	21 3.8
30 M	0 30 18.8	9 29.6	9 23.6	9♎ 3.8	19 54.5	0 13.7	7 26.1	21 5.5	25 4.6	14 27.6	22 52.6	21 2.9
31 T	0 34 15.3	10 28.8	9 20.4	21 10.1	19 48.0	29♈54.3	8 9.5	21 17.8	25 0.2	14 28.0	22 51.0	21 2.1

DECLINATION at NOON

DAY	EPHEMERIS SIDEREAL TIME	☉	☊	☽	☿	♀	♂	♃	♄	♅	♆	♇
1 S	22 35 58.7	7S35.2	17S29.7	1N48.0	0N49.6	13N 4.0	6N 9.4	15N44.9	7S49.4	23N 4.7	7S32.9	23N25.2
4 W	22 47 48.4	6 26.4	17 32.3	13S58.4	2 32.4	14 9.4	7 2.7	15 53.9	7 46.0	23 5.0	7 31.5	23 26.5
7 S	22 59 38.0	5 16.8	17 34.9	25 14.7	3 41.2	15 9.9	7 55.3	16 3.1	7 42.4	23 5.3	7 30.1	23 27.7
10 T	23 11 27.7	4 6.5	17 37.5	25 35.6	4 9.9	16 4.8	8 47.1	16 12.5	7 38.5	23 5.5	7 28.5	23 28.8
13 F	23 23 17.3	2 55.7	17 40.1	12 9.4	3 56.1	16 53.3	9 38.0	16 22.0	7 34.4	23 5.6	7 27.0	23 29.9
16 M	23 35 7.0	1 44.7	17 42.6	8N 8.1	3 3.8	17 34.8	10 28.1	16 31.7	7 30.1	23 5.7	7 25.3	23 30.9
19 T	23 46 56.7	0 33.5	17 45.2	23 37.1	1 43.2	18 8.0	11 17.1	16 41.6	7 25.7	23 5.8	7 23.7	23 31.7
22 S	23 58 46.3	0N37.6	17 47.8	26 33.4	0 9.6	18 31.9	12 5.2	16 51.5	7 21.0	23 5.7	7 22.0	23 32.5
25 W	0 10 36.0	1 48.5	17 50.3	17 55.0	1S21.8	18 45.3	12 52.1	17 1.6	7 16.3	23 5.7	7 20.2	23 33.2
28 S	0 22 25.6	2 59.0	17 52.9	3 11.1	2 39.3	18 46.9	13 37.8	17 11.6	7 11.4	23 5.6	7 18.4	23 33.8
31 T	0 34 15.3	4 9.0	17 55.4	12S41.1	3 36.4	18 35.7	14 22.3	17 21.8	7 6.4	23 5.4	7 16.6	23 34.3

APRIL 1953

LONGITUDE at NOON

DAY	EPHEMERIS SIDEREAL TIME	☉	☊	☽	☿	♀	♂	♃	♄	♅	♆	♇
1 W	0 38 11.9	11♈28.0	9♒17.2	3♏25.2	19♓47.2	29♈32.6	8♉52.8	21♉30.2	24♎55.8	14♋28.5	22♎49.4	21♌ 1.2
2 T	0 42 8.4	12 27.1	9 14.0	15 50.0	19D51.9	29R 8.6	9 36.0	21 42.7	24R51.4	14 29.1	22R47.8	21R 0.4
3 F	0 46 5.0	13 26.2	9 10.8	28 25.4	20 2.0	28 42.5	10 19.3	21 55.2	24 46.9	14 29.7	22 46.2	20 59.6
4 S	0 50 1.5	14 25.3	9 7.7	11♐12.7	20 17.2	28 14.4	11 2.4	22 7.8	24 42.4	14 30.3	22 44.6	20 58.8
5 S	0 53 58.1	15 24.4	9 4.5	24 13.8	20 37.3	27 44.4	11 45.6	22 20.5	24 37.9	14 31.0	22 42.9	20 58.1
6 M	0 57 54.6	16 23.4	9 1.3	7♑30.5	21 2.1	27 12.7	12 28.6	22 33.2	24 33.4	14 31.8	22 41.3	20 57.3
7 T	1 1 51.2	17 22.4	8 58.1	21 5.0	21 31.5	26 39.5	13 11.7	22 46.0	24 28.8	14 32.6	22 39.7	20 56.6
8 W	1 5 47.7	18 21.4	8 55.0	4♒58.9	22 5.1	26 5.0	13 54.7	22 58.8	24 24.2	14 33.5	22 38.0	20 56.0
9 T	1 9 44.3	19 20.3	8 51.8	19 13.1	22 42.7	25 29.4	14 37.6	23 11.7	24 19.7	14 34.4	22 36.4	20 55.3
10 F	1 13 40.8	20 19.2	8 48.6	3♓46.2	23 24.2	24 52.8	15 20.5	23 24.7	24 15.1	14 35.3	22 34.7	20 54.7
11 S	1 17 37.4	21 18.1	8 45.4	18 34.8	24 9.3	24 15.7	16 3.4	23 37.7	24 10.4	14 36.4	22 33.1	20 54.1
12 S	1 21 33.9	22 17.0	8 42.2	3♈32.8	24 58.0	23 38.1	16 46.2	23 50.8	24 5.9	14 37.5	22 31.5	20 53.6
13 M	1 25 30.5	23 15.8	8 39.1	18 31.5	25 49.9	23 0.3	17 29.0	24 3.9	24 1.3	14 38.6	22 29.8	20 53.0
14 T	1 29 27.1	24 14.6	8 35.9	3♉21.8	26 44.9	22 22.6	18 11.7	24 17.1	23 56.6	14 39.8	22 28.2	20 52.5
15 W	1 33 23.6	25 13.3	8 32.7	17 54.8	27 42.9	21 45.3	18 54.4	24 30.3	23 52.0	14 41.0	22 26.5	20 52.0
16 T	1 37 20.2	26 12.1	8 29.5	2♊ 3.9	28 43.7	21 8.4	19 37.0	24 43.5	23 47.4	14 42.3	22 24.9	20 51.5
17 F	1 41 16.7	27 10.7	8 26.4	15 45.4	29 47.3	20 32.4	20 19.6	24 56.9	23 42.8	14 43.6	22 23.3	20 51.1
18 S	1 45 13.3	28 9.4	8 23.2	28 58.8	0♈53.4	19 57.4	21 2.2	25 10.2	23 38.2	14 45.0	22 21.6	20 50.7
19 S	1 49 9.8	29 8.0	8 20.0	11♋46.0	2 2.1	19 23.6	21 44.6	25 23.6	23 33.6	14 46.4	22 20.0	20 50.3
20 M	1 53 6.4	0♉ 6.6	8 16.8	24 10.9	3 13.2	18 51.3	22 27.1	25 37.0	23 29.0	14 47.9	22 18.4	20 49.9
21 T	1 57 2.9	1 5.1	8 13.6	6♌18.4	4 26.6	18 20.5	23 9.5	25 50.5	23 24.5	14 49.4	22 16.7	20 49.6
22 W	2 0 59.5	2 3.6	8 10.5	18 14.1	5 42.2	17 51.5	23 51.8	26 4.0	23 19.9	14 51.0	22 15.1	20 49.3
23 T	2 4 56.0	3 2.1	8 7.3	0♍ 3.4	7 0.1	17 24.5	24 34.1	26 17.6	23 15.4	14 52.6	22 13.5	20 49.0
24 F	2 8 52.6	4 0.5	8 4.1	11 51.2	8 20.0	16 59.5	25 16.4	26 31.2	23 10.9	14 54.3	22 11.9	20 48.8
25 S	2 12 49.2	4 58.9	8 0.9	23 42.0	9 42.1	16 36.7	25 58.6	26 44.8	23 6.4	14 56.0	22 10.3	20 48.6
26 S	2 16 45.7	5 57.3	7 57.8	5♎39.4	11 6.1	16 16.1	26 40.7	26 58.4	23 2.0	14 57.7	22 8.7	20 48.4
27 M	2 20 42.3	6 55.6	7 54.6	17 46.2	12 32.2	15 57.9	27 22.8	27 12.1	22 57.5	14 59.5	22 7.1	20 48.2
28 T	2 24 38.8	7 53.9	7 51.4	0♏ 3.9	14 0.3	15 42.0	28 4.9	27 25.8	22 53.2	15 1.4	22 5.5	20 48.1
29 W	2 28 35.4	8 52.2	7 48.2	12 33.6	15 30.2	15 28.5	28 46.9	27 39.6	22 48.8	15 3.3	22 4.0	20 48.0
30 T	2 32 31.9	9 50.4	7 45.0	25 15.2	17 2.2	15 17.5	29 28.9	27 53.3	22 44.5	15 5.2	22 2.4	20 47.9

DECLINATION at NOON

DAY	EPHEMERIS SIDEREAL TIME	☉	☊	☽	☿	♀	♂	♃	♄	♅	♆	♇
1 W	0 38 11.9	4N32.2	17S56.2	17S22.5	3S50.4	18N29.0	14N36.9	17N25.1	7S 4.8	23N 5.3	7S16.0	23N34.5
4 S	0 50 1.5	5 41.2	17 58.7	26 25.0	4 17.0	17 60.0	15 19.7	17 35.3	6 59.7	23 5.1	7 14.2	23 34.9
7 T	1 1 51.2	6 49.4	18 1.3	23 24.3	4 21.4	17 17.8	16 1.1	17 45.5	6 54.6	23 4.8	7 12.3	23 35.1
10 F	1 13 40.8	7 56.5	18 3.8	8 12.4	4 5.4	16 23.9	16 41.2	17 55.6	6 49.5	23 4.4	7 10.5	23 35.3
13 M	1 25 30.5	9 2.5	18 6.3	11N36.3	3 30.8	15 20.4	17 19.9	18 5.7	6 44.4	23 4.0	7 8.6	23 35.4
16 T	1 37 20.2	10 7.1	18 8.7	25 6.6	2 39.7	14 10.4	17 57.0	18 15.8	6 39.3	23 3.6	7 6.8	23 35.4
19 S	1 49 9.8	11 10.2	18 11.2	25 12.1	1 33.7	12 57.7	18 32.6	18 25.8	6 34.3	23 3.1	7 5.0	23 35.3
22 W	2 0 59.5	12 11.6	18 13.7	14 33.6	0 14.4	11 45.8	19 6.7	18 35.7	6 29.4	23 2.6	7 3.2	23 35.1
25 S	2 12 49.2	13 11.2	18 16.2	0S46.8	1N16.8	10 38.2	19 39.1	18 45.5	6 24.6	23 2.0	7 1.4	23 34.8
28 T	2 24 38.8	14 8.8	18 18.6	16 7.7	2 58.9	9 37.6	20 9.8	18 55.3	6 19.9	23 1.3	6 59.7	23 34.4

MAY 1953

LONGITUDE at NOON

DAY	EPHEMERIS SIDEREAL TIME h m s	☉ ° ′	☊ ° ′	☽ ° ′	☿ ° ′	♀ ° ′	♂ ° ′	♃ ° ′	♄ ° ′	♅ ° ′	♆ ° ′	♇ ° ′
1 F	2 36 28.5	10♉48.6	7♒41.9	8♐ 8.6	18♈36.0	15♈ 9.0	0♊10.8	28♉ 7.1	22♎40.2	15♋ 7.2	22♎ 0.9	20♌47.8
2 S	2 40 25.0	11 46.8	7 38.7	21 13.3	20 11.7	15R 2.9	0 52.7	28 20.9	22R36.0	15 9.2	21R59.3	20 47.8
3 S	2 44 21.6	12 45.0	7 35.5	4♑29.3	21 49.4	14 59.3	1 34.5	28 34.8	22 31.8	15 11.3	21 57.9	20D47.9
4 M	2 48 18.2	13 43.1	7 32.3	17 56.5	23 28.9	14 58.0	2 16.3	28 48.7	22 27.7	15 13.5	21 56.4	20 47.9
5 T	2 52 14.7	14 41.2	7 29.2	1♒35.7	25 10.3	14D59.2	2 58.1	29 2.6	22 23.6	15 15.6	21 54.9	20 48.0
6 W	2 56 11.3	15 39.3	7 26.0	15 27.5	26 53.6	15 2.6	3 39.8	29 16.5	22 19.5	15 17.8	21 53.4	20 48.0
7 T	3 0 7.8	16 37.4	7 22.8	29 32.3	28 38.8	15 8.4	4 21.5	29 30.5	22 15.5	15 20.1	21 51.9	20 48.2
8 F	3 4 4.4	17 35.4	7 19.6	13♓49.6	0♉25.9	15 16.3	5 3.1	29 44.4	22 11.6	15 22.3	21 50.5	20 48.3
9 S	3 8 0.9	18 33.5	7 16.5	28 17.4	2 14.9	15 26.5	5 44.7	29 58.4	22 7.7	15 24.7	21 49.0	20 48.5
10 S	3 11 57.5	19 31.5	7 13.3	12♈51.7	4 5.8	15 38.7	6 26.2	0♊12.4	22 3.8	15 27.0	21 47.6	20 48.7
11 M	3 15 54.0	20 29.4	7 10.1	27 27.0	5 58.6	15 53.0	7 7.7	0 26.4	22 0.0	15 29.4	21 46.2	20 48.9
12 T	3 19 50.6	21 27.4	7 6.9	11♉56.3	7 53.3	16 9.3	7 49.2	0 40.4	21 56.3	15 31.9	21 44.8	20 49.2
13 W	3 23 47.2	22 25.3	7 3.7	26 12.8	9 49.9	16 27.5	8 30.6	0 54.4	21 52.7	15 34.3	21 43.5	20 49.5
14 T	3 27 43.7	23 23.2	7 0.6	10♊10.5	11 48.3	16 47.5	9 11.9	1 8.5	21 49.1	15 36.9	21 42.1	20 49.8
15 F	3 31 40.3	24 21.1	6 57.4	23 45.5	13 48.6	17 9.3	9 53.3	1 22.5	21 45.5	15 39.4	21 40.8	20 50.1
16 S	3 35 36.8	25 18.9	6 54.2	6♋56.1	15 50.5	17 32.9	10 34.6	1 36.6	21 42.1	15 42.0	21 39.5	20 50.5
17 S	3 39 33.4	26 16.8	6 51.0	19 43.3	17 54.2	17 58.1	11 15.8	1 50.7	21 38.7	15 44.6	21 38.2	20 50.9
18 M	3 43 29.9	27 14.5	6 47.9	2♌ 9.5	19 59.5	18 24.9	11 57.0	2 4.7	21 35.4	15 47.3	21 36.9	20 51.3
19 T	3 47 26.5	28 12.3	6 44.7	14 19.0	22 6.2	18 53.2	12 38.2	2 18.8	21 32.1	15 50.0	21 35.6	20 51.8
20 W	3 51 23.1	29 10.1	6 41.5	26 16.6	24 14.3	19 23.0	13 19.3	2 32.9	21 28.9	15 52.7	21 34.4	20 52.3
21 T	3 55 19.6	0♊ 7.8	6 38.3	8♍ 7.7	26 23.6	19 54.3	14 0.3	2 47.0	21 25.9	15 55.5	21 33.2	20 52.8
22 F	3 59 16.2	1 5.5	6 35.2	19 57.6	28 33.8	20 26.9	14 41.4	3 1.1	21 22.8	15 58.3	21 32.0	20 53.3
23 S	4 3 12.7	2 3.1	6 32.0	1♎51.2	0♊44.8	21 0.9	15 22.4	3 15.2	21 19.9	16 1.1	21 30.8	20 53.9
24 S	4 7 9.3	3 0.8	6 28.8	13 53.0	2 56.4	21 36.2	16 3.3	3 29.3	21 17.1	16 4.1	21 29.7	20 54.6
25 M	4 11 5.8	3 58.4	6 25.6	26 6.5	5 8.2	22 12.6	16 44.2	3 43.4	21 14.3	16 6.9	21 28.6	20 55.2
26 T	4 15 2.4	4 56.0	6 22.4	8♏34.3	7 20.0	22 50.3	17 25.1	3 57.5	21 11.6	16 9.9	21 27.5	20 55.8
27 W	4 18 59.0	5 53.6	6 19.3	21 17.7	9 31.5	23 29.1	18 5.9	4 11.6	21 9.0	16 12.8	21 26.5	20 56.5
28 T	4 22 55.5	6 51.1	6 16.1	4♐16.8	11 42.5	24 9.0	18 46.7	4 25.6	21 6.5	16 15.8	21 25.4	20 57.2
29 F	4 26 52.1	7 48.6	6 12.9	17 30.8	13 52.7	24 49.9	19 27.4	4 39.7	21 4.0	16 18.8	21 24.4	20 57.9
30 S	4 30 48.6	8 46.2	6 9.7	0♑58.0	16 1.8	25 31.9	20 8.1	4 53.8	21 1.7	16 21.9	21 23.4	20 58.7
31 S	4 34 45.2	9 43.6	6 6.6	14 36.5	18 9.6	26 14.8	20 48.8	5 7.8	20 59.4	16 24.9	21 22.4	20 59.5

DECLINATION at NOON

DAY	EPHEMERIS SIDEREAL TIME h m s	☉	☊	☽	☿	♀	♂	♃	♄	♅	♆	♇
1 F	2 36 28.5	15N 4.4	18S21.1	25S54.8	4N50.4	8N45.7	20N38.9	19N 4.9	6S15.4	23N 0.6	6S58.0	23N34.0
4 M	2 48 18.2	15 57.7	18 23.5	23 52.2	6 50.4	8 3.6	21 6.2	19 14.4	6 11.0	22 59.9	6 56.3	23 33.4
7 T	3 0 7.8	16 48.6	18 25.9	9 48.9	8 57.2	7 31.8	21 31.8	19 23.7	6 6.9	22 59.1	6 54.8	23 32.7
10 S	3 11 57.5	17 37.1	18 28.3	9N18.8	11 9.3	7 10.0	21 55.6	19 32.9	6 2.9	22 58.3	6 53.2	23 32.0
13 W	3 23 47.2	18 22.9	18 30.8	23 53.8	13 24.5	6 57.7	22 17.6	19 41.9	5 59.2	22 57.4	6 51.7	23 31.1
16 S	3 35 36.8	19 5.9	18 33.2	25 42.1	15 39.9	6 54.4	22 37.7	19 50.7	5 55.7	22 56.5	6 50.3	23 30.2
19 T	3 47 26.5	19 46.0	18 35.6	15 48.5	17 51.7	6 59.2	22 56.0	19 59.4	5 52.5	22 55.5	6 49.0	23 29.3
22 F	3 59 16.2	20 23.0	18 38.0	0 42.6	19 55.1	7 11.3	23 12.4	20 7.9	5 49.6	22 54.5	6 47.7	23 28.2
25 M	4 11 5.8	20 56.9	18 40.3	14S44.3	21 44.7	7 29.9	23 26.9	20 16.2	5 46.9	22 53.4	6 46.6	23 27.0
28 T	4 22 55.5	21 27.6	18 42.7	25 21.0	23 15.3	7 54.4	23 39.6	20 24.2	5 44.6	22 52.3	6 45.5	23 25.8
31 S	4 34 45.2	21 54.9	18 45.1	24 22.7	24 23.1	8 23.8	23 50.3	20 32.1	5 42.6	22 51.2	6 44.5	23 24.6

JUNE 1953

LONGITUDE at NOON

DAY	EPHEMERIS SIDEREAL TIME h m s	☉ ° ′	☊ ° ′	☽ ° ′	☿ ° ′	♀ ° ′	♂ ° ′	♃ ° ′	♄ ° ′	♅ ° ′	♆ ° ′	♇ ° ′
1 M	4 38 41.7	10♊41.1	6♒ 3.4	28♑24.3	20♊15.8	26♈58.7	21♊29.4	5♊21.9	20♎57.2	16♋28.0	21♎21.5	21♌ 0.3
2 T	4 42 38.3	11 38.6	6 0.2	12♒19.7	22 20.3	27 43.5	22 10.0	5 35.9	20R55.1	16 31.2	21R20.6	21 1.1
3 W	4 46 34.9	12 36.0	5 57.0	26 21.4	24 22.9	28 29.2	22 50.5	5 49.9	20 53.1	16 34.3	21 19.7	21 2.0
4 T	4 50 31.4	13 33.5	5 53.9	10♓28.3	26 23.5	29 15.7	23 31.1	6 3.9	20 51.2	16 37.5	21 18.8	21 2.9
5 F	4 54 28.0	14 30.9	5 50.7	24 39.2	28 21.9	0♉ 3.0	24 11.5	6 17.9	20 49.4	16 40.7	21 17.9	21 3.8
6 S	4 58 24.5	15 28.4	5 47.5	8♈52.4	0♋18.1	0 51.0	24 52.0	6 31.9	20 47.6	16 43.9	21 17.1	21 4.7
7 S	5 2 21.1	16 25.8	5 44.3	23 5.4	2 11.9	1 39.9	25 32.4	6 45.9	20 46.0	16 47.2	21 16.3	21 5.7
8 M	5 6 17.7	17 23.2	5 41.2	7♉15.0	4 3.3	2 29.4	26 12.7	6 59.8	20 44.5	16 50.4	21 15.6	21 6.6
9 T	5 10 14.2	18 20.6	5 38.0	21 17.3	5 52.2	3 19.6	26 53.1	7 13.8	20 43.0	16 53.7	21 14.9	21 7.6
10 W	5 14 10.8	19 17.9	5 34.8	5♊ 8.1	7 38.7	4 10.5	27 33.4	7 27.7	20 41.7	16 57.0	21 14.2	21 8.7
11 T	5 18 7.3	20 15.3	5 31.6	18 43.9	9 22.6	5 2.0	28 13.6	7 41.6	20 40.4	17 0.4	21 13.5	21 9.7
12 F	5 22 3.9	21 12.7	5 28.4	2♋ 1.9	11 4.0	5 54.1	28 53.9	7 55.4	20 39.3	17 3.7	21 12.8	21 10.8
13 S	5 26 0.4	22 10.0	5 25.3	15 0.7	12 42.9	6 46.8	29 34.1	8 9.3	20 38.2	17 7.1	21 12.2	21 11.9
14 S	5 29 57.0	23 7.4	5 22.1	27 40.7	14 19.2	7 40.0	0♋14.3	8 23.2	20 37.3	17 10.5	21 11.7	21 13.1
15 M	5 33 53.6	24 4.7	5 18.9	10♌ 3.5	15 52.8	8 33.8	0 54.4	8 37.0	20 36.4	17 14.0	21 11.1	21 14.2
16 T	5 37 50.1	25 2.0	5 15.7	22 11.9	17 23.8	9 28.1	1 34.5	8 50.7	20 35.6	17 17.4	21 10.6	21 15.4
17 W	5 41 46.7	25 59.3	5 12.6	4♍ 9.9	18 52.2	10 23.0	2 14.5	9 4.5	20 35.0	17 20.8	21 10.1	21 16.6
18 T	5 45 43.2	26 56.6	5 9.4	16 1.9	20 18.0	11 18.3	2 54.5	9 18.2	20 34.4	17 24.3	21 9.7	21 17.8
19 F	5 49 39.8	27 53.9	5 6.2	27 52.9	21 41.0	12 14.0	3 34.5	9 31.9	20 34.0	17 27.8	21 9.2	21 19.0
20 S	5 53 36.4	28 51.1	5 3.0	9♎47.9	23 1.3	13 10.3	4 14.5	9 45.5	20 33.6	17 31.3	21 8.8	21 20.3
21 S	5 57 32.9	29 48.4	4 59.9	21 51.6	24 18.8	14 6.9	4 54.4	9 59.2	20 33.3	17 34.8	21 8.5	21 21.6
22 M	6 1 29.5	0♋45.6	4 56.7	4♏ 8.4	25 33.5	15 4.0	5 34.2	10 12.7	20 33.1	17 38.3	21 8.1	21 22.9
23 T	6 5 26.0	1 42.8	4 53.5	16 41.7	26 45.3	16 1.5	6 14.1	10 26.3	20 33.1	17 41.8	21 7.8	21 24.2
24 W	6 9 22.6	2 40.0	4 50.3	29 33.9	27 54.1	16 59.5	6 53.9	10 39.8	20 33.1	17 45.4	21 7.5	21 25.5
25 T	6 13 19.1	3 37.3	4 47.2	12♐46.0	29 0.0	17 57.8	7 33.6	10 53.3	20D33.2	17 48.9	21 7.3	21 26.9
26 F	6 17 15.7	4 34.5	4 44.0	26 17.6	0♌ 2.8	18 56.5	8 13.4	11 6.7	20 33.5	17 52.5	21 7.1	21 28.3
27 S	6 21 12.3	5 31.6	4 40.8	10♑ 6.7	1 2.4	19 55.5	8 53.1	11 20.1	20 33.8	17 56.1	21 6.9	21 29.7
28 S	6 25 8.8	6 28.8	4 37.6	24 10.1	1 58.7	20 54.9	9 32.7	11 33.5	20 34.2	17 59.6	21 6.7	21 31.1
29 M	6 29 5.4	7 26.0	4 34.5	8♒23.9	2 51.7	21 54.7	10 12.4	11 46.8	20 34.7	18 3.2	21 6.6	21 32.5
30 T	6 33 1.9	8 23.2	4 31.3	22 43.7	3 41.2	22 54.8	10 52.0	12 0.1	20 35.4	18 6.8	21 6.5	21 34.0

DECLINATION at NOON

DAY	EPHEMERIS SIDEREAL TIME h m s	☉	☊	☽	☿	♀	♂	♃	♄	♅	♆	♇
1 M	4 38 41.7	22N 3.3	18S45.9	21S 1.1	24N40.3	8N34.6	23N53.5	20N34.7	5S42.0	22N50.8	6S44.1	23N24.1
4 T	4 50 31.4	22 26.0	18 48.2	4 50.8	25 15.4	9 9.7	24 1.7	20 42.2	5 40.4	22 49.7	6 43.3	23 22.8
7 S	5 2 21.1	22 45.3	18 50.5	13N38.5	25 27.1	9 48.1	24 8.0	20 49.6	5 39.1	22 48.4	6 42.5	23 21.3
10 W	5 14 10.8	23 0.9	18 52.9	25 29.3	25 17.6	10 29.3	24 12.4	20 56.7	5 38.1	22 47.2	6 41.8	23 19.9
13 S	5 26 0.4	23 12.9	18 55.2	24 15.5	24 50.2	11 12.7	24 14.9	21 3.6	5 37.5	22 45.9	6 41.2	23 18.3
16 T	5 37 50.1	23 21.2	18 57.5	12 33.7	24 8.0	11 57.6	24 15.5	21 10.2	5 37.3	22 44.6	6 40.7	23 16.7
19 F	5 49 39.8	23 25.8	18 59.8	3S 1.4	23 14.3	12 43.6	24 14.3	21 16.6	5 37.3	22 43.3	6 40.3	23 15.1
22 M	6 1 29.5	23 26.6	19 2.1	17 47.3	22 12.2	13 30.3	24 11.3	21 22.8	5 37.8	22 41.9	6 40.0	23 13.4
25 T	6 13 19.1	23 23.8	19 4.4	26 20.3	21 4.4	14 17.0	24 6.4	21 28.7	5 38.5	22 40.5	6 39.9	23 11.7
28 S	6 25 8.8	23 17.3	19 6.7	22 6.7	19 54.0	15 3.4	23 59.8	21 34.4	5 39.6	22 39.1	6 39.8	23 10.0

JULY 1953

DAY	EPHEMERIS SIDEREAL TIME	☉	☊	☽	☿	♀	♂	♃	♄	♅	♆	♇
	h m s	° ′	° ′	° ′	° ′	° ′	° ′	° ′	° ′	° ′	° ′	° ′
LONGITUDE at NOON												
1 W	6 36 58.5	9♋20.4	4♒28.1	7♓ 5.6	4♌27.1	23♉55.2	11♋31.6	12♊13.3	20♎36.1	18♋10.5	21♎ 6.5	21♌35.4
2 T	6 40 55.1	10 17.6	4 24.9	21 25.9	5 9.3	24 56.0	12 11.1	12 26.5	20 36.9	18 14.1	21R 6.4	21 36.9
3 F	6 44 51.6	11 14.8	4 21.7	5♈41.6	5 47.7	25 57.0	12 50.6	12 39.7	20 37.8	18 17.7	21 6.4	21 38.4
4 S	6 48 48.2	12 12.0	4 18.6	19 50.3	6 22.2	26 58.4	13 30.1	12 52.8	20 38.9	18 21.3	21D 6.5	21 40.0
5 S	6 52 44.7	13 9.3	4 15.4	3♉50.3	6 52.6	28 0.1	14 9.6	13 5.9	20 40.0	18 25.0	21 6.6	21 41.5
6 M	6 56 41.3	14 6.5	4 12.2	17 39.8	7 18.8	29 2.0	14 49.1	13 18.9	20 41.2	18 28.6	21 6.7	21 43.1
7 T	7 0 37.9	15 3.7	4 9.0	1♊17.4	7 40.6	0♊ 4.2	15 28.5	13 31.8	20 42.5	18 32.3	21 6.9	21 44.7
8 W	7 4 34.4	16 0.9	4 5.9	14 42.0	7 58.0	1 6.6	16 7.9	13 44.7	20 44.0	18 35.9	21 7.0	21 46.3
9 T	7 8 31.0	16 58.1	4 2.7	27 52.6	8 10.8	2 9.3	16 47.2	13 57.6	20 45.5	18 39.6	21 7.2	21 47.9
10 F	7 12 27.5	17 55.4	3 59.5	10♋48.6	8 18.9	3 12.3	17 26.6	14 10.3	20 47.1	18 43.2	21 7.5	21 49.5
11 S	7 16 24.1	18 52.6	3 56.3	23 29.9	8 22.4	4 15.5	18 5.9	14 23.1	20 48.8	18 46.9	21 7.7	21 51.1
12 S	7 20 20.6	19 49.8	3 53.2	5♌57.2	8R 21.0	5 18.9	18 45.1	14 35.7	20 50.6	18 50.5	21 8.0	21 52.8
13 M	7 24 17.2	20 47.1	3 50.0	18 11.8	8 14.9	6 22.6	19 24.4	14 48.4	20 52.5	18 54.2	21 8.4	21 54.4
14 T	7 28 13.8	21 44.3	3 46.8	0♍15.6	8 4.1	7 26.4	20 3.6	15 0.9	20 54.5	18 57.8	21 8.7	21 56.1
15 W	7 32 10.3	22 41.6	3 43.6	12 11.4	7 48.6	8 30.5	20 42.8	15 13.4	20 56.6	19 1.5	21 9.1	21 57.8
16 T	7 36 6.9	23 38.8	3 40.5	24 2.8	7 28.6	9 34.8	21 21.9	15 25.8	20 58.7	19 5.1	21 9.5	21 59.5
17 F	7 40 3.4	24 36.1	3 37.3	5♎53.6	7 4.2	10 39.3	22 1.1	15 38.2	21 1.0	19 8.7	21 10.0	22 1.2
18 S	7 43 60.0	25 33.3	3 34.1	17 48.2	6 35.8	11 44.0	22 40.2	15 50.5	21 3.4	19 12.4	21 10.5	22 2.9
19 S	7 47 56.5	26 30.6	3 30.9	29 51.3	6 3.8	12 48.9	23 19.2	16 2.7	21 5.8	19 16.0	21 11.0	22 4.7
20 M	7 51 53.1	27 27.9	3 27.7	12♏ 7.3	5 28.5	13 53.9	23 58.3	16 14.8	21 8.4	19 19.6	21 11.6	22 6.4
21 T	7 55 49.7	28 25.1	3 24.6	24 40.5	4 50.4	14 59.2	24 37.3	16 26.9	21 11.0	19 23.2	21 12.2	22 8.2
22 W	7 59 46.2	29 22.4	3 21.4	7♐34.4	4 10.2	16 4.7	25 16.3	16 38.9	21 13.8	19 26.8	21 12.8	22 9.9
23 T	8 3 42.8	0♌19.7	3 18.2	20 51.3	3 28.4	17 10.3	25 55.3	16 50.9	21 16.6	19 30.5	21 13.4	22 11.7
24 F	8 7 39.3	1 17.0	3 15.0	4♑32.2	2 45.9	18 16.1	26 34.2	17 2.7	21 19.5	19 34.0	21 14.1	22 13.5
25 S	8 11 35.9	2 14.3	3 11.9	18 35.9	2 3.2	19 22.1	27 13.1	17 14.5	21 22.5	19 37.6	21 14.8	22 15.3
26 S	8 15 32.4	3 11.6	3 8.7	2♒59.4	1 21.3	20 28.3	27 52.0	17 26.3	21 25.6	19 41.3	21 15.6	22 17.2
27 M	8 19 29.0	4 8.9	3 5.5	17 37.4	0 40.8	21 34.6	28 30.9	17 37.9	21 28.8	19 44.8	21 16.4	22 19.0
28 T	8 23 25.6	5 6.2	3 2.3	2♓23.5	0 2.4	22 41.1	29 9.8	17 49.5	21 32.1	19 48.4	21 17.2	22 20.8
29 W	8 27 22.1	6 3.6	2 59.2	17 10.7	29♋27.1	23 47.7	29 48.6	18 1.0	21 35.4	19 51.9	21 18.0	22 22.6
30 T	8 31 18.7	7 0.9	2 56.0	1♈52.1	28 55.3	24 54.5	0♌27.4	18 12.3	21 38.8	19 55.4	21 18.9	22 24.5
31 F	8 35 15.2	7 58.3	2 52.8	16 22.2	28 27.8	26 1.5	1 6.1	18 23.7	21 42.3	19 59.0	21 19.8	22 26.3
DECLINATION at NOON												
1 W	6 36 58.5	23N 7.0	19S 9.0	6S 12.1	18N 43.5	15N 49.1	23N 51.3	21N 39.8	5S 41.0	22N 37.7	6S 39.9	23N 8.2
4 S	6 48 48.2	22 53.2	19 11.3	12N 28.8	17 35.9	16 33.5	23 41.2	21 45.0	5 42.8	22 36.2	6 40.0	23 6.4
7 T	7 0 37.9	22 35.7	19 13.5	24 57.9	16 34.1	17 16.3	23 29.3	21 50.0	5 44.9	22 34.7	6 40.3	23 4.6
10 F	7 12 27.5	22 14.7	19 15.8	25 0.8	15 41.1	17 57.1	23 15.7	21 54.7	5 47.3	22 33.2	6 40.7	23 2.8
13 M	7 24 17.2	21 50.3	19 18.0	14 4.9	14 59.9	18 35.5	23 0.5	21 59.1	5 50.1	22 31.8	6 41.2	23 0.9
16 T	7 36 6.9	21 22.5	19 20.2	1S 23.8	14 33.2	19 11.2	22 43.7	22 3.3	5 53.1	22 30.2	6 41.7	22 59.0
19 S	7 47 56.5	20 51.5	19 22.5	16 21.2	14 22.9	19 43.7	22 25.3	22 7.3	5 56.5	22 28.7	6 42.4	22 57.2
22 W	7 59 46.2	20 17.3	19 24.7	25 53.4	14 29.6	20 12.9	22 5.5	22 11.1	6 0.1	22 27.2	6 43.2	22 55.3
25 S	8 11 35.9	19 40.0	19 26.9	23 29.1	14 51.9	20 38.3	21 44.1	22 14.6	6 4.1	22 25.7	6 44.1	22 53.4
28 T	8 23 25.6	18 59.8	19 29.1	8 13.1	15 26.7	20 59.7	21 21.3	22 17.9	6 8.3	22 24.2	6 45.2	22 51.5
31 F	8 35 15.2	18 16.8	19 31.3	11N 6.2	16 9.6	21 16.9	20 57.1	22 21.0	6 12.8	22 22.7	6 46.3	22 49.7

AUGUST 1953

DAY	EPHEMERIS SIDEREAL TIME	☉	☊	☽	☿	♀	♂	♃	♄	♅	♆	♇
LONGITUDE at NOON												
1 S	8 39 11.8	8♌55.7	2♒49.6	0♉36.9	28♋ 5.1	27♊ 8.7	1♌44.9	18♊34.9	21♎45.9	20♋ 2.5	21♎20.7	22♌28.2
2 S	8 43 8.3	9 53.1	2 46.4	14 34.1	27R 47.7	28 15.9	2 23.6	18 46.0	21 49.6	20 6.0	21 21.6	22 30.0
3 M	8 47 4.9	10 50.6	2 43.3	28 12.9	27 36.1	29 23.4	3 2.4	18 57.1	21 53.4	20 9.4	21 22.6	22 31.9
4 T	8 51 1.5	11 48.0	2 40.1	11♊33.7	27 30.5	0♋31.0	3 41.0	19 8.0	21 57.2	20 12.9	21 23.6	22 33.8
5 W	8 54 58.0	12 45.5	2 36.9	24 37.9	27D 31.2	1 38.7	4 19.7	19 18.9	22 1.2	20 16.3	21 24.7	22 35.6
6 T	8 58 54.6	13 43.0	2 33.7	7♋26.8	27 38.5	2 46.5	4 58.4	19 29.6	22 5.2	20 19.8	21 25.7	22 37.5
7 F	9 2 51.1	14 40.5	2 30.6	20 2.1	27 52.5	3 54.5	5 37.0	19 40.3	22 9.2	20 23.2	21 26.8	22 39.4
8 S	9 6 47.7	15 38.1	2 27.4	2♌25.6	28 13.2	5 2.7	6 15.6	19 50.9	22 13.4	20 26.6	21 28.0	22 41.3
9 S	9 10 44.2	16 35.6	2 24.2	14 38.7	28 40.8	6 10.9	6 54.2	20 1.4	22 17.6	20 29.9	21 29.1	22 43.2
10 M	9 14 40.8	17 33.2	2 21.0	26 43.2	29 15.2	7 19.3	7 32.8	20 11.8	22 22.0	20 33.3	21 30.3	22 45.1
11 T	9 18 37.3	18 30.8	2 17.9	8♍40.8	29 56.3	8 27.8	8 11.3	20 22.0	22 26.4	20 36.6	21 31.5	22 47.0
12 W	9 22 33.9	19 28.4	2 14.7	20 33.4	0♌44.1	9 36.4	8 49.9	20 32.2	22 30.8	20 39.9	21 32.8	22 48.8
13 T	9 26 30.5	20 26.0	2 11.5	2♎23.6	1 38.5	10 45.2	9 28.4	20 42.3	22 35.4	20 43.2	21 34.0	22 50.7
14 F	9 30 27.0	21 23.7	2 8.3	14 14.2	2 39.2	11 54.0	10 6.9	20 52.2	22 40.0	20 46.5	21 35.3	22 52.6
15 S	9 34 23.6	22 21.3	2 5.1	26 8.5	3 46.2	13 3.0	10 45.3	21 2.1	22 44.7	20 49.7	21 36.7	22 54.5
16 S	9 38 20.1	23 19.0	2 2.0	8♏10.3	4 59.1	14 12.2	11 23.8	21 11.9	22 49.5	20 53.0	21 38.0	22 56.5
17 M	9 42 16.7	24 16.7	1 58.8	20 23.8	6 17.7	15 21.4	12 2.2	21 21.5	22 54.3	20 56.2	21 39.4	22 58.4
18 T	9 46 13.2	25 14.5	1 55.6	2♐53.2	7 41.7	16 30.7	12 40.6	21 31.0	22 59.2	20 59.4	21 40.8	23 0.3
19 W	9 50 9.8	26 12.2	1 52.4	15 42.9	9 10.7	17 40.2	13 19.0	21 40.4	23 4.2	21 2.5	21 42.2	23 2.2
20 T	9 54 6.3	27 9.9	1 49.3	28 56.4	10 44.5	18 49.7	13 57.4	21 49.7	23 9.2	21 5.6	21 43.7	23 4.1
21 F	9 58 2.9	28 7.7	1 46.1	12♑36.1	12 22.5	19 59.4	14 35.7	21 58.8	23 14.3	21 8.7	21 45.2	23 6.0
22 S	10 1 59.4	29 5.5	1 42.9	26 42.8	14 4.4	21 9.1	15 14.0	22 7.8	23 19.5	21 11.8	21 46.7	23 7.9
23 S	10 5 56.0	0♍ 3.3	1 39.7	11♒14.6	15 49.7	22 19.0	15 52.3	22 16.8	23 24.7	21 14.8	21 48.2	23 9.8
24 M	10 9 52.6	1 1.1	1 36.5	26 6.8	17 38.0	23 29.0	16 30.6	22 25.6	23 30.0	21 17.9	21 49.7	23 11.7
25 T	10 13 49.1	1 59.0	1 33.4	11♓12.3	19 28.9	24 39.1	17 8.9	22 34.2	23 35.3	21 20.8	21 51.3	23 13.5
26 W	10 17 45.7	2 56.9	1 30.2	26 21.7	21 21.9	25 49.3	17 47.1	22 42.8	23 40.7	21 23.8	21 52.9	23 15.4
27 T	10 21 42.2	3 54.8	1 27.0	11♈25.4	23 16.5	26 59.6	18 25.4	22 51.2	23 46.2	21 26.7	21 54.5	23 17.3
28 F	10 25 38.8	4 52.7	1 23.8	26 14.5	25 12.5	28 10.0	19 3.6	22 59.5	23 51.8	21 29.6	21 56.2	23 19.2
29 S	10 29 35.3	5 50.7	1 20.7	10♉42.6	27 9.4	29 20.5	19 41.8	23 7.6	23 57.3	21 32.5	21 57.8	23 21.0
30 S	10 33 31.9	6 48.7	1 17.5	24 46.2	29 6.9	0♌31.1	20 20.0	23 15.6	24 3.0	21 35.3	21 59.5	23 22.9
31 M	10 37 28.4	7 46.7	1 14.3	8♊24.4	1♍ 4.7	1 41.8	20 58.2	23 23.5	24 8.7	21 38.1	22 1.2	23 24.7
DECLINATION at NOON												
1 S	8 39 11.8	18N 1.9	19S 32.0	16N 37.8	16N 24.7	21N 21.6	20N 48.8	22N 22.0	6S 14.4	22N 22.2	6S 46.7	22N 49.1
4 T	8 51 1.5	17 15.3	19 34.2	26 17.3	17 10.2	21 32.7	20 22.8	22 24.8	6 19.2	22 20.7	6 47.9	22 47.2
7 F	9 2 51.1	16 26.1	19 36.3	23 9.2	17 51.6	21 39.1	19 55.5	22 27.4	6 24.3	22 19.2	6 49.2	22 45.4
10 M	9 14 40.8	15 34.6	19 38.5	10 38.3	18 23.6	21 40.5	19 27.0	22 29.8	6 29.6	22 17.7	6 50.7	22 43.6
13 T	9 26 30.5	14 40.9	19 40.7	5S 5.6	18 41.4	21 36.9	18 57.4	22 32.0	6 35.1	22 16.3	6 52.2	22 41.8
16 S	9 38 20.1	13 45.0	19 42.8	19 10.6	18 40.3	21 28.1	18 26.5	22 34.1	6 40.9	22 14.8	6 53.8	22 40.0
19 W	9 50 9.8	12 47.2	19 44.9	26 31.4	18 16.3	21 14.2	17 54.6	22 35.9	6 46.9	22 13.4	6 55.5	22 38.3
22 S	10 1 59.4	11 47.6	19 47.1	21 23.8	17 27.4	20 55.1	17 21.6	22 37.6	6 53.0	22 12.1	6 57.2	22 36.7
25 T	10 13 49.1	10 46.3	19 49.2	4 22.8	16 13.6	20 30.8	16 47.7	22 39.1	6 59.4	22 10.7	6 59.1	22 35.0
28 F	10 25 38.8	9 43.5	19 51.3	14N 56.6	14 37.5	20 1.3	16 12.8	22 40.5	7 5.9	22 9.4	7 1.0	22 33.4
31 M	10 37 28.4	8 39.3	19 53.4	25 53.6	12 43.6	19 26.8	15 36.9	22 41.7	7 12.6	22 8.1	7 2.9	22 31.9

SEPTEMBER 1953

DAY	EPHEMERIS SIDEREAL TIME	☉	☊	☽	☿	♀	♂	♃	♄	♅	♆	♇
	h m s	° ′	° ′	° ′	° ′	° ′	° ′	° ′	° ′	° ′	° ′	° ′
LONGITUDE at NOON												
1 T	10 41 25.0	8♍44.8	1♒11.1	21♊38.5	3♍ 2.6	2♌52.7	21♌36.3	23♊31.2	24♎14.5	21♋40.8	22♎ 2.9	23♌26.6
2 W	10 45 21.5	9 42.9	1 7.9	4♋31.3	5 0.3	4 3.6	22 14.5	23 38.8	24 20.3	21 43.6	22 4.7	23 28.4
3 T	10 49 18.1	10 41.0	1 4.8	17 6.2	6 57.5	5 14.6	22 52.6	23 46.3	24 26.2	21 46.2	22 6.5	23 30.3
4 F	10 53 14.7	11 39.2	1 1.6	29 26.8	8 54.3	6 25.7	23 30.7	23 53.6	24 32.1	21 48.9	22 8.2	23 32.1
5 S	10 57 11.2	12 37.4	0 58.4	11♌36.3	10 50.3	7 36.9	24 8.8	24 0.8	24 38.1	21 51.5	22 10.0	23 33.9
6 S	11 1 7.8	13 35.6	0 55.2	23 37.9	12 45.7	8 48.2	24 47.0	24 7.9	24 44.2	21 54.2	22 11.9	23 35.8
7 M	11 5 4.3	14 33.9	0 52.1	5♍33.8	14 40.0	9 59.6	25 25.0	24 14.7	24 50.2	21 56.7	22 13.8	23 37.6
8 T	11 9 0.9	15 32.2	0 48.9	17 26.1	16 33.5	11 11.1	26 3.1	24 21.4	24 56.4	21 59.2	22 15.6	23 39.4
9 W	11 12 57.4	16 30.5	0 45.7	29 16.7	18 25.9	12 22.6	26 41.1	24 28.0	25 2.6	22 1.7	22 17.5	23 41.2
10 T	11 16 54.0	17 28.8	0 42.5	11♎ 7.3	20 17.3	13 34.3	27 19.1	24 34.4	25 8.8	22 4.1	22 19.4	23 42.9
11 F	11 20 50.5	18 27.2	0 39.3	22 59.8	22 7.6	14 46.0	27 57.1	24 40.7	25 15.1	22 6.5	22 21.3	23 44.7
12 S	11 24 47.1	19 25.6	0 36.2	4♏56.3	23 56.9	15 57.8	28 35.1	24 46.8	25 21.4	22 8.8	22 23.3	23 46.4
13 S	11 28 43.6	20 24.0	0 33.0	16 59.5	25 45.0	17 9.6	29 13.1	24 52.7	25 27.8	22 11.2	22 25.2	23 48.2
14 M	11 32 40.2	21 22.5	0 29.8	29 12.6	27 32.1	18 21.6	29 51.1	24 58.5	25 34.2	22 13.4	22 27.2	23 49.9
15 T	11 36 36.7	22 21.0	0 26.6	11♐39.4	29 18.1	19 33.6	0♍29.0	25 4.1	25 40.6	22 15.7	22 29.2	23 51.6
16 W	11 40 33.3	23 19.5	0 23.5	24 23.8	1♎ 3.0	20 45.8	1 6.9	25 9.5	25 47.1	22 17.8	22 31.2	23 53.3
17 T	11 44 29.8	24 18.0	0 20.3	7♑29.9	2 46.8	21 57.9	1 44.8	25 14.8	25 53.6	22 20.0	22 33.2	23 55.0
18 F	11 48 26.4	25 16.6	0 17.1	21 1.2	4 29.6	23 10.2	2 22.7	25 19.9	26 0.2	22 22.1	22 35.2	23 56.7
19 S	11 52 23.0	26 15.2	0 13.9	5♒ 0.1	6 11.3	24 22.6	3 0.6	25 24.8	26 6.8	22 24.1	22 37.2	23 58.4
20 S	11 56 19.5	27 13.8	0 10.7	19 26.6	7 52.1	25 35.0	3 38.5	25 29.6	26 13.5	22 26.1	22 39.3	24 0.0
21 M	12 0 16.1	28 12.4	0 7.6	4♓17.9	9 31.8	26 47.5	4 16.3	25 34.2	26 20.1	22 28.1	22 41.4	24 1.6
22 T	12 4 12.6	29 11.1	0 4.4	19 27.8	11 10.5	28 0.0	4 54.2	25 38.6	26 26.8	22 30.0	22 43.4	24 3.3
23 W	12 8 9.2	0♎ 9.8	0 1.2	4♈47.0	12 48.3	29 12.7	5 32.0	25 42.8	26 33.6	22 31.9	22 45.5	24 4.9
24 T	12 12 5.7	1 8.6	29♑58.0	20 4.3	14 25.1	0♍25.4	6 9.8	25 46.9	26 40.4	22 33.7	22 47.6	24 6.4
25 F	12 16 2.3	2 7.3	29 54.9	5♉ 8.6	16 1.0	1 38.2	6 47.6	25 50.8	26 47.2	22 35.5	22 49.7	24 8.0
26 S	12 19 58.8	3 6.2	29 51.7	19 50.9	17 35.9	2 51.0	7 25.4	25 54.5	26 54.0	22 37.3	22 51.9	24 9.6
27 S	12 23 55.4	4 5.1	29 48.5	4♊ 5.6	19 10.0	4 4.0	8 3.2	25 58.0	27 0.9	22 39.0	22 54.1	24 11.2
28 M	12 27 51.9	5 4.0	29 45.3	17 50.7	20 43.2	5 17.0	8 40.9	26 1.4	27 7.8	22 40.7	22 56.2	24 12.7
29 T	12 31 48.5	6 2.9	29 42.1	1♋ 7.1	22 15.4	6 30.1	9 18.7	26 4.5	27 14.8	22 42.3	22 58.3	24 14.2
30 W	12 35 45.0	7 1.8	29 39.0	13 58.0	23 46.8	7 43.2	9 56.4	26 7.5	27 21.7	22 43.8	23 0.5	24 15.7
DECLINATION at NOON												
1 T	10 41 25.0	8N17.6	19S54.1	26N36.3	12N 2.5	19N14.2	15N24.8	22N42.1	7S14.8	22N 7.7	7S 3.6	22N31.4
4 F	10 53 14.7	7 11.7	19 56.2	20 34.5	9 52.2	18 33.1	14 47.8	22 43.2	7 21.7	22 6.5	7 5.7	22 29.9
7 M	11 5 4.3	6 4.7	19 58.2	6 52.2	7 34.7	17 47.2	14 10.1	22 44.1	7 28.7	22 5.3	7 7.8	22 28.5
10 T	11 16 54.0	4 56.9	20 0.3	8S47.7	5 13.4	16 56.8	13 31.5	22 44.9	7 35.9	22 4.2	7 10.0	22 27.2
13 S	11 28 43.6	3 48.3	20 2.4	21 39.3	2 50.9	16 2.0	12 52.3	22 45.7	7 43.1	22 3.2	7 12.2	22 25.9
16 W	11 40 33.3	2 39.1	20 4.4	26 26.9	0 29.2	15 3.1	12 12.5	22 46.3	7 50.5	22 2.2	7 14.5	22 24.7
19 S	11 52 23.0	1 29.4	20 6.4	18 45.1	1S50.4	14 0.4	11 32.0	22 46.8	7 57.9	22 1.2	7 16.8	22 23.5
22 T	12 4 12.6	0 19.5	20 8.5	0 42.4	4 6.8	12 53.9	10 50.9	22 47.3	8 5.4	22 0.4	7 19.1	22 22.5
25 F	12 16 2.3	0S50.7	20 10.5	18N 0.0	6 19.0	11 44.1	10 9.4	22 47.7	8 13.0	21 59.5	7 21.5	22 21.5
28 M	12 27 51.9	2 0.8	20 12.5	26 21.3	8 26.5	10 31.2	9 27.3	22 48.0	8 20.6	21 58.8	7 23.9	22 20.6

OCTOBER 1953

DAY	EPHEMERIS SIDEREAL TIME	☉	☊	☽	☿	♀	♂	♃	♄	♅	♆	♇
LONGITUDE at NOON												
1 T	12 39 41.6	8♎ 0.8	29♑35.8	26♋27.8	25♎17.3	8♍56.4	10♍34.1	26♊10.3	27♎28.7	22♋45.3	23♎ 2.7	24♌17.1
2 F	12 43 38.1	8 59.9	29 32.6	8♌41.4	26 47.0	10 9.7	11 11.9	26 12.9	27 35.7	22 46.8	23 4.9	24 18.6
3 S	12 47 34.7	9 59.0	29 29.4	20 43.3	28 15.7	11 23.1	11 49.6	26 15.2	27 42.7	22 48.2	23 7.0	24 20.0
4 S	12 51 31.3	10 58.1	29 26.3	2♍38.0	29 43.6	12 36.5	12 27.2	26 17.4	27 49.8	22 49.5	23 9.2	24 21.4
5 M	12 55 27.8	11 57.2	29 23.1	14 28.8	1♏10.6	13 49.9	13 4.9	26 19.4	27 56.9	22 50.8	23 11.4	24 22.8
6 T	12 59 24.4	12 56.4	29 19.9	26 18.7	2 36.7	15 3.5	13 42.6	26 21.3	28 4.0	22 52.1	23 13.6	24 24.2
7 W	13 3 20.9	13 55.7	29 16.7	8♎ 9.8	4 1.8	16 17.0	14 20.2	26 22.9	28 11.1	22 53.3	23 15.9	24 25.5
8 T	13 7 17.5	14 54.9	29 13.5	20 3.7	5 26.1	17 30.7	14 57.9	26 24.3	28 18.2	22 54.4	23 18.1	24 26.9
9 F	13 11 14.0	15 54.2	29 10.4	2♏ 1.7	6 49.3	18 44.4	15 35.5	26 25.5	28 25.4	22 55.5	23 20.3	24 28.2
10 S	13 15 10.6	16 53.5	29 7.2	14 5.1	8 11.6	19 58.1	16 13.1	26 26.5	28 32.5	22 56.5	23 22.5	24 29.5
11 S	13 19 7.1	17 52.9	29 4.0	26 15.4	9 32.8	21 11.9	16 50.7	26 27.3	28 39.7	22 57.5	23 24.7	24 30.7
12 M	13 23 3.7	18 52.3	29 0.8	8♐34.3	10 52.9	22 25.8	17 28.3	26 28.0	28 46.9	22 58.5	23 27.0	24 32.0
13 T	13 27 0.2	19 51.7	28 57.7	21 4.5	12 11.8	23 39.7	18 5.8	26 28.4	28 54.1	22 59.4	23 29.2	24 33.2
14 W	13 30 56.8	20 51.2	28 54.5	3♑48.9	13 29.5	24 53.6	18 43.4	26 28.6	29 1.3	23 0.2	23 31.4	24 34.4
15 T	13 34 53.3	21 50.7	28 51.3	16 51.0	14 46.0	26 7.6	19 20.9	26 28.6	29 8.5	23 1.0	23 33.7	24 35.6
16 F	13 38 49.9	22 50.2	28 48.1	0♒14.2	16 1.0	27 21.7	19 58.4	26R28.4	29 15.8	23 1.7	23 35.9	24 36.7
17 S	13 42 46.4	23 49.7	28 44.9	14 1.5	17 14.5	28 35.8	20 35.9	26 28.0	29 23.0	23 2.4	23 38.2	24 37.9
18 S	13 46 43.0	24 49.3	28 41.8	28 14.3	18 26.5	29 49.9	21 13.4	26 27.5	29 30.3	23 3.0	23 40.4	24 39.0
19 M	13 50 39.6	25 48.9	28 38.6	12♓51.6	19 36.6	1♎ 4.1	21 50.9	26 26.7	29 37.6	23 3.6	23 42.7	24 40.1
20 T	13 54 36.1	26 48.5	28 35.4	27 49.4	20 44.8	2 18.4	22 28.4	26 25.7	29 44.8	23 4.1	23 44.9	24 41.1
21 W	13 58 32.7	27 48.2	28 32.2	13♈ 0.3	21 51.0	3 32.6	23 5.8	26 24.5	29 52.1	23 4.6	23 47.1	24 42.2
22 T	14 2 29.2	28 47.9	28 29.1	28 14.3	22 54.8	4 46.9	23 43.2	26 23.1	29 59.4	23 5.0	23 49.4	24 43.2
23 F	14 6 25.8	29 47.6	28 25.9	13♉20.2	23 56.1	6 1.3	24 20.7	26 21.5	0♏ 6.6	23 5.3	23 51.6	24 44.2
24 S	14 10 22.3	0♏47.4	28 22.7	28 8.0	24 54.6	7 15.7	24 58.1	26 19.8	0 13.9	23 5.6	23 53.8	24 45.1
25 S	14 14 18.9	1 47.2	28 19.5	12♊30.2	25 50.1	8 30.1	25 35.5	26 17.8	0 21.2	23 5.9	23 56.1	24 46.1
26 M	14 18 15.4	2 47.0	28 16.4	26 22.9	26 42.1	9 44.6	26 12.8	26 15.6	0 28.4	23 6.1	23 58.3	24 47.0
27 T	14 22 12.0	3 46.8	28 13.2	9♋45.8	27 30.3	10 59.1	26 50.2	26 13.2	0 35.7	23 6.2	24 0.5	24 47.8
28 W	14 26 8.6	4 46.7	28 10.0	22 41.2	28 14.3	12 13.7	27 27.6	26 10.6	0 42.9	23 6.3	24 2.7	24 48.7
29 T	14 30 5.1	5 46.7	28 6.8	5♌13.3	28 53.6	13 28.3	28 4.9	26 7.8	0 50.2	23 6.3	24 4.9	24 49.5
30 F	14 34 1.7	6 46.7	28 3.6	17 27.0	29 27.7	14 43.0	28 42.2	26 4.9	0 57.4	23 6.3	24 7.1	24 50.3
31 S	14 37 58.2	7 46.7	28 0.5	29 27.7	29 56.1	15 57.6	29 19.6	26 1.7	1 4.7	23R 6.2	24 9.3	24 51.1
DECLINATION at NOON												
1 T	12 39 41.6	3S10.8	20S14.5	21N15.6	10S28.6	9N15.4	8N44.8	22N48.3	8S28.3	21N58.1	7S26.3	22N19.7
4 S	12 51 31.3	4 20.5	20 16.5	8 3.3	12 24.7	7 57.1	8 1.9	22 48.5	8 36.0	21 57.5	7 28.8	22 19.0
7 W	13 3 20.9	5 29.8	20 18.5	7S30.0	14 14.2	6 36.6	7 18.7	22 48.7	8 43.7	21 57.0	7 31.2	22 18.3
10 S	13 15 10.6	6 38.4	20 20.4	20 41.7	15 56.3	5 14.2	6 35.1	22 48.8	8 51.5	21 56.5	7 33.7	22 17.8
13 T	13 27 0.2	7 46.2	20 22.4	26 15.2	17 30.5	3 50.3	5 51.3	22 48.9	8 59.2	21 56.1	7 36.2	22 17.3
16 F	13 38 49.9	8 53.0	20 24.4	20 1.1	18 55.7	2 25.0	5 7.3	22 48.9	9 6.9	21 55.8	7 38.6	22 16.9
19 M	13 50 39.6	9 58.7	20 26.3	3 31.4	20 10.9	0 58.8	4 23.1	22 48.9	9 14.6	21 55.6	7 41.1	22 16.6
22 T	14 2 29.2	11 3.0	20 28.2	15N30.9	21 14.7	0S28.0	3 38.8	22 48.9	9 22.3	21 55.5	7 43.5	22 16.4
25 S	14 14 18.9	12 5.9	20 30.2	25 51.7	22 5.5	1 55.1	2 54.4	22 48.8	9 29.9	21 55.4	7 46.0	22 16.3
28 W	14 26 8.6	13 7.1	20 32.1	21 59.8	22 41.0	3 22.3	2 9.9	22 48.7	9 37.4	21 55.5	7 48.4	22 16.4
31 S	14 37 58.2	14 6.5	20 34.0	9 11.5	22 58.0	4 49.0	1 25.4	22 48.5	9 44.9	21 55.6	7 50.7	22 16.5

NOVEMBER 1953

DAY	EPHEMERIS SIDEREAL TIME	☉	☊	☽	☿	♀	♂	♃	♄	♅	♆	♇
	h m s	° ′	° ′	° ′	° ′	° ′	° ′	° ′	° ′	° ′	° ′	° ′
						LONGITUDE at NOON						
1 S	14 41 54.8	8♏46.7	27♑57.3	11♍20.6	0♐18.2	17♎12.4	29♍56.9	25♊58.3	1♏11.9	23♋ 6.0	24♎11.5	24♌51.8
2 M	14 45 51.3	9 46.8	27 54.1	23 10.2	0 33.2	18 27.1	0♎34.1	25R54.8	1 19.1	23R 5.8	24 13.7	24 52.5
3 T	14 49 47.9	10 46.9	27 50.9	5♎ 0.4	0 40.7	19 41.9	1 11.4	25 51.1	1 26.4	23 5.6	24 15.8	24 53.2
4 W	14 53 44.4	11 47.1	27 47.8	16 54.1	0R39.8	20 56.7	1 48.7	25 47.1	1 33.6	23 5.3	24 18.0	24 53.9
5 T	14 57 41.0	12 47.2	27 44.6	28 53.5	0 30.1	22 11.6	2 25.9	25 43.0	1 40.7	23 4.9	24 20.1	24 54.5
6 F	15 1 37.5	13 47.4	27 41.4	11♏ 0.1	0 11.0	23 26.4	3 3.2	25 38.7	1 47.9	23 4.5	24 22.3	24 55.1
7 S	15 5 34.1	14 47.7	27 38.2	23 14.8	29♏42.2	24 41.3	3 40.4	25 34.2	1 55.1	23 4.1	24 24.4	24 55.7
8 S	15 9 30.7	15 48.0	27 35.0	5♐38.2	29 3.5	25 56.3	4 17.6	25 29.6	2 2.3	23 3.6	24 26.6	24 56.3
9 M	15 13 27.2	16 48.3	27 31.9	18 11.0	28 15.0	27 11.3	4 54.8	25 24.8	2 9.4	23 3.0	24 28.7	24 56.8
10 T	15 17 23.8	17 48.6	27 28.7	0♑53.9	27 17.3	28 26.3	5 31.9	25 19.8	2 16.5	23 2.4	24 30.8	24 57.3
11 W	15 21 20.3	18 49.0	27 25.5	13 48.5	26 11.3	29 41.3	6 9.1	25 14.6	2 23.6	23 1.7	24 32.9	24 57.8
12 T	15 25 16.9	19 49.3	27 22.3	26 56.6	24 58.5	0♏56.3	6 46.2	25 9.3	2 30.6	23 1.0	24 34.9	24 58.2
13 F	15 29 13.4	20 49.7	27 19.2	10♒20.4	23 40.8	2 11.3	7 23.3	25 3.8	2 37.7	23 0.2	24 37.0	24 58.6
14 S	15 33 10.0	21 50.2	27 16.0	24 1.9	22 20.4	3 26.4	8 0.4	24 58.1	2 44.7	22 59.4	24 39.0	24 59.0
15 S	15 37 6.6	22 50.6	27 12.8	8♓ 2.4	21 0.1	4 41.5	8 37.4	24 52.3	2 51.7	22 58.5	24 41.1	24 59.3
16 M	15 41 3.1	23 51.1	27 9.6	22 22.0	19 42.3	5 56.6	9 14.5	24 46.3	2 58.7	22 57.5	24 43.1	24 59.6
17 T	15 44 59.7	24 51.5	27 6.5	6♈58.3	18 29.7	7 11.7	9 51.5	24 40.2	3 5.6	22 56.6	24 45.1	24 59.9
18 W	15 48 56.2	25 52.1	27 3.3	21 46.7	17 24.5	8 26.8	10 28.5	24 34.0	3 12.5	22 55.5	24 47.1	25 0.2
19 T	15 52 52.8	26 52.6	27 0.1	6♉39.9	16 28.6	9 42.0	11 5.5	24 27.6	3 19.4	22 54.4	24 49.0	25 0.4
20 F	15 56 49.3	27 53.1	26 56.9	21 29.4	15 43.3	10 57.2	11 42.4	24 21.0	3 26.2	22 53.3	24 51.0	25 0.6
21 S	16 0 45.9	28 53.7	26 53.7	6♊ 6.4	15 9.4	12 12.4	12 19.4	24 14.4	3 33.1	22 52.1	24 52.9	25 0.8
22 S	16 4 42.5	29 54.3	26 50.6	20 23.6	14 47.1	13 27.6	12 56.3	24 7.6	3 39.8	22 50.9	24 54.8	25 0.9
23 M	16 8 39.0	0♐54.9	26 47.4	4♋16.2	14 36.4	14 42.8	13 33.2	24 0.7	3 46.6	22 49.6	24 56.7	25 1.0
24 T	16 12 35.6	1 55.6	26 44.2	17 42.2	14D36.9	15 58.1	14 10.1	23 53.7	3 53.3	22 48.3	24 58.6	25 1.1
25 W	16 16 32.1	2 56.3	26 41.0	0♌42.2	14 48.0	17 13.3	14 47.0	23 46.6	3 60.0	22 46.9	25 0.5	25 1.1
26 T	16 20 28.7	3 57.0	26 37.9	13 18.9	15 8.7	18 28.6	15 23.9	23 39.3	4 6.6	22 45.5	25 2.3	25 1.1
27 F	16 24 25.2	4 57.7	26 34.7	25 36.7	15 38.3	19 43.9	16 0.7	23 32.0	4 13.2	22 44.0	25 4.1	25 1.1
28 S	16 28 21.8	5 58.5	26 31.5	7♍40.2	16 15.9	20 59.2	16 37.5	23 24.5	4 19.8	22 42.5	25 6.0	25 1.1
29 S	16 32 18.4	6 59.3	26 28.3	19 34.9	17 0.7	22 14.6	17 14.4	23 17.1	4 26.4	22 41.0	25 7.8	25 1.1
30 M	16 36 14.9	8 0.1	26 25.2	1♎25.7	17 51.6	23 29.9	17 51.2	23 9.4	4 32.9	22 39.4	25 9.5	25R 1.0
						DECLINATION at NOON						
1 S	14 41 54.8	14S 25.8	20S 34.6	4N 6.4	22S 58.9	5S 17.8	1N 10.5	22N 48.4	9S 47.4	21N 55.6	7S 51.5	22N 16.5
4 W	14 53 44.4	15 22.5	20 36.5	11S 11.2	22 44.4	6 43.6	0 26.1	22 48.2	9 54.8	21 55.9	7 53.8	22 16.8
7 S	15 5 34.1	16 16.8	20 38.4	22 55.9	21 59.9	8 8.2	0S 18.3	22 47.9	10 2.1	21 56.2	7 56.1	22 17.1
10 T	15 17 23.8	17 8.8	20 40.3	25 36.8	20 41.2	9 31.2	1 2.6	22 47.6	10 9.3	21 56.5	7 58.4	22 17.5
13 F	15 29 13.4	17 58.0	20 42.1	16 27.6	18 52.1	10 52.4	1 46.7	22 47.2	10 16.3	21 57.0	8 0.6	22 18.1
16 M	15 41 3.1	18 44.4	20 44.0	0N 50.8	16 51.6	12 11.4	2 30.6	22 46.7	10 23.3	21 57.5	8 2.7	22 18.7
19 T	15 52 52.8	19 27.9	20 45.8	18 26.3	15 9.3	13 27.8	3 14.2	22 46.2	10 30.1	21 58.1	8 4.8	22 19.4
22 S	16 4 42.5	20 8.2	20 47.7	26 0.9	14 8.2	14 41.2	3 57.5	22 45.6	10 36.7	21 58.8	8 6.8	22 20.2
25 W	16 16 32.1	20 45.1	20 49.5	19 31.8	13 53.4	15 51.3	4 40.6	22 44.9	10 43.3	21 59.6	8 8.8	22 21.2
28 S	16 28 21.8	21 18.6	20 51.3	5 28.5	14 17.1	16 57.8	5 23.3	22 44.1	10 49.6	22 0.4	8 10.7	22 22.2

DECEMBER 1953

DAY	EPHEMERIS SIDEREAL TIME	☉	☊	☽	☿	♀	♂	♃	♄	♅	♆	♇
						LONGITUDE at NOON						
1 T	16 40 11.5	9♐ 0.9	26♑22.0	13♎17.4	18♏48.1	24♏45.3	18♎27.9	23♊ 1.7	4♏39.3	22♋37.8	25♎11.3	25♌ 0.8
2 W	16 44 8.0	10 1.8	26 18.8	25 13.9	19 49.4	26 0.7	19 4.7	22R54.0	4 45.7	22R36.1	25 13.0	25R 0.7
3 T	16 48 4.6	11 2.7	26 15.6	7♏18.5	20 54.8	27 16.1	19 41.4	22 46.1	4 52.1	22 34.4	25 14.7	25 0.5
4 F	16 52 1.1	12 3.6	26 12.5	19 33.6	22 3.9	28 31.5	20 18.1	22 38.2	4 58.4	22 32.6	25 16.4	25 0.3
5 S	16 55 57.7	13 4.5	26 9.3	2♐ 0.6	23 16.1	29 46.9	20 54.7	22 30.3	5 4.6	22 30.8	25 18.0	25 0.0
6 S	16 59 54.3	14 5.4	26 6.1	14 40.1	24 31.0	1♐ 2.3	21 31.4	22 22.3	5 10.8	22 28.9	25 19.7	24 59.7
7 M	17 3 50.8	15 6.4	26 2.9	27 32.1	25 48.2	2 17.7	22 8.0	22 14.2	5 17.0	22 27.1	25 21.3	24 59.4
8 T	17 7 47.4	16 7.3	25 59.7	10♑36.1	27 7.4	3 33.1	22 44.6	22 6.1	5 23.1	22 25.1	25 22.8	24 59.1
9 W	17 11 43.9	17 8.3	25 56.6	23 51.8	28 28.4	4 48.5	23 21.1	21 58.0	5 29.1	22 23.2	25 24.4	24 58.7
10 T	17 15 40.5	18 9.3	25 53.4	7♒18.6	29 50.8	6 4.0	23 57.6	21 49.9	5 35.1	22 21.2	25 25.9	24 58.3
11 F	17 19 37.1	19 10.3	25 50.2	20 56.5	1♐14.5	7 19.4	24 34.1	21 41.7	5 41.1	22 19.1	25 27.4	24 57.9
12 S	17 23 33.6	20 11.3	25 47.0	4♓45.2	2 39.3	8 34.9	25 10.6	21 33.5	5 47.0	22 17.1	25 28.9	24 57.5
13 S	17 27 30.2	21 12.3	25 43.9	18 44.5	4 5.1	9 50.3	25 47.0	21 25.3	5 52.8	22 15.0	25 30.3	24 57.0
14 M	17 31 26.7	22 13.4	25 40.7	2♈53.8	5 31.7	11 5.8	26 23.5	21 17.2	5 58.6	22 12.8	25 31.8	24 56.5
15 T	17 35 23.3	23 14.4	25 37.5	17 11.3	6 59.1	12 21.2	26 59.8	21 9.0	6 4.3	22 10.7	25 33.2	24 55.9
16 W	17 39 19.8	24 15.4	25 34.3	1♉34.3	8 27.0	13 36.7	27 36.2	21 0.8	6 9.9	22 8.5	25 34.5	24 55.4
17 T	17 43 16.4	25 16.5	25 31.2	15 58.6	9 55.6	14 52.1	28 12.5	20 52.7	6 15.5	22 6.3	25 35.9	24 54.8
18 F	17 47 13.0	26 17.5	25 28.0	0♊19.2	11 24.6	16 7.6	28 48.8	20 44.6	6 21.0	22 4.0	25 37.2	24 54.2
19 S	17 51 9.5	27 18.6	25 24.8	14 30.6	12 54.0	17 23.0	29 25.1	20 36.5	6 26.5	22 1.7	25 38.5	24 53.5
20 S	17 55 6.1	28 19.7	25 21.6	28 27.9	14 24.0	18 38.6	0♏ 1.3	20 28.5	6 32.0	21 59.5	25 39.8	24 52.9
21 M	17 59 2.6	29 20.8	25 18.5	12♋ 7.1	15 54.2	19 54.0	0 37.5	20 20.6	6 37.3	21 57.2	25 41.0	24 52.2
22 T	18 2 59.2	0♑21.9	25 15.3	25 25.9	17 24.8	21 9.5	1 13.7	20 12.6	6 42.5	21 54.8	25 42.2	24 51.5
23 W	18 6 55.8	1 23.0	25 12.1	8♌23.6	18 55.7	22 25.0	1 49.8	20 4.7	6 47.7	21 52.4	25 43.3	24 50.8
24 T	18 10 52.3	2 24.1	25 8.9	21 1.4	20 26.9	23 40.4	2 26.0	19 56.9	6 52.9	21 50.0	25 44.5	24 50.0
25 F	18 14 48.9	3 25.2	25 5.7	3♍21.9	21 58.4	24 55.9	3 2.0	19 49.2	6 57.9	21 47.6	25 45.6	24 49.2
26 S	18 18 45.4	4 26.3	25 2.6	15 28.5	23 30.2	26 11.4	3 38.1	19 41.5	7 2.9	21 45.2	25 46.7	24 48.4
27 S	18 22 42.0	5 27.5	24 59.4	27 25.7	25 2.3	27 26.9	4 14.1	19 33.9	7 7.8	21 42.7	25 47.7	24 47.5
28 M	18 26 38.5	6 28.6	24 56.2	9♎18.2	26 34.7	28 42.4	4 50.1	19 26.4	7 12.7	21 40.2	25 48.7	24 46.7
29 T	18 30 35.1	7 29.8	24 53.0	21 10.9	28 7.4	29 57.9	5 26.0	19 18.9	7 17.4	21 37.7	25 49.7	24 45.8
30 W	18 34 31.7	8 30.9	24 49.9	3♏ 8.4	29 40.4	1♑13.4	6 1.9	19 11.6	7 22.1	21 35.2	25 50.6	24 44.9
31 T	18 38 28.2	9 32.1	24 46.7	15 15.0	1♑13.7	2 28.9	6 37.8	19 4.4	7 26.7	21 32.7	25 51.6	24 43.9
						DECLINATION at NOON						
1 T	16 40 11.5	21S 48.5	20S 53.1	9S 52.3	15S 7.4	18S 0.3	6S 5.6	22N 43.3	10S 55.8	22N 1.2	8S 12.5	22N 23.2
4 F	16 52 1.1	22 14.6	20 54.9	22 6.8	16 13.2	18 58.4	6 47.4	22 42.3	11 1.8	22 2.2	8 14.2	22 24.4
7 M	17 3 50.8	22 36.8	20 56.7	25 45.9	17 26.3	19 51.7	7 28.8	22 41.3	11 7.6	22 3.2	8 15.9	22 25.7
10 T	17 15 40.5	22 55.1	20 58.5	17 19.3	18 41.0	20 40.1	8 9.6	22 40.3	11 13.2	22 4.2	8 17.4	22 27.0
13 S	17 27 30.2	23 9.2	21 0.2	0 33.5	19 53.3	21 23.1	8 49.9	22 39.1	11 18.6	22 5.3	8 18.9	22 28.4
16 W	17 39 19.8	23 19.3	21 2.0	16N 51.7	21 0.4	22 0.4	9 29.6	22 37.9	11 23.8	22 6.4	8 20.3	22 29.9
19 S	17 51 9.5	23 25.1	21 3.8	25 51.4	22 0.5	22 31.9	10 8.6	22 36.7	11 28.8	22 7.5	8 21.5	22 31.5
22 T	18 2 59.2	23 26.7	21 5.5	20 56.1	22 52.1	22 57.4	10 47.1	22 35.5	11 33.5	22 8.7	8 22.7	22 33.1
25 F	18 14 48.9	23 24.1	21 7.2	7 10.0	23 34.3	23 16.5	11 24.8	22 34.2	11 38.0	22 9.9	8 23.8	22 34.7
28 M	18 26 38.5	23 17.2	21 8.9	8S 21.6	24 6.0	23 29.3	12 1.7	22 32.9	11 42.3	22 11.1	8 24.8	22 36.5
31 T	18 38 28.2	23 6.2	21 10.6	21 6.2	24 26.6	23 35.5	12 38.0	22 31.7	11 46.3	22 12.4	8 25.7	22 38.2

JANUARY 1954

LONGITUDE at NOON

DAY	EPHEMERIS SIDEREAL TIME h m s	☉ ° ′	☊ ° ′	☽ ° ′	☿ ° ′	♀ ° ′	♂ ° ′	♃ ° ′	♄ ° ′	♅ ° ′	♆ ° ′	♇ ° ′
1 F	18 42 24.8	10♑33.3	24♑43.5	27♏34.5	2♑47.3	3♑44.4	7♏13.6	18♊57.3	7♏31.3	21♋30.2	25♎52.5	24♌43.0
2 S	18 46 21.3	11 34.4	24 40.3	10♐ 9.6	4 21.2	4 59.9	7 49.4	18R50.3	7 35.7	21R27.6	25 53.3	24R42.0
3 S	18 50 17.9	12 35.6	24 37.2	23 1.9	5 55.5	6 15.4	8 25.1	18 43.4	7 40.1	21 25.0	25 54.1	24 41.0
4 M	18 54 14.5	13 36.8	24 34.0	6♑12.0	7 30.1	7 30.9	9 0.8	18 36.6	7 44.4	21 22.5	25 54.9	24 39.9
5 T	18 58 11.0	14 38.0	24 30.8	19 39.1	9 5.1	8 46.4	9 36.5	18 30.0	7 48.6	21 19.9	25 55.7	24 38.9
6 W	19 2 7.6	15 39.1	24 27.6	3♒21.4	10 40.4	10 1.9	10 12.1	18 23.5	7 52.7	21 17.3	25 56.4	24 37.8
7 T	19 6 4.1	16 40.3	24 24.5	17 16.2	12 16.1	11 17.4	10 47.7	18 17.1	7 56.8	21 14.7	25 57.1	24 36.7
8 F	19 10 0.7	17 41.5	24 21.3	1♓20.4	13 52.3	12 32.8	11 23.2	18 10.9	8 0.7	21 12.1	25 57.7	24 35.6
9 S	19 13 57.2	18 42.6	24 18.1	15 30.6	15 28.8	13 48.3	11 58.6	18 4.8	8 4.6	21 9.5	25 58.4	24 34.5
10 S	19 17 53.8	19 43.8	24 14.9	29 43.8	17 5.9	15 3.8	12 34.1	17 58.9	8 8.5	21 6.9	25 59.0	24 33.4
11 M	19 21 50.4	20 45.0	24 11.7	13♈57.1	18 43.3	16 19.3	13 9.5	17 53.2	8 12.1	21 4.3	25 59.6	24 32.2
12 T	19 25 46.9	21 46.1	24 8.6	28 7.9	20 21.2	17 34.8	13 44.8	17 47.6	8 15.8	21 1.7	26 0.1	24 31.0
13 W	19 29 43.5	22 47.2	24 5.4	12♉14.3	21 59.6	18 50.2	14 20.1	17 42.1	8 19.3	20 59.1	26 0.6	24 29.8
14 T	19 33 40.0	23 48.3	24 2.2	26 14.1	23 38.4	20 5.7	14 55.3	17 36.8	8 22.7	20 56.5	26 1.0	24 28.6
15 F	19 37 36.6	24 49.4	23 59.0	10♊ 5.6	25 17.7	21 21.1	15 30.4	17 31.7	8 26.0	20 53.9	26 1.4	24 27.4
16 S	19 41 33.1	25 50.5	23 55.9	23 46.8	26 57.6	22 36.6	16 5.6	17 26.8	8 29.3	20 51.3	26 1.8	24 26.1
17 S	19 45 29.7	26 51.6	23 52.7	7♋16.1	28 37.9	23 52.0	16 40.6	17 22.0	8 32.4	20 48.7	26 2.2	24 24.9
18 M	19 49 26.3	27 52.6	23 49.5	20 31.8	0♒18.8	25 7.4	17 15.6	17 17.4	8 35.5	20 46.1	26 2.5	24 23.6
19 T	19 53 22.8	28 53.7	23 46.3	3♌33.0	2 0.2	26 22.8	17 50.6	17 13.0	8 38.5	20 43.5	26 2.8	24 22.3
20 W	19 57 19.4	29 54.7	23 43.2	16 19.2	3 42.0	27 38.2	18 25.5	17 8.7	8 41.4	20 41.0	26 3.0	24 21.0
21 T	20 1 15.9	0♒55.8	23 40.0	28 50.6	5 24.4	28 53.6	19 0.3	17 4.7	8 44.1	20 38.4	26 3.2	24 19.7
22 F	20 5 12.5	1 56.8	23 36.8	11♍ 8.5	7 7.2	0♒ 9.0	19 35.1	17 0.8	8 46.8	20 35.8	26 3.4	24 18.3
23 S	20 9 9.0	2 57.8	23 33.6	23 15.1	8 50.5	1 24.4	20 9.9	16 57.1	8 49.4	20 33.3	26 3.6	24 17.0
24 S	20 13 5.6	3 58.8	23 30.4	5♎13.0	10 34.2	2 39.8	20 44.6	16 53.7	8 51.9	20 30.8	26 3.7	24 15.6
25 M	20 17 2.2	4 59.8	23 27.3	17 6.2	12 18.3	3 55.2	21 19.2	16 50.4	8 54.3	20 28.3	26 3.7	24 14.2
26 T	20 20 58.7	6 0.8	23 24.1	28 58.6	14 2.7	5 10.6	21 53.7	16 47.3	8 56.6	20 25.8	26 3.8	24 12.9
27 W	20 24 55.3	7 1.8	23 20.9	10♏54.9	15 47.2	6 26.0	22 28.2	16 44.3	8 58.8	20 23.3	26 3.8	24 11.5
28 T	20 28 51.8	8 2.7	23 17.7	22 60.0	17 32.0	7 41.3	23 2.7	16 41.6	9 0.9	20 20.9	26 3.8	24 10.1
29 F	20 32 48.4	9 3.7	23 14.6	5♐18.3	19 16.7	8 56.7	23 37.0	16 39.1	9 2.9	20 18.4	26R 3.7	24 8.7
30 S	20 36 44.9	10 4.6	23 11.4	17 54.1	21 1.3	10 12.0	24 11.3	16 36.8	9 4.7	20 16.0	26 3.6	24 7.2
31 S	20 40 41.5	11 5.6	23 8.2	0♑50.8	22 45.7	11 27.4	24 45.6	16 34.7	9 6.6	20 13.7	26 3.5	24 5.9

DECLINATION at NOON

DAY	EPHEMERIS SIDEREAL TIME h m s	☉	☊	☽	☿	♀	♂	♃	♄	♅	♆	♇
1 F	18 42 24.8	23S 1.6	21S11.2	23S53.9	24S30.9	23S36.1	12S49.9	22N31.3	11S47.5	22N12.8	8S25.9	22N38.8
4 M	18 54 14.5	22 45.0	21 12.9	24 54.8	24 35.8	23 33.5	13 25.0	22 30.1	11 51.2	22 14.0	8 26.7	22 40.6
7 T	19 6 4.1	22 24.3	21 14.6	13 40.1	24 28.2	23 24.4	13 59.3	22 29.0	11 54.6	22 15.3	8 27.3	22 42.5
10 S	19 17 53.8	21 59.7	21 16.3	4N18.8	24 7.7	23 8.8	14 32.7	22 27.9	11 57.7	22 16.5	8 27.8	22 44.4
13 W	19 29 43.5	21 31.2	21 17.9	20 17.3	23 34.0	22 46.7	15 5.2	22 27.0	12 0.5	22 17.8	8 28.2	22 46.3
16 S	19 41 33.1	20 59.0	21 19.6	25 57.8	22 46.6	22 18.3	15 36.8	22 26.1	12 3.1	22 19.0	8 28.5	22 48.2
19 T	19 53 22.8	20 23.2	21 21.2	18 30.8	21 45.4	21 43.9	16 7.4	22 25.4	12 5.3	22 20.2	8 28.7	22 50.1
22 F	20 5 12.5	19 43.9	21 22.9	3 48.2	20 30.2	21 3.5	16 37.1	22 24.8	12 7.3	22 21.4	8 28.7	22 52.0
25 M	20 17 2.2	19 1.4	21 24.5	11S33.1	19 1.1	20 17.5	17 5.7	22 24.4	12 9.0	22 22.5	8 28.7	22 53.9
28 T	20 28 51.8	18 15.6	21 26.1	22 59.1	17 18.5	19 26.1	17 33.4	22 24.1	12 10.4	22 23.6	8 28.5	22 55.8
31 S	20 40 41.5	17 27.0	21 27.7	25 31.0	15 23.7	18 29.7	17 60.0	22 24.0	12 11.5	22 24.7	8 28.2	22 57.7

FEBRUARY 1954

LONGITUDE at NOON

DAY	EPHEMERIS SIDEREAL TIME h m s	☉ ° ′	☊ ° ′	☽ ° ′	☿ ° ′	♀ ° ′	♂ ° ′	♃ ° ′	♄ ° ′	♅ ° ′	♆ ° ′	♇ ° ′
1 M	20 44 38.1	12♒ 6.5	23♑ 5.0	14♑10.4	24♒29.5	12♒42.8	25♏19.7	16♊32.8	9♏ 8.3	20♋11.3	26♎ 3.4	24♌ 4.4
2 T	20 48 34.6	13 7.4	23 1.9	27 53.3	26 12.6	13 58.1	25 53.8	16R31.1	9 9.9	20R 8.9	26R 3.2	24R 3.0
3 W	20 52 31.2	14 8.3	22 58.7	11♒57.8	27 54.7	15 13.4	26 27.8	16 29.6	9 11.3	20 6.6	26 2.9	24 1.5
4 T	20 56 27.7	15 9.1	22 55.5	26 20.0	29 35.5	16 28.7	27 1.7	16 28.3	9 12.7	20 4.3	26 2.7	24 0.1
5 F	21 0 24.3	16 10.0	22 52.3	10♓54.5	1♓14.5	17 44.0	27 35.6	16 27.2	9 14.0	20 2.0	26 2.4	23 58.6
6 S	21 4 20.8	17 10.8	22 49.1	25 34.4	2 51.4	18 59.3	28 9.3	16 26.3	9 15.2	19 59.8	26 2.0	23 57.1
7 S	21 8 17.4	18 11.6	22 46.0	10♈12.8	4 25.7	20 14.6	28 43.0	16 25.6	9 16.2	19 57.6	26 1.7	23 55.7
8 M	21 12 13.9	19 12.4	22 42.8	24 43.8	5 56.9	21 29.9	29 16.6	16 25.1	9 17.2	19 55.4	26 1.3	23 54.2
9 T	21 16 10.5	20 13.1	22 39.6	9♉ 2.8	7 24.3	22 45.1	29 50.1	16 24.8	9 18.0	19 53.2	26 0.8	23 52.7
10 W	21 20 7.1	21 13.8	22 36.4	23 6.9	8 47.4	24 0.4	0♐23.5	16 24.8	9 18.8	19 51.1	26 0.4	23 51.3
11 T	21 24 3.6	22 14.5	22 33.3	6♊55.2	10 5.4	25 15.6	0 56.8	16D24.9	9 19.4	19 49.0	25 59.9	23 49.8
12 F	21 28 0.2	23 15.2	22 30.1	20 27.7	11 17.6	26 30.8	1 30.1	16 25.2	9 20.0	19 46.9	25 59.4	23 48.3
13 S	21 31 56.7	24 15.8	22 26.9	3♋45.4	12 23.4	27 45.9	2 3.2	16 25.7	9 20.4	19 44.9	25 58.8	23 46.8
14 S	21 35 53.3	25 16.4	22 23.7	16 49.4	13 21.9	29 1.1	2 36.3	16 26.5	9 20.7	19 42.9	25 58.2	23 45.3
15 M	21 39 49.8	26 17.0	22 20.6	29 40.9	14 12.6	0♓16.3	3 9.2	16 27.4	9 21.0	19 41.0	25 57.6	23 43.9
16 T	21 43 46.4	27 17.6	22 17.4	12♌21.0	14 54.6	1 31.4	3 42.1	16 28.5	9 21.1	19 39.1	25 56.9	23 42.4
17 W	21 47 42.9	28 18.1	22 14.2	24 50.4	15 27.6	2 46.5	4 14.9	16 29.9	9 21.1	19 37.2	25 56.3	23 40.9
18 T	21 51 39.5	29 18.6	22 11.0	7♍ 9.8	15 50.9	4 1.6	4 47.5	16 31.4	9R21.0	19 35.4	25 55.5	23 39.4
19 F	21 55 36.1	0♓19.1	22 7.8	19 20.1	16 4.2	5 16.7	5 20.1	16 33.1	9 20.9	19 33.6	25 54.8	23 38.0
20 S	21 59 32.6	1 19.5	22 4.7	1♎22.6	16 7.4	6 31.8	5 52.6	16 35.0	9 20.6	19 31.8	25 54.0	23 36.5
21 S	22 3 29.2	2 20.0	22 1.5	13 19.0	16R 0.4	7 46.9	6 25.0	16 37.2	9 20.2	19 30.1	25 53.3	23 35.1
22 M	22 7 25.7	3 20.4	21 58.3	25 11.5	15 43.5	9 1.9	6 57.3	16 39.5	9 19.7	19 28.4	25 52.5	23 33.6
23 T	22 11 22.3	4 20.8	21 55.1	7♏ 3.3	15 17.0	10 17.0	7 29.4	16 42.0	9 19.1	19 26.8	25 51.6	23 32.2
24 W	22 15 18.8	5 21.1	21 52.0	18 58.1	14 41.7	11 32.0	8 1.5	16 44.7	9 18.4	19 25.2	25 50.7	23 30.7
25 T	22 19 15.4	6 21.5	21 48.8	1♐ 0.3	13 58.4	12 47.0	8 33.4	16 47.6	9 17.6	19 23.7	25 49.8	23 29.3
26 F	22 23 11.9	7 21.8	21 45.6	13 14.6	13 8.3	14 2.0	9 5.2	16 50.6	9 16.7	19 22.2	25 48.9	23 27.9
27 S	22 27 8.5	8 22.1	21 42.4	25 45.9	12 12.7	15 16.9	9 36.9	16 53.9	9 15.7	19 20.7	25 47.9	23 26.4
28 S	22 31 5.0	9 22.3	21 39.2	8♑38.9	11 13.1	16 31.9	10 8.5	16 57.4	9 14.6	19 19.3	25 46.9	23 25.0

DECLINATION at NOON

DAY	EPHEMERIS SIDEREAL TIME h m s	☉	☊	☽	☿	♀	♂	♃	♄	♅	♆	♇
1 M	20 44 38.1	17S10.1	21S28.3	23S35.2	14S43.0	18S 9.8	18S 8.6	22N24.0	12S11.8	22N25.0	8S28.1	22N58.4
4 T	20 56 27.7	16 17.7	21 29.9	10 5.7	12 35.1	17 7.0	18 33.8	22 24.1	12 12.5	22 26.1	8 27.7	23 0.2
7 S	21 8 17.4	15 22.8	21 31.4	8N43.2	10 22.0	15 59.9	18 57.9	22 24.4	12 12.9	22 27.0	8 27.2	23 2.0
10 W	21 20 7.1	14 25.6	21 33.0	22 58.0	8 10.1	14 48.8	19 21.0	22 24.9	12 13.1	22 28.0	8 26.5	23 3.8
13 S	21 31 56.7	13 26.2	21 34.6	25 11.1	6 8.1	13 34.1	19 43.0	22 25.6	12 12.9	22 28.9	8 25.8	23 5.6
16 T	21 43 46.4	12 24.9	21 36.1	15 30.5	4 26.8	12 16.1	20 3.8	22 26.4	12 12.4	22 29.7	8 25.0	23 7.3
19 F	21 55 36.1	11 21.8	21 37.7	0 17.2	3 17.1	10 55.2	20 23.7	22 27.4	12 11.6	22 30.5	8 24.1	23 9.0
22 M	22 7 25.7	10 17.0	21 39.2	14S32.5	2 47.9	9 31.6	20 42.4	22 28.6	12 10.6	22 31.2	8 23.1	23 10.5
25 T	22 19 15.4	9 10.9	21 40.7	24 20.8	3 2.3	8 5.8	21 0.1	22 29.9	12 9.2	22 31.8	8 22.0	23 12.1
28 S	22 31 5.0	8 3.5	21 42.2	24 26.7	3 55.3	6 38.0	21 16.7	22 31.4	12 7.6	22 32.4	8 20.8	23 13.5

MARCH 1954

DAY	EPHEMERIS SIDEREAL TIME	☉	☊	☽	☿	♀	♂	♃	♄	♅	♆	♇
	h m s	° '	° '	° '	° '	° '	° '	° '	° '	° '	° '	° '
						LONGITUDE at NOON						
1 M	22 35 1.6	10♓22.5	21♑36.1	21♑57.3	10♓10.9	17♓46.8	10♐39.9	17♊ 1.0	9♏13.3	19♋17.9	25♎45.9	23♌23.6
2 T	22 38 58.1	11 22.7	21 32.9	5♒43.4	9R 7.8	19 1.7	11 11.2	17 4.8	9R12.0	19R16.6	25R44.8	23R22.2
3 W	22 42 54.7	12 22.9	21 29.7	19 56.9	8 5.2	20 16.6	11 42.4	17 8.8	9 10.6	19 15.3	25 43.8	23 20.8
4 T	22 46 51.3	13 23.1	21 26.5	4♓35.0	7 4.5	21 31.5	12 13.4	17 13.0	9 9.1	19 14.1	25 42.7	23 19.5
5 F	22 50 47.8	14 23.2	21 23.4	19 31.2	6 7.0	22 46.4	12 44.3	17 17.3	9 7.5	19 12.9	25 41.5	23 18.1
6 S	22 54 44.4	15 23.3	21 20.2	4♈36.8	5 13.7	24 1.2	13 15.0	17 21.9	9 5.8	19 11.8	25 40.4	23 16.7
7 S	22 58 40.9	16 23.4	21 17.0	19 41.6	4 25.4	25 16.0	13 45.6	17 26.6	9 4.0	19 10.7	25 39.2	23 15.4
8 M	23 2 37.5	17 23.4	21 13.8	4♉36.2	3 42.8	26 30.8	14 16.0	17 31.5	9 2.1	19 9.7	25 38.0	23 14.1
9 T	23 6 34.0	18 23.4	21 10.6	19 13.0	3 6.4	27 45.6	14 46.3	17 36.5	9 0.1	19 8.7	25 36.8	23 12.7
10 W	23 10 30.6	19 23.3	21 7.5	3♊27.5	2 36.5	29 0.4	15 16.4	17 41.8	8 58.0	19 7.7	25 35.6	23 11.4
11 T	23 14 27.1	20 23.2	21 4.3	17 18.1	2 13.1	0♈15.1	15 46.4	17 47.2	8 55.8	19 6.9	25 34.3	23 10.1
12 F	23 18 23.7	21 23.1	21 1.1	0♋45.4	1 56.4	1 29.8	16 16.2	17 52.7	8 53.6	19 6.0	25 33.0	23 8.9
13 S	23 22 20.2	22 22.9	20 57.9	13 52.0	1 46.1	2 44.5	16 45.8	17 58.5	8 51.2	19 5.2	25 31.7	23 7.6
14 S	23 26 16.8	23 22.8	20 54.8	26 41.0	1 42.3	3 59.2	17 15.3	18 4.4	8 48.8	19 4.6	25 30.5	23 6.4
15 M	23 30 13.3	24 22.6	20 51.6	9♌15.6	1D44.6	5 13.8	17 44.6	18 10.5	8 46.3	19 3.9	25 29.1	23 5.2
16 T	23 34 9.9	25 22.3	20 48.4	21 38.7	1 52.7	6 28.4	18 13.8	18 16.7	8 43.6	19 3.3	25 27.8	23 4.0
17 W	23 38 6.4	26 22.0	20 45.2	3♍52.8	2 6.4	7 43.0	18 42.7	18 23.0	8 40.9	19 2.7	25 26.4	23 2.8
18 T	23 42 3.0	27 21.6	20 42.0	15 59.9	2 25.5	8 57.5	19 11.5	18 29.6	8 38.2	19 2.2	25 25.0	23 1.6
19 F	23 45 59.6	28 21.3	20 38.9	28 1.3	2 49.6	10 12.0	19 40.1	18 36.2	8 35.3	19 1.7	25 23.6	23 0.4
20 S	23 49 56.1	29 20.9	20 35.7	9♎58.3	3 18.4	11 26.5	20 8.5	18 43.1	8 32.3	19 1.3	25 22.1	22 59.3
21 S	23 53 52.7	0♈20.4	20 32.5	21 52.1	3 51.7	12 41.0	20 36.6	18 50.0	8 29.3	19 1.0	25 20.7	22 58.2
22 M	23 57 49.2	1 20.0	20 29.3	3♏44.2	4 29.2	13 55.4	21 4.6	18 57.2	8 26.2	19 0.6	25 19.2	22 57.0
23 T	0 1 45.8	2 19.4	20 26.2	15 36.6	5 10.6	15 9.8	21 32.4	19 4.4	8 23.0	19 0.4	25 17.8	22 56.0
24 W	0 5 42.3	3 18.9	20 23.0	27 32.0	5 55.7	16 24.2	22 0.0	19 11.8	8 19.8	19 0.2	25 16.3	22 54.9
25 T	0 9 38.9	4 18.3	20 19.8	9♐33.8	6 44.3	17 38.6	22 27.4	19 19.4	8 16.5	19 0.0	25 14.8	22 53.8
26 F	0 13 35.4	5 17.8	20 16.6	21 46.1	7 36.3	18 52.9	22 54.5	19 27.1	8 13.1	18 60.0	25 13.3	22 52.8
27 S	0 17 32.0	6 17.1	20 13.4	4♑13.4	8 31.3	20 7.2	23 21.5	19 34.9	8 9.6	18 59.9	25 11.7	22 51.8
28 S	0 21 28.5	7 16.5	20 10.3	17 0.6	9 29.2	21 21.5	23 48.1	19 42.9	8 6.1	18 59.9	25 10.2	22 50.8
29 M	0 25 25.1	8 15.8	20 7.1	0♒12.4	10 29.9	22 35.8	24 14.6	19 51.0	8 2.5	19D 0.0	25 8.6	22 49.9
30 T	0 29 21.6	9 15.1	20 3.9	13 52.1	11 33.2	23 50.1	24 40.8	19 59.2	7 58.8	19 0.1	25 7.1	22 48.9
31 W	0 33 18.2	10 14.3	20 0.7	28 1.5	12 39.1	25 4.3	25 6.7	20 7.6	7 55.1	19 0.3	25 5.5	22 48.0
						DECLINATION at NOON						
1 M	22 35 1.6	7S40.8	21S42.7	21S45.2	4S19.5	6S 8.4	21S22.0	22N31.9	12S 7.0	22N32.6	8S20.4	23N14.0
4 T	22 46 51.3	6 32.0	21 44.2	6 39.7	5 42.7	4 38.6	21 37.3	22 33.6	12 5.1	22 33.1	8 19.1	23 15.4
7 S	22 58 40.9	5 22.3	21 45.7	12N24.6	7 8.9	3 7.7	21 51.5	22 35.4	12 2.8	22 33.5	8 17.7	23 16.7
10 W	23 10 30.6	4 12.1	21 47.2	24 37.3	8 24.9	1 36.0	22 4.8	22 37.3	12 0.3	22 33.9	8 16.3	23 17.9
13 S	23 22 20.2	3 1.4	21 48.7	23 27.8	9 23.3	0 3.9	22 17.1	22 39.3	11 57.6	22 34.2	8 14.8	23 19.0
16 T	23 34 9.9	1 50.4	21 50.1	11 55.6	10 1.2	1N28.4	22 28.5	22 41.4	11 54.7	22 34.4	8 13.2	23 20.0
19 F	23 45 59.6	0 39.3	21 51.6	3S26.4	10 18.6	3 0.4	22 39.1	22 43.6	11 51.5	22 34.6	8 11.6	23 21.0
22 M	23 57 49.2	0N31.8	21 53.0	17 22.3	10 16.6	4 31.9	22 48.9	22 45.8	11 48.1	22 34.7	8 10.0	23 21.9
25 T	0 9 38.9	1 42.7	21 54.4	25 10.3	9 56.8	6 2.6	22 57.8	22 48.0	11 44.6	22 34.7	8 8.3	23 22.6
28 S	0 21 28.5	2 53.3	21 55.8	22 40.7	9 20.5	7 32.1	23 6.1	22 50.3	11 40.9	22 34.7	8 6.5	23 23.3
31 W	0 33 18.2	4 3.3	21 57.2	9 17.0	8 29.3	9 0.0	23 13.8	22 52.6	11 37.0	22 34.6	8 4.8	23 23.9

APRIL 1954

DAY	EPHEMERIS SIDEREAL TIME	☉	☊	☽	☿	♀	♂	♃	♄	♅	♆	♇
						LONGITUDE at NOON						
1 T	0 37 14.7	11♈13.6	19♑57.6	12♓39.3	13♓47.3	26♈18.5	25♐32.4	20♊16.1	7♏51.3	19♋ 0.5	25♎ 3.9	22♌47.1
2 F	0 41 11.3	12 12.8	19 54.4	27 40.4	14 57.8	27 32.6	25 57.8	20 24.7	7R47.4	19 0.8	25R 2.3	22R46.2
3 S	0 45 7.8	13 11.9	19 51.2	12♈56.4	16 10.4	28 46.8	26 23.0	20 33.4	7 43.5	19 1.2	25 0.7	22 45.4
4 S	0 49 4.4	14 11.1	19 48.0	28 16.2	17 25.2	0♉ 0.9	26 47.9	20 42.3	7 39.6	19 1.6	24 59.2	22 44.6
5 M	0 53 1.0	15 10.2	19 44.8	13♉28.0	18 42.0	1 15.0	27 12.5	20 51.3	7 35.6	19 2.1	24 57.6	22 43.8
6 T	0 56 57.5	16 9.3	19 41.7	28 22.0	20 0.7	2 29.1	27 36.7	21 0.5	7 31.6	19 2.6	24 55.9	22 43.0
7 W	1 0 54.1	17 8.3	19 38.5	12♊51.0	21 21.3	3 43.1	28 0.7	21 9.7	7 27.5	19 3.1	24 54.3	22 42.3
8 T	1 4 50.6	18 7.3	19 35.3	26 51.9	22 43.8	4 57.1	28 24.4	21 19.0	7 23.3	19 3.7	24 52.7	22 41.5
9 F	1 8 47.2	19 6.2	19 32.1	10♋24.7	24 8.0	6 11.0	28 47.8	21 28.5	7 19.1	19 4.4	24 51.0	22 40.8
10 S	1 12 43.7	20 5.1	19 29.0	23 31.8	25 34.0	7 24.9	29 10.8	21 38.1	7 14.9	19 5.1	24 49.4	22 40.1
11 S	1 16 40.3	21 4.0	19 25.8	6♌17.0	27 1.7	8 38.8	29 33.5	21 47.7	7 10.6	19 5.9	24 47.8	22 39.5
12 M	1 20 36.8	22 2.8	19 22.6	18 44.7	28 31.1	9 52.7	29 55.9	21 57.5	7 6.3	19 6.7	24 46.1	22 38.9
13 T	1 24 33.4	23 1.6	19 19.4	0♍59.1	0♈ 2.2	11 6.5	0♑18.0	22 7.4	7 2.0	19 7.6	24 44.5	22 38.3
14 W	1 28 29.9	24 0.4	19 16.2	13 4.1	1 34.9	12 20.3	0 39.7	22 17.4	6 57.6	19 8.5	24 42.8	22 37.7
15 T	1 32 26.5	24 59.1	19 13.1	25 2.8	3 9.3	13 34.0	1 1.1	22 27.5	6 53.2	19 9.5	24 41.2	22 37.1
16 F	1 36 23.0	25 57.8	19 9.9	6♎57.6	4 45.3	14 47.8	1 22.1	22 37.7	6 48.8	19 10.5	24 39.5	22 36.6
17 S	1 40 19.6	26 56.4	19 6.7	18 50.6	6 23.0	16 1.5	1 42.7	22 48.0	6 44.4	19 11.6	24 37.9	22 36.1
18 S	1 44 16.2	27 55.0	19 3.5	0♏43.3	8 2.3	17 15.1	2 3.0	22 58.4	6 39.9	19 12.7	24 36.3	22 35.7
19 M	1 48 12.7	28 53.6	19 0.4	12 36.8	9 43.3	18 28.7	2 22.9	23 8.9	6 35.4	19 13.9	24 34.6	22 35.2
20 T	1 52 9.3	29 52.2	18 57.2	24 32.8	11 25.9	19 42.3	2 42.4	23 19.5	6 30.9	19 15.2	24 33.0	22 34.8
21 W	1 56 5.8	0♉50.7	18 54.0	6♐33.0	13 10.1	20 55.9	3 1.5	23 30.2	6 26.4	19 16.4	24 31.3	22 34.4
22 T	2 0 2.4	1 49.2	18 50.8	18 39.6	14 56.0	22 9.4	3 20.1	23 41.0	6 21.8	19 17.8	24 29.7	22 34.1
23 F	2 3 58.9	2 47.7	18 47.6	0♑55.8	16 43.6	23 22.9	3 38.3	23 51.8	6 17.3	19 19.2	24 28.1	22 33.7
24 S	2 7 55.5	3 46.1	18 44.5	13 25.0	18 32.9	24 36.3	3 56.1	24 2.8	6 12.7	19 20.6	24 26.5	22 33.4
25 S	2 11 52.0	4 44.6	18 41.3	26 11.3	20 23.9	25 49.8	4 13.5	24 13.8	6 8.2	19 22.1	24 24.9	22 33.2
26 M	2 15 48.6	5 42.9	18 38.1	9♒18.8	22 16.5	27 3.2	4 30.4	24 24.9	6 3.7	19 23.7	24 23.3	22 32.9
27 T	2 19 45.1	6 41.3	18 34.9	22 51.2	24 10.8	28 16.6	4 46.8	24 36.1	5 59.1	19 25.2	24 21.7	22 32.7
28 W	2 23 41.7	7 39.6	18 31.8	6♓50.7	26 6.8	29 29.9	5 2.8	24 47.4	5 54.5	19 26.9	24 20.1	22 32.5
29 T	2 27 38.3	8 38.0	18 28.6	21 17.4	28 4.4	0♊43.2	5 18.2	24 58.8	5 50.0	19 28.5	24 18.5	22 32.4
30 F	2 31 34.8	9 36.2	18 25.4	6♈ 8.2	0♉ 3.7	1 56.5	5 33.1	25 10.2	5 45.4	19 30.3	24 16.9	22 32.2
						DECLINATION at NOON						
1 T	0 37 14.7	4N26.6	21S57.7	3S 8.5	8S 9.1	9N29.0	23S16.2	22N53.4	11S35.6	22N34.5	8S 4.2	23N24.0
4 S	0 49 4.4	5 35.7	21 59.1	15N28.9	6 59.7	10 54.4	23 23.1	22 55.7	11 31.6	22 34.3	8 2.4	23 24.4
7 W	1 0 54.1	6 44.0	22 0.5	25 19.4	5 37.9	12 17.5	23 29.6	22 57.9	11 27.4	22 34.1	8 0.6	23 24.8
10 S	1 12 43.7	7 51.2	22 1.9	21 2.3	4 4.5	13 37.9	23 35.7	23 0.2	11 23.1	22 33.7	7 58.8	23 25.0
13 T	1 24 33.4	8 57.2	22 3.2	7 60.0	2 20.3	14 55.4	23 41.4	23 2.4	11 18.8	22 33.3	7 56.9	23 25.2
16 F	1 36 23.0	10 1.9	22 4.6	7S15.1	0 26.0	16 9.5	23 47.0	23 4.5	11 14.3	22 32.8	7 55.1	23 25.2
19 M	1 48 12.7	11 5.0	22 5.9	19 57.6	1N37.6	17 20.0	23 52.5	23 6.5	11 9.9	22 32.3	7 53.3	23 25.1
22 T	2 0 2.4	12 6.6	22 7.2	25 23.9	3 49.5	18 26.5	23 58.0	23 8.5	11 5.4	22 31.7	7 51.5	23 25.0
25 S	2 11 52.0	13 6.3	22 8.5	20 10.5	6 8.8	19 28.7	24 3.6	23 10.4	11 1.0	22 31.0	7 49.8	23 24.7
28 W	2 23 41.7	14 4.2	22 9.8	5 26.2	8 33.9	20 26.2	24 9.4	23 12.1	10 56.5	22 30.3	7 48.1	23 24.3

MAY 1954

DAY	EPHEMERIS SIDEREAL TIME	☉	☊	☽	☿	♀	♂	♃	♄	♅	♆	♇
	h m s	° ′	° ′	° ′	° ′	° ′	° ′	° ′	° ′	° ′	° ′	° ′
						LONGITUDE at NOON						
1 S	2 35 31.4	10♉34.5	18♑22.2	21♈16.6	2♉ 4.6	3♊ 9.7	5♑47.5	25♊21.7	5♏40.9	19♋32.0	24♎15.3	22♌32.1
2 S	2 39 27.9	11 32.7	18 19.1	6♉33.0	4 7.0	4 22.9	6 1.4	25 33.3	5R36.3	19 33.9	24R13.8	22 32.1
3 M	2 43 24.5	12 30.9	18 15.9	21 46.2	6 10.9	5 36.1	6 14.7	25 45.0	5 31.8	19 35.7	24 12.2	22 32.0
4 T	2 47 21.0	13 29.1	18 12.7	6♊45.6	8 16.3	6 49.2	6 27.4	25 56.8	5 27.3	19 37.6	24 10.7	22 32.0
5 W	2 51 17.6	14 27.3	18 9.5	21 22.8	10 22.9	8 2.3	6 39.6	26 8.6	5 22.8	19 39.6	24 9.2	22 32.0
6 T	2 55 14.1	15 25.4	18 6.3	5♋32.7	12 30.6	9 15.4	6 51.3	26 20.4	5 18.3	19 41.6	24 7.7	22 32.0
7 F	2 59 10.7	16 23.5	18 3.2	19 13.8	14 39.4	10 28.4	7 2.3	26 32.4	5 13.9	19 43.6	24 6.2	22D32.1
8 S	3 3 7.3	17 21.5	17 60.0	2♌27.2	16 49.0	11 41.4	7 12.7	26 44.4	5 9.5	19 45.7	24 4.7	22 32.2
9 S	3 7 3.8	18 19.5	17 56.8	15 16.2	18 59.2	12 54.4	7 22.6	26 56.5	5 5.1	19 47.8	24 3.2	22 32.3
10 M	3 11 0.4	19 17.5	17 53.6	27 45.0	21 9.7	14 7.3	7 31.8	27 8.6	5 0.7	19 50.0	24 1.8	22 32.5
11 T	3 14 56.9	20 15.5	17 50.5	9♍58.3	23 20.4	15 20.1	7 40.5	27 20.8	4 56.4	19 52.2	24 0.3	22 32.7
12 W	3 18 53.5	21 13.4	17 47.3	22 0.6	25 30.9	16 33.0	7 48.5	27 33.1	4 52.1	19 54.5	23 58.9	22 32.9
13 T	3 22 50.0	22 11.3	17 44.1	3♎56.1	27 41.0	17 45.7	7 55.8	27 45.4	4 47.9	19 56.8	23 57.5	22 33.1
14 F	3 26 46.6	23 9.2	17 40.9	15 48.3	29 50.4	18 58.5	8 2.5	27 57.8	4 43.6	19 59.1	23 56.1	22 33.4
15 S	3 30 43.1	24 7.0	17 37.7	27 40.2	1♊58.7	20 11.2	8 8.5	28 10.2	4 39.5	20 1.5	23 54.7	22 33.7
16 S	3 34 39.7	25 4.9	17 34.6	9♏34.1	4 5.9	21 23.9	8 14.0	28 22.7	4 35.4	20 3.9	23 53.4	22 34.0
17 M	3 38 36.3	26 2.7	17 31.4	21 31.7	6 11.4	22 36.5	8 18.6	28 35.2	4 31.3	20 6.4	23 52.1	22 34.4
18 T	3 42 32.8	27 0.4	17 28.2	3♐34.6	8 15.2	23 49.1	8 22.6	28 47.8	4 27.2	20 8.9	23 50.7	22 34.8
19 W	3 46 29.4	27 58.2	17 25.0	15 44.1	10 16.9	25 1.6	8 25.9	29 0.5	4 23.2	20 11.4	23 49.4	22 35.2
20 T	3 50 25.9	28 55.9	17 21.9	28 1.6	12 16.4	26 14.1	8 28.5	29 13.1	4 19.3	20 14.0	23 48.2	22 35.6
21 F	3 54 22.5	29 53.6	17 18.7	10♑29.1	14 13.6	27 26.5	8 30.4	29 25.9	4 15.4	20 16.6	23 46.9	22 36.1
22 S	3 58 19.0	0♊51.3	17 15.5	23 8.7	16 8.3	28 39.0	8 31.5	29 38.6	4 11.6	20 19.2	23 45.7	22 36.6
23 S	4 2 15.6	1 48.9	17 12.3	6♒ 2.9	18 0.3	29 51.3	8 31.9	29 51.5	4 7.8	20 21.9	23 44.4	22 37.1
24 M	4 6 12.2	2 46.6	17 9.2	19 14.4	19 49.7	1♋ 3.6	8R31.5	0♋ 4.3	4 4.1	20 24.6	23 43.2	22 37.6
25 T	4 10 8.7	3 44.2	17 6.0	2♓45.7	21 36.2	2 15.9	8 30.4	0 17.2	4 0.4	20 27.3	23 42.1	22 38.2
26 W	4 14 5.3	4 41.8	17 2.8	16 38.4	23 19.8	3 28.2	8 28.6	0 30.2	3 56.8	20 30.1	23 40.9	22 38.8
27 T	4 18 1.8	5 39.4	16 59.6	0♈52.7	25 0.5	4 40.4	8 25.9	0 43.2	3 53.3	20 32.9	23 39.8	22 39.4
28 F	4 21 58.4	6 37.0	16 56.4	15 25.8	26 38.3	5 52.5	8 22.5	0 56.2	3 49.8	20 35.8	23 38.7	22 40.1
29 S	4 25 54.9	7 34.6	16 53.3	0♉16.2	28 13.0	7 4.7	8 18.4	1 9.3	3 46.4	20 38.6	23 37.6	22 40.8
30 S	4 29 51.5	8 32.2	16 50.1	15 14.1	29 44.7	8 16.7	8 13.4	1 22.4	3 43.0	20 41.5	23 36.5	22 41.5
31 M	4 33 48.1	9 29.7	16 46.9	0♊11.8	1♋13.3	9 28.8	8 7.7	1 35.5	3 39.8	20 44.5	23 35.5	22 42.2
						DECLINATION at NOON						
1 S	2 35 31.4	14N59.9	22S11.1	12N57.5	11N 2.9	21N18.9	24S15.5	23N13.8	10S52.1	22N29.5	7S46.4	23N23.9
4 T	2 47 21.0	15 53.5	22 12.4	24 39.2	13 32.8	22 6.3	24 22.1	23 15.3	10 47.8	22 28.7	7 44.7	23 23.3
7 F	2 59 10.7	16 44.6	22 13.7	21 50.1	15 59.8	22 48.2	24 29.2	23 16.6	10 43.6	22 27.7	7 43.1	23 22.7
10 M	3 11 0.4	17 33.3	22 15.0	9 6.1	18 19.0	23 24.4	24 36.9	23 17.8	10 39.5	22 26.8	7 41.5	23 22.0
13 T	3 22 50.0	18 19.2	22 16.2	6S 7.5	20 25.0	23 54.7	24 45.3	23 18.8	10 35.5	22 25.7	7 40.0	23 21.2
16 S	3 34 39.7	19 2.5	22 17.5	19 6.3	22 12.7	24 18.8	24 54.5	23 19.7	10 31.7	22 24.6	7 38.6	23 20.2
19 W	3 46 29.4	19 42.8	22 18.7	25 13.2	23 38.3	24 36.7	25 4.4	23 20.4	10 28.0	22 23.5	7 37.2	23 19.2
22 S	3 58 19.0	20 20.1	22 19.9	20 46.8	24 40.5	24 48.2	25 15.2	23 20.9	10 24.5	22 22.3	7 35.9	23 18.2
25 T	4 10 8.7	20 54.3	22 21.1	6 56.6	25 19.6	24 53.3	25 26.8	23 21.3	10 21.2	22 21.1	7 34.7	23 17.0
28 F	4 21 58.4	21 25.2	22 22.3	10N50.8	25 37.5	24 51.9	25 39.2	23 21.4	10 18.1	22 19.7	7 33.5	23 15.8
31 M	4 33 48.1	21 52.8	22 23.5	23 46.6	25 36.7	24 44.1	25 52.3	23 21.3	10 15.3	22 18.4	7 32.5	23 14.5

JUNE 1954

DAY	EPHEMERIS SIDEREAL TIME	☉	☊	☽	☿	♀	♂	♃	♄	♅	♆	♇
						LONGITUDE at NOON						
1 T	4 37 44.6	10♊27.2	16♑43.7	15♊ 0.5	2♋38.8	10♋40.8	8♑ 1.3	1♋48.7	3♏36.6	20♋47.4	23♎34.5	22♌43.0
2 W	4 41 41.2	11 24.7	16 40.6	29 32.5	4 1.1	11 52.7	7R54.1	2 1.9	3R33.4	20 50.4	23R33.5	22 43.8
3 T	4 45 37.7	12 22.2	16 37.4	13♋41.9	5 20.3	13 4.6	7 46.1	2 15.1	3 30.4	20 53.4	23 32.5	22 44.6
4 F	4 49 34.3	13 19.7	16 34.2	27 25.8	6 36.2	14 16.4	7 37.5	2 28.4	3 27.4	20 56.5	23 31.6	22 45.4
5 S	4 53 30.8	14 17.1	16 31.0	10♌43.8	7 48.9	15 28.2	7 28.1	2 41.7	3 24.5	20 59.6	23 30.7	22 46.3
6 S	4 57 27.4	15 14.6	16 27.9	23 37.7	8 58.3	16 40.0	7 18.0	2 55.1	3 21.8	21 2.8	23 29.9	22 47.2
7 M	5 1 24.0	16 12.0	16 24.7	6♍10.6	10 4.2	17 51.7	7 7.3	3 8.4	3 19.0	21 5.9	23 29.0	22 48.2
8 T	5 5 20.5	17 9.4	16 21.5	18 26.6	11 6.6	19 3.3	6 55.8	3 21.8	3 16.4	21 9.1	23 28.2	22 49.1
9 W	5 9 17.1	18 6.8	16 18.3	0♎30.2	12 5.6	20 14.9	6 43.7	3 35.2	3 13.8	21 12.3	23 27.4	22 50.1
10 T	5 13 13.6	19 4.2	16 15.2	12 26.2	13 0.9	21 26.4	6 31.0	3 48.6	3 11.3	21 15.5	23 26.6	22 51.1
11 F	5 17 10.2	20 1.5	16 12.0	24 18.6	13 52.5	22 37.9	6 17.7	4 2.0	3 8.9	21 18.7	23 25.9	22 52.1
12 S	5 21 6.7	20 58.8	16 8.8	6♏11.5	14 40.3	23 49.3	6 3.8	4 15.5	3 6.6	21 22.0	23 25.2	22 53.1
13 S	5 25 3.3	21 56.2	16 5.6	18 8.2	15 24.2	25 0.7	5 49.4	4 28.9	3 4.4	21 25.2	23 24.5	22 54.2
14 M	5 28 59.9	22 53.5	16 2.4	0♐11.3	16 4.1	26 12.0	5 34.4	4 42.4	3 2.2	21 28.6	23 23.8	22 55.3
15 T	5 32 56.4	23 50.7	15 59.3	12 22.9	16 39.9	27 23.2	5 18.9	4 55.9	3 0.2	21 31.9	23 23.2	22 56.4
16 W	5 36 53.0	24 48.0	15 56.1	24 44.7	17 11.6	28 34.3	5 2.9	5 9.5	2 58.2	21 35.2	23 22.6	22 57.5
17 T	5 40 49.5	25 45.3	15 52.9	7♑17.9	17 39.0	29 45.4	4 46.6	5 23.0	2 56.3	21 38.6	23 22.0	22 58.7
18 F	5 44 46.1	26 42.5	15 49.7	20 3.2	18 2.0	0♌56.5	4 29.8	5 36.5	2 54.5	21 42.0	23 21.5	22 59.9
19 S	5 48 42.7	27 39.8	15 46.6	3♒ 1.4	18 20.6	2 7.5	4 12.6	5 50.1	2 52.8	21 45.4	23 21.0	23 1.1
20 S	5 52 39.2	28 37.0	15 43.4	16 13.2	18 34.7	3 18.4	3 55.1	6 3.7	2 51.2	21 48.8	23 20.5	23 2.3
21 M	5 56 35.8	29 34.3	15 40.2	29 39.0	18 44.2	4 29.2	3 37.3	6 17.3	2 49.7	21 52.2	23 20.1	23 3.5
22 T	6 0 32.3	0♋31.5	15 37.0	13♓19.2	18 49.2	5 40.0	3 19.2	6 30.9	2 48.3	21 55.7	23 19.6	23 4.8
23 W	6 4 28.9	1 28.7	15 33.9	27 13.7	18 49.6	6 50.8	3 1.0	6 44.5	2 47.0	21 59.2	23 19.3	23 6.1
24 T	6 8 25.4	2 26.0	15 30.7	11♈21.8	18R45.4	8 1.4	2 42.5	6 58.1	2 45.7	22 2.7	23 18.9	23 7.4
25 F	6 12 22.0	3 23.2	15 27.5	25 41.7	18 36.9	9 12.0	2 23.9	7 11.7	2 44.6	22 6.2	23 18.6	23 8.7
26 S	6 16 18.6	4 20.5	15 24.3	10♉10.4	18 24.0	10 22.5	2 5.3	7 25.3	2 43.5	22 9.7	23 18.3	23 10.1
27 S	6 20 15.1	5 17.7	15 21.2	24 43.5	18 7.0	11 33.1	1 46.6	7 39.0	2 42.7	22 13.3	23 18.1	23 11.5
28 M	6 24 11.7	6 15.0	15 18.0	9♊15.7	17 46.0	12 43.5	1 27.9	7 52.6	2 41.8	22 16.8	23 17.8	23 12.9
29 T	6 28 8.2	7 12.2	15 14.8	23 41.3	17 21.4	13 53.8	1 9.3	8 6.2	2 41.1	22 20.4	23 17.6	23 14.3
30 W	6 32 4.8	8 9.4	15 11.6	7♋54.8	16 53.5	15 4.0	0 50.8	8 19.9	2 40.4	22 23.9	23 17.5	23 15.7
						DECLINATION at NOON						
1 T	4 37 44.6	22N 1.3	22S23.9	25N11.4	25N32.8	24N40.0	25S56.8	23N21.2	10S14.4	22N17.9	7S32.1	23N14.1
4 F	4 49 34.3	22 24.3	22 25.1	19 34.8	25 11.7	24 23.7	26 10.6	23 20.9	10 11.9	22 16.5	7 31.2	23 12.7
7 M	5 1 24.0	22 43.8	22 26.2	5 27.9	24 38.8	24 1.2	26 24.8	23 20.4	10 9.6	22 15.1	7 30.4	23 11.2
10 T	5 13 13.6	22 59.7	22 27.4	9S42.9	23 56.9	23 32.6	26 39.1	23 19.6	10 7.6	22 13.5	7 29.6	23 9.7
13 S	5 25 3.3	23 12.0	22 28.5	21 26.1	23 8.9	22 58.1	26 53.3	23 18.6	10 5.9	22 12.0	7 29.0	23 8.2
16 W	5 36 53.0	23 20.6	22 29.7	25 8.3	22 17.3	22 18.1	27 7.1	23 17.5	10 4.5	22 10.4	7 28.4	23 6.6
19 S	5 48 42.7	23 25.5	22 30.8	17 52.7	21 24.8	21 32.6	27 20.3	23 16.1	10 3.4	22 8.8	7 27.9	23 4.9
22 T	6 0 32.3	23 26.7	22 31.9	2 24.2	20 34.0	20 41.9	27 32.5	23 14.5	10 2.5	22 7.1	7 27.6	23 3.2
25 F	6 12 22.0	23 24.1	22 33.0	14N44.8	19 47.3	19 46.5	27 43.7	23 12.6	10 2.0	22 5.5	7 27.3	23 1.4
28 M	6 24 11.7	23 17.9	22 34.1	24 52.5	19 7.2	18 46.4	27 53.5	23 10.6	10 1.8	22 3.7	7 27.2	22 59.6

JULY 1954

LONGITUDE at NOON

DAY	EPHEMERIS SIDEREAL TIME	☉	☊	☽	☿	♀	♂	♃	♄	♅	♆	♇
	h m s	° ′	° ′	° ′	° ′	° ′	° ′	° ′	° ′	° ′	° ′	° ′
1 T	6 36 1.4	9♋ 6.7	15♑ 8.4	21♋51.5	16♋22.8	16♌14.2	0♑32.5	8♋33.5	2♏39.8	22♋27.5	23♎17.3	23♌17.2
2 F	6 39 57.9	10 3.9	15 5.3	5♌28.2	15R49.7	17 24.3	0R14.4	8 47.1	2R39.4	22 31.1	23R17.2	23 18.7
3 S	6 43 54.5	11 1.1	15 2.1	18 43.5	15 14.6	18 34.4	29♐56.5	9 0.7	2 39.0	22 34.7	23 17.2	23 20.1
4 S	6 47 51.0	11 58.3	14 58.9	1♍37.6	14 38.3	19 44.3	29 39.0	9 14.3	2 38.8	22 38.3	23 17.1	23 21.6
5 M	6 51 47.6	12 55.6	14 55.7	14 12.3	14 1.2	20 54.2	29 21.8	9 28.0	2 38.6	22 41.9	23 17.1	23 23.2
6 T	6 55 44.1	13 52.8	14 52.6	26 30.5	13 24.1	22 3.9	29 5.0	9 41.6	2 38.6	22 45.6	23 17.1	23 24.7
7 W	6 59 40.7	14 50.0	14 49.4	8♎36.0	12 47.5	23 13.6	28 48.6	9 55.1	2 38.6	22 49.2	23D17.2	23 26.3
8 T	7 3 37.3	15 47.2	14 46.2	20 33.1	12 12.0	24 23.2	28 32.8	10 8.7	2D38.7	22 52.8	23 17.3	23 27.8
9 F	7 7 33.8	16 44.4	14 43.0	2♏26.4	11 38.4	25 32.8	28 17.4	10 22.3	2 39.0	22 56.5	23 17.4	23 29.4
10 S	7 11 30.4	17 41.6	14 39.9	14 20.3	11 7.3	26 42.2	28 2.6	10 35.9	2 39.3	23 0.1	23 17.6	23 31.0
11 S	7 15 26.9	18 38.8	14 36.7	26 19.2	10 39.0	27 51.5	27 48.3	10 49.4	2 39.7	23 3.8	23 17.8	23 32.6
12 M	7 19 23.5	19 36.0	14 33.5	8♐26.8	10 14.3	29 0.7	27 34.7	11 2.9	2 40.3	23 7.4	23 18.0	23 34.3
13 T	7 23 20.1	20 33.2	14 30.3	20 46.4	9 53.5	0♍ 9.8	27 21.7	11 16.4	2 40.9	23 11.1	23 18.2	23 35.9
14 W	7 27 16.6	21 30.4	14 27.2	3♑20.2	9 37.1	1 18.9	27 9.3	11 29.9	2 41.6	23 14.7	23 18.5	23 37.6
15 T	7 31 13.2	22 27.6	14 24.0	16 10.0	9 25.4	2 27.8	26 57.7	11 43.4	2 42.4	23 18.4	23 18.8	23 39.3
16 F	7 35 9.7	23 24.8	14 20.8	29 16.1	9 18.6	3 36.6	26 46.7	11 56.9	2 43.4	23 22.1	23 19.2	23 41.0
17 S	7 39 6.3	24 22.1	14 17.6	12♒38.1	9 17.1	4 45.3	26 36.5	12 10.3	2 44.4	23 25.7	23 19.6	23 42.7
18 S	7 43 2.8	25 19.3	14 14.4	26 14.7	9D21.1	5 54.0	26 27.1	12 23.8	2 45.6	23 29.4	23 20.0	23 44.4
19 M	7 46 59.4	26 16.6	14 11.3	10♓ 4.0	9 30.6	7 2.4	26 18.3	12 37.2	2 46.8	23 33.1	23 20.5	23 46.1
20 T	7 50 56.0	27 13.8	14 8.1	24 3.3	9 45.7	8 10.8	26 10.4	12 50.6	2 48.1	23 36.7	23 20.9	23 47.9
21 W	7 54 52.5	28 11.1	14 4.9	8♈10.2	10 6.5	9 19.1	26 3.2	13 3.9	2 49.5	23 40.4	23 21.4	23 49.6
22 T	7 58 49.1	29 8.4	14 1.7	22 21.9	10 33.1	10 27.2	25 56.8	13 17.3	2 51.0	23 44.0	23 22.0	23 51.4
23 F	8 2 45.6	0♌ 5.7	13 58.6	6♉35.8	11 5.5	11 35.3	25 51.3	13 30.6	2 52.6	23 47.7	23 22.5	23 53.2
24 S	8 6 42.2	1 3.0	13 55.4	20 49.5	11 43.6	12 43.2	25 46.5	13 43.8	2 54.3	23 51.3	23 23.1	23 55.0
25 S	8 10 38.7	2 0.3	13 52.2	5♊ 0.5	12 27.4	13 51.0	25 42.6	13 57.1	2 56.1	23 55.0	23 23.8	23 56.8
26 M	8 14 35.3	2 57.6	13 49.0	19 6.4	13 16.8	14 58.7	25 39.5	14 10.3	2 57.9	23 58.6	23 24.4	23 58.6
27 T	8 18 31.9	3 55.0	13 45.9	3♋ 4.6	14 11.8	16 6.3	25 37.3	14 23.5	2 59.9	24 2.2	23 25.1	24 0.4
28 W	8 22 28.4	4 52.4	13 42.7	16 52.4	15 12.3	17 13.7	25 35.9	14 36.7	3 2.0	24 5.8	23 25.9	24 2.2
29 T	8 26 25.0	5 49.8	13 39.5	0♌27.5	16 18.2	18 21.0	25 35.3	14 49.8	3 4.2	24 9.5	23 26.6	24 4.0
30 F	8 30 21.5	6 47.1	13 36.3	13 47.8	17 29.4	19 28.2	25D35.6	15 2.9	3 6.4	24 13.1	23 27.4	24 5.9
31 S	8 34 18.1	7 44.6	13 33.1	26 51.9	18 45.8	20 35.2	25 36.8	15 15.9	3 8.8	24 16.6	23 28.2	24 7.7

DECLINATION at NOON

DAY	EPHEMERIS SIDEREAL TIME	☉	☊	☽	☿	♀	♂	♃	♄	♅	♆	♇
1 T	6 36 1.4	23N 7.9	22S 35.2	21N 1.4	18N35.7	17N42.1	28S 1.9	23N 8.4	10S 1.8	22N 2.0	7S 27.2	22N57.8
4 S	6 47 51.0	22 54.3	22 36.2	7 17.4	18 14.8	16 33.9	28 8.7	23 5.9	10 2.2	22 0.2	7 27.2	22 56.0
7 W	6 59 40.7	22 37.2	22 37.3	8S 14.1	18 5.4	15 22.2	28 14.0	23 3.3	10 2.9	21 58.4	7 27.4	22 54.1
10 S	7 11 30.4	22 16.5	22 38.3	20 31.8	18 7.9	14 7.1	28 17.9	23 0.4	10 3.9	21 56.6	7 27.7	22 52.2
13 T	7 23 20.1	21 52.4	22 39.4	25 16.3	18 21.6	12 49.1	28 20.5	22 57.4	10 5.2	21 54.8	7 28.1	22 50.3
16 F	7 35 9.7	21 24.9	22 40.4	19 1.0	18 44.8	11 28.5	28 21.9	22 54.1	10 6.8	21 52.9	7 28.6	22 48.3
19 M	7 46 59.4	20 54.1	22 41.4	3 46.8	19 14.9	10 5.6	28 22.2	22 50.7	10 8.7	21 51.1	7 29.2	22 46.4
22 T	7 58 49.1	20 20.1	22 42.4	13N32.6	19 48.5	8 40.7	28 21.8	22 47.1	10 10.9	21 49.2	7 29.9	22 44.4
25 S	8 10 38.7	19 43.1	22 43.4	24 26.9	20 21.5	7 14.0	28 20.6	22 43.4	10 13.4	21 47.4	7 30.7	22 42.5
28 W	8 22 28.4	19 3.1	22 44.4	22 11.2	20 49.4	5 45.9	28 18.8	22 39.5	10 16.2	21 45.5	7 31.6	22 40.6
31 S	8 34 18.1	18 20.3	22 45.3	9 15.1	21 7.3	4 16.7	28 16.6	22 35.4	10 19.2	21 43.6	7 32.7	22 38.6

AUGUST 1954

LONGITUDE at NOON

DAY	EPHEMERIS SIDEREAL TIME	☉	☊	☽	☿	♀	♂	♃	♄	♅	♆	♇
1 S	8 38 14.6	8♌42.0	13♑30.0	9♍39.3	20♋ 7.1	21♍42.1	25♐38.8	15♋29.0	3♏11.2	24♋20.2	23♎29.1	24♌ 9.6
2 M	8 42 11.2	9 39.4	13 26.8	22 10.6	21 33.3	22 48.8	25 41.7	15 41.9	3 13.8	24 23.8	23 30.0	24 11.4
3 T	8 46 7.7	10 36.9	13 23.6	4♎27.4	23 4.0	23 55.4	25 45.4	15 54.9	3 16.4	24 27.4	23 30.9	24 13.3
4 W	8 50 4.3	11 34.3	13 20.4	16 32.4	24 39.2	25 1.8	25 49.9	16 7.8	3 19.1	24 30.9	23 31.8	24 15.2
5 T	8 54 0.9	12 31.8	13 17.3	28 29.2	26 18.5	26 8.1	25 55.2	16 20.6	3 21.9	24 34.4	23 32.8	24 17.1
6 F	8 57 57.4	13 29.3	13 14.1	10♏22.0	28 1.6	27 14.2	26 1.4	16 33.4	3 24.8	24 38.0	23 33.8	24 19.0
7 S	9 1 54.0	14 26.8	13 10.9	22 15.3	29 48.3	28 20.2	26 8.4	16 46.2	3 27.8	24 41.5	23 34.8	24 20.9
8 S	9 5 50.5	15 24.3	13 7.7	4♐14.1	1♌38.2	29 26.0	26 16.2	16 58.9	3 30.9	24 45.0	23 35.9	24 22.8
9 M	9 9 47.1	16 21.8	13 4.6	16 23.0	3 30.9	0♎31.6	26 24.8	17 11.6	3 34.1	24 48.5	23 37.0	24 24.7
10 T	9 13 43.6	17 19.4	13 1.4	28 46.5	5 26.0	1 37.0	26 34.1	17 24.2	3 37.3	24 51.9	23 38.1	24 26.6
11 W	9 17 40.2	18 16.9	12 58.2	11♑28.2	7 23.2	2 42.2	26 44.2	17 36.8	3 40.6	24 55.4	23 39.3	24 28.5
12 T	9 21 36.7	19 14.5	12 55.0	24 30.6	9 22.0	3 47.2	26 55.1	17 49.3	3 44.0	24 58.8	23 40.4	24 30.4
13 F	9 25 33.3	20 12.1	12 51.8	7♒54.7	11 22.2	4 52.0	27 6.6	18 1.8	3 47.5	25 2.2	23 41.6	24 32.3
14 S	9 29 29.9	21 9.7	12 48.7	21 39.8	13 23.3	5 56.6	27 18.9	18 14.2	3 51.1	25 5.6	23 42.9	24 34.2
15 S	9 33 26.4	22 7.3	12 45.5	5♓43.2	15 25.1	7 1.0	27 31.9	18 26.5	3 54.8	25 8.9	23 44.1	24 36.2
16 M	9 37 23.0	23 4.9	12 42.3	20 0.5	17 27.2	8 5.2	27 45.6	18 38.8	3 58.5	25 12.3	23 45.4	24 38.1
17 T	9 41 19.5	24 2.6	12 39.1	4♈26.3	19 29.3	9 9.2	28 0.0	18 51.1	4 2.3	25 15.6	23 46.7	24 40.0
18 W	9 45 16.1	25 0.3	12 36.0	18 54.6	21 31.1	10 12.9	28 15.1	19 3.3	4 6.2	25 18.9	23 48.0	24 41.9
19 T	9 49 12.6	25 58.0	12 32.8	3♉20.1	23 32.6	11 16.4	28 30.8	19 15.4	4 10.2	25 22.2	23 49.4	24 43.8
20 F	9 53 9.2	26 55.8	12 29.6	17 38.7	25 33.5	12 19.7	28 47.2	19 27.5	4 14.3	25 25.5	23 50.8	24 45.7
21 S	9 57 5.7	27 53.6	12 26.4	1♊47.6	27 33.5	13 22.8	29 4.2	19 39.5	4 18.4	25 28.7	23 52.2	24 47.7
22 S	10 1 2.3	28 51.4	12 23.2	15 45.3	29 32.7	14 25.6	29 21.8	19 51.4	4 22.6	25 31.9	23 53.6	24 49.6
23 M	10 4 58.8	29 49.2	12 20.1	29 31.3	1♍30.9	15 28.1	29 40.1	20 3.3	4 26.9	25 35.1	23 55.1	24 51.5
24 T	10 8 55.4	0♍47.1	12 16.9	13♋ 5.7	3 28.0	16 30.4	29 58.9	20 15.1	4 31.3	25 38.2	23 56.6	24 53.4
25 W	10 12 52.0	1 44.9	12 13.7	26 28.6	5 23.9	17 32.4	0♑18.4	20 26.8	4 35.7	25 41.4	23 58.1	24 55.3
26 T	10 16 48.5	2 42.9	12 10.5	9♌39.9	7 18.7	18 34.2	0 38.4	20 38.5	4 40.2	25 44.5	23 59.6	24 57.2
27 F	10 20 45.1	3 40.8	12 7.4	22 39.3	9 12.2	19 35.7	0 59.1	20 50.1	4 44.8	25 47.6	24 1.2	24 59.1
28 S	10 24 41.6	4 38.8	12 4.2	5♍26.7	11 4.5	20 36.9	1 20.3	21 1.6	4 49.5	25 50.6	24 2.8	25 1.0
29 S	10 28 38.2	5 36.8	12 1.0	18 1.6	12 55.5	21 37.8	1 42.1	21 13.1	4 54.3	25 53.7	24 4.4	25 3.0
30 M	10 32 34.7	6 34.9	11 57.8	0♎24.3	14 45.2	22 38.4	2 4.4	21 24.4	4 59.1	25 56.7	24 6.1	25 4.9
31 T	10 36 31.3	7 32.9	11 54.6	12 35.7	16 33.7	23 38.6	2 27.2	21 35.7	5 3.9	25 59.7	24 7.7	25 6.8

DECLINATION at NOON

DAY	EPHEMERIS SIDEREAL TIME	☉	☊	☽	☿	♀	♂	♃	♄	♅	♆	♇
1 S	8 38 14.6	18N 5.4	22S 45.7	3N58.7	21N10.1	3N46.8	28S 15.8	22N34.0	10S 20.3	21N43.0	7S 33.0	22N38.0
4 W	8 50 4.3	17 19.0	22 46.6	11S 18.9	21 6.6	2 16.6	28 13.1	22 29.7	10 23.6	21 41.2	7 34.2	22 36.0
7 S	9 1 54.0	16 30.1	22 47.6	22 19.3	20 42.0	0 45.9	28 10.1	22 25.4	10 27.3	21 39.3	7 35.4	22 34.1
10 T	9 13 43.6	15 38.8	22 48.5	24 51.1	19 53.9	0S 44.9	28 6.9	22 20.8	10 31.2	21 37.5	7 36.8	22 32.2
13 F	9 25 33.3	14 45.3	22 49.4	16 17.6	18 42.3	2 15.6	28 3.3	22 16.2	10 35.3	21 35.7	7 38.2	22 30.4
16 M	9 37 23.0	13 49.6	22 50.3	0N22.4	17 9.5	3 45.8	27 59.4	22 11.5	10 39.7	21 33.9	7 39.7	22 28.6
19 T	9 49 12.6	12 52.0	22 51.2	17 12.0	15 19.5	5 15.4	27 55.1	22 6.7	10 44.3	21 32.2	7 41.3	22 26.8
22 S	10 1 2.3	11 52.5	22 52.1	25 6.6	13 16.6	6 44.1	27 50.4	22 1.9	10 49.0	21 30.5	7 43.0	22 25.0
25 W	10 12 52.0	10 51.3	22 53.0	19 46.0	11 5.1	8 11.6	27 45.2	21 57.0	10 54.0	21 28.8	7 44.7	22 23.3
28 S	10 24 41.6	9 48.6	22 53.9	5 47.1	8 48.3	9 37.6	27 39.3	21 52.0	10 59.2	21 27.1	7 46.5	22 21.6
31 T	10 36 31.3	8 44.4	22 54.7	9S 39.4	6 28.8	11 1.9	27 32.7	21 47.0	11 4.6	21 25.5	7 48.4	22 20.0

SEPTEMBER 1954

DAY	EPHEMERIS SIDEREAL TIME	☉	☊	☽	☿	♀	♂	♃	♄	♅	♆	♇
	h m s	° ′	° ′	° ′	° ′	° ′	° ′	° ′	° ′	° ′	° ′	° ′
LONGITUDE at NOON												
1 W	10 40 27.8	8♍31.0	11♑51.5	24♎37.3	18♍20.9	24♎38.5	2♑50.6	21♋46.9	5♏ 8.9	26♋ 2.6	24♎ 9.4	25♌ 8.6
2 T	10 44 24.4	9 29.1	11 48.3	6♏31.7	20 6.8	25 38.1	3 14.5	21 58.0	5 13.9	26 5.5	24 11.1	25 10.5
3 F	10 48 20.9	10 27.2	11 45.1	18 22.4	21 51.5	26 37.3	3 38.9	22 9.1	5 18.9	26 8.4	24 12.8	25 12.4
4 S	10 52 17.5	11 25.3	11 41.9	0♐13.5	23 34.9	27 36.1	4 3.7	22 20.0	5 24.1	26 11.2	24 14.5	25 14.2
5 S	10 56 14.0	12 23.5	11 38.8	12 9.9	25 17.2	28 34.5	4 29.1	22 30.9	5 29.3	26 14.0	24 16.3	25 16.1
6 M	11 0 10.6	13 21.7	11 35.6	24 16.6	26 58.2	29 32.6	4 54.9	22 41.7	5 34.5	26 16.8	24 18.1	25 17.9
7 T	11 4 7.1	14 19.9	11 32.4	6♑38.9	28 38.0	0♏30.2	5 21.1	22 52.4	5 39.9	26 19.5	24 19.9	25 19.8
8 W	11 8 3.7	15 18.2	11 29.2	19 21.7	0♎16.7	1 27.4	5 47.9	23 3.0	5 45.3	26 22.2	24 21.7	25 21.6
9 T	11 12 0.3	16 16.4	11 26.0	2♒28.7	1 54.2	2 24.1	6 15.0	23 13.5	5 50.7	26 24.9	24 23.5	25 23.4
10 F	11 15 56.8	17 14.7	11 22.9	16 2.4	3 30.6	3 20.4	6 42.6	23 23.9	5 56.2	26 27.5	24 25.4	25 25.2
11 S	11 19 53.4	18 13.1	11 19.7	0♓ 2.7	5 5.9	4 16.2	7 10.5	23 34.2	6 1.8	26 30.1	24 27.3	25 27.0
12 S	11 23 49.9	19 11.4	11 16.5	14 26.8	6 40.0	5 11.5	7 38.9	23 44.4	6 7.4	26 32.6	24 29.2	25 28.8
13 M	11 27 46.5	20 9.8	11 13.3	29 9.0	8 13.0	6 6.3	8 7.6	23 54.6	6 13.1	26 35.1	24 31.1	25 30.6
14 T	11 31 43.0	21 8.2	11 10.2	14♈ 1.5	9 44.9	7 0.6	8 36.8	24 4.6	6 18.8	26 37.6	24 33.0	25 32.4
15 W	11 35 39.6	22 6.7	11 7.0	28 55.3	11 15.8	7 54.3	9 6.3	24 14.5	6 24.6	26 40.1	24 34.9	25 34.1
16 T	11 39 36.1	23 5.1	11 3.8	13♉41.9	12 45.5	8 47.5	9 36.1	24 24.3	6 30.4	26 42.5	24 36.9	25 35.9
17 F	11 43 32.7	24 3.7	11 0.6	28 15.0	14 14.1	9 40.0	10 6.4	24 34.0	6 36.3	26 44.8	24 38.9	25 37.6
18 S	11 47 29.2	25 2.2	10 57.4	12♊30.3	15 41.6	10 32.0	10 36.9	24 43.6	6 42.3	26 47.1	24 40.9	25 39.3
19 S	11 51 25.8	26 0.9	10 54.3	26 26.4	17 8.0	11 23.3	11 7.9	24 53.2	6 48.3	26 49.5	24 42.9	25 41.1
20 M	11 55 22.3	26 59.5	10 51.1	10♋ 3.6	18 33.3	12 14.0	11 39.1	25 2.6	6 54.4	26 51.7	24 44.9	25 42.8
21 T	11 59 18.9	27 58.2	10 47.9	23 23.6	19 57.4	13 4.0	12 10.7	25 11.8	7 0.5	26 53.9	24 47.0	25 44.5
22 W	12 3 15.4	28 56.9	10 44.7	6♌28.3	21 20.3	13 53.3	12 42.6	25 21.0	7 6.6	26 56.1	24 49.0	25 46.1
23 T	12 7 12.0	29 55.6	10 41.6	19 19.9	22 42.1	14 41.9	13 14.8	25 30.1	7 12.8	26 58.2	24 51.1	25 47.8
24 F	12 11 8.5	0♎54.4	10 38.4	2♍ 0.1	24 2.5	15 29.7	13 47.4	25 39.0	7 19.0	27 0.2	24 53.2	25 49.4
25 S	12 15 5.1	1 53.2	10 35.2	14 30.0	25 21.7	16 16.8	14 20.2	25 47.8	7 25.3	27 2.3	24 55.2	25 51.0
26 S	12 19 1.7	2 52.0	10 32.0	26 50.5	26 39.6	17 3.0	14 53.4	25 56.5	7 31.7	27 4.2	24 57.3	25 52.6
27 M	12 22 58.2	3 50.9	10 28.8	9♎ 2.1	27 56.0	17 48.3	15 26.8	26 5.0	7 38.0	27 6.2	24 59.5	25 54.2
28 T	12 26 54.8	4 49.8	10 25.7	21 5.7	29 11.0	18 32.8	16 0.5	26 13.5	7 44.4	27 8.0	25 1.6	25 55.8
29 W	12 30 51.3	5 48.8	10 22.5	3♏ 2.3	0♏24.4	19 16.4	16 34.5	26 21.8	7 50.9	27 9.9	25 3.7	25 57.4
30 T	12 34 47.9	6 47.7	10 19.3	14 53.7	1 36.2	19 59.0	17 8.8	26 29.9	7 57.4	27 11.7	25 5.8	25 58.9
DECLINATION at NOON												
1 W	10 40 27.8	8N22.7	22S55.0	14S10.4	5N42.1	11S29.6	27S30.3	21N45.3	11S 6.4	21N25.0	7S49.1	22N19.5
4 S	10 52 17.5	7 16.9	22 55.8	23 34.8	3 22.3	12 51.2	27 22.6	21 40.3	11 12.0	21 23.4	7 51.1	22 17.9
7 T	11 4 7.1	6 10.1	22 56.7	23 49.7	1 3.9	14 10.5	27 14.0	21 35.4	11 17.8	21 21.9	7 53.1	22 16.4
10 F	11 15 56.8	5 2.4	22 57.5	13 22.4	1S11.9	15 27.1	27 4.4	21 30.4	11 23.7	21 20.5	7 55.2	22 15.0
13 M	11 27 46.5	3 53.9	22 58.3	4N 9.7	3 24.3	16 40.9	26 53.7	21 25.5	11 29.7	21 19.1	7 57.4	22 13.6
16 T	11 39 36.1	2 44.7	22 59.1	20 2.5	5 32.3	17 51.5	26 41.8	21 20.6	11 35.8	21 17.8	7 59.6	22 12.3
19 S	11 51 25.8	1 35.1	22 59.9	24 44.1	7 35.4	18 58.8	26 28.6	21 15.8	11 42.1	21 16.5	8 1.8	22 11.1
22 W	12 3 15.4	0 25.1	23 0.6	16 36.7	9 32.8	20 2.5	26 14.1	21 11.2	11 48.5	21 15.4	8 4.1	22 9.9
25 S	12 15 5.1	0S45.0	23 1.4	1 58.8	11 23.6	21 2.4	25 58.1	21 6.6	11 54.9	21 14.3	8 6.4	22 8.8
28 T	12 26 54.8	1 55.2	23 2.2	12S46.9	13 6.9	21 58.2	25 40.7	21 2.2	12 1.5	21 13.2	8 8.8	22 7.9

OCTOBER 1954

DAY	EPHEMERIS SIDEREAL TIME	☉	☊	☽	☿	♀	♂	♃	♄	♅	♆	♇
LONGITUDE at NOON												
1 F	12 38 44.4	7♎46.7	10♑16.1	26♏42.4	2♏46.2	20♏40.5	17♑43.3	26♋38.0	8♏ 3.9	27♋13.4	25♎ 8.0	26♌ 0.4
2 S	12 42 41.0	8 45.8	10 13.0	8♐31.7	3 54.3	21 21.1	18 18.1	26 45.9	8 10.5	27 15.1	25 10.2	26 1.9
3 S	12 46 37.5	9 44.9	10 9.8	20 25.7	5 0.5	22 0.5	18 53.1	26 53.7	8 17.1	27 16.8	25 12.3	26 3.4
4 M	12 50 34.1	10 44.0	10 6.6	2♑29.4	6 4.4	22 38.8	19 28.4	27 1.3	8 23.7	27 18.4	25 14.5	26 4.9
5 T	12 54 30.6	11 43.1	10 3.4	14 47.9	7 6.1	23 15.9	20 4.0	27 8.8	8 30.4	27 19.9	25 16.7	26 6.3
6 W	12 58 27.2	12 42.2	10 0.2	27 26.5	8 5.1	23 51.8	20 39.7	27 16.2	8 37.1	27 21.4	25 18.9	26 7.7
7 T	13 2 23.7	13 41.4	9 57.1	10♒30.2	9 1.5	24 26.4	21 15.7	27 23.4	8 43.9	27 22.9	25 21.1	26 9.1
8 F	13 6 20.3	14 40.6	9 53.9	24 2.5	9 54.8	24 59.6	21 51.9	27 30.5	8 50.6	27 24.3	25 23.3	26 10.5
9 S	13 10 16.8	15 39.9	9 50.7	8♓ 5.0	10 44.9	25 31.4	22 28.3	27 37.4	8 57.4	27 25.6	25 25.5	26 11.9
10 S	13 14 13.4	16 39.2	9 47.5	22 36.1	11 31.4	26 1.8	23 5.0	27 44.2	9 4.3	27 27.0	25 27.7	26 13.3
11 M	13 18 10.0	17 38.5	9 44.4	7♈30.7	12 13.9	26 30.7	23 41.8	27 50.9	9 11.2	27 28.2	25 30.0	26 14.6
12 T	13 22 6.5	18 37.9	9 41.2	22 40.4	12 52.1	26 58.0	24 18.9	27 57.4	9 18.1	27 29.4	25 32.2	26 15.9
13 W	13 26 3.1	19 37.2	9 38.0	7♉54.6	13 25.6	27 23.7	24 56.1	28 3.7	9 25.0	27 30.6	25 34.4	26 17.2
14 T	13 29 59.6	20 36.6	9 34.8	23 2.4	13 53.9	27 47.7	25 33.5	28 9.9	9 31.9	27 31.7	25 36.6	26 18.5
15 F	13 33 56.2	21 36.1	9 31.6	7♊54.5	14 16.6	28 9.9	26 11.0	28 15.9	9 38.9	27 32.7	25 38.9	26 19.7
16 S	13 37 52.7	22 35.6	9 28.5	22 24.7	14 33.1	28 30.4	26 48.8	28 21.8	9 45.8	27 33.7	25 41.1	26 20.9
17 S	13 41 49.3	23 35.1	9 25.3	6♋30.0	14 42.9	28 48.9	27 26.7	28 27.5	9 52.9	27 34.6	25 43.3	26 22.1
18 M	13 45 45.8	24 34.7	9 22.1	20 10.3	14 45.5	29 5.6	28 4.8	28 33.0	9 59.9	27 35.5	25 45.6	26 23.3
19 T	13 49 42.4	25 34.3	9 18.9	3♌27.5	14R40.4	29 20.3	28 43.1	28 38.4	10 6.9	27 36.4	25 47.8	26 24.4
20 W	13 53 38.9	26 33.9	9 15.8	16 24.6	14 27.0	29 32.9	29 21.5	28 43.6	10 14.0	27 37.1	25 50.1	26 25.5
21 T	13 57 35.5	27 33.6	9 12.6	29 5.1	14 5.1	29 43.5	0♒ 0.1	28 48.7	10 21.1	27 37.9	25 52.3	26 26.6
22 F	14 1 32.0	28 33.3	9 9.4	11♍32.2	13 34.3	29 51.9	0 38.8	28 53.6	10 28.2	27 38.5	25 54.5	26 27.7
23 S	14 5 28.6	29 33.0	9 6.2	23 48.7	12 54.7	29 58.0	1 17.7	28 58.3	10 35.3	27 39.2	25 56.8	26 28.7
24 S	14 9 25.2	0♏32.8	9 3.0	5♎56.8	12 6.3	0♐ 2.0	1 56.8	29 2.8	10 42.4	27 39.7	25 59.0	26 29.7
25 M	14 13 21.7	1 32.6	8 59.9	17 58.3	11 9.7	0 3.6	2 36.0	29 7.2	10 49.5	27 40.2	26 1.2	26 30.7
26 T	14 17 18.3	2 32.5	8 56.7	29 54.5	10 5.7	0R 2.8	3 15.4	29 11.4	10 56.7	27 40.7	26 3.5	26 31.7
27 W	14 21 14.8	3 32.4	8 53.5	11♏46.7	8 55.7	29♏59.7	3 54.9	29 15.4	11 3.9	27 41.1	26 5.7	26 32.7
28 T	14 25 11.4	4 32.3	8 50.3	23 36.4	7 41.3	29 54.2	4 34.5	29 19.2	11 11.0	27 41.4	26 7.9	26 33.6
29 F	14 29 7.9	5 32.3	8 47.2	5♐25.4	6 24.5	29 46.3	5 14.3	29 22.9	11 18.2	27 41.7	26 10.1	26 34.5
30 S	14 33 4.5	6 32.2	8 44.0	17 16.1	5 7.6	29 35.9	5 54.2	29 26.4	11 25.4	27 42.0	26 12.4	26 35.3
31 S	14 37 1.0	7 32.3	8 40.8	29 11.8	3 53.0	29 23.1	6 34.2	29 29.7	11 32.7	27 42.2	26 14.6	26 36.2
DECLINATION at NOON												
1 F	12 38 44.4	3S 5.2	23S 2.9	22S47.0	14S41.7	22S49.5	25S21.8	20N57.9	12S 8.1	21N12.3	8S11.2	22N 7.0
4 M	12 50 34.1	4 15.0	23 3.6	24 4.8	16 6.6	23 36.3	25 1.3	20 53.8	12 14.8	21 11.4	8 13.6	22 6.1
7 T	13 2 23.7	5 24.2	23 4.3	15 8.4	17 19.8	24 18.0	24 39.3	20 49.9	12 21.5	21 10.6	8 16.0	22 5.4
10 S	13 14 13.4	6 32.8	23 5.1	1N28.1	18 18.8	24 54.4	24 15.6	20 46.2	12 28.2	21 9.9	8 18.4	22 4.7
13 W	13 26 3.1	7 40.7	23 5.7	18 18.3	19 0.5	25 25.1	23 50.3	20 42.7	12 35.0	21 9.3	8 20.8	22 4.2
16 S	13 37 52.7	8 47.5	23 6.4	24 39.0	19 20.4	25 49.5	23 23.4	20 39.5	12 41.8	21 8.8	8 23.3	22 3.7
19 T	13 49 42.4	9 53.3	23 7.1	17 19.6	19 12.4	26 7.2	22 54.9	20 36.5	12 48.6	21 8.4	8 25.7	22 3.4
22 F	14 1 32.0	10 57.8	23 7.8	3 5.0	18 29.8	26 17.5	22 24.8	20 33.9	12 55.4	21 8.0	8 28.1	22 3.1
25 M	14 13 21.7	12 0.8	23 8.4	11S37.7	17 7.9	26 19.5	21 53.1	20 31.5	13 2.2	21 7.8	8 30.5	22 3.0
28 T	14 25 11.4	13 2.2	23 9.0	22 4.3	15 10.4	26 12.4	21 19.7	20 29.4	13 8.9	21 7.7	8 32.9	22 2.9
31 S	14 37 1.0	14 1.8	23 9.7	24 9.1	12 56.5	25 55.4	20 44.8	20 27.7	13 15.7	21 7.6	8 35.3	22 3.0

NOVEMBER 1954

LONGITUDE at NOON

DAY	EPHEMERIS SIDEREAL TIME	☉	☊	☽	☿	♀	♂	♃	♄	♅	♆	♇
	h m s	° ′	° ′	° ′	° ′	° ′	° ′	° ′	° ′	° ′	° ′	° ′
1 M	14 40 57.6	8♏32.3	8♑37.6	11♑15.9	2♏43.0	29♏ 7.9	7♒14.4	29♋32.8	11♏39.9	27♋42.3	26♎16.8	26♌37.0
2 T	14 44 54.1	9 32.4	8 34.5	23 33.2	1R39.8	28R50.3	7 54.7	29 35.7	11 47.1	27 42.4	26 19.0	26 37.8
3 W	14 48 50.7	10 32.5	8 31.3	6♒ 8.3	0 45.3	28 30.4	8 35.0	29 38.4	11 54.3	27 42.4	26 21.2	26 38.5
4 T	14 52 47.3	11 32.6	8 28.1	19 5.9	0 0.8	28 8.3	9 15.5	29 41.0	12 1.5	27 42.4	26 23.4	26 39.3
5 F	14 56 43.8	12 32.7	8 24.9	2♓30.3	29♎27.4	27 44.0	9 56.1	29 43.3	12 8.7	27R42.3	26 25.5	26 40.0
6 S	15 0 40.4	13 32.9	8 21.7	16 23.9	29 5.5	27 17.6	10 36.8	29 45.5	12 15.9	27 42.1	26 27.7	26 40.6
7 S	15 4 36.9	14 33.1	8 18.6	0♈46.9	28 55.3	26 49.4	11 17.6	29 47.5	12 23.1	27 41.9	26 29.9	26 41.3
8 M	15 8 33.5	15 33.3	8 15.4	15 36.2	28D56.5	26 19.4	11 58.5	29 49.3	12 30.3	27 41.7	26 32.0	26 41.9
9 T	15 12 30.0	16 33.6	8 12.2	0♉45.2	29 8.6	25 47.8	12 39.5	29 50.8	12 37.5	27 41.4	26 34.1	26 42.5
10 W	15 16 26.6	17 33.8	8 9.0	16 4.2	29 30.9	25 14.8	13 20.6	29 52.2	12 44.7	27 41.0	26 36.3	26 43.0
11 T	15 20 23.1	18 34.1	8 5.9	1♊21.9	0♏ 2.5	24 40.6	14 1.8	29 53.4	12 51.9	27 40.6	26 38.4	26 43.6
12 F	15 24 19.7	19 34.5	8 2.7	16 27.7	0 42.6	24 5.5	14 43.0	29 54.4	12 59.0	27 40.1	26 40.5	26 44.0
13 S	15 28 16.3	20 34.8	7 59.5	1♋13.0	1 30.4	23 29.6	15 24.3	29 55.3	13 6.2	27 39.6	26 42.6	26 44.5
14 S	15 32 12.8	21 35.2	7 56.3	15 32.4	2 24.8	22 53.3	16 5.7	29 55.9	13 13.4	27 39.0	26 44.6	26 45.0
15 M	15 36 9.4	22 35.6	7 53.1	29 24.0	3 25.1	22 16.8	16 47.2	29 56.3	13 20.5	27 38.4	26 46.7	26 45.4
16 T	15 40 5.9	23 36.1	7 50.0	12♌48.6	4 30.6	21 40.3	17 28.8	29 56.5	13 27.7	27 37.7	26 48.8	26 45.7
17 W	15 44 2.5	24 36.6	7 46.8	25 48.6	5 40.5	21 4.1	18 10.4	29 56.5	13 34.8	27 37.0	26 50.8	26 46.1
18 T	15 47 59.0	25 37.1	7 43.6	8♍27.8	6 54.2	20 28.5	18 52.1	29R56.3	13 41.9	27 36.2	26 52.8	26 46.4
19 F	15 51 55.6	26 37.6	7 40.4	20 50.3	8 11.1	19 53.6	19 33.9	29 56.0	13 49.0	27 35.3	26 54.8	26 46.7
20 S	15 55 52.2	27 38.2	7 37.3	3♎ 0.1	9 30.8	19 19.8	20 15.7	29 55.4	13 56.1	27 34.5	26 56.8	26 47.0
21 S	15 59 48.7	28 38.9	7 34.1	15 0.7	10 53.0	18 47.2	20 57.7	29 54.6	14 3.2	27 33.6	26 58.9	26 47.3
22 M	16 3 45.3	29 39.5	7 30.9	26 55.4	12 17.0	18 16.0	21 39.7	29 53.7	14 10.3	27 32.6	27 0.8	26 47.5
23 T	16 7 41.8	0♐40.2	7 27.7	8♏46.6	13 42.7	17 46.4	22 21.7	29 52.5	14 17.3	27 31.5	27 2.8	26 47.6
24 W	16 11 38.4	1 40.8	7 24.6	20 36.6	15 9.8	17 18.7	23 3.8	29 51.1	14 24.3	27 30.4	27 4.7	26 47.8
25 T	16 15 34.9	2 41.6	7 21.4	2♐27.3	16 38.0	16 52.8	23 46.0	29 49.5	14 31.3	27 29.3	27 6.6	26 47.9
26 F	16 19 31.5	3 42.3	7 18.2	14 20.3	18 7.2	16 29.0	24 28.2	29 47.7	14 38.2	27 28.1	27 8.5	26 48.0
27 S	16 23 28.1	4 43.0	7 15.0	26 17.5	19 37.2	16 7.4	25 10.5	29 45.7	14 45.2	27 26.8	27 10.4	26 48.0
28 S	16 27 24.6	5 43.8	7 11.8	8♑21.0	21 7.8	15 48.1	25 52.9	29 43.6	14 52.1	27 25.5	27 12.2	26 48.0
29 M	16 31 21.2	6 44.6	7 8.7	20 33.2	22 39.0	15 31.1	26 35.3	29 41.2	14 59.0	27 24.2	27 14.0	26 48.0
30 T	16 35 17.7	7 45.4	7 5.5	2♒57.1	24 10.6	15 16.4	27 17.7	29 38.6	15 5.8	27 22.8	27 15.9	26 48.0

DECLINATION at NOON

DAY	EPHEMERIS SIDEREAL TIME	☉	☊	☽	☿	♀	♂	♃	♄	♅	♆	♇
1 M	14 40 57.6	14S21.2	23S 9.9	22S36.1	12S13.5	25S47.4	20S32.9	20N27.2	13S17.9	21N 7.6	8S36.1	22N 3.0
4 T	14 52 47.3	15 18.0	23 10.5	11 50.5	10 26.0	25 16.0	19 55.9	20 26.0	13 24.5	21 7.7	8 38.4	22 3.2
7 S	15 4 36.9	16 12.5	23 11.1	4N58.3	9 25.5	24 33.5	19 17.6	20 25.1	13 31.1	21 7.9	8 40.7	22 3.5
10 W	15 16 26.6	17 4.6	23 11.7	20 26.2	9 16.1	23 40.5	18 37.8	20 24.5	13 37.7	21 8.2	8 42.9	22 3.9
13 S	15 28 16.3	17 54.0	23 12.3	23 54.4	9 49.0	22 38.5	17 56.7	20 24.4	13 44.1	21 8.6	8 45.1	22 4.4
16 T	15 40 5.9	18 40.7	23 12.8	14 1.3	10 51.8	21 30.0	17 14.3	20 24.6	13 50.5	21 9.0	8 47.2	22 4.9
19 F	15 51 55.6	19 24.4	23 13.4	0S57.0	12 12.8	20 18.1	16 30.6	20 25.2	13 56.8	21 9.6	8 49.3	22 5.6
22 M	16 3 45.3	20 5.0	23 13.9	14 53.0	13 43.2	19 6.5	15 45.7	20 26.2	14 2.9	21 10.3	8 51.4	22 6.4
25 T	16 15 34.9	20 42.2	23 14.5	23 27.6	15 16.9	17 58.4	14 59.7	20 27.6	14 9.0	21 11.0	8 53.4	22 7.3
28 S	16 27 24.6	21 16.0	23 15.0	22 56.3	16 49.5	16 56.9	14 12.6	20 29.3	14 14.9	21 11.8	8 55.3	22 8.3

DECEMBER 1954

LONGITUDE at NOON

DAY	EPHEMERIS SIDEREAL TIME	☉	☊	☽	☿	♀	♂	♃	♄	♅	♆	♇
1 W	16 39 14.3	8♐46.2	7♑ 2.3	15♒35.9	25♏42.5	15♏ 4.3	28♒ 0.2	29♋35.9	15♏12.6	27♋21.4	27♎17.6	26♌47.9
2 T	16 43 10.8	9 47.1	6 59.1	28 33.1	27 14.7	14R54.5	28 42.7	29R32.9	15 19.4	27R19.9	27 19.4	26R47.8
3 F	16 47 7.4	10 47.9	6 56.0	11♓51.8	28 47.2	14 47.3	29 25.3	29 29.8	15 26.2	27 18.4	27 21.2	26 47.7
4 S	16 51 4.0	11 48.8	6 52.8	25 34.5	0♐19.8	14 42.5	0♓ 7.9	29 26.4	15 32.9	27 16.8	27 22.9	26 47.5
5 S	16 55 0.5	12 49.7	6 49.6	9♈42.2	1 52.6	14 40.2	0 50.6	29 22.9	15 39.6	27 15.2	27 24.6	26 47.3
6 M	16 58 57.1	13 50.6	6 46.4	24 13.5	3 25.5	14D40.4	1 33.2	29 19.2	15 46.3	27 13.6	27 26.3	26 47.1
7 T	17 2 53.6	14 51.5	6 43.3	9♉ 4.6	4 58.5	14 42.9	2 16.0	29 15.3	15 52.9	27 11.9	27 27.9	26 46.9
8 W	17 6 50.2	15 52.4	6 40.1	24 8.7	6 31.6	14 47.9	2 58.7	29 11.3	15 59.5	27 10.1	27 29.6	26 46.6
9 T	17 10 46.7	16 53.3	6 36.9	9♊17.2	8 4.8	14 55.1	3 41.5	29 7.0	16 6.0	27 8.3	27 31.2	26 46.3
10 F	17 14 43.3	17 54.3	6 33.7	24 20.4	9 38.0	15 4.7	4 24.3	29 2.6	16 12.5	27 6.5	27 32.8	26 45.9
11 S	17 18 39.9	18 55.2	6 30.6	9♋ 9.4	11 11.4	15 16.5	5 7.1	28 58.0	16 19.0	27 4.7	27 34.3	26 45.6
12 S	17 22 36.4	19 56.3	6 27.4	23 37.2	12 44.8	15 30.6	5 50.0	28 53.3	16 25.5	27 2.8	27 35.9	26 45.2
13 M	17 26 33.0	20 57.2	6 24.2	7♌39.4	14 18.3	15 46.7	6 32.8	28 48.3	16 31.8	27 0.9	27 37.4	26 44.8
14 T	17 30 29.5	21 58.3	6 21.0	21 14.5	15 51.9	16 4.9	7 15.7	28 43.2	16 38.2	26 58.9	27 38.9	26 44.4
15 W	17 34 26.1	22 59.3	6 17.8	4♍23.3	17 25.6	16 25.1	7 58.6	28 38.0	16 44.5	26 56.9	27 40.4	26 43.9
16 T	17 38 22.6	24 0.3	6 14.7	17 8.4	18 59.4	16 47.2	8 41.6	28 32.6	16 50.7	26 54.9	27 41.8	26 43.4
17 F	17 42 19.2	25 1.4	6 11.5	29 33.6	20 33.3	17 11.2	9 24.5	28 27.0	16 56.9	26 52.8	27 43.2	26 42.8
18 S	17 46 15.8	26 2.5	6 8.3	11♎43.2	22 7.4	17 37.0	10 7.5	28 21.2	17 3.1	26 50.7	27 44.6	26 42.3
19 S	17 50 12.3	27 3.6	6 5.1	23 41.8	23 41.6	18 4.5	10 50.5	28 15.3	17 9.2	26 48.6	27 46.0	26 41.7
20 M	17 54 8.9	28 4.7	6 2.0	5♏33.8	25 15.9	18 33.7	11 33.5	28 9.3	17 15.2	26 46.4	27 47.3	26 41.1
21 T	17 58 5.4	29 5.8	5 58.8	17 22.9	26 50.4	19 4.5	12 16.5	28 3.1	17 21.2	26 44.2	27 48.6	26 40.4
22 W	18 2 2.0	0♑ 6.9	5 55.6	29 12.9	28 25.2	19 36.8	12 59.5	27 56.8	17 27.2	26 41.9	27 49.8	26 39.8
23 T	18 5 58.6	1 8.0	5 52.4	11♐ 6.5	0♑ 0.1	20 10.6	13 42.6	27 50.4	17 33.1	26 39.7	27 51.1	26 39.1
24 F	18 9 55.1	2 9.2	5 49.3	23 6.2	1 35.2	20 45.9	14 25.7	27 43.8	17 38.9	26 37.4	27 52.3	26 38.3
25 S	18 13 51.7	3 10.3	5 46.1	5♑14.0	3 10.6	21 22.5	15 8.7	27 37.1	17 44.7	26 35.1	27 53.5	26 37.6
26 S	18 17 48.2	4 11.5	5 42.9	17 31.3	4 46.2	22 0.4	15 51.8	27 30.2	17 50.4	26 32.7	27 54.6	26 36.8
27 M	18 21 44.8	5 12.7	5 39.7	29 59.6	6 22.1	22 39.6	16 34.9	27 23.3	17 56.0	26 30.4	27 55.7	26 36.0
28 T	18 25 41.3	6 13.8	5 36.6	12♒39.9	7 58.3	23 20.0	17 18.0	27 16.3	18 1.6	26 28.0	27 56.8	26 35.2
29 W	18 29 37.9	7 15.0	5 33.4	25 33.6	9 34.7	24 1.6	18 1.2	27 9.1	18 7.2	26 25.6	27 57.9	26 34.3
30 T	18 33 34.5	8 16.2	5 30.2	8♓41.8	11 11.5	24 44.2	18 44.3	27 1.8	18 12.6	26 23.1	27 58.9	26 33.5
31 F	18 37 31.0	9 17.3	5 27.0	22 5.5	12 48.5	25 28.0	19 27.4	26 54.5	18 18.0	26 20.7	27 59.9	26 32.6

DECLINATION at NOON

DAY	EPHEMERIS SIDEREAL TIME	☉	☊	☽	☿	♀	♂	♃	♄	♅	♆	♇
1 W	16 39 14.3	21S46.1	23S15.5	12S56.6	18S18.1	16S 3.9	13S24.5	20N31.5	14S20.7	21N12.7	8S57.1	22N 9.3
4 S	16 51 4.0	22 12.5	23 16.0	2N59.1	19 40.8	15 20.7	12 35.5	20 34.0	14 26.4	21 13.7	8 58.9	22 10.5
7 T	17 2 53.6	22 35.1	23 16.5	18 40.7	20 56.1	14 47.8	11 45.7	20 36.8	14 31.9	21 14.8	9 0.6	22 11.8
10 F	17 14 43.3	22 53.7	23 17.0	24 20.9	22 2.8	14 25.0	10 55.1	20 39.9	14 37.3	21 15.9	9 2.2	22 13.1
13 M	17 26 33.0	23 8.2	23 17.4	15 38.5	23 0.0	14 11.8	10 3.7	20 43.4	14 42.5	21 17.1	9 3.7	22 14.5
16 T	17 38 22.6	23 18.6	23 17.9	0 27.6	23 47.0	14 7.3	9 11.8	20 47.1	14 47.6	21 18.3	9 5.1	22 16.0
19 S	17 50 12.3	23 24.7	23 18.3	13S51.9	24 23.2	14 10.5	8 19.2	20 51.1	14 52.5	21 19.6	9 6.4	22 17.5
22 W	18 2 2.0	23 26.7	23 18.7	23 2.9	24 47.7	14 20.5	7 26.2	20 55.3	14 57.2	21 20.9	9 7.7	22 19.1
25 S	18 13 51.7	23 24.4	23 19.2	23 22.1	25 0.1	14 36.0	6 32.7	20 59.7	15 1.7	21 22.3	9 8.8	22 20.8
28 T	18 25 41.3	23 17.9	23 19.6	13 56.3	24 59.9	14 56.2	5 38.9	21 4.3	15 6.0	21 23.7	9 9.9	22 22.5
31 F	18 37 31.0	23 7.2	23 20.0	1N35.6	24 46.5	15 20.1	4 44.8	21 9.0	15 10.1	21 25.2	9 10.8	22 24.3

JANUARY 1955

DAY	EPHEMERIS SIDEREAL TIME	☉	☊	☽	☿	♀	♂	♃	♄	♅	♆	♇
	h m s	° ′	° ′	° ′	° ′	° ′	° ′	° ′	° ′	° ′	° ′	° ′
						LONGITUDE at NOON						
1 S	18 41 27.6	10♑18.5	5♑23.8	5♈45.7	14♑25.8	26♏12.8	20♓10.5	26♋47.1	18♏23.4	26♋18.2	28♎ 0.9	26♌31.6
2 S	18 45 24.1	11 19.7	5 20.7	19 42.7	16 3.5	26 58.6	20 53.7	26R39.6	18 28.7	26R15.8	28 1.8	26R30.8
3 M	18 49 20.7	12 20.8	5 17.5	3♉55.8	17 41.5	27 45.3	21 36.8	26 32.0	18 33.9	26 13.3	28 2.7	26 29.8
4 T	18 53 17.3	13 22.0	5 14.3	18 22.9	19 19.8	28 33.0	22 19.9	26 24.3	18 39.1	26 10.7	28 3.6	26 28.8
5 W	18 57 13.8	14 23.1	5 11.1	3♊ 0.6	20 58.3	29 21.5	23 3.0	26 16.6	18 44.1	26 8.2	28 4.4	26 27.8
6 T	19 1 10.4	15 24.3	5 8.0	17 43.9	22 37.1	0♐10.9	23 46.2	26 8.8	18 49.1	26 5.7	28 5.2	26 26.8
7 F	19 5 6.9	16 25.4	5 4.8	2♋26.3	24 16.2	1 1.1	24 29.2	26 1.0	18 54.1	26 3.1	28 6.0	26 25.7
8 S	19 9 3.5	17 26.5	5 1.6	17 1.2	25 55.5	1 52.1	25 12.3	25 53.1	18 58.9	26 0.5	28 6.7	26 24.6
9 S	19 13 0.0	18 27.6	4 58.4	1♌22.0	27 35.0	2 43.8	25 55.4	25 45.1	19 3.7	25 57.9	28 7.5	26 23.5
10 M	19 16 56.6	19 28.8	4 55.3	15 23.5	29 14.7	3 36.3	26 38.5	25 37.2	19 8.4	25 55.4	28 8.1	26 22.4
11 T	19 20 53.2	20 29.9	4 52.1	29 2.2	0♒54.4	4 29.5	27 21.5	25 29.1	19 13.0	25 52.8	28 8.8	26 21.3
12 W	19 24 49.7	21 31.0	4 48.9	12♍17.0	2 34.1	5 23.4	28 4.6	25 21.1	19 17.6	25 50.2	28 9.4	26 20.1
13 T	19 28 46.3	22 32.1	4 45.7	25 8.3	4 13.7	6 18.0	28 47.6	25 13.1	19 22.1	25 47.6	28 9.9	26 19.0
14 F	19 32 42.8	23 33.2	4 42.6	7♎38.7	5 53.1	7 13.1	29 30.7	25 5.0	19 26.5	25 44.9	28 10.5	26 17.8
15 S	19 36 39.4	24 34.3	4 39.4	19 51.7	7 32.2	8 8.9	0♈13.7	24 56.9	19 30.8	25 42.3	28 11.0	26 16.6
16 S	19 40 35.9	25 35.4	4 36.2	1♏51.8	9 10.7	9 5.2	0 56.7	24 48.8	19 35.1	25 39.7	28 11.4	26 15.3
17 M	19 44 32.5	26 36.6	4 33.0	13 44.0	10 48.5	10 2.1	1 39.7	24 40.8	19 39.2	25 37.1	28 11.9	26 14.1
18 T	19 48 29.1	27 37.7	4 29.8	25 33.0	12 25.4	10 59.6	2 22.7	24 32.7	19 43.3	25 34.5	28 12.3	26 12.8
19 W	19 52 25.6	28 38.7	4 26.7	7♐23.7	14 1.0	11 57.5	3 5.6	24 24.6	19 47.3	25 31.9	28 12.6	26 11.6
20 T	19 56 22.2	29 39.8	4 23.5	19 20.3	15 35.1	12 56.0	3 48.6	24 16.6	19 51.2	25 29.3	28 13.0	26 10.3
21 F	20 0 18.7	0♒40.9	4 20.3	1♑26.5	17 7.3	13 54.9	4 31.5	24 8.6	19 55.1	25 26.7	28 13.3	26 9.0
22 S	20 4 15.3	1 42.0	4 17.1	13 45.1	18 37.1	14 54.3	5 14.5	24 0.7	19 58.8	25 24.1	28 13.6	26 7.7
23 S	20 8 11.8	2 43.1	4 14.0	26 18.1	20 4.1	15 54.1	5 57.5	23 52.8	20 2.5	25 21.5	28 13.8	26 6.4
24 M	20 12 8.4	3 44.1	4 10.8	9♒ 6.4	21 27.6	16 54.3	6 40.4	23 44.9	20 6.1	25 18.9	28 14.0	26 5.0
25 T	20 16 5.0	4 45.2	4 7.6	22 9.9	22 47.1	17 54.9	7 23.3	23 37.1	20 9.5	25 16.4	28 14.2	26 3.7
26 W	20 20 1.5	5 46.2	4 4.4	5♓27.8	24 2.0	18 56.0	8 6.1	23 29.3	20 12.9	25 13.8	28 14.3	26 2.3
27 T	20 23 58.1	6 47.2	4 1.3	18 58.6	25 11.4	19 57.3	8 49.0	23 21.6	20 16.2	25 11.2	28 14.4	26 0.9
28 F	20 27 54.6	7 48.2	3 58.1	2♈40.7	26 14.5	20 59.1	9 31.8	23 14.0	20 19.4	25 8.7	28 14.4	25 59.5
29 S	20 31 51.2	8 49.1	3 54.9	16 32.1	27 10.7	22 1.2	10 14.7	23 6.5	20 22.6	25 6.2	28 14.4	25 58.1
30 S	20 35 47.7	9 50.1	3 51.7	0♉31.3	27 59.0	23 3.6	10 57.5	22 59.0	20 25.6	25 3.7	28 14.4	25 56.7
31 M	20 39 44.3	10 51.0	3 48.5	14 36.8	28 38.7	24 6.4	11 40.2	22 51.6	20 28.5	25 1.2	28 14.4	25 55.3
						DECLINATION at NOON						
1 S	18 41 27.6	23S 2.6	23S 20.1	7N 8.8	24S 39.0	15S 28.7	4S 26.7	21N 10.6	15S 11.4	21N 25.6	9S 11.1	22N 24.9
4 T	18 53 17.3	22 46.4	23 20.5	21 2.0	24 7.4	15 56.1	3 32.3	21 15.4	15 15.3	21 27.1	9 11.9	22 26.8
7 F	19 5 6.9	22 26.1	23 20.9	23 42.7	23 21.8	16 25.2	2 37.8	21 20.2	15 18.9	21 28.6	9 12.6	22 28.7
10 M	19 16 56.6	22 1.8	23 21.2	12 59.2	22 22.1	16 55.3	1 43.3	21 25.1	15 22.4	21 30.1	9 13.2	22 30.6
13 T	19 28 46.3	21 33.7	23 21.6	2S 49.6	21 8.4	17 25.5	0 48.8	21 29.9	15 25.6	21 31.6	9 13.6	22 32.5
16 S	19 40 35.9	21 1.8	23 21.9	16 32.7	19 41.7	17 55.4	0N 5.7	21 34.7	15 28.5	21 33.1	9 14.0	22 34.5
19 W	19 52 25.6	20 26.2	23 22.2	23 59.6	18 3.3	18 24.2	0 59.9	21 39.4	15 31.3	21 34.5	9 14.3	22 36.4
22 S	20 4 15.3	19 47.2	23 22.5	21 59.0	16 16.1	18 51.4	1 54.0	21 44.0	15 33.8	21 36.0	9 14.4	22 38.4
25 T	20 16 5.0	19 4.8	23 22.8	10 31.4	14 25.1	19 16.5	2 47.8	21 48.4	15 36.1	21 37.4	9 14.5	22 40.4
28 F	20 27 54.6	18 19.4	23 23.1	5N 49.9	12 37.6	19 39.0	3 41.3	21 52.7	15 38.2	21 38.8	9 14.4	22 42.3
31 M	20 39 44.3	17 30.9	23 23.4	20 3.3	11 3.6	19 58.5	4 34.3	21 56.7	15 40.0	21 40.2	9 14.2	22 44.3

FEBRUARY 1955

DAY	EPHEMERIS SIDEREAL TIME	☉	☊	☽	☿	♀	♂	♃	♄	♅	♆	♇
						LONGITUDE at NOON						
1 T	20 43 40.8	11♒51.9	3♑45.4	28♉47.2	29♒ 8.9	25♐ 9.4	12♈23.0	22♋44.4	20♏31.3	24♋58.7	28♎14.3	25♌53.8
2 W	20 47 37.4	12 52.8	3 42.2	13♊ 0.9	29 29.0	26 12.8	13 5.7	22R37.2	20 34.1	24R56.2	28R14.2	25R52.4
3 T	20 51 34.0	13 53.6	3 39.0	27 15.8	29 38.5	27 16.5	13 48.4	22 30.1	20 36.7	24 53.8	28 14.0	25 51.0
4 F	20 55 30.5	14 54.5	3 35.8	11♋29.1	29R37.0	28 20.4	14 31.1	22 23.1	20 39.3	24 51.4	28 13.9	25 49.5
5 S	20 59 27.1	15 55.3	3 32.7	25 37.3	29 24.5	29 24.6	15 13.7	22 16.3	20 41.7	24 49.0	28 13.6	25 48.1
6 S	21 3 23.6	16 56.1	3 29.5	9♌36.4	29 0.9	0♑29.1	15 56.4	22 9.5	20 44.1	24 46.6	28 13.4	25 46.6
7 M	21 7 20.2	17 56.8	3 26.3	23 22.4	28 27.0	1 33.9	16 39.0	22 2.9	20 46.4	24 44.3	28 13.1	25 45.1
8 T	21 11 16.7	18 57.6	3 23.1	6♍51.8	27 43.3	2 38.9	17 21.5	21 56.4	20 48.5	24 42.0	28 12.8	25 43.6
9 W	21 15 13.3	19 58.3	3 19.9	20 2.2	26 51.1	3 44.1	18 4.1	21 50.1	20 50.6	24 39.7	28 12.4	25 42.2
10 T	21 19 9.8	20 59.0	3 16.8	2♎52.8	25 51.9	4 49.6	18 46.6	21 43.8	20 52.5	24 37.4	28 12.1	25 40.7
11 F	21 23 6.4	21 59.7	3 13.6	15 24.5	24 47.2	5 55.3	19 29.1	21 37.8	20 54.4	24 35.1	28 11.6	25 39.2
12 S	21 27 3.0	23 0.4	3 10.4	27 39.4	23 38.9	7 1.3	20 11.6	21 31.9	20 56.2	24 33.0	28 11.2	25 37.8
13 S	21 30 59.5	24 1.1	3 7.2	9♏41.0	22 29.0	8 7.5	20 54.0	21 26.1	20 57.9	24 30.8	28 10.8	25 36.3
14 M	21 34 56.1	25 1.7	3 4.1	21 33.9	21 19.3	9 13.9	21 36.4	21 20.4	20 59.5	24 28.6	28 10.3	25 34.8
15 T	21 38 52.6	26 2.3	3 0.9	3♐23.1	20 11.5	10 20.4	22 18.8	21 14.9	21 0.9	24 26.5	28 9.7	25 33.3
16 W	21 42 49.2	27 2.9	2 57.7	15 13.9	19 7.3	11 27.2	23 1.2	21 9.6	21 2.3	24 24.4	28 9.1	25 31.8
17 T	21 46 45.7	28 3.5	2 54.5	27 11.6	18 7.9	12 34.1	23 43.5	21 4.4	21 3.5	24 22.4	28 8.5	25 30.3
18 F	21 50 42.3	29 4.0	2 51.4	9♑21.1	17 14.5	13 41.2	24 25.8	20 59.3	21 4.7	24 20.4	28 7.9	25 28.8
19 S	21 54 38.8	0♓ 4.5	2 48.2	21 46.6	16 27.7	14 48.5	25 8.1	20 54.5	21 5.7	24 18.4	28 7.2	25 27.4
20 S	21 58 35.4	1 5.1	2 45.0	4♒31.2	15 48.1	15 56.0	25 50.3	20 49.8	21 6.7	24 16.4	28 6.5	25 25.9
21 M	22 2 31.9	2 5.5	2 41.8	17 36.5	15 16.0	17 3.6	26 32.6	20 45.3	21 7.5	24 14.5	28 5.8	25 24.4
22 T	22 6 28.5	3 6.0	2 38.6	1♓ 2.3	14 51.3	18 11.3	27 14.8	20 40.9	21 8.3	24 12.6	28 5.0	25 22.9
23 W	22 10 25.1	4 6.4	2 35.5	14 46.6	14 34.2	19 19.2	27 56.9	20 36.8	21 8.9	24 10.8	28 4.2	25 21.4
24 T	22 14 21.6	5 6.8	2 32.3	28 45.7	14 24.3	20 27.3	28 39.1	20 32.8	21 9.5	24 9.0	28 3.4	25 20.0
25 F	22 18 18.2	6 7.2	2 29.1	12♈55.0	14 21.4	21 35.5	29 21.2	20 29.0	21 9.9	24 7.2	28 2.6	25 18.5
26 S	22 22 14.7	7 7.5	2 25.9	27 9.6	14D25.2	22 43.8	0♉ 3.3	20 25.4	21 10.2	24 5.5	28 1.7	25 17.1
27 S	22 26 11.3	8 7.8	2 22.8	11♉25.0	14 35.3	23 52.2	0 45.3	20 21.9	21 10.4	24 3.9	28 0.8	25 15.6
28 M	22 30 7.8	9 8.1	2 19.6	25 37.7	14 51.3	25 0.8	1 27.3	20 18.7	21 10.6	24 2.2	27 59.9	25 14.2
						DECLINATION at NOON						
1 T	20 43 40.8	17S 14.1	23S 23.5	22N 53.8	10S 37.3	20S 4.2	4N 51.9	21N 58.0	15S 40.5	21N 40.6	9S 14.1	22N 44.9
4 F	20 55 30.5	16 22.0	23 23.8	22 22.1	9 39.3	20 19.1	5 44.3	22 1.8	15 42.0	21 41.9	9 13.8	22 46.9
7 M	21 7 20.2	15 27.4	23 24.0	10 4.9	9 19.4	20 30.2	6 36.1	22 5.4	15 43.3	21 43.2	9 13.3	22 48.8
10 T	21 19 9.8	14 30.4	23 24.3	5S 51.2	9 39.2	20 37.1	7 27.3	22 8.7	15 44.3	21 44.4	9 12.8	22 50.6
13 S	21 30 59.5	13 31.1	23 24.5	18 41.3	10 30.9	20 39.6	8 17.9	22 11.7	15 45.1	21 45.6	9 12.2	22 52.4
16 W	21 42 49.2	12 29.9	23 24.7	24 17.4	11 39.4	20 37.5	9 7.7	22 14.5	15 45.6	21 46.7	9 11.4	22 54.2
19 S	21 54 38.8	11 26.9	23 24.9	20 9.3	12 49.1	20 30.7	9 56.7	22 17.0	15 45.9	21 47.7	9 10.6	22 55.9
22 T	22 6 28.5	10 22.2	23 25.1	7 7.0	13 49.5	20 19.1	10 44.9	22 19.2	15 46.0	21 48.7	9 9.7	22 57.6
25 F	22 18 18.2	9 16.1	23 25.3	9N 41.8	14 35.3	20 2.6	11 32.2	22 21.2	15 45.8	21 49.6	9 8.7	22 59.2
28 M	22 30 7.8	8 8.8	23 25.5	22 10.4	15 4.8	19 41.2	12 18.6	22 22.9	15 45.3	21 50.5	9 7.6	23 0.8

MARCH 1955

DAY	EPHEMERIS SIDEREAL TIME h m s	☉ ° ′	☊ ° ′	☽ ° ′	☿ ° ′	♀ ° ′	♂ ° ′	♃ ° ′	♄ ° ′	♅ ° ′	♆ ° ′	♇ ° ′
LONGITUDE at NOON												
1 T	22 34 4.4	10♓ 8.3	2♑16.4	9♊45.7	15♒12.9	26♑ 9.5	2♉ 9.3	20♋15.6	21♏10.6	24♋ 0.6	27♎58.9	25♌12.7
2 W	22 38 0.9	11 8.5	2 13.2	23 47.7	15 39.7	27 18.3	2 51.3	20R12.7	21R10.5	23R59.1	27R57.9	25R11.3
3 T	22 41 57.5	12 8.7	2 10.0	7♋43.3	16 11.3	28 27.2	3 33.2	20 10.1	21 10.3	23 57.6	27 56.9	25 9.9
4 F	22 45 54.0	13 8.8	2 6.9	21 32.0	16 47.4	29 36.2	4 15.1	20 7.6	21 10.0	23 56.1	27 55.9	25 8.5
5 S	22 49 50.6	14 9.0	2 3.7	5♌13.3	17 27.7	0♒45.4	4 57.0	20 5.3	21 9.7	23 54.8	27 54.9	25 7.1
6 S	22 53 47.1	15 9.0	2 0.5	18 45.7	18 11.9	1 54.7	5 38.8	20 3.2	21 9.2	23 53.4	27 53.8	25 5.8
7 M	22 57 43.7	16 9.1	1 57.3	2♍ 7.8	18 59.7	3 4.0	6 20.6	20 1.3	21 8.6	23 52.1	27 52.7	25 4.4
8 T	23 1 40.2	17 9.0	1 54.2	15 17.5	19 50.9	4 13.5	7 2.3	19 59.6	21 7.9	23 50.8	27 51.5	25 3.0
9 W	23 5 36.8	18 9.0	1 51.0	28 13.3	20 45.3	5 23.0	7 44.0	19 58.1	21 7.1	23 49.6	27 50.4	25 1.7
10 T	23 9 33.4	19 8.9	1 47.8	10♎54.0	21 42.6	6 32.6	8 25.7	19 56.7	21 6.2	23 48.4	27 49.2	25 0.3
11 F	23 13 29.9	20 8.8	1 44.6	23 19.7	22 42.7	7 42.4	9 7.4	19 55.6	21 5.2	23 47.3	27 48.0	24 59.0
12 S	23 17 26.5	21 8.7	1 41.4	5♏31.4	23 45.4	8 52.2	9 49.0	19 54.6	21 4.1	23 46.2	27 46.8	24 57.7
13 S	23 21 23.0	22 8.6	1 38.3	17 31.6	24 50.5	10 2.1	10 30.6	19 53.9	21 2.9	23 45.2	27 45.5	24 56.4
14 M	23 25 19.6	23 8.4	1 35.1	29 23.7	25 57.9	11 12.2	11 12.1	19 53.3	21 1.6	23 44.2	27 44.3	24 55.1
15 T	23 29 16.1	24 8.2	1 31.9	11♐12.2	27 7.5	12 22.2	11 53.6	19 53.0	21 0.2	23 43.3	27 43.0	24 53.8
16 W	23 33 12.7	25 7.9	1 28.7	23 2.1	28 19.2	13 32.4	12 35.1	19 52.8	20 58.7	23 42.4	27 41.7	24 52.6
17 T	23 37 9.2	26 7.6	1 25.6	4♑59.0	29 32.8	14 42.7	13 16.5	19 52.8	20 57.2	23 41.6	27 40.3	24 51.3
18 F	23 41 5.8	27 7.3	1 22.4	17 8.2	0♓48.4	15 53.0	13 58.0	19D53.1	20 55.5	23 40.8	27 39.0	24 50.1
19 S	23 45 2.3	28 7.0	1 19.2	29 35.2	2 5.8	17 3.4	14 39.4	19 53.5	20 53.7	23 40.1	27 37.6	24 48.9
20 S	23 48 58.9	29 6.7	1 16.0	12♒24.1	3 24.9	18 13.9	15 20.7	19 54.1	20 51.8	23 39.5	27 36.2	24 47.7
21 M	23 52 55.4	0♈ 6.3	1 12.8	25 37.9	4 45.7	19 24.4	16 2.0	19 54.9	20 49.9	23 38.8	27 34.8	24 46.5
22 T	23 56 52.0	1 5.9	1 9.7	9♓17.3	6 8.1	20 35.0	16 43.3	19 55.9	20 47.8	23 38.3	27 33.4	24 45.4
23 W	0 0 48.5	2 5.4	1 6.5	23 20.8	7 32.1	21 45.7	17 24.6	19 57.1	20 45.7	23 37.8	27 32.0	24 44.3
24 T	0 4 45.1	3 4.9	1 3.3	7♈43.8	8 57.7	22 56.4	18 5.8	19 58.5	20 43.5	23 37.3	27 30.5	24 43.1
25 F	0 8 41.6	4 4.4	1 0.1	22 19.9	10 24.7	24 7.2	18 47.0	20 0.0	20 41.1	23 36.9	27 29.1	24 42.1
26 S	0 12 38.2	5 3.9	0 57.0	7♉ 1.5	11 53.3	25 18.1	19 28.2	20 1.8	20 38.8	23 36.6	27 27.6	24 41.0
27 S	0 16 34.8	6 3.3	0 53.8	21 41.1	13 23.4	26 29.0	20 9.4	20 3.8	20 36.3	23 36.3	27 26.1	24 40.0
28 M	0 20 31.3	7 2.7	0 50.6	6♊12.6	14 54.8	27 39.9	20 50.5	20 5.9	20 33.7	23 36.1	27 24.6	24 38.9
29 T	0 24 27.9	8 2.0	0 47.4	20 31.8	16 27.7	28 50.9	21 31.5	20 8.3	20 31.0	23 35.9	27 23.1	24 37.9
30 W	0 28 24.4	9 1.3	0 44.2	4♋36.8	18 2.1	0♓ 1.9	22 12.6	20 10.8	20 28.3	23 35.7	27 21.6	24 36.9
31 T	0 32 21.0	10 0.5	0 41.1	18 27.0	19 37.8	1 13.0	22 53.6	20 13.5	20 25.5	23 35.7	27 20.0	24 36.0
DECLINATION at NOON												
1 T	22 34 4.4	7S46.1	23S25.5	23N54.6	15S11.0	19S32.9	12N33.8	22N23.4	15S45.1	21N50.7	9S 7.2	23N 1.2
4 F	22 45 54.0	6 37.4	23 25.7	20 8.1	15 18.8	19 5.0	13 18.8	22 24.7	15 44.4	21 51.5	9 6.0	23 2.7
7 M	22 57 43.7	5 27.9	23 25.8	6 40.4	15 11.3	18 32.2	14 2.7	22 25.8	15 43.4	21 52.1	9 4.7	23 4.0
10 T	23 9 33.4	4 17.7	23 26.0	8S52.3	14 49.1	17 54.8	14 45.4	22 26.5	15 42.2	21 52.7	9 3.3	23 5.3
13 S	23 21 23.0	3 7.1	23 26.1	20 25.8	14 13.1	17 12.7	15 27.0	22 27.1	15 40.8	21 53.2	9 1.9	23 6.5
16 W	23 33 12.7	1 56.1	23 26.2	24 0.4	13 23.8	16 26.2	16 7.3	22 27.3	15 39.2	21 53.6	9 0.4	23 7.6
19 S	23 45 2.3	0 44.9	23 26.3	17 54.8	12 21.9	15 35.5	16 46.4	22 27.3	15 37.3	21 54.0	8 58.9	23 8.7
22 T	23 56 52.0	0N26.2	23 26.4	3 46.4	11 8.0	14 40.8	17 24.1	22 27.0	15 35.3	21 54.2	8 57.3	23 9.6
25 F	0 8 41.6	1 37.2	23 26.5	13N 0.5	9 42.5	13 42.3	18 0.5	22 26.5	15 33.1	21 54.4	8 55.6	23 10.4
28 M	0 20 31.3	2 47.8	23 26.6	23 22.1	8 5.7	12 40.3	18 35.4	22 25.6	15 30.6	21 54.5	8 54.0	23 11.1
31 T	0 32 21.0	3 57.9	23 26.6	20 35.9	6 18.3	11 35.0	19 8.9	22 24.6	15 28.1	21 54.5	8 52.3	23 11.8

APRIL 1955

DAY	EPHEMERIS SIDEREAL TIME h m s	☉ ° ′	☊ ° ′	☽ ° ′	☿ ° ′	♀ ° ′	♂ ° ′	♃ ° ′	♄ ° ′	♅ ° ′	♆ ° ′	♇ ° ′
LONGITUDE at NOON												
1 F	0 36 17.5	10♈59.8	0♑37.9	2♌ 3.3	21♓15.0	2♓24.1	23♉34.5	20♋16.3	20♏22.6	23♋35.6	27♎18.5	24♌35.0
2 S	0 40 14.1	11 58.9	0 34.7	15 26.4	22 53.5	3 35.3	24 15.5	20 19.4	20R19.6	23D35.7	27R16.9	24R34.1
3 S	0 44 10.6	12 58.1	0 31.5	28 37.5	24 33.5	4 46.5	24 56.3	20 22.6	20 16.5	23 35.7	27 15.3	24 33.2
4 M	0 48 7.2	13 57.2	0 28.3	11♍37.1	26 14.9	5 57.7	25 37.2	20 26.0	20 13.4	23 35.9	27 13.7	24 32.3
5 T	0 52 3.7	14 56.2	0 25.2	24 25.3	27 57.8	7 9.0	26 18.0	20 29.6	20 10.2	23 36.1	27 12.1	24 31.5
6 W	0 56 0.3	15 55.3	0 22.0	7♎ 2.2	29 42.1	8 20.4	26 58.8	20 33.4	20 6.9	23 36.3	27 10.5	24 30.6
7 T	0 59 56.8	16 54.3	0 18.8	19 27.7	1♈27.9	9 31.7	27 39.6	20 37.3	20 3.6	23 36.6	27 8.9	24 29.8
8 F	1 3 53.4	17 53.2	0 15.6	1♏42.2	3 15.1	10 43.2	28 20.3	20 41.4	20 0.1	23 37.0	27 7.3	24 29.0
9 S	1 7 49.9	18 52.1	0 12.5	13 46.4	5 3.8	11 54.6	29 0.9	20 45.7	19 56.7	23 37.4	27 5.7	24 28.3
10 S	1 11 46.5	19 51.0	0 9.3	25 42.2	6 54.0	13 6.1	29 41.6	20 50.1	19 53.1	23 37.8	27 4.1	24 27.6
11 M	1 15 43.0	20 49.9	0 6.1	7♐32.1	8 45.7	14 17.7	0♊22.2	20 54.7	19 49.5	23 38.3	27 2.4	24 26.8
12 T	1 19 39.6	21 48.7	0 2.9	19 19.5	10 38.9	15 29.3	1 2.8	20 59.5	19 45.8	23 38.9	27 0.8	24 26.2
13 W	1 23 36.2	22 47.5	29♐59.7	1♑ 8.7	12 33.6	16 40.9	1 43.3	21 4.4	19 42.1	23 39.5	26 59.2	24 25.5
14 T	1 27 32.7	23 46.3	29 56.6	13 4.6	14 29.7	17 52.5	2 23.9	21 9.5	19 38.3	23 40.2	26 57.5	24 24.9
15 F	1 31 29.3	24 45.1	29 53.4	25 12.4	16 27.4	19 4.2	3 4.3	21 14.8	19 34.5	23 40.9	26 55.9	24 24.3
16 S	1 35 25.8	25 43.8	29 50.2	7♒37.5	18 26.6	20 16.0	3 44.9	21 20.2	19 30.6	23 41.7	26 54.3	24 23.7
17 S	1 39 22.4	26 42.5	29 47.0	20 24.9	20 27.1	21 27.8	4 25.3	21 25.8	19 26.7	23 42.6	26 52.6	24 23.2
18 M	1 43 18.9	27 41.2	29 43.9	3♓38.4	22 29.0	22 39.5	5 5.7	21 31.5	19 22.7	23 43.5	26 51.0	24 22.7
19 T	1 47 15.5	28 39.8	29 40.7	17 20.1	24 32.2	23 51.4	5 46.0	21 37.4	19 18.7	23 44.4	26 49.4	24 22.2
20 W	1 51 12.0	29 38.4	29 37.5	1♈29.8	26 36.6	25 3.2	6 26.4	21 43.4	19 14.6	23 45.4	26 47.7	24 21.7
21 T	1 55 8.6	0♉37.0	29 34.3	16 4.0	28 42.2	26 15.1	7 6.7	21 49.6	19 10.4	23 46.4	26 46.1	24 21.2
22 F	1 59 5.1	1 35.5	29 31.2	0♉56.3	0♉48.7	27 27.0	7 47.0	21 56.0	19 6.3	23 47.5	26 44.4	24 20.8
23 S	2 3 1.7	2 34.1	29 28.0	15 58.1	2 56.0	28 38.9	8 27.2	22 2.4	19 2.0	23 48.7	26 42.8	24 20.4
24 S	2 6 58.2	3 32.5	29 24.8	0♊59.8	5 4.0	29 50.8	9 7.4	22 9.1	18 57.8	23 49.8	26 41.2	24 20.1
25 M	2 10 54.8	4 31.0	29 21.6	15 52.9	7 12.5	1♈ 2.8	9 47.6	22 15.8	18 53.5	23 51.1	26 39.5	24 19.7
26 T	2 14 51.4	5 29.4	29 18.4	0♋30.6	9 21.1	2 14.8	10 27.8	22 22.7	18 49.2	23 52.4	26 37.9	24 19.4
27 W	2 18 47.9	6 27.8	29 1..3	14 48.9	11 29.6	3 26.8	11 7.9	22 29.8	18 44.9	23 53.7	26 36.3	24 19.2
28 T	2 22 44.5	7 26.1	29 12.1	28 46.0	13 37.8	4 38.8	11 48.0	22 37.0	18 40.5	23 55.1	26 34.7	24 18.9
29 F	2 26 41.0	8 24.4	29 8.9	12♌22.3	15 45.4	5 50.9	12 28.1	22 44.3	18 36.1	23 56.6	26 33.1	24 18.7
30 S	2 30 37.6	9 22.7	29 5.7	25 39.3	17 52.0	7 2.9	13 8.1	22 51.7	18 31.7	23 58.1	26 31.5	24 18.5
DECLINATION at NOON												
1 F	0 36 17.5	4N21.1	23S26.6	17N 6.1	5S40.2	11S12.5	19N19.7	22N24.2	15S27.2	21N54.5	8S51.7	23N12.0
4 M	0 48 7.2	5 30.3	23 26.7	2 47.5	3 39.1	10 3.3	19 51.2	22 22.8	15 24.3	21 54.4	8 50.0	23 12.5
7 T	0 59 56.8	6 38.6	23 26.7	11S58.5	1 28.5	8 51.4	20 21.1	22 21.1	15 21.4	21 54.2	8 48.2	23 12.9
10 S	1 11 46.5	7 45.9	23 26.7	21 52.0	0N51.2	7 37.1	20 49.5	22 19.2	15 18.3	21 53.9	8 46.4	23 13.1
13 W	1 23 36.2	8 52.0	23 26.7	23 12.6	3 18.9	6 20.7	21 16.2	22 17.0	15 15.1	21 53.6	8 44.6	23 13.3
16 S	1 35 25.8	9 56.8	23 26.7	15 15.4	5 53.3	5 2.5	21 41.3	22 14.6	15 11.8	21 53.1	8 42.9	23 13.4
19 T	1 47 15.5	11 0.1	23 26.7	0 24.3	8 32.4	3 42.8	22 4.7	22 12.0	15 8.3	21 52.6	8 41.1	23 13.4
22 F	1 59 5.1	12 1.9	23 26.7	15N48.1	11 13.3	2 21.9	22 26.4	22 9.0	15 4.8	21 52.0	8 39.3	23 13.3
25 M	2 10 54.8	13 1.8	23 26.6	23 44.2	13 52.0	1 0.1	22 46.3	22 5.9	15 1.3	21 51.3	8 37.5	23 13.0
28 T	2 22 44.5	13 59.8	23 26.6	17 48.3	16 23.3	0N22.3	23 4.5	22 2.4	14 57.6	21 50.5	8 35.8	23 12.7

MAY 1955

DAY	EPHEMERIS SIDEREAL TIME	☉	☊	☽	☿	♀	♂	♃	♄	♅	♆	♇
	h m s	° ′	° ′	° ′	° ′	° ′	° ′	° ′	° ′	° ′	° ′	° ′
						LONGITUDE at NOON						
1 S	2 34 34.1	10♉20.9	29♐ 2.6	8♍39.0	19♉57.4	8♈15.0	13♊48.1	22♋59.3	18♏27.2	23♋59.6	26♎29.9	24♌18.4
2 M	2 38 30.7	11 19.1	28 59.4	21 23.8	22 1.3	9 27.1	14 28.1	23 7.1	18R22.8	24 1.2	26R28.3	24R18.2
3 T	2 42 27.2	12 17.3	28 56.2	3♎55.5	24 3.2	10 39.2	15 8.0	23 14.9	18 18.3	24 2.8	26 26.7	24 18.1
4 W	2 46 23.8	13 15.4	28 53.0	16 16.1	26 3.1	11 51.3	15 47.9	23 22.9	18 13.8	24 4.5	26 25.2	24 18.0
5 T	2 50 20.3	14 13.6	28 49.8	28 27.1	28 0.6	13 3.5	16 27.8	23 31.0	18 9.3	24 6.3	26 23.6	24 18.0
6 F	2 54 16.9	15 11.6	28 46.7	10♏29.8	29 55.6	14 15.7	17 7.6	23 39.2	18 4.8	24 8.0	26 22.1	24 18.0
7 S	2 58 13.5	16 9.7	28 43.5	22 25.8	1♊47.7	15 27.9	17 47.5	23 47.6	18 0.4	24 9.9	26 20.6	24 18.0
8 S	3 2 10.0	17 7.8	28 40.3	4♐16.7	3 36.9	16 40.1	18 27.2	23 56.0	17 55.8	24 11.8	26 19.1	24D18.1
9 M	3 6 6.6	18 5.8	28 37.1	16 4.7	5 22.9	17 52.4	19 7.0	24 4.6	17 51.3	24 13.7	26 17.6	24 18.1
10 T	3 10 3.1	19 3.7	28 34.0	27 52.4	7 5.6	19 4.6	19 46.7	24 13.3	17 46.8	24 15.7	26 16.1	24 18.2
11 W	3 13 59.7	20 1.7	28 30.8	9♑43.2	8 45.0	20 16.9	20 26.4	24 22.1	17 42.3	24 17.7	26 14.6	24 18.4
12 T	3 17 56.2	20 59.6	28 27.6	21 40.7	10 21.0	21 29.2	21 6.1	24 31.0	17 37.8	24 19.7	26 13.2	24 18.5
13 F	3 21 52.8	21 57.5	28 24.4	3♒49.4	11 53.4	22 41.5	21 45.7	24 40.0	17 33.3	24 21.8	26 11.7	24 18.7
14 S	3 25 49.3	22 55.4	28 21.2	16 13.9	13 22.2	23 53.8	22 25.3	24 49.2	17 28.8	24 23.9	26 10.3	24 18.9
15 S	3 29 45.9	23 53.3	28 18.1	28 58.7	14 47.3	25 6.2	23 4.9	24 58.4	17 24.3	24 26.1	26 8.9	24 19.1
16 M	3 33 42.5	24 51.1	28 14.9	12♓ 7.8	16 8.8	26 18.5	23 44.5	25 7.8	17 19.8	24 28.3	26 7.5	24 19.4
17 T	3 37 39.0	25 48.9	28 11.7	25 44.2	17 26.4	27 30.9	24 24.0	25 17.2	17 15.4	24 30.6	26 6.1	24 19.7
18 W	3 41 35.6	26 46.8	28 8.5	9♈48.8	18 40.2	28 43.3	25 3.5	25 26.8	17 11.0	24 32.9	26 4.7	24 20.0
19 T	3 45 32.1	27 44.5	28 5.4	24 19.8	19 50.2	29 55.8	25 43.0	25 36.4	17 6.5	24 35.2	26 3.4	24 20.4
20 F	3 49 28.7	28 42.3	28 2.2	9♉12.7	20 56.2	1♉ 8.2	26 22.5	25 46.2	17 2.2	24 37.6	26 2.0	24 20.8
21 S	3 53 25.2	29 40.1	27 59.0	24 19.9	21 58.2	2 20.6	27 1.9	25 56.0	16 57.8	24 40.0	26 0.7	24 21.2
22 S	3 57 21.8	0♊37.8	27 55.8	9♊32.1	22 56.1	3 33.1	27 41.4	26 6.0	16 53.5	24 42.5	25 59.4	24 21.6
23 M	4 1 18.3	1 35.5	27 52.7	24 39.5	23 49.9	4 45.6	28 20.8	26 16.0	16 49.2	24 45.0	25 58.2	24 22.1
24 T	4 5 14.9	2 33.2	27 49.5	9♋33.3	24 39.5	5 58.1	29 0.1	26 26.2	16 44.9	24 47.5	25 56.9	24 22.6
25 W	4 9 11.5	3 30.8	27 46.3	24 7.0	25 24.8	7 10.6	29 39.5	26 36.4	16 40.7	24 50.1	25 55.7	24 23.1
26 T	4 13 8.0	4 28.4	27 43.1	8♌16.8	26 5.8	8 23.1	0♋18.8	26 46.8	16 36.5	24 52.7	25 54.5	24 23.7
27 F	4 17 4.6	5 26.1	27 39.9	22 1.4	26 42.4	9 35.6	0 58.1	26 57.2	16 32.3	24 55.4	25 53.3	24 24.3
28 S	4 21 1.1	6 23.7	27 36.8	5♍21.6	27 14.5	10 48.2	1 37.4	27 7.7	16 28.2	24 58.1	25 52.2	24 24.9
29 S	4 24 57.7	7 21.2	27 33.6	18 19.6	27 42.0	12 0.8	2 16.6	27 18.3	16 24.2	25 0.8	25 51.0	24 25.5
30 M	4 28 54.2	8 18.8	27 30.4	0♎58.3	28 4.9	13 13.3	2 55.8	27 29.0	16 20.1	25 3.6	25 49.9	24 26.2
31 T	4 32 50.8	9 16.3	27 27.2	13 21.3	28 23.2	14 25.9	3 35.0	27 39.7	16 16.2	25 6.4	25 48.8	24 26.9
						DECLINATION at NOON						
1 S	2 34 34.1	14N55.7	23S26.5	3N49.0	18N41.8	1N45.0	23N21.0	21N58.8	14S54.0	21N49.7	8S34.1	23N12.3
4 W	2 46 23.8	15 49.3	23 26.4	10S52.9	20 42.5	3 7.7	23 35.6	21 54.8	14 50.3	21 48.8	8 32.5	23 11.8
7 S	2 58 13.5	16 40.7	23 26.3	21 12.6	22 22.0	4 30.2	23 48.5	21 50.6	14 46.7	21 47.8	8 30.9	23 11.1
10 T	3 10 3.1	17 29.5	23 26.2	23 19.6	23 38.9	5 52.1	23 59.5	21 46.2	14 43.0	21 46.7	8 29.3	23 10.4
13 F	3 21 52.8	18 15.7	23 26.1	16 14.4	24 33.6	7 13.1	24 8.7	21 41.5	14 39.4	21 45.6	8 27.8	23 9.6
16 M	3 33 42.5	18 59.1	23 26.0	2 20.4	25 7.6	8 33.0	24 16.1	21 36.6	14 35.9	21 44.4	8 26.3	23 8.7
19 T	3 45 32.1	19 39.7	23 25.9	13N44.1	25 23.0	9 51.3	24 21.7	21 31.4	14 32.4	21 43.1	8 24.9	23 7.7
22 S	3 57 21.8	20 17.3	23 25.7	23 24.1	25 22.2	11 7.9	24 25.4	21 25.9	14 29.0	21 41.8	8 23.6	23 6.7
25 W	4 9 11.5	20 51.7	23 25.6	18 53.3	25 7.4	12 22.3	24 27.4	21 20.2	14 25.7	21 40.3	8 22.3	23 5.5
28 S	4 21 1.1	21 22.9	23 25.4	4 58.7	24 40.9	13 34.3	24 27.5	21 14.3	14 22.6	21 38.9	8 21.1	23 4.3
31 T	4 32 50.8	21 50.8	23 25.2	9S54.7	24 4.8	14 43.6	24 25.8	21 8.1	14 19.5	21 37.3	8 20.0	23 3.0

JUNE 1955

DAY	EPHEMERIS SIDEREAL TIME	☉	☊	☽	☿	♀	♂	♃	♄	♅	♆	♇
						LONGITUDE at NOON						
1 W	4 36 47.4	10♊13.8	27♐24.1	25♎31.6	28♊36.8	15♉38.5	4♋14.2	27♋50.5	16♏12.2	25♋ 9.2	25♎47.8	24♌27.6
2 T	4 40 43.9	11 11.2	27 20.9	7♏32.5	28 45.8	16 51.1	4 53.3	28 1.4	16R 8.3	25 12.1	25R46.7	24 28.4
3 F	4 44 40.5	12 8.7	27 17.7	19 26.7	28 50.1	18 3.7	5 32.4	28 12.4	16 4.5	25 14.9	25 45.7	24 29.1
4 S	4 48 37.0	13 6.1	27 14.5	1♐16.8	28R49.9	19 16.3	6 11.5	28 23.5	16 0.7	25 17.9	25 44.7	24 29.9
5 S	4 52 33.6	14 3.5	27 11.4	13 5.0	28 45.2	20 29.0	6 50.6	28 34.6	15 57.0	25 20.8	25 43.7	24 30.8
6 M	4 56 30.2	15 0.9	27 8.2	24 53.6	28 36.1	21 41.7	7 29.6	28 45.8	15 53.4	25 23.8	25 42.8	24 31.6
7 T	5 0 26.7	15 58.3	27 5.0	6♑44.8	28 22.9	22 54.3	8 8.7	28 57.1	15 49.8	25 26.8	25 41.9	24 32.5
8 W	5 4 23.3	16 55.7	27 1.8	18 41.2	28 5.7	24 7.0	8 47.7	29 8.4	15 46.2	25 29.8	25 41.0	24 33.4
9 T	5 8 19.8	17 53.1	26 58.7	0♒45.4	27 45.0	25 19.8	9 26.6	29 19.8	15 42.8	25 32.9	25 40.1	24 34.3
10 F	5 12 16.4	18 50.4	26 55.5	13 0.4	27 20.9	26 32.5	10 5.6	29 31.3	15 39.3	25 36.0	25 39.3	24 35.3
11 S	5 16 12.9	19 47.8	26 52.3	25 29.4	26 54.0	27 45.2	10 44.5	29 42.9	15 36.0	25 39.1	25 38.5	24 36.2
12 S	5 20 9.5	20 45.1	26 49.1	8♓15.8	26 24.6	28 58.0	11 23.5	29 54.5	15 32.7	25 42.2	25 37.7	24 37.2
13 M	5 24 6.1	21 42.4	26 45.9	21 22.8	25 53.2	0♊10.8	12 2.4	0♌ 6.2	15 29.5	25 45.4	25 36.9	24 38.3
14 T	5 28 2.6	22 39.7	26 42.8	4♈52.9	25 20.5	1 23.6	12 41.2	0 17.9	15 26.4	25 48.6	25 36.2	24 39.3
15 W	5 31 59.2	23 37.1	26 39.6	18 47.6	24 46.8	2 36.5	13 20.1	0 29.7	15 23.3	25 51.8	25 35.5	24 40.4
16 T	5 35 55.7	24 34.4	26 36.4	3♉ 6.6	24 12.8	3 49.3	13 59.0	0 41.5	15 20.3	25 55.1	25 34.8	24 41.5
17 F	5 39 52.3	25 31.7	26 33.2	17 47.4	23 39.1	5 2.2	14 37.8	0 53.5	15 17.4	25 58.4	25 34.2	24 42.6
18 S	5 43 48.8	26 29.0	26 30.1	2♊44.8	23 6.3	6 15.1	15 16.7	1 5.5	15 14.6	26 1.7	25 33.6	24 43.8
19 S	5 47 45.4	27 26.3	26 26.9	17 51.6	22 34.9	7 28.0	15 55.5	1 17.5	15 11.8	26 5.0	25 33.0	24 45.0
20 M	5 51 42.0	28 23.6	26 23.7	2♋58.9	22 5.4	8 41.0	16 34.2	1 29.6	15 9.2	26 8.3	25 32.5	24 46.2
21 T	5 55 38.5	29 20.9	26 20.5	17 57.6	21 38.3	9 53.9	17 13.0	1 41.7	15 6.6	26 11.7	25 32.0	24 47.4
22 W	5 59 35.1	0♋18.1	26 17.4	2♌39.8	21 14.2	11 6.8	17 51.8	1 53.9	15 4.0	26 15.1	25 31.5	24 48.6
23 T	6 3 31.6	1 15.4	26 14.2	16 59.5	20 53.3	12 19.8	18 30.5	2 6.1	15 1.6	26 18.5	25 31.0	24 49.9
24 F	6 7 28.2	2 12.6	26 11.0	0♍53.4	20 36.2	13 32.8	19 9.2	2 18.4	14 59.3	26 21.9	25 30.6	24 51.1
25 S	6 11 24.7	3 9.9	26 7.8	14 20.5	20 23.0	14 45.8	19 47.9	2 30.8	14 57.0	26 25.3	25 30.2	24 52.5
26 S	6 15 21.3	4 7.1	26 4.7	27 22.3	20 14.1	15 58.8	20 26.6	2 43.1	14 54.8	26 28.8	25 29.8	24 53.8
27 M	6 19 17.9	5 4.3	26 1.5	10♎ 1.6	20 9.7	17 11.9	21 5.2	2 55.6	14 52.7	26 32.3	25 29.5	24 55.1
28 T	6 23 14.4	6 1.5	25 58.3	22 22.2	20D 9.9	18 24.9	21 43.9	3 8.0	14 50.7	26 35.7	25 29.2	24 56.5
29 W	6 27 11.0	6 58.7	25 55.1	4♏28.4	20 14.8	19 38.0	22 22.5	3 20.5	14 48.8	26 39.2	25 28.9	24 57.9
30 T	6 31 7.5	7 55.9	25 51.9	16 24.5	20 24.6	20 51.1	23 1.1	3 33.1	14 47.0	26 42.8	25 28.7	24 59.3
						DECLINATION at NOON						
1 W	4 36 47.4	21N59.3	23S25.2	14S 9.4	23N50.9	15N 6.0	24N24.9	21N 5.9	14S18.6	21N36.8	8S19.7	23N 2.5
4 S	4 48 37.0	22 22.6	23 25.0	22 36.9	23 5.1	16 11.0	24 20.9	20 59.4	14 15.7	21 35.2	8 18.7	23 1.1
7 T	5 0 26.7	22 42.4	23 24.8	22 19.0	22 14.6	17 12.6	24 15.1	20 52.6	14 13.1	21 33.5	8 17.8	22 59.7
10 F	5 12 16.4	22 58.6	23 24.5	13 13.0	21 22.1	18 10.4	24 7.5	20 45.6	14 10.6	21 31.8	8 16.9	22 58.2
13 M	5 24 6.1	23 11.1	23 24.3	1N25.9	20 30.9	19 4.1	23 58.3	20 38.4	14 8.3	21 30.0	8 16.2	22 56.6
16 T	5 35 55.7	23 20.0	23 24.1	16 32.5	19 44.9	19 53.4	23 47.4	20 30.9	14 6.2	21 28.2	8 15.6	22 54.9
19 S	5 47 45.4	23 25.2	23 23.8	23 40.5	19 7.8	20 38.0	23 34.8	20 23.1	14 4.4	21 26.3	8 15.1	22 53.2
22 W	5 59 35.1	23 26.7	23 23.6	16 30.7	18 43.0	21 17.6	23 20.5	20 15.1	14 2.8	21 24.4	8 14.7	22 51.5
25 S	6 11 24.7	23 24.4	23 23.3	1 23.1	18 32.4	21 52.0	23 4.7	20 6.9	14 1.4	21 22.5	8 14.3	22 49.7
28 T	6 23 14.4	23 18.5	23 23.0	13S 7.3	18 36.5	22 20.9	22 47.3	19 58.5	14 0.2	21 20.5	8 14.1	22 47.8

JULY 1955

DAY	EPHEMERIS SIDEREAL TIME	☉	☊	☽	☿	♀	♂	♃	♄	♅	♆	♇
	h m s	° ′	° ′	° ′	° ′	° ′	° ′	° ′	° ′	° ′	° ′	° ′
						LONGITUDE at NOON						
1 F	6 35 4.1	8♋53.1	25♐48.8	28♏14.5	20♊39.2	22♊ 4.2	23♋39.7	3♌45.6	14♏45.2	26♋46.3	25♎28.4	25♌ 0.7
2 S	6 39 0.7	9 50.3	25 45.6	10♐ 2.2	20 58.8	23 17.3	24 18.2	3 58.3	14R43.6	26 49.8	25R28.3	25 2.1
3 S	6 42 57.2	10 47.5	25 42.4	21 50.9	21 23.3	24 30.4	24 56.8	4 10.9	14 42.0	26 53.4	25 28.1	25 3.6
4 M	6 46 53.8	11 44.7	25 39.2	3♑43.3	21 52.7	25 43.6	25 35.3	4 23.6	14 40.6	26 57.0	25 28.0	25 5.1
5 T	6 50 50.3	12 41.8	25 36.1	15 41.8	22 27.1	26 56.8	26 13.8	4 36.3	14 39.2	27 0.5	25 27.9	25 6.6
6 W	6 54 46.9	13 39.0	25 32.9	27 48.4	23 6.2	28 10.0	26 52.4	4 49.1	14 37.9	27 4.1	25 27.8	25 8.1
7 T	6 58 43.4	14 36.2	25 29.7	10♒ 4.9	23 50.2	29 23.2	27 30.9	5 1.9	14 36.7	27 7.7	25 27.8	25 9.6
8 F	7 2 40.0	15 33.4	25 26.5	22 32.9	24 38.9	0♋36.5	28 9.3	5 14.7	14 35.6	27 11.3	25 27.8	25 11.2
9 S	7 6 36.6	16 30.6	25 23.4	5♓14.0	25 32.4	1 49.8	28 47.9	5 27.6	14 34.7	27 15.0	25D27.9	25 12.8
10 S	7 10 33.1	17 27.8	25 20.2	18 9.6	26 30.4	3 3.1	29 26.3	5 40.5	14 33.8	27 18.6	25 28.0	25 14.4
11 M	7 14 29.7	18 25.0	25 17.0	1♈21.3	27 33.1	4 16.4	0♌ 4.8	5 53.4	14 33.0	27 22.3	25 28.1	25 16.0
12 T	7 18 26.2	19 22.2	25 13.8	14 50.6	28 40.3	5 29.8	0 43.2	6 6.3	14 32.3	27 25.9	25 28.2	25 17.6
13 W	7 22 22.8	20 19.4	25 10.6	28 38.2	29 51.9	6 43.2	1 21.6	6 19.3	14 31.7	27 29.6	25 28.4	25 19.2
14 T	7 26 19.3	21 16.7	25 7.5	12♉44.4	1♋ 8.0	7 56.5	2 0.1	6 32.3	14 31.1	27 33.2	25 28.6	25 20.9
15 F	7 30 15.9	22 13.9	25 4.3	27 8.1	2 28.3	9 10.0	2 38.5	6 45.3	14 30.7	27 36.9	25 28.8	25 22.6
16 S	7 34 12.5	23 11.2	25 1.1	11♊46.6	3 52.9	10 23.4	3 16.9	6 58.3	14 30.4	27 40.5	25 29.1	25 24.2
17 S	7 38 9.0	24 8.4	24 57.9	26 35.4	5 21.7	11 36.9	3 55.3	7 11.4	14 30.2	27 44.2	25 29.4	25 25.9
18 M	7 42 5.6	25 5.7	24 54.8	11♋28.0	6 54.4	12 50.4	4 33.6	7 24.5	14 30.0	27 47.9	25 29.7	25 27.6
19 T	7 46 2.1	26 3.0	24 51.6	26 17.0	8 31.1	14 3.9	5 12.0	7 37.6	14 30.0	27 51.6	25 30.1	25 29.3
20 W	7 49 58.7	27 0.2	24 48.4	10♌54.7	10 11.6	15 17.4	5 50.4	7 50.7	14D30.1	27 55.2	25 30.5	25 31.1
21 T	7 53 55.2	27 57.5	24 45.2	25 14.4	11 55.6	16 31.0	6 28.7	8 3.8	14 30.3	27 58.9	25 30.9	25 32.8
22 F	7 57 51.8	28 54.8	24 42.1	9♍11.2	13 43.1	17 44.6	7 7.1	8 17.0	14 30.5	28 2.6	25 31.4	25 34.6
23 S	8 1 48.4	29 52.1	24 38.9	22 42.4	15 33.7	18 58.2	7 45.4	8 30.1	14 30.9	28 6.3	25 31.9	25 36.4
24 S	8 5 44.9	0♌49.4	24 35.7	5♎47.9	17 27.2	20 11.8	8 23.7	8 43.3	14 31.3	28 9.9	25 32.4	25 38.1
25 M	8 9 41.5	1 46.8	24 32.5	18 29.8	19 23.4	21 25.5	9 2.1	8 56.5	14 31.9	28 13.6	25 33.0	25 39.9
26 T	8 13 38.0	2 44.1	24 29.3	0♏51.3	21 21.9	22 39.1	9 40.4	9 9.7	14 32.6	28 17.3	25 33.6	25 41.7
27 W	8 17 34.6	3 41.4	24 26.2	12 57.1	23 22.5	23 52.8	10 18.7	9 22.8	14 33.3	28 20.9	25 34.2	25 43.5
28 T	8 21 31.1	4 38.7	24 23.0	24 52.0	25 24.7	25 6.5	10 56.9	9 36.1	14 34.2	28 24.6	25 34.8	25 45.4
29 F	8 25 27.7	5 36.1	24 19.8	6♐41.1	27 28.3	26 20.2	11 35.2	9 49.3	14 35.1	28 28.3	25 35.5	25 47.2
30 S	8 29 24.3	6 33.5	24 16.6	18 29.1	29 32.9	27 34.0	12 13.5	10 2.5	14 36.2	28 32.0	25 36.3	25 49.1
31 S	8 33 20.8	7 30.9	24 13.5	0♑20.3	1♌38.2	28 47.8	12 51.8	10 15.7	14 37.4	28 35.6	25 37.0	25 50.9
						DECLINATION at NOON						
1 F	6 35 4.1	23N 8.8	23S22.7	22S12.7	18N54.2	22N44.2	22N28.4	19N49.9	13S59.3	21N18.4	8S14.0	22N46.0
4 M	6 46 53.8	22 55.5	23 22.4	22 43.3	19 23.2	23 1.7	22 8.0	19 41.0	13 58.7	21 16.4	8 14.0	22 44.1
7 T	6 58 43.4	22 38.7	23 22.1	14 12.9	20 0.4	23 13.3	21 46.1	19 32.0	13 58.3	21 14.3	8 14.1	22 42.1
10 S	7 10 33.1	22 18.3	23 21.7	0N 6.4	20 42.0	23 18.7	21 22.8	19 22.7	13 58.1	21 12.2	8 14.3	22 40.2
13 W	7 22 22.8	21 54.4	23 21.4	15 7.9	21 23.8	23 18.1	20 58.1	19 13.3	13 58.3	21 10.0	8 14.6	22 38.2
16 S	7 34 12.5	21 27.2	23 21.1	23 30.3	22 1.0	23 11.2	20 32.1	19 3.6	13 58.6	21 7.9	8 15.0	22 36.2
19 T	7 46 2.1	20 56.6	23 20.7	18 19.4	22 28.4	22 58.3	20 4.8	18 53.8	13 59.3	21 5.7	8 15.5	22 34.2
22 F	7 57 51.8	20 22.9	23 20.3	3 30.2	22 40.7	22 39.2	19 36.2	18 43.8	14 0.2	21 3.5	8 16.1	22 32.2
25 M	8 9 41.5	19 46.1	23 19.9	11S41.4	22 33.1	22 14.1	19 6.4	18 33.7	14 1.3	21 1.3	8 16.8	22 30.1
28 T	8 21 31.1	19 6.4	23 19.5	21 35.4	22 2.4	21 43.2	18 35.5	18 23.4	14 2.8	20 59.1	8 17.7	22 28.1
31 S	8 33 20.8	18 23.8	23 19.1	23 2.4	21 7.9	21 6.6	18 3.4	18 12.9	14 4.5	20 56.9	8 18.6	22 26.1

AUGUST 1955

DAY	EPHEMERIS SIDEREAL TIME	☉	☊	☽	☿	♀	♂	♃	♄	♅	♆	♇
						LONGITUDE at NOON						
1 M	8 37 17.4	8♌28.2	24♐10.3	12♑18.5	3♌43.8	0♌ 1.6	13♌30.0	10♌29.0	14♏38.6	28♋39.2	25♎37.8	25♌52.8
2 T	8 41 13.9	9 25.6	24 7.1	24 26.5	5 49.5	1 15.4	14 8.3	10 42.2	14 39.9	28 42.9	25 38.6	25 54.7
3 W	8 45 10.5	10 23.0	24 3.9	6♒46.4	7 55.1	2 29.2	14 46.5	10 55.4	14 41.4	28 46.5	25 39.4	25 56.5
4 T	8 49 7.0	11 20.4	24 0.8	19 19.5	10 0.2	3 43.1	15 24.8	11 8.6	14 42.9	28 50.1	25 40.3	25 58.4
5 F	8 53 3.6	12 17.9	23 57.6	2♓ 6.3	12 4.7	4 57.0	16 3.0	11 21.9	14 44.5	28 53.7	25 41.2	26 0.3
6 S	8 57 0.1	13 15.3	23 54.4	15 6.6	14 8.4	6 10.9	16 41.2	11 35.1	14 46.2	28 57.3	25 42.1	26 2.2
7 S	9 0 56.7	14 12.8	23 51.2	28 19.9	16 11.1	7 24.8	17 19.4	11 48.3	14 48.1	29 0.9	25 43.1	26 4.1
8 M	9 4 53.3	15 10.3	23 48.0	11♈45.6	18 12.8	8 38.7	17 57.6	12 1.5	14 50.0	29 4.4	25 44.0	26 6.0
9 T	9 8 49.8	16 7.8	23 44.9	25 23.0	20 13.2	9 52.7	18 35.9	12 14.7	14 52.0	29 8.0	25 45.1	26 7.9
10 W	9 12 46.4	17 5.3	23 41.7	9♉11.8	22 12.4	11 6.7	19 14.1	12 27.9	14 54.0	29 11.6	25 46.1	26 9.8
11 T	9 16 42.9	18 2.9	23 38.5	23 11.6	24 10.3	12 20.7	19 52.3	12 41.1	14 56.2	29 15.1	25 47.2	26 11.7
12 F	9 20 39.5	19 0.5	23 35.3	7♊21.7	26 6.8	13 34.8	20 30.5	12 54.3	14 58.5	29 18.6	25 48.3	26 13.7
13 S	9 24 36.0	19 58.1	23 32.2	21 40.9	28 1.8	14 48.9	21 8.7	13 7.5	15 0.9	29 22.1	25 49.4	26 15.6
14 S	9 28 32.6	20 55.7	23 29.0	6♋ 7.0	29 55.5	16 3.0	21 46.9	13 20.7	15 3.3	29 25.6	25 50.6	26 17.5
15 M	9 32 29.1	21 53.4	23 25.8	20 36.3	1♍47.7	17 17.1	22 25.1	13 33.8	15 5.9	29 29.1	25 51.8	26 19.4
16 T	9 36 25.7	22 51.0	23 22.6	5♌ 4.0	3 38.4	18 31.2	23 3.3	13 47.0	15 8.5	29 32.5	25 53.0	26 21.4
17 W	9 40 22.2	23 48.7	23 19.5	19 24.4	5 27.7	19 45.4	23 41.5	14 0.1	15 11.2	29 36.0	25 54.2	26 23.3
18 T	9 44 18.8	24 46.5	23 16.3	3♍31.5	7 15.6	20 59.6	24 19.7	14 13.2	15 14.1	29 39.4	25 55.5	26 25.3
19 F	9 48 15.4	25 44.2	23 13.1	17 20.3	9 2.0	22 13.8	24 57.9	14 26.3	15 17.0	29 42.8	25 56.8	26 27.2
20 S	9 52 11.9	26 42.0	23 9.9	0♎47.5	10 47.0	23 28.1	25 36.1	14 39.4	15 20.0	29 46.2	25 58.1	26 29.2
21 S	9 56 8.5	27 39.8	23 6.7	13 51.6	12 30.6	24 42.3	26 14.3	14 52.5	15 23.1	29 49.6	25 59.5	26 31.1
22 M	10 0 5.0	28 37.6	23 3.6	26 33.3	14 12.8	25 56.6	26 52.5	15 5.5	15 26.3	29 52.9	26 0.9	26 33.1
23 T	10 4 1.6	29 35.4	23 0.4	8♏55.2	15 53.6	27 10.8	27 30.7	15 18.5	15 29.5	29 56.2	26 2.3	26 35.0
24 W	10 7 58.1	0♍33.3	22 57.2	21 1.2	17 33.0	28 25.1	28 8.9	15 31.5	15 32.9	29 59.5	26 3.7	26 36.9
25 T	10 11 54.7	1 31.2	22 54.0	2♐56.1	19 11.1	29 39.4	28 47.0	15 44.5	15 36.3	0♌ 2.8	26 5.2	26 38.9
26 F	10 15 51.2	2 29.0	22 50.9	14 45.2	20 47.8	0♍53.7	29 25.2	15 57.4	15 39.8	0 6.0	26 6.6	26 40.8
27 S	10 19 47.8	3 27.0	22 47.7	26 34.0	22 23.2	2 8.1	0♍ 3.4	16 10.3	15 43.4	0 9.3	26 8.1	26 42.7
28 S	10 23 44.3	4 24.9	22 44.5	8♑27.6	23 57.3	3 22.4	0 41.6	16 23.2	15 47.0	0 12.5	26 9.7	26 44.6
29 M	10 27 40.9	5 22.8	22 41.3	20 30.7	25 30.0	4 36.8	1 19.7	16 36.0	15 50.8	0 15.6	26 11.2	26 46.6
30 T	10 31 37.4	6 20.8	22 38.1	2♒47.2	27 1.4	5 51.2	1 57.9	16 48.9	15 54.6	0 18.8	26 12.8	26 48.5
31 W	10 35 34.0	7 18.8	22 35.0	15 19.8	28 31.5	7 5.6	2 36.1	17 1.6	15 58.5	0 21.9	26 14.4	26 50.4
						DECLINATION at NOON						
1 M	8 37 17.4	18N 9.0	23S19.0	21S24.8	20N44.6	20N53.1	17N52.5	18N 9.4	14S 5.1	20N56.2	8S18.9	22N25.4
4 T	8 49 7.0	17 22.8	23 18.6	11 5.3	19 21.1	20 9.2	17 19.0	17 58.8	14 7.1	20 54.0	8 20.0	22 23.4
7 S	9 0 56.7	16 34.2	23 18.1	4N 1.8	17 40.1	19 20.0	16 44.5	17 48.0	14 9.3	20 51.8	8 21.1	22 21.5
10 W	9 12 46.4	15 43.1	23 17.7	18 3.0	15 45.8	18 25.9	16 8.9	17 37.2	14 11.8	20 49.7	8 22.4	22 19.5
13 S	9 24 36.0	14 49.7	23 17.2	23 28.9	13 42.1	17 27.0	15 32.5	17 26.2	14 14.5	20 47.5	8 23.7	22 17.6
16 T	9 36 25.7	13 54.1	23 16.7	15 48.6	11 32.1	16 23.8	14 55.1	17 15.1	14 17.5	20 45.4	8 25.1	22 15.7
19 F	9 48 15.4	12 56.6	23 16.3	0 22.0	9 18.6	15 16.4	14 16.9	17 4.0	14 20.6	20 43.3	8 26.6	22 13.8
22 M	10 0 5.0	11 57.3	23 15.8	14S14.2	7 3.7	14 5.2	13 37.9	16 52.8	14 24.0	20 41.2	8 28.3	22 11.9
25 T	10 11 54.7	10 56.2	23 15.3	22 32.5	4 48.9	12 50.6	12 58.1	16 41.6	14 27.6	20 39.1	8 29.9	22 10.1
28 S	10 23 44.3	9 53.6	23 14.7	21 54.0	2 35.7	11 32.7	12 17.7	16 30.3	14 31.3	20 37.2	8 31.7	22 8.4
31 W	10 35 34.0	8 49.6	23 14.2	12 27.6	0 25.1	10 12.1	11 36.5	16 19.0	14 35.3	20 35.2	8 33.5	22 6.6

SEPTEMBER 1955

LONGITUDE at NOON

DAY	EPHEMERIS SIDEREAL TIME	☉	☊	☽	☿	♀	♂	♃	♄	♅	♆	♇
	h m s	° ′	° ′	° ′	° ′	° ′	° ′	° ′	° ′	° ′	° ′	° ′
1 T	10 39 30.6	8♍16.8	22♐31.8	28♒ 9.9	0♎ 0.2	8♍20.0	3♍14.3	17♌14.4	16♏ 2.5	0♌25.0	26♎16.0	26♌52.3
2 F	10 43 27.1	9 14.9	22 28.6	11♓17.4	1 27.6	9 34.4	3 52.4	17 27.1	16 6.6	0 28.1	26 17.6	26 54.2
3 S	10 47 23.7	10 13.0	22 25.4	24 41.1	2 53.6	10 48.9	4 30.6	17 39.8	16 10.7	0 31.1	26 19.3	26 56.1
4 S	10 51 20.2	11 11.1	22 22.3	8♈18.5	4 18.2	12 3.3	5 8.8	17 52.4	16 15.0	0 34.1	26 21.0	26 58.0
5 M	10 55 16.8	12 9.2	22 19.1	22 6.6	5 41.5	13 17.8	5 47.0	18 5.0	16 19.2	0 37.1	26 22.7	26 59.9
6 T	10 59 13.3	13 7.4	22 15.9	6♉ 2.4	7 3.3	14 32.3	6 25.1	18 17.6	16 23.6	0 40.0	26 24.4	27 1.8
7 W	11 3 9.9	14 5.6	22 12.7	20 3.2	8 23.7	15 46.8	7 3.3	18 30.1	16 28.1	0 42.9	26 26.2	27 3.6
8 T	11 7 6.4	15 3.8	22 9.5	4♊ 7.2	9 42.5	17 1.3	7 41.5	18 42.6	16 32.6	0 45.8	26 27.9	27 5.5
9 F	11 11 3.0	16 2.1	22 6.4	18 13.3	10 59.8	18 15.9	8 19.7	18 55.1	16 37.2	0 48.7	26 29.7	27 7.4
10 S	11 14 59.5	17 0.5	22 3.2	2♋20.5	12 15.6	19 30.5	8 58.0	19 7.5	16 41.9	0 51.5	26 31.6	27 9.3
11 S	11 18 56.1	17 58.8	22 0.0	16 27.8	13 29.7	20 45.1	9 36.2	19 19.9	16 46.6	0 54.3	26 33.4	27 11.1
12 M	11 22 52.6	18 57.2	21 56.8	0♌33.8	14 42.0	21 59.7	10 14.4	19 32.2	16 51.4	0 57.0	26 35.3	27 12.9
13 T	11 26 49.2	19 55.6	21 53.7	14 36.1	15 52.5	23 14.3	10 52.6	19 44.4	16 56.3	0 59.8	26 37.1	27 14.7
14 W	11 30 45.7	20 54.1	21 50.5	28 31.5	17 1.0	24 28.9	11 30.8	19 56.6	17 1.2	1 2.4	26 39.0	27 16.6
15 T	11 34 42.3	21 52.5	21 47.3	12♍16.3	18 7.6	25 43.5	12 9.1	20 8.8	17 6.2	1 5.1	26 40.9	27 18.4
16 F	11 38 38.8	22 51.0	21 44.1	25 47.0	19 12.0	26 58.1	12 47.3	20 20.9	17 11.3	1 7.7	26 42.8	27 20.1
17 S	11 42 35.4	23 49.6	21 40.9	9♎ 0.6	20 14.1	28 12.8	13 25.5	20 32.9	17 16.4	1 10.2	26 44.8	27 21.9
18 S	11 46 31.9	24 48.2	21 37.8	21 55.4	21 13.8	29 27.5	14 3.8	20 44.9	17 21.6	1 12.8	26 46.7	27 23.7
19 M	11 50 28.5	25 46.8	21 34.6	4♏31.4	22 10.8	0♎42.1	14 42.0	20 56.9	17 26.9	1 15.3	26 48.7	27 25.4
20 T	11 54 25.1	26 45.4	21 31.4	16 50.1	23 5.1	1 56.8	15 20.3	21 8.7	17 32.2	1 17.7	26 50.7	27 27.2
21 W	11 58 21.6	27 44.1	21 28.2	28 54.3	23 56.3	3 11.5	15 58.5	21 20.6	17 37.6	1 20.1	26 52.7	27 28.9
22 T	12 2 18.2	28 42.8	21 25.0	10♐48.3	24 44.3	4 26.2	16 36.8	21 32.3	17 43.0	1 22.5	26 54.7	27 30.6
23 F	12 6 14.7	29 41.5	21 21.9	22 36.8	25 28.7	5 40.9	17 15.0	21 44.0	17 48.5	1 24.8	26 56.7	27 32.3
24 S	12 10 11.3	0♎40.2	21 18.7	4♑25.4	26 9.4	6 55.6	17 53.3	21 55.6	17 54.1	1 27.1	26 58.8	27 34.0
25 S	12 14 7.8	1 39.0	21 15.5	16 19.4	26 45.9	8 10.3	18 31.6	22 7.2	17 59.7	1 29.3	27 0.8	27 35.7
26 M	12 18 4.4	2 37.8	21 12.3	28 24.3	27 18.0	9 25.0	19 9.8	22 18.7	18 5.4	1 31.5	27 2.9	27 37.3
27 T	12 22 0.9	3 36.6	21 9.2	10♒44.9	27 45.3	10 39.7	19 48.1	22 30.1	18 11.1	1 33.7	27 5.0	27 39.0
28 W	12 25 57.5	4 35.5	21 6.0	23 24.9	28 7.3	11 54.5	20 26.4	22 41.4	18 16.9	1 35.8	27 7.1	27 40.6
29 T	12 29 54.0	5 34.4	21 2.8	6♓26.6	28 23.8	13 9.2	21 4.7	22 52.7	18 22.7	1 37.9	27 9.2	27 42.2
30 F	12 33 50.6	6 33.3	20 59.6	19 50.7	28 34.2	14 23.9	21 43.0	23 3.9	18 28.6	1 39.9	27 11.3	27 43.8

DECLINATION at NOON

DAY	EPHEMERIS SIDEREAL TIME	☉	☊	☽	☿	♀	♂	♃	♄	♅	♆	♇
1 T	10 39 30.6	8N28.0	23S14.0	7S50.7	0S17.6	9N44.6	11N22.6	16N15.2	14S36.6	20N34.6	8S34.1	22N 6.1
4 S	10 51 20.2	7 22.4	23 13.5	7N44.5	2 23.1	8 20.7	10 40.7	16 3.9	14 40.8	20 32.7	8 36.0	22 4.5
7 W	11 3 9.9	6 15.6	23 12.9	20 22.3	4 23.6	6 54.7	9 58.1	15 52.6	14 45.1	20 30.8	8 38.0	22 2.9
10 S	11 14 59.5	5 7.9	23 12.4	22 33.7	6 18.2	5 26.9	9 14.9	15 41.3	14 49.7	20 29.0	8 40.0	22 1.3
13 T	11 26 49.2	3 59.4	23 11.8	12 39.1	8 5.6	3 57.7	8 31.3	15 30.1	14 54.3	20 27.3	8 42.1	21 59.9
16 F	11 38 38.8	2 50.3	23 11.2	2S54.4	9 44.5	2 27.4	7 47.2	15 19.0	14 59.1	20 25.7	8 44.2	21 58.5
19 M	11 50 28.5	1 40.7	23 10.6	16 28.6	11 13.1	0 56.3	7 2.7	15 7.9	15 4.0	20 24.1	8 46.4	21 57.2
22 T	12 2 18.2	0 30.7	23 10.0	22 57.6	12 29.1	0S35.2	6 17.8	14 56.9	15 9.0	20 22.6	8 48.6	21 55.9
25 S	12 14 7.8	0S39.4	23 9.4	20 17.7	13 29.4	2 6.8	5 32.6	14 46.0	15 14.1	20 21.2	8 50.9	21 54.8
28 W	12 25 57.5	1 49.5	23 8.8	9 29.1	14 9.8	3 38.1	4 47.2	14 35.3	15 19.3	20 19.8	8 53.2	21 53.7

OCTOBER 1955

LONGITUDE at NOON

DAY	EPHEMERIS SIDEREAL TIME	☉	☊	☽	☿	♀	♂	♃	♄	♅	♆	♇
1 S	12 37 47.1	7♎32.3	20♐56.4	3♈35.5	28♎38.1	15♎38.7	22♍21.3	23♌15.1	18♏34.6	1♌41.9	27♎13.5	27♌45.4
2 S	12 41 43.7	8 31.3	20 53.3	17 37.6	28R35.1	16 53.5	22 59.6	23 26.1	18 40.6	1 43.9	27 15.6	27 47.0
3 M	12 45 40.2	9 30.4	20 50.1	1♉52.0	28 24.9	18 8.2	23 37.9	23 37.1	18 46.6	1 45.8	27 17.8	27 48.5
4 T	12 49 36.8	10 29.4	20 46.9	16 13.3	28 7.1	19 23.0	24 16.3	23 48.0	18 52.7	1 47.6	27 19.9	27 50.0
5 W	12 53 33.3	11 28.5	20 43.7	0♊36.2	27 41.5	20 37.7	24 54.6	23 58.8	18 58.9	1 49.4	27 22.1	27 51.5
6 T	12 57 29.9	12 27.7	20 40.6	14 56.4	27 7.9	21 52.5	25 32.9	24 9.5	19 5.0	1 51.2	27 24.3	27 53.0
7 F	13 1 26.4	13 26.8	20 37.4	29 10.9	26 26.5	23 7.3	26 11.3	24 20.1	19 11.3	1 52.9	27 26.4	27 54.5
8 S	13 5 23.0	14 26.1	20 34.2	13♋18.1	25 37.6	24 22.0	26 49.7	24 30.7	19 17.5	1 54.5	27 28.6	27 55.9
9 S	13 9 19.6	15 25.3	20 31.0	27 16.9	24 41.7	25 36.8	27 28.0	24 41.2	19 23.9	1 56.1	27 30.8	27 57.3
10 M	13 13 16.1	16 24.6	20 27.8	11♌ 7.1	23 39.6	26 51.6	28 6.4	24 51.6	19 30.2	1 57.7	27 33.0	27 58.7
11 T	13 17 12.7	17 23.9	20 24.7	24 48.0	22 32.6	28 6.4	28 44.8	25 1.8	19 36.6	1 59.2	27 35.2	28 0.1
12 W	13 21 9.2	18 23.3	20 21.5	8♍19.0	21 22.1	29 21.2	29 23.2	25 12.0	19 43.0	2 0.7	27 37.4	28 1.5
13 T	13 25 5.8	19 22.7	20 18.3	21 38.8	20 9.8	0♏36.1	0♎ 1.6	25 22.1	19 49.5	2 2.1	27 39.7	28 2.8
14 F	13 29 2.3	20 22.2	20 15.1	4♎46.1	18 57.8	1 50.9	0 40.0	25 32.1	19 56.0	2 3.4	27 41.9	28 4.1
15 S	13 32 58.9	21 21.6	20 12.0	17 39.7	17 48.1	3 5.7	1 18.4	25 42.0	20 2.6	2 4.7	27 44.1	28 5.4
16 S	13 36 55.4	22 21.2	20 8.8	0♏18.9	16 42.7	4 20.5	1 56.9	25 51.9	20 9.2	2 6.0	27 46.3	28 6.7
17 M	13 40 52.0	23 20.7	20 5.6	12 43.6	15 43.7	5 35.3	2 35.3	26 1.6	20 15.8	2 7.2	27 48.6	28 8.0
18 T	13 44 48.5	24 20.3	20 2.4	24 54.8	14 52.6	6 50.2	3 13.8	26 11.2	20 22.5	2 8.3	27 50.8	28 9.2
19 W	13 48 45.1	25 19.9	19 59.2	6♐54.7	14 10.9	8 5.0	3 52.2	26 20.6	20 29.2	2 9.4	27 53.1	28 10.4
20 T	13 52 41.6	26 19.5	19 56.1	18 46.2	13 39.5	9 19.8	4 30.7	26 30.0	20 35.9	2 10.5	27 55.3	28 11.6
21 F	13 56 38.2	27 19.2	19 52.9	0♑33.3	13 19.2	10 34.6	5 9.2	26 39.3	20 42.6	2 11.5	27 57.5	28 12.7
22 S	14 0 34.7	28 19.0	19 49.7	12 20.7	13 10.2	11 49.5	5 47.7	26 48.5	20 49.5	2 12.5	27 59.8	28 13.9
23 S	14 4 31.3	29 18.7	19 46.5	24 13.4	13D12.4	13 4.3	6 26.2	26 57.6	20 56.3	2 13.3	28 2.1	28 15.0
24 M	14 8 27.9	0♏18.4	19 43.4	6♒16.9	13 25.5	14 19.2	7 4.7	27 6.5	21 3.1	2 14.2	28 4.3	28 16.1
25 T	14 12 24.4	1 18.2	19 40.2	18 36.2	13 48.9	15 34.0	7 43.2	27 15.3	21 10.0	2 15.0	28 6.5	28 17.1
26 W	14 16 21.0	2 18.0	19 37.0	1♓16.1	14 22.0	16 48.8	8 21.7	27 24.0	21 16.9	2 15.7	28 8.8	28 18.2
27 T	14 20 17.5	3 17.9	19 33.8	14 20.2	15 4.0	18 3.6	9 0.2	27 32.6	21 23.8	2 16.3	28 11.0	28 19.2
28 F	14 24 14.1	4 17.8	19 30.6	27 50.2	15 54.1	19 18.4	9 38.7	27 41.0	21 30.7	2 17.0	28 13.2	28 20.2
29 S	14 28 10.6	5 17.7	19 27.5	11♈45.8	16 51.3	20 33.2	10 17.3	27 49.4	21 37.7	2 17.5	28 15.5	28 21.1
30 S	14 32 7.2	6 17.6	19 24.3	26 4.2	17 54.8	21 48.1	10 55.8	27 57.6	21 44.6	2 18.0	28 17.7	28 22.0
31 M	14 36 3.7	7 17.6	19 21.1	10♉40.0	19 3.9	23 2.9	11 34.4	28 5.7	21 51.6	2 18.5	28 19.9	28 22.9

DECLINATION at NOON

DAY	EPHEMERIS SIDEREAL TIME	☉	☊	☽	☿	♀	♂	♃	♄	♅	♆	♇
1 S	12 37 47.1	2S59.5	23S 8.1	5N55.2	14S24.9	5S 8.9	4N 1.4	14N24.7	15S24.6	20N18.5	8S55.5	21N52.7
4 T	12 49 36.8	4 9.2	23 7.5	19 22.4	14 8.1	6 38.8	3 15.5	14 14.2	15 30.0	20 17.4	8 57.9	21 51.8
7 F	13 1 26.4	5 18.5	23 6.8	22 36.0	13 13.1	8 7.5	2 29.4	14 4.0	15 35.5	20 16.3	9 0.2	21 51.0
10 M	13 13 16.1	6 27.2	23 6.1	13 36.7	11 38.0	9 34.6	1 43.1	13 54.0	15 41.0	20 15.3	9 2.6	21 50.3
13 T	13 25 5.8	7 35.2	23 5.4	1S20.7	9 31.6	10 59.7	0 56.8	13 44.2	15 46.5	20 14.4	9 5.0	21 49.6
16 S	13 36 55.4	8 42.2	23 4.7	15 9.2	7 16.5	12 22.6	0 10.4	13 34.6	15 52.1	20 13.7	9 7.4	21 49.1
19 W	13 48 45.1	9 48.1	23 4.0	22 29.2	5 22.7	13 42.8	0S36.0	13 25.4	15 57.7	20 13.0	9 9.8	21 48.7
22 S	14 0 34.7	10 52.7	23 3.3	20 47.4	4 13.1	15 0.1	1 22.4	13 16.4	16 3.3	20 12.4	9 12.2	21 48.3
25 T	14 12 24.4	11 55.8	23 2.5	10 59.6	3 55.3	16 13.9	2 8.6	13 7.7	16 9.0	20 12.0	9 14.5	21 48.1
28 F	14 24 14.1	12 57.3	23 1.8	3N48.2	4 24.1	17 24.1	2 54.7	12 59.4	16 14.6	20 11.6	9 16.9	21 48.0
31 M	14 36 3.7	13 56.9	23 1.0	18 0.2	5 28.4	18 30.1	3 40.7	12 51.5	16 20.2	20 11.4	9 19.2	21 48.0

NOVEMBER 1955

DAY	EPHEMERIS SIDEREAL TIME	☉	☊	☽	☿	♀	♂	♃	♄	♅	♆	♇
	h m s	° ′	° ′	° ′	° ′	° ′	° ′	° ′	° ′	° ′	° ′	° ′
LONGITUDE at NOON												
1 T	14 40 0.3	8 ♏ 17.6	19 ♐ 17.9	25 ♉ 26.3	20 ♎ 17.8	24 ♏ 17.7	12 ♎ 12.9	28 ♌ 13.6	21 ♏ 58.6	2 ♌ 18.9	28 ♎ 22.1	28 ♌ 23.8
2 W	14 43 56.8	9 17.6	19 14.8	10 ♊ 15.4	21 35.8	25 32.5	12 51.5	28 21.5	22 5.7	2 19.2	28 24.3	28 24.7
3 T	14 47 53.4	10 17.6	19 11.6	25 0.1	22 57.2	26 47.3	13 30.1	28 29.2	22 12.7	2 19.5	28 26.5	28 25.5
4 F	14 51 50.0	11 17.7	19 8.4	9 ♋ 34.4	24 21.7	28 2.1	14 8.7	28 36.7	22 19.8	2 19.8	28 28.7	28 26.3
5 S	14 55 46.5	12 17.9	19 5.2	23 54.5	25 48.5	29 16.9	14 47.3	28 44.1	22 26.8	2 19.9	28 30.9	28 27.0
6 S	14 59 43.1	13 18.0	19 2.1	7 ♌ 58.2	27 17.5	0 ♐ 31.7	15 26.0	28 51.4	22 33.9	2 20.1	28 33.1	28 27.8
7 M	15 3 39.6	14 18.2	18 58.9	21 44.8	28 48.1	1 46.5	16 4.6	28 58.6	22 41.0	2 20.1	28 35.3	28 28.5
8 T	15 7 36.2	15 18.5	18 55.7	5 ♍ 14.7	0 ♏ 20.0	3 1.3	16 43.3	29 5.6	22 48.1	2 20.1	28 37.5	28 29.2
9 W	15 11 32.7	16 18.7	18 52.5	18 28.8	1 53.1	4 16.1	17 21.9	29 12.5	22 55.3	2 20.1	28 39.6	28 29.8
10 T	15 15 29.3	17 19.0	18 49.3	1 ♎ 28.2	3 27.0	5 30.9	18 0.6	29 19.2	23 2.4	2 R 20.0	28 41.8	28 30.4
11 F	15 19 25.8	18 19.4	18 46.2	14 13.9	5 1.6	6 45.7	18 39.3	29 25.8	23 9.5	2 19.9	28 43.9	28 31.0
12 S	15 23 22.4	19 19.8	18 43.0	26 47.1	6 36.7	8 0.6	19 18.1	29 32.2	23 16.7	2 19.7	28 46.1	28 31.7
13 S	15 27 19.0	20 20.2	18 39.8	9 ♏ 8.5	8 12.1	9 15.4	19 56.8	29 38.5	23 23.9	2 19.4	28 48.2	28 32.2
14 M	15 31 15.5	21 20.6	18 36.6	21 19.3	9 47.8	10 30.2	20 35.5	29 44.6	23 31.0	2 19.1	28 50.3	28 32.7
15 T	15 35 12.1	22 21.1	18 33.5	3 ♐ 20.9	11 23.7	11 45.0	21 14.2	29 50.6	23 38.2	2 18.8	28 52.4	28 33.2
16 W	15 39 8.6	23 21.5	18 30.3	15 14.9	12 59.6	12 59.8	21 53.0	29 56.4	23 45.4	2 18.3	28 54.5	28 33.6
17 T	15 43 5.2	24 22.0	18 27.1	27 3.6	14 35.6	14 14.6	22 31.7	0 ♍ 2.0	23 52.5	2 17.9	28 56.6	28 34.0
18 F	15 47 1.7	25 22.6	18 23.9	8 ♑ 49.9	16 11.5	15 29.4	23 10.5	0 7.5	23 59.7	2 17.3	28 58.6	28 34.4
19 S	15 50 58.3	26 23.1	18 20.7	20 37.2	17 47.4	16 44.2	23 49.2	0 12.8	24 6.8	2 16.7	29 0.7	28 34.8
20 S	15 54 54.8	27 23.7	18 17.6	2 ♒ 29.5	19 23.2	17 59.0	24 28.0	0 18.0	24 14.0	2 16.1	29 2.7	28 35.1
21 M	15 58 51.4	28 24.3	18 14.4	14 31.4	20 58.9	19 13.8	25 6.8	0 23.0	24 21.1	2 15.4	29 4.7	28 35.4
22 T	16 2 48.0	29 24.9	18 11.2	26 47.5	22 34.4	20 28.5	25 45.6	0 27.8	24 28.3	2 14.7	29 6.7	28 35.7
23 W	16 6 44.5	0 ♐ 25.5	18 8.0	9 ♓ 22.6	24 9.8	21 43.3	26 24.4	0 32.5	24 35.4	2 13.9	29 8.7	28 35.9
24 T	16 10 41.1	1 26.2	18 4.9	22 20.8	25 45.1	22 58.1	27 3.2	0 37.0	24 42.5	2 13.0	29 10.7	28 36.1
25 F	16 14 37.6	2 26.8	18 1.7	5 ♈ 45.3	27 20.2	24 12.8	27 42.0	0 41.3	24 49.7	2 12.1	29 12.6	28 36.3
26 S	16 18 34.2	3 27.5	17 58.5	19 37.6	28 55.2	25 27.6	28 20.8	0 45.4	24 56.8	2 11.2	29 14.6	28 36.4
27 S	16 22 30.7	4 28.2	17 55.3	3 ♉ 56.8	0 ♐ 30.1	26 42.3	28 59.7	0 49.4	25 3.9	2 10.1	29 16.5	28 36.6
28 M	16 26 27.3	5 29.0	17 52.2	18 39.3	2 4.8	27 57.0	29 38.5	0 53.2	25 11.0	2 9.1	29 18.4	28 36.6
29 T	16 30 23.9	6 29.7	17 49.0	3 ♊ 38.9	3 39.4	29 11.7	0 ♏ 17.4	0 56.8	25 18.0	2 8.0	29 20.3	28 36.7
30 W	16 34 20.4	7 30.5	17 45.8	18 47.1	5 13.9	0 ♑ 26.4	0 56.3	1 0.3	25 25.1	2 6.8	29 22.1	28 36.7
DECLINATION at NOON												
1 T	14 40 0.3	14 S 16.4	23 S 0.8	21 N 2.9	5 S 55.6	18 S 51.2	3 S 56.0	12 N 48.9	16 S 22.1	20 N 11.3	9 S 20.0	21 N 48.0
4 F	14 51 50.0	15 13.4	23 0.0	21 10.2	7 29.3	19 51.2	4 41.6	12 41.5	16 27.6	20 11.2	9 22.3	21 48.1
7 M	15 3 39.6	16 8.1	22 59.2	9 49.3	9 14.4	20 46.4	5 27.1	12 34.4	16 33.2	20 11.3	9 24.6	21 48.4
10 T	15 15 29.3	17 0.4	22 58.4	5 S 13.8	11 4.3	21 36.4	6 12.2	12 27.9	16 38.7	20 11.4	9 26.8	21 48.7
13 S	15 27 19.0	17 50.1	22 57.6	17 37.3	12 54.6	22 20.9	6 56.9	12 21.7	16 44.2	20 11.6	9 29.0	21 49.1
16 W	15 39 8.6	18 37.0	22 56.8	22 49.2	14 42.1	22 59.5	7 41.3	12 16.1	16 49.6	20 12.0	9 31.2	21 49.7
19 S	15 50 58.3	19 21.0	22 56.0	18 60.0	16 24.9	23 32.1	8 25.2	12 10.9	16 54.9	20 12.5	9 33.3	21 50.3
22 T	16 2 48.0	20 1.8	22 55.1	7 56.1	18 1.3	23 58.4	9 8.6	12 6.3	17 0.2	20 13.0	9 35.3	21 51.0
25 F	16 14 37.6	20 39.3	22 54.3	6 N 53.3	19 30.2	24 18.3	9 51.5	12 2.2	17 5.4	20 13.7	9 37.3	21 51.9
28 M	16 26 27.3	21 13.3	22 53.4	19 49.4	20 50.8	24 31.5	10 33.8	11 58.6	17 10.5	20 14.5	9 39.2	21 52.8

DECEMBER 1955

DAY	EPHEMERIS SIDEREAL TIME	☉	☊	☽	☿	♀	♂	♃	♄	♅	♆	♇
LONGITUDE at NOON												
1 T	16 38 17.0	8 ♐ 31.3	17 ♐ 42.6	3 ♋ 54.6	6 ♐ 48.3	1 ♑ 41.1	1 ♏ 35.1	1 ♍ 3.5	25 ♏ 32.1	2 ♌ 5.6	29 ♎ 24.0	28 ♌ 36.7
2 F	16 42 13.5	9 32.1	17 39.4	18 52.6	8 22.7	2 55.8	2 14.0	1 6.6	25 39.2	2 R 4.4	29 25.8	28 36.7
3 S	16 46 10.1	10 32.9	17 36.3	3 ♌ 33.7	9 57.0	4 10.5	2 53.0	1 9.6	25 46.2	2 3.1	29 27.6	28 36.7
4 S	16 50 6.6	11 33.8	17 33.1	17 53.2	11 31.2	5 25.2	3 31.9	1 12.3	25 53.2	2 1.8	29 29.4	28 R 36.6
5 M	16 54 3.2	12 34.7	17 29.9	1 ♍ 48.7	13 5.4	6 39.9	4 10.9	1 14.8	26 0.2	2 0.4	29 31.2	28 36.4
6 T	16 57 59.8	13 35.6	17 26.7	15 20.2	14 39.6	7 54.5	4 49.8	1 17.1	26 7.1	1 59.0	29 32.9	28 36.3
7 W	17 1 56.3	14 36.5	17 23.6	28 29.0	16 13.8	9 9.2	5 28.8	1 19.3	26 14.1	1 57.5	29 34.6	28 36.1
8 T	17 5 52.9	15 37.4	17 20.4	11 ♎ 17.8	17 48.1	10 23.8	6 7.7	1 21.3	26 21.0	1 55.9	29 36.3	28 35.9
9 F	17 9 49.4	16 38.4	17 17.2	23 49.6	19 22.3	11 38.5	6 46.7	1 23.1	26 27.9	1 54.4	29 38.0	28 35.6
10 S	17 13 46.0	17 39.4	17 14.0	6 ♏ 7.4	20 56.6	12 53.1	7 25.7	1 24.6	26 34.7	1 52.7	29 39.6	28 35.4
11 S	17 17 42.5	18 40.4	17 10.9	18 14.3	22 31.0	14 7.7	8 4.7	1 26.0	26 41.5	1 51.1	29 41.3	28 35.1
12 M	17 21 39.1	19 41.4	17 7.7	0 ♐ 12.9	24 5.4	15 22.3	8 43.7	1 27.2	26 48.3	1 49.4	29 42.9	28 34.7
13 T	17 25 35.7	20 42.4	17 4.5	12 5.5	25 39.9	16 36.9	9 22.8	1 28.2	26 55.1	1 47.6	29 44.4	28 34.4
14 W	17 29 32.2	21 43.5	17 1.3	23 54.5	27 14.5	17 51.5	10 1.8	1 29.1	27 1.8	1 45.8	29 46.0	28 34.0
15 T	17 33 28.8	22 44.5	16 58.2	5 ♑ 41.9	28 49.2	19 6.1	10 40.8	1 29.7	27 8.6	1 44.0	29 47.5	28 33.5
16 F	17 37 25.3	23 45.6	16 55.0	17 29.8	0 ♑ 24.0	20 20.6	11 19.9	1 30.1	27 15.2	1 42.1	29 49.0	28 33.1
17 S	17 41 21.9	24 46.7	16 51.8	29 20.5	1 58.9	21 35.2	11 58.9	1 30.3	27 21.9	1 40.2	29 50.5	28 32.6
18 S	17 45 18.5	25 47.8	16 48.6	11 ♒ 16.7	3 33.9	22 49.7	12 38.0	1 30.3	27 28.5	1 38.3	29 51.9	28 32.1
19 M	17 49 15.0	26 48.9	16 45.4	23 21.4	5 9.0	24 4.2	13 17.1	1 R 30.2	27 35.0	1 36.3	29 53.3	28 31.6
20 T	17 53 11.6	27 50.0	16 42.3	5 ♓ 38.1	6 44.2	25 18.7	13 56.1	1 29.8	27 41.6	1 34.3	29 54.7	28 31.0
21 W	17 57 8.1	28 51.1	16 39.1	18 10.3	8 19.4	26 33.2	14 35.2	1 29.3	27 48.1	1 32.2	29 56.1	28 30.4
22 T	18 1 4.7	29 52.2	16 35.9	1 ♈ 1.9	9 54.8	27 47.6	15 14.3	1 28.5	27 54.5	1 30.1	29 57.4	28 29.8
23 F	18 5 1.2	0 ♑ 53.3	16 32.7	14 16.3	11 30.1	29 2.0	15 53.4	1 27.6	28 0.9	1 28.0	29 58.7	28 29.2
24 S	18 8 57.8	1 54.4	16 29.6	27 56.2	13 5.5	0 ♒ 16.5	16 32.6	1 26.5	28 7.3	1 25.9	0 ♏ 0.1	28 28.5
25 S	18 12 54.4	2 55.6	16 26.4	12 ♉ 2.6	14 40.8	1 30.8	17 11.7	1 25.1	28 13.7	1 23.7	0 1.3	28 27.8
26 M	18 16 50.9	3 56.7	16 23.2	26 34.7	16 16.0	2 45.2	17 50.8	1 23.6	28 19.9	1 21.5	0 2.5	28 27.1
27 T	18 20 47.5	4 57.8	16 20.0	11 ♊ 28.7	17 51.0	3 59.5	18 30.0	1 21.9	28 26.2	1 19.3	0 3.7	28 26.3
28 W	18 24 44.0	5 58.9	16 16.9	26 38.1	19 25.7	5 13.8	19 9.1	1 19.9	28 32.3	1 17.0	0 4.9	28 25.6
29 T	18 28 40.6	7 0.0	16 13.7	11 ♋ 54.0	21 0.1	6 28.1	19 48.2	1 17.8	28 38.5	1 14.7	0 6.0	28 24.8
30 F	18 32 37.1	8 1.2	16 10.5	27 6.1	22 34.1	7 42.3	20 27.4	1 15.5	28 44.6	1 12.4	0 7.1	28 23.9
31 S	18 36 33.7	9 2.3	16 7.3	12 ♌ 4.8	24 7.4	8 56.5	21 6.6	1 13.0	28 50.6	1 10.0	0 8.2	28 23.1
DECLINATION at NOON												
1 T	16 38 17.0	21 S 43.8	22 S 52.6	21 N 52.3	22 S 2.3	24 S 38.0	11 S 15.4	11 N 55.6	17 S 15.5	20 N 15.4	9 S 41.1	21 N 53.9
4 S	16 50 6.6	22 10.5	22 51.7	11 4.4	23 3.9	24 37.7	11 56.5	11 53.2	17 20.4	20 16.3	9 42.9	21 55.0
7 W	17 1 56.3	22 33.4	22 50.8	4 S 10.2	23 55.1	24 30.7	12 36.8	11 51.4	17 25.2	20 17.4	9 44.6	21 56.2
10 S	17 13 46.0	22 52.3	22 49.9	16 51.9	24 35.2	24 16.8	13 16.3	11 50.3	17 29.9	20 18.5	9 46.2	21 57.5
13 T	17 25 35.7	23 7.1	22 49.0	22 43.8	25 3.6	23 56.4	13 55.0	11 49.7	17 34.5	20 19.8	9 47.8	21 58.9
16 F	17 37 25.3	23 17.8	22 48.0	19 39.4	25 19.7	23 29.4	14 32.8	11 49.8	17 38.9	20 21.1	9 49.3	22 0.4
19 M	17 49 15.0	23 24.4	22 47.1	9 9.8	25 22.9	22 56.0	15 9.8	11 50.5	17 43.2	20 22.5	9 50.6	22 2.0
22 T	18 1 4.7	23 26.7	22 46.2	5 N 7.4	25 12.8	22 16.6	15 45.7	11 51.8	17 47.4	20 23.9	9 51.9	22 3.6
25 S	18 12 54.4	23 24.7	22 45.2	18 21.6	24 49.0	21 31.2	16 20.7	11 53.7	17 51.5	20 25.4	9 53.1	22 5.3
28 W	18 24 44.0	23 18.6	22 44.2	22 32.8	24 11.3	20 40.2	16 54.6	11 56.3	17 55.3	20 27.0	9 54.2	22 7.0
31 S	18 36 33.7	23 8.2	22 43.3	13 2.4	23 20.0	19 44.0	17 27.5	11 59.5	17 59.1	20 28.5	9 55.2	22 8.8

JANUARY 1956

LONGITUDE at NOON

DAY	EPHEMERIS SIDEREAL TIME h m s	☉ ° ′	☊ ° ′	☾ ° ′	☿ ° ′	♀ ° ′	♂ ° ′	♃ ° ′	♄ ° ′	♅ ° ′	♆ ° ′	♇ ° ′
1 S	18 40 30.3	10♑ 3.4	16♐ 4.2	26♌41.9	25♑39.9	10♒10.7	21♏45.8	1♍10.4	28♏56.6	1♌ 7.7	0♏ 9.2	28♌22.2
2 M	18 44 26.8	11 4.6	16 1.0	10♍52.5	27 11.4	11 24.9	22 25.0	1R 7.5	29 2.5	1R 5.3	0 10.2	28R21.3
3 T	18 48 23.4	12 5.7	15 57.8	24 34.5	28 41.7	12 39.0	23 4.2	1 4.4	29 8.4	1 2.9	0 11.2	28 20.4
4 W	18 52 19.9	13 6.9	15 54.6	7♎48.5	0♒10.5	13 53.1	23 43.4	1 1.2	29 14.2	1 0.4	0 12.1	28 19.4
5 T	18 56 16.5	14 8.0	15 51.4	20 37.4	1 37.5	15 7.1	24 22.6	0 57.8	29 20.0	0 58.0	0 13.1	28 18.5
6 F	19 0 13.0	15 9.2	15 48.3	3♏ 5.0	3 2.3	16 21.2	25 1.9	0 54.2	29 25.7	0 55.5	0 13.9	28 17.5
7 S	19 4 9.6	16 10.4	15 45.1	15 16.0	4 24.4	17 35.2	25 41.1	0 50.4	29 31.4	0 53.0	0 14.8	28 16.5
8 S	19 8 6.2	17 11.5	15 41.9	27 15.0	5 43.4	18 49.2	26 20.3	0 46.4	29 37.0	0 50.5	0 15.6	28 15.4
9 M	19 12 2.7	18 12.7	15 38.7	9♐ 6.2	6 58.7	20 3.1	26 59.6	0 42.3	29 42.5	0 47.9	0 16.4	28 14.4
10 T	19 15 59.3	19 13.8	15 35.6	20 53.4	8 9.7	21 17.0	27 38.9	0 37.9	29 48.0	0 45.4	0 17.1	28 13.3
11 W	19 19 55.8	20 15.0	15 32.4	2♑40.0	9 15.6	22 30.9	28 18.1	0 33.5	29 53.4	0 42.8	0 17.9	28 12.2
12 T	19 23 52.4	21 16.2	15 29.2	14 28.6	10 15.7	23 44.7	28 57.4	0 28.8	29 58.8	0 40.3	0 18.5	28 11.0
13 F	19 27 48.9	22 17.3	15 26.0	26 21.2	11 9.2	24 58.5	29 36.7	0 24.0	0♐ 4.1	0 37.7	0 19.2	28 9.9
14 S	19 31 45.5	23 18.5	15 22.9	8♒19.7	11 55.2	26 12.3	0♐16.0	0 19.0	0 9.3	0 35.2	0 19.9	28 8.8
15 S	19 35 42.1	24 19.7	15 19.7	20 25.5	12 32.8	27 26.0	0 55.3	0 13.9	0 14.5	0 32.6	0 20.4	28 7.6
16 M	19 39 38.6	25 20.8	15 16.5	2♓40.2	13 1.1	28 39.6	1 34.6	0 8.6	0 19.6	0 29.9	0 21.0	28 6.4
17 T	19 43 35.2	26 21.9	15 13.3	15 5.3	13 19.3	29 53.3	2 13.9	0 3.1	0 24.6	0 27.3	0 21.5	28 5.2
18 W	19 47 31.7	27 23.0	15 10.1	27 43.0	13 26.7	1♓ 6.8	2 53.2	29♌57.5	0 29.5	0 24.7	0 22.0	28 4.0
19 T	19 51 28.3	28 24.1	15 7.0	10♈35.4	13R22.7	2 20.3	3 32.5	29 51.7	0 34.4	0 22.1	0 22.4	28 2.7
20 F	19 55 24.8	29 25.2	15 3.8	23 45.1	13 7.1	3 33.8	4 11.8	29 45.8	0 39.2	0 19.5	0 22.8	28 1.4
21 S	19 59 21.4	0♒26.2	15 0.6	7♉14.5	12 39.9	4 47.2	4 51.1	29 39.8	0 43.9	0 16.9	0 23.2	28 0.2
22 S	20 3 18.0	1 27.3	14 57.4	21 5.6	12 1.5	6 0.5	5 30.5	29 33.6	0 48.6	0 14.2	0 23.6	27 58.9
23 M	20 7 14.5	2 28.3	14 54.3	5♊19.1	11 12.6	7 13.8	6 9.8	29 27.3	0 53.1	0 11.6	0 23.9	27 57.6
24 T	20 11 11.1	3 29.3	14 51.1	19 53.9	10 14.5	8 27.0	6 49.1	29 20.9	0 57.6	0 9.0	0 24.2	27 56.2
25 W	20 15 7.6	4 30.3	14 47.9	4♋46.6	9 8.9	9 40.2	7 28.4	29 14.4	1 2.1	0 6.4	0 24.4	27 54.9
26 T	20 19 4.2	5 31.3	14 44.7	19 50.7	7 57.6	10 53.3	8 7.8	29 7.7	1 6.4	0 3.8	0 24.6	27 53.5
27 F	20 23 0.7	6 32.3	14 41.6	4♌57.7	6 43.0	12 6.3	8 47.1	29 0.9	1 10.7	0 1.2	0 24.8	27 52.2
28 S	20 26 57.3	7 33.2	14 38.4	19 57.7	5 27.2	13 19.3	9 26.5	28 54.1	1 14.9	29♋58.6	0 24.9	27 50.8
29 S	20 30 53.9	8 34.1	14 35.2	4♍41.4	4 12.4	14 32.1	10 5.8	28 47.1	1 19.0	29 56.0	0 25.0	27 49.4
30 M	20 34 50.4	9 35.1	14 32.0	19 1.3	3 0.8	15 45.0	10 45.2	28 40.0	1 23.0	29 53.4	0 25.1	27 48.0
31 T	20 38 47.0	10 36.0	14 28.8	2♎53.1	1 54.0	16 57.7	11 24.5	28 32.8	1 26.9	29 50.9	0 25.1	27 46.6

DECLINATION at NOON

DAY	SIDEREAL TIME	☉	☊	☾	☿	♀	♂	♃	♄	♅	♆	♇
1 S	18 40 30.3	23S 3.8	22S42.9	7N59.0	22S60.0	19S24.1	17S38.2	12N 0.7	18S 0.3	20N29.1	9S55.5	22N 9.4
4 W	18 52 19.9	22 47.9	22 41.9	7S36.7	21 51.8	18 21.2	18 9.5	12 4.6	18 3.8	20 30.7	9 56.4	22 11.3
7 S	19 4 9.6	22 27.9	22 40.9	19 4.2	20 33.4	17 13.8	18 39.6	12 9.2	18 7.2	20 32.4	9 57.2	22 13.2
10 T	19 15 59.3	22 3.9	22 39.9	22 47.5	19 8.6	16 2.2	19 8.4	12 14.3	18 10.4	20 34.1	9 57.8	22 15.1
13 F	19 27 48.9	21 36.0	22 38.9	17 38.9	17 43.6	14 46.8	19 36.0	12 19.9	18 13.5	20 35.8	9 58.3	22 17.1
16 M	19 39 38.6	21 4.4	22 37.8	5 50.4	16 27.1	13 27.8	20 2.3	12 26.0	18 16.4	20 37.5	9 58.8	22 19.1
19 T	19 51 28.3	20 29.1	22 36.8	8N31.9	15 29.6	12 5.8	20 27.2	12 32.5	18 19.1	20 39.2	9 59.1	22 21.1
22 S	20 3 18.0	19 50.4	22 35.7	20 10.2	15 0.2	10 41.0	20 50.7	12 39.5	18 21.6	20 40.9	9 59.4	22 23.1
25 W	20 15 7.6	19 8.4	22 34.7	21 44.0	15 2.4	9 13.8	21 12.7	12 46.8	18 24.0	20 42.6	9 59.5	22 25.1
28 S	20 26 57.3	18 23.2	22 33.6	10 27.9	15 30.7	7 44.5	21 33.3	12 54.4	18 26.2	20 44.3	9 59.5	22 27.2
31 T	20 38 47.0	17 35.0	22 32.5	5S37.7	16 13.8	6 13.5	21 52.4	13 2.3	18 28.2	20 46.0	9 59.4	22 29.2

FEBRUARY 1956

LONGITUDE at NOON

DAY	SIDEREAL TIME	☉	☊	☾	☿	♀	♂	♃	♄	♅	♆	♇
1 W	20 42 43.5	11♒36.9	14♐25.7	16♎15.6	0♒53.5	18♓10.4	12♐ 3.9	28♌25.6	1♐30.8	29♋48.3	0♏25.1	27♌45.2
2 T	20 46 40.1	12 37.8	14 22.5	29 10.5	0R 0.4	19 23.0	12 43.3	28R18.2	1 34.6	29R45.8	0 25.1	27R43.7
3 F	20 50 36.6	13 38.6	14 19.3	11♏41.4	29♑15.2	20 35.6	13 22.7	28 10.8	1 38.3	29 43.3	0R25.0	27 42.3
4 S	20 54 33.2	14 39.5	14 16.1	23 53.1	28 38.5	21 48.1	14 2.1	28 3.3	1 41.9	29 40.8	0 25.0	27 40.9
5 S	20 58 29.7	15 40.4	14 13.0	5♐50.9	28 10.3	23 0.4	14 41.5	27 55.8	1 45.4	29 38.3	0 24.8	27 39.5
6 M	21 2 26.3	16 41.2	14 9.8	17 40.3	27 50.5	24 12.8	15 20.9	27 48.1	1 48.9	29 35.8	0 24.7	27 38.0
7 T	21 6 22.8	17 42.0	14 6.6	29 26.3	27 38.9	25 25.0	16 0.3	27 40.4	1 52.2	29 33.4	0 24.5	27 36.5
8 W	21 10 19.4	18 42.8	14 3.4	11♑13.4	27 35.1	26 37.1	16 39.7	27 32.7	1 55.5	29 30.9	0 24.2	27 35.0
9 T	21 14 16.0	19 43.6	14 0.2	23 5.2	27D38.7	27 49.2	17 19.1	27 24.9	1 58.6	29 28.5	0 24.0	27 33.6
10 F	21 18 12.5	20 44.3	13 57.1	5♒ 4.6	27 49.2	29 1.2	17 58.5	27 17.1	2 1.7	29 26.1	0 23.7	27 32.1
11 S	21 22 9.1	21 45.1	13 53.9	17 13.5	28 6.2	0♈13.1	18 37.8	27 9.2	2 4.7	29 23.7	0 23.3	27 30.6
12 S	21 26 5.6	22 45.8	13 50.7	29 33.0	28 29.1	1 24.9	19 17.2	27 1.3	2 7.6	29 21.4	0 23.0	27 29.1
13 M	21 30 2.2	23 46.4	13 47.5	12♓ 3.5	28 57.5	2 36.6	19 56.6	26 53.4	2 10.3	29 19.1	0 22.6	27 27.6
14 T	21 33 58.7	24 47.1	13 44.4	24 45.3	29 31.0	3 48.2	20 36.0	26 45.5	2 13.0	29 16.8	0 22.1	27 26.1
15 W	21 37 55.3	25 47.7	13 41.2	7♈38.4	0♒ 9.2	4 59.7	21 15.4	26 37.6	2 15.7	29 14.5	0 21.7	27 24.6
16 T	21 41 51.8	26 48.4	13 38.0	20 43.1	0 51.6	6 11.1	21 54.8	26 29.6	2 18.2	29 12.2	0 21.2	27 23.1
17 F	21 45 48.4	27 48.9	13 34.8	3♉59.9	1 38.0	7 22.4	22 34.1	26 21.7	2 20.6	29 10.0	0 20.6	27 21.6
18 S	21 49 44.9	28 49.5	13 31.7	17 29.9	2 27.9	8 33.6	23 13.5	26 13.8	2 22.9	29 7.9	0 20.1	27 20.1
19 S	21 53 41.5	29 50.0	13 28.5	1♊14.5	3 21.3	9 44.7	23 52.9	26 5.9	2 25.1	29 5.7	0 19.5	27 18.6
20 M	21 57 38.1	0♓50.5	13 25.3	15 14.4	4 17.7	10 55.7	24 32.2	25 58.0	2 27.2	29 3.6	0 18.9	27 17.1
21 T	22 1 34.6	1 50.9	13 22.1	29 29.9	5 16.9	12 6.5	25 11.6	25 50.1	2 29.2	29 1.5	0 18.2	27 15.6
22 W	22 5 31.2	2 51.4	13 18.9	13♋59.5	6 18.8	13 17.2	25 50.9	25 42.3	2 31.2	28 59.4	0 17.5	27 14.1
23 T	22 9 27.7	3 51.8	13 15.8	28 39.6	7 23.1	14 27.8	26 30.3	25 34.5	2 33.0	28 57.4	0 16.8	27 12.6
24 F	22 13 24.3	4 52.1	13 12.6	13♌24.6	8 29.8	15 38.3	27 9.6	25 26.7	2 34.7	28 55.4	0 16.1	27 11.2
25 S	22 17 20.8	5 52.5	13 9.4	28 7.1	9 38.6	16 48.7	27 49.0	25 19.1	2 36.4	28 53.6	0 15.3	27 9.7
26 S	22 21 17.4	6 52.8	13 6.2	12♍38.9	10 49.4	17 58.9	28 28.4	25 11.4	2 37.9	28 51.6	0 14.5	27 8.3
27 M	22 25 13.9	7 53.1	13 3.1	26 52.8	12 2.1	19 8.9	29 7.7	25 3.8	2 39.4	28 49.8	0 13.7	27 6.8
28 T	22 29 10.5	8 53.3	12 59.9	10♎43.4	13 16.6	20 18.9	29 47.1	24 56.3	2 40.7	28 47.9	0 12.8	27 5.3
29 W	22 33 7.0	9 53.5	12 56.7	24 8.0	14 32.8	21 28.7	0♑26.4	24 48.8	2 41.9	28 46.2	0 12.0	27 3.9

DECLINATION at NOON

DAY	SIDEREAL TIME	☉	☊	☾	☿	♀	♂	♃	♄	♅	♆	♇
1 W	20 42 43.5	17S18.3	22S32.1	10S27.5	16S29.4	5S42.8	21S58.4	13N 5.0	18S28.8	20N46.5	9S59.3	22N29.8
4 S	20 54 33.2	16 26.4	22 31.0	20 34.9	17 15.4	4 10.1	22 15.4	13 13.2	18 30.6	20 48.1	9 59.1	22 31.8
7 T	21 6 22.8	15 31.9	22 29.9	22 13.0	17 56.0	2 36.4	22 30.9	13 21.5	18 32.2	20 49.7	9 58.8	22 33.8
10 F	21 18 12.5	14 35.0	22 28.8	15 14.9	18 27.8	1 2.1	22 44.7	13 29.9	18 33.6	20 51.2	9 58.3	22 35.7
13 M	21 30 2.2	13 35.9	22 27.6	2 23.4	18 49.4	0N32.5	22 57.0	13 38.4	18 34.8	20 52.6	9 57.8	22 37.6
16 T	21 41 51.8	12 34.8	22 26.5	11N50.6	18 59.9	2 7.0	23 7.6	13 46.8	18 35.8	20 54.0	9 57.1	22 39.4
19 S	21 53 41.5	11 32.0	22 25.3	21 30.5	18 58.9	3 41.2	23 16.6	13 55.1	18 36.7	20 55.3	9 56.4	22 41.2
22 W	22 5 31.2	10 27.5	22 24.1	20 11.7	18 46.1	5 14.6	23 23.9	14 3.3	18 37.4	20 56.6	9 55.5	22 43.0
25 S	22 17 20.8	9 21.5	22 23.0	7 35.5	18 21.5	6 47.1	23 29.6	14 11.3	18 37.9	20 57.8	9 54.6	22 44.6
28 T	22 29 10.5	8 14.3	22 21.8	8S19.7	17 45.0	8 18.2	23 33.6	14 19.1	18 38.2	20 58.9	9 53.6	22 46.3

MARCH 1956

LONGITUDE at NOON

DAY	EPHEMERIS SIDEREAL TIME	☉	☊	☽	☿	♀	♂	♃	♄	♅	♆	♇
	h m s	° ′	° ′	° ′	° ′	° ′	° ′	° ′	° ′	° ′	° ′	° ′
1 T	22 37 3.6	10♓53.7	12♐53.5	7♏ 6.5	15♒50.6	22♈38.3	1♑ 5.8	24♌41.5	2♐43.1	28♋44.4	0♏11.0	27♌ 2.4
2 F	22 41 0.1	11 53.9	12 50.3	19 41.3	17 10.0	23 47.8	1 45.1	24R34.2	2 44.1	28R42.7	0R10.1	27R 1.0
3 S	22 44 56.7	12 54.1	12 47.2	1♐56.4	18 30.8	24 57.2	2 24.4	24 26.9	2 45.0	28 41.0	0 9.1	26 59.5
4 S	22 48 53.2	13 54.2	12 44.0	13 56.7	19 53.1	26 6.4	3 3.7	24 19.8	2 45.8	28 39.4	0 8.1	26 58.1
5 M	22 52 49.8	14 54.3	12 40.8	25 47.8	21 16.8	27 15.4	3 43.1	24 12.8	2 46.6	28 37.8	0 7.1	26 56.7
6 T	22 56 46.4	15 54.3	12 37.6	7♑35.4	22 41.9	28 24.3	4 22.4	24 5.8	2 47.2	28 36.3	0 6.1	26 55.3
7 W	23 0 42.9	16 54.4	12 34.5	19 24.5	24 8.3	29 33.1	5 1.7	23 59.0	2 47.7	28 34.8	0 5.0	26 53.9
8 T	23 4 39.5	17 54.4	12 31.3	1♒20.1	25 35.9	0♉41.7	5 41.0	23 52.2	2 48.1	28 33.3	0 3.9	26 52.5
9 F	23 8 36.0	18 54.4	12 28.1	13 25.8	27 4.9	1 50.1	6 20.2	23 45.6	2 48.5	28 31.9	0 2.8	26 51.1
10 S	23 12 32.6	19 54.3	12 24.9	25 44.4	28 35.1	2 58.3	6 59.5	23 39.1	2 48.7	28 30.6	0 1.6	26 49.8
11 S	23 16 29.1	20 54.2	12 21.7	8♓17.5	0♓ 6.5	4 6.4	7 38.8	23 32.8	2 48.8	28 29.2	0 0.4	26 48.4
12 M	23 20 25.7	21 54.1	12 18.6	21 5.5	1 39.1	5 14.3	8 18.0	23 26.5	2 48.8	28 28.0	29♎59.3	26 47.1
13 T	23 24 22.2	22 54.0	12 15.4	4♈ 7.8	3 13.0	6 22.0	8 57.2	23 20.4	2R48.7	28 26.8	29 58.0	26 45.8
14 W	23 28 18.8	23 53.8	12 12.2	17 22.9	4 48.1	7 29.5	9 36.4	23 14.4	2 48.5	28 25.6	29 56.8	26 44.4
15 T	23 32 15.3	24 53.6	12 9.0	0♉49.3	6 24.4	8 36.8	10 15.6	23 8.5	2 48.2	28 24.5	29 55.5	26 43.1
16 F	23 36 11.9	25 53.3	12 5.8	14 25.2	8 1.9	9 43.9	10 54.8	23 2.8	2 47.8	28 23.4	29 54.3	26 41.9
17 S	23 40 8.4	26 53.1	12 2.7	28 9.5	9 40.7	10 50.9	11 34.0	22 57.3	2 47.3	28 22.4	29 53.0	26 40.7
18 S	23 44 5.0	27 52.8	11 59.5	12♊ 1.5	11 20.6	11 57.6	12 13.1	22 51.9	2 46.7	28 21.5	29 51.7	26 39.4
19 M	23 48 1.5	28 52.4	11 56.3	26 1.0	13 1.8	13 4.0	12 52.3	22 46.7	2 46.0	28 20.6	29 50.3	26 38.2
20 T	23 51 58.1	29 52.0	11 53.1	10♋ 7.5	14 44.3	14 10.3	13 31.4	22 41.6	2 45.3	28 19.7	29 49.0	26 37.0
21 W	23 55 54.6	0♈51.6	11 50.0	24 20.3	16 28.0	15 16.3	14 10.5	22 36.6	2 44.4	28 18.9	29 47.6	26 35.8
22 T	23 59 51.2	1 51.1	11 46.8	8♌37.4	18 13.0	16 22.1	14 49.5	22 31.8	2 43.4	28 18.1	29 46.2	26 34.6
23 F	0 3 47.7	2 50.6	11 43.6	22 55.7	19 59.2	17 27.6	15 28.6	22 27.2	2 42.3	28 17.4	29 44.8	26 33.4
24 S	0 7 44.3	3 50.0	11 40.4	7♍10.7	21 46.8	18 32.9	16 7.6	22 22.7	2 41.1	28 16.7	29 43.4	26 32.3
25 S	0 11 40.9	4 49.4	11 37.2	21 17.3	23 35.6	19 37.9	16 46.6	22 18.4	2 39.8	28 16.1	29 41.9	26 31.2
26 M	0 15 37.4	5 48.8	11 34.1	5♎10.4	25 25.8	20 42.6	17 25.6	22 14.3	2 38.4	28 15.6	29 40.5	26 30.1
27 T	0 19 34.0	6 48.2	11 30.9	18 45.8	27 17.3	21 47.1	18 4.6	22 10.4	2 36.9	28 15.1	29 39.0	26 29.0
28 W	0 23 30.5	7 47.5	11 27.7	2♏ 0.6	29 10.1	22 51.3	18 43.5	22 6.6	2 35.4	28 14.6	29 37.5	26 27.9
29 T	0 27 27.1	8 46.7	11 24.5	14 54.1	1♈ 4.3	23 55.2	19 22.5	22 3.0	2 33.7	28 14.2	29 36.0	26 26.9
30 F	0 31 23.6	9 46.0	11 21.4	27 27.4	2 59.8	24 58.8	20 1.4	21 59.5	2 31.9	28 13.9	29 34.5	26 25.9
31 S	0 35 20.2	10 45.2	11 18.2	9♐43.1	4 56.6	26 2.1	20 40.3	21 56.3	2 30.1	28 13.6	29 33.0	26 24.9

DECLINATION at NOON

DAY	EPHEMERIS SIDEREAL TIME	☉	☊	☽	☿	♀	♂	♃	♄	♅	♆	♇
1 T	22 37 3.6	7S28.9	22S21.0	16S39.7	17S14.1	9N18.0	23S35.3	14N24.1	18S38.4	20N59.6	9S52.9	22N47.3
4 S	22 48 53.2	6 20.0	22 19.7	22 21.8	16 17.9	10 46.3	23 36.5	14 31.4	18 38.4	21 0.6	9 51.7	22 48.8
7 W	23 0 42.9	5 10.3	22 18.5	19 2.7	15 10.1	12 12.4	23 36.1	14 38.3	18 38.2	21 1.5	9 50.5	22 50.2
10 S	23 12 32.6	3 59.9	22 17.3	8 24.8	13 50.8	13 36.1	23 34.0	14 44.9	18 37.9	21 2.3	9 49.2	22 51.5
13 T	23 24 22.2	2 49.1	22 16.0	5N53.2	12 20.2	14 57.1	23 30.3	14 51.0	18 37.4	21 3.0	9 47.8	22 52.8
16 F	23 36 11.9	1 38.1	22 14.8	18 19.8	10 38.4	16 15.1	23 25.0	14 56.6	18 36.8	21 3.6	9 46.4	22 53.9
19 M	23 48 1.5	0 26.9	22 13.5	22 4.1	8 45.6	17 29.8	23 18.1	15 1.8	18 36.0	21 4.1	9 44.9	22 55.0
22 T	23 59 51.2	0N44.2	22 12.3	13 58.7	6 42.2	18 41.0	23 9.7	15 6.5	18 35.0	21 4.6	9 43.4	22 56.0
25 S	0 11 40.9	1 55.0	22 11.0	1S 6.1	4 28.5	19 48.4	22 59.7	15 10.6	18 33.9	21 4.9	9 41.8	22 56.8
28 W	0 23 30.5	3 5.5	22 9.7	15 6.2	2 4.9	20 51.7	22 48.2	15 14.3	18 32.6	21 5.1	9 40.1	22 57.6
31 S	0 35 20.2	4 15.4	22 8.4	21 55.2	0N27.6	21 50.8	22 35.3	15 17.3	18 31.1	21 5.3	9 38.5	22 58.3

APRIL 1956

LONGITUDE at NOON

DAY	EPHEMERIS SIDEREAL TIME	☉	☊	☽	☿	♀	♂	♃	♄	♅	♆	♇
1 S	0 39 16.7	11♈44.4	11♐15.0	21♐45.1	6♈54.6	27♉ 5.1	21♑19.2	21♌53.2	2♐28.2	28♋13.4	29♎31.4	26♌23.9
2 M	0 43 13.3	12 43.5	11 11.8	3♑38.3	8 53.9	28 7.7	21 58.0	21R50.3	2R26.1	28R13.2	29R29.9	26R22.9
3 T	0 47 9.8	13 42.7	11 8.6	15 27.7	10 54.4	29 10.1	22 36.8	21 47.6	2 24.0	28 13.0	29 28.3	26 22.0
4 W	0 51 6.4	14 41.8	11 5.5	27 18.8	12 56.1	0♊12.1	23 15.6	21 45.0	2 21.8	28 13.0	29 26.8	26 21.1
5 T	0 55 2.9	15 40.8	11 2.3	9♒16.7	14 58.7	1 13.8	23 54.4	21 42.7	2 19.5	28 12.9	29 25.2	26 20.2
6 F	0 58 59.5	16 39.9	10 59.1	21 26.0	17 2.3	2 15.1	24 33.1	21 40.5	2 17.1	28D13.0	29 23.6	26 19.4
7 S	1 2 56.0	17 38.9	10 55.9	3♓50.5	19 6.7	3 16.1	25 11.8	21 38.6	2 14.7	28 13.1	29 22.0	26 18.6
8 S	1 6 52.6	18 37.9	10 52.8	16 32.8	21 11.7	4 16.7	25 50.5	21 36.8	2 12.2	28 13.2	29 20.4	26 17.8
9 M	1 10 49.1	19 36.8	10 49.6	29 34.2	23 17.2	5 16.9	26 29.1	21 35.2	2 9.5	28 13.4	29 18.8	26 17.0
10 T	1 14 45.7	20 35.7	10 46.4	12♈54.3	25 22.9	6 16.7	27 7.7	21 33.8	2 6.8	28 13.7	29 17.2	26 16.2
11 W	1 18 42.2	21 34.6	10 43.2	26 31.4	27 28.6	7 16.1	27 46.2	21 32.5	2 4.0	28 14.0	29 15.6	26 15.5
12 T	1 22 38.8	22 33.5	10 40.0	10♉22.5	29 34.0	8 15.1	28 24.7	21 31.5	2 1.1	28 14.4	29 14.0	26 14.7
13 F	1 26 35.4	23 32.3	10 36.9	24 24.2	1♉38.8	9 13.6	29 3.2	21 30.6	1 58.2	28 14.8	29 12.3	26 14.1
14 S	1 30 31.9	24 31.0	10 33.7	8♊32.6	3 42.7	10 11.7	29 41.6	21 30.0	1 55.2	28 15.2	29 10.7	26 13.4
15 S	1 34 28.5	25 29.8	10 30.5	22 44.6	5 45.4	11 9.3	0♒19.9	21 29.5	1 52.1	28 15.7	29 9.1	26 12.8
16 M	1 38 25.0	26 28.5	10 27.3	6♋57.3	7 46.6	12 6.4	0 58.2	21 29.2	1 48.9	28 16.3	29 7.4	26 12.2
17 T	1 42 21.6	27 27.1	10 24.2	21 8.8	9 45.8	13 3.1	1 36.5	21 29.1	1 45.6	28 17.0	29 5.8	26 11.6
18 W	1 46 18.1	28 25.8	10 21.0	5♌17.2	11 42.8	13 59.1	2 14.7	21D29.2	1 42.3	28 17.6	29 4.1	26 11.0
19 T	1 50 14.7	29 24.3	10 17.8	19 21.1	13 37.3	14 54.7	2 52.9	21 29.5	1 39.0	28 18.4	29 2.5	26 10.5
20 F	1 54 11.2	0♉22.9	10 14.6	3♍18.7	15 28.9	15 49.7	3 31.0	21 29.9	1 35.5	28 19.2	29 0.8	26 10.0
21 S	1 58 7.8	1 21.4	10 11.4	17 8.1	17 17.3	16 44.0	4 9.1	21 30.6	1 32.0	28 20.0	28 59.2	26 9.5
22 S	2 2 4.3	2 19.9	10 8.3	0♎47.0	19 2.4	17 37.8	4 47.1	21 31.4	1 28.4	28 20.9	28 57.6	26 9.1
23 M	2 6 0.9	3 18.3	10 5.1	14 13.4	20 43.9	18 31.0	5 25.0	21 32.4	1 24.8	28 21.8	28 55.9	26 8.7
24 T	2 9 57.4	4 16.7	10 1.9	27 25.2	22 21.6	19 23.5	6 2.9	21 33.6	1 21.1	28 22.8	28 54.3	26 8.3
25 W	2 13 54.0	5 15.1	9 58.7	10♏21.3	23 55.3	20 15.3	6 40.8	21 35.0	1 17.4	28 23.9	28 52.7	26 7.9
26 T	2 17 50.5	6 13.5	9 55.6	23 1.4	25 24.9	21 6.5	7 18.6	21 36.6	1 13.6	28 25.0	28 51.0	26 7.6
27 F	2 21 47.1	7 11.8	9 52.4	5♐26.2	26 50.2	21 56.9	7 56.3	21 38.3	1 9.7	28 26.1	28 49.4	26 7.3
28 S	2 25 43.7	8 10.1	9 49.2	17 37.4	28 11.3	22 46.6	8 34.1	21 40.3	1 5.9	28 27.4	28 47.8	26 7.0
29 S	2 29 40.2	9 8.4	9 46.0	29 37.8	29 27.7	23 35.6	9 11.7	21 42.4	1 1.9	28 28.6	28 46.2	26 6.8
30 M	2 33 36.8	10 6.6	9 42.8	11♑31.0	0♊39.7	24 23.7	9 49.2	21 44.6	0 57.9	28 29.9	28 44.6	26 6.6

DECLINATION at NOON

DAY	EPHEMERIS SIDEREAL TIME	☉	☊	☽	☿	♀	♂	♃	♄	♅	♆	♇
1 S	0 39 16.7	4N38.6	22S 7.9	22S 7.7	1N20.2	22N 9.5	22S30.7	15N18.3	18S30.6	21N 5.3	9S37.9	22N58.5
4 W	0 51 6.4	5 47.6	22 6.6	16 59.6	4 2.4	23 2.7	22 15.9	15 20.6	18 29.0	21 5.3	9 36.2	22 59.0
7 S	1 2 56.0	6 55.7	22 5.3	5 21.5	6 49.3	23 51.1	21 59.7	15 22.4	18 27.2	21 5.2	9 34.5	22 59.4
10 T	1 14 45.7	8 2.7	22 3.9	9N 1.1	9 37.2	24 34.8	21 42.2	15 23.6	18 25.4	21 5.0	9 32.8	22 59.7
13 F	1 26 35.4	9 8.5	22 2.6	20 7.6	12 21.4	25 13.6	21 23.5	15 24.3	18 23.4	21 4.7	9 31.0	22 59.9
16 M	1 38 25.0	10 13.0	22 1.2	20 49.5	14 56.3	25 47.4	21 3.6	15 24.4	18 21.2	21 4.3	9 29.3	23 0.0
19 T	1 50 14.7	11 15.9	21 59.8	10 22.8	17 16.5	26 16.2	20 42.6	15 24.0	18 19.0	21 3.8	9 27.5	23 0.0
22 S	2 2 4.3	12 17.1	21 58.4	4S42.7	19 17.4	26 40.1	20 20.5	15 23.0	18 16.7	21 3.3	9 25.8	22 59.9
25 W	2 13 54.0	13 16.5	21 57.0	17 15.1	20 56.5	26 59.1	19 57.4	15 21.5	18 14.3	21 2.6	9 24.1	22 59.7
28 S	2 25 43.7	14 14.0	21 55.6	22 1.5	22 12.8	27 13.2	19 33.4	15 19.4	18 11.8	21 1.8	9 22.4	22 59.3

MAY 1956

DAY	EPHEMERIS SIDEREAL TIME	☉	☊	☽	☿	♀	♂	♃	♄	♅	♆	♇
	h m s	° ′	° ′	° ′	° ′	° ′	° ′	° ′	° ′	° ′	° ′	° ′
						LONGITUDE at NOON						
1 T	2 37 33.3	11♉ 4.9	9♐39.7	23♑21.1	1♊46.9	25♊11.0	10♒26.7	21♌47.1	0♐53.9	28♋31.3	28♎43.0	26♌ 6.4
2 W	2 41 29.9	12 3.0	9 36.5	5♒13.0	2 49.5	25 57.4	11 4.1	21 49.7	0R49.8	28 32.7	28R41.4	26R 6.2
3 T	2 45 26.4	13 1.2	9 33.3	17 11.4	3 47.2	26 43.0	11 41.5	21 52.5	0 45.7	28 34.1	28 39.9	26 6.1
4 F	2 49 23.0	13 59.4	9 30.1	29 21.1	4 40.1	27 27.7	12 18.7	21 55.5	0 41.5	28 35.6	28 38.3	26 6.0
5 S	2 53 19.5	14 57.5	9 27.0	11♓46.6	5 28.1	28 11.4	12 55.9	21 58.6	0 37.3	28 37.2	28 36.7	26 5.9
6 S	2 57 16.1	15 55.6	9 23.8	24 31.6	6 11.1	28 54.1	13 33.0	22 2.0	0 33.1	28 38.8	28 35.2	26 5.8
7 M	3 1 12.6	16 53.6	9 20.6	7♈38.5	6 49.1	29 35.8	14 10.0	22 5.4	0 28.8	28 40.4	28 33.6	26 5.8
8 T	3 5 9.2	17 51.7	9 17.4	21 8.3	7 22.0	0♋16.4	14 47.0	22 9.1	0 24.5	28 42.1	28 32.1	26 5.8
9 W	3 9 5.8	18 49.7	9 14.2	5♉ 0.2	7 49.9	0 55.9	15 23.8	22 12.9	0 20.2	28 43.8	28 30.6	26D 5.9
10 T	3 13 2.3	19 47.7	9 11.1	19 11.2	8 12.5	1 34.3	16 0.5	22 16.9	0 15.8	28 45.6	28 29.0	26 5.9
11 F	3 16 58.9	20 45.7	9 7.9	3♊37.1	8 30.1	2 11.5	16 37.1	22 21.1	0 11.4	28 47.4	28 27.6	26 6.0
12 S	3 20 55.4	21 43.6	9 4.7	18 12.0	8 42.6	2 47.5	17 13.7	22 25.4	0 7.0	28 49.3	28 26.1	26 6.2
13 S	3 24 52.0	22 41.5	9 1.5	2♋49.9	8 50.0	3 22.1	17 50.1	22 29.9	0 2.6	28 51.2	28 24.6	26 6.3
14 M	3 28 48.5	23 39.4	8 58.4	17 25.0	8 52.5	3 55.4	18 26.4	22 34.5	29♏58.2	28 53.2	28 23.1	26 6.5
15 T	3 32 45.1	24 37.2	8 55.2	1♌52.5	8R50.1	4 27.4	19 2.6	22 39.3	29 53.8	28 55.2	28 21.7	26 6.7
16 W	3 36 41.6	25 35.1	8 52.0	16 8.8	8 43.1	4 57.8	19 38.7	22 44.3	29 49.3	28 57.3	28 20.3	26 7.0
17 T	3 40 38.2	26 32.9	8 48.8	0♍11.4	8 31.5	5 26.8	20 14.6	22 49.4	29 44.8	28 59.4	28 18.9	26 7.2
18 F	3 44 34.8	27 30.6	8 45.7	13 59.1	8 15.8	5 54.2	20 50.5	22 54.6	29 40.4	29 1.5	28 17.5	26 7.5
19 S	3 48 31.3	28 28.4	8 42.5	27 31.7	7 56.2	6 20.0	21 26.3	23 0.1	29 35.9	29 3.8	28 16.2	26 7.9
20 S	3 52 27.9	29 26.1	8 39.3	10♎49.0	7 33.0	6 44.1	22 1.9	23 5.7	29 31.5	29 6.0	28 14.8	26 8.3
21 M	3 56 24.4	0♊23.8	8 36.1	23 51.6	7 6.7	7 6.4	22 37.4	23 11.4	29 27.0	29 8.3	28 13.5	26 8.7
22 T	4 0 21.0	1 21.5	8 32.9	6♏40.3	6 37.8	7 27.0	23 12.8	23 17.2	29 22.5	29 10.6	28 12.2	26 9.1
23 W	4 4 17.5	2 19.1	8 29.8	19 15.7	6 6.7	7 45.6	23 48.0	23 23.2	29 18.0	29 12.9	28 10.9	26 9.5
24 T	4 8 14.1	3 16.8	8 26.6	1♐39.1	5 34.1	8 2.4	24 23.1	23 29.4	29 13.6	29 15.3	28 9.6	26 10.0
25 F	4 12 10.7	4 14.4	8 23.4	13 51.6	5 0.4	8 17.1	24 58.1	23 35.7	29 9.1	29 17.7	28 8.3	26 10.5
26 S	4 16 7.2	5 11.9	8 20.2	25 54.9	4 26.4	8 29.8	25 32.9	23 42.1	29 4.7	29 20.2	28 7.1	26 11.0
27 S	4 20 3.8	6 9.5	8 17.1	7♑51.0	3 52.5	8 40.5	26 7.6	23 48.7	29 0.2	29 22.7	28 5.9	26 11.6
28 M	4 24 0.3	7 7.0	8 13.9	19 42.6	3 19.4	8 48.9	26 42.1	23 55.4	28 55.8	29 25.3	28 4.7	26 12.2
29 T	4 27 56.9	8 4.6	8 10.7	1♒32.7	2 47.6	8 55.2	27 16.5	24 2.2	28 51.4	29 27.8	28 3.5	26 12.8
30 W	4 31 53.4	9 2.1	8 7.5	13 24.9	2 17.7	8 59.2	27 50.7	24 9.2	28 47.1	29 30.5	28 2.4	26 13.4
31 T	4 35 50.0	9 59.6	8 4.4	25 23.2	1 50.2	9 1.0	28 24.8	24 16.3	28 42.7	29 33.1	28 1.2	26 14.1
						DECLINATION at NOON						
1 T	2 37 33.3	15N 9.3	21S54.2	17S46.0	23N 6.7	27N22.8	19S 8.4	15N16.8	18S 9.2	21N 0.9	9S20.7	22N58.9
4 F	2 49 23.0	16 2.5	21 52.8	6 50.6	23 39.2	27 27.8	18 42.7	15 13.7	18 6.6	20 60.0	9 19.0	22 58.4
7 M	3 1 12.6	16 53.2	21 51.4	7N14.1	23 51.6	27 28.5	18 16.3	15 10.1	18 4.0	20 58.9	9 17.4	22 57.8
10 T	3 13 2.3	17 41.4	21 49.9	19 10.4	23 45.1	27 25.2	17 49.3	15 6.0	18 1.3	20 57.8	9 15.9	22 57.1
13 S	3 24 52.0	18 26.9	21 48.5	21 12.5	23 21.0	27 18.1	17 21.8	15 1.5	17 58.6	20 56.6	9 14.4	22 56.2
16 W	3 36 41.6	19 9.6	21 47.0	11 19.5	22 40.8	27 7.5	16 53.8	14 56.4	17 55.8	20 55.3	9 12.9	22 55.3
19 S	3 48 31.3	19 49.4	21 45.5	3S35.3	21 47.0	26 53.7	16 25.4	14 50.9	17 53.1	20 53.9	9 11.5	22 54.3
22 T	4 0 21.0	20 26.2	21 44.0	16 21.2	20 43.1	26 37.0	15 56.7	14 44.9	17 50.4	20 52.4	9 10.2	22 53.2
25 F	4 12 10.7	20 59.8	21 42.5	21 56.5	19 34.7	26 17.4	15 27.9	14 38.5	17 47.8	20 50.9	9 8.9	22 52.0
28 M	4 24 0.3	21 30.2	21 41.0	18 31.0	18 28.1	25 55.3	14 58.9	14 31.6	17 45.1	20 49.3	9 7.7	22 50.8
31 T	4 35 50.0	21 57.2	21 39.5	8 11.7	17 30.1	25 30.5	14 30.0	14 24.4	17 42.6	20 47.6	9 6.6	22 49.5

JUNE 1956

DAY	EPHEMERIS SIDEREAL TIME	☉	☊	☽	☿	♀	♂	♃	♄	♅	♆	♇
						LONGITUDE at NOON						
1 F	4 39 46.6	10♊57.1	8♐ 1.2	7♓31.9	1♊25.4	9♋ 0.4	28♒58.7	24♌23.5	28♏38.4	29♋35.8	28♎ 0.1	26♌14.8
2 S	4 43 43.1	11 54.5	7 58.0	19 55.4	1R 3.9	8R57.5	29 32.4	24 30.9	28R34.1	29 38.5	27R59.1	26 15.5
3 S	4 47 39.7	12 52.0	7 54.8	2♈37.9	0 45.9	8 52.1	0♓ 5.9	24 38.3	28 29.8	29 41.3	27 58.0	26 16.2
4 M	4 51 36.2	13 49.4	7 51.6	15 42.9	0 31.7	8 44.4	0 39.2	24 46.0	28 25.5	29 44.1	27 57.0	26 17.0
5 T	4 55 32.8	14 46.9	7 48.5	29 12.9	0 21.5	8 34.3	1 12.3	24 53.7	28 21.3	29 46.9	27 56.0	26 17.8
6 W	4 59 29.3	15 44.3	7 45.3	13♉ 8.5	0 15.6	8 21.8	1 45.2	25 1.6	28 17.1	29 49.8	27 55.0	26 18.7
7 T	5 3 25.9	16 41.7	7 42.1	27 28.5	0 14.0	8 6.9	2 18.0	25 9.5	28 13.0	29 52.7	27 54.0	26 19.5
8 F	5 7 22.5	17 39.1	7 38.9	12♊ 8.9	0D16.9	7 49.7	2 50.4	25 17.6	28 8.9	29 55.6	27 53.1	26 20.4
9 S	5 11 19.0	18 36.6	7 35.8	27 3.6	0 24.3	7 30.2	3 22.8	25 25.9	28 4.9	29 58.6	27 52.2	26 21.3
10 S	5 15 15.6	19 33.9	7 32.6	12♋ 4.5	0 36.2	7 8.5	3 54.8	25 34.2	28 0.9	0♌ 1.6	27 51.4	26 22.3
11 M	5 19 12.1	20 31.3	7 29.4	27 3.1	0 52.7	6 44.5	4 26.6	25 42.7	27 56.9	0 4.6	27 50.5	26 23.2
12 T	5 23 8.7	21 28.6	7 26.2	11♌51.3	1 13.6	6 18.5	4 58.2	25 51.3	27 53.0	0 7.7	27 49.7	26 24.2
13 W	5 27 5.2	22 26.0	7 23.1	26 23.0	1 38.9	5 50.5	5 29.5	25 59.9	27 49.1	0 10.7	27 48.9	26 25.2
14 T	5 31 1.8	23 23.3	7 19.9	10♍33.8	2 8.7	5 20.7	6 0.6	26 8.7	27 45.3	0 13.8	27 48.1	26 26.3
15 F	5 34 58.4	24 20.6	7 16.7	24 22.1	2 42.8	4 49.2	6 31.4	26 17.6	27 41.5	0 17.0	27 47.4	26 27.3
16 S	5 38 54.9	25 17.9	7 13.5	7♎48.1	3 21.1	4 16.2	7 1.9	26 26.6	27 37.8	0 20.1	27 46.7	26 28.4
17 S	5 42 51.5	26 15.1	7 10.4	20 53.3	4 3.7	3 41.8	7 32.2	26 35.7	27 34.2	0 23.3	27 46.0	26 29.5
18 M	5 46 48.0	27 12.4	7 7.2	3♏40.3	4 50.4	3 6.4	8 2.2	26 44.9	27 30.6	0 26.5	27 45.3	26 30.7
19 T	5 50 44.6	28 9.6	7 4.0	16 11.7	5 41.1	2 30.0	8 32.0	26 54.2	27 27.0	0 29.7	27 44.7	26 31.8
20 W	5 54 41.1	29 6.9	7 0.8	28 30.6	6 35.7	1 53.0	9 1.4	27 3.6	27 23.6	0 33.0	27 44.1	26 33.0
21 T	5 58 37.7	0♋ 4.1	6 57.6	10♐39.3	7 34.3	1 15.5	9 30.6	27 13.1	27 20.2	0 36.3	27 43.5	26 34.2
22 F	6 2 34.3	1 1.3	6 54.5	22 40.4	8 36.8	0 37.8	9 59.5	27 22.7	27 16.8	0 39.6	27 43.0	26 35.4
23 S	6 6 30.8	1 58.5	6 51.3	4♑36.0	9 43.0	0 0.2	10 28.0	27 32.4	27 13.5	0 42.9	27 42.5	26 36.7
24 S	6 10 27.4	2 55.7	6 48.1	16 27.9	10 53.0	29♊22.8	10 56.2	27 42.1	27 10.3	0 46.2	27 42.0	26 37.9
25 M	6 14 23.9	3 52.9	6 44.9	28 18.3	12 6.7	28 46.1	11 24.1	27 52.0	27 7.2	0 49.6	27 41.6	26 39.2
26 T	6 18 20.5	4 50.1	6 41.8	10♒ 9.3	13 24.1	28 10.0	11 51.7	28 2.0	27 4.1	0 53.0	27 41.2	26 40.5
27 W	6 22 17.0	5 47.3	6 38.6	22 3.4	14 45.0	27 35.0	12 18.9	28 12.0	27 1.1	0 56.4	27 40.8	26 41.9
28 T	6 26 13.6	6 44.5	6 35.4	4♓ 3.4	16 9.5	27 1.2	12 45.8	28 22.2	26 58.2	0 59.8	27 40.4	26 43.2
29 F	6 30 10.2	7 41.7	6 32.2	16 12.7	17 37.6	26 28.9	13 12.3	28 32.4	26 55.4	1 3.3	27 40.1	26 44.6
30 S	6 34 6.7	8 39.0	6 29.1	28 34.9	19 9.1	25 58.1	13 38.5	28 42.7	26 52.6	1 6.8	27 39.9	26 46.0
						DECLINATION at NOON						
1 F	4 39 46.6	22N 5.4	21S39.0	3S49.8	17N13.7	25N21.7	14S20.4	14N21.8	17S41.7	20N47.0	9S 6.2	22N49.0
4 M	4 51 36.2	22 27.8	21 37.4	10N 3.4	16 35.3	24 53.6	13 51.6	14 14.0	17 39.3	20 45.2	9 5.2	22 47.6
7 T	5 3 25.9	22 46.7	21 35.9	20 33.5	16 15.1	24 22.9	13 23.1	14 5.8	17 36.9	20 43.3	9 4.3	22 46.1
10 S	5 15 15.6	23 2.0	21 34.4	19 57.4	16 13.6	23 49.5	12 55.1	13 57.2	17 34.6	20 41.4	9 3.4	22 44.5
13 W	5 27 5.2	23 13.7	21 32.8	7 51.8	16 29.7	23 13.5	12 27.5	13 48.2	17 32.4	20 39.4	9 2.7	22 42.8
16 S	5 38 54.9	23 21.6	21 31.2	7S18.2	17 1.3	22 35.3	12 0.5	13 38.9	17 30.3	20 37.4	9 2.0	22 41.2
19 T	5 50 44.6	23 25.9	21 29.6	18 34.4	17 45.5	21 55.5	11 34.2	13 29.2	17 28.4	20 35.3	9 1.5	22 39.4
22 F	6 2 34.3	23 26.4	21 28.0	21 55.4	18 39.1	21 15.0	11 8.7	13 19.2	17 26.6	20 33.1	9 1.0	22 37.6
25 M	6 14 23.9	23 23.2	21 26.4	16 33.6	19 38.7	20 35.2	10 44.2	13 8.9	17 25.0	20 30.9	9 0.6	22 35.8
28 T	6 26 13.6	23 16.3	21 24.8	5 10.2	20 40.4	19 57.6	10 20.7	12 58.2	17 23.5	20 28.7	9 0.4	22 33.9

JULY 1956

DAY	EPHEMERIS SIDEREAL TIME	☉	☊	☽	☿	♀	♂	♃	♄	♅	♆	♇
	h m s	° ′	° ′	° ′	° ′	° ′	° ′	° ′	° ′	° ′	° ′	° ′
						LONGITUDE at NOON						
1 S	6 38 3.3	9♋36.2	6♐25.9	11♈13.9	20♊44.1	25♊29.1	14♓ 4.2	28♌53.1	26♏49.9	1♌10.3	27♎39.6	26♌47.5
2 M	6 41 59.8	10 33.4	6 22.7	24 13.6	22 22.4	25R 1.9	14 29.5	29 3.6	26R47.3	1 13.8	27R39.4	26 48.9
3 T	6 45 56.4	11 30.6	6 19.5	7♉37.4	24 4.0	24 36.8	14 54.4	29 14.2	26 44.8	1 17.3	27 39.2	26 50.4
4 W	6 49 52.9	12 27.8	6 16.3	21 27.6	25 48.8	24 13.7	15 18.9	29 24.8	26 42.3	1 20.8	27 39.0	26 51.8
5 T	6 53 49.5	13 25.0	6 13.2	5♊44.5	27 36.7	23 52.9	15 42.9	29 35.5	26 40.0	1 24.3	27 38.9	26 53.3
6 F	6 57 46.1	14 22.2	6 10.0	20 26.0	29 27.6	23 34.4	16 6.5	29 46.3	26 37.7	1 27.9	27 38.8	26 54.8
7 S	7 1 42.6	15 19.4	6 6.8	5♋27.0	1♋21.4	23 18.1	16 29.6	29 57.2	26 35.5	1 31.5	27 38.7	26 56.4
8 S	7 5 39.2	16 16.7	6 3.6	20 39.4	3 17.8	23 4.2	16 52.3	0♍ 8.1	26 33.3	1 35.1	27 38.7	26 57.9
9 M	7 9 35.7	17 13.9	6 0.5	5♌53.4	5 16.6	22 52.7	17 14.5	0 19.1	26 31.3	1 38.6	27 38.6	26 59.5
10 T	7 13 32.3	18 11.1	5 57.3	20 58.4	7 17.7	22 43.6	17 36.1	0 30.2	26 29.4	1 42.3	27D38.7	27 1.1
11 W	7 17 28.8	19 8.4	5 54.1	5♍45.6	9 20.7	22 36.9	17 57.3	0 41.3	26 27.5	1 45.9	27 38.7	27 2.7
12 T	7 21 25.4	20 5.6	5 50.9	20 8.4	11 25.4	22 32.5	18 17.9	0 52.6	26 25.7	1 49.5	27 38.8	27 4.3
13 F	7 25 22.0	21 2.8	5 47.8	4♎ 3.8	13 31.5	22 30.4	18 38.0	1 3.8	26 24.1	1 53.1	27 38.9	27 5.9
14 S	7 29 18.5	22 0.0	5 44.6	17 31.6	15 38.7	22D30.7	18 57.6	1 15.2	26 22.5	1 56.8	27 39.1	27 7.6
15 S	7 33 15.1	22 57.3	5 41.4	0♏33.8	17 46.6	22 33.2	19 16.7	1 26.6	26 21.0	2 0.4	27 39.3	27 9.2
16 M	7 37 11.6	23 54.5	5 38.2	13 13.9	19 55.1	22 38.0	19 35.2	1 38.1	26 19.6	2 4.1	27 39.5	27 10.9
17 T	7 41 8.2	24 51.7	5 35.1	25 36.3	22 3.7	22 44.9	19 53.1	1 49.6	26 18.3	2 7.7	27 39.8	27 12.6
18 W	7 45 4.7	25 49.0	5 31.9	7♐45.2	24 12.2	22 54.1	20 10.4	2 1.2	26 17.1	2 11.4	27 40.0	27 14.3
19 T	7 49 1.3	26 46.2	5 28.7	19 44.7	26 20.4	23 5.3	20 27.1	2 12.8	26 15.9	2 15.1	27 40.4	27 16.0
20 F	7 52 57.9	27 43.5	5 25.5	1♑38.3	28 27.9	23 18.5	20 43.3	2 24.5	26 14.9	2 18.7	27 40.7	27 17.8
21 S	7 56 54.4	28 40.8	5 22.3	13 29.1	0♌34.7	23 33.8	20 58.9	2 36.4	26 14.0	2 22.5	27 41.1	27 19.6
22 S	8 0 51.0	29 38.0	5 19.2	25 19.2	2 40.5	23 51.0	21 13.7	2 48.2	26 13.2	2 26.2	27 41.6	27 21.3
23 M	8 4 47.5	0♌35.3	5 16.0	7♒10.8	4 45.2	24 10.0	21 28.0	3 0.0	26 12.4	2 29.8	27 42.0	27 23.1
24 T	8 8 44.1	1 32.6	5 12.8	19 5.5	6 48.6	24 30.9	21 41.6	3 12.0	26 11.8	2 33.5	27 42.5	27 24.9
25 W	8 12 40.6	2 29.9	5 9.6	1♓ 4.8	8 50.6	24 53.5	21 54.5	3 23.9	26 11.2	2 37.2	27 43.0	27 26.7
26 T	8 16 37.2	3 27.2	5 6.5	13 10.7	10 51.2	25 17.8	22 6.7	3 35.9	26 10.8	2 40.9	27 43.5	27 28.5
27 F	8 20 33.8	4 24.5	5 3.3	25 25.0	12 50.3	25 43.7	22 18.3	3 48.0	26 10.4	2 44.6	27 44.1	27 30.3
28 S	8 24 30.3	5 21.9	5 0.1	7♈50.3	14 47.8	26 11.2	22 29.1	4 0.1	26 10.2	2 48.3	27 44.7	27 32.1
29 S	8 28 26.9	6 19.2	4 56.9	20 29.7	16 43.7	26 40.3	22 39.2	4 12.3	26 10.0	2 52.0	27 45.3	27 34.0
30 M	8 32 23.4	7 16.6	4 53.7	3♉26.5	18 38.1	27 10.8	22 48.5	4 24.5	26 9.9	2 55.6	27 46.0	27 35.8
31 T	8 36 20.0	8 14.0	4 50.6	16 44.0	20 30.8	27 42.7	22 57.1	4 36.7	26 9.9	2 59.3	27 46.7	27 37.7
						DECLINATION at NOON						
1 S	6 38 3.3	23N 5.8	21S23.2	8N26.8	21N39.9	19N23.6	9S58.5	12N47.3	17S22.3	20N26.4	9S 0.2	22N31.9
4 W	6 49 52.9	22 51.6	21 21.6	19 32.6	22 32.3	18 54.4	9 37.6	12 36.0	17 21.1	20 24.0	9 0.2	22 30.0
7 S	7 1 42.6	22 33.8	21 19.9	20 55.0	23 12.4	18 30.8	9 18.2	12 24.5	17 20.2	20 21.7	9 0.2	22 28.0
10 T	7 13 32.3	22 12.5	21 18.3	9 48.6	23 35.0	18 13.0	9 0.5	12 12.6	17 19.5	20 19.3	9 0.4	22 26.0
13 F	7 25 22.0	21 47.8	21 16.6	5S50.8	23 35.6	18 1.1	8 44.5	12 0.6	17 18.9	20 16.8	9 0.6	22 23.9
16 M	7 37 11.6	21 19.7	21 14.9	17 49.2	23 12.0	17 54.5	8 30.3	11 48.2	17 18.6	20 14.4	9 1.0	22 21.9
19 T	7 49 1.3	20 48.4	21 13.3	21 56.2	22 24.2	17 52.7	8 18.0	11 35.7	17 18.4	20 11.9	9 1.4	22 19.8
22 S	8 0 51.0	20 13.9	21 11.6	17 19.6	21 14.5	17 54.9	8 7.8	11 22.8	17 18.5	20 9.4	9 2.0	22 17.7
25 W	8 12 40.6	19 36.4	21 9.9	6 21.5	19 46.7	18 0.3	7 59.8	11 9.8	17 18.7	20 6.9	9 2.7	22 15.6
28 S	8 24 30.3	18 55.9	21 8.1	7N 5.2	18 4.6	18 8.0	7 54.0	10 56.6	17 19.2	20 4.4	9 3.4	22 13.5
31 T	8 36 20.0	18 12.6	21 6.4	18 27.5	16 12.0	18 17.3	7 50.6	10 43.2	17 19.9	20 1.9	9 4.3	22 11.4

AUGUST 1956

DAY	EPHEMERIS SIDEREAL TIME	☉	☊	☽	☿	♀	♂	♃	♄	♅	♆	♇
						LONGITUDE at NOON						
1 W	8 40 16.5	9♌11.4	4♐47.4	0♊25.2	22♌21.9	28♊16.0	23♓ 5.0	4♍49.0	26♏10.1	3♌ 3.0	27♎47.4	27♌39.5
2 T	8 44 13.1	10 8.8	4 44.2	14 31.6	24 11.3	28 50.6	23 12.0	5 1.3	26D10.3	3 6.7	27 48.2	27 41.4
3 F	8 48 9.6	11 6.3	4 41.0	29 3.1	25 59.2	29 26.4	23 18.3	5 13.7	26 10.6	3 10.3	27 49.0	27 43.3
4 S	8 52 6.2	12 3.7	4 37.9	13♋56.2	27 45.4	0♋ 3.5	23 23.7	5 26.1	26 11.0	3 14.0	27 49.8	27 45.2
5 S	8 56 2.8	13 1.2	4 34.7	29 4.6	29 30.0	0 41.7	23 28.4	5 38.6	26 11.5	3 17.6	27 50.6	27 47.1
6 M	8 59 59.3	13 58.7	4 31.5	14♌19.0	1♍13.0	1 21.0	23 32.2	5 51.1	26 12.1	3 21.3	27 51.5	27 49.0
7 T	9 3 55.9	14 56.3	4 28.3	29 28.6	2 54.5	2 1.4	23 35.2	6 3.6	26 12.9	3 24.9	27 52.4	27 50.9
8 W	9 7 52.4	15 53.8	4 25.2	14♍23.0	4 34.3	2 42.9	23 37.4	6 16.1	26 13.7	3 28.5	27 53.4	27 52.8
9 T	9 11 49.0	16 51.4	4 22.0	28 54.0	6 12.6	3 25.3	23 38.8	6 28.7	26 14.6	3 32.2	27 54.3	27 54.7
10 F	9 15 45.5	17 48.9	4 18.8	12♎56.8	7 49.3	4 8.7	23 39.3	6 41.3	26 15.6	3 35.8	27 55.3	27 56.7
11 S	9 19 42.1	18 46.6	4 15.6	26 29.9	9 24.5	4 53.1	23R39.1	6 54.0	26 16.7	3 39.4	27 56.4	27 58.7
12 S	9 23 38.6	19 44.2	4 12.4	9♏34.8	10 58.1	5 38.3	23 38.0	7 6.7	26 17.9	3 43.0	27 57.5	28 0.6
13 M	9 27 35.2	20 41.8	4 9.3	22 15.1	12 30.2	6 24.3	23 36.1	7 19.4	26 19.2	3 46.6	27 58.6	28 2.5
14 T	9 31 31.7	21 39.4	4 6.1	4♐35.5	14 0.6	7 11.2	23 33.4	7 32.1	26 20.6	3 50.1	27 59.7	28 4.5
15 W	9 35 28.3	22 37.1	4 2.9	16 41.1	15 29.5	7 58.9	23 29.9	7 44.9	26 22.1	3 53.7	28 0.8	28 6.4
16 T	9 39 24.9	23 34.7	3 59.7	28 36.9	16 56.9	8 47.3	23 25.6	7 57.6	26 23.6	3 57.2	28 2.0	28 8.4
17 F	9 43 21.4	24 32.4	3 56.6	10♑27.6	18 22.6	9 36.5	23 20.6	8 10.4	26 25.3	4 0.7	28 3.2	28 10.3
18 S	9 47 18.0	25 30.1	3 53.4	22 17.0	19 46.6	10 26.5	23 14.7	8 23.3	26 27.1	4 4.2	28 4.4	28 12.3
19 S	9 51 14.5	26 27.8	3 50.2	4♒ 8.3	21 9.0	11 17.1	23 8.1	8 36.1	26 28.9	4 7.7	28 5.7	28 14.2
20 M	9 55 11.1	27 25.6	3 47.0	16 3.8	22 29.8	12 8.4	23 0.7	8 49.0	26 30.9	4 11.2	28 7.0	28 16.2
21 T	9 59 7.6	28 23.4	3 43.8	28 5.3	23 48.8	13 0.4	22 52.6	9 1.8	26 32.9	4 14.6	28 8.3	28 18.2
22 W	10 3 4.2	29 21.1	3 40.7	10♓13.9	25 6.0	13 53.0	22 43.8	9 14.7	26 35.1	4 18.1	28 9.6	28 20.1
23 T	10 7 0.7	0♍19.0	3 37.5	22 30.6	26 21.4	14 46.2	22 34.2	9 27.6	26 37.3	4 21.5	28 11.0	28 22.1
24 F	10 10 57.3	1 16.8	3 34.3	4♈56.2	27 35.0	15 40.0	22 24.0	9 40.5	26 39.6	4 24.9	28 12.4	28 24.0
25 S	10 14 53.8	2 14.7	3 31.1	17 32.0	28 46.5	16 34.4	22 13.1	9 53.5	26 42.0	4 28.2	28 13.8	28 26.0
26 S	10 18 50.4	3 12.6	3 28.0	0♉19.4	29 56.1	17 29.3	22 1.6	10 6.4	26 44.5	4 31.6	28 15.2	28 27.9
27 M	10 22 46.9	4 10.5	3 24.8	13 20.6	1♎ 3.5	18 24.8	21 49.4	10 19.4	26 47.1	4 34.9	28 16.7	28 29.9
28 T	10 26 43.5	5 8.5	3 21.6	26 38.0	2 8.7	19 20.8	21 36.7	10 32.3	26 49.8	4 38.2	28 18.2	28 31.8
29 W	10 30 40.0	6 6.4	3 18.4	10♊13.9	3 11.6	20 17.3	21 23.4	10 45.3	26 52.6	4 41.5	28 19.7	28 33.8
30 T	10 34 36.6	7 4.5	3 15.2	24 10.2	4 12.0	21 14.3	21 9.6	10 58.3	26 55.4	4 44.8	28 21.2	28 35.7
31 F	10 38 33.2	8 2.5	3 12.1	8♋27.4	5 9.8	22 11.8	20 55.3	11 11.3	26 58.4	4 48.0	28 22.8	28 37.6
						DECLINATION at NOON						
1 W	8 40 16.5	17N57.6	21S 5.8	20N44.0	15N32.7	18N20.6	7S50.0	10N38.7	17S20.2	20N 1.1	9S 4.6	22N10.7
4 S	8 52 6.2	17 10.8	21 4.1	19 36.7	13 31.1	18 30.7	7 49.8	10 25.0	17 21.1	19 58.5	9 5.6	22 8.7
7 T	9 3 55.9	16 21.4	21 2.4	6 57.4	11 25.7	18 40.6	7 52.0	10 11.2	17 22.3	19 56.0	9 6.7	22 6.6
10 F	9 15 45.5	15 29.7	21 0.6	8S47.3	9 18.5	18 49.7	7 56.5	9 57.2	17 23.6	19 53.5	9 7.9	22 4.6
13 M	9 27 35.2	14 35.8	20 58.8	19 25.1	7 11.2	18 57.4	8 3.3	9 43.1	17 25.2	19 51.0	9 9.2	22 2.6
16 T	9 39 24.9	13 39.8	20 57.1	21 24.6	5 5.4	19 3.2	8 12.1	9 28.8	17 26.9	19 48.6	9 10.5	22 0.6
19 S	9 51 14.5	12 41.8	20 55.3	15 1.5	3 2.3	19 6.6	8 22.8	9 14.5	17 28.9	19 46.1	9 12.0	21 58.6
22 W	10 3 4.2	11 42.1	20 53.5	3 7.8	1 3.4	19 7.3	8 35.1	9 0.0	17 31.0	19 43.7	9 13.5	21 56.7
25 S	10 14 53.8	10 40.6	20 51.7	10N12.9	0S50.1	19 4.7	8 48.7	8 45.4	17 33.3	19 41.4	9 15.1	21 54.8
28 T	10 26 43.5	9 37.7	20 49.9	19 58.5	2 36.6	18 58.7	9 3.2	8 30.8	17 35.7	19 39.0	9 16.8	21 53.0
31 F	10 38 33.2	8 33.3	20 48.0	20 16.4	4 14.4	18 49.0	9 18.4	8 16.1	17 38.4	19 36.7	9 18.5	21 51.2

SEPTEMBER 1956

DAY	EPHEMERIS SIDEREAL TIME	☉	☊	☽	☿	♀	♂	♃	♄	♅	♆	♇
	h m s	° ′	° ′	° ′	° ′	° ′	° ′	° ′	° ′	° ′	° ′	° ′
						LONGITUDE at NOON						
1 S	10 42 29.7	9♍ 0.7	3♐ 8.9	23♋ 4.0	6♎ 4.9	23♋ 9.8	20♓40.6	11♍24.3	27♏ 1.5	4♌51.3	28♎24.4	28♌39.6
2 S	10 46 26.3	9 58.8	3 5.7	7♌55.4	6 57.1	24 8.1	20R25.4	11 37.3	27 4.6	4 54.5	28 26.0	28 41.6
3 M	10 50 22.8	10 56.9	3 2.5	22 54.6	7 46.1	25 6.9	20 9.9	11 50.4	27 7.8	4 57.6	28 27.7	28 43.5
4 T	10 54 19.4	11 55.1	2 59.4	7♍52.8	8 31.9	26 6.1	19 54.1	12 3.4	27 11.1	5 0.8	28 29.3	28 45.4
5 W	10 58 15.9	12 53.3	2 56.2	22 40.1	9 14.1	27 5.7	19 38.0	12 16.4	27 14.4	5 3.9	28 31.0	28 47.3
6 T	11 2 12.5	13 51.6	2 53.0	7♎ 8.4	9 52.5	28 5.7	19 21.8	12 29.4	27 17.9	5 6.9	28 32.7	28 49.2
7 F	11 6 9.0	14 49.8	2 49.8	21 11.7	10 26.9	29 6.1	19 5.3	12 42.4	27 21.5	5 10.0	28 34.4	28 51.1
8 S	11 10 5.6	15 48.1	2 46.6	4♏47.3	10 56.9	0♌ 6.8	18 48.8	12 55.4	27 25.1	5 13.0	28 36.2	28 53.0
9 S	11 14 2.1	16 46.4	2 43.5	17 55.4	11 22.3	1 7.9	18 32.1	13 8.4	27 28.8	5 16.0	28 37.9	28 54.9
10 M	11 17 58.7	17 44.8	2 40.3	0♐38.5	11 42.7	2 9.4	18 15.5	13 21.4	27 32.6	5 19.0	28 39.7	28 56.8
11 T	11 21 55.2	18 43.1	2 37.1	13 0.8	11 57.9	3 11.1	17 59.0	13 34.4	27 36.4	5 21.9	28 41.5	28 58.6
12 W	11 25 51.8	19 41.5	2 33.9	25 7.5	12 7.4	4 13.2	17 42.5	13 47.3	27 40.4	5 24.8	28 43.3	29 0.5
13 T	11 29 48.3	20 39.9	2 30.8	7♑ 3.7	12 11.0	5 15.7	17 26.1	14 0.3	27 44.4	5 27.6	28 45.2	29 2.4
14 F	11 33 44.9	21 38.4	2 27.6	18 54.7	12R 8.4	6 18.4	17 10.0	14 13.3	27 48.5	5 30.5	28 47.0	29 4.2
15 S	11 37 41.4	22 36.9	2 24.4	0♒45.2	11 59.2	7 21.4	16 54.1	14 26.2	27 52.7	5 33.3	28 48.9	29 6.0
16 S	11 41 38.0	23 35.4	2 21.2	12 39.2	11 43.2	8 24.8	16 38.4	14 39.1	27 57.0	5 36.0	28 50.8	29 7.8
17 M	11 45 34.5	24 33.9	2 18.0	24 39.9	11 20.3	9 28.4	16 23.1	14 52.0	28 1.3	5 38.7	28 52.7	29 9.6
18 T	11 49 31.1	25 32.5	2 14.9	6♓49.6	10 50.4	10 32.3	16 8.1	15 4.9	28 5.7	5 41.4	28 54.7	29 11.4
19 W	11 53 27.7	26 31.1	2 11.7	19 9.6	10 13.6	11 36.5	15 53.5	15 17.8	28 10.2	5 44.1	28 56.6	29 13.2
20 T	11 57 24.2	27 29.7	2 8.5	1♈40.8	9 30.1	12 41.0	15 39.4	15 30.7	28 14.7	5 46.7	28 58.6	29 15.0
21 F	12 1 20.8	28 28.3	2 5.3	14 23.1	8 40.4	13 45.8	15 25.7	15 43.5	28 19.3	5 49.3	29 0.5	29 16.8
22 S	12 5 17.3	29 27.1	2 2.2	27 16.7	7 45.0	14 50.8	15 12.6	15 56.4	28 24.1	5 51.8	29 2.6	29 18.5
23 S	12 9 13.9	0♎25.8	1 59.0	10♉21.3	6 44.9	15 56.1	14 59.9	16 9.2	28 28.8	5 54.3	29 4.6	29 20.3
24 M	12 13 10.4	1 24.6	1 55.8	23 37.1	5 41.2	17 1.6	14 47.8	16 22.0	28 33.7	5 56.8	29 6.6	29 22.0
25 T	12 17 7.0	2 23.4	1 52.6	7♊ 4.9	4 35.3	18 7.4	14 36.3	16 34.7	28 38.6	5 59.2	29 8.7	29 23.7
26 W	12 21 3.5	3 22.2	1 49.4	20 45.4	3 28.6	19 13.4	14 25.4	16 47.5	28 43.5	6 1.6	29 10.7	29 25.4
27 T	12 25 0.1	4 21.1	1 46.3	4♋39.3	2 22.9	20 19.6	14 15.2	17 0.2	28 48.5	6 3.9	29 12.8	29 27.1
28 F	12 28 56.6	5 20.0	1 43.1	18 46.7	1 19.9	21 26.1	14 5.6	17 12.9	28 53.6	6 6.2	29 14.8	29 28.7
29 S	12 32 53.2	6 18.9	1 39.9	3♌ 6.6	0 21.2	22 32.8	13 56.7	17 25.5	28 58.8	6 8.5	29 16.9	29 30.4
30 S	12 36 49.7	7 17.9	1 36.7	17 36.1	29♍28.6	23 39.7	13 48.5	17 38.1	29 4.0	6 10.7	29 19.0	29 32.0
						DECLINATION at NOON						
1 S	10 42 29.7	8N11.6	20S47.4	17N40.7	4S44.7	18N44.8	9S23.4	8N11.2	17S39.3	19N36.0	9S19.2	21N50.6
4 T	10 54 19.4	7 5.6	20 45.6	3 58.9	6 7.2	18 29.8	9 38.5	7 56.4	17 42.1	19 33.8	9 21.0	21 48.9
7 F	11 6 9.0	5 58.5	20 43.7	11S20.0	7 14.8	18 10.6	9 53.0	7 41.6	17 45.1	19 31.6	9 22.9	21 47.3
10 M	11 17 58.7	4 50.6	20 41.9	20 24.7	8 3.3	17 47.2	10 6.4	7 26.8	17 48.3	19 29.5	9 24.9	21 45.7
13 T	11 29 48.3	3 42.0	20 40.0	20 21.0	8 27.7	17 19.6	10 18.1	7 11.9	17 51.6	19 27.4	9 26.9	21 44.2
16 S	11 41 38.0	2 32.8	20 38.1	12 26.2	8 22.0	16 47.6	10 27.8	6 57.1	17 55.0	19 25.5	9 29.0	21 42.7
19 W	11 53 27.7	1 23.1	20 36.3	0N 7.5	7 40.7	16 11.3	10 35.2	6 42.4	17 58.5	19 23.6	9 31.1	21 41.3
22 S	12 5 17.3	0 13.1	20 34.4	13 7.1	6 21.5	15 30.7	10 40.1	6 27.6	18 2.1	19 21.7	9 33.3	21 40.0
25 T	12 17 7.0	0S57.0	20 32.5	20 55.7	4 30.3	14 45.9	10 42.3	6 12.9	18 5.8	19 20.0	9 35.5	21 38.8
28 F	12 28 56.6	2 7.2	20 30.5	18 21.1	2 23.5	13 57.1	10 41.6	5 58.3	18 9.6	19 18.4	9 37.7	21 37.7

OCTOBER 1956

DAY	EPHEMERIS SIDEREAL TIME	☉	☊	☽	☿	♀	♂	♃	♄	♅	♆	♇
						LONGITUDE at NOON						
1 M	12 40 46.3	8♎17.0	1♐33.5	2♍10.8	28♍43.4	24♌46.8	13♓41.1	17♍50.7	29♏ 9.3	6♌12.9	29♎21.1	29♌33.6
2 T	12 44 42.8	9 16.0	1 30.4	16 44.6	28R 6.8	25 54.1	13R34.3	18 3.3	29 14.6	6 15.0	29 23.3	29 35.2
3 W	12 48 39.4	10 15.1	1 27.2	1♎10.7	27 39.7	27 1.6	13 28.4	18 15.8	29 20.1	6 17.1	29 25.4	29 36.8
4 T	12 52 35.9	11 14.3	1 24.0	15 22.5	27 22.8	28 9.3	13 23.2	18 28.3	29 25.5	6 19.1	29 27.6	29 38.3
5 F	12 56 32.5	12 13.4	1 20.8	29 14.7	27 16.5	29 17.2	13 18.8	18 40.8	29 31.1	6 21.1	29 29.7	29 39.9
6 S	13 0 29.0	13 12.6	1 17.7	12♏44.3	27D20.8	0♍25.3	13 15.3	18 53.2	29 36.6	6 23.0	29 31.9	29 41.4
7 S	13 4 25.6	14 11.9	1 14.5	25 50.4	27 35.6	1 33.6	13 12.5	19 5.5	29 42.3	6 24.9	29 34.0	29 42.9
8 M	13 8 22.1	15 11.1	1 11.3	8♐34.0	28 0.6	2 42.0	13 10.5	19 17.9	29 48.0	6 26.8	29 36.2	29 44.4
9 T	13 12 18.7	16 10.4	1 8.1	20 58.1	28 35.1	3 50.6	13 9.4	19 30.2	29 53.7	6 28.6	29 38.4	29 45.8
10 W	13 16 15.3	17 9.8	1 4.9	3♑ 6.8	29 18.7	4 59.4	13 9.0	19 42.4	29 59.5	6 30.3	29 40.6	29 47.3
11 T	13 20 11.8	18 9.1	1 1.8	15 4.9	0♎10.5	6 8.3	13D 9.5	19 54.6	0♐ 5.4	6 32.1	29 42.8	29 48.7
12 F	13 24 8.4	19 8.5	0 58.6	26 57.3	1 9.9	7 17.4	13 10.8	20 6.7	0 11.3	6 33.7	29 45.0	29 50.1
13 S	13 28 4.9	20 8.0	0 55.4	8♒49.2	2 16.0	8 26.7	13 12.9	20 18.9	0 17.3	6 35.4	29 47.3	29 51.5
14 S	13 32 1.5	21 7.4	0 52.2	20 45.2	3 28.0	9 36.1	13 15.8	20 30.9	0 23.3	6 36.9	29 49.5	29 52.9
15 M	13 35 58.0	22 6.9	0 49.1	2♓49.3	4 45.3	10 45.7	13 19.4	20 42.9	0 29.4	6 38.4	29 51.7	29 54.2
16 T	13 39 54.6	23 6.4	0 45.9	15 5.1	6 7.0	11 55.4	13 23.8	20 54.9	0 35.5	6 39.9	29 53.9	29 55.5
17 W	13 43 51.1	24 5.9	0 42.7	27 34.7	7 32.6	13 5.2	13 29.0	21 6.8	0 41.6	6 41.3	29 56.2	29 56.8
18 T	13 47 47.7	25 5.5	0 39.5	10♈19.6	9 1.4	14 15.3	13 35.0	21 18.6	0 47.8	6 42.7	29 58.4	29 58.1
19 F	13 51 44.2	26 5.1	0 36.3	23 20.0	10 32.8	15 25.4	13 41.7	21 30.4	0 54.1	6 44.0	0♏ 0.6	29 59.3
20 S	13 55 40.8	27 4.7	0 33.2	6♉35.1	12 6.5	16 35.7	13 49.1	21 42.1	1 0.3	6 45.2	0 2.9	0♍ 0.5
21 S	13 59 37.3	28 4.4	0 30.0	20 3.6	13 42.0	17 46.1	13 57.3	21 53.7	1 6.7	6 46.4	0 5.1	0 1.7
22 M	14 3 33.9	29 4.1	0 26.8	3♊43.7	15 19.0	18 56.7	14 6.1	22 5.3	1 13.0	6 47.6	0 7.3	0 2.9
23 T	14 7 30.4	0♏ 3.8	0 23.6	17 33.5	16 57.0	20 7.4	14 15.7	22 16.9	1 19.4	6 48.7	0 9.6	0 4.0
24 W	14 11 27.0	1 3.6	0 20.5	1♋31.2	18 35.9	21 18.2	14 25.9	22 28.3	1 25.9	6 49.7	0 11.8	0 5.2
25 T	14 15 23.6	2 3.4	0 17.3	15 35.2	20 15.3	22 29.2	14 36.9	22 39.7	1 32.3	6 50.7	0 14.1	0 6.3
26 F	14 19 20.1	3 3.3	0 14.1	29 43.8	21 55.2	23 40.3	14 48.5	22 51.1	1 38.9	6 51.7	0 16.3	0 7.3
27 S	14 23 16.7	4 3.2	0 10.9	13♌55.3	23 35.4	24 51.5	15 0.7	23 2.3	1 45.4	6 52.6	0 18.5	0 8.4
28 S	14 27 13.2	5 3.1	0 7.7	28 7.6	25 15.6	26 2.8	15 13.6	23 13.5	1 52.0	6 53.4	0 20.8	0 9.4
29 M	14 31 9.8	6 3.1	0 4.6	12♍18.2	26 55.9	27 14.3	15 27.2	23 24.7	1 58.6	6 54.2	0 23.0	0 10.4
30 T	14 35 6.3	7 3.1	0 1.4	26 23.8	28 36.0	28 25.8	15 41.3	23 35.7	2 5.3	6 54.9	0 25.2	0 11.4
31 W	14 39 2.9	8 3.1	29♏58.2	10♎21.0	0♏16.0	29 37.5	15 56.1	23 46.7	2 12.0	6 55.6	0 27.5	0 12.3
						DECLINATION at NOON						
1 M	12 40 46.3	3S17.1	20S28.6	5N55.9	0S25.6	13N 4.5	10S38.1	5N43.8	18S13.6	19N16.8	9S40.0	21N36.6
4 T	12 52 35.9	4 26.8	20 26.7	9S22.5	1N 0.1	12 8.0	10 31.6	5 29.3	18 17.5	19 15.4	9 42.3	21 35.7
7 S	13 4 25.6	5 36.0	20 24.7	19 34.1	1 40.4	11 8.1	10 22.3	5 15.0	18 21.6	19 14.0	9 44.6	21 34.8
10 W	13 16 15.3	6 44.5	20 22.8	20 33.9	1 33.1	10 4.9	10 10.1	5 0.9	18 25.7	19 12.7	9 46.9	21 34.0
13 S	13 28 4.9	7 52.2	20 20.8	13 23.4	0 44.3	8 58.5	9 55.3	4 46.8	18 29.8	19 11.6	9 49.3	21 33.3
16 T	13 39 54.6	8 58.9	20 18.9	1 16.5	0S36.3	7 49.4	9 37.9	4 33.0	18 34.0	19 10.6	9 51.6	21 32.8
19 F	13 51 44.2	10 4.5	20 16.9	11N54.2	2 18.7	6 37.7	9 18.2	4 19.4	18 38.3	19 9.6	9 54.0	21 32.3
22 M	14 3 33.9	11 8.7	20 14.9	20 29.7	4 14.3	5 23.7	8 56.3	4 5.9	18 42.5	19 8.8	9 56.3	21 31.9
25 T	14 15 23.6	12 11.4	20 12.9	18 46.0	6 16.5	4 7.6	8 32.3	3 52.7	18 46.8	19 8.2	9 58.7	21 31.7
28 S	14 27 13.2	13 12.5	20 10.9	7 12.5	8 20.7	2 49.8	8 6.5	3 39.7	18 51.0	19 7.6	10 1.0	21 31.5
31 W	14 39 2.9	14 11.7	20 8.9	7S43.6	10 23.6	1 30.6	7 38.8	3 27.0	18 55.3	19 7.2	10 3.3	21 31.5

NOVEMBER 1956

LONGITUDE at NOON

DAY	EPHEMERIS SIDEREAL TIME h m s	☉ ° ′	☊ ° ′	☽ ° ′	☿ ° ′	♀ ° ′	♂ ° ′	♃ ° ′	♄ ° ′	♅ ° ′	♆ ° ′	♇ ° ′
1 T	14 42 59.4	9♏ 3.2	29♏55.0	24♎ 6.3	1♏55.8	0♎49.3	16♓11.5	23♍57.6	2♐18.7	6♌56.2	0♏29.7	0♍13.2
2 F	14 46 56.0	10 3.3	29 51.9	7♏36.8	3 35.3	2 1.1	16 27.5	24 8.4	2 25.4	6 56.8	0 31.9	0 14.1
3 S	14 50 52.5	11 3.4	29 48.7	20 50.4	5 14.6	3 13.2	16 44.1	24 19.2	2 32.3	6 57.3	0 34.2	0 15.0
4 S	14 54 49.1	12 3.6	29 45.5	3♐46.2	6 53.5	4 25.2	17 1.2	24 29.9	2 39.1	6 57.8	0 36.4	0 15.8
5 M	14 58 45.6	13 3.8	29 42.3	16 24.3	8 32.1	5 37.4	17 18.9	24 40.4	2 45.9	6 58.2	0 38.6	0 16.6
6 T	15 2 42.2	14 4.0	29 39.1	28 46.3	10 10.3	6 49.7	17 37.2	24 50.9	2 52.8	6 58.5	0 40.8	0 17.4
7 W	15 6 38.8	15 4.2	29 36.0	10♑55.0	11 48.1	8 2.0	17 56.0	25 1.3	2 59.6	6 58.8	0 43.0	0 18.2
8 T	15 10 35.3	16 4.5	29 32.8	22 53.8	13 25.6	9 14.4	18 15.3	25 11.6	3 6.5	6 59.0	0 45.2	0 18.9
9 F	15 14 31.9	17 4.8	29 29.6	4♒46.9	15 2.7	10 26.9	18 35.1	25 21.8	3 13.5	6 59.2	0 47.3	0 19.6
10 S	15 18 28.4	18 5.1	29 26.4	16 38.8	16 39.5	11 39.5	18 55.4	25 31.9	3 20.4	6 59.3	0 49.5	0 20.2
11 S	15 22 25.0	19 5.5	29 23.3	28 34.4	18 15.9	12 52.2	19 16.2	25 42.0	3 27.4	6 59.4	0 51.7	0 20.9
12 M	15 26 21.5	20 5.8	29 20.1	10♓38.4	19 52.1	14 4.9	19 37.4	25 51.9	3 34.4	6 59.4	0 53.8	0 21.5
13 T	15 30 18.1	21 6.2	29 16.9	22 55.1	21 27.9	15 17.8	19 59.2	26 1.7	3 41.4	6 59.4	0 55.9	0 22.0
14 W	15 34 14.6	22 6.6	29 13.7	5♈28.1	23 3.3	16 30.7	20 21.3	26 11.5	3 48.4	6R59.3	0 58.1	0 22.6
15 T	15 38 11.2	23 7.1	29 10.6	18 20.3	24 38.6	17 43.7	20 43.9	26 21.1	3 55.4	6 59.1	1 0.2	0 23.1
16 F	15 42 7.8	24 7.5	29 7.4	1♉33.0	26 13.5	18 56.7	21 6.9	26 30.6	4 2.4	6 58.9	1 2.3	0 23.6
17 S	15 46 4.3	25 8.0	29 4.2	15 6.3	27 48.2	20 9.9	21 30.3	26 40.1	4 9.5	6 58.6	1 4.4	0 24.0
18 S	15 50 0.9	26 8.5	29 1.0	28 58.4	29 22.6	21 23.1	21 54.2	26 49.4	4 16.6	6 58.3	1 6.4	0 24.5
19 M	15 53 57.4	27 9.0	28 57.8	13♊ 6.1	0♐56.8	22 36.3	22 18.4	26 58.6	4 23.6	6 57.9	1 8.5	0 24.9
20 T	15 57 54.0	28 9.6	28 54.7	27 25.2	2 30.8	23 49.7	22 42.9	27 7.7	4 30.7	6 57.5	1 10.6	0 25.2
21 W	16 1 50.5	29 10.2	28 51.5	11♋50.6	4 4.6	25 3.1	23 7.9	27 16.7	4 37.8	6 57.0	1 12.6	0 25.6
22 T	16 5 47.1	0♐10.8	28 48.3	26 17.4	5 38.3	26 16.5	23 33.2	27 25.6	4 44.9	6 56.5	1 14.6	0 25.9
23 F	16 9 43.7	1 11.4	28 45.1	10♌40.9	7 11.8	27 30.1	23 58.8	27 34.3	4 52.0	6 55.9	1 16.6	0 26.2
24 S	16 13 40.2	2 12.2	28 42.0	24 57.5	8 45.1	28 43.7	24 24.9	27 43.0	4 59.2	6 55.3	1 18.7	0 26.4
25 S	16 17 36.8	3 12.9	28 38.8	9♍ 4.5	10 18.3	29 57.4	24 51.2	27 51.5	5 6.3	6 54.6	1 20.6	0 26.7
26 M	16 21 33.3	4 13.6	28 35.6	23 0.2	11 51.4	1♏11.1	25 17.9	27 60.0	5 13.4	6 53.8	1 22.6	0 26.8
27 T	16 25 29.9	5 14.3	28 32.4	6♎43.6	13 24.4	2 24.9	25 44.8	28 8.2	5 20.5	6 53.0	1 24.5	0 27.0
28 W	16 29 26.4	6 15.1	28 29.3	20 14.3	14 57.2	3 38.7	26 12.1	28 16.4	5 27.7	6 52.2	1 26.5	0 27.1
29 T	16 33 23.0	7 15.9	28 26.1	3♏32.1	16 30.0	4 52.6	26 39.7	28 24.4	5 34.8	6 51.3	1 28.4	0 27.2
30 F	16 37 19.5	8 16.7	28 22.9	16 36.8	18 2.6	6 6.5	27 7.6	28 32.3	5 41.9	6 50.3	1 30.3	0 27.3

DECLINATION at NOON

DAY	EPHEMERIS SIDEREAL TIME	☉	☊	☽	☿	♀	♂	♃	♄	♅	♆	♇
1 T	14 42 59.4	14S31.0	20S 8.2	12S 8.9	11S 3.9	1N 3.9	7S29.2	3N22.9	18S56.7	19N 7.0	10S 4.1	21N31.5
4 S	14 54 49.1	15 27.4	20 6.2	20 28.6	13 1.7	0S16.8	6 59.2	3 10.5	19 1.0	19 6.8	10 6.3	21 31.5
7 W	15 6 38.8	16 21.6	20 4.1	19 28.7	14 54.0	1 38.1	6 27.8	2 58.5	19 5.2	19 6.6	10 8.6	21 31.7
10 S	15 18 28.4	17 13.2	20 2.1	10 55.6	16 39.6	2 59.8	5 54.9	2 46.8	19 9.5	19 6.6	10 10.8	21 32.0
13 T	15 30 18.1	18 2.2	20 0.0	1N37.7	18 17.8	4 21.6	5 20.7	2 35.5	19 13.6	19 6.7	10 13.0	21 32.5
16 F	15 42 7.8	18 48.4	19 57.9	14 18.4	19 47.9	5 43.0	4 45.3	2 24.5	19 17.8	19 6.9	10 15.1	21 33.0
19 M	15 53 57.4	19 31.5	19 55.9	21 5.7	21 9.2	7 3.9	4 8.8	2 14.0	19 21.9	19 7.3	10 17.2	21 33.6
22 T	16 5 47.1	20 11.5	19 53.8	16 31.4	22 21.1	8 23.7	3 31.4	2 3.8	19 25.9	19 7.8	10 19.2	21 34.4
25 S	16 17 36.8	20 48.2	19 51.7	3 20.3	23 23.0	9 42.3	2 53.0	1 54.0	19 29.9	19 8.4	10 21.2	21 35.2
28 W	16 29 26.4	21 21.3	19 49.6	10S58.9	24 14.2	10 59.2	2 13.8	1 44.7	19 33.8	19 9.1	10 23.1	21 36.1

DECEMBER 1956

LONGITUDE at NOON

DAY	EPHEMERIS SIDEREAL TIME h m s	☉ ° ′	☊ ° ′	☽ ° ′	☿ ° ′	♀ ° ′	♂ ° ′	♃ ° ′	♄ ° ′	♅ ° ′	♆ ° ′	♇ ° ′
1 S	16 41 16.1	9♐17.6	28♏19.7	29♏28.5	19♐35.2	7♏20.5	27♓35.8	28♍40.1	5♐49.0	6♌49.3	1♏32.1	0♍27.3
2 S	16 45 12.7	10 18.5	28 16.5	12♐ 7.3	21 7.6	8 34.5	28 4.2	28 47.8	5 56.1	6R48.2	1 34.0	0 27.3
3 M	16 49 9.2	11 19.3	28 13.4	24 33.8	22 39.9	9 48.6	28 33.0	28 55.3	6 3.2	6 47.1	1 35.8	0 27.3
4 T	16 53 5.8	12 20.3	28 10.2	6♑48.8	24 12.1	11 2.7	29 2.0	29 2.7	6 10.3	6 46.0	1 37.6	0R27.2
5 W	16 57 2.3	13 21.2	28 7.0	18 53.9	25 44.1	12 16.9	29 31.3	29 9.9	6 17.4	6 44.8	1 39.4	0 27.1
6 T	17 0 58.9	14 22.1	28 3.8	0♒51.3	27 15.9	13 31.0	0♈ 0.8	29 17.0	6 24.5	6 43.5	1 41.2	0 27.0
7 F	17 4 55.4	15 23.0	28 0.7	12 43.8	28 47.6	14 45.3	0 30.6	29 23.9	6 31.6	6 42.2	1 42.9	0 26.8
8 S	17 8 52.0	16 24.0	27 57.5	24 34.8	0♑18.9	15 59.5	1 0.7	29 30.7	6 38.6	6 40.8	1 44.7	0 26.7
9 S	17 12 48.6	17 25.0	27 54.3	6♓28.6	1 50.0	17 13.8	1 30.9	29 37.4	6 45.7	6 39.4	1 46.4	0 26.4
10 M	17 16 45.1	18 26.0	27 51.1	18 29.6	3 20.7	18 28.1	2 1.4	29 43.9	6 52.7	6 38.0	1 48.0	0 26.2
11 T	17 20 41.7	19 27.0	27 48.0	0♈42.4	4 51.0	19 42.5	2 32.1	29 50.3	6 59.7	6 36.5	1 49.7	0 25.9
12 W	17 24 38.2	20 28.0	27 44.8	13 11.9	6 20.7	20 56.9	3 3.1	29 56.5	7 6.7	6 34.9	1 51.3	0 25.6
13 T	17 28 34.8	21 29.0	27 41.6	26 2.1	7 49.8	22 11.3	3 34.2	0♎ 2.6	7 13.7	6 33.3	1 52.9	0 25.3
14 F	17 32 31.3	22 30.0	27 38.4	9♉16.4	9 18.2	23 25.7	4 5.6	0 8.5	7 20.7	6 31.7	1 54.5	0 24.9
15 S	17 36 27.9	23 31.1	27 35.2	22 56.5	10 45.7	24 40.3	4 37.1	0 14.3	7 27.7	6 30.1	1 56.1	0 24.6
16 S	17 40 24.5	24 32.1	27 32.1	7♊ 2.0	12 12.0	25 54.8	5 8.9	0 19.9	7 34.6	6 28.4	1 57.7	0 24.2
17 M	17 44 21.0	25 33.1	27 28.9	21 30.0	13 37.0	27 9.3	5 40.8	0 25.4	7 41.5	6 26.6	1 59.2	0 23.7
18 T	17 48 17.6	26 34.2	27 25.7	6♋15.2	15 0.5	28 23.9	6 12.8	0 30.6	7 48.4	6 24.8	2 0.7	0 23.2
19 W	17 52 14.1	27 35.2	27 22.5	21 9.9	16 22.2	29 38.5	6 45.1	0 35.8	7 55.2	6 23.0	2 2.1	0 22.7
20 T	17 56 10.7	28 36.3	27 19.4	6♌ 5.6	17 41.7	0♐53.1	7 17.5	0 40.7	8 2.1	6 21.1	2 3.5	0 22.2
21 F	18 0 7.2	29 37.4	27 16.2	20 54.0	18 58.7	2 7.7	7 50.1	0 45.5	8 8.9	6 19.2	2 4.9	0 21.6
22 S	18 4 3.8	0♑38.5	27 13.0	5♍28.2	20 12.7	3 22.4	8 22.8	0 50.2	8 15.6	6 17.2	2 6.3	0 21.0
23 S	18 8 0.4	1 39.6	27 9.8	19 43.8	21 23.2	4 37.1	8 55.7	0 54.6	8 22.4	6 15.3	2 7.7	0 20.4
24 M	18 11 56.9	2 40.7	27 6.7	3♎38.7	22 29.7	5 51.8	9 28.8	0 58.9	8 29.1	6 13.2	2 9.0	0 19.8
25 T	18 15 53.5	3 41.9	27 3.5	17 12.8	23 31.5	7 6.5	10 2.0	1 3.1	8 35.8	6 11.2	2 10.3	0 19.1
26 W	18 19 50.0	4 43.0	27 0.3	0♏27.7	24 27.9	8 21.3	10 35.3	1 7.0	8 42.5	6 9.1	2 11.5	0 18.4
27 T	18 23 46.6	5 44.2	26 57.1	13 25.7	25 18.1	9 36.1	11 8.8	1 10.8	8 49.1	6 6.9	2 12.8	0 17.7
28 F	18 27 43.2	6 45.3	26 54.0	26 9.1	26 1.3	10 50.9	11 42.4	1 14.4	8 55.7	6 4.8	2 14.0	0 16.9
29 S	18 31 39.7	7 46.5	26 50.8	8♐40.3	26 36.5	12 5.7	12 16.2	1 17.8	9 2.2	6 2.6	2 15.1	0 16.1
30 S	18 35 36.3	8 47.7	26 47.6	21 1.4	27 2.9	13 20.5	12 50.1	1 21.1	9 8.7	6 0.4	2 16.3	0 15.3
31 M	18 39 32.8	9 48.8	26 44.4	3♑13.8	27 19.6	14 35.4	13 24.1	1 24.1	9 15.2	5 58.1	2 17.4	0 14.5

DECLINATION at NOON

DAY	EPHEMERIS SIDEREAL TIME	☉	☊	☽	☿	♀	♂	♃	♄	♅	♆	♇
1 S	16 41 16.1	21S50.9	19S47.5	20S 0.3	24S54.1	12S14.1	1S33.9	1N35.9	19S37.6	19N 9.9	10S25.0	21N37.2
4 T	16 53 5.8	22 16.6	19 45.4	20 2.4	25 22.2	13 26.6	0 53.2	1 27.6	19 41.4	19 10.8	10 26.8	21 38.3
7 F	17 4 55.4	22 38.5	19 43.2	12 8.5	25 37.8	14 36.3	0 11.9	1 19.7	19 45.1	19 11.9	10 28.5	21 39.5
10 M	17 16 45.1	22 56.4	19 41.1	0N 0.5	25 40.5	15 42.9	0N29.9	1 12.5	19 48.7	19 13.1	10 30.1	21 40.9
13 T	17 28 34.8	23 10.2	19 38.9	12 42.9	25 29.9	16 46.1	1 12.1	1 5.7	19 52.2	19 14.3	10 31.7	21 42.3
16 S	17 40 24.5	23 19.8	19 36.8	20 45.5	25 6.1	17 45.4	1 54.8	0 59.5	19 55.6	19 15.7	10 33.2	21 43.7
19 W	17 52 14.1	23 25.3	19 34.6	17 41.6	24 29.5	18 40.6	2 37.8	0 53.9	19 58.9	19 17.1	10 34.5	21 45.3
22 S	18 4 3.8	23 26.5	19 32.4	4 41.6	23 41.4	19 31.3	3 21.0	0 48.9	20 2.1	19 18.6	10 35.8	21 46.9
25 T	18 15 53.5	23 23.5	19 30.3	9S56.6	22 44.6	20 17.2	4 4.3	0 44.5	20 5.2	19 20.2	10 37.0	21 48.6
28 F	18 27 43.2	23 16.3	19 28.1	19 30.7	21 43.2	20 58.0	4 47.8	0 40.7	20 8.2	19 21.9	10 38.2	21 50.4
31 M	18 39 32.8	23 4.8	19 25.9	20 27.8	20 43.7	21 33.4	5 31.4	0 37.6	20 11.0	19 23.6	10 39.2	21 52.3

JANUARY 1957

DAY	EPHEMERIS SIDEREAL TIME	☉	☊	☽	☿	♀	♂	♃	♄	♅	♆	♇
	h m s	° ′	° ′	° ′	° ′	° ′	° ′	° ′	° ′	° ′	° ′	° ′
LONGITUDE at NOON												
1 T	18 43 29.4	10♑50.0	26♏41.2	15♑19.1	27♑25.7	15♐50.3	13♈58.3	1♎27.0	9♐21.7	5♌55.8	2♏18.5	0♍13.7
2 W	18 47 25.9	11 51.2	26 38.1	27 18.3	27R20.6	17 5.1	14 32.6	1 29.7	9 28.1	5R53.5	2 19.5	0R12.8
3 T	18 51 22.5	12 52.4	26 34.9	9♒12.9	27 3.7	18 20.0	15 7.0	1 32.2	9 34.4	5 51.2	2 20.6	0 11.9
4 F	18 55 19.1	13 53.6	26 31.7	21 4.5	26 35.0	19 34.9	15 41.5	1 34.6	9 40.7	5 48.8	2 21.6	0 10.9
5 S	18 59 15.6	14 54.8	26 28.5	2♓55.4	25 54.7	20 49.9	16 16.2	1 36.8	9 47.0	5 46.5	2 22.6	0 10.0
6 S	19 3 12.2	15 55.9	26 25.4	14 48.5	25 3.3	22 4.8	16 50.9	1 38.7	9 53.3	5 44.1	2 23.5	0 9.0
7 M	19 7 8.7	16 57.1	26 22.2	26 47.3	24 2.2	23 19.7	17 25.8	1 40.5	9 59.4	5 41.7	2 24.4	0 8.0
8 T	19 11 5.3	17 58.2	26 19.0	8♈56.1	22 52.9	24 34.7	18 0.7	1 42.1	10 5.6	5 39.2	2 25.2	0 7.0
9 W	19 15 1.8	18 59.4	26 15.8	21 19.5	21 37.7	25 49.6	18 35.8	1 43.5	10 11.7	5 36.7	2 26.1	0 6.0
10 T	19 18 58.4	20 0.5	26 12.7	4♉ 2.3	20 18.8	27 4.5	19 10.9	1 44.7	10 17.7	5 34.3	2 26.9	0 4.9
11 F	19 22 55.0	21 1.7	26 9.5	17 9.2	18 58.8	28 19.5	19 46.2	1 45.7	10 23.7	5 31.8	2 27.6	0 3.8
12 S	19 26 51.5	22 2.8	26 6.3	0♊43.6	17 40.4	29 34.4	20 21.5	1 46.5	10 29.6	5 29.2	2 28.4	0 2.7
13 S	19 30 48.1	23 3.9	26 3.1	14 47.3	16 25.7	0♑49.4	20 56.9	1 47.2	10 35.5	5 26.7	2 29.1	0 1.6
14 M	19 34 44.6	24 5.0	25 59.9	29 19.3	15 16.8	2 4.4	21 32.4	1 47.6	10 41.3	5 24.2	2 29.7	0 0.4
15 T	19 38 41.2	25 6.1	25 56.8	14♋15.4	14 15.2	3 19.3	22 8.0	1 47.9	10 47.1	5 21.6	2 30.4	29♌59.3
16 W	19 42 37.7	26 7.1	25 53.6	29 27.5	13 22.1	4 34.3	22 43.6	1 47.9	10 52.8	5 19.0	2 30.9	29 58.1
17 T	19 46 34.3	27 8.2	25 50.4	14♌45.4	12 38.2	5 49.3	23 19.3	1R47.8	10 58.4	5 16.4	2 31.5	29 56.9
18 F	19 50 30.8	28 9.3	25 47.2	29 57.6	12 3.7	7 4.3	23 55.1	1 47.5	11 4.0	5 13.8	2 32.0	29 55.7
19 S	19 54 27.4	29 10.3	25 44.1	14♍53.9	11 38.6	8 19.3	24 31.0	1 47.0	11 9.6	5 11.2	2 32.5	29 54.4
20 S	19 58 24.0	0♒11.4	25 40.9	29 26.9	11 22.8	9 34.3	25 6.9	1 46.3	11 15.0	5 8.6	2 33.0	29 53.2
21 M	20 2 20.5	1 12.4	25 37.7	13♎32.9	11 15.9	10 49.3	25 42.9	1 45.4	11 20.5	5 6.0	2 33.4	29 51.9
22 T	20 6 17.1	2 13.4	25 34.5	27 11.2	11D17.3	12 4.3	26 19.0	1 44.3	11 25.8	5 3.4	2 33.8	29 50.6
23 W	20 10 13.6	3 14.5	25 31.4	10♏23.9	11 26.4	13 19.3	26 55.1	1 43.0	11 31.1	5 0.8	2 34.2	29 49.3
24 T	20 14 10.2	4 15.5	25 28.2	23 14.4	11 42.8	14 34.4	27 31.3	1 41.6	11 36.3	4 58.2	2 34.5	29 48.0
25 F	20 18 6.7	5 16.5	25 25.0	5♐46.8	12 5.7	15 49.4	28 7.6	1 39.9	11 41.5	4 55.5	2 34.8	29 46.7
26 S	20 22 3.3	6 17.5	25 21.8	18 5.4	12 34.7	17 4.5	28 43.9	1 38.1	11 46.6	4 53.0	2 35.1	29 45.4
27 S	20 25 59.9	7 18.5	25 18.6	0♑13.8	13 9.1	18 19.5	29 20.3	1 36.1	11 51.7	4 50.3	2 35.3	29 44.0
28 M	20 29 56.4	8 19.5	25 15.5	12 15.0	13 48.5	19 34.5	29 56.7	1 33.8	11 56.6	4 47.7	2 35.5	29 42.6
29 T	20 33 53.0	9 20.5	25 12.3	24 11.6	14 32.5	20 49.6	0♉33.2	1 31.4	12 1.5	4 45.1	2 35.7	29 41.2
30 W	20 37 49.5	10 21.4	25 9.1	6♒ 5.3	15 20.6	22 4.6	1 9.8	1 28.8	12 6.3	4 42 5	2 35.8	29 39.8
31 T	20 41 46.1	11 22.3	25 5.9	17 57.6	16 12.4	23 19.7	1 46.4	1 26.0	12 11.1	4 39.9	2 35.9	29 38.4
DECLINATION at NOON												
1 T	18 43 29.4	23S 0.1	19S 25.1	18S 49.6	20S 25.6	21S 44.0	5N 45.9	0N 36.7	20S 12.0	19N 24.2	10S 39.5	21N 52.9
4 F	18 55 19.1	22 43.1	19 22.9	9 39.1	19 40.3	22 11.8	6 29.5	0 34.5	20 14.7	19 26.0	10 40.4	21 54.8
7 M	19 7 8.7	22 22.1	19 20.7	2N 50.0	19 12.2	22 33.7	7 13.0	0 32.9	20 17.3	19 27.8	10 41.2	21 56.7
10 T	19 18 58.4	21 57.1	19 18.5	14 47.9	19 2.1	22 49.6	7 56.3	0 32.0	20 19.8	19 29.7	10 41.9	21 58.7
13 S	19 30 48.1	21 28.3	19 16.2	21 4.3	19 7.0	22 59.2	8 39.4	0 31.7	20 22.1	19 31.6	10 42.4	22 0.7
16 W	19 42 37.7	20 55.8	19 14.0	15 52.6	19 22.8	23 2.6	9 22.2	0 32.2	20 24.4	19 33.5	10 42.9	22 2.7
19 S	19 54 27.4	20 19.6	19 11.7	1 30.1	19 45.5	22 59.6	10 4.7	0 33.3	20 26.5	19 35.4	10 43.3	22 4.8
22 T	20 6 17.1	19 40.1	19 9.5	12S 48.4	20 11.5	22 50.3	10 46.8	0 35.2	20 28.5	19 37.3	10 43.6	22 6.8
25 F	20 18 6.7	18 57.2	19 7.2	20 28.8	20 37.1	22 34.7	11 28.4	0 37.7	20 30.4	19 39.3	10 43.7	22 8.9
28 M	20 29 56.4	18 11.2	19 4.9	19 16.9	20 59.0	22 12.9	12 9.6	0 40.8	20 32.2	19 41.2	10 43.8	22 11.0
31 T	20 41 46.1	17 22.2	19 2.6	10 43.8	21 14.9	21 45.0	12 50.2	0 44.7	20 33.8	19 43.1	10 43.7	22 13.0

FEBRUARY 1957

DAY	EPHEMERIS SIDEREAL TIME	☉	☊	☽	☿	♀	♂	♃	♄	♅	♆	♇
LONGITUDE at NOON												
1 F	20 45 42.6	12♒23.3	25♏ 2.8	29♒49.6	17♑ 7.6	24♑34.7	2♉23.0	1♎23.1	12♐15.7	4♌37.3	2♏35.9	29♌37.0
2 S	20 49 39.2	13 24.1	24 59.6	11♓42.8	18 5.8	25 49.7	2 59.7	1R19.9	12 20.3	4R34.7	2 35.9	29R35.6
3 S	20 53 35.7	14 25.0	24 56.4	23 38.9	19 7.0	27 4.7	3 36.5	1 16.6	12 24.9	4 32.1	2 35.9	29 34.1
4 M	20 57 32.3	15 25.9	24 53.2	5♈40.2	20 10.6	28 19.8	4 13.3	1 13.0	12 29.3	4 29.5	2 35.9	29 32.7
5 T	21 1 28.8	16 26.7	24 50.1	17 49.9	21 16.7	29 34.8	4 50.1	1 9.4	12 33.7	4 27.0	2R35.8	29 31.2
6 W	21 5 25.4	17 27.5	24 46.9	0♉11.6	22 25.0	0♒49.8	5 27.0	1 5.5	12 38.0	4 24.4	2 35.7	29 29.8
7 T	21 9 22.0	18 28.3	24 43.7	12 49.8	23 35.2	2 4.8	6 3.9	1 1.5	12 42.2	4 21.9	2 35.5	29 28.3
8 F	21 13 18.5	19 29.0	24 40.5	25 48.8	24 47.3	3 19.8	6 40.9	0 57.3	12 46.3	4 19.4	2 35.3	29 26.8
9 S	21 17 15.1	20 29.8	24 37.3	9♊12.9	26 1.2	4 34.8	7 17.9	0 52.9	12 50.3	4 16.9	2 35.1	29 25.3
10 S	21 21 11.6	21 30.5	24 34.2	23 5.3	27 16.7	5 49.8	7 54.9	0 48.4	12 54.3	4 14.4	2 34.8	29 23.8
11 M	21 25 8.2	22 31.1	24 31.0	7♋26.8	28 33.7	7 4.8	8 32.0	0 43.7	12 58.2	4 12.0	2 34.6	29 22.3
12 T	21 29 4.7	23 31.8	24 27.8	22 15.3	29 52.2	8 19.7	9 9.1	0 38.8	13 2.0	4 9.5	2 34.2	29 20.9
13 W	21 33 1.3	24 32.4	24 24.6	7♌24.8	1♒12.1	9 34.7	9 46.2	0 33.8	13 5.7	4 7.1	2 33.9	29 19.4
14 T	21 36 57.8	25 33.0	24 21.5	22 46.0	2 33.2	10 49.7	10 23.3	0 28.6	13 9.3	4 4.7	2 33.5	29 17.8
15 F	21 40 54.4	26 33.6	24 18.3	8♍ 7.0	3 55.6	12 4.6	11 0.5	0 23.3	13 12.9	4 2.3	2 33.1	29 16.3
16 S	21 44 50.9	27 34.2	24 15.1	23 16.2	5 19.3	13 19.6	11 37.8	0 17.9	13 16.4	4 0.0	2 32.7	29 14.9
17 S	21 48 47.5	28 34.7	24 11.9	8♎ 3.7	6 44.0	14 34.6	12 15.0	0 12.3	13 19.8	3 57.7	2 32.2	29 13.4
18 M	21 52 44.1	29 35.2	24 8.7	22 23.4	8 9.9	15 49.5	12 52.2	0 6.6	13 23.1	3 55.4	2 31.7	29 11.9
19 T	21 56 40.6	0♓35.7	24 5.6	6♏12.8	9 36.9	17 4.5	13 29.5	0 0.7	13 26.3	3 53.2	2 31.1	29 10.4
20 W	22 0 37.2	1 36.1	24 2.4	19 32.9	11 5.0	18 19.4	14 6.8	29♍54.7	13 29.4	3 50.9	2 30.6	29 8.9
21 T	22 4 33.7	2 36.6	23 59.2	2♐26.9	12 34.1	19 34.4	14 44.1	29 48.6	13 32.4	3 48.7	2 29.9	29 7.3
22 F	22 8 30.3	3 37.0	23 56.0	14 59.2	14 4.3	20 49.3	15 21.5	29 42.3	13 35.3	3 46.5	2 29.3	29 5.8
23 S	22 12 26.8	4 37.4	23 52.9	27 14.7	15 35.5	22 4.2	15 58.8	29 35.9	13 38.2	3 44.4	2 28.6	29 4.3
24 S	22 16 23.4	5 37.7	23 49.7	9♑18.3	17 7.7	23 19.2	16 36.2	29 29.4	13 40.9	3 42.3	2 27.9	29 2.8
25 M	22 20 19.9	6 38.1	23 46.5	21 14.2	18 41.0	24 34.1	17 13.7	29 22.8	13 43.6	3 40.2	2 27.2	29 1.3
26 T	22 24 16.5	7 38.4	23 43.3	3♒ 6.2	20 15.3	25 49.0	17 51.1	29 16.1	13 46.1	3 38.1	2 26.4	28 59.8
27 W	22 28 13.0	8 38.7	23 40.1	14 57.1	21 50.6	27 3.9	18 28.6	29 9.3	13 48.6	3 36.1	2 25.7	28 58.4
28 T	22 32 9.6	9 39.0	23 37.0	26 49.0	23 26.9	28 18.8	19 6.0	29 2.4	13 51.0	3 34.1	2 24.8	28 56.9
DECLINATION at NOON												
1 F	20 45 42.6	17S 5.3	19S 1.8	6S 51.7	21S 18.5	21S 34.3	13N 3.6	0N 46.1	20S 34.3	19N 43.7	10S 43.7	22N 13.7
4 M	20 57 32.3	16 12.7	18 59.5	5N 44.9	21 23.6	20 58.6	13 43.3	0 50.7	20 35.8	19 45.6	10 43.5	22 15.8
7 T	21 9 22.0	15 17.6	18 57.2	16 41.3	21 19.1	20 17.3	14 22.4	0 56.0	20 37.1	19 47.4	10 43.2	22 17.8
10 S	21 21 11.6	14 20.2	18 54.9	20 52.5	21 4.3	19 30.6	15 0.7	1 1.9	20 38.3	19 49.2	10 42.8	22 19.8
13 W	21 33 1.3	13 20.7	18 52.6	13 47.4	20 38.6	18 38.7	15 38.1	1 8.3	20 39.4	19 50.9	10 42.3	22 21.7
16 S	21 44 50.9	12 19.1	18 50.3	1S 20.2	20 1.7	17 42.0	16 14.8	1 15.2	20 40.4	19 52.5	10 41.7	22 23.6
19 T	21 56 40.6	11 15.9	18 47.9	15 0.8	19 13.4	16 40.8	16 50.5	1 22.6	20 41.3	19 54.1	10 41.0	22 25.4
22 F	22 8 30.3	10 11.0	18 45.6	20 45.7	18 13.4	15 35.3	17 25.2	1 30.4	20 42.1	19 55.7	10 40.3	22 27.2
25 M	22 20 19.9	9 4.7	18 43.2	17 33.6	17 1.7	14 26.0	17 59.0	1 38.6	20 42.7	19 57.1	10 39.4	22 29.0
28 T	22 32 9.6	7 57.2	18 40.8	7 52.6	15 38.3	13 13.1	18 31.7	1 47.2	20 43.2	19 58.5	10 38.4	22 30.6

MARCH 1957

DAY	EPHEMERIS SIDEREAL TIME	☉	☊	☽	☿	♀	♂	♃	♄	♅	♆	♇
	h m s	° ′	° ′	° ′	° ′	° ′	° ′	° ′	° ′	° ′	° ′	° ′
LONGITUDE at NOON												
1 F	22 36 6.1	10♓39.2	23♏33.8	8♓43.6	25♒ 4.2	29♒33.7	19♉43.5	28♍55.3	13♐53.2	3♌32.2	2♏24.0	28♌55.4
2 S	22 40 2.7	11 39.4	23 30.6	20 42.1	26 42.6	0♓48.5	20 21.1	28R48.2	13 55.4	3R30.3	2R23.1	28R53.9
3 S	22 43 59.2	12 39.6	23 27.4	2♈45.7	28 22.0	2 3.4	20 58.6	28 41.1	13 57.5	3 28.4	2 22.2	28 52.5
4 M	22 47 55.8	13 39.7	23 24.3	14 55.8	0♓ 2.5	3 18.2	21 36.1	28 33.8	13 59.5	3 26.6	2 21.3	28 51.0
5 T	22 51 52.3	14 39.8	23 21.1	27 14.1	1 44.1	4 33.1	22 13.7	28 26.4	14 1.4	3 24.8	2 20.3	28 49.6
6 W	22 55 48.9	15 39.9	23 17.9	9♉43.0	3 26.7	5 47.9	22 51.3	28 19.0	14 3.2	3 23.0	2 19.3	28 48.1
7 T	22 59 45.5	16 39.9	23 14.7	22 25.5	5 10.5	7 2.7	23 28.9	28 11.6	14 4.9	3 21.3	2 18.3	28 46.7
8 F	23 3 42.0	17 39.9	23 11.5	5♊24.9	6 55.3	8 17.5	24 6.5	28 4.1	14 6.4	3 19.7	2 17.3	28 45.3
9 S	23 7 38.6	18 40.0	23 8.4	18 44.5	8 41.3	9 32.4	24 44.2	27 56.5	14 8.0	3 18.1	2 16.3	28 43.9
10 S	23 11 35.1	19 39.9	23 5.2	2♋27.3	10 28.4	10 47.1	25 21.8	27 48.9	14 9.4	3 16.5	2 15.2	28 42.5
11 M	23 15 31.7	20 39.8	23 2.0	16 34.7	12 16.7	12 1.9	25 59.4	27 41.2	14 10.7	3 15.0	2 14.1	28 41.2
12 T	23 19 28.2	21 39.6	22 58.8	1♌ 6.0	14 6.1	13 16.6	26 37.0	27 33.6	14 11.9	3 13.5	2 12.9	28 39.8
13 W	23 23 24.8	22 39.5	22 55.6	15 57.7	15 56.6	14 31.4	27 14.7	27 25.8	14 13.0	3 12.0	2 11.8	28 38.4
14 T	23 27 21.3	23 39.2	22 52.5	1♍ 2.8	17 48.3	15 46.1	27 52.3	27 18.1	14 14.0	3 10.6	2 10.6	28 37.1
15 F	23 31 17.9	24 39.0	22 49.3	16 12.2	19 41.2	17 0.8	28 30.0	27 10.3	14 14.9	3 9.3	2 9.4	28 35.7
16 S	23 35 14.4	25 38.7	22 46.1	1♎15.3	21 35.2	18 15.5	29 7.7	27 2.6	14 15.7	3 8.0	2 8.2	28 34.4
17 S	23 39 11.0	26 38.4	22 42.9	16 2.6	23 30.4	19 30.2	29 45.3	26 54.8	14 16.4	3 6.7	2 6.9	28 33.1
18 M	23 43 7.5	27 38.0	22 39.8	0♏26.6	25 26.6	20 44.8	0♊23.0	26 47.0	14 17.0	3 5.5	2 5.7	28 31.8
19 T	23 47 4.1	28 37.7	22 36.6	14 23.1	27 23.9	21 59.5	1 0.7	26 39.2	14 17.5	3 4.3	2 4.4	28 30.6
20 W	23 51 0.6	29 37.3	22 33.4	27 51.3	29 22.2	23 14.1	1 38.3	26 31.4	14 17.9	3 3.2	2 3.1	28 29.3
21 T	23 54 57.2	0♈36.8	22 30.2	10♐52.6	1♈21.4	24 28.8	2 16.0	26 23.7	14 18.1	3 2.2	2 1.7	28 28.1
22 F	23 58 53.7	1 36.4	22 27.0	23 30.6	3 21.5	25 43.4	2 53.7	26 15.9	14 18.3	3 1.2	2 0.4	28 26.8
23 S	0 2 50.3	2 35.9	22 23.9	5♑49.8	5 22.3	26 58.0	3 31.4	26 8.2	14 18.4	3 0.2	1 59.0	28 25.6
24 S	0 6 46.8	3 35.3	22 20.7	17 55.0	7 23.7	28 12.6	4 9.1	26 0.5	14 18.4	2 59.3	1 57.6	28 24.5
25 M	0 10 43.4	4 34.8	22 17.5	29 51.2	9 25.4	29 27.2	4 46.8	25 52.9	14R18.3	2 58.4	1 56.2	28 23.3
26 T	0 14 39.9	5 34.2	22 14.3	11♒42.8	11 27.5	0♈41.8	5 24.5	25 45.3	14 18.1	2 57.6	1 54.8	28 22.1
27 W	0 18 36.5	6 33.6	22 11.2	23 33.8	13 29.5	1 56.3	6 2.2	25 37.7	14 17.8	2 56.8	1 53.4	28 21.0
28 T	0 22 33.1	7 32.9	22 8.0	5♓27.4	15 31.2	3 10.9	6 39.9	25 30.2	14 17.4	2 56.1	1 51.9	28 19.9
29 F	0 26 29.6	8 32.3	22 4.8	17 26.2	17 32.3	4 25.4	7 17.7	25 22.7	14 16.9	2 55.5	1 50.5	28 18.8
30 S	0 30 26.2	9 31.6	22 1.6	29 32.0	19 32.7	5 40.0	7 55.4	25 15.4	14 16.3	2 54.9	1 49.0	28 17.8
31 S	0 34 22.7	10 30.8	21 58.4	11♈46.2	21 31.7	6 54.5	8 33.2	25 8.1	14 15.6	2 54.3	1 47.5	28 16.7
DECLINATION at NOON												
1 F	22 36 6.1	7S34.4	18S40.0	3S50.1	15S 7.9	12S48.0	18N42.3	1N50.1	20S43.4	19N58.9	10S38.1	22N31.2
4 M	22 47 55.8	6 25.5	18 37.6	8N41.1	13 28.9	11 30.9	19 13.5	1 59.1	20 43.7	20 0.2	10 37.0	22 32.8
7 T	22 59 45.5	5 15.9	18 35.3	18 19.4	11 38.3	10 11.0	19 43.6	2 8.2	20 44.0	20 1.4	10 35.9	22 34.3
10 S	23 11 35.1	4 5.6	18 32.9	20 6.1	9 36.2	8 48.6	20 12.4	2 17.5	20 44.2	20 2.4	10 34.7	22 35.6
13 W	23 23 24.8	2 54.9	18 30.4	11 13.7	7 22.9	7 24.1	20 40.0	2 26.8	20 44.2	20 3.4	10 33.4	22 37.0
16 S	23 35 14.4	1 43.9	18 28.0	4S 4.2	4 59.0	5 57.9	21 6.2	2 36.2	20 44.1	20 4.3	10 32.0	22 38.2
19 T	23 47 4.1	0 32.8	18 25.6	16 42.8	2 25.2	4 30.2	21 31.2	2 45.6	20 44.0	20 5.1	10 30.6	22 39.3
22 F	23 58 53.7	0N38.3	18 23.2	20 30.9	0N17.0	3 1.4	21 54.7	2 54.9	20 43.7	20 5.8	10 29.2	22 40.4
25 M	0 10 43.4	1 49.2	18 20.7	15 29.6	3 5.1	1 31.8	22 16.8	3 4.0	20 43.4	20 6.3	10 27.6	22 41.3
28 T	0 22 33.1	2 59.8	18 18.3	4 53.5	5 55.7	0 1.7	22 37.5	3 13.0	20 42.9	20 6.8	10 26.1	22 42.2
31 S	0 34 22.7	4 9.8	18 15.8	7N36.3	8 43.9	1N28.5	22 56.7	3 21.6	20 42.4	20 7.1	10 24.5	22 42.9

APRIL 1957

DAY	EPHEMERIS SIDEREAL TIME	☉	☊	☽	☿	♀	♂	♃	♄	♅	♆	♇
LONGITUDE at NOON												
1 M	0 38 19.3	11♈30.1	21♏55.3	24♈ 9.8	23♈29.2	8♈ 9.0	9♊10.9	25♍ 0.8	14♐14.8	2♌53.9	1♏46.0	28♌15.7
2 T	0 42 15.8	12 29.3	21 52.1	6♉43.7	25 24.7	9 23.5	9 48.6	24R53.6	14R13.9	2R53.4	1R44.5	28R14.7
3 W	0 46 12.4	13 28.4	21 48.9	19 28.9	27 17.9	10 38.0	10 26.4	24 46.6	14 12.9	2 53.0	1 43.0	28 13.7
4 T	0 50 8.9	14 27.5	21 45.7	2♊26.5	29 8.3	11 52.4	11 4.1	24 39.6	14 11.8	2 52.7	1 41.4	28 12.8
5 F	0 54 5.5	15 26.6	21 42.6	15 37.9	0♉55.6	13 6.8	11 41.8	24 32.7	14 10.6	2 52.4	1 39.9	28 11.8
6 S	0 58 2.0	16 25.6	21 39.4	29 4.6	2 39.4	14 21.3	12 19.6	24 25.8	14 9.4	2 52.2	1 38.3	28 10.9
7 S	1 1 58.6	17 24.6	21 36.2	12♋47.9	4 19.3	15 35.6	12 57.3	24 19.1	14 8.0	2 52.0	1 36.7	28 10.0
8 M	1 5 55.1	18 23.6	21 33.0	26 48.2	5 55.1	16 50.0	13 35.1	24 12.5	14 6.5	2 51.9	1 35.1	28 9.1
9 T	1 9 51.7	19 22.5	21 29.8	11♌ 5.0	7 26.5	18 4.4	14 12.8	24 6.1	14 4.9	2 51.8	1 33.6	28 8.3
10 W	1 13 48.2	20 21.4	21 26.7	25 35.7	8 53.2	19 18.7	14 50.5	23 59.7	14 3.3	2 51.8	1 32.0	28 7.5
11 T	1 17 44.8	21 20.2	21 23.5	10♍16.2	10 14.9	20 33.0	15 28.2	23 53.4	14 1.5	2 51.8	1 30.4	28 6.7
12 F	1 21 41.3	22 19.0	21 20.3	25 0.3	11 31.5	21 47.3	16 5.9	23 47.3	13 59.7	2D51.9	1 28.7	28 5.9
13 S	1 25 37.9	23 17.8	21 17.1	9♎40.9	12 42.7	23 1.6	16 43.7	23 41.3	13 57.7	2 52.1	1 27.1	28 5.2
14 S	1 29 34.4	24 16.6	21 14.0	24 10.7	13 48.5	24 15.9	17 21.4	23 35.4	13 55.7	2 52.3	1 25.5	28 4.5
15 M	1 33 31.0	25 15.3	21 10.8	8♏23.6	14 48.7	25 30.1	17 59.1	23 29.7	13 53.6	2 52.5	1 23.9	28 3.8
16 T	1 37 27.5	26 13.9	21 7.6	22 15.1	15 43.1	26 44.4	18 36.8	23 24.1	13 51.4	2 52.8	1 22.2	28 3.1
17 W	1 41 24.1	27 12.6	21 4.4	5♐43.0	16 31.7	27 58.6	19 14.5	23 18.6	13 49.1	2 53.2	1 20.6	28 2.5
18 T	1 45 20.7	28 11.2	21 1.2	18 47.3	17 14.4	29 12.8	19 52.2	23 13.3	13 46.8	2 53.6	1 19.0	28 1.8
19 F	1 49 17.2	29 9.8	20 58.1	1♑29.7	17 51.1	0♉27.0	20 29.9	23 8.1	13 44.3	2 54.1	1 17.3	28 1.3
20 S	1 53 13.8	0♉ 8.4	20 54.9	13 53.4	18 21.9	1 41.2	21 7.6	23 3.1	13 41.8	2 54.6	1 15.7	28 0.7
21 S	1 57 10.3	1 6.9	20 51.7	26 2.5	18 46.7	2 55.4	21 45.3	22 58.2	13 39.2	2 55.2	1 14.1	28 0.2
22 M	2 1 6.9	2 5.4	20 48.5	8♒ 1.4	19 5.4	4 9.6	22 23.0	22 53.5	13 36.5	2 55.8	1 12.5	27 59.7
23 T	2 5 3.4	3 3.9	20 45.4	19 54.8	19 18.2	5 23.7	23 0.7	22 48.9	13 33.8	2 56.5	1 10.8	27 59.2
24 W	2 8 60.0	4 2.3	20 42.2	1♓47.3	19 25.2	6 37.8	23 38.4	22 44.5	13 30.9	2 57.3	1 9.2	27 58.8
25 T	2 12 56.5	5 0.8	20 39.0	13 43.1	19 26.5	7 51.9	24 16.0	22 40.2	13 28.0	2 58.0	1 7.5	27 58.3
26 F	2 16 53.1	5 59.2	20 35.8	25 45.7	19R22.3	9 6.0	24 53.7	22 36.1	13 25.0	2 58.9	1 5.9	27 58.0
27 S	2 20 49.6	6 57.5	20 32.6	7♈58.3	19 12.7	10 20.1	25 31.4	22 32.2	13 21.9	2 59.8	1 4.3	27 57.6
28 S	2 24 46.2	7 55.9	20 29.5	20 23.0	18 58.2	11 34.2	26 9.1	22 28.4	13 18.8	3 0.7	1 2.6	27 57.2
29 M	2 28 42.7	8 54.2	20 26.3	3♉ 1.3	18 38.9	12 48.3	26 46.8	22 24.8	13 15.5	3 1.7	1 1.0	27 56.9
30 T	2 32 39.3	9 52.4	20 23.1	15 53.9	18 15.5	14 2.3	27 24.4	22 21.4	13 12.3	3 2.8	0 59.4	27 56.7
DECLINATION at NOON												
1 M	0 38 19.3	4N33.0	18S15.0	11N28.5	9N38.4	1N58.6	23N 2.8	3N24.4	20S42.2	20N 7.2	10S23.9	22N43.1
4 T	0 50 8.9	5 42.0	18 12.5	19 33.1	12 14.0	3 28.5	23 20.0	3 32.7	20 41.5	20 7.4	10 22.3	22 43.7
7 S	1 1 58.6	6 50.2	18 10.1	18 41.7	14 33.4	4 57.8	23 35.6	3 40.5	20 40.7	20 7.5	10 20.6	22 44.2
10 W	1 13 48.2	7 57.3	18 7.6	8 6.2	16 31.9	6 26.1	23 49.7	3 48.0	20 39.9	20 7.4	10 18.9	22 44.6
13 S	1 25 37.9	9 3.2	18 5.1	6S56.0	18 6.4	7 53.2	24 2.2	3 54.9	20 38.9	20 7.3	10 17.2	22 44.8
16 T	1 37 27.5	10 7.7	18 2.6	18 6.7	19 15.4	9 18.7	24 13.1	4 1.4	20 37.9	20 7.0	10 15.5	22 45.0
19 F	1 49 17.2	11 10.7	18 0.1	19 56.0	19 58.1	10 42.3	24 22.4	4 7.3	20 36.8	20 6.7	10 13.8	22 45.0
22 M	2 1 6.9	12 12.1	17 57.6	13 17.2	20 14.5	12 3.6	24 30.0	4 12.6	20 35.7	20 6.2	10 12.1	22 45.0
25 T	2 12 56.5	13 11.7	17 55.0	1 57.8	20 4.7	13 22.4	24 36.0	4 17.4	20 34.4	20 5.6	10 10.4	22 44.8
28 S	2 24 46.2	14 9.3	17 52.5	10N21.3	19 29.9	14 38.2	24 40.3	4 21.5	20 33.1	20 4.9	10 8.7	22 44.5

MAY 1957

DAY	EPHEMERIS SIDEREAL TIME	☉	☊	☽	☿	♀	♂	♃	♄	♅	♆	♇
	h m s	° ′	° ′	° ′	° ′	° ′	° ′	° ′	° ′	° ′	° ′	° ′
						LONGITUDE at NOON						
1 W	2 36 35.9	10♉50.7	20♏19.9	29♉ 0.9	17♉48.3	15♉16.3	28♊ 2.1	22♍18.1	13♐ 8.9	3♌ 3.9	0♏57.8	27♌56.4
2 T	2 40 32.4	11 48.9	20 16.8	12♊21.7	17R17.8	16 30.3	28 39.8	22R15.0	13R 5.5	3 5.0	0R56.2	27R56.2
3 F	2 44 29.0	12 47.1	20 13.6	25 55.5	16 44.6	17 44.3	29 17.5	22 12.1	13 2.0	3 6.2	0 54.6	27 56.0
4 S	2 48 25.5	13 45.3	20 10.4	9♋41.1	16 9.4	18 58.3	29 55.1	22 9.4	12 58.5	3 7.5	0 53.0	27 55.8
5 S	2 52 22.1	14 43.4	20 7.2	23 37.2	15 32.9	20 12.3	0♋32.8	22 6.9	12 54.9	3 8.8	0 51.4	27 55.7
6 M	2 56 18.6	15 41.5	20 4.0	7♌42.2	14 55.5	21 26.2	1 10.5	22 4.5	12 51.2	3 10.2	0 49.8	27 55.6
7 T	3 0 15.2	16 39.5	20 0.9	21 54.2	14 18.1	22 40.1	1 48.1	22 2.3	12 47.5	3 11.6	0 48.3	27 55.5
8 W	3 4 11.7	17 37.6	19 57.7	6♍10.9	13 41.3	23 54.0	2 25.8	22 0.3	12 43.7	3 13.0	0 46.7	27 55.5
9 T	3 8 8.3	18 35.6	19 54.5	20 29.5	13 5.7	25 7.9	3 3.4	21 58.5	12 39.9	3 14.5	0 45.1	27 55.4
10 F	3 12 4.8	19 33.5	19 51.3	4♎46.6	12 32.0	26 21.8	3 41.0	21 56.8	12 36.0	3 16.1	0 43.6	27 55.4
11 S	3 16 1.4	20 31.5	19 48.2	18 58.5	12 0.6	27 35.7	4 18.7	21 55.4	12 32.2	3 17.7	0 42.1	27D55.5
12 S	3 19 58.0	21 29.4	19 45.0	3♏ 1.3	11 32.1	28 49.5	4 56.4	21 54.1	12 28.2	3 19.4	0 40.6	27 55.6
13 M	3 23 54.5	22 27.3	19 41.8	16 51.4	11 6.8	0♊ 3.4	5 34.0	21 53.0	12 24.2	3 21.1	0 39.1	27 55.7
14 T	3 27 51.1	23 25.1	19 38.6	0♐25.8	10 45.1	1 17.2	6 11.6	21 52.1	12 20.1	3 22.8	0 37.6	27 55.8
15 W	3 31 47.6	24 23.0	19 35.4	13 42.5	10 27.4	2 31.0	6 49.2	21 51.4	12 16.0	3 24.6	0 36.2	27 56.0
16 T	3 35 44.2	25 20.8	19 32.3	26 40.9	10 13.9	3 44.7	7 26.8	21 50.8	12 11.9	3 26.5	0 34.7	27 56.2
17 F	3 39 40.7	26 18.5	19 29.1	9♑21.2	10 4.7	4 58.5	8 4.4	21 50.4	12 7.7	3 28.3	0 33.3	27 56.4
18 S	3 43 37.3	27 16.3	19 25.9	21 45.3	10 0.0	6 12.3	8 42.0	21 50.2	12 3.5	3 30.3	0 31.8	27 56.6
19 S	3 47 33.8	28 14.0	19 22.7	3♒55.8	9 59.8	7 26.0	9 19.6	21 50.2	11 59.3	3 32.2	0 30.4	27 56.9
20 M	3 51 30.4	29 11.8	19 19.6	15 56.3	10D 4.2	8 39.7	9 57.2	21D50.4	11 55.0	3 34.2	0 29.0	27 57.2
21 T	3 55 27.0	0♊ 9.5	19 16.4	27 50.9	10 13.1	9 53.4	10 34.8	21 50.7	11 50.8	3 36.3	0 27.6	27 57.5
22 W	3 59 23.5	1 7.2	19 13.2	9♓44.2	10 26.6	11 7.2	11 12.4	21 51.3	11 46.4	3 38.4	0 26.3	27 57.9
23 T	4 3 20.1	2 4.8	19 10.0	21 40.9	10 44.5	12 20.8	11 50.0	21 52.0	11 42.1	3 40.6	0 24.9	27 58.3
24 F	4 7 16.6	3 2.5	19 6.9	3♈45.3	11 6.7	13 34.5	12 27.6	21 52.9	11 37.7	3 42.8	0 23.6	27 58.7
25 S	4 11 13.2	4 0.1	19 3.7	16 1.7	11 33.3	14 48.2	13 5.2	21 53.9	11 33.3	3 45.0	0 22.3	27 59.1
26 S	4 15 9.7	4 57.7	19 0.5	28 33.5	12 4.1	16 1.9	13 42.8	21 55.2	11 28.9	3 47.3	0 21.0	27 59.6
27 M	4 19 6.3	5 55.4	18 57.3	11♉23.3	12 38.9	17 15.5	14 20.4	21 56.6	11 24.5	3 49.6	0 19.8	28 0.1
28 T	4 23 2.8	6 52.9	18 54.1	24 32.5	13 17.7	18 29.1	14 58.0	21 58.2	11 20.1	3 51.9	0 18.5	28 0.6
29 W	4 26 59.4	7 50.5	18 51.0	8♊ 1.0	14 0.4	19 42.8	15 35.6	21 60.0	11 15.7	3 54.3	0 17.3	28 1.2
30 T	4 30 56.0	8 48.1	18 47.8	21 47.3	14 46.8	20 56.4	16 13.2	22 1.9	11 11.2	3 56.8	0 16.1	28 1.8
31 F	4 34 52.5	9 45.6	18 44.6	5♋48.5	15 36.9	22 10.0	16 50.8	22 4.1	11 6.8	3 59.2	0 14.9	28 2.4
						DECLINATION at NOON						
1 W	2 36 35.9	15N 4.9	17S50.0	19N 6.0	18N33.2	15N50.7	24N42.9	4N25.1	20S31.8	20N 4.1	10S 7.1	22N44.1
4 S	2 48 25.5	15 58.2	17 47.4	19 2.9	17 20.0	16 59.7	24 43.9	4 27.9	20 30.3	20 3.2	10 5.4	22 43.6
7 T	3 0 15.2	16 49.1	17 44.9	9 12.5	15 58.1	18 4.8	24 43.3	4 30.2	20 28.9	20 2.1	10 3.8	22 43.0
10 F	3 12 4.8	17 37.5	17 42.3	5S 19.5	14 37.0	19 5.6	24 40.9	4 31.7	20 27.4	20 1.0	10 2.2	22 42.3
13 M	3 23 54.5	18 23.2	17 39.7	17 7.5	13 25.6	20 1.8	24 37.0	4 32.6	20 25.8	19 59.8	10 0.7	22 41.5
16 T	3 35 44.2	19 6.2	17 37.1	20 13.1	12 30.8	20 53.2	24 31.3	4 32.9	20 24.2	19 58.5	9 59.3	22 40.6
19 S	3 47 33.8	19 46.2	17 34.6	14 20.0	11 56.4	21 39.4	24 24.1	4 32.5	20 22.6	19 57.0	9 57.8	22 39.7
22 W	3 59 23.5	20 23.2	17 32.0	3 19.6	11 43.6	22 20.1	24 15.2	4 31.5	20 20.9	19 55.5	9 56.5	22 38.6
25 S	4 11 13.2	20 57.1	17 29.4	9N 0.3	11 51.6	22 55.2	24 4.8	4 29.8	20 19.3	19 53.9	9 55.2	22 37.4
28 T	4 23 2.8	21 27.7	17 26.8	18 28.5	12 18.6	23 24.4	23 52.7	4 27.5	20 17.6	19 52.2	9 54.0	22 36.2
31 F	4 34 52.5	21 55.0	17 24.1	19 31.8	13 2.2	23 47.5	23 39.1	4 24.5	20 16.0	19 50.4	9 52.8	22 34.8

JUNE 1957

DAY	EPHEMERIS SIDEREAL TIME	☉	☊	☽	☿	♀	♂	♃	♄	♅	♆	♇
						LONGITUDE at NOON						
1 S	4 38 49.1	10♊43.1	18♏41.4	20♋ 0.8	16♉30.6	23♊23.6	17♋28.4	22♍ 6.4	11♐ 2.4	4♌ 1.8	0♏13.8	28♌ 3.1
2 S	4 42 45.6	11 40.6	18 38.3	4♌19.4	17 27.7	24 37.2	18 6.0	22 8.9	10R57.9	4 4.4	0R12.6	28 3.8
3 M	4 46 42.2	12 38.1	18 35.1	18 40.1	18 28.1	25 50.7	18 43.6	22 11.6	10 53.5	4 6.9	0 11.5	28 4.5
4 T	4 50 38.7	13 35.6	18 31.9	2♍58.8	19 31.9	27 4.3	19 21.2	22 14.4	10 49.0	4 9.6	0 10.4	28 5.2
5 W	4 54 35.3	14 33.0	18 28.7	17 12.3	20 38.9	28 17.8	19 58.8	22 17.4	10 44.6	4 12.2	0 9.4	28 6.0
6 T	4 58 31.9	15 30.4	18 25.6	1♎18.4	21 49.1	29 31.3	20 36.4	22 20.5	10 40.2	4 14.9	0 8.3	28 6.8
7 F	5 2 28.4	16 27.8	18 22.4	15 15.4	23 2.4	0♋44.8	21 13.9	22 23.9	10 35.7	4 17.7	0 7.3	28 7.6
8 S	5 6 25.0	17 25.2	18 19.2	29 2.3	24 18.8	1 58.3	21 51.5	22 27.4	10 31.3	4 20.4	0 6.3	28 8.4
9 S	5 10 21.5	18 22.5	18 16.0	12♏38.2	25 38.2	3 11.8	22 29.1	22 31.0	10 26.9	4 23.2	0 5.3	28 9.3
10 M	5 14 18.1	19 1..8	18 12.8	26 2.4	27 0.6	4 25.2	23 6.7	22 34.8	10 22.6	4 26.1	0 4.4	28 10.1
11 T	5 18 14.6	20 17.2	18 9.7	9♐14.0	28 25.9	5 38.6	23 44.2	22 38.8	10 18.2	4 28.9	0 3.5	28 11.1
12 W	5 22 11.2	21 14.5	18 6.5	22 12.5	29 54.2	6 52.0	24 21.8	22 42.9	10 13.9	4 31.8	0 2.6	28 12.0
13 T	5 26 7.8	22 11.8	18 3.3	4♑57.5	1♊25.4	8 5.4	24 59.4	22 47.2	10 9.6	4 34.8	0 1.7	28 13.0
14 F	5 30 4.3	23 9.1	18 0.1	17 29.0	2 59.6	9 18.8	25 37.0	22 51.7	10 5.3	4 37.7	0 0.9	28 14.0
15 S	5 34 0.9	24 6.3	17 57.0	29 47.9	4 36.5	10 32.2	26 14.5	22 56.3	10 1.1	4 40.7	0 0.1	28 15.0
16 S	5 37 57.4	25 3.6	17 53.8	11♒55.8	6 16.4	11 45.6	26 52.1	23 1.1	9 56.8	4 43.7	29♎59.3	28 16.0
17 M	5 41 54.0	26 0.9	17 50.6	23 55.0	7 59.0	12 58.9	27 29.7	23 6.0	9 52.6	4 46.8	29 58.6	28 17.1
18 T	5 45 50.5	26 58.1	17 47.4	5♓48.9	9 44.5	14 12.2	28 7.2	23 11.1	9 48.5	4 49.9	29 57.8	28 18.2
19 W	5 49 47.1	27 55.4	17 44.3	17 41.4	11 32.7	15 25.6	28 44.8	23 16.3	9 44.4	4 53.0	29 57.1	28 19.3
20 T	5 53 43.7	28 52.7	17 41.1	29 37.0	13 23.6	16 38.9	29 22.4	23 21.6	9 40.3	4 56.1	29 56.5	28 20.4
21 F	5 57 40.2	29 49.9	17 37.9	11♈40.4	15 17.0	17 52.2	29 60.0	23 27.2	9 36.2	4 59.3	29 55.8	28 21.6
22 S	6 [illegible] 36.8	0♋47.2	17 34.7	23 56.8	17 13.1	19 5.5	0♌37.6	23 32.9	9 32.3	5 2.5	29 55.3	28 22.8
23 S	6 5 33.3	1 44.4	17 31.5	6♉30.5	19 11.5	20 18.8	1 15.2	23 38.7	9 28.3	5 5.7	29 54.7	28 24.0
24 M	6 9 29.9	2 41.7	17 28.4	19 25.5	21 12.1	21 32.1	1 52.8	23 44.6	9 24.4	5 9.0	29 54.1	28 25.3
25 T	6 13 26.4	3 38.9	17 25.2	2♊44.4	23 14.8	22 45.3	2 30.4	23 50.7	9 20.5	5 12.2	29 53.6	28 26.5
26 W	6 17 23.0	4 36.2	17 22.0	16 28.1	25 19.4	23 58.6	3 8.0	23 56.9	9 16.7	5 15.5	29 53.1	28 27.8
27 T	6 21 19.6	5 33.4	17 18.8	0♋35.0	27 25.7	25 11.8	3 45.6	24 3.3	9 13.0	5 18.9	29 52.7	28 29.1
28 F	6 25 16.1	6 30.6	17 15.7	15 1.3	29 33.4	26 25.0	4 23.3	24 9.8	9 9.3	5 22.2	29 52.2	28 30.4
29 S	6 29 12.7	7 27.9	17 12.5	29 40.7	1♋42.3	27 38.2	5 0.9	24 16.5	9 5.6	5 25.5	29 51.8	28 31.8
30 S	6 33 9.2	8 25.1	17 9.3	14♌25.8	3 52.0	28 51.4	5 38.5	24 23.3	9 2.0	5 28.9	29 51.5	28 33.2
						DECLINATION at NOON						
1 S	4 38 49.1	22N 3.4	17S 23.3	17N26.3	13N20.0	23N53.8	23N34.2	4N23.4	20S 15.4	19N49.8	9S 52.4	22N34.3
4 T	4 50 38.7	22 26.1	17 20.6	5 39.5	14 21.4	24 8.6	23 18.6	4 19.6	20 13.8	19 47.9	9 51.4	22 32.9
7 F	5 2 28.4	22 45.3	17 18.0	8S 43.7	15 33.1	24 17.0	23 1.4	4 15.2	20 12.1	19 45.9	9 50.4	22 31.4
10 M	5 14 18.1	23 0.8	17 15.4	18 41.4	16 52.3	24 18.9	22 42.8	4 10.3	20 10.5	19 43.9	9 49.5	22 29.8
13 T	5 26 7.8	23 12.8	17 12.7	19 38.4	18 15.8	24 14.3	22 22.8	4 4.7	20 9.0	19 41.8	9 48.7	22 28.2
16 S	5 37 57.4	23 21.0	17 10.1	12 16.6	19 40.2	24 3.4	22 1.3	3 58.7	20 7.5	19 39.6	9 48.0	22 26.4
19 W	5 49 47.1	23 25.6	17 7.4	0 40.9	21 1.5	23 46.0	21 38.4	3 52.1	20 6.0	19 37.3	9 47.4	22 24.7
22 S	6 1 36.8	23 26.4	17 4.7	11N19.7	22 15.1	23 22.4	21 14.2	3 44.9	20 4.6	19 34.9	9 46.8	22 22.8
25 T	6 13 26.4	23 23.5	17 2.0	19 30.2	23 15.7	22 52.6	20 48.6	3 37.3	20 3.3	19 32.6	9 46.4	22 20.9
28 F	6 25 16.1	23 17.0	16 59.4	18 21.5	23 58.0	22 16.9	20 21.8	3 29.1	20 2.1	19 30.1	9 46.1	22 19.0

JULY 1957

LONGITUDE at NOON

DAY	EPHEMERIS SIDEREAL TIME h m s	☉ ° ′	☊ ° ′	☽ ° ′	☿ ° ′	♀ ° ′	♂ ° ′	♃ ° ′	♄ ° ′	♅ ° ′	♆ ° ′	♇ ° ′
1 M	6 37 5.8	9♋22.3	17♏ 6.1	29♌ 8.8	6♋ 2.3	0♌ 4.6	6♌16.1	24♍30.2	8♐58.5	5♌32.3	29♎51.1	28♌34.5
2 T	6 41 2.3	10 19.5	17 3.0	13♍43.0	8 13.0	1 17.7	6 53.8	24 37.2	8R55.0	5 35.7	29R50.8	28 35.9
3 W	6 44 58.9	11 16.7	16 59.8	28 3.8	10 23.6	2 30.8	7 31.4	24 44.4	8 51.6	5 39.2	29 50.5	28 37.4
4 T	6 48 55.5	12 13.9	16 56.6	12♎ 8.3	12 34.0	3 43.9	8 9.0	24 51.7	8 48.3	5 42.6	29 50.3	28 38.8
5 F	6 52 52.0	13 11.1	16 53.4	25 55.9	14 43.9	4 57.0	8 46.7	24 59.1	8 45.0	5 46.1	29 50.1	28 40.3
6 S	6 56 48.6	14 8.3	16 50.3	9♏27.1	16 53.0	6 10.1	9 24.3	25 6.7	8 41.8	5 49.6	29 49.9	28 41.8
7 S	7 0 45.1	15 5.5	16 47.1	22 43.2	19 1.2	7 23.2	10 2.0	25 14.3	8 38.7	5 53.1	29 49.7	28 43.3
8 M	7 4 41.7	16 2.7	16 43.9	5♐45.8	21 8.3	8 36.2	10 39.6	25 22.1	8 35.6	5 56.6	29 49.6	28 44.8
9 T	7 8 38.2	16 59.9	16 40.7	18 36.3	23 14.0	9 49.2	11 17.3	25 30.0	8 32.6	6 0.2	29 49.5	28 46.4
10 W	7 12 34.8	17 57.1	16 37.5	1♑15.7	25 18.4	11 2.2	11 54.9	25 38.1	8 29.7	6 3.7	29 49.5	28 47.9
11 T	7 16 31.4	18 54.3	16 34.4	13 44.8	27 21.2	12 15.1	12 32.6	25 46.2	8 26.8	6 7.3	29 49.5	28 49.5
12 F	7 20 27.9	19 51.4	16 31.2	26 4.1	29 22.3	13 28.1	13 10.3	25 54.5	8 24.0	6 10.8	29 49.5	28 51.1
13 S	7 24 24.5	20 48.7	16 28.0	8♒14.4	1♌21.9	14 41.1	13 48.0	26 2.9	8 21.4	6 14.5	29D49.6	28 52.8
14 S	7 28 21.0	21 45.9	16 24.8	20 16.6	3 19.6	15 54.0	14 25.7	26 11.4	8 18.8	6 18.1	29 49.6	28 54.4
15 M	7 32 17.6	22 43.1	16 21.7	2♓12.5	5 15.6	17 6.9	15 3.4	26 20.0	8 16.2	6 21.7	29 49.8	28 56.0
16 T	7 36 14.1	23 40.3	16 18.5	14 4.4	7 9.8	18 19.7	15 41.1	26 28.7	8 13.8	6 25.3	29 49.9	28 57.7
17 W	7 40 10.7	24 37.6	16 15.3	25 55.3	9 2.2	19 32.6	16 18.8	26 37.5	8 11.4	6 29.0	29 50.1	28 59.4
18 T	7 44 7.3	25 34.8	16 12.1	7♈49.1	10 52.8	20 45.4	16 56.5	26 46.4	8 9.1	6 32.6	29 50.3	29 1.1
19 F	7 48 3.8	26 32.0	16 9.0	19 50.5	12 41.5	21 58.2	17 34.2	26 55.4	8 6.9	6 36.3	29 50.5	29 2.8
20 S	7 52 0.4	27 29.3	16 5.8	2♉ 4.3	14 28.4	23 11.0	18 11.9	27 4.5	8 4.7	6 39.9	29 50.8	29 4.5
21 S	7 55 56.9	28 26.6	16 2.6	14 35.7	16 13.5	24 23.8	18 49.7	27 13.8	8 2.7	6 43.6	29 51.1	29 6.2
22 M	7 59 53.5	29 23.9	15 59.4	27 29.6	17 56.8	25 36.5	19 27.4	27 23.1	8 0.7	6 47.3	29 51.4	29 8.0
23 T	8 3 50.0	0♌21.2	15 56.2	10♊49.9	19 38.3	26 49.2	20 5.2	27 32.5	7 58.9	6 50.9	29 51.8	29 9.7
24 W	8 7 46.6	1 18.5	15 53.1	24 38.6	21 18.0	28 1.9	20 43.0	27 42.0	7 57.1	6 54.6	29 52.2	29 11.5
25 T	8 11 43.1	2 15.8	15 49.9	8♋55.3	22 55.9	29 14.6	21 20.7	27 51.6	7 55.4	6 58.3	29 52.6	29 13.3
26 F	8 15 39.7	3 13.2	15 46.7	23 36.6	24 32.0	0♍27.3	21 58.5	28 1.3	7 53.8	7 2.0	29 53.1	29 15.1
27 S	8 19 36.3	4 10.5	15 43.5	8♌35.3	26 6.3	1 39.9	22 36.4	28 11.2	7 52.3	7 5.7	29 53.5	29 16.9
28 S	8 23 32.8	5 7.9	15 40.4	23 42.3	27 38.8	2 52.5	23 14.2	28 21.0	7 50.8	7 9.4	29 54.1	29 18.7
29 M	8 27 29.4	6 5.3	15 37.2	8♍47.2	29 9.4	4 5.1	23 52.0	28 31.0	7 49.5	7 13.1	29 54.6	29 20.6
30 T	8 31 25.9	7 2.7	15 34.0	23 40.5	0♍38.3	5 17.7	24 29.8	28 41.1	7 48.3	7 16.8	29 55.2	29 22.4
31 W	8 35 22.5	8 0.1	15 30.8	8♎15.3	2 5.3	6 30.2	25 7.7	28 51.3	7 47.1	7 20.5	29 55.8	29 24.3

DECLINATION at NOON

DAY	EPHEMERIS SIDEREAL TIME h m s	☉	☊	☽	☿	♀	♂	♃	♄	♅	♆	♇
1 M	6 37 5.8	23N 6.7	16S56.7	7N 3.6	24N17.7	21N35.5	19N53.8	3N20.5	20S 0.9	19N27.6	9S45.8	22N17.0
4 T	6 48 55.5	22 52.8	16 54.0	7S34.8	24 12.6	20 48.7	19 24.5	3 11.5	19 59.8	19 25.0	9 45.7	22 15.0
7 S	7 0 45.1	22 35.3	16 51.2	18 4.2	23 42.7	19 56.6	18 54.0	3 2.0	19 58.9	19 22.4	9 45.7	22 13.0
10 W	7 12 34.8	22 14.3	16 48.5	19 57.7	22 50.3	18 59.6	18 22.5	2 52.1	19 58.0	19 19.8	9 45.7	22 10.9
13 S	7 24 24.5	21 49.9	16 45.8	13 23.6	21 38.9	17 57.9	17 49.8	2 41.7	19 57.3	19 17.1	9 45.9	22 8.8
16 T	7 36 14.1	21 22.1	16 43.1	2 6.5	20 12.4	16 51.9	17 16.1	2 31.0	19 56.7	19 14.4	9 46.2	22 6.7
19 F	7 48 3.8	20 51.0	16 40.3	9N53.8	18 34.2	15 41.9	16 41.3	2 19.9	19 56.2	19 11.7	9 46.6	22 4.6
22 M	7 59 53.5	20 16.8	16 37.6	18 41.6	16 47.7	14 28.3	16 5.6	2 8.5	19 55.8	19 8.9	9 47.0	22 2.4
25 T	8 11 43.1	19 39.5	16 34.8	19 10.2	14 55.6	13 11.2	15 29.0	1 56.7	19 55.6	19 6.1	9 47.6	22 0.3
28 S	8 23 32.8	18 59.2	16 32.1	8 55.3	13 0.3	11 51.1	14 51.4	1 44.6	19 55.5	19 3.3	9 48.3	21 58.1
31 W	8 35 22.5	18 16.2	16 29.3	6S 5.8	11 3.7	10 28.4	14 13.0	1 32.2	19 55.6	19 0.5	9 49.1	21 55.9

AUGUST 1957

LONGITUDE at NOON

DAY	EPHEMERIS SIDEREAL TIME h m s	☉ ° ′	☊ ° ′	☽ ° ′	☿ ° ′	♀ ° ′	♂ ° ′	♃ ° ′	♄ ° ′	♅ ° ′	♆ ° ′	♇ ° ′
1 T	8 39 19.0	8♌57.5	15♏27.7	22♎27.6	3♍30.4	7♍42.8	25♌45.6	29♍ 1.5	7♐46.1	7♌24.2	29♎56.5	29♌26.1
2 F	8 43 15.6	9 54.9	15 24.5	6♏16.3	4 53.7	8 55.2	26 23.4	29 11.9	7R45.1	7 27.9	29 57.2	29 28.0
3 S	8 47 12.1	10 52.4	15 21.3	19 42.6	6 15.0	10 7.7	27 1.3	29 22.3	7 44.3	7 31.6	29 57.9	29 30.0
4 S	8 51 8.7	11 49.8	15 18.1	2♐49.0	7 34.4	11 20.1	27 39.2	29 32.8	7 43.6	7 35.3	29 58.7	29 31.8
5 M	8 55 5.3	12 47.3	15 14.9	15 38.5	8 51.7	12 32.5	28 17.1	29 43.4	7 42.9	7 39.0	29 59.5	29 33.7
6 T	8 59 1.8	13 44.8	15 11.8	28 14.0	10 7.0	13 44.9	28 55.0	29 54.0	7 42.3	7 42.7	0♏ 0.3	29 35.7
7 W	9 2 58.4	14 42.2	15 8.6	10♑38.4	11 20.2	14 57.2	29 33.0	0♎ 4.8	7 41.8	7 46.4	0 1.1	29 37.6
8 T	9 6 54.9	15 39.7	15 5.4	22 53.6	12 31.1	16 9.5	0♍10.9	0 15.6	7 41.5	7 50.1	0 2.0	29 39.5
9 F	9 10 51.5	16 37.2	15 2.2	5♒ 1.4	13 39.8	17 21.7	0 48.8	0 26.4	7 41.2	7 53.7	0 2.9	29 41.4
10 S	9 14 48.0	17 34.8	14 59.1	17 2.9	14 46.2	18 33.9	1 26.8	0 37.4	7 41.0	7 57.4	0 3.8	29 43.4
11 S	9 18 44.6	18 32.3	14 55.9	28 59.3	15 50.1	19 46.1	2 4.8	0 48.4	7 40.9	8 1.1	0 4.7	29 45.3
12 M	9 22 41.1	19 29.9	14 52.7	10♓52.0	16 51.4	20 58.3	2 42.7	0 59.5	7 40.9	8 4.7	0 5.7	29 47.2
13 T	9 26 37.7	20 27.5	14 49.5	22 42.6	17 50.1	22 10.4	3 20.7	1 10.6	7D41.0	8 8.4	0 6.7	29 49.2
14 W	9 30 34.2	21 25.1	14 46.3	4♈33.4	18 46.0	23 22.5	3 58.7	1 21.8	7 41.2	8 12.0	0 7.8	29 51.2
15 T	9 34 30.8	22 22.7	14 43.2	16 27.6	19 38.9	24 34.5	4 36.8	1 33.1	7 41.5	8 15.6	0 8.9	29 53.1
16 F	9 38 27.4	23 20.4	14 40.0	28 28.7	20 28.7	25 46.5	5 14.8	1 44.5	7 41.9	8 19.2	0 10.0	29 55.1
17 S	9 42 23.9	24 18.1	14 36.8	10♉41.3	21 15.3	26 58.5	5 52.9	1 55.9	7 42.4	8 22.8	0 11.1	29 57.0
18 S	9 46 20.5	25 15.8	14 33.6	23 10.2	21 58.4	28 10.4	6 30.9	2 7.4	7 43.0	8 26.4	0 12.2	29 59.0
19 M	9 50 17.0	26 13.5	14 30.5	6♊ 0.3	22 37.9	29 22.3	7 9.0	2 18.9	7 43.6	8 30.0	0 13.4	0♍ 1.0
20 T	9 54 13.6	27 11.3	14 27.3	19 16.0	23 13.5	0♎34.2	7 47.1	2 30.5	7 44.4	8 33.5	0 14.7	0 3.0
21 W	9 58 10.1	28 9.1	14 24.1	3♋ 0.6	23 45.1	1 46.1	8 25.3	2 42.2	7 45.3	8 37.1	0 15.9	0 4.9
22 T	10 2 6.7	29 6.9	14 20.9	17 14.9	24 12.3	2 57.9	9 3.4	2 53.9	7 46.3	8 40.6	0 17.2	0 6.9
23 F	10 6 3.2	0♍ 4.8	14 17.7	1♌56.7	24 34.9	4 9.6	9 41.6	3 5.7	7 47.3	8 44.1	0 18.5	0 8.9
24 S	10 9 59.8	1 2.7	14 14.6	17 0.3	24 52.8	5 21.4	10 19.8	3 17.5	7 48.6	8 47.7	0 19.8	0 10.9
25 S	10 13 56.3	2 0.6	14 11.4	2♍16.4	25 5.6	6 33.1	10 58.0	3 29.4	7 49.8	8 51.2	0 21.2	0 12.9
26 M	10 17 52.9	2 58.5	14 8.2	17 33.9	25 13.1	7 44.8	11 36.2	3 41.4	7 51.2	8 54.6	0 22.6	0 14.9
27 T	10 21 49.4	3 56.5	14 5.0	2♎41.6	25 15.0	8 56.4	12 14.4	3 53.3	7 52.6	8 58.1	0 24.0	0 16.8
28 W	10 25 46.0	4 54.5	14 1.9	17 30.6	25R11.1	10 8.0	12 52.7	4 5.4	7 54.2	9 1.5	0 25.4	0 18.8
29 T	10 29 42.5	5 52.5	13 58.7	1♏54.9	25 1.2	11 19.5	13 31.0	4 17.5	7 55.8	9 4.9	0 26.9	0 20.8
30 F	10 33 39.1	6 50.5	13 55.5	15 52.1	24 45.2	12 31.0	14 9.2	4 29.6	7 57.6	9 8.3	0 28.3	0 22.7
31 S	10 37 35.7	7 48.5	13 52.3	29 22.6	24 23.1	13 42.4	14 47.5	4 41.8	7 59.4	9 11.7	0 29.8	0 24.7

DECLINATION at NOON

DAY	EPHEMERIS SIDEREAL TIME h m s	☉	☊	☽	☿	♀	♂	♃	♄	♅	♆	♇
1 T	8 39 19.0	18N 1.2	16S28.4	10S35.7	10N24.9	10N 0.2	13N60.0	1N28.0	19S55.6	18N59.6	9S49.3	21N55.2
4 S	8 51 8.7	17 14.6	16 25.6	19 16.2	8 29.6	8 34.3	13 20.4	1 15.2	19 55.9	18 56.7	9 50.3	21 53.1
7 W	9 2 58.4	16 25.5	16 22.8	18 54.9	6 37.3	7 6.5	12 40.2	1 2.2	19 56.2	18 53.9	9 51.3	21 50.9
10 S	9 14 48.0	15 34.0	16 20.0	10 58.0	4 49.8	5 37.0	11 59.2	0 48.9	19 56.8	18 51.1	9 52.3	21 48.8
13 T	9 26 37.7	14 40.3	16 17.2	0N43.0	3 9.1	4 6.2	11 17.5	0 35.3	19 57.4	18 48.3	9 53.5	21 46.7
16 F	9 38 27.4	13 44.5	16 14.4	12 11.9	1 37.3	2 34.4	10 35.1	0 21.6	19 58.2	18 45.5	9 54.8	21 44.7
19 M	9 50 17.0	12 46.6	16 11.6	19 26.5	0 17.3	1 1.9	9 52.2	0 7.6	19 59.2	18 42.8	9 56.2	21 42.6
22 T	10 2 6.7	11 47.0	16 8.8	17 51.4	0S47.7	0S31.1	9 8.6	0S 6.5	20 0.3	18 40.0	9 57.6	21 40.6
25 S	10 13 56.3	10 45.6	16 6.0	6 13.0	1 33.5	2 4.1	8 24.5	0 20.9	20 1.5	18 37.3	9 59.1	21 38.7
28 W	10 25 46.0	9 42.8	16 3.1	8S53.2	1 55.4	3 37.0	7 40.0	0 35.4	20 2.9	18 34.6	10 0.7	21 36.7
31 S	10 37 35.7	8 38.5	16 0.3	18 36.6	1 48.4	5 9.3	6 54.9	0 50.0	20 4.3	18 32.0	10 2.4	21 34.9

SEPTEMBER 1957

DAY	EPHEMERIS SIDEREAL TIME	☉	☊	☽	☿	♀	♂	♃	♄	♅	♆	♇
	h m s	° ′	° ′	° ′	° ′	° ′	° ′	° ′	° ′	° ′	° ′	° ′
						LONGITUDE at NOON						
1 S	10 41 32.2	8♍46.6	13♏49.1	12♐28.9	23♍54.8	14♎53.8	15♍25.9	4♎54.0	8♐ 1.3	9♌15.0	0♏31.4	0♍26.7
2 M	10 45 28.8	9 44.7	13 46.0	25 14.4	23R20.5	16 5.1	16 4.2	5 6.2	8 3.4	9 18.3	0 32.9	0 28.6
3 T	10 49 25.3	10 42.8	13 42.8	7♑43.2	22 40.4	17 16.4	16 42.5	5 18.5	8 5.5	9 21.6	0 34.5	0 30.6
4 W	10 53 21.9	11 40.9	13 39.6	19 59.0	21 55.0	18 27.7	17 20.9	5 30.9	8 7.7	9 24.9	0 36.1	0 32.5
5 T	10 57 18.4	12 39.1	13 36.4	2♒ 5.4	21 4.8	19 38.9	17 59.3	5 43.3	8 10.0	9 28.2	0 37.7	0 34.5
6 F	11 1 15.0	13 37.3	13 33.3	14 4.9	20 10.5	20 50.0	18 37.7	5 55.7	8 12.4	9 31.4	0 39.4	0 36.4
7 S	11 5 11.5	14 35.5	13 30.1	26 0.1	19 13.2	22 1.1	19 16.1	6 8.1	8 14.9	9 34.6	0 41.0	0 38.3
8 S	11 9 8.1	15 33.8	13 26.9	7♓52.7	18 13.8	23 12.1	19 54.6	6 20.6	8 17.4	9 37.7	0 42.7	0 40.3
9 M	11 13 4.6	16 32.0	13 23.7	19 44.2	17 13.6	24 23.1	20 33.0	6 33.1	8 20.1	9 40.9	0 44.4	0 42.2
10 T	11 17 1.2	17 30.3	13 20.5	1♈36.4	16 13.9	25 34.0	21 11.5	6 45.7	8 22.8	9 44.0	0 46.2	0 44.1
11 W	11 20 57.7	18 28.7	13 17.4	13 30.9	15 16.2	26 44.8	21 50.0	6 58.3	8 25.7	9 47.1	0 47.9	0 46.0
12 T	11 24 54.3	19 27.0	13 14.2	25 29.9	14 21.7	27 55.6	22 28.5	7 10.9	8 28.6	9 50.2	0 49.7	0 47.9
13 F	11 28 50.8	20 25.4	13 11.0	7♉36.1	13 31.9	29 6.4	23 7.1	7 23.5	8 31.6	9 53.2	0 51.5	0 49.8
14 S	11 32 47.4	21 23.9	13 7.8	19 52.9	12 48.1	0♏17.1	23 45.7	7 36.2	8 34.8	9 56.2	0 53.3	0 51.7
15 S	11 36 43.9	22 22.4	13 4.6	2♊23.9	12 11.2	1 27.8	24 24.3	7 48.9	8 37.9	9 59.2	0 55.2	0 53.6
16 M	11 40 40.5	23 20.9	13 1.5	15 13.3	11 42.3	2 38.3	25 2.9	8 1.7	8 41.2	10 2.1	0 57.0	0 55.4
17 T	11 44 37.0	24 19.4	12 58.3	28 24.9	11 22.0	3 48.9	25 41.5	8 14.4	8 44.6	10 5.1	0 58.9	0 57.3
18 W	11 48 33.6	25 18.0	12 55.1	12♋ 1.9	11 11.0	4 59.3	26 20.2	8 27.2	8 48.0	10 7.9	1 0.8	0 59.1
19 T	11 52 30.1	26 16.6	12 51.9	26 6.0	11 9.6	6 9.7	26 58.9	8 40.0	8 51.5	10 10.8	1 2.7	1 1.0
20 F	11 56 26.7	27 15.3	12 48.8	10♌36.3	11D17.9	7 20.1	27 37.6	8 52.8	8 55.1	10 13.6	1 4.6	1 2.8
21 S	12 0 23.2	28 14.0	12 45.6	25 29.0	11 35.9	8 30.3	28 16.3	9 5.7	8 58.8	10 16.3	1 6.5	1 4.6
22 S	12 4 19.8	29 12.7	12 42.4	10♍37.1	12 3.4	9 40.6	28 55.1	9 18.5	9 2.6	10 19.1	1 8.5	1 6.4
23 M	12 8 16.4	0♎11.5	12 39.2	25 50.9	12 40.1	10 50.7	29 33.8	9 31.4	9 6.4	10 21.8	1 10.5	1 8.2
24 T	12 12 12.9	1 10.3	12 36.0	11♎ 0.1	13 25.4	12 0.8	0♎12.7	9 44.3	9 10.4	10 24.4	1 12.5	1 9.9
25 W	12 16 9.5	2 9.1	12 32.9	25 54.7	14 19.0	13 10.8	0 51.5	9 57.2	9 14.4	10 27.1	1 14.5	1 11.7
26 T	12 20 6.0	3 7.9	12 29.7	10♏27.5	15 20.2	14 20.8	1 30.3	10 10.1	9 18.5	10 29.6	1 16.5	1 13.4
27 F	12 24 2.6	4 6.8	12 26.5	24 33.9	16 28.2	15 30.6	2 9.2	10 23.1	9 22.6	10 32.2	1 18.5	1 15.1
28 S	12 27 59.1	5 5.7	12 23.3	8♐12.8	17 42.5	16 40.4	2 48.1	10 36.0	9 26.9	10 34.7	1 20.6	1 16.8
29 S	12 31 55.7	6 4.7	12 20.2	21 25.2	19 2.4	17 50.1	3 27.0	10 49.0	9 31.2	10 37.2	1 22.6	1 18.5
30 M	12 35 52.2	7 3.7	12 17.0	4♑14.1	20 27.1	18 59.8	4 6.0	11 2.0	9 35.6	10 39.6	1 24.7	1 20.2

DAY	EPHEMERIS SIDEREAL TIME	☉	☊	☽	☿	♀	♂	♃	♄	♅	♆	♇
						DECLINATION at NOON						
1 S	10 41 32.2	8N16.8	15S59.3	19S48.1	1S38.9	5S39.9	6N39.8	0S54.9	20S 4.9	18N31.1	10S 3.0	21N34.3
4 W	10 53 21.9	7 11.0	15 56.5	17 19.5	0 48.0	7 11.1	5 54.3	1 9.7	20 6.5	18 28.6	10 4.7	21 32.5
7 S	11 5 11.5	6 4.1	15 53.6	8 12.8	0N34.1	8 41.0	5 8.4	1 24.7	20 8.3	18 26.1	10 6.5	21 30.7
10 T	11 17 1.2	4 56.3	15 50.8	3N39.5	2 18.2	10 9.4	4 22.1	1 39.7	20 10.1	18 23.6	10 8.4	21 29.1
13 F	11 28 50.8	3 47.7	15 47.9	14 23.2	4 7.8	11 35.9	3 35.6	1 54.7	20 12.1	18 21.2	10 10.4	21 27.4
16 M	11 40 40.5	2 38.5	15 45.0	19 46.9	5 43.6	13 0.3	2 48.8	2 9.9	20 14.2	18 18.9	10 12.4	21 25.9
19 T	11 52 30.1	1 28.8	15 42.1	16 3.1	6 49.8	14 22.3	2 1.9	2 25.1	20 16.4	18 16.6	10 14.4	21 24.4
22 S	12 4 19.8	0 18.8	15 39.2	3 25.4	7 17.1	15 41.4	1 14.7	2 40.3	20 18.7	18 14.5	10 16.5	21 23.0
25 W	12 16 9.5	0S51.4	15 36.4	11S16.4	7 3.3	16 57.4	0 27.5	2 55.6	20 21.0	18 12.4	10 18.7	21 21.7
28 S	12 27 59.1	2 1.5	15 33.4	19 19.7	6 11.8	18 10.1	0S19.9	3 10.9	20 23.5	18 10.4	10 20.8	21 20.5

OCTOBER 1957

DAY	EPHEMERIS SIDEREAL TIME	☉	☊	☽	☿	♀	♂	♃	♄	♅	♆	♇
						LONGITUDE at NOON						
1 T	12 39 48.8	8♎ 2.7	12♏13.8	16♑43.3	21♍56.1	20♏ 9.3	4♎44.9	11♎14.9	9♐40.0	10♌42.0	1♏26.8	1♍21.9
2 W	12 43 45.3	9 1.7	12 10.6	28 57.1	23 28.7	21 18.8	5 23.9	11 27.9	9 44.6	10 44.3	1 28.9	1 23.5
3 T	12 47 41.9	10 0.8	12 7.4	10♒59.9	25 4.3	22 28.1	6 2.9	11 40.9	9 49.2	10 46.6	1 31.0	1 25.1
4 F	12 51 38.4	10 59.9	12 4.3	22 55.6	26 42.4	23 37.4	6 41.9	11 53.9	9 53.9	10 48.9	1 33.1	1 26.8
5 S	12 55 35.0	11 59.0	12 1.1	4♓47.6	28 22.6	24 46.6	7 21.1	12 6.9	9 58.6	10 51.2	1 35.3	1 28.4
6 S	12 59 31.5	12 58.2	11 57.9	16 38.9	0♎ 4.3	25 55.7	8 0.1	12 19.9	10 3.5	10 53.3	1 37.4	1 30.0
7 M	13 3 28.1	13 57.4	11 54.7	28 31.9	1 47.3	27 4.7	8 39.2	12 32.9	10 8.3	10 55.5	1 39.6	1 31.5
8 T	13 7 24.6	14 56.6	11 51.6	10♈28.7	3 31.2	28 13.6	9 18.4	12 45.9	10 13.3	10 57.6	1 41.7	1 33.1
9 W	13 11 21.2	15 55.9	11 48.4	22 31.0	5 15.7	29 22.4	9 57.5	12 58.8	10 18.3	10 59.6	1 43.9	1 34.6
10 T	13 15 17.7	16 55.1	11 45.2	4♉40.5	7 0.6	0♐31.1	10 36.7	13 11.8	10 23.4	11 1.6	1 46.1	1 36.1
11 F	13 19 14.3	17 54.5	11 42.0	16 58.8	8 45.8	1 39.6	11 15.9	13 24.8	10 28.5	11 3.6	1 48.3	1 37.6
12 S	13 23 10.8	18 53.8	11 38.8	29 27.9	10 30.9	2 48.1	11 55.2	13 37.8	10 33.7	11 5.5	1 50.5	1 39.0
13 S	13 27 7.4	19 53.2	11 35.7	12♊ 9.9	12 15.9	3 56.4	12 34.4	13 50.7	10 39.0	11 7.3	1 52.7	1 40.4
14 M	13 31 3.9	20 52.7	11 32.5	25 7.1	14 0.7	5 4.6	13 13.7	14 3.7	10 44.3	11 9.1	1 54.9	1 41.9
15 T	13 35 0.5	21 52.1	11 29.3	8♋21.7	15 45.2	6 12.8	13 53.1	14 16.6	10 49.7	11 10.9	1 57.1	1 43.3
16 W	13 38 57.1	22 51.7	11 26.1	21 55.8	17 29.3	7 20.7	14 32.4	14 29.6	10 55.2	11 12.6	1 59.3	1 44.6
17 T	13 42 53.6	23 51.2	11 23.0	5♌50.3	19 13.0	8 28.6	15 11.8	14 42.5	11 0.7	11 14.3	2 1.5	1 46.0
18 F	13 46 50.2	24 50.8	11 19.8	20 5.2	20 56.2	9 36.4	15 51.2	14 55.4	11 6.3	11 15.9	2 3.7	1 47.3
19 S	13 50 46.7	25 50.4	11 16.6	4♍38.1	22 38.8	10 44.0	16 30.7	15 8.3	11 11.9	11 17.5	2 6.0	1 48.6
20 S	13 54 43.3	26 50.1	11 13.4	19 24.8	24 20.9	11 51.4	17 10.1	15 21.2	11 17.6	11 19.0	2 8.2	1 49.9
21 M	13 58 39.8	27 49.8	11 10.2	4♎18.8	26 2.5	12 58.8	17 49.6	15 34.0	11 23.3	11 20.4	2 10.4	1 51.2
22 T	14 2 36.4	28 49.5	11 7.1	19 12.5	27 43.5	14 6.0	18 29.2	15 46.9	11 29.1	11 21.9	2 12.7	1 52.4
23 W	14 6 32.9	29 49.3	11 3.9	3♏57.6	29 23.9	15 13.1	19 8.7	15 59.7	11 35.0	11 23.2	2 14.9	1 53.6
24 T	14 10 29.5	0♏49.1	11 0.7	18 26.9	1♏ 3.7	16 20.0	19 48.3	16 12.5	11 40.9	11 24.5	2 17.1	1 54.8
25 F	14 14 26.0	1 48.9	10 57.5	2♐35.1	2 43.0	17 26.7	20 27.9	16 25.3	11 46.8	11 25.8	2 19.4	1 56.0
26 S	14 18 22.6	2 48.9	10 54.4	16 18.9	4 21.8	18 33.4	21 7.6	16 38.1	11 52.9	11 27.1	2 21.7	1 57.2
27 S	14 22 19.1	3 48.8	10 51.2	29 37.4	5 60.0	19 39.8	21 47.3	16 50.8	11 58.9	11 28.2	2 23.9	1 58.3
28 M	14 26 15.7	4 48.7	10 48.0	12♑32.0	7 37.6	20 46.0	22 27.0	17 3.5	12 5.0	11 29.3	2 26.2	1 59.4
29 T	14 30 12.2	5 48.6	10 44.8	25 5.4	9 14.8	21 52.1	23 6.7	17 16.2	12 11.1	11 30.4	2 28.4	2 0.4
30 W	14 34 8.8	6 48.6	10 41.6	7♒21.6	10 51.4	22 57.9	23 46.4	17 28.8	12 17.3	11 31.4	2 30.6	2 1.5
31 T	14 38 5.4	7 48.6	10 38.5	19 24.8	12 27.5	24 3.6	24 26.2	17 41.4	12 23.5	11 32.3	2 32.9	2 2.5

DAY	EPHEMERIS SIDEREAL TIME	☉	☊	☽	☿	♀	♂	♃	♄	♅	♆	♇
						DECLINATION at NOON						
1 T	12 39 48.8	3S11.5	15S30.5	17S41.1	4N49.2	19S19.0	1S 7.2	3S26.1	20S26.0	18N 8.5	10S23.0	21N19.4
4 F	12 51 38.4	4 21.2	15 27.6	9 3.4	3 3.6	20 23.8	1 54.6	3 41.3	20 28.5	18 6.7	10 25.3	21 18.3
7 M	13 3 28.1	5 30.4	15 24.7	2N38.1	1 2.8	21 24.4	2 41.9	3 56.5	20 31.1	18 5.0	10 27.5	21 17.3
10 T	13 15 17.7	6 38.9	15 21.8	13 35.3	1S 6.9	22 20.3	3 29.1	4 11.6	20 33.8	18 3.4	10 29.8	21 16.5
13 S	13 27 7.4	7 46.7	15 18.8	19 31.0	3 20.4	23 11.3	4 16.1	4 26.7	20 36.5	18 2.0	10 32.1	21 15.7
16 W	13 38 57.1	8 53.5	15 15.9	16 43.6	5 34.4	23 57.2	5 3.0	4 41.7	20 39.2	18 0.6	10 34.4	21 15.1
19 S	13 50 46.7	9 59.2	15 12.9	5 19.5	7 46.3	24 37.7	5 49.6	4 56.5	20 42.0	17 59.4	10 36.7	21 14.5
22 T	14 2 36.4	11 3.5	15 10.0	9S18.0	9 54.5	25 12.7	6 36.0	5 11.3	20 44.8	17 58.3	10 39.0	21 14.1
25 F	14 14 26.0	12 6.4	15 7.0	18 43.6	11 57.6	25 42.0	7 22.0	5 25.9	20 47.6	17 57.3	10 41.3	21 13.7
28 M	14 26 15.7	13 7.6	15 4.0	18 11.9	13 54.8	26 5.4	8 7.7	5 40.4	20 50.4	17 56.5	10 43.6	21 13.5
31 T	14 38 5.4	14 7.0	15 1.1	10 1.7	15 45.4	26 22.9	8 52.9	5 54.8	20 53.2	17 55.8	10 45.9	21 13.3

NOVEMBER 1957

LONGITUDE at NOON

DAY	EPHEMERIS SIDEREAL TIME h m s	☉ ° ′	☊ ° ′	☽ ° ′	☿ ° ′	♀ ° ′	♂ ° ′	♃ ° ′	♄ ° ′	♅ ° ′	♆ ° ′	♇ ° ′
1 F	14 42 1.9	8♏48.6	10♏35.3	1♓19.8	14♏ 3.2	25♐ 9.1	25♎ 6.0	17♎54.0	12♐29.8	11♌33.2	2♏35.1	2♍ 3.4
2 S	14 45 58.5	9 48.7	10 32.1	13 10.9	15 38.4	26 14.3	25 45.8	18 6.5	12 36.1	11 34.0	2 37.3	2 4.4
3 S	14 49 55.0	10 48.8	10 28.9	25 2.4	17 13.2	27 19.3	26 25.7	18 19.0	12 42.5	11 34.8	2 39.6	2 5.3
4 M	14 53 51.6	11 48.9	10 25.8	6♈57.8	18 47.6	28 24.1	27 5.6	18 31.5	12 48.9	11 35.5	2 41.8	2 6.2
5 T	14 57 48.1	12 49.0	10 22.6	19 0.4	20 21.6	29 28.7	27 45.5	18 43.9	12 55.3	11 36.2	2 44.0	2 7.1
6 W	15 1 44.7	13 49.2	10 19.4	1♉12.5	21 55.2	0♑33.0	28 25.4	18 56.3	13 1.8	11 36.8	2 46.2	2 7.9
7 T	15 5 41.2	14 49.4	10 16.2	13 36.0	23 28.4	1 37.1	29 5.4	19 8.6	13 8.3	11 37.4	2 48.4	2 8.8
8 F	15 9 37.8	15 49.6	10 13.0	26 12.0	25 1.2	2 40.9	29 45.4	19 20.9	13 14.8	11 37.9	2 50.6	2 9.5
9 S	15 13 34.3	16 49.9	10 9.9	9♊ 1.2	26 33.7	3 44.4	0♏25.5	19 33.2	13 21.4	11 38.3	2 52.8	2 10.3
10 S	15 17 30.9	17 50.2	10 6.7	22 3.9	28 5.9	4 47.6	1 5.5	19 45.4	13 28.0	11 38.7	2 55.0	2 11.0
11 M	15 21 27.5	18 50.5	10 3.5	5♋20.0	29 37.7	5 50.6	1 45.6	19 57.6	13 34.7	11 39.1	2 57.2	2 11.7
12 T	15 25 24.0	19 50.9	10 0.3	18 49.2	1♐ 9.3	6 53.3	2 25.8	20 9.7	13 41.3	11 39.4	2 59.3	2 12.4
13 W	15 29 20.6	20 51.2	9 57.2	2♌31.3	2 40.5	7 55.6	3 5.9	20 21.8	13 48.0	11 39.6	3 1.5	2 13.1
14 T	15 33 17.1	21 51.7	9 54.0	16 25.5	4 11.3	8 57.7	3 46.1	20 33.8	13 54.8	11 39.8	3 3.7	2 13.7
15 F	15 37 13.7	22 52.1	9 50.8	0♍31.0	5 41.9	9 59.4	4 26.4	20 45.8	14 1.5	11 39.9	3 5.8	2 14.3
16 S	15 41 10.2	23 52.6	9 47.6	14 46.1	7 12.2	11 0.8	5 6.7	20 57.7	14 8.4	11 40.0	3 8.0	2 14.9
17 S	15 45 6.8	24 53.1	9 44.4	29 8.5	8 42.1	12 1.9	5 47.0	21 9.6	14 15.2	11 40.0	3 10.1	2 15.4
18 M	15 49 3.3	25 53.7	9 41.3	13♎35.0	10 11.7	13 2.6	6 27.3	21 21.4	14 22.0	11 40.0	3 12.2	2 15.9
19 T	15 52 59.9	26 54.3	9 38.1	28 1.3	11 40.9	14 2.9	7 7.7	21 33.2	14 28.9	11R39.9	3 14.3	2 16.4
20 W	15 56 56.5	27 54.9	9 34.9	12♏22.7	13 9.7	15 2.8	7 48.1	21 44.8	14 35.8	11 39.7	3 16.4	2 16.8
21 T	16 0 53.0	28 55.5	9 31.7	26 34.0	14 38.1	16 2.3	8 28.5	21 56.5	14 42.7	11 39.5	3 18.5	2 17.2
22 F	16 4 49.6	29 56.1	9 28.6	10♐30.5	16 6.0	17 1.4	9 8.9	22 8.0	14 49.6	11 39.2	3 20.5	2 17.6
23 S	16 8 46.1	0♐56.8	9 25.4	24 8.7	17 33.4	18 0.0	9 49.4	22 19.5	14 56.5	11 38.9	3 22.6	2 17.9
24 S	16 12 42.7	1 57.5	9 22.2	7♑26.2	19 0.3	18 58.2	10 29.9	22 30.9	15 3.5	11 38.5	3 24.6	2 18.2
25 M	16 16 39.2	2 58.2	9 19.0	20 22.5	20 26.5	19 55.9	11 10.5	22 42.3	15 10.5	11 38.1	3 26.6	2 18.5
26 T	16 20 35.8	3 58.9	9 15.9	2♒58.7	21 52.0	20 53.2	11 51.1	22 53.6	15 17.5	11 37.6	3 28.6	2 18.8
27 W	16 24 32.4	4 59.7	9 12.7	15 17.4	23 16.6	21 49.8	12 31.7	23 4.8	15 24.5	11 37.0	3 30.6	2 19.0
28 T	16 28 28.9	6 0.5	9 9.5	27 22.2	24 40.3	22 46.0	13 12.3	23 15.9	15 31.5	11 36.4	3 32.6	2 19.2
29 F	16 32 25.5	7 1.2	9 6.3	9♓17.6	26 3.0	23 41.6	13 53.0	23 27.0	15 38.6	11 35.8	3 34.5	2 19.3
30 S	16 36 22.0	8 2.0	9 3.1	21 8.4	27 24.4	24 36.6	14 33.7	23 38.0	15 45.6	11 35.1	3 36.4	2 19.5

DECLINATION at NOON

DAY	h m s	☉	☊	☽	☿	♀	♂	♃	♄	♅	♆	♇
1 F	14 42 1.9	14S26.3	15S 0.1	6S22.4	16S20.6	26S27.4	9S 7.9	5S59.5	20S54.1	17N55.5	10S46.6	21N13.3
4 M	14 53 51.6	15 22.9	14 57.1	5N27.5	18 1.2	26 36.9	9 52.5	6 13.6	20 56.9	17 55.0	10 48.9	21 13.4
7 T	15 5 41.2	16 17.2	14 54.1	15 39.3	19 33.8	26 40.5	10 36.5	6 27.5	20 59.7	17 54.6	10 51.1	21 13.5
10 S	15 17 30.9	17 9.0	14 51.1	19 42.2	20 57.7	26 38.2	11 19.9	6 41.2	21 2.5	17 54.4	10 53.3	21 13.7
13 W	15 29 20.6	17 58.3	14 48.1	14 30.2	22 12.3	26 30.2	12 2.7	6 54.6	21 5.2	17 54.2	10 55.5	21 14.1
16 S	15 41 10.2	18 44.7	14 45.1	1 58.1	23 17.1	26 16.5	12 44.8	7 7.9	21 7.9	17 54.2	10 57.6	21 14.5
19 T	15 52 59.9	19 28.1	14 42.1	11S50.5	24 11.4	25 57.4	13 26.1	7 20.8	21 10.5	17 54.4	10 59.7	21 15.1
22 F	16 4 49.6	20 8.4	14 39.0	19 25.2	24 54.5	25 33.2	14 6.6	7 33.6	21 13.2	17 54.7	11 1.7	21 15.8
25 M	16 16 39.2	20 45.3	14 36.0	17 1.3	25 25.9	25 4.1	14 46.2	7 46.0	21 15.7	17 55.1	11 3.7	21 16.6
28 T	16 28 28.9	21 18.8	14 33.0	7 40.6	25 45.0	24 30.5	15 24.9	7 58.1	21 18.2	17 55.7	11 5.6	21 17.5

DECEMBER 1957

LONGITUDE at NOON

DAY	EPHEMERIS SIDEREAL TIME h m s	☉ ° ′	☊ ° ′	☽ ° ′	☿ ° ′	♀ ° ′	♂ ° ′	♃ ° ′	♄ ° ′	♅ ° ′	♆ ° ′	♇ ° ′
1 S	16 40 18.6	9♐ 2.8	8♏60.0	2♈59.6	28♐44.3	25♑31.0	15♏14.4	23♎48.9	15♐52.7	11♌34.3	3♏38.4	2♍19.6
2 M	16 44 15.1	10 3.7	8 56.8	14 56.2	0♑ 2.6	26 24.8	15 55.1	23 59.7	15 59.7	11R33.5	3 40.3	2 19.6
3 T	16 48 11.7	11 4.5	8 53.6	27 2.4	1 19.1	27 17.9	16 35.9	24 10.5	16 6.8	11 32.7	3 42.1	2 19.7
4 W	16 52 8.2	12 5.4	8 50.4	9♉22.1	2 33.3	28 10.3	17 16.7	24 21.1	16 13.9	11 31.7	3 44.0	2 19.7
5 T	16 56 4.8	13 6.3	8 47.3	21 58.1	3 45.0	29 1.9	17 57.6	24 31.7	16 21.0	11 30.8	3 45.8	2R19.6
6 F	17 0 1.4	14 7.1	8 44.1	4♊51.8	4 53.8	29 52.9	18 38.5	24 42.2	16 28.1	11 29.8	3 47.6	2 19.6
7 S	17 3 57.9	15 8.1	8 40.9	18 3.8	5 59.3	0♒43.1	19 19.4	24 52.7	16 35.2	11 28.7	3 49.5	2 19.6
8 S	17 7 54.5	16 9.0	8 37.7	1♋32.7	7 0.8	1 32.4	20 0.4	25 3.0	16 42.3	11 27.6	3 51.3	2 19.4
9 M	17 11 51.0	17 10.0	8 34.6	15 16.2	7 57.9	2 20.9	20 41.4	25 13.2	16 49.4	11 26.4	3 53.0	2 19.3
10 T	17 15 47.6	18 10.9	8 31.4	29 11.2	8 50.0	3 8.5	21 22.4	25 23.3	16 56.5	11 25.2	3 54.8	2 19.1
11 W	17 19 44.1	19 11.9	8 28.2	13♌14.1	9 36.2	3 55.3	22 3.4	25 33.4	17 3.6	11 24.0	3 56.5	2 18.9
12 T	17 23 40.7	20 12.9	8 25.0	27 21.6	10 15.9	4 41.0	22 44.5	25 43.3	17 10.7	11 22.6	3 58.2	2 18.7
13 F	17 27 37.3	21 13.9	8 21.8	11♍30.7	10 48.1	5 25.8	23 25.6	25 53.2	17 17.7	11 21.3	3 59.8	2 18.4
14 S	17 31 33.8	22 14.9	8 18.7	25 39.2	11 12.1	6 9.6	24 6.8	26 2.9	17 24.8	11 19.9	4 1.5	2 18.1
15 S	17 35 30.4	23 16.0	8 15.5	9♎45.7	11 26.9	6 52.3	24 48.0	26 12.6	17 31.9	11 18.4	4 3.1	2 17.8
16 M	17 39 26.9	24 17.0	8 12.3	23 48.9	11 31.7	7 33.9	25 29.2	26 22.1	17 39.0	11 16.9	4 4.7	2 17.4
17 T	17 43 23.5	25 18.1	8 9.1	7♏47.6	11R25.8	8 14.4	26 10.4	26 31.5	17 46.0	11 15.4	4 6.3	2 17.0
18 W	17 47 20.0	26 19.2	8 6.0	21 40.2	11 8.5	8 53.7	26 51.7	26 40.9	17 53.1	11 13.8	4 7.8	2 16.6
19 T	17 51 16.6	27 20.3	8 2.8	5♐24.6	10 39.5	9 31.7	27 33.1	26 50.1	18 0.1	11 12.1	4 9.3	2 16.2
20 F	17 55 13.2	28 21.4	7 59.6	18 58.6	9 58.9	10 8.4	28 14.4	26 59.2	18 7.2	11 10.5	4 10.8	2 15.7
21 S	17 59 9.7	29 22.6	7 56.4	2♑19.5	9 7.2	10 43.8	28 55.8	27 8.2	18 14.2	11 8.7	4 12.3	2 15.2
22 S	18 3 6.3	0♑23.7	7 53.3	15 25.4	8 5.3	11 17.7	29 37.2	27 17.1	18 21.2	11 7.0	4 13.7	2 14.6
23 M	18 7 2.8	1 24.8	7 50.1	28 14.9	6 54.8	11 50.2	0♐18.6	27 25.8	18 28.2	11 5.2	4 15.1	2 14.1
24 T	18 10 59.4	2 26.0	7 46.9	10♒47.8	5 37.8	12 21.2	1 0.1	27 34.5	18 35.1	11 3.3	4 16.5	2 13.5
25 W	18 14 55.9	3 27.1	7 43.7	23 5.3	4 16.8	12 50.6	1 41.6	27 43.0	18 42.1	11 1.4	4 17.9	2 12.9
26 T	18 18 52.5	4 28.3	7 40.6	5♓ 9.7	2 54.4	13 18.3	2 23.2	27 51.4	18 49.0	10 59.5	4 19.2	2 12.2
27 F	18 22 49.1	5 29.4	7 37.4	17 4.6	1 33.5	13 44.3	3 4.7	27 59.7	18 55.9	10 57.5	4 20.5	2 11.5
28 S	18 26 45.6	6 30.6	7 34.2	28 54.5	0 16.6	14 8.5	3 46.4	28 7.9	19 2.9	10 55.6	4 21.8	2 10.9
29 S	18 30 42.2	7 31.8	7 31.0	10♈44.2	29♐ 5.8	14 30.9	4 28.0	28 15.9	19 9.7	10 53.5	4 23.1	2 10.2
30 M	18 34 38.7	8 32.9	7 27.8	22 39.3	28 3.1	14 51.3	5 9.7	28 23.8	19 16.6	10 51.5	4 24.3	2 9.4
31 T	18 38 35.3	9 34.0	7 24.7	4♉45.1	27 9.6	15 9.7	5 51.4	28 31.6	19 23.4	10 49.4	4 25.5	2 8.6

DECLINATION at NOON

DAY	h m s	☉	☊	☽	☿	♀	♂	♃	♄	♅	♆	♇
1 S	16 40 18.6	21S48.6	14S29.9	4N 6.4	25S51.4	23S52.8	16S 2.6	8S 9.9	21S20.7	17N56.4	11S 7.5	21N18.5
4 W	16 52 8.2	22 14.6	14 26.9	14 42.0	25 44.9	23 11.4	16 39.2	8 21.4	21 23.1	17 57.2	11 9.3	21 19.6
7 S	17 3 57.9	22 36.8	14 23.8	19 43.9	25 26.1	22 26.8	17 14.8	8 32.5	21 25.4	17 58.2	11 11.0	21 20.8
10 T	17 15 47.6	22 55.0	14 20.8	15 21.0	24 55.9	21 39.3	17 49.1	8 43.3	21 27.6	17 59.2	11 12.7	21 22.1
13 F	17 27 37.3	23 9.2	14 17.7	3 10.6	24 16.5	20 49.6	18 22.3	8 53.8	21 29.8	18 0.4	11 14.2	21 23.5
16 M	17 39 26.9	23 19.1	14 14.6	10S34.0	23 30.6	19 58.1	18 54.2	9 3.8	21 31.9	18 1.7	11 15.7	21 24.9
19 T	17 51 16.6	23 24.9	14 11.6	19 0.7	22 42.0	19 5.3	19 24.7	9 13.4	21 33.9	18 3.2	11 17.2	21 26.5
22 S	18 3 6.3	23 26.5	14 8.5	17 54.8	21 53.6	18 12.0	19 53.8	9 22.7	21 35.9	18 4.7	11 18.5	21 28.1
25 W	18 14 55.9	23 23.8	14 5.4	9 8.8	21 9.1	17 18.8	20 21.4	9 31.5	21 37.8	18 6.3	11 19.8	21 29.8
28 S	18 26 45.6	23 16.9	14 2.3	2N34.1	20 34.1	16 26.4	20 47.6	9 39.8	21 39.5	18 8.0	11 20.9	21 31.6
31 T	18 38 35.3	23 5.8	13 59.2	13 26.2	20 14.9	15 35.5	21 12.1	9 47.7	21 41.2	18 9.7	11 22.0	21 33.4

JANUARY 1958

DAY	EPHEMERIS SIDEREAL TIME	☉	☊	☽	☿	♀	♂	♃	♄	♅	♆	♇
	h m s	° ′	° ′	° ′	° ′	° ′	° ′	° ′	° ′	° ′	° ′	° ′
						LONGITUDE at NOON						
1 W	18 42 31.8	10♑35.2	7♏21.5	17♉ 6.7	26♐26.1	15♒26.1	6♐33.1	28♎39.2	19♐30.2	10♌47.2	4♏26.6	2♍ 7.8
2 T	18 46 28.4	11 36.3	7 18.3	29 48.3	25R53.0	15 40.3	7 14.8	28 46.7	19 36.9	10R45.1	4 27.8	2R 7.0
3 F	18 50 25.0	12 37.5	7 15.1	12♊52.8	25 30.3	15 52.3	7 56.6	28 54.1	19 43.7	10 42.9	4 28.9	2 6.1
4 S	18 54 21.5	13 38.6	7 12.0	26 21.4	25 17.5	16 2.1	8 38.4	29 1.3	19 50.4	10 40.6	4 29.9	2 5.2
5 S	18 58 18.1	14 39.7	7 8.8	10♋13.0	25 14.2	16 9.6	9 20.3	29 8.4	19 57.1	10 38.4	4 31.0	2 4.3
6 M	19 2 14.6	15 40.9	7 5.6	24 23.8	25D19.8	16 14.8	10 2.2	29 15.4	20 3.7	10 36.1	4 32.0	2 3.4
7 T	19 6 11.2	16 42.0	7 2.4	8♌48.5	25 33.7	16 17.5	10 44.1	29 22.2	20 10.3	10 33.8	4 32.9	2 2.4
8 W	19 10 7.7	17 43.1	6 59.3	23 20.3	25 55.0	16 17.8	11 26.1	29 28.8	20 16.9	10 31.4	4 33.9	2 1.5
9 T	19 14 4.3	18 44.2	6 56.1	7♍52.4	26 23.1	16R15.6	12 8.0	29 35.3	20 23.4	10 29.1	4 34.8	2 0.5
10 F	19 18 0.9	19 45.4	6 52.9	22 19.1	26 57.4	16 10.9	12 50.1	29 41.7	20 30.0	10 26.7	4 35.7	1 59.4
11 S	19 21 57.4	20 46.5	6 49.7	6♎36.2	27 37.3	16 3.7	13 32.1	29 47.9	20 36.4	10 24.3	4 36.5	1 58.4
12 S	19 25 54.0	21 47.6	6 46.5	20 41.7	28 22.1	15 54.0	14 14.2	29 54.0	20 42.9	10 21.8	4 37.3	1 57.3
13 M	19 29 50.5	22 48.7	6 43.4	4♏34.9	29 11.4	15 41.7	14 56.3	29 59.9	20 49.2	10 19.4	4 38.1	1 56.2
14 T	19 33 47.1	23 49.9	6 40.2	18 16.2	0♑ 4.7	15 27.1	15 38.5	0♏ 5.7	20 55.6	10 16.9	4 38.8	1 55.1
15 W	19 37 43.6	24 51.0	6 37.0	1♐46.3	1 1.6	15 10.0	16 20.7	0 11.3	21 1.9	10 14.4	4 39.6	1 54.0
16 T	19 41 40.2	25 52.1	6 33.8	15 5.8	2 1.7	14 50.5	17 2.9	0 16.7	21 8.2	10 11.9	4 40.2	1 52.8
17 F	19 45 36.8	26 53.2	6 30.7	28 14.9	3 4.7	14 28.7	17 45.2	0 22.0	21 14.4	10 9.4	4 40.9	1 51.6
18 S	19 49 33.3	27 54.4	6 27.5	11♑13.4	4 10.4	14 4.7	18 27.5	0 27.2	21 20.6	10 6.9	4 41.5	1 50.5
19 S	19 53 29.9	28 55.5	6 24.3	24 0.5	5 18.4	13 38.6	19 9.8	0 32.2	21 26.8	10 4.3	4 42.1	1 49.3
20 M	19 57 26.4	29 56.5	6 21.1	6♒35.6	6 28.5	13 10.5	19 52.1	0 37.0	21 32.8	10 1.8	4 42.7	1 48.1
21 T	20 1 23.0	0♒57.6	6 18.0	18 58.5	7 40.5	12 40.6	20 34.5	0 41.6	21 38.9	9 59.2	4 43.2	1 46.8
22 W	20 5 19.5	1 58.7	6 14.8	1♓ 9.6	8 54.3	12 9.0	21 16.9	0 46.1	21 44.9	9 56.6	4 43.7	1 45.6
23 T	20 9 16.1	2 59.7	6 11.6	13 10.2	10 9.8	11 35.9	21 59.4	0 50.4	21 50.8	9 54.0	4 44.1	1 44.3
24 F	20 13 12.6	4 0.8	6 8.4	25 2.9	11 26.7	11 1.6	22 41.8	0 54.5	21 56.7	9 51.4	4 44.5	1 43.0
25 S	20 17 9.2	5 1.8	6 5.2	6♈51.0	12 45.0	10 26.2	23 24.3	0 58.4	22 2.5	9 48.8	4 44.9	1 41.7
26 S	20 21 5.8	6 2.8	6 2.1	18 38.8	14 4.6	9 50.0	24 6.8	1 2.2	22 8.3	9 46.2	4 45.2	1 40.3
27 M	20 25 2.3	7 3.8	5 58.9	0♉31.3	15 25.4	9 13.2	24 49.4	1 5.8	22 14.0	9 43.5	4 45.5	1 39.0
28 T	20 28 58.9	8 4.7	5 55.7	12 34.1	16 47.4	8 36.1	25 32.0	1 9.2	22 19.7	9 40.9	4 45.8	1 37.6
29 W	20 32 55.4	9 5.7	5 52.5	24 52.7	18 10.4	7 59.0	26 14.6	1 12.5	22 25.3	9 38.3	4 46.0	1 36.3
30 T	20 36 52.0	10 6.6	5 49.4	7♊32.5	19 34.4	7 22.1	26 57.2	1 15.5	22 30.8	9 35.6	4 46.2	1 34.9
31 F	20 40 48.5	11 7.5	5 46.2	20 37.6	20 59.3	6 45.6	27 39.9	1 18.4	22 36.3	9 33.0	4 46.4	1 33.5
						DECLINATION at NOON						
1 W	18 42 31.8	23S 1.2	13S58.2	16N13.7	20S12.6	15S19.1	21S20.0	9S50.3	21S41.8	18N10.4	11S22.3	21N34.0
4 S	18 54 21.5	22 44.6	13 55.0	19 38.3	20 17.6	14 31.5	21 42.4	9 57.6	21 43.4	18 12.2	11 23.3	21 36.0
7 T	19 6 11.2	22 23.9	13 51.9	13 11.7	20 36.6	13 47.5	22 3.0	10 4.4	21 44.9	18 14.2	11 24.1	21 37.9
10 F	19 18 0.9	21 59.3	13 48.8	0S14.8	21 3.7	13 7.7	22 22.0	10 10.7	21 46.3	18 16.2	11 24.9	21 39.9
13 M	19 29 50.5	21 30.8	13 45.7	13 17.3	21 33.4	12 33.0	22 39.1	10 16.5	21 47.6	18 18.2	11 25.5	21 42.0
16 T	19 41 40.2	20 58.5	13 42.6	19 32.6	22 1.3	12 4.0	22 54.4	10 21.8	21 48.9	18 20.3	11 26.0	21 44.0
19 S	19 53 29.9	20 22.6	13 39.4	16 30.3	22 24.2	11 41.4	23 7.9	10 26.5	21 50.0	18 22.4	11 26.5	21 46.1
22 W	20 5 19.5	19 43.3	13 36.3	6 49.1	22 40.1	11 25.7	23 19.4	10 30.8	21 51.1	18 24.5	11 26.8	21 48.2
25 S	20 17 9.2	19 0.7	13 33.1	4N57.4	22 47.3	11 16.7	23 29.0	10 34.4	21 52.1	18 26.6	11 27.1	21 50.3
28 T	20 28 58.9	18 15.0	13 30.0	15 1.9	22 44.7	11 14.4	23 36.6	10 37.6	21 53.0	18 28.8	11 27.2	21 52.4
31 F	20 40 48.5	17 26.3	13 26.8	19 33.1	22 31.5	11 18.1	23 42.2	10 40.1	21 53.9	18 30.9	11 27.2	21 54.6

FEBRUARY 1958

DAY	EPHEMERIS SIDEREAL TIME	☉	☊	☽	☿	♀	♂	♃	♄	♅	♆	♇
						LONGITUDE at NOON						
1 S	20 44 45.1	12♒ 8.4	5♏43.0	4♋10.9	22♑25.3	6♒ 9.8	28♐22.6	1♏21.2	22♐41.7	9♌30.4	4♏46.5	1♍32.1
2 S	20 48 41.6	13 9.2	5 39.8	18 12.4	23 52.1	5R35.0	29 5.3	1 23.7	22 47.1	9R27.8	4 46.6	1R30.7
3 M	20 52 38.2	14 10.0	5 36.6	2♌39.3	25 19.8	5 1.4	29 48.1	1 26.0	22 52.4	9 25.2	4 46.7	1 29.2
4 T	20 56 34.8	15 10.9	5 33.5	17 25.7	26 48.3	4 29.2	0♑30.9	1 28.2	22 57.6	9 22.5	4 46.7	1 27.8
5 W	21 0 31.3	16 11.7	5 30.3	2♍23.0	28 17.7	3 58.5	1 13.7	1 30.2	23 2.8	9 19.9	4 46.7	1 26.4
6 T	21 4 27.9	17 12.4	5 27.1	17 21.7	29 47.9	3 29.7	1 56.5	1 32.0	23 7.9	9 17.3	4 46.7	1 24.9
7 F	21 8 24.4	18 13.2	5 23.9	2♎13.1	1♒19.0	3 2.8	2 39.4	1 33.6	23 12.9	9 14.7	4R46.6	1 23.4
8 S	21 12 21.0	19 14.0	5 20.8	16 50.2	2 50.9	2 38.1	3 22.4	1 35.1	23 17.9	9 12.2	4 46.6	1 22.0
9 S	21 16 17.5	20 14.7	5 17.6	1♏ 8.8	4 23.6	2 15.5	4 5.3	1 36.3	23 22.8	9 9.6	4 46.4	1 20.5
10 M	21 20 14.1	21 15.4	5 14.4	15 7.2	5 57.2	1 55.2	4 48.3	1 37.4	23 27.7	9 7.1	4 46.2	1 19.0
11 T	21 24 10.6	22 16.1	5 11.2	28 46.0	7 31.5	1 37.3	5 31.3	1 38.3	23 32.4	9 4.5	4 46.0	1 17.5
12 W	21 28 7.2	23 16.8	5 8.1	12♐ 6.8	9 6.7	1 21.9	6 14.4	1 39.0	23 37.1	9 2.0	4 45.8	1 16.0
13 T	21 32 3.7	24 17.4	5 4.9	25 11.6	10 42.7	1 8.9	6 57.4	1 39.4	23 41.7	8 59.5	4 45.5	1 14.5
14 F	21 36 0.3	25 18.1	5 1.7	8♑ 2.8	12 19.6	0 58.3	7 40.5	1 39.7	23 46.3	8 57.0	4 45.2	1 13.0
15 S	21 39 56.8	26 18.7	4 58.5	20 41.9	13 57.3	0 50.3	8 23.7	1 39.9	23 50.8	8 54.5	4 44.9	1 11.5
16 S	21 43 53.4	27 19.3	4 55.3	3♒10.5	15 35.9	0 44.8	9 6.8	1R39.8	23 55.2	8 52.0	4 44.5	1 10.0
17 M	21 47 50.0	28 19.9	4 52.2	15 29.3	17 15.4	0 41.7	9 50.0	1 39.5	23 59.5	8 49.6	4 44.1	1 8.5
18 T	21 51 46.5	29 20.4	4 49.0	27 39.2	18 55.7	0 41.1	10 33.2	1 39.0	24 3.7	8 47.2	4 43.7	1 7.0
19 W	21 55 43.1	0♓20.9	4 45.8	9♓40.9	20 37.0	0D42.8	11 16.4	1 38.4	24 7.9	8 44.8	4 43.2	1 5.5
20 T	21 59 39.6	1 21.4	4 42.6	21 35.8	22 19.2	0 47.0	11 59.7	1 37.6	24 12.0	8 42.4	4 42.7	1 3.9
21 F	22 3 36.2	2 21.9	4 39.5	3♈25.5	24 2.3	0 53.4	12 43.0	1 36.5	24 16.0	8 40.1	4 42.2	1 2.4
22 S	22 7 32.7	3 22.3	4 36.3	15 12.4	25 46.4	1 2.1	13 26.3	1 35.3	24 19.9	8 37.7	4 41.6	1 0.9
23 S	22 11 29.3	4 22.7	4 33.1	26 60.0	27 31.5	1 13.0	14 9.6	1 33.9	24 23.7	8 35.4	4 41.0	0 59.4
24 M	22 15 25.8	5 23.1	4 29.9	8♉52.1	29 17.5	1 26.0	14 53.0	1 32.3	24 27.5	8 33.2	4 40.4	0 57.9
25 T	22 19 22.4	6 23.5	4 26.7	20 53.5	1♓ 4.5	1 41.2	15 36.4	1 30.5	24 31.1	8 30.9	4 39.7	0 56.3
26 W	22 23 18.9	7 23.8	4 23.6	3♊ 9.2	2 52.5	1 58.3	16 19.8	1 28.5	24 34.7	8 28.7	4 39.0	0 54.8
27 T	22 27 15.5	8 24.1	4 20.4	15 44.5	4 41.5	2 17.4	17 3.2	1 26.4	24 38.2	8 26.5	4 38.3	0 53.3
28 F	22 31 12.0	9 24.3	4 17.2	28 44.2	6 31.5	2 38.3	17 46.7	1 24.1	24 41.6	8 24.4	4 37.6	0 51.8
						DECLINATION at NOON						
1 S	20 44 45.1	17S 9.4	13S25.8	19N 4.9	22S24.7	11S20.5	23S43.6	10S40.8	21S54.1	18N31.6	11S27.2	21N55.3
4 T	20 56 34.8	16 17.1	13 22.6	10 56.8	21 56.5	11 30.8	23 46.5	10 42.6	21 54.9	18 33.7	11 27.1	21 57.4
7 F	21 8 24.4	15 22.2	13 19.4	3S21.0	21 16.7	11 44.7	23 47.3	10 43.9	21 55.5	18 35.8	11 26.9	21 59.4
10 M	21 20 14.1	14 25.0	13 16.2	15 28.0	20 25.0	12 1.0	23 46.0	10 44.5	21 56.1	18 37.8	11 26.6	22 1.5
13 T	21 32 3.7	13 25.6	13 13.0	19 25.9	19 21.1	12 18.7	23 42.7	10 44.6	21 56.6	18 39.8	11 26.2	22 3.5
16 S	21 43 53.4	12 24.2	13 9.9	14 32.7	18 4.9	12 36.7	23 37.3	10 44.1	21 57.1	18 41.7	11 25.7	22 5.4
19 W	21 55 43.1	11 21.0	13 6.7	4 10.1	16 36.3	12 54.0	23 29.8	10 42.9	21 57.5	18 43.6	11 25.1	22 7.4
22 S	22 7 32.7	10 16.3	13 3.5	7N25.0	14 55.4	13 10.0	23 20.3	10 41.3	21 57.8	18 45.5	11 24.4	22 9.2
25 T	22 19 22.4	9 10.1	13 0.3	16 26.5	13 2.0	13 23.9	23 8.7	10 39.0	21 58.1	18 47.2	11 23.6	22 11.1
28 F	22 31 12.0	8 2.7	12 57.0	19 11.1	10 56.6	13 35.1	22 55.1	10 36.2	21 58.4	18 48.9	11 22.7	22 12.8

MARCH 1958

DAY	EPHEMERIS SIDEREAL TIME	☉	☊	☽	☿	♀	♂	♃	♄	♅	♆	♇
	h m s	° ′	° ′	° ′	° ′	° ′	° ′	° ′	° ′	° ′	° ′	° ′
						LONGITUDE at NOON						
1 S	22 35 8.6	10♓24.6	4♏14.0	12♋12.0	8♓22.4	3♒ 1.2	18♑30.2	1♏21.6	24♐45.0	8♌22.3	4♏36.8	0♍50.4
2 S	22 39 5.1	11 24.7	4 10.8	26 9.7	10 14.4	3 25.8	19 13.7	1R18.9	24 48.2	8R20.2	4R36.0	0R48.9
3 M	22 43 1.7	12 24.9	4 7.7	10♌36.1	12 7.2	3 52.0	19 57.2	1 16.0	24 51.4	8 18.2	4 35.2	0 47.4
4 T	22 46 58.2	13 25.0	4 4.5	25 26.9	14 0.9	4 20.0	20 40.8	1 13.0	24 54.4	8 16.2	4 34.3	0 45.9
5 W	22 50 54.8	14 25.1	4 1.3	10♍34.5	15 55.5	4 49.5	21 24.3	1 9.7	24 57.4	8 14.2	4 33.4	0 44.5
6 T	22 54 51.4	15 25.1	3 58.1	25 48.9	17 50.9	5 20.5	22 7.9	1 6.3	25 0.3	8 12.3	4 32.5	0 43.0
7 F	22 58 47.9	16 25.1	3 55.0	10♎59.6	19 47.0	5 53.0	22 51.6	1 2.8	25 3.1	8 10.4	4 31.6	0 41.5
8 S	23 2 44.5	17 25.1	3 51.8	25 57.2	21 43.7	6 27.0	23 35.2	0 59.0	25 5.8	8 8.5	4 30.6	0 40.1
9 S	23 6 41.0	18 25.1	3 48.6	10♏34.7	23 40.9	7 2.3	24 18.9	0 55.1	25 8.4	8 6.7	4 29.6	0 38.7
10 M	23 10 37.6	19 25.0	3 45.4	24 48.2	25 38.4	7 38.9	25 2.6	0 51.0	25 10.9	8 4.9	4 28.6	0 37.2
11 T	23 14 34.1	20 24.9	3 42.2	8♐36.7	27 36.1	8 16.7	25 46.3	0 46.8	25 13.3	8 3.1	4 27.5	0 35.8
12 W	23 18 30.7	21 24.8	3 39.1	22 1.0	29 33.7	8 55.8	26 30.1	0 42.3	25 15.7	8 1.4	4 26.5	0 34.4
13 T	23 22 27.2	22 24.6	3 35.9	5♑ 3.6	1♈31.1	9 36.1	27 13.9	0 37.8	25 17.9	7 59.8	4 25.4	0 33.0
14 F	23 26 23.8	23 24.5	3 32.7	17 47.7	3 27.8	10 17.4	27 57.7	0 33.0	25 20.1	7 58.1	4 24.2	0 31.6
15 S	23 30 20.3	24 24.2	3 29.5	0♒16.2	5 23.6	10 59.8	28 41.5	0 28.2	25 22.1	7 56.6	4 23.1	0 30.3
16 S	23 34 16.9	25 24.0	3 26.4	12 32.4	7 18.1	11 43.2	29 25.3	0 23.1	25 24.0	7 55.0	4 21.9	0 28.9
17 M	23 38 13.4	26 23.7	3 23.2	24 38.8	9 11.0	12 27.6	0♒ 9.2	0 17.9	25 25.9	7 53.5	4 20.7	0 27.6
18 T	23 42 10.0	27 23.5	3 20.0	6♓37.7	11 1.9	13 13.0	0 53.1	0 12.6	25 27.7	7 52.1	4 19.5	0 26.2
19 W	23 46 6.5	28 23.1	3 16.8	18 31.1	12 50.2	13 59.2	1 37.0	0 7.1	25 29.3	7 50.7	4 18.3	0 24.9
20 T	23 50 3.1	29 22.8	3 13.6	0♈20.9	14 35.6	14 46.3	2 20.9	0 1.5	25 30.9	7 49.3	4 17.0	0 23.6
21 F	23 53 59.6	0♈22.4	3 10.5	12 8.9	16 17.6	15 34.2	3 4.8	29♎55.8	25 32.3	7 48.0	4 15.7	0 22.3
22 S	23 57 56.2	1 22.0	3 7.3	23 57.1	17 55.8	16 23.0	3 48.8	29 49.9	25 33.7	7 46.8	4 14.5	0 21.1
23 S	0 1 52.7	2 21.5	3 4.1	5♉48.0	19 29.6	17 12.4	4 32.8	29 43.9	25 35.0	7 45.6	4 13.2	0 19.9
24 M	0 5 49.3	3 21.0	3 0.9	17 44.4	20 58.7	18 2.6	5 16.7	29 37.8	25 36.2	7 44.5	4 11.8	0 18.6
25 T	0 9 45.8	4 20.5	2 57.8	29 49.8	22 22.7	18 53.5	6 0.7	29 31.5	25 37.2	7 43.3	4 10.5	0 17.4
26 W	0 13 42.4	5 19.9	2 54.6	12♊ 7.9	23 41.1	19 45.1	6 44.7	29 25.2	25 38.2	7 42.3	4 9.1	0 16.2
27 T	0 17 38.9	6 19.3	2 51.4	24 43.0	24 53.6	20 37.3	7 28.7	29 18.7	25 39.1	7 41.3	4 7.7	0 15.0
28 F	0 21 35.5	7 18.7	2 48.2	7♋39.0	26 0.0	21 30.2	8 12.8	29 12.1	25 39.8	7 40.3	4 6.3	0 13.9
29 S	0 25 32.0	8 18.0	2 45.0	20 59.5	27 0.0	22 23.6	8 56.8	29 5.4	25 40.5	7 39.4	4 4.9	0 12.7
30 S	0 29 28.6	9 17.2	2 41.9	4♌46.9	27 53.3	23 17.7	9 40.8	28 58.7	25 41.1	7 38.5	4 3.4	0 11.6
31 M	0 33 25.2	10 16.5	2 38.7	19 1.5	28 39.8	24 12.2	10 24.9	28 51.8	25 41.5	7 37.7	4 2.0	0 10.5
						DECLINATION at NOON						
1 S	22 35 8.6	7S39.9	12S56.0	18N 6.1	10S12.1	13S38.2	22S50.1	10S35.1	21S58.4	18N49.4	11S22.4	22N13.3
4 T	22 46 58.2	6 31.2	12 52.7	8 35.6	7 51.1	13 45.2	22 33.8	10 31.6	21 58.6	18 51.0	11 21.5	22 15.0
7 F	22 58 47.9	5 21.6	12 49.5	6S 3.6	5 19.7	13 48.4	22 15.6	10 27.5	21 58.7	18 52.4	11 20.4	22 16.6
10 M	23 10 37.6	4 11.4	12 46.3	17 1.5	2 39.4	13 47.7	21 55.4	10 22.9	21 58.8	18 53.8	11 19.3	22 18.1
13 T	23 22 27.2	3 0.7	12 43.1	18 43.8	0N 6.7	13 42.9	21 33.2	10 17.9	21 58.8	18 55.1	11 18.1	22 19.5
16 S	23 34 16.9	1 49.7	12 39.8	12 9.3	2 54.4	13 33.6	21 9.2	10 12.3	21 58.8	18 56.2	11 16.8	22 20.8
19 W	23 46 6.5	0 38.5	12 36.6	1 16.3	5 37.9	13 19.9	20 43.4	10 6.3	21 58.8	18 57.3	11 15.5	22 22.0
22 S	23 57 56.2	0N32.6	12 33.3	9N55.5	8 10.5	13 1.8	20 15.8	9 59.9	21 58.7	18 58.2	11 14.1	22 23.1
25 T	0 9 45.8	1 43.5	12 30.1	17 40.2	10 25.2	12 39.2	19 46.6	9 53.2	21 58.6	18 59.0	11 12.6	22 24.1
28 F	0 21 35.5	2 54.1	12 26.8	18 25.1	12 16.1	12 12.1	19 15.6	9 46.0	21 58.5	18 59.7	11 11.1	22 25.0
31 M	0 33 25.2	4 4.1	12 23.5	10 21.1	13 38.7	11 40.7	18 43.1	9 38.6	21 58.3	19 0.3	11 9.6	22 25.8

APRIL 1958

DAY	EPHEMERIS SIDEREAL TIME	☉	☊	☽	☿	♀	♂	♃	♄	♅	♆	♇
						LONGITUDE at NOON						
1 T	0 37 21.7	11♈15.7	2♏35.5	3♍41.1	29♈19.3	25♒ 7.4	11♒ 9.0	28♎44.8	25♐41.9	7♌37.0	4♏ 0.5	0♍ 9.4
2 W	0 41 18.3	12 14.8	2 32.3	18 40.6	29 51.6	26 3.0	11 53.1	28R37.8	25 42.2	7R36.3	3R59.0	0R 8.4
3 T	0 45 14.8	13 13.9	2 29.1	3♎52.1	0♉16.9	26 59.2	12 37.2	28 30.7	25 42.4	7 35.6	3 57.5	0 7.3
4 F	0 49 11.4	14 13.0	2 26.0	19 6.0	0 35.0	27 55.8	13 21.3	28 23.5	25 42.4	7 35.0	3 56.0	0 6.3
5 S	0 53 7.9	15 12.1	2 22.8	4♏12.4	0 46.0	28 53.0	14 5.4	28 16.2	25 42.4	7 34.5	3 54.5	0 5.3
6 S	0 57 4.5	16 11.1	2 19.6	19 2.6	0 50.1	29 50.5	14 49.6	28 8.9	25R42.3	7 34.0	3 52.9	0 4.4
7 M	1 1 1.0	17 10.1	2 16.4	3♐30.2	0R47.4	0♓48.6	15 33.7	28 1.5	25 42.1	7 33.5	3 51.4	0 3.4
8 T	1 4 57.6	18 9.0	2 13.3	17 31.7	0 38.2	1 47.0	16 17.9	27 54.1	25 41.7	7 33.1	3 49.8	0 2.5
9 W	1 8 54.1	19 8.0	2 10.1	1♑ 6.3	0 22.8	2 45.8	17 2.1	27 46.6	25 41.3	7 32.8	3 48.3	0 1.6
10 T	1 12 50.7	20 6.9	2 6.9	14 15.1	0 1.7	3 45.1	17 46.3	27 39.0	25 40.8	7 32.5	3 46.7	0 0.7
11 F	1 16 47.2	21 5.7	2 3.7	27 1.1	29♈35.4	4 44.7	18 30.5	27 31.5	25 40.2	7 32.3	3 45.1	29♌59.9
12 S	1 20 43.8	22 4.6	2 0.5	9♒27.9	29 4.4	5 44.8	19 14.7	27 23.9	25 39.5	7 32.2	3 43.6	29 59.1
13 S	1 24 40.3	23 3.4	1 57.4	21 39.4	28 29.4	6 45.1	19 58.9	27 16.3	25 38.7	7 32.0	3 42.0	29 58.3
14 M	1 28 36.9	24 2.2	1 54.2	3♓39.6	27 51.1	7 45.8	20 43.1	27 8.6	25 37.8	7 32.0	3 40.3	29 57.5
15 T	1 32 33.4	25 1.0	1 51.0	15 32.5	27 10.4	8 46.8	21 27.4	27 0.9	25 36.8	7 32.0	3 38.7	29 56.8
16 W	1 36 30.0	25 59.7	1 47.8	27 21.1	26 27.9	9 48.1	22 11.6	26 53.3	25 35.7	7 32.0	3 37.1	29 56.0
17 T	1 40 26.5	26 58.4	1 44.7	9♈ 8.7	25 44.6	10 49.7	22 55.8	26 45.6	25 34.5	7D32.1	3 35.5	29 55.3
18 F	1 44 23.1	27 57.1	1 41.5	20 57.6	25 1.2	11 51.6	23 40.0	26 37.9	25 33.2	7 32.2	3 33.9	29 54.7
19 S	1 48 19.6	28 55.7	1 38.3	2♉50.3	24 18.5	12 53.8	24 24.2	26 30.2	25 31.8	7 32.4	3 32.2	29 54.0
20 S	1 52 16.2	29 54.3	1 35.1	14 48.8	23 37.3	13 56.3	25 8.4	26 22.5	25 30.4	7 32.7	3 30.6	29 53.4
21 M	1 56 12.8	0♉52.9	1 31.9	26 55.2	22 58.3	14 59.0	25 52.6	26 14.8	25 28.8	7 33.0	3 29.0	29 52.8
22 T	2 0 9.3	1 51.4	1 28.8	9♊11.5	22 22.1	16 2.0	26 36.9	26 7.2	25 27.1	7 33.4	3 27.3	29 52.2
23 W	2 4 5.9	2 49.9	1 25.6	21 40.0	21 49.2	17 5.2	27 21.1	25 59.6	25 25.4	7 33.8	3 25.7	29 51.7
24 T	2 8 2.4	3 48.4	1 22.4	4♋23.1	21 20.0	18 8.6	28 5.2	25 52.0	25 23.5	7 34.3	3 24.0	29 51.2
25 F	2 11 59.0	4 46.8	1 19.2	17 23.2	20 55.0	19 12.3	28 49.4	25 44.5	25 21.6	7 34.8	3 22.4	29 50.7
26 S	2 15 55.5	5 45.2	1 16.1	0♌42.6	20 34.5	20 16.2	29 33.6	25 37.0	25 19.6	7 35.4	3 20.8	29 50.2
27 S	2 19 52.1	6 43.6	1 12.9	14 22.7	20 18.6	21 20.3	0♓17.8	25 29.5	25 17.5	7 36.0	3 19.1	29 49.8
28 M	2 23 48.6	7 41.9	1 9.7	28 24.5	20 7.4	22 24.6	1 1.9	25 22.1	25 15.3	7 36.7	3 17.5	29 49.4
29 T	2 27 45.2	8 40.2	1 6.5	12♍47.0	20 1.2	23 29.2	1 46.1	25 14.8	25 13.0	7 37.4	3 15.8	29 49.1
30 W	2 31 41.7	9 38.4	1 3.3	27 27.5	19 59.8	24 33.9	2 30.2	25 7.5	25 10.6	7 38.2	3 14.2	29 48.7
						DECLINATION at NOON						
1 T	0 37 21.7	4N27.3	12S22.4	6N 0.5	13N59.3	11S29.3	18S31.9	9S36.1	21S58.2	19N 0.5	11S 9.1	22N26.1
4 F	0 49 11.4	5 36.4	12 19.2	8S30.7	14 39.3	10 52.2	17 57.3	9 28.4	21 58.0	19 0.9	11 7.5	22 26.8
7 M	1 1 1.0	6 44.6	12 15.9	18 5.1	14 45.5	10 11.0	17 21.2	9 20.4	21 57.8	19 1.2	11 5.9	22 27.3
10 T	1 12 50.7	7 51.8	12 12.6	17 39.1	14 18.5	9 26.0	16 43.8	9 12.4	21 57.6	19 1.4	11 4.2	22 27.8
13 S	1 24 40.3	8 57.8	12 9.3	9 35.2	13 21.9	8 37.2	16 5.0	9 4.2	21 57.3	19 1.4	11 2.6	22 28.1
16 W	1 36 30.0	10 2.5	12 6.0	1N39.7	12 3.0	7 45.0	15 25.0	8 56.0	21 57.0	19 1.4	11 0.9	22 28.3
19 S	1 48 19.6	11 5.7	12 2.7	12 19.3	10 32.5	6 49.5	14 43.8	8 47.8	21 56.7	19 1.2	10 59.3	22 28.4
22 T	2 0 9.3	12 7.2	11 59.4	18 36.4	9 2.5	5 51.1	14 1.5	8 39.7	21 56.4	19 0.8	10 57.6	22 28.4
25 F	2 11 59.0	13 7.0	11 56.1	17 12.6	7 43.7	4 50.0	13 18.2	8 31.7	21 56.1	19 0.4	10 55.9	22 28.3
28 M	2 23 48.6	14 4.8	11 52.8	7 36.1	6 43.4	3 46.4	12 33.9	8 23.8	21 55.7	18 59.8	10 54.2	22 28.0

MAY 1958

DAY	EPHEMERIS SIDEREAL TIME	☉	☊	☽	☿	♀	♂	♃	♄	♅	♆	♇
	h m s	° ′	° ′	° ′	° ′	° ′	° ′	° ′	° ′	° ′	° ′	° ′
						LONGITUDE at NOON						
1 T	2 35 38.3	10♉36.6	1♏ 0.2	12♎21.0	20♈ 3.2	25♓38.8	3♓14.4	25♎ 0.3	25♐ 8.2	7♌39.1	3♏12.6	29♌48.4
2 F	2 39 34.8	11 34.8	0 57.0	27 20.8	20D11.5	26 43.9	3 58.5	24R53.2	25R 5.7	7 40.0	3R11.0	29R48.1
3 S	2 43 31.4	12 33.0	0 53.8	12♏18.9	20 24.5	27 49.2	4 42.7	24 46.2	25 3.1	7 41.0	3 9.4	29 47.9
4 S	2 47 28.0	13 31.2	0 50.6	27 6.9	20 42.1	28 54.7	5 26.8	24 39.2	25 0.4	7 42.0	3 7.8	29 47.7
5 M	2 51 24.5	14 29.3	0 47.5	11♐37.5	21 4.2	0♈ 0.3	6 10.9	24 32.3	24 57.7	7 43.0	3 6.2	29 47.5
6 T	2 55 21.1	15 27.3	0 44.3	25 45.3	21 30.6	1 6.2	6 55.0	24 25.6	24 54.8	7 44.1	3 4.6	29 47.3
7 W	2 59 17.6	16 25.4	0 41.1	9♑27.5	22 1.2	2 12.1	7 39.0	24 18.9	24 51.9	7 45.3	3 3.0	29 47.2
8 T	3 3 14.2	17 23.4	0 37.9	22 43.4	22 35.9	3 18.3	8 23.1	24 12.2	24 48.9	7 46.5	3 1.4	29 47.1
9 F	3 7 10.7	18 21.4	0 34.7	5♒34.6	23 14.5	4 24.6	9 7.1	24 5.7	24 45.9	7 47.8	2 59.9	29 47.0
10 S	3 11 7.3	19 19.4	0 31.6	18 4.3	23 56.9	5 31.0	9 51.2	23 59.4	24 42.8	7 49.1	2 58.3	29 46.9
11 S	3 15 3.8	20 17.4	0 28.4	0♓16.4	24 42.9	6 37.6	10 35.2	23 53.1	24 39.6	7 50.4	2 56.8	29 46.9
12 M	3 19 0.4	21 15.3	0 25.2	12 15.7	25 32.4	7 44.4	11 19.2	23 46.9	24 36.3	7 51.8	2 55.2	29 46.9
13 T	3 22 56.9	22 13.2	0 22.0	24 6.9	26 25.2	8 51.2	12 3.1	23 40.9	24 33.0	7 53.3	2 53.7	29 46.9
14 W	3 26 53.5	23 11.1	0 18.9	5♈54.5	27 21.4	9 58.2	12 47.1	23 34.9	24 29.6	7 54.8	2 52.2	29D47.0
15 T	3 30 50.1	24 9.0	0 15.7	17 42.6	28 20.6	11 5.4	13 31.0	23 29.1	24 26.1	7 56.4	2 50.7	29 47.1
16 F	3 34 46.6	25 6.9	0 12.5	29 35.0	29 22.9	12 12.6	14 14.8	23 23.5	24 22.6	7 58.0	2 49.2	29 47.2
17 S	3 38 43.2	26 4.7	0 9.3	11♉34.6	0♉28.1	13 20.0	14 58.7	23 17.9	24 19.0	7 59.6	2 47.7	29 47.4
18 S	3 42 39.7	27 2.5	0 6.2	23 43.9	1 36.2	14 27.5	15 42.5	23 12.5	24 15.4	8 1.3	2 46.2	29 47.6
19 M	3 46 36.3	28 0.3	0 3.0	6♊ 4.5	2 47.1	15 35.1	16 26.3	23 7.3	24 11.7	8 3.1	2 44.8	29 47.8
20 T	3 50 32.8	28 58.1	29♎59.8	18 37.6	4 0.6	16 42.8	17 10.1	23 2.2	24 7.9	8 4.8	2 43.3	29 48.0
21 W	3 54 29.4	29 55.8	29 56.6	1♋23.9	5 16.9	17 50.7	17 53.8	22 57.2	24 4.1	8 6.7	2 41.9	29 48.3
22 T	3 58 25.9	0♊53.5	29 53.4	14 24.0	6 35.7	18 58.6	18 37.4	22 52.4	24 0.2	8 8.6	2 40.5	29 48.6
23 F	4 2 22.5	1 51.2	29 50.3	27 37.9	7 57.1	20 6.6	19 21.1	22 47.7	23 56.3	8 10.5	2 39.1	29 48.9
24 S	4 6 19.1	2 48.9	29 47.1	11♌ 5.9	9 21.1	21 14.8	20 4.7	22 43.2	23 52.4	8 12.5	2 37.8	29 49.4
25 S	4 10 15.6	3 46.6	29 43.9	24 47.9	10 47.5	22 23.0	20 48.3	22 38.9	23 48.5	8 14.6	2 36.4	29 49.7
26 M	4 14 12.2	4 44.2	29 40.7	8♍43.9	12 16.3	23 31.3	21 31.8	22 34.7	23 44.4	8 16.6	2 35.1	29 50.2
27 T	4 18 8.7	5 41.8	29 37.6	22 53.3	13 47.6	24 39.7	22 15.3	22 30.7	23 40.4	8 18.7	2 33.8	29 50.6
28 W	4 22 5.3	6 39.3	29 34.4	7♎14.5	15 21.4	25 48.2	22 58.7	22 26.8	23 36.2	8 20.9	2 32.5	29 51.1
29 T	4 26 1.8	7 36.9	29 31.2	21 45.2	16 57.6	26 56.7	23 42.1	22 23.1	23 32.1	8 23.1	2 31.2	29 51.6
30 F	4 29 58.4	8 34.4	29 28.0	6♏21.5	18 36.2	28 5.4	24 25.4	22 19.5	23 27.9	8 25.3	2 30.0	29 52.1
31 S	4 33 54.9	9 31.9	29 24.8	20 58.1	20 17.2	29 14.2	25 8.7	22 16.2	23 23.7	8 27.6	2 28.7	29 52.7
						DECLINATION at NOON						
1 T	2 35 38.3	15N 0.5	11S49.5	6S28.0	6N 5.4	2S40.7	11S48.8	8S16.2	21S55.3	18N59.1	10S52.6	22N27.7
4 S	2 47 28.0	15 53.9	11 46.1	17 16.1	5 50.5	1 33.0	11 2.8	8 8.9	21 54.9	18 58.3	10 51.0	22 27.2
7 W	2 59 17.6	16 45.0	11 42.8	18 12.8	5 57.7	0 23.7	10 16.2	8 1.8	21 54.5	18 57.3	10 49.4	22 26.7
10 S	3 11 7.3	17 33.6	11 39.5	10 36.4	6 25.1	0N47.0	9 28.9	7 55.1	21 54.1	18 56.3	10 47.8	22 26.0
13 T	3 22 56.9	18 19.6	11 36.1	0N35.1	7 10.3	1 58.6	8 41.0	7 48.8	21 53.7	18 55.1	10 46.3	22 25.2
16 F	3 34 46.6	19 2.8	11 32.8	11 28.2	8 11.0	3 11.1	7 52.6	7 42.9	21 53.2	18 53.8	10 44.8	22 24.4
19 M	3 46 36.3	19 43.1	11 29.5	18 22.2	9 25.0	4 23.9	7 3.9	7 37.5	21 52.8	18 52.4	10 43.4	22 23.4
22 T	3 58 25.9	20 20.4	11 26.1	17 41.5	10 50.1	5 36.9	6 14.9	7 32.6	21 52.3	18 50.9	10 42.0	22 22.3
25 S	4 10 15.6	20 54.5	11 22.7	8 45.6	12 24.1	6 49.7	5 25.6	7 28.3	21 51.8	18 49.3	10 40.7	22 21.2
28 W	4 22 5.3	21 25.4	11 19.4	4S47.6	14 4.8	8 2.0	4 36.1	7 24.4	21 51.3	18 47.5	10 39.5	22 19.9
31 S	4 33 54.9	21 53.0	11 16.0	16 16.4	15 49.9	9 13.6	3 46.6	7 21.2	21 50.8	18 45.7	10 38.3	22 18.6

JUNE 1958

DAY	EPHEMERIS SIDEREAL TIME	☉	☊	☽	☿	♀	♂	♃	♄	♅	♆	♇
						LONGITUDE at NOON						
1 S	4 37 51.5	10♊29.4	29♎21.7	5♐29.2	22♉ 0.5	0♉23.0	25♓51.9	22♎13.0	23♐19.5	8♌29.9	2♏27.5	29♌53.3
2 M	4 41 48.1	11 26.8	29 18.5	19 48.3	23 46.3	1 31.9	26 35.1	22R 9.9	23R15.2	8 32.3	2R26.3	29 53.9
3 T	4 45 44.6	12 24.3	29 15.3	3♑49.9	25 34.5	2 40.9	27 18.3	22 7.1	23 10.9	8 34.7	2 25.2	29 54.6
4 W	4 49 41.2	13 21.7	29 12.1	17 30.1	27 25.0	3 50.0	28 1.4	22 4.4	23 6.6	8 37.1	2 24.0	29 55.2
5 T	4 53 37.7	14 19.1	29 9.0	0♒46.8	29 17.9	4 59.2	28 44.4	22 1.9	23 2.3	8 39.6	2 22.9	29 55.9
6 F	4 57 34.3	15 16.5	29 5.8	13 40.1	1♊13.0	6 8.4	29 27.4	21 59.5	22 57.9	8 42.1	2 21.8	29 56.7
7 S	5 1 30.8	16 13.9	29 2.6	26 11.9	3 10.4	7 17.7	0♈10.3	21 57.3	22 53.5	8 44.7	2 20.7	29 57.4
8 S	5 5 27.4	17 11.3	28 59.4	8♓25.7	5 9.9	8 27.2	0 53.2	21 55.4	22 49.1	8 47.3	2 19.7	29 58.2
9 M	5 9 24.0	18 8.7	28 56.3	20 25.8	7 11.5	9 36.6	1 36.0	21 53.5	22 44.7	8 49.9	2 18.6	29 59.0
10 T	5 13 20.5	19 6.0	28 53.1	2♈17.5	9 15.0	10 46.2	2 18.8	21 51.9	22 40.3	8 52.6	2 17.6	29 59.9
11 W	5 17 17.1	20 3.4	28 49.9	14 5.7	11 20.4	11 55.8	3 1.5	21 50.4	22 35.9	8 55.3	2 16.6	0♍ 0.7
12 T	5 21 13.6	21 0.7	28 46.7	25 55.7	13 27.3	13 5.5	3 44.1	21 49.2	22 31.5	8 58.0	2 15.7	0 1.6
13 F	5 25 10.2	21 58.1	28 43.6	7♉52.1	15 35.7	14 15.3	4 26.6	21 48.1	22 27.0	9 0.8	2 14.8	0 2.6
14 S	5 29 6.7	22 55.5	28 40.4	19 58.9	17 45.3	15 25.1	5 9.1	21 47.2	22 22.6	9 3.6	2 13.9	0 3.5
15 S	5 33 3.3	23 52.8	28 37.2	2♊19.2	19 55.9	16 35.0	5 51.5	21 46.5	22 18.2	9 6.5	2 13.0	0 4.5
16 M	5 36 59.9	24 50.1	28 34.0	14 55.1	22 7.1	17 45.0	6 33.8	21 45.9	22 13.8	9 9.3	2 12.2	0 5.5
17 T	5 40 56.4	25 47.4	28 30.8	27 47.4	24 18.8	18 55.0	7 16.1	21 45.5	22 9.4	9 12.3	2 11.3	0 6.5
18 W	5 44 53.0	26 44.7	28 27.7	10♋55.8	26 30.7	20 5.1	7 58.2	21 45.3	22 4.9	9 15.2	2 10.6	0 7.6
19 T	5 48 49.5	27 42.0	28 24.5	24 19.0	28 42.4	21 15.2	8 40.3	21 45.3	22 0.5	9 18.2	2 9.8	0 8.7
20 F	5 52 46.1	28 39.3	28 21.3	7♌54.8	0♋53.8	22 25.4	9 22.2	21D45.5	21 56.2	9 21.2	2 9.0	0 9.8
21 S	5 56 42.6	29 36.5	28 18.1	21 41.1	3 4.5	23 35.7	10 4.1	21 45.8	21 51.8	9 24.2	2 8.3	0 10.9
22 S	6 0 39.2	0♋33.8	28 15.0	5♍35.5	5 14.3	24 46.0	10 45.9	21 46.4	21 47.4	9 27.3	2 7.7	0 12.0
23 M	6 4 35.8	1 31.0	28 11.8	19 36.3	7 23.0	25 56.3	11 27.6	21 47.1	21 43.1	9 30.3	2 7.0	0 13.2
24 T	6 8 32.3	2 28.3	28 8.6	3♎42.0	9 30.4	27 6.7	12 9.2	21 48.0	21 38.8	9 33.5	2 6.4	0 14.4
25 W	6 12 28.9	3 25.5	28 5.4	17 51.6	11 36.3	28 17.2	12 50.7	21 49.0	21 34.5	9 36.6	2 5.8	0 15.6
26 T	6 16 25.4	4 22.7	28 2.3	2♏ 3.8	13 40.7	29 27.7	13 32.1	21 50.3	21 30.2	9 39.8	2 5.2	0 16.9
27 F	6 20 22.0	5 19.9	27 59.1	16 16.9	15 43.3	0♊38.3	14 13.4	21 51.7	21 26.0	9 43.0	2 4.7	0 18.1
28 S	6 24 18.5	6 17.1	27 55.9	0♐28.3	17 44.1	1 48.9	14 54.6	21 53.3	21 21.7	9 46.2	2 4.2	0 19.4
29 S	6 28 15.1	7 14.3	27 52.7	14 34.6	19 43.1	2 59.6	15 35.7	21 55.1	21 17.6	9 49.4	2 3.7	0 20.7
30 M	6 32 11.7	8 11.5	27 49.5	28 31.9	21 40.1	4 10.3	16 16.7	21 57.0	21 13.4	9 52.7	2 3.3	0 22.1
						DECLINATION at NOON						
1 S	4 37 51.5	22N 1.4	11S14.9	18S18.8	16N25.4	9N37.2	3S30.1	7S20.2	21S50.6	18N45.1	10S37.9	22N18.1
4 W	4 49 41.2	22 24.4	11 11.5	17 18.6	18 11.7	10 47.3	2 40.6	7 17.7	21 50.1	18 43.1	10 36.8	22 16.7
7 S	5 1 30.8	22 43.8	11 8.1	8 24.9	19 54.7	11 55.8	1 51.2	7 15.8	21 49.5	18 41.1	10 35.8	22 15.2
10 T	5 13 20.5	22 59.7	11 4.8	3N 7.8	21 29.6	13 2.6	1 1.9	7 14.5	21 49.0	18 39.0	10 34.9	22 13.6
13 F	5 25 10.2	23 11.9	11 1.4	13 29.1	22 51.2	14 7.2	0 12.9	7 13.9	21 48.5	18 36.7	10 34.0	22 11.9
16 M	5 36 59.9	23 20.5	10 58.0	19 0.3	23 54.4	15 9.4	0N35.7	7 13.8	21 47.9	18 34.4	10 33.2	22 10.1
19 T	5 48 49.5	23 25.3	10 54.6	16 16.3	24 34.7	16 8.8	1 24.0	7 14.3	21 47.4	18 32.0	10 32.6	22 8.3
22 S	6 0 39.2	23 26.4	10 51.2	5 38.8	24 49.9	17 5.2	2 11.7	7 15.5	21 46.9	18 29.6	10 32.0	22 6.5
25 W	6 12 28.9	23 23.9	10 47.8	7S55.9	24 40.2	17 58.1	2 58.9	7 17.2	21 46.4	18 27.0	10 31.5	22 4.6
28 S	6 24 18.5	23 17.6	10 44.4	17 39.9	24 7.6	18 47.4	3 45.5	7 19.6	21 45.9	18 24.4	10 31.1	22 2.6

JULY 1958

DAY	EPHEMERIS SIDEREAL TIME	☉	☊	☽	☿	♀	♂	♃	♄	♅	♆	♇
	h m s	° ′	° ′	° ′	° ′	° ′	° ′	° ′	° ′	° ′	° ′	° ′
					LONGITUDE at NOON							
1 T	6 36 8.2	9♋ 8.7	27♎46.4	12♑16.0	23♋35.1	5♊21.1	16♈57.6	21♎59.2	21♐ 9.3	9♌56.0	2♏ 2.8	0♍23.4
2 W	6 40 4.8	10 5.8	27 43.2	25 43.3	25 28.1	6 32.0	17 38.3	22 1.5	21R 5.2	9 59.3	2R 2.5	0 24.8
3 T	6 44 1.3	11 3.0	27 40.0	8♒51.5	27 19.1	7 42.9	18 19.0	22 3.9	21 1.2	10 2.7	2 2.1	0 26.2
4 F	6 47 57.9	12 0.2	27 36.8	21 39.8	29 8.0	8 53.8	18 59.5	22 6.6	20 57.2	10 6.0	2 1.8	0 27.6
5 S	6 51 54.4	12 57.4	27 33.7	4♓ 9.1	0♌54.9	10 4.9	19 40.0	22 9.4	20 53.3	10 9.5	2 1.5	0 29.1
6 S	6 55 51.0	13 54.6	27 30.5	16 21.8	2 39.7	11 16.0	20 20.3	22 12.4	20 49.4	10 12.9	2 1.3	0 30.6
7 M	6 59 47.6	14 51.8	27 27.3	28 21.7	4 22.5	12 27.1	21 0.5	22 15.5	20 45.6	10 16.3	2 1.1	0 32.0
8 T	7 3 44.1	15 49.0	27 24.1	10♈13.3	6 3.2	13 38.3	21 40.6	22 18.8	20 41.8	10 19.7	2 0.9	0 33.5
9 W	7 7 40.7	16 46.2	27 21.0	22 1.9	7 41.8	14 49.5	22 20.5	22 22.3	20 38.0	10 23.2	2 0.7	0 35.1
10 T	7 11 37.2	17 43.4	27 17.8	3♉52.9	9 18.4	16 0.8	23 0.3	22 25.9	20 34.3	10 26.7	2 0.6	0 36.6
11 F	7 15 33.8	18 40.7	27 14.6	15 51.7	10 52.9	17 12.2	23 40.0	22 29.7	20 30.7	10 30.2	2 0.5	0 38.2
12 S	7 19 30.3	19 37.9	27 11.4	28 3.2	12 25.4	18 23.5	24 19.5	22 33.7	20 27.1	10 33.7	2 0.4	0 39.7
13 S	7 23 26.9	20 35.1	27 8.2	10♊31.5	13 55.7	19 35.0	24 58.8	22 37.8	20 23.6	10 37.2	2 0.3	0 41.3
14 M	7 27 23.5	21 32.4	27 5.1	23 19.4	15 24.0	20 46.5	25 38.1	22 42.1	20 20.1	10 40.8	2 0.3	0 42.9
15 T	7 31 20.0	22 29.6	27 1.9	6♋28.3	16 50.1	21 58.0	26 17.1	22 46.6	20 16.7	10 44.3	2D 0.4	0 44.6
16 W	7 35 16.6	23 26.9	26 58.7	19 57.6	18 14.1	23 9.6	26 56.0	22 51.2	20 13.3	10 47.9	2 0.4	0 46.2
17 T	7 39 13.1	24 24.1	26 55.5	3♌44.8	19 35.9	24 21.3	27 34.7	22 55.9	20 10.0	10 51.5	2 0.5	0 47.9
18 F	7 43 9.7	25 21.4	26 52.4	17 46.3	20 55.4	25 33.0	28 13.3	23 0.8	20 6.8	10 55.1	2 0.6	0 49.5
19 S	7 47 6.2	26 18.7	26 49.2	1♍57.1	22 12.7	26 44.7	28 51.7	23 5.9	20 3.7	10 58.7	2 0.8	0 51.2
20 S	7 51 2.8	27 15.9	26 46.0	16 12.5	23 27.7	27 56.5	29 29.9	23 11.1	20 0.6	11 2.3	2 1.0	0 52.9
21 M	7 54 59.3	28 13.2	26 42.8	0♎28.5	24 40.3	29 8.3	0♉ 8.0	23 16.5	19 57.6	11 6.0	2 1.2	0 54.7
22 T	7 58 55.9	29 10.5	26 39.7	14 41.9	25 50.4	0♋20.2	0 45.8	23 22.0	19 54.7	11 9.6	2 1.5	0 56.4
23 W	8 2 52.5	0♌ 7.8	26 36.5	28 50.8	26 58.0	1 32.1	1 23.5	23 27.7	19 51.8	11 13.3	2 1.7	0 58.2
24 T	8 6 49.0	1 5.1	26 33.3	12♏54.2	28 3.0	2 44.1	2 1.0	23 33.5	19 49.1	11 16.9	2 2.1	0 59.9
25 F	8 10 45.6	2 2.4	26 30.1	26 51.4	29 5.3	3 56.1	2 38.3	23 39.5	19 46.4	11 20.6	2 2.4	1 1.7
26 S	8 14 42.1	2 59.8	26 26.9	10♐41.7	0♍ 4.8	5 8.2	3 15.5	23 45.6	19 43.8	11 24.3	2 2.8	1 3.5
27 S	8 18 38.7	3 57.1	26 23.8	24 23.9	1 1.3	6 20.3	3 52.5	23 51.8	19 41.2	11 28.0	2 3.3	1 5.3
28 M	8 22 35.2	4 54.4	26 20.6	7♑56.5	1 54.8	7 32.4	4 29.2	23 58.2	19 38.8	11 31.7	2 3.7	1 7.2
29 T	8 26 31.8	5 51.7	26 17.4	21 17.4	2 45.1	8 44.6	5 5.7	24 4.7	19 36.4	11 35.4	2 4.2	1 9.0
30 W	8 30 28.3	6 49.1	26 14.2	4♒24.8	3 32.1	9 56.9	5 42.1	24 11.4	19 34.1	11 39.1	2 4.7	1 10.8
31 T	8 34 24.9	7 46.4	26 11.1	17 17.2	4 15.6	11 9.2	6 18.2	24 18.2	19 31.9	11 42.8	2 5.2	1 12.7
					DECLINATION at NOON							
1 T	6 36 8.2	23N 7.6	10S41.0	18S 3.6	23N15.4	19N32.7	4N31.4	7S22.5	21S45.5	18N21.7	10S30.8	22N 0.6
4 F	6 47 57.9	22 54.0	10 37.6	9 54.2	22 7.2	20 13.7	5 16.6	7 26.0	21 45.0	18 19.0	10 30.6	21 58.5
7 M	6 59 47.6	22 36.8	10 34.1	1N38.4	20 46.5	20 50.3	6 1.0	7 30.1	21 44.6	18 16.2	10 30.5	21 56.4
10 T	7 11 37.2	22 16.1	10 30.7	12 18.7	19 16.5	21 22.0	6 44.5	7 34.7	21 44.3	18 13.4	10 30.4	21 54.3
13 S	7 23 26.9	21 51.9	10 27.3	18 38.1	17 40.2	21 48.7	7 27.1	7 39.8	21 44.0	18 10.5	10 30.5	21 52.2
16 W	7 35 16.6	21 24.3	10 23.8	17 2.3	15 60.0	22 10.2	8 8.7	7 45.5	21 43.7	18 7.6	10 30.7	21 50.0
19 S	7 47 6.2	20 53.5	10 20.4	6 56.8	14 18.3	22 26.2	8 49.2	7 51.6	21 43.4	18 4.6	10 31.0	21 47.8
22 T	7 58 55.9	20 19.5	10 17.0	6S44.6	12 37.3	22 36.7	9 28.6	7 58.3	21 43.3	18 1.6	10 31.4	21 45.6
25 F	8 10 45.6	19 42.5	10 13.5	16 58.0	10 59.3	22 41.6	10 6.9	8 5.4	21 43.1	17 58.5	10 31.9	21 43.4
28 M	8 22 35.2	19 2.5	10 10.1	18 26.5	9 26.7	22 40.6	10 44.1	8 12.9	21 43.1	17 55.5	10 32.5	21 41.1
31 T	8 34 24.9	18 19.7	10 6.6	11 12.4	8 2.1	22 33.9	11 20.0	8 20.9	21 43.1	17 52.4	10 33.2	21 38.9

AUGUST 1958

DAY	EPHEMERIS SIDEREAL TIME	☉	☊	☽	☿	♀	♂	♃	♄	♅	♆	♇
					LONGITUDE at NOON							
1 F	8 38 21.5	8♌43.8	26♎ 7.9	29♒53.8	4♍55.5	12♋21.5	6♉54.1	24♎25.1	19♐29.8	11♌46.5	2♏ 5.8	1♍14.5
2 S	8 42 18.0	9 41.2	26 4.7	12♓15.1	5 31.6	13 33.9	7 29.8	24 32.2	19R27.7	11 50.2	2 6.4	1 16.4
3 S	8 46 14.6	10 38.6	26 1.5	24 22.9	6 3.6	14 46.4	8 5.2	24 39.3	19 25.7	11 53.9	2 7.0	1 18.3
4 M	8 50 11.1	11 36.0	25 58.4	6♈19.9	6 31.5	15 58.9	8 40.5	24 46.7	19 23.9	11 57.6	2 7.7	1 20.2
5 T	8 54 7.7	12 33.5	25 55.2	18 10.0	6 55.0	17 11.4	9 15.5	24 54.1	19 22.1	12 1.4	2 8.4	1 22.1
6 W	8 58 4.2	13 31.0	25 52.0	29 57.7	7 13.9	18 24.0	9 50.2	25 1.7	19 20.4	12 5.1	2 9.1	1 24.0
7 T	9 2 0.8	14 28.4	25 48.8	11♉48.3	7 28.0	19 36.7	10 24.8	25 9.4	19 18.8	12 8.8	2 9.9	1 25.9
8 F	9 5 57.3	15 26.0	25 45.6	23 47.2	7 37.2	20 49.4	10 59.0	25 17.2	19 17.2	12 12.5	2 10.7	1 27.8
9 S	9 9 53.9	16 23.5	25 42.5	5♊59.7	7 41.3	22 2.1	11 33.0	25 25.1	19 15.8	12 16.2	2 11.5	1 29.8
10 S	9 13 50.4	17 21.0	25 39.3	18 30.7	7R40.1	23 14.9	12 6.7	25 33.2	19 14.5	12 19.9	2 12.4	1 31.7
11 M	9 17 47.0	18 18.6	25 36.1	1♋24.0	7 33.6	24 27.7	12 40.2	25 41.4	19 13.2	12 23.6	2 13.2	1 33.7
12 T	9 21 43.6	19 16.2	25 32.9	14 42.0	7 21.5	25 40.6	13 13.4	25 49.6	19 12.1	12 27.3	2 14.1	1 35.6
13 W	9 25 40.1	20 13.8	25 29.8	28 24.8	7 4.0	26 53.6	13 46.3	25 58.1	19 11.0	12 31.0	2 15.1	1 37.6
14 T	9 29 36.7	21 11.5	25 26.6	12♌30.2	6 41.0	28 6.5	14 18.9	26 6.6	19 10.1	12 34.7	2 16.1	1 39.5
15 F	9 33 33.2	22 9.2	25 23.4	26 53.8	6 12.7	29 19.6	14 51.2	26 15.2	19 9.2	12 38.3	2 17.1	1 41.5
16 S	9 37 29.8	23 6.9	25 20.2	11♍29.3	5 39.4	0♌32.7	15 23.2	26 24.0	19 8.5	12 42.1	2 18.1	1 43.5
17 S	9 41 26.3	24 4.6	25 17.0	26 9.4	5 1.2	1 45.8	15 54.9	26 32.9	19 7.8	12 45.7	2 19.2	1 45.5
18 M	9 45 22.9	25 2.3	25 13.9	10♎47.5	4 18.7	2 58.9	16 26.2	26 41.9	19 7.2	12 49.4	2 20.3	1 47.5
19 T	9 49 19.4	26 0.1	25 10.7	25 18.1	3 32.5	4 12.1	16 57.2	26 51.0	19 6.7	12 53.0	2 21.4	1 49.5
20 W	9 53 16.0	26 57.8	25 7.5	9♏37.5	2 43.1	5 25.4	17 27.9	27 0.1	19 6.3	12 56.7	2 22.6	1 51.5
21 T	9 57 12.5	27 55.6	25 4.3	23 43.6	1 51.5	6 38.6	17 58.3	27 9.4	19 6.0	13 0.3	2 23.7	1 53.5
22 F	10 1 9.1	28 53.4	25 1.2	7♐35.7	0 58.6	7 52.0	18 28.3	27 18.8	19 5.8	13 3.9	2 24.9	1 55.5
23 S	10 5 5.6	29 51.2	24 58.0	21 13.9	0 5.4	9 5.3	18 57.9	27 28.3	19 5.7	13 7.5	2 26.2	1 57.4
24 S	10 9 2.2	0♍49.1	24 54.8	4♑38.7	29♌12.9	10 18.7	19 27.2	27 37.9	19 5.7	13 11.1	2 27.4	1 59.4
25 M	10 12 58.8	1 46.9	24 51.6	17 50.4	28 22.2	11 32.2	19 56.2	27 47.6	19D 5.8	13 14.7	2 28.7	2 1.4
26 T	10 16 55.3	2 44.8	24 48.4	0♒49.3	27 34.5	12 45.6	20 24.7	27 57.4	19 6.0	13 18.2	2 30.0	2 3.4
27 W	10 20 51.9	3 42.7	24 45.3	13 35.6	26 50.8	13 59.2	20 52.9	28 7.3	19 6.3	13 21.8	2 31.4	2 5.4
28 T	10 24 48.4	4 40.6	24 42.1	26 9.3	26 12.1	15 12.7	21 20.7	28 17.2	19 6.7	13 25.3	2 32.7	2 7.4
29 F	10 28 45.0	5 38.6	24 38.9	8♓30.9	25 39.3	16 26.3	21 48.1	28 27.3	19 7.2	13 28.8	2 34.1	2 9.4
30 S	10 32 41.5	6 36.5	24 35.7	20 41.2	25 13.1	17 40.0	22 15.1	28 37.4	19 7.8	13 32.3	2 35.5	2 11.4
31 S	10 36 38.1	7 34.6	24 32.6	2♈41.5	24 54.4	18 53.7	22 41.7	28 47.7	19 8.5	13 35.8	2 37.0	2 13.4
					DECLINATION at NOON							
1 F	8 38 21.5	18N 4.8	10S 5.5	7S37.5	7N36.1	22N30.3	11N31.8	8S23.7	21S43.1	17N51.4	10S33.4	21N38.2
4 M	8 50 11.1	17 18.4	10 2.0	4N 0.5	6 26.8	22 15.8	12 6.0	8 32.2	21 43.1	17 48.3	10 34.2	21 36.0
7 T	9 2 0.8	16 29.5	9 58.5	13 58.5	5 33.1	21 55.5	12 39.1	8 41.1	21 43.3	17 45.2	10 35.1	21 33.8
10 S	9 13 50.4	15 38.2	9 55.1	18 52.3	4 58.9	21 29.5	13 10.8	8 50.3	21 43.5	17 42.1	10 36.1	21 31.6
13 W	9 25 40.1	14 44.6	9 51.6	15 31.8	4 48.3	20 57.9	13 41.2	8 59.9	21 43.8	17 39.0	10 37.2	21 29.4
16 S	9 37 29.8	13 48.9	9 48.1	4 4.2	5 4.3	20 20.8	14 10.2	9 9.9	21 44.1	17 35.9	10 38.4	21 27.2
19 T	9 49 19.4	12 51.2	9 44.6	9S40.3	5 47.7	19 38.5	14 37.9	9 20.1	21 44.6	17 32.8	10 39.7	21 25.1
22 F	10 1 9.1	11 51.7	9 41.2	18 5.0	6 55.0	18 51.1	15 4.3	9 30.7	21 45.1	17 29.8	10 41.0	21 23.0
25 M	10 12 58.8	10 50.5	9 37.7	17 12.5	8 17.7	17 58.8	15 29.3	9 41.5	21 45.7	17 26.7	10 42.5	21 21.0
28 T	10 24 48.4	9 47.8	9 34.2	8 44.7	9 43.8	17 1.9	15 53.0	9 52.5	21 46.3	17 23.7	10 44.0	21 19.0
31 S	10 36 38.1	8 43.7	9 30.7	2N42.9	11 0.3	16 0.7	16 15.4	10 3.8	21 47.0	17 20.8	10 45.5	21 17.0

SEPTEMBER 1958

LONGITUDE at NOON

DAY	EPHEMERIS SIDEREAL TIME	☉	☊	☽	☿	♀	♂	♃	♄	♅	♆	♇
	h m s	° ′	° ′	° ′	° ′	° ′	° ′	° ′	° ′	° ′	° ′	° ′
1 M	10 40 34.6	8♍32.6	24♎29.4	14♈34.1	24♌43.5	20♌ 7.4	23♉ 7.8	28♎58.0	19♐ 9.2	13♌39.2	2♏38.4	2♍15.4
2 T	10 44 31.2	9 30.7	24 26.2	26 22.0	24R40.8	21 21.2	23 33.6	29 8.4	19 10.1	13 42.7	2 39.9	2 17.4
3 W	10 48 27.7	10 28.8	24 23.0	8♉ 8.7	24D46.6	22 35.0	23 58.8	29 18.9	19 11.1	13 46.1	2 41.4	2 19.4
4 T	10 52 24.3	11 26.9	24 19.8	19 58.8	25 1.1	23 48.9	24 23.7	29 29.5	19 12.1	13 49.5	2 43.0	2 21.3
5 F	10 56 20.8	12 25.0	24 16.7	1♊56.8	25 24.2	25 2.8	24 48.0	29 40.2	19 13.3	13 52.9	2 44.6	2 23.3
6 S	11 0 17.4	13 23.3	24 13.5	14 8.1	25 55.9	26 16.8	25 11.9	29 51.0	19 14.6	13 56.3	2 46.2	2 25.3
7 S	11 4 13.9	14 21.5	24 10.3	26 37.3	26 35.9	27 30.7	25 35.3	0♏ 1.8	19 15.9	13 59.6	2 47.8	2 27.3
8 M	11 8 10.5	15 19.8	24 7.1	9♋29.1	27 24.0	28 44.8	25 58.2	0 12.7	19 17.4	14 2.9	2 49.4	2 29.2
9 T	11 12 7.0	16 18.1	24 3.9	22 46.8	28 19.8	29 58.8	26 20.6	0 23.7	19 18.9	14 6.2	2 51.1	2 31.2
10 W	11 16 3.6	17 16.4	24 0.8	6♌ @.8	29 22.8	1♍12.9	26 42.4	0 34.7	19 20.6	14 9.5	2 52.8	2 33.1
11 T	11 20 0.1	18 14.8	23 57.6	20 43.5	0♍32.7	2 27.1	27 3.7	0 45.9	19 22.3	14 12.7	2 54.5	2 35.1
12 F	11 23 56.7	19 13.2	23 54.4	5♍18.2	1 48.9	3 41.2	27 24.4	0 57.1	19 24.1	14 15.9	2 56.2	2 37.0
13 S	11 27 53.2	20 11.6	23 51.2	20 9.7	3 10.7	4 55.5	27 44.6	1 8.3	19 26.1	14 19.1	2 57.9	2 38.9
14 S	11 31 49.8	21 10.0	23 48.1	5♎10.0	4 37.7	6 9.7	28 4.1	1 19.7	19 28.1	14 22.3	2 59.7	2 40.9
15 M	11 35 46.3	22 8.5	23 44.9	20 10.2	6 9.3	7 24.0	28 23.1	1 31.1	19 30.2	14 25.4	3 1.5	2 42.8
16 T	11 39 42.9	23 7.1	23 41.7	5♏ 2.3	7 44.8	8 38.3	28 41.5	1 42.6	19 32.4	14 28.5	3 3.3	2 44.7
17 W	11 43 39.5	24 5.6	23 38.5	19 39.8	9 23.7	9 52.6	28 59.3	1 54.2	19 34.7	14 31.6	3 5.1	2 46.6
18 T	11 47 36.0	25 4.2	23 35.3	3♐58.6	11 5.5	11 7.0	29 16.5	2 5.8	19 37.1	14 34.6	3 7.0	2 48.4
19 F	11 51 32.6	26 2.8	23 32.2	17 56.6	12 49.7	12 21.4	29 33.0	2 17.4	19 39.6	14 37.6	3 8.8	2 50.3
20 S	11 55 29.1	27 1.4	23 29.0	1♑33.6	14 35.8	13 35.8	29 48.9	2 29.2	19 42.2	14 40.6	3 10.7	2 52.2
21 S	11 59 25.7	28 0.1	23 25.8	14 50.7	16 23.4	14 50.3	0♊ 4.1	2 41.0	19 44.8	14 43.6	3 12.6	2 54.0
22 M	12 3 22.2	28 58.7	23 22.6	27 49.8	18 12.1	16 4.8	0 18.7	2 52.8	19 47.6	14 46.5	3 14.5	2 55.8
23 T	12 7 18.8	29 57.5	23 19.5	10♒32.8	20 1.5	17 19.3	0 32.5	3 4.7	19 50.4	14 49.4	3 16.5	2 57.7
24 W	12 11 15.3	0♎56.2	23 16.3	23 2.0	21 51.5	18 33.8	0 45.7	3 16.7	19 53.3	14 52.2	3 18.4	2 59.5
25 T	12 15 11.9	1 55.0	23 13.1	5♓19.4	23 41.7	19 48.4	0 58.2	3 28.7	19 56.4	14 55.0	3 20.4	3 1.3
26 F	12 19 8.4	2 53.8	23 9.9	17 26.8	25 31.9	21 3.0	1 10.0	3 40.8	19 59.5	14 57.8	3 22.4	3 3.1
27 S	12 23 5.0	3 52.7	23 6.7	29 26.2	27 22.0	22 17.6	1 21.1	3 53.0	20 2.7	15 0.6	3 24.4	3 4.9
28 S	12 27 1.5	4 51.5	23 3.6	11♈19.3	29 11.7	23 32.3	1 31.4	4 5.2	20 6.0	15 3.3	3 26.4	3 6.6
29 M	12 30 58.1	5 50.4	23 0.4	23 8.3	1♎ 1.1	24 47.0	1 40.9	4 17.4	20 9.3	15 6.0	3 28.4	3 8.4
30 T	12 34 54.6	6 49.4	22 57.2	4♉55.3	2 49.9	26 1.7	1 49.7	4 29.7	20 12.8	15 8.6	3 30.5	3 10.1

DECLINATION at NOON

DAY	EPHEMERIS SIDEREAL TIME	☉	☊	☽	☿	♀	♂	♃	♄	♅	♆	♇
1 M	10 40 34.6	8N22.1	9S29.5	6N26.3	11N21.6	15N39.4	16N22.6	10S 7.6	21S47.3	17N19.8	10S46.1	21N16.4
4 T	10 52 24.3	7 16.3	9 26.0	15 27.5	12 8.7	14 32.8	16 43.2	10 19.2	21 48.1	17 16.9	10 47.7	21 14.5
7 S	11 4 13.9	6 9.4	9 22.5	18 44.3	12 25.7	13 22.5	17 2.6	10 31.0	21 48.9	17 14.1	10 49.5	21 12.7
10 W	11 16 3.6	5 1.7	9 19.0	13 44.9	12 9.7	12 8.8	17 20.8	10 42.9	21 49.9	17 11.3	10 51.3	21 10.9
13 S	11 27 53.2	3 53.1	9 15.5	1 19.3	11 21.1	10 52.1	17 37.7	10 55.0	21 50.9	17 8.5	10 53.2	21 9.2
16 T	11 39 42.9	2 43.9	9 12.0	12S 7.7	10 3.1	9 32.6	17 53.4	11 7.3	21 51.9	17 5.9	10 55.1	21 7.5
19 F	11 51 32.6	1 34.3	9 8.5	18 35.4	8 21.2	8 10.6	18 7.9	11 19.6	21 53.0	17 3.3	10 57.1	21 6.0
22 M	12 3 22.2	0 24.4	9 4.9	15 28.4	6 21.8	6 46.6	18 21.3	11 32.1	21 54.2	17 0.8	10 59.1	21 4.5
25 T	12 15 11.9	0S45.7	9 1.4	5 58.5	4 10.9	5 20.7	18 33.6	11 44.7	21 55.4	16 58.4	11 1.1	21 3.1
28 S	12 27 1.5	1 55.9	8 57.9	5N24.1	1 53.6	3 53.4	18 44.8	11 57.3	21 56.6	16 56.0	11 3.2	21 1.8

OCTOBER 1958

LONGITUDE at NOON

DAY	EPHEMERIS SIDEREAL TIME	☉	☊	☽	☿	♀	♂	♃	♄	♅	♆	♇
1 W	12 38 51.2	7♎48.3	22♎54.0	16♉43.2	4♎38.1	27♍16.4	1♊57.7	4♏42.0	20♐16.3	15♌11.2	3♏32.5	3♍11.8
2 T	12 42 47.7	8 47.3	22 50.9	28 35.1	6 25.7	28 31.1	2 4.8	4 54.4	20 19.9	15 13.8	3 34.6	3 13.5
3 F	12 46 44.3	9 46.4	22 47.7	10♊34.7	8 12.6	29 45.9	2 11.2	5 6.8	20 23.6	15 16.3	3 36.7	3 15.2
4 S	12 50 40.8	10 45.5	22 44.5	22 46.0	9 58.7	1♎ 0.7	2 16.8	5 19.2	20 27.4	15 18.8	3 38.8	3 16.9
5 S	12 54 37.4	11 44.6	22 41.3	5♋13.3	11 44.1	2 15.6	2 21.5	5 31.7	20 31.2	15 21.2	3 40.9	3 18.5
6 M	12 58 33.9	12 43.8	22 38.1	18 0.7	13 28.7	3 30.4	2 25.3	5 44.3	20 35.1	15 23.6	3 43.0	3 20.1
7 T	13 2 30.5	13 43.0	22 35.0	1♌11.9	15 12.6	4 45.3	2 28.3	5 56.9	20 39.2	15 26.0	3 45.1	3 21.8
8 W	13 6 27.0	14 42.2	22 31.8	14 49.5	16 55.7	6 0.2	2 30.5	6 9.5	20 43.2	15 28.3	3 47.3	3 23.4
9 T	13 10 23.6	15 41.5	22 28.6	28 54.3	18 38.0	7 15.2	2 31.7	6 22.1	20 47.4	15 30.6	3 49.4	3 24.9
10 F	13 14 20.1	16 40.8	22 25.4	13♍25.0	20 19.5	8 30.1	2 32.1	6 34.8	20 51.7	15 32.8	3 51.6	3 26.5
11 S	13 18 16.7	17 40.2	22 22.2	28 17.2	22 0.3	9 45.1	2R31.6	6 47.6	20 56.0	15 35.0	3 53.7	3 28.0
12 S	13 22 13.3	18 39.5	22 19.1	13♎23.9	23 40.3	11 0.1	2 30.1	7 0.3	21 0.4	15 37.1	3 55.9	3 29.5
13 M	13 26 9.8	19 39.0	22 15.9	28 36.4	25 19.7	12 15.1	2 27.8	7 13.1	21 4.8	15 39.2	3 58.1	3 31.0
14 T	13 30 6.4	20 38.4	22 12.7	13♏44.9	26 58.3	13 30.1	2 24.5	7 26.0	21 9.4	15 41.3	4 0.3	3 32.5
15 W	13 34 2.9	21 37.9	22 9.5	28 40.5	28 36.2	14 45.2	2 20.4	7 38.8	21 14.0	15 43.3	4 2.5	3 34.0
16 T	13 37 59.5	22 37.4	22 6.4	13♐16.0	0♏13.4	16 0.2	2 15.3	7 51.7	21 18.7	15 45.2	4 4.7	3 35.4
17 F	13 41 56.0	23 37.0	22 3.2	27 27.2	1 49.9	17 15.3	2 9.4	8 4.6	21 23.4	15 47.1	4 6.9	3 36.8
18 S	13 45 52.6	24 36.6	22 0.0	11♑12.3	3 25.9	18 30.4	2 2.6	8 17.6	21 28.3	15 49.0	4 9.1	3 38.3
19 S	13 49 49.1	25 36.2	21 56.8	24 31.6	5 1.2	19 45.5	1 54.9	8 30.6	21 33.2	15 50.9	4 11.4	3 39.6
20 M	13 53 45.7	26 35.9	21 53.6	7♒27.6	6 35.8	21 0.7	1 46.3	8 43.5	21 38.2	15 52.6	4 13.6	3 41.0
21 T	13 57 42.2	27 35.5	21 50.5	20 3.3	8 9.9	22 15.8	1 36.9	8 56.5	21 43.2	15 54.3	4 15.8	3 42.3
22 W	14 1 38.8	28 35.2	21 47.3	2♓22.6	9 43.4	23 30.9	1 26.6	9 9.6	21 48.3	15 56.0	4 18.1	3 43.6
23 T	14 5 35.3	29 34.9	21 44.1	14 29.2	11 16.3	24 46.1	1 15.4	9 22.6	21 53.4	15 57.6	4 20.3	3 44.9
24 F	14 9 31.9	0♏34.7	21 40.9	26 26.6	12 48.6	26 1.2	1 3.5	9 35.7	21 58.7	15 59.2	4 22.5	3 46.1
25 S	14 13 28.4	1 34.5	21 37.8	8♈18.0	14 20.4	27 16.4	0 50.7	9 48.7	22 3.9	16 0.7	4 24.8	3 47.4
26 S	14 17 25.0	2 34.3	21 34.6	20 6.4	15 51.7	28 31.6	0 37.1	10 1.8	22 9.3	16 2.2	4 27.0	3 48.6
27 M	14 21 21.5	3 34.1	21 31.4	1♉54.1	17 22.4	29 46.8	0 22.8	10 14.9	22 14.7	16 3.6	4 29.2	3 49.7
28 T	14 25 18.1	4 34.0	21 28.2	13 43.3	18 52.6	1♏ 2.0	0 7.7	10 28.1	22 20.2	16 5.0	4 31.5	3 50.9
29 W	14 29 14.7	5 33.9	21 25.0	25 36.3	20 22.2	2 17.2	29♉52.0	10 41.2	22 25.7	16 6.3	4 33.7	3 52.0
30 T	14 33 11.2	6 33.9	21 21.9	7♊35.0	21 51.3	3 32.5	29 35.5	10 54.3	22 31.3	16 7.6	4 36.0	3 53.1
31 F	14 37 7.8	7 33.8	21 18.7	19 41.7	23 19.9	4 47.7	29 18.3	11 7.5	22 36.9	16 8.8	4 38.2	3 54.2

DECLINATION at NOON

DAY	EPHEMERIS SIDEREAL TIME	☉	☊	☽	☿	♀	♂	♃	♄	♅	♆	♇
1 W	12 38 51.2	3S 5.8	8S54.3	14N43.8	0S26.4	2N24.9	18N55.0	12S10.0	21S57.9	16N53.8	11S 5.4	21N 0.5
4 S	12 50 40.8	4 15.5	8 50.8	18 38.5	2 46.2	0 55.6	19 4.1	12 22.7	21 59.2	16 51.6	11 7.5	20 59.4
7 T	13 2 30.5	5 24.8	8 47.3	14 47.1	5 3.9	0S34.2	19 12.1	12 35.4	22 0.5	16 49.6	11 9.7	20 58.4
10 F	13 14 20.1	6 33.4	8 43.7	3 26.5	7 18.0	2 4.2	19 19.1	12 48.2	22 1.9	16 47.7	11 12.0	20 57.4
13 M	13 26 9.8	7 41.3	8 40.2	10S26.0	9 27.6	3 34.0	19 24.9	13 0.9	22 3.2	16 45.9	11 14.2	20 56.6
16 T	13 37 59.5	8 48.2	8 36.6	18 18.0	11 31.7	5 3.2	19 29.6	13 13.7	22 4.6	16 44.2	11 16.4	20 55.8
19 S	13 49 49.1	9 53.9	8 33.0	16 0.0	13 29.7	6 31.6	19 33.2	13 26.4	22 6.0	16 42.6	11 18.7	20 55.2
22 W	14 1 38.8	10 58.4	8 29.5	6 50.1	15 21.1	7 58.8	19 35.5	13 39.0	22 7.4	16 41.2	11 20.9	20 54.6
25 S	14 13 28.4	12 1.4	8 25.9	4N28.6	17 5.3	9 24.5	19 36.6	13 51.6	22 8.7	16 39.9	11 23.2	20 54.2
28 T	14 25 18.1	13 2.7	8 22.4	14 6.9	18 41.8	10 48.2	19 36.5	14 4.1	22 10.1	16 38.8	11 25.4	20 53.9
31 F	14 37 7.8	14 2.2	8 18.8	18 36.4	20 10.0	12 9.7	19 35.0	14 16.5	22 11.4	16 37.7	11 27.7	20 53.7

NOVEMBER 1958

DAY	EPHEMERIS SIDEREAL TIME h m s	☉ ° ′	☊ ° ′	☽ ° ′	☿ ° ′	♀ ° ′	♂ ° ′	♃ ° ′	♄ ° ′	♅ ° ′	♆ ° ′	♇ ° ′
LONGITUDE at NOON												
1 S	14 41 4.3	8♏33.9	21♎15.5	1♋59.0	24♏47.9	6♏ 2.9	29♉ 0.5	11♏20.6	22♐42.6	16♌ 9.9	4♏40.5	3♍55.3
2 S	14 45 0.9	9 33.9	21 12.3	14 29.5	26 15.3	7 18.2	28R42.2	11 33.8	22 48.3	16 11.0	4 42.7	3 56.3
3 M	14 48 57.4	10 34.0	21 9.2	27 16.3	27 42.2	8 33.5	28 23.2	11 46.9	22 54.1	16 12.1	4 44.9	3 57.3
4 T	14 52 54.0	11 34.1	21 6.0	10♌22.2	29 8.4	9 48.8	28 3.7	12 0.1	22 60.0	16 13.1	4 47.2	3 58.3
5 W	14 56 50.5	12 34.3	21 2.8	23 50.0	0♐34.0	11 4.1	27 43.8	12 13.3	23 5.9	16 14.1	4 49.4	3 59.2
6 T	15 0 47.1	13 34.4	20 59.6	7♍41.4	1 58.9	12 19.4	27 23.4	12 26.5	23 11.8	16 14.9	4 51.6	4 0.1
7 F	15 4 43.6	14 34.7	20 56.4	21 56.8	3 23.1	13 34.7	27 2.6	12 39.7	23 17.8	16 15.8	4 53.8	4 1.0
8 S	15 8 40.2	15 35.0	20 53.3	6♎34.6	4 46.6	14 50.1	26 41.5	12 52.9	23 23.9	16 16.6	4 56.1	4 1.9
9 S	15 12 36.8	16 35.3	20 50.1	21 30.5	6 9.1	16 5.4	26 20.1	13 6.1	23 30.0	16 17.3	4 58.3	4 2.7
10 M	15 16 33.3	17 35.6	20 46.9	6♏37.7	7 30.7	17 20.8	25 58.4	13 19.2	23 36.2	16 18.0	5 0.5	4 3.5
11 T	15 20 29.9	18 35.9	20 43.7	21 47.4	8 51.3	18 36.1	25 36.6	13 32.4	23 42.4	16 18.6	5 2.7	4 4.3
12 W	15 24 26.4	19 36.3	20 40.6	6♐50.0	10 10.7	19 51.5	25 14.6	13 45.6	23 48.6	16 19.2	5 4.9	4 5.1
13 T	15 28 23.0	20 36.7	20 37.4	21 36.4	11 28.9	21 6.8	24 52.5	13 58.7	23 54.9	16 19.7	5 7.1	4 5.8
14 F	15 32 19.5	21 37.1	20 34.2	5♑59.6	12 45.6	22 22.2	24 30.4	14 11.8	24 1.2	16 20.2	5 9.3	4 6.5
15 S	15 36 16.1	22 37.6	20 31.0	19 55.5	14 0.8	23 37.6	24 8.4	14 25.0	24 7.6	16 20.5	5 11.4	4 7.1
16 S	15 40 12.6	23 38.1	20 27.9	3♒22.9	15 14.1	24 52.9	23 46.4	14 38.1	24 14.0	16 20.9	5 13.6	4 7.7
17 M	15 44 9.2	24 38.6	20 24.7	16 23.1	16 25.5	26 8.3	23 24.6	14 51.2	24 20.4	16 21.2	5 15.7	4 8.3
18 T	15 48 5.7	25 39.1	20 21.5	28 59.5	17 34.5	27 23.7	23 2.9	15 4.3	24 26.9	16 21.4	5 17.9	4 8.9
19 W	15 52 2.3	26 39.6	20 18.3	11♓16.4	18 40.9	28 39.1	22 41.5	15 17.4	24 33.4	16 21.6	5 20.0	4 9.5
20 T	15 55 58.9	27 40.2	20 15.1	23 18.8	19 44.4	29 54.4	22 20.4	15 30.4	24 40.0	16 21.7	5 22.1	4 10.0
21 F	15 59 55.4	28 40.8	20 12.0	5♈11.5	20 44.6	1♐ 9.8	21 59.6	15 43.4	24 46.6	16 21.7	5 24.2	4 10.4
22 S	16 3 52.0	29 41.4	20 8.8	16 59.1	21 40.9	2 25.2	21 39.2	15 56.5	24 53.2	16 21.7	5 26.3	4 10.9
23 S	16 7 48.5	0♐42.0	20 5.6	28 45.8	22 33.0	3 40.6	21 19.2	16 9.4	24 59.8	16 21.7	5 28.4	4 11.3
24 M	16 11 45.1	1 42.6	20 2.4	10♉35.0	23 20.2	4 56.0	20 59.7	16 22.4	25 6.5	16R21.6	5 30.4	4 11.7
25 T	16 15 41.6	2 43.3	19 59.3	22 29.4	24 1.9	6 11.3	20 40.6	16 35.4	25 13.2	16 21.4	5 32.5	4 12.0
26 W	16 19 38.2	3 44.0	19 56.1	4♊31.1	24 37.4	7 26.7	20 22.1	16 48.3	25 19.9	16 21.2	5 34.5	4 12.4
27 T	16 23 34.7	4 44.7	19 52.9	16 41.7	25 5.9	8 42.1	20 4.2	17 1.2	25 26.7	16 20.9	5 36.5	4 12.7
28 F	16 27 31.3	5 45.4	19 49.7	29 2.1	25 26.7	9 57.5	19 46.8	17 14.0	25 33.5	16 20.6	5 38.5	4 12.9
29 S	16 31 27.9	6 46.2	19 46.5	11♋33.4	25 39.0	11 12.9	19 30.2	17 26.9	25 40.4	16 20.3	5 40.6	4 13.2
30 S	16 35 24.4	7 47.0	19 43.4	24 16.3	25 41.9	12 28.3	19 14.1	17 39.7	25 47.2	16 19.8	5 42.6	4 13.4
DECLINATION at NOON												
1 S	14 41 4.3	14S21.6	8S17.6	18N28.8	20S37.4	12S36.3	19N34.3	14S20.6	22S11.9	16N37.4	11S28.4	20N53.7
4 T	14 52 54.0	15 18.3	8 14.0	12 49.1	21 53.5	13 54.2	19 31.1	14 32.8	22 13.2	16 36.6	11 30.6	20 53.6
7 F	15 4 43.6	16 12.8	8 10.5	0 45.2	22 59.8	15 9.0	19 26.8	14 45.0	22 14.5	16 35.9	11 32.8	20 53.7
10 M	15 16 33.3	17 4.9	8 6.9	12S29.5	23 55.6	16 20.3	19 21.4	14 57.0	22 15.8	16 35.4	11 35.0	20 53.8
13 T	15 28 23.0	17 54.4	8 3.3	18 40.4	24 40.1	17 27.8	19 15.1	15 8.8	22 17.0	16 35.0	11 37.2	20 54.1
16 S	15 40 12.6	18 41.0	7 59.7	14 25.0	25 12.5	18 31.2	19 8.1	15 20.5	22 18.2	16 34.7	11 39.3	20 54.5
19 W	15 52 2.3	19 24.7	7 56.1	4 11.3	25 32.1	19 29.9	19 0.7	15 32.1	22 19.3	16 34.7	11 41.3	20 55.0
22 S	16 3 52.0	20 5.2	7 52.5	7N 5.2	25 38.3	20 23.9	18 53.3	15 43.4	22 20.4	16 34.7	11 43.3	20 55.7
25 T	16 15 41.6	20 42.4	7 48.9	15 50.3	25 30.4	21 12.6	18 46.0	15 54.6	22 21.5	16 34.9	11 45.3	20 56.4
28 F	16 27 31.3	21 16.1	7 45.3	18 41.1	25 7.8	21 55.8	18 39.2	16 5.5	22 22.5	16 35.3	11 47.2	20 57.3

DECEMBER 1958

DAY	EPHEMERIS SIDEREAL TIME h m s	☉ ° ′	☊ ° ′	☽ ° ′	☿ ° ′	♀ ° ′	♂ ° ′	♃ ° ′	♄ ° ′	♅ ° ′	♆ ° ′	♇ ° ′
LONGITUDE at NOON												
1 M	16 39 21.0	8♐47.8	19♎40.2	7♌11.8	25♐34.8	13♐43.7	18♉58.7	17♏52.5	25♐54.1	16♌19.3	5♏44.5	4♍13.6
2 T	16 43 17.5	9 48.6	19 37.0	20 21.3	25R16.9	14 59.1	18R44.0	18 5.2	26 0.9	16R18.8	5 46.5	4 13.7
3 W	16 47 14.1	10 49.5	19 33.8	3♍46.2	24 47.9	16 14.5	18 30.0	18 17.9	26 7.8	16 18.2	5 48.4	4 13.8
4 T	16 51 10.6	11 50.4	19 30.7	17 27.9	24 7.8	17 29.9	18 16.8	18 30.6	26 14.8	16 17.5	5 50.3	4 13.9
5 F	16 55 7.2	12 51.3	19 27.5	1♎27.6	23 16.8	18 45.3	18 4.3	18 43.2	26 21.7	16 16.8	5 52.2	4 13.9
6 S	16 59 3.8	13 52.2	19 24.3	15 45.3	22 15.7	20 0.8	17 52.6	18 55.8	26 28.7	16 16.1	5 54.0	4 13.9
7 S	17 3 0.3	14 53.1	19 21.1	0♏19.2	21 5.8	21 16.2	17 41.7	19 8.4	26 35.7	16 15.3	5 55.9	4 13.9
8 M	17 6 56.9	15 54.1	19 18.0	15 5.7	19 49.2	22 31.6	17 31.5	19 20.9	26 42.7	16 14.4	5 57.7	4 13.9
9 T	17 10 53.4	16 55.1	19 14.8	29 58.6	18 28.0	23 47.0	17 22.2	19 33.3	26 49.7	16 13.5	5 59.5	4R13.8
10 W	17 14 50.0	17 56.1	19 11.6	14♐50.1	17 5.0	25 2.4	17 13.8	19 45.7	26 56.7	16 12.5	6 1.3	4 13.7
11 T	17 18 46.5	18 57.1	19 8.4	29 31.6	15 43.0	26 17.8	17 6.1	19 58.1	27 3.7	16 11.5	6 3.1	4 13.5
12 F	17 22 43.1	19 58.1	19 5.3	13♑55.3	14 24.7	27 33.3	16 59.3	20 10.4	27 10.8	16 10.4	6 4.8	4 13.4
13 S	17 26 39.7	20 59.1	19 2.1	27 55.1	13 12.6	28 48.7	16 53.3	20 22.7	27 17.8	16 9.3	6 6.5	4 13.2
14 S	17 30 36.2	22 0.2	18 58.9	11♒28.0	12 8.8	0♑ 4.1	16 48.2	20 34.9	27 24.9	16 8.1	6 8.2	4 12.9
15 M	17 34 32.8	23 1.2	18 55.7	24 33.6	11 14.6	1 19.5	16 43.8	20 47.1	27 31.9	16 6.9	6 9.9	4 12.7
16 T	17 38 29.3	24 2.3	18 52.5	7♓14.2	10 31.0	2 34.9	16 40.4	20 59.2	27 39.0	16 5.6	6 11.6	4 12.4
17 W	17 42 25.9	25 3.3	18 49.4	19 33.5	9 58.5	3 50.3	16 37.7	21 11.2	27 46.1	16 4.3	6 13.2	4 12.0
18 T	17 46 22.4	26 4.4	18 46.2	1♈36.7	9 37.0	5 5.7	16 35.9	21 23.2	27 53.2	16 2.9	6 14.8	4 11.7
19 F	17 50 19.0	27 5.5	18 43.0	13 29.1	9 26.2	6 21.0	16 34.9	21 35.2	28 0.3	16 1.5	6 16.4	4 11.3
20 S	17 54 15.6	28 6.6	18 39.8	25 16.4	9 25.7	7 36.5	16 34.7	21 47.1	28 7.4	16 0.1	6 18.0	4 10.9
21 S	17 58 12.1	29 7.7	18 36.7	7♉ 3.6	9D34.6	8 51.8	16D35.2	21 58.9	28 14.5	15 58.6	6 19.5	4 10.5
22 M	18 2 8.7	0♑ 8.8	18 33.5	18 55.4	9 52.2	10 7.2	16 36.6	22 10.6	28 21.6	15 57.0	6 21.0	4 10.0
23 T	18 6 5.2	1 9.9	18 30.3	0♊55.7	10 17.8	11 22.6	16 38.7	22 22.3	28 28.6	15 55.4	6 22.5	4 9.5
24 W	18 10 1.8	2 11.0	18 27.1	13 7.1	10 50.4	12 37.9	16 41.6	22 33.9	28 35.7	15 53.8	6 24.0	4 9.0
25 T	18 13 58.3	3 12.1	18 24.0	25 31.4	11 29.5	13 53.3	16 45.2	22 45.4	28 42.8	15 52.1	6 25.4	4 8.4
26 F	18 17 54.9	4 13.2	18 20.8	8♋ 9.3	12 14.3	15 8.6	16 49.6	22 56.9	28 49.8	15 50.3	6 26.8	4 7.8
27 S	18 21 51.5	5 14.3	18 17.6	21 0.5	13 4.1	16 24.0	16 54.7	23 8.3	28 56.9	15 48.6	6 28.2	4 7.2
28 S	18 25 48.0	6 15.5	18 14.4	4♌ 4.1	13 58.4	17 39.3	17 0.4	23 19.6	29 4.0	15 46.8	6 29.5	4 6.5
29 M	18 29 44.6	7 16.6	18 11.2	17 19.1	14 56.7	18 54.6	17 6.9	23 30.9	29 11.0	15 44.9	6 30.8	4 5.9
30 T	18 33 41.1	8 17.7	18 8.1	0♍44.4	15 58.5	20 9.9	17 14.1	23 42.1	29 18.0	15 43.0	6 32.1	4 5.2
31 W	18 37 37.7	9 18.9	18 4.9	14 19.3	17 3.4	21 25.2	17 21.9	23 53.2	29 25.1	15 41.1	6 33.4	4 4.4
DECLINATION at NOON												
1 M	16 39 21.0	21S46.2	7S41.7	13N41.8	24S29.7	22S33.2	18N33.1	16S16.3	22S23.4	16N35.8	11S49.1	20N58.2
4 T	16 51 10.6	22 12.6	7 38.1	2 20.0	23 35.3	23 4.6	18 28.1	16 26.8	22 24.3	16 36.5	11 50.9	20 59.3
7 S	17 3 0.3	22 35.1	7 34.5	10S48.3	22 25.7	23 29.8	18 24.2	16 37.1	22 25.1	16 37.3	11 52.7	21 0.4
10 W	17 14 50.0	22 53.6	7 30.9	18 28.7	21 8.1	23 48.5	18 21.7	16 47.1	22 25.8	16 38.2	11 54.3	21 1.7
13 S	17 26 39.7	23 8.1	7 27.3	15 38.6	19 58.5	24 0.6	18 20.7	16 56.9	22 26.5	16 39.3	11 55.9	21 3.0
16 T	17 38 29.3	23 18.4	7 23.7	5 38.4	19 13.2	24 6.1	18 21.4	17 6.5	22 27.1	16 40.5	11 57.5	21 4.5
19 F	17 50 19.0	23 24.6	7 20.1	5N51.1	18 58.7	24 4.9	18 23.6	17 15.8	22 27.7	16 41.8	11 58.9	21 6.0
22 M	18 2 8.7	23 26.5	7 16.4	15 4.8	19 11.0	23 56.9	18 27.5	17 24.8	22 28.2	16 43.3	12 0.3	21 7.6
25 T	18 13 58.3	23 24.2	7 12.8	18 46.4	19 41.8	23 42.2	18 32.9	17 33.5	22 28.6	16 44.8	12 1.6	21 9.3
28 S	18 25 48.0	23 17.6	7 9.2	14 32.1	20 22.7	23 21.0	18 39.8	17 42.0	22 28.9	16 46.5	12 2.8	21 11.1
31 W	18 37 37.7	23 6.9	7 5.5	3 33.8	21 7.0	22 53.3	18 48.2	17 50.1	22 29.2	16 48.3	12 3.9	21 12.9

JANUARY 1959

DAY	EPHEMERIS SIDEREAL TIME	☉	☊	☽	☿	♀	♂	♃	♄	♅	♆	♇
	h m s	° ′	° ′	° ′	° ′	° ′	° ′	° ′	° ′	° ′	° ′	° ′
						LONGITUDE at NOON						
1 T	18 41 34.2	10♑20.0	18♎ 1.7	28♍ 3.8	18♐11.1	22♑40.6	17♉30.4	24♏ 4.2	29♐32.1	15♌39.1	6♏34.6	4♍ 3.7
2 F	18 45 30.8	11 21.2	17 58.5	11♎58.1	19 21.2	23 55.9	17 39.6	24 15.1	29 39.1	15R37.1	6 35.8	4R 2.9
3 S	18 49 27.4	12 22.3	17 55.4	26 2.3	20 33.5	25 11.2	17 49.3	24 26.0	29 46.0	15 35.1	6 36.9	4 2.1
4 S	18 53 23.9	13 23.5	17 52.2	10♏16.1	21 47.7	26 26.5	17 59.7	24 36.7	29 53.0	15 33.0	6 38.1	4 1.3
5 M	18 57 20.5	14 24.7	17 49.0	24 37.8	23 3.7	27 41.8	18 10.7	24 47.4	29 59.9	15 30.9	6 39.2	4 0.4
6 T	19 1 17.0	15 25.8	17 45.8	9♐ 4.1	24 21.2	28 57.0	18 22.3	24 58.0	0♑ 6.9	15 28.7	6 40.3	3 59.5
7 W	19 5 13.6	16 27.0	17 42.7	23 30.4	25 40.1	0♒12.3	18 34.5	25 8.5	0 13.8	15 26.6	6 41.3	3 58.6
8 T	19 9 10.1	17 28.2	17 39.5	7♑50.5	27 0.2	1 27.6	18 47.3	25 18.9	0 20.7	15 24.4	6 42.3	3 57.7
9 F	19 13 6.7	18 29.3	17 36.3	21 58.1	28 21.6	2 42.8	19 0.7	25 29.3	0 27.5	15 22.1	6 43.3	3 56.7
10 S	19 17 3.3	19 30.6	17 33.1	5♒47.8	29 44.0	3 58.1	19 14.6	25 39.5	0 34.4	15 19.9	6 44.3	3 55.8
11 S	19 20 59.8	20 31.7	17 29.9	19 15.6	1♑ 7.3	5 13.4	19 29.1	25 49.6	0 41.3	15 17.6	6 45.2	3 54.8
12 M	19 24 56.4	21 32.9	17 26.8	2♓19.9	2 31.6	6 28.6	19 44.0	25 59.7	0 48.0	15 15.3	6 46.1	3 53.7
13 T	19 28 52.9	22 34.0	17 23.6	15 1.4	3 56.6	7 43.8	19 59.5	26 9.6	0 54.8	15 12.9	6 47.0	3 52.7
14 W	19 32 49.5	23 35.1	17 20.4	27 22.7	5 22.5	8 59.0	20 15.5	26 19.4	1 1.6	15 10.6	6 47.8	3 51.6
15 T	19 36 46.0	24 36.3	17 17.2	9♈27.8	6 49.1	10 14.2	20 32.0	26 29.1	1 8.3	15 8.2	6 48.6	3 50.5
16 F	19 40 42.6	25 37.4	17 14.1	21 21.7	8 16.4	11 29.4	20 49.0	26 38.7	1 14.9	15 5.7	6 49.4	3 49.4
17 S	19 44 39.1	26 38.5	17 10.9	3♉10.0	9 44.4	12 44.5	21 6.4	26 48.2	1 21.6	15 3.3	6 50.1	3 48.3
18 S	19 48 35.7	27 39.6	17 7.7	14 58.4	11 13.1	13 59.7	21 24.3	26 57.6	1 28.2	15 0.8	6 50.8	3 47.1
19 M	19 52 32.3	28 40.6	17 4.5	26 52.1	12 42.4	15 14.8	21 42.7	27 6.9	1 34.8	14 58.4	6 51.4	3 45.9
20 T	19 56 28.8	29 41.7	17 1.4	8♊55.9	14 12.3	16 29.9	22 1.4	27 16.1	1 41.3	14 55.9	6 52.1	3 44.7
21 W	20 0 25.4	0♒42.7	16 58.2	21 13.9	15 42.9	17 45.0	22 20.6	27 25.1	1 47.8	14 53.3	6 52.7	3 43.5
22 T	20 4 21.9	1 43.8	16 55.0	3♋48.7	17 14.0	19 0.0	22 40.2	27 34.1	1 54.3	14 50.8	6 53.2	3 42.3
23 F	20 8 18.5	2 44.8	16 51.8	16 41.6	18 45.8	20 15.1	23 0.2	27 42.9	2 0.7	14 48.3	6 53.7	3 41.0
24 S	20 12 15.0	3 45.8	16 48.6	29 52.4	20 18.2	21 30.1	23 20.6	27 51.6	2 7.1	14 45.7	6 54.2	3 39.8
25 S	20 16 11.6	4 46.7	16 45.5	13♌19.3	21 51.2	22 45.1	23 41.4	28 0.2	2 13.5	14 43.1	6 54.7	3 38.5
26 M	20 20 8.1	5 47.7	16 42.3	26 59.7	23 24.9	24 0.1	24 2.5	28 8.6	2 19.8	14 40.6	6 55.1	3 37.2
27 T	20 24 4.7	6 48.7	16 39.1	10♍50.3	24 59.1	25 15.1	24 24.0	28 17.0	2 26.1	14 38.0	6 55.5	3 35.8
28 W	20 28 1.3	7 49.6	16 35.9	24 47.8	26 34.0	26 30.0	24 45.8	28 25.2	2 32.3	14 35.4	6 55.8	3 34.5
29 T	20 31 57.8	8 50.6	16 32.8	8♎49.7	28 9.6	27 44.9	25 7.9	28 33.3	2 38.5	14 32.7	6 56.2	3 33.2
30 F	20 35 54.4	9 51.5	16 29.6	22 53.9	29 45.8	28 59.8	25 30.4	28 41.2	2 44.6	14 30.1	6 56.5	3 31.8
31 S	20 39 50.9	10 52.5	16 26.4	6♏59.4	1♒22.8	0♓14.8	25 53.3	28 49.1	2 50.8	14 27.6	6 56.8	3 30.5
						DECLINATION at NOON						
1 T	18 41 34.2	23S 2.4	7S 4.3	0S50.1	21S21.7	22S42.7	18N51.3	17S52.8	22S29.3	16N48.9	12S 4.2	21N13.6
4 S	18 53 23.9	22 46.1	7 0.7	13 6.3	22 3.6	22 6.7	19 1.3	18 0.6	22 29.4	16 50.8	12 5.2	21 15.5
7 W	19 5 13.6	22 25.7	6 57.1	18 43.5	22 40.1	21 24.8	19 12.6	18 8.0	22 29.6	16 52.8	12 6.1	21 17.5
10 S	19 17 3.3	22 1.4	6 53.4	14 12.9	23 9.1	20 37.1	19 24.9	18 15.2	22 29.6	16 54.8	12 6.9	21 19.5
13 T	19 28 52.9	21 33.2	6 49.8	3 26.5	23 29.2	19 44.0	19 38.2	18 22.1	22 29.6	16 56.9	12 7.6	21 21.5
16 F	19 40 42.6	21 1.2	6 46.1	7N57.6	23 39.3	18 45.7	19 52.3	18 28.6	22 29.5	16 59.1	12 8.3	21 23.6
19 M	19 52 32.3	20 25.6	6 42.5	16 17.3	23 38.7	17 42.7	20 7.1	18 34.9	22 29.4	17 1.3	12 8.8	21 25.7
22 T	20 4 21.9	19 46.6	6 38.8	18 28.9	23 26.6	16 35.2	20 22.5	18 40.8	22 29.2	17 3.6	12 9.2	21 27.9
25 S	20 16 11.6	19 4.3	6 35.2	12 32.6	23 2.7	15 23.6	20 38.4	18 46.4	22 29.0	17 5.9	12 9.5	21 30.0
28 W	20 28 1.3	18 18.8	6 31.5	0 25.9	22 26.5	14 8.2	20 54.6	18 51.6	22 28.7	17 8.2	12 9.7	21 32.2
31 S	20 39 50.9	17 30.4	6 27.9	12S 4.1	21 37.7	12 49.4	21 11.0	18 56.6	22 28.4	17 10.5	12 9.8	21 34.3

FEBRUARY 1959

DAY	EPHEMERIS SIDEREAL TIME	☉	☊	☽	☿	♀	♂	♃	♄	♅	♆	♇
						LONGITUDE at NOON						
1 S	20 43 47.5	11♒53.4	16♎23.2	21♏ 5.1	3♒ 0.4	1♓29.6	26♉16.5	28♏56.8	2♑56.8	14♌24.9	6♏57.0	3♍29.1
2 M	20 47 44.0	12 54.2	16 20.0	5♐10.3	4 38.7	2 44.5	26 39.9	29 4.3	3 2.8	14R22.3	6 57.2	3R27.7
3 T	20 51 40.6	13 55.1	16 16.9	19 13.4	6 17.7	3 59.3	27 3.7	29 11.8	3 8.8	14 19.7	6 57.3	3 26.3
4 W	20 55 37.1	14 56.0	16 13.7	3♑12.2	7 57.5	5 14.1	27 27.7	29 19.0	3 14.7	14 17.0	6 57.4	3 24.8
5 T	20 59 33.7	15 56.8	16 10.5	17 3.8	9 38.0	6 28.9	27 52.1	29 26.2	3 20.5	14 14.4	6 57.5	3 23.4
6 F	21 3 30.3	16 57.7	16 7.3	0♒44.8	11 19.2	7 43.7	28 16.7	29 33.2	3 26.3	14 11.8	6 57.5	3 22.0
7 S	21 7 26.8	17 58.5	16 4.2	14 12.0	13 1.3	8 58.4	28 41.7	29 40.0	3 32.0	14 9.1	6 57.6	3 20.5
8 S	21 11 23.4	18 59.3	16 1.0	27 22.6	14 44.1	10 13.1	29 6.8	29 46.7	3 37.7	14 6.5	6R57.5	3 19.0
9 M	21 15 19.9	20 0.0	15 57.8	10♓15.3	16 27.7	11 27.8	29 32.3	29 53.3	3 43.3	14 3.9	6 57.5	3 17.6
10 T	21 19 16.5	21 0.8	15 54.6	22 50.0	18 12.2	12 42.5	29 58.0	29 59.7	3 48.9	14 1.3	6 57.4	3 16.1
11 W	21 23 13.0	22 1.5	15 51.5	5♈ 8.2	19 57.4	13 57.1	0♊24.0	0♐ 6.0	3 54.4	13 58.7	6 57.3	3 14.6
12 T	21 27 9.6	23 2.2	15 48.3	17 12.5	21 43.5	15 11.7	0 50.2	0 12.1	3 59.9	13 56.1	6 57.1	3 13.1
13 F	21 31 6.1	24 2.8	15 45.1	29 6.9	23 30.3	16 26.2	1 16.6	0 18.0	4 5.2	13 53.5	6 56.9	3 11.6
14 S	21 35 2.7	25 3.5	15 41.9	10♉55.9	25 18.0	17 40.8	1 43.3	0 23.8	4 10.6	13 50.9	6 56.7	3 10.1
15 S	21 38 59.2	26 4.1	15 38.7	22 44.7	27 6.4	18 55.3	2 10.2	0 29.4	4 15.8	13 48.4	6 56.4	3 8.6
16 M	21 42 55.8	27 4.7	15 35.6	4♊38.6	28 55.6	20 9.7	2 37.4	0 34.9	4 21.0	13 45.8	6 56.1	3 7.0
17 T	21 46 52.3	28 5.2	15 32.4	16 42.9	0♓45.5	21 24.1	3 4.7	0 40.2	4 26.1	13 43.3	6 55.8	3 5.5
18 W	21 50 48.9	29 5.8	15 29.2	29 2.2	2 36.2	22 38.5	3 32.3	0 45.4	4 31.2	13 40.8	6 55.4	3 4.0
19 T	21 54 45.4	0♓ 6.2	15 26.0	11♋40.5	4 27.4	23 52.9	4 0.0	0 50.4	4 36.2	13 38.3	6 55.1	3 2.5
20 F	21 58 42.0	1 6.7	15 22.9	24 40.4	6 19.2	25 7.2	4 27.9	0 55.2	4 41.1	13 35.8	6 54.6	3 0.9
21 S	22 2 38.6	2 7.2	15 19.7	8♌ 2.9	8 11.5	26 21.5	4 56.1	0 59.9	4 46.0	13 33.4	6 54.2	2 59.5
22 S	22 6 35.1	3 7.6	15 16.5	21 46.8	10 4.1	27 35.7	5 24.4	1 4.4	4 50.8	13 30.9	6 53.7	2 57.9
23 M	22 10 31.7	4 8.0	15 13.3	5♍49.4	11 56.9	28 49.9	5 52.9	1 8.8	4 55.5	13 28.5	6 53.2	2 56.4
24 T	22 14 28.2	5 8.3	15 10.1	20 6.1	13 49.7	0♈ 4.1	6 21.6	1 12.9	5 0.2	13 26.1	6 52.7	2 54.9
25 W	22 18 24.8	6 8.6	15 7.0	4♎31.6	15 42.4	1 18.2	6 50.5	1 16.9	5 4.7	13 23.8	6 52.1	2 53.3
26 T	22 22 21.3	7 8.9	15 3.8	19 0.3	17 34.6	2 32.2	7 19.5	1 20.8	5 9.2	13 21.4	6 51.5	2 51.8
27 F	22 26 17.9	8 9.2	15 0.6	3♏27.3	19 26.2	3 46.3	7 48.6	1 24.4	5 13.7	13 19.1	6 50.8	2 50.3
28 S	22 30 14.4	9 9.5	14 57.4	17 48.7	21 16.8	5 0.2	8 18.0	1 27.9	5 18.0	13 16.8	6 50.2	2 48.8
						DECLINATION at NOON						
1 S	20 43 47.5	17S13.6	6S26.7	15S 9.3	21S18.6	12S22.4	21N16.5	18S58.2	22S28.3	17N11.3	12S 9.8	21N35.1
4 W	20 55 37.1	16 21.4	6 23.0	18 26.2	20 12.7	10 59.6	21 33.0	19 2.7	22 27.9	17 13.6	12 9.8	21 37.2
7 S	21 7 26.8	15 26.7	6 19.3	12 20.1	18 53.7	9 34.2	21 49.6	19 6.9	22 27.5	17 15.9	12 9.6	21 39.3
10 T	21 19 16.5	14 29.7	6 15.7	1 7.5	17 21.5	8 6.5	22 6.0	19 10.7	22 27.0	17 18.2	12 9.4	21 41.5
13 F	21 31 6.1	13 30.4	6 12.0	9N55.0	15 36.2	6 37.0	22 22.2	19 14.2	22 26.5	17 20.4	12 9.1	21 43.5
16 M	21 42 55.8	12 29.2	6 8.3	17 9.2	13 38.1	5 5.9	22 38.1	19 17.4	22 26.0	17 22.7	12 8.7	21 45.6
19 T	21 54 45.4	11 26.2	6 4.6	17 47.9	11 27.6	3 33.6	22 53.6	19 20.3	22 25.5	17 24.8	12 8.1	21 47.6
22 S	22 6 35.1	10 21.6	6 1.0	10 23.6	9 5.7	2 0.4	23 8.6	19 22.8	22 25.0	17 26.9	12 7.6	21 49.5
25 W	22 18 24.8	9 15.5	5 57.3	2S32.5	6 34.5	0 26.8	23 23.1	19 25.0	22 24.4	17 28.9	12 6.9	21 51.4
28 S	22 30 14.4	8 8.2	5 53.6	14 18.9	3 57.0	1N 7.1	23 37.0	19 26.9	22 23.9	17 30.9	12 6.1	21 53.2

MARCH 1959

LONGITUDE at NOON

DAY	EPHEMERIS SIDEREAL TIME h m s	☉ ° ′	☊ ° ′	☽ ° ′	☿ ° ′	♀ ° ′	♂ ° ′	♃ ° ′	♄ ° ′	♅ ° ′	♆ ° ′	♇ ° ′
1 S	22 34 11.0	10♓ 9.7	14♎54.3	2♐ 1.8	23♓ 6.1	6♈14.2	8♊47.5	1♐31.2	5♑22.3	13♌14.5	6♏49.5	2♍47.3
2 M	22 38 7.5	11 9.9	14 51.1	16 4.7	24 53.6	7 28.1	9 17.1	1 34.3	5 26.5	13R12.3	6R48.7	2R45.7
3 T	22 42 4.1	12 10.1	14 47.9	29 56.5	26 38.9	8 42.0	9 46.9	1 37.2	5 30.6	13 10.1	6 48.0	2 44.2
4 W	22 46 0.6	13 10.2	14 44.7	13♑36.5	28 21.6	9 55.8	10 16.8	1 40.0	5 34.6	13 7.9	6 47.2	2 42.7
5 T	22 49 57.2	14 10.3	14 41.5	27 4.1	0♈ 1.1	11 9.6	10 46.9	1 42.6	5 38.6	13 5.7	6 46.4	2 41.2
6 F	22 53 53.7	15 10.4	14 38.4	10♒18.9	1 36.9	12 23.3	11 17.2	1 45.0	5 42.5	13 3.6	6 45.5	2 39.7
7 S	22 57 50.3	16 10.5	14 35.2	23 20.5	3 8.5	13 37.0	11 47.6	1 47.2	5 46.3	13 1.5	6 44.6	2 38.3
8 S	23 1 46.8	17 10.5	14 32.0	6♓ 8.5	4 35.2	14 50.6	12 18.1	1 49.2	5 50.0	12 59.5	6 43.7	2 36.8
9 M	23 5 43.4	18 10.5	14 28.8	18 42.9	5 56.7	16 4.2	12 48.7	1 51.1	5 53.6	12 57.5	6 42.8	2 35.3
10 T	23 9 39.9	19 10.5	14 25.6	1♈ 4.3	7 12.3	17 17.8	13 19.5	1 52.8	5 57.2	12 55.5	6 41.8	2 33.9
11 W	23 13 36.5	20 10.5	14 22.5	13 14.0	8 21.4	18 31.3	13 50.4	1 54.2	6 0.6	12 53.5	6 40.8	2 32.4
12 T	23 17 33.1	21 10.4	14 19.3	25 13.7	9 23.8	19 44.7	14 21.4	1 55.5	6 4.0	12 51.6	6 39.8	2 31.0
13 F	23 21 29.6	22 10.2	14 16.1	7♉ 6.2	10 18.9	20 58.1	14 52.6	1 56.6	6 7.3	12 49.8	6 38.8	2 29.5
14 S	23 25 26.2	23 10.1	14 12.9	18 55.0	11 6.4	22 11.5	15 23.9	1 57.6	6 10.5	12 48.0	6 37.8	2 28.2
15 S	23 29 22.7	24 9.9	14 9.8	0♊43.9	11 45.9	23 24.8	15 55.3	1 58.3	6 13.7	12 46.2	6 36.7	2 26.8
16 M	23 33 19.3	25 9.7	14 6.6	12 37.4	12 17.3	24 38.0	16 26.8	1 58.9	6 16.7	12 44.5	6 35.6	2 25.4
17 T	23 37 15.8	26 9.4	14 3.4	24 40.4	12 40.3	25 51.2	16 58.4	1 59.2	6 19.6	12 42.8	6 34.4	2 24.0
18 W	23 41 12.4	27 9.1	14 0.2	6♋57.5	12 55.0	27 4.3	17 30.1	1 59.4	6 22.5	12 41.1	6 33.3	2 22.6
19 T	23 45 8.9	28 8.8	13 57.0	19 33.4	13 1.3	28 17.4	18 1.9	1R59.3	6 25.2	12 39.5	6 32.1	2 21.3
20 F	23 49 5.5	29 8.4	13 53.9	2♌31.6	12R59.5	29 30.4	18 33.8	1 59.1	6 27.9	12 37.9	6 30.9	2 19.9
21 S	23 53 2.0	0♈ 8.0	13 50.7	15 54.7	12 49.6	0♉43.3	19 5.8	1 58.7	6 30.4	12 36.4	6 29.7	2 18.6
22 S	23 56 58.6	1 7.5	13 47.5	29 43.5	12 32.3	1 56.2	19 37.9	1 58.2	6 32.9	12 34.9	6 28.4	2 17.3
23 M	0 0 55.1	2 7.0	13 44.3	13♍56.4	12 7.8	3 9.0	20 10.1	1 57.4	6 35.3	12 33.4	6 27.1	2 16.0
24 T	0 4 51.7	3 6.5	13 41.2	28 29.7	11 36.9	4 21.7	20 42.4	1 56.4	6 37.6	12 32.1	6 25.9	2 14.7
25 W	0 8 48.2	4 5.9	13 38.0	13♎17.2	11 0.3	5 34.4	21 14.8	1 55.3	6 39.8	12 30.7	6 24.5	2 13.5
26 T	0 12 44.8	5 5.3	13 34.8	28 11.8	10 18.8	6 47.0	21 47.2	1 54.0	6 41.9	12 29.4	6 23.2	2 12.2
27 F	0 16 41.3	6 4.7	13 31.6	13♏ 5.4	9 33.5	7 59.5	22 19.7	1 52.4	6 43.9	12 28.1	6 21.9	2 11.0
28 S	0 20 37.9	7 4.0	13 28.4	27 50.8	8 45.2	9 12.0	22 52.4	1 50.7	6 45.9	12 26.9	6 20.5	2 9.8
29 S	0 24 34.4	8 3.3	13 25.3	12♐22.3	7 55.0	10 24.4	23 25.1	1 48.9	6 47.7	12 25.8	6 19.1	2 8.6
30 M	0 28 31.0	9 2.6	13 22.1	26 35.9	7 4.0	11 36.7	23 57.8	1 46.8	6 49.4	12 24.7	6 17.7	2 7.4
31 T	0 32 27.5	10 1.9	13 18.9	10♑29.7	6 13.3	12 49.0	24 30.7	1 44.5	6 51.0	12 23.6	6 16.3	2 6.3

DECLINATION at NOON

DAY	SIDEREAL TIME	☉	☊	☽	☿	♀	♂	♃	♄	♅	♆	♇
1 S	22 34 11.0	7S45.5	5S52.4	16S44.1	3S 3.9	1N38.4	23N41.4	19S27.4	22S23.7	17N31.5	12S 5.8	21N53.8
4 W	22 46 0.6	6 36.8	5 48.7	17 33.4	0 25.9	3 12.0	23 54.3	19 28.9	22 23.2	17 33.4	12 4.9	21 55.5
7 S	22 57 50.3	5 27.3	5 45.0	9 57.5	2N 4.3	4 45.0	24 6.4	19 30.0	22 22.6	17 35.2	12 3.9	21 57.2
10 T	23 9 39.9	4 17.1	5 41.3	1N25.9	4 18.5	6 17.2	24 17.6	19 30.7	22 22.1	17 36.8	12 2.9	21 58.7
13 F	23 21 29.6	3 6.4	5 37.6	11 51.4	6 8.3	7 48.1	24 27.9	19 31.1	22 21.6	17 38.4	12 1.8	22 0.2
16 M	23 33 19.3	1 55.4	5 33.9	17 48.1	7 26.5	9 17.5	24 37.3	19 31.3	22 21.1	17 39.8	12 0.6	22 1.6
19 T	23 45 8.9	0 44.3	5 30.2	16 49.4	8 7.5	10 44.9	24 45.6	19 31.0	22 20.6	17 41.2	11 59.3	22 2.9
22 S	23 56 58.6	0N26.8	5 26.5	8 9.9	8 8.5	12 10.2	24 52.9	19 30.5	22 20.2	17 42.4	11 58.0	22 4.1
25 W	0 8 48.2	1 37.8	5 22.8	5S13.6	7 31.0	13 32.8	24 59.0	19 29.6	22 19.8	17 43.5	11 56.6	22 5.2
28 S	0 20 37.9	2 48.3	5 19.1	16 2.5	6 21.4	14 52.6	25 4.0	19 28.4	22 19.4	17 44.5	11 55.2	22 6.2
31 T	0 32 27.5	3 58.4	5 15.4	17 45.1	4 51.8	16 9.2	25 7.8	19 26.9	22 19.1	17 45.4	11 53.7	22 7.1

APRIL 1959

LONGITUDE at NOON

DAY	SIDEREAL TIME	☉	☊	☽	☿	♀	♂	♃	♄	♅	♆	♇
1 W	0 36 24.1	11♈ 1.1	13♎15.7	24♑ 3.4	5♈23.7	14♉ 1.2	25♊ 3.6	1♐42.1	6♑52.6	12♌22.6	6♏14.9	2♍ 5.2
2 T	0 40 20.6	12 0.3	13 12.5	7♒18.0	4R36.3	15 13.4	25 36.6	1R39.5	6 54.0	12R21.6	6R13.4	2R 4.0
3 F	0 44 17.2	12 59.4	13 9.4	20 15.1	3 51.8	16 25.4	26 9.7	1 36.7	6 55.3	12 20.7	6 12.0	2 3.0
4 S	0 48 13.7	13 58.6	13 6.2	2♓56.7	3 10.9	17 37.5	26 42.9	1 33.8	6 56.6	12 19.9	6 10.5	2 1.9
5 S	0 52 10.3	14 57.7	13 3.0	15 24.8	2 34.1	18 49.4	27 16.2	1 30.6	6 57.8	12 19.1	6 9.0	2 0.9
6 M	0 56 6.8	15 56.8	12 59.8	27 41.4	2 1.9	20 1.3	27 49.5	1 27.3	6 58.8	12 18.3	6 7.5	1 59.9
7 T	1 0 3.4	16 55.8	12 56.7	9♈48.5	1 34.8	21 13.1	28 22.9	1 23.8	6 59.8	12 17.6	6 6.0	1 58.9
8 W	1 3 60.0	17 54.8	12 53.5	21 47.8	1 12.8	22 24.8	28 56.3	1 20.2	7 0.6	12 17.0	6 4.5	1 57.9
9 T	1 7 56.5	18 53.8	12 50.3	3♉41.4	0 56.2	23 36.4	29 29.8	1 16.3	7 1.4	12 16.4	6 2.9	1 56.9
10 F	1 11 53.1	19 52.7	12 47.1	15 31.3	0 45.1	24 48.0	0♋ 3.4	1 12.3	7 2.0	12 15.8	6 1.4	1 56.0
11 S	1 15 49.6	20 51.6	12 43.9	27 19.8	0 39.3	25 59.4	0 37.1	1 8.1	7 2.6	12 15.3	5 59.8	1 55.1
12 S	1 19 46.2	21 50.5	12 40.8	9♊ 9.9	0 38.9	27 10.8	1 10.8	1 3.8	7 3.0	12 14.9	5 58.2	1 54.2
13 M	1 23 42.7	22 49.3	12 37.6	21 4.6	0D43.7	28 22.2	1 44.5	0 59.3	7 3.4	12 14.5	5 56.7	1 53.3
14 T	1 27 39.3	23 48.1	12 34.4	3♋ 7.7	0 53.7	29 33.4	2 18.4	0 54.7	7 3.6	12 14.2	5 55.1	1 52.5
15 W	1 31 35.8	24 46.9	12 31.2	15 23.2	1 8.6	0♊44.5	2 52.3	0 49.9	7 3.8	12 13.9	5 53.5	1 51.7
16 T	1 35 32.4	25 45.6	12 28.1	27 55.2	1 28.3	1 55.6	3 26.2	0 44.9	7 3.8	12 13.7	5 51.9	1 50.9
17 F	1 39 28.9	26 44.3	12 24.9	10♌47.8	1 52.6	3 6.5	4 0.2	0 39.8	7 3.8	12 13.5	5 50.3	1 50.1
18 S	1 43 25.5	27 42.9	12 21.7	24 4.4	2 21.2	4 17.4	4 34.3	0 34.6	7R 3.6	12 13.4	5 48.6	1 49.4
19 S	1 47 22.0	28 41.5	12 18.5	7♍47.3	2 54.1	5 28.1	5 8.4	0 29.2	7 3.4	12 13.3	5 47.0	1 48.7
20 M	1 51 18.6	29 40.1	12 15.3	21 57.2	3 31.0	6 38.8	5 42.5	0 23.7	7 3.1	12 13.3	5 45.4	1 48.0
21 T	1 55 15.1	0♉38.6	12 12.2	6♎32.1	4 11.7	7 49.4	6 16.7	0 18.1	7 2.6	12 13.3	5 43.8	1 47.4
22 W	1 59 11.7	1 37.1	12 9.0	21 27.4	4 56.1	8 59.8	6 51.0	0 12.3	7 2.1	12D13.4	5 42.1	1 46.7
23 T	2 3 8.2	2 35.6	12 5.8	6♏35.8	5 44.0	10 10.2	7 25.3	0 6.4	7 1.5	12 13.6	5 40.5	1 46.1
24 F	2 7 4.8	3 34.0	12 2.6	21 48.1	6 35.3	11 20.5	7 59.6	0 0.3	7 0.8	12 13.8	5 38.9	1 45.6
25 S	2 11 1.3	4 32.5	11 59.5	6♐54.5	7 29.8	12 30.7	8 34.0	29♏54.2	6 60.0	12 14.1	5 37.3	1 45.1
26 S	2 14 57.9	5 30.9	11 56.3	21 46.0	8 27.3	13 40.7	9 8.5	29 48.0	6 59.1	12 14.4	5 35.6	1 44.6
27 M	2 18 54.5	6 29.2	11 53.1	6♑15.8	9 27.7	14 50.7	9 42.9	29 41.6	6 58.1	12 14.8	5 34.0	1 44.1
28 T	2 22 51.0	7 27.5	11 49.9	20 20.3	10 31.0	16 0.5	10 17.5	29 35.1	6 57.0	12 15.2	5 32.4	1 43.6
29 W	2 26 47.6	8 25.8	11 46.7	3♒58.1	11 37.0	17 10.2	10 52.0	29 28.5	6 55.8	12 15.7	5 30.7	1 43.2
30 T	2 30 44.1	9 24.1	11 43.6	17 10.6	12 45.6	18 19.9	11 26.7	29 21.8	6 54.5	12 16.2	5 29.1	1 42.8

DECLINATION at NOON

DAY	SIDEREAL TIME	☉	☊	☽	☿	♀	♂	♃	♄	♅	♆	♇
1 W	0 36 24.1	4N21.6	5S14.2	16S10.6	4N20.0	16N34.0	25N 8.8	19S26.3	22S19.0	17N45.6	11S53.2	22N 7.3
4 S	0 48 13.7	5 30.8	5 10.5	7 13.9	2 46.0	17 45.8	25 11.0	19 24.4	22 18.7	17 46.3	11 51.7	22 8.1
7 T	1 0 3.4	6 39.2	5 6.8	4N10.0	1 23.4	18 53.7	25 11.8	19 22.1	22 18.5	17 46.8	11 50.2	22 8.7
10 F	1 11 53.1	7 46.5	5 3.0	13 46.1	0 20.1	19 57.3	25 11.4	19 19.6	22 18.3	17 47.3	11 48.6	22 9.2
13 M	1 23 42.7	8 52.6	4 59.3	18 14.9	0S20.4	20 56.4	25 9.7	19 16.8	22 18.2	17 47.5	11 47.0	22 9.6
16 T	1 35 32.4	9 57.4	4 55.6	15 34.4	0 37.6	21 50.6	25 6.7	19 13.7	22 18.1	17 47.7	11 45.4	22 9.9
19 S	1 47 22.0	11 0.6	4 51.9	5 48.9	0 32.7	22 39.7	25 2.3	19 10.3	22 18.1	17 47.7	11 43.8	22 10.1
22 W	1 59 11.7	12 2.3	4 48.2	7S39.1	0 7.5	23 23.5	24 56.6	19 6.7	22 18.1	17 47.6	11 42.1	22 10.1
25 S	2 11 1.3	13 2.2	4 44.5	17 16.4	0N35.7	24 1.7	24 49.4	19 2.8	22 18.1	17 47.3	11 40.5	22 10.0
28 T	2 22 51.0	14 0.1	4 40.7	16 45.2	1 35.0	24 34.1	24 41.0	18 58.7	22 18.3	17 46.9	11 38.9	22 9.9

MAY 1959

DAY	EPHEMERIS SIDEREAL TIME	☉	☊	☽	☿	♀	♂	♃	♄	♅	♆	♇
	h m s	° ′	° ′	° ′	° ′	° ′	° ′	° ′	° ′	° ′	° ′	° ′
						LONGITUDE at NOON						
1 F	2 34 40.7	10♉22.4	11♎40.4	0♓ 0.6	13♈56.7	19♊29.4	12♋ 1.3	29♏15.0	6♑53.1	12♌16.8	5♏27.5	1♍42.4
2 S	2 38 37.2	11 20.6	11 37.2	12 31.5	15 10.3	20 38.8	12 36.0	29R 8.2	6R51.6	12 17.4	5R25.8	1R42.0
3 S	2 42 33.8	12 18.8	11 34.0	24 47.3	16 26.3	21 48.1	13 10.8	29 1.2	6 50.0	12 18.1	5 24.2	1 41.7
4 M	2 46 30.3	13 17.0	11 30.9	6♈51.7	17 44.6	22 57.2	13 45.6	28 54.2	6 48.4	12 18.8	5 22.6	1 41.4
5 T	2 50 26.9	14 15.1	11 27.7	18 48.2	19 5.1	24 6.3	14 20.4	28 47.0	6 46.6	12 19.6	5 21.0	1 41.2
6 W	2 54 23.4	15 13.2	11 24.5	0♉39.7	20 27.9	25 15.2	14 55.3	28 39.8	6 44.8	12 20.5	5 19.4	1 40.9
7 T	2 58 20.0	16 11.3	11 21.3	12 28.8	21 52.8	26 24.0	15 30.2	28 32.6	6 42.9	12 21.4	5 17.7	1 40.7
8 F	3 2 16.5	17 9.4	11 18.1	24 17.5	23 19.9	27 32.7	16 5.2	28 25.2	6 40.8	12 22.3	5 16.1	1 40.6
9 S	3 6 13.1	18 7.5	11 15.0	6♊ 7.9	24 49.0	28 41.3	16 40.2	28 17.9	6 38.7	12 23.3	5 14.6	1 40.4
10 S	3 10 9.7	19 5.5	11 11.8	18 1.9	26 20.3	29 49.7	17 15.2	28 10.4	6 36.5	12 24.4	5 13.0	1 40.3
11 M	3 14 6.2	20 3.5	11 8.6	0♋ 1.4	27 53.7	0♋58.0	17 50.3	28 3.0	6 34.3	12 25.5	5 11.4	1 40.2
12 T	3 18 2.8	21 1.4	11 5.4	12 8.9	29 29.1	2 6.1	18 25.4	27 55.4	6 31.9	12 26.7	5 9.8	1 40.2
13 W	3 21 59.3	21 59.3	11 2.3	24 27.2	1♉ 6.6	3 14.1	19 0.6	27 47.9	6 29.5	12 27.9	5 8.3	1 40.1
14 T	3 25 55.9	22 57.2	10 59.1	6♌59.2	2 46.1	4 21.9	19 35.7	27 40.3	6 27.0	12 29.1	5 6.7	1D40.2
15 F	3 29 52.4	23 55.1	10 55.9	19 48.5	4 27.7	5 29.6	20 11.0	27 32.7	6 24.4	12 30.4	5 5.2	1 40.2
16 S	3 33 49.0	24 53.0	10 52.7	2♍58.5	6 11.4	6 37.2	20 46.3	27 25.1	6 21.7	12 31.8	5 3.7	1 40.3
17 S	3 37 45.5	25 50.8	10 49.5	16 32.1	7 57.1	7 44.6	21 21.6	27 17.5	6 19.0	12 33.3	5 2.2	1 40.4
18 M	3 41 42.1	26 48.6	10 46.4	0♎31.4	9 44.8	8 51.8	21 56.9	27 9.9	6 16.1	12 34.7	5 0.7	1 40.5
19 T	3 45 38.7	27 46.4	10 43.2	14 56.3	11 34.6	9 58.8	22 32.2	27 2.2	6 13.2	12 36.2	4 59.2	1 40.7
20 W	3 49 35.2	28 44.1	10 40.0	29 44.5	13 26.5	11 5.7	23 7.6	26 54.6	6 10.2	12 37.8	4 57.8	1 40.9
21 T	3 53 31.8	29 41.8	10 36.8	14♏50.4	15 20.4	12 12.4	23 43.0	26 47.0	6 7.2	12 39.4	4 56.3	1 41.1
22 F	3 57 28.3	0♊39.5	10 33.7	0♐ 5.5	17 16.3	13 18.9	24 18.5	26 39.3	6 4.1	12 41.0	4 54.9	1 41.3
23 S	4 1 24.9	1 37.1	10 30.5	15 19.6	19 14.2	14 25.2	24 54.0	26 31.7	6 0.9	12 42.7	4 53.4	1 41.6
24 S	4 5 21.4	2 34.8	10 27.3	0♑22.1	21 14.0	15 31.3	25 29.5	26 24.2	5 57.6	12 44.5	4 52.0	1 41.9
25 M	4 9 18.0	3 32.4	10 24.1	15 4.0	23 15.7	16 37.3	26 5.0	26 16.6	5 54.3	12 46.3	4 50.6	1 42.2
26 T	4 13 14.5	4 30.0	10 21.0	29 19.3	25 19.2	17 43.0	26 40.6	26 9.1	5 50.9	12 48.1	4 49.3	1 42.6
27 W	4 17 11.1	5 27.6	10 17.8	13♒ 5.1	27 24.4	18 48.6	27 16.2	26 1.6	5 47.5	12 50.0	4 47.9	1 43.0
28 T	4 21 7.7	6 25.1	10 14.6	26 22.0	29 31.2	19 53.9	27 51.8	25 54.2	5 44.0	12 51.9	4 46.6	1 43.4
29 F	4 25 4.2	7 22.7	10 11.4	9♓12.6	1♊39.3	20 59.0	28 27.5	25 46.8	5 40.4	12 53.9	4 45.2	1 43.8
30 S	4 29 0.8	8 20.2	10 8.2	21 41.2	3 48.7	22 4.0	29 3.2	25 39.5	5 36.8	12 55.9	4 43.9	1 44.3
31 S	4 32 57.3	9 17.8	10 5.1	3♈52.7	5 59.2	23 8.7	29 38.9	25 32.2	5 33.1	12 58.0	4 42.6	1 44.8
						DECLINATION at NOON						
1 F	2 34 40.7	14N56.0	4S37.0	8S 7.3	2N48.5	25N 0.6	24N31.1	18S54.4	22S18.4	17N46.3	11S37.3	22N 9.6
4 M	2 46 30.3	15 49.7	4 33.3	3N14.0	4 14.4	25 21.1	24 19.8	18 50.0	22 18.7	17 45.7	11 35.7	22 9.2
7 T	2 58 20.0	16 41.0	4 29.5	13 7.7	5 51.3	25 35.5	24 7.2	18 45.4	22 18.9	17 44.9	11 34.1	22 8.6
10 S	3 10 9.7	17 29.8	4 25.8	18 12.5	7 37.5	25 43.8	23 53.2	18 40.6	22 19.3	17 43.9	11 32.5	22 8.0
13 W	3 21 59.3	18 16.0	4 22.1	16 15.0	9 31.6	25 46.0	23 37.9	18 35.8	22 19.6	17 42.8	11 31.0	22 7.3
16 S	3 33 49.0	18 59.4	4 18.4	7 21.2	11 31.9	25 42.0	23 21.2	18 30.9	22 20.0	17 41.6	11 29.6	22 6.4
19 T	3 45 38.7	19 39.9	4 14.6	5S39.7	13 36.3	25 32.1	23 3.1	18 25.9	22 20.5	17 40.3	11 28.1	22 5.5
22 F	3 57 28.3	20 17.4	4 10.9	16 26.3	15 42.1	25 16.4	22 43.8	18 21.0	22 20.9	17 38.9	11 26.7	22 4.4
25 M	4 9 18.0	20 51.8	4 7.1	17 30.6	17 46.2	24 54.9	22 23.1	18 16.1	22 21.4	17 37.3	11 25.4	22 3.3
28 T	4 21 7.7	21 23.0	4 3.4	9 18.2	19 44.2	24 28.0	22 1.2	18 11.2	22 22.0	17 35.6	11 24.1	22 2.1
31 S	4 32 57.3	21 50.8	3 59.7	2N10.1	21 30.9	23 55.8	21 38.0	18 6.4	22 22.5	17 33.8	11 22.9	22 0.7

JUNE 1959

DAY	EPHEMERIS SIDEREAL TIME	☉	☊	☽	☿	♀	♂	♃	♄	♅	♆	♇
						LONGITUDE at NOON						
1 M	4 36 53.9	10♊15.3	10♎ 1.9	15♈51.8	8♊10.4	24♋13.2	0♌14.6	25♏25.0	5♑29.4	13♌ 0.1	4♏41.4	1♍45.4
2 T	4 40 50.4	11 12.8	9 58.7	27 43.4	10 22.2	25 17.4	0 50.4	25R17.8	5R25.6	13 2.3	4R40.1	1 45.9
3 W	4 44 47.0	12 10.3	9 55.5	9♉31.5	12 34.2	26 21.5	1 26.3	25 10.8	5 21.7	13 4.5	4 38.9	1 46.5
4 T	4 48 43.5	13 7.7	9 52.4	21 19.4	14 46.3	27 25.2	2 2.1	25 3.8	5 17.8	13 6.7	4 37.7	1 47.1
5 F	4 52 40.1	14 5.2	9 49.2	3♊ 9.9	16 58.2	28 28.8	2 38.0	24 56.8	5 13.9	13 9.0	4 36.5	1 47.8
6 S	4 56 36.7	15 2.7	9 46.0	15 5.2	19 9.5	29 32.1	3 14.0	24 50.1	5 10.0	13 11.4	4 35.4	1 48.5
7 S	5 0 33.2	16 0.1	9 42.8	27 6.5	21 20.1	0♌35.1	3 49.9	24 43.3	5 6.0	13 13.7	4 34.3	1 49.2
8 M	5 4 29.8	16 57.5	9 39.7	9♋15.3	23 29.5	1 37.9	4 25.9	24 36.7	5 1.9	13 16.1	4 33.2	1 50.0
9 T	5 8 26.3	17 54.9	9 36.5	21 32.8	25 37.8	2 40.4	5 1.9	24 30.2	4 57.8	13 18.6	4 32.1	1 50.7
10 W	5 12 22.9	18 52.3	9 33.3	4♌ 0.3	27 44.5	3 42.6	5 37.9	24 23.8	4 53.7	13 21.1	4 31.0	1 51.5
11 T	5 16 19.4	19 49.7	9 30.1	16 39.5	29 49.6	4 44.4	6 14.0	24 17.4	4 49.5	13 23.6	4 30.0	1 52.3
12 F	5 20 16.0	20 47.0	9 26.9	29 32.6	1♋52.9	5 46.0	6 50.1	24 11.2	4 45.3	13 26.1	4 28.9	1 53.2
13 S	5 24 12.6	21 44.4	9 23.8	12♍42.0	3 54.2	6 47.3	7 26.2	24 5.2	4 41.1	13 28.7	4 28.0	1 54.1
14 S	5 28 9.1	22 41.7	9 20.6	26 10.4	5 53.5	7 48.2	8 2.4	23 59.2	4 36.8	13 31.4	4 27.0	1 55.0
15 M	5 32 5.7	23 39.0	9 17.4	9♎59.9	7 50.7	8 48.8	8 38.5	23 53.4	4 32.5	13 34.1	4 26.0	1 55.9
16 T	5 36 2.2	24 36.3	9 14.2	24 11.6	9 45.7	9 49.1	9 14.7	23 47.7	4 28.2	13 36.8	4 25.1	1 56.8
17 W	5 39 58.8	25 33.6	9 11.1	8♏44.6	11 38.5	10 49.0	9 50.9	23 42.1	4 23.9	13 39.5	4 24.2	1 57.8
18 T	5 43 55.3	26 30.8	9 7.9	23 35.5	13 29.0	11 48.5	10 27.2	23 36.6	4 19.5	13 42.3	4 23.4	1 58.8
19 F	5 47 51.9	27 28.1	9 4.7	8♐38.0	15 17.1	12 47.6	11 3.5	23 31.3	4 15.2	13 45.1	4 22.5	1 59.9
20 S	5 51 48.5	28 25.3	9 1.5	23 43.2	17 3.0	13 46.3	11 39.8	23 26.2	4 10.8	13 47.9	4 21.7	2 0.9
21 S	5 55 45.0	29 22.5	8 58.4	8♑41.4	18 46.5	14 44.7	12 16.1	23 21.2	4 6.4	13 50.8	4 21.0	2 2.0
22 M	5 59 41.6	0♋19.7	8 55.2	23 23.0	20 27.6	15 42.6	12 52.4	23 16.3	4 2.0	13 53.7	4 20.2	2 3.1
23 T	6 3 38.1	1 17.0	8 52.0	7♒40.8	22 6.4	16 40.0	13 28.8	23 11.6	3 57.6	13 56.7	4 19.5	2 4.2
24 W	6 7 34.7	2 14.2	8 48.8	21 30.7	23 42.8	17 37.1	14 5.2	23 7.0	3 53.2	13 59.6	4 18.8	2 5.4
25 T	6 11 31.2	3 11.4	8 45.6	4♓51.7	25 16.8	18 33.6	14 41.7	23 2.6	3 48.8	14 2.6	4 18.1	2 6.6
26 F	6 15 27.8	4 8.6	8 42.5	17 45.7	26 48.4	19 29.7	15 18.1	22 58.3	3 44.3	14 5.7	4 17.5	2 7.8
27 S	6 19 24.4	5 5.9	8 39.3	0♈16.4	28 17.6	20 25.4	15 54.7	22 54.2	3 40.0	14 8.8	4 16.9	2 9.0
28 S	6 23 20.9	6 3.1	8 36.1	12 28.6	29 44.4	21 20.5	16 31.2	22 50.3	3 35.5	14 11.9	4 16.3	2 10.3
29 M	6 27 17.5	7 0.3	8 32.9	24 27.7	1♌ 8.7	22 15.1	17 7.7	22 46.5	3 31.1	14 15.0	4 15.8	2 11.6
30 T	6 31 14.0	7 57.5	8 29.8	6♉19.0	2 30.5	23 9.1	17 44.3	22 42.9	3 26.7	14 18.1	4 15.3	2 12.9
						DECLINATION at NOON						
1 M	4 36 53.9	21N59.3	3S58.4	5N53.1	22N 3.1	23N43.9	21N30.0	18S 4.9	22S22.7	17N33.2	11S22.5	22N 0.3
4 T	4 48 43.5	22 22.6	3 54.7	14 56.4	23 26.6	23 5.2	21 5.1	18 0.3	22 23.3	17 31.2	11 21.4	21 58.8
7 S	5 0 33.2	22 42.3	3 50.9	18 30.6	24 27.5	22 21.8	20 39.0	17 55.9	22 23.9	17 29.1	11 20.4	21 57.3
10 W	5 12 22.9	22 58.5	3 47.2	14 45.5	25 3.6	21 34.2	20 11.8	17 51.6	22 24.5	17 27.0	11 19.4	21 55.7
13 S	5 24 12.6	23 11.0	3 43.4	4 38.3	25 15.0	20 42.6	19 43.3	17 47.6	22 25.1	17 24.7	11 18.5	21 54.0
16 T	5 36 2.2	23 19.9	3 39.7	8S14.0	25 3.7	19 47.5	19 13.8	17 43.9	22 25.7	17 22.3	11 17.7	21 52.3
19 F	5 47 51.9	23 25.0	3 35.9	17 29.5	24 32.6	18 49.1	18 43.1	17 40.5	22 26.4	17 19.9	11 16.9	21 50.4
22 M	5 59 41.6	23 26.5	3 32.2	16 36.9	23 45.1	17 47.9	18 11.4	17 37.4	22 27.0	17 17.3	11 16.3	21 48.6
25 T	6 11 31.2	23 24.2	3 28.4	7 5.6	22 44.6	16 44.2	17 38.7	17 34.6	22 27.6	17 14.7	11 15.7	21 46.6
28 S	6 23 20.9	23 18.2	3 24.7	4N38.4	21 34.2	15 38.4	17 4.9	17 32.2	22 28.2	17 12.0	11 15.3	21 44.6

JULY 1959

DAY	EPHEMERIS SIDEREAL TIME	☉	☊	☽	☿	♀	♂	♃	♄	♅	♆	♇
	h m s	° ′	° ′	° ′	° ′	° ′	° ′	° ′	° ′	° ′	° ′	° ′
LONGITUDE at NOON												
1 W	6 35 10.6	8♋54.7	8♎26.6	18♉ 7.3	3♌49.7	24♌ 2.6	18♌20.9	22♏39.5	3♑22.3	14♌21.3	4♏14.8	2♍14.2
2 T	6 39 7.1	9 51.9	8 23.4	29 57.1	5 6.4	24 55.5	18 57.6	22R36.2	3R17.9	14 24.5	4R14.3	2 15.5
3 F	6 43 3.7	10 49.1	8 20.2	11♊51.6	6 20.5	25 47.9	19 34.2	22 33.1	3 13.6	14 27.8	4 13.9	2 16.9
4 S	6 47 0.3	11 46.4	8 17.1	23 53.7	7 31.8	26 39.6	20 10.9	22 30.1	3 9.2	14 31.0	4 13.5	2 18.3
5 S	6 50 56.8	12 43.6	8 13.9	6♋ 4.9	8 40.4	27 30.7	20 47.7	22 27.4	3 4.9	14 34.3	4 13.1	2 19.7
6 M	6 54 53.4	13 40.8	8 10.7	18 26.4	9 46.2	28 21.1	21 24.4	22 24.8	3 0.6	14 37.6	4 12.8	2 21.1
7 T	6 58 49.9	14 38.0	8 7.5	0♌58.7	10 49.1	29 10.8	22 1.2	22 22.4	2 56.3	14 40.9	4 12.5	2 22.6
8 W	7 2 46.5	15 35.2	8 4.4	13 41.8	11 48.9	29 59.8	22 38.0	22 20.1	2 52.0	14 44.3	4 12.2	2 24.0
9 T	7 6 43.0	16 32.5	8 1.2	26 36.1	12 45.7	0♍48.1	23 14.9	22 18.1	2 47.8	14 47.6	4 11.9	2 25.5
10 F	7 10 39.6	17 29.7	7 58.0	9♍42.0	13 39.2	1 35.6	23 51.7	22 16.2	2 43.5	14 51.0	4 11.7	2 27.0
11 S	7 14 36.2	18 26.9	7 54.8	23 0.5	14 29.4	2 22.3	24 28.6	22 14.5	2 39.4	14 54.4	4 11.6	2 28.6
12 S	7 18 32.7	19 24.1	7 51.6	6♎32.7	15 16.1	3 8.2	25 5.5	22 13.0	2 35.2	14 57.9	4 11.4	2 30.1
13 M	7 22 29.3	20 21.3	7 48.5	20 20.0	15 59.2	3 53.2	25 42.5	22 11.6	2 31.1	15 1.3	4 11.3	2 31.7
14 T	7 26 25.8	21 18.6	7 45.3	4♏23.0	16 38.6	4 37.3	26 19.5	22 10.5	2 27.0	15 4.8	4 11.2	2 33.3
15 W	7 30 22.4	22 15.8	7 42.1	18 41.5	17 14.1	5 20.5	26 56.5	22 9.5	2 23.0	15 8.3	4 11.2	2 34.9
16 T	7 34 18.9	23 13.0	7 38.9	3♐13.3	17 45.6	6 2.6	27 33.5	22 8.7	2 19.0	15 11.8	4 11.1	2 36.5
17 F	7 38 15.5	24 10.2	7 35.8	17 54.3	18 12.9	6 43.8	28 10.6	22 8.1	2 15.1	15 15.3	4 11.1	2 38.1
18 S	7 42 12.0	25 7.5	7 32.6	2♑38.2	18 36.0	7 24.0	28 47.7	22 7.8	2 11.2	15 18.9	4D11.2	2 39.8
19 S	7 46 8.6	26 4.7	7 29.4	17 17.5	18 54.5	8 3.0	29 24.8	22 7.5	2 7.4	15 22.5	4 11.3	2 41.5
20 M	7 50 5.2	27 1.9	7 26.2	1♒44.4	19 8.3	8 40.9	0♍ 1.9	22 7.5	2 3.6	15 26.0	4 11.4	2 43.2
21 T	7 54 1.7	27 59.2	7 23.0	15 52.3	19 17.5	9 17.6	0 39.1	22D 7.6	1 59.8	15 29.6	4 11.6	2 44.9
22 W	7 57 58.3	28 56.4	7 19.9	29 36.7	19 21.8	9 53.1	1 16.3	22 7.9	1 56.1	15 33.2	4 11.7	2 46.6
23 T	8 1 54.8	29 53.7	7 16.7	12♓55.8	19R21.1	10 27.3	1 53.5	22 8.4	1 52.5	15 36.8	4 11.9	2 48.4
24 F	8 5 51.4	0♌51.0	7 13.5	25 50.2	19 15.5	11 0.2	2 30.8	22 9.0	1 48.9	15 40.4	4 12.2	2 50.1
25 S	8 9 47.9	1 48.3	7 10.3	8♈22.4	19 4.9	11 31.7	3 8.1	22 9.9	1 45.4	15 44.1	4 12.4	2 51.9
26 S	8 13 44.5	2 45.6	7 7.2	20 36.6	18 49.4	12 1.9	3 45.4	22 10.9	1 41.9	15 47.7	4 12.7	2 53.7
27 M	8 17 41.0	3 42.9	7 4.0	2♉37.5	18 29.0	12 30.6	4 22.7	22 12.1	1 38.5	15 51.4	4 13.1	2 55.4
28 T	8 21 37.6	4 40.2	7 0.8	14 30.5	18 4.0	12 57.7	5 0.1	22 13.5	1 35.2	15 55.0	4 13.4	2 57.3
29 W	8 25 34.2	5 37.6	6 57.6	26 20.8	17 34.5	13 23.3	5 37.5	22 15.1	1 31.9	15 58.7	4 13.8	2 59.1
30 T	8 29 30.7	6 35.0	6 54.5	8♊13.2	17 0.9	13 47.3	6 15.0	22 16.8	1 28.7	16 2.4	4 14.3	3 0.9
31 F	8 33 27.3	7 32.4	6 51.3	20 11.9	16 23.7	14 9.6	6 52.4	22 18.7	1 25.5	16 6.1	4 14.7	3 2.7
DECLINATION at NOON												
1 W	6 35 10.6	23N 8.5	3S20.9	14N 9.7	20N16.9	14N30.8	16N30.1	17S30.1	22S28.8	17N 9.2	11S14.9	21N42.6
4 S	6 47 0.3	22 55.2	3 17.2	18 27.5	18 55.5	13 22.0	15 54.4	17 28.4	22 29.4	17 6.3	11 14.6	21 40.5
7 T	6 58 49.9	22 38.3	3 13.4	15 26.9	17 32.7	12 12.2	15 17.8	17 27.2	22 30.0	17 3.4	11 14.5	21 38.3
10 F	7 10 39.6	22 17.8	3 9.6	5 46.0	16 11.0	11 2.0	14 40.3	17 26.3	22 30.6	17 0.4	11 14.4	21 36.2
13 M	7 22 29.3	21 53.9	3 5.9	6S52.9	14 53.2	9 51.7	14 1.9	17 25.9	22 31.2	16 57.3	11 14.4	21 34.0
16 T	7 34 18.9	21 26.7	3 2.1	16 41.4	13 42.3	8 42.0	13 22.8	17 25.8	22 31.8	16 54.2	11 14.5	21 31.8
19 S	7 46 8.6	20 56.1	2 58.3	17 24.8	12 41.4	7 33.2	12 42.8	17 26.2	22 32.3	16 51.1	11 14.7	21 29.5
22 W	7 57 58.3	20 22.4	2 54.6	8 46.6	11 53.8	6 26.0	12 2.1	17 27.1	22 32.9	16 47.9	11 15.0	21 27.2
25 S	8 9 47.9	19 45.6	2 50.8	3N 8.2	11 22.8	5 21.0	11 20.8	17 28.3	22 33.4	16 44.6	11 15.4	21 25.0
28 T	8 21 37.6	19 5.8	2 47.0	13 9.8	11 11.1	4 18.9	10 38.7	17 29.9	22 33.9	16 41.3	11 15.9	21 22.7
31 F	8 33 27.3	18 23.2	2 43.3	18 11.8	11 20.2	3 20.3	9 56.0	17 32.0	22 34.4	16 38.0	11 16.5	21 20.4

AUGUST 1959

DAY	EPHEMERIS SIDEREAL TIME	☉	☊	☽	☿	♀	♂	♃	♄	♅	♆	♇
LONGITUDE at NOON												
1 S	8 37 23.8	8♌29.8	6♎48.1	2♋20.4	15♌43.3	14♍30.1	7♍29.9	22♏20.8	1♑22.4	16♌ 9.8	4♏15.2	3♍ 4.6
2 S	8 41 20.4	9 27.2	6 44.9	14 41.3	15R 0.3	14 48.9	8 7.5	22 23.1	1R19.4	16 13.5	4 15.7	3 6.5
3 M	8 45 16.9	10 24.6	6 41.7	27 15.9	14 15.4	15 5.8	8 45.1	22 25.6	1 16.5	16 17.2	4 16.3	3 8.4
4 T	8 49 13.5	11 22.1	6 38.6	10♌ 4.7	13 29.4	15 20.8	9 22.7	22 28.2	1 13.6	16 20.9	4 16.9	3 10.2
5 W	8 53 10.0	12 19.6	6 35.4	23 7.2	12 43.1	15 33.7	10 0.3	22 31.0	1 10.9	16 24.6	4 17.5	3 12.1
6 T	8 57 6.6	13 17.1	6 32.2	6♍22.6	11 57.3	15 44.7	10 38.0	22 34.0	1 8.1	16 28.3	4 18.1	3 14.0
7 F	9 1 3.2	14 14.6	6 29.0	19 49.6	11 12.8	15 53.5	11 15.7	22 37.1	1 5.5	16 32.0	4 18.8	3 16.0
8 S	9 4 59.7	15 12.1	6 25.9	3♎27.1	10 30.7	16 0.3	11 53.4	22 40.5	1 3.0	16 35.8	4 19.6	3 17.9
9 S	9 8 56.3	16 9.7	6 22.7	17 14.1	9 51.6	16 4.8	12 31.2	22 44.0	1 0.6	16 39.5	4 20.3	3 19.9
10 M	9 12 52.8	17 7.2	6 19.5	1♏ 9.9	9 16.4	16 7.0	13 9.0	22 47.7	0 58.2	16 43.3	4 21.1	3 21.8
11 T	9 16 49.4	18 4.8	6 16.3	15 14.0	8 45.8	16R 6.9	13 46.8	22 51.5	0 55.9	16 47.0	4 21.9	3 23.8
12 W	9 20 45.9	19 2.3	6 13.1	29 25.2	8 20.5	16 4.5	14 24.7	22 55.5	0 53.6	16 50.7	4 22.8	3 25.7
13 T	9 24 42.5	19 59.9	6 10.0	13♐41.9	8 1.0	15 59.7	15 2.5	22 59.7	0 51.5	16 54.4	4 23.6	3 27.7
14 F	9 28 39.0	20 57.5	6 6.8	28 1.2	7 47.8	15 52.5	15 40.5	23 4.0	0 49.5	16 58.1	4 24.5	3 29.7
15 S	9 32 35.6	21 55.1	6 3.6	12♑19.5	7 41.4	15 42.9	16 18.4	23 8.5	0 47.5	17 1.9	4 25.5	3 31.6
16 S	9 36 32.1	22 52.8	6 0.4	26 32.0	7D42.0	15 30.9	16 56.4	23 13.1	0 45.6	17 5.6	4 26.4	3 33.6
17 M	9 40 28.7	23 50.4	5 57.3	10♒33.9	7 49.9	15 16.6	17 34.4	23 17.9	0 43.8	17 9.3	4 27.4	3 35.6
18 T	9 44 25.2	24 48.1	5 54.1	24 20.8	8 5.1	14 59.8	18 12.4	23 22.9	0 42.1	17 13.0	4 28.4	3 37.6
19 W	9 48 21.8	25 45.8	5 50.9	7♓49.4	8 27.9	14 40.8	18 50.5	23 28.0	0 40.5	17 16.7	4 29.5	3 39.6
20 T	9 52 18.4	26 43.5	5 47.7	20 58.0	8 58.1	14 19.5	19 28.6	23 33.3	0 39.0	17 20.4	4 30.5	3 41.6
21 F	9 56 14.9	27 41.3	5 44.5	3♈46.3	9 35.8	13 56.1	20 6.7	23 38.7	0 37.6	17 24.0	4 31.6	3 43.6
22 S	10 0 11.5	28 39.0	5 41.4	16 16.0	10 20.7	13 30.6	20 44.9	23 44.3	0 36.2	17 27.7	4 32.8	3 45.6
23 S	10 4 8.0	29 36.8	5 38.2	28 29.8	11 12.9	13 3.1	21 23.1	23 50.0	0 35.0	17 31.4	4 33.9	3 47.6
24 M	10 8 4.6	0♍34.7	5 35.0	10♉31.6	12 11.9	12 33.8	22 1.4	23 55.9	0 33.8	17 35.0	4 35.1	3 49.6
25 T	10 12 1.1	1 32.5	5 31.8	22 25.9	13 17.5	12 2.9	22 39.6	24 1.9	0 32.8	17 38.7	4 36.3	3 51.7
26 W	10 15 57.7	2 30.4	5 28.7	4♊17.5	14 29.6	11 30.5	23 17.9	24 8.1	0 31.8	17 42.3	4 37.6	3 53.7
27 T	10 19 54.2	3 28.3	5 25.5	16 11.3	15 47.5	10 56.7	23 56.3	24 14.4	0 30.9	17 46.0	4 38.9	3 55.7
28 F	10 23 50.8	4 26.3	5 22.3	28 12.0	17 11.1	10 21.9	24 34.7	24 20.9	0 30.2	17 49.6	4 40.2	3 57.7
29 S	10 27 47.3	5 24.3	5 19.1	10♋24.0	18 39.9	9 46.2	25 13.2	24 27.6	0 29.5	17 53.2	4 41.5	3 59.8
30 S	10 31 43.9	6 22.3	5 15.9	22 50.6	20 13.3	9 9.7	25 51.6	24 34.3	0 28.9	17 56.8	4 42.9	4 1.8
31 M	10 35 40.4	7 20.3	5 12.8	5♌34.4	21 50.9	8 32.8	26 30.1	24 41.2	0 28.5	18 0.4	4 44.3	4 3.8
DECLINATION at NOON												
1 S	8 37 23.8	18N 8.4	2S42.0	18N20.9	11N27.8	3N 1.7	9N41.6	17S32.7	22S34.6	16N36.9	11S16.7	21N19.6
4 T	8 49 13.5	17 22.2	2 38.3	13 41.2	12 3.2	2 9.2	8 58.2	17 35.3	22 35.1	16 33.6	11 17.4	21 17.3
7 F	9 1 3.2	16 33.5	2 34.5	2 47.5	12 53.5	1 22.3	8 14.1	17 38.3	22 35.6	16 30.3	11 18.3	21 15.0
10 M	9 12 52.8	15 42.4	2 30.7	9S44.8	13 52.0	0 42.3	7 29.5	17 41.6	22 36.1	16 26.9	11 19.2	21 12.8
13 T	9 24 42.5	14 49.0	2 26.9	17 40.8	14 51.2	0 10.1	6 44.5	17 45.3	22 36.6	16 23.5	11 20.2	21 10.5
16 S	9 36 32.1	13 53.5	2 23.2	16 9.0	15 43.5	0S13.1	5 59.0	17 49.4	22 37.0	16 20.2	11 21.3	21 8.3
19 W	9 48 21.8	12 56.0	2 19.4	6 28.8	16 22.4	0 26.4	5 13.1	17 53.7	22 37.5	16 16.8	11 22.4	21 6.1
22 S	10 0 11.5	11 56.7	2 15.6	5N24.4	16 42.4	0 29.0	4 26.9	17 58.4	22 38.0	16 13.5	11 23.7	21 3.9
25 T	10 12 1.1	10 55.6	2 11.8	14 37.6	16 39.1	0 20.7	3 40.3	18 3.4	22 38.5	16 10.2	11 25.0	21 1.8
28 F	10 23 50.8	9 53.0	2 8.1	18 14.6	16 9.4	0 2.0	2 53.5	18 8.7	22 38.9	16 6.9	11 26.4	20 59.7
31 M	10 35 40.4	8 49.0	2 4.3	14 33.0	15 12.5	0N26.2	2 6.3	18 14.2	22 39.4	16 3.6	11 27.9	20 57.6

SEPTEMBER 1959

LONGITUDE at NOON

DAY	EPHEMERIS SIDEREAL TIME	☉	☊	☽	☿	♀	♂	♃	♄	♅	♆	♇
	h m s	° ′	° ′	° ′	° ′	° ′	° ′	° ′	° ′	° ′	° ′	° ′
1 T	10 39 37.0	8♍18.4	5♎ 9.6	18♌36.6	23♌32.2	7♍55.7	27♍ 8.7	24♏48.3	0♑28.1	18♌ 3.9	4♏45.7	4♍ 5.8
2 W	10 43 33.5	9 16.5	5 6.4	1♍57.1	25 16.8	7R18.7	27 47.2	24 55.4	0R27.8	18 7.5	4 47.1	4 7.8
3 T	10 47 30.1	10 14.6	5 3.2	15 34.7	27 4.1	6 41.8	28 25.8	25 2.7	0 27.6	18 11.0	4 48.6	4 9.8
4 F	10 51 26.6	11 12.8	5 0.1	29 26.8	28 53.7	6 5.5	29 4.5	25 10.2	0 27.5	18 14.5	4 50.0	4 11.8
5 S	10 55 23.2	12 10.9	4 56.9	13♎30.3	0♍45.2	5 29.9	29 43.2	25 17.8	0 27.5	18 18.0	4 51.5	4 13.8
6 S	10 59 19.7	13 9.1	4 53.7	27 41.5	2 38.1	4 55.2	0♎21.9	25 25.5	0D27.6	18 21.5	4 53.1	4 15.8
7 M	11 3 16.3	14 7.4	4 50.5	11♏57.0	4 32.0	4 21.6	1 0.6	25 33.3	0 27.8	18 24.9	4 54.6	4 17.8
8 T	11 7 12.9	15 5.6	4 47.3	26 13.7	6 26.6	3 49.4	1 39.4	25 41.3	0 28.1	18 28.4	4 56.2	4 19.8
9 W	11 11 9.4	16 3.9	4 44.2	10♐28.6	8 21.7	3 18.8	2 18.3	25 49.4	0 28.5	18 31.8	4 57.8	4 21.8
10 T	11 15 6.0	17 2.2	4 41.0	24 39.5	10 16.8	2 49.8	2 57.1	25 57.6	0 29.0	18 35.2	4 59.4	4 23.8
11 F	11 19 2.5	18 0.5	4 37.8	8♑44.1	12 11.9	2 22.6	3 36.0	26 5.9	0 29.5	18 38.5	5 1.1	4 25.8
12 S	11 22 59.1	18 58.9	4 34.6	22 40.4	14 6.7	1 57.5	4 14.9	26 14.4	0 30.2	18 41.9	5 2.8	4 27.7
13 S	11 26 55.6	19 57.3	4 31.5	6♒26.7	16 1.1	1 34.4	4 53.9	26 23.0	0 31.0	18 45.2	5 4.4	4 29.7
14 M	11 30 52.2	20 55.7	4 28.3	20 1.0	17 54.9	1 13.5	5 32.9	26 31.7	0 31.9	18 48.5	5 6.2	4 31.6
15 T	11 34 48.7	21 54.1	4 25.1	3♓21.9	19 48.0	0 54.9	6 12.0	26 40.5	0 32.9	18 51.8	5 7.9	4 33.6
16 W	11 38 45.3	22 52.6	4 21.9	16 28.2	21 40.3	0 38.7	6 51.0	26 49.4	0 34.0	18 55.0	5 9.6	4 35.5
17 T	11 42 41.8	23 51.1	4 18.7	29 19.4	23 31.8	0 24.8	7 30.1	26 58.5	0 35.1	18 58.3	5 11.4	4 37.4
18 F	11 46 38.4	24 49.6	4 15.6	11♈55.5	25 22.4	0 13.3	8 9.3	27 7.6	0 36.4	19 1.5	5 13.2	4 39.4
19 S	11 50 34.9	25 48.2	4 12.4	24 17.7	27 12.1	0 4.4	8 48.5	27 17.0	0 37.8	19 4.7	5 15.1	4 41.3
20 S	11 54 31.5	26 46.8	4 9.2	6♉27.5	29 0.9	29♌57.8	9 27.8	27 26.3	0 39.3	19 7.8	5 16.9	4 43.2
21 M	11 58 28.0	27 45.5	4 6.0	18 27.7	0♎48.6	29 53.7	10 7.0	27 35.8	0 40.8	19 10.9	5 18.8	4 45.1
22 T	12 2 24.6	28 44.1	4 2.8	0♊21.5	2 35.4	29 52.0	10 46.4	27 45.4	0 42.5	19 14.0	5 20.6	4 47.0
23 W	12 6 21.1	29 42.8	3 59.7	12 13.0	4 21.2	29D52.6	11 25.7	27 55.1	0 44.2	19 17.1	5 22.5	4 48.9
24 T	12 10 17.7	0♎41.6	3 56.5	24 6.3	6 6.0	29 55.6	12 5.1	28 4.9	0 46.1	19 20.1	5 24.4	4 50.7
25 F	12 14 14.2	1 40.3	3 53.3	6♋ 6.2	7 49.9	0♍ 1.0	12 44.5	28 14.8	0 48.0	19 23.1	5 26.4	4 52.6
26 S	12 18 10.8	2 39.2	3 50.1	18 17.2	9 32.8	0 8.6	13 24.0	28 24.8	0 50.0	19 26.0	5 28.3	4 54.4
27 S	12 22 7.3	3 38.0	3 47.0	0♌43.7	11 14.8	0 18.4	14 3.5	28 34.9	0 52.2	19 29.0	5 30.3	4 56.2
28 M	12 26 3.9	4 36.9	3 43.8	13 29.3	12 55.9	0 30.3	14 43.1	28 45.1	0 54.4	19 31.9	5 32.2	4 58.0
29 T	12 30 0.4	5 35.8	3 40.6	26 36.9	14 36.0	0 44.4	15 22.7	28 55.4	0 56.7	19 34.7	5 34.2	4 59.8
30 W	12 33 57.0	6 34.8	3 37.4	10♍ 7.8	16 15.3	1 0.5	16 2.4	29 5.8	0 59.1	19 37.6	5 36.2	5 1.6

DECLINATION at NOON

DAY	EPHEMERIS SIDEREAL TIME	☉	☊	☽	☿	♀	♂	♃	♄	♅	♆	♇
1 T	10 39 37.0	8N27.3	2S 3.0	11N41.7	14N47.7	0N37.4	1N50.6	18S 16.1	22S 39.5	16N 2.5	11S 28.5	20N 57.0
4 F	10 51 26.6	7 21.7	1 59.2	0S 10.0	13 17.6	1 15.5	1 3.2	18 22.0	22 40.0	15 59.3	11 30.0	20 55.0
7 M	11 3 16.3	6 14.9	1 55.5	12 20.5	11 27.6	1 58.4	0 15.6	18 28.1	22 40.5	15 56.1	11 31.7	20 53.1
10 T	11 15 6.0	5 7.2	1 51.7	18 8.7	9 22.8	2 43.6	0S 32.0	18 34.4	22 40.9	15 53.0	11 33.4	20 51.2
13 S	11 26 55.6	3 58.7	1 47.9	14 21.1	7 8.3	3 28.8	1 19.7	18 40.9	22 41.4	15 50.0	11 35.2	20 49.4
16 W	11 38 45.3	2 49.7	1 44.1	3 52.5	4 48.2	4 11.9	2 7.5	18 47.5	22 41.8	15 47.0	11 37.0	20 47.7
19 S	11 50 34.9	1 40.1	1 40.3	7N42.5	2 25.9	4 51.1	2 55.2	18 54.4	22 42.2	15 44.0	11 38.9	20 46.0
22 T	12 2 24.6	0 30.2	1 36.5	15 55.0	0 3.6	5 25.2	3 42.9	19 1.3	22 42.7	15 41.2	11 40.9	20 44.4
25 F	12 14 14.2	0S 39.9	1 32.8	18 1.2	2S 16.9	5 53.4	4 30.4	19 8.4	22 43.1	15 38.4	11 42.8	20 42.9
28 M	12 26 3.9	1 50.1	1 29.0	12 51.3	4 34.4	6 15.1	5 17.8	19 15.5	22 43.5	15 35.8	11 44.9	20 41.5

OCTOBER 1959

LONGITUDE at NOON

DAY	EPHEMERIS SIDEREAL TIME	☉	☊	☽	☿	♀	♂	♃	♄	♅	♆	♇
1 T	12 37 53.5	7♎33.8	3♎34.2	24♍ 1.3	17♎53.7	1♍18.5	16♎42.0	29♏16.3	1♑ 1.6	19♌40.4	5♏38.3	5♍ 3.4
2 F	12 41 50.1	8 32.9	3 31.1	8♎15.0	19 31.2	1 38.5	17 21.8	29 26.8	1 4.2	19 43.1	5 40.3	5 5.1
3 S	12 45 46.6	9 31.9	3 27.9	22 44.5	21 7.9	2 0.3	18 1.6	29 37.5	1 6.9	19 45.8	5 42.3	5 6.9
4 S	12 49 43.2	10 31.0	3 24.7	7♏23.9	22 43.7	2 23.9	18 41.4	29 48.3	1 9.6	19 48.5	5 44.4	5 8.6
5 M	12 53 39.7	11 30.2	3 21.5	22 6.3	24 18.8	2 49.2	19 21.2	29 59.1	1 12.5	19 51.2	5 46.5	5 10.3
6 T	12 57 36.3	12 29.3	3 18.4	6♐45.4	25 53.0	3 16.2	20 1.1	0♐10.1	1 15.4	19 53.8	5 48.6	5 12.0
7 W	13 1 32.9	13 28.5	3 15.2	21 15.3	27 26.5	3 44.8	20 41.0	0 21.1	1 18.5	19 56.3	5 50.7	5 13.6
8 T	13 5 29.4	14 27.8	3 12.0	5♑32.0	28 59.2	4 15.0	21 21.0	0 32.2	1 21.6	19 58.9	5 52.8	5 15.3
9 F	13 9 26.0	15 27.0	3 8.8	19 33.0	0♏31.1	4 46.6	22 1.0	0 43.3	1 24.8	20 1.4	5 54.9	5 16.9
10 S	13 13 22.5	16 26.4	3 5.6	3♒17.2	2 2.3	5 19.7	22 41.1	0 54.6	1 28.2	20 3.9	5 57.1	5 18.6
11 S	13 17 19.1	17 25.7	3 2.5	16 44.8	3 32.7	5 54.2	23 21.2	1 6.0	1 31.5	20 6.3	5 59.2	5 20.2
12 M	13 21 15.6	18 25.0	2 59.3	29 56.5	5 2.3	6 30.1	24 1.4	1 17.4	1 35.0	20 8.6	6 1.4	5 21.7
13 T	13 25 12.2	19 24.4	2 56.1	12♓53.6	6 31.2	7 7.2	24 41.5	1 28.9	1 38.6	20 10.9	6 3.5	5 23.3
14 W	13 29 8.7	20 23.8	2 52.9	25 37.5	7 59.4	7 45.6	25 21.8	1 40.4	1 42.2	20 13.2	6 5.7	5 24.8
15 T	13 33 5.3	21 23.2	2 49.8	8♈ 9.2	9 26.7	8 25.2	26 2.0	1 52.1	1 45.9	20 15.5	6 7.9	5 26.3
16 F	13 37 1.8	22 22.7	2 46.6	20 30.2	10 53.3	9 6.0	26 42.3	2 3.8	1 49.7	20 17.6	6 10.1	5 27.8
17 S	13 40 58.4	23 22.2	2 43.4	2♉41.6	12 19.1	9 47.9	27 22.7	2 15.5	1 53.6	20 19.8	6 12.3	5 29.3
18 S	13 44 54.9	24 21.7	2 40.2	14 44.8	13 44.1	10 30.9	28 3.1	2 27.4	1 57.5	20 21.9	6 14.5	5 30.8
19 M	13 48 51.5	25 21.3	2 37.0	26 41.5	15 8.2	11 14.9	28 43.5	2 39.3	2 1.6	20 24.0	6 16.7	5 32.2
20 T	13 52 48.0	26 20.9	2 33.9	8♊34.0	16 31.5	11 60.0	29 24.0	2 51.3	2 5.7	20 26.0	6 18.9	5 33.6
21 W	13 56 44.6	27 20.6	2 30.7	20 24.9	17 53.8	12 46.0	0♏ 4.5	3 3.3	2 9.9	20 27.9	6 21.1	5 35.0
22 T	14 0 41.1	28 20.3	2 27.5	2♋17.4	19 15.2	13 32.9	0 45.1	3 15.4	2 14.1	20 29.9	6 23.3	5 36.4
23 F	14 4 37.7	29 20.0	2 24.3	14 15.5	20 35.6	14 20.8	1 25.7	3 27.5	2 18.5	20 31.7	6 25.6	5 37.7
24 S	14 8 34.2	0♏19.7	2 21.2	26 23.3	21 54.8	15 9.6	2 6.3	3 39.8	2 22.9	20 33.6	6 27.8	5 39.0
25 S	14 12 30.8	1 19.5	2 18.0	8♌45.3	23 12.9	15 59.1	2 47.0	3 52.0	2 27.4	20 35.3	6 30.0	5 40.3
26 M	14 16 27.4	2 19.4	2 14.8	21 26.2	24 29.8	16 49.5	3 27.8	4 4.4	2 32.0	20 37.1	6 32.3	5 41.6
27 T	14 20 23.9	3 19.2	2 11.6	4♍30.0	25 45.3	17 40.7	4 8.6	4 16.8	2 36.6	20 38.7	6 34.5	5 42.8
28 W	14 24 20.5	4 19.2	2 8.4	17 59.7	26 59.3	18 32.6	4 49.4	4 29.2	2 41.3	20 40.4	6 36.8	5 44.1
29 T	14 28 17.0	5 19.1	2 5.3	1♎56.6	28 11.6	19 25.2	5 30.3	4 41.7	2 46.1	20 41.9	6 39.0	5 45.3
30 F	14 32 13.6	6 19.1	2 2.1	16 19.9	29 22.2	20 18.6	6 11.2	4 54.3	2 50.9	20 43.5	6 41.2	5 46.4
31 S	14 36 10.1	7 19.1	1 58.9	1♏ 5.5	0♐30.8	21 12.6	6 52.3	5 6.9	2 55.9	20 45.0	6 43.5	5 47.6

DECLINATION at NOON

DAY	EPHEMERIS SIDEREAL TIME	☉	☊	☽	☿	♀	♂	♃	♄	♅	♆	♇
1 T	12 37 53.5	3S 0.1	1S 25.2	1N31.7	6S 47.8	6N30.2	6S 5.0	19S 22.8	22S 43.8	15N33.2	11S 46.9	20N40.2
4 S	12 49 43.2	4 9.8	1 21.4	11S 13.6	8 56.4	6 38.5	6 52.0	19 30.1	22 44.2	15 30.7	11 49.0	20 39.0
7 W	13 1 32.9	5 19.1	1 17.6	18 0.8	10 59.6	6 40.3	7 38.6	19 37.4	22 44.5	15 28.3	11 51.1	20 37.8
10 S	13 13 22.5	6 27.8	1 13.8	14 56.3	12 56.8	6 35.5	8 24.9	19 44.8	22 44.9	15 26.1	11 53.3	20 36.8
13 T	13 25 12.2	7 35.7	1 10.0	4 57.5	14 47.4	6 24.4	9 10.8	19 52.2	22 45.2	15 23.9	11 55.5	20 35.8
16 F	13 37 1.8	8 42.7	1 6.2	6N37.5	16 30.8	6 7.3	9 56.2	19 59.6	22 45.4	15 21.9	11 57.7	20 35.0
19 M	13 48 51.5	9 48.5	1 2.5	15 21.2	18 6.5	5 44.4	10 41.1	20 7.0	22 45.6	15 20.0	11 59.9	20 34.3
22 T	14 0 41.1	10 53.1	0 58.7	18 11.5	19 33.7	5 16.1	11 25.5	20 14.4	22 45.8	15 18.2	12 2.1	20 33.7
25 S	14 12 30.8	11 56.2	0 54.9	13 56.0	20 51.6	4 42.5	12 9.2	20 21.7	22 46.0	15 16.6	12 4.3	20 33.1
28 W	14 24 20.5	12 57.7	0 51.1	3 26.3	21 59.4	4 4.1	12 52.2	20 28.9	22 46.1	15 15.1	12 6.5	20 32.7
31 S	14 36 10.1	13 57.3	0 47.3	9S 36.5	22 56.0	3 21.3	13 34.4	20 36.1	22 46.1	15 13.7	12 8.7	20 32.4

NOVEMBER 1959

DAY	EPHEMERIS SIDEREAL TIME	☉	☊	☽	☿	♀	♂	♃	♄	♅	♆	♇
	h m s	° ′	° ′	° ′	° ′	° ′	° ′	° ′	° ′	° ′	° ′	° ′
LONGITUDE at NOON												
1 S	14 40 6.7	8 ♏ 19.2	1 ♎ 55.7	16 ♏ 6.6	1 ♐ 37.2	22 ♍ 7.2	7 ♏ 33.3	5 ♐ 19.6	3 ♑ 0.9	20 ♌ 46.4	6 ♏ 45.8	5 ♍ 48.8
2 M	14 44 3.2	9 19.3	1 52.6	1 ♐ 14.3	2 41.1	23 2.5	8 14.3	5 32.3	3 5.9	20 47.8	6 48.0	5 49.9
3 T	14 47 59.8	10 19.4	1 49.4	16 18.6	3 42.4	23 58.3	8 55.5	5 45.1	3 11.1	20 49.1	6 50.3	5 50.9
4 W	14 51 56.3	11 19.5	1 46.2	1 ♑ 10.4	4 40.5	24 54.8	9 36.6	5 57.9	3 16.3	20 50.4	6 52.5	5 52.0
5 T	14 55 52.9	12 19.7	1 43.0	15 42.8	5 35.3	25 51.8	10 17.8	6 10.7	3 21.5	20 51.6	6 54.7	5 53.0
6 F	14 59 49.4	13 19.8	1 39.8	29 51.7	6 26.3	26 49.3	10 59.1	6 23.6	3 26.8	20 52.8	6 57.0	5 54.0
7 S	15 3 46.0	14 20.1	1 36.7	13 ♒ 35.8	7 13.0	27 47.3	11 40.3	6 36.5	3 32.2	20 53.9	6 59.2	5 54.9
8 S	15 7 42.6	15 20.3	1 33.5	26 56.4	7 55.0	28 45.9	12 21.7	6 49.5	3 37.6	20 54.9	7 1.4	5 55.9
9 M	15 11 39.1	16 20.5	1 30.3	9 ♓ 55.7	8 31.7	29 44.9	13 3.0	7 2.5	3 43.1	20 55.9	7 3.7	5 56.8
10 T	15 15 35.7	17 20.8	1 27.1	22 37.2	9 2.4	0 ♎ 44.4	13 44.4	7 15.5	3 48.7	20 56.9	7 5.9	5 57.6
11 W	15 19 32.2	18 21.1	1 24.0	5 ♈ 4.3	9 26.5	1 44.4	14 25.9	7 28.6	3 54.3	20 57.8	7 8.1	5 58.5
12 T	15 23 28.8	19 21.5	1 20.8	17 20.2	9 43.4	2 44.8	15 7.4	7 41.7	3 59.9	20 58.6	7 10.3	5 59.3
13 F	15 27 25.3	20 21.8	1 17.6	29 27.5	9 52.2	3 45.7	15 48.9	7 54.8	4 5.7	20 59.4	7 12.5	6 0.1
14 S	15 31 21.9	21 22.2	1 14.4	11 ♉ 28.4	9 52.4	4 46.9	16 30.5	8 8.0	4 11.4	21 0.1	7 14.7	6 0.8
15 S	15 35 18.4	22 22.6	1 11.2	23 24.9	9R 43.2	5 48.6	17 12.2	8 21.2	4 17.3	21 0.8	7 16.9	6 1.6
16 M	15 39 15.0	23 23.1	1 8.1	5 ♊ 18.3	9 24.1	6 50.7	17 53.9	8 34.4	4 23.1	21 1.4	7 19.1	6 2.3
17 T	15 43 11.6	24 23.5	1 4.9	17 10.1	8 54.7	7 53.2	18 35.6	8 47.6	4 29.1	21 2.0	7 21.2	6 2.9
18 W	15 47 8.1	25 24.0	1 1.7	29 2.0	8 14.9	8 56.0	19 17.4	9 0.9	4 35.1	21 2.5	7 23.4	6 3.6
19 T	15 51 4.7	26 24.5	0 58.5	10 ♋ 56.1	7 24.8	9 59.2	19 59.2	9 14.2	4 41.1	21 2.9	7 25.5	6 4.2
20 F	15 55 1.2	27 25.1	0 55.4	22 55.0	6 25.2	11 2.8	20 41.0	9 27.6	4 47.2	21 3.3	7 27.7	6 4.8
21 S	15 58 57.8	28 25.7	0 52.2	5 ♌ 1.9	5 17.1	12 6.7	21 23.0	9 41.0	4 53.3	21 3.7	7 29.9	6 5.4
22 S	16 2 54.3	29 26.3	0 49.0	17 20.6	4 2.2	13 10.9	22 5.0	9 54.3	4 59.5	21 4.0	7 32.0	6 5.9
23 M	16 6 50.9	0 ♐ 27.0	0 45.8	29 55.6	2 42.5	14 15.5	22 47.0	10 7.7	5 5.7	21 4.2	7 34.1	6 6.4
24 T	16 10 47.4	1 27.6	0 42.7	12 ♍ 51.2	1 20.7	15 20.3	23 29.0	10 21.1	5 12.0	21 4.4	7 36.2	6 6.8
25 W	16 14 44.0	2 28.3	0 39.5	26 11.8	29 ♏ 59.3	16 25.5	24 11.2	10 34.6	5 18.3	21 4.5	7 38.3	6 7.3
26 T	16 18 40.6	3 29.1	0 36.3	10 ♎ 0.3	28 41.2	17 30.9	24 53.3	10 48.0	5 24.6	21 4.6	7 40.3	6 7.7
27 F	16 22 37.1	4 29.8	0 33.1	24 17.7	27 28.8	18 36.6	25 35.5	11 1.5	5 31.0	21 4.6	7 42.4	6 8.0
28 S	16 26 33.7	5 30.6	0 29.9	9 ♏ 2.3	26 24.4	19 42.6	26 17.8	11 15.0	5 37.4	21R 4.5	7 44.4	6 8.4
29 S	16 30 30.2	6 31.4	0 26.8	24 8.6	25 29.7	20 48.8	27 0.0	11 28.4	5 43.9	21 4.4	7 46.5	6 8.7
30 M	16 34 26.8	7 32.2	0 23.6	9 ♐ 27.5	24 45.7	21 55.3	27 42.4	11 41.9	5 50.4	21 4.3	7 48.5	6 8.9
DECLINATION at NOON												
1 S	14 40 6.7	14S 16.8	0S 46.0	13S 17.9	23S 12.1	3N 6.1	13S 48.4	20S 38.5	22S 46.1	15N 13.3	12S 9.4	20N 32.4
4 W	14 51 56.3	15 13.8	0 42.2	18 15.8	23 51.5	2 17.9	14 29.5	20 45.5	22 46.1	15 12.2	12 11.6	20 32.2
7 S	15 3 46.0	16 8.5	0 38.4	12 57.3	24 16.1	1 26.0	15 9.8	20 52.5	22 46.1	15 11.2	12 13.7	20 32.2
10 T	15 15 35.7	17 0.7	0 34.7	2 2.8	24 23.3	0 30.9	15 49.1	20 59.3	22 46.0	15 10.3	12 15.9	20 32.3
13 F	15 27 25.3	17 50.4	0 30.9	9N 9.3	24 10.1	0S 27.1	16 27.3	21 6.0	22 45.8	15 9.7	12 18.0	20 32.6
16 M	15 39 15.0	18 37.3	0 27.1	16 44.1	23 32.2	1 27.7	17 4.5	21 12.6	22 45.6	15 9.1	12 20.1	20 32.9
19 T	15 51 4.7	19 21.2	0 23.3	17 58.5	22 25.8	2 30.4	17 40.5	21 19.0	22 45.3	15 8.8	12 22.1	20 33.3
22 S	16 2 54.3	20 1.9	0 19.5	12 12.6	20 52.2	3 35.0	18 15.3	21 25.2	22 44.9	15 8.5	12 24.1	20 33.9
25 W	16 14 44.0	20 39.4	0 15.7	1 1.9	19 4.8	4 41.0	18 48.8	21 31.3	22 44.5	15 8.5	12 26.1	20 34.6
28 S	16 26 33.7	21 13.5	0 11.9	11S 36.7	17 28.9	5 48.1	19 20.9	21 37.2	22 44.0	15 8.6	12 28.0	20 35.4

DECEMBER 1959

DAY	EPHEMERIS SIDEREAL TIME	☉	☊	☽	☿	♀	♂	♃	♄	♅	♆	♇
LONGITUDE at NOON												
1 T	16 38 23.3	8 ♐ 33.0	0 ♎ 20.4	24 ♐ 47.8	24 ♏ 13.2	23 ♎ 2.0	28 ♏ 24.8	11 ♐ 55.5	5 ♑ 57.0	21 ♌ 4.0	7 ♏ 50.5	6 ♍ 9.2
2 W	16 42 19.9	9 33.9	0 17.2	9 ♑ 57.9	23R 52.2	24 9.0	29 7.2	12 9.0	6 3.5	21R 3.8	7 52.5	6 9.4
3 T	16 46 16.4	10 34.8	0 14.1	24 47.8	23 42.5	25 16.1	29 49.7	12 22.5	6 10.1	21 3.4	7 54.4	6 9.6
4 F	16 50 13.0	11 35.6	0 10.9	9 ♒ 11.0	23D 43.7	26 23.5	0 ♐ 32.2	12 36.0	6 16.8	21 3.0	7 56.4	6 9.7
5 S	16 54 9.6	12 36.5	0 7.7	23 4.8	23 54.9	27 31.1	1 14.8	12 49.6	6 23.4	21 2.6	7 58.3	6 9.8
6 S	16 58 6.1	13 37.5	0 4.5	6 ♓ 29.5	24 15.5	28 38.9	1 57.4	13 3.1	6 30.1	21 2.1	8 0.2	6 9.9
7 M	17 2 2.7	14 38.4	0 1.3	19 28.1	24 44.4	29 47.0	2 40.0	13 16.6	6 36.9	21 1.6	8 2.1	6 10.0
8 T	17 5 59.2	15 39.3	29 ♍ 58.2	2 ♈ 4.8	25 21.0	0 ♏ 55.2	3 22.7	13 30.1	6 43.6	21 0.9	8 4.0	6 10.0
9 W	17 9 55.8	16 40.3	29 55.0	14 24.4	26 4.3	2 3.5	4 5.4	13 43.7	6 50.4	21 0.3	8 5.8	6 10.0
10 T	17 13 52.3	17 41.2	29 51.8	26 31.4	26 53.5	3 12.1	4 48.2	13 57.2	6 57.2	20 59.6	8 7.7	6R 9.9
11 F	17 17 48.9	18 42.2	29 48.6	8 ♉ 30.2	27 48.0	4 20.9	5 31.0	14 10.7	7 4.1	20 58.8	8 9.5	6 9.9
12 S	17 21 45.5	19 43.2	29 45.5	20 24.2	28 47.2	5 29.9	6 13.9	14 24.3	7 11.0	20 58.0	8 11.3	6 9.8
13 S	17 25 42.0	20 44.2	29 42.3	2 ♊ 16.1	29 50.3	6 39.0	6 56.9	14 37.8	7 17.8	20 57.2	8 13.1	6 9.7
14 M	17 29 38.6	21 45.2	29 39.1	14 7.9	0 ♐ 57.0	7 48.2	7 39.8	14 51.3	7 24.7	20 56.2	8 14.9	6 9.5
15 T	17 33 35.1	22 46.3	29 35.9	26 1.2	2 6.7	8 57.7	8 22.8	15 4.8	7 31.7	20 55.3	8 16.6	6 9.3
16 W	17 37 31.7	23 47.3	29 32.8	7 ♋ 57.2	3 19.1	10 7.2	9 5.9	15 18.2	7 38.6	20 54.2	8 18.3	6 9.1
17 T	17 41 28.2	24 48.3	29 29.6	19 57.1	4 33.8	11 17.0	9 49.0	15 31.7	7 45.6	20 53.1	8 20.0	6 8.8
18 F	17 45 24.8	25 49.4	29 26.4	2 ♌ 2.2	5 50.5	12 26.9	10 32.1	15 45.1	7 52.5	20 52.0	8 21.7	6 8.5
19 S	17 49 21.4	26 50.5	29 23.2	14 14.6	7 9.0	13 36.9	11 15.3	15 58.6	7 59.5	20 50.8	8 23.3	6 8.2
20 S	17 53 17.9	27 51.5	29 20.1	26 36.9	8 29.1	14 47.1	11 58.5	16 12.0	8 6.5	20 49.6	8 24.9	6 7.8
21 M	17 57 14.5	28 52.6	29 16.9	9 ♍ 12.1	9 50.6	15 57.4	12 41.8	16 25.4	8 13.6	20 48.3	8 26.5	6 7.5
22 T	18 1 11.0	29 53.7	29 13.7	22 4.2	11 13.2	17 7.8	13 25.1	16 38.8	8 20.6	20 47.0	8 28.1	6 7.1
23 W	18 5 7.6	0 ♑ 54.9	29 10.5	5 ♎ 17.0	12 36.9	18 18.4	14 8.5	16 52.1	8 27.6	20 45.6	8 29.6	6 6.6
24 T	18 9 4.1	1 56.0	29 7.3	18 53.9	14 1.5	19 29.1	14 51.9	17 5.5	8 34.7	20 44.2	8 31.1	6 6.1
25 F	18 13 0.7	2 57.1	29 4.2	2 ♏ 57.2	15 27.0	20 39.9	15 35.4	17 18.8	8 41.7	20 42.7	8 32.6	6 5.6
26 S	18 16 57.3	3 58.3	29 1.0	17 27.0	16 53.2	21 50.8	16 18.9	17 32.1	8 48.8	20 41.2	8 34.1	6 5.1
27 S	18 20 53.8	4 59.5	28 57.8	2 ♐ 20.1	18 20.1	23 1.9	17 2.4	17 45.4	8 55.9	20 39.7	8 35.5	6 4.5
28 M	18 24 50.4	6 0.6	28 54.6	17 29.9	19 47.6	24 13.0	17 46.0	17 58.6	9 3.0	20 38.1	8 36.9	6 4.0
29 T	18 28 46.9	7 1.8	28 51.5	2 ♑ 46.6	21 15.7	25 24.3	18 29.6	18 11.8	9 10.0	20 36.4	8 38.3	6 3.3
30 W	18 32 43.5	8 3.0	28 48.3	17 58.9	22 44.3	26 35.6	19 13.3	18 25.0	9 17.1	20 34.7	8 39.7	6 2.7
31 T	18 36 40.0	9 4.2	28 45.1	2 ♒ 55.7	24 13.4	27 47.0	19 57.1	18 38.2	9 24.2	20 33.0	8 41.0	6 2.0
DECLINATION at NOON												
1 T	16 38 23.3	21S 43.9	0S 8.1	18S 20.1	16S 27.4	6S 55.7	19S 51.6	21S 43.0	22S 43.4	15N 8.9	12S 29.9	20N 36.3
4 F	16 50 13.0	22 10.6	0 4.3	14 7.1	16 7.7	8 3.7	20 20.8	21 48.5	22 42.8	15 9.3	12 31.7	20 37.3
7 M	17 2 2.7	22 33.4	0 0.5	3 14.1	16 23.8	9 11.6	20 48.5	21 53.9	22 42.1	15 9.9	12 33.4	20 38.4
10 T	17 13 52.3	22 52.3	0N 3.3	8N 12.0	17 4.8	10 18.9	21 14.5	21 59.0	22 41.3	15 10.7	12 35.1	20 39.6
13 S	17 25 42.0	23 7.1	0 7.1	16 17.7	18 0.4	11 25.4	21 38.8	22 3.9	22 40.5	15 11.6	12 36.7	20 40.9
16 W	17 37 31.7	23 17.7	0 10.8	18 16.3	19 2.6	12 30.7	22 1.3	22 8.7	22 39.5	15 12.6	12 38.3	20 42.4
19 S	17 49 21.4	23 24.2	0 14.6	13 9.5	20 5.7	13 34.3	22 22.0	22 13.2	22 38.6	15 13.8	12 39.7	20 43.9
22 T	18 1 11.0	23 26.5	0 18.4	2 34.8	21 5.9	14 35.9	22 40.8	22 17.5	22 37.5	15 15.2	12 41.1	20 45.5
25 F	18 13 0.7	23 24.5	0 22.2	9S 51.3	22 0.4	15 35.1	22 57.7	22 21.5	22 36.4	15 16.6	12 42.4	20 47.2
28 M	18 24 50.4	23 18.3	0 26.0	17 57.7	22 47.5	16 31.5	23 12.6	22 25.4	22 35.2	15 18.2	12 43.7	20 48.9
31 T	18 36 40.0	23 7.9	0 29.8	15 29.5	23 25.7	17 24.8	23 25.5	22 29.0	22 33.9	15 19.9	12 44.8	20 50.8

JANUARY 1960

DAY	EPHEMERIS SIDEREAL TIME	☉	☊	☽	☿	♀	♂	♃	♄	♅	♆	♇
	h m s	° ′	° ′	° ′	° ′	° ′	° ′	° ′	° ′	° ′	° ′	° ′
LONGITUDE at NOON												
1 F	18 40 36.6	10♑ 5.3	28♍41.9	17♒28.6	25♐43.0	28♏58.6	20♐40.8	18♐51.3	9♑31.3	20♌31.2	8♏42.3	6♍ 1.3
2 S	18 44 33.2	11 6.6	28 38.8	1♓32.7	27 13.0	0♐10.2	21 24.7	19 4.4	9 38.5	20R 29.4	8 43.6	6R 0.6
3 S	18 48 29.7	12 7.7	28 35.6	15 6.6	28 43.5	1 21.9	22 8.5	19 17.4	9 45.5	20 27.6	8 44.9	5 59.9
4 M	18 52 26.3	13 8.9	28 32.4	28 12.0	0♑14.3	2 33.7	22 52.4	19 30.4	9 52.6	20 25.7	8 46.1	5 59.1
5 T	18 56 22.8	14 10.1	28 29.2	10♈52.8	1 45.6	3 45.5	23 36.3	19 43.4	9 59.7	20 23.7	8 47.2	5 58.3
6 W	19 0 19.4	15 11.2	28 26.0	23 13.6	3 17.2	4 57.4	24 20.3	19 56.3	10 6.8	20 21.7	8 48.4	5 57.5
7 T	19 4 15.9	16 12.4	28 22.9	5♉19.8	4 49.3	6 9.4	25 4.3	20 9.2	10 13.8	20 19.7	8 49.5	5 56.6
8 F	19 8 12.5	17 13.5	28 19.7	17 16.3	6 21.8	7 21.5	25 48.4	20 22.0	10 20.9	20 17.7	8 50.6	5 55.7
9 S	19 12 9.1	18 14.7	28 16.5	29 7.9	7 54.7	8 33.6	26 32.4	20 34.8	10 27.9	20 15.6	8 51.7	5 54.8
10 S	19 16 5.6	19 15.8	28 13.3	10♊58.3	9 28.0	9 45.9	27 16.6	20 47.6	10 35.0	20 13.5	8 52.7	5 53.9
11 M	19 20 2.2	20 16.9	28 10.2	22 50.7	11 1.7	10 58.1	28 0.7	21 0.3	10 42.0	20 11.3	8 53.7	5 52.9
12 T	19 23 58.7	21 18.1	28 7.0	4♋47.3	12 35.9	12 10.5	28 44.9	21 12.9	10 49.0	20 9.2	8 54.7	5 51.9
13 W	19 27 55.3	22 19.2	28 3.8	16 49.7	14 10.5	13 22.9	29 29.2	21 25.5	10 56.0	20 6.9	8 55.6	5 50.9
14 T	19 31 51.8	23 20.3	28 0.6	28 59.1	15 45.6	14 35.4	0♑13.5	21 38.0	11 3.0	20 4.7	8 56.5	5 49.9
15 F	19 35 48.4	24 21.4	27 57.5	11♌16.1	17 21.1	15 47.9	0 57.8	21 50.5	11 10.0	20 2.4	8 57.4	5 48.8
16 S	19 39 44.9	25 22.5	27 54.3	23 41.6	18 57.2	17 0.5	1 42.2	22 3.0	11 16.9	20 0.1	8 58.2	5 47.7
17 S	19 43 41.5	26 23.5	27 51.1	6♍16.9	20 33.8	18 13.1	2 26.6	22 15.3	11 23.9	19 57.8	8 59.0	5 46.6
18 M	19 47 38.1	27 24.6	27 47.9	19 3.3	22 10.9	19 25.8	3 11.1	22 27.7	11 30.8	19 55.5	8 59.8	5 45.5
19 T	19 51 34.6	28 25.7	27 44.7	2♎ 2.9	23 48.5	20 38.6	3 55.6	22 39.9	11 37.7	19 53.1	9 0.5	5 44.4
20 W	19 55 31.2	29 26.8	27 41.6	15 18.2	25 26.7	21 51.4	4 40.1	22 52.1	11 44.6	19 50.7	9 1.2	5 43.2
21 T	19 59 27.7	0♒27.8	27 38.4	28 51.5	27 5.4	23 4.3	5 24.7	23 4.2	11 51.4	19 48.3	9 1.9	5 42.0
22 F	20 3 24.3	1 28.9	27 35.2	12♏44.6	28 44.8	24 17.3	6 9.3	23 16.4	11 58.3	19 45.9	9 2.6	5 40.9
23 S	20 7 20.8	2 30.0	27 32.0	26 57.9	0♒24.7	25 30.2	6 54.0	23 28.4	12 5.1	19 43.4	9 3.2	5 39.7
24 S	20 11 17.4	3 31.0	27 28.9	11♐30.0	2 5.2	26 43.3	7 38.7	23 40.3	12 11.9	19 40.9	9 3.8	5 38.4
25 M	20 15 13.9	4 32.1	27 25.7	26 16.7	3 46.4	27 56.3	8 23.4	23 52.2	12 18.7	19 38.4	9 4.3	5 37.2
26 T	20 19 10.5	5 33.1	27 22.5	11♑11.4	5 28.1	29 9.4	9 8.2	24 4.0	12 25.4	19 35.9	9 4.8	5 35.9
27 W	20 23 7.1	6 34.1	27 19.3	26 5.7	7 10.5	0♑22.5	9 53.0	24 15.7	12 32.1	19 33.3	9 5.3	5 34.6
28 T	20 27 3.6	7 35.1	27 16.2	10♒50.4	8 53.5	1 35.7	10 37.9	24 27.4	12 38.7	19 30.8	9 5.7	5 33.3
29 F	20 31 0.2	8 36.1	27 13.0	25 17.7	10 37.2	2 48.9	11 22.8	24 39.0	12 45.4	19 28.2	9 6.1	5 32.0
30 S	20 34 56.7	9 37.0	27 9.8	9♓21.7	12 21.4	4 2.1	12 7.7	24 50.5	12 52.0	19 25.7	9 6.5	5 30.6
31 S	20 38 53.3	10 38.0	27 6.6	22 59.4	14 6.2	5 15.4	12 52.6	25 1.9	12 58.5	19 23.1	9 6.8	5 29.3
DECLINATION at NOON												
1 F	18 40 36.6	23S 3.5	0N31.1	12S 28.9	23S 36.3	17S 41.8	23S 29.3	22S 30.2	22S 33.5	15N 20.5	12S 45.2	20N 51.4
4 M	18 52 26.3	22 47.5	0 34.8	0 44.8	24 1.2	18 30.4	23 39.4	22 33.5	22 32.2	15 22.4	12 46.3	20 53.3
7 T	19 4 15.9	22 27.5	0 38.6	10N23.5	24 15.0	19 15.0	23 47.4	22 36.6	22 30.8	15 24.4	12 47.2	20 55.3
10 S	19 16 5.6	22 3.5	0 42.4	17 18.6	24 17.3	19 55.3	23 53.1	22 39.5	22 29.3	15 26.4	12 48.0	20 57.3
13 W	19 27 55.3	21 35.6	0 46.2	17 41.1	24 7.5	20 31.1	23 56.7	22 42.2	22 27.8	15 28.6	12 48.8	20 59.4
16 S	19 39 44.9	21 4.0	0 50.0	11 2.2	23 45.0	21 1.9	23 58.0	22 44.7	22 26.3	15 30.8	12 49.5	21 1.5
19 T	19 51 34.6	20 28.7	0 53.8	0S 20.2	23 9.7	21 27.7	23 57.0	22 46.9	22 24.7	15 33.1	12 50.0	21 3.6
22 F	20 3 24.3	19 49.9	0 57.6	12 7.4	22 21.0	21 48.1	23 53.8	22 49.0	22 23.0	15 35.4	12 50.5	21 5.8
25 M	20 15 13.9	19 7.8	1 1.4	18 17.2	21 18.7	22 3.0	23 48.3	22 50.9	22 21.3	15 37.8	12 50.9	21 8.0
28 T	20 27 3.6	18 22.6	1 5.2	14 2.4	20 2.8	22 12.3	23 40.6	22 52.5	22 19.6	15 40.3	12 51.2	21 10.2
31 S	20 38 53.3	17 34.3	1 8.9	2 34.9	18 33.1	22 15.7	23 30.5	22 54.0	22 17.9	15 42.7	12 51.3	21 12.4

FEBRUARY 1960

DAY	EPHEMERIS SIDEREAL TIME	☉	☊	☽	☿	♀	♂	♃	♄	♅	♆	♇
LONGITUDE at NOON												
1 M	20 42 49.8	11♒38.9	27♍ 3.4	6♈10.7	15♒51.7	6♑28.7	13♑37.6	25♐13.2	13♑ 5.1	19♌20.5	9♏ 7.1	5♍27.9
2 T	20 46 46.4	12 39.8	27 0.3	18 57.6	17 37.6	7 42.0	14 22.6	25 24.5	13 11.6	19R 17.9	9 7.4	5R 26.5
3 W	20 50 42.9	13 40.7	26 57.1	1♉23.8	19 24.0	8 55.4	15 7.7	25 35.6	13 18.0	19 15.2	9 7.6	5 25.1
4 T	20 54 39.5	14 41.6	26 53.9	13 33.8	21 10.9	10 8.7	15 52.8	25 46.7	13 24.4	19 12.6	9 7.8	5 23.7
5 F	20 58 36.1	15 42.4	26 50.7	25 32.7	22 58.2	11 22.1	16 37.9	25 57.7	13 30.8	19 10.0	9 8.0	5 22.3
6 S	21 2 32.6	16 43.2	26 47.6	7♊25.5	24 45.7	12 35.5	17 23.0	26 8.6	13 37.1	19 7.4	9 8.1	5 20.8
7 S	21 6 29.2	17 44.0	26 44.4	19 16.8	26 33.4	13 49.0	18 8.2	26 19.5	13 43.4	19 4.7	9 8.2	5 19.4
8 M	21 10 25.7	18 44.8	26 41.2	1♋10.8	28 21.1	15 2.5	18 53.4	26 30.2	13 49.7	19 2.1	9 8.2	5 17.9
9 T	21 14 22.3	19 45.5	26 38.0	13 10.8	0♓ 8.7	16 15.9	19 38.6	26 40.8	13 55.9	18 59.5	9 8.3	5 16.5
10 W	21 18 18.8	20 46.2	26 34.8	25 19.6	1 56.0	17 29.5	20 23.9	26 51.4	14 2.1	18 56.8	9 8.3	5 15.0
11 T	21 22 15.4	21 46.9	26 31.7	7♌39.0	3 42.7	18 43.0	21 9.2	27 1.8	14 8.2	18 54.2	9R 8.2	5 13.5
12 F	21 26 11.9	22 47.6	26 28.5	20 10.0	5 28.6	19 56.6	21 54.6	27 12.2	14 14.3	18 51.6	9 8.2	5 12.1
13 S	21 30 8.5	23 48.2	26 25.3	2♍53.2	7 13.4	21 10.2	22 40.0	27 22.4	14 20.3	18 49.0	9 8.1	5 10.6
14 S	21 34 5.0	24 48.9	26 22.1	15 48.6	8 56.7	22 23.8	23 25.4	27 32.6	14 26.3	18 46.4	9 7.9	5 9.1
15 M	21 38 1.6	25 49.5	26 19.0	28 56.1	10 38.1	23 37.4	24 10.8	27 42.6	14 32.2	18 43.8	9 7.8	5 7.6
16 T	21 41 58.1	26 50.0	26 15.8	12♎15.7	12 17.1	24 51.0	24 56.3	27 52.6	14 38.1	18 41.2	9 7.6	5 6.0
17 W	21 45 54.7	27 50.6	26 12.6	25 47.2	13 53.3	26 4.7	25 41.8	28 2.4	14 43.9	18 38.6	9 7.3	5 4.5
18 T	21 49 51.3	28 51.1	26 9.4	9♏30.8	15 26.2	27 18.4	26 27.3	28 12.1	14 49.6	18 36.0	9 7.0	5 3.0
19 F	21 53 47.8	29 51.6	26 6.2	23 26.2	16 55.0	28 32.1	27 12.9	28 21.7	14 55.4	18 33.4	9 6.7	5 1.5
20 S	21 57 44.4	0♓52.1	26 3.1	7♐32.7	18 19.2	29 45.8	27 58.4	28 31.3	15 1.0	18 30.8	9 6.4	4 59.9
21 S	22 1 40.9	1 52.6	25 59.9	21 49.0	19 38.1	0♒59.6	28 44.1	28 40.6	15 6.6	18 28.3	9 6.0	4 58.4
22 M	22 5 37.5	2 53.0	25 56.7	6♑12.4	20 51.1	2 13.3	29 29.7	28 49.9	15 12.1	18 25.8	9 5.6	4 56.8
23 T	22 9 34.0	3 53.5	25 53.5	20 39.1	21 57.6	3 27.1	0♒15.4	28 59.1	15 17.6	18 23.2	9 5.2	4 55.3
24 W	22 13 30.6	4 53.9	25 50.4	5♒ 4.0	22 56.8	4 40.9	1 1.1	29 8.1	15 23.0	18 20.7	9 4.7	4 53.8
25 T	22 17 27.1	5 54.2	25 47.2	19 22.0	23 48.2	5 54.7	1 46.8	29 17.1	15 28.4	18 18.3	9 4.2	4 52.2
26 F	22 21 23.7	6 54.6	25 44.0	3♓27.5	24 31.2	7 8.5	2 32.6	29 25.9	15 33.7	18 15.8	9 3.6	4 50.7
27 S	22 25 20.2	7 54.9	25 40.8	17 16.4	25 5.4	8 22.3	3 18.3	29 34.5	15 38.9	18 13.3	9 3.1	4 49.1
28 S	22 29 16.8	8 55.2	25 37.6	0♈45.5	25 30.4	9 36.1	4 4.1	29 43.1	15 44.1	18 10.9	9 2.5	4 47.6
29 M	22 33 13.3	9 55.5	25 34.5	13 53.6	25 46.0	10 49.9	4 49.9	29 51.5	15 49.2	18 8.5	9 1.8	4 46.1
DECLINATION at NOON												
1 M	20 42 49.8	17S 17.6	1N10.2	1N34.0	18S 0.2	22S 15.6	23S 26.7	22S 54.5	22S 17.3	15N 43.6	12S 51.4	21N 13.1
4 T	20 54 39.5	16 25.7	1 14.0	12 13.8	16 12.5	22 11.2	23 13.6	22 55.7	22 15.5	15 46.1	12 51.4	21 15.3
7 S	21 6 29.2	15 31.2	1 17.8	17 52.9	14 12.3	22 0.9	22 58.4	22 56.8	22 13.8	15 48.5	12 51.4	21 17.5
10 W	21 18 18.8	14 34.3	1 21.6	16 40.2	12 0.8	21 44.8	22 40.9	22 57.7	22 12.0	15 51.0	12 51.2	21 19.7
13 S	21 30 8.5	13 35.3	1 25.4	8 37.6	9 40.8	21 22.9	22 21.2	22 58.5	22 10.2	15 53.5	12 51.0	21 21.8
16 T	21 41 58.1	12 34.2	1 29.1	3S 23.8	7 16.6	20 55.2	21 59.3	22 59.1	22 8.4	15 55.9	12 50.6	21 23.9
19 F	21 53 47.8	11 31.3	1 32.9	14 17.9	4 54.4	20 22.1	21 35.4	22 59.6	22 6.6	15 58.3	12 50.2	21 26.0
22 M	22 5 37.5	10 26.8	1 36.7	18 9.8	2 42.8	19 43.5	21 9.3	23 0.0	22 4.9	16 0.7	12 49.7	21 28.0
25 T	22 17 27.1	9 20.8	1 40.5	12 7.5	0 51.8	18 59.8	20 41.3	23 0.3	22 3.1	16 3.0	12 49.1	21 30.0
28 S	22 29 16.8	8 13.6	1 44.3	0 12.9	0N28.5	18 11.1	20 11.3	23 0.5	22 1.4	16 5.2	12 48.4	21 31.9

MARCH 1960

DAY	EPHEMERIS SIDEREAL TIME	☉	☊	☽	☿	♀	♂	♃	♄	♅	♆	♇
	h m s	° ′	° ′	° ′	° ′	° ′	° ′	° ′	° ′	° ′	° ′	° ′
LONGITUDE at NOON												
1 T	22 37 9.9	10♓55.7	25♍31.3	26♈41.2	25♓52.0	12♒ 3.7	5♒35.8	29♐59.8	15♑54.2	18♌ 6.2	9♏ 1.2	4♍44.5
2 W	22 41 6.4	11 55.9	25 28.1	9♉10.1	25R48.5	13 17.6	6 21.6	0♑ 8.0	15 59.2	18R 3.8	9R 0.5	4R43.0
3 T	22 45 3.0	12 56.0	25 24.9	21 23.6	25 35.6	14 31.4	7 7.5	0 16.0	16 4.1	18 1.5	8 59.8	4 41.5
4 F	22 48 59.5	13 56.2	25 21.8	3♊25.5	25 13.9	15 45.3	7 53.5	0 23.9	16 9.0	17 59.2	8 59.1	4 40.0
5 S	22 52 56.1	14 56.3	25 18.6	15 20.4	24 43.9	16 59.2	8 39.4	0 31.7	16 13.7	17 57.0	8 58.3	4 38.5
6 S	22 56 52.6	15 56.4	25 15.4	27 13.0	24 6.2	18 13.0	9 25.3	0 39.3	16 18.4	17 54.7	8 57.5	4 37.0
7 M	23 0 49.2	16 56.4	25 12.2	9♋ 7.9	23 22.0	19 26.9	10 11.3	0 46.8	16 23.0	17 52.5	8 56.6	4 35.5
8 T	23 4 45.8	17 56.4	25 9.0	21 9.6	22 32.2	20 40.7	10 57.2	0 54.2	16 27.6	17 50.3	8 55.8	4 34.0
9 W	23 8 42.3	18 56.3	25 5.9	3♌21.8	21 38.2	21 54.6	11 43.2	1 1.4	16 32.0	17 48.2	8 54.9	4 32.5
10 T	23 12 38.9	19 56.2	25 2.7	15 47.9	20 41.3	23 8.4	12 29.2	1 8.4	16 36.4	17 46.1	8 54.0	4 31.0
11 F	23 16 35.4	20 56.1	24 59.5	28 30.0	19 42.7	24 22.3	13 15.3	1 15.3	16 40.8	17 44.0	8 53.0	4 29.6
12 S	23 20 32.0	21 55.9	24 56.3	11♍29.3	18 43.9	25 36.2	14 1.3	1 22.1	16 45.0	17 41.9	8 52.0	4 28.1
13 S	23 24 28.5	22 55.7	24 53.1	24 45.8	17 46.2	26 50.1	14 47.4	1 28.7	16 49.2	17 39.9	8 51.0	4 26.6
14 M	23 28 25.1	23 55.5	24 50.0	8♎18.5	16 50.6	28 3.9	15 33.4	1 35.2	16 53.3	17 38.0	8 50.0	4 25.2
15 T	23 32 21.6	24 55.3	24 46.8	22 5.3	15 58.2	29 17.8	16 19.5	1 41.5	16 57.3	17 36.0	8 49.0	4 23.8
16 W	23 36 18.2	25 55.0	24 43.6	6♏ 3.5	15 10.0	0♓31.7	17 5.6	1 47.7	17 1.2	17 34.1	8 47.9	4 22.4
17 T	23 40 14.7	26 54.7	24 40.4	20 10.1	14 26.5	1 45.6	17 51.8	1 53.7	17 5.1	17 32.2	8 46.8	4 21.0
18 F	23 44 11.3	27 54.3	24 37.3	4♐21.8	13 48.5	2 59.5	18 37.9	1 59.6	17 8.8	17 30.4	8 45.7	4 19.6
19 S	23 48 7.8	28 53.9	24 34.1	18 35.7	13 16.2	4 13.4	19 24.1	2 5.3	17 12.5	17 28.6	8 44.5	4 18.2
20 S	23 52 4.4	29 53.5	24 30.9	2♑48.9	12 50.0	5 27.3	20 10.2	2 10.8	17 16.1	17 26.9	8 43.3	4 16.8
21 M	23 56 0.9	0♈53.1	24 27.7	16 59.0	12 29.8	6 41.2	20 56.4	2 16.2	17 19.6	17 25.2	8 42.1	4 15.5
22 T	23 59 57.5	1 52.7	24 24.5	1♒ 4.0	12 15.8	7 55.1	21 42.6	2 21.5	17 23.1	17 23.5	8 40.9	4 14.1
23 W	0 3 54.0	2 52.2	24 21.4	15 1.6	12 7.9	9 9.0	22 28.8	2 26.5	17 26.4	17 21.9	8 39.7	4 12.8
24 T	0 7 50.6	3 51.6	24 18.2	28 50.0	12 6.0	10 22.9	23 15.0	2 31.4	17 29.7	17 20.3	8 38.4	4 11.5
25 F	0 11 47.1	4 51.1	24 15.0	12♓27.3	12D 9.9	11 36.9	24 1.3	2 36.2	17 32.9	17 18.8	8 37.2	4 10.3
26 S	0 15 43.7	5 50.6	24 11.8	25 51.5	12 19.2	12 50.8	24 47.5	2 40.7	17 36.0	17 17.3	8 35.9	4 9.0
27 S	0 19 40.2	6 49.9	24 8.7	9♈ 1.5	12 33.9	14 4.7	25 33.8	2 45.1	17 39.0	17 15.9	8 34.6	4 7.7
28 M	0 23 36.8	7 49.3	24 5.5	21 56.3	12 53.7	15 18.6	26 20.0	2 49.3	17 41.9	17 14.5	8 33.2	4 6.5
29 T	0 27 33.3	8 48.6	24 2.3	4♉35.9	13 18.3	16 32.5	27 6.3	2 53.4	17 44.8	17 13.2	8 31.9	4 5.3
30 W	0 31 29.9	9 47.9	23 59.1	17 1.1	13 47.4	17 46.4	27 52.5	2 57.3	17 47.5	17 11.9	8 30.5	4 4.1
31 T	0 35 26.4	10 47.1	23 55.9	29 13.4	14 20.9	19 0.3	28 38.8	3 1.0	17 50.1	17 10.6	8 29.1	4 2.9

DAY	EPHEMERIS SIDEREAL TIME	☉	☊	☽	☿	♀	♂	♃	♄	♅	♆	♇
DECLINATION at NOON												
1 T	22 37 9.9	7S28.1	1N46.8	7N40.6	1N 0.6	17S36.0	19S50.2	23S 0.6	22S 0.3	16N 6.7	12S47.9	21N33.1
4 F	22 48 59.5	6 19.2	1 50.6	16 0.5	1 13.1	16 39.7	19 17.1	23 0.6	21 58.7	16 8.7	12 47.0	21 34.8
7 M	23 0 49.2	5 9.5	1 54.4	18 1.6	0 42.7	15 39.1	18 42.2	23 0.6	21 57.1	16 10.8	12 46.1	21 36.5
10 T	23 12 38.9	3 59.2	1 58.2	12 55.8	0S23.0	14 34.6	18 5.5	23 0.5	21 55.5	16 12.7	12 45.1	21 38.2
13 S	23 24 28.5	2 48.4	2 1.9	2 5.4	1 50.2	13 26.5	17 27.2	23 0.4	21 54.1	16 14.5	12 44.1	21 39.7
16 W	23 36 18.2	1 37.4	2 5.7	10S14.1	3 22.3	12 15.0	16 47.3	23 0.3	21 52.7	16 16.3	12 42.9	21 41.1
19 S	23 48 7.8	0 26.3	2 9.5	17 43.0	4 45.2	11 0.5	16 5.9	23 0.1	21 51.3	16 17.9	12 41.7	21 42.5
22 T	23 59 57.5	0N44.8	2 13.3	15 46.1	5 50.3	9 43.3	15 23.0	22 59.9	21 50.1	16 19.4	12 40.5	21 43.7
25 F	0 11 47.1	1 55.7	2 17.0	5 51.1	6 33.7	8 23.7	14 38.8	22 59.7	21 48.9	16 20.7	12 39.2	21 44.9
28 M	0 23 36.8	3 6.2	2 20.8	6N18.2	6 55.0	7 2.0	13 53.3	22 59.5	21 47.8	16 21.9	12 37.8	21 45.9
31 T	0 35 26.4	4 16.2	2 24.6	15 20.6	6 55.2	5 38.6	13 6.7	22 59.4	21 46.8	16 23.1	12 36.4	21 46.8

APRIL 1960

DAY	EPHEMERIS SIDEREAL TIME	☉	☊	☽	☿	♀	♂	♃	♄	♅	♆	♇
LONGITUDE at NOON												
1 F	0 39 23.0	11♈46.3	23♍52.8	11♊15.6	14♓58.5	20♓14.2	29♒25.0	3♑ 4.5	17♑52.7	17♌ 9.4	8♏27.7	4♍ 1.7
2 S	0 43 19.5	12 45.5	23 49.6	23 11.0	15 39.9	21 28.1	0♓11.3	3 7.8	17 55.1	17R 8.2	8R26.3	4R 0.6
3 S	0 47 16.1	13 44.6	23 46.4	5♋ 3.6	16 25.0	22 42.0	0 57.5	3 11.0	17 57.5	17 7.1	8 24.8	3 59.5
4 M	0 51 12.6	14 43.7	23 43.2	16 58.0	17 13.6	23 55.8	1 43.8	3 14.0	17 59.8	17 6.1	8 23.4	3 58.4
5 T	0 55 9.2	15 42.8	23 40.1	28 58.7	18 5.4	25 9.7	2 30.0	3 16.8	18 2.0	17 5.1	8 21.9	3 57.3
6 W	0 59 5.8	16 41.8	23 36.9	11♌10.6	19 0.4	26 23.6	3 16.3	3 19.4	18 4.1	17 4.1	8 20.4	3 56.3
7 T	1 3 2.3	17 40.8	23 33.7	23 38.0	19 58.3	27 37.4	4 2.5	3 21.8	18 6.0	17 3.2	8 18.9	3 55.2
8 F	1 6 58.9	18 39.7	23 30.5	6♍24.6	20 59.0	28 51.3	4 48.8	3 24.1	18 7.9	17 2.3	8 17.4	3 54.2
9 S	1 10 55.4	19 38.6	23 27.3	19 33.1	22 2.4	0♈ 5.1	5 35.0	3 26.2	18 9.7	17 1.5	8 15.9	3 53.2
10 S	1 14 52.0	20 37.5	23 24.2	3♎ 4.5	23 8.4	1 18.9	6 21.3	3 28.1	18 11.5	17 0.8	8 14.4	3 52.3
11 M	1 18 48.5	21 36.3	23 21.0	16 58.0	24 16.8	2 32.8	7 7.5	3 29.8	18 13.1	17 0.1	8 12.8	3 51.3
12 T	1 22 45.1	22 35.1	23 17.8	1♏10.7	25 27.5	3 46.6	7 53.7	3 31.3	18 14.6	16 59.4	8 11.2	3 50.4
13 W	1 26 41.6	23 33.9	23 14.6	15 37.9	26 40.6	5 0.4	8 40.0	3 32.7	18 16.0	16 58.8	8 9.7	3 49.5
14 T	1 30 38.2	24 32.6	23 11.4	0♐13.4	27 55.8	6 14.3	9 26.2	3 33.8	18 17.3	16 58.3	8 8.1	3 48.6
15 F	1 34 34.7	25 31.4	23 8.3	14 50.5	29 13.1	7 28.1	10 12.5	3 34.9	18 18.6	16 57.8	8 6.6	3 47.8
16 S	1 38 31.3	26 30.0	23 5.1	29 23.0	0♈32.5	8 41.9	10 58.7	3 35.6	18 19.7	16 57.4	8 5.0	3 47.0
17 S	1 42 27.8	27 28.7	23 1.9	13♑45.9	1 53.9	9 55.8	11 44.9	3 36.2	18 20.8	16 57.0	8 3.4	3 46.2
18 M	1 46 24.4	28 27.3	22 58.7	27 55.9	3 17.3	11 9.6	12 31.1	3 36.6	18 21.7	16 56.7	8 1.8	3 45.5
19 T	1 50 20.9	29 25.9	22 55.6	11♒51.4	4 42.5	12 23.4	13 17.3	3 36.9	18 22.5	16 56.4	8 0.2	3 44.7
20 W	1 54 17.5	0♉24.5	22 52.4	25 31.9	6 9.6	13 37.2	14 3.5	3 36.9	18 23.3	16 56.1	7 58.5	3 44.0
21 T	1 58 14.0	1 23.0	22 49.2	8♓58.2	7 38.6	14 51.0	14 49.7	3R36.7	18 23.9	16 56.0	7 56.9	3 43.3
22 F	2 2 10.6	2 21.5	22 46.0	22 10.8	9 9.4	16 4.8	15 35.9	3 36.4	18 24.5	16 55.8	7 55.3	3 42.6
23 S	2 6 7.1	3 20.0	22 42.8	5♈10.9	10 42.0	17 18.6	16 22.0	3 35.9	18 24.9	16 55.8	7 53.7	3 42.0
24 S	2 10 3.7	4 18.4	22 39.7	17 59.1	12 16.4	18 32.4	17 8.2	3 35.1	18 25.3	16 55.8	7 52.0	3 41.4
25 M	2 14 0.3	5 16.9	22 36.5	0♉36.0	13 52.6	19 46.2	17 54.3	3 34.2	18 25.5	16 55.8	7 50.4	3 40.8
26 T	2 17 56.8	6 15.3	22 33.3	13 2.1	15 30.5	20 60.0	18 40.4	3 33.1	18 25.7	16D55.9	7 48.8	3 40.3
27 W	2 21 53.4	7 13.6	22 30.1	25 18.0	17 10.3	22 13.8	19 26.5	3 31.8	18 25.7	16 56.1	7 47.1	3 39.7
28 T	2 25 49.9	8 11.9	22 27.0	7♊24.7	18 51.8	23 27.5	20 12.6	3 30.3	18 25.7	16 56.3	7 45.5	3 39.2
29 F	2 29 46.5	9 10.2	22 23.8	19 23.8	20 35.0	24 41.3	20 58.6	3 28.7	18R25.5	16 56.5	7 43.8	3 38.8
30 S	2 33 43.0	10 8.5	22 20.6	1♋17.6	22 20.1	25 55.0	21 44.6	3 26.8	18 25.3	16 56.8	7 42.2	3 38.3

DAY	EPHEMERIS SIDEREAL TIME	☉	☊	☽	☿	♀	♂	♃	♄	♅	♆	♇
DECLINATION at NOON												
1 F	0 39 23.0	4N39.3	2N25.9	17N 3.8	6S50.9	5S10.5	12S50.9	22S59.3	21S46.5	16N23.4	12S35.9	21N47.1
4 M	0 51 12.6	5 48.3	2 29.6	17 32.7	6 25.8	3 45.2	12 2.8	22 59.2	21 45.7	16 24.3	12 34.5	21 47.9
7 T	1 3 2.3	6 56.3	2 33.4	11 5.6	5 43.7	2 19.0	11 13.7	22 59.1	21 44.9	16 25.1	12 33.0	21 48.6
10 S	1 14 52.0	8 3.3	2 37.2	0S30.6	4 46.3	0 52.0	10 23.7	22 59.0	21 44.3	16 25.7	12 31.5	21 49.1
13 W	1 26 41.6	9 9.1	2 40.9	12 37.8	3 35.0	0N35.3	9 32.9	22 59.0	21 43.8	16 26.2	12 29.9	21 49.5
16 S	1 38 31.3	10 13.5	2 44.7	18 15.5	2 11.0	2 2.8	8 41.4	22 59.1	21 43.4	16 26.6	12 28.3	21 49.8
19 T	1 50 20.9	11 16.4	2 48.5	13 51.8	0 35.4	3 29.9	7 49.2	22 59.2	21 43.1	16 26.8	12 26.8	21 50.0
22 F	2 2 10.6	12 17.6	2 52.3	2 55.8	1N10.6	4 56.6	6 56.4	22 59.3	21 42.9	16 26.9	12 25.2	21 50.1
25 M	2 14 0.3	13 17.0	2 56.0	8N48.4	3 6.2	6 22.4	6 3.2	22 59.5	21 42.9	16 26.8	12 23.6	21 50.1
28 T	2 25 49.9	14 14.5	2 59.8	16 41.4	5 10.2	7 47.0	5 9.6	22 59.8	21 43.0	16 26.5	12 22.0	21 49.9

MAY 1960

LONGITUDE at NOON

DAY	EPHEMERIS SIDEREAL TIME h m s	☉ ° ′	☊ ° ′	☽ ° ′	☿ ° ′	♀ ° ′	♂ ° ′	♃ ° ′	♄ ° ′	♅ ° ′	♆ ° ′	♇ ° ′
1 S	2 37 39.6	11♉ 6.7	22♍17.4	13♋ 9.1	24♈ 7.0	27♈ 8.8	22♓30.6	3♑24.8	18♑24.9	16♌57.2	7♏40.6	3♍37.9
2 M	2 41 36.1	12 4.9	22 14.2	25 1.9	25 55.6	28 22.5	23 16.6	3R22.6	18R24.5	16 57.6	7R38.9	3R37.5
3 T	2 45 32.7	13 3.1	22 11.1	7♌ 0.5	27 46.0	29 36.3	24 2.6	3 20.2	18 24.0	16 58.1	7 37.3	3 37.2
4 W	2 49 29.2	14 1.2	22 7.9	19 9.7	29 38.3	0♉50.0	24 48.5	3 17.6	18 23.3	16 58.6	7 35.7	3 36.9
5 T	2 53 25.8	14 59.3	22 4.7	1♍34.4	1♉32.3	2 3.7	25 34.4	3 14.8	18 22.6	16 59.2	7 34.1	3 36.6
6 F	2 57 22.3	15 57.5	22 1.5	14 19.4	3 28.2	3 17.5	26 20.4	3 12.0	18 21.8	16 59.9	7 32.5	3 36.3
7 S	3 1 18.9	16 55.5	21 58.4	27 28.7	5 25.8	4 31.2	27 6.2	3 8.9	18 20.9	17 0.6	7 30.9	3 36.1
8 S	3 5 15.5	17 53.5	21 55.2	11♎ 5.0	7 25.1	5 44.9	27 52.0	3 5.6	18 19.9	17 1.3	7 29.3	3 35.9
9 M	3 9 12.0	18 51.5	21 52.0	25 8.7	9 26.2	6 58.6	28 37.8	3 2.1	18 18.8	17 2.1	7 27.7	3 35.7
10 T	3 13 8.6	19 49.4	21 48.8	9♏37.5	11 28.9	8 12.3	29 23.6	2 58.5	18 17.6	17 3.0	7 26.1	3 35.6
11 W	3 17 5.1	20 47.4	21 45.6	24 26.1	13 33.2	9 26.0	0♈ 9.4	2 54.7	18 16.3	17 3.9	7 24.5	3 35.5
12 T	3 21 1.7	21 45.2	21 42.5	9♐26.3	15 38.9	10 39.6	0 55.1	2 50.7	18 14.9	17 4.8	7 22.9	3 35.4
13 F	3 24 58.2	22 43.1	21 39.3	24 28.8	17 46.1	11 53.3	1 40.8	2 46.6	18 13.4	17 5.8	7 21.3	3 35.3
14 S	3 28 54.8	23 41.0	21 36.1	9♑23.9	19 54.4	13 7.0	2 26.4	2 42.3	18 11.9	17 6.9	7 19.8	3 35.3
15 S	3 32 51.3	24 38.8	21 32.9	24 4.0	22 3.8	14 20.7	3 12.1	2 37.9	18 10.2	17 8.0	7 18.2	3 35.3
16 M	3 36 47.9	25 36.6	21 29.8	8♒24.1	24 14.1	15 34.4	3 57.7	2 33.3	18 8.5	17 9.1	7 16.7	3 35.3
17 T	3 40 44.4	26 34.4	21 26.6	22 21.9	26 25.0	16 48.1	4 43.3	2 28.5	18 6.6	17 10.3	7 15.2	3D35.4
18 W	3 44 41.0	27 32.2	21 23.4	5♓57.6	28 36.3	18 1.7	5 28.8	2 23.6	18 4.7	17 11.6	7 13.7	3 35.5
19 T	3 48 37.6	28 29.9	21 20.2	19 13.1	0♊47.8	19 15.4	6 14.3	2 18.5	18 2.7	17 12.9	7 12.2	3 35.6
20 F	3 52 34.1	29 27.7	21 17.1	2♈10.8	2 59.1	20 29.1	6 59.8	2 13.3	18 0.6	17 14.3	7 10.7	3 35.7
21 S	3 56 30.7	0♊25.4	21 13.9	14 53.8	5 10.0	21 42.8	7 45.2	2 8.0	17 58.4	17 15.7	7 9.2	3 35.9
22 S	4 0 27.2	1 23.1	21 10.7	27 24.7	7 20.3	22 56.4	8 30.6	2 2.5	17 56.1	17 17.1	7 7.7	3 36.1
23 M	4 4 23.8	2 20.8	21 7.5	9♉45.5	9 29.5	24 10.1	9 16.0	1 56.8	17 53.8	17 18.6	7 6.3	3 36.4
24 T	4 8 20.3	3 18.4	21 4.3	21 58.0	11 37.6	25 23.8	10 1.3	1 51.1	17 51.4	17 20.2	7 4.8	3 36.6
25 W	4 12 16.9	4 16.1	21 1.2	4♊ 3.4	13 44.2	26 37.5	10 46.5	1 45.2	17 48.8	17 21.8	7 3.4	3 36.9
26 T	4 16 13.5	5 13.7	20 58.0	16 3.0	15 49.1	27 51.2	11 31.8	1 39.1	17 46.2	17 23.4	7 2.0	3 37.3
27 F	4 20 10.0	6 11.3	20 54.8	27 57.9	17 52.2	29 4.9	12 17.0	1 33.0	17 43.6	17 25.2	7 0.7	3 37.7
28 S	4 24 6.6	7 8.9	20 51.6	9♋49.6	19 53.1	0♊18.5	13 2.1	1 26.8	17 40.9	17 26.9	6 59.3	3 38.1
29 S	4 28 3.1	8 6.5	20 48.5	21 40.2	21 51.9	1 32.2	13 47.2	1 20.4	17 38.0	17 28.7	6 58.0	3 38.5
30 M	4 31 59.7	9 4.0	20 45.3	3♌32.7	23 48.3	2 45.9	14 32.2	1 13.9	17 35.1	17 30.6	6 56.6	3 38.9
31 T	4 35 56.2	10 1.5	20 42.1	15 30.5	25 42.3	3 59.5	15 17.2	1 7.3	17 32.2	17 32.5	6 55.3	3 39.4

DECLINATION at NOON

DAY	EPHEMERIS SIDEREAL TIME h m s	☉	☊	☽	☿	♀	♂	♃	♄	♅	♆	♇
1 S	2 37 39.6	15N 9.8	3N 3.6	17N59.0	7N21.5	9N10.1	4S 15.6	23S 0.1	21S 43.2	16N26.1	12S 20.4	21N49.6
4 W	2 49 29.2	16 2.9	3 7.3	12 20.0	9 38.5	10 31.3	3 21.5	23 0.5	21 43.5	16 25.6	12 18.8	21 49.2
7 S	3 1 18.9	16 53.6	3 11.1	1 20.5	11 59.4	11 50.5	2 27.2	23 0.9	21 43.9	16 24.9	12 17.3	21 48.7
10 T	3 13 8.6	17 41.7	3 14.8	11S 11.6	14 21.4	13 7.1	1 32.9	23 1.3	21 44.5	16 24.1	12 15.8	21 48.1
13 F	3 24 58.2	18 27.2	3 18.6	18 15.7	16 40.9	14 20.9	0 38.6	23 1.8	21 45.2	16 23.1	12 14.3	21 47.4
16 M	3 36 47.9	19 9.9	3 22.4	14 44.8	18 53.2	15 31.7	0N15.6	23 2.3	21 46.0	16 22.0	12 12.9	21 46.5
19 T	3 48 37.6	19 49.7	3 26.1	4 0.2	20 53.0	16 38.9	1 9.6	23 2.8	21 46.9	16 20.8	12 11.4	21 45.6
22 S	4 0 27.2	20 26.4	3 29.9	7N50.4	22 35.0	17 42.4	2 3.4	23 3.3	21 47.9	16 19.4	12 10.1	21 44.5
25 W	4 12 16.9	20 60.0	3 33.6	16 15.9	23 55.1	18 41.8	2 56.8	23 3.8	21 49.0	16 17.9	12 8.7	21 43.4
28 S	4 24 6.6	21 30.3	3 37.4	18 20.1	24 51.2	19 36.8	3 49.8	23 4.3	21 50.2	16 16.2	12 7.5	21 42.1
31 T	4 35 56.2	21 57.3	3 41.1	13 23.8	25 23.5	20 27.1	4 42.2	23 4.8	21 51.5	16 14.4	12 6.3	21 40.8

JUNE 1960

LONGITUDE at NOON

DAY	EPHEMERIS SIDEREAL TIME h m s	☉ ° ′	☊ ° ′	☽ ° ′	☿ ° ′	♀ ° ′	♂ ° ′	♃ ° ′	♄ ° ′	♅ ° ′	♆ ° ′	♇ ° ′
1 W	4 39 52.8	10♊59.0	20♍38.9	27♌37.9	27♊33.7	5♊13.2	16♈ 2.2	1♑ 0.6	17♑29.1	17♌34.4	6♏54.0	3♍39.9
2 T	4 43 49.3	11 56.5	20 35.8	9♍59.6	29 22.6	6 26.9	16 47.1	0R53.8	17R26.0	17 36.4	6R52.7	3 40.5
3 F	4 47 45.9	12 53.9	20 32.6	22 40.7	1♋ 8.9	7 40.5	17 31.9	0 47.0	17 22.8	17 38.4	6 51.5	3 41.0
4 S	4 51 42.5	13 51.4	20 29.4	5♎45.8	2 52.5	8 54.2	18 16.7	0 40.0	17 19.6	17 40.5	6 50.3	3 41.6
5 S	4 55 39.0	14 48.8	20 26.2	19 18.7	4 33.3	10 7.8	19 1.4	0 32.9	17 16.2	17 42.6	6 49.0	3 42.3
6 M	4 59 35.6	15 46.2	20 23.0	3♏21.4	6 11.5	11 21.5	19 46.1	0 25.8	17 12.9	17 44.8	6 47.9	3 42.9
7 T	5 3 32.1	16 43.5	20 19.9	17 52.8	7 46.8	12 35.1	20 30.7	0 18.6	17 9.4	17 47.0	6 46.7	3 43.6
8 W	5 7 28.7	17 40.9	20 16.7	2♐48.6	9 19.4	13 48.8	21 15.3	0 11.4	17 5.9	17 49.2	6 45.5	3 44.3
9 T	5 11 25.2	18 38.2	20 13.5	18 0.7	10 49.2	15 2.4	21 59.8	0 4.0	17 2.3	17 51.5	6 44.4	3 45.0
10 F	5 15 21.8	19 35.6	20 10.3	3♑18.7	12 16.1	16 16.1	22 44.2	29♐56.7	16 58.7	17 53.8	6 43.3	3 45.8
11 S	5 19 18.4	20 32.9	20 7.2	18 31.1	13 40.2	17 29.8	23 28.6	29 49.2	16 55.1	17 56.2	6 42.2	3 46.6
12 S	5 23 14.9	21 30.2	20 4.0	3♒27.8	15 1.4	18 43.4	24 13.0	29 41.7	16 51.3	17 58.6	6 41.2	3 47.4
13 M	5 27 11.5	22 27.5	20 0.8	18 1.6	16 19.7	19 57.1	24 57.3	29 34.2	16 47.5	18 1.0	6 40.2	3 48.3
14 T	5 31 8.0	23 24.8	19 57.6	2♓ 8.8	17 34.9	21 10.8	25 41.5	29 26.7	16 43.7	18 3.5	6 39.2	3 49.1
15 W	5 35 4.6	24 22.1	19 54.5	15 49.0	18 47.2	22 24.4	26 25.7	29 19.1	16 39.8	18 6.0	6 38.2	3 50.0
16 T	5 39 1.1	25 19.4	19 51.3	29 4.0	19 56.4	23 38.1	27 9.8	29 11.4	16 35.9	18 8.6	6 37.2	3 51.0
17 F	5 42 57.7	26 16.7	19 48.1	11♈57.2	21 2.4	24 51.9	27 53.9	29 3.8	16 32.0	18 11.2	6 36.3	3 52.0
18 S	5 46 54.3	27 14.0	19 44.9	24 32.4	22 5.2	26 5.6	28 37.9	28 56.2	16 28.0	18 13.9	6 35.4	3 53.0
19 S	5 50 50.8	28 11.2	19 41.7	6♉53.4	23 4.8	27 19.3	29 21.9	28 48.5	16 23.9	18 16.5	6 34.6	3 54.0
20 M	5 54 47.4	29 8.5	19 38.6	19 3.9	24 0.9	28 33.0	0♉ 5.7	28 40.8	16 19.8	18 19.2	6 33.7	3 55.0
21 T	5 58 43.9	0♋ 5.8	19 35.4	1♊ 6.8	24 53.5	29 46.7	0 49.5	28 33.2	16 15.7	18 22.0	6 32.9	3 56.1
22 W	6 2 40.5	1 3.0	19 32.2	13 4.3	25 42.6	1♋ 0.4	1 33.2	28 25.5	16 11.5	18 24.8	6 32.1	3 57.2
23 T	6 6 37.0	2 0.3	19 29.0	24 58.2	26 28.0	2 14.1	2 16.9	28 17.8	16 7.3	18 27.6	6 31.3	3 58.3
24 F	6 10 33.6	2 57.5	19 25.9	6♋50.1	27 9.6	3 27.9	3 0.5	28 10.2	16 3.1	18 30.4	6 30.6	3 59.4
25 S	6 14 30.2	3 54.8	19 22.7	18 41.4	27 47.2	4 41.6	3 44.0	28 2.6	15 58.8	18 33.3	6 29.9	4 0.6
26 S	6 18 26.7	4 52.0	19 19.5	0♌33.7	28 20.9	5 55.3	4 27.4	27 55.0	15 54.5	18 36.2	6 29.2	4 1.8
27 M	6 22 23.3	5 49.2	19 16.3	12 29.1	28 50.4	7 9.1	5 10.7	27 47.4	15 50.2	18 39.2	6 28.5	4 3.0
28 T	6 26 19.8	6 46.5	19 13.2	24 30.1	29 15.6	8 22.8	5 54.0	27 39.9	15 45.9	18 42.1	6 27.9	4 4.2
29 W	6 30 16.4	7 43.7	19 10.0	6♍40.2	29 36.5	9 36.6	6 37.2	27 32.4	15 41.5	18 45.2	6 27.3	4 5.5
30 T	6 34 12.9	8 40.9	19 6.8	19 3.1	29 52.9	10 50.3	7 20.3	27 25.0	15 37.2	18 48.2	6 26.8	4 6.7

DECLINATION at NOON

DAY	EPHEMERIS SIDEREAL TIME h m s	☉	☊	☽	☿	♀	♂	♃	♄	♅	♆	♇
1 W	4 39 52.8	22N 5.6	3N42.4	10N25.6	25N29.2	20N42.8	4N59.6	23S 5.0	21S51.9	16N13.8	12S 5.9	21N40.3
4 S	4 51 42.5	22 28.0	3 46.1	1S 5.5	25 32.5	21 26.3	5 51.3	23 5.4	21 53.3	16 11.9	12 4.8	21 38.8
7 T	5 3 32.1	22 46.8	3 49.9	13 6.2	25 17.3	22 4.5	6 42.3	23 5.8	21 54.8	16 9.8	12 3.7	21 37.3
10 F	5 15 21.8	23 2.0	3 53.6	18 31.6	24 46.8	22 37.1	7 32.5	23 6.2	21 56.3	16 7.6	12 2.7	21 35.6
13 M	5 27 11.5	23 13.6	3 57.3	12 54.6	24 4.1	23 3.8	8 22.0	23 6.5	21 57.9	16 5.3	12 1.8	21 33.9
16 T	5 39 1.1	23 21.6	4 1.1	1 7.8	23 12.2	23 24.6	9 10.6	23 6.8	21 59.5	16 2.9	12 1.0	21 32.2
19 S	5 50 50.8	23 25.8	4 4.8	10N19.0	22 14.1	23 39.2	9 58.3	23 7.0	22 1.2	16 0.4	12 0.2	21 30.3
22 W	6 2 40.5	23 26.3	4 8.6	17 25.7	21 12.6	23 47.6	10 44.9	23 7.2	22 2.9	15 57.8	11 59.6	21 28.4
25 S	6 14 30.2	23 23.0	4 12.3	17 50.6	20 10.4	23 49.7	11 30.5	23 7.3	22 4.6	15 55.1	11 59.0	21 26.4
28 T	6 26 19.8	23 16.1	4 16.0	11 27.1	19 10.4	23 45.4	12 14.9	23 7.4	22 6.4	15 52.3	11 58.5	21 24.3

DAY	EPHEMERIS SIDEREAL TIME	☉	☊	☽	☿	♀	♂	♃	♄	♅	♆	♇
	h m s	° ′	° ′	° ′	° ′	° ′	° ′	° ′	° ′	° ′	° ′	° ′
						LONGITUDE at NOON						
1 F	6 38 9.5	9♋38.1	19♍ 3.6	1♎43.2	0♌ 4.8	12♋ 4.1	8♉ 3.4	27♐17.6	15♑32.8	18♌51.3	6♏26.2	4♍ 8.0
2 S	6 42 6.1	10 35.3	19 0.4	14 44.9	0 12.0	13 17.8	8 46.3	27R 10.3	15R 28.4	18 54.4	6R 25.7	4 9.4
3 S	6 46 2.6	11 32.5	18 57.3	28 12.0	0 14.5	14 31.6	9 29.2	27 3.0	15 24.0	18 57.5	6 25.2	4 10.7
4 M	6 49 59.2	12 29.7	18 54.1	12♏ 7.1	0R 12.4	15 45.3	10 12.0	26 55.9	15 19.6	19 0.6	6 24.8	4 12.1
5 T	6 53 55.7	13 26.8	18 50.9	26 30.4	0 5.7	16 59.1	10 54.7	26 48.8	15 15.2	19 3.8	6 24.4	4 13.5
6 W	6 57 52.3	14 24.0	18 47.7	11♐19.2	29♋54.3	18 12.9	11 37.3	26 41.8	15 10.7	19 7.0	6 24.0	4 14.9
7 T	7 1 48.8	15 21.2	18 44.6	26 27.1	29 38.5	19 26.6	12 19.9	26 34.8	15 6.3	19 10.3	6 23.6	4 16.4
8 F	7 5 45.4	16 18.4	18 41.4	11♑44.7	29 18.5	20 40.5	13 2.4	26 28.0	15 2.0	19 13.6	6 23.4	4 17.9
9 S	7 9 42.0	17 15.6	18 38.2	27 0.8	28 54.4	21 54.2	13 44.7	26 21.3	14 57.5	19 16.8	6 23.1	4 19.3
10 S	7 13 38.5	18 12.8	18 35.0	12♒ 4.7	28 26.5	23 8.0	14 27.0	26 14.6	14 53.1	19 20.2	6 22.8	4 20.8
11 M	7 17 35.1	19 10.0	18 31.9	26 47.6	27 55.3	24 21.8	15 9.2	26 8.1	14 48.7	19 23.5	6 22.6	4 22.4
12 T	7 21 31.6	20 7.2	18 28.7	11♓ 4.2	27 21.2	25 35.6	15 51.4	26 1.6	14 44.3	19 26.8	6 22.4	4 23.9
13 W	7 25 28.2	21 4.4	18 25.5	24 52.5	26 44.6	26 49.4	16 33.4	25 55.3	14 39.9	19 30.2	6 22.2	4 25.5
14 T	7 29 24.7	22 1.6	18 22.3	8♈13.2	26 6.3	28 3.2	17 15.3	25 49.0	14 35.6	19 33.6	6 22.1	4 27.0
15 F	7 33 21.3	22 58.8	18 19.1	21 9.1	25 26.7	29 17.0	17 57.2	25 42.9	14 31.2	19 37.0	6 22.0	4 28.6
16 S	7 37 17.8	23 56.0	18 16.0	3♉44.2	24 46.6	0♌30.9	18 38.9	25 36.9	14 26.9	19 40.5	6 21.9	4 30.2
17 S	7 41 14.4	24 53.3	18 12.8	16 2.9	24 6.6	1 44.7	19 20.6	25 31.1	14 22.5	19 43.9	6 21.9	4 31.9
18 M	7 45 11.0	25 50.5	18 9.6	28 9.4	23 27.5	2 58.6	20 2.2	25 25.3	14 18.2	19 47.4	6 21.9	4 33.5
19 T	7 49 7.5	26 47.8	18 6.4	10♊ 7.6	22 49.9	4 12.4	20 43.6	25 19.7	14 14.0	19 50.9	6 21.9	4 35.2
20 W	7 53 4.1	27 45.1	18 3.3	22 1.0	22 14.5	5 26.3	21 25.0	25 14.3	14 9.7	19 54.4	6D 22.0	4 36.9
21 T	7 57 0.6	28 42.4	18 0.1	3♋52.4	21 42.1	6 40.1	22 6.2	25 8.9	14 5.5	19 57.9	6 22.1	4 38.6
22 F	8 0 57.2	29 39.7	17 56.9	15 44.0	21 13.1	7 54.0	22 47.4	25 3.8	14 1.3	20 1.5	6 22.2	4 40.3
23 S	8 4 53.7	0♌37.0	17 53.7	27 37.7	20 48.2	9 7.9	23 28.4	24 58.7	13 57.2	20 5.1	6 22.3	4 42.0
24 S	8 8 50.3	1 34.3	17 50.6	9♌35.2	20 27.8	10 21.7	24 9.4	24 53.8	13 53.0	20 8.6	6 22.5	4 43.8
25 M	8 12 46.8	2 31.6	17 47.4	21 38.0	20 12.4	11 35.6	24 50.2	24 49.1	13 49.0	20 12.2	6 22.7	4 45.6
26 T	8 16 43.4	3 29.0	17 44.2	3♍48.1	20 2.3	12 49.5	25 30.9	24 44.5	13 44.9	20 15.8	6 23.0	4 47.3
27 W	8 20 40.0	4 26.3	17 41.0	16 7.5	19 57.8	14 3.4	26 11.5	24 40.1	13 40.9	20 19.4	6 23.3	4 49.1
28 T	8 24 36.5	5 23.7	17 37.8	28 39.0	19D 59.2	15 17.3	26 52.0	24 35.9	13 37.0	20 23.1	6 23.6	4 50.9
29 F	8 28 33.1	6 21.1	17 34.7	11♎25.4	20 6.7	16 31.2	27 32.4	24 31.8	13 33.1	20 26.8	6 24.0	4 52.8
30 S	8 32 29.6	7 18.5	17 31.5	24 29.8	20 20.4	17 45.1	28 12.7	24 27.9	13 29.2	20 30.4	6 24.4	4 54.7
31 S	8 36 26.2	8 15.9	17 28.3	7♏55.0	20 40.4	18 59.0	28 52.8	24 24.2	13 25.4	20 34.1	6 24.8	4 56.5

DAY	EPHEMERIS SIDEREAL TIME	☉	☊	☽	☿	♀	♂	♃	♄	♅	♆	♇
						DECLINATION at NOON						
1 F	6 38 9.5	23N 5.5	4N19.8	0N25.6	18N15.4	23N34.7	12N58.2	23S 7.4	22S 8.2	15N49.4	11S58.1	21N22.3
4 M	6 49 59.2	22 51.3	4 23.5	11S33.0	17 28.3	23 17.8	13 40.2	23 7.4	22 9.9	15 46.4	11 57.8	21 20.1
7 T	7 1 48.8	22 33.5	4 27.2	18 23.6	16 51.7	22 54.6	14 20.9	23 7.3	22 11.7	15 43.4	11 57.6	21 17.9
10 S	7 13 38.5	22 12.2	4 31.0	14 21.7	16 27.6	22 25.4	15 0.3	23 7.2	22 13.4	15 40.2	11 57.5	21 15.7
13 W	7 25 28.2	21 47.4	4 34.7	2 40.6	16 17.6	21 50.3	15 38.4	23 7.1	22 15.1	15 37.0	11 57.4	21 13.4
16 S	7 37 17.8	21 19.3	4 38.4	9N15.3	16 21.5	21 9.4	16 15.0	23 7.0	22 16.8	15 33.8	11 57.5	21 11.2
19 T	7 49 7.5	20 48.0	4 42.1	16 56.8	16 38.4	20 23.1	16 50.2	23 6.9	22 18.5	15 30.5	11 57.6	21 8.9
22 F	8 0 57.2	20 13.4	4 45.9	18 4.6	17 5.8	19 31.6	17 23.8	23 6.8	22 20.1	15 27.1	11 57.9	21 6.5
25 M	8 12 46.8	19 35.9	4 49.6	12 16.2	17 40.3	18 35.1	17 56.0	23 6.7	22 21.6	15 23.7	11 58.3	21 4.2
28 T	8 24 36.5	18 55.4	4 53.3	1 34.7	18 18.1	17 34.0	18 26.7	23 6.7	22 23.2	15 20.2	11 58.7	21 1.8
31 S	8 36 26.2	18 12.1	4 57.0	10S16.8	18 55.0	16 28.5	18 55.8	23 6.7	22 24.6	15 16.7	11 59.3	20 59.5

AUGUST 1960

DAY	EPHEMERIS SIDEREAL TIME	☉	☊	☽	☿	♀	♂	♃	♄	♅	♆	♇
						LONGITUDE at NOON						
1 M	8 40 22.7	9♌13.3	17♍25.1	21♏43.2	21♋ 6.7	20♌12.9	29♉32.8	24♐20.6	13♑21.7	20♌37.8	6♏25.2	4♍58.4
2 T	8 44 19.3	10 10.7	17 22.0	5♐55.0	21 39.3	21 26.8	0♊12.7	24R 17.2	13R 18.0	20 41.4	6 25.7	5 0.2
3 W	8 48 15.8	11 8.1	17 18.8	20 28.5	22 18.2	22 40.7	0 52.5	24 13.9	13 14.3	20 45.1	6 26.2	5 2.1
4 T	8 52 12.4	12 5.5	17 15.6	5♑19.7	23 3.4	23 54.6	1 32.1	24 10.9	13 10.7	20 48.8	6 26.8	5 4.0
5 F	8 56 9.0	13 3.0	17 12.4	20 21.5	23 54.8	25 8.5	2 11.7	24 8.0	13 7.2	20 52.5	6 27.3	5 5.9
6 S	9 0 5.5	14 0.4	17 9.2	5♒25.2	24 52.3	26 22.4	2 51.1	24 5.3	13 3.7	20 56.2	6 27.9	5 7.8
7 S	9 4 2.1	14 57.9	17 6.1	20 21.5	25 55.8	27 36.3	3 30.3	24 2.7	13 0.3	20 60.0	6 28.6	5 9.8
8 M	9 7 58.6	15 55.4	17 2.9	5♓ 2.0	27 5.0	28 50.2	4 9.5	24 0.4	12 56.9	21 3.7	6 29.2	5 11.7
9 T	9 11 55.2	16 52.9	16 59.7	19 20.4	28 19.9	0♍ 4.1	4 48.5	23 58.2	12 53.7	21 7.4	6 29.9	5 13.6
10 W	9 15 51.7	17 50.4	16 56.5	3♈13.2	29 40.2	1 18.0	5 27.4	23 56.2	12 50.4	21 11.1	6 30.7	5 15.6
11 T	9 19 48.3	18 48.0	16 53.4	16 39.5	1♌ 5.6	2 31.9	6 6.2	23 54.4	12 47.3	21 14.9	6 31.4	5 17.5
12 F	9 23 44.8	19 45.6	16 50.2	29 40.7	2 35.9	3 45.8	6 44.8	23 52.8	12 44.2	21 18.6	6 32.2	5 19.5
13 S	9 27 41.4	20 43.2	16 47.0	12♉19.7	4 10.7	4 59.7	7 23.4	23 51.4	12 41.2	21 22.3	6 33.0	5 21.5
14 S	9 31 37.9	21 40.8	16 43.8	24 40.6	5 49.8	6 13.6	8 1.7	23 50.1	12 38.3	21 26.1	6 33.9	5 23.5
15 M	9 35 34.5	22 38.4	16 40.7	6♊47.6	7 32.7	7 27.5	8 39.9	23 49.0	12 35.4	21 29.8	6 34.8	5 25.5
16 T	9 39 31.0	23 36.1	16 37.5	18 45.3	9 19.1	8 41.4	9 18.0	23 48.2	12 32.6	21 33.5	6 35.7	5 27.5
17 W	9 43 27.6	24 33.8	16 34.3	0♋37.9	11 8.5	9 55.3	9 55.9	23 47.5	12 29.9	21 37.3	6 36.6	5 29.5
18 T	9 47 24.2	25 31.5	16 31.1	12 29.2	13 0.5	11 9.2	10 33.7	23 47.0	12 27.2	21 41.0	6 37.6	5 31.5
19 F	9 51 20.7	26 29.3	16 27.9	24 22.6	14 54.9	12 23.2	11 11.4	23 46.7	12 24.7	21 44.8	6 38.7	5 33.5
20 S	9 55 17.3	27 27.1	16 24.8	6♌20.7	16 51.0	13 37.1	11 48.9	23 46.6	12 22.3	21 48.5	6 39.7	5 35.5
21 S	9 59 13.8	28 24.9	16 21.6	18 26.0	18 48.5	14 51.0	12 26.2	23 46.6	12 19.9	21 52.2	6 40.8	5 37.6
22 M	10 3 10.4	29 22.8	16 18.4	0♍40.0	20 47.0	16 4.9	13 3.3	23D 46.9	12 17.5	21 55.9	6 41.8	5 39.6
23 T	10 7 6.9	0♍20.6	16 15.2	13 4.4	22 46.3	17 18.8	13 40.3	23 47.3	12 15.3	21 59.6	6 43.0	5 41.6
24 W	10 11 3.5	1 18.5	16 12.1	25 40.1	24 46.0	18 32.7	14 17.1	23 47.9	12 13.2	22 3.3	6 44.1	5 43.6
25 T	10 15 0.0	2 16.4	16 8.9	8♎28.5	26 45.7	19 46.6	14 53.8	23 48.8	12 11.1	22 7.0	6 45.3	5 45.7
26 F	10 18 56.6	3 14.3	16 5.7	21 30.5	28 45.3	21 0.5	15 30.3	23 49.8	12 9.1	22 10.7	6 46.5	5 47.7
27 S	10 22 53.1	4 12.3	16 2.5	4♏47.2	0♍44.6	22 14.4	16 6.6	23 50.9	12 7.3	22 14.4	6 47.7	5 49.7
28 S	10 26 49.7	5 10.2	15 59.3	18 19.5	2 43.3	23 28.3	16 42.7	23 52.3	12 5.5	22 18.1	6 49.0	5 51.8
29 M	10 30 46.2	6 8.2	15 56.2	2♐ 7.8	4 41.4	24 42.1	17 18.7	23 53.9	12 3.8	22 21.7	6 50.3	5 53.8
30 T	10 34 42.8	7 6.2	15 53.0	16 12.0	6 38.6	25 56.0	17 54.4	23 55.6	12 2.2	22 25.4	6 51.6	5 55.9
31 W	10 38 39.3	8 4.2	15 49.8	0♑30.5	8 34.9	27 9.9	18 30.0	23 57.6	12 0.6	22 29.0	6 52.9	5 57.9

DAY	EPHEMERIS SIDEREAL TIME	☉	☊	☽	☿	♀	♂	♃	♄	♅	♆	♇
						DECLINATION at NOON						
1 M	8 40 22.7	17N57.0	4N58.3	13S37.4	19N 6.3	16N 5.7	19N 5.1	23S 6.7	22S25.1	15N15.5	11S59.5	20N58.7
4 T	8 52 12.4	17 10.2	5 2.0	18 26.3	19 34.9	14 54.9	19 32.1	23 6.8	22 26.5	15 12.0	12 0.1	20 56.3
7 S	9 4 2.1	16 20.9	5 5.7	12 34.8	19 51.4	13 40.5	19 57.5	23 6.9	22 27.8	15 8.4	12 0.9	20 54.0
10 W	9 15 51.7	15 29.2	5 9.4	0 10.1	19 51.1	12 22.8	20 21.3	23 7.1	22 29.1	15 4.8	12 1.7	20 51.6
13 S	9 27 41.4	14 35.3	5 13.1	11N22.0	19 29.7	11 2.2	20 43.6	23 7.3	22 30.3	15 1.3	12 2.7	20 49.3
16 T	9 39 31.0	13 39.3	5 16.8	17 45.0	18 44.5	9 38.9	21 4.2	23 7.6	22 31.4	14 57.7	12 3.7	20 47.0
19 F	9 51 20.7	12 41.2	5 20.5	17 12.8	17 34.9	8 13.2	21 23.4	23 8.0	22 32.5	14 54.0	12 4.8	20 44.7
22 M	10 3 10.4	11 41.5	5 24.2	9 58.6	16 3.2	6 45.6	21 41.0	23 8.5	22 33.5	14 50.5	12 6.0	20 42.5
25 T	10 15 0.0	10 40.0	5 27.9	1S27.7	14 13.1	5 16.4	21 57.0	23 9.0	22 34.4	14 46.9	12 7.3	20 40.3
28 S	10 26 49.7	9 37.0	5 31.6	12 45.9	12 9.4	3 45.8	22 11.6	23 9.6	22 35.2	14 43.3	12 8.6	20 38.1
31 W	10 38 39.3	8 32.7	5 35.3	18 20.3	9 56.4	2 14.2	22 24.8	23 10.3	22 36.0	14 39.8	12 10.0	20 36.0

SEPTEMBER 1960

DAY	EPHEMERIS SIDEREAL TIME	☉	☊	☽	☿	♀	♂	♃	♄	♅	♆	♇
	h m s	° ′	° ′	° ′	° ′	° ′	° ′	° ′	° ′	° ′	° ′	° ′
						LONGITUDE at NOON						
1 T	10 42 35.9	9♍ 2.3	15♍46.6	15♑ 0.7	10♍30.2	28♍23.7	19♊ 5.4	23♐59.7	11♑59.2	22♌32.6	6♏54.3	5♍59.9
2 F	10 46 32.4	10 0.4	15 43.4	29 38.3	12 24.5	29 37.6	19 40.7	24 2.0	11R57.9	22 36.2	6 55.7	6 2.0
3 S	10 50 29.0	10 58.5	15 40.3	14♒17.7	14 17.6	0≏51.4	20 15.7	24 4.5	11 56.6	22 39.8	6 57.1	6 4.0
4 S	10 54 25.5	11 56.6	15 37.1	28 52.7	16 9.7	2 5.2	20 50.6	24 7.1	11 55.5	22 43.4	6 58.5	6 6.0
5 M	10 58 22.1	12 54.8	15 33.9	13♓17.0	18 0.5	3 19.0	21 25.2	24 10.0	11 54.4	22 47.0	7 0.0	6 8.0
6 T	11 2 18.7	13 52.9	15 30.7	27 25.2	19 50.3	4 32.9	21 59.7	24 13.0	11 53.5	22 50.5	7 1.5	6 10.1
7 W	11 6 15.2	14 51.2	15 27.6	11♈13.3	21 38.8	5 46.7	22 33.9	24 16.2	11 52.6	22 54.1	7 3.0	6 12.1
8 T	11 10 11.8	15 49.4	15 24.4	24 39.1	23 26.2	7 0.5	23 8.0	24 19.6	11 51.8	22 57.6	7 4.6	6 14.1
9 F	11 14 8.3	16 47.7	15 21.2	7♉42.4	25 12.4	8 14.3	23 41.9	24 23.2	11 51.2	23 1.2	7 6.2	6 16.2
10 S	11 18 4.9	17 46.0	15 18.0	20 24.5	26 57.5	9 28.1	24 15.5	24 26.9	11 50.6	23 4.6	7 7.8	6 18.2
11 S	11 22 1.4	18 44.4	15 14.8	2♊48.2	28 41.5	10 41.9	24 49.0	24 30.8	11 50.2	23 8.1	7 9.4	6 20.2
12 M	11 25 58.0	19 42.8	15 11.7	14 57.3	0≏24.3	11 55.6	25 22.2	24 34.9	11 49.8	23 11.5	7 11.0	6 22.2
13 T	11 29 54.5	20 41.2	15 8.5	26 56.0	2 6.0	13 9.4	25 55.1	24 39.1	11 49.5	23 15.0	7 12.7	6 24.1
14 W	11 33 51.1	21 39.6	15 5.3	8♋48.9	3 46.6	14 23.2	26 27.9	24 43.5	11 49.3	23 18.4	7 14.4	6 26.1
15 T	11 37 47.6	22 38.1	15 2.1	20 40.8	5 26.2	15 36.9	27 0.4	24 48.1	11 49.2	23 21.8	7 16.1	6 28.1
16 F	11 41 44.2	23 36.6	14 59.0	2♌35.9	7 4.7	16 50.7	27 32.7	24 52.9	11 49.2	23 25.1	7 17.8	6 30.1
17 S	11 45 40.7	24 35.2	14 55.8	14 38.2	8 42.1	18 4.4	28 4.7	24 57.8	11D49.3	23 28.5	7 19.5	6 32.0
18 S	11 49 37.3	25 33.8	14 52.6	26 51.0	10 18.6	19 18.2	28 36.5	25 2.9	11 49.5	23 31.8	7 21.3	6 34.0
19 M	11 53 33.8	26 32.4	14 49.4	9♍16.8	11 54.0	20 31.9	29 8.0	25 8.1	11 49.8	23 35.1	7 23.1	6 35.9
20 T	11 57 30.4	27 31.1	14 46.2	21 57.4	13 28.4	21 45.6	29 39.3	25 13.6	11 50.2	23 38.3	7 24.9	6 37.9
21 W	12 1 26.9	28 29.8	14 43.1	4≏53.5	15 1.9	22 59.3	0♋10.3	25 19.1	11 50.7	23 41.6	7 26.7	6 39.8
22 T	12 5 23.5	29 28.5	14 39.9	18 5.1	16 34.3	24 13.0	0 41.1	25 24.9	11 51.3	23 44.8	7 28.6	6 41.7
23 F	12 9 20.0	0≏27.3	14 36.7	1♏31.2	18 5.8	25 26.7	1 11.5	25 30.8	11 52.0	23 48.0	7 30.4	6 43.6
24 S	12 13 16.6	1 26.1	14 33.5	15 10.3	19 36.4	26 40.4	1 41.7	25 36.8	11 52.8	23 51.1	7 32.3	6 45.5
25 S	12 17 13.1	2 24.9	14 30.4	29 0.6	21 5.9	27 54.1	2 11.6	25 43.0	11 53.7	23 54.2	7 34.2	6 47.4
26 M	12 21 9.7	3 23.7	14 27.2	12♐60.0	22 34.5	29 7.7	2 41.2	25 49.4	11 54.7	23 57.3	7 36.2	6 49.2
27 T	12 25 6.2	4 22.6	14 24.0	27 6.3	24 2.0	0♏21.4	3 10.5	25 55.9	11 55.8	24 0.4	7 38.1	6 51.1
28 W	12 29 2.8	5 21.5	14 20.8	11♑17.4	25 28.6	1 35.0	3 39.5	26 2.6	11 57.0	24 3.4	7 40.0	6 52.9
29 T	12 32 59.3	6 20.4	14 17.6	25 31.3	26 54.2	2 48.6	4 8.3	26 9.4	11 58.3	24 6.4	7 42.0	6 54.8
30 F	12 36 55.9	7 19.4	14 14.5	9♒45.6	28 18.8	4 2.3	4 36.7	26 16.4	11 59.8	24 9.5	7 44.0	6 56.6
						DECLINATION at NOON						
1 T	10 42 35.9	8N10.9	5N36.5	18S 1.4	9N10.7	1N43.5	22N28.8	23S10.6	22S36.2	14N38.6	12S10.5	20N35.3
4 S	10 54 25.5	7 5.0	5 40.2	10 26.7	6 50.9	0 11.1	22 40.1	23 11.3	22 36.9	14 35.1	12 12.0	20 33.3
7 W	11 6 15.2	5 58.0	5 43.9	2N19.4	4 29.3	1S21.5	22 50.1	23 12.2	22 37.5	14 31.7	12 13.6	20 31.3
10 S	11 18 4.9	4 50.1	5 47.6	13 13.8	2 7.9	2 54.1	22 58.8	23 13.0	22 38.0	14 28.3	12 15.3	20 29.3
13 T	11 29 54.5	3 41.5	5 51.3	18 13.6	0S12.0	4 26.3	23 6.2	23 13.9	22 38.4	14 25.0	12 17.0	20 27.5
16 F	11 41 44.2	2 32.2	5 55.0	16 4.2	2 29.1	5 57.7	23 12.6	23 14.9	22 38.7	14 21.7	12 18.8	20 25.7
19 M	11 53 33.8	1 22.5	5 58.7	7 33.4	4 42.5	7 28.2	23 17.8	23 15.8	22 39.0	14 18.5	12 20.6	20 23.9
22 T	12 5 23.5	0 12.5	6 2.4	4S28.0	6 51.5	8 57.2	23 22.1	23 16.8	22 39.2	14 15.3	12 22.5	20 22.3
25 S	12 17 13.1	0S57.6	6 6.0	15 0.8	8 55.5	10 24.6	23 25.5	23 17.8	22 39.3	14 12.3	12 24.4	20 20.7
28 W	12 29 2.8	2 7.7	6 9.7	18 14.9	10 53.6	11 49.8	23 28.1	23 18.8	22 39.3	14 9.3	12 26.3	20 19.2

OCTOBER 1960

DAY	EPHEMERIS SIDEREAL TIME	☉	☊	☽	☿	♀	♂	♃	♄	♅	♆	♇
						LONGITUDE at NOON						
1 S	12 40 52.4	8≏18.4	14♍11.3	23♒57.7	29≏42.3	5♏15.9	5♋ 4.8	26♐23.5	12♑ 1.2	24♌12.4	7♏46.0	6♍58.4
2 S	12 44 49.0	9 17.5	14 8.1	8♓ 4.7	1♏ 4.7	6 29.4	5 32.6	26 30.8	12 2.8	24 15.3	7 48.1	7 0.2
3 M	12 48 45.6	10 16.5	14 4.9	22 3.5	2 26.1	7 43.0	6 0.0	26 38.2	12 4.5	24 18.2	7 50.1	7 2.0
4 T	12 52 42.1	11 15.6	14 1.7	5♈50.6	3 46.2	8 56.5	6 27.1	26 45.7	12 6.3	24 21.0	7 52.1	7 3.7
5 W	12 56 38.7	12 14.7	13 58.6	19 23.3	5 5.1	10 10.0	6 53.9	26 53.4	12 8.1	24 23.8	7 54.2	7 5.5
6 T	13 0 35.2	13 13.9	13 55.4	2♉39.3	6 22.8	11 23.5	7 20.4	27 1.2	12 10.1	24 26.6	7 56.3	7 7.2
7 F	13 4 31.8	14 13.1	13 52.2	15 37.3	7 39.1	12 37.0	7 46.5	27 9.2	12 12.2	24 29.3	7 58.3	7 8.9
8 S	13 8 28.3	15 12.3	13 49.0	28 17.4	8 54.1	13 50.5	8 12.2	27 17.3	12 14.3	24 32.0	8 0.4	7 10.6
9 S	13 12 24.9	16 11.5	13 45.9	10♊40.9	10 7.5	15 4.0	8 37.5	27 25.5	12 16.6	24 34.7	8 2.5	7 12.3
10 M	13 16 21.4	17 10.8	13 42.7	22 50.3	11 19.3	16 17.4	9 2.5	27 33.8	12 18.9	24 37.3	8 4.7	7 13.9
11 T	13 20 18.0	18 10.2	13 39.5	4♋49.2	12 29.3	17 30.9	9 27.1	27 42.3	12 21.3	24 39.9	8 6.8	7 15.5
12 W	13 24 14.5	19 9.6	13 36.3	16 41.9	13 37.5	18 44.3	9 51.3	27 50.9	12 23.9	24 42.4	8 8.9	7 17.2
13 T	13 28 11.1	20 9.0	13 33.1	28 33.2	14 43.7	19 57.7	10 15.1	27 59.7	12 26.5	24 44.9	8 11.1	7 18.8
14 F	13 32 7.6	21 8.4	13 30.0	10♌28.0	15 47.6	21 11.1	10 38.5	28 8.5	12 29.2	24 47.4	8 13.2	7 20.3
15 S	13 36 4.2	22 7.9	13 26.8	22 31.4	16 49.2	22 24.5	11 1.5	28 17.5	12 32.0	24 49.8	8 15.4	7 21.9
16 S	13 40 0.7	23 7.5	13 23.6	4♍47.9	17 48.1	23 37.9	11 24.0	28 26.6	12 34.9	24 52.1	8 17.6	7 23.4
17 M	13 43 57.3	24 7.0	13 20.4	17 21.4	18 44.1	24 51.3	11 46.1	28 35.8	12 37.8	24 54.5	8 19.8	7 24.9
18 T	13 47 53.8	25 6.6	13 17.3	0≏14.7	19 36.9	26 4.6	12 7.7	28 45.2	12 40.9	24 56.8	8 22.0	7 26.4
19 W	13 51 50.4	26 6.3	13 14.1	13 29.1	20 26.2	27 18.0	12 28.9	28 54.7	12 44.1	24 59.0	8 24.2	7 27.9
20 T	13 55 46.9	27 5.9	13 10.9	27 4.1	21 11.6	28 31.3	12 49.6	29 4.2	12 47.3	25 1.2	8 26.4	7 29.4
21 F	13 59 43.5	28 5.7	13 7.7	10♏57.6	21 52.7	29 44.7	13 9.9	29 14.0	12 50.7	25 3.4	8 28.6	7 30.9
22 S	14 3 40.1	29 5.4	13 4.5	25 5.4	22 29.1	0♐58.0	13 29.6	29 23.8	12 54.1	25 5.5	8 30.8	7 32.3
23 S	14 7 36.6	0♏ 5.2	13 1.4	9♐22.7	23 0.3	2 11.2	13 48.8	29 33.7	12 57.6	25 7.6	8 33.1	7 33.6
24 M	14 11 33.2	1 5.0	12 58.2	23 44.0	23 25.6	3 24.5	14 7.6	29 43.8	13 1.2	25 9.6	8 35.3	7 35.0
25 T	14 15 29.7	2 4.9	12 55.0	8♑ 4.6	23 44.7	4 37.7	14 25.7	29 53.9	13 4.9	25 11.6	8 37.5	7 36.3
26 W	14 19 26.3	3 4.7	12 51.8	22 20.5	23 56.8	5 50.9	14 43.4	0♑ 4.2	13 8.6	25 13.5	8 39.8	7 37.7
27 T	14 23 22.8	4 4.6	12 48.7	6♒29.3	24 1.4	7 4.1	15 0.5	0 14.5	13 12.5	25 15.4	8 42.0	7 39.0
28 F	14 27 19.4	5 4.5	12 45.5	20 29.5	23R57.9	8 17.3	15 17.1	0 25.0	13 16.4	25 17.2	8 44.2	7 40.2
29 S	14 31 15.9	6 4.4	12 42.3	4♓20.6	23 45.8	9 30.4	15 33.1	0 35.5	13 20.4	25 19.0	8 46.5	7 41.5
30 S	14 35 12.5	7 4.4	12 39.1	18 2.4	23 24.5	10 43.5	15 48.5	0 46.2	13 24.5	25 20.7	8 48.7	7 42.7
31 M	14 39 9.0	8 4.4	12 35.9	1♈34.4	22 53.9	11 56.6	16 3.4	0 56.9	13 28.6	25 22.4	8 51.0	7 43.9
						DECLINATION at NOON						
1 S	12 40 52.4	3S17.7	6N13.4	11S43.1	12S45.4	13S12.7	23N30.0	23S19.8	22S39.2	14N 6.4	12S28.3	20N17.8
4 T	12 52 42.1	4 27.3	6 17.0	0N38.5	14 30.1	14 32.9	23 31.2	23 20.7	22 39.1	14 3.6	12 30.4	20 16.5
7 F	13 4 31.8	5 36.4	6 20.7	12 10.7	16 6.7	15 49.9	23 32.0	23 21.6	22 38.9	14 0.9	12 32.4	20 15.3
10 M	13 16 21.4	6 44.9	6 24.4	18 5.9	17 34.4	17 3.5	23 32.4	23 22.4	22 38.6	13 58.4	12 34.5	20 14.2
13 T	13 28 11.1	7 52.6	6 28.0	16 45.2	18 51.9	18 13.3	23 32.6	23 23.2	22 38.2	13 55.9	12 36.6	20 13.2
16 S	13 40 0.7	8 59.3	6 31.7	8 53.5	19 57.6	19 18.9	23 32.6	23 23.9	22 37.7	13 53.6	12 38.7	20 12.3
19 W	13 51 50.4	10 4.9	6 35.4	3S 2.9	20 49.3	20 20.1	23 32.7	23 24.5	22 37.1	13 51.4	12 40.9	20 11.6
22 S	14 3 40.1	11 9.1	6 39.0	14 20.3	21 24.2	21 16.5	23 32.8	23 25.0	22 36.4	13 49.3	12 43.0	20 10.9
25 T	14 15 29.7	12 11.9	6 42.7	18 30.0	21 38.2	22 7.8	23 33.3	23 25.4	22 35.7	13 47.4	12 45.2	20 10.3
28 F	14 27 19.4	13 12.9	6 46.3	12 41.2	21 25.9	22 53.6	23 34.1	23 25.7	22 34.8	13 45.6	12 47.3	20 9.9
31 M	14 39 9.0	14 12.1	6 50.0	0 46.1	20 41.0	23 33.8	23 35.4	23 25.9	22 33.9	13 43.9	12 49.5	20 9.5

NOVEMBER 1960

LONGITUDE at NOON

DAY	EPHEMERIS SIDEREAL TIME h m s	☉ ° ′	☊ ° ′	☽ ° ′	☿ ° ′	♀ ° ′	♂ ° ′	♃ ° ′	♄ ° ′	♅ ° ′	♆ ° ′	♇ ° ′
1 T	14 43 5.6	9♏ 4.4	12♍32.8	14♈56.2	22♏13.7	13♐ 9.7	16♋17.7	1♑ 7.8	13♑32.8	25♌24.1	8♏53.2	7♍45.0
2 W	14 47 2.1	10 4.5	12 29.6	28 6.8	21R24.3	14 22.7	16 31.3	1 18.7	13 37.2	25 25.6	8 55.5	7 46.2
3 T	14 50 58.7	11 4.6	12 26.4	11♉ 5.2	20 26.1	15 35.7	16 44.4	1 29.8	13 41.5	25 27.2	8 57.7	7 47.3
4 F	14 54 55.2	12 4.7	12 23.2	23 50.4	19 20.1	16 48.7	16 56.8	1 40.9	13 46.0	25 28.6	8 59.9	7 48.4
5 S	14 58 51.8	13 4.8	12 20.1	6♊22.0	18 7.7	18 1.7	17 8.6	1 52.1	13 50.5	25 30.1	9 2.2	7 49.4
6 S	15 2 48.4	14 5.0	12 16.9	18 40.3	16 50.9	19 14.6	17 19.7	2 3.4	13 55.1	25 31.5	9 4.4	7 50.5
7 M	15 6 44.9	15 5.2	12 13.7	0♋46.9	15 31.7	20 27.5	17 30.1	2 14.8	13 59.8	25 32.8	9 6.7	7 51.5
8 T	15 10 41.5	16 5.5	12 10.5	12 43.9	14 12.8	21 40.4	17 39.9	2 26.3	14 4.6	25 34.1	9 8.9	7 52.4
9 W	15 14 38.0	17 5.7	12 7.3	24 35.0	12 56.5	22 53.2	17 49.0	2 37.8	14 9.4	25 35.3	9 11.1	7 53.4
10 T	15 18 34.6	18 6.0	12 4.2	6♌24.3	11 45.5	24 6.0	17 57.3	2 49.5	14 14.3	25 36.4	9 13.4	7 54.3
11 F	15 22 31.1	19 6.4	12 1.0	18 16.9	10 41.9	25 18.9	18 5.0	3 1.3	14 19.3	25 37.6	9 15.6	7 55.2
12 S	15 26 27.7	20 6.8	11 57.8	0♍17.9	9 47.5	26 31.6	18 11.9	3 13.1	14 24.3	25 38.7	9 17.8	7 56.1
13 S	15 30 24.2	21 7.2	11 54.6	12 33.0	9 3.7	27 44.3	18 18.1	3 25.0	14 29.4	25 39.7	9 20.0	7 56.9
14 M	15 34 20.8	22 7.6	11 51.5	25 7.1	8 31.2	28 57.0	18 23.5	3 36.9	14 34.6	25 40.6	9 22.3	7 57.7
15 T	15 38 17.4	23 8.1	11 48.3	8♎ 4.5	8 10.4	0♑ 9.7	18 28.1	3 49.0	14 39.8	25 41.5	9 24.5	7 58.5
16 W	15 42 13.9	24 8.6	11 45.1	21 28.0	8 1.3	1 22.3	18 31.9	4 1.1	14 45.1	25 42.4	9 26.6	7 59.3
17 T	15 46 10.5	25 9.1	11 41.9	5♏18.0	8D 3.4	2 34.9	18 35.0	4 13.3	14 50.5	25 43.2	9 28.8	7 60.0
18 F	15 50 7.0	26 9.7	11 38.8	19 32.3	8 16.1	3 47.5	18 37.2	4 25.5	14 55.9	25 43.9	9 31.0	8 0.7
19 S	15 54 3.6	27 10.3	11 35.6	4♐ 6.0	8 38.7	5 0.0	18 38.6	4 37.8	15 1.4	25 44.6	9 33.2	8 1.3
20 S	15 58 0.1	28 10.9	11 32.4	18 51.5	9 10.3	6 12.5	18 39.2	4 50.2	15 6.9	25 45.2	9 35.3	8 2.0
21 M	16 1 56.7	29 11.5	11 29.2	3♑40.5	9 49.9	7 24.9	18R38.9	5 2.7	15 12.5	25 45.7	9 37.5	8 2.5
22 T	16 5 53.2	0♐12.2	11 26.0	18 24.8	10 36.8	8 37.3	18 37.9	5 15.2	15 18.1	25 46.2	9 39.6	8 3.1
23 W	16 9 49.8	1 12.8	11 22.9	2♒57.7	11 30.0	9 49.7	18 35.9	5 27.8	15 23.9	25 46.7	9 41.7	8 3.6
24 T	16 13 46.4	2 13.5	11 19.7	17 15.1	12 28.8	11 2.0	18 33.1	5 40.5	15 29.6	25 47.1	9 43.8	8 4.1
25 F	16 17 42.9	3 14.2	11 16.5	1♓15.2	13 32.4	12 14.2	18 29.5	5 53.2	15 35.4	25 47.4	9 45.9	8 4.6
26 S	16 21 39.5	4 14.9	11 13.3	14 58.1	14 40.2	13 26.4	18 25.0	6 5.9	15 41.3	25 47.7	9 48.0	8 5.1
27 S	16 25 36.0	5 15.7	11 10.2	28 25.0	15 51.6	14 38.6	18 19.7	6 18.8	15 47.2	25 47.9	9 50.1	8 5.5
28 M	16 29 32.6	6 16.4	11 7.0	11♈37.8	17 6.1	15 50.7	18 13.5	6 31.7	15 53.2	25 48.1	9 52.2	8 5.8
29 T	16 33 29.1	7 17.2	11 3.8	24 38.1	18 23.3	17 2.7	18 6.5	6 44.6	15 59.2	25 48.2	9 54.2	8 6.2
30 W	16 37 25.7	8 18.0	11 0.6	7♉27.2	19 42.8	18 14.7	17 58.6	6 57.6	16 5.3	25 48.3	9 56.3	8 6.5

DECLINATION at NOON

DAY	EPHEMERIS SIDEREAL TIME h m s	☉ ° ′	☊ ° ′	☽ ° ′	☿ ° ′	♀ ° ′	♂ ° ′	♃ ° ′	♄ ° ′	♅ ° ′	♆ ° ′	♇ ° ′
1 T	14 43 5.6	14S 31.3	6N51.2	3N28.8	20S 17.9	23S 45.8	23N36.0	23S 25.9	22S 33.5	13N43.4	12S 50.2	20N 9.4
4 F	14 54 55.2	15 27.7	6 54.8	14 6.9	18 43.9	24 17.9	23 38.3	23 25.8	22 32.5	13 42.0	12 52.3	20 9.3
7 M	15 6 44.9	16 21.8	6 58.5	18 36.4	16 41.8	24 43.8	23 41.4	23 25.6	22 31.3	13 40.7	12 54.4	20 9.2
10 T	15 18 34.6	17 13.4	7 2.1	15 43.9	14 36.7	25 3.2	23 45.4	23 25.3	22 30.1	13 39.6	12 56.5	20 9.3
13 S	15 30 24.2	18 2.4	7 5.7	6 48.7	12 59.5	25 16.1	23 50.5	23 24.7	22 28.7	13 38.6	12 58.6	20 9.4
16 W	15 42 13.9	18 48.6	7 9.4	5S 26.9	12 9.0	25 22.4	23 56.7	23 24.0	22 27.3	13 37.9	13 0.6	20 9.7
19 S	15 54 3.6	19 31.7	7 13.0	16 5.2	12 6.3	25 21.9	24 4.1	23 23.1	22 25.7	13 37.2	13 2.6	20 10.2
22 T	16 5 53.2	20 11.7	7 16.6	18 10.0	12 41.4	25 14.8	24 12.7	23 22.0	22 24.1	13 36.8	13 4.6	20 10.7
25 F	16 17 42.9	20 48.4	7 20.2	10 10.0	13 41.7	25 1.1	24 22.4	23 20.7	22 22.3	13 36.5	13 6.5	20 11.4
28 M	16 29 32.6	21 21.5	7 23.8	2N17.2	14 56.6	24 40.8	24 33.4	23 19.2	22 20.5	13 36.4	13 8.4	20 12.1

DECEMBER 1960

LONGITUDE at NOON

DAY	EPHEMERIS SIDEREAL TIME h m s	☉ ° ′	☊ ° ′	☽ ° ′	☿ ° ′	♀ ° ′	♂ ° ′	♃ ° ′	♄ ° ′	♅ ° ′	♆ ° ′	♇ ° ′
1 T	16 41 22.2	9♐18.8	10♍57.4	20♉ 5.9	21♏ 4.3	19♑26.6	17♋49.8	7♑10.6	16♑11.4	25♌48.3	9♏58.3	8♍ 6.8
2 F	16 45 18.8	10 19.7	10 54.3	2♊34.6	22 27.4	20 38.4	17R40.3	7 23.7	16 17.6	25 48.3	10 0.3	8 7.1
3 S	16 49 15.4	11 20.5	10 51.1	14 53.4	23 51.9	21 50.2	17 29.8	7 36.9	16 23.9	25R48.2	10 2.3	8 7.3
4 S	16 53 11.9	12 21.4	10 47.9	27 2.8	25 17.6	23 1.9	17 18.6	7 50.1	16 30.1	25 48.0	10 4.3	8 7.5
5 M	16 57 8.5	13 22.3	10 44.7	9♋ 3.6	26 44.3	24 13.5	17 6.5	8 3.3	16 36.4	25 47.8	10 6.2	8 7.6
6 T	17 1 5.0	14 23.2	10 41.6	20 57.3	28 11.9	25 25.1	16 53.5	8 16.6	16 42.8	25 47.5	10 8.2	8 7.8
7 W	17 5 1.6	15 24.1	10 38.4	2♌46.4	29 40.3	26 36.6	16 39.8	8 29.9	16 49.1	25 47.2	10 10.1	8 7.9
8 T	17 8 58.1	16 25.0	10 35.2	14 34.2	1♐ 9.2	27 48.0	16 25.3	8 43.2	16 55.6	25 46.8	10 12.0	8 7.9
9 F	17 12 54.7	17 26.0	10 32.0	26 24.7	2 38.8	28 59.3	16 10.0	8 56.6	17 2.0	25 46.3	10 13.9	8 8.0
10 S	17 16 51.3	18 27.0	10 28.9	8♍22.9	4 8.7	0♒10.6	15 53.9	9 10.1	17 8.5	25 45.8	10 15.8	8 8.0
11 S	17 20 47.8	19 28.0	10 25.7	20 34.1	5 39.1	1 21.7	15 37.1	9 23.5	17 15.1	25 45.3	10 17.6	8R 7.9
12 M	17 24 44.4	20 29.0	10 22.5	3♎ 3.8	7 9.9	2 32.8	15 19.6	9 37.1	17 21.6	25 44.7	10 19.4	8 7.9
13 T	17 28 40.9	21 30.0	10 19.3	15 57.1	8 40.9	3 43.8	15 1.4	9 50.6	17 28.2	25 44.0	10 21.2	8 7.8
14 W	17 32 37.5	22 31.1	10 16.2	29 18.2	10 12.2	4 54.7	14 42.5	10 4.2	17 34.9	25 43.3	10 23.0	8 7.6
15 T	17 36 34.0	23 32.1	10 13.0	13♏ 9.2	11 43.8	6 5.5	14 23.0	10 17.8	17 41.6	25 42.5	10 24.8	8 7.5
16 F	17 40 30.6	24 33.2	10 9.8	27 29.5	13 15.6	7 16.3	14 2.9	10 31.5	17 48.3	25 41.7	10 26.5	8 7.3
17 S	17 44 27.2	25 34.3	10 6.6	12♐14.9	14 47.6	8 26.9	13 42.2	10 45.1	17 55.0	25 40.8	10 28.2	8 7.1
18 S	17 48 23.7	26 35.4	10 3.4	27 17.9	16 19.8	9 37.4	13 21.0	10 58.8	18 1.8	25 39.9	10 29.9	8 6.8
19 M	17 52 20.3	27 36.5	10 0.3	12♑28.7	17 52.2	10 47.9	12 59.4	11 12.6	18 8.6	25 38.9	10 31.6	8 6.5
20 T	17 56 16.8	28 37.7	9 57.1	27 36.5	19 24.8	11 58.2	12 37.3	11 26.3	18 15.4	25 37.9	10 33.3	8 6.2
21 W	18 0 13.4	29 38.8	9 53.9	12♒31.8	20 57.6	13 8.4	12 14.8	11 40.1	18 22.2	25 36.8	10 34.9	8 5.9
22 T	18 4 9.9	0♑39.9	9 50.7	27 7.6	22 30.7	14 18.4	11 51.9	11 53.9	18 29.1	25 35.7	10 36.5	8 5.5
23 F	18 8 6.5	1 41.1	9 47.6	11♓20.4	24 3.9	15 28.5	11 28.9	12 7.8	18 36.0	25 34.5	10 38.1	8 5.1
24 S	18 12 3.1	2 42.2	9 44.4	25 9.2	25 37.3	16 38.3	11 5.5	12 21.6	18 43.0	25 33.3	10 39.7	8 4.7
25 S	18 15 59.6	3 43.4	9 41.2	8♈35.3	27 11.0	17 48.0	10 41.9	12 35.5	18 49.9	25 32.0	10 41.2	8 4.2
26 M	18 19 56.2	4 44.5	9 38.0	21 41.3	28 44.9	18 57.5	10 18.2	12 49.4	18 56.8	25 30.7	10 42.7	8 3.7
27 T	18 23 52.7	5 45.7	9 34.9	4♉30.2	0♑19.0	20 6.9	9 54.4	13 3.2	19 3.8	25 29.3	10 44.2	8 3.2
28 W	18 27 49.3	6 46.8	9 31.7	17 5.0	1 53.4	21 16.2	9 30.5	13 17.1	19 10.8	25 27.9	10 45.6	8 2.6
29 T	18 31 45.8	7 47.9	9 28.5	29 28.3	3 28.0	22 25.3	9 6.7	13 31.1	19 17.8	25 26.4	10 47.0	8 2.1
30 F	18 35 42.4	8 49.1	9 25.3	11♊42.2	5 3.0	23 34.2	8 42.8	13 45.0	19 24.8	25 24.9	10 48.4	8 1.4
31 S	18 39 39.0	9 50.2	9 22.1	23 48.4	6 38.3	24 43.0	8 19.1	13 58.9	19 31.9	25 23.3	10 49.8	8 0.8

DECLINATION at NOON

DAY	EPHEMERIS SIDEREAL TIME h m s	☉ ° ′	☊ ° ′	☽ ° ′	☿ ° ′	♀ ° ′	♂ ° ′	♃ ° ′	♄ ° ′	♅ ° ′	♆ ° ′	♇ ° ′
1 T	16 41 22.2	21S 51.0	7N27.5	13N16.5	16S 18.2	24S 14.1	24N45.3	23S 17.4	22S 18.6	13N36.5	13S 10.3	20N 13.0
4 S	16 53 11.9	22 16.7	7 31.1	18 37.1	17 41.0	23 41.3	24 58.2	23 15.5	22 16.6	13 36.7	13 12.0	20 14.0
7 W	17 5 1.6	22 38.5	7 34.7	16 34.3	19 1.2	23 2.4	25 11.8	23 13.3	22 14.5	13 37.1	13 13.8	20 15.1
10 S	17 16 51.3	22 56.4	7 38.3	8 18.1	20 16.2	22 17.9	25 25.9	23 10.9	22 12.3	13 37.7	13 15.4	20 16.3
13 T	17 28 40.9	23 10.2	7 41.9	3S 31.7	21 24.3	21 27.9	25 40.2	23 8.3	22 10.0	13 38.4	13 17.0	20 17.6
16 F	17 40 30.6	23 19.8	7 45.5	14 48.5	22 24.0	20 32.7	25 54.3	23 5.5	22 7.6	13 39.3	13 18.6	20 19.0
19 M	17 52 20.3	23 25.2	7 49.1	18 40.3	23 14.4	19 32.8	26 8.0	23 2.4	22 5.1	13 40.4	13 20.0	20 20.6
22 T	18 4 9.9	23 26.4	7 52.7	11 30.7	23 54.5	18 28.4	26 20.9	22 59.1	22 2.6	13 41.6	13 21.4	20 22.2
25 S	18 15 59.6	23 23.4	7 56.3	1N 4.5	24 23.8	17 19.9	26 32.8	22 55.6	21 60.0	13 42.9	13 22.7	20 23.8
28 W	18 27 49.3	23 16.1	7 59.9	12 24.4	24 41.4	16 7.6	26 43.3	22 51.8	21 57.3	13 44.4	13 24.0	20 25.6
31 S	18 39 39.0	23 4.6	8 3.5	18 25.6	24 47.0	14 52.0	26 52.3	22 47.9	21 54.5	13 46.1	13 25.1	20 27.5

JANUARY 1961

DAY	EPHEMERIS SIDEREAL TIME	☉	☊	☽	☿	♀	♂	♃	♄	♅	♆	♇
	h m s	° ′	° ′	° ′	° ′	° ′	° ′	° ′	° ′	° ′	° ′	° ′
						LONGITUDE at NOON						
1 S	18 43 35.5	10♑51.4	9♍19.0	5♋48.1	8♑13.8	25♒51.6	7♋55.5	14♑12.9	19♑38.9	25♌21.7	10♏51.1	8♍ 0.1
2 M	18 47 32.1	11 52.5	9 15.8	17 42.6	9 49.7	27 0.0	7R32.1	14 26.8	19 46.0	25R20.0	10 52.4	7R59.4
3 T	18 51 28.6	12 53.6	9 12.6	29 33.2	11 26.0	28 8.3	7 8.9	14 40.8	19 53.0	25 18.4	10 53.7	7 58.7
4 W	18 55 25.2	13 54.8	9 9.4	11♌21.9	13 2.6	29 16.4	6 46.1	14 54.7	20 0.1	25 16.6	10 55.0	7 57.9
5 T	18 59 21.7	14 55.9	9 6.3	23 10.8	14 39.6	0♓24.3	6 23.5	15 8.7	20 7.2	25 14.8	10 56.2	7 57.2
6 F	19 3 18.3	15 57.1	9 3.1	5♍ 3.0	16 17.1	1 31.9	6 1.3	15 22.7	20 14.3	25 13.0	10 57.4	7 56.4
7 S	19 7 14.9	16 58.2	8 59.9	17 2.3	17 54.9	2 39.4	5 39.5	15 36.6	20 21.4	25 11.1	10 58.6	7 55.5
8 S	19 11 11.4	17 59.4	8 56.7	29 13.0	19 33.1	3 46.7	5 18.1	15 50.6	20 28.5	25 9.2	10 59.7	7 54.7
9 M	19 15 8.0	19 0.5	8 53.6	11♎39.9	21 11.7	4 53.8	4 57.2	16 4.6	20 35.6	25 7.3	11 0.8	7 53.8
10 T	19 19 4.5	20 1.7	8 50.4	24 27.7	22 50.8	6 0.6	4 36.8	16 18.5	20 42.7	25 5.3	11 1.9	7 52.9
11 W	19 23 1.1	21 2.8	8 47.2	7♏41.0	24 30.3	7 7.2	4 17.0	16 32.5	20 49.8	25 3.3	11 2.9	7 51.9
12 T	19 26 57.6	22 3.9	8 44.0	21 22.7	26 10.2	8 13.6	3 57.8	16 46.5	20 56.9	25 1.3	11 3.9	7 51.0
13 F	19 30 54.2	23 5.1	8 40.8	5♐34.0	27 50.6	9 19.9	3 39.2	17 0.4	21 4.0	24 59.2	11 4.9	7 50.0
14 S	19 34 50.8	24 6.3	8 37.7	20 12.8	29 31.4	10 25.8	3 21.2	17 14.4	21 11.1	24 57.1	11 5.9	7 49.0
15 S	19 38 47.3	25 7.4	8 34.5	5♑13.9	1♒12.6	11 31.4	3 3.9	17 28.3	21 18.2	24 54.9	11 6.8	7 48.0
16 M	19 42 43.9	26 8.5	8 31.3	20 28.6	2 54.1	12 36.8	2 47.3	17 42.2	21 25.3	24 52.8	11 7.7	7 46.9
17 T	19 46 40.4	27 9.7	8 28.1	5♒46.4	4 35.9	13 42.0	2 31.4	17 56.1	21 32.4	24 50.5	11 8.5	7 45.8
18 W	19 50 37.0	28 10.8	8 25.0	20 56.4	6 18.1	14 46.8	2 16.3	18 10.0	21 39.5	24 48.3	11 9.4	7 44.7
19 T	19 54 33.5	29 11.9	8 21.8	5♓49.5	8 0.5	15 51.4	2 1.9	18 23.9	21 46.6	24 46.0	11 10.1	7 43.6
20 F	19 58 30.1	0♒13.0	8 18.6	20 19.2	9 43.0	16 55.7	1 48.3	18 37.8	21 53.7	24 43.7	11 10.9	7 42.5
21 S	20 2 26.6	1 14.0	8 15.4	4♈22.3	11 25.6	17 59.6	1 35.4	18 51.6	22 0.7	24 41.4	11 11.6	7 41.3
22 S	20 6 23.2	2 15.1	8 12.3	17 58.5	13 8.1	19 3.2	1 23.4	19 5.4	22 7.7	24 39.0	11 12.3	7 40.1
23 M	20 10 19.8	3 16.1	8 9.1	1♉ 9.4	14 50.5	20 6.5	1 12.2	19 19.2	22 14.8	24 36.6	11 13.0	7 38.9
24 T	20 14 16.3	4 17.2	8 5.9	13 58.3	16 32.5	21 9.5	1 1.7	19 33.0	22 21.8	24 34.2	11 13.6	7 37.7
25 W	20 18 12.9	5 18.2	8 2.7	26 28.9	18 14.1	22 12.0	0 52.1	19 46.7	22 28.8	24 31.8	11 14.2	7 36.4
26 T	20 22 9.4	6 19.1	7 59.5	8♊44.9	19 54.8	23 14.2	0 43.4	20 0.5	22 35.8	24 29.4	11 14.7	7 35.2
27 F	20 26 6.0	7 20.1	7 56.4	20 50.1	21 34.6	24 16.0	0 35.4	20 14.2	22 42.7	24 26.9	11 15.2	7 33.9
28 S	20 30 2.5	8 21.1	7 53.2	2♋47.6	23 13.0	25 17.4	0 28.2	20 27.8	22 49.7	24 24.4	11 15.7	7 32.6
29 S	20 33 59.1	9 22.0	7 50.0	14 40.3	24 49.8	26 18.4	0 21.9	20 41.5	22 56.6	24 21.9	11 16.2	7 31.3
30 M	20 37 55.6	10 22.9	7 46.8	26 30.3	26 24.5	27 19.0	0 16.3	20 55.1	23 3.5	24 19.4	11 16.6	7 29.9
31 T	20 41 52.2	11 23.8	7 43.7	8♌19.8	27 56.6	28 19.1	0 11.6	21 8.7	23 10.4	24 16.8	11 17.0	7 28.6
						DECLINATION at NOON						
1 S	18 43 35.5	22S59.9	8N 4.7	18N50.2	24S46.0	14S26.1	26N54.9	22S46.5	21S53.6	13N46.6	13S25.5	20N28.1
4 W	18 55 25.2	22 42.9	8 8.2	15 12.7	24 34.6	13 6.5	27 1.7	22 42.2	21 50.7	13 48.5	13 26.5	20 30.0
7 S	19 7 14.9	22 21.9	8 11.8	5 55.5	24 9.9	11 44.4	27 6.9	22 37.8	21 47.8	13 50.4	13 27.5	20 32.0
10 T	19 19 4.5	21 56.9	8 15.4	5S57.4	23 31.5	10 20.2	27 10.5	22 33.1	21 44.8	13 52.4	13 28.3	20 34.1
13 F	19 30 54.2	21 28.0	8 19.0	16 9.6	22 39.2	8 54.0	27 12.7	22 28.2	21 41.7	13 54.6	13 29.1	20 36.2
16 M	19 42 43.9	20 55.4	8 22.5	18 10.7	21 32.9	7 26.5	27 13.5	22 23.1	21 38.6	13 56.8	13 29.8	20 38.3
19 T	19 54 33.5	20 19.2	8 26.1	9 18.2	20 12.6	5 57.8	27 13.1	22 17.9	21 35.5	13 59.1	13 30.4	20 40.5
22 S	20 6 23.2	19 39.6	8 29.7	3N52.1	18 38.7	4 28.4	27 11.9	22 12.4	21 32.3	14 1.5	13 30.9	20 42.7
25 W	20 18 12.9	18 56.7	8 33.2	14 22.6	16 52.5	2 58.5	27 9.8	22 6.8	21 29.1	14 4.0	13 31.3	20 44.9
28 S	20 30 2.5	18 10.7	8 36.8	18 44.0	14 56.0	1 28.6	27 7.2	22 1.1	21 25.9	14 6.5	13 31.6	20 47.2
31 T	20 41 52.2	17 21.8	8 40.3	15 48.4	12 52.9	0N 0.9	27 4.2	21 55.1	21 22.6	14 9.1	13 31.8	20 49.4

FEBRUARY 1961

DAY	EPHEMERIS SIDEREAL TIME	☉	☊	☽	☿	♀	♂	♃	♄	♅	♆	♇
						LONGITUDE at NOON						
1 W	20 45 48.8	12♒24.7	7♍40.5	20♌10.7	29♒25.6	29♓18.8	0♋ 7.6	21♑22.2	23♑17.2	24♌14.3	11♏17.3	7♍27.2
2 T	20 49 45.3	13 25.5	7 37.3	2♍ 4.9	0♓51.0	0♈17.9	0R 4.5	21 35.7	23 24.1	24R11.7	11 17.6	7R25.9
3 F	20 53 41.9	14 26.4	7 34.1	14 4.5	2 12.1	1 16.7	0 2.1	21 49.2	23 30.9	24 9.2	11 18.0	7 24.5
4 S	20 57 38.4	15 27.2	7 30.9	26 11.9	3 28.2	2 14.9	0 0.5	22 2.7	23 37.7	24 6.6	11 18.2	7 23.1
5 S	21 1 35.0	16 28.0	7 27.8	8♎30.0	4 38.6	3 12.5	29♊59.7	22 16.0	23 44.5	24 4.0	11 18.4	7 21.7
6 M	21 5 31.5	17 28.8	7 24.6	21 1.9	5 42.6	4 9.6	29 59.6	22 29.4	23 51.2	24 1.4	11 18.6	7 20.3
7 T	21 9 28.1	18 29.6	7 21.4	3♏51.0	6 39.2	5 6.2	0♋ 0.2	22 42.7	23 57.9	23 58.8	11 18.7	7 18.8
8 W	21 13 24.6	19 30.4	7 18.2	17 0.6	7 27.9	6 2.2	0D 1.6	22 56.0	24 4.5	23 56.2	11 18.8	7 17.4
9 T	21 17 21.2	20 31.1	7 15.1	0♐33.4	8 7.8	6 57.6	0 3.8	23 9.2	24 11.2	23 53.5	11 18.9	7 15.9
10 F	21 21 17.7	21 31.8	7 11.9	14 30.8	8 38.4	7 52.3	0 6.6	23 22.4	24 17.8	23 50.9	11 19.0	7 14.4
11 S	21 25 14.3	22 32.5	7 8.7	28 52.6	8 59.0	8 46.5	0 10.2	23 35.5	24 24.3	23 48.3	11 19.0	7 13.0
12 S	21 29 10.8	23 33.2	7 5.5	13♑35.8	9 9.3	9 39.9	0 14.4	23 48.6	24 30.9	23 45.6	11R18.9	7 11.5
13 M	21 33 7.4	24 33.9	7 2.3	28 35.1	9R 9.1	10 32.7	0 19.4	24 1.7	24 37.4	23 43.0	11 18.9	7 10.0
14 T	21 37 4.0	25 34.5	6 59.2	13♒42.5	8 58.3	11 24.8	0 25.0	24 14.7	24 43.8	23 40.3	11 18.8	7 8.5
15 W	21 41 0.5	26 35.2	6 56.0	28 49.0	8 37.1	12 16.1	0 31.3	24 27.6	24 50.2	23 37.7	11 18.6	7 6.9
16 T	21 44 57.1	27 35.8	6 52.8	13♓45.1	8 6.0	13 6.7	0 38.2	24 40.5	24 56.6	23 35.1	11 18.5	7 5.4
17 F	21 48 53.6	28 36.3	6 49.6	28 23.1	7 25.9	13 56.4	0 45.8	24 53.3	25 3.0	23 32.4	11 18.3	7 3.9
18 S	21 52 50.2	29 36.9	6 46.5	12♈37.4	6 37.7	14 45.3	0 54.0	25 6.1	25 9.2	23 29.8	11 18.1	7 2.4
19 S	21 56 46.7	0♓37.4	6 43.3	26 25.1	5 42.7	15 33.4	1 2.9	25 18.8	25 15.5	23 27.2	11 17.8	7 0.8
20 M	22 0 43.3	1 37.9	6 40.1	9♉46.0	4 42.5	16 20.5	1 12.3	25 31.4	25 21.7	23 24.6	11 17.5	6 59.3
21 T	22 4 39.8	2 38.3	6 36.9	22 41.9	3 38.6	17 6.7	1 22.4	25 44.0	25 27.9	23 22.0	11 17.2	6 57.7
22 W	22 8 36.4	3 38.8	6 33.7	5♊16.0	2 32.7	17 51.9	1 33.0	25 56.5	25 34.0	23 19.4	11 16.8	6 56.2
23 T	22 12 32.9	4 39.1	6 30.6	17 32.3	1 26.6	18 36.1	1 44.2	26 8.9	25 40.0	23 16.8	11 16.4	6 54.6
24 F	22 16 29.5	5 39.5	6 27.4	29 35.5	0 21.8	19 19.3	1 56.0	26 21.4	25 46.1	23 14.3	11 16.0	6 53.1
25 S	22 20 26.0	6 39.9	6 24.2	11♋29.7	29♒19.8	20 1.3	2 8.2	26 33.7	25 52.1	23 11.8	11 15.6	6 51.6
26 S	22 24 22.6	7 40.2	6 21.0	23 19.1	28 21.7	20 42.2	2 21.1	26 45.9	25 58.0	23 9.3	11 15.1	6 50.0
27 M	22 28 19.1	8 40.4	6 17.9	5♌ 7.6	27 28.8	21 21.9	2 34.4	26 58.1	26 3.8	23 6.7	11 14.5	6 48.5
28 T	22 32 15.7	9 40.7	6 14.7	16 58.3	26 41.7	22 0.4	2 48.2	27 10.2	26 9.6	23 4.2	11 14.0	6 46.9
						DECLINATION at NOON						
1 W	20 45 48.8	17S 4.9	8N41.5	13N22.7	12S11.3	0N30.7	27N 3.1	21S53.1	21S21.6	14N10.0	13S31.9	20N50.2
4 S	20 57 38.4	16 12.3	8 45.0	3 9.9	10 8.8	1 59.3	26 59.6	21 47.0	21 18.3	14 12.5	13 32.0	20 52.4
7 T	21 9 28.1	15 17.2	8 48.6	8S36.3	8 17.3	3 26.9	26 56.0	21 40.8	21 15.0	14 15.2	13 31.9	20 54.6
10 F	21 21 17.7	14 19.7	8 52.1	17 21.1	6 47.9	4 52.9	26 52.1	21 34.5	21 11.7	14 17.8	13 31.8	20 56.8
13 M	21 33 7.4	13 20.1	8 55.7	17 16.8	5 51.8	6 17.2	26 48.2	21 28.1	21 8.5	14 20.4	13 31.6	20 59.0
16 T	21 44 57.1	12 18.6	8 59.2	7 2.1	5 37.1	7 39.3	26 44.1	21 21.6	21 5.3	14 23.1	13 31.3	21 1.2
19 S	21 56 46.7	11 15.2	9 2.7	6N23.7	6 4.4	8 58.8	26 39.9	21 15.0	21 2.1	14 25.7	13 31.0	21 3.3
22 W	22 8 36.4	10 10.3	9 6.3	15 58.0	7 5.3	10 15.3	26 35.6	21 8.4	20 58.9	14 28.2	13 30.5	21 5.3
25 S	22 20 26.0	9 4.0	9 9.8	18 37.8	8 24.1	11 28.4	26 31.1	21 1.7	20 55.8	14 30.7	13 30.0	21 7.3
28 T	22 32 15.7	7 56.5	9 13.3	14 4.8	9 44.1	12 37.5	26 26.3	20 55.0	20 52.7	14 33.2	13 29.3	21 9.3

MARCH 1961

DAY	EPHEMERIS SIDEREAL TIME	☉	☊	☽	☿	♀	♂	♃	♄	♅	♆	♇
	h m s	° ′	° ′	° ′	° ′	° ′	° ′	° ′	° ′	° ′	° ′	° ′
LONGITUDE at NOON												
1 W	22 36 12.3	10 ♓ 40.8	6 ♍ 11.5	28 ♌ 53.9	26 ♒ 1.0	22 ♈ 37.5	3 ♋ 2.5	27 ♑ 22.2	26 ♑ 15.4	23 ♌ 1.8	11 ♏ 13.4	6 ♍ 45.4
2 T	22 40 8.8	11 41.0	6 8.3	10 ♍ 56.6	25 R 27.1	23 13.3	3 17.3	27 34.2	26 21.1	22 R 59.3	11 R 12.8	6 R 43.8
3 F	22 44 5.4	12 41.1	6 5.1	23 8.3	25 0.2	23 47.7	3 32.6	27 46.1	26 26.7	22 56.9	11 12.1	6 42.3
4 S	22 48 1.9	13 41.3	6 2.0	5 ♎ 30.4	24 40.3	24 20.7	3 48.3	27 57.9	26 32.3	22 54.4	11 11.5	6 40.8
5 S	22 51 58.5	14 41.3	5 58.8	18 4.4	24 27.3	24 52.2	4 4.5	28 9.6	26 37.8	22 52.0	11 10.8	6 39.2
6 M	22 55 55.0	15 41.4	5 55.6	0 ♏ 51.5	24 21.0	25 22.1	4 21.1	28 21.2	26 43.3	22 49.7	11 10.0	6 37.7
7 T	22 59 51.6	16 41.4	5 52.4	13 52.8	24 D 21.2	25 50.5	4 38.1	28 32.8	26 48.7	22 47.3	11 9.3	6 36.2
8 W	23 3 48.1	17 41.4	5 49.3	27 9.6	24 27.6	26 17.1	4 55.6	28 44.2	26 54.1	22 45.0	11 8.5	6 34.6
9 T	23 7 44.7	18 41.4	5 46.1	10 ♐ 42.8	24 39.9	26 42.1	5 13.4	28 55.6	26 59.4	22 42.7	11 7.6	6 33.1
10 F	23 11 41.2	19 41.3	5 42.9	24 33.0	24 57.8	27 5.2	5 31.7	29 6.9	27 4.6	22 40.4	11 6.8	6 31.6
11 S	23 15 37.8	20 41.2	5 39.7	8 ♑ 39.9	25 20.9	27 26.6	5 50.3	29 18.1	27 9.7	22 38.2	11 5.9	6 30.1
12 S	23 19 34.3	21 41.1	5 36.5	23 2.4	25 48.9	27 46.0	6 9.3	29 29.3	27 14.8	22 36.0	11 5.0	6 28.6
13 M	23 23 30.9	22 40.9	5 33.4	7 ♒ 37.4	26 21.5	28 3.4	6 28.8	29 40.3	27 19.9	22 33.8	11 4.1	6 27.2
14 T	23 27 27.4	23 40.8	5 30.2	22 20.7	26 58.5	28 18.9	6 48.5	29 51.2	27 24.8	22 31.6	11 3.1	6 25.7
15 W	23 31 24.0	24 40.6	5 27.0	7 ♓ 6.3	27 39.4	28 32.2	7 8.7	0 ♒ 2.1	27 29.7	22 29.5	11 2.1	6 24.2
16 T	23 35 20.5	25 40.3	5 23.8	21 47.3	28 24.2	28 43.4	7 29.1	0 12.8	27 34.5	22 27.4	11 1.1	6 22.8
17 F	23 39 17.1	26 40.1	5 20.7	6 ♈ 17.0	29 12.5	28 52.5	7 50.0	0 23.5	27 39.4	22 25.4	11 0.1	6 21.4
18 S	23 43 13.6	27 39.8	5 17.5	20 29.1	0 ♓ 4.1	28 59.2	8 11.2	0 34.1	27 44.0	22 23.4	10 59.0	6 19.9
19 S	23 47 10.2	28 39.5	5 14.3	4 ♉ 19.2	0 58.8	29 3.6	8 32.7	0 44.5	27 48.6	22 21.4	10 57.9	6 18.5
20 M	23 51 6.7	29 39.1	5 11.1	17 45.2	1 56.4	29 5.6	8 54.5	0 54.8	27 53.2	22 19.5	10 56.8	6 17.1
21 T	23 55 3.3	0 ♈ 38.7	5 7.9	0 ♊ 46.8	2 56.8	29 R 5.2	9 16.6	1 5.1	27 57.6	22 17.6	10 55.7	6 15.7
22 W	23 58 59.8	1 38.2	5 4.8	13 25.8	3 59.8	29 2.4	9 39.1	1 15.2	28 2.0	22 15.7	10 54.5	6 14.4
23 T	0 2 56.4	2 37.8	5 1.6	25 45.5	5 5.2	28 57.0	10 1.8	1 25.2	28 6.3	22 13.9	10 53.4	6 13.0
24 F	0 6 52.9	3 37.2	4 58.4	7 ♋ 50.2	6 13.0	28 49.2	10 24.8	1 35.1	28 10.6	22 12.1	10 52.1	6 11.6
25 S	0 10 49.5	4 36.7	4 55.2	19 44.7	7 23.0	28 38.9	10 48.1	1 44.9	28 14.7	22 10.4	10 50.9	6 10.3
26 S	0 14 46.1	5 36.1	4 52.1	1 ♌ 33.9	8 35.1	28 26.0	11 11.7	1 54.6	28 18.8	22 8.7	10 49.7	6 9.0
27 M	0 18 42.6	6 35.4	4 48.9	13 22.8	9 49.3	28 10.7	11 35.6	2 4.1	28 22.8	22 7.0	10 48.4	6 7.7
28 T	0 22 39.2	7 34.8	4 45.7	25 15.7	11 5.5	27 52.9	11 59.7	2 13.6	28 26.7	22 5.4	10 47.1	6 6.4
29 W	0 26 35.7	8 34.0	4 42.5	7 ♍ 16.6	12 23.5	27 32.8	12 24.0	2 22.9	28 30.6	22 3.8	10 45.8	6 5.1
30 T	0 30 32.3	9 33.3	4 39.3	19 28.6	13 43.3	27 10.3	12 48.7	2 32.1	28 34.4	22 2.3	10 44.5	6 3.9
31 F	0 34 28.8	10 32.5	4 36.2	1 ♎ 53.9	15 5.0	26 45.6	13 13.5	2 41.2	28 38.0	22 0.8	10 43.1	6 2.7
DECLINATION at NOON												
1 W	22 36 12.3	7 S 33.8	9 N 14.5	11 N 13.3	10 S 8.8	12 N 59.5	26 N 24.7	20 S 52.8	20 S 51.7	14 N 34.0	13 S 29.1	21 N 9.9
4 S	22 48 1.9	6 24.9	9 18.0	0 11.5	11 12.8	14 2.4	26 19.5	20 46.1	20 48.7	14 36.4	13 28.3	21 11.8
7 T	22 59 51.6	5 15.3	9 21.5	11 S 20.1	11 58.8	14 59.8	26 14.0	20 39.5	20 45.7	14 38.7	13 27.5	21 13.6
10 F	23 11 41.2	4 5.0	9 25.0	18 19.2	12 25.5	15 51.2	26 8.1	20 32.8	20 42.9	14 40.9	13 26.6	21 15.3
13 M	23 23 30.9	2 54.3	9 28.5	15 55.2	12 33.6	16 35.5	26 1.7	20 26.3	20 40.1	14 43.0	13 25.6	21 16.9
16 T	23 35 20.5	1 43.2	9 32.0	4 33.6	12 24.2	17 12.0	25 54.8	20 19.8	20 37.5	14 45.0	13 24.6	21 18.4
19 S	23 47 10.2	0 32.0	9 35.5	8 N 45.2	11 58.7	17 39.4	25 47.3	20 13.4	20 34.9	14 46.9	13 23.5	21 19.8
22 W	23 58 59.8	0 N 39.1	9 39.0	17 15.1	11 18.3	17 56.6	25 39.2	20 7.1	20 32.5	14 48.7	13 22.3	21 21.2
25 S	0 10 49.5	1 50.0	9 42.5	18 14.4	10 23.9	18 2.2	25 30.3	20 0.9	20 30.1	14 50.4	13 21.1	21 22.4
28 T	0 22 39.2	3 0.5	9 46.0	12 10.9	9 16.5	17 55.3	25 20.7	19 54.9	20 27.9	14 51.9	13 19.8	21 23.5
31 F	0 34 28.8	4 10.4	9 49.4	1 20.2	7 56.8	17 34.9	25 10.4	19 49.1	20 25.9	14 53.3	13 18.4	21 24.5

APRIL 1961

DAY	EPHEMERIS SIDEREAL TIME	☉	☊	☽	☿	♀	♂	♃	♄	♅	♆	♇
LONGITUDE at NOON												
1 S	0 38 25.4	11 ♈ 31.7	4 ♍ 33.0	14 ♎ 34.0	16 ♓ 28.3	26 ♈ 18.8	13 ♋ 38.6	2 ♒ 50.2	28 ♑ 41.6	21 ♌ 59.4	10 ♏ 41.8	6 ♍ 1.5
2 S	0 42 21.9	12 30.8	4 29.8	27 29.1	17 53.4	25 R 50.0	14 3.9	2 59.0	28 45.1	21 R 58.0	10 R 40.4	6 R 0.3
3 M	0 46 18.5	13 29.9	4 26.6	10 ♏ 38.9	19 20.1	25 19.4	14 29.5	3 7.8	28 48.6	21 56.6	10 39.0	5 59.1
4 T	0 50 15.0	14 29.0	4 23.4	24 2.2	20 48.4	24 47.1	14 55.2	3 16.4	28 51.9	21 55.3	10 37.6	5 57.9
5 W	0 54 11.6	15 28.1	4 20.3	7 ♐ 37.5	22 18.3	24 13.3	15 21.2	3 24.8	28 55.2	21 54.1	10 36.1	5 56.8
6 T	0 58 8.1	16 27.1	4 17.1	21 23.4	23 49.8	23 38.3	15 47.4	3 33.2	28 58.4	21 52.9	10 34.7	5 55.7
7 F	1 2 4.7	17 26.1	4 13.9	5 ♑ 18.5	25 22.9	23 2.3	16 13.9	3 41.4	29 1.5	21 51.7	10 33.3	5 54.7
8 S	1 6 1.2	18 25.1	4 10.7	19 21.5	26 57.5	22 25.4	16 40.5	3 49.5	29 4.5	21 50.6	10 31.8	5 53.6
9 S	1 9 57.8	19 24.0	4 7.6	3 ♒ 31.1	28 33.7	21 48.0	17 7.3	3 57.4	29 7.4	21 49.6	10 30.3	5 52.5
10 M	1 13 54.3	20 22.9	4 4.4	17 46.0	0 ♈ 11.4	21 10.3	17 34.3	4 5.2	29 10.2	21 48.6	10 28.8	5 51.5
11 T	1 17 50.9	21 21.8	4 1.2	2 ♓ 4.1	1 50.7	20 32.5	18 1.5	4 12.9	29 13.0	21 47.6	10 27.3	5 50.5
12 W	1 21 47.4	22 20.6	3 58.0	16 22.7	3 31.5	19 54.8	18 28.9	4 20.4	29 15.6	21 46.7	10 25.7	5 49.5
13 T	1 25 44.0	23 19.5	3 54.8	0 ♈ 38.1	5 13.8	19 17.6	18 56.4	4 27.7	29 18.2	21 45.8	10 24.2	5 48.6
14 F	1 29 40.5	24 18.2	3 51.7	14 45.8	6 57.7	18 41.1	19 24.2	4 35.0	29 20.6	21 45.0	10 22.6	5 47.7
15 S	1 33 37.1	25 17.0	3 48.5	28 41.3	8 43.2	18 5.4	19 52.2	4 42.0	29 23.0	21 44.3	10 21.1	5 46.8
16 S	1 37 33.6	26 15.7	3 45.3	12 ♉ 20.5	10 30.2	17 30.8	20 20.3	4 49.0	29 25.3	21 43.5	10 19.5	5 45.9
17 M	1 41 30.2	27 14.4	3 42.1	25 40.4	12 18.9	16 57.6	20 48.6	4 55.8	29 27.5	21 42.9	10 17.9	5 45.0
18 T	1 45 26.8	28 13.0	3 39.0	8 ♊ 39.7	14 9.1	16 25.9	21 17.0	5 2.4	29 29.5	21 42.3	10 16.3	5 44.2
19 W	1 49 23.3	29 11.7	3 35.8	21 18.6	16 0.9	15 55.8	21 45.7	5 8.9	29 31.5	21 41.7	10 14.7	5 43.4
20 T	1 53 19.9	0 ♉ 10.2	3 32.6	3 ♋ 39.2	17 54.3	15 27.6	22 14.4	5 15.2	29 33.4	21 41.2	10 13.1	5 42.6
21 F	1 57 16.4	1 8.8	3 29.4	15 44.9	19 49.3	15 1.3	22 43.4	5 21.4	29 35.2	21 40.8	10 11.5	5 41.9
22 S	2 1 13.0	2 7.3	3 26.2	27 40.0	21 45.9	14 37.2	23 12.5	5 27.4	29 36.9	21 40.4	10 9.9	5 41.1
23 S	2 5 9.5	3 5.8	3 23.1	9 ♌ 29.6	23 44.1	14 15.2	23 41.7	5 33.2	29 38.6	21 40.1	10 8.3	5 40.4
24 M	2 9 6.1	4 4.2	3 19.9	21 19.0	25 43.8	13 55.5	24 11.1	5 38.9	29 40.1	21 39.8	10 6.7	5 39.8
25 T	2 13 2.6	5 2.6	3 16.7	3 ♍ 13.5	27 45.0	13 38.1	24 40.7	5 44.4	29 41.5	21 39.6	10 5.0	5 39.1
26 W	2 16 59.2	6 1.0	3 13.5	15 18.1	29 47.7	13 23.2	25 10.3	5 49.8	29 42.8	21 39.4	10 3.4	5 38.5
27 T	2 20 55.7	6 59.3	3 10.4	27 37.0	1 ♉ 51.7	13 10.6	25 40.1	5 55.0	29 44.1	21 39.3	10 1.8	5 37.9
28 F	2 24 52.3	7 57.6	3 7.2	10 ♎ 13.5	3 57.1	13 0.5	26 10.1	6 0.1	29 45.2	21 39.3	10 0.2	5 37.4
29 S	2 28 48.8	8 55.9	3 4.0	23 9.4	6 3.6	12 52.8	26 40.2	6 5.0	29 46.3	21 39.2	9 58.6	5 36.9
30 S	2 32 45.4	9 54.1	3 0.8	6 ♏ 25.1	8 11.2	12 47.6	27 10.4	6 9.7	29 47.2	21 D 39.3	9 56.9	5 36.4
DECLINATION at NOON												
1 S	0 38 25.4	4 N 33.6	9 N 50.6	2 S 44.8	7 S 27.6	17 N 25.1	25 N 6.7	19 S 47.1	20 S 25.2	14 N 53.8	13 S 18.0	21 N 24.8
4 T	0 50 15.0	5 42.6	9 54.1	13 52.1	5 52.7	16 46.8	24 55.2	19 41.6	20 23.3	14 55.0	13 16.6	21 25.7
7 F	1 2 4.7	6 50.8	9 57.5	18 51.2	4 6.9	15 56.1	24 42.9	19 36.2	20 21.6	14 56.1	13 15.2	21 26.4
10 M	1 13 54.3	7 57.9	10 1.0	14 0.9	2 11.0	14 55.2	24 29.6	19 31.0	20 20.0	14 57.0	13 13.7	21 27.0
13 T	1 25 44.0	9 3.7	10 4.5	1 45.9	0 5.7	13 47.0	24 15.4	19 26.1	20 18.6	14 57.8	13 12.2	21 27.5
16 S	1 37 33.6	10 8.3	10 7.9	11 N 2.7	2 N 8.4	12 35.2	24 0.2	19 21.5	20 17.4	14 58.4	13 10.7	21 27.9
19 W	1 49 23.3	11 11.3	10 11.4	18 16.3	4 30.3	11 23.4	23 44.0	19 17.2	20 16.3	14 58.9	13 9.2	21 28.2
22 S	2 1 13.0	12 12.7	10 14.8	17 37.2	6 58.6	10 15.0	23 26.8	19 13.2	20 15.4	14 59.2	13 7.7	21 28.3
25 T	2 13 2.6	13 12.3	10 18.3	10 13.3	9 31.6	9 12.9	23 8.6	19 9.5	20 14.7	14 59.4	13 6.1	21 28.4
28 F	2 24 52.3	14 9.9	10 21.7	1 S 18.5	12 6.5	8 19.0	22 49.3	19 6.2	20 14.2	14 59.4	13 4.6	21 28.2

MAY 1961

DAY	EPHEMERIS SIDEREAL TIME	☉	☊	☽	☿	♀	♂	♃	♄	♅	♆	♇
	h m s	° ′	° ′	° ′	° ′	° ′	° ′	° ′	° ′	° ′	° ′	° ′
LONGITUDE at NOON												
1 M	2 36 41.9	10♉52.4	2♍57.6	19♏59.2	10♉19.7	12♈44.8	27♋40.7	6♒14.2	29♑48.0	21♌39.4	9♏55.3	5♍35.9
2 T	2 40 38.5	11 50.5	2 54.5	3♐48.7	12 28.8	12R44.4	28 11.2	6 18.6	29 48.8	21 39.5	9R53.6	5R35.4
3 W	2 44 35.1	12 48.7	2 51.3	17 49.8	14 38.5	12D46.3	28 41.7	6 22.8	29 49.4	21 39.7	9 52.0	5 35.0
4 T	2 48 31.6	13 46.8	2 48.1	1♑58.0	16 48.3	12 50.6	29 12.4	6 26.8	29 50.0	21 40.0	9 50.4	5 34.6
5 F	2 52 28.2	14 44.9	2 44.9	16 9.5	18 58.2	12 57.1	29 43.2	6 30.6	29 50.4	21 40.3	9 48.8	5 34.3
6 S	2 56 24.7	15 43.0	2 41.8	0♒21.0	21 7.7	13 5.8	0♌14.2	6 34.3	29 50.8	21 40.7	9 47.1	5 33.9
7 S	3 0 21.3	16 41.0	2 38.6	14 30.3	23 16.7	13 16.7	0 45.2	6 37.8	29 51.1	21 41.1	9 45.5	5 33.6
8 M	3 4 17.8	17 39.1	2 35.4	28 36.1	25 24.8	13 29.7	1 16.3	6 41.1	29 51.2	21 41.5	9 43.9	5 33.4
9 T	3 8 14.4	18 37.1	2 32.2	12♓37.6	27 31.7	13 44.8	1 47.6	6 44.3	29 51.3	21 42.1	9 42.3	5 33.1
10 W	3 12 10.9	19 35.1	2 29.0	26 34.0	29 37.1	14 1.8	2 19.0	6 47.2	29R51.2	21 42.6	9 40.7	5 32.9
11 T	3 16 7.5	20 33.0	2 25.9	10♈24.0	1♊40.9	14 20.7	2 50.5	6 50.0	29 51.1	21 43.3	9 39.0	5 32.7
12 F	3 20 4.0	21 31.0	2 22.7	24 6.0	3 42.6	14 41.4	3 22.1	6 52.6	29 50.9	21 44.0	9 37.5	5 32.6
13 S	3 24 0.6	22 28.9	2 19.5	7♉37.6	5 42.2	15 3.9	3 53.8	6 55.0	29 50.5	21 44.7	9 35.9	5 32.4
14 S	3 27 57.2	23 26.8	2 16.3	20 56.6	7 39.3	15 28.2	4 25.6	6 57.2	29 50.1	21 45.5	9 34.3	5 32.3
15 M	3 31 53.7	24 24.7	2 13.2	4♊ 0.7	9 33.9	15 54.0	4 57.5	6 59.2	29 49.6	21 46.3	9 32.7	5 32.3
16 T	3 35 50.3	25 22.5	2 10.0	16 48.6	11 25.8	16 21.4	5 29.5	7 1.1	29 49.0	21 47.2	9 31.1	5 32.2
17 W	3 39 46.8	26 20.4	2 6.8	29 20.2	13 14.8	16 50.4	6 1.6	7 2.7	29 48.2	21 48.2	9 29.6	5 32.2
18 T	3 43 43.4	27 18.1	2 3.6	11♋36.4	15 0.9	17 20.8	6 33.8	7 4.2	29 47.4	21 49.2	9 28.0	5D32.3
19 F	3 47 39.9	28 16.0	2 0.5	23 39.7	16 43.9	17 52.7	7 6.2	7 5.5	29 46.6	21 50.3	9 26.6	5 32.4
20 S	3 51 36.5	29 13.7	1 57.3	5♌33.5	18 23.8	18 25.9	7 38.6	7 6.6	29 45.5	21 51.4	9 25.0	5 32.5
21 S	3 55 33.0	0♊11.4	1 54.1	17 22.3	20 0.5	19 0.4	8 11.1	7 7.5	29 44.4	21 52.6	9 23.5	5 32.6
22 M	3 59 29.6	1 9.1	1 50.9	29 11.3	21 34.0	19 36.1	8 43.6	7 8.2	29 43.3	21 53.8	9 22.0	5 32.7
23 T	4 3 26.2	2 6.8	1 47.7	11♍ 5.7	23 4.2	20 13.1	9 16.3	7 8.7	29 42.0	21 55.0	9 20.5	5 32.9
24 W	4 7 22.7	3 4.4	1 44.6	23 11.2	24 31.0	20 51.2	9 49.1	7 9.1	29 40.6	21 56.3	9 19.1	5 33.1
25 T	4 11 19.3	4 2.0	1 41.4	5♎32.8	25 54.5	21 30.4	10 21.9	7 9.2	29 39.1	21 57.7	9 17.6	5 33.4
26 F	4 15 15.8	4 59.6	1 38.2	18 14.8	27 14.6	22 10.7	10 54.8	7 9.2	29 37.6	21 59.1	9 16.2	5 33.6
27 S	4 19 12.4	5 57.2	1 35.0	1♏20.2	28 31.3	22 52.0	11 27.8	7R 8.9	29 35.9	22 0.6	9 14.8	5 33.9
28 S	4 23 8.9	6 54.7	1 31.9	14 49.9	29 44.4	23 34.4	12 0.9	7 8.5	29 34.2	22 2.1	9 13.4	5 34.3
29 M	4 27 5.5	7 52.3	1 28.7	28 42.9	0♋54.0	24 17.7	12 34.1	7 7.9	29 32.3	22 3.6	9 12.0	5 34.6
30 T	4 31 2.0	8 49.8	1 25.5	12♐55.5	1 60.0	25 1.9	13 7.3	7 7.1	29 30.4	22 5.2	9 10.6	5 35.0
31 W	4 34 58.6	9 47.3	1 22.3	27 22.2	3 2.3	25 47.0	13 40.6	7 6.1	29 28.4	22 6.9	9 9.2	5 35.4

DAY	EPHEMERIS SIDEREAL TIME	☉	☊	☽	☿	♀	♂	♃	♄	♅	♆	♇
DECLINATION at NOON												
1 M	2 36 41.9	15N 5.4	10N25.2	13S 0.9	14N39.6	7N34.6	22N29.0	19S 3.2	20S13.8	14N59.3	13S 3.0	21N28.0
4 T	2 48 31.6	15 58.6	10 28.6	18 59.4	17 6.2	7 0.3	22 7.6	19 0.6	20 13.6	14 59.0	13 1.5	21 27.7
7 S	3 0 21.3	16 49.5	10 32.0	14 55.3	19 20.9	6 36.0	21 45.2	18 58.4	20 13.7	14 58.5	12 60.0	21 27.2
10 W	3 12 10.9	17 37.9	10 35.4	3 12.3	21 18.3	6 21.5	21 21.8	18 56.6	20 13.9	14 57.9	12 58.5	21 26.6
13 S	3 24 0.6	18 23.6	10 38.9	9N45.4	22 54.6	6 16.1	20 57.3	18 55.2	20 14.3	14 57.1	12 57.0	21 26.0
16 T	3 35 50.3	19 6.5	10 42.3	17 57.5	24 8.1	6 19.0	20 31.7	18 54.2	20 14.9	14 56.2	12 55.6	21 25.2
19 F	3 47 39.9	19 46.6	10 45.7	18 17.9	24 58.7	6 29.5	20 5.1	18 53.6	20 15.7	14 55.1	12 54.2	21 24.2
22 M	3 59 29.6	20 23.6	10 49.1	11 32.9	25 27.9	6 46.7	19 37.4	18 53.5	20 16.6	14 53.9	12 52.8	21 23.2
25 T	4 11 19.3	20 57.4	10 52.5	0 22.9	25 38.2	7 9.8	19 8.8	18 53.8	20 17.7	14 52.5	12 51.5	21 22.1
28 S	4 23 8.9	21 28.0	10 55.9	11S41.0	25 32.1	7 38.3	18 39.1	18 54.6	20 19.0	14 51.0	12 50.2	21 20.9
31 W	4 34 58.6	21 55.2	10 59.3	18 55.6	25 12.6	8 11.2	18 8.5	18 55.8	20 20.5	14 49.3	12 49.0	21 19.5

JUNE 1961

DAY	EPHEMERIS SIDEREAL TIME	☉	☊	☽	☿	♀	♂	♃	♄	♅	♆	♇
LONGITUDE at NOON												
1 T	4 38 55.2	10♊44.7	1♍19.1	11♑56.2	4♋ 0.8	26♈32.9	14♌14.0	7♒ 4.9	29♑26.3	22♌ 8.6	9♏ 7.9	5♍35.9
2 F	4 42 51.7	11 42.2	1 16.0	26 30.9	4 55.6	27 19.7	14 47.5	7R 3.5	29R24.2	22 10.3	9R 6.6	5 36.3
3 S	4 46 48.3	12 39.6	1 12.8	11♒ 0.5	5 46.5	28 7.3	15 21.1	7 2.0	29 21.9	22 12.1	9 5.3	5 36.9
4 S	4 50 44.8	13 37.1	1 9.6	25 21.1	6 33.4	28 55.7	15 54.7	7 0.2	29 19.6	22 14.0	9 4.0	5 37.4
5 M	4 54 41.4	14 34.5	1 6.4	9♓30.1	7 16.2	29 44.8	16 28.4	6 58.3	29 17.1	22 15.8	9 2.7	5 38.0
6 T	4 58 37.9	15 31.9	1 3.3	23 26.9	7 55.0	0♉34.6	17 2.2	6 56.1	29 14.6	22 17.8	9 1.5	5 38.6
7 W	5 2 34.5	16 29.3	1 0.1	7♈11.3	8 29.5	1 25.1	17 36.0	6 53.8	29 12.1	22 19.7	9 0.2	5 39.2
8 T	5 6 31.1	17 26.7	0 56.9	20 43.7	8 59.7	2 16.2	18 9.9	6 51.3	29 9.4	22 21.8	8 59.0	5 39.8
9 F	5 10 27.6	18 24.2	0 53.7	4♉ 4.4	9 25.6	3 8.0	18 44.0	6 48.7	29 6.7	22 23.9	8 57.9	5 40.6
10 S	5 14 24.2	19 21.5	0 50.6	17 13.4	9 47.0	4 0.4	19 18.1	6 45.8	29 3.9	22 26.0	8 56.8	5 41.3
11 S	5 18 20.7	20 18.9	0 47.4	0♊10.3	10 3.8	4 53.3	19 52.2	6 42.8	29 1.0	22 28.1	8 55.6	5 42.0
12 M	5 22 17.3	21 16.2	0 44.2	12 54.7	10 16.2	5 46.8	20 26.4	6 39.6	28 58.0	22 30.3	8 54.5	5 42.8
13 T	5 26 13.8	22 13.6	0 41.0	25 26.5	10 24.0	6 40.8	21 0.7	6 36.2	28 55.0	22 32.6	8 53.4	5 43.6
14 W	5 30 10.4	23 10.9	0 37.9	7♋45.7	10 27.2	7 35.4	21 35.1	6 32.6	28 51.9	22 34.9	8 52.3	5 44.4
15 T	5 34 7.0	24 8.2	0 34.7	19 53.2	10R25.9	8 30.4	22 9.5	6 28.9	28 48.7	22 37.2	8 51.3	5 45.2
16 F	5 38 3.5	25 5.6	0 31.5	1♌51.0	10 20.1	9 26.0	22 44.0	6 24.9	28 45.4	22 39.6	8 50.3	5 46.1
17 S	5 42 0.1	26 2.9	0 28.3	13 41.7	10 10.0	10 21.9	23 18.6	6 20.8	28 42.1	22 42.0	8 49.3	5 47.0
18 S	5 45 56.6	27 0.1	0 25.1	25 28.8	9 55.8	11 18.4	23 53.2	6 16.6	28 38.7	22 44.4	8 48.3	5 48.0
19 M	5 49 53.2	27 57.4	0 22.0	7♍16.7	9 37.6	12 15.2	24 27.9	6 12.2	28 35.3	22 46.9	8 47.4	5 48.9
20 T	5 53 49.7	28 54.7	0 18.8	19 10.3	9 15.7	13 12.5	25 2.7	6 7.6	28 31.8	22 49.4	8 46.5	5 49.9
21 W	5 57 46.3	29 51.9	0 15.6	1♎14.9	8 50.4	14 10.2	25 37.5	6 2.8	28 28.2	22 52.0	8 45.6	5 50.9
22 T	6 1 42.9	0♋49.2	0 12.4	13 35.8	8 22.2	15 8.3	26 12.4	5 57.9	28 24.6	22 54.6	8 44.7	5 52.0
23 F	6 5 39.4	1 46.4	0 9.3	26 17.9	7 51.5	16 6.8	26 47.4	5 52.9	28 20.9	22 57.2	8 43.9	5 53.0
24 S	6 9 36.0	2 43.6	0 6.1	9♏24.9	7 18.7	17 5.6	27 22.4	5 47.7	28 17.2	22 59.9	8 43.1	5 54.1
25 S	6 13 32.5	3 40.8	0 2.9	22 59.1	6 44.4	18 4.8	27 57.4	5 42.3	28 13.4	23 2.6	8 42.3	5 55.2
26 M	6 17 29.1	4 38.0	29♌59.7	7♐ 0.4	6 9.2	19 4.3	28 32.6	5 36.8	28 9.6	23 5.4	8 41.6	5 56.4
27 T	6 21 25.6	5 35.2	29 56.6	21 25.9	5 33.6	20 4.2	29 7.8	5 31.2	28 5.7	23 8.1	8 40.8	5 57.6
28 W	6 25 22.2	6 32.4	29 53.4	6♑10.0	4 58.3	21 4.4	29 43.0	5 25.4	28 1.8	23 10.9	8 40.1	5 58.8
29 T	6 29 18.8	7 29.6	29 50.2	21 5.0	4 23.9	22 4.9	0♍18.3	5 19.5	27 57.8	23 13.8	8 39.5	5 60.0
30 F	6 33 15.3	8 26.8	29 47.0	6♒ 2.2	3 51.1	23 5.8	0 53.7	5 13.6	27 53.8	23 16.7	8 38.9	6 1.3

DAY	EPHEMERIS SIDEREAL TIME	☉	☊	☽	☿	♀	♂	♃	♄	♅	♆	♇
DECLINATION at NOON												
1 T	4 38 55.2	22N 3.6	11N 0.4	19S 8.5	25N 3.5	8N23.1	17N58.1	18S56.3	20S21.0	14N48.7	12S48.6	21N19.1
4 S	4 50 44.8	22 26.2	11 3.8	12 39.1	24 30.0	9 1.1	17 26.2	18 58.1	20 22.7	14 46.9	12 47.5	21 17.6
7 W	5 2 34.5	22 45.4	11 7.2	0N 3.9	23 49.1	9 42.2	16 53.3	19 0.3	20 24.5	14 44.9	12 46.4	21 16.1
10 S	5 14 24.2	23 0.9	11 10.6	12 15.6	23 3.1	10 25.7	16 19.5	19 2.9	20 26.5	14 42.8	12 45.4	21 14.4
13 T	5 26 13.8	23 12.8	11 13.9	18 49.6	22 14.5	11 11.1	15 44.8	19 5.9	20 28.6	14 40.6	12 44.4	21 12.7
16 F	5 38 3.5	23 21.0	11 17.3	17 28.7	21 25.6	11 57.8	15 9.2	19 9.4	20 30.8	14 38.2	12 43.6	21 10.9
19 M	5 49 53.2	23 25.6	11 20.7	9 31.4	20 38.9	12 45.3	14 32.8	19 13.1	20 33.2	14 35.7	12 42.8	21 9.1
22 T	6 1 42.9	23 26.4	11 24.0	2S 3.1	19 56.7	13 33.2	13 55.5	19 17.2	20 35.6	14 33.1	12 42.1	21 7.1
25 S	6 13 32.5	23 23.5	11 27.4	13 36.0	19 21.7	14 21.0	13 17.5	19 21.7	20 38.1	14 30.4	12 41.4	21 5.1
28 W	6 25 22.2	23 16.8	11 30.7	19 15.3	18 56.2	15 8.2	12 38.6	19 26.4	20 40.7	14 27.6	12 40.9	21 3.1

JULY 1961

DAY	EPHEMERIS SIDEREAL TIME	☉	☊	☽	☿	♀	♂	♃	♄	♅	♆	♇
	h m s	° ′	° ′	° ′	° ′	° ′	° ′	° ′	° ′	° ′	° ′	° ′
						LONGITUDE at NOON						
1 S	6 37 11.9	9♋24.0	29♌43.8	20♒53.3	3♋20.2	24♉ 7.0	1♍29.2	5♒ 7.4	27♑49.8	23♌19.6	8♏38.3	6♍ 2.5
2 S	6 41 8.4	10 21.2	29 40.7	5♓32.0	2R52.0	25 8.4	2 4.6	5R 1.1	27R45.7	23 22.6	8R37.7	6 3.8
3 M	6 45 5.0	11 18.4	29 37.5	19 53.8	2 26.8	26 10.2	2 40.2	4 54.7	27 41.5	23 25.6	8 37.1	6 5.1
4 T	6 49 1.5	12 15.6	29 34.3	3♈56.7	2 5.2	27 12.2	3 15.8	4 48.2	27 37.4	23 28.6	8 36.6	6 6.5
5 W	6 52 58.1	13 12.8	29 31.1	17 40.2	1 47.5	28 14.5	3 51.5	4 41.6	27 33.2	23 31.6	8 36.1	6 7.8
6 T	6 56 54.7	14 10.0	29 28.0	1♉ 5.3	1 34.1	29 17.0	4 27.2	4 34.9	27 28.9	23 34.7	8 35.7	6 9.2
7 F	7 0 51.2	15 7.2	29 24.8	14 13.4	1 25.2	0♊19.8	5 3.0	4 28.0	27 24.7	23 37.8	8 35.2	6 10.6
8 S	7 4 47.8	16 4.4	29 21.6	27 6.1	1 21.2	1 22.9	5 38.8	4 21.1	27 20.4	23 40.9	8 34.8	6 12.0
9 S	7 8 44.3	17 1.6	29 18.4	9♊45.2	1D22.1	2 26.1	6 14.7	4 14.1	27 16.0	23 44.1	8 34.5	6 13.5
10 M	7 12 40.9	17 58.8	29 15.3	22 12.0	1 28.2	3 29.7	6 50.7	4 7.0	27 11.7	23 47.3	8 34.1	6 14.9
11 T	7 16 37.4	18 56.1	29 12.1	4♋27.9	1 39.5	4 33.4	7 26.7	3 59.8	27 7.3	23 50.5	8 33.8	6 16.4
12 W	7 20 34.0	19 53.3	29 8.9	16 34.1	1 56.1	5 37.4	8 2.8	3 52.5	27 3.0	23 53.7	8 33.5	6 17.9
13 T	7 24 30.6	20 50.6	29 5.7	28 32.2	2 18.0	6 41.5	8 38.9	3 45.2	26 58.6	23 57.0	8 33.3	6 19.5
14 F	7 28 27.1	21 47.8	29 2.5	10♌24.0	2 45.3	7 45.9	9 15.1	3 37.8	26 54.2	24 0.3	8 33.1	6 21.0
15 S	7 32 23.7	22 45.1	28 59.4	22 11.6	3 18.0	8 50.5	9 51.4	3 30.3	26 49.8	24 3.6	8 32.9	6 22.6
16 S	7 36 20.2	23 42.3	28 56.2	3♍57.8	3 55.9	9 55.3	10 27.7	3 22.8	26 45.3	24 6.9	8 32.7	6 24.2
17 M	7 40 16.8	24 39.6	28 53.0	15 46.1	4 39.2	11 0.2	11 4.1	3 15.2	26 40.9	24 10.3	8 32.6	6 25.8
18 T	7 44 13.3	25 36.8	28 49.8	27 40.5	5 27.7	12 5.4	11 40.5	3 7.6	26 36.5	24 13.6	8 32.5	6 27.4
19 W	7 48 9.9	26 34.1	28 46.7	9♎45.2	6 21.3	13 10.7	12 17.0	2 59.9	26 32.0	24 17.1	8 32.5	6 29.1
20 T	7 52 6.4	27 31.4	28 43.5	22 5.1	7 20.1	14 16.2	12 53.5	2 52.2	26 27.6	24 20.5	8 32.5	6 30.7
21 F	7 56 3.0	28 28.7	28 40.3	4♏44.8	8 24.1	15 21.9	13 30.1	2 44.6	26 23.2	24 24.0	8 32.5	6 32.5
22 S	7 59 59.6	29 26.0	28 37.1	17 48.3	9 32.9	16 27.8	14 6.8	2 36.8	26 18.8	24 27.4	8D32.6	6 34.2
23 S	8 3 56.1	0♌23.2	28 34.0	1♐18.6	10 46.6	17 33.8	14 43.5	2 29.1	26 14.3	24 30.9	8 32.7	6 35.9
24 M	8 7 52.7	1 20.5	28 30.8	15 17.0	12 5.1	18 40.0	15 20.2	2 21.3	26 9.9	24 34.4	8 32.8	6 37.6
25 T	8 11 49.2	2 17.8	28 27.6	29 42.2	13 28.3	19 46.3	15 57.0	2 13.5	26 5.5	24 37.9	8 32.9	6 39.4
26 W	8 15 45.8	3 15.1	28 24.4	14♑30.1	14 55.9	20 52.9	16 33.9	2 5.8	26 1.1	24 41.5	8 33.1	6 41.1
27 T	8 19 42.3	4 12.4	28 21.2	29 33.6	16 28.0	21 59.5	17 10.8	1 58.0	25 56.8	24 45.0	8 33.3	6 42.9
28 F	8 23 38.9	5 9.8	28 18.1	14♒44.0	18 4.2	23 6.4	17 47.7	1 50.3	25 52.4	24 48.6	8 33.5	6 44.7
29 S	8 27 35.4	6 7.1	28 14.9	29 51.7	19 44.4	24 13.4	18 24.7	1 42.5	25 48.1	24 52.2	8 33.8	6 46.5
30 S	8 31 32.0	7 4.4	28 11.7	14♓48.1	21 28.3	25 20.5	19 1.8	1 34.8	25 43.8	24 55.8	8 34.1	6 48.3
31 M	8 35 28.6	8 1.8	28 8.5	29 26.2	23 15.8	26 27.8	19 38.9	1 27.1	25 39.5	24 59.4	8 34.4	6 50.2
						DECLINATION at NOON						
1 S	6 37 11.9	23N 6.5	11N34.1	13S54.8	18N42.1	15N54.5	11N59.0	19S31.3	20S43.4	14N24.7	12S40.4	21N 0.9
4 T	6 49 1.5	22 52.6	11 37.4	1 12.3	18 40.4	16 39.4	11 18.7	19 36.5	20 46.1	14 21.7	12 40.1	20 58.8
7 F	7 0 51.2	22 35.1	11 40.7	11N19.1	18 50.9	17 22.6	10 37.7	19 41.9	20 48.9	14 18.6	12 39.8	20 56.5
10 M	7 12 40.9	22 14.0	11 44.1	18 30.8	19 12.1	18 3.6	9 56.1	19 47.4	20 51.7	14 15.4	12 39.6	20 54.3
13 T	7 24 30.6	21 49.5	11 47.4	17 59.2	19 41.5	18 42.1	9 13.8	19 53.0	20 54.5	14 12.1	12 39.5	20 52.0
16 S	7 36 20.2	21 21.7	11 50.7	10 36.6	20 15.8	19 17.6	8 30.9	19 58.7	20 57.3	14 8.8	12 39.5	20 49.7
19 W	7 48 9.9	20 50.6	11 54.0	0S37.3	20 51.0	19 50.0	7 47.5	20 4.5	21 0.1	14 5.4	12 39.6	20 47.3
22 S	7 59 59.6	20 16.3	11 57.3	12 10.7	21 22.4	20 18.9	7 3.4	20 10.2	21 2.9	14 1.9	12 39.8	20 44.9
25 T	8 11 49.2	19 39.0	12 0.7	19 0.5	21 45.2	20 43.9	6 19.0	20 15.9	21 5.6	13 58.3	12 40.0	20 42.5
28 F	8 23 38.9	18 58.8	12 4.0	15 19.3	21 53.9	21 4.8	5 34.0	20 21.6	21 8.3	13 54.7	12 40.4	20 40.1
31 M	8 35 28.6	18 15.7	12 7.3	2 48.2	21 43.7	21 21.4	4 48.7	20 27.1	21 11.0	13 51.1	12 40.9	20 37.7

AUGUST 1961

DAY	EPHEMERIS SIDEREAL TIME	☉	☊	☽	☿	♀	♂	♃	♄	♅	♆	♇
						LONGITUDE at NOON						
1 T	8 39 25.1	8♌59.2	28♌ 5.4	13♈41.8	25♋ 6.3	27♊35.2	20♍16.1	1♒19.5	25♑35.2	25♌ 3.0	8♏34.8	6♍52.0
2 W	8 43 21.7	9 56.6	28 2.2	27 33.0	26 59.8	28 42.8	20 53.3	1R11.8	25R31.0	25 6.6	8 35.2	6 53.9
3 T	8 47 18.2	10 54.0	27 59.0	11♉ 0.0	28 55.8	29 50.6	21 30.6	1 4.3	25 26.8	25 10.3	8 35.6	6 55.7
4 F	8 51 14.8	11 51.5	27 55.8	24 4.7	0♌53.9	0♋58.4	22 7.9	0 56.7	25 22.6	25 14.0	8 36.1	6 57.6
5 S	8 55 11.3	12 49.0	27 52.6	6♊49.7	2 53.8	2 6.4	22 45.3	0 49.2	25 18.5	25 17.6	8 36.6	6 59.5
6 S	8 59 7.9	13 46.4	27 49.5	19 18.0	4 55.2	3 14.6	23 22.8	0 41.8	25 14.4	25 21.3	8 37.1	7 1.4
7 M	9 3 4.4	14 44.0	27 46.3	1♋32.7	6 57.7	4 22.8	24 0.3	0 34.5	25 10.3	25 25.0	8 37.6	7 3.4
8 T	9 7 1.0	15 41.5	27 43.1	13 36.8	9 0.9	5 31.2	24 37.8	0 27.2	25 6.3	25 28.7	8 38.2	7 5.3
9 W	9 10 57.6	16 39.0	27 39.9	25 33.1	11 4.5	6 39.8	25 15.5	0 20.0	25 2.3	25 32.4	8 38.8	7 7.2
10 T	9 14 54.1	17 36.6	27 36.8	7♌23.9	13 8.3	7 48.4	25 53.1	0 12.9	24 58.4	25 36.1	8 39.5	7 9.2
11 F	9 18 50.7	18 34.2	27 33.6	19 11.7	15 12.0	8 57.2	26 30.9	0 5.9	24 54.5	25 39.9	8 40.2	7 11.2
12 S	9 22 47.2	19 31.9	27 30.4	0♍58.5	17 15.2	10 6.1	27 8.7	29♑58.9	24 50.7	25 43.6	8 40.9	7 13.2
13 S	9 26 43.8	20 29.5	27 27.2	12 46.9	19 17.9	11 15.1	27 46.5	29 52.1	24 46.9	25 47.3	8 41.7	7 15.1
14 M	9 30 40.3	21 27.1	27 24.1	24 39.3	21 19.9	12 24.2	28 24.4	29 45.3	24 43.2	25 51.1	8 42.5	7 17.1
15 T	9 34 36.9	22 24.8	27 20.9	6♎38.5	23 21.0	13 33.4	29 2.4	29 38.7	24 39.5	25 54.8	8 43.3	7 19.1
16 W	9 38 33.4	23 22.5	27 17.7	18 47.8	25 21.0	14 42.8	29 40.4	29 32.2	24 35.9	25 58.6	8 44.1	7 21.1
17 T	9 42 30.0	24 20.2	27 14.5	1♏10.4	27 19.9	15 52.2	0♎18.4	29 25.7	24 32.3	26 2.3	8 45.0	7 23.1
18 F	9 46 26.5	25 17.9	27 11.3	13 50.0	29 17.7	17 1.8	0 56.5	29 19.5	24 28.9	26 6.0	8 45.9	7 25.2
19 S	9 50 23.1	26 15.6	27 8.2	26 50.1	1♍14.2	18 11.4	1 34.7	29 13.3	24 25.4	26 9.8	8 46.8	7 27.2
20 S	9 54 19.6	27 13.4	27 5.0	10♐13.7	3 9.4	19 21.2	2 12.9	29 7.2	24 22.0	26 13.5	8 47.8	7 29.2
21 M	9 58 16.2	28 11.2	27 1.8	24 2.5	5 3.3	20 31.0	2 51.2	29 1.3	24 18.7	26 17.3	8 48.8	7 31.2
22 T	10 2 12.7	29 9.0	26 58.6	8♑16.9	6 55.8	21 41.0	3 29.5	28 55.6	24 15.5	26 21.0	8 49.8	7 33.3
23 W	10 6 9.3	0♍ 6.8	26 55.5	22 54.8	8 47.0	22 51.1	4 7.8	28 49.9	24 12.3	26 24.8	8 50.8	7 35.3
24 T	10 10 5.9	1 4.6	26 52.3	7♒51.6	10 36.9	24 1.2	4 46.3	28 44.4	24 9.2	26 28.5	8 51.9	7 37.3
25 F	10 14 2.4	2 2.4	26 49.1	23 0.2	12 25.4	25 11.5	5 24.7	28 39.1	24 6.2	26 32.2	8 53.0	7 39.4
26 S	10 17 59.0	3 0.3	26 45.9	8♓11.6	14 12.5	26 21.9	6 3.2	28 33.9	24 3.3	26 36.0	8 54.1	7 41.4
27 S	10 21 55.5	3 58.2	26 42.7	23 16.5	15 58.4	27 32.4	6 41.8	28 28.8	24 0.4	26 39.7	8 55.3	7 43.5
28 M	10 25 52.1	4 56.2	26 39.6	8♈ 6.2	17 42.9	28 43.0	7 20.4	28 24.0	23 57.6	26 43.4	8 56.5	7 45.5
29 T	10 29 48.6	5 54.1	26 36.4	22 34.0	19 26.1	29 53.6	7 59.1	28 19.2	23 54.9	26 47.1	8 57.7	7 47.6
30 W	10 33 45.2	6 52.1	26 33.2	6♉35.8	21 8.0	1♌ 4.4	8 37.9	28 14.7	23 52.2	26 50.8	8 59.0	7 49.7
31 T	10 37 41.7	7 50.1	26 30.0	20 10.3	22 48.7	2 15.3	9 16.7	28 10.2	23 49.6	26 54.5	9 0.2	7 51.7
						DECLINATION at NOON						
1 T	8 39 25.1	18N 0.7	12N 8.4	1N52.7	21N35.5	21N25.9	4N33.5	20S28.9	21S11.9	13N49.9	12S41.0	20N36.9
4 F	8 51 14.8	17 14.1	12 11.6	13 41.0	20 55.0	21 36.3	3 47.6	20 34.2	21 14.4	13 46.2	12 41.6	20 34.5
7 M	9 3 4.4	16 25.0	12 14.9	19 4.1	19 50.9	21 41.9	3 1.4	20 39.3	21 16.9	13 42.4	12 42.3	20 32.0
10 T	9 14 54.1	15 33.4	12 18.2	16 41.4	18 25.1	21 42.5	2 14.8	20 44.3	21 19.3	13 38.7	12 43.0	20 29.6
13 S	9 26 43.8	14 39.6	12 21.5	8 5.0	16 41.2	21 38.1	1 28.0	20 48.9	21 21.6	13 34.9	12 43.9	20 27.2
16 W	9 38 33.4	13 43.8	12 24.8	3S30.9	14 43.6	21 28.4	0 40.9	20 53.4	21 23.8	13 31.1	12 44.8	20 24.8
19 S	9 50 23.1	12 45.9	12 28.0	14 17.4	12 36.4	21 13.6	0S 6.3	20 57.5	21 25.9	13 27.3	12 45.8	20 22.5
22 T	10 2 12.7	11 46.3	12 31.3	19 11.4	10 22.9	20 53.5	0 53.7	21 1.4	21 27.8	13 23.5	12 46.9	20 20.2
25 F	10 14 2.4	10 45.0	12 34.5	13 28.9	8 6.0	20 28.2	1 41.1	21 4.9	21 29.7	13 19.7	12 48.1	20 17.9
28 M	10 25 52.1	9 42.1	12 37.8	0N 1.4	5 47.8	19 57.8	2 28.7	21 8.1	21 31.4	13 15.9	12 49.4	20 15.6
31 T	10 37 41.7	8 37.9	12 41.0	12 43.4	3 30.0	19 22.3	3 16.2	21 11.0	21 33.0	13 12.1	12 50.7	20 13.4

SEPTEMBER 1961

DAY	EPHEMERIS SIDEREAL TIME	☉	☊	☽	☿	♀	♂	♃	♄	♅	♆	♇
	h m s	° ′	° ′	° ′	° ′	° ′	° ′	° ′	° ′	° ′	° ′	° ′
						LONGITUDE at NOON						
1 F	10 41 38.3	8 ♍ 48.2	26 ♌ 26.8	3 ♓ 18.5	24 ♍ 28.2	3 ♌ 26.3	9 ♎ 55.6	28 ♑ 6.1	23 ♑ 47.2	26 ♌ 58.2	9 ♏ 1.6	7 ♍ 53.8
2 S	10 45 34.8	9 46.3	26 23.7	16 3.1	26 6.3	4 37.4	10 34.5	28R 2.0	23R 44.8	27 1.9	9 2.9	7 55.9
3 S	10 49 31.4	10 44.5	26 20.5	28 27.8	27 43.3	5 48.6	11 13.4	27 58.1	23 42.5	27 5.6	9 4.3	7 57.9
4 M	10 53 27.9	11 42.6	26 17.3	10 ♋ 36.9	29 19.0	6 59.8	11 52.5	27 54.4	23 40.2	27 9.3	9 5.6	7 60.0
5 T	10 57 24.5	12 40.8	26 14.1	22 34.6	0 ♎ 53.5	8 11.2	12 31.5	27 50.8	23 38.1	27 12.9	9 7.0	8 2.0
6 W	11 1 21.0	13 39.0	26 11.0	4 ♌ 25.3	2 26.8	9 22.6	13 10.7	27 47.4	23 36.0	27 16.5	9 8.5	8 4.1
7 T	11 5 17.6	14 37.3	26 7.8	16 12.4	3 59.0	10 34.1	13 49.8	27 44.2	23 34.0	27 20.2	9 9.9	8 6.1
8 F	11 9 14.1	15 35.5	26 4.6	27 59.3	5 29.9	11 45.8	14 29.1	27 41.2	23 32.1	27 23.8	9 11.4	8 8.2
9 S	11 13 10.7	16 33.8	26 1.4	9 ♍ 48.8	6 59.6	12 57.4	15 8.4	27 38.4	23 30.3	27 27.4	9 12.9	8 10.2
10 S	11 17 7.2	17 32.2	25 58.2	21 43.1	8 28.2	14 9.2	15 47.8	27 35.8	23 28.6	27 31.0	9 14.5	8 12.3
11 M	11 21 3.8	18 30.6	25 55.1	3 ♎ 44.3	9 55.5	15 21.1	16 27.2	27 33.3	23 27.0	27 34.5	9 16.0	8 14.3
12 T	11 25 0.4	19 29.0	25 51.9	15 54.2	11 21.6	16 33.0	17 6.6	27 31.1	23 25.5	27 38.1	9 17.6	8 16.3
13 W	11 28 56.9	20 27.4	25 48.7	28 14.5	12 46.5	17 45.0	17 46.2	27 29.0	23 24.1	27 41.6	9 19.2	8 18.3
14 T	11 32 53.5	21 25.9	25 45.5	10 ♏ 47.0	14 10.1	18 57.1	18 25.7	27 27.1	23 22.7	27 45.1	9 20.8	8 20.4
15 F	11 36 50.0	22 24.3	25 42.4	23 33.6	15 32.4	20 9.3	19 5.4	27 25.4	23 21.5	27 48.6	9 22.5	8 22.4
16 S	11 40 46.6	23 22.9	25 39.2	6 ♐ 36.2	16 53.4	21 21.5	19 45.1	27 24.0	23 20.3	27 52.1	9 24.2	8 24.4
17 S	11 44 43.1	24 21.4	25 36.0	19 56.8	18 13.0	22 33.8	20 24.8	27 22.7	23 19.3	27 55.6	9 25.9	8 26.4
18 M	11 48 39.7	25 20.0	25 32.8	3 ♑ 37.0	19 31.3	23 46.2	21 4.6	27 21.6	23 18.3	27 59.0	9 27.6	8 28.4
19 T	11 52 36.2	26 18.6	25 29.6	17 37.7	20 48.0	24 58.7	21 44.5	27 20.7	23 17.5	28 2.4	9 29.3	8 30.3
20 W	11 56 32.8	27 17.2	25 26.5	1 ♒ 58.5	22 3.3	26 11.2	22 24.4	27 20.0	23 16.7	28 5.8	9 31.1	8 32.3
21 T	12 0 29.3	28 15.8	25 23.3	16 37.1	23 16.9	27 23.8	23 4.3	27 1..4	23 16.0	28 9.2	9 32.8	8 34.3
22 F	12 4 25.9	29 14.5	25 20.1	1 ♓ 29.3	24 28.9	28 36.5	23 44.4	27 19.2	23 15.5	28 12.6	9 34.7	8 36.3
23 S	12 8 22.4	0 ♎ 13.3	25 16.9	16 28.6	25 39.1	29 49.3	24 24.4	27 19.1	23 15.0	28 15.9	9 36.5	8 38.2
24 S	12 12 19.0	1 12.0	25 13.8	1 ♈ 26.8	26 47.4	1 ♍ 2.1	25 4.6	27 19.1	23 14.7	28 19.2	9 38.3	8 40.2
25 M	12 16 15.5	2 10.8	25 10.6	16 15.4	27 53.7	2 15.0	25 44.7	27D 19.4	23 14.4	28 22.5	9 40.2	8 42.1
26 T	12 20 12.1	3 9.6	25 7.4	0 ♉ 46.5	28 57.8	3 27.9	26 25.0	27 19.9	23 14.2	28 25.7	9 42.1	8 44.0
27 W	12 24 8.6	4 8.4	25 4.2	14 54.1	29 59.6	4 41.0	27 5.2	27 20.5	23 14.1	28 28.9	9 44.0	8 45.9
28 T	12 28 5.2	5 7.3	25 1.0	28 35.0	0 ♏ 59.0	5 54.1	27 45.6	27 21.4	23D 14.2	28 32.1	9 45.9	8 47.8
29 F	12 32 1.7	6 6.2	24 57.9	11 ♊ 48.6	1 55.7	7 7.2	28 26.0	27 22.4	23 14.3	28 35.3	9 47.8	8 49.7
30 S	12 35 58.3	7 5.2	24 54.7	24 36.6	2 49.6	8 20.5	29 6.4	27 23.7	23 14.5	28 38.4	9 49.8	8 51.5
						DECLINATION at NOON						
1 F	10 41 38.3	8N 16.2	12N 42.1	15N 39.2	2N 44.4	19N 9.3	3S 32.1	21S 11.9	21S 33.5	13N 10.8	12S 51.2	20N 12.7
4 M	10 53 27.9	7 10.3	12 45.3	19 11.1	0 29.1	18 27.3	4 19.6	21 14.3	21 34.9	13 7.1	12 52.6	20 10.6
7 T	11 5 17.6	6 3.4	12 48.6	15 0.9	1S 43.1	17 40.5	5 7.0	21 16.4	21 36.1	13 3.4	12 54.1	20 8.5
10 S	11 17 7.2	4 55.5	12 51.8	5 17.6	3 51.4	16 49.2	5 54.3	21 18.1	21 37.2	12 59.7	12 55.7	20 6.4
13 W	11 28 56.9	3 46.9	12 55.0	6S 33.2	5 54.9	15 53.6	6 41.4	21 19.5	21 38.2	12 56.1	12 57.3	20 4.5
16 S	11 40 46.6	2 37.7	12 58.2	16 19.4	7 52.8	14 53.8	7 28.3	21 20.5	21 39.0	12 52.5	12 59.0	20 2.6
19 T	11 52 36.2	1 28.0	13 1.5	18 59.3	9 44.1	13 50.2	8 14.9	21 21.1	21 39.7	12 49.0	13 0.7	20 0.8
22 F	12 4 25.9	0 18.1	13 4.7	11 20.1	11 28.0	12 43.0	9 1.1	21 21.4	21 40.2	12 45.6	13 2.5	19 59.0
25 M	12 16 15.5	0S 52.0	13 7.9	2N 44.6	13 2.9	11 32.5	9 46.9	21 21.3	21 40.6	12 42.2	13 4.3	19 57.3
28 T	12 28 5.2	2 2.1	13 11.1	14 47.2	14 27.4	10 18.9	10 32.3	21 20.9	21 40.8	12 38.9	13 6.2	19 55.8

OCTOBER 1961

DAY	EPHEMERIS SIDEREAL TIME	☉	☊	☽	☿	♀	♂	♃	♄	♅	♆	♇
						LONGITUDE at NOON						
1 S	12 39 54.8	8 ♎ 4.2	24 ♌ 51.5	7 ♋ 2.6	3 ♏ 40.3	9 ♍ 33.7	29 ♎ 46.9	27 ♑ 25.1	23 ♑ 14.8	28 ♌ 41.5	9 ♏ 51.7	8 ♍ 53.4
2 M	12 43 51.4	9 3.2	24 48.3	19 11.1	4 27.6	10 47.1	0 ♏ 27.5	27 26.7	23 15.2	28 44.6	9 53.7	8 55.2
3 T	12 47 47.9	10 2.3	24 45.1	1 ♌ 7.2	5 11.1	12 0.5	1 8.2	27 28.5	23 15.8	28 47.7	9 55.7	8 57.0
4 W	12 51 44.5	11 1.4	24 42.0	12 56.1	5 50.7	13 14.0	1 48.8	27 30.6	23 16.4	28 50.7	9 57.7	8 58.8
5 T	12 55 41.0	12 0.5	24 38.8	24 42.6	6 25.9	14 27.6	2 29.6	27 32.8	23 17.1	28 53.7	9 59.7	9 0.6
6 F	12 59 37.6	12 59.7	24 35.6	6 ♍ 31.1	6 56.2	15 41.2	3 10.4	27 35.2	23 17.9	28 56.6	10 1.8	9 2.4
7 S	13 3 34.2	13 58.9	24 32.4	18 25.3	7 21.4	16 54.8	3 51.3	27 37.8	23 18.8	28 59.5	10 3.8	9 4.2
8 S	13 7 30.7	14 58.2	24 29.3	0 ♎ 28.2	7 40.8	18 8.6	4 32.2	27 40.5	23 19.9	29 2.4	10 5.9	9 5.9
9 M	13 11 27.3	15 57.5	24 26.1	12 41.6	7 54.2	19 22.3	5 13.2	27 43.5	23 21.0	29 5.3	10 8.0	9 7.6
10 T	13 15 23.8	16 56.8	24 22.9	25 7.0	8 0.8	20 36.1	5 54.2	27 46.7	23 22.2	29 8.1	10 10.0	9 9.4
11 W	13 19 20.4	17 56.2	24 19.7	7 ♏ 44.8	8R 0.4	21 50.0	6 35.3	27 50.0	23 23.5	29 10.9	10 12.2	9 11.0
12 T	13 23 16.9	18 55.5	24 16.5	20 35.2	7 52.3	23 4.0	7 16.4	27 53.6	23 24.9	29 13.6	10 14.3	9 12.7
13 F	13 27 13.5	19 55.0	24 13.4	3 ♐ 38.0	7 36.4	24 18.0	7 57.7	27 57.3	23 26.5	29 16.4	10 16.4	9 14.4
14 S	13 31 10.0	20 54.5	24 10.2	16 53.0	7 12.1	25 32.0	8 39.0	28 1.2	23 28.1	29 19.0	10 18.6	9 16.1
15 S	13 35 6.6	21 54.0	24 7.0	0 ♑ 20.3	6 39.3	26 46.1	9 20.3	28 5.3	23 29.8	29 21.6	10 20.7	9 17.7
16 M	13 39 3.1	22 53.5	24 3.8	14 0.2	5 58.0	28 0.2	10 1.6	28 9.6	23 31.6	29 24.2	10 22.9	9 19.3
17 T	13 42 59.7	23 53.0	24 0.7	27 53.0	5 8.6	29 14.3	10 43.1	28 14.0	23 33.5	29 26.8	10 25.1	9 20.9
18 W	13 46 56.2	24 52.6	23 57.5	11 ♒ 59.0	4 11.5	0 ♎ 28.5	11 24.6	28 18.6	23 35.5	29 29.3	10 27.2	9 22.4
19 T	13 50 52.8	25 52.2	23 54.3	26 17.4	3 7.6	1 42.8	12 6.1	28 23.5	23 37.6	29 31.7	10 29.4	9 24.0
20 F	13 54 49.3	26 51.8	23 51.1	10 ♓ 46.3	1 58.2	2 57.0	12 47.7	28 28.4	23 39.8	29 34.2	10 31.6	9 25.5
21 S	13 58 45.9	27 51.5	23 47.9	25 22.0	0 45.0	4 11.4	13 29.3	28 33.6	23 42.1	29 36.6	10 33.8	9 27.0
22 S	14 2 42.4	28 51.1	23 44.8	9 ♈ 59.2	29 ♎ 29.8	5 25.7	14 11.0	28 38.9	23 44.5	29 38.9	10 36.0	9 28.4
23 M	14 6 39.0	29 50.9	23 41.6	24 31.4	28 14.9	6 40.1	14 52.8	28 44.4	23 46.9	29 41.2	10 38.2	9 29.9
24 T	14 10 35.5	0 ♏ 50.6	23 38.4	8 ♉ 51.4	27 2.5	7 54.6	15 34.6	28 50.1	23 49.5	29 43.4	10 40.4	9 31.3
25 W	14 14 32.1	1 50.4	23 35.2	22 53.2	25 54.8	9 9.1	16 16.5	28 55.9	23 52.2	29 45.7	10 42.6	9 32.7
26 T	14 18 28.7	2 50.2	23 32.1	6 ♊ 32.3	24 53.9	10 23.6	16 58.4	29 1.9	23 54.9	29 47.8	10 44.9	9 34.1
27 F	14 22 25.2	3 50.1	23 28.9	19 46.7	24 1.5	11 38.2	17 40.4	29 8.0	23 57.7	29 49.9	10 47.1	9 35.5
28 S	14 26 21.8	4 50.0	23 25.7	2 ♋ 36.7	23 19.1	12 52.8	18 22.4	29 14.3	24 0.7	29 52.0	10 49.3	9 36.8
29 S	14 30 18.3	5 49.9	23 22.5	15 4.7	22 47.6	14 7.4	19 4.5	29 20.8	24 3.7	29 54.0	10 51.6	9 38.1
30 M	14 34 14.9	6 49.8	23 19.3	27 14.7	22 27.5	15 22.1	19 46.7	29 27.5	24 6.8	29 56.0	10 53.8	9 39.4
31 T	14 38 11.4	7 49.8	23 16.2	9 ♌ 11.5	22 19.0	16 36.8	20 28.9	29 34.3	24 10.0	29 58.0	10 56.0	9 40.7
						DECLINATION at NOON						
1 S	12 39 54.8	3S 12.1	13N 14.2	19N 19.1	15S 39.3	9N 2.6	11S 17.1	21S 20.2	21S 40.8	12N 35.7	13S 8.1	19N 54.3
4 W	12 51 44.5	4 21.7	13 17.4	15 46.1	16 35.8	7 43.8	12 1.4	21 19.0	21 40.7	12 32.6	13 10.1	19 52.9
7 S	13 3 34.2	5 31.0	13 20.6	6 21.4	17 12.9	6 22.8	12 45.0	21 17.6	21 40.5	12 29.6	13 12.0	19 51.6
10 T	13 15 23.8	6 39.5	13 23.8	5S 38.2	17 25.4	4 60.0	13 27.9	21 15.7	21 40.1	12 26.7	13 14.1	19 50.4
13 F	13 27 13.5	7 47.3	13 26.9	15 55.2	17 6.5	3 35.6	14 10.1	21 13.6	21 39.5	12 23.9	13 16.1	19 49.3
16 M	13 39 3.1	8 54.1	13 30.1	19 20.5	16 9.8	2 10.1	14 51.5	21 11.0	21 38.8	12 21.2	13 18.2	19 48.3
19 T	13 50 52.8	9 59.8	13 33.3	12 49.8	14 33.0	0 43.6	15 31.9	21 8.2	21 37.9	12 18.7	13 20.2	19 47.4
22 S	14 2 42.4	11 4.1	13 36.4	0N 40.2	12 24.9	0S 43.4	16 11.3	21 5.0	21 36.9	12 16.3	13 22.3	19 46.6
25 W	14 14 32.1	12 6.9	13 39.6	13 36.6	10 10.1	2 10.6	16 49.7	21 1.4	21 35.7	12 14.0	13 24.4	19 46.0
28 S	14 26 21.8	13 8.1	13 42.7	19 26.5	8 20.0	3 37.8	17 27.0	20 57.5	21 34.4	12 11.9	13 26.5	19 45.4
31 T	14 38 11.4	14 7.4	13 45.8	16 41.3	7 16.8	5 4.5	18 3.1	20 53.3	21 32.9	12 9.9	13 28.6	19 45.0

NOVEMBER 1961

LONGITUDE at NOON

DAY	EPHEMERIS SIDEREAL TIME	☉	☊	☽	☿	♀	♂	♃	♄	♅	♆	♇
	h m s	° ′	° ′	° ′	° ′	° ′	° ′	° ′	° ′	° ′	° ′	° ′
1 W	14 42 8.0	8♏49.9	23♌13.0	21♌ 0.8	22♎21.8	17♎51.6	21♏11.1	29♑41.2	24♑13.3	29♌59.8	10♏58.3	9♍41.9
2 T	14 46 4.5	9 49.9	23 9.8	2♍48.0	22D35.5	19 6.4	21 53.5	29 48.3	24 16.7	0♍ 1.7	11 0.5	9 43.1
3 F	14 50 1.1	10 50.1	23 6.6	14 38.5	22 59.5	20 21.2	22 35.9	29 55.6	24 20.2	0 3.5	11 2.8	9 44.3
4 S	14 53 57.6	11 50.2	23 3.5	26 37.0	23 32.9	21 36.1	23 18.4	0♒ 3.1	24 23.7	0 5.3	11 5.1	9 45.5
5 S	14 57 54.2	12 50.4	23 0.3	8♎47.4	24 14.9	22 51.0	24 0.9	0 10.6	24 27.4	0 6.9	11 7.3	9 46.6
6 M	15 1 50.8	13 50.6	22 57.1	21 12.5	25 4.5	24 5.9	24 43.4	0 18.4	24 31.1	0 8.6	11 9.6	9 47.7
7 T	15 5 47.3	14 50.8	22 53.9	3♏53.9	26 1.0	25 20.8	25 26.1	0 26.2	24 34.9	0 10.2	11 11.8	9 48.8
8 W	15 9 43.9	15 51.1	22 50.7	16 51.7	27 3.4	26 35.8	26 8.7	0 34.2	24 38.8	0 11.7	11 14.1	9 49.9
9 T	15 13 40.4	16 51.4	22 47.6	0♐ 4.8	28 11.1	27 50.8	26 51.5	0 42.4	24 42.7	0 13.2	11 16.3	9 50.9
10 F	15 17 37.0	17 51.7	22 44.4	13 31.3	29 23.2	29 5.8	27 34.3	0 50.7	24 46.8	0 14.6	11 18.5	9 51.9
11 S	15 21 33.5	18 52.1	22 41.2	27 8.6	0♏39.2	0♏20.8	28 17.1	0 59.1	24 50.9	0 16.0	11 20.8	9 52.9
12 S	15 25 30.1	19 52.5	22 38.0	10♑54.4	1 58.5	1 35.9	28 60.0	1 7.7	24 55.1	0 17.3	11 23.0	9 53.8
13 M	15 29 26.6	20 52.9	22 34.9	24 46.7	3 20.5	2 51.0	29 42.9	1 16.4	24 59.4	0 18.6	11 25.2	9 54.7
14 T	15 33 23.2	21 53.3	22 31.7	8♒44.3	4 44.9	4 6.1	0♐26.0	1 25.3	25 3.8	0 19.8	11 27.4	9 55.6
15 W	15 37 19.7	22 53.7	22 28.5	22 46.3	6 11.2	5 21.2	1 9.0	1 34.3	25 8.2	0 21.0	11 29.7	9 56.4
16 T	15 41 16.3	23 54.2	22 25.3	6♓52.4	7 39.1	6 36.3	1 52.1	1 43.4	25 12.7	0 22.1	11 31.9	9 57.3
17 F	15 45 12.9	24 54.7	22 22.2	21 1.8	9 8.3	7 51.4	2 35.3	1 52.6	25 17.3	0 23.2	11 34.1	9 58.0
18 S	15 49 9.4	25 55.2	22 19.0	5♈12.9	10 38.7	9 6.6	3 18.5	2 2.0	25 22.0	0 24.2	11 36.3	9 58.8
19 S	15 53 6.0	26 55.7	22 15.8	19 23.1	12 9.9	10 21.8	4 1.8	2 11.5	25 26.7	0 25.1	11 38.4	9 59.5
20 M	15 57 2.5	27 56.3	22 12.6	3♉28.7	13 41.8	11 37.0	4 45.1	2 21.1	25 31.5	0 26.0	11 40.6	10 0.2
21 T	16 0 59.1	28 56.8	22 9.4	17 25.3	15 14.3	12 52.2	5 28.5	2 30.8	25 36.4	0 26.9	11 42.8	10 0.9
22 W	16 4 55.6	29 57.4	22 6.3	1♊ 8.3	16 47.3	14 7.4	6 11.9	2 40.7	25 41.3	0 27.7	11 44.9	10 1.5
23 T	16 8 52.2	0♐58.0	22 3.1	14 33.9	18 20.5	15 22.7	6 55.4	2 50.7	25 46.4	0 28.4	11 47.1	10 2.2
24 F	16 12 48.7	1 58.7	21 59.9	27 39.9	19 54.1	16 38.0	7 39.0	3 0.8	25 51.5	0 29.1	11 49.3	10 2.8
25 S	16 16 45.3	2 59.4	21 56.7	10♋25.4	21 27.9	17 53.3	8 22.6	3 11.0	25 56.6	0 29.8	11 51.4	10 3.3
26 S	16 20 41.9	4 0.1	21 53.6	22 51.6	23 1.8	19 8.6	9 6.2	3 21.3	26 1.9	0 30.3	11 53.5	10 3.9
27 M	16 24 38.4	5 0.8	21 50.4	5♌ 1.4	24 35.7	20 23.9	9 49.9	3 31.8	26 7.1	0 30.8	11 55.6	10 4.3
28 T	16 28 35.0	6 1.6	21 47.2	16 58.7	26 9.8	21 39.2	10 33.7	3 42.3	26 12.5	0 31.3	11 57.7	10 4.8
29 W	16 32 31.5	7 2.3	21 44.0	28 48.5	27 43.9	22 54.5	11 17.5	3 53.0	26 17.9	0 31.7	11 59.8	10 5.2
30 T	16 36 28.1	8 3.1	21 40.9	10♍36.1	29 17.9	24 9.9	12 1.4	4 3.7	26 23.4	0 32.0	12 1.9	10 5.6

DECLINATION at NOON

DAY	EPHEMERIS SIDEREAL TIME	☉	☊	☽	☿	♀	♂	♃	♄	♅	♆	♇
1 W	14 42 8.0	14S 26.7	13N 46.9	14N 13.6	7S 7.5	5S 33.3	18S 14.8	20S 51.8	21S 32.4	12N 9.3	13S 29.3	19N 44.9
4 S	14 53 57.6	15 23.3	13 50.0	3 50.3	7 12.2	6 58.9	18 49.2	20 47.1	21 30.7	12 7.5	13 31.4	19 44.6
7 T	15 5 47.3	16 17.6	13 53.1	8S 22.5	7 57.3	8 23.3	19 22.3	20 42.1	21 28.9	12 5.9	13 33.4	19 44.5
10 F	15 17 37.0	17 9.4	13 56.2	17 46.0	9 10.2	9 46.2	19 53.9	20 36.8	21 26.9	12 4.4	13 35.5	19 44.5
13 M	15 29 26.6	17 58.7	13 59.3	18 51.3	10 40.0	11 7.0	20 24.0	20 31.1	21 24.8	12 3.1	13 37.5	19 44.6
16 T	15 41 16.3	18 45.0	14 2.4	10 8.9	12 18.3	12 25.6	20 52.5	20 25.1	21 22.5	12 2.0	13 39.5	19 44.8
19 S	15 53 6.0	19 28.4	14 5.5	3N41.2	13 59.4	13 41.6	21 19.4	20 18.7	21 20.1	12 1.1	13 41.5	19 45.1
22 W	16 4 55.6	20 8.6	14 8.6	15 33.0	15 39.2	14 54.5	21 44.5	20 12.1	21 17.6	12 0.3	13 43.4	19 45.6
25 S	16 16 45.3	20 45.5	14 11.7	19 44.8	17 15.1	16 4.0	22 7.8	20 5.1	21 14.9	11 59.7	13 45.3	19 46.2
28 T	16 28 35.0	21 18.9	14 14.8	15 24.2	18 45.0	17 9.8	22 29.3	19 57.7	21 12.1	11 59.3	13 47.2	19 46.9

DECEMBER 1961

LONGITUDE at NOON

DAY	EPHEMERIS SIDEREAL TIME	☉	☊	☽	☿	♀	♂	♃	♄	♅	♆	♇
1 F	16 40 24.6	9♐ 4.0	21♌37.7	22♍27.1	0♐52.0	25♏25.3	12♐45.3	4♒14.6	26♑28.9	0♍32.3	12♏ 3.9	10♍ 6.0
2 S	16 44 21.2	10 4.8	21 34.5	4♎27.1	2 26.1	26 40.6	13 29.3	4 25.5	26 34.5	0 32.5	12 6.0	10 6.3
3 S	16 48 17.8	11 5.7	21 31.3	16 40.8	4 0.2	27 56.0	14 13.3	4 36.6	26 40.1	0 32.7	12 8.0	10 6.6
4 M	16 52 14.3	12 6.6	21 28.1	29 12.2	5 34.2	29 11.4	14 57.4	4 47.8	26 45.8	0 32.8	12 10.0	10 6.9
5 T	16 56 10.9	13 7.5	21 25.0	12♏ 3.9	7 8.2	0♐26.9	15 41.5	4 59.1	26 51.6	0 32.9	12 12.0	10 7.1
6 W	17 0 7.4	14 8.4	21 21.8	25 16.9	8 42.3	1 42.3	16 25.7	5 10.4	26 57.4	0 32.9	12 14.0	10 7.3
7 T	17 4 4.0	15 9.4	21 18.6	8♐50.2	10 16.3	2 57.7	17 10.0	5 21.9	27 3.3	0R32.8	12 16.0	10 7.5
8 F	17 8 0.5	16 10.3	21 15.4	22 41.0	11 50.3	4 13.1	17 54.3	5 33.5	27 9.2	0 32.7	12 17.9	10 7.6
9 S	17 11 57.1	17 11.3	21 12.3	6♑45.2	13 24.4	5 28.6	18 38.6	5 45.1	27 15.2	0 32.6	12 19.8	10 7.7
10 S	17 15 53.7	18 12.3	21 9.1	20 57.8	14 58.5	6 44.0	19 23.0	5 56.9	27 21.2	0 32.3	12 21.8	10 7.8
11 M	17 19 50.2	19 13.3	21 5.9	5♒14.2	16 32.6	7 59.5	20 7.5	6 8.7	27 27.3	0 32.0	12 23.6	10 7.8
12 T	17 23 46.8	20 14.3	21 2.7	19 30.4	18 6.8	9 14.9	20 52.0	6 20.6	27 33.5	0 31.7	12 25.5	10 7.8
13 W	17 27 43.3	21 15.3	20 59.6	3♓43.5	19 41.1	10 30.4	21 36.5	6 32.6	27 39.6	0 31.3	12 27.4	10 7.8
14 T	17 31 39.9	22 16.4	20 56.4	17 51.7	21 15.4	11 45.9	22 21.1	6 44.7	27 45.9	0 30.9	12 29.2	10R 7.7
15 F	17 35 36.4	23 17.5	20 53.2	1♈54.0	22 49.9	13 1.4	23 5.8	6 56.9	27 52.2	0 30.4	12 31.1	10 7.7
16 S	17 39 33.0	24 18.5	20 50.0	15 49.5	24 24.4	14 16.8	23 50.5	7 9.2	27 58.5	0 29.9	12 32.9	10 7.6
17 S	17 43 29.6	25 19.6	20 46.8	29 37.6	25 59.1	15 32.3	24 35.2	7 21.5	28 4.8	0 29.3	12 34.6	10 7.4
18 M	17 47 26.1	26 20.6	20 43.7	13♉17.0	27 34.0	16 47.8	25 20.0	7 33.9	28 11.2	0 28.6	12 36.4	10 7.2
19 T	17 51 22.7	27 21.7	20 40.5	26 46.2	29 9.0	18 3.2	26 4.8	7 46.4	28 17.7	0 27.9	12 38.1	10 7.0
20 W	17 55 19.2	28 22.8	20 37.3	10♊ 3.5	0♑44.1	19 18.7	26 49.7	7 58.9	28 24.2	0 27.1	12 39.8	10 6.8
21 T	17 59 15.8	29 23.8	20 34.1	23 7.0	2 19.5	20 34.2	27 34.6	8 11.5	28 30.7	0 26.3	12 41.5	10 6.5
22 F	18 3 12.3	0♑24.9	20 31.0	5♋55.6	3 55.0	21 49.7	28 19.6	8 24.2	28 37.2	0 25.4	12 43.2	10 6.2
23 S	18 7 8.9	1 26.0	20 27.8	18 29.0	5 30.8	23 5.1	29 4.6	8 37.0	28 43.8	0 24.5	12 44.8	10 5.9
24 S	18 11 5.5	2 27.1	20 24.6	0♌47.7	7 6.8	24 20.6	29 49.6	8 49.8	28 50.4	0 23.5	12 46.4	10 5.5
25 M	18 15 2.0	3 28.2	20 21.4	12 53.5	8 43.0	25 36.1	0♑34.7	9 2.7	28 57.1	0 22.4	12 48.0	10 5.1
26 T	18 18 58.6	4 29.4	20 18.3	24 49.2	10 19.4	26 51.6	1 19.9	9 15.6	29 3.8	0 21.4	12 49.6	10 4.7
27 W	18 22 55.1	5 30.5	20 15.1	6♍38.5	11 56.0	28 7.1	2 5.1	9 28.7	29 10.5	0 20.2	12 51.1	10 4.2
28 T	18 26 51.7	6 31.6	20 11.9	18 25.9	13 32.9	29 22.6	2 50.3	9 41.7	29 17.3	0 19.0	12 52.6	10 3.7
29 F	18 30 48.2	7 32.8	20 8.7	0♎16.4	15 10.0	0♑38.1	3 35.6	9 54.9	29 24.0	0 17.8	12 54.1	10 3.2
30 S	18 34 44.8	8 33.9	20 5.5	12 15.3	16 47.3	1 53.6	4 21.0	10 8.1	29 30.9	0 16.5	12 55.5	10 2.6
31 S	18 38 41.4	9 35.1	20 2.4	24 27.6	18 24.7	3 9.1	5 6.4	10 21.3	29 37.7	0 15.2	12 57.0	10 2.0

DECLINATION at NOON

DAY	EPHEMERIS SIDEREAL TIME	☉	☊	☽	☿	♀	♂	♃	♄	♅	♆	♇
1 F	16 40 24.6	21S 48.7	14N 17.8	5N 25.5	20S 7.7	18S 11.6	22S 48.8	19S 50.1	21S 9.1	11N 59.0	13S 49.0	19N 47.7
4 M	16 52 14.3	22 14.8	14 20.9	6S 47.5	21 22.1	19 8.8	23 6.3	19 42.2	21 6.0	11 59.0	13 50.8	19 48.6
7 T	17 4 4.0	22 36.9	14 24.0	17 2.6	22 27.2	20 1.4	23 21.8	19 33.9	21 2.8	11 59.1	13 52.5	19 49.7
10 S	17 15 53.7	22 55.1	14 27.0	19 22.7	23 22.5	20 48.8	23 35.1	19 25.3	20 59.5	11 59.4	13 54.2	19 50.8
13 W	17 27 43.3	23 9.2	14 30.1	11 17.7	24 7.0	21 30.8	23 46.3	19 16.4	20 56.0	11 59.9	13 55.8	19 52.1
16 S	17 39 33.0	23 19.2	14 33.1	2N18.5	24 40.3	22 7.2	23 55.3	19 7.2	20 52.5	12 0.5	13 57.3	19 53.5
19 T	17 51 22.7	23 25.0	14 36.1	14 30.5	25 1.8	22 37.6	24 2.0	18 57.7	20 48.8	12 1.3	13 58.8	19 55.0
22 F	18 3 12.3	23 26.5	14 39.2	19 48.7	25 10.8	23 2.0	24 6.4	18 48.0	20 45.0	12 2.3	14 0.2	19 56.5
25 M	18 15 2.0	23 23.8	14 42.2	16 26.4	25 6.8	23 20.0	24 8.5	18 37.9	20 41.1	12 3.5	14 1.5	19 58.2
28 T	18 26 51.7	23 16.9	14 45.2	6 56.6	24 49.3	23 31.5	24 8.3	18 27.6	20 37.1	12 4.8	14 2.8	19 59.9
31 S	18 38 41.4	23 5.7	14 48.2	5S 4.4	24 18.1	23 36.6	24 5.6	18 17.0	20 33.0	12 6.3	14 3.9	20 1.8

JANUARY 1962

DAY	EPHEMERIS SIDEREAL TIME	☉	☊	☽	☿	♀	♂	♃	♄	♅	♆	♇
	h m s	° ′	° ′	° ′	° ′	° ′	° ′	° ′	° ′	° ′	° ′	° ′
						LONGITUDE at NOON						
1 M	18 42 37.9	10♑36.2	19♌59.2	6♏58.3	20♑ 2.3	4♑24.6	5♑51.8	10♒34.7	29♑44.6	0♍13.8	12♏58.4	10♍ 1.4
2 T	18 46 34.5	11 37.4	19 56.0	19 51.1	21 40.0	5 40.1	6 37.3	10 48.0	29 51.4	0R12.4	12 59.8	10R 0.8
3 W	18 50 31.0	12 38.6	19 52.8	3♐ 8.5	23 17.8	6 55.6	7 22.8	11 1.5	29 58.4	0 10.9	13 1.1	10 0.1
4 T	18 54 27.6	13 39.8	19 49.7	16 51.0	24 55.5	8 11.1	8 8.3	11 14.9	0♒ 5.3	0 9.4	13 2.4	9 59.4
5 F	18 58 24.1	14 41.0	19 46.5	0♑56.7	26 33.3	9 26.6	8 54.0	11 28.5	0 12.3	0 7.8	13 3.8	9 58.8
6 S	19 2 20.7	15 42.2	19 43.3	15 21.6	28 10.8	10 42.1	9 39.6	11 42.1	0 19.3	0 6.2	13 5.0	9 58.0
7 S	19 6 17.3	16 43.3	19 40.1	29 59.7	29 48.0	11 57.6	10 25.3	11 55.7	0 26.3	0 4.6	13 6.3	9 57.2
8 M	19 10 13.8	17 44.5	19 37.0	14♒43.9	1♒24.8	13 13.1	11 11.0	12 9.4	0 33.3	0 2.9	13 7.5	9 56.4
9 T	19 14 10.4	18 45.7	19 33.8	29 27.2	3 1.1	14 28.6	11 56.8	12 23.1	0 40.3	0 1.1	13 8.7	9 55.6
10 W	19 18 6.9	19 46.8	19 30.6	14♓ 3.5	4 36.6	15 44.1	12 42.6	12 36.8	0 47.4	29♌59.3	13 9.8	9 54.7
11 T	19 22 3.5	20 48.0	19 27.4	28 28.2	6 11.0	16 59.6	13 28.4	12 50.6	0 54.4	29 57.5	13 10.9	9 53.8
12 F	19 26 0.0	21 49.1	19 24.3	12♈38.4	7 44.3	18 15.0	14 14.3	13 4.4	1 1.5	29 55.6	13 12.0	9 52.9
13 S	19 29 56.6	22 50.3	19 21.1	26 32.9	9 16.0	19 30.5	15 0.2	13 18.3	1 8.6	29 53.7	13 13.0	9 52.0
14 S	19 33 53.2	23 51.4	19 17.9	10♉11.2	10 45.7	20 45.9	15 46.2	13 32.2	1 15.7	29 51.8	13 14.1	9 51.0
15 M	19 37 49.7	24 52.5	19 14.7	23 33.9	12 13.1	22 1.4	16 32.2	13 46.1	1 22.8	29 49.8	13 15.1	9 50.0
16 T	19 41 46.3	25 53.6	19 11.5	6♊41.8	13 37.7	23 16.8	17 18.2	14 0.1	1 29.9	29 47.8	13 16.0	9 49.0
17 W	19 45 42.8	26 54.6	19 8.4	19 35.6	14 59.0	24 32.3	18 4.2	14 14.1	1 37.0	29 45.7	13 16.9	9 48.0
18 T	19 49 39.4	27 55.7	19 5.2	2♋16.4	16 16.3	25 47.7	18 50.3	14 28.1	1 44.2	29 43.6	13 17.8	9 46.9
19 F	19 53 35.9	28 56.8	19 2.0	14 44.9	17 28.9	27 3.1	19 36.4	14 42.2	1 51.3	29 41.5	13 18.7	9 45.9
20 S	19 57 32.5	29 57.8	18 58.8	27 2.2	18 36.3	28 18.5	20 22.6	14 56.3	1 58.4	29 39.4	13 19.5	9 44.7
21 S	20 1 29.0	0♒58.9	18 55.7	9♌ 9.5	19 37.4	29 33.9	21 8.8	15 10.4	2 5.6	29 37.2	13 20.3	9 43.6
22 M	20 5 25.6	1 59.9	18 52.5	21 8.2	20 31.6	0♒49.3	21 55.0	15 24.5	2 12.7	29 35.0	13 21.1	9 42.5
23 T	20 9 22.2	3 0.9	18 49.3	3♍ 0.5	21 18.0	2 4.7	22 41.3	15 38.7	2 19.8	29 32.7	13 21.8	9 41.3
24 W	20 13 18.7	4 1.9	18 46.1	14 49.0	21 55.7	3 20.1	23 27.5	15 52.9	2 27.0	29 30.4	13 22.5	9 40.1
25 T	20 17 15.3	5 2.9	18 42.9	26 36.8	22 23.9	4 35.5	24 13.9	16 7.1	2 34.1	29 28.1	13 23.2	9 38.9
26 F	20 21 11.8	6 3.9	18 39.8	8♎27.8	22 41.9	5 50.9	25 0.3	16 21.4	2 41.3	29 25.9	13 23.9	9 37.7
27 S	20 25 8.4	7 4.9	18 36.6	20 26.0	22 49.1	7 6.3	25 46.6	16 35.6	2 48.4	29 23.5	13 24.5	9 36.5
28 S	20 29 4.9	8 5.9	18 33.4	2♏36.0	22R45.0	8 21.7	26 33.1	16 49.9	2 55.6	29 21.1	13 25.0	9 35.2
29 M	20 33 1.5	9 6.8	18 30.2	15 2.6	22 29.6	9 37.0	27 19.5	17 4.1	3 2.7	29 18.7	13 25.6	9 33.9
30 T	20 36 58.0	10 7.7	18 27.1	27 49.9	22 2.9	10 52.4	28 6.0	17 18.4	3 9.8	29 16.3	13 26.1	9 32.6
31 W	20 40 54.6	11 8.7	18 23.9	11♐ 1.7	21 25.6	12 7.7	28 52.5	17 32.7	3 16.9	29 13.8	13 26.5	9 31.3
						DECLINATION at NOON						
1 M	18 42 37.9	23S 1.1	14N49.2	9S 2.1	24S 4.6	23S36.8	24S 4.2	18S13.4	20S31.6	12N 6.8	14S 4.3	20N 2.4
4 T	18 54 27.6	22 44.4	14 52.2	18 14.4	23 14.6	23 33.0	23 58.4	18 2.4	20 27.4	12 8.5	14 5.4	20 4.3
7 S	19 6 17.3	22 23.7	14 55.2	18 33.1	22 10.8	23 22.7	23 50.2	17 51.2	20 23.1	12 10.3	14 6.4	20 6.3
10 W	19 18 6.9	21 59.0	14 58.2	8 22.9	20 53.9	23 5.9	23 39.6	17 39.8	20 18.7	12 12.2	14 7.3	20 8.3
13 S	19 29 56.6	21 30.5	15 1.2	5N41.6	19 25.5	22 42.7	23 26.6	17 28.1	20 14.3	12 14.3	14 8.1	20 10.5
16 T	19 41 46.3	20 58.2	15 4.2	16 31.3	17 48.5	22 13.2	23 11.3	17 16.2	20 9.8	12 16.4	14 8.8	20 12.6
19 F	19 53 35.9	20 22.4	15 7.1	19 45.0	16 7.9	21 37.6	22 53.6	17 4.1	20 5.2	12 18.7	14 9.5	20 14.8
22 M	20 5 25.6	19 43.0	15 10.1	14 43.8	14 31.4	20 56.2	22 33.6	16 51.8	20 0.6	12 21.1	14 10.0	20 17.0
25 T	20 17 15.3	19 0.4	15 13.0	4 22.8	13 8.9	20 9.2	22 11.4	16 39.3	19 56.0	12 23.6	14 10.5	20 19.3
28 S	20 29 4.9	18 14.7	15 16.0	7S34.6	12 12.1	19 16.8	21 46.9	16 26.6	19 51.3	12 26.1	14 10.8	20 21.5
31 W	20 40 54.6	17 25.9	15 18.9	17 16.0	11 49.9	18 19.4	21 20.2	16 13.7	19 46.6	12 28.7	14 11.1	20 23.8

FEBRUARY 1962

DAY	EPHEMERIS SIDEREAL TIME	☉	☊	☽	☿	♀	♂	♃	♄	♅	♆	♇
						LONGITUDE at NOON						
1 T	20 44 51.2	12♒ 9.6	18♌20.7	24♐40.2	20♒38.3	13♒23.1	29♑39.0	17♒47.1	3♒24.0	29♌11.4	13♏27.0	9♍30.0
2 F	20 48 47.7	13 10.5	18 17.5	8♑45.6	19R42.4	14 38.4	0♒25.6	18 1.4	3 31.1	29R 8.9	13 27.4	9R28.6
3 S	20 52 44.3	14 11.4	18 14.4	23 15.8	18 39.4	15 53.7	1 12.2	18 15.7	3 38.1	29 6.4	13 27.7	9 27.3
4 S	20 56 40.8	15 12.2	18 11.2	8♒ 5.9	17 31.2	17 9.0	1 58.8	18 30.1	3 45.2	29 3.8	13 28.1	9 25.9
5 M	21 0 37.4	16 13.1	18 8.0	23 8.6	16 19.8	18 24.3	2 45.5	18 44.4	3 52.2	29 1.3	13 28.4	9 24.5
6 T	21 4 33.9	17 13.9	18 4.8	8♓15.2	15 7.2	19 39.6	3 32.1	18 58.8	3 59.3	28 58.7	13 28.6	9 23.1
7 W	21 8 30.5	18 14.7	18 1.6	23 16.5	13 55.4	20 54.9	4 18.8	19 13.2	4 6.3	28 56.2	13 28.8	9 21.6
8 T	21 12 27.0	19 15.5	17 58.5	8♈ 4.5	12 46.3	22 10.2	5 5.6	19 27.5	4 13.3	28 53.6	13 29.0	9 20.2
9 F	21 16 23.6	20 16.3	17 55.3	22 33.3	11 41.5	23 25.4	5 52.3	19 41.9	4 20.2	28 51.0	13 29.2	9 18.7
10 S	21 20 20.1	21 17.0	17 52.1	6♉39.3	10 42.3	24 40.6	6 39.0	19 56.2	4 27.2	28 48.4	13 29.3	9 17.3
11 S	21 24 16.7	22 17.7	17 48.9	20 21.4	9 49.7	25 55.9	7 25.8	20 10.6	4 34.1	28 45.8	13 29.4	9 15.8
12 M	21 28 13.3	23 18.4	17 45.8	3♊40.4	9 4.5	27 11.1	8 12.6	20 25.0	4 41.0	28 43.2	13 29.4	9 14.3
13 T	21 32 9.8	24 19.0	17 42.6	16 38.4	8 27.0	28 26.2	8 59.4	20 39.3	4 47.9	28 40.5	13 29.5	9 12.8
14 W	21 36 6.4	25 19.6	17 39.4	29 18.1	7 57.4	29 41.4	9 46.2	20 53.7	4 54.7	28 37.9	13 29.5	9 11.3
15 T	21 40 2.9	26 20.2	17 36.2	11♋42.7	7 35.8	0♓56.6	10 33.1	21 8.0	5 1.6	28 35.3	13R29.4	9 9.8
16 F	21 43 59.5	27 20.8	17 33.0	23 55.3	7 21.9	2 11.8	11 20.0	21 22.4	5 8.4	28 32.7	13 29.4	9 8.4
17 S	21 47 56.0	28 21.4	17 29.9	5♌58.5	7 15.5	3 26.9	12 6.9	21 36.7	5 15.2	28 30.0	13 29.3	9 6.8
18 S	21 51 52.6	29 21.9	17 26.7	17 54.9	7D16.2	4 42.0	12 53.8	21 51.0	5 21.9	28 27.4	13 29.1	9 5.3
19 M	21 55 49.1	0♓22.4	17 23.5	29 46.6	7 23.7	5 57.1	13 40.7	22 5.3	5 28.7	28 24.8	13 28.9	9 3.8
20 T	21 59 45.7	1 22.8	17 20.3	11♍35.9	7 37.4	7 12.1	14 27.6	22 19.6	5 35.3	28 22.1	13 28.7	9 2.2
21 W	22 3 42.2	2 23.3	17 17.2	23 24.6	7 57.1	8 27.2	15 14.5	22 33.8	5 42.0	28 19.5	13 28.5	9 0.7
22 T	22 7 38.8	3 23.7	17 14.0	5♎15.1	8 22.3	9 42.2	16 1.5	22 48.1	5 48.6	28 16.9	13 28.2	8 59.1
23 F	22 11 35.3	4 24.0	17 10.8	17 9.6	8 52.6	10 57.2	16 48.5	23 2.3	5 55.2	28 14.3	13 27.9	8 57.6
24 S	22 15 31.9	5 24.4	17 7.6	29 11.1	9 27.6	12 12.2	17 35.4	23 16.5	6 1.7	28 11.7	13 27.5	8 56.0
25 S	22 19 28.5	6 24.7	17 4.4	11♏22.8	10 7.0	13 27.2	18 22.4	23 30.7	6 8.2	28 9.1	13 27.1	8 54.5
26 M	22 23 25.0	7 25.0	17 1.3	23 48.0	10 50.5	14 42.2	19 9.5	23 44.9	6 14.7	28 6.5	13 26.7	8 52.9
27 T	22 27 21.6	8 25.3	16 58.1	6♐30.8	11 37.7	15 57.2	19 56.5	23 59.1	6 21.2	28 3.9	13 26.3	8 51.4
28 W	22 31 18.1	9 25.6	16 54.9	19 34.6	12 28.3	17 12.1	20 43.5	24 13.2	6 27.5	28 1.3	13 25.8	8 49.8
						DECLINATION at NOON						
1 T	20 44 51.2	17S 9.1	15N19.9	19S 5.0	11S50.9	17S59.2	21S10.9	16S 9.4	19S45.0	12N29.6	14S11.2	20N24.6
4 S	20 56 40.8	16 16.7	15 22.9	17 21.5	12 16.6	16 55.6	20 41.4	15 56.3	19 40.3	12 32.2	14 11.3	20 26.9
7 W	21 8 30.5	15 21.8	15 25.8	5 29.1	13 7.4	15 47.8	20 9.9	15 43.1	19 35.6	12 35.0	14 11.4	20 29.1
10 S	21 20 20.1	14 24.5	15 28.7	8N49.5	14 8.5	14 36.0	19 36.3	15 29.8	19 30.8	12 37.7	14 11.4	20 31.4
13 T	21 32 9.8	13 25.1	15 31.6	18 8.3	15 7.3	13 20.6	19 0.9	15 16.4	19 26.1	12 40.5	14 11.2	20 33.7
16 F	21 43 59.5	12 23.7	15 34.5	19 11.1	15 56.3	12 2.0	18 23.6	15 2.8	19 21.4	12 43.2	14 11.0	20 35.8
19 M	21 55 49.1	11 20.5	15 37.4	12 33.4	16 32.2	10 40.5	17 44.6	14 49.2	19 16.7	12 46.0	14 10.7	20 38.0
22 T	22 7 38.8	10 15.8	15 40.3	1 28.3	16 54.1	9 16.4	17 3.9	14 35.5	19 12.1	12 48.7	14 10.3	20 40.2
25 S	22 19 28.5	9 9.6	15 43.2	10S16.0	17 1.8	7 50.2	16 21.6	14 21.8	19 7.5	12 51.4	14 9.9	20 42.2
28 W	22 31 18.1	8 2.2	15 46.1	18 33.9	16 55.7	6 22.1	15 37.8	14 8.0	19 2.9	12 54.1	14 9.3	20 44.3

MARCH 1962

DAY	EPHEMERIS SIDEREAL TIME	☉	☊	☽	☿	♀	♂	♃	♄	♅	♆	♇
	h m s	° ′	° ′	° ′	° ′	° ′	° ′	° ′	° ′	° ′	° ′	° ′
LONGITUDE at NOON												
1 T	22 35 14.7	10♓25.8	16♌51.7	3♑ 2.6	13♒22.2	18♓27.0	21♒30.6	24♒27.3	6♒33.9	27♌58.7	13♏25.3	8♍48.2
2 F	22 39 11.2	11 26.0	16 48.6	16 56.8	14 19.1	19 41.9	22 17.6	24 41.4	6 40.2	27R56.2	13R24.7	8R46.7
3 S	22 43 7.8	12 26.2	16 45.4	1♒17.3	15 18.8	20 56.8	23 4.7	24 55.4	6 46.5	27 53.6	13 24.2	8 45.1
4 S	22 47 4.3	13 26.4	16 42.2	16 1.8	16 21.1	22 11.7	23 51.7	25 9.5	6 52.7	27 51.1	13 23.6	8 43.6
5 M	22 51 0.9	14 26.5	16 39.0	1♓ 5.1	17 25.8	23 26.5	24 38.8	25 23.5	6 58.9	27 48.6	13 22.9	8 42.0
6 T	22 54 57.4	15 26.6	16 35.8	16 18.9	18 32.8	24 41.4	25 25.9	25 37.4	7 5.0	27 46.1	13 22.3	8 40.5
7 W	22 58 54.0	16 26.6	16 32.7	1♈33.5	19 42.0	25 56.2	26 13.0	25 51.4	7 11.1	27 43.7	13 21.6	8 38.9
8 T	23 2 50.5	17 26.7	16 29.5	16 38.5	20 53.2	27 11.0	27 0.1	26 5.2	7 17.1	27 41.2	13 20.9	8 37.4
9 F	23 6 47.1	18 26.7	16 26.3	1♉24.9	22 6.4	28 25.8	27 47.2	26 19.2	7 23.1	27 38.9	13 20.1	8 35.9
10 S	23 10 43.6	19 26.7	16 23.1	15 46.4	23 21.4	29 40.5	28 34.3	26 33.0	7 29.1	27 36.5	13 19.4	8 34.3
11 S	23 14 40.2	20 26.6	16 20.0	29 39.8	24 38.2	0♈55.3	29 21.4	26 46.8	7 35.0	27 34.1	13 18.5	8 32.8
12 M	23 18 36.7	21 26.5	16 16.8	13♊ 4.8	25 56.6	2 9.9	0♓ 8.5	27 0.5	7 40.8	27 31.7	13 17.7	8 31.3
13 T	23 22 33.3	22 26.4	16 13.6	26 3.6	27 16.7	3 24.6	0 55.6	27 14.2	7 46.5	27 29.4	13 16.8	8 29.8
14 W	23 26 29.8	23 26.2	16 10.4	8♋39.7	28 38.3	4 39.2	1 42.6	27 27.8	7 52.3	27 27.1	13 15.9	8 28.3
15 T	23 30 26.4	24 26.0	16 7.2	20 57.6	0♓ 1.5	5 53.9	2 29.7	27 41.5	7 57.9	27 24.9	13 15.0	8 26.8
16 F	23 34 22.9	25 25.7	16 4.1	3♌ 1.9	1 26.1	7 8.4	3 16.8	27 55.0	8 3.5	27 22.6	13 14.1	8 25.3
17 S	23 38 19.5	26 25.4	16 0.9	14 56.9	2 52.2	8 23.0	4 3.9	28 8.5	8 9.1	27 20.4	13 13.1	8 23.8
18 S	23 42 16.1	27 25.1	15 57.7	26 46.6	4 19.7	9 37.5	4 50.9	28 22.0	8 14.5	27 18.2	13 12.1	8 22.4
19 M	23 46 12.6	28 24.7	15 54.5	8♍34.3	5 48.6	10 52.0	5 38.0	28 35.4	8 20.0	27 16.1	13 11.1	8 20.9
20 T	23 50 9.2	29 24.3	15 51.4	20 22.8	7 18.8	12 6.5	6 25.1	28 48.8	8 25.3	27 14.0	13 10.0	8 19.5
21 W	23 54 5.7	0♈23.9	15 48.2	2♎14.3	8 50.4	13 21.0	7 12.1	29 2.1	8 30.6	27 11.9	13 8.9	8 18.0
22 T	23 58 2.3	1 23.4	15 45.0	14 10.6	10 23.4	14 35.4	7 59.1	29 15.4	8 35.9	27 9.8	13 7.8	8 16.6
23 F	0 1 58.8	2 22.9	15 41.8	26 13.1	11 57.7	15 49.8	8 46.2	29 28.6	8 41.0	27 7.8	13 6.7	8 15.2
24 S	0 5 55.4	3 22.4	15 38.6	8♏23.5	13 33.3	17 4.1	9 33.2	29 41.8	8 46.1	27 5.8	13 5.6	8 13.8
25 S	0 9 51.9	4 21.8	15 35.5	20 43.4	15 10.3	18 18.5	10 20.2	29 54.9	8 51.2	27 3.9	13 4.4	8 12.5
26 M	0 13 48.5	5 21.2	15 32.3	3♐14.7	16 48.6	19 32.8	11 7.3	0♓ 7.9	8 56.2	27 2.0	13 3.2	8 11.1
27 T	0 17 45.0	6 20.6	15 29.1	15 59.9	18 28.2	20 47.1	11 54.3	0 20.9	9 1.1	27 0.1	13 2.0	8 9.8
28 W	0 21 41.6	7 19.9	15 25.9	29 1.6	20 9.2	22 1.4	12 41.3	0 33.8	9 5.9	26 58.3	13 0.7	8 8.4
29 T	0 25 38.1	8 19.2	15 22.7	12♑22.6	21 51.6	23 15.6	13 28.3	0 46.7	9 10.7	26 56.5	12 59.5	8 7.1
30 F	0 29 34.7	9 18.6	15 19.6	26 5.3	23 35.3	24 29.9	14 15.3	0 59.6	9 15.4	26 54.8	12 58.2	8 5.9
31 S	0 33 31.2	10 17.8	15 16.4	10♒11.0	25 20.4	25 44.0	15 2.2	1 12.3	9 20.1	26 53.1	12 56.9	8 4.6
DECLINATION at NOON												
1 T	22 35 14.7	7S39.5	15N47.1	19S41.6	16S50.7	5S52.4	15S22.8	14S 3.4	19S 1.4	12N55.0	14S 9.1	20N44.9
4 S	22 47 4.3	6 30.7	15 49.9	15 52.1	16 26.8	4 22.3	14 37.1	13 49.6	18 57.0	12 57.6	14 8.4	20 46.9
7 W	22 58 54.0	5 21.0	15 52.8	2 42.0	15 50.1	2 51.2	13 50.0	13 35.7	18 52.6	13 0.1	14 7.7	20 48.7
10 S	23 10 43.6	4 10.8	15 55.7	11N34.0	15 0.9	1 19.3	13 1.7	13 21.9	18 48.3	13 2.6	14 6.9	20 50.5
13 T	23 22 33.3	3 0.0	15 58.5	19 17.9	13 59.5	0N12.9	12 12.3	13 8.2	18 44.1	13 5.0	14 6.0	20 52.2
16 F	23 34 22.9	1 49.0	16 1.4	18 12.3	12 46.4	1 45.2	11 21.8	12 54.5	18 40.0	13 7.3	14 5.0	20 53.8
19 M	23 46 12.6	0 37.9	16 4.2	10 4.8	11 21.8	3 17.2	10 30.4	12 40.8	18 36.0	13 9.5	14 4.0	20 55.3
22 T	23 58 2.3	0N33.2	16 7.0	1S36.9	9 46.0	4 48.7	9 38.1	12 27.2	18 32.2	13 11.5	14 2.9	20 56.7
25 S	0 9 51.9	1 44.1	16 9.9	12 59.7	7 59.4	6 19.2	8 45.1	12 13.8	18 28.5	13 13.5	14 1.7	20 58.0
28 W	0 21 41.6	2 54.6	16 12.7	19 38.5	6 2.2	7 48.4	7 51.3	12 0.4	18 24.9	13 15.4	14 0.5	20 59.2
31 S	0 33 31.2	4 4.7	16 15.5	17 8.2	3 54.9	9 16.1	6 56.9	11 47.2	18 21.5	13 17.1	13 59.3	21 0.3

APRIL 1962

DAY	EPHEMERIS SIDEREAL TIME	☉	☊	☽	☿	♀	♂	♃	♄	♅	♆	♇
LONGITUDE at NOON												
1 S	0 37 27.8	11♈17.1	15♌13.2	24♒39.5	27♓ 6.9	26♈58.2	15♓49.2	1♓25.0	9♒24.6	26♌51.5	12♏55.6	8♍ 3.3
2 M	0 41 24.3	12 16.3	15 10.0	9♓28.0	28 54.8	28 12.3	16 36.1	1 37.6	9 29.1	26R49.8	12R54.3	8R 2.1
3 T	0 45 20.9	13 15.4	15 6.9	24 30.9	0♈44.1	29 26.5	17 23.1	1 50.1	9 33.5	26 48.3	12 52.9	8 0.9
4 W	0 49 17.4	14 14.6	15 3.7	9♈39.9	2 34.7	0♉40.5	18 10.0	2 2.6	9 37.9	26 46.7	12 51.5	7 59.7
5 T	0 53 14.0	15 13.7	15 0.5	24 45.1	4 26.9	1 54.6	18 56.9	2 14.9	9 42.1	26 45.2	12 50.1	7 58.5
6 F	0 57 10.5	16 12.7	14 57.3	9♉36.4	6 20.4	3 8.6	19 43.7	2 27.3	9 46.3	26 43.8	12 48.7	7 57.3
7 S	1 1 7.1	17 11.8	14 54.1	24 5.6	8 15.4	4 22.6	20 30.6	2 39.5	9 50.4	26 42.4	12 47.3	7 56.2
8 S	1 5 3.6	18 10.8	14 51.0	8♊ 7.5	10 11.7	5 36.6	21 17.4	2 51.7	9 54.4	26 41.0	12 45.9	7 55.0
9 M	1 9 0.2	19 9.7	14 47.8	21 40.0	12 9.5	6 50.5	22 4.2	3 3.7	9 58.4	26 39.7	12 44.4	7 53.9
10 T	1 12 56.8	20 8.6	14 44.6	4♋44.1	14 8.6	8 4.4	22 51.0	3 15.7	10 2.2	26 38.5	12 42.9	7 52.9
11 W	1 16 53.3	21 7.5	14 41.4	17 23.1	16 9.1	9 18.2	23 37.7	3 27.6	10 6.0	26 37.3	12 41.5	7 51.8
12 T	1 20 49.9	22 6.3	14 38.3	29 41.4	18 10.8	10 32.1	24 24.5	3 39.5	10 9.7	26 36.1	12 40.0	7 50.8
13 F	1 24 46.4	23 5.1	14 35.1	11♌44.5	20 13.7	11 45.8	25 11.2	3 51.2	10 13.3	26 35.0	12 38.4	7 49.8
14 S	1 28 43.0	24 3.9	14 31.9	23 37.5	22 17.8	12 59.6	25 57.9	4 2.9	10 16.8	26 34.0	12 36.9	7 48.8
15 S	1 32 39.5	25 2.6	14 28.7	5♍25.5	24 22.8	14 13.3	26 44.5	4 14.5	10 20.3	26 32.9	12 35.4	7 47.8
16 M	1 36 36.1	26 1.3	14 25.5	17 12.9	26 28.7	15 27.0	27 31.1	4 26.0	10 23.7	26 32.0	12 33.8	7 46.9
17 T	1 40 32.6	26 60.0	14 22.4	29 3.4	28 35.3	16 40.7	28 17.7	4 37.4	10 26.9	26 31.1	12 32.3	7 46.0
18 W	1 44 29.2	27 58.6	14 19.2	10♎60.0	0♉42.4	17 54.3	29 4.3	4 48.7	10 30.1	26 30.2	12 30.7	7 45.1
19 T	1 48 25.7	28 57.2	14 16.0	23 4.5	2 49.8	19 7.9	29 50.9	4 59.9	10 33.2	26 29.4	12 29.1	7 44.2
20 F	1 52 22.3	29 55.8	14 12.8	5♏18.5	4 57.3	20 21.4	0♈37.4	5 11.0	10 36.3	26 28.7	12 27.6	7 43.4
21 S	1 56 18.8	0♉54.3	14 9.7	17 42.6	7 4.6	21 35.0	1 23.9	5 22.1	10 39.2	26 28.0	12 26.0	7 42.6
22 S	2 0 15.4	1 52.8	14 6.5	0♐17.2	9 11.3	22 48.4	2 10.4	5 33.0	10 42.1	26 27.3	12 24.4	7 41.8
23 M	2 4 11.9	2 51.3	14 3.3	13 2.8	11 17.2	24 1.9	2 56.8	5 43.8	10 44.8	26 26.7	12 22.8	7 41.0
24 T	2 8 8.5	3 49.7	14 0.1	25 59.9	13 21.9	25 15.3	3 43.3	5 54.6	10 47.5	26 26.2	12 21.2	7 40.3
25 W	2 12 5.0	4 48.1	13 56.9	9♑ 9.7	15 25.2	26 28.7	4 29.6	6 5.2	10 50.1	26 25.7	12 19.6	7 39.6
26 T	2 16 1.6	5 46.5	13 53.8	22 33.4	17 26.8	27 42.0	5 16.0	6 15.7	10 52.6	26 25.2	12 18.0	7 38.9
27 F	2 19 58.2	6 44.9	13 50.6	6♒12.7	19 26.3	28 55.3	6 2.3	6 26.1	10 55.0	26 24.8	12 16.3	7 38.3
28 S	2 23 54.7	7 43.2	13 47.4	20 8.9	21 23.4	0♊ 8.6	6 48.6	6 36.5	10 57.3	26 24.5	12 14.7	7 37.6
29 S	2 27 51.3	8 41.5	13 44.2	4♓22.2	23 17.9	1 21.8	7 34.9	6 46.7	10 59.5	26 24.2	12 13.1	7 37.0
30 M	2 31 47.8	9 39.8	13 41.1	18 51.6	25 9.6	2 35.0	8 21.1	6 56.8	11 1.6	26 24.0	12 11.4	7 36.5
DECLINATION at NOON												
1 S	0 37 27.8	4N27.9	16N16.4	13S58.7	3S10.3	9N44.9	6S38.7	11S42.8	18S20.4	13N17.6	13S58.9	21N 0.6
4 W	0 49 17.4	5 37.0	16 19.2	0N 4.6	0 50.3	11 10.0	5 43.7	11 29.8	18 17.2	13 19.1	13 57.5	21 1.6
7 S	1 1 7.1	6 45.3	16 22.0	13 55.3	1N38.3	12 32.7	4 48.3	11 17.0	18 14.2	13 20.5	13 56.2	21 2.4
10 T	1 12 56.8	7 52.5	16 24.8	20 1.0	4 14.3	13 52.6	3 52.6	11 4.4	18 11.3	13 21.8	13 54.8	21 3.1
13 F	1 24 46.4	8 58.5	16 27.6	16 55.8	6 55.8	15 9.6	2 56.7	10 52.0	18 8.7	13 22.9	13 53.4	21 3.7
16 M	1 36 36.1	10 3.1	16 30.3	7 29.8	9 40.0	16 23.1	2 0.7	10 39.9	18 6.2	13 23.8	13 51.9	21 4.2
19 T	1 48 25.7	11 6.2	16 33.1	4S38.6	12 23.0	17 32.9	1 4.6	10 28.0	18 4.0	13 24.6	13 50.5	21 4.5
22 S	2 0 15.4	12 7.7	16 35.9	15 29.4	14 59.8	18 38.7	0 8.6	10 16.4	18 1.9	13 25.2	13 49.0	21 4.7
25 W	2 12 5.0	13 7.4	16 38.6	20 14.5	17 24.9	19 40.1	0N47.3	10 5.0	18 0.1	13 25.7	13 47.5	21 4.8
28 S	2 23 54.7	14 5.2	16 41.4	15 16.6	19 33.1	20 36.8	1 43.0	9 54.0	17 58.5	13 26.0	13 46.0	21 4.7

MAY 1962

DAY	EPHEMERIS SIDEREAL TIME	☉	☊	☽	☿	♀	♂	♃	♄	♅	♆	♇
	h m s	° ′	° ′	° ′	° ′	° ′	° ′	° ′	° ′	° ′	° ′	° ′
LONGITUDE at NOON												
1 T	2 35 44.4	10 ♉ 38.1	13 ♌ 37.9	3 ♈ 33.7	26 ♉ 58.2	3 ♊ 48.2	9 ♈ 7.3	7 ♓ 6.7	11 ♒ 3.6	26 ♌ 23.8	12 ♏ 9.8	7 ♍ 35.9
2 W	2 39 40.9	11 36.3	13 34.7	18 22.7	28 43.5	5 1.4	9 53.4	7 16.6	11 5.5	26 R 23.7	12 R 8.2	7 R 35.4
3 T	2 43 37.5	12 34.5	13 31.5	3 ♉ 11.0	0 ♊ 25.4	6 14.5	10 39.5	7 26.4	11 7.4	26 23.6	12 6.5	7 34.9
4 F	2 47 34.0	13 32.7	13 28.3	17 50.2	2 3.7	7 27.6	11 25.6	7 36.0	11 9.1	26 23.6	12 4.9	7 34.5
5 S	2 51 30.6	14 30.8	13 25.2	2 ♊ 12.2	3 38.4	8 40.6	12 11.7	7 45.5	11 10.7	26 23.6	12 3.3	7 34.0
6 S	2 55 27.1	15 28.9	13 22.0	16 11.4	5 9.2	9 53.6	12 57.7	7 54.9	11 12.3	26 D 23.7	12 1.6	7 33.6
7 M	2 59 23.7	16 27.0	13 18.8	29 44.3	6 36.2	11 6.6	13 43.6	8 4.2	11 13.7	26 23.9	11 60.0	7 33.3
8 T	3 3 20.3	17 25.1	13 15.6	12 ♋ 50.6	7 59.2	12 19.5	14 29.5	8 13.3	11 15.1	26 24.1	11 58.4	7 32.9
9 W	3 7 16.8	18 23.1	13 12.5	25 32.3	9 18.1	13 32.4	15 15.4	8 22.4	11 16.3	26 24.3	11 56.7	7 32.6
10 T	3 11 13.4	19 21.1	13 9.3	7 ♌ 53.3	10 33.0	14 45.2	16 1.2	8 31.3	11 17.5	26 24.6	11 55.1	7 32.3
11 F	3 15 9.9	20 19.1	13 6.1	19 58.3	11 43.8	15 58.1	16 47.1	8 40.1	11 18.6	26 25.0	11 53.5	7 32.1
12 S	3 19 6.5	21 17.1	13 2.9	1 ♍ 52.8	12 50.2	17 10.8	17 32.8	8 48.7	11 19.6	26 25.4	11 51.9	7 31.9
13 S	3 23 3.0	22 15.0	12 59.7	13 42.1	13 52.4	18 23.6	18 18.5	8 57.2	11 20.4	26 25.9	11 50.3	7 31.7
14 M	3 26 59.6	23 12.8	12 56.6	25 31.5	14 50.2	19 36.2	19 4.1	9 5.6	11 21.2	26 26.4	11 48.7	7 31.6
15 T	3 30 56.1	24 10.7	12 53.4	7 ♎ 25.4	15 43.6	20 48.9	19 49.7	9 13.9	11 21.9	26 27.0	11 47.1	7 31.4
16 W	3 34 52.7	25 8.5	12 50.2	19 27.6	16 32.5	22 1.4	20 35.3	9 22.0	11 22.4	26 27.6	11 45.6	7 31.3
17 T	3 38 49.2	26 6.3	12 47.0	1 ♏ 40.8	17 16.8	23 14.0	21 20.8	9 29.9	11 22.9	26 28.3	11 44.0	7 31.3
18 F	3 42 45.8	27 4.1	12 43.9	14 6.8	17 56.6	24 26.5	22 6.3	9 37.8	11 23.3	26 29.1	11 42.4	7 31.2
19 S	3 46 42.4	28 1.8	12 40.7	26 46.4	18 31.6	25 38.9	22 51.7	9 45.5	11 23.6	26 29.9	11 40.9	7 31.2
20 S	3 50 38.9	28 59.5	12 37.5	9 ♐ 39.3	19 2.0	26 51.4	23 37.1	9 53.0	11 23.8	26 30.7	11 39.3	7 31.2
21 M	3 54 35.5	29 57.2	12 34.3	22 44.9	19 27.6	28 3.7	24 22.4	10 0.4	11 23.8	26 31.6	11 37.8	7 D 31.3
22 T	3 58 32.0	0 ♊ 54.9	12 31.2	6 ♑ 2.0	19 48.4	29 16.0	25 7.7	10 7.7	11 23.8	26 32.5	11 36.2	7 31.4
23 W	4 2 28.6	1 52.6	12 28.0	19 29.7	20 4.3	0 ♋ 28.3	25 52.9	10 14.8	11 R 23.7	26 33.5	11 34.7	7 31.5
24 T	4 6 25.1	2 50.2	12 24.8	3 ♒ 7.6	20 15.5	1 40.6	26 38.1	10 21.7	11 23.5	26 34.6	11 33.2	7 31.6
25 F	4 10 21.7	3 47.8	12 21.6	16 55.2	20 22.0	2 52.7	27 23.3	10 28.6	11 23.2	26 35.7	11 31.7	7 31.8
26 S	4 14 18.3	4 45.4	12 18.4	0 ♓ 52.6	20 23.7	4 4.9	28 8.3	10 35.2	11 22.8	26 36.8	11 30.3	7 32.0
27 S	4 18 14.8	5 43.0	12 15.3	14 59.5	20 R 20.9	5 17.0	28 53.4	10 41.7	11 22.3	26 38.0	11 28.8	7 32.2
28 M	4 22 11.4	6 40.6	12 12.1	29 15.0	20 13.6	6 29.1	29 38.4	10 48.1	11 21.7	26 39.3	11 27.4	7 32.5
29 T	4 26 7.9	7 38.2	12 8.9	13 ♈ 36.9	20 2.1	7 41.1	0 ♉ 23.3	10 54.3	11 21.0	26 40.6	11 25.9	7 32.8
30 W	4 30 4.5	8 35.7	12 5.7	28 1.6	19 46.5	8 53.0	1 8.2	11 0.3	11 20.2	26 41.9	11 24.5	7 33.1
31 T	4 34 1.0	9 33.3	12 2.6	12 ♉ 24.3	19 27.2	10 5.0	1 53.1	11 6.2	11 19.4	26 43.3	11 23.1	7 33.5

DAY	EPHEMERIS SIDEREAL TIME	☉	☊	☽	☿	♀	♂	♃	♄	♅	♆	♇
DECLINATION at NOON												
1 T	2 35 44.4	15 N 0.9	16 N 44.1	2 S 6.0	21 N 20.7	21 N 28.5	2 N 38.4	9 S 43.4	17 S 57.1	13 N 26.1	13 S 44.5	21 N 4.6
4 F	2 47 34.0	15 54.4	16 46.8	12 N 21.1	22 46.0	22 15.0	3 33.4	9 33.1	17 56.0	13 26.0	13 43.0	21 4.3
7 M	2 59 23.7	16 45.5	16 49.5	19 59.8	23 49.1	22 56.0	4 27.9	9 23.2	17 55.1	13 25.8	13 41.5	21 3.9
10 T	3 11 13.4	17 34.1	16 52.3	17 52.9	24 31.0	23 31.2	5 21.9	9 13.7	17 54.5	13 25.5	13 40.0	21 3.4
13 S	3 23 3.0	18 20.0	16 55.0	8 48.6	24 53.5	24 0.4	6 15.4	9 4.6	17 54.0	13 24.9	13 38.6	21 2.7
16 W	3 34 52.7	19 3.2	16 57.7	3 S 19.8	24 58.6	24 23.4	7 8.1	8 55.9	17 53.9	13 24.2	13 37.2	21 2.0
19 S	3 46 42.4	19 43.4	17 0.4	14 42.9	24 48.1	24 40.2	8 0.0	8 47.8	17 53.9	13 23.4	13 35.8	21 1.1
22 T	3 58 32.0	20 20.7	17 3.0	20 23.0	24 23.8	24 50.6	8 51.1	8 40.1	17 54.3	13 22.3	13 34.4	21 0.1
25 F	4 10 21.7	20 54.8	17 5.7	16 14.7	23 47.4	24 54.5	9 41.4	8 32.8	17 54.8	13 21.2	13 33.1	20 59.0
28 M	4 22 11.4	21 25.6	17 8.4	3 45.8	23 1.0	24 52.0	10 30.6	8 26.2	17 55.6	13 19.8	13 31.9	20 57.8
31 T	4 34 1.0	21 53.2	17 11.0	10 N 44.1	22 6.9	24 43.1	11 18.9	8 20.0	17 56.7	13 18.3	13 30.6	20 56.5

JUNE 1962

DAY	EPHEMERIS SIDEREAL TIME	☉	☊	☽	☿	♀	♂	♃	♄	♅	♆	♇
LONGITUDE at NOON												
1 F	4 37 57.6	10 ♊ 30.8	11 ♌ 59.4	26 ♉ 39.4	19 ♊ 4.5	11 ♋ 16.9	2 ♉ 37.9	11 ♓ 12.0	11 ♒ 18.4	26 ♌ 44.9	11 ♏ 21.8	7 ♍ 33.9
2 S	4 41 54.1	11 28.3	11 56.2	10 ♊ 41.0	18 R 38.8	12 28.7	3 22.6	11 17.5	11 R 17.3	26 46.4	11 R 20.4	7 34.3
3 S	4 45 50.7	12 25.8	11 53.0	24 24.6	18 10.4	13 40.5	4 7.3	11 22.9	11 16.2	26 47.9	11 19.0	7 34.8
4 M	4 49 47.3	13 23.3	11 49.9	7 ♋ 47.2	17 40.0	14 52.3	4 51.9	11 28.1	11 14.9	26 49.5	11 17.7	7 35.3
5 T	4 53 43.8	14 20.7	11 46.7	20 47.7	17 8.0	16 3.9	5 36.5	11 33.1	11 13.6	26 51.2	11 16.4	7 35.8
6 W	4 57 40.4	15 18.2	11 43.5	3 ♌ 27.0	16 34.9	17 15.6	6 21.0	11 38.0	11 12.1	26 52.9	11 15.1	7 36.3
7 T	5 1 36.9	16 15.6	11 40.3	15 47.8	16 1.4	18 27.1	7 5.4	11 42.7	11 10.6	26 54.6	11 13.8	7 36.9
8 F	5 5 33.5	17 13.0	11 37.1	27 53.8	15 28.0	19 38.7	7 49.8	11 47.3	11 8.9	26 56.4	11 12.6	7 37.5
9 S	5 9 30.0	18 10.4	11 34.0	9 ♍ 49.8	14 55.2	20 50.1	8 34.1	11 51.6	11 7.2	26 58.2	11 11.4	7 38.1
10 S	5 13 26.6	19 7.8	11 30.8	21 40.9	14 23.7	22 1.5	9 18.4	11 55.8	11 5.4	27 0.1	11 10.1	7 38.7
11 M	5 17 23.2	20 5.1	11 27.6	3 ♎ 32.1	13 54.0	23 12.9	10 2.6	11 59.8	11 3.5	27 2.1	11 8.9	7 39.4
12 T	5 21 19.7	21 2.4	11 24.4	15 28.6	13 26.6	24 24.2	10 46.7	12 3.6	11 1.5	27 4.0	11 7.8	7 40.1
13 W	5 25 16.3	21 59.7	11 21.3	27 34.6	13 1.8	25 35.4	11 30.8	12 7.3	10 59.4	27 6.1	11 6.6	7 40.9
14 T	5 29 12.8	22 57.0	11 18.1	9 ♏ 54.0	12 40.3	26 46.5	12 14.8	12 10.7	10 57.3	27 8.1	11 5.5	7 41.6
15 F	5 33 9.4	23 54.3	11 14.9	22 29.3	12 22.2	27 57.6	12 58.8	12 14.0	10 55.0	27 10.2	11 4.4	7 42.4
16 S	5 37 5.9	24 51.6	11 11.7	5 ♐ 21.9	12 8.0	29 8.7	13 42.7	12 17.1	10 52.7	27 12.4	11 3.3	7 43.3
17 S	5 41 2.5	25 48.9	11 8.6	18 32.0	11 57.8	0 ♌ 19.6	14 26.5	12 20.1	10 50.3	27 14.6	11 2.3	7 44.1
18 M	5 44 59.1	26 46.1	11 5.4	1 ♑ 58.4	11 51.9	1 30.5	15 10.3	12 22.8	10 47.8	27 16.8	11 1.3	7 45.0
19 T	5 48 55.6	27 43.4	11 2.2	15 39.1	11 50.4	2 41.4	15 54.0	12 25.4	10 45.2	27 19.1	11 0.3	7 45.9
20 W	5 52 52.2	28 40.6	10 59.0	29 31.3	11 D 53.6	3 52.1	16 37.7	12 27.7	10 42.6	27 21.4	10 59.3	7 46.8
21 T	5 56 48.7	29 37.8	10 55.8	13 ♒ 32.1	12 1.3	5 2.8	17 21.3	12 29.9	10 39.9	27 23.8	10 58.3	7 47.8
22 F	6 0 45.3	0 ♋ 35.1	10 52.7	27 39.0	12 13.8	6 13.5	18 4.9	12 32.0	10 37.1	27 26.2	10 57.4	7 48.8
23 S	6 4 41.8	1 32.3	10 49.5	11 ♓ 49.4	12 31.0	7 24.0	18 48.3	12 33.8	10 34.2	27 28.7	10 56.5	7 49.9
24 S	6 8 38.4	2 29.6	10 46.3	26 1.3	12 52.8	8 34.5	19 31.7	12 35.4	10 31.3	27 31.1	10 55.7	7 50.9
25 M	6 12 35.0	3 26.8	10 43.1	10 ♈ 12.9	13 19.4	9 45.0	20 15.1	12 36.8	10 28.2	27 33.7	10 54.8	7 52.0
26 T	6 16 31.5	4 24.0	10 40.0	24 22.1	13 50.6	10 55.3	20 58.4	12 38.0	10 25.1	27 36.2	10 54.0	7 53.1
27 W	6 20 28.1	5 21.2	10 36.8	8 ♉ 26.9	14 26.4	12 5.6	21 41.6	12 39.1	10 22.0	27 38.8	10 53.2	7 54.2
28 T	6 24 24.6	6 18.5	10 33.6	22 24.5	15 6.7	13 15.8	22 24.7	12 39.9	10 18.7	27 41.5	10 52.4	7 55.3
29 F	6 28 21.2	7 15.7	10 30.4	6 ♊ 12.4	15 51.5	14 25.9	23 7.8	12 40.6	10 15.4	27 44.1	10 51.7	7 56.5
30 S	6 32 17.7	8 12.9	10 27.3	19 47.6	16 40.8	15 36.0	23 50.9	12 41.0	10 12.0	27 46.8	10 51.0	7 57.7

DAY	EPHEMERIS SIDEREAL TIME	☉	☊	☽	☿	♀	♂	♃	♄	♅	♆	♇
DECLINATION at NOON												
1 F	4 37 57.6	22 N 1.6	17 N 11.9	14 N 39.9	21 N 47.8	24 N 38.7	11 N 34.7	8 S 18.1	17 S 57.1	13 N 17.8	13 S 30.3	20 N 56.0
4 M	4 49 47.3	22 24.6	17 14.6	20 28.3	20 48.9	24 21.4	12 21.5	8 12.7	17 58.4	13 16.1	13 29.1	20 54.6
7 T	5 1 36.9	22 44.0	17 17.2	16 34.6	19 51.7	23 57.8	13 7.0	8 7.9	18 0.0	13 14.2	13 28.0	20 53.1
10 S	5 13 26.6	22 59.8	17 19.9	6 25.5	19 1.4	23 28.2	13 51.3	8 3.7	18 1.8	13 12.2	13 27.0	20 51.5
13 W	5 25 16.3	23 12.0	17 22.5	5 S 55.9	18 22.5	22 52.8	14 34.3	8 0.1	18 3.8	13 10.1	13 26.0	20 49.8
16 S	5 37 5.9	23 20.6	17 25.1	16 38.2	17 58.6	22 11.8	15 15.9	7 57.1	18 6.1	13 7.9	13 25.1	20 48.0
19 T	5 48 55.6	23 25.4	17 27.7	20 26.8	17 51.0	21 25.5	15 56.1	7 54.8	18 8.5	13 5.5	13 24.3	20 46.1
22 F	6 0 45.3	23 26.5	17 30.3	13 48.9	17 59.7	20 34.1	16 34.9	7 53.1	18 11.1	13 2.9	13 23.5	20 44.1
25 M	6 12 35.0	23 23.8	17 32.9	0 7.6	18 22.8	19 37.9	17 12.1	7 52.0	18 13.9	13 0.3	13 22.9	20 42.1
28 T	6 24 24.6	23 17.5	17 35.5	13 N 28.7	18 57.9	18 37.2	17 47.8	7 51.6	18 16.8	12 57.5	13 22.3	20 40.0

JULY 1962

DAY	EPHEMERIS SIDEREAL TIME	☉	☊	☽	☿	♀	♂	♃	♄	♅	♆	♇
	h m s	° ′	° ′	° ′	° ′	° ′	° ′	° ′	° ′	° ′	° ′	° ′
					LONGITUDE at NOON							
1 S	6 36 14.3	9♋10.2	10♌24.1	3♋ 8.0	17♊34.4	16♌46.0	24♉33.8	12♓41.3	10♒ 8.6	27♌49.6	10♏50.3	7♍58.9
2 M	6 40 10.9	10 7.4	10 20.9	16 12.0	18 32.3	17 55.9	25 16.7	12 41.4	10R 5.1	27 52.4	10R49.6	8 0.2
3 T	6 44 7.4	11 4.6	10 17.7	28 58.9	19 34.4	19 5.7	25 59.5	12R41.2	10 1.5	27 55.2	10 49.0	8 1.4
4 W	6 48 4.0	12 1.8	10 14.6	11♌29.5	20 40.8	20 15.5	26 42.2	12 40.9	9 57.9	27 58.0	10 48.4	8 2.7
5 T	6 52 0.5	12 59.0	10 11.4	23 45.4	21 51.3	21 25.1	27 24.9	12 40.4	9 54.2	28 0.9	10 47.9	8 4.1
6 F	6 55 57.1	13 56.3	10 8.2	5♍49.3	23 5.9	22 34.7	28 7.5	12 39.7	9 50.5	28 3.8	10 47.3	8 5.4
7 S	6 59 53.7	14 53.5	10 5.0	17 44.9	24 24.5	23 44.2	28 50.0	12 38.8	9 46.7	28 6.8	10 46.8	8 6.8
8 S	7 3 50.2	15 50.7	10 1.8	29 36.2	25 47.1	24 53.6	29 32.4	12 37.6	9 42.9	28 9.8	10 46.3	8 8.2
9 M	7 7 46.8	16 47.9	9 58.7	11♎27.9	27 13.6	26 2.8	0♊14.8	12 36.3	9 39.0	28 12.8	10 45.9	8 9.6
10 T	7 11 43.3	17 45.1	9 55.5	23 24.9	28 43.9	27 12.0	0 57.1	12 34.9	9 35.0	28 15.8	10 45.5	8 11.0
11 W	7 15 39.9	18 42.3	9 52.3	5♏31.7	0♋18.0	28 21.1	1 39.3	12 33.2	9 31.1	28 18.9	10 45.1	8 12.5
12 T	7 19 36.4	19 39.5	9 49.1	17 52.7	1 55.8	29 30.1	2 21.5	12 31.3	9 27.0	28 22.0	10 44.7	8 13.9
13 F	7 23 33.0	20 36.8	9 46.0	0♐31.6	3 37.1	0♍39.1	3 3.6	12 29.3	9 23.0	28 25.2	10 44.5	8 15.5
14 S	7 27 29.5	21 34.0	9 42.8	13 31.0	5 21.9	1 47.8	3 45.6	12 27.0	9 18.9	28 28.3	10 44.2	8 17.0
15 S	7 31 26.1	22 31.2	9 39.6	26 52.0	7 9.9	2 56.5	4 27.5	12 24.6	9 14.8	28 31.5	10 43.9	8 18.6
16 M	7 35 22.7	23 28.4	9 36.4	10♑34.3	9 1.0	4 5.0	5 9.4	12 22.0	9 10.6	28 34.7	10 43.7	8 20.1
17 T	7 39 19.2	24 25.6	9 33.3	24 35.7	10 54.9	5 13.5	5 51.2	12 19.1	9 6.4	28 38.0	10 43.5	8 21.7
18 W	7 43 15.8	25 22.8	9 30.1	8♒52.5	12 51.6	6 21.8	6 32.9	12 16.1	9 2.1	28 41.3	10 43.3	8 23.3
19 T	7 47 12.3	26 20.1	9 26.9	23 20.0	14 50.6	7 30.0	7 14.5	12 13.0	8 57.8	28 44.5	10 43.2	8 24.9
20 F	7 51 8.9	27 17.3	9 23.7	7♓52.5	16 51.7	8 38.1	7 56.1	12 9.6	8 53.5	28 47.9	10 43.1	8 26.6
21 S	7 55 5.4	28 14.6	9 20.5	22 24.9	18 54.6	9 46.1	8 37.6	12 6.1	8 49.2	28 51.2	10 43.0	8 28.2
22 S	7 59 2.0	29 11.8	9 17.4	6♈52.2	20 58.9	10 53.9	9 19.0	12 2.3	8 44.9	28 54.6	10 43.0	8 29.9
23 M	8 2 58.6	0♌ 9.1	9 14.2	21 10.7	23 4.5	12 1.6	10 0.3	11 58.4	8 40.5	28 57.9	10 43.0	8 31.6
24 T	8 6 55.1	1 6.4	9 11.0	5♉17.7	25 10.8	13 9.2	10 41.6	11 54.3	8 36.1	29 1.3	10 43.0	8 33.3
25 W	8 10 51.7	2 3.7	9 7.8	19 11.5	27 17.7	14 16.7	11 22.7	11 50.1	8 31.7	29 4.8	10D43.1	8 35.0
26 T	8 14 48.2	3 1.1	9 4.7	2♊51.1	29 24.7	15 24.1	12 3.8	11 45.7	8 27.3	29 8.2	10 43.2	8 36.8
27 F	8 18 44.8	3 58.4	9 1.5	16 16.3	1♌31.7	16 31.3	12 44.9	11 41.1	8 22.8	29 11.7	10 43.3	8 38.5
28 S	8 22 41.3	4 55.8	8 58.3	29 26.9	3 38.4	17 38.3	13 25.8	11 36.3	8 18.4	29 15.2	10 43.4	8 40.3
29 S	8 26 37.9	5 53.1	8 55.1	12♋23.4	5 44.5	18 45.3	14 6.7	11 31.4	8 13.9	29 18.7	10 43.6	8 42.1
30 M	8 30 34.4	6 50.5	8 52.0	25 6.2	7 49.9	19 52.1	14 47.4	11 26.3	8 9.5	29 22.2	10 43.8	8 43.9
31 T	8 34 31.0	7 47.9	8 48.8	7♌36.1	9 54.4	20 58.7	15 28.1	11 21.1	8 5.0	29 25.8	10 44.1	8 45.7
					DECLINATION at NOON							
1 S	6 36 14.3	23N 7.5	17N38.1	20N20.4	19N41.6	17N32.3	18N21.9	7S 51.9	18S 19.9	12N54.6	13S 21.8	20N37.9
4 W	6 48 4.0	22 53.9	17 40.7	17 33.2	20 30.2	16 23.6	18 54.3	7 52.9	18 23.1	12 51.6	13 21.3	20 35.7
7 S	6 59 53.7	22 36.6	17 43.2	7 52.0	21 19.6	15 11.4	19 25.1	7 54.6	18 26.5	12 48.5	13 21.0	20 33.5
10 T	7 11 43.3	22 15.9	17 45.8	4S 23.5	22 5.0	13 55.9	19 54.1	7 56.9	18 29.9	12 45.3	13 20.7	20 31.2
13 F	7 23 33.0	21 51.7	17 48.4	15 28.6	22 41.4	12 37.6	20 21.5	7 59.8	18 33.5	12 42.0	13 20.6	20 28.8
16 M	7 35 22.7	21 24.1	17 50.9	20 31.3	23 3.3	11 16.7	20 47.0	8 3.4	18 37.1	12 38.7	13 20.5	20 26.4
19 T	7 47 12.3	20 53.3	17 53.4	14 59.1	23 6.0	9 53.6	21 10.8	8 7.6	18 40.8	12 35.2	13 20.5	20 24.0
22 S	7 59 2.0	20 19.3	17 56.0	1 23.2	22 45.7	8 28.5	21 32.8	8 12.5	18 44.5	12 31.7	13 20.6	20 21.6
25 W	8 10 51.7	19 42.2	17 58.5	12N31.1	22 1.3	7 1.8	21 53.0	8 17.9	18 48.2	12 28.0	13 20.8	20 19.2
28 S	8 22 41.3	19 2.2	18 1.0	20 4.5	20 53.9	5 33.7	22 11.3	8 23.9	18 52.0	12 24.4	13 21.1	20 16.7
31 T	8 34 31.0	18 19.3	18 3.5	18 15.2	19 26.8	4 4.5	22 27.9	8 30.4	18 55.7	12 20.6	13 21.5	20 14.2

AUGUST 1962

DAY	EPHEMERIS SIDEREAL TIME	☉	☊	☽	☿	♀	♂	♃	♄	♅	♆	♇
					LONGITUDE at NOON							
1 W	8 38 27.6	8♌45.4	8♌45.6	19♌54.1	11♌57.8	22♍ 5.2	16♊ 8.7	11♓15.7	8♒ 0.5	29♌29.3	10♏44.4	8♍47.6
2 T	8 42 24.1	9 42.8	8 42.4	2♍ 1.6	13 59.9	23 11.5	16 49.3	11R10.1	7R56.1	29 32.9	10 44.7	8 49.4
3 F	8 46 20.7	10 40.3	8 39.2	14 0.9	16 0.9	24 17.8	17 29.7	11 4.5	7 51.6	29 36.5	10 45.1	8 51.3
4 S	8 50 17.2	11 37.7	8 36.1	25 54.1	18 0.4	25 23.8	18 10.1	10 58.6	7 47.2	29 40.1	10 45.5	8 53.2
5 S	8 54 13.8	12 35.2	8 32.9	7♎44.6	19 58.5	26 29.6	18 50.3	10 52.7	7 42.7	29 43.8	10 45.9	8 55.1
6 M	8 58 10.3	13 32.7	8 29.7	19 35.8	21 55.2	27 35.3	19 30.5	10 46.6	7 38.3	29 47.4	10 46.3	8 57.0
7 T	9 2 6.9	14 30.2	8 26.5	1♏31.8	23 50.3	28 40.8	20 10.6	10 40.3	7 33.9	29 51.0	10 46.8	8 58.9
8 W	9 6 3.4	15 27.7	8 23.4	13 37.1	25 43.9	29 46.1	20 50.6	10 33.9	7 29.5	29 54.7	10 47.3	9 0.8
9 T	9 9 60.0	16 25.2	8 20.2	25 55.9	27 36.0	0♎51.2	21 30.5	10 27.4	7 25.1	29 58.4	10 47.9	9 2.8
10 F	9 13 56.5	17 22.8	8 17.0	8♐32.7	29 26.6	1 56.1	22 10.3	10 20.8	7 20.7	0♍ 2.0	10 48.4	9 4.7
11 S	9 17 53.1	18 20.3	8 13.8	21 31.1	1♍15.6	3 0.9	22 50.0	10 14.1	7 16.4	0 5.7	10 49.0	9 6.7
12 S	9 21 49.7	19 17.9	8 10.6	4♑53.8	3 3.2	4 5.4	23 29.6	10 7.3	7 12.1	0 9.4	10 49.7	9 8.6
13 M	9 25 46.2	20 15.5	8 7.5	18 42.1	4 49.2	5 9.7	24 9.2	10 0.4	7 7.8	0 13.1	10 50.3	9 10.6
14 T	9 29 42.8	21 13.1	8 4.3	2♒54.8	6 33.7	6 13.7	24 48.6	9 53.3	7 3.5	0 16.8	10 51.0	9 12.6
15 W	9 33 39.3	22 10.7	8 1.1	17 28.8	8 16.7	7 17.6	25 28.0	9 46.2	6 59.3	0 20.6	10 51.8	9 14.6
16 T	9 37 35.9	23 8.3	7 57.9	2♓18.4	9 58.3	8 21.2	26 7.3	9 39.0	6 55.1	0 24.3	10 52.5	9 16.6
17 F	9 41 32.4	24 6.0	7 54.8	17 16.0	11 38.4	9 24.6	26 46.4	9 31.7	6 50.9	0 28.0	10 53.3	9 18.6
18 S	9 45 29.0	25 3.7	7 51.6	2♈13.2	13 17.0	10 27.7	27 25.5	9 24.3	6 46.8	0 31.7	10 54.2	9 20.6
19 S	9 49 25.5	26 1.4	7 48.4	17 2.1	14 54.2	11 30.6	28 4.5	9 16.8	6 42.7	0 35.5	10 55.0	9 22.7
20 M	9 53 22.1	26 59.1	7 45.2	1♉36.0	16 30.0	12 33.2	28 43.4	9 9.3	6 38.7	0 39.2	10 55.9	9 24.7
21 T	9 57 18.6	27 56.9	7 42.0	15 50.7	18 4.3	13 35.6	29 22.2	9 1.7	6 34.7	0 43.0	10 56.8	9 26.7
22 W	10 1 15.2	28 54.7	7 38.9	29 43.8	19 37.3	14 37.7	0♋ 0.9	8 54.0	6 30.7	0 46.7	10 57.7	9 28.8
23 T	10 5 11.8	29 52.5	7 35.7	13♊15.4	21 8.8	15 39.6	0 39.5	8 46.3	6 26.8	0 50.5	10 58.7	9 30.8
24 F	10 9 8.3	0♍50.4	7 32.5	26 26.7	22 38.9	16 41.2	1 18.1	8 38.6	6 23.0	0 54.3	10 59.8	9 32.9
25 S	10 13 4.9	1 48.3	7 29.3	9♋19.9	24 7.5	17 42.5	1 56.5	8 30.8	6 19.1	0 58.0	11 0.8	9 35.0
26 S	10 17 1.4	2 46.2	7 26.2	21 57.6	25 34.7	18 43.4	2 34.8	8 23.0	6 15.4	1 1.8	11 1.9	9 37.0
27 M	10 20 58.0	3 44.2	7 23.0	4♌22.2	27 0.5	19 44.1	3 13.0	8 15.1	6 11.7	1 5.5	11 3.0	9 39.1
28 T	10 24 54.5	4 42.1	7 19.8	16 36.3	28 24.8	20 44.4	3 51.1	8 7.2	6 8.0	1 9.3	11 4.1	9 41.2
29 W	10 28 51.1	5 40.1	7 16.6	28 41.8	29 47.5	21 44.5	4 29.1	7 59.3	6 4.4	1 13.0	11 5.2	9 43.2
30 T	10 32 47.6	6 38.2	7 13.4	10♍40.6	1♎ 8.8	22 44.2	5 7.0	7 51.3	6 0.9	1 16.8	11 6.4	9 45.3
31 F	10 36 44.2	7 36.2	7 10.3	22 34.7	2 28.4	23 43.5	5 44.8	7 43.4	5 57.4	1 20.5	11 7.6	9 47.4
					DECLINATION at NOON							
1 W	8 38 27.6	18N 4.4	18N 4.3	15N48.2	18N54.0	3N34.6	22N33.0	8S 32.6	18S 56.9	12N19.4	13S 21.6	20N13.4
4 S	8 50 17.2	17 18.0	18 6.8	5 10.7	17 6.6	2 4.5	22 47.2	8 39.8	19 0.6	12 15.5	13 22.1	20 10.9
7 T	9 2 6.9	16 29.0	18 9.3	7S 5.2	15 8.8	0 34.0	22 59.5	8 47.4	19 4.3	12 11.7	13 22.7	20 8.4
10 F	9 13 56.5	15 37.7	18 11.8	17 11.4	13 3.7	0S 56.6	23 10.1	8 55.3	19 7.8	12 7.8	13 23.4	20 5.9
13 M	9 25 46.2	14 44.1	18 14.3	20 19.3	10 54.2	2 27.0	23 18.9	9 3.6	19 11.3	12 3.9	13 24.2	20 3.5
16 T	9 37 35.9	13 48.4	18 16.7	12 36.5	8 42.5	3 56.9	23 26.0	9 12.2	19 14.8	11 59.9	13 25.0	20 1.0
19 S	9 49 25.5	12 50.7	18 19.2	2N10.6	6 30.4	5 26.2	23 31.3	9 21.0	19 18.1	11 55.9	13 25.9	19 58.6
22 W	10 1 15.2	11 51.2	18 21.6	15 17.5	4 19.3	6 54.4	23 35.0	9 30.0	19 21.2	11 52.0	13 26.9	19 56.2
25 S	10 13 4.9	10 50.0	18 24.1	20 31.5	2 10.4	8 21.4	23 37.0	9 39.1	19 24.3	11 48.0	13 28.0	19 53.8
28 T	10 24 54.5	9 47.3	18 26.5	16 32.0	0 4.9	9 46.8	23 37.3	9 48.2	19 27.2	11 44.0	13 29.2	19 51.5
31 F	10 36 44.2	8 43.1	18 28.9	6 15.7	1S 56.1	11 10.6	23 36.2	9 57.4	19 30.0	11 40.0	13 30.4	19 49.2

SEPTEMBER 1962

DAY	EPHEMERIS SIDEREAL TIME	☉	☊	☽	☿	♀	♂	♃	♄	♅	♆	♇
	h m s	° ′	° ′	° ′	° ′	° ′	° ′	° ′	° ′	° ′	° ′	° ′
						LONGITUDE at NOON						
1 S	10 40 40.7	8♍34.3	7♌ 7.1	4♎25.7	3♎46.5	24♎42.5	6♋22.5	7♓35.5	5♒54.0	1♍24.3	11♏ 8.8	9♍49.5
2 S	10 44 37.3	9 32.4	7 3.9	16 15.9	5 2.8	25 41.1	7 0.0	7R27.5	5R50.7	1 28.0	11 10.1	9 51.6
3 M	10 48 33.8	10 30.5	7 0.7	28 7.6	6 17.5	26 39.3	7 37.5	7 19.6	5 47.4	1 31.7	11 11.4	9 53.6
4 T	10 52 30.4	11 28.7	6 57.6	10♏ 3.8	7 30.3	27 37.1	8 14.8	7 11.7	5 44.2	1 35.4	11 12.7	9 55.7
5 W	10 56 26.9	12 26.8	6 54.4	22 8.0	8 41.3	28 34.5	8 52.0	7 3.8	5 41.1	1 39.1	11 14.1	9 57.8
6 T	11 0 23.5	13 25.0	6 51.2	4♐24.1	9 50.3	29 31.4	9 29.1	6 56.0	5 38.1	1 42.8	11 15.4	9 59.9
7 F	11 4 20.0	14 23.3	6 48.0	16 56.3	10 57.2	0♏27.9	10 6.1	6 48.2	5 35.1	1 46.5	11 16.8	10 1.9
8 S	11 8 16.6	15 21.5	6 44.8	29 48.9	12 2.0	1 24.0	10 43.0	6 40.4	5 32.2	1 50.2	11 18.2	10 4.0
9 S	11 12 13.1	16 19.8	6 41.7	13♑ 5.6	13 4.5	2 19.5	11 19.7	6 32.7	5 29.4	1 53.9	11 19.7	10 6.1
10 M	11 16 9.7	17 18.1	6 38.5	26 49.2	14 4.5	3 14.5	11 56.4	6 25.1	5 26.6	1 57.5	11 21.2	10 8.1
11 T	11 20 6.3	18 16.4	6 35.3	11♒ 0.6	15 2.0	4 9.1	12 32.9	6 17.4	5 23.9	2 1.2	11 22.7	10 10.2
12 W	11 24 2.8	19 14.8	6 32.1	25 38.2	15 56.6	5 3.0	13 9.3	6 9.9	5 21.3	2 4.8	11 24.2	10 12.3
13 T	11 27 59.4	20 13.1	6 29.0	10♓37.3	16 48.4	5 56.4	13 45.5	6 2.4	5 18.8	2 8.4	11 25.7	10 14.3
14 F	11 31 55.9	21 11.6	6 25.8	25 49.8	17 37.0	6 49.3	14 21.7	5 55.1	5 16.5	2 12.1	11 27.3	10 16.4
15 S	11 35 52.5	22 10.0	6 22.6	11♈ 5.8	18 22.1	7 41.5	14 57.8	5 47.8	5 14.1	2 15.7	11 28.9	10 18.5
16 S	11 39 49.0	23 8.5	6 19.4	26 14.5	19 3.6	8 33.1	15 33.7	5 40.5	5 11.9	2 19.3	11 30.6	10 20.5
17 M	11 43 45.6	24 7.0	6 16.2	11♉ 6.4	19 41.1	9 24.1	16 9.5	5 33.4	5 9.7	2 22.8	11 32.2	10 22.5
18 T	11 47 42.1	25 5.6	6 13.1	25 34.6	20 14.4	10 14.3	16 45.1	5 26.4	5 7.6	2 26.4	11 33.9	10 24.5
19 W	11 51 38.7	26 4.1	6 9.9	9♊35.6	20 43.2	11 3.9	17 20.6	5 19.4	5 5.6	2 29.9	11 35.5	10 26.6
20 T	11 55 35.2	27 2.8	6 6.7	23 8.9	21 7.0	11 52.8	17 56.0	5 12.6	5 3.7	2 33.4	11 37.2	10 28.6
21 F	11 59 31.8	28 1.4	6 3.5	6♋16.4	21 25.6	12 40.9	18 31.3	5 5.8	5 1.9	2 36.9	11 39.0	10 30.6
22 S	12 3 28.3	29 0.1	6 0.4	19 1.7	21 38.5	13 28.3	19 6.4	4 59.2	5 0.2	2 40.4	11 40.7	10 32.6
23 S	12 7 24.9	29 58.8	5 57.2	1♌28.8	21 45.4	14 14.8	19 41.4	4 52.7	4 58.6	2 43.8	11 42.5	10 34.6
24 M	12 11 21.4	0♎57.6	5 54.0	13 41.9	21 45.8	15 0.5	20 16.2	4 46.4	4 57.0	2 47.2	11 44.3	10 36.5
25 T	12 15 18.0	1 56.4	5 50.8	25 45.0	21R39.6	15 45.4	20 50.9	4 40.1	4 55.6	2 50.6	11 46.1	10 38.5
26 W	12 19 14.5	2 55.3	5 47.6	7♍41.4	21 26.2	16 29.3	21 25.4	4 34.0	4 54.2	2 54.0	11 47.9	10 40.5
27 T	12 23 11.1	3 54.1	5 44.5	19 33.9	21 5.5	17 12.3	21 59.8	4 28.1	4 53.0	2 57.4	11 49.8	10 42.4
28 F	12 27 7.6	4 53.0	5 41.3	1♎24.6	20 37.3	17 54.3	22 34.1	4 22.2	4 51.8	3 0.7	11 51.6	10 44.4
29 S	12 31 4.2	5 52.0	5 38.1	13 15.4	20 1.6	18 35.3	23 8.2	4 16.6	4 50.8	3 4.0	11 53.5	10 46.3
30 S	12 35 0.7	6 51.0	5 34.9	25 7.7	19 18.6	19 15.2	23 42.1	4 11.0	4 49.8	3 7.3	11 55.4	10 48.2
						DECLINATION at NOON						
1 S	10 40 40.7	8N21.4	18N29.7	2N11.4	2S35.2	11S38.0	23N35.4	10S 0.4	19S30.8	11N38.7	13S30.9	19N48.4
4 T	10 52 30.4	7 15.6	18 32.1	9S54.2	4 28.5	12 59.0	23 32.3	10 9.4	19 33.4	11 34.7	13 32.2	19 46.2
7 F	11 4 20.0	6 8.8	18 34.5	18 45.3	6 14.3	14 17.5	23 27.6	10 18.3	19 35.7	11 30.8	13 33.6	19 44.0
10 M	11 16 9.7	5 1.0	18 36.9	19 46.4	7 51.0	15 33.4	23 21.6	10 27.0	19 37.9	11 26.8	13 35.1	19 41.9
13 T	11 27 59.4	3 52.5	18 39.3	10 8.4	9 16.7	16 46.4	23 14.3	10 35.4	19 39.9	11 23.0	13 36.6	19 39.8
16 S	11 39 49.0	2 43.4	18 41.7	5N26.2	10 28.6	17 56.1	23 5.7	10 43.4	19 41.6	11 19.1	13 38.2	19 37.8
19 W	11 51 38.7	1 33.8	18 44.1	17 34.0	11 23.0	19 2.4	22 55.8	10 51.1	19 43.2	11 15.4	13 39.8	19 35.9
22 S	12 3 28.3	0 23.8	18 46.4	20 27.1	11 55.3	20 5.0	22 44.9	10 58.4	19 44.6	11 11.6	13 41.5	19 34.1
25 T	12 15 18.0	0S46.3	18 48.8	14 25.6	11 59.5	21 3.7	22 32.9	11 5.2	19 45.8	11 8.0	13 43.3	19 32.3
28 F	12 27 7.6	1 56.5	18 51.1	3 12.3	11 29.3	21 58.1	22 20.0	11 11.5	19 46.7	11 4.4	13 45.1	19 30.6

OCTOBER 1962

DAY	EPHEMERIS SIDEREAL TIME	☉	☊	☽	☿	♀	♂	♃	♄	♅	♆	♇
						LONGITUDE at NOON						
1 M	12 38 57.3	7♎50.0	5♌31.7	7♏ 3.1	18♎28.6	19♏54.1	24♋15.9	4♓ 5.7	4♒48.9	3♍10.6	11♏57.4	10♍50.1
2 T	12 42 53.8	8 49.0	5 28.6	19 3.5	17R32.3	20 31.7	24 49.5	4R 0.5	4R48.2	3 13.8	11 59.3	10 52.0
3 W	12 46 50.4	9 48.1	5 25.4	1♐10.9	16 30.5	21 8.2	25 22.9	3 55.4	4 47.5	3 17.0	12 1.3	10 53.8
4 T	12 50 47.0	10 47.2	5 22.2	13 28.4	15 24.4	21 43.4	25 56.2	3 50.5	4 46.9	3 20.2	12 3.2	10 55.7
5 F	12 54 43.5	11 46.4	5 19.0	25 59.2	14 15.6	22 17.4	26 29.4	3 45.9	4 46.5	3 23.4	12 5.3	10 57.6
6 S	12 58 40.1	12 45.5	5 15.9	8♑47.1	13 5.5	22 49.9	27 2.3	3 41.3	4 46.1	3 26.5	12 7.3	10 59.4
7 S	13 2 36.6	13 44.7	5 12.7	21 56.0	11 56.1	23 21.1	27 35.1	3 37.0	4 45.9	3 29.6	12 9.3	11 1.2
8 M	13 6 33.2	14 43.9	5 9.5	5♒29.6	10 49.4	23 50.7	28 7.7	3 32.8	4 45.7	3 32.6	12 11.3	11 3.0
9 T	13 10 29.7	15 43.2	5 6.3	19 30.2	9 47.2	24 18.8	28 40.1	3 28.8	4 45.6	3 35.7	12 13.4	11 4.8
10 W	13 14 26.3	16 42.5	5 3.1	3♓58.0	8 51.3	24 45.3	29 12.3	3 25.0	4D45.7	3 38.7	12 15.4	11 6.6
11 T	13 18 22.8	17 41.8	4 60.0	18 50.3	8 3.3	25 10.2	29 44.4	3 21.3	4 45.8	3 41.6	12 17.5	11 8.3
12 F	13 22 19.4	18 41.1	4 56.8	4♈ 0.8	7 24.5	25 33.3	0♌16.3	3 17.9	4 46.1	3 44.6	12 19.6	11 10.1
13 S	13 26 15.9	19 40.5	4 53.6	19 20.1	6 55.8	25 54.7	0 48.0	3 14.6	4 46.4	3 47.4	12 21.7	11 11.8
14 S	13 30 12.5	20 39.9	4 50.4	4♉36.8	6 37.9	26 14.2	1 19.5	3 11.5	4 46.8	3 50.3	12 23.8	11 13.5
15 M	13 34 9.0	21 39.3	4 47.3	19 39.6	6 30.9	26 31.8	1 50.8	3 8.6	4 47.4	3 53.1	12 25.9	11 15.2
16 T	13 38 5.6	22 38.8	4 44.1	4♊19.5	6D35.1	26 47.4	2 21.9	3 5.9	4 48.0	3 55.9	12 28.0	11 16.8
17 W	13 42 2.1	23 38.3	4 40.9	18 30.9	6 49.9	27 1.1	2 52.8	3 3.4	4 48.7	3 58.7	12 30.2	11 18.5
18 T	13 45 58.7	24 37.9	4 37.7	2♋11.8	7 15.1	27 12.6	3 23.5	3 1.1	4 49.6	4 1.4	12 32.3	11 20.1
19 F	13 49 55.2	25 37.5	4 34.5	15 23.6	7 49.8	27 22.0	3 54.0	2 59.0	4 50.5	4 4.0	12 34.5	11 21.7
20 S	13 53 51.8	26 37.1	4 31.4	28 9.8	8 33.5	27 29.3	4 24.3	2 57.1	4 51.6	4 6.7	12 36.7	11 23.3
21 S	13 57 48.4	27 36.8	4 28.2	10♌34.9	9 25.3	27 34.3	4 54.4	2 55.4	4 52.7	4 9.3	12 38.9	11 24.8
22 M	14 1 44.9	28 36.5	4 25.0	22 44.2	10 24.3	27 37.0	5 24.3	2 53.9	4 53.9	4 11.8	12 41.0	11 26.4
23 T	14 5 41.5	29 36.2	4 21.8	4♍42.6	11 29.7	27 37.4	5 53.9	2 52.5	4 55.3	4 14.4	12 43.2	11 27.9
24 W	14 9 38.0	0♏36.0	4 18.7	16 34.7	12 40.7	27R35.5	6 23.3	2 51.4	4 56.7	4 16.8	12 45.4	11 29.4
25 T	14 13 34.6	1 35.8	4 15.5	28 24.3	13 56.7	27 31.1	6 52.5	2 50.5	4 58.3	4 19.3	12 47.6	11 30.9
26 F	14 17 31.1	2 35.7	4 12.3	10♎14.6	15 16.9	27 24.4	7 21.5	2 49.9	4 59.9	4 21.7	12 49.9	11 32.4
27 S	14 21 27.7	3 35.6	4 9.1	22 7.7	16 40.5	27 15.3	7 50.1	2 49.4	5 1.7	4 24.1	12 52.1	11 33.8
28 S	14 25 24.2	4 35.5	4 5.9	4♏ 5.2	18 7.2	27 3.7	8 18.6	2 49.1	5 3.5	4 26.4	12 54.4	11 35.2
29 M	14 29 20.8	5 35.4	4 2.8	16 8.3	19 36.4	26 49.8	8 46.7	2 49.0	5 5.5	4 28.6	12 56.6	11 36.6
30 T	14 33 17.3	6 35.4	3 59.6	28 18.1	21 7.6	26 33.4	9 14.7	2D49.1	5 7.5	4 30.8	12 58.8	11 37.9
31 W	14 37 13.9	7 35.4	3 56.4	10♐35.5	22 40.5	26 14.7	9 42.3	2 49.4	5 9.6	4 33.0	13 1.1	11 39.3
						DECLINATION at NOON						
1 M	12 38 57.3	3S 6.5	18N53.4	9S 5.3	10S19.9	22S48.0	22N 6.1	11S17.3	19S47.4	11N 0.9	13S46.9	19N29.1
4 T	12 50 47.0	4 16.2	18 55.8	18 24.1	8 33.1	23 33.1	21 51.5	11 22.5	19 47.9	10 57.5	13 48.8	19 27.6
7 S	13 2 36.6	5 25.4	18 58.1	20 24.2	6 22.7	24 12.9	21 36.1	11 27.1	19 48.2	10 54.2	13 50.7	19 26.1
10 W	13 14 26.3	6 34.0	19 0.4	12 14.5	4 14.0	24 47.1	21 20.0	11 31.1	19 48.3	10 51.0	13 52.6	19 24.8
13 S	13 26 15.9	7 41.9	19 2.7	3N 6.6	2 34.4	25 15.0	21 3.4	11 34.5	19 48.1	10 47.9	13 54.6	19 23.7
16 T	13 38 5.6	8 48.7	19 5.0	16 40.8	1 41.5	25 36.2	20 46.4	11 37.2	19 47.7	10 44.9	13 56.6	19 22.6
19 F	13 49 55.2	9 54.4	19 7.3	20 50.9	1 39.0	25 49.9	20 29.0	11 39.2	19 47.1	10 42.0	13 58.6	19 21.6
22 M	14 1 44.9	10 58.9	19 9.5	15 22.5	2 20.3	25 55.3	20 11.3	11 40.6	19 46.3	10 39.3	14 0.6	19 20.7
25 T	14 13 34.6	12 1.8	19 11.8	4 19.6	3 34.6	25 51.6	19 53.5	11 41.3	19 45.3	10 36.7	14 2.6	19 20.0
28 S	14 25 24.2	13 3.2	19 14.1	8S11.1	5 10.8	25 37.8	19 35.6	11 41.3	19 44.0	10 34.2	14 4.7	19 19.3
31 W	14 37 13.9	14 2.7	19 16.3	18 4.5	6 60.0	25 13.2	19 17.7	11 40.7	19 42.5	10 31.8	14 6.7	19 18.8

NOVEMBER 1962

LONGITUDE at NOON

DAY	EPHEMERIS SIDEREAL TIME	☉	☊	☽	☿	♀	♂	♃	♄	♅	♆	♇
	h m s	° ′	° ′	° ′	° ′	° ′	° ′	° ′	° ′	° ′	° ′	° ′
1 T	14 41 10.4	8♏35.5	3♌53.2	23♐ 1.9	24♎14.7	25♏53.8	10♌ 9.7	2♓50.0	5♒11.8	4♍35.1	13♏ 3.3	11♍40.6
2 F	14 45 7.0	9 35.5	3 50.1	5♑39.4	25 50.0	25R30.7	10 36.8	2 50.7	5 14.2	4 37.2	13 5.5	11 41.9
3 S	14 49 3.6	10 35.6	3 46.9	18 30.4	27 26.0	25 5.4	11 3.6	2 51.6	5 16.6	4 39.3	13 7.8	11 43.1
4 S	14 53 0.1	11 35.7	3 43.7	1♒37.9	29 2.7	24 38.2	11 30.1	2 52.8	5 19.1	4 41.2	13 10.0	11 44.4
5 M	14 56 56.7	12 35.9	3 40.5	15 5.0	0♏39.8	24 9.2	11 56.4	2 54.1	5 21.7	4 43.2	13 12.3	11 45.6
6 T	15 0 53.2	13 36.1	3 37.3	28 54.1	2 17.2	23 38.5	12 22.4	2 55.7	5 24.4	4 45.1	13 14.5	11 46.7
7 W	15 4 49.8	14 36.2	3 34.2	13♓ 6.4	3 54.8	23 6.3	12 48.0	2 57.4	5 27.2	4 46.9	13 16.8	11 47.9
8 T	15 8 46.3	15 36.5	3 31.0	27 40.9	5 32.4	22 32.7	13 13.4	2 59.4	5 30.1	4 48.7	13 19.0	11 49.0
9 F	15 12 42.9	16 36.7	3 27.8	12♈33.8	7 10.1	21 58.1	13 38.4	3 1.5	5 33.1	4 50.4	13 21.3	11 50.1
10 S	15 16 39.4	17 37.0	3 24.6	27 38.0	8 47.6	21 22.6	14 3.1	3 3.9	5 36.1	4 52.1	13 23.5	11 51.2
11 S	15 20 36.0	18 37.3	3 21.5	12♉44.1	10 25.1	20 46.5	14 27.5	3 6.4	5 39.3	4 53.8	13 25.7	11 52.2
12 M	15 24 32.5	19 37.6	3 18.3	27 41.8	12 2.4	20 10.0	14 51.6	3 9.2	5 42.6	4 55.4	13 28.0	11 53.2
13 T	15 28 29.1	20 38.0	3 15.1	12♊21.7	13 39.5	19 33.4	15 15.3	3 12.1	5 45.9	4 56.9	13 30.2	11 54.2
14 W	15 32 25.7	21 38.3	3 11.9	26 36.8	15 16.5	18 56.9	15 38.7	3 15.3	5 49.3	4 58.4	13 32.4	11 55.2
15 T	15 36 22.2	22 38.7	3 8.8	10♋23.6	16 53.2	18 20.9	16 1.8	3 18.6	5 52.8	4 59.8	13 34.7	11 56.1
16 F	15 40 18.8	23 39.2	3 5.6	23 41.7	18 29.7	17 45.5	16 24.5	3 22.2	5 56.5	5 1.3	13 36.9	11 57.0
17 S	15 44 15.3	24 39.7	3 2.4	6♌33.2	20 6.0	17 11.0	16 46.9	3 25.9	6 0.2	5 2.6	13 39.2	11 57.9
18 S	15 48 11.9	25 40.2	2 59.2	19 2.2	21 42.0	16 37.6	17 8.8	3 29.8	6 3.9	5 3.9	13 41.4	11 58.8
19 M	15 52 8.4	26 40.8	2 56.0	1♍13.6	23 17.8	16 5.5	17 30.4	3 33.9	6 7.8	5 5.1	13 43.6	11 59.6
20 T	15 56 5.0	27 41.3	2 52.9	13 12.8	24 53.4	15 35.0	17 51.5	3 38.2	6 11.7	5 6.3	13 45.8	12 0.3
21 W	16 0 1.5	28 41.9	2 49.7	25 5.0	26 28.8	15 6.2	18 12.3	3 42.6	6 15.7	5 7.4	13 48.0	12 1.1
22 T	16 3 58.1	29 42.5	2 46.5	6♎54.8	28 3.9	14 39.2	18 32.7	3 47.3	6 19.8	5 8.5	13 50.1	12 1.8
23 F	16 7 54.7	0♐43.2	2 43.3	18 46.4	29 38.9	14 14.3	18 52.6	3 52.1	6 24.0	5 9.5	13 52.3	12 2.5
24 S	16 11 51.2	1 43.9	2 40.2	0♏43.1	1♐13.7	13 51.5	19 12.1	3 57.1	6 28.3	5 10.5	13 54.5	12 3.2
25 S	16 15 47.8	2 44.6	2 37.0	12 47.1	2 48.4	13 30.9	19 31.1	4 2.3	6 32.6	5 11.4	13 56.6	12 3.8
26 M	16 19 44.3	3 45.3	2 33.8	25 0.1	4 22.9	13 12.6	19 49.7	4 7.7	6 37.1	5 12.2	13 58.8	12 4.4
27 T	16 23 40.9	4 46.0	2 30.6	7♐22.9	5 57.2	12 56.7	20 7.9	4 13.3	6 41.6	5 13.0	14 0.9	12 5.0
28 W	16 27 37.4	5 46.8	2 27.5	19 55.9	7 31.5	12 43.3	20 25.6	4 19.0	6 46.1	5 13.7	14 3.0	12 5.5
29 T	16 31 34.0	6 47.6	2 24.3	2♑39.5	9 5.6	12 32.3	20 42.8	4 24.9	6 50.8	5 14.4	14 5.2	12 6.0
30 F	16 35 30.6	7 48.4	2 21.1	15 33.8	10 39.7	12 23.7	20 59.5	4 31.0	6 55.5	5 15.0	14 7.3	12 6.5

DECLINATION at NOON

DAY	EPHEMERIS SIDEREAL TIME	☉	☊	☽	☿	♀	♂	♃	♄	♅	♆	♇
1 T	14 41 10.4	14S22.1	19N17.1	20S 0.2	7S38.0	25S 2.5	19N11.8	11S40.3	19S42.0	10N31.1	14S 7.4	19N18.6
4 S	14 53 0.1	15 18.8	19 19.3	19 39.1	9 34.2	24 22.8	18 54.2	11 38.8	19 40.2	10 29.0	14 9.4	19 18.3
7 W	15 4 49.8	16 13.3	19 21.5	9 37.1	11 30.5	23 32.0	18 36.9	11 36.5	19 38.2	10 27.0	14 11.4	19 18.1
10 S	15 16 39.4	17 5.3	19 23.7	5N57.8	13 24.1	22 31.5	18 20.1	11 33.7	19 36.0	10 25.2	14 13.4	19 18.0
13 T	15 28 29.1	17 54.7	19 25.9	18 27.0	15 13.0	21 23.6	18 3.7	11 30.2	19 33.6	10 23.6	14 15.4	19 18.0
16 F	15 40 18.8	18 41.3	19 28.1	20 37.6	16 55.8	20 11.4	17 48.1	11 26.0	19 31.0	10 22.1	14 17.4	19 18.1
19 M	15 52 8.4	19 25.0	19 30.3	13 20.9	18 31.4	18 58.6	17 33.2	11 21.2	19 28.2	10 20.8	14 19.3	19 18.3
22 T	16 3 58.1	20 5.5	19 32.5	1 28.3	19 59.0	17 48.7	17 19.2	11 15.8	19 25.2	10 19.7	14 21.2	19 18.7
25 S	16 15 47.8	20 42.6	19 34.7	10S56.6	21 17.8	16 44.8	17 6.4	11 9.8	19 22.1	10 18.8	14 23.1	19 19.2
28 W	16 27 37.4	21 16.4	19 36.9	19 43.6	22 27.1	15 49.2	16 54.7	11 3.2	19 18.7	10 18.0	14 24.9	19 19.9

DECEMBER 1962

LONGITUDE at NOON

DAY	EPHEMERIS SIDEREAL TIME	☉	☊	☽	☿	♀	♂	♃	♄	♅	♆	♇
1 S	16 39 27.1	8♐49.2	2♌17.9	28♑39.5	12♐13.7	12♏17.6	21♌15.7	4♓37.3	7♒ 0.3	5♍15.6	14♏ 9.4	12♍ 6.9
2 S	16 43 23.7	9 50.1	2 14.7	11♒57.7	13 47.6	12R14.0	21 31.4	4 43.7	7 5.2	5 16.1	14 11.4	12 7.3
3 M	16 47 20.2	10 50.9	2 11.6	25 29.5	15 21.5	12 12.9	21 46.6	4 50.3	7 10.1	5 16.6	14 13.5	12 7.7
4 T	16 51 16.8	11 51.8	2 8.4	9♓16.2	16 55.3	12D14.1	22 1.2	4 57.0	7 15.1	5 17.0	14 15.5	12 8.0
5 W	16 55 13.3	12 52.7	2 5.2	23 18.4	18 29.2	12 17.8	22 15.3	5 4.0	7 20.2	5 17.3	14 17.6	12 8.3
6 T	16 59 9.9	13 53.6	2 2.0	7♈35.5	20 3.0	12 23.8	22 28.9	5 11.0	7 25.4	5 17.6	14 19.6	12 8.6
7 F	17 3 6.5	14 54.5	1 58.9	22 5.2	21 36.9	12 32.1	22 41.9	5 18.3	7 30.6	5 17.9	14 21.6	12 8.9
8 S	17 7 3.0	15 55.5	1 55.7	6♉43.3	23 10.7	12 42.7	22 54.4	5 25.7	7 35.9	5 18.0	14 23.6	12 9.1
9 S	17 10 59.6	16 56.4	1 52.5	21 23.6	24 44.5	12 55.5	23 6.2	5 33.3	7 41.3	5 18.1	14 25.6	12 9.3
10 M	17 14 56.1	17 57.3	1 49.3	5♊58.8	26 18.4	13 10.4	23 17.5	5 41.0	7 46.7	5 18.2	14 27.5	12 9.4
11 T	17 18 52.7	18 58.3	1 46.2	20 21.9	27 52.2	13 27.4	23 28.2	5 48.9	7 52.1	5 18.2	14 29.5	12 9.6
12 W	17 22 49.2	19 59.3	1 43.0	4♋26.6	29 26.1	13 46.4	23 38.3	5 56.9	7 57.7	5 18.2	14 31.4	12 9.6
13 T	17 26 45.8	21 0.3	1 39.8	18 8.9	0♑60.0	14 7.4	23 47.7	6 5.0	8 3.3	5R18.0	14 33.3	12 9.7
14 F	17 30 42.4	22 1.3	1 36.6	1♌27.1	2 33.8	14 30.3	23 56.5	6 13.4	8 8.9	5 17.9	14 35.2	12 9.7
15 S	17 34 38.9	23 2.3	1 33.4	14 21.5	4 7.7	14 55.1	24 4.7	6 21.8	8 14.6	5 17.7	14 37.0	12 9.7
16 S	17 38 35.5	24 3.3	1 30.3	26 54.7	5 41.4	15 21.6	24 12.1	6 30.4	8 20.4	5 17.4	14 38.9	12 9.7
17 M	17 42 32.0	25 4.4	1 27.1	9♍10.3	7 15.1	15 49.8	24 19.0	6 39.1	8 26.2	5 17.0	14 40.7	12R 9.6
18 T	17 46 28.6	26 5.4	1 23.9	21 12.8	8 48.6	16 19.7	24 25.1	6 48.0	8 32.1	5 16.7	14 42.5	12 9.5
19 W	17 50 25.1	27 6.5	1 20.7	3♎ 7.2	10 22.0	16 51.2	24 30.5	6 57.0	8 38.0	5 16.2	14 44.3	12 9.3
20 T	17 54 21.7	28 7.6	1 17.6	14 58.6	11 55.1	17 24.2	24 35.2	7 6.2	8 44.0	5 15.7	14 46.1	12 9.2
21 F	17 58 18.3	29 8.7	1 14.4	26 51.8	13 27.9	17 58.6	24 39.2	7 15.5	8 50.1	5 15.2	14 47.8	12 9.0
22 S	18 2 14.8	0♑ 9.8	1 11.2	8♏50.8	15 0.2	18 34.5	24 42.4	7 24.9	8 56.2	5 14.5	14 49.5	12 8.7
23 S	18 6 11.4	1 11.0	1 8.0	20 59.5	16 32.0	19 11.7	24 44.9	7 34.4	9 2.3	5 13.9	14 51.2	12 8.4
24 M	18 10 7.9	2 12.1	1 4.9	3♐20.3	18 3.1	19 50.3	24 46.7	7 44.1	9 8.5	5 13.2	14 52.9	12 8.1
25 T	18 14 4.5	3 13.2	1 1.7	15 55.2	19 33.3	20 30.0	24 47.6	7 53.9	9 14.7	5 12.4	14 54.5	12 7.8
26 W	18 18 1.0	4 14.4	0 58.5	28 44.8	21 2.5	21 11.0	24 47.8	8 3.9	9 21.0	5 11.6	14 56.1	12 7.5
27 T	18 21 57.6	5 15.6	0 55.3	11♑49.0	22 30.4	21 53.1	24R47.2	8 13.9	9 27.4	5 10.7	14 57.7	12 7.1
28 F	18 25 54.2	6 16.8	0 52.2	25 7.1	23 56.8	22 36.4	24 45.9	8 24.1	9 33.8	5 9.8	14 59.4	12 6.7
29 S	18 29 50.7	7 17.9	0 49.0	8♒37.6	25 21.4	23 20.6	24 43.7	8 34.4	9 40.2	5 8.8	15 0.9	12 6.2
30 S	18 33 47.3	8 19.1	0 45.8	22 19.0	26 43.7	24 5.9	24 40.7	8 44.9	9 46.7	5 7.8	15 2.4	12 5.7
31 M	18 37 43.8	9 20.3	0 42.6	6♓ 9.9	28 3.4	24 52.2	24 37.0	8 55.4	9 53.2	5 6.7	15 3.9	12 5.2

DECLINATION at NOON

DAY	EPHEMERIS SIDEREAL TIME	☉	☊	☽	☿	♀	♂	♃	♄	♅	♆	♇
1 S	16 39 27.1	21S46.5	19N39.0	20S14.8	23S26.3	15S 3.2	16N44.4	10S56.0	19S15.1	10N17.5	14S26.7	19N20.6
4 T	16 51 16.8	22 12.8	19 41.2	11 3.7	24 14.8	14 27.5	16 35.6	10 48.3	19 11.4	10 17.1	14 28.4	19 21.5
7 F	17 3 6.5	22 35.3	19 43.3	3N53.2	24 51.9	14 2.0	16 28.3	10 40.0	19 7.5	10 16.9	14 30.2	19 22.5
10 M	17 14 56.1	22 53.8	19 45.4	17 11.1	25 17.1	13 46.3	16 22.9	10 31.1	19 3.4	10 16.9	14 31.8	19 23.6
13 T	17 26 45.8	23 8.2	19 47.5	21 8.7	25 29.8	13 39.7	16 19.3	10 21.8	18 59.2	10 17.1	14 33.4	19 24.8
16 S	17 38 35.5	23 18.5	19 49.6	14 44.9	25 29.4	13 41.3	16 17.7	10 12.0	18 54.8	10 17.4	14 34.9	19 26.1
19 W	17 50 25.1	23 24.6	19 51.8	3 0.9	25 15.6	13 49.9	16 18.2	10 1.7	18 50.2	10 18.0	14 36.4	19 27.6
22 S	18 2 14.8	23 26.5	19 53.8	9S34.2	24 48.1	14 4.6	16 21.0	9 50.9	18 45.5	10 18.7	14 37.8	19 29.1
25 T	18 14 4.5	23 24.2	19 55.9	19 5.7	24 7.2	14 24.4	16 26.1	9 39.6	18 40.7	10 19.6	14 39.1	19 30.7
28 F	18 25 54.2	23 17.6	19 58.0	20 42.1	23 13.5	14 48.2	16 33.6	9 27.9	18 35.7	10 20.7	14 40.4	19 32.4
31 M	18 37 43.8	23 6.8	20 0.1	12 9.4	22 8.8	15 15.2	16 43.6	9 15.8	18 30.6	10 22.0	14 41.6	19 34.2

JANUARY 1963

LONGITUDE at NOON

DAY	EPHEMERIS SIDEREAL TIME h m s	☉ ° ′	☊ ° ′	☽ ° ′	☿ ° ′	♀ ° ′	♂ ° ′	♃ ° ′	♄ ° ′	♅ ° ′	♆ ° ′	♇ ° ′
1 T	18 41 40.4	10♑21.4	0♌39.4	20♓ 8.7	29♑19.9	25♏39.3	24♌32.4	9♓ 6.0	9♒59.7	5♍ 5.5	15♏ 5.4	12♍ 4.7
2 W	18 45 37.0	11 22.6	0 36.3	4♈14.1	0♒32.8	26 27.4	24R26.9	9 16.8	10 6.3	5R 4.3	15 6.8	12R 4.1
3 T	18 49 33.5	12 23.8	0 33.1	18 24.4	1 41.4	27 16.4	24 20.7	9 27.7	10 12.9	5 3.1	15 8.2	12 3.5
4 F	18 53 30.1	13 24.9	0 29.9	2♉37.7	2 45.0	28 6.1	24 13.7	9 38.6	10 19.6	5 1.8	15 9.6	12 2.9
5 S	18 57 26.6	14 26.1	0 26.7	16 51.3	3 43.0	28 56.7	24 5.8	9 49.7	10 26.2	5 0.5	15 11.0	12 2.2
6 S	19 1 23.2	15 27.2	0 23.6	1♊ 2.2	4 34.3	29 48.1	23 57.1	10 0.9	10 33.0	4 59.1	15 12.3	12 1.5
7 M	19 5 19.7	16 28.3	0 20.4	15 6.8	5 18.2	0♐40.1	23 47.7	10 12.2	10 39.7	4 57.7	15 13.6	12 0.8
8 T	19 9 16.3	17 29.5	0 17.2	29 1.5	5 53.9	1 33.0	23 37.4	10 23.6	10 46.5	4 56.2	15 14.9	12 0.0
9 W	19 13 12.9	18 30.6	0 14.0	12♋42.7	6 20.2	2 26.5	23 26.3	10 35.0	10 53.3	4 54.7	15 16.1	11 59.3
10 T	19 17 9.4	19 31.7	0 10.9	26 7.7	6 36.5	3 20.6	23 14.4	10 46.6	11 0.1	4 53.1	15 17.4	11 58.5
11 F	19 21 6.0	20 32.8	0 7.7	9♌15.1	6 42.0	4 15.4	23 1.8	10 58.3	11 7.0	4 51.5	15 18.5	11 57.6
12 S	19 25 2.5	21 33.9	0 4.5	22 4.2	6R36.1	5 10.9	22 48.4	11 10.1	11 13.9	4 49.8	15 19.7	11 56.8
13 S	19 28 59.1	22 35.0	0 1.3	4♍36.1	6 18.4	6 6.9	22 34.2	11 21.9	11 20.8	4 48.1	15 20.8	11 55.9
14 M	19 32 55.6	23 36.1	29♋58.1	16 52.8	5 48.9	7 3.5	22 19.2	11 33.9	11 27.8	4 46.4	15 21.9	11 55.0
15 T	19 36 52.2	24 37.3	29 55.0	28 57.5	5 8.1	8 0.7	22 3.5	11 45.9	11 34.7	4 44.6	15 23.0	11 54.0
16 W	19 40 48.7	25 38.4	29 51.8	10♎53.8	4 16.6	8 58.3	21 47.1	11 58.0	11 41.7	4 42.8	15 24.0	11 53.1
17 T	19 44 45.3	26 39.4	29 48.6	22 46.4	3 15.9	9 56.5	21 30.0	12 10.2	11 48.7	4 40.9	15 25.0	11 52.1
18 F	19 48 41.9	27 40.6	29 45.4	4♏39.8	2 7.7	10 55.3	21 12.2	12 22.6	11 55.8	4 39.0	15 26.1	11 51.1
19 S	19 52 38.4	28 41.7	29 42.3	16 38.8	0 54.0	11 54.4	20 53.7	12 35.0	12 2.9	4 37.1	15 27.0	11 50.1
20 S	19 56 35.0	29 42.8	29 39.1	28 47.9	29♑37.1	12 54.0	20 34.6	12 47.4	12 9.9	4 35.1	15 27.9	11 49.0
21 M	20 0 31.5	0♒43.8	29 35.9	11♐11.2	28 19.4	13 54.1	20 14.9	12 60.0	12 17.0	4 33.1	15 28.8	11 48.0
22 T	20 4 28.1	1 44.9	29 32.7	23 51.9	27 3.3	14 54.5	19 54.7	13 12.6	12 24.1	4 31.0	15 29.6	11 46.9
23 W	20 8 24.6	2 46.0	29 29.6	6♑52.1	25 50.9	15 55.4	19 33.8	13 25.3	12 31.2	4 28.9	15 30.4	11 45.7
24 T	20 12 21.2	3 47.0	29 26.4	20 12.8	24 43.9	16 56.6	19 12.5	13 38.0	12 38.4	4 26.8	15 31.2	11 44.6
25 F	20 16 17.8	4 48.0	29 23.2	3♒53.0	23 43.9	17 58.3	18 50.7	13 50.9	12 45.5	4 24.7	15 32.0	11 43.4
26 S	20 20 14.3	5 49.1	29 20.0	17 50.5	22 51.8	19 0.2	18 28.5	14 3.8	12 52.7	4 22.5	15 32.7	11 42.2
27 S	20 24 10.9	6 50.1	29 16.8	2♓ 1.5	22 8.3	20 2.5	18 5.9	14 16.7	12 59.8	4 20.2	15 33.4	11 41.0
28 M	20 28 7.4	7 51.1	29 13.7	16 21.5	21 33.7	21 5.2	17 43.0	14 29.8	13 7.0	4 18.0	15 34.0	11 39.8
29 T	20 32 4.0	8 52.0	29 10.5	0♈45.5	21 7.9	22 8.1	17 19.8	14 42.9	13 14.2	4 15.7	15 34.6	11 38.5
30 W	20 36 0.5	9 53.0	29 7.3	15 8.7	20 51.0	23 11.4	16 56.3	14 56.1	13 21.3	4 13.4	15 35.2	11 37.3
31 T	20 39 57.1	10 53.9	29 4.1	29 27.2	20 42.4	24 15.0	16 32.6	15 9.3	13 28.5	4 11.1	15 35.7	11 36.0

DECLINATION at NOON

DAY	EPHEMERIS SIDEREAL TIME h m s	☉	☊	☽	☿	♀	♂	♃	♄	♅	♆	♇
1 T	18 41 40.4	23S 2.3	20N 0.8	7S 38.0	21S 45.3	15S 24.7	16N47.4	9S 11.7	18S 28.8	10N22.4	14S 42.0	19N34.9
4 F	18 53 30.1	22 46.0	20 2.8	7N26.7	20 31.2	15 54.6	17 0.5	8 59.1	18 23.6	10 23.9	14 43.1	19 36.8
7 M	19 5 19.7	22 25.6	20 4.9	18 56.0	19 16.8	16 25.7	17 15.8	8 46.1	18 18.2	10 25.5	14 44.1	19 38.7
10 T	19 17 9.4	22 1.3	20 6.9	20 36.6	18 10.4	16 57.4	17 33.3	8 32.7	18 12.7	10 27.3	14 45.0	19 40.8
13 S	19 28 59.1	21 33.0	20 8.9	12 38.8	17 21.5	17 29.0	17 52.8	8 19.0	18 7.1	10 29.2	14 45.9	19 42.9
16 W	19 40 48.7	21 1.1	20 10.9	0 17.7	16 57.4	17 59.9	18 13.9	8 4.9	18 1.5	10 31.3	14 46.6	19 45.1
19 S	19 52 38.4	20 25.5	20 12.9	11S 57.7	16 59.2	18 29.5	18 36.4	7 50.5	17 55.7	10 33.4	14 47.3	19 47.2
22 T	20 4 28.1	19 46.4	20 14.9	20 12.3	17 20.9	18 57.3	18 60.0	7 35.9	17 49.9	10 35.7	14 47.9	19 49.5
25 F	20 16 17.8	19 4.0	20 16.9	19 39.7	17 53.5	19 22.7	19 24.1	7 20.9	17 44.0	10 38.1	14 48.4	19 51.8
28 M	20 28 7.4	18 18.5	20 18.9	8 55.5	18 29.3	19 45.4	19 48.2	7 5.7	17 38.1	10 40.6	14 48.9	19 54.1
31 T	20 39 57.1	17 30.0	20 20.9	6N20.4	19 3.3	20 4.8	20 12.0	6 50.2	17 32.1	10 43.2	14 49.2	19 56.4

FEBRUARY 1963

LONGITUDE at NOON

DAY	EPHEMERIS SIDEREAL TIME h m s	☉ ° ′	☊ ° ′	☽ ° ′	☿ ° ′	♀ ° ′	♂ ° ′	♃ ° ′	♄ ° ′	♅ ° ′	♆ ° ′	♇ ° ′
1 F	20 43 53.6	11♒54.8	29♋ 1.0	13♉37.9	20♑41.7	25♐18.8	16♌ 8.8	15♓22.6	13♒35.7	4♍ 8.7	15♏36.3	11♍34.7
2 S	20 47 50.2	12 55.7	28 57.8	27 38.9	20D48.6	26 23.0	15R44.9	15 36.0	13 42.9	4R 6.3	15 36.7	11R33.3
3 S	20 51 46.8	13 56.6	28 54.6	11♊28.8	21 2.4	27 27.3	15 20.9	15 49.4	13 50.1	4 3.9	15 37.2	11 32.0
4 M	20 55 43.3	14 57.4	28 51.4	25 7.0	21 22.7	28 32.0	14 56.8	16 2.8	13 57.3	4 1.5	15 37.6	11 30.6
5 T	20 59 39.9	15 58.2	28 48.2	8♋33.1	21 48.8	29 36.9	14 32.9	16 16.3	14 4.5	3 59.0	15 38.0	11 29.3
6 W	21 3 36.4	16 59.0	28 45.1	21 46.8	22 20.5	0♑42.1	14 8.9	16 29.9	14 11.6	3 56.6	15 38.3	11 27.9
7 T	21 7 33.0	17 59.8	28 41.9	4♌48.0	22 57.0	1 47.5	13 45.1	16 43.5	14 18.8	3 54.1	15 38.6	11 26.5
8 F	21 11 29.5	19 0.6	28 38.7	17 36.5	23 38.2	2 53.1	13 21.5	16 57.2	14 26.0	3 51.6	15 38.9	11 25.1
9 S	21 15 26.1	20 1.3	28 35.5	0♍12.3	24 23.6	3 59.0	12 58.1	17 11.0	14 33.2	3 49.1	15 39.2	11 23.7
10 S	21 19 22.6	21 2.0	28 32.4	12 35.9	25 12.7	5 5.1	12 34.9	17 24.7	14 40.4	3 46.6	15 39.4	11 22.2
11 M	21 23 19.2	22 2.7	28 29.2	24 48.4	26 5.3	6 11.4	12 12.0	17 38.5	14 47.5	3 44.0	15 39.5	11 20.8
12 T	21 27 15.7	23 3.4	28 26.0	6♎51.5	27 1.1	7 17.8	11 49.5	17 52.4	14 54.7	3 41.4	15 39.7	11 19.3
13 W	21 31 12.3	24 4.0	28 22.8	18 47.6	27 59.9	8 24.5	11 27.3	18 6.3	15 1.8	3 38.9	15 39.8	11 17.8
14 T	21 35 8.9	25 4.7	28 19.7	0♏40.1	29 1.4	9 31.4	11 5.5	18 20.2	15 8.9	3 36.3	15 39.9	11 16.4
15 F	21 39 5.4	26 5.3	28 16.5	12 32.7	0♒ 5.4	10 38.5	10 44.1	18 34.2	15 16.1	3 33.7	15 39.9	11 14.9
16 S	21 43 2.0	27 5.9	28 13.3	24 29.8	1 11.7	11 45.7	10 23.3	18 48.2	15 23.2	3 31.1	15 39.9	11 13.4
17 S	21 46 58.5	28 6.4	28 10.1	6♐36.1	2 20.2	12 53.1	10 2.9	19 2.3	15 30.2	3 28.4	15 39.9	11 11.8
18 M	21 50 55.1	29 7.0	28 6.9	18 56.6	3 30.6	14 0.7	9 43.1	19 16.4	15 37.3	3 25.8	15R39.8	11 10.3
19 T	21 54 51.6	0♓ 7.5	28 3.8	1♑35.6	4 43.0	15 8.5	9 23.9	19 30.5	15 44.4	3 23.2	15 39.7	11 8.8
20 W	21 58 48.2	1 8.0	28 0.6	14 37.1	5 57.2	16 16.4	9 5.3	19 44.7	15 51.4	3 20.6	15 39.6	11 7.2
21 T	22 2 44.7	2 8.5	27 57.4	28 3.6	7 13.0	17 24.4	8 47.3	19 58.8	15 58.4	3 17.9	15 39.4	11 5.7
22 F	22 6 41.3	3 8.9	27 54.2	11♒55.8	8 30.4	18 32.6	8 29.9	20 13.1	16 5.4	3 15.3	15 39.2	11 4.2
23 S	22 10 37.8	4 9.4	27 51.1	26 11.9	9 49.2	19 40.9	8 13.3	20 27.3	16 12.4	3 12.6	15 38.9	11 2.6
24 S	22 14 34.4	5 9.8	27 47.9	10♓47.6	11 9.6	20 49.4	7 57.3	20 41.6	16 19.3	3 10.0	15 38.7	11 1.0
25 M	22 18 30.9	6 10.1	27 44.7	25 36.1	12 31.3	21 57.9	7 42.1	20 55.9	16 26.2	3 7.4	15 38.4	10 59.5
26 T	22 22 27.5	7 10.5	27 41.5	10♈29.3	13 54.3	23 6.6	7 27.6	21 10.2	16 33.1	3 4.7	15 38.0	10 57.9
27 W	22 26 24.1	8 10.8	27 38.3	25 18.6	15 18.6	24 15.5	7 13.9	21 24.6	16 40.0	3 2.1	15 37.7	10 56.3
28 T	22 30 20.6	9 11.1	27 35.2	9♉56.9	16 44.2	25 24.4	7 0.9	21 39.0	16 46.9	2 59.5	15 37.3	10 54.8

DECLINATION at NOON

DAY	EPHEMERIS SIDEREAL TIME h m s	☉	☊	☽	☿	♀	♂	♃	♄	♅	♆	♇
1 F	20 43 53.6	17S 13.2	20N21.5	11N 2.6	19S 13.6	20S 10.5	20N19.8	6S 45.0	17S 30.1	10N44.1	14S 49.3	19N57.1
4 M	20 55 43.3	16 21.1	20 23.5	20 21.6	19 40.2	20 25.2	20 42.3	6 29.2	17 24.1	10 46.8	14 49.5	19 59.5
7 T	21 7 33.0	15 26.4	20 25.4	19 31.4	19 59.0	20 35.8	21 3.5	6 13.2	17 18.0	10 49.5	14 49.6	20 1.8
10 S	21 19 22.6	14 29.3	20 27.4	10 8.3	20 8.6	20 42.2	21 22.8	5 57.0	17 12.0	10 52.3	14 49.7	20 4.1
13 W	21 31 12.3	13 30.0	20 29.3	2S 36.4	20 8.1	20 44.1	21 40.1	5 40.7	17 5.9	10 55.1	14 49.6	20 6.4
16 S	21 43 2.0	12 28.8	20 31.2	14 18.3	19 56.8	20 41.4	21 55.2	5 24.1	16 59.8	10 58.0	14 49.5	20 8.6
19 T	21 54 51.6	11 25.8	20 33.1	20 59.8	19 34.5	20 33.9	22 7.9	5 7.5	16 53.8	11 0.8	14 49.2	20 10.9
22 F	22 6 41.3	10 21.1	20 35.0	18 18.3	19 0.7	20 21.4	22 18.1	4 50.7	16 47.7	11 3.7	14 48.9	20 13.1
25 M	22 18 30.9	9 15.0	20 36.9	5 42.4	18 15.4	20 4.0	22 25.9	4 33.7	16 41.8	11 6.6	14 48.5	20 15.2
28 T	22 30 20.6	8 7.6	20 38.8	9N58.9	17 18.5	19 41.7	22 31.2	4 16.7	16 35.8	11 9.4	14 48.0	20 17.3

MARCH 1963

LONGITUDE at NOON

DAY	EPHEMERIS SIDEREAL TIME h m s	☉ ° ′	☊ ° ′	☽ ° ′	☿ ° ′	♀ ° ′	♂ ° ′	♃ ° ′	♄ ° ′	♅ ° ′	♆ ° ′	♇ ° ′
1 F	22 34 17.2	10 ♓ 11.4	27 ♋ 32.0	24 ♉ 18.8	18 ♒ 11.0	26 ♑ 33.5	6 ♌ 48.8	21 ♓ 53.4	16 ♒ 53.7	2 ♍ 56.9	15 ♏ 36.9	10 ♍ 53.2
2 S	22 38 13.7	11 11.6	27 28.8	8 ♊ 21.4	19 39.0	27 42.6	6 R 37.4	22 7.8	17 0.5	2 R 54.3	15 R 36.4	10 R 51.7
3 S	22 42 10.3	12 11.8	27 25.6	22 4.2	21 8.2	28 51.9	6 26.7	22 22.2	17 7.3	2 51.7	15 35.9	10 50.1
4 M	22 46 6.8	13 11.9	27 22.5	5 ♋ 28.2	22 38.5	0 ♒ 1.2	6 16.9	22 36.7	17 14.0	2 49.1	15 35.4	10 48.5
5 T	22 50 3.4	14 12.0	27 19.3	18 35.2	24 9.9	1 10.7	6 7.9	22 51.1	17 20.7	2 46.6	15 34.8	10 47.0
6 W	22 53 59.9	15 12.1	27 16.1	1 ♌ 27.6	25 42.5	2 20.2	5 59.6	23 5.6	17 27.3	2 44.0	15 34.2	10 45.4
7 T	22 57 56.5	16 12.1	27 12.9	14 7.4	27 16.2	3 29.9	5 52.2	23 20.1	17 34.0	2 41.5	15 33.6	10 43.8
8 F	23 1 53.0	17 12.1	27 9.7	26 36.5	28 51.0	4 39.6	5 45.5	23 34.6	17 40.5	2 38.9	15 33.0	10 42.3
9 S	23 5 49.6	18 12.1	27 6.6	8 ♍ 56.4	0 ♓ 27.0	5 49.5	5 39.7	23 49.1	17 47.1	2 36.4	15 32.3	10 40.7
10 S	23 9 46.1	19 12.0	27 3.4	21 8.2	2 4.1	6 59.4	5 34.6	24 3.6	17 53.6	2 33.9	15 31.6	10 39.2
11 M	23 13 42.7	20 11.9	27 0.2	3 ♎ 12.9	3 42.4	8 9.4	5 30.3	24 18.1	18 0.1	2 31.4	15 30.8	10 37.6
12 T	23 17 39.2	21 11.8	26 57.0	15 11.6	5 21.8	9 19.5	5 26.7	24 32.6	18 6.5	2 29.0	15 30.1	10 36.1
13 W	23 21 35.8	22 11.7	26 53.9	27 5.9	7 2.4	10 29.7	5 23.9	24 47.2	18 12.9	2 26.5	15 29.3	10 34.5
14 T	23 25 32.3	23 11.5	26 50.7	8 ♏ 57.8	8 44.1	11 39.9	5 21.9	25 1.7	18 19.2	2 24.1	15 28.4	10 33.0
15 F	23 29 28.9	24 11.3	25 47.5	20 50.0	10 27.0	12 50.3	5 20.6	25 16.2	18 25.5	2 21.7	15 27.6	10 31.5
16 S	23 33 25.4	25 11.0	26 44.3	2 ♐ 45.9	12 11.2	14 0.7	5 20.1	25 30.8	18 31.8	2 19.4	15 26.7	10 30.0
17 S	23 37 22.0	26 10.8	26 41.1	14 49.8	13 56.5	15 11.2	5 D 20.3	25 45.3	18 38.0	2 17.0	15 25.8	10 28.5
18 M	23 41 18.6	27 10.5	26 38.0	27 6.3	15 43.0	16 21.7	5 21.2	25 59.8	18 44.2	2 14.7	15 24.9	10 27.0
19 T	23 45 15.1	28 10.1	26 34.8	9 ♑ 40.2	17 30.8	17 32.3	5 22.9	26 14.4	18 50.3	2 12.4	15 23.9	10 25.5
20 W	23 49 11.7	29 9.8	26 31.6	22 36.5	19 19.9	18 43.0	5 25.2	26 28.9	18 56.4	2 10.1	15 22.9	10 24.0
21 T	23 53 8.2	0 ♈ 9.4	26 28.4	5 ♒ 59.2	21 10.2	19 53.8	5 28.3	26 43.4	19 2.4	2 7.9	15 21.9	10 22.5
22 F	23 57 4.8	1 9.0	26 25.2	19 50.6	23 1.8	21 4.7	5 32.1	26 58.0	19 8.4	2 5.7	15 20.9	10 21.1
23 S	0 1 1.3	2 8.6	26 22.1	4 ♓ 10.9	24 54.6	22 15.5	5 36.5	27 12.5	19 14.3	2 3.5	15 19.8	10 19.7
24 S	0 4 57.9	3 8.1	26 18.9	18 56.6	26 48.6	23 26.5	5 41.6	27 27.0	19 20.2	2 1.4	15 18.7	10 18.3
25 M	0 8 54.4	4 7.6	26 15.7	4 ♈ 1.2	28 43.9	24 37.5	5 47.3	27 41.5	19 26.0	1 59.3	15 17.6	10 16.8
26 T	0 12 51.0	5 7.0	26 12.5	19 15.0	0 ♈ 40.5	25 48.5	5 53.8	27 56.0	19 31.8	1 57.2	15 16.5	10 15.4
27 W	0 16 47.5	6 6.4	26 9.4	4 ♉ 26.9	2 38.2	26 59.6	6 0.8	28 10.5	19 37.5	1 55.1	15 15.3	10 14.1
28 T	0 20 44.1	7 5.8	26 6.2	19 26.6	4 37.1	28 10.7	6 8.5	28 24.9	19 43.1	1 53.1	15 14.1	10 12.7
29 F	0 24 40.6	8 5.2	26 3.0	4 ♊ 5.9	6 37.0	29 21.9	6 16.8	28 39.4	19 48.7	1 51.2	15 12.9	10 11.3
30 S	0 28 37.2	9 4.5	25 59.8	18 20.3	8 38.0	0 ♓ 33.1	6 25.6	28 53.8	19 54.2	1 49.2	15 11.7	10 10.0
31 S	0 32 33.7	10 3.8	25 56.6	2 ♋ 8.2	10 39.9	1 44.3	6 35.1	29 8.2	19 59.7	1 47.3	15 10.4	10 8.7

DECLINATION at NOON

DAY	EPHEMERIS SIDEREAL TIME h m s	☉ ° ′	☊ ° ′	☽ ° ′	☿ ° ′	♀ ° ′	♂ ° ′	♃ ° ′	♄ ° ′	♅ ° ′	♆ ° ′	♇ ° ′
1 F	22 34 17.2	7 S 44.9	20 N 39.4	14 N 19.3	16 S 57.0	19 S 33.1	22 N 32.5	4 S 11.0	16 S 33.8	11 N 10.4	14 S 47.9	20 N 18.0
4 M	22 46 6.8	6 36.2	20 41.3	21 16.6	15 44.7	19 4.2	22 34.8	3 53.9	16 27.9	11 13.2	14 47.3	20 20.0
7 T	22 57 56.5	5 26.7	20 43.2	17 53.4	14 21.0	18 30.5	22 34.9	3 36.7	16 22.2	11 15.9	14 46.6	20 21.9
10 S	23 9 46.1	4 16.5	20 45.0	7 14.3	12 45.9	17 52.1	22 33.0	3 19.5	16 16.4	11 18.6	14 45.9	20 23.8
13 W	23 21 35.8	3 5.8	20 46.9	5 S 41.6	10 59.4	17 9.1	22 29.3	3 2.3	16 10.8	11 21.2	14 45.1	20 25.5
16 S	23 33 25.4	1 54.8	20 48.7	16 37.3	9 1.9	16 21.7	22 23.8	2 45.0	16 5.3	11 23.8	14 44.2	20 27.2
19 T	23 45 15.1	0 43.7	20 50.5	21 31.0	6 53.5	15 30.1	22 16.6	2 27.8	15 59.9	11 26.2	14 43.2	20 28.8
22 F	23 57 4.8	0 N 27.5	20 52.3	16 41.3	4 34.6	14 34.5	22 7.9	2 10.5	15 54.6	11 28.6	14 42.2	20 30.3
25 M	0 8 54.4	1 38.4	20 54.1	2 39.3	2 5.9	13 35.1	21 57.7	1 53.3	15 49.4	11 30.8	14 41.2	20 31.7
28 T	0 20 44.1	2 49.0	20 55.9	13 N 6.6	0 N 31.6	12 32.2	21 46.1	1 36.2	15 44.4	11 32.9	14 40.0	20 33.0
31 S	0 32 33.7	3 59.2	20 57.7	21 19.6	3 16.1	11 26.2	21 33.2	1 19.1	15 39.5	11 35.0	14 38.9	20 34.2

APRIL 1963

LONGITUDE at NOON

DAY	EPHEMERIS SIDEREAL TIME h m s	☉ ° ′	☊ ° ′	☽ ° ′	☿ ° ′	♀ ° ′	♂ ° ′	♃ ° ′	♄ ° ′	♅ ° ′	♆ ° ′	♇ ° ′
1 M	0 36 30.3	11 ♈ 3.0	25 ♋ 53.5	15 ♋ 30.9	12 ♈ 42.6	2 ♓ 55.6	6 ♌ 45.2	29 ♓ 22.6	20 ♒ 5.1	1 ♍ 45.4	15 ♏ 9.2	10 ♍ 7.4
2 T	0 40 26.8	12 2.2	25 50.3	28 31.3	14 45.9	4 7.0	6 55.8	29 36.9	20 10.4	1 R 43.6	15 R 7.9	10 R 6.1
3 W	0 44 23.4	13 1.3	25 47.1	11 ♌ 13.1	16 49.8	5 18.4	7 7.0	29 51.3	20 15.7	1 41.8	15 6.6	10 4.8
4 T	0 48 19.9	14 0.4	25 43.9	23 40.2	18 53.9	6 29.8	7 18.7	0 ♈ 5.6	20 20.9	1 40.1	15 5.2	10 3.5
5 F	0 52 16.5	14 59.5	25 40.8	5 ♍ 56.0	20 58.2	7 41.2	7 31.0	0 19.9	20 26.1	1 38.4	15 3.9	10 2.3
6 S	0 56 13.0	15 58.5	25 37.6	18 3.5	23 2.2	8 52.7	7 43.7	0 34.2	20 31.2	1 36.7	15 2.5	10 1.1
7 S	1 0 9.6	16 57.5	25 34.4	0 ♎ 4.9	25 5.8	10 4.3	7 57.0	0 48.4	20 36.2	1 35.1	15 1.1	9 59.9
8 M	1 4 6.2	17 56.5	25 31.2	12 2.1	27 8.5	11 15.8	8 10.8	1 2.6	20 41.1	1 33.5	14 59.7	9 58.7
9 T	1 8 2.7	18 55.4	25 28.0	23 56.5	29 10.2	12 27.4	8 25.0	1 16.8	20 46.0	1 32.0	14 58.3	9 57.6
10 W	1 11 59.3	19 54.3	25 24.9	5 ♏ 49.2	1 ♉ 10.4	13 39.1	8 39.7	1 31.0	20 50.8	1 30.5	14 56.9	9 56.4
11 T	1 15 55.8	20 53.2	25 21.7	17 41.7	3 8.8	14 50.8	8 54.9	1 45.1	20 55.6	1 29.1	14 55.4	9 55.3
12 F	1 19 52.4	21 52.1	25 18.5	29 35.9	5 5.1	16 2.5	9 10.6	1 59.3	21 0.3	1 27.7	14 54.0	9 54.3
13 S	1 23 48.9	22 50.9	25 15.3	11 ♐ 34.1	6 58.8	17 14.3	9 26.7	2 13.3	21 4.9	1 26.4	14 52.5	9 53.2
14 S	1 27 45.5	23 49.7	25 12.2	23 39.4	8 49.6	18 26.1	9 43.2	2 27.4	21 9.4	1 25.1	14 51.0	9 52.2
15 M	1 31 42.0	24 48.4	25 9.0	5 ♑ 55.7	10 37.3	19 37.9	10 0.1	2 41.3	21 13.9	1 23.8	14 49.5	9 51.1
16 T	1 35 38.6	25 47.1	25 5.8	18 27.4	12 21.4	20 49.7	10 17.5	2 55.3	21 18.3	1 22.6	14 48.0	9 50.1
17 W	1 39 35.1	26 45.8	25 2.6	1 ♒ 19.0	14 1.9	22 1.6	10 35.3	3 9.2	21 22.6	1 21.4	14 46.5	9 49.2
18 T	1 43 31.7	27 44.5	24 59.4	14 34.9	15 38.3	23 13.5	10 53.4	3 23.1	21 26.8	1 20.3	14 45.0	9 48.2
19 F	1 47 28.2	28 43.1	24 56.3	28 18.5	17 10.6	24 25.5	11 12.0	3 36.9	21 30.9	1 19.3	14 43.4	9 47.3
20 S	1 51 24.8	29 41.7	24 53.1	12 ♓ 31.4	18 38.4	25 37.4	11 30.9	3 50.7	21 35.0	1 18.2	14 41.8	9 46.4
21 S	1 55 21.3	0 ♉ 40.3	24 49.9	27 11.9	20 1.7	26 49.4	11 50.3	4 4.5	21 39.0	1 17.3	14 40.3	9 45.5
22 M	1 59 17.9	1 38.9	24 46.7	12 ♈ 15.0	21 20.3	28 1.4	12 10.0	4 18.2	21 42.9	1 16.4	14 38.7	9 44.6
23 T	2 3 14.4	2 37.4	24 43.6	27 32.1	22 34.1	29 13.5	12 30.0	4 31.9	21 46.7	1 15.5	14 37.1	9 43.8
24 W	2 7 11.0	3 35.9	24 40.4	12 ♉ 52.0	23 42.9	0 ♈ 25.5	12 50.4	4 45.5	21 50.5	1 14.7	14 35.5	9 43.0
25 T	2 11 7.6	4 34.3	24 37.2	28 3.1	24 46.6	1 37.6	13 11.2	4 59.1	21 54.2	1 13.9	14 33.9	9 42.2
26 F	2 15 4.1	5 32.7	24 34.0	12 ♊ 55.4	25 45.3	2 49.7	13 32.3	5 12.6	21 57.7	1 13.2	14 32.3	9 41.5
27 S	2 19 0.7	6 31.1	24 30.8	27 22.1	26 38.7	4 1.8	13 53.8	5 26.1	22 1.2	1 12.6	14 30.7	9 40.8
28 S	2 22 57.2	7 29.5	24 27.7	11 ♋ 20.1	27 26.8	5 14.0	14 15.5	5 39.5	22 4.7	1 11.9	14 29.1	9 40.1
29 M	2 26 53.8	8 27.8	24 24.5	24 49.4	28 9.5	6 26.1	14 37.6	5 52.8	22 8.0	1 11.4	14 27.4	9 39.4
30 T	2 30 50.3	9 26.1	24 21.3	7 ♌ 52.8	28 46.8	7 38.3	15 0.0	6 6.1	22 11.2	1 10.9	14 25.8	9 38.8

DECLINATION at NOON

DAY	EPHEMERIS SIDEREAL TIME h m s	☉ ° ′	☊ ° ′	☽ ° ′	☿ ° ′	♀ ° ′	♂ ° ′	♃ ° ′	♄ ° ′	♅ ° ′	♆ ° ′	♇ ° ′
1 M	0 36 30.3	4 N 22.4	20 N 58.3	21 N 34.3	4 N 12.1	11 S 3.5	21 N 28.7	1 S 13.4	15 S 37.9	11 N 35.6	14 S 38.5	20 N 34.5
4 T	0 48 19.9	5 31.6	21 0.1	15 48.1	7 1.5	9 53.5	21 14.1	0 56.5	15 33.3	11 37.4	14 37.2	20 35.6
7 S	1 0 9.6	6 39.8	21 1.8	4 5.4	9 49.9	8 40.9	20 58.4	0 39.6	15 28.8	11 39.1	14 35.9	20 36.5
10 W	1 11 59.3	7 47.1	21 3.6	8 S 49.5	12 31.8	7 26.0	20 41.5	0 22.9	15 24.6	11 40.7	14 34.6	20 37.3
13 S	1 23 48.9	8 53.2	21 5.3	18 45.5	15 1.3	6 9.1	20 23.4	0 6.3	15 20.5	11 42.1	14 33.3	20 37.9
16 T	1 35 38.6	9 58.0	21 7.0	21 37.2	17 13.4	4 50.4	20 4.3	0 N 10.2	15 16.6	11 43.3	14 31.9	20 38.4
19 F	1 47 28.2	11 1.2	21 8.8	14 40.6	19 4.2	3 30.3	19 44.1	0 26.5	15 13.0	11 44.4	14 30.5	20 38.9
22 M	1 59 17.9	12 2.9	21 10.5	0 N 19.9	20 31.9	2 9.0	19 22.8	0 42.6	15 9.5	11 45.4	14 29.1	20 39.1
25 T	2 11 7.6	13 2.8	21 12.2	15 40.7	21 36.1	0 46.9	19 0.5	0 58.5	15 6.4	11 46.1	14 27.6	20 39.3
28 S	2 22 57.2	14 0.8	21 13.9	21 53.2	22 17.0	0 N 35.8	18 37.1	1 14.2	15 3.4	11 46.7	14 26.2	20 39.3

MAY 1963

DAY	EPHEMERIS SIDEREAL TIME	☉	☊	☽	☿	♀	♂	♃	♄	♅	♆	♇
	h m s	° ′	° ′	° ′	° ′	° ′	° ′	° ′	° ′	° ′	° ′	° ′
LONGITUDE at NOON												
1 W	2 34 46.9	10♉24.3	24♋18.1	20♌34.0	29♉18.7	8♈50.5	15♌22.7	6♈19.4	22♒14.4	1♍10.4	14♏24.2	9♍38.2
2 T	2 38 43.4	11 22.6	24 15.0	2♍57.5	29 45.2	10 2.6	15 45.7	6 32.6	22 17.4	1R10.1	14R22.6	9R37.6
3 F	2 42 40.0	12 20.8	24 11.8	15 8.0	0♊ 6.2	11 14.9	16 9.0	6 45.8	22 20.5	1 9.8	14 21.0	9 37.1
4 S	2 46 36.5	13 18.9	24 8.6	27 9.3	0 21.7	12 27.1	16 32.6	6 58.8	22 23.4	1 9.5	14 19.3	9 36.6
5 S	2 50 33.1	14 17.1	24 5.4	9♎ 4.9	0 31.9	13 39.4	16 56.4	7 11.8	22 26.2	1 9.2	14 17.7	9 36.1
6 M	2 54 29.7	15 15.1	24 2.2	20 57.8	0 36.7	14 51.7	17 20.6	7 24.8	22 28.9	1 9.1	14 16.1	9 35.6
7 T	2 58 26.2	16 13.2	23 59.1	2♏50.0	0R36.4	16 3.9	17 44.9	7 37.7	22 31.5	1 8.9	14 14.4	9 35.2
8 W	3 2 22.8	17 11.2	23 55.9	14 43.3	0 31.1	17 16.2	18 9.6	7 50.5	22 34.0	1 8.9	14 12.8	9 34.8
9 T	3 6 19.3	18 9.2	23 52.7	26 39.1	0 20.9	18 28.6	18 34.5	8 3.2	22 36.5	1 8.8	14 11.2	9 34.4
10 F	3 10 15.9	19 7.2	23 49.5	8♐38.8	0 6.3	19 40.9	18 59.6	8 15.9	22 38.8	1D 8.9	14 9.5	9 34.0
11 S	3 14 12.4	20 5.2	23 46.4	20 44.0	29♉47.4	20 53.2	19 25.0	8 28.5	22 41.1	1 9.0	14 7.9	9 33.7
12 S	3 18 9.0	21 3.1	23 43.2	2♑57.0	29 24.7	22 5.6	19 50.6	8 41.1	22 43.3	1 9.1	14 6.3	9 33.4
13 M	3 22 5.5	22 1.0	23 40.0	15 20.1	28 58.6	23 18.0	20 16.4	8 53.5	22 45.3	1 9.3	14 4.7	9 33.2
14 T	3 26 2.1	22 58.9	23 36.8	27 56.7	28 29.6	24 30.4	20 42.5	9 5.9	22 47.3	1 9.5	14 3.0	9 32.9
15 W	3 29 58.6	23 56.7	23 33.7	10♒50.2	27 58.2	25 42.8	21 8.8	9 18.3	22 49.2	1 9.9	14 1.4	9 32.7
16 T	3 33 55.2	24 54.6	23 30.5	24 4.1	27 25.0	26 55.3	21 35.3	9 30.5	22 51.0	1 10.2	13 59.8	9 32.6
17 F	3 37 51.8	25 52.4	23 27.3	7♓41.5	26 50.6	28 7.7	22 2.1	9 42.7	22 52.7	1 10.6	13 58.2	9 32.4
18 S	3 41 48.3	26 50.2	23 24.1	21 44.0	26 15.6	29 20.2	22 29.1	9 54.8	22 54.3	1 11.1	13 56.7	9 32.3
19 S	3 45 44.9	27 48.0	23 20.9	6♈11.4	25 40.7	0♉32.7	22 56.2	10 6.8	22 55.8	1 11.6	13 55.1	9 32.2
20 M	3 49 41.4	28 45.8	23 17.8	21 0.2	25 6.3	1 45.2	23 23.6	10 18.7	22 57.2	1 12.2	13 53.5	9 32.2
21 T	3 53 38.0	29 43.5	23 14.6	6♉ 4.2	24 33.2	2 57.7	23 51.2	10 30.6	22 58.5	1 12.8	13 51.9	9 32.2
22 W	3 57 34.5	0♊41.2	23 11.4	21 14.2	24 1.8	4 10.3	24 19.0	10 42.3	22 59.7	1 13.5	13 50.4	9 32.2
23 T	4 1 31.1	1 38.9	23 8.2	6♊20.0	23 32.6	5 22.8	24 47.0	10 54.0	23 0.8	1 14.2	13 48.8	9 32.2
24 F	4 5 27.7	2 36.7	23 5.1	21 11.9	23 6.3	6 35.4	25 15.2	11 5.7	23 1.9	1 15.0	13 47.4	9D32.4
25 S	4 9 24.2	3 34.3	23 1.9	5♋42.0	22 43.0	7 48.0	25 43.6	11 17.1	23 2.8	1 15.9	13 45.8	9 32.5
26 S	4 13 20.8	4 32.0	22 58.7	19 45.9	22 23.2	9 0.6	26 12.2	11 28.6	23 3.6	1 16.8	13 44.3	9 32.6
27 M	4 17 17.3	5 29.6	22 55.5	3♌22.0	22 7.2	10 13.2	26 41.0	11 39.9	23 4.3	1 17.7	13 42.8	9 32.8
28 T	4 21 13.9	6 27.2	22 52.3	16 31.3	21 55.3	11 25.8	27 9.9	11 51.1	23 4.9	1 18.7	13 41.4	9 33.0
29 W	4 25 10.4	7 24.7	22 49.2	29 17.0	21 47.5	12 38.4	27 39.0	12 2.2	23 5.5	1 19.7	13 39.9	9 33.2
30 T	4 29 7.0	8 22.3	22 46.0	11♍43.0	21 44.0	13 51.0	28 8.3	12 13.2	23 5.9	1 20.8	13 38.4	9 33.5
31 F	4 33 3.6	9 19.8	22 42.8	23 53.9	21D45.0	15 3.7	28 37.8	12 24.2	23 6.2	1 22.0	13 37.0	9 33.8
DECLINATION at NOON												
1 W	2 34 46.9	14N56.6	21N15.5	16N48.8	22N35.2	1N58.7	18N12.8	1N29.7	15S 0.7	11N47.1	14S 24.7	20N39.2
4 S	2 46 36.5	15 50.3	21 17.2	5 16.7	22 31.5	3 21.7	17 47.3	1 45.0	14 58.3	11 47.4	14 23.3	20 39.0
7 T	2 58 26.2	16 41.6	21 18.9	7S 47.9	22 6.8	4 44.2	17 20.9	1 60.0	14 56.1	11 47.5	14 21.9	20 38.7
10 F	3 10 15.9	17 30.3	21 20.5	18 17.8	21 22.9	6 6.1	16 53.6	2 14.7	14 54.2	11 47.4	14 20.4	20 38.2
13 M	3 22 5.5	18 16.5	21 22.2	21 58.0	20 23.0	7 27.1	16 25.2	2 29.1	14 52.5	11 47.1	14 19.0	20 37.6
16 T	3 33 55.2	18 59.8	21 23.8	16 3.4	19 11.9	8 46.9	15 55.9	2 43.2	14 51.2	11 46.7	14 17.6	20 36.9
19 S	3 45 44.9	19 40.3	21 25.4	2 3.1	17 56.8	10 5.1	15 25.7	2 57.1	14 50.1	11 46.1	14 16.3	20 36.1
22 W	3 57 34.5	20 17.8	21 27.0	13N46.9	16 45.5	11 21.4	14 54.5	3 10.5	14 49.3	11 45.3	14 14.9	20 35.1
25 S	4 9 24.2	20 52.2	21 28.6	21 56.0	15 45.3	12 35.6	14 22.4	3 23.7	14 48.8	11 44.3	14 13.6	20 34.1
28 T	4 21 13.9	21 23.4	21 30.2	17 59.0	15 1.7	13 47.2	13 49.5	3 36.5	14 48.6	11 43.2	14 12.4	20 32.9
31 F	4 33 3.6	21 51.2	21 31.8	6 37.7	14 37.5	14 56.1	13 15.6	3 48.9	14 48.7	11 41.9	14 11.1	20 31.6

JUNE 1963

DAY	EPHEMERIS SIDEREAL TIME	☉	☊	☽	☿	♀	♂	♃	♄	♅	♆	♇
LONGITUDE at NOON												
1 S	4 37 0.1	10♊17.3	22♋39.6	5♎54.4	21♉50.4	16♉16.3	29♌ 7.4	12♈35.0	23♒ 6.4	1♍23.2	13♏35.6	9♍34.1
2 S	4 40 56.7	11 14.8	22 36.5	17 48.8	22 0.4	17 29.0	29 37.2	12 45.7	23 6.6	1 24.4	13R34.2	9 34.4
3 M	4 44 53.2	12 12.2	22 33.3	29 40.7	22 14.8	18 41.7	0♍ 7.1	12 56.3	23 6.6	1 25.7	13 32.8	9 34.8
4 T	4 48 49.8	13 9.7	22 30.1	11♏33.3	22 33.6	19 54.4	0 37.2	13 6.8	23R 6.5	1 27.1	13 31.4	9 35.2
5 W	4 52 46.3	14 7.1	22 26.9	23 29.4	22 56.9	21 7.1	1 7.4	13 17.2	23 6.4	1 28.5	13 30.0	9 35.7
6 T	4 56 42.9	15 4.5	22 23.8	5♐30.9	23 24.5	22 19.8	1 37.9	13 27.6	23 6.1	1 30.0	13 28.7	9 36.2
7 F	5 0 39.5	16 1.9	22 20.6	17 39.4	23 56.3	23 32.5	2 8.4	13 37.7	23 5.8	1 31.4	13 27.4	9 36.7
8 S	5 4 36.0	16 59.2	22 17.4	29 56.3	24 32.3	24 45.3	2 39.1	13 47.8	23 5.3	1 33.0	13 26.1	9 37.2
9 S	5 8 32.6	17 56.6	22 14.2	12♑22.9	25 12.3	25 58.1	3 9.9	13 57.8	23 4.8	1 34.6	13 24.8	9 37.8
10 M	5 12 29.1	18 53.9	22 11.1	25 0.7	25 56.4	27 10.8	3 40.9	14 7.7	23 4.1	1 36.2	13 23.5	9 38.3
11 T	5 16 25.7	19 51.3	22 7.9	7♒51.1	26 44.4	28 23.6	4 12.1	14 17.4	23 3.4	1 37.9	13 22.3	9 39.0
12 W	5 20 22.2	20 48.6	22 4.7	20 56.0	27 36.2	29 36.5	4 43.3	14 27.0	23 2.5	1 39.7	13 21.1	9 39.6
13 T	5 24 18.8	21 45.9	22 1.5	4♓17.1	28 31.8	0♊49.3	5 14.7	14 36.6	23 1.6	1 41.5	13 19.9	9 40.3
14 F	5 28 15.4	22 43.3	21 58.3	17 56.0	29 31.0	2 2.2	5 46.3	14 46.0	23 0.6	1 43.3	13 18.7	9 41.1
15 S	5 32 11.9	23 40.6	21 55.2	1♈53.4	0♊33.9	3 15.1	6 18.0	14 55.3	22 59.5	1 45.2	13 17.6	9 41.8
16 S	5 36 8.5	24 37.9	21 52.0	16 8.6	1 40.2	4 28.0	6 49.8	15 4.4	22 58.3	1 47.1	13 16.4	9 42.6
17 M	5 40 5.0	25 35.2	21 48.8	0♉39.6	2 50.1	5 40.9	7 21.7	15 13.4	22 57.0	1 49.1	13 15.3	9 43.4
18 T	5 44 1.6	26 32.5	21 45.6	15 22.0	4 3.4	6 53.8	7 53.8	15 22.3	22 55.6	1 51.1	13 14.2	9 44.2
19 W	5 47 58.1	27 29.8	21 42.5	0♊ 9.7	5 20.0	8 6.8	8 26.0	15 31.1	22 54.0	1 53.2	13 13.2	9 45.0
20 T	5 51 54.7	28 27.1	21 39.3	14 55.5	6 40.0	9 19.8	8 58.4	15 39.7	22 52.5	1 55.3	13 12.1	9 45.9
21 F	5 55 51.3	29 24.3	21 36.1	29 31.7	8 3.4	10 32.7	9 30.8	15 48.2	22 50.8	1 57.5	13 11.1	9 46.8
22 S	5 59 47.8	0♋21.6	21 32.9	13♋51.9	9 30.0	11 45.7	10 3.4	15 56.6	22 49.0	1 59.6	13 10.1	9 47.8
23 S	6 3 44.4	1 18.9	21 29.8	27 51.2	10 59.8	12 58.8	10 36.1	16 4.8	22 47.1	2 1.9	13 9.2	9 48.7
24 M	6 7 40.9	2 16.1	21 26.6	11♌26.9	12 32.8	14 11.8	11 9.0	16 12.9	22 45.2	2 4.2	13 8.2	9 49.7
25 T	6 11 37.5	3 13.3	21 23.4	24 38.6	14 9.0	15 24.8	11 41.9	16 20.8	22 43.1	2 6.5	13 7.3	9 50.8
26 W	6 15 34.0	4 10.6	21 20.2	7♍27.8	15 48.4	16 37.9	12 15.0	16 28.7	22 41.0	2 8.8	13 6.4	9 51.8
27 T	6 19 30.6	5 7.8	21 17.0	19 57.2	17 30.8	17 51.0	12 48.2	16 36.3	22 38.8	2 11.2	13 5.5	9 52.9
28 F	6 23 27.2	6 5.0	21 13.9	2♎10.9	19 16.2	19 4.1	13 21.5	16 43.8	22 36.5	2 13.7	13 4.7	9 54.0
29 S	6 27 23.7	7 2.2	21 10.7	14 13.0	21 4.6	20 17.2	13 54.9	16 51.2	22 34.1	2 16.2	13 3.9	9 55.1
30 S	6 31 20.3	7 59.4	21 7.5	26 8.2	22 55.8	21 30.3	14 28.5	16 58.4	22 31.6	2 18.7	13 3.1	9 56.3
DECLINATION at NOON												
1 S	4 37 0.1	21N59.7	21N32.3	2N13.3	14N33.9	15N18.3	13N 4.1	3N52.9	14S 48.8	11N41.4	14S 10.7	20N31.2
4 T	4 48 49.8	22 22.9	21 33.9	10S 41.9	14 36.3	16 22.9	12 29.2	4 4.8	14 49.3	11 39.9	14 9.6	20 29.8
7 F	5 0 39.5	22 42.6	21 35.4	20 2.9	14 57.1	17 23.9	11 53.4	4 16.2	14 50.0	11 38.3	14 8.5	20 28.3
10 M	5 12 29.1	22 58.7	21 37.0	21 31.5	15 33.8	18 21.0	11 16.8	4 27.3	14 51.1	11 36.5	14 7.4	20 26.7
13 T	5 24 18.8	23 11.2	21 38.5	13 17.9	16 23.9	19 14.0	10 39.4	4 37.9	14 52.4	11 34.5	14 6.5	20 25.0
16 S	5 36 8.5	23 20.0	21 40.0	1N32.2	17 24.2	20 2.5	10 1.3	4 48.0	14 54.0	11 32.4	14 5.6	20 23.2
19 W	5 47 58.1	23 25.1	21 41.5	16 14.5	18 31.4	20 46.2	9 22.4	4 57.7	14 55.9	11 30.1	14 4.7	20 21.3
22 S	5 59 47.8	23 26.5	21 43.0	22 7.2	19 42.2	21 25.0	8 42.9	5 6.9	14 58.1	11 27.7	14 3.9	20 19.3
25 T	6 11 37.5	23 24.2	21 44.5	16 5.9	20 52.7	21 58.4	8 2.7	5 15.5	15 0.5	11 25.1	14 3.2	20 17.3
28 F	6 23 27.2	23 18.2	21 46.0	3 43.2	21 58.3	22 26.4	7 21.8	5 23.7	15 3.1	11 22.5	14 2.6	20 15.2

JULY 1963

DAY	EPHEMERIS SIDEREAL TIME	☉	☊	☽	☿	♀	♂	♃	♄	♅	♆	♇
	h m s	° ′	° ′	° ′	° ′	° ′	° ′	° ′	° ′	° ′	° ′	° ′
						LONGITUDE at NOON						
1 M	6 35 16.8	8♋56.6	21♋ 4.3	8♏ 0.8	24♓49.8	22♓43.5	15♍ 2.1	17♈ 5.5	22♒29.1	2♍21.3	13♏ 2.4	9♍57.4
2 T	6 39 13.4	9 53.8	21 1.2	19 55.1	26 46.3	23 56.6	15 35.8	17 12.4	22R26.4	2 23.8	13R 1.6	9 58.6
3 W	6 43 9.9	10 51.0	20 58.0	1♐54.5	28 45.3	25 9.8	16 9.7	17 19.2	22 23.7	2 26.5	13 1.0	9 59.9
4 T	6 47 6.5	11 48.2	20 54.8	14 2.2	0♋46.5	26 23.0	16 43.6	17 25.8	22 20.9	2 29.2	13 0.3	10 1.1
5 F	6 51 3.1	12 45.4	20 51.6	26 20.6	2 49.7	27 36.3	17 17.8	17 32.4	22 18.1	2 31.9	12 59.7	10 2.4
6 S	6 54 59.6	13 42.6	20 48.5	8♑51.3	4 54.7	28 49.5	17 51.9	17 38.7	22 15.2	2 34.7	12 59.1	10 3.7
7 S	6 58 56.2	14 39.7	20 45.3	21 35.5	7 1.2	0♋ 2.8	18 26.2	17 44.8	22 12.2	2 37.4	12 58.5	10 5.1
8 M	7 2 52.7	15 36.9	20 42.1	4♒33.6	9 8.8	1 16.1	19 0.5	17 50.8	22 9.1	2 40.2	12 58.0	10 6.4
9 T	7 6 49.3	16 34.1	20 38.9	17 45.7	11 17.4	2 29.4	19 35.0	17 56.6	22 5.9	2 43.1	12 57.4	10 7.8
10 W	7 10 45.8	17 31.3	20 35.8	1♓11.3	13 26.6	3 42.7	20 9.6	18 2.3	22 2.7	2 46.0	12 56.9	10 9.2
11 T	7 14 42.4	18 28.5	20 32.6	14 49.9	15 36.1	4 56.1	20 44.2	18 7.8	21 59.4	2 48.9	12 56.5	10 10.6
12 F	7 18 39.0	19 25.7	20 29.4	28 40.6	17 45.7	6 9.4	21 19.0	18 13.1	21 56.1	2 51.8	12 56.1	10 12.0
13 S	7 22 35.5	20 22.9	20 26.2	12♈42.1	19 55.1	7 22.8	21 53.8	18 18.3	21 52.6	2 54.8	12 55.7	10 13.5
14 S	7 26 32.1	21 20.1	20 23.0	26 52.7	22 3.9	8 36.3	22 28.8	18 23.3	21 49.1	2 57.8	12 55.3	10 15.0
15 M	7 30 28.6	22 17.3	20 19.9	11♉10.2	24 12.0	9 49.7	23 3.9	18 28.1	21 45.6	3 0.9	12 54.9	10 16.5
16 T	7 34 25.2	23 14.6	20 16.7	25 31.9	26 19.3	11 3.2	23 39.0	18 32.8	21 42.0	3 3.9	12 54.6	10 18.0
17 W	7 38 21.7	24 11.8	20 13.5	9♊54.1	28 25.4	12 16.7	24 14.3	18 37.3	21 38.3	3 7.0	12 54.4	10 19.6
18 T	7 42 18.3	25 9.1	20 10.3	24 12.9	0♌30.3	13 30.2	24 49.6	18 41.6	21 34.5	3 10.2	12 54.1	10 21.1
19 F	7 46 14.9	26 6.3	20 7.2	8♋23.9	2 33.9	14 43.8	25 25.1	18 45.7	21 30.8	3 13.3	12 53.9	10 22.7
20 S	7 50 11.4	27 3.6	20 4.0	22 22.9	4 36.0	15 57.3	26 0.6	18 49.6	21 26.9	3 16.5	12 53.7	10 24.3
21 S	7 54 8.0	28 0.9	20 0.8	6♌ 6.5	6 36.6	17 10.9	26 36.3	18 53.4	21 23.0	3 19.7	12 53.6	10 26.0
22 M	7 58 4.5	28 58.2	19 57.6	19 32.1	8 35.5	18 24.5	27 12.0	18 57.0	21 19.1	3 23.0	12 53.5	10 27.6
23 T	8 2 1.1	29 55.5	19 54.5	2♍38.4	10 32.9	19 38.1	27 47.8	19 0.3	21 15.1	3 26.3	12 53.4	10 29.3
24 W	8 5 57.6	0♌52.8	19 51.3	15 25.6	12 28.5	20 51.8	28 23.7	19 3.5	21 11.0	3 29.6	12 53.3	10 31.0
25 T	8 9 54.2	1 50.1	19 48.1	27 55.2	14 22.5	22 5.5	28 59.7	19 6.6	21 7.0	3 32.9	12 53.3	10 32.7
26 F	8 13 50.8	2 47.5	19 44.9	10♎ 9.7	16 14.8	23 19.2	29 35.9	19 9.4	21 2.9	3 36.3	12D53.4	10 34.5
27 S	8 17 47.3	3 44.8	19 41.7	22 12.8	18 5.3	24 32.9	0♎12.1	19 12.1	20 58.7	3 39.6	12 53.4	10 36.2
28 S	8 21 43.9	4 42.2	19 38.6	4♏ 8.5	19 54.1	25 46.6	0 48.4	19 14.5	20 54.5	3 43.0	12 53.5	10 38.0
29 M	8 25 40.4	5 39.5	19 35.4	16 1.4	21 41.2	27 0.4	1 24.7	19 16.8	20 50.3	3 46.4	12 53.6	10 39.7
30 T	8 29 37.0	6 36.9	19 32.2	27 56.1	23 26.7	28 14.2	2 1.2	19 18.9	20 46.0	3 49.9	12 53.7	10 41.5
31 W	8 33 33.5	7 34.3	19 29.0	9♐57.3	25 10.4	29 28.0	2 37.7	19 20.7	20 41.7	3 53.3	12 53.9	10 43.3
						DECLINATION at NOON						
1 M	6 35 16.8	23N 8.5	21N47.5	9S25.4	22N54.0	22N48.7	6N40.3	5N31.3	15S 6.0	11N19.7	14S 2.0	20N13.1
4 T	6 47 6.5	22 55.1	21 49.0	19 22.6	23 34.5	23 5.1	5 58.2	5 38.4	15 9.2	11 16.7	14 1.5	20 10.9
7 S	6 58 56.2	22 38.2	21 50.4	21 49.1	23 54.9	23 15.5	5 15.6	5 44.9	15 12.5	11 13.7	14 1.2	20 8.6
10 W	7 10 45.8	22 17.7	21 51.9	14 16.8	23 51.7	23 19.9	4 32.5	5 50.9	15 16.0	11 10.5	14 0.9	20 6.3
13 S	7 22 35.5	21 53.8	21 53.3	0N11.7	23 23.6	23 18.1	3 48.9	5 56.2	15 19.7	11 7.3	14 0.6	20 3.9
16 T	7 34 25.2	21 26.5	21 54.7	14 56.6	22 32.1	23 10.1	3 4.8	6 1.0	15 23.6	11 3.9	14 0.5	20 1.5
19 F	7 46 14.9	20 55.9	21 56.1	22 4.4	21 19.9	22 56.0	2 20.3	6 5.1	15 27.6	11 0.4	14 0.4	19 59.0
22 M	7 58 4.5	20 22.1	21 57.5	17 24.1	19 51.1	22 35.8	1 35.5	6 8.6	15 31.7	10 56.9	14 0.5	19 56.6
25 T	8 9 54.2	19 45.3	21 58.9	5 17.7	18 9.5	22 9.6	0 50.3	6 11.5	15 36.0	10 53.3	14 0.6	19 54.1
28 S	8 21 43.9	19 5.5	22 0.3	8S 4.9	16 18.5	21 37.6	0 4.7	6 13.7	15 40.3	10 49.5	14 0.8	19 51.5
31 W	8 33 33.5	18 22.8	22 1.7	18 33.8	14 21.1	20 59.9	0S41.0	6 15.3	15 44.7	10 45.8	14 1.1	19 49.0

AUGUST 1963

DAY	EPHEMERIS SIDEREAL TIME	☉	☊	☽	☿	♀	♂	♃	♄	♅	♆	♇
						LONGITUDE at NOON						
1 T	8 37 30.1	8♌31.6	19♋25.9	22♐ 9.0	26♌52.4	0♌41.8	3♎14.3	19♈22.4	20♒37.4	3♍56.8	12♏54.1	10♍45.1
2 F	8 41 26.6	9 29.0	19 22.7	4♑34.9	28 32.8	1 55.6	3 51.0	19 23.9	20R33.1	4 0.3	12 54.3	10 47.0
3 S	8 45 23.2	10 26.4	19 19.5	17 17.6	0♍11.5	3 9.5	4 27.8	19 25.2	20 28.7	4 3.8	12 54.6	10 48.8
4 S	8 49 19.8	11 23.8	19 16.3	0♒18.6	1 48.5	4 23.3	5 4.7	19 26.3	20 24.3	4 7.3	12 54.9	10 50.7
5 M	8 53 16.3	12 21.2	19 13.2	13 38.4	3 23.9	5 37.2	5 41.6	19 27.2	20 19.9	4 10.9	12 55.2	10 52.6
6 T	8 57 12.9	13 18.7	19 10.0	27 15.6	4 57.6	6 51.1	6 18.6	19 27.9	20 15.4	4 14.4	12 55.6	10 54.5
7 W	9 1 9.4	14 16.1	19 6.8	11♓ 8.1	6 29.6	8 5.1	6 55.7	19 28.5	20 11.0	4 18.0	12 56.0	10 56.4
8 T	9 5 6.0	15 13.6	19 3.6	25 12.4	7 60.0	9 19.0	7 32.9	19 28.8	20 6.5	4 21.6	12 56.4	10 58.3
9 F	9 9 2.5	16 11.1	19 0.4	9♈24.5	9 28.7	10 33.0	8 10.2	19 28.9	20 2.0	4 25.2	12 56.9	11 0.2
10 S	9 12 59.1	17 8.7	18 57.3	23 40.5	10 55.7	11 47.0	8 47.6	19R28.8	19 57.6	4 28.8	12 57.4	11 2.1
11 S	9 16 55.6	18 6.2	18 54.1	7♉56.7	12 21.0	13 1.1	9 25.0	19 28.6	19 53.1	4 32.5	12 57.9	11 4.1
12 M	9 20 52.2	19 3.8	18 50.9	22 10.1	13 44.5	14 15.1	10 2.5	19 28.1	19 48.6	4 36.1	12 58.5	11 6.1
13 T	9 24 48.8	20 1.4	18 47.7	6♊18.5	15 6.3	15 29.2	10 40.1	19 27.4	19 44.1	4 39.8	12 59.1	11 8.0
14 W	9 28 45.3	20 59.0	18 44.6	20 20.2	16 26.3	16 43.3	11 17.8	19 26.5	19 39.6	4 43.4	12 59.7	11 10.0
15 T	9 32 41.9	21 56.6	18 41.4	4♋13.8	17 44.5	17 57.4	11 55.6	19 25.5	19 35.1	4 47.1	13 0.3	11 12.0
16 F	9 36 38.4	22 54.4	18 38.2	17 58.0	19 0.8	19 11.6	12 33.5	19 24.2	19 30.6	4 50.9	13 1.1	11 14.1
17 S	9 40 35.0	23 52.1	18 35.0	1♌31.4	20 15.1	20 25.8	13 11.4	19 22.8	19 26.2	4 54.6	13 1.8	11 16.1
18 S	9 44 31.5	24 49.8	18 31.8	14 52.6	21 27.4	21 40.0	13 49.5	19 21.1	19 21.7	4 58.3	13 2.5	11 18.1
19 M	9 48 28.1	25 47.5	18 28.7	28 0.4	22 37.6	22 54.2	14 27.6	19 19.2	19 17.2	5 2.0	13 3.3	11 20.1
20 T	9 52 24.6	26 45.3	18 25.5	10♍53.9	23 45.6	24 8.4	15 5.7	19 17.1	19 12.8	5 5.7	13 4.1	11 22.2
21 W	9 56 21.2	27 43.1	18 22.3	23 32.6	24 51.4	25 22.7	15 44.0	19 14.9	19 8.3	5 9.5	13 5.0	11 24.2
22 T	10 0 17.7	28 40.9	18 19.1	5♎57.1	25 54.8	26 37.0	16 22.3	19 12.4	19 3.9	5 13.2	13 5.8	11 26.3
23 F	10 4 14.3	29 38.7	18 16.0	18 8.9	26 55.7	27 51.2	17 0.8	19 9.8	18 59.5	5 17.0	13 6.7	11 28.3
24 S	10 8 10.8	0♍36.5	18 12.8	0♏10.3	27 54.0	29 5.5	17 39.3	19 6.9	18 55.2	5 20.7	13 7.7	11 30.4
25 S	10 12 7.4	1 34.4	18 9.6	12 4.7	28 49.6	0♍19.9	18 17.8	19 3.9	18 50.8	5 24.5	13 8.6	11 32.5
26 M	10 16 4.0	2 32.3	18 6.4	23 56.2	29 42.2	1 34.2	18 56.5	19 0.7	18 46.5	5 28.2	13 9.6	11 34.5
27 T	10 20 0.5	3 30.2	18 3.2	5♐49.4	0♎31.7	2 48.5	19 35.2	18 57.3	18 42.2	5 32.0	13 10.6	11 36.6
28 W	10 23 57.1	4 28.2	18 0.1	17 49.4	1 18.0	4 2.9	20 14.0	18 53.7	18 38.0	5 35.7	13 11.7	11 38.7
29 T	10 27 53.6	5 26.1	17 56.9	0♑ 1.1	2 0.8	5 17.3	20 52.9	18 49.9	18 33.8	5 39.5	13 12.8	11 40.8
30 F	10 31 50.2	6 24.1	17 53.7	12 29.3	2 39.8	6 31.7	21 31.9	18 45.9	18 29.6	5 43.3	13 13.9	11 42.9
31 S	10 35 46.7	7 22.1	17 50.5	25 18.0	3 14.9	7 46.1	22 10.9	18 41.8	18 25.5	5 47.0	13 15.0	11 44.9
						DECLINATION at NOON						
1 T	8 37 30.1	18N 8.0	22N 2.1	20S43.2	13N41.0	20N46.1	0S56.3	6N15.7	15S46.2	10N44.5	14S 1.2	19N48.2
4 S	8 49 19.8	17 21.8	22 3.5	20 58.2	11 39.0	20 1.1	1 42.4	6 16.4	15 50.7	10 40.6	14 1.6	19 45.6
7 W	9 1 9.4	16 33.1	22 4.8	11 8.4	9 35.7	19 11.0	2 28.6	6 16.4	15 55.2	10 36.7	14 2.1	19 43.1
10 S	9 12 59.1	15 42.0	22 6.2	4N20.7	7 33.0	18 16.0	3 14.9	6 15.8	15 59.7	10 32.7	14 2.7	19 40.5
13 T	9 24 48.8	14 48.5	22 7.5	17 47.8	5 32.3	17 16.2	4 1.3	6 14.5	16 4.2	10 28.7	14 3.4	19 38.0
16 F	9 36 38.4	13 53.0	22 8.8	22 2.1	3 35.0	16 12.2	4 47.7	6 12.6	16 8.7	10 24.6	14 4.2	19 35.4
19 M	9 48 28.1	12 55.5	22 10.1	15 9.4	1 42.8	15 4.0	5 34.2	6 9.9	16 13.1	10 20.5	14 5.0	19 32.9
22 T	10 0 17.7	11 56.1	22 11.4	2 14.2	0S 2.7	13 52.2	6 20.5	6 6.7	16 17.4	10 16.4	14 5.9	19 30.5
25 S	10 12 7.4	10 55.0	22 12.7	10S55.2	1 39.6	12 36.9	7 6.8	6 2.7	16 21.7	10 12.2	14 6.9	19 28.0
28 W	10 23 57.1	9 52.4	22 14.0	20 10.9	3 5.4	11 18.5	7 52.8	5 58.2	16 25.8	10 8.1	14 8.0	19 25.6
31 S	10 35 46.7	8 48.4	22 15.2	21 35.4	4 17.1	9 57.3	8 38.6	5 53.1	16 29.8	10 3.9	14 9.1	19 23.2

SEPTEMBER 1963

DAY	EPHEMERIS SIDEREAL TIME	☉	☊	☽	☿	♀	♂	♃	♄	♅	♆	♇
	h m s	° ′	° ′	° ′	° ′	° ′	° ′	° ′	° ′	° ′	° ′	° ′
LONGITUDE at NOON												
1 S	10 39 43.3	8 ♍ 20.1	17 ♋ 47.4	8 ♒ 29.9	3 ♎ 45.8	9 ♍ 0.5	22 ♎ 50.0	18 ♈ 37.5	18 ♒ 21.4	5 ♍ 50.8	13 ♏ 16.2	11 ♍ 47.0
2 M	10 43 39.8	9 18.2	17 44.2	22 6.1	4 12.3	10 14.9	23 29.2	18 R 33.0	18 R 17.3	5 54.5	13 17.4	11 49.1
3 T	10 47 36.4	10 16.2	17 41.0	6 ♓ 5.3	4 34.0	11 29.3	24 8.4	18 28.3	18 13.3	5 58.3	13 18.6	11 51.2
4 W	10 51 32.9	11 14.3	17 37.8	20 24.0	4 50.6	12 43.8	24 47.8	18 23.5	18 9.4	6 2.0	13 19.8	11 53.3
5 T	10 55 29.5	12 12.5	17 34.6	4 ♈ 56.4	5 1.9	13 58.3	25 27.2	18 18.5	18 5.5	6 5.8	13 21.1	11 55.4
6 F	10 59 26.0	13 10.7	17 31.5	19 35.6	5 7.6	15 12.8	26 6.7	18 13.4	18 1.6	6 9.6	13 22.5	11 57.6
7 S	11 3 22.6	14 8.9	17 28.3	4 ♉ 14.3	5 R 7.4	16 27.3	26 46.2	18 8.0	17 57.8	6 13.3	13 23.8	11 59.7
8 S	11 7 19.1	15 7.1	17 25.1	18 46.1	5 1.0	17 41.8	27 25.9	18 2.5	17 54.1	6 17.0	13 25.1	12 1.8
9 M	11 11 15.7	16 5.4	17 21.9	3 ♊ 6.4	4 48.2	18 56.4	28 5.6	17 56.9	17 50.4	6 20.8	13 26.5	12 3.9
10 T	11 15 12.2	17 3.7	17 18.8	17 12.7	4 28.8	20 10.9	28 45.4	17 51.1	17 46.8	6 24.5	13 27.9	12 5.9
11 W	11 19 8.8	18 2.0	17 15.6	1 ♋ 4.0	4 2.9	21 25.5	29 25.2	17 45.2	17 43.2	6 28.2	13 29.4	12 8.0
12 T	11 23 5.4	19 0.4	17 12.4	14 40.7	3 30.4	22 40.1	0 ♏ 5.1	17 39.1	17 39.7	6 31.9	13 30.8	12 10.1
13 F	11 27 1.9	19 58.8	17 9.2	28 3.8	2 51.4	23 54.6	0 45.2	17 32.9	17 36.2	6 35.6	13 32.3	12 12.2
14 S	11 30 58.5	20 57.2	17 6.0	11 ♌ 14.3	2 6.4	25 9.3	1 25.2	17 26.5	17 32.9	6 39.3	13 33.8	12 14.3
15 S	11 34 55.0	21 55.7	17 2.9	24 13.2	1 15.8	26 23.9	2 5.4	17 20.0	17 29.5	6 42.9	13 35.4	12 16.4
16 M	11 38 51.6	22 54.2	16 59.7	7 ♍ 0.9	0 20.4	27 38.5	2 45.6	17 13.4	17 26.3	6 46.6	13 36.9	12 18.4
17 T	11 42 48.1	23 52.7	16 56.5	19 37.6	29 ♍ 21.0	28 53.1	3 25.9	17 6.6	17 23.1	6 50.2	13 38.5	12 20.5
18 W	11 46 44.7	24 51.3	16 53.3	2 ♎ 3.4	28 18.8	0 ♎ 7.8	4 6.3	16 59.7	17 20.0	6 53.9	13 40.1	12 22.6
19 T	11 50 41.2	25 49.9	16 50.2	14 18.8	27 15.1	1 22.5	4 46.8	16 52.8	17 17.0	6 57.5	13 41.7	12 24.6
20 F	11 54 37.8	26 48.5	16 47.0	26 24.5	26 11.3	2 37.1	5 27.3	16 45.7	17 14.1	7 1.1	13 43.4	12 26.7
21 S	11 58 34.3	27 47.2	16 43.8	8 ♏ 22.0	25 9.0	3 51.8	6 7.9	16 38.5	17 11.2	7 4.7	13 45.1	12 28.7
22 S	12 2 30.9	28 45.9	16 40.6	20 13.7	24 9.9	5 6.5	6 48.6	16 31.2	17 8.4	7 8.3	13 46.8	12 30.8
23 M	12 6 27.4	29 44.6	16 37.4	2 ♐ 2.9	23 15.4	6 21.2	7 29.4	16 23.8	17 5.7	7 11.8	13 48.5	12 32.8
24 T	12 10 24.0	0 ♎ 43.4	16 34.3	13 53.6	22 26.9	7 35.9	8 10.2	16 16.3	17 3.1	7 15.3	13 50.2	12 34.8
25 W	12 14 20.5	1 42.2	16 31.1	25 50.6	21 45.8	8 50.6	8 51.1	16 8.8	17 0.5	7 18.9	13 52.0	12 36.8
26 T	12 18 17.1	2 41.0	16 27.9	7 ♑ 59.2	21 13.1	10 5.3	9 32.1	16 1.1	16 58.1	7 22.4	13 53.8	12 38.8
27 F	12 22 13.6	3 39.9	16 24.7	20 24.7	20 49.7	11 20.0	10 13.1	15 53.5	16 55.7	7 25.9	13 55.6	12 40.8
28 S	12 26 10.2	4 38.7	16 21.6	3 ♒ 12.1	20 36.1	12 34.7	10 54.3	15 45.7	16 53.5	7 29.3	13 57.4	12 42.8
29 S	12 30 6.7	5 37.6	16 18.4	16 25.6	20 32.7	13 49.5	11 35.4	15 37.9	16 51.3	7 32.8	13 59.3	12 44.8
30 M	12 34 3.3	6 36.6	16 15.2	0 ♓ 7.5	20 D 39.6	15 4.2	12 16.7	15 30.0	16 49.2	7 36.2	14 1.2	12 46.8
DECLINATION at NOON												
1 S	10 39 43.3	8 N 26.7	22 N 15.6	19 S 45.3	4 S 37.3	9 N 29.7	8 S 53.8	5 N 51.2	16 S 31.1	10 N 2.6	14 S 9.5	19 N 22.4
4 W	10 51 32.9	7 21.1	22 16.9	7 54.7	5 24.1	8 5.3	9 39.3	5 45.3	16 34.9	9 58.4	14 10.8	19 20.1
7 S	11 3 22.6	6 14.3	22 18.1	8 N 18.4	5 46.5	6 38.9	10 24.3	5 38.9	16 38.5	9 54.3	14 12.1	19 17.8
10 T	11 15 12.2	5 6.6	22 19.3	20 10.3	5 38.9	5 10.8	11 9.0	5 32.0	16 42.0	9 50.2	14 13.5	19 15.6
13 F	11 27 1.9	3 58.2	22 20.6	21 21.8	4 56.6	3 41.4	11 53.1	5 24.6	16 45.2	9 46.1	14 14.9	19 13.5
16 M	11 38 51.6	2 49.0	22 21.8	12 27.2	3 38.5	2 10.9	12 36.7	5 16.7	16 48.3	9 42.0	14 16.4	19 11.4
19 T	11 50 41.2	1 39.4	22 23.0	1 S 0.9	1 51.2	0 39.7	13 19.7	5 8.5	16 51.1	9 38.0	14 18.0	19 9.4
22 S	12 2 30.9	0 29.5	22 24.1	13 43.1	0 N 9.4	0 S 51.9	14 2.1	4 59.9	16 53.7	9 34.1	14 19.6	19 7.4
25 W	12 14 20.5	0 S 40.6	22 25.3	21 32.0	2 0.9	2 23.5	14 43.6	4 51.1	16 56.0	9 30.2	14 21.2	19 5.6
28 S	12 26 10.2	1 50.8	22 26.5	20 48.1	3 22.6	3 54.9	15 24.4	4 42.1	16 58.1	9 26.3	14 23.0	19 3.8

OCTOBER 1963

DAY	EPHEMERIS SIDEREAL TIME	☉	☊	☽	☿	♀	♂	♃	♄	♅	♆	♇
LONGITUDE at NOON												
1 T	12 37 59.8	7 ♎ 35.5	16 ♋ 12.0	14 ♓ 17.8	20 ♍ 56.6	16 ♎ 18.9	12 ♏ 58.0	15 ♈ 22.1	16 ♒ 47.1	7 ♍ 39.6	14 ♏ 3.0	12 ♍ 48.7
2 W	12 41 56.4	8 34.5	16 8.8	28 53.2	21 23.5	17 33.6	13 39.4	15 R 14.1	16 R 45.2	7 43.0	14 4.9	12 50.6
3 T	12 45 53.0	9 33.5	16 5.7	13 ♈ 47.2	21 59.9	18 48.4	14 20.8	15 6.1	16 43.4	7 46.3	14 6.8	12 52.6
4 F	12 49 49.5	10 32.6	16 2.5	28 50.8	22 45.1	20 3.1	15 2.3	14 58.1	16 41.6	7 49.6	14 8.8	12 54.5
5 S	12 53 46.1	11 31.7	15 59.3	13 ♉ 53.8	23 38.5	21 17.8	15 43.9	14 50.1	16 40.0	7 52.9	14 10.7	12 56.4
6 S	12 57 42.6	12 30.8	15 56.1	28 47.1	24 39.4	22 32.6	16 25.6	14 42.0	16 38.4	7 56.2	14 12.7	12 58.2
7 M	13 1 39.2	13 30.0	15 52.9	13 ♊ 23.5	25 47.1	23 47.3	17 7.3	14 33.9	16 37.0	7 59.4	14 14.7	13 0.1
8 T	13 5 35.7	14 29.2	15 49.8	27 38.9	27 0.9	25 2.1	17 49.1	14 25.8	16 35.6	8 2.6	14 16.7	13 2.0
9 W	13 9 32.3	15 28.4	15 46.6	11 ♋ 32.0	28 19.9	26 16.9	18 31.0	14 17.7	16 34.3	8 5.8	14 18.7	13 3.8
10 T	13 13 28.8	16 27.7	15 43.4	25 3.7	29 43.5	27 31.6	19 13.0	14 9.7	16 33.1	8 9.0	14 20.7	13 5.6
11 F	13 17 25.4	17 27.0	15 40.2	8 ♌ 16.2	1 ♎ 11.0	28 46.4	19 55.0	14 1.6	16 32.1	8 12.1	14 22.7	13 7.4
12 S	13 21 21.9	18 26.4	15 37.1	21 12.2	2 41.9	0 ♏ 1.2	20 37.1	13 53.5	16 31.1	8 15.2	14 24.8	13 9.2
13 S	13 25 18.5	19 25.8	15 33.9	3 ♍ 54.4	4 15.6	1 16.0	21 19.2	13 45.5	16 30.2	8 18.3	14 26.9	13 11.0
14 M	13 29 15.0	20 25.2	15 30.7	16 25.1	5 51.5	2 30.8	22 1.5	13 37.5	16 29.4	8 21.3	14 29.0	13 12.8
15 T	13 33 11.6	21 24.7	15 27.5	28 46.0	7 29.2	3 45.6	22 43.8	13 29.6	16 28.8	8 24.3	14 31.0	13 14.5
16 W	13 37 8.1	22 24.2	15 24.3	10 ♎ 58.5	9 8.4	5 0.3	23 26.1	13 21.7	16 28.2	8 27.3	14 33.2	13 16.2
17 T	13 41 4.7	23 23.8	15 21.2	23 3.6	10 48.7	6 15.1	24 8.6	13 13.8	16 27.7	8 30.2	14 35.3	13 17.9
18 F	13 45 1.2	24 23.4	15 18.0	5 ♏ 2.1	12 29.8	7 30.0	24 51.1	13 6.1	16 27.4	8 33.2	14 37.4	13 19.7
19 S	13 48 57.8	25 23.0	15 14.8	16 55.3	14 11.5	8 44.8	25 33.7	12 58.3	16 27.1	8 36.0	14 39.6	13 21.3
20 S	13 52 54.4	26 22.6	15 11.6	28 44.8	15 53.6	9 59.6	26 16.4	12 50.7	16 26.9	8 38.9	14 41.7	13 23.0
21 M	13 56 50.9	27 22.3	15 8.5	10 ♐ 33.0	17 35.8	11 14.4	26 59.1	12 43.1	16 26.9	8 41.7	14 43.9	13 24.6
22 T	14 0 47.5	28 22.0	15 5.3	22 23.0	19 18.1	12 29.2	27 41.9	12 35.6	16 26.9	8 44.4	14 46.1	13 26.2
23 W	14 4 44.0	29 21.8	15 2.1	4 ♑ 18.8	21 0.4	13 44.0	28 24.7	12 28.2	16 D 27.0	8 47.2	14 48.2	13 27.8
24 T	14 8 40.6	0 ♏ 21.5	14 58.9	16 24.9	22 42.4	14 58.8	29 7.6	12 20.8	16 27.3	8 49.8	14 50.4	13 29.4
25 F	14 12 37.1	1 21.3	14 55.7	28 46.5	24 24.2	16 13.6	29 50.6	12 13.6	16 27.6	8 52.5	14 52.6	13 30.9
26 S	14 16 33.7	2 21.1	14 52.6	11 ♒ 28.8	26 5.7	17 28.4	0 ♐ 33.7	12 6.5	16 28.1	8 55.1	14 54.8	13 32.4
27 S	14 20 30.2	3 21.0	14 49.4	24 36.5	27 46.9	18 43.2	1 16.8	11 59.5	16 28.6	8 57.6	14 57.0	13 33.9
28 M	14 24 26.8	4 20.9	14 46.2	8 ♓ 13.3	29 27.7	19 58.0	1 59.9	11 52.6	16 29.3	9 0.2	14 59.2	13 35.4
29 T	14 28 23.3	5 20.8	14 43.0	22 20.6	1 ♏ 8.0	21 12.8	2 43.2	11 45.8	16 30.0	9 2.7	15 1.5	13 36.8
30 W	14 32 19.9	6 20.7	14 39.9	6 ♈ 56.8	2 47.9	22 27.6	3 26.5	11 39.1	16 30.9	9 5.1	15 3.7	13 38.3
31 T	14 36 16.5	7 20.6	14 36.7	21 56.6	4 27.4	23 42.3	4 9.8	11 32.6	16 31.8	9 7.5	15 5.9	13 39.7
DECLINATION at NOON												
1 T	12 37 59.8	3 S 0.8	22 N 27.6	10 S 4.8	4 N 2.0	5 S 25.6	16 S 4.2	4 N 32.9	16 S 60.0	9 N 22.6	14 S 24.7	19 N 2.1
4 F	12 49 49.5	4 10.5	22 28.8	6 N 29.5	3 56.2	6 55.3	16 43.1	4 23.6	17 1.5	9 18.9	14 26.5	19 0.5
7 M	13 1 39.2	5 19.7	22 29.9	19 43.0	3 9.4	8 23.7	17 20.9	4 14.2	17 2.9	9 15.3	14 28.3	18 59.0
10 T	13 13 28.8	6 28.4	22 31.0	21 54.5	1 50.1	9 50.5	17 57.6	4 4.9	17 3.9	9 11.8	14 30.2	18 57.6
13 S	13 25 18.5	7 36.3	22 32.1	13 33.4	0 7.4	11 15.3	18 33.2	3 55.7	17 4.7	9 8.4	14 32.1	18 56.3
16 W	13 37 8.1	8 43.3	22 33.2	0 14.4	1 S 50.0	12 37.7	19 7.4	3 46.7	17 5.1	9 5.1	14 34.0	18 55.1
19 S	13 48 57.8	9 49.2	22 34.3	12 S 49.8	3 55.6	13 57.5	19 40.3	3 37.9	17 5.3	9 1.9	14 35.9	18 54.0
22 T	14 0 47.5	10 53.7	22 35.4	21 20.9	6 4.2	15 14.1	20 11.8	3 29.3	17 5.3	8 58.8	14 37.8	18 53.1
25 F	14 12 37.1	11 56.8	22 36.4	21 39.8	8 12.5	16 27.4	20 41.7	3 21.2	17 4.9	8 55.9	14 39.8	18 52.2
28 M	14 24 26.8	12 58.3	22 37.5	12 17.5	10 18.0	17 36.9	21 10.1	3 13.4	17 4.2	8 53.1	14 41.8	18 51.5
31 T	14 36 16.5	13 57.9	22 38.5	3 N 54.7	12 19.1	18 42.2	21 36.7	3 6.1	17 3.3	8 50.5	14 43.7	18 50.9

NOVEMBER 1963

LONGITUDE at NOON

DAY	EPHEMERIS SIDEREAL TIME	☉	☊	☽	☿	♀	♂	♃	♄	♅	♆	♇
	h m s	° ′	° ′	° ′	° ′	° ′	° ′	° ′	° ′	° ′	° ′	° ′
1 F	14 40 13.0	8♏20.6	14♋33.5	7♉11.3	6♏ 6.4	24♏57.1	4♐53.3	11♈26.2	16♒32.9	9♍ 9.8	15♏ 8.1	13♍41.0
2 S	14 44 9.6	9 20.7	14 30.3	22 30.0	7 45.0	26 11.9	5 36.8	11R20.0	16 34.1	9 12.2	15 10.4	13 42.4
3 S	14 48 6.1	10 20.7	14 27.2	7♊41.4	9 23.2	27 26.7	6 20.3	11 13.8	16 35.3	9 14.4	15 12.6	13 43.7
4 M	14 52 2.7	11 20.8	14 24.0	22 35.9	11 0.9	28 41.4	7 3.9	11 7.9	16 36.7	9 16.7	15 14.9	13 45.0
5 T	14 55 59.2	12 20.9	14 20.8	7♋ 7.1	12 38.1	29 56.2	7 47.6	11 2.0	16 38.1	9 18.8	15 17.1	13 46.3
6 W	14 59 55.8	13 21.1	14 17.6	21 11.8	14 15.0	1♐11.0	8 31.3	10 56.4	16 39.7	9 21.0	15 19.4	13 47.6
7 T	15 3 52.3	14 21.3	14 14.4	4♌50.0	15 51.5	2 25.7	9 15.1	10 50.9	16 41.4	9 23.1	15 21.6	13 48.8
8 F	15 7 48.9	15 21.5	14 11.3	18 3.6	17 27.6	3 40.6	9 59.1	10 45.6	16 43.2	9 25.1	15 23.9	13 50.0
9 S	15 11 45.4	16 21.8	14 8.1	0♍56.0	19 3.3	4 55.3	10 43.0	10 40.4	16 45.0	9 27.1	15 26.1	13 51.2
10 S	15 15 42.0	17 22.1	14 4.9	13 30.7	20 38.6	6 10.1	11 27.0	10 35.4	16 47.0	9 29.1	15 28.4	13 52.4
11 M	15 19 38.6	18 22.4	14 1.7	25 51.5	22 13.7	7 24.9	12 11.1	10 30.5	16 49.1	9 31.0	15 30.6	13 53.5
12 T	15 23 35.1	19 22.8	13 58.6	8♎ 1.6	23 48.3	8 39.7	12 55.2	10 25.9	16 51.2	9 32.8	15 32.9	13 54.6
13 W	15 27 31.7	20 23.2	13 55.4	20 3.9	25 22.7	9 54.4	13 39.4	10 21.4	16 53.5	9 34.6	15 35.1	13 55.6
14 T	15 31 28.2	21 23.6	13 52.2	2♏ 0.5	26 56.8	11 9.2	14 23.6	10 17.1	16 55.8	9 36.4	15 37.4	13 56.7
15 F	15 35 24.8	22 24.0	13 49.0	13 53.2	28 30.6	12 24.0	15 8.0	10 12.9	16 58.3	9 38.1	15 39.6	13 57.7
16 S	15 39 21.3	23 24.5	13 45.8	25 43.6	0♐ 4.2	13 38.7	15 52.3	10 9.0	17 0.8	9 39.7	15 41.8	13 58.7
17 S	15 43 17.9	24 25.0	13 42.7	7♐33.2	1 37.5	14 53.5	16 36.8	10 5.2	17 3.5	9 41.3	15 44.1	13 59.6
18 M	15 47 14.4	25 25.5	13 39.5	19 24.0	3 10.5	16 8.2	17 21.3	10 1.7	17 6.2	9 42.9	15 46.3	14 0.5
19 T	15 51 11.0	26 26.1	13 36.3	1♑17.9	4 43.3	17 23.0	18 5.8	9 58.3	17 9.1	9 44.4	15 48.5	14 1.4
20 W	15 55 7.6	27 26.7	13 33.1	13 17.9	6 16.0	18 37.8	18 50.4	9 55.2	17 12.0	9 45.8	15 50.7	14 2.3
21 T	15 59 4.1	28 27.3	13 30.0	25 27.4	7 48.4	19 52.5	19 35.1	9 52.2	17 15.0	9 47.2	15 52.9	14 3.1
22 F	16 3 0.7	29 27.9	13 26.8	7♒50.1	9 20.6	21 7.2	20 19.8	9 49.4	17 18.1	9 48.5	15 55.1	14 3.9
23 S	16 6 57.2	0♐28.5	13 23.6	20 30.5	10 52.6	22 22.0	21 4.6	9 46.9	17 21.3	9 49.8	15 57.3	14 4.7
24 S	16 10 53.8	1 29.2	13 20.4	3♓32.7	12 24.4	23 36.7	21 49.4	9 44.5	17 24.6	9 51.1	15 59.5	14 5.4
25 M	16 14 50.3	2 29.8	13 17.3	17 0.3	13 56.0	24 51.4	22 34.3	9 42.4	17 28.0	9 52.2	16 1.7	14 6.1
26 T	16 18 46.9	3 30.5	13 14.1	0♈55.6	15 27.4	26 6.1	23 19.3	9 40.4	17 31.5	9 53.4	16 3.9	14 6.8
27 W	16 22 43.5	4 31.2	13 10.9	15 18.6	16 58.6	27 20.8	24 4.3	9 38.7	17 35.1	9 54.4	16 6.0	14 7.4
28 T	16 26 40.0	5 32.0	13 7.7	0♉ 6.4	18 29.5	28 35.5	24 49.3	9 37.1	17 38.7	9 55.4	16 8.2	14 8.0
29 F	16 30 36.6	6 32.8	13 4.5	15 12.8	20 0.3	29 50.2	25 34.4	9 35.9	17 42.5	9 56.4	16 10.4	14 8.7
30 S	16 34 33.1	7 33.5	13 1.4	0♊28.6	21 30.7	1♑ 4.9	26 19.6	9 34.7	17 46.3	9 57.3	16 12.5	14 9.2

DECLINATION at NOON

DAY	EPHEMERIS SIDEREAL TIME	☉	☊	☽	☿	♀	♂	♃	♄	♅	♆	♇
1 F	14 40 13.0	14S17.3	22N38.9	9N32.2	12S58.3	19S 2.9	21S45.2	3N 3.8	17S 2.9	8N49.6	14S44.4	18N50.7
4 M	14 52 2.7	15 14.2	22 39.9	21 27.2	14 51.6	20 2.2	22 9.6	2 57.2	17 1.6	8 47.1	14 46.3	18 50.2
7 T	15 3 52.3	16 8.9	22 40.9	20 53.8	16 38.1	20 56.5	22 32.0	2 51.1	17 0.1	8 44.8	14 48.3	18 49.9
10 S	15 15 42.0	17 1.2	22 41.9	10 34.8	18 17.0	21 45.5	22 52.6	2 45.7	16 58.2	8 42.7	14 50.2	18 49.7
13 W	15 27 31.7	17 50.8	22 42.9	3S 9.8	19 47.8	22 29.0	23 11.2	2 40.9	16 56.1	8 40.7	14 52.2	18 49.6
16 S	15 39 21.3	18 37.7	22 43.9	15 35.2	21 9.8	23 6.6	23 27.7	2 36.7	16 53.7	8 38.9	14 54.1	18 49.6
19 T	15 51 11.0	19 21.6	22 44.9	22 29.2	22 22.4	23 38.2	23 42.0	2 33.3	16 51.1	8 37.2	14 56.0	18 49.8
22 F	16 3 0.7	20 2.4	22 45.8	20 30.4	23 24.9	24 3.4	23 54.2	2 30.6	16 48.1	8 35.8	14 57.8	18 50.1
25 M	16 14 50.3	20 39.8	22 46.8	9 27.9	24 16.9	24 22.1	24 4.2	2 28.6	16 45.0	8 34.5	14 59.7	18 50.6
28 T	16 26 40.0	21 13.8	22 47.7	6N53.8	24 57.6	24 34.1	24 11.9	2 27.3	16 41.6	8 33.4	15 1.5	18 51.1

DECEMBER 1963

LONGITUDE at NOON

DAY	EPHEMERIS SIDEREAL TIME	☉	☊	☽	☿	♀	♂	♃	♄	♅	♆	♇
1 S	16 38 29.7	8♐34.3	12♋58.2	15♊43.3	23♐ 0.8	2♑19.5	27♐ 4.8	9♈33.8	17♒50.2	9♍58.2	16♏14.6	14♍ 9.7
2 M	16 42 26.2	9 35.1	12 55.0	0♋46.6	24 30.6	3 34.2	27 50.1	9R33.1	17 54.2	9 59.0	16 16.7	14 10.2
3 T	16 46 22.8	10 35.9	12 51.8	15 30.0	25 60.0	4 48.8	28 35.4	9 32.6	17 58.3	9 59.7	16 18.8	14 10.7
4 W	16 50 19.4	11 36.8	12 48.7	29 48.1	27 28.9	6 3.4	29 20.7	9 32.3	18 2.5	10 0.4	16 20.9	14 11.1
5 T	16 54 15.9	12 37.6	12 45.5	13♌38.4	28 57.3	7 18.0	0♑ 6.2	9 32.2	18 6.7	10 1.0	16 23.0	14 11.5
6 F	16 58 12.5	13 38.5	12 42.3	27 1.4	0♑25.1	8 32.6	0 51.6	9D32.3	18 11.0	10 1.6	16 25.0	14 11.9
7 S	17 2 9.0	14 39.4	12 39.1	9♍59.3	1 52.1	9 47.2	1 37.1	9 32.7	18 15.4	10 2.1	16 27.1	14 12.2
8 S	17 6 5.6	15 40.4	12 36.0	22 35.7	3 18.3	11 1.8	2 22.7	9 33.2	18 19.9	10 2.6	16 29.1	14 12.5
9 M	17 10 2.1	16 41.3	12 32.8	4♎54.9	4 43.6	12 16.4	3 8.3	9 34.0	18 24.4	10 3.0	16 31.1	14 12.7
10 T	17 13 58.7	17 42.3	12 29.6	17 1.0	6 7.6	13 31.0	3 54.0	9 34.9	18 29.1	10 3.3	16 33.1	14 13.0
11 W	17 17 55.3	18 43.3	12 26.4	28 58.1	7 30.3	14 45.5	4 39.7	9 36.1	18 33.8	10 3.6	16 35.1	14 13.2
12 T	17 21 51.8	19 44.3	12 23.3	10♏49.9	8 51.4	16 0.1	5 25.5	9 37.5	18 38.6	10 3.8	16 37.0	14 13.3
13 F	17 25 48.4	20 45.3	12 20.1	22 39.5	10 10.6	17 14.6	6 11.3	9 39.0	18 43.4	10 4.0	16 39.0	14 13.5
14 S	17 29 44.9	21 46.4	12 16.9	4♐29.4	11 27.6	18 29.2	6 57.2	9 40.8	18 48.4	10 4.1	16 40.9	14 13.6
15 S	17 33 41.5	22 47.4	12 13.7	16 22.0	12 42.1	19 43.7	7 43.1	9 42.8	18 53.4	10 4.2	16 42.8	14 13.6
16 M	17 37 38.0	23 48.5	12 10.5	28 19.0	13 53.5	20 58.2	8 29.1	9 45.0	18 58.4	10 4.2	16 44.7	14 13.7
17 T	17 41 34.6	24 49.6	12 7.4	10♑22.4	15 1.5	22 12.7	9 15.1	9 47.4	19 3.6	10R 4.1	16 46.6	14 13.7
18 W	17 45 31.2	25 50.7	12 4.2	22 33.7	16 5.5	23 27.1	10 1.2	9 50.0	19 8.8	10 4.0	16 48.4	14R13.6
19 T	17 49 27.7	26 51.8	12 1.0	4♒55.1	17 4.8	24 41.6	10 47.3	9 52.8	19 14.1	10 3.9	16 50.3	14 13.6
20 F	17 53 24.3	27 52.9	11 57.8	17 28.6	17 58.9	25 56.1	11 33.4	9 55.9	19 19.5	10 3.7	16 52.1	14 13.5
21 S	17 57 20.8	28 54.0	11 54.7	0♓16.7	18 46.7	27 10.5	12 19.6	9 59.1	19 24.9	10 3.4	16 53.9	14 13.4
22 S	18 1 17.4	29 55.1	11 51.5	13 21.8	19 27.7	28 24.9	13 5.8	10 2.5	19 30.3	10 3.1	16 55.7	14 13.2
23 M	18 5 14.0	0♑56.2	11 48.3	26 46.2	20 0.8	29 39.2	13 52.1	10 6.1	19 35.9	10 2.7	16 57.4	14 13.0
24 T	18 9 10.5	1 57.4	11 45.1	10♈31.6	20 25.2	0♒53.6	14 38.4	10 9.8	19 41.5	10 2.2	16 59.1	14 12.8
25 W	18 13 7.1	2 58.5	11 42.0	24 38.4	20 40.0	2 7.9	15 24.7	10 13.8	19 47.2	10 1.7	17 0.8	14 12.5
26 T	18 17 3.6	3 59.6	11 38.8	9♉ 5.3	20 44.4	3 22.2	16 11.1	10 18.0	19 52.9	10 1.2	17 2.5	14 12.2
27 F	18 21 0.2	5 0.7	11 35.6	23 48.9	20R37.5	4 36.4	16 57.5	10 22.4	19 58.7	10 0.6	17 4.2	14 11.9
28 S	18 24 56.7	6 1.8	11 32.4	8♊43.6	20 19.1	5 50.7	17 44.0	10 26.9	20 4.5	9 59.9	17 5.8	14 11.6
29 S	18 28 53.3	7 3.0	11 29.2	23 42.0	19 48.7	7 4.9	18 30.5	10 31.7	20 10.4	9 59.2	17 7.4	14 11.2
30 M	18 32 49.9	8 4.1	11 26.1	8♋35.7	19 6.7	8 19.0	19 17.0	10 36.6	20 16.3	9 58.4	17 9.0	14 10.8
31 T	18 36 46.4	9 5.2	11 22.9	23 16.7	18 13.7	9 33.2	20 3.5	10 41.7	20 22.3	9 57.6	17 10.5	14 10.3

DECLINATION at NOON

DAY	EPHEMERIS SIDEREAL TIME	☉	☊	☽	☿	♀	♂	♃	♄	♅	♆	♇
1 S	16 38 29.7	21S44.2	22N48.7	20N25.3	25S26.5	24S39.4	24S17.2	2N26.8	16S37.9	8N32.5	15S 3.3	18N51.8
4 W	16 50 19.4	22 10.8	22 49.6	21 48.4	25 42.9	24 38.0	24 20.2	2 27.1	16 34.0	8 31.8	15 5.0	18 52.6
7 S	17 2 9.0	22 33.6	22 50.5	11 57.5	25 46.5	24 29.7	24 20.7	2 28.1	16 29.9	8 31.3	15 6.7	18 53.5
10 T	17 13 58.7	22 52.5	22 51.4	1S52.0	25 37.0	24 14.8	24 18.9	2 29.8	16 25.6	8 30.9	15 8.3	18 54.5
13 F	17 25 48.4	23 7.2	22 52.3	14 37.4	25 14.7	23 53.2	24 14.6	2 32.2	16 21.0	8 30.8	15 9.9	18 55.7
16 M	17 37 38.0	23 17.9	22 53.1	22 15.5	24 40.4	23 25.1	24 7.9	2 35.4	16 16.2	8 30.9	15 11.4	18 57.0
19 T	17 49 27.7	23 24.3	22 54.0	21 6.4	23 56.0	22 50.7	23 58.7	2 39.3	16 11.3	8 31.1	15 12.9	18 58.4
22 S	18 1 17.4	23 26.6	22 54.8	10 51.4	23 4.7	22 10.2	23 47.0	2 43.9	16 6.1	8 31.5	15 14.3	18 59.8
25 W	18 13 7.1	23 24.6	22 55.7	4N45.4	22 11.5	21 23.8	23 32.9	2 49.2	16 0.7	8 32.2	15 15.6	19 1.4
28 S	18 24 56.7	23 18.3	22 56.5	18 56.9	21 22.1	20 31.9	23 16.4	2 55.1	15 55.2	8 33.0	15 16.9	19 3.1
31 T	18 36 46.4	23 7.9	22 57.3	22 31.9	20 41.9	19 34.8	22 57.5	3 1.7	15 49.5	8 34.0	15 18.1	19 4.9

JANUARY 1964

DAY	EPHEMERIS SIDEREAL TIME	☉	☊	☽	☿	♀	♂	♃	♄	♅	♆	♇
	h m s	° ′	° ′	° ′	° ′	° ′	° ′	° ′	° ′	° ′	° ′	° ′
						LONGITUDE at NOON						
1 W	18 40 43.0	10♑ 6.3	11♋19.7	7♌38.3	17♑10.9	10♒47.3	20♑50.1	10♈47.0	20♒28.4	9♍56.7	17♏12.1	14♍ 9.8
2 T	18 44 39.5	11 7.5	11 16.5	21 36.0	15R60.0	12 1.4	21 36.8	10 52.4	20 34.5	9R55.8	17 13.6	14R 9.3
3 F	18 48 36.1	12 8.6	11 13.4	5♍ 7.9	14 43.1	13 15.4	22 23.4	10 58.1	20 40.7	9 54.8	17 15.1	14 8.8
4 S	18 52 32.6	13 9.8	11 10.2	18 14.3	13 22.7	14 29.4	23 10.1	11 3.9	20 46.9	9 53.8	17 16.5	14 8.2
5 S	18 56 29.2	14 10.9	11 7.0	0♎57.3	12 1.6	15 43.4	23 56.9	11 9.9	20 53.1	9 52.7	17 17.9	14 7.6
6 M	19 0 25.8	15 12.1	11 3.8	13 20.4	10 42.2	16 57.4	24 43.6	11 16.1	20 59.4	9 51.5	17 19.3	14 7.0
7 T	19 4 22.3	16 13.2	11 0.7	25 28.0	9 27.1	18 11.3	25 30.4	11 22.4	21 5.8	9 50.3	17 20.7	14 6.4
8 W	19 8 18.9	17 14.4	10 57.5	7♏24.8	8 18.2	19 25.2	26 17.2	11 28.9	21 12.2	9 49.1	17 22.1	14 5.7
9 T	19 12 15.4	18 15.5	10 54.3	19 15.3	7 17.2	20 39.0	27 4.1	11 35.6	21 18.6	9 47.8	17 23.4	14 5.0
10 F	19 16 12.0	19 16.7	10 51.1	1♐ 4.2	6 25.1	21 52.9	27 51.1	11 42.5	21 25.1	9 46.5	17 24.7	14 4.3
11 S	19 20 8.5	20 17.9	10 48.0	12 55.2	5 42.7	23 6.6	28 38.0	11 49.5	21 31.7	9 45.1	17 26.0	14 3.5
12 S	19 24 5.1	21 19.0	10 44.8	24 51.9	5 10.1	24 20.4	29 24.9	11 56.6	21 38.2	9 43.7	17 27.2	14 2.7
13 M	19 28 1.7	22 20.2	10 41.6	6♑57.0	4 47.3	25 34.1	0♒11.9	12 3.9	21 44.8	9 42.2	17 28.4	14 1.9
14 T	19 31 58.2	23 21.3	10 38.4	19 12.6	4 34.1	26 47.7	0 58.9	12 11.4	21 51.5	9 40.7	17 29.6	14 1.0
15 W	19 35 54.8	24 22.5	10 35.2	1♒40.3	4 29.9	28 1.3	1 46.0	12 19.1	21 58.2	9 39.1	17 30.7	14 0.1
16 T	19 39 51.3	25 23.6	10 32.1	14 20.8	4D34.1	29 14.9	2 33.0	12 26.9	22 4.9	9 37.5	17 31.8	13 59.2
17 F	19 43 47.9	26 24.7	10 28.9	27 14.6	4 46.3	0♓28.4	3 20.1	12 34.8	22 11.6	9 35.9	17 32.9	13 58.3
18 S	19 47 44.4	27 25.8	10 25.7	10♓21.9	5 5.6	1 41.8	4 7.2	12 42.9	22 18.4	9 34.1	17 33.9	13 57.3
19 S	19 51 41.0	28 26.9	10 22.5	23 42.5	5 31.6	2 55.2	4 54.3	12 51.2	22 25.2	9 32.4	17 35.0	13 56.3
20 M	19 55 37.6	29 28.0	10 19.4	7♈16.4	6 3.6	4 8.6	5 41.5	12 59.6	22 32.1	9 30.6	17 35.9	13 55.3
21 T	19 59 34.1	0♒29.1	10 16.2	21 3.1	6 40.9	5 21.9	6 28.6	13 8.1	22 39.0	9 28.8	17 36.9	13 54.3
22 W	20 3 30.7	1 30.1	10 13.0	5♉ 2.1	7 23.2	6 35.1	7 15.8	13 16.8	22 45.9	9 26.9	17 37.8	13 53.2
23 T	20 7 27.2	2 31.2	10 9.8	19 12.6	8 10.0	7 48.3	8 3.0	13 25.6	22 52.8	9 25.0	17 38.7	13 52.2
24 F	20 11 23.8	3 32.2	10 6.7	3♊32.7	9 0.7	9 1.4	8 50.2	13 34.5	22 59.8	9 23.1	17 39.6	13 51.1
25 S	20 15 20.3	4 33.2	10 3.5	17 59.8	9 55.0	10 14.4	9 37.5	13 43.6	23 6.8	9 21.1	17 40.4	13 49.9
26 S	20 19 16.9	5 34.2	10 0.3	2♋30.0	10 52.7	11 27.4	10 24.7	13 52.9	23 13.8	9 19.1	17 41.2	13 48.8
27 M	20 23 13.5	6 35.1	9 57.1	16 58.5	11 53.3	12 40.3	11 12.0	14 2.2	23 20.8	9 17.0	17 41.9	13 47.6
28 T	20 27 10.0	7 36.1	9 53.9	1♌20.0	12 56.6	13 53.1	11 59.3	14 11.7	23 27.9	9 14.9	17 42.7	13 46.4
29 W	20 31 6.6	8 37.0	9 50.8	15 28.8	14 2.3	15 5.9	12 46.6	14 21.3	23 34.9	9 12.8	17 43.4	13 45.2
30 T	20 35 3.1	9 37.9	9 47.6	29 20.4	15 10.3	16 18.6	13 33.9	14 31.0	23 42.0	9 10.6	17 44.0	13 44.0
31 F	20 38 59.7	10 38.9	9 44.4	12♍51.5	16 20.5	17 31.3	14 21.2	14 41.0	23 49.2	9 8.5	17 44.7	13 42.8
						DECLINATION at NOON						
1 W	18 40 43.0	23S 3.5	22N57.6	20N38.8	20S31.1	19S14.6	22S50.7	3N 4.0	15S47.6	8N34.3	15S18.5	19N 5.5
4 S	18 52 32.6	22 47.5	22 58.4	9 8.3	20 7.2	18 11.0	22 28.7	3 11.4	15 41.6	8 35.6	15 19.6	19 7.3
7 T	19 4 22.3	22 27.4	22 59.2	5S 4.0	19 56.1	17 2.8	22 4.3	3 19.4	15 35.6	8 37.0	15 20.6	19 9.3
10 F	19 16 12.0	22 3.4	22 60.0	17 1.8	19 57.9	15 50.6	21 37.8	3 28.0	15 29.3	8 38.5	15 21.6	19 11.3
13 M	19 28 1.7	21 35.5	23 0.8	22 51.8	20 11.3	14 34.5	21 9.0	3 37.1	15 23.0	8 40.2	15 22.5	19 13.4
16 T	19 39 51.3	21 3.8	23 1.5	19 17.4	20 32.7	13 15.1	20 38.0	3 46.7	15 16.5	8 42.1	15 23.3	19 15.6
19 S	19 51 41.0	20 28.5	23 2.3	7 6.5	20 57.9	11 52.5	20 5.0	3 56.9	15 9.9	8 44.1	15 24.0	19 17.8
22 W	20 3 30.7	19 49.7	23 3.0	8N40.0	21 22.5	10 27.3	19 30.0	4 7.5	15 3.2	8 46.3	15 24.6	19 20.0
25 S	20 15 20.3	19 7.6	23 3.7	20 50.6	21 43.3	8 59.7	18 53.1	4 18.6	14 56.4	8 48.6	15 25.2	19 22.3
28 T	20 27 10.0	18 22.4	23 4.4	21 38.1	21 57.7	7 30.1	18 14.3	4 30.1	14 49.5	8 51.0	15 25.6	19 24.6
31 F	20 38 59.7	17 34.1	23 5.1	10 59.0	22 4.0	5 58.8	17 33.8	4 42.0	14 42.6	8 53.5	15 26.0	19 26.9

FEBRUARY 1964

DAY	EPHEMERIS SIDEREAL TIME	☉	☊	☽	☿	♀	♂	♃	♄	♅	♆	♇
						LONGITUDE at NOON						
1 S	20 42 56.2	11♒39.8	9♋41.2	26♍ 0.4	17♑32.4	18♓43.8	15♒ 8.6	14♈50.9	23♒56.3	9♍ 6.3	17♏45.3	13♍41.5
2 S	20 46 52.8	12 40.6	9 38.1	8♎47.3	18 46.2	19 56.3	15 55.9	15 1.0	24 3.5	9R 4.0	17 45.8	13R40.2
3 M	20 50 49.3	13 41.5	9 34.9	21 14.4	20 1.5	21 8.6	16 43.3	15 11.3	24 10.6	9 1.8	17 46.4	13 38.9
4 T	20 54 45.9	14 42.3	9 31.7	3♏25.0	21 18.4	22 20.9	17 30.6	15 21.6	24 17.8	8 59.5	17 46.9	13 37.6
5 W	20 58 42.5	15 43.2	9 28.5	15 23.5	22 36.7	23 33.2	18 18.0	15 32.0	24 25.0	8 57.1	17 47.3	13 36.2
6 T	21 2 39.0	16 44.0	9 25.4	27 14.6	23 56.3	24 45.3	19 5.4	15 42.6	24 32.2	8 54.8	17 47.8	13 34.9
7 F	21 6 35.6	17 44.8	9 22.2	9♐ 3.6	25 17.2	25 57.4	19 52.8	15 53.3	24 39.4	8 52.4	17 48.1	13 33.5
8 S	21 10 32.1	18 45.6	9 19.0	20 55.6	26 39.3	27 9.3	20 40.2	16 4.1	24 46.6	8 50.0	17 48.5	13 32.1
9 S	21 14 28.7	19 46.4	9 15.8	2♑55.2	28 2.5	28 21.2	21 27.6	16 15.0	24 53.8	8 47.6	17 48.8	13 30.7
10 M	21 18 25.2	20 47.1	9 12.6	15 6.6	29 26.8	29 33.0	22 15.0	16 26.0	25 1.1	8 45.1	17 49.1	13 29.3
11 T	21 22 21.8	21 47.8	9 9.5	27 33.0	0♒52.2	0♈44.7	23 2.5	16 37.1	25 8.3	8 42.6	17 49.4	13 27.9
12 W	21 26 18.3	22 48.5	9 6.3	10♒16.4	2 18.7	1 56.4	23 49.9	16 48.3	25 15.6	8 40.1	17 49.6	13 26.4
13 T	21 30 14.9	23 49.2	9 3.1	23 17.6	3 46.1	3 7.9	24 37.3	16 59.6	25 22.8	8 37.6	17 49.8	13 24.9
14 F	21 34 11.4	24 49.9	8 59.9	6♓36.0	5 14.5	4 19.3	25 24.8	17 11.0	25 30.1	8 35.1	17 49.9	13 23.5
15 S	21 38 8.0	25 50.5	8 56.8	20 9.8	6 43.8	5 30.6	26 12.2	17 22.5	25 37.3	8 32.6	17 50.0	13 22.0
16 S	21 42 4.6	26 51.1	8 53.6	3♈56.2	8 14.1	6 41.8	26 59.7	17 34.1	25 44.6	8 30.0	17 50.1	13 20.5
17 M	21 46 1.1	27 51.7	8 50.4	17 52.0	9 45.4	7 52.9	27 47.1	17 45.8	25 51.8	8 27.4	17 50.2	13 19.0
18 T	21 49 57.7	28 52.3	8 47.2	1♉54.0	11 17.5	9 3.9	28 34.5	17 57.5	25 59.1	8 24.9	17 50.2	13 17.5
19 W	21 53 54.2	29 52.8	8 44.0	15 59.6	12 50.6	10 14.7	29 21.9	18 9.4	26 6.3	8 22.3	17 50.2	13 16.0
20 T	21 57 50.8	0♓53.3	8 40.9	0♊ 6.7	14 24.7	11 25.5	0♓ 9.4	18 21.4	26 13.5	8 19.7	17R50.1	13 14.4
21 F	22 1 47.3	1 53.8	8 37.7	14 14.1	15 59.7	12 36.2	0 56.8	18 33.4	26 20.8	8 17.1	17 50.1	13 12.9
22 S	22 5 43.9	2 54.3	8 34.5	28 20.3	17 35.6	13 46.7	1 44.2	18 45.6	26 28.1	8 14.5	17 49.9	13 11.4
23 S	22 9 40.4	3 54.7	8 31.3	12♋24.3	19 12.4	14 57.0	2 31.7	18 57.8	26 35.3	8 11.9	17 49.8	13 9.8
24 M	22 13 37.0	4 55.0	8 28.2	26 24.3	20 50.2	16 7.3	3 19.0	19 10.1	26 42.5	8 9.3	17 49.6	13 8.3
25 T	22 17 33.5	5 55.4	8 25.0	10♌18.0	22 29.0	17 17.3	4 6.4	19 22.4	26 49.7	8 6.6	17 49.4	13 6.7
26 W	22 21 30.1	6 55.7	8 21.8	24 2.6	24 8.8	18 27.3	4 53.8	19 34.8	26 56.8	8 4.0	17 49.1	13 5.2
27 T	22 25 26.6	7 55.9	8 18.6	7♍35.0	25 49.5	19 37.1	5 41.2	19 47.4	27 4.0	8 1.4	17 48.8	13 3.6
28 F	22 29 23.2	8 56.2	8 15.4	20 52.5	27 31.3	20 46.8	6 28.5	19 59.9	27 11.2	7 58.7	17 48.5	13 2.0
29 S	22 33 19.8	9 56.4	8 12.3	3♎53.0	29 14.0	21 56.3	7 15.9	20 12.6	27 18.3	7 56.1	17 48.2	13 0.4
						DECLINATION at NOON						
1 S	20 42 56.2	17S17.4	23N 5.4	6N12.6	22S 4.0	5S28.1	17S19.9	4N46.1	14S40.2	8N54.3	15S26.1	19N27.7
4 T	20 54 45.9	16 25.5	23 6.1	8S 7.9	21 57.6	3 55.2	16 37.1	4 58.5	14 33.2	8 56.9	15 26.4	19 30.1
7 F	21 6 35.6	15 31.0	23 6.7	19 6.5	21 40.8	2 21.4	15 52.8	5 11.3	14 26.1	8 59.7	15 26.6	19 32.4
10 M	21 18 25.2	14 34.1	23 7.4	22 58.9	21 12.9	0 47.1	15 7.0	5 24.4	14 19.0	9 2.4	15 26.7	19 34.8
13 T	21 30 14.9	13 35.0	23 8.1	17 3.5	20 33.7	0N47.5	14 19.7	5 37.8	14 11.8	9 5.3	15 26.7	19 37.1
16 S	21 42 4.6	12 33.9	23 8.7	3 6.9	19 42.8	2 22.0	13 31.2	5 51.4	14 4.6	9 8.2	15 26.6	19 39.4
19 W	21 53 54.2	11 31.0	23 9.3	12N38.9	18 40.2	3 56.0	12 41.5	6 5.4	13 57.4	9 11.1	15 26.5	19 41.7
22 S	22 5 43.9	10 26.4	23 10.0	22 24.0	17 25.6	5 29.3	11 50.7	6 19.6	13 50.2	9 14.0	15 26.2	19 44.0
25 T	22 17 33.5	9 20.4	23 10.6	20 9.3	15 59.2	7 1.5	10 58.9	6 34.0	13 43.1	9 17.0	15 25.9	19 46.2
28 F	22 29 23.2	8 13.2	23 11.2	8 2.0	14 20.7	8 32.4	10 6.1	6 48.6	13 35.9	9 20.0	15 25.5	19 48.3

MARCH 1964

LONGITUDE at NOON

DAY	EPHEMERIS SIDEREAL TIME h m s	☉ ° ′	☊ ° ′	☽ ° ′	☿ ° ′	♀ ° ′	♂ ° ′	♃ ° ′	♄ ° ′	♅ ° ′	♆ ° ′	♇ ° ′
1 S	22 37 16.3	10♓56.6	8♋ 9.1	16♎35.8	0♓57.8	23♈ 5.6	8♓ 3.2	20♈25.3	27♒25.4	7♍53.5	17♏47.8	12♍58.9
2 M	22 41 12.9	11 56.8	8 5.9	29 1.4	2 42.7	24 14.9	8 50.6	20 38.1	27 32.5	7R50.8	17R47.4	12R57.3
3 T	22 45 9.4	12 56.9	8 2.7	11♏12.0	4 28.6	25 23.9	9 37.9	20 51.0	27 39.6	7 48.2	17 46.9	12 55.7
4 W	22 49 6.0	13 57.0	7 59.6	23 10.7	6 15.6	26 32.8	10 25.2	21 3.9	27 46.7	7 45.6	17 46.4	12 54.1
5 T	22 53 2.5	14 57.1	7 56.4	5♐ 2.0	8 3.7	27 41.5	11 12.5	21 16.9	27 53.8	7 43.0	17 45.9	12 52.5
6 F	22 56 59.1	15 57.2	7 53.2	16 50.8	9 52.8	28 50.1	11 59.8	21 29.9	28 0.8	7 40.4	17 45.4	12 51.0
7 S	23 0 55.6	16 57.2	7 50.0	28 42.5	11 43.1	29 58.5	12 47.1	21 43.0	28 7.8	7 37.8	17 44.8	12 49.4
8 S	23 4 52.2	17 57.2	7 46.8	10♑42.7	13 34.5	1♉ 6.7	13 34.3	21 56.2	28 14.8	7 35.2	17 44.2	12 47.8
9 M	23 8 48.7	18 57.2	7 43.7	22 56.4	15 26.9	2 14.8	14 21.5	22 9.4	28 21.7	7 32.6	17 43.5	12 46.2
10 T	23 12 45.3	19 57.1	7 40.5	5♒28.2	17 20.4	3 22.7	15 8.8	22 22.7	28 28.7	7 30.1	17 42.9	12 44.7
11 W	23 16 41.8	20 57.1	7 37.3	18 21.3	19 14.9	4 30.3	15 56.0	22 36.1	28 35.6	7 27.5	17 42.2	12 43.1
12 T	23 20 38.4	21 56.9	7 34.1	1♓37.6	21 10.5	5 37.8	16 43.2	22 49.5	28 42.5	7 25.0	17 41.5	12 41.5
13 F	23 24 34.9	22 56.9	7 31.0	15 16.5	23 7.0	6 45.2	17 30.4	23 3.0	28 49.4	7 22.5	17 40.7	12 40.0
14 S	23 28 31.5	23 56.7	7 27.8	29 15.4	25 4.5	7 52.3	18 17.5	23 16.5	28 56.2	7 20.0	17 40.0	12 38.5
15 S	23 32 28.1	24 56.5	7 24.6	13♈29.6	27 2.7	8 59.2	19 4.7	23 30.0	29 3.0	7 17.6	17 39.1	12 36.9
16 M	23 36 24.6	25 56.2	7 21.4	27 53.3	29 1.6	10 5.9	19 51.8	23 43.6	29 9.7	7 15.1	17 38.3	12 35.4
17 T	23 40 21.2	26 56.0	7 18.2	12♉20.2	1♈ 1.1	11 12.3	20 38.9	23 57.3	29 16.4	7 12.7	17 37.4	12 33.9
18 W	23 44 17.7	27 55.7	7 15.1	26 44.8	3 1.1	12 18.6	21 25.9	24 11.0	29 23.1	7 10.3	17 36.5	12 32.4
19 T	23 48 14.3	28 55.3	7 11.9	11♊ 2.9	5 1.3	13 24.6	22 13.0	24 24.7	29 29.8	7 7.9	17 35.6	12 30.9
20 F	23 52 10.8	29 54.9	7 8.7	25 12.1	7 1.6	14 30.4	22 60.0	24 38.5	29 36.4	7 5.5	17 34.6	12 29.4
21 S	23 56 7.4	0♈54.5	7 5.5	9♋11.3	9 1.6	15 35.9	23 46.9	24 52.3	29 42.9	7 3.1	17 33.7	12 27.9
22 S	0 0 3.9	1 54.0	7 2.4	23 0.4	11 1.2	16 41.2	24 33.9	25 6.1	29 49.5	7 0.8	17 32.7	12 26.4
23 M	0 4 0.5	2 53.5	6 59.2	6♌39.7	12 60.0	17 46.2	25 20.8	25 20.0	29 56.0	6 58.5	17 31.6	12 24.9
24 T	0 7 57.0	3 53.0	6 56.0	20 9.2	14 57.6	18 50.9	26 7.7	25 33.9	0♓ 2.4	6 56.3	17 30.6	12 23.5
25 W	0 11 53.6	4 52.4	6 52.8	3♍28.6	16 53.8	19 55.3	26 54.6	25 47.9	0 8.8	6 54.0	17 29.5	12 22.0
26 T	0 15 50.1	5 51.8	6 49.6	16 37.3	18 48.1	20 59.5	27 41.4	26 1.9	0 15.2	6 51.8	17 28.4	12 20.6
27 F	0 19 46.7	6 51.1	6 46.5	29 34.2	20 40.1	22 3.4	28 28.2	26 15.9	0 21.5	6 49.6	17 27.3	12 19.2
28 S	0 23 43.2	7 50.4	6 43.3	12♎18.3	22 29.3	23 7.0	29 15.0	26 29.9	0 27.8	6 47.5	17 26.1	12 17.8
29 S	0 27 39.8	8 49.7	6 40.1	24 49.0	24 15.5	24 10.3	0♈ 1.7	26 44.0	0 34.0	6 45.4	17 24.9	12 16.4
30 M	0 31 36.3	9 49.0	6 36.9	7♏ 6.7	25 58.2	25 13.2	0 48.4	26 58.1	0 40.2	6 43.3	17 23.7	12 15.0
31 T	0 35 32.9	10 48.2	6 33.8	19 12.5	27 36.9	26 15.9	1 35.1	27 12.2	0 46.3	6 41.3	17 22.5	12 13.7

DECLINATION at NOON

DAY	EPHEMERIS SIDEREAL TIME h m s	☉ ° ′	☊ ° ′	☽ ° ′	☿ ° ′	♀ ° ′	♂ ° ′	♃ ° ′	♄ ° ′	♅ ° ′	♆ ° ′	♇ ° ′
1 S	22 37 16.3	7S27.8	23N11.6	1S53.1	13S 8.4	9N32.0	9S30.5	6N58.4	13S31.2	9N21.9	15S25.2	19N49.7
4 W	22 49 6.0	6 18.9	23 12.2	15 3.4	11 10.2	10 59.9	8 36.5	7 13.3	13 24.1	9 24.9	15 24.7	19 51.8
7 S	23 0 55.6	5 9.2	23 12.7	22 33.3	9 0.3	12 25.7	7 41.7	7 28.3	13 17.0	9 27.8	15 24.0	19 53.8
10 T	23 12 45.3	3 58.8	23 13.3	21 7.5	6 39.2	13 48.9	6 46.4	7 43.4	13 10.1	9 30.6	15 23.4	19 55.7
13 F	23 24 34.9	2 48.0	23 13.8	10 4.1	4 7.8	15 9.5	5 50.6	7 58.7	13 3.1	9 33.4	15 22.6	19 57.5
16 M	23 36 24.6	1 36.9	23 14.4	6N19.3	1 27.4	16 27.0	4 54.4	8 14.0	12 56.3	9 36.1	15 21.8	19 59.2
19 T	23 48 14.3	0 25.7	23 14.9	19 53.2	1N19.6	17 41.2	3 57.9	8 29.4	12 49.6	9 38.8	15 20.9	20 0.9
22 S	0 0 3.9	0N45.4	23 15.4	22 49.6	4 9.6	18 51.9	3 1.2	8 44.8	12 43.0	9 41.4	15 20.0	20 2.4
25 W	0 11 53.6	1 56.2	23 15.9	14 7.4	6 57.7	19 58.7	2 4.4	9 0.3	12 36.6	9 43.8	15 19.0	20 3.9
28 S	0 23 43.2	3 6.7	23 16.4	0S 17.0	9 37.8	21 1.4	1 7.5	9 15.8	12 30.2	9 46.2	15 17.9	20 5.2
31 T	0 35 32.9	4 16.6	23 16.9	14 0.6	12 3.6	21 59.9	0 10.7	9 31.2	12 24.0	9 48.4	15 16.8	20 6.4

APRIL 1964

LONGITUDE at NOON

DAY	EPHEMERIS SIDEREAL TIME h m s	☉ ° ′	☊ ° ′	☽ ° ′	☿ ° ′	♀ ° ′	♂ ° ′	♃ ° ′	♄ ° ′	♅ ° ′	♆ ° ′	♇ ° ′
1 W	0 39 29.4	11♈47.4	6♋30.6	1♐ 8.7	29♈11.4	27♉18.2	2♈21.8	27♈26.4	0♓52.4	6♍39.2	17♏21.3	12♍12.4
2 T	0 43 26.0	12 46.5	6 27.4	12 58.6	0♉41.2	28 20.1	3 8.4	27 40.6	0 58.5	6R37.3	17R20.0	12R11.0
3 F	0 47 22.6	13 45.7	6 24.2	24 46.5	2 6.1	29 21.8	3 55.0	27 54.8	1 4.5	6 35.4	17 18.8	12 9.8
4 S	0 51 19.1	14 44.8	6 21.0	6♑37.2	3 25.8	0♊23.0	4 41.6	28 9.1	1 10.4	6 33.5	17 17.5	12 8.5
5 S	0 55 15.7	15 43.8	6 17.9	18 36.2	4 39.9	1 23.9	5 28.1	28 23.3	1 16.3	6 31.6	17 16.2	12 7.2
6 M	0 59 12.2	16 42.9	6 14.7	0♒49.0	5 48.4	2 24.4	6 14.6	28 37.6	1 22.1	6 29.8	17 14.8	12 6.0
7 T	1 3 8.8	17 41.9	6 11.5	13 20.7	6 50.9	3 24.6	7 1.1	28 51.9	1 27.9	6 28.0	17 13.5	12 4.7
8 W	1 7 5.3	18 40.9	6 8.3	26 15.9	7 47.4	4 24.3	7 47.5	29 6.2	1 33.6	6 26.2	17 12.1	12 3.5
9 T	1 11 1.9	19 39.8	6 5.2	9♓37.5	8 37.7	5 23.6	8 33.9	29 20.5	1 39.3	6 24.5	17 10.7	12 2.3
10 F	1 14 58.4	20 38.7	6 2.0	23 26.2	9 21.7	6 22.4	9 20.2	29 34.8	1 44.9	6 22.9	17 9.3	12 1.2
11 S	1 18 55.0	21 37.6	5 58.8	7♈40.1	9 59.3	7 20.9	10 6.5	29 49.2	1 50.4	6 21.3	17 7.9	12 0.0
12 S	1 22 51.5	22 36.5	5 55.6	22 14.4	10 30.4	8 18.8	10 52.8	0♉ 3.5	1 55.9	6 19.7	17 6.4	11 58.9
13 M	1 26 48.1	23 35.3	5 52.4	7♉ 1.8	10 55.1	9 16.4	11 39.0	0 17.9	2 1.3	6 18.1	17 5.0	11 57.8
14 T	1 30 44.6	24 34.1	5 49.3	21 53.9	11 13.3	10 13.4	12 25.2	0 32.3	2 6.6	6 16.7	17 3.5	11 56.7
15 W	1 34 41.2	25 32.8	5 46.1	6♊42.3	11 25.2	11 9.9	13 11.4	0 46.7	2 11.9	6 15.2	17 2.0	11 55.7
16 T	1 38 37.7	26 31.5	5 42.9	21 20.2	11 30.8	12 5.9	13 57.5	1 1.1	2 17.1	6 13.8	17 0.5	11 54.6
17 F	1 42 34.3	27 30.2	5 39.7	5♋43.1	11R30.2	13 1.3	14 43.6	1 15.4	2 22.3	6 12.5	16 59.0	11 53.6
18 S	1 46 30.8	28 28.8	5 36.6	19 48.7	11 23.7	13 56.2	15 29.6	1 29.8	2 27.4	6 11.2	16 57.5	11 52.6
19 S	1 50 27.4	29 27.4	5 33.4	3♌36.5	11 11.6	14 50.5	16 15.6	1 44.2	2 32.4	6 9.9	16 55.9	11 51.7
20 M	1 54 24.0	0♉26.0	5 30.2	17 7.5	10 54.2	15 44.1	17 1.5	1 58.7	2 37.4	6 8.7	16 54.4	11 50.7
21 T	1 58 20.5	1 24.5	5 27.0	0♍23.0	10 31.9	16 37.2	17 47.4	2 13.1	2 42.2	6 7.5	16 52.8	11 49.8
22 W	2 2 17.1	2 23.0	5 23.8	13 24.5	10 5.3	17 29.5	18 33.2	2 27.5	2 47.1	6 6.4	16 51.3	11 48.9
23 T	2 6 13.6	3 21.5	5 20.7	26 13.4	9 34.8	18 21.2	19 19.0	2 41.9	2 51.8	6 5.3	16 49.7	11 48.1
24 F	2 10 10.2	4 19.9	5 17.5	8♎50.7	9 1.0	19 12.3	20 4.8	2 56.3	2 56.5	6 4.4	16 48.2	11 47.3
25 S	2 14 6.7	5 18.3	5 14.3	21 17.0	8 24.7	20 2.6	20 50.6	3 10.7	3 1.1	6 3.4	16 46.6	11 46.5
26 S	2 18 3.3	6 16.7	5 11.1	3♏33.0	7 46.5	20 52.1	21 36.2	3 25.1	3 5.6	6 2.5	16 45.0	11 45.7
27 M	2 21 59.8	7 15.0	5 8.0	15 39.6	7 7.1	21 40.8	22 21.8	3 39.4	3 10.1	6 1.6	16 43.4	11 44.9
28 T	2 25 56.4	8 13.3	5 4.8	27 38.0	6 27.3	22 28.8	23 7.4	3 53.8	3 14.5	6 0.8	16 41.8	11 44.2
29 W	2 29 52.9	9 11.6	5 1.6	9♐29.9	5 47.8	23 15.8	23 52.9	4 8.2	3 18.8	6 0.1	16 40.1	11 43.5
30 T	2 33 49.5	10 9.8	4 58.4	21 17.9	5 9.2	24 2.1	24 38.4	4 22.5	3 23.0	5 59.3	16 38.5	11 42.8

DECLINATION at NOON

DAY	EPHEMERIS SIDEREAL TIME h m s	☉ ° ′	☊ ° ′	☽ ° ′	☿ ° ′	♀ ° ′	♂ ° ′	♃ ° ′	♄ ° ′	♅ ° ′	♆ ° ′	♇ ° ′
1 W	0 39 29.4	4N39.8	23N17.0	17S35.3	12N48.0	22N18.4	0N 8.2	9N36.4	12S22.0	9N49.2	15S16.4	20N 6.8
4 S	0 51 19.1	5 48.7	23 17.5	23 21.8	14 46.1	23 10.9	1 4.8	9 51.8	12 16.0	9 51.2	15 15.2	20 7.9
7 T	1 3 8.8	6 56.8	23 17.9	19 46.9	16 18.9	23 58.8	2 1.2	10 7.2	12 10.2	9 53.2	15 14.0	20 8.8
10 F	1 14 58.4	8 3.8	23 18.4	7 7.6	17 24.1	24 41.9	2 57.3	10 22.6	12 4.5	9 55.0	15 12.8	20 9.6
13 M	1 26 48.1	9 9.6	23 18.8	9N49.9	18 0.4	25 20.1	3 52.9	10 37.9	11 59.1	9 56.6	15 11.5	20 10.4
16 T	1 38 37.7	10 14.1	23 19.2	22 0.6	18 7.2	25 53.5	4 48.1	10 53.0	11 53.8	9 58.2	15 10.1	20 10.9
19 S	1 50 27.4	11 17.0	23 19.6	21 45.7	17 44.8	26 21.9	5 42.7	11 8.1	11 48.8	9 59.5	15 8.8	20 11.4
22 W	2 2 17.1	12 18.2	23 20.0	10 53.8	16 55.8	26 45.4	6 36.6	11 23.1	11 44.0	10 0.7	15 7.4	20 11.7
25 S	2 14 6.7	13 17.6	23 20.4	3S48.9	15 45.1	27 4.0	7 29.9	11 38.0	11 39.4	10 1.7	15 6.1	20 11.9
28 T	2 25 56.4	14 15.0	23 20.8	16 43.9	14 21.1	27 17.9	8 22.3	11 52.7	11 35.1	10 2.5	15 4.7	20 12.0

MAY 1964

DAY	EPHEMERIS SIDEREAL TIME	☉	☊	☽	☿	♀	♂	♃	♄	♅	♆	♇
	h m s	° ′	° ′	° ′	° ′	° ′	° ′	° ′	° ′	° ′	° ′	° ′
LONGITUDE at NOON												
1 F	2 37 46.1	11♉ 8.0	4♋55.2	3♑ 5.4	4♉32.3	24♊47.4	25♈23.9	4♉36.9	3♓27.1	5♍58.7	16♏36.9	11♍42.2
2 S	2 41 42.6	12 6.2	4 52.1	14 56.2	3R57.6	25 31.8	26 9.3	4 51.2	3 31.2	5R58.1	16R35.3	11R41.5
3 S	2 45 39.2	13 4.4	4 48.9	26 55.0	3 25.8	26 15.2	26 54.6	5 5.5	3 35.2	5 57.5	16 33.6	11 40.9
4 M	2 49 35.7	14 2.5	4 45.7	9♒ 6.7	2 57.1	26 57.6	27 39.9	5 19.8	3 39.1	5 57.0	16 32.0	11 40.4
5 T	2 53 32.3	15 0.6	4 42.5	21 36.5	2 32.2	27 39.0	28 25.2	5 34.1	3 42.9	5 56.5	16 30.4	11 39.8
6 W	2 57 28.8	15 58.7	4 39.4	4♓29.0	2 11.2	28 19.3	29 10.4	5 48.4	3 46.7	5 56.1	16 28.7	11 39.3
7 T	3 1 25.4	16 56.8	4 36.2	17 48.1	1 54.4	28 58.5	29 55.5	6 2.7	3 50.4	5 55.8	16 27.1	11 38.9
8 F	3 5 21.9	17 54.8	4 33.0	1♈35.6	1 42.1	29 36.5	0♉40.6	6 16.9	3 53.9	5 55.5	16 25.5	11 38.4
9 S	3 9 18.5	18 52.9	4 29.8	15 51.1	1 34.4	0♋13.3	1 25.7	6 31.1	3 57.4	5 55.3	16 23.8	11 38.0
10 S	3 13 15.0	19 50.9	4 26.6	0♉31.2	1 31.2	0 48.9	2 10.7	6 45.3	4 0.8	5 55.1	16 22.2	11 37.6
11 M	3 17 11.6	20 48.8	4 23.5	15 29.3	1D32.8	1 23.1	2 55.7	6 59.5	4 4.2	5 54.9	16 20.6	11 37.2
12 T	3 21 8.2	21 46.8	4 20.3	0♊36.6	1 39.0	1 56.1	3 40.6	7 13.6	4 7.4	5 54.9	16 18.9	11 36.9
13 W	3 25 4.7	22 44.7	4 17.1	15 43.5	1 49.8	2 27.6	4 25.4	7 27.8	4 10.6	5 54.8	16 17.3	11 36.6
14 T	3 29 1.3	23 42.6	4 13.9	0♋40.9	2 5.1	2 57.6	5 10.2	7 41.9	4 13.6	5D54.9	16 15.7	11 36.3
15 F	3 32 57.8	24 40.5	4 10.8	15 21.7	2 24.9	3 26.2	5 55.0	7 56.0	4 16.6	5 55.0	16 14.1	11 36.2
16 S	3 36 54.4	25 38.4	4 7.6	29 41.3	2 49.0	3 53.1	6 39.7	8 10.0	4 19.5	5 55.1	16 12.5	11 36.0
17 S	3 40 50.9	26 36.2	4 4.4	13♌37.9	3 17.4	4 18.5	7 24.4	8 24.0	4 22.3	5 55.3	16 10.9	11 35.8
18 M	3 44 47.5	27 34.0	4 1.2	27 11.6	3 49.8	4 42.1	8 8.9	8 38.0	4 25.0	5 55.6	16 9.3	11 35.6
19 T	3 48 44.1	28 31.7	3 58.1	10♍24.1	4 26.3	5 3.9	8 53.5	8 52.0	4 27.6	5 55.9	16 7.7	11 35.5
20 W	3 52 40.6	29 29.4	3 54.9	23 17.6	5 6.6	5 24.0	9 38.0	9 5.9	4 30.2	5 56.2	16 6.1	11 35.4
21 T	3 56 37.2	0♊27.1	3 51.7	5♎54.8	5 50.7	5 42.1	10 22.4	9 19.7	4 32.6	5 56.6	16 4.6	11 35.4
22 F	4 0 33.7	1 24.8	3 48.5	18 18.5	6 38.4	5 58.3	11 6.7	9 33.6	4 34.9	5 57.1	16 3.0	11 35.4
23 S	4 4 30.3	2 22.5	3 45.3	0♏31.1	7 29.6	6 12.5	11 51.0	9 47.4	4 37.2	5 57.6	16 1.4	11 35.4
24 S	4 8 26.8	3 20.1	3 42.2	12 34.8	8 24.2	6 24.6	12 35.3	10 1.2	4 39.3	5 58.2	15 59.9	11 35.4
25 M	4 12 23.4	4 17.7	3 39.0	24 31.5	9 22.2	6 34.6	13 19.5	10 14.9	4 41.4	5 58.8	15 58.4	11D35.5
26 T	4 16 20.0	5 15.3	3 35.8	6♐23.2	10 23.3	6 42.4	14 3.7	10 28.6	4 43.3	5 59.5	15 56.8	11 35.6
27 W	4 20 16.5	6 12.8	3 32.6	18 11.9	11 27.6	6 48.0	14 47.8	10 42.2	4 45.2	6 0.2	15 55.3	11 35.7
28 T	4 24 13.1	7 10.4	3 29.5	29 59.7	12 35.0	6 51.4	15 31.8	10 55.8	4 47.0	6 1.0	15 53.8	11 35.9
29 F	4 28 9.6	8 7.9	3 26.3	11♑49.2	13 45.4	6 52.4	16 15.8	11 9.4	4 48.7	6 1.8	15 52.3	11 36.1
30 S	4 32 6.2	9 5.4	3 23.1	23 43.5	14 58.7	6R51.0	16 59.7	11 22.9	4 50.2	6 2.7	15 50.9	11 36.3
31 S	4 36 2.7	10 2.9	3 19.9	5♒45.8	16 14.8	6 47.3	17 43.6	11 36.4	4 51.7	6 3.6	15 49.4	11 36.5
DECLINATION at NOON												
1 F	2 37 46.1	15N10.3	23N21.1	23S24.0	12N54.2	27N27.2	9N13.9	12N 7.2	11S31.0	10N 3.2	15S 3.3	20N11.9
4 M	2 49 35.7	16 3.3	23 21.5	20 54.0	11 34.5	27 32.1	10 4.6	12 21.6	11 27.2	10 3.7	15 1.9	20 11.7
7 T	3 1 25.4	16 54.0	23 21.8	9 23.7	10 30.4	27 32.8	10 54.2	12 35.8	11 23.6	10 4.1	15 0.5	20 11.4
10 S	3 13 15.0	17 42.2	23 22.1	7N22.4	9 46.6	27 29.5	11 42.8	12 49.9	11 20.4	10 4.2	14 59.1	20 10.9
13 W	3 25 4.7	18 27.7	23 22.5	21 10.8	9 25.1	27 22.5	12 30.3	13 3.7	11 17.4	10 4.2	14 57.7	20 10.4
16 S	3 36 54.4	19 10.4	23 22.8	22 32.4	9 25.5	27 12.1	13 16.6	13 17.3	11 14.7	10 4.0	14 56.4	20 9.7
19 T	3 48 44.1	19 50.1	23 23.0	12 7.6	9 46.3	26 58.3	14 1.6	13 30.7	11 12.3	10 3.6	14 55.1	20 8.8
22 F	4 0 33.7	20 26.8	23 23.3	2S32.7	10 25.1	26 41.5	14 45.3	13 43.9	11 10.2	10 3.0	14 53.8	20 7.9
25 M	4 12 23.4	21 0.4	23 23.6	15 48.2	11 19.6	26 21.7	15 27.6	13 56.9	11 8.4	10 2.3	14 52.5	20 6.9
28 T	4 24 13.1	21 30.7	23 23.9	23 15.0	12 27.1	25 59.0	16 8.4	14 9.5	11 7.0	10 1.3	14 51.3	20 5.7
31 S	4 36 2.7	21 57.6	23 24.1	21 39.8	13 45.3	25 33.3	16 47.8	14 22.0	11 5.8	10 0.2	14 50.1	20 4.4

JUNE 1964

DAY	EPHEMERIS SIDEREAL TIME	☉	☊	☽	☿	♀	♂	♃	♄	♅	♆	♇
LONGITUDE at NOON												
1 M	4 39 59.3	11♊ 0.4	3♋16.8	18♒ 0.2	17♉33.9	6♋41.2	18♉27.4	11♉49.8	4♓53.1	6♍ 4.6	15♏48.0	11♍36.8
2 T	4 43 55.9	11 57.9	3 13.6	0♓30.7	18 55.7	6R32.7	19 11.2	12 3.2	4 54.4	6 5.7	15R46.5	11 37.1
3 W	4 47 52.4	12 55.3	3 10.4	13 21.2	20 20.3	6 21.8	19 54.9	12 16.5	4 55.6	6 6.7	15 45.1	11 37.5
4 T	4 51 49.0	13 52.8	3 7.2	26 35.5	21 47.6	6 8.5	20 38.6	12 29.8	4 56.7	6 7.9	15 43.7	11 37.9
5 F	4 55 45.5	14 50.3	3 4.0	10♈15.9	23 17.7	5 52.8	21 22.2	12 43.0	4 57.8	6 9.1	15 42.4	11 38.3
6 S	4 59 42.1	15 47.7	3 0.9	24 23.3	24 50.4	5 34.8	22 5.8	12 56.2	4 58.7	6 10.4	15 41.0	11 38.8
7 S	5 3 38.6	16 45.1	2 57.7	8♉55.8	26 25.8	5 14.5	22 49.3	13 9.3	4 59.5	6 11.7	15 39.7	11 39.2
8 M	5 7 35.2	17 42.5	2 54.5	23 49.2	28 3.9	4 52.0	23 32.7	13 22.4	5 0.2	6 13.0	15 38.3	11 39.7
9 T	5 11 31.8	18 39.9	2 51.3	8♊56.3	29 44.6	4 27.4	24 16.1	13 35.4	5 0.8	6 14.4	15 37.0	11 40.3
10 W	5 15 28.3	19 37.3	2 48.2	24 8.1	1♊28.0	4 0.8	24 59.4	13 48.3	5 1.3	6 15.9	15 35.7	11 40.8
11 T	5 19 24.9	20 34.6	2 45.0	9♋15.1	3 13.9	3 32.2	25 42.7	14 1.2	5 1.7	6 17.3	15 34.5	11 41.4
12 F	5 23 21.4	21 32.0	2 41.8	24 8.5	5 2.5	3 1.9	26 25.9	14 14.0	5 2.0	6 18.9	15 33.2	11 42.0
13 S	5 27 18.0	22 29.3	2 38.6	8♌41.4	6 53.5	2 29.9	27 9.0	14 26.8	5 2.2	6 20.5	15 32.0	11 42.7
14 S	5 31 14.5	23 26.7	2 35.5	22 49.8	8 47.1	1 56.5	27 52.1	14 39.5	5 2.3	6 22.1	15 30.8	11 43.4
15 M	5 35 11.1	24 24.0	2 32.3	6♍32.0	10 43.0	1 21.9	28 35.2	14 52.1	5 2.3	6 23.8	15 29.6	11 44.1
16 T	5 39 7.7	25 21.3	2 29.1	19 48.8	12 41.3	0 46.1	29 18.1	15 4.6	5R 2.2	6 25.6	15 28.4	11 44.8
17 W	5 43 4.2	26 18.6	2 25.9	2♎42.3	14 41.8	0 9.6	0♊ 1.0	15 17.1	5 2.0	6 27.3	15 27.3	11 45.6
18 T	5 47 0.8	27 15.8	2 22.8	15 15.9	16 44.3	29♊32.4	0 43.9	15 29.5	5 1.7	6 29.2	15 26.1	11 46.4
19 F	5 50 57.3	28 13.1	2 19.6	27 33.3	18 48.7	28 54.9	1 26.7	15 41.9	5 1.3	6 31.0	15 25.0	11 47.2
20 S	5 54 53.9	29 10.3	2 16.4	9♏38.2	20 54.9	28 17.2	2 9.4	15 54.1	5 0.9	6 33.0	15 24.0	11 48.1
21 S	5 58 50.4	0♋ 7.5	2 13.2	21 34.3	23 2.5	27 39.7	2 52.1	16 6.3	5 0.3	6 34.9	15 22.9	11 48.9
22 M	6 2 47.0	1 4.8	2 10.0	3♐25.0	25 11.5	27 2.5	3 34.7	16 18.5	4 59.6	6 36.9	15 21.9	11 49.8
23 T	6 6 43.6	2 2.0	2 6.9	15 13.1	27 21.4	26 25.9	4 17.2	16 30.5	4 58.8	6 39.0	15 20.9	11 50.8
24 W	6 10 40.1	2 59.2	2 3.7	27 1.4	29 32.0	25 50.2	4 59.7	16 42.5	4 58.0	6 41.1	15 19.9	11 51.7
25 T	6 14 36.7	3 56.4	2 0.5	8♑52.2	1♋43.1	25 15.5	5 42.1	16 54.4	4 57.0	6 43.3	15 18.9	11 52.7
26 F	6 18 33.2	4 53.6	1 57.3	20 47.8	3 54.4	24 42.1	6 24.6	17 6.2	4 56.0	6 45.5	15 18.1	11 53.8
27 S	6 22 29.8	5 50.8	1 54.2	2♒50.3	6 5.6	24 10.2	7 6.9	17 18.0	4 54.8	6 47.7	15 17.2	11 54.9
28 S	6 26 26.4	6 48.0	1 51.0	15 1.9	8 16.3	23 39.8	7 49.1	17 29.6	4 53.6	6 50.0	15 16.3	11 55.9
29 M	6 30 22.9	7 45.2	1 47.8	27 25.2	10 26.5	23 11.3	8 31.3	17 41.2	4 52.2	6 52.3	15 15.4	11 57.0
30 T	6 34 19.5	8 42.4	1 44.6	10♓ 2.6	12 35.8	22 44.7	9 13.5	17 52.6	4 50.8	6 54.7	15 14.6	11 58.2
DECLINATION at NOON												
1 M	4 39 59.3	22N 5.8	23N24.2	19S 2.1	14N13.2	25N24.1	17N 0.6	14N26.1	11S 5.5	9N59.8	14S49.7	20N 4.0
4 T	4 51 49.0	22 28.2	23 24.4	6 10.0	15 41.5	24 54.5	17 38.0	14 38.1	11 4.8	9 58.5	14 48.5	20 2.6
7 S	5 3 38.6	22 47.0	23 24.6	10N28.2	17 14.3	24 21.7	18 13.7	14 50.0	11 4.4	9 57.0	14 47.5	20 1.0
10 W	5 15 28.3	23 2.2	23 24.8	22 35.1	18 48.3	23 45.8	18 47.8	15 1.5	11 4.4	9 55.4	14 46.4	19 59.4
13 S	5 27 18.0	23 13.8	23 25.0	21 8.4	20 19.8	23 7.1	19 20.2	15 12.7	11 4.7	9 53.5	14 45.5	19 57.7
16 T	5 39 7.7	23 21.7	23 25.2	8 47.3	21 44.3	22 26.0	19 50.9	15 23.7	11 5.3	9 51.6	14 44.5	19 55.9
19 F	5 50 57.3	23 25.9	23 25.4	6S 8.3	22 56.6	21 43.5	20 19.8	15 34.3	11 6.2	9 49.4	14 43.7	19 54.0
22 M	6 2 47.0	23 26.3	23 25.6	18 20.6	23 51.5	21 1.1	20 47.0	15 44.6	11 7.4	9 47.1	14 42.9	19 52.0
25 T	6 14 36.7	23 23.1	23 25.7	23 46.4	24 24.3	20 20.3	21 12.3	15 54.6	11 9.0	9 44.7	14 42.2	19 50.0
28 S	6 26 26.4	23 16.1	23 25.8	19 46.7	24 32.3	19 42.8	21 35.7	16 4.3	11 10.9	9 42.1	14 41.6	19 47.8

JULY 1964

LONGITUDE at NOON

DAY	EPHEMERIS SIDEREAL TIME	☉	☊	☽	☿	♀	♂	♃	♄	♅	♆	♇
	h m s	° ′	° ′	° ′	° ′	° ′	° ′	° ′	° ′	° ′	° ′	° ′
1 W	6 38 16.0	9♋39.6	1♋41.5	22♓56.7	14♋44.0	22♊20.2	9♊55.6	18♉ 4.0	4♓49.2	6♍57.1	15♏13.8	11♍59.3
2 T	6 42 12.6	10 36.8	1 38.3	6♈10.1	16 51.0	21R57.8	10 37.6	18 15.3	4R47.6	6 59.5	15R13.1	12 0.5
3 F	6 46 9.1	11 34.0	1 35.1	19 44.5	18 56.5	21 37.6	11 19.6	18 26.5	4 45.9	7 2.0	15 12.3	12 1.7
4 S	6 50 5.7	12 31.2	1 31.9	3♉41.2	21 0.6	21 19.8	12 1.5	18 37.6	4 44.1	7 4.5	15 11.6	12 2.9
5 S	6 54 2.3	13 28.4	1 28.8	17 59.7	23 3.0	21 4.3	12 43.3	18 48.7	4 42.2	7 7.0	15 10.9	12 4.2
6 M	6 57 58.8	14 25.6	1 25.6	2♊37.7	25 3.8	20 51.2	13 25.1	18 59.6	4 40.2	7 9.6	15 10.3	12 5.5
7 T	7 1 55.4	15 22.8	1 22.4	17 30.7	27 2.7	20 40.5	14 6.9	19 10.4	4 38.1	7 12.3	15 9.6	12 6.8
8 W	7 5 51.9	16 20.1	1 19.2	2♋32.1	28 59.8	20 32.1	14 48.5	19 21.2	4 35.9	7 14.9	15 9.1	12 8.1
9 T	7 9 48.5	17 17.3	1 16.0	17 33.7	0♌55.1	20 26.2	15 30.2	19 31.8	4 33.7	7 17.6	15 8.5	12 9.5
10 F	7 13 45.0	18 14.5	1 12.9	2♌27.1	2 48.4	20 22.6	16 11.7	19 42.3	4 31.3	7 20.4	15 8.0	12 10.8
11 S	7 17 41.6	19 11.8	1 9.7	17 4.3	4 39.9	20 21.3	16 53.2	19 52.7	4 28.9	7 23.2	15 7.4	12 12.3
12 S	7 21 38.2	20 9.0	1 6.5	1♍19.3	6 29.4	20D22.4	17 34.6	20 3.1	4 26.4	7 26.0	15 7.0	12 13.7
13 M	7 25 34.7	21 6.2	1 3.3	15 8.7	8 17.1	20 25.7	18 16.0	20 13.3	4 23.8	7 28.8	15 6.5	12 15.1
14 T	7 29 31.3	22 3.5	1 0.2	28 31.5	10 2.8	20 31.2	18 57.3	20 23.4	4 21.1	7 31.7	15 6.1	12 16.6
15 W	7 33 27.8	23 0.7	0 57.0	11♎28.8	11 46.6	20 38.9	19 38.5	20 33.3	4 18.4	7 34.6	15 5.7	12 18.1
16 T	7 37 24.4	23 57.9	0 53.8	24 3.6	13 28.4	20 48.7	20 19.7	20 43.2	4 15.5	7 37.6	15 5.4	12 19.6
17 F	7 41 20.9	24 55.2	0 50.6	6♏20.0	15 8.5	21 0.7	21 0.9	20 53.0	4 12.7	7 40.6	15 5.1	12 21.2
18 S	7 45 17.5	25 52.5	0 47.5	18 22.4	16 46.5	21 14.6	21 41.9	21 2.7	4 9.7	7 43.6	15 4.8	12 22.7
19 S	7 49 14.1	26 49.7	0 44.3	0♐15.5	18 22.7	21 30.5	22 22.9	21 12.2	4 6.6	7 46.7	15 4.6	12 24.3
20 M	7 53 10.6	27 47.0	0 41.1	12 3.9	19 56.9	21 48.2	23 3.8	21 21.6	4 3.5	7 49.7	15 4.3	12 25.9
21 T	7 57 7.2	28 44.2	0 37.9	23 51.7	21 29.2	22 7.8	23 44.7	21 30.9	4 0.3	7 52.8	15 4.1	12 27.5
22 W	8 1 3.7	29 41.5	0 34.7	5♑42.4	22 59.5	22 29.2	24 25.5	21 40.1	3 57.0	7 56.0	15 4.0	12 29.2
23 T	8 5 0.3	0♌38.8	0 31.6	17 39.2	24 28.0	22 52.3	25 6.3	21 49.1	3 53.6	7 59.1	15 3.8	12 30.8
24 F	8 8 56.8	1 36.0	0 28.4	29 44.2	25 54.4	23 17.1	25 46.9	21 58.1	3 50.2	8 2.3	15 3.7	12 32.5
25 S	8 12 53.4	2 33.3	0 25.2	11♒59.5	27 18.9	23 43.5	26 27.6	22 6.9	3 46.7	8 5.5	15 3.7	12 34.2
26 S	8 16 50.0	3 30.6	0 22.0	24 26.2	28 41.4	24 11.5	27 8.1	22 15.5	3 43.2	8 8.8	15 3.6	12 35.9
27 M	8 20 46.5	4 27.9	0 18.9	7♓ 5.3	0♍ 1.8	24 40.9	27 48.6	22 24.1	3 39.6	8 12.0	15 3.6	12 37.7
28 T	8 24 43.1	5 25.3	0 15.7	19 57.6	1 20.1	25 11.9	28 29.1	22 32.5	3 35.9	8 15.3	15D 3.7	12 39.4
29 W	8 28 39.6	6 22.6	0 12.5	3♈ 3.6	2 36.2	25 44.2	29 9.4	22 40.7	3 32.2	8 18.6	15 3.7	12 41.2
30 T	8 32 36.2	7 20.0	0 9.3	16 24.0	3 50.2	26 17.8	29 49.8	22 48.9	3 28.4	8 22.0	15 3.8	12 43.0
31 F	8 36 32.7	8 17.4	0 6.2	29 59.4	5 1.9	26 52.8	0♋30.0	22 56.9	3 24.6	8 25.3	15 3.9	12 44.8

DECLINATION at NOON

DAY	EPHEMERIS SIDEREAL TIME	☉	☊	☽	☿	♀	♂	♃	♄	♅	♆	♇
1 W	6 38 16.0	23N 5.5	23N26.0	7S35.7	24N15.3	19N10.0	21N57.3	16N13.7	11S13.0	9N39.4	14S41.0	19N45.7
4 S	6 50 5.7	22 51.2	23 26.1	8N30.4	23 35.0	18 42.8	22 17.1	16 22.7	11 15.5	9 36.5	14 40.5	19 43.4
7 T	7 1 55.4	22 33.4	23 26.2	21 31.9	22 34.7	18 21.7	22 34.9	16 31.4	11 18.3	9 33.6	14 40.1	19 41.1
10 F	7 13 45.0	22 12.0	23 26.3	22 13.1	21 18.2	18 6.7	22 50.8	16 39.7	11 21.3	9 30.5	14 39.7	19 38.7
13 M	7 25 34.7	21 47.2	23 26.4	10 29.8	19 49.0	17 57.5	23 4.8	16 47.7	11 24.6	9 27.2	14 39.5	19 36.3
16 T	7 37 24.4	21 19.1	23 26.4	4S47.9	18 10.5	17 53.6	23 16.9	16 55.4	11 28.2	9 23.9	14 39.3	19 33.9
19 S	7 49 14.1	20 47.7	23 26.5	17 30.2	16 25.5	17 54.2	23 27.1	17 2.6	11 31.9	9 20.4	14 39.2	19 31.4
22 W	8 1 3.7	20 13.1	23 26.5	23 39.7	14 36.5	17 58.5	23 35.4	17 9.6	11 35.9	9 16.9	14 39.2	19 28.8
25 S	8 12 53.4	19 35.6	23 26.6	20 25.6	12 45.8	18 5.7	23 41.8	17 16.1	11 40.1	9 13.3	14 39.3	19 26.3
28 T	8 24 43.1	18 55.0	23 26.6	8 39.2	10 55.4	18 14.9	23 46.3	17 22.3	11 44.5	9 9.5	14 39.5	19 23.7
31 F	8 36 32.7	18 11.7	23 26.6	7N11.5	9 7.2	18 25.3	23 49.0	17 28.1	11 49.1	9 5.7	14 39.7	19 21.1

AUGUST 1964

LONGITUDE at NOON

DAY	EPHEMERIS SIDEREAL TIME	☉	☊	☽	☿	♀	♂	♃	♄	♅	♆	♇
1 S	8 40 29.3	9♌14.8	0♋ 3.0	13♉50.2	6♍11.3	27♊29.0	1♋10.2	23♉ 4.8	3♓20.7	8♍28.7	15♏ 4.1	12♍46.6
2 S	8 44 25.9	10 12.2	29♊59.8	27 56.2	7 18.2	28 6.4	1 50.3	23 12.5	3R16.7	8 32.1	15 4.3	12 48.4
3 M	8 48 22.4	11 9.6	29 56.6	12♊16.5	8 22.7	28 45.0	2 30.4	23 20.1	3 12.7	8 35.6	15 4.5	12 50.3
4 T	8 52 19.0	12 7.1	29 53.4	26 48.8	9 24.6	29 24.7	3 10.4	23 27.5	3 8.7	8 39.0	15 4.7	12 52.1
5 W	8 56 15.5	13 4.6	29 50.3	11♋29.3	10 23.7	0♋ 5.4	3 50.4	23 34.8	3 4.6	8 42.5	15 5.0	12 54.0
6 T	9 0 12.1	14 2.1	29 47.1	26 12.5	11 20.1	0 47.2	4 30.3	23 42.0	3 0.5	8 46.0	15 5.3	12 55.9
7 F	9 4 8.6	14 59.7	29 43.9	10♌51.7	12 13.5	1 30.0	5 10.1	23 49.0	2 56.4	8 49.6	15 5.7	12 57.8
8 S	9 8 5.2	15 57.2	29 40.7	25 19.8	13 3.7	2 13.7	5 49.9	23 55.8	2 52.1	8 53.1	15 6.1	12 59.8
9 S	9 12 1.7	16 54.7	29 37.6	9♍30.6	13 50.7	2 58.3	6 29.6	24 2.5	2 47.9	8 56.7	15 6.5	13 1.7
10 M	9 15 58.3	17 52.3	29 34.4	23 19.3	14 34.2	3 43.8	7 9.2	24 9.1	2 43.6	9 0.2	15 7.0	13 3.6
11 T	9 19 54.8	18 49.9	29 31.2	6♎43.4	15 14.1	4 30.1	7 48.8	24 15.4	2 39.3	9 3.8	15 7.5	13 5.6
12 W	9 23 51.4	19 47.5	29 28.0	19 42.7	15 50.2	5 17.2	8 28.3	24 21.6	2 34.9	9 7.4	15 8.0	13 7.6
13 T	9 27 48.0	20 45.1	29 24.9	2♏19.3	16 22.3	6 5.1	9 7.7	24 27.7	2 30.5	9 11.0	15 8.5	13 9.5
14 F	9 31 44.5	21 42.8	29 21.7	14 36.4	16 50.1	6 53.8	9 47.0	24 33.6	2 26.1	9 14.6	15 9.1	13 11.5
15 S	9 35 41.1	22 40.4	29 18.5	26 38.9	17 13.5	7 43.2	10 26.3	24 39.3	2 21.7	9 18.3	15 9.7	13 13.5
16 S	9 39 37.6	23 38.1	29 15.3	8♐31.6	17 32.1	8 33.4	11 5.6	24 44.9	2 17.3	9 21.9	15 10.3	13 15.5
17 M	9 43 34.2	24 35.8	29 12.1	20 19.9	17 45.9	9 24.2	11 44.7	24 50.3	2 12.8	9 25.6	15 11.0	13 17.6
18 T	9 47 30.7	25 33.5	29 9.0	2♑ 8.9	17 54.5	10 15.6	12 23.8	24 55.5	2 8.3	9 29.3	15 11.7	13 19.6
19 W	9 51 27.3	26 31.2	29 5.8	14 3.2	17 57.7	11 7.8	13 2.8	25 0.5	2 3.8	9 33.0	15 12.4	13 21.6
20 T	9 55 23.8	27 28.9	29 2.6	26 6.6	17R55.4	12 0.5	13 41.8	25 5.4	1 59.3	9 36.7	15 13.2	13 23.7
21 F	9 59 20.4	28 26.7	28 59.4	8♒22.3	17 47.4	12 53.8	14 20.7	25 10.1	1 54.8	9 40.4	15 14.0	13 25.7
22 S	10 3 16.9	29 24.5	28 56.3	20 52.2	17 33.6	13 47.8	14 59.5	25 14.7	1 50.2	9 44.1	15 14.8	13 27.8
23 S	10 7 13.5	0♍22.3	28 53.1	3♓37.2	17 13.9	14 42.2	15 38.3	25 19.1	1 45.7	9 47.8	15 15.7	13 29.9
24 M	10 11 10.1	1 20.1	28 49.9	16 37.2	16 48.3	15 37.3	16 17.0	25 23.2	1 41.2	9 51.6	15 16.6	13 31.9
25 T	10 15 6.6	2 18.0	28 46.7	29 51.2	16 17.1	16 32.9	16 55.6	25 27.2	1 36.6	9 55.3	15 17.5	13 34.0
26 W	10 19 3.2	3 15.9	28 43.5	13♈17.6	15 40.3	17 28.9	17 34.1	25 31.1	1 32.1	9 59.0	15 18.4	13 36.1
27 T	10 22 59.7	4 13.8	28 40.4	26 54.7	14 58.5	18 25.5	18 12.6	25 34.7	1 27.5	10 2.8	15 19.4	13 38.2
28 F	10 26 56.3	5 11.8	28 37.2	10♉41.1	14 12.0	19 22.7	18 51.1	25 38.2	1 23.1	10 6.6	15 20.5	13 40.3
29 S	10 30 52.8	6 9.8	28 34.0	24 35.6	13 21.5	20 20.2	19 29.5	25 41.5	1 18.5	10 10.4	15 21.5	13 42.4
30 S	10 34 49.4	7 7.8	28 30.8	8♊37.3	12 27.8	21 18.2	20 7.8	25 44.6	1 14.0	10 14.1	15 22.6	13 44.5
31 M	10 38 45.9	8 5.8	28 27.7	22 45.6	11 31.9	22 16.7	20 46.0	25 47.5	1 9.5	10 17.9	15 23.7	13 46.7

DECLINATION at NOON

DAY	EPHEMERIS SIDEREAL TIME	☉	☊	☽	☿	♀	♂	♃	♄	♅	♆	♇
1 S	8 40 29.3	17N56.7	23N26.6	12N19.5	8N32.0	18N28.9	23N49.5	17N30.0	11S50.7	9N 4.4	14S39.9	19N20.3
4 T	8 52 19.0	17 9.8	23 26.6	22 58.9	6 49.8	18 39.8	23 49.7	17 35.3	11 55.4	9 0.5	14 40.2	19 17.7
7 F	9 4 8.6	16 20.4	23 26.6	20 40.0	5 14.7	18 50.2	23 48.1	17 40.2	12 0.2	8 56.5	14 40.7	19 15.0
10 M	9 15 58.3	15 28.7	23 26.6	7 19.5	3 49.3	18 59.5	23 44.8	17 44.7	12 5.2	8 52.5	14 41.2	19 12.4
13 T	9 27 48.0	14 34.7	23 26.6	8S 9.6	2 36.6	19 7.3	23 39.8	17 48.9	12 10.2	8 48.4	14 41.8	19 9.8
16 S	9 39 37.6	13 38.7	23 26.5	19 48.2	1 40.2	19 12.9	23 33.0	17 52.6	12 15.3	8 44.3	14 42.5	19 7.3
19 W	9 51 27.3	12 40.7	23 26.5	23 52.5	1 4.4	19 15.9	23 24.6	17 56.0	12 20.4	8 40.1	14 43.3	19 4.7
22 S	10 3 16.9	11 40.9	23 26.4	18 14.9	0 53.9	19 16.0	23 14.7	17 58.9	12 25.6	8 35.9	14 44.2	19 2.1
25 T	10 15 6.6	10 39.4	23 26.3	4 42.1	1 12.5	19 12.9	23 3.1	18 1.5	12 30.6	8 31.6	14 45.1	18 59.6
28 F	10 26 56.3	9 36.4	23 26.2	11N23.5	2 2.1	19 6.1	22 50.1	18 3.7	12 35.7	8 27.3	14 46.1	18 57.1
31 M	10 38 45.9	8 32.1	23 26.1	22 38.5	3 19.7	18 55.6	22 35.6	18 5.4	12 40.7	8 23.1	14 47.2	18 54.7

SEPTEMBER 1964

DAY	EPHEMERIS SIDEREAL TIME	☉	☊	☽	☿	♀	♂	♃	♄	♅	♆	♇
	h m s	° ′	° ′	° ′	° ′	° ′	° ′	° ′	° ′	° ′	° ′	° ′
					LONGITUDE at NOON							
1 T	10 42 42.5	9♍ 3.9	28♓24.5	6♋59.4	10♍34.8	23♋15.5	21♋24.1	25♉50.2	1♓ 5.0	10♍21.6	15♏24.8	13♍48.8
2 W	10 46 39.0	10 2.0	28 21.3	21 17.0	9R37.8	24 14.8	22 2.2	25 52.7	1R 0.6	10 25.4	15 25.9	13 50.9
3 T	10 50 35.6	11 0.2	28 18.1	5♌35.6	8 41.9	25 14.5	22 40.3	25 55.1	0 56.1	10 29.2	15 27.1	13 53.0
4 F	10 54 32.1	11 58.3	28 14.9	19 51.0	7 48.6	26 14.6	23 18.2	25 57.2	0 51.7	10 33.0	15 28.3	13 55.1
5 S	10 58 28.7	12 56.5	28 11.8	3♍58.4	6 59.0	27 15.0	23 56.1	25 59.1	0 47.3	10 36.7	15 29.6	13 57.2
6 S	11 2 25.2	13 54.8	28 8.6	17 52.9	6 14.3	28 15.8	24 33.9	26 0.9	0 42.9	10 40.5	15 30.8	13 59.3
7 M	11 6 21.8	14 53.0	28 5.4	1♎30.0	5 35.6	29 17.0	25 11.6	26 2.4	0 38.6	10 44.3	15 32.1	14 1.5
8 T	11 10 18.4	15 51.3	28 2.2	14 46.8	5 3.9	0♌18.5	25 49.2	26 3.8	0 34.3	10 48.0	15 33.4	14 3.6
9 W	11 14 14.9	16 49.6	27 59.1	27 42.2	4 40.0	1 20.3	26 26.8	26 4.9	0 30.0	10 51.8	15 34.8	14 5.7
10 T	11 18 11.5	17 48.0	27 55.9	10♏16.9	4 24.4	2 22.5	27 4.3	26 5.9	0 25.8	10 55.5	15 36.1	14 7.8
11 F	11 22 8.0	18 46.3	27 52.7	22 33.3	4 17.7	3 24.9	27 41.7	26 6.6	0 21.6	10 59.3	15 37.5	14 9.9
12 S	11 26 4.6	19 44.7	27 49.5	4♐35.4	4D20.1	4 27.7	28 19.1	26 7.2	0 17.4	11 3.0	15 39.0	14 12.0
13 S	11 30 1.1	20 43.2	27 46.3	16 28.0	4 31.8	5 30.8	28 56.3	26 7.5	0 13.3	11 6.8	15 40.4	14 14.2
14 M	11 33 57.7	21 41.6	27 43.2	28 16.3	4 52.7	6 34.2	29 33.5	26 7.7	0 9.2	11 10.5	15 41.9	14 16.3
15 T	11 37 54.2	22 40.1	27 40.0	10♑ 6.0	5 22.8	7 37.8	0♌10.6	26R 7.6	0 5.2	11 14.2	15 43.4	14 18.4
16 W	11 41 50.8	23 38.6	27 36.8	22 2.4	6 1.6	8 41.8	0 47.6	26 7.4	0 1.2	11 17.9	15 44.9	14 20.5
17 T	11 45 47.3	24 37.1	27 33.6	4♒10.3	6 48.9	9 46.0	1 24.6	26 6.9	29♒57.3	11 21.6	15 46.5	14 22.6
18 F	11 49 43.9	25 35.7	27 30.5	16 33.8	7 44.2	10 50.5	2 1.5	26 6.3	29 53.5	11 25.3	15 48.1	14 24.7
19 S	11 53 40.4	26 34.3	27 27.3	29 15.6	8 46.9	11 55.2	2 38.3	26 5.5	29 49.7	11 29.0	15 49.7	14 26.8
20 S	11 57 37.0	27 32.9	27 24.1	12♓17.1	9 56.4	13 0.2	3 15.0	26 4.4	29 45.9	11 32.7	15 51.3	14 28.9
21 M	12 1 33.5	28 31.6	27 20.9	25 38.0	11 12.1	14 5.5	3 51.6	26 3.2	29 42.2	11 36.3	15 53.0	14 30.9
22 T	12 5 30.1	29 30.3	27 17.7	9♈16.0	12 33.5	15 11.0	4 28.2	26 1.7	29 38.6	11 40.0	15 54.6	14 33.0
23 W	12 9 26.6	0♎29.0	27 14.6	23 7.9	13 59.8	16 16.7	5 4.6	26 0.1	29 35.0	11 43.6	15 56.3	14 35.1
24 T	12 13 23.2	1 27.7	27 11.4	7♉ 9.6	15 30.4	17 22.7	5 41.0	25 58.2	29 31.5	11 47.2	15 58.0	14 37.1
25 F	12 17 19.8	2 26.5	27 8.2	21 17.0	17 4.7	18 28.9	6 17.3	25 56.1	29 28.1	11 50.8	15 59.7	14 39.1
26 S	12 21 16.3	3 25.3	27 5.0	5♊26.6	18 42.2	19 35.4	6 53.5	25 53.9	29 24.7	11 54.4	16 1.5	14 41.2
27 S	12 25 12.9	4 24.2	27 1.9	19 35.9	20 22.2	20 42.1	7 29.7	25 51.5	29 21.4	11 57.9	16 3.3	14 43.2
28 M	12 29 9.4	5 23.1	26 58.7	3♋43.3	22 4.4	21 48.9	8 5.7	25 48.8	29 18.2	12 1.5	16 5.1	14 45.2
29 T	12 33 6.0	6 22.1	26 55.5	17 47.9	23 48.3	22 56.0	8 41.7	25 46.0	29 15.0	12 5.0	16 6.9	14 47.2
30 W	12 37 2.5	7 21.0	26 52.3	1♌48.9	25 33.4	24 3.3	9 17.6	25 42.9	29 12.0	12 8.5	16 8.7	14 49.2
					DECLINATION at NOON							
1 T	10 42 42.5	8N10.3	23N26.1	23N54.7	3N50.4	18N51.2	22N30.4	18N 5.9	12S42.3	8N21.6	14S47.6	18N53.9
4 F	10 54 32.1	7 4.4	23 25.9	18 33.2	5 29.7	18 35.2	22 14.0	18 7.1	12 47.2	8 17.4	14 48.7	18 51.5
7 M	11 6 21.8	5 57.3	23 25.8	4 0.4	7 7.2	18 15.0	21 56.4	18 7.9	12 51.9	8 13.1	14 50.0	18 49.1
10 T	11 18 11.5	4 49.4	23 25.7	11S20.3	8 27.0	17 50.6	21 37.4	18 8.3	12 56.5	8 8.8	14 51.3	18 46.9
13 S	11 30 1.1	3 40.7	23 25.5	21 43.6	9 17.1	17 21.8	21 17.2	18 8.3	13 0.9	8 4.6	14 52.7	18 44.6
16 W	11 41 50.8	2 31.5	23 25.4	23 39.4	9 30.9	16 48.7	20 55.9	18 7.8	13 5.2	8 0.4	14 54.1	18 42.5
19 S	11 53 40.4	1 21.8	23 25.2	15 51.4	9 7.0	16 11.3	20 33.5	18 7.0	13 9.2	7 56.2	14 55.6	18 40.4
22 T	12 5 30.1	0 11.8	23 25.0	0 49.8	8 8.4	15 29.7	20 10.1	18 5.7	13 13.1	7 52.0	14 57.1	18 38.4
25 F	12 17 19.8	0S58.3	23 24.8	15N15.4	6 40.8	14 43.9	19 45.7	18 4.1	13 16.7	7 47.9	14 58.7	18 36.4
28 M	12 29 9.4	2 8.4	23 24.6	24 0.3	4 51.5	13 54.1	19 20.4	18 2.0	13 20.1	7 43.9	15 0.3	18 34.6

OCTOBER 1964

DAY	EPHEMERIS SIDEREAL TIME	☉	☊	☽	☿	♀	♂	♃	♄	♅	♆	♇
					LONGITUDE at NOON							
1 T	12 40 59.1	8♎20.1	26♓49.1	15♌45.3	27♍19.5	25♌10.8	9♌53.4	25♉39.7	29♒ 8.9	12♍12.0	16♏10.6	14♍51.2
2 F	12 44 55.6	9 19.1	26 46.0	29 35.4	29 6.3	26 18.5	10 29.1	25R36.3	29R 6.0	12 15.5	16 12.4	14 53.2
3 S	12 48 52.2	10 18.2	26 42.8	13♍17.1	0♎53.4	27 26.4	11 4.7	25 32.7	29 3.2	12 18.9	16 14.3	14 55.1
4 S	12 52 48.7	11 17.3	26 39.6	26 47.7	2 40.7	28 34.5	11 40.2	25 28.9	29 0.4	12 22.4	16 16.2	14 57.1
5 M	12 56 45.3	12 16.5	26 36.4	10♎ 4.5	4 28.0	29 42.7	12 15.6	25 24.9	28 57.7	12 25.8	16 18.2	14 59.0
6 T	13 0 41.8	13 15.7	26 33.2	23 5.5	6 15.2	0♍51.2	12 51.0	25 20.7	28 55.1	12 29.1	16 20.1	15 0.9
7 W	13 4 38.4	14 14.9	26 30.1	5♏49.5	8 2.1	1 59.8	13 26.2	25 16.3	28 52.6	12 32.5	16 22.1	15 2.8
8 T	13 8 34.9	15 14.2	26 26.9	18 16.8	9 48.6	3 8.5	14 1.3	25 11.8	28 50.2	12 35.8	16 24.0	15 4.7
9 F	13 12 31.5	16 13.5	26 23.7	0♐28.9	11 34.6	4 17.5	14 36.4	25 7.1	28 47.9	12 39.2	16 26.1	15 6.7
10 S	13 16 28.0	17 12.9	26 20.5	12 28.5	13 20.2	5 26.6	15 11.3	25 2.3	28 45.7	12 42.5	16 28.1	15 8.5
11 S	13 20 24.6	18 12.2	26 17.4	24 19.7	15 5.1	6 35.8	15 46.2	24 57.2	28 43.5	12 45.7	16 30.1	15 10.4
12 M	13 24 21.2	19 11.6	26 14.2	6♑ 7.2	16 49.4	7 45.2	16 20.9	24 52.0	28 41.4	12 48.9	16 32.1	15 12.2
13 T	13 28 17.7	20 11.0	26 11.0	17 56.1	18 33.1	8 54.8	16 55.5	24 46.6	28 39.5	12 52.1	16 34.2	15 14.0
14 W	13 32 14.3	21 10.5	26 7.8	29 51.9	20 16.1	10 4.5	17 30.0	24 41.0	28 37.6	12 55.3	16 36.3	15 15.8
15 T	13 36 10.8	22 10.0	26 4.6	12♒ 0.2	21 58.5	11 14.3	18 4.4	24 35.3	28 35.8	12 58.4	16 38.3	15 17.6
16 F	13 40 7.4	23 9.5	26 1.5	24 25.7	23 40.2	12 24.3	18 38.7	24 29.5	28 34.1	13 1.5	16 40.4	15 19.4
17 S	13 44 3.9	24 9.0	25 58.3	7♓12.3	25 21.3	13 34.4	19 12.9	24 23.5	28 32.5	13 4.6	16 42.5	15 21.1
18 S	13 48 0.5	25 8.6	25 55.1	20 22.5	27 1.7	14 44.7	19 47.0	24 17.3	28 31.0	13 7.7	16 44.6	15 22.8
19 M	13 51 57.0	26 8.2	25 51.9	3♈56.9	28 41.5	15 55.1	20 20.9	24 11.0	28 29.6	13 10.7	16 46.8	15 24.6
20 T	13 55 53.6	27 7.8	25 48.8	17 53.6	0♏20.6	17 5.6	20 54.8	24 4.6	28 28.3	13 13.6	16 48.9	15 26.2
21 W	13 59 50.1	28 7.5	25 45.6	2♉ 8.7	1 59.1	18 16.3	21 28.5	23 58.0	28 27.1	13 16.6	16 51.1	15 27.9
22 T	14 3 46.7	29 7.2	25 42.4	16 36.5	3 37.0	19 27.1	22 2.2	23 51.3	28 26.0	13 19.5	16 53.2	15 29.6
23 F	14 7 43.2	0♏ 6.9	25 39.2	1♊10.5	5 14.3	20 38.0	22 35.7	23 44.5	28 25.0	13 22.4	16 55.4	15 31.2
24 S	14 11 39.8	1 6.7	25 36.1	15 44.5	6 51.1	21 49.0	23 9.1	23 37.6	28 24.1	13 25.2	16 57.6	15 32.8
25 S	14 15 36.4	2 6.5	25 32.9	0♋13.2	8 27.2	23 0.2	23 42.4	23 30.5	28 23.3	13 28.0	16 59.7	15 34.4
26 M	14 19 32.9	3 6.3	25 29.7	14 32.9	10 2.9	24 11.5	24 15.5	23 23.3	28 22.6	13 30.8	17 1.9	15 35.9
27 T	14 23 29.5	4 6.2	25 26.5	28 41.3	11 38.0	25 22.9	24 48.6	23 16.1	28 22.0	13 33.5	17 4.1	15 37.5
28 W	14 27 26.0	5 6.1	25 23.3	12♌37.6	13 12.7	26 34.4	25 21.5	23 8.7	28 21.5	13 36.2	17 6.3	15 39.0
29 T	14 31 22.6	6 6.0	25 20.2	26 21.3	14 46.8	27 46.1	25 54.3	23 1.2	28 21.1	13 38.9	17 8.5	15 40.5
30 F	14 35 19.1	7 6.1	25 17.0	9♍52.7	16 20.6	28 57.9	26 27.0	22 53.7	28 20.9	13 41.5	17 10.8	15 42.0
31 S	14 39 15.7	8 6.1	25 13.8	23 11.7	17 53.8	0♎ 9.7	26 59.5	22 46.1	28 20.7	13 44.1	17 13.0	15 43.5
					DECLINATION at NOON							
1 T	12 40 59.1	3S18.4	23N24.3	19N45.1	2N47.6	13N 0.3	18N54.3	17N59.5	13S23.2	7N39.9	15S 2.0	18N32.8
4 S	12 52 48.7	4 28.0	23 24.1	5 52.8	0 35.0	12 2.9	18 27.4	17 56.7	13 26.0	7 36.0	15 3.7	18 31.2
7 W	13 4 38.4	5 37.2	23 23.9	9S49.8	1S41.5	11 2.0	17 59.8	17 53.4	13 28.5	7 32.2	15 5.5	18 29.6
10 S	13 16 28.0	6 45.7	23 23.6	21 10.5	3 58.6	9 57.9	17 31.6	17 49.8	13 30.8	7 28.4	15 7.3	18 28.1
13 T	13 28 17.7	7 53.4	23 23.3	24 11.4	6 13.9	8 50.7	17 2.8	17 45.9	13 32.7	7 24.8	15 9.1	18 26.7
16 F	13 40 7.4	9 0.1	23 23.1	17 30.1	8 25.6	7 40.7	16 33.6	17 41.6	13 34.4	7 21.3	15 10.9	18 25.5
19 M	13 51 57.0	10 5.6	23 22.8	3 2.1	10 32.8	6 28.3	16 3.9	17 36.9	13 35.7	7 17.8	15 12.8	18 24.3
22 T	14 3 46.7	11 9.8	23 22.5	13N48.2	12 34.3	5 13.5	15 33.8	17 32.0	13 36.7	7 14.5	15 14.6	18 23.3
25 S	14 15 36.4	12 12.5	23 22.1	23 58.8	14 29.5	3 56.9	15 3.5	17 26.9	13 37.4	7 11.3	15 16.5	18 22.4
28 W	14 27 26.0	13 13.5	23 21.8	20 42.6	16 17.7	2 38.5	14 32.9	17 21.4	13 37.7	7 8.3	15 18.4	18 21.6
31 S	14 39 15.7	14 12.7	23 21.5	7 25.1	17 58.6	1 18.7	14 2.1	17 15.8	13 37.7	7 5.3	15 20.3	18 20.9

NOVEMBER 1964

LONGITUDE at NOON

DAY	EPHEMERIS SIDEREAL TIME h m s	☉ ° ′	☊ ° ′	☽ ° ′	☿ ° ′	♀ ° ′	♂ ° ′	♃ ° ′	♄ ° ′	♅ ° ′	♆ ° ′	♇ ° ′
1 S	14 43 12.2	9♏ 6.2	25♓10.6	6♎18.1	19♏26.6	1♎21.7	27♌31.9	22♉38.3	28♒20.6	13♍46.6	17♏15.3	15♍44.9
2 M	14 47 8.8	10 6.3	25 7.5	19 11.9	20 58.9	2 33.7	28 4.1	22R30.5	28 20.6	13 49.1	17 17.5	15 46.3
3 T	14 51 5.3	11 6.4	25 4.3	1♏52.6	22 30.8	3 45.9	28 36.2	22 22.7	28D20.7	13 51.6	17 19.7	15 47.7
4 W	14 55 1.9	12 6.5	25 1.1	14 20.4	24 2.3	4 58.1	29 8.2	22 14.8	28 21.0	13 54.0	17 22.0	15 49.1
5 T	14 58 58.5	13 6.7	24 57.9	26 35.8	25 33.4	6 10.4	29 40.0	22 6.8	28 21.3	13 56.3	17 24.2	15 50.4
6 F	15 2 55.0	14 6.9	24 54.7	8♐40.1	27 4.1	7 22.9	0♍11.7	21 58.7	28 21.7	13 58.7	17 26.5	15 51.7
7 S	15 6 51.6	15 7.2	24 51.6	20 35.3	28 34.4	8 35.4	0 43.2	21 50.7	28 22.3	14 0.9	17 28.7	15 53.0
8 S	15 10 48.1	16 7.5	24 48.4	2♑24.3	0♐ 4.3	9 48.0	1 14.5	21 42.6	28 22.9	14 3.2	17 31.0	15 54.2
9 M	15 14 44.7	17 7.8	24 45.2	14 10.6	1 33.7	11 0.6	1 45.7	21 34.4	28 23.7	14 5.3	17 33.2	15 55.4
10 T	15 18 41.2	18 8.1	24 42.0	25 58.5	3 2.7	12 13.4	2 16.8	21 26.3	28 24.5	14 7.5	17 35.4	15 56.6
11 W	15 22 37.8	19 8.4	24 38.9	7♒52.9	4 31.3	13 26.2	2 47.7	21 18.1	28 25.5	14 9.6	17 37.7	15 57.8
12 T	15 26 34.4	20 8.8	24 35.7	19 58.8	5 59.4	14 39.1	3 18.4	21 9.9	28 26.5	14 11.6	17 39.9	15 58.9
13 F	15 30 30.9	21 9.2	24 32.5	2♓21.3	7 27.0	15 52.1	3 48.9	21 1.8	28 27.7	14 13.6	17 42.2	16 0.0
14 S	15 34 27.5	22 9.6	24 29.3	15 4.9	8 54.1	17 5.1	4 19.3	20 53.6	28 29.0	14 15.6	17 44.4	16 1.1
15 S	15 38 24.0	23 10.0	24 26.2	28 13.5	10 20.6	18 18.2	4 49.5	20 45.4	28 30.4	14 17.5	17 46.7	16 2.2
16 M	15 42 20.6	24 10.5	24 23.0	11♈48.9	11 46.5	19 31.4	5 19.6	20 37.3	28 31.8	14 19.3	17 48.9	16 3.2
17 T	15 46 17.1	25 11.0	24 19.8	25 51.2	13 11.7	20 44.6	5 49.4	20 29.1	28 33.4	14 21.1	17 51.2	16 4.2
18 W	15 50 13.7	26 11.5	24 16.6	10♉17.5	14 36.2	21 58.0	6 19.1	20 21.0	28 35.1	14 22.9	17 53.4	16 5.2
19 T	15 54 10.2	27 12.0	24 13.4	25 2.6	15 59.8	23 11.3	6 48.6	20 13.0	28 36.9	14 24.6	17 55.6	16 6.1
20 F	15 58 6.8	28 12.6	24 10.3	9♊59.1	17 22.6	24 24.8	7 18.0	20 5.0	28 38.8	14 26.3	17 57.9	16 7.1
21 S	16 2 3.4	29 13.2	24 7.1	24 58.4	18 44.3	25 38.4	7 47.1	19 57.0	28 40.8	14 27.9	18 0.1	16 8.0
22 S	16 5 59.9	0♐13.8	24 3.9	9♋52.3	20 4.8	26 51.9	8 16.0	19 49.1	28 42.9	14 29.4	18 2.3	16 8.8
23 M	16 9 56.5	1 14.5	24 0.7	24 34.1	21 24.0	28 5.6	8 44.8	19 41.2	28 45.1	14 30.9	18 4.5	16 9.6
24 T	16 13 53.0	2 15.1	23 57.6	8♌58.7	22 41.6	29 19.3	9 13.3	19 33.4	28 47.3	14 32.4	18 6.7	16 10.4
25 W	16 17 49.6	3 15.8	23 54.4	23 3.6	23 57.6	0♏33.0	9 41.6	19 25.7	28 49.7	14 33.8	18 8.9	16 11.2
26 T	16 21 46.1	4 16.5	23 51.2	6♍47.8	25 11.6	1 46.8	10 9.8	19 18.0	28 52.2	14 35.1	18 11.1	16 11.9
27 F	16 25 42.7	5 17.3	23 48.0	20 12.0	26 23.3	3 0.7	10 37.7	19 10.5	28 54.8	14 36.4	18 13.3	16 12.6
28 S	16 29 39.3	6 18.0	23 44.9	3♎17.7	27 32.4	4 14.6	11 5.4	19 3.0	28 57.4	14 37.7	18 15.4	16 13.3
29 S	16 33 35.8	7 18.8	23 41.7	16 6.8	28 38.6	5 28.6	11 32.9	18 55.6	29 0.2	14 38.8	18 17.6	16 13.9
30 M	16 37 32.4	8 19.7	23 38.5	28 41.5	29 41.4	6 42.6	12 0.1	18 48.3	29 3.1	14 40.0	18 19.7	16 14.5

DECLINATION at NOON

DAY	EPHEMERIS SIDEREAL TIME h m s	☉ ° ′	☊ ° ′	☽ ° ′	☿ ° ′	♀ ° ′	♂ ° ′	♃ ° ′	♄ ° ′	♅ ° ′	♆ ° ′	♇ ° ′
1 S	14 43 12.2	14S31.9	23N21.4	2N 6.5	18S30.4	0N51.9	13N51.9	17N13.9	13S37.6	7N 4.4	15S20.9	18N20.7
4 W	14 55 1.9	15 28.3	23 21.0	13S 1.3	20 0.4	0S29.2	13 21.0	17 8.0	13 37.2	7 1.7	15 22.8	18 20.2
7 S	15 6 51.6	16 22.5	23 20.6	22 51.3	21 21.5	1 50.9	12 50.2	17 2.0	13 36.4	6 59.1	15 24.7	18 19.8
10 T	15 18 41.2	17 14.1	23 20.3	23 43.2	22 33.2	3 12.8	12 19.5	16 56.0	13 35.3	6 56.7	15 26.6	18 19.6
13 F	15 30 30.9	18 3.0	23 19.9	15 11.0	23 34.8	4 34.8	11 48.9	16 49.9	13 33.9	6 54.4	15 28.5	18 19.4
16 M	15 42 20.6	18 49.1	23 19.5	0N 6.5	24 25.7	5 56.4	11 18.6	16 43.8	13 32.2	6 52.3	15 30.3	18 19.4
19 T	15 54 10.2	19 32.2	23 19.1	16 37.8	25 5.2	7 17.3	10 48.6	16 37.7	13 30.1	6 50.4	15 32.2	18 19.6
22 S	16 5 59.9	20 12.2	23 18.7	24 35.7	25 32.8	8 37.2	10 18.9	16 31.8	13 27.7	6 48.6	15 34.0	18 19.8
25 W	16 17 49.6	20 48.7	23 18.2	18 8.3	25 47.8	9 55.6	9 49.7	16 26.0	13 25.0	6 47.1	15 35.8	18 20.2
28 S	16 29 39.3	21 21.8	23 17.8	3 27.0	25 50.0	11 12.4	9 21.0	16 20.4	13 22.0	6 45.7	15 37.5	18 20.7

DECEMBER 1964

LONGITUDE at NOON

DAY	EPHEMERIS SIDEREAL TIME h m s	☉ ° ′	☊ ° ′	☽ ° ′	☿ ° ′	♀ ° ′	♂ ° ′	♃ ° ′	♄ ° ′	♅ ° ′	♆ ° ′	♇ ° ′
1 T	16 41 28.9	9♐20.5	23♓35.3	11♏ 3.7	0♑40.4	7♏56.7	12♍27.1	18♉41.1	29♒ 6.0	14♍41.0	18♏21.9	16♍15.1
2 W	16 45 25.5	10 21.4	23 32.1	23 15.3	1 34.9	9 10.8	12 53.9	18R34.0	29 9.1	14 42.1	18 24.0	16 15.6
3 T	16 49 22.0	11 22.3	23 29.0	5♐18.0	2 24.3	10 25.0	13 20.4	18 27.0	29 12.2	14 43.0	18 26.1	16 16.1
4 F	16 53 18.6	12 23.2	23 25.8	17 13.6	3 8.0	11 39.2	13 46.6	18 20.2	29 15.5	14 43.9	18 28.2	16 16.6
5 S	16 57 15.2	13 24.1	23 22.6	29 4.0	3 45.3	12 53.4	14 12.7	18 13.5	29 18.8	14 44.8	18 30.3	16 17.0
6 S	17 1 11.7	14 25.0	23 19.4	10♑51.3	4 15.2	14 7.7	14 38.4	18 6.9	29 22.2	14 45.6	18 32.4	16 17.4
7 M	17 5 8.3	15 26.0	23 16.3	22 38.2	4 37.0	15 22.0	15 3.9	18 0.5	29 25.8	14 46.3	18 34.4	16 17.8
8 T	17 9 4.8	16 26.9	23 13.1	4♒27.5	4 49.8	16 36.3	15 29.1	17 54.2	29 29.4	14 47.0	18 36.5	16 18.2
9 W	17 13 1.4	17 27.9	23 9.9	16 22.9	4 52.8	17 50.7	15 54.1	17 48.0	29 33.1	14 47.6	18 38.5	16 18.5
10 T	17 16 58.0	18 28.9	23 6.7	28 28.2	4R45.2	19 5.1	16 18.7	17 42.0	29 36.8	14 48.2	18 40.5	16 18.7
11 F	17 20 54.5	19 29.9	23 3.6	10♓47.8	4 26.5	20 19.6	16 43.1	17 36.2	29 40.8	14 48.8	18 42.6	16 19.0
12 S	17 24 51.1	20 30.9	23 0.4	23 25.9	3 56.2	21 34.0	17 7.2	17 30.5	29 44.7	14 49.2	18 44.6	16 19.2
13 S	17 28 47.6	21 32.0	22 57.2	6♈26.5	3 14.5	22 48.5	17 31.0	17 25.0	29 48.8	14 49.6	18 46.5	16 19.4
14 M	17 32 44.2	22 33.0	22 54.0	19 52.9	2 21.7	24 3.0	17 54.5	17 19.6	29 52.9	14 50.0	18 48.5	16 19.6
15 T	17 36 40.7	23 34.0	22 50.9	3♉46.7	1 18.9	25 17.6	18 17.6	17 14.4	29 57.1	14 50.3	18 50.4	16 19.7
16 W	17 40 37.3	24 35.0	22 47.7	18 7.7	0 7.6	26 32.1	18 40.5	17 9.4	0♓ 1.4	14 50.5	18 52.3	16 19.8
17 T	17 44 33.9	25 36.1	22 44.5	2♊52.6	28♐49.8	27 46.7	19 3.0	17 4.5	0 5.7	14 50.7	18 54.2	16 19.8
18 F	17 48 30.4	26 37.1	22 41.3	17 55.7	27 28.1	29 1.4	19 25.2	16 59.9	0 10.2	14 50.8	18 56.1	16 19.8
19 S	17 52 27.0	27 38.2	22 38.1	3♋ 8.7	26 5.2	0♐16.0	19 47.1	16 55.4	0 14.7	14 50.8	18 58.0	16 19.8
20 S	17 56 23.5	28 39.3	22 35.0	18 21.6	24 43.8	1 30.7	20 8.7	16 51.1	0 19.3	14 50.8	18 59.8	16R19.7
21 M	18 0 20.1	29 40.4	22 31.8	3♌25.0	23 26.7	2 45.4	20 29.8	16 46.9	0 24.0	14 50.8	19 1.6	16 19.7
22 T	18 4 16.6	0♑41.5	22 28.6	18 10.5	22 16.1	4 0.1	20 50.7	16 43.0	0 28.8	14R50.7	19 3.4	16 19.5
23 W	18 8 13.2	1 42.6	22 25.4	2♍32.5	21 13.9	5 14.8	21 11.1	16 39.3	0 33.6	14 50.5	19 5.2	16 19.4
24 T	18 12 9.8	2 43.7	22 22.3	16 28.2	20 21.3	6 29.6	21 31.2	16 35.7	0 38.5	14 50.3	19 7.0	16 19.2
25 F	18 16 6.3	3 44.8	22 19.1	29 57.3	19 39.1	7 44.4	21 50.9	16 32.3	0 43.5	14 50.0	19 8.7	16 19.0
26 S	18 20 2.9	4 45.9	22 15.9	13♎ 1.5	19 7.5	8 59.2	22 10.3	16 29.2	0 48.6	14 49.7	19 10.4	16 18.8
27 S	18 23 59.4	5 47.1	22 12.7	25 44.0	18 46.7	10 14.0	22 29.2	16 26.2	0 53.7	14 49.3	19 12.1	16 18.5
28 M	18 27 56.0	6 48.2	22 9.6	8♏ 8.4	18 36.1	11 28.9	22 47.7	16 23.4	0 58.9	14 48.9	19 13.8	16 18.2
29 T	18 31 52.6	7 49.4	22 6.4	20 18.8	18 35.2	12 43.7	23 5.7	16 20.9	1 4.2	14 48.4	19 15.4	16 17.8
30 W	18 35 49.1	8 50.6	22 3.2	2♐18.8	18D43.4	13 58.6	23 23.4	16 18.5	1 9.5	14 47.8	19 17.0	16 17.5
31 T	18 39 45.7	9 51.7	22 0.0	14 11.8	18 59.9	15 13.5	23 40.6	16 16.3	1 14.9	14 47.2	19 18.6	16 17.1

DECLINATION at NOON

DAY	EPHEMERIS SIDEREAL TIME h m s	☉ ° ′	☊ ° ′	☽ ° ′	☿ ° ′	♀ ° ′	♂ ° ′	♃ ° ′	♄ ° ′	♅ ° ′	♆ ° ′	♇ ° ′
1 T	16 41 28.9	21S51.3	23N17.3	11S47.3	25S39.4	12S27.0	8N53.0	16N15.0	13S18.7	6N44.5	15S39.2	18N21.3
4 F	16 53 18.6	22 17.0	23 16.9	22 18.2	25 16.6	13 39.2	8 25.6	16 9.8	13 15.1	6 43.5	15 40.9	18 22.1
7 M	17 5 8.3	22 38.8	23 16.4	24 8.1	24 42.5	14 48.6	7 59.1	16 5.0	13 11.2	6 42.7	15 42.5	18 23.0
10 T	17 16 58.0	22 56.7	23 15.9	16 31.7	23 58.7	15 54.8	7 33.4	16 0.6	13 7.1	6 42.1	15 44.1	18 24.0
13 S	17 28 47.6	23 10.4	23 15.4	2 10.7	23 6.8	16 57.4	7 8.7	15 56.5	13 2.6	6 41.7	15 45.7	18 25.1
16 W	17 40 37.3	23 20.0	23 14.9	14N18.8	22 9.2	17 56.1	6 45.0	15 52.9	12 57.9	6 41.5	15 47.2	18 26.4
19 S	17 52 27.0	23 25.3	23 14.4	24 20.4	21 11.8	18 50.6	6 22.5	15 49.7	12 52.9	6 41.5	15 48.6	18 27.7
22 T	18 4 16.6	23 26.5	23 13.8	19 31.2	20 25.1	19 40.6	6 1.2	15 47.0	12 47.7	6 41.6	15 50.0	18 29.2
25 F	18 16 6.3	23 23.4	23 13.3	4 50.3	19 59.2	20 25.7	5 41.3	15 44.8	12 42.3	6 42.0	15 51.3	18 30.8
28 M	18 27 56.0	23 16.1	23 12.7	10S41.1	19 56.8	21 5.6	5 22.8	15 43.0	12 36.6	6 42.6	15 52.5	18 32.4
31 T	18 39 45.7	23 4.6	23 12.1	21 41.9	20 13.6	21 40.1	5 5.8	15 41.8	12 30.7	6 43.3	15 53.7	18 34.2

JANUARY 1965

DAY	EPHEMERIS SIDEREAL TIME	☉	☊	☽	☿	♀	♂	♃	♄	♅	♆	♇
	h m s	° '	° '	° '	° '	° '	° '	° '	° '	° '	° '	° '
LONGITUDE at NOON												
1 F	18 43 42.2	10♑53.0	21♊56.9	26♐ 0.7	19♐24.1	16♐28.5	23♍57.4	16♉14.4	1♓20.4	14♍46.6	19♏20.2	16♍16.7
2 S	18 47 38.8	11 54.1	21 53.7	7♑48.1	19 55.0	17 43.4	24 13.7	16R12.7	1 26.0	14R45.9	19 21.8	16R16.2
3 S	18 51 35.3	12 55.3	21 50.5	19 36.1	20 32.1	18 58.3	24 29.5	16 11.1	1 31.6	14 45.1	19 23.3	16 15.7
4 M	18 55 31.9	13 56.5	21 47.3	1♒26.7	21 14.7	20 13.3	24 44.9	16 9.8	1 37.2	14 44.3	19 24.8	16 15.2
5 T	18 59 28.5	14 57.7	21 44.1	13 21.9	22 2.3	21 28.2	24 59.7	16 8.7	1 42.9	14 43.4	19 26.2	16 14.6
6 W	19 3 25.0	15 58.8	21 41.0	25 23.7	22 54.3	22 43.2	25 14.1	16 7.8	1 48.7	14 42.4	19 27.7	16 14.0
7 T	19 7 21.6	16 60.0	21 37.8	7♓34.6	23 50.1	23 58.2	25 27.9	16 7.1	1 54.6	14 41.5	19 29.1	16 13.4
8 F	19 11 18.1	18 1.2	21 34.6	19 57.2	24 49.5	25 13.1	25 41.2	16 6.6	2 0.5	14 40.4	19 30.5	16 12.8
9 S	19 15 14.7	19 2.3	21 31.4	2♈34.6	25 52.0	26 28.1	25 54.0	16 6.3	2 6.4	14 39.3	19 31.8	16 12.1
10 S	19 19 11.2	20 3.4	21 28.3	15 30.0	26 57.2	27 43.1	26 6.3	16 6.2	2 12.5	14 38.2	19 33.1	16 11.4
11 M	19 23 7.8	21 4.6	21 25.1	28 46.4	28 5.0	28 58.1	26 18.0	16D 6.3	2 18.5	14 37.0	19 34.4	16 10.6
12 T	19 27 4.4	22 5.7	21 21.9	12♉26.4	29 15.0	0♑13.1	26 29.1	16 6.7	2 24.6	14 35.8	19 35.7	16 9.9
13 W	19 31 0.9	23 6.8	21 18.7	26 31.5	0♑27.0	1 28.1	26 39.7	16 7.2	2 30.8	14 34.5	19 37.0	16 9.1
14 T	19 34 57.5	24 7.9	21 15.6	11♊ 1.1	1 40.9	2 43.1	26 49.7	16 8.0	2 37.0	14 33.1	19 38.2	16 8.3
15 F	19 38 54.0	25 9.0	21 12.4	25 52.2	2 56.4	3 58.1	26 59.1	16 8.9	2 43.3	14 31.8	19 39.3	16 7.4
16 S	19 42 50.6	26 10.1	21 9.2	10♋59.0	4 13.4	5 13.1	27 7.9	16 10.1	2 49.6	14 30.3	19 40.5	16 6.5
17 S	19 46 47.2	27 11.1	21 6.0	26 12.8	5 31.8	6 28.1	27 16.1	16 11.4	2 56.0	14 28.8	19 41.6	16 5.6
18 M	19 50 43.7	28 12.2	21 2.8	11♌23.7	6 51.5	7 43.1	27 23.7	16 13.0	3 2.4	14 27.3	19 42.7	16 4.7
19 T	19 54 40.3	29 13.3	20 59.7	26 21.5	8 12.3	8 58.2	27 30.7	16 14.8	3 8.9	14 25.8	19 43.8	16 3.8
20 W	19 58 36.8	0♒14.3	20 56.5	10♍57.9	9 34.3	10 13.2	27 37.0	16 16.8	3 15.4	14 24.1	19 44.8	16 2.8
21 T	20 2 33.4	1 15.3	20 53.3	25 7.2	10 57.3	11 28.2	27 42.6	16 18.9	3 21.9	14 22.5	19 45.8	16 1.8
22 F	20 6 29.9	2 16.4	20 50.1	8♎47.1	12 21.3	12 43.3	27 47.6	16 21.4	3 28.6	14 20.8	19 46.8	16 0.8
23 S	20 10 26.5	3 17.4	20 47.0	21 58.2	13 46.1	13 58.4	27 51.9	16 23.9	3 35.2	14 19.1	19 47.7	15 59.7
24 S	20 14 23.0	4 18.4	20 43.8	4♏43.4	15 11.9	15 13.4	27 55.5	16 26.7	3 41.9	14 17.3	19 48.7	15 58.7
25 M	20 18 19.6	5 19.4	20 40.6	17 6.9	16 38.5	16 28.5	27 58.4	16 29.7	3 48.6	14 15.5	19 49.5	15 57.6
26 T	20 22 16.2	6 20.4	20 37.4	29 13.7	18 5.9	17 43.5	28 0.5	16 32.8	3 55.3	14 13.6	19 50.4	15 56.4
27 W	20 26 12.7	7 21.4	20 34.3	11♐ 9.0	19 34.0	18 58.6	28 2.0	16 36.2	4 2.1	14 11.7	19 51.2	15 55.3
28 T	20 30 9.3	8 22.4	20 31.1	22 57.4	21 3.0	20 13.6	28 2.7	16 39.7	4 8.9	14 9.8	19 51.9	15 54.1
29 F	20 34 5.8	9 23.3	20 27.9	4♑43.4	22 32.7	21 28.7	28R 2.6	16 43.5	4 15.8	14 7.8	19 52.7	15 52.9
30 S	20 38 2.4	10 24.3	20 24.7	16 30.5	24 3.1	22 43.8	28 1.8	16 47.4	4 22.7	14 5.8	19 53.4	15 51.7
31 S	20 41 58.9	11 25.2	20 21.5	28 21.7	25 34.3	23 58.8	28 0.3	16 51.5	4 29.6	14 3.7	19 54.1	15 50.5
DECLINATION at NOON												
1 F	18 43 42.2	22S59.9	23N12.0	23S39.5	20S22.3	21S50.4	5N 0.5	15N41.6	12S28.7	6N43.6	15S54.2	18N34.8
4 M	18 55 31.9	22 42.9	23 11.4	23 2.0	20 53.7	22 17.3	4 45.8	15 41.1	12 22.5	6 44.6	15 55.3	18 36.7
7 T	19 7 21.6	22 21.8	23 10.8	13 25.0	21 28.6	22 38.2	4 32.9	15 41.1	12 16.2	6 45.8	15 56.3	18 38.6
10 S	19 19 11.2	21 56.7	23 10.2	1N38.7	22 2.4	22 52.9	4 22.0	15 41.7	12 9.6	6 47.2	15 57.2	18 40.7
13 W	19 31 0.9	21 27.9	23 9.6	17 7.9	22 31.7	23 1.5	4 13.0	15 42.8	12 2.9	6 48.7	15 58.1	18 42.8
16 S	19 42 50.6	20 55.3	23 8.9	24 37.4	22 54.1	23 3.7	4 6.2	15 44.5	11 56.0	6 50.4	15 58.9	18 44.9
19 T	19 54 40.3	20 19.1	23 8.3	17 6.6	23 8.0	22 59.6	4 1.5	15 46.7	11 48.9	6 52.3	15 59.6	18 47.1
22 F	20 6 29.9	19 39.4	23 7.6	1 5.2	23 12.3	22 49.1	3 59.2	15 49.4	11 41.7	6 54.3	16 0.3	18 49.4
25 M	20 18 19.6	18 56.5	23 7.0	14S 5.0	23 6.1	22 32.4	3 59.4	15 52.6	11 34.3	6 56.4	16 0.8	18 51.7
28 T	20 30 9.3	18 10.5	23 6.3	23 19.3	22 48.7	22 9.5	4 2.0	15 56.2	11 26.9	6 58.7	16 1.3	18 54.0
31 S	20 41 58.9	17 21.5	23 5.6	23 28.0	22 19.7	21 40.5	4 7.2	16 0.4	11 19.3	7 1.1	16 1.7	18 56.4

FEBRUARY 1965

DAY	EPHEMERIS SIDEREAL TIME	☉	☊	☽	☿	♀	♂	♃	♄	♅	♆	♇
LONGITUDE at NOON												
1 M	20 45 55.5	12♒26.1	20♊18.4	10♒19.1	27♑ 6.2	25♑13.9	27♍57.9	16♉55.8	4♓36.5	14♍ 1.6	19♏54.7	15♍49.2
2 T	20 49 52.1	13 27.0	20 15.2	22 24.2	28 38.9	26 28.9	27R54.8	17 0.3	4 43.5	13R59.5	19 55.3	15R48.0
3 W	20 53 48.6	14 27.9	20 12.0	4♓38.3	0♒12.2	27 44.0	27 50.9	17 5.0	4 50.5	13 57.4	19 55.9	15 46.7
4 T	20 57 45.2	15 28.7	20 8.8	17 2.2	1 46.3	28 59.1	27 46.2	17 9.9	4 57.5	13 55.2	19 56.4	15 45.4
5 F	21 1 41.7	16 29.6	20 5.7	29 36.8	3 21.2	0♒14.1	27 40.8	17 14.9	5 4.6	13 52.9	19 56.9	15 44.0
6 S	21 5 38.3	17 30.4	20 2.5	12♈23.3	4 56.8	1 29.1	27 34.5	17 20.1	5 11.7	13 50.7	19 57.4	15 42.7
7 S	21 9 34.8	18 31.2	19 59.3	25 23.3	6 33.2	2 44.2	27 27.4	17 25.5	5 18.8	13 48.4	19 57.8	15 41.3
8 M	21 13 31.4	19 31.9	19 56.1	8♉38.5	8 10.3	3 59.2	27 19.6	17 31.1	5 25.9	13 46.1	19 58.2	15 39.9
9 T	21 17 27.9	20 32.7	19 53.0	22 10.9	9 48.2	5 14.2	27 11.0	17 36.8	5 33.1	13 43.8	19 58.6	15 38.6
10 W	21 21 24.5	21 33.4	19 49.8	6♊ 2.2	11 26.9	6 29.2	27 1.6	17 42.7	5 40.2	13 41.4	19 58.9	15 37.1
11 T	21 25 21.1	22 34.1	19 46.6	20 13.3	13 6.5	7 44.2	26 51.4	17 48.8	5 47.4	13 39.1	19 59.2	15 35.7
12 F	21 29 17.6	23 34.8	19 43.4	4♋43.3	14 46.9	8 59.3	26 40.5	17 55.1	5 54.7	13 36.7	19 59.6	15 34.3
13 S	21 33 14.2	24 35.4	19 40.2	19 29.1	16 28.1	10 14.3	26 28.8	18 1.5	6 1.9	13 34.3	19 59.8	15 32.9
14 S	21 37 10.7	25 36.0	19 37.1	4♌25.2	18 10.1	11 29.3	26 16.4	18 8.1	6 9.1	13 31.8	19 60.0	15 31.4
15 M	21 41 7.3	26 36.6	19 33.9	19 23.6	19 53.0	12 44.2	26 3.1	18 14.8	6 16.3	13 29.4	20 0.2	15 29.9
16 T	21 45 3.8	27 37.1	19 30.7	4♍15.2	21 36.8	13 59.2	25 49.2	18 21.7	6 23.6	13 26.9	20 0.3	15 28.5
17 W	21 49 0.4	28 37.6	19 27.5	18 51.1	23 21.5	15 14.2	25 34.5	18 28.7	6 30.9	13 24.4	20 0.4	15 27.0
18 T	21 52 56.9	29 38.1	19 24.4	3♎ 4.1	25 7.2	16 29.1	25 19.1	18 35.9	6 38.1	13 21.9	20 0.4	15 25.5
19 F	21 56 53.5	0♓38.6	19 21.2	16 50.1	26 53.7	17 44.1	25 3.0	18 43.3	6 45.4	13 19.3	20 0.5	15 23.9
20 S	22 0 50.0	1 39.0	19 18.0	0♏ 7.7	28 41.1	18 59.0	24 46.2	18 50.8	6 52.7	13 16.8	20 0.5	15 22.4
21 S	22 4 46.6	2 39.5	19 14.8	12 58.5	0♓29.5	20 14.0	24 28.8	18 58.4	7 0.0	13 14.2	20R 0.4	15 20.9
22 M	22 8 43.2	3 39.9	19 11.6	25 26.0	2 18.8	21 28.9	24 10.7	19 6.2	7 7.3	13 11.6	20 0.4	15 19.3
23 T	22 12 39.7	4 40.3	19 8.5	7♐35.0	4 9.0	22 43.9	23 52.0	19 14.2	7 14.6	13 9.1	20 0.3	15 17.8
24 W	22 16 36.3	5 40.6	19 5.3	19 31.1	6 0.0	23 58.8	23 32.8	19 22.3	7 22.0	13 6.5	20 0.1	15 16.2
25 T	22 20 32.8	6 41.0	19 2.1	1♑19.7	7 51.9	25 13.7	23 12.9	19 30.5	7 29.3	13 3.9	19 59.9	15 14.7
26 F	22 24 29.4	7 41.3	18 58.9	13 6.2	9 44.6	26 28.7	22 52.5	19 38.9	7 36.6	13 1.2	19 59.7	15 13.1
27 S	22 28 25.9	8 41.6	18 55.8	24 55.3	11 38.1	27 43.6	22 31.7	19 47.4	7 43.9	12 58.6	19 59.5	15 11.5
28 S	22 32 22.5	9 41.8	18 52.6	6♒51.0	13 32.2	28 58.5	22 10.3	19 56.0	7 51.2	12 56.0	19 59.2	15 9.9
DECLINATION at NOON												
1 M	20 45 55.5	17S 4.5	23N 5.4	21S20.3	22S 7.4	21S29.5	4N 9.5	16N 1.8	11S16.8	7N 2.0	16S 1.8	18N57.2
4 T	20 57 45.2	16 11.9	23 4.7	9 47.5	21 22.4	20 52.7	4 18.3	16 6.6	11 9.1	7 4.5	16 2.1	18 59.5
7 S	21 9 34.8	15 16.8	23 4.0	5N53.7	20 25.1	20 10.3	4 29.6	16 11.7	11 1.3	7 7.2	16 2.3	19 1.9
10 W	21 21 24.5	14 19.3	23 3.3	20 1.0	19 15.2	19 22.6	4 43.4	16 17.3	10 53.4	7 9.9	16 2.5	19 4.3
13 S	21 33 14.2	13 19.7	23 2.5	24 25.8	17 52.7	18 29.8	4 59.7	16 23.2	10 45.5	7 12.7	16 2.5	19 6.7
16 T	21 45 3.8	12 18.2	23 1.8	14 27.5	16 17.6	17 32.2	5 18.2	16 29.6	10 37.5	7 15.6	16 2.5	19 9.0
19 F	21 56 53.5	11 14.8	23 1.0	2S26.8	14 29.7	16 30.1	5 38.9	16 36.2	10 29.5	7 18.6	16 2.4	19 11.3
22 M	22 8 43.2	10 10.0	23 0.3	17 5.0	12 29.2	15 23.9	6 1.4	16 43.1	10 21.5	7 21.5	16 2.2	19 13.6
25 T	22 20 32.8	9 3.6	22 59.5	24 26.7	10 16.6	14 13.8	6 25.4	16 50.4	10 13.4	7 24.6	16 1.9	19 15.9
28 S	22 32 22.5	7 56.1	22 58.7	22 8.0	7 52.7	13 0.2	6 50.6	16 57.9	10 5.3	7 27.6	16 1.5	19 18.1

MARCH 1965

LONGITUDE at NOON

DAY	EPHEMERIS SIDEREAL TIME h m s	☉ ° ′	☊ ° ′	☾ ° ′	☿ ° ′	♀ ° ′	♂ ° ′	♃ ° ′	♄ ° ′	♅ ° ′	♆ ° ′	♇ ° ′
1 M	22 36 19.0	10♓42.1	18♊49.4	18♒56.1	15♓26.9	0♓13.4	21♍48.6	20♉ 4.8	7♓58.6	12♍53.4	19♏58.9	15♍ 8.3
2 T	22 40 15.6	11 42.3	18 46.2	1♓12.7	17 22.1	1 28.3	21R26.4	20 13.7	8 5.9	12R50.7	19R58.6	15R 6.8
3 W	22 44 12.1	12 42.4	18 43.0	13 41.8	19 17.6	2 43.1	21 3.9	20 22.7	8 13.2	12 48.1	19 58.2	15 5.2
4 T	22 48 8.7	13 42.6	18 39.9	26 23.4	21 13.3	3 58.0	20 41.1	20 31.9	8 20.5	12 45.5	19 57.8	15 3.6
5 F	22 52 5.2	14 42.8	18 36.7	9♈17.2	23 9.0	5 12.9	20 18.1	20 41.2	8 27.8	12 42.9	19 57.4	15 2.0
6 S	22 56 1.8	15 42.8	18 33.5	22 22.5	25 4.4	6 27.8	19 54.8	20 50.6	8 35.1	12 40.3	19 56.9	15 0.4
7 S	22 59 58.3	16 42.9	18 30.3	5♉38.5	26 59.3	7 42.6	19 31.4	21 0.2	8 42.4	12 37.7	19 56.4	14 58.9
8 M	23 3 54.9	17 42.9	18 27.2	19 5.3	28 53.3	8 57.4	19 7.8	21 9.8	8 49.7	12 35.0	19 55.9	14 57.3
9 T	23 7 51.5	18 42.9	18 24.0	2♊43.0	0♈46.1	10 12.2	18 44.1	21 19.6	8 56.9	12 32.4	19 55.3	14 55.7
10 W	23 11 48.0	19 42.8	18 20.8	16 32.1	2 37.4	11 27.0	18 20.4	21 29.5	9 4.2	12 29.8	19 54.8	14 54.1
11 T	23 15 44.6	20 42.7	18 17.6	0♋33.3	4 26.7	12 41.8	17 56.8	21 39.5	9 11.4	12 27.2	19 54.1	14 52.5
12 F	23 19 41.1	21 42.6	18 14.4	14 46.3	6 13.5	13 56.5	17 33.2	21 49.6	9 18.6	12 24.6	19 53.5	14 50.9
13 S	23 23 37.7	22 42.4	18 11.3	29 9.7	7 57.5	15 11.3	17 9.7	21 59.8	9 25.8	12 22.0	19 52.8	14 49.4
14 S	23 27 34.2	23 42.2	18 8.1	13♌40.4	9 38.1	16 26.0	16 46.3	22 10.2	9 33.0	12 19.5	19 52.1	14 47.8
15 M	23 31 30.8	24 42.0	18 4.9	28 13.4	11 14.8	17 40.7	16 23.1	22 20.6	9 40.2	12 16.9	19 51.3	14 46.2
16 T	23 35 27.3	25 41.7	18 1.7	12♍42.5	12 47.2	18 55.4	16 0.2	22 31.1	9 47.3	12 14.4	19 50.6	14 44.7
17 W	23 39 23.9	26 41.4	17 58.6	27 0.6	14 14.7	20 10.1	15 37.5	22 41.8	9 54.4	12 11.9	19 49.8	14 43.1
18 T	23 43 20.4	27 41.0	17 55.4	11♎ 1.6	15 36.9	21 24.8	15 15.2	22 52.5	10 1.5	12 9.4	19 48.9	14 41.6
19 F	23 47 17.0	28 40.6	17 52.2	24 40.9	16 53.3	22 39.4	14 53.2	23 3.4	10 8.6	12 6.9	19 48.1	14 40.0
20 S	23 51 13.5	29 40.2	17 49.0	7♏56.2	18 3.6	23 54.1	14 31.5	23 14.3	10 15.7	12 4.4	19 47.2	14 38.5
21 S	23 55 10.1	0♈39.8	17 45.8	20 47.6	19 7.3	25 8.7	14 10.3	23 25.3	10 22.7	12 1.9	19 46.3	14 37.0
22 M	23 59 6.6	1 39.3	17 42.7	3♐17.3	20 4.3	26 23.4	13 49.6	23 36.5	10 29.7	11 59.5	19 45.3	14 35.5
23 T	0 3 3.2	2 38.8	17 39.5	15 29.1	20 54.1	27 38.0	13 29.3	23 47.7	10 36.7	11 57.1	19 44.4	14 34.0
24 W	0 6 59.7	3 38.3	17 36.3	27 27.7	21 36.5	28 52.6	13 9.6	23 59.0	10 43.6	11 54.7	19 43.4	14 32.5
25 T	0 10 56.3	4 37.7	17 33.1	9♑18.6	22 11.5	0♈ 7.2	12 50.4	24 10.4	10 50.6	11 52.3	19 42.4	14 31.0
26 F	0 14 52.9	5 37.2	17 30.0	21 7.2	22 38.9	1 21.8	12 31.9	24 21.9	10 57.5	11 50.0	19 41.4	14 29.6
27 S	0 18 49.4	6 36.6	17 26.8	2♒58.7	22 58.6	2 36.4	12 13.9	24 33.5	11 4.4	11 47.7	19 40.3	14 28.1
28 S	0 22 46.0	7 35.9	17 23.6	14 58.1	23 10.7	3 50.9	11 56.5	24 45.1	11 11.2	11 45.4	19 39.2	14 26.7
29 M	0 26 42.5	8 35.2	17 20.4	27 9.2	23 15.3	5 5.5	11 39.8	24 56.9	11 18.0	11 43.1	19 38.1	14 25.3
30 T	0 30 39.1	9 34.5	17 17.2	9♓35.0	23R12.5	6 20.0	11 23.8	25 8.7	11 24.8	11 40.9	19 36.9	14 23.9
31 W	0 34 35.6	10 33.8	17 14.1	22 17.2	23 2.6	7 34.5	11 8.4	25 20.6	11 31.5	11 38.7	19 35.8	14 22.5

DECLINATION at NOON

DAY	h m s	☉	☊	☾	☿	♀	♂	♃	♄	♅	♆	♇
1 M	22 36 19.0	7S33.4	22N58.4	19S15.1	7S 2.4	12S35.0	6N59.1	17N 0.5	10S 2.7	7N28.6	16S 1.4	19N18.8
4 T	22 48 8.7	6 24.5	22 57.6	5 58.8	4 25.8	11 17.2	7 25.1	17 8.3	9 54.6	7 31.6	16 0.9	19 20.9
7 S	22 59 58.3	5 14.7	22 56.8	10N11.6	1 42.9	9 56.7	7 51.2	17 16.4	9 46.6	7 34.6	16 0.4	19 23.0
10 W	23 11 48.0	4 4.4	22 56.0	22 37.4	1N 1.9	8 33.9	8 16.8	17 24.6	9 38.6	7 37.6	15 59.8	19 24.9
13 S	23 23 37.7	2 53.7	22 55.2	23 34.0	3 42.6	7 9.0	8 41.5	17 33.0	9 30.6	7 40.6	15 59.1	19 26.8
16 T	23 35 27.3	1 42.7	22 54.3	11 23.8	6 11.9	5 42.4	9 4.8	17 41.6	9 22.8	7 43.5	15 58.4	19 28.7
19 F	23 47 17.0	0 31.6	22 53.5	5S51.4	8 22.5	4 14.4	9 26.3	17 50.3	9 15.0	7 46.3	15 57.6	19 30.4
22 M	23 59 6.6	0N39.5	22 52.6	19 39.4	10 7.5	2 45.3	9 45.8	17 59.1	9 7.3	7 49.1	15 56.7	19 32.0
25 T	0 10 56.3	1 50.4	22 51.7	25 3.5	11 21.5	1 15.6	10 2.9	18 8.0	8 59.6	7 51.8	15 55.8	19 33.6
28 S	0 22 46.0	3 0.9	22 50.8	20 27.6	12 0.9	0N14.7	10 17.4	18 17.0	8 52.1	7 54.4	15 54.8	19 35.0
31 W	0 34 35.6	4 10.9	22 49.9	7 39.9	12 3.7	1 45.0	10 29.2	18 26.0	8 44.7	7 56.9	15 53.8	19 36.3

APRIL 1965

LONGITUDE at NOON

DAY	h m s	☉	☊	☾	☿	♀	♂	♃	♄	♅	♆	♇
1 T	0 38 32.2	11♈33.0	17♊10.9	5♈16.0	22♈46.1	8♈49.0	10♍53.8	25♉32.6	11♓38.2	11♍36.5	19♏34.6	14♍21.1
2 F	0 42 28.7	12 32.2	17 7.7	18 30.7	22R23.3	10 3.5	10R40.0	25 44.6	11 44.9	11R34.4	19R33.4	14R19.7
3 S	0 46 25.3	13 31.3	17 4.5	1♉59.2	21 54.8	11 18.0	10 26.8	25 56.7	11 51.5	11 32.3	19 32.2	14 18.4
4 S	0 50 21.8	14 30.5	17 1.4	15 39.1	21 21.2	12 32.4	10 14.5	26 8.9	11 58.1	11 30.2	19 30.9	14 17.0
5 M	0 54 18.4	15 29.5	16 58.2	29 28.1	20 43.4	13 46.9	10 2.9	26 21.2	12 4.6	11 28.1	19 29.6	14 15.7
6 T	0 58 14.9	16 28.6	16 55.0	13♊23.9	20 2.1	15 1.3	9 52.1	26 33.5	12 11.1	11 26.1	19 28.3	14 14.4
7 W	1 2 11.5	17 27.6	16 51.8	27 24.9	19 18.1	16 15.7	9 42.1	26 45.9	12 17.5	11 24.1	19 27.0	14 13.1
8 T	1 6 8.0	18 26.6	16 48.6	11♋29.9	18 32.4	17 30.1	9 32.9	26 58.4	12 24.0	11 22.2	19 25.7	14 11.9
9 F	1 10 4.6	19 25.5	16 45.5	25 38.0	17 45.9	18 44.4	9 24.4	27 10.9	12 30.3	11 20.3	19 24.3	14 10.6
10 S	1 14 1.2	20 24.4	16 42.3	9♌47.9	16 59.4	19 58.8	9 16.8	27 23.5	12 36.6	11 18.4	19 23.0	14 9.4
11 S	1 17 57.7	21 23.3	16 39.1	23 57.7	16 13.9	21 13.1	9 10.0	27 36.2	12 42.9	11 16.6	19 21.6	14 8.2
12 M	1 21 54.3	22 22.1	16 35.9	8♍ 4.9	15 30.1	22 27.4	9 3.9	27 48.9	12 49.1	11 14.8	19 20.2	14 7.0
13 T	1 25 50.8	23 20.9	16 32.8	22 5.9	14 48.9	23 41.7	8 58.6	28 1.7	12 55.3	11 13.1	19 18.8	14 5.9
14 W	1 29 47.4	24 19.6	16 29.6	5♎57.0	14 10.7	24 56.0	8 54.1	28 14.5	13 1.4	11 11.4	19 17.3	14 4.7
15 T	1 33 43.9	25 18.3	16 26.4	19 34.3	13 36.3	26 10.2	8 50.4	28 27.4	13 7.5	11 9.7	19 15.9	14 3.6
16 F	1 37 40.5	26 17.0	16 23.2	2♏55.0	13 6.0	27 24.5	8 47.5	28 40.4	13 13.6	11 8.2	19 14.5	14 2.6
17 S	1 41 37.0	27 15.7	16 20.0	15 57.2	12 40.2	28 38.7	8 45.3	28 53.3	13 19.5	11 6.6	19 13.0	14 1.5
18 S	1 45 33.6	28 14.3	16 16.9	28 40.6	12 19.1	29 52.9	8 43.9	29 6.4	13 25.4	11 5.0	19 11.5	14 0.5
19 M	1 49 30.1	29 12.9	16 13.7	11♐ 6.4	12 3.0	1♉ 7.1	8 43.2	29 19.5	13 31.3	11 3.6	19 10.0	13 59.4
20 T	1 53 26.7	0♉11.4	16 10.5	23 17.0	11 52.0	2 21.3	8D43.3	29 32.6	13 37.1	11 2.1	19 8.5	13 58.4
21 W	1 57 23.2	1 10.0	16 7.3	5♑16.3	11 46.1	3 35.5	8 44.1	29 45.8	13 42.9	11 0.7	19 7.0	13 57.4
22 T	2 1 19.8	2 8.5	16 4.2	17 8.4	11 45.3	4 49.6	8 45.6	29 59.0	13 48.5	10 59.4	19 5.4	13 56.5
23 F	2 5 16.4	3 6.9	16 1.0	28 58.5	11D49.5	6 3.7	8 47.9	0♊12.3	13 54.2	10 58.0	19 3.9	13 55.6
24 S	2 9 12.9	4 5.4	15 57.8	10♒51.5	11 58.6	7 17.9	8 50.8	0 25.6	13 59.7	10 56.8	19 2.3	13 54.7
25 S	2 13 9.5	5 3.8	15 54.6	22 52.5	12 12.5	8 32.0	8 54.5	0 39.0	14 5.3	10 55.6	19 0.7	13 53.8
26 M	2 17 6.0	6 2.2	15 51.4	5♓ 6.1	12 31.2	9 46.1	8 58.8	0 52.4	14 10.7	10 54.4	18 59.2	13 52.9
27 T	2 21 2.6	7 0.6	15 48.3	17 36.2	12 54.3	11 0.1	9 3.8	1 5.8	14 16.1	10 53.3	18 57.6	13 52.1
28 W	2 24 59.1	7 58.9	15 45.1	0♈25.6	13 21.9	12 14.2	9 9.5	1 19.3	14 21.4	10 52.2	18 56.0	13 51.3
29 T	2 28 55.7	8 57.2	15 41.9	13 35.8	13 53.6	13 28.3	9 15.9	1 32.8	14 26.7	10 51.2	18 54.4	13 50.5
30 F	2 32 52.2	9 55.5	15 38.7	27 6.3	14 29.3	14 42.3	9 22.9	1 46.3	14 31.9	10 50.2	18 52.8	13 49.8

DECLINATION at NOON

DAY	h m s	☉	☊	☾	☿	♀	♂	♃	♄	♅	♆	♇
1 T	0 38 32.2	4N34.1	22N49.6	2S16.8	11N56.5	2N15.0	10N32.5	18N29.0	8S42.3	7N57.7	15S53.4	19N36.7
4 S	0 50 21.8	5 43.2	22 48.7	14N 6.3	11 12.6	3 44.9	10 40.5	18 38.0	8 35.0	8 0.0	15 52.3	19 37.8
7 W	1 2 11.5	6 51.4	22 47.8	24 28.9	10 0.5	5 14.2	10 45.7	18 47.1	8 28.0	8 2.3	15 51.2	19 38.9
10 S	1 14 1.2	7 58.5	22 46.8	21 48.0	8 31.1	6 42.4	10 48.1	18 56.1	8 21.0	8 4.3	15 50.0	19 39.8
13 T	1 25 50.8	9 4.3	22 45.9	7 47.2	6 57.2	8 9.3	10 47.7	19 5.1	8 14.3	8 6.3	15 48.8	19 40.6
16 F	1 37 40.5	10 8.9	22 44.9	9S16.3	5 31.3	9 34.5	10 44.6	19 14.1	8 7.7	8 8.1	15 47.6	19 41.2
19 M	1 49 30.1	11 11.9	22 43.9	21 48.3	4 22.4	10 57.7	10 39.0	19 23.0	8 1.3	8 9.7	15 46.3	19 41.8
22 T	2 1 19.8	12 13.2	22 42.9	25 6.8	3 35.3	12 18.7	10 31.1	19 31.8	7 55.2	8 11.2	15 45.0	19 42.2
25 S	2 13 9.5	13 12.8	22 41.9	18 26.3	3 11.6	13 37.0	10 20.8	19 40.6	7 49.2	8 12.6	15 43.7	19 42.4
28 W	2 24 59.1	14 10.4	22 40.9	4 23.8	3 10.7	14 52.3	10 8.4	19 49.2	7 43.5	8 13.8	15 42.4	19 42.6

MAY 1965

DAY	EPHEMERIS SIDEREAL TIME	☉	☊	☽	☿	♀	♂	♃	♄	♅	♆	♇
	h m s	° ′	° ′	° ′	° ′	° ′	° ′	° ′	° ′	° ′	° ′	° ′
						LONGITUDE at NOON						
1 S	2 36 48.8	10♉53.7	15♊35.6	10♉55.4	15♈ 8.9	15♉56.3	9♍30.5	1♊59.9	14♓37.0	10♍49.3	18♏51.2	13♍49.1
2 S	2 40 45.3	11 52.0	15 32.4	24 59.8	15 52.2	17 10.3	9 38.8	2 13.5	14 42.1	10R48.4	18R49.6	13R48.4
3 M	2 44 41.9	12 50.2	15 29.2	9♊15.1	16 39.1	18 24.3	9 47.7	2 27.2	14 47.0	10 47.6	18 47.9	13 47.7
4 T	2 48 38.5	13 48.3	15 26.0	23 36.6	17 29.4	19 38.3	9 57.2	2 40.8	14 52.0	10 46.8	18 46.3	13 47.1
5 W	2 52 35.0	14 46.5	15 22.9	7♋60.0	18 23.0	20 52.3	10 7.3	2 54.5	14 56.8	10 46.1	18 44.7	13 46.5
6 T	2 56 31.6	15 44.6	15 19.7	22 21.3	19 19.7	22 6.2	10 18.1	3 8.3	15 1.6	10 45.5	18 43.0	13 45.9
7 F	3 0 28.1	16 42.7	15 16.5	6♌37.5	20 19.5	23 20.2	10 29.4	3 22.1	15 6.3	10 44.9	18 41.5	13 45.4
8 S	3 4 24.7	17 40.7	15 13.3	20 46.3	21 22.2	24 34.1	10 41.2	3 35.9	15 11.0	10 44.3	18 39.8	13 44.9
9 S	3 8 21.2	18 38.7	15 10.1	4♍46.0	22 27.7	25 48.0	10 53.6	3 49.7	15 15.5	10 43.8	18 38.2	13 44.4
10 M	3 12 17.8	19 36.7	15 7.0	18 35.2	23 36.0	27 1.8	11 6.6	4 3.5	15 20.0	10 43.4	18 36.6	13 44.0
11 T	3 16 14.3	20 34.7	15 3.8	2♎12.8	24 46.9	28 15.7	11 20.1	4 17.3	15 24.4	10 43.0	18 34.9	13 43.5
12 W	3 20 10.9	21 32.6	15 0.6	15 37.8	26 0.4	29 29.5	11 34.0	4 31.2	15 28.8	10 42.6	18 33.3	13 43.1
13 T	3 24 7.5	22 30.5	14 57.4	28 49.2	27 16.4	0♊43.3	11 48.5	4 45.1	15 33.0	10 42.3	18 31.7	13 42.8
14 F	3 28 4.0	23 28.3	14 54.3	11♏46.5	28 34.9	1 57.1	12 3.5	4 59.0	15 37.2	10 42.1	18 30.0	13 42.4
15 S	3 32 0.6	24 26.1	14 51.1	24 29.4	29 55.9	3 10.9	12 19.0	5 12.9	15 41.3	10 41.9	18 28.4	13 42.1
16 S	3 35 57.1	25 24.0	14 47.9	6♐58.5	1♉19.2	4 24.7	12 35.0	5 26.8	15 45.3	10 41.8	18 26.8	13 41.8
17 M	3 39 53.7	26 21.7	14 44.7	19 14.7	2 44.8	5 38.4	12 51.4	5 40.7	15 49.2	10 41.7	18 25.2	13 41.6
18 T	3 43 50.2	27 19.5	14 41.6	1♑20.0	4 12.8	6 52.2	13 8.3	5 54.7	15 53.1	10 41.6	18 23.6	13 41.4
19 W	3 47 46.8	28 17.2	14 38.4	13 16.8	5 43.1	8 5.9	13 25.6	6 8.6	15 56.9	10D41.7	18 22.0	13 41.2
20 T	3 51 43.4	29 15.0	14 35.2	25 8.5	7 15.7	9 19.6	13 43.3	6 22.6	16 0.6	10 41.7	18 20.4	13 41.0
21 F	3 55 39.9	0♊12.7	14 32.0	6♒58.8	8 50.5	10 33.3	14 1.5	6 36.6	16 4.2	10 41.9	18 18.8	13 40.9
22 S	3 59 36.5	1 10.4	14 28.8	18 52.1	10 27.6	11 47.0	14 20.1	6 50.6	16 7.7	10 42.1	18 17.2	13 40.8
23 S	4 3 33.0	2 8.0	14 25.7	0♓53.0	12 7.0	13 0.7	14 39.2	7 4.6	16 11.1	10 42.3	18 15.6	13 40.7
24 M	4 7 29.6	3 5.7	14 22.5	13 6.0	13 48.6	14 14.3	14 58.6	7 18.6	16 14.5	10 42.6	18 14.0	13 40.7
25 T	4 11 26.1	4 3.3	14 19.3	25 35.6	15 32.4	15 28.0	15 18.4	7 32.6	16 17.8	10 42.9	18 12.5	13 40.7
26 W	4 15 22.7	5 0.9	14 16.1	8♈25.4	17 18.5	16 41.6	15 38.6	7 46.6	16 20.9	10 43.3	18 10.9	13 40.7
27 T	4 19 19.3	5 58.5	14 13.0	21 38.4	19 6.9	17 55.3	15 59.3	8 0.7	16 24.0	10 43.8	18 9.4	13D40.8
28 F	4 23 15.8	6 56.2	14 9.8	5♉15.6	20 57.5	19 8.9	16 20.3	8 14.7	16 27.1	10 44.3	18 7.9	13 40.9
29 S	4 27 12.4	7 53.8	14 6.6	19 16.3	22 50.2	20 22.5	16 41.7	8 28.7	16 30.0	10 44.9	18 6.4	13 41.1
30 S	4 31 8.9	8 51.3	14 3.4	3♊37.7	24 45.2	21 36.1	17 3.4	8 42.8	16 32.8	10 45.5	18 4.9	13 41.2
31 M	4 35 5.5	9 48.9	14 0.3	18 14.9	26 42.2	22 49.7	17 25.5	8 56.8	16 35.5	10 46.2	18 3.4	13 41.4
						DECLINATION at NOON						
1 S	2 36 48.8	15N 5.9	22N39.9	12N23.9	3N30.9	16N 4.3	9N53.8	19N57.7	7S 38.0	8N14.8	15S41.0	19N42.6
4 T	2 48 38.5	15 59.2	22 38.9	24 9.7	4 9.8	17 12.6	9 37.3	20 6.1	7 32.7	8 15.6	15 39.7	19 42.5
7 F	3 0 28.1	16 50.1	22 37.8	22 38.6	5 5.3	18 17.0	9 18.9	20 14.4	7 27.7	8 16.2	15 38.4	19 42.2
10 M	3 12 17.8	17 38.4	22 36.8	9 18.8	6 15.2	19 17.0	8 58.8	20 22.5	7 22.9	8 16.7	15 37.0	19 41.8
13 T	3 24 7.5	18 24.1	22 35.7	7S 34.9	7 37.6	20 12.4	8 36.9	20 30.4	7 18.5	8 17.0	15 35.7	19 41.3
16 S	3 35 57.1	19 7.0	22 34.7	20 51.7	9 10.5	21 2.8	8 13.5	20 38.2	7 14.3	8 17.1	15 34.4	19 40.7
19 W	3 47 46.8	19 47.0	22 33.6	25 22.1	10 52.2	21 48.1	7 48.7	20 45.8	7 10.4	8 17.0	15 33.1	19 39.9
22 S	3 59 36.5	20 23.9	22 32.5	19 42.9	12 40.7	22 27.9	7 22.4	20 53.2	7 6.8	8 16.7	15 31.8	19 39.1
25 T	4 11 26.1	20 57.8	22 31.4	6 29.7	14 33.7	23 1.9	6 54.8	21 0.4	7 3.5	8 16.3	15 30.6	19 38.1
28 F	4 23 15.8	21 28.4	22 30.3	10N10.0	16 28.7	23 30.1	6 25.9	21 7.4	7 0.6	8 15.6	15 29.4	19 36.9
31 M	4 35 5.5	21 55.6	22 29.1	23 20.0	18 22.5	23 52.0	5 55.8	21 14.2	6 57.9	8 14.8	15 28.2	19 35.7

JUNE 1965

DAY	EPHEMERIS SIDEREAL TIME	☉	☊	☽	☿	♀	♂	♃	♄	♅	♆	♇
						LONGITUDE at NOON						
1 T	4 39 2.0	10♊46.4	13♊57.1	3♋ 1.6	28♉41.4	24♊ 3.3	17♍47.9	9♊10.8	16♓38.2	10♍46.9	18♏ 1.9	13♍41.6
2 W	4 42 58.6	11 43.9	13 53.9	17 50.5	0♊42.5	25 16.8	18 10.7	9 24.8	16 40.7	10 47.7	18R 0.4	13 41.9
3 T	4 46 55.2	12 41.4	13 50.7	2♌34.7	2 45.6	26 30.4	18 33.8	9 38.8	16 43.2	10 48.5	17 59.0	13 42.2
4 F	4 50 51.7	13 38.8	13 47.5	17 8.1	4 50.4	27 43.9	18 57.3	9 52.8	16 45.5	10 49.4	17 57.5	13 42.5
5 S	4 54 48.3	14 36.3	13 44.4	1♍26.5	6 56.9	28 57.4	19 21.0	10 6.8	16 47.8	10 50.3	17 56.1	13 42.8
6 S	4 58 44.8	15 33.7	13 41.2	15 27.2	9 4.8	0♋10.9	19 45.1	10 20.8	16 50.0	10 51.3	17 54.7	13 43.2
7 M	5 2 41.4	16 31.1	13 38.0	29 9.2	11 14.1	1 24.4	20 9.5	10 34.7	16 52.0	10 52.3	17 53.3	13 43.6
8 T	5 6 37.9	17 28.5	13 34.8	12♎32.8	13 24.4	2 37.8	20 34.3	10 48.7	16 54.0	10 53.4	17 52.0	13 44.0
9 W	5 10 34.5	18 25.8	13 31.7	25 39.2	15 35.5	3 51.3	20 59.3	11 2.6	16 55.9	10 54.5	17 50.6	13 44.5
10 T	5 14 31.1	19 23.2	13 28.5	8♏29.7	17 47.3	5 4.7	21 24.5	11 16.6	16 57.7	10 55.7	17 49.3	13 45.0
11 F	5 18 27.6	20 20.5	13 25.3	21 6.3	19 59.3	6 18.1	21 50.1	11 30.5	16 59.4	10 57.0	17 47.9	13 45.5
12 S	5 22 24.2	21 17.8	13 22.1	3♐30.6	22 11.3	7 31.5	22 16.0	11 44.4	17 1.0	10 58.3	17 46.6	13 46.1
13 S	5 26 20.7	22 15.1	13 19.0	15 44.4	24 23.1	8 44.9	22 42.1	11 58.2	17 2.5	10 59.6	17 45.4	13 46.6
14 M	5 30 17.3	23 12.4	13 15.8	27 49.4	26 34.3	9 58.2	23 8.5	12 12.1	17 3.9	11 1.0	17 44.1	13 47.3
15 T	5 34 13.9	24 9.7	13 12.6	9♑47.5	28 44.8	11 11.6	23 35.1	12 25.9	17 5.2	11 2.4	17 42.9	13 47.9
16 W	5 38 10.4	25 7.0	13 9.4	21 40.6	0♋54.3	12 24.9	24 2.0	12 39.8	17 6.4	11 3.9	17 41.6	13 48.6
17 T	5 42 7.0	26 4.2	13 6.3	3♒31.1	3 2.6	13 38.2	24 29.2	12 53.6	17 7.5	11 5.4	17 40.4	13 49.3
18 F	5 46 3.5	27 1.6	13 3.1	15 21.8	5 9.5	14 51.6	24 56.7	13 7.4	17 8.6	11 7.1	17 39.3	13 50.1
19 S	5 50 0.1	27 58.8	12 59.9	27 15.8	7 14.8	16 4.9	25 24.3	13 21.1	17 9.5	11 8.7	17 38.1	13 50.8
20 S	5 53 56.6	28 56.1	12 56.7	9♓16.7	9 18.3	17 18.1	25 52.2	13 34.9	17 10.3	11 10.4	17 37.0	13 51.6
21 M	5 57 53.2	29 53.3	12 53.5	21 28.6	11 20.1	18 31.4	26 20.4	13 48.6	17 11.0	11 12.1	17 35.9	13 52.5
22 T	6 1 49.8	0♋50.5	12 50.4	3♈55.5	13 19.9	19 44.6	26 48.7	14 2.3	17 11.6	11 13.9	17 34.8	13 53.3
23 W	6 5 46.3	1 47.8	12 47.2	16 41.7	15 17.7	20 57.9	27 17.3	14 15.9	17 12.1	11 15.7	17 33.8	13 54.2
24 T	6 9 42.9	2 45.0	12 44.0	29 50.7	17 13.5	22 11.1	27 46.2	14 29.5	17 12.6	11 17.6	17 32.7	13 55.1
25 F	6 13 39.4	3 42.3	12 40.8	13♉25.1	19 7.2	23 24.3	28 15.2	14 43.1	17 12.9	11 19.5	17 31.7	13 56.0
26 S	6 17 36.0	4 39.5	12 37.7	27 26.1	20 58.8	24 37.5	28 44.5	14 56.7	17 13.1	11 21.5	17 30.7	13 57.0
27 S	6 21 32.6	5 36.7	12 34.5	11♊52.4	22 48.2	25 50.7	29 14.0	15 10.2	17 13.2	11 23.5	17 29.7	13 58.0
28 M	6 25 29.1	6 34.0	12 31.3	26 40.1	24 35.5	27 3.9	29 43.7	15 23.7	17 13.2	11 25.5	17 28.8	13 59.0
29 T	6 29 25.7	7 31.2	12 28.1	11♋42.6	26 20.6	28 17.0	0♎13.7	15 37.2	17R13.1	11 27.6	17 27.9	14 0.1
30 W	6 33 22.2	8 28.5	12 25.0	26 51.3	28 3.6	29 30.2	0 43.8	15 50.6	17 12.9	11 29.8	17 27.0	14 1.1
						DECLINATION at NOON						
1 T	4 39 2.0	22N 3.9	22N28.8	25N 9.3	18N59.4	23N58.0	5N45.5	21N16.5	6S 57.1	8N14.5	15S 27.8	19N35.2
4 F	4 50 51.7	22 26.6	22 27.6	20 12.2	20 44.8	24 11.6	5 13.8	21 23.0	6 54.9	8 13.4	15 26.7	19 33.9
7 M	5 2 41.4	22 45.7	22 26.5	5 1.0	22 18.0	24 18.8	4 41.1	21 29.3	6 53.0	8 12.2	15 25.6	19 32.4
10 T	5 14 31.1	23 1.2	22 25.3	11S 26.1	23 33.7	24 19.5	4 7.4	21 35.3	6 51.5	8 10.8	15 24.5	19 30.8
13 S	5 26 20.7	23 13.1	22 24.1	22 51.3	24 27.3	24 13.8	3 32.7	21 41.2	6 50.3	8 9.2	15 23.6	19 29.1
16 W	5 38 10.4	23 21.3	22 23.0	24 53.9	24 56.1	24 1.7	2 57.1	21 46.8	6 49.5	8 7.4	15 22.6	19 27.3
19 S	5 50 0.1	23 25.7	22 21.8	17 9.8	24 59.8	23 43.2	2 20.6	21 52.2	6 49.0	8 5.5	15 21.8	19 25.4
22 T	6 1 49.8	23 26.5	22 20.6	2 58.5	24 40.2	23 18.4	1 43.4	21 57.3	6 48.8	8 3.4	15 21.0	19 23.5
25 F	6 13 39.4	23 23.6	22 19.3	13N19.9	24 0.1	22 47.6	1 5.4	22 2.2	6 49.0	8 1.2	15 20.2	19 21.4
28 M	6 25 29.1	23 16.9	22 18.1	24 34.6	23 3.2	22 10.8	0 26.8	22 6.9	6 49.6	7 58.8	15 19.6	19 19.3

JULY 1965

LONGITUDE at NOON

DAY	EPHEMERIS SIDEREAL TIME	☉	☊	☽	☿	♀	♂	♃	♄	♅	♆	♇
	h m s	° ′	° ′	° ′	° ′	° ′	° ′	° ′	° ′	° ′	° ′	° ′
1 T	6 37 18.8	9♋25.7	12♊21.8	11♌56.4	29♋44.3	0♌43.3	1♎14.2	16♊ 4.0	17♓12.7	11♍31.9	17♏26.1	14♍ 2.2
2 F	6 41 15.3	10 22.9	12 18.6	26 49.2	1♌22.9	1 56.4	1 44.7	16 17.3	17R12.3	11 34.2	17R25.3	14 3.4
3 S	6 45 11.9	11 20.1	12 15.4	11♍22.5	2 59.3	3 9.5	2 15.5	16 30.6	17 11.8	11 36.4	17 24.5	14 4.5
4 S	6 49 8.5	12 17.3	12 12.3	25 32.0	4 33.5	4 22.5	2 46.5	16 43.9	17 11.2	11 38.7	17 23.7	14 5.7
5 M	6 53 5.0	13 14.5	12 9.1	9♎16.2	6 5.4	5 35.6	3 17.6	16 57.1	17 10.5	11 41.1	17 23.0	14 6.9
6 T	6 57 1.6	14 11.7	12 5.9	22 35.7	7 35.2	6 48.6	3 48.9	17 10.3	17 9.7	11 43.5	17 22.2	14 8.2
7 W	7 0 58.1	15 8.9	12 2.7	5♏32.9	9 2.7	8 1.6	4 20.5	17 23.4	17 8.8	11 45.9	17 21.5	14 9.4
8 T	7 4 54.7	16 6.1	11 59.5	18 11.0	10 27.9	9 14.6	4 52.2	17 36.5	17 7.9	11 48.4	17 20.9	14 10.7
9 F	7 8 51.2	17 3.4	11 56.4	0♐33.8	11 50.9	10 27.6	5 24.1	17 49.5	17 6.8	11 51.0	17 20.3	14 12.1
10 S	7 12 47.8	18 0.6	11 53.2	12 44.5	13 11.4	11 40.5	5 56.1	18 2.5	17 5.7	11 53.5	17 19.7	14 13.4
11 S	7 16 44.4	18 57.8	11 50.0	24 46.5	14 29.6	12 53.4	6 28.4	18 15.5	17 4.4	11 56.1	17 19.1	14 14.8
12 M	7 20 40.9	19 55.0	11 46.8	6♑42.4	15 45.4	14 6.3	7 0.8	18 28.3	17 3.0	11 58.7	17 18.5	14 16.1
13 T	7 24 37.5	20 52.2	11 43.7	18 34.7	16 58.7	15 19.2	7 33.3	18 41.2	17 1.6	12 1.4	17 18.0	14 17.6
14 W	7 28 34.0	21 49.4	11 40.5	0♒25.4	18 9.4	16 32.0	8 6.1	18 53.9	17 0.0	12 4.1	17 17.5	14 19.0
15 T	7 32 30.6	22 46.6	11 37.3	12 16.3	19 17.6	17 44.9	8 39.0	19 6.7	16 58.4	12 6.8	17 17.1	14 20.4
16 F	7 36 27.2	23 43.8	11 34.1	24 9.3	20 23.0	18 57.7	9 12.0	19 19.3	16 56.7	12 9.6	17 16.7	14 21.9
17 S	7 40 23.7	24 41.0	11 31.0	6♓ 6.6	21 25.6	20 10.4	9 45.2	19 31.9	16 54.8	12 12.4	17 16.3	14 23.4
18 S	7 44 20.3	25 38.3	11 27.8	18 10.5	22 25.4	21 23.2	10 18.6	19 44.5	16 52.9	12 15.3	17 15.9	14 24.9
19 M	7 48 16.8	26 35.5	11 24.6	0♈24.0	23 22.2	22 35.9	10 52.1	19 57.0	16 50.9	12 18.1	17 15.5	14 26.5
20 T	7 52 13.4	27 32.8	11 21.4	12 50.4	24 15.9	23 48.6	11 25.8	20 9.4	16 48.8	12 21.1	17 15.2	14 28.0
21 W	7 56 9.9	28 30.0	11 18.3	25 33.4	25 6.3	25 1.3	11 59.7	20 21.8	16 46.6	12 24.0	17 15.0	14 29.6
22 T	8 0 6.5	29 27.3	11 15.1	8♉36.8	25 53.4	26 14.0	12 33.7	20 34.1	16 44.3	12 27.0	17 14.7	14 31.2
23 F	8 4 3.1	0♌24.6	11 11.9	22 3.9	26 37.0	27 26.7	13 7.8	20 46.3	16 42.0	12 30.0	17 14.5	14 32.9
24 S	8 7 59.6	1 21.9	11 8.7	5♊57.0	27 17.0	28 39.3	13 42.1	20 58.5	16 39.5	12 33.0	17 14.3	14 34.5
25 S	8 11 56.2	2 19.3	11 5.5	20 16.8	27 53.1	29 51.9	14 16.6	21 10.6	16 37.0	12 36.1	17 14.2	14 36.2
26 M	8 15 52.7	3 16.6	11 2.4	5♋ 1.1	28 25.2	1♍ 4.5	14 51.2	21 22.6	16 34.4	12 39.2	17 14.1	14 37.9
27 T	8 19 49.3	4 14.0	10 59.2	20 4.9	28 53.2	2 17.0	15 25.9	21 34.6	16 31.6	12 42.3	17 14.0	14 39.6
28 W	8 23 45.8	5 11.3	10 56.0	5♌19.7	29 16.9	3 29.6	16 0.8	21 46.5	16 28.9	12 45.5	17 13.9	14 41.3
29 T	8 27 42.4	6 8.7	10 52.8	20 35.2	29 36.0	4 42.1	16 35.9	21 58.3	16 26.0	12 48.7	17 13.9	14 43.0
30 F	8 31 38.9	7 6.2	10 49.7	5♍40.7	29 50.6	5 54.6	17 11.1	22 10.1	16 23.1	12 51.9	17D14.0	14 44.8
31 S	8 35 35.5	8 3.6	10 46.5	20 26.7	0♍ 0.2	7 7.1	17 46.4	22 21.7	16 20.1	12 55.2	17 14.0	14 46.6

DECLINATION at NOON

DAY	EPHEMERIS SIDEREAL TIME	☉	☊	☽	☿	♀	♂	♃	♄	♅	♆	♇
1 T	6 37 18.8	23N 6.6	22N16.9	21N29.2	21N52.8	21N28.4	0S 12.6	22N11.3	6S 50.5	7N56.2	15S 19.0	19N17.1
4 S	6 49 8.5	22 52.6	22 15.6	6 27.9	20 32.3	20 40.6	0 52.6	22 15.5	6 51.8	7 53.5	15 18.4	19 14.8
7 W	7 0 58.1	22 35.0	22 14.4	10S 20.3	19 4.7	19 47.6	1 33.1	22 19.5	6 53.4	7 50.7	15 18.0	19 12.5
10 S	7 12 47.8	22 14.0	22 13.1	22 15.4	17 32.5	18 49.6	2 14.1	22 23.2	6 55.3	7 47.7	15 17.6	19 10.1
13 T	7 24 37.5	21 49.4	22 11.8	25 6.6	15 58.4	17 47.2	2 55.6	22 26.7	6 57.5	7 44.6	15 17.3	19 7.7
16 F	7 36 27.2	21 21.6	22 10.6	18 3.8	14 24.8	16 40.5	3 37.4	22 30.0	7 0.1	7 41.4	15 17.1	19 5.2
19 M	7 48 16.8	20 50.5	22 9.3	4 20.7	12 54.0	15 29.8	4 19.6	22 33.1	7 3.0	7 38.1	15 16.9	19 2.7
22 T	8 0 6.5	20 16.2	22 7.9	11N37.9	11 28.7	14 15.5	5 2.0	22 35.9	7 6.2	7 34.6	15 16.9	19 0.1
25 S	8 11 56.2	19 38.8	22 6.6	23 45.6	10 11.8	12 57.9	5 44.7	22 38.5	7 9.6	7 31.1	15 16.9	18 57.5
28 W	8 23 45.8	18 58.5	22 5.3	22 53.0	9 6.3	11 37.3	6 27.6	22 40.9	7 13.4	7 27.4	15 17.0	18 54.9
31 S	8 35 35.5	18 15.4	22 4.0	8 25.2	8 15.8	10 14.1	7 10.7	22 43.1	7 17.4	7 23.6	15 17.2	18 52.3

AUGUST 1965

LONGITUDE at NOON

DAY	EPHEMERIS SIDEREAL TIME	☉	☊	☽	☿	♀	♂	♃	♄	♅	♆	♇
	h m s	° ′	° ′	° ′	° ′	° ′	° ′	° ′	° ′	° ′	° ′	° ′
1 S	8 39 32.1	9♌ 1.0	10♊43.3	4♎46.8	0♍ 4.8	8♍19.5	18♎21.9	22♊33.3	16♓17.0	12♍58.4	17♏14.1	14♍48.4
2 M	8 43 28.6	9 58.4	10 40.1	18 37.9	0R 4.4	9 31.9	18 57.5	22 44.8	16R13.8	13 1.7	17 14.2	14 50.2
3 T	8 47 25.2	10 55.9	10 37.0	2♏ 0.4	29♌58.7	10 44.2	19 33.3	22 56.2	16 10.5	13 5.1	17 14.3	14 52.1
4 W	8 51 21.7	11 53.3	10 33.8	14 56.6	29 47.8	11 56.6	20 9.1	23 7.5	16 7.2	13 8.4	17 14.5	14 53.9
5 T	8 55 18.3	12 50.8	10 30.6	27 30.6	29 31.6	13 8.8	20 45.1	23 18.8	16 3.8	13 11.8	17 14.7	14 55.8
6 F	8 59 14.8	13 48.2	10 27.4	9♐47.2	29 10.2	14 21.1	21 21.3	23 29.9	16 0.4	13 15.2	17 15.0	14 57.6
7 S	9 3 11.4	14 45.7	10 24.2	21 51.0	28 43.7	15 33.3	21 57.5	23 41.0	15 56.9	13 18.6	17 15.2	14 59.5
8 S	9 7 8.0	15 43.2	10 21.1	3♑46.5	28 12.4	16 45.5	22 33.9	23 52.0	15 53.3	13 22.0	17 15.5	15 1.4
9 M	9 11 4.5	16 40.7	10 17.9	15 37.5	27 36.6	17 57.7	23 10.4	24 2.9	15 49.6	13 25.5	17 15.9	15 3.4
10 T	9 15 1.1	17 38.3	10 14.7	27 27.3	26 56.7	19 9.8	23 47.0	24 13.7	15 45.9	13 28.9	17 16.2	15 5.3
11 W	9 18 57.6	18 35.8	10 11.5	9♒18.3	26 13.2	20 21.9	24 23.8	24 24.4	15 42.1	13 32.4	17 16.6	15 7.2
12 T	9 22 54.2	19 33.4	10 8.4	21 12.4	25 26.8	21 33.9	25 0.6	24 35.0	15 38.3	13 35.9	17 17.1	15 9.2
13 F	9 26 50.7	20 31.0	10 5.2	3♓11.1	24 38.2	22 45.9	25 37.6	24 45.5	15 34.4	13 39.5	17 17.5	15 11.2
14 S	9 30 47.3	21 28.6	10 2.0	15 15.8	23 48.3	23 57.9	26 14.7	24 55.9	15 30.5	13 43.0	17 18.0	15 13.1
15 S	9 34 43.8	22 26.2	9 58.8	27 27.8	22 58.0	25 9.8	26 52.0	25 6.2	15 26.5	13 46.6	17 18.5	15 15.1
16 M	9 38 40.4	23 23.9	9 55.6	9♈48.6	22 8.2	26 21.7	27 29.3	25 16.4	15 22.4	13 50.2	17 19.1	15 17.1
17 T	9 42 36.9	24 21.5	9 52.5	22 20.5	21 19.9	27 33.6	28 6.8	25 26.6	15 18.4	13 53.8	17 19.7	15 19.2
18 W	9 46 33.5	25 19.2	9 49.3	5♉ 5.9	20 34.2	28 45.4	28 44.4	25 36.6	15 14.2	13 57.4	17 20.3	15 21.2
19 T	9 50 30.1	26 17.0	9 46.1	18 7.9	19 52.0	29 57.2	29 22.1	25 46.5	15 10.0	14 1.0	17 21.0	15 23.2
20 F	9 54 26.6	27 14.8	9 42.9	1♊29.5	19 14.2	1♎ 8.9	29 59.9	25 56.3	15 5.9	14 4.7	17 21.7	15 25.3
21 S	9 58 23.2	28 12.6	9 39.8	15 13.5	18 41.6	2 20.7	0♏37.8	26 6.0	15 1.6	14 8.4	17 22.4	15 27.4
22 S	10 2 19.7	29 10.4	9 36.6	29 21.3	18 15.0	3 32.3	1 15.9	26 15.6	14 57.3	14 12.0	17 23.2	15 29.4
23 M	10 6 16.3	0♍ 8.2	9 33.4	13♋52.5	17 55.0	4 44.0	1 54.1	26 25.0	14 52.9	14 15.7	17 24.0	15 31.5
24 T	10 10 12.8	1 6.1	9 30.2	28 43.9	17 42.1	5 55.5	2 32.3	26 34.4	14 48.6	14 19.4	17 24.8	15 33.6
25 W	10 14 9.4	2 4.0	9 27.0	13♌49.1	17 36.8	7 7.1	3 10.7	26 43.6	14 44.2	14 23.1	17 25.6	15 35.7
26 T	10 18 5.9	3 1.9	9 23.9	28 59.0	17D39.4	8 18.6	3 49.2	26 52.7	14 39.7	14 26.8	17 26.5	15 37.8
27 F	10 22 2.5	3 59.9	9 20.7	14♍ 3.2	17 50.0	9 30.1	4 27.9	27 1.7	14 35.3	14 30.6	17 27.4	15 39.9
28 S	10 25 59.0	4 57.8	9 17.5	28 51.5	18 8.7	10 41.5	5 6.6	27 10.5	14 30.8	14 34.3	17 28.3	15 42.0
29 S	10 29 55.6	5 55.8	9 14.3	13♎16.2	18 35.6	11 52.9	5 45.4	27 19.3	14 26.3	14 38.0	17 29.3	15 44.1
30 M	10 33 52.2	6 53.9	9 11.2	27 12.7	19 10.5	13 4.2	6 24.4	27 27.9	14 21.7	14 41.8	17 30.3	15 46.2
31 T	10 37 48.7	7 51.9	9 8.0	10♏39.9	19 53.3	14 15.5	7 3.4	27 36.3	14 17.2	14 45.5	17 31.3	15 48.3

DECLINATION at NOON

DAY	EPHEMERIS SIDEREAL TIME	☉	☊	☽	☿	♀	♂	♃	♄	♅	♆	♇
1 S	8 39 32.1	18N 0.4	22N 3.5	2N25.2	8N 2.9	9N45.8	7S 25.0	22N43.8	7S 18.8	7N22.3	15S 17.3	18N51.4
4 W	8 51 21.7	17 13.7	22 2.2	14S 5.9	7 38.2	8 19.6	8 8.2	22 45.8	7 23.1	7 18.5	15 17.6	18 48.7
7 S	9 3 11.4	16 24.6	22 0.8	24 3.9	7 36.7	6 51.4	8 51.3	22 47.5	7 27.6	7 14.5	15 17.9	18 46.1
10 T	9 15 1.1	15 33.0	21 59.4	24 13.2	7 59.9	5 21.7	9 34.3	22 49.1	7 32.4	7 10.5	15 18.4	18 43.4
13 F	9 26 50.7	14 39.2	21 58.0	14 58.4	8 46.7	3 50.7	10 17.2	22 50.5	7 37.3	7 6.4	15 18.9	18 40.8
16 M	9 38 40.4	13 43.4	21 56.6	0 9.4	9 51.6	2 18.8	10 59.9	22 51.8	7 42.4	7 2.2	15 19.6	18 38.1
19 T	9 50 30.1	12 45.5	21 55.2	15N23.3	11 6.1	0 46.2	11 42.3	22 52.9	7 47.6	6 58.0	15 20.2	18 35.5
22 S	10 2 19.7	11 45.9	21 53.8	25 4.9	12 19.5	0S 46.8	12 24.4	22 53.8	7 52.9	6 53.7	15 21.0	18 32.8
25 W	10 14 9.4	10 44.5	21 52.4	20 59.0	13 21.6	2 19.8	13 6.1	22 54.6	7 58.3	6 49.4	15 21.9	18 30.2
28 S	10 25 59.0	9 41.6	21 50.9	4 47.7	14 4.2	3 52.6	13 47.3	22 55.3	8 3.8	6 45.1	15 22.8	18 27.7
31 T	10 37 48.7	8 37.3	21 49.5	12S 43.8	14 21.3	5 24.8	14 28.1	22 55.9	8 9.3	6 40.7	15 23.8	18 25.1

SEPTEMBER 1965

LONGITUDE at NOON

DAY	EPHEMERIS SIDEREAL TIME h m s	☉ ° ′	☊ ° ′	☾ ° ′	☿ ° ′	♀ ° ′	♂ ° ′	♃ ° ′	♄ ° ′	♅ ° ′	♆ ° ′	♇ ° ′
1 W	10 41 45.3	8♍50.0	9♓ 4.8	23♏39.4	20♌43.8	15♎26.8	7♏42.6	27♊44.7	14♓12.6	14♍49.3	17♏32.3	15♍50.4
2 T	10 45 41.8	9 48.1	9 1.6	6♐14.9	21 41.6	16 38.0	8 21.9	27 52.9	14R 8.1	14 53.1	17 33.4	15 52.6
3 F	10 49 38.4	10 46.2	8 58.5	18 31.4	22 46.4	17 49.1	9 1.2	28 1.0	14 3.5	14 56.8	17 34.5	15 54.7
4 S	10 53 34.9	11 44.3	8 55.3	0♑33.9	23 57.8	19 0.2	9 40.7	28 8.9	13 58.9	15 0.6	17 35.7	15 56.8
5 S	10 57 31.5	12 42.5	8 52.1	12 27.8	25 15.4	20 11.2	10 20.3	28 16.7	13 54.3	15 4.4	17 36.8	15 59.0
6 M	11 1 28.0	13 40.7	8 48.9	24 17.9	26 38.6	21 22.2	10 59.9	28 24.4	13 49.7	15 8.1	17 38.0	16 1.1
7 T	11 5 24.6	14 38.9	8 45.7	6♒ 8.1	28 6.8	22 33.1	11 39.7	28 31.9	13 45.1	15 11.9	17 39.3	16 3.2
8 W	11 9 21.1	15 37.2	8 42.6	18 1.8	29 39.7	23 44.0	12 19.6	28 39.3	13 40.5	15 15.7	17 40.5	16 5.4
9 T	11 13 17.7	16 35.4	8 39.4	0♓ 1.4	1♍16.6	24 54.8	12 59.5	28 46.6	13 35.9	15 19.5	17 41.8	16 7.5
10 F	11 17 14.2	17 33.8	8 36.2	12 8.7	2 57.1	26 5.5	13 39.7	28 53.7	13 31.4	15 23.3	17 43.2	16 9.7
11 S	11 21 10.8	18 32.1	8 33.0	24 24.6	4 40.5	27 16.2	14 19.8	29 0.7	13 26.8	15 27.0	17 44.5	16 11.8
12 S	11 25 7.3	19 30.5	8 29.9	6♈49.8	6 26.4	28 26.8	15 0.1	29 7.5	13 22.3	15 30.8	17 45.8	16 14.0
13 M	11 29 3.9	20 28.8	8 26.7	19 24.8	8 14.3	29 37.4	15 40.4	29 14.1	13 17.7	15 34.6	17 47.2	16 16.1
14 T	11 33 0.5	21 27.3	8 23.5	2♉10.2	10 3.8	0♏47.9	16 20.9	29 20.6	13 13.2	15 38.3	17 48.6	16 18.2
15 W	11 36 57.0	22 25.7	8 20.3	15 6.9	11 54.4	1 58.3	17 1.4	29 27.0	13 8.7	15 42.1	17 50.1	16 20.4
16 T	11 40 53.6	23 24.2	8 17.1	28 16.6	13 46.0	3 8.7	17 42.1	29 33.2	13 4.2	15 45.9	17 51.5	16 22.5
17 F	11 44 50.1	24 22.8	8 14.0	11♊40.9	15 38.0	4 19.0	18 22.8	29 39.2	12 59.7	15 49.6	17 53.0	16 24.6
18 S	11 48 46.7	25 21.3	8 10.8	25 21.7	17 30.4	5 29.2	19 3.6	29 45.1	12 55.3	15 53.3	17 54.5	16 26.8
19 S	11 52 43.2	26 19.9	8 7.6	9♋20.3	19 22.7	6 39.4	19 44.6	29 50.8	12 50.9	15 57.1	17 56.1	16 28.9
20 M	11 56 39.8	27 18.6	8 4.4	23 36.7	21 15.0	7 49.5	20 25.6	29 56.4	12 46.5	16 0.8	17 57.6	16 31.0
21 T	12 0 36.3	28 17.2	8 1.2	8♌ 9.2	23 6.8	8 59.6	21 6.7	0♋ 1.7	12 42.2	16 4.5	17 59.2	16 33.1
22 W	12 4 32.9	29 16.0	7 58.1	22 53.6	24 58.3	10 9.6	21 47.9	0 7.0	12 37.8	16 8.2	18 0.8	16 35.2
23 T	12 8 29.4	0♎14.7	7 54.9	7♍43.4	26 49.2	11 19.5	22 29.2	0 12.0	12 33.6	16 11.9	18 2.5	16 37.3
24 F	12 12 26.0	1 13.5	7 51.7	22 30.4	28 39.4	12 29.3	23 10.6	0 16.9	12 29.3	16 1..6	18 4.1	16 39.4
25 S	12 16 22.5	2 12.3	7 48.5	7♎ 6.2	0♎28.9	13 39.1	23 52.1	0 21.6	12 25.1	16 19.3	18 5.8	16 41.5
26 S	12 20 19.1	3 11.2	7 45.4	21 23.4	2 17.7	14 48.8	24 33.7	0 26.1	12 21.0	16 23.0	18 7.5	16 43.5
27 M	12 24 15.6	4 10.1	7 42.2	5♏16.8	4 5.6	15 58.4	25 15.4	0 30.4	12 16.9	16 26.6	18 9.2	16 45.6
28 T	12 28 12.2	5 9.0	7 39.0	18 44.2	5 52.7	17 7.9	25 57.2	0 34.6	12 12.8	16 30.2	18 11.0	16 47.7
29 W	12 32 8.8	6 7.9	7 35.8	1♐45.7	7 38.9	18 17.4	26 39.0	0 38.6	12 8.8	16 33.9	18 12.8	16 49.7
30 T	12 36 5.3	7 6.9	7 32.6	14 23.9	9 24.3	19 26.8	27 21.0	0 42.4	12 4.9	16 37.5	18 14.5	16 51.7

DECLINATION at NOON

DAY	SIDEREAL TIME	☉	☊	☾	☿	♀	♂	♃	♄	♅	♆	♇
1 W	10 41 45.3	8N15.6	21N49.0	17S22.5	14N20.6	5S55.4	14S41.5	22N56.1	8S11.1	6N39.3	15S24.1	18N24.3
4 S	10 53 34.9	7 9.7	21 47.5	25 16.8	13 58.5	7 26.4	15 21.4	22 56.5	8 16.6	6 34.9	15 25.2	18 21.8
7 T	11 5 24.6	6 2.8	21 46.1	22 49.4	13 6.3	8 56.1	16 0.5	22 56.9	8 22.1	6 30.5	15 26.4	18 19.4
10 F	11 17 14.2	4 54.9	21 44.6	11 36.7	11 46.5	10 24.2	16 38.9	22 57.1	8 27.5	6 26.1	15 27.6	18 17.0
13 M	11 29 3.9	3 46.4	21 43.1	4N 7.4	10 3.7	11 50.4	17 16.3	22 57.3	8 32.9	6 21.8	15 28.9	18 14.7
16 T	11 40 53.6	2 37.2	21 41.6	18 59.2	8 3.7	13 14.4	17 52.9	22 57.5	8 38.1	6 17.4	15 30.2	18 12.5
19 S	11 52 43.2	1 27.5	21 40.1	25 46.8	5 52.2	14 35.8	18 28.3	22 57.6	8 43.3	6 13.1	15 31.6	18 10.3
22 W	12 4 32.9	0 17.5	21 38.5	18 30.0	3 33.9	15 54.5	19 2.7	22 57.7	8 48.3	6 8.7	15 33.0	18 8.2
25 S	12 16 22.5	0S52.6	21 37.0	1 11.2	1 12.6	17 10.1	19 35.9	22 57.7	8 53.1	6 4.5	15 34.5	18 6.1
28 T	12 28 12.2	2 2.8	21 35.5	15S54.5	1S 8.9	18 22.1	20 7.7	22 57.7	8 57.7	6 0.3	15 36.1	18 4.2

OCTOBER 1965

LONGITUDE at NOON

DAY	SIDEREAL TIME	☉	☊	☾	☿	♀	♂	♃	♄	♅	♆	♇
1 F	12 40 1.9	8♎ 6.0	7♓29.5	26♐42.9	11♎ 8.9	20♏36.1	28♏ 3.0	0♋46.1	12♓ 1.0	16♍41.1	18♏16.4	16♍53.8
2 S	12 43 58.4	9 5.0	7 26.3	8♑47.3	12 52.5	21 45.3	28 45.2	0 49.5	11R57.2	16 44.7	18 18.2	16 55.8
3 S	12 47 55.0	10 4.1	7 23.1	20 42.5	14 35.3	22 54.4	29 27.4	0 52.8	11 53.4	16 48.2	18 20.1	16 57.8
4 M	12 51 51.5	11 3.1	7 19.9	2♒33.6	16 17.2	24 3.4	0♐ 9.7	0 55.9	11 49.7	16 51.8	18 21.9	16 59.8
5 T	12 55 48.1	12 2.3	7 16.8	14 25.5	17 58.3	25 12.2	0 52.0	0 58.7	11 46.1	16 55.3	18 23.8	17 1.8
6 W	12 59 44.6	13 1.4	7 13.6	26 22.2	19 38.6	26 21.0	1 34.5	1 1.4	11 42.5	16 58.8	18 25.7	17 3.8
7 T	13 3 41.2	14 0.6	7 10.4	8♓27.3	21 18.1	27 29.7	2 17.0	1 4.0	11 39.0	17 2.2	18 27.6	17 5.8
8 F	13 7 37.7	14 59.8	7 7.2	20 43.0	22 56.8	28 38.3	2 59.6	1 6.3	11 35.5	17 5.7	18 29.6	17 7.7
9 S	13 11 34.3	15 59.1	7 4.0	3♈11.1	24 34.7	29 46.7	3 42.3	1 8.4	11 32.1	17 9.1	18 31.5	17 9.6
10 S	13 15 30.8	16 58.4	7 0.9	15 52.0	26 11.9	0♐55.1	4 25.1	1 10.3	11 28.8	17 12.5	18 33.5	17 11.6
11 M	13 19 27.4	17 57.7	6 57.7	28 45.7	27 48.3	2 3.3	5 7.9	1 12.1	11 25.6	17 15.9	18 35.5	17 13.5
12 T	13 23 23.9	18 57.0	6 54.5	11♉51.7	29 24.0	3 11.4	5 50.9	1 13.6	11 22.5	17 19.3	18 37.5	17 15.3
13 W	13 27 20.5	19 56.4	6 51.3	25 9.1	0♏59.0	4 19.4	6 33.9	1 15.0	11 19.4	17 22.6	18 39.5	17 17.2
14 T	13 31 17.1	20 55.8	6 48.2	8♊37.5	2 33.3	5 27.2	7 17.0	1 16.1	11 16.4	17 25.9	18 41.5	17 19.1
15 F	13 35 13.6	21 55.3	6 45.0	22 16.4	4 7.0	6 35.0	8 0.1	1 17.1	11 13.5	17 29.2	18 43.6	17 20.9
16 S	13 39 10.2	22 54.8	6 41.8	6♋ 5.5	5 40.0	7 42.6	8 43.4	1 17.8	11 10.6	17 32.5	18 45.6	17 22.7
17 S	13 43 6.7	23 54.3	6 38.6	20 4.7	7 12.3	8 50.0	9 26.7	1 18.4	11 7.9	17 35.7	18 47.7	17 24.6
18 M	13 47 3.3	24 53.9	6 35.5	4♌13.3	8 44.1	9 57.3	10 10.1	1 18.8	11 5.2	17 38.9	18 49.8	17 26.3
19 T	13 50 59.8	25 53.5	6 32.3	18 29.8	10 15.1	11 4.5	10 53.6	1 18.9	11 2.6	17 42.1	18 51.9	17 28.1
20 W	13 54 56.4	26 53.2	6 29.1	2♍51.6	11 45.6	12 11.6	11 37.1	1 18.9	11 0.1	17 45.2	18 54.0	17 29.9
21 T	13 58 52.9	27 52.9	6 25.9	17 14.7	13 15.5	13 18.5	12 20.8	1R18.6	10 57.7	17 48.4	18 56.1	17 31.6
22 F	14 2 49.5	28 52.7	6 22.7	1♎34.3	14 44.7	14 25.3	13 4.6	1 18.2	10 55.4	17 51.5	18 58.3	17 33.4
23 S	14 6 46.0	29 52.4	6 19.6	15 45.0	16 13.3	15 31.8	13 48.4	1 17.6	10 53.2	17 54.5	19 0.5	17 35.1
24 S	14 10 42.6	0♏52.2	6 16.4	29 41.6	17 41.3	16 38.3	14 32.2	1 16.7	10 51.1	17 57.6	19 2.6	17 36.7
25 M	14 14 39.2	1 52.0	6 13.2	13♏20.3	19 8.6	17 44.5	15 16.2	1 15.7	10 49.0	18 0.6	19 4.8	17 38.4
26 T	14 18 35.7	2 51.9	6 10.0	26 38.6	20 35.2	18 50.6	16 0.2	1 14.4	10 47.1	18 3.5	19 6.9	17 40.0
27 W	14 22 32.3	3 51.8	6 6.9	9♐35.8	22 1.2	19 56.5	16 44.3	1 12.9	10 45.2	18 6.4	19 9.1	17 41.6
28 T	14 26 28.8	4 51.7	6 3.7	22 13.0	23 26.4	21 2.2	17 28.4	1 11.3	10 43.5	18 9.3	19 11.3	17 43.2
29 F	14 30 25.4	5 51.7	6 0.5	4♑32.9	24 50.9	22 7.7	18 12.7	1 9.4	10 41.8	18 12.2	19 13.5	17 44.8
30 S	14 34 21.9	6 51.7	5 57.3	16 39.0	26 14.6	23 13.0	18 57.0	1 7.3	10 40.3	18 15.0	19 15.7	17 46.3
31 S	14 38 18.5	7 51.7	5 54.1	28 35.7	27 37.5	24 18.1	19 41.4	1 5.1	10 38.8	18 17.7	19 17.9	17 47.9

DECLINATION at NOON

DAY	SIDEREAL TIME	☉	☊	☾	☿	♀	♂	♃	♄	♅	♆	♇
1 F	12 40 1.9	3S12.8	21N33.9	25S10.5	3S28.7	19S30.5	20S38.3	22N57.7	9S 2.1	5N56.1	15S37.7	18N 2.3
4 M	12 51 51.5	4 22.5	21 32.3	23 43.2	5 45.2	20 34.8	21 7.3	22 57.8	9 6.3	5 52.0	15 39.3	18 0.6
7 T	13 3 41.2	5 31.7	21 30.8	13 7.1	7 57.6	21 34.7	21 34.8	22 57.8	9 10.2	5 47.9	15 41.0	17 58.9
10 S	13 15 30.8	6 40.2	21 29.2	2N38.2	10 4.9	22 29.9	22 0.7	22 57.8	9 13.8	5 44.0	15 42.7	17 57.3
13 W	13 27 20.5	7 47.9	21 27.6	18 10.0	12 6.5	23 20.3	22 24.8	22 57.9	9 17.2	5 40.1	15 44.4	17 55.8
16 S	13 39 10.2	8 54.7	21 26.0	25 56.7	14 1.9	24 5.5	22 47.2	22 57.9	9 20.3	5 36.3	15 46.1	17 54.5
19 T	13 50 59.8	10 0.3	21 24.3	19 59.2	15 50.5	24 45.3	23 7.7	22 58.0	9 23.0	5 32.6	15 47.9	17 53.2
22 F	14 2 49.5	11 4.7	21 22.7	3 37.6	17 31.7	25 19.7	23 26.3	22 58.1	9 25.4	5 29.0	15 49.7	17 52.1
25 M	14 14 39.2	12 7.5	21 21.1	14S 1.1	19 5.0	25 48.3	23 42.8	22 58.3	9 27.5	5 25.5	15 51.5	17 51.0
28 T	14 26 28.8	13 8.7	21 19.4	24 46.3	20 29.7	26 11.1	23 57.3	22 58.5	9 29.3	5 22.2	15 53.3	17 50.1
31 S	14 38 18.5	14 8.1	21 17.8	24 34.5	21 45.2	26 28.1	24 9.6	22 58.7	9 30.7	5 19.0	15 55.1	17 49.4

NOVEMBER 1965

DAY	EPHEMERIS SIDEREAL TIME	☉	☊	☽	☿	♀	♂	♃	♄	♅	♆	♇
	h m s	° ′	° ′	° ′	° ′	° ′	° ′	° ′	° ′	° ′	° ′	° ′
					LONGITUDE at NOON							
1 M	14 42 15.0	8♏51.7	5♓51.0	10♒28.0	28♏59.4	25♐23.0	20♐25.8	1♋ 2.6	10♓37.5	18♍20.5	19♏20.1	17♍49.4
2 T	14 46 11.6	9 51.8	5 47.8	22 20.7	0♐20.4	26 27.6	21 10.3	0R60.0	10R36.2	18 23.2	19 22.4	17 50.8
3 W	14 50 8.1	10 51.9	5 44.6	4♓18.5	1 40.4	27 32.0	21 54.9	0 57.1	10 35.1	18 25.8	19 24.6	17 52.3
4 T	14 54 4.7	11 52.0	5 41.4	16 25.7	2 59.2	28 36.1	22 39.5	0 54.1	10 34.0	18 28.4	19 26.8	17 53.7
5 F	14 58 1.3	12 52.1	5 38.3	28 46.1	4 16.7	29 40.0	23 24.2	0 50.8	10 33.1	18 31.0	19 29.1	17 55.1
6 S	15 1 57.8	13 52.3	5 35.1	11♈22.3	5 32.9	0♑43.7	24 9.0	0 47.4	10 32.2	18 33.6	19 31.3	17 56.5
7 S	15 5 54.4	14 52.5	5 31.9	24 15.9	6 47.5	1 47.0	24 53.8	0 43.8	10 31.5	18 36.1	19 33.5	17 57.9
8 M	15 9 50.9	15 52.7	5 28.7	7♉27.2	8 0.4	2 50.1	25 38.7	0 40.0	10 30.8	18 38.5	19 35.8	17 59.2
9 T	15 13 47.5	16 52.9	5 25.5	20 55.5	9 11.4	3 52.8	26 23.6	0 36.0	10 30.3	18 40.9	19 38.0	18 0.5
10 W	15 17 44.0	17 53.2	5 22.4	4♊38.8	10 20.4	4 55.3	27 8.6	0 31.9	10 29.9	18 43.3	19 40.3	18 1.8
11 T	15 21 40.6	18 53.5	5 19.2	18 34.3	11 26.9	5 57.5	27 53.7	0 27.5	10 29.5	18 45.6	19 42.5	18 3.0
12 F	15 25 37.1	19 53.9	5 16.0	2♋39.0	12 30.8	6 59.3	28 38.9	0 23.0	10 29.4	18 47.9	19 44.8	18 4.3
13 S	15 29 33.7	20 54.3	5 12.8	16 49.5	13 31.6	8 0.8	29 24.1	0 18.3	10 29.2	18 50.2	19 47.1	18 5.5
14 S	15 33 30.3	21 54.7	5 9.7	1♌ 2.8	14 29.1	9 2.0	0♑ 9.3	0 13.5	10 29.2	18 52.4	19 49.3	18 6.6
15 M	15 37 26.8	22 55.1	5 6.5	15 16.3	15 22.7	10 2.8	0 54.6	0 8.4	10D29.3	18 54.5	19 51.6	18 7.8
16 T	15 41 23.4	23 55.6	5 3.3	29 27.5	16 12.0	11 3.2	1 40.0	0 3.2	10 29.5	18 56.6	19 53.8	18 8.9
17 W	15 45 19.9	24 56.1	5 0.1	13♍34.3	16 56.4	12 3.2	2 25.5	29♊57.8	10 29.8	18 58.7	19 56.1	18 9.9
18 T	15 49 16.5	25 56.6	4 57.0	27 34.6	17 35.3	13 2.8	3 10.9	29 52.3	10 30.2	19 0.7	19 58.3	18 11.0
19 F	15 53 13.0	26 57.2	4 53.8	11♎26.4	18 8.2	14 2.1	3 56.5	29 46.6	10 30.7	19 2.6	20 0.5	18 12.0
20 S	15 57 9.6	27 57.8	4 50.6	25 7.8	18 34.1	15 0.9	4 42.1	29 40.7	10 31.4	19 4.5	20 2.8	18 13.0
21 S	16 1 6.2	28 58.4	4 47.4	8♏36.9	18 52.5	15 59.2	5 27.8	29 34.7	10 32.1	19 6.4	20 5.0	18 14.0
22 M	16 5 2.7	29 59.1	4 44.3	21 52.1	19 2.4	16 57.1	6 13.5	29 28.6	10 32.9	19 8.2	20 7.2	18 14.9
23 T	16 8 59.3	0♐59.7	4 41.1	4♐52.3	19 3.3	17 54.5	6 59.3	29 22.3	10 33.9	19 10.0	20 9.5	18 15.8
24 W	16 12 55.8	2 0.4	4 37.9	17 37.2	18R54.2	18 51.5	7 45.1	29 15.8	10 34.9	19 11.7	20 11.7	18 16.7
25 T	16 16 52.4	3 1.1	4 34.7	0♑ 7.2	18 34.8	19 47.9	8 31.0	29 9.3	10 36.1	19 13.3	20 13.9	18 17.5
26 F	16 20 48.9	4 1.9	4 31.5	12 23.6	18 4.6	20 43.7	9 16.9	29 2.6	10 37.3	19 15.0	20 16.1	18 18.3
27 S	16 24 45.5	5 2.6	4 28.4	24 28.7	17 23.4	21 39.0	10 2.9	28 55.7	10 38.7	19 16.5	20 18.3	18 19.1
28 S	16 28 42.1	6 3.4	4 25.2	6♒25.5	16 31.7	22 33.7	10 48.9	28 48.8	10 40.2	19 18.0	20 20.5	18 19.9
29 M	16 32 38.6	7 4.2	4 22.0	18 17.7	15 30.2	23 27.8	11 35.0	28 41.7	10 41.7	19 19.5	20 22.7	18 20.6
30 T	16 36 35.2	8 5.0	4 18.8	0♓ 9.7	14 20.1	24 21.2	12 21.1	28 34.6	10 43.4	19 20.9	20 24.8	18 21.3
					DECLINATION at NOON							
1 M	14 42 15.0	14S27.4	21N17.2	22S12.1	22S 8.2	26S32.4	24S13.2	22N58.7	9S31.0	5N17.9	15S55.8	17N49.1
4 T	14 54 4.7	15 23.9	21 15.6	10 4.8	23 10.1	26 41.4	24 22.5	22 59.0	9 31.9	5 14.9	15 57.6	17 48.5
7 S	15 5 54.4	16 18.2	21 13.9	6N14.3	24 1.0	26 44.5	24 29.6	22 59.2	9 32.5	5 12.0	15 59.4	17 48.0
10 W	15 17 44.0	17 10.0	21 12.2	21 4.3	24 39.7	26 41.8	24 34.3	22 59.4	9 32.7	5 9.3	16 1.2	17 47.7
13 S	15 29 33.7	17 59.2	21 10.5	25 54.0	25 5.4	26 33.4	24 36.6	22 59.7	9 32.5	5 6.7	16 3.0	17 47.4
16 T	15 41 23.4	18 45.5	21 8.8	16 34.7	25 16.8	26 19.6	24 36.6	22 59.9	9 31.9	5 4.3	16 4.8	17 47.3
19 F	15 53 13.0	19 28.9	21 7.1	0S37.8	25 12.5	26 0.4	24 34.1	23 0.2	9 31.0	5 2.0	16 6.6	17 47.4
22 M	16 5 2.7	20 9.1	21 5.3	17 6.3	24 50.6	25 36.2	24 29.1	23 0.4	9 29.7	4 59.9	16 8.4	17 47.5
25 T	16 16 52.4	20 46.0	21 3.6	25 43.3	24 8.7	25 7.3	24 21.7	23 0.6	9 28.1	4 58.0	16 10.1	17 47.8
28 S	16 28 42.1	21 19.4	21 1.8	23 10.7	23 4.9	24 34.0	24 11.8	23 0.7	9 26.1	4 56.3	16 11.8	17 48.2

DECEMBER 1965

DAY	EPHEMERIS SIDEREAL TIME	☉	☊	☽	☿	♀	♂	♃	♄	♅	♆	♇
					LONGITUDE at NOON							
1 W	16 40 31.7	9♐ 5.8	4♓15.7	12♓ 6.0	13♐ 3.4	25♑14.0	13♑ 7.3	28♊27.3	10♓45.2	19♍22.2	20♏27.0	18♍21.9
2 T	16 44 28.3	10 6.6	4 12.5	24 11.4	11R42.3	26 6.0	13 53.5	28R19.9	10 47.1	19 23.5	20 29.1	18 22.5
3 F	16 48 24.9	11 7.5	4 9.3	6♈30.5	10 19.5	26 57.4	14 39.8	28 12.5	10 49.1	19 24.8	20 31.3	18 23.2
4 S	16 52 21.4	12 8.4	4 6.1	19 7.2	8 57.8	27 48.0	15 26.1	28 5.0	10 51.2	19 26.0	20 33.5	18 23.7
5 S	16 56 18.0	13 9.3	4 3.0	2♉ 4.8	7 39.9	28 37.8	16 12.5	27 57.3	10 53.4	19 27.1	20 35.6	18 24.3
6 M	17 0 14.5	14 10.2	3 59.8	15 25.3	6 28.3	29 26.7	16 58.8	27 49.6	10 55.7	19 28.2	20 37.7	18 24.7
7 T	17 4 11.1	15 11.1	3 56.6	29 8.9	5 25.0	0♒14.8	17 45.3	27 41.9	10 58.1	19 29.2	20 39.8	18 25.2
8 W	17 8 7.6	16 12.0	3 53.4	13♊13.9	4 31.7	1 2.0	18 31.7	27 34.0	11 0.6	19 30.2	20 41.8	18 25.6
9 T	17 12 4.2	17 12.9	3 50.2	27 36.5	3 49.1	1 48.3	19 18.2	27 26.1	11 3.2	19 31.1	20 43.9	18 26.0
10 F	17 16 0.8	18 13.9	3 47.1	12♋11.1	3 17.9	2 33.6	20 4.7	27 18.2	11 5.8	19 31.9	20 46.0	18 26.4
11 S	17 19 57.3	19 14.8	3 43.9	26 51.3	2 57.9	3 17.9	20 51.3	27 10.2	11 8.6	19 32.7	20 48.0	18 26.7
12 S	17 23 53.9	20 15.8	3 40.7	11♌30.3	2 48.9	4 1.1	21 37.9	27 2.1	11 11.5	19 33.5	20 50.0	18 27.0
13 M	17 27 50.4	21 16.8	3 37.5	26 2.1	2D50.3	4 43.3	22 24.6	26 54.0	11 14.5	19 34.1	20 52.0	18 27.3
14 T	17 31 47.0	22 17.9	3 34.4	10♍22.1	3 1.4	5 24.3	23 11.3	26 45.9	11 17.5	19 34.8	20 54.0	18 27.5
15 W	17 35 43.6	23 18.9	3 31.2	24 27.5	3 21.4	6 4.2	23 58.0	26 37.8	11 20.7	19 35.4	20 56.0	18 27.7
16 T	17 39 40.1	24 19.9	3 28.0	8♎16.8	3 49.4	6 42.9	24 44.8	26 29.6	11 24.0	19 35.9	20 58.0	18 27.9
17 F	17 43 36.7	25 21.0	3 24.8	21 50.1	4 24.7	7 20.2	25 31.6	26 21.5	11 27.3	19 36.3	20 59.9	18 28.0
18 S	17 47 33.2	26 22.1	3 21.7	5♏ 8.1	5 6.4	7 56.3	26 18.4	26 13.3	11 30.8	19 36.7	21 1.8	18 28.1
19 S	17 51 29.8	27 23.2	3 18.5	18 12.0	5 53.8	8 31.0	27 5.3	26 5.1	11 34.3	19 37.1	21 3.7	18 28.2
20 M	17 55 26.3	28 24.3	3 15.3	1♐ 2.9	6 46.2	9 4.2	27 52.2	25 57.0	11 37.9	19 37.4	21 5.6	18 28.2
21 T	17 59 22.9	29 25.4	3 12.1	13 41.8	7 43.1	9 36.0	28 39.1	25 48.8	11 41.7	19 37.6	21 7.5	18 28.2
22 W	18 3 19.5	0♑26.6	3 9.0	26 9.7	8 43.9	10 6.2	29 26.0	25 40.7	11 45.5	19 37.8	21 9.3	18 28.2
23 T	18 7 16.0	1 27.7	3 5.8	8♑27.6	9 48.2	10 34.8	0♒13.0	25 32.6	11 49.4	19 37.9	21 11.2	18R28.1
24 F	18 11 12.6	2 28.9	3 2.6	20 36.4	10 55.6	11 1.8	1 0.1	25 24.6	11 53.4	19 38.0	21 13.0	18 28.0
25 S	18 15 9.1	3 30.1	2 59.4	2♒37.4	12 5.5	11 26.9	1 47.1	25 16.6	11 57.5	19 38.0	21 14.8	18 27.9
26 S	18 19 5.7	4 31.2	2 56.2	14 32.4	13 17.8	11 50.3	2 34.2	25 8.6	12 1.6	19 38.0	21 16.6	18 27.7
27 M	18 23 2.3	5 32.4	2 53.1	26 23.9	14 32.2	12 11.8	3 21.3	25 0.7	12 5.9	19R37.9	21 18.3	18 27.5
28 T	18 26 58.8	6 33.5	2 49.9	8♓14.9	15 48.4	12 31.4	4 8.4	24 52.8	12 10.2	19 37.7	21 20.0	18 27.3
29 W	18 30 55.4	7 34.7	2 46.7	20 9.2	17 6.3	12 48.9	4 55.6	24 45.0	12 14.6	19 37.5	21 21.7	18 27.0
30 T	18 34 51.9	8 35.8	2 43.5	2♈11.0	18 25.5	13 4.4	5 42.7	24 37.3	12 19.1	19 37.2	21 23.4	18 26.7
31 F	18 38 48.5	9 37.0	2 40.4	14 25.0	19 46.1	13 17.7	6 29.9	24 29.6	12 23.7	19 36.9	21 25.1	18 26.4
					DECLINATION at NOON							
1 W	16 40 31.7	21S49.2	21N 0.1	11S51.7	21S41.3	23S56.8	23S59.5	23N 0.8	9S23.7	4N54.8	16S13.5	17N48.8
4 S	16 52 21.4	22 15.2	20 58.3	3N59.4	20 10.4	23 16.0	23 44.7	23 0.8	9 21.0	4 53.4	16 15.1	17 49.5
7 T	17 4 11.1	22 37.3	20 56.5	19 28.3	18 53.5	22 32.1	23 27.4	23 0.8	9 17.9	4 52.3	16 16.7	17 50.3
10 F	17 16 0.8	22 55.4	20 54.7	26 5.0	18 8.1	21 45.6	23 7.8	23 0.7	9 14.5	4 51.3	16 18.3	17 51.2
13 M	17 27 50.4	23 9.5	20 52.9	17 43.8	17 58.2	20 57.1	22 45.8	23 0.6	9 10.8	4 50.6	16 19.8	17 52.3
16 T	17 39 40.1	23 19.4	20 51.1	0 44.4	18 17.4	20 7.1	22 21.5	23 0.4	9 6.8	4 50.0	16 21.3	17 53.5
19 S	17 51 29.8	23 25.1	20 49.3	15S49.4	18 55.6	19 16.1	21 54.9	23 0.1	9 2.4	4 49.6	16 22.7	17 54.7
22 W	18 3 19.5	23 26.7	20 47.5	25 18.7	19 44.1	18 24.8	21 26.0	22 59.8	8 57.8	4 49.5	16 24.0	17 56.2
25 S	18 15 9.1	23 23.9	20 45.7	23 53.0	20 36.1	17 33.8	20 55.0	22 59.4	8 52.8	4 49.5	16 25.4	17 57.6
28 T	18 26 58.8	23 17.0	20 43.8	13 16.8	21 26.9	16 44.0	20 21.9	22 59.0	8 47.5	4 49.8	16 26.6	17 59.3
31 F	18 38 48.5	23 5.8	20 42.0	2N 1.7	22 13.2	15 55.9	19 46.8	22 58.6	8 42.0	4 50.2	16 27.8	18 1.0

JANUARY 1966

LONGITUDE at NOON

DAY	EPHEMERIS SIDEREAL TIME h m s	☉ ° ′	☊ ° ′	☽ ° ′	☿ ° ′	♀ ° ′	♂ ° ′	♃ ° ′	♄ ° ′	♅ ° ′	♆ ° ′	♇ ° ′
1 S	18 42 45.0	10♑38.1	2♊37.2	26♈56.1	21♐ 7.8	13♒28.8	7♒17.1	24♊22.1	12♓28.3	19♍36.5	21♏26.7	18♍26.0
2 S	18 46 41.6	11 39.3	2 34.0	9♉48.8	22 30.6	13 37.6	8 4.3	24R14.6	12 33.0	19R36.0	21 28.3	18R25.6
3 M	18 50 38.2	12 40.4	2 30.8	23 6.9	23 54.3	13 44.1	8 51.5	24 7.2	12 37.9	19 35.5	21 29.9	18 25.2
4 T	18 54 34.7	13 41.6	2 27.7	6♊52.5	25 18.9	13 48.2	9 38.8	23 59.9	12 42.7	19 35.0	21 31.4	18 24.8
5 W	18 58 31.3	14 42.7	2 24.5	21 5.6	26 44.3	13 49.9	10 26.0	23 52.8	12 47.7	19 34.4	21 33.0	18 24.3
6 T	19 2 27.8	15 43.8	2 21.3	5♋43.5	28 10.4	13R49.1	11 13.3	23 45.7	12 52.7	19 33.7	21 34.5	18 23.8
7 F	19 6 24.4	16 44.9	2 18.1	20 40.0	29 37.2	13 45.8	12 0.6	23 38.7	12 57.8	19 33.0	21 35.9	18 23.2
8 S	19 10 21.0	17 46.1	2 15.0	5♌46.6	1♑ 4.7	13 39.9	12 47.9	23 31.9	13 3.0	19 32.2	21 37.4	18 22.6
9 S	19 14 17.5	18 47.2	2 11.8	20 53.3	2 32.7	13 31.6	13 35.2	23 25.2	13 8.2	19 31.4	21 38.8	18 22.0
10 M	19 18 14.1	19 48.3	2 8.6	5♍50.3	4 1.4	13 20.7	14 22.5	23 18.6	13 13.6	19 30.5	21 40.2	18 21.4
11 T	19 22 10.6	20 49.4	2 5.4	20 29.8	5 30.6	13 7.4	15 9.8	23 12.2	13 18.9	19 29.6	21 41.6	18 20.7
12 W	19 26 7.2	21 50.6	2 2.2	4♎46.8	7 0.4	12 51.5	15 57.2	23 5.8	13 24.4	19 28.6	21 42.9	18 20.0
13 T	19 30 3.7	22 51.7	1 59.1	18 39.4	8 30.8	12 33.3	16 44.5	22 59.7	13 29.9	19 27.6	21 44.2	18 19.3
14 F	19 34 0.3	23 52.8	1 55.9	2♏ 8.2	10 1.7	12 12.7	17 32.0	22 53.7	13 35.5	19 26.5	21 45.5	18 18.6
15 S	19 37 56.9	24 54.0	1 52.7	15 15.3	11 33.1	11 49.9	18 19.3	22 47.8	13 41.2	19 25.4	21 46.8	18 17.8
16 S	19 41 53.4	25 55.1	1 49.5	28 3.9	13 5.0	11 24.9	19 6.7	22 42.1	13 46.9	19 24.2	21 48.0	18 17.0
17 M	19 45 50.0	26 56.2	1 46.4	10♐37.5	14 37.5	10 57.8	19 54.1	22 36.5	13 52.7	19 23.0	21 49.2	18 16.1
18 T	19 49 46.5	27 57.3	1 43.2	22 59.2	16 10.5	10 28.9	20 41.5	22 31.1	13 58.5	19 21.7	21 50.4	18 15.3
19 W	19 53 43.1	28 58.4	1 40.0	5♑11.7	17 44.0	9 58.2	21 28.9	22 25.8	14 4.4	19 20.4	21 51.5	18 14.4
20 T	19 57 39.6	29 59.5	1 36.8	17 17.0	19 18.1	9 25.9	22 16.3	22 20.8	14 10.4	19 19.0	21 52.6	18 13.5
21 F	20 1 36.2	1♒ 0.5	1 33.7	29 16.9	20 52.7	8 52.3	23 3.7	22 15.8	14 16.4	19 17.6	21 53.7	18 12.5
22 S	20 5 32.8	2 1.6	1 30.5	11♒12.6	22 27.9	8 17.5	23 51.1	22 11.1	14 22.4	19 16.1	21 54.7	18 11.5
23 S	20 9 29.3	3 2.6	1 27.3	23 5.4	24 3.7	7 41.8	24 38.6	22 6.6	14 28.6	19 14.6	21 55.7	18 10.5
24 M	20 13 25.9	4 3.7	1 24.1	4♓56.8	25 40.1	7 5.4	25 26.0	22 2.2	14 34.7	19 13.0	21 56.7	18 9.5
25 T	20 17 22.4	5 4.7	1 21.0	16 48.7	27 17.1	6 28.6	26 13.4	21 58.0	14 41.0	19 11.4	21 57.7	18 8.5
26 W	20 21 19.0	6 5.7	1 17.8	28 43.5	28 54.7	5 51.6	27 0.8	21 54.0	14 47.3	19 9.7	21 58.6	18 7.4
27 T	20 25 15.5	7 6.7	1 14.6	10♈44.5	0♒32.9	5 14.6	27 48.2	21 50.2	14 53.6	19 8.0	21 59.5	18 6.3
28 F	20 29 12.1	8 7.7	1 11.4	22 55.6	2 11.8	4 38.0	28 35.6	21 46.5	14 60.0	19 6.3	22 0.3	18 5.2
29 S	20 33 8.7	9 8.6	1 8.2	5♉21.4	3 51.3	4 1.9	29 23.0	21 43.1	15 6.4	19 4.5	22 1.1	18 4.0
30 S	20 37 5.2	10 9.5	1 5.1	18 6.5	5 31.5	3 26.6	0♓10.4	21 39.8	15 12.9	19 2.7	22 1.9	18 2.8
31 M	20 41 1.8	11 10.5	1 1.9	1♊15.6	7 12.4	2 52.4	0 57.7	21 36.8	15 19.4	19 0.8	22 2.7	18 1.7

DECLINATION at NOON

DAY	SIDEREAL TIME	☉	☊	☽	☿	♀	♂	♃	♄	♅	♆	♇
1 S	18 42 45.0	23S 1.1	20N41.3	7N27.0	22S27.2	15S40.4	19S34.6	22N58.4	8S40.1	4N50.4	16S28.2	18N 1.6
4 T	18 54 34.7	22 44.4	20 39.5	21 42.4	23 4.0	14 56.1	18 56.9	22 58.0	8 34.3	4 51.1	16 29.3	18 3.4
7 F	19 6 24.4	22 23.7	20 37.6	25 33.5	23 32.0	14 15.5	18 17.4	22 57.5	8 28.1	4 52.0	16 30.3	18 5.3
10 M	19 18 14.1	21 59.0	20 35.7	14 8.1	23 50.1	13 39.4	17 36.1	22 57.0	8 21.8	4 53.1	16 31.3	18 7.3
13 T	19 30 3.7	21 30.4	20 33.8	3S57.4	23 57.4	13 8.5	16 53.1	22 56.6	8 15.2	4 54.3	16 32.2	18 9.4
16 S	19 41 53.4	20 58.1	20 31.9	19 15.6	23 53.4	12 43.3	16 8.5	22 56.1	8 8.4	4 55.8	16 33.0	18 11.6
19 W	19 53 43.1	20 22.2	20 30.0	26 1.7	23 37.4	12 24.4	15 22.4	22 55.7	8 1.4	4 57.4	16 33.7	18 13.8
22 S	20 5 32.8	19 42.8	20 28.1	21 55.7	23 9.1	12 11.7	14 35.0	22 55.4	7 54.2	4 59.2	16 34.4	18 16.0
25 T	20 17 22.4	19 0.1	20 26.1	9 42.5	22 28.1	12 5.3	13 46.2	22 55.2	7 46.8	5 1.1	16 35.0	18 18.3
28 F	20 29 12.1	18 14.3	20 24.2	5N56.7	21 34.1	12 4.6	12 56.2	22 55.0	7 39.2	5 3.2	16 35.5	18 20.7
31 M	20 41 1.8	17 25.6	20 22.2	20 21.2	20 26.9	12 9.2	12 5.1	22 54.9	7 31.5	5 5.4	16 36.0	18 23.0

FEBRUARY 1966

LONGITUDE at NOON

DAY	SIDEREAL TIME	☉	☊	☽	☿	♀	♂	♃	♄	♅	♆	♇
1 T	20 44 58.3	12♒11.3	0♊58.7	14♊52.5	8♒54.0	2♒19.5	1♓45.1	21♊33.9	15♓26.0	18♍58.9	22♏ 3.4	18♍ 0.5
2 W	20 48 54.9	13 12.2	0 55.5	28 59.1	10 36.3	1R48.1	2 32.5	21R31.3	15 32.6	18R57.0	22 4.1	17R59.2
3 T	20 52 51.4	14 13.0	0 52.4	13♋34.7	12 19.4	1 18.3	3 19.8	21 28.8	15 39.2	18 55.0	22 4.7	17 58.0
4 F	20 56 48.0	15 13.9	0 49.2	28 35.0	14 3.2	0 50.4	4 7.2	21 26.6	15 46.0	18 53.0	22 5.4	17 56.7
5 S	21 0 44.5	16 14.7	0 46.0	13♌51.8	15 47.7	0 24.5	4 54.5	21 24.5	15 52.7	18 51.0	22 6.0	17 55.5
6 S	21 4 41.1	17 15.5	0 42.8	29 14.1	17 32.9	0 0.7	5 41.8	21 22.7	15 59.5	18 48.9	22 6.5	17 54.1
7 M	21 8 37.7	18 16.2	0 39.7	14♍30.0	19 18.9	29♑39.1	6 29.1	21 21.0	16 6.3	18 46.8	22 7.1	17 52.8
8 T	21 12 34.2	19 17.0	0 36.5	29 28.8	21 5.6	29 19.9	7 16.4	21 19.5	16 13.1	18 44.6	22 7.6	17 51.5
9 W	21 16 30.8	20 17.7	0 33.3	14♎ 2.7	22 52.9	29 3.1	8 3.7	21 18.3	16 20.0	18 42.4	22 8.0	17 50.1
10 T	21 20 27.3	21 18.4	0 30.1	28 7.7	24 41.0	28 48.7	8 50.9	21 17.2	16 26.9	18 40.2	22 8.4	17 48.7
11 F	21 24 23.9	22 19.1	0 26.9	11♏43.6	26 29.6	28 36.8	9 38.2	21 16.3	16 33.9	18 38.0	22 8.8	17 47.3
12 S	21 28 20.4	23 19.8	0 23.8	24 52.5	28 18.9	28 27.5	10 25.4	21 15.7	16 40.9	18 35.7	22 9.2	17 45.9
13 S	21 32 17.0	24 20.4	0 20.6	7♐38.2	0♓ 8.6	28 20.6	11 12.6	21 15.2	16 47.9	18 33.4	22 9.5	17 44.5
14 M	21 36 13.5	25 21.0	0 17.4	20 5.3	1 58.8	28 16.2	11 59.8	21 14.9	16 54.9	18 31.1	22 9.8	17 43.1
15 T	21 40 10.1	26 21.7	0 14.2	2♑18.5	3 49.2	28 14.3	12 47.0	21 14.9	17 2.0	18 28.7	22 10.0	17 41.6
16 W	21 44 6.7	27 22.3	0 11.1	14 21.7	5 39.9	28D14.9	13 34.1	21D15.0	17 9.1	18 26.4	22 10.2	17 40.1
17 T	21 48 3.2	28 22.8	0 7.9	26 18.7	7 30.6	28 17.8	14 21.3	21 15.4	17 16.2	18 24.0	22 10.4	17 38.7
18 F	21 51 59.8	29 23.4	0 4.7	8♒12.1	9 21.1	28 23.1	15 8.4	21 15.9	17 23.3	18 21.5	22 10.5	17 37.2
19 S	21 55 56.3	0♓23.9	0 1.5	20 4.0	11 11.3	28 30.6	15 55.5	21 16.7	17 30.5	18 19.1	22 10.7	17 35.7
20 S	21 59 52.9	1 24.4	29♉58.3	1♓55.9	13 0.8	28 40.5	16 42.6	21 17.6	17 37.7	18 16.6	22 10.7	17 34.2
21 M	22 3 49.4	2 24.9	29 55.2	13 49.3	14 49.4	28 52.5	17 29.7	21 18.8	17 44.9	18 14.2	22 10.8	17 32.6
22 T	22 7 46.0	3 25.3	29 52.0	25 45.2	16 36.7	29 6.6	18 16.7	21 20.1	17 52.2	18 11.7	22 10.8	17 31.1
23 W	22 11 42.5	4 25.7	29 48.8	7♈45.2	18 22.3	29 22.7	19 3.7	21 21.7	17 59.4	18 9.1	22 10.8	17 29.6
24 T	22 15 39.1	5 26.1	29 45.6	19 51.4	20 5.8	29 40.9	19 50.7	21 23.4	18 6.7	18 6.6	22R10.7	17 28.0
25 F	22 19 35.6	6 26.5	29 42.5	2♉ 6.5	21 46.8	0♒ 1.0	20 37.7	21 25.4	18 14.0	18 4.1	22 10.7	17 26.5
26 S	22 23 32.2	7 26.8	29 39.3	14 33.6	23 24.6	0 22.9	21 24.6	21 27.6	18 21.3	18 1.6	22 10.5	17 24.9
27 S	22 27 28.8	8 27.1	29 36.1	27 16.8	24 58.8	0 46.6	22 11.5	21 29.9	18 28.6	17 59.0	22 10.4	17 23.4
28 M	22 31 25.3	9 27.4	29 32.9	10♊20.3	26 28.8	1 12.1	22 58.4	21 32.4	18 36.0	17 56.4	22 10.2	17 21.8

DECLINATION at NOON

DAY	SIDEREAL TIME	☉	☊	☽	☿	♀	♂	♃	♄	♅	♆	♇
1 T	20 44 58.3	17S 8.7	20N21.6	23N42.6	20S 1.5	12S11.7	11S47.8	22N54.9	7S28.9	5N 6.2	16S36.1	18N23.8
4 F	20 56 48.0	16 16.3	20 19.6	24 34.1	18 36.5	12 21.7	10 55.4	22 55.0	7 21.0	5 8.6	16 36.4	18 26.2
7 M	21 8 37.7	15 21.4	20 17.6	10 36.1	16 58.0	12 34.8	10 2.1	22 55.1	7 13.0	5 11.1	16 36.7	18 28.6
10 T	21 20 27.3	14 24.1	20 15.6	8S15.9	15 6.4	12 49.7	9 8.0	22 55.4	7 4.8	5 13.7	16 36.9	18 31.0
13 S	21 32 17.0	13 24.7	20 13.6	22 10.8	13 2.0	13 5.5	8 13.2	22 55.8	6 56.6	5 16.4	16 37.0	18 33.4
16 W	21 44 6.7	12 23.3	20 11.6	26 7.0	10 46.1	13 21.4	7 17.7	22 56.3	6 48.3	5 19.2	16 37.0	18 35.8
19 S	21 55 56.3	11 20.1	20 9.6	19 26.9	8 20.4	13 36.3	6 21.8	22 56.9	6 39.8	5 22.1	16 36.9	18 38.2
22 T	22 7 46.0	10 15.3	20 7.6	5 47.5	5 48.4	13 49.8	5 25.4	22 57.6	6 31.4	5 25.1	16 36.8	18 40.5
25 F	22 19 35.6	9 9.0	20 5.6	10N 4.6	3 15.0	14 1.0	4 28.6	22 58.4	6 22.8	5 28.1	16 36.6	18 42.8
28 M	22 31 25.3	8 1.6	20 3.5	22 59.9	0 47.3	14 9.6	3 31.7	22 59.4	6 14.2	5 31.1	16 36.3	18 45.1

MARCH 1966

DAY	EPHEMERIS SIDEREAL TIME	☉	☊	☽	☿	♀	♂	♃	♄	♅	♆	♇
	h m s	° ′	° ′	° ′	° ′	° ′	° ′	° ′	° ′	° ′	° ′	° ′
LONGITUDE at NOON												
1 T	22 35 21.9	10♓27.6	29♉29.7	23♊47.7	27♓53.9	1♒39.2	23♓45.2	21♊35.1	18♓43.3	17♍53.8	22♏10.0	17♍20.2
2 W	22 39 18.4	11 27.8	29 26.6	7♋42.0	29 13.7	2 7.9	24 32.0	21 38.0	18 50.7	17R51.2	22R 9.7	17R18.6
3 T	22 43 15.0	12 27.9	29 23.4	22 4.0	0♈27.4	2 38.2	25 18.8	21 41.1	18 58.0	17 48.6	22 9.4	17 17.0
4 F	22 47 11.5	13 28.0	29 20.2	6♌51.3	1 34.5	3 9.9	26 5.6	21 44.4	19 5.4	17 46.0	22 9.1	17 15.4
5 S	22 51 8.1	14 28.1	29 17.0	21 58.3	2 34.6	3 43.1	26 52.3	21 47.9	19 12.8	17 43.4	22 8.7	17 13.8
6 S	22 55 4.6	15 28.2	29 13.9	7♍15.7	3 27.0	4 17.7	27 38.9	21 51.5	19 20.2	17 40.8	22 8.3	17 12.2
7 M	22 59 1.2	16 28.2	29 10.7	22 32.4	4 11.4	4 53.7	28 25.6	21 55.3	19 27.5	17 38.1	22 7.9	17 10.6
8 T	23 2 57.7	17 28.2	29 7.5	7♎37.0	4 47.4	5 30.9	29 12.2	21 59.3	19 34.9	17 35.5	22 7.5	17 9.0
9 W	23 6 54.3	18 28.1	29 4.3	22 20.3	5 14.8	6 9.3	29 58.8	22 3.5	19 42.3	17 32.9	22 7.0	17 7.5
10 T	23 10 50.8	19 28.0	29 1.1	6♏36.1	5 33.3	6 49.0	0♈45.3	22 7.9	19 49.7	17 30.3	22 6.5	17 5.9
11 F	23 14 47.4	20 27.9	28 58.0	20 22.2	5 43.0	7 29.7	1 31.8	22 12.4	19 57.1	17 27.6	22 5.9	17 4.3
12 S	23 18 44.0	21 27.8	28 54.8	3♐39.4	5 43.8	8 11.6	2 18.3	22 17.1	20 4.5	17 25.0	22 5.3	17 2.7
13 S	23 22 40.5	22 27.7	28 51.6	16 30.6	5R35.9	8 54.5	3 4.8	22 22.0	20 11.9	17 22.4	22 4.7	17 1.1
14 M	23 26 37.1	23 27.5	28 48.4	29 0.4	5 19.8	9 38.5	3 51.2	22 27.0	20 19.3	17 19.8	22 4.1	16 59.5
15 T	23 30 33.6	24 27.3	28 45.3	11♑13.5	4 55.9	10 23.4	4 37.6	22 32.2	20 26.7	17 17.2	22 3.4	16 57.9
16 W	23 34 30.2	25 27.0	28 42.1	23 15.0	4 24.8	11 9.2	5 23.9	22 37.6	20 34.1	17 14.6	22 2.7	16 56.3
17 T	23 38 26.7	26 26.8	28 38.9	5♒ 9.2	3 47.2	11 55.9	6 10.2	22 43.2	20 41.4	17 12.0	22 2.0	16 54.7
18 F	23 42 23.3	27 26.5	28 35.7	17 0.3	3 4.2	12 43.5	6 56.5	22 48.9	20 48.9	17 9.5	22 1.3	16 53.2
19 S	23 46 19.8	28 26.2	28 32.5	28 51.2	2 16.7	13 31.9	7 42.7	22 54.8	20 56.2	17 6.9	22 0.5	16 51.7
20 S	23 50 16.4	29 25.8	28 29.4	10♓44.5	1 25.8	14 21.0	8 28.9	23 0.8	21 3.6	17 4.4	21 59.7	16 50.1
21 M	23 54 12.9	0♈25.4	28 26.2	22 41.9	0 32.6	15 10.9	9 15.1	23 7.0	21 10.9	17 1.8	21 58.8	16 48.5
22 T	23 58 9.5	1 25.0	28 23.0	4♈45.0	29♓38.4	16 1.5	10 1.2	23 13.4	21 18.3	16 59.3	21 57.9	16 47.0
23 W	0 2 6.0	2 24.5	28 19.8	16 54.7	28 44.3	16 52.8	10 47.3	23 19.9	21 25.6	16 56.8	21 57.0	16 45.5
24 T	0 6 2.6	3 24.0	28 16.7	29 12.4	27 51.4	17 44.8	11 33.3	23 26.6	21 32.9	16 54.3	21 56.1	16 44.0
25 F	0 9 59.1	4 23.5	28 13.5	11♉39.5	27 0.6	18 37.4	12 19.3	23 33.4	21 40.2	16 51.8	21 55.2	16 42.4
26 S	0 13 55.7	5 22.9	28 10.3	24 17.7	26 12.9	19 30.6	13 5.2	23 40.3	21 47.4	16 49.4	21 54.2	16 40.9
27 S	0 17 52.2	6 22.3	28 7.1	7♊ 9.5	25 29.1	20 24.4	13 51.2	23 47.4	21 54.7	16 46.9	21 53.2	16 39.4
28 M	0 21 48.8	7 21.7	28 3.9	20 17.3	24 49.7	21 18.8	14 37.0	23 54.7	22 1.9	16 44.5	21 52.1	16 38.0
29 T	0 25 45.4	8 21.0	28 0.8	3♋43.8	24 15.2	22 13.7	15 22.8	24 2.1	22 9.1	16 42.1	21 51.1	16 36.5
30 W	0 29 41.9	9 20.3	27 57.6	17 31.0	23 46.0	23 9.2	16 8.6	24 9.6	22 16.3	16 39.8	21 50.0	16 35.1
31 T	0 33 38.5	10 19.5	27 54.4	1♌39.8	23 22.3	24 5.1	16 54.3	24 17.3	22 23.5	16 37.4	21 48.9	16 33.6
DECLINATION at NOON												
1 T	22 35 21.9	7S38.8	20N 2.9	25N25.6	0S 0.7	14S11.8	3S12.7	22N59.7	6S11.3	5N32.1	16S36.2	18N45.8
4 F	22 47 11.5	6 30.1	20 0.8	23 4.5	2N 6.0	14 16.2	2 15.5	23 0.8	6 2.7	5 35.2	16 35.8	18 48.0
7 M	22 59 1.2	5 20.5	19 58.7	7 9.7	3 46.2	14 17.0	1 18.4	23 1.9	5 54.1	5 38.3	16 35.4	18 50.1
10 T	23 10 50.8	4 10.2	19 56.7	11S59.7	4 51.9	14 13.8	0 21.3	23 3.1	5 45.5	5 41.3	16 34.8	18 52.2
13 S	23 22 40.5	2 59.5	19 54.6	24 23.4	5 17.5	14 6.5	0N35.7	23 4.3	5 36.9	5 44.4	16 34.2	18 54.1
16 W	23 34 30.2	1 48.5	19 52.5	25 33.9	5 1.2	13 54.9	1 32.5	23 5.7	5 28.3	5 47.4	16 33.6	18 56.0
19 S	23 46 19.8	0 37.3	19 50.4	16 36.5	4 7.1	13 38.9	2 29.0	23 7.0	5 19.7	5 50.4	16 32.9	18 57.8
22 T	23 58 9.5	0N33.8	19 48.3	1 47.0	2 45.6	13 18.5	3 25.1	23 8.4	5 11.2	5 53.3	16 32.1	18 59.5
25 F	0 9 59.1	1 44.8	19 46.2	14N 5.7	1 11.4	12 53.7	4 20.8	23 9.8	5 2.7	5 56.2	16 31.2	19 1.2
28 M	0 21 48.8	2 55.3	19 44.0	25 10.3	0S20.3	12 24.6	5 16.0	23 11.2	4 54.4	5 59.0	16 30.3	19 2.7
31 T	0 33 38.5	4 5.4	19 41.9	24 20.8	1 38.1	11 51.1	6 10.5	23 12.6	4 46.1	6 1.7	16 29.4	19 4.1

APRIL 1966

DAY	EPHEMERIS SIDEREAL TIME	☉	☊	☽	☿	♀	♂	♃	♄	♅	♆	♇
LONGITUDE at NOON												
1 F	0 37 35.0	11♈18.7	27♉51.2	16♌ 8.9	23♓ 4.3	25♒ 1.6	17♈40.0	24♊25.1	22♓30.7	16♍35.1	21♏47.8	16♍32.2
2 S	0 41 31.6	12 17.9	27 48.1	0♍54.8	22R52.0	25 58.5	18 25.6	24 33.0	22 37.8	16R32.8	21R46.6	16R30.8
3 S	0 45 28.1	13 17.0	27 44.9	15 51.1	22 45.4	26 55.9	19 11.2	24 41.1	22 44.9	16 30.6	21 45.4	16 29.4
4 M	0 49 24.7	14 16.1	27 41.7	0♎49.7	22 44.4	27 53.7	19 56.7	24 49.3	22 52.0	16 28.3	21 44.2	16 28.0
5 T	0 53 21.2	15 15.2	27 38.5	15 41.4	22D48.9	28 51.9	20 42.2	24 57.7	22 59.0	16 26.1	21 43.0	16 26.6
6 W	0 57 17.8	16 14.2	27 35.3	0♏17.8	22 58.7	29 50.6	21 27.7	25 6.1	23 6.0	16 24.0	21 41.8	16 25.3
7 T	1 1 14.3	17 13.2	27 32.2	14 32.4	23 13.5	0♓49.7	22 13.1	25 14.7	23 13.0	16 21.8	21 40.5	16 24.0
8 F	1 5 10.9	18 12.2	27 29.0	28 21.5	23 33.4	1 49.2	22 58.5	25 23.5	23 20.0	16 19.8	21 39.3	16 22.7
9 S	1 9 7.4	19 11.1	27 25.8	11♐44.2	23 57.8	2 49.0	23 43.8	25 32.3	23 27.0	16 17.7	21 38.0	16 21.4
10 S	1 13 4.0	20 10.0	27 22.6	24 41.6	24 26.8	3 49.2	24 29.0	25 41.2	23 33.9	16 15.6	21 36.7	16 20.1
11 M	1 17 0.6	21 8.9	27 19.5	7♑17.0	24 60.0	4 49.7	25 14.2	25 50.3	23 40.7	16 13.6	21 35.3	16 18.9
12 T	1 20 57.1	22 7.7	27 16.3	19 34.5	25 37.2	5 50.6	25 59.4	25 59.5	23 47.6	16 11.6	21 34.0	16 17.6
13 W	1 24 53.7	23 6.5	27 13.1	1♒38.7	26 18.3	6 51.8	26 44.5	26 8.8	23 54.3	16 9.7	21 32.6	16 16.4
14 T	1 28 50.2	24 5.3	27 9.9	13 34.4	27 3.1	7 53.3	27 29.6	26 18.2	24 1.1	16 7.8	21 31.2	16 15.2
15 F	1 32 46.8	25 4.0	27 6.7	25 26.3	27 51.4	8 55.2	28 14.6	26 27.7	24 7.8	16 5.9	21 29.8	16 14.1
16 S	1 36 43.3	26 2.8	27 3.6	7♓18.4	28 42.9	9 57.3	28 59.6	26 37.4	24 14.5	16 4.1	21 28.4	16 12.9
17 S	1 40 39.9	27 1.5	27 0.4	19 14.2	29 37.7	10 59.7	29 44.5	26 47.1	24 21.2	16 2.3	21 26.9	16 11.8
18 M	1 44 36.4	28 0.1	26 57.2	1♈16.7	0♈35.4	12 2.3	0♉29.4	26 57.0	24 27.8	16 0.6	21 25.5	16 10.7
19 T	1 48 33.0	28 58.8	26 54.0	13 28.0	1 36.0	13 5.2	1 14.2	27 6.9	24 34.3	15 58.9	21 24.0	16 9.6
20 W	1 52 29.5	29 57.4	26 50.9	25 49.7	2 39.4	14 8.4	1 59.0	27 17.0	24 40.8	15 57.2	21 22.5	16 8.5
21 T	1 56 26.1	0♉55.9	26 47.7	8♉22.8	3 45.4	15 11.8	2 43.8	27 27.1	24 47.3	15 55.6	21 21.0	16 7.5
22 F	2 0 22.6	1 54.5	26 44.5	21 8.0	4 53.9	16 15.4	3 28.4	27 37.4	24 53.8	15 54.0	21 19.5	16 6.5
23 S	2 4 19.2	2 53.0	26 41.3	4♊ 5.7	6 4.9	17 19.3	4 13.1	27 47.7	25 0.1	15 52.5	21 18.0	16 5.5
24 S	2 8 15.8	3 51.5	26 38.2	17 16.4	7 18.2	18 23.4	4 57.7	27 58.2	25 6.5	15 51.0	21 16.5	16 4.5
25 M	2 12 12.3	4 49.9	26 35.0	0♋40.4	8 33.8	19 27.6	5 42.2	28 8.7	25 12.8	15 49.5	21 14.9	16 3.6
26 T	2 16 8.9	5 48.3	26 31.8	14 18.0	9 51.7	20 32.1	6 26.7	28 19.4	25 19.0	15 48.1	21 13.4	16 2.6
27 W	2 20 5.4	6 46.7	26 28.6	28 9.3	11 11.6	21 36.8	7 11.1	28 30.1	25 25.2	15 46.8	21 11.8	16 1.7
28 T	2 24 2.0	7 45.0	26 25.4	12♌13.8	12 33.8	22 41.7	7 55.5	28 40.9	25 31.3	15 45.5	21 10.2	16 0.9
29 F	2 27 58.5	8 43.3	26 22.3	26 30.2	13 58.0	23 46.8	8 39.8	28 51.9	25 37.5	15 44.2	21 8.7	16 0.1
30 S	2 31 55.1	9 41.6	26 19.1	10♍55.8	15 24.2	24 52.0	9 24.1	29 2.8	25 43.5	15 43.0	21 7.1	15 59.3
DECLINATION at NOON												
1 F	0 37 35.0	4N28.6	19N41.2	20N49.3	1S59.7	11S39.1	6N28.5	23N13.1	4S43.4	6N 2.6	16S29.1	19N 4.5
4 M	0 49 24.7	5 37.7	19 39.0	3 32.9	2 49.4	11 0.1	7 22.1	23 14.5	4 35.2	6 5.2	16 28.0	19 5.7
7 T	1 1 14.3	6 45.9	19 36.9	15S14.3	3 16.0	10 17.2	8 14.9	23 15.8	4 27.2	6 7.7	16 27.0	19 6.9
10 S	1 13 4.0	7 53.0	19 34.7	25 51.1	3 20.2	9 30.5	9 6.9	23 17.1	4 19.2	6 10.0	16 25.9	19 7.9
13 W	1 24 53.7	8 59.0	19 32.5	24 25.3	3 3.8	8 40.1	9 57.9	23 18.3	4 11.5	6 12.2	16 24.8	19 8.7
16 S	1 36 43.3	10 3.7	19 30.4	13 33.2	2 28.7	7 46.4	10 48.0	23 19.4	4 3.8	6 14.3	16 23.6	19 9.5
19 T	1 48 33.0	11 6.9	19 28.2	2N 5.8	1 36.9	6 49.5	11 37.0	23 20.5	3 56.3	6 16.3	16 22.4	19 10.1
22 F	2 0 22.6	12 8.4	19 26.0	17 40.5	0 30.2	5 49.7	12 25.0	23 21.4	3 49.0	6 18.1	16 21.2	19 10.6
25 M	2 12 12.3	13 8.1	19 23.8	26 29.0	0N49.7	4 47.3	13 11.7	23 22.3	3 41.9	6 19.7	16 19.9	19 11.0
28 T	2 24 2.0	14 5.9	19 21.5	22 2.4	2 21.6	3 42.5	13 57.2	23 23.0	3 35.0	6 21.2	16 18.6	19 11.2

MAY 1966

DAY	EPHEMERIS SIDEREAL TIME	☉	☊	☽	☿	♀	♂	♃	♄	♅	♆	♇
	h m s	° ′	° ′	° ′	° ′	° ′	° ′	° ′	° ′	° ′	° ′	° ′
						LONGITUDE at NOON						
1 S	2 35 51.6	10♉39.8	26♉15.9	25♍26.6	16♈52.4	25♓57.4	10♉ 8.3	29♊13.9	25♓49.5	15♍41.9	21♏ 5.5	15♍58.5
2 M	2 39 48.2	11 38.0	26 12.7	9♎57.8	18 22.6	27 3.0	10 52.5	29 25.1	25 55.4	15R40.7	21R 3.9	15R57.7
3 T	2 43 44.8	12 36.2	26 9.6	24 23.6	19 54.7	28 8.8	11 36.6	29 36.3	26 1.3	15 39.7	21 2.3	15 57.0
4 W	2 47 41.3	13 34.3	26 6.4	8♏38.5	21 28.8	29 14.7	12 20.6	29 47.6	26 7.1	15 38.7	21 0.7	15 56.3
5 T	2 51 37.9	14 32.4	26 3.2	22 37.6	23 4.9	0♈20.8	13 4.6	29 59.0	26 12.8	15 37.7	20 59.1	15 55.6
6 F	2 55 34.4	15 30.5	26 0.0	6♐17.3	24 42.8	1 27.1	13 48.6	0♋10.4	26 18.5	15 36.8	20 57.5	15 55.0
7 S	2 59 31.0	16 28.6	25 56.8	19 35.9	26 22.7	2 33.5	14 32.5	0 22.0	26 24.2	15 35.9	20 55.8	15 54.4
8 S	3 3 27.5	17 26.6	25 53.7	2♑33.3	28 4.6	3 40.0	15 16.3	0 33.6	26 29.7	15 35.1	20 54.2	15 53.8
9 M	3 7 24.1	18 24.6	25 50.5	15 10.9	29 48.4	4 46.7	16 0.1	0 45.3	26 35.2	15 34.3	20 52.6	15 53.2
10 T	3 11 20.6	19 22.6	25 47.3	27 31.4	1♉34.1	5 53.5	16 43.9	0 57.0	26 40.7	15 33.6	20 50.9	15 52.7
11 W	3 15 17.2	20 20.5	25 44.1	9♒38.6	3 21.7	7 0.5	17 27.6	1 8.8	26 46.1	15 32.9	20 49.3	15 52.2
12 T	3 19 13.8	21 18.5	25 41.0	21 36.7	5 11.3	8 7.6	18 11.2	1 20.7	26 51.4	15 32.3	20 47.7	15 51.7
13 F	3 23 10.3	22 16.4	25 37.8	3♓30.1	7 2.9	9 14.9	18 54.8	1 32.7	26 56.7	15 31.7	20 46.0	15 51.3
14 S	3 27 6.9	23 14.3	25 34.6	15 23.6	8 56.4	10 22.2	19 38.3	1 44.7	27 1.8	15 31.2	20 44.4	15 50.9
15 S	3 31 3.4	24 12.2	25 31.4	27 21.5	10 51.8	11 29.7	20 21.8	1 56.7	27 7.0	15 30.7	20 42.8	15 50.5
16 M	3 34 60.0	25 10.0	25 28.3	9♈27.7	12 49.1	12 37.3	21 5.3	2 8.9	27 12.0	15 30.3	20 41.2	15 50.1
17 T	3 38 56.5	26 7.8	25 25.1	21 45.7	14 48.3	13 45.0	21 48.7	2 21.1	27 17.0	15 30.0	20 39.5	15 49.8
18 W	3 42 53.1	27 5.7	25 21.9	4♉17.9	16 49.2	14 52.8	22 32.0	2 33.3	27 21.9	15 29.7	20 37.9	15 49.5
19 T	3 46 49.7	28 3.4	25 18.7	17 6.1	18 52.0	16 0.8	23 15.3	2 45.7	27 26.8	15 29.4	20 36.3	15 49.3
20 F	3 50 46.2	29 1.3	25 15.5	0♊10.9	20 56.5	17 8.8	23 58.6	2 58.1	27 31.6	15 29.3	20 34.7	15 49.1
21 S	3 54 42.8	29 59.0	25 12.4	13 31.9	23 2.4	18 17.0	24 41.8	3 10.5	27 36.3	15 29.1	20 33.1	15 48.9
22 S	3 58 39.3	0♊56.7	25 9.2	27 8.0	25 9.9	19 25.2	25 24.9	3 23.0	27 40.9	15 29.0	20 31.5	15 48.7
23 M	4 2 35.9	1 54.4	25 6.0	10♋56.9	27 18.6	20 33.5	26 8.0	3 35.5	27 45.5	15 29.0	20 29.9	15 48.6
24 T	4 6 32.4	2 52.1	25 2.8	24 56.3	29 28.4	21 41.9	26 51.0	3 48.1	27 49.9	15 29.0	20 28.3	15 48.5
25 W	4 10 29.0	3 49.8	24 59.7	9♌ 3.4	1♊39.1	22 50.4	27 34.0	4 0.7	27 54.3	15D29.1	20 26.7	15 48.4
26 T	4 14 25.6	4 47.4	24 56.5	23 15.3	3 50.5	23 59.0	28 16.9	4 13.4	27 58.6	15 29.2	20 25.2	15 48.4
27 F	4 18 22.1	5 45.0	24 53.3	7♍29.3	6 2.3	25 7.6	28 59.7	4 26.1	28 2.9	15 29.4	20 23.6	15 48.4
28 S	4 22 18.7	6 42.6	24 50.1	21 42.9	8 14.2	26 16.4	29 42.5	4 38.9	28 7.0	15 29.6	20 22.1	15 48.4
29 S	4 26 15.2	7 40.1	24 47.0	5♎53.6	10 26.0	27 25.2	0♊25.3	4 51.7	28 11.1	15 29.9	20 20.5	15 48.4
30 M	4 30 11.8	8 37.6	24 43.8	19 59.0	12 37.5	28 34.1	1 8.0	5 4.5	28 15.1	15 30.2	20 19.0	15D48.5
31 T	4 34 8.3	9 35.1	24 40.6	3♏56.6	14 48.2	29 43.1	1 50.6	5 17.4	28 19.0	15 30.6	20 17.5	15 48.6
						DECLINATION at NOON						
1 S	2 35 51.6	15N 1.6	19N19.3	5N59.3	4N 3.9	2S35.7	14N41.4	23N23.6	3S28.3	6N22.5	16S17.4	19N11.3
4 W	2 47 41.3	15 55.0	19 17.1	12S57.1	5 55.6	1 27.1	15 24.2	23 24.0	3 21.8	6 23.6	16 16.1	19 11.2
7 S	2 59 31.0	16 46.1	19 14.8	25 12.4	7 55.1	0 16.9	16 5.6	23 24.3	3 15.5	6 24.6	16 14.8	19 11.0
10 T	3 11 20.6	17 34.6	19 12.6	25 14.3	10 1.2	0N54.5	16 45.6	23 24.5	3 9.4	6 25.4	16 13.5	19 10.7
13 F	3 23 10.3	18 20.5	19 10.3	15 5.4	12 11.9	2 6.9	17 24.0	23 24.4	3 3.6	6 26.0	16 12.3	19 10.3
16 M	3 34 60.0	19 3.7	19 8.0	0N15.6	14 24.8	3 20.0	18 0.9	23 24.2	2 58.1	6 26.4	16 11.0	19 9.7
19 T	3 46 49.7	19 43.9	19 5.8	16 13.1	16 36.9	4 33.4	18 36.2	23 23.9	2 52.8	6 26.6	16 9.7	19 9.0
22 S	3 58 39.3	20 21.2	19 3.5	26 11.9	18 44.0	5 46.9	19 9.9	23 23.3	2 47.8	6 26.7	16 8.5	19 8.2
25 W	4 10 29.0	20 55.3	19 1.2	22 52.4	20 41.1	7 0.1	19 41.8	23 22.5	2 43.0	6 26.5	16 7.3	19 7.2
28 S	4 22 18.7	21 26.1	18 58.9	7 37.4	22 22.7	8 12.7	20 12.0	23 21.6	2 38.6	6 26.2	16 6.1	19 6.2
31 T	4 34 8.3	21 53.6	18 56.6	11S 1.5	23 44.0	9 24.5	20 40.4	23 20.4	2 34.5	6 25.7	16 4.9	19 5.0

JUNE 1966

DAY	EPHEMERIS SIDEREAL TIME	☉	☊	☽	☿	♀	♂	♃	♄	♅	♆	♇
						LONGITUDE at NOON						
1 W	4 38 4.9	10♊32.6	24♉37.4	17♏44.1	16♊58.1	0♉52.2	2♊33.2	5♋30.3	28♓22.9	15♍31.1	20♏15.9	15♍48.8
2 T	4 42 1.5	11 30.1	24 34.3	1♐19.2	19 6.7	2 1.3	3 15.7	5 43.3	28 26.6	15 31.6	20R14.4	15 49.0
3 F	4 45 58.0	12 27.5	24 31.1	14 39.9	21 14.0	3 10.5	3 58.2	5 56.3	28 30.3	15 32.1	20 13.0	15 49.2
4 S	4 49 54.6	13 25.0	24 27.9	27 45.0	23 19.6	4 19.8	4 40.6	6 9.3	28 33.9	15 32.7	20 11.5	15 49.4
5 S	4 53 51.1	14 22.4	24 24.7	10♑33.9	25 23.5	5 29.2	5 23.0	6 22.4	28 37.4	15 33.4	20 10.0	15 49.7
6 M	4 57 47.7	15 19.8	24 21.5	23 7.1	27 25.4	6 38.7	6 5.3	6 35.5	28 40.8	15 34.1	20 8.6	15 50.0
7 T	5 1 44.2	16 17.2	24 18.4	5♒26.0	29 25.3	7 48.2	6 47.6	6 48.6	28 44.1	15 34.9	20 7.2	15 50.3
8 W	5 5 40.8	17 14.6	24 15.2	17 33.1	1♋22.9	8 57.8	7 29.9	7 1.8	28 47.3	15 35.7	20 5.7	15 50.7
9 T	5 9 37.4	18 11.9	24 12.0	29 31.5	3 18.4	10 7.5	8 12.0	7 15.0	28 50.5	15 36.6	20 4.4	15 51.1
10 F	5 13 33.9	19 9.4	24 8.8	11♓25.2	5 11.5	11 17.3	8 54.2	7 28.3	28 53.6	15 37.5	20 3.0	15 51.6
11 S	5 17 30.5	20 6.7	24 5.7	23 18.7	7 2.2	12 27.1	9 36.3	7 41.5	28 56.6	15 38.5	20 1.7	15 52.0
12 S	5 21 27.0	21 4.1	24 2.5	5♈16.6	8 50.5	13 36.9	10 18.3	7 54.8	28 59.5	15 39.5	20 0.3	15 52.5
13 M	5 25 23.6	22 1.4	23 59.3	17 23.6	10 36.3	14 46.9	11 0.3	8 8.1	29 2.2	15 40.6	19 59.0	15 53.0
14 T	5 29 20.2	22 58.7	23 56.1	29 44.3	12 19.7	15 56.9	11 42.2	8 21.5	29 4.9	15 41.7	19 57.7	15 53.6
15 W	5 33 16.7	23 56.1	23 53.0	12♉22.5	14 0.5	17 7.0	12 24.1	8 34.8	29 7.5	15 42.9	19 56.4	15 54.1
16 T	5 37 13.3	24 53.4	23 49.8	25 21.0	15 38.9	18 17.1	13 5.9	8 48.2	29 10.1	15 44.1	19 55.1	15 54.8
17 F	5 41 9.8	25 50.7	23 46.6	8♊41.3	17 14.7	19 27.3	13 47.7	9 1.6	29 12.5	15 45.4	19 53.9	15 55.4
18 S	5 45 6.4	26 48.0	23 43.4	22 23.2	18 48.0	20 37.5	14 29.5	9 15.0	29 14.8	15 46.7	19 52.6	15 56.1
19 S	5 49 3.0	27 45.3	23 40.3	6♋24.5	20 18.7	21 47.8	15 11.1	9 28.4	29 17.0	15 48.1	19 51.4	15 56.8
20 M	5 52 59.5	28 42.6	23 37.1	20 41.3	21 46.8	22 58.2	15 52.8	9 41.9	29 19.2	15 49.6	19 50.2	15 57.5
21 T	5 56 56.1	29 39.8	23 33.9	5♌ 8.0	23 12.4	24 8.6	16 34.3	9 55.3	29 21.2	15 51.0	19 49.1	15 58.3
22 W	6 0 52.6	0♋37.1	23 30.7	19 38.8	24 35.3	25 19.1	17 15.9	10 8.8	29 23.1	15 52.6	19 47.9	15 59.1
23 T	6 4 49.2	1 34.4	23 27.5	4♍ 7.9	25 55.5	26 29.6	17 57.3	10 22.3	29 25.0	15 54.1	19 46.8	15 59.9
24 F	6 8 45.7	2 31.6	23 24.4	18 30.4	27 13.0	27 40.1	18 38.8	10 35.8	29 26.7	15 55.8	19 45.7	16 0.7
25 S	6 12 42.3	3 28.8	23 21.2	2♎43.0	28 27.7	28 50.8	19 20.1	10 49.3	29 28.4	15 57.5	19 44.6	16 1.6
26 S	6 16 38.9	4 26.1	23 18.0	16 43.7	29 39.6	0♊ 1.4	20 1.4	11 2.8	29 29.9	15 59.2	19 43.6	16 2.5
27 M	6 20 35.4	5 23.3	23 14.8	0♏31.7	0♌48.6	1 12.1	20 42.7	11 16.4	29 31.4	16 0.9	19 42.5	16 3.5
28 T	6 24 32.0	6 20.5	23 11.7	14 7.0	1 54.7	2 22.9	21 23.9	11 29.9	29 32.7	16 2.8	19 41.5	16 4.4
29 W	6 28 28.5	7 17.7	23 8.5	27 29.9	2 57.7	3 33.7	22 5.1	11 43.5	29 34.0	16 4.6	19 40.6	16 5.4
30 T	6 32 25.1	8 14.9	23 5.3	10♐40.6	3 57.6	4 44.6	22 46.2	11 57.0	29 35.1	16 6.5	19 39.6	16 6.4
						DECLINATION at NOON						
1 W	4 38 4.9	22N 2.0	18N55.8	16S27.2	24N 6.0	9N48.2	20N49.5	23N20.0	2S33.2	6N25.5	16S 4.6	19N 4.6
4 S	4 49 54.6	22 24.9	18 53.5	26 14.8	24 55.4	10 58.3	21 15.5	23 18.6	2 29.5	6 24.7	16 3.5	19 3.2
7 T	5 1 44.2	22 44.3	18 51.1	23 41.6	25 20.2	12 6.9	21 39.6	23 16.9	2 26.1	6 23.8	16 2.4	19 1.8
10 F	5 13 33.9	23 0.1	18 48.8	11 55.5	25 22.1	13 13.6	22 1.9	23 15.1	2 23.0	6 22.6	16 1.4	19 0.2
13 M	5 25 23.6	23 12.3	18 46.4	3N52.1	25 3.7	14 18.1	22 22.3	23 13.0	2 20.3	6 21.3	16 0.4	18 58.5
16 T	5 37 13.3	23 20.8	18 44.1	19 7.4	24 28.1	15 20.1	22 40.9	23 10.8	2 17.9	6 19.8	15 59.5	18 56.8
19 S	5 49 3.0	23 25.6	18 41.7	26 43.2	23 38.9	16 19.3	22 57.5	23 8.3	2 15.8	6 18.1	15 58.6	18 54.9
22 W	6 0 52.6	23 26.6	18 39.3	19 49.1	22 39.0	17 15.3	23 12.1	23 5.6	2 14.1	6 16.3	15 57.8	18 53.0
25 S	6 12 42.3	23 24.0	18 37.0	2 40.0	21 31.5	18 7.8	23 24.9	23 2.7	2 12.8	6 14.3	15 57.0	18 50.9
28 T	6 24 32.0	23 17.6	18 34.6	15S10.0	20 19.4	18 56.6	23 35.7	22 59.6	2 11.8	6 12.1	15 56.3	18 48.8

JULY 1966

LONGITUDE at NOON

DAY	EPHEMERIS SIDEREAL TIME	☉	☊	☽	☿	♀	♂	♃	♄	♅	♆	♇
	h m s	° ′	° ′	° ′	° ′	° ′	° ′	° ′	° ′	° ′	° ′	° ′
1 F	6 36 21.7	9♋12.1	23♉ 2.1	23♐39.4	4♌54.3	5♊55.6	23♊27.3	12♋10.6	29♓36.2	16♍ 8.5	19♏38.7	16♍ 7.5
2 S	6 40 18.2	10 9.3	22 59.0	6♑26.3	5 47.6	7 6.5	24 8.3	12 24.2	29 37.2	16 10.5	19R37.8	16 8.6
3 S	6 44 14.8	11 6.5	22 55.8	19 1.3	6 37.6	8 17.6	24 49.3	12 37.7	29 38.0	16 12.6	19 37.0	16 9.7
4 M	6 48 11.3	12 3.7	22 52.6	1♒24.7	7 24.0	9 28.7	25 30.2	12 51.3	29 38.8	16 14.7	19 36.1	16 10.8
5 T	6 52 7.9	13 0.9	22 49.4	13 37.4	8 6.7	10 39.8	26 11.1	13 4.8	29 39.4	16 16.8	19 35.3	16 12.0
6 W	6 56 4.4	13 58.0	22 46.3	25 40.7	8 45.6	11 51.0	26 51.9	13 18.4	29 40.0	16 19.0	19 34.5	16 13.2
7 T	7 0 1.0	14 55.2	22 43.1	7♓36.9	9 20.6	13 2.2	27 32.7	13 31.9	29 40.4	16 21.2	19 33.7	16 14.4
8 F	7 3 57.6	15 52.4	22 39.9	19 29.1	9 51.6	14 13.5	28 13.4	13 45.5	29 40.8	16 23.5	19 33.0	16 15.6
9 S	7 7 54.1	16 49.6	22 36.7	1♈21.1	10 18.3	15 24.9	28 54.1	13 59.0	29 41.0	16 25.8	19 32.3	16 16.9
10 S	7 11 50.7	17 46.8	22 33.5	13 17.3	10 40.8	16 36.3	29 34.7	14 12.6	29 41.2	16 28.1	19 31.6	16 18.2
11 M	7 15 47.2	18 44.1	22 30.4	25 22.5	10 58.8	17 47.7	0♋15.3	14 26.1	29 41.2	16 30.5	19 31.0	16 19.5
12 T	7 19 43.8	19 41.3	22 27.2	7♉42.0	11 12.2	18 59.2	0 55.9	14 39.6	29 41.2	16 32.9	19 30.3	16 20.8
13 W	7 23 40.4	20 38.5	22 24.0	20 20.5	11 21.0	20 10.8	1 36.4	14 53.1	29R41.0	16 35.4	19 29.7	16 22.2
14 T	7 27 36.9	21 35.8	22 20.8	3♊22.1	11 25.0	21 22.4	2 16.8	15 6.6	29 40.8	16 37.9	19 29.2	16 23.6
15 F	7 31 33.5	22 33.0	22 17.7	16 49.8	11R24.2	22 34.0	2 57.2	15 20.1	29 40.4	16 40.4	19 28.6	16 25.0
16 S	7 35 30.0	23 30.3	22 14.5	0♋44.1	11 18.6	23 45.7	3 37.6	15 33.6	29 40.0	16 43.0	19 28.1	16 26.4
17 S	7 39 26.6	24 27.5	22 11.3	15 3.4	11 8.2	24 57.5	4 17.9	15 47.1	29 39.4	16 45.6	19 27.7	16 27.9
18 M	7 43 23.1	25 24.8	22 8.1	29 42.7	10 53.1	26 9.3	4 58.2	16 0.6	29 38.7	16 48.3	19 27.2	16 29.4
19 T	7 47 19.7	26 22.1	22 5.0	14♌34.7	10 33.4	27 21.1	5 38.4	16 14.0	29 38.0	16 51.0	19 26.8	16 30.9
20 W	7 51 16.3	27 19.4	22 1.8	29 30.7	10 9.2	28 33.0	6 18.6	16 27.4	29 37.1	16 53.7	19 26.4	16 32.4
21 T	7 55 12.8	28 16.7	21 58.6	14♍21.7	9 40.9	29 44.9	6 58.7	16 40.8	29 36.2	16 56.5	19 26.1	16 34.0
22 F	7 59 9.4	29 14.0	21 55.4	29 0.4	9 8.8	0♋57.0	7 38.8	16 54.3	29 35.2	16 59.4	19 25.8	16 35.6
23 S	8 3 5.9	0♌11.3	21 52.3	13♎21.7	8 33.3	2 9.0	8 18.8	17 7.6	29 34.0	17 2.2	19 25.5	16 37.2
24 S	8 7 2.5	1 8.6	21 49.1	27 23.2	7 54.8	3 21.0	8 58.8	17 21.0	29 32.7	17 5.1	19 25.3	16 38.8
25 M	8 10 59.0	2 5.9	21 45.9	11♏ 4.7	7 14.1	4 33.1	9 38.7	17 34.3	29 31.4	17 8.0	19 25.0	16 40.4
26 T	8 14 55.6	3 3.2	21 42.7	24 27.7	6 31.7	5 45.3	10 18.6	17 47.6	29 29.9	17 10.9	19 24.8	16 42.1
27 W	8 18 52.2	4 0.6	21 39.5	7♐34.1	5 48.3	6 57.5	10 58.5	18 0.8	29 28.4	17 13.9	19 24.7	16 43.7
28 T	8 22 48.7	4 57.9	21 36.4	20 26.3	5 4.7	8 9.7	11 38.2	18 14.1	29 26.8	17 16.9	19 24.5	16 45.4
29 F	8 26 45.3	5 55.2	21 33.2	3♑ 6.4	4 21.6	9 22.0	12 18.0	18 27.3	29 25.0	17 20.0	19 24.4	16 47.2
30 S	8 30 41.8	6 52.6	21 30.0	15 36.0	3 39.9	10 34.3	12 57.7	18 40.4	29 23.2	17 23.0	19 24.4	16 48.9
31 S	8 34 38.4	7 50.0	21 26.8	27 56.3	3 0.4	11 46.7	13 37.3	18 53.6	29 21.3	17 26.1	19 24.3	16 50.6

DECLINATION at NOON

DAY	EPHEMERIS SIDEREAL TIME	☉	☊	☽	☿	♀	♂	♃	♄	♅	♆	♇
1 F	6 36 21.7	23N 7.5	18N32.2	25S47.2	19N 5.3	19N41.3	23N44.5	22N56.3	2S11.1	6N 9.8	15S55.7	18N46.6
4 M	6 48 11.3	22 53.9	18 29.8	24 26.4	17 52.0	20 21.7	23 51.4	22 52.7	2 10.9	6 7.3	15 55.2	18 44.3
7 T	7 0 1.0	22 36.6	18 27.3	13 19.0	16 42.5	20 57.5	23 56.5	22 49.0	2 11.0	6 4.7	15 54.7	18 42.0
10 S	7 11 50.7	22 15.8	18 24.9	2N10.9	15 39.5	21 28.4	23 59.5	22 45.1	2 11.4	6 1.9	15 54.3	18 39.6
13 W	7 23 40.4	21 51.6	18 22.5	17 32.5	14 46.3	21 54.3	24 0.8	22 41.0	2 12.2	5 58.9	15 53.9	18 37.2
16 S	7 35 30.0	21 23.9	18 20.0	26 30.5	14 5.9	22 14.9	24 0.1	22 36.7	2 13.4	5 55.9	15 53.6	18 34.7
19 T	7 47 19.7	20 53.0	18 17.6	21 14.2	13 41.0	22 30.0	23 57.6	22 32.2	2 14.9	5 52.7	15 53.4	18 32.1
22 F	7 59 9.4	20 19.0	18 15.1	4 8.8	13 33.6	22 39.5	23 53.2	22 27.6	2 16.8	5 49.3	15 53.3	18 29.5
25 M	8 10 59.0	19 41.8	18 12.7	14S10.4	13 44.2	22 43.3	23 47.1	22 22.8	2 19.0	5 45.9	15 53.3	18 26.9
28 T	8 22 48.7	19 1.8	18 10.2	25 26.5	14 11.1	22 41.3	23 39.1	22 17.8	2 21.5	5 42.3	15 53.3	18 24.3
31 S	8 34 38.4	18 18.9	18 7.7	25 3.0	14 50.8	22 33.5	23 29.5	22 12.7	2 24.4	5 38.7	15 53.5	18 21.6

AUGUST 1966

LONGITUDE at NOON

DAY	EPHEMERIS SIDEREAL TIME	☉	☊	☽	☿	♀	♂	♃	♄	♅	♆	♇
1 M	8 38 34.9	8♌47.3	21♉23.7	10♒ 8.2	2♌23.8	12♋59.1	14♋16.9	19♋ 6.7	29♓19.3	17♍29.3	19♏24.3	16♍52.4
2 T	8 42 31.5	9 44.7	21 20.5	22 12.6	1R50.8	14 11.6	14 56.5	19 19.8	29R17.2	17 32.4	19D24.4	16 54.2
3 W	8 46 28.1	10 42.1	21 17.3	4♓10.5	1 22.1	15 24.1	15 36.0	19 32.8	29 15.0	17 35.6	19 24.4	16 56.0
4 T	8 50 24.6	11 39.6	21 14.1	16 3.7	0 58.3	16 36.7	16 15.5	19 45.9	29 12.7	17 38.8	19 24.5	16 57.8
5 F	8 54 21.2	12 37.0	21 11.0	27 54.1	0 39.9	17 49.3	16 54.9	19 58.8	29 10.3	17 42.0	19 24.6	16 59.7
6 S	8 58 17.7	13 34.5	21 7.8	9♈44.9	0 27.3	19 2.0	17 34.3	20 11.8	29 7.9	17 45.3	19 24.8	17 1.5
7 S	9 2 14.3	14 32.0	21 4.6	21 39.7	0 20.9	20 14.7	18 13.6	20 24.7	29 5.3	17 48.6	19 25.0	17 3.4
8 M	9 6 10.8	15 29.5	21 1.4	3♉43.1	0D21.0	21 27.5	18 52.9	20 37.6	29 2.7	17 51.9	19 25.2	17 5.3
9 T	9 10 7.4	16 27.0	20 58.2	15 59.8	0 27.8	22 40.3	19 32.2	20 50.4	28 60.0	17 55.3	19 25.5	17 7.2
10 W	9 14 3.9	17 24.5	20 55.1	28 35.2	0 41.5	23 53.2	20 11.4	21 3.2	28 57.2	17 58.6	19 25.8	17 9.1
11 T	9 18 0.5	18 22.1	20 51.9	11♊34.1	1 2.2	25 6.1	20 50.6	21 15.9	28 54.3	18 2.0	19 26.1	17 11.0
12 F	9 21 57.1	19 19.8	20 48.7	25 0.4	1 29.9	26 19.1	21 29.7	21 28.7	28 51.4	18 5.5	19 26.5	17 13.0
13 S	9 25 53.6	20 17.4	20 45.5	8♋56.2	2 4.5	27 32.1	22 8.8	21 41.3	28 48.4	18 8.9	19 26.9	17 15.0
14 S	9 29 50.2	21 15.0	20 42.4	23 20.8	2 46.1	28 45.1	22 47.9	21 53.9	28 45.2	18 12.4	19 27.3	17 16.9
15 M	9 33 46.7	22 12.7	20 39.2	8♌10.3	3 34.4	29 58.2	23 26.8	22 6.5	28 42.0	18 15.8	19 27.7	17 18.9
16 T	9 37 43.3	23 10.4	20 36.0	23 17.0	4 29.5	1♌11.3	24 5.8	22 19.0	28 38.8	18 19.3	19 28.2	17 20.9
17 W	9 41 39.8	24 8.1	20 32.8	8♍30.8	5 31.0	2 24.5	24 44.7	22 31.4	28 35.4	18 22.9	19 28.7	17 22.9
18 T	9 45 36.4	25 5.8	20 29.7	23 40.8	6 38.8	3 37.7	25 23.6	22 43.8	28 32.0	18 26.4	19 29.3	17 25.0
19 F	9 49 32.9	26 3.6	20 26.5	8♎37.1	7 52.6	4 51.0	26 2.4	22 56.2	28 28.5	18 29.9	19 29.8	17 27.0
20 S	9 53 29.5	27 1.3	20 23.3	23 12.4	9 12.1	6 4.3	26 41.1	23 8.5	28 25.0	18 33.5	19 30.4	17 29.0
21 S	9 57 26.1	27 59.1	20 20.1	7♏23.1	10 37.0	7 17.6	27 19.9	23 20.7	28 21.3	18 37.1	19 31.1	17 31.1
22 M	10 1 22.6	28 56.9	20 16.9	21 8.2	12 6.9	8 31.0	27 58.5	23 32.9	28 17.6	18 40.7	19 31.8	17 33.1
23 T	10 5 19.2	29 54.7	20 13.8	4♐29.3	13 41.4	9 44.4	28 37.1	23 45.0	28 13.9	18 44.3	19 32.5	17 35.2
24 W	10 9 15.7	0♍52.6	20 10.6	17 29.4	15 20.2	10 57.9	29 15.7	23 57.0	28 10.1	18 48.0	19 33.2	17 37.3
25 T	10 13 12.3	1 50.5	20 7.4	0♑11.8	17 2.6	12 11.4	29 54.3	24 9.0	28 6.2	18 51.6	19 34.0	17 39.4
26 F	10 17 8.8	2 48.3	20 4.2	12 40.1	18 48.4	13 24.9	0♌32.7	24 20.9	28 2.3	18 55.3	19 34.8	17 41.5
27 S	10 21 5.4	3 46.2	20 1.1	24 57.3	20 37.0	14 38.5	1 11.2	24 32.8	27 58.3	18 58.9	19 35.6	17 43.6
28 S	10 25 1.9	4 44.2	19 57.9	7♒ 5.9	22 28.0	15 52.1	1 49.6	24 44.6	27 54.3	19 2.6	19 36.5	17 45.7
29 M	10 28 58.5	5 42.1	19 54.7	19 8.0	24 21.0	17 5.8	2 27.9	24 56.3	27 50.2	19 6.3	19 37.3	17 47.8
30 T	10 32 55.0	6 40.1	19 51.5	1♓ 5.2	26 15.5	18 19.5	3 6.3	25 7.9	27 46.0	19 10.0	19 38.3	17 49.9
31 W	10 36 51.6	7 38.1	19 48.3	12 58.7	28 11.2	19 33.2	3 44.5	25 19.5	27 41.9	19 13.7	19 39.2	17 52.1

DECLINATION at NOON

DAY	EPHEMERIS SIDEREAL TIME	☉	☊	☽	☿	♀	♂	♃	♄	♅	♆	♇
1 M	8 38 34.9	18N 4.0	18N 6.9	22S25.1	15N 6.0	22N29.6	23N25.9	22N10.9	2S25.4	5N37.4	15S53.5	18N20.7
4 T	8 50 24.6	17 17.6	18 4.4	9 41.9	15 54.6	22 14.0	23 14.0	22 5.7	2 28.7	5 33.6	15 53.7	18 18.0
7 S	9 2 14.3	16 28.6	18 1.9	6N 8.4	16 43.0	21 52.6	23 0.5	22 0.2	2 32.2	5 29.8	15 54.0	18 15.3
10 W	9 14 3.9	15 37.2	17 59.4	20 29.3	17 25.5	21 25.5	22 45.4	21 54.7	2 36.1	5 25.8	15 54.4	18 12.5
13 S	9 25 53.6	14 43.6	17 56.9	26 51.9	17 56.8	20 52.9	22 28.7	21 49.1	2 40.2	5 21.7	15 54.9	18 9.8
16 T	9 37 43.3	13 47.8	17 54.3	18 28.5	18 11.9	20 14.8	22 10.6	21 43.3	2 44.6	5 17.6	15 55.4	18 7.1
19 F	9 49 32.9	12 50.1	17 51.8	0S21.5	18 6.2	19 31.4	21 50.9	21 37.5	2 49.2	5 13.4	15 56.0	18 4.4
22 M	10 1 22.6	11 50.6	17 49.3	18 8.8	17 36.4	18 43.0	21 29.9	21 31.6	2 54.0	5 9.1	15 56.7	18 1.7
25 T	10 13 12.3	10 49.3	17 46.7	26 42.3	16 40.9	17 49.8	21 7.5	21 25.7	2 59.1	5 4.8	15 57.5	17 59.0
28 S	10 25 1.9	9 46.6	17 44.2	23 14.1	15 20.8	16 52.0	20 43.9	21 19.8	3 4.2	5 0.5	15 58.3	17 56.4
31 W	10 36 51.6	8 42.4	17 41.6	10 55.1	13 39.2	15 50.0	20 18.9	21 13.8	3 9.6	4 56.1	15 59.2	17 53.8

SEPTEMBER 1966

LONGITUDE at NOON

DAY	EPHEMERIS SIDEREAL TIME h m s	☉ ° ′	☊ ° ′	☽ ° ′	☿ ° ′	♀ ° ′	♂ ° ′	♃ ° ′	♄ ° ′	♅ ° ′	♆ ° ′	♇ ° ′
1 T	10 40 48.1	8♍36.1	19♉45.2	24♓50.0	0♍ 7.6	20♌47.0	4♌22.8	25♋31.0	27♓37.6	19♍17.5	19♏40.2	17♍54.2
2 F	10 44 44.7	9 34.2	19 42.0	6♈40.8	2 4.6	22 0.9	5 1.0	25 42.5	27R33.4	19 21.2	19 41.2	17 56.4
3 S	10 48 41.3	10 32.3	19 38.8	18 33.2	4 1.8	23 14.7	5 39.1	25 53.9	27 29.1	19 25.0	19 42.3	17 58.5
4 S	10 52 37.8	11 30.5	19 35.6	0♉30.1	5 58.9	24 28.6	6 17.2	26 5.1	27 24.7	19 28.7	19 43.4	18 0.7
5 M	10 56 34.4	12 28.6	19 32.5	12 35.0	7 55.8	25 42.5	6 55.3	26 16.4	27 20.4	19 32.5	19 44.4	18 2.8
6 T	11 0 30.9	13 26.8	19 29.3	24 52.0	9 52.2	26 56.5	7 33.3	26 27.5	27 15.9	19 36.2	19 45.6	18 5.0
7 W	11 4 27.5	14 25.0	19 26.1	7♊25.7	11 48.1	28 10.5	8 11.2	26 38.5	27 11.5	19 40.0	19 46.7	18 7.1
8 T	11 8 24.0	15 23.3	19 22.9	20 20.7	13 43.2	29 24.6	8 49.2	26 49.5	27 7.0	19 43.8	19 47.9	18 9.3
9 F	11 12 20.6	16 21.6	19 19.7	3♋41.1	15 37.5	0♍38.7	9 27.0	27 0.4	27 2.5	19 47.5	19 49.1	18 11.4
10 S	11 16 17.1	17 19.9	19 16.6	17 30.0	17 31.0	1 52.8	10 4.9	27 11.2	26 57.9	19 51.3	19 50.4	18 13.6
11 S	11 20 13.7	18 18.2	19 13.4	1♌47.8	19 23.5	3 7.0	10 42.7	27 21.9	26 53.4	19 55.1	19 51.6	18 15.8
12 M	11 24 10.2	19 16.6	19 10.2	16 32.3	21 15.0	4 21.2	11 20.4	27 32.5	26 48.8	19 58.9	19 52.9	18 17.9
13 T	11 28 6.8	20 15.0	19 7.0	1♍37.4	23 5.5	5 35.5	11 58.1	27 43.0	26 44.2	20 2.7	19 54.2	18 20.1
14 W	11 32 3.3	21 13.5	19 3.9	16 54.0	24 55.0	6 49.7	12 35.8	27 53.4	26 39.6	20 6.4	19 55.6	18 22.2
15 T	11 35 59.9	22 12.0	19 0.7	2♎11.1	26 43.4	8 4.1	13 13.4	28 3.8	26 35.0	20 10.2	19 57.0	18 24.4
16 F	11 39 56.5	23 10.5	18 57.5	17 17.8	28 30.7	9 18.4	13 50.9	28 14.0	26 30.3	20 14.0	19 58.4	18 26.6
17 S	11 43 53.0	24 9.1	18 54.3	2♏ 5.2	0♎17.0	10 32.8	14 28.5	28 24.1	26 25.7	20 17.8	19 59.8	18 28.7
18 S	11 47 49.6	25 7.6	18 51.1	16 27.3	2 2.2	11 47.2	15 5.9	28 34.2	26 21.0	20 21.6	20 1.3	18 30.9
19 M	11 51 46.1	26 6.2	18 48.0	0♐21.8	3 46.4	13 1.6	15 43.3	28 44.1	26 16.4	20 25.3	20 2.7	18 33.0
20 T	11 55 42.7	27 4.9	18 44.8	13 49.0	5 29.5	14 16.1	16 20.7	28 53.9	26 11.7	20 29.1	20 4.2	18 35.2
21 W	11 59 39.2	28 3.5	18 41.6	26 51.5	7 11.7	15 30.5	16 58.0	29 3.7	26 7.0	20 32.9	20 5.8	18 37.3
22 T	12 3 35.8	29 2.2	18 38.4	9♑32.8	8 52.8	16 45.0	17 35.3	29 13.3	26 2.4	20 36.6	20 7.3	18 39.4
23 F	12 7 32.3	0♎ 1.0	18 35.3	21 57.1	10 33.0	17 59.6	18 12.5	29 22.8	25 57.8	20 40.4	20 9.0	18 41.6
24 S	12 11 28.9	0 59.7	18 32.1	4♒ 8.4	12 12.1	19 14.2	18 49.7	29 32.2	25 53.2	20 44.1	20 10.6	18 43.7
25 S	12 15 25.4	1 58.5	18 28.9	16 10.4	13 50.3	20 28.8	19 26.8	29 41.5	25 48.6	20 47.9	20 12.2	18 45.9
26 M	12 19 22.0	2 57.3	18 25.7	28 6.5	15 27.6	21 43.4	20 3.9	29 50.7	25 44.0	20 51.6	20 13.8	18 48.0
27 T	12 23 18.5	3 56.1	18 22.5	9♓59.1	17 4.0	22 58.0	20 40.9	29 59.8	25 39.4	20 55.3	20 15.5	18 50.1
28 W	12 27 15.1	4 55.0	18 19.4	21 50.6	18 39.5	24 12.7	21 17.9	0♌ 8.7	25 34.8	20 59.0	20 17.2	18 52.2
29 T	12 31 11.6	5 53.9	18 16.2	3♈42.7	20 14.0	25 27.4	21 54.8	0 17.5	25 30.3	21 2.7	20 18.9	18 54.3
30 F	12 35 8.2	6 52.8	18 13.0	15 37.3	21 47.7	26 42.1	22 31.7	0 26.2	25 25.7	21 6.4	20 20.6	18 56.3

DECLINATION at NOON

DAY	SIDEREAL TIME	☉	☊	☽	☿	♀	♂	♃	♄	♅	♆	♇
1 T	10 40 48.1	8N20.8	17N40.7	5S47.0	13N 1.4	15N28.4	20N10.4	21N11.8	3S11.4	4N54.6	15S59.5	17N52.9
4 S	10 52 37.8	7 15.0	17 38.2	10N11.6	10 58.6	14 21.0	19 43.9	21 5.8	3 16.8	4 50.2	16 0.6	17 50.4
7 W	11 4 27.5	6 8.1	17 35.6	23 12.1	8 45.6	13 10.0	19 16.2	20 59.9	3 22.4	4 45.7	16 1.6	17 47.9
10 S	11 16 17.1	5 0.4	17 33.0	26 38.1	6 26.4	11 55.7	18 47.5	20 53.9	3 28.1	4 41.3	16 2.7	17 45.4
13 T	11 28 6.8	3 51.8	17 30.4	15 30.3	4 4.3	10 38.3	18 17.8	20 48.0	3 33.8	4 36.8	16 3.9	17 43.0
16 F	11 39 56.5	2 42.6	17 27.8	4S24.9	1 41.7	9 18.2	17 47.1	20 42.2	3 39.5	4 32.4	16 5.2	17 40.7
19 M	11 51 46.1	1 32.9	17 25.2	21 21.3	0S39.6	7 55.8	17 15.5	20 36.5	3 45.2	4 27.9	16 6.5	17 38.4
22 T	12 3 35.8	0 23.0	17 22.5	27 8.8	2 58.3	6 31.3	16 43.1	20 30.9	3 50.8	4 23.5	16 7.8	17 36.2
25 S	12 15 25.4	0S47.2	17 19.9	20 53.0	5 13.4	5 5.0	16 9.8	20 25.4	3 56.3	4 19.1	16 9.2	17 34.0
28 W	12 27 15.1	1 57.3	17 17.3	7 6.5	7 24.1	3 37.4	15 35.9	20 20.0	4 1.8	4 14.7	16 10.7	17 32.0

OCTOBER 1966

LONGITUDE at NOON

DAY	SIDEREAL TIME	☉	☊	☽	☿	♀	♂	♃	♄	♅	♆	♇
1 S	12 39 4.8	7♎51.8	18♉ 9.8	27♈35.9	23♎20.6	27♍56.9	23♌ 8.5	0♌34.8	25♓21.3	21♍10.0	20♏22.4	18♍58.4
2 S	12 43 1.3	8 50.8	18 6.7	9♉40.5	24 52.5	29 11.6	23 45.3	0 43.3	25R16.8	21 13.7	20 24.2	19 0.5
3 M	12 46 57.9	9 49.8	18 3.5	21 53.6	26 23.7	0♎26.4	24 22.0	0 51.6	25 12.4	21 17.3	20 26.0	19 2.5
4 T	12 50 54.4	10 48.9	18 0.3	4♊17.8	27 54.0	1 41.2	24 58.7	0 59.8	25 8.0	21 21.0	20 27.8	19 4.6
5 W	12 54 51.0	11 48.0	17 57.1	16 56.5	29 23.4	2 56.1	25 35.4	1 7.9	25 3.6	21 24.6	20 29.6	19 6.6
6 T	12 58 47.5	12 47.2	17 53.9	29 52.9	0♏52.0	4 11.0	26 11.9	1 15.9	24 59.3	21 28.2	20 31.5	19 8.6
7 F	13 2 44.1	13 46.4	17 50.8	13♋10.3	2 19.8	5 25.8	26 48.5	1 23.7	24 55.0	21 31.8	20 33.4	19 10.6
8 S	13 6 40.6	14 45.6	17 47.6	26 51.1	3 46.7	6 40.8	27 25.0	1 31.4	24 50.8	21 35.3	20 35.3	19 12.6
9 S	13 10 37.2	15 44.9	17 44.4	10♌56.6	5 12.7	7 55.7	28 1.4	1 38.9	24 46.6	21 38.9	20 37.2	19 14.6
10 M	13 14 33.7	16 44.2	17 41.2	25 25.6	6 37.8	9 10.7	28 37.8	1 46.3	24 42.4	21 42.4	20 39.1	19 16.6
11 T	13 18 30.3	17 43.5	17 38.1	10♍14.5	8 2.0	10 25.6	29 14.1	1 53.6	24 38.3	21 45.9	20 41.0	19 18.5
12 W	13 22 26.8	18 42.9	17 34.9	25 16.7	9 25.3	11 40.6	29 50.4	2 0.7	24 34.3	21 49.4	20 43.0	19 20.5
13 T	13 26 23.4	19 42.3	17 31.7	10♎23.7	10 47.6	12 55.7	0♍26.6	2 7.7	24 30.3	21 52.8	20 45.0	19 22.4
14 F	13 30 20.0	20 41.8	17 28.5	25 25.8	12 8.9	14 10.7	1 2.8	2 14.5	24 26.4	21 56.3	20 47.0	19 24.4
15 S	13 34 16.5	21 41.3	17 25.3	10♏14.0	13 29.2	15 25.8	1 38.9	2 21.2	24 22.5	21 59.7	20 49.0	19 26.3
16 S	13 38 13.1	22 40.8	17 22.2	24 41.3	14 48.2	16 40.9	2 14.9	2 27.7	24 18.7	22 3.1	20 51.1	19 28.2
17 M	13 42 9.6	23 40.4	17 19.0	8♐43.4	16 6.1	17 55.9	2 50.9	2 34.1	24 15.0	22 6.5	20 53.1	19 30.0
18 T	13 46 6.2	24 39.9	17 15.8	22 18.7	17 22.7	19 11.0	3 26.9	2 40.3	24 11.3	22 9.8	20 55.2	19 31.9
19 W	13 50 2.7	25 39.5	17 12.6	5♑28.1	18 37.9	20 26.2	4 2.7	2 46.4	24 7.7	22 13.2	20 57.2	19 33.7
20 T	13 53 59.3	26 39.2	17 9.5	18 14.0	19 51.6	21 41.3	4 38.5	2 52.3	24 4.1	22 16.5	20 59.3	19 35.5
21 F	13 57 55.8	27 38.8	17 6.3	0♒40.4	21 3.7	22 56.4	5 14.3	2 58.1	24 0.6	22 19.7	21 1.4	19 37.3
22 S	14 1 52.4	28 38.5	17 3.1	12 51.5	22 14.1	24 11.5	5 49.9	3 3.6	23 57.2	22 23.0	21 3.5	19 39.1
23 S	14 5 48.9	29 38.3	16 59.9	24 51.7	23 22.5	25 26.7	6 25.5	3 9.1	23 53.9	22 26.2	21 5.6	19 40.9
24 M	14 9 45.5	0♏38.0	16 56.7	6♓45.3	24 28.9	26 41.9	7 1.1	3 14.3	23 50.7	22 29.4	21 7.8	19 42.6
25 T	14 13 42.1	1 37.8	16 53.6	18 36.3	25 32.9	27 57.0	7 36.6	3 19.4	23 47.5	22 32.5	21 9.9	19 44.3
26 W	14 17 38.6	2 37.6	16 50.4	0♈27.9	26 34.4	29 12.2	8 12.0	3 24.3	23 44.4	22 35.6	21 12.1	19 46.0
27 T	14 21 35.2	3 37.4	16 47.2	12 23.0	27 33.0	0♏27.4	8 47.4	3 29.1	23 41.4	22 38.7	21 14.2	19 47.7
28 F	14 25 31.7	4 37.3	16 44.0	24 23.9	28 28.5	1 42.6	9 22.7	3 33.7	23 38.4	22 41.8	21 16.4	19 49.4
29 S	14 29 28.3	5 37.2	16 40.9	6♉32.7	29 20.5	2 57.8	9 57.9	3 38.1	23 35.6	22 44.8	21 18.6	19 51.0
30 S	14 33 24.8	6 37.2	16 37.7	18 50.7	0♐ 8.6	4 13.1	10 33.1	3 42.4	23 32.8	22 47.8	21 20.8	19 52.6
31 M	14 37 21.4	7 37.1	16 34.5	1♊19.3	0 52.4	5 28.3	11 8.2	3 46.4	23 30.2	22 50.7	21 23.0	19 54.2

DECLINATION at NOON

DAY	SIDEREAL TIME	☉	☊	☽	☿	♀	♂	♃	♄	♅	♆	♇
1 S	12 39 4.8	3S 7.2	17N14.6	9N 2.8	9S29.6	2N 8.7	15N 1.2	20N14.8	4S 7.1	4N10.4	16S12.2	17N30.0
4 T	12 50 54.4	4 16.9	17 12.0	22 34.3	11 29.6	0 39.2	14 25.9	20 9.8	4 12.3	4 6.1	16 13.7	17 28.2
7 F	13 2 44.1	5 26.1	17 9.3	27 7.6	13 23.2	0S50.7	13 50.0	20 5.0	4 17.4	4 1.9	16 15.3	17 26.4
10 M	13 14 33.7	6 34.7	17 6.6	17 53.6	15 10.0	2 20.7	13 13.6	20 0.4	4 22.2	3 57.7	16 16.9	17 24.7
13 T	13 26 23.4	7 42.6	17 4.0	1S17.4	16 49.3	3 50.5	12 36.7	19 56.0	4 26.8	3 53.7	16 18.5	17 23.1
16 S	13 38 13.1	8 49.5	17 1.3	19 41.6	18 20.3	5 19.7	11 59.4	19 51.9	4 31.1	3 49.6	16 20.2	17 21.7
19 W	13 50 2.7	9 55.3	16 58.6	27 18.6	19 42.2	6 48.0	11 21.7	19 48.1	4 35.2	3 45.7	16 21.9	17 20.3
22 S	14 1 52.4	10 59.7	16 55.9	21 59.1	20 53.8	8 15.0	10 43.7	19 44.6	4 39.1	3 41.9	16 23.6	17 19.1
25 T	14 13 42.1	12 2.6	16 53.2	8 36.0	21 54.0	9 40.4	10 5.4	19 41.5	4 42.6	3 38.2	16 25.3	17 17.9
28 F	14 25 31.7	13 3.9	16 50.5	7N38.2	22 40.9	11 3.7	9 26.9	19 38.6	4 45.8	3 34.6	16 27.0	17 16.9
31 M	14 37 21.4	14 3.3	16 47.8	21 47.2	23 12.5	12 24.8	8 48.3	19 36.1	4 48.6	3 31.2	16 28.8	17 16.0

NOVEMBER 1966

LONGITUDE at NOON

DAY	EPHEMERIS SIDEREAL TIME	☉	☊	☽	☿	♀	♂	♃	♄	♅	♆	♇
	h m s	° '	° '	° '	° '	° '	° '	° '	° '	° '	° '	° '
1 T	14 41 17.9	8♏37.1	16♉31.3	13♓59.8	1♐31.5	6♏43.5	11♍43.3	3♌50.3	23♓27.6	22♍53.7	21♏25.2	19♍55.8
2 W	14 45 14.5	9 37.2	16 28.2	26 53.5	2 5.1	7 58.8	12 18.3	3 54.0	23R25.1	22 56.6	21 27.4	19 57.3
3 T	14 49 11.1	10 37.2	16 25.0	10♋ 1.6	2 32.9	9 14.1	12 53.2	3 57.6	23 22.7	22 59.4	21 29.6	19 58.9
4 F	14 53 7.6	11 37.4	16 21.8	23 25.3	2 54.2	10 29.4	13 28.1	4 1.0	23 20.4	23 2.3	21 31.8	20 0.4
5 S	14 57 4.2	12 37.5	16 18.6	7♌ 5.5	3 8.3	11 44.7	14 2.9	4 4.1	23 18.2	23 5.1	21 34.1	20 1.9
6 S	15 1 0.7	13 37.7	16 15.4	21 2.5	3 14.5	12 60.0	14 37.6	4 7.1	23 16.1	23 7.8	21 36.3	20 3.3
7 M	15 4 57.3	14 37.9	16 12.3	5♍15.6	3R12.2	14 15.3	15 12.2	4 9.9	23 14.0	23 10.5	21 38.5	20 4.8
8 T	15 8 53.8	15 38.1	16 9.1	19 42.6	3 0.8	15 30.6	15 46.8	4 12.5	23 12.1	23 13.2	21 40.8	20 6.2
9 W	15 12 50.4	16 38.4	16 5.9	4♎20.0	2 39.9	16 45.9	16 21.3	4 15.0	23 10.2	23 15.8	21 43.0	20 7.5
10 T	15 16 46.9	17 38.7	16 2.7	19 2.4	2 9.0	18 1.3	16 55.7	4 17.2	23 8.5	23 18.4	21 45.3	20 8.9
11 F	15 20 43.5	18 39.1	15 59.6	3♏43.7	1 28.0	19 16.6	17 30.0	4 19.2	23 6.9	23 20.9	21 47.5	20 10.2
12 S	15 24 40.1	19 39.5	15 56.4	18 16.9	0 37.3	20 32.0	18 4.3	4 21.1	23 5.3	23 23.4	21 49.8	20 11.5
13 S	15 28 36.6	20 39.9	15 53.2	2♐35.8	29♏37.4	21 47.3	18 38.4	4 22.7	23 3.9	23 25.9	21 52.0	20 12.8
14 M	15 32 33.2	21 40.3	15 50.0	16 35.5	28 29.4	23 2.7	19 12.5	4 24.2	23 2.6	23 28.3	21 54.3	20 14.0
15 T	15 36 29.7	22 40.7	15 46.9	0♑12.7	27 14.9	24 18.0	19 46.5	4 25.4	23 1.3	23 30.7	21 56.5	20 15.3
16 W	15 40 26.3	23 41.2	15 43.7	13 26.4	25 56.0	25 33.4	20 20.4	4 26.5	23 0.2	23 33.0	21 58.8	20 16.4
17 T	15 44 22.8	24 41.7	15 40.5	26 17.2	24 35.0	26 48.8	20 54.3	4 27.4	22 59.2	23 35.3	22 1.0	20 17.6
18 F	15 48 19.4	25 42.2	15 37.3	8♒47.7	23 14.7	28 4.1	21 28.0	4 28.1	22 58.3	23 37.5	22 3.3	20 18.7
19 S	15 52 16.0	26 42.8	15 34.1	21 1.4	21 57.6	29 19.5	22 1.7	4 28.5	22 57.4	23 39.7	22 5.5	20 19.8
20 S	15 56 12.5	27 43.3	15 31.0	3♓ 2.6	20 46.4	0♐34.9	22 35.2	4 28.8	22 56.7	23 41.9	22 7.8	20 20.9
21 M	16 0 9.1	28 43.9	15 27.8	14 56.1	19 43.0	1 50.2	23 8.7	4 28.9	22 56.1	23 44.0	22 10.0	20 22.0
22 T	16 4 5.6	29 44.5	15 24.6	26 46.7	18 49.4	3 5.6	23 42.1	4R28.8	22 55.6	23 46.0	22 12.2	20 23.0
23 W	16 8 2.2	0♐45.1	15 21.4	8♈38.8	18 6.6	4 21.0	24 15.4	4 28.5	22 55.3	23 48.0	22 14.5	20 24.0
24 T	16 11 58.7	1 45.8	15 18.3	20 36.7	17 35.3	5 36.4	24 48.6	4 27.9	22 55.0	23 50.0	22 16.7	20 24.9
25 F	16 15 55.3	2 46.5	15 15.1	2♉43.9	17 15.7	6 51.8	25 21.7	4 27.3	22 54.9	23 52.0	22 19.0	20 25.9
26 S	16 19 51.9	3 47.2	15 11.9	15 3.2	17 7.5	8 7.2	25 54.7	4 26.4	22 54.8	23 53.8	22 21.2	20 26.8
27 S	16 23 48.4	4 47.9	15 8.7	27 36.5	17D10.2	9 22.5	26 27.6	4 25.3	22 54.8	23 55.6	22 23.4	20 27.7
28 M	16 27 45.0	5 48.6	15 5.6	10♊24.8	17 23.3	10 37.9	27 0.4	4 23.9	22D55.0	23 57.4	22 25.6	20 28.5
29 T	16 31 41.5	6 49.4	15 2.4	23 28.2	17 45.8	11 53.3	27 33.1	4 22.4	22 55.2	23 59.1	22 27.8	20 29.3
30 W	16 35 38.1	7 50.1	14 59.2	6♋46.1	18 16.9	13 8.7	28 5.7	4 20.7	22 55.6	24 0.8	22 30.0	20 30.1

DECLINATION at NOON

DAY	EPHEMERIS SIDEREAL TIME	☉	☊	☽	☿	♀	♂	♃	♄	♅	♆	♇
1 T	14 41 17.9	14S22.7	16N46.9	24N56.5	23S19.1	12S51.2	8N35.4	19N35.4	4S49.5	3N30.0	16S29.4	17N15.8
4 F	14 53 7.6	15 19.4	16 44.1	26 13.1	23 25.4	14 8.7	7 56.6	19 33.4	4 51.9	3 26.7	16 31.1	17 15.0
7 M	15 4 57.3	16 13.9	16 41.4	14 13.9	23 7.5	15 22.9	7 17.7	19 31.8	4 54.0	3 23.5	16 32.9	17 14.4
10 T	15 16 46.9	17 5.9	16 38.6	5S13.2	22 20.2	16 33.6	6 38.8	19 30.5	4 55.7	3 20.5	16 34.6	17 14.0
13 S	15 28 36.6	17 55.4	16 35.9	22 9.2	20 60.0	17 40.4	5 60.0	19 29.7	4 57.0	3 17.6	16 36.4	17 13.6
16 W	15 40 26.3	18 42.0	16 33.1	27 11.5	19 11.6	18 43.0	5 21.3	19 29.4	4 57.9	3 14.9	16 38.1	17 13.4
19 S	15 52 16.0	19 25.6	16 30.4	19 28.3	17 14.9	19 41.0	4 42.7	19 29.4	4 58.5	3 12.3	16 39.8	17 13.4
22 T	16 4 5.6	20 6.0	16 27.6	4 57.7	15 38.8	20 34.0	4 4.4	19 29.9	4 58.6	3 9.9	16 41.5	17 13.4
25 F	16 15 55.3	20 43.2	16 24.8	11N16.0	14 44.1	21 21.8	3 26.2	19 30.8	4 58.4	3 7.7	16 43.2	17 13.6
28 M	16 27 45.0	21 16.8	16 22.0	24 9.1	14 34.2	22 4.0	2 48.4	19 32.1	4 57.8	3 5.6	16 44.9	17 14.0

DECEMBER 1966

LONGITUDE at NOON

DAY	EPHEMERIS SIDEREAL TIME	☉	☊	☽	☿	♀	♂	♃	♄	♅	♆	♇
1 T	16 39 34.6	8♐50.9	14♉56.0	20♋17.2	18♏55.7	14♐24.0	28♍38.2	4♌18.8	22♓56.1	24♍ 2.4	22♏32.2	20♍30.8
2 F	16 43 31.2	9 51.7	14 52.9	3♌59.7	19 41.3	15 39.4	29 10.6	4R16.8	22 56.6	24 3.9	22 34.4	20 31.5
3 S	16 47 27.8	10 52.6	14 49.7	17 51.9	20 32.9	16 54.8	29 42.9	4 14.5	22 57.3	24 5.4	22 36.5	20 32.2
4 S	16 51 24.3	11 53.4	14 46.5	1♍52.1	21 29.9	18 10.2	0♎15.1	4 12.0	22 58.1	24 6.9	22 38.7	20 32.8
5 M	16 55 20.9	12 54.3	14 43.3	15 58.5	22 31.5	19 25.6	0 47.2	4 9.3	22 59.0	24 8.3	22 40.8	20 33.4
6 T	16 59 17.4	13 55.2	14 40.1	0♎ 9.6	23 37.1	20 41.0	1 19.1	4 6.4	23 0.0	24 9.7	22 43.0	20 34.0
7 W	17 3 14.0	14 56.1	14 37.0	14 23.5	24 46.2	21 56.4	1 51.0	4 3.4	23 1.1	24 11.0	22 45.1	20 34.6
8 T	17 7 10.6	15 57.1	14 33.8	28 38.0	25 58.3	23 11.8	2 22.7	4 0.1	23 2.4	24 12.2	22 47.2	20 35.1
9 F	17 11 7.1	16 58.1	14 30.6	12♏50.2	27 13.0	24 27.2	2 54.3	3 56.7	23 3.7	24 13.4	22 49.3	20 35.6
10 S	17 15 3.7	17 59.1	14 27.4	26 56.8	28 30.0	25 42.6	3 25.8	3 53.1	23 5.1	24 14.5	22 51.4	20 36.0
11 S	17 19 0.2	19 0.1	14 24.3	10♐53.8	29 49.0	26 58.0	3 57.1	3 49.2	23 6.7	24 15.6	22 53.5	20 36.4
12 M	17 22 56.8	20 1.1	14 21.1	24 37.7	1♐ 9.6	28 13.4	4 28.3	3 45.2	23 8.3	24 16.6	22 55.5	20 36.8
13 T	17 26 53.3	21 2.1	14 17.9	8♑ 5.2	2 31.7	29 28.8	4 59.4	3 41.1	23 10.1	24 17.6	22 57.6	20 37.1
14 W	17 30 49.9	22 3.2	14 14.7	21 14.3	3 55.0	0♑44.2	5 30.3	3 36.7	23 11.9	24 18.5	22 59.6	20 37.5
15 T	17 34 46.5	23 4.2	14 11.6	4♒ 4.0	5 19.5	1 59.6	6 1.1	3 32.2	23 13.9	24 19.4	23 1.6	20 37.7
16 F	17 38 43.0	24 5.3	14 8.4	16 35.4	6 45.0	3 15.0	6 31.9	3 27.5	23 16.0	24 20.2	23 3.7	20 38.0
17 S	17 42 39.6	25 6.4	14 5.2	28 50.4	8 11.2	4 30.4	7 2.4	3 22.7	23 18.2	24 20.9	23 5.6	20 38.3
18 S	17 46 36.1	26 7.5	14 2.0	10♓52.5	9 38.2	5 45.8	7 32.7	3 17.6	23 20.5	24 21.6	23 7.6	20 38.4
19 M	17 50 32.7	27 8.6	13 58.9	22 46.1	11 5.8	7 1.1	8 3.0	3 12.4	23 22.8	24 22.3	23 9.6	20 38.6
20 T	17 54 29.3	28 9.6	13 55.7	4♈36.0	12 34.0	8 16.5	8 33.0	3 7.0	23 25.3	24 22.8	23 11.5	20 38.7
21 W	17 58 25.8	29 10.7	13 52.5	16 27.4	14 2.7	9 31.9	9 2.9	3 1.5	23 27.9	24 23.4	23 13.4	20 38.8
22 T	18 2 22.4	0♑11.8	13 49.3	28 25.6	15 31.9	10 47.2	9 32.7	2 55.9	23 30.6	24 23.8	23 15.3	20 38.8
23 F	18 6 18.9	1 12.9	13 46.1	10♉35.3	17 1.5	12 2.6	10 2.3	2 50.0	23 33.3	24 24.2	23 17.2	20 38.8
24 S	18 10 15.5	2 14.0	13 43.0	23 0.9	18 31.5	13 17.9	10 31.8	2 44.1	23 36.2	24 24.6	23 19.0	20 38.8
25 S	18 14 12.1	3 15.1	13 39.8	5♊45.3	20 1.8	14 33.3	11 1.0	2 38.0	23 39.2	24 24.9	23 20.9	20 38.8
26 M	18 18 8.6	4 16.3	13 36.6	18 50.5	21 32.5	15 48.6	11 30.2	2 31.7	23 42.2	24 25.1	23 22.7	20R38.7
27 T	18 22 5.2	5 17.4	13 33.4	2♋16.4	23 3.6	17 3.9	11 59.1	2 25.3	23 45.4	24 25.3	23 24.5	20 38.6
28 W	18 26 1.7	6 18.5	13 30.3	16 1.1	24 35.0	18 19.2	12 27.9	2 18.8	23 48.7	24 25.4	23 26.3	20 38.4
29 T	18 29 58.3	7 19.6	13 27.1	0♌ 1.2	26 6.7	19 34.5	12 56.5	2 12.2	23 52.0	24 25.5	23 28.0	20 38.2
30 F	18 33 54.8	8 20.7	13 23.9	14 12.1	27 38.7	20 49.8	13 24.9	2 5.4	23 55.5	24 25.5	23 29.7	20 38.0
31 S	18 37 51.4	9 21.9	13 20.7	28 28.5	29 11.0	22 5.1	13 53.2	1 58.6	23 59.0	24R25.4	23 31.4	20 37.8

DECLINATION at NOON

DAY	EPHEMERIS SIDEREAL TIME	☉	☊	☽	☿	♀	♂	♃	♄	♅	♆	♇
1 T	16 39 34.6	21S46.9	16N19.2	26N34.6	15S 0.5	22S40.4	2N10.9	19N33.9	4S56.7	3N 3.8	16S46.5	17N14.4
4 S	16 51 24.3	22 13.2	16 16.4	15 30.4	15 51.1	23 10.7	1 33.8	19 36.1	4 55.4	3 2.1	16 48.1	17 15.0
7 W	17 3 14.0	22 35.6	16 13.6	3S 8.8	16 55.7	23 34.7	0 57.1	19 38.7	4 53.6	3 0.6	16 49.7	17 15.7
10 S	17 15 3.7	22 54.1	16 10.8	20 26.8	18 6.3	23 52.3	0 20.8	19 41.7	4 51.4	2 59.3	16 51.2	17 16.6
13 T	17 26 53.3	23 8.5	16 8.0	27 17.6	19 17.7	24 3.2	0S14.9	19 45.0	4 48.9	2 58.2	16 52.7	17 17.6
16 F	17 38 43.0	23 18.8	16 5.2	20 47.5	20 25.9	24 7.5	0 50.0	19 48.7	4 46.0	2 57.3	16 54.1	17 18.7
19 M	17 50 32.7	23 24.9	16 2.3	6 38.7	21 28.6	24 5.0	1 24.5	19 52.8	4 42.7	2 56.6	16 55.5	17 19.9
22 T	18 2 22.4	23 26.7	15 59.5	9N30.5	22 23.8	23 55.8	1 58.3	19 57.1	4 39.1	2 56.1	16 56.8	17 21.2
25 S	18 14 12.1	23 24.3	15 56.6	23 2.3	23 10.2	23 40.0	2 31.4	20 1.8	4 35.1	2 55.8	16 58.1	17 22.7
28 W	18 26 1.7	23 17.7	15 53.8	26 54.9	23 46.8	23 17.6	3 3.7	20 6.6	4 30.8	2 55.7	16 59.3	17 24.2
31 S	18 37 51.4	23 6.9	15 50.9	16 38.4	24 12.9	22 48.7	3 35.3	20 11.7	4 26.2	2 55.8	17 0.5	17 25.9

JANUARY 1967

DAY	EPHEMERIS SIDEREAL TIME	☉	☊	☽	☿	♀	♂	♃	♄	♅	♆	♇
	h m s	° ′	° ′	° ′	° ′	° ′	° ′	° ′	° ′	° ′	° ′	° ′
LONGITUDE at NOON												
1 S	18 41 48.0	10♑23.0	13♉17.6	12♍45.8	0♑43.7	23♑20.4	14♎21.2	1♌51.6	24♓ 2.6	24♍25.3	23♏33.1	20♍37.5
2 M	18 45 44.5	11 24.2	13 14.4	27 0.1	2 16.7	24 35.7	14 49.1	1R44.5	24 6.4	24R25.2	23 34.8	20R37.2
3 T	18 49 41.1	12 25.3	13 11.2	11♎ 9.0	3 50.0	25 51.0	15 16.7	1 37.3	24 10.2	24 24.9	23 36.4	20 36.8
4 W	18 53 37.6	13 26.5	13 8.0	25 11.2	5 23.7	27 6.3	15 44.2	1 30.0	24 14.1	24 24.7	23 38.0	20 36.4
5 T	18 57 34.2	14 27.6	13 4.9	9♏ 6.0	6 57.8	28 21.5	16 11.5	1 22.6	24 18.1	24 24.3	23 39.6	20 36.0
6 F	19 1 30.8	15 28.8	13 1.7	22 53.2	8 32.2	29 36.9	16 38.6	1 15.2	24 22.2	24 24.0	23 41.2	20 35.6
7 S	19 5 27.3	16 30.0	12 58.5	6♐32.3	10 7.0	0♒52.1	17 5.4	1 7.7	24 26.4	24 23.6	23 42.8	20 35.2
8 S	19 9 23.9	17 31.2	12 55.3	20 2.4	11 42.2	2 7.4	17 32.0	1 0.0	24 30.6	24 23.1	23 44.3	20 34.6
9 M	19 13 20.4	18 32.3	12 52.1	3♑22.3	13 17.8	3 22.6	17 58.4	0 52.3	24 35.0	24 22.5	23 45.8	20 34.1
10 T	19 17 17.0	19 33.5	12 49.0	16 30.3	14 53.8	4 37.8	18 24.5	0 44.6	24 39.4	24 21.9	23 47.2	20 33.5
11 W	19 21 13.5	20 34.7	12 45.8	29 24.8	16 30.3	5 53.0	18 50.5	0 36.8	24 43.9	24 21.2	23 48.7	20 32.9
12 T	19 25 10.1	21 35.8	12 42.6	12♒ 4.9	18 7.2	7 8.3	19 16.1	0 28.9	24 48.5	24 20.5	23 50.1	20 32.3
13 F	19 29 6.7	22 37.0	12 39.4	24 30.5	19 44.6	8 23.5	19 41.5	0 21.0	24 53.2	24 19.8	23 51.5	20 31.7
14 S	19 33 3.2	23 38.1	12 36.3	6♓42.4	21 22.5	9 38.6	20 6.7	0 13.0	24 57.9	24 18.9	23 52.8	20 31.0
15 S	19 36 59.8	24 39.2	12 33.1	18 42.9	23 0.8	10 53.8	20 31.6	0 5.0	25 2.7	24 18.1	23 54.1	20 30.2
16 M	19 40 56.3	25 40.4	12 29.9	0♈35.3	24 39.7	12 9.0	20 56.3	29♋57.0	25 7.6	24 17.1	23 55.4	20 29.5
17 T	19 44 52.9	26 41.5	12 26.7	12 23.7	26 19.0	13 24.1	21 20.7	29 49.0	25 12.6	24 16.1	23 56.7	20 28.7
18 W	19 48 49.5	27 42.5	12 23.6	24 13.1	27 58.9	14 39.2	21 44.8	29 40.9	25 17.7	24 15.1	23 57.9	20 27.9
19 T	19 52 46.0	28 43.6	12 20.4	6♉ 9.1	29 39.4	15 54.3	22 8.6	29 32.9	25 22.8	24 14.0	23 59.1	20 27.1
20 F	19 56 42.6	29 44.7	12 17.2	18 17.1	1♒20.4	17 9.4	22 32.2	29 24.8	25 28.0	24 12.9	24 0.3	20 26.2
21 S	20 0 39.1	0♒45.7	12 14.0	0♊42.5	3 1.9	18 24.5	22 55.4	29 16.8	25 33.3	24 11.7	24 1.5	20 25.3
22 S	20 4 35.7	1 46.8	12 10.9	13 29.9	4 43.9	19 39.5	23 18.4	29 8.7	25 38.6	24 10.5	24 2.6	20 24.4
23 M	20 8 32.2	2 47.8	12 7.7	26 42.5	6 26.5	20 54.5	23 41.1	29 0.7	25 44.1	24 9.2	24 3.7	20 23.5
24 T	20 12 28.8	3 48.8	12 4.5	10♋21.4	8 9.6	22 9.5	24 3.4	28 52.7	25 49.5	24 7.9	24 4.7	20 22.5
25 W	20 16 25.4	4 49.8	12 1.3	24 25.2	9 53.2	23 24.5	24 25.5	28 44.7	25 55.1	24 6.5	24 5.7	20 21.5
26 T	20 20 21.9	5 50.8	11 58.1	8♌49.9	11 37.2	24 39.5	24 47.2	28 36.8	26 0.7	24 5.1	24 6.7	20 20.5
27 F	20 24 18.5	6 51.8	11 55.0	23 28.9	13 21.7	25 54.4	25 8.7	28 28.9	26 6.4	24 3.6	24 7.7	20 19.5
28 S	20 28 15.0	7 52.7	11 51.8	8♍14.1	15 6.5	27 9.4	25 29.8	28 21.0	26 12.2	24 2.1	24 8.7	20 18.4
29 S	20 32 11.6	8 53.6	11 48.6	22 57.5	16 51.7	28 24.3	25 50.5	28 13.2	26 18.0	24 0.5	24 9.6	20 17.3
30 M	20 36 8.1	9 54.6	11 45.4	7♎32.2	18 37.1	29 39.1	26 10.9	28 5.5	26 23.9	23 58.9	24 10.4	20 16.2
31 T	20 40 4.7	10 55.5	11 42.3	21 53.8	20 22.6	0♓54.0	26 30.9	27 57.8	26 29.8	23 57.3	24 11.3	20 15.1
DECLINATION at NOON												
1 S	18 41 48.0	23S 2.3	15N50.0	10N55.0	24S19.1	22S37.7	3S45.6	20N13.4	4S24.6	2N55.9	17S 0.9	17N26.5
4 W	18 53 37.6	22 46.0	15 47.1	8S10.8	24 30.0	22 0.7	4 16.0	20 18.7	4 19.5	2 56.2	17 2.0	17 28.3
7 S	19 5 27.3	22 25.6	15 44.2	23 17.7	24 28.8	21 17.6	4 45.6	20 24.1	4 14.1	2 56.8	17 3.0	17 30.1
10 T	19 17 17.0	22 1.2	15 41.3	26 51.8	24 15.0	20 28.9	5 14.1	20 29.6	4 8.5	2 57.6	17 4.0	17 32.1
13 F	19 29 6.7	21 32.9	15 38.4	18 0.3	23 48.3	19 34.8	5 41.6	20 35.1	4 2.6	2 58.5	17 4.9	17 34.2
16 M	19 40 56.3	21 0.9	15 35.5	2 53.7	23 8.2	18 35.7	6 8.1	20 40.7	3 56.4	2 59.7	17 5.7	17 36.3
19 T	19 52 46.0	20 25.2	15 32.6	13N 0.7	22 14.4	17 31.7	6 33.5	20 46.2	3 49.9	3 1.0	17 6.5	17 38.5
22 S	20 4 35.7	19 46.1	15 29.7	24 58.7	21 6.8	16 23.4	6 57.7	20 51.6	3 43.2	3 2.5	17 7.2	17 40.7
25 W	20 16 25.4	19 3.7	15 26.8	25 55.5	19 45.3	15 11.1	7 20.7	20 56.9	3 36.3	3 4.2	17 7.8	17 43.0
28 S	20 28 15.0	18 18.2	15 23.9	12 38.5	18 10.1	13 55.0	7 42.5	21 2.0	3 29.1	3 6.0	17 8.4	17 45.3
31 T	20 40 4.7	17 29.7	15 21.0	6S57.5	16 21.7	12 35.6	8 3.1	21 7.0	3 21.8	3 8.0	17 8.8	17 47.7

FEBRUARY 1967

DAY	EPHEMERIS SIDEREAL TIME	☉	☊	☽	☿	♀	♂	♃	♄	♅	♆	♇
LONGITUDE at NOON												
1 W	20 44 1.3	11♒56.4	11♉39.1	5♏59.8	22♒ 8.1	2♓ 8.8	26♎50.6	27♋50.1	26♓35.8	23♍55.6	24♏12.1	20♍13.9
2 T	20 47 57.8	12 57.3	11 35.9	19 49.7	23 53.4	3 23.6	27 9.9	27R42.6	26 41.8	23R53.9	24 12.8	20R12.7
3 F	20 51 54.4	13 58.1	11 32.7	3♐24.5	25 38.4	4 38.4	27 28.8	27 35.1	26 47.9	23 52.1	24 13.6	20 11.5
4 S	20 55 50.9	14 59.0	11 29.6	16 45.6	27 22.9	5 53.2	27 47.3	27 27.7	26 54.1	23 50.3	24 14.3	20 10.3
5 S	20 59 47.5	15 59.8	11 26.4	29 54.2	29 6.5	7 7.9	28 5.3	27 20.4	27 0.3	23 48.4	24 14.9	20 9.0
6 M	21 3 44.0	17 0.7	11 23.2	12♑51.4	0♓49.1	8 22.7	28 23.0	27 13.2	27 6.6	23 46.5	24 15.6	20 7.8
7 T	21 7 40.6	18 1.5	11 20.0	25 37.7	2 30.2	9 37.4	28 40.3	27 6.1	27 12.9	23 44.6	24 16.2	20 6.5
8 W	21 11 37.1	19 2.3	11 16.8	8♒13.4	4 9.5	10 52.0	28 57.1	26 59.0	27 19.3	23 42.6	24 16.7	20 5.2
9 T	21 15 33.7	20 3.0	11 13.7	20 38.3	5 46.5	12 6.7	29 13.5	26 52.1	27 25.7	23 40.6	24 17.3	20 3.9
10 F	21 19 30.3	21 3.8	11 10.5	2♓52.8	7 20.7	13 21.3	29 29.4	26 45.4	27 32.2	23 38.5	24 17.8	20 2.5
11 S	21 23 26.8	22 4.5	11 7.3	14 57.3	8 51.7	14 35.9	29 44.8	26 38.7	27 38.7	23 36.5	24 18.2	20 1.1
12 S	21 27 23.4	23 5.2	11 4.1	26 53.4	10 18.7	15 50.4	29 59.8	26 32.1	27 45.3	23 34.3	24 18.7	19 59.8
13 M	21 31 19.9	24 5.9	11 1.0	8♈43.4	11 41.1	17 4.9	0♏14.3	26 25.7	27 51.9	23 32.2	24 19.1	19 58.4
14 T	21 35 16.5	25 6.5	10 57.8	20 30.3	12 58.3	18 19.4	0 28.3	26 19.5	27 58.6	23 30.0	24 19.4	19 57.0
15 W	21 39 13.0	26 7.1	10 54.6	2♉18.3	14 9.5	19 33.9	0 41.8	26 13.3	28 5.3	23 27.8	24 19.8	19 55.5
16 T	21 43 9.6	27 7.7	10 51.4	14 12.2	15 14.1	20 48.3	0 54.8	26 7.3	28 12.1	23 25.6	24 20.1	19 54.1
17 F	21 47 6.1	28 8.3	10 48.3	26 17.3	16 11.3	22 2.7	1 7.4	26 1.5	28 18.9	23 23.3	24 20.4	19 52.7
18 S	21 51 2.7	29 8.9	10 45.1	8♊39.1	17 0.5	23 17.1	1 19.3	25 55.8	28 25.7	23 21.0	24 20.6	19 51.2
19 S	21 54 59.3	0♓ 9.4	10 41.9	21 22.9	17 41.1	24 31.4	1 30.7	25 50.2	28 32.6	23 18.7	24 20.8	19 49.7
20 M	21 58 55.8	1 9.9	10 38.7	4♋33.0	18 12.4	25 45.6	1 41.6	25 44.8	28 39.5	23 16.4	24 21.0	19 48.2
21 T	22 2 52.4	2 10.3	10 35.5	18 12.1	18 34.2	26 59.8	1 51.9	25 39.6	28 46.4	23 14.0	24 21.1	19 46.7
22 W	22 6 48.9	3 10.7	10 32.4	2♌20.4	18 46.0	28 14.0	2 1.6	25 34.5	28 53.4	23 11.6	24 21.2	19 45.2
23 T	22 10 45.5	4 11.1	10 29.2	16 55.1	18 47.9	29 28.2	2 10.8	25 29.6	29 0.4	23 9.2	24 21.2	19 43.7
24 F	22 14 42.0	5 11.4	10 26.0	1♍49.8	18R39.7	0♈42.3	2 19.3	25 24.8	29 7.4	23 6.8	24 21.3	19 42.1
25 S	22 18 38.6	6 11.8	10 22.8	16 55.7	18 21.8	1 56.3	2 27.3	25 20.3	29 14.5	23 4.3	24R21.2	19 40.6
26 S	22 22 35.1	7 12.1	10 19.7	2♎ 2.6	17 54.6	3 10.3	2 34.7	25 15.9	29 21.6	23 1.8	24 21.2	19 39.0
27 M	22 26 31.7	8 12.3	10 16.5	17 0.9	17 18.9	4 24.3	2 41.4	25 11.6	29 28.7	22 59.3	24 21.1	19 37.5
28 T	22 30 28.2	9 12.6	10 13.3	1♏43.2	16 35.5	5 38.2	2 47.4	25 7.5	29 35.9	22 56.8	24 21.0	19 35.9
DECLINATION at NOON												
1 W	20 44 1.3	17S12.9	15N20.0	13S 3.8	15S42.9	12S 8.4	8S 9.6	21N 8.6	3S19.3	3N 8.7	17S 9.0	17N48.5
4 S	20 55 50.9	16 20.7	15 17.0	25 40.7	13 39.1	10 45.1	8 28.3	21 13.4	3 11.7	3 10.9	17 9.4	17 50.9
7 T	21 7 40.6	15 26.0	15 14.1	25 45.4	11 26.6	9 19.2	8 45.7	21 17.8	3 3.9	3 13.2	17 9.7	17 53.3
10 F	21 19 30.3	14 28.8	15 11.1	14 45.5	9 10.1	7 51.1	9 1.5	21 22.1	2 56.0	3 15.7	17 9.9	17 55.8
13 M	21 31 19.9	13 29.5	15 8.2	1N 3.6	6 56.2	6 21.2	9 15.8	21 26.0	2 47.9	3 18.3	17 10.0	17 58.2
16 T	21 43 9.6	12 28.3	15 5.2	16 28.9	4 53.9	4 49.8	9 28.5	21 29.7	2 39.6	3 20.9	17 10.1	18 0.6
19 S	21 54 59.3	11 25.2	15 2.2	26 31.8	3 14.0	3 17.3	9 39.7	21 33.1	2 31.3	3 23.7	17 10.1	18 3.0
22 W	22 6 48.9	10 20.5	14 59.3	24 31.3	2 7.1	1 44.0	9 49.1	21 36.1	2 22.8	3 26.6	17 10.0	18 5.4
25 S	22 18 38.6	9 14.4	14 56.3	8 50.3	1 41.5	0 10.2	9 56.9	21 38.9	2 14.2	3 29.5	17 9.9	18 7.7
28 T	22 30 28.2	8 7.1	14 53.3	11S29.7	1 59.6	1N23.7	10 2.8	21 41.3	2 5.6	3 32.5	17 9.7	18 10.1

MARCH 1967

LONGITUDE at NOON

DAY	EPHEMERIS SIDEREAL TIME	☉	☊	☽	☿	♀	♂	♃	♄	♅	♆	♇
	h m s	° ′	° ′	° ′	° ′	° ′	° ′	° ′	° ′	° ′	° ′	° ′
1 W	22 34 24.8	10♓12.8	10♉10.1	16♏ 4.8	15♓45.7	6♈52.1	2♏52.9	25♋ 3.7	29♓43.1	22♍54.3	24♏20.9	19♍34.3
2 T	22 38 21.4	11 13.0	10 6.9	0♐ 3.8	14R50.6	8 5.9	2 57.6	24R59.9	29 50.3	22R51.8	24R20.7	19R32.8
3 F	22 42 17.9	12 13.2	10 3.8	13 40.6	13 51.7	9 19.7	3 1.7	24 56.4	29 57.5	22 49.2	24 20.5	19 31.2
4 S	22 46 14.5	13 13.3	10 0.6	26 57.0	12 50.4	10 33.5	3 5.1	24 53.1	0♈ 4.8	22 46.7	24 20.2	19 29.6
5 S	22 50 11.0	14 13.4	9 57.4	9♑55.5	11 48.4	11 47.2	3 7.8	24 49.9	0 12.0	22 44.1	24 20.0	19 28.0
6 M	22 54 7.6	15 13.5	9 54.2	22 38.7	10 47.0	13 0.8	3 9.8	24 46.9	0 19.3	22 41.5	24 19.7	19 26.4
7 T	22 58 4.1	16 13.6	9 51.1	5♒ 9.1	9 47.5	14 14.5	3 11.1	24 44.2	0 26.7	22 38.9	24 19.3	19 24.8
8 W	23 2 0.7	17 13.6	9 47.9	17 28.6	8 51.1	15 28.0	3 11.6	24 41.6	0 34.0	22 36.3	24 18.9	19 23.2
9 T	23 5 57.2	18 13.6	9 44.7	29 38.9	7 58.9	16 41.6	3R11.4	24 39.2	0 41.4	22 33.7	24 18.5	19 21.6
10 F	23 9 53.8	19 13.7	9 41.5	11♓41.5	7 11.7	17 55.1	3 10.5	24 37.0	0 48.8	22 31.1	24 18.1	19 20.0
11 S	23 13 50.3	20 13.6	9 38.3	23 37.6	6 30.1	19 8.5	3 8.8	24 35.0	0 56.2	22 28.5	24 17.7	19 18.4
12 S	23 17 46.9	21 13.5	9 35.2	5♈28.6	5 54.5	20 21.9	3 6.4	24 33.1	1 3.6	22 25.9	24 17.2	19 16.8
13 M	23 21 43.4	22 13.4	9 32.0	17 16.6	5 25.3	21 35.2	3 3.2	24 31.5	1 11.0	22 23.3	24 16.6	19 15.2
14 T	23 25 40.0	23 13.3	9 28.8	29 3.7	5 2.5	22 48.4	2 59.2	24 30.1	1 18.4	22 20.6	24 16.1	19 13.6
15 W	23 29 36.6	24 13.1	9 25.6	10♉53.1	4 46.2	24 1.6	2 54.4	24 28.8	1 25.8	22 18.0	24 15.5	19 12.0
16 T	23 33 33.1	25 12.8	9 22.5	22 48.5	4 36.3	25 14.8	2 48.9	24 27.8	1 33.3	22 15.4	24 14.8	19 10.4
17 F	23 37 29.7	26 12.6	9 19.3	4♊54.0	4 32.6	26 27.9	2 42.6	24 26.9	1 40.7	22 12.8	24 14.2	19 8.8
18 S	23 41 26.2	27 12.3	9 16.1	17 14.4	4D35.0	27 40.9	2 35.6	24 26.3	1 48.2	22 10.2	24 13.5	19 7.2
19 S	23 45 22.8	28 11.9	9 12.9	29 54.4	4 43.2	28 53.9	2 27.7	24 25.8	1 55.7	22 7.6	24 12.8	19 5.6
20 M	23 49 19.3	29 11.6	9 9.7	12♋58.5	4 56.9	0♉ 6.8	2 19.1	24 25.5	2 3.1	22 5.0	24 12.0	19 4.0
21 T	23 53 15.9	0♈11.2	9 6.6	26 30.1	5 15.9	1 19.6	2 9.8	24 25.5	2 10.6	22 2.4	24 11.3	19 2.4
22 W	23 57 12.4	1 10.7	9 3.4	10♌30.7	5 39.8	2 32.4	1 59.6	24D25.6	2 18.1	21 59.8	24 10.5	19 0.9
23 T	0 1 9.0	2 10.2	9 0.2	24 59.4	6 8.5	3 45.1	1 48.8	24 25.9	2 25.6	21 57.2	24 9.6	18 59.3
24 F	0 5 5.5	3 9.7	8 57.0	9♍51.9	6 41.6	4 57.7	1 37.1	24 26.4	2 33.1	21 54.7	24 8.8	18 57.8
25 S	0 9 2.1	4 9.1	8 53.9	25 0.9	7 18.9	6 10.3	1 24.8	24 27.1	2 40.5	21 52.1	24 7.9	18 56.2
26 S	0 12 58.6	5 8.5	8 50.7	10♎16.8	8 0.1	7 22.8	1 11.7	24 28.0	2 48.0	21 49.6	24 7.0	18 54.7
27 M	0 16 55.2	6 7.9	8 47.5	25 29.1	8 45.0	8 35.2	0 57.9	24 29.1	2 55.5	21 47.1	24 6.0	18 53.2
28 T	0 20 51.7	7 7.2	8 44.3	10♏28.3	9 33.4	9 47.6	0 43.4	24 30.3	3 2.9	21 44.6	24 5.1	18 51.7
29 W	0 24 48.3	8 6.5	8 41.1	25 7.2	10 25.1	10 59.9	0 28.2	24 31.8	3 10.4	21 42.1	24 4.1	18 50.2
30 T	0 28 44.9	9 5.8	8 38.0	9♐21.4	11 20.0	12 12.1	0 12.3	24 33.4	3 17.9	21 39.6	24 3.1	18 48.7
31 F	0 32 41.4	10 5.1	8 34.8	23 9.4	12 17.8	13 24.3	29♎55.8	24 35.3	3 25.4	21 37.2	24 2.1	18 47.2

DECLINATION at NOON

DAY	EPHEMERIS SIDEREAL TIME	☉	☊	☽	☿	♀	♂	♃	♄	♅	♆	♇
1 W	22 34 24.8	7S44.4	14N52.3	17S17.1	2S14.7	1N55.0	10S 4.4	21N42.1	2S 2.7	3N33.5	17S 9.6	18N10.8
4 S	22 46 14.5	6 35.7	14 49.3	27 13.6	3 20.9	3 28.6	10 7.9	21 44.1	1 54.0	3 36.5	17 9.3	18 13.1
7 T	22 58 4.1	5 26.1	14 46.3	23 55.2	4 46.4	5 1.5	10 9.5	21 45.7	1 45.2	3 39.6	17 8.9	18 15.3
10 F	23 9 53.8	4 15.9	14 43.3	11 6.6	6 14.1	6 33.5	10 9.1	21 47.1	1 36.3	3 42.7	17 8.4	18 17.4
13 M	23 21 43.4	3 5.2	14 40.2	5N 7.8	7 31.1	8 4.3	10 6.7	21 48.1	1 27.5	3 45.8	17 7.9	18 19.4
16 T	23 33 33.1	1 54.1	14 37.2	19 48.0	8 29.8	9 33.4	10 2.3	21 48.8	1 18.6	3 48.9	17 7.3	18 21.4
19 S	23 45 22.8	0 43.0	14 34.2	27 33.5	9 7.7	11 0.5	9 55.9	21 49.2	1 9.7	3 52.0	17 6.7	18 23.3
22 W	23 57 12.4	0N28.1	14 31.1	22 35.4	9 24.6	12 25.4	9 47.4	21 49.2	1 0.8	3 55.0	17 6.0	18 25.0
25 S	0 9 2.1	1 39.1	14 28.1	5 11.7	9 21.7	13 47.6	9 37.1	21 49.0	0 52.0	3 58.0	17 5.2	18 26.7
28 T	0 20 51.7	2 49.6	14 25.0	15S15.3	9 0.7	15 7.0	9 25.0	21 48.4	0 43.2	4 1.0	17 4.4	18 28.3
31 F	0 32 41.4	3 59.7	14 22.0	27 2.1	8 23.0	16 23.0	9 11.1	21 47.5	0 34.4	4 3.9	17 3.5	18 29.8

APRIL 1967

LONGITUDE at NOON

DAY	EPHEMERIS SIDEREAL TIME	☉	☊	☽	☿	♀	♂	♃	♄	♅	♆	♇
1 S	0 36 38.0	11♈ 4.3	8♉31.6	6♑32.0	13♓18.4	14♉36.4	29♎38.7	24♋37.3	3♈32.8	21♍34.8	24♏ 1.0	18♍45.8
2 S	0 40 34.5	12 3.5	8 28.4	19 31.4	14 21.6	15 48.4	29R20.9	24 39.5	3 40.2	21R32.4	23R59.9	18R44.3
3 M	0 44 31.1	13 2.7	8 25.3	2♒10.9	15 27.3	17 0.3	29 2.5	24 41.9	3 47.7	21 30.0	23 58.8	18 42.9
4 T	0 48 27.6	14 1.8	8 22.1	14 34.1	16 35.5	18 12.2	28 43.6	24 44.4	3 55.1	21 27.6	23 57.6	18 41.4
5 W	0 52 24.2	15 0.9	8 18.9	26 44.4	17 45.9	19 24.0	28 24.1	24 47.2	4 2.5	21 25.3	23 56.5	18 40.0
6 T	0 56 20.7	15 60.0	8 15.7	8♓45.1	18 58.6	20 35.7	28 4.1	24 50.1	4 9.8	21 23.0	23 55.3	18 38.6
7 F	1 0 17.3	16 59.0	8 12.5	20 39.1	20 13.3	21 47.4	27 43.7	24 53.2	4 17.2	21 20.7	23 54.1	18 37.3
8 S	1 4 13.8	17 58.0	8 9.4	2♈29.0	21 30.1	22 58.9	27 22.8	24 56.5	4 24.6	21 18.4	23 52.9	18 35.9
9 S	1 8 10.4	18 57.0	8 6.2	14 16.9	22 48.9	24 10.4	27 1.5	24 60.0	4 31.9	21 16.2	23 51.6	18 34.6
10 M	1 12 6.9	19 55.9	8 3.0	26 5.2	24 9.6	25 21.8	26 39.9	25 3.6	4 39.2	21 14.0	23 50.3	18 33.2
11 T	1 16 3.5	20 54.8	7 59.8	7♉55.7	25 32.2	26 33.2	26 18.0	25 7.4	4 46.5	21 11.8	23 49.0	18 31.9
12 W	1 20 0.1	21 53.7	7 56.7	19 50.9	26 56.6	27 44.4	25 55.8	25 11.4	4 53.8	21 9.7	23 47.7	18 30.6
13 T	1 23 56.6	22 52.5	7 53.5	1♊53.3	28 22.8	28 55.5	25 33.4	25 15.5	5 1.1	21 7.6	23 46.4	18 29.4
14 F	1 27 53.2	23 51.3	7 50.3	14 5.7	29 50.7	0♊ 6.6	25 10.8	25 19.9	5 8.3	21 5.5	23 45.0	18 28.1
15 S	1 31 49.7	24 50.1	7 47.1	26 31.4	1♈20.4	1 17.6	24 48.0	25 24.3	5 15.5	21 3.4	23 43.7	18 26.9
16 S	1 35 46.3	25 48.8	7 43.9	9♋13.8	2 51.8	2 28.5	24 25.2	25 29.0	5 22.7	21 1.4	23 42.3	18 25.7
17 M	1 39 42.8	26 47.5	7 40.8	22 16.2	4 24.8	3 39.3	24 2.4	25 33.8	5 29.8	20 59.5	23 40.9	18 24.5
18 T	1 43 39.4	27 46.2	7 37.6	5♌41.4	5 59.6	4 49.9	23 39.5	25 38.8	5 37.0	20 57.5	23 39.5	18 23.3
19 W	1 47 35.9	28 44.8	7 34.4	19 31.2	7 36.0	6 0.5	23 16.7	25 43.9	5 44.1	20 55.6	23 38.0	18 22.2
20 T	1 51 32.5	29 43.4	7 31.2	3♍45.9	9 14.1	7 11.0	22 54.0	25 49.2	5 51.2	20 53.8	23 36.6	18 21.0
21 F	1 55 29.0	0♉42.0	7 28.1	18 23.5	10 53.9	8 21.5	22 31.5	25 54.7	5 58.2	20 52.0	23 35.2	18 20.0
22 S	1 59 25.6	1 40.5	7 24.9	3♎19.1	12 35.3	9 31.7	22 9.2	26 0.4	6 5.3	20 50.2	23 33.7	18 18.9
23 S	2 3 22.2	2 38.9	7 21.7	18 25.8	14 18.4	10 41.9	21 47.0	26 6.1	6 12.2	20 48.4	23 32.2	18 17.9
24 M	2 7 18.7	3 37.4	7 18.5	3♏34.7	16 3.2	11 52.0	21 25.1	26 12.0	6 19.2	20 46.7	23 30.7	18 16.8
25 T	2 11 15.3	4 35.8	7 15.4	18 36.6	17 49.7	13 1.9	21 3.5	26 18.1	6 26.1	20 45.1	23 29.2	18 15.8
26 W	2 15 11.8	5 34.2	7 12.2	3♐23.1	19 37.9	14 11.8	20 42.3	26 24.3	6 33.0	20 43.5	23 27.7	18 14.8
27 T	2 19 8.4	6 32.5	7 9.0	17 47.7	21 27.8	15 21.5	20 21.4	26 30.7	6 39.8	20 41.9	23 26.1	18 13.9
28 F	2 23 4.9	7 30.8	7 5.8	1♑46.6	23 19.4	16 31.1	20 1.0	26 37.2	6 46.6	20 40.3	23 24.6	18 13.0
29 S	2 27 1.5	8 29.1	7 2.6	15 18.6	25 12.8	17 40.6	19 41.0	26 43.8	6 53.4	20 38.8	23 23.0	18 12.1
30 S	2 30 58.0	9 27.4	6 59.5	28 24.5	27 7.8	18 50.0	19 21.5	26 50.6	7 0.1	20 37.4	23 21.5	18 11.2

DECLINATION at NOON

DAY	EPHEMERIS SIDEREAL TIME	☉	☊	☽	☿	♀	♂	♃	♄	♅	♆	♇
1 S	0 36 38.0	4N22.9	14N21.0	27S47.3	8S 7.1	16N47.6	9S 6.1	21N47.1	0S31.5	4N 4.8	17S 3.2	18N30.3
4 T	0 48 27.6	5 32.1	14 17.9	21 25.9	7 9.5	17 58.8	8 50.0	21 45.9	0 22.8	4 7.6	17 2.3	18 31.6
7 F	1 0 17.3	6 40.4	14 14.8	7 11.9	5 58.5	19 6.0	8 32.7	21 44.3	0 14.2	4 10.3	17 1.3	18 32.8
10 M	1 12 6.9	7 47.7	14 11.7	9N 9.2	4 35.0	20 8.9	8 14.4	21 42.4	0 5.7	4 12.8	17 0.3	18 33.9
13 T	1 23 56.6	8 53.9	14 8.7	22 44.1	3 0.1	21 7.2	7 55.4	21 40.2	0N 2.7	4 15.3	16 59.3	18 34.9
16 S	1 35 46.3	9 58.6	14 5.6	27 47.8	1 14.4	22 0.7	7 36.2	21 37.7	0 11.1	4 17.6	16 58.2	18 35.7
19 W	1 47 35.9	11 1.9	14 2.5	19 51.9	0N41.0	22 49.0	7 17.1	21 34.9	0 19.2	4 19.9	16 57.0	18 36.4
22 S	1 59 25.6	12 3.6	13 59.4	1 22.4	2 45.5	23 31.9	6 58.5	21 31.8	0 27.3	4 21.9	16 55.9	18 37.0
25 T	2 11 15.3	13 3.4	13 56.3	18S24.1	4 57.9	24 9.2	6 40.9	21 28.5	0 35.2	4 23.8	16 54.7	18 37.4
28 F	2 23 4.9	14 1.3	13 53.1	27 46.0	7 17.2	24 40.7	6 24.4	21 24.8	0 43.0	4 25.6	16 53.5	18 37.7

MAY 1967

DAY	EPHEMERIS SIDEREAL TIME	☉	☊	☽	☿	♀	♂	♃	♄	♅	♆	♇
	h m s	° ′	° ′	° ′	° ′	° ′	° ′	° ′	° ′	° ′	° ′	° ′
							LONGITUDE at NOON					
1 M	2 34 54.6	10♉25.6	6♉56.3	11♒ 7.2	29♈ 4.6	19♊59.3	19♎ 2.5	26♋57.5	7♈ 6.8	20♍36.0	23♏19.9	18♍10.3
2 T	2 38 51.1	11 23.9	6 53.1	23 30.4	1♉ 3.0	21 8.4	18R44.1	27 4.6	7 13.5	20R34.6	23R18.3	18R 9.5
3 W	2 42 47.7	12 22.1	6 49.9	5♓38.2	3 3.1	22 17.5	18 26.2	27 11.8	7 20.1	20 33.3	23 16.7	18 8.7
4 T	2 46 44.3	13 20.2	6 46.8	17 35.2	5 4.7	23 26.4	18 9.0	27 19.1	7 26.6	20 32.0	23 15.1	18 7.9
5 F	2 50 40.8	14 18.4	6 43.6	29 25.4	7 8.0	24 35.1	17 52.4	27 26.6	7 33.1	20 30.8	23 13.5	18 7.2
6 S	2 54 37.4	15 16.5	6 40.4	11♈12.8	9 12.7	25 43.8	17 36.4	27 34.2	7 39.6	20 29.6	23 11.9	18 6.5
7 S	2 58 33.9	16 14.6	6 37.2	23 0.7	11 18.8	26 52.3	17 21.2	27 41.9	7 46.0	20 28.5	23 10.3	18 5.8
8 M	3 2 30.5	17 12.7	6 34.0	4♉52.0	13 26.1	28 0.7	17 6.6	27 49.7	7 52.4	20 27.4	23 8.7	18 5.1
9 T	3 6 27.0	18 10.7	6 30.9	16 49.3	15 34.5	29 9.0	16 52.8	27 57.7	7 58.7	20 26.4	23 7.1	18 4.5
10 W	3 10 23.6	19 8.7	6 27.7	28 54.6	17 43.9	0♋17.1	16 39.8	28 5.8	8 5.0	20 25.4	23 5.4	18 3.9
11 T	3 14 20.2	20 6.7	6 24.5	11♊ 9.7	19 54.0	1 25.1	16 27.5	28 14.1	8 11.3	20 24.5	23 3.8	18 3.3
12 F	3 18 16.7	21 4.7	6 21.3	23 36.2	22 4.7	2 33.0	16 16.0	28 22.5	8 17.5	20 23.7	23 2.2	18 2.8
13 S	3 22 13.3	22 2.7	6 18.2	6♋15.5	24 15.6	3 40.6	16 5.2	28 30.9	8 23.6	20 22.8	23 0.6	18 2.3
14 S	3 26 9.8	23 0.6	6 15.0	19 9.1	26 26.5	4 48.2	15 55.3	28 39.5	8 29.7	20 22.1	22 59.0	18 1.8
15 M	3 30 6.4	23 58.5	6 11.8	2♌18.5	28 37.1	5 55.5	15 46.2	28 48.2	8 35.7	20 21.3	22 57.3	18 1.4
16 T	3 34 2.9	24 56.3	6 8.6	15 45.0	0♊47.1	7 2.7	15 37.9	28 57.0	8 41.6	20 20.7	22 55.7	18 0.9
17 W	3 37 59.5	25 54.1	6 5.5	29 29.6	2 56.4	8 9.7	15 30.3	29 6.0	8 47.5	20 20.0	22 54.1	18 0.5
18 T	3 41 56.1	26 51.9	6 2.3	13♍32.3	5 4.4	9 16.6	15 23.6	29 15.0	8 53.4	20 19.5	22 52.4	18 0.2
19 F	3 45 52.6	27 49.7	5 59.1	27 52.4	7 11.2	10 23.3	15 17.8	29 24.1	8 59.2	20 19.0	22 50.8	17 59.8
20 S	3 49 49.2	28 47.4	5 55.9	12♎27.3	9 16.2	11 29.8	15 12.7	29 33.4	9 4.9	20 18.5	22 49.2	17 59.5
21 S	3 53 45.7	29 45.1	5 52.7	27 13.0	11 19.4	12 36.1	15 8.4	29 42.7	9 10.6	20 18.1	22 47.6	17 59.3
22 M	3 57 42.3	0♊42.8	5 49.6	12♏ 3.5	13 20.6	13 42.2	15 5.0	29 52.2	9 16.2	20 17.7	22 46.0	17 59.0
23 T	4 1 38.8	1 40.5	5 46.4	26 51.9	15 19.5	14 48.1	15 2.3	0♌ 1.7	9 21.7	20 17.4	22 44.4	17 58.8
24 W	4 5 35.4	2 38.1	5 43.2	11♐30.7	17 16.0	15 53.8	15 0.4	0 11.4	9 27.2	20 17.1	22 42.8	17 58.6
25 T	4 9 32.0	3 35.7	5 40.0	25 53.2	19 10.0	16 59.3	14 59.3	0 21.1	9 32.6	20 16.9	22 41.2	17 58.5
26 F	4 13 28.5	4 33.3	5 36.9	9♑54.0	21 1.4	18 4.6	14 59.0	0 31.0	9 37.9	20 16.8	22 39.6	17 58.4
27 S	4 17 25.1	5 30.9	5 33.7	23 30.1	22 50.0	19 9.7	14D59.5	0 40.9	9 43.2	20 16.7	22 38.0	17 58.3
28 S	4 21 21.6	6 28.5	5 30.5	6♒40.8	24 35.9	20 14.5	15 0.7	0 51.0	9 48.4	20 16.7	22 36.4	17 58.2
29 M	4 25 18.2	7 26.0	5 27.3	19 27.6	26 19.0	21 19.2	15 2.7	1 1.1	9 53.6	20 16.7	22 34.8	17 58.2
30 T	4 29 14.7	8 23.6	5 24.2	1♓53.4	27 59.2	22 23.6	15 5.5	1 11.3	9 58.7	20 16.7	22 33.3	17 58.2
31 W	4 33 11.3	9 21.1	5 21.0	14 2.3	29 36.5	23 27.8	15 8.9	1 21.6	10 3.7	20D16.8	22 31.7	17D58.3
							DECLINATION at NOON					
1 M	2 34 54.6	14N57.1	13N50.0	22S30.8	9N41.7	25N 6.4	6S 9.6	21N20.9	0N50.6	4N27.2	16S52.3	18N37.9
4 T	2 46 44.3	15 50.8	13 46.9	8 36.4	12 9.1	25 26.0	5 56.6	21 16.7	0 58.0	4 28.7	16 51.1	18 38.0
7 S	2 58 33.9	16 42.1	13 43.8	7N45.6	14 36.4	25 39.5	5 45.8	21 12.2	1 5.3	4 30.0	16 49.9	18 37.9
10 W	3 10 23.6	17 30.9	13 40.6	21 51.0	16 59.4	25 46.9	5 37.3	21 7.4	1 12.3	4 31.1	16 48.7	18 37.6
13 S	3 22 13.3	18 17.0	13 37.5	27 49.7	19 13.1	25 48.2	5 31.3	21 2.3	1 19.2	4 32.0	16 47.4	18 37.2
16 T	3 34 2.9	19 0.4	13 34.3	21 4.7	21 11.8	25 43.5	5 28.0	20 57.0	1 25.8	4 32.7	16 46.2	18 36.7
19 F	3 45 52.6	19 40.9	13 31.2	3 53.1	22 50.8	25 32.8	5 27.2	20 51.3	1 32.2	4 33.3	16 45.0	18 36.1
22 M	3 57 42.3	20 18.3	13 28.0	15S54.8	24 7.1	25 16.3	5 29.0	20 45.4	1 38.3	4 33.6	16 43.8	18 35.4
25 T	4 9 32.0	20 52.6	13 24.9	27 20.4	24 59.6	24 54.2	5 33.4	20 39.3	1 44.2	4 33.8	16 42.7	18 34.5
28 S	4 21 21.6	21 23.7	13 21.7	23 39.4	25 29.3	24 26.7	5 40.3	20 32.8	1 49.9	4 33.8	16 41.5	18 33.5
31 W	4 33 11.3	21 51.5	13 18.5	10 6.2	25 38.4	23 54.0	5 49.5	20 26.2	1 55.2	4 33.6	16 40.4	18 32.3

JUNE 1967

DAY	EPHEMERIS SIDEREAL TIME	☉	☊	☽	☿	♀	♂	♃	♄	♅	♆	♇
							LONGITUDE at NOON					
1 T	4 37 7.9	10♊18.6	5♉17.8	25♓59.2	1♋10.8	24♋31.7	15♎13.2	1♌32.0	10♈ 8.6	20♍17.0	22♏30.2	17♍58.3
2 F	4 41 4.4	11 16.2	5 14.6	7♈49.1	2 42.2	25 35.5	15 18.2	1 42.5	10 13.5	20 17.3	22R28.7	17 58.5
3 S	4 45 1.0	12 13.6	5 11.5	19 36.7	4 10.6	26 39.0	15 23.8	1 53.1	10 18.3	20 17.6	22 27.2	17 58.6
4 S	4 48 57.5	13 11.1	5 8.3	1♉26.7	5 35.9	27 42.2	15 30.2	2 3.8	10 23.0	20 17.9	22 25.7	17 58.8
5 M	4 52 54.1	14 8.6	5 5.1	13 22.9	6 58.1	28 45.1	15 37.3	2 14.5	10 27.7	20 18.3	22 24.2	17 59.0
6 T	4 56 50.7	15 6.0	5 1.9	25 28.6	8 17.2	29 47.8	15 45.1	2 25.3	10 32.2	20 18.7	22 22.7	17 59.2
7 W	5 0 47.2	16 3.5	4 58.7	7♊46.3	9 33.2	0♌50.1	15 53.5	2 36.2	10 36.7	20 19.2	22 21.3	17 59.5
8 T	5 4 43.8	17 0.9	4 55.6	20 17.5	10 45.9	1 52.2	16 2.6	2 47.2	10 41.2	20 19.7	22 19.8	17 59.8
9 F	5 8 40.3	17 58.3	4 52.4	3♋ 3.0	11 55.4	2 54.0	16 12.4	2 58.2	10 45.5	20 20.3	22 18.4	18 0.1
10 S	5 12 36.9	18 55.7	4 49.2	16 2.6	13 1.6	3 55.5	16 22.9	3 9.3	10 49.7	20 21.0	22 17.0	18 0.5
11 S	5 16 33.4	19 53.0	4 46.0	29 15.8	14 4.4	4 56.7	16 34.0	3 20.5	10 53.9	20 21.7	22 15.6	18 0.8
12 M	5 20 30.0	20 50.4	4 42.9	12♌41.9	15 3.7	5 57.6	16 45.7	3 31.8	10 58.0	20 22.4	22 14.2	18 1.3
13 T	5 24 26.6	21 47.7	4 39.7	26 19.8	15 59.5	6 58.1	16 58.0	3 43.1	11 2.0	20 23.2	22 12.8	18 1.7
14 W	5 28 23.1	22 45.1	4 36.5	10♍ 8.8	16 51.7	7 58.2	17 10.9	3 54.5	11 6.0	20 24.1	22 11.4	18 2.2
15 T	5 32 19.7	23 42.4	4 33.3	24 8.1	17 40.1	8 58.0	17 24.5	4 6.0	11 9.8	20 25.0	22 10.1	18 2.7
16 F	5 36 16.2	24 39.7	4 30.2	8♎16.8	18 24.7	9 57.4	17 38.6	4 17.5	11 13.6	20 26.0	22 8.8	18 3.3
17 S	5 40 12.8	25 37.0	4 27.0	22 33.7	19 5.3	10 56.5	17 53.3	4 29.1	11 17.2	20 27.0	22 7.5	18 3.8
18 S	5 44 9.4	26 34.2	4 23.8	6♏56.7	19 42.0	11 55.1	18 8.5	4 40.8	11 20.8	20 28.1	22 6.2	18 4.4
19 M	5 48 5.9	27 31.5	4 20.6	21 22.7	20 14.4	12 53.3	18 24.3	4 52.5	11 24.3	20 29.2	22 5.0	18 5.1
20 T	5 52 2.5	28 28.7	4 17.5	5♐47.6	20 42.7	13 51.1	18 40.6	5 4.3	11 27.7	20 30.4	22 3.7	18 5.7
21 W	5 55 59.0	29 26.0	4 14.3	20 6.2	21 6.6	14 48.4	18 57.5	5 16.1	11 31.1	20 31.6	22 2.5	18 6.4
22 T	5 59 55.6	0♋23.2	4 11.1	4♑13.1	21 26.1	15 45.3	19 14.9	5 28.0	11 34.3	20 32.9	22 1.3	18 7.2
23 F	6 3 52.1	1 20.5	4 7.9	18 3.5	21 41.2	16 41.8	19 32.8	5 40.0	11 37.5	20 34.2	22 0.2	18 8.0
24 S	6 7 48.7	2 17.7	4 4.8	1♒33.7	21 51.7	17 37.7	19 51.1	5 52.0	11 40.6	20 35.6	21 59.0	18 8.7
25 S	6 11 45.3	3 14.9	4 1.6	14 41.9	21 57.5	18 33.2	20 10.0	6 4.0	11 43.6	20 37.0	21 57.9	18 9.6
26 M	6 15 41.8	4 12.1	3 58.4	27 28.2	21 58.8	19 28.1	20 29.3	6 16.1	11 46.4	20 38.5	21 56.8	18 10.4
27 T	6 19 38.4	5 9.3	3 55.2	9♓54.4	21R55.6	20 22.5	20 49.1	6 28.3	11 49.2	20 40.0	21 55.7	18 11.3
28 W	6 23 34.9	6 6.5	3 52.0	22 4.0	21 47.8	21 16.4	21 9.3	6 40.5	11 51.9	20 41.6	21 54.6	18 12.2
29 T	6 27 31.5	7 3.7	3 48.9	4♈ 1.5	21 35.6	22 9.6	21 30.0	6 52.7	11 54.5	20 43.2	21 53.6	18 13.1
30 F	6 31 28.1	8 0.9	3 45.7	15 51.8	21 19.2	23 2.3	21 51.1	7 5.0	11 57.0	20 44.9	21 52.6	18 14.1
							DECLINATION at NOON					
1 T	4 37 7.9	22N 0.0	13N17.5	4S42.7	25N37.3	23N42.0	5S53.1	20N23.9	1N57.0	4N33.5	16S40.0	18N31.9
4 S	4 48 57.5	22 23.2	13 14.3	11N32.6	25 23.2	23 2.9	6 5.4	20 16.8	2 2.0	4 33.1	16 38.9	18 30.6
7 W	5 0 47.2	22 42.9	13 11.1	24 16.0	24 55.3	22 19.3	6 19.8	20 9.5	2 6.7	4 32.4	16 37.9	18 29.2
10 S	5 12 36.9	22 59.0	13 7.9	27 16.8	24 16.5	21 31.4	6 36.4	20 1.9	2 11.2	4 31.6	16 36.9	18 27.7
13 T	5 24 26.6	23 11.5	13 4.7	17 16.4	23 29.7	20 39.8	6 54.8	19 54.1	2 15.3	4 30.6	16 35.9	18 26.1
16 F	5 36 16.2	23 20.3	13 1.5	1S 5.6	22 37.6	19 44.6	7 15.1	19 46.0	2 19.1	4 29.4	16 35.0	18 24.3
19 M	5 48 5.9	23 25.3	12 58.3	19 26.4	21 43.1	18 46.4	7 37.1	19 37.7	2 22.6	4 28.0	16 34.1	18 22.5
22 T	5 59 55.6	23 26.7	12 55.1	27 43.9	20 48.7	17 45.4	8 0.6	19 29.2	2 25.8	4 26.4	16 33.3	18 20.6
25 S	6 11 45.3	23 24.3	12 51.8	21 13.3	19 57.1	16 42.1	8 25.6	19 20.4	2 28.7	4 24.7	16 32.5	18 18.5
28 W	6 23 34.9	23 18.3	12 48.6	6 20.1	19 11.0	15 36.8	8 51.8	19 11.3	2 31.2	4 22.8	16 31.8	18 16.4

JULY 1967

DAY	EPHEMERIS SIDEREAL TIME	☉	☊	☽	☿	♀	♂	♃	♄	♅	♆	♇
	h m s	° ′	° ′	° ′	° ′	° ′	° ′	° ′	° ′	° ′	° ′	° ′
						LONGITUDE at NOON						
1 S	6 35 24.6	8♋58.1	3♉42.5	27♈40.3	20♋58.7	23♌54.4	22♎12.7	7♌17.4	11♈59.4	20♍46.6	21♏51.6	18♍15.1
2 S	6 39 21.2	9 55.3	3 39.3	9♉32.4	20R34.6	24 45.9	22 34.7	7 29.8	12 1.8	20 48.3	21R50.6	18 16.1
3 M	6 43 17.7	10 52.6	3 36.2	21 32.8	20 7.0	25 36.7	22 57.1	7 42.2	12 4.0	20 50.1	21 49.7	18 17.1
4 T	6 47 14.3	11 49.8	3 33.0	3♊45.9	19 36.3	26 26.9	23 19.9	7 54.7	12 6.1	20 52.0	21 48.8	18 18.2
5 W	6 51 10.9	12 47.0	3 29.8	16 14.9	19 3.1	27 16.3	23 43.1	8 7.2	12 8.1	20 53.9	21 47.9	18 19.3
6 T	6 55 7.4	13 44.2	3 26.6	29 1.7	18 27.9	28 5.1	24 6.8	8 19.7	12 10.1	20 55.8	21 47.0	18 20.4
7 F	6 59 4.0	14 41.4	3 23.5	12♋ 6.9	17 51.2	28 53.1	24 30.8	8 32.3	12 11.9	20 57.8	21 46.2	18 21.6
8 S	7 3 0.5	15 38.7	3 20.3	25 29.5	17 13.5	29 40.3	24 55.2	8 45.0	12 13.6	20 59.9	21 45.4	18 22.8
9 S	7 6 57.1	16 35.9	3 17.1	9♌ 7.2	16 35.7	0♍26.7	25 20.0	8 57.6	12 15.3	21 2.0	21 44.6	18 24.0
10 M	7 10 53.6	17 33.1	3 13.9	22 57.0	15 58.2	1 12.3	25 45.2	9 10.4	12 16.8	21 4.1	21 43.9	18 25.2
11 T	7 14 50.2	18 30.4	3 10.8	6♍55.3	15 21.8	1 56.9	26 10.7	9 23.1	12 18.2	21 6.3	21 43.1	18 26.5
12 W	7 18 46.8	19 27.6	3 7.6	20 59.1	14 47.1	2 40.7	26 36.6	9 35.9	12 19.6	21 8.5	21 42.4	18 27.8
13 T	7 22 43.3	20 24.8	3 4.4	5♎ 5.8	14 14.6	3 23.6	27 2.8	9 48.7	12 20.8	21 10.7	21 41.8	18 29.1
14 F	7 26 39.9	21 22.1	3 1.2	19 13.6	13 45.2	4 5.5	27 29.4	10 1.5	12 22.0	21 13.1	21 41.2	18 30.5
15 S	7 30 36.4	22 19.3	2 58.0	3♏21.3	13 19.1	4 46.3	27 56.3	10 14.4	12 23.0	21 15.4	21 40.6	18 31.9
16 S	7 34 33.0	23 16.5	2 54.9	17 27.8	12 56.9	5 26.0	28 23.6	10 27.3	12 23.9	21 17.8	21 40.0	18 33.2
17 M	7 38 29.6	24 13.8	2 51.7	1♐32.1	12 39.1	6 4.7	28 51.1	10 40.2	12 24.7	21 20.2	21 39.5	18 34.7
18 T	7 42 26.1	25 11.0	2 48.5	15 32.2	12 26.0	6 42.2	29 19.0	10 53.1	12 25.5	21 22.7	21 38.9	18 36.1
19 W	7 46 22.7	26 8.2	2 45.3	29 25.6	12 18.0	7 18.5	29 47.2	11 6.1	12 26.1	21 25.2	21 38.5	18 37.6
20 T	7 50 19.2	27 5.5	2 42.2	13♑ 9.2	12 15.3	7 53.5	0♏15.7	11 19.0	12 26.6	21 27.7	21 38.0	18 39.0
21 F	7 54 15.8	28 2.7	2 39.0	26 39.8	12D18.1	8 27.3	0 44.4	11 32.0	12 27.0	21 30.3	21 37.6	18 40.5
22 S	7 58 12.3	28 60.0	2 35.8	9♒54.5	12 26.6	8 59.7	1 13.5	11 45.0	12 27.4	21 32.9	21 37.2	18 42.1
23 S	8 2 8.9	29 57.3	2 32.6	22 51.6	12 40.8	9 30.7	1 42.9	11 58.1	12 27.6	21 35.6	21 36.8	18 43.6
24 M	8 6 5.5	0♌54.5	2 29.5	5♓30.6	13 0.9	10 0.3	2 12.5	12 11.1	12 27.7	21 38.3	21 36.5	18 45.2
25 T	8 10 2.0	1 51.8	2 26.3	17 52.5	13 26.9	10 28.4	2 42.4	12 24.2	12 27.7	21 41.0	21 36.2	18 46.8
26 W	8 13 58.6	2 49.1	2 23.1	29 59.7	13 58.8	10 55.0	3 12.6	12 37.3	12R27.6	21 43.7	21 35.9	18 48.4
27 T	8 17 55.1	3 46.4	2 19.9	11♈56.0	14 36.6	11 20.0	3 43.0	12 50.4	12 27.4	21 46.5	21 35.6	18 50.1
28 F	8 21 51.7	4 43.8	2 16.8	23 45.7	15 20.2	11 43.3	4 13.7	13 3.5	12 27.1	21 49.4	21 35.4	18 51.7
29 S	8 25 48.2	5 41.1	2 13.6	5♉34.2	16 9.7	12 4.9	4 44.7	13 16.6	12 26.7	21 52.2	21 35.3	18 53.4
30 S	8 29 44.8	6 38.5	2 10.4	17 26.8	17 4.8	12 24.7	5 16.0	13 29.8	12 26.2	21 55.1	21 35.1	18 55.1
31 M	8 33 41.4	7 35.9	2 7.2	29 29.0	18 5.6	12 42.7	5 47.4	13 42.9	12 25.6	21 58.1	21 35.0	18 56.8
						DECLINATION at NOON						
1 S	6 35 24.6	23N 8.5	12N45.4	10N 3.1	18N32.7	14N30.0	9S 19.3	19N 2.1	2N33.4	4N20.7	16S 31.2	18N14.3
4 T	6 47 14.3	22 55.1	12 42.2	23 19.5	18 4.3	13 22.0	9 47.8	18 52.6	2 35.3	4 18.5	16 30.6	18 12.0
7 F	6 59 4.0	22 38.1	12 38.9	27 32.1	17 47.2	12 13.3	10 17.3	18 43.0	2 36.7	4 16.1	16 30.1	18 9.7
10 M	7 10 53.6	22 17.6	12 35.7	18 21.6	17 42.3	11 4.3	10 47.8	18 33.1	2 37.9	4 13.5	16 29.6	18 7.3
13 T	7 22 43.3	21 53.6	12 32.4	0 11.3	17 49.3	9 55.5	11 19.0	18 23.0	2 38.7	4 10.8	16 29.2	18 4.8
16 S	7 34 33.0	21 26.3	12 29.2	18S 12.9	18 7.1	8 47.4	11 50.9	18 12.7	2 39.1	4 7.9	16 28.9	18 2.3
19 W	7 46 22.7	20 55.7	12 25.9	27 36.8	18 33.4	7 40.6	12 23.4	18 2.2	2 39.2	4 4.9	16 28.7	17 59.7
22 S	7 58 12.3	20 21.9	12 22.6	22 33.1	19 5.5	6 35.7	12 56.4	17 51.6	2 38.9	4 1.7	16 28.5	17 57.1
25 T	8 10 2.0	19 45.0	12 19.4	8 2.0	19 39.7	5 33.5	13 29.7	17 40.8	2 38.2	3 58.5	16 28.5	17 54.5
28 F	8 21 51.7	19 5.2	12 16.1	8N32.6	20 11.7	4 34.4	14 3.2	17 29.9	2 37.2	3 55.1	16 28.4	17 51.8
31 M	8 33 41.4	18 22.5	12 12.8	22 19.1	20 37.0	3 39.5	14 37.0	17 18.8	2 35.9	3 51.5	16 28.5	17 49.1

AUGUST 1967

DAY	EPHEMERIS SIDEREAL TIME	☉	☊	☽	☿	♀	♂	♃	♄	♅	♆	♇
						LONGITUDE at NOON						
1 T	8 37 37.9	8♌33.3	2♉ 4.0	11♊45.8	19♋12.0	12♍58.9	6♏19.2	13♌56.1	12♈24.9	22♍ 1.1	21♏34.9	18♍58.6
2 W	8 41 34.5	9 30.7	2 0.9	24 21.4	20 23.7	13 13.1	6 51.2	14 9.3	12R24.1	22 4.1	21 34.9	19 0.3
3 T	8 45 31.0	10 28.2	1 57.7	7♋18.8	21 40.6	13 25.3	7 23.4	14 22.4	12 23.2	22 7.1	21 34.8	19 2.1
4 F	8 49 27.6	11 25.7	1 54.5	20 39.0	23 2.7	13 35.4	7 55.9	14 35.7	12 22.2	22 10.2	21D34.9	19 3.9
5 S	8 53 24.1	12 23.1	1 51.3	4♌21.1	24 29.6	13 43.5	8 28.6	14 48.9	12 21.1	22 13.3	21 34.9	19 5.8
6 S	8 57 20.7	13 20.6	1 48.2	18 22.1	26 1.1	13 49.3	9 1.6	15 2.0	12 19.9	22 16.4	21 35.0	19 7.6
7 M	9 1 17.3	14 18.1	1 45.0	2♍37.3	27 37.1	13 53.0	9 34.8	15 15.2	12 18.6	22 19.6	21 35.1	19 9.4
8 T	9 5 13.8	15 15.7	1 41.8	17 0.9	29 17.1	13 54.4	10 8.2	15 28.4	12 17.2	22 22.8	21 35.3	19 11.3
9 W	9 9 10.4	16 13.2	1 38.6	1♎27.2	1♌ 0.9	13R53.4	10 41.8	15 41.6	12 15.7	22 26.0	21 35.5	19 13.2
10 T	9 13 6.9	17 10.8	1 35.5	15 51.1	2 48.2	13 50.2	11 15.6	15 54.8	12 14.1	22 29.2	21 35.7	19 15.1
11 F	9 17 3.5	18 8.3	1 32.3	0♏ 9.2	4 38.5	13 44.5	11 49.7	16 8.0	12 12.4	22 32.5	21 35.9	19 17.0
12 S	9 21 0.0	19 5.9	1 29.1	14 19.1	6 31.6	13 36.5	12 24.0	16 21.2	12 10.6	22 35.8	21 36.2	19 18.9
13 S	9 24 56.6	20 3.5	1 25.9	28 19.8	8 27.0	13 26.1	12 58.5	16 34.4	12 8.7	22 39.1	21 36.5	19 20.9
14 M	9 28 53.1	21 1.1	1 22.7	12♐10.8	10 24.2	13 13.2	13 33.2	16 47.5	12 6.7	22 42.4	21 36.8	19 22.8
15 T	9 32 49.7	21 58.8	1 19.6	25 51.9	12 23.1	12 58.0	14 8.0	17 0.7	12 4.6	22 45.8	21 37.2	19 24.8
16 W	9 36 46.3	22 56.4	1 16.4	9♑22.7	14 23.1	12 40.5	14 43.1	17 13.8	12 2.5	22 49.2	21 37.6	19 26.8
17 T	9 40 42.8	23 54.1	1 13.2	22 42.4	16 23.9	12 20.6	15 18.4	17 27.0	12 0.2	22 52.6	21 38.0	19 28.8
18 F	9 44 39.4	24 51.7	1 10.0	5♒49.9	18 25.2	11 58.5	15 53.9	17 40.1	11 57.8	22 56.0	21 38.5	19 30.8
19 S	9 48 35.9	25 49.4	1 6.9	18 44.2	20 26.7	11 34.3	16 29.5	17 53.2	11 55.4	22 59.5	21 39.0	19 32.8
20 S	9 52 32.5	26 47.2	1 3.7	1♓24.6	22 28.2	11 8.1	17 5.3	18 6.3	11 52.9	23 2.9	21 39.5	19 34.9
21 M	9 56 29.0	27 44.9	1 0.5	13 51.0	24 29.3	10 39.9	17 41.3	18 19.4	11 50.3	23 6.4	21 40.1	19 36.9
22 T	10 0 25.6	28 42.7	0 57.3	26 4.2	26 30.0	10 9.9	18 17.5	18 32.5	11 47.5	23 9.9	21 40.7	19 39.0
23 W	10 4 22.1	29 40.5	0 54.1	8♈ 6.0	28 29.9	9 38.3	18 53.9	18 45.6	11 44.8	23 13.5	21 41.3	19 41.0
24 T	10 8 18.7	0♍38.3	0 51.0	19 59.0	0♍29.1	9 5.3	19 30.5	18 58.6	11 41.9	23 17.0	21 42.0	19 43.1
25 F	10 12 15.2	1 36.2	0 47.8	1♉47.1	2 27.4	8 31.1	20 7.2	19 11.7	11 39.0	23 20.6	21 42.7	19 45.2
26 S	10 16 11.8	2 34.1	0 44.6	13 34.6	4 24.6	7 55.8	20 44.1	19 24.7	11 35.9	23 24.2	21 43.4	19 47.3
27 S	10 20 8.4	3 32.0	0 41.4	25 26.5	6 20.8	7 19.7	21 21.2	19 37.7	11 32.8	23 27.8	21 44.2	19 49.4
28 M	10 24 4.9	4 29.9	0 38.3	7♊28.0	8 15.7	6 43.0	21 58.4	19 50.6	11 29.6	23 31.5	21 44.9	19 51.5
29 T	10 28 1.5	5 27.9	0 35.1	19 44.5	10 9.5	6 5.9	22 35.8	20 3.6	11 26.3	23 35.1	21 45.8	19 53.7
30 W	10 31 58.0	6 25.9	0 31.9	2♋20.8	12 2.1	5 28.7	23 13.4	20 16.5	11 23.0	23 38.7	21 46.6	19 55.8
31 T	10 35 54.6	7 23.9	0 28.7	15 20.7	13 53.5	4 51.6	23 51.1	20 29.4	11 19.6	23 42.4	21 47.5	19 57.9
						DECLINATION at NOON						
1 T	8 37 37.9	18N 7.7	12N11.7	25N24.1	20N43.1	3N22.2	14S 48.2	17N15.0	2N35.4	3N50.3	16S 28.5	17N48.1
4 F	8 49 27.6	17 21.4	12 8.4	26 43.7	20 51.5	2 34.1	15 22.1	17 3.7	2 33.6	3 46.7	16 28.7	17 45.4
7 M	9 1 17.3	16 32.6	12 5.1	14 32.2	20 41.6	1 52.3	15 55.9	16 52.3	2 31.4	3 42.9	16 28.9	17 42.6
10 T	9 13 6.9	15 41.4	12 1.8	5S 2.1	20 9.7	1 17.8	16 29.5	16 40.8	2 29.0	3 39.0	16 29.2	17 39.9
13 S	9 24 56.6	14 48.0	11 58.5	22 5.0	19 13.8	0 51.8	17 3.0	16 29.2	2 26.2	3 35.0	16 29.6	17 37.1
16 W	9 36 46.3	13 52.4	11 55.2	27 48.8	17 54.8	0 35.3	17 36.1	16 17.4	2 23.1	3 31.0	16 30.1	17 34.3
19 S	9 48 35.9	12 54.9	11 51.9	19 45.5	16 15.6	0 29.1	18 8.7	16 5.6	2 19.7	3 26.9	16 30.6	17 31.6
22 T	10 0 25.6	11 55.5	11 48.6	4 8.6	14 20.4	0 33.5	18 40.8	15 53.8	2 16.0	3 22.7	16 31.2	17 28.8
25 F	10 12 15.2	10 54.4	11 45.2	12N17.6	12 13.7	0 48.3	19 12.3	15 41.8	2 12.0	3 18.4	16 31.9	17 26.1
28 M	10 24 4.9	9 51.8	11 41.9	24 40.8	9 59.4	1 12.7	19 43.0	15 29.9	2 7.8	3 14.1	16 32.7	17 23.4
31 T	10 35 54.6	8 47.7	11 38.6	27 30.0	7 40.8	1 45.1	20 12.9	15 17.9	2 3.3	3 9.7	16 33.5	17 20.7

SEPTEMBER 1967

DAY	EPHEMERIS SIDEREAL TIME	☉	☊	☽	☿	♀	♂	♃	♄	♅	♆	♇
	h m s	° ′	° ′	° ′	° ′	° ′	° ′	° ′	° ′	° ′	° ′	° ′
						LONGITUDE at NOON						
1 F	10 39 51.1	8♍22.0	0♉25.6	28♋46.6	15♍43.6	4♍14.9	24♏29.0	20♌42.2	11♈16.1	23♍46.1	21♏48.4	20♍ 0.1
2 S	10 43 47.7	9 20.1	0 22.4	12♌38.6	17 32.5	3R38.8	25 7.0	20 55.1	11R12.5	23 49.8	21 49.3	20 2.2
3 S	10 47 44.2	10 18.2	0 19.2	26 54.4	19 20.1	3 3.5	25 45.3	21 7.9	11 8.9	23 53.5	21 50.3	20 4.4
4 M	10 51 40.8	11 16.4	0 16.0	11♍28.9	21 6.5	2 29.2	26 23.6	21 20.6	11 5.2	23 57.2	21 51.3	20 6.5
5 T	10 55 37.3	12 14.6	0 12.8	26 15.3	22 51.6	1 56.2	27 2.2	21 33.4	11 1.4	24 0.9	21 52.3	20 8.7
6 W	10 59 33.9	13 12.8	0 9.7	11♎ 5.6	24 35.6	1 24.6	27 40.8	21 46.1	10 57.5	24 4.6	21 53.4	20 10.8
7 T	11 3 30.5	14 11.0	0 6.5	25 52.4	26 18.4	0 54.6	28 19.7	21 58.8	10 53.6	24 8.4	21 54.5	20 13.0
8 F	11 7 27.0	15 9.3	0 3.3	10♏29.4	27 60.0	0 26.3	28 58.7	22 11.4	10 49.7	24 12.1	21 55.6	20 15.2
9 S	11 11 23.6	16 7.6	0 0.1	24 52.2	29 40.4	29♌59.9	29 37.8	22 24.0	10 45.7	24 15.9	21 56.7	20 17.4
10 S	11 15 20.1	17 5.9	29♈57.0	8♐58.5	1♎19.7	29 35.5	0♐17.1	22 36.5	10 41.6	24 19.6	21 57.9	20 19.5
11 M	11 19 16.7	18 4.2	29 53.8	22 47.5	2 57.8	29 13.2	0 56.5	22 49.1	10 37.5	24 23.4	21 59.1	20 21.7
12 T	11 23 13.2	19 2.6	29 50.6	6♑19.6	4 34.8	28 53.2	1 36.0	23 1.5	10 33.3	24 27.1	22 0.3	20 23.9
13 W	11 27 9.8	20 0.9	29 47.4	19 35.6	6 10.7	28 35.4	2 15.7	23 13.9	10 29.1	24 30.9	22 1.6	20 26.1
14 T	11 31 6.3	20 59.4	29 44.2	2♒36.7	7 45.5	28 20.0	2 55.5	23 26.3	10 24.8	24 34.7	22 2.9	20 28.3
15 F	11 35 2.9	21 57.9	29 41.1	15 24.1	9 19.3	28 7.0	3 35.5	23 38.7	10 20.6	24 38.5	22 4.2	20 30.5
16 S	11 38 59.4	22 56.3	29 37.9	27 58.8	10 52.0	27 56.4	4 15.6	23 51.0	10 16.2	24 42.3	22 5.5	20 32.7
17 S	11 42 56.0	23 54.8	29 34.7	10♓21.7	12 23.5	27 48.2	4 55.8	24 3.2	10 11.8	24 46.1	22 6.9	20 34.8
18 M	11 46 52.5	24 53.4	29 31.5	22 33.9	13 54.1	27 42.4	5 36.1	24 15.4	10 7.4	24 49.9	22 8.3	20 37.0
19 T	11 50 49.1	25 51.9	29 28.4	4♈36.7	15 23.5	27 39.1	6 16.6	24 27.6	10 2.9	24 53.6	22 9.7	20 39.2
20 W	11 54 45.7	26 50.5	29 25.2	16 31.7	16 51.9	27 38.1	6 57.2	24 39.7	9 58.4	24 57.4	22 11.2	20 41.4
21 T	11 58 42.2	27 49.1	29 22.0	28 21.2	18 19.2	27D39.6	7 37.9	24 51.7	9 53.9	25 1.2	22 12.6	20 43.5
22 F	12 2 38.8	28 47.8	29 18.8	10♉ 8.0	19 45.4	27 43.3	8 18.7	25 3.7	9 49.3	25 5.0	22 14.1	20 45.7
23 S	12 6 35.3	29 46.5	29 15.6	21 55.4	21 10.5	27 49.4	8 59.6	25 15.6	9 44.7	25 8.8	22 15.6	20 47.9
24 S	12 10 31.9	0♎45.2	29 12.5	3♊47.3	22 34.5	27 57.7	9 40.7	25 27.5	9 40.1	25 12.5	22 17.2	20 50.0
25 M	12 14 28.4	1 44.0	29 9.3	15 48.4	23 57.3	28 8.2	10 21.9	25 39.3	9 35.5	25 16.3	22 18.8	20 52.2
26 T	12 18 25.0	2 42.8	29 6.1	28 3.2	25 18.9	28 20.8	11 3.2	25 51.0	9 30.8	25 20.1	22 20.3	20 54.3
27 W	12 22 21.5	3 41.7	29 2.9	10♋36.5	26 39.4	28 35.5	11 44.6	26 2.7	9 26.2	25 23.8	22 22.0	20 56.5
28 T	12 26 18.1	4 40.6	28 59.8	23 32.5	27 58.5	28 52.3	12 26.1	26 14.3	9 21.5	25 27.6	22 23.6	20 58.6
29 F	12 30 14.6	5 39.5	28 56.6	6♌54.5	29 16.4	29 11.0	13 7.8	26 25.9	9 16.8	25 31.3	22 25.3	21 0.7
30 S	12 34 11.2	6 38.4	28 53.4	20 44.2	0♏32.9	29 31.6	13 49.6	26 37.4	9 12.1	25 35.1	22 26.9	21 2.9
						DECLINATION at NOON						
1 F	10 39 51.1	8N26.1	11N37.5	25N25.2	6N54.1	1N57.3	20S22.7	15N13.9	2N 1.8	3N 8.2	16S33.8	17N19.8
4 M	10 51 40.8	7 20.4	11 34.1	10 45.3	4 33.4	2 37.2	20 51.3	15 1.9	1 57.0	3 3.8	16 34.7	17 17.2
7 T	11 3 30.5	6 13.5	11 30.8	9S45.8	2 13.4	3 19.9	21 19.0	14 49.9	1 52.1	2 59.4	16 35.7	17 14.6
10 S	11 15 20.1	5 5.8	11 27.4	25 6.8	0S 4.8	4 3.2	21 45.4	14 37.9	1 46.9	2 54.9	16 36.7	17 12.0
13 W	11 27 9.8	3 57.3	11 24.1	27 4.4	2 20.0	4 45.1	22 10.6	14 26.0	1 41.7	2 50.4	16 37.8	17 9.5
16 S	11 38 59.4	2 48.2	11 20.7	16 24.4	4 31.4	5 23.8	22 34.5	14 14.1	1 36.3	2 45.9	16 39.0	17 7.1
19 T	11 50 49.1	1 38.6	11 17.3	0 4.7	6 38.2	5 58.0	22 56.9	14 2.3	1 30.8	2 41.4	16 40.2	17 4.7
22 F	12 2 38.8	0 28.7	11 14.0	15N54.0	8 39.7	6 26.8	23 17.7	13 50.6	1 25.2	2 36.9	16 41.4	17 2.4
25 M	12 14 28.4	0S41.4	11 10.6	26 33.2	10 35.2	6 49.5	23 36.9	13 39.0	1 19.6	2 32.4	16 42.7	17 0.2
28 T	12 26 18.1	1 51.5	11 7.2	26 33.0	12 24.0	7 5.9	23 54.4	13 27.5	1 14.0	2 27.9	16 44.1	16 58.1

OCTOBER 1967

DAY	EPHEMERIS SIDEREAL TIME	☉	☊	☽	☿	♀	♂	♃	♄	♅	♆	♇
						LONGITUDE at NOON						
1 S	12 38 7.7	7♎37.4	28♈50.2	5♍ 0.9	1♏47.9	29♌54.0	14♐31.4	26♌48.8	9♈ 7.3	25♍38.8	22♏28.6	21♍ 5.0
2 M	12 42 4.3	8 36.5	28 47.0	19 41.2	3 1.4	0♍18.2	15 13.4	27 0.1	9R 2.6	25 42.5	22 30.4	21 7.1
3 T	12 46 0.8	9 35.5	28 43.9	4♎38.9	4 13.2	0 44.1	15 55.5	27 11.4	8 57.9	25 46.2	22 32.1	21 9.2
4 W	12 49 57.4	10 34.7	28 40.7	19 45.7	5 23.4	1 11.6	16 37.7	27 22.6	8 53.2	25 49.9	22 33.9	21 11.3
5 T	12 53 54.0	11 33.8	28 37.5	4♏52.4	6 31.6	1 40.8	17 20.1	27 33.7	8 48.5	25 53.6	22 35.7	21 13.3
6 F	12 57 50.5	12 33.0	28 34.3	19 50.3	7 38.0	2 11.5	18 2.5	27 44.8	8 43.8	25 57.3	22 37.5	21 15.5
7 S	13 1 47.1	13 32.2	28 31.2	4♐32.0	8 42.1	2 43.6	18 45.1	27 55.8	8 39.1	26 1.0	22 39.4	21 17.5
8 S	13 5 43.6	14 31.4	28 28.0	18 52.7	9 43.8	3 17.2	19 27.7	28 6.7	8 34.4	26 4.6	22 41.2	21 19.6
9 M	13 9 40.2	15 30.7	28 24.8	2♑50.1	10 43.1	3 52.1	20 10.4	28 17.5	8 29.8	26 8.3	22 43.1	21 21.6
10 T	13 13 36.7	16 30.0	28 21.6	16 23.8	11 39.5	4 28.4	20 53.3	28 28.2	8 25.1	26 11.9	22 45.0	21 23.6
11 W	13 17 33.3	17 29.3	28 18.4	29 35.3	12 32.9	5 5.9	21 36.2	28 38.9	8 20.5	26 15.5	22 46.9	21 25.6
12 T	13 21 29.8	18 28.7	28 15.3	12♒26.8	13 23.0	5 44.6	22 19.2	28 49.4	8 15.9	26 19.1	22 48.8	21 27.6
13 F	13 25 26.4	19 28.0	28 12.1	25 1.2	14 9.5	6 24.6	23 2.3	28 59.9	8 11.3	26 22.6	22 50.8	21 29.6
14 S	13 29 22.9	20 27.4	28 8.9	7♓21.4	14 52.0	7 5.7	23 45.5	29 10.3	8 6.7	26 26.2	22 52.7	21 31.6
15 S	13 33 19.5	21 26.9	28 5.7	19 30.3	15 30.1	7 47.9	24 28.8	29 20.6	8 2.2	26 29.7	22 54.7	21 33.5
16 M	13 37 16.1	22 26.4	28 2.6	1♈30.5	16 3.3	8 31.2	25 12.2	29 30.8	7 57.7	26 33.2	22 56.7	21 35.5
17 T	13 41 12.6	23 25.9	27 59.4	13 24.3	16 31.3	9 15.5	25 55.7	29 40.9	7 53.3	26 36.7	22 58.7	21 37.4
18 W	13 45 9.2	24 25.4	27 56.2	25 14.0	16 53.5	10 0.8	26 39.2	29 50.9	7 48.8	26 40.2	23 0.7	21 39.3
19 T	13 49 5.7	25 25.0	27 53.0	7♉ 1.7	17 9.4	10 47.0	27 22.9	0♍ 0.8	7 44.5	26 43.6	23 2.7	21 41.2
20 F	13 53 2.3	26 24.6	27 49.8	18 49.6	17 18.5	11 34.2	28 6.6	0 10.6	7 40.1	26 47.0	23 4.8	21 43.1
21 S	13 56 58.8	27 24.2	27 46.7	0♊40.2	17 20.1	12 22.3	28 50.4	0 20.3	7 35.8	26 50.4	23 6.9	21 44.9
22 S	14 0 55.4	28 23.9	27 43.5	12 36.2	17R13.8	13 11.2	29 34.3	0 29.9	7 31.6	26 53.8	23 8.9	21 46.8
23 M	14 4 51.9	29 23.6	27 40.3	24 40.7	16 59.1	14 1.0	0♑18.2	0 39.4	7 27.4	26 57.2	23 11.0	21 48.6
24 T	14 8 48.5	0♏23.3	27 37.1	6♋57.1	16 35.6	14 51.5	1 2.3	0 48.8	7 23.2	27 0.5	23 13.1	21 50.4
25 W	14 12 45.0	1 23.1	27 34.0	19 29.1	16 3.1	15 42.9	1 46.4	0 58.1	7 19.1	27 3.8	23 15.2	21 52.2
26 T	14 16 41.6	2 23.0	27 30.8	2♌20.5	15 21.6	16 35.0	2 30.6	1 7.2	7 15.1	27 7.1	23 17.4	21 54.0
27 F	14 20 38.2	3 22.9	27 27.6	15 34.6	14 31.3	17 27.8	3 14.9	1 16.3	7 11.1	27 10.3	23 19.6	21 55.7
28 S	14 24 34.7	4 22.8	27 24.4	29 13.8	13 32.7	18 21.3	3 59.3	1 25.3	7 7.2	27 13.6	23 21.7	21 57.5
29 S	14 28 31.3	5 22.7	27 21.3	13♍19.3	12 27.0	19 15.4	4 43.7	1 34.1	7 3.3	27 16.8	23 23.9	21 59.2
30 M	14 32 27.8	6 22.7	27 18.1	27 50.0	11 15.3	20 10.2	5 28.2	1 42.9	6 59.5	27 19.9	23 26.0	22 0.9
31 T	14 36 24.4	7 22.7	27 14.9	12♎42.0	9 59.6	21 5.7	6 12.8	1 51.5	6 55.8	27 23.0	23 28.2	22 2.5
						DECLINATION at NOON						
1 S	12 38 7.7	3S 1.5	11N 3.8	13N35.0	14S 5.2	7N15.7	24S10.1	13N16.2	1N 8.3	2N23.5	16S45.5	16N56.0
4 W	12 49 57.4	4 11.3	11 0.5	7S 2.1	15 37.6	7 19.0	24 24.0	13 5.0	1 2.7	2 19.1	16 46.9	16 54.1
7 S	13 1 47.1	5 20.6	10 57.1	24 9.1	16 60.0	7 16.0	24 35.9	12 54.0	0 57.2	2 14.7	16 48.4	16 52.2
10 T	13 13 36.7	6 29.3	10 53.7	27 34.7	18 10.4	7 6.9	24 45.7	12 43.2	0 51.7	2 10.4	16 49.9	16 50.4
13 F	13 25 26.4	7 37.2	10 50.3	17 37.1	19 6.7	6 51.7	24 53.5	12 32.7	0 46.4	2 6.2	16 51.5	16 48.7
16 M	13 37 16.1	8 44.1	10 46.9	1 33.9	19 45.4	6 30.9	24 59.1	12 22.3	0 41.2	2 2.0	16 53.1	16 47.1
19 T	13 49 5.7	9 49.9	10 43.4	14N39.5	20 2.2	6 4.5	25 2.5	12 12.3	0 36.1	1 57.9	16 54.7	16 45.7
22 S	14 0 55.4	10 54.5	10 40.0	26 0.7	19 51.1	5 32.9	25 3.6	12 2.5	0 31.3	1 53.9	16 56.3	16 44.3
25 W	14 12 45.0	11 57.5	10 36.6	27 12.8	19 5.5	4 56.4	25 2.4	11 53.0	0 26.7	1 50.0	16 57.9	16 43.1
28 S	14 24 34.7	12 59.0	10 33.2	15 58.9	17 41.0	4 15.3	24 58.9	11 43.9	0 22.3	1 46.2	16 59.6	16 41.9
31 T	14 36 24.4	13 58.6	10 29.8	3S44.0	15 42.2	3 29.9	24 53.1	11 35.1	0 18.2	1 42.5	17 1.2	16 40.9

DAY	EPHEMERIS SIDEREAL TIME	☉	☊	☾	☿	♀	♂	♃	♄	♅	♆	♇
	h m s	° ′	° ′	° ′	° ′	° ′	° ′	° ′	° ′	° ′	° ′	° ′
						LONGITUDE at NOON						
1 W	14 40 20.9	8♏22.7	27♈11.7	27♎49.0	8♏42.0	22♍ 1.7	6♑57.5	1♍59.9	6♈52.1	27♍26.1	23♏30.4	22♍ 4.2
2 T	14 44 17.5	9 22.8	27 8.5	13♏ 2.4	7R24.8	22 58.3	7 42.2	2 8.3	6R48.5	27 29.2	23 32.6	22 5.8
3 F	14 48 14.0	10 22.9	27 5.4	28 12.3	6 10.5	23 55.4	8 27.1	2 16.5	6 45.0	27 32.2	23 34.8	22 7.4
4 S	14 52 10.6	11 23.0	27 2.2	13♐ 9.2	5 1.4	24 53.1	9 11.9	2 24.6	6 41.6	27 35.2	23 37.0	22 9.0
5 S	14 56 7.2	12 23.2	26 59.0	27 45.6	3 59.6	25 51.2	9 56.9	2 32.6	6 38.2	27 38.2	23 39.2	22 10.5
6 M	15 0 3.7	13 23.4	26 55.8	11♑56.4	3 7.0	26 49.9	10 41.9	2 40.4	6 34.9	27 41.1	23 41.4	22 12.1
7 T	15 4 0.3	14 23.6	26 52.7	25 39.5	2 24.8	27 49.1	11 27.0	2 48.1	6 31.7	27 44.0	23 43.7	22 13.6
8 W	15 7 56.8	15 23.8	26 49.5	8♒55.4	1 53.8	28 48.7	12 12.1	2 55.7	6 28.6	27 46.9	23 45.9	22 15.0
9 T	15 11 53.4	16 24.1	26 46.3	21 46.6	1 34.5	29 48.8	12 57.3	3 3.1	6 25.5	27 49.7	23 48.1	22 16.5
10 F	15 15 49.9	17 24.4	26 43.1	4♓16.7	1 26.8	0♎49.3	13 42.6	3 10.4	6 22.5	27 52.5	23 50.4	22 17.9
11 S	15 19 46.5	18 24.7	26 39.9	16 30.1	1D30.4	1 50.2	14 27.9	3 17.6	6 19.7	27 55.2	23 52.6	22 19.3
12 S	15 23 43.1	19 25.0	26 36.8	28 31.0	1 44.7	2 51.6	15 13.3	3 24.6	6 16.9	27 57.9	23 54.8	22 20.7
13 M	15 27 39.6	20 25.4	26 33.6	10♈23.8	2 9.0	3 53.3	15 58.7	3 31.5	6 14.2	28 0.6	23 57.1	22 22.0
14 T	15 31 36.2	21 25.7	26 30.4	22 12.1	2 42.4	4 55.5	16 44.2	3 38.2	6 11.6	28 3.2	23 59.3	22 23.4
15 W	15 35 32.7	22 26.1	26 27.2	3♉59.3	3 23.9	5 58.0	17 29.7	3 44.8	6 9.0	28 5.8	24 1.6	22 24.7
16 T	15 39 29.3	23 26.6	26 24.1	15 48.0	4 12.8	7 0.9	18 15.3	3 51.2	6 6.6	28 8.4	24 3.8	22 25.9
17 F	15 43 25.8	24 27.1	26 20.9	27 40.6	5 8.2	8 4.2	19 0.9	3 57.6	6 4.3	28 10.9	24 6.2	22 27.2
18 S	15 47 22.4	25 27.6	26 17.7	9♊38.8	6 9.2	9 7.8	19 46.6	4 3.7	6 2.1	28 13.4	24 8.4	22 28.4
19 S	15 51 19.0	26 28.1	26 14.5	21 44.5	7 15.1	10 11.7	20 32.4	4 9.7	5 60.0	28 15.8	24 10.7	22 29.6
20 M	15 55 15.5	27 28.6	26 11.4	3♋59.1	8 25.2	11 16.0	21 18.1	4 15.5	5 57.9	28 18.2	24 12.9	22 30.8
21 T	15 59 12.1	28 29.2	26 8.2	16 24.6	9 39.0	12 20.5	22 4.0	4 21.2	5 56.0	28 20.5	24 15.2	22 31.9
22 W	16 3 8.6	29 29.8	26 5.0	29 2.8	10 55.9	13 25.4	22 49.8	4 26.7	5 54.1	28 22.8	24 17.4	22 33.0
23 T	16 7 5.2	0♐30.4	26 1.8	11♌56.0	12 15.4	14 30.6	23 35.7	4 32.0	5 52.4	28 25.0	24 19.6	22 34.1
24 F	16 11 1.7	1 31.1	25 58.7	25 6.4	13 37.2	15 36.1	24 21.7	4 37.2	5 50.7	28 27.2	24 21.9	22 35.1
25 S	16 14 58.3	2 31.7	25 55.5	8♍36.3	15 0.9	16 41.8	25 7.7	4 42.3	5 49.2	28 29.4	24 24.1	22 36.1
26 S	16 18 54.9	3 32.5	25 52.3	22 27.4	16 26.3	17 47.8	25 53.7	4 47.1	5 47.7	28 31.5	24 26.4	22 37.1
27 M	16 22 51.4	4 33.2	25 49.1	6♎40.2	17 52.9	18 54.1	26 39.8	4 51.8	5 46.4	28 33.6	24 28.6	22 38.1
28 T	16 26 48.0	5 34.0	25 45.9	21 13.6	19 20.7	20 0.6	27 26.0	4 56.3	5 45.2	28 35.6	24 30.8	22 39.0
29 W	16 30 44.5	6 34.7	25 42.8	6♏ 4.1	20 49.4	21 7.4	28 12.1	5 0.7	5 44.0	28 37.5	24 33.0	22 39.9
30 T	16 34 41.1	7 35.6	25 39.6	21 5.6	22 18.9	22 14.4	28 58.4	5 4.9	5 43.0	28 39.4	24 35.2	22 40.7
						DECLINATION at NOON						
1 W	14 40 20.9	14S 18.1	10N28.6	10S41.3	14S58.1	3N13.9	24S50.6	11N32.2	0N16.8	1N41.3	17S 1.8	16N40.6
4 S	14 52 10.6	15 15.0	10 25.2	26 6.5	12 47.9	2 23.4	24 41.6	11 24.0	0 13.1	1 37.7	17 3.5	16 39.8
7 T	15 4 0.3	16 9.7	10 21.8	26 11.7	11 5.5	1 29.5	24 30.1	11 16.1	0 9.6	1 34.3	17 5.2	16 39.1
10 F	15 15 49.9	17 1.9	10 18.3	13 53.7	10 10.9	0 32.5	24 16.3	11 8.6	0 6.5	1 31.0	17 6.8	16 38.5
13 M	15 27 39.6	17 51.5	10 14.9	2N39.5	10 6.3	0S 27.2	24 0.2	11 1.6	0 3.7	1 27.9	17 8.5	16 38.1
16 T	15 39 29.3	18 38.3	10 11.4	18 7.1	10 42.1	1 29.3	23 41.6	10 55.1	0 1.3	1 24.9	17 10.2	16 37.8
19 S	15 51 19.0	19 22.2	10 8.0	27 24.3	11 45.8	2 33.5	23 20.8	10 49.0	0S 0.8	1 22.0	17 11.8	16 37.6
22 W	16 3 8.6	20 2.9	10 4.5	25 26.6	13 6.0	3 39.3	22 57.6	10 43.5	0 2.5	1 19.3	17 13.5	16 37.6
25 S	16 14 58.3	20 40.3	10 1.0	11 58.7	14 34.5	4 46.4	22 32.2	10 38.5	0 3.8	1 16.8	17 15.1	16 37.7
28 T	16 26 48.0	21 14.3	9 57.6	7S45.7	16 5.3	5 54.4	22 4.6	10 34.0	0 4.8	1 14.4	17 16.7	16 37.9

DECEMBER 1967

DAY	EPHEMERIS SIDEREAL TIME	☉	☊	☾	☿	♀	♂	♃	♄	♅	♆	♇
						LONGITUDE at NOON						
1 F	16 38 37.6	8♐36.4	25♈36.4	6♐ 9.9	23♏49.1	23♎21.7	29♑44.6	5♍ 8.9	5♈42.1	28♍41.3	24♏37.4	22♍41.6
2 S	16 42 34.2	9 37.2	25 33.2	21 7.6	25 19.7	24 29.1	0♒30.9	5 12.7	5R41.3	28 43.1	24 39.6	22 42.4
3 S	16 46 30.8	10 38.1	25 30.1	5♑49.7	26 50.9	25 36.8	1 17.2	5 16.3	5 40.6	28 44.9	24 41.8	22 43.1
4 M	16 50 27.3	11 39.0	25 26.9	20 9.1	28 22.4	26 44.6	2 3.6	5 19.8	5 40.0	28 46.6	24 44.0	22 43.9
5 T	16 54 23.9	12 39.9	25 23.7	4♒ 1.3	29 54.2	27 52.7	2 50.0	5 23.1	5 39.5	28 48.3	24 46.2	22 44.6
6 W	16 58 20.4	13 40.8	25 20.5	17 24.9	1♐26.2	29 1.0	3 36.4	5 26.2	5 39.2	28 49.9	24 48.3	22 45.2
7 T	17 2 17.0	14 41.7	25 17.4	0♓21.3	2 58.4	0♏ 9.4	4 22.8	5 29.1	5 38.9	28 51.4	24 50.5	22 45.9
8 F	17 6 13.6	15 42.7	25 14.2	12 53.9	4 30.9	1 18.1	5 9.4	5 31.9	5 38.8	28 53.0	24 52.7	22 46.5
9 S	17 10 10.1	16 43.7	25 11.0	25 7.0	6 3.5	2 26.9	5 55.9	5 34.4	5 38.8	28 54.5	24 54.8	22 47.1
10 S	17 14 6.7	17 44.6	25 7.8	7♈ 6.1	7 36.2	3 35.8	6 42.4	5 36.8	5 38.8	28 55.9	24 56.9	22 47.6
11 M	17 18 3.2	18 45.6	25 4.7	18 56.5	9 9.0	4 45.0	7 28.9	5 39.0	5D39.0	28 57.2	24 59.0	22 48.1
12 T	17 21 59.8	19 46.6	25 1.5	0♉43.0	10 41.9	5 54.3	8 15.5	5 41.0	5 39.3	28 58.5	25 1.1	22 48.6
13 W	17 25 56.3	20 47.6	24 58.3	12 30.3	12 15.0	7 3.7	9 2.1	5 42.8	5 39.7	28 59.7	25 3.2	22 49.0
14 T	17 29 52.9	21 48.6	24 55.1	24 22.1	13 48.1	8 13.4	9 48.7	5 44.4	5 40.2	29 0.9	25 5.3	22 49.4
15 F	17 33 49.5	22 49.6	24 51.9	6♊21.4	15 21.4	9 23.1	10 35.3	5 45.8	5 40.8	29 2.1	25 7.3	22 49.8
16 S	17 37 46.0	23 50.6	24 48.8	18 30.3	16 54.7	10 33.0	11 22.0	5 47.1	5 41.5	29 3.1	25 9.4	22 50.1
17 S	17 41 42.6	24 51.7	24 45.6	0♋50.0	18 28.2	11 43.1	12 8.6	5 48.1	5 42.4	29 4.2	25 11.4	22 50.4
18 M	17 45 39.1	25 52.7	24 42.4	13 21.1	20 1.8	12 53.3	12 55.3	5 49.0	5 43.3	29 5.1	25 13.4	22 50.7
19 T	17 49 35.7	26 53.8	24 39.2	26 3.9	21 35.6	14 3.6	13 42.0	5 49.6	5 44.3	29 6.1	25 15.4	22 50.9
20 W	17 53 32.3	27 54.9	24 36.1	8♌58.1	23 9.5	15 14.1	14 28.7	5 50.1	5 45.5	29 6.9	25 17.3	22 51.1
21 T	17 57 28.8	28 55.9	24 32.9	22 4.0	24 43.6	16 24.7	15 15.4	5 50.3	5 46.8	29 7.7	25 19.3	22 51.3
22 F	18 1 25.4	29 57.0	24 29.7	5♍22.0	26 17.8	17 35.4	16 2.2	5 50.4	5 48.1	29 8.5	25 21.2	22 51.4
23 S	18 5 21.9	0♑58.1	24 26.5	18 52.7	27 52.3	18 46.2	16 48.9	5R50.3	5 49.6	29 9.2	25 23.2	22 51.5
24 S	18 9 18.5	1 59.3	24 23.4	2♎37.2	29 26.9	19 57.2	17 35.7	5 50.0	5 51.2	29 9.8	25 25.1	22 51.6
25 M	18 13 15.1	3 0.4	24 20.2	16 36.2	1♑ 1.8	21 8.3	18 22.4	5 49.5	5 52.9	29 10.4	25 27.0	22 51.6
26 T	18 17 11.6	4 1.5	24 17.0	0♏49.8	2 36.9	22 19.4	19 9.2	5 48.8	5 54.7	29 10.9	25 28.8	22 51.6
27 W	18 21 8.2	5 2.7	24 13.8	15 16.8	4 12.3	23 30.7	19 56.0	5 47.9	5 56.6	29 11.4	25 30.7	22 51.6
28 T	18 25 4.7	6 3.8	24 10.7	29 54.0	5 48.0	24 42.1	20 42.8	5 46.8	5 58.6	29 11.8	25 32.5	22R51.5
29 F	18 29 1.3	7 5.1	24 7.5	14♐36.3	7 23.9	25 53.6	21 29.7	5 45.5	6 0.8	29 12.2	25 34.3	22 51.5
30 S	18 32 57.8	8 6.2	24 4.3	29 16.5	9 0.2	27 5.2	22 16.5	5 44.0	6 3.0	29 12.5	25 36.1	22 51.3
31 S	18 36 54.4	9 7.4	24 1.1	13♑47.1	10 36.7	28 16.9	23 3.3	5 42.3	6 5.3	29 12.7	25 37.9	22 51.2
						DECLINATION at NOON						
1 F	16 38 37.6	21S 44.7	9N54.1	24S32.2	17S34.4	7S 3.0	21S34.8	10N30.1	0S 5.3	1N12.2	17S18.2	16N38.3
4 M	16 50 27.3	22 11.3	9 50.6	26 59.2	18 59.0	8 11.7	21 2.9	10 26.8	0 5.5	1 10.2	17 19.8	16 38.8
7 T	17 2 17.0	22 34.0	9 47.2	15 21.8	20 17.3	9 20.1	20 29.0	10 24.1	0 5.3	1 8.4	17 21.3	16 39.4
10 S	17 14 6.7	22 52.8	9 43.7	1N13.5	21 27.8	10 28.0	19 53.1	10 22.0	0 4.6	1 6.7	17 22.8	16 40.2
13 W	17 25 56.3	23 7.5	9 40.2	16 55.3	22 29.4	11 34.8	19 15.3	10 20.5	0 3.6	1 5.3	17 24.2	16 41.1
16 S	17 37 46.0	23 18.1	9 36.7	26 56.5	23 21.3	12 40.3	18 35.7	10 19.7	0 2.2	1 4.1	17 25.6	16 42.1
19 T	17 49 35.7	23 24.5	9 33.2	25 54.5	24 2.7	13 44.1	17 54.4	10 19.5	0 0.3	1 3.0	17 27.0	16 43.2
22 F	18 1 25.4	23 26.7	9 29.7	13 10.0	24 33.0	14 45.7	17 11.5	10 19.9	0N 1.8	1 2.2	17 28.3	16 44.5
25 M	18 13 15.1	23 24.7	9 26.2	5S48.5	24 51.5	15 44.9	16 27.0	10 21.0	0 4.4	1 1.5	17 29.5	16 45.9
28 T	18 25 4.7	23 18.4	9 22.7	22 56.2	24 57.7	16 41.2	15 41.0	10 22.8	0 7.4	1 1.1	17 30.8	16 47.4
31 S	18 36 54.4	23 7.9	9 19.2	27 38.0	24 51.0	17 34.2	14 53.7	10 25.1	0 10.7	1 0.8	17 31.9	16 49.0

JANUARY 1968

LONGITUDE at NOON

DAY	EPHEMERIS SIDEREAL TIME h m s	☉ ° ′	☊ ° ′	☽ ° ′	☿ ° ′	♀ ° ′	♂ ° ′	♃ ° ′	♄ ° ′	♅ ° ′	♆ ° ′	♇ ° ′
1 M	18 40 51.0	10♑ 8.6	23♈58.0	28♑ 0.7	12♑13.5	29♏28.6	23♒50.1	5♍40.4	6♈ 7.8	29♍12.9	25♏39.6	22♍51.0
2 T	18 44 47.5	11 9.8	23 54.8	11♒51.9	13 50.7	0♐40.4	24 37.0	5R38.4	6 10.3	29 13.0	25 41.4	22R50.7
3 W	18 48 44.1	12 11.0	23 51.6	25 17.6	15 28.2	1 52.3	25 23.8	5 36.1	6 12.9	29 13.1	25 43.0	22 50.5
4 T	18 52 40.6	13 12.1	23 48.4	8♓17.5	17 6.1	3 4.3	26 10.6	5 33.6	6 15.7	29 13.1	25 44.7	22 50.2
5 F	18 56 37.2	14 13.3	23 45.2	20 53.5	18 44.3	4 16.4	26 57.5	5 31.0	6 18.5	29R13.0	25 46.4	22 49.8
6 S	19 0 33.8	15 14.5	23 42.1	3♈ 9.5	20 22.8	5 28.5	27 44.3	5 28.2	6 21.4	29 12.9	25 48.0	22 49.5
7 S	19 4 30.3	16 15.6	23 38.9	15 10.3	22 1.6	6 40.7	28 31.1	5 25.1	6 24.5	29 12.7	25 49.6	22 49.1
8 M	19 8 26.9	17 16.8	23 35.7	27 1.5	23 40.8	7 52.9	29 17.9	5 21.9	6 27.6	29 12.5	25 51.2	22 48.6
9 T	19 12 23.4	18 17.9	23 32.5	8♉48.7	25 20.3	9 5.2	0♓ 4.7	5 18.5	6 30.8	29 12.3	25 52.7	22 48.2
10 W	19 16 20.0	19 19.1	23 29.4	20 37.3	27 0.1	10 17.6	0 51.5	5 15.0	6 34.2	29 11.9	25 54.2	22 47.7
11 T	19 20 16.6	20 20.2	23 26.2	2♊32.2	28 40.1	11 30.1	1 38.3	5 11.2	6 37.6	29 11.5	25 55.7	22 47.1
12 F	19 24 13.1	21 21.3	23 23.0	14 37.5	0♒20.3	12 42.6	2 25.1	5 7.3	6 41.1	29 11.1	25 57.2	22 46.6
13 S	19 28 9.7	22 22.4	23 19.8	26 56.0	2 0.6	13 55.2	3 11.9	5 3.2	6 44.7	29 10.6	25 58.6	22 46.0
14 S	19 32 6.2	23 23.5	23 16.7	9♋29.6	3 41.1	15 7.8	3 58.6	4 58.9	6 48.4	29 10.1	26 0.1	22 45.4
15 M	19 36 2.8	24 24.6	23 13.5	22 18.8	5 21.5	16 20.5	4 45.4	4 54.5	6 52.2	29 9.4	26 1.5	22 44.7
16 T	19 39 59.3	25 25.7	23 10.3	5♌22.9	7 1.8	17 33.2	5 32.1	4 49.9	6 56.1	29 8.8	26 2.8	22 44.1
17 W	19 43 55.9	26 26.8	23 7.1	18 40.3	8 41.9	18 46.0	6 18.8	4 45.1	7 0.1	29 8.1	26 4.1	22 43.4
18 T	19 47 52.5	27 27.8	23 4.0	2♍ 9.0	10 21.6	19 58.9	7 5.5	4 40.2	7 4.2	29 7.3	26 5.5	22 42.6
19 F	19 51 49.0	28 29.0	23 0.8	15 46.9	12 0.9	21 11.8	7 52.3	4 35.1	7 8.4	29 6.5	26 6.8	22 41.9
20 S	19 55 45.6	29 30.0	22 57.6	29 32.4	13 39.3	22 24.8	8 38.9	4 29.9	7 12.6	29 5.7	26 8.0	22 41.1
21 S	19 59 42.1	0♒31.1	22 54.4	13♎24.6	15 16.7	23 37.8	9 25.6	4 24.5	7 16.9	29 4.7	26 9.2	22 40.3
22 M	20 3 38.7	1 32.1	22 51.2	27 23.0	16 52.7	24 50.8	10 12.2	4 18.9	7 21.3	29 3.8	26 10.4	22 39.4
23 T	20 7 35.2	2 33.2	22 48.1	11♏27.4	18 27.1	26 3.9	10 58.9	4 13.2	7 25.8	29 2.7	26 11.6	22 38.6
24 W	20 11 31.8	3 34.2	22 44.9	25 37.1	19 59.5	27 17.0	11 45.5	4 7.4	7 30.4	29 1.7	26 12.7	22 37.6
25 T	20 15 28.4	4 35.2	22 41.7	9♐50.7	21 29.4	28 30.2	12 32.1	4 1.4	7 35.1	29 0.5	26 13.8	22 36.7
26 F	20 19 24.9	5 36.2	22 38.5	24 5.7	22 56.3	29 43.4	13 18.7	3 55.2	7 39.8	28 59.3	26 14.9	22 35.8
27 S	20 23 21.5	6 37.3	22 35.4	8♑18.2	24 19.6	0♑56.7	14 5.2	3 49.0	7 44.6	28 58.1	26 15.9	22 34.8
28 S	20 27 18.0	7 38.3	22 32.2	22 23.3	25 38.6	2 10.0	14 51.8	3 42.6	7 49.5	28 56.8	26 16.9	22 33.8
29 M	20 31 14.6	8 39.2	22 29.0	6♒16.1	26 52.8	3 23.3	15 38.3	3 36.1	7 54.5	28 55.5	26 17.9	22 32.7
30 T	20 35 11.1	9 40.2	22 25.8	19 52.0	28 1.3	4 36.6	16 24.8	3 29.5	7 59.6	28 54.1	26 18.9	22 31.6
31 W	20 39 7.7	10 41.1	22 22.7	3♓ 8.0	29 3.4	5 50.0	17 11.3	3 22.7	8 4.7	28 52.7	26 19.8	22 30.6

DECLINATION at NOON

DAY	EPHEMERIS SIDEREAL TIME h m s	☉	☊	☽	☿	♀	♂	♃	♄	♅	♆	♇
1 M	18 40 51.0	23S 3.5	9N18.0	25S28.3	24S45.9	17S51.1	14S37.6	10N26.1	0N11.9	1N 0.8	17S32.3	16N49.5
4 T	18 52 40.6	22 47.4	9 14.5	11 49.2	24 21.4	18 39.3	13 48.5	10 29.3	0 15.7	1 0.8	17 33.4	16 51.3
7 S	19 4 30.3	22 27.3	9 11.0	5N15.2	23 43.0	19 23.4	12 58.3	10 33.2	0 19.8	1 1.1	17 34.4	16 53.1
10 W	19 16 20.0	22 3.2	9 7.5	20 5.4	22 50.7	20 3.1	12 7.0	10 37.6	0 24.3	1 1.5	17 35.4	16 55.0
13 S	19 28 9.7	21 35.3	9 4.0	27 52.9	21 44.3	20 38.2	11 14.7	10 42.6	0 29.1	1 2.1	17 36.3	16 57.1
16 T	19 39 59.3	21 3.5	9 0.4	23 39.5	20 24.1	21 8.4	10 21.6	10 48.2	0 34.2	1 3.0	17 37.1	16 59.1
19 F	19 51 49.0	20 28.2	8 56.9	8 22.7	18 51.0	21 33.4	9 27.7	10 54.2	0 39.6	1 4.0	17 37.9	17 1.3
22 M	20 3 38.7	19 49.4	8 53.4	10S57.4	17 6.9	21 53.0	8 33.1	11 0.8	0 45.3	1 5.2	17 38.6	17 3.5
25 T	20 15 28.4	19 7.2	8 49.8	25 36.5	15 14.8	22 7.0	7 37.8	11 7.8	0 51.3	1 6.6	17 39.2	17 5.8
28 S	20 27 18.0	18 21.9	8 46.3	26 32.0	13 20.0	22 15.3	6 42.1	11 15.2	0 57.5	1 8.1	17 39.8	17 8.1
31 W	20 39 7.7	17 33.6	8 42.8	13 51.4	11 30.4	22 17.8	5 45.9	11 22.9	1 4.0	1 9.8	17 40.3	17 10.5

FEBRUARY 1968

LONGITUDE at NOON

DAY	EPHEMERIS SIDEREAL TIME h m s	☉ ° ′	☊ ° ′	☽ ° ′	☿ ° ′	♀ ° ′	♂ ° ′	♃ ° ′	♄ ° ′	♅ ° ′	♆ ° ′	♇ ° ′
1 T	20 43 4.3	11♒42.1	22♈19.5	16♓ 2.9	29♒58.2	7♑ 3.4	17♓57.8	3♍15.9	8♈ 9.9	28♍51.2	26♏20.6	22♍29.4
2 F	20 47 0.8	12 43.0	22 16.3	28 37.3	0♓44.9	8 16.9	18 44.2	3R 8.9	8 15.2	28R49.7	26 21.5	22R28.3
3 S	20 50 57.4	13 43.9	22 13.1	10♈53.7	1 22.9	9 30.3	19 30.6	3 1.9	8 20.5	28 48.1	26 22.3	22 27.2
4 S	20 54 53.9	14 44.7	22 9.9	22 55.8	1 51.2	10 43.8	20 17.0	2 54.7	8 26.0	28 46.5	26 23.1	22 26.0
5 M	20 58 50.5	15 45.6	22 6.8	4♉48.3	2 9.4	11 57.3	21 3.4	2 47.5	8 31.5	28 44.9	26 23.8	22 24.8
6 T	21 2 47.0	16 46.4	22 3.6	16 36.7	2 16.9	13 10.8	21 49.7	2 40.2	8 37.0	28 43.2	26 24.5	22 23.5
7 W	21 6 43.6	17 47.2	22 0.4	28 26.2	2R13.5	14 24.4	22 36.0	2 32.8	8 42.7	28 41.5	26 25.2	22 22.3
8 T	21 10 40.2	18 48.0	21 57.2	10♊22.5	1 59.1	15 37.9	23 22.2	2 25.3	8 48.4	28 39.7	26 25.9	22 21.0
9 F	21 14 36.7	19 48.8	21 54.1	22 30.4	1 34.1	16 51.6	24 8.5	2 17.8	8 54.2	28 37.9	26 26.5	22 19.8
10 S	21 18 33.3	20 49.5	21 50.9	4♋53.9	0 58.8	18 5.2	24 54.7	2 10.2	8 60.0	28 36.1	26 27.1	22 18.5
11 S	21 22 29.8	21 50.2	21 47.7	17 36.0	0 14.2	19 18.8	25 40.9	2 2.6	9 5.9	28 34.2	26 27.7	22 17.2
12 M	21 26 26.4	22 50.8	21 44.5	0♌38.2	29♒21.4	20 32.4	26 27.0	1 54.9	9 11.8	28 32.2	26 28.2	22 15.8
13 T	21 30 22.9	23 51.5	21 41.4	14 0.2	28 22.0	21 46.1	27 13.1	1 47.1	9 17.8	28 30.3	26 28.7	22 14.5
14 W	21 34 19.5	24 52.1	21 38.2	27 40.0	27 17.5	22 59.8	27 59.2	1 39.3	9 23.9	28 28.3	26 29.1	22 13.1
15 T	21 38 16.0	25 52.7	21 35.0	11♍34.4	26 9.7	24 13.5	28 45.2	1 31.5	9 30.0	28 26.2	26 29.5	22 11.7
16 F	21 42 12.6	26 53.3	21 31.8	25 39.4	25 0.6	25 27.2	29 31.2	1 23.7	9 36.2	28 24.1	26 29.9	22 10.3
17 S	21 46 9.2	27 53.8	21 28.6	9♎50.5	23 52.0	26 41.0	0♈17.2	1 15.8	9 42.5	28 22.0	26 30.3	22 8.8
18 S	21 50 5.7	28 54.3	21 25.5	24 4.1	22 45.5	27 54.7	1 3.1	1 7.9	9 48.8	28 19.9	26 30.6	22 7.4
19 M	21 54 2.3	29 54.9	21 22.3	8♏17.3	21 42.6	29 8.5	1 49.0	0 60.0	9 55.1	28 17.7	26 30.8	22 5.9
20 T	21 57 58.8	0♓55.3	21 19.1	22 27.8	20 44.6	0♒22.3	2 34.9	0 52.1	10 1.5	28 15.5	26 31.1	22 4.5
21 W	22 1 55.4	1 55.8	21 15.9	6♐34.2	19 52.5	1 36.1	3 20.7	0 44.2	10 8.0	28 13.3	26 31.3	22 3.0
22 T	22 5 51.9	2 56.2	21 12.8	20 35.4	19 7.0	2 49.9	4 6.5	0 36.3	10 14.5	28 11.0	26 31.5	22 1.5
23 F	22 9 48.5	3 56.7	21 9.6	4♑30.2	18 28.6	4 3.8	4 52.3	0 28.4	10 21.0	28 8.7	26 31.6	21 60.0
24 S	22 13 45.0	4 57.1	21 6.4	18 17.1	17 57.5	5 17.6	5 38.0	0 20.5	10 27.6	28 6.4	26 31.7	21 58.5
25 S	22 17 41.6	5 57.4	21 3.2	1♒54.3	17 33.8	6 31.5	6 23.7	0 12.6	10 34.3	28 4.1	26 31.8	21 56.9
26 M	22 21 38.1	6 57.8	21 0.0	15 19.7	17 17.4	7 45.3	7 9.3	0 4.8	10 41.0	28 1.7	26 31.8	21 55.4
27 T	22 25 34.7	7 58.1	20 56.9	28 31.4	17 8.1	8 59.2	7 54.9	29♌57.0	10 47.7	27 59.3	26 31.8	21 53.8
28 W	22 29 31.3	8 58.4	20 53.7	11♓27.9	17 5.7	10 13.1	8 40.5	29 49.3	10 54.5	27 56.9	26 31.8	21 52.3
29 T	22 33 27.8	9 58.7	20 50.5	24 8.7	17D 9.9	11 27.0	9 26.0	29 41.5	11 1.3	27 54.5	26R31.7	21 50.7

DECLINATION at NOON

DAY	EPHEMERIS SIDEREAL TIME h m s	☉	☊	☽	☿	♀	♂	♃	♄	♅	♆	♇
1 T	20 43 4.3	17S16.9	8N41.6	8S10.9	10S56.8	22S17.3	5S27.1	11N25.6	1N 6.3	1N10.5	17S40.5	17N11.3
4 S	20 54 53.9	16 24.9	8 38.0	9N 4.8	9 30.6	22 11.9	4 30.5	11 33.7	1 13.1	1 12.4	17 40.9	17 13.7
7 W	21 6 43.6	15 30.3	8 34.5	22 50.4	8 35.5	22 0.5	3 33.7	11 42.1	1 20.1	1 14.5	17 41.2	17 16.1
10 S	21 18 33.3	14 33.4	8 30.9	28 14.3	8 19.7	21 43.4	2 36.7	11 50.6	1 27.4	1 16.7	17 41.5	17 18.6
13 T	21 30 22.9	13 34.3	8 27.3	21 4.8	8 44.5	21 20.4	1 39.7	11 59.3	1 34.8	1 19.1	17 41.7	17 21.0
16 F	21 42 12.6	12 33.2	8 23.8	3 39.3	9 40.8	20 51.7	0 42.8	12 8.0	1 42.4	1 21.6	17 41.8	17 23.5
19 M	21 54 2.3	11 30.3	8 20.2	15S48.9	10 53.0	20 17.5	0N14.1	12 16.7	1 50.2	1 24.2	17 41.8	17 25.9
22 T	22 5 51.9	10 25.8	8 16.6	27 35.4	12 5.4	19 38.0	1 10.7	12 25.4	1 58.1	1 26.9	17 41.8	17 28.3
25 S	22 17 41.6	9 19.8	8 13.1	24 37.9	13 7.4	18 53.3	2 7.1	12 33.9	2 6.2	1 29.7	17 41.7	17 30.7
28 W	22 29 31.3	8 12.5	8 9.5	10 11.5	13 53.7	18 3.6	3 3.2	12 42.3	2 14.4	1 32.6	17 41.6	17 33.1

MARCH 1968

DAY	EPHEMERIS SIDEREAL TIME	☉	☊	☽	☿	♀	♂	♃	♄	♅	♆	♇
	h m s	° ′	° ′	° ′	° ′	° ′	° ′	° ′	° ′	° ′	° ′	° ′
LONGITUDE at NOON												
1 F	22 37 24.4	10 ♓ 58.9	20 ♈ 47.3	6 ♈ 34.1	17 ♒ 20.4	12 ♒ 41.0	10 ♈ 11.6	29 ♌ 33.9	11 ♈ 8.2	27 ♍ 52.1	26 ♏ 31.7	21 ♍ 49.2
2 S	22 41 20.9	11 59.2	20 44.2	18 45.5	17 36.6	13 54.9	10 57.0	29 R 26.3	11 15.1	27 R 49.6	26 R 31.6	21 R 47.6
3 S	22 45 17.5	12 59.3	20 41.0	0 ♉ 45.7	17 58.3	15 8.8	11 42.4	29 18.8	11 22.1	27 47.1	26 31.4	21 46.0
4 M	22 49 14.0	13 59.5	20 37.8	12 37.9	18 25.2	16 22.7	12 27.8	29 11.3	11 29.1	27 44.6	26 31.2	21 44.4
5 T	22 53 10.6	14 59.6	20 34.6	24 26.6	18 56.8	17 36.6	13 13.1	29 3.9	11 36.1	27 42.1	26 31.0	21 42.8
6 W	22 57 7.1	15 59.6	20 31.5	6 ♊ 16.3	19 32.9	18 50.5	13 58.4	28 56.6	11 43.1	27 39.6	26 30.7	21 41.2
7 T	23 1 3.7	16 59.6	20 28.3	18 12.3	20 13.2	20 4.4	14 43.7	28 49.4	11 50.2	27 37.0	26 30.4	21 39.6
8 F	23 5 0.2	17 59.6	20 25.1	0 ♋ 19.4	20 57.3	21 18.4	15 28.9	28 42.3	11 57.3	27 34.5	26 30.1	21 38.0
9 S	23 8 56.8	18 59.6	20 21.9	12 42.5	21 45.1	22 32.3	16 14.0	28 35.2	12 4.5	27 31.9	26 29.7	21 36.4
10 S	23 12 53.4	19 59.5	20 18.7	25 25.6	22 36.2	23 46.2	16 59.1	28 28.3	12 11.7	27 29.3	26 29.3	21 34.8
11 M	23 16 49.9	20 59.4	20 15.6	8 ♌ 31.5	23 30.5	25 0.1	17 44.2	28 21.4	12 18.9	27 26.7	26 28.9	21 33.1
12 T	23 20 46.5	21 59.3	20 12.4	22 1.3	24 27.7	26 14.1	18 29.2	28 14.7	12 26.1	27 24.1	26 28.5	21 31.5
13 W	23 24 43.0	22 59.1	20 9.2	5 ♍ 54.4	25 27.6	27 28.0	19 14.1	28 8.1	12 33.4	27 21.5	26 28.0	21 29.9
14 T	23 28 39.6	23 58.8	20 6.0	20 7.8	26 30.2	28 41.9	19 59.1	28 1.6	12 40.6	27 18.9	26 27.4	21 28.3
15 F	23 32 36.1	24 58.6	20 2.9	4 ♎ 36.7	27 35.3	29 55.9	20 43.9	27 55.2	12 47.9	27 16.3	26 26.9	21 26.7
16 S	23 36 32.7	25 58.3	19 59.7	19 15.1	28 42.6	1 ♓ 9.8	21 28.8	27 48.9	12 55.3	27 13.7	26 26.3	21 25.1
17 S	23 40 29.2	26 58.0	19 56.5	3 ♏ 56.3	29 52.2	2 23.7	22 13.5	27 42.8	13 2.6	27 11.1	26 25.7	21 23.5
18 M	23 44 25.8	27 57.6	19 53.3	18 34.2	1 ♓ 3.9	3 37.7	22 58.3	27 36.8	13 10.0	27 8.5	26 25.1	21 21.9
19 T	23 48 22.3	28 57.3	19 50.1	3 ♐ 3.7	2 17.5	4 51.6	23 43.0	27 30.9	13 17.4	27 5.9	26 24.4	21 20.3
20 W	23 52 18.9	29 56.9	19 47.0	17 21.1	3 33.1	6 5.6	24 27.6	27 25.2	13 24.8	27 3.2	26 23.7	21 18.7
21 T	23 56 15.4	0 ♈ 56.4	19 43.8	1 ♑ 24.1	4 50.6	7 19.5	25 12.2	27 19.6	13 32.2	27 0.6	26 23.0	21 17.1
22 F	0 0 12.0	1 56.0	19 40.6	15 11.7	6 9.8	8 33.5	25 56.8	27 14.2	13 39.7	26 58.1	26 22.3	21 15.5
23 S	0 4 8.6	2 55.5	19 37.4	28 43.5	7 30.7	9 47.5	26 41.3	27 8.9	13 47.2	26 55.5	26 21.5	21 14.0
24 S	0 8 5.1	3 55.0	19 34.3	12 ♒ 0.1	8 53.3	11 1.5	27 25.8	27 3.7	13 54.7	26 52.9	26 20.6	21 12.4
25 M	0 12 1.7	4 54.5	19 31.1	25 2.0	10 17.5	12 15.4	28 10.2	26 58.8	14 2.2	26 50.3	26 19.8	21 10.8
26 T	0 15 58.2	5 53.9	19 27.9	7 ♓ 50.1	11 43.2	13 29.4	28 54.6	26 53.9	14 9.7	26 47.7	26 18.9	21 9.3
27 W	0 19 54.8	6 53.3	19 24.7	20 25.1	13 10.5	14 43.3	29 38.9	26 49.2	14 17.2	26 45.1	26 18.0	21 7.7
28 T	0 23 51.3	7 52.6	19 21.5	2 ♈ 48.0	14 39.3	15 57.3	0 ♉ 23.2	26 44.7	14 24.7	26 42.6	26 17.1	21 6.2
29 F	0 27 47.9	8 51.9	19 18.4	15 0.1	16 9.7	17 11.2	1 7.4	26 40.4	14 32.3	26 40.0	26 16.1	21 4.7
30 S	0 31 44.4	9 51.2	19 15.2	27 2.8	17 41.5	18 25.2	1 51.6	26 36.2	14 39.8	26 37.5	26 15.2	21 3.1
31 S	0 35 41.0	10 50.5	19 12.0	8 ♉ 58.1	19 14.7	19 39.1	2 35.8	26 32.2	14 47.4	26 35.0	26 14.2	21 1.6
DECLINATION at NOON												
1 F	22 37 24.4	7 S 27.0	8 N 7.1	1 N 34.4	14 S 15.0	17 S 27.9	3 N 40.3	12 N 47.8	2 N 20.0	1 N 34.6	17 S 41.4	17 N 34.6
4 M	22 49 14.0	6 18.0	8 3.5	17 37.2	14 32.7	16 30.7	4 35.6	12 55.8	2 28.4	1 37.6	17 41.2	17 36.9
7 T	23 1 3.7	5 8.2	7 59.9	27 23.1	14 33.9	15 29.3	5 30.4	13 3.5	2 36.9	1 40.6	17 40.8	17 39.1
10 S	23 12 53.4	3 57.9	7 56.3	26 9.4	14 19.5	14 24.0	6 24.5	13 10.8	2 45.4	1 43.7	17 40.4	17 41.3
13 W	23 24 43.0	2 47.1	7 52.8	12 39.8	13 50.4	13 15.1	7 17.9	13 17.8	2 54.1	1 46.8	17 40.0	17 43.4
16 S	23 36 32.7	1 36.1	7 49.2	7 S 34.8	13 7.5	12 3.0	8 10.6	13 24.3	3 2.7	1 49.9	17 39.4	17 45.4
19 T	23 48 22.3	0 25.0	7 45.6	24 23.0	12 11.4	10 47.9	9 2.4	13 30.4	3 11.5	1 53.0	17 38.8	17 47.3
22 F	0 0 12.0	0 N 46.1	7 42.0	27 48.0	11 2.9	9 30.0	9 53.4	13 36.0	3 20.2	1 56.1	17 38.2	17 49.1
25 M	0 12 1.7	1 57.0	7 38.3	17 10.9	9 42.4	8 9.9	10 43.4	13 41.1	3 29.0	1 59.2	17 37.5	17 50.9
28 T	0 23 51.3	3 7.5	7 34.7	0 12.8	8 10.6	6 47.8	11 32.3	13 45.6	3 37.8	2 2.2	17 36.7	17 52.5
31 S	0 35 41.0	4 17.5	7 31.1	16 N 14.0	6 27.8	5 24.0	12 20.2	13 49.7	3 46.5	2 5.2	17 35.9	17 54.0

APRIL 1968

DAY	EPHEMERIS SIDEREAL TIME	☉	☊	☽	☿	♀	♂	♃	♄	♅	♆	♇
LONGITUDE at NOON												
1 M	0 39 37.5	11 ♈ 49.7	19 ♈ 8.8	20 ♉ 48.5	20 ♓ 49.4	20 ♓ 53.0	3 ♉ 19.9	26 ♌ 28.4	14 ♈ 54.9	26 ♍ 32.5	26 ♏ 13.1	21 ♍ 0.1
2 T	0 43 34.1	12 48.9	19 5.7	2 ♊ 37.0	22 25.6	22 7.0	4 3.9	26 R 24.7	15 2.5	26 R 30.0	26 R 12.1	20 R 58.7
3 W	0 47 30.6	13 48.0	19 2.5	14 27.1	24 3.2	23 20.9	4 47.9	26 21.2	15 10.0	26 27.6	26 11.0	20 57.2
4 T	0 51 27.2	14 47.1	18 59.3	26 22.9	25 42.2	24 34.8	5 31.8	26 17.9	15 17.6	26 25.1	26 9.9	20 55.7
5 F	0 55 23.7	15 46.2	18 56.1	8 ♋ 28.7	27 22.7	25 48.7	6 15.7	26 14.8	15 25.1	26 22.7	26 8.7	20 54.3
6 S	0 59 20.3	16 45.2	18 52.9	20 49.0	29 4.7	27 2.6	6 59.6	26 11.8	15 32.7	26 20.3	26 7.6	20 52.9
7 S	1 3 16.9	17 44.2	18 49.8	3 ♌ 28.2	0 ♈ 48.1	28 16.5	7 43.4	26 9.1	15 40.3	26 17.9	26 6.4	20 51.5
8 M	1 7 13.4	18 43.1	18 46.6	16 30.1	2 33.0	29 30.4	8 27.1	26 6.5	15 47.8	26 15.5	26 5.2	20 50.1
9 T	1 11 10.0	19 42.0	18 43.4	29 57.4	4 19.4	0 ♈ 44.3	9 10.8	26 4.1	15 55.4	26 13.2	26 4.0	20 48.7
10 W	1 15 6.5	20 40.9	18 40.2	13 ♍ 51.1	6 7.3	1 58.2	9 54.4	26 1.9	16 2.9	26 10.9	26 2.8	20 47.3
11 T	1 19 3.1	21 39.7	18 37.1	28 10.1	7 56.7	3 12.0	10 38.0	25 59.8	16 10.5	26 8.6	26 1.5	20 46.0
12 F	1 22 59.6	22 38.6	18 33.9	12 ♎ 50.8	9 47.7	4 25.9	11 21.6	25 58.0	16 18.0	26 6.4	26 0.3	20 44.7
13 S	1 26 56.2	23 37.4	18 30.7	27 46.9	11 40.1	5 39.8	12 5.1	25 56.4	16 25.6	26 4.2	25 59.0	20 43.4
14 S	1 30 52.7	24 36.1	18 27.5	12 ♏ 50.6	13 34.1	6 53.6	12 48.5	25 54.9	16 33.1	26 2.0	25 57.7	20 42.1
15 M	1 34 49.3	25 34.8	18 24.3	27 53.1	15 29.5	8 7.5	13 31.9	25 53.6	16 40.6	25 59.8	25 56.3	20 40.9
16 T	1 38 45.8	26 33.5	18 21.2	12 ♐ 45.8	17 26.5	9 21.3	14 15.2	25 52.5	16 48.1	25 57.7	25 55.0	20 39.6
17 W	1 42 42.4	27 32.1	18 18.0	27 22.0	19 25.0	10 35.2	14 58.5	25 51.6	16 55.6	25 55.6	25 53.6	20 38.4
18 T	1 46 39.0	28 30.7	18 14.8	11 ♑ 37.2	21 24.9	11 49.0	15 41.8	25 50.8	17 3.0	25 53.5	25 52.2	20 37.2
19 F	1 50 35.5	29 29.3	18 11.6	25 29.2	23 26.3	13 2.9	16 25.0	25 50.3	17 10.5	25 51.4	25 50.8	20 36.0
20 S	1 54 32.1	0 ♉ 27.9	18 8.5	8 ♒ 58.1	25 29.0	14 16.7	17 8.1	25 49.9	17 17.9	25 49.4	25 49.4	20 34.9
21 S	1 58 28.6	1 26.4	18 5.3	22 5.3	27 33.1	15 30.5	17 51.2	25 49.7	17 25.3	25 47.4	25 47.9	20 33.7
22 M	2 2 25.2	2 24.9	18 2.1	4 ♓ 53.2	29 38.3	16 44.4	18 34.3	25 D 49.8	17 32.8	25 45.5	25 46.5	20 32.6
23 T	2 6 21.7	3 23.4	17 58.9	17 24.9	1 ♉ 44.6	17 58.2	19 17.3	25 50.0	17 40.1	25 43.6	25 45.0	20 31.5
24 W	2 10 18.3	4 21.9	17 55.7	29 43.3	3 51.8	19 12.0	20 0.2	25 50.3	17 47.5	25 41.7	25 43.5	20 30.4
25 T	2 14 14.8	5 20.3	17 52.6	11 ♈ 51.2	5 59.8	20 25.8	20 43.1	25 50.9	17 54.9	25 39.9	25 42.0	20 29.4
26 F	2 18 11.4	6 18.7	17 49.4	23 51.1	8 8.3	21 39.7	21 26.0	25 51.6	18 2.2	25 38.1	25 40.5	20 28.4
27 S	2 22 7.9	7 17.0	17 46.2	5 ♉ 45.2	10 17.2	22 53.5	22 8.8	25 52.6	18 9.5	25 36.4	25 39.0	20 27.4
28 S	2 26 4.5	8 15.4	17 43.0	17 35.8	12 26.2	24 7.3	22 51.6	25 53.7	18 16.8	25 34.7	25 37.5	20 26.4
29 M	2 30 1.1	9 13.7	17 39.9	29 24.7	14 35.0	25 21.1	23 34.3	25 55.0	18 24.0	25 33.0	25 35.9	20 25.4
30 T	2 33 57.6	10 11.9	17 36.7	11 ♊ 14.2	16 43.4	26 34.8	24 17.0	25 56.5	18 31.2	25 31.4	25 34.4	20 24.5
DECLINATION at NOON												
1 M	0 39 37.5	4 N 40.7	7 N 29.9	20 N 40.7	5 S 51.3	4 S 55.7	12 N 36.0	13 N 50.9	3 N 49.4	2 N 6.2	17 S 35.7	17 N 54.5
4 T	0 51 27.2	5 49.7	7 26.3	28 17.5	3 54.7	3 30.1	13 22.3	13 54.1	3 58.2	2 9.1	17 34.8	17 55.9
7 S	1 3 16.9	6 57.7	7 22.7	24 21.5	1 48.5	2 3.6	14 7.5	13 56.8	4 6.8	2 11.9	17 33.9	17 57.2
10 W	1 15 6.5	8 4.7	7 19.1	9 9.0	0 N 26.9	0 36.4	14 51.3	13 58.9	4 15.5	2 14.6	17 32.9	17 58.3
13 S	1 26 56.2	9 10.4	7 15.4	11 S 28.0	2 50.5	0 N 51.1	15 33.8	14 0.4	4 24.1	2 17.2	17 31.9	17 59.3
16 T	1 38 45.8	10 14.8	7 11.8	26 34.9	5 21.3	2 18.6	16 14.9	14 1.4	4 32.6	2 19.8	17 30.9	18 0.2
19 F	1 50 35.5	11 17.7	7 8.2	26 12.2	7 57.5	3 45.8	16 54.6	14 1.7	4 41.0	2 22.2	17 29.9	18 0.9
22 M	2 2 25.2	12 18.9	7 4.6	13 7.6	10 36.5	5 12.4	17 32.8	14 1.5	4 49.3	2 24.4	17 28.8	18 1.6
25 T	2 14 14.8	13 18.3	7 0.9	4 N 6.2	13 14.9	6 38.1	18 9.5	14 0.7	4 57.5	2 26.6	17 27.7	18 2.1
28 S	2 26 4.5	14 15.7	6 57.3	19 31.5	15 48.0	8 2.6	18 44.6	13 59.4	5 5.6	2 28.6	17 26.5	18 2.4

MAY 1968

DAY	EPHEMERIS SIDEREAL TIME	☉	☊	☽	☿	♀	♂	♃	♄	♅	♆	♇
	h m s	° ′	° ′	° ′	° ′	° ′	° ′	° ′	° ′	° ′	° ′	° ′
LONGITUDE at NOON												
1 W	2 37 54.2	11 ♉ 10.2	17 ♈ 33.5	23 ♊ 6.7	18 ♉ 51.0	27 ♈ 48.6	24 ♉ 59.6	25 ♌ 58.2	18 ♈ 38.4	25 ♍ 29.8	25 ♏ 32.8	20 ♍ 23.6
2 T	2 41 50.7	12 8.4	17 30.3	5 ♋ 4.9	20 57.5	29 2.4	25 42.2	26 0.0	18 45.6	25 R 28.2	25 R 31.3	20 R 22.8
3 F	2 45 47.3	13 6.6	17 27.2	17 12.1	23 2.7	0 ♉ 16.2	26 24.7	26 2.1	18 52.8	25 26.8	25 29.7	20 22.0
4 S	2 49 43.8	14 4.8	17 24.0	29 31.8	25 6.2	1 30.0	27 7.2	26 4.3	18 59.9	25 25.3	25 28.1	20 21.2
5 S	2 53 40.4	15 2.9	17 20.8	12 ♌ 7.7	27 7.8	2 43.7	27 49.6	26 6.7	19 7.0	25 23.9	25 26.5	20 20.4
6 M	2 57 37.0	16 1.0	17 17.6	25 3.7	29 7.2	3 57.5	28 32.0	26 9.2	19 14.0	25 22.6	25 24.9	20 19.6
7 T	3 1 33.5	16 59.0	17 14.4	8 ♍ 23.3	1 ♊ 4.1	5 11.2	29 14.3	26 12.0	19 21.1	25 21.3	25 23.3	20 18.9
8 W	3 5 30.1	17 57.0	17 11.3	22 8.9	2 58.4	6 24.9	29 56.6	26 14.9	19 28.0	25 20.0	25 21.7	20 18.2
9 T	3 9 26.6	18 55.0	17 8.1	6 ♎ 21.3	4 49.9	7 38.6	0 ♊ 38.8	26 18.0	19 35.0	25 18.8	25 20.1	20 17.5
10 F	3 13 23.2	19 53.0	17 4.9	20 59.0	6 38.4	8 52.4	1 21.0	26 21.2	19 41.9	25 17.6	25 18.5	20 16.8
11 S	3 17 19.7	20 50.9	17 1.7	5 ♏ 57.6	8 23.8	10 6.1	2 3.1	26 24.6	19 48.7	25 16.5	25 16.9	20 16.2
12 S	3 21 16.3	21 48.8	16 58.6	21 9.5	10 6.0	11 19.8	2 45.2	26 28.2	19 55.6	25 15.4	25 15.3	20 15.6
13 M	3 25 12.8	22 46.6	16 55.4	6 ♐ 25.3	11 44.9	12 33.5	3 27.3	26 32.0	20 2.4	25 14.4	25 13.6	20 15.1
14 T	3 29 9.4	23 44.5	16 52.2	21 34.4	13 20.3	13 47.2	4 9.2	26 35.9	20 9.1	25 13.4	25 12.0	20 14.6
15 W	3 33 6.0	24 42.3	16 49.0	6 ♑ 27.4	14 52.3	15 0.9	4 51.2	26 39.9	20 15.8	25 12.4	25 10.4	20 14.1
16 T	3 37 2.5	25 40.1	16 45.9	20 57.1	16 20.8	16 14.6	5 33.1	26 44.2	20 22.5	25 11.6	25 8.7	20 13.6
17 F	3 40 59.1	26 37.9	16 42.7	4 ♒ 59.5	17 45.6	17 28.3	6 14.9	26 48.6	20 29.1	25 10.7	25 7.1	20 13.1
18 S	3 44 55.6	27 35.7	16 39.5	18 33.5	19 6.9	18 41.9	6 56.7	26 53.1	20 35.7	25 9.9	25 5.5	20 12.7
19 S	3 48 52.2	28 33.4	16 36.3	1 ♓ 40.7	20 24.4	19 55.6	7 38.5	26 57.9	20 42.2	25 9.2	25 3.9	20 12.4
20 M	3 52 48.7	29 31.2	16 33.1	14 24.4	21 38.2	21 9.3	8 20.2	27 2.7	20 48.7	25 8.5	25 2.2	20 12.0
21 T	3 56 45.3	0 ♊ 28.9	16 30.0	26 48.8	22 48.3	22 23.0	9 1.9	27 7.8	20 55.1	25 7.9	25 0.6	20 11.7
22 W	4 0 41.9	1 26.6	16 26.8	8 ♈ 58.4	23 54.5	23 36.7	9 43.5	27 12.9	21 1.5	25 7.3	24 59.0	20 11.4
23 T	4 4 38.4	2 24.2	16 23.6	20 57.4	24 56.8	24 50.4	10 25.1	27 18.3	21 7.8	25 6.8	24 57.4	20 11.1
24 F	4 8 35.0	3 21.9	16 20.4	2 ♉ 49.7	25 55.1	26 4.2	11 6.7	27 23.8	21 14.2	25 6.3	24 55.8	20 11.0
25 S	4 12 31.5	4 19.6	16 17.3	14 38.7	26 49.4	27 17.8	11 48.2	27 29.4	21 20.4	25 5.9	24 54.2	20 10.8
26 S	4 16 28.1	5 17.2	16 14.1	26 27.0	27 39.6	28 31.5	12 29.6	27 35.2	21 26.6	25 5.6	24 52.6	20 10.6
27 M	4 20 24.7	6 14.8	16 10.9	8 ♊ 16.9	28 25.6	29 45.2	13 11.0	27 41.1	21 32.7	25 5.2	24 51.0	20 10.5
28 T	4 24 21.2	7 12.4	16 7.7	20 10.2	29 7.4	0 ♊ 58.9	13 52.4	27 47.2	21 38.8	25 5.0	24 49.4	20 10.4
29 W	4 28 17.8	8 10.0	16 4.6	2 ♋ 8.5	29 44.8	2 12.6	14 33.7	27 53.4	21 44.8	25 4.8	24 47.8	20 10.3
30 T	4 32 14.3	9 7.5	16 1.4	14 13.6	0 ♋ 17.8	3 26.3	15 15.0	27 59.8	21 50.8	25 4.6	24 46.3	20 10.3
31 F	4 36 10.9	10 5.0	15 58.2	26 27.2	0 46.3	4 40.0	15 56.2	28 6.3	21 56.7	25 4.5	24 44.7	20 10.3
DECLINATION at NOON												
1 W	2 37 54.2	15 N 11.1	6 N 53.6	27 N 59.5	18 N 10.3	9 N 25.5	19 N 18.1	13 N 57.4	5 N 13.6	2 N 30.4	17 S 25.4	18 N 2.6
4 S	2 49 43.8	16 4.1	6 50.0	25 16.4	20 16.5	10 46.5	19 49.9	13 54.9	5 21.4	2 32.1	17 24.3	18 2.7
7 T	3 1 33.5	16 54.8	6 46.3	11 33.0	22 2.5	12 5.3	20 20.0	13 51.9	5 29.1	2 33.6	17 23.1	18 2.6
10 F	3 13 23.2	17 42.8	6 42.7	8 S 24.3	23 26.1	13 21.5	20 48.4	13 48.4	5 36.6	2 35.0	17 21.9	18 2.4
13 M	3 25 12.8	18 28.3	6 39.0	25 11.9	24 27.0	14 34.9	21 15.0	13 44.3	5 44.0	2 36.1	17 20.8	18 2.1
16 T	3 37 2.5	19 10.9	6 35.4	26 55.7	25 6.5	15 45.0	21 39.8	13 39.7	5 51.2	2 37.1	17 19.6	18 1.6
19 S	3 48 52.2	19 50.6	6 31.7	14 23.2	25 26.7	16 51.7	22 2.8	13 34.6	5 58.2	2 38.0	17 18.5	18 1.0
22 W	4 0 41.9	20 27.3	6 28.1	2 N 48.3	25 29.9	17 54.5	22 23.9	13 29.1	6 5.0	2 38.6	17 17.3	18 0.3
25 S	4 12 31.5	21 0.9	6 24.4	18 26.6	25 18.5	18 53.2	22 43.2	13 23.0	6 11.6	2 39.0	17 16.2	17 59.4
28 T	4 24 21.2	21 31.1	6 20.8	27 36.2	24 55.1	19 47.4	23 0.6	13 16.5	6 18.0	2 39.3	17 15.1	17 58.4
31 F	4 36 10.9	21 58.1	6 17.1	25 48.4	24 21.7	20 36.8	23 16.1	13 9.5	6 24.2	2 39.4	17 14.0	17 57.3

JUNE 1968

DAY	EPHEMERIS SIDEREAL TIME	☉	☊	☽	☿	♀	♂	♃	♄	♅	♆	♇
LONGITUDE at NOON												
1 S	4 40 7.4	11 ♊ 2.5	15 ♈ 55.0	8 ♌ 51.7	1 ♋ 10.4	5 ♊ 53.6	16 ♊ 37.4	28 ♌ 12.9	22 ♈ 2.5	25 ♍ 4.4	24 ♏ 43.2	20 ♍ 10.3
2 S	4 44 4.0	12 0.0	15 51.9	21 29.6	1 29.8	7 7.3	17 18.6	28 19.7	22 8.3	25 4.4	24 R 41.6	20 D 10.4
3 M	4 48 0.6	12 57.5	15 48.7	4 ♍ 24.1	1 44.6	8 21.0	17 59.7	28 26.6	22 14.0	25 D 4.5	24 40.1	20 10.5
4 T	4 51 57.1	13 54.9	15 45.5	17 38.2	1 54.8	9 34.7	18 40.7	28 33.6	22 19.7	25 4.6	24 38.6	20 10.6
5 W	4 55 53.7	14 52.3	15 42.3	1 ♎ 14.8	2 0.3	10 48.3	19 21.7	28 40.8	22 25.3	25 4.8	24 37.1	20 10.7
6 T	4 59 50.2	15 49.7	15 39.1	15 15.7	2 1.3	12 2.0	20 2.7	28 48.1	22 30.8	25 5.0	24 35.6	20 10.9
7 F	5 3 46.8	16 47.1	15 36.0	29 41.1	1 R 57.8	13 15.7	20 43.6	28 55.5	22 36.3	25 5.3	24 34.1	20 11.2
8 S	5 7 43.4	17 44.5	15 32.8	14 ♏ 28.6	1 49.9	14 29.3	21 24.5	29 3.1	22 41.7	25 5.6	24 32.6	20 11.4
9 S	5 11 39.9	18 41.8	15 29.6	29 32.9	1 37.8	15 43.0	22 5.3	29 10.7	22 47.0	25 6.0	24 31.2	20 11.7
10 M	5 15 36.5	19 39.2	15 26.4	14 ♐ 45.5	1 21.7	16 56.7	22 46.1	29 18.5	22 52.2	25 6.4	24 29.7	20 12.0
11 T	5 19 33.0	20 36.5	15 23.3	29 56.2	1 1.8	18 10.3	23 26.9	29 26.4	22 57.4	25 6.9	24 28.3	20 12.4
12 W	5 23 29.6	21 33.8	15 20.1	14 ♑ 54.6	0 38.6	19 24.0	24 7.6	29 34.5	23 2.6	25 7.4	24 26.9	20 12.7
13 T	5 27 26.1	22 31.1	15 16.9	29 31.8	0 12.3	20 37.7	24 48.2	29 42.6	23 7.6	25 8.0	24 25.5	20 13.1
14 F	5 31 22.7	23 28.4	15 13.7	13 ♒ 42.0	29 ♊ 43.4	21 51.4	25 28.9	29 50.9	23 12.7	25 8.7	24 24.2	20 13.6
15 S	5 35 19.3	24 25.7	15 10.6	27 22.5	29 12.3	23 5.1	26 9.5	29 59.3	23 17.6	25 9.4	24 22.8	20 14.1
16 S	5 39 15.8	25 23.0	15 7.4	10 ♓ 34.0	28 39.6	24 18.8	26 50.0	0 ♍ 7.8	23 22.4	25 10.1	24 21.5	20 14.6
17 M	5 43 12.4	26 20.2	15 4.2	23 19.6	28 5.9	25 32.4	27 30.6	0 16.4	23 27.2	25 10.9	24 20.1	20 15.1
18 T	5 47 8.9	27 17.5	15 1.0	5 ♈ 43.6	27 31.6	26 46.1	28 11.0	0 25.1	23 31.9	25 11.8	24 18.8	20 15.7
19 W	5 51 5.5	28 14.8	14 57.9	17 51.1	26 57.4	27 59.8	28 51.5	0 33.9	23 36.5	25 12.7	24 17.5	20 16.3
20 T	5 55 2.1	29 12.0	14 54.7	29 47.3	26 23.9	29 13.6	29 31.9	0 42.8	23 41.0	25 13.6	24 16.3	20 16.9
21 F	5 58 58.6	0 ♋ 9.3	14 51.5	11 ♉ 37.2	25 51.7	0 ♋ 27.3	0 ♋ 12.2	0 51.9	23 45.5	25 14.6	24 15.0	20 17.6
22 S	6 2 55.2	1 6.6	14 48.3	23 25.0	25 21.2	1 41.0	0 52.6	1 1.0	23 49.9	25 15.7	24 13.8	20 18.3
23 S	6 6 51.7	2 3.8	14 45.2	5 ♊ 14.3	24 53.0	2 54.7	1 32.9	1 10.2	23 54.2	25 16.8	24 12.6	20 19.0
24 M	6 10 48.3	3 1.0	14 42.0	17 8.0	24 27.7	4 8.5	2 13.1	1 19.6	23 58.4	25 17.9	24 11.4	20 19.7
25 T	6 14 44.9	3 58.3	14 38.8	29 7.9	24 5.6	5 22.2	2 53.3	1 29.0	24 2.5	25 19.2	24 10.2	20 20.5
26 W	6 18 41.4	4 55.5	14 35.6	11 ♋ 15.7	23 47.1	6 35.9	3 33.5	1 38.6	24 6.6	25 20.4	24 9.1	20 21.3
27 T	6 22 38.0	5 52.8	14 32.4	23 32.1	23 32.5	7 49.7	4 13.6	1 48.2	24 10.6	25 21.7	24 8.0	20 22.2
28 F	6 26 34.5	6 50.0	14 29.3	5 ♌ 58.1	23 22.2	9 3.4	4 53.7	1 57.9	24 14.5	25 23.1	24 6.9	20 23.0
29 S	6 30 31.1	7 47.2	14 26.1	18 34.5	23 16.4	10 17.2	5 33.8	2 7.7	24 18.3	25 24.5	24 5.8	20 23.9
30 S	6 34 27.6	8 44.4	14 22.9	1 ♍ 22.4	23 15.2	11 30.9	6 13.8	2 17.7	24 22.0	25 26.0	24 4.7	20 24.9
DECLINATION at NOON												
1 S	4 40 7.4	22 N 6.3	6 N 15.9	22 N 37.0	24 N 8.8	20 N 52.2	23 N 20.8	13 N 7.1	6 N 26.2	2 N 39.3	17 S 13.7	17 N 56.9
4 T	4 51 57.1	22 28.6	6 12.2	7 11.6	23 25.6	21 34.8	23 33.8	12 59.5	6 32.0	2 39.1	17 12.6	17 55.6
7 F	5 3 46.8	22 47.3	6 8.5	12 S 25.0	22 37.6	22 11.9	23 44.8	12 51.6	6 37.6	2 38.8	17 11.6	17 54.2
10 M	5 15 36.5	23 2.5	6 4.9	26 50.7	21 47.2	22 43.5	23 53.9	12 43.2	6 43.0	2 38.2	17 10.6	17 52.7
13 T	5 27 26.1	23 14.0	6 1.2	25 3.8	20 57.0	23 9.2	24 1.1	12 34.4	6 48.1	2 37.4	17 9.7	17 51.1
16 S	5 39 15.8	23 21.9	5 57.5	10 19.9	20 10.2	23 28.8	24 6.3	12 25.2	6 52.9	2 36.5	17 8.8	17 49.4
19 W	5 51 5.5	23 26.0	5 53.8	7 N 9.5	19 30.3	23 42.3	24 9.7	12 15.7	6 57.5	2 35.4	17 8.0	17 47.5
22 S	6 2 55.2	23 26.5	5 50.1	21 36.5	19 0.7	23 49.5	24 11.2	12 5.8	7 1.7	2 34.0	17 7.2	17 45.6
25 T	6 14 44.9	23 23.2	5 46.4	28 15.0	18 43.8	23 50.4	24 10.8	11 55.5	7 5.7	2 32.5	17 6.4	17 43.6
28 F	6 26 34.5	23 16.2	5 42.8	23 18.2	18 40.8	23 44.9	24 8.5	11 44.9	7 9.4	2 30.9	17 5.7	17 41.5

JULY 1968

LONGITUDE at NOON

DAY	EPHEMERIS SIDEREAL TIME h m s	☉ ° ′	☊ ° ′	☽ ° ′	☿ ° ′	♀ ° ′	♂ ° ′	♃ ° ′	♄ ° ′	♅ ° ′	♆ ° ′	♇ ° ′
1 M	6 38 24.2	9♋41.6	14♈19.7	14♍23.5	23♊18.8	12♋44.7	6♋53.8	2♍27.7	24♈25.6	25♍27.5	24♏ 3.7	20♍25.8
2 T	6 42 20.8	10 38.8	14 16.6	27 39.8	23D27.2	13 58.4	7 33.8	2 37.7	24 29.1	25 29.0	24R 2.7	20 26.8
3 W	6 46 17.3	11 36.0	14 13.4	11♎13.3	23 40.7	15 12.2	8 13.7	2 47.9	24 32.6	25 30.7	24 1.7	20 27.8
4 T	6 50 13.9	12 33.2	14 10.2	25 5.8	23 59.1	16 26.0	8 53.5	2 58.2	24 36.0	25 32.3	24 0.8	20 28.9
5 F	6 54 10.4	13 30.5	14 7.0	9♏18.1	24 22.7	17 39.8	9 33.4	3 8.6	24 39.3	25 34.1	23 59.9	20 30.0
6 S	6 58 7.0	14 27.7	14 3.9	23 49.1	24 51.2	18 53.6	10 13.2	3 19.0	24 42.5	25 35.8	23 59.0	20 31.1
7 S	7 2 3.6	15 24.9	14 0.7	8♐35.4	25 24.6	20 7.3	10 53.0	3 29.5	24 45.6	25 37.6	23 58.1	20 32.2
8 M	7 6 0.1	16 22.0	13 57.5	23 30.9	26 3.1	21 21.1	11 32.7	3 40.1	24 48.6	25 39.5	23 57.3	20 33.4
9 T	7 9 56.7	17 19.2	13 54.3	8♑27.4	26 46.5	22 34.9	12 12.4	3 50.7	24 51.5	25 41.4	23 56.5	20 34.6
10 W	7 13 53.2	18 16.4	13 51.2	23 15.7	27 34.7	23 48.7	12 52.1	4 1.5	24 54.3	25 43.3	23 55.7	20 35.8
11 T	7 17 49.8	19 13.6	13 48.0	7♒47.3	28 27.8	25 2.4	13 31.7	4 12.3	24 57.0	25 45.3	23 54.9	20 37.0
12 F	7 21 46.4	20 10.8	13 44.8	21 55.5	29 25.7	26 16.2	14 11.3	4 23.2	24 59.6	25 47.3	23 54.2	20 38.3
13 S	7 25 42.9	21 8.0	13 41.6	5♓36.9	0♋28.2	27 30.0	14 50.8	4 34.1	25 2.2	25 49.4	23 53.5	20 39.5
14 S	7 29 39.5	22 5.2	13 38.4	18 50.7	1 35.4	28 43.8	15 30.4	4 45.2	25 4.6	25 51.5	23 52.8	20 40.9
15 M	7 33 36.0	23 2.4	13 35.3	1♈38.9	2 47.2	29 57.6	16 9.9	4 56.3	25 7.0	25 53.6	23 52.2	20 42.2
16 T	7 37 32.6	23 59.6	13 32.1	14 5.1	4 3.5	1♌11.5	16 49.3	5 7.4	25 9.2	25 55.8	23 51.5	20 43.6
17 W	7 41 29.1	24 56.9	13 28.9	26 14.2	5 24.3	2 25.3	17 28.8	5 18.7	25 11.3	25 58.1	23 50.9	20 45.0
18 T	7 45 25.7	25 54.1	13 25.7	8♉11.6	6 49.3	3 39.1	18 8.2	5 29.9	25 13.4	26 0.4	23 50.4	20 46.4
19 F	7 49 22.3	26 51.4	13 22.6	20 2.4	8 18.6	4 52.9	18 47.5	5 41.3	25 15.3	26 2.7	23 49.8	20 47.8
20 S	7 53 18.8	27 48.7	13 19.4	1♊51.7	9 52.0	6 6.8	19 26.9	5 52.7	25 17.2	26 5.1	23 49.3	20 49.3
21 S	7 57 15.4	28 45.9	13 16.2	13 43.9	11 29.3	7 20.6	20 6.2	6 4.2	25 19.0	26 7.5	23 48.9	20 50.8
22 M	8 1 11.9	29 43.2	13 13.0	25 42.6	13 10.5	8 34.5	20 45.5	6 15.8	25 20.6	26 9.9	23 48.4	20 52.3
23 T	8 5 8.5	0♌40.6	13 9.9	7♋50.4	14 55.2	9 48.4	21 24.7	6 27.4	25 22.2	26 12.4	23 48.0	20 53.8
24 W	8 9 5.0	1 37.9	13 6.7	20 9.2	16 43.3	11 2.2	22 4.0	6 39.1	25 23.6	26 15.0	23 47.6	20 55.4
25 T	8 13 1.6	2 35.2	13 3.5	2♌39.7	18 34.6	12 16.1	22 43.1	6 50.8	25 24.9	26 17.5	23 47.3	20 56.9
26 F	8 16 58.2	3 32.6	13 0.3	15 22.4	20 28.7	13 30.0	23 22.4	7 2.6	25 26.2	26 20.2	23 47.0	20 58.6
27 S	8 20 54.7	4 30.0	12 57.2	28 16.8	22 25.3	14 43.9	24 1.5	7 14.5	25 27.4	26 22.9	23 46.7	21 0.2
28 S	8 24 51.3	5 27.3	12 54.0	11♍22.6	24 24.2	15 57.8	24 40.6	7 26.3	25 28.4	26 25.5	23 46.5	21 1.9
29 M	8 28 47.8	6 24.7	12 50.8	24 39.8	26 25.0	17 11.6	25 19.6	7 38.3	25 29.3	26 28.3	23 46.2	21 3.5
30 T	8 32 44.4	7 22.1	12 47.6	8♎ 8.4	28 27.4	18 25.5	25 58.7	7 50.3	25 30.2	26 31.0	23 46.1	21 5.2
31 W	8 36 40.9	8 19.5	12 44.4	21 48.9	0♌30.9	19 39.4	26 37.7	8 2.3	25 30.9	26 33.8	23 45.9	21 6.9

DECLINATION at NOON

DAY	EPHEMERIS SIDEREAL TIME h m s	☉ ° ′	☊ ° ′	☽ ° ′	☿ ° ′	♀ ° ′	♂ ° ′	♃ ° ′	♄ ° ′	♅ ° ′	♆ ° ′	♇ ° ′
1 M	6 38 24.2	23N 5.5	5N39.1	8N28.1	18N51.5	23N33.0	24N 4.4	11N34.0	7N12.8	2N29.0	17S 5.1	17N39.3
4 T	6 50 13.9	22 51.2	5 35.4	10S35.6	19 14.2	23 14.9	23 58.5	11 22.8	7 15.9	2 27.0	17 4.5	17 37.0
7 S	7 2 3.6	22 33.3	5 31.7	25 46.4	19 46.3	22 50.6	23 50.7	11 11.2	7 18.7	2 24.8	17 4.0	17 34.6
10 W	7 13 53.2	22 11.9	5 28.0	26 18.2	20 24.3	22 20.2	23 41.3	10 59.4	7 21.1	2 22.4	17 3.5	17 32.2
13 S	7 25 42.9	21 47.1	5 24.3	12 18.7	21 4.2	21 44.0	23 30.1	10 47.3	7 23.2	2 19.9	17 3.1	17 29.7
16 T	7 37 32.6	21 18.9	5 20.6	5N38.1	21 41.4	21 2.1	23 17.2	10 34.9	7 25.0	2 17.2	17 2.8	17 27.2
19 F	7 49 22.3	20 47.5	5 16.9	20 40.9	22 10.8	20 14.8	23 2.7	10 22.3	7 26.5	2 14.4	17 2.6	17 24.6
22 M	8 1 11.9	20 12.9	5 13.2	28 10.8	22 27.2	19 22.3	22 46.5	10 9.4	7 27.7	2 11.4	17 2.4	17 22.0
25 T	8 13 1.6	19 35.2	5 9.5	24 9.1	22 25.5	18 24.9	22 28.8	9 56.3	7 28.5	2 8.3	17 2.3	17 19.3
28 S	8 24 51.3	18 54.7	5 5.8	9 39.9	22 1.7	17 22.9	22 9.5	9 43.0	7 29.0	2 5.0	17 2.2	17 16.5
31 W	8 36 40.9	18 11.3	5 2.0	9S20.4	21 14.2	16 16.6	21 48.8	9 29.5	7 29.1	2 1.6	17 2.3	17 13.8

AUGUST 1968

LONGITUDE at NOON

DAY	EPHEMERIS SIDEREAL TIME h m s	☉ ° ′	☊ ° ′	☽ ° ′	☿ ° ′	♀ ° ′	♂ ° ′	♃ ° ′	♄ ° ′	♅ ° ′	♆ ° ′	♇ ° ′
1 T	8 40 37.5	9♌16.9	12♈41.3	5♏41.8	2♌35.3	20♌53.3	27♋16.7	8♍14.4	25♈31.5	26♍36.6	23♏45.8	21♍ 8.6
2 F	8 44 34.1	10 14.3	12 38.1	19 47.3	4 40.3	22 7.2	27 55.6	8 26.5	25 32.0	26 39.5	23R45.7	21 10.4
3 S	8 48 30.6	11 11.7	12 34.9	4♐ 4.4	6 45.6	23 21.0	28 34.5	8 38.7	25 32.5	26 42.4	23 45.6	21 12.2
4 S	8 52 27.2	12 9.2	12 31.7	18 31.0	8 50.8	24 34.9	29 13.4	8 50.9	25 32.8	26 45.3	23 45.6	21 13.9
5 M	8 56 23.7	13 6.6	12 28.6	3♑ 3.1	10 55.7	25 48.8	29 52.2	9 3.2	25 33.0	26 48.3	23 45.6	21 15.8
6 T	9 0 20.3	14 4.1	12 25.4	17 35.2	13 0.1	27 2.7	0♌31.1	9 15.5	25 33.1	26 51.3	23 45.6	21 17.6
7 W	9 4 16.8	15 1.6	12 22.2	2♒ 0.9	15 3.8	28 16.5	1 9.9	9 27.8	25 33.1	26 54.3	23D45.7	21 19.4
8 T	9 8 13.4	15 59.1	12 19.0	16 13.6	17 6.6	29 30.4	1 48.6	9 40.2	25R33.0	26 57.4	23 45.8	21 21.3
9 F	9 12 10.0	16 56.6	12 15.9	0♓ 7.9	19 8.5	0♍44.3	2 27.4	9 52.6	25 32.8	27 0.5	23 45.9	21 23.1
10 S	9 16 6.5	17 54.1	12 12.7	13 40.5	21 9.2	1 58.2	3 6.1	10 5.1	25 32.5	27 3.6	23 46.0	21 25.0
11 S	9 20 3.1	18 51.7	12 9.5	26 49.7	23 8.7	3 12.0	3 44.8	10 17.5	25 32.1	27 6.7	23 46.2	21 26.9
12 M	9 23 59.6	19 49.2	12 6.3	9♈36.5	25 6.9	4 25.9	4 23.4	10 30.1	25 31.5	27 9.9	23 46.5	21 28.9
13 T	9 27 56.2	20 46.8	12 3.1	22 3.3	27 3.8	5 39.8	5 2.1	10 42.6	25 30.9	27 13.1	23 46.7	21 30.8
14 W	9 31 52.7	21 44.5	11 60.0	4♉13.9	28 59.3	6 53.7	5 40.7	10 55.2	25 30.2	27 16.4	23 47.0	21 32.8
15 T	9 35 49.3	22 42.1	11 56.8	16 13.0	0♍53.4	8 7.5	6 19.3	11 7.8	25 29.4	27 19.6	23 47.3	21 34.7
16 F	9 39 45.8	23 39.8	11 53.6	28 5.6	2 46.2	9 21.5	6 57.9	11 20.5	25 28.5	27 22.9	23 47.7	21 36.8
17 S	9 43 42.4	24 37.5	11 50.4	9♊56.8	4 37.5	10 35.3	7 36.4	11 33.2	25 27.5	27 26.3	23 48.1	21 38.7
18 S	9 47 39.0	25 35.3	11 47.3	21 51.5	6 27.4	11 49.2	8 14.9	11 45.9	25 26.3	27 29.6	23 48.5	21 40.8
19 M	9 51 35.5	26 33.0	11 44.1	3♋54.0	8 15.8	13 3.1	8 53.4	11 58.6	25 25.1	27 33.0	23 49.0	21 42.8
20 T	9 55 32.1	27 30.8	11 40.9	16 7.8	10 2.9	14 17.0	9 31.9	12 11.4	25 23.7	27 36.3	23 49.5	21 44.8
21 W	9 59 28.6	28 28.6	11 37.7	28 35.7	11 48.5	15 30.8	10 10.3	12 24.2	25 22.3	27 39.7	23 50.0	21 46.9
22 T	10 3 25.2	29 26.4	11 34.5	11♌19.2	13 32.8	16 44.7	10 48.8	12 37.0	25 20.8	27 43.2	23 50.5	21 48.9
23 F	10 7 21.7	0♍24.3	11 31.4	24 18.7	15 15.7	17 58.6	11 27.2	12 49.8	25 19.1	27 46.6	23 51.1	21 51.0
24 S	10 11 18.3	1 22.2	11 28.2	7♍33.6	16 57.2	19 12.5	12 5.5	13 2.6	25 17.4	27 50.1	23 51.7	21 53.1
25 S	10 15 14.8	2 20.1	11 25.0	21 2.4	18 37.4	20 26.3	12 43.9	13 15.5	25 15.6	27 53.6	23 52.4	21 55.2
26 M	10 19 11.4	3 18.0	11 21.8	4♎43.2	20 16.2	21 40.2	13 22.2	13 28.4	25 13.6	27 57.1	23 53.0	21 57.3
27 T	10 23 8.0	4 15.9	11 18.7	18 34.0	21 53.8	22 54.0	14 0.5	13 41.3	25 11.6	28 0.7	23 53.7	21 59.4
28 W	10 27 4.5	5 13.9	11 15.5	2♏32.6	23 30.0	24 7.9	14 38.7	13 54.2	25 9.5	28 4.2	23 54.5	22 1.5
29 T	10 31 1.1	6 11.9	11 12.3	16 37.4	25 4.9	25 21.7	15 17.0	14 7.1	25 7.2	28 7.8	23 55.2	22 3.6
30 F	10 34 57.6	7 9.9	11 9.1	0♐46.6	26 38.5	26 35.6	15 55.2	14 20.0	25 4.9	28 11.4	23 56.0	22 5.8
31 S	10 38 54.2	8 8.0	11 6.0	14 58.6	28 10.8	27 49.4	16 33.4	14 33.0	25 2.5	28 15.0	23 56.9	22 7.9

DECLINATION at NOON

DAY	EPHEMERIS SIDEREAL TIME h m s	☉ ° ′	☊ ° ′	☽ ° ′	☿ ° ′	♀ ° ′	♂ ° ′	♃ ° ′	♄ ° ′	♅ ° ′	♆ ° ′	♇ ° ′
1 T	8 40 37.5	17N56.2	5N 0.8	15S23.1	20N53.1	15N53.6	21N41.6	9N24.9	7N29.1	2N 0.5	17S 2.3	17N12.9
4 S	8 52 27.2	17 9.3	4 57.1	27 36.6	19 35.4	14 42.0	21 18.9	9 11.1	7 28.7	1 57.0	17 2.4	17 10.1
7 W	9 4 16.8	16 20.0	4 53.4	24 20.4	17 58.7	13 27.0	20 54.9	8 57.2	7 28.1	1 53.3	17 2.6	17 7.3
10 S	9 16 6.5	15 28.2	4 49.7	8 34.5	16 7.3	12 8.7	20 29.5	8 43.1	7 27.1	1 49.6	17 2.9	17 4.5
13 T	9 27 56.2	14 34.3	4 45.9	9N31.9	14 5.1	10 47.5	20 2.9	8 28.8	7 25.8	1 45.7	17 3.2	17 1.7
16 F	9 39 45.8	13 38.2	4 42.2	23 26.0	11 55.7	9 23.7	19 35.0	8 14.4	7 24.2	1 41.7	17 3.7	16 58.8
19 M	9 51 35.5	12 40.1	4 38.5	28 29.7	9 42.1	7 57.6	19 5.9	7 59.8	7 22.2	1 37.7	17 4.1	16 56.0
22 T	10 3 25.2	11 40.3	4 34.8	21 37.6	7 26.4	6 29.7	18 35.6	7 45.2	7 20.0	1 33.6	17 4.7	16 53.2
25 S	10 15 14.8	10 38.8	4 31.0	5 6.2	5 10.4	5 0.1	18 4.3	7 30.4	7 17.4	1 29.4	17 5.3	16 50.4
28 W	10 27 4.5	9 35.7	4 27.3	14S14.1	2 55.6	3 29.3	17 31.9	7 15.6	7 14.5	1 25.1	17 6.0	16 47.7
31 S	10 38 54.2	8 31.3	4 23.6	27 17.3	0 43.1	1 57.5	16 58.6	7 0.6	7 11.3	1 20.8	17 6.8	16 44.9

SEPTEMBER 1968

DAY	EPHEMERIS SIDEREAL TIME	☉	☊	☽	☿	♀	♂	♃	♄	♅	♆	♇
	h m s	° ′	° ′	° ′	° ′	° ′	° ′	° ′	° ′	° ′	° ′	° ′
						LONGITUDE at NOON						
1 S	10 42 50.7	9♍ 6.0	11♈ 2.8	29♐11.3	29♍41.8	29♍ 3.2	17♌11.5	14♍45.9	25♈ 0.0	28♍18.6	23♏57.7	22♍10.0
2 M	10 46 47.3	10 4.1	10 59.6	13♑22.1	1♎11.6	0♎17.0	17 49.7	14 58.9	24R57.4	28 22.2	23 58.6	22 12.2
3 T	10 50 43.8	11 2.2	10 56.4	27 28.1	2 40.0	1 30.8	18 27.8	15 11.9	24 54.8	28 25.9	23 59.6	22 14.4
4 W	10 54 40.4	12 0.4	10 53.2	11♒25.9	4 7.1	2 44.6	19 5.9	15 24.9	24 52.0	28 29.5	24 0.5	22 16.5
5 T	10 58 36.9	12 58.5	10 50.1	25 12.0	5 32.8	3 58.4	19 43.9	15 37.8	24 49.2	28 33.2	24 1.5	22 18.7
6 F	11 2 33.5	13 56.8	10 46.9	8♓43.5	6 57.3	5 12.2	20 22.0	15 50.9	24 46.3	28 36.9	24 2.6	22 20.9
7 S	11 6 30.0	14 55.0	10 43.7	21 58.0	8 20.4	6 26.0	21 0.0	16 3.9	24 43.3	28 40.6	24 3.6	22 23.1
8 S	11 10 26.6	15 53.2	10 40.5	4♈54.8	9 42.0	7 39.7	21 38.0	16 16.9	24 40.2	28 44.3	24 4.7	22 25.3
9 M	11 14 23.2	16 51.5	10 37.4	17 33.9	11 2.3	8 53.5	22 16.0	16 29.9	24 37.0	28 48.0	24 5.8	22 27.5
10 T	11 18 19.7	17 49.8	10 34.2	29 56.8	12 21.0	10 7.2	22 53.9	16 42.8	24 33.7	28 51.8	24 6.9	22 29.7
11 W	11 22 16.3	18 48.2	10 31.0	12♉ 6.2	13 38.3	11 20.9	23 31.9	16 55.8	24 30.4	28 55.5	24 8.1	22 31.9
12 T	11 26 12.8	19 46.5	10 27.8	24 5.4	14 53.9	12 34.7	24 9.8	17 8.8	24 27.0	28 59.3	24 9.2	22 34.1
13 F	11 30 9.4	20 44.9	10 24.6	5♊58.6	16 7.9	13 48.4	24 47.7	17 21.8	24 23.5	29 3.0	24 10.5	22 36.3
14 S	11 34 5.9	21 43.4	10 21.5	17 50.4	17 20.2	15 2.1	25 25.5	17 34.8	24 19.9	29 6.8	24 11.7	22 38.5
15 S	11 38 2.5	22 41.9	10 18.3	29 45.5	18 30.7	16 15.8	26 3.4	17 47.8	24 16.3	29 10.5	24 13.0	22 40.7
16 M	11 41 59.0	23 40.4	10 15.1	11♋48.7	19 39.3	17 29.5	26 41.2	18 0.8	24 12.6	29 14.3	24 14.3	22 42.9
17 T	11 45 55.6	24 39.0	10 11.9	24 4.2	20 45.9	18 43.2	27 19.0	18 13.7	24 8.8	29 18.1	24 15.6	22 45.1
18 W	11 49 52.1	25 37.5	10 8.8	6♌35.9	21 50.4	19 56.8	27 56.8	18 26.7	24 5.0	29 21.9	24 16.9	22 47.3
19 T	11 53 48.7	26 36.2	10 5.6	19 26.5	22 52.6	21 10.5	28 34.6	18 39.6	24 1.1	29 25.6	24 18.3	22 49.5
20 F	11 57 45.2	27 34.8	10 2.4	2♍37.6	23 52.3	22 24.2	29 12.3	18 52.6	23 57.1	29 29.4	24 19.7	22 51.7
21 S	12 1 41.8	28 33.5	9 59.2	16 9.1	24 49.4	23 37.8	29 50.0	19 5.5	23 53.1	29 33.2	24 21.2	22 53.9
22 S	12 5 38.4	29 32.3	9 56.0	29 59.7	25 43.8	24 51.5	0♍27.7	19 18.4	23 49.0	29 37.0	24 22.6	22 56.1
23 M	12 9 34.9	0♎31.0	9 52.9	14♎ 6.2	26 35.1	26 5.1	1 5.4	19 31.3	23 44.8	29 40.8	24 24.1	22 58.3
24 T	12 13 31.5	1 29.8	9 49.7	28 24.5	27 23.1	27 18.7	1 43.0	19 44.1	23 40.6	29 44.6	24 25.6	23 0.4
25 W	12 17 28.0	2 28.7	9 46.5	12♏49.8	28 7.6	28 32.3	2 20.7	19 57.0	23 36.4	29 48.4	24 27.1	23 2.6
26 T	12 21 24.6	3 27.5	9 43.3	27 17.0	28 48.3	29 45.9	2 58.3	20 9.8	23 32.1	29 52.1	24 28.7	23 4.8
27 F	12 25 21.1	4 26.4	9 40.2	11♐41.7	29 24.9	0♏59.6	3 35.9	20 22.7	23 27.8	29 56.0	24 30.3	23 7.0
28 S	12 29 17.7	5 25.4	9 37.0	26 0.2	29 56.9	2 13.2	4 13.4	20 35.5	23 23.4	29 59.8	24 31.9	23 9.2
29 S	12 33 14.2	6 24.3	9 33.8	10♑ 9.5	0♏24.0	3 26.7	4 51.0	20 48.2	23 19.0	0♎ 3.5	24 33.6	23 11.3
30 M	12 37 10.8	7 23.3	9 30.6	24 7.8	0 45.8	4 40.3	5 28.5	21 1.0	23 14.5	0 7.3	24 35.2	23 13.5
						DECLINATION at NOON						
1 S	10 42 50.7	8N 9.6	4N22.3	28S33.5	0S 0.4	1N26.8	16N47.2	6N55.7	7N10.2	1N19.3	17S 7.0	16N44.0
4 W	10 54 40.4	7 3.6	4 18.6	21 37.3	2 8.2	0S 5.7	16 12.6	6 40.7	7 6.7	1 14.9	17 7.9	16 41.3
7 S	11 6 30.0	5 56.6	4 14.9	4 39.2	4 11.4	1 38.4	15 37.2	6 25.6	7 2.9	1 10.5	17 8.8	16 38.7
10 T	11 18 19.7	4 48.7	4 11.1	13N 9.7	6 9.0	3 11.0	15 0.9	6 10.6	6 58.9	1 6.0	17 9.8	16 36.1
13 F	11 30 9.4	3 40.0	4 7.4	25 37.1	8 0.1	4 43.1	14 23.8	5 55.5	6 54.7	1 1.5	17 10.8	16 33.5
16 M	11 41 59.0	2 30.8	4 3.6	28 9.4	9 43.4	6 14.4	13 45.9	5 40.4	6 50.2	0 57.0	17 11.9	16 31.0
19 T	11 53 48.7	1 21.1	3 59.9	18 50.2	11 17.5	7 44.7	13 7.4	5 25.4	6 45.6	0 52.5	17 13.0	16 28.6
22 S	12 5 38.4	0 11.0	3 56.2	0 48.7	12 40.4	9 13.5	12 28.2	5 10.3	6 40.8	0 48.0	17 14.2	16 26.2
25 W	12 17 28.0	0S59.1	3 52.4	18S27.2	13 49.6	10 40.5	11 48.5	4 55.3	6 35.8	0 43.4	17 15.4	16 23.9
28 S	12 29 17.7	2 9.3	3 48.7	28 31.1	14 41.8	12 5.4	11 8.1	4 40.4	6 30.7	0 38.9	17 16.7	16 21.7

OCTOBER 1968

DAY	EPHEMERIS SIDEREAL TIME	☉	☊	☽	☿	♀	♂	♃	♄	♅	♆	♇
						LONGITUDE at NOON						
1 T	12 41 7.3	8♎22.3	9♈27.4	7♒53.8	1♏ 1.8	5♏53.8	6♍ 5.9	21♍13.7	23♈10.0	0♎11.1	24♏36.9	23♍15.6
2 W	12 45 3.9	9 21.3	9 24.3	21 26.8	1 11.8	7 7.3	6 43.4	21 26.3	23R 5.5	0 14.8	24 38.6	23 17.8
3 T	12 49 0.4	10 20.4	9 21.1	4♓46.4	1 15.1	8 20.8	7 20.8	21 39.0	23 0.9	0 18.6	24 40.3	23 19.9
4 F	12 52 57.0	11 19.4	9 17.9	17 52.4	1R11.4	9 34.3	7 58.2	21 51.6	22 56.3	0 22.3	24 42.1	23 22.0
5 S	12 56 53.6	12 18.6	9 14.7	0♈44.7	1 0.2	10 47.7	8 35.6	22 4.2	22 51.6	0 26.0	24 43.8	23 24.1
6 S	13 0 50.1	13 17.7	9 11.6	13 23.8	0 41.4	12 1.2	9 13.0	22 16.8	22 47.0	0 29.7	24 45.6	23 26.2
7 M	13 4 46.7	14 16.9	9 8.4	25 50.2	0 14.5	13 14.6	9 50.3	22 29.3	22 42.3	0 33.5	24 47.4	23 28.3
8 T	13 8 43.2	15 16.1	9 5.2	8♉ 5.0	29♎39.6	14 28.0	10 27.7	22 41.8	22 37.6	0 37.2	24 49.2	23 30.4
9 W	13 12 39.8	16 15.4	9 2.0	20 9.8	28 56.7	15 41.4	11 5.0	22 54.2	22 32.9	0 40.8	24 51.1	23 32.5
10 T	13 16 36.3	17 14.7	8 58.8	2♊ 7.0	28 6.1	16 54.8	11 42.2	23 6.6	22 28.1	0 44.5	24 52.9	23 34.5
11 F	13 20 32.9	18 14.0	8 55.7	13 59.5	27 8.6	18 8.1	12 19.5	23 19.0	22 23.4	0 48.2	24 54.8	23 36.6
12 S	13 24 29.4	19 13.4	8 52.5	25 50.7	26 4.9	19 21.5	12 56.7	23 31.3	22 18.6	0 51.8	24 56.7	23 38.6
13 S	13 28 26.0	20 12.8	8 49.3	7♋44.6	24 56.4	20 34.8	13 33.9	23 43.6	22 13.9	0 55.5	24 58.6	23 40.7
14 M	13 32 22.5	21 12.3	8 46.1	19 45.8	23 44.7	21 48.1	14 11.1	23 55.9	22 9.1	0 59.1	25 0.6	23 42.7
15 T	13 36 19.1	22 11.8	8 43.0	1♌58.6	22 31.5	23 1.5	14 48.3	24 8.1	22 4.3	1 2.7	25 2.5	23 44.7
16 W	13 40 15.6	23 11.3	8 39.8	14 27.8	21 19.0	24 14.7	15 25.5	24 20.2	21 59.5	1 6.3	25 4.5	23 46.6
17 T	13 44 12.2	24 10.8	8 36.6	27 17.2	20 9.2	25 28.0	16 2.6	24 32.4	21 54.8	1 ..9	25 6.5	23 48.6
18 F	13 48 8.8	25 10.5	8 33.4	10♍30.2	19 4.4	26 41.3	16 39.7	24 44.5	21 50.0	1 13.5	25 8.5	23 50.6
19 S	13 52 5.3	26 10.1	8 30.2	24 8.3	18 6.2	27 54.6	17 16.8	24 56.5	21 45.3	1 17.0	25 10.5	23 52.5
20 S	13 56 1.9	27 9.8	8 27.1	8♎11.4	17 16.6	29 7.8	17 53.9	25 8.4	21 40.5	1 20.5	25 12.6	23 54.5
21 M	13 59 58.4	28 9.5	8 23.9	22 36.7	16 36.6	0♐21.0	18 30.9	25 20.3	21 35.8	1 24.0	25 14.6	23 56.4
22 T	14 3 55.0	29 9.3	8 20.7	7♏19.3	16 7.3	1 34.2	19 7.9	25 32.2	21 31.1	1 27.5	25 16.7	23 58.3
23 W	14 7 51.5	0♏ 9.0	8 17.5	22 12.0	15 49.3	2 47.4	19 44.9	25 44.0	21 26.4	1 30.9	25 18.7	24 0.1
24 T	14 11 48.1	1 8.8	8 14.4	7♐ 6.7	15 42.6	4 0.6	20 21.8	25 55.7	21 21.7	1 34.3	25 20.8	24 2.0
25 F	14 15 44.6	2 8.7	8 11.2	21 55.2	15D47.1	5 13.7	20 58.8	26 7.4	21 17.0	1 37.8	25 22.9	24 3.8
26 S	14 19 41.2	3 8.5	8 8.0	6♑30.8	16 2.5	6 26.9	21 35.7	26 19.0	21 12.4	1 41.1	25 25.0	24 5.6
27 S	14 23 37.8	4 8.4	8 4.8	20 48.8	16 28.0	7 40.0	22 12.5	26 30.5	21 7.8	1 44.5	25 27.2	24 7.4
28 M	14 27 34.3	5 8.4	8 1.7	4♒46.6	17 3.1	8 53.0	22 49.4	26 42.0	21 3.2	1 47.8	25 29.3	24 9.2
29 T	14 31 30.9	6 8.3	7 58.5	18 23.8	17 46.7	10 6.1	23 26.2	26 53.4	20 58.7	1 51.1	25 31.5	24 10.9
30 W	14 35 27.4	7 8.3	7 55.3	1♓41.6	18 38.1	11 19.1	24 2.9	27 4.8	20 54.2	1 54.4	25 33.6	24 12.7
31 T	14 39 24.0	8 8.3	7 52.1	14 41.8	19 36.5	12 32.1	24 39.7	27 16.0	20 49.7	1 57.6	25 35.8	24 14.4
						DECLINATION at NOON						
1 T	12 41 7.3	3S19.3	3N44.9	22S47.6	15S12.1	13S27.9	10N27.4	4N25.6	6N25.5	0N34.4	17S18.0	16N19.6
4 F	12 52 57.0	4 28.9	3 41.2	6 36.1	15 14.8	14 47.5	9 46.1	4 10.8	6 20.3	0 30.0	17 19.4	16 17.5
7 M	13 4 46.7	5 38.0	3 37.4	11N21.6	14 42.9	16 4.0	9 4.5	3 56.2	6 15.0	0 25.5	17 20.8	16 15.6
10 T	13 16 36.3	6 46.4	3 33.7	24 41.7	13 31.2	17 17.0	8 22.4	3 41.7	6 9.7	0 21.2	17 22.2	16 13.7
13 S	13 28 26.0	7 54.1	3 29.9	28 28.8	11 41.1	18 26.1	7 40.1	3 27.3	6 4.3	0 16.8	17 23.7	16 12.0
16 W	13 40 15.6	9 0.8	3 26.1	20 38.0	9 27.2	19 31.0	6 57.5	3 13.1	5 59.0	0 12.5	17 25.2	16 10.4
19 S	13 52 5.3	10 6.4	3 22.4	3 37.3	7 17.2	20 31.5	6 14.6	2 59.0	5 53.8	0 8.3	17 26.7	16 8.8
22 T	14 3 55.0	11 10.6	3 18.6	16S16.2	5 40.1	21 27.1	5 31.5	2 45.2	5 48.6	0 4.2	17 28.2	16 7.4
25 F	14 15 44.6	12 13.3	3 14.9	28 11.1	4 52.8	22 17.5	4 48.3	2 31.6	5 43.5	0 0.2	17 29.8	16 6.1
28 M	14 27 34.3	13 14.3	3 11.1	23 39.9	4 56.3	23 2.4	4 5.0	2 18.2	5 38.6	0S 3.8	17 31.4	16 4.9
31 T	14 39 24.0	14 13.4	3 7.3	8 3.1	5 41.6	23 41.5	3 21.6	2 5.1	5 33.8	0 7.7	17 32.9	16 3.8

NOVEMBER 1968

DAY	EPHEMERIS SIDEREAL TIME	☉	☊	☽	☿	♀	♂	♃	♄	♅	♆	♇
	h m s	° ′	° ′	° ′	° ′	° ′	° ′	° ′	° ′	° ′	° ′	° ′
LONGITUDE at NOON												
1 F	14 43 20.5	9♏ 8.3	7♈48.9	27♓26.9	20♎40.9	13♐45.1	25♍16.4	27♍27.2	20♈45.3	2♎ 0.9	25♏37.9	24♍16.1
2 S	14 47 17.1	10 8.4	7 45.8	9♈59.0	21 50.6	14 58.0	25 53.1	27 38.4	20R41.0	2 4.0	25 40.1	24 17.7
3 S	14 51 13.6	11 8.4	7 42.6	22 20.4	23 4.9	16 10.9	26 29.8	27 49.4	20 36.6	2 7.2	25 42.3	24 19.4
4 M	14 55 10.2	12 8.6	7 39.4	4♉32.7	24 23.1	17 23.8	27 6.4	28 0.4	20 32.4	2 10.3	25 44.5	24 21.0
5 T	14 59 6.8	13 8.7	7 36.2	16 37.5	25 44.7	18 36.6	27 43.1	28 11.3	20 28.2	2 13.4	25 46.7	24 22.6
6 W	15 3 3.3	14 8.9	7 33.1	28 36.3	27 9.0	19 49.4	28 19.7	28 22.1	20 24.0	2 16.5	25 48.9	24 24.2
7 T	15 6 59.9	15 9.1	7 29.9	10♊30.6	28 35.6	21 2.2	28 56.2	28 32.9	20 19.9	2 19.5	25 51.2	24 25.8
8 F	15 10 56.4	16 9.4	7 26.7	22 22.2	0♏ 4.3	22 15.0	29 32.8	28 43.6	20 15.9	2 22.6	25 53.4	24 27.3
9 S	15 14 53.0	17 9.6	7 23.5	4♋13.5	1 34.5	23 27.7	0♎ 9.3	28 54.2	20 11.9	2 25.5	25 55.7	24 28.8
10 S	15 18 49.5	18 9.9	7 20.4	16 7.1	3 6.0	24 40.4	0 45.8	29 4.7	20 7.9	2 28.5	25 57.9	24 30.3
11 M	15 22 46.1	19 10.3	7 17.2	28 6.7	4 38.5	25 53.1	1 22.2	29 15.1	20 4.1	2 31.4	26 0.1	24 31.8
12 T	15 26 42.7	20 10.6	7 14.0	10♌16.2	6 11.8	27 5.7	1 58.7	29 25.4	20 0.3	2 34.2	26 2.4	24 33.2
13 W	15 30 39.2	21 11.0	7 10.8	22 40.1	7 45.8	28 18.3	2 35.1	29 35.7	19 56.6	2 37.1	26 4.6	24 34.6
14 T	15 34 35.8	22 11.4	7 7.6	5♍22.9	9 20.3	29 30.8	3 11.4	29 45.8	19 52.9	2 39.8	26 6.9	24 36.0
15 F	15 38 32.3	23 11.9	7 4.5	18 29.1	10 55.1	0♑43.4	3 47.8	29 55.8	19 49.3	2 42.6	26 9.1	24 37.3
16 S	15 42 28.9	24 12.4	7 1.3	2♎ 2.1	12 30.3	1 55.9	4 24.1	0♎ 5.8	19 45.8	2 45.3	26 11.4	24 38.7
17 S	15 46 25.4	25 12.9	6 58.1	16 3.5	14 5.5	3 8.3	5 0.3	0 15.7	19 42.4	2 48.0	26 13.6	24 40.0
18 M	15 50 22.0	26 13.5	6 54.9	0♏32.7	15 40.9	4 20.7	5 36.6	0 25.4	19 39.0	2 50.6	26 15.9	24 41.2
19 T	15 54 18.6	27 14.0	6 51.8	15 25.8	17 16.3	5 33.1	6 12.8	0 35.1	19 35.7	2 53.2	26 18.1	24 42.5
20 W	15 58 15.1	28 14.6	6 48.6	0♐35.3	18 51.8	6 45.4	6 48.9	0 44.6	19 32.5	2 55.8	26 20.4	24 43.7
21 T	16 2 11.7	29 15.3	6 45.4	15 51.3	20 27.1	7 57.7	7 25.1	0 54.1	19 29.4	2 58.3	26 22.6	24 44.9
22 F	16 6 8.2	0♐15.9	6 42.2	1♑ 2.8	22 2.5	9 10.0	8 1.2	1 3.4	19 26.4	3 0.7	26 24.9	24 46.0
23 S	16 10 4.8	1 16.6	6 39.1	15 59.7	23 37.7	10 22.2	8 37.2	1 12.6	19 23.5	3 3.2	26 27.1	24 47.2
24 S	16 14 1.3	2 17.3	6 35.9	0♒34.3	25 12.8	11 34.3	9 13.2	1 21.8	19 20.6	3 5.5	26 29.4	24 48.2
25 M	16 17 57.9	3 18.0	6 32.7	14 42.5	26 47.9	12 46.4	9 49.2	1 30.8	19 17.9	3 7.9	26 31.6	24 49.3
26 T	16 21 54.5	4 18.7	6 29.5	28 23.1	28 22.8	13 58.4	10 25.1	1 39.6	19 15.2	3 10.2	26 33.9	24 50.4
27 W	16 25 51.0	5 19.5	6 26.3	11♓37.9	29 57.6	15 10.4	11 1.0	1 48.4	19 12.6	3 12.4	26 36.1	24 51.4
28 T	16 29 47.6	6 20.2	6 23.2	24 30.1	1♐32.3	16 22.3	11 36.9	1 57.1	19 10.2	3 14.6	26 38.3	24 52.3
29 F	16 33 44.1	7 21.1	6 20.0	7♈ 3.8	3 6.9	17 34.2	12 12.8	2 5.7	19 7.8	3 16.8	26 40.6	24 53.3
30 S	16 37 40.7	8 21.8	6 16.8	19 22.9	4 41.4	18 46.0	12 48.5	2 14.1	19 5.6	3 18.9	26 42.8	24 54.2
DECLINATION at NOON												
1 F	14 43 20.5	14S32.7	3N 6.1	2S 0.9	6S 3.9	23S53.3	3N 7.2	2N 0.7	5N32.3	0S 8.9	17S33.5	16N 3.5
4 M	14 55 10.2	15 29.0	3 2.3	15N 7.2	7 26.3	24 24.4	2 23.8	1 48.0	5 27.8	0 12.6	17 35.1	16 2.6
7 T	15 6 59.9	16 23.1	2 58.6	26 31.1	9 4.2	24 49.2	1 40.5	1 35.5	5 23.5	0 16.2	17 36.7	16 1.9
10 S	15 18 49.5	17 14.7	2 54.8	27 33.2	10 50.0	25 7.6	0 57.2	1 23.3	5 19.4	0 19.7	17 38.3	16 1.2
13 W	15 30 39.2	18 3.6	2 51.0	17 28.7	12 38.0	25 19.5	0 14.0	1 11.4	5 15.6	0 23.0	17 39.9	16 0.7
16 S	15 42 28.9	18 49.7	2 47.3	0S 15.3	14 24.6	25 24.7	0S 29.0	0 59.9	5 12.1	0 26.2	17 41.4	16 0.3
19 T	15 54 18.6	19 32.8	2 43.5	19 24.1	16 7.3	25 23.2	1 11.8	0 48.8	5 8.8	0 29.3	17 43.0	16 0.1
22 F	16 6 8.2	20 12.7	2 39.7	28 30.1	17 44.2	25 15.0	1 54.4	0 38.0	5 5.9	0 32.2	17 44.6	16 0.0
25 M	16 17 57.9	20 49.3	2 36.0	20 20.4	19 14.0	25 0.3	2 36.7	0 27.7	5 3.3	0 35.0	17 46.1	16 0.1
28 T	16 29 47.6	21 22.3	2 32.2	3 16.7	20 35.6	24 39.0	3 18.6	0 17.8	5 1.0	0 37.5	17 47.7	16 0.2

DECEMBER 1968

DAY	EPHEMERIS SIDEREAL TIME	☉	☊	☽	☿	♀	♂	♃	♄	♅	♆	♇
LONGITUDE at NOON												
1 S	16 41 37.3	9♐22.7	6♈13.6	1♉31.5	6♐15.9	19♑57.7	13♎24.3	2♎22.4	19♈ 3.4	3♎21.0	26♏45.0	24♍55.1
2 M	16 45 33.8	10 23.5	6 10.5	13 32.7	7 50.2	21 9.4	13 60.0	2 30.6	19R 1.3	3 23.0	26 47.3	24 56.0
3 T	16 49 30.4	11 24.3	6 7.3	25 29.0	9 24.5	22 21.0	14 35.6	2 38.6	18 59.3	3 24.9	26 49.5	24 56.8
4 W	16 53 26.9	12 25.2	6 4.1	7♊22.6	10 58.8	23 32.5	15 11.2	2 46.5	18 57.4	3 26.9	26 51.6	24 57.6
5 T	16 57 23.5	13 26.1	6 0.9	19 14.9	12 33.0	24 43.9	15 46.8	2 54.3	18 55.7	3 28.7	26 53.8	24 58.3
6 F	17 1 20.0	14 26.9	5 57.8	1♋ 7.4	14 7.2	25 55.2	16 22.3	3 2.0	18 54.0	3 30.5	26 56.0	24 59.1
7 S	17 5 16.6	15 27.9	5 54.6	13 1.2	15 41.4	27 6.5	16 57.8	3 9.5	18 52.4	3 32.3	26 58.2	24 59.7
8 S	17 9 13.2	16 28.8	5 51.4	24 58.3	17 15.7	28 17.7	17 33.3	3 16.9	18 50.9	3 34.0	27 0.3	25 0.4
9 M	17 13 9.7	17 29.7	5 48.2	7♌ 0.6	18 50.0	29 28.8	18 8.7	3 24.2	18 49.6	3 35.7	27 2.5	25 1.0
10 T	17 17 6.3	18 30.7	5 45.1	19 11.2	20 24.3	0♒39.8	18 44.0	3 31.3	18 48.3	3 37.3	27 4.6	25 1.6
11 W	17 21 2.8	19 31.7	5 41.9	1♍33.5	21 58.7	1 50.7	19 19.4	3 38.3	18 47.2	3 38.9	27 6.7	25 2.2
12 T	17 24 59.4	20 32.7	5 38.7	14 11.6	23 33.1	3 1.6	19 54.6	3 45.1	18 46.1	3 40.4	27 8.8	25 2.7
13 F	17 28 56.0	21 33.7	5 35.5	27 9.9	25 7.7	4 12.3	20 29.8	3 51.8	18 45.2	3 41.8	27 10.9	25 3.2
14 S	17 32 52.5	22 34.8	5 32.4	10♎32.4	26 42.4	5 23.0	21 5.0	3 58.3	18 44.4	3 43.2	27 13.0	25 3.7
15 S	17 36 49.1	23 35.8	5 29.2	24 22.4	28 17.2	6 33.5	21 40.1	4 4.7	18 43.7	3 44.6	27 15.1	25 4.1
16 M	17 40 45.6	24 36.9	5 26.0	8♏41.0	29 52.1	7 44.0	22 15.2	4 11.0	18 43.0	3 45.9	27 17.2	25 4.5
17 T	17 44 42.2	25 38.0	5 22.8	23 26.5	1♑27.1	8 54.3	22 50.2	4 17.1	18 42.5	3 47.1	27 19.2	25 4.8
18 W	17 48 38.7	26 39.1	5 19.6	8♐33.5	3 2.3	10 4.6	23 25.2	4 23.0	18 42.2	3 48.3	27 21.2	25 5.2
19 T	17 52 35.3	27 40.2	5 16.5	23 53.1	4 37.6	11 14.7	24 0.1	4 28.8	18 41.9	3 49.5	27 23.2	25 5.4
20 F	17 56 31.9	28 41.3	5 13.3	9♑13.8	6 13.1	12 24.8	24 35.0	4 34.5	18 41.8	3 50.6	27 25.3	25 5.7
21 S	18 0 28.4	29 42.5	5 10.1	24 23.7	7 48.7	13 34.7	25 9.8	4 40.0	18 41.7	3 51.6	27 27.3	25 6.0
22 S	18 4 25.0	0♑43.6	5 6.9	9♒12.8	9 24.4	14 44.4	25 44.5	4 45.3	18D41.8	3 52.6	27 29.2	25 6.2
23 M	18 8 21.5	1 44.7	5 3.8	23 34.4	11 0.2	15 54.1	26 19.2	4 50.4	18 41.9	3 53.5	27 31.2	25 6.3
24 T	18 12 18.1	2 45.9	5 0.6	7♓25.7	12 36.0	17 3.6	26 53.8	4 55.4	18 42.2	3 54.4	27 33.1	25 6.4
25 W	18 16 14.7	3 47.0	4 57.4	20 47.3	14 12.0	18 12.9	27 28.3	5 0.2	18 42.6	3 55.2	27 35.0	25 6.5
26 T	18 20 11.2	4 48.2	4 54.2	3♈42.1	15 47.9	19 22.1	28 2.8	5 4.9	18 43.1	3 55.9	27 36.9	25 6.6
27 F	18 24 7.8	5 49.3	4 51.1	16 14.8	17 23.8	20 31.2	28 37.2	5 9.4	18 43.7	3 56.6	27 38.8	25 6.6
28 S	18 28 4.3	6 50.5	4 47.9	28 30.3	18 59.6	21 40.1	29 11.6	5 13.7	18 44.5	3 57.2	27 40.7	25 6.6
29 S	18 32 0.9	7 51.6	4 44.7	10♉33.6	20 35.3	22 48.8	29 45.9	5 17.8	18 45.3	3 57.8	27 42.5	25R 6.5
30 M	18 35 57.5	8 52.7	4 41.5	22 29.2	22 10.7	23 57.4	0♏20.1	5 21.8	18 46.3	3 58.3	27 44.3	25 6.4
31 T	18 39 54.0	9 53.9	4 38.4	4♊20.9	23 45.7	25 5.8	0 54.2	5 25.6	18 47.3	3 58.8	27 46.1	25 6.3
DECLINATION at NOON												
1 S	16 41 37.3	21S51.7	2N28.4	13N55.0	21S48.4	24S11.4	4S 0.2	0N 8.3	4N59.1	0S40.0	17S49.2	16N 0.5
4 W	16 53 26.9	22 17.4	2 24.6	25 50.5	22 51.5	23 37.6	4 41.5	0S 0.7	4 57.5	0 42.2	17 50.6	16 1.0
7 S	17 5 16.6	22 39.1	2 20.9	27 46.6	23 44.3	22 58.0	5 22.2	0 9.2	4 56.4	0 44.3	17 52.1	16 1.6
10 T	17 17 6.3	22 56.9	2 17.1	18 35.2	24 26.2	22 12.6	6 2.6	0 17.2	4 55.5	0 46.2	17 53.5	16 2.3
13 F	17 28 56.0	23 10.6	2 13.3	1 51.9	24 56.5	21 21.9	6 42.4	0 24.7	4 55.1	0 47.9	17 54.9	16 3.1
16 M	17 40 45.6	23 20.2	2 9.5	16S57.4	25 14.6	20 26.1	7 21.7	0 31.7	4 55.0	0 49.4	17 56.2	16 4.1
19 T	17 52 35.3	23 25.5	2 5.8	28 11.6	25 20.1	19 25.6	8 0.5	0 38.1	4 55.4	0 50.7	17 57.5	16 5.2
22 S	18 4 25.0	23 26.6	2 2.0	21 57.8	25 12.2	18 20.7	8 38.6	0 43.9	4 56.1	0 51.8	17 58.8	16 6.4
25 W	18 16 14.7	23 23.5	1 58.2	4 47.7	24 50.8	17 11.7	9 16.0	0 49.1	4 57.2	0 52.7	18 0.0	16 7.8
28 S	18 28 4.3	23 16.1	1 54.4	12N49.2	24 15.5	15 59.1	9 52.8	0 53.7	4 58.7	0 53.5	18 1.2	16 9.2
31 T	18 39 54.0	23 4.6	1 50.6	25 15.5	23 26.3	14 43.1	10 28.8	0 57.7	5 0.5	0 54.0	18 2.3	16 10.8

JANUARY 1969

DAY	EPHEMERIS SIDEREAL TIME	☉	☊	☽	☿	♀	♂	♃	♄	♅	♆	♇
	h m s	° ′	° ′	° ′	° ′	° ′	° ′	° ′	° ′	° ′	° ′	° ′
						LONGITUDE at NOON						
1 W	18 43 50.6	10♑55.0	4♈35.2	16♓11.9	25♑20.3	26♒14.0	1♏28.3	5♎29.2	18♈48.5	3♎59.2	27♏47.9	25♍ 6.2
2 T	18 47 47.1	11 56.1	4 32.0	28 4.3	26 54.2	27 22.0	2 2.3	5 32.7	18 49.8	3 59.5	27 49.6	25R 6.0
3 F	18 51 43.7	12 57.3	4 28.8	9♋59.8	28 27.3	28 29.8	2 36.3	5 35.9	18 51.1	3 59.8	27 51.3	25 5.8
4 S	18 55 40.3	13 58.4	4 25.6	21 59.6	29 59.4	29 37.4	3 10.2	5 39.0	18 52.6	4 0.1	27 53.0	25 5.5
5 S	18 59 36.8	14 59.6	4 22.5	4♌ 4.8	1♒30.2	0♓44.8	3 44.0	5 41.9	18 54.2	4 0.3	27 54.7	25 5.2
6 M	19 3 33.4	16 0.7	4 19.3	16 16.3	2 59.4	1 52.1	4 17.7	5 44.7	18 56.0	4 0.4	27 56.4	25 4.9
7 T	19 7 29.9	17 1.8	4 16.1	28 35.8	4 26.6	2 59.1	4 51.4	5 47.2	18 57.8	4 0.4	27 58.0	25 4.6
8 W	19 11 26.5	18 3.0	4 12.9	11♍ 5.4	5 51.6	4 5.8	5 25.0	5 49.6	18 59.7	4 0.5	27 59.6	25 4.2
9 T	19 15 23.0	19 4.1	4 9.8	23 47.6	7 13.8	5 12.4	5 58.5	5 51.8	19 1.7	4R 0.4	28 1.2	25 3.8
10 F	19 19 19.6	20 5.3	4 6.6	6♎45.8	8 32.7	6 18.7	6 32.0	5 53.8	19 3.9	4 0.4	28 2.8	25 3.4
11 S	19 23 16.2	21 6.4	4 3.4	20 3.2	9 47.7	7 24.8	7 5.3	5 55.6	19 6.2	4 0.2	28 4.4	25 2.9
12 S	19 27 12.7	22 7.5	4 0.2	3♏42.9	10 58.2	8 30.6	7 38.6	5 57.2	19 8.5	3 60.0	28 5.9	25 2.4
13 M	19 31 9.3	23 8.7	3 57.1	17 46.7	12 3.4	9 36.2	8 11.8	5 58.7	19 11.0	3 59.7	28 7.3	25 1.8
14 T	19 35 5.8	24 9.8	3 53.9	2♐14.4	13 2.5	10 41.5	8 44.9	5 59.9	19 13.5	3 59.4	28 8.8	25 1.3
15 W	19 39 2.4	25 10.9	3 50.7	17 3.0	13 54.8	11 46.5	9 17.9	6 1.0	19 16.2	3 59.0	28 10.2	25 0.7
16 T	19 42 59.0	26 12.1	3 47.5	2♑ 6.2	14 39.3	12 51.3	9 50.8	6 1.8	19 18.9	3 58.6	28 11.6	25 0.0
17 F	19 46 55.5	27 13.2	3 44.4	17 15.1	15 15.1	13 55.8	10 23.6	6 2.5	19 21.8	3 58.1	28 13.0	24 59.4
18 S	19 50 52.1	28 14.3	3 41.2	2♒19.1	15 41.4	14 59.9	10 56.3	6 3.0	19 24.8	3 57.5	28 14.4	24 58.7
19 S	19 54 48.6	29 15.4	3 38.0	17 8.1	15 57.5	16 3.8	11 28.9	6 3.3	19 27.8	3 56.9	28 15.7	24 57.9
20 M	19 58 45.2	0♒16.5	3 34.8	1♓34.3	16 2.6	17 7.3	12 1.5	6 3.4	19 31.0	3 56.3	28 17.0	24 57.2
21 T	20 2 41.7	1 17.5	3 31.7	15 32.9	15R56.3	18 10.5	12 33.9	6R 3.3	19 34.3	3 55.5	28 18.2	24 56.4
22 W	20 6 38.3	2 18.6	3 28.5	29 2.6	15 38.3	19 13.4	13 6.2	6 3.0	19 37.6	3 54.8	28 19.5	24 55.6
23 T	20 10 34.9	3 19.6	3 25.3	12♈ 4.9	15 8.9	20 15.8	13 38.4	6 2.5	19 41.1	3 54.0	28 20.7	24 54.7
24 F	20 14 31.4	4 20.7	3 22.1	24 43.1	14 28.6	21 17.9	14 10.5	6 1.8	19 44.6	3 53.1	28 21.8	24 53.9
25 S	20 18 28.0	5 21.7	3 18.9	7♉ 2.1	13 38.1	22 19.7	14 42.5	6 1.0	19 48.3	3 52.2	28 23.0	24 53.0
26 S	20 22 24.5	6 22.7	3 15.8	19 6.8	12 38.9	23 21.0	15 14.4	5 59.9	19 52.0	3 51.2	28 24.1	24 52.0
27 M	20 26 21.1	7 23.6	3 12.6	1♊ 2.4	11 32.6	24 21.9	15 46.1	5 58.7	19 55.8	3 50.2	28 25.2	24 51.1
28 T	20 30 17.6	8 24.6	3 9.4	12 53.7	10 21.2	25 22.3	16 17.8	5 57.2	19 59.8	3 49.1	28 26.2	24 50.1
29 W	20 34 14.2	9 25.5	3 6.2	24 44.7	9 6.9	26 22.4	16 49.3	5 55.6	20 3.8	3 47.9	28 27.2	24 49.1
30 T	20 38 10.8	10 26.4	3 3.1	6♋38.8	7 51.9	27 21.9	17 20.7	5 53.8	20 7.9	3 46.8	28 28.2	24 48.1
31 F	20 42 7.3	11 27.4	2 59.9	18 38.6	6 38.4	28 21.0	17 52.1	5 51.8	20 12.1	3 45.6	28 29.2	24 47.1
						DECLINATION at NOON						
1 W	18 43 50.6	22S59.8	1N49.4	27N26.6	23S 6.9	14S17.2	10S40.7	0S58.9	5N 1.2	0S54.1	18S 2.7	16N11.4
4 S	18 55 40.3	22 42.7	1 45.6	26 19.7	22 0.2	12 57.4	11 15.8	1 2.1	5 3.6	0 54.3	18 3.7	16 13.1
7 T	19 7 29.9	22 21.6	1 41.8	14 38.8	20 42.1	11 35.2	11 50.1	1 4.6	5 6.3	0 54.4	18 4.7	16 14.9
10 F	19 19 19.6	21 56.5	1 38.0	2S58.8	19 15.6	10 10.9	12 23.6	1 6.4	5 9.4	0 54.2	18 5.6	16 16.8
13 M	19 31 9.3	21 27.6	1 34.3	20 32.8	17 45.7	8 44.9	12 56.3	1 7.6	5 12.8	0 53.9	18 6.5	16 18.8
16 T	19 42 59.0	20 55.0	1 30.5	28 27.9	16 20.1	7 17.4	13 28.1	1 8.1	5 16.6	0 53.3	18 7.3	16 20.8
19 S	19 54 48.6	20 18.7	1 26.7	19 7.1	15 8.8	5 49.0	13 59.1	1 7.9	5 20.6	0 52.6	18 8.1	16 23.0
22 W	20 6 38.3	19 39.0	1 22.9	0 37.6	14 22.5	4 19.8	14 29.1	1 7.0	5 25.1	0 51.6	18 8.8	16 25.2
25 S	20 18 28.0	18 56.0	1 19.1	16N37.9	14 8.5	2 50.4	14 58.2	1 5.5	5 29.8	0 50.5	18 9.4	16 27.5
28 T	20 30 17.6	18 10.0	1 15.3	27 7.7	14 26.3	1 21.0	15 26.4	1 3.2	5 34.8	0 49.2	18 10.0	16 29.8
31 F	20 42 7.3	17 20.9	1 11.5	26 58.2	15 6.8	0N 8.1	15 53.6	1 0.4	5 40.1	0 47.7	18 10.5	16 32.2

FEBRUARY 1969

DAY	EPHEMERIS SIDEREAL TIME	☉	☊	☽	☿	♀	♂	♃	♄	♅	♆	♇
						LONGITUDE at NOON						
1 S	20 46 3.9	12♒28.2	2♈56.7	0♌46.0	5♒28.2	29♓19.6	18♏23.2	5♎49.6	20♈16.4	3♎44.3	28♏30.1	24♍46.0
2 S	20 50 0.4	13 29.1	2 53.5	13 2.1	4R23.0	0♈17.7	18 54.3	5R47.3	20 20.8	3R43.0	28 31.0	24R44.9
3 M	20 53 57.0	14 29.9	2 50.4	25 27.7	3 24.2	1 15.2	19 25.2	5 44.7	20 25.2	3 41.6	28 31.9	24 43.8
4 T	20 57 53.5	15 30.7	2 47.2	8♍ 3.4	2 32.7	2 12.2	19 56.0	5 42.0	20 29.8	3 40.2	28 32.7	24 42.6
5 W	21 1 50.1	16 31.5	2 44.0	20 49.8	1 49.2	3 8.6	20 26.7	5 39.0	20 34.4	3 38.7	28 33.5	24 41.4
6 T	21 5 46.7	17 32.3	2 40.8	3♎47.7	1 13.9	4 4.4	20 57.2	5 35.9	20 39.1	3 37.2	28 34.3	24 40.2
7 F	21 9 43.2	18 33.1	2 37.6	16 58.4	0 47.0	4 59.6	21 27.6	5 32.6	20 43.9	3 35.7	28 35.0	24 39.0
8 S	21 13 39.8	19 33.8	2 34.5	0♏23.2	0 28.4	5 54.1	21 57.8	5 29.2	20 48.7	3 34.1	28 35.7	24 37.8
9 S	21 17 36.3	20 34.6	2 31.3	14 3.6	0 17.8	6 48.1	22 27.9	5 25.5	20 53.7	3 32.4	28 36.4	24 36.5
10 M	21 21 32.9	21 35.3	2 28.1	28 0.3	0 14.8	7 41.3	22 57.9	5 21.7	20 58.7	3 30.7	28 37.0	24 35.2
11 T	21 25 29.4	22 36.0	2 24.9	12♐13.1	0D19.1	8 33.9	23 27.7	5 17.7	21 3.8	3 29.0	28 37.6	24 33.9
12 W	21 29 26.0	23 36.7	2 21.8	26 40.3	0 30.2	9 25.7	23 57.3	5 13.6	21 9.0	3 27.2	28 38.2	24 32.6
13 T	21 33 22.5	24 37.3	2 18.6	11♑17.9	0 47.6	10 16.8	24 26.8	5 9.2	21 14.2	3 25.4	28 38.7	24 31.3
14 F	21 37 19.1	25 38.0	2 15.4	26 0.4	1 10.8	11 7.0	24 56.1	5 4.7	21 19.6	3 23.6	28 39.2	24 29.9
15 S	21 41 15.7	26 38.6	2 12.2	10♒40.5	1 39.5	11 56.5	25 25.3	5 0.1	21 25.0	3 21.7	28 39.7	24 28.5
16 S	21 45 12.2	27 39.2	2 9.0	25 11.0	2 13.2	12 45.2	25 54.2	4 55.3	21 30.4	3 19.7	28 40.1	24 27.1
17 M	21 49 8.8	28 39.8	2 5.9	9♓25.3	2 51.4	13 33.0	26 23.0	4 50.3	21 36.0	3 17.8	28 40.5	24 25.7
18 T	21 53 5.3	29 40.3	2 2.7	23 18.3	3 33.9	14 19.8	26 51.6	4 45.2	21 41.6	3 15.8	28 40.8	24 24.3
19 W	21 57 1.9	0♓40.8	1 59.5	6♈47.7	4 20.3	15 5.7	27 20.1	4 39.9	21 47.3	3 13.7	28 41.2	24 22.8
20 T	22 0 58.4	1 41.3	1 56.3	19 53.1	5 10.3	15 50.6	27 48.3	4 34.5	21 53.0	3 11.7	28 41.5	24 21.4
21 F	22 4 55.0	2 41.8	1 53.2	2♉36.1	6 3.6	16 34.6	28 16.4	4 28.9	21 58.9	3 9.6	28 41.8	24 20.0
22 S	22 8 51.5	3 42.3	1 50.0	14 59.9	6 60.0	17 17.4	28 44.2	4 23.2	22 4.8	3 7.5	28 42.0	24 18.5
23 S	22 12 48.1	4 42.6	1 46.8	27 8.7	7 59.2	17 59.1	29 11.9	4 17.4	22 10.7	3 5.3	28 42.2	24 17.0
24 M	22 16 44.6	5 43.0	1 43.6	9♊ 7.2	9 1.0	18 39.7	29 39.3	4 11.4	22 16.7	3 3.1	28 42.3	24 15.5
25 T	22 20 41.2	6 43.3	1 40.5	21 0.2	10 5.3	19 19.0	0♐ 6.5	4 5.3	22 22.8	3 0.9	28 42.4	24 13.9
26 W	22 24 37.8	7 43.6	1 37.3	2♋52.4	11 11.9	19 57.1	0 33.6	3 59.1	22 28.9	2 58.6	28 42.5	24 12.4
27 T	22 28 34.3	8 43.9	1 34.1	14 48.2	12 20.6	20 33.9	1 0.4	3 52.7	22 35.1	2 56.3	28 42.6	24 10.9
28 F	22 32 30.9	9 44.1	1 30.9	26 51.4	13 31.4	21 9.3	1 27.0	3 46.3	22 41.3	2 54.0	28 42.6	24 9.3
						DECLINATION at NOON						
1 S	20 46 3.9	17S 4.0	1N10.3	24N19.6	15S23.1	0N37.6	16S 2.5	0S59.3	5N41.9	0S47.1	18S10.6	16N33.0
4 T	20 57 53.5	16 11.4	1 6.5	10 24.5	16 14.0	2 5.5	16 28.5	0 55.5	5 47.6	0 45.4	18 11.0	16 35.4
7 F	21 9 43.2	15 16.2	1 2.7	7S59.6	17 1.5	3 32.1	16 53.5	0 51.1	5 53.5	0 43.5	18 11.4	16 37.8
10 M	21 21 32.9	14 18.7	0 58.9	23 57.2	17 40.7	4 57.2	17 17.5	0 46.1	5 59.6	0 41.5	18 11.7	16 40.3
13 T	21 33 22.5	13 19.1	0 55.1	28 2.0	18 9.1	6 20.3	17 40.5	0 40.5	6 6.0	0 39.3	18 11.9	16 42.8
16 S	21 45 12.2	12 17.5	0 51.3	15 57.7	18 25.8	7 41.1	18 2.6	0 34.4	6 12.6	0 37.0	18 12.0	16 45.2
19 W	21 57 1.9	11 14.1	0 47.5	3N13.7	18 30.4	8 59.1	18 23.7	0 27.7	6 19.4	0 34.6	18 12.1	16 47.7
22 S	22 8 51.5	10 9.1	0 43.8	19 50.7	18 22.9	10 13.9	18 43.8	0 20.6	6 26.5	0 32.0	18 12.1	16 50.1
25 T	22 20 41.2	9 2.8	0 40.0	28 17.4	18 3.1	11 24.9	19 3.0	0 12.9	6 33.6	0 29.3	18 12.0	16 52.5
28 F	22 32 30.9	7 55.3	0 36.2	25 23.5	17 31.2	12 31.6	19 21.2	0 4.9	6 41.0	0 26.6	18 11.9	16 54.9

MARCH 1969

DAY	EPHEMERIS SIDEREAL TIME	☉	☊	☽	☿	♀	♂	♃	♄	♅	♆	♇
	h m s	° ′	° ′	° ′	° ′	° ′	° ′	° ′	° ′	° ′	° ′	° ′
						LONGITUDE at NOON						
1 S	22 36 27.4	10♓44.3	1♈27.7	9♌ 4.9	14♒44.1	21♈43.3	1♐53.3	3♎39.7	22♈47.6	2♎51.7	28♏42.6	24♍ 7.7
2 S	22 40 24.0	11 44.5	1 24.6	21 31.0	15 58.6	22 15.8	2 19.5	3R33.0	22 54.0	2R49.3	28R42.5	24R 6.2
3 M	22 44 20.5	12 44.6	1 21.4	4♍11.0	17 14.8	22 46.8	2 45.4	3 26.2	23 0.4	2 47.0	28 42.5	24 4.6
4 T	22 48 17.1	13 44.7	1 18.2	17 5.4	18 32.6	23 16.3	3 11.0	3 19.4	23 6.8	2 44.6	28 42.4	24 3.0
5 W	22 52 13.6	14 44.8	1 15.0	0♎14.1	19 52.1	23 44.1	3 36.5	3 12.4	23 13.3	2 42.1	28 42.2	24 1.4
6 T	22 56 10.2	15 44.9	1 11.9	13 36.2	21 13.0	24 10.2	4 1.6	3 5.3	23 19.9	2 39.7	28 42.0	23 59.8
7 F	23 0 6.7	16 44.9	1 8.7	27 10.6	22 35.4	24 34.5	4 26.5	2 58.2	23 26.5	2 37.2	28 41.8	23 58.2
8 S	23 4 3.3	17 44.9	1 5.5	10♏56.2	23 59.3	24 57.0	4 51.2	2 50.9	23 33.1	2 34.7	28 41.6	23 56.6
9 S	23 7 59.9	18 44.8	1 2.3	24 51.4	25 24.5	25 17.7	5 15.6	2 43.6	23 39.8	2 32.2	28 41.3	23 55.0
10 M	23 11 56.4	19 44.8	0 59.1	8♐54.7	26 51.0	25 36.4	5 39.7	2 36.3	23 46.6	2 29.7	28 41.0	23 53.4
11 T	23 15 53.0	20 44.7	0 56.0	23 4.6	28 18.9	25 53.2	6 3.5	2 28.8	23 53.4	2 27.2	28 40.6	23 51.7
12 W	23 19 49.5	21 44.5	0 52.8	7♑18.9	29 48.1	26 7.8	6 27.1	2 21.4	24 0.2	2 24.7	28 40.3	23 50.1
13 T	23 23 46.1	22 44.4	0 49.6	21 35.1	1♓18.6	26 20.4	6 50.3	2 13.8	24 7.1	2 22.1	28 39.8	23 48.5
14 F	23 27 42.6	23 44.3	0 46.4	5♒50.1	2 50.3	26 30.9	7 13.3	2 6.3	24 14.1	2 19.6	28 39.4	23 46.9
15 S	23 31 39.2	24 44.1	0 43.3	20 0.3	4 23.3	26 39.0	7 35.9	1 58.6	24 21.0	2 17.0	28 39.0	23 45.3
16 S	23 35 35.7	25 43.8	0 40.1	4♓ 1.9	5 57.6	26 44.9	7 58.2	1 50.9	24 28.0	2 14.4	28 38.5	23 43.7
17 M	23 39 32.3	26 43.6	0 36.9	17 51.3	7 33.0	26 48.5	8 20.1	1 43.2	24 35.1	2 11.8	28 37.9	23 42.0
18 T	23 43 28.8	27 43.3	0 33.7	1♈25.5	9 9.8	26 49.7	8 41.7	1 35.5	24 42.1	2 9.2	28 37.4	23 40.4
19 W	23 47 25.4	28 42.9	0 30.5	14 42.3	10 47.8	26R48.4	9 3.0	1 27.7	24 49.3	2 6.6	28 36.8	23 38.8
20 T	23 51 21.9	29 42.6	0 27.4	27 40.9	12 27.0	26 44.7	9 23.9	1 20.0	24 56.4	2 4.0	28 36.1	23 37.2
21 F	23 55 18.5	0♈42.2	0 24.2	10♉21.5	14 7.5	26 38.6	9 44.4	1 12.2	25 3.6	2 1.4	28 35.5	23 35.6
22 S	23 59 15.1	1 41.7	0 21.0	22 45.8	15 49.2	26 29.9	10 4.6	1 4.4	25 10.8	1 58.8	28 34.8	23 34.0
23 S	0 3 11.6	2 41.2	0 17.8	4♊56.3	17 32.3	26 18.7	10 24.4	0 56.6	25 18.0	1 56.2	28 34.1	23 32.4
24 M	0 7 8.2	3 40.7	0 14.7	16 56.8	19 16.6	26 5.1	10 43.9	0 48.9	25 25.3	1 53.6	28 33.3	23 30.8
25 T	0 11 4.7	4 40.2	0 11.5	28 51.1	21 2.2	25 48.9	11 2.9	0 41.1	25 32.6	1 51.0	28 32.6	23 29.2
26 W	0 15 1.3	5 39.6	0 8.3	10♋44.0	22 49.2	25 30.4	11 21.5	0 33.4	25 39.9	1 48.4	28 31.7	23 27.6
27 T	0 18 57.8	6 39.0	0 5.1	22 40.1	24 37.4	25 9.5	11 39.7	0 25.7	25 47.3	1 45.8	28 30.9	23 26.0
28 F	0 22 54.4	7 38.3	0 1.9	4♌44.0	26 27.0	24 46.2	11 57.5	0 18.0	25 54.6	1 43.2	28 30.1	23 24.4
29 S	0 26 50.9	8 37.6	29♓58.8	16 59.9	28 18.0	24 20.8	12 14.9	0 10.4	26 2.0	1 40.6	28 29.2	23 22.9
30 S	0 30 47.5	9 36.8	29 55.6	29 31.3	0♈10.3	23 53.3	12 31.9	0 2.8	26 9.5	1 38.0	28 28.3	23 21.3
31 M	0 34 44.0	10 36.1	29 52.4	12♍21.0	2 3.9	23 23.9	12 48.4	29♍55.2	26 16.9	1 35.5	28 27.3	23 19.8
						DECLINATION at NOON						
1 S	22 36 27.4	7S32.5	0N34.9	21N56.0	17S17.9	12N52.8	19S27.1	0S 2.2	6N43.4	0S25.6	18S11.9	16N55.7
4 T	22 48 17.1	6 23.6	0 31.1	6 12.2	16 30.1	13 52.7	19 44.2	0N 6.3	6 51.0	0 22.8	18 11.6	16 58.1
7 F	23 0 6.7	5 14.0	0 27.3	12S42.0	15 30.5	14 46.7	20 0.3	0 15.1	6 58.6	0 19.8	18 11.4	17 0.3
10 M	23 11 56.4	4 3.7	0 23.5	26 38.6	14 19.2	15 33.9	20 15.7	0 24.1	7 6.4	0 16.8	18 11.0	17 2.6
13 T	23 23 46.1	2 52.9	0 19.7	26 34.0	12 56.4	16 13.5	20 30.2	0 33.3	7 14.3	0 13.8	18 10.6	17 4.7
16 S	23 35 35.7	1 41.9	0 16.0	12 12.6	11 22.4	16 44.3	20 43.9	0 42.5	7 22.2	0 10.7	18 10.2	17 6.8
19 W	23 47 25.4	0 30.7	0 12.2	7N 0.9	9 37.3	17 5.1	20 56.9	0 51.9	7 30.3	0 7.6	18 9.7	17 8.8
22 S	23 59 15.1	0N40.5	0 8.4	22 31.2	7 41.5	17 14.7	21 9.2	1 1.3	7 38.4	0 4.5	18 9.1	17 10.7
25 T	0 11 4.7	1 51.4	0 4.6	28 43.1	5 35.3	17 11.8	21 20.8	1 10.6	7 46.6	0 1.4	18 8.5	17 12.5
28 F	0 22 54.4	3 1.9	0 0.8	23 18.6	3 19.0	16 55.7	21 31.8	1 19.7	7 54.8	0N 1.7	18 7.8	17 14.2
31 M	0 34 44.0	4 11.9	0S 3.0	8 26.0	0 53.2	16 25.9	21 42.3	1 28.7	8 3.0	0 4.7	18 7.1	17 15.8

APRIL 1969

DAY	EPHEMERIS SIDEREAL TIME	☉	☊	☽	☿	♀	♂	♃	♄	♅	♆	♇
						LONGITUDE at NOON						
1 T	0 38 40.6	11♈35.2	29♓49.2	25♍30.3	3♈58.9	22♈52.7	13♐ 4.4	29♍47.7	26♈24.4	1♎32.9	28♏26.3	23♍18.3
2 W	0 42 37.1	12 34.4	29 46.1	8♎59.5	5 55.2	22R19.8	13 20.0	29R40.3	26 31.8	1R30.4	28R25.4	23R16.8
3 T	0 46 33.7	13 33.5	29 42.9	22 46.9	7 52.9	21 45.6	13 35.1	29 32.9	26 39.3	1 27.8	28 24.3	23 15.2
4 F	0 50 30.3	14 32.6	29 39.7	6♏49.7	9 51.9	21 10.2	13 49.8	29 25.6	26 46.9	1 25.3	28 23.3	23 13.8
5 S	0 54 26.8	15 31.7	29 36.5	21 3.8	11 52.0	20 33.7	14 4.0	29 18.4	26 54.4	1 22.8	28 22.3	23 12.3
6 S	0 58 23.4	16 30.7	29 33.3	5♐24.5	13 53.4	19 56.6	14 17.6	29 11.2	27 2.0	1 20.3	28 21.2	23 10.9
7 M	1 2 19.9	17 29.7	29 30.2	19 47.1	15 55.8	19 18.9	14 30.7	29 4.1	27 9.5	1 17.9	28 20.1	23 9.4
8 T	1 6 16.5	18 28.6	29 27.0	4♑ 7.4	17 59.3	18 41.1	14 43.3	28 57.1	27 17.1	1 15.4	28 18.9	23 8.0
9 W	1 10 13.0	19 27.6	29 23.8	18 22.0	20 3.7	18 3.2	14 55.3	28 50.2	27 24.7	1 13.0	28 17.8	23 6.5
10 T	1 14 9.6	20 26.5	29 20.6	2♒28.3	22 8.8	17 25.7	15 6.8	28 43.4	27 32.3	1 10.5	28 16.6	23 5.1
11 F	1 18 6.1	21 25.3	29 17.5	16 24.8	24 14.5	16 48.6	15 17.7	28 36.7	27 39.9	1 8.1	28 15.4	23 3.7
12 S	1 22 2.7	22 24.2	29 14.3	0♓10.5	26 20.5	16 12.3	15 28.0	28 30.1	27 47.5	1 5.7	28 14.1	23 2.4
13 S	1 25 59.2	23 23.0	29 11.1	13 44.7	28 26.7	15 37.0	15 37.8	28 23.6	27 55.1	1 3.4	28 12.9	23 1.0
14 M	1 29 55.8	24 21.8	29 7.9	27 6.9	0♉32.8	15 3.0	15 46.9	28 17.2	28 2.8	1 1.1	28 11.6	22 59.7
15 T	1 33 52.3	25 20.5	29 4.8	10♈16.6	2 38.5	14 30.3	15 55.4	28 10.9	28 10.4	0 58.7	28 10.3	22 58.3
16 W	1 37 48.9	26 19.3	29 1.6	23 13.4	4 43.5	13 59.2	16 3.2	28 4.7	28 18.0	0 56.5	28 9.0	22 57.0
17 T	1 41 45.5	27 17.9	28 58.4	5♉57.1	6 47.5	13 29.8	16 10.5	27 58.7	28 25.7	0 54.2	28 7.7	22 55.8
18 F	1 45 42.0	28 16.6	28 55.2	18 27.8	8 50.1	13 2.4	16 17.0	27 52.8	28 33.3	0 52.0	28 6.3	22 54.5
19 S	1 49 38.6	29 15.2	28 52.0	0♊46.3	10 51.0	12 37.0	16 22.9	27 47.0	28 40.9	0 49.8	28 5.0	22 53.3
20 S	1 53 35.1	0♉13.8	28 48.9	12 54.1	12 49.9	12 13.7	16 28.2	27 41.4	28 48.6	0 47.6	28 3.6	22 52.0
21 M	1 57 31.7	1 12.4	28 45.7	24 53.4	14 46.5	11 52.6	16 32.8	27 35.9	28 56.2	0 45.5	28 2.2	22 50.8
22 T	2 1 28.2	2 10.9	28 42.5	6♋47.2	16 40.5	11 33.8	16 36.7	27 30.5	29 3.8	0 43.4	28 0.8	22 49.7
23 W	2 5 24.8	3 9.4	28 39.3	18 39.4	18 31.5	11 17.4	16 39.8	27 25.3	29 11.5	0 41.3	27 59.4	22 48.5
24 T	2 9 21.3	4 7.8	28 36.2	0♌34.1	20 19.4	11 3.4	16 42.3	27 20.2	29 19.1	0 39.2	27 57.9	22 47.4
25 F	2 13 17.9	5 6.3	28 33.0	12 36.3	22 3.9	10 51.9	16 44.2	27 15.4	29 26.8	0 37.3	27 56.5	22 46.3
26 S	2 17 14.5	6 4.7	28 29.8	24 50.6	23 44.8	10 42.7	16 45.2	27 10.6	29 34.4	0 35.3	27 55.0	22 45.2
27 S	2 21 11.0	7 3.0	28 26.6	7♍21.9	25 21.9	10 36.0	16 45.6	27 6.0	29 42.0	0 33.4	27 53.5	22 44.2
28 M	2 25 7.6	8 1.3	28 23.4	20 14.0	26 55.1	10 31.7	16R45.2	27 1.5	29 49.6	0 31.5	27 52.0	22 43.1
29 T	2 29 4.1	8 59.6	28 20.3	3♎30.2	28 24.2	10 29.7	16 44.1	26 57.3	29 57.1	0 29.6	27 50.5	22 42.1
30 W	2 33 0.7	9 57.8	28 17.1	17 11.5	29 49.1	10D30.2	16 42.2	26 53.1	0♉ 4.7	0 27.8	27 49.0	22 41.1
						DECLINATION at NOON						
1 T	0 38 40.6	4N35.0	0S 4.3	2N11.5	0S 2.7	16N12.9	21S45.7	1N31.7	8N 5.8	0N 5.7	18S 6.8	17N16.4
4 F	0 50 30.3	5 44.0	0 8.1	16S45.6	2N34.0	15 25.8	21 55.6	1 40.3	8 14.0	0 8.7	18 6.0	17 17.8
7 M	1 2 19.9	6 52.2	0 11.9	28 12.2	5 17.0	14 27.8	22 5.1	1 48.7	8 22.3	0 11.7	18 5.2	17 19.2
10 T	1 14 9.6	7 59.2	0 15.7	23 56.2	8 3.6	13 21.7	22 14.2	1 56.7	8 30.5	0 14.5	18 4.3	17 20.4
13 S	1 25 59.2	9 5.1	0 19.5	7 46.2	10 50.1	12 11.0	22 22.9	2 4.3	8 38.7	0 17.3	18 3.4	17 21.5
16 W	1 37 48.9	10 9.7	0 23.2	10N55.7	13 31.3	10 59.5	22 31.4	2 11.4	8 46.9	0 20.0	18 2.5	17 22.5
19 S	1 49 38.6	11 12.7	0 27.0	24 45.5	16 1.8	9 50.6	22 39.6	2 18.1	8 55.1	0 22.6	18 1.5	17 23.3
22 T	2 1 28.2	12 14.1	0 30.8	28 25.3	18 16.1	8 47.3	22 47.6	2 24.2	9 3.2	0 25.1	18 0.5	17 24.0
25 F	2 13 17.9	13 13.6	0 34.6	20 40.9	20 10.4	7 51.7	22 55.4	2 29.8	9 11.2	0 27.4	17 59.5	17 24.6
28 M	2 25 7.6	14 11.2	0 38.4	4 39.6	21 42.5	7 5.2	23 3.1	2 34.8	9 19.1	0 29.7	17 58.4	17 25.0

MAY 1969

DAY	EPHEMERIS SIDEREAL TIME	☉	☊	☽	☿	♀	♂	♃	♄	♅	♆	♇
	h m s	° ′	° ′	° ′	° ′	° ′	° ′	° ′	° ′	° ′	° ′	° ′
						LONGITUDE at NOON						
1 T	2 36 57.2	10♉56.0	28♓13.9	1♏17.1	1♊ 9.7	10♈33.0	16♐39.6	26♍49.2	0♉12.3	0♎26.0	27♏47.5	22♍40.2
2 F	2 40 53.8	11 54.2	28 10.7	15 43.6	2 25.9	10 38.1	16R36.2	26R45.4	0 19.8	0R24.2	27R45.9	22R39.2
3 S	2 44 50.3	12 52.4	28 7.6	0♐25.0	3 37.7	10 45.4	16 32.1	26 41.7	0 27.3	0 22.5	27 44.4	22 38.3
4 S	2 48 46.9	13 50.5	28 4.4	15 13.7	4 44.9	10 55.0	16 27.3	26 38.3	0 34.9	0 20.9	27 42.8	22 37.4
5 M	2 52 43.5	14 48.6	28 1.2	0♑ 1.7	5 47.6	11 6.6	16 21.6	26 35.0	0 42.3	0 19.2	27 41.2	22 36.6
6 T	2 56 40.0	15 46.7	27 58.0	14 41.5	6 45.6	11 20.4	16 15.2	26 31.9	0 49.8	0 17.6	27 39.7	22 35.7
7 W	3 0 36.6	16 44.7	27 54.9	29 7.5	7 38.8	11 36.2	16 8.1	26 28.9	0 57.3	0 16.1	27 38.1	22 34.9
8 T	3 4 33.1	17 42.7	27 51.7	13♒16.3	8 27.2	11 53.9	16 0.2	26 26.2	1 4.7	0 14.6	27 36.5	22 34.1
9 F	3 8 29.7	18 40.7	27 48.5	27 6.7	9 10.8	12 13.5	15 51.5	26 23.6	1 12.1	0 13.1	27 34.9	22 33.4
10 S	3 12 26.2	19 38.7	27 45.3	10♓39.2	9 49.5	12 35.0	15 42.1	26 21.1	1 19.5	0 11.7	27 33.3	22 32.7
11 S	3 16 22.8	20 36.7	27 42.1	23 55.1	10 23.2	12 58.2	15 31.9	26 18.9	1 26.9	0 10.4	27 31.7	22 32.0
12 M	3 20 19.4	21 34.6	27 39.0	6♈56.3	10 52.0	13 23.0	15 21.0	26 16.8	1 34.3	0 9.0	27 30.0	22 31.3
13 T	3 24 15.9	22 32.6	27 35.8	19 44.7	11 15.7	13 49.6	15 9.3	26 14.9	1 41.6	0 7.8	27 28.4	22 30.7
14 W	3 28 12.5	23 30.5	27 32.6	2♉21.7	11 34.4	14 17.6	14 57.0	26 13.2	1 48.9	0 6.5	27 26.8	22 30.1
15 T	3 32 9.0	24 28.3	27 29.4	14 48.5	11 48.1	14 47.2	14 43.9	26 11.7	1 56.2	0 5.4	27 25.2	22 29.5
16 F	3 36 5.6	25 26.2	27 26.3	27 6.1	11 56.9	15 18.3	14 30.3	26 10.4	2 3.5	0 4.3	27 23.6	22 29.0
17 S	3 40 2.1	26 24.1	27 23.1	9♊15.3	12 0.7	15 50.7	14 15.9	26 9.3	2 10.7	0 3.2	27 22.0	22 28.5
18 S	3 43 58.7	27 21.9	27 19.9	21 17.0	11R59.7	16 24.5	14 0.9	26 8.3	2 17.9	0 2.1	27 20.3	22 28.0
19 M	3 47 55.2	28 19.6	27 16.7	3♋12.9	11 54.1	16 59.5	13 45.3	26 7.5	2 25.0	0 1.2	27 18.7	22 27.5
20 T	3 51 51.8	29 17.4	27 13.6	15 4.8	11 43.9	17 35.8	13 29.1	26 6.9	2 32.1	0 0.2	27 17.1	22 27.1
21 W	3 55 48.4	0♊15.1	27 10.4	26 55.7	11 29.6	18 13.3	13 12.4	26 6.5	2 39.2	29♍59.3	27 15.4	22 26.7
22 T	3 59 44.9	1 12.8	27 7.2	8♌49.0	11 11.3	18 51.9	12 55.2	26 6.2	2 46.3	29 58.5	27 13.8	22 26.4
23 F	4 3 41.5	2 10.5	27 4.0	20 49.0	10 49.4	19 31.5	12 37.5	26 6.2	2 53.3	29 57.7	27 12.2	22 26.0
24 S	4 7 38.0	3 8.2	27 0.8	3♍ 0.5	10 24.3	20 12.3	12 19.4	26D 6.3	3 0.3	29 57.0	27 10.6	22 25.7
25 S	4 11 34.6	4 5.8	26 57.7	15 28.4	9 56.4	20 54.1	12 0.8	26 6.6	3 7.2	29 56.3	27 9.0	22 25.5
26 M	4 15 31.2	5 3.4	26 54.5	28 17.7	9 26.2	21 36.8	11 41.9	26 7.1	3 14.1	29 55.6	27 7.4	22 25.2
27 T	4 19 27.7	6 1.0	26 51.3	11♎32.6	8 54.3	22 20.5	11 22.6	26 7.7	3 21.0	29 55.1	27 5.8	22 25.0
28 W	4 23 24.3	6 58.5	26 48.1	25 15.8	8 21.1	23 5.1	11 3.1	26 8.6	3 27.8	29 54.5	27 4.2	22 24.8
29 T	4 27 20.8	7 56.0	26 45.0	9♏27.9	7 47.4	23 50.5	10 43.3	26 9.6	3 34.6	29 54.0	27 2.6	22 24.7
30 F	4 31 17.4	8 53.5	26 41.8	24 6.0	7 13.6	24 36.8	10 23.3	26 10.8	3 41.3	29 53.6	27 1.0	22 24.6
31 S	4 35 13.9	9 51.0	26 38.6	9♐ 4.3	6 40.4	25 23.9	10 3.1	26 12.2	3 48.0	29 53.2	26 59.4	22 24.5
						DECLINATION at NOON						
1 T	2 36 57.2	15N 6.6	0S42.2	14S27.6	22N52.0	6N28.5	23S10.5	2N39.1	9N27.0	0N31.8	17S57.4	17N25.3
4 S	2 48 46.9	15 59.8	0 46.0	27 34.5	23 39.6	6 1.9	23 17.6	2 42.9	9 34.7	0 33.7	17 56.3	17 25.5
7 W	3 0 36.6	16 50.7	0 49.8	24 41.5	24 6.7	5 45.1	23 24.5	2 46.1	9 42.4	0 35.5	17 55.2	17 25.5
10 S	3 12 26.2	17 39.0	0 53.6	9 5.1	24 14.7	5 37.6	23 30.9	2 48.6	9 49.9	0 37.2	17 54.1	17 25.4
13 T	3 24 15.9	18 24.7	0 57.4	9N23.6	24 4.9	5 38.6	23 36.8	2 50.4	9 57.4	0 38.6	17 53.0	17 25.2
16 F	3 36 5.6	19 7.6	1 1.2	23 42.9	23 38.9	5 47.4	23 42.2	2 51.6	10 4.7	0 39.9	17 51.9	17 24.8
19 M	3 47 55.2	19 47.6	1 4.9	28 26.7	22 58.2	6 3.1	23 46.9	2 52.1	10 11.8	0 41.1	17 50.8	17 24.2
22 T	3 59 44.9	20 24.5	1 8.7	21 45.5	22 5.1	6 25.0	23 50.7	2 52.0	10 18.8	0 42.0	17 49.7	17 23.6
25 S	4 11 34.6	20 58.3	1 12.5	6 44.0	21 3.1	6 52.4	23 53.8	2 51.2	10 25.6	0 42.8	17 48.6	17 22.8
28 W	4 23 24.3	21 28.8	1 16.3	11S56.9	19 57.2	7 24.5	23 55.9	2 49.7	10 32.3	0 43.4	17 47.6	17 21.9
31 S	4 35 13.9	21 56.0	1 20.1	26 31.6	18 53.2	8 0.8	23 57.1	2 47.6	10 38.8	0 43.7	17 46.5	17 20.8

JUNE 1969

DAY	EPHEMERIS SIDEREAL TIME	☉	☊	☽	☿	♀	♂	♃	♄	♅	♆	♇
	h m s	° ′	° ′	° ′	° ′	° ′	° ′	° ′	° ′	° ′	° ′	° ′
						LONGITUDE at NOON						
1 S	4 39 10.5	10♊48.5	26♓35.4	24♐13.7	6♊ 8.3	26♈11.8	9♐42.8	26♍13.7	3♉54.7	29♍52.9	26♏57.8	22♍24.4
2 M	4 43 7.1	11 46.0	26 32.3	9♑23.7	5R37.9	27 0.4	9R22.4	26 15.5	4 1.3	29R52.6	26R56.3	22 24.4
3 T	4 47 3.6	12 43.4	26 29.1	24 24.0	5 9.6	27 49.8	9 2.0	26 17.4	4 7.8	29 52.4	26 54.7	22 24.4
4 W	4 51 0.2	13 40.8	26 25.9	9♒ 6.6	4 44.0	28 39.9	8 41.6	26 19.5	4 14.3	29 52.2	26 53.2	22D24.5
5 T	4 54 56.7	14 38.3	26 22.7	23 26.3	4 21.5	29 30.6	8 21.2	26 21.7	4 20.8	29 52.1	26 51.6	22 24.6
6 F	4 58 53.3	15 35.7	26 19.6	7♓21.1	4 2.4	0♉22.0	8 0.9	26 24.2	4 27.2	29 52.1	26 50.1	22 24.7
7 S	5 2 49.9	16 33.1	26 16.4	20 51.7	3 47.0	1 14.1	7 40.7	26 26.8	4 33.6	29 52.1	26 48.6	22 24.9
8 S	5 6 46.4	17 30.5	26 13.2	4♈ 0.4	3 35.6	2 6.7	7 20.7	26 29.5	4 39.9	29D52.2	26 47.1	22 25.0
9 M	5 10 43.0	18 27.9	26 10.0	16 50.6	3 28.4	2 59.9	7 1.0	26 32.5	4 46.2	29 52.2	26 45.6	22 25.2
10 T	5 14 39.5	19 25.3	26 6.8	29 25.5	3 25.5	3 53.6	6 41.5	26 35.6	4 52.4	29 52.4	26 44.2	22 25.5
11 W	5 18 36.1	20 22.6	26 3.7	11♉48.3	3D27.0	4 47.9	6 22.3	26 38.8	4 58.5	29 52.6	26 42.7	22 25.8
12 T	5 22 32.6	21 20.0	26 0.5	24 1.7	3 33.1	5 42.6	6 3.5	26 42.3	5 4.6	29 52.9	26 41.3	22 26.1
13 F	5 26 29.2	22 17.3	25 57.3	6♊ 7.7	3 43.7	6 37.9	5 45.1	26 45.9	5 10.7	29 53.2	26 39.8	22 26.4
14 S	5 30 25.8	23 14.6	25 54.1	18 7.9	3 58.9	7 33.7	5 27.1	26 49.6	5 16.6	29 53.5	26 38.4	22 26.8
15 S	5 34 22.3	24 12.0	25 51.0	0♋ 3.6	4 18.6	8 29.9	5 9.7	26 53.6	5 22.5	29 54.0	26 37.0	22 27.2
16 M	5 38 18.9	25 9.3	25 47.8	11 56.1	4 42.8	9 26.5	4 52.7	26 57.7	5 28.4	29 54.4	26 35.6	22 27.6
17 T	5 42 15.4	26 6.6	25 44.6	23 46.9	5 11.5	10 23.6	4 36.4	27 1.9	5 34.2	29 54.9	26 34.2	22 28.0
18 W	5 46 12.0	27 3.9	25 41.4	5♌38.1	5 44.6	11 21.1	4 20.6	27 6.3	5 39.9	29 55.5	26 32.9	22 28.5
19 T	5 50 8.6	28 1.2	25 38.3	17 32.2	6 22.0	12 19.0	4 5.4	27 10.9	5 45.6	29 56.2	26 31.6	22 29.1
20 F	5 54 5.1	28 58.4	25 35.1	29 32.8	7 3.7	13 17.3	3 50.9	27 15.6	5 51.2	29 56.8	26 30.2	22 29.6
21 S	5 58 1.7	29 55.7	25 31.9	11♍43.7	7 49.6	14 15.9	3 37.1	27 20.5	5 56.7	29 57.6	26 28.9	22 30.2
22 S	6 1 58.2	0♋52.9	25 28.7	24 9.6	8 39.7	15 14.9	3 24.0	27 25.5	6 2.2	29 58.4	26 27.7	22 30.8
23 M	6 5 54.8	1 50.2	25 25.6	6♎55.3	9 33.8	16 14.2	3 11.7	27 30.7	6 7.6	29 59.2	26 26.4	22 31.5
24 T	6 9 51.4	2 47.4	25 22.4	20 5.5	10 31.9	17 13.9	3 0.0	27 36.0	6 13.0	0♎ 0.1	26 25.2	22 32.2
25 W	6 13 47.9	3 44.6	25 19.2	3♏43.6	11 34.0	18 14.0	2 49.2	27 41.5	6 18.2	0 1.0	26 24.0	22 32.9
26 T	6 17 44.5	4 41.8	25 16.0	17 51.3	12 40.0	19 14.3	2 39.1	27 47.1	6 23.4	0 2.0	26 22.8	22 33.6
27 F	6 21 41.0	5 39.1	25 12.9	2♐27.6	13 49.9	20 15.0	2 29.9	27 52.9	6 28.6	0 3.1	26 21.6	22 34.4
28 S	6 25 37.6	6 36.2	25 9.7	17 27.5	15 3.5	21 16.0	2 21.4	27 58.8	6 33.7	0 4.2	26 20.5	22 35.2
29 S	6 29 34.2	7 33.4	25 6.5	2♑42.9	16 20.8	22 17.2	2 13.8	28 4.9	6 38.6	0 5.4	26 19.4	22 36.1
30 M	6 33 30.7	8 30.6	25 3.3	18 2.7	17 41.9	23 18.8	2 6.9	28 11.1	6 43.5	0 6.6	26 18.2	22 36.9
						DECLINATION at NOON						
1 S	4 39 10.5	22N 4.3	1S21.3	28S19.7	18N33.5	8N13.7	23S57.2	2N46.8	10N40.9	0N43.8	17S46.2	17N20.4
4 W	4 51 0.2	22 26.9	1 25.1	21 34.6	17 42.0	8 54.5	23 57.2	2 43.8	10 47.1	0 44.0	17 45.2	17 19.2
7 S	5 2 49.9	22 45.9	1 28.9	4 6.1	17 5.5	9 38.0	23 56.3	2 40.3	10 53.2	0 43.9	17 44.2	17 17.9
10 T	5 14 39.5	23 1.4	1 32.7	13N48.9	16 46.6	10 23.6	23 54.8	2 36.1	10 59.0	0 43.7	17 43.3	17 16.4
13 F	5 26 29.2	23 13.3	1 36.5	25 57.2	16 45.8	11 10.9	23 52.7	2 31.4	11 4.7	0 43.3	17 42.3	17 14.8
16 M	5 38 18.9	23 21.4	1 40.3	27 40.8	17 2.1	11 59.2	23 50.4	2 26.1	11 10.1	0 42.6	17 41.5	17 13.1
19 T	5 50 8.6	23 25.8	1 44.1	18 29.9	17 33.2	12 48.0	23 48.0	2 20.2	11 15.3	0 41.8	17 40.6	17 11.4
22 S	6 1 58.2	23 26.5	1 47.8	2 23.3	18 16.3	13 37.1	23 45.9	2 13.8	11 20.2	0 40.8	17 39.8	17 9.5
25 W	6 13 47.9	23 23.5	1 51.6	15S43.8	19 8.1	14 25.8	23 44.1	2 6.8	11 25.0	0 39.6	17 39.1	17 7.5
28 S	6 25 37.6	23 16.8	1 55.4	27 48.5	20 5.0	15 13.8	23 43.0	1 59.3	11 29.5	0 38.3	17 38.4	17 5.4

JULY 1969

DAY	EPHEMERIS SIDEREAL TIME	☉	☊	☽	☿	♀	♂	♃	♄	♅	♆	♇
	h m s	° ′	° ′	° ′	° ′	° ′	° ′	° ′	° ′	° ′	° ′	° ′
						LONGITUDE at NOON						
1 T	6 37 27.3	9♋27.8	25♓ 0.1	3♒15.6	19♊ 6.6	24♉20.6	2♐ 0.9	28♍17.4	6♉48.4	0♎ 7.8	26♏17.2	22♍37.8
2 W	6 41 23.8	10 25.0	24 57.0	18 11.5	20 35.0	25 22.7	1R55.7	28 23.9	6 53.1	0 9.1	26R16.1	22 38.7
3 T	6 45 20.4	11 22.2	24 53.8	2♓43.4	22 6.9	26 25.1	1 51.3	28 30.5	6 57.8	0 10.5	26 15.1	22 39.7
4 F	6 49 16.9	12 19.3	24 50.6	16 47.6	23 42.3	27 27.7	1 47.8	28 37.2	7 2.4	0 11.9	26 14.1	22 40.7
5 S	6 53 13.5	13 16.5	24 47.4	0♈24.0	25 21.1	28 30.6	1 45.1	28 44.1	7 7.0	0 13.3	26 13.1	22 41.7
6 S	6 57 10.1	14 13.7	24 44.3	13 34.6	27 3.3	29 33.7	1 43.2	28 51.1	7 11.4	0 14.8	26 12.1	22 42.7
7 M	7 1 6.6	15 10.9	24 41.1	26 22.9	28 48.8	0♊37.1	1 42.1	28 58.2	7 15.8	0 16.4	26 11.2	22 43.8
8 T	7 5 3.2	16 8.2	24 37.9	8♉53.0	0♋37.3	1 40.7	1 41.9	29 5.4	7 20.1	0 18.0	26 10.3	22 44.9
9 W	7 8 59.7	17 5.4	24 34.7	21 9.1	2 28.9	2 44.5	1D42.5	29 12.8	7 24.3	0 19.6	26 9.4	22 46.0
10 T	7 12 56.3	18 2.6	24 31.6	3♊14.9	4 23.3	3 48.6	1 44.0	29 20.3	7 28.4	0 21.3	26 8.5	22 47.1
11 F	7 16 52.9	18 59.8	24 28.4	15 13.6	6 20.2	4 52.8	1 46.3	29 28.0	7 32.5	0 23.1	26 7.7	22 48.3
12 S	7 20 49.4	19 57.1	24 25.2	27 7.9	8 19.6	5 57.3	1 49.4	29 35.7	7 36.4	0 24.9	26 6.9	22 49.5
13 S	7 24 46.0	20 54.3	24 22.0	8♋59.9	10 21.1	7 1.9	1 53.3	29 43.6	7 40.3	0 26.7	26 6.1	22 50.8
14 M	7 28 42.5	21 51.5	24 18.9	20 51.2	12 24.5	8 6.8	1 58.0	29 51.6	7 44.1	0 28.6	26 5.3	22 52.0
15 T	7 32 39.1	22 48.8	24 15.7	2♌43.5	14 29.5	9 11.8	2 3.5	29 59.7	7 47.8	0 30.5	26 4.6	22 53.3
16 W	7 36 35.6	23 46.0	24 12.5	14 38.4	16 35.7	10 17.1	2 9.9	0♎ 7.9	7 51.4	0 32.5	26 3.9	22 54.6
17 T	7 40 32.2	24 43.3	24 9.3	26 37.7	18 42.9	11 22.5	2 17.0	0 16.3	7 54.9	0 34.5	26 3.3	22 56.0
18 F	7 44 28.8	25 40.6	24 6.1	8♍44.0	20 50.8	12 28.1	2 24.9	0 24.8	7 58.4	0 36.6	26 2.7	22 57.4
19 S	7 48 25.3	26 37.9	24 3.0	21 0.1	22 59.0	13 33.9	2 33.6	0 33.4	8 1.7	0 38.7	26 2.1	22 58.8
20 S	7 52 21.9	27 35.2	23 59.8	3♎29.6	25 7.3	14 39.8	2 43.0	0 42.0	8 4.9	0 40.9	26 1.5	23 0.2
21 M	7 56 18.4	28 32.4	23 56.6	16 16.3	27 15.3	15 45.9	2 53.1	0 50.8	8 8.1	0 43.1	26 0.9	23 1.6
22 T	8 0 15.0	29 29.7	23 53.4	29 24.2	29 22.9	16 52.1	3 4.0	0 59.7	8 11.1	0 45.3	26 0.4	23 3.1
23 W	8 4 11.6	0♌27.0	23 50.3	12♏56.5	1♌29.7	17 58.5	3 15.7	1 8.7	8 14.1	0 47.6	25 59.9	23 4.6
24 T	8 8 8.1	1 24.3	23 47.1	26 55.3	3 35.7	19 5.1	3 28.0	1 17.8	8 17.0	0 49.9	25 59.5	23 6.1
25 F	8 12 4.7	2 21.6	23 43.9	11♐20.4	5 40.7	20 11.8	3 41.0	1 27.0	8 19.8	0 52.3	25 59.1	23 7.6
26 S	8 16 1.2	3 18.9	23 40.7	26 8.8	7 44.5	21 18.6	3 54.7	1 36.3	8 22.4	0 54.7	25 58.7	23 9.2
27 S	8 19 57.8	4 16.2	23 37.6	11♑14.1	9 47.0	22 25.6	4 9.0	1 45.7	8 25.0	0 57.1	25 58.3	23 10.8
28 M	8 23 54.3	5 13.6	23 34.4	26 27.4	11 48.1	23 32.8	4 24.0	1 55.2	8 27.5	0 59.6	25 58.0	23 12.4
29 T	8 27 50.9	6 10.9	23 31.2	11♒38.1	13 47.7	24 40.1	4 39.7	2 4.8	8 29.9	1 2.1	25 57.7	23 14.0
30 W	8 31 47.5	7 8.2	23 28.0	26 36.2	15 45.9	25 47.6	4 55.9	2 14.5	8 32.2	1 4.7	25 57.4	23 15.6
31 T	8 35 44.0	8 5.6	23 24.9	11♓13.6	17 42.5	26 55.2	5 12.8	2 24.3	8 34.4	1 7.3	25 57.2	23 17.3
						DECLINATION at NOON						
1 T	6 37 27.3	23N 6.4	1S59.2	23S13.5	21N 3.0	16N 0.7	23S42.5	1N51.3	11N33.7	0N36.7	17S37.8	17N 3.2
4 F	6 49 16.9	22 52.4	2 3.0	5 47.6	21 57.7	16 46.0	23 43.0	1 42.9	11 37.7	0 35.0	17 37.2	17 0.9
7 M	7 1 6.6	22 34.9	2 6.7	12N43.2	22 43.9	17 29.5	23 44.4	1 34.0	11 41.4	0 33.1	17 36.6	16 58.6
10 T	7 12 56.3	22 13.7	2 10.5	25 27.1	23 16.4	18 10.7	23 46.7	1 24.6	11 44.9	0 31.0	17 36.2	16 56.2
13 S	7 24 46.0	21 49.2	2 14.3	27 58.9	23 30.1	18 49.2	23 50.1	1 14.8	11 48.1	0 28.8	17 35.7	16 53.7
16 W	7 36 35.6	21 21.2	2 18.1	19 26.2	23 21.0	19 24.6	23 54.6	1 4.7	11 51.0	0 26.3	17 35.4	16 51.2
19 S	7 48 25.3	20 50.0	2 21.8	3 41.3	22 47.6	19 56.8	24 0.0	0 54.0	11 53.6	0 23.8	17 35.1	16 48.6
22 T	8 0 15.0	20 15.7	2 25.6	14S 8.8	21 50.6	20 25.3	24 6.4	0 43.1	11 56.0	0 21.0	17 34.9	16 45.9
25 F	8 12 4.7	19 38.3	2 29.4	27 7.3	20 32.8	20 49.9	24 13.5	0 31.8	11 58.0	0 18.2	17 34.7	16 43.2
28 M	8 23 54.3	18 58.0	2 33.2	25 1.2	18 58.1	21 10.2	24 21.4	0 20.1	11 59.8	0 15.2	17 34.7	16 40.5
31 T	8 35 44.0	18 14.9	2 36.9	8 14.2	17 10.4	21 26.2	24 29.9	0 8.1	12 1.3	0 12.0	17 34.6	16 37.7

AUGUST 1969

DAY	EPHEMERIS SIDEREAL TIME	☉	☊	☽	☿	♀	♂	♃	♄	♅	♆	♇
						LONGITUDE at NOON						
1 F	8 39 40.6	9♌ 3.0	23♓21.7	25♓25.1	19♌37.5	28♊ 2.9	5♐30.3	2♎34.1	8♉36.5	1♎ 9.9	25♏56.9	23♍19.0
2 S	8 43 37.1	10 0.4	23 18.5	9♈ 8.8	21 30.9	29 10.8	5 48.4	2 44.1	8 38.5	1 12.6	25R56.8	23 20.7
3 S	8 47 33.7	10 57.8	23 15.3	22 25.5	23 22.8	0♋18.8	6 7.0	2 54.1	8 40.4	1 15.3	25 56.6	23 22.4
4 M	8 51 30.2	11 55.3	23 12.1	5♉17.8	25 13.0	1 26.9	6 26.3	3 4.3	8 42.2	1 18.1	25 56.5	23 24.2
5 T	8 55 26.8	12 52.7	23 9.0	17 49.5	27 1.6	2 35.2	6 46.1	3 14.5	8 43.9	1 20.9	25 56.4	23 26.0
6 W	8 59 23.3	13 50.2	23 5.8	0♊ 5.0	28 48.7	3 43.6	7 6.4	3 24.8	8 45.5	1 23.7	25 56.4	23 27.8
7 T	9 3 19.9	14 47.7	23 2.6	12 8.7	0♍34.1	4 52.1	7 27.3	3 35.2	8 47.0	1 26.5	25 56.4	23 29.6
8 F	9 7 16.5	15 45.3	22 59.4	24 4.8	2 18.1	6 0.8	7 48.8	3 45.7	8 48.4	1 29.5	25 56.4	23 31.4
9 S	9 11 13.0	16 42.8	22 56.3	5♋56.8	4 0.4	7 9.6	8 10.7	3 56.3	8 49.7	1 32.4	25D56.5	23 33.3
10 S	9 15 9.6	17 40.4	22 53.1	17 47.9	5 41.2	8 18.5	8 33.2	4 6.9	8 50.9	1 35.4	25 56.5	23 35.2
11 M	9 19 6.1	18 38.0	22 49.9	29 40.7	7 20.4	9 27.5	8 56.2	4 17.6	8 51.9	1 38.3	25 56.7	23 37.0
12 T	9 23 2.7	19 35.6	22 46.7	11♌37.3	8 58.1	10 36.6	9 19.6	4 28.4	8 52.9	1 41.4	25 56.8	23 38.9
13 W	9 26 59.2	20 33.2	22 43.6	23 39.5	10 34.3	11 45.9	9 43.6	4 39.3	8 53.8	1 44.4	25 57.0	23 40.9
14 T	9 30 55.8	21 30.9	22 40.4	5♍48.9	12 9.0	12 55.2	10 8.0	4 50.2	8 54.5	1 47.5	25 57.2	23 42.8
15 F	9 34 52.4	22 28.5	22 37.2	18 7.1	13 42.1	14 4.7	10 33.0	5 1.2	8 55.2	1 50.6	25 57.4	23 44.7
16 S	9 38 48.9	23 26.2	22 34.0	0♎35.9	15 13.7	15 14.2	10 58.3	5 12.3	8 55.7	1 53.8	25 57.7	23 46.7
17 S	9 42 45.5	24 23.9	22 30.8	13 17.3	16 43.8	16 23.9	11 24.2	5 23.5	8 56.2	1 56.9	25 58.0	23 48.7
18 M	9 46 42.0	25 21.7	22 27.7	26 13.5	18 12.3	17 33.7	11 50.4	5 34.7	8 56.5	2 0.1	25 58.4	23 50.7
19 T	9 50 38.6	26 19.4	22 24.5	9♏26.8	19 39.3	18 43.5	12 17.1	5 46.0	8 56.7	2 3.4	25 58.7	23 52.7
20 W	9 54 35.1	27 17.2	22 21.3	22 59.0	21 4.7	19 53.5	12 44.2	5 57.3	8 56.8	2 6.6	25 59.1	23 54.7
21 T	9 58 31.7	28 15.0	22 18.1	6♐51.5	22 28.6	21 3.6	13 11.8	6 8.7	8 56.9	2 9.9	25 59.6	23 56.7
22 F	10 2 28.2	29 12.8	22 15.0	21 4.1	23 50.8	22 13.7	13 39.7	6 20.2	8R56.8	2 13.2	26 0.0	23 58.8
23 S	10 6 24.8	0♍10.6	22 11.8	5♑34.9	25 11.3	23 24.0	14 8.0	6 31.7	8 56.6	2 16.6	26 0.5	24 0.8
24 S	10 10 21.3	1 8.4	22 8.6	20 19.8	26 30.1	24 34.3	14 36.7	6 43.3	8 56.3	2 19.9	26 1.1	24 2.9
25 M	10 14 17.9	2 6.3	22 5.4	5♒12.7	27 47.2	25 44.8	15 5.8	6 55.0	8 55.9	2 23.3	26 1.6	24 5.0
26 T	10 18 14.5	3 4.2	22 2.2	20 5.9	29 2.5	26 55.4	15 35.3	7 6.7	8 55.4	2 26.7	26 2.2	24 7.1
27 W	10 22 11.0	4 2.1	21 59.1	4♓51.3	0♎16.0	28 6.0	16 5.1	7 18.5	8 54.7	2 30.1	26 2.9	24 9.2
28 T	10 26 7.6	4 60.0	21 55.9	19 21.7	1 27.5	29 16.8	16 35.2	7 30.3	8 54.0	2 33.6	26 3.5	24 11.3
29 F	10 30 4.1	5 58.0	21 52.7	3♈31.5	2 37.1	0♌27.6	17 5.7	7 42.2	8 53.2	2 37.1	26 4.3	24 13.5
30 S	10 34 0.7	6 56.0	21 49.5	17 17.3	3 44.5	1 38.6	17 36.6	7 54.1	8 52.3	2 40.6	26 5.0	24 15.6
31 S	10 37 57.2	7 54.0	21 46.4	0♉38.1	4 49.7	2 49.6	18 7.7	8 6.1	8 51.3	2 44.1	26 5.7	24 17.7
						DECLINATION at NOON						
1 F	8 39 40.6	17N59.9	2S38.2	1S31.4	16N32.3	21N30.5	24S32.8	0N 4.1	12N 1.7	0N10.9	17S34.6	16N36.8
4 M	8 51 30.2	17 13.2	2 42.0	16N38.8	14 32.9	21 40.2	24 41.8	0S 8.3	12 2.8	0 7.6	17 34.7	16 34.0
7 T	9 3 19.9	16 24.0	2 45.7	27 18.6	12 28.2	21 45.0	24 51.1	0 21.0	12 3.6	0 4.1	17 34.9	16 31.1
10 S	9 15 9.6	15 32.4	2 49.5	26 52.0	10 20.4	21 44.8	25 0.6	0 33.9	12 4.1	0 0.6	17 35.1	16 28.3
13 W	9 26 59.2	14 38.6	2 53.3	15 55.1	8 11.6	21 39.5	25 10.0	0 47.1	12 4.3	0S 3.1	17 35.3	16 25.4
16 S	9 38 48.9	13 42.6	2 57.0	1S 1.3	6 3.2	21 28.9	25 19.4	1 0.5	12 4.2	0 6.9	17 35.7	16 22.5
19 T	9 50 38.6	12 44.7	3 0.8	18 20.8	3 56.7	21 13.0	25 28.5	1 14.2	12 3.8	0 10.8	17 36.1	16 19.7
22 F	10 2 28.2	11 45.0	3 4.6	28 22.5	1 53.3	20 52.0	25 37.1	1 28.0	12 3.1	0 14.8	17 36.6	16 16.8
25 M	10 14 17.9	10 43.7	3 8.3	22 37.9	0S 5.6	20 25.7	25 45.2	1 42.1	12 2.1	0 18.8	17 37.1	16 14.0
28 T	10 26 7.6	9 40.8	3 12.1	4 21.6	1 58.7	19 54.3	25 52.6	1 56.3	12 0.9	0 23.0	17 37.7	16 11.1
31 S	10 37 57.2	8 36.5	3 15.8	14N50.5	3 44.7	19 17.8	25 59.2	2 10.7	11 59.3	0 27.2	17 38.4	16 8.3

SEPTEMBER 1969

DAY	EPHEMERIS SIDEREAL TIME	☉	☊	☽	☿	♀	♂	♃	♄	♅	♆	♇
	h m s	° ′	° ′	° ′	° ′	° ′	° ′	° ′	° ′	° ′	° ′	° ′
						LONGITUDE at NOON						
1 M	10 41 53.8	8 ♍ 52.1	21 ♓ 43.2	13 ♉ 35.0	5 ♎ 52.6	4 ♌ 0.8	18 ♐ 39.2	8 ♎ 18.1	8 ♉ 50.1	2 ♎ 47.6	26 ♏ 6.5	24 ♍ 19.9
2 T	10 45 50.3	9 50.1	21 40.0	26 10.7	6 53.0	5 12.0	19 11.0	8 30.2	8 R 48.9	2 51.2	26 7.3	24 22.0
3 W	10 49 46.9	10 48.3	21 36.8	8 ♊ 28.8	7 50.9	6 23.3	19 43.1	8 42.3	8 47.6	2 54.7	26 8.2	24 24.2
4 T	10 53 43.4	11 46.4	21 33.6	20 33.7	8 46.0	7 34.7	20 15.5	8 54.5	8 46.1	2 58.3	26 9.1	24 26.4
5 F	10 57 40.0	12 44.6	21 30.5	2 ♋ 29.9	9 38.2	8 46.2	20 48.2	9 6.7	8 44.6	3 1.9	26 10.0	24 28.6
6 S	11 1 36.6	13 42.8	21 27.3	14 21.8	10 27.4	9 57.8	21 21.2	9 19.0	8 42.9	3 5.5	26 10.9	24 30.7
7 S	11 5 33.1	14 41.0	21 24.1	26 13.7	11 13.1	11 9.4	21 54.5	9 31.3	8 41.2	3 9.2	26 11.9	24 32.9
8 M	11 9 29.7	15 39.3	21 20.9	8 ♌ 9.1	11 55.4	12 21.2	22 28.1	9 43.6	8 39.3	3 12.8	26 12.9	24 35.1
9 T	11 13 26.2	16 37.6	21 17.8	20 11.2	12 33.9	13 33.0	23 2.0	9 56.0	8 37.4	3 16.5	26 13.9	24 37.3
10 W	11 17 22.8	17 36.0	21 14.6	2 ♍ 22.5	13 8.2	14 44.9	23 36.1	10 8.5	8 35.3	3 20.1	26 15.0	24 39.5
11 T	11 21 19.3	18 34.3	21 11.4	14 45.0	13 38.3	15 56.9	24 10.5	10 20.9	8 33.2	3 23.8	26 16.0	24 41.7
12 F	11 25 15.9	19 32.8	21 8.2	27 19.9	14 3.6	17 9.0	24 45.2	10 33.4	8 30.9	3 27.5	26 17.2	24 44.0
13 S	11 29 12.4	20 31.2	21 5.1	10 ♎ 8.1	14 23.9	18 21.1	25 20.1	10 46.0	8 28.6	3 31.2	26 18.3	24 46.2
14 S	11 33 9.0	21 29.7	21 1.9	23 9.8	14 38.9	19 33.3	25 55.3	10 58.5	8 26.2	3 35.0	26 19.5	24 48.4
15 M	11 37 5.5	22 28.1	20 58.7	6 ♏ 25.3	14 48.3	20 45.6	26 30.8	11 11.1	8 23.6	3 38.7	26 20.7	24 50.6
16 T	11 41 2.1	23 26.7	20 55.5	19 54.4	14 51.5	21 58.0	27 6.5	11 23.8	8 21.0	3 42.4	26 21.9	24 52.8
17 W	11 44 58.6	24 25.2	20 52.3	3 ♐ 36.7	14 R 48.5	23 10.4	27 42.4	11 36.4	8 18.3	3 46.2	26 23.2	24 55.1
18 T	11 48 55.2	25 23.8	20 49.2	17 31.5	14 38.7	24 22.9	28 18.6	11 49.1	8 15.5	3 49.9	26 24.5	24 57.3
19 F	11 52 51.8	26 22.4	20 46.0	1 ♑ 37.9	14 22.2	25 35.6	28 55.0	12 1.9	8 12.7	3 53.7	26 25.8	24 59.5
20 S	11 56 48.3	27 21.1	20 42.8	15 53.9	13 58.5	26 48.2	29 31.7	12 14.6	8 9.7	3 57.5	26 27.2	25 1.8
21 S	12 0 44.9	28 19.7	20 39.6	0 ♒ 17.1	13 27.6	28 0.9	0 ♑ 8.5	12 27.4	8 6.7	4 1.3	26 28.5	25 4.0
22 M	12 4 41.4	29 18.4	20 36.5	14 43.9	12 49.7	29 13.7	0 45.5	12 40.2	8 3.5	4 5.0	26 29.9	25 6.2
23 T	12 8 38.0	0 ♎ 17.1	20 33.3	29 10.3	12 5.1	0 ♍ 26.5	1 22.8	12 53.0	8 0.3	4 8.8	26 31.4	25 8.4
24 W	12 12 34.5	1 15.9	20 30.1	13 ♓ 31.2	11 14.0	1 39.5	2 0.2	13 5.8	7 57.0	4 12.6	26 32.8	25 10.6
25 T	12 16 31.1	2 14.7	20 26.9	27 41.8	10 17.3	2 52.4	2 37.9	13 18.7	7 53.6	4 16.4	26 34.3	25 12.8
26 F	12 20 27.6	3 13.5	20 23.7	11 ♈ 37.7	9 15.9	4 5.5	3 15.7	13 31.5	7 50.1	4 20.2	26 35.8	25 15.0
27 S	12 24 24.2	4 12.3	20 20.6	25 15.5	8 11.0	5 18.6	3 53.7	13 44.4	7 46.6	4 24.0	26 37.3	25 17.2
28 S	12 28 20.7	5 11.2	20 17.4	8 ♉ 33.0	7 3.9	6 31.8	4 31.9	13 57.3	7 43.0	4 27.7	26 38.8	25 19.4
29 M	12 32 17.3	6 10.1	20 14.2	21 29.9	5 56.4	7 45.0	5 10.3	14 10.3	7 39.3	4 31.5	26 40.4	25 21.6
30 T	12 36 13.8	7 9.1	20 11.0	4 ♊ 7.2	4 50.0	8 58.4	5 48.9	14 23.2	7 35.6	4 35.3	26 42.0	25 23.8
						DECLINATION at NOON						
1 M	10 41 53.8	8 N 14.8	3 S 17.1	19 N 54.5	4 S 18.1	19 N 4.5	26 S 1.2	2 S 15.5	11 N 58.7	0 S 28.6	17 S 38.7	16 N 7.4
4 T	10 53 43.4	7 8.9	3 20.9	28 22.2	5 51.7	18 21.5	26 6.5	2 30.0	11 56.8	0 32.9	17 39.4	16 4.6
7 S	11 5 33.1	6 2.0	3 24.6	25 9.2	7 13.1	17 33.8	26 10.7	2 44.7	11 54.6	0 37.3	17 40.2	16 1.9
10 W	11 17 22.8	4 54.1	3 28.4	12 13.1	8 19.4	16 41.5	26 13.7	2 59.5	11 52.1	0 41.7	17 41.1	15 59.2
13 S	11 29 12.4	3 45.4	3 32.1	5 S 36.1	9 6.4	15 45.0	26 15.4	3 14.3	11 49.4	0 46.1	17 42.1	15 56.6
16 T	11 41 2.1	2 36.2	3 35.9	22 4.3	9 28.9	14 44.4	26 15.7	3 29.3	11 46.4	0 50.6	17 43.1	15 54.0
19 F	11 52 51.8	1 26.5	3 39.6	28 37.7	9 20.8	13 39.9	26 14.4	3 44.3	11 43.2	0 55.1	17 44.1	15 51.5
22 M	12 4 41.4	0 16.5	3 43.4	19 25.0	8 36.5	12 32.0	26 11.6	3 59.4	11 39.7	0 59.6	17 45.2	15 49.1
25 T	12 16 31.1	0 S 53.6	3 47.1	0 21.7	7 13.9	11 20.7	26 7.0	4 14.4	11 36.1	1 4.1	17 46.3	15 46.7
28 S	12 28 20.7	2 3.7	3 50.9	18 N 1.8	5 19.3	10 6.5	26 0.7	4 29.5	11 32.3	1 8.7	17 47.5	15 44.4

OCTOBER 1969

DAY	EPHEMERIS SIDEREAL TIME	☉	☊	☽	☿	♀	♂	♃	♄	♅	♆	♇
						LONGITUDE at NOON						
1 W	12 40 10.4	8 ♎ 8.0	20 ♓ 7.9	16 ♊ 27.3	3 ♎ 46.7	10 ♍ 11.7	6 ♑ 27.6	14 ♎ 36.1	7 ♉ 31.7	4 ♎ 39.1	26 ♏ 43.6	25 ♍ 26.0
2 T	12 44 7.0	9 7.1	20 4.7	28 33.6	2 R 48.1	11 25.2	7 6.5	14 49.1	7 R 27.8	4 42.9	26 45.3	25 28.2
3 F	12 48 3.5	10 6.1	20 1.5	10 ♋ 30.5	1 55.9	12 38.7	7 45.6	15 2.1	7 23.9	4 46.7	26 46.9	25 30.4
4 S	12 52 0.1	11 5.2	19 58.3	22 22.6	1 11.5	13 52.3	8 24.8	15 15.1	7 19.9	4 50.4	26 48.6	25 32.5
5 S	12 55 56.6	12 4.4	19 55.1	4 ♌ 14.7	0 36.1	15 5.9	9 4.3	15 28.1	7 15.8	4 54.2	26 50.3	25 34.7
6 M	12 59 53.2	13 3.6	19 52.0	16 11.4	0 10.6	16 19.6	9 43.8	15 41.1	7 11.6	4 58.0	26 52.1	25 36.8
7 T	13 3 49.7	14 2.8	19 48.8	28 17.2	29 ♍ 55.4	17 33.3	10 23.6	15 54.1	7 7.4	5 1.7	26 53.8	25 39.0
8 W	13 7 46.3	15 2.0	19 45.6	10 ♍ 35.8	29 51.0	18 47.1	11 3.4	16 7.1	7 3.2	5 5.5	26 55.6	25 41.1
9 T	13 11 42.8	16 1.3	19 42.4	23 10.1	29 D 57.4	20 0.9	11 43.5	16 20.1	6 58.9	5 9.2	26 57.4	25 43.2
10 F	13 15 39.4	17 0.7	19 39.3	6 ♎ 1.9	0 ♎ 14.3	21 14.9	12 23.7	16 33.1	6 54.6	5 13.0	26 59.3	25 45.4
11 S	13 19 35.9	18 0.1	19 36.1	19 11.6	0 41.2	22 28.8	13 4.1	16 46.2	6 50.2	5 16.7	27 1.1	25 47.4
12 S	13 23 32.5	18 59.5	19 32.9	2 ♏ 38.6	1 17.7	23 42.8	13 44.6	16 59.2	6 45.7	5 20.4	27 3.0	25 49.5
13 M	13 27 29.0	19 58.9	19 29.7	16 20.8	2 3.0	24 56.9	14 25.2	17 12.2	6 41.2	5 24.2	27 4.8	25 51.6
14 T	13 31 25.6	20 58.4	19 26.5	0 ♐ 15.4	2 56.4	26 11.0	15 5.9	17 25.2	6 36.7	5 27.8	27 6.7	25 53.7
15 W	13 35 22.2	21 57.9	19 23.4	14 18.9	3 57.0	27 25.1	15 46.8	17 38.2	6 32.1	5 31.5	27 8.6	25 55.7
16 T	13 39 18.7	22 57.4	19 20.2	28 27.9	5 4.2	28 39.3	16 27.9	17 51.2	6 27.5	5 35.2	27 10.6	25 57.8
17 F	13 43 15.3	23 56.9	19 17.0	12 ♑ 39.1	6 17.1	29 53.5	17 9.0	18 4.2	6 22.8	5 38.8	27 12.5	25 59.8
18 S	13 47 11.8	24 56.5	19 13.8	26 50.2	7 35.0	1 ♎ 7.8	17 50.3	18 17.2	6 18.2	5 42.5	27 14.5	26 1.8
19 S	13 51 8.4	25 56.1	19 10.7	10 ♒ 59.0	8 57.1	2 22.1	18 31.7	18 30.1	6 13.5	5 46.1	27 16.5	26 3.8
20 M	13 55 4.9	26 55.8	19 7.5	25 4.1	10 22.9	3 36.4	19 13.2	18 43.1	6 8.7	5 49.7	27 18.4	26 5.7
21 T	13 59 1.5	27 55.4	19 4.3	9 ♓ 3.8	11 51.7	4 50.8	19 54.9	18 56.0	6 4.0	5 53.3	27 20.5	26 7.7
22 W	14 2 58.0	28 55.1	19 1.1	22 56.6	13 23.1	6 5.2	20 36.6	19 9.0	5 59.2	5 56.9	27 22.5	26 9.7
23 T	14 6 54.6	29 54.8	18 57.9	6 ♈ 40.6	14 56.5	7 19.7	21 18.4	19 21.9	5 54.4	6 0.4	27 24.5	26 11.6
24 F	14 10 51.2	0 ♏ 54.6	18 54.8	20 13.6	16 31.6	8 34.2	22 0.4	19 34.8	5 49.6	6 4.0	27 26.6	26 13.5
25 S	14 14 47.7	1 54.4	18 51.6	3 ♉ 33.5	18 8.1	9 48.7	22 42.4	19 47.7	5 44.8	6 7.5	27 28.6	26 15.4
26 S	14 18 44.3	2 54.2	18 48.4	16 38.6	19 45.6	11 3.3	23 24.6	20 0.5	5 40.0	6 11.0	27 30.7	26 17.3
27 M	14 22 40.8	3 54.1	18 45.2	29 27.8	21 23.8	12 17.9	24 6.8	20 13.4	5 35.2	6 14.4	27 32.8	26 19.1
28 T	14 26 37.4	4 53.9	18 42.1	12 ♊ 1.0	23 2.6	13 32.6	24 49.1	20 26.2	5 30.4	6 17.9	27 34.9	26 21.0
29 W	14 30 33.9	5 53.9	18 38.9	24 19.3	24 41.9	14 47.2	25 31.6	20 39.0	5 25.5	6 21.3	27 37.0	26 22.8
30 T	14 34 30.5	6 53.8	18 35.7	6 ♋ 24.9	26 21.3	16 2.0	26 14.1	20 51.8	5 20.7	6 24.7	27 39.2	26 24.6
31 F	14 38 27.0	7 53.9	18 32.5	18 21.2	28 0.9	17 16.8	26 56.7	21 4.6	5 15.9	6 28.1	27 41.4	26 26.4
						DECLINATION at NOON						
1 W	12 40 10.4	3 S 13.6	3 S 54.6	27 N 58.2	3 S 10.3	8 N 49.6	25 S 52.7	4 S 44.6	11 N 28.2	1 S 13.2	17 S 48.8	15 N 42.2
4 S	12 52 0.1	4 23.3	3 58.4	26 0.9	1 12.7	7 30.2	25 42.7	4 59.7	11 24.1	1 17.7	17 50.0	15 40.0
7 T	13 3 49.7	5 32.5	4 2.1	13 58.8	0 N 10.5	6 8.7	25 30.9	5 14.7	11 19.7	1 22.1	17 51.3	15 38.0
10 F	13 15 39.4	6 41.1	4 5.9	3 S 38.4	0 46.4	4 45.4	25 17.1	5 29.7	11 15.3	1 26.6	17 52.7	15 36.0
13 M	13 27 29.0	7 48.9	4 9.6	20 50.3	0 34.6	3 20.7	25 1.4	5 44.7	11 10.7	1 31.0	17 54.0	15 34.2
16 T	13 39 18.7	8 55.7	4 13.3	28 35.3	0 S 18.0	1 54.8	24 43.7	5 59.5	11 6.1	1 35.3	17 55.4	15 32.4
19 S	13 51 8.4	10 1.3	4 17.1	20 40.4	1 41.1	0 28.2	24 24.0	6 14.3	11 1.4	1 39.6	17 56.9	15 30.8
22 W	14 2 58.0	11 5.6	4 20.8	2 36.9	3 24.5	0 S 59.0	24 2.3	6 29.0	10 56.7	1 43.9	17 58.3	15 29.2
25 S	14 14 47.7	12 8.4	4 24.5	16 N 0.7	5 19.9	2 26.4	23 38.6	6 43.5	10 52.0	1 48.0	17 59.8	15 27.8
28 T	14 26 37.4	13 9.5	4 28.3	27 16.2	7 20.9	3 53.6	23 13.0	6 57.9	10 47.2	1 52.1	18 1.3	15 26.5
31 F	14 38 27.0	14 8.8	4 32.0	26 39.6	9 23.1	5 20.3	22 45.4	7 12.2	10 42.6	1 56.1	18 2.8	15 25.4

NOVEMBER 1969

DAY	EPHEMERIS SIDEREAL TIME	☉	☊	☽	☿	♀	♂	♃	♄	♅	♆	♇
	h m s	° ′	° ′	° ′	° ′	° ′	° ′	° ′	° ′	° ′	° ′	° ′
					LONGITUDE at NOON							
1 S	14 42 23.6	8♏53.9	18♓29.4	0♌12.2	29♎40.4	18♎31.6	27♑39.4	21♎17.3	5♉11.1	6♎31.5	27♏43.5	26♍28.2
2 S	14 46 20.2	9 54.0	18 26.2	12 2.9	1♏19.9	19 46.4	28 22.2	21 30.0	5R 6.3	6 34.8	27 45.7	26 29.9
3 M	14 50 16.7	10 54.1	18 23.0	23 58.4	2 59.2	21 1.2	29 5.1	21 42.7	5 1.5	6 38.1	27 47.9	26 31.6
4 T	14 54 13.3	11 54.2	18 19.8	6♍ 3.9	4 38.4	22 16.1	29 48.0	21 55.3	4 56.7	6 41.4	27 50.0	26 33.3
5 W	14 58 9.8	12 54.4	18 16.6	18 24.5	6 17.2	23 31.1	0♒31.0	22 7.9	4 51.9	6 44.7	27 52.2	26 35.0
6 T	15 2 6.4	13 54.6	18 13.5	1♎ 4.4	7 55.8	24 46.0	1 14.1	22 20.5	4 47.2	6 47.9	27 54.4	26 36.7
7 F	15 6 2.9	14 54.8	18 10.3	14 6.7	9 34.2	26 1.0	1 57.3	22 33.0	4 42.4	6 51.1	27 56.6	26 38.3
8 S	15 9 59.5	15 55.1	18 7.1	27 32.8	11 12.2	27 16.0	2 40.6	22 45.5	4 37.7	6 54.2	27 58.8	26 39.9
9 S	15 13 56.0	16 55.4	18 3.9	11♏22.0	12 49.8	28 31.0	3 23.9	22 58.0	4 33.0	6 57.4	28 1.1	26 41.5
10 M	15 17 52.6	17 55.7	18 0.8	25 31.0	14 27.2	29 46.1	4 7.3	23 10.4	4 28.4	7 0.5	28 3.3	26 43.0
11 T	15 21 49.2	18 56.1	17 57.6	9♐54.8	16 4.2	1♏ 1.1	4 50.8	23 22.8	4 23.8	7 3.5	28 5.5	26 44.6
12 W	15 25 45.7	19 56.4	17 54.4	24 26.8	17 41.0	2 16.2	5 34.3	23 35.1	4 19.2	7 6.6	28 7.7	26 46.1
13 T	15 29 42.3	20 56.8	17 51.2	9♑ 0.1	19 17.4	3 31.3	6 18.0	23 47.4	4 14.7	7 9.6	28 10.0	26 47.6
14 F	15 33 38.8	21 57.3	17 48.1	23 28.7	20 53.4	4 46.5	7 1.6	23 59.7	4 10.2	7 12.6	28 12.2	26 49.0
15 S	15 37 35.4	22 57.7	17 44.9	7♒48.1	22 29.2	6 1.6	7 45.4	24 11.9	4 5.7	7 15.5	28 14.5	26 50.5
16 S	15 41 31.9	23 58.2	17 41.7	21 55.7	24 4.8	7 16.8	8 29.2	24 24.0	4 1.3	7 18.4	28 16.7	26 51.9
17 M	15 45 28.5	24 58.7	17 38.5	5♓50.6	25 40.0	8 31.9	9 13.0	24 36.2	3 57.0	7 21.2	28 19.0	26 53.2
18 T	15 49 25.1	25 59.2	17 35.3	19 32.9	27 15.0	9 47.1	9 56.9	24 48.2	3 52.7	7 24.1	28 21.2	26 54.6
19 W	15 53 21.6	26 59.7	17 32.2	3♈ 3.4	28 49.8	11 2.3	10 40.8	25 0.2	3 48.4	7 26.9	28 23.5	26 55.9
20 T	15 57 18.2	28 0.3	17 29.0	16 22.7	0♐24.3	12 17.6	11 24.8	25 12.1	3 44.3	7 29.6	28 25.7	26 57.2
21 F	16 1 14.7	29 0.9	17 25.8	29 31.3	1 58.7	13 32.8	12 8.9	25 24.1	3 40.2	7 32.4	28 28.0	26 58.5
22 S	16 5 11.3	0♐ 1.5	17 22.6	12♉29.2	3 32.8	14 48.1	12 53.0	25 35.9	3 36.1	7 35.0	28 30.3	26 59.8
23 S	16 9 7.8	1 2.1	17 19.5	25 15.8	5 6.8	16 3.4	13 37.1	25 47.7	3 32.1	7 37.7	28 32.5	27 1.0
24 M	16 13 4.4	2 2.8	17 16.3	7♊50.9	6 40.6	17 18.6	14 21.3	25 59.4	3 28.2	7 40.3	28 34.8	27 2.2
25 T	16 17 1.0	3 3.5	17 13.1	20 14.2	8 14.2	18 33.9	15 5.5	26 11.0	3 24.3	7 42.8	28 37.0	27 3.3
26 W	16 20 57.5	4 4.2	17 9.9	2♋26.1	9 47.8	19 49.3	15 49.7	26 22.6	3 20.5	7 45.3	28 39.3	27 4.4
27 T	16 24 54.1	5 4.9	17 6.8	14 27.9	11 21.2	21 4.6	16 34.0	26 34.2	3 16.7	7 47.8	28 41.5	27 5.5
28 F	16 28 50.6	6 5.6	17 3.6	26 21.7	12 54.5	22 19.9	17 18.3	26 45.6	3 13.1	7 50.2	28 43.8	27 6.6
29 S	16 32 47.2	7 6.4	17 0.4	8♌10.9	14 27.7	23 35.3	18 2.6	26 57.0	3 9.5	7 52.6	28 46.0	27 7.6
30 S	16 36 43.8	8 7.2	16 57.2	19 59.4	16 0.9	24 50.6	18 47.0	27 8.3	3 6.0	7 54.9	28 48.3	27 8.6
					DECLINATION at NOON							
1 S	14 42 23.6	14S28.1	4S33.2	23N56.3	10S 3.6	5S49.1	22S35.8	7S16.9	10N41.0	1S57.4	18S 3.3	15N25.0
4 T	14 54 13.3	15 24.6	4 37.0	10 25.7	12 2.8	7 14.6	22 5.7	7 31.0	10 36.4	2 1.3	18 4.8	15 24.0
7 F	15 6 2.9	16 18.9	4 40.7	7S30.3	13 57.5	8 38.9	21 33.8	7 44.9	10 31.9	2 5.1	18 6.3	15 23.1
10 M	15 17 52.6	17 10.7	4 44.4	23 38.5	15 46.2	10 1.5	21 0.0	7 58.5	10 27.5	2 8.7	18 7.8	15 22.4
13 T	15 29 42.3	17 59.9	4 48.1	27 53.3	17 28.0	11 22.1	20 24.5	8 12.0	10 23.2	2 12.3	18 9.3	15 21.8
16 S	15 41 31.9	18 46.2	4 51.9	16 22.7	19 2.1	12 40.3	19 47.2	8 25.3	10 19.1	2 15.7	18 10.8	15 21.3
19 W	15 53 21.6	19 29.5	4 55.6	2N21.6	20 27.7	13 55.8	19 8.3	8 38.2	10 15.2	2 19.0	18 12.3	15 21.0
22 S	16 5 11.3	20 9.6	4 59.3	19 27.5	21 44.3	15 8.2	18 27.8	8 51.0	10 11.5	2 22.1	18 13.8	15 20.7
25 T	16 17 1.0	20 46.4	5 3.0	28 4.5	22 51.2	16 17.1	17 45.9	9 3.5	10 8.0	2 25.1	18 15.3	15 20.7
28 F	16 28 50.6	21 19.8	5 6.7	24 43.2	23 47.7	17 22.2	17 2.5	9 15.7	10 4.8	2 28.0	18 16.8	15 20.7

DECEMBER 1969

DAY	EPHEMERIS SIDEREAL TIME	☉	☊	☽	☿	♀	♂	♃	♄	♅	♆	♇
					LONGITUDE at NOON							
1 M	16 40 40.3	9♐ 8.0	16♓54.1	1♍52.2	17♐33.9	26♏ 6.0	19♒31.4	27♎19.6	3♉ 2.5	7♎57.2	28♏50.5	27♍ 9.6
2 T	16 44 36.9	10 8.8	16 50.9	13 54.6	19 6.9	27 21.4	20 15.8	27 30.8	2R59.2	7 59.5	28 52.7	27 10.5
3 W	16 48 33.4	11 9.7	16 47.7	26 12.1	20 39.8	28 36.8	21 0.3	27 41.9	2 55.9	8 1.7	28 54.9	27 11.4
4 T	16 52 30.0	12 10.6	16 44.5	8♎50.1	22 12.7	29 52.2	21 44.8	27 52.9	2 52.7	8 3.8	28 57.1	27 12.3
5 F	16 56 26.5	13 11.5	16 41.3	21 53.1	23 45.4	1♐ 7.7	22 29.3	28 3.8	2 49.6	8 5.9	28 59.3	27 13.2
6 S	17 0 23.1	14 12.4	16 38.2	5♏23.9	25 18.1	2 23.1	23 13.9	28 14.7	2 46.6	8 8.0	29 1.5	27 14.0
7 S	17 4 19.7	15 13.3	16 35.0	19 23.3	26 50.7	3 38.5	23 58.5	28 25.5	2 43.7	8 10.0	29 3.7	27 14.8
8 M	17 8 16.2	16 14.3	16 31.8	3♐48.6	28 23.1	4 54.0	24 43.1	28 36.2	2 40.9	8 12.0	29 5.9	27 15.5
9 T	17 12 12.8	17 15.3	16 28.6	18 34.3	29 55.4	6 9.4	25 27.7	28 46.8	2 38.2	8 13.9	29 8.1	27 16.2
10 W	17 16 9.3	18 16.3	16 25.5	3♑32.0	1♑27.5	7 24.9	26 12.3	28 57.4	2 35.5	8 15.7	29 10.2	27 16.9
11 T	17 20 5.9	19 17.3	16 22.3	18 32.0	2 59.4	8 40.4	26 57.0	29 7.8	2 33.0	8 17.6	29 12.4	27 17.6
12 F	17 24 2.5	20 18.4	16 19.1	3♒25.1	4 31.1	9 55.9	27 41.8	29 18.2	2 30.6	8 19.4	29 14.6	27 18.2
13 S	17 27 59.0	21 19.4	16 15.9	18 3.8	6 2.3	11 11.4	28 26.5	29 28.5	2 28.2	8 21.1	29 16.7	27 18.8
14 S	17 31 55.6	22 20.4	16 12.8	2♓23.8	7 33.2	12 26.8	29 11.2	29 38.6	2 26.0	8 22.8	29 18.8	27 19.3
15 M	17 35 52.1	23 21.5	16 9.6	16 23.1	9 3.5	13 42.3	29 55.9	29 48.7	2 23.8	8 24.4	29 20.9	27 19.9
16 T	17 39 48.7	24 22.5	16 6.4	0♈ 2.1	10 33.1	14 57.8	0♓40.7	29 58.7	2 21.8	8 25.9	29 23.0	27 20.3
17 W	17 43 45.3	25 23.6	16 3.2	13 22.6	12 2.0	16 13.3	1 25.4	0♏ 8.6	2 19.8	8 27.4	29 25.1	27 20.8
18 T	17 47 41.8	26 24.7	16 0.1	26 26.9	13 29.9	17 28.8	2 10.2	0 18.4	2 18.0	8 28.9	29 27.2	27 21.2
19 F	17 51 38.4	27 25.7	15 56.9	9♉17.5	14 56.8	18 44.2	2 54.9	0 28.0	2 16.3	8 30.3	29 29.2	27 21.6
20 S	17 55 34.9	28 26.8	15 53.7	21 56.3	16 22.3	19 59.7	3 39.7	0 37.6	2 14.6	8 31.6	29 31.3	27 21.9
21 S	17 59 31.5	29 27.9	15 50.5	4♊24.8	17 46.2	21 15.2	4 24.5	0 47.1	2 13.1	8 32.9	29 33.3	27 22.2
22 M	18 3 28.0	0♑29.0	15 47.3	16 44.1	19 8.2	22 30.7	5 9.3	0 56.4	2 11.7	8 34.2	29 35.3	27 22.5
23 T	18 7 24.6	1 30.1	15 44.2	28 54.8	20 27.9	23 46.2	5 54.0	1 5.7	2 10.4	8 35.4	29 37.3	27 22.8
24 W	18 11 21.2	2 31.2	15 41.0	10♋57.8	21 45.1	25 1.7	6 38.8	1 14.8	2 9.2	8 36.5	29 39.2	27 23.0
25 T	18 15 17.7	3 32.3	15 37.8	22 54.0	22 59.1	26 17.1	7 23.6	1 23.9	2 8.1	8 37.6	29 41.2	27 23.1
26 F	18 19 14.3	4 33.4	15 34.6	4♌45.0	24 9.4	27 32.6	8 8.3	1 32.8	2 7.1	8 38.6	29 43.1	27 23.3
27 S	18 23 10.8	5 34.5	15 31.5	16 33.0	25 15.6	28 48.1	8 53.1	1 41.6	2 6.2	8 39.6	29 45.1	27 23.4
28 S	18 27 7.4	6 35.6	15 28.3	28 21.1	26 16.8	0♑ 3.6	9 37.9	1 50.3	2 5.5	8 40.5	29 47.0	27 23.5
29 M	18 31 4.0	7 36.8	15 25.1	10♍13.1	27 12.5	1 19.1	10 22.6	1 58.8	2 4.8	8 41.4	29 48.8	27 23.5
30 T	18 35 0.5	8 37.9	15 21.9	22 13.6	28 1.6	2 34.6	11 7.4	2 7.3	2 4.3	8 42.2	29 50.7	27 23.5
31 W	18 38 57.1	9 39.1	15 18.8	4♎27.7	28 43.5	3 50.1	11 52.1	2 15.6	2 3.8	8 42.9	29 52.5	27 23.5
					DECLINATION at NOON							
1 M	16 40 40.3	21S49.5	5S10.4	12N 3.4	24S33.3	18S23.2	16S17.7	9S27.6	10N 1.8	2S30.6	18S18.2	15N21.0
4 T	16 52 30.0	22 15.5	5 14.1	5S13.2	25 7.3	19 19.7	15 31.7	9 39.2	9 59.1	2 33.2	18 19.6	15 21.3
7 S	17 4 19.7	22 37.6	5 17.8	21 51.3	25 29.2	20 11.4	14 44.4	9 50.5	9 56.7	2 35.5	18 21.0	15 21.8
10 W	17 16 9.3	22 55.6	5 21.5	28 10.3	25 38.4	20 57.9	13 56.0	10 1.4	9 54.6	2 37.7	18 22.4	15 22.4
13 S	17 27 59.0	23 9.7	5 25.2	17 39.2	25 34.4	21 38.9	13 6.5	10 12.1	9 52.9	2 39.7	18 23.7	15 23.2
16 T	17 39 48.7	23 19.5	5 28.9	1N 9.2	25 17.1	22 14.2	12 16.0	10 22.3	9 51.4	2 41.5	18 25.0	15 24.1
19 F	17 51 38.4	23 25.2	5 32.6	18 25.7	24 46.5	22 43.6	11 24.7	10 32.2	9 50.3	2 43.1	18 26.2	15 25.1
22 M	18 3 28.0	23 26.6	5 36.3	27 45.8	24 3.3	23 6.8	10 32.6	10 41.6	9 49.5	2 44.6	18 27.5	15 26.2
25 T	18 15 17.7	23 23.9	5 40.0	25 23.0	23 9.1	23 23.6	9 39.7	10 50.7	9 49.1	2 45.8	18 28.6	15 27.5
28 S	18 27 7.4	23 16.8	5 43.7	13 20.5	22 7.1	23 34.0	8 46.2	10 59.4	9 49.0	2 46.8	18 29.8	15 28.9
31 W	18 38 57.1	23 5.6	5 47.4	3S24.4	21 2.0	23 37.8	7 52.2	11 7.6	9 49.2	2 47.7	18 30.9	15 30.4

JANUARY 1970

LONGITUDE at NOON

DAY	EPHEMERIS SIDEREAL TIME	☉	☊	☽	☿	♀	♂	♃	♄	♅	♆	♇
	h m s	° ′	° ′	° ′	° ′	° ′	° ′	° ′	° ′	° ′	° ′	° ′
1 T	18 42 53.6	10♑40.2	15♓15.6	17♎ 0.8	29♑17.1	5♑ 5.6	12♓36.9	2♏23.8	2♉ 3.5	8♎43.6	29♏54.4	27♍23.4
2 F	18 46 50.2	11 41.4	15 12.4	29 57.8	29 41.7	6 21.1	13 21.7	2 31.9	2R 3.4	8 44.3	29 56.2	27 23.4
3 S	18 50 46.8	12 42.6	15 9.2	13♏22.8	29 56.2	7 36.6	14 6.4	2 39.9	2 3.3	8 44.9	29 58.0	27R 23.2
4 S	18 54 43.3	13 43.8	15 6.1	27 17.9	29 60.0	8 52.1	14 51.1	2 47.7	2 3.3	8 45.4	29 59.8	27 23.1
5 M	18 58 39.9	14 44.9	15 2.9	11♐42.6	29R 52.3	10 7.7	15 35.9	2 55.4	2D 3.4	8 45.8	0♐ 1.5	27 22.9
6 T	19 2 36.4	15 46.1	14 59.7	26 32.8	29 32.9	11 23.2	16 20.6	3 2.9	2 3.7	8 46.2	0 3.2	27 22.6
7 W	19 6 33.0	16 47.3	14 56.5	11♑40.9	29 1.6	12 38.6	17 5.3	3 10.3	2 4.0	8 46.6	0 4.9	27 22.4
8 T	19 10 29.5	17 48.5	14 53.4	26 56.8	28 18.8	13 54.1	17 50.0	3 17.6	2 4.5	8 46.9	0 6.6	27 22.1
9 F	19 14 26.1	18 49.6	14 50.2	12♒ 9.5	27 25.4	15 9.6	18 34.7	3 24.7	2 5.1	8 47.1	0 8.2	27 21.7
10 S	19 18 22.7	19 50.8	14 47.0	27 9.0	26 22.5	16 25.1	19 19.4	3 31.7	2 5.8	8 47.3	0 9.8	27 21.4
11 S	19 22 19.2	20 51.9	14 43.8	11♓48.0	25 12.1	17 40.6	20 4.0	3 38.6	2 6.6	8 47.4	0 11.4	27 21.0
12 M	19 26 15.8	21 53.1	14 40.6	26 2.4	23 56.3	18 56.1	20 48.7	3 45.3	2 7.5	8 47.5	0 13.0	27 20.5
13 T	19 30 12.3	22 54.2	14 37.5	9♈51.0	22 37.5	20 11.5	21 33.3	3 51.8	2 8.5	8 47.5	0 14.6	27 20.1
14 W	19 34 8.9	23 55.3	14 34.3	23 15.0	21 18.2	21 27.0	22 17.9	3 58.2	2 9.7	8 47.5	0 16.1	27 19.6
15 T	19 38 5.5	24 56.4	14 31.1	6♉17.1	20 0.9	22 42.5	23 2.5	4 4.5	2 10.9	8R 47.3	0 17.6	27 19.1
16 F	19 42 2.0	25 57.5	14 27.9	19 0.6	18 47.8	23 57.9	23 47.1	4 10.6	2 12.3	8 47.2	0 19.0	27 18.5
17 S	19 45 58.6	26 58.6	14 24.8	1♊28.9	17 40.7	25 13.3	24 31.6	4 16.6	2 13.7	8 47.0	0 20.5	27 17.9
18 S	19 49 55.1	27 59.7	14 21.6	13 45.2	16 41.2	26 28.8	25 16.2	4 22.4	2 15.3	8 46.7	0 21.9	27 17.3
19 M	19 53 51.7	29 0.8	14 18.4	25 52.2	15 50.1	27 44.2	26 0.7	4 28.0	2 17.0	8 46.4	0 23.3	27 16.6
20 T	19 57 48.2	0♒ 1.8	14 15.2	7♋52.2	15 8.1	28 59.6	26 45.1	4 33.5	2 18.8	8 46.0	0 24.6	27 16.0
21 W	20 1 44.8	1 2.8	14 12.1	19 47.0	14 35.4	0♒15.0	27 29.6	4 38.8	2 20.7	8 45.5	0 26.0	27 15.2
22 T	20 5 41.4	2 3.8	14 8.9	1♌38.3	14 12.0	1 30.4	28 14.0	4 44.0	2 22.7	8 45.1	0 27.3	27 14.5
23 F	20 9 37.9	3 4.9	14 5.7	13 27.7	13 57.8	2 45.8	28 58.5	4 49.1	2 24.9	8 44.6	0 28.6	27 13.8
24 S	20 13 34.5	4 5.9	14 2.5	25 17.1	13 52.1	4 1.2	29 42.9	4 53.9	2 27.1	8 44.0	0 29.8	27 13.0
25 S	20 17 31.0	5 6.9	13 59.4	7♍ 8.6	13D 54.5	5 16.6	0♈27.2	4 58.6	2 29.5	8 43.3	0 31.0	27 12.1
26 M	20 21 27.6	6 7.9	13 56.2	19 4.9	14 4.6	6 32.0	1 11.6	5 3.1	2 31.9	8 42.6	0 32.2	27 11.3
27 T	20 25 24.1	7 8.8	13 53.0	1♎ 9.4	14 21.6	7 47.3	1 55.9	5 7.4	2 34.5	8 41.8	0 33.4	27 10.4
28 W	20 29 20.7	8 9.8	13 49.8	13 25.8	14 45.1	9 2.7	2 40.1	5 11.6	2 37.1	8 41.0	0 34.5	27 9.5
29 T	20 33 17.3	9 10.7	13 46.6	25 58.4	15 14.5	10 18.0	3 24.4	5 15.6	2 39.9	8 40.1	0 35.6	27 8.5
30 F	20 37 13.8	10 11.6	13 43.5	8♏51.2	15 49.2	11 33.4	4 8.6	5 19.5	2 42.7	8 39.2	0 36.7	27 7.6
31 S	20 41 10.4	11 12.6	13 40.3	22 8.3	16 28.9	12 48.7	4 52.8	5 23.1	2 45.7	8 38.2	0 37.7	27 6.6

DECLINATION at NOON

DAY	EPHEMERIS SIDEREAL TIME	☉	☊	☽	☿	♀	♂	♃	♄	♅	♆	♇
1 T	18 42 53.6	23S 1.0	5S 48.6	9S 14.8	20S 40.8	23S 37.6	7S 34.1	11S 10.3	9N 49.4	2S 47.9	18S 31.2	15N 30.9
4 S	18 54 43.3	22 44.2	5 52.3	24 17.9	19 43.0	23 32.7	6 39.4	11 17.9	9 50.2	2 48.5	18 32.2	15 32.5
7 W	19 6 33.0	22 23.4	5 56.0	27 23.6	18 59.8	23 21.1	5 44.3	11 25.1	9 51.2	2 48.9	18 33.2	15 34.3
10 S	19 18 22.7	21 58.6	5 59.7	13 47.3	18 36.6	23 3.1	4 49.0	11 31.9	9 52.7	2 49.1	18 34.1	15 36.1
13 T	19 30 12.3	21 30.0	6 3.3	6N 1.9	18 33.2	22 38.7	3 53.4	11 38.1	9 54.5	2 49.1	18 35.0	15 38.1
16 F	19 42 2.0	20 57.6	6 7.0	21 59.1	18 45.0	22 8.0	2 57.6	11 43.9	9 56.6	2 48.8	18 35.8	15 40.1
19 M	19 53 51.7	20 21.7	6 10.7	28 22.8	19 6.5	21 31.3	2 1.9	11 49.2	9 59.0	2 48.4	18 36.6	15 42.2
22 T	20 5 41.4	19 42.3	6 14.4	23 5.0	19 33.1	20 48.8	1 6.1	11 54.0	10 1.8	2 47.8	18 37.2	15 44.4
25 S	20 17 31.0	18 59.6	6 18.0	9 18.8	20 0.8	20 0.7	0 10.4	11 58.3	10 4.9	2 47.0	18 37.9	15 46.6
28 W	20 29 20.7	18 13.8	6 21.7	7S 47.9	20 26.4	19 7.4	0N 45.1	12 2.0	10 8.3	2 46.0	18 38.5	15 48.9
31 S	20 41 10.4	17 25.0	6 25.4	23 2.7	20 46.9	18 9.1	1 40.4	12 5.2	10 12.0	2 44.8	18 39.0	15 51.3

FEBRUARY 1970

LONGITUDE at NOON

DAY	EPHEMERIS SIDEREAL TIME	☉	☊	☽	☿	♀	♂	♃	♄	♅	♆	♇
1 S	20 45 6.9	12♒13.5	13♓37.1	5♐52.2	17♑13.0	14♒ 4.1	5♈37.0	5♏26.6	2♉48.7	8♎37.2	0♐38.7	27♍ 5.6
2 M	20 49 3.5	13 14.4	13 33.9	20 3.9	18 1.1	15 19.4	6 21.1	5 29.9	2 51.9	8R 36.1	0 39.7	27R 4.5
3 T	20 53 0.0	14 15.2	13 30.8	4♑41.6	18 52.9	16 34.7	7 5.2	5 33.1	2 55.1	8 35.0	0 40.6	27 3.4
4 W	20 56 56.6	15 16.1	13 27.6	19 40.2	19 48.1	17 50.0	7 49.3	5 36.0	2 58.5	8 33.8	0 41.5	27 2.3
5 T	21 0 53.2	16 16.9	13 24.4	4♒52.1	20 46.4	19 5.3	8 33.4	5 38.8	3 1.9	8 32.6	0 42.4	27 1.2
6 F	21 4 49.7	17 17.8	13 21.2	20 7.2	21 47.4	20 20.6	9 17.4	5 41.4	3 5.5	8 31.3	0 43.2	27 0.1
7 S	21 8 46.3	18 18.6	13 18.1	5♓15.2	22 51.1	21 35.9	10 1.4	5 43.8	3 9.1	8 30.0	0 44.0	26 58.9
8 S	21 12 42.8	19 19.4	13 14.9	20 7.1	23 57.1	22 51.1	10 45.4	5 46.0	3 12.9	8 28.6	0 44.8	26 57.7
9 M	21 16 39.4	20 20.1	13 11.7	4♈36.3	25 5.2	24 6.4	11 29.4	5 48.0	3 16.7	8 27.2	0 45.5	26 56.5
10 T	21 20 35.9	21 20.8	13 8.5	18 38.9	26 15.4	25 21.6	12 13.3	5 49.9	3 20.6	8 25.8	0 46.3	26 55.3
11 W	21 24 32.5	22 21.6	13 5.3	2♉14.3	27 27.5	26 36.8	12 57.2	5 51.5	3 24.6	8 24.3	0 46.9	26 54.0
12 T	21 28 29.0	23 22.2	13 2.2	15 23.7	28 41.3	27 52.0	13 41.0	5 53.0	3 28.8	8 22.7	0 47.6	26 52.7
13 F	21 32 25.6	24 22.9	12 59.0	28 10.2	29 56.8	29 7.2	14 24.9	5 54.3	3 33.0	8 21.1	0 48.2	26 51.5
14 S	21 36 22.2	25 23.6	12 55.8	10♊37.4	1♒13.8	0♓22.4	15 8.6	5 55.5	3 37.3	8 19.5	0 48.8	26 50.1
15 S	21 40 18.7	26 24.2	12 52.6	22 49.6	2 32.3	1 37.6	15 52.4	5 56.4	3 41.7	8 17.8	0 49.4	26 48.8
16 M	21 44 15.3	27 24.7	12 49.5	4♋50.7	3 52.2	2 52.7	16 36.1	5 57.1	3 46.1	8 16.1	0 49.9	26 47.4
17 T	21 48 11.8	28 25.3	12 46.3	16 44.5	5 13.3	4 7.8	17 19.8	5 57.6	3 50.7	8 14.3	0 50.3	26 46.1
18 W	21 52 8.4	29 25.8	12 43.1	28 34.4	6 35.8	5 22.9	18 3.4	5 58.0	3 55.3	8 12.5	0 50.8	26 44.7
19 T	21 56 4.9	0♓26.2	12 39.9	10♌23.2	7 59.5	6 38.0	18 47.0	5 58.2	4 0.0	8 10.7	0 51.2	26 43.3
20 F	22 0 1.5	1 26.7	12 36.7	22 13.5	9 24.4	7 53.0	19 30.5	5R 58.1	4 4.8	8 8.8	0 51.6	26 41.8
21 S	22 3 58.0	2 27.1	12 33.6	4♍ 7.2	10 50.4	9 8.1	20 14.0	5 57.9	4 9.7	8 6.9	0 51.9	26 40.4
22 S	22 7 54.6	3 27.5	12 30.4	16 6.5	12 17.5	10 23.1	20 57.5	5 57.5	4 14.6	8 4.9	0 52.2	26 38.9
23 M	22 11 51.2	4 27.9	12 27.2	28 13.1	13 45.8	11 38.1	21 40.9	5 56.9	4 19.7	8 2.9	0 52.5	26 37.5
24 T	22 15 47.7	5 28.3	12 24.0	10♎29.2	15 15.1	12 53.1	22 24.3	5 56.2	4 24.8	8 0.9	0 52.7	26 36.0
25 W	22 19 44.3	6 28.6	12 20.9	22 56.8	16 45.5	14 8.1	23 7.7	5 55.2	4 30.0	7 58.8	0 52.9	26 34.5
26 T	22 23 40.8	7 28.9	12 17.7	5♏38.2	18 17.0	15 23.0	23 51.0	5 54.0	4 35.2	7 56.7	0 53.1	26 33.0
27 F	22 27 37.4	8 29.1	12 14.5	18 36.0	19 49.5	16 38.0	24 34.3	5 52.7	4 40.6	7 54.6	0 53.2	26 31.5
28 S	22 31 33.9	9 29.4	12 11.3	1♐52.4	21 23.1	17 52.9	25 17.6	5 51.2	4 46.0	7 52.4	0 53.3	26 29.9

DECLINATION at NOON

DAY	EPHEMERIS SIDEREAL TIME	☉	☊	☽	☿	♀	♂	♃	♄	♅	♆	♇
1 S	20 45 6.9	17S 8.1	6S 26.6	26S 24.0	20S 52.2	17S 48.6	1N 58.8	12S 6.2	10N 13.3	2S 44.4	18S 39.1	15N 52.1
4 W	20 56 56.6	16 15.7	6 30.2	26 6.1	21 3.0	16 44.1	2 53.7	12 8.7	10 17.4	2 43.0	18 39.6	15 54.5
7 S	21 8 46.3	15 20.7	6 33.9	10 9.3	21 4.7	15 35.5	3 48.2	12 10.7	10 21.8	2 41.4	18 39.9	15 56.9
10 T	21 20 35.9	14 23.4	6 37.6	10N 13.4	20 56.4	14 22.9	4 42.3	12 12.1	10 26.4	2 39.6	18 40.2	15 59.4
13 F	21 32 25.6	13 23.9	6 41.2	24 44.4	20 37.5	13 6.8	5 35.8	12 12.9	10 31.3	2 37.8	18 40.5	16 1.8
16 M	21 44 15.3	12 22.4	6 44.9	28 12.4	20 7.6	11 47.6	6 28.8	12 13.2	10 36.5	2 35.7	18 40.7	16 4.3
19 T	21 56 4.9	11 19.2	6 48.5	20 17.6	19 26.4	10 25.6	7 21.1	12 13.0	10 41.8	2 33.5	18 40.8	16 6.8
22 S	22 7 54.6	10 14.4	6 52.1	5 6.8	18 33.6	9 1.0	8 12.6	12 12.2	10 47.4	2 31.2	18 40.8	16 9.3
25 W	22 19 44.3	9 8.2	6 55.8	12S 9.6	17 29.3	7 34.4	9 3.4	12 10.8	10 53.2	2 28.7	18 40.8	16 11.7
28 S	22 31 33.9	8 0.8	6 59.4	25 38.9	16 13.4	6 5.9	9 53.4	12 8.9	10 59.1	2 26.1	18 40.7	16 14.2

MARCH 1970

LONGITUDE at NOON

DAY	EPHEMERIS SIDEREAL TIME	☉	☊	☽	☿	♀	♂	♃	♄	♅	♆	♇
	h m s	° ′	° ′	° ′	° ′	° ′	° ′	° ′	° ′	° ′	° ′	° ′
1 S	22 35 30.5	10♓29.6	12♓ 8.2	15♐29.4	22♒57.7	19♓ 7.8	26♈ 0.8	5♏49.5	4♉51.5	7♎50.2	0♐53.4	26♍28.4
2 M	22 39 27.0	11 29.8	12 5.0	29 27.7	24 33.3	20 22.7	26 43.9	5R47.6	4 57.0	7R48.0	0 53.5	26R26.8
3 T	22 43 23.6	12 30.0	12 1.8	13♑46.9	26 10.1	21 37.6	27 27.1	5 45.5	5 2.6	7 45.8	0 53.5	26 25.2
4 W	22 47 20.1	13 30.1	11 58.6	28 24.5	27 47.9	22 52.4	28 10.2	5 43.2	5 8.3	7 43.5	0R53.4	26 23.7
5 T	22 51 16.7	14 30.3	11 55.4	13♒15.8	29 26.7	24 7.3	28 53.3	5 40.7	5 14.1	7 41.2	0 53.4	26 22.1
6 F	22 55 13.3	15 30.4	11 52.3	28 14.3	1♓ 6.7	25 22.1	29 36.3	5 38.1	5 20.0	7 38.9	0 53.3	26 20.5
7 S	22 59 9.8	16 30.5	11 49.1	13♓11.7	2 47.8	26 36.9	0♉19.3	5 35.3	5 25.9	7 36.6	0 53.2	26 18.9
8 S	23 3 6.4	17 30.5	11 45.9	27 59.9	4 29.9	27 51.7	1 2.3	5 32.3	5 31.8	7 34.2	0 53.0	26 17.3
9 M	23 7 2.9	18 30.5	11 42.7	12♈31.4	6 13.2	29 6.4	1 45.2	5 29.1	5 37.8	7 31.8	0 52.8	26 15.7
10 T	23 10 59.5	19 30.5	11 39.6	26 40.8	7 57.5	0♈21.2	2 28.1	5 25.8	5 43.9	7 29.4	0 52.6	26 14.1
11 W	23 14 56.0	20 30.4	11 36.4	10♉24.8	9 43.1	1 35.9	3 10.9	5 22.3	5 50.1	7 26.9	0 52.3	26 12.5
12 T	23 18 52.6	21 30.3	11 33.2	23 42.7	11 29.7	2 50.6	3 53.7	5 18.6	5 56.3	7 24.5	0 52.0	26 10.9
13 F	23 22 49.1	22 30.2	11 30.0	6♊35.9	13 17.6	4 5.2	4 36.5	5 14.7	6 2.6	7 22.0	0 51.7	26 9.2
14 S	23 26 45.7	23 30.0	11 26.8	19 7.4	15 6.6	5 19.8	5 19.2	5 10.7	6 8.9	7 19.5	0 51.3	26 7.6
15 S	23 30 42.2	24 29.8	11 23.7	1♋21.3	16 56.8	6 34.4	6 1.9	5 6.5	6 15.2	7 17.0	0 50.9	26 6.0
16 M	23 34 38.8	25 29.5	11 20.5	13 22.0	18 48.1	7 49.0	6 44.5	5 2.1	6 21.7	7 14.5	0 50.5	26 4.4
17 T	23 38 35.3	26 29.2	11 17.3	25 14.3	20 40.7	9 3.5	7 27.1	4 57.6	6 28.2	7 11.9	0 50.0	26 2.7
18 W	23 42 31.9	27 28.9	11 14.1	7♌ 2.8	22 34.4	10 18.1	8 9.6	4 52.9	6 34.7	7 9.4	0 49.6	26 1.1
19 T	23 46 28.5	28 28.6	11 11.0	18 51.7	24 29.3	11 32.5	8 52.1	4 48.1	6 41.3	7 6.8	0 49.0	25 59.5
20 F	23 50 25.0	29 28.2	11 7.8	0♍44.6	26 25.3	12 47.0	9 34.6	4 43.1	6 47.9	7 4.3	0 48.5	25 57.8
21 S	23 54 21.6	0♈27.7	11 4.6	12 44.6	28 22.5	14 1.4	10 17.0	4 37.9	6 54.6	7 1.7	0 47.9	25 56.2
22 S	23 58 18.1	1 27.3	11 1.4	24 54.2	0♈20.7	15 15.8	10 59.4	4 32.7	7 1.3	6 59.1	0 47.3	25 54.6
23 M	0 2 14.7	2 26.8	10 58.2	7♎15.1	2 19.9	16 30.2	11 41.7	4 27.2	7 8.1	6 56.5	0 46.6	25 53.0
24 T	0 6 11.2	3 26.2	10 55.1	19 48.5	4 19.9	17 44.6	12 24.0	4 21.7	7 14.9	6 53.9	0 46.0	25 51.3
25 W	0 10 7.8	4 25.6	10 51.9	2♏35.2	6 20.9	18 58.9	13 6.3	4 16.0	7 21.8	6 51.3	0 45.3	25 49.7
26 T	0 14 4.3	5 25.0	10 48.7	15 35.4	8 22.4	20 13.2	13 48.5	4 10.2	7 28.7	6 48.7	0 44.5	25 48.1
27 F	0 18 0.9	6 24.4	10 45.5	28 49.2	10 24.6	21 27.4	14 30.7	4 4.2	7 35.6	6 46.1	0 43.8	25 46.5
28 S	0 21 57.4	7 23.8	10 42.4	12♐16.6	12 27.0	22 41.7	15 12.8	3 58.2	7 42.6	6 43.5	0 43.0	25 44.9
29 S	0 25 54.0	8 23.1	10 39.2	25 57.6	14 29.6	23 55.9	15 54.9	3 52.0	7 49.7	6 40.9	0 42.2	25 43.3
30 M	0 29 50.5	9 22.3	10 36.0	9♑51.8	16 32.2	25 10.0	16 36.9	3 45.6	7 56.7	6 38.3	0 41.3	25 41.7
31 T	0 33 47.1	10 21.6	10 32.8	23 58.5	18 34.3	26 24.3	17 19.0	3 39.3	8 3.9	6 35.8	0 40.5	25 40.2

DECLINATION at NOON

DAY	EPHEMERIS SIDEREAL TIME	☉	☊	☽	☿	♀	♂	♃	♄	♅	♆	♇
1 S	22 35 30.5	7S38.1	7S 0.6	27S54.4	15S45.4	5S36.1	10N 9.8	12S 8.1	11N 1.2	2S25.3	18S40.7	16N15.0
4 W	22 47 20.1	6 29.3	7 4.3	24 3.2	14 14.0	4 5.8	10 58.6	12 5.5	11 7.4	2 22.5	18 40.5	16 17.3
7 S	22 59 9.8	5 19.6	7 7.9	6 29.4	12 30.9	2 34.4	11 46.4	12 2.4	11 13.7	2 19.8	18 40.3	16 19.6
10 T	23 10 59.5	4 9.3	7 11.5	13N46.2	10 36.4	1 2.4	12 33.2	11 58.7	11 20.2	2 16.9	18 40.0	16 21.9
13 F	23 22 49.1	2 58.5	7 15.2	26 36.1	8 30.7	0N30.0	13 18.9	11 54.6	11 26.9	2 14.0	18 39.7	16 24.1
16 M	23 34 38.8	1 47.5	7 18.8	27 15.3	6 14.1	2 2.3	14 3.4	11 49.9	11 33.7	2 11.0	18 39.4	16 26.3
19 T	23 46 28.5	0 36.4	7 22.4	17 8.2	3 47.1	3 34.3	14 46.8	11 44.8	11 40.6	2 8.0	18 38.9	16 28.3
22 S	23 58 18.1	0N34.7	7 26.0	0 56.0	1 10.8	5 5.7	15 28.8	11 39.3	11 47.5	2 4.9	18 38.4	16 30.3
25 W	0 10 7.8	1 45.6	7 29.6	16S11.4	1N33.2	6 36.0	16 9.6	11 33.3	11 54.6	2 1.8	18 37.8	16 32.2
28 S	0 21 57.4	2 56.1	7 33.3	27 27.5	4 22.2	8 5.1	16 49.1	11 27.0	12 1.7	1 58.7	18 37.2	16 34.0
31 T	0 33 47.1	4 6.2	7 36.9	25 7.5	7 12.6	9 32.5	17 27.1	11 20.4	12 8.9	1 55.7	18 36.6	16 35.7

APRIL 1970

LONGITUDE at NOON

DAY	EPHEMERIS SIDEREAL TIME	☉	☊	☽	☿	♀	♂	♃	♄	♅	♆	♇
1 W	0 37 43.6	11♈20.9	10♓29.6	8♒16.5	20♈35.8	27♈38.4	18♉ 1.0	3♏32.7	8♉11.0	6♎33.2	0♐39.6	25♍38.7
2 T	0 41 40.2	12 20.1	10 26.5	22 43.5	22 36.3	28 52.5	18 42.9	3R26.1	8 18.2	6R30.6	0R38.7	25R37.1
3 F	0 45 36.8	13 19.2	10 23.3	7♓15.9	24 35.4	0♉ 6.6	19 24.8	3 19.3	8 25.4	6 28.0	0 37.7	25 35.6
4 S	0 49 33.3	14 18.4	10 20.1	21 49.1	26 32.8	1 20.6	20 6.6	3 12.5	8 32.7	6 25.4	0 36.7	25 34.0
5 S	0 53 29.9	15 17.5	10 16.9	6♈17.6	28 28.0	2 34.6	20 48.5	3 5.6	8 40.0	6 22.9	0 35.7	25 32.5
6 M	0 57 26.4	16 16.5	10 13.8	20 35.3	0♉20.9	3 48.6	21 30.3	2 58.6	8 47.3	6 20.3	0 34.7	25 31.0
7 T	1 1 23.0	17 15.6	10 10.6	4♉37.0	2 10.8	5 2.6	22 12.0	2 51.5	8 54.6	6 17.8	0 33.6	25 29.5
8 W	1 5 19.5	18 14.6	10 7.4	18 18.4	3 57.6	6 16.5	22 53.7	2 44.3	9 2.0	6 15.2	0 32.6	25 28.0
9 T	1 9 16.1	19 13.5	10 4.2	1♊37.3	5 40.7	7 30.4	23 35.4	2 37.0	9 9.4	6 12.7	0 31.4	25 26.6
10 F	1 13 12.6	20 12.4	10 1.0	14 33.2	7 20.0	8 44.3	24 17.0	2 29.7	9 16.8	6 10.2	0 30.3	25 25.1
11 S	1 17 9.2	21 11.3	9 57.9	27 7.8	8 55.2	9 58.1	24 58.6	2 22.4	9 24.2	6 7.7	0 29.2	25 23.7
12 S	1 21 5.7	22 10.2	9 54.7	9♋24.1	10 25.9	11 11.9	25 40.1	2 14.9	9 31.7	6 5.2	0 28.0	25 22.2
13 M	1 25 2.3	23 9.0	9 51.5	21 26.3	11 51.9	12 25.6	26 21.6	2 7.5	9 39.2	6 2.8	0 26.8	25 20.8
14 T	1 28 58.9	24 7.8	9 48.3	3♌19.3	13 13.0	13 39.4	27 3.1	1 60.0	9 46.7	6 0.3	0 25.6	25 19.4
15 W	1 32 55.4	25 6.5	9 45.2	15 8.1	14 29.1	14 53.0	27 44.5	1 52.4	9 54.2	5 57.9	0 24.3	25 18.1
16 T	1 36 52.0	26 5.2	9 42.0	26 58.0	15 40.0	16 6.7	28 25.9	1 44.8	10 1.8	5 55.5	0 23.1	25 16.7
17 F	1 40 48.5	27 3.9	9 38.8	8♍53.7	16 45.4	17 20.3	29 7.2	1 37.2	10 9.4	5 53.1	0 21.8	25 15.4
18 S	1 44 45.1	28 2.5	9 35.6	20 59.5	17 45.4	18 33.9	29 48.5	1 29.6	10 16.9	5 50.8	0 20.5	25 14.1
19 S	1 48 41.6	29 1.1	9 32.4	3♎18.8	18 39.8	19 47.4	0♊29.7	1 21.9	10 24.5	5 48.5	0 19.2	25 12.8
20 M	1 52 38.2	29 59.7	9 29.3	15 54.0	19 28.5	21 0.9	1 10.9	1 14.3	10 32.2	5 46.2	0 17.8	25 11.5
21 T	1 56 34.7	0♉58.2	9 26.1	28 46.2	20 11.5	22 14.4	1 52.2	1 6.6	10 39.8	5 43.9	0 16.5	25 10.3
22 W	2 0 31.3	1 56.7	9 22.9	11♏55.3	20 48.6	23 27.9	2 33.3	0 59.0	10 47.5	5 41.7	0 15.2	25 9.0
23 T	2 4 27.8	2 55.2	9 19.7	25 20.0	21 19.9	24 41.3	3 14.4	0 51.3	10 55.1	5 39.4	0 13.8	25 7.8
24 F	2 8 24.4	3 53.6	9 16.6	8♐58.0	21 45.3	25 54.6	3 55.4	0 43.6	11 2.8	5 37.3	0 12.4	25 6.6
25 S	2 12 21.0	4 52.0	9 13.4	22 46.8	22 4.9	27 7.9	4 36.5	0 36.0	11 10.5	5 35.1	0 11.0	25 5.4
26 S	2 16 17.5	5 50.4	9 10.2	6♑43.5	22 18.7	28 21.2	5 17.4	0 28.4	11 18.1	5 32.9	0 9.5	25 4.3
27 M	2 20 14.1	6 48.8	9 7.0	20 45.9	22 26.7	29 34.5	5 58.4	0 20.8	11 25.8	5 30.8	0 8.1	25 3.2
28 T	2 24 10.6	7 47.1	9 3.9	4♒52.0	22 29.2	0♊47.7	6 39.3	0 13.2	11 33.5	5 28.8	0 6.6	25 2.1
29 W	2 28 7.2	8 45.4	9 0.7	19 0.4	22R26.2	2 0.9	7 20.1	0 5.6	11 41.2	5 26.7	0 5.1	25 1.0
30 T	2 32 3.7	9 43.7	8 57.5	3♓ 9.9	22 18.0	3 14.1	8 1.0	29♎58.1	11 48.9	5 24.7	0 3.6	24 59.9

DECLINATION at NOON

DAY	EPHEMERIS SIDEREAL TIME	☉	☊	☽	☿	♀	♂	♃	♄	♅	♆	♇
1 W	0 37 43.6	4N29.4	7S38.1	20S58.6	8N 8.8	10N 1.2	17N39.5	11S18.1	12N11.3	1S54.7	18S36.4	16N36.2
4 S	0 49 33.3	5 38.5	7 41.7	2 23.5	10 52.6	11 25.9	18 15.6	11 11.0	12 18.6	1 51.6	18 35.7	16 37.8
7 T	1 1 23.0	6 46.8	7 45.3	16N58.5	13 24.7	12 48.2	18 50.3	11 3.7	12 25.8	1 48.6	18 34.9	16 39.2
10 F	1 13 12.6	7 54.0	7 48.9	27 41.0	15 39.3	14 7.7	19 23.4	10 56.2	12 33.1	1 45.7	18 34.1	16 40.5
13 M	1 25 2.3	8 60.0	7 52.5	25 38.0	17 32.5	15 24.1	19 54.9	10 48.5	12 40.5	1 42.8	18 33.3	16 41.7
16 T	1 36 52.0	10 4.6	7 56.1	13 42.6	19 1.7	16 37.0	20 24.8	10 40.7	12 47.8	1 40.0	18 32.4	16 42.8
19 S	1 48 41.6	11 7.7	7 59.7	3S 6.8	20 5.9	17 46.1	20 53.0	10 32.9	12 55.1	1 37.2	18 31.5	16 43.7
22 W	2 0 31.3	12 9.2	8 3.2	19 40.4	20 44.6	18 51.2	21 19.6	10 25.0	13 2.4	1 34.6	18 30.6	16 44.5
25 S	2 12 21.0	13 8.8	8 6.8	28 13.2	20 58.0	19 51.8	21 44.4	10 17.2	13 9.6	1 32.0	18 29.7	16 45.2
28 T	2 24 10.6	14 6.6	8 10.4	21 55.0	20 46.5	20 47.7	22 7.5	10 9.5	13 16.8	1 29.6	18 28.7	16 45.7

MAY 1970

DAY	EPHEMERIS SIDEREAL TIME	☉	☊	☽	☿	♀	♂	♃	♄	♅	♆	♇
	h m s	° ′	° ′	° ′	° ′	° ′	° ′	° ′	° ′	° ′	° ′	° ′
						LONGITUDE at NOON						
1 F	2 36 0.3	10♉41.9	8♓54.3	17♓19.2	22♉ 4.9	4♊27.2	8♊41.8	29♎50.7	11♉56.6	5♎22.7	0♐ 2.1	24♍58.9
2 S	2 39 56.8	11 40.2	8 51.1	1♈26.3	21R47.1	5 40.3	9 22.5	29R43.3	12 4.3	5R20.8	0R 0.6	24R57.9
3 S	2 43 53.4	12 38.4	8 48.0	15 28.4	21 25.1	6 53.3	10 3.3	29 35.9	12 12.0	5 18.9	29♏59.1	24 56.9
4 M	2 47 50.0	13 36.5	8 44.8	29 22.3	20 59.3	8 6.3	10 44.0	29 28.6	12 19.7	5 17.0	29 57.5	24 55.9
5 T	2 51 46.5	14 34.7	8 41.6	13♉ 4.3	20 30.2	9 19.3	11 24.6	29 21.4	12 27.4	5 15.2	29 56.0	24 55.0
6 W	2 55 43.1	15 32.8	8 38.4	26 31.1	19 58.3	10 32.2	12 5.3	29 14.2	12 35.1	5 13.4	29 54.4	24 54.1
7 T	2 59 39.6	16 30.9	8 35.3	9♊40.1	19 24.3	11 45.1	12 45.8	29 7.1	12 42.8	5 11.6	29 52.9	24 53.2
8 F	3 3 36.2	17 29.0	8 32.1	22 30.3	18 48.7	12 58.0	13 26.4	29 0.1	12 50.5	5 9.9	29 51.3	24 52.4
9 S	3 7 32.7	18 27.0	8 28.9	5♋ 2.0	18 12.2	14 10.8	14 6.9	28 53.2	12 58.2	5 8.3	29 49.7	24 51.6
10 S	3 11 29.3	19 25.0	8 25.7	17 17.1	17 35.5	15 23.6	14 47.4	28 46.4	13 5.9	5 6.6	29 48.1	24 50.8
11 M	3 15 25.8	20 23.0	8 22.5	29 19.0	16 59.2	16 36.3	15 27.8	28 39.7	13 13.6	5 5.0	29 46.5	24 50.0
12 T	3 19 22.4	21 21.0	8 19.4	11♌11.9	16 24.0	17 49.1	16 8.3	28 33.1	13 21.3	5 3.5	29 45.0	24 49.3
13 W	3 23 19.0	22 18.9	8 16.2	23 0.7	15 50.3	19 1.7	16 48.7	28 26.6	13 28.9	5 2.0	29 43.4	24 48.6
14 T	3 27 15.5	23 16.8	8 13.0	4♍50.9	15 18.8	20 14.3	17 29.0	28 20.1	13 36.6	5 0.6	29 41.7	24 47.9
15 F	3 31 12.1	24 14.6	8 9.8	16 48.0	14 50.0	21 26.9	18 9.3	28 13.8	13 44.2	4 59.2	29 40.1	24 47.3
16 S	3 35 8.6	25 12.5	8 6.7	28 56.9	14 24.3	22 39.4	18 49.6	28 7.6	13 51.8	4 57.8	29 38.5	24 46.6
17 S	3 39 5.2	26 10.3	8 3.5	11♎22.3	14 2.1	23 51.9	19 29.8	28 1.6	13 59.4	4 56.5	29 36.9	24 46.0
18 M	3 43 1.7	27 8.0	8 0.3	24 7.6	13 43.7	25 4.3	20 10.0	27 55.6	14 7.0	4 55.2	29 35.3	24 45.5
19 T	3 46 58.3	28 5.8	7 57.1	7♏14.5	13 29.3	26 16.7	20 50.2	27 49.8	14 14.6	4 54.0	29 33.6	24 44.9
20 W	3 50 54.9	29 3.5	7 54.0	20 43.1	13 19.2	27 29.0	21 30.3	27 44.1	14 22.1	4 52.8	29 32.0	24 44.4
21 T	3 54 51.4	0♊ 1.2	7 50.8	4♐31.4	13 13.4	28 41.3	22 10.4	27 38.5	14 29.7	4 51.6	29 30.4	24 44.0
22 F	3 58 48.0	0 58.9	7 47.6	18 35.6	13 12.1	29 53.5	22 50.4	27 33.1	14 37.2	4 50.6	29 28.8	24 43.5
23 S	4 2 44.5	1 56.5	7 44.4	2♑50.7	13D15.4	1♋ 5.7	23 30.4	27 27.8	14 44.7	4 49.5	29 27.1	24 43.1
24 S	4 6 41.1	2 54.2	7 41.3	17 11.1	13 23.2	2 17.9	24 10.4	27 22.7	14 52.1	4 48.5	29 25.5	24 42.7
25 M	4 10 37.6	3 51.8	7 38.1	1♒31.9	13 35.5	3 30.0	24 50.4	27 17.7	14 59.6	4 47.6	29 23.9	24 42.4
26 T	4 14 34.2	4 49.4	7 34.9	15 49.2	13 52.3	4 42.0	25 30.3	27 12.8	15 7.0	4 46.7	29 22.3	24 42.1
27 W	4 18 30.8	5 47.0	7 31.7	0♓ 0.4	14 13.5	5 54.0	26 10.2	27 8.1	15 14.4	4 45.8	29 20.6	24 41.8
28 T	4 22 27.3	6 44.6	7 28.5	14 4.3	14 39.0	7 6.0	26 50.1	27 3.5	15 21.8	4 45.0	29 19.0	24 41.5
29 F	4 26 23.9	7 42.1	7 25.4	28 0.3	15 8.7	8 17.9	27 30.0	26 59.1	15 29.1	4 44.3	29 17.4	24 41.3
30 S	4 30 20.4	8 39.7	7 22.2	11♈48.0	15 42.6	9 29.8	28 9.8	26 54.8	15 36.5	4 43.6	29 15.8	24 41.1
31 S	4 34 17.0	9 37.2	7 19.0	25 27.0	16 20.5	10 41.6	28 49.6	26 50.8	15 43.7	4 42.9	29 14.2	24 40.9
						DECLINATION at NOON						
1 F	2 36 0.3	15N 2.2	8S14.0	4S25.2	20N11.4	21N38.5	22N28.8	10S 1.8	13N24.0	1S27.3	18S27.7	16N46.1
4 M	2 47 50.0	15 55.7	8 17.6	14N51.2	19 15.5	22 24.0	22 48.4	9 54.4	13 31.1	1 25.1	18 26.7	16 46.4
7 T	2 59 39.6	16 46.8	8 21.1	26 53.6	18 3.8	23 4.0	23 6.1	9 47.2	13 38.1	1 23.1	18 25.7	16 46.5
10 S	3 11 29.3	17 35.3	8 24.7	26 15.9	16 43.8	23 38.1	23 22.0	9 40.3	13 45.0	1 21.2	18 24.6	16 46.5
13 W	3 23 19.0	18 21.2	8 28.3	15 9.4	15 24.5	24 6.3	23 36.1	9 33.7	13 51.9	1 19.5	18 23.6	16 46.3
16 S	3 35 8.6	19 4.3	8 31.8	1S11.0	14 14.5	24 28.2	23 48.3	9 27.5	13 58.7	1 17.9	18 22.6	16 46.0
19 T	3 46 58.3	19 44.5	8 35.4	17 59.3	13 20.5	24 43.9	23 58.7	9 21.6	14 5.3	1 16.4	18 21.5	16 45.6
22 F	3 58 48.0	20 21.6	8 38.9	27 51.7	12 46.4	24 53.2	24 7.2	9 16.3	14 11.9	1 15.2	18 20.5	16 45.0
25 M	4 10 37.6	20 55.7	8 42.5	22 42.6	12 33.5	24 56.0	24 13.8	9 11.3	14 18.3	1 14.1	18 19.5	16 44.3
28 T	4 22 27.3	21 26.5	8 46.0	5 43.9	12 41.3	24 52.4	24 18.6	9 6.9	14 24.6	1 13.2	18 18.5	16 43.4
31 S	4 34 17.0	21 53.9	8 49.6	13N19.6	13 7.7	24 42.4	24 21.5	9 3.0	14 30.8	1 12.5	18 17.5	16 42.4

JUNE 1970

DAY	EPHEMERIS SIDEREAL TIME	☉	☊	☽	☿	♀	♂	♃	♄	♅	♆	♇
						LONGITUDE at NOON						
1 M	4 38 13.6	10♊34.7	7♓15.8	8♉56.2	17♉ 2.3	11♋53.3	29♊29.3	26♎46.8	15♉51.0	4♎42.3	29♏12.6	24♍40.8
2 T	4 42 10.1	11 32.3	7 12.7	22 14.5	17 48.0	13 5.1	0♋ 9.1	26R43.1	15 58.3	4R41.9	29R11.1	24R40.7
3 W	4 46 6.7	12 29.8	7 9.5	5♊20.2	18 37.3	14 16.8	0 48.8	26 39.5	16 5.5	4 41.4	29 9.5	24 40.7
4 T	4 50 3.2	13 27.2	7 6.3	18 11.9	19 30.3	15 28.4	1 28.5	26 36.1	16 12.7	4 40.9	29 7.9	24 40.6
5 F	4 53 59.8	14 24.7	7 3.1	0♋49.0	20 26.8	16 40.0	2 8.1	26 32.8	16 19.8	4 40.5	29 6.4	24 40.6
6 S	4 57 56.3	15 22.1	6 60.0	13 11.6	21 26.8	17 51.5	2 47.7	26 29.7	16 26.9	4 40.2	29 4.8	24D40.7
7 S	5 1 52.9	16 19.6	6 56.8	25 20.9	22 30.1	19 2.9	3 27.3	26 26.8	16 33.9	4 39.9	29 3.3	24 40.7
8 M	5 5 49.5	17 17.0	6 53.6	7♌19.2	23 36.8	20 14.3	4 6.9	26 24.0	16 41.0	4 39.7	29 1.8	24 40.8
9 T	5 9 46.0	18 14.4	6 50.4	19 10.1	24 46.7	21 25.7	4 46.4	26 21.5	16 48.0	4 39.5	29 0.3	24 41.0
10 W	5 13 42.6	19 11.7	6 47.3	0♍57.7	25 59.7	22 36.9	5 25.9	26 19.1	16 54.9	4 39.4	28 58.7	24 41.1
11 T	5 17 39.1	20 9.1	6 44.1	12 47.2	27 16.0	23 48.2	6 5.4	26 16.9	17 1.8	4 39.3	28 57.3	24 41.3
12 F	5 21 35.7	21 6.4	6 40.9	24 43.7	28 35.3	24 59.3	6 44.8	26 14.8	17 8.7	4 39.3	28 55.8	24 41.5
13 S	5 25 32.3	22 3.8	6 37.7	6♎52.9	29 57.7	26 10.4	7 24.2	26 13.0	17 15.5	4 39.3	28 54.3	24 41.8
14 S	5 29 28.8	23 1.1	6 34.5	19 19.7	1♊23.2	27 21.4	8 3.6	26 11.3	17 22.3	4D39.4	28 52.8	24 42.1
15 M	5 33 25.4	23 58.4	6 31.4	2♏ 8.6	2 51.6	28 32.4	8 43.0	26 9.8	17 29.0	4 39.6	28 51.4	24 42.4
16 T	5 37 21.9	24 55.6	6 28.2	15 22.5	4 23.1	29 43.3	9 22.3	26 8.4	17 35.7	4 39.8	28 50.0	24 42.8
17 W	5 41 18.5	25 52.9	6 25.0	29 2.4	5 57.5	0♌54.1	10 1.6	26 7.3	17 42.3	4 40.0	28 48.6	24 43.2
18 T	5 45 15.1	26 50.2	6 21.8	13♐ 6.6	7 34.9	2 4.8	10 40.9	26 6.3	17 48.9	4 40.3	28 47.2	24 43.6
19 F	5 49 11.6	27 47.4	6 18.7	27 31.2	9 15.2	3 15.5	11 20.1	26 5.5	17 55.4	4 40.7	28 45.8	24 44.0
20 S	5 53 8.2	28 44.6	6 15.5	12♑ 9.8	10 58.3	4 26.1	11 59.4	26 4.9	18 1.9	4 41.1	28 44.5	24 44.5
21 S	5 57 4.7	29 41.9	6 12.3	26 54.8	12 44.3	5 36.7	12 38.6	26 4.5	18 8.4	4 41.6	28 43.1	24 45.0
22 M	6 1 1.3	0♋39.1	6 9.1	11♒38.8	14 33.1	6 47.1	13 17.7	26 4.3	18 14.8	4 42.1	28 41.8	24 45.6
23 T	6 4 57.8	1 36.4	6 6.0	26 15.3	16 24.7	7 57.6	13 56.9	26 4.2	18 21.2	4 42.7	28 40.5	24 46.2
24 W	6 8 54.4	2 33.6	6 2.8	10♓39.8	18 18.8	9 7.9	14 36.1	26D 4.3	18 27.4	4 43.3	28 39.2	24 46.8
25 T	6 12 51.0	3 30.8	5 59.6	24 49.7	20 15.4	10 18.1	15 15.2	26 4.6	18 33.7	4 44.0	28 38.0	24 47.4
26 F	6 16 47.5	4 28.0	5 56.4	8♈44.0	22 14.4	11 28.3	15 54.3	26 5.1	18 39.8	4 44.7	28 36.7	24 48.1
27 S	6 20 44.1	5 25.2	5 53.3	22 22.9	24 15.7	12 38.4	16 33.3	26 5.7	18 46.0	4 45.5	28 35.5	24 48.8
28 S	6 24 40.6	6 22.5	5 50.1	5♉47.2	26 18.9	13 48.4	17 12.4	26 6.6	18 52.0	4 46.3	28 34.3	24 49.5
29 M	6 28 37.2	7 19.7	5 46.9	18 57.8	28 24.0	14 58.3	17 51.4	26 7.6	18 58.0	4 47.2	28 33.1	24 50.3
30 T	6 32 33.8	8 16.9	5 43.7	1♊55.4	0♋30.7	16 8.2	18 30.4	26 8.8	19 4.0	4 48.1	28 31.9	24 51.1
						DECLINATION at NOON						
1 M	4 38 13.6	22N 2.3	8S50.7	18N39.7	13N20.3	24N37.6	24N22.1	9S 1.8	14N32.8	1S12.3	18S17.2	16N42.1
4 T	4 50 3.2	22 25.2	8 54.3	27 48.3	14 7.8	24 1.2	24 22.6	8 58.6	14 38.8	1 11.9	18 16.2	16 40.9
7 S	5 1 52.9	22 44.6	8 57.8	24 18.3	15 8.0	23 54.6	24 21.2	8 55.9	14 44.7	1 11.6	18 15.3	16 39.6
10 W	5 13 42.6	23 0.3	9 1.3	11 20.7	16 17.9	23 24.0	24 18.0	8 53.9	14 50.4	1 11.5	18 14.3	16 38.2
13 S	5 25 32.3	23 12.5	9 4.9	5S 7.9	17 34.6	22 47.6	24 13.1	8 52.4	14 55.9	1 11.6	18 13.4	16 36.7
16 T	5 37 21.9	23 20.9	9 8.4	20 58.5	18 54.9	22 5.7	24 6.3	8 51.5	15 1.2	1 11.9	18 12.6	16 35.1
19 F	5 49 11.6	23 25.6	9 11.9	28 5.5	20 15.2	21 18.5	23 57.8	8 51.2	15 6.4	1 12.4	18 11.8	16 33.3
22 M	6 1 1.3	23 26.6	9 15.4	19 13.2	21 31.2	20 26.3	23 47.6	8 51.5	15 11.4	1 13.0	18 11.0	16 31.5
25 T	6 12 51.0	23 23.9	9 18.9	0 26.9	22 38.0	19 29.4	23 35.7	8 52.4	15 16.3	1 13.9	18 10.3	16 29.5
28 S	6 24 40.6	23 17.5	9 22.4	17N39.4	23 30.5	18 28.0	23 22.2	8 53.9	15 20.9	1 14.9	18 9.6	16 27.5

JULY 1970

LONGITUDE at NOON

DAY	EPHEMERIS SIDEREAL TIME h m s	☉ ° ′	☊ ° ′	☽ ° ′	☿ ° ′	♀ ° ′	♂ ° ′	♃ ° ′	♄ ° ′	♅ ° ′	♆ ° ′	♇ ° ′
1 W	6 36 30.3	9♋14.1	5♓40.6	14♊40.5	2♋38.7	17♌18.0	19♋ 9.4	26♎10.1	19♉ 9.9	4♎49.1	28♏30.8	24♍51.9
2 T	6 40 26.9	10 11.4	5 37.4	27 13.5	4 47.7	18 27.7	19 48.4	26 11.7	19 15.7	4 50.1	28R29.7	24 52.8
3 F	6 44 23.4	11 8.6	5 34.2	9♋34.8	6 57.5	19 37.3	20 27.3	26 13.4	19 21.4	4 51.2	28 28.6	24 53.6
4 S	6 48 20.0	12 5.8	5 31.0	21 45.3	9 7.8	20 46.8	21 6.2	26 15.3	19 27.1	4 52.4	28 27.5	24 54.6
5 S	6 52 16.6	13 3.0	5 27.8	3♌46.0	11 18.2	21 56.2	21 45.1	26 17.3	19 32.8	4 53.5	28 26.5	24 55.5
6 M	6 56 13.1	14 0.2	5 24.7	15 39.1	13 28.5	23 5.6	22 24.0	26 19.6	19 38.3	4 54.8	28 25.4	24 56.5
7 T	7 0 9.7	14 57.5	5 21.5	27 27.1	15 38.5	24 14.8	23 2.9	26 22.0	19 43.8	4 56.1	28 24.4	24 57.5
8 W	7 4 6.2	15 54.7	5 18.3	9♍13.5	17 47.9	25 24.0	23 41.7	26 24.6	19 49.2	4 57.4	28 23.5	24 58.5
9 T	7 8 2.8	16 51.9	5 15.1	21 2.4	19 56.4	26 33.0	24 20.5	26 27.4	19 54.6	4 58.8	28 22.5	24 59.6
10 F	7 11 59.3	17 49.1	5 12.0	2♎58.4	22 3.9	27 42.0	24 59.3	26 30.3	19 59.9	5 0.3	28 21.6	25 0.7
11 S	7 15 55.9	18 46.3	5 8.8	15 6.5	24 10.1	28 50.8	25 38.1	26 33.4	20 5.1	5 1.7	28 20.7	25 1.8
12 S	7 19 52.5	19 43.5	5 5.6	27 31.9	26 15.1	29 59.6	26 16.9	26 36.7	20 10.2	5 3.3	28 19.8	25 2.9
13 M	7 23 49.0	20 40.7	5 2.4	10♏19.3	28 18.6	1♍ 8.2	26 55.6	26 40.1	20 15.3	5 4.9	28 19.0	25 4.1
14 T	7 27 45.6	21 38.0	4 59.3	23 32.3	0♌20.5	2 16.8	27 34.4	26 43.7	20 20.4	5 6.6	28 18.2	25 5.3
15 W	7 31 42.1	22 35.2	4 56.1	7♐13.1	2 20.8	3 25.2	28 13.1	26 47.5	20 25.3	5 8.2	28 17.4	25 6.6
16 T	7 35 38.7	23 32.4	4 52.9	21 21.5	4 19.4	4 33.4	28 51.8	26 51.4	20 30.1	5 10.0	28 16.7	25 7.8
17 F	7 39 35.3	24 29.7	4 49.7	5♑54.4	6 16.3	5 41.6	29 30.4	26 55.5	20 34.9	5 11.8	28 15.9	25 9.1
18 S	7 43 31.8	25 26.9	4 46.6	20 46.1	8 11.4	6 49.6	0♌ 9.1	26 59.8	20 39.6	5 13.6	28 15.2	25 10.4
19 S	7 47 28.4	26 24.1	4 43.4	5♒48.5	10 4.8	7 57.5	0 47.7	27 4.2	20 44.2	5 15.5	28 14.5	25 11.8
20 M	7 51 24.9	27 21.3	4 40.2	20 52.4	11 56.3	9 5.3	1 26.3	27 8.7	20 48.7	5 17.4	28 13.9	25 13.1
21 T	7 55 21.5	28 18.6	4 37.0	5♓49.3	13 46.1	10 13.0	2 4.9	27 13.4	20 53.2	5 19.3	28 13.3	25 14.5
22 W	7 59 18.0	29 15.9	4 33.8	20 32.0	15 34.0	11 20.5	2 43.5	27 18.3	20 57.6	5 21.3	28 12.7	25 15.9
23 T	8 3 14.6	0♌13.1	4 30.7	4♈55.8	17 20.2	12 27.9	3 22.0	27 23.3	21 1.9	5 23.4	28 12.1	25 17.3
24 F	8 7 11.2	1 10.4	4 27.5	18 58.1	19 4.6	13 35.1	4 0.6	27 28.5	21 6.1	5 25.5	28 11.6	25 18.8
25 S	8 11 7.7	2 7.7	4 24.3	2♉38.7	20 47.2	14 42.3	4 39.1	27 33.8	21 10.2	5 27.6	28 11.1	25 20.3
26 S	8 15 4.3	3 5.0	4 21.1	15 58.4	22 28.0	15 49.2	5 17.7	27 39.3	21 14.2	5 29.8	28 10.6	25 21.8
27 M	8 19 0.8	4 2.4	4 18.0	28 59.2	24 7.1	16 56.1	5 56.2	27 44.9	21 18.2	5 32.0	28 10.2	25 23.3
28 T	8 22 57.4	4 59.7	4 14.8	11♊43.4	25 44.4	18 2.8	6 34.7	27 50.7	21 22.1	5 34.3	28 9.8	25 24.9
29 W	8 26 53.9	5 57.1	4 11.6	24 13.1	27 20.0	19 9.3	7 13.2	27 56.6	21 25.8	5 36.6	28 9.4	25 26.5
30 T	8 30 50.5	6 54.5	4 8.4	6♋30.7	28 53.8	20 15.7	7 51.7	28 2.7	21 29.5	5 39.0	28 9.0	25 28.1
31 F	8 34 47.1	7 51.9	4 5.3	18 38.2	0♍25.8	21 21.9	8 30.1	28 8.9	21 33.1	5 41.4	28 8.7	25 29.7

DECLINATION at NOON

DAY	SIDEREAL TIME	☉	☊	☽	☿	♀	♂	♃	♄	♅	♆	♇
1 W	6 36 30.3	23N 7.4	9S25.9	27N32.2	24N 3.3	17N22.6	23N 7.0	8S55.9	15N25.3	1S16.2	18S 8.9	16N25.3
4 S	6 48 20.0	22 53.7	9 29.4	25 4.6	24 12.8	16 13.3	22 50.2	8 58.5	15 29.6	1 17.6	18 8.4	16 23.1
7 T	7 0 9.7	22 36.4	9 32.9	12 53.2	23 57.2	15 0.6	22 31.8	9 1.7	15 33.6	1 19.2	18 7.8	16 20.8
10 F	7 11 59.3	22 15.5	9 36.4	3S30.4	23 17.4	13 44.8	22 11.9	9 5.5	15 37.5	1 20.9	18 7.3	16 18.4
13 M	7 23 49.0	21 51.2	9 39.9	19 25.4	22 16.2	12 26.1	21 50.6	9 9.7	15 41.1	1 22.9	18 6.9	16 15.9
16 T	7 35 38.7	21 23.6	9 43.4	28 4.6	20 57.2	11 4.9	21 27.8	9 14.6	15 44.5	1 25.0	18 6.5	16 13.4
19 S	7 47 28.4	20 52.7	9 46.9	21 8.7	19 24.2	9 41.6	21 3.6	9 19.9	15 47.7	1 27.3	18 6.2	16 10.8
22 W	7 59 18.0	20 18.6	9 50.4	2 19.1	17 40.8	8 16.3	20 38.1	9 25.6	15 50.7	1 29.7	18 6.0	16 8.1
25 S	8 11 7.7	19 41.5	9 53.8	16N36.8	15 50.1	6 49.6	20 11.2	9 31.9	15 53.4	1 32.3	18 5.8	16 5.4
28 T	8 22 57.4	19 1.4	9 57.3	27 18.7	13 54.6	5 21.5	19 43.1	9 38.6	15 55.9	1 35.1	18 5.6	16 2.7
31 F	8 34 47.1	18 18.4	10 0.8	25 46.3	11 56.7	3 52.4	19 13.7	9 45.8	15 58.2	1 38.0	18 5.6	15 59.9

AUGUST 1970

LONGITUDE at NOON

DAY	SIDEREAL TIME	☉	☊	☽	☿	♀	♂	♃	♄	♅	♆	♇
1 S	8 38 43.6	8♌49.3	4♓ 2.1	0♌37.4	1♍56.1	22♍28.0	9♌ 8.6	28♎15.3	21♉36.6	5♎43.8	28♏ 8.4	25♍31.4
2 S	8 42 40.2	9 46.7	3 58.9	12 30.4	3 24.5	23 33.9	9 47.0	28 21.7	21 40.1	5 46.3	28R 8.2	25 33.0
3 M	8 46 36.7	10 44.2	3 55.7	24 18.9	4 51.2	24 39.7	10 25.4	28 28.4	21 43.4	5 48.8	28 7.9	25 34.7
4 T	8 50 33.3	11 41.7	3 52.5	6♍ 5.5	6 16.1	25 45.3	11 3.9	28 35.2	21 46.7	5 51.4	28 7.8	25 36.5
5 W	8 54 29.8	12 39.2	3 49.4	17 52.7	7 39.1	26 50.7	11 42.3	28 42.1	21 49.8	5 54.0	28 7.6	25 38.2
6 T	8 58 26.4	13 36.7	3 46.2	29 43.6	9 0.2	27 55.9	12 20.7	28 49.1	21 52.9	5 56.6	28 7.5	25 40.0
7 F	9 2 23.0	14 34.2	3 43.0	11♎41.7	10 19.3	29 0.9	12 59.1	28 56.3	21 55.8	5 59.3	28 7.4	25 41.8
8 S	9 6 19.5	15 31.7	3 39.8	23 51.2	11 36.5	0♎ 5.7	13 37.4	29 3.6	21 58.7	6 2.0	28 7.3	25 43.6
9 S	9 10 16.1	16 29.2	3 36.7	6♏16.1	12 51.7	1 10.3	14 15.8	29 11.0	22 1.4	6 4.7	28 7.3	25 45.4
10 M	9 14 12.6	17 26.8	3 33.5	19 0.7	14 4.7	2 14.7	14 54.1	29 18.6	22 4.1	6 7.5	28 7.3	25 47.2
11 T	9 18 9.2	18 24.3	3 30.3	2♐ 8.8	15 15.6	3 18.9	15 32.5	29 26.2	22 6.6	6 10.3	28 7.3	25 49.1
12 W	9 22 5.7	19 21.9	3 27.1	15 43.2	16 24.3	4 22.9	16 10.8	29 34.0	22 9.1	6 13.2	28D 7.4	25 50.9
13 T	9 26 2.3	20 19.5	3 24.0	29 44.9	17 30.7	5 26.6	16 49.1	29 42.0	22 11.5	6 16.1	28 7.5	25 52.8
14 F	9 29 58.8	21 17.1	3 20.8	14♑12.7	18 34.6	6 30.1	17 27.4	29 50.0	22 13.7	6 19.0	28 7.6	25 54.7
15 S	9 33 55.4	22 14.7	3 17.6	29 2.8	19 36.0	7 33.4	18 5.7	29 58.2	22 15.9	6 21.9	28 7.8	25 56.6
16 S	9 37 52.0	23 12.3	3 14.4	14♒ 8.4	20 34.7	8 36.4	18 43.9	0♏ 6.5	22 17.9	6 24.9	28 8.0	25 58.6
17 M	9 41 48.5	24 10.0	3 11.2	29 20.9	21 30.7	9 39.1	19 22.2	0 14.9	22 19.9	6 27.9	28 8.2	26 0.5
18 T	9 45 45.1	25 7.7	3 8.1	14♓30.7	22 23.7	10 41.6	20 0.4	0 23.4	22 21.8	6 31.0	28 8.5	26 2.5
19 W	9 49 41.6	26 5.4	3 4.9	29 28.7	23 13.6	11 43.8	20 38.7	0 32.0	22 23.5	6 34.1	28 8.8	26 4.5
20 T	9 53 38.2	27 3.1	3 1.7	14♈ 7.7	24 0.3	12 45.8	21 16.9	0 40.7	22 25.2	6 37.2	28 9.1	26 6.5
21 F	9 57 34.7	28 0.9	2 58.5	28 22.8	24 43.6	13 47.4	21 55.2	0 49.6	22 26.7	6 40.3	28 9.4	26 8.5
22 S	10 1 31.3	28 58.7	2 55.4	12♉12.0	25 23.2	14 48.8	22 33.4	0 58.5	22 28.2	6 43.5	28 9.8	26 10.5
23 S	10 5 27.8	29 56.5	2 52.2	25 35.4	25 58.9	15 49.9	23 11.6	1 7.6	22 29.5	6 46.7	28 10.3	26 12.6
24 M	10 9 24.4	0♍54.3	2 49.0	8♊35.0	26 30.6	16 50.7	23 49.8	1 16.8	22 30.8	6 49.9	28 10.7	26 14.6
25 T	10 13 20.9	1 52.3	2 45.8	21 13.9	26 57.9	17 51.2	24 28.1	1 26.1	22 31.9	6 53.2	28 11.2	26 16.8
26 W	10 17 17.5	2 50.2	2 42.6	3♋35.5	27 20.7	18 51.3	25 6.3	1 35.5	22 33.0	6 56.5	28 11.8	26 18.8
27 T	10 21 14.1	3 48.1	2 39.5	15 43.6	27 38.5	19 51.1	25 44.5	1 45.0	22 33.9	6 59.8	28 12.3	26 20.9
28 F	10 25 10.6	4 46.1	2 36.3	27 41.9	27 51.3	20 50.5	26 22.7	1 54.5	22 34.7	7 3.1	28 12.9	26 23.0
29 S	10 29 7.2	5 44.0	2 33.1	9♌33.5	27 58.7	21 49.7	27 0.9	2 4.2	22 35.4	7 6.4	28 13.5	26 25.2
30 S	10 33 3.7	6 42.1	2 29.9	21 21.4	28 0.5	22 48.4	27 39.1	2 14.0	22 36.0	7 9.8	28 14.1	26 27.3
31 M	10 37 0.3	7 40.1	2 26.8	3♍ 8.3	27R56.4	23 46.7	28 17.2	2 23.9	22 36.5	7 13.2	28 14.8	26 29.4

DECLINATION at NOON

DAY	SIDEREAL TIME	☉	☊	☽	☿	♀	♂	♃	♄	♅	♆	♇
1 S	8 38 43.6	18N 3.5	10S 1.9	22N45.3	11N17.1	3N22.5	19N 3.7	9S48.3	15N59.0	1S39.0	18S 5.6	15N58.9
4 T	8 50 33.3	17 17.0	10 5.4	8 59.9	9 18.7	1 52.5	18 32.7	9 56.0	16 0.9	1 42.1	18 5.6	15 56.1
7 F	9 2 23.0	16 28.0	10 8.8	7S40.5	7 22.1	0 22.1	18 0.7	10 4.1	16 2.7	1 45.3	18 5.7	15 53.2
10 M	9 14 12.6	15 36.6	10 12.3	22 24.2	5 28.9	1S 8.2	17 27.6	10 12.6	16 4.2	1 48.6	18 5.8	15 50.3
13 T	9 26 2.3	14 42.9	10 15.7	28 9.5	3 40.8	2 38.4	16 53.5	10 21.4	16 5.5	1 52.1	18 6.1	15 47.4
16 S	9 37 52.0	13 47.2	10 19.2	18 12.8	1 59.8	4 8.0	16 18.4	10 30.6	16 6.5	1 55.7	18 6.4	15 44.5
19 W	9 49 41.6	12 49.5	10 22.6	1N58.7	0 28.2	5 36.8	15 42.3	10 40.1	16 7.3	1 59.4	18 6.7	15 41.6
22 S	10 1 31.3	11 50.0	10 26.1	20 13.0	0S51.4	7 4.5	15 5.4	10 49.9	16 7.8	2 3.1	18 7.1	15 38.7
25 T	10 13 20.9	10 48.7	10 29.5	28 10.2	1 55.7	8 31.0	14 27.5	11 0.0	16 8.1	2 7.1	18 7.6	15 35.8
28 F	10 25 10.6	9 45.9	10 32.9	23 37.1	2 40.4	9 55.9	13 48.9	11 10.4	16 8.2	2 11.0	18 8.1	15 32.9
31 M	10 37 0.3	8 41.7	10 36.3	10 19.8	3 0.6	11 19.0	13 9.5	11 21.0	16 8.0	2 15.1	18 8.7	15 30.1

SEPTEMBER 1970

DAY	EPHEMERIS SIDEREAL TIME	☉	☊	☽	☿	♀	♂	♃	♄	♅	♆	♇
	h m s	° ′	° ′	° ′	° ′	° ′	° ′	° ′	° ′	° ′	° ′	° ′
						LONGITUDE at NOON						
1 T	10 40 56.8	8 ♍ 38.2	2 ♓ 23.6	14 ♍ 56.5	27 ♍ 46.2	24 ♎ 44.7	28 ♌ 55.4	2 ♏ 33.9	22 ♉ 36.9	7 ♎ 16.7	28 ♏ 15.5	26 ♍ 31.6
2 W	10 44 53.4	9 36.3	2 20.4	26 48.3	27 R 29.9	25 42.3	29 33.6	2 43.9	22 37.1	7 20.1	28 16.3	26 33.7
3 T	10 48 49.9	10 34.4	2 17.2	8 ♎ 45.8	27 7.3	26 39.4	0 ♍ 11.7	2 54.1	22 37.3	7 23.6	28 17.0	26 35.9
4 F	10 52 46.5	11 32.6	2 14.1	20 51.5	26 38.4	27 36.1	0 49.9	3 4.3	22 37.4	7 27.1	28 17.8	26 38.1
5 S	10 56 43.0	12 30.8	2 10.9	3 ♏ 7.8	26 3.4	28 32.3	1 28.0	3 14.7	22 R 37.3	7 30.6	28 18.7	26 40.2
6 S	11 0 39.6	13 29.0	2 7.7	15 37.6	25 22.5	29 28.1	2 6.2	3 25.1	22 37.1	7 34.1	28 19.5	26 42.4
7 M	11 4 36.2	14 27.2	2 4.5	28 23.7	24 36.2	0 ♏ 23.4	2 44.3	3 35.6	22 36.9	7 37.6	28 20.4	26 44.6
8 T	11 8 32.7	15 25.4	2 1.3	11 ♐ 29.0	23 45.0	1 18.1	3 22.5	3 46.2	22 36.5	7 41.2	28 21.4	26 46.8
9 W	11 12 29.3	16 23.7	1 58.2	24 55.9	22 49.7	2 12.4	4 0.6	3 56.9	22 36.0	7 44.8	28 22.3	26 49.0
10 T	11 16 25.8	17 22.0	1 55.0	8 ♑ 46.3	21 51.2	3 6.0	4 38.7	4 7.7	22 35.4	7 48.4	28 23.3	26 51.2
11 F	11 20 22.4	18 20.4	1 51.8	23 0.3	20 50.8	3 59.1	5 16.8	4 18.5	22 34.7	7 52.0	28 24.3	26 53.5
12 S	11 24 18.9	19 18.7	1 48.6	7 ♒ 36.2	19 49.6	4 51.7	5 54.9	4 29.4	22 33.9	7 55.6	28 25.4	26 55.7
13 S	11 28 15.5	20 17.1	1 45.5	22 29.9	18 49.0	5 43.6	6 33.0	4 40.4	22 33.0	7 59.3	28 26.4	26 57.9
14 M	11 32 12.0	21 15.5	1 42.3	7 ♓ 35.0	17 50.6	6 34.8	7 11.1	4 51.5	22 32.0	8 2.9	28 27.5	27 0.1
15 T	11 36 8.6	22 14.0	1 39.1	22 43.1	16 55.6	7 25.4	7 49.3	5 2.7	22 30.9	8 6.6	28 28.7	27 2.4
16 W	11 40 5.1	23 12.5	1 35.9	7 ♈ 44.9	16 5.6	8 15.3	8 27.4	5 13.9	22 29.7	8 10.3	28 29.9	27 4.6
17 T	11 44 1.7	24 11.0	1 32.7	22 31.6	15 21.7	9 4.5	9 5.5	5 25.2	22 28.4	8 14.0	28 31.1	27 6.9
18 F	11 47 58.2	25 9.5	1 29.6	6 ♉ 56.5	14 45.2	9 53.0	9 43.5	5 36.5	22 27.0	8 17.7	28 32.3	27 9.1
19 S	11 51 54.8	26 8.1	1 26.4	20 55.1	14 16.8	10 40.7	10 21.6	5 47.9	22 25.4	8 21.4	28 33.5	27 11.4
20 S	11 55 51.4	27 6.7	1 23.2	4 ♊ 25.8	13 57.5	11 27.5	10 59.7	5 59.4	22 23.8	8 25.2	28 34.8	27 13.6
21 M	11 59 47.9	28 5.4	1 20.0	17 29.7	13 47.6	12 13.6	11 37.8	6 11.0	22 22.1	8 28.9	28 36.1	27 15.8
22 T	12 3 44.5	29 4.0	1 16.9	0 ♋ 9.6	13 47.5	12 58.8	12 15.9	6 22.6	22 20.2	8 32.6	28 37.4	27 18.1
23 W	12 7 41.0	0 ♎ 2.8	1 13.7	12 29.6	13 D 57.4	13 43.1	12 54.0	6 34.3	22 18.3	8 36.4	28 38.8	27 20.3
24 T	12 11 37.6	1 1.5	1 10.5	24 34.2	14 17.0	14 26.5	13 32.1	6 46.1	22 16.2	8 40.2	28 40.2	27 22.6
25 F	12 15 34.1	2 0.3	1 7.3	6 ♌ 28.3	14 46.1	15 9.0	14 10.2	6 57.9	22 14.1	8 43.9	28 41.6	27 24.8
26 S	12 19 30.7	2 59.2	1 4.1	18 16.5	15 24.4	15 50.4	14 48.3	7 9.8	22 11.8	8 47.7	28 43.0	27 27.0
27 S	12 23 27.2	3 58.0	1 1.0	0 ♍ 2.9	16 11.4	16 30.8	15 26.4	7 21.7	22 9.5	8 51.5	28 44.5	27 29.3
28 M	12 27 23.8	4 56.9	0 57.8	11 51.1	17 6.5	17 10.1	16 4.4	7 33.7	22 7.1	8 55.2	28 46.0	27 31.5
29 T	12 31 20.3	5 55.9	0 54.6	23 44.1	18 9.0	17 48.3	16 42.5	7 45.7	22 4.5	8 59.0	28 47.5	27 33.7
30 W	12 35 16.9	6 54.9	0 51.4	5 ♎ 44.2	19 18.3	18 25.3	17 20.6	7 57.8	22 1.9	9 2.8	28 49.0	27 35.9
						DECLINATION at NOON						
1 T	10 40 56.8	8 N 20.0	10 S 37.5	4 N 54.4	3 S 1.1	11 S 46.3	12 N 56.3	11 S 24.6	16 N 7.9	2 S 16.5	18 S 8.9	15 N 29.1
4 F	10 52 46.5	7 14.2	10 40.9	11 S 47.3	2 40.9	13 6.5	12 15.9	11 35.4	16 7.4	2 20.6	18 9.6	15 26.3
7 M	11 4 36.2	6 7.3	10 44.3	24 56.3	1 46.8	14 24.3	11 34.9	11 46.5	16 6.7	2 24.9	18 10.4	15 23.5
10 T	11 16 25.8	4 59.5	10 47.7	27 25.2	0 20.8	15 39.4	10 53.4	11 57.8	16 5.7	2 29.1	18 11.1	15 20.8
13 S	11 28 15.5	3 51.0	10 51.1	14 54.7	1 N 27.1	16 51.4	10 11.2	12 9.2	16 4.5	2 33.5	18 12.0	15 18.1
16 W	11 40 5.1	2 41.8	10 54.5	5 N 50.9	3 19.4	18 0.2	9 28.5	12 20.8	16 3.1	2 37.9	18 12.9	15 15.4
19 S	11 51 54.8	1 32.2	10 57.9	22 56.5	4 56.0	19 5.4	8 45.3	12 32.6	16 1.5	2 42.3	18 13.9	15 12.8
22 T	12 3 44.5	0 22.3	11 1.3	28 5.9	6 0.5	20 6.8	8 1.7	12 44.4	15 59.6	2 46.7	18 14.9	15 10.3
25 F	12 15 34.1	0 S 47.9	11 4.7	20 53.9	6 24.3	21 4.1	7 17.7	12 56.3	15 57.5	2 51.2	18 15.9	15 7.8
28 M	12 27 23.8	1 58.0	11 8.1	6 20.7	6 6.1	21 57.1	6 33.3	13 8.3	15 55.2	2 55.7	18 17.0	15 5.4

OCTOBER 1970

DAY	EPHEMERIS SIDEREAL TIME	☉	☊	☽	☿	♀	♂	♃	♄	♅	♆	♇
						LONGITUDE at NOON						
1 T	12 39 13.4	7 ♎ 53.9	0 ♓ 48.3	17 ♎ 53.2	20 ♍ 33.6	19 ♏ 1.1	17 ♍ 58.7	8 ♏ 10.0	21 ♉ 59.2	9 ♎ 6.6	28 ♏ 50.6	27 ♍ 38.2
2 F	12 43 10.0	8 52.9	0 45.1	0 ♏ 12.4	21 54.3	19 35.7	18 36.8	8 22.2	21 R 56.4	9 10.4	28 52.2	27 40.4
3 S	12 47 6.5	9 52.0	0 41.9	12 42.9	23 19.7	20 8.9	19 14.9	8 34.5	21 53.5	9 14.2	28 53.8	27 42.6
4 S	12 51 3.1	10 51.1	0 38.7	25 25.7	24 49.1	20 40.7	19 53.0	8 46.8	21 50.5	9 18.0	28 55.4	27 44.8
5 M	12 54 59.7	11 50.2	0 35.5	8 ♐ 21.7	26 21.9	21 11.1	20 31.0	8 59.1	21 47.4	9 21.8	28 57.1	27 47.0
6 T	12 58 56.2	12 49.5	0 32.4	21 32.1	27 57.6	21 40.0	21 9.2	9 11.6	21 44.3	9 25.6	28 58.8	27 49.2
7 W	13 2 52.8	13 48.7	0 29.2	4 ♑ 58.1	29 35.6	22 7.4	21 47.2	9 24.0	21 41.0	9 29.4	29 0.5	27 51.4
8 T	13 6 49.3	14 47.9	0 26.0	18 40.8	1 ♎ 15.4	22 33.1	22 25.3	9 36.5	21 37.7	9 33.1	29 2.2	27 53.5
9 F	13 10 45.9	15 47.1	0 22.8	2 ♒ 41.0	2 56.8	22 57.1	23 3.4	9 49.1	21 34.3	9 36.9	29 4.0	27 55.7
10 S	13 14 42.4	16 46.4	0 19.7	16 58.3	4 39.3	23 19.4	23 41.4	10 1.6	21 30.8	9 40.7	29 5.8	27 57.8
11 S	13 18 39.0	17 45.7	0 16.5	1 ♓ 31.1	6 22.6	23 39.9	24 19.5	10 14.3	21 27.2	9 44.5	29 7.5	27 60.0
12 M	13 22 35.5	18 45.1	0 13.3	16 15.8	8 6.5	23 58.5	24 57.6	10 26.9	21 23.6	9 48.2	29 9.3	28 2.1
13 T	13 26 32.1	19 44.5	0 10.1	1 ♈ 6.5	9 50.7	24 15.2	25 35.6	10 39.6	21 19.9	9 52.0	29 11.2	28 4.2
14 W	13 30 28.6	20 43.9	0 6.9	15 56.0	11 35.1	24 29.8	26 13.7	10 52.3	21 16.1	9 55.7	29 13.0	28 6.3
15 T	13 34 25.2	21 43.3	0 3.8	0 ♉ 36.2	13 19.4	24 42.5	26 51.8	11 5.1	21 12.2	9 59.4	29 14.9	28 8.4
16 F	13 38 21.8	22 42.8	0 0.6	14 59.6	15 3.7	24 53.0	27 29.9	11 17.9	21 8.3	10 3.2	29 16.8	28 10.5
17 S	13 42 18.3	23 42.3	29 ♒ 57.4	29 0.4	16 47.7	25 1.3	28 7.9	11 30.7	21 4.3	10 6.9	29 18.7	28 12.6
18 S	13 46 14.9	24 41.9	29 54.2	12 ♊ 35.1	18 31.4	25 7.4	28 46.0	11 43.6	21 0.2	10 10.6	29 20.6	28 14.7
19 M	13 50 11.4	25 41.4	29 51.1	25 43.3	20 14.7	25 11.3	29 24.1	11 56.4	20 56.1	10 14.3	29 22.5	28 16.7
20 T	13 54 8.0	26 41.1	29 47.9	8 ♋ 26.5	21 57.6	25 12.8	0 ♎ 2.2	12 9.4	20 51.9	10 17.9	29 24.5	28 18.7
21 W	13 58 4.5	27 40.7	29 44.7	20 48.4	23 40.1	25 R 12.0	0 40.2	12 22.3	20 47.7	10 21.6	29 26.5	28 20.8
22 T	14 2 1.1	28 40.4	29 41.5	2 ♌ 53.6	25 22.0	25 8.8	1 18.3	12 35.3	20 43.4	10 25.3	29 28.5	28 22.8
23 F	14 5 57.6	29 40.2	29 38.3	14 47.3	27 3.4	25 3.3	1 56.4	12 48.3	20 39.0	10 28.9	29 30.5	28 24.8
24 S	14 9 54.2	0 ♏ 39.9	29 35.2	26 35.1	28 44.3	24 55.3	2 34.5	13 1.3	20 34.6	10 32.5	29 32.5	28 26.7
25 S	14 13 50.7	1 39.8	29 32.0	8 ♍ 22.0	0 ♏ 24.7	24 44.9	3 12.6	13 14.3	20 30.2	10 36.1	29 34.5	28 28.7
26 M	14 17 47.3	2 39.6	29 28.8	20 12.9	2 4.5	24 32.1	3 50.7	13 27.4	20 25.7	10 39.7	29 36.6	28 30.6
27 T	14 21 43.9	3 39.5	29 25.6	2 ♎ 11.8	3 43.8	24 17.0	4 28.9	13 40.5	20 21.2	10 43.4	29 38.7	28 32.6
28 W	14 25 40.4	4 39.5	29 22.5	14 21.5	5 22.5	23 59.5	5 7.0	13 53.6	20 16.6	10 46.9	29 40.8	28 34.5
29 T	14 29 37.0	5 39.4	29 19.3	26 44.1	7 0.8	23 39.7	5 45.1	14 6.8	20 12.0	10 50.4	29 42.8	28 36.4
30 F	14 33 33.5	6 39.4	29 16.1	9 ♏ 20.6	8 38.5	23 17.8	6 23.2	14 19.9	20 7.3	10 54.0	29 44.9	28 38.2
31 S	14 37 30.1	7 39.4	29 12.9	22 11.0	10 15.7	22 53.6	7 1.3	14 33.0	20 2.6	10 57.5	29 47.1	28 40.1
						DECLINATION at NOON						
1 T	12 39 13.4	3 S 8.1	11 S 11.5	10 S 26.1	5 N 10.2	22 S 45.3	5 N 48.6	13 S 20.4	15 N 52.8	3 S 0.2	18 S 18.1	15 N 3.1
4 S	12 51 3.1	4 17.8	11 14.8	24 6.3	3 44.1	23 28.4	5 3.6	13 32.5	15 50.1	3 4.6	18 19.3	15 0.9
7 W	13 2 52.8	5 27.0	11 18.2	27 41.3	1 56.2	24 5.9	4 18.3	13 44.6	15 47.3	3 9.1	18 20.5	14 58.7
10 S	13 14 42.4	6 35.6	11 21.6	17 1.8	0 S 5.6	24 37.2	3 32.9	13 56.8	15 44.3	3 13.6	18 21.8	14 56.7
13 T	13 26 32.1	7 43.4	11 24.9	2 N 44.7	2 15.2	25 1.9	2 47.4	14 8.9	15 41.1	3 18.0	18 23.1	14 54.7
16 F	13 38 21.8	8 50.2	11 28.3	21 1.1	4 27.8	25 19.1	2 1.7	14 21.1	15 37.8	3 22.4	18 24.4	14 52.9
19 M	13 50 11.4	9 55.9	11 31.6	28 1.8	6 40.1	25 27.9	1 16.0	14 33.2	15 34.4	3 26.7	18 25.7	14 51.1
22 T	14 2 1.1	11 0.4	11 35.0	21 52.7	8 49.9	25 27.6	0 30.2	14 45.2	15 30.9	3 31.0	18 27.0	14 49.5
25 S	14 13 50.7	12 3.3	11 38.3	7 50.2	10 55.5	25 17.2	0 S 15.6	14 57.2	15 27.3	3 35.3	18 28.4	14 48.0
28 W	14 25 40.4	13 4.6	11 41.7	8 S 52.5	12 55.7	24 55.8	1 1.4	15 9.2	15 23.6	3 39.5	18 29.8	14 46.6
31 S	14 37 30.1	14 4.1	11 45.0	23 7.9	14 49.7	24 22.8	1 47.0	15 21.0	15 19.8	3 43.6	18 31.2	14 45.3

NOVEMBER 1970

DAY	EPHEMERIS SIDEREAL TIME	☉	☊	☽	☿	♀	♂	♃	♄	♅	♆	♇
	h m s	° ′	° ′	° ′	° ′	° ′	° ′	° ′	° ′	° ′	° ′	° ′
LONGITUDE at NOON												
1 S	14 41 26.6	8♏39.4	29♒ 9.8	5♐14.6	11♏52.5	22♏27.5	7♎39.4	14♏46.2	19♉57.9	11♎ 0.9	29♏49.2	28♍41.9
2 M	14 45 23.2	9 39.5	29 6.6	18 30.1	13 28.8	21R59.4	8 17.5	14 59.4	19R53.2	11 4.4	29 51.3	28 43.7
3 T	14 49 19.7	10 39.6	29 3.4	1♑56.5	15 4.6	21 29.6	8 55.6	15 12.6	19 48.4	11 7.8	29 53.5	28 45.5
4 W	14 53 16.3	11 39.8	29 0.2	15 32.9	16 40.0	20 58.3	9 33.7	15 25.8	19 43.6	11 11.2	29 55.6	28 47.3
5 T	14 57 12.9	12 39.9	28 57.0	29 18.7	18 15.0	20 25.5	10 11.7	15 39.0	19 38.7	11 14.6	29 57.8	28 49.0
6 F	15 1 9.4	13 40.1	28 53.9	13♒14.0	19 49.6	19 51.4	10 49.8	15 52.2	19 33.9	11 18.0	29 60.0	28 50.8
7 S	15 5 6.0	14 40.3	28 50.7	27 18.6	21 23.8	19 16.5	11 27.9	16 5.4	19 29.1	11 21.3	0♐ 2.2	28 52.5
8 S	15 9 2.5	15 40.5	28 47.5	11♓32.0	22 57.7	18 40.7	12 6.0	16 18.6	19 24.2	11 24.6	0 4.4	28 54.1
9 M	15 12 59.1	16 40.8	28 44.3	25 52.6	24 31.2	18 4.4	12 44.1	16 31.8	19 19.3	11 27.9	0 6.6	28 55.8
10 T	15 16 55.6	17 41.1	28 41.2	10♈17.6	26 4.3	17 27.8	13 22.2	16 45.0	19 14.4	11 31.1	0 8.8	28 57.4
11 W	15 20 52.2	18 41.4	28 38.0	24 42.5	27 37.1	16 51.3	14 0.3	16 58.3	19 9.6	11 34.3	0 11.0	28 59.0
12 T	15 24 48.8	19 41.7	28 34.8	9♉ 1.6	29 9.6	16 14.9	14 38.4	17 11.5	19 4.7	11 37.5	0 13.2	29 0.6
13 F	15 28 45.3	20 42.1	28 31.6	23 8.9	0♐41.8	15 39.1	15 16.5	17 24.7	18 59.8	11 40.7	0 15.4	29 2.2
14 S	15 32 41.9	21 42.4	28 28.5	6♊59.0	2 13.7	15 4.0	15 54.6	17 37.9	18 54.9	11 43.8	0 17.7	29 3.7
15 S	15 36 38.4	22 42.9	28 25.3	20 28.0	3 45.3	14 29.9	16 32.7	17 51.1	18 50.0	11 46.9	0 19.9	29 5.2
16 M	15 40 35.0	23 43.3	28 22.1	3♋34.0	5 16.7	13 57.0	17 10.8	18 4.3	18 45.2	11 50.0	0 22.2	29 6.7
17 T	15 44 31.5	24 43.8	28 18.9	16 17.4	6 47.8	13 25.6	17 49.0	18 17.6	18 40.4	11 53.1	0 24.5	29 8.2
18 W	15 48 28.1	25 44.3	28 15.7	28 40.4	8 18.5	12 55.7	18 27.1	18 30.7	18 35.5	11 56.1	0 26.7	29 9.7
19 T	15 52 24.7	26 44.9	28 12.6	10♌46.8	9 49.0	12 27.7	19 5.2	18 43.9	18 30.7	11 59.0	0 29.0	29 11.1
20 F	15 56 21.2	27 45.4	28 9.4	22 41.5	11 19.1	12 1.6	19 43.3	18 57.1	18 25.9	12 2.0	0 31.2	29 12.5
21 S	16 0 17.8	28 46.0	28 6.2	4♍30.0	12 49.0	11 37.5	20 21.4	19 10.2	18 21.2	12 4.9	0 33.5	29 13.8
22 S	16 4 14.3	29 46.6	28 3.0	16 17.8	14 18.5	11 15.6	20 59.6	19 23.4	18 16.4	12 7.7	0 35.7	29 15.1
23 M	16 8 10.9	0♐47.3	27 59.9	28 10.5	15 47.6	10 56.1	21 37.7	19 36.5	18 11.7	12 10.6	0 38.0	29 16.4
24 T	16 12 7.4	1 48.0	27 56.7	10♎13.0	17 16.3	10 38.9	22 15.8	19 49.6	18 7.0	12 13.3	0 40.2	29 17.7
25 W	16 16 4.0	2 48.7	27 53.5	22 29.4	18 44.6	10 24.1	22 53.9	20 2.7	18 2.4	12 16.1	0 42.5	29 18.9
26 T	16 20 0.6	3 49.4	27 50.3	5♏ 2.8	20 12.4	10 11.7	23 32.0	20 15.8	17 57.7	12 18.8	0 44.7	29 20.1
27 F	16 23 57.1	4 50.1	27 47.2	17 54.7	21 39.7	10 1.8	24 10.2	20 28.8	17 53.2	12 21.5	0 47.0	29 21.3
28 S	16 27 53.7	5 50.9	27 44.0	1♐ 4.9	23 6.3	9 54.5	24 48.3	20 41.9	17 48.6	12 24.1	0 49.2	29 22.5
29 S	16 31 50.2	6 51.7	27 40.8	14 32.0	24 32.3	9 49.5	25 26.4	20 54.9	17 44.1	12 26.7	0 51.5	29 23.6
30 M	16 35 46.8	7 52.5	27 37.6	28 13.0	25 57.4	9 47.1	26 4.5	21 7.8	17 39.7	12 29.2	0 53.7	29 24.7
DECLINATION at NOON												
1 S	14 41 26.6	14S 23.5	11S 46.1	26S 6.8	15S 26.2	24S 9.2	2S 2.2	15S 24.9	15N 18.5	3S 44.9	18S 31.7	14N 44.9
4 W	14 53 16.3	15 20.2	11 49.4	26 2.5	17 10.8	23 20.9	2 47.6	15 36.6	15 14.7	3 48.9	18 33.1	14 43.8
7 S	15 5 6.0	16 14.6	11 52.7	12 36.5	18 47.5	22 22.2	3 32.9	15 48.2	15 10.9	3 52.8	18 34.5	14 42.8
10 T	15 16 55.6	17 6.6	11 56.0	7N 5.9	20 15.8	21 15.3	4 17.9	15 59.7	15 7.1	3 56.6	18 36.0	14 41.9
13 F	15 28 45.3	17 55.9	11 59.4	23 22.8	21 35.2	20 3.2	5 2.6	16 11.0	15 3.3	4 0.3	18 37.4	14 41.2
16 M	15 40 35.0	18 42.5	12 2.7	27 30.5	22 45.0	18 49.6	5 47.0	16 22.1	14 59.5	4 3.8	18 38.8	14 40.6
19 T	15 52 24.7	19 26.1	12 5.9	18 59.8	23 44.7	17 38.1	6 31.1	16 33.2	14 55.8	4 7.3	18 40.2	14 40.2
22 S	16 4 14.3	20 6.5	12 9.2	3 57.8	24 33.6	16 32.0	7 14.8	16 44.0	14 52.2	4 10.7	18 41.7	14 39.9
25 W	16 16 4.0	20 43.6	12 12.5	12S 32.8	25 11.0	15 33.8	7 58.0	16 54.6	14 48.7	4 13.8	18 43.1	14 39.7
28 S	16 27 53.7	21 17.2	12 15.8	25 15.9	25 36.4	14 45.1	8 40.8	17 5.1	14 45.3	4 16.9	18 44.4	14 39.7

DECEMBER 1970

DAY	EPHEMERIS SIDEREAL TIME	☉	☊	☽	☿	♀	♂	♃	♄	♅	♆	♇
LONGITUDE at NOON												
1 T	16 39 43.3	8♐53.4	27♒34.5	12♑ 4.5	27♐21.5	9♏47.1	26♎42.6	21♏20.8	17♉35.3	12♎31.8	0♐56.0	29♍25.7
2 W	16 43 39.9	9 54.2	27 31.3	26 3.1	28 44.6	9D49.5	27 20.7	21 33.7	17R31.0	12 34.2	0 58.2	29 26.8
3 T	16 47 36.5	10 55.1	27 28.1	10♒ 5.7	0♑ 6.4	9 54.3	27 58.9	21 46.6	17 26.7	12 36.6	1 0.5	29 27.8
4 F	16 51 33.0	11 56.0	27 24.9	24 10.2	1 26.8	10 1.3	28 37.0	21 59.5	17 22.5	12 39.0	1 2.7	29 28.7
5 S	16 55 29.6	12 56.9	27 21.7	8♓15.4	2 45.5	10 10.7	29 15.1	22 12.3	17 18.3	12 41.4	1 4.9	29 29.7
6 S	16 59 26.1	13 57.8	27 18.6	22 20.3	4 2.2	10 22.3	29 53.2	22 25.1	17 14.2	12 43.6	1 7.1	29 30.6
7 M	17 3 22.7	14 58.7	27 15.4	6♈24.4	5 16.7	10 36.0	0♏31.3	22 37.8	17 10.2	12 45.9	1 9.3	29 31.4
8 T	17 7 19.3	15 59.7	27 12.2	20 26.3	6 28.7	10 51.9	1 9.4	22 50.6	17 6.3	12 48.1	1 11.6	29 32.3
9 W	17 11 15.8	17 0.6	27 9.0	4♉24.3	7 37.5	11 9.8	1 47.5	23 3.3	17 2.4	12 50.3	1 13.8	29 33.1
10 T	17 15 12.4	18 1.6	27 5.9	18 15.6	8 42.9	11 29.7	2 25.6	23 15.9	16 58.6	12 52.4	1 16.0	29 33.9
11 F	17 19 8.9	19 2.5	27 2.7	1♊56.9	9 44.3	11 51.5	3 3.7	23 28.5	16 54.8	12 54.4	1 18.1	29 34.6
12 S	17 23 5.5	20 3.5	26 59.5	15 25.0	10 41.0	12 15.2	3 41.7	23 41.1	16 51.1	12 56.5	1 20.3	29 35.4
13 S	17 27 2.0	21 4.5	26 56.3	28 37.1	11 32.5	12 40.7	4 19.8	23 53.6	16 47.5	12 58.4	1 22.4	29 36.0
14 M	17 30 58.6	22 5.5	26 53.2	11♋31.4	12 17.9	13 8.0	4 57.9	24 6.0	16 44.0	13 0.3	1 24.6	29 36.7
15 T	17 34 55.2	23 6.5	26 50.0	24 7.7	12 56.5	13 36.9	5 36.0	24 18.5	16 40.6	13 2.2	1 26.7	29 37.3
16 W	17 38 51.7	24 7.6	26 46.8	6♌27.2	13 27.4	14 7.4	6 14.1	24 30.8	16 37.2	13 4.0	1 28.8	29 37.9
17 T	17 42 48.3	25 8.6	26 43.6	18 32.4	13 49.8	14 39.6	6 52.2	24 43.1	16 33.9	13 5.8	1 31.0	29 38.4
18 F	17 46 44.8	26 9.7	26 40.5	0♍27.1	14 2.7	15 13.2	7 30.2	24 55.4	16 30.8	13 7.5	1 33.1	29 38.9
19 S	17 50 41.4	27 10.7	26 37.3	12 15.8	14 5.3	15 48.3	8 8.3	25 7.6	16 27.7	13 9.2	1 35.1	29 39.4
20 S	17 54 38.0	28 11.8	26 34.1	24 3.7	13R56.9	16 24.7	8 46.4	25 19.8	16 24.6	13 10.8	1 37.2	29 39.8
21 M	17 58 34.5	29 12.9	26 30.9	5♎56.3	13 37.0	17 2.5	9 24.5	25 31.9	16 21.7	13 12.3	1 39.3	29 40.2
22 T	18 2 31.1	0♑14.0	26 27.7	17 59.0	13 5.3	17 41.6	10 2.5	25 44.0	16 18.9	13 13.8	1 41.3	29 40.6
23 W	18 6 27.6	1 15.2	26 24.6	0♏16.8	12 22.0	18 21.9	10 40.6	25 56.0	16 16.2	13 15.3	1 43.3	29 40.9
24 T	18 10 24.2	2 16.3	26 21.4	12 53.8	11 27.8	19 3.4	11 18.7	26 7.9	16 13.5	13 16.7	1 45.4	29 41.2
25 F	18 14 20.8	3 17.5	26 18.2	25 52.8	10 23.8	19 46.1	11 56.7	26 19.8	16 11.0	13 18.0	1 47.4	29 41.5
26 S	18 18 17.3	4 18.6	26 15.0	9♐14.9	9 11.8	20 29.8	12 34.8	26 31.6	16 8.6	13 19.3	1 49.3	29 41.7
27 S	18 22 13.9	5 19.8	26 11.9	22 59.2	7 53.8	21 14.6	13 12.8	26 43.3	16 6.2	13 20.6	1 51.3	29 41.9
28 M	18 26 10.4	6 21.0	26 8.7	7♑ 2.7	6 32.4	22 0.3	13 50.9	26 55.0	16 4.0	13 21.8	1 53.2	29 42.1
29 T	18 30 7.0	7 22.2	26 5.5	21 20.6	5 10.5	22 47.1	14 28.9	27 6.7	16 1.9	13 22.9	1 55.2	29 42.3
30 W	18 34 3.5	8 23.3	26 2.3	5♒47.1	3 50.5	23 34.7	15 7.0	27 18.2	15 59.8	13 24.0	1 57.1	29 42.4
31 T	18 38 0.1	9 24.5	25 59.2	20 16.4	2 35.1	24 23.2	15 45.0	27 29.7	15 57.9	13 25.0	1 59.0	29 42.4
DECLINATION at NOON												
1 T	16 39 43.3	21S 47.3	12S 19.1	26S 25.5	25S 49.2	14S 6.6	9S 23.0	17S 15.3	14N 42.1	4S 19.8	18S 45.8	14N 39.8
4 F	16 51 33.0	22 13.5	12 22.4	13 40.5	25 49.3	13 38.5	10 4.7	17 25.3	14 39.0	4 22.6	18 47.2	14 40.0
7 M	17 3 22.7	22 35.9	12 25.6	5N 31.1	25 36.6	13 20.4	10 45.7	17 35.1	14 36.1	4 25.2	18 48.5	14 40.4
10 T	17 15 12.4	22 54.3	12 28.9	22 3.5	25 11.8	13 11.7	11 26.1	17 44.7	14 33.4	4 27.6	18 49.8	14 40.9
13 S	17 27 2.0	23 8.7	12 32.2	27 40.9	24 36.3	13 11.4	12 5.7	17 54.1	14 30.9	4 29.9	18 51.1	14 41.6
16 W	17 38 51.7	23 18.9	12 35.4	20 15.9	23 52.8	13 18.7	12 44.7	18 3.2	14 28.6	4 32.0	18 52.3	14 42.4
19 S	17 50 41.4	23 24.9	12 38.7	5 34.9	23 4.9	13 32.3	13 22.8	18 12.0	14 26.6	4 33.9	18 53.5	14 43.3
22 T	18 2 31.1	23 26.7	12 41.9	10S 49.2	22 16.7	13 51.5	14 0.2	18 20.6	14 24.8	4 35.6	18 54.7	14 44.3
25 F	18 14 20.8	23 24.3	12 45.1	24 11.5	21 31.8	14 15.0	14 36.6	18 28.9	14 23.3	4 37.1	18 55.8	14 45.5
28 M	18 26 10.4	23 17.6	12 48.4	27 2.3	20 53.5	14 42.1	15 12.2	18 37.0	14 22.1	4 38.5	18 56.9	14 46.8
31 T	18 38 0.1	23 6.7	12 51.6	15 5.0	20 25.9	15 11.9	15 46.8	18 44.8	14 21.1	4 39.7	18 58.0	14 48.2

JANUARY 1971

DAY	EPHEMERIS SIDEREAL TIME h m s	☉ ° ′	☊ ° ′	☽ ° ′	☿ ° ′	♀ ° ′	♂ ° ′	♃ ° ′	♄ ° ′	♅ ° ′	♆ ° ′	♇ ° ′
					LONGITUDE at NOON							
1 F	18 41 56.7	10♑25.7	25♒56.0	4♓43.4	1♑26.3	25♏12.6	16♏23.0	27♏41.0	15♉56.1	13♎26.0	2♐ 0.9	29♍42.4
2 S	18 45 53.2	11 26.9	25 52.8	19 4.2	0R25.7	26 2.8	17 1.0	27 52.4	15R54.4	13 26.9	2 2.7	29 42.4
3 S	18 49 49.8	12 28.0	25 49.6	3♈16.1	29♐34.6	26 53.8	17 38.9	28 3.6	15 52.8	13 27.8	2 4.6	29 42.4
4 M	18 53 46.3	13 29.2	25 46.5	17 17.8	28 53.4	27 45.5	18 16.9	28 14.8	15 51.3	13 28.6	2 6.4	29R42.3
5 T	18 57 42.9	14 30.4	25 43.3	1♉ 8.3	28 22.5	28 37.9	18 54.9	28 25.8	15 49.9	13 29.3	2 8.2	29 42.2
6 W	19 1 39.5	15 31.5	25 40.1	14 47.5	28 1.7	29 31.1	19 32.8	28 36.8	15 48.6	13 30.0	2 9.9	29 42.0
7 T	19 5 36.0	16 32.6	25 36.9	28 14.9	27 50.8	0♐24.9	20 10.8	28 47.7	15 47.4	13 30.6	2 11.7	29 41.9
8 F	19 9 32.6	17 33.8	25 33.7	11♊30.2	27 49.1	1 19.3	20 48.7	28 58.6	15 46.4	13 31.2	2 13.4	29 41.7
9 S	19 13 29.1	18 34.9	25 30.6	24 32.8	27D56.0	2 14.4	21 26.7	29 9.3	15 45.4	13 31.7	2 15.1	29 41.4
10 S	19 17 25.7	19 36.0	25 27.4	7♋22.1	28 10.9	3 10.1	22 4.6	29 20.0	15 44.6	13 32.2	2 16.8	29 41.1
11 M	19 21 22.2	20 37.2	25 24.2	19 58.1	28 33.2	4 6.4	22 42.5	29 30.5	15 43.8	13 32.6	2 18.4	29 40.8
12 T	19 25 18.8	21 38.3	25 21.0	2♌21.1	29 2.0	5 3.3	23 20.4	29 41.0	15 43.2	13 32.9	2 20.1	29 40.5
13 W	19 29 15.4	22 39.4	25 17.9	14 31.9	29 36.8	6 0.7	23 58.3	29 51.4	15 42.7	13 33.2	2 21.7	29 40.1
14 T	19 33 11.9	23 40.5	25 14.7	26 32.3	0♑17.1	6 58.6	24 36.2	0♐ 1.7	15 42.3	13 33.5	2 23.3	29 39.7
15 F	19 37 8.5	24 41.6	25 11.5	8♍25.0	1 2.2	7 57.0	25 14.1	0 11.8	15 42.0	13 33.6	2 24.8	29 39.2
16 S	19 41 5.0	25 42.7	25 8.3	20 13.3	1 51.6	8 55.9	25 51.9	0 21.9	15 41.9	13 33.8	2 26.3	29 38.7
17 S	19 45 1.6	26 43.8	25 5.2	2♎ 1.2	2 45.0	9 55.3	26 29.8	0 31.9	15 41.8	13 33.8	2 27.9	29 38.2
18 M	19 48 58.2	27 44.8	25 2.0	13 53.3	3 41.9	10 55.1	27 7.7	0 41.8	15D41.9	13 33.8	2 29.3	29 37.7
19 T	19 52 54.7	28 46.0	24 58.8	25 54.5	4 42.0	11 55.4	27 45.5	0 51.7	15 42.1	13 33.8	2 30.8	29 37.2
20 W	19 56 51.3	29 47.0	24 55.6	8♏ 9.7	5 44.9	12 56.1	28 23.4	1 1.3	15 42.4	13R33.7	2 32.3	29 36.6
21 T	20 0 47.8	0♒48.1	24 52.5	20 43.6	6 50.4	13 57.2	29 1.2	1 10.9	15 42.8	13 33.6	2 33.7	29 35.9
22 F	20 4 44.4	1 49.2	24 49.3	3♐40.3	7 58.3	14 58.6	29 39.0	1 20.4	15 43.3	13 33.4	2 35.0	29 35.3
23 S	20 8 40.9	2 50.2	24 46.1	17 2.3	9 8.3	16 0.5	0♐16.8	1 29.7	15 43.9	13 33.1	2 36.4	29 34.6
24 S	20 12 37.5	3 51.3	24 42.9	0♑50.6	10 20.2	17 2.7	0 54.6	1 39.0	15 44.6	13 32.8	2 37.7	29 33.8
25 M	20 16 34.1	4 52.3	24 39.7	15 3.7	11 33.9	18 5.2	1 32.3	1 48.1	15 45.5	13 32.4	2 39.0	29 33.1
26 T	20 20 30.6	5 53.3	24 36.6	29 37.6	12 49.2	19 8.0	2 10.1	1 57.1	15 46.5	13 31.9	2 40.2	29 32.3
27 W	20 24 27.2	6 54.3	24 33.4	14♒26.0	14 6.0	20 11.2	2 47.8	2 6.0	15 47.5	13 31.5	2 41.4	29 31.5
28 T	20 28 23.7	7 55.3	24 30.2	29 21.3	15 24.2	21 14.7	3 25.5	2 14.8	15 48.7	13 30.9	2 42.6	29 30.6
29 F	20 32 20.3	8 56.3	24 27.0	14♓15.4	16 43.7	22 18.4	4 3.2	2 23.5	15 50.0	13 30.3	2 43.8	29 29.7
30 S	20 36 16.8	9 57.3	24 23.9	29 1.1	18 4.5	23 22.5	4 40.8	2 32.0	15 51.4	13 29.6	2 44.9	29 28.8
31 S	20 40 13.4	10 58.2	24 20.7	13♈32.5	19 26.4	24 26.8	5 18.5	2 40.4	15 53.0	13 28.9	2 46.1	29 27.9
					DECLINATION at NOON							
1 F	18 41 56.7	23S 2.1	12S52.7	8S54.9	20S19.9	15S22.3	15S58.1	18S47.3	14N20.9	4S40.0	18S58.3	14N48.7
4 M	18 53 46.3	22 45.7	12 55.9	10N36.5	20 13.2	15 54.3	16 31.4	18 54.7	14 20.3	4 40.9	18 59.3	14 50.3
7 T	19 5 36.0	22 25.2	12 59.1	24 48.3	20 22.3	16 27.3	17 3.6	19 1.8	14 20.0	4 41.6	19 0.2	14 52.0
10 S	19 17 25.7	22 0.8	13 2.3	27 0.5	20 43.0	17 0.5	17 34.8	19 8.7	14 20.0	4 42.1	19 1.1	14 53.8
13 W	19 29 15.4	21 32.5	13 5.5	17 16.9	21 9.8	17 33.4	18 4.8	19 15.2	14 20.3	4 42.4	19 2.0	14 55.7
16 S	19 41 5.0	21 0.4	13 8.7	1 43.4	21 37.7	18 5.2	18 33.7	19 21.5	14 20.9	4 42.5	19 2.8	14 57.6
19 T	19 52 54.7	20 24.7	13 11.9	14S19.9	22 2.7	18 35.5	19 1.4	19 27.5	14 21.8	4 42.5	19 3.5	14 59.7
22 F	20 4 44.4	19 45.6	13 15.1	25 58.3	22 22.0	19 3.7	19 27.9	19 33.1	14 23.0	4 42.2	19 4.2	15 1.8
25 M	20 16 34.1	19 3.1	13 18.3	25 51.7	22 33.7	19 29.3	19 53.2	19 38.5	14 24.5	4 41.7	19 4.8	15 4.0
28 T	20 28 23.7	18 17.5	13 21.4	11 12.3	22 36.3	19 52.0	20 17.1	19 43.6	14 26.3	4 41.1	19 5.4	15 6.3
31 S	20 40 13.4	17 28.9	13 24.6	9N 4.3	22 28.9	20 11.3	20 39.8	19 48.4	14 28.3	4 40.2	19 5.9	15 8.6

FEBRUARY 1971

DAY	EPHEMERIS SIDEREAL TIME h m s	☉ ° ′	☊ ° ′	☽ ° ′	☿ ° ′	♀ ° ′	♂ ° ′	♃ ° ′	♄ ° ′	♅ ° ′	♆ ° ′	♇ ° ′
					LONGITUDE at NOON							
1 M	20 44 10.0	11♒59.1	24♒17.5	27♈45.9	20♑49.3	25♐31.4	5♐56.1	2♐48.7	15♉54.6	13♎28.2	2♐47.1	29♍26.9
2 T	20 48 6.5	13 0.0	24 14.3	11♉39.7	22 13.3	26 36.2	6 33.7	2 56.9	15 56.3	13R27.3	2 48.2	29R26.0
3 W	20 52 3.1	14 0.9	24 11.2	25 13.5	23 38.3	27 41.3	7 11.3	3 4.9	15 58.2	13 26.5	2 49.2	29 24.9
4 T	20 55 59.6	15 1.7	24 8.0	8♊28.5	25 4.3	28 46.6	7 48.8	3 12.8	16 0.2	13 25.6	2 50.2	29 23.9
5 F	20 59 56.2	16 2.6	24 4.8	21 26.2	26 31.2	29 52.2	8 26.4	3 20.5	16 2.2	13 24.6	2 51.1	29 22.8
6 S	21 3 52.7	17 3.3	24 1.6	4♋ 8.6	27 59.0	0♑57.9	9 3.9	3 28.2	16 4.4	13 23.6	2 52.0	29 21.8
7 S	21 7 49.3	18 4.1	23 58.4	16 37.8	29 27.6	2 3.9	9 41.4	3 35.7	16 6.7	13 22.5	2 52.9	29 20.6
8 M	21 11 45.8	19 4.9	23 55.3	28 55.4	0♒57.2	3 10.1	10 18.9	3 43.0	16 9.1	13 21.4	2 53.8	29 19.5
9 T	21 15 42.4	20 5.7	23 52.1	11♌ 3.5	2 27.6	4 16.6	10 56.4	3 50.3	16 11.6	13 20.2	2 54.6	29 18.4
10 W	21 19 39.0	21 6.4	23 48.9	23 3.6	3 58.9	5 23.2	11 33.8	3 57.3	16 14.2	13 19.0	2 55.4	29 17.2
11 T	21 23 35.5	22 7.0	23 45.7	4♍57.7	5 31.0	6 30.0	12 11.2	4 4.3	16 16.9	13 17.7	2 56.2	29 16.0
12 F	21 27 32.1	23 7.7	23 42.6	16 47.7	7 3.9	7 37.0	12 48.6	4 11.1	16 19.7	13 16.4	2 56.9	29 14.8
13 S	21 31 28.6	24 8.3	23 39.4	28 36.0	8 37.7	8 44.2	13 26.0	4 17.7	16 22.6	13 15.0	2 57.6	29 13.5
14 S	21 35 25.2	25 9.0	23 36.2	10♎25.4	10 12.4	9 51.5	14 3.4	4 24.2	16 25.6	13 13.6	2 58.3	29 12.2
15 M	21 39 21.7	26 9.6	23 33.0	22 19.0	11 47.9	10 59.1	14 40.7	4 30.5	16 28.7	13 12.2	2 58.9	29 10.9
16 T	21 43 18.3	27 10.1	23 29.9	4♏20.6	13 24.3	12 6.8	15 18.0	4 36.7	16 32.0	13 10.7	2 59.5	29 9.6
17 W	21 47 14.8	28 10.7	23 26.7	16 34.2	15 1.6	13 14.6	15 55.3	4 42.8	16 35.3	13 9.1	3 0.0	29 8.3
18 T	21 51 11.4	29 11.2	23 23.5	29 4.0	16 39.8	14 22.6	16 32.5	4 48.7	16 38.7	13 7.5	3 0.6	29 6.9
19 F	21 55 8.0	0♓11.8	23 20.3	11♐54.1	18 18.8	15 30.8	17 9.7	4 54.4	16 42.2	13 5.9	3 1.1	29 5.6
20 S	21 59 4.5	1 12.3	23 17.1	25 8.2	19 58.8	16 39.1	17 46.9	4 60.0	16 45.8	13 4.2	3 1.5	29 4.2
21 S	22 3 1.1	2 12.7	23 14.0	8♑48.8	21 39.7	17 47.5	18 24.1	5 5.4	16 49.5	13 2.5	3 1.9	29 2.8
22 M	22 6 57.6	3 13.2	23 10.8	22 56.4	23 21.6	18 56.1	19 1.2	5 10.6	16 53.2	13 0.7	3 2.3	29 1.3
23 T	22 10 54.2	4 13.6	23 7.6	7♒29.5	25 4.4	20 4.8	19 38.3	5 15.7	16 57.1	12 58.9	3 2.7	28 59.9
24 W	22 14 50.7	5 14.0	23 4.4	22 23.5	26 48.2	21 13.7	20 15.4	5 20.7	17 1.1	12 57.1	3 3.0	28 58.4
25 T	22 18 47.3	6 14.4	23 1.3	7♓31.4	28 32.9	22 22.6	20 52.4	5 25.4	17 5.2	12 55.2	3 3.3	28 57.0
26 F	22 22 43.8	7 14.7	22 58.1	22 43.8	0♓18.7	23 31.7	21 29.4	5 30.0	17 9.3	12 53.3	3 3.6	28 55.5
27 S	22 26 40.4	8 15.0	22 54.9	7♈51.1	2 5.4	24 40.8	22 6.4	5 34.4	17 13.6	12 51.3	3 3.8	28 54.0
28 S	22 30 36.9	9 15.3	22 51.7	22 44.2	3 53.2	25 50.1	22 43.3	5 38.7	17 17.9	12 49.3	3 4.0	28 52.5
					DECLINATION at NOON							
1 M	20 44 10.0	17S12.1	13S25.7	15N 7.1	22S24.1	20S17.0	20S47.0	19S49.9	14N29.1	4S39.9	19S 6.1	15N 9.4
4 T	20 55 59.6	16 19.9	13 28.8	26 46.2	22 2.2	20 31.3	21 7.9	19 54.3	14 31.5	4 38.8	19 6.5	15 11.8
7 S	21 7 49.3	15 25.1	13 32.0	25 34.5	21 29.0	20 41.5	21 27.5	19 58.4	14 34.2	4 37.5	19 6.9	15 14.2
10 W	21 19 39.0	14 28.0	13 35.1	13 52.9	20 44.1	20 47.4	21 45.6	20 2.2	14 37.2	4 36.1	19 7.2	15 16.7
13 S	21 31 28.6	13 28.7	13 38.3	2S14.0	19 47.3	20 48.6	22 2.4	20 5.7	14 40.4	4 34.5	19 7.5	15 19.1
16 T	21 43 18.3	12 27.4	13 41.4	17 40.3	18 38.4	20 45.2	22 17.7	20 8.9	14 43.8	4 32.7	19 7.7	15 21.6
19 F	21 55 8.0	11 24.4	13 44.6	27 12.2	17 17.3	20 36.8	22 31.7	20 11.9	14 47.5	4 30.8	19 7.8	15 24.1
22 M	22 6 57.6	10 19.6	13 47.7	24 9.7	15 43.9	20 23.5	22 44.2	20 14.5	14 51.4	4 28.7	19 7.9	15 26.6
25 T	22 18 47.3	9 13.5	13 50.8	7 34.2	13 58.2	20 5.2	22 55.3	20 16.8	14 55.5	4 26.5	19 8.0	15 29.1
28 S	22 30 36.9	8 6.1	13 53.9	13N 2.9	12 0.4	19 41.9	23 5.0	20 18.9	14 59.8	4 24.2	19 7.9	15 31.6

MARCH 1971

DAY	EPHEMERIS SIDEREAL TIME	☉	☊	☽	☿	♀	♂	♃	♄	♅	♆	♇
	h m s	° ′	° ′	° ′	° ′	° ′	° ′	° ′	° ′	° ′	° ′	° ′
LONGITUDE at NOON												
1 M	22 34 33.5	10♓15.6	22♒48.5	7♉16.3	5♓42.0	26♑59.5	23♐20.1	5♐42.8	17♉22.4	12♎47.3	3♐ 4.1	28♍50.9
2 T	22 38 30.1	11 15.8	22 45.4	21 23.1	7 31.8	28 9.0	23 57.0	5 46.7	17 26.9	12R45.3	3 4.3	28R49.5
3 W	22 42 26.6	12 16.0	22 42.2	5♊ 3.4	9 22.6	29 18.6	24 33.8	5 50.5	17 31.5	12 43.2	3 4.4	28 47.9
4 T	22 46 23.2	13 16.2	22 39.0	18 18.1	11 14.4	0♒28.2	25 10.5	5 54.0	17 36.2	12 41.1	3 4.4	28 46.3
5 F	22 50 19.7	14 16.3	22 35.8	1♋ 9.9	13 7.2	1 38.0	25 47.2	5 57.4	17 41.0	12 38.9	3 4.4	28 44.8
6 S	22 54 16.3	15 16.4	22 32.7	13 42.3	15 1.0	2 47.8	26 23.9	6 0.6	17 45.8	12 36.7	3 4.4	28 43.2
7 S	22 58 12.8	16 16.4	22 29.5	25 59.2	16 55.6	3 57.7	27 0.5	6 3.7	17 50.7	12 34.5	3 4.4	28 41.6
8 M	23 2 9.4	17 16.4	22 26.3	8♌ 4.3	18 51.1	5 7.7	27 37.1	6 6.5	17 55.7	12 32.3	3R 4.3	28 40.0
9 T	23 6 5.9	18 16.4	22 23.1	20 1.2	20 47.4	6 17.8	28 13.6	6 9.2	18 0.8	12 30.0	3 4.2	28 38.4
10 W	23 10 2.5	19 16.3	22 19.9	1♍52.9	22 44.3	7 28.0	28 50.1	6 11.7	18 6.0	12 27.7	3 4.0	28 36.8
11 T	23 13 59.0	20 16.2	22 16.8	13 42.0	24 41.9	8 38.3	29 26.6	6 14.0	18 11.2	12 25.4	3 3.8	28 35.2
12 F	23 17 55.6	21 16.1	22 13.6	25 30.8	26 39.9	9 48.6	0♑ 3.0	6 16.1	18 16.5	12 23.0	3 3.6	28 33.6
13 S	23 21 52.1	22 15.9	22 10.4	7♎21.1	28 38.1	10 59.0	0 39.3	6 18.1	18 21.9	12 20.7	3 3.3	28 31.9
14 S	23 25 48.7	23 15.7	22 7.2	19 15.0	0♈36.5	12 9.5	1 15.7	6 19.8	18 27.4	12 18.3	3 3.1	28 30.3
15 M	23 29 45.3	24 15.5	22 4.1	1♏14.3	2 34.7	13 20.1	1 51.9	6 21.4	18 32.9	12 15.9	3 2.8	28 28.7
16 T	23 33 41.8	25 15.3	22 0.9	13 21.4	4 32.5	14 30.7	2 28.1	6 22.8	18 38.5	12 13.4	3 2.4	28 27.0
17 W	23 37 38.4	26 15.0	21 57.7	25 38.8	6 29.7	15 41.4	3 4.3	6 24.0	18 44.2	12 11.0	3 2.0	28 25.4
18 T	23 41 34.9	27 14.7	21 54.5	8♐ 9.5	8 25.7	16 52.2	3 40.4	6 25.0	18 49.9	12 8.5	3 1.6	28 23.8
19 F	23 45 31.5	28 14.3	21 51.3	20 56.8	10 20.4	18 3.0	4 16.4	6 25.9	18 55.7	12 6.0	3 1.2	28 22.1
20 S	23 49 28.0	29 14.0	21 48.2	4♑ 3.8	12 13.3	19 13.9	4 52.4	6 26.5	19 1.6	12 3.5	3 0.7	28 20.5
21 S	23 53 24.6	0♈13.6	21 45.0	17 33.8	14 4.1	20 24.8	5 28.4	6 27.0	19 7.6	12 1.0	3 0.2	28 18.8
22 M	23 57 21.1	1 13.2	21 41.8	1♒28.6	15 52.1	21 35.9	6 4.3	6 27.3	19 13.6	11 58.5	2 59.7	28 17.2
23 T	0 1 17.7	2 12.7	21 38.6	15 48.7	17 37.2	22 47.0	6 40.1	6 27.4	19 19.7	11 56.0	2 59.1	28 15.6
24 W	0 5 14.2	3 12.3	21 35.5	0♓32.2	19 18.6	23 58.1	7 15.9	6R27.3	19 25.8	11 53.4	2 58.5	28 14.0
25 T	0 9 10.8	4 11.7	21 32.3	15 34.2	20 56.1	25 9.3	7 51.5	6 27.0	19 32.0	11 50.9	2 57.9	28 12.3
26 F	0 13 7.3	5 11.2	21 29.1	0♈47.0	22 29.2	26 20.5	8 27.1	6 26.5	19 38.3	11 48.3	2 57.2	28 10.7
27 S	0 17 3.9	6 10.6	21 25.9	16 0.6	23 57.5	27 31.7	9 2.7	6 25.8	19 44.6	11 45.7	2 56.6	28 9.1
28 S	0 21 0.5	7 10.0	21 22.7	1♉ 4.7	25 20.7	28 43.0	9 38.1	6 25.0	19 50.9	11 43.1	2 55.8	28 7.5
29 M	0 24 57.0	8 9.3	21 19.6	15 49.8	26 38.3	29 54.4	10 13.5	6 23.9	19 57.4	11 40.6	2 55.1	28 5.8
30 T	0 28 53.6	9 8.7	21 16.4	0♊ 9.3	27 50.1	1♓ 5.8	10 48.8	6 22.7	20 3.8	11 38.0	2 54.3	28 4.2
31 W	0 32 50.1	10 7.9	21 13.2	13 59.9	28 55.8	2 17.2	11 24.0	6 21.3	20 10.4	11 35.4	2 53.5	28 2.6
DECLINATION at NOON												
1 M	22 34 33.5	7S43.4	13S55.0	18N43.2	11S18.4	19S33.0	23S 7.9	20S19.5	15N 1.3	4S23.3	19S 7.9	15N32.4
4 T	22 46 23.2	6 34.6	13 58.1	27 41.9	9 4.8	19 3.1	23 15.7	20 21.1	15 5.8	4 20.9	19 7.8	15 34.8
7 S	22 58 12.8	5 25.0	14 1.2	23 21.2	6 40.0	18 28.4	23 22.1	20 22.5	15 10.6	4 18.3	19 7.6	15 37.1
10 W	23 10 2.5	4 14.8	14 4.3	10 6.0	4 5.3	17 49.0	23 27.1	20 23.6	15 15.4	4 15.6	19 7.4	15 39.5
13 S	23 21 52.1	3 4.2	14 7.4	6S14.7	1 22.5	17 5.0	23 30.7	20 24.4	15 20.5	4 12.8	19 7.1	15 41.7
16 T	23 33 41.8	1 53.2	14 10.5	20 44.0	1N25.2	16 16.7	23 33.0	20 24.9	15 25.6	4 10.0	19 6.8	15 43.9
19 F	23 45 31.5	0 42.0	14 13.5	27 43.4	4 13.2	15 24.1	23 33.9	20 25.2	15 30.9	4 7.1	19 6.4	15 46.1
22 M	23 57 21.1	0N29.1	14 16.6	21 42.2	6 55.7	14 27.6	23 33.5	20 25.1	15 36.3	4 4.1	19 6.0	15 48.1
25 T	0 9 10.8	1 40.1	14 19.7	3 51.5	9 25.8	13 27.4	23 31.9	20 24.8	15 41.9	4 1.1	19 5.5	15 50.1
28 S	0 21 0.5	2 50.7	14 22.7	16N19.9	11 37.1	12 23.7	23 29.0	20 24.2	15 47.5	3 58.1	19 5.0	15 51.9
31 W	0 32 50.1	4 0.8	14 25.8	27 14.4	13 24.0	11 16.8	23 25.0	20 23.3	15 53.1	3 55.1	19 4.4	15 53.7

APRIL 1971

DAY	EPHEMERIS SIDEREAL TIME	☉	☊	☽	☿	♀	♂	♃	♄	♅	♆	♇
LONGITUDE at NOON												
1 T	0 36 46.7	11♈ 7.2	21♒10.0	27♊21.3	29♈55.1	3♓28.7	11♑59.1	6♐19.7	20♉16.9	11♎32.8	2♐52.7	28♍ 1.0
2 F	0 40 43.2	12 6.4	21 6.9	10♋15.7	0♉48.0	4 40.2	12 34.2	6R17.9	20 23.6	11R30.2	2R51.8	27R59.5
3 S	0 44 39.8	13 5.5	21 3.7	22 47.2	1 34.1	5 51.7	13 9.2	6 15.9	20 30.3	11 27.6	2 50.9	27 57.9
4 S	0 48 36.3	14 4.6	21 0.5	5♌ 0.6	2 13.3	7 3.3	13 44.1	6 13.7	20 37.0	11 25.0	2 50.0	27 56.3
5 M	0 52 32.9	15 3.7	20 57.3	17 0.8	2 45.7	8 14.9	14 18.9	6 11.4	20 43.8	11 22.4	2 49.1	27 54.8
6 T	0 56 29.4	16 2.8	20 54.1	28 52.6	3 11.1	9 26.5	14 53.6	6 8.9	20 50.6	11 19.8	2 48.1	27 53.2
7 W	1 0 26.0	17 1.8	20 51.0	10♍40.5	3 29.5	10 38.2	15 28.2	6 6.2	20 57.5	11 17.2	2 47.1	27 51.7
8 T	1 4 22.5	18 0.7	20 47.8	22 28.0	3 41.0	11 49.9	16 2.8	6 3.3	21 4.4	11 14.6	2 46.1	27 50.2
9 F	1 8 19.1	18 59.7	20 44.6	4♎18.1	3 45.7	13 1.6	16 37.2	6 0.2	21 11.3	11 12.1	2 45.0	27 48.6
10 S	1 12 15.6	19 58.6	20 41.4	16 13.2	3R43.9	14 13.4	17 11.6	5 57.0	21 18.3	11 9.5	2 44.0	27 47.1
11 S	1 16 12.2	20 57.4	20 38.3	28 14.9	3 35.6	15 25.2	17 45.8	5 53.6	21 25.4	11 7.0	2 42.9	27 45.7
12 M	1 20 8.8	21 56.3	20 35.1	10♏24.4	3 21.4	16 37.1	18 20.0	5 50.1	21 32.4	11 4.4	2 41.8	27 44.2
13 T	1 24 5.3	22 55.1	20 31.9	22 42.9	3 1.5	17 49.0	18 54.1	5 46.4	21 39.6	11 2.0	2 40.7	27 42.8
14 W	1 28 1.9	23 53.9	20 28.7	5♐11.3	2 36.4	19 0.9	19 28.1	5 42.5	21 46.7	10 59.4	2 39.5	27 41.4
15 T	1 31 58.4	24 52.6	20 25.6	17 51.1	2 6.8	20 12.8	20 1.9	5 38.4	21 53.9	10 56.9	2 38.3	27 39.9
16 F	1 35 55.0	25 51.3	20 22.4	0♑44.0	1 33.1	21 24.8	20 35.7	5 34.2	22 1.2	10 54.5	2 37.1	27 38.5
17 S	1 39 51.5	26 50.0	20 19.2	13 52.1	0 56.1	22 36.8	21 9.3	5 29.8	22 8.4	10 52.0	2 35.9	27 37.1
18 S	1 43 48.1	27 48.6	20 16.0	27 17.6	0 16.6	23 48.8	21 42.8	5 25.2	22 15.7	10 49.5	2 34.6	27 35.8
19 M	1 47 44.6	28 47.3	20 12.8	11♒ 2.6	29♈35.4	25 0.8	22 16.2	5 20.5	22 23.0	10 47.1	2 33.4	27 34.4
20 T	1 51 41.2	29 45.9	20 9.7	25 8.5	28 53.1	26 12.9	22 49.4	5 15.6	22 30.4	10 44.7	2 32.1	27 33.1
21 W	1 55 37.7	0♉44.4	20 6.5	9♓34.9	28 10.7	27 25.0	23 22.6	5 10.6	22 37.8	10 42.3	2 30.8	27 31.8
22 T	1 59 34.3	1 43.0	20 3.3	24 19.2	27 28.8	28 37.1	23 55.6	5 5.5	22 45.2	10 39.9	2 29.4	27 30.5
23 F	2 3 30.9	2 41.5	20 0.1	9♈16.1	26 48.3	29 49.3	24 28.4	5 0.2	22 52.6	10 37.6	2 28.1	27 29.2
24 S	2 7 27.4	3 40.0	19 57.0	24 18.0	26 9.8	1♈ 1.4	25 1.1	4 54.7	23 0.1	10 35.2	2 26.7	27 27.9
25 S	2 11 24.0	4 38.4	19 53.8	9♉15.3	25 33.8	2 13.6	25 33.7	4 49.1	23 7.6	10 32.9	2 25.4	27 26.7
26 M	2 15 20.5	5 36.9	19 50.6	23 58.6	25 1.1	3 25.8	26 6.1	4 43.4	23 15.1	10 30.6	2 24.0	27 25.5
27 T	2 19 17.1	6 35.3	19 47.4	8♊20.2	24 31.9	4 38.0	26 38.4	4 37.6	23 22.6	10 28.4	2 22.5	27 24.3
28 W	2 23 13.6	7 33.6	19 44.2	22 15.1	24 6.8	5 50.3	27 10.4	4 31.6	23 30.2	10 26.2	2 21.1	27 23.1
29 T	2 27 10.2	8 31.9	19 41.1	5♋41.5	23 45.9	7 2.5	27 42.4	4 25.5	23 37.8	10 24.0	2 19.7	27 22.0
30 F	2 31 6.7	9 30.2	19 37.9	18 40.3	23 29.6	8 14.8	28 14.2	4 19.3	23 45.4	10 21.8	2 18.2	27 20.8
DECLINATION at NOON												
1 T	0 36 46.7	4N24.1	14S26.8	27N38.6	13N53.5	10S53.8	23S23.4	20S23.0	15N55.0	3S54.1	19S 4.2	15N54.3
4 S	0 48 36.3	5 33.2	14 29.9	20 31.0	15 2.1	9 43.2	23 17.8	20 21.7	16 0.8	3 51.0	19 3.6	15 55.9
7 W	1 0 26.0	6 41.5	14 32.9	6 4.7	15 39.1	8 29.9	23 11.2	20 20.2	16 6.6	3 48.0	19 2.9	15 57.4
10 S	1 12 15.6	7 48.7	14 35.9	10S10.7	15 43.4	7 14.4	23 3.6	20 18.5	16 12.5	3 45.0	19 2.2	15 58.8
13 T	1 24 5.3	8 54.8	14 39.0	23 20.5	15 15.7	5 56.9	22 55.0	20 16.5	16 18.4	3 42.1	19 1.4	16 0.1
16 F	1 35 55.0	9 59.5	14 42.0	27 21.3	14 19.3	4 37.8	22 45.6	20 14.2	16 24.3	3 39.2	19 0.6	16 1.3
19 M	1 47 44.6	11 2.8	14 45.0	18 19.0	13 1.3	3 17.2	22 35.3	20 11.7	16 30.3	3 36.4	18 59.8	16 2.3
22 T	1 59 34.3	12 4.4	14 48.0	0N17.6	11 31.9	1 55.5	22 24.3	20 8.9	16 36.2	3 33.6	18 59.0	16 3.2
25 S	2 11 24.0	13 4.3	14 51.0	19 14.9	10 2.8	0 33.1	22 12.6	20 5.9	16 42.1	3 30.9	18 58.1	16 4.0
28 W	2 23 13.6	14 2.2	14 54.0	27 28.6	8 44.6	0N49.9	22 0.4	20 2.7	16 48.0	3 28.4	18 57.2	16 4.6

MAY 1971

DAY	EPHEMERIS SIDEREAL TIME	☉	☊	☽	☿	♀	♂	♃	♄	♅	♆	♇
	h m s	° ′	° ′	° ′	° ′	° ′	° ′	° ′	° ′	° ′	° ′	° ′
						LONGITUDE at NOON						
1 S	2 35 3.3	10♉28.5	19♒34.7	1♌14.9	23♈18.0	9♈27.0	28♑45.8	4♐13.0	23♉53.0	10♎19.7	2♐16.7	27♍19.7
2 S	2 38 59.9	11 26.7	19 31.5	13 29.9	23R11.1	10 39.3	29 17.2	4R 6.5	24 0.6	10R17.6	2R15.3	27R18.7
3 M	2 42 56.4	12 24.9	19 28.4	25 30.5	23 9.0	11 51.6	29 48.5	3 60.0	24 8.3	10 15.5	2 13.8	27 17.6
4 T	2 46 53.0	13 23.1	19 25.2	7♍22.3	23D11.8	13 4.0	0♒19.6	3 53.4	24 16.0	10 13.5	2 12.3	27 16.6
5 W	2 50 49.5	14 21.2	19 22.0	19 10.4	23 19.3	14 16.3	0 50.5	3 46.7	24 23.7	10 11.5	2 10.8	27 15.6
6 T	2 54 46.1	15 19.3	19 18.8	0♎59.3	23 31.4	15 28.7	1 21.2	3 39.8	24 31.3	10 9.5	2 9.2	27 14.7
7 F	2 58 42.6	16 17.4	19 15.7	12 53.0	23 48.2	16 41.1	1 51.7	3 32.9	24 39.0	10 7.6	2 7.7	27 13.7
8 S	3 2 39.2	17 15.4	19 12.5	24 54.5	24 9.5	17 53.4	2 22.1	3 25.9	24 46.8	10 5.7	2 6.1	27 12.8
9 S	3 6 35.7	18 13.4	19 9.3	7♏ 5.8	24 35.0	19 5.8	2 52.2	3 18.8	24 54.5	10 3.8	2 4.6	27 11.9
10 M	3 10 32.3	19 11.4	19 6.1	19 28.2	25 4.9	20 18.2	3 22.2	3 11.7	25 2.2	10 2.0	2 3.0	27 11.0
11 T	3 14 28.9	20 9.3	19 2.9	2♐ 2.1	25 38.8	21 30.7	3 51.9	3 4.5	25 9.9	10 0.2	2 1.4	27 10.2
12 W	3 18 25.4	21 7.3	18 59.8	14 47.5	26 16.6	22 43.1	4 21.4	2 57.2	25 17.7	9 58.4	1 59.8	27 9.4
13 T	3 22 22.0	22 5.2	18 56.6	27 44.2	26 58.2	23 55.6	4 50.7	2 49.9	25 25.4	9 56.7	1 58.3	27 8.6
14 F	3 26 18.5	23 3.0	18 53.4	10♑52.3	27 43.5	25 8.0	5 19.8	2 42.5	25 33.2	9 55.1	1 56.7	27 7.8
15 S	3 30 15.1	24 0.9	18 50.2	24 11.9	28 32.3	26 20.5	5 48.6	2 35.0	25 40.9	9 53.4	1 55.1	27 7.1
16 S	3 34 11.6	24 58.7	18 47.1	7♒43.8	29 24.6	27 33.0	6 17.2	2 27.5	25 48.7	9 51.8	1 53.4	27 6.4
17 M	3 38 8.2	25 56.6	18 43.9	21 29.0	0♉20.1	28 45.6	6 45.5	2 20.0	25 56.5	9 50.3	1 51.8	27 5.7
18 T	3 42 4.8	26 54.4	18 40.7	5♓28.0	1 18.9	29 58.1	7 13.6	2 12.5	26 4.2	9 48.8	1 50.2	27 5.1
19 W	3 46 1.3	27 52.1	18 37.5	19 41.0	2 20.7	1♉10.7	7 41.4	2 4.9	26 12.0	9 47.3	1 48.6	27 4.5
20 T	3 49 57.9	28 49.9	18 34.4	4♈ 6.6	3 25.5	2 23.3	8 9.0	1 57.3	26 19.7	9 45.9	1 47.0	27 3.9
21 F	3 53 54.4	29 47.6	18 31.2	18 41.4	4 33.3	3 35.8	8 36.2	1 49.6	26 27.5	9 44.5	1 45.3	27 3.3
22 S	3 57 51.0	0♊45.4	18 28.0	3♉20.2	5 43.9	4 48.5	9 3.2	1 42.0	26 35.2	9 43.2	1 43.7	27 2.8
23 S	4 1 47.5	1 43.1	18 24.8	17 56.4	6 57.2	6 1.1	9 29.8	1 34.3	26 43.0	9 41.9	1 42.1	27 2.3
24 M	4 5 44.1	2 40.7	18 21.6	2♊22.4	8 13.3	7 13.7	9 56.2	1 26.7	26 50.7	9 40.7	1 40.5	27 1.8
25 T	4 9 40.7	3 38.5	18 18.5	16 31.6	9 32.1	8 26.4	10 22.3	1 19.1	26 58.5	9 39.5	1 38.9	27 1.5
26 W	4 13 37.2	4 36.1	18 15.3	0♋18.9	10 53.4	9 39.0	10 48.0	1 11.4	27 6.2	9 38.4	1 37.3	27 1.1
27 T	4 17 33.8	5 33.7	18 12.1	13 41.8	12 17.3	10 51.7	11 13.4	1 3.8	27 14.0	9 37.3	1 35.6	27 0.7
28 F	4 21 30.3	6 31.3	18 8.9	26 40.1	13 43.8	12 4.4	11 38.4	0 56.2	27 21.7	9 36.2	1 34.0	27 0.4
29 S	4 25 26.9	7 28.9	18 5.8	9♌15.9	15 12.8	13 17.1	12 3.2	0 48.7	27 29.3	9 35.2	1 32.4	27 0.0
30 S	4 29 23.4	8 26.4	18 2.6	21 32.7	16 44.3	14 29.7	12 27.5	0 41.1	27 37.0	9 34.3	1 30.8	26 59.8
31 M	4 33 20.0	9 24.0	17 59.4	3♍35.3	18 18.3	15 42.5	12 51.5	0 33.6	27 44.7	9 33.4	1 29.2	26 59.5
						DECLINATION at NOON						
1 S	2 35 3.3	14N58.0	14S57.0	21N28.0	7N44.4	2N13.0	21S47.8	19S59.3	16N53.9	3S25.9	18S56.3	16N 5.1
4 T	2 46 53.0	15 51.6	14 60.0	7 23.7	7 6.3	3 36.1	21 34.7	19 55.7	16 59.8	3 23.5	18 55.4	16 5.4
7 F	2 58 42.6	16 42.8	15 3.0	8S47.5	6 51.1	4 58.7	21 21.4	19 51.9	17 5.6	3 21.3	18 54.4	16 5.6
10 M	3 10 32.3	17 31.6	15 5.9	22 24.3	6 57.9	6 20.7	21 7.8	19 48.0	17 11.3	3 19.2	18 53.5	16 5.7
13 T	3 22 22.0	18 17.6	15 8.9	27 18.5	7 24.8	7 41.6	20 54.2	19 44.0	17 17.0	3 17.2	18 52.5	16 5.6
16 S	3 34 11.6	19 1.0	15 11.9	19 13.9	8 9.5	9 1.3	20 40.7	19 39.8	17 22.7	3 15.4	18 51.5	16 5.4
19 W	3 46 1.3	19 41.4	15 14.8	1 39.7	9 9.6	10 19.3	20 27.3	19 35.6	17 28.2	3 13.7	18 50.6	16 5.0
22 S	3 57 51.0	20 18.8	15 17.8	17N11.6	10 22.8	11 35.4	20 14.2	19 31.3	17 33.7	3 12.2	18 49.6	16 4.5
25 T	4 9 40.7	20 53.1	15 20.7	27 8.0	11 46.7	12 49.3	20 1.5	19 27.0	17 39.1	3 10.8	18 48.6	16 3.9
28 F	4 21 30.3	21 24.2	15 23.6	22 33.6	13 19.2	14 0.5	19 49.4	19 22.7	17 44.4	3 9.6	18 47.7	16 3.1
31 M	4 33 20.0	21 51.9	15 26.6	8 50.4	14 57.9	15 8.9	19 38.0	19 18.4	17 49.6	3 8.6	18 46.7	16 2.2

JUNE 1971

DAY	EPHEMERIS SIDEREAL TIME	☉	☊	☽	☿	♀	♂	♃	♄	♅	♆	♇
						LONGITUDE at NOON						
1 T	4 37 16.6	10♊21.5	17♒56.2	15♍28.8	19♉54.8	16♉55.2	13♒15.2	0♐26.2	27♉52.3	9♎32.5	1♐27.6	26♍59.3
2 W	4 41 13.1	11 19.0	17 53.1	27 18.7	21 33.7	18 7.9	13 38.4	0R18.7	27 60.0	9R31.7	1R26.0	26R59.1
3 T	4 45 9.7	12 16.4	17 49.9	9♎10.1	23 15.1	19 20.6	14 1.3	0 11.4	28 7.6	9 31.0	1 24.4	26 59.0
4 F	4 49 6.2	13 13.9	17 46.7	21 7.5	24 59.0	20 33.4	14 23.8	0 4.1	28 15.2	9 30.3	1 22.8	26 58.9
5 S	4 53 2.8	14 11.3	17 43.5	3♏14.7	26 45.3	21 46.1	14 45.9	29♏56.8	28 22.8	9 29.6	1 21.2	26 58.8
6 S	4 56 59.4	15 8.7	17 40.4	15 34.8	28 34.1	22 58.9	15 7.6	29 49.7	28 30.3	9 29.0	1 19.6	26 58.7
7 M	5 0 55.9	16 6.1	17 37.2	28 9.4	0♊25.2	24 11.7	15 28.8	29 42.6	28 37.9	9 28.5	1 18.1	26 58.7
8 T	5 4 52.5	17 3.4	17 34.0	10♐59.1	2 18.7	25 24.5	15 49.6	29 35.5	28 45.4	9 28.0	1 16.5	26 58.7
9 W	5 8 49.0	18 0.8	17 30.8	24 3.7	4 14.5	26 37.3	16 10.0	29 28.6	28 52.9	9 27.5	1 15.0	26D58.8
10 T	5 12 45.6	18 58.2	17 27.6	7♑21.9	6 12.5	27 50.2	16 30.0	29 21.7	29 0.3	9 27.1	1 13.4	26 58.9
11 F	5 16 42.1	19 55.5	17 24.5	20 52.1	8 12.7	29 3.0	16 49.5	29 15.0	29 7.8	9 26.8	1 11.9	26 59.0
12 S	5 20 38.7	20 52.8	17 21.3	4♒32.6	10 14.9	0♊15.9	17 8.5	29 8.3	29 15.2	9 26.5	1 10.4	26 59.1
13 S	5 24 35.3	21 50.1	17 18.1	18 21.9	12 19.1	1 28.8	17 27.0	29 1.7	29 22.6	9 26.3	1 8.9	26 59.3
14 M	5 28 31.8	22 47.4	17 14.9	2♓18.8	14 25.0	2 41.7	17 45.0	28 55.2	29 29.9	9 26.1	1 7.4	26 59.5
15 T	5 32 28.4	23 44.8	17 11.8	16 22.4	16 32.5	3 54.6	18 2.5	28 48.9	29 37.3	9 26.0	1 6.0	26 59.8
16 W	5 36 24.9	24 42.1	17 8.6	0♈31.8	18 41.3	5 7.6	18 19.5	28 42.6	29 44.6	9 25.9	1 4.5	27 0.1
17 T	5 40 21.5	25 39.4	17 5.4	14 45.3	20 51.2	6 20.5	18 35.9	28 36.5	29 51.9	9 25.9	1 3.1	27 0.4
18 F	5 44 18.1	26 36.7	17 2.2	29 1.0	23 2.0	7 33.5	18 51.7	28 30.5	29 59.2	9 25.9	1 1.7	27 0.7
19 S	5 48 14.6	27 33.9	16 59.1	13♉15.5	25 13.3	8 46.5	19 7.0	28 24.6	0♊ 6.4	9D26.0	1 0.2	27 1.1
20 S	5 52 11.2	28 31.2	16 55.9	27 25.0	27 25.0	9 59.5	19 21.7	28 18.8	0 13.5	9 26.1	0 58.8	27 1.5
21 M	5 56 7.7	29 28.5	16 52.7	11♊24.9	29 36.7	11 12.6	19 35.8	28 13.1	0 20.7	9 26.3	0 57.5	27 1.9
22 T	6 0 4.3	0♋25.8	16 49.5	25 11.0	1♋48.2	12 25.6	19 49.3	28 7.6	0 27.8	9 26.6	0 56.1	27 2.4
23 W	6 4 0.8	1 23.0	16 46.4	8♋40.0	3 59.2	13 38.7	20 2.2	28 2.2	0 34.8	9 26.8	0 54.7	27 2.9
24 T	6 7 57.4	2 20.3	16 43.2	21 49.7	6 9.4	14 51.8	20 14.4	27 57.0	0 41.9	9 27.2	0 53.4	27 3.4
25 F	6 11 54.0	3 17.5	16 40.0	4♌39.7	8 18.6	16 4.8	20 26.0	27 51.9	0 48.9	9 27.6	0 52.1	27 4.0
26 S	6 15 50.5	4 14.7	16 36.8	17 11.0	10 26.7	17 18.0	20 37.0	27 46.9	0 55.8	9 28.0	0 50.8	27 4.6
27 S	6 19 47.1	5 12.0	16 33.6	29 26.2	12 33.4	18 31.1	20 47.2	27 42.1	1 2.7	9 28.5	0 49.5	27 5.2
28 M	6 23 43.6	6 9.2	16 30.5	11♍28.9	14 38.6	19 44.2	20 56.9	27 37.5	1 9.6	9 29.1	0 48.3	27 5.9
29 T	6 27 40.2	7 6.4	16 27.3	23 23.4	16 42.1	20 57.4	21 5.8	27 33.0	1 16.4	9 29.7	0 47.0	27 6.5
30 W	6 31 36.8	8 3.6	16 24.1	5♎14.5	18 43.9	22 10.6	21 14.1	27 28.6	1 23.1	9 30.4	0 45.8	27 7.3
						DECLINATION at NOON						
1 T	4 37 16.6	22N 0.4	15S27.5	3N29.3	15N31.8	15N31.0	19S34.4	19S17.0	17N51.4	3S 8.3	18S46.4	16N 1.9
4 F	4 49 6.2	22 23.5	15 30.5	12S28.4	17 14.7	16 35.0	19 24.2	19 12.8	17 56.4	3 7.5	18 45.5	16 0.8
7 M	5 0 55.9	22 43.1	15 33.4	24 34.9	18 57.0	17 35.4	19 15.0	19 8.7	18 1.4	3 6.9	18 44.6	15 59.6
10 T	5 12 45.6	22 59.2	15 36.3	26 24.7	20 34.6	18 31.9	19 6.9	19 4.7	18 6.2	3 6.5	18 43.7	15 58.3
13 S	5 24 35.3	23 11.6	15 39.2	15 6.6	22 2.8	19 24.1	19 0.1	19 0.9	18 10.9	3 6.3	18 42.9	15 56.8
16 W	5 36 24.9	23 20.3	15 42.0	3N31.4	23 16.3	20 11.9	18 54.8	18 57.3	18 15.5	3 6.3	18 42.1	15 55.2
19 S	5 48 14.6	23 25.3	15 44.9	20 41.8	24 9.8	20 54.8	18 51.1	18 53.9	18 20.0	3 6.4	18 41.3	15 53.5
22 T	6 0 4.3	23 26.6	15 47.8	27 17.9	24 39.6	21 32.6	18 49.2	18 50.8	18 24.3	3 6.8	18 40.5	15 51.7
25 F	6 11 54.0	23 24.2	15 50.7	20 0.7	24 44.1	22 5.1	18 49.2	18 47.9	18 28.5	3 7.3	18 39.8	15 49.8
28 M	6 23 43.6	23 18.1	15 53.5	5 7.3	24 24.1	22 32.0	18 51.2	18 45.3	18 32.6	3 8.0	18 39.1	15 47.8

JULY 1971

LONGITUDE at NOON

DAY	EPHEMERIS SIDEREAL TIME (h m s)	☉ (° ′)	☊ (° ′)	☽ (° ′)	☿ (° ′)	♀ (° ′)	♂ (° ′)	♃ (° ′)	♄ (° ′)	♅ (° ′)	♆ (° ′)	♇ (° ′)
1 T	6 35 33.3	9♋ 0.8	16♒20.9	17♎ 7.2	20♋43.9	23♓23.8	21♒21.6	27♏24.5	1♓29.9	9♎31.1	0♐44.6	27♍ 8.0
2 F	6 39 29.9	9 58.0	16 17.8	29 6.4	22 42.0	24 37.0	21 28.5	27R20.4	1 36.5	9 31.9	0R43.4	27 8.8
3 S	6 43 26.4	10 55.2	16 14.6	11♏16.5	24 38.2	25 50.2	21 34.6	27 16.6	1 43.2	9 32.7	0 42.3	27 9.6
4 S	6 47 23.0	11 52.4	16 11.4	23 41.4	26 32.4	27 3.4	21 40.0	27 12.9	1 49.7	9 33.5	0 41.2	27 10.5
5 M	6 51 19.6	12 49.6	16 8.2	6♐23.9	28 24.6	28 16.7	21 44.8	27 9.4	1 56.3	9 34.5	0 40.1	27 11.3
6 T	6 55 16.1	13 46.8	16 5.1	19 25.5	0♌14.9	29 30.0	21 48.8	27 6.1	2 2.8	9 35.5	0 39.0	27 12.3
7 W	6 59 12.7	14 44.0	16 1.9	2♑46.3	2 3.1	0♋43.3	21 52.0	27 2.9	2 9.2	9 36.5	0 38.0	27 13.2
8 T	7 3 9.2	15 41.1	15 58.7	16 25.0	3 49.3	1 56.6	21 54.5	26 59.9	2 15.6	9 37.6	0 36.9	27 14.2
9 F	7 7 5.8	16 38.3	15 55.5	0♒19.2	5 33.4	3 10.0	21 56.2	26 57.0	2 21.9	9 38.7	0 35.9	27 15.2
10 S	7 11 2.3	17 35.5	15 52.4	14 25.4	7 15.5	4 23.3	21 57.2	26 54.4	2 28.2	9 39.9	0 34.9	27 16.2
11 S	7 14 58.9	18 32.7	15 49.2	28 39.7	8 55.7	5 36.7	21 57.4	26 51.9	2 34.4	9 41.1	0 34.0	27 17.3
12 M	7 18 55.5	19 29.9	15 46.0	12♓58.2	10 33.7	6 50.1	21R56.8	26 49.5	2 40.5	9 42.4	0 33.0	27 18.3
13 T	7 22 52.0	20 27.1	15 42.8	27 17.4	12 9.8	8 3.5	21 55.5	26 47.4	2 46.6	9 43.7	0 32.1	27 19.4
14 W	7 26 48.6	21 24.3	15 39.6	11♈34.3	13 43.8	9 17.0	21 53.4	26 45.4	2 52.7	9 45.1	0 31.2	27 20.6
15 T	7 30 45.1	22 21.5	15 36.5	25 46.3	15 15.9	10 30.5	21 50.5	26 43.6	2 58.6	9 46.5	0 30.4	27 21.7
16 F	7 34 41.7	23 18.8	15 33.3	9♉51.3	16 45.8	11 44.0	21 46.8	26 42.0	3 4.5	9 48.0	0 29.5	27 22.9
17 S	7 38 38.3	24 16.0	15 30.1	23 47.5	18 13.7	12 57.5	21 42.4	26 40.6	3 10.4	9 49.6	0 28.7	27 24.2
18 S	7 42 34.8	25 13.2	15 26.9	7♊33.1	19 39.5	14 11.0	21 37.2	26 39.4	3 16.2	9 51.1	0 28.0	27 25.4
19 M	7 46 31.4	26 10.5	15 23.8	21 6.6	21 3.2	15 24.6	21 31.2	26 38.3	3 21.9	9 52.8	0 27.2	27 26.7
20 T	7 50 27.9	27 7.8	15 20.6	4♋26.7	22 24.8	16 38.2	21 24.5	26 37.4	3 27.6	9 54.4	0 26.5	27 28.0
21 W	7 54 24.5	28 5.1	15 17.4	17 32.2	23 44.1	17 51.8	21 17.1	26 36.7	3 33.2	9 56.1	0 25.8	27 29.3
22 T	7 58 21.0	29 2.4	15 14.2	0♌22.7	25 1.3	19 5.5	21 9.0	26 36.2	3 38.7	9 57.9	0 25.1	27 30.7
23 F	8 2 17.6	29 59.7	15 11.1	12 58.3	26 16.1	20 19.1	21 0.1	26 35.9	3 44.1	9 59.7	0 24.5	27 32.1
24 S	8 6 14.2	0♌57.0	15 7.9	25 20.1	27 28.6	21 32.8	20 50.6	26 35.8	3 49.5	10 1.6	0 23.9	27 33.5
25 S	8 10 10.7	1 54.3	15 4.7	7♍29.6	28 38.7	22 46.5	20 40.5	26 35.8	3 54.8	10 3.5	0 23.3	27 34.9
26 M	8 14 7.3	2 51.6	15 1.5	19 29.4	29 46.3	24 0.2	20 29.7	26D36.0	4 0.1	10 5.4	0 22.8	27 36.4
27 T	8 18 3.8	3 49.0	14 58.4	1♎22.9	0♍51.4	25 14.0	20 18.4	26 36.5	4 5.3	10 7.5	0 22.3	27 37.9
28 W	8 22 0.4	4 46.4	14 55.2	13 13.7	1 53.8	26 27.8	20 6.5	26 37.1	4 10.4	10 9.5	0 21.8	27 39.4
29 T	8 25 56.9	5 43.7	14 52.0	25 6.2	2 53.4	27 41.5	19 54.1	26 37.8	4 15.4	10 11.6	0 21.4	27 40.9
30 F	8 29 53.5	6 41.1	14 48.8	7♏ 4.9	3 50.1	28 55.3	19 41.2	26 38.8	4 20.3	10 13.8	0 20.9	27 42.5
31 S	8 33 50.1	7 38.4	14 45.6	19 14.5	4 43.7	0♌ 9.2	19 27.8	26 39.9	4 25.2	10 15.9	0 20.5	27 44.1

DECLINATION at NOON

DAY	EPHEMERIS SIDEREAL TIME (h m s)	☉	☊	☽	☿	♀	♂	♃	♄	♅	♆	♇
1 T	6 35 33.3	23N 8.3	15S56.4	10S57.7	23N42.2	22N53.2	18S55.2	18S43.0	18N36.5	3S 8.9	18S38.5	15N45.7
4 S	6 47 23.0	22 54.8	15 59.3	23 40.1	22 41.7	23 8.5	19 1.3	18 41.0	18 40.2	3 10.0	18 37.9	15 43.5
7 W	6 59 12.7	22 37.8	16 2.1	26 54.2	21 26.4	23 17.8	19 9.5	18 39.4	18 43.9	3 11.3	18 37.4	15 41.2
10 S	7 11 2.3	22 17.3	16 4.9	16 31.7	19 59.8	23 21.0	19 19.7	18 38.1	18 47.3	3 12.7	18 36.9	15 38.8
13 T	7 22 52.0	21 53.3	16 7.8	2N11.0	18 24.9	23 18.1	19 31.9	18 37.2	18 50.6	3 14.3	18 36.5	15 36.4
16 F	7 34 41.7	21 25.9	16 10.6	19 43.4	16 44.4	23 8.9	19 46.1	18 36.7	18 53.8	3 16.1	18 36.1	15 33.8
19 M	7 46 31.4	20 55.2	16 13.4	27 21.6	15 0.9	22 53.6	20 2.0	18 36.5	18 56.8	3 18.1	18 35.7	15 31.2
22 T	7 58 21.0	20 21.3	16 16.2	21 19.9	13 16.5	22 32.3	20 19.4	18 36.7	18 59.6	3 20.2	18 35.5	15 28.6
25 S	8 10 10.7	19 44.4	16 19.0	6 50.6	11 33.4	22 5.0	20 37.9	18 37.3	19 2.3	3 22.5	18 35.2	15 25.9
28 W	8 22 0.4	19 4.5	16 21.8	9S22.8	9 53.8	21 31.8	20 57.0	18 38.3	19 4.8	3 25.0	18 35.1	15 23.1
31 S	8 33 50.1	18 21.8	16 24.6	22 35.9	8 20.1	20 53.0	21 16.3	18 39.7	19 7.1	3 27.6	18 35.0	15 20.3

AUGUST 1971

LONGITUDE at NOON

DAY	EPHEMERIS SIDEREAL TIME (h m s)	☉ (° ′)	☊ (° ′)	☽ (° ′)	☿ (° ′)	♀ (° ′)	♂ (° ′)	♃ (° ′)	♄ (° ′)	♅ (° ′)	♆ (° ′)	♇ (° ′)
1 S	8 37 46.6	8♌35.8	14♒42.5	1♐39.2	5♍34.3	1♌23.0	19♒14.0	26♏41.3	4♓30.0	10♎18.2	0♐20.2	27♍45.7
2 M	8 41 43.2	9 33.2	14 39.3	14 23.0	6 21.5	2 36.8	18R59.8	26 42.8	4 34.7	10 20.4	0R19.8	27 47.3
3 T	8 45 39.7	10 30.6	14 36.1	27 28.7	7 5.2	3 50.7	18 45.2	26 44.4	4 39.3	10 22.7	0 19.5	27 49.0
4 W	8 49 36.3	11 28.0	14 32.9	10♑57.7	7 45.4	5 4.6	18 30.3	26 46.3	4 43.9	10 25.1	0 19.3	27 50.6
5 T	8 53 32.8	12 25.5	14 29.8	24 49.9	8 21.7	6 18.5	18 15.2	26 48.3	4 48.3	10 27.5	0 19.0	27 52.3
6 F	8 57 29.4	13 22.9	14 26.6	9♒ 3.0	8 54.0	7 32.5	17 59.8	26 50.6	4 52.7	10 29.9	0 18.8	27 54.1
7 S	9 1 25.9	14 20.4	14 23.4	23 32.7	9 22.1	8 46.4	17 44.3	26 52.9	4 57.0	10 32.3	0 18.6	27 55.8
8 S	9 5 22.5	15 17.8	14 20.2	8♓13.3	9 45.9	10 0.4	17 28.6	26 55.5	5 1.2	10 34.8	0 18.5	27 57.5
9 M	9 9 19.1	16 15.3	14 17.1	22 58.1	10 5.0	11 14.4	17 12.7	26 58.2	5 5.4	10 37.4	0 18.4	27 59.3
10 T	9 13 15.6	17 12.8	14 13.9	7♈40.4	10 19.4	12 28.4	16 56.8	27 1.2	5 9.4	10 40.0	0 18.3	28 1.1
11 W	9 17 12.2	18 10.4	14 10.7	22 14.3	10 28.8	13 42.4	16 40.9	27 4.2	5 13.4	10 42.6	0 18.3	28 2.9
12 T	9 21 8.7	19 7.9	14 7.5	6♉35.1	10 33.0	14 56.5	16 25.0	27 7.5	5 17.2	10 45.3	0 18.2	28 4.8
13 F	9 25 5.3	20 5.5	14 4.3	20 39.9	10R31.9	16 10.6	16 9.2	27 10.9	5 21.0	10 48.0	0D18.3	28 6.6
14 S	9 29 1.8	21 3.1	14 1.2	4♊27.5	10 25.4	17 24.7	15 53.5	27 14.5	5 24.7	10 50.7	0 18.3	28 8.5
15 S	9 32 58.4	22 0.8	13 58.0	17 57.5	10 13.3	18 38.8	15 37.9	27 18.3	5 28.3	10 53.5	0 18.4	28 10.4
16 M	9 36 54.9	22 58.4	13 54.8	1♋10.8	9 55.6	19 53.0	15 22.6	27 22.2	5 31.8	10 56.3	0 18.5	28 12.3
17 T	9 40 51.5	23 56.2	13 51.6	14 8.5	9 32.5	21 7.2	15 7.5	27 26.3	5 35.3	10 59.2	0 18.7	28 14.3
18 W	9 44 48.1	24 53.9	13 48.5	26 52.1	9 3.8	22 21.4	14 52.7	27 30.6	5 38.6	11 2.0	0 18.9	28 16.2
19 T	9 48 44.6	25 51.6	13 45.3	9♌23.0	8 30.0	23 35.6	14 38.3	27 35.0	5 41.9	11 4.9	0 19.1	28 18.2
20 F	9 52 41.2	26 49.4	13 42.1	21 42.7	7 51.2	24 49.9	14 24.2	27 39.6	5 45.0	11 7.9	0 19.3	28 20.2
21 S	9 56 37.7	27 47.2	13 38.9	3♍52.6	7 8.0	26 4.1	14 10.6	27 44.4	5 48.0	11 10.9	0 19.6	28 22.2
22 S	10 0 34.3	28 45.0	13 35.7	15 54.3	6 21.0	27 18.4	13 57.4	27 49.3	5 51.0	11 13.9	0 19.9	28 24.2
23 M	10 4 30.8	29 42.8	13 32.6	27 49.8	5 30.7	28 32.7	13 44.8	27 54.4	5 53.8	11 16.9	0 20.2	28 26.2
24 T	10 8 27.4	0♍40.7	13 29.4	9♎41.2	4 38.2	29 47.0	13 32.7	27 59.6	5 56.6	11 20.0	0 20.6	28 28.2
25 W	10 12 23.9	1 38.5	13 26.2	21 31.4	3 44.3	1♍ 1.3	13 21.1	28 5.0	5 59.2	11 23.1	0 21.0	28 30.3
26 T	10 16 20.5	2 36.4	13 23.0	3♏23.4	2 50.0	2 15.7	13 10.2	28 10.5	6 1.8	11 26.2	0 21.5	28 32.4
27 F	10 20 17.0	3 34.3	13 19.9	15 21.0	1 56.5	3 30.0	12 60.0	28 16.2	6 4.2	11 29.4	0 21.9	28 34.4
28 S	10 24 13.6	4 32.3	13 16.7	27 28.3	1 5.0	4 44.4	12 50.4	28 22.1	6 6.6	11 32.6	0 22.4	28 36.5
29 S	10 28 10.2	5 30.2	13 13.5	9♐49.7	0 16.4	5 58.8	12 41.5	28 28.1	6 8.8	11 35.8	0 23.0	28 38.6
30 M	10 32 6.7	6 28.2	13 10.3	22 29.4	29♌32.0	7 13.1	12 33.3	28 34.2	6 10.9	11 39.0	0 23.5	28 40.7
31 T	10 36 3.3	7 26.2	13 7.1	5♑31.5	28 52.8	8 27.6	12 25.8	28 40.5	6 13.0	11 42.3	0 24.1	28 42.9

DECLINATION at NOON

DAY	EPHEMERIS SIDEREAL TIME (h m s)	☉	☊	☽	☿	♀	♂	♃	♄	♅	♆	♇
1 S	8 37 46.6	18N 7.0	16S25.5	25S26.4	7N50.5	20N38.8	21S22.7	18S40.2	19N 7.9	3S28.5	18S35.0	15N19.4
4 W	8 49 36.3	17 20.7	16 28.3	25 54.6	6 28.7	19 52.9	21 41.6	18 42.1	19 10.0	3 31.3	18 34.9	15 16.5
7 S	9 1 25.9	16 31.9	16 31.1	12 53.5	5 19.3	19 1.7	21 59.5	18 44.3	19 12.0	3 34.3	18 35.0	15 13.7
10 T	9 13 15.6	15 40.8	16 33.8	6N55.9	4 26.0	18 5.7	22 16.0	18 46.8	19 13.7	3 37.3	18 35.1	15 10.8
13 F	9 25 5.3	14 47.3	16 36.6	22 58.9	3 53.0	17 5.1	22 30.8	18 49.7	19 15.4	3 40.6	18 35.3	15 7.8
16 M	9 36 54.9	13 51.7	16 39.3	27 4.3	3 44.2	16 0.2	22 43.4	18 52.9	19 16.8	3 43.9	18 35.5	15 4.9
19 T	9 48 44.6	12 54.1	16 42.1	18 22.3	4 3.0	14 51.3	22 53.5	18 56.5	19 18.1	3 47.4	18 35.8	15 1.9
22 S	10 0 34.3	11 54.7	16 44.8	3 1.8	4 50.0	13 38.7	23 0.8	19 0.3	19 19.2	3 50.9	18 36.1	14 59.0
25 W	10 12 23.9	10 53.6	16 47.5	12S52.6	6 1.6	12 22.8	23 5.1	19 4.5	19 20.2	3 54.6	18 36.5	14 56.0
28 S	10 24 13.6	9 50.9	16 50.3	24 34.6	7 28.8	11 3.8	23 6.4	19 8.9	19 21.0	3 58.4	18 37.0	14 53.1
31 T	10 36 3.3	8 46.9	16 53.0	26 37.5	8 58.4	9 42.0	23 4.7	19 13.5	19 21.6	4 2.3	18 37.5	14 50.2

SEPTEMBER 1971

DAY	EPHEMERIS SIDEREAL TIME	☉	☊	☽	☿	♀	♂	♃	♄	♅	♆	♇
	h m s	° ′	° ′	° ′	° ′	° ′	° ′	° ′	° ′	° ′	° ′	° ′
LONGITUDE at NOON												
1 W	10 39 59.8	8♍24.2	13♒ 4.0	18♑59.0	28♌19.7	9♍42.0	12♒19.1	28♏47.0	6♊14.9	11♎45.6	0♐24.8	28♍45.0
2 T	10 43 56.4	9 22.3	13 0.8	2♒53.3	27R53.4	10 56.4	12R13.2	28 53.5	6 16.8	11 48.9	0 25.4	28 47.2
3 F	10 47 52.9	10 20.4	12 57.6	17 13.7	27 34.7	12 10.8	12 8.0	29 0.3	6 18.5	11 52.3	0 26.1	28 49.3
4 S	10 51 49.5	11 18.5	12 54.4	1♓56.8	27 24.1	13 25.3	12 3.6	29 7.1	6 20.1	11 55.6	0 26.8	28 51.5
5 S	10 55 46.0	12 16.6	12 51.3	16 56.3	27 22.0	14 39.8	11 60.0	29 14.1	6 21.6	11 59.0	0 27.6	28 53.7
6 M	10 59 42.6	13 14.8	12 48.1	2♈ 3.7	27D28.6	15 54.2	11 57.1	29 21.3	6 23.0	12 2.5	0 28.4	28 55.8
7 T	11 3 39.1	14 13.0	12 44.9	17 9.6	27 44.0	17 8.8	11 55.1	29 28.6	6 24.4	12 5.9	0 29.3	28 58.1
8 W	11 7 35.7	15 11.2	12 41.7	2♉ 4.6	28 8.2	18 23.3	11 53.9	29 36.0	6 25.6	12 9.4	0 30.1	29 0.3
9 T	11 11 32.3	16 9.5	12 38.6	16 41.4	28 41.0	19 37.8	11 53.4	29 43.6	6 26.7	12 12.9	0 31.0	29 2.5
10 F	11 15 28.8	17 7.8	12 35.4	0♊55.3	29 22.3	20 52.3	11D53.7	29 51.3	6 27.7	12 16.4	0 31.9	29 4.7
11 S	11 19 25.4	18 6.1	12 32.2	14 44.5	0♍11.7	22 6.9	11 54.9	29 59.1	6 28.6	12 19.9	0 32.8	29 6.9
12 S	11 23 21.9	19 4.4	12 29.0	28 9.3	1 8.8	23 21.5	11 56.8	0♐ 7.0	6 29.3	12 23.4	0 33.8	29 9.2
13 M	11 27 18.5	20 2.8	12 25.8	11♋12.0	2 13.2	24 36.0	11 59.5	0 15.1	6 30.0	12 27.0	0 34.8	29 11.4
14 T	11 31 15.0	21 1.3	12 22.7	23 55.6	3 24.2	25 50.6	12 3.1	0 23.3	6 30.5	12 30.6	0 35.8	29 13.6
15 W	11 35 11.6	21 59.7	12 19.5	6♌23.5	4 41.4	27 5.2	12 7.4	0 31.6	6 31.0	12 34.2	0 36.9	29 15.9
16 T	11 39 8.1	22 58.2	12 16.3	18 39.1	6 4.2	28 19.8	12 12.5	0 40.0	6 31.3	12 37.8	0 38.0	29 18.1
17 F	11 43 4.7	23 56.8	12 13.1	0♍45.4	7 32.0	29 34.5	12 18.4	0 48.6	6 31.5	12 41.4	0 39.1	29 20.4
18 S	11 47 1.2	24 55.3	12 10.0	12 44.9	9 4.2	0♎49.1	12 25.1	0 57.3	6 31.7	12 45.1	0 40.3	29 22.6
19 S	11 50 57.8	25 53.9	12 6.8	24 39.6	10 40.2	2 3.7	12 32.6	1 6.1	6 31.7	12 48.7	0 41.4	29 24.9
20 M	11 54 54.3	26 52.6	12 3.6	6♎31.4	12 19.4	3 18.4	12 40.8	1 15.0	6R31.6	12 52.4	0 42.6	29 27.1
21 T	11 58 50.9	27 51.2	12 0.4	18 22.0	14 1.2	4 33.1	12 49.8	1 24.1	6 31.3	12 56.1	0 43.9	29 29.4
22 W	12 2 47.4	28 49.9	11 57.2	0♏13.1	15 45.4	5 47.7	12 59.6	1 33.2	6 31.0	12 59.8	0 45.1	29 31.6
23 T	12 6 44.0	29 48.6	11 54.1	12 6.8	17 31.2	7 2.4	13 10.1	1 42.5	6 30.6	13 3.5	0 46.4	29 33.9
24 F	12 10 40.6	0♎47.4	11 50.9	24 5.8	19 18.4	8 17.1	13 21.3	1 51.9	6 30.0	13 7.2	0 47.8	29 36.2
25 S	12 14 37.1	1 46.2	11 47.7	6♐13.0	21 6.6	9 31.8	13 33.3	2 1.3	6 29.4	13 10.9	0 49.1	29 38.4
26 S	12 18 33.7	2 45.0	11 44.5	18 32.1	22 55.5	10 46.5	13 45.9	2 10.9	6 28.6	13 14.6	0 50.5	29 40.7
27 M	12 22 30.2	3 43.8	11 41.4	1♑ 7.2	24 44.8	12 1.2	13 59.3	2 20.6	6 27.8	13 18.4	0 51.9	29 42.9
28 T	12 26 26.8	4 42.8	11 38.2	14 2.5	26 34.3	13 15.9	14 13.4	2 30.5	6 26.8	13 22.2	0 53.3	29 45.2
29 W	12 30 23.3	5 41.7	11 35.0	27 21.9	28 23.8	14 30.6	14 28.1	2 40.4	6 25.7	13 25.9	0 54.8	29 47.5
30 T	12 34 19.9	6 40.6	11 31.8	11♒ 8.3	0♎13.0	15 45.3	14 43.4	2 50.4	6 24.6	13 29.7	0 56.3	29 49.7
DECLINATION at NOON												
1 W	10 39 59.8	8N25.2	16S53.9	24S20.0	9N26.4	9N14.3	23S 3.5	19S15.1	19N21.7	4S 3.6	18S37.7	14N49.2
4 S	10 51 49.5	7 19.5	16 56.6	9 18.6	10 38.3	7 49.5	22 57.9	19 20.1	19 22.1	4 7.6	18 38.3	14 46.4
7 T	11 3 39.1	6 12.8	16 59.3	11N 1.4	11 24.3	6 22.7	22 49.6	19 25.3	19 22.4	4 11.6	18 39.0	14 43.5
10 F	11 15 28.8	5 5.1	17 2.0	25 13.3	11 38.2	4 54.3	22 38.6	19 30.7	19 22.4	4 15.8	18 39.7	14 40.7
13 M	11 27 18.5	3 56.6	17 4.6	25 47.6	11 17.6	3 24.6	22 25.3	19 36.3	19 22.3	4 19.9	18 40.5	14 37.9
16 T	11 39 8.1	2 47.4	17 7.3	14 51.0	10 24.2	1 53.9	22 9.5	19 42.0	19 22.1	4 24.2	18 41.3	14 35.2
19 S	11 50 57.8	1 37.8	17 10.0	0S57.8	9 1.6	0 22.5	21 51.6	19 47.9	19 21.7	4 28.5	18 42.1	14 32.5
22 W	12 2 47.4	0 27.9	17 12.6	16 12.8	7 16.0	1S 9.1	21 31.6	19 53.9	19 21.1	4 32.8	18 43.0	14 29.9
25 S	12 14 37.1	0S42.3	17 15.3	25 59.9	5 14.1	2 40.7	21 9.6	20 0.1	19 20.3	4 37.2	18 44.0	14 27.4
28 T	12 26 26.8	1 52.4	17 17.9	25 11.4	3 1.8	4 12.0	20 45.7	20 6.3	19 19.5	4 41.6	18 45.0	14 24.9

OCTOBER 1971

DAY	EPHEMERIS SIDEREAL TIME	☉	☊	☽	☿	♀	♂	♃	♄	♅	♆	♇
LONGITUDE at NOON												
1 F	12 38 16.4	7♎39.6	11♒28.6	25♒22.9	2♎ 1.9	17♎ 0.0	14♒59.4	3♐ 0.5	6♊23.3	13♎33.5	0♐57.8	29♍52.0
2 S	12 42 13.0	8 38.6	11 25.5	10♓ 4.2	3 50.4	18 14.7	15 16.0	3 10.7	6R21.9	13 37.2	0 59.3	29 54.2
3 S	12 46 9.5	9 37.6	11 22.3	25 7.4	5 38.4	19 29.4	15 33.3	3 21.0	6 20.3	13 41.0	1 0.9	29 56.5
4 M	12 50 6.1	10 36.6	11 19.1	10♈24.3	7 25.8	20 44.2	15 51.1	3 31.4	6 18.7	13 44.8	1 2.4	29 58.7
5 T	12 54 2.6	11 35.7	11 15.9	25 44.0	9 12.5	21 58.9	16 9.5	3 41.9	6 17.0	13 48.6	1 4.0	0♎ 0.9
6 W	12 57 59.2	12 34.8	11 12.8	10♉55.3	10 58.6	23 13.6	16 28.4	3 52.5	6 15.2	13 52.4	1 5.6	0 3.1
7 T	13 1 55.7	13 34.0	11 9.6	25 48.1	12 43.9	24 28.3	16 47.9	4 3.2	6 13.3	13 56.1	1 7.3	0 5.3
8 F	13 5 52.3	14 33.2	11 6.4	10♊15.2	14 28.5	25 43.1	17 8.0	4 13.9	6 11.3	13 59.9	1 9.0	0 7.6
9 S	13 9 48.9	15 32.4	11 3.2	24 13.2	16 12.4	26 57.8	17 28.5	4 24.8	6 9.1	14 3.7	1 10.7	0 9.8
10 S	13 13 45.4	16 31.7	11 0.0	7♋42.0	17 55.5	28 12.5	17 49.6	4 35.7	6 6.9	14 7.5	1 12.4	0 11.9
11 M	13 17 42.0	17 31.0	10 56.9	20 44.0	19 37.9	29 27.3	18 11.2	4 46.7	6 4.6	14 11.3	1 14.1	0 14.1
12 T	13 21 38.5	18 30.4	10 53.7	3♌23.1	21 19.5	0♏42.0	18 33.4	4 57.8	6 2.2	14 15.1	1 15.9	0 16.3
13 W	13 25 35.1	19 29.8	10 50.5	15 43.9	23 0.4	1 56.8	18 55.9	5 9.0	5 59.6	14 18.8	1 17.6	0 18.5
14 T	13 29 31.6	20 29.2	10 47.3	27 51.3	24 40.6	3 11.6	19 19.0	5 20.3	5 57.0	14 22.6	1 19.4	0 20.6
15 F	13 33 28.2	21 28.7	10 44.2	9♍49.6	26 20.1	4 26.3	19 42.6	5 31.6	5 54.3	14 26.4	1 21.3	0 22.8
16 S	13 37 24.7	22 28.2	10 41.0	21 42.5	27 58.9	5 41.1	20 6.6	5 43.1	5 51.5	14 30.1	1 23.1	0 24.9
17 S	13 41 21.3	23 27.7	10 37.8	3♎33.0	29 37.0	6 55.9	20 31.0	5 54.6	5 48.6	14 33.9	1 25.0	0 27.0
18 M	13 45 17.8	24 27.3	10 34.6	15 23.5	1♏14.5	8 10.6	20 55.9	6 6.2	5 45.6	14 37.7	1 26.8	0 29.1
19 T	13 49 14.4	25 26.9	10 31.4	27 15.7	2 51.3	9 25.5	21 21.3	6 17.9	5 42.6	14 41.4	1 28.8	0 31.3
20 W	13 53 11.0	26 26.6	10 28.3	9♏11.0	4 27.5	10 40.2	21 47.0	6 29.6	5 39.4	14 45.2	1 30.7	0 33.4
21 T	13 57 7.5	27 26.3	10 25.1	21 10.7	6 3.1	11 55.0	22 13.2	6 41.4	5 36.2	14 48.9	1 32.6	0 35.4
22 F	14 1 4.1	28 26.0	10 21.9	3♐16.1	7 38.1	13 9.8	22 39.8	6 53.3	5 32.8	14 52.6	1 34.6	0 37.5
23 S	14 5 0.6	29 25.7	10 18.7	15 29.1	9 12.5	14 24.6	23 6.7	7 5.2	5 29.4	14 56.3	1 36.6	0 39.6
24 S	14 8 57.2	0♏25.5	10 15.6	27 52.0	10 46.3	15 39.3	23 34.0	7 17.2	5 25.9	15 0.0	1 38.5	0 41.6
25 M	14 12 53.7	1 25.3	10 12.4	10♑27.8	12 19.6	16 54.1	24 1.7	7 29.3	5 22.3	15 3.7	1 40.5	0 43.6
26 T	14 16 50.3	2 25.1	10 9.2	23 20.1	13 52.4	18 8.9	24 29.8	7 41.4	5 18.7	15 7.4	1 42.6	0 45.6
27 W	14 20 46.8	3 25.0	10 6.0	6♒32.4	15 24.6	19 23.7	24 58.2	7 53.6	5 14.9	15 11.0	1 44.6	0 47.6
28 T	14 24 43.4	4 24.9	10 2.8	20 8.2	16 56.3	20 38.4	25 27.0	8 5.9	5 11.1	15 14.6	1 46.6	0 49.5
29 F	14 28 39.9	5 24.8	9 59.7	4♓ 9.7	18 27.5	21 53.2	25 56.0	8 18.2	5 7.2	15 18.3	1 48.7	0 51.5
30 S	14 32 36.5	6 24.7	9 56.5	18 37.2	19 58.2	23 7.9	26 25.4	8 30.6	5 3.3	15 21.9	1 50.8	0 53.4
31 S	14 36 33.1	7 24.7	9 53.3	3♈28.0	21 28.4	24 22.7	26 55.2	8 43.0	4 59.3	15 25.5	1 52.8	0 55.3
DECLINATION at NOON												
1 F	12 38 16.4	3S 2.4	17S20.6	12S 2.6	0N44.1	5S42.6	20S20.1	20S12.6	19N18.4	4S46.0	18S46.1	14N22.5
4 M	12 50 6.1	4 12.1	17 23.2	8N 3.6	1S35.3	7 12.1	19 52.9	20 19.0	19 17.2	4 50.4	18 47.1	14 20.2
7 T	13 1 55.7	5 21.3	17 25.8	24 0.2	3 54.0	8 40.3	19 24.2	20 25.4	19 15.9	4 54.8	18 48.3	14 17.9
10 S	13 13 45.4	6 30.0	17 28.4	26 6.3	6 10.1	10 6.8	18 54.0	20 31.8	19 14.5	4 59.2	18 49.4	14 15.8
13 W	13 25 35.1	7 37.8	17 31.0	15 49.9	8 22.2	11 31.2	18 22.4	20 38.3	19 12.9	5 3.6	18 50.6	14 13.7
16 S	13 37 24.7	8 44.8	17 33.6	0 20.0	10 29.4	12 53.2	17 49.5	20 44.7	19 11.1	5 8.0	18 51.8	14 11.8
19 T	13 49 14.4	9 50.7	17 36.2	15S 1.3	12 30.8	14 12.4	17 15.2	20 51.2	19 9.3	5 12.4	18 53.0	14 9.9
22 F	14 1 4.1	10 55.2	17 38.8	25 21.5	14 25.9	15 28.5	16 39.7	20 57.5	19 7.3	5 16.7	18 54.3	14 8.2
25 M	14 12 53.7	11 58.3	17 41.4	25 33.1	16 14.1	16 41.1	16 2.9	21 3.9	19 5.2	5 20.9	18 55.6	14 6.6
28 T	14 24 43.4	12 59.7	17 43.9	13 58.4	17 54.8	17 49.9	15 25.0	21 10.2	19 3.0	5 25.2	18 56.9	14 5.1
31 S	14 36 33.1	13 59.3	17 46.5	5N 3.6	19 27.4	18 54.4	14 46.0	21 16.4	19 0.8	5 29.3	18 58.2	14 3.7

NOVEMBER 1971

DAY	EPHEMERIS SIDEREAL TIME	☉	☊	☽	☿	♀	♂	♃	♄	♅	♆	♇
	h m s	° ′	° ′	° ′	° ′	° ′	° ′	° ′	° ′	° ′	° ′	° ′
					LONGITUDE at NOON							
1 M	14 40 29.6	8♏24.7	9♒50.1	18♈35.9	22♏58.1	25♏37.4	27♒25.2	8♐55.5	4♊55.2	15≏29.0	1♐54.9	0≏57.2
2 T	14 44 26.2	9 24.7	9 47.0	3♉51.8	24 27.3	26 52.2	27 55.5	9 8.0	4R51.0	15 32.6	1 57.1	0 59.1
3 W	14 48 22.7	10 24.7	9 43.8	19 4.4	25 55.9	28 6.9	28 26.0	9 20.6	4 46.8	15 36.1	1 59.2	1 1.0
4 T	14 52 19.3	11 24.8	9 40.6	4♊ 2.8	27 24.1	29 21.7	28 56.9	9 33.2	4 42.6	15 39.6	2 1.3	1 2.8
5 F	14 56 15.8	12 24.9	9 37.4	18 38.1	28 51.7	0♐36.4	29 28.0	9 45.9	4 38.2	15 43.1	2 3.5	1 4.6
6 S	15 0 12.4	13 25.1	9 34.3	2♋45.0	0♐18.7	1 51.1	29 59.4	9 58.6	4 33.9	15 46.6	2 5.6	1 6.4
7 S	15 4 8.9	14 25.3	9 31.1	16 21.6	1 45.2	3 5.9	0♓31.0	10 11.4	4 29.4	15 50.0	2 7.8	1 8.2
8 M	15 8 5.5	15 25.5	9 27.9	29 29.3	3 11.0	4 20.6	1 2.9	10 24.3	4 25.0	15 53.5	2 10.0	1 9.9
9 T	15 12 2.1	16 25.8	9 24.7	12♌11.6	4 36.2	5 35.4	1 35.1	10 37.2	4 20.5	15 56.9	2 12.2	1 11.7
10 W	15 15 58.6	17 26.1	9 21.5	24 33.3	6 0.7	6 50.1	2 7.4	10 50.1	4 15.9	16 0.3	2 14.4	1 13.4
11 T	15 19 55.2	18 26.4	9 18.4	6♍39.6	7 24.4	8 4.9	2 40.0	11 3.1	4 11.3	16 3.7	2 16.6	1 15.1
12 F	15 23 51.7	19 26.8	9 15.2	18 35.7	8 47.2	9 19.6	3 12.9	11 16.1	4 6.6	16 7.0	2 18.8	1 16.8
13 S	15 27 48.3	20 27.1	9 12.0	0≏26.6	10 9.1	10 34.3	3 45.9	11 29.1	4 1.9	16 10.3	2 21.0	1 18.4
14 S	15 31 44.8	21 27.6	9 8.8	12 16.1	11 30.1	11 49.1	4 19.2	11 42.2	3 57.2	16 13.6	2 23.2	1 20.0
15 M	15 35 41.4	22 28.0	9 5.7	24 7.6	12 49.8	13 3.8	4 52.6	11 55.3	3 52.4	16 16.8	2 25.4	1 21.6
16 T	15 39 38.0	23 28.5	9 2.5	6♏ 3.6	14 8.3	14 18.5	5 26.3	12 8.5	3 47.6	16 20.0	2 27.7	1 23.2
17 W	15 43 34.5	24 29.0	8 59.3	18 5.7	15 25.4	15 33.3	6 0.2	12 21.6	3 42.8	16 23.2	2 29.9	1 24.7
18 T	15 47 31.1	25 29.5	8 56.1	0♐15.1	16 40.9	16 48.0	6 34.3	12 34.9	3 38.0	16 26.4	2 32.2	1 26.2
19 F	15 51 27.6	26 30.1	8 53.0	12 32.4	17 54.5	18 2.7	7 8.6	12 48.1	3 33.1	16 29.5	2 34.4	1 27.7
20 S	15 55 24.2	27 30.7	8 49.8	24 58.5	19 6.1	19 17.4	7 43.0	13 1.4	3 28.2	16 32.6	2 36.7	1 29.2
21 S	15 59 20.7	28 31.3	8 46.6	7♑34.1	20 15.3	20 32.1	8 17.7	13 14.7	3 23.3	16 35.7	2 38.9	1 30.6
22 M	16 3 17.3	29 31.9	8 43.4	20 20.7	21 21.9	21 46.8	8 52.5	13 28.0	3 18.4	16 38.7	2 41.2	1 32.0
23 T	16 7 13.9	0♐32.5	8 40.2	3♒20.1	22 25.5	23 1.5	9 27.5	13 41.4	3 13.5	16 41.7	2 43.4	1 33.4
24 W	16 11 10.4	1 33.2	8 37.1	16 34.6	23 25.7	24 16.2	10 2.7	13 54.8	3 8.6	16 44.7	2 45.7	1 34.8
25 T	16 15 7.0	2 33.9	8 33.9	0♓ 6.6	24 21.9	25 30.9	10 38.0	14 8.2	3 3.7	16 47.6	2 47.9	1 36.1
26 F	16 19 3.5	3 34.6	8 30.7	13 58.0	25 13.7	26 45.6	11 13.5	14 21.6	2 58.7	16 50.5	2 50.2	1 37.4
27 S	16 23 0.1	4 35.3	8 27.5	28 9.6	26 0.5	28 0.2	11 49.1	14 35.1	2 53.8	16 53.4	2 52.4	1 38.6
28 S	16 26 56.6	5 36.0	8 24.4	12♈40.1	26 41.6	29 14.9	12 24.8	14 48.5	2 48.9	16 56.2	2 54.7	1 39.9
29 M	16 30 53.2	6 36.8	8 21.2	27 25.8	27 16.2	0♑29.5	13 0.8	15 2.0	2 44.0	16 59.0	2 57.0	1 41.1
30 T	16 34 49.8	7 37.6	8 18.0	12♉20.5	27 43.7	1 44.2	13 36.8	15 15.5	2 39.1	17 1.8	2 59.3	1 42.3

DAY	EPHEMERIS SIDEREAL TIME	☉	☊	☽	☿	♀	♂	♃	♄	♅	♆	♇
					DECLINATION at NOON							
1 M	14 40 29.6	14S18.7	17S47.3	11N35.4	19S56.4	19S14.9	14S32.7	21S18.4	18N60.0	5S30.7	18S58.6	14N 3.3
4 T	14 52 19.3	15 15.5	17 49.9	25 26.2	21 17.5	20 13.3	13 52.3	21 24.5	18 57.6	5 34.7	18 60.0	14 2.0
7 S	15 4 8.9	16 10.2	17 52.4	24 23.5	22 29.1	21 6.7	13 11.0	21 30.5	18 55.2	5 38.7	19 1.3	14 0.9
10 W	15 15 58.6	17 2.4	17 55.0	12 5.0	23 30.7	21 54.8	12 28.7	21 36.3	18 52.7	5 42.6	19 2.6	13 60.0
13 S	15 27 48.3	17 52.0	17 57.5	3S46.6	24 21.4	22 37.3	11 45.5	21 42.0	18 50.1	5 46.4	19 4.0	13 59.1
16 T	15 39 38.0	18 38.8	17 60.0	18 15.3	25 0.6	23 13.9	11 1.4	21 47.6	18 47.5	5 50.1	19 5.3	13 58.4
19 F	15 51 27.6	19 22.6	18 2.5	26 24.0	25 27.6	23 44.3	10 16.6	21 53.0	18 44.9	5 53.7	19 6.6	13 57.9
22 M	16 3 17.3	20 3.3	18 5.0	23 23.0	25 41.7	24 8.3	9 31.0	21 58.3	18 42.3	5 57.2	19 8.0	13 57.5
25 T	16 15 7.0	20 40.7	18 7.5	9 36.2	25 42.6	24 25.9	8 44.7	22 3.4	18 39.7	6 0.5	19 9.3	13 57.2
28 S	16 26 56.6	21 14.6	18 10.0	9N14.7	25 29.8	24 36.7	7 57.8	22 8.3	18 37.1	6 3.7	19 10.6	13 57.0

DECEMBER 1971

DAY	EPHEMERIS SIDEREAL TIME	☉	☊	☽	☿	♀	♂	♃	♄	♅	♆	♇
					LONGITUDE at NOON							
1 W	16 38 46.3	8♐38.4	8♒14.8	27♉15.5	28♐ 3.2	2♑58.8	14♓13.0	15♐29.1	2♊34.2	17≏ 4.5	3♐ 1.5	1≏43.5
2 T	16 42 42.9	9 39.2	8 11.7	12♊ 1.9	28 13.8	4 13.4	14 49.3	15 42.6	2R29.4	17 7.1	3 3.8	1 44.6
3 F	16 46 39.4	10 40.0	8 8.5	26 31.2	28 14.8	5 28.0	15 25.7	15 56.1	2 24.5	17 9.8	3 6.0	1 45.7
4 S	16 50 36.0	11 40.9	8 5.3	10♋37.3	28R 5.4	6 42.6	16 2.2	16 9.7	2 19.7	17 12.3	3 8.2	1 46.7
5 S	16 54 32.5	12 41.7	8 2.1	24 16.9	27 45.1	7 57.2	16 38.9	16 23.2	2 14.9	17 14.9	3 10.5	1 47.7
6 M	16 58 29.1	13 42.6	7 59.0	7♌29.6	27 13.6	9 11.7	17 15.6	16 36.8	2 10.1	17 17.4	3 12.7	1 48.7
7 T	17 2 25.7	14 43.5	7 55.8	20 17.3	26 30.8	10 26.3	17 52.5	16 50.4	2 5.3	17 19.9	3 14.9	1 49.7
8 W	17 6 22.2	15 44.5	7 52.6	2♍43.7	25 37.3	11 40.8	18 29.4	17 3.9	2 0.6	17 22.3	3 17.1	1 50.6
9 T	17 10 18.8	16 45.4	7 49.4	14 53.5	24 33.9	12 55.4	19 6.5	17 17.5	1 55.9	17 24.7	3 19.4	1 51.5
10 F	17 14 15.3	17 46.4	7 46.2	26 51.8	23 22.1	14 9.9	19 43.7	17 31.1	1 51.3	17 27.0	3 21.6	1 52.4
11 S	17 18 11.9	18 47.4	7 43.1	8≏43.9	22 4.0	15 24.4	20 21.0	17 44.7	1 46.7	17 29.3	3 23.8	1 53.2
12 S	17 22 8.5	19 48.4	7 39.9	20 34.5	20 42.0	16 38.9	20 58.3	17 58.3	1 42.1	17 31.5	3 25.9	1 54.0
13 M	17 26 5.0	20 49.4	7 36.7	2♏28.0	19 19.0	17 53.4	21 35.8	18 11.9	1 37.6	17 33.7	3 28.1	1 54.8
14 T	17 30 1.6	21 50.5	7 33.5	14 27.8	17 57.7	19 7.9	22 13.4	18 25.5	1 33.1	17 35.9	3 30.3	1 55.5
15 W	17 33 58.1	22 51.5	7 30.4	26 36.7	16 40.7	20 22.3	22 51.0	18 39.0	1 28.7	17 38.0	3 32.5	1 56.2
16 T	17 37 54.7	23 52.6	7 27.2	8♐56.4	15 30.5	21 36.8	23 28.7	18 52.6	1 24.3	17 40.0	3 34.6	1 56.9
17 F	17 41 51.2	24 53.7	7 24.0	21 28.0	14 28.9	22 51.2	24 6.6	19 6.2	1 20.0	17 42.0	3 36.8	1 57.5
18 S	17 45 47.8	25 54.8	7 20.8	4♑11.7	13 37.2	24 5.6	24 44.5	19 19.8	1 15.7	17 44.0	3 38.9	1 58.1
19 S	17 49 44.4	26 55.9	7 17.7	17 7.4	12 56.1	25 20.0	25 22.5	19 33.3	1 11.5	17 45.9	3 41.0	1 58.7
20 M	17 53 40.9	27 57.0	7 14.5	0♒14.7	12 26.1	26 34.4	26 0.5	19 46.9	1 7.4	17 47.8	3 43.1	1 59.2
21 T	17 57 37.5	28 58.2	7 11.3	13 33.6	12 7.0	27 48.8	26 38.7	20 0.4	1 3.4	17 49.6	3 45.2	1 59.8
22 W	18 1 34.0	29 59.3	7 8.1	27 3.8	11 58.3	29 3.1	27 16.9	20 14.0	0 59.4	17 51.4	3 47.3	2 0.2
23 T	18 5 30.6	1♑ 0.4	7 5.0	10♓45.5	11D59.6	0♒17.5	27 55.2	20 27.5	0 55.5	17 53.1	3 49.4	2 0.7
24 F	18 9 27.2	2 1.5	7 1.8	24 38.8	12 10.2	1 31.7	28 33.6	20 41.0	0 51.6	17 54.7	3 51.4	2 1.1
25 S	18 13 23.7	3 2.7	6 58.6	8♈43.4	12 29.2	2 46.0	29 12.0	20 54.4	0 47.9	17 56.4	3 53.5	2 1.4
26 S	18 17 20.3	4 3.8	6 55.4	22 58.1	12 55.8	4 0.2	29 50.5	21 7.9	0 44.2	17 57.9	3 55.5	2 1.7
27 M	18 21 16.8	5 4.9	6 52.2	7♉20.6	13 29.4	5 14.4	0♈29.0	21 21.3	0 40.5	17 59.4	3 57.5	2 2.0
28 T	18 25 13.4	6 6.1	6 49.1	21 47.2	14 9.1	6 28.6	1 7.6	21 34.7	0 37.0	18 0.9	3 59.5	2 2.3
29 W	18 29 10.0	7 7.2	6 45.9	6♊13.0	14 54.4	7 42.7	1 46.2	21 48.1	0 33.5	18 2.3	4 1.5	2 2.5
30 T	18 33 6.5	8 8.3	6 42.7	20 32.4	15 44.6	8 56.9	2 24.9	22 1.4	0 30.2	18 3.6	4 3.4	2 2.7
31 F	18 37 3.1	9 9.5	6 39.5	4♋39.7	16 39.1	10 10.9	3 3.6	22 14.8	0 26.9	18 4.9	4 5.3	2 2.9

DAY	EPHEMERIS SIDEREAL TIME	☉	☊	☽	☿	♀	♂	♃	♄	♅	♆	♇
					DECLINATION at NOON							
1 W	16 38 46.3	21S44.9	18S12.4	24N10.6	25S 3.2	24S40.8	7S10.3	22S13.1	18N34.5	6S 6.9	19S11.9	13N57.0
4 S	16 50 36.0	22 11.5	18 14.9	25 14.9	24 22.6	24 38.2	6 22.3	22 17.6	18 32.0	6 9.8	19 13.2	13 57.2
7 T	17 2 25.7	22 34.2	18 17.4	13 34.0	23 27.8	24 28.8	5 33.8	22 22.0	18 29.6	6 12.6	19 14.4	13 57.4
10 F	17 14 15.3	22 52.9	18 19.8	2S23.0	22 20.6	24 12.6	4 45.0	22 26.1	18 27.2	6 15.3	19 15.7	13 57.9
13 M	17 26 5.0	23 7.6	18 22.3	17 7.9	21 8.4	23 49.8	3 55.8	22 30.1	18 24.9	6 17.8	19 16.9	13 58.4
16 T	17 37 54.7	23 18.2	18 24.7	26 3.3	20 6.1	23 20.6	3 6.3	22 33.8	18 22.7	6 20.1	19 18.0	13 59.1
19 S	17 49 44.4	23 24.5	18 27.1	23 58.8	19 27.8	22 45.1	2 16.6	22 37.3	18 20.7	6 22.2	19 19.2	13 59.9
22 W	18 1 34.0	23 26.7	18 29.5	10 42.2	19 18.5	22 3.5	1 26.7	22 40.6	18 18.8	6 24.3	19 20.3	14 0.9
25 S	18 13 23.7	23 24.5	18 31.9	7N43.5	19 33.4	21 16.1	0 36.6	22 43.7	18 17.0	6 26.1	19 21.4	14 2.0
28 T	18 25 13.4	23 18.2	18 34.3	23 2.4	20 4.4	20 23.3	0N13.5	22 46.5	18 15.4	6 27.7	19 22.4	14 3.2
31 F	18 37 3.1	23 7.7	18 36.7	26 1.8	20 43.8	19 25.3	1 3.6	22 49.2	18 14.0	6 29.1	19 23.4	14 4.5

JANUARY 1972

DAY	EPHEMERIS SIDEREAL TIME	☉	☊	☽	☿	♀	♂	♃	♄	♅	♆	♇
	h m s	° ′	° ′	° ′	° ′	° ′	° ′	° ′	° ′	° ′	° ′	° ′
						LONGITUDE at NOON						
1 S	18 40 59.6	10♑10.6	6♒36.4	18♋30.4	17♐37.5	11♒25.0	3♈42.4	22♐28.1	0♊23.7	18♎ 6.1	4♐ 7.3	2♎ 3.0
2 S	18 44 56.2	11 11.7	6 33.2	2♌ 1.1	18 39.3	12 39.0	4 21.2	22 41.3	0R20.6	18 7.3	4 9.2	2 3.1
3 M	18 48 52.7	12 12.9	6 30.0	15 10.4	19 44.1	13 53.0	5 0.1	22 54.6	0 17.5	18 8.4	4 11.0	2 3.1
4 T	18 52 49.3	13 14.0	6 26.8	27 58.7	20 51.6	15 6.9	5 39.0	23 7.8	0 14.6	18 9.5	4 12.9	2 3.1
5 W	18 56 45.9	14 15.2	6 23.7	10♍27.8	22 1.6	16 20.8	6 17.9	23 21.0	0 11.8	18 10.5	4 14.7	2 3.1
6 T	19 0 42.4	15 16.3	6 20.5	22 41.1	23 13.7	17 34.7	6 56.9	23 34.1	0 9.0	18 11.5	4 16.6	2R 3.0
7 F	19 4 39.0	16 17.5	6 17.3	4♎42.6	24 27.7	18 48.5	7 35.9	23 47.2	0 6.4	18 12.4	4 18.4	2 3.0
8 S	19 8 35.5	17 18.6	6 14.1	16 37.0	25 43.4	20 2.3	8 15.0	24 0.3	0 3.8	18 13.3	4 20.1	2 2.8
9 S	19 12 32.1	18 19.8	6 11.0	28 29.0	27 0.7	21 16.0	8 54.1	24 13.4	0 1.4	18 14.1	4 21.9	2 2.7
10 M	19 16 28.7	19 20.9	6 7.8	10♏23.4	28 19.3	22 29.8	9 33.2	24 26.4	29♉59.0	18 14.8	4 23.6	2 2.5
11 T	19 20 25.2	20 22.1	6 4.6	22 24.9	29 39.3	23 43.5	10 12.4	24 39.4	29 56.8	18 15.5	4 25.4	2 2.3
12 W	19 24 21.8	21 23.3	6 1.4	4♐37.1	1♑ 0.5	24 57.1	10 51.6	24 52.3	29 54.7	18 16.2	4 27.1	2 2.0
13 T	19 28 18.3	22 24.5	5 58.2	17 3.4	2 22.7	26 10.7	11 30.9	25 5.1	29 52.7	18 16.7	4 28.7	2 1.7
14 F	19 32 14.9	23 25.6	5 55.1	29 45.8	3 45.8	27 24.3	12 10.1	25 18.0	29 50.7	18 17.3	4 30.4	2 1.4
15 S	19 36 11.4	24 26.7	5 51.9	12♑45.4	5 9.9	28 37.8	12 49.4	25 30.7	29 48.9	18 17.7	4 32.0	2 1.1
16 S	19 40 8.0	25 27.9	5 48.7	26 2.1	6 34.9	29 51.2	13 28.7	25 43.5	29 47.2	18 18.1	4 33.6	2 0.7
17 M	19 44 4.6	26 29.0	5 45.5	9♒34.6	8 0.7	1♓ 4.6	14 8.1	25 56.2	29 45.6	18 18.5	4 35.1	2 0.2
18 T	19 48 1.1	27 30.1	5 42.4	23 20.9	9 27.2	2 18.0	14 47.4	26 8.8	29 44.1	18 18.7	4 36.7	1 59.8
19 W	19 51 57.7	28 31.2	5 39.2	7♓18.1	10 54.5	3 31.3	15 26.9	26 21.4	29 42.7	18 19.0	4 38.2	1 59.3
20 T	19 55 54.2	29 32.3	5 36.0	21 23.3	12 22.4	4 44.5	16 6.3	26 33.9	29 41.4	18 19.2	4 39.7	1 58.7
21 F	19 59 50.8	0♒33.4	5 32.8	5♈33.5	13 51.1	5 57.7	16 45.7	26 46.3	29 40.2	18 19.3	4 41.2	1 58.2
22 S	20 3 47.3	1 34.5	5 29.7	19 45.8	15 20.5	7 10.8	17 25.2	26 58.7	29 39.1	18 19.3	4 42.6	1 57.6
23 S	20 7 43.9	2 35.5	5 26.5	3♉57.8	16 50.4	8 23.9	18 4.7	27 11.1	29 38.2	18 19.3	4 44.0	1 57.0
24 M	20 11 40.5	3 36.5	5 23.3	18 7.2	18 21.1	9 36.9	18 44.2	27 23.3	29 37.4	18 19.3	4 45.4	1 56.3
25 T	20 15 37.0	4 37.6	5 20.1	2♊11.9	19 52.4	10 49.8	19 23.7	27 35.6	29 36.6	18R19.2	4 46.7	1 55.6
26 W	20 19 33.6	5 38.6	5 17.0	16 9.8	21 24.3	12 2.7	20 3.2	27 47.7	29 36.0	18 19.0	4 48.1	1 54.9
27 T	20 23 30.1	6 39.5	5 13.8	29 58.7	22 56.9	13 15.4	20 42.7	27 59.8	29 35.5	18 18.8	4 49.4	1 54.2
28 F	20 27 26.7	7 40.5	5 10.6	13♋36.7	24 30.1	14 28.1	21 22.3	28 11.8	29 35.1	18 18.5	4 50.6	1 53.4
29 S	20 31 23.2	8 41.4	5 7.4	27 1.9	26 4.0	15 40.8	22 1.8	28 23.8	29 34.9	18 18.2	4 51.9	1 52.6
30 S	20 35 19.8	9 42.3	5 4.2	10♌12.7	27 38.5	16 53.3	22 41.4	28 35.6	29 34.7	18 17.8	4 53.1	1 51.8
31 M	20 39 16.4	10 43.3	5 1.1	23 8.2	29 13.7	18 5.8	23 20.9	28 47.4	29 34.7	18 17.4	4 54.2	1 50.9
						DECLINATION at NOON						
1 S	18 40 59.6	23S 3.2	18S37.5	23N40.0	20S57.7	19S 4.8	1N20.3	22S50.0	18N13.5	6S29.6	19S23.8	14N 5.0
4 T	18 52 49.3	22 47.2	18 39.9	10 16.5	21 39.0	18 0.4	2 10.3	22 52.4	18 12.4	6 30.8	19 24.7	14 6.5
7 F	19 4 39.0	22 27.0	18 42.3	6S 1.6	22 17.0	16 51.5	3 0.1	22 54.5	18 11.3	6 31.8	19 25.6	14 8.1
10 M	19 16 28.7	22 2.9	18 44.7	19 54.5	22 49.1	15 38.5	3 49.8	22 56.4	18 10.5	6 32.6	19 26.5	14 9.8
13 T	19 28 18.3	21 34.9	18 47.0	26 43.5	23 13.3	14 21.8	4 39.2	22 58.1	18 10.0	6 33.3	19 27.3	14 11.6
16 S	19 40 8.0	21 3.1	18 49.4	21 46.5	23 28.3	13 1.8	5 28.4	22 59.7	18 9.6	6 33.7	19 28.1	14 13.5
19 W	19 51 57.7	20 27.7	18 51.7	6 13.2	23 33.0	11 38.7	6 17.2	23 1.0	18 9.4	6 33.9	19 28.8	14 15.5
22 S	20 3 47.3	19 48.8	18 54.0	12N26.5	23 26.9	10 13.1	7 5.6	23 2.1	18 9.5	6 34.0	19 29.5	14 17.6
25 T	20 15 37.0	19 6.6	18 56.4	25 13.3	23 9.2	8 45.1	7 53.5	23 3.0	18 9.7	6 33.8	19 30.1	14 19.8
28 F	20 27 26.7	18 21.3	18 58.7	24 41.5	22 39.6	7 15.2	8 40.9	23 3.7	18 10.2	6 33.5	19 30.7	14 22.0
31 M	20 39 16.4	17 33.0	19 1.0	12 16.3	21 57.8	5 43.7	9 27.7	23 4.3	18 10.9	6 33.0	19 31.2	14 24.3

FEBRUARY 1972

DAY	EPHEMERIS SIDEREAL TIME	☉	☊	☽	☿	♀	♂	♃	♄	♅	♆	♇
						LONGITUDE at NOON						
1 T	20 43 12.9	11♒44.2	4♒57.9	5♍48.5	0♒49.6	19♓18.2	24♈ 0.6	28♐59.2	29♉34.8	18♎16.9	4♐55.4	1♎50.1
2 W	20 47 9.5	12 45.1	4 54.7	18 14.0	2 26.2	20 30.6	24 40.1	29 10.9	29D35.0	18R16.4	4 56.6	1R49.2
3 T	20 51 6.0	13 45.9	4 51.5	0♎26.7	4 3.5	21 42.8	25 19.7	29 22.5	29 35.3	18 15.8	4 57.6	1 48.2
4 F	20 55 2.6	14 46.8	4 48.4	12 29.0	5 41.5	22 54.9	25 59.3	29 34.0	29 35.7	18 15.1	4 58.7	1 47.2
5 S	20 58 59.1	15 47.6	4 45.2	24 24.3	7 20.3	24 7.0	26 38.9	29 45.4	29 36.2	18 14.4	4 59.7	1 46.2
6 S	21 2 55.7	16 48.4	4 42.0	6♏16.7	8 59.8	25 19.0	27 18.5	29 56.8	29 36.8	18 13.7	5 0.7	1 45.2
7 M	21 6 52.2	17 49.2	4 38.8	18 10.6	10 40.1	26 30.8	27 58.1	0♑ 8.0	29 37.6	18 12.8	5 1.7	1 44.1
8 T	21 10 48.8	18 50.0	4 35.6	0♐10.8	12 21.1	27 42.6	28 37.7	0 19.2	29 38.4	18 12.0	5 2.6	1 43.1
9 W	21 14 45.4	19 50.8	4 32.5	12 22.0	14 3.0	28 54.3	29 17.3	0 30.3	29 39.4	18 11.1	5 3.5	1 42.0
10 T	21 18 41.9	20 51.5	4 29.3	24 48.5	15 45.6	0♈ 5.9	29 56.9	0 41.3	29 40.5	18 10.1	5 4.4	1 40.8
11 F	21 22 38.5	21 52.2	4 26.1	7♑34.1	17 29.1	1 17.5	0♉36.5	0 52.3	29 41.7	18 9.1	5 5.2	1 39.7
12 S	21 26 35.0	22 52.9	4 22.9	20 41.5	19 13.4	2 28.9	1 16.1	1 3.1	29 43.0	18 8.0	5 6.0	1 38.5
13 S	21 30 31.6	23 53.6	4 19.8	4♒11.8	20 58.5	3 40.2	1 55.7	1 13.8	29 44.4	18 6.9	5 6.8	1 37.3
14 M	21 34 28.1	24 54.3	4 16.6	18 4.3	22 44.5	4 51.4	2 35.4	1 24.5	29 46.0	18 5.7	5 7.6	1 36.1
15 T	21 38 24.7	25 54.9	4 13.4	2♓16.3	24 31.3	6 2.5	3 15.0	1 35.0	29 47.6	18 4.5	5 8.3	1 34.8
16 W	21 42 21.2	26 55.6	4 10.2	16 43.0	26 19.0	7 13.5	3 54.6	1 45.5	29 49.4	18 3.2	5 8.9	1 33.6
17 T	21 46 17.8	27 56.2	4 7.1	1♈18.4	28 7.4	8 24.4	4 34.2	1 55.8	29 51.2	18 1.9	5 9.6	1 32.3
18 F	21 50 14.4	28 56.7	4 3.9	15 55.8	29 56.7	9 35.1	5 13.9	2 6.1	29 53.2	18 0.5	5 10.2	1 31.0
19 S	21 54 10.9	29 57.3	4 0.7	0♉29.0	1♓46.8	10 45.8	5 53.5	2 16.2	29 55.3	17 59.1	5 10.7	1 29.6
20 S	21 58 7.5	0♓57.8	3 57.5	14 52.8	3 37.6	11 56.3	6 33.1	2 26.3	29 57.5	17 57.6	5 11.3	1 28.3
21 M	22 2 4.0	1 58.2	3 54.3	29 3.7	5 29.1	13 6.7	7 12.7	2 36.2	29 59.8	17 56.1	5 11.8	1 26.9
22 T	22 6 0.6	2 58.7	3 51.2	13♊ 0.0	7 21.2	14 17.0	7 52.4	2 46.1	0♊ 2.2	17 54.6	5 12.3	1 25.6
23 W	22 9 57.1	3 59.1	3 48.0	26 41.1	9 13.9	15 27.1	8 32.0	2 55.8	0 4.7	17 53.0	5 12.7	1 24.2
24 T	22 13 53.7	4 59.5	3 44.8	10♋ 7.6	11 7.0	16 37.1	9 11.6	3 5.4	0 7.4	17 51.4	5 13.1	1 22.7
25 F	22 17 50.2	5 59.9	3 41.6	23 20.2	13 0.4	17 46.9	9 51.1	3 14.9	0 10.1	17 49.7	5 13.5	1 21.3
26 S	22 21 46.8	7 0.2	3 38.5	6♌20.0	14 54.0	18 56.6	10 30.7	3 24.3	0 12.9	17 48.0	5 13.9	1 19.9
27 S	22 25 43.3	8 0.5	3 35.3	19 7.9	16 47.5	20 6.1	11 10.3	3 33.6	0 15.8	17 46.3	5 14.2	1 18.4
28 M	22 29 39.9	9 0.7	3 32.1	1♍44.5	18 40.9	21 15.5	11 49.8	3 42.7	0 18.9	17 44.5	5 14.4	1 16.9
29 T	22 33 36.5	10 0.9	3 28.9	14 10.6	20 33.7	22 24.7	12 29.3	3 51.7	0 22.0	17 42.6	5 14.7	1 15.4
						DECLINATION at NOON						
1 T	20 43 12.9	17S16.2	19S 1.7	6N52.9	21S41.0	5S12.9	9N43.2	23S 4.5	18N11.2	6S32.8	19S31.4	14N25.1
4 F	20 55 2.6	16 24.2	19 4.0	9S24.7	20 42.3	3 39.8	10 29.1	23 4.8	18 12.2	6 32.0	19 31.8	14 27.4
7 M	21 6 52.2	15 29.7	19 6.3	22 10.5	19 30.8	2 6.0	11 14.3	23 5.0	18 13.5	6 31.1	19 32.2	14 29.8
10 T	21 18 41.9	14 32.7	19 8.6	26 45.6	18 6.3	0 31.6	11 58.8	23 5.0	18 14.9	6 29.9	19 32.5	14 32.3
13 S	21 30 31.6	13 33.5	19 10.9	19 18.4	16 28.8	1N 3.0	12 42.5	23 5.0	18 16.5	6 28.6	19 32.8	14 34.7
16 W	21 42 21.2	12 32.4	19 13.1	2 2.3	14 38.3	2 37.4	13 25.3	23 4.7	18 18.4	6 27.2	19 33.0	14 37.2
19 S	21 54 10.9	11 29.4	19 15.4	16N31.2	12 35.1	4 11.3	14 7.2	23 4.4	18 20.4	6 25.5	19 33.2	14 39.7
22 T	22 6 0.6	10 24.8	19 17.6	26 27.2	10 19.9	5 44.5	14 48.2	23 4.0	18 22.7	6 23.8	19 33.3	14 42.2
25 F	22 17 50.2	9 18.8	19 19.9	22 28.3	7 53.9	7 16.5	15 28.1	23 3.5	18 25.1	6 21.9	19 33.4	14 44.7
28 M	22 29 39.9	8 11.6	19 22.1	8 40.2	5 19.2	8 47.0	16 6.9	23 2.9	18 27.7	6 19.8	19 33.4	14 47.2

MARCH 1972

LONGITUDE at NOON

DAY	EPHEMERIS SIDEREAL TIME h m s	☉ ° ′	☊ ° ′	☽ ° ′	☿ ° ′	♀ ° ′	♂ ° ′	♃ ° ′	♄ ° ′	♅ ° ′	♆ ° ′	♇ ° ′
1 W	22 37 33.0	11♓ 1.1	3♒25.7	26♍26.7	22♓25.8	23♈33.8	13♉ 8.9	4♑ 0.6	0♊25.2	17♎40.7	5♐14.9	1♎13.9
2 T	22 41 29.6	12 1.3	3 22.6	8♎33.9	24 16.7	24 42.7	13 48.4	4 9.4	0 28.5	17R38.8	5 15.0	1R12.4
3 F	22 45 26.1	13 1.4	3 19.4	20 33.7	26 6.2	25 51.4	14 27.9	4 18.1	0 31.9	17 36.9	5 15.2	1 10.8
4 S	22 49 22.7	14 1.5	3 16.2	2♏28.1	27 53.8	26 60.0	15 7.4	4 26.6	0 35.5	17 34.9	5 15.3	1 9.3
5 S	22 53 19.2	15 1.6	3 13.0	14 20.0	29 39.0	28 8.3	15 46.9	4 35.1	0 39.1	17 32.9	5 15.3	1 7.7
6 M	22 57 15.8	16 1.7	3 9.9	26 12.8	1♈21.5	29 16.6	16 26.3	4 43.4	0 42.8	17 30.8	5 15.4	1 6.1
7 T	23 1 12.3	17 1.7	3 6.7	8♐10.8	3 0.6	0♉24.6	17 5.8	4 51.5	0 46.6	17 28.7	5 15.4	1 4.6
8 W	23 5 8.9	18 1.7	3 3.5	20 18.7	4 35.9	1 32.4	17 45.2	4 59.5	0 50.5	17 26.6	5R15.3	1 3.0
9 T	23 9 5.4	19 1.7	3 0.3	2♑41.3	6 6.8	2 40.1	18 24.7	5 7.4	0 54.5	17 24.5	5 15.3	1 1.4
10 F	23 13 2.0	20 1.6	2 57.1	15 23.4	7 32.7	3 47.6	19 4.1	5 15.2	0 58.5	17 22.3	5 15.2	0 59.8
11 S	23 16 58.5	21 1.5	2 54.0	28 29.2	8 53.3	4 54.9	19 43.5	5 22.8	1 2.7	17 20.1	5 15.0	0 58.2
12 S	23 20 55.1	22 1.4	2 50.8	12♒ 1.7	10 7.8	6 1.9	20 22.9	5 30.3	1 7.0	17 17.8	5 14.8	0 56.5
13 M	23 24 51.7	23 1.3	2 47.6	26 1.9	11 16.0	7 8.8	21 2.3	5 37.6	1 11.3	17 15.6	5 14.6	0 54.9
14 T	23 28 48.2	24 1.1	2 44.4	10♓27.9	12 17.4	8 15.5	21 41.8	5 44.9	1 15.8	17 13.3	5 14.5	0 53.3
15 W	23 32 44.8	25 0.9	2 41.3	25 14.9	13 11.4	9 21.9	22 21.2	5 51.9	1 20.3	17 11.0	5 14.2	0 51.7
16 T	23 36 41.3	26 0.7	2 38.1	10♈15.3	13 58.0	10 28.2	23 0.5	5 58.8	1 24.9	17 8.7	5 13.9	0 50.0
17 F	23 40 37.9	27 0.4	2 34.9	25 19.4	14 36.7	11 34.2	23 39.9	6 5.6	1 29.6	17 6.3	5 13.6	0 48.4
18 S	23 44 34.4	28 0.1	2 31.7	10♉17.7	15 7.3	12 39.9	24 19.2	6 12.2	1 34.4	17 3.9	5 13.2	0 46.7
19 S	23 48 31.0	28 59.8	2 28.5	25 1.7	15 29.9	13 45.4	24 58.6	6 18.6	1 39.3	17 1.5	5 12.8	0 45.1
20 M	23 52 27.5	29 59.4	2 25.4	9♊25.7	15 44.2	14 50.7	25 37.9	6 24.9	1 44.2	16 59.1	5 12.4	0 43.5
21 T	23 56 24.1	0♈59.0	2 22.2	23 26.9	15 50.4	15 55.7	26 17.2	6 31.1	1 49.2	16 56.6	5 11.9	0 41.8
22 W	0 0 20.6	1 58.5	2 19.0	7♋ 5.1	15R48.6	17 0.4	26 56.5	6 37.1	1 54.3	16 54.2	5 11.4	0 40.2
23 T	0 4 17.2	2 58.0	2 15.8	20 21.9	15 39.1	18 4.8	27 35.7	6 42.9	1 59.5	16 51.7	5 10.9	0 38.5
24 F	0 8 13.7	3 57.5	2 12.7	3♌20.2	15 22.2	19 9.0	28 15.0	6 48.6	2 4.8	16 49.2	5 10.3	0 36.9
25 S	0 12 10.3	4 56.9	2 9.5	16 2.9	14 58.4	20 12.9	28 54.2	6 54.1	2 10.1	16 46.7	5 9.7	0 35.2
26 S	0 16 6.8	5 56.3	2 6.3	28 33.0	14 28.4	21 16.4	29 33.4	6 59.5	2 15.5	16 44.2	5 9.1	0 33.6
27 M	0 20 3.4	6 55.7	2 3.1	10♍53.1	13 52.8	22 19.7	0♊12.6	7 4.7	2 21.0	16 41.6	5 8.5	0 31.9
28 T	0 23 59.9	7 55.0	1 59.9	23 5.0	13 12.4	23 22.6	0 51.8	7 9.7	2 26.5	16 39.1	5 7.8	0 30.3
29 W	0 27 56.5	8 54.2	1 56.8	5♎10.3	12 28.2	24 25.2	1 31.0	7 14.6	2 32.1	16 36.6	5 7.1	0 28.7
30 T	0 31 53.1	9 53.5	1 53.6	17 10.2	11 41.2	25 27.5	2 10.1	7 19.3	2 37.8	16 34.0	5 6.4	0 27.0
31 F	0 35 49.6	10 52.7	1 50.4	29 5.9	10 52.2	26 29.4	2 49.2	7 23.8	2 43.6	16 31.4	5 5.6	0 25.4

DECLINATION at NOON

DAY	h m s	☉	☊	☽	☿	♀	♂	♃	♄	♅	♆	♇
1 W	22 37 33.0	7S26.1	19S23.6	2S18.6	3S32.9	9N46.5	16N32.2	23S 2.5	18N29.5	6S18.3	19S33.4	14N48.8
4 S	22 49 22.7	6 17.2	19 25.8	17 9.9	0 52.1	11 14.0	17 9.2	23 1.8	18 32.4	6 16.1	19 33.3	14 51.3
7 T	23 1 12.3	5 7.4	19 28.0	25 54.4	1N44.4	12 39.3	17 44.9	23 1.1	18 35.4	6 13.7	19 33.1	14 53.7
10 F	23 13 2.0	3 57.1	19 30.2	24 13.2	4 9.1	14 2.2	18 19.5	23 0.3	18 38.6	6 11.2	19 33.0	14 56.0
13 M	23 24 51.7	2 46.2	19 32.4	11 3.1	6 13.7	15 22.2	18 52.7	22 59.5	18 41.9	6 8.6	19 32.7	14 58.3
16 T	23 36 41.3	1 35.1	19 34.5	8N21.2	7 50.6	16 39.2	19 24.7	22 58.7	18 45.3	6 5.9	19 32.4	15 0.5
19 S	23 48 31.0	0 23.9	19 36.7	23 37.7	8 53.7	17 52.9	19 55.3	22 57.9	18 48.8	6 3.1	19 32.1	15 2.7
22 W	0 0 20.6	0N47.2	19 38.8	25 31.6	9 18.8	19 2.9	20 24.5	22 57.2	18 52.5	6 0.3	19 31.7	15 4.8
25 S	0 12 10.3	1 58.0	19 41.0	14 58.3	9 4.7	20 9.1	20 52.2	22 56.5	18 56.2	5 57.4	19 31.3	15 6.8
28 T	0 23 59.9	3 8.5	19 43.1	0S48.0	8 14.5	21 11.3	21 18.4	22 55.8	19 0.1	5 54.5	19 30.8	15 8.7
31 F	0 35 49.6	4 18.4	19 45.3	15 50.3	6 56.4	22 9.1	21 43.2	22 55.2	19 4.0	5 51.6	19 30.3	15 10.5

APRIL 1972

LONGITUDE at NOON

DAY	h m s	☉	☊	☽	☿	♀	♂	♃	♄	♅	♆	♇
1 S	0 39 46.2	11♈51.9	1♒47.2	10♏58.7	10♈ 2.4	27♉30.9	3♊28.4	7♑28.2	2♊49.4	16♎28.8	5♐ 4.8	0♎23.8
2 S	0 43 42.7	12 51.0	1 44.1	22 50.6	9R12.7	28 32.1	4 7.4	7 32.4	2 55.3	16R26.3	5R 4.0	0R22.2
3 M	0 47 39.3	13 50.1	1 40.9	4♐43.8	8 24.2	29 32.9	4 46.5	7 36.4	3 1.2	16 23.7	5 3.1	0 20.6
4 T	0 51 35.8	14 49.3	1 37.7	16 41.8	7 37.6	0♊33.4	5 25.6	7 40.3	3 7.3	16 21.1	5 2.3	0 19.1
5 W	0 55 32.4	15 48.3	1 34.5	28 48.2	6 53.7	1 33.4	6 4.7	7 44.0	3 13.4	16 18.6	5 1.4	0 17.5
6 T	0 59 28.9	16 47.4	1 31.3	11♑ 7.6	6 13.3	2 33.1	6 43.7	7 47.5	3 19.5	16 16.0	5 0.5	0 15.9
7 F	1 3 25.5	17 46.3	1 28.2	23 45.0	5 37.0	3 32.2	7 22.7	7 50.8	3 25.7	16 13.4	4 59.5	0 14.4
8 S	1 7 22.0	18 45.3	1 25.0	6♒45.0	5 5.1	4 31.0	8 1.7	7 54.0	3 32.0	16 10.8	4 58.6	0 12.8
9 S	1 11 18.6	19 44.3	1 21.8	20 11.8	4 38.1	5 29.3	8 40.7	7 56.9	3 38.3	16 8.2	4 57.5	0 11.3
10 M	1 15 15.1	20 43.2	1 18.6	4♓ 7.9	4 16.1	6 27.2	9 19.7	7 59.7	3 44.6	16 5.6	4 56.5	0 9.7
11 T	1 19 11.7	21 42.0	1 15.5	18 33.2	3 59.4	7 24.6	9 58.6	8 2.3	3 51.1	16 3.0	4 55.5	0 8.2
12 W	1 23 8.3	22 40.9	1 12.3	3♈24.4	3 48.1	8 21.4	10 37.6	8 4.8	3 57.6	16 0.5	4 54.4	0 6.7
13 T	1 27 4.8	23 39.7	1 9.1	18 34.3	3 42.0	9 17.8	11 16.5	8 7.0	4 4.1	15 57.9	4 53.3	0 5.2
14 F	1 31 1.4	24 38.5	1 5.9	3♉52.9	3 41.3	10 13.7	11 55.4	8 9.0	4 10.7	15 55.3	4 52.1	0 3.8
15 S	1 34 57.9	25 37.2	1 2.7	19 8.6	3D45.7	11 9.0	12 34.3	8 10.9	4 17.3	15 52.8	4 51.0	0 2.3
16 S	1 38 54.5	26 36.0	0 59.6	4♊10.4	3 55.2	12 3.7	13 13.2	8 12.6	4 24.0	15 50.3	4 49.8	0 0.9
17 M	1 42 51.0	27 34.6	0 56.4	18 50.2	4 9.7	12 57.9	13 52.1	8 14.1	4 30.8	15 47.7	4 48.6	29♍59.5
18 T	1 46 47.6	28 33.3	0 53.2	3♋ 3.3	4 28.9	13 51.4	14 31.0	8 15.4	4 37.6	15 45.2	4 47.4	29 58.0
19 W	1 50 44.1	29 31.9	0 50.0	16 48.4	4 52.6	14 44.3	15 9.8	8 16.5	4 44.4	15 42.7	4 46.2	29 56.7
20 T	1 54 40.7	0♉30.5	0 46.9	0♌ 7.0	5 20.8	15 36.6	15 48.6	8 17.5	4 51.3	15 40.3	4 44.9	29 55.3
21 F	1 58 37.2	1 29.0	0 43.7	13 2.3	5 53.1	16 28.1	16 27.4	8 18.2	4 58.2	15 37.8	4 43.6	29 53.9
22 S	2 2 33.8	2 27.5	0 40.5	25 38.5	6 29.5	17 19.0	17 6.2	8 18.8	5 5.2	15 35.3	4 42.3	29 52.6
23 S	2 6 30.3	3 25.9	0 37.3	7♍59.8	7 9.8	18 9.1	17 45.0	8 19.1	5 12.2	15 32.9	4 41.0	29 51.3
24 M	2 10 26.9	4 24.4	0 34.2	20 10.0	7 53.7	18 58.4	18 23.7	8 19.3	5 19.3	15 30.5	4 39.7	29 50.0
25 T	2 14 23.5	5 22.8	0 31.0	2♎12.5	8 41.2	19 47.0	19 2.5	8 19.4	5 26.4	15 28.2	4 38.4	29 48.8
26 W	2 18 20.0	6 21.2	0 27.8	14 9.9	9 32.0	20 34.8	19 41.2	8R19.2	5 33.5	15 25.8	4 37.0	29 47.5
27 T	2 22 16.6	7 19.5	0 24.6	26 4.1	10 26.0	21 21.7	20 19.9	8 18.8	5 40.7	15 23.4	4 35.6	29 46.3
28 F	2 26 13.1	8 17.8	0 21.4	7♏56.9	11 23.2	22 7.7	20 58.6	8 18.2	5 47.9	15 21.1	4 34.2	29 45.1
29 S	2 30 9.7	9 16.0	0 18.3	19 49.6	12 23.3	22 52.7	21 37.2	8 17.5	5 55.1	15 18.8	4 32.8	29 43.9
30 S	2 34 6.2	10 14.3	0 15.1	1♐43.6	13 26.2	23 36.9	22 15.9	8 16.5	6 2.4	15 16.6	4 31.3	29 42.7

DECLINATION at NOON

DAY	h m s	☉	☊	☽	☿	♀	♂	♃	♄	♅	♆	♇
1 S	0 39 46.2	4N41.5	19S46.0	19S50.4	6N26.4	22N27.5	21N51.1	22S55.0	19N 5.3	5S50.6	19S30.1	15N11.1
4 T	0 51 35.8	5 50.5	19 48.1	26 20.9	4 51.5	23 19.4	22 13.7	22 54.5	19 9.3	5 47.6	19 29.5	15 12.7
7 F	1 3 25.5	6 58.5	19 50.2	22 3.8	3 20.2	24 6.6	22 34.8	22 54.0	19 13.3	5 44.7	19 28.9	15 14.3
10 M	1 15 15.1	8 5.5	19 52.3	7 29.2	2 3.4	24 49.1	22 54.3	22 53.6	19 17.4	5 41.7	19 28.3	15 15.8
13 T	1 27 4.8	9 11.3	19 54.4	11N47.4	1 7.3	25 26.8	23 12.1	22 53.4	19 21.5	5 38.8	19 27.6	15 17.1
16 S	1 38 54.5	10 15.7	19 56.5	25 6.3	0 34.5	25 59.6	23 28.3	22 53.2	19 25.7	5 35.9	19 26.8	15 18.3
19 W	1 50 44.1	11 18.6	19 58.5	23 35.5	0 24.8	26 27.5	23 42.8	22 53.2	19 29.8	5 33.0	19 26.1	15 19.4
22 S	2 2 33.8	12 19.7	20 0.6	10 58.4	0 36.7	26 50.6	23 55.6	22 53.2	19 34.0	5 30.2	19 25.3	15 20.3
25 T	2 14 23.5	13 19.1	20 2.7	4S55.5	1 8.2	27 8.9	24 6.7	22 53.4	19 38.2	5 27.5	19 24.5	15 21.1
28 F	2 26 13.1	14 16.4	20 4.7	18 49.9	1 57.2	27 22.5	24 16.0	22 53.7	19 42.4	5 24.8	19 23.7	15 21.8

MAY 1972

DAY	EPHEMERIS SIDEREAL TIME h m s	☉ ° ′	☊ ° ′	☽ ° ′	☿ ° ′	♀ ° ′	♂ ° ′	♃ ° ′	♄ ° ′	♅ ° ′	♆ ° ′	♇ ° ′
LONGITUDE at NOON												
1 M	2 38 2.8	11♉12.5	0♒11.9	13♐40.6	14♈31.9	24♊20.0	22♊54.5	8♑15.4	6♊ 9.7	15♎14.3	4♐29.9	29♍41.6
2 T	2 41 59.3	12 10.7	0 8.7	25 42.8	15 40.3	25 2.2	23 33.1	8R14.1	6 17.1	15R12.1	4R28.4	29R40.5
3 W	2 45 55.9	13 8.8	0 5.6	7♑53.0	16 51.2	25 43.2	24 11.7	8 12.6	6 24.4	15 9.9	4 27.0	29 39.4
4 T	2 49 52.5	14 7.0	0 2.4	20 14.8	18 4.6	26 23.2	24 50.3	8 10.9	6 31.8	15 7.7	4 25.5	29 38.3
5 F	2 53 49.0	15 5.1	29♑59.2	2♒52.0	19 20.5	27 2.0	25 28.9	8 9.0	6 39.3	15 5.6	4 24.0	29 37.2
6 S	2 57 45.6	16 3.1	29 56.0	15 49.1	20 38.7	27 39.7	26 7.4	8 7.0	6 46.7	15 3.5	4 22.4	29 36.2
7 S	3 1 42.1	17 1.2	29 52.8	29 10.0	21 59.2	28 16.1	26 45.9	8 4.7	6 54.2	15 1.4	4 20.9	29 35.2
8 M	3 5 38.7	17 59.2	29 49.7	12♓57.6	23 21.9	28 51.3	27 24.5	8 2.3	7 1.7	14 59.4	4 19.4	29 34.2
9 T	3 9 35.2	18 57.3	29 46.5	27 13.2	24 46.9	29 25.1	28 3.0	7 59.7	7 9.2	14 57.4	4 17.8	29 33.3
10 W	3 13 31.8	19 55.3	29 43.3	11♈54.9	26 14.1	29 57.6	28 41.5	7 56.9	7 16.8	14 55.4	4 16.3	29 32.4
11 T	3 17 28.3	20 53.2	29 40.1	26 57.6	27 43.4	0♋28.6	29 20.0	7 54.0	7 24.4	14 53.4	4 14.7	29 31.5
12 F	3 21 24.9	21 51.2	29 37.0	12♉12.7	29 14.9	0 58.2	29 58.5	7 50.8	7 32.0	14 51.5	4 13.1	29 30.6
13 S	3 25 21.5	22 49.1	29 33.8	27 29.3	0♉48.5	1 26.3	0♋36.9	7 47.5	7 39.6	14 49.7	4 11.5	29 29.8
14 S	3 29 18.0	23 47.0	29 30.6	12♊36.4	2 24.2	1 52.8	1 15.4	7 44.0	7 47.3	14 47.8	4 10.0	29 29.0
15 M	3 33 14.6	24 44.9	29 27.4	27 24.3	4 2.1	2 17.6	1 53.8	7 40.4	7 54.9	14 46.0	4 8.4	29 28.2
16 T	3 37 11.1	25 42.8	29 24.3	11♋46.8	5 42.0	2 40.7	2 32.3	7 36.6	8 2.6	14 44.3	4 6.8	29 27.5
17 W	3 41 7.7	26 40.6	29 21.1	25 40.6	7 24.1	3 2.1	3 10.7	7 32.6	8 10.3	14 42.6	4 5.2	29 26.8
18 T	3 45 4.2	27 38.4	29 17.9	9♌ 6.2	9 8.2	3 21.6	3 49.1	7 28.4	8 18.0	14 41.0	4 3.6	29 26.1
19 F	3 49 0.8	28 36.1	29 14.7	22 5.9	10 54.4	3 39.2	4 27.5	7 24.1	8 25.8	14 39.3	4 2.0	29 25.4
20 S	3 52 57.4	29 33.9	29 11.5	4♍43.7	12 42.7	3 54.8	5 5.9	7 19.6	8 33.5	14 37.7	4 0.4	29 24.8
21 S	3 56 53.9	0♊31.6	29 8.4	17 4.0	14 33.2	4 8.4	5 44.2	7 14.9	8 41.2	14 36.2	3 58.7	29 24.2
22 M	4 0 50.5	1 29.2	29 5.2	29 11.4	16 25.7	4 20.0	6 22.6	7 10.1	8 49.0	14 34.7	3 57.1	29 23.6
23 T	4 4 47.0	2 26.9	29 2.0	11♎10.1	18 20.2	4 29.4	7 0.9	7 5.2	8 56.7	14 33.2	3 55.5	29 23.1
24 W	4 8 43.6	3 24.5	28 58.8	23 3.9	20 16.8	4 36.5	7 39.2	7 0.1	9 4.5	14 31.8	3 53.9	29 22.6
25 T	4 12 40.1	4 22.1	28 55.7	4♏55.8	22 15.4	4 41.5	8 17.5	6 54.9	9 12.3	14 30.4	3 52.2	29 22.1
26 F	4 16 36.7	5 19.7	28 52.5	16 48.4	24 16.0	4 44.1	8 55.8	6 49.5	9 20.1	14 29.1	3 50.6	29 21.6
27 S	4 20 33.3	6 17.3	28 49.3	28 43.4	26 18.4	4 44.4	9 34.0	6 44.0	9 27.9	14 27.8	3 49.0	29 21.2
28 S	4 24 29.8	7 14.8	28 46.1	10♐42.6	28 22.6	4R42.4	10 12.3	6 38.3	9 35.6	14 26.6	3 47.4	29 20.8
29 M	4 28 26.4	8 12.3	28 43.0	22 47.3	0♊28.4	4 37.9	10 50.5	6 32.5	9 43.4	14 25.4	3 45.7	29 20.5
30 T	4 32 22.9	9 9.8	28 39.8	4♑59.1	2 35.8	4 31.0	11 28.8	6 26.6	9 51.2	14 24.2	3 44.1	29 20.1
31 W	4 36 19.5	10 7.3	28 36.6	17 19.9	4 44.5	4 21.8	12 7.0	6 20.6	9 59.0	14 23.1	3 42.5	29 19.9
DECLINATION at NOON												
1 M	2 38 2.8	15N11.7	20S 6.7	25S 60.0	3N 1.5	27N31.6	24N23.7	22S54.0	19N46.5	5S22.3	19S22.9	15N22.3
4 T	2 49 52.5	16 4.7	20 8.8	22 40.4	4 19.4	27 36.4	24 29.6	22 54.5	19 50.6	5 19.8	19 22.0	15 22.7
7 S	3 1 42.1	16 55.3	20 10.8	9 22.4	5 49.1	27 37.0	24 33.7	22 55.2	19 54.7	5 17.4	19 21.1	15 23.0
10 W	3 13 31.8	17 43.4	20 12.8	9N 9.2	7 28.9	27 33.7	24 36.1	22 55.9	19 58.8	5 15.2	19 20.2	15 23.1
13 S	3 25 21.5	18 28.8	20 14.8	23 53.4	9 17.3	27 26.6	24 36.8	22 56.7	20 2.8	5 13.1	19 19.3	15 23.1
16 T	3 37 11.1	19 11.5	20 16.8	24 20.0	11 12.6	27 16.0	24 35.8	22 57.6	20 6.8	5 11.1	19 18.5	15 22.9
19 F	3 49 0.8	19 51.1	20 18.8	12 10.0	13 12.8	27 2.1	24 33.0	22 58.6	20 10.7	5 9.2	19 17.5	15 22.5
22 M	4 0 50.5	20 27.8	20 20.7	3S46.7	15 15.4	26 44.8	24 28.5	22 59.6	20 14.5	5 7.5	19 16.6	15 22.1
25 T	4 12 40.1	21 1.2	20 22.7	17 54.8	17 17.6	26 24.4	24 22.3	23 0.7	20 18.3	5 6.0	19 15.8	15 21.5
28 S	4 24 29.8	21 31.4	20 24.6	25 42.8	19 15.4	26 0.7	24 14.5	23 1.9	20 22.0	5 4.6	19 14.9	15 20.8
31 W	4 36 19.5	21 58.3	20 26.6	23 9.6	21 3.8	25 33.6	24 5.0	23 3.1	20 25.6	5 3.3	19 14.0	15 19.9

JUNE 1972

DAY	EPHEMERIS SIDEREAL TIME h m s	☉ ° ′	☊ ° ′	☽ ° ′	☿ ° ′	♀ ° ′	♂ ° ′	♃ ° ′	♄ ° ′	♅ ° ′	♆ ° ′	♇ ° ′
LONGITUDE at NOON												
1 T	4 40 16.0	11♊ 4.8	28♑33.4	29♑51.7	6♊54.4	4♋10.0	12♋45.2	6♑14.4	10♊ 6.8	14♎22.1	3♐40.9	29♍19.6
2 F	4 44 12.6	12 2.3	28 30.2	12♒37.2	9 5.2	3R55.9	13 23.4	6R 8.1	10 14.6	14R21.0	3R39.3	29R19.4
3 S	4 48 9.2	12 59.7	28 27.1	25 39.3	11 16.7	3 39.5	14 1.6	6 1.7	10 22.4	14 20.1	3 37.7	29 19.2
4 S	4 52 5.7	13 57.2	28 23.9	9♓ 0.6	13 28.7	3 20.7	14 39.8	5 55.2	10 30.2	14 19.2	3 36.1	29 19.0
5 M	4 56 2.3	14 54.6	28 20.7	22 43.5	15 40.8	2 59.6	15 18.0	5 48.6	10 38.0	14 18.3	3 34.5	29 18.9
6 T	4 59 58.8	15 52.1	28 17.5	6♈49.1	17 52.9	2 36.4	15 56.2	5 41.9	10 45.8	14 17.6	3 33.0	29 18.8
7 W	5 3 55.4	16 49.5	28 14.4	21 16.1	20 4.5	2 11.1	16 34.3	5 35.1	10 53.6	14 16.8	3 31.4	29 18.7
8 T	5 7 52.0	17 46.9	28 11.2	6♉ 1.3	22 15.5	1 43.7	17 12.5	5 28.2	11 1.4	14 16.1	3 29.8	29 18.7
9 F	5 11 48.5	18 44.3	28 8.0	20 58.6	24 25.6	1 14.6	17 50.6	5 21.2	11 9.1	14 15.4	3 28.3	29 18.7
10 S	5 15 45.1	19 41.6	28 4.8	5♊59.8	26 34.6	0 43.7	18 28.8	5 14.2	11 16.9	14 14.8	3 26.7	29 18.7
11 S	5 19 41.6	20 39.0	28 1.7	20 55.7	28 42.2	0 11.3	19 6.9	5 7.0	11 24.6	14 14.3	3 25.2	29D18.8
12 M	5 23 38.2	21 36.4	27 58.5	5♋37.6	0♋48.3	29♊37.5	19 45.0	4 59.8	11 32.3	14 13.8	3 23.7	29 18.9
13 T	5 27 34.7	22 33.7	27 55.3	19 58.9	2 52.7	29 2.5	20 23.1	4 52.5	11 40.1	14 13.3	3 22.1	29 19.0
14 W	5 31 31.3	23 31.0	27 52.1	3♌55.3	4 55.3	28 26.5	21 1.3	4 45.1	11 47.8	14 12.9	3 20.6	29 19.2
15 T	5 35 27.9	24 28.3	27 49.0	17 25.4	6 55.9	27 49.8	21 39.4	4 37.7	11 55.4	14 12.6	3 19.1	29 19.3
16 F	5 39 24.4	25 25.6	27 45.8	0♍30.2	8 54.4	27 12.5	22 17.4	4 30.3	12 3.1	14 12.3	3 17.7	29 19.6
17 S	5 43 21.0	26 22.9	27 42.6	13 12.3	10 50.8	26 35.0	22 55.5	4 22.8	12 10.8	14 12.0	3 16.2	29 19.8
18 S	5 47 17.5	27 20.2	27 39.4	25 35.7	12 45.1	25 57.4	23 33.6	4 15.2	12 18.4	14 11.8	3 14.7	29 20.1
19 M	5 51 14.1	28 17.5	27 36.3	7♎44.6	14 37.1	25 20.0	24 11.7	4 7.6	12 26.0	14 11.7	3 13.3	29 20.4
20 T	5 55 10.7	29 14.7	27 33.1	19 43.7	16 26.9	24 43.0	24 49.7	4 0.0	12 33.6	14 11.6	3 11.9	29 20.8
21 W	5 59 7.2	0♋11.9	27 29.9	1♏37.3	18 14.4	24 6.7	25 27.8	3 52.4	12 41.2	14 11.6	3 10.5	29 21.2
22 T	6 3 3.8	1 9.2	27 26.7	13 29.4	19 59.6	23 31.3	26 5.8	3 44.7	12 48.7	14 11.6	3 9.1	29 21.6
23 F	6 7 0.3	2 6.4	27 23.5	25 23.6	21 42.5	22 57.0	26 43.8	3 37.1	12 56.3	14 11.6	3 7.7	29 22.1
24 S	6 10 56.9	3 3.6	27 20.4	7♐22.7	23 23.1	22 24.0	27 21.9	3 29.4	13 3.8	14D11.8	3 6.3	29 22.5
25 S	6 14 53.4	4 0.8	27 17.2	19 28.9	25 1.4	21 52.5	27 59.9	3 21.7	13 11.2	14 11.9	3 5.0	29 23.1
26 M	6 18 50.0	4 58.0	27 14.0	1♑44.2	26 37.4	21 22.7	28 37.9	3 14.0	13 18.7	14 12.2	3 3.7	29 23.6
27 T	6 22 46.6	5 55.2	27 10.8	14 10.0	28 11.0	20 54.8	29 16.0	3 6.4	13 26.2	14 12.5	3 2.4	29 24.2
28 W	6 26 43.1	6 52.4	27 7.7	26 47.1	29 42.3	20 28.8	29 54.0	2 58.7	13 33.5	14 12.8	3 1.1	29 24.8
29 T	6 30 39.7	7 49.6	27 4.5	9♒36.7	1♌11.2	20 4.9	0♌32.0	2 51.1	13 40.9	14 13.2	2 59.9	29 25.5
30 F	6 34 36.2	8 46.8	27 1.3	22 39.5	2 37.6	19 43.1	1 10.0	2 43.5	13 48.2	14 13.7	2 58.6	29 26.2
DECLINATION at NOON												
1 T	4 40 16.0	22N 6.5	20S27.2	19S54.7	21N37.0	25N23.7	24N 1.4	23S 3.5	20N26.8	5S 3.0	19S13.7	15N19.6
4 S	4 52 5.7	22 28.8	20 29.1	4 58.2	23 4.8	24 51.9	23 49.8	23 4.7	20 30.4	5 2.0	19 12.8	15 18.5
7 W	5 3 55.4	22 47.5	20 31.1	13N 3.5	24 11.4	24 16.3	23 36.5	23 5.9	20 33.8	5 1.1	19 12.0	15 17.3
10 S	5 15 45.1	23 2.6	20 33.0	25 14.6	24 53.7	23 37.3	23 21.6	23 7.1	20 37.1	5 0.5	19 11.2	15 16.0
13 T	5 27 34.7	23 14.1	20 34.9	22 31.6	25 10.9	22 55.2	23 5.1	23 8.3	20 40.4	5 0.0	19 10.4	15 14.6
16 F	5 39 24.4	23 21.9	20 36.8	8 33.1	25 4.4	22 11.2	22 47.2	23 9.5	20 43.5	4 59.7	19 9.6	15 13.0
19 M	5 51 14.1	23 26.0	20 38.6	7S36.9	24 36.9	21 26.4	22 27.7	23 10.6	20 46.6	4 59.6	19 8.9	15 11.4
22 T	6 3 3.8	23 26.3	20 40.5	20 38.6	23 51.7	20 42.8	22 6.8	23 11.7	20 49.5	4 59.7	19 8.1	15 9.6
25 S	6 14 53.4	23 23.0	20 42.4	26 8.5	22 52.3	20 1.9	21 44.5	23 12.8	20 52.4	4 59.9	19 7.5	15 7.7
28 W	6 26 43.1	23 15.9	20 44.2	20 44.0	21 41.9	19 25.5	21 20.8	23 13.7	20 55.1	5 0.4	19 6.8	15 5.7

JULY 1972

LONGITUDE at NOON

DAY	EPHEMERIS SIDEREAL TIME	☉	☊	☽	☿	♀	♂	♃	♄	♅	♆	♇
	h m s	° ′	° ′	° ′	° ′	° ′	° ′	° ′	° ′	° ′	° ′	° ′
1 S	6 38 32.8	9♋44.0	26♑58.1	5♓56.4	4♌ 1.7	19♊23.6	1♌47.9	2♑35.9	13♊55.6	14♎14.2	2♐57.4	29♍26.9
2 S	6 42 29.4	10 41.2	26 55.0	19 28.2	5 23.3	19R 6.5	2 25.9	2R28.3	14 2.8	14 14.7	2R56.2	29 27.6
3 M	6 46 25.9	11 38.4	26 51.8	3♈15.1	6 42.5	18 51.7	3 3.9	2 20.8	14 10.1	14 15.3	2 55.0	29 28.4
4 T	6 50 22.5	12 35.6	26 48.6	17 16.9	7 59.1	18 39.3	3 41.9	2 13.4	14 17.3	14 15.9	2 53.8	29 29.2
5 W	6 54 19.0	13 32.8	26 45.4	1♉32.4	9 13.1	18 29.3	4 19.9	2 5.9	14 24.4	14 16.6	2 52.7	29 30.0
6 T	6 58 15.6	14 30.0	26 42.3	15 59.2	10 24.4	18 21.7	4 57.9	1 58.6	14 31.6	14 17.4	2 51.6	29 30.9
7 F	7 2 12.1	15 27.2	26 39.1	0♊33.3	11 33.1	18 16.5	5 35.9	1 51.2	14 38.7	14 18.2	2 50.5	29 31.8
8 S	7 6 8.7	16 24.4	26 35.9	15 9.5	12 39.0	18 13.7	6 13.8	1 44.0	14 45.7	14 19.1	2 49.4	29 32.7
9 S	7 10 5.3	17 21.6	26 32.7	29 41.9	13 42.0	18 13.2	6 51.8	1 36.8	14 52.8	14 20.0	2 48.4	29 33.6
10 M	7 14 1.8	18 18.9	26 29.5	14♋ 4.5	14 42.0	18D15.1	7 29.8	1 29.7	14 59.7	14 20.9	2 47.3	29 34.6
11 T	7 17 58.4	19 16.1	26 26.4	28 11.9	15 39.0	18 19.1	8 7.8	1 22.7	15 6.7	14 22.0	2 46.3	29 35.6
12 W	7 21 54.9	20 13.3	26 23.2	12♌ 0.2	16 32.8	18 25.4	8 45.8	1 15.8	15 13.6	14 23.0	2 45.4	29 36.7
13 T	7 25 51.5	21 10.6	26 20.0	25 26.9	17 23.3	18 33.9	9 23.7	1 8.9	15 20.4	14 24.1	2 44.4	29 37.7
14 F	7 29 48.1	22 7.8	26 16.8	8♍31.6	18 10.4	18 44.4	10 1.7	1 2.2	15 27.2	14 25.3	2 43.5	29 38.8
15 S	7 33 44.6	23 5.0	26 13.7	21 15.6	18 53.9	18 57.0	10 39.7	0 55.5	15 34.0	14 26.5	2 42.6	29 40.0
16 S	7 37 41.2	24 2.3	26 10.5	3♎41.2	19 33.8	19 11.6	11 17.7	0 49.0	15 40.7	14 27.8	2 41.7	29 41.1
17 M	7 41 37.7	24 59.5	26 7.3	15 52.2	20 9.7	19 28.1	11 55.6	0 42.5	15 47.3	14 29.1	2 40.9	29 42.3
18 T	7 45 34.3	25 56.8	26 4.1	27 52.7	20 41.7	19 46.5	12 33.7	0 36.3	15 54.0	14 30.5	2 40.1	29 43.6
19 W	7 49 30.8	26 54.1	26 1.0	9♏47.1	21 9.6	20 6.7	13 11.6	0 30.1	16 0.6	14 32.0	2 39.3	29 44.8
20 T	7 53 27.4	27 51.3	25 57.8	21 40.0	21 33.0	20 28.7	13 49.6	0 24.0	16 7.1	14 33.4	2 38.5	29 46.1
21 F	7 57 24.0	28 48.6	25 54.6	3♐35.8	21 52.0	20 52.3	14 27.6	0 18.0	16 13.5	14 35.0	2 37.8	29 47.4
22 S	8 1 20.5	29 45.9	25 51.4	15 38.4	22 6.4	21 17.6	15 5.5	0 12.2	16 19.9	14 36.5	2 37.1	29 48.7
23 S	8 5 17.1	0♌43.1	25 48.2	27 51.2	22 16.1	21 44.5	15 43.5	0 6.5	16 26.3	14 38.1	2 36.4	29 50.1
24 M	8 9 13.6	1 40.4	25 45.1	10♑16.9	22 20.8	22 12.9	16 21.5	0 0.9	16 32.6	14 39.8	2 35.8	29 51.5
25 T	8 13 10.2	2 37.7	25 41.9	22 57.4	22R20.6	22 42.8	16 59.5	29♐55.5	16 38.8	14 41.5	2 35.2	29 52.9
26 W	8 17 6.7	3 35.0	25 38.7	5♒53.6	22 15.3	23 14.1	17 37.4	29 50.2	16 45.0	14 43.3	2 34.6	29 54.3
27 T	8 21 3.3	4 32.3	25 35.5	19 5.6	22 5.0	23 46.9	18 15.4	29 45.1	16 51.1	14 45.1	2 34.0	29 55.7
28 F	8 24 59.9	5 29.7	25 32.4	2♓32.7	21 49.7	24 20.9	18 53.4	29 40.1	16 57.1	14 46.9	2 33.5	29 57.2
29 S	8 28 56.4	6 27.0	25 29.2	16 13.2	21 29.4	24 56.2	19 31.4	29 35.2	17 3.1	14 48.8	2 33.0	29 58.7
30 S	8 32 53.0	7 24.3	25 26.0	0♈ 5.3	21 4.3	25 32.8	20 9.3	29 30.5	17 9.1	14 50.8	2 32.5	0♎ 0.3
31 M	8 36 49.5	8 21.7	25 22.8	14 6.6	20 34.7	26 10.5	20 47.3	29 26.0	17 15.0	14 52.7	2 32.1	0 1.8

DECLINATION at NOON

DAY	EPHEMERIS SIDEREAL TIME	☉	☊	☽	☿	♀	♂	♃	♄	♅	♆	♇
1 S	6 38 32.8	23N 5.2	20S46.1	6S11.3	20N23.7	18N54.6	20N55.7	23S14.6	20N57.8	5S 1.0	19S 6.2	15N 3.6
4 T	6 50 22.5	22 50.9	20 47.9	11N35.5	19 0.3	18 30.0	20 29.4	23 15.5	21 0.3	5 1.8	19 5.7	15 1.4
7 F	7 2 12.1	22 32.9	20 49.7	24 31.1	17 34.4	18 11.9	20 1.7	23 16.2	21 2.7	5 2.8	19 5.1	14 59.1
10 M	7 14 1.8	22 11.5	20 51.6	23 47.2	16 8.7	17 60.0	19 32.9	23 17.0	21 5.0	5 4.0	19 4.7	14 56.7
13 T	7 25 51.5	21 46.6	20 53.4	10 35.4	14 45.8	17 53.8	19 2.8	23 17.6	21 7.2	5 5.3	19 4.2	14 54.3
16 S	7 37 41.2	21 18.3	20 55.2	5S57.0	13 28.3	17 52.6	18 31.5	23 18.2	21 9.3	5 6.9	19 3.9	14 51.8
19 W	7 49 30.8	20 46.8	20 56.9	19 36.6	12 19.5	17 55.7	17 59.2	23 18.7	21 11.3	5 8.6	19 3.5	14 49.1
22 S	8 1 20.5	20 12.2	20 58.7	26 4.7	11 22.4	18 2.1	17 25.8	23 19.2	21 13.1	5 10.5	19 3.3	14 46.5
25 T	8 13 10.2	19 34.6	21 0.5	21 46.3	10 40.6	18 11.0	16 51.3	23 19.7	21 14.9	5 12.5	19 3.0	14 43.8
28 F	8 24 59.9	18 54.0	21 2.2	7 38.2	10 17.3	18 21.6	16 15.9	23 20.1	21 16.5	5 14.7	19 2.9	14 41.0
31 M	8 36 49.5	18 10.6	21 4.0	10N18.7	10 15.0	18 33.1	15 39.5	23 20.5	21 18.1	5 17.0	19 2.8	14 38.2

AUGUST 1972

LONGITUDE at NOON

DAY	EPHEMERIS SIDEREAL TIME	☉	☊	☽	☿	♀	♂	♃	♄	♅	♆	♇
1 T	8 40 46.1	9♌19.1	25♑19.7	28♈14.7	20♌ 0.8	26♊49.4	21♌25.3	29♐21.6	17♊20.8	14♎54.8	2♐31.6	0♎ 3.4
2 W	8 44 42.6	10 16.5	25 16.5	12♉27.3	19R23.1	27 29.4	22 3.3	29R17.4	17 26.5	14 56.8	2R31.3	0 5.0
3 T	8 48 39.2	11 14.0	25 13.3	26 41.8	18 42.2	28 10.4	22 41.3	29 13.3	17 32.2	14 59.0	2 30.9	0 6.6
4 F	8 52 35.7	12 11.4	25 10.1	10♊55.8	17 58.5	28 52.5	23 19.4	29 9.4	17 37.8	15 1.1	2 30.6	0 8.3
5 S	8 56 32.3	13 8.9	25 6.9	25 6.7	17 12.8	29 35.5	23 57.4	29 5.7	17 43.3	15 3.3	2 30.3	0 9.9
6 S	9 0 28.9	14 6.4	25 3.8	9♋11.7	16 25.9	0♋19.5	24 35.4	29 2.2	17 48.8	15 5.6	2 30.1	0 11.6
7 M	9 4 25.4	15 3.9	25 0.6	23 7.9	15 38.6	1 4.4	25 13.5	28 58.8	17 54.2	15 7.9	2 29.8	0 13.3
8 T	9 8 22.0	16 1.5	24 57.4	6♌52.5	14 51.7	1 50.2	25 51.5	28 55.6	17 59.6	15 10.3	2 29.7	0 15.1
9 W	9 12 18.5	16 59.0	24 54.2	20 22.9	14 6.2	2 36.8	26 29.6	28 52.6	18 4.9	15 12.6	2 29.5	0 16.9
10 T	9 16 15.1	17 56.6	24 51.1	3♍37.1	13 22.9	3 24.2	27 7.7	28 49.8	18 10.1	15 15.1	2 29.4	0 18.7
11 F	9 20 11.6	18 54.2	24 47.9	16 34.1	12 42.7	4 12.4	27 45.7	28 47.1	18 15.2	15 17.5	2 29.3	0 20.5
12 S	9 24 8.2	19 51.8	24 44.7	29 14.1	12 6.5	5 1.3	28 23.8	28 44.6	18 20.2	15 20.0	2 29.2	0 22.3
13 S	9 28 4.7	20 49.4	24 41.5	11♎38.2	11 35.0	5 50.9	29 1.9	28 42.3	18 25.2	15 22.6	2 29.2	0 24.1
14 M	9 32 1.3	21 47.1	24 38.4	23 48.7	11 8.8	6 41.3	29 39.9	28 40.2	18 30.1	15 25.1	2 29.2	0 26.0
15 T	9 35 57.9	22 44.7	24 35.2	5♏49.0	10 48.6	7 32.3	0♍18.0	28 38.3	18 34.9	15 27.7	2 29.2	0 27.9
16 W	9 39 54.4	23 42.4	24 32.0	17 43.1	10 35.0	8 23.9	0 56.1	28 36.5	18 39.6	15 30.4	2D29.3	0 29.8
17 T	9 43 51.0	24 40.1	24 28.8	29 35.4	10 28.2	9 16.2	1 34.2	28 35.0	18 44.2	15 33.1	2 29.4	0 31.7
18 F	9 47 47.5	25 37.8	24 25.6	11♐30.9	10D28.7	10 9.1	2 12.3	28 33.6	18 48.8	15 35.8	2 29.5	0 33.6
19 S	9 51 44.1	26 35.5	24 22.5	23 34.3	10 36.6	11 2.6	2 50.5	28 32.4	18 53.3	15 38.6	2 29.7	0 35.6
20 S	9 55 40.6	27 33.3	24 19.3	5♑50.1	10 52.0	11 56.7	3 28.6	28 31.4	18 57.7	15 41.4	2 29.9	0 37.5
21 M	9 59 37.2	28 31.0	24 16.1	18 22.3	11 15.2	12 51.3	4 6.7	28 30.6	19 2.0	15 44.2	2 30.1	0 39.5
22 T	10 3 33.7	29 28.8	24 12.9	1♒13.9	11 46.0	13 46.4	4 44.8	28 30.0	19 6.2	15 47.1	2 30.4	0 41.5
23 W	10 7 30.3	0♍26.6	24 9.8	14 26.5	12 24.3	14 42.1	5 23.0	28 29.5	19 10.3	15 50.0	2 30.7	0 43.5
24 T	10 11 26.8	1 24.5	24 6.6	28 0.1	13 10.1	15 38.3	6 1.1	28 29.3	19 14.4	15 52.9	2 31.0	0 45.6
25 F	10 15 23.4	2 22.3	24 3.4	11♓53.0	14 3.1	16 35.0	6 39.3	28 29.2	19 18.3	15 55.9	2 31.3	0 47.6
26 S	10 19 20.0	3 20.2	24 0.2	26 1.5	15 3.1	17 32.1	7 17.5	28D29.4	19 22.2	15 58.9	2 31.7	0 49.7
27 S	10 23 16.5	4 18.1	23 57.0	10♈20.8	16 9.8	18 29.7	7 55.7	28 29.7	19 26.0	16 1.9	2 32.2	0 51.7
28 M	10 27 13.1	5 16.1	23 53.9	24 45.4	17 22.8	19 27.8	8 33.9	28 30.2	19 29.7	16 5.0	2 32.6	0 53.8
29 T	10 31 9.6	6 14.1	23 50.7	9♉10.1	18 41.9	20 26.4	9 12.1	28 30.9	19 33.4	16 8.1	2 33.1	0 56.0
30 W	10 35 6.2	7 12.1	23 47.5	23 30.4	20 6.4	21 25.3	9 50.3	28 31.8	19 36.9	16 11.2	2 33.7	0 58.1
31 T	10 39 2.7	8 10.1	23 44.3	7♊43.0	21 35.9	22 24.6	10 28.6	28 32.9	19 40.3	16 14.4	2 34.2	1 0.2

DECLINATION at NOON

DAY	EPHEMERIS SIDEREAL TIME	☉	☊	☽	☿	♀	♂	♃	♄	♅	♆	♇
1 T	8 40 46.1	17N55.6	21S 4.6	15N45.6	10N19.2	18N37.0	15N27.2	23S20.6	21N18.6	5S17.8	19S 2.7	14N37.3
4 F	8 52 35.7	17 8.6	21 6.3	25 46.8	10 46.0	18 48.5	14 49.6	23 21.0	21 20.0	5 20.4	19 2.7	14 34.4
7 M	9 4 25.4	16 19.2	21 8.0	21 43.3	11 31.6	18 59.3	14 11.1	23 21.4	21 21.3	5 23.1	19 2.7	14 31.5
10 T	9 16 15.1	15 27.4	21 9.7	7 11.7	12 30.2	19 8.8	13 31.8	23 21.7	21 22.5	5 26.0	19 2.8	14 28.5
13 S	9 28 4.7	14 33.3	21 11.4	9S15.7	13 34.1	19 16.5	12 51.8	23 22.1	21 23.6	5 28.9	19 2.9	14 25.6
16 W	9 39 54.4	13 37.2	21 13.1	21 45.8	14 34.7	19 21.9	12 11.0	23 22.4	21 24.6	5 32.1	19 3.1	14 22.6
19 S	9 51 44.1	12 39.2	21 14.8	26 4.0	15 24.3	19 24.6	11 29.5	23 22.8	21 25.5	5 35.3	19 3.4	14 19.6
22 T	10 3 33.7	11 39.4	21 16.5	19 24.2	15 56.5	19 24.2	10 47.4	23 23.2	21 26.3	5 38.6	19 3.7	14 16.7
25 F	10 15 23.4	10 37.9	21 18.2	3 38.7	16 6.1	19 20.4	10 4.7	23 23.6	21 27.0	5 42.1	19 4.0	14 13.7
28 M	10 27 13.1	9 34.9	21 19.8	14N23.1	15 49.6	19 12.9	9 21.4	23 24.0	21 27.6	5 45.7	19 4.5	14 10.7
31 T	10 39 2.7	8 30.5	21 21.5	25 21.5	15 5.1	19 1.4	8 37.5	23 24.4	21 28.2	5 49.4	19 4.9	14 7.8

SEPTEMBER 1972

DAY	EPHEMERIS SIDEREAL TIME	☉	☊	☽	☿	♀	♂	♃	♄	♅	♆	♇
	h m s	° '	° '	° '	° '	° '	° '	° '	° '	° '	° '	° '
						LONGITUDE at NOON						
1 F	10 42 59.3	9♍ 8.2	23♑41.2	21♊46.0	23♌10.1	23♋24.4	11♍ 6.8	28♐34.1	19♊43.6	16♎17.6	2♐34.8	1♎ 2.3
2 S	10 46 55.8	10 6.3	23 38.0	5♋38.6	24 48.3	24 24.5	11 45.1	28 35.6	19 46.8	16 20.8	2 35.4	1 4.5
3 S	10 50 52.4	11 4.4	23 34.8	19 20.4	26 30.1	25 25.0	12 23.4	28 37.2	19 50.0	16 24.0	2 36.1	1 6.6
4 M	10 54 48.9	12 2.6	23 31.6	2♌51.2	28 15.0	26 25.9	13 1.7	28 39.0	19 53.0	16 27.3	2 36.7	1 8.8
5 T	10 58 45.5	13 0.8	23 28.4	16 10.9	0♍ 2.5	27 27.1	13 40.0	28 41.0	19 55.9	16 30.6	2 37.4	1 11.0
6 W	11 2 42.0	13 59.0	23 25.3	29 18.9	1 52.1	28 28.7	14 18.3	28 43.2	19 58.8	16 33.9	2 38.2	1 13.2
7 T	11 6 38.6	14 57.2	23 22.1	12♍14.7	3 43.4	29 30.6	14 56.6	28 45.6	20 1.5	16 37.2	2 39.0	1 15.4
8 F	11 10 35.2	15 55.5	23 18.9	24 57.8	5 35.9	0♌32.8	15 35.0	28 48.1	20 4.1	16 40.6	2 39.8	1 17.6
9 S	11 14 31.7	16 53.8	23 15.7	7♎28.0	7 29.4	1 35.3	16 13.3	28 50.9	20 6.7	16 44.0	2 40.6	1 19.8
10 S	11 18 28.3	17 52.2	23 12.6	19 45.7	9 23.5	2 38.2	16 51.7	28 53.8	20 9.1	16 47.4	2 41.5	1 22.0
11 M	11 22 24.8	18 50.6	23 9.4	1♏52.4	11 17.9	3 41.3	17 30.1	28 56.9	20 11.4	16 50.9	2 42.4	1 24.3
12 T	11 26 21.4	19 49.0	23 6.2	13 50.1	13 12.4	4 44.7	18 8.5	29 0.2	20 13.7	16 54.3	2 43.3	1 26.5
13 W	11 30 17.9	20 47.4	23 3.0	25 42.2	15 6.7	5 48.4	18 46.9	29 3.6	20 15.8	16 57.8	2 44.3	1 28.7
14 T	11 34 14.5	21 45.8	22 59.8	7♐32.4	17 0.7	6 52.4	19 25.3	29 7.3	20 17.8	17 1.3	2 45.2	1 31.0
15 F	11 38 11.0	22 44.3	22 56.7	19 25.5	18 54.2	7 56.6	20 3.8	29 11.1	20 19.7	17 4.8	2 46.3	1 33.2
16 S	11 42 7.6	23 42.8	22 53.5	1♑26.6	20 47.1	9 1.1	20 42.2	29 15.1	20 21.5	17 8.3	2 47.3	1 35.5
17 S	11 46 4.1	24 41.4	22 50.3	13 41.0	22 39.3	10 5.9	21 20.7	29 19.2	20 23.2	17 11.9	2 48.4	1 37.8
18 M	11 50 0.7	25 39.9	22 47.1	26 13.6	24 30.8	11 10.9	21 59.1	29 23.6	20 24.8	17 15.5	2 49.5	1 40.0
19 T	11 53 57.2	26 38.6	22 44.0	9♒ 8.8	26 21.4	12 16.2	22 37.7	29 28.1	20 26.4	17 19.1	2 50.7	1 42.3
20 W	11 57 53.8	27 37.2	22 40.8	22 29.5	28 11.1	13 21.7	23 16.2	29 32.8	20 27.8	17 22.7	2 51.8	1 44.6
21 T	12 1 50.3	28 35.8	22 37.6	6♓16.9	29 59.9	14 27.4	23 54.7	29 37.6	20 29.0	17 26.3	2 53.0	1 46.9
22 F	12 5 46.9	29 34.5	22 34.4	20 29.1	1♎47.8	15 33.4	24 33.2	29 42.7	20 30.2	17 30.0	2 54.3	1 49.1
23 S	12 9 43.4	0♎33.2	22 31.2	5♈ 1.9	3 34.7	16 39.6	25 11.8	29 47.8	20 31.3	17 33.6	2 55.5	1 51.4
24 S	12 13 40.0	1 32.0	22 28.1	19 48.3	5 20.7	17 46.0	25 50.4	29 53.2	20 32.2	17 37.3	2 56.8	1 53.7
25 M	12 17 36.6	2 30.7	22 24.9	4♉39.8	7 5.8	18 52.6	26 29.0	29 58.7	20 33.0	17 41.0	2 58.1	1 56.0
26 T	12 21 33.1	3 29.6	22 21.7	19 27.9	8 49.8	19 59.5	27 7.6	0♑ 4.3	20 33.8	17 44.6	2 59.4	1 58.3
27 W	12 25 29.7	4 28.4	22 18.5	4♊ 5.4	10 33.0	21 6.6	27 46.2	0 10.1	20 34.4	17 48.3	3 0.8	2 0.5
28 T	12 29 26.2	5 27.3	22 15.4	18 27.4	12 15.2	22 13.8	28 24.8	0 16.1	20 34.9	17 52.1	3 2.2	2 2.8
29 F	12 33 22.8	6 26.2	22 12.2	2♋31.5	13 56.6	23 21.3	29 3.5	0 22.3	20 35.3	17 55.8	3 3.6	2 5.1
30 S	12 37 19.3	7 25.2	22 9.0	16 17.2	15 37.0	24 29.0	29 42.2	0 28.6	20 35.6	17 59.5	3 5.0	2 7.4
						DECLINATION at NOON						
1 F	10 42 59.3	8N 8.8	21S 22.0	26N 1.9	14N 44.2	18N 56.7	8N 22.8	23S 24.6	21N 28.4	5S 50.6	19S 5.1	14N 6.8
4 M	10 54 48.9	7 2.7	21 23.6	18 51.6	13 24.2	18 39.8	7 38.3	23 25.0	21 28.8	5 54.4	19 5.7	14 3.9
7 T	11 6 38.6	5 55.7	21 25.3	3 29.9	11 41.9	18 18.6	6 53.4	23 25.4	21 29.1	5 58.3	19 6.3	14 1.0
10 S	11 18 28.3	4 47.7	21 26.9	12S 25.3	9 42.5	17 53.1	6 8.1	23 25.9	21 29.4	6 2.2	19 6.9	13 58.1
13 W	11 30 17.9	3 39.1	21 28.5	23 24.5	7 31.3	17 23.3	5 22.4	23 26.3	21 29.6	6 6.3	19 7.6	13 55.3
16 S	11 42 7.6	2 29.8	21 30.1	25 24.5	5 13.0	16 49.1	4 36.5	23 26.7	21 29.7	6 10.4	19 8.4	13 52.5
19 T	11 53 57.2	1 20.1	21 31.6	16 41.9	2 51.3	16 10.6	3 50.2	23 27.1	21 29.7	6 14.5	19 9.2	13 49.8
22 F	12 5 46.9	0 10.1	21 33.2	0N 6.5	0 28.8	15 27.9	3 3.7	23 27.5	21 29.7	6 18.7	19 10.0	13 47.1
25 M	12 17 36.6	0S 60.0	21 34.8	17 43.5	1S 52.3	14 41.0	2 17.0	23 27.9	21 29.6	6 22.9	19 10.9	13 44.5
28 T	12 29 26.2	2 10.1	21 36.3	25 48.4	4 10.7	13 50.1	1 30.2	23 28.2	21 29.4	6 27.2	19 11.8	13 42.0

OCTOBER 1972

DAY	EPHEMERIS SIDEREAL TIME	☉	☊	☽	☿	♀	♂	♃	♄	♅	♆	♇
						LONGITUDE at NOON						
1 S	12 41 15.9	8♎24.2	22♑ 5.8	29♋45.6	17♎16.6	25♌36.9	0♎20.9	0♑35.0	20♊35.8	18♎ 3.2	3♐ 6.5	2♎ 9.6
2 M	12 45 12.4	9 23.3	22 2.6	12♌58.6	18 55.3	26 44.9	0 59.6	0 41.6	20 35.9	18 7.0	3 8.0	2 11.9
3 T	12 49 9.0	10 22.3	21 59.5	25 58.1	20 33.2	27 53.2	1 38.3	0 48.4	20R35.8	18 10.7	3 9.5	2 14.1
4 W	12 53 5.5	11 21.5	21 56.3	8♍45.8	22 10.3	29 1.6	2 17.1	0 55.3	20 35.7	18 14.5	3 11.0	2 16.4
5 T	12 57 2.1	12 20.6	21 53.1	21 22.7	23 46.5	0♍10.2	2 55.9	1 2.3	20 35.4	18 18.3	3 12.6	2 18.7
6 F	13 0 58.6	13 19.8	21 49.9	3♎49.6	25 22.0	1 18.9	3 34.7	1 9.5	20 35.0	18 22.0	3 14.2	2 20.9
7 S	13 4 55.2	14 19.0	21 46.8	16 7.1	26 56.7	2 27.8	4 13.5	1 16.8	20 34.5	18 25.8	3 15.8	2 23.2
8 S	13 8 51.7	15 18.3	21 43.6	28 15.6	28 30.6	3 36.9	4 52.3	1 24.3	20 33.9	18 29.6	3 17.4	2 25.4
9 M	13 12 48.3	16 17.6	21 40.4	10♏16.1	0♏ 3.8	4 46.2	5 31.2	1 32.0	20 33.2	18 33.4	3 19.1	2 27.6
10 T	13 16 44.9	17 17.0	21 37.2	22 10.1	1 36.3	5 55.6	6 10.1	1 39.8	20 32.4	18 37.2	3 20.8	2 29.9
11 W	13 20 41.4	18 16.3	21 34.0	3♐59.6	3 8.0	7 5.1	6 49.0	1 47.7	20 31.5	18 41.0	3 22.5	2 32.1
12 T	13 24 38.0	19 15.7	21 30.9	15 47.9	4 39.0	8 14.8	7 27.9	1 55.7	20 30.5	18 44.8	3 24.3	2 34.3
13 F	13 28 34.5	20 15.1	21 27.7	27 38.8	6 9.3	9 24.7	8 6.9	2 3.9	20 29.3	18 48.6	3 26.0	2 36.5
14 S	13 32 31.1	21 14.6	21 24.5	9♑36.9	7 38.8	10 34.6	8 45.8	2 12.2	20 28.1	18 52.3	3 27.8	2 38.7
15 S	13 36 27.6	22 14.1	21 21.3	21 47.6	9 7.7	11 44.7	9 24.8	2 20.7	20 26.7	18 56.1	3 29.6	2 40.9
16 M	13 40 24.2	23 13.6	21 18.2	4♒16.1	10 35.8	12 55.0	10 3.8	2 29.3	20 25.2	18 59.9	3 31.4	2 43.0
17 T	13 44 20.7	24 13.1	21 15.0	17 7.6	12 3.1	14 5.3	10 42.8	2 38.0	20 23.7	19 3.7	3 33.2	2 45.2
18 W	13 48 17.3	25 12.7	21 11.8	0♓26.5	13 29.7	15 15.8	11 21.8	2 46.8	20 22.0	19 7.4	3 35.1	2 47.4
19 T	13 52 13.8	26 12.3	21 8.6	14 15.0	14 55.6	16 26.5	12 0.8	2 55.8	20 20.2	19 11.2	3 37.0	2 49.5
20 F	13 56 10.4	27 11.9	21 5.4	28 33.2	16 20.7	17 37.2	12 39.9	3 4.9	20 18.3	19 15.0	3 38.8	2 51.6
21 S	14 0 6.9	28 11.6	21 2.3	13♈17.3	17 44.9	18 48.1	13 19.0	3 14.1	20 16.3	19 18.7	3 40.7	2 53.7
22 S	14 4 3.5	29 11.3	20 59.1	28 20.3	19 8.3	19 59.1	13 58.1	3 23.4	20 14.2	19 22.5	3 42.7	2 55.8
23 M	14 8 0.1	0♏11.0	20 55.9	13♉32.5	20 30.8	21 10.3	14 37.2	3 32.8	20 12.0	19 26.2	3 44.6	2 57.9
24 T	14 11 56.6	1 10.8	20 52.7	28 42.8	21 52.3	22 21.5	15 16.3	3 42.4	20 9.7	19 29.9	3 46.6	2 60.0
25 W	14 15 53.2	2 10.6	20 49.6	13♊41.4	23 12.9	23 32.9	15 55.5	3 52.0	20 7.3	19 33.7	3 48.6	3 2.0
26 T	14 19 49.7	3 10.4	20 46.4	28 20.7	24 32.3	24 44.4	16 34.7	4 1.8	20 4.8	19 37.4	3 50.5	3 4.1
27 F	14 23 46.3	4 10.3	20 43.2	12♋36.5	25 50.6	25 56.0	17 13.9	4 11.7	20 2.2	19 41.1	3 52.6	3 6.1
28 S	14 27 42.8	5 10.2	20 40.0	26 27.5	27 7.7	27 7.7	17 53.2	4 21.7	19 59.5	19 44.8	3 54.6	3 8.1
29 S	14 31 39.4	6 10.1	20 36.9	9♌55.1	28 23.4	28 19.5	18 32.4	4 31.9	19 56.8	19 48.4	3 56.6	3 10.1
30 M	14 35 35.9	7 10.1	20 33.7	23 1.6	29 37.6	29 31.4	19 11.7	4 42.1	19 53.9	19 52.1	3 58.7	3 12.1
31 T	14 39 32.5	8 10.1	20 30.5	5♍50.5	0♐50.3	0♎43.5	19 51.1	4 52.5	19 50.9	19 55.8	4 0.8	3 14.1
						DECLINATION at NOON						
1 S	12 41 15.9	3S 20.0	21S 37.9	19N 37.6	6S 25.4	12N 55.4	0N 43.3	23S 28.5	21N 29.2	6S 31.5	19S 12.8	13N 39.5
4 W	12 53 5.5	4 29.6	21 39.4	4 56.3	8 35.4	11 57.0	0S 3.8	23 28.7	21 28.9	6 35.8	19 13.8	13 37.2
7 S	13 4 55.2	5 38.8	21 40.9	10S 55.2	10 40.0	10 55.1	0 50.8	23 28.8	21 28.5	6 40.1	19 14.8	13 34.9
10 T	13 16 44.9	6 47.3	21 42.4	22 28.8	12 38.8	9 50.0	1 37.9	23 28.8	21 28.1	6 44.5	19 15.9	13 32.6
13 F	13 28 34.5	7 55.0	21 43.9	25 26.8	14 31.2	8 42.0	2 24.9	23 28.8	21 27.6	6 48.8	19 17.0	13 30.5
16 M	13 40 24.2	9 1.6	21 45.4	18 5.4	16 16.5	7 31.3	3 11.7	23 28.7	21 27.1	6 53.1	19 18.1	13 28.5
19 T	13 52 13.8	10 7.1	21 46.9	2 29.2	17 54.2	6 18.1	3 58.4	23 28.4	21 26.5	6 57.4	19 19.3	13 26.6
22 S	14 4 3.5	11 11.3	21 48.3	15N 31.0	19 23.6	5 2.7	4 45.0	23 28.0	21 25.8	7 1.6	19 20.4	13 24.8
25 W	14 15 53.2	12 13.9	21 49.8	25 25.1	20 44.0	3 45.4	5 31.3	23 27.5	21 25.1	7 5.9	19 21.6	13 23.1
28 S	14 27 42.8	13 14.9	21 51.3	20 18.6	21 54.7	2 26.5	6 17.3	23 26.9	21 24.4	7 10.1	19 22.8	13 21.6
31 T	14 39 32.5	14 14.0	21 52.7	5 59.8	22 54.7	1 6.2	7 3.0	23 26.1	21 23.6	7 14.2	19 24.1	13 20.1

NOVEMBER 1972

LONGITUDE at NOON

DAY	EPHEMERIS SIDEREAL TIME h m s	☉ ° ′	☊ ° ′	☽ ° ′	☿ ° ′	♀ ° ′	♂ ° ′	♃ ° ′	♄ ° ′	♅ ° ′	♆ ° ′	♇ ° ′
1 W	14 43 29.1	9♏10.2	20♑27.3	18♍24.8	2♐ 1.1	1♎55.6	20♎30.4	5♑ 2.9	19♓47.9	19♎59.4	4♐ 2.9	3♎16.0
2 T	14 47 25.6	10 10.3	20 24.1	0♎47.3	3 9.9	3 7.8	21 9.8	5 13.4	19R44.7	20 3.1	4 5.0	3 17.9
3 F	14 51 22.2	11 10.4	20 21.0	13 0.5	4 16.4	4 20.1	21 49.2	5 24.1	19 41.5	20 6.7	4 7.1	3 19.8
4 S	14 55 18.7	12 10.6	20 17.8	25 6.1	5 20.5	5 32.5	22 28.6	5 34.8	19 38.2	20 10.2	4 9.2	3 21.7
5 S	14 59 15.3	13 10.7	20 14.6	7♏ 5.5	6 21.9	6 45.0	23 8.0	5 45.7	19 34.7	20 13.8	4 11.3	3 23.6
6 M	15 3 11.8	14 11.0	20 11.4	18 59.9	7 20.1	7 57.6	23 47.5	5 56.6	19 31.2	20 17.4	4 13.5	3 25.4
7 T	15 7 8.4	15 11.2	20 8.3	0♐50.7	8 14.9	9 10.3	24 26.9	6 7.7	19 27.7	20 20.9	4 15.6	3 27.3
8 W	15 11 4.9	16 11.5	20 5.1	12 39.5	9 5.8	10 23.0	25 6.4	6 18.8	19 24.0	20 24.4	4 17.8	3 29.1
9 T	15 15 1.5	17 11.8	20 1.9	24 28.5	9 52.3	11 35.8	25 45.9	6 30.0	19 20.3	20 27.9	4 20.0	3 30.8
10 F	15 18 58.1	18 12.1	19 58.7	6♑20.5	10 33.9	12 48.7	26 25.5	6 41.3	19 16.4	20 31.4	4 22.1	3 32.6
11 S	15 22 54.6	19 12.4	19 55.5	18 19.3	11 10.1	14 1.7	27 5.0	6 52.7	19 12.6	20 34.8	4 24.3	3 34.3
12 S	15 26 51.2	20 12.8	19 52.4	0♒29.1	11 40.1	15 14.7	27 44.6	7 4.2	19 8.6	20 38.2	4 26.5	3 36.0
13 M	15 30 47.7	21 13.2	19 49.2	12 54.7	12 3.4	16 27.8	28 24.2	7 15.8	19 4.6	20 41.6	4 28.7	3 37.7
14 T	15 34 44.3	22 13.6	19 46.0	25 40.9	12 19.1	17 41.0	29 3.9	7 27.4	19 0.5	20 45.0	4 30.9	3 39.4
15 W	15 38 40.8	23 14.1	19 42.8	8♓52.3	12 26.6	18 54.2	29 43.5	7 39.2	18 56.3	20 48.4	4 33.2	3 41.0
16 T	15 42 37.4	24 14.6	19 39.7	22 32.3	12R25.2	20 7.5	0♏23.2	7 51.0	18 52.1	20 51.7	4 35.4	3 42.7
17 F	15 46 33.9	25 15.0	19 36.5	6♈42.3	12 14.2	21 20.9	1 2.9	8 2.9	18 47.8	20 55.0	4 37.6	3 44.3
18 S	15 50 30.5	26 15.6	19 33.3	21 20.6	11 53.0	22 34.3	1 42.6	8 14.9	18 43.5	20 58.3	4 39.9	3 45.8
19 S	15 54 27.1	27 16.1	19 30.1	6♉22.0	11 21.3	23 47.8	2 22.3	8 26.9	18 39.1	21 1.5	4 42.1	3 47.4
20 M	15 58 23.6	28 16.6	19 27.0	21 38.0	10 39.1	25 1.4	3 2.1	8 39.0	18 34.7	21 4.7	4 44.3	3 48.9
21 T	16 2 20.2	29 17.3	19 23.8	6♊57.8	9 46.7	26 15.0	3 41.9	8 51.3	18 30.2	21 8.0	4 46.6	3 50.4
22 W	16 6 16.7	0♐17.9	19 20.6	22 10.2	8 44.8	27 28.7	4 21.7	9 3.5	18 25.7	21 11.1	4 48.9	3 51.9
23 T	16 10 13.3	1 18.5	19 17.4	7♋ 5.4	7 34.6	28 42.4	5 1.6	9 15.9	18 21.1	21 14.2	4 51.1	3 53.3
24 F	16 14 9.8	2 19.2	19 14.2	21 36.9	6 18.0	29 56.2	5 41.4	9 28.3	18 16.4	21 17.3	4 53.4	3 54.7
25 S	16 18 6.4	3 19.8	19 11.1	5♌41.3	4 57.3	1♏10.1	6 21.3	9 40.8	18 11.8	21 20.4	4 55.7	3 56.1
26 S	16 22 3.0	4 20.6	19 7.9	19 18.1	3 35.0	2 24.0	7 1.3	9 53.3	18 7.1	21 23.4	4 57.9	3 57.5
27 M	16 25 59.5	5 21.3	19 4.7	2♍29.3	2 13.9	3 38.0	7 41.2	10 5.9	18 2.3	21 26.4	5 0.2	3 58.8
28 T	16 29 56.1	6 22.1	19 1.5	15 18.1	0 56.8	4 52.0	8 21.2	10 18.6	17 57.5	21 29.4	5 2.4	4 0.1
29 W	16 33 52.6	7 22.8	18 58.4	27 48.4	29♏46.0	6 6.0	9 1.2	10 31.3	17 52.7	21 32.3	5 4.7	4 1.3
30 T	16 37 49.2	8 23.7	18 55.2	10♎ 4.3	28 43.7	7 20.1	9 41.2	10 44.1	17 47.9	21 35.2	5 6.9	4 2.6

DECLINATION at NOON

DAY	EPHEMERIS SIDEREAL TIME h m s	☉	☊	☽	☿	♀	♂	♃	♄	♅	♆	♇
1 W	14 43 29.1	14S33.2	21S53.2	0N37.4	23S12.1	0N39.2	7S18.2	23S25.8	21N23.3	7S15.6	19S24.5	13N19.6
4 S	14 55 18.7	15 29.6	21 54.6	14S22.1	23 55.9	0S42.2	8 3.4	23 24.8	21 22.4	7 19.6	19 25.7	13 18.4
7 T	15 7 8.4	16 23.6	21 56.0	24 0.0	24 26.1	2 4.2	8 48.1	23 23.6	21 21.5	7 23.6	19 26.9	13 17.2
10 F	15 18 58.1	17 15.2	21 57.4	24 21.6	24 40.8	3 26.5	9 32.4	23 22.3	21 20.6	7 27.5	19 28.2	13 16.2
13 M	15 30 47.7	18 4.1	21 58.8	14 54.1	24 37.6	4 48.6	10 16.1	23 20.7	21 19.6	7 31.4	19 29.4	13 15.3
16 T	15 42 37.4	18 50.1	22 0.2	1N16.2	24 13.2	6 10.3	10 59.2	23 19.0	21 18.6	7 35.1	19 30.7	13 14.5
19 S	15 54 27.1	19 33.1	22 1.5	18 13.3	23 23.8	7 31.2	11 41.7	23 17.0	21 17.5	7 38.7	19 31.9	13 13.9
22 W	16 6 16.7	20 13.0	22 2.9	25 25.7	22 7.3	8 51.1	12 23.6	23 14.9	21 16.4	7 42.3	19 33.2	13 13.4
25 S	16 18 6.4	20 49.5	22 4.2	17 18.0	20 29.0	10 9.4	13 4.6	23 12.5	21 15.3	7 45.7	19 34.4	13 13.0
28 T	16 29 56.1	21 22.5	22 5.6	1 45.7	18 47.4	11 26.0	13 44.9	23 9.9	21 14.2	7 49.0	19 35.6	13 12.8

DECEMBER 1972

LONGITUDE at NOON

DAY	EPHEMERIS SIDEREAL TIME h m s	☉ ° ′	☊ ° ′	☽ ° ′	☿ ° ′	♀ ° ′	♂ ° ′	♃ ° ′	♄ ° ′	♅ ° ′	♆ ° ′	♇ ° ′
1 F	16 41 45.8	9♐24.5	18♑52.0	22♎ 9.4	27♏51.3	8♏34.3	10♏21.2	10♑56.9	17♓43.0	21♎38.0	5♐ 9.2	4♎ 3.8
2 S	16 45 42.3	10 25.4	18 48.8	4♏ 7.0	27R10.0	9 48.5	11 1.3	11 9.8	17R38.1	21 40.9	5 11.4	4 5.0
3 S	16 49 38.9	11 26.2	18 45.7	15 59.9	26 40.0	11 2.7	11 41.4	11 22.8	17 33.2	21 43.6	5 13.7	4 6.1
4 M	16 53 35.4	12 27.1	18 42.5	27 50.3	26 21.6	12 17.0	12 21.5	11 35.8	17 28.3	21 46.4	5 15.9	4 7.2
5 T	16 57 32.0	13 28.1	18 39.3	9♐40.1	26 14.3	13 31.3	13 1.7	11 48.9	17 23.4	21 49.1	5 18.2	4 8.3
6 W	17 1 28.5	14 29.0	18 36.1	21 31.1	26D17.6	14 45.6	13 41.9	12 2.0	17 18.4	21 51.8	5 20.4	4 9.4
7 T	17 5 25.1	15 30.0	18 33.0	3♑25.1	26 30.8	16 0.0	14 22.1	12 15.2	17 13.5	21 54.4	5 22.7	4 10.4
8 F	17 9 21.7	16 30.9	18 29.8	15 24.1	26 52.9	17 14.4	15 2.3	12 28.4	17 8.5	21 57.0	5 24.9	4 11.4
9 S	17 13 18.2	17 31.9	18 26.6	27 30.5	27 23.2	18 28.9	15 42.5	12 41.7	17 3.5	21 59.5	5 27.1	4 12.3
10 S	17 17 14.8	18 32.9	18 23.4	9♒47.0	28 0.9	19 43.4	16 22.8	12 55.0	16 58.6	22 2.0	5 29.3	4 13.3
11 M	17 21 11.3	19 33.9	18 20.2	22 17.1	28 45.0	20 57.9	17 3.1	13 8.3	16 53.6	22 4.5	5 31.5	4 14.2
12 T	17 25 7.9	20 35.0	18 17.1	5♓ 4.2	29 34.9	22 12.4	17 43.4	13 21.8	16 48.7	22 6.9	5 33.8	4 15.1
13 W	17 29 4.4	21 36.0	18 13.9	18 11.7	0♐29.8	23 27.0	18 23.8	13 35.2	16 43.8	22 9.3	5 36.0	4 15.9
14 T	17 33 1.0	22 37.0	18 10.7	1♈42.7	1 29.2	24 41.6	19 4.1	13 48.7	16 38.9	22 11.6	5 38.2	4 16.7
15 F	17 36 57.6	23 38.1	18 7.5	15 38.9	2 32.5	25 56.2	19 44.5	14 2.2	16 34.0	22 13.9	5 40.3	4 17.5
16 S	17 40 54.1	24 39.1	18 4.4	0♉ 0.2	3 39.1	27 10.8	20 24.9	14 15.7	16 29.1	22 16.1	5 42.5	4 18.2
17 S	17 44 50.7	25 40.2	18 1.2	14 43.8	4 48.8	28 25.5	21 5.3	14 29.3	16 24.2	22 18.3	5 44.7	4 18.9
18 M	17 48 47.2	26 41.2	17 58.0	29 44.3	6 1.0	29 40.1	21 45.8	14 42.9	16 19.4	22 20.5	5 46.8	4 19.5
19 T	17 52 43.8	27 42.3	17 54.8	14♊53.4	7 15.5	0♐54.8	22 26.3	14 56.6	16 14.6	22 22.6	5 48.9	4 20.2
20 W	17 56 40.4	28 43.4	17 51.7	0♋ 1.7	8 32.0	2 9.6	23 6.8	15 10.3	16 9.8	22 24.6	5 51.1	4 20.8
21 T	18 0 36.9	29 44.5	17 48.5	14 59.6	9 50.2	3 24.3	23 47.3	15 24.0	16 5.1	22 26.6	5 53.2	4 21.3
22 F	18 4 33.5	0♑45.6	17 45.3	29 39.1	11 10.0	4 39.1	24 27.9	15 37.7	16 0.3	22 28.6	5 55.3	4 21.8
23 S	18 8 30.0	1 46.7	17 42.1	13♌54.4	12 31.1	5 53.9	25 8.5	15 51.5	15 55.7	22 30.5	5 57.3	4 22.3
24 S	18 12 26.6	2 47.8	17 39.0	27 42.8	13 53.4	7 8.7	25 49.1	16 5.3	15 51.0	22 32.3	5 59.4	4 22.8
25 M	18 16 23.1	3 48.9	17 35.8	11♍ 4.1	15 16.7	8 23.5	26 29.7	16 19.1	15 46.4	22 34.1	6 1.5	4 23.2
26 T	18 20 19.7	4 50.0	17 32.6	24 0.2	16 41.0	9 38.4	27 10.4	16 32.9	15 41.9	22 35.9	6 3.5	4 23.6
27 W	18 24 16.3	5 51.2	17 29.4	6♎34.5	18 6.2	10 53.3	27 51.1	16 46.8	15 37.4	22 37.6	6 5.5	4 23.9
28 T	18 28 12.8	6 52.3	17 26.2	18 51.1	19 32.1	12 8.1	28 31.8	17 0.7	15 32.9	22 39.2	6 7.6	4 24.3
29 F	18 32 9.4	7 53.5	17 23.1	0♏54.5	20 58.7	13 23.1	29 12.5	17 14.6	15 28.5	22 40.8	6 9.5	4 24.5
30 S	18 36 5.9	8 54.6	17 19.9	12 49.1	22 26.0	14 38.0	29 53.3	17 28.5	15 24.2	22 42.4	6 11.5	4 24.8
31 S	18 40 2.5	9 55.8	17 16.7	24 39.0	23 53.9	15 52.9	0♐34.1	17 42.5	15 19.9	22 43.9	6 13.5	4 25.0

DECLINATION at NOON

DAY	EPHEMERIS SIDEREAL TIME h m s	☉	☊	☽	☿	♀	♂	♃	♄	♅	♆	♇
1 F	16 41 45.8	21S51.9	22S 6.9	13S24.3	17S28.1	12S40.4	14S24.4	23S 7.1	21N13.0	7S52.2	19S36.8	13N12.8
4 M	16 53 35.4	22 17.5	22 8.2	23 30.8	16 46.9	13 52.2	15 2.9	23 4.1	21 11.9	7 55.3	19 38.0	13 12.8
7 T	17 5 25.1	22 39.3	22 9.5	24 37.3	16 44.6	15 1.1	15 40.5	23 0.9	21 10.7	7 58.2	19 39.2	13 13.1
10 S	17 17 14.8	22 57.0	22 10.8	15 50.2	17 12.2	16 6.8	16 17.1	22 57.4	21 9.6	8 1.0	19 40.4	13 13.4
13 W	17 29 4.4	23 10.6	22 12.1	0 25.8	17 58.9	17 8.9	16 52.6	22 53.6	21 8.4	8 3.6	19 41.5	13 13.9
16 S	17 40 54.1	23 20.1	22 13.4	16N15.4	18 55.6	18 7.0	17 27.0	22 49.7	21 7.3	8 6.1	19 42.6	13 14.5
19 T	17 52 43.8	23 25.4	22 14.7	25 21.4	19 55.6	19 0.8	18 0.2	22 45.5	21 6.2	8 8.4	19 43.7	13 15.3
22 F	18 4 33.5	23 26.5	22 15.9	19 4.6	20 54.4	19 50.0	18 32.2	22 41.1	21 5.2	8 10.6	19 44.7	13 16.2
25 M	18 16 23.1	23 23.3	22 17.2	3 26.7	21 48.6	20 34.2	19 2.9	22 36.5	21 4.1	8 12.6	19 45.7	13 17.2
28 T	18 28 12.8	23 15.9	22 18.4	12S16.0	22 36.1	21 13.2	19 32.2	22 31.6	21 3.2	8 14.4	19 46.7	13 18.4
31 S	18 40 2.5	23 4.3	22 19.6	22 59.1	23 15.2	21 46.7	20 0.2	22 26.5	21 2.3	8 16.1	19 47.6	13 19.7

JANUARY 1973

DAY	EPHEMERIS SIDEREAL TIME	☉	☊	☽	☿	♀	♂	♃	♄	♅	♆	♇
	h m s	° ′	° ′	° ′	° ′	° ′	° ′	° ′	° ′	° ′	° ′	° ′
LONGITUDE at NOON												
1 M	18 43 59.1	10♑57.0	17♑13.5	6♐27.9	25♐22.3	17♐ 7.9	1♐14.9	17♑56.4	15♊15.7	22♎45.3	6♐15.4	4♎25.2
2 T	18 47 55.6	11 58.2	17 10.4	18 18.9	26 51.2	18 22.9	1 55.8	18 10.4	15R11.6	22 46.8	6 17.4	4 25.4
3 W	18 51 52.2	12 59.4	17 7.2	0♑14.6	28 20.7	19 37.9	2 36.7	18 24.4	15 7.5	22 48.1	6 19.3	4 25.5
4 T	18 55 48.7	14 0.6	17 4.0	12 17.0	29 50.6	20 52.8	3 17.6	18 38.4	15 3.5	22 49.4	6 21.2	4 25.5
5 F	18 59 45.3	15 1.8	17 0.8	24 28.0	1♑20.9	22 7.8	3 58.5	18 52.4	14 59.5	22 50.6	6 23.1	4 25.6
6 S	19 3 41.8	16 2.9	16 57.7	6♒49.1	2 51.7	23 22.8	4 39.5	19 6.4	14 55.6	22 51.8	6 24.9	4 25.6
7 S	19 7 38.4	17 4.1	16 54.5	19 21.5	4 23.0	24 37.9	5 20.4	19 20.4	14 51.8	22 52.9	6 26.7	4R25.5
8 M	19 11 35.0	18 5.3	16 51.3	2♓ 6.7	5 54.6	25 52.9	6 1.4	19 34.5	14 48.1	22 54.0	6 28.6	4 25.5
9 T	19 15 31.5	19 6.5	16 48.1	15 5.9	7 26.7	27 7.9	6 42.4	19 48.5	14 44.5	22 55.0	6 30.3	4 25.4
10 W	19 19 28.1	20 7.6	16 45.0	28 20.6	8 59.3	28 22.9	7 23.5	20 2.5	14 40.9	22 56.0	6 32.1	4 25.2
11 T	19 23 24.6	21 8.8	16 41.8	11♈51.8	10 32.3	29 38.0	8 4.5	20 16.5	14 37.4	22 56.9	6 33.8	4 25.1
12 F	19 27 21.2	22 9.9	16 38.6	25 40.4	12 5.7	0♑53.0	8 45.6	20 30.6	14 34.0	22 57.7	6 35.6	4 24.9
13 S	19 31 17.7	23 11.0	16 35.4	9♉46.2	13 39.6	2 8.0	9 26.7	20 44.6	14 30.7	22 58.5	6 37.3	4 24.6
14 S	19 35 14.3	24 12.1	16 32.2	24 8.0	15 14.0	3 23.1	10 7.8	20 58.6	14 27.5	22 59.2	6 38.9	4 24.3
15 M	19 39 10.9	25 13.2	16 29.1	8♊42.9	16 48.8	4 38.1	10 49.0	21 12.6	14 24.3	22 59.9	6 40.6	4 24.0
16 T	19 43 7.4	26 14.3	16 25.9	23 26.5	18 24.2	5 53.1	11 30.1	21 26.6	14 21.3	23 0.5	6 42.2	4 23.7
17 W	19 47 4.0	27 15.4	16 22.7	8♋12.6	20 0.0	7 8.2	12 11.3	21 40.6	14 18.4	23 1.1	6 43.8	4 23.3
18 T	19 51 0.5	28 16.5	16 19.5	22 54.5	21 36.4	8 23.2	12 52.6	21 54.6	14 15.5	23 1.6	6 45.4	4 22.9
19 F	19 54 57.1	29 17.5	16 16.4	7♌25.0	23 13.3	9 38.3	13 33.8	22 8.6	14 12.7	23 2.1	6 46.9	4 22.5
20 S	19 58 53.6	0♒18.6	16 13.2	21 38.2	24 50.8	10 53.4	14 15.1	22 22.6	14 10.1	23 2.5	6 48.5	4 22.0
21 S	20 2 50.2	1 19.6	16 10.0	5♍29.6	26 28.8	12 8.4	14 56.4	22 36.5	14 7.5	23 2.8	6 50.0	4 21.5
22 M	20 6 46.8	2 20.6	16 6.8	18 56.8	28 7.5	13 23.5	15 37.7	22 50.5	14 5.0	23 3.1	6 51.4	4 20.9
23 T	20 10 43.3	3 21.7	16 3.7	1♎59.8	29 46.7	14 38.6	16 19.1	23 4.5	14 2.7	23 3.4	6 52.9	4 20.4
24 W	20 14 39.9	4 22.7	16 0.5	14 40.1	1♒26.6	15 53.7	17 0.5	23 18.4	14 0.5	23 3.5	6 54.4	4 19.8
25 T	20 18 36.4	5 23.7	15 57.3	27 1.1	3 7.0	17 8.8	17 41.9	23 32.3	13 58.3	23 3.7	6 55.7	4 19.2
26 F	20 22 33.0	6 24.7	15 54.1	9♏ 6.8	4 48.1	18 23.9	18 23.3	23 46.2	13 56.2	23 3.7	6 57.1	4 18.5
27 S	20 26 29.5	7 25.7	15 50.9	21 2.0	6 29.9	19 38.9	19 4.8	24 0.1	13 54.3	23 3.7	6 58.4	4 17.8
28 S	20 30 26.1	8 26.7	15 47.8	2♐51.7	8 12.3	20 54.0	19 46.3	24 13.9	13 52.4	23 3.7	6 59.8	4 17.1
29 M	20 34 22.7	9 27.6	15 44.6	14 40.7	9 55.3	22 9.1	20 27.8	24 27.7	13 50.7	23R 3.6	7 1.0	4 16.3
30 T	20 38 19.2	10 28.6	15 41.4	26 33.5	11 39.0	23 24.2	21 9.3	24 41.5	13 49.1	23 3.4	7 2.3	4 15.5
31 W	20 42 15.8	11 29.5	15 38.2	8♑33.9	13 23.4	24 39.3	21 50.8	24 55.3	13 47.5	23 3.2	7 3.5	4 14.7
DECLINATION at NOON												
1 M	18 43 59.1	22S59.5	22S20.0	24S46.1	23S26.2	21S56.6	20S 9.2	22S24.8	21N 2.0	8S16.6	19S47.9	13N20.2
4 T	18 55 48.7	22 42.4	22 21.2	23 17.4	23 52.4	22 22.5	20 35.3	22 19.4	21 1.2	8 18.0	19 48.8	13 21.6
7 S	19 7 38.4	22 21.2	22 22.4	12 18.2	24 8.0	22 42.3	20 59.9	22 13.8	21 0.5	8 19.2	19 49.7	13 23.2
10 W	19 19 28.1	21 56.1	22 23.6	3N56.9	24 12.2	22 56.0	21 22.9	22 8.0	20 59.8	8 20.3	19 50.5	13 24.8
13 S	19 31 17.7	21 27.1	22 24.8	19 21.7	24 4.5	23 3.4	21 44.2	22 1.9	20 59.3	8 21.1	19 51.3	13 26.6
16 T	19 43 7.4	20 54.4	22 26.0	25 22.8	23 44.5	23 4.4	22 4.0	21 55.7	20 58.8	8 21.8	19 52.0	13 28.5
19 F	19 54 57.1	20 18.1	22 27.1	16 37.0	23 11.7	22 59.2	22 22.0	21 49.4	20 58.5	8 22.3	19 52.7	13 30.5
22 M	20 6 46.8	19 38.4	22 28.2	0 4.8	22 25.7	22 47.5	22 38.4	21 42.8	20 58.3	8 22.6	19 53.3	13 32.5
25 T	20 18 36.4	18 55.4	22 29.4	15S14.4	21 26.4	22 29.6	22 52.9	21 36.0	20 58.1	8 22.7	19 53.9	13 34.6
28 S	20 30 26.1	18 9.3	22 30.5	24 18.8	20 13.6	22 5.5	23 5.7	21 29.1	20 58.1	8 22.6	19 54.4	13 36.8
31 W	20 42 15.8	17 20.3	22 31.6	23 54.8	18 47.0	21 35.4	23 16.6	21 22.1	20 58.3	8 22.4	19 54.9	13 39.1

FEBRUARY 1973

DAY	EPHEMERIS SIDEREAL TIME	☉	☊	☽	☿	♀	♂	♃	♄	♅	♆	♇
LONGITUDE at NOON												
1 T	20 46 12.3	12♒30.4	15♑35.1	20♑45.1	15♒ 8.4	25♑54.4	22♐32.4	25♑ 9.0	13♊46.1	23♎ 2.9	7♐ 4.7	4♎13.9
2 F	20 50 8.9	13 31.3	15 31.9	3♒ 9.5	16 54.0	27 9.5	23 14.0	25 22.8	13R44.8	23R 2.6	7 5.9	4R13.0
3 S	20 54 5.4	14 32.2	15 28.7	15 48.4	18 40.2	28 24.5	23 55.6	25 36.4	13 43.6	23 2.2	7 7.0	4 12.1
4 S	20 58 2.0	15 33.1	15 25.5	28 42.4	20 26.9	29 39.6	24 37.3	25 50.1	13 42.6	23 1.8	7 8.1	4 11.2
5 M	21 1 58.6	16 33.9	15 22.4	11♓51.0	22 14.2	0♒54.7	25 18.9	26 3.7	13 41.6	23 1.3	7 9.2	4 10.2
6 T	21 5 55.1	17 34.7	15 19.2	25 13.2	24 1.9	2 9.8	26 0.6	26 17.3	13 40.7	23 0.7	7 10.2	4 9.2
7 W	21 9 51.7	18 35.5	15 16.0	8♈47.5	25 50.0	3 24.8	26 42.3	26 30.9	13 40.0	23 0.1	7 11.2	4 8.2
8 T	21 13 48.2	19 36.3	15 12.8	22 32.6	27 38.3	4 39.9	27 24.0	26 44.4	13 39.4	22 59.4	7 12.2	4 7.2
9 F	21 17 44.8	20 37.1	15 9.6	6♉26.7	29 26.8	5 54.9	28 5.8	26 57.9	13 38.8	22 58.7	7 13.1	4 6.1
10 S	21 21 41.3	21 37.8	15 6.5	20 28.7	1♓15.3	7 10.0	28 47.5	27 11.3	13 38.4	22 58.0	7 14.0	4 5.0
11 S	21 25 37.9	22 38.5	15 3.3	4♊37.2	3 3.6	8 25.0	29 29.3	27 24.7	13 38.2	22 57.1	7 14.9	4 3.9
12 M	21 29 34.4	23 39.1	15 0.1	18 50.8	4 51.6	9 40.0	0♑11.1	27 38.0	13 38.0	22 56.3	7 15.8	4 2.7
13 T	21 33 31.0	24 39.8	14 56.9	3♋ 7.6	6 38.9	10 55.1	0 53.0	27 51.4	13 38.0	22 55.4	7 16.6	4 1.6
14 W	21 37 27.5	25 40.4	14 53.8	17 24.8	8 25.3	12 10.1	1 34.8	28 4.6	13 38.0	22 54.4	7 17.4	4 0.4
15 T	21 41 24.1	26 41.0	14 50.6	1♌39.0	10 10.5	13 25.1	2 16.7	28 17.9	13D38.2	22 53.4	7 18.2	3 59.2
16 F	21 45 20.7	27 41.6	14 47.4	15 46.1	11 54.1	14 40.1	2 58.6	28 31.0	13 38.5	22 52.3	7 18.9	3 58.0
17 S	21 49 17.2	28 42.1	14 44.2	29 41.7	13 35.6	15 55.1	3 40.5	28 44.1	13 38.9	22 51.2	7 19.6	3 56.7
18 S	21 53 13.8	29 42.6	14 41.0	13♍21.8	15 14.6	17 10.1	4 22.4	28 57.2	13 39.4	22 50.0	7 20.2	3 55.4
19 M	21 57 10.3	0♓43.1	14 37.9	26 43.4	16 50.7	18 25.0	5 4.4	29 10.2	13 40.0	22 48.8	7 20.9	3 54.1
20 T	22 1 6.9	1 43.5	14 34.7	9♎44.8	18 23.1	19 40.0	5 46.3	29 23.2	13 40.7	22 47.6	7 21.4	3 52.8
21 W	22 5 3.4	2 44.0	14 31.5	22 26.2	19 51.4	20 55.0	6 28.4	29 36.1	13 41.6	22 46.2	7 22.0	3 51.5
22 T	22 8 60.0	3 44.4	14 28.3	4♏49.1	21 14.8	22 9.9	7 10.4	29 48.9	13 42.5	22 44.9	7 22.5	3 50.1
23 F	22 12 56.5	4 44.7	14 25.2	16 56.8	22 32.9	23 24.9	7 52.4	0♒ 1.7	13 43.6	22 43.5	7 23.0	3 48.7
24 S	22 16 53.1	5 45.1	14 22.0	28 53.2	23 44.8	24 39.8	8 34.5	0 14.5	13 44.8	22 42.0	7 23.5	3 47.3
25 S	22 20 49.6	6 45.4	14 18.8	10♐43.4	24 50.0	25 54.8	9 16.6	0 27.2	13 46.1	22 40.5	7 23.9	3 45.9
26 M	22 24 46.2	7 45.8	14 15.6	22 32.7	25 47.9	27 9.7	9 58.7	0 39.8	13 47.5	22 39.0	7 24.3	3 44.5
27 T	22 28 42.8	8 46.0	14 12.5	4♑26.2	26 38.0	28 24.6	10 40.8	0 52.3	13 49.0	22 37.4	7 24.6	3 43.0
28 W	22 32 39.3	9 46.3	14 9.3	16 29.1	27 19.6	29 39.6	11 23.0	1 4.8	13 50.6	22 35.8	7 24.9	3 41.5
DECLINATION at NOON												
1 T	20 46 12.3	17S 3.3	22S32.0	21S28.6	18S15.2	21S24.0	23S19.8	21S19.7	20N58.3	8S22.2	19S55.1	13N39.9
4 S	20 58 2.0	16 10.6	22 33.1	8 38.4	16 30.6	20 46.1	23 28.3	21 12.5	20 58.6	8 21.7	19 55.5	13 42.2
7 W	21 9 51.7	15 15.4	22 34.2	8N13.4	14 33.1	20 2.7	23 34.8	21 5.1	20 59.0	8 21.0	19 55.9	13 44.6
10 S	21 21 41.3	14 17.8	22 35.2	22 1.1	12 23.8	19 14.0	23 39.4	20 57.7	20 59.6	8 20.2	19 56.2	13 47.1
13 T	21 33 31.0	13 18.2	22 36.3	24 35.5	10 4.6	18 20.2	23 42.1	20 50.1	21 0.2	8 19.2	19 56.5	13 49.5
16 F	21 45 20.7	12 16.6	22 37.4	13 40.5	7 39.1	17 21.7	23 42.9	20 42.5	21 1.0	8 18.0	19 56.7	13 52.0
19 M	21 57 10.3	11 13.2	22 38.4	3S 9.2	5 12.3	16 18.8	23 41.7	20 34.8	21 1.9	8 16.6	19 56.9	13 54.5
22 T	22 8 60.0	10 8.3	22 39.4	17 41.7	2 51.8	15 11.7	23 38.5	20 27.0	21 2.9	8 15.1	19 57.0	13 57.0
25 S	22 20 49.6	9 2.0	22 40.5	24 57.7	0 46.7	14 0.9	23 33.4	20 19.3	21 4.1	8 13.4	19 57.1	13 59.5
28 W	22 32 39.3	7 54.4	22 41.5	22 20.2	0N52.9	12 46.6	23 26.4	20 11.5	21 5.3	8 11.6	19 57.1	14 2.0

MARCH 1973

LONGITUDE at NOON

DAY	EPHEMERIS SIDEREAL TIME h m s	☉ ° ′	☊ ° ′	☽ ° ′	☿ ° ′	♀ ° ′	♂ ° ′	♃ ° ′	♄ ° ′	♅ ° ′	♆ ° ′	♇ ° ′
1 T	22 36 35.9	10♓46.5	14♑ 6.1	28♑46.0	27♓52.5	0♓54.5	12♑ 5.2	1♒17.2	13♊52.3	22♎34.1	7♐25.2	3♎40.1
2 F	22 40 32.4	11 46.7	14 2.9	11♒20.2	28 16.2	2 9.4	12 47.3	1 29.6	13 54.2	22R32.4	7 25.5	3R38.6
3 S	22 44 29.0	12 46.9	13 59.7	24 14.1	28 30.6	3 24.3	13 29.5	1 41.9	13 56.1	22 30.6	7 25.7	3 37.0
4 S	22 48 25.5	13 47.1	13 56.6	7♓28.2	28 35.6	4 39.2	14 11.8	1 54.1	13 58.2	22 28.8	7 25.9	3 35.5
5 M	22 52 22.1	14 47.2	13 53.4	21 1.5	28R31.3	5 54.0	14 54.0	2 6.2	14 0.4	22 27.0	7 26.0	3 34.0
6 T	22 56 18.6	15 47.3	13 50.2	4♈51.1	28 18.0	7 8.9	15 36.3	2 18.3	14 2.7	22 25.2	7 26.2	3 32.5
7 W	23 0 15.2	16 47.4	13 47.0	18 53.0	27 56.0	8 23.8	16 18.6	2 30.3	14 5.1	22 23.2	7 26.2	3 30.9
8 T	23 4 11.7	17 47.4	13 43.9	3♉ 2.6	27 25.9	9 38.6	17 0.9	2 42.2	14 7.6	22 21.3	7 26.3	3 29.3
9 F	23 8 8.3	18 47.4	13 40.7	17 15.4	26 48.5	10 53.5	17 43.1	2 54.1	14 10.2	22 19.3	7 26.3	3 27.8
10 S	23 12 4.8	19 47.4	13 37.5	1♊27.9	26 4.8	12 8.3	18 25.5	3 5.8	14 12.9	22 17.3	7 26.3	3 26.2
11 S	23 16 1.4	20 47.3	13 34.3	15 37.5	25 15.8	13 23.0	19 7.8	3 17.5	14 15.7	22 15.3	7R26.2	3 24.6
12 M	23 19 57.9	21 47.2	13 31.1	29 42.7	24 22.7	14 37.8	19 50.1	3 29.1	14 18.6	22 13.2	7 26.1	3 23.0
13 T	23 23 54.5	22 47.0	13 28.0	13♋42.7	23 26.8	15 52.6	20 32.5	3 40.6	14 21.6	22 11.1	7 26.0	3 21.3
14 W	23 27 51.1	23 46.8	13 24.8	27 36.9	22 29.4	17 7.3	21 14.8	3 52.0	14 24.7	22 8.9	7 25.9	3 19.7
15 T	23 31 47.6	24 46.6	13 21.6	11♌24.7	21 31.8	18 22.1	21 57.2	4 3.3	14 27.9	22 6.7	7 25.7	3 18.1
16 F	23 35 44.2	25 46.3	13 18.4	25 4.6	20 35.2	19 36.8	22 39.6	4 14.5	14 31.2	22 4.5	7 25.5	3 16.4
17 S	23 39 40.7	26 46.0	13 15.3	8♍35.1	19 40.7	20 51.5	23 22.0	4 25.7	14 34.6	22 2.3	7 25.2	3 14.8
18 S	23 43 37.3	27 45.6	13 12.1	21 53.8	18 49.3	22 6.2	24 4.4	4 36.7	14 38.1	22 0.0	7 24.9	3 13.2
19 M	23 47 33.8	28 45.3	13 8.9	4♎58.9	18 2.0	23 20.8	24 46.9	4 47.7	14 41.7	21 57.8	7 24.6	3 11.5
20 T	23 51 30.4	29 44.9	13 5.7	17 48.7	17 19.4	24 35.5	25 29.3	4 58.6	14 45.4	21 55.5	7 24.2	3 9.9
21 W	23 55 26.9	0♈44.4	13 2.5	0♏22.8	16 42.0	25 50.1	26 11.8	5 9.3	14 49.1	21 53.1	7 23.9	3 8.2
22 T	23 59 23.5	1 43.9	12 59.4	12 41.7	16 10.2	27 4.8	26 54.3	5 20.0	14 53.0	21 50.8	7 23.4	3 6.5
23 F	0 3 20.0	2 43.4	12 56.2	24 47.5	15 44.4	28 19.4	27 36.8	5 30.6	14 57.0	21 48.4	7 23.0	3 4.9
24 S	0 7 16.6	3 42.9	12 53.0	6♐43.1	15 24.5	29 34.0	28 19.3	5 41.0	15 1.0	21 46.0	7 22.5	3 3.2
25 S	0 11 13.1	4 42.3	12 49.8	18 32.8	15 10.6	0♈48.6	29 1.8	5 51.4	15 5.2	21 43.6	7 22.0	3 1.6
26 M	0 15 9.7	5 41.8	12 46.7	0♑21.5	15 2.8	2 3.2	29 44.4	6 1.7	15 9.4	21 41.1	7 21.5	2 59.9
27 T	0 19 6.2	6 41.2	12 43.5	12 14.5	15 0.8	3 17.8	0♒27.0	6 11.9	15 13.8	21 38.7	7 21.0	2 58.3
28 W	0 23 2.8	7 40.5	12 40.3	24 17.3	15D 4.6	4 32.4	1 9.5	6 21.9	15 18.2	21 36.3	7 20.4	2 56.7
29 T	0 26 59.3	8 39.8	12 37.1	6♒35.2	15 13.8	5 46.9	1 52.1	6 31.9	15 22.7	21 33.8	7 19.7	2 55.0
30 F	0 30 55.9	9 39.1	12 33.9	19 13.1	15 28.3	7 1.4	2 34.7	6 41.7	15 27.3	21 31.3	7 19.1	2 53.4
31 S	0 34 52.5	10 38.4	12 30.8	2♓14.4	15 47.8	8 16.0	3 17.3	6 51.4	15 32.0	21 28.8	7 18.4	2 51.7

DECLINATION at NOON

DAY	EPHEMERIS SIDEREAL TIME h m s	☉	☊	☽	☿	♀	♂	♃	♄	♅	♆	♇
1 T	22 36 35.9	7S31.6	22S41.8	19S15.3	1N18.8	12S21.2	23S23.6	20S 8.8	21N 5.8	8S10.9	19S57.1	14N 2.8
4 S	22 48 25.5	6 22.7	22 42.8	5 2.1	2 10.6	11 2.8	23 14.0	20 1.0	21 7.2	8 8.9	19 57.0	14 5.2
7 W	23 0 15.2	5 13.0	22 43.8	12N 3.8	2 19.8	9 41.8	23 2.5	19 53.3	21 8.7	8 6.8	19 57.0	14 7.7
10 S	23 12 4.8	4 2.6	22 44.8	23 50.6	1 46.7	8 18.5	22 49.1	19 45.5	21 10.3	8 4.5	19 56.8	14 10.0
13 T	23 23 54.5	2 51.9	22 45.7	22 47.6	0 39.0	6 53.2	22 33.8	19 37.8	21 11.9	8 2.2	19 56.6	14 12.4
16 F	23 35 44.2	1 40.9	22 46.7	10 3.0	0S49.6	5 26.2	22 16.7	19 30.2	21 13.7	7 59.7	19 56.4	14 14.7
19 M	23 47 33.8	0 29.7	22 47.6	6S31.8	2 22.6	3 57.9	21 57.8	19 22.7	21 15.6	7 57.2	19 56.1	14 16.9
22 T	23 59 23.5	0N41.3	22 48.6	19 48.7	3 46.2	2 28.7	21 37.2	19 15.3	21 17.5	7 54.5	19 55.8	14 19.0
25 S	0 11 13.1	1 52.2	22 49.5	25 1.3	4 51.7	0 58.7	21 14.8	19 8.0	21 19.5	7 51.8	19 55.4	14 21.1
28 W	0 23 2.8	3 2.8	22 50.4	20 16.1	5 35.2	0N31.6	20 50.7	19 0.9	21 21.5	7 49.1	19 55.0	14 23.0
31 S	0 34 52.5	4 12.8	22 51.3	7 6.0	5 56.2	2 2.0	20 25.0	18 54.0	21 23.6	7 46.3	19 54.5	14 24.9

APRIL 1973

LONGITUDE at NOON

DAY	EPHEMERIS SIDEREAL TIME h m s	☉ ° ′	☊ ° ′	☽ ° ′	☿ ° ′	♀ ° ′	♂ ° ′	♃ ° ′	♄ ° ′	♅ ° ′	♆ ° ′	♇ ° ′
1 S	0 38 49.0	11♈37.6	12♑27.6	15♓40.7	16♓12.1	9♈30.5	3♒59.9	7♒ 1.0	15♊36.7	21♎26.2	7♐17.6	2♎50.1
2 M	0 42 45.6	12 36.8	12 24.4	29 31.5	16 41.0	10 45.0	4 42.5	7 10.5	15 41.5	21R23.7	7R16.9	2R48.5
3 T	0 46 42.1	13 36.0	12 21.2	13♈43.6	17 14.3	11 59.4	5 25.1	7 19.8	15 46.5	21 21.1	7 16.1	2 46.8
4 W	0 50 38.7	14 35.1	12 18.0	28 11.5	17 51.6	13 13.9	6 7.7	7 29.1	15 51.4	21 18.6	7 15.3	2 45.2
5 T	0 54 35.2	15 34.2	12 14.9	12♉48.2	18 32.7	14 28.3	6 50.3	7 38.2	15 56.5	21 16.0	7 14.5	2 43.6
6 F	0 58 31.8	16 33.2	12 11.7	27 26.4	19 17.6	15 42.8	7 32.9	7 47.2	16 1.7	21 13.5	7 13.6	2 42.0
7 S	1 2 28.3	17 32.3	12 8.5	11♊59.6	20 5.9	16 57.2	8 15.5	7 56.1	16 6.9	21 10.9	7 12.7	2 40.4
8 S	1 6 24.9	18 31.2	12 5.3	26 23.0	20 57.5	18 11.6	8 58.1	8 4.8	16 12.2	21 8.3	7 11.8	2 38.8
9 M	1 10 21.4	19 30.2	12 2.2	10♋33.9	21 52.3	19 25.9	9 40.7	8 13.4	16 17.6	21 5.7	7 10.9	2 37.2
10 T	1 14 18.0	20 29.1	11 59.0	24 31.2	22 50.0	20 40.3	10 23.3	8 21.9	16 23.0	21 3.1	7 9.9	2 35.7
11 W	1 18 14.5	21 27.9	11 55.8	8♌15.1	23 50.5	21 54.6	11 5.9	8 30.3	16 28.6	21 0.6	7 8.9	2 34.1
12 T	1 22 11.1	22 26.8	11 52.6	21 46.2	24 53.7	23 8.9	11 48.5	8 38.5	16 34.2	20 58.0	7 7.9	2 32.6
13 F	1 26 7.6	23 25.5	11 49.4	5♍ 5.3	25 59.6	24 23.2	12 31.1	8 46.6	16 39.8	20 55.4	7 6.8	2 31.1
14 S	1 30 4.2	24 24.3	11 46.3	18 13.0	27 7.8	25 37.5	13 13.7	8 54.5	16 45.5	20 52.8	7 5.8	2 29.5
15 S	1 34 0.8	25 23.0	11 43.1	1♎ 9.3	28 18.5	26 51.7	13 56.3	9 2.4	16 51.3	20 50.2	7 4.7	2 28.0
16 M	1 37 57.3	26 21.7	11 39.9	13 54.0	29 31.5	28 6.0	14 38.9	9 10.0	16 57.2	20 47.7	7 3.6	2 26.6
17 T	1 41 53.9	27 20.4	11 36.7	26 26.9	0♈46.7	29 20.2	15 21.6	9 17.6	17 3.2	20 45.2	7 2.5	2 25.1
18 W	1 45 50.4	28 19.0	11 33.6	8♏48.0	2 4.0	0♉34.4	16 4.2	9 25.0	17 9.2	20 42.6	7 1.3	2 23.7
19 T	1 49 47.0	29 17.6	11 30.4	20 58.0	3 23.5	1 48.6	16 46.8	9 32.3	17 15.2	20 40.1	7 0.1	2 22.2
20 F	1 53 43.5	0♉16.1	11 27.2	2♐58.1	4 44.9	3 2.8	17 29.4	9 39.4	17 21.3	20 37.5	6 58.9	2 20.8
21 S	1 57 40.1	1 14.7	11 24.0	14 50.6	6 8.3	4 16.9	18 12.0	9 46.3	17 27.5	20 35.0	6 57.7	2 19.4
22 S	2 1 36.6	2 13.1	11 20.9	26 38.8	7 33.7	5 31.1	18 54.6	9 53.2	17 33.7	20 32.5	6 56.4	2 18.0
23 M	2 5 33.2	3 11.6	11 17.7	8♑26.6	9 1.0	6 45.2	19 37.1	9 59.8	17 40.0	20 30.0	6 55.2	2 16.7
24 T	2 9 29.7	4 10.1	11 14.5	20 18.8	10 30.1	7 59.3	20 19.7	10 6.3	17 46.4	20 27.5	6 53.9	2 15.3
25 W	2 13 26.3	5 8.5	11 11.3	2♒20.5	12 1.2	9 13.4	21 2.3	10 12.7	17 52.8	20 25.0	6 52.6	2 14.0
26 T	2 17 22.8	6 6.8	11 8.1	14 37.2	13 34.0	10 27.5	21 44.8	10 18.9	17 59.3	20 22.5	6 51.2	2 12.7
27 F	2 21 19.4	7 5.2	11 5.0	27 13.9	15 8.7	11 41.6	22 27.4	10 24.9	18 5.8	20 20.1	6 49.9	2 11.4
28 S	2 25 16.0	8 3.5	11 1.8	10♓15.0	16 45.3	12 55.6	23 9.9	10 30.8	18 12.4	20 17.7	6 48.5	2 10.1
29 S	2 29 12.5	9 1.8	10 58.6	23 43.5	18 23.6	14 9.7	23 52.4	10 36.6	18 19.0	20 15.3	6 47.2	2 8.8
30 M	2 33 9.1	10 0.1	10 55.4	7♈40.0	20 3.8	15 23.7	24 34.9	10 42.1	18 25.7	20 12.9	6 45.8	2 7.6

DECLINATION at NOON

DAY	EPHEMERIS SIDEREAL TIME h m s	☉	☊	☽	☿	♀	♂	♃	♄	♅	♆	♇
1 S	0 38 49.0	4N35.9	22S51.6	1S31.0	5S58.4	2N32.0	20S16.0	18S51.7	21N24.3	7S45.4	19S54.4	14N25.5
4 W	0 50 38.7	5 45.0	22 52.5	15N19.1	5 51.3	4 1.9	19 48.2	18 45.0	21 26.4	7 42.5	19 53.9	14 27.3
7 S	1 2 28.3	6 53.1	22 53.3	24 41.5	5 25.3	5 31.0	19 18.9	18 38.6	21 28.6	7 39.6	19 53.3	14 28.9
10 T	1 14 18.0	8 0.2	22 54.2	20 5.6	4 42.3	6 59.1	18 48.2	18 32.3	21 30.8	7 36.7	19 52.8	14 30.5
13 F	1 26 7.6	9 6.0	22 55.0	5 51.8	3 43.8	8 25.7	18 16.1	18 26.4	21 33.0	7 33.8	19 52.1	14 31.9
16 M	1 37 57.3	10 10.5	22 55.9	10S 5.9	2 31.4	9 50.6	17 42.6	18 20.7	21 35.2	7 31.0	19 51.5	14 33.2
19 T	1 49 47.0	11 13.5	22 56.7	21 40.9	1 6.4	11 13.5	17 7.9	18 15.3	21 37.5	7 28.1	19 50.8	14 34.3
22 S	2 1 36.6	12 14.8	22 57.5	24 34.0	0N30.0	12 34.0	16 32.0	18 10.2	21 39.7	7 25.3	19 50.1	14 35.3
25 W	2 13 26.3	13 14.3	22 58.3	17 44.4	2 16.8	13 51.8	15 54.9	18 5.5	21 41.9	7 22.6	19 49.4	14 36.3
28 S	2 25 16.0	14 11.8	22 59.1	3 37.3	4 12.8	15 6.6	15 16.8	18 1.2	21 44.1	7 19.9	19 48.7	14 37.0

MAY 1973

LONGITUDE at NOON

DAY	EPHEMERIS SIDEREAL TIME h m s	☉ ° ′	☊ ° ′	☽ ° ′	☿ ° ′	♀ ° ′	♂ ° ′	♃ ° ′	♄ ° ′	♅ ° ′	♆ ° ′	♇ ° ′
1 T	2 37 5.6	10♉58.4	10♑52.3	22♈ 2.4	21♈45.7	16♉37.7	25♒17.4	10♒47.5	18♊32.4	20♎10.5	6♐44.3	2♎ 6.4
2 W	2 41 2.2	11 56.6	10 49.1	6♉45.6	23 29.5	17 51.7	25 59.9	10 52.8	18 39.1	20R 8.2	6R42.9	2R 5.2
3 T	2 44 58.7	12 54.8	10 45.9	21 41.9	25 15.2	19 5.7	26 42.3	10 57.8	18 46.0	20 5.8	6 41.5	2 4.0
4 F	2 48 55.3	13 53.0	10 42.7	6♊42.3	27 2.6	20 19.7	27 24.7	11 2.7	18 52.8	20 3.5	6 40.0	2 2.9
5 S	2 52 51.8	14 51.1	10 39.5	21 37.8	28 51.9	21 33.6	28 7.1	11 7.5	18 59.7	20 1.3	6 38.5	2 1.8
6 S	2 56 48.4	15 49.2	10 36.4	6♋21.1	0♉43.0	22 47.5	28 49.4	11 12.0	19 6.7	19 59.0	6 37.1	2 0.7
7 M	3 0 45.0	16 47.3	10 33.2	20 47.1	2 35.9	24 1.5	29 31.8	11 16.4	19 13.7	19 56.8	6 35.6	1 59.6
8 T	3 4 41.5	17 45.4	10 30.0	4♌53.4	4 30.7	25 15.4	0♓14.1	11 20.7	19 20.8	19 54.7	6 34.1	1 58.6
9 W	3 8 38.1	18 43.4	10 26.8	18 39.2	6 27.3	26 29.3	0 56.4	11 24.7	19 27.9	19 52.5	6 32.6	1 57.6
10 T	3 12 34.6	19 41.4	10 23.7	2♍ 5.7	8 25.7	27 43.1	1 38.6	11 28.6	19 35.0	19 50.4	6 31.0	1 56.6
11 F	3 16 31.2	20 39.3	10 20.5	15 14.5	10 25.8	28 57.0	2 20.8	11 32.3	19 42.1	19 48.3	6 29.5	1 55.7
12 S	3 20 27.7	21 37.2	10 17.3	28 7.7	12 27.6	0♊10.8	3 3.0	11 35.8	19 49.3	19 46.2	6 27.9	1 54.7
13 S	3 24 24.3	22 35.1	10 14.1	10♎47.1	14 31.1	1 24.6	3 45.1	11 39.1	19 56.6	19 44.2	6 26.4	1 53.8
14 M	3 28 20.8	23 33.0	10 11.0	23 14.6	16 36.1	2 38.4	4 27.3	11 42.3	20 3.8	19 42.2	6 24.8	1 52.9
15 T	3 32 17.4	24 30.8	10 7.8	5♏31.5	18 42.6	3 52.2	5 9.3	11 45.3	20 11.1	19 40.2	6 23.2	1 52.1
16 W	3 36 14.0	25 28.6	10 4.6	17 39.2	20 50.4	5 5.9	5 51.4	11 48.1	20 18.5	19 38.2	6 21.7	1 51.3
17 T	3 40 10.5	26 26.4	10 1.4	29 39.0	22 59.4	6 19.7	6 33.4	11 50.7	20 25.8	19 36.3	6 20.1	1 50.5
18 F	3 44 7.1	27 24.2	9 58.2	11♐32.6	25 9.3	7 33.4	7 15.4	11 53.1	20 33.2	19 34.5	6 18.5	1 49.7
19 S	3 48 3.6	28 21.9	9 55.1	23 21.7	27 20.1	8 47.1	7 57.3	11 55.4	20 40.6	19 32.7	6 16.9	1 48.9
20 S	3 52 0.2	29 19.6	9 51.9	5♑ 9.1	29 31.3	10 0.8	8 39.2	11 57.4	20 48.1	19 30.9	6 15.3	1 48.2
21 M	3 55 56.7	0♊17.3	9 48.7	16 57.7	1♊42.9	11 14.5	9 21.1	11 59.3	20 55.5	19 29.1	6 13.6	1 47.5
22 T	3 59 53.3	1 15.0	9 45.5	28 51.2	3 54.5	12 28.1	10 2.9	12 1.0	21 3.0	19 27.4	6 12.0	1 46.9
23 W	4 3 49.9	2 12.7	9 42.4	10♒54.0	6 5.8	13 41.8	10 44.7	12 2.5	21 10.6	19 25.7	6 10.4	1 46.3
24 T	4 7 46.4	3 10.3	9 39.2	23 10.5	8 16.6	14 55.4	11 26.4	12 3.8	21 18.1	19 24.1	6 8.8	1 45.7
25 F	4 11 43.0	4 7.9	9 36.0	5♓45.5	10 26.6	16 9.1	12 8.1	12 4.9	21 25.7	19 22.5	6 7.2	1 45.1
26 S	4 15 39.5	5 5.6	9 32.8	18 43.3	12 35.5	17 22.7	12 49.7	12 5.9	21 33.3	19 20.9	6 5.5	1 44.6
27 S	4 19 36.1	6 3.2	9 29.7	2♈ 7.3	14 43.1	18 36.3	13 31.2	12 6.6	21 40.9	19 19.4	6 3.9	1 44.1
28 M	4 23 32.6	7 0.7	9 26.5	15 59.5	16 49.2	19 49.9	14 12.7	12 7.2	21 48.6	19 17.9	6 2.3	1 43.6
29 T	4 27 29.2	7 58.4	9 23.3	0♉19.2	18 53.6	21 3.5	14 54.2	12 7.6	21 56.3	19 16.6	6 0.7	1 43.2
30 W	4 31 25.8	8 55.9	9 20.1	15 2.9	20 55.9	22 17.1	15 35.6	12 7.7	22 3.9	19 15.2	5 59.1	1 42.8
31 T	4 35 22.3	9 53.4	9 16.9	0♊ 4.2	22 56.2	23 30.6	16 16.9	12 7.7	22 11.6	19 13.8	5 57.5	1 42.4

DECLINATION at NOON

DAY	h m s	☉	☊	☽	☿	♀	♂	♃	♄	♅	♆	♇
1 T	2 37 5.6	15N 7.3	22S59.9	13N11.0	6N17.0	16N17.9	14S37.7	17S57.2	21N46.3	7S17.2	19S47.9	14N37.7
4 F	2 48 55.3	16 0.5	23 0.7	24 7.6	8 27.9	17 25.6	13 57.7	17 53.6	21 48.5	7 14.6	19 47.1	14 38.1
7 M	3 0 45.0	16 51.3	23 1.4	20 47.5	10 44.0	18 29.2	13 16.9	17 50.4	21 50.6	7 12.2	19 46.3	14 38.5
10 T	3 12 34.6	17 39.6	23 2.2	6 53.1	13 3.1	19 28.4	12 35.3	17 47.6	21 52.7	7 9.8	19 45.5	14 38.7
13 S	3 24 24.3	18 25.2	23 2.9	8S59.2	15 22.2	20 22.9	11 53.0	17 45.3	21 54.7	7 7.5	19 44.7	14 38.7
16 W	3 36 14.0	19 8.0	23 3.6	20 55.3	17 37.5	21 12.4	11 10.2	17 43.4	21 56.7	7 5.4	19 43.9	14 38.7
19 S	3 48 3.6	19 47.9	23 4.3	24 35.7	19 44.1	21 56.7	10 26.8	17 42.0	21 58.7	7 3.3	19 43.0	14 38.4
22 T	3 59 53.3	20 24.8	23 5.0	18 34.8	21 36.5	22 35.5	9 42.9	17 41.0	22 0.5	7 1.4	19 42.2	14 38.1
25 F	4 11 43.0	20 58.6	23 5.7	5 17.8	23 9.7	23 8.4	8 58.6	17 40.5	22 2.4	6 59.7	19 41.4	14 37.6
28 M	4 23 32.6	21 29.1	23 6.4	11N 3.4	24 20.0	23 35.4	8 14.1	17 40.5	22 4.1	6 58.0	19 40.5	14 36.9
31 T	4 35 22.3	21 56.2	23 7.1	23 18.1	25 6.0	23 56.2	7 29.4	17 41.0	22 5.8	6 56.6	19 39.7	14 36.1

JUNE 1973

LONGITUDE at NOON

DAY	h m s	☉	☊	☽	☿	♀	♂	♃	♄	♅	♆	♇
1 F	4 39 18.9	10♊51.0	9♑13.8	15♊14.6	24♊54.3	24♊44.2	16♓58.1	12♒ 7.5	22♊19.3	19♎12.6	5♐55.8	1♎42.1
2 S	4 43 15.4	11 48.5	9 10.6	0♋24.2	26 50.0	25 57.7	17 39.3	12R 7.1	22 27.1	19R11.3	5R54.2	1R41.7
3 S	4 47 12.0	12 45.9	9 7.4	15 23.9	28 43.3	27 11.2	18 20.4	12 6.5	22 34.8	19 10.1	5 52.6	1 41.5
4 M	4 51 8.5	13 43.4	9 4.2	0♌ 6.3	0♋34.1	28 24.7	19 1.4	12 5.7	22 42.6	19 9.0	5 51.0	1 41.2
5 T	4 55 5.1	14 40.9	9 1.1	14 26.3	2 22.4	29 38.2	19 42.3	12 4.7	22 50.3	19 7.9	5 49.4	1 41.0
6 W	4 59 1.7	15 38.3	8 57.9	28 21.9	4 8.0	0♋51.7	20 23.2	12 3.6	22 58.1	19 6.8	5 47.8	1 40.8
7 T	5 2 58.2	16 35.7	8 54.7	11♍52.9	5 51.0	2 5.1	21 3.9	12 2.2	23 5.9	19 5.8	5 46.2	1 40.6
8 F	5 6 54.8	17 33.1	8 51.5	25 1.1	7 31.4	3 18.5	21 44.6	12 0.6	23 13.7	19 4.8	5 44.6	1 40.5
9 S	5 10 51.3	18 30.4	8 48.4	7♎48.9	9 9.1	4 31.9	22 25.2	11 58.9	23 21.5	19 3.9	5 43.0	1 40.4
10 S	5 14 47.9	19 27.8	8 45.2	20 19.6	10 44.1	5 45.3	23 5.7	11 57.0	23 29.3	19 3.1	5 41.5	1 40.4
11 M	5 18 44.4	20 25.1	8 42.0	2♏36.4	12 16.3	6 58.7	23 46.1	11 54.9	23 37.1	19 2.2	5 39.9	1 40.4
12 T	5 22 41.0	21 22.4	8 38.8	14 42.2	13 45.8	8 12.1	24 26.4	11 52.6	23 44.9	19 1.5	5 38.4	1 40.4
13 W	5 26 37.6	22 19.8	8 35.6	26 40.0	15 12.6	9 25.4	25 6.7	11 50.1	23 52.7	19 0.8	5 36.8	1 40.4
14 T	5 30 34.1	23 17.0	8 32.5	8♐32.2	16 36.5	10 38.8	25 46.8	11 47.4	24 0.5	19 0.1	5 35.3	1D40.5
15 F	5 34 30.7	24 14.3	8 29.3	20 21.2	17 57.6	11 52.1	26 26.9	11 44.6	24 8.3	18 59.5	5 33.8	1 40.6
16 S	5 38 27.2	25 11.6	8 26.1	2♑ 9.1	19 15.9	13 5.4	27 6.8	11 41.6	24 16.1	18 58.9	5 32.2	1 40.7
17 S	5 42 23.8	26 8.9	8 22.9	13 58.4	20 31.2	14 18.6	27 46.6	11 38.4	24 23.9	18 58.4	5 30.7	1 40.9
18 M	5 46 20.4	27 6.1	8 19.8	25 51.3	21 43.5	15 31.9	28 26.4	11 35.0	24 31.7	18 57.9	5 29.3	1 41.1
19 T	5 50 16.9	28 3.4	8 16.6	7♒50.6	22 52.9	16 45.2	29 6.1	11 31.5	24 39.6	18 57.6	5 27.8	1 41.4
20 W	5 54 13.5	29 0.6	8 13.4	19 59.2	23 59.1	17 58.4	29 45.6	11 27.8	24 47.4	18 57.2	5 26.4	1 41.7
21 T	5 58 10.0	29 57.9	8 10.2	2♓20.4	25 2.2	19 11.6	0♈25.0	11 23.9	24 55.2	18 56.9	5 24.9	1 42.0
22 F	6 2 6.6	0♋55.1	8 7.1	14 57.7	26 2.0	20 24.8	1 4.2	11 19.8	25 3.0	18 56.7	5 23.5	1 42.3
23 S	6 6 3.1	1 52.3	8 3.9	27 54.5	26 58.5	21 38.0	1 43.4	11 15.5	25 10.8	18 56.5	5 22.1	1 42.7
24 S	6 9 59.7	2 49.6	8 0.7	11♈13.8	27 51.5	22 51.2	2 22.4	11 11.1	25 18.5	18 56.3	5 20.7	1 43.1
25 M	6 13 56.3	3 46.8	7 57.5	24 57.6	28 41.1	24 4.4	3 1.3	11 6.6	25 26.3	18 56.2	5 19.3	1 43.5
26 T	6 17 52.8	4 44.0	7 54.4	9♉ 6.6	29 27.0	25 17.5	3 40.1	11 1.8	25 34.1	18 56.2	5 17.9	1 44.0
27 W	6 21 49.4	5 41.3	7 51.2	23 39.0	0♌ 9.1	26 30.7	4 18.7	10 57.0	25 41.8	18 56.2	5 16.6	1 44.5
28 T	6 25 45.9	6 38.5	7 48.0	8♊30.9	0 47.4	27 43.8	4 57.1	10 51.9	25 49.5	18 56.2	5 15.2	1 45.0
29 F	6 29 42.5	7 35.7	7 44.8	23 35.6	1 21.7	28 56.9	5 35.4	10 46.7	25 57.3	18D56.3	5 13.9	1 45.6
30 S	6 33 39.1	8 33.0	7 41.6	8♋44.8	1 51.9	0♌10.0	6 13.6	10 41.4	26 5.0	18 56.5	5 12.6	1 46.2

DECLINATION at NOON

DAY	h m s	☉	☊	☽	☿	♀	♂	♃	♄	♅	♆	♇
1 F	4 39 18.9	22N 4.5	23S 7.3	24N37.6	25N16.0	24N 1.8	7S14.4	17S41.3	22N 6.3	6S56.1	19S39.5	14N35.8
4 M	4 51 8.5	22 27.0	23 8.0	18 10.6	25 30.8	24 14.2	6 29.6	17 42.4	22 7.9	6 54.9	19 38.7	14 34.9
7 T	5 2 58.2	22 46.1	23 8.6	2 43.8	25 25.1	24 20.2	5 44.7	17 44.0	22 9.4	6 53.8	19 37.9	14 33.8
10 S	5 14 47.9	23 1.5	23 9.2	12S41.7	25 1.7	24 19.7	4 59.9	17 46.1	22 10.9	6 52.8	19 37.1	14 32.5
13 W	5 26 37.6	23 13.2	23 9.9	22 46.8	24 23.9	24 12.8	4 15.2	17 48.7	22 12.2	6 52.1	19 36.3	14 31.2
16 S	5 38 27.2	23 21.3	23 10.5	23 55.8	23 34.8	23 59.5	3 30.7	17 51.7	22 13.5	6 51.5	19 35.6	14 29.7
19 T	5 50 16.9	23 25.7	23 11.1	15 43.9	22 37.5	23 39.8	2 46.5	17 55.1	22 14.7	6 51.1	19 34.9	14 28.1
22 F	6 2 6.6	23 26.4	23 11.7	1 24.9	21 34.9	23 13.9	2 2.7	17 59.0	22 15.8	6 50.8	19 34.2	14 26.3
25 M	6 13 56.3	23 23.3	23 12.2	14N21.9	20 29.7	22 42.0	1 19.3	18 3.3	22 16.8	6 50.8	19 33.6	14 24.5
28 T	6 25 45.9	23 16.6	23 12.8	24 16.8	19 24.7	22 4.1	0 36.5	18 7.9	22 17.7	6 50.9	19 33.0	14 22.6

JULY 1973

DAY	EPHEMERIS SIDEREAL TIME	☉	☊	☽	☿	♀	♂	♃	♄	♅	♆	♇
	h m s	° ′	° ′	° ′	° ′	° ′	° ′	° ′	° ′	° ′	° ′	° ′
						LONGITUDE at NOON						
1 S	6 37 35.6	9♋30.2	7♑38.5	23♋49.1	2♌17.9	1♌23.0	6♈51.6	10♒35.9	26♊12.6	18♎56.7	5♐11.3	1♎46.8
2 M	6 41 32.2	10 27.4	7 35.3	8♌40.1	2 39.5	2 36.1	7 29.4	10R30.2	26 20.3	18 57.0	5R10.1	1 47.5
3 T	6 45 28.7	11 24.6	7 32.1	23 10.6	2 56.7	3 49.1	8 7.0	10 24.5	26 28.0	18 57.3	5 8.8	1 48.1
4 W	6 49 25.3	12 21.8	7 28.9	7♍16.3	3 9.3	5 2.1	8 44.5	10 18.5	26 35.6	18 57.7	5 7.6	1 48.9
5 T	6 53 21.8	13 19.1	7 25.8	20 55.3	3 17.3	6 15.1	9 21.8	10 12.5	26 43.2	18 58.1	5 6.4	1 49.6
6 F	6 57 18.4	14 16.3	7 22.6	4♎ 8.3	3 20.6	7 28.1	9 58.9	10 6.3	26 50.8	18 58.6	5 5.3	1 50.4
7 S	7 1 15.0	15 13.5	7 19.4	16 57.4	3R19.2	8 41.1	10 35.8	10 0.1	26 58.4	18 59.2	5 4.1	1 51.2
8 S	7 5 11.5	16 10.7	7 16.2	29 26.1	3 13.1	9 54.0	11 12.6	9 53.6	27 5.9	18 59.7	5 3.0	1 52.1
9 M	7 9 8.1	17 7.9	7 13.1	11♏38.6	3 2.4	11 6.9	11 49.1	9 47.1	27 13.4	19 0.4	5 1.9	1 53.0
10 T	7 13 4.6	18 5.1	7 9.9	23 39.1	2 47.2	12 19.8	12 25.6	9 40.5	27 21.0	19 1.1	5 0.8	1 53.9
11 W	7 17 1.2	19 2.3	7 6.7	5♐31.6	2 27.5	13 32.7	13 1.7	9 33.8	27 28.5	19 1.9	4 59.8	1 54.9
12 T	7 20 57.7	19 59.5	7 3.5	17 20.1	2 3.7	14 45.5	13 37.7	9 27.0	27 35.9	19 2.7	4 58.7	1 55.8
13 F	7 24 54.3	20 56.7	7 0.4	29 7.8	1 36.0	15 58.3	14 13.4	9 20.1	27 43.3	19 3.5	4 57.7	1 56.8
14 S	7 28 50.9	21 53.9	6 57.2	10♑57.7	1 4.8	17 11.1	14 49.0	9 13.0	27 50.7	19 4.4	4 56.7	1 57.9
15 S	7 32 47.4	22 51.1	6 54.0	22 52.3	0 30.5	18 23.8	15 24.3	9 5.9	27 58.1	19 5.4	4 55.8	1 58.9
16 M	7 36 44.0	23 48.3	6 50.8	4♒53.8	29♋53.7	19 36.6	15 59.4	8 58.7	28 5.4	19 6.4	4 54.8	2 0.0
17 T	7 40 40.5	24 45.5	6 47.6	17 4.0	29 14.8	20 49.3	16 34.3	8 51.5	28 12.7	19 7.4	4 53.9	2 1.1
18 W	7 44 37.1	25 42.8	6 44.5	29 24.7	28 34.6	22 2.0	17 9.0	8 44.1	28 19.9	19 8.6	4 53.0	2 2.3
19 T	7 48 33.6	26 40.0	6 41.3	11♓57.7	27 53.6	23 14.6	17 43.4	8 36.7	28 27.1	19 9.7	4 52.2	2 3.5
20 F	7 52 30.2	27 37.3	6 38.1	24 44.5	27 12.7	24 27.3	18 17.5	8 29.2	28 34.3	19 10.9	4 51.4	2 4.7
21 S	7 56 26.8	28 34.5	6 34.9	7♈47.1	26 32.5	25 39.9	18 51.4	8 21.7	28 41.5	19 12.2	4 50.6	2 5.9
22 S	8 0 23.3	29 31.8	6 31.8	21 7.0	25 53.7	26 52.5	19 25.1	8 14.1	28 48.6	19 13.5	4 49.8	2 7.2
23 M	8 4 19.9	0♌29.1	6 28.6	4♉45.6	25 17.1	28 5.0	19 58.4	8 6.5	28 55.7	19 14.8	4 49.0	2 8.4
24 T	8 8 16.4	1 26.4	6 25.4	18 43.7	24 43.3	29 17.6	20 31.5	7 58.8	29 2.7	19 16.2	4 48.3	2 9.8
25 W	8 12 13.0	2 23.7	6 22.2	3♊ 0.7	24 13.0	0♍30.1	21 4.3	7 51.1	29 9.7	19 17.7	4 47.6	2 11.1
26 T	8 16 9.5	3 21.1	6 19.1	17 34.7	23 46.8	1 42.6	21 36.9	7 43.4	29 16.7	19 19.2	4 46.9	2 12.5
27 F	8 20 6.1	4 18.4	6 15.9	2♋21.8	23 25.2	2 55.0	22 9.1	7 35.6	29 23.6	19 20.8	4 46.3	2 13.9
28 S	8 24 2.7	5 15.8	6 12.7	17 16.1	23 8.6	4 7.5	22 41.0	7 27.9	29 30.4	19 22.4	4 45.7	2 15.3
29 S	8 27 59.2	6 13.2	6 9.5	2♌10.2	22 57.4	5 19.9	23 12.5	7 20.1	29 37.3	19 24.0	4 45.1	2 16.7
30 M	8 31 55.8	7 10.6	6 6.3	16 56.3	22 52.0	6 32.3	23 43.8	7 12.3	29 44.0	19 25.7	4 44.6	2 18.2
31 T	8 35 52.3	8 8.0	6 3.2	1♍26.7	22D52.7	7 44.7	24 14.7	7 4.5	29 50.8	19 27.5	4 44.1	2 19.8
						DECLINATION at NOON						
1 S	6 37 35.6	23N 6.1	23S13.3	19N53.2	18N22.9	21N20.7	0N 5.7	18S12.9	22N18.6	6S51.2	19S32.4	14N20.5
4 W	6 49 25.3	22 52.1	23 13.9	4 35.7	17 27.1	20 31.9	0 47.2	18 18.2	22 19.4	6 51.7	19 31.8	14 18.4
7 S	7 1 15.0	22 34.4	23 14.4	11S29.0	16 40.2	19 37.9	1 27.9	18 23.7	22 20.1	6 52.3	19 31.3	14 16.1
10 T	7 13 4.6	22 13.2	23 14.9	22 15.1	16 4.9	18 39.2	2 7.8	18 29.5	22 20.7	6 53.2	19 30.9	14 13.8
13 F	7 24 54.3	21 48.7	23 15.5	24 13.8	15 43.4	17 35.9	2 46.8	18 35.5	22 21.2	6 54.2	19 30.4	14 11.3
16 M	7 36 44.0	21 20.7	23 15.9	16 42.0	15 37.0	16 28.4	3 24.9	18 41.7	22 21.6	6 55.4	19 30.1	14 8.9
19 T	7 48 33.6	20 49.5	23 16.4	2 41.4	15 45.5	15 17.1	4 1.9	18 48.0	22 22.0	6 56.8	19 29.7	14 6.3
22 S	8 0 23.3	20 15.1	23 16.9	12N58.1	16 7.2	14 2.2	4 37.9	18 54.4	22 22.3	6 58.3	19 29.4	14 3.6
25 W	8 12 13.0	19 37.7	23 17.4	23 41.1	16 39.2	12 44.1	5 12.7	19 0.8	22 22.5	6 60.0	19 29.2	14 0.9
28 S	8 24 2.7	18 57.3	23 17.8	21 26.8	17 17.5	11 23.0	5 46.2	19 7.2	22 22.7	7 1.9	19 29.0	13 58.2
31 T	8 35 52.3	18 14.1	23 18.3	7 0.6	17 57.9	9 59.3	6 18.4	19 13.5	22 22.8	7 3.9	19 28.9	13 55.4

AUGUST 1973

DAY	EPHEMERIS SIDEREAL TIME	☉	☊	☽	☿	♀	♂	♃	♄	♅	♆	♇
						LONGITUDE at NOON						
1 W	8 39 48.9	9♌ 5.4	5♑60.0	15♍35.5	22♋59.5	8♍57.0	24♈45.3	6♒56.7	29♊57.5	19♎29.3	4♐43.6	2♎21.3
2 T	8 43 45.4	10 2.9	5 56.8	29 19.1	23 12.6	10 9.3	25 15.5	6R48.9	0♋ 4.1	19 31.1	4R43.2	2 22.9
3 F	8 47 42.0	11 0.3	5 53.6	12♎36.4	23 32.2	11 21.6	25 45.4	6 41.2	0 10.7	19 33.0	4 42.7	2 24.4
4 S	8 51 38.5	11 57.8	5 50.5	25 28.7	23 58.3	12 33.8	26 14.9	6 33.4	0 17.2	19 35.0	4 42.3	2 26.0
5 S	8 55 35.1	12 55.2	5 47.3	7♏58.9	24 30.8	13 46.0	26 44.0	6 25.7	0 23.7	19 36.9	4 42.0	2 27.7
6 M	8 59 31.7	13 52.7	5 44.1	20 11.2	25 9.9	14 58.2	27 12.8	6 18.0	0 30.1	19 39.0	4 41.6	2 29.3
7 T	9 3 28.2	14 50.2	5 40.9	2♐10.4	25 55.4	16 10.3	27 41.1	6 10.4	0 36.5	19 41.0	4 41.3	2 31.0
8 W	9 7 24.8	15 47.7	5 37.8	14 1.4	26 47.2	17 22.4	28 9.1	6 2.8	0 42.8	19 43.2	4 41.1	2 32.7
9 T	9 11 21.3	16 45.2	5 34.6	25 49.1	27 45.2	18 34.5	28 36.7	5 55.3	0 49.0	19 45.3	4 40.8	2 34.4
10 F	9 15 17.9	17 42.7	5 31.4	7♑38.1	28 49.3	19 46.5	29 3.8	5 47.8	0 55.2	19 47.5	4 40.6	2 36.1
11 S	9 19 14.4	18 40.3	5 28.2	19 32.1	29 59.3	20 58.4	29 30.5	5 40.3	1 1.4	19 49.8	4 40.4	2 37.9
12 S	9 23 11.0	19 37.9	5 25.0	1♒34.4	1♌14.9	22 10.4	29 56.9	5 33.0	1 7.4	19 52.0	4 40.3	2 39.6
13 M	9 27 7.5	20 35.4	5 21.9	13 47.3	2 36.0	23 22.3	0♉22.7	5 25.7	1 13.4	19 54.4	4 40.2	2 41.4
14 T	9 31 4.1	21 33.0	5 18.7	26 12.5	4 2.3	24 34.1	0 48.1	5 18.5	1 19.4	19 56.7	4 40.1	2 43.3
15 W	9 35 0.7	22 30.7	5 15.5	8♓50.8	5 33.4	25 45.9	1 13.1	5 11.3	1 25.3	19 59.1	4 40.1	2 45.1
16 T	9 38 57.2	23 28.3	5 12.3	21 42.2	7 9.0	26 57.7	1 37.6	5 4.3	1 31.1	20 1.6	4 40.0	2 47.0
17 F	9 42 53.8	24 26.0	5 9.2	4♈46.8	8 48.7	28 9.4	2 1.6	4 57.3	1 36.9	20 4.1	4D40.1	2 48.8
18 S	9 46 50.3	25 23.7	5 6.0	18 4.1	10 32.3	29 21.1	2 25.1	4 50.5	1 42.5	20 6.6	4 40.1	2 50.7
19 S	9 50 46.9	26 21.4	5 2.8	1♉33.7	12 19.1	0♎32.8	2 48.1	4 43.7	1 48.2	20 9.2	4 40.2	2 52.7
20 M	9 54 43.4	27 19.1	4 59.6	15 15.5	14 8.9	1 44.4	3 10.5	4 37.1	1 53.7	20 11.8	4 40.3	2 54.6
21 T	9 58 40.0	28 17.0	4 56.4	29 9.4	16 1.3	2 56.0	3 32.5	4 30.6	1 59.3	20 14.5	4 40.5	2 56.6
22 W	10 2 36.5	29 14.8	4 53.3	13♊14.9	17 55.6	4 7.5	3 53.9	4 24.1	2 4.7	20 17.1	4 40.7	2 58.6
23 T	10 6 33.1	0♍12.6	4 50.1	27 31.3	19 51.6	5 19.0	4 14.7	4 17.8	2 10.0	20 19.9	4 40.9	3 0.6
24 F	10 10 29.6	1 10.5	4 46.9	11♋56.8	21 49.0	6 30.5	4 34.9	4 11.6	2 15.3	20 22.6	4 41.1	3 2.6
25 S	10 14 26.2	2 8.4	4 43.7	26 28.1	23 47.2	7 41.9	4 54.5	4 5.6	2 20.5	20 25.4	4 41.4	3 4.6
26 S	10 18 22.8	3 6.3	4 40.6	11♌ 0.6	25 46.0	8 53.2	5 13.5	3 59.6	2 25.6	20 28.2	4 41.7	3 6.6
27 M	10 22 19.3	4 4.2	4 37.4	25 28.5	27 45.1	10 4.6	5 31.9	3 53.8	2 30.6	20 31.1	4 42.0	3 8.7
28 T	10 26 15.9	5 2.2	4 34.2	9♍45.4	29 44.1	11 15.8	5 49.7	3 48.2	2 35.6	20 34.0	4 42.4	3 10.7
29 W	10 30 12.4	6 0.2	4 31.0	23 45.7	1♍43.0	12 27.1	6 6.8	3 42.7	2 40.5	20 36.9	4 42.8	3 12.8
30 T	10 34 9.0	6 58.2	4 27.8	7♎25.0	3 41.5	13 38.3	6 23.2	3 37.3	2 45.3	20 39.9	4 43.3	3 14.9
31 F	10 38 5.5	7 56.3	4 24.7	20 40.9	5 39.4	14 49.4	6 39.0	3 32.1	2 50.0	20 42.9	4 43.7	3 17.0
						DECLINATION at NOON						
1 W	8 39 48.9	17N59.1	23S18.4	1N12.9	18N11.0	9N30.9	6N28.8	19S15.6	22N22.8	7S 4.6	19S28.9	13N54.4
4 S	8 51 38.5	17 12.4	23 18.8	14S27.2	18 46.9	8 4.3	6 59.2	19 21.8	22 22.8	7 6.9	19 28.8	13 51.5
7 T	9 3 28.2	16 23.2	23 19.3	23 31.6	19 13.9	6 35.9	7 28.2	19 27.9	22 22.8	7 9.3	19 28.8	13 48.6
10 F	9 15 17.9	15 31.6	23 19.7	23 10.9	19 27.1	5 5.9	7 55.8	19 33.8	22 22.7	7 11.8	19 28.8	13 45.7
13 M	9 27 7.5	14 37.8	23 20.1	13 43.8	19 21.7	3 34.8	8 21.8	19 39.5	22 22.5	7 14.5	19 28.9	13 42.7
16 T	9 38 57.2	13 41.9	23 20.4	1N15.9	18 54.0	2 2.7	8 46.3	19 44.9	22 22.4	7 17.3	19 29.1	13 39.8
19 S	9 50 46.9	12 44.0	23 20.8	16 22.2	18 1.7	0 30.1	9 9.3	19 50.1	22 22.1	7 20.2	19 29.2	13 36.8
22 W	10 2 36.5	11 44.3	23 21.2	24 23.5	16 45.3	1S 2.9	9 30.6	19 55.0	22 21.9	7 23.3	19 29.5	13 33.7
25 S	10 14 26.2	10 42.9	23 21.5	19 7.8	15 7.4	2 35.9	9 50.1	19 59.5	22 21.6	7 26.5	19 29.8	13 30.7
28 T	10 26 15.9	9 39.9	23 21.8	3 41.2	13 12.4	4 8.5	10 8.0	20 3.8	22 21.2	7 29.8	19 30.2	13 27.7
31 F	10 38 5.5	8 35.6	23 22.2	12S36.7	11 4.9	5 40.6	10 24.1	20 7.6	22 20.9	7 33.2	19 30.6	13 24.7

SEPTEMBER 1973

DAY	EPHEMERIS SIDEREAL TIME	☉	☊	☽	☿	♀	♂	♃	♄	♅	♆	♇
	h m s	° ′	° ′	° ′	° ′	° ′	° ′	° ′	° ′	° ′	° ′	° ′
LONGITUDE at NOON												
1 S	10 42 2.1	8 ♍ 54.4	4 ♑ 21.5	3 ♏ 33.3	7 ♍ 36.5	16 ♎ 0.5	6 ♉ 54.1	3 ♒ 27.0	2 ♋ 54.7	20 ♎ 45.9	4 ♐ 44.2	3 ♎ 19.1
2 S	10 45 58.6	9 52.4	4 18.3	16 4.1	9 32.8	17 11.5	7 8.5	3 R 22.1	2 59.2	20 49.0	4 44.8	3 21.3
3 M	10 49 55.2	10 50.6	4 15.1	28 16.9	11 28.2	18 22.5	7 22.2	3 17.4	3 3.7	20 52.0	4 45.3	3 23.4
4 T	10 53 51.7	11 48.7	4 12.0	10 ♐ 16.1	13 22.6	19 33.4	7 35.2	3 12.8	3 8.1	20 55.2	4 45.9	3 25.6
5 W	10 57 48.3	12 46.9	4 8.8	22 7.1	15 16.0	20 44.2	7 47.5	3 8.4	3 12.4	20 58.3	4 46.6	3 27.7
6 T	11 1 44.8	13 45.1	4 5.6	3 ♑ 55.2	17 8.2	21 55.0	7 59.0	3 4.2	3 16.6	21 1.5	4 47.2	3 29.9
7 F	11 5 41.4	14 43.3	4 2.4	15 45.8	18 59.3	23 5.8	8 9.7	3 0.1	3 20.8	21 4.7	4 47.9	3 32.1
8 S	11 9 37.9	15 41.5	3 59.2	27 43.6	20 49.3	24 16.5	8 19.7	2 56.2	3 24.8	21 7.9	4 48.7	3 34.3
9 S	11 13 34.5	16 39.8	3 56.1	9 ♒ 53.0	22 38.2	25 27.1	8 29.0	2 52.5	3 28.8	21 11.2	4 49.4	3 36.5
10 M	11 17 31.0	17 38.1	3 52.9	22 16.9	24 25.9	26 37.6	8 37.4	2 48.9	3 32.6	21 14.5	4 50.2	3 38.7
11 T	11 21 27.6	18 36.5	3 49.7	4 ♓ 57.3	26 12.5	27 48.2	8 45.1	2 45.6	3 36.5	21 17.8	4 51.1	3 41.0
12 W	11 25 24.2	19 34.8	3 46.5	17 54.8	27 58.0	28 58.6	8 51.9	2 42.4	3 40.1	21 21.2	4 51.9	3 43.2
13 T	11 29 20.7	20 33.2	3 43.4	1 ♈ 8.7	29 42.3	0 ♏ 9.0	8 57.9	2 39.4	3 43.7	21 24.5	4 52.8	3 45.5
14 F	11 33 17.3	21 31.6	3 40.2	14 36.9	1 ♎ 25.6	1 19.2	9 3.1	2 36.6	3 47.2	21 27.9	4 53.7	3 47.7
15 S	11 37 13.8	22 30.1	3 37.0	28 17.0	3 7.7	2 29.5	9 7.5	2 34.0	3 50.6	21 31.3	4 54.7	3 50.0
16 S	11 41 10.4	23 28.6	3 33.8	12 ♉ 6.2	4 48.8	3 39.6	9 10.9	2 31.6	3 54.0	21 34.7	4 55.6	3 52.2
17 M	11 45 6.9	24 27.1	3 30.6	26 2.0	6 28.8	4 49.7	9 13.6	2 29.3	3 57.2	21 38.2	4 56.7	3 54.5
18 T	11 49 3.5	25 25.6	3 27.5	10 ♊ 2.6	8 7.8	5 59.7	9 15.3	2 27.3	4 0.3	21 41.6	4 57.7	3 56.8
19 W	11 53 0.0	26 24.2	3 24.3	24 6.6	9 45.7	7 9.7	9 16.2	2 25.4	4 3.3	21 45.1	4 58.7	3 59.0
20 T	11 56 56.6	27 22.9	3 21.1	8 ♋ 13.3	11 22.7	8 19.5	9 R 16.1	2 23.7	4 6.2	21 48.7	4 59.8	4 1.3
21 F	12 0 53.1	28 21.5	3 17.9	22 21.8	12 58.7	9 29.4	9 15.2	2 22.2	4 9.0	21 52.2	5 1.0	4 3.6
22 S	12 4 49.7	29 20.2	3 14.8	6 ♌ 30.8	14 33.7	10 39.1	9 13.4	2 20.9	4 11.8	21 55.7	5 2.1	4 5.9
23 S	12 8 46.2	0 ♎ 19.0	3 11.6	20 38.1	16 7.7	11 48.8	9 10.6	2 19.8	4 14.4	21 59.3	5 3.3	4 8.2
24 M	12 12 42.8	1 17.8	3 8.4	4 ♍ 40.6	17 40.8	12 58.3	9 7.0	2 18.9	4 16.9	22 2.9	5 4.5	4 10.5
25 T	12 16 39.3	2 16.6	3 5.2	18 34.3	19 12.9	14 7.8	9 2.5	2 18.2	4 19.3	22 6.5	5 5.7	4 12.8
26 W	12 20 35.9	3 15.4	3 2.0	2 ♎ 15.1	20 44.1	15 17.3	8 57.0	2 17.7	4 21.6	22 10.1	5 7.0	4 15.1
27 T	12 24 32.4	4 14.3	2 58.9	15 39.6	22 14.4	16 26.6	8 50.7	2 17.4	4 23.8	22 13.7	5 8.3	4 17.4
28 F	12 28 29.0	5 13.2	2 55.7	28 45.4	23 43.7	17 35.9	8 43.5	2 17.3	4 25.9	22 17.4	5 9.6	4 19.7
29 S	12 32 25.6	6 12.2	2 52.5	11 ♏ 31.4	25 12.1	18 45.1	8 35.5	2 D 17.4	4 27.9	22 21.0	5 11.0	4 22.0
30 S	12 36 22.1	7 11.2	2 49.3	23 58.7	26 39.6	19 54.1	8 26.5	2 17.7	4 29.8	22 24.7	5 12.3	4 24.2
DECLINATION at NOON												
1 S	10 42 2.1	8 N 13.9	23 S 22.3	16 S 54.7	10 N 20.4	6 S 11.1	10 N 29.0	20 S 8.8	22 N 20.8	7 S 34.4	19 S 30.7	13 N 23.7
4 T	10 53 51.7	7 8.0	23 22.6	24 7.4	8 3.0	7 41.8	10 42.8	20 12.2	22 20.4	7 37.9	19 31.2	13 20.8
7 F	11 5 41.4	6 1.1	23 22.9	21 35.4	5 42.0	9 11.3	10 54.7	20 15.2	22 20.0	7 41.6	19 31.7	13 17.8
10 M	11 17 31.0	4 53.2	23 23.2	10 34.7	3 19.9	10 39.0	11 4.8	20 17.7	22 19.7	7 45.3	19 32.3	13 14.9
13 T	11 29 20.7	3 44.6	23 23.4	5 N 3.1	0 58.5	12 4.9	11 13.1	20 19.9	22 19.3	7 49.1	19 32.9	13 12.0
16 S	11 41 10.4	2 35.4	23 23.7	19 14.2	1 S 20.8	13 28.5	11 19.5	20 21.7	22 18.9	7 53.0	19 33.6	13 9.2
19 W	11 53 0.0	1 25.8	23 23.9	24 9.9	3 37.0	14 49.5	11 24.0	20 23.0	22 18.5	7 56.9	19 34.3	13 6.4
22 S	12 4 49.7	0 15.8	23 24.2	16 0.4	5 49.1	16 7.7	11 26.6	20 24.0	22 18.2	8 0.9	19 35.1	13 3.7
25 T	12 16 39.3	0 S 54.3	23 24.4	0 3.8	7 56.5	17 22.7	11 27.3	20 24.5	22 17.9	8 5.0	19 35.9	13 1.0
28 F	12 28 29.0	2 4.5	23 24.6	15 S 14.5	9 58.6	18 34.2	11 26.1	20 24.7	22 17.6	8 9.1	19 36.7	12 58.4

OCTOBER 1973

DAY	EPHEMERIS SIDEREAL TIME	☉	☊	☽	☿	♀	♂	♃	♄	♅	♆	♇
LONGITUDE at NOON												
1 M	12 40 18.7	8 ♎ 10.2	2 ♑ 46.2	6 ♐ 9.7	28 ♎ 6.0	21 ♏ 3.1	8 ♉ 16.8	2 ♒ 18.2	4 ♋ 31.6	22 ♎ 28.4	5 ♐ 13.8	4 ♎ 26.5
2 T	12 44 15.2	9 9.2	2 43.0	18 8.1	29 31.6	22 12.1	8 R 6.3	2 18.9	4 33.3	22 32.2	5 15.2	4 28.9
3 W	12 48 11.8	10 8.3	2 39.8	29 58.6	0 ♏ 56.1	23 20.9	7 54.9	2 19.8	4 34.8	22 35.9	5 16.7	4 31.2
4 T	12 52 8.3	11 7.4	2 36.6	11 ♑ 46.4	2 19.6	24 29.5	7 42.8	2 20.9	4 36.3	22 39.6	5 18.2	4 33.5
5 F	12 56 4.9	12 6.5	2 33.4	23 37.2	3 42.0	25 38.1	7 29.9	2 22.2	4 37.6	22 43.3	5 19.7	4 35.7
6 S	13 0 1.4	13 5.7	2 30.3	5 ♒ 36.3	5 3.3	26 46.6	7 16.3	2 23.6	4 38.9	22 47.0	5 21.2	4 38.0
7 S	13 3 58.0	14 4.9	2 27.1	17 48.8	6 23.5	27 54.9	7 2.0	2 25.3	4 40.0	22 50.8	5 22.8	4 40.3
8 M	13 7 54.5	15 4.1	2 23.9	0 ♓ 19.0	7 42.6	29 3.2	6 47.0	2 27.2	4 41.0	22 54.5	5 24.3	4 42.6
9 T	13 11 51.1	16 3.3	2 20.7	13 9.6	9 0.3	0 ♐ 11.3	6 31.4	2 29.2	4 41.9	22 58.3	5 25.9	4 44.8
10 W	13 15 47.6	17 2.6	2 17.6	26 22.0	10 16.8	1 19.3	6 15.2	2 31.5	4 42.7	23 2.0	5 27.6	4 47.1
11 T	13 19 44.2	18 1.9	2 14.4	9 ♈ 55.5	11 31.8	2 27.1	5 58.4	2 33.9	4 43.4	23 5.8	5 29.2	4 49.3
12 F	13 23 40.7	19 1.3	2 11.2	23 47.4	12 45.4	3 34.9	5 41.1	2 36.5	4 44.0	23 9.6	5 30.9	4 51.6
13 S	13 27 37.3	20 0.7	2 8.0	7 ♉ 53.6	13 57.3	4 42.5	5 23.3	2 39.3	4 44.4	23 13.3	5 32.6	4 53.8
14 S	13 31 33.9	21 0.1	2 4.8	22 9.0	15 7.6	5 49.9	5 5.1	2 42.4	4 44.8	23 17.1	5 34.3	4 56.0
15 M	13 35 30.4	21 59.5	2 1.7	6 ♊ 28.5	16 15.9	6 57.2	4 46.4	2 45.6	4 45.0	23 20.9	5 36.0	4 58.3
16 T	13 39 27.0	22 59.0	1 58.5	20 47.5	17 22.2	8 4.4	4 27.3	2 48.9	4 45.1	23 24.7	5 37.8	5 0.5
17 W	13 43 23.5	23 58.5	1 55.3	5 ♋ 2.8	18 26.3	9 11.4	4 8.0	2 52.5	4 45.2	23 28.5	5 39.6	5 2.7
18 T	13 47 20.1	24 58.1	1 52.1	19 12.4	19 28.0	10 18.3	3 48.3	2 56.3	4 R 45.1	23 32.2	5 41.4	5 4.9
19 F	13 51 16.6	25 57.7	1 49.0	3 ♌ 15.1	20 27.0	11 25.1	3 28.5	3 0.2	4 44.9	23 36.0	5 43.2	5 7.0
20 S	13 55 13.2	26 57.4	1 45.8	17 10.4	21 23.0	12 31.6	3 8.4	3 4.3	4 44.5	23 39.8	5 45.1	5 9.2
21 S	13 59 9.7	27 57.0	1 42.6	0 ♍ 57.5	22 15.9	13 38.0	2 48.2	3 8.6	4 44.1	23 43.6	5 46.9	5 11.4
22 M	14 3 6.3	28 56.8	1 39.4	14 35.7	23 5.1	14 44.3	2 28.0	3 13.1	4 43.6	23 47.3	5 48.8	5 13.5
23 T	14 7 2.8	29 56.6	1 36.2	28 3.8	23 50.5	15 50.4	2 7.7	3 17.8	4 43.0	23 51.2	5 50.8	5 15.7
24 W	14 10 59.4	0 ♏ 56.3	1 33.1	11 ♎ 20.0	24 31.4	16 56.3	1 47.5	3 22.6	4 42.2	23 54.9	5 52.7	5 17.8
25 T	14 14 55.9	1 56.2	1 29.9	24 22.9	25 7.5	18 2.0	1 27.3	3 27.7	4 41.3	23 58.7	5 54.6	5 19.9
26 F	14 18 52.5	2 56.0	1 26.7	7 ♏ 11.2	25 38.2	19 7.6	1 7.3	3 32.8	4 40.3	24 2.4	5 56.6	5 22.0
27 S	14 22 49.1	3 55.9	1 23.5	19 44.4	26 3.0	20 12.9	0 47.5	3 38.2	4 39.2	24 6.2	5 58.5	5 24.1
28 S	14 26 45.6	4 55.8	1 20.4	2 ♐ 3.1	26 21.3	21 18.0	0 27.9	3 43.8	4 38.0	24 9.9	6 0.5	5 26.2
29 M	14 30 42.2	5 55.8	1 17.2	14 8.8	26 32.6	22 22.9	0 8.6	3 49.5	4 36.7	24 13.6	6 2.5	5 28.2
30 T	14 34 38.7	6 55.8	1 14.0	26 4.3	26 36.1	23 27.6	29 ♈ 49.7	3 55.3	4 35.3	24 17.3	6 4.5	5 30.3
31 W	14 38 35.3	7 55.8	1 10.8	7 ♑ 53.2	26 R 31.2	24 32.1	29 31.1	4 1.4	4 33.7	24 21.1	6 6.6	5 32.3
DECLINATION at NOON												
1 M	12 40 18.7	3 S 14.5	23 S 24.8	23 S 32.3	11 S 54.7	19 S 41.9	11 N 23.2	20 S 24.4	22 N 17.3	8 S 13.2	19 S 37.6	12 N 55.9
4 T	12 52 8.3	4 24.1	23 25.0	22 5.5	13 44.1	20 45.6	11 18.7	20 23.6	22 17.0	8 17.4	19 38.5	12 53.4
7 S	13 3 58.0	5 33.3	23 25.2	12 3.4	15 26.2	21 44.8	11 12.7	20 22.5	22 16.8	8 21.6	19 39.4	12 51.0
10 W	13 15 47.6	6 41.8	23 25.4	3 N 8.9	17 0.1	22 39.4	11 5.3	20 21.0	22 16.6	8 25.8	19 40.4	12 48.7
13 S	13 27 37.3	7 49.5	23 25.5	17 58.0	18 24.8	23 29.1	10 56.8	20 19.1	22 16.5	8 30.0	19 41.4	12 46.5
16 T	13 39 27.0	8 56.2	23 25.7	24 1.1	19 39.1	24 13.6	10 47.3	20 16.7	22 16.4	8 34.2	19 42.5	12 44.4
19 F	13 51 16.6	10 1.8	23 25.8	16 47.1	20 41.4	24 52.8	10 37.3	20 14.0	22 16.3	8 38.4	19 43.5	12 42.4
22 M	14 3 6.3	11 6.1	23 25.9	1 34.1	21 29.7	25 26.4	10 26.9	20 10.9	22 16.3	8 42.5	19 44.6	12 40.5
25 T	14 14 55.9	12 8.9	23 26.1	13 S 45.5	22 1.1	25 54.4	10 16.7	20 7.4	22 16.3	8 46.7	19 45.7	12 38.7
28 S	14 26 45.6	13 10.0	23 26.2	22 54.8	22 11.6	26 16.6	10 6.9	20 3.5	22 16.3	8 50.9	19 46.8	12 37.1
31 W	14 38 35.3	14 9.3	23 26.2	22 28.7	21 56.0	26 32.9	9 57.9	19 59.2	22 16.5	8 54.9	19 47.9	12 35.5

NOVEMBER 1973

LONGITUDE at NOON

DAY	EPHEMERIS SIDEREAL TIME h m s	☉ ° ′	☊ ° ′	☽ ° ′	☿ ° ′	♀ ° ′	♂ ° ′	♃ ° ′	♄ ° ′	♅ ° ′	♆ ° ′	♇ ° ′
1 T	14 42 31.8	8♏55.8	1♑ 7.6	19♑40.0	26♏17.6	25♐36.3	29♈13.0	4♒ 7.6	4♋32.1	24♎24.8	6♐ 8.6	5♎34.3
2 F	14 46 28.4	9 55.9	1 4.5	1♒29.6	25R54.6	26 40.3	28R55.3	4 14.0	4R30.3	24 28.4	6 10.7	5 36.3
3 S	14 50 24.9	10 56.0	1 1.3	13 27.4	25 22.0	27 44.0	28 38.2	4 20.5	4 28.5	24 32.1	6 12.8	5 38.2
4 S	14 54 21.5	11 56.1	0 58.1	25 38.6	24 39.8	28 47.4	28 21.6	4 27.2	4 26.5	24 35.8	6 14.9	5 40.2
5 M	14 58 18.0	12 56.2	0 54.9	8♓ 8.3	23 48.2	29 50.6	28 5.6	4 34.1	4 24.4	24 39.4	6 17.0	5 42.1
6 T	15 2 14.6	13 56.4	0 51.8	21 0.4	22 48.0	0♑53.5	27 50.2	4 41.1	4 22.3	24 43.0	6 19.1	5 44.0
7 W	15 6 11.2	14 56.6	0 48.6	4♈17.5	21 40.1	1 56.1	27 35.5	4 48.3	4 20.0	24 46.7	6 21.2	5 45.9
8 T	15 10 7.7	15 56.8	0 45.4	18 0.4	20 26.1	2 58.3	27 21.4	4 55.6	4 17.6	24 50.3	6 23.3	5 47.8
9 F	15 14 4.3	16 57.1	0 42.2	2♉ 7.1	19 8.0	4 0.3	27 8.0	5 3.1	4 15.2	24 53.8	6 25.5	5 49.6
10 S	15 18 0.8	17 57.4	0 39.1	16 33.6	17 48.2	5 1.9	26 55.4	5 10.7	4 12.6	24 57.4	6 27.6	5 51.5
11 S	15 21 57.4	18 57.7	0 35.9	1♊13.6	16 29.1	6 3.2	26 43.4	5 18.5	4 9.9	25 0.9	6 29.8	5 53.3
12 M	15 25 53.9	19 58.0	0 32.7	15 59.7	15 13.4	7 4.1	26 32.2	5 26.4	4 7.2	25 4.5	6 32.0	5 55.1
13 T	15 29 50.5	20 58.4	0 29.5	0♋44.7	14 3.6	8 4.7	26 21.8	5 34.5	4 4.4	25 8.0	6 34.2	5 56.9
14 W	15 33 47.0	21 58.8	0 26.3	15 22.3	13 1.7	9 4.8	26 12.1	5 42.7	4 1.4	25 11.5	6 36.4	5 58.6
15 T	15 37 43.6	22 59.2	0 23.2	29 47.8	12 9.5	10 4.6	26 3.2	5 51.0	3 58.4	25 15.0	6 38.6	6 0.3
16 F	15 41 40.2	23 59.7	0 20.0	13♌58.5	11 28.1	11 4.0	25 55.1	5 59.5	3 55.3	25 18.4	6 40.8	6 2.0
17 S	15 45 36.7	25 0.2	0 16.8	27 53.0	10 58.1	12 2.9	25 47.7	6 8.2	3 52.0	25 21.8	6 43.1	6 3.7
18 S	15 49 33.3	26 0.7	0 13.6	11♍31.3	10 40.0	13 1.4	25 41.2	6 16.9	3 48.7	25 25.2	6 45.3	6 5.3
19 M	15 53 29.8	27 1.2	0 10.5	24 54.0	10 33.3	13 59.5	25 35.5	6 25.8	3 45.3	25 28.6	6 47.5	6 7.0
20 T	15 57 26.4	28 1.8	0 7.3	8♎ 1.9	10D37.8	14 57.0	25 30.6	6 34.8	3 41.8	25 31.9	6 49.7	6 8.6
21 W	16 1 22.9	29 2.4	0 4.1	20 55.9	10 52.7	15 54.1	25 26.5	6 44.0	3 38.3	25 35.3	6 52.0	6 10.1
22 T	16 5 19.5	0♐ 3.1	0 0.9	3♏36.8	11 17.1	16 50.7	25 23.2	6 53.3	3 34.6	25 38.6	6 54.2	6 11.7
23 F	16 9 16.1	1 3.7	29♐57.8	16 5.5	11 50.2	17 46.8	25 20.8	7 2.7	3 30.9	25 41.8	6 56.5	6 13.2
24 S	16 13 12.6	2 4.4	29 54.6	28 22.8	12 31.2	18 42.3	25 19.1	7 12.3	3 27.1	25 45.1	6 58.7	6 14.7
25 S	16 17 9.2	3 5.1	29 51.4	10♐29.9	13 19.1	19 37.3	25 18.3	7 22.0	3 23.2	25 48.3	7 1.0	6 16.2
26 M	16 21 5.7	4 5.9	29 48.2	22 28.1	14 13.0	20 31.6	25 18.3	7 31.8	3 19.3	25 51.5	7 3.2	6 17.6
27 T	16 25 2.3	5 6.6	29 45.0	4♑19.6	15 12.4	21 25.3	25D19.1	7 41.7	3 15.3	25 54.6	7 5.5	6 19.0
28 W	16 28 58.8	6 7.4	29 41.9	16 6.9	16 16.4	22 18.4	25 20.7	7 51.7	3 11.2	25 57.7	7 7.8	6 20.4
29 T	16 32 55.4	7 8.2	29 38.7	27 53.3	17 24.4	23 10.8	25 23.1	8 1.9	3 7.0	26 0.8	7 10.0	6 21.7
30 F	16 36 52.0	8 9.0	29 35.5	9♒42.6	18 35.8	24 2.5	25 26.3	8 12.1	3 2.8	26 3.9	7 12.3	6 23.1

DECLINATION at NOON

DAY	EPHEMERIS SIDEREAL TIME h m s	☉	☊	☽	☿	♀	♂	♃	♄	♅	♆	♇
1 T	14 42 31.8	14S28.6	23S26.3	20S15.7	21S44.0	26S37.1	9N55.1	19S57.7	22N16.5	8S56.3	19S48.3	12N35.0
4 S	14 54 21.5	15 25.1	23 26.3	8 56.9	20 44.3	26 45.6	9 47.8	19 52.9	22 16.7	9 0.3	19 49.4	12 33.6
7 W	15 6 11.2	16 19.3	23 26.4	6N25.0	19 8.8	26 48.3	9 42.0	19 47.7	22 16.9	9 4.3	19 50.6	12 32.4
10 S	15 18 0.8	17 11.0	23 26.5	20 8.7	17 7.6	26 45.2	9 38.0	19 42.1	22 17.1	9 8.2	19 51.7	12 31.2
13 T	15 29 50.5	18 0.1	23 26.5	23 17.2	15 6.4	26 36.6	9 35.9	19 36.2	22 17.4	9 12.1	19 52.9	12 30.2
16 F	15 41 40.2	18 46.4	23 26.5	13 6.5	13 35.2	26 22.6	9 35.8	19 29.9	22 17.7	9 15.8	19 54.1	12 29.3
19 M	15 53 29.8	19 29.7	23 26.5	2S44.7	12 50.8	26 3.4	9 37.8	19 23.3	22 18.0	9 19.5	19 55.2	12 28.6
22 T	16 5 19.5	20 9.8	23 26.6	16 45.1	12 52.6	25 39.2	9 42.0	19 16.3	22 18.4	9 23.1	19 56.4	12 28.0
25 S	16 17 9.2	20 46.6	23 26.5	23 38.6	13 29.8	25 10.5	9 48.3	19 8.9	22 18.7	9 26.6	19 57.5	12 27.5
28 W	16 28 58.8	21 20.0	23 26.5	20 53.7	14 30.3	24 37.6	9 56.9	19 1.2	22 19.2	9 30.0	19 58.6	12 27.2

DECEMBER 1973

LONGITUDE at NOON

DAY	EPHEMERIS SIDEREAL TIME h m s	☉	☊	☽	☿	♀	♂	♃	♄	♅	♆	♇
1 S	16 40 48.5	9♐ 9.8	29♐32.3	21♒39.3	19♏50.3	24♑53.5	25♈30.2	8♒22.5	2♋58.5	26♎ 6.9	7♐14.5	6♎24.4
2 S	16 44 45.1	10 10.6	29 29.2	3♓47.9	21 7.3	25 43.7	25 34.9	8 33.0	2R54.2	26 9.9	7 16.8	6 25.6
3 M	16 48 41.6	11 11.5	29 26.0	16 13.3	22 26.6	26 33.1	25 40.3	8 43.6	2 49.8	26 12.8	7 19.0	6 26.9
4 T	16 52 38.2	12 12.4	29 22.8	29 0.1	23 47.8	27 21.7	25 46.6	8 54.4	2 45.4	26 15.8	7 21.3	6 28.1
5 W	16 56 34.7	13 13.3	29 19.6	12♈11.7	25 10.5	28 9.4	25 53.4	9 5.2	2 40.9	26 18.7	7 23.6	6 29.3
6 T	17 0 31.3	14 14.2	29 16.5	25 50.6	26 34.6	28 56.2	26 1.0	9 16.2	2 36.4	26 21.5	7 25.8	6 30.4
7 F	17 4 27.9	15 15.1	29 13.3	9♉57.0	27 59.9	29 42.0	26 9.3	9 27.2	2 31.8	26 24.3	7 28.1	6 31.6
8 S	17 8 24.4	16 16.0	29 10.1	24 28.6	29 26.2	0♒26.8	26 18.3	9 38.3	2 27.1	26 27.1	7 30.3	6 32.6
9 S	17 12 21.0	17 16.9	29 6.9	9♊20.2	0♐53.4	1 10.6	26 27.9	9 49.5	2 22.5	26 29.8	7 32.6	6 33.7
10 M	17 16 17.5	18 17.9	29 3.7	24 24.3	2 21.3	1 53.4	26 38.2	10 0.9	2 17.7	26 32.5	7 34.8	6 34.7
11 T	17 20 14.1	19 18.9	29 0.6	9♋32.0	3 49.8	2 35.0	26 49.1	10 12.3	2 13.0	26 35.2	7 37.0	6 35.7
12 W	17 24 10.6	20 19.8	28 57.4	24 34.1	5 18.9	3 15.5	27 0.6	10 23.8	2 8.2	26 37.8	7 39.2	6 36.6
13 T	17 28 7.2	21 20.8	28 54.2	9♌22.7	6 48.5	3 54.8	27 12.8	10 35.4	2 3.4	26 40.4	7 41.5	6 37.6
14 F	17 32 3.8	22 21.8	28 51.0	23 52.0	8 18.5	4 32.8	27 25.5	10 47.1	1 58.5	26 42.9	7 43.7	6 38.5
15 S	17 36 0.3	23 22.9	28 47.9	7♍58.4	9 48.8	5 9.5	27 38.8	10 58.9	1 53.7	26 45.4	7 45.9	6 39.3
16 S	17 39 56.9	24 23.9	28 44.7	21 41.0	11 19.6	5 44.9	27 52.7	11 10.8	1 48.8	26 47.9	7 48.0	6 40.1
17 M	17 43 53.4	25 25.0	28 41.5	5♎ 0.5	12 50.6	6 18.8	28 7.1	11 22.7	1 43.9	26 50.3	7 50.2	6 40.9
18 T	17 47 50.0	26 26.1	28 38.3	17 59.1	14 21.9	6 51.3	28 22.1	11 34.8	1 38.9	26 52.6	7 52.4	6 41.7
19 W	17 51 46.6	27 27.2	28 35.2	0♏39.5	15 53.4	7 22.3	28 37.6	11 46.9	1 34.0	26 54.9	7 54.5	6 42.4
20 T	17 55 43.1	28 28.3	28 32.0	13 4.7	17 25.2	7 51.8	28 53.7	11 59.2	1 29.0	26 57.2	7 56.7	6 43.1
21 F	17 59 39.7	29 29.4	28 28.8	25 17.5	18 57.2	8 19.6	29 10.2	12 11.5	1 24.1	26 59.5	7 58.8	6 43.8
22 S	18 3 36.2	0♑30.5	28 25.6	7♐20.8	20 29.5	8 45.7	29 27.3	12 23.8	1 19.1	27 1.6	8 1.0	6 44.4
23 S	18 7 32.8	1 31.6	28 22.5	19 16.9	22 2.0	9 10.0	29 44.9	12 36.3	1 14.1	27 3.8	8 3.1	6 45.0
24 M	18 11 29.3	2 32.8	28 19.3	1♑ 8.0	23 34.7	9 32.5	0♉ 2.9	12 48.8	1 9.2	27 5.9	8 5.2	6 45.5
25 T	18 15 25.9	3 34.0	28 16.1	12 56.2	25 7.7	9 53.1	0 21.5	13 1.5	1 4.2	27 8.0	8 7.3	6 46.1
26 W	18 19 22.5	4 35.1	28 12.9	24 43.6	26 40.9	10 11.8	0 40.5	13 14.2	0 59.3	27 9.9	8 9.4	6 46.6
27 T	18 23 19.0	5 36.3	28 9.7	6♒32.4	28 14.3	10 28.4	0 59.9	13 26.9	0 54.3	27 11.9	8 11.5	6 47.0
28 F	18 27 15.6	6 37.5	28 6.6	18 25.2	29 48.0	10 42.9	1 19.8	13 39.7	0 49.4	27 13.8	8 13.5	6 47.4
29 S	18 31 12.1	7 38.6	28 3.4	0♓24.9	1♑22.0	10 55.2	1 40.1	13 52.6	0 44.5	27 15.6	8 15.5	6 47.8
30 S	18 35 8.7	8 39.8	28 0.2	12 34.8	2 56.2	11 5.3	2 0.9	14 5.6	0 39.6	27 17.4	8 17.6	6 48.1
31 M	18 39 5.3	9 40.9	27 57.0	24 58.5	4 30.8	11 13.1	2 22.0	14 18.6	0 34.7	27 19.2	8 19.6	6 48.4

DECLINATION at NOON

DAY	EPHEMERIS SIDEREAL TIME h m s	☉	☊	☽	☿	♀	♂	♃	♄	♅	♆	♇
1 S	16 40 48.5	21S49.6	23S26.5	10S17.6	15S43.8	24S 0.9	10N 7.4	18S53.1	22N19.6	9S33.3	19S59.8	12N27.0
4 T	16 52 38.2	22 15.5	23 26.5	4N26.7	17 2.8	23 20.8	10 20.0	18 44.7	22 20.0	9 36.5	20 0.9	12 27.0
7 F	17 4 27.9	22 37.6	23 26.4	18 34.0	18 22.2	22 37.8	10 34.4	18 35.9	22 20.4	9 39.5	20 2.0	12 27.1
10 M	17 16 17.5	22 55.6	23 26.3	23 42.6	19 38.4	21 52.5	10 50.6	18 26.8	22 20.9	9 42.4	20 3.0	12 27.3
13 T	17 28 7.2	23 9.6	23 26.3	14 33.8	20 49.0	21 5.3	11 8.3	18 17.4	22 21.3	9 45.2	20 4.1	12 27.7
16 S	17 39 56.9	23 19.4	23 26.2	1S32.3	21 52.2	20 16.9	11 27.5	18 7.7	22 21.8	9 47.8	20 5.1	12 28.2
19 W	17 51 46.6	23 25.1	23 26.1	15 54.7	22 46.8	19 27.7	11 48.1	17 57.7	22 22.3	9 50.3	20 6.1	12 28.9
22 S	18 3 36.2	23 26.5	23 26.0	23 26.4	23 31.8	18 38.5	12 9.8	17 47.3	22 22.7	9 52.7	20 7.1	12 29.7
25 T	18 15 25.9	23 23.6	23 25.9	21 30.3	24 6.3	17 49.9	12 32.7	17 36.7	22 23.1	9 54.9	20 8.1	12 30.6
28 F	18 27 15.6	23 16.6	23 25.7	11 27.3	24 29.6	17 2.6	12 56.6	17 25.7	22 23.6	9 56.9	20 9.0	12 31.7
31 M	18 39 5.3	23 5.3	23 25.6	2N50.9	24 41.2	16 17.5	13 21.3	17 14.5	22 24.0	9 58.8	20 9.9	12 32.9

JANUARY 1974

LONGITUDE at NOON

DAY	EPHEMERIS SIDEREAL TIME h m s	☉ ° ′	☊ ° ′	☽ ° ′	☿ ° ′	♀ ° ′	♂ ° ′	♃ ° ′	♄ ° ′	♅ ° ′	♆ ° ′	♇ ° ′
1 T	18 43 1.8	10♑42.1	27♐53.9	7♈40.0	6♑ 5.6	11♒18.6	2♉43.5	14♒31.6	0♋29.8	27♎20.9	8♐21.5	6♎48.7
2 W	18 46 58.4	11 43.3	27 50.7	20 42.9	7 40.8	11 21.7	3 5.4	14 44.8	0R25.0	27 22.5	8 23.5	6 49.0
3 T	18 50 54.9	12 44.4	27 47.5	4♉10.3	9 16.3	11 22.3	3 27.7	14 58.0	0 20.2	27 24.1	8 25.5	6 49.2
4 F	18 54 51.5	13 45.6	27 44.3	18 4.3	10 52.2	11R20.5	3 50.3	15 11.2	0 15.4	27 25.6	8 27.4	6 49.3
5 S	18 58 48.0	14 46.7	27 41.2	2♊24.9	12 28.4	11 16.1	4 13.3	15 24.5	0 10.7	27 27.1	8 29.3	6 49.4
6 S	19 2 44.6	15 47.8	27 38.0	17 9.7	14 5.0	11 9.2	4 36.7	15 37.9	0 6.0	27 28.6	8 31.2	6 49.5
7 M	19 6 41.2	16 49.0	27 34.8	2♋13.3	15 42.0	10 59.7	5 0.4	15 51.3	0 1.4	27 30.0	8 33.1	6 49.6
8 T	19 10 37.7	17 50.1	27 31.6	17 27.7	17 19.4	10 47.7	5 24.4	16 4.8	29♊56.8	27 31.3	8 34.9	6 49.6
9 W	19 14 34.3	18 51.2	27 28.5	2♌43.2	18 57.2	10 33.2	5 48.7	16 18.3	29 52.2	27 32.6	8 36.8	6 49.6
10 T	19 18 30.8	19 52.3	27 25.3	17 49.3	20 35.5	10 16.3	6 13.3	16 31.9	29 47.7	27 33.8	8 38.6	6 49.6
11 F	19 22 27.4	20 53.4	27 22.1	2♍37.3	22 14.2	9 57.0	6 38.2	16 45.5	29 43.2	27 35.0	8 40.4	6R49.5
12 S	19 26 23.9	21 54.6	27 18.9	17 0.7	23 53.4	9 35.3	7 3.4	16 59.1	29 38.8	27 36.1	8 42.2	6 49.4
13 S	19 30 20.5	22 55.7	27 15.7	0♎56.0	25 33.0	9 11.4	7 28.9	17 12.8	29 34.4	27 37.1	8 43.9	6 49.2
14 M	19 34 17.1	23 56.8	27 12.6	14 22.9	27 13.1	8 45.4	7 54.6	17 26.6	29 30.2	27 38.1	8 45.6	6 49.1
15 T	19 38 13.6	24 57.9	27 9.4	27 23.3	28 53.7	8 17.4	8 20.7	17 40.4	29 26.0	27 39.2	8 47.4	6 48.9
16 W	19 42 10.2	25 59.1	27 6.2	10♏ 0.7	0♒34.7	7 47.6	8 47.0	17 54.2	29 21.8	27 40.0	8 49.1	6 48.6
17 T	19 46 6.7	27 0.2	27 3.0	22 19.4	2 16.1	7 16.2	9 13.6	18 8.1	29 17.7	27 40.9	8 50.7	6 48.4
18 F	19 50 3.3	28 1.3	26 59.9	4♐24.0	3 58.0	6 43.3	9 40.4	18 22.0	29 13.6	27 41.7	8 52.4	6 48.0
19 S	19 53 59.8	29 2.4	26 56.7	16 18.9	5 40.2	6 9.1	10 7.5	18 36.0	29 9.7	27 42.4	8 54.0	6 47.7
20 S	19 57 56.4	0♒ 3.4	26 53.5	28 8.0	7 22.8	5 33.9	10 34.8	18 50.0	29 5.8	27 43.1	8 55.6	6 47.3
21 M	20 1 53.0	1 4.5	26 50.3	9♑54.8	9 5.7	4 57.8	11 2.3	19 4.0	29 1.9	27 43.7	8 57.1	6 46.9
22 T	20 5 49.5	2 5.6	26 47.2	21 42.1	10 48.8	4 21.3	11 30.1	19 18.0	28 58.2	27 44.3	8 58.7	6 46.4
23 W	20 9 46.1	3 6.6	26 44.0	3♒32.3	12 32.1	3 44.4	11 58.1	19 32.1	28 54.5	27 44.8	9 0.2	6 45.9
24 T	20 13 42.6	4 7.7	26 40.8	15 27.1	14 15.5	3 7.4	12 26.3	19 46.2	28 50.9	27 45.2	9 1.7	6 45.4
25 F	20 17 39.2	5 8.7	26 37.6	27 28.2	15 58.8	2 30.7	12 54.8	20 0.3	28 47.4	27 45.6	9 3.1	6 44.9
26 S	20 21 35.7	6 9.7	26 34.4	9♓37.2	17 41.9	1 54.4	13 23.4	20 14.5	28 44.0	27 45.9	9 4.6	6 44.3
27 S	20 25 32.3	7 10.7	26 31.3	21 55.8	19 24.6	1 18.8	13 52.3	20 28.7	28 40.6	27 46.2	9 6.0	6 43.7
28 M	20 29 28.8	8 11.7	26 28.1	4♈25.8	21 6.7	0 44.1	14 21.3	20 42.9	28 37.4	27 46.4	9 7.3	6 43.0
29 T	20 33 25.4	9 12.7	26 24.9	17 9.6	22 48.1	0 10.6	14 50.6	20 57.1	28 34.2	27 46.6	9 8.7	6 42.3
30 W	20 37 22.0	10 13.6	26 21.7	0♉ 9.8	24 28.4	29♑38.4	15 20.0	21 11.4	28 31.2	27 46.7	9 10.0	6 41.6
31 T	20 41 18.5	11 14.5	26 18.6	13 29.1	26 7.2	29 7.9	15 49.6	21 25.6	28 28.2	27 46.8	9 11.3	6 40.9

DECLINATION at NOON

DAY	EPHEMERIS SIDEREAL TIME h m s	☉	☊	☽	☿	♀	♂	♃	♄	♅	♆	♇
1 T	18 43 1.8	23S 0.6	23S25.5	7N50.2	24S42.4	16S 3.0	13N29.7	17S10.7	22N24.2	9S59.4	20S10.1	12N33.3
4 F	18 54 51.5	22 43.9	23 25.4	20 30.8	24 37.5	15 21.9	13 55.4	16 59.1	22 24.6	10 1.0	20 11.0	12 34.7
7 M	19 6 41.2	22 23.0	23 25.2	23 5.3	24 19.7	14 44.7	14 21.7	16 47.3	22 25.0	10 2.5	20 11.8	12 36.2
10 T	19 18 30.8	21 58.3	23 25.0	11 41.3	23 48.5	14 12.0	14 48.4	16 35.2	22 25.4	10 3.8	20 12.6	12 37.8
13 S	19 30 20.5	21 29.6	23 24.8	5S11.1	23 3.6	13 44.5	15 15.4	16 22.9	22 25.8	10 4.9	20 13.3	12 39.4
16 W	19 42 10.2	20 57.2	23 24.6	18 32.6	22 4.8	13 22.5	15 42.7	16 10.3	22 26.2	10 5.9	20 14.0	12 41.2
19 S	19 53 59.8	20 21.2	23 24.4	23 50.0	20 51.9	13 6.3	16 10.2	15 57.5	22 26.6	10 6.7	20 14.6	12 43.1
22 T	20 5 49.5	19 41.8	23 24.2	19 39.1	19 25.2	12 55.9	16 37.7	15 44.5	22 27.1	10 7.3	20 15.2	12 45.1
25 F	20 17 39.2	18 59.0	23 24.0	8 9.7	17 45.3	12 51.1	17 5.2	15 31.3	22 27.5	10 7.7	20 15.8	12 47.2
28 M	20 29 28.8	18 13.1	23 23.7	6N28.2	15 53.3	12 51.4	17 32.6	15 17.9	22 27.9	10 7.9	20 16.3	12 49.4
31 T	20 41 18.5	17 24.3	23 23.5	19 19.5	13 51.7	12 56.1	17 59.8	15 4.3	22 28.3	10 7.9	20 16.8	12 51.6

FEBRUARY 1974

LONGITUDE at NOON

DAY	EPHEMERIS SIDEREAL TIME h m s	☉ ° ′	☊ ° ′	☽ ° ′	☿ ° ′	♀ ° ′	♂ ° ′	♃ ° ′	♄ ° ′	♅ ° ′	♆ ° ′	♇ ° ′
1 F	20 45 15.1	12♒15.4	26♐15.4	27♉ 9.7	27♒44.3	28♑39.0	16♉19.4	21♒39.9	28♊25.3	27♎46.8	9♐12.6	6♎40.1
2 S	20 49 11.6	13 16.3	26 12.2	11♊13.2	29 19.1	28R12.1	16 49.4	21 54.2	28R22.5	27R46.7	9 13.8	6R39.3
3 S	20 53 8.2	14 17.2	26 9.0	25 39.5	0♓51.2	27 47.2	17 19.5	22 8.5	28 19.8	27 46.6	9 15.0	6 38.5
4 M	20 57 4.7	15 18.0	26 5.9	10♋26.0	2 20.1	27 24.4	17 49.8	22 22.9	28 17.2	27 46.4	9 16.2	6 37.6
5 T	21 1 1.3	16 18.8	26 2.7	25 27.6	3 45.1	27 4.0	18 20.3	22 37.2	28 14.8	27 46.3	9 17.4	6 36.8
6 W	21 4 57.8	17 19.6	25 59.5	10♌36.3	5 5.6	26 45.9	18 50.9	22 51.6	28 12.4	27 46.0	9 18.5	6 35.8
7 T	21 8 54.4	18 20.4	25 56.3	25 42.4	6 20.9	26 30.2	19 21.6	23 5.9	28 10.1	27 45.6	9 19.5	6 34.9
8 F	21 12 51.0	19 21.1	25 53.1	10♍36.0	7 30.3	26 17.0	19 52.5	23 20.3	28 7.9	27 45.3	9 20.6	6 33.9
9 S	21 16 47.5	20 21.9	25 50.0	25 8.6	8 33.0	26 6.2	20 23.5	23 34.7	28 5.9	27 44.8	9 21.6	6 32.9
10 S	21 20 44.1	21 22.6	25 46.8	9♎14.4	9 28.3	25 58.0	20 54.7	23 49.1	28 3.9	27 44.3	9 22.6	6 31.9
11 M	21 24 40.6	22 23.3	25 43.6	22 50.8	10 15.3	25 52.3	21 26.0	24 3.5	28 2.0	27 43.8	9 23.6	6 30.8
12 T	21 28 37.2	23 23.9	25 40.4	5♏58.4	10 53.6	25 49.0	21 57.4	24 17.8	28 0.2	27 43.2	9 24.5	6 29.8
13 W	21 32 33.7	24 24.6	25 37.3	18 40.0	11 22.4	25 48.3	22 28.9	24 32.2	27 58.6	27 42.5	9 25.4	6 28.6
14 T	21 36 30.3	25 25.2	25 34.1	1♐ 0.2	11 41.2	25D50.0	23 0.6	24 46.6	27 57.0	27 41.8	9 26.3	6 27.5
15 F	21 40 26.8	26 25.8	25 30.9	13 4.0	11 49.8	25 54.0	23 32.4	25 1.0	27 55.6	27 41.0	9 27.1	6 26.4
16 S	21 44 23.4	27 26.4	25 27.7	24 56.8	11R47.9	26 0.4	24 4.3	25 15.4	27 54.2	27 40.2	9 27.9	6 25.2
17 S	21 48 19.9	28 27.0	25 24.5	6♑44.0	11 35.6	26 9.1	24 36.4	25 29.8	27 53.0	27 39.3	9 28.7	6 24.0
18 M	21 52 16.5	29 27.5	25 21.4	18 30.1	11 13.1	26 20.0	25 8.5	25 44.2	27 51.9	27 38.4	9 29.4	6 22.7
19 T	21 56 13.1	0♓28.1	25 18.2	0♒19.1	10 41.2	26 33.0	25 40.8	25 58.6	27 50.9	27 37.4	9 30.1	6 21.5
20 W	22 0 9.6	1 28.6	25 15.0	12 14.0	10 0.4	26 48.2	26 13.2	26 13.0	27 50.0	27 36.4	9 30.8	6 20.2
21 T	22 4 6.2	2 29.0	25 11.8	24 17.3	9 11.9	27 5.4	26 45.6	26 27.3	27 49.2	27 35.4	9 31.4	6 18.9
22 F	22 8 2.7	3 29.5	25 8.7	6♓30.2	8 17.1	27 24.5	27 18.2	26 41.7	27 48.6	27 34.2	9 32.0	6 17.6
23 S	22 11 59.3	4 29.9	25 5.5	18 53.7	7 17.2	27 45.6	27 50.9	26 56.0	27 48.0	27 33.1	9 32.6	6 16.3
24 S	22 15 55.8	5 30.3	25 2.3	1♈28.0	6 14.1	28 8.5	28 23.7	27 10.4	27 47.6	27 31.8	9 33.1	6 14.9
25 M	22 19 52.4	6 30.7	24 59.1	14 13.3	5 9.1	28 33.1	28 56.6	27 24.7	27 47.2	27 30.6	9 33.6	6 13.5
26 T	22 23 48.9	7 31.1	24 55.9	27 10.2	4 4.2	28 59.5	29 29.7	27 39.0	27 47.1	27 29.3	9 34.1	6 12.2
27 W	22 27 45.5	8 31.4	24 52.8	10♉19.2	3 0.6	29 27.4	0♊ 2.7	27 53.3	27 47.0	27 27.9	9 34.5	6 10.8
28 T	22 31 42.0	9 31.6	24 49.6	23 41.4	1 59.9	29 57.0	0 35.9	28 7.6	27 47.0	27 26.5	9 34.9	6 9.3

DECLINATION at NOON

DAY	EPHEMERIS SIDEREAL TIME h m s	☉	☊	☽	☿	♀	♂	♃	♄	♅	♆	♇
1 F	20 45 15.1	17S 7.4	23S23.4	22N 5.0	13S 9.6	12S58.6	18N 8.8	14S59.8	22N28.5	10S 7.9	20S16.9	12N52.3
4 M	20 57 4.7	16 15.0	23 23.1	21 53.7	11 1.8	13 8.1	18 35.6	14 46.0	22 28.9	10 7.7	20 17.4	12 54.6
7 T	21 8 54.4	15 20.0	23 22.8	8 50.8	8 57.1	13 20.0	19 2.0	14 32.1	22 29.4	10 7.4	20 17.7	12 57.0
10 S	21 20 44.1	14 22.7	23 22.5	8S15.1	7 5.3	13 33.4	19 27.9	14 18.0	22 29.8	10 6.8	20 18.1	12 59.4
13 W	21 32 33.7	13 23.2	23 22.2	20 25.4	5 37.5	13 47.4	19 53.2	14 3.9	22 30.3	10 6.1	20 18.3	13 1.8
16 S	21 44 23.4	12 21.8	23 21.9	23 30.8	4 44.6	14 1.1	20 18.0	13 49.6	22 30.8	10 5.2	20 18.6	13 4.3
19 T	21 56 13.1	11 18.5	23 21.5	17 20.2	4 33.9	14 13.9	20 42.1	13 35.2	22 31.3	10 4.2	20 18.7	13 6.8
22 F	22 8 2.7	10 13.7	23 21.2	4 42.9	5 5.4	14 25.1	21 5.4	13 20.8	22 31.9	10 2.9	20 18.9	13 9.3
25 M	22 19 52.4	9 7.4	23 20.8	10N 0.3	6 9.9	14 34.1	21 27.9	13 6.3	22 32.4	10 1.6	20 19.0	13 11.8
28 T	22 31 42.0	7 59.9	23 20.5	21 15.9	7 31.4	14 40.3	21 49.6	12 51.7	22 33.0	10 0.1	20 19.0	13 14.2

MARCH 1974

DAY	EPHEMERIS SIDEREAL TIME	☉	☊	☽	☿	♀	♂	♃	♄	♅	♆	♇
	h m s	° ′	° ′	° ′	° ′	° ′	° ′	° ′	° ′	° ′	° ′	° ′
LONGITUDE at NOON												
1 F	22 35 38.6	10♓31.9	24♐46.4	7♊18.2	1♓ 3.2	0♒28.0	1♊ 9.2	28♒21.8	27♊47.1	27♎25.1	9♐35.3	6♎ 7.9
2 S	22 39 35.1	11 32.1	24 43.2	21 11.0	0R11.5	1 0.6	1 42.5	28 36.1	27D47.4	27R23.6	9 35.6	6R 6.4
3 S	22 43 31.7	12 32.2	24 40.1	5♋20.3	29♒25.5	1 34.5	2 15.9	28 50.3	27 47.7	27 22.0	9 35.9	6 5.0
4 M	22 47 28.3	13 32.4	24 36.9	19 45.4	28 45.9	2 9.8	2 49.4	29 4.4	27 48.2	27 20.4	9 36.2	6 3.5
5 T	22 51 24.8	14 32.4	24 33.7	4♌23.7	28 12.9	2 46.3	3 23.0	29 18.6	27 48.8	27 18.8	9 36.4	6 2.0
6 W	22 55 21.4	15 32.5	24 30.5	19 10.2	27 46.7	3 24.2	3 56.7	29 32.7	27 49.5	27 17.1	9 36.6	6 0.4
7 T	22 59 17.9	16 32.5	24 27.3	3♍57.7	27 27.4	4 3.2	4 30.4	29 46.8	27 50.3	27 15.4	9 36.8	5 58.9
8 F	23 3 14.5	17 32.5	24 24.2	18 38.0	27 14.9	4 43.4	5 4.2	0♓ 0.9	27 51.2	27 13.7	9 36.9	5 57.3
9 S	23 7 11.0	18 32.5	24 21.0	3♎ 3.2	27 8.9	5 24.7	5 38.0	0 15.0	27 52.2	27 11.9	9 37.0	5 55.8
10 S	23 11 7.6	19 32.4	24 17.8	17 6.7	27D 9.4	6 7.1	6 11.9	0 29.0	27 53.4	27 10.1	9 37.1	5 54.2
11 M	23 15 4.1	20 32.3	24 14.6	0♏44.5	27 16.0	6 50.6	6 45.9	0 43.0	27 54.6	27 8.2	9 37.1	5 52.6
12 T	23 19 0.7	21 32.2	24 11.5	13 55.7	27 28.4	7 35.0	7 20.0	0 56.9	27 56.0	27 6.3	9 37.1	5 51.0
13 W	23 22 57.2	22 32.0	24 8.3	26 41.5	27 46.3	8 20.3	7 54.1	1 10.8	27 57.5	27 4.4	9R37.0	5 49.4
14 T	23 26 53.8	23 31.9	24 5.1	9♐ 5.3	28 9.3	9 6.6	8 28.3	1 24.7	27 59.0	27 2.4	9 37.0	5 47.8
15 F	23 30 50.3	24 31.6	24 1.9	21 12.0	28 37.3	9 53.8	9 2.5	1 38.6	28 0.7	27 0.4	9 36.9	5 46.2
16 S	23 34 46.9	25 31.4	23 58.7	3♑ 6.9	29 9.8	10 41.8	9 36.8	1 52.4	28 2.5	26 58.3	9 36.7	5 44.6
17 S	23 38 43.4	26 31.1	23 55.6	14 55.5	29 46.6	11 30.6	10 11.1	2 6.1	28 4.4	26 56.3	9 36.6	5 42.9
18 M	23 42 40.0	27 30.8	23 52.4	26 43.3	0♓27.5	12 20.1	10 45.5	2 19.9	28 6.4	26 54.1	9 36.3	5 41.3
19 T	23 46 36.5	28 30.6	23 49.2	8♒35.2	1 12.1	13 10.5	11 20.0	2 33.6	28 8.6	26 52.1	9 36.2	5 39.7
20 W	23 50 33.1	29 30.2	23 46.0	20 35.3	2 0.3	14 1.5	11 54.6	2 47.3	28 10.8	26 49.9	9 35.9	5 38.1
21 T	23 54 29.7	0♈29.8	23 42.9	2♓46.6	2 51.7	14 53.2	12 29.1	3 0.9	28 13.2	26 47.7	9 35.6	5 36.4
22 F	23 58 26.2	1 29.4	23 39.7	15 11.4	3 46.3	15 45.6	13 3.8	3 14.4	28 15.6	26 45.5	9 35.2	5 34.7
23 S	0 2 22.8	2 28.9	23 36.5	27 50.4	4 43.9	16 38.6	13 38.5	3 27.9	28 18.1	26 43.2	9 34.9	5 33.1
24 S	0 6 19.3	3 28.5	23 33.3	10♈43.6	5 44.2	17 32.2	14 13.2	3 41.4	28 20.8	26 40.9	9 34.5	5 31.4
25 M	0 10 15.9	4 27.9	23 30.1	23 49.9	6 47.1	18 26.4	14 48.0	3 54.8	28 23.5	26 38.6	9 34.0	5 29.8
26 T	0 14 12.4	5 27.4	23 27.0	7♉ 8.1	7 52.5	19 21.1	15 22.8	4 8.2	28 26.4	26 36.3	9 33.6	5 28.1
27 W	0 18 9.0	6 26.8	23 23.8	20 36.6	9 0.2	20 16.4	15 57.7	4 21.5	28 29.3	26 33.9	9 33.1	5 26.4
28 T	0 22 5.5	7 26.2	23 20.6	4♊14.5	10 10.2	21 12.1	16 32.6	4 34.7	28 32.4	26 31.6	9 32.6	5 24.8
29 F	0 26 2.1	8 25.5	23 17.4	18 1.1	11 22.4	22 8.4	17 7.6	4 47.9	28 35.6	26 29.2	9 32.0	5 23.1
30 S	0 29 58.6	9 24.8	23 14.3	1♋56.3	12 36.6	23 5.1	17 42.6	5 1.0	28 38.8	26 26.8	9 31.4	5 21.4
31 S	0 33 55.2	10 24.0	23 11.1	15 59.8	13 52.8	24 2.4	18 17.7	5 14.1	28 42.2	26 24.3	9 30.8	5 19.8
DECLINATION at NOON												
1 F	22 35 38.6	7S37.2	23S20.4	23N 4.4	7S59.4	14S41.8	21N56.6	12S46.9	22N33.2	9S59.5	20S19.0	13N15.1
4 M	22 47 28.3	6 28.4	23 20.0	19 54.8	9 18.6	14 43.8	22 17.0	12 32.3	22 33.8	9 57.8	20 19.0	13 17.5
7 T	22 59 17.9	5 18.8	23 19.6	5 41.3	10 23.6	14 42.3	22 36.4	12 17.7	22 34.4	9 56.0	20 19.0	13 20.0
10 S	23 11 7.6	4 8.5	23 19.2	10S59.4	11 9.8	14 36.8	22 54.7	12 3.1	22 35.0	9 54.0	20 18.9	13 22.4
13 W	23 22 57.2	2 57.8	23 18.8	21 40.1	11 36.1	14 27.3	23 11.9	11 48.6	22 35.6	9 51.9	20 18.7	13 24.8
16 S	23 34 46.9	1 46.8	23 18.3	22 35.8	11 43.3	14 13.5	23 28.0	11 34.1	22 36.3	9 49.7	20 18.5	13 27.1
19 T	23 46 36.5	0 35.6	23 17.9	14 41.4	11 32.5	13 55.3	23 42.9	11 19.6	22 36.9	9 47.4	20 18.3	13 29.3
22 F	23 58 26.2	0N35.6	23 17.4	1 15.8	11 5.4	13 32.8	23 56.6	11 5.2	22 37.6	9 45.0	20 18.0	13 31.5
25 M	0 10 15.9	1 46.5	23 17.0	13N14.2	10 23.0	13 6.0	24 9.0	10 51.0	22 38.2	9 42.5	20 17.7	13 33.6
28 T	0 22 5.5	2 57.1	23 16.5	22 32.1	9 26.6	12 34.9	24 20.0	10 36.8	22 38.8	9 40.0	20 17.3	13 35.7
31 S	0 33 55.2	4 7.1	23 16.0	20 27.4	8 17.1	11 59.6	24 29.8	10 22.8	22 39.4	9 37.3	20 16.9	13 37.6

APRIL 1974

DAY	EPHEMERIS SIDEREAL TIME	☉	☊	☽	☿	♀	♂	♃	♄	♅	♆	♇
LONGITUDE at NOON												
1 M	0 37 51.7	11♈23.3	23♐ 7.9	0♌11.1	15♓10.9	25♒ 0.0	18♊52.8	5♓27.1	28♊45.6	26♎21.9	9♐30.1	5♎18.1
2 T	0 41 48.3	12 22.4	23 4.7	14 28.7	16 30.9	25 58.1	19 27.9	5 40.1	28 49.1	26R19.4	9R29.5	5R16.5
3 W	0 45 44.8	13 21.6	23 1.5	28 49.9	17 52.7	26 56.6	20 3.1	5 53.0	28 52.8	26 16.9	9 28.8	5 14.8
4 T	0 49 41.4	14 20.7	22 58.4	13♍10.4	19 16.2	27 55.5	20 38.3	6 5.8	28 56.5	26 14.5	9 28.0	5 13.2
5 F	0 53 37.9	15 19.7	22 55.2	27 24.9	20 41.4	28 54.8	21 13.5	6 18.5	29 0.3	26 12.0	9 27.3	5 11.5
6 S	0 57 34.5	16 18.8	22 52.0	11♎27.9	22 8.3	29 54.5	21 48.8	6 31.2	29 4.2	26 9.4	9 26.5	5 9.9
7 S	1 1 31.0	17 17.8	22 48.8	25 14.4	23 36.9	0♓54.5	22 24.1	6 43.9	29 8.2	26 6.9	9 25.6	5 8.3
8 M	1 5 27.6	18 16.7	22 45.7	8♏41.0	25 7.1	1 54.9	22 59.4	6 56.4	29 12.3	26 4.4	9 24.8	5 6.7
9 T	1 9 24.2	19 15.7	22 42.5	21 45.8	26 38.9	2 55.7	23 34.8	7 8.9	29 16.6	26 1.9	9 24.0	5 5.1
10 W	1 13 20.7	20 14.6	22 39.3	4♐29.2	28 12.3	3 56.8	24 10.2	7 21.4	29 20.8	25 59.3	9 23.1	5 3.5
11 T	1 17 17.3	21 13.5	22 36.1	16 53.2	29 47.3	4 58.2	24 45.6	7 33.7	29 25.2	25 56.8	9 22.1	5 1.9
12 F	1 21 13.8	22 12.3	22 32.9	29 1.4	1♈23.8	5 59.9	25 21.1	7 46.0	29 29.6	25 54.2	9 21.2	5 0.4
13 S	1 25 10.4	23 11.1	22 29.8	10♑58.3	3 2.0	7 1.9	25 56.6	7 58.2	29 34.2	25 51.6	9 20.2	4 58.8
14 S	1 29 6.9	24 9.9	22 26.6	22 49.1	4 41.7	8 4.2	26 32.1	8 10.3	29 38.8	25 49.0	9 19.2	4 57.2
15 M	1 33 3.5	25 8.6	22 23.4	4♒38.9	6 23.0	9 6.7	27 7.6	8 22.3	29 43.5	25 46.5	9 18.1	4 55.7
16 T	1 37 0.0	26 7.3	22 20.2	16 33.0	8 5.9	10 9.6	27 43.2	8 34.3	29 48.2	25 43.9	9 17.1	4 54.2
17 W	1 40 56.6	27 6.0	22 17.1	28 36.4	9 50.3	11 12.7	28 18.8	8 46.2	29 53.1	25 41.3	9 16.0	4 52.6
18 T	1 44 53.1	28 4.7	22 13.9	10♓52.9	11 36.4	12 16.0	28 54.5	8 57.9	29 58.0	25 38.7	9 14.9	4 51.1
19 F	1 48 49.7	29 3.3	22 10.7	23 25.7	13 24.1	13 19.6	29 30.1	9 9.7	0♋ 3.1	25 36.2	9 13.8	4 49.7
20 S	1 52 46.2	0♉ 1.9	22 7.5	6♈16.6	15 13.4	14 23.4	0♋ 5.8	9 21.3	0 8.1	25 33.6	9 12.6	4 48.2
21 S	1 56 42.8	1 0.5	22 4.3	19 26.0	17 4.3	15 27.4	0 41.6	9 32.8	0 13.3	25 31.0	9 11.4	4 46.7
22 M	2 0 39.3	1 59.1	22 1.2	2♉52.7	18 56.9	16 31.7	1 17.3	9 44.2	0 18.6	25 28.5	9 10.2	4 45.3
23 T	2 4 35.9	2 57.6	21 58.0	16 34.5	20 51.1	17 36.2	1 53.1	9 55.6	0 23.9	25 25.9	9 9.0	4 43.9
24 W	2 8 32.5	3 56.1	21 54.8	0♊28.2	22 46.9	18 40.8	2 28.9	10 6.8	0 29.3	25 23.4	9 7.8	4 42.5
25 T	2 12 29.0	4 54.5	21 51.6	14 30.6	24 44.3	19 45.7	3 4.8	10 18.0	0 34.8	25 20.9	9 6.5	4 41.1
26 F	2 16 25.6	5 52.9	21 48.5	28 38.5	26 43.3	20 50.7	3 40.6	10 29.1	0 40.3	25 18.3	9 5.2	4 39.7
27 S	2 20 22.1	6 51.3	21 45.3	12♋49.1	28 43.8	21 55.9	4 16.5	10 40.0	0 45.9	25 15.8	9 3.9	4 38.3
28 S	2 24 18.7	7 49.6	21 42.1	27 0.3	0♉45.9	23 1.3	4 52.4	10 50.9	0 51.6	25 13.3	9 2.6	4 37.0
29 M	2 28 15.2	8 47.9	21 38.9	11♌10.4	2 49.4	24 6.9	5 28.3	11 1.7	0 57.3	25 10.8	9 1.3	4 35.7
30 T	2 32 11.8	9 46.3	21 35.7	25 17.8	4 54.3	25 12.6	6 4.3	11 12.4	1 3.2	25 8.4	8 60.0	4 34.5
DECLINATION at NOON												
1 M	0 37 51.7	4N30.3	23S15.9	17N 4.1	7S51.2	11S46.9	24N32.7	10S18.1	22N39.7	9S36.5	20S16.8	13N38.3
4 T	0 49 41.4	5 39.4	23 15.4	2 0.3	6 25.6	11 6.2	24 40.6	10 4.3	22 40.3	9 33.8	20 16.4	13 40.1
7 S	1 1 31.0	6 47.5	23 14.8	13S40.6	4 48.7	10 21.6	24 47.1	9 50.6	22 40.9	9 31.0	20 15.9	13 41.8
10 W	1 13 20.7	7 54.7	23 14.3	22 28.6	3 1.2	9 33.3	24 52.2	9 37.1	22 41.4	9 28.3	20 15.4	13 43.4
13 S	1 25 10.4	9 0.7	23 13.8	21 15.2	1 3.8	8 41.4	24 55.8	9 23.9	22 42.0	9 25.5	20 14.8	13 44.9
16 T	1 37 0.0	10 5.3	23 13.2	11 51.1	1N 2.9	7 46.2	24 57.9	9 10.8	22 42.5	9 22.7	20 14.3	13 46.3
19 F	1 48 49.7	11 8.4	23 12.7	2N 4.6	3 17.9	6 47.9	24 58.6	8 58.1	22 43.0	9 19.9	20 13.7	13 47.5
22 M	2 0 39.3	12 9.9	23 12.1	16 1.1	5 40.3	5 46.9	24 57.8	8 45.5	22 43.4	9 17.2	20 13.1	13 48.6
25 T	2 12 29.0	13 9.6	23 11.5	23 2.8	8 8.5	4 43.3	24 55.5	8 33.3	22 43.8	9 14.4	20 12.4	13 49.6
28 S	2 24 18.7	14 7.3	23 10.9	17 42.6	10 40.5	3 37.5	24 51.7	8 21.4	22 44.1	9 11.7	20 11.7	13 50.5

MAY 1974

DAY	EPHEMERIS SIDEREAL TIME	☉	☊	☽	☿	♀	♂	♃	♄	♅	♆	♇
	h m s	° ′	° ′	° ′	° ′	° ′	° ′	° ′	° ′	° ′	° ′	° ′
						LONGITUDE at NOON						
1 W	2 36 8.3	10♉44.5	21♐32.6	9♍20.7	7♉ 0.4	26♓18.5	6♋40.3	11♓22.9	1♋ 9.1	25♎ 6.0	8♐58.6	4♎33.2
2 T	2 40 4.9	11 42.7	21 29.4	23 16.9	9 7.7	27 24.6	7 16.3	11 33.4	1 15.0	25R 3.5	8R57.2	4R31.9
3 F	2 44 1.4	12 40.9	21 26.2	7♎ 4.0	11 16.0	28 30.8	7 52.3	11 43.7	1 21.0	25 1.1	8 55.8	4 30.7
4 S	2 47 58.0	13 39.0	21 23.0	20 39.6	13 25.0	29 37.2	8 28.3	11 54.0	1 27.1	24 58.7	8 54.4	4 29.5
5 S	2 51 54.6	14 37.1	21 19.9	4♏ 1.3	15 34.7	0♈43.7	9 4.4	12 4.1	1 33.2	24 56.3	8 53.0	4 28.3
6 M	2 55 51.1	15 35.2	21 16.7	17 7.4	17 44.8	1 50.3	9 40.4	12 14.1	1 39.4	24 54.0	8 51.5	4 27.2
7 T	2 59 47.7	16 33.3	21 13.5	29 56.9	19 54.9	2 57.1	10 16.5	12 24.0	1 45.6	24 51.6	8 50.1	4 26.0
8 W	3 3 44.2	17 31.3	21 10.3	12♐30.1	22 5.0	4 4.0	10 52.6	12 33.8	1 51.9	24 49.3	8 48.6	4 24.9
9 T	3 7 40.8	18 29.3	21 7.1	24 48.4	24 14.6	5 11.1	11 28.7	12 43.5	1 58.3	24 47.0	8 47.1	4 23.8
10 F	3 11 37.3	19 27.3	21 4.0	6♑54.1	26 23.5	6 18.3	12 4.8	12 53.1	2 4.7	24 44.8	8 45.6	4 22.8
11 S	3 15 33.9	20 25.2	21 0.8	18 50.6	28 31.4	7 25.6	12 41.0	13 2.5	2 11.2	24 42.5	8 44.1	4 21.7
12 S	3 19 30.4	21 23.2	20 57.6	0♒42.0	0♊38.1	8 33.1	13 17.2	13 11.8	2 17.7	24 40.3	8 42.5	4 20.7
13 M	3 23 27.0	22 21.1	20 54.4	12 32.7	2 43.1	9 40.7	13 53.4	13 21.0	2 24.3	24 38.1	8 41.0	4 19.7
14 T	3 27 23.6	23 19.0	20 51.3	24 27.7	4 46.4	10 48.4	14 29.6	13 30.1	2 30.9	24 35.9	8 39.5	4 18.8
15 W	3 31 20.1	24 16.8	20 48.1	6♓31.7	6 47.6	11 56.2	15 5.8	13 39.1	2 37.6	24 33.8	8 37.9	4 17.8
16 T	3 35 16.7	25 14.7	20 44.9	18 49.4	8 46.6	13 4.1	15 42.1	13 47.9	2 44.3	24 31.7	8 36.3	4 16.9
17 F	3 39 13.2	26 12.5	20 41.7	1♈24.7	10 43.1	14 12.1	16 18.3	13 56.6	2 51.0	24 29.6	8 34.8	4 16.0
18 S	3 43 9.8	27 10.3	20 38.6	14 20.6	12 37.0	15 20.2	16 54.6	14 5.1	2 57.9	24 27.6	8 33.2	4 15.2
19 S	3 47 6.3	28 8.1	20 35.4	27 38.7	14 28.2	16 28.4	17 30.9	14 13.6	3 4.7	24 25.6	8 31.6	4 14.4
20 M	3 51 2.9	29 5.9	20 32.2	11♉18.8	16 16.6	17 36.8	18 7.3	14 21.9	3 11.6	24 23.6	8 30.0	4 13.6
21 T	3 54 59.4	0♊ 3.7	20 29.0	25 19.2	18 2.1	18 45.2	18 43.7	14 30.1	3 18.6	24 21.7	8 28.4	4 12.9
22 W	3 58 56.0	1 1.4	20 25.8	9♊36.0	19 44.6	19 53.7	19 20.0	14 38.1	3 25.6	24 19.8	8 26.8	4 12.1
23 T	4 2 52.6	1 59.1	20 22.7	24 4.4	21 24.0	21 2.3	19 56.4	14 46.0	3 32.7	24 18.0	8 25.2	4 11.4
24 F	4 6 49.1	2 56.8	20 19.5	8♋38.6	23 0.2	22 11.0	20 32.8	14 53.7	3 39.8	24 16.1	8 23.6	4 10.7
25 S	4 10 45.7	3 54.4	20 16.3	23 13.0	24 33.3	23 19.7	21 9.2	15 1.3	3 46.9	24 14.3	8 22.0	4 10.1
26 S	4 14 42.2	4 52.1	20 13.1	7♌42.5	26 3.2	24 28.6	21 45.7	15 8.8	3 54.0	24 12.6	8 20.4	4 9.5
27 M	4 18 38.8	5 49.7	20 10.0	22 3.2	27 29.9	25 37.5	22 22.1	15 16.1	4 1.2	24 10.9	8 18.7	4 8.9
28 T	4 22 35.3	6 47.2	20 6.8	6♍12.1	28 53.3	26 46.5	22 58.6	15 23.2	4 8.5	24 9.2	8 17.1	4 8.3
29 W	4 26 31.9	7 44.8	20 3.6	20 7.5	0♋13.3	27 55.5	23 35.1	15 30.2	4 15.7	24 7.6	8 15.5	4 7.8
30 T	4 30 28.5	8 42.3	20 0.4	3♎48.6	1 30.0	29 4.7	24 11.6	15 37.1	4 23.0	24 6.0	8 13.9	4 7.3
31 F	4 34 25.0	9 39.8	19 57.3	17 14.9	2 43.2	0♉13.9	24 48.1	15 43.8	4 30.3	24 4.4	8 12.2	4 6.9
						DECLINATION at NOON						
1 W	2 36 8.3	15N 2.9	23S 10.3	3N21.3	13N13.4	2S 29.7	24N46.4	8S 9.7	22N44.4	9S 9.1	20S 11.1	13N51.2
4 S	2 47 58.0	15 56.3	23 9.7	12S 11.3	15 43.1	1 20.1	24 39.5	7 58.5	22 44.7	9 6.5	20 10.4	13 51.8
7 T	2 59 47.7	16 47.3	23 9.1	21 51.5	18 4.7	0 9.1	24 31.2	7 47.6	22 44.9	9 3.9	20 9.6	13 52.2
10 F	3 11 37.3	17 35.7	23 8.5	21 42.4	20 12.6	1N 3.0	24 21.4	7 37.1	22 45.0	9 1.5	20 8.9	13 52.5
13 M	3 23 27.0	18 21.6	23 7.8	13 1.7	22 2.0	2 16.1	24 10.2	7 27.0	22 45.1	8 59.1	20 8.2	13 52.7
16 T	3 35 16.7	19 4.7	23 7.2	0N24.0	23 29.5	3 29.7	23 57.4	7 17.3	22 45.1	8 56.8	20 7.4	13 52.7
19 S	3 47 6.3	19 44.8	23 6.5	14 29.3	24 33.7	4 43.6	23 43.2	7 8.1	22 45.0	8 54.7	20 6.7	13 52.6
22 W	3 58 56.0	20 22.0	23 5.8	22 46.9	25 15.2	5 57.5	23 27.5	6 59.3	22 44.8	8 52.6	20 5.9	13 52.3
25 S	4 10 45.7	20 56.0	23 5.1	18 32.9	25 35.9	7 11.0	23 10.4	6 51.0	22 44.6	8 50.7	20 5.1	13 51.9
28 T	4 22 35.3	21 26.7	23 4.4	4 27.6	25 38.3	8 23.9	22 52.0	6 43.2	22 44.3	8 48.9	20 4.4	13 51.3
31 F	4 34 25.0	21 54.1	23 3.7	11S 5.1	25 25.3	9 35.8	22 32.1	6 35.9	22 43.9	8 47.2	20 3.6	13 50.6

JUNE 1974

DAY	EPHEMERIS SIDEREAL TIME	☉	☊	☽	☿	♀	♂	♃	♄	♅	♆	♇
						LONGITUDE at NOON						
1 S	4 38 21.6	10♊37.3	19♐54.1	0♏26.7	3♋53.0	1♉23.2	25♋24.6	15♓50.4	4♋37.7	24♎ 2.9	8♐10.6	4♎ 6.4
2 S	4 42 18.1	11 34.8	19 50.9	13 24.2	4 59.3	2 32.5	26 1.2	15 56.8	4 45.1	24R 1.4	8R 9.0	4R 6.0
3 M	4 46 14.7	12 32.3	19 47.7	26 8.1	6 1.9	3 42.0	26 37.7	16 3.0	4 52.5	24 0.0	8 7.4	4 5.7
4 T	4 50 11.2	13 29.7	19 44.5	8♐39.0	7 0.9	4 51.5	27 14.3	16 9.1	4 59.9	23 58.6	8 5.8	4 5.3
5 W	4 54 7.8	14 27.1	19 41.4	20 58.1	7 56.2	6 1.1	27 50.9	16 15.0	5 7.4	23 57.3	8 4.1	4 5.0
6 T	4 58 4.4	15 24.5	19 38.2	3♑ 6.8	8 47.7	7 10.7	28 27.5	16 20.8	5 14.9	23 56.0	8 2.5	4 4.7
7 F	5 2 0.9	16 21.9	19 35.0	15 6.9	9 35.2	8 20.4	29 4.1	16 26.4	5 22.4	23 54.8	8 0.9	4 4.5
8 S	5 5 57.5	17 19.3	19 31.8	27 0.8	10 18.8	9 30.2	29 40.7	16 31.8	5 30.0	23 53.6	7 59.3	4 4.3
9 S	5 9 54.0	18 16.6	19 28.7	8♒51.5	10 58.3	10 40.0	0♌17.3	16 37.1	5 37.5	23 52.4	7 57.7	4 4.1
10 M	5 13 50.6	19 14.0	19 25.5	20 42.4	11 33.7	11 50.0	0 54.0	16 42.2	5 45.1	23 51.3	7 56.1	4 4.0
11 T	5 17 47.1	20 11.4	19 22.3	2♓37.4	12 4.8	12 60.0	1 30.7	16 47.2	5 52.8	23 50.3	7 54.6	4 3.9
12 W	5 21 43.7	21 8.7	19 19.1	14 40.8	12 31.6	14 10.0	2 7.4	16 52.0	6 0.4	23 49.3	7 53.0	4 3.8
13 T	5 25 40.3	22 6.0	19 16.0	26 57.0	12 53.9	15 20.1	2 44.1	16 56.6	6 8.1	23 48.3	7 51.5	4 3.8
14 F	5 29 36.8	23 3.4	19 12.8	9♈30.3	13 11.8	16 30.3	3 20.9	17 1.0	6 15.7	23 47.4	7 49.9	4 3.8
15 S	5 33 33.4	24 0.7	19 9.6	22 24.6	13 25.2	17 40.5	3 57.6	17 5.2	6 23.4	23 46.5	7 48.4	4 3.8
16 S	5 37 29.9	24 58.0	19 6.4	5♉42.7	13 34.0	18 50.8	4 34.4	17 9.3	6 31.1	23 45.7	7 46.8	4 3.8
17 M	5 41 26.5	25 55.3	19 3.3	19 26.2	13 38.3	20 1.2	5 11.2	17 13.2	6 38.9	23 44.9	7 45.3	4D 3.9
18 T	5 45 23.1	26 52.6	19 0.1	3♊34.6	13R38.0	21 11.6	5 48.0	17 16.9	6 46.6	23 44.2	7 43.8	4 4.0
19 W	5 49 19.6	27 49.9	18 56.9	18 5.1	13 33.3	22 22.0	6 24.8	17 20.4	6 54.3	23 43.5	7 42.3	4 4.2
20 T	5 53 16.2	28 47.2	18 53.7	2♋52.4	13 24.1	23 32.6	7 1.6	17 23.8	7 2.1	23 42.9	7 40.8	4 4.4
21 F	5 57 12.7	29 44.4	18 50.5	17 49.5	13 10.8	24 43.1	7 38.5	17 26.9	7 9.9	23 42.3	7 39.3	4 4.6
22 S	6 1 9.3	0♋41.7	18 47.4	2♌48.0	12 53.4	25 53.7	8 15.4	17 29.9	7 17.6	23 41.8	7 37.8	4 4.9
23 S	6 5 5.8	1 39.0	18 44.2	17 39.8	12 32.2	27 4.4	8 52.3	17 32.7	7 25.4	23 41.3	7 36.4	4 5.1
24 M	6 9 2.4	2 36.2	18 41.0	2♍18.0	12 7.5	28 15.1	9 29.2	17 35.3	7 33.2	23 40.9	7 34.9	4 5.5
25 T	6 12 59.0	3 33.5	18 37.8	16 37.5	11 39.7	29 25.9	10 6.1	17 37.7	7 41.0	23 40.6	7 33.5	4 5.8
26 W	6 16 55.5	4 30.7	18 34.7	0♎35.7	11 9.2	0♊36.7	10 43.1	17 40.0	7 48.8	23 40.2	7 32.1	4 6.2
27 T	6 20 52.1	5 27.9	18 31.5	14 12.0	10 36.5	1 47.5	11 20.0	17 42.0	7 56.6	23 40.0	7 30.7	4 6.6
28 F	6 24 48.6	6 25.1	18 28.3	27 27.2	10 2.1	2 58.4	11 57.0	17 43.9	8 4.4	23 39.8	7 29.3	4 7.1
29 S	6 28 45.2	7 22.3	18 25.1	10♏23.5	9 26.6	4 9.4	12 34.0	17 45.5	8 12.2	23 39.6	7 28.0	4 7.5
30 S	6 32 41.7	8 19.5	18 22.0	23 3.4	8 50.6	5 20.4	13 11.0	17 47.0	8 20.0	23 39.5	7 26.6	4 8.1
						DECLINATION at NOON						
1 S	4 38 21.6	22N 2.5	23S 3.5	15S 21.6	25N18.0	9N59.6	22N25.2	6S 33.6	22N43.8	8S 46.7	20S 3.4	13N50.3
4 T	4 50 11.2	22 25.3	23 2.7	22 43.4	24 48.8	11 9.8	22 3.5	6 27.1	22 43.3	8 45.2	20 2.6	13 49.5
7 F	5 2 0.9	22 44.6	23 2.0	20 17.9	24 10.6	12 18.3	21 40.5	6 21.1	22 42.8	8 43.9	20 1.9	13 48.4
10 M	5 13 50.6	23 0.3	23 1.2	10 11.2	23 26.1	13 24.9	21 16.3	6 15.8	22 42.1	8 42.7	20 1.2	13 47.3
13 T	5 25 40.3	23 12.4	23 0.5	3N36.0	22 37.6	14 29.3	20 50.7	6 11.0	22 41.4	8 41.7	20 0.5	13 46.0
16 S	5 37 29.9	23 20.8	22 59.7	16 52.6	21 47.8	15 31.0	20 23.9	6 6.8	22 40.6	8 40.8	19 59.8	13 44.6
19 W	5 49 19.6	23 25.4	22 58.9	23 1.9	20 59.0	16 29.8	19 55.9	6 3.2	22 39.7	8 40.1	19 59.1	13 43.0
22 S	6 1 9.3	23 26.4	22 58.1	15 60.0	20 13.6	17 25.3	19 26.7	6 0.4	22 38.8	8 39.6	19 58.5	13 41.4
25 T	6 12 59.0	23 23.6	22 57.3	0 25.5	19 34.0	18 17.4	18 56.4	5 58.1	22 37.7	8 39.2	19 57.9	13 39.6
28 F	6 24 48.6	23 17.2	22 56.5	14S 26.4	19 2.5	19 5.6	18 25.0	5 56.6	22 36.6	8 39.0	19 57.3	13 37.7

JULY 1974

LONGITUDE at NOON

DAY	EPHEMERIS SIDEREAL TIME h m s	☉ ° ′	☊ ° ′	☽ ° ′	☿ ° ′	♀ ° ′	♂ ° ′	♃ ° ′	♄ ° ′	♅ ° ′	♆ ° ′	♇ ° ′
1 M	6 36 38.3	9♋16.7	18♐18.8	5♐29.4	8♋14.6	6♊31.4	13♌48.0	17♓48.3	8♋27.8	23♎39.5	7♐25.3	4♎ 8.6
2 T	6 40 34.9	10 13.9	18 15.6	17 44.3	7R39.4	7 42.5	14 25.1	17 49.4	8 35.7	23 39.5	7R24.0	4 9.2
3 W	6 44 31.4	11 11.1	18 12.4	29 50.1	7 5.5	8 53.7	15 2.1	17 50.3	8 43.5	23D39.6	7 22.7	4 9.8
4 T	6 48 28.0	12 8.3	18 9.3	11♑49.2	6 33.5	10 4.9	15 39.2	17 51.0	8 51.3	23 39.7	7 21.5	4 10.5
5 F	6 52 24.5	13 5.5	18 6.1	23 43.4	6 3.9	11 16.1	16 16.3	17 51.5	8 59.1	23 39.8	7 20.2	4 11.2
6 S	6 56 21.1	14 2.7	18 2.9	5♒34.7	5 37.4	12 27.4	16 53.4	17 51.9	9 6.9	23 40.0	7 19.0	4 11.9
7 S	7 0 17.6	14 59.8	17 59.7	17 25.2	5 14.3	13 38.8	17 30.5	17 52.0	9 14.7	23 40.3	7 17.8	4 12.6
8 M	7 4 14.2	15 57.0	17 56.5	29 17.3	4 55.2	14 50.2	18 7.6	17R51.9	9 22.4	23 40.6	7 16.6	4 13.4
9 T	7 8 10.8	16 54.2	17 53.4	11♓13.7	4 40.3	16 1.6	18 44.8	17 51.6	9 30.2	23 41.0	7 15.5	4 14.2
10 W	7 12 7.3	17 51.4	17 50.2	23 17.8	4 30.0	17 13.1	19 22.0	17 51.2	9 38.0	23 41.4	7 14.3	4 15.0
11 T	7 16 3.9	18 48.6	17 47.0	5♈33.1	4 24.6	18 24.7	19 59.2	17 50.5	9 45.7	23 41.9	7 13.2	4 15.9
12 F	7 20 0.4	19 45.8	17 43.8	18 3.5	4 24.2	19 36.3	20 36.4	17 49.7	9 53.5	23 42.4	7 12.1	4 16.8
13 S	7 23 57.0	20 43.0	17 40.7	0♉53.2	4D29.0	20 47.9	21 13.6	17 48.6	10 1.2	23 43.0	7 11.0	4 17.7
14 S	7 27 53.6	21 40.3	17 37.5	14 5.8	4 39.1	21 59.6	21 50.9	17 47.4	10 8.9	23 43.6	7 10.0	4 18.7
15 M	7 31 50.1	22 37.5	17 34.3	27 44.0	4 54.7	23 11.4	22 28.2	17 46.0	10 16.6	23 44.3	7 8.9	4 19.6
16 T	7 35 46.7	23 34.8	17 31.1	11♊49.3	5 15.7	24 23.2	23 5.5	17 44.3	10 24.3	23 45.0	7 7.9	4 20.7
17 W	7 39 43.2	24 32.0	17 28.0	26 20.5	5 42.3	25 35.0	23 42.8	17 42.5	10 32.0	23 45.8	7 7.0	4 21.7
18 T	7 43 39.8	25 29.3	17 24.8	11♋13.7	6 14.3	26 46.9	24 20.2	17 40.5	10 39.6	23 46.7	7 6.0	4 22.8
19 F	7 47 36.3	26 26.6	17 21.6	26 22.0	6 51.7	27 58.8	24 57.5	17 38.3	10 47.3	23 47.6	7 5.1	4 23.9
20 S	7 51 32.9	27 23.9	17 18.4	11♌36.0	7 34.6	29 10.8	25 34.9	17 35.9	10 54.9	23 48.5	7 4.2	4 25.0
21 S	7 55 29.4	28 21.2	17 15.2	26 45.5	8 22.9	0♋22.8	26 12.3	17 33.3	11 2.5	23 49.5	7 3.3	4 26.2
22 M	7 59 26.0	29 18.5	17 12.1	11♍40.7	9 16.5	1 34.9	26 49.8	17 30.5	11 10.0	23 50.5	7 2.5	4 27.4
23 T	8 3 22.6	0♌15.8	17 8.9	26 14.1	10 15.5	2 47.0	27 27.3	17 27.6	11 17.6	23 51.7	7 1.7	4 28.7
24 W	8 7 19.1	1 13.1	17 5.7	10♎21.3	11 19.5	3 59.2	28 4.7	17 24.4	11 25.1	23 52.8	7 0.9	4 29.9
25 T	8 11 15.7	2 10.4	17 2.5	24 0.9	12 28.7	5 11.4	28 42.2	17 21.1	11 32.6	23 54.0	7 0.1	4 31.2
26 F	8 15 12.2	3 7.7	16 59.4	7♏14.2	13 42.8	6 23.6	29 19.7	17 17.6	11 40.1	23 55.3	6 59.4	4 32.5
27 S	8 19 8.8	4 5.1	16 56.2	20 †.2	15 1.8	7 35.9	29 57.3	17 13.9	11 47.6	23 56.6	6 58.7	4 33.8
28 S	8 23 5.3	5 2.4	16 53.0	2♐34.8	16 25.6	8 48.2	0♍34.8	17 10.0	11 55.0	23 57.9	6 58.0	4 35.2
29 M	8 27 1.9	5 59.8	16 49.8	14 50.2	17 53.9	10 0.6	1 12.4	17 6.0	12 2.3	23 59.3	6 57.4	4 36.6
30 T	8 30 58.5	6 57.1	16 46.7	26 54.5	19 26.7	11 13.0	1 50.0	17 1.7	12 9.7	24 0.8	6 56.8	4 38.0
31 W	8 34 55.0	7 54.5	16 43.5	8♑51.4	21 3.6	12 25.4	2 27.6	16 57.3	12 17.0	24 2.3	6 56.2	4 39.5

DECLINATION at NOON

DAY	EPHEMERIS SIDEREAL TIME h m s	☉ ° ′	☊ ° ′	☽ ° ′	☿ ° ′	♀ ° ′	♂ ° ′	♃ ° ′	♄ ° ′	♅ ° ′	♆ ° ′	♇ ° ′
1 M	6 36 38.3	23N 7.0	22S55.7	22S28.2	18N41.2	19N49.6	17N52.5	5S55.7	22N35.4	8S39.0	19S56.8	13N35.7
4 T	6 48 28.0	22 53.2	22 54.8	20 55.2	18 31.3	20 29.3	17 19.0	5 55.4	22 34.1	8 39.2	19 56.2	13 33.6
7 S	7 0 17.6	22 35.9	22 54.0	11 22.8	18 33.5	21 4.3	16 44.4	5 55.9	22 32.8	8 39.6	19 55.7	13 31.4
10 W	7 12 7.3	22 15.0	22 53.1	2N 7.1	18 47.1	21 34.4	16 8.9	5 57.0	22 31.4	8 40.1	19 55.3	13 29.1
13 S	7 23 57.0	21 50.7	22 52.2	15 25.5	19 10.5	21 59.4	15 32.5	5 58.8	22 29.9	8 40.8	19 54.9	13 26.8
16 T	7 35 46.7	21 23.0	22 51.4	22 51.5	19 40.9	22 19.0	14 55.1	6 1.3	22 28.3	8 41.6	19 54.5	13 24.3
19 F	7 47 36.3	20 52.0	22 50.5	17 47.1	20 14.8	22 33.2	14 16.9	6 4.5	22 26.7	8 42.7	19 54.2	13 21.8
22 M	7 59 26.0	20 17.8	22 49.6	2 26.3	20 48.2	22 41.7	13 37.9	6 8.4	22 25.1	8 43.9	19 53.9	13 19.2
25 T	8 11 15.7	19 40.6	22 48.6	13S13.8	21 16.4	22 44.4	12 58.0	6 12.8	22 23.4	8 45.2	19 53.6	13 16.5
28 S	8 23 5.3	19 0.5	22 47.7	22 4.5	21 34.3	22 41.3	12 17.4	6 17.9	22 21.6	8 46.8	19 53.4	13 13.7
31 W	8 34 55.0	18 17.6	22 46.8	21 21.8	21 36.6	22 32.4	11 36.1	6 23.6	22 19.8	8 48.5	19 53.3	13 10.9

AUGUST 1974

LONGITUDE at NOON

DAY	EPHEMERIS SIDEREAL TIME h m s	☉ ° ′	☊ ° ′	☽ ° ′	☿ ° ′	♀ ° ′	♂ ° ′	♃ ° ′	♄ ° ′	♅ ° ′	♆ ° ′	♇ ° ′
1 T	8 38 51.6	8♌51.8	16♐40.3	20♑43.9	22♋44.5	13♋37.9	3♍ 5.2	16♓52.8	12♋24.3	24♎ 3.8	6♐55.6	4♎40.9
2 F	8 42 48.1	9 49.2	16 37.1	2♒34.5	24 29.1	14 50.5	3 42.9	16R48.1	12 31.6	24 5.4	6R55.1	4 42.4
3 S	8 46 44.7	10 46.6	16 33.9	14 25.3	26 17.2	16 3.1	4 20.6	16 43.2	12 38.8	24 7.1	6 54.6	4 43.9
4 S	8 50 41.2	11 44.1	16 30.8	26 18.0	28 8.3	17 15.7	4 58.3	16 38.1	12 46.0	24 8.8	6 54.1	4 45.5
5 M	8 54 37.8	12 41.5	16 27.6	8♓14.2	0♌ 2.2	18 28.4	5 36.0	16 32.9	12 53.1	24 10.5	6 53.7	4 47.1
6 T	8 58 34.3	13 38.9	16 24.4	20 15.8	1 58.4	19 41.1	6 13.7	16 27.6	13 0.2	24 12.3	6 53.2	4 48.6
7 W	9 2 30.9	14 36.4	16 21.2	2♈24.6	3 56.8	20 53.9	6 51.5	16 22.0	13 7.3	24 14.1	6 52.9	4 50.3
8 T	9 6 27.5	15 33.9	16 18.1	14 43.2	5 56.7	22 6.7	7 29.3	16 16.4	13 14.3	24 16.0	6 52.5	4 51.9
9 F	9 10 24.0	16 31.4	16 14.9	27 14.5	7 58.0	23 19.6	8 7.1	16 10.6	13 21.3	24 17.9	6 52.2	4 53.6
10 S	9 14 20.6	17 29.0	16 11.7	10♉ 2.0	10 0.3	24 32.5	8 44.9	16 4.6	13 28.3	24 19.9	6 51.9	4 55.3
11 S	9 18 17.1	18 26.5	16 8.5	23 9.2	12 3.1	25 45.5	9 22.8	15 58.5	13 35.2	24 21.9	6 51.6	4 57.0
12 M	9 22 13.7	19 24.1	16 5.3	6♊39.3	14 6.3	26 58.5	10 0.7	15 52.3	13 42.0	24 23.9	6 51.4	4 58.7
13 T	9 26 10.2	20 21.8	16 2.2	20 34.9	16 9.5	28 11.6	10 38.7	15 46.0	13 48.9	24 26.1	6 51.3	5 0.5
14 W	9 30 6.8	21 19.4	15 59.0	4♋56.4	18 12.5	29 24.7	11 16.6	15 39.5	13 55.7	24 28.2	6 51.1	5 2.3
15 T	9 34 3.3	22 17.1	15 55.8	19 41.8	20 15.0	0♌37.9	11 54.6	15 32.9	14 2.4	24 30.4	6 51.0	5 4.1
16 F	9 37 59.9	23 14.7	15 52.6	4♌45.9	22 16.9	1 51.1	12 32.6	15 26.2	14 9.1	24 32.7	6 50.9	5 5.9
17 S	9 41 56.4	24 12.4	15 49.5	20 0.4	24 18.0	3 4.3	13 10.7	15 19.4	14 15.7	24 34.9	6 50.8	5 7.7
18 S	9 45 53.0	25 10.2	15 46.3	5♍14.7	26 18.1	4 17.6	13 48.7	15 12.4	14 22.3	24 37.3	6 50.8	5 9.6
19 M	9 49 49.6	26 7.9	15 43.1	20 17.8	28 17.2	5 30.9	14 26.8	15 5.4	14 28.8	24 39.6	6 50.8	5 11.5
20 T	9 53 46.1	27 5.7	15 39.9	5♎ 0.4	0♍15.2	6 44.2	15 4.9	14 58.3	14 35.3	24 42.0	6 50.8	5 13.4
21 W	9 57 42.7	28 3.5	15 36.8	19 16.2	2 12.0	7 57.6	15 43.1	14 51.0	14 41.7	24 44.5	6D50.9	5 15.3
22 T	10 1 39.2	29 1.3	15 33.6	3♏ 2.4	4 7.6	9 11.1	16 21.2	14 43.7	14 48.1	24 46.9	6 51.0	5 17.2
23 F	10 5 35.8	29 59.1	15 30.4	16 19.4	6 1.9	10 24.6	16 59.4	14 36.3	14 54.4	24 49.5	6 51.1	5 19.2
24 S	10 9 32.3	0♍57.0	15 27.2	29 10.2	7 54.8	11 38.1	17 37.6	14 28.9	15 0.6	24 52.0	6 51.3	5 21.2
25 S	10 13 28.9	1 54.8	15 24.0	11♐39.0	9 46.5	12 51.6	18 15.9	14 21.3	15 6.8	24 54.6	6 51.5	5 23.2
26 M	10 17 25.4	2 52.7	15 20.9	23 50.9	11 36.8	14 5.2	18 54.1	14 13.7	15 12.9	24 57.3	6 51.7	5 25.2
27 T	10 21 22.0	3 50.6	15 17.7	5♑51.0	13 25.8	15 18.8	19 32.4	14 6.0	15 19.0	24 59.9	6 52.0	5 27.2
28 W	10 25 18.5	4 48.6	15 14.5	17 43.9	15 13.5	16 32.5	20 10.7	13 58.3	15 25.0	25 2.6	6 52.3	5 29.2
29 T	10 29 15.1	5 46.5	15 11.3	29 33.7	16 59.9	17 46.2	20 49.1	13 50.5	15 30.9	25 5.4	6 52.6	5 31.3
30 F	10 33 11.6	6 44.5	15 8.2	11♒23.9	18 44.9	18 59.9	21 27.4	13 42.7	15 36.8	25 8.2	6 52.9	5 33.4
31 S	10 37 8.2	7 42.5	15 5.0	23 17.0	20 28.7	20 13.7	22 5.8	13 34.9	15 42.6	25 11.0	6 53.3	5 35.4

DECLINATION at NOON

DAY	EPHEMERIS SIDEREAL TIME h m s	☉ ° ′	☊ ° ′	☽ ° ′	☿ ° ′	♀ ° ′	♂ ° ′	♃ ° ′	♄ ° ′	♅ ° ′	♆ ° ′	♇ ° ′
1 T	8 38 51.6	18N 2.7	22S46.5	19S 8.2	21N33.1	22N28.2	11N22.2	6S25.6	22N19.2	8S49.1	19S53.3	13N10.0
4 S	8 50 41.2	17 16.2	22 45.5	8 18.0	21 7.9	22 11.5	10 40.0	6 32.0	22 17.3	8 51.0	19 53.2	13 7.1
7 W	9 2 30.9	16 27.2	22 44.5	5N28.1	20 19.2	21 49.0	9 57.2	6 38.9	22 15.5	8 53.1	19 53.1	13 4.2
10 S	9 14 20.6	15 35.8	22 43.6	17 45.7	19 7.1	21 20.8	9 13.8	6 46.3	22 13.6	8 55.3	19 53.1	13 1.3
13 T	9 26 10.2	14 42.1	22 42.6	22 49.4	17 34.3	20 47.1	8 29.8	6 54.2	22 11.6	8 57.6	19 53.2	12 58.3
16 F	9 37 59.9	13 46.3	22 41.6	15 26.8	15 44.6	20 7.9	7 45.3	7 2.4	22 9.7	9 0.1	19 53.3	12 55.3
19 M	9 49 49.6	12 48.5	22 40.6	0S47.0	13 42.5	19 23.6	7 0.3	7 11.0	22 7.8	9 2.8	19 53.4	12 52.3
22 T	10 1 39.2	11 48.9	22 39.6	15 47.4	11 31.9	18 34.2	6 14.9	7 19.8	22 5.8	9 5.5	19 53.7	12 49.3
25 S	10 13 28.9	10 47.7	22 38.5	22 35.8	9 16.1	17 40.1	5 29.1	7 28.9	22 3.9	9 8.4	19 53.9	12 46.2
28 W	10 25 18.5	9 44.9	22 37.5	19 39.3	6 57.7	16 41.4	4 42.9	7 38.1	22 2.0	9 11.4	19 54.2	12 43.2
31 S	10 37 8.2	8 40.8	22 36.4	9 23.3	4 38.8	15 38.5	3 56.5	7 47.5	22 0.1	9 14.6	19 54.6	12 40.2

SEPTEMBER 1974

DAY	EPHEMERIS SIDEREAL TIME	☉	☊	☽	☿	♀	♂	♃	♄	♅	♆	♇
	h m s	° ′	° ′	° ′	° ′	° ′	° ′	° ′	° ′	° ′	° ′	° ′
LONGITUDE at NOON												
1 S	10 41 4.7	8♍40.5	15♐1.8	5♓14.8	22♍11.2	21♌27.5	22♍44.3	13♓27.0	15♋48.4	25♎13.8	6♐53.8	5♎37.5
2 M	10 45 1.3	9 38.6	14 58.6	17 18.9	23 52.5	22 41.4	23 22.7	13R19.1	15 54.0	25 16.7	6 54.2	5 39.7
3 T	10 48 57.9	10 36.7	14 55.4	29 30.1	25 32.6	23 55.3	24 1.3	13 11.2	15 59.7	25 19.7	6 54.7	5 41.8
4 W	10 52 54.4	11 34.8	14 52.3	11♈49.5	27 11.4	25 9.3	24 39.8	13 3.3	16 5.2	25 22.6	6 55.3	5 44.0
5 T	10 56 51.0	12 33.0	14 49.1	24 18.1	28 49.0	26 23.2	25 18.3	12 55.4	16 10.7	25 25.6	6 55.8	5 46.1
6 F	11 0 47.5	13 31.1	14 45.9	6♉57.7	0♎25.4	27 37.3	25 56.9	12 47.4	16 16.1	25 28.7	6 56.4	5 48.3
7 S	11 4 44.1	14 29.3	14 42.7	19 50.3	2 0.7	28 51.3	26 35.5	12 39.5	16 21.4	25 31.7	6 57.0	5 50.5
8 S	11 8 40.6	15 27.6	14 39.5	2♊58.4	3 34.7	0♍5.4	27 14.1	12 31.5	16 26.7	25 34.8	6 57.7	5 52.6
9 M	11 12 37.2	16 25.9	14 36.4	16 24.7	5 7.6	1 19.5	27 52.8	12 23.6	16 31.9	25 37.9	6 58.3	5 54.8
10 T	11 16 33.7	17 24.2	14 33.2	0♋11.5	6 39.3	2 33.7	28 31.5	12 15.7	16 37.0	25 41.0	6 59.1	5 57.0
11 W	11 20 30.3	18 22.5	14 30.0	14 20.0	8 9.9	3 47.9	29 10.2	12 7.8	16 42.0	25 44.2	6 59.8	5 59.3
12 T	11 24 26.8	19 20.9	14 26.8	28 49.8	9 39.3	5 2.1	29 49.0	11 60.0	16 47.0	25 47.4	7 0.6	6 1.5
13 F	11 28 23.4	20 19.3	14 23.7	13♌37.4	11 7.6	6 16.4	0♎27.8	11 52.2	16 51.8	25 50.6	7 1.4	6 3.7
14 S	11 32 19.9	21 17.8	14 20.5	28 36.8	12 34.7	7 30.7	1 6.6	11 44.4	16 56.6	25 53.9	7 2.2	6 6.0
15 S	11 36 16.5	22 16.3	14 17.3	13♍39.4	14 0.6	8 45.1	1 45.5	11 36.7	17 1.3	25 57.1	7 3.1	6 8.2
16 M	11 40 13.0	23 14.8	14 14.1	28 35.2	15 25.2	9 59.4	2 24.4	11 29.1	17 5.9	26 0.5	7 4.0	6 10.5
17 T	11 44 9.6	24 13.3	14 10.9	13♎14.9	16 48.7	11 13.8	3 3.3	11 21.5	17 10.5	26 3.8	7 4.9	6 12.8
18 W	11 48 6.1	25 11.9	14 7.8	27 31.4	18 10.9	12 28.3	3 42.3	11 14.0	17 15.0	26 7.1	7 5.9	6 15.0
19 T	11 52 2.7	26 10.5	14 4.6	11♏20.6	19 31.8	13 42.7	4 21.3	11 6.5	17 19.3	26 10.5	7 6.9	6 17.3
20 F	11 55 59.2	27 9.1	14 1.4	24 41.4	20 51.4	14 57.2	5 0.3	10 59.2	17 23.6	26 13.9	7 7.9	6 19.6
21 S	11 59 55.8	28 7.8	13 58.2	7♐35.6	22 9.6	16 11.7	5 39.4	10 51.9	17 27.8	26 17.3	7 8.9	6 21.9
22 S	12 3 52.4	29 6.5	13 55.1	20 6.9	23 26.3	17 26.3	6 18.4	10 44.7	17 31.9	26 20.8	7 10.0	6 24.2
23 M	12 7 48.9	0♎5.2	13 51.9	2♑20.2	24 41.6	18 40.8	6 57.6	10 37.6	17 35.9	26 24.3	7 11.1	6 26.5
24 T	12 11 45.5	1 4.0	13 48.7	14 20.6	25 55.3	19 55.5	7 36.8	10 30.7	17 39.9	26 27.8	7 12.3	6 28.8
25 W	12 15 42.0	2 2.8	13 45.5	26 13.5	27 7.3	21 10.1	8 15.9	10 23.8	17 43.7	26 31.3	7 13.5	6 31.1
26 T	12 19 38.6	3 1.6	13 42.3	8♒3.7	28 17.6	22 24.7	8 55.1	10 17.1	17 47.5	26 34.8	7 14.7	6 33.4
27 F	12 23 35.1	4 0.4	13 39.2	19 55.5	29 26.0	23 39.4	9 34.4	10 10.4	17 51.1	26 38.4	7 15.9	6 35.7
28 S	12 27 31.7	4 59.3	13 36.0	1♓52.3	0♏32.4	24 54.1	10 13.7	10 3.9	17 54.7	26 41.9	7 17.2	6 38.1
29 S	12 31 28.2	5 58.2	13 32.8	13 56.8	1 36.6	26 8.8	10 53.0	9 57.5	17 58.2	26 45.5	7 18.4	6 40.4
30 M	12 35 24.8	6 57.1	13 29.6	26 10.6	2 38.6	27 23.5	11 32.3	9 51.3	18 1.5	26 49.1	7 19.8	6 42.7
DECLINATION at NOON												
1 S	10 41 4.7	8N19.1	22S36.1	5S 0.6	3N52.6	15N16.7	3N40.9	7S50.6	21N59.5	9S15.6	19S54.7	12N39.2
4 W	10 52 54.4	7 13.3	22 35.0	8N47.1	1 35.1	14 8.5	2 54.0	7 60.0	21 57.6	9 18.9	19 55.1	12 36.2
7 S	11 4 44.1	6 6.4	22 33.9	19 44.0	0S39.9	12 56.8	2 6.9	8 9.3	21 55.8	9 22.3	19 55.6	12 33.2
10 T	11 16 33.7	4 58.6	22 32.9	22 5.0	2 51.4	11 41.8	1 19.6	8 18.5	21 54.1	9 25.7	19 56.1	12 30.2
13 F	11 28 23.4	3 50.1	22 31.8	12 36.0	4 58.7	10 23.9	0 32.2	8 27.6	21 52.4	9 29.3	19 56.6	12 27.3
16 M	11 40 13.0	2 40.9	22 30.6	3S53.1	7 0.9	9 3.3	0S15.4	8 36.4	21 50.7	9 32.9	19 57.2	12 24.4
19 T	11 52 2.7	1 31.2	22 29.5	17 47.1	8 57.3	7 40.4	1 3.0	8 45.0	21 49.2	9 36.6	19 57.8	12 21.6
22 S	12 3 52.4	0 21.3	22 28.4	22 28.8	10 47.0	6 15.5	1 50.6	8 53.2	21 47.7	9 40.4	19 58.5	12 18.8
25 W	12 15 42.0	0S48.8	22 27.2	17 31.3	12 28.9	4 48.9	2 38.3	9 0.9	21 46.2	9 44.2	19 59.2	12 16.0
28 S	12 27 31.7	1 58.9	22 26.1	6 11.2	14 1.8	3 21.0	3 25.8	9 8.3	21 44.9	9 48.1	19 60.0	12 13.3

OCTOBER 1974

DAY	EPHEMERIS SIDEREAL TIME	☉	☊	☽	☿	♀	♂	♃	♄	♅	♆	♇
LONGITUDE at NOON												
1 T	12 39 21.3	7♎56.1	13♐26.5	8♈34.7	3♏38.1	28♍38.3	12♎11.7	9♓45.1	18♋4.8	26♎52.7	7♐21.1	6♎45.0
2 W	12 43 17.9	8 55.1	13 23.3	21 9.5	4 34.9	29 53.0	12 51.1	9R39.2	18 8.0	26 56.3	7 22.5	6 47.3
3 T	12 47 14.4	9 54.1	13 20.1	3♉55.1	5 28.8	1♎7.8	13 30.6	9 33.3	18 11.1	26 60.0	7 23.8	6 49.6
4 F	12 51 11.0	10 53.2	13 16.9	16 51.6	6 19.5	2 22.7	14 10.0	9 27.6	18 14.0	27 3.6	7 25.3	6 51.9
5 S	12 55 7.5	11 52.3	13 13.7	29 59.3	7 6.8	3 37.5	14 49.6	9 22.0	18 16.9	27 7.3	7 26.7	6 54.2
6 S	12 59 4.1	12 51.4	13 10.6	13♊18.9	7 50.4	4 52.4	15 29.1	9 16.6	18 19.7	27 11.0	7 28.2	6 56.5
7 M	13 3 0.6	13 50.6	13 7.4	26 51.4	8 29.8	6 7.3	16 8.7	9 11.4	18 22.4	27 14.7	7 29.7	6 58.8
8 T	13 6 57.2	14 49.8	13 4.2	10♋37.9	9 4.8	7 22.2	16 48.3	9 6.3	18 24.9	27 18.4	7 31.2	7 1.1
9 W	13 10 53.7	15 49.0	13 1.0	24 38.9	9 34.9	8 37.2	17 28.0	9 1.4	18 27.4	27 22.1	7 32.7	7 3.4
10 T	13 14 50.3	16 48.3	12 57.9	8♌54.1	9 59.7	9 52.1	18 7.7	8 56.6	18 29.8	27 25.8	7 34.3	7 5.7
11 F	13 18 46.9	17 47.7	12 54.7	23 21.4	10 18.7	11 7.1	18 47.5	8 52.1	18 32.0	27 29.5	7 35.9	7 8.0
12 S	13 22 43.4	18 47.0	12 51.5	7♍57.0	10 31.4	12 22.1	19 27.2	8 47.7	18 34.2	27 33.3	7 37.5	7 10.3
13 S	13 26 40.0	19 46.5	12 48.3	22 35.2	10 37.3	13 37.1	20 7.1	8 43.4	18 36.3	27 37.0	7 39.1	7 12.5
14 M	13 30 36.5	20 45.9	12 45.1	7♎8.9	10R36.0	14 52.2	20 46.9	8 39.4	18 38.2	27 40.8	7 40.8	7 14.8
15 T	13 34 33.1	21 45.4	12 42.0	21 31.0	10 26.9	16 7.3	21 26.9	8 35.6	18 40.1	27 44.6	7 42.5	7 17.1
16 W	13 38 29.6	22 44.9	12 38.8	5♏35.4	10 9.6	17 22.4	22 6.8	8 31.9	18 41.8	27 48.3	7 44.3	7 19.4
17 T	13 42 26.2	23 44.5	12 35.6	19 17.7	9 43.9	18 37.4	22 46.8	8 28.4	18 43.4	27 52.1	7 46.0	7 21.6
18 F	13 46 22.7	24 44.1	12 32.4	2♐36.1	9 9.5	19 52.6	23 26.8	8 25.1	18 44.9	27 55.9	7 47.7	7 23.8
19 S	13 50 19.3	25 43.7	12 29.3	15 30.9	8 26.6	21 7.7	24 6.8	8 22.0	18 46.3	27 59.6	7 49.5	7 26.1
20 S	13 54 15.8	26 43.3	12 26.1	28 4.2	7 35.3	22 22.8	24 46.9	8 19.0	18 47.6	28 3.4	7 51.3	7 28.3
21 M	13 58 12.4	27 43.0	12 22.9	10♑19.9	6 36.4	23 37.9	25 27.0	8 16.3	18 48.8	28 7.2	7 53.1	7 30.5
22 T	14 2 8.9	28 42.7	12 19.7	22 22.5	5 30.9	24 53.1	26 7.2	8 13.8	18 49.9	28 11.0	7 55.0	7 32.7
23 W	14 6 5.5	29 42.4	12 16.5	4♒17.1	4 20.0	26 8.2	26 47.4	8 11.5	18 50.8	28 14.7	7 56.8	7 34.9
24 T	14 10 2.0	0♏42.2	12 13.4	16 8.6	3 5.6	27 23.4	27 27.6	8 9.3	18 51.7	28 18.5	7 58.7	7 37.0
25 F	14 13 58.6	1 41.9	12 10.2	28 1.9	1 49.6	28 38.6	28 7.8	8 7.4	18 52.4	28 22.3	8 0.6	7 39.2
26 S	14 17 55.2	2 41.8	12 7.0	10♓1.4	0 34.4	29 53.8	28 48.1	8 5.7	18 53.0	28 26.0	8 2.5	7 41.3
27 S	14 21 51.7	3 41.6	12 3.8	22 10.7	29♎22.2	1♏9.0	29 28.5	8 4.2	18 53.5	28 29.8	8 4.4	7 43.5
28 M	14 25 48.3	4 41.5	12 0.7	4♈32.5	28 15.2	2 24.2	0♏8.8	8 2.8	18 53.9	28 33.6	8 6.4	7 45.6
29 T	14 29 44.8	5 41.4	11 57.5	17 8.6	27 15.6	3 39.4	0 49.2	8 1.7	18 54.2	28 37.3	8 8.3	7 47.7
30 W	14 33 41.4	6 41.3	11 54.3	29 59.7	26 25.0	4 54.6	1 29.7	8 0.8	18 54.4	28 41.1	8 10.3	7 49.8
31 T	14 37 37.9	7 41.3	11 51.1	13♉5.4	25 44.7	6 9.8	2 10.2	8 0.1	18 54.4	28 44.8	8 12.3	7 51.9
DECLINATION at NOON												
1 T	12 39 21.3	3S 8.9	22S24.9	7N33.6	15S24.1	1N52.1	4S13.3	9S15.1	21N43.7	9S52.1	20S 0.8	12N10.7
4 F	12 51 11.0	4 18.5	22 23.8	18 56.6	16 33.6	0 22.5	5 0.5	9 21.5	21 42.6	9 56.0	20 1.6	12 8.2
7 M	13 3 0.6	5 27.7	22 22.6	22 5.0	17 27.6	1S 7.5	5 47.6	9 27.3	21 41.6	10 0.0	20 2.5	12 5.7
10 T	13 14 50.3	6 36.3	22 21.4	13 53.7	18 2.0	2 37.6	6 34.5	9 32.4	21 40.7	10 4.1	20 3.3	12 3.4
13 S	13 26 40.0	7 44.1	22 20.2	1S39.6	18 11.6	4 7.3	7 21.0	9 37.0	21 40.0	10 8.1	20 4.2	12 1.1
16 W	13 38 29.6	8 51.0	22 18.9	16 12.1	17 49.7	5 36.4	8 7.2	9 40.9	21 39.3	10 12.2	20 5.2	11 58.9
19 S	13 50 19.3	9 56.7	22 17.7	22 15.4	16 50.0	7 4.5	8 53.0	9 44.1	21 38.8	10 16.2	20 6.1	11 56.8
22 T	14 2 8.9	11 1.0	22 16.5	18 12.7	15 10.5	8 31.2	9 38.3	9 46.7	21 38.5	10 20.3	20 7.1	11 54.8
25 F	14 13 58.6	12 3.9	22 15.2	7 25.5	13 1.3	9 56.3	10 23.1	9 48.6	21 38.3	10 24.4	20 8.1	11 52.9
28 M	14 25 48.3	13 5.2	22 14.0	6N 9.2	10 48.1	11 19.3	11 7.4	9 49.7	21 38.2	10 28.4	20 9.1	11 51.1
31 T	14 37 37.9	14 4.5	22 12.7	18 3.2	9 2.3	12 39.9	11 51.0	9 50.2	21 38.2	10 32.4	20 10.2	11 49.5

NOVEMBER 1974

DAY	EPHEMERIS SIDEREAL TIME	☉	☊	☽	☿	♀	♂	♃	♄	♅	♆	♇
	h m s	° ′	° ′	° ′	° ′	° ′	° ′	° ′	° ′	° ′	° ′	° ′
						LONGITUDE at NOON						
1 F	14 41 34.5	8♏41.3	11♐47.9	26♉24.9	25♎15.5	7♏25.1	2♏50.7	7♓59.6	18♋54.4	28♎48.6	8♐14.3	7♎53.9
2 S	14 45 31.0	9 41.3	11 44.8	9♊56.6	24R57.8	8 40.3	3 31.3	7R59.3	18R54.2	28 52.3	8 16.4	7 56.0
3 S	14 49 27.6	10 41.3	11 41.6	23 39.0	24 51.8	9 55.6	4 11.9	7 59.2	18 54.0	28 56.0	8 18.4	7 58.0
4 M	14 53 24.1	11 41.4	11 38.4	7♋30.4	24D57.0	11 10.8	4 52.5	7D59.3	18 53.6	28 59.7	8 20.5	8 0.0
5 T	14 57 20.7	12 41.6	11 35.2	21 29.6	25 13.0	12 26.2	5 33.2	7 59.6	18 53.1	29 3.5	8 22.6	8 2.0
6 W	15 1 17.3	13 41.8	11 32.1	5♌34.9	25 38.9	13 41.4	6 14.0	8 0.1	18 52.5	29 7.2	8 24.7	8 4.0
7 T	15 5 13.8	14 42.0	11 28.9	19 44.9	26 14.1	14 56.7	6 54.7	8 0.8	18 51.8	29 10.8	8 26.8	8 6.0
8 F	15 9 10.4	15 42.2	11 25.7	3♍57.9	26 57.5	16 12.1	7 35.5	8 1.8	18 51.0	29 14.5	8 28.9	8 7.9
9 S	15 13 6.9	16 42.5	11 22.5	18 11.2	27 48.4	17 27.4	8 16.4	8 2.9	18 50.0	29 18.1	8 31.0	8 9.8
10 S	15 17 3.5	17 42.8	11 19.3	2♎21.9	28 45.9	18 42.7	8 57.3	8 4.2	18 48.9	29 21.8	8 33.1	8 11.7
11 M	15 21 0.0	18 43.1	11 16.2	16 26.3	29 49.1	19 58.0	9 38.2	8 5.7	18 47.8	29 25.4	8 35.3	8 13.6
12 T	15 24 56.6	19 43.5	11 13.0	0♏20.7	0♏57.2	21 13.4	10 19.2	8 7.5	18 46.5	29 29.0	8 37.4	8 15.5
13 W	15 28 53.1	20 43.9	11 9.8	14 1.5	2 9.7	22 28.7	11 0.2	8 9.4	18 45.1	29 32.6	8 39.6	8 17.3
14 T	15 32 49.7	21 44.3	11 6.6	27 25.9	3 25.8	23 44.0	11 41.3	8 11.5	18 43.6	29 36.2	8 41.8	8 19.1
15 F	15 36 46.3	22 44.7	11 3.5	10♐32.4	4 45.1	24 59.4	12 22.4	8 13.9	18 42.0	29 39.8	8 44.0	8 20.9
16 S	15 40 42.8	23 45.2	11 0.3	23 20.5	6 7.0	26 14.8	13 3.5	8 16.4	18 40.3	29 43.3	8 46.2	8 22.7
17 S	15 44 39.4	24 45.7	10 57.1	5♑51.2	7 31.1	27 30.1	13 44.7	8 19.2	18 38.5	29 46.8	8 48.4	8 24.4
18 M	15 48 35.9	25 46.2	10 53.9	18 6.7	8 57.0	28 45.5	14 25.9	8 22.1	18 36.5	29 50.3	8 50.6	8 26.2
19 T	15 52 32.5	26 46.8	10 50.8	0♒10.3	10 24.6	0♐ 0.8	15 7.1	8 25.2	18 34.5	29 53.8	8 52.8	8 27.9
20 W	15 56 29.0	27 47.3	10 47.6	12 5.8	11 53.4	1 16.2	15 48.4	8 28.6	18 32.4	29 57.2	8 55.0	8 29.5
21 T	16 0 25.6	28 47.9	10 44.4	23 57.9	13 23.2	2 31.6	16 29.8	8 32.1	18 30.1	0♏ 0.7	8 57.2	8 31.2
22 F	16 4 22.1	29 48.5	10 41.2	5♓51.1	14 53.9	3 46.9	17 11.1	8 35.8	18 27.8	0 4.1	8 59.5	8 32.8
23 S	16 8 18.7	0♐49.2	10 38.0	17 50.4	16 25.3	5 2.3	17 52.5	8 39.7	18 25.3	0 7.5	9 1.7	8 34.4
24 S	16 12 15.3	1 49.8	10 34.9	0D 0.2	17 57.3	6 17.7	18 34.0	8 43.8	18 22.8	0 10.8	9 3.9	8 36.0
25 M	16 16 11.8	2 50.5	10 31.7	12♈24.4	19 29.7	7 33.0	19 15.5	8 48.1	18 20.1	0 14.2	9 6.2	8 37.5
26 T	16 20 8.4	3 51.2	10 28.5	25 6.4	21 2.5	8 48.4	19 57.1	8 52.6	18 17.5	0 17.5	9 8.5	8 39.1
27 W	16 24 4.9	4 51.9	10 25.3	8♉ 7.9	22 35.6	10 3.8	20 38.6	8 57.3	18 14.6	0 20.8	9 10.7	8 40.6
28 T	16 28 1.5	5 52.6	10 22.2	21 29.7	24 8.8	11 19.2	21 20.2	9 2.1	18 11.7	0 24.1	9 13.0	8 42.1
29 F	16 31 58.0	6 53.4	10 19.0	5♊10.9	25 42.2	12 34.5	22 1.9	9 7.2	18 8.7	0 27.3	9 15.3	8 43.5
30 S	16 35 54.6	7 54.1	10 15.8	19 9.1	27 15.7	13 49.9	22 43.6	9 12.4	18 5.6	0 30.5	9 17.5	8 44.9
						DECLINATION at NOON						
1 F	14 41 34.5	14S23.9	22S12.3	20N35.1	8S37.3	13S 6.2	12S 5.4	9S50.2	21N38.3	10S33.7	20S10.5	11N49.0
4 M	14 53 24.1	15 20.6	22 11.0	20 51.0	7 57.2	14 23.1	12 48.1	9 49.8	21 38.6	10 37.7	20 11.5	11 47.5
7 T	15 5 13.8	16 15.0	22 9.7	10 14.4	8 6.4	15 36.7	13 30.0	9 48.6	21 39.0	10 41.6	20 12.6	11 46.1
10 S	15 17 3.5	17 6.9	22 8.4	5S23.9	8 54.1	16 46.8	14 11.2	9 46.7	21 39.5	10 45.5	20 13.7	11 44.8
13 W	15 28 53.1	17 56.3	22 7.1	18 16.2	10 7.8	17 52.8	14 51.5	9 44.2	21 40.2	10 49.3	20 14.7	11 43.7
16 S	15 40 42.8	18 42.8	22 5.7	22 4.7	11 36.8	18 54.6	15 30.8	9 41.0	21 41.0	10 53.0	20 15.8	11 42.7
19 T	15 52 32.5	19 26.3	22 4.4	16 10.0	13 13.2	19 51.7	16 9.1	9 37.1	21 42.0	10 56.7	20 16.8	11 41.9
22 F	16 4 22.1	20 6.7	22 3.0	4 28.1	14 51.5	20 43.8	16 46.4	9 32.5	21 43.1	11 0.3	20 17.9	11 41.2
25 M	16 16 11.8	20 43.7	22 1.7	9N 1.3	16 27.9	21 30.5	17 22.5	9 27.3	21 44.3	11 3.8	20 19.0	11 40.6
28 T	16 28 1.5	21 17.3	22 0.3	19 47.0	17 59.9	22 11.7	17 57.5	9 21.5	21 45.6	11 7.2	20 20.0	11 40.1

DECEMBER 1974

DAY	EPHEMERIS SIDEREAL TIME	☉	☊	☽	☿	♀	♂	♃	♄	♅	♆	♇
						LONGITUDE at NOON						
1 S	16 39 51.2	8♐54.9	10♐12.6	3♋20.5	28♏49.3	15♐ 5.2	23♏25.3	9♓17.7	18♋ 2.4	0♏33.7	9♐19.8	8♎46.3
2 M	16 43 47.7	9 55.7	10 9.5	17 40.7	0♐23.0	16 20.6	24 7.1	9 23.3	17R59.1	0 36.8	9 22.0	8 47.6
3 T	16 47 44.3	10 56.5	10 6.3	2♌ 4.9	1 56.7	17 36.0	24 48.9	9 29.0	17 55.7	0 39.9	9 24.3	8 49.0
4 W	16 51 40.8	11 57.4	10 3.1	16 28.3	3 30.4	18 51.4	25 30.7	9 35.0	17 52.3	0 43.0	9 26.5	8 50.3
5 T	16 55 37.4	12 58.3	9 59.9	0♍47.2	5 4.1	20 6.7	26 12.7	9 41.0	17 48.7	0 46.1	9 28.8	8 51.5
6 F	16 59 33.9	13 59.2	9 56.7	14 58.5	6 37.9	21 22.1	26 54.6	9 47.3	17 45.1	0 49.1	9 31.1	8 52.8
7 S	17 3 30.5	15 0.1	9 53.6	29 0.1	8 11.7	22 37.5	27 36.6	9 53.7	17 41.4	0 52.1	9 33.3	8 54.0
8 S	17 7 27.1	16 1.0	9 50.4	12♎50.7	9 45.5	23 52.9	28 18.6	10 0.3	17 37.6	0 55.0	9 35.6	8 55.2
9 M	17 11 23.6	17 2.0	9 47.2	26 29.3	11 19.4	25 8.2	29 0.7	10 7.1	17 33.8	0 57.9	9 37.8	8 56.3
10 T	17 15 20.2	18 3.0	9 44.0	9♏55.6	12 53.2	26 23.6	29 42.8	10 14.0	17 29.8	1 0.8	9 40.1	8 57.4
11 W	17 19 16.7	19 4.0	9 40.9	23 9.1	14 27.2	27 39.0	0♐25.0	10 21.1	17 25.8	1 3.6	9 42.3	8 58.5
12 T	17 23 13.3	20 5.0	9 37.7	6♐ 9.5	16 1.1	28 54.4	1 7.2	10 28.3	17 21.8	1 6.4	9 44.5	8 59.5
13 F	17 27 9.8	21 6.0	9 34.5	18 56.9	17 35.2	0♑ 9.8	1 49.4	10 35.7	17 17.6	1 9.2	9 46.8	9 0.6
14 S	17 31 6.4	22 7.0	9 31.3	1♑31.3	19 9.3	1 25.1	2 31.7	10 43.3	17 13.4	1 11.9	9 49.0	9 1.5
15 S	17 35 3.0	23 8.1	9 28.2	13 53.3	20 43.5	2 40.5	3 14.0	10 51.0	17 9.2	1 14.6	9 51.2	9 2.5
16 M	17 38 59.5	24 9.2	9 25.0	26 4.2	22 17.8	3 55.9	3 56.4	10 58.9	17 4.8	1 17.3	9 53.4	9 3.4
17 T	17 42 56.1	25 10.3	9 21.8	8♒ 5.9	23 52.3	5 11.3	4 38.8	11 7.0	17 0.5	1 19.9	9 55.7	9 4.3
18 W	17 46 52.6	26 11.4	9 18.6	20 0.8	25 26.9	6 26.7	5 21.3	11 15.1	16 56.1	1 22.5	9 57.8	9 5.2
19 T	17 50 49.2	27 12.4	9 15.5	1♓52.3	27 1.6	7 42.0	6 3.7	11 23.5	16 51.6	1 25.0	10 0.0	9 6.0
20 F	17 54 45.8	28 13.5	9 12.3	13 44.3	28 36.5	8 57.4	6 46.3	11 31.9	16 47.0	1 27.5	10 2.2	9 6.8
21 S	17 58 42.3	29 14.6	9 9.1	25 41.2	0♑11.5	10 12.8	7 28.8	11 40.5	16 42.5	1 29.9	10 4.4	9 7.5
22 S	18 2 38.9	0♑15.7	9 5.9	7♈47.6	1 46.8	11 28.1	8 11.4	11 49.3	16 37.8	1 32.3	10 6.5	9 8.3
23 M	18 6 35.4	1 16.8	9 2.7	20 8.3	3 22.3	12 43.4	8 54.1	11 58.2	16 33.2	1 34.7	10 8.7	9 8.9
24 T	18 10 32.0	2 17.9	8 59.6	2♉47.7	4 57.9	13 58.8	9 36.7	12 7.2	16 28.5	1 37.0	10 10.8	9 9.6
25 W	18 14 28.5	3 19.1	8 56.4	15 49.7	6 33.8	15 14.1	10 19.4	12 16.4	16 23.7	1 39.2	10 12.9	9 10.2
26 T	18 18 25.1	4 20.2	8 53.2	29 16.6	8 10.0	16 29.4	11 2.2	12 25.7	16 18.9	1 41.5	10 15.0	9 10.8
27 F	18 22 21.7	5 21.3	8 50.0	13♊ 9.1	9 46.4	17 44.7	11 45.0	12 35.1	16 14.1	1 43.6	10 17.1	9 11.3
28 S	18 26 18.2	6 22.4	8 46.9	27 25.4	11 23.0	18 60.0	12 27.8	12 44.7	16 9.3	1 45.8	10 19.2	9 11.8
29 S	18 30 14.8	7 23.5	8 43.7	12♋ 1.4	12 59.9	20 15.3	13 10.7	12 54.4	16 4.4	1 47.8	10 21.3	9 12.3
30 M	18 34 11.3	8 24.6	8 40.5	26 50.5	14 37.1	21 30.6	13 53.6	13 4.2	15 59.5	1 49.9	10 23.3	9 12.8
31 T	18 38 7.9	9 25.8	8 37.3	11♌44.6	16 14.5	22 45.8	14 36.6	13 14.1	15 54.6	1 51.8	10 25.4	9 13.2
						DECLINATION at NOON						
1 S	16 39 51.2	21S47.3	21S58.9	21N19.3	19S25.5	22S47.0	18S31.2	9S15.0	21N47.1	11S10.6	20S21.0	11N39.9
4 W	16 51 40.8	22 13.5	21 57.5	11 16.7	20 43.6	23 16.2	19 3.6	9 8.0	21 48.6	11 13.8	20 22.1	11 39.7
7 S	17 3 30.5	22 35.9	21 56.1	4S11.8	21 53.0	23 39.0	19 34.5	9 0.3	21 50.3	11 16.9	20 23.1	11 39.7
10 T	17 15 20.2	22 54.2	21 54.7	17 19.8	22 53.0	23 55.4	20 4.1	8 52.1	21 52.0	11 19.9	20 24.1	11 39.8
13 F	17 27 9.8	23 8.5	21 53.3	22 11.3	23 42.7	24 5.1	20 32.1	8 43.3	21 53.8	11 22.8	20 25.0	11 40.1
16 M	17 38 59.5	23 18.7	21 51.9	17 13.3	24 21.5	24 8.1	20 58.6	8 34.0	21 55.7	11 25.5	20 26.0	11 40.5
19 T	17 50 49.2	23 24.7	21 50.4	5 56.6	24 48.8	24 4.4	21 23.4	8 24.2	21 57.6	11 28.2	20 26.9	11 41.1
22 S	18 2 38.9	23 26.4	21 49.0	7N22.1	25 4.0	23 54.0	21 46.5	8 13.8	21 59.6	11 30.7	20 27.8	11 41.8
25 W	18 14 28.5	23 24.0	21 47.5	18 39.1	25 6.6	23 37.0	22 7.8	8 3.0	22 1.6	11 33.0	20 28.7	11 42.6
28 S	18 26 18.2	23 17.3	21 46.1	21 51.6	24 56.1	23 13.4	22 27.4	7 51.7	22 3.6	11 35.2	20 29.6	11 43.6
31 T	18 38 7.9	23 6.4	21 44.6	12 51.0	24 31.9	22 43.4	22 45.0	7 40.0	22 5.7	11 37.2	20 30.4	11 44.7

JANUARY 1975

DAY	EPHEMERIS SIDEREAL TIME	☉	☊	☽	☿	♀	♂	♃	♄	♅	♆	♇
	h m s	° ′	° ′	° ′	° ′	° ′	° ′	° ′	° ′	° ′	° ′	° ′
						LONGITUDE at NOON						
1 W	18 42 4.4	10♑26.9	8♐34.2	26♌35.2	17♑52.1	24♑ 1.1	15♐19.6	13♓24.2	15♋49.7	1♏53.8	10♐27.4	9♎13.5
2 T	18 46 1.0	11 28.0	8 31.0	11♍15.0	19 30.0	25 16.4	16 2.6	13 34.4	15R44.8	1 55.7	10 29.4	9 13.9
3 F	18 49 57.6	12 29.2	8 27.8	25 38.6	21 8.0	26 31.6	16 45.7	13 44.7	15 39.8	1 57.5	10 31.4	9 14.2
4 S	18 53 54.1	13 30.3	8 24.6	9♎42.9	22 46.3	27 46.9	17 28.8	13 55.1	15 34.9	1 59.3	10 33.4	9 14.4
5 S	18 57 50.7	14 31.5	8 21.5	23 26.9	24 24.6	29 2.1	18 12.0	14 5.6	15 29.9	2 1.0	10 35.3	9 14.7
6 M	19 1 47.2	15 32.6	8 18.3	6♏51.5	26 3.0	0♒17.4	18 55.2	14 16.3	15 25.0	2 2.7	10 37.3	9 14.9
7 T	19 5 43.8	16 33.8	8 15.1	19 58.6	27 41.5	1 32.6	19 38.5	14 27.1	15 20.0	2 4.4	10 39.2	9 15.1
8 W	19 9 40.3	17 35.0	8 11.9	2♐50.4	29 19.9	2 47.8	20 21.8	14 37.9	15 15.1	2 6.0	10 41.1	9 15.2
9 T	19 13 36.9	18 36.2	8 8.7	15 29.2	0♒58.0	4 3.1	21 5.1	14 48.9	15 10.1	2 7.5	10 43.0	9 15.3
10 F	19 17 33.5	19 37.3	8 5.6	27 56.9	2 35.9	5 18.3	21 48.5	14 60.0	15 5.2	2 9.0	10 44.9	9 15.3
11 S	19 21 30.0	20 38.5	8 2.4	10♑15.2	4 13.4	6 33.5	22 31.9	15 11.2	15 0.2	2 10.4	10 46.7	9 15.3
12 S	19 25 26.6	21 39.6	7 59.2	22 25.4	5 50.3	7 48.6	23 15.3	15 22.5	14 55.3	2 11.8	10 48.5	9 15.3
13 M	19 29 23.1	22 40.8	7 56.0	4♒28.5	7 26.3	9 3.8	23 58.8	15 33.9	14 50.4	2 13.1	10 50.3	9 15.3
14 T	19 33 19.7	23 41.9	7 52.9	16 26.0	9 1.4	10 19.0	24 42.3	15 45.4	14 45.5	2 14.4	10 52.1	9R15.2
15 W	19 37 16.2	24 43.1	7 49.7	28 19.2	10 35.1	11 34.1	25 25.9	15 57.0	14 40.7	2 15.6	10 53.9	9 15.0
16 T	19 41 12.8	25 44.2	7 46.5	10♓10.2	12 7.1	12 49.2	26 9.5	16 8.6	14 35.8	2 16.8	10 55.6	9 14.9
17 F	19 45 9.4	26 45.3	7 43.3	22 1.7	13 37.1	14 4.4	26 53.1	16 20.4	14 31.0	2 17.9	10 57.3	9 14.7
18 S	19 49 5.9	27 46.4	7 40.2	3♈56.9	15 4.6	15 19.5	27 36.8	16 32.3	14 26.3	2 18.9	10 59.0	9 14.5
19 S	19 53 2.5	28 47.5	7 37.0	16 0.1	16 29.2	16 34.5	28 20.5	16 44.3	14 21.5	2 19.9	11 0.7	9 14.2
20 M	19 56 59.0	29 48.5	7 33.8	28 15.6	17 50.3	17 49.6	29 4.3	16 56.3	14 16.8	2 20.9	11 2.3	9 13.9
21 T	20 0 55.6	0♒49.6	7 30.6	10♉48.4	19 7.2	19 4.6	29 48.0	17 8.4	14 12.2	2 21.8	11 4.0	9 13.6
22 W	20 4 52.1	1 50.7	7 27.4	23 43.3	20 19.3	20 19.7	0♑31.9	17 20.7	14 7.6	2 22.6	11 5.6	9 13.3
23 T	20 8 48.7	2 51.7	7 24.3	7♊ 4.3	21 25.8	21 34.7	1 15.7	17 33.0	14 3.0	2 23.4	11 7.2	9 12.9
24 F	20 12 45.3	3 52.7	7 21.1	20 54.0	22 25.9	22 49.7	1 59.6	17 45.4	13 58.5	2 24.1	11 8.7	9 12.4
25 S	20 16 41.8	4 53.7	7 17.9	5♋12.8	23 18.7	24 4.6	2 43.5	17 57.9	13 54.0	2 24.8	11 10.2	9 12.0
26 S	20 20 38.4	5 54.7	7 14.7	19 57.9	24 3.5	25 19.6	3 27.5	18 10.4	13 49.6	2 25.4	11 11.7	9 11.5
27 M	20 24 34.9	6 55.6	7 11.6	5♌ 2.8	24 39.4	26 34.5	4 11.5	18 23.0	13 45.3	2 26.0	11 13.2	9 10.9
28 T	20 28 31.5	7 56.6	7 8.4	20 18.3	25 5.6	27 49.4	4 55.5	18 35.7	13 41.0	2 26.5	11 14.6	9 10.4
29 W	20 32 28.0	8 57.5	7 5.2	5♍33.1	25 21.5	29 4.2	5 39.6	18 48.5	13 36.7	2 26.9	11 16.1	9 9.8
30 T	20 36 24.6	9 58.4	7 2.0	20 36.6	25 26.4	0♓19.1	6 23.7	19 1.3	13 32.5	2 27.3	11 17.5	9 9.1
31 F	20 40 21.1	10 59.3	6 58.9	5♎19.9	25R20.2	1 33.9	7 7.8	19 14.2	13 28.4	2 27.6	11 18.8	9 8.5
						DECLINATION at NOON						
1 W	18 42 4.4	23S 1.8	21S44.1	7N53.0	24S20.8	22S32.0	22S50.5	7S36.0	22N 6.3	11S37.9	20S30.7	11N45.0
4 S	18 53 54.1	22 45.4	21 42.6	7S60.0	23 38.0	21 53.8	23 5.6	7 23.7	22 8.4	11 39.7	20 31.4	11 46.3
7 T	19 5 43.8	22 24.9	21 41.1	19 26.5	22 41.3	21 9.7	23 18.8	7 10.9	22 10.4	11 41.4	20 32.2	11 47.7
10 F	19 17 33.5	22 0.4	21 39.6	21 48.9	21 30.8	20 20.0	23 29.8	6 57.8	22 12.4	11 43.0	20 32.9	11 49.2
13 M	19 29 23.1	21 32.0	21 38.0	15 3.4	20 7.4	19 25.0	23 38.9	6 44.3	22 14.4	11 44.3	20 33.6	11 50.8
16 T	19 41 12.8	20 59.9	21 36.5	3 0.6	18 33.0	18 24.9	23 45.8	6 30.5	22 16.3	11 45.5	20 34.3	11 52.5
19 S	19 53 2.5	20 24.2	21 34.9	10N 4.1	16 50.9	17 20.1	23 50.6	6 16.3	22 18.2	11 46.5	20 34.9	11 54.3
22 W	20 4 52.1	19 45.1	21 33.4	20 0.2	15 6.5	16 11.0	23 53.2	6 1.8	22 20.1	11 47.4	20 35.5	11 56.2
25 S	20 16 41.8	19 2.6	21 31.8	21 4.2	13 27.9	14 58.0	23 53.6	5 47.0	22 21.8	11 48.1	20 36.0	11 58.2
28 T	20 28 31.5	18 17.0	21 30.2	10 8.7	12 5.7	13 41.2	23 51.9	5 31.9	22 23.6	11 48.6	20 36.5	12 0.3
31 F	20 40 21.1	17 28.5	21 28.6	6S15.3	11 11.4	12 21.2	23 47.9	5 16.6	22 25.2	11 48.9	20 36.9	12 2.5

FEBRUARY 1975

DAY	EPHEMERIS SIDEREAL TIME	☉	☊	☽	☿	♀	♂	♃	♄	♅	♆	♇
						LONGITUDE at NOON						
1 S	20 44 17.7	12♒ 0.2	6♐55.7	19♎38.0	25♒ 2.7	2♓48.7	7♑52.0	19♓27.2	13♋24.4	2♏27.9	11♐20.1	9♎ 7.8
2 S	20 48 14.3	13 1.1	6 52.5	3♏28.7	24R34.1	4 3.5	8 36.3	19 40.2	13R20.4	2 28.1	11 21.4	9R 7.1
3 M	20 52 10.8	14 2.0	6 49.3	16 53.2	23 55.1	5 18.2	9 20.5	19 53.3	13 16.5	2 28.3	11 22.7	9 6.3
4 T	20 56 7.4	15 2.8	6 46.1	29 54.2	23 6.6	6 32.9	10 4.8	20 6.5	13 12.6	2 28.4	11 24.0	9 5.5
5 W	21 0 3.9	16 3.7	6 43.0	12♐35.7	22 9.9	7 47.6	10 49.1	20 19.7	13 8.9	2 28.4	11 25.2	9 4.7
6 T	21 4 0.5	17 4.5	6 39.8	25 1.6	21 6.5	9 2.3	11 33.5	20 33.0	13 5.2	2 28.4	11 26.4	9 3.9
7 F	21 7 57.0	18 5.3	6 36.6	7♑15.7	19 58.4	10 17.0	12 17.9	20 46.4	13 1.6	2 28.4	11 27.5	9 3.0
8 S	21 11 53.6	19 6.1	6 33.4	19 21.4	18 47.5	11 31.6	13 2.3	20 59.8	12 58.1	2R28.2	11 28.6	9 2.1
9 S	21 15 50.1	20 6.9	6 30.3	1♒21.1	17 35.7	12 46.2	13 46.8	21 13.3	12 54.6	2 28.1	11 29.7	9 1.2
10 M	21 19 46.7	21 7.6	6 27.1	13 16.9	16 25.1	14 0.8	14 31.3	21 26.8	12 51.3	2 27.8	11 30.8	9 0.2
11 T	21 23 43.2	22 8.3	6 23.9	25 10.2	15 17.4	15 15.3	15 15.8	21 40.3	12 48.0	2 27.6	11 31.8	8 59.2
12 W	21 27 39.8	23 9.1	6 20.7	7♓ 2.3	14 14.2	16 29.9	16 0.4	21 54.0	12 44.9	2 27.3	11 32.9	8 58.2
13 T	21 31 36.4	24 9.8	6 17.5	18 54.4	13 16.5	17 44.4	16 45.0	22 7.7	12 41.8	2 26.9	11 33.9	8 57.2
14 F	21 35 32.9	25 10.4	6 14.4	0♈48.2	12 25.5	18 58.8	17 29.7	22 21.4	12 38.8	2 26.4	11 34.8	8 56.1
15 S	21 39 29.5	26 11.1	6 11.2	12 45.9	11 41.7	20 13.2	18 14.3	22 35.2	12 35.9	2 25.9	11 35.7	8 55.0
16 S	21 43 26.0	27 11.7	6 8.0	24 50.4	11 5.6	21 27.6	18 59.0	22 49.0	12 33.1	2 25.4	11 36.6	8 53.9
17 M	21 47 22.6	28 12.3	6 4.8	7♉ 5.1	10 37.2	22 41.9	19 43.7	23 2.9	12 30.3	2 24.8	11 37.4	8 52.8
18 T	21 51 19.1	29 12.8	6 1.7	19 34.4	10 16.6	23 56.2	20 28.4	23 16.8	12 27.7	2 24.1	11 38.2	8 51.6
19 W	21 55 15.7	0♓13.3	5 58.5	2♊22.8	10 3.6	25 10.5	21 13.2	23 30.7	12 25.2	2 23.4	11 39.0	8 50.4
20 T	21 59 12.2	1 13.8	5 55.3	15 34.8	9 57.9	26 24.7	21 58.0	23 44.7	12 22.8	2 22.6	11 39.8	8 49.2
21 F	22 3 8.8	2 14.3	5 52.1	29 14.1	9D59.2	27 38.9	22 42.8	23 58.7	12 20.5	2 21.8	11 40.5	8 48.0
22 S	22 7 5.3	3 14.7	5 48.9	13♋22.7	10 7.1	28 53.0	23 27.7	24 12.8	12 18.3	2 20.9	11 41.2	8 46.7
23 S	22 11 1.9	4 15.1	5 45.8	27 59.9	10 21.3	0♈ 7.1	24 12.5	24 26.9	12 16.2	2 20.0	11 41.8	8 45.4
24 M	22 14 58.4	5 15.4	5 42.6	13♌ 1.4	10 41.2	1 21.1	24 57.5	24 41.0	12 14.2	2 19.0	11 42.4	8 44.1
25 T	22 18 55.0	6 15.8	5 39.4	28 19.0	11 6.6	2 35.1	25 42.4	24 55.1	12 12.3	2 18.0	11 43.0	8 42.8
26 W	22 22 51.6	7 16.1	5 36.2	13♍41.7	11 37.0	3 49.1	26 27.4	25 9.3	12 10.5	2 16.9	11 43.6	8 41.4
27 T	22 26 48.1	8 16.3	5 33.1	28 57.6	12 12.0	5 3.0	27 12.3	25 23.5	12 8.8	2 15.8	11 44.1	8 40.1
28 F	22 30 44.7	9 16.6	5 29.9	13♎55.7	12 51.4	6 16.9	27 57.4	25 37.8	12 7.2	2 14.6	11 44.5	8 38.7
						DECLINATION at NOON						
1 S	20 44 17.7	17S11.7	21S28.1	11S11.4	11S 1.2	11S53.9	23S46.1	5S11.4	22N25.7	11S49.0	20S37.1	12N 3.2
4 T	20 56 7.4	16 19.4	21 26.5	20 49.4	10 56.5	10 30.0	23 39.2	4 55.7	22 27.3	11 49.1	20 37.5	12 5.5
7 F	21 7 57.0	15 24.6	21 24.9	20 45.7	11 27.6	9 3.7	23 30.1	4 39.8	22 28.7	11 49.0	20 37.8	12 7.8
10 M	21 19 46.7	14 27.5	21 23.3	12 26.7	12 23.4	7 35.2	23 18.8	4 23.7	22 30.1	11 48.8	20 38.1	12 10.2
13 T	21 31 36.4	13 28.1	21 21.6	0N 6.6	13 28.4	6 5.0	23 5.3	4 7.3	22 31.4	11 48.4	20 38.4	12 12.5
16 S	21 43 26.0	12 26.8	21 20.0	12 42.5	14 29.8	4 33.4	22 49.7	3 50.8	22 32.6	11 47.8	20 38.7	12 15.0
19 W	21 55 15.7	11 23.7	21 18.4	20 57.4	15 20.1	3 0.6	22 31.9	3 34.2	22 33.7	11 47.1	20 38.8	12 17.4
22 S	22 7 5.3	10 19.0	21 16.7	19 43.7	15 56.3	1 27.2	22 12.0	3 17.4	22 34.8	11 46.2	20 39.0	12 19.9
25 T	22 18 55.0	9 12.9	21 15.0	7 24.1	16 17.4	0N 6.7	21 50.0	3 0.5	22 35.7	11 45.1	20 39.1	12 22.4
28 F	22 30 44.7	8 5.6	21 13.3	9S 5.4	16 23.6	1 40.6	21 26.0	2 43.5	22 36.6	11 43.9	20 39.2	12 24.9

MARCH 1975

DAY	EPHEMERIS SIDEREAL TIME	☉	☊	☽	☿	♀	♂	♃	♄	♅	♆	♇
	h m s	° ′	° ′	° ′	° ′	° ′	° ′	° ′	° ′	° ′	° ′	° ′
						LONGITUDE at NOON						
1 S	22 34 41.2	10♓16.8	5♐26.7	28♎28.3	13♒34.8	7♈30.7	28♑42.4	25♓52.0	12♋ 5.7	2♏13.4	11♐45.0	8♎37.3
2 S	22 38 37.8	11 17.0	5 23.5	12♏31.4	14 22.0	8 44.4	29 27.5	26 6.3	12R 4.3	2R12.2	11 45.4	8R35.8
3 M	22 42 34.3	12 17.2	5 20.3	26 4.7	15 12.6	9 58.2	0♒12.6	26 20.6	12 3.1	2 10.8	11 45.8	8 34.4
4 T	22 46 30.9	13 17.3	5 17.2	9♐10.5	16 6.4	11 11.9	0 57.7	26 35.0	12 1.9	2 9.5	11 46.1	8 32.9
5 W	22 50 27.4	14 17.5	5 14.0	21 52.8	17 3.3	12 25.5	1 43.0	26 49.4	12 0.9	2 8.1	11 46.5	8 31.5
6 T	22 54 24.0	15 17.6	5 10.8	4♑16.2	18 2.9	13 39.1	2 28.1	27 3.8	11 60.0	2 6.7	11 46.8	8 30.0
7 F	22 58 20.5	16 17.6	5 7.6	16 25.5	19 5.1	14 52.7	3 13.4	27 18.2	11 59.2	2 5.2	11 47.0	8 28.5
8 S	23 2 17.1	17 17.7	5 4.5	28 25.4	20 9.8	16 6.2	3 58.6	27 32.6	11 58.5	2 3.6	11 47.2	8 27.0
9 S	23 6 13.6	18 17.7	5 1.3	10♒19.5	21 16.8	17 19.6	4 43.9	27 47.0	11 57.9	2 2.1	11 47.4	8 25.5
10 M	23 10 10.2	19 17.7	4 58.1	22 11.0	22 26.0	18 33.0	5 29.1	28 1.5	11 57.4	2 0.4	11 47.6	8 23.9
11 T	23 14 6.7	20 17.6	4 54.9	4♓ 2.3	23 37.2	19 46.3	6 14.5	28 16.0	11 57.0	1 58.8	11 47.7	8 22.4
12 W	23 18 3.3	21 17.5	4 51.7	15 55.1	24 50.4	20 59.6	6 59.8	28 30.5	11 56.7	1 57.1	11 47.7	8 20.8
13 T	23 21 59.8	22 17.4	4 48.6	27 50.9	26 5.4	22 12.9	7 45.1	28 45.0	11 56.6	1 55.3	11 47.8	8 19.2
14 F	23 25 56.4	23 17.3	4 45.4	9♈50.7	27 22.3	23 26.0	8 30.5	28 59.5	11 56.6	1 53.5	11 47.8	8 17.6
15 S	23 29 52.9	24 17.1	4 42.2	21 56.1	28 40.8	24 39.2	9 15.9	29 14.0	11 56.6	1 51.7	11 47.8	8 16.0
16 S	23 33 49.5	25 16.9	4 39.0	4♉ 8.6	0♓ 1.0	25 52.2	10 1.3	29 28.5	11D56.8	1 49.8	11R47.7	8 14.4
17 M	23 37 46.1	26 16.7	4 35.9	16 30.7	1 22.8	27 5.2	10 46.7	29 43.0	11 57.1	1 47.9	11 47.6	8 12.8
18 T	23 41 42.6	27 16.4	4 32.7	29 5.1	2 46.1	28 18.2	11 32.1	29 57.5	11 57.5	1 46.0	11 47.5	8 11.2
19 W	23 45 39.2	28 16.0	4 29.5	11♊55.1	4 11.0	29 31.0	12 17.6	0♈12.1	11 58.1	1 44.0	11 47.3	8 9.5
20 T	23 49 35.7	29 15.7	4 26.3	25 4.5	5 37.3	0♉43.9	13 3.0	0 26.6	11 58.7	1 42.0	11 47.1	8 7.9
21 F	23 53 32.3	0♈15.3	4 23.1	8♋36.4	7 5.0	1 56.6	13 48.5	0 41.1	11 59.5	1 40.0	11 46.9	8 6.2
22 S	23 57 28.8	1 14.9	4 20.0	22 33.1	8 34.2	3 9.3	14 34.0	0 55.7	12 0.3	1 37.9	11 46.6	8 4.6
23 S	0 1 25.4	2 14.4	4 16.8	6♌54.9	10 4.7	4 21.9	15 19.5	1 10.2	12 1.3	1 35.8	11 46.4	8 2.9
24 M	0 5 21.9	3 13.9	4 13.6	21 39.6	11 36.6	5 34.4	16 5.0	1 24.7	12 2.4	1 33.7	11 46.0	8 1.3
25 T	0 9 18.5	4 13.3	4 10.4	6♍41.4	13 10.0	6 46.9	16 50.6	1 39.3	12 3.6	1 31.5	11 45.7	7 59.6
26 W	0 13 15.0	5 12.8	4 7.3	21 51.9	14 44.7	7 59.3	17 36.2	1 53.8	12 4.9	1 29.4	11 45.3	7 58.0
27 T	0 17 11.6	6 12.1	4 4.1	7♎ 0.7	16 20.7	9 11.7	18 21.7	2 8.3	12 6.3	1 27.1	11 44.9	7 56.3
28 F	0 21 8.1	7 11.5	4 0.9	21 57.4	17 58.1	10 23.9	19 7.3	2 22.8	12 7.9	1 24.9	11 44.5	7 54.6
29 S	0 25 4.7	8 10.8	3 57.7	6♏33.5	19 36.9	11 36.1	19 52.9	2 37.3	12 9.5	1 22.6	11 44.0	7 53.0
30 S	0 29 1.2	9 10.1	3 54.5	20 43.4	21 17.0	12 48.2	20 38.5	2 51.8	12 11.2	1 20.3	11 43.5	7 51.3
31 M	0 32 57.8	10 9.3	3 51.4	4♐24.8	22 58.6	14 0.2	21 24.1	3 6.3	12 13.1	1 18.0	11 42.9	7 49.6
						DECLINATION at NOON						
1 S	22 34 41.2	7S42.9	21S12.8	13S43.3	16S22.4	2N11.9	21S17.5	2S37.8	22N36.8	11S43.5	20S39.2	12N25.7
4 T	22 46 30.9	6 34.1	21 11.1	21 26.9	16 9.6	3 45.4	20 50.9	2 20.6	22 37.6	11 42.1	20 39.2	12 28.2
7 F	22 58 20.5	5 24.5	21 9.4	19 6.3	15 43.1	5 18.2	20 22.3	2 3.4	22 38.2	11 40.5	20 39.2	12 30.7
10 M	23 10 10.2	4 14.3	21 7.7	9 28.8	15 3.5	6 50.1	19 51.8	1 46.2	22 38.7	11 38.8	20 39.1	12 33.1
13 T	23 21 59.8	3 3.5	21 5.9	3N20.5	14 11.3	8 20.5	19 19.5	1 28.9	22 39.2	11 37.0	20 39.0	12 35.5
16 S	23 33 49.5	1 52.5	21 4.2	15 12.6	13 7.0	9 49.3	18 45.5	1 11.5	22 39.6	11 35.1	20 38.8	12 37.8
19 W	23 45 39.2	0 41.4	21 2.5	21 26.5	11 50.9	11 16.1	18 9.8	0 54.2	22 39.8	11 33.1	20 38.6	12 40.1
22 S	23 57 28.8	0N29.8	21 0.7	17 44.2	10 23.3	12 40.6	17 32.5	0 36.9	22 40.0	11 30.9	20 38.4	12 42.4
25 T	0 9 18.5	1 40.7	20 58.9	4 21.1	8 44.7	14 2.4	16 53.6	0 19.6	22 40.1	11 28.7	20 38.1	12 44.5
28 F	0 21 8.1	2 51.3	20 57.2	11S36.9	6 55.4	15 21.2	16 13.3	0 2.4	22 40.1	11 26.4	20 37.8	12 46.6
31 M	0 32 57.8	4 1.3	20 55.4	20 49.7	4 55.8	16 36.7	15 31.6	0N14.8	22 40.0	11 24.0	20 37.5	12 48.6

APRIL 1975

DAY	EPHEMERIS SIDEREAL TIME	☉	☊	☽	☿	♀	♂	♃	♄	♅	♆	♇
						LONGITUDE at NOON						
1 T	0 36 54.3	11♈ 8.5	3♐48.2	17♐38.4	24♓41.5	15♉12.2	22♒ 9.8	3♈20.7	12♋15.0	1♏15.7	11♐42.4	7♎47.9
2 W	0 40 50.9	12 7.7	3 45.0	0♑26.9	26 25.8	16 24.1	22 55.4	3 35.2	12 17.1	1R13.3	11R41.8	7R46.3
3 T	0 44 47.4	13 6.9	3 41.8	12 54.5	28 11.5	17 35.9	23 41.1	3 49.6	12 19.2	1 10.9	11 41.1	7 44.6
4 F	0 48 44.0	14 6.0	3 38.6	25 5.9	29 58.6	18 47.6	24 26.7	4 4.0	12 21.5	1 8.5	11 40.5	7 43.0
5 S	0 52 40.5	15 5.1	3 35.5	7♒ 6.1	1♈47.2	19 59.3	25 12.4	4 18.4	12 23.9	1 6.1	11 39.8	7 41.3
6 S	0 56 37.1	16 4.2	3 32.3	18 59.6	3 37.2	21 10.8	25 58.1	4 32.8	12 26.3	1 3.7	11 39.0	7 39.6
7 M	1 0 33.7	17 3.2	3 29.1	0♓50.6	5 28.6	22 22.3	26 43.8	4 47.2	12 28.9	1 1.2	11 38.3	7 38.0
8 T	1 4 30.2	18 2.2	3 25.9	12 42.4	7 21.5	23 33.8	27 29.5	5 1.5	12 31.6	0 58.7	11 37.5	7 36.4
9 W	1 8 26.8	19 1.2	3 22.8	24 37.9	9 15.9	24 45.1	28 15.2	5 15.9	12 34.4	0 56.2	11 36.7	7 34.7
10 T	1 12 23.3	20 0.2	3 19.6	6♈39.1	11 11.7	25 56.3	29 0.9	5 30.2	12 37.2	0 53.7	11 35.9	7 33.1
11 F	1 16 19.9	20 59.1	3 16.4	18 47.7	13 8.9	27 7.5	29 46.6	5 44.4	12 40.2	0 51.2	11 35.0	7 31.5
12 S	1 20 16.4	21 58.0	3 13.2	1♉ 4.8	15 7.5	28 18.6	0♓32.3	5 58.7	12 43.3	0 48.7	11 34.1	7 29.9
13 S	1 24 13.0	22 56.8	3 10.0	13 31.6	17 7.5	29 29.6	1 18.0	6 12.9	12 46.5	0 46.2	11 33.2	7 28.3
14 M	1 28 9.5	23 55.6	3 6.9	26 8.9	19 8.9	0♊40.5	2 3.7	6 27.1	12 49.7	0 43.6	11 32.2	7 26.7
15 T	1 32 6.1	24 54.4	3 3.7	8♊58.3	21 11.5	1 51.3	2 49.4	6 41.3	12 53.1	0 41.1	11 31.3	7 25.1
16 W	1 36 2.6	25 53.2	3 0.5	22 1.1	23 15.3	3 2.1	3 35.1	6 55.4	12 56.6	0 38.6	11 30.3	7 23.6
17 T	1 39 59.2	26 51.9	2 57.3	5♋19.0	25 20.2	4 12.7	4 20.8	7 9.5	13 0.2	0 36.0	11 29.3	7 22.0
18 F	1 43 55.7	27 50.6	2 54.2	18 53.7	27 26.0	5 23.2	5 6.5	7 23.6	13 3.8	0 33.5	11 28.3	7 20.5
19 S	1 47 52.3	28 49.2	2 51.0	2♌46.2	29 32.6	6 33.6	5 52.2	7 37.6	13 7.6	0 30.9	11 27.2	7 18.9
20 S	1 51 48.8	29 47.8	2 47.8	16 56.5	1♉39.9	7 43.9	6 37.9	7 51.6	13 11.4	0 28.3	11 26.1	7 17.4
21 M	1 55 45.4	0♉46.3	2 44.6	1♍22.9	3 47.6	8 54.1	7 23.5	8 5.6	13 15.4	0 25.8	11 25.0	7 15.9
22 T	1 59 41.9	1 44.9	2 41.4	16 2.0	5 55.5	10 4.2	8 9.2	8 19.5	13 19.4	0 23.2	11 23.8	7 14.4
23 W	2 3 38.5	2 43.3	2 38.3	0♎47.9	8 3.3	11 14.1	8 54.9	8 33.4	13 23.5	0 20.6	11 22.7	7 13.0
24 T	2 7 35.1	3 41.8	2 35.1	15 33.8	10 10.7	12 24.0	9 40.5	8 47.2	13 27.7	0 18.1	11 21.5	7 11.5
25 F	2 11 31.6	4 40.2	2 31.9	0♏12.0	12 17.6	13 33.7	10 26.2	9 1.0	13 32.0	0 15.5	11 20.3	7 10.1
26 S	2 15 28.2	5 38.6	2 28.7	14 35.5	14 23.5	14 43.4	11 11.8	9 14.7	13 36.3	0 13.0	11 19.0	7 8.6
27 S	2 19 24.7	6 36.9	2 25.6	28 39.0	16 28.1	15 52.9	11 57.4	9 28.4	13 40.8	0 10.4	11 17.8	7 7.2
28 M	2 23 21.3	7 35.3	2 22.4	12♐19.1	18 31.2	17 2.3	12 43.0	9 42.1	13 45.3	0 7.9	11 16.5	7 5.8
29 T	2 27 17.8	8 33.6	2 19.2	25 35.0	20 32.4	18 11.5	13 28.7	9 55.7	13 49.9	0 5.3	11 15.2	7 4.5
30 W	2 31 14.4	9 31.8	2 16.0	8♑27.8	22 31.4	19 20.7	14 14.3	10 9.3	13 54.6	0 2.8	11 13.9	7 3.1
						DECLINATION at NOON						
1 T	0 36 54.3	4N24.5	20S54.8	21S30.1	4S13.7	17N 1.0	15S17.4	0N20.5	22N39.9	11S23.2	20S37.4	12N49.3
4 F	0 48 44.0	5 33.7	20 53.0	17 4.8	2 1.0	18 11.6	14 33.9	0 37.6	22 39.7	11 20.7	20 37.0	12 51.1
7 M	1 0 33.7	6 42.0	20 51.2	6 22.4	0N20.8	19 18.1	13 49.2	0 54.6	22 39.3	11 18.1	20 36.6	12 52.9
10 T	1 12 23.3	7 49.3	20 49.4	6N30.4	2 50.7	20 20.3	13 3.3	1 11.5	22 38.9	11 15.5	20 36.2	12 54.6
13 S	1 24 13.0	8 55.4	20 47.5	17 24.6	5 27.4	21 17.8	12 16.4	1 28.2	22 38.4	11 12.9	20 35.7	12 56.2
16 W	1 36 2.6	10 0.1	20 45.7	21 21.6	8 8.8	22 10.4	11 28.5	1 44.9	22 37.7	11 10.3	20 35.2	12 57.6
19 S	1 47 52.3	11 3.4	20 43.8	15 5.0	10 51.8	22 57.8	10 39.8	2 1.3	22 37.0	11 7.6	20 34.7	12 58.9
22 T	1 59 41.9	12 4.9	20 42.0	0 51.9	13 32.2	23 39.9	9 50.2	2 17.6	22 36.2	11 4.9	20 34.1	13 0.2
25 F	2 11 31.6	13 4.7	20 40.1	14S 3.2	16 4.8	24 16.3	8 60.0	2 33.7	22 35.2	11 2.3	20 33.5	13 1.2
28 M	2 23 21.3	14 2.6	20 38.2	21 15.0	18 24.1	24 46.9	8 9.0	2 49.7	22 34.2	10 59.6	20 32.9	13 2.2

MAY 1975

LONGITUDE at NOON

DAY	EPHEMERIS SIDEREAL TIME	☉	☊	☾	☿	♀	♂	♃	♄	♅	♆	♇
	h m s	° ′	° ′	° ′	° ′	° ′	° ′	° ′	° ′	° ′	° ′	° ′
1 T	2 35 10.9	10♉30.1	2♐12.8	20♑60.0	24♉28.0	20♊29.7	14♓59.9	10♈22.8	13♋59.4	0♏ 0.3	11♐12.6	7♎ 1.8
2 F	2 39 7.5	11 28.3	2 9.7	3♒15.5	26 22.0	21 38.6	15 45.4	10 36.3	14 4.3	29♎57.8	11R11.3	7R 0.5
3 S	2 43 4.0	12 26.5	2 6.5	15 18.7	28 13.0	22 47.4	16 31.0	10 49.7	14 9.2	29R55.3	11 9.9	6 59.2
4 S	2 47 0.6	13 24.7	2 3.3	27 14.1	0♊ 1.0	23 56.0	17 16.6	11 3.1	14 14.2	29 52.8	11 8.5	6 57.9
5 M	2 50 57.2	14 22.8	2 0.1	9♓ 6.5	1 45.6	25 4.5	18 2.1	11 16.4	14 19.3	29 50.4	11 7.1	6 56.7
6 T	2 54 53.7	15 20.9	1 57.0	21 0.0	3 26.9	26 12.9	18 47.6	11 29.6	14 24.5	29 47.9	11 5.7	6 55.4
7 W	2 58 50.3	16 19.1	1 53.8	2♈58.6	5 4.8	27 21.2	19 33.2	11 42.9	14 29.7	29 45.5	11 4.3	6 54.3
8 T	3 2 46.8	17 17.2	1 50.6	15 5.3	6 38.9	28 29.2	20 18.6	11 56.0	14 35.1	29 43.1	11 2.9	6 53.1
9 F	3 6 43.4	18 15.2	1 47.4	27 22.7	8 9.3	29 37.2	21 4.1	12 9.1	14 40.5	29 40.7	11 1.4	6 51.9
10 S	3 10 39.9	19 13.2	1 44.3	9♉52.7	9 35.9	0♋45.0	21 49.5	12 22.1	14 45.9	29 38.3	10 59.9	6 50.8
11 S	3 14 36.5	20 11.2	1 41.1	22 36.3	10 58.7	1 52.7	22 34.9	12 35.1	14 51.4	29 36.0	10 58.5	6 49.7
12 M	3 18 33.0	21 9.2	1 37.9	5♊33.9	12 17.5	3 0.1	23 20.3	12 48.0	14 57.0	29 33.6	10 57.0	6 48.6
13 T	3 22 29.6	22 7.2	1 34.7	18 45.4	13 32.3	4 7.5	24 5.7	13 0.8	15 2.7	29 31.3	10 55.4	6 47.6
14 W	3 26 26.1	23 5.1	1 31.5	2♋10.3	14 43.1	5 14.7	24 51.0	13 13.6	15 8.4	29 29.0	10 53.9	6 46.5
15 T	3 30 22.7	24 3.0	1 28.4	15 48.0	15 49.7	6 21.7	25 36.3	13 26.3	15 14.2	29 26.8	10 52.4	6 45.5
16 F	3 34 19.3	25 0.8	1 25.2	29 37.4	16 52.2	7 28.5	26 21.6	13 38.9	15 20.1	29 24.5	10 50.8	6 44.5
17 S	3 38 15.8	25 58.6	1 22.0	13♌37.2	17 50.4	8 35.2	27 6.8	13 51.5	15 26.0	29 22.3	10 49.3	6 43.6
18 S	3 42 12.4	26 56.5	1 18.8	27 45.9	18 44.2	9 41.6	27 52.0	14 3.9	15 32.0	29 20.2	10 47.7	6 42.7
19 M	3 46 8.9	27 54.2	1 15.7	12♍ 1.6	19 33.8	10 47.9	28 37.2	14 16.4	15 38.1	29 18.0	10 46.2	6 41.8
20 T	3 50 5.5	28 52.0	1 12.5	26 21.4	20 18.8	11 54.0	29 22.3	14 28.7	15 44.2	29 15.9	10 44.6	6 40.9
21 W	3 54 2.0	29 49.7	1 9.3	10♎42.1	20 59.4	12 59.9	0♈ 7.4	14 40.9	15 50.4	29 13.8	10 43.0	6 40.0
22 T	3 57 58.6	0♊47.4	1 6.1	24 59.9	21 35.3	14 5.6	0 52.5	14 53.1	15 56.6	29 11.7	10 41.4	6 39.2
23 F	4 1 55.2	1 45.1	1 2.9	9♏10.6	22 6.7	15 11.1	1 37.5	15 5.2	16 2.9	29 9.7	10 39.8	6 38.4
24 S	4 5 51.7	2 42.7	0 59.8	23 10.1	22 33.3	16 16.4	2 22.5	15 17.2	16 9.2	29 7.7	10 38.2	6 37.7
25 S	4 9 48.3	3 40.3	0 56.6	6♐54.8	22 55.3	17 21.4	3 7.5	15 29.2	16 15.6	29 5.7	10 36.6	6 37.0
26 M	4 13 44.8	4 37.9	0 53.4	20 22.2	23 12.5	18 26.2	3 52.4	15 41.0	16 22.1	29 3.8	10 35.0	6 36.3
27 T	4 17 41.4	5 35.5	0 50.2	3♑30.9	23 24.9	19 30.8	4 37.3	15 52.8	16 28.6	29 1.9	10 33.4	6 35.6
28 W	4 21 37.9	6 33.1	0 47.1	16 20.7	23 32.7	20 35.2	5 22.2	16 4.5	16 35.2	29 0.1	10 31.8	6 35.0
29 T	4 25 34.5	7 30.7	0 43.9	28 52.9	23 35.8	21 39.4	6 7.0	16 16.2	16 41.8	28 58.2	10 30.2	6 34.4
30 F	4 29 31.0	8 28.2	0 40.7	11♒ 9.8	23R34.3	22 43.2	6 51.8	16 27.7	16 48.4	28 56.4	10 28.6	6 33.8
31 S	4 33 27.6	9 25.7	0 37.5	23 14.7	23 28.3	23 46.9	7 36.6	16 39.1	16 55.1	28 54.7	10 26.9	6 33.2

DECLINATION at NOON

DAY	EPHEMERIS SIDEREAL TIME	☉	☊	☾	☿	♀	♂	♃	♄	♅	♆	♇
1 T	2 35 10.9	14N58.4	20S36.4	17S49.3	20N25.3	25N11.6	7S17.5	3N 5.4	22N33.1	10S57.0	20S32.3	13N 3.0
4 S	2 47 0.6	15 52.0	20 34.5	7 30.1	22 5.2	25 30.3	6 25.5	3 20.9	22 31.8	10 54.4	20 31.7	13 3.7
7 W	2 58 50.3	16 43.2	20 32.6	5N16.7	23 22.6	25 43.0	5 33.1	3 36.1	22 30.5	10 51.9	20 31.1	13 4.2
10 S	3 10 39.9	17 31.9	20 30.6	16 34.4	24 18.0	25 49.5	4 40.5	3 51.1	22 29.0	10 49.4	20 30.4	13 4.6
13 T	3 22 29.6	18 18.0	20 28.7	21 20.9	24 52.8	25 49.9	3 47.5	4 5.8	22 27.5	10 47.0	20 29.8	13 4.9
16 F	3 34 19.3	19 1.3	20 26.8	15 48.8	25 9.0	25 44.4	2 54.5	4 20.2	22 25.8	10 44.7	20 29.1	13 5.0
19 M	3 46 8.9	19 41.7	20 24.9	2 15.3	25 8.8	25 32.9	2 1.4	4 34.4	22 24.1	10 42.4	20 28.4	13 4.9
22 T	3 57 58.6	20 19.0	20 22.9	12S34.0	24 54.0	25 15.7	1 8.3	4 48.2	22 22.2	10 40.3	20 27.7	13 4.8
25 S	4 9 48.3	20 53.3	20 20.9	20 55.3	24 26.7	24 53.0	0 15.3	5 1.7	22 20.2	10 38.2	20 27.0	13 4.4
28 W	4 21 37.9	21 24.3	20 19.0	18 42.1	23 48.8	24 24.9	0N37.5	5 14.9	22 18.1	10 36.3	20 26.3	13 3.9
31 S	4 33 27.6	21 52.0	20 17.0	8 49.6	23 2.1	23 51.8	1 30.1	5 27.7	22 15.9	10 34.5	20 25.7	13 3.3

JUNE 1975

LONGITUDE at NOON

DAY	EPHEMERIS SIDEREAL TIME	☉	☊	☾	☿	♀	♂	♃	♄	♅	♆	♇
1 S	4 37 24.2	10♊23.2	0♐34.4	5♓11.6	23♊18.0	24♋50.2	8♈21.3	16♈50.4	17♋ 1.9	28♎53.0	10♐25.3	6♎32.7
2 M	4 41 20.7	11 20.7	0 31.2	17 4.9	23R 3.6	25 53.4	9 5.9	17 1.7	17 8.7	28R51.3	10R23.7	6R32.2
3 T	4 45 17.3	12 18.2	0 28.0	28 59.3	22 45.4	26 56.2	9 50.5	17 12.8	17 15.5	28 49.7	10 22.1	6 31.8
4 W	4 49 13.8	13 15.7	0 24.8	10♈59.3	22 23.6	27 58.8	10 35.1	17 23.9	17 22.4	28 48.1	10 20.4	6 31.4
5 T	4 53 10.4	14 13.1	0 21.6	23 9.1	21 58.8	29 1.1	11 19.6	17 34.8	17 29.3	28 46.5	10 18.8	6 31.0
6 F	4 57 6.9	15 10.6	0 18.5	5♉32.6	21 31.2	0♌ 3.0	12 4.0	17 45.7	17 36.3	28 45.0	10 17.2	6 30.6
7 S	5 1 3.5	16 8.0	0 15.3	18 12.6	21 1.3	1 4.7	12 48.4	17 56.4	17 43.3	28 43.5	10 15.6	6 30.3
8 S	5 5 0.1	17 5.4	0 12.1	1♊11.1	20 29.7	2 6.1	13 32.8	18 7.1	17 50.3	28 42.1	10 14.0	6 30.0
9 M	5 8 56.6	18 2.8	0 8.9	14 28.5	19 56.9	3 7.2	14 17.1	18 17.6	17 57.4	28 40.7	10 12.3	6 29.7
10 T	5 12 53.2	19 0.2	0 5.8	28 4.1	19 23.4	4 7.9	15 1.3	18 28.1	18 4.6	28 39.4	10 10.7	6 29.5
11 W	5 16 49.7	19 57.6	0 2.6	11♋55.8	18 49.8	5 8.4	15 45.4	18 38.4	18 11.7	28 38.1	10 9.1	6 29.3
12 T	5 20 46.3	20 55.0	29♏59.4	26 0.2	18 16.8	6 8.4	16 29.6	18 48.6	18 18.9	28 36.8	10 7.5	6 29.1
13 F	5 24 42.8	21 52.3	29 56.2	10♌13.4	17 44.7	7 8.1	17 13.6	18 58.7	18 26.2	28 35.6	10 6.0	6 29.0
14 S	5 28 39.4	22 49.6	29 53.1	24 31.2	17 14.3	8 7.4	17 57.6	19 8.7	18 33.4	28 34.5	10 4.4	6 28.9
15 S	5 32 36.0	23 47.0	29 49.9	8♍49.5	16 45.9	9 6.3	18 41.5	19 18.6	18 40.7	28 33.3	10 2.8	6 28.8
16 M	5 36 32.5	24 44.3	29 46.7	23 5.0	16 20.2	10 4.9	19 25.3	19 28.4	18 48.1	28 32.3	10 1.2	6 28.8
17 T	5 40 29.1	25 41.6	29 43.5	7♎15.1	15 57.5	11 3.0	20 9.1	19 38.0	18 55.4	28 31.3	9 59.7	6 28.8
18 W	5 44 25.6	26 38.9	29 40.4	21 17.9	15 38.2	12 0.7	20 52.9	19 47.6	19 2.9	28 30.3	9 58.2	6D28.9
19 T	5 48 22.2	27 36.1	29 37.2	5♏11.8	15 22.6	12 57.9	21 36.5	19 57.0	19 10.3	28 29.4	9 56.7	6 28.9
20 F	5 52 18.7	28 33.4	29 34.0	18 55.8	15 11.0	13 54.7	22 20.1	20 6.3	19 17.7	28 28.6	9 55.1	6 29.0
21 S	5 56 15.3	29 30.6	29 30.8	2♐28.6	15 3.7	14 51.0	23 3.6	20 15.5	19 25.2	28 27.7	9 53.6	6 29.2
22 S	6 0 11.9	0♋27.8	29 27.6	15 49.3	15 0.8	15 46.8	23 47.1	20 24.5	19 32.7	28 27.0	9 52.1	6 29.3
23 M	6 4 8.4	1 25.1	29 24.5	28 56.8	15D 2.5	16 42.1	24 30.4	20 33.4	19 40.2	28 26.2	9 50.6	6 29.5
24 T	6 8 5.0	2 22.3	29 21.3	11♑50.5	15 8.9	17 36.8	25 13.7	20 42.2	19 47.8	28 25.6	9 49.2	6 29.8
25 W	6 12 1.5	3 19.5	29 18.1	24 30.2	15 20.0	18 31.0	25 57.0	20 50.9	19 55.3	28 24.9	9 47.7	6 30.0
26 T	6 15 58.1	4 16.7	29 14.9	6♒56.1	15 35.8	19 24.7	26 40.1	20 59.4	20 2.9	28 24.4	9 46.3	6 30.3
27 F	6 19 54.7	5 13.9	29 11.8	19 9.7	15 56.5	20 17.8	27 23.2	21 7.8	20 10.5	28 23.8	9 44.8	6 30.7
28 S	6 23 51.2	6 11.1	29 8.6	1♓13.0	16 21.9	21 10.3	28 6.2	21 16.1	20 18.1	28 23.4	9 43.4	6 31.0
29 S	6 27 47.8	7 8.3	29 5.4	13 9.1	16 52.0	22 2.1	28 49.1	21 24.2	20 25.8	28 22.9	9 42.0	6 31.4
30 M	6 31 44.3	8 5.5	29 2.2	25 1.7	17 26.8	22 53.3	29 32.0	21 32.2	20 33.4	28 22.6	9 40.6	6 31.8

DECLINATION at NOON

DAY	EPHEMERIS SIDEREAL TIME	☉	☊	☾	☿	♀	♂	♃	♄	♅	♆	♇
1 S	4 37 24.2	22N 0.5	20S16.3	4S42.5	22N45.0	23N39.7	1N47.6	5N31.8	22N15.2	10S33.9	20S25.4	13N 3.1
4 W	4 49 13.8	22 23.6	20 14.3	8N 3.8	21 50.5	23 0.2	2 39.7	5 44.2	22 12.9	10 32.2	20 24.8	13 2.3
7 S	5 1 3.5	22 43.2	20 12.3	18 22.3	20 54.2	22 16.3	3 31.4	5 56.1	22 10.4	10 30.7	20 24.1	13 1.4
10 T	5 12 53.2	22 59.2	20 10.3	21 1.6	20 0.1	21 28.3	4 22.6	6 7.6	22 7.9	10 29.3	20 23.4	13 0.3
13 F	5 24 42.8	23 11.5	20 8.3	12 57.1	19 13.0	20 36.6	5 13.2	6 18.7	22 5.3	10 28.1	20 22.8	12 59.1
16 M	5 36 32.5	23 20.2	20 6.3	1S42.4	18 37.2	19 41.5	6 3.1	6 29.4	22 2.5	10 27.0	20 22.2	12 57.8
19 T	5 48 22.2	23 25.2	20 4.2	15 23.3	18 15.7	18 43.5	6 52.4	6 39.6	21 59.7	10 26.0	20 21.5	12 56.3
22 S	6 0 11.9	23 26.4	20 2.2	21 20.3	18 10.0	17 42.9	7 40.8	6 49.4	21 56.8	10 25.3	20 21.0	12 54.7
25 W	6 12 1.5	23 24.0	20 0.1	17 5.4	18 19.8	16 40.0	8 28.4	6 58.7	21 53.8	10 24.6	20 20.4	12 53.0
28 S	6 23 51.2	23 17.8	19 58.1	6 11.7	18 43.3	15 35.4	9 15.1	7 7.5	21 50.7	10 24.2	20 19.8	12 51.2

JULY 1975

DAY	EPHEMERIS SIDEREAL TIME	☉	☊	☽	☿	♀	♂	♃	♄	♅	♆	♇
	h m s	° ′	° ′	° ′	° ′	° ′	° ′	° ′	° ′	° ′	° ′	° ′
LONGITUDE at NOON												
1 T	6 35 40.9	9♋ 2.7	28♏59.1	6♈55.2	18♊ 6.3	23♌43.9	0♉14.7	21♈40.1	20♋41.1	28♎22.2	9♐39.3	6♎32.3
2 W	6 39 37.4	9 59.9	28 55.9	18 54.3	18 50.4	24 33.8	0 57.4	21 47.8	20 48.8	28R22.0	9R37.9	6 32.8
3 T	6 43 34.0	10 57.1	28 52.7	1♉ 4.0	19 39.1	25 23.0	1 40.0	21 55.3	20 56.5	28 21.8	9 36.6	6 33.3
4 F	6 47 30.6	11 54.3	28 49.5	13 28.9	20 32.2	26 11.4	2 22.5	22 2.7	21 4.2	28 21.6	9 35.3	6 33.9
5 S	6 51 27.1	12 51.5	28 46.3	26 13.3	21 29.8	26 59.1	3 4.9	22 10.0	21 12.0	28 21.5	9 34.0	6 34.5
6 S	6 55 23.7	13 48.7	28 43.2	9♊20.3	22 31.7	27 46.0	3 47.2	22 17.1	21 19.7	28 21.4	9 32.7	6 35.1
7 M	6 59 20.2	14 46.0	28 40.0	22 51.6	23 37.9	28 32.1	4 29.5	22 24.1	21 27.4	28 21.4	9 31.4	6 35.8
8 T	7 3 16.8	15 43.2	28 36.8	6♋46.5	24 48.4	29 17.3	5 11.6	22 30.9	21 35.2	28D21.5	9 30.2	6 36.5
9 W	7 7 13.3	16 40.5	28 33.6	21 2.3	26 3.1	0♍ 1.7	5 53.7	22 37.6	21 43.0	28 21.6	9 29.0	6 37.2
10 T	7 11 9.9	17 37.7	28 30.5	5♌33.8	27 22.0	0 45.2	6 35.6	22 44.2	21 50.8	28 21.8	9 27.8	6 38.0
11 F	7 15 6.5	18 34.9	28 27.3	20 14.2	28 44.9	1 27.7	7 17.4	22 50.5	21 58.6	28 22.0	9 26.6	6 38.8
12 S	7 19 3.0	19 32.2	28 24.1	4♍56.1	0♋11.8	2 9.1	7 59.1	22 56.7	22 6.3	28 22.2	9 25.5	6 39.6
13 S	7 22 59.6	20 29.4	28 20.9	19 32.4	1 42.6	2 49.6	8 40.7	23 2.7	22 14.1	28 22.5	9 24.3	6 40.4
14 M	7 26 56.1	21 26.6	28 17.8	3♎58.0	3 17.2	3 29.0	9 22.2	23 8.6	22 21.9	28 22.9	9 23.2	6 41.3
15 T	7 30 52.7	22 23.8	28 14.6	18 9.2	4 55.6	4 7.3	10 3.6	23 14.3	22 29.7	28 23.3	9 22.2	6 42.2
16 W	7 34 49.2	23 21.1	28 11.4	2♏ 4.5	6 37.6	4 44.4	10 44.9	23 19.8	22 37.5	28 23.8	9 21.1	6 43.2
17 T	7 38 45.8	24 18.3	28 8.2	15 44.1	8 23.0	5 20.2	11 26.1	23 25.2	22 45.3	28 24.3	9 20.1	6 44.1
18 F	7 42 42.4	25 15.5	28 5.1	29 8.7	10 11.6	5 54.9	12 7.2	23 30.4	22 53.0	28 24.9	9 19.0	6 45.1
19 S	7 46 38.9	26 12.8	28 1.9	12♐19.7	12 3.4	6 28.2	12 48.1	23 35.4	23 0.8	28 25.5	9 18.1	6 46.2
20 S	7 50 35.5	27 10.0	27 58.7	25 18.3	13 57.9	7 0.1	13 28.9	23 40.3	23 8.6	28 26.2	9 17.1	6 47.2
21 M	7 54 32.0	28 7.3	27 55.5	8♑ 5.3	15 55.1	7 30.7	14 9.7	23 45.0	23 16.3	28 26.9	9 16.2	6 48.3
22 T	7 58 28.6	29 4.5	27 52.3	20 41.5	17 54.5	7 59.7	14 50.3	23 49.5	23 24.1	28 27.7	9 15.2	6 49.5
23 W	8 2 25.1	0♌ 1.8	27 49.2	3♒ 7.3	19 55.9	8 27.3	15 30.7	23 53.8	23 31.9	28 28.5	9 14.4	6 50.6
24 T	8 6 21.7	0 59.0	27 46.0	15 23.2	21 59.0	8 53.3	16 11.1	23 58.0	23 39.6	28 29.4	9 13.5	6 51.8
25 F	8 10 18.2	1 56.3	27 42.8	27 30.0	24 3.4	9 17.7	16 51.3	24 2.0	23 47.3	28 30.3	9 12.7	6 53.0
26 S	8 14 14.8	2 53.6	27 39.6	9♓29.2	26 8.9	9 40.3	17 31.5	24 5.8	23 55.1	28 31.3	9 11.9	6 54.3
27 S	8 18 11.4	3 50.9	27 36.5	21 22.7	28 15.0	10 1.3	18 11.5	24 9.4	24 2.8	28 32.4	9 11.1	6 55.5
28 M	8 22 7.9	4 48.3	27 33.3	3♈13.5	0♌21.5	10 20.4	18 51.3	24 12.8	24 10.5	28 33.4	9 10.3	6 56.8
29 T	8 26 4.5	5 45.6	27 30.1	15 5.2	2 28.1	10 37.7	19 31.1	24 16.1	24 18.2	28 34.6	9 9.6	6 58.1
30 W	8 30 1.0	6 43.0	27 26.9	27 2.3	4 34.6	10 53.1	20 10.7	24 19.2	24 25.9	28 35.8	9 9.0	6 59.5
31 T	8 33 57.6	7 40.4	27 23.7	9♉ 9.6	6 40.6	11 6.5	20 50.2	24 22.1	24 33.6	28 37.1	9 8.3	7 0.9
DECLINATION at NOON												
1 T	6 35 40.9	23N 8.0	19S56.0	6N33.9	19N17.9	14N29.4	10N 0.9	7N15.8	21N47.5	10S23.9	20S19.3	12N49.3
4 F	6 47 30.6	22 54.5	19 53.9	17 18.8	20 0.2	13 22.4	10 45.6	7 23.7	21 44.2	10 23.7	20 18.8	12 47.2
7 M	6 59 20.2	22 37.4	19 51.8	21 16.0	20 46.4	12 14.8	11 29.2	7 30.9	21 40.9	10 23.8	20 18.4	12 45.1
10 T	7 11 9.9	22 16.8	19 49.7	14 21.2	21 32.1	11 7.2	12 11.7	7 37.7	21 37.5	10 24.0	20 17.9	12 42.8
13 S	7 22 59.6	21 52.7	19 47.6	0S17.3	22 12.5	10 0.0	12 52.9	7 43.9	21 34.0	10 24.4	20 17.5	12 40.5
16 W	7 34 49.2	21 25.3	19 45.5	14 25.0	22 42.5	8 53.9	13 32.9	7 49.5	21 30.4	10 24.9	20 17.2	12 38.1
19 S	7 46 38.9	20 54.6	19 43.4	21 9.2	22 56.7	7 49.3	14 11.7	7 54.5	21 26.8	10 25.6	20 16.9	12 35.6
22 T	7 58 28.6	20 20.7	19 41.2	17 55.8	22 50.5	6 47.0	14 49.1	7 59.0	21 23.1	10 26.5	20 16.6	12 33.0
25 F	8 10 18.2	19 43.8	19 39.1	7 35.7	22 21.0	5 47.7	15 25.2	8 2.9	21 19.4	10 27.6	20 16.3	12 30.4
28 M	8 22 7.9	19 3.9	19 36.9	5N 5.6	21 27.4	4 52.2	15 60.0	8 6.1	21 15.7	10 28.8	20 16.1	12 27.7
31 T	8 33 57.6	18 21.2	19 34.8	16 7.3	20 11.8	4 1.2	16 33.3	8 8.8	21 11.9	10 30.1	20 16.0	12 24.9

AUGUST 1975

DAY	EPHEMERIS SIDEREAL TIME	☉	☊	☽	☿	♀	♂	♃	♄	♅	♆	♇
LONGITUDE at NOON												
1 F	8 37 54.1	8♌37.8	27♏20.6	21♉32.3	8♌46.0	11♍17.9	21♉29.5	24♈24.8	24♋41.2	28♎38.4	9♐ 7.7	7♎ 2.3
2 S	8 41 50.7	9 35.2	27 17.4	4♊15.4	10 50.6	11 27.2	22 8.7	24 27.3	24 48.8	28 39.7	9R 7.1	7 3.8
3 S	8 45 47.2	10 32.6	27 14.2	17 23.3	12 54.2	11 34.4	22 47.7	24 29.6	24 56.4	28 41.1	9 6.5	7 5.2
4 M	8 49 43.8	11 30.1	27 11.0	0♋58.9	14 56.6	11 39.4	23 26.6	24 31.7	25 4.0	28 42.5	9 5.9	7 6.7
5 T	8 53 40.4	12 27.5	27 7.9	15 2.8	16 57.9	11 42.2	24 5.3	24 33.7	25 11.6	28 44.0	9 5.4	7 8.2
6 W	8 57 36.9	13 25.0	27 4.7	29 32.8	18 57.9	11 42.7	24 43.9	24 35.4	25 19.1	28 45.5	9 4.9	7 9.8
7 T	9 1 33.5	14 22.5	27 1.5	14♌23.3	20 56.4	11R40.9	25 22.3	24 36.9	25 26.7	28 47.1	9 4.5	7 11.3
8 F	9 5 30.0	15 20.0	26 58.3	29 26.0	22 53.6	11 36.7	26 0.6	24 38.3	25 34.2	28 48.8	9 4.0	7 12.9
9 S	9 9 26.6	16 17.6	26 55.2	14♍30.8	24 49.3	11 30.2	26 38.7	24 39.4	25 41.6	28 50.4	9 3.6	7 14.5
10 S	9 13 23.1	17 15.1	26 52.0	29 28.1	26 43.5	11 21.3	27 16.6	24 40.4	25 49.1	28 52.2	9 3.3	7 16.2
11 M	9 17 19.7	18 12.7	26 48.8	14♎10.0	28 36.2	11 10.0	27 54.4	24 41.1	25 56.5	28 53.9	9 2.9	7 17.8
12 T	9 21 16.2	19 10.3	26 45.6	28 31.2	0♍27.5	10 56.4	28 32.0	24 41.7	26 3.9	28 55.8	9 2.6	7 19.5
13 W	9 25 12.8	20 7.9	26 42.4	12♏29.7	2 17.2	10 40.4	29 9.4	24 42.0	26 11.2	28 57.6	9 2.4	7 21.2
14 T	9 29 9.3	21 5.5	26 39.3	26 5.9	4 5.4	10 22.0	29 46.6	24 42.2	26 18.6	28 59.6	9 2.1	7 22.9
15 F	9 33 5.9	22 3.1	26 36.1	9♐21.6	5 52.2	10 1.4	0♊23.7	24R42.1	26 25.9	29 1.5	9 1.9	7 24.7
16 S	9 37 2.5	23 0.8	26 32.9	22 19.6	7 37.4	9 38.6	1 0.5	24 41.9	26 33.1	29 3.5	9 1.7	7 26.5
17 S	9 40 59.0	23 58.4	26 29.7	5♑ 2.8	9 21.2	9 13.6	1 37.2	24 41.4	26 40.4	29 5.6	9 1.6	7 28.3
18 M	9 44 55.6	24 56.1	26 26.6	17 33.9	11 3.6	8 46.7	2 13.7	24 40.8	26 47.6	29 7.7	9 1.5	7 30.1
19 T	9 48 52.1	25 53.8	26 23.4	29 54.9	12 44.5	8 17.8	2 50.1	24 39.9	26 54.7	29 9.8	9 1.4	7 31.9
20 W	9 52 48.7	26 51.6	26 20.2	12♒ 7.6	14 24.0	7 47.3	3 26.2	24 39.0	27 1.9	29 12.0	9 1.4	7 33.8
21 T	9 56 45.2	27 49.3	26 17.0	24 13.2	16 2.0	7 15.2	4 2.2	24 37.7	27 9.0	29 14.3	9 1.4	7 35.7
22 F	10 0 41.8	28 47.1	26 13.8	6♓12.6	17 38.7	6 41.7	4 37.9	24 36.3	27 16.0	29 16.5	9 1.4	7 37.6
23 S	10 4 38.3	29 44.9	26 10.7	18 7.2	19 13.9	6 6.9	5 13.5	24 34.7	27 23.0	29 18.8	9D 1.5	7 39.5
24 S	10 8 34.9	0♍42.7	26 7.5	29 58.4	20 47.8	5 31.3	5 48.8	24 32.8	27 30.0	29 21.2	9 1.5	7 41.4
25 M	10 12 31.4	1 40.5	26 4.3	11♈48.4	22 20.3	4 54.8	6 24.0	24 30.8	27 36.9	29 23.6	9 1.6	7 43.4
26 T	10 16 28.0	2 38.4	26 1.1	23 40.0	23 51.4	4 17.9	6 58.9	24 28.6	27 43.8	29 26.0	9 1.8	7 45.4
27 W	10 20 24.5	3 36.3	25 58.0	5♉36.7	25 21.1	3 40.6	7 33.6	24 26.2	27 50.6	29 28.5	9 2.0	7 47.4
28 T	10 24 21.1	4 34.2	25 54.8	17 42.8	26 49.3	3 3.4	8 8.1	24 23.6	27 57.4	29 31.0	9 2.2	7 49.4
29 F	10 28 17.6	5 32.2	25 51.6	0♊ 3.1	28 16.2	2 26.3	8 42.4	24 20.8	28 4.1	29 33.5	9 2.4	7 51.4
30 S	10 32 14.2	6 30.2	25 48.4	12 42.7	29 41.7	1 49.7	9 16.4	24 17.8	28 10.8	29 36.1	9 2.7	7 53.4
31 S	10 36 10.8	7 28.2	25 45.2	25 46.3	1♎ 5.7	1 13.8	9 50.2	24 14.6	28 17.5	29 38.8	9 3.0	7 55.5
DECLINATION at NOON												
1 F	8 37 54.1	18N 6.3	19S34.0	18N43.2	19N42.2	3N45.3	16N44.1	8N 9.5	21N10.6	10S30.6	20S15.9	12N23.9
4 M	8 49 43.8	17 20.0	19 31.9	20 41.8	18 2.7	3 2.0	17 15.5	8 11.3	21 6.7	10 32.2	20 15.8	12 21.1
7 T	9 1 33.5	16 31.2	19 29.7	11 50.3	16 10.0	2 25.5	17 45.5	8 12.5	21 2.9	10 33.9	20 15.8	12 18.2
10 S	9 13 23.1	15 39.9	19 27.5	3S41.4	14 8.0	1 57.0	18 14.0	8 13.0	20 59.0	10 35.8	20 15.7	12 15.3
13 W	9 25 12.8	14 46.4	19 25.3	16 48.0	11 59.8	1 37.4	18 41.0	8 12.9	20 55.1	10 37.9	20 15.8	12 12.3
16 S	9 37 2.5	13 50.8	19 23.1	21 4.1	9 48.1	1 27.7	19 6.6	8 12.1	20 51.2	10 40.0	20 15.8	12 9.3
19 T	9 48 52.1	12 53.3	19 20.9	15 48.0	7 34.9	1 28.3	19 30.8	8 10.7	20 47.4	10 42.3	20 15.9	12 6.3
22 F	10 0 41.8	11 53.9	19 18.6	4 39.6	5 21.7	1 39.2	19 53.5	8 8.6	20 43.5	10 44.8	20 16.1	12 3.2
25 M	10 12 31.4	10 52.8	19 16.4	7N51.8	3 10.1	1 59.6	20 14.8	8 5.9	20 39.7	10 47.4	20 16.3	12 0.2
28 T	10 24 21.1	9 50.1	19 14.1	17 45.4	1 1.2	2 28.3	20 34.7	8 2.6	20 35.9	10 50.1	20 16.6	11 57.1
31 S	10 36 10.8	8 46.1	19 11.9	20 48.5	1S 4.0	3 3.3	20 53.3	7 58.7	20 32.1	10 52.9	20 16.9	11 54.1

SEPTEMBER 1975

DAY	EPHEMERIS SIDEREAL TIME	☉	☊	☽	☿	♀	♂	♃	♄	♅	♆	♇
	h m s	° ′	° ′	° ′	° ′	° ′	° ′	° ′	° ′	° ′	° ′	° ′
LONGITUDE at NOON												
1 M	10 40 7.3	8 ♍ 26.2	25 ♏ 42.1	9 ♋ 17.9	2 ♎ 28.2	0 ♍ 38.7	10 ♊ 23.7	24 ♈ 11.2	28 ♋ 24.1	29 ♎ 41.4	9 ♐ 3.4	7 ♎ 57.6
2 T	10 44 3.9	9 24.3	25 38.9	23 19.2	3 49.3	0 R 4.8	10 57.1	24 R 7.7	28 30.6	29 44.1	9 3.7	7 59.7
3 W	10 48 0.4	10 22.4	25 35.7	7 ♌ 49.6	5 8.7	29 ♌ 32.3	11 30.1	24 3.9	28 37.1	29 46.9	9 4.1	8 1.8
4 T	10 51 57.0	11 20.6	25 32.5	22 44.6	6 26.6	29 1.2	12 2.9	23 60.0	28 43.6	29 49.6	9 4.6	8 3.9
5 F	10 55 53.5	12 18.8	25 29.4	7 ♍ 56.2	7 42.9	28 31.8	12 35.5	23 55.9	28 50.0	29 52.4	9 5.0	8 6.0
6 S	10 59 50.1	13 17.0	25 26.2	23 14.1	8 57.5	28 4.2	13 7.7	23 51.6	28 56.3	29 55.3	9 5.6	8 8.2
7 S	11 3 46.6	14 15.2	25 23.0	8 ♎ 26.7	10 10.3	27 38.5	13 39.7	23 47.1	29 2.6	29 58.2	9 6.1	8 10.3
8 M	11 7 43.2	15 13.5	25 19.8	23 24.1	11 21.2	27 14.9	14 11.4	23 42.4	29 8.8	0 ♏ 1.1	9 6.7	8 12.5
9 T	11 11 39.7	16 11.8	25 16.6	7 ♏ 59.1	12 30.3	26 53.5	14 42.9	23 37.6	29 14.9	0 4.0	9 7.3	8 14.7
10 W	11 15 36.3	17 10.1	25 13.5	22 7.9	13 37.3	26 34.3	15 14.1	23 32.7	29 21.1	0 7.1	9 7.9	8 16.9
11 T	11 19 32.8	18 8.5	25 10.3	5 ♐ 49.9	14 42.1	26 17.4	15 44.9	23 27.5	29 27.1	0 10.1	9 8.6	8 19.1
12 F	11 23 29.4	19 6.8	25 7.1	19 6.7	15 44.6	26 2.9	16 15.5	23 22.2	29 33.1	0 13.1	9 9.3	8 21.3
13 S	11 27 25.9	20 5.2	25 3.9	2 ♑ 1.6	16 44.8	25 50.7	16 45.7	23 16.7	29 39.0	0 16.2	9 10.0	8 23.6
14 S	11 31 22.5	21 3.6	25 0.8	14 38.2	17 42.3	25 40.9	17 15.7	23 11.1	29 44.8	0 19.3	9 10.8	8 25.8
15 M	11 35 19.0	22 2.1	24 57.6	27 0.4	18 37.0	25 33.6	17 45.3	23 5.3	29 50.6	0 22.4	9 11.6	8 28.0
16 T	11 39 15.6	23 0.5	24 54.4	9 ♒ 11.7	19 28.9	25 28.6	18 14.6	22 59.4	29 56.3	0 25.6	9 12.4	8 30.3
17 W	11 43 12.1	23 59.0	24 51.2	21 15.0	20 17.5	25 26.0	18 43.6	22 53.3	0 ♌ 1.9	0 28.8	9 13.3	8 32.6
18 T	11 47 8.7	24 57.6	24 48.0	3 ♓ 12.7	21 2.7	25 25.9	19 12.3	22 47.1	0 7.5	0 32.0	9 14.2	8 34.8
19 F	11 51 5.3	25 56.1	24 44.9	15 6.6	21 44.2	25 D 28.0	19 40.6	22 40.7	0 13.0	0 35.2	9 15.1	8 37.1
20 S	11 55 1.8	26 54.7	24 41.7	26 58.4	22 21.8	25 32.5	20 8.6	22 34.3	0 18.4	0 38.5	9 16.0	8 39.4
21 S	11 58 58.4	27 53.3	24 38.5	8 ♈ 49.6	22 55.0	25 39.3	20 36.2	22 27.7	0 23.8	0 41.8	9 17.0	8 41.7
22 M	12 2 54.9	28 52.0	24 35.3	20 41.9	23 23.7	25 48.3	21 3.5	22 20.9	0 29.1	0 45.1	9 18.0	8 44.0
23 T	12 6 51.5	29 50.7	24 32.1	2 ♉ 37.4	23 47.3	25 59.4	21 30.4	22 14.1	0 34.3	0 48.5	9 19.0	8 46.3
24 W	12 10 48.0	0 ♎ 49.4	24 29.0	14 38.6	24 5.7	26 12.7	21 57.0	22 7.1	0 39.4	0 51.9	9 20.1	8 48.6
25 T	12 14 44.6	1 48.2	24 25.8	26 48.7	24 18.2	26 28.0	22 23.1	22 0.0	0 44.5	0 55.2	9 21.2	8 50.9
26 F	12 18 41.1	2 47.0	24 22.6	9 ♊ 11.4	24 24.6	26 45.4	22 48.9	21 52.8	0 49.5	0 58.7	9 22.3	8 53.2
27 S	12 22 37.7	3 45.8	24 19.4	21 50.8	24 R 24.5	27 4.6	23 14.3	21 45.6	0 54.4	1 2.1	9 23.5	8 55.5
28 S	12 26 34.2	4 44.7	24 16.3	4 ♋ 51.2	24 17.5	27 25.8	23 39.2	21 38.2	0 59.2	1 5.6	9 24.7	8 57.8
29 M	12 30 30.8	5 43.6	24 13.1	18 16.2	24 3.3	27 48.8	24 3.8	21 30.7	1 3.9	1 9.0	9 25.9	9 0.2
30 T	12 34 27.3	6 42.5	24 9.9	2 ♌ 8.2	23 41.6	28 13.5	24 27.9	21 23.2	1 8.6	1 12.5	9 27.1	9 2.5
DECLINATION at NOON												
1 M	10 40 7.3	8 N 24.4	19 S 11.1	19 N 36.7	1 S 44.8	3 N 16.0	20 N 59.2	7 N 57.2	20 N 30.9	10 S 53.9	20 S 17.0	11 N 53.1
4 T	10 51 57.0	7 18.7	19 8.9	9 10.8	3 43.4	3 56.2	21 16.0	7 52.5	20 27.2	10 56.8	20 17.3	11 50.0
7 S	11 3 46.6	6 11.9	19 6.6	6 S 41.0	5 35.7	4 37.5	21 31.6	7 47.2	20 23.6	10 59.9	20 17.7	11 47.0
10 W	11 15 36.3	5 4.1	19 4.3	18 28.8	7 20.5	5 17.9	21 45.9	7 41.3	20 20.0	11 3.1	20 18.2	11 44.0
13 S	11 27 25.9	3 55.6	19 2.0	20 18.4	8 56.0	5 55.9	21 59.2	7 35.0	20 16.6	11 6.3	20 18.7	11 41.0
16 T	11 39 15.6	2 46.5	18 59.7	13 13.6	10 20.2	6 29.9	22 11.3	7 28.1	20 13.2	11 9.7	20 19.2	11 38.1
19 F	11 51 5.3	1 37.0	18 57.4	1 31.1	11 30.4	6 59.0	22 22.5	7 20.8	20 9.9	11 13.1	20 19.7	11 35.2
22 M	12 2 54.9	0 27.1	18 55.1	10 N 36.7	12 23.0	7 22.5	22 32.8	7 13.1	20 6.8	11 16.6	20 20.3	11 32.3
25 T	12 14 44.6	0 S 43.0	18 52.8	19 6.0	12 53.3	7 40.0	22 42.2	7 5.0	20 3.7	11 20.2	20 21.0	11 29.6
28 S	12 26 34.2	1 53.1	18 50.4	19 54.2	12 55.1	7 51.3	22 50.9	6 56.7	20 0.8	11 23.9	20 21.6	11 26.8

OCTOBER 1975

DAY	EPHEMERIS SIDEREAL TIME	☉	☊	☽	☿	♀	♂	♃	♄	♅	♆	♇
LONGITUDE at NOON												
1 W	12 38 23.9	7 ♎ 41.6	24 ♏ 6.7	16 ♌ 27.7	23 ♎ 12.3	28 ♌ 40.0	24 ♊ 51.6	21 ♈ 15.6	1 ♌ 13.2	1 ♏ 16.1	9 ♐ 28.4	9 ♎ 4.9
2 T	12 42 20.4	8 40.6	24 3.5	1 ♍ 12.1	22 R 35.3	29 8.1	25 14.8	21 R 7.9	1 17.7	1 19.6	9 29.7	9 7.2
3 F	12 46 17.0	9 39.7	24 0.4	16 15.6	21 50.9	29 37.7	25 37.6	21 0.1	1 22.1	1 23.2	9 31.1	9 9.5
4 S	12 50 13.5	10 38.8	23 57.2	1 ♎ 29.4	20 59.5	0 ♍ 8.9	25 59.9	20 52.2	1 26.4	1 26.8	9 32.4	9 11.9
5 S	12 54 10.1	11 37.9	23 54.0	16 43.1	20 1.7	0 41.5	26 21.7	20 44.4	1 30.7	1 30.4	9 33.8	9 14.2
6 M	12 58 6.6	12 37.1	23 50.8	1 ♏ 46.2	18 58.5	1 15.5	26 43.0	20 36.4	1 34.8	1 34.0	9 35.2	9 16.5
7 T	13 2 3.2	13 36.3	23 47.7	16 30.2	17 51.1	1 50.9	27 3.8	20 28.4	1 38.9	1 37.6	9 36.6	9 18.8
8 W	13 5 59.7	14 35.5	23 44.5	0 ♐ 49.3	16 41.0	2 27.5	27 24.1	20 20.4	1 42.8	1 41.2	9 38.1	9 21.2
9 T	13 9 56.3	15 34.8	23 41.3	14 40.8	15 30.1	3 5.4	27 43.8	20 12.4	1 46.7	1 44.9	9 39.6	9 23.5
10 F	13 13 52.8	16 34.1	23 38.1	28 5.2	14 20.3	3 44.6	28 3.1	20 4.3	1 50.5	1 48.5	9 41.1	9 25.8
11 S	13 17 49.4	17 33.4	23 34.9	11 ♑ 4.5	13 13.5	4 24.9	28 21.8	19 56.2	1 54.2	1 52.2	9 42.6	9 28.1
12 S	13 21 46.0	18 32.7	23 31.8	23 42.4	12 11.7	5 6.3	28 39.9	19 48.1	1 57.8	1 55.9	9 44.2	9 30.4
13 M	13 25 42.5	19 32.1	23 28.6	6 ♒ 3.1	11 16.6	5 48.8	28 57.5	19 40.0	2 1.3	1 59.6	9 45.8	9 32.7
14 T	13 29 39.1	20 31.5	23 25.4	18 10.8	10 29.8	6 32.4	29 14.5	19 31.9	2 4.7	2 3.3	9 47.4	9 35.0
15 W	13 33 35.6	21 31.0	23 22.2	0 ♓ 9.5	9 52.6	7 16.9	29 31.0	19 23.8	2 8.0	2 7.0	9 49.0	9 37.3
16 T	13 37 32.2	22 30.4	23 19.1	12 2.9	9 25.8	8 2.5	29 46.8	19 15.7	2 11.2	2 10.7	9 50.6	9 39.6
17 F	13 41 28.7	23 29.9	23 15.9	23 54.1	9 9.9	8 49.0	0 ♋ 2.0	19 7.6	2 14.3	2 14.5	9 52.3	9 41.9
18 S	13 45 25.3	24 29.5	23 12.7	5 ♈ 45.6	9 5.2	9 36.4	0 16.7	18 59.6	2 17.3	2 18.2	9 54.0	9 44.1
19 S	13 49 21.8	25 29.0	23 9.5	17 39.7	9 D 11.5	10 24.6	0 30.7	18 51.6	2 20.2	2 22.0	9 55.7	9 46.4
20 M	13 53 18.4	26 28.6	23 6.3	29 38.0	9 28.6	11 13.7	0 44.0	18 43.6	2 23.0	2 25.7	9 57.5	9 48.7
21 T	13 57 14.9	27 28.3	23 3.2	11 ♉ 42.4	9 55.8	12 3.7	0 56.7	18 35.7	2 25.7	2 29.5	9 59.3	9 50.9
22 W	14 1 11.5	28 28.0	22 60.0	23 54.6	10 32.4	12 54.5	1 8.8	18 27.9	2 28.4	2 33.3	10 1.1	9 53.2
23 T	14 5 8.0	29 27.7	22 56.8	6 ♊ 16.4	11 17.8	13 45.9	1 20.1	18 20.1	2 30.9	2 37.0	10 2.9	9 55.4
24 F	14 9 4.6	0 ♏ 27.4	22 53.6	18 50.1	12 10.9	14 38.2	1 30.8	18 12.3	2 33.3	2 40.8	10 4.7	9 57.6
25 S	14 13 1.1	1 27.2	22 50.5	1 ♋ 38.0	13 11.1	15 31.1	1 40.7	18 4.7	2 35.6	2 44.6	10 6.6	9 59.8
26 S	14 16 57.7	2 27.0	22 47.3	14 42.7	14 17.4	16 24.7	1 50.0	17 57.0	2 37.7	2 48.3	10 8.4	10 2.0
27 M	14 20 54.3	3 26.9	22 44.1	28 6.5	15 29.2	17 19.0	1 58.4	17 49.5	2 39.8	2 52.1	10 10.3	10 4.2
28 T	14 24 50.8	4 26.8	22 40.9	11 ♌ 51.0	16 45.6	18 14.0	2 6.2	17 42.1	2 41.8	2 55.9	10 12.2	10 6.4
29 W	14 28 47.4	5 26.7	22 37.7	25 56.9	18 6.0	19 9.5	2 13.1	17 34.7	2 43.7	2 59.6	10 14.2	10 8.6
30 T	14 32 43.9	6 26.6	22 34.6	10 ♍ 22.9	19 29.8	20 5.7	2 19.3	17 27.4	2 45.4	3 3.4	10 16.1	10 10.7
31 F	14 36 40.5	7 26.6	22 31.4	25 5.6	20 56.4	21 2.4	2 24.7	17 20.3	2 47.1	3 7.2	10 18.1	10 12.8
DECLINATION at NOON												
1 W	12 38 23.9	3 S 3.2	18 S 48.1	11 N 1.0	12 S 21.9	7 N 56.2	22 N 59.0	6 N 48.0	19 N 58.1	11 S 27.6	20 S 22.4	11 N 24.1
4 S	12 50 13.5	4 12.9	18 45.7	4 S 16.3	11 9.2	7 55.0	23 6.5	6 39.2	19 55.4	11 31.3	20 23.1	11 21.5
7 T	13 2 3.2	5 22.1	18 43.4	17 16.5	9 19.4	7 47.7	23 13.7	6 30.2	19 53.0	11 35.1	20 23.9	11 19.0
10 F	13 13 52.8	6 30.8	18 41.0	20 22.9	7 7.1	7 34.6	23 20.4	6 21.1	19 50.7	11 38.9	20 24.6	11 16.5
13 M	13 25 42.5	7 38.6	18 38.6	13 54.8	4 58.9	7 15.7	23 27.0	6 12.0	19 48.6	11 42.8	20 25.5	11 14.2
16 T	13 37 32.2	8 45.5	18 36.2	2 30.7	3 22.3	6 51.4	23 33.5	6 3.0	19 46.7	11 46.6	20 26.3	11 11.9
19 S	13 49 21.8	9 51.3	18 33.8	9 N 39.1	2 34.1	6 21.8	23 39.9	5 54.1	19 45.0	11 50.5	20 27.2	11 9.7
22 W	14 1 11.5	10 55.8	18 31.4	18 33.8	2 36.3	5 47.2	23 46.5	5 45.3	19 43.4	11 54.4	20 28.1	11 7.6
25 S	14 13 1.1	11 58.8	18 29.0	20 3.4	3 21.3	5 7.9	23 53.2	5 36.8	19 42.1	11 58.3	20 29.0	11 5.6
28 T	14 24 50.8	13 0.2	18 26.6	12 14.8	4 37.7	4 24.3	24 0.3	5 28.6	19 41.0	12 2.2	20 29.9	11 3.8
31 F	14 36 40.5	13 59.8	18 24.2	2 S 6.0	6 14.5	3 36.6	24 7.7	5 20.7	19 40.1	12 6.1	20 30.8	11 2.0

NOVEMBER 1975

DAY	EPHEMERIS SIDEREAL TIME	☉	☊	☽	☿	♀	♂	♃	♄	♅	♆	♇
	h m s	° ′	° ′	° ′	° ′	° ′	° ′	° ′	° ′	° ′	° ′	° ′
	LONGITUDE at NOON											
1 S	14 40 37.0	8♏26.7	22♏28.2	9♎59.3	22♎25.4	21♍59.6	2♋29.3	17♈13.2	2♌48.6	3♏10.9	10♐20.0	10♎14.9
2 S	14 44 33.6	9 26.7	22 25.0	24 56.5	23 56.3	22 57.4	2 33.1	17R 6.3	2 50.1	3 14.7	10 22.0	10 17.0
3 M	14 48 30.1	10 26.8	22 21.9	9♏48.9	25 28.8	23 55.8	2 36.0	16 59.5	2 51.4	3 18.4	10 24.0	10 19.1
4 T	14 52 26.7	11 27.0	22 18.7	24 28.5	27 2.5	24 54.6	2 38.1	16 52.8	2 52.6	3 22.2	10 26.1	10 21.2
5 W	14 56 23.2	12 27.1	22 15.5	8♐48.8	28 37.2	25 53.8	2 39.4	16 46.2	2 53.7	3 25.9	10 28.1	10 23.3
6 T	15 0 19.8	13 27.3	22 12.3	22 45.4	0♏12.7	26 53.6	2 39.8	16 39.8	2 54.7	3 29.6	10 30.1	10 25.3
7 F	15 4 16.4	14 27.5	22 9.1	6♑16.5	1 48.8	27 53.8	2R39.4	16 33.5	2 55.5	3 33.4	10 32.2	10 27.3
8 S	15 8 12.9	15 27.8	22 6.0	19 22.6	3 25.3	28 54.4	2 38.1	16 27.3	2 56.3	3 37.1	10 34.3	10 29.3
9 S	15 12 9.5	16 28.0	22 2.8	2♒ 5.8	5 2.1	29 55.4	2 35.9	16 21.3	2 56.9	3 40.8	10 36.4	10 31.3
10 M	15 16 6.0	17 28.3	21 59.6	14 29.6	6 39.0	0♎56.8	2 32.9	16 15.5	2 57.5	3 44.5	10 38.5	10 33.3
11 T	15 20 2.6	18 28.6	21 56.4	26 38.3	8 16.0	1 58.7	2 29.0	16 9.8	2 57.9	3 48.2	10 40.6	10 35.2
12 W	15 23 59.1	19 29.0	21 53.3	8♓36.6	9 53.1	3 0.9	2 24.3	16 4.3	2 58.3	3 51.9	10 42.8	10 37.2
13 T	15 27 55.7	20 29.4	21 50.1	20 28.7	11 30.1	4 3.5	2 18.6	15 58.9	2 58.5	3 55.5	10 44.9	10 39.1
14 F	15 31 52.2	21 29.8	21 46.9	2♈19.2	13 7.0	5 6.5	2 12.1	15 53.7	2 58.5	3 59.2	10 47.1	10 41.0
15 S	15 35 48.8	22 30.2	21 43.7	14 11.8	14 43.8	6 9.8	2 4.7	15 48.7	2 58.5	4 2.8	10 49.2	10 42.8
16 S	15 39 45.3	23 30.6	21 40.6	26 9.8	16 20.4	7 13.4	1 56.5	15 43.8	2R58.4	4 6.4	10 51.4	10 44.7
17 M	15 43 41.9	24 31.1	21 37.4	8♉16.0	17 56.8	8 17.4	1 47.4	15 39.1	2 58.1	4 10.0	10 53.6	10 46.5
18 T	15 47 38.5	25 31.5	21 34.2	20 32.4	19 33.0	9 21.7	1 37.4	15 34.6	2 57.7	4 13.6	10 55.8	10 48.3
19 W	15 51 35.0	26 32.0	21 31.0	3♊ 0.4	21 9.1	10 26.3	1 26.6	15 30.3	2 57.3	4 17.2	10 58.0	10 50.1
20 T	15 55 31.6	27 32.6	21 27.8	15 41.1	22 44.9	11 31.2	1 14.9	15 26.1	2 56.7	4 20.7	11 0.2	10 51.8
21 F	15 59 28.1	28 33.1	21 24.7	28 34.9	24 20.5	12 36.4	1 2.4	15 22.2	2 56.0	4 24.2	11 2.4	10 53.6
22 S	16 3 24.7	29 33.7	21 21.5	11♋42.0	25 56.0	13 41.9	0 49.0	15 18.4	2 55.2	4 27.8	11 4.6	10 55.3
23 S	16 7 21.2	0♐34.3	21 18.3	25 2.7	27 31.3	14 47.7	0 34.9	15 14.8	2 54.2	4 31.3	11 6.9	10 56.9
24 M	16 11 17.8	1 35.0	21 15.1	8♌36.7	29 6.3	15 53.7	0 20.0	15 11.4	2 53.2	4 34.7	11 9.1	10 58.6
25 T	16 15 14.4	2 35.7	21 12.0	22 23.7	0♐41.3	17 0.0	0 4.3	15 8.2	2 52.1	4 38.2	11 11.3	11 0.2
26 W	16 19 10.9	3 36.4	21 8.8	6♍23.3	2 16.0	18 6.6	29♊47.8	15 5.2	2 50.8	4 41.6	11 13.6	11 1.8
27 T	16 23 7.5	4 37.1	21 5.6	20 34.2	3 50.7	19 13.4	29 30.7	15 2.4	2 49.4	4 45.0	11 15.8	11 3.4
28 F	16 27 4.0	5 37.8	21 2.4	4♎54.6	5 25.2	20 20.5	29 12.8	14 59.8	2 48.0	4 48.4	11 18.1	11 5.0
29 S	16 31 0.6	6 38.6	20 59.2	19 21.5	6 59.5	21 27.7	28 54.2	14 57.4	2 46.4	4 51.7	11 20.3	11 6.5
30 S	16 34 57.1	7 39.4	20 56.1	3♏51.1	8 33.8	22 35.2	28 35.1	14 55.2	2 44.7	4 55.1	11 22.6	11 8.0
	DECLINATION at NOON											
1 S	14 40 37.0	14S 19.2	18S 23.4	7S 11.6	6S 49.7	3N 19.9	24N 10.2	5N 18.2	19N 39.9	12S 7.4	20S 31.1	11N 1.5
4 T	14 52 26.7	15 16.1	18 20.9	18 38.8	8 40.5	2 27.3	24 18.1	5 10.9	19 39.3	12 11.2	20 32.1	10 59.9
7 F	15 4 16.4	16 10.7	18 18.5	19 35.0	10 34.7	1 31.5	24 26.5	5 4.1	19 39.0	12 15.0	20 33.0	10 58.4
10 M	15 16 6.0	17 2.8	18 16.0	11 27.4	12 28.3	0 32.8	24 35.2	4 57.8	19 38.9	12 18.8	20 34.0	10 57.0
13 T	15 27 55.7	17 52.4	18 13.5	0N 30.0	14 18.8	0S 28.5	24 44.3	4 52.1	19 39.0	12 22.5	20 35.0	10 55.8
16 S	15 39 45.3	18 39.1	18 11.1	12 14.4	16 4.1	1 32.0	24 53.7	4 46.9	19 39.3	12 26.2	20 35.9	10 54.7
19 W	15 51 35.0	19 22.9	18 8.6	19 45.0	17 43.0	2 37.5	25 3.1	4 42.4	19 39.9	12 29.8	20 36.9	10 53.8
22 S	16 3 24.7	20 3.5	18 6.1	18 53.6	19 14.3	3 44.4	25 12.6	4 38.6	19 40.8	12 33.3	20 37.8	10 52.9
25 T	16 15 14.4	20 40.8	18 3.6	9 2.9	20 37.3	4 52.5	25 21.8	4 35.5	19 41.8	12 36.8	20 38.8	10 52.2
28 F	16 27 4.0	21 14.7	18 1.1	5S 29.4	21 51.2	6 1.4	25 30.6	4 33.0	19 43.1	12 40.2	20 39.8	10 51.7

DECEMBER 1975

DAY	EPHEMERIS SIDEREAL TIME	☉	☊	☽	☿	♀	♂	♃	♄	♅	♆	♇
	LONGITUDE at NOON											
1 M	16 38 53.7	8♐40.2	20♏52.9	18♏18.4	10♐ 8.1	23♎43.0	28♊15.3	14♈53.2	2♌42.9	4♏58.4	11♐24.8	11♎ 9.5
2 T	16 42 50.2	9 41.1	20 49.7	2♐38.1	11 42.2	24 50.9	27R54.9	14R51.4	2R41.0	5 1.6	11 27.1	11 10.9
3 W	16 46 46.8	10 42.0	20 46.5	16 45.1	13 16.3	25 59.0	27 34.1	14 49.9	2 39.0	5 4.9	11 29.4	11 12.4
4 T	16 50 43.4	11 42.9	20 43.4	0♑34.8	14 50.4	27 7.4	27 12.7	14 48.6	2 36.9	5 8.2	11 31.7	11 13.7
5 F	16 54 39.9	12 43.8	20 40.2	14 4.1	16 24.4	28 15.9	26 51.0	14 47.4	2 34.7	5 11.4	11 33.9	11 15.1
6 S	16 58 36.5	13 44.7	20 37.0	27 11.8	17 58.5	29 24.5	26 28.8	14 46.4	2 32.4	5 14.5	11 36.2	11 16.4
7 S	17 2 33.0	14 45.6	20 33.8	9♒58.2	19 32.5	0♏33.4	26 6.3	14 45.7	2 29.9	5 17.7	11 38.4	11 17.7
8 M	17 6 29.6	15 46.6	20 30.7	22 25.3	21 6.5	1 42.4	25 43.5	14 45.2	2 27.4	5 20.8	11 40.7	11 19.0
9 T	17 10 26.1	16 47.5	20 27.5	4♓36.4	22 40.6	2 51.6	25 20.4	14 44.9	2 24.8	5 23.8	11 42.9	11 20.2
10 W	17 14 22.7	17 48.5	20 24.3	16 35.6	24 14.7	4 0.9	24 57.2	14 44.8	2 22.1	5 26.9	11 45.2	11 21.4
11 T	17 18 19.3	18 49.5	20 21.1	28 27.8	25 48.8	5 10.4	24 33.8	14D44.9	2 1..3	5 29.9	11 47.5	11 22.6
12 F	17 22 15.8	19 50.5	20 18.0	10♈17.9	27 23.0	6 20.1	24 10.4	14 45.2	2 16.4	5 32.8	11 49.7	11 23.7
13 S	17 26 12.4	20 51.5	20 14.8	22 10.9	28 57.2	7 29.9	23 46.9	14 45.7	2 13.4	5 35.8	11 51.9	11 24.8
14 S	17 30 8.9	21 52.5	20 11.6	4♉11.4	0♑31.5	8 39.8	23 23.4	14 46.4	2 10.3	5 38.7	11 54.2	11 25.9
15 M	17 34 5.5	22 53.5	20 8.4	16 23.4	2 5.8	9 49.9	23 0.0	14 47.4	2 7.1	5 41.5	11 56.4	11 27.0
16 T	17 38 2.0	23 54.5	20 5.2	28 50.2	3 40.1	11 0.1	22 36.7	14 48.5	2 3.8	5 44.4	11 58.6	11 28.0
17 W	17 41 58.6	24 55.5	20 2.1	11♊33.7	5 14.4	12 10.5	22 13.6	14 49.9	2 0.5	5 47.1	12 0.8	11 29.0
18 T	17 45 55.2	25 56.6	19 58.9	24 35.0	6 48.8	13 21.0	21 50.6	14 51.4	1 57.0	5 49.9	12 3.1	11 29.9
19 F	17 49 51.7	26 57.6	19 55.7	7♋53.6	8 23.1	14 31.6	21 27.9	14 53.2	1 53.5	5 52.6	12 5.3	11 30.8
20 S	17 53 48.3	27 58.7	19 52.5	21 27.7	9 57.3	15 42.3	21 5.6	14 55.2	1 49.9	5 55.3	12 7.5	11 31.7
21 S	17 57 44.8	28 59.8	19 49.4	5♌14.7	11 31.4	16 53.2	20 43.5	14 57.3	1 46.2	5 57.9	12 9.6	11 32.6
22 M	18 1 41.4	0♑ 0.9	19 46.2	19 11.4	13 5.3	18 4.1	20 21.8	14 59.7	1 42.5	6 0.5	12 11.8	11 33.4
23 T	18 5 38.0	1 2.0	19 43.0	3♍14.6	14 39.0	19 15.2	20 0.6	15 2.3	1 38.6	6 3.1	12 14.0	11 34.2
24 W	18 9 34.5	2 3.1	19 39.8	17 21.5	16 12.4	20 26.5	19 39.9	15 5.1	1 34.8	6 5.6	12 16.2	11 34.9
25 T	18 13 31.1	3 4.2	19 36.7	1♎29.6	17 45.3	21 37.8	19 19.6	15 8.1	1 30.8	6 8.1	12 18.3	11 35.7
26 F	18 17 27.6	4 5.4	19 33.5	15 37.3	19 17.6	22 49.2	18 59.8	15 11.2	1 26.8	6 10.5	12 20.5	11 36.3
27 S	18 21 24.2	5 6.5	19 30.3	29 43.3	20 49.3	24 0.7	18 40.6	15 14.6	1 22.6	6 12.9	12 22.6	11 37.0
28 S	18 25 20.7	6 7.7	19 27.1	13♏46.2	22 20.1	25 12.3	18 22.0	15 18.2	1 18.5	6 15.3	12 24.7	11 37.6
29 M	18 29 17.3	7 8.8	19 23.9	27 44.6	23 49.8	26 24.0	18 4.1	15 21.9	1 14.2	6 17.6	12 26.8	11 38.2
30 T	18 33 13.9	8 10.0	19 20.8	11♐36.3	25 18.2	27 35.8	17 46.8	15 25.9	1 9.9	6 19.8	12 28.9	11 38.7
31 W	18 37 10.4	9 11.2	19 17.6	25 18.8	26 44.9	28 47.7	17 30.2	15 30.0	1 5.6	6 22.0	12 31.0	11 39.2
	DECLINATION at NOON											
1 M	16 38 53.7	21S 45.0	17S 58.6	17S 35.3	22S 55.3	7S 10.7	25N 38.8	4N 31.3	19N 44.6	12S 43.6	20S 40.7	10N 51.3
4 T	16 50 43.4	22 11.5	17 56.1	20 8.4	23 49.1	8 20.0	25 46.1	4 30.3	19 46.4	12 46.8	20 41.6	10 51.0
7 S	17 2 33.0	22 34.2	17 53.6	12 47.8	24 31.8	9 29.0	25 52.3	4 30.1	19 48.3	12 49.9	20 42.6	10 50.9
10 W	17 14 22.7	22 52.9	17 51.0	0 54.8	25 3.0	10 37.2	25 57.2	4 30.5	19 50.4	12 53.0	20 43.5	10 50.9
13 S	17 26 12.4	23 7.5	17 48.5	11N 1.4	25 21.9	11 44.4	26 0.8	4 31.8	19 52.8	12 55.9	20 44.4	10 51.1
16 T	17 38 2.0	23 18.0	17 45.9	19 15.4	25 28.1	12 50.0	26 3.1	4 33.7	19 55.3	12 58.7	20 45.2	10 51.4
19 F	17 49 51.7	23 24.3	17 43.4	19 27.0	25 21.0	13 53.9	26 4.1	4 36.4	19 57.9	13 1.4	20 46.1	10 51.8
22 M	18 1 41.4	23 26.4	17 40.8	10 9.3	25 0.4	14 55.5	26 3.9	4 39.7	20 0.8	13 4.0	20 46.9	10 52.4
25 T	18 13 31.1	23 24.3	17 38.2	4S 12.3	24 26.0	15 54.5	26 2.6	4 43.8	20 3.7	13 6.5	20 47.7	10 53.1
28 S	18 25 20.7	23 17.9	17 35.6	16 35.7	23 38.2	16 50.5	26 0.6	4 48.5	20 6.8	13 8.8	20 48.5	10 54.0
31 W	18 37 10.4	23 7.3	17 33.1	20 27.4	22 37.9	17 43.3	25 57.9	4 53.9	20 10.0	13 11.0	20 49.3	10 55.0

JANUARY 1976

DAY	EPHEMERIS SIDEREAL TIME	☉	☊	☽	☿	♀	♂	♃	♄	♅	♆	♇
	h m s	° ′	° ′	° ′	° ′	° ′	° ′	° ′	° ′	° ′	° ′	° ′
						LONGITUDE at NOON						
1 T	18 41 7.0	10♑12.3	19♏14.4	8♑49.2	28♑ 9.8	29♏59.7	17♊14.3	15♈34.3	1♌ 1.1	6♏24.2	12♐33.0	11♎39.7
2 F	18 45 3.5	11 13.5	19 11.2	22 5.1	29 32.3	1♐11.7	16R59.2	15 38.9	0R56.7	6 26.3	12 35.1	11 40.1
3 S	18 49 0.1	12 14.7	19 8.1	5♒ 4.6	0♒52.0	2 23.8	16 44.8	15 43.6	0 52.2	6 28.4	12 37.1	11 40.5
4 S	18 52 56.6	13 15.9	19 4.9	17 46.9	2 8.5	3 36.0	16 31.2	15 48.5	0 47.6	6 30.4	12 39.1	11 40.9
5 M	18 56 53.2	14 17.0	19 1.7	0♓12.5	3 21.2	4 48.2	16 18.4	15 53.6	0 43.0	6 32.4	12 41.1	11 41.2
6 T	19 0 49.8	15 18.2	18 58.5	12 23.3	4 29.4	6 0.5	16 6.4	15 58.8	0 38.3	6 34.3	12 43.1	11 41.5
7 W	19 4 46.3	16 19.4	18 55.4	24 22.5	5 32.4	7 12.9	15 55.2	16 4.3	0 33.6	6 36.2	12 45.1	11 41.8
8 T	19 8 42.9	17 20.5	18 52.2	6♈14.2	6 29.4	8 25.3	15 44.8	16 9.9	0 28.9	6 38.0	12 47.0	11 42.0
9 F	19 12 39.4	18 21.7	18 49.0	18 3.2	7 19.6	9 37.8	15 35.2	16 15.7	0 24.2	6 39.8	12 49.0	11 42.2
10 S	19 16 36.0	19 22.8	18 45.8	29 54.9	8 2.1	10 50.4	15 26.5	16 21.7	0 19.4	6 41.5	12 50.9	11 42.3
11 S	19 20 32.5	20 24.0	18 42.7	11♉54.6	8 36.0	12 3.0	15 18.5	16 27.8	0 14.6	6 43.2	12 52.8	11 42.4
12 M	19 24 29.1	21 25.1	18 39.5	24 7.7	9 0.4	13 15.7	15 11.5	16 34.1	0 9.7	6 44.8	12 54.6	11 42.5
13 T	19 28 25.7	22 26.2	18 36.3	6♊38.8	9 14.6	14 28.4	15 5.2	16 40.6	0 4.9	6 46.4	12 56.5	11 42.5
14 W	19 32 22.2	23 27.3	18 33.1	19 31.3	9 17.7	15 41.2	14 59.8	16 47.3	0 0.0	6 47.9	12 58.4	11 42.6
15 T	19 36 18.8	24 28.4	18 29.9	2♋47.1	9R 9.3	16 54.1	14 55.1	16 54.1	29♋55.1	6 49.4	13 0.2	11 42.6
16 F	19 40 15.3	25 29.5	18 26.8	16 26.2	8 49.1	18 6.9	14 51.3	17 1.1	29 50.2	6 50.8	13 2.0	11R42.5
17 S	19 44 11.9	26 30.6	18 23.6	0♌26.0	8 17.3	19 19.9	14 48.3	17 8.3	29 45.3	6 52.2	13 3.7	11 42.4
18 S	19 48 8.4	27 31.7	18 20.4	14 42.1	7 34.3	20 32.8	14 46.0	17 15.6	29 40.3	6 53.5	13 5.5	11 42.3
19 M	19 52 5.0	28 32.7	18 17.2	29 8.2	6 41.0	21 45.9	14 44.6	17 23.0	29 35.4	6 54.7	13 7.2	11 42.1
20 T	19 56 1.5	29 33.8	18 14.1	13♍38.0	5 39.0	22 59.0	14 43.9	17 30.6	29 30.5	6 56.0	13 8.9	11 41.9
21 W	19 59 58.1	0♒34.8	18 10.9	28 5.3	4 29.9	24 12.1	14D44.0	17 38.4	29 25.5	6 57.1	13 10.6	11 41.7
22 T	20 3 54.7	1 35.9	18 7.7	12♎25.5	3 15.8	25 25.3	14 44.8	17 46.3	29 20.6	6 58.2	13 12.2	11 41.4
23 F	20 7 51.2	2 36.9	18 4.5	26 35.8	1 59.2	26 38.5	14 46.4	17 54.4	29 15.7	6 59.2	13 13.9	11 41.1
24 S	20 11 47.8	3 37.9	18 1.3	10♏34.9	0 42.3	27 51.7	14 48.7	18 2.6	29 10.7	7 0.2	13 15.5	11 40.7
25 S	20 15 44.3	4 38.9	17 58.2	24 22.8	29♑27.3	29 5.0	14 51.8	18 10.9	29 5.8	7 1.2	13 17.1	11 40.4
26 M	20 19 40.9	5 40.0	17 55.0	8♐ 0.1	28 16.4	0♑18.3	14 55.5	18 19.4	29 0.9	7 2.0	13 18.6	11 40.0
27 T	20 23 37.4	6 41.0	17 51.8	21 27.1	27 11.2	1 31.7	15 0.0	18 28.1	28 56.0	7 2.9	13 20.1	11 39.5
28 W	20 27 34.0	7 41.9	17 48.6	4♑43.9	26 13.0	2 45.1	15 5.2	18 36.8	28 51.2	7 3.6	13 21.7	11 39.0
29 T	20 31 30.5	8 42.9	17 45.5	17 50.4	25 22.8	3 58.5	15 11.1	18 45.8	28 46.3	7 4.4	13 23.1	11 38.5
30 F	20 35 27.1	9 43.9	17 42.3	0♒45.6	24 41.0	5 12.0	15 17.6	18 54.8	28 41.5	7 5.0	13 24.6	11 38.0
31 S	20 39 23.7	10 44.8	17 39.1	13 28.7	24 8.0	6 25.5	15 24.8	19 4.0	28 36.7	7 5.6	13 26.0	11 37.4
						DECLINATION at NOON						
1 T	18 41 7.0	23S 2.9	17S 32.2	19S 20.8	22S 15.3	18S 0.0	25N 56.9	4N 55.9	20N 11.0	13S 11.6	20S 49.5	10N 55.3
4 S	18 52 56.6	22 46.8	17 29.6	10 38.9	21 1.8	18 47.7	25 53.7	5 2.1	20 14.3	13 13.6	20 50.2	10 56.5
7 W	19 4 46.3	22 26.6	17 27.0	1N 38.3	19 43.1	19 31.3	25 50.4	5 9.0	20 17.7	13 15.5	20 50.9	10 57.8
10 S	19 16 36.0	22 2.4	17 24.4	13 4.9	18 25.7	20 10.5	25 47.3	5 16.4	20 21.1	13 17.2	20 51.6	10 59.2
13 T	19 28 25.7	21 34.4	17 21.7	19 58.4	17 18.8	20 44.9	25 44.4	5 24.5	20 24.5	13 18.7	20 52.2	11 0.7
16 F	19 40 15.3	21 2.6	17 19.1	18 13.8	16 32.1	21 14.3	25 41.9	5 33.0	20 28.0	13 20.1	20 52.8	11 2.3
19 M	19 52 5.0	20 27.2	17 16.5	7 7.3	16 12.8	21 38.5	25 39.9	5 42.1	20 31.4	13 21.4	20 53.4	11 4.1
22 T	20 3 54.7	19 48.3	17 13.8	7S 40.1	16 20.8	21 57.2	25 38.3	5 51.7	20 34.8	13 22.4	20 53.9	11 5.9
25 S	20 15 44.3	19 6.1	17 11.2	18 22.8	16 49.0	22 10.3	25 37.3	6 1.8	20 38.2	13 23.3	20 54.4	11 7.8
28 W	20 27 34.0	18 20.7	17 8.5	19 43.7	17 27.0	22 17.6	25 36.9	6 12.3	20 41.5	13 24.1	20 54.8	11 9.8
31 S	20 39 23.7	17 32.4	17 5.8	11 59.8	18 6.6	22 19.0	25 36.9	6 23.3	20 44.7	13 24.7	20 55.3	11 11.9

FEBRUARY 1976

DAY	EPHEMERIS SIDEREAL TIME	☉	☊	☽	☿	♀	♂	♃	♄	♅	♆	♇
						LONGITUDE at NOON						
1 S	20 43 20.2	11♒45.8	17♏35.9	25♒59.2	23♑43.8	7♑39.0	15♊32.7	19♈13.3	28♋32.0	7♏ 6.2	13♐27.4	11♎36.8
2 M	20 47 16.8	12 46.7	17 32.8	8♓17.0	23R28.1	8 52.5	15 41.2	19 22.8	28R27.2	7 6.6	13 28.8	11R36.2
3 T	20 51 13.3	13 47.6	17 29.6	20 23.2	23 20.7	10 6.1	15 50.3	19 32.4	28 22.5	7 7.1	13 30.1	11 35.5
4 W	20 55 9.9	14 48.5	17 26.4	2♈19.8	23D21.1	11 19.7	16 0.1	19 42.1	28 18.0	7 7.5	13 31.5	11 34.8
5 T	20 59 6.4	15 49.3	17 23.2	14 9.7	23 28.7	12 33.3	16 10.4	19 52.0	28 13.3	7 7.8	13 32.8	11 34.1
6 F	21 3 3.0	16 50.2	17 20.0	25 57.1	23 43.2	13 46.9	16 21.4	20 1.9	28 8.8	7 8.1	13 34.0	11 33.3
7 S	21 6 59.5	17 51.0	17 16.9	7♉46.7	24 3.9	15 0.6	16 32.9	20 12.0	28 4.3	7 8.3	13 35.3	11 32.5
8 S	21 10 56.1	18 51.7	17 13.7	19 44.0	24 30.5	16 14.2	16 44.9	20 22.2	27 59.8	7 8.5	13 36.5	11 31.7
9 M	21 14 52.7	19 52.5	17 10.5	1♊54.4	25 2.4	17 27.9	16 57.6	20 32.5	27 55.4	7 8.5	13 37.6	11 30.9
10 T	21 18 49.2	20 53.2	17 7.3	14 23.5	25 39.2	18 41.6	17 10.7	20 42.9	27 51.1	7 8.6	13 38.8	11 30.0
11 W	21 22 45.8	21 53.9	17 4.2	27 16.1	26 20.4	19 55.3	17 24.4	20 53.5	27 46.8	7 8.6	13 39.9	11 29.1
12 T	21 26 42.3	22 54.6	17 1.0	10♋35.5	27 5.8	21 9.1	17 38.6	21 4.1	27 42.5	7R 8.5	13 40.9	11 28.1
13 F	21 30 38.9	23 55.2	16 57.8	24 23.0	27 54.9	22 22.8	17 53.2	21 14.9	27 38.4	7 8.4	13 42.0	11 27.1
14 S	21 34 35.4	24 55.8	16 54.6	8♌37.1	28 47.5	23 36.6	18 8.4	21 25.7	27 34.3	7 8.2	13 43.0	11 26.1
15 S	21 38 32.0	25 56.4	16 51.4	23 13.2	29 43.3	24 50.3	18 24.0	21 36.7	27 30.2	7 8.0	13 44.0	11 25.1
16 M	21 42 28.5	26 57.0	16 48.3	8♍ 4.1	0♒42.0	26 4.1	18 40.1	21 47.8	27 26.2	7 7.7	13 44.9	11 24.1
17 T	21 46 25.1	27 57.6	16 45.1	23 0.6	1 43.4	27 17.9	18 56.7	21 58.9	27 22.3	7 7.3	13 45.9	11 23.0
18 W	21 50 21.6	28 58.1	16 41.9	7♎53.8	2 47.3	28 31.8	19 13.7	22 10.2	27 18.5	7 6.9	13 46.7	11 21.9
19 T	21 54 18.2	29 58.6	16 38.7	22 36.1	3 53.6	29 45.6	19 31.1	22 21.5	27 14.7	7 6.5	13 47.6	11 20.8
20 F	21 58 14.7	0♓59.1	16 35.6	7♏ 2.1	5 2.0	0♒59.5	19 48.9	22 33.0	27 11.1	7 6.0	13 48.4	11 19.6
21 S	22 2 11.3	1 59.5	16 32.4	21 9.4	6 12.4	2 13.4	20 7.1	22 44.6	27 7.5	7 5.4	13 49.2	11 18.4
22 S	22 6 7.9	2 60.0	16 29.2	4♐57.5	7 24.7	3 27.2	20 25.8	22 56.2	27 3.9	7 4.8	13 50.0	11 17.2
23 M	22 10 4.4	4 0.4	16 26.0	18 27.4	8 38.8	4 41.1	20 44.8	23 7.9	27 0.5	7 4.2	13 50.7	11 16.0
24 T	22 14 1.0	5 0.8	16 22.8	1♑41.1	9 54.6	5 55.1	21 4.2	23 19.8	26 57.1	7 3.4	13 51.4	11 14.7
25 W	22 17 57.5	6 1.2	16 19.7	14 40.6	11 12.1	7 9.0	21 24.1	23 31.7	26 53.9	7 2.7	13 52.1	11 13.5
26 T	22 21 54.1	7 1.5	16 16.5	27 27.4	12 31.0	8 23.0	21 44.2	23 43.7	26 50.7	7 1.9	13 52.7	11 12.2
27 F	22 25 50.6	8 1.8	16 13.3	10♒ 2.9	13 51.4	9 36.9	22 4.7	23 55.8	26 47.6	7 1.0	13 53.3	11 10.9
28 S	22 29 47.2	9 2.1	16 10.1	22 28.2	15 13.2	10 50.9	22 25.6	24 8.0	26 44.6	7 0.1	13 53.9	11 9.6
29 S	22 33 43.7	10 2.4	16 7.0	4♓43.8	16 36.4	12 4.8	22 46.8	24 20.2	26 41.7	6 59.1	13 54.4	11 8.2
						DECLINATION at NOON						
1 S	20 43 20.2	17S 15.6	17S 5.0	8S 11.8	18S 19.1	22S 18.2	25N 37.0	6N 27.0	20N 45.8	13S 24.8	20S 55.4	11N 12.7
4 W	20 55 9.9	16 23.6	17 2.3	4N 10.6	18 53.0	22 11.8	25 37.6	6 38.6	20 48.9	13 25.2	20 55.8	11 14.8
7 S	21 6 59.5	15 29.0	16 59.6	14 52.0	19 19.4	21 59.4	25 38.6	6 50.4	20 52.0	13 25.4	20 56.1	11 17.1
10 T	21 18 49.2	14 32.0	16 56.9	20 12.6	19 36.8	21 41.2	25 39.9	7 2.6	20 54.9	13 25.5	20 56.4	11 19.4
13 F	21 30 38.9	13 32.9	16 54.2	16 40.0	19 44.2	21 17.1	25 41.4	7 15.2	20 57.7	13 25.3	20 56.7	11 21.8
16 M	21 42 28.5	12 31.8	16 51.5	4 13.6	19 40.8	20 47.4	25 43.0	7 28.0	21 0.3	13 25.1	20 56.9	11 24.2
19 T	21 54 18.2	11 28.9	16 48.8	10S 37.8	19 26.2	20 12.2	25 44.6	7 41.1	21 2.8	13 24.6	20 57.1	11 26.6
22 S	22 6 7.9	10 24.3	16 46.1	19 28.3	19 0.2	19 31.7	25 46.3	7 54.5	21 5.1	13 24.0	20 57.2	11 29.1
25 W	22 17 57.5	9 18.2	16 43.3	18 19.1	18 22.6	18 46.0	25 47.7	8 8.1	21 7.3	13 23.3	20 57.3	11 31.5
28 S	22 29 47.2	8 10.9	16 40.6	9 17.7	17 33.5	17 55.4	25 48.9	8 21.9	21 9.3	13 22.4	20 57.4	11 34.0

MARCH 1976

LONGITUDE at NOON

DAY	EPHEMERIS SIDEREAL TIME	☉	☊	☽	☿	♀	♂	♃	♄	♅	♆	♇
	h m s	° ′	° ′	° ′	° ′	° ′	° ′	° ′	° ′	° ′	° ′	° ′
1 M	22 37 40.3	11♓ 2.6	16♏ 3.8	16♓50.4	18♒ 0.8	13♒18.8	23♊ 8.4	24♈32.5	26♋38.9	6♏58.1	13♐54.9	11♎ 6.8
2 T	22 41 36.8	12 2.8	16 0.6	28 49.0	19 26.6	14 32.8	23 30.2	24 44.9	26R36.1	6R57.0	13 55.4	11R 5.4
3 W	22 45 33.4	13 3.0	15 57.4	10♈41.2	20 53.5	15 46.7	23 52.4	24 57.4	26 33.5	6 55.9	13 55.8	11 4.0
4 T	22 49 29.9	14 3.2	15 54.2	22 29.2	22 21.7	17 0.7	24 15.0	25 9.9	26 31.0	6 54.7	13 56.2	11 2.6
5 F	22 53 26.5	15 3.3	15 51.1	4♉15.9	23 51.1	18 14.7	24 37.8	25 22.6	26 28.5	6 53.5	13 56.6	11 1.1
6 S	22 57 23.0	16 3.3	15 47.9	16 5.1	25 21.7	19 28.7	25 0.9	25 35.3	26 26.2	6 52.2	13 56.9	10 59.7
7 S	23 1 19.6	17 3.4	15 44.7	28 1.4	26 53.5	20 42.6	25 24.3	25 48.0	26 23.9	6 50.9	13 57.2	10 58.2
8 M	23 5 16.1	18 3.4	15 41.5	10♊ 9.7	28 26.4	21 56.6	25 48.0	26 0.8	26 21.8	6 49.6	13 57.4	10 56.7
9 T	23 9 12.7	19 3.4	15 38.4	22 35.3	0♓ 0.5	23 10.6	26 11.9	26 13.7	26 19.8	6 48.2	13 57.7	10 55.2
10 W	23 13 9.2	20 3.3	15 35.2	5♋23.3	1 35.7	24 24.6	26 36.2	26 26.7	26 17.9	6 46.7	13 57.9	10 53.6
11 T	23 17 5.8	21 3.2	15 32.0	18 37.8	3 12.1	25 38.6	27 0.6	26 39.7	26 16.0	6 45.2	13 58.0	10 52.1
12 F	23 21 2.4	22 3.0	15 28.8	2♌21.6	4 49.7	26 52.5	27 25.4	26 52.8	26 14.3	6 43.7	13 58.1	10 50.5
13 S	23 24 58.9	23 2.9	15 25.6	16 34.8	6 28.4	28 6.5	27 50.4	27 5.9	26 12.7	6 42.1	13 58.2	10 49.0
14 S	23 28 55.5	24 2.6	15 22.5	1♍14.5	8 8.3	29 20.5	28 15.6	27 19.1	26 11.2	6 40.5	13 58.3	10 47.4
15 M	23 32 52.0	25 2.4	15 19.3	16 14.4	9 49.4	0♓34.5	28 41.0	27 32.3	26 9.8	6 38.8	13 58.3	10 45.8
16 T	23 36 48.6	26 2.1	15 16.1	1♎25.6	11 31.7	1 48.5	29 6.7	27 45.6	26 8.5	6 37.1	13 58.3	10 44.2
17 W	23 40 45.1	27 1.8	15 12.9	16 37.7	13 15.3	3 2.5	29 32.7	27 59.0	26 7.4	6 35.4	13 58.3	10 42.6
18 T	23 44 41.7	28 1.5	15 9.8	1♏40.7	15 0.0	4 16.5	29 58.8	28 12.4	26 6.3	6 33.6	13R58.2	10 41.0
19 F	23 48 38.2	29 1.1	15 6.6	16 26.8	16 46.0	5 30.5	0♋25.1	28 25.9	26 5.3	6 31.8	13 58.1	10 39.4
20 S	23 52 34.8	0♈ 0.7	15 3.4	0♐50.7	18 33.2	6 44.5	0 51.7	28 39.4	26 4.5	6 30.0	13 58.0	10 37.8
21 S	23 56 31.3	1 0.3	15 0.2	14 50.4	20 21.7	7 58.5	1 18.4	28 52.9	26 3.7	6 28.1	13 57.8	10 36.1
22 M	0 0 27.9	1 59.8	14 57.0	28 25.8	22 11.5	9 12.5	1 45.4	29 6.5	26 3.1	6 26.1	13 57.6	10 34.5
23 T	0 4 24.4	2 59.3	14 53.9	11♑38.9	24 2.6	10 26.5	2 12.5	29 20.2	26 2.5	6 24.2	13 57.3	10 32.8
24 W	0 8 21.0	3 58.8	14 50.7	24 32.2	25 54.9	11 40.5	2 39.8	29 33.8	26 2.1	6 22.2	13 57.1	10 31.1
25 T	0 12 17.5	4 58.2	14 47.5	7♒ 8.9	27 48.6	12 54.5	3 7.4	29 47.6	26 1.8	6 20.1	13 56.8	10 29.5
26 F	0 16 14.1	5 57.7	14 44.3	19 31.9	29 43.5	14 8.5	3 35.1	0♉ 1.3	26 1.6	6 18.1	13 56.4	10 27.8
27 S	0 20 10.6	6 57.1	14 41.1	1♓43.9	1♈39.6	15 22.4	4 2.9	0 15.1	26 1.5	6 16.0	13 56.0	10 26.1
28 S	0 24 7.2	7 56.4	14 38.0	13 47.1	3 37.0	16 36.4	4 31.0	0 29.0	26 1.5	6 13.8	13 55.6	10 24.5
29 M	0 28 3.7	8 55.7	14 34.8	25 43.6	5 35.6	17 50.4	4 59.3	0 42.9	26D 1.7	6 11.7	13 55.2	10 22.8
30 T	0 32 0.3	9 55.0	14 31.6	7♈35.3	7 35.4	19 4.4	5 27.7	0 56.8	26 1.9	6 9.5	13 54.7	10 21.1
31 W	0 35 56.8	10 54.3	14 28.4	19 23.9	9 36.2	20 18.4	5 56.3	1 10.7	26 2.3	6 7.3	13 54.2	10 19.4

DECLINATION at NOON

DAY	EPHEMERIS SIDEREAL TIME	☉	☊	☽	☿	♀	♂	♃	♄	♅	♆	♇
1 M	22 37 40.3	7S25.5	16S38.8	1S15.5	16S54.2	17S19.1	25N49.6	8N31.2	21N10.6	13S21.7	20S57.5	11N35.6
4 T	22 49 29.9	6 16.5	16 36.0	10N29.9	15 45.8	16 21.0	25 50.3	8 45.3	21 12.3	13 20.6	20 57.5	11 38.1
7 S	23 1 19.6	5 6.7	16 33.2	18 30.9	14 25.9	15 18.8	25 50.5	8 59.6	21 13.8	13 19.3	20 57.4	11 40.6
10 W	23 13 9.2	3 56.4	16 30.5	19 19.7	12 54.6	14 12.8	25 50.2	9 14.0	21 15.2	13 17.9	20 57.4	11 43.0
13 S	23 24 58.9	2 45.6	16 27.7	10 59.0	11 12.1	13 3.2	25 49.3	9 28.5	21 16.4	13 16.3	20 57.3	11 45.4
16 T	23 36 48.6	1 34.6	16 24.9	3S43.6	9 18.5	11 50.4	25 47.7	9 43.1	21 17.4	13 14.6	20 57.2	11 47.8
19 F	23 48 38.2	0 23.4	16 22.1	16 29.2	7 14.1	10 34.6	25 45.5	9 57.8	21 18.1	13 12.9	20 57.0	11 50.0
22 M	0 0 27.9	0N47.7	16 19.4	19 45.6	4 59.2	9 16.3	25 42.4	10 12.6	21 18.7	13 11.0	20 56.8	11 52.3
25 T	0 12 17.5	1 58.5	16 16.5	13 30.1	2 34.4	7 55.7	25 38.5	10 27.3	21 19.2	13 9.0	20 56.6	11 54.5
28 S	0 24 7.2	3 9.0	16 13.7	2 15.7	0 0.5	6 33.2	25 33.7	10 42.1	21 19.4	13 6.9	20 56.3	11 56.6
31 W	0 35 56.8	4 19.0	16 10.9	9N30.3	2N41.0	5 9.0	25 28.0	10 57.0	21 19.4	13 4.7	20 56.0	11 58.6

APRIL 1976

LONGITUDE at NOON

DAY	EPHEMERIS SIDEREAL TIME	☉	☊	☽	☿	♀	♂	♃	♄	♅	♆	♇
1 T	0 39 53.4	11♈53.5	14♏25.3	1♉11.4	11♈38.0	21♓32.4	6♋25.0	1♉24.7	26♋ 2.7	6♏ 5.1	13♐53.7	10♎17.8
2 F	0 43 49.9	12 52.7	14 22.1	13 0.2	13 40.8	22 46.3	6 53.9	1 38.7	26 3.3	6R 2.8	13R53.1	10R16.1
3 S	0 47 46.5	13 51.8	14 18.9	24 53.0	15 44.2	24 0.3	7 23.0	1 52.7	26 4.0	6 0.5	13 52.6	10 14.4
4 S	0 51 43.0	14 51.0	14 15.7	6♊53.0	17 48.4	25 14.3	7 52.2	2 6.8	26 4.8	5 58.2	13 51.9	10 12.7
5 M	0 55 39.6	15 50.0	14 12.5	19 4.1	19 52.9	26 28.2	8 21.5	2 20.9	26 5.7	5 55.8	13 51.3	10 11.1
6 T	0 59 36.2	16 49.1	14 9.4	1♋30.4	21 57.6	27 42.2	8 51.0	2 35.0	26 6.7	5 53.5	13 50.6	10 9.4
7 W	1 3 32.7	17 48.1	14 6.2	14 16.2	24 2.4	28 56.1	9 20.7	2 49.2	26 7.9	5 51.2	13 49.9	10 7.8
8 T	1 7 29.3	18 47.1	14 3.0	27 25.2	26 6.8	0♈10.1	9 50.5	3 3.4	26 9.2	5 48.8	13 49.2	10 6.1
9 F	1 11 25.8	19 46.0	13 59.8	11♌ 0.4	28 10.7	1 24.0	10 20.4	3 17.6	26 10.5	5 46.3	13 48.4	10 4.5
10 S	1 15 22.4	20 44.9	13 56.7	25 3.1	0♉13.6	2 37.9	10 50.5	3 31.8	26 12.0	5 43.9	13 47.6	10 2.8
11 S	1 19 18.9	21 43.7	13 53.5	9♍32.4	2 15.3	3 51.8	11 20.7	3 46.0	26 13.5	5 41.5	13 46.8	10 1.2
12 M	1 23 15.5	22 42.5	13 50.3	24 24.2	4 15.4	5 5.7	11 51.0	4 0.2	26 15.2	5 39.0	13 46.0	9 59.6
13 T	1 27 12.0	23 41.3	13 47.1	9♎31.7	6 13.5	6 19.6	12 21.4	4 14.5	26 17.0	5 36.5	13 45.1	9 57.9
14 W	1 31 8.6	24 40.1	13 43.9	24 46.0	8 9.4	7 33.5	12 51.9	4 28.7	26 18.8	5 34.0	13 44.2	9 56.3
15 T	1 35 5.1	25 38.8	13 40.8	9♏56.9	10 2.6	8 47.4	13 22.6	4 43.0	26 20.8	5 31.5	13 43.2	9 54.7
16 F	1 39 1.7	26 37.4	13 37.6	24 55.2	11 52.9	10 1.2	13 53.3	4 57.3	26 22.9	5 29.0	13 42.3	9 53.1
17 S	1 42 58.2	27 36.1	13 34.4	9♐33.4	13 39.9	11 15.1	14 24.2	5 11.6	26 25.1	5 26.5	13 41.3	9 51.6
18 S	1 46 54.8	28 34.7	13 31.2	23 46.9	15 23.5	12 29.0	14 55.2	5 25.9	26 27.4	5 24.0	13 40.3	9 50.0
19 M	1 50 51.3	29 33.3	13 28.1	7♑33.6	17 3.3	13 42.8	15 26.3	5 40.3	26 29.8	5 21.4	13 39.3	9 48.4
20 T	1 54 47.9	0♉31.9	13 24.9	20 54.1	18 39.1	14 56.7	15 57.5	5 54.6	26 32.3	5 18.9	13 38.2	9 46.9
21 W	1 58 44.4	1 30.4	13 21.7	3♒50.5	20 10.7	16 10.6	16 28.8	6 8.9	26 34.9	5 16.4	13 37.1	9 45.4
22 T	2 2 41.0	2 28.9	13 18.5	16 26.0	21 38.0	17 24.4	17 0.2	6 23.3	26 37.5	5 13.8	13 36.0	9 43.8
23 F	2 6 37.6	3 27.4	13 15.3	28 44.6	23 0.8	18 38.3	17 31.7	6 37.7	26 40.3	5 11.2	13 34.9	9 42.3
24 S	2 10 34.1	4 25.8	13 12.2	10♓50.2	24 18.9	19 52.1	18 3.4	6 52.0	26 43.2	5 8.7	13 33.7	9 40.8
25 S	2 14 30.7	5 24.3	13 9.0	22 46.5	25 32.4	21 6.0	18 35.1	7 6.4	26 46.2	5 6.1	13 32.5	9 39.4
26 M	2 18 27.2	6 22.7	13 5.8	4♈37.1	26 41.0	22 19.8	19 6.9	7 20.7	26 49.3	5 3.6	13 31.4	9 37.9
27 T	2 22 23.8	7 21.0	13 2.6	16 24.9	27 44.7	23 33.7	19 38.8	7 35.1	26 52.5	5 1.0	13 30.1	9 36.5
28 W	2 26 20.3	8 19.4	12 59.5	28 12.4	28 43.4	24 47.5	20 10.9	7 49.5	26 55.8	4 58.5	13 28.9	9 35.1
29 T	2 30 16.9	9 17.7	12 56.3	10♉ 2.7	29 37.0	26 1.4	20 43.0	8 3.9	26 59.2	4 55.9	13 27.7	9 33.7
30 F	2 34 13.4	10 16.0	12 53.1	21 57.2	0♊25.4	27 15.2	21 15.2	8 18.2	27 2.7	4 53.4	13 26.4	9 32.3

DECLINATION at NOON

DAY	EPHEMERIS SIDEREAL TIME	☉	☊	☽	☿	♀	♂	♃	♄	♅	♆	♇
1 T	0 39 53.4	4N42.1	16S10.0	12N52.0	3N36.2	4S40.6	25N25.9	11N 1.9	21N19.4	13S 4.0	20S55.9	11N59.3
4 S	0 51 43.0	5 51.1	16 7.2	19 20.1	6 24.3	3 14.7	25 18.9	11 16.7	21 19.1	13 1.7	20 55.6	12 1.2
7 W	1 3 32.7	6 59.1	16 4.3	18 4.8	9 13.1	1 47.9	25 10.8	11 31.4	21 18.7	12 59.4	20 55.2	12 3.0
10 S	1 15 22.4	8 6.1	16 1.5	8 19.7	11 57.5	0 20.6	25 1.7	11 46.1	21 18.1	12 57.0	20 54.8	12 4.7
13 T	1 27 12.0	9 11.8	15 58.6	6S25.2	14 32.0	1N 7.0	24 51.6	12 0.8	21 17.3	12 54.5	20 54.4	12 6.3
16 F	1 39 1.7	10 16.1	15 55.8	17 53.8	16 51.1	2 34.6	24 40.3	12 15.3	21 16.3	12 52.0	20 54.0	12 7.8
19 M	1 50 51.3	11 19.0	15 52.9	18 53.9	18 50.3	4 1.8	24 27.9	12 29.8	21 15.2	12 49.5	20 53.5	12 9.1
22 T	2 2 41.0	12 20.1	15 50.1	10 52.4	20 27.3	5 28.3	24 14.4	12 44.2	21 13.9	12 47.0	20 53.0	12 10.4
25 S	2 14 30.7	13 19.5	15 47.2	0N50.9	21 41.0	6 53.9	23 59.8	12 58.4	21 12.3	12 44.4	20 52.5	12 11.5
28 W	2 26 20.3	14 16.9	15 44.3	12 3.8	22 31.9	8 18.2	23 43.9	13 12.5	21 10.6	12 41.9	20 52.0	12 12.5

MAY 1976

DAY	EPHEMERIS SIDEREAL TIME	☉	☊	☽	☿	♀	♂	♃	♄	♅	♆	♇
	h m s	° ′	° ′	° ′	° ′	° ′	° ′	° ′	° ′	° ′	° ′	° ′
LONGITUDE at NOON												
1 S	2 38 10.0	11♉14.3	12♏49.9	3♊58.4	1♊ 8.6	28♈29.0	21♋47.5	8♉32.6	27♋ 6.3	4♏50.9	13♐25.1	9♎30.9
2 S	2 42 6.5	12 12.5	12 46.7	16 8.4	1 46.6	29 42.8	22 19.9	8 46.9	27 9.9	4R48.3	13R23.8	9R29.6
3 M	2 46 3.1	13 10.7	12 43.6	28 29.5	2 19.2	0♉56.6	22 52.3	9 1.3	27 13.7	4 45.8	13 22.4	9 28.2
4 T	2 49 59.6	14 8.8	12 40.4	11♋ 4.3	2 46.6	2 10.4	23 24.9	9 15.6	27 17.5	4 43.3	13 21.1	9 26.9
5 W	2 53 56.2	15 6.9	12 37.2	23 55.1	3 8.6	3 24.1	23 57.5	9 29.9	27 21.4	4 40.8	13 19.7	9 25.6
6 T	2 57 52.8	16 5.0	12 34.0	7♌ 4.7	3 25.2	4 37.9	24 30.2	9 44.2	27 25.4	4 38.3	13 18.3	9 24.4
7 F	3 1 49.3	17 3.1	12 30.9	20 35.0	3 36.6	5 51.7	25 3.0	9 58.5	27 29.6	4 35.8	13 16.9	9 23.1
8 S	3 5 45.9	18 1.1	12 27.7	4♍27.3	3 42.8	7 5.4	25 35.9	10 12.8	27 33.7	4 33.3	13 15.5	9 21.9
9 S	3 9 42.4	18 59.1	12 24.5	18 41.5	3 43.8	8 19.2	26 8.8	10 27.0	27 38.0	4 30.9	13 14.1	9 20.7
10 M	3 13 39.0	19 57.1	12 21.3	3♎15.7	3R39.9	9 32.9	26 41.8	10 41.3	27 42.4	4 28.4	13 12.6	9 19.5
11 T	3 17 35.5	20 55.0	12 18.1	18 5.9	3 31.2	10 46.6	27 14.9	10 55.5	27 46.8	4 26.0	13 11.1	9 18.4
12 W	3 21 32.1	21 52.9	12 15.0	3♏ 5.7	3 18.0	12 0.4	27 48.1	11 9.7	27 51.3	4 23.6	13 9.7	9 17.2
13 T	3 25 28.6	22 50.8	12 11.8	18 7.5	3 0.6	13 14.1	28 21.3	11 23.9	27 56.0	4 21.2	13 8.2	9 16.1
14 F	3 29 25.2	23 48.7	12 8.6	3♐ 2.5	2 39.2	14 27.8	28 54.6	11 38.1	28 0.6	4 18.8	13 6.7	9 15.1
15 S	3 33 21.7	24 46.5	12 5.4	17 43.0	2 14.4	15 41.5	29 28.0	11 52.2	28 5.4	4 16.5	13 5.2	9 14.0
16 S	3 37 18.3	25 44.3	12 2.3	2♑ 2.6	1 46.6	16 55.2	0♌ 1.4	12 6.4	28 10.2	4 14.2	13 3.6	9 13.0
17 M	3 41 14.9	26 42.1	11 59.1	15 57.1	1 16.3	18 9.0	0 34.9	12 20.5	28 15.2	4 11.9	13 2.1	9 12.0
18 T	3 45 11.4	27 39.9	11 55.9	29 25.1	0 44.0	19 22.7	1 8.5	12 34.6	28 20.2	4 9.6	13 0.6	9 11.0
19 W	3 49 8.0	28 37.7	11 52.7	12♒27.4	0 10.4	20 36.4	1 42.2	12 48.7	28 25.3	4 7.4	12 59.0	9 10.1
20 T	3 53 4.5	29 35.4	11 49.6	25 6.5	29♉35.9	21 50.1	2 1..9	13 2.7	28 30.4	4 5.1	12 57.5	9 9.2
21 F	3 57 1.1	0♊33.1	11 46.4	7♓26.1	29 1.3	23 3.8	2 49.6	13 16.7	28 35.6	4 2.9	12 55.9	9 8.3
22 S	4 0 57.6	1 30.8	11 43.2	19 30.8	28 27.1	24 17.6	3 23.5	13 30.7	28 40.9	4 0.8	12 54.3	9 7.4
23 S	4 4 54.2	2 28.5	11 40.0	1♈25.1	27 53.9	25 31.3	3 57.4	13 44.6	28 46.3	3 58.6	12 52.7	9 6.6
24 M	4 8 50.8	3 26.1	11 36.8	13 13.8	27 22.3	26 45.0	4 31.3	13 58.5	28 51.7	3 56.5	12 51.1	9 5.8
25 T	4 12 47.3	4 23.8	11 33.7	25 1.0	26 52.7	27 58.7	5 5.4	14 12.4	28 57.2	3 54.4	12 49.5	9 5.0
26 W	4 16 43.9	5 21.4	11 30.5	6♉50.6	26 25.7	29 12.4	5 39.4	14 26.3	29 2.8	3 52.3	12 47.9	9 4.2
27 T	4 20 40.4	6 19.0	11 27.3	18 45.8	26 1.7	0♊26.1	6 13.6	14 40.1	29 8.5	3 50.3	12 46.3	9 3.5
28 F	4 24 37.0	7 16.6	11 24.1	0♊49.1	25 41.1	1 39.8	6 47.8	14 53.9	29 14.2	3 48.3	12 44.7	9 2.8
29 S	4 28 33.5	8 14.2	11 21.0	13 2.7	25 24.2	2 53.5	7 22.1	15 7.6	29 19.9	3 46.3	12 43.1	9 2.1
30 S	4 32 30.1	9 11.7	11 17.8	25 28.0	25 11.1	4 7.2	7 56.4	15 21.3	29 25.8	3 44.4	12 41.5	9 1.5
31 M	4 36 26.6	10 9.2	11 14.6	8♋ 5.9	25 2.2	5 20.9	8 30.8	15 35.0	29 31.7	3 42.5	12 39.8	9 0.9
DECLINATION at NOON												
1 S	2 38 10.0	15N12.1	15S41.4	19N 2.2	23N 0.4	9N40.8	23N26.9	13N26.5	21N 8.8	12S39.4	20S51.5	12N13.4
4 T	2 49 59.6	16 5.1	15 38.5	18 28.3	23 7.7	11 1.5	23 8.7	13 40.3	21 6.7	12 36.9	20 50.9	12 14.1
7 F	3 1 49.3	16 55.7	15 35.6	9 39.1	22 54.7	12 19.9	22 49.4	13 53.9	21 4.5	12 34.4	20 50.3	12 14.7
10 M	3 13 39.0	17 43.7	15 32.7	4S22.7	22 22.5	13 35.6	22 28.9	14 7.4	21 2.1	12 32.0	20 49.8	12 15.1
13 T	3 25 28.6	18 29.1	15 29.8	16 44.1	21 33.3	14 48.5	22 7.3	14 20.7	20 59.6	12 29.6	20 49.2	12 15.4
16 S	3 37 18.3	19 11.6	15 26.9	19 24.2	20 30.4	15 58.1	21 44.5	14 33.7	20 56.8	12 27.3	20 48.6	12 15.6
19 W	3 49 8.0	19 51.3	15 24.0	11 59.8	19 19.3	17 4.1	21 20.5	14 46.6	20 53.9	12 25.1	20 48.0	12 15.6
22 S	4 0 57.6	20 27.9	15 21.0	0 16.5	18 6.9	18 6.2	20 55.5	14 59.2	20 50.9	12 22.9	20 47.4	12 15.4
25 T	4 12 47.3	21 1.3	15 18.1	11N 9.6	17 0.7	19 4.1	20 29.3	15 11.6	20 47.7	12 20.8	20 46.7	12 15.2
28 F	4 24 37.0	21 31.5	15 15.2	18 42.3	16 7.2	19 57.4	20 2.0	15 23.8	20 44.4	12 18.8	20 46.1	12 14.7
31 M	4 36 26.6	21 58.4	15 12.2	18 52.8	15 30.9	20 45.9	19 33.6	15 35.7	20 40.9	12 16.9	20 45.5	12 14.2

JUNE 1976

DAY	EPHEMERIS SIDEREAL TIME	☉	☊	☽	☿	♀	♂	♃	♄	♅	♆	♇
LONGITUDE at NOON												
1 T	4 40 23.2	11♊ 6.8	11♏11.4	20♋57.2	24♉57.6	6♊34.6	9♌ 5.3	15♉48.6	29♋37.6	3♏40.6	12♐38.2	9♎ 0.3
2 W	4 44 19.8	12 4.3	11 8.3	4♌ 2.4	24R57.4	7 48.3	9 39.8	16 2.1	29 43.6	3R38.8	12R36.6	8R59.8
3 T	4 48 16.3	13 1.7	11 5.1	17 21.9	25D 1.6	9 2.0	10 14.3	16 15.7	29 49.7	3 37.0	12 35.0	8 59.3
4 F	4 52 12.9	13 59.2	11 1.9	0♍56.1	25 10.3	10 15.7	10 49.0	16 29.2	29 55.9	3 35.3	12 33.3	8 58.8
5 S	4 56 9.4	14 56.6	10 58.7	14 45.1	25 23.5	11 29.4	11 23.6	16 42.6	0♌ 2.1	3 33.6	12 31.7	8 58.3
6 S	5 0 6.0	15 54.0	10 55.5	28 48.7	25 41.2	12 43.0	11 58.3	16 56.0	0 8.3	3 31.9	12 30.1	8 57.9
7 M	5 4 2.5	16 51.4	10 52.4	13♎ 6.0	26 3.2	13 56.7	12 33.1	17 9.3	0 14.6	3 30.3	12 28.5	8 57.6
8 T	5 7 59.1	17 48.8	10 49.2	27 34.9	26 29.7	15 10.4	13 8.0	17 22.6	0 21.0	3 28.7	12 26.8	8 57.2
9 W	5 11 55.7	18 46.2	10 46.0	12♏12.0	27 0.5	16 24.1	13 42.9	17 35.9	0 27.5	3 27.2	12 25.3	8 56.9
10 T	5 15 52.2	19 43.5	10 42.8	26 52.3	27 35.5	17 37.8	14 17.8	17 49.1	0 33.9	3 25.7	12 23.7	8 56.6
11 F	5 19 48.8	20 40.8	10 39.7	11♐29.8	28 14.6	18 51.5	14 52.8	18 2.2	0 40.4	3 24.2	12 22.1	8 56.4
12 S	5 23 45.3	21 38.2	10 36.5	25 57.8	28 57.8	20 5.2	15 27.8	18 15.3	0 47.0	3 22.8	12 20.5	8 56.2
13 S	5 27 41.9	22 35.5	10 33.3	10♑10.3	29 45.0	21 18.8	16 2.9	18 28.3	0 53.6	3 21.4	12 18.9	8 56.0
14 M	5 31 38.4	23 32.7	10 30.1	24 2.3	0♊36.1	22 32.5	16 38.0	18 41.3	1 0.3	3 20.0	12 17.3	8 55.8
15 T	5 35 35.0	24 30.0	10 27.0	7♒30.8	1 31.0	23 46.2	17 13.2	18 54.2	1 7.0	3 18.7	12 15.7	8 55.7
16 W	5 39 31.6	25 27.3	10 23.8	20 35.2	2 29.7	24 59.9	17 48.4	19 7.1	1 13.7	3 17.5	12 14.1	8 55.6
17 T	5 43 28.1	26 24.6	10 20.6	3♓16.6	3 32.0	26 13.6	18 23.7	19 19.8	1 20.5	3 16.3	12 12.6	8 55.5
18 F	5 47 24.7	27 21.8	10 17.4	15 38.1	4 38.1	27 27.3	18 59.0	19 32.6	1 27.4	3 15.1	12 11.0	8 55.5
19 S	5 51 21.2	28 19.1	10 14.2	27 43.8	5 47.6	28 41.0	19 34.3	19 45.2	1 34.3	3 14.0	12 9.4	8 55.5
20 S	5 55 17.8	29 16.4	10 11.1	9♈38.5	7 0.7	29 54.7	20 9.8	19 57.8	1 41.2	3 12.9	12 7.9	8D55.6
21 M	5 59 14.3	0♋13.6	10 7.9	21 27.5	8 17.3	1♋ 8.4	20 45.2	20 10.4	1 48.2	3 11.9	12 6.4	8 55.6
22 T	6 3 10.9	1 10.9	10 4.7	3♉15.9	9 37.4	2 22.2	21 20.8	20 22.8	1 55.2	3 10.9	12 4.9	8 55.8
23 W	6 7 7.5	2 8.1	10 1.5	15 8.4	11 0.8	3 35.9	21 56.3	20 35.2	2 2.2	3 10.0	12 3.4	8 55.9
24 T	6 11 4.0	3 5.4	9 58.4	27 9.4	12 27.6	4 49.6	22 31.9	20 47.6	2 9.3	3 9.1	12 1.9	8 56.1
25 F	6 15 0.6	4 2.6	9 55.2	9♊22.2	13 57.7	6 3.4	23 7.6	20 59.8	2 16.4	3 8.3	12 0.4	8 56.3
26 S	6 18 57.1	4 59.8	9 52.0	21 49.3	15 31.1	7 17.1	23 43.3	21 12.0	2 23.6	3 7.5	11 58.9	8 56.5
27 S	6 22 53.7	5 57.1	9 48.8	4♋32.1	17 7.8	8 30.9	24 19.1	21 24.1	2 30.8	3 6.8	11 57.5	8 56.8
28 M	6 26 50.2	6 54.3	9 45.7	17 30.6	18 47.6	9 44.6	24 54.9	21 36.1	2 38.0	3 6.1	11 56.0	8 57.1
29 T	6 30 46.8	7 51.5	9 42.5	0♌44.3	20 30.6	10 58.4	25 30.8	21 48.1	2 45.3	3 5.5	11 54.6	8 57.5
30 W	6 34 43.4	8 48.8	9 39.3	14 11.4	22 16.7	12 12.2	26 6.7	22 0.0	2 52.6	3 5.0	11 53.2	8 57.9
DECLINATION at NOON												
1 T	4 40 23.2	22N 6.5	15S11.2	16N60.0	15N23.1	21N 1.0	19N23.9	15N39.7	20N39.7	12S16.3	20S45.3	12N14.0
4 F	4 52 12.9	22 28.8	15 8.3	6 31.2	15 12.8	21 42.6	18 54.1	15 51.3	20 36.0	12 14.6	20 44.7	12 13.2
7 M	5 4 2.5	22 47.5	15 5.3	7S30.4	15 21.5	22 18.8	18 23.3	16 2.6	20 32.2	12 12.9	20 44.1	12 12.3
10 T	5 15 52.2	23 2.6	15 2.3	18 10.2	15 47.5	22 49.3	17 51.5	16 13.6	20 28.2	12 11.4	20 43.5	12 11.3
13 S	5 27 41.9	23 14.0	14 59.3	18 39.9	16 28.1	23 13.8	17 18.7	16 24.4	20 24.1	12 10.1	20 42.9	12 10.1
16 W	5 39 31.6	23 21.7	14 56.4	9 47.3	17 20.4	23 32.3	16 44.9	16 34.9	20 19.8	12 8.8	20 42.4	12 8.8
19 S	5 51 21.2	23 25.8	14 53.4	2N22.8	18 21.3	23 44.7	16 10.2	16 45.1	20 15.5	12 7.7	20 41.8	12 7.4
22 T	6 3 10.9	23 26.1	14 50.4	13 18.1	19 27.3	23 50.7	15 34.6	16 55.0	20 11.0	12 6.8	20 41.3	12 5.9
25 F	6 15 0.6	23 22.7	14 47.4	19 28.9	20 34.7	23 50.3	14 58.1	17 4.6	20 6.4	12 6.0	20 40.8	12 4.2
28 M	6 26 50.2	23 15.6	14 44.4	17 39.9	21 39.1	23 43.6	14 20.8	17 13.9	20 1.7	12 5.3	20 40.3	12 2.4

JULY 1976

DAY	EPHEMERIS SIDEREAL TIME	☉	☊	☽	☿	♀	♂	♃	♄	♅	♆	♇
	h m s	° ′	° ′	° ′	° ′	° ′	° ′	° ′	° ′	° ′	° ′	° ′
						LONGITUDE at NOON						
1 T	6 38 39.9	9♋46.0	9♏36.1	27♌50.1	24♊ 5.7	13♋25.9	26♌42.7	22♉11.8	2♌59.9	3♏ 4.4	11♐51.8	8♎58.3
2 F	6 42 36.5	10 43.2	9 33.0	11♍38.3	25 57.6	14 39.7	27 18.7	22 23.5	3 7.3	3R 4.0	11R50.5	8 58.7
3 S	6 46 33.0	11 40.4	9 29.8	25 34.4	27 52.2	15 53.5	27 54.7	22 35.1	3 14.7	3 3.5	11 49.1	8 59.2
4 S	6 50 29.6	12 37.7	9 26.6	9♎37.0	29 49.4	17 7.2	28 30.8	22 46.7	3 22.1	3 3.2	11 47.7	8 59.7
5 M	6 54 26.1	13 34.9	9 23.4	23 45.1	1♋48.9	18 21.0	29 7.0	22 58.1	3 29.5	3 2.8	11 46.4	9 0.3
6 T	6 58 22.7	14 32.0	9 20.2	7♏57.5	3 50.7	19 34.8	29 43.1	23 9.5	3 37.0	3 2.6	11 45.1	9 0.8
7 W	7 2 19.3	15 29.2	9 17.1	22 12.8	5 54.3	20 48.5	0♍19.4	23 20.8	3 44.4	3 2.4	11 43.8	9 1.4
8 T	7 6 15.8	16 26.4	9 13.9	6♐28.4	7 59.6	22 2.3	0 55.6	23 32.0	3 51.9	3 2.2	11 42.6	9 2.1
9 F	7 10 12.4	17 23.6	9 10.7	20 41.1	10 6.3	23 16.1	1 31.9	23 43.0	3 59.5	3 2.1	11 41.3	9 2.7
10 S	7 14 8.9	18 20.8	9 7.5	4♑46.6	12 14.1	24 29.8	2 8.3	23 54.0	4 7.0	3 2.0	11 40.1	9 3.4
11 S	7 18 5.5	19 18.0	9 4.4	18 40.5	14 22.7	25 43.6	2 44.7	24 4.9	4 14.6	3 2.0	11 38.9	9 4.2
12 M	7 22 2.0	20 15.2	9 1.2	2♒18.5	16 31.7	26 57.4	3 21.1	24 15.8	4 22.1	3 2.0	11 37.7	9 5.0
13 T	7 25 58.6	21 12.4	8 58.0	15 37.7	18 41.0	28 11.2	3 57.6	24 26.5	4 29.7	3D 2.1	11 36.5	9 5.8
14 W	7 29 55.2	22 9.6	8 54.8	28 36.5	20 50.1	29 25.0	4 34.1	24 37.1	4 37.3	3 2.3	11 35.4	9 6.6
15 T	7 33 51.7	23 6.8	8 51.7	11♓15.1	22 59.0	0♌38.8	5 10.7	24 47.6	4 45.0	3 2.5	11 34.3	9 7.4
16 F	7 37 48.3	24 4.0	8 48.5	23 35.3	25 7.2	1 52.6	5 47.3	24 58.0	4 52.6	3 2.7	11 33.2	9 8.3
17 S	7 41 44.8	25 1.2	8 45.3	5♈40.6	27 14.7	3 6.4	6 23.9	25 8.3	5 0.3	3 3.0	11 32.1	9 9.3
18 S	7 45 41.4	25 58.5	8 42.1	17 35.3	29 21.1	4 20.2	7 0.6	25 18.5	5 7.9	3 3.4	11 31.0	9 10.2
19 M	7 49 37.9	26 55.7	8 38.9	29 24.6	1♌26.4	5 34.0	7 37.4	25 28.6	5 15.6	3 3.8	11 30.0	9 11.2
20 T	7 53 34.5	27 53.0	8 35.8	11♉13.7	3 30.5	6 47.8	8 14.2	25 38.6	5 23.3	3 4.2	11 29.0	9 12.2
21 W	7 57 31.0	28 50.3	8 32.6	23 8.2	5 33.2	8 1.7	8 51.1	25 48.5	5 31.1	3 4.8	11 28.1	9 13.3
22 T	8 1 27.6	29 47.6	8 29.4	5♊13.1	7 34.4	9 15.6	9 27.9	25 58.2	5 38.8	3 5.4	11 27.1	9 14.4
23 F	8 5 24.2	0♌44.9	8 26.2	17 32.8	9 34.0	10 29.4	10 4.9	26 7.9	5 46.5	3 6.0	11 26.2	9 15.5
24 S	8 9 20.7	1 42.2	8 23.1	0♋10.6	11 32.0	11 43.2	10 41.8	26 17.4	5 54.2	3 6.7	11 25.3	9 16.7
25 S	8 13 17.3	2 39.6	8 19.9	13 8.5	13 28.5	12 57.1	11 18.9	26 26.8	6 2.0	3 7.4	11 24.4	9 17.8
26 M	8 17 13.8	3 36.9	8 16.7	26 26.5	15 23.2	14 10.9	11 55.9	26 36.1	6 9.7	3 8.1	11 23.6	9 19.0
27 T	8 21 10.4	4 34.3	8 13.5	10♌ 3.3	17 16.3	15 24.8	12 33.1	26 45.3	6 17.4	3 9.0	11 22.8	9 20.2
28 W	8 25 6.9	5 31.6	8 10.3	23 55.6	19 7.7	16 38.7	13 10.2	26 54.3	6 25.2	3 9.9	11 22.0	9 21.5
29 T	8 29 3.5	6 29.0	8 7.2	7♍59.2	20 57.4	17 52.5	13 47.4	27 3.2	6 32.9	3 10.8	11 21.2	9 22.8
30 F	8 33 0.0	7 26.4	8 4.0	22 9.6	22 45.5	19 6.4	14 24.7	27 12.0	6 40.7	3 11.8	11 20.5	9 24.1
31 S	8 36 56.6	8 23.8	8 0.8	6♎22.7	24 31.9	20 20.3	15 2.0	27 20.7	6 48.4	3 12.8	11 19.8	9 25.4
						DECLINATION at NOON						
1 T	6 38 39.9	23N 4.8	14S 41.3	7N39.5	22N35.7	23N30.6	13N42.6	17N23.0	19N56.8	12S 4.8	20S39.8	12N 0.5
4 S	6 50 29.6	22 50.4	14 38.3	6S 13.0	23 19.3	23 11.3	13 3.6	17 31.6	19 51.9	12 4.5	20 39.4	11 58.5
7 W	7 2 19.3	22 32.5	14 35.3	17 19.3	23 44.6	22 45.8	12 23.9	17 40.0	19 46.9	12 4.3	20 39.0	11 56.4
10 S	7 14 8.9	22 11.0	14 32.3	19 14.3	23 47.6	22 14.3	11 43.4	17 48.0	19 41.8	12 4.3	20 38.6	11 54.2
13 T	7 25 58.6	21 46.1	14 29.2	11 21.5	23 26.0	21 37.0	11 2.3	17 55.8	19 36.6	12 4.4	20 38.2	11 51.9
16 F	7 37 48.3	21 17.9	14 26.2	0N46.9	22 40.2	20 54.1	10 20.5	18 3.2	19 31.3	12 4.7	20 37.9	11 49.5
19 M	7 49 37.9	20 46.4	14 23.1	12 4.4	21 32.7	20 5.7	9 38.0	18 10.2	19 25.9	12 5.2	20 37.6	11 47.0
22 T	8 1 27.6	20 11.7	14 20.1	18 59.1	20 7.1	19 12.3	8 55.0	18 17.0	19 20.5	12 5.8	20 37.3	11 44.4
25 S	8 13 17.3	19 34.0	14 17.0	18 17.2	18 27.4	18 14.0	8 11.3	18 23.4	19 15.0	12 6.6	20 37.1	11 41.8
28 W	8 25 6.9	18 53.3	14 13.9	8 59.2	16 37.3	17 11.1	7 27.2	18 29.4	19 9.5	12 7.5	20 36.9	11 39.1
31 S	8 36 56.6	18 9.9	14 10.8	4S57.0	14 40.0	16 4.1	6 42.5	18 35.1	19 3.9	12 8.6	20 36.8	11 36.3

AUGUST 1976

DAY	EPHEMERIS SIDEREAL TIME	☉	☊	☽	☿	♀	♂	♃	♄	♅	♆	♇
						LONGITUDE at NOON						
1 S	8 40 53.2	9♌21.2	7♏57.6	20♎35.3	26♌16.6	21♌34.1	15♍39.3	27♉29.2	6♌56.1	3♏13.9	11♐19.1	9♎26.8
2 M	8 44 49.7	10 18.6	7 54.5	4♏45.2	27 59.6	22 48.0	16 16.7	27 37.6	7 3.9	3 15.0	11R18.4	9 28.2
3 T	8 48 46.3	11 16.1	7 51.3	18 51.2	29 41.0	24 1.8	16 54.1	27 45.8	7 11.6	3 16.2	11 17.8	9 29.6
4 W	8 52 42.8	12 13.5	7 48.1	2♐52.5	1♍20.8	25 15.7	17 31.6	27 54.0	7 19.3	3 17.4	11 17.2	9 31.1
5 T	8 56 39.4	13 11.0	7 44.9	16 48.2	2 58.9	26 29.5	18 9.1	28 2.0	7 27.0	3 18.7	11 16.7	9 32.6
6 F	9 0 35.9	14 8.4	7 41.8	0♑37.1	4 35.4	27 43.4	18 46.6	28 9.8	7 34.7	3 20.0	11 16.1	9 34.1
7 S	9 4 32.5	15 5.9	7 38.6	14 17.6	6 10.2	28 57.2	19 24.2	28 17.5	7 42.4	3 21.4	11 15.6	9 35.6
8 S	9 8 29.0	16 3.4	7 35.4	27 47.5	7 43.5	0♍11.1	20 1.8	28 25.1	7 50.1	3 22.9	11 15.1	9 37.1
9 M	9 12 25.6	17 0.9	7 32.2	11♒ 4.3	9 15.1	1 24.9	20 39.5	28 32.5	7 57.8	3 24.3	11 14.7	9 38.7
10 T	9 16 22.2	17 58.4	7 29.0	24 6.3	10 45.0	2 38.8	21 17.2	28 39.8	8 5.5	3 25.9	11 14.3	9 40.3
11 W	9 20 18.7	18 56.0	7 25.9	6♓52.1	12 13.4	3 52.7	21 55.1	28 47.0	8 13.2	3 27.5	11 14.0	9 42.0
12 T	9 24 15.3	19 53.6	7 22.7	19 21.7	13 40.1	5 6.5	22 32.9	28 53.9	8 20.8	3 29.1	11 13.6	9 43.7
13 F	9 28 11.8	20 51.2	7 19.5	1♈36.3	15 5.1	6 20.3	23 10.7	29 0.8	8 28.4	3 30.8	11 13.3	9 45.3
14 S	9 32 8.4	21 48.8	7 16.3	13 38.3	16 28.3	7 34.2	23 48.6	29 7.5	8 36.1	3 32.5	11 13.0	9 47.0
15 S	9 36 4.9	22 46.4	7 13.2	25 31.2	17 49.9	8 48.0	24 26.6	29 14.0	8 43.6	3 34.3	11 12.7	9 48.8
16 M	9 40 1.5	23 44.1	7 10.0	7♉19.4	19 9.7	10 1.8	25 4.6	29 20.4	8 51.2	3 36.1	11 12.5	9 50.5
17 T	9 43 58.0	24 41.8	7 6.8	19 8.1	20 27.6	11 15.7	25 42.6	29 26.6	8 58.8	3 37.9	11 12.3	9 52.3
18 W	9 47 54.6	25 39.5	7 3.6	1♊ 2.5	21 43.7	12 29.5	26 20.7	29 32.6	9 6.3	3 39.9	11 12.2	9 54.1
19 T	9 51 51.1	26 37.2	7 0.4	13 8.2	22 57.9	13 43.4	26 58.8	29 38.5	9 13.8	3 41.8	11 12.0	9 55.9
20 F	9 55 47.7	27 35.0	6 57.3	25 30.1	24 10.1	14 57.2	27 37.0	29 44.3	9 21.3	3 43.8	11 11.9	9 57.7
21 S	9 59 44.2	28 32.8	6 54.1	8♋12.6	25 20.2	16 11.0	28 15.2	29 49.8	9 28.8	3 45.8	11 11.9	9 59.6
22 S	10 3 40.8	29 30.6	6 50.9	21 18.5	26 28.2	17 24.8	28 53.5	29 55.2	9 36.3	3 47.9	11 11.8	10 1.4
23 M	10 7 37.3	0♍28.5	6 47.7	4♌49.1	27 34.0	18 38.7	29 31.8	0♊ 0.4	9 43.7	3 50.1	11 11.8	10 3.3
24 T	10 11 33.9	1 26.3	6 44.6	18 42.9	28 37.4	19 52.5	0♎10.2	0 5.5	9 51.1	3 52.2	11D11.9	10 5.2
25 W	10 15 30.5	2 24.2	6 41.4	2♍56.7	29 38.4	21 6.3	0 48.6	0 10.4	9 58.5	3 54.4	11 11.9	10 7.2
26 T	10 19 27.0	3 22.2	6 38.2	17 24.7	0♎36.7	22 20.1	1 27.1	0 15.1	10 5.8	3 56.7	11 12.0	10 9.1
27 F	10 23 23.6	4 20.1	6 35.0	2♎ 0.4	1 32.4	23 34.0	2 5.6	0 19.6	10 13.1	3 59.0	11 12.2	10 11.1
28 S	10 27 20.1	5 18.1	6 31.8	16 37.1	2 25.1	24 47.8	2 44.2	0 24.0	10 20.4	4 1.4	11 12.3	10 13.1
29 S	10 31 16.7	6 16.1	6 28.7	1♏ 8.9	3 14.7	26 1.6	3 22.8	0 28.1	10 27.6	4 3.7	11 12.5	10 15.1
30 M	10 35 13.2	7 14.1	6 25.5	15 31.8	4 1.1	27 15.4	4 1.4	0 32.1	10 34.9	4 6.2	11 12.8	10 17.1
31 T	10 39 9.8	8 12.1	6 22.3	29 43.0	4 44.0	28 29.1	4 40.1	0 35.9	10 42.0	4 8.6	11 13.0	10 19.2
						DECLINATION at NOON						
1 S	8 40 53.2	17N54.8	14S 9.8	9S25.6	13N59.7	15N40.8	6N27.5	18N37.0	19N 2.0	12S 9.0	20S36.7	11N35.4
4 W	8 52 42.8	17 7.9	14 6.7	18 37.9	11 56.8	14 28.6	5 42.2	18 42.2	18 56.4	12 10.3	20 36.6	11 32.5
7 S	9 4 32.5	16 18.5	14 3.6	18 5.0	9 52.0	13 12.9	4 56.6	18 47.2	18 50.7	12 11.8	20 36.5	11 29.6
10 T	9 16 22.2	15 26.7	14 0.5	8 57.5	7 47.2	11 54.0	4 10.5	18 51.7	18 45.1	12 13.4	20 36.5	11 26.7
13 F	9 28 11.8	14 32.7	13 57.4	3N17.3	5 44.0	10 32.3	3 24.1	18 56.0	18 39.4	12 15.1	20 36.5	11 23.7
16 M	9 40 1.5	13 36.6	13 54.3	13 52.4	3 43.6	9 8.1	2 37.4	18 59.8	18 33.7	12 17.0	20 36.6	11 20.7
19 T	9 51 51.1	12 38.5	13 51.2	19 21.0	1 47.7	7 41.6	1 50.5	19 3.4	18 28.0	12 19.1	20 36.7	11 17.7
22 S	10 3 40.8	11 38.7	13 48.1	16 54.8	0S 2.5	6 13.4	1 3.3	19 6.6	18 22.3	12 21.2	20 36.8	11 14.6
25 W	10 15 30.5	10 37.1	13 45.0	6 13.3	1 45.0	4 43.6	0 15.9	19 9.4	18 16.6	12 23.5	20 37.0	11 11.6
28 S	10 27 20.1	9 34.1	13 41.8	8S 2.3	3 17.9	3 12.6	0S31.6	19 11.9	18 11.0	12 25.9	20 37.2	11 8.5
31 T	10 39 9.8	8 29.7	13 38.7	18 0.7	4 38.7	1 40.7	1 19.3	19 14.0	18 5.5	12 28.4	20 37.5	11 5.5

SEPTEMBER 1976

DAY	EPHEMERIS SIDEREAL TIME	☉	☊	☽	☿	♀	♂	♃	♄	♅	♆	♇
	h m s	° ′	° ′	° ′	° ′	° ′	° ′	° ′	° ′	° ′	° ′	° ′
LONGITUDE at NOON												
1 W	10 43 6.3	9 ♍ 10.3	6 ♏ 19.1	13 ♐ 41.5	5 ♎ 23.2	29 ♍ 43.0	5 ♎ 18.9	0 ♊ 39.6	10 ♌ 49.2	4 ♏ 11.2	11 ♐ 13.4	10 ♎ 21.3
2 T	10 47 2.9	10 8.3	6 16.0	27 26.8	5 58.4	0 ♎ 56.7	5 57.7	0 43.1	10 56.3	4 13.7	11 13.7	10 23.4
3 F	10 50 59.4	11 6.4	6 12.8	10 ♑ 59.3	6 29.4	2 10.5	6 36.5	0 46.3	11 3.4	4 16.3	11 14.0	10 25.5
4 S	10 54 56.0	12 4.6	6 9.6	24 19.1	6 55.9	3 24.2	7 15.4	0 49.4	11 10.4	4 18.9	11 14.4	10 27.6
5 S	10 58 52.5	13 2.7	6 6.4	7 ♒ 26.4	7 17.6	4 38.0	7 54.3	0 52.3	11 17.4	4 21.6	11 14.9	10 29.7
6 M	11 2 49.1	14 0.9	6 3.2	20 21.0	7 34.2	5 51.7	8 33.3	0 55.0	11 24.4	4 24.3	11 15.3	10 31.8
7 T	11 6 45.6	14 59.1	6 0.1	3 ♓ 2.8	7 45.4	7 5.4	9 12.3	0 57.5	11 31.3	4 27.0	11 15.8	10 34.0
8 W	11 10 42.2	15 57.4	5 56.9	15 31.9	7 50.8	8 19.1	9 51.4	0 59.8	11 38.2	4 29.8	11 16.3	10 36.1
9 T	11 14 38.7	16 55.6	5 53.7	27 48.8	7 R 50.3	9 32.8	10 30.5	1 1.9	11 45.0	4 32.6	11 16.9	10 38.3
10 F	11 18 35.3	17 53.9	5 50.5	9 ♈ 54.5	7 43.5	10 46.5	11 9.7	1 3.9	11 51.8	4 35.4	11 17.5	10 40.5
11 S	11 22 31.8	18 52.3	5 47.4	21 51.0	7 30.2	12 0.1	11 48.9	1 5.6	11 58.5	4 38.3	11 18.1	10 42.7
12 S	11 26 28.4	19 50.6	5 44.2	3 ♉ 41.0	7 10.3	13 13.8	12 28.1	1 7.2	12 5.2	4 41.2	11 18.7	10 44.9
13 M	11 30 24.9	20 49.0	5 41.0	15 27.8	6 43.6	14 27.4	13 7.4	1 8.5	12 11.8	4 44.1	11 19.4	10 47.1
14 T	11 34 21.5	21 47.5	5 37.8	27 15.7	6 10.1	15 41.1	13 46.8	1 9.7	12 18.4	4 47.1	11 20.1	10 49.4
15 W	11 38 18.1	22 45.9	5 34.6	9 ♊ 9.3	5 30.2	16 54.7	14 26.2	1 10.6	12 24.9	4 50.1	11 20.9	10 51.6
16 T	11 42 14.6	23 44.4	5 31.5	21 13.7	4 44.1	18 8.4	15 5.6	1 11.4	12 31.4	4 53.2	11 21.7	10 53.9
17 F	11 46 11.2	24 43.0	5 28.3	3 ♋ 34.0	3 52.3	19 22.0	15 45.1	1 11.9	12 37.9	4 56.2	11 22.5	10 56.1
18 S	11 50 7.7	25 41.6	5 25.1	16 14.9	2 55.6	20 35.6	16 24.7	1 12.3	12 44.2	4 59.3	11 23.3	10 58.4
19 S	11 54 4.3	26 40.2	5 21.9	29 20.4	1 55.0	21 49.2	17 4.3	1 12.4	12 50.6	5 2.4	11 24.2	11 0.7
20 M	11 58 0.8	27 38.8	5 18.7	12 ♌ 52.6	0 51.6	23 2.8	17 44.0	1 12.4	12 56.8	5 5.6	11 25.1	11 3.0
21 T	12 1 57.4	28 37.5	5 15.6	26 51.9	29 ♍ 46.9	24 16.4	18 23.7	1 R 12.1	13 3.0	5 8.8	11 26.0	11 5.2
22 W	12 5 53.9	29 36.3	5 12.4	11 ♍ 15.8	28 42.3	25 30.0	19 3.5	1 11.7	13 9.2	5 12.0	11 27.0	11 7.6
23 T	12 9 50.5	0 ♎ 35.1	5 9.2	25 59.3	27 39.4	26 43.6	19 43.3	1 11.0	13 15.3	5 15.3	11 28.0	11 9.9
24 F	12 13 47.0	1 33.8	5 6.0	10 ♎ 54.9	26 40.0	27 57.1	20 23.1	1 10.2	13 21.4	5 18.6	11 29.0	11 12.2
25 S	12 17 43.6	2 32.7	5 2.9	25 54.2	25 45.4	29 10.7	21 3.1	1 9.1	13 27.3	5 21.8	11 30.1	11 14.5
26 S	12 21 40.1	3 31.5	4 59.7	10 ♏ 48.9	24 57.3	0 ♏ 24.2	21 43.0	1 7.8	13 33.2	5 25.2	11 31.2	11 16.9
27 M	12 25 36.7	4 30.4	4 56.5	25 32.0	24 16.9	1 37.7	22 23.0	1 6.4	13 39.1	5 28.5	11 32.3	11 19.2
28 T	12 29 33.2	5 29.3	4 53.3	9 ♐ 58.4	23 45.2	2 51.2	23 3.1	1 4.7	13 44.8	5 31.9	11 33.4	11 21.5
29 W	12 33 29.8	6 28.3	4 50.1	24 5.2	23 23.1	4 4.7	23 43.2	1 2.8	13 50.5	5 35.3	11 34.6	11 23.9
30 T	12 37 26.3	7 27.2	4 47.0	7 ♑ 51.6	23 11.1	5 18.2	24 23.3	1 0.7	13 56.2	5 38.7	11 35.8	11 26.2
DECLINATION at NOON												
1 W	10 43 6.3	8N 7.9	13S 37.6	19S 16.6	5S 2.3	1N 9.9	1S 35.2	19N 14.6	18N 3.6	12S 29.3	20S 37.6	11N 4.4
4 S	10 54 56.0	7 1.9	13 34.5	16 18.4	6 1.5	0S 22.7	2 22.9	19 16.3	17 58.1	12 32.0	20 37.9	11 1.4
7 T	11 6 45.6	5 54.9	13 31.3	6 11.0	6 39.3	1 55.4	3 10.5	19 17.6	17 52.7	12 34.8	20 38.3	10 58.3
10 F	11 18 35.3	4 47.0	13 28.2	5N 53.0	6 50.4	3 27.9	3 58.2	19 18.5	17 47.3	12 37.7	20 38.7	10 55.3
13 M	11 30 24.9	3 38.4	13 25.0	15 30.2	6 29.1	4 59.8	4 45.7	19 19.1	17 42.1	12 40.7	20 39.1	10 52.3
16 T	11 42 14.6	2 29.1	13 21.8	19 21.3	5 31.5	6 31.0	5 33.1	19 19.3	17 36.9	12 43.8	20 39.6	10 49.3
19 S	11 54 4.3	1 19.4	13 18.7	15 13.4	3 58.7	8 1.0	6 20.3	19 19.2	17 31.9	12 47.0	20 40.1	10 46.4
22 W	12 5 53.9	0 9.4	13 15.5	3 30.5	2 1.4	9 29.5	7 7.3	19 18.7	17 26.9	12 50.2	20 40.6	10 43.5
25 S	12 17 43.6	1S 0.7	13 12.3	10S 40.6	0N 0.7	10 56.2	7 54.0	19 17.8	17 22.1	12 53.5	20 41.2	10 40.7
28 T	12 29 33.2	2 10.8	13 9.1	18 52.8	1 43.8	12 20.7	8 40.4	19 16.6	17 17.5	12 56.9	20 41.8	10 37.9

OCTOBER 1976

DAY	EPHEMERIS SIDEREAL TIME	☉	☊	☽	☿	♀	♂	♃	♄	♅	♆	♇
LONGITUDE at NOON												
1 F	12 41 22.9	8 ♎ 26.2	4 ♏ 43.8	21 ♑ 18.2	23 ♍ 9.4	6 ♏ 31.7	25 ♎ 3.5	0 ♊ 58.5	14 ♌ 1.7	5 ♏ 42.1	11 ♐ 37.0	11 ♎ 28.5
2 S	12 45 19.4	9 25.3	4 40.6	4 ♒ 26.2	23 D 18.1	7 45.1	25 43.8	0 R 56.0	14 7.2	5 45.6	11 38.3	11 30.9
3 S	12 49 16.0	10 24.3	4 37.4	17 17.7	23 37.0	8 58.5	26 24.1	0 53.3	14 12.7	5 49.0	11 39.6	11 33.2
4 M	12 53 12.5	11 23.4	4 34.3	29 54.5	24 5.8	10 11.9	27 4.4	0 50.5	14 18.0	5 52.5	11 40.9	11 35.6
5 T	12 57 9.1	12 22.5	4 31.1	12 ♓ 18.6	24 43.9	11 25.3	27 44.8	0 47.4	14 23.3	5 56.0	11 42.2	11 37.9
6 W	13 1 5.6	13 21.7	4 27.9	24 31.9	25 30.8	12 38.7	28 25.3	0 44.2	14 28.5	5 59.6	11 43.6	11 40.2
7 T	13 5 2.2	14 20.9	4 24.7	6 ♈ 35.9	26 25.7	13 52.0	29 5.8	0 40.8	14 33.6	6 3.1	11 45.0	11 42.6
8 F	13 8 58.8	15 20.1	4 21.5	18 32.6	27 28.0	15 5.4	29 46.3	0 37.1	14 38.7	6 6.7	11 46.4	11 44.9
9 S	13 12 55.3	16 19.3	4 18.4	0 ♉ 23.7	28 36.8	16 18.7	0 ♏ 26.9	0 33.3	14 43.7	6 10.3	11 47.9	11 47.3
10 S	13 16 51.9	17 18.6	4 15.2	12 11.4	29 51.4	17 32.0	1 7.6	0 29.3	14 48.6	6 13.9	11 49.3	11 49.6
11 M	13 20 48.4	18 17.9	4 12.0	23 58.4	1 ♎ 11.1	18 45.3	1 48.3	0 25.2	14 53.4	6 17.5	11 50.8	11 51.9
12 T	13 24 45.0	19 17.3	4 8.8	5 ♊ 47.6	2 35.1	19 58.5	2 29.0	0 20.8	14 58.1	6 21.1	11 52.4	11 54.3
13 W	13 28 41.5	20 16.8	4 5.7	17 42.7	4 3.0	21 11.8	3 9.9	0 16.3	15 2.8	6 24.8	11 54.0	11 56.6
14 T	13 32 38.1	21 16.2	4 2.5	29 47.5	5 33.9	22 25.1	3 50.7	0 11.6	15 7.4	6 28.5	11 55.5	11 59.0
15 F	13 36 34.6	22 15.7	3 59.3	12 ♋ 6.3	7 7.4	23 38.3	4 31.7	0 6.7	15 11.9	6 32.1	11 57.1	12 1.3
16 S	13 40 31.2	23 15.2	3 56.1	24 43.5	8 43.1	24 51.5	5 12.6	0 1.7	15 16.3	6 35.8	11 58.7	12 3.6
17 S	13 44 27.7	24 14.7	3 52.9	7 ♌ 43.0	10 20.5	26 4.7	5 53.6	29 ♉ 56.4	15 20.6	6 39.5	12 0.4	12 5.9
18 M	13 48 24.3	25 14.3	3 49.8	21 8.2	11 59.2	27 17.8	6 34.7	29 51.0	15 24.9	6 43.2	12 2.1	12 8.2
19 T	13 52 20.8	26 13.9	3 46.6	5 ♍ 0.6	13 39.0	28 31.0	7 15.8	29 45.5	15 29.0	6 46.9	12 3.7	12 10.5
20 W	13 56 17.4	27 13.6	3 43.4	19 19.9	15 19.5	29 44.1	7 57.0	29 39.8	15 33.1	6 50.6	12 5.5	12 12.8
21 T	14 0 13.9	28 13.3	3 40.2	4 ♎ 3.0	17 0.5	0 ♐ 57.2	8 38.3	29 33.9	15 37.0	6 54.3	12 7.2	12 15.0
22 F	14 4 10.5	29 13.0	3 37.1	19 4.1	18 41.9	2 10.3	9 19.5	29 27.9	15 40.9	6 58.1	12 9.0	12 17.3
23 S	14 8 7.0	0 ♏ 12.8	3 33.9	4 ♏ 15.0	20 23.5	3 23.4	10 0.9	29 21.7	15 44.7	7 1.8	12 10.7	12 19.6
24 S	14 12 3.6	1 12.6	3 30.7	19 26.2	22 5.0	4 36.5	10 42.3	29 15.4	15 48.4	7 5.6	12 12.5	12 21.8
25 M	14 16 0.1	2 12.5	3 27.5	4 ♐ 28.3	23 46.5	5 49.5	11 23.7	29 8.9	15 52.0	7 9.3	12 14.4	12 24.1
26 T	14 19 56.7	3 12.3	3 24.3	19 13.3	25 27.9	7 2.6	12 5.2	29 2.3	15 55.5	7 13.1	12 16.2	12 26.3
27 W	14 23 53.3	4 12.2	3 21.2	3 ♑ 35.6	27 9.0	8 15.6	12 46.8	28 55.6	15 58.9	7 16.8	12 18.1	12 28.5
28 T	14 27 49.8	5 12.1	3 18.0	17 32.4	28 49.8	9 28.5	13 28.3	28 48.8	16 2.2	7 20.6	12 19.9	12 30.7
29 F	14 31 46.4	6 12.1	3 14.8	1 ♒ 3.2	0 ♏ 30.3	10 41.5	14 10.0	28 41.8	16 5.4	7 24.3	12 21.8	12 32.9
30 S	14 35 42.9	7 12.1	3 11.6	14 9.8	2 10.4	11 54.4	14 51.7	28 34.7	16 8.5	7 28.1	12 23.8	12 35.1
31 S	14 39 39.5	8 12.1	3 8.5	26 54.8	3 50.1	13 7.3	15 33.4	28 27.6	16 11.5	7 31.9	12 25.7	12 37.3
DECLINATION at NOON												
1 F	12 41 22.9	3S 20.8	13S 5.9	16S 41.5	2N 49.7	13S 42.6	9S 26.3	19N 15.1	17N 13.0	13S 0.4	20S 42.4	10N 35.2
4 M	12 53 12.5	4 30.3	13 2.7	7 5.3	3 9.8	15 1.8	10 11.8	19 13.2	17 8.7	13 3.9	20 43.1	10 32.6
7 T	13 5 2.2	5 39.4	12 59.5	4N 48.9	2 45.1	16 17.7	10 56.8	19 10.9	17 4.6	13 7.4	20 43.8	10 30.0
10 S	13 16 51.9	6 47.9	12 56.3	14 44.0	1 42.7	17 30.0	11 41.2	19 8.3	17 0.6	13 11.0	20 44.5	10 27.5
13 W	13 28 41.5	7 55.5	12 53.1	19 11.7	0 12.0	18 38.4	12 25.0	19 5.4	16 56.8	13 14.7	20 45.2	10 25.1
16 S	13 40 31.2	9 2.1	12 49.8	16 1.8	1S 37.6	19 42.6	13 8.1	19 2.2	16 53.3	13 18.3	20 46.0	10 22.7
19 T	13 52 20.8	10 7.6	12 46.6	5 27.7	3 38.4	20 42.3	13 50.4	18 58.6	16 50.0	13 22.0	20 46.8	10 20.5
22 F	14 4 10.5	11 11.8	12 43.4	8S 41.8	5 44.4	21 37.0	14 32.0	18 54.8	16 46.9	13 25.7	20 47.6	10 18.4
25 M	14 16 0.1	12 14.4	12 40.1	18 21.0	7 51.5	22 26.5	15 12.6	18 50.7	16 44.1	13 29.4	20 48.4	10 16.4
28 T	14 27 49.8	13 15.4	12 36.9	17 14.0	9 56.8	23 10.5	15 52.3	18 46.3	16 41.5	13 33.0	20 49.2	10 14.4
31 S	14 39 39.5	14 14.5	12 33.6	7 57.6	11 58.3	23 48.7	16 31.0	18 41.7	16 39.2	13 36.7	20 50.0	10 12.6

NOVEMBER 1976

LONGITUDE at NOON

DAY	EPHEMERIS SIDEREAL TIME h m s	☉ ° ′	☊ ° ′	☽ ° ′	☿ ° ′	♀ ° ′	♂ ° ′	♃ ° ′	♄ ° ′	♅ ° ′	♆ ° ′	♇ ° ′
1 M	14 43 36.0	9♏12.1	3♏ 5.3	9♓21.8	5♏29.5	14♐20.1	16♏15.2	28♉20.3	16♌14.4	7♏35.6	12♐27.6	12♎39.4
2 T	14 47 32.6	10 12.1	3 2.1	21 34.5	7 8.4	15 33.0	16 57.1	28R 12.9	16 17.2	7 39.4	12 29.6	12 41.6
3 W	14 51 29.1	11 12.3	2 58.9	3♈36.5	8 46.9	16 45.8	17 39.0	28 5.5	16 19.9	7 43.2	12 31.6	12 43.7
4 T	14 55 25.7	12 12.4	2 55.7	15 30.9	10 25.0	17 58.6	18 21.0	27 57.9	16 22.5	7 46.9	12 33.6	12 45.8
5 F	14 59 22.2	13 12.5	2 52.6	27 20.8	12 2.7	19 11.3	19 3.0	27 50.2	16 25.0	7 50.7	12 35.7	12 47.9
6 S	15 3 18.8	14 12.7	2 49.4	9♉ 8.7	13 39.9	20 24.0	19 45.0	27 42.5	16 27.4	7 54.4	12 37.7	12 50.0
7 S	15 7 15.4	15 12.9	2 46.2	20 56.8	15 16.8	21 36.7	20 27.1	27 34.7	16 29.7	7 58.2	12 39.7	12 52.1
8 M	15 11 11.9	16 13.1	2 43.0	2♊47.2	16 53.3	22 49.3	21 9.3	27 26.9	16 31.9	8 1.9	12 41.8	12 54.1
9 T	15 15 8.5	17 13.4	2 39.9	14 42.2	18 29.4	24 1.9	21 51.5	27 18.9	16 34.0	8 5.6	12 43.9	12 56.2
10 W	15 19 5.0	18 13.7	2 36.7	26 43.8	20 5.1	25 14.5	22 33.8	27 11.0	16 36.0	8 9.4	12 46.0	12 58.2
11 T	15 23 1.6	19 14.0	2 33.5	8♋54.6	21 40.6	26 27.0	23 16.1	27 2.9	16 37.8	8 13.1	12 48.1	13 0.2
12 F	15 26 58.1	20 14.3	2 30.3	21 17.3	23 15.7	27 39.5	23 58.4	26 54.9	16 39.6	8 16.8	12 50.2	13 2.1
13 S	15 30 54.7	21 14.7	2 27.1	3♌54.9	24 50.5	28 51.9	24 40.9	26 46.8	16 41.2	8 20.5	12 52.3	13 4.1
14 S	15 34 51.2	22 15.1	2 24.0	16 50.6	26 25.0	0♑ 4.3	25 23.3	26 38.6	16 42.8	8 24.2	12 54.4	13 6.0
15 M	15 38 47.8	23 15.6	2 20.8	0♍ 7.3	27 59.2	1 16.7	26 5.9	26 30.5	16 44.2	8 27.8	12 56.6	13 7.9
16 T	15 42 44.3	24 16.1	2 17.6	13 47.3	29 33.2	2 29.1	26 48.4	26 22.3	16 45.5	8 31.5	12 58.8	13 9.8
17 W	15 46 40.9	25 16.6	2 14.4	27 52.0	1♐ 6.9	3 41.4	27 31.1	26 14.1	16 46.7	8 35.1	13 0.9	13 11.7
18 T	15 50 37.5	26 17.1	2 11.3	12♎20.5	2 40.5	4 53.6	28 13.8	26 5.9	16 47.8	8 38.8	13 3.1	13 13.5
19 F	15 54 34.0	27 17.7	2 8.1	27 9.9	4 13.8	6 5.8	28 56.5	25 57.7	16 48.8	8 42.4	13 5.3	13 15.4
20 S	15 58 30.6	28 18.3	2 4.9	12♏14.3	5 46.9	7 18.0	29 39.3	25 49.6	16 49.7	8 46.0	13 7.5	13 17.2
21 S	16 2 27.1	29 18.9	2 1.7	27 25.5	7 19.8	8 30.1	0♐22.2	25 41.4	16 50.4	8 49.6	13 9.7	13 19.0
22 M	16 6 23.7	0♐19.6	1 58.6	12♐34.0	8 52.5	9 42.2	1 5.1	25 33.2	16 51.1	8 53.2	13 11.9	13 20.7
23 T	16 10 20.2	1 20.2	1 55.4	27 29.9	10 25.1	10 54.2	1 48.0	25 25.1	16 51.6	8 56.7	13 14.1	13 22.4
24 W	16 14 16.8	2 21.0	1 52.2	12♑ 5.3	11 57.5	12 6.3	2 31.1	25 17.1	16 52.1	9 0.3	13 16.4	13 24.2
25 T	16 18 13.4	3 21.7	1 49.0	26 14.6	13 29.7	13 18.2	3 14.1	25 9.1	16 52.4	9 3.9	13 18.6	13 25.9
26 F	16 22 9.9	4 22.4	1 45.8	9♒55.3	15 1.8	14 30.0	3 57.2	25 1.1	16 52.6	9 7.4	13 20.9	13 27.5
27 S	16 26 6.5	5 23.2	1 42.7	23 7.9	16 33.6	15 41.9	4 40.4	24 53.1	16 52.7	9 10.8	13 23.1	13 29.2
28 S	16 30 3.0	6 23.9	1 39.5	5♓54.9	18 5.3	16 53.6	5 23.6	24 45.3	16R 52.6	9 14.3	13 25.4	13 30.8
29 M	16 33 59.6	7 24.7	1 36.3	18 20.4	19 36.9	18 5.3	6 6.8	24 37.5	16 52.5	9 17.7	13 27.6	13 32.4
30 T	16 37 56.1	8 25.5	1 33.1	0♈29.0	21 8.2	19 16.9	6 50.1	24 29.7	16 52.2	9 21.1	13 29.9	13 33.9

DECLINATION at NOON

DAY	SIDEREAL TIME	☉	☊	☽	☿	♀	♂	♃	♄	♅	♆	♇
1 M	14 43 36.0	14S 33.7	12S 32.5	4S 4.1	12S 37.6	24S 0.1	16S 43.6	18N 40.1	16N 38.5	13S 38.0	20S 50.3	10N 12.0
4 T	14 55 25.7	15 30.0	12 29.3	7N 37.7	14 31.8	24 30.2	17 20.8	18 35.2	16 36.5	13 41.6	20 51.2	10 10.4
7 S	15 7 15.4	16 24.0	12 26.0	16 28.1	16 19.3	24 54.0	17 56.8	18 30.2	16 34.8	13 45.3	20 52.0	10 8.8
10 W	15 19 5.0	17 15.5	12 22.8	19 10.3	17 59.5	25 11.4	18 31.5	18 25.0	16 33.5	13 48.9	20 52.9	10 7.4
13 S	15 30 54.7	18 4.3	12 19.5	14 8.9	19 31.5	25 22.2	19 5.0	18 19.7	16 32.4	13 52.5	20 53.8	10 6.1
16 T	15 42 44.3	18 50.3	12 16.2	2 39.9	20 54.9	25 26.3	19 37.0	18 14.3	16 31.6	13 56.0	20 54.6	10 5.0
19 F	15 54 34.0	19 33.3	12 12.9	11S 0.2	22 9.1	25 23.8	20 7.5	18 8.9	16 31.1	13 59.5	20 55.5	10 4.0
22 M	16 6 23.7	20 13.2	12 9.6	19 1.0	23 13.3	25 14.6	20 36.5	18 3.6	16 30.9	14 3.0	20 56.4	10 3.1
25 T	16 18 13.4	20 49.7	12 6.3	15 48.3	24 7.0	24 58.9	21 3.9	17 58.2	16 31.0	14 6.4	20 57.2	10 2.3
28 S	16 30 3.0	21 22.7	12 3.0	5 15.1	24 49.6	24 36.6	21 29.7	17 53.0	16 31.4	14 9.7	20 58.1	10 1.7

DECEMBER 1976

LONGITUDE at NOON

DAY	EPHEMERIS SIDEREAL TIME h m s	☉ ° ′	☊ ° ′	☽ ° ′	☿ ° ′	♀ ° ′	♂ ° ′	♃ ° ′	♄ ° ′	♅ ° ′	♆ ° ′	♇ ° ′
1 W	16 41 52.7	9♐26.3	1♏30.0	12♈25.8	22♐39.3	20♑28.4	7♐33.5	24♉22.1	16♌51.9	9♏24.5	13♐32.1	13♎35.4
2 T	16 45 49.2	10 27.2	1 26.8	24 15.4	24 10.1	21 39.8	8 16.9	24R 14.5	16R 51.4	9 27.9	13 34.4	13 36.9
3 F	16 49 45.8	11 28.0	1 23.6	6♉ 2.0	25 40.7	22 51.2	9 0.3	24 7.0	16 50.8	9 31.3	13 36.6	13 38.4
4 S	16 53 42.4	12 28.9	1 20.4	17 49.5	27 10.9	24 2.5	9 43.8	23 59.6	16 50.1	9 34.6	13 38.9	13 39.9
5 S	16 57 38.9	13 29.7	1 17.3	29 40.7	28 40.8	25 13.7	10 27.4	23 52.4	16 49.3	9 37.9	13 41.1	13 41.3
6 M	17 1 35.5	14 30.6	1 14.1	11♊38.0	0♑10.2	26 24.9	11 11.0	23 45.2	16 48.3	9 41.1	13 43.4	13 42.7
7 T	17 5 32.0	15 31.5	1 10.9	23 43.1	1 39.1	27 35.9	11 54.6	23 38.1	16 47.3	9 44.4	13 45.7	13 44.0
8 W	17 9 28.6	16 32.5	1 7.7	5♋57.2	3 7.4	28 46.9	12 38.3	23 31.2	16 46.2	9 47.6	13 47.9	13 45.3
9 T	17 13 25.1	17 33.4	1 4.5	18 21.4	4 34.9	29 57.7	13 22.1	23 24.3	16 44.9	9 50.8	13 50.2	13 46.6
10 F	17 17 21.7	18 34.4	1 1.4	0♌56.7	6 1.6	1♒ 8.5	14 5.9	23 17.6	16 43.5	9 53.9	13 52.4	13 47.9
11 S	17 21 18.3	19 35.3	0 58.2	13 44.0	7 27.3	2 19.2	14 49.7	23 11.1	16 42.1	9 57.0	13 54.7	13 49.1
12 S	17 25 14.8	20 36.3	0 55.0	26 44.8	8 51.8	3 29.7	15 33.6	23 4.6	16 40.5	10 0.1	13 56.9	13 50.3
13 M	17 29 11.4	21 37.3	0 51.8	10♍ 0.7	10 14.9	4 40.2	16 17.5	22 58.3	16 38.8	10 3.2	13 59.2	13 51.5
14 T	17 33 7.9	22 38.4	0 48.7	23 33.5	11 36.4	5 50.6	17 1.5	22 52.2	16 37.0	10 6.2	14 1.4	13 52.7
15 W	17 37 4.5	23 39.5	0 45.5	7♎24.5	12 55.9	7 0.9	17 45.6	22 46.2	16 35.2	10 9.2	14 3.7	13 53.8
16 T	17 41 1.0	24 40.5	0 42.3	21 34.4	14 13.2	8 11.1	18 29.7	22 40.4	16 33.2	10 12.2	14 6.0	13 54.9
17 F	17 44 57.6	25 41.6	0 39.1	6♏ 2.5	15 27.8	9 21.1	19 13.9	22 34.7	16 31.0	10 15.1	14 8.2	13 55.9
18 S	17 48 54.2	26 42.7	0 36.0	20 45.8	16 39.3	10 31.1	19 58.1	22 29.1	16 28.8	10 18.0	14 10.4	13 57.0
19 S	17 52 50.7	27 43.8	0 32.8	5♐39.1	17 47.1	11 40.9	20 42.3	22 23.8	16 26.5	10 20.9	14 12.6	13 57.9
20 M	17 56 47.3	28 44.9	0 29.6	20 35.0	18 50.8	12 50.6	21 26.6	22 18.6	16 24.1	10 23.7	14 14.8	13 58.9
21 T	18 0 43.8	29 46.1	0 26.4	5♑24.7	19 49.7	14 0.1	22 11.0	22 13.5	16 21.6	10 26.5	14 17.0	13 59.8
22 W	18 4 40.4	0♑47.2	0 23.2	19 59.7	20 42.9	15 9.6	22 55.4	22 8.7	16 19.0	10 29.2	14 19.2	14 0.7
23 T	18 8 36.9	1 48.3	0 20.1	4♒12.7	21 29.9	16 18.9	23 39.8	22 4.0	16 16.3	10 31.9	14 21.4	14 1.5
24 F	18 12 33.5	2 49.5	0 16.9	17 59.4	22 9.6	17 28.0	24 24.3	21 59.5	16 13.5	10 34.6	14 23.6	14 2.3
25 S	18 16 30.1	3 50.6	0 13.7	1♓18.3	22 41.3	18 37.0	25 8.8	21 55.2	16 10.6	10 37.2	14 25.7	14 3.1
26 S	18 20 26.6	4 51.8	0 10.5	14 10.5	23 3.9	19 45.9	25 53.4	21 51.1	16 7.6	10 39.8	14 27.9	14 3.8
27 M	18 24 23.2	5 52.9	0 7.4	26 39.3	23 16.6	20 54.5	26 38.0	21 47.1	16 4.5	10 42.3	14 30.0	14 4.6
28 T	18 28 19.7	6 54.1	0 4.2	8♈49.5	23 18.7	22 3.0	27 22.6	21 43.4	16 1.3	10 44.8	14 32.2	14 5.2
29 W	18 32 16.3	7 55.2	0 1.0	20 46.2	23R 9.4	23 11.4	28 7.3	21 39.8	15 58.1	10 47.3	14 34.3	14 5.9
30 T	18 36 12.8	8 56.3	29♎57.8	2♉35.2	22 48.3	24 19.5	28 52.1	21 36.5	15 54.7	10 49.7	14 36.4	14 6.5
31 F	18 40 9.4	9 57.5	29 54.7	14 21.7	22 15.3	25 27.5	29 36.8	21 33.3	15 51.3	10 52.1	14 38.5	14 7.0

DECLINATION at NOON

DAY	SIDEREAL TIME	☉	☊	☽	☿	♀	♂	♃	♄	♅	♆	♇
1 W	16 41 52.7	21S 52.0	11S 59.7	6N 36.9	25S 20.4	24S 8.1	21S 53.6	17N 47.9	16N 32.2	14S 12.9	20S 58.9	10N 1.2
4 S	16 53 42.4	22 17.6	11 56.4	15 52.8	25 38.9	23 33.5	22 15.7	17 42.9	16 33.2	14 16.1	20 59.8	10 0.9
7 T	17 5 32.0	22 39.2	11 53.1	19 17.9	25 44.6	22 53.0	22 36.0	17 38.2	16 34.6	14 19.2	21 0.6	10 0.7
10 F	17 17 21.7	22 56.9	11 49.8	14 56.0	25 37.3	22 7.0	22 54.3	17 33.7	16 36.2	14 22.2	21 1.4	10 0.7
13 M	17 29 11.4	23 10.5	11 46.5	4 2.7	25 16.8	21 15.6	23 10.6	17 29.6	16 38.2	14 25.0	21 2.2	10 0.8
16 T	17 41 1.0	23 20.0	11 43.2	9S 17.7	24 43.9	20 19.2	23 24.8	17 25.7	16 40.4	14 27.9	21 3.0	10 1.0
19 S	17 52 50.7	23 25.2	11 39.8	18 28.1	24 0.0	19 18.1	23 36.9	17 22.2	16 42.9	14 30.6	21 3.8	10 1.4
22 W	18 4 40.4	23 26.2	11 36.5	17 1.7	23 7.8	18 12.7	23 46.9	17 19.1	16 45.6	14 33.1	21 4.5	10 1.9
25 S	18 16 30.1	23 23.0	11 33.1	6 53.2	22 11.8	17 3.4	23 54.6	17 16.4	16 48.7	14 35.6	21 5.2	10 2.5
28 T	18 28 19.7	23 15.6	11 29.8	5N 17.1	21 18.0	15 50.4	24 0.1	17 14.1	16 51.9	14 37.9	21 5.9	10 3.3
31 F	18 40 9.4	23 4.0	11 26.5	15 2.4	20 32.8	14 34.2	24 3.3	17 12.3	16 55.4	14 40.2	21 6.6	10 4.3

JANUARY 1977

DAY	EPHEMERIS SIDEREAL TIME	☉	☊	☽	☿	♀	♂	♃	♄	♅	♆	♇
	h m s	° ′	° ′	° ′	° ′	° ′	° ′	° ′	° ′	° ′	° ′	° ′
						LONGITUDE at NOON						
1 S	18 44 6.0	10♑58.6	29♎51.5	26♉10.6	21♑30.9	26♒35.3	0♑21.7	21♉30.4	15♌47.8	10♏54.4	14♐40.6	14♎ 7.6
2 S	18 48 2.5	11 59.8	29 48.3	8♊ 6.0	20R35.6	27 42.9	1 6.5	21R27.6	15R44.2	10 56.7	14 42.6	14 8.1
3 M	18 51 59.1	13 0.9	29 45.1	20 11.0	19 31.0	28 50.2	1 51.5	21 25.1	15 40.5	10 58.9	14 44.7	14 8.5
4 T	18 55 55.6	14 2.0	29 41.9	2♋27.8	18 18.7	29 57.4	2 36.4	21 22.7	15 36.8	11 1.1	14 46.7	14 9.0
5 W	18 59 52.2	15 3.2	29 38.8	14 57.5	17 1.2	1♓ 4.4	3 21.5	21 20.6	15 33.0	11 3.3	14 48.8	14 9.4
6 T	19 3 48.7	16 4.3	29 35.6	27 40.3	15 40.8	2 11.1	4 6.5	21 18.6	15 29.1	11 5.4	14 50.8	14 9.8
7 F	19 7 45.3	17 5.5	29 32.4	10♌35.5	14 20.2	3 17.5	4 51.6	21 16.9	15 25.2	11 7.4	14 52.8	14 10.1
8 S	19 11 41.9	18 6.6	29 29.2	23 42.5	13 2.0	4 23.8	5 36.7	21 15.4	15 21.2	11 9.5	14 54.8	14 10.4
9 S	19 15 38.4	19 7.7	29 26.1	7♍ 0.2	11 48.4	5 29.8	6 21.9	21 14.0	15 17.1	11 11.4	14 56.7	14 10.6
10 M	19 19 35.0	20 8.9	29 22.9	20 28.1	10 41.4	6 35.5	7 7.1	21 12.9	15 12.9	11 13.3	14 58.6	14 10.8
11 T	19 23 31.5	21 10.0	29 19.7	4♎ 6.3	9 42.5	7 41.0	7 52.3	21 12.0	15 8.7	11 15.2	15 0.6	14 11.0
12 W	19 27 28.1	22 11.1	29 16.5	17 54.8	8 52.5	8 46.2	8 37.6	21 11.3	15 4.4	11 17.0	15 2.5	14 11.2
13 T	19 31 24.6	23 12.2	29 13.4	1♏54.3	8 12.1	9 51.1	9 23.0	21 10.8	15 0.1	11 18.8	15 4.3	14 11.3
14 F	19 35 21.2	24 13.4	29 10.2	16 4.7	7 41.5	10 55.8	10 8.4	21 10.5	14 55.7	11 20.5	15 6.2	14 11.3
15 S	19 39 17.8	25 14.5	29 7.0	0♐24.8	7 20.5	12 0.1	10 53.8	21 10.4	14 51.3	11 22.1	15 8.0	14 11.4
16 S	19 43 14.3	26 15.6	29 3.8	14 52.1	7 8.8	13 4.2	11 39.2	21D10.5	14 46.8	11 23.8	15 9.9	14 11.4
17 M	19 47 10.9	27 16.7	29 0.6	29 22.2	7 6.0	14 7.9	12 24.7	21 10.8	14 42.2	11 25.3	15 11.7	14R11.3
18 T	19 51 7.4	28 17.8	28 57.5	13♑49.2	7D11.4	15 11.3	13 10.3	21 11.3	14 37.7	11 26.8	15 13.4	14 11.3
19 W	19 55 4.0	29 18.9	28 54.3	28 6.4	7 24.6	16 14.4	13 55.9	21 12.1	14 33.0	11 28.3	15 15.2	14 11.2
20 T	19 59 0.5	0♒20.0	28 51.1	12♒ 7.6	7 44.7	17 17.2	14 41.5	21 13.0	14 28.4	11 29.7	15 16.9	14 11.0
21 F	20 2 57.1	1 21.1	28 47.9	25 47.9	8 11.3	18 19.5	15 27.1	21 14.2	14 23.7	11 31.0	15 18.6	14 10.8
22 S	20 6 53.6	2 22.1	28 44.8	9♓ 4.8	8 43.7	19 21.5	16 12.8	21 15.5	14 18.9	11 32.3	15 20.3	14 10.6
23 S	20 10 50.2	3 23.2	28 41.6	21 57.7	9 21.5	20 23.2	16 58.5	21 17.1	14 14.2	11 33.6	15 22.0	14 10.4
24 M	20 14 46.8	4 24.2	28 38.4	4♈28.6	10 4.0	21 24.4	17 44.3	21 18.8	14 9.4	11 34.8	15 23.6	14 10.1
25 T	20 18 43.3	5 25.2	28 35.2	16 41.1	10 50.9	22 25.2	18 30.1	21 20.8	14 4.6	11 35.9	15 25.3	14 9.8
26 W	20 22 39.9	6 26.3	28 32.1	28 39.9	11 41.8	23 25.6	19 15.9	21 23.0	13 59.8	11 37.1	15 26.9	14 9.5
27 T	20 26 36.4	7 27.2	28 28.9	10♉30.3	12 36.2	24 25.5	20 1.8	21 25.4	13 54.9	11 38.1	15 28.5	14 9.1
28 F	20 30 33.0	8 28.2	28 25.7	22 18.0	13 33.8	25 24.9	20 47.7	21 28.0	13 50.1	11 39.1	15 30.0	14 8.7
29 S	20 34 29.5	9 29.1	28 22.5	4♊ 8.4	14 34.3	26 23.9	21 33.6	21 30.7	13 45.2	11 40.0	15 31.5	14 8.2
30 S	20 38 26.1	10 30.1	28 19.3	16 6.7	15 37.5	27 22.3	22 19.5	21 33.7	13 40.3	11 40.8	15 33.0	14 7.7
31 M	20 42 22.6	11 31.0	28 16.2	28 17.1	16 43.2	28 20.3	23 5.5	21 36.9	13 35.4	11 41.7	15 34.5	14 7.2
						DECLINATION at NOON						
1 S	18 44 6.0	22S59.2	11S25.3	17N12.5	20S20.5	14S 8.2	24S 3.9	17N11.8	16N56.6	14S40.9	21S 6.8	10N 4.6
4 T	18 55 55.6	22 42.0	11 22.0	18 59.3	19 53.6	12 48.3	24 4.0	17 10.6	17 0.3	14 42.9	21 7.4	10 5.7
7 F	19 7 45.3	22 20.8	11 18.6	12 49.9	19 40.9	11 26.0	24 1.8	17 9.9	17 4.2	14 44.8	21 8.1	10 6.9
10 M	19 19 35.0	21 55.7	11 15.3	0 50.9	19 41.3	10 1.8	23 57.3	17 9.7	17 8.2	14 46.6	21 8.7	10 8.2
13 T	19 31 24.6	21 26.7	11 11.9	11S56.5	19 52.8	8 35.9	23 50.4	17 9.9	17 12.4	14 48.3	21 9.2	10 9.7
16 S	19 43 14.3	20 54.0	11 8.5	19 1.2	20 12.8	7 8.6	23 41.2	17 10.6	17 16.7	14 49.8	21 9.7	10 11.3
19 W	19 55 4.0	20 17.7	11 5.1	15 38.1	20 37.2	5 40.5	23 29.6	17 11.9	17 21.1	14 51.1	21 10.2	10 13.0
22 S	20 6 53.6	19 37.9	11 1.7	4 38.1	21 2.0	4 11.7	23 15.7	17 13.6	17 25.6	14 52.3	21 10.7	10 14.7
25 T	20 18 43.3	18 54.9	10 58.4	7N29.0	21 23.8	2 42.7	22 59.5	17 15.7	17 30.1	14 53.4	21 11.1	10 16.6
28 F	20 30 33.0	18 8.8	10 55.0	16 20.1	21 39.8	1 13.9	22 40.9	17 18.4	17 34.7	14 54.3	21 11.6	10 18.6
31 M	20 42 22.6	17 19.7	10 51.6	19 2.8	21 48.2	0N14.4	22 20.2	17 21.5	17 39.2	14 55.1	21 11.9	10 20.6

FEBRUARY 1977

DAY	EPHEMERIS SIDEREAL TIME	☉	☊	☽	☿	♀	♂	♃	♄	♅	♆	♇
						LONGITUDE at NOON						
1 T	20 46 19.2	12♒31.8	28♎13.0	10♋42.7	17♑51.1	29♓17.7	23♑51.5	21♉40.2	13♌30.5	11♏42.4	15♐35.9	14♎ 6.7
2 W	20 50 15.8	13 32.7	28 9.8	23 25.4	19 1.1	0♈14.5	24 37.5	21 43.7	13R25.6	11 43.1	15 37.3	14R 6.1
3 T	20 54 12.3	14 33.5	28 6.6	6♌25.7	20 12.9	1 10.8	25 23.6	21 47.5	13 20.7	11 43.8	15 38.7	14 5.5
4 F	20 58 8.9	15 34.3	28 3.5	19 42.6	21 26.5	2 6.4	26 9.7	21 51.4	13 15.8	11 44.4	15 40.1	14 4.8
5 S	21 2 5.4	16 35.1	28 0.3	3♍13.9	22 41.8	3 1.5	26 55.8	21 55.5	13 10.9	11 44.9	15 41.4	14 4.1
6 S	21 6 2.0	17 35.9	27 57.1	16 56.8	23 58.6	3 55.8	27 42.0	21 59.8	13 6.0	11 45.4	15 42.7	14 3.4
7 M	21 9 58.5	18 36.7	27 53.9	0♎48.2	25 16.8	4 49.6	28 28.2	22 4.2	13 1.1	11 45.8	15 43.9	14 2.7
8 T	21 13 55.1	19 37.4	27 50.7	14 45.6	26 36.3	5 42.6	29 14.4	22 8.9	12 56.2	11 46.2	15 45.2	14 1.9
9 W	21 17 51.6	20 38.1	27 47.6	28 46.9	27 57.2	6 34.9	0♒ 0.6	22 13.7	12 51.4	11 46.5	15 46.4	14 1.1
10 T	21 21 48.2	21 38.8	27 44.4	12♏50.9	29 19.3	7 26.5	0 46.9	22 18.7	12 46.6	11 46.7	15 47.6	14 0.3
11 F	21 25 44.7	22 39.5	27 41.2	26 56.7	0♒42.5	8 17.3	1 33.2	22 23.9	12 41.8	11 46.9	15 48.7	13 59.4
12 S	21 29 41.3	23 40.2	27 38.0	11♐ 3.4	2 6.9	9 7.3	2 19.6	22 29.3	12 37.0	11 47.1	15 49.8	13 58.5
13 S	21 33 37.8	24 40.9	27 34.9	25 9.8	3 32.4	9 56.5	3 5.9	22 34.8	12 32.2	11 47.2	15 50.9	13 57.6
14 M	21 37 34.4	25 41.5	27 31.7	9♑13.6	4 58.9	10 44.9	3 52.3	22 40.5	12 27.5	11 47.2	15 52.0	13 56.6
15 T	21 41 31.0	26 42.1	27 28.5	23 12.2	6 26.4	11 32.4	4 38.7	22 46.4	12 22.8	11 47.2	15 53.0	13 55.6
16 W	21 45 27.5	27 42.8	27 25.3	7♒ 1.8	7 55.1	12 19.0	5 25.2	22 52.5	12 18.2	11 47.2	15 54.1	13 54.7
17 T	21 49 24.1	28 43.3	27 22.1	20 38.8	9 24.6	13 4.6	6 11.7	22 58.7	12 13.6	11R47.0	15 55.0	13 53.6
18 F	21 53 20.6	29 43.9	27 19.0	3♓60.0	10 55.1	13 49.1	6 58.1	23 5.1	12 9.0	11 46.9	15 56.0	13 52.6
19 S	21 57 17.2	0♓44.4	27 15.8	17 3.2	12 26.6	14 32.7	7 44.6	23 11.6	12 4.5	11 46.6	15 56.9	13 51.5
20 S	22 1 13.7	1 44.9	27 12.6	29 47.8	13 59.1	15 15.2	8 31.2	23 18.3	12 0.0	11 46.3	15 57.7	13 50.4
21 M	22 5 10.3	2 45.3	27 9.4	12♈14.6	15 32.5	15 56.5	9 17.7	23 25.2	11 55.6	11 46.0	15 58.6	13 49.2
22 T	22 9 6.8	3 45.8	27 6.3	24 25.8	17 6.9	16 36.7	10 4.3	23 32.2	11 51.2	11 45.6	15 59.4	13 48.1
23 W	22 13 3.4	4 46.2	27 3.1	6♉24.8	18 42.2	17 15.7	10 50.8	23 39.4	11 46.9	11 45.1	16 0.2	13 46.9
24 T	22 16 59.9	5 46.6	26 59.9	18 16.1	20 18.5	17 53.4	11 37.4	23 46.7	11 42.6	11 44.6	16 0.9	13 45.7
25 F	22 20 56.5	6 46.9	26 56.7	0♊ 4.6	21 55.8	18 29.8	12 24.0	23 54.2	11 38.4	11 44.0	16 1.6	13 44.4
26 S	22 24 53.0	7 47.2	26 53.5	11 55.7	23 34.0	19 4.8	13 10.6	24 1.8	11 34.2	11 43.4	16 2.3	13 43.2
27 S	22 28 49.6	8 47.5	26 50.4	23 54.5	25 13.3	19 38.3	13 57.3	24 9.5	11 30.2	11 42.7	16 2.9	13 41.9
28 M	22 32 46.1	9 47.7	26 47.2	6♋ 6.1	26 53.6	20 10.4	14 43.9	24 17.5	11 26.1	11 42.0	16 3.5	13 40.6
						DECLINATION at NOON						
1 T	20 46 19.2	17S 2.8	10S50.4	18N12.8	21S49.0	0N43.7	22S12.8	17N22.6	17N40.7	14S55.3	21S12.0	10N21.3
4 F	20 58 8.9	16 10.1	10 47.0	10 29.7	21 45.0	2 10.8	21 49.1	17 26.2	17 45.2	14 55.8	21 12.4	10 23.5
7 M	21 9 58.5	15 14.9	10 43.6	2S20.7	21 30.8	3 36.4	21 23.2	17 30.3	17 49.7	14 56.2	21 12.7	10 25.7
10 T	21 21 48.2	14 17.4	10 40.2	14 20.0	21 5.8	5 0.4	20 55.3	17 34.7	17 54.1	14 56.5	21 12.9	10 28.0
13 S	21 33 37.8	13 17.7	10 36.8	19 0.7	20 29.5	6 22.2	20 25.3	17 39.6	17 58.4	14 56.5	21 13.2	10 30.3
16 W	21 45 27.5	12 16.1	10 33.4	13 41.4	19 41.7	7 41.5	19 53.2	17 44.8	18 2.5	14 56.5	21 13.4	10 32.6
19 S	21 57 17.2	11 12.7	10 29.9	2 10.8	18 42.3	8 57.7	19 19.3	17 50.3	18 6.6	14 56.3	21 13.5	10 35.0
22 T	22 9 6.8	10 7.7	10 26.5	9N33.2	17 31.1	10 10.5	18 43.5	17 56.1	18 10.5	14 55.9	21 13.7	10 37.5
25 F	22 20 56.5	9 1.4	10 23.1	17 18.0	16 8.0	11 19.2	18 6.0	18 2.2	18 14.2	14 55.4	21 13.8	10 39.9
28 M	22 32 46.1	7 53.8	10 19.6	18 26.3	14 33.1	12 23.2	17 26.7	18 8.6	18 17.7	14 54.7	21 13.8	10 42.4

MARCH 1977

DAY	EPHEMERIS SIDEREAL TIME	☉	☊	☽	☿	♀	♂	♃	♄	♅	♆	♇
	h m s	° ′	° ′	° ′	° ′	° ′	° ′	° ′	° ′	° ′	° ′	° ′
						LONGITUDE at NOON						
1 T	22 36 42.7	10♓47.9	26♎44.0	18♋34.7	28♒34.9	20♈41.0	15♒30.6	24♉25.5	11♌22.2	11♏41.3	16♐4.1	13♎39.3
2 W	22 40 39.2	11 48.1	26 40.8	1♌23.4	0♓17.2	21 9.9	16 17.3	24 33.7	11R18.3	11R40.4	16 4.7	13R37.9
3 T	22 44 35.8	12 48.2	26 37.7	14 33.8	2 0.6	21 37.2	17 4.0	24 42.0	11 14.5	11 39.6	16 5.2	13 36.5
4 F	22 48 32.4	13 48.3	26 34.5	28 5.9	3 45.0	22 2.7	17 50.7	24 50.5	11 10.7	11 38.6	16 5.6	13 35.2
5 S	22 52 28.9	14 48.4	26 31.3	11♍57.6	5 30.6	22 26.5	18 37.4	24 59.1	11 7.1	11 37.7	16 6.1	13 33.8
6 S	22 56 25.5	15 48.4	26 28.1	26 5.2	7 17.2	22 48.4	19 24.1	25 7.8	11 3.5	11 36.6	16 6.5	13 32.3
7 M	23 0 22.0	16 48.5	26 24.9	10♎24.0	9 4.9	23 8.5	20 10.8	25 16.7	10 60.0	11 35.6	16 6.9	13 30.9
8 T	23 4 18.6	17 48.4	26 21.8	24 48.7	10 53.7	23 26.5	20 57.6	25 25.7	10 56.6	11 34.4	16 7.2	13 29.4
9 W	23 8 15.1	18 48.4	26 18.6	9♏14.5	12 43.7	23 42.6	21 44.4	25 34.8	10 53.3	11 33.3	16 7.6	13 28.0
10 T	23 12 11.7	19 48.4	26 15.4	23 37.0	14 34.7	23 56.5	22 31.2	25 44.1	10 50.0	11 32.1	16 7.8	13 26.5
11 F	23 16 8.2	20 48.3	26 12.2	7♐53.3	16 26.9	24 8.3	23 18.0	25 53.4	10 46.8	11 30.8	16 8.1	13 25.0
12 S	23 20 4.8	21 48.1	26 9.1	22 1.2	18 20.2	24 17.9	24 4.8	26 2.9	10 43.7	11 29.5	16 8.3	13 23.5
13 S	23 24 1.3	22 48.0	26 5.9	5♑59.3	20 14.5	24 25.2	24 51.6	26 12.5	10 40.7	11 28.2	16 8.4	13 21.9
14 M	23 27 57.9	23 47.8	26 2.7	19 46.7	22 10.0	24 30.3	25 38.4	26 22.3	10 37.8	11 26.8	16 8.6	13 20.4
15 T	23 31 54.4	24 47.6	25 59.5	3♒22.5	24 6.4	24 33.0	26 25.2	26 32.1	10 35.0	11 25.3	16 8.7	13 18.8
16 W	23 35 51.0	25 47.4	25 56.3	16 46.0	26 3.8	24 33.2	27 12.1	26 42.0	10 32.2	11 23.8	16 8.8	13 17.3
17 T	23 39 47.5	26 47.1	25 53.2	29 56.5	28 2.1	24R31.1	27 58.9	26 52.1	10 29.6	11 22.3	16 8.8	13 15.7
18 F	23 43 44.1	27 46.8	25 50.0	12♓53.4	0♈1.1	24 26.5	28 45.7	27 2.3	10 27.1	11 20.7	16 8.8	13 14.1
19 S	23 47 40.6	28 46.5	25 46.8	25 36.4	2 0.9	24 19.5	29 32.6	27 12.6	10 24.6	11 19.1	16 8.8	13 12.5
20 S	23 51 37.2	29 46.1	25 43.6	8♈5.6	4 1.2	24 9.9	0♓19.4	27 22.9	10 22.3	11 17.4	16R 8.7	13 10.8
21 M	23 55 33.7	0♈45.7	25 40.5	20 22.0	6 1.9	23 57.9	1 6.2	27 33.4	10 20.0	11 15.7	16 8.6	13 9.2
22 T	23 59 30.3	1 45.3	25 37.3	2♉27.1	8 2.8	23 43.4	1 53.1	27 44.0	10 17.9	11 14.0	16 8.5	13 7.6
23 W	0 3 26.8	2 44.8	25 34.1	14 23.3	10 3.6	23 26.4	2 39.9	27 54.7	10 15.8	11 12.2	16 8.3	13 5.9
24 T	0 7 23.4	3 44.3	25 30.9	26 13.9	12 4.2	23 7.0	3 26.8	28 5.5	10 13.9	11 10.4	16 8.1	13 4.3
25 F	0 11 19.9	4 43.7	25 27.7	8♊2.5	14 4.2	22 45.3	4 13.6	28 16.4	10 12.1	11 8.5	16 7.9	13 2.6
26 S	0 15 16.5	5 43.2	25 24.6	19 53.5	16 3.2	22 21.4	5 0.4	28 27.4	10 10.3	11 6.6	16 7.6	13 1.0
27 S	0 19 13.0	6 42.5	25 21.4	1♋51.7	18 1.0	21 55.3	5 47.2	28 38.5	10 8.7	11 4.7	16 7.3	12 59.3
28 M	0 23 9.6	7 41.9	25 18.2	14 1.8	19 57.2	21 27.1	6 34.1	28 49.7	10 7.2	11 2.7	16 7.0	12 57.6
29 T	0 27 6.2	8 41.2	25 15.0	26 28.4	21 51.3	20 57.1	7 20.9	29 0.9	10 5.7	11 0.8	16 6.7	12 56.0
30 W	0 31 2.7	9 40.5	25 11.8	9♌15.7	23 43.1	20 25.4	8 7.7	29 12.3	10 4.5	10 58.8	16 6.3	12 54.3
31 T	0 34 59.3	10 39.7	25 8.7	22 26.6	25 32.0	19 52.1	8 54.5	29 23.7	10 3.3	10 56.7	16 5.9	12 52.7
						DECLINATION at NOON						
1 T	22 36 42.7	7S31.1	10S18.5	17N 4.9	13S58.9	12N43.3	17S13.3	18N10.7	18N18.9	14S54.5	21S13.9	10N43.2
4 F	22 48 32.4	6 22.2	10 15.0	8 4.4	12 8.3	13 39.9	16 31.8	18 17.4	18 22.1	14 53.6	21 13.9	10 45.7
7 M	23 0 22.0	5 12.5	10 11.6	5S18.2	10 6.1	14 30.0	15 48.9	18 24.3	18 25.2	14 52.7	21 13.9	10 48.1
10 T	23 12 11.7	4 2.2	10 8.1	16 14.2	7 52.4	15 12.6	15 4.5	18 31.5	18 28.0	14 51.6	21 13.8	10 50.5
13 S	23 24 1.3	2 51.5	10 4.7	18 22.3	5 28.0	15 46.6	14 18.7	18 38.7	18 30.6	14 50.3	21 13.8	10 52.9
16 W	23 35 51.0	1 40.4	10 1.2	11 11.9	2 53.7	16 10.9	13 31.7	18 46.2	18 33.0	14 48.9	21 13.7	10 55.3
19 S	23 47 40.6	0 29.2	9 57.8	0N34.4	0 11.0	16 24.2	12 43.5	18 53.7	18 35.1	14 47.5	21 13.5	10 57.6
22 T	23 59 30.3	0N41.9	9 54.3	11 37.6	2N37.3	16 25.4	11 54.2	19 1.4	18 36.9	14 45.8	21 13.4	10 59.9
25 F	0 11 19.9	1 52.8	9 50.8	18 3.2	5 27.6	16 13.4	11 3.9	19 9.1	18 38.5	14 44.1	21 13.2	11 2.1
28 M	0 23 9.6	3 3.3	9 47.3	17 32.4	8 14.5	15 47.9	10 12.7	19 17.0	18 39.8	14 42.3	21 13.0	11 4.3
31 T	0 34 59.3	4 13.2	9 43.9	9 37.3	10 52.0	15 8.9	9 20.6	19 24.8	18 40.9	14 40.4	21 12.7	11 6.3

APRIL 1977

DAY	EPHEMERIS SIDEREAL TIME	☉	☊	☽	☿	♀	♂	♃	♄	♅	♆	♇
						LONGITUDE at NOON						
1 F	0 38 55.8	11♈38.9	25♎5.5	6♍2.7	27♈17.7	19♈17.4	9♓41.3	29♉35.3	10♌2.2	10♏54.6	16♐5.4	12♎51.0
2 S	0 42 52.4	12 38.1	25 2.3	20 3.3	28 59.7	18R41.6	10 28.1	29 46.9	10R 1.2	10R52.5	16R 5.0	12R49.3
3 S	0 46 48.9	13 37.2	24 59.1	4♎25.9	0♉37.8	18 4.8	11 14.8	29 58.5	10 0.3	10 50.4	16 4.4	12 47.6
4 M	0 50 45.5	14 36.3	24 56.0	19 5.4	2 11.5	17 27.4	12 1.6	0♊10.3	9 59.5	10 48.2	16 3.9	12 45.9
5 T	0 54 42.0	15 35.3	24 52.8	3♏55.1	3 40.6	16 49.6	12 48.4	0 22.1	9 58.8	10 46.0	16 3.3	12 44.2
6 W	0 58 38.6	16 34.3	24 49.6	18 47.6	5 4.7	16 11.7	13 35.1	0 34.0	9 58.3	10 43.7	16 2.7	12 42.6
7 T	1 2 35.1	17 33.3	24 46.4	3♐35.4	6 23.7	15 33.9	14 21.8	0 46.0	9 57.8	10 41.5	16 2.1	12 40.9
8 F	1 6 31.7	18 32.3	24 43.2	18 12.3	7 37.2	14 56.4	15 8.6	0 58.1	9 57.5	10 39.2	16 1.4	12 39.2
9 S	1 10 28.2	19 31.2	24 40.1	2♑33.6	8 45.1	14 19.5	15 55.3	1 10.2	9 57.2	10 36.9	16 0.7	12 37.6
10 S	1 14 24.8	20 30.1	24 36.9	16 36.5	9 47.2	13 43.5	16 42.0	1 22.4	9 57.1	10 34.6	15 60.0	12 35.9
11 M	1 18 21.3	21 29.0	24 33.7	0♒20.1	10 43.4	13 8.6	17 28.7	1 34.7	9 57.1	10 32.2	15 59.2	12 34.2
12 T	1 22 17.9	22 27.8	24 30.5	13 44.6	11 33.5	12 35.0	18 15.4	1 47.0	9 57.1	10 29.9	15 58.5	12 32.6
13 W	1 26 14.4	23 26.6	24 27.4	26 51.2	12 17.4	12 2.8	19 2.0	1 59.4	9D57.3	10 27.5	15 57.6	12 30.9
14 T	1 30 11.0	24 25.4	24 24.2	9♓41.6	12 55.1	11 32.3	19 48.7	2 11.9	9 57.6	10 25.1	15 56.8	12 29.3
15 F	1 34 7.5	25 24.1	24 21.0	22 17.7	13 26.5	11 3.7	20 35.3	2 24.4	9 58.1	10 22.7	15 55.9	12 27.7
16 S	1 38 4.1	26 22.9	24 17.8	4♈41.3	13 51.7	10 37.0	21 21.9	2 37.0	9 58.6	10 20.2	15 55.1	12 26.0
17 S	1 42 0.6	27 21.6	24 14.6	16 54.3	14 10.5	10 12.4	22 8.5	2 49.7	9 59.2	10 17.8	15 54.1	12 24.4
18 M	1 45 57.2	28 20.2	24 11.5	28 58.4	14 23.1	9 50.0	22 55.1	3 2.4	9 59.9	10 15.3	15 53.2	12 22.8
19 T	1 49 53.8	29 18.8	24 8.3	10♉55.4	14 29.6	9 29.8	23 41.7	3 15.2	10 0.8	10 12.8	15 52.2	12 21.2
20 W	1 53 50.3	0♉17.5	24 5.1	22 47.4	14 30.2	9 12.1	24 28.2	3 28.1	10 1.8	10 10.4	15 51.3	12 19.7
21 T	1 57 46.9	1 16.1	24 1.9	4♊36.6	14R24.9	8 56.6	25 14.7	3 40.9	10 2.9	10 7.9	15 50.2	12 18.1
22 F	2 1 43.4	2 14.6	23 58.8	16 25.7	14 14.1	8 43.6	26 1.2	3 53.9	10 4.0	10 5.3	15 49.2	12 16.5
23 S	2 5 40.0	3 13.1	23 55.6	28 17.8	13 58.1	8 33.0	26 47.7	4 6.9	10 5.3	10 2.8	15 48.1	12 15.0
24 S	2 9 36.5	4 11.5	23 52.4	10♋16.4	13 37.3	8 24.8	27 34.1	4 19.9	10 6.7	10 0.3	15 47.0	12 13.5
25 M	2 13 33.1	5 10.0	23 49.2	22 25.5	13 12.1	8 19.0	28 20.5	4 33.0	10 8.2	9 57.8	15 45.9	12 11.9
26 T	2 17 29.6	6 8.3	23 46.0	4♌49.3	12 43.0	8 15.7	29 6.9	4 46.1	10 9.8	9 55.2	15 44.8	12 10.4
27 W	2 21 26.2	7 6.7	23 42.9	17 32.0	12 10.6	8 14.7	29 53.2	4 59.3	10 11.5	9 52.7	15 43.6	12 9.0
28 T	2 25 22.7	8 5.0	23 39.7	0♍37.2	11 35.6	8D16.1	0♈39.5	5 12.5	10 13.3	9 50.1	15 42.4	12 7.5
29 F	2 29 19.3	9 3.3	23 36.5	14 7.9	10 58.6	8 19.8	1 25.8	5 25.7	10 15.2	9 47.6	15 41.2	12 6.0
30 S	2 33 15.8	10 1.6	23 33.3	28 5.5	10 20.3	8 25.8	2 12.1	5 39.0	10 17.2	9 45.0	15 40.0	12 4.6
						DECLINATION at NOON						
1 F	0 38 55.8	4N36.4	9S42.7	5N37.3	11N41.4	14N53.1	9S 3.1	19N27.5	18N41.2	14S39.8	21S12.6	11N 7.0
4 M	0 50 45.5	5 45.4	9 39.2	7S55.3	13 56.9	13 58.3	8 10.1	19 35.4	18 41.9	14 37.8	21 12.4	11 8.9
7 T	1 2 35.1	6 53.5	9 35.7	17 34.5	15 50.2	12 54.6	7 16.5	19 43.3	18 42.3	14 35.7	21 12.0	11 10.8
10 S	1 14 24.8	8 0.5	9 32.2	17 11.9	17 18.3	11 45.4	6 22.3	19 51.2	18 42.4	14 33.5	21 11.7	11 12.6
13 W	1 26 14.4	9 6.4	9 28.7	8 21.4	18 19.3	10 34.3	5 27.7	19 59.1	18 42.3	14 31.3	21 11.4	11 14.3
16 S	1 38 4.1	10 10.8	9 25.2	3N30.2	18 52.3	9 25.1	4 32.7	20 6.9	18 42.0	14 29.0	21 11.0	11 15.8
19 T	1 49 53.8	11 13.8	9 21.7	13 39.9	18 56.9	8 20.8	3 37.5	20 14.7	18 41.3	14 26.7	21 10.6	11 17.3
22 F	2 1 43.4	12 15.2	9 18.2	18 35.6	18 33.7	7 23.8	2 42.0	20 22.4	18 40.4	14 24.4	21 10.2	11 18.6
25 M	2 13 33.1	13 14.6	9 14.7	16 21.7	17 44.9	6 35.4	1 46.5	20 30.0	18 39.2	14 22.0	21 9.7	11 19.8
28 T	2 25 22.7	14 12.2	9 11.2	7 16.0	16 35.4	5 56.7	0 51.0	20 37.5	18 37.8	14 19.6	21 9.3	11 20.9

MAY 1977

DAY	EPHEMERIS SIDEREAL TIME	☉	☊	☽	☿	♀	♂	♃	♄	♅	♆	♇
	h m s	° ′	° ′	° ′	° ′	° ′	° ′	° ′	° ′	° ′	° ′	° ′
						LONGITUDE at NOON						
1 S	2 37 12.4	10♉59.8	23♎30.2	12♎29.1	9♉41.3	8♈33.9	2♈58.3	5♊52.4	10♌19.3	9♏42.5	15♐38.7	12♎ 3.2
2 M	2 41 8.9	11 58.0	23 27.0	27 15.3	9R 2.5	8 44.3	3 44.5	6 5.7	10 21.5	9R39.9	15R37.5	12R 1.8
3 T	2 45 5.5	12 56.1	23 23.8	12♏17.9	8 24.5	8 56.7	4 30.7	6 19.1	10 23.9	9 37.4	15 36.2	12 0.4
4 W	2 49 2.1	13 54.2	23 20.6	27 28.4	7 47.9	9 11.2	5 16.8	6 32.6	10 26.3	9 34.9	15 34.9	11 59.0
5 T	2 52 58.6	14 52.3	23 17.4	12♐37.3	7 13.4	9 27.7	6 2.9	6 46.1	10 28.8	9 32.3	15 33.5	11 57.7
6 F	2 56 55.2	15 50.4	23 14.3	27 35.2	6 41.5	9 46.2	6 49.0	6 59.6	10 31.4	9 29.8	15 32.2	11 56.3
7 S	3 0 51.7	16 48.5	23 11.1	12♑14.4	6 12.7	10 6.5	7 35.0	7 13.1	10 34.1	9 27.3	15 30.8	11 55.0
8 S	3 4 48.3	17 46.5	23 7.9	26 29.9	5 47.3	10 28.6	8 21.1	7 26.7	10 36.9	9 24.7	15 29.4	11 53.7
9 M	3 8 44.8	18 44.5	23 4.7	10♒19.5	5 25.8	10 52.4	9 7.0	7 40.3	10 39.8	9 22.2	15 28.0	11 52.5
10 T	3 12 41.4	19 42.5	23 1.6	23 43.4	5 8.5	11 18.0	9 53.0	7 53.9	10 42.8	9 19.7	15 26.6	11 51.2
11 W	3 16 37.9	20 40.5	22 58.4	6♓43.9	4 55.5	11 45.1	10 38.9	8 7.6	10 46.0	9 17.3	15 25.3	11 50.0
12 T	3 20 34.5	21 38.4	22 55.2	19 24.0	4 46.9	12 13.8	11 24.8	8 21.3	10 49.2	9 14.8	15 23.8	11 48.8
13 F	3 24 31.0	22 36.4	22 52.0	1♈47.4	4 42.9	12 44.0	12 10.7	8 35.0	10 52.5	9 12.4	15 22.3	11 47.7
14 S	3 28 27.6	23 34.3	22 48.8	13 57.9	4D43.5	13 15.6	12 56.5	8 48.8	10 55.9	9 9.9	15 20.9	11 46.5
15 S	3 32 24.2	24 32.1	22 45.7	25 58.8	4 48.8	13 48.6	13 42.2	9 2.5	10 59.3	9 7.5	15 19.4	11 45.4
16 M	3 36 20.7	25 30.0	22 42.5	7♉53.3	4 58.6	14 23.0	14 27.9	9 16.3	11 2.9	9 5.1	15 17.9	11 44.3
17 T	3 40 17.3	26 27.8	22 39.3	19 44.0	5 13.0	14 58.5	15 13.6	9 30.1	11 6.5	9 2.7	15 16.4	11 43.2
18 W	3 44 13.8	27 25.6	22 36.1	1♊33.0	5 31.8	15 35.3	15 59.2	9 44.0	11 10.3	9 0.3	15 14.9	11 42.2
19 T	3 48 10.4	28 23.4	22 33.0	13 22.4	5 55.0	16 13.3	16 44.8	9 57.8	11 14.1	8 57.9	15 13.3	11 41.1
20 F	3 52 6.9	29 21.2	22 29.8	25 14.1	6 22.4	16 52.4	17 30.4	10 11.7	11 18.1	8 55.6	15 11.8	11 40.1
21 S	3 56 3.5	0♊18.9	22 26.6	7♋10.2	6 54.0	17 32.6	18 15.9	10 25.5	11 22.1	8 53.3	15 10.2	11 39.2
22 S	4 0 0.0	1 16.6	22 23.4	19 12.9	7 29.6	18 13.8	19 1.3	10 39.4	11 26.2	8 51.0	15 8.7	11 38.2
23 M	4 3 56.6	2 14.3	22 20.3	1♌24.9	8 9.1	18 56.0	19 46.7	10 53.3	11 30.3	8 48.7	15 7.1	11 37.3
24 T	4 7 53.2	3 12.0	22 17.1	13 49.5	8 52.4	19 39.2	20 32.1	11 7.2	11 34.6	8 46.4	15 5.5	11 36.4
25 W	4 11 49.7	4 9.6	22 13.9	26 29.9	9 39.4	20 23.3	21 17.4	11 21.1	11 39.0	8 44.2	15 3.9	11 35.5
26 T	4 15 46.3	5 7.2	22 10.7	9♍29.8	10 29.9	21 8.2	22 2.7	11 35.1	11 43.4	8 42.0	15 2.3	11 34.7
27 F	4 19 42.8	6 4.8	22 7.5	22 52.5	11 23.9	21 54.1	22 47.9	11 49.0	11 47.9	8 39.8	15 0.7	11 33.9
28 S	4 23 39.4	7 2.4	22 4.4	6♎40.5	12 21.3	22 40.7	23 33.0	12 2.9	11 52.5	8 37.7	14 59.1	11 33.1
29 S	4 27 35.9	7 59.9	22 1.2	20 54.8	13 22.0	23 28.1	24 18.1	12 16.9	11 57.2	8 35.6	14 57.5	11 32.4
30 M	4 31 32.5	8 57.5	21 58.0	5♏34.0	14 25.8	24 16.3	25 3.2	12 30.8	12 1.9	8 33.5	14 55.9	11 31.7
31 T	4 35 29.1	9 55.0	21 54.8	20 33.8	15 32.8	25 5.3	25 48.2	12 44.8	12 6.7	8 31.4	14 54.3	11 31.0
						DECLINATION at NOON						
1 S	2 37 12.4	15N 7.6	9S 7.7	5S55.9	15N13.1	5N27.9	0N 4.5	20N44.9	18N36.1	14S 17.2	21S 8.8	11N21.8
4 W	2 49 2.1	16 0.7	9 4.1	16 47.1	13 47.6	5 8.8	0 59.8	20 52.2	18 34.1	14 14.9	21 8.3	11 22.6
7 S	3 0 51.7	16 51.5	9 0.6	17 45.5	12 29.1	4 59.0	1 54.9	20 59.3	18 31.9	14 12.5	21 7.9	11 23.3
10 T	3 12 41.4	17 39.8	8 57.1	9 17.8	11 25.5	4 58.0	2 49.7	21 6.3	18 29.5	14 10.1	21 7.4	11 23.8
13 F	3 24 31.0	18 25.4	8 53.5	2N32.8	10 41.9	5 4.9	3 44.1	21 13.1	18 26.8	14 7.8	21 6.8	11 24.2
16 M	3 36 20.7	19 8.2	8 50.0	12 58.0	10 20.3	5 19.0	4 38.0	21 19.8	18 23.9	14 5.5	21 6.3	11 24.5
19 T	3 48 10.4	19 48.1	8 46.5	18 29.4	10 20.4	5 39.6	5 31.3	21 26.3	18 20.8	14 3.3	21 5.8	11 24.6
22 S	4 0 0.0	20 25.0	8 42.9	16 57.1	10 40.7	6 5.8	6 24.1	21 32.6	18 17.4	14 1.1	21 5.3	11 24.5
25 W	4 11 49.7	20 58.7	8 39.4	8 35.5	11 18.8	6 37.1	7 16.1	21 38.7	18 13.8	13 59.0	21 4.7	11 24.3
28 S	4 23 39.4	21 29.1	8 35.8	4S 1.8	12 12.4	7 12.6	8 7.3	21 44.6	18 10.0	13 57.0	21 4.2	11 24.0
31 T	4 35 29.1	21 56.2	8 32.3	15 37.6	13 18.7	7 51.9	8 57.7	21 50.3	18 6.0	13 55.1	21 3.6	11 23.6

JUNE 1977

DAY	EPHEMERIS SIDEREAL TIME	☉	☊	☽	☿	♀	♂	♃	♄	♅	♆	♇
						LONGITUDE at NOON						
1 W	4 39 25.6	10♊52.5	21♎51.7	5♐46.8	16♉42.9	25♈55.0	26♈33.2	12♊58.8	12♌11.7	8♏29.5	14♐52.7	11♎30.4
2 T	4 43 22.2	11 50.0	21 48.5	21 3.2	17 55.9	26 45.3	27 18.1	13 12.7	12 16.7	8R27.5	14R51.1	11R29.7
3 F	4 47 18.7	12 47.4	21 45.3	6♑12.2	19 11.9	27 36.3	28 2.9	13 26.7	12 21.7	8 25.5	14 49.5	11 29.1
4 S	4 51 15.3	13 44.8	21 42.1	21 4.1	20 30.8	28 27.9	28 47.7	13 40.6	12 26.8	8 23.6	14 47.9	11 28.6
5 S	4 55 11.8	14 42.2	21 39.0	5♒31.4	21 52.6	29 20.2	29 32.5	13 54.6	12 32.0	8 21.7	14 46.2	11 28.0
6 M	4 59 8.4	15 39.7	21 35.8	19 30.1	23 17.2	0♉13.0	0♉17.2	14 8.5	12 37.3	8 19.8	14 44.6	11 27.5
7 T	5 3 4.9	16 37.1	21 32.6	2♓59.5	24 44.6	1 6.4	1 1.8	14 22.5	12 42.6	8 18.0	14 43.0	11 27.1
8 W	5 7 1.5	17 34.4	21 29.4	16 1.5	26 14.8	2 0.4	1 46.4	14 36.4	12 48.0	8 16.2	14 41.4	11 26.6
9 T	5 10 58.1	18 31.8	21 26.2	28 39.6	27 47.8	2 54.9	2 31.0	14 50.4	12 53.5	8 14.5	14 39.8	11 26.2
10 F	5 14 54.6	19 29.2	21 23.1	10♈58.6	29 23.5	3 49.9	3 15.5	15 4.3	12 59.0	8 12.8	14 38.1	11 25.8
11 S	5 18 51.2	20 26.6	21 19.9	23 3.3	1♊ 1.9	4 45.4	3 59.9	15 18.2	13 4.6	8 11.1	14 36.5	11 25.5
12 S	5 22 47.7	21 23.9	21 16.7	4♉58.4	2 43.1	5 41.4	4 44.3	15 32.1	13 10.3	8 9.5	14 34.9	11 25.2
13 M	5 26 44.3	22 21.3	21 13.5	16 48.1	4 26.9	6 37.8	5 28.6	15 46.0	13 16.0	8 7.9	14 33.3	11 24.9
14 T	5 30 40.8	23 18.6	21 10.4	28 36.1	6 13.4	7 34.7	6 12.8	15 59.9	13 21.8	8 6.3	14 31.7	11 24.7
15 W	5 34 37.4	24 15.9	21 7.2	10♊25.2	8 2.6	8 31.9	6 57.0	16 13.8	13 27.7	8 4.8	14 30.1	11 24.4
16 T	5 38 34.0	25 13.2	21 4.0	22 17.6	9 54.3	9 29.6	7 41.1	16 27.6	13 33.6	8 3.3	14 28.5	11 24.3
17 F	5 42 30.5	26 10.6	21 0.8	4♋15.2	11 48.5	10 27.7	8 25.2	16 41.5	13 39.6	8 1.9	14 26.9	11 24.1
18 S	5 46 27.1	27 7.9	20 57.7	16 19.2	13 45.1	11 26.2	9 9.2	16 55.3	13 45.7	8 0.5	14 25.3	11 24.0
19 S	5 50 23.6	28 5.1	20 54.5	28 30.9	15 44.1	12 25.0	9 53.1	17 9.1	13 51.8	7 59.2	14 23.8	11 23.9
20 M	5 54 20.2	29 2.4	20 51.3	10♌51.8	17 45.2	13 24.2	10 37.0	17 22.9	13 57.9	7 57.9	14 22.2	11 23.9
21 T	5 58 16.7	29 59.7	20 48.1	23 23.6	19 48.3	14 23.7	11 20.8	17 36.7	14 4.1	7 56.7	14 20.6	11 23.9
22 W	6 2 13.3	0♋57.0	20 44.9	6♍ 8.5	21 53.4	15 23.6	12 4.5	17 50.5	14 10.5	7 55.5	14 19.1	11 23.9
23 T	6 6 9.9	1 54.2	20 41.8	19 9.0	24 0.0	16 23.8	12 48.2	18 4.2	14 16.8	7 54.3	14 17.6	11D24.0
24 F	6 10 6.4	2 51.5	20 38.6	2♎27.9	26 8.1	17 24.3	13 31.8	18 17.9	14 23.1	7 53.2	14 16.1	11 24.1
25 S	6 14 3.0	3 48.7	20 35.4	16 7.8	28 17.3	18 25.1	14 15.3	18 31.6	14 29.6	7 52.2	14 14.6	11 24.2
26 S	6 17 59.5	4 45.9	20 32.2	0♏10.3	0♋27.4	19 26.2	14 58.8	18 45.2	14 36.0	7 51.1	14 13.1	11 24.3
27 M	6 21 56.1	5 43.1	20 29.1	14 35.5	2 38.1	20 27.6	15 42.1	18 58.8	14 42.6	7 50.2	14 11.6	11 24.5
28 T	6 25 52.6	6 40.3	20 25.9	29 21.1	4 49.1	21 29.2	16 25.5	19 12.4	14 49.1	7 49.3	14 10.1	11 24.7
29 W	6 29 49.2	7 37.5	20 22.7	14♐21.7	7 0.2	22 31.2	17 8.7	19 26.0	14 55.8	7 48.4	14 8.7	11 25.0
30 T	6 33 45.8	8 34.7	20 19.5	29 29.2	9 11.0	23 33.4	17 51.9	19 39.5	15 2.4	7 47.5	14 7.2	11 25.3
						DECLINATION at NOON						
1 W	4 39 25.6	22N 4.5	8S31.1	17S51.4	13N43.2	8N 5.8	9N14.4	21N52.2	18N 4.6	13S 54.5	21S 3.5	11N23.4
4 S	4 51 15.3	22 27.0	8 27.5	16 43.7	15 2.6	8 49.1	10 3.5	21 57.6	18 0.3	13 52.6	21 2.9	11 22.7
7 T	5 3 4.9	22 46.0	8 24.0	6 44.6	16 28.6	9 34.8	10 51.7	22 2.8	17 55.8	13 50.9	21 2.4	11 21.9
10 F	5 14 54.6	23 1.4	8 20.4	5N18.9	17 58.3	10 22.3	11 38.8	22 7.8	17 51.2	13 49.3	21 1.9	11 21.0
13 M	5 26 44.3	23 13.1	8 16.8	14 51.9	19 28.3	11 11.2	12 24.8	22 12.5	17 46.3	13 47.8	21 1.4	11 19.9
16 T	5 38 34.0	23 21.2	8 13.2	18 50.7	20 54.6	12 1.0	13 9.6	22 17.0	17 41.3	13 46.4	21 0.9	11 18.7
19 S	5 50 23.6	23 25.5	8 9.7	15 32.9	22 12.6	12 51.1	13 53.2	22 21.3	17 36.1	13 45.1	21 0.4	11 17.4
22 W	6 2 13.3	23 26.2	8 6.1	5 54.5	23 17.0	13 41.2	14 35.4	22 25.4	17 30.7	13 44.0	20 59.9	11 15.9
25 S	6 14 3.0	23 23.1	8 2.5	6S46.6	24 2.5	14 30.7	15 16.3	22 29.3	17 25.2	13 43.0	20 59.4	11 14.3
28 T	6 25 52.6	23 16.3	7 58.9	16 58.4	24 25.0	15 19.4	15 55.7	22 32.9	17 19.5	13 42.2	20 59.0	11 12.6

JULY 1977

DAY	EPHEMERIS SIDEREAL TIME	☉	☊	☽	☿	♀	♂	♃	♄	♅	♆	♇
	h m s	° ′	° ′	° ′	° ′	° ′	° ′	° ′	° ′	° ′	° ′	° ′
LONGITUDE at NOON												
1 F	6 37 42.3	9♋31.9	20♎16.4	14♑63.7	11♋21.3	24♉35.8	18♉35.0	19♊53.0	15♌ 9.1	7♏46.8	14♐ 5.8	11♎25.6
2 S	6 41 38.9	10 29.1	20 13.2	29 25.3	13 30.9	25 38.5	19 18.0	20 6.5	15 15.9	7R46.0	14R 4.4	11 25.9
3 S	6 45 35.4	11 26.3	20 10.0	13♒55.3	15 39.6	26 41.5	20 1.0	20 19.9	15 22.7	7 45.4	14 3.0	11 26.3
4 M	6 49 32.0	12 23.4	20 6.8	27 58.5	17 47.1	27 44.7	20 43.9	20 33.3	15 29.5	7 44.7	14 1.6	11 26.8
5 T	6 53 28.5	13 20.6	20 3.6	11♓32.5	19 53.3	28 48.2	21 26.7	20 46.7	15 36.4	7 44.1	14 0.2	11 27.2
6 W	6 57 25.1	14 17.8	20 0.5	24 38.2	21 58.1	29 51.9	22 9.5	21 0.0	15 43.3	7 43.6	13 58.8	11 27.7
7 T	7 1 21.7	15 15.0	19 57.3	7♈18.7	24 1.3	0♊55.8	22 52.1	21 13.3	15 50.3	7 43.1	13 57.5	11 28.2
8 F	7 5 18.2	16 12.2	19 54.1	19 38.6	26 2.8	1 59.9	23 34.8	21 26.5	15 57.3	7 42.7	13 56.2	11 28.8
9 S	7 9 14.8	17 9.5	19 50.9	1♉43.1	28 2.7	3 4.2	24 17.3	21 39.8	16 4.3	7 42.3	13 54.9	11 29.3
10 S	7 13 11.3	18 6.7	19 47.8	13 37.4	0♌ 0.8	4 8.8	24 59.7	21 52.9	16 11.4	7 42.0	13 53.6	11 30.0
11 M	7 17 7.9	19 3.9	19 44.6	25 26.7	1 57.0	5 13.5	25 42.1	22 6.0	16 18.5	7 41.7	13 52.4	11 30.6
12 T	7 21 4.4	20 1.1	19 41.4	7♊15.3	3 51.4	6 18.4	26 24.4	22 19.1	16 25.6	7 41.5	13 51.1	11 31.3
13 W	7 25 1.0	20 58.4	19 38.2	19 7.1	5 44.0	7 23.6	27 6.7	22 32.2	16 32.9	7 41.4	13 49.9	11 32.1
14 T	7 28 57.6	21 55.7	19 35.1	1♋ 4.9	7 34.7	8 28.9	27 48.8	22 45.2	16 40.1	7 41.3	13 48.7	11 32.8
15 F	7 32 54.1	22 52.9	19 31.9	13 10.7	9 23.5	9 34.4	28 30.9	22 58.1	16 47.3	7 41.2	13 47.6	11 33.6
16 S	7 36 50.7	23 50.2	19 28.7	25 25.9	11 10.4	10 40.1	29 12.9	23 11.0	16 54.6	7 41.2	13 46.4	11 34.4
17 S	7 40 47.2	24 47.4	19 25.5	7♌51.1	12 55.4	11 45.9	29 54.8	23 23.8	17 1.9	7 41.2	13 45.3	11 35.3
18 M	7 44 43.8	25 44.7	19 22.3	20 26.7	14 38.5	12 51.9	0♊36.6	23 36.6	17 9.2	7D41.3	13 44.2	11 36.1
19 T	7 48 40.3	26 42.0	19 19.2	3♍13.1	16 19.8	13 58.0	1 18.3	23 49.4	17 16.5	7 41.4	13 43.1	11 37.0
20 W	7 52 36.9	27 39.3	19 16.0	16 10.9	17 59.2	15 4.3	1 59.9	24 2.0	17 23.9	7 41.6	13 42.0	11 38.0
21 T	7 56 33.4	28 36.6	19 12.8	29 21.2	19 36.7	16 10.8	2 41.5	24 14.6	17 31.3	7 41.9	13 41.0	11 38.9
22 F	8 0 30.0	29 33.9	19 9.6	12♎45.2	21 12.4	17 17.4	3 22.9	24 27.2	17 38.8	7 42.2	13 40.0	11 40.0
23 S	8 4 26.6	0♌31.2	19 6.5	26 24.5	22 46.2	18 24.2	4 4.3	24 39.7	17 46.2	7 42.5	13 39.0	11 41.0
24 S	8 8 23.1	1 28.5	19 3.3	10♏20.3	24 18.0	19 31.1	4 45.6	24 52.1	17 53.7	7 42.9	13 38.0	11 42.0
25 M	8 12 19.7	2 25.8	19 0.1	24 33.0	25 48.0	20 38.1	5 26.8	25 4.5	18 1.2	7 43.4	13 37.1	11 43.1
26 T	8 16 16.2	3 23.1	18 56.9	9♐ 1.1	27 16.1	21 45.3	6 7.9	25 16.8	18 8.7	7 43.9	13 36.2	11 44.3
27 W	8 20 12.8	4 20.4	18 53.8	23 41.4	28 42.3	22 52.7	6 48.9	25 29.0	18 16.2	7 44.5	13 35.3	11 45.4
28 T	8 24 9.3	5 17.7	18 50.6	8♑28.0	0♍ 6.5	24 0.1	7 29.8	25 41.2	18 23.7	7 45.1	13 34.4	11 46.6
29 F	8 28 5.9	6 15.1	18 47.4	23 13.6	1 28.7	25 7.7	8 10.7	25 53.3	18 31.3	7 45.7	13 33.6	11 47.8
30 S	8 32 2.4	7 12.4	18 44.2	7♒49.9	2 48.9	26 15.5	8 51.4	26 5.4	18 38.9	7 46.4	13 32.8	11 49.1
31 S	8 35 59.0	8 9.8	18 41.0	22 9.4	4 7.0	27 23.4	9 32.0	26 17.3	18 46.4	7 47.2	13 32.0	11 50.3
DECLINATION at NOON												
1 F	6 37 42.3	23N 5.8	7S55.3	17S40.9	24N22.5	16N 6.8	16N33.7	22N36.3	17N13.7	13S41.5	20S58.6	11N10.8
4 M	6 49 32.0	22 51.7	7 51.7	8 25.6	23 55.3	16 52.5	17 10.2	22 39.4	17 7.7	13 40.9	20 58.2	11 8.8
7 T	7 1 21.7	22 34.1	7 48.1	3N56.6	23 5.7	17 36.1	17 45.2	22 42.3	17 1.6	13 40.5	20 57.8	11 6.8
10 S	7 13 11.3	22 12.9	7 44.5	14 0.8	21 57.3	18 17.4	18 18.5	22 45.0	16 55.4	13 40.2	20 57.4	11 4.6
13 W	7 25 1.0	21 48.2	7 40.9	18 42.0	20 33.8	18 55.8	18 50.3	22 47.5	16 49.0	13 40.1	20 57.1	11 2.4
16 S	7 36 50.7	21 20.2	7 37.3	16 9.8	18 58.8	19 31.1	19 20.4	22 49.8	16 42.6	13 40.1	20 56.8	11 0.0
19 T	7 48 40.3	20 48.9	7 33.7	6 58.6	17 15.6	20 3.0	19 48.8	22 51.8	16 36.0	13 40.3	20 56.5	10 57.6
22 F	8 0 30.0	20 14.5	7 30.1	5S30.6	15 26.7	20 31.1	20 15.6	22 53.7	16 29.3	13 40.6	20 56.3	10 55.1
25 M	8 12 19.7	19 37.1	7 26.5	16 1.4	13 34.7	20 55.2	20 40.6	22 55.3	16 22.6	13 41.1	20 56.1	10 52.5
28 T	8 24 9.3	18 56.7	7 22.9	18 13.2	11 41.6	21 15.0	21 3.9	22 56.7	16 15.8	13 41.7	20 55.9	10 49.8
31 S	8 35 59.0	18 13.5	7 19.3	10 11.0	9 49.3	21 30.3	21 25.4	22 58.0	16 8.9	13 42.5	20 55.7	10 47.1

AUGUST 1977

DAY	EPHEMERIS SIDEREAL TIME	☉	☊	☽	☿	♀	♂	♃	♄	♅	♆	♇
LONGITUDE at NOON												
1 M	8 39 55.6	9♌ 7.2	18♎37.9	6♓ 6.6	5♍23.1	28♊31.4	10♊12.6	26♊29.2	18♌54.0	7♏48.0	13♐31.3	11♎51.6
2 T	8 43 52.1	10 4.6	18 34.7	19 38.3	6 36.9	29 39.5	10 53.1	26 41.1	19 1.6	7 48.9	13R30.5	11 52.9
3 W	8 47 48.7	11 2.0	18 31.5	2♈44.4	7 48.6	0♋47.9	11 33.5	26 52.9	19 9.3	7 49.9	13 29.9	11 54.4
4 T	8 51 45.2	11 59.5	18 28.3	15 26.6	8 57.9	1 56.3	12 13.8	27 4.6	19 17.0	7 50.8	13 29.2	11 55.7
5 F	8 55 41.8	12 56.9	18 25.2	27 48.5	10 4.9	3 4.8	12 54.0	27 16.2	19 24.6	7 51.9	13 28.6	11 57.1
6 S	8 59 38.3	13 54.4	18 22.0	9♉54.9	11 ×.4	4 13.5	13 34.1	27 27.7	19 32.2	7 52.9	13 28.0	11 58.6
7 S	9 3 34.9	14 51.9	18 18.8	21 50.9	12 11.3	5 22.2	14 14.1	27 39.1	19 39.9	7 54.1	13 27.4	12 0.0
8 M	9 7 31.4	15 49.4	18 15.6	3♊41.8	13 10.5	6 31.1	14 54.0	27 50.5	19 47.6	7 55.2	13 26.8	12 1.5
9 T	9 11 28.0	16 46.9	18 12.4	15 32.6	14 6.9	7 40.2	15 33.8	28 1.8	19 55.2	7 56.5	13 26.3	12 3.1
10 W	9 15 24.5	17 44.5	18 9.3	27 27.7	15 0.4	8 49.3	16 13.5	28 13.0	20 2.9	7 57.7	13 25.8	12 4.6
11 T	9 19 21.1	18 42.1	18 6.1	9♋30.9	15 50.8	9 58.5	16 53.1	28 24.1	20 10.6	7 59.1	13 25.4	12 6.2
12 F	9 23 17.7	19 39.7	18 2.9	21 44.9	16 37.9	11 7.9	17 32.5	28 35.1	20 18.3	8 0.4	13 25.0	12 7.8
13 S	9 27 14.2	20 37.3	17 59.7	4♌11.7	17 21.6	12 17.3	18 11.9	28 46.1	20 26.0	8 1.9	13 24.6	12 9.4
14 S	9 31 10.8	21 35.0	17 56.6	16 51.9	18 1.7	13 26.9	18 51.2	28 56.9	20 33.6	8 3.3	13 24.2	12 11.0
15 M	9 35 7.3	22 32.6	17 53.4	29 45.6	18 38.0	14 36.6	19 30.4	29 7.7	20 41.3	8 4.9	13 23.9	12 12.7
16 T	9 39 3.9	23 30.3	17 50.2	12♍52.2	19 10.3	15 46.3	20 9.4	29 18.3	20 49.0	8 6.4	13 23.6	12 14.4
17 W	9 43 0.4	24 28.0	17 47.0	26 10.8	19 38.3	16 56.2	20 48.3	29 28.9	20 56.7	8 8.1	13 23.3	12 16.1
18 T	9 46 57.0	25 25.8	17 43.8	9♎40.3	20 1.8	18 6.2	21 27.2	29 39.3	21 4.3	8 9.7	13 23.0	12 17.8
19 F	9 50 53.5	26 23.5	17 40.7	23 20.2	20 20.7	19 16.2	22 5.9	29 49.7	21 12.0	8 11.4	13 22.8	12 19.6
20 S	9 54 50.1	27 21.3	17 37.5	7♏ 9.8	20 34.6	20 26.4	22 44.5	29 60.0	21 19.7	8 13.2	13 22.7	12 21.4
21 S	9 58 46.6	28 19.1	17 34.3	21 9.0	20 43.3	21 36.7	23 22.9	0♋10.1	21 27.3	8 15.0	13 22.5	12 23.2
22 M	10 2 43.2	29 16.9	17 31.1	5♐16.9	20 46.6	22 47.0	24 1.3	0 20.2	21 34.9	8 16.9	13 22.4	12 25.0
23 T	10 6 39.7	0♍14.7	17 28.0	19 32.2	20R44.2	23 57.5	24 39.5	0 30.1	21 42.6	8 18.8	13 22.3	12 26.9
24 W	10 10 36.3	1 12.6	17 24.8	3♑52.8	20 36.2	25 8.0	25 17.7	0 40.0	21 50.2	8 20.8	13 22.3	12 28.8
25 T	10 14 32.8	2 10.4	17 21.6	18 14.8	20 22.2	26 18.7	25 55.7	0 49.7	21 57.8	8 22.8	13 22.3	12 30.7
26 F	10 18 29.4	3 8.3	17 18.4	2♒33.8	20 2.2	27 29.4	26 33.6	0 59.4	22 5.4	8 24.8	13 22.3	12 32.6
27 S	10 22 26.0	4 6.2	17 15.2	16 44.5	19 36.3	28 40.2	27 11.3	1 8.9	22 13.0	8 26.9	13D22.4	12 34.5
28 S	10 26 22.5	5 4.2	17 12.1	0♓41.9	19 4.5	29 51.1	27 49.0	1 18.3	22 20.6	8 29.0	13 22.5	12 36.5
29 M	10 30 19.1	6 2.1	17 8.9	14 22.0	18 27.1	1♌ 2.1	28 26.5	1 27.5	22 28.1	8 31.2	13 22.6	12 38.5
30 T	10 34 15.6	7 0.1	17 5.7	27 42.0	17 44.5	2 13.2	29 3.9	1 36.7	22 35.6	8 33.4	13 22.7	12 40.5
31 W	10 38 12.2	7 58.1	17 2.5	10♈41.2	16 57.1	3 24.4	29 41.2	1 45.8	22 43.1	8 35.6	13 22.9	12 42.5
DECLINATION at NOON												
1 M	8 39 55.6	17N58.5	7S18.1	6S 9.2	9N12.4	21N34.4	21N32.2	22N58.4	16N 6.6	13S42.8	20S55.7	10N46.2
4 T	8 51 45.2	17 11.8	7 14.4	6N14.7	7 24.1	21 43.4	21 51.4	22 59.4	15 59.6	13 43.8	20 55.6	10 43.4
7 S	9 3 34.9	16 22.5	7 10.8	15 26.6	5 41.2	21 47.4	22 8.9	23 0.2	15 52.6	13 44.9	20 55.5	10 40.5
10 W	9 15 24.5	15 30.9	7 7.2	18 38.0	4 5.6	21 46.3	22 24.6	23 0.9	15 45.5	13 46.2	20 55.5	10 37.6
13 S	9 27 14.2	14 37.0	7 3.5	14 29.7	2 40.1	21 40.0	22 38.6	23 1.4	15 38.4	13 47.6	20 55.5	10 34.6
16 T	9 39 3.9	13 41.1	6 59.9	4 7.1	1 27.7	21 28.5	22 51.0	23 1.8	15 31.3	13 49.2	20 55.5	10 31.6
19 F	9 50 53.5	12 43.2	6 56.3	8S28.6	0 31.9	21 11.7	23 1.6	23 2.0	15 24.1	13 50.9	20 55.6	10 28.6
22 M	10 2 43.2	11 43.4	6 52.6	17 21.2	0S 2.7	20 49.7	23 10.6	23 2.1	15 17.0	13 52.7	20 55.7	10 25.6
25 T	10 14 32.8	10 42.1	6 49.0	17 6.0	0 11.5	20 22.4	23 17.9	23 2.1	15 9.8	13 54.7	20 55.9	10 22.5
28 S	10 26 22.5	9 39.2	6 45.3	7 48.0	0N 9.7	19 50.0	23 23.6	23 2.0	15 2.7	13 56.7	20 56.1	10 19.4
31 W	10 38 12.2	8 34.9	6 41.7	4N38.7	1 2.8	19 12.5	23 27.9	23 1.8	14 55.6	13 58.9	20 56.3	10 16.4

SEPTEMBER 1977

DAY	EPHEMERIS SIDEREAL TIME	☉	☊	☽	☿	♀	♂	♃	♄	♅	♆	♇
	h m s	° ′	° ′	° ′	° ′	° ′	° ′	° ′	° ′	° ′	° ′	° ′
						LONGITUDE at NOON						
1 T	10 42 8.7	8♍56.1	16♎59.4	23♈20.3	16♍ 5.6	4♌35.7	0♋18.3	1♋54.7	22♌50.6	8♏37.9	13♐23.1	12♎44.5
2 F	10 46 5.3	9 54.2	16 56.2	5♉41.7	15R10.9	5 47.0	0 55.3	2 3.5	22 58.1	8 40.2	13 23.4	12 46.5
3 S	10 50 1.8	10 52.3	16 53.0	17 48.9	14 13.9	6 58.5	1 32.2	2 12.2	23 5.5	8 42.6	13 23.6	12 48.6
4 S	10 53 58.4	11 50.5	16 49.8	29 46.3	13 15.7	8 10.0	2 9.0	2 20.7	23 13.0	8 45.0	13 24.0	12 50.7
5 M	10 57 54.9	12 48.6	16 46.6	11♊38.6	12 17.6	9 21.6	2 45.6	2 29.1	23 20.4	8 47.5	13 24.3	12 52.7
6 T	11 1 51.5	13 46.8	16 43.5	23 30.8	11 20.9	10 33.3	3 22.1	2 37.4	23 27.8	8 50.0	13 24.7	12 54.9
7 W	11 5 48.0	14 45.1	16 40.3	5♋27.6	10 26.8	11 45.1	3 58.4	2 45.6	23 35.1	8 52.5	13 25.1	12 57.0
8 T	11 9 44.6	15 43.3	16 37.1	17 33.6	9 36.6	12 57.0	4 34.6	2 53.6	23 42.4	8 55.1	13 25.5	12 59.1
9 F	11 13 41.1	16 41.6	16 33.9	29 52.5	8 51.5	14 9.0	5 10.6	3 1.5	23 49.7	8 57.7	13 26.0	13 1.3
10 S	11 17 37.7	17 40.0	16 30.8	12♌27.2	8 12.8	15 21.0	5 46.5	3 9.3	23 57.0	9 0.4	13 26.5	13 3.4
11 S	11 21 34.2	18 38.3	16 27.6	25 19.3	7 41.2	16 33.1	6 22.3	3 16.9	24 4.2	9 3.1	13 27.0	13 5.6
12 M	11 25 30.8	19 36.7	16 24.4	8♍29.5	7 17.7	17 45.3	6 57.9	3 24.4	24 11.4	9 5.8	13 27.6	13 7.8
13 T	11 29 27.3	20 35.2	16 21.2	21 57.0	7 2.8	18 57.6	7 33.4	3 31.7	24 18.6	9 8.6	13 28.2	13 10.0
14 W	11 33 23.9	21 33.7	16 18.0	5♎39.8	6 57.0	20 10.0	8 8.7	3 39.0	24 25.8	9 11.4	13 28.9	13 12.3
15 T	11 37 20.4	22 32.2	16 14.9	19 35.2	7D 0.6	21 22.4	8 43.8	3 46.0	24 32.9	9 14.2	13 29.6	13 14.5
16 F	11 41 17.0	23 30.7	16 11.7	3♏40.1	7 13.5	22 34.8	9 18.8	3 52.9	24 40.0	9 17.1	13 30.3	13 16.7
17 S	11 45 13.5	24 29.2	16 8.5	17 51.1	7 35.9	23 47.4	9 53.6	3 59.6	24 47.0	9 20.0	13 31.0	13 19.0
18 S	11 49 10.1	25 27.8	16 5.3	2♐ 5.4	8 7.4	25 0.0	10 28.2	4 6.2	24 54.0	9 22.9	13 31.8	13 21.3
19 M	11 53 6.7	26 26.4	16 2.2	16 20.0	8 47.8	26 12.7	11 2.7	4 12.6	25 1.0	9 25.9	13 32.6	13 23.5
20 T	11 57 3.2	27 25.0	15 59.0	0♑32.5	9 36.5	27 25.4	11 37.0	4 18.9	25 7.9	9 28.9	13 33.4	13 25.8
21 W	12 0 59.8	28 23.7	15 55.8	14 40.9	10 33.2	28 38.3	12 11.1	4 25.0	25 14.7	9 31.9	13 34.2	13 28.1
22 T	12 4 56.3	29 22.4	15 52.6	28 42.8	11 37.2	29 51.1	12 45.1	4 31.0	25 21.6	9 35.0	13 35.1	13 30.4
23 F	12 8 52.9	0♎21.1	15 49.4	12♒36.2	12 47.9	1♍ 4.1	13 18.9	4 36.8	25 28.3	9 38.1	13 36.1	13 32.7
24 S	12 12 49.4	1 19.8	15 46.3	26 19.0	14 4.7	2 17.1	13 52.5	4 42.5	25 35.1	9 41.2	13 37.0	13 35.0
25 S	12 16 46.0	2 18.6	15 43.1	9♓49.2	15 26.9	3 30.2	14 25.9	4 47.9	25 41.8	9 44.4	13 38.0	13 37.3
26 M	12 20 42.5	3 17.4	15 39.9	23 5.3	16 53.9	4 43.3	14 59.1	4 53.2	25 48.4	9 47.5	13 39.0	13 39.6
27 T	12 24 39.1	4 16.3	15 36.7	6♈ 6.1	18 24.9	5 56.5	15 32.2	4 58.4	25 55.0	9 50.7	13 40.0	13 42.0
28 W	12 28 35.6	5 15.1	15 33.5	18 51.4	19 59.5	7 9.8	16 5.0	5 3.4	26 1.6	9 54.0	13 41.1	13 44.3
29 T	12 32 32.2	6 14.0	15 30.4	1♉21.5	21 37.1	8 23.1	16 37.7	5 8.2	26 8.1	9 57.2	13 42.2	13 46.6
30 F	12 36 28.7	7 13.0	15 27.2	13 38.1	23 17.0	9 36.5	17 10.2	5 12.8	26 14.5	10 0.5	13 43.3	13 49.0
						DECLINATION at NOON						
1 T	10 42 8.7	8N13.2	6S40.5	8N25.2	1N27.1	18N59.0	23N28.9	23N 1.7	14N53.3	13S59.7	20S56.4	10N15.3
4 S	10 53 58.4	7 7.3	6 36.8	16 33.3	2 56.5	18 15.0	23 31.1	23 1.5	14 46.2	14 2.1	20 56.6	10 12.3
7 W	11 5 48.0	6 0.3	6 33.2	18 12.0	4 39.7	17 26.3	23 31.9	23 1.1	14 39.2	14 4.5	20 56.9	10 9.2
10 S	11 17 37.7	4 52.4	6 29.5	12 35.9	6 19.7	16 33.2	23 31.3	23 0.7	14 32.3	14 7.1	20 57.3	10 6.2
13 T	11 29 27.3	3 43.8	6 25.8	1 16.8	7 40.0	15 35.8	23 29.4	23 0.3	14 25.4	14 9.8	20 57.6	10 3.1
16 F	11 41 17.0	2 34.6	6 22.2	11S10.7	8 28.3	14 34.3	23 26.3	22 59.8	14 18.7	14 12.6	20 58.1	10 0.1
19 M	11 53 6.7	1 24.9	6 18.5	18 9.5	8 38.4	13 29.1	23 22.0	22 59.3	14 12.0	14 15.4	20 58.5	9 57.2
22 T	12 4 56.3	0 15.0	6 14.8	15 24.1	8 10.1	12 20.5	23 16.5	22 58.8	14 5.4	14 18.4	20 59.0	9 54.2
25 S	12 16 46.0	0S55.1	6 11.2	5 3.1	7 6.9	11 8.5	23 10.1	22 58.4	13 59.0	14 21.4	20 59.5	9 51.4
28 W	12 28 35.6	2 5.2	6 7.5	7N 4.5	5 35.7	9 53.7	23 2.7	22 57.9	13 52.7	14 24.5	20 60.0	9 48.5

OCTOBER 1977

DAY	EPHEMERIS SIDEREAL TIME	☉	☊	☽	☿	♀	♂	♃	♄	♅	♆	♇
						LONGITUDE at NOON						
1 S	12 40 25.3	8♎11.9	15♎24.0	25♉43.2	24♍59.0	10♍49.9	17♋42.5	5♋17.3	26♌20.9	10♏ 3.8	13♐44.5	13♎51.3
2 S	12 44 21.8	9 11.0	15 20.8	7♊40.1	26 42.5	12 3.4	18 14.6	5 21.6	26 27.2	10 7.2	13 45.7	13 53.7
3 M	12 48 18.4	10 10.0	15 17.7	19 32.4	28 27.2	13 17.0	18 46.5	5 25.7	26 33.5	10 10.5	13 46.9	13 56.0
4 T	12 52 14.9	11 9.1	15 14.5	1♋24.4	0♎12.7	14 30.6	19 18.1	5 29.6	26 39.7	10 13.9	13 48.1	13 58.4
5 W	12 56 11.5	12 8.3	15 11.3	13 20.6	1 58.8	15 44.4	19 49.7	5 33.4	26 46.0	10 17.4	13 49.5	14 0.8
6 T	13 0 8.0	13 7.4	15 8.1	25 25.7	3 45.2	16 58.1	20 20.9	5 37.0	26 52.1	10 20.8	13 50.8	14 3.1
7 F	13 4 4.6	14 6.6	15 4.9	7♌44.2	5 31.8	18 11.9	20 51.9	5 40.3	26 58.1	10 24.2	13 52.1	14 5.5
8 S	13 8 1.1	15 5.9	15 1.8	20 20.1	7 18.3	19 25.8	21 22.7	5 43.5	27 4.1	10 27.7	13 53.4	14 7.8
9 S	13 11 57.7	16 5.2	14 58.6	3♍16.5	9 4.7	20 39.7	21 53.3	5 46.5	27 10.1	10 31.2	13 54.8	14 10.2
10 M	13 15 54.2	17 4.5	14 55.4	16 35.5	10 50.7	21 53.7	22 23.6	5 49.4	27 15.9	10 34.7	13 56.2	14 12.6
11 T	13 19 50.8	18 3.8	14 52.2	0♎17.2	12 36.4	23 7.7	22 53.7	5 52.0	27 21.7	10 38.2	13 57.7	14 14.9
12 W	13 23 47.3	19 3.2	14 49.1	14 20.1	14 21.6	24 21.7	23 23.5	5 54.4	27 27.5	10 41.8	13 59.1	14 17.3
13 T	13 27 43.9	20 2.7	14 45.9	28 40.7	16 6.4	25 35.8	23 53.1	5 56.7	27 33.1	10 45.3	14 0.6	14 19.6
14 F	13 31 40.5	21 2.1	14 42.7	13♏13.7	17 50.5	26 50.0	24 22.4	5 58.7	27 38.7	10 48.9	14 2.1	14 22.0
15 S	13 35 37.0	22 1.6	14 39.5	27 52.9	19 34.1	28 4.2	24 51.5	6 0.6	27 44.3	10 52.5	14 3.7	14 24.3
16 S	13 39 33.6	23 1.1	14 36.3	12♐31.8	21 17.1	29 18.4	25 20.3	6 2.3	27 49.7	10 56.1	14 5.2	14 26.7
17 M	13 43 30.1	24 0.7	14 33.2	27 4.6	22 59.4	0♎32.7	25 48.8	6 3.7	27 55.1	10 59.7	14 6.8	14 29.0
18 T	13 47 26.7	25 0.2	14 30.0	11♑26.4	24 41.1	1 47.0	26 17.1	6 5.0	28 0.4	11 3.4	14 8.4	14 31.3
19 W	13 51 23.2	25 59.9	14 26.8	25 34.3	26 22.2	3 1.4	26 45.0	6 6.1	28 5.7	11 7.0	14 10.1	14 33.6
20 T	13 55 19.8	26 59.5	14 23.6	9♒26.5	28 2.7	4 15.8	27 12.7	6 6.9	28 10.8	11 10.7	14 11.7	14 36.0
21 F	13 59 16.3	27 59.2	14 20.5	23 2.7	29 42.5	5 30.2	27 40.1	6 7.6	28 15.9	11 14.3	14 13.4	14 38.3
22 S	14 3 12.9	28 58.8	14 17.3	6♓23.3	1♏21.7	6 44.7	28 7.3	6 8.1	28 20.9	11 18.0	14 15.1	14 40.6
23 S	14 7 9.4	29 58.6	14 14.1	19 29.1	3 0.4	7 59.2	28 34.1	6 8.4	28 25.9	11 21.7	14 16.9	14 42.9
24 M	14 11 6.0	0♏58.3	14 10.9	2♈21.2	4 38.4	9 13.7	29 0.6	6 8.4	28 30.7	11 25.4	14 18.6	14 45.2
25 T	14 15 2.5	1 58.1	14 7.7	15 0.7	6 15.9	10 28.3	29 26.8	6R 8.3	28 35.5	11 29.1	14 20.4	14 47.4
26 W	14 18 59.1	2 58.0	14 4.6	27 28.8	7 52.8	11 42.9	29 52.7	6 8.1	28 40.3	11 32.9	14 22.2	14 49.8
27 T	14 22 55.6	3 57.8	14 1.4	9♉46.3	9 29.2	12 57.6	0♌18.3	6 7.5	28 44.9	11 36.6	14 24.0	14 52.0
28 F	14 26 52.2	4 57.7	13 58.2	21 54.6	11 5.0	14 12.3	0 43.5	6 6.8	28 49.4	11 40.3	14 25.9	14 54.3
29 S	14 30 48.7	5 57.6	13 55.0	3♊55.2	12 40.4	15 27.0	1 8.4	6 5.9	28 53.9	11 44.1	14 27.7	14 56.5
30 S	14 34 45.3	6 57.5	13 51.9	15 49.9	14 15.3	16 41.8	1 33.0	6 4.8	28 58.2	11 47.8	14 29.6	14 58.7
31 M	14 38 41.9	7 57.5	13 48.7	27 41.4	15 49.7	17 56.5	1 57.2	6 3.4	29 2.5	11 51.6	14 31.5	15 1.0
						DECLINATION at NOON						
1 S	12 40 25.3	3S15.1	6S 3.8	15N50.9	3N43.9	8N36.2	22N54.5	22N57.5	13N46.5	14S27.6	21S 0.5	9N45.8
4 T	12 52 14.9	4 24.8	6 0.2	18 17.8	1 38.6	7 16.3	22 45.5	22 57.2	13 40.5	14 30.8	21 1.1	9 43.1
7 F	13 4 4.6	5 33.9	5 56.5	13 36.3	0S34.1	5 54.4	22 35.8	22 56.9	13 34.7	14 34.1	21 1.7	9 40.4
10 M	13 15 54.2	6 42.4	5 52.8	2 56.9	2 49.9	4 30.7	22 25.6	22 56.6	13 29.0	14 37.4	21 2.4	9 37.9
13 T	13 27 43.9	7 50.2	5 49.1	9S51.4	5 5.7	3 5.7	22 14.9	22 56.4	13 23.6	14 40.8	21 3.0	9 35.4
16 S	13 39 33.6	8 56.9	5 45.4	17 53.2	7 19.1	1 39.6	22 3.8	22 56.3	13 18.3	14 44.2	21 3.7	9 33.0
19 W	13 51 23.2	10 2.5	5 41.7	15 55.1	9 28.6	0 12.7	21 52.6	22 56.3	13 13.3	14 47.6	21 4.4	9 30.7
22 S	14 3 12.9	11 6.7	5 38.0	6 5.0	11 33.0	1S14.7	21 41.1	22 56.4	13 8.5	14 51.1	21 5.1	9 28.5
25 T	14 15 2.5	12 9.5	5 34.3	5N56.3	13 31.6	2 42.1	21 29.7	22 56.6	13 4.0	14 54.5	21 5.8	9 26.4
28 F	14 26 52.2	13 10.6	5 30.6	15 12.5	15 23.5	4 9.3	21 18.4	22 56.8	12 59.7	14 58.0	21 6.5	9 24.3
31 M	14 38 41.9	14 9.8	5 26.9	18 25.3	17 8.2	5 36.0	21 7.2	22 57.2	12 55.6	15 1.5	21 7.3	9 22.4

NOVEMBER 1977

DAY	EPHEMERIS SIDEREAL TIME h m s	☉ ° ′	☊ ° ′	☽ ° ′	☿ ° ′	♀ ° ′	♂ ° ′	♃ ° ′	♄ ° ′	♅ ° ′	♆ ° ′	♇ ° ′
LONGITUDE at NOON												
1 T	14 42 38.4	8♏57.5	13♎45.5	9♋32.7	17♏23.6	19♎11.4	2♌21.1	6♋ 1.9	29♌ 6.7	11♏55.3	14♐33.4	15♎ 3.2
2 W	14 46 35.0	9 57.6	13 42.3	21 27.5	18 57.1	20 26.2	2 44.6	6R 0.2	29 10.8	11 59.1	14 35.3	15 5.4
3 T	14 50 31.5	10 57.7	13 39.1	3♌29.8	20 30.2	21 41.1	3 7.7	5 58.3	29 14.8	12 2.8	14 37.3	15 7.5
4 F	14 54 28.1	11 57.8	13 36.0	15 44.3	22 2.9	22 56.0	3 30.4	5 56.2	29 18.8	12 6.6	14 39.2	15 9.7
5 S	14 58 24.6	12 57.9	13 32.8	28 15.5	23 35.2	24 11.0	3 52.8	5 53.8	29 22.6	12 10.3	14 41.2	15 11.8
6 S	15 2 21.2	13 58.1	13 29.6	11♍ 7.8	25 7.1	25 25.9	4 14.7	5 51.3	29 26.3	12 14.1	14 43.2	15 14.0
7 M	15 6 17.7	14 58.4	13 26.4	24 24.7	26 38.6	26 40.9	4 36.2	5 48.6	29 30.0	12 17.8	14 45.2	15 16.1
8 T	15 10 14.3	15 58.6	13 23.3	8♎ 8.6	28 9.7	27 56.0	4 57.3	5 45.7	29 33.5	12 21.6	14 47.2	15 18.2
9 W	15 14 10.8	16 58.9	13 20.1	22 19.3	29 40.5	29 11.0	5 18.0	5 42.6	29 37.0	12 25.3	14 49.3	15 20.3
10 T	15 18 7.4	17 59.2	13 16.9	6♏54.4	1♐10.9	0♏26.1	5 38.3	5 39.3	29 40.3	12 29.1	14 51.3	15 22.4
11 F	15 22 4.0	18 59.6	13 13.7	21 48.1	2 40.9	1 41.2	5 58.1	5 35.8	29 43.6	12 32.8	14 53.4	15 24.4
12 S	15 26 0.5	19 59.9	13 10.5	6♐52.5	4 10.5	2 56.3	6 17.4	5 32.1	29 46.8	12 36.5	14 55.5	15 26.5
13 S	15 29 57.1	21 0.4	13 7.4	21 58.0	5 39.7	4 11.4	6 36.2	5 28.2	29 49.8	12 40.3	14 57.6	15 28.5
14 M	15 33 53.6	22 0.8	13 4.2	6♑55.0	7 8.5	5 26.6	6 54.6	5 24.2	29 52.8	12 44.0	14 59.7	15 30.5
15 T	15 37 50.2	23 1.2	13 1.0	21 35.6	8 36.9	6 41.7	7 12.5	5 19.9	29 55.7	12 47.7	15 1.8	15 32.5
16 W	15 41 46.7	24 1.8	12 57.8	5♒54.7	10 4.8	7 57.0	7 30.0	5 15.6	29 58.5	12 51.5	15 4.0	15 34.5
17 T	15 45 43.3	25 2.3	12 54.7	19 49.8	11 32.2	9 12.2	7 46.9	5 11.0	0♍ 1.1	12 55.2	15 6.2	15 36.4
18 F	15 49 39.8	26 2.8	12 51.5	3♓21.1	12 59.1	10 27.4	8 3.3	5 6.2	0 3.7	12 58.8	15 8.3	15 38.3
19 S	15 53 36.4	27 3.3	12 48.3	16 30.5	14 25.3	11 42.6	8 19.1	5 1.3	0 6.2	13 2.5	15 10.5	15 40.2
20 S	15 57 33.0	28 3.9	12 45.1	29 21.0	15 50.9	12 57.9	8 34.5	4 56.2	0 8.5	13 6.2	15 12.7	15 42.1
21 M	16 1 29.5	29 4.4	12 41.9	11♈55.7	17 15.8	14 13.1	8 49.3	4 50.9	0 10.7	13 9.8	15 14.8	15 44.0
22 T	16 5 26.1	0♐ 5.0	12 38.8	24 18.0	18 39.8	15 28.4	9 3.5	4 45.5	0 12.9	13 13.5	15 17.0	15 45.8
23 W	16 9 22.6	1 5.7	12 35.6	6♉30.6	20 3.0	16 43.7	9 17.2	4 39.9	0 14.9	13 17.1	15 19.2	15 47.6
24 T	16 13 19.2	2 6.3	12 32.4	18 35.7	21 25.1	17 59.0	9 30.3	4 34.1	0 16.8	13 20.7	15 21.4	15 49.4
25 F	16 17 15.7	3 7.0	12 29.2	0♊35.3	22 46.0	19 14.3	9 42.8	4 28.2	0 18.7	13 24.3	15 23.7	15 51.1
26 S	16 21 12.3	4 7.7	12 26.1	12 30.7	24 5.5	20 29.6	9 54.7	4 22.2	0 20.4	13 27.9	15 25.9	15 52.9
27 S	16 25 8.8	5 8.4	12 22.9	24 23.5	25 23.6	21 44.9	10 6.0	4 16.0	0 22.0	13 31.4	15 28.1	15 54.6
28 M	16 29 5.4	6 9.1	12 19.7	6♋15.2	26 39.8	23 0.3	10 16.7	4 9.7	0 23.5	13 35.0	15 30.3	15 56.3
29 T	16 33 2.0	7 9.8	12 16.5	18 7.6	27 54.1	24 15.7	10 26.7	4 3.2	0 24.9	13 38.5	15 32.6	15 57.9
30 W	16 36 58.5	8 10.6	12 13.4	0♌ 3.2	29 6.0	25 31.0	10 36.1	3 56.6	0 26.1	13 42.0	15 34.8	15 59.6
DECLINATION at NOON												
1 T	14 42 38.4	14S29.1	5S25.7	17N53.9	17S41.5	6S 4.7	21N 3.6	22N57.3	12N54.4	15S 2.6	21S 7.5	9N21.8
4 F	14 54 28.1	15 25.5	5 22.0	11 49.1	19 15.7	7 30.1	20 53.0	22 57.8	12 50.7	15 6.1	21 8.3	9 20.1
7 M	15 6 17.7	16 19.7	5 18.3	0 31.8	20 41.4	8 54.1	20 43.0	22 58.3	12 47.3	15 9.6	21 9.0	9 18.4
10 T	15 18 7.4	17 11.4	5 14.6	11S58.8	21 58.0	10 16.4	20 33.6	22 59.0	12 44.3	15 13.0	21 9.8	9 16.9
13 S	15 29 57.1	18 0.5	5 10.9	18 25.6	23 4.8	11 36.6	20 25.1	22 59.7	12 41.5	15 16.4	21 10.6	9 15.5
16 W	15 41 46.7	18 46.8	5 7.2	14 6.9	24 1.3	12 54.4	20 17.6	23 0.5	12 39.1	15 19.8	21 11.4	9 14.3
19 S	15 53 36.4	19 30.0	5 3.5	3 4.7	24 46.8	14 9.4	20 11.1	23 1.3	12 37.0	15 23.2	21 12.1	9 13.1
22 T	16 5 26.1	20 10.1	4 59.8	8N36.5	25 20.6	15 21.3	20 5.9	23 2.2	12 35.2	15 26.5	21 12.9	9 12.1
25 F	16 17 15.7	20 46.8	4 56.0	16 39.3	25 42.3	16 29.6	20 2.1	23 3.0	12 33.8	15 29.7	21 13.7	9 11.3
28 M	16 29 5.4	21 20.1	4 52.3	18 15.0	25 51.3	17 34.0	19 59.8	23 4.0	12 32.7	15 32.9	21 14.4	9 10.6

DECEMBER 1977

DAY	EPHEMERIS SIDEREAL TIME h m s	☉ ° ′	☊ ° ′	☽ ° ′	☿ ° ′	♀ ° ′	♂ ° ′	♃ ° ′	♄ ° ′	♅ ° ′	♆ ° ′	♇ ° ′
LONGITUDE at NOON												
1 T	16 40 55.1	9♐11.4	12♎10.2	12♌ 5.1	0♑15.3	26♏46.4	10♌44.8	3♋49.9	0♍27.3	13♏45.5	15♐37.1	16♎ 1.2
2 F	16 44 51.6	10 12.3	12 7.0	24 16.9	1 21.6	28 1.8	10 52.9	3R43.0	0 28.4	13 49.0	15 39.3	16 2.8
3 S	16 48 48.2	11 13.1	12 3.8	6♍43.0	2 24.3	29 17.2	11 0.3	3 36.0	0 29.3	13 52.4	15 41.6	16 4.3
4 S	16 52 44.7	12 14.0	12 0.6	19 27.9	3 23.0	0♐32.6	11 6.9	3 29.0	0 30.2	13 55.9	15 43.8	16 5.9
5 M	16 56 41.3	13 14.9	11 57.5	2♎36.2	4 17.1	1 48.1	11 12.9	3 21.8	0 30.9	13 59.3	15 46.1	16 7.4
6 T	17 0 37.9	14 15.8	11 54.3	16 11.3	5 6.0	3 3.5	11 18.1	3 14.5	0 31.5	14 2.6	15 48.4	16 8.8
7 W	17 4 34.4	15 16.8	11 51.1	0♏15.6	5 49.0	4 19.0	11 22.6	3 7.1	0 32.0	14 6.1	15 50.7	16 10.3
8 T	17 8 31.0	16 17.7	11 47.9	14 48.4	6 25.3	5 34.5	11 26.4	2 59.6	0 32.4	14 9.4	15 52.9	16 11.7
9 F	17 12 27.5	17 18.7	11 44.8	29 45.8	6 54.0	6 49.9	11 29.3	2 52.1	0 32.7	14 12.7	15 55.2	16 13.1
10 S	17 16 24.1	18 19.7	11 41.6	15♐ 0.3	7 14.2	8 5.4	11 31.5	2 44.4	0 32.9	14 16.0	15 57.5	16 14.5
11 S	17 20 20.6	19 20.7	11 38.4	0♑21.4	7 25.2	9 20.9	11 33.0	2 36.7	0 32.9	14 19.2	15 59.7	16 15.8
12 M	17 24 17.2	20 21.7	11 35.2	15 37.2	7 26.1	10 36.4	11 33.6	2 28.9	0R32.8	14 22.5	16 2.0	16 17.1
13 T	17 28 13.8	21 22.8	11 32.1	0♒37.0	7R16.1	11 51.8	11R33.4	2 21.0	0 32.7	14 25.7	16 4.2	16 18.4
14 W	17 32 10.3	22 23.8	11 28.9	15 12.6	6 54.9	13 7.3	11 32.5	2 13.1	0 32.4	14 28.8	16 6.5	16 19.6
15 T	17 36 6.9	23 24.9	11 25.7	29 19.6	6 22.0	14 22.8	11 30.7	2 5.1	0 32.0	14 32.0	16 8.7	16 20.8
16 F	17 40 3.4	24 25.9	11 22.5	12♓57.4	5 37.6	15 38.3	11 28.1	1 57.1	0 31.4	14 35.1	16 11.0	16 22.0
17 S	17 43 60.0	25 27.0	11 19.3	26 7.7	4 42.4	16 53.8	11 24.7	1 49.0	0 30.8	14 38.1	16 13.2	16 23.1
18 S	17 47 56.5	26 28.0	11 16.2	8♈54.5	3 37.5	18 9.3	11 20.4	1 40.9	0 30.1	14 41.2	16 15.5	16 24.2
19 M	17 51 53.1	27 29.1	11 13.0	21 22.1	2 24.5	19 24.8	11 15.4	1 32.8	0 29.2	14 44.2	16 17.7	16 25.3
20 T	17 55 49.6	28 30.2	11 9.8	3♉35.3	1 5.6	20 40.3	11 9.5	1 24.7	0 28.3	14 47.2	16 19.9	16 26.4
21 W	17 59 46.2	29 31.3	11 6.6	15 38.4	29♐43.5	21 55.8	11 2.8	1 16.6	0 27.2	14 50.1	16 22.1	16 27.4
22 T	18 3 42.8	0♑32.4	11 3.5	27 35.1	28 20.8	23 11.2	10 55.3	1 8.4	0 26.0	14 53.0	16 24.4	16 28.3
23 F	18 7 39.3	1 33.5	11 0.3	9♊28.4	27 0.4	24 26.7	10 46.9	1 0.3	0 24.8	14 55.9	16 26.6	16 29.3
24 S	18 11 35.9	2 34.6	10 57.1	21 20.4	25 44.8	25 42.2	10 37.7	0 52.1	0 23.4	14 58.7	16 28.7	16 30.2
25 S	18 15 32.4	3 35.7	10 53.9	3♋12.8	24 36.2	26 57.7	10 27.7	0 44.0	0 21.9	15 1.5	16 30.9	16 31.1
26 M	18 19 29.0	4 36.8	10 50.8	15 6.9	23 36.2	28 13.2	10 16.9	0 35.8	0 20.3	15 4.3	16 33.1	16 31.9
27 T	18 23 25.5	5 37.9	10 47.6	27 3.9	22 45.9	29 28.7	10 5.2	0 27.8	0 18.6	15 7.0	16 35.3	16 32.7
28 W	18 27 22.1	6 39.1	10 44.4	9♌ 5.3	22 6.1	0♑44.2	9 52.8	0 19.7	0 16.8	15 9.8	16 37.5	16 33.5
29 T	18 31 18.7	7 40.2	10 41.2	21 12.6	21 36.8	1 59.7	9 39.6	0 11.7	0 14.9	15 12.4	16 39.6	16 34.3
30 F	18 35 15.2	8 41.3	10 38.1	3♍28.4	21 18.0	3 15.2	9 25.5	0 3.7	0 12.8	15 15.0	16 41.8	16 35.0
31 S	18 39 11.8	9 42.5	10 34.9	15 55.8	21 9.3	4 30.7	9 10.7	29♊55.8	0 10.7	15 17.6	16 43.9	16 35.7
DECLINATION at NOON												
1 T	16 40 55.1	21S49.7	4S48.6	12N52.2	25S47.5	18S34.2	19N59.2	23N 4.9	12N32.0	15S36.1	21S15.2	9N10.0
4 S	16 52 44.7	22 15.6	4 44.9	2 16.0	25 31.3	19 29.9	20 0.4	23 5.8	12 31.6	15 39.1	21 15.9	9 9.5
7 W	17 4 34.4	22 37.6	4 41.2	10S10.4	25 3.4	20 20.7	20 3.4	23 6.7	12 31.6	15 42.2	21 16.6	9 9.2
10 S	17 16 24.1	22 55.6	4 37.4	18 9.8	24 25.6	21 6.2	20 8.5	23 7.6	12 31.9	15 45.1	21 17.4	9 9.1
13 T	17 28 13.8	23 9.5	4 33.7	15 20.0	23 40.0	21 46.3	20 15.7	23 8.4	12 32.6	15 47.9	21 18.1	9 9.0
16 F	17 40 3.4	23 19.3	4 30.0	4 24.1	22 48.9	22 20.5	20 24.9	23 9.2	12 33.7	15 50.7	21 18.8	9 9.2
19 M	17 51 53.1	23 24.9	4 26.3	7N35.4	21 55.1	22 48.8	20 36.2	23 9.9	12 35.1	15 53.4	21 19.4	9 9.4
22 T	18 3 42.8	23 26.3	4 22.5	16 7.6	21 4.1	23 10.8	20 49.5	23 10.6	12 36.9	15 55.9	21 20.1	9 9.8
25 S	18 15 32.4	23 23.4	4 18.8	18 27.7	20 25.0	23 26.5	21 4.7	23 11.2	12 39.0	15 58.4	21 20.7	9 10.4
28 W	18 27 22.1	23 16.3	4 15.1	13 44.1	20 5.8	23 35.7	21 21.6	23 11.7	12 41.4	16 0.8	21 21.4	9 11.0
31 S	18 39 11.8	23 5.0	4 11.3	3 37.6	20 7.9	23 38.4	21 40.1	23 12.2	12 44.2	16 3.1	21 21.9	9 11.9

JANUARY 1978

LONGITUDE at NOON

DAY	EPHEMERIS SIDEREAL TIME h m s	☉ ° '	☊ ° '	☾ ° '	☿ ° '	♀ ° '	♂ ° '	♃ ° '	♄ ° '	♅ ° '	♆ ° '	♇ ° '
1 S	18 43 8.3	10♑43.6	10♎31.7	28♍38.4	21♐10.1	5♑46.2	8♌55.2	29♊47.9	0♍ 8.5	15♏20.1	16♐46.0	16♎36.3
2 M	18 47 4.9	11 44.8	10 28.5	11♎40.3	21D19.6	7 1.7	8R38.9	29R40.0	0R 6.2	15 22.6	16 48.1	16 36.9
3 T	18 51 1.4	12 45.9	10 25.3	25 5.4	21 37.3	8 17.2	8 21.9	29 32.3	0 3.7	15 25.0	16 50.2	16 37.5
4 W	18 54 58.0	13 47.1	10 22.2	8♏56.6	22 2.3	9 32.7	8 4.1	29 24.6	0 1.2	15 27.4	16 52.3	16 38.0
5 T	18 58 54.6	14 48.2	10 19.0	23 15.1	22 34.0	10 48.2	7 45.7	29 17.0	29♌58.6	15 29.8	16 54.3	16 38.5
6 F	19 2 51.1	15 49.4	10 15.8	7♐59.2	23 11.7	12 3.7	7 26.7	29 9.4	29 55.9	15 32.1	16 56.4	16 39.0
7 S	19 6 47.7	16 50.6	10 12.6	23 3.7	23 54.8	13 19.2	7 7.1	29 2.0	29 53.1	15 34.4	16 58.4	16 39.4
8 S	19 10 44.2	17 51.8	10 9.5	8♑20.0	24 42.6	14 34.7	6 46.8	28 54.6	29 50.2	15 36.6	17 0.4	16 39.8
9 M	19 14 40.8	18 52.9	10 6.3	23 36.9	25 34.7	15 50.2	6 26.0	28 47.4	29 47.2	15 38.8	17 2.4	16 40.1
10 T	19 18 37.3	19 54.1	10 3.1	8♒42.9	26 30.7	17 5.7	6 4.7	28 40.2	29 44.1	15 40.9	17 4.4	16 40.4
11 W	19 22 33.9	20 55.2	9 59.9	23 28.3	27 30.1	18 21.2	5 42.9	28 33.2	29 40.9	15 43.0	17 6.3	16 40.7
12 T	19 26 30.5	21 56.4	9 56.8	7♓46.4	28 32.5	19 36.7	5 20.7	28 26.3	29 37.7	15 45.0	17 8.3	16 40.9
13 F	19 30 27.0	22 57.5	9 53.6	21 34.5	29 37.7	20 52.2	4 58.2	28 19.5	29 34.3	15 47.0	17 10.2	16 41.2
14 S	19 34 23.6	23 58.7	9 50.4	4♈53.0	0♑45.3	22 7.6	4 35.2	28 12.8	29 30.9	15 49.0	17 12.1	16 41.3
15 S	19 38 20.1	24 59.8	9 47.2	17 45.0	1 55.2	23 23.1	4 12.0	28 6.3	29 27.4	15 50.9	17 14.0	16 41.5
16 M	19 42 16.7	26 0.9	9 44.0	0♉14.8	3 7.1	24 38.5	3 48.5	27 59.9	29 23.8	15 52.7	17 15.9	16 41.6
17 T	19 46 13.2	27 2.0	9 40.9	12 27.6	4 20.8	25 54.0	3 24.8	27 53.6	29 20.1	15 54.5	17 17.7	16 41.6
18 W	19 50 9.8	28 3.1	9 37.7	24 28.6	5 36.1	27 9.4	3 1.0	27 47.5	29 16.5	15 56.3	17 19.6	16 41.7
19 T	19 54 6.4	29 4.2	9 34.5	6♊22.4	6 53.0	28 24.9	2 37.1	27 41.5	29 12.7	15 58.0	17 21.4	16 41.7
20 F	19 58 2.9	0♒ 5.2	9 31.3	18 13.2	8 11.2	29 40.3	2 13.1	27 35.7	29 8.8	15 59.7	17 23.2	16R41.6
21 S	20 1 59.5	1 6.2	9 28.2	0♋ 4.3	9 30.8	0♒55.7	1 49.0	27 30.0	29 4.8	16 1.3	17 25.0	16 41.6
22 S	20 5 56.0	2 7.3	9 25.0	11 58.3	10 51.5	2 11.1	1 25.0	27 24.5	29 0.8	16 2.8	17 26.7	16 41.5
23 M	20 9 52.6	3 8.3	9 21.8	23 57.0	12 13.3	3 26.5	1 1.1	27 19.2	28 56.7	16 4.3	17 28.4	16 41.3
24 T	20 13 49.1	4 9.3	9 18.6	6♌ 1.7	13 36.2	4 41.9	0 37.2	27 14.0	28 52.6	16 5.7	17 30.1	16 41.1
25 W	20 17 45.7	5 10.3	9 15.5	18 13.3	15 0.0	5 57.2	0 13.6	27 9.0	28 48.4	16 7.1	17 31.8	16 40.9
26 T	20 21 42.2	6 11.2	9 12.3	0♍32.7	16 24.8	7 12.6	29♋50.1	27 4.1	28 44.2	16 8.5	17 33.4	16 40.6
27 F	20 25 38.8	7 12.2	9 9.1	13 1.1	17 50.5	8 28.0	29 26.9	26 59.5	28 39.9	16 9.8	17 35.1	16 40.4
28 S	20 29 35.3	8 13.1	9 5.9	25 39.9	19 17.1	9 43.3	29 4.0	26 55.0	28 35.5	16 11.0	17 36.7	16 40.0
29 S	20 33 31.9	9 14.1	9 2.7	8♎31.2	20 44.5	10 58.7	28 41.4	26 50.6	28 31.1	16 12.2	17 38.3	16 39.7
30 M	20 37 28.5	10 15.0	8 59.6	21 37.4	22 12.7	12 14.0	28 19.2	26 46.5	28 26.6	16 13.3	17 39.8	16 39.3
31 T	20 41 25.0	11 15.9	8 56.4	5♏ 1.2	23 41.7	13 29.3	27 57.5	26 42.5	28 22.1	16 14.4	17 41.3	16 38.9

DECLINATION at NOON

DAY	EPHEMERIS SIDEREAL TIME h m s	☉	☊	☾	☿	♀	♂	♃	♄	♅	♆	♇
1 S	18 43 8.3	23S 0.4	4S10.1	0S23.9	20S12.6	23S37.8	21N46.5	23N12.4	12N45.2	16S 3.8	21S22.1	9N12.2
4 W	18 54 58.0	22 43.5	4 6.4	12 11.3	20 35.4	23 31.6	22 6.7	23 12.7	12 48.3	16 5.9	21 22.7	9 13.1
7 S	19 6 47.7	22 22.7	4 2.6	18 28.3	21 6.0	23 18.9	22 27.6	23 13.1	12 51.8	16 7.9	21 23.3	9 14.3
10 T	19 18 37.3	21 57.8	3 58.9	13 51.4	21 38.7	22 59.6	22 48.8	23 13.4	12 55.5	16 9.7	21 23.8	9 15.5
13 F	19 30 27.0	21 29.1	3 55.1	1 56.5	22 9.3	22 34.0	23 10.0	23 13.6	12 59.5	16 11.5	21 24.3	9 16.9
16 M	19 42 16.7	20 56.7	3 51.4	9N50.6	22 34.6	22 2.3	23 30.7	23 13.8	13 3.7	16 13.1	21 24.7	9 18.3
19 T	19 54 6.4	20 20.7	3 47.6	17 10.8	22 52.6	21 24.5	23 50.5	23 14.0	13 8.1	16 14.6	21 25.2	9 19.9
22 S	20 5 56.0	19 41.3	3 43.9	17 54.0	23 1.8	20 40.9	24 8.9	23 14.2	13 12.8	16 15.9	21 25.6	9 21.6
25 W	20 17 45.7	18 58.5	3 40.1	11 42.3	23 1.1	19 51.8	24 25.7	23 14.3	13 17.6	16 17.1	21 26.0	9 23.4
28 S	20 29 35.3	18 12.7	3 36.4	0 45.9	22 49.7	18 57.5	24 40.7	23 14.5	13 22.5	16 18.2	21 26.3	9 25.3
31 T	20 41 25.0	17 23.8	3 32.6	10S57.7	22 27.0	17 58.3	24 53.6	23 14.7	13 27.6	16 19.1	21 26.7	9 27.2

FEBRUARY 1978

LONGITUDE at NOON

DAY	EPHEMERIS SIDEREAL TIME h m s	☉ ° '	☊ ° '	☾ ° '	☿ ° '	♀ ° '	♂ ° '	♃ ° '	♄ ° '	♅ ° '	♆ ° '	♇ ° '
1 W	20 45 21.6	12♒16.8	8♎53.2	18♏44.7	25♑11.5	14♒44.7	27♋36.1	26♊38.8	28♌17.6	16♏15.4	17♐42.8	16♎38.4
2 T	20 49 18.1	13 17.7	8 50.0	2♐49.3	26 42.1	15 60.0	27R15.3	26R35.2	28R13.0	16 16.4	17 44.3	16R37.9
3 F	20 53 14.7	14 18.5	8 46.9	17 14.3	28 13.5	17 15.3	26 54.9	26 31.8	28 8.4	16 17.3	17 45.8	16 37.4
4 S	20 57 11.2	15 19.4	8 43.7	1♑56.8	29 45.6	18 30.6	26 35.2	26 28.6	28 3.7	16 18.1	17 47.2	16 36.8
5 S	21 1 7.8	16 20.2	8 40.5	16 51.0	1♒18.4	19 45.9	26 16.0	26 25.6	27 59.0	16 18.9	17 48.6	16 36.2
6 M	21 5 4.3	17 21.1	8 37.3	1♒49.0	2 52.1	21 1.2	25 57.4	26 22.8	27 54.3	16 19.7	17 49.9	16 35.6
7 T	21 9 0.9	18 21.9	8 34.1	16 41.4	4 26.5	22 16.4	25 39.5	26 20.1	27 49.5	16 20.4	17 51.3	16 34.9
8 W	21 12 57.5	19 22.7	8 31.0	1♓19.6	6 1.7	23 31.7	25 22.3	26 17.8	27 44.8	16 21.1	17 52.6	16 34.3
9 T	21 16 54.0	20 23.5	8 27.8	15 36.4	7 37.6	24 47.0	25 5.8	26 15.5	27 40.0	16 21.6	17 53.9	16 33.6
10 F	21 20 50.6	21 24.2	8 24.6	29 27.6	9 14.4	26 2.2	24 49.9	26 13.5	27 35.2	16 22.2	17 55.2	16 32.8
11 S	21 24 47.1	22 24.9	8 21.4	12♈51.9	10 51.9	27 17.4	24 34.9	26 11.7	27 30.4	16 22.6	17 56.4	16 32.0
12 S	21 28 43.7	23 25.6	8 18.3	25 50.4	12 30.3	28 32.6	24 20.5	26 10.1	27 25.5	16 23.0	17 57.6	16 31.2
13 M	21 32 40.2	24 26.3	8 15.1	8♉26.2	14 9.5	29 47.8	24 6.9	26 8.6	27 20.7	16 23.4	17 58.7	16 30.4
14 T	21 36 36.8	25 26.9	8 11.9	20 43.6	15 49.6	1♓ 3.0	23 54.1	26 7.4	27 15.8	16 23.7	17 59.9	16 29.5
15 W	21 40 33.3	26 27.5	8 8.7	2♊47.4	17 30.5	2 18.1	23 42.1	26 6.4	27 10.9	16 23.9	18 1.0	16 28.6
16 T	21 44 29.9	27 28.1	8 5.5	14 42.7	19 12.3	3 33.2	23 30.9	26 5.6	27 6.1	16 24.1	18 2.0	16 27.7
17 F	21 48 26.4	28 28.6	8 2.4	26 34.3	20 54.9	4 48.3	23 20.4	26 5.0	27 1.2	16 24.3	18 3.1	16 26.7
18 S	21 52 23.0	29 29.1	7 59.2	8♋26.4	22 38.5	6 3.4	23 10.8	26 4.6	26 56.4	16 24.4	18 4.1	16 25.7
19 S	21 56 19.5	0♓29.6	7 56.0	20 22.7	24 23.0	7 18.5	23 2.0	26 4.4	26 51.5	16 24.4	18 5.1	16 24.7
20 M	22 0 16.1	1 30.1	7 52.8	2♌26.2	26 8.4	8 33.6	22 53.9	26 4.4	26 46.7	16 24.4	18 6.0	16 23.7
21 T	22 4 12.6	2 30.5	7 49.7	14 39.0	27 54.7	9 48.6	22 46.7	26D 4.5	26 41.8	16R24.3	18 6.9	16 22.6
22 W	22 8 9.2	3 30.9	7 46.5	27 2.6	29 42.0	11 3.6	22 40.2	26 4.9	26 37.0	16 24.1	18 7.8	16 21.5
23 T	22 12 5.8	4 31.3	7 43.3	9♍37.7	1♓30.2	12 18.6	22 34.5	26 5.5	26 32.2	16 23.9	18 8.7	16 20.4
24 F	22 16 2.3	5 31.6	7 40.1	22 24.8	3 19.4	13 33.6	22 29.7	26 6.3	26 27.5	16 23.7	18 9.5	16 19.2
25 S	22 19 58.9	6 31.9	7 36.9	5♎23.9	5 9.5	14 48.6	22 25.6	26 7.3	26 22.7	16 23.4	18 10.3	16 18.1
26 S	22 23 55.4	7 32.2	7 33.8	18 35.1	7 0.5	16 3.5	22 22.2	26 8.5	26 18.0	16 23.0	18 11.0	16 16.9
27 M	22 27 52.0	8 32.5	7 30.6	1♏58.6	8 52.4	17 18.4	22 19.7	26 9.9	26 13.3	16 22.6	18 11.8	16 15.6
28 T	22 31 48.5	9 32.8	7 27.4	15 34.7	10 45.1	18 33.3	22 17.9	26 11.4	26 8.6	16 22.2	18 12.4	16 14.4

DECLINATION at NOON

DAY	EPHEMERIS SIDEREAL TIME h m s	☉	☊	☾	☿	♀	♂	♃	♄	♅	♆	♇
1 W	20 45 21.6	17S 6.9	3S31.4	14S 9.1	22S16.9	17S37.6	24N57.4	23N14.7	13N29.3	16S19.4	21S26.8	9N27.9
4 S	20 57 11.2	16 14.5	3 27.6	18 20.5	21 38.6	16 32.3	25 7.5	23 14.9	13 34.5	16 20.2	21 27.1	9 30.0
7 T	21 9 0.9	15 19.4	3 23.9	12 4.7	20 48.2	15 22.8	25 15.3	23 15.2	13 39.8	16 20.8	21 27.3	9 32.1
10 F	21 20 50.6	14 22.1	3 20.1	0N22.9	19 45.6	14 9.6	25 21.1	23 15.5	13 45.1	16 21.2	21 27.6	9 34.3
13 M	21 32 40.2	13 22.6	3 16.4	11 44.1	18 30.5	12 52.9	25 24.7	23 15.8	13 50.4	16 21.6	21 27.8	9 36.6
16 T	21 44 29.9	12 21.1	3 12.6	17 47.7	17 2.9	11 33.1	25 26.5	23 16.1	13 55.7	16 21.7	21 28.0	9 38.9
19 S	21 56 19.5	11 17.9	3 8.8	16 55.6	15 22.8	10 10.5	25 26.5	23 16.5	14 0.9	16 21.8	21 28.1	9 41.3
22 W	22 8 9.2	10 13.1	3 5.1	9 24.8	13 30.1	8 45.5	25 25.0	23 17.0	14 6.1	16 21.7	21 28.2	9 43.7
25 S	22 19 58.9	9 6.9	3 1.3	2S11.8	11 25.1	7 18.5	25 21.9	23 17.5	14 11.1	16 21.4	21 28.3	9 46.1
28 T	22 31 48.5	7 59.4	2 57.5	13 18.6	9 8.3	5 49.7	25 17.6	23 18.0	14 16.1	16 21.0	21 28.4	9 48.5

MARCH 1978

DAY	EPHEMERIS SIDEREAL TIME	☉	☊	☽	☿	♀	♂	♃	♄	♅	♆	♇
	h m s	° ′	° ′	° ′	° ′	° ′	° ′	° ′	° ′	° ′	° ′	° ′
LONGITUDE at NOON												
1 W	22 35 45.1	10♓33.0	7♎24.2	29♏23.6	12♓38.8	19♓48.3	22♋16.9	26♊13.2	26♌ 4.0	16♏21.7	18♐13.2	16♎13.2
2 T	22 39 41.6	11 33.2	7 21.1	13♐24.9	14 33.1	21 3.1	22R16.5	26 15.2	25R59.4	16R21.1	18 13.8	16R11.9
3 F	22 43 38.2	12 33.4	7 17.9	27 37.7	16 28.1	22 18.0	22D17.0	26 17.4	25 54.8	16 20.5	18 14.4	16 10.6
4 S	22 47 34.7	13 33.5	7 14.7	11♑59.8	18 23.6	23 32.8	22 18.1	26 19.7	25 50.3	16 19.9	18 14.9	16 9.2
5 S	22 51 31.3	14 33.6	7 11.5	26 27.8	20 19.6	24 47.6	22 20.0	26 22.2	25 45.8	16 19.1	18 15.5	16 7.9
6 M	22 55 27.8	15 33.7	7 8.3	10♒57.0	22 15.9	26 2.4	22 22.6	26 25.0	25 41.4	16 18.4	18 15.9	16 6.5
7 T	22 59 24.4	16 33.8	7 5.2	25 21.8	24 12.3	27 17.2	22 25.9	26 27.9	25 37.0	16 17.5	18 16.4	16 5.1
8 W	23 3 20.9	17 33.8	7 2.0	9♓36.6	26 8.6	28 32.0	22 29.9	26 31.0	25 32.7	16 16.6	18 16.8	16 3.7
9 T	23 7 17.5	18 33.8	6 58.8	23 36.2	28 4.6	29 46.7	22 34.6	26 34.3	25 28.4	16 15.7	18 17.2	16 2.3
10 F	23 11 14.0	19 33.8	6 55.6	7♈16.9	29 59.9	1♈ 1.4	22 39.9	26 37.7	25 24.2	16 14.7	18 17.6	16 0.8
11 S	23 15 10.6	20 33.7	6 52.5	20 36.6	1♈54.3	2 16.1	22 45.9	26 41.4	25 20.0	16 13.7	18 17.9	15 59.3
12 S	23 19 7.1	21 33.6	6 49.3	3♉34.8	3 47.3	3 30.8	22 52.5	26 45.2	25 15.9	16 12.6	18 18.2	15 57.9
13 M	23 23 3.7	22 33.5	6 46.1	16 13.1	5 38.7	4 45.4	22 59.8	26 49.3	25 11.8	16 11.5	18 18.4	15 56.4
14 T	23 27 0.2	23 33.3	6 42.9	28 34.0	7 28.0	5 60.0	23 7.7	26 53.5	25 7.8	16 10.3	18 18.6	15 54.8
15 W	23 30 56.8	24 33.1	6 39.7	10♊41.2	9 14.6	7 14.6	23 16.3	26 57.8	25 3.9	16 9.1	18 18.8	15 53.3
16 T	23 34 53.3	25 32.9	6 36.6	22 39.1	10 58.3	8 29.1	23 25.4	27 2.4	25 0.1	16 7.9	18 19.0	15 51.8
17 F	23 38 49.9	26 32.6	6 33.4	4♋32.3	12 38.4	9 43.7	23 35.1	27 7.1	24 56.3	16 6.5	18 19.1	15 50.2
18 S	23 42 46.5	27 32.3	6 30.2	16 25.5	14 14.5	10 58.1	23 45.4	27 12.0	24 52.6	16 5.2	18 19.2	15 48.6
19 S	23 46 43.0	28 31.9	6 27.0	28 23.2	15 46.2	12 12.6	23 56.2	27 17.0	24 49.0	16 3.8	18 19.2	15 47.1
20 M	23 50 39.6	29 31.5	6 23.8	10♌29.5	17 12.9	13 27.0	24 7.6	27 22.3	24 45.4	16 2.3	18 19.3	15 45.5
21 T	23 54 36.1	0♈31.1	6 20.7	22 47.8	18 34.2	14 41.5	24 19.5	27 27.7	24 41.9	16 0.8	18R19.2	15 43.9
22 W	23 58 32.7	1 30.7	6 17.5	5♍20.7	19 49.8	15 55.9	24 32.0	27 33.3	24 38.6	15 59.4	18 19.2	15 42.3
23 T	0 2 29.2	2 30.2	6 14.3	18 9.9	20 59.2	17 10.2	24 45.0	27 39.0	24 35.3	15 57.8	18 19.2	15 40.7
24 F	0 6 25.8	3 29.7	6 11.1	1♎16.0	22 2.1	18 24.5	24 58.4	27 44.9	24 32.1	15 56.2	18 19.1	15 39.1
25 S	0 10 22.3	4 29.1	6 8.0	14 38.4	22 58.2	19 38.8	25 12.4	27 50.9	24 28.9	15 54.5	18 18.9	15 37.4
26 S	0 14 18.9	5 28.5	6 4.8	28 15.8	23 47.3	20 53.1	25 26.8	27 57.1	24 25.8	15 52.8	18 18.7	15 35.8
27 M	0 18 15.4	6 27.9	6 1.6	12♏ 6.0	24 29.2	22 7.3	25 41.7	28 3.4	24 22.9	15 51.1	18 18.5	15 34.1
28 T	0 22 12.0	7 27.2	5 58.4	26 6.3	25 3.7	23 21.5	25 57.0	28 9.9	24 20.0	15 49.3	18 18.3	15 32.4
29 W	0 26 8.5	8 26.5	5 55.2	10♐13.8	25 30.8	24 35.7	26 12.8	28 16.6	24 17.2	15 47.5	18 18.0	15 30.8
30 T	0 30 5.1	9 25.8	5 52.1	24 25.6	25 50.5	25 49.9	26 29.1	28 23.4	24 14.5	15 45.6	18 17.7	15 29.1
31 F	0 34 1.6	10 25.0	5 48.9	8♑39.0	26 2.6	27 4.0	26 45.7	28 30.3	24 11.8	15 43.8	18 17.3	15 27.4
DECLINATION at NOON												
1 W	22 35 45.1	7S36.7	2S56.3	15S54.8	8S20.1	5S19.8	25N15.8	23N18.2	14N17.7	16S20.9	21S28.4	9N49.3
4 S	22 47 34.7	6 27.8	2 52.5	17 42.4	5 49.1	3 49.2	25 9.9	23 18.8	14 22.4	16 20.3	21 28.4	9 51.7
7 T	22 59 24.4	5 18.2	2 48.8	9 50.7	3 9.5	2 17.7	25 2.8	23 19.5	14 27.0	16 19.6	21 28.4	9 54.2
10 F	23 11 14.0	4 7.9	2 45.0	2N46.3	0 24.6	0 45.6	24 54.6	23 20.1	14 31.4	16 18.8	21 28.4	9 56.6
13 M	23 23 3.7	2 57.2	2 41.2	13 24.8	2N21.0	0N46.8	24 45.5	23 20.8	14 35.6	16 17.8	21 28.4	9 59.0
16 T	23 34 53.3	1 46.2	2 37.5	18 6.4	5 1.1	2 19.2	24 35.5	23 21.5	14 39.6	16 16.8	21 28.3	10 1.4
19 S	23 46 43.0	0 35.0	2 33.7	15 42.1	7 28.4	3 51.1	24 24.5	23 22.2	14 43.3	16 15.6	21 28.2	10 3.7
22 W	23 58 32.7	0N36.1	2 29.9	7 2.8	9 35.9	5 22.4	24 12.7	23 22.9	14 46.7	16 14.3	21 28.0	10 6.0
25 S	0 10 22.3	1 47.0	2 26.1	5S 1.6	11 17.3	6 52.5	24 0.0	23 23.5	14 49.8	16 12.9	21 27.9	10 8.2
28 T	0 22 12.0	2 57.5	2 22.4	15 19.5	12 27.8	8 21.3	23 46.5	23 24.2	14 52.7	16 11.3	21 27.7	10 10.4
31 F	0 34 1.6	4 7.5	2 18.6	17 53.4	13 4.3	9 48.4	23 32.0	23 24.8	14 55.3	16 9.7	21 27.5	10 12.5

APRIL 1978

DAY	EPHEMERIS SIDEREAL TIME	☉	☊	☽	☿	♀	♂	♃	♄	♅	♆	♇
LONGITUDE at NOON												
1 S	0 37 58.2	11♈24.2	5♎45.7	22♑51.5	26♈ 7.5	28♈18.1	27♋ 2.8	28♊37.4	24♌ 9.3	15♏41.8	18♐17.0	15♎25.8
2 S	0 41 54.7	12 23.4	5 42.5	7♒ 0.7	26R 5.2	29 32.1	27 20.3	28 44.6	24R 6.9	15R39.9	18R16.6	15R24.1
3 M	0 45 51.3	13 22.6	5 39.4	21 4.3	25 56.0	0♉46.2	27 38.2	28 52.0	24 4.5	15 37.9	18 16.1	15 22.4
4 T	0 49 47.8	14 21.7	5 36.2	5♓ 0.1	25 40.3	2 0.2	27 56.5	28 59.5	24 2.3	15 35.9	18 15.6	15 20.7
5 W	0 53 44.4	15 20.8	5 33.0	18 45.8	25 18.5	3 14.2	28 15.2	29 7.1	24 0.2	15 33.8	18 15.1	15 19.0
6 T	0 57 40.9	16 19.9	5 29.8	2♈19.4	24 51.1	4 28.1	28 34.3	29 14.9	23 58.1	15 31.7	18 14.6	15 17.3
7 F	1 1 37.5	17 18.9	5 26.6	15 39.0	24 18.8	5 42.0	28 53.7	29 22.9	23 56.2	15 29.6	18 14.1	15 15.6
8 S	1 5 34.0	18 17.9	5 23.5	28 43.3	23 42.3	6 55.9	29 13.5	29 30.9	23 54.3	15 27.5	18 13.5	15 14.0
9 S	1 9 30.6	19 16.9	5 20.3	11♉31.9	23 2.3	8 9.8	29 33.7	29 39.1	23 52.6	15 25.3	18 12.8	15 12.3
10 M	1 13 27.1	20 15.8	5 17.1	24 5.1	22 19.6	9 23.6	29 54.2	29 47.4	23 51.0	15 23.1	18 12.2	15 10.6
11 T	1 17 23.7	21 14.7	5 13.9	6♊24.2	21 35.1	10 37.4	0♌15.0	29 55.9	23 49.4	15 20.9	18 11.5	15 8.9
12 W	1 21 20.2	22 13.6	5 10.7	18 31.5	20 49.8	11 51.2	0 36.3	0♋ 4.5	23 48.0	15 18.7	18 10.8	15 7.3
13 T	1 25 16.8	23 12.4	5 7.6	0♋30.0	20 4.5	13 4.9	0 57.8	0 13.2	23 46.7	15 16.4	18 10.1	15 5.6
14 F	1 29 13.4	24 11.2	5 4.4	12 23.6	19 19.9	14 18.6	1 19.6	0 22.0	23 45.5	15 14.1	18 9.3	15 4.0
15 S	1 33 9.9	25 10.0	5 1.2	24 16.6	18 36.9	15 32.2	1 41.7	0 30.9	23 44.4	15 11.8	18 8.5	15 2.3
16 S	1 37 6.5	26 8.7	4 58.0	6♌13.8	17 56.2	16 45.9	2 4.2	0 40.0	23 43.4	15 9.5	18 7.7	15 0.7
17 M	1 41 3.0	27 7.3	4 54.9	18 19.7	17 18.5	17 59.4	2 26.9	0 49.1	23 42.5	15 7.1	18 6.9	14 59.0
18 T	1 44 59.6	28 6.0	4 51.7	0♍39.0	16 44.3	19 13.0	2 49.9	0 58.4	23 41.7	15 4.7	18 6.0	14 57.4
19 W	1 48 56.1	29 4.6	4 48.5	13 15.7	16 14.1	20 26.5	3 13.2	1 7.8	23 41.0	15 2.3	18 5.1	14 55.8
20 T	1 52 52.7	0♉ 3.1	4 45.3	26 12.7	15 48.3	21 39.9	3 36.8	1 17.3	23 40.4	14 59.9	18 4.1	14 54.2
21 F	1 56 49.2	1 1.7	4 42.1	9♎31.9	15 27.1	22 53.3	4 0.6	1 26.9	23 39.9	14 57.5	18 3.2	14 52.5
22 S	2 0 45.8	2 0.2	4 39.0	23 13.3	15 10.7	24 6.7	4 24.7	1 36.6	23 39.5	14 55.0	18 2.2	14 51.0
23 S	2 4 42.3	2 58.6	4 35.8	7♏15.0	14 59.2	25 20.1	4 49.1	1 46.4	23 39.3	14 52.6	18 1.2	14 49.4
24 M	2 8 38.9	3 57.1	4 32.6	21 33.3	14 52.8	26 33.4	5 13.7	1 56.3	23 39.1	14 50.1	18 0.1	14 47.8
25 T	2 12 35.4	4 55.5	4 29.4	6♐ 2.6	14 51.4	27 46.7	5 38.6	2 6.4	23 39.1	14 47.6	17 59.1	14 46.2
26 W	2 16 32.0	5 53.8	4 26.3	20 36.8	14D55.0	28 59.9	6 3.6	2 16.5	23 39.1	14 45.1	17 58.0	14 44.7
27 T	2 20 28.5	6 52.2	4 23.1	5♑ 9.6	15 3.4	0♊13.1	6 29.0	2 26.7	23D39.3	14 42.6	17 56.9	14 43.2
28 F	2 24 25.1	7 50.5	4 19.9	19 35.8	15 16.7	1 26.2	6 54.5	2 37.0	23 39.6	14 40.1	17 55.8	14 41.6
29 S	2 28 21.6	8 48.8	4 16.7	3♒51.3	15 34.6	2 39.4	7 20.3	2 47.4	23 39.9	14 37.6	17 54.6	14 40.1
30 S	2 32 18.2	9 47.1	4 13.5	17 53.8	15 57.1	3 52.5	7 46.3	2 57.9	23 40.4	14 35.1	17 53.4	14 38.6
DECLINATION at NOON												
1 S	0 37 58.2	4N30.7	2S17.3	16S30.9	13N 8.5	10N17.0	23N27.0	23N25.0	14N56.1	16S 9.2	21S27.4	10N13.2
4 T	0 49 47.8	5 39.8	2 13.5	7 8.7	12 57.5	11 41.3	23 11.4	23 25.5	14 58.3	16 7.4	21 27.2	10 15.2
7 F	1 1 37.5	6 48.0	2 9.8	5N20.1	12 13.1	13 3.1	22 54.9	23 26.0	15 0.2	16 5.6	21 26.9	10 17.1
10 M	1 13 27.1	7 55.1	2 6.0	14 59.0	11 1.3	14 22.1	22 37.5	23 26.4	15 1.7	16 3.7	21 26.7	10 18.9
13 T	1 25 16.8	9 1.1	2 2.2	18 12.2	9 32.6	15 37.9	22 19.2	23 26.7	15 3.0	16 1.7	21 26.4	10 20.7
16 S	1 37 6.5	10 5.7	1 58.4	14 19.3	7 59.5	16 50.2	21 60.0	23 26.9	15 3.9	15 59.7	21 26.0	10 22.3
19 W	1 48 56.1	11 8.8	1 54.6	4 43.0	6 34.0	17 58.7	21 39.8	23 27.1	15 4.4	15 57.6	21 25.7	10 23.8
22 S	2 0 45.8	12 10.2	1 50.9	7S33.9	5 25.1	19 3.0	21 18.7	23 27.1	15 4.7	15 55.5	21 25.4	10 25.2
25 T	2 12 35.4	13 9.8	1 47.1	16 51.0	4 37.9	20 2.8	20 56.7	23 27.0	15 4.6	15 53.4	21 25.0	10 26.5
28 F	2 24 25.1	14 7.5	1 43.3	17 0.6	4 14.0	20 57.8	20 33.7	23 26.7	15 4.2	15 51.2	21 24.6	10 27.6

MAY 1978

LONGITUDE at NOON

DAY	EPHEMERIS SIDEREAL TIME h m s	☉ ° ′	☊ ° ′	☽ ° ′	☿ ° ′	♀ ° ′	♂ ° ′	♃ ° ′	♄ ° ′	♅ ° ′	♆ ° ′	♇ ° ′
1 M	2 36 14.8	10♉45.3	4♎10.4	1♓42.5	16♈23.9	5♊ 5.5	8♌12.5	3♋ 8.5	23♌41.0	14♏32.6	17♐52.2	14♎37.2
2 T	2 40 11.3	11 43.6	4 7.2	15 17.2	16 55.0	6 18.5	8 39.0	3 19.2	23 41.7	14R30.0	17R51.0	14R35.7
3 W	2 44 7.9	12 41.8	4 4.0	28 38.6	17 30.1	7 31.6	9 5.7	3 30.0	23 42.5	14 27.5	17 49.8	14 34.3
4 T	2 48 4.4	13 40.0	4 0.8	11♈47.2	18 9.1	8 44.5	9 32.6	3 40.9	23 43.4	14 25.0	17 48.6	14 32.9
5 F	2 52 1.0	14 38.1	3 57.7	24 43.7	18 51.8	9 57.4	9 59.6	3 51.8	23 44.5	14 22.4	17 47.3	14 31.5
6 S	2 55 57.5	15 36.3	3 54.5	7♉28.4	19 38.2	11 10.3	10 26.9	4 2.8	23 45.6	14 19.9	17 46.0	14 30.1
7 S	2 59 54.1	16 34.4	3 51.3	20 1.6	20 27.9	12 23.1	10 54.4	4 13.9	23 46.8	14 17.4	17 44.7	14 28.7
8 M	3 3 50.6	17 32.4	3 48.1	2♊24.0	21 21.0	13 35.9	11 22.0	4 25.1	23 48.1	14 14.8	17 43.3	14 27.4
9 T	3 7 47.2	18 30.5	3 44.9	14 36.1	22 17.3	14 48.7	11 49.9	4 36.4	23 49.6	14 12.3	17 42.0	14 26.0
10 W	3 11 43.7	19 28.5	3 41.8	26 39.3	23 16.7	16 1.4	12 17.9	4 47.8	23 51.1	14 9.8	17 40.6	14 24.7
11 T	3 15 40.3	20 26.5	3 38.6	8♋35.7	24 19.0	17 14.1	12 46.1	4 59.2	23 52.7	14 7.2	17 39.2	14 23.5
12 F	3 19 36.9	21 24.4	3 35.4	20 28.0	25 24.2	18 26.7	13 14.5	5 10.7	23 54.5	14 4.7	17 37.8	14 22.2
13 S	3 23 33.4	22 22.3	3 32.2	2♌19.7	26 32.2	19 39.3	13 43.1	5 22.2	23 56.3	14 2.2	17 36.4	14 21.0
14 S	3 27 30.0	23 20.2	3 29.1	14 15.1	27 42.9	20 51.8	14 11.9	5 33.9	23 58.3	13 59.7	17 35.0	14 19.7
15 M	3 31 26.5	24 18.1	3 25.9	26 18.7	28 56.2	22 4.3	14 40.8	5 45.6	24 0.3	13 57.2	17 33.5	14 18.5
16 T	3 35 23.1	25 15.9	3 22.7	8♍35.6	0♉12.1	23 16.7	15 9.9	5 57.4	24 2.5	13 54.8	17 32.0	14 17.4
17 W	3 39 19.6	26 13.8	3 19.5	21 10.7	1 30.5	24 29.1	15 39.1	6 9.2	24 4.7	13 52.3	17 30.6	14 16.2
18 T	3 43 16.2	27 11.5	3 16.4	4♎ 8.3	2 51.4	25 41.5	16 8.5	6 21.1	24 7.1	13 49.8	17 29.1	14 15.1
19 F	3 47 12.7	28 9.3	3 13.2	17 31.6	4 14.7	26 53.8	16 38.0	6 33.1	24 9.5	13 47.4	17 27.6	14 14.0
20 S	3 51 9.3	29 7.0	3 10.0	1♏22.2	5 40.4	28 6.0	17 7.7	6 45.1	24 12.1	13 45.0	17 26.1	14 12.9
21 S	3 55 5.9	0♊ 4.7	3 6.8	15 38.8	7 8.5	29 18.2	17 37.6	6 57.2	24 14.7	13 42.6	17 24.5	14 11.9
22 M	3 59 2.4	1 2.4	3 3.6	0♐17.4	8 38.9	0♋30.4	18 7.5	7 9.3	24 17.5	13 40.2	17 23.0	14 10.9
23 T	4 2 59.0	2 0.1	3 0.5	15 11.2	10 11.7	1 42.5	18 37.7	7 21.5	24 20.3	13 37.8	17 21.5	14 9.9
24 W	4 6 55.5	2 57.7	2 57.3	0♑11.2	11 46.8	2 54.6	19 8.0	7 33.9	24 23.3	13 35.5	17 19.9	14 8.9
25 T	4 10 52.1	3 55.4	2 54.1	15 8.1	13 24.2	4 6.6	19 38.4	7 46.2	24 26.3	13 33.2	17 18.4	14 8.0
26 F	4 14 48.6	4 53.0	2 50.9	29 53.6	15 3.9	5 18.5	20 8.9	7 58.5	24 29.4	13 30.9	17 16.8	14 7.1
27 S	4 18 45.2	5 50.6	2 47.8	14♒21.6	16 46.0	6 30.4	20 39.6	8 11.0	24 32.6	13 28.6	17 15.2	14 6.2
28 S	4 22 41.7	6 48.1	2 44.6	28 28.8	18 30.3	7 42.3	21 10.4	8 23.4	24 35.9	13 26.3	17 13.6	14 5.3
29 M	4 26 38.3	7 45.7	2 41.4	12♓14.4	20 16.9	8 54.1	21 41.3	8 36.0	24 39.3	13 24.1	17 12.1	14 4.5
30 T	4 30 34.9	8 43.2	2 38.2	25 39.6	22 5.8	10 5.8	22 12.4	8 48.5	24 42.8	13 21.9	17 10.5	14 3.7
31 W	4 34 31.4	9 40.8	2 35.1	8♈46.6	23 57.0	11 17.5	22 43.6	9 1.2	24 46.4	13 19.7	17 8.8	14 2.9

DECLINATION at NOON

DAY	SIDEREAL TIME	☉	☊	☽	☿	♀	♂	♃	♄	♅	♆	♇
1 M	2 36 14.8	15N 3.1	1S39.5	8S 9.5	4N12.8	21N47.7	20N 9.8	23N26.3	15N 3.5	15S49.0	21S24.2	10N28.7
4 T	2 48 4.4	15 56.5	1 35.7	4N 8.3	4 32.7	22 32.3	19 44.9	23 25.8	15 2.5	15 46.8	21 23.8	10 29.5
7 S	2 59 54.1	16 47.5	1 32.0	14 15.1	5 11.4	23 11.2	19 19.0	23 25.1	15 1.1	15 44.5	21 23.4	10 30.3
10 W	3 11 43.7	17 36.0	1 28.2	18 19.1	6 6.6	23 44.3	18 52.2	23 24.2	14 59.4	15 42.3	21 23.0	10 30.9
13 S	3 23 33.4	18 21.8	1 24.4	15 12.2	7 16.2	24 11.4	18 24.4	23 23.2	14 57.4	15 40.1	21 22.5	10 31.4
16 T	3 35 23.1	19 4.8	1 20.6	6 15.1	8 37.9	24 32.3	17 55.7	23 22.0	14 55.2	15 37.9	21 22.1	10 31.7
19 F	3 47 12.7	19 45.0	1 16.8	5S49.4	10 10.0	24 46.8	17 26.1	23 20.6	14 52.6	15 35.8	21 21.6	10 32.0
22 M	3 59 2.4	20 22.0	1 13.0	16 5.4	11 50.4	24 55.0	16 55.5	23 19.0	14 49.7	15 33.7	21 21.2	10 32.0
25 T	4 10 52.1	20 56.0	1 9.2	17 37.9	13 37.1	24 56.7	16 24.1	23 17.2	14 46.5	15 31.6	21 20.7	10 31.9
28 S	4 22 41.7	21 26.7	1 5.4	9 14.4	15 27.8	24 52.0	15 51.7	23 15.2	14 43.1	15 29.6	21 20.3	10 31.7
31 W	4 34 31.4	21 54.1	1 1.7	3N 4.3	17 19.5	24 40.9	15 18.5	23 13.0	14 39.3	15 27.7	21 19.8	10 31.3

JUNE 1978

LONGITUDE at NOON

DAY	SIDEREAL TIME	☉	☊	☽	☿	♀	♂	♃	♄	♅	♆	♇
1 T	4 38 28.0	10♊38.3	2♎31.9	21♈37.9	25♉50.4	12♋29.2	23♌14.9	9♋13.8	24♌50.0	13♏17.5	17♐ 7.2	14♎ 2.2
2 F	4 42 24.5	11 35.8	2 28.7	4♉16.2	27 46.0	13 40.8	23 46.4	9 26.5	24 53.8	13R15.4	17R 5.6	14R 1.5
3 S	4 46 21.1	12 33.3	2 25.5	16 43.6	29 43.7	14 52.3	24 18.0	9 39.3	24 57.6	13 13.3	17 4.0	14 0.8
4 S	4 50 17.6	13 30.8	2 22.3	29 1.8	1♊43.6	16 3.8	24 49.7	9 52.1	25 1.5	13 11.2	17 2.4	14 0.1
5 M	4 54 14.2	14 28.2	2 19.2	11♊12.0	3 45.4	17 15.3	25 21.5	10 4.9	25 5.5	13 9.1	17 0.8	13 59.5
6 T	4 58 10.8	15 25.7	2 16.0	23 15.3	5 49.2	18 26.7	25 53.4	10 17.8	25 9.6	13 7.1	16 59.1	13 58.9
7 W	5 2 7.3	16 23.1	2 12.8	5♋12.9	7 54.6	19 38.0	26 25.5	10 30.7	25 13.8	13 5.1	16 57.5	13 58.4
8 T	5 6 3.9	17 20.5	2 9.6	17 6.0	10 1.7	20 49.3	26 57.7	10 43.7	25 18.1	13 3.2	16 55.9	13 57.8
9 F	5 10 0.4	18 17.9	2 6.5	28 56.8	12 10.2	22 0.5	27 30.0	10 56.7	25 22.4	13 1.2	16 54.3	13 57.3
10 S	5 13 57.0	19 15.3	2 3.3	10♌47.7	14 19.9	23 11.6	28 2.4	11 9.7	25 26.8	12 59.4	16 52.6	13 56.9
11 S	5 17 53.5	20 12.7	2 0.1	22 42.2	16 30.6	24 22.7	28 34.9	11 22.8	25 31.3	12 57.5	16 51.0	13 56.4
12 M	5 21 50.1	21 10.0	1 56.9	4♍44.2	18 42.0	25 33.8	29 7.5	11 35.8	25 35.9	12 55.7	16 49.4	13 56.0
13 T	5 25 46.6	22 7.4	1 53.8	16 58.6	20 53.8	26 44.7	29 40.2	11 49.0	25 40.6	12 53.9	16 47.8	13 55.7
14 W	5 29 43.2	23 4.7	1 50.6	29 30.3	23 5.9	27 55.6	0♍13.1	12 2.2	25 45.3	12 52.2	16 46.2	13 55.4
15 T	5 33 39.8	24 2.0	1 47.4	12♎24.1	25 17.8	29 6.5	0 46.1	12 15.3	25 50.2	12 50.5	16 44.6	13 55.1
16 F	5 37 36.3	24 59.3	1 44.2	25 44.4	27 29.3	0♌17.2	1 19.1	12 28.5	25 55.0	12 48.8	16 43.0	13 54.8
17 S	5 41 32.9	25 56.6	1 41.0	9♏33.9	29 40.2	1 27.9	1 52.2	12 41.8	26 0.0	12 47.2	16 41.4	13 54.6
18 S	5 45 29.4	26 53.9	1 37.9	23 52.9	1♋50.2	2 38.5	2 25.5	12 55.0	26 5.0	12 45.6	16 39.8	13 54.4
19 M	5 49 26.0	27 51.1	1 34.7	8♐38.4	3 59.1	3 49.0	2 58.8	13 8.3	26 10.1	12 44.1	16 38.2	13 54.2
20 T	5 53 22.5	28 48.3	1 31.5	23 43.8	6 6.8	4 59.5	3 32.2	13 21.6	26 15.3	12 42.6	16 36.6	13 54.0
21 W	5 57 19.1	29 45.6	1 28.3	8♑59.5	8 12.9	6 9.8	4 5.7	13 34.9	26 20.5	12 41.1	16 35.0	13 53.9
22 T	6 1 15.7	0♋42.8	1 25.2	24 14.3	10 17.4	7 20.1	4 39.3	13 48.2	26 25.9	12 39.7	16 33.5	13 53.9
23 F	6 5 12.2	1 40.0	1 22.0	9♒17.5	12 20.2	8 30.3	5 13.0	14 1.6	26 31.2	12 38.3	16 31.9	13 53.8
24 S	6 9 8.8	2 37.2	1 18.8	24 0.7	14 21.2	9 40.5	5 46.8	14 15.0	26 36.7	12 37.0	16 30.4	13 53.8
25 S	6 13 5.3	3 34.5	1 15.6	8♓18.9	16 20.2	10 50.5	6 20.7	14 28.4	26 42.2	12 35.7	16 28.8	13 53.8
26 M	6 17 1.9	4 31.7	1 12.5	22 10.5	18 17.2	12 0.5	6 54.7	14 41.8	26 47.8	12 34.4	16 27.3	13D53.9
27 T	6 20 58.4	5 28.9	1 9.3	5♈36.4	20 12.2	13 10.4	7 28.8	14 55.2	26 53.4	12 33.2	16 25.8	13 54.0
28 W	6 24 55.0	6 26.1	1 6.1	18 39.4	22 5.1	14 20.2	8 2.9	15 8.6	26 59.1	12 32.1	16 24.3	13 54.1
29 T	6 28 51.6	7 23.3	1 2.9	1♉23.1	23 55.9	15 30.0	8 37.2	15 22.1	27 4.9	12 31.0	16 22.8	13 54.3
30 F	6 32 48.1	8 20.6	0 59.7	13 51.3	25 44.6	16 39.6	9 11.5	15 35.5	27 10.7	12 29.9	16 21.3	13 54.5

DECLINATION at NOON

DAY	SIDEREAL TIME	☉	☊	☽	☿	♀	♂	♃	♄	♅	♆	♇
1 T	4 38 28.0	22N 2.5	1S 0.4	6N59.1	17N56.4	24N35.8	15N 7.2	23N12.2	14N38.0	15S27.0	21S19.6	10N31.2
4 S	4 50 17.6	22 25.3	0 56.6	15 53.1	19 43.9	24 16.3	14 32.8	23 9.7	14 34.0	15 25.2	21 19.2	10 30.6
7 W	5 2 7.3	22 44.6	0 52.8	18 19.8	21 23.0	23 50.7	13 57.6	23 7.0	14 29.6	15 23.4	21 18.7	10 29.9
10 S	5 13 57.0	23 0.3	0 49.0	13 43.8	22 48.3	23 19.2	13 21.5	23 4.1	14 25.0	15 21.7	21 18.3	10 29.1
13 T	5 25 46.6	23 12.3	0 45.2	3 55.4	23 54.7	22 41.9	12 44.7	23 1.0	14 20.2	15 20.2	21 17.8	10 28.1
16 F	5 37 36.3	23 20.7	0 41.5	8S 3.8	24 37.9	21 59.1	12 7.0	22 57.7	14 15.1	15 18.7	21 17.4	10 26.9
19 M	5 49 26.0	23 25.3	0 37.7	17 11.4	24 56.1	21 11.1	11 28.6	22 54.2	14 9.8	15 17.3	21 17.0	10 25.7
22 T	6 1 15.7	23 26.2	0 33.9	16 43.2	24 49.4	20 18.1	10 49.5	22 50.4	14 4.3	15 16.1	21 16.6	10 24.3
25 S	6 13 5.3	23 23.5	0 30.1	6 38.7	24 20.1	19 20.5	10 9.7	22 46.5	13 58.6	15 14.9	21 16.2	10 22.8
28 W	6 24 55.0	23 17.0	0 26.3	5N53.5	23 31.4	18 18.6	9 29.2	22 42.3	13 52.6	15 13.9	21 15.8	10 21.2

JULY 1978

LONGITUDE at NOON

DAY	EPHEMERIS SIDEREAL TIME h m s	☉ ° ′	☊ ° ′	☽ ° ′	☿ ° ′	♀ ° ′	♂ ° ′	♃ ° ′	♄ ° ′	♅ ° ′	♆ ° ′	♇ ° ′
1 S	6 36 44.7	9♋17.8	0♎56.6	26♉ 7.6	27♋31.2	17♌49.2	9♍46.0	15♋49.0	27♌16.6	12♏28.9	16♐19.8	13♎54.7
2 S	6 40 41.2	10 15.0	0 53.4	8♊15.0	29 15.7	18 58.6	10 20.5	16 2.5	27 22.5	12R27.9	16R18.4	13 55.0
3 M	6 44 37.8	11 12.2	0 50.2	20 15.8	0♌58.0	20 8.0	10 55.1	16 16.0	27 28.5	12 27.0	16 16.9	13 55.3
4 T	6 48 34.3	12 9.5	0 47.0	2♋12.0	2 38.2	21 17.3	11 29.8	16 29.5	27 34.6	12 26.1	16 15.5	13 55.6
5 W	6 52 30.9	13 6.7	0 43.9	14 5.0	4 16.3	22 26.6	12 4.6	16 43.0	27 40.8	12 25.3	16 14.2	13 56.0
6 T	6 56 27.5	14 4.0	0 40.7	25 56.3	5 52.2	23 35.7	12 39.5	16 56.5	27 47.0	12 24.5	16 12.8	13 56.4
7 F	7 0 24.0	15 1.2	0 37.5	7♌47.4	7 26.0	24 44.7	13 14.5	17 10.0	27 53.2	12 23.8	16 11.4	13 56.8
8 S	7 4 20.6	15 58.4	0 34.3	19 40.3	8 57.6	25 53.6	13 49.5	17 23.5	27 59.5	12 23.1	16 10.0	13 57.3
9 S	7 8 17.1	16 55.6	0 31.2	1♍37.3	10 27.0	27 2.4	14 24.6	17 37.0	28 5.8	12 22.5	16 8.7	13 57.8
10 M	7 12 13.7	17 52.9	0 28.0	13 41.8	11 54.2	28 11.1	14 59.8	17 50.6	28 12.2	12 21.9	16 7.4	13 58.3
11 T	7 16 10.2	18 50.1	0 24.8	25 57.4	13 19.2	29 19.7	15 35.1	18 4.1	28 18.6	12 21.4	16 6.0	13 58.9
12 W	7 20 6.8	19 47.3	0 21.6	8♎28.5	14 41.9	0♍28.2	16 10.5	18 17.6	28 25.1	12 20.9	16 4.8	13 59.5
13 T	7 24 3.4	20 44.5	0 18.4	21 19.6	16 2.3	1 36.6	16 45.9	18 31.1	28 31.6	12 20.5	16 3.5	14 0.1
14 F	7 27 59.9	21 41.8	0 15.3	4♏35.0	17 20.4	2 44.8	17 21.5	18 44.6	28 38.2	12 20.1	16 2.2	14 0.8
15 S	7 31 56.5	22 39.0	0 12.1	18 17.8	18 36.1	3 52.9	17 57.1	18 58.0	28 44.8	12 19.8	16 1.0	14 1.5
16 S	7 35 53.0	23 36.2	0 8.9	2♐29.6	19 49.4	5 0.9	18 32.7	19 11.5	28 51.5	12 19.5	15 59.8	14 2.2
17 M	7 39 49.6	24 33.4	0 5.7	17 8.7	21 0.1	6 8.8	19 8.5	19 25.0	28 58.2	12 19.3	15 58.6	14 3.0
18 T	7 43 46.1	25 30.7	0 2.6	2♑10.1	22 8.3	7 16.5	19 44.3	19 38.4	29 4.9	12 19.1	15 57.5	14 3.8
19 W	7 47 42.7	26 27.9	29♍59.4	17 25.5	23 13.8	8 24.1	20 20.2	19 51.9	29 11.7	12 19.0	15 56.3	14 4.6
20 T	7 51 39.2	27 25.2	29 56.2	2♒44.1	24 16.6	9 31.6	20 56.2	20 5.3	29 18.6	12 18.9	15 55.2	14 5.4
21 F	7 55 35.8	28 22.4	29 53.0	17 54.8	25 16.5	10 38.9	21 32.3	20 18.7	29 25.4	12 18.9	15 54.1	14 6.3
22 S	7 59 32.4	29 19.7	29 49.9	2♓47.7	26 13.5	11 46.1	22 8.4	20 32.2	29 32.3	12 18.9	15 53.0	14 7.2
23 S	8 3 28.9	0♌16.9	29 46.7	17 16.1	27 7.3	12 53.1	22 44.6	20 45.6	29 39.3	12D19.0	15 52.0	14 8.2
24 M	8 7 25.5	1 14.2	29 43.5	1♈16.7	27 58.0	14 0.0	23 20.9	20 58.9	29 46.3	12 19.1	15 50.9	14 9.2
25 T	8 11 22.0	2 11.5	29 40.3	14 49.3	28 45.4	15 6.8	23 57.2	21 12.3	29 53.3	12 19.3	15 49.9	14 10.2
26 W	8 15 18.6	3 8.9	29 37.1	27 55.9	29 29.3	16 13.4	24 33.7	21 25.7	0♍ 0.4	12 19.6	15 49.0	14 11.3
27 T	8 19 15.1	4 6.2	29 34.0	10♉40.1	0♍ 9.6	17 19.9	25 10.2	21 39.0	0 7.5	12 19.9	15 48.1	14 12.4
28 F	8 23 11.7	5 3.6	29 30.8	23 6.1	0 46.0	18 26.2	25 46.7	21 52.3	0 14.6	12 20.3	15 47.1	14 13.5
29 S	8 27 8.2	6 0.9	29 27.6	5♊18.1	1 18.5	19 32.3	26 23.4	22 5.6	0 21.7	12 20.7	15 46.2	14 14.6
30 S	8 31 4.8	6 58.3	29 24.4	17 20.2	1 46.8	20 38.3	27 0.1	22 18.9	0 28.9	12 21.1	15 45.4	14 15.8
31 M	8 35 1.4	7 55.7	29 21.3	29 16.0	2 10.9	21 44.1	27 36.9	22 32.1	0 36.1	12 21.6	15 44.5	14 17.0

DECLINATION at NOON

DAY	h m s	☉	☊	☽	☿	♀	♂	♃	♄	♅	♆	♇
1 S	6 36 44.7	23N 6.8	0S22.5	15N16.0	22N26.9	17N12.6	8N48.1	22N37.9	13N46.5	15S13.0	21S15.4	10N19.5
4 T	6 48 34.3	22 53.0	0 18.7	18 25.2	21 10.1	16 2.8	8 6.4	22 33.3	13 40.2	15 12.2	21 15.1	10 17.6
7 F	7 0 24.0	22 35.6	0 14.9	14 30.0	19 44.2	14 49.7	7 24.0	22 28.6	13 33.7	15 11.6	21 14.7	10 15.6
10 M	7 12 13.7	22 14.7	0 11.1	5 9.1	18 12.0	13 33.5	6 41.1	22 23.6	13 27.0	15 11.1	21 14.4	10 13.5
13 T	7 24 3.4	21 50.3	0 7.3	6S32.9	16 36.1	12 14.5	5 57.6	22 18.4	13 20.2	15 10.8	21 14.1	10 11.4
16 S	7 35 53.0	21 22.6	0 3.5	16 13.0	14 58.9	10 53.1	5 13.7	22 13.1	13 13.2	15 10.5	21 13.8	10 9.1
19 W	7 47 42.7	20 51.6	0N 0.2	17 32.7	13 22.8	9 29.6	4 29.3	22 7.6	13 6.1	15 10.5	21 13.6	10 6.7
22 S	7 59 32.4	20 17.5	0 4.0	8 25.1	11 50.2	8 4.3	3 44.5	22 1.9	12 58.8	15 10.5	21 13.4	10 4.3
25 T	8 11 22.0	19 40.3	0 7.8	4N30.1	10 23.6	6 37.5	2 59.3	21 56.1	12 51.4	15 10.7	21 13.2	10 1.7
28 F	8 23 11.7	19 0.1	0 11.6	14 30.0	9 5.9	5 9.4	2 13.7	21 50.1	12 43.9	15 11.1	21 13.0	9 59.1
31 M	8 35 1.4	18 17.1	0 15.4	18 19.8	8 0.2	3 40.4	1 27.8	21 43.9	12 36.3	15 11.6	21 12.9	9 56.4

AUGUST 1978

LONGITUDE at NOON

DAY	h m s	☉	☊	☽	☿	♀	♂	♃	♄	♅	♆	♇
1 T	8 38 57.9	8♌53.1	29♍18.1	11♋ 8.2	2♍30.4	22♍49.7	28♍13.8	22♋45.3	0♍43.4	12♏22.2	15♐43.7	14♎18.2
2 W	8 42 54.5	9 50.6	29 14.9	22 59.4	2 45.2	23 55.2	28 50.7	22 58.5	0 50.6	12 22.8	15R42.9	14 19.4
3 T	8 46 51.0	10 48.0	29 11.7	4♌51.5	2 55.1	25 0.5	29 27.8	23 11.7	0 57.9	12 23.4	15 42.1	14 20.7
4 F	8 50 47.6	11 45.5	29 8.6	16 46.1	3 0.1	26 5.5	0♎ 4.9	23 24.8	1 5.3	12 24.1	15 41.4	14 22.0
5 S	8 54 44.1	12 43.0	29 5.4	28 44.9	2R59.8	27 10.4	0 42.0	23 37.9	1 12.6	12 24.9	15 40.7	14 23.4
6 S	8 58 40.7	13 40.5	29 2.2	10♍49.8	2 54.4	28 15.2	1 19.3	23 51.0	1 20.0	12 25.7	15 40.0	14 24.7
7 M	9 2 37.2	14 38.0	28 59.0	23 2.9	2 43.6	29 19.7	1 56.6	24 4.0	1 27.4	12 26.6	15 39.4	14 26.1
8 T	9 6 33.8	15 35.5	28 55.8	5♎26.7	2 27.4	0♎23.9	2 33.9	24 17.0	1 34.8	12 27.5	15 38.7	14 27.6
9 W	9 10 30.3	16 33.0	28 52.7	18 4.2	2 6.0	1 28.0	3 11.4	24 30.0	1 42.2	12 28.5	15 38.1	14 29.0
10 T	9 14 26.9	17 30.6	28 49.5	0♏58.7	1 39.4	2 31.9	3 48.9	24 42.9	1 49.6	12 29.5	15 37.6	14 30.5
11 F	9 18 23.5	18 28.2	28 46.3	14 13.4	1 7.9	3 35.5	4 26.5	24 55.8	1 57.1	12 30.6	15 37.1	14 32.0
12 S	9 22 20.0	19 25.8	28 43.1	27 50.9	0 31.7	4 38.9	5 4.2	25 8.6	2 4.6	12 31.7	15 36.5	14 33.5
13 S	9 26 16.6	20 23.3	28 40.0	11♐52.6	29♌51.2	5 42.0	5 41.9	25 21.4	2 12.1	12 32.9	15 36.1	14 35.1
14 M	9 30 13.1	21 21.0	28 36.8	26 18.0	29 7.1	6 44.9	6 19.7	25 34.2	2 19.6	12 34.1	15 35.6	14 36.7
15 T	9 34 9.7	22 18.6	28 33.6	11♑ 3.7	28 19.9	7 47.5	6 57.6	25 46.9	2 27.1	12 35.4	15 35.2	14 38.3
16 W	9 38 6.2	23 16.3	28 30.4	26 3.8	27 30.5	8 49.9	7 35.5	25 59.6	2 34.7	12 36.7	15 34.9	14 40.0
17 T	9 42 2.8	24 13.9	28 27.2	11♒10.0	26 39.6	9 52.0	8 13.5	26 12.3	2 42.2	12 38.1	15 34.5	14 41.6
18 F	9 45 59.3	25 11.6	28 24.1	26 12.7	25 48.3	10 53.8	8 51.6	26 24.9	2 49.8	12 39.5	15 34.2	14 43.3
19 S	9 49 55.9	26 9.3	28 20.9	11♓ 2.8	24 57.4	11 55.3	9 29.7	26 37.4	2 57.4	12 41.0	15 33.9	14 45.0
20 S	9 53 52.4	27 7.1	28 17.7	25 33.0	24 8.1	12 56.5	10 7.9	26 49.9	3 4.9	12 42.5	15 33.7	14 46.8
21 M	9 57 49.0	28 4.8	28 14.5	9♈38.4	23 21.3	13 57.4	10 46.2	27 2.3	3 12.5	12 44.1	15 33.5	14 48.5
22 T	10 1 45.5	29 2.6	28 11.4	23 17.1	22 38.1	14 58.0	11 24.5	27 14.7	3 20.1	12 45.7	15 33.3	14 50.3
23 W	10 5 42.1	0♍ 0.4	28 8.2	6♉29.6	21 59.5	15 58.2	12 2.9	27 27.1	3 27.7	12 47.3	15 33.1	14 52.1
24 T	10 9 38.7	0 58.2	28 5.0	19 18.4	21 26.2	16 58.2	12 41.4	27 39.3	3 35.3	12 49.0	15 33.0	14 53.9
25 F	10 13 35.2	1 56.1	28 1.8	1♊47.1	20 59.1	17 57.7	13 19.9	27 51.6	3 42.9	12 50.8	15 32.9	14 55.7
26 S	10 17 31.8	2 54.0	27 58.6	13 59.9	20 38.7	18 57.0	13 58.5	28 3.7	3 50.5	12 52.6	15 32.8	14 57.6
27 S	10 21 28.3	3 51.9	27 55.5	26 1.4	20 25.8	19 55.8	14 37.2	28 15.9	3 58.1	12 54.4	15 32.8	14 59.5
28 M	10 25 24.9	4 49.9	27 52.3	7♋55.8	20 20.6	20 54.3	15 15.9	28 27.9	4 5.7	12 56.3	15 32.8	15 1.4
29 T	10 29 21.4	5 47.9	27 49.1	19 47.1	20D23.4	21 52.4	15 54.7	28 39.9	4 13.3	12 58.3	15 32.8	15 3.3
30 W	10 33 18.0	6 45.9	27 45.9	1♌38.8	20 34.5	22 50.1	16 33.6	28 51.8	4 20.9	13 0.3	15D32.9	15 5.3
31 T	10 37 14.5	7 43.9	27 42.8	13 33.7	20 54.0	23 47.4	17 12.6	29 3.7	4 28.5	13 2.3	15 33.0	15 7.2

DECLINATION at NOON

DAY	h m s	☉	☊	☽	☿	♀	♂	♃	♄	♅	♆	♇
1 T	8 38 57.9	18N 2.2	0N16.7	18N 0.8	7N41.5	3N10.5	1N12.4	21N41.8	12N33.8	15S11.8	21S12.8	9N55.5
4 F	8 50 47.6	17 15.7	0 20.5	12 36.6	6 57.5	1 40.7	0 26.2	21 35.5	12 26.0	15 12.5	21 12.7	9 52.7
7 M	9 2 37.2	16 26.6	0 24.3	2 24.3	6 34.2	0 10.6	0S20.3	21 29.1	12 18.2	15 13.3	21 12.7	9 49.9
10 T	9 14 26.9	15 35.2	0 28.0	9S 6.9	6 34.9	1S19.5	1 7.0	21 22.5	12 10.3	15 14.3	21 12.6	9 47.0
13 S	9 26 16.6	14 41.5	0 31.8	17 15.2	7 1.4	2 49.2	1 53.8	21 15.9	12 2.3	15 15.4	21 12.6	9 44.1
16 W	9 38 6.2	13 45.7	0 35.6	16 27.9	7 52.2	4 18.5	2 40.8	21 9.1	11 54.3	15 16.6	21 12.7	9 41.1
19 S	9 49 55.9	12 48.0	0 39.4	6 5.7	9 1.9	5 46.8	3 27.8	21 2.3	11 46.3	15 18.0	21 12.7	9 38.1
22 T	10 1 45.5	11 48.4	0 43.2	6N53.2	10 20.8	7 14.1	4 14.7	20 55.5	11 38.2	15 19.5	21 12.7	9 35.1
25 F	10 13 35.2	10 47.2	0 47.0	15 52.3	11 37.4	8 40.0	5 1.7	20 48.5	11 30.0	15 21.1	21 12.8	9 32.0
28 M	10 25 24.9	9 44.4	0 50.8	18 4.0	12 41.0	10 4.3	5 48.6	20 41.6	11 21.9	15 22.9	21 12.9	9 29.0
31 T	10 37 14.5	8 40.2	0 54.6	13 18.0	13 22.9	11 26.6	6 35.3	20 34.6	11 13.8	15 24.8	21 13.1	9 25.9

SEPTEMBER 1978

LONGITUDE at NOON

DAY	EPHEMERIS SIDEREAL TIME h m s	☉ ° ′	☊ ° ′	☾ ° ′	☿ ° ′	♀ ° ′	♂ ° ′	♃ ° ′	♄ ° ′	♅ ° ′	♆ ° ′	♇ ° ′
1 F	10 41 11.1	8♍42.0	27♍39.6	25♌34.4	21♌21.7	24♎44.3	17♎51.6	29♋15.5	4♍36.1	13♏ 4.4	15♐33.1	15♎ 9.2
2 S	10 45 7.6	9 40.1	27 36.4	7♍42.7	21 57.6	25 40.7	18 30.7	29 27.2	4 43.7	13 6.5	15 33.3	15 11.2
3 S	10 49 4.2	10 38.2	27 33.2	20 0.2	22 41.5	26 36.6	19 9.9	29 38.9	4 51.3	13 8.6	15 33.5	15 13.3
4 M	10 53 0.7	11 36.4	27 30.0	2♎28.3	23 33.2	27 32.1	19 49.1	29 50.5	4 58.9	13 10.9	15 33.7	15 15.3
5 T	10 56 57.3	12 34.6	27 26.9	15 8.2	24 32.2	28 27.1	20 28.4	0♌ 2.0	5 6.5	13 13.1	15 34.0	15 17.4
6 W	11 0 53.8	13 32.8	27 23.7	28 1.3	25 38.3	29 21.6	21 7.8	0 13.5	5 14.1	13 15.4	15 34.3	15 19.5
7 T	11 4 50.4	14 31.1	27 20.5	11♏ 8.8	26 50.8	0♏15.5	21 47.2	0 24.9	5 21.6	13 17.8	15 34.7	15 21.6
8 F	11 8 46.9	15 29.3	27 17.3	24 31.9	28 9.4	1 8.9	22 26.7	0 36.2	5 29.2	13 20.1	15 35.0	15 23.7
9 S	11 12 43.5	16 27.6	27 14.1	8♐11.5	29 33.5	2 1.7	23 6.3	0 47.4	5 36.7	13 22.6	15 35.4	15 25.8
10 S	11 16 40.0	17 25.9	27 11.0	22 8.0	1♍ 2.7	2 53.9	23 45.9	0 58.5	5 44.2	13 25.0	15 35.8	15 27.9
11 M	11 20 36.6	18 24.3	27 7.8	6♑20.5	2 36.2	3 45.5	24 25.6	1 9.6	5 51.7	13 27.5	15 36.3	15 30.1
12 T	11 24 33.1	19 22.6	27 4.6	20 47.1	4 13.6	4 36.4	25 5.4	1 20.5	5 59.2	13 30.0	15 36.8	15 32.3
13 W	11 28 29.7	20 21.0	27 1.4	5♒24.0	5 54.3	5 26.6	25 45.2	1 31.4	6 6.6	13 32.6	15 37.3	15 34.4
14 T	11 32 26.2	21 19.4	26 58.3	20 6.1	7 37.9	6 16.2	26 25.1	1 42.2	6 14.1	13 35.2	15 37.9	15 36.6
15 F	11 36 22.8	22 17.9	26 55.1	4♓46.9	9 23.7	7 5.0	27 5.0	1 52.9	6 21.5	13 37.9	15 38.5	15 38.8
16 S	11 40 19.4	23 16.3	26 51.9	19 19.8	11 11.5	7 53.0	27 45.0	2 3.5	6 28.9	13 40.6	15 39.1	15 41.1
17 S	11 44 15.9	24 14.8	26 48.7	3♈38.7	13 0.6	8 40.3	28 25.1	2 14.1	6 36.3	13 43.3	15 39.7	15 43.3
18 M	11 48 12.5	25 13.4	26 45.5	17 38.6	14 50.9	9 26.7	29 5.3	2 24.5	6 43.6	13 46.0	15 40.4	15 45.5
19 T	11 52 9.0	26 11.9	26 42.4	1♉16.5	16 41.8	10 12.3	29 45.5	2 34.9	6 51.0	13 48.8	15 41.1	15 47.8
20 W	11 56 5.6	27 10.5	26 39.2	14 31.2	18 33.2	10 57.0	0♏25.7	2 45.1	6 58.3	13 51.6	15 41.9	15 50.1
21 T	12 0 2.1	28 9.2	26 36.0	27 23.4	20 24.8	11 40.8	1 6.1	2 55.3	7 5.5	13 54.5	15 42.7	15 52.3
22 F	12 3 58.7	29 7.8	26 32.8	9♊55.6	22 16.4	12 23.7	1 46.5	3 5.4	7 12.8	13 57.4	15 43.5	15 54.6
23 S	12 7 55.2	0♎ 6.6	26 29.7	22 11.0	24 7.8	13 5.5	2 27.0	3 15.3	7 20.0	14 0.3	15 44.3	15 56.9
24 S	12 11 51.8	1 5.3	26 26.5	4♋13.8	25 58.9	13 46.4	3 7.5	3 25.2	7 27.2	14 3.3	15 45.2	15 59.2
25 M	12 15 48.3	2 4.1	26 23.3	16 8.7	27 49.4	14 26.2	3 48.1	3 34.9	7 34.4	14 6.3	15 46.1	16 1.5
26 T	12 19 44.9	3 2.9	26 20.1	28 0.2	29 39.4	15 4.9	4 28.8	3 44.6	7 41.5	14 9.3	15 47.0	16 3.8
27 W	12 23 41.4	4 1.8	26 16.9	9♌52.9	1♎28.8	15 42.4	5 9.6	3 54.2	7 48.7	14 12.4	15 48.1	16 6.2
28 T	12 27 38.0	5 0.7	26 13.8	21 50.8	3 17.5	16 18.8	5 50.4	4 3.6	7 55.8	14 15.5	15 49.1	16 8.5
29 F	12 31 34.5	5 59.7	26 10.6	3♍57.4	5 5.4	16 53.9	6 31.3	4 13.0	8 2.8	14 18.6	15 50.1	16 10.9
30 S	12 35 31.1	6 58.6	26 7.4	16 15.6	6 52.5	17 27.7	7 12.2	4 22.2	8 9.8	14 21.7	15 51.1	16 13.2

DECLINATION at NOON

DAY	EPHEMERIS SIDEREAL TIME h m s	☉ ° ′	☊ ° ′	☾ ° ′	☿ ° ′	♀ ° ′	♂ ° ′	♃ ° ′	♄ ° ′	♅ ° ′	♆ ° ′	♇ ° ′
1 F	10 41 11.1	8N18.5	0N55.8	10N25.6	13N30.9	11S53.6	6S50.9	20N32.3	11N11.1	15S25.4	21S13.3	9N24.9
4 M	10 53 0.7	7 12.6	0 59.6	0S29.8	13 35.2	13 13.1	7 37.4	20 25.3	11 2.9	15 27.4	21 13.6	9 21.8
7 T	11 4 50.4	6 5.7	1 3.4	11 39.2	13 8.3	14 30.0	8 23.6	20 18.4	10 54.8	15 29.6	21 13.8	9 18.7
10 S	11 16 40.0	4 57.9	1 7.2	17 57.0	12 10.9	15 44.1	9 9.6	20 11.5	10 46.7	15 31.8	21 14.1	9 15.6
13 W	11 28 29.7	3 49.4	1 11.0	14 54.6	10 46.1	16 55.2	9 55.1	20 4.6	10 38.7	15 34.2	21 14.4	9 12.6
16 S	11 40 19.4	2 40.3	1 14.8	3 35.7	8 59.2	18 2.8	10 40.3	19 57.8	10 30.8	15 36.6	21 14.8	9 9.6
19 T	11 52 9.0	1 30.7	1 18.6	9N 5.9	6 56.4	19 6.8	11 24.9	19 51.1	10 22.9	15 39.1	21 15.2	9 6.6
22 F	12 3 58.7	0 20.7	1 22.4	16 55.7	4 43.1	20 6.9	12 9.0	19 44.5	10 15.1	15 41.8	21 15.6	9 3.6
25 M	12 15 48.3	0S49.4	1 26.2	17 30.5	2 24.2	21 2.6	12 52.5	19 38.1	10 7.4	15 44.5	21 16.0	9 0.7
28 T	12 27 38.0	1 59.5	1 29.9	11 21.2	0 3.1	21 53.8	13 35.4	19 31.8	9 59.7	15 47.2	21 16.5	8 57.8

OCTOBER 1978

LONGITUDE at NOON

DAY	EPHEMERIS SIDEREAL TIME h m s	☉ ° ′	☊ ° ′	☾ ° ′	☿ ° ′	♀ ° ′	♂ ° ′	♃ ° ′	♄ ° ′	♅ ° ′	♆ ° ′	♇ ° ′
1 S	12 39 27.6	7♎57.6	26♍ 4.2	28♍47.5	8♎38.7	18♏ 0.2	7♏53.3	4♌31.3	8♍16.8	14♏24.9	15♐52.2	16♎15.6
2 M	12 43 24.2	8 56.7	26 1.0	11♎34.2	10 24.2	18 31.2	8 34.3	4 40.2	8 23.7	14 28.1	15 53.3	16 17.9
3 T	12 47 20.7	9 55.8	25 57.9	24 36.1	12 8.8	19 0.8	9 15.5	4 49.1	8 30.6	14 31.3	15 54.5	16 20.3
4 W	12 51 17.3	10 54.9	25 54.7	7♏52.8	13 52.6	19 28.9	9 56.7	4 57.8	8 37.5	14 34.6	15 55.7	16 22.6
5 T	12 55 13.8	11 54.0	25 51.5	21 23.1	15 35.5	19 55.5	10 38.0	5 6.5	8 44.3	14 37.9	15 56.9	16 25.0
6 F	12 59 10.4	12 53.2	25 48.3	5♐ 5.5	17 17.7	20 20.4	11 19.3	5 15.0	8 51.0	14 41.2	15 58.1	16 27.4
7 S	13 3 6.9	13 52.4	25 45.2	18 58.4	18 59.0	20 43.5	12 0.7	5 23.3	8 57.7	14 44.5	15 59.4	16 29.7
8 S	13 7 3.5	14 51.6	25 42.0	2♑59.9	20 39.5	21 5.0	12 42.2	5 31.6	9 4.4	14 47.9	16 0.7	16 32.1
9 M	13 11 0.0	15 50.8	25 38.8	17 8.2	22 19.2	21 24.6	13 23.7	5 39.7	9 11.0	14 51.2	16 2.0	16 34.5
10 T	13 14 56.6	16 50.1	25 35.6	1♒21.1	23 58.2	21 42.2	14 5.3	5 47.7	9 17.6	14 54.6	16 3.3	16 36.8
11 W	13 18 53.1	17 49.4	25 32.4	15 36.6	25 36.4	21 58.0	14 47.0	5 55.5	9 24.1	14 58.1	16 4.7	16 39.2
12 T	13 22 49.7	18 48.8	25 29.3	29 52.2	27 13.9	22 11.7	15 28.7	6 3.2	9 30.6	15 1.5	16 6.1	16 41.6
13 F	13 26 46.3	19 48.2	25 26.1	14♓ 4.8	28 50.6	22 23.3	16 10.5	6 10.8	9 37.0	15 5.0	16 7.5	16 44.0
14 S	13 30 42.8	20 47.6	25 22.9	28 11.0	0♏26.6	22 32.8	16 52.4	6 18.2	9 43.4	15 8.5	16 9.0	16 46.3
15 S	13 34 39.4	21 47.0	25 19.7	12♈ 7.2	2 2.0	22 40.0	17 34.3	6 25.6	9 49.7	15 12.0	16 10.4	16 48.7
16 M	13 38 35.9	22 46.5	25 16.6	25 50.1	3 36.7	22 45.0	18 16.2	6 32.7	9 56.0	15 15.5	16 12.0	16 51.0
17 T	13 42 32.5	23 46.0	25 13.4	9♉16.8	5 10.8	22 47.8	18 58.3	6 39.7	10 2.2	15 19.0	16 13.5	16 53.4
18 W	13 46 29.0	24 45.6	25 10.2	22 25.4	6 44.2	22 48.2	19 40.4	6 46.7	10 8.4	15 22.6	16 15.1	16 55.8
19 T	13 50 25.6	25 45.1	25 7.0	5♊15.3	8 17.0	22R46.2	20 22.6	6 53.4	10 14.5	15 26.2	16 16.7	16 58.2
20 F	13 54 22.1	26 44.7	25 3.8	17 47.3	9 49.2	22 41.8	21 4.8	6 60.0	10 20.6	15 29.8	16 18.3	17 0.5
21 S	13 58 18.7	27 44.4	25 0.7	0♋ 3.5	11 20.7	22 35.0	21 47.1	7 6.4	10 26.5	15 33.4	16 19.9	17 2.8
22 S	14 2 15.2	28 44.1	24 57.5	12 7.0	12 51.7	22 25.8	22 29.5	7 12.7	10 32.5	15 37.0	16 21.5	17 5.2
23 M	14 6 11.8	29 43.8	24 54.3	24 1.9	14 22.1	22 14.2	23 11.9	7 18.8	10 38.3	15 40.6	16 23.2	17 7.5
24 T	14 10 8.3	0♏43.6	24 51.1	5♌53.0	15 51.9	22 0.2	23 54.4	7 24.8	10 44.1	15 44.2	16 24.9	17 9.8
25 W	14 14 4.9	1 43.4	24 48.0	17 45.3	17 21.1	21 43.9	24 36.9	7 30.6	10 49.8	15 47.9	16 26.6	17 12.2
26 T	14 18 1.4	2 43.2	24 44.8	29 43.6	18 49.7	21 25.2	25 19.5	7 36.2	10 55.5	15 51.6	16 28.4	17 14.5
27 F	14 21 58.0	3 43.1	24 41.6	11♍52.9	20 17.7	21 4.3	26 2.2	7 41.7	11 1.1	15 55.2	16 30.1	17 16.8
28 S	14 25 54.5	4 43.0	24 38.4	24 17.3	21 45.0	20 41.2	26 45.0	7 47.0	11 6.6	15 58.9	16 31.9	17 19.1
29 S	14 29 51.1	5 42.9	24 35.2	6♎60.0	23 11.8	20 16.1	27 27.8	7 52.2	11 12.1	16 2.6	16 33.7	17 21.3
30 M	14 33 47.7	6 42.9	24 32.1	20 2.9	24 37.9	19 49.0	28 10.7	7 57.2	11 17.5	16 6.3	16 35.5	17 23.6
31 T	14 37 44.2	7 42.9	24 28.9	3♏26.5	26 3.3	19 20.1	28 53.6	8 2.0	11 22.8	16 10.0	16 37.4	17 25.9

DECLINATION at NOON

DAY	EPHEMERIS SIDEREAL TIME h m s	☉ ° ′	☊ ° ′	☾ ° ′	☿ ° ′	♀ ° ′	♂ ° ′	♃ ° ′	♄ ° ′	♅ ° ′	♆ ° ′	♇ ° ′
1 S	12 39 27.6	3S 9.5	1N33.7	0N39.0	2S17.6	22S39.9	14S17.5	19N25.6	9N52.2	15S50.1	21S16.9	8N55.0
4 W	12 51 17.3	4 19.2	1 37.5	10S51.1	4 36.0	23 20.6	14 58.7	19 19.7	9 44.9	15 53.0	21 17.4	8 52.3
7 S	13 3 6.9	5 28.4	1 41.3	17 47.2	6 50.9	23 55.3	15 39.1	19 13.9	9 37.7	15 56.0	21 18.0	8 49.6
10 T	13 14 56.6	6 36.9	1 45.1	15 38.1	9 1.1	24 23.3	16 18.6	19 8.4	9 30.6	15 59.0	21 18.5	8 47.0
13 F	13 26 46.3	7 44.7	1 48.9	5 12.2	11 6.0	24 44.0	16 57.0	19 3.2	9 23.7	16 2.1	21 19.1	8 44.4
16 M	13 38 35.9	8 51.5	1 52.6	7N36.1	13 5.0	24 56.3	17 34.3	18 58.2	9 17.0	16 5.2	21 19.7	8 41.9
19 T	13 50 25.6	9 57.1	1 56.4	16 23.6	14 57.4	24 59.5	18 10.5	18 53.4	9 10.5	16 8.3	21 20.3	8 39.6
22 S	14 2 15.2	11 1.5	2 0.2	17 53.7	16 42.7	24 52.4	18 45.4	18 49.0	9 4.2	16 11.5	21 20.9	8 37.3
25 W	14 14 4.9	12 4.4	2 4.0	12 25.1	18 20.4	24 34.2	19 18.9	18 45.0	8 58.1	16 14.7	21 21.5	8 35.1
28 S	14 25 54.5	13 5.6	2 7.8	2 6.0	19 49.8	24 4.3	19 51.1	18 41.3	8 52.2	16 17.9	21 22.2	8 33.0
31 T	14 37 44.2	14 5.0	2 11.5	9S43.3	21 10.5	23 22.4	20 21.8	18 37.9	8 46.6	16 21.1	21 22.8	8 31.0

NOVEMBER 1978

DAY	EPHEMERIS SIDEREAL TIME	☉	☊	☽	☿	♀	♂	♃	♄	♅	♆	♇
	h m s	° ′	° ′	° ′	° ′	° ′	° ′	° ′	° ′	° ′	° ′	° ′
					LONGITUDE at NOON							
1 W	14 41 40.8	8♏42.9	24♍25.7	17♏ 9.2	27♏28.0	18♏49.5	29♏36.6	8♌ 6.7	11♍28.1	16♏13.8	16♐39.3	17♎28.1
2 T	14 45 37.3	9 43.0	24 22.5	1♐ 7.9	28 51.9	18R17.5	0♐19.7	8 11.1	11 33.2	16 17.5	16 41.1	17 30.4
3 F	14 49 33.9	10 43.1	24 19.4	15 18.3	0♐15.0	17 44.1	1 2.8	8 15.4	11 38.3	16 21.2	16 43.0	17 32.6
4 S	14 53 30.4	11 43.2	24 16.2	29 35.4	1 37.2	17 9.7	1 46.0	8 19.6	11 43.3	16 24.9	16 45.0	17 34.8
5 S	14 57 27.0	12 43.4	24 13.0	13♑54.2	2 58.5	16 34.4	2 29.2	8 23.5	11 48.3	16 28.7	16 46.9	17 37.0
6 M	15 1 23.5	13 43.6	24 9.8	28 10.7	4 18.7	15 58.4	3 12.5	8 27.3	11 53.1	16 32.4	16 48.9	17 39.2
7 T	15 5 20.1	14 43.8	24 6.6	12♒21.9	5 37.8	15 22.0	3 55.9	8 30.9	11 57.9	16 36.2	16 50.8	17 41.4
8 W	15 9 16.6	15 44.0	24 3.5	26 26.2	6 55.7	14 45.5	4 39.4	8 34.3	12 2.7	16 39.9	16 52.9	17 43.6
9 T	15 13 13.2	16 44.3	24 0.3	10♓22.6	8 12.2	14 9.0	5 22.8	8 37.6	12 7.3	16 43.7	16 54.9	17 45.7
10 F	15 17 9.8	17 44.6	23 57.1	24 10.6	9 27.1	13 32.9	6 6.4	8 40.6	12 11.8	16 47.4	16 56.9	17 47.8
11 S	15 21 6.3	18 44.9	23 53.9	7♈49.8	10 40.4	12 57.4	6 50.0	8 43.5	12 16.3	16 51.2	16 58.9	17 50.0
12 S	15 25 2.9	19 45.2	23 50.8	21 19.5	11 51.7	12 22.7	7 33.6	8 46.1	12 20.7	16 54.9	17 1.0	17 52.0
13 M	15 28 59.4	20 45.6	23 47.6	4♉38.6	13 0.8	11 49.1	8 17.3	8 48.6	12 24.9	16 58.7	17 3.1	17 54.1
14 T	15 32 56.0	21 45.9	23 44.4	17 45.7	14 7.5	11 16.8	9 1.1	8 50.9	12 29.1	17 2.4	17 5.1	17 56.2
15 W	15 36 52.5	22 46.3	23 41.2	0♊39.8	15 11.5	10 46.0	9 45.0	8 53.0	12 33.2	17 6.1	17 7.2	17 58.2
16 T	15 40 49.1	23 46.8	23 38.0	13 19.8	16 12.4	10 16.8	10 28.8	8 55.0	12 37.3	17 9.9	17 9.3	18 0.3
17 F	15 44 45.6	24 47.2	23 34.9	25 45.8	17 9.8	9 49.6	11 12.8	8 56.7	12 41.2	17 13.6	17 11.5	18 2.3
18 S	15 48 42.2	25 47.7	23 31.7	7♋58.6	18 3.3	9 24.3	11 56.8	8 58.2	12 45.0	17 17.3	17 13.6	18 4.2
19 S	15 52 38.8	26 48.2	23 28.5	20 0.2	18 52.3	9 1.1	12 40.9	8 59.6	12 48.8	17 21.0	17 15.7	18 6.2
20 M	15 56 35.3	27 48.8	23 25.3	1♌53.8	19 36.3	8 40.2	13 25.0	9 0.7	12 52.5	17 24.7	17 17.9	18 8.2
21 T	16 0 31.9	28 49.4	23 22.2	13 43.3	20 14.6	8 21.6	14 9.2	9 1.7	12 56.0	17 28.4	17 20.0	18 10.1
22 W	16 4 28.4	29 50.0	23 19.0	25 33.4	20 46.6	8 5.4	14 53.4	9 2.4	12 59.5	17 32.1	17 22.2	18 12.0
23 T	16 8 25.0	0♐50.6	23 15.8	7♍29.6	21 11.5	7 51.6	15 37.7	9 3.0	13 2.9	17 35.8	17 24.4	18 13.9
24 F	16 12 21.5	1 51.3	23 12.6	19 37.1	21 28.6	7 40.3	16 22.1	9 3.4	13 6.2	17 39.4	17 26.6	18 15.7
25 S	16 16 18.1	2 51.9	23 9.5	2♎ 1.3	21 37.0	7 31.5	17 6.5	9 3.5	13 9.3	17 43.1	17 28.8	18 17.6
26 S	16 20 14.6	3 52.7	23 6.3	14 46.9	21R36.0	7 25.3	17 51.0	9 3.5	13 12.4	17 46.7	17 31.0	18 19.4
27 M	16 24 11.2	4 53.4	23 3.1	27 57.3	21 24.9	7 21.4	18 35.5	9R 3.2	13 15.4	17 50.4	17 33.2	18 21.2
28 T	16 28 7.8	5 54.2	22 59.9	11♏33.9	21 3.2	7 20.1	19 20.1	9 2.8	13 18.3	17 54.0	17 35.4	18 22.9
29 W	16 32 4.3	6 55.0	22 56.7	25 35.8	20 30.5	7D21.2	20 4.8	9 2.2	13 21.1	17 57.6	17 37.7	18 24.7
30 T	16 36 0.9	7 55.8	22 53.6	9♐59.1	19 46.9	7 24.7	20 49.5	9 1.4	13 23.8	18 1.2	17 39.9	18 26.5
					DECLINATION at NOON							
1 W	14 41 40.8	14S24.4	2N12.8	13S 6.6	21S35.3	23S 5.9	20S31.7	18N36.9	8N44.8	16S22.2	21S23.0	8N30.4
4 S	14 53 30.4	15 21.0	2 16.6	18 18.9	22 43.1	22 9.4	21 0.2	18 34.1	8 39.5	16 25.4	21 23.7	8 28.5
7 T	15 5 20.1	16 15.4	2 20.3	13 42.4	23 40.3	21 4.0	21 27.2	18 31.7	8 34.6	16 28.7	21 24.3	8 26.8
10 F	15 17 9.8	17 7.3	2 24.1	2 11.7	24 26.3	19 52.5	21 52.4	18 29.7	8 29.8	16 31.9	21 25.0	8 25.2
13 M	15 28 59.4	17 56.6	2 27.9	10N 1.9	24 60.0	18 38.5	22 15.7	18 28.1	8 25.4	16 35.1	21 25.7	8 23.7
16 T	15 40 49.1	18 43.1	2 31.7	17 28.4	25 20.6	17 25.7	22 37.2	18 27.0	8 21.3	16 38.3	21 26.4	8 22.3
19 S	15 52 38.8	19 26.6	2 35.4	17 25.1	25 27.0	16 17.6	22 56.7	18 26.3	8 17.6	16 41.4	21 27.0	8 21.1
22 W	16 4 28.4	20 6.9	2 39.2	10 41.6	25 18.2	15 16.9	23 14.2	18 26.2	8 14.1	16 44.6	21 27.7	8 20.0
25 S	16 16 18.1	20 43.9	2 43.0	0S10.7	24 52.6	14 25.5	23 29.7	18 26.5	8 11.0	16 47.7	21 28.4	8 19.1
28 T	16 28 7.8	21 17.5	2 46.7	11 45.8	24 8.5	13 44.3	23 42.9	18 27.2	8 8.2	16 50.7	21 29.0	8 18.2

DECEMBER 1978

DAY	EPHEMERIS SIDEREAL TIME	☉	☊	☽	☿	♀	♂	♃	♄	♅	♆	♇
					LONGITUDE at NOON							
1 F	16 39 57.4	8♐56.7	22♍50.4	24♐37.6	18♐52.7	7♏30.6	21♐34.2	9♌ 0.4	13♍26.4	18♏ 4.8	17♐42.2	18♎28.1
2 S	16 43 54.0	9 57.5	22 47.2	9♑23.3	17R48.9	7 38.7	22 19.0	8R59.1	13 28.9	18 8.3	17 44.4	18 29.8
3 S	16 47 50.5	10 58.4	22 44.0	24 8.0	16 36.9	7 49.1	23 3.9	8 57.7	13 31.2	18 11.9	17 46.7	18 31.5
4 M	16 51 47.1	11 59.2	22 40.9	8♒44.5	15 18.7	8 1.7	23 48.8	8 56.1	13 33.5	18 15.4	17 48.9	18 33.1
5 T	16 55 43.6	13 0.1	22 37.7	23 7.8	13 56.9	8 16.4	24 33.8	8 54.2	13 35.7	18 18.9	17 51.2	18 34.7
6 W	16 59 40.2	14 1.0	22 34.5	7♓15.2	12 33.9	8 33.2	25 18.8	8 52.2	13 37.7	18 22.3	17 53.4	18 36.2
7 T	17 3 36.8	15 2.0	22 31.3	21 6.0	11 12.8	8 52.0	26 3.8	8 50.0	13 39.7	18 25.8	17 55.7	18 37.7
8 F	17 7 33.3	16 2.9	22 28.2	4♈41.1	9 56.2	9 12.8	26 49.0	8 47.6	13 41.5	18 29.2	17 58.0	18 39.2
9 S	17 11 29.9	17 3.8	22 25.0	18 1.9	8 46.4	9 35.4	27 34.1	8 45.0	13 43.3	18 32.7	18 0.2	18 40.7
10 S	17 15 26.4	18 4.8	22 21.8	1♉10.0	7 45.4	9 59.9	28 19.3	8 42.2	13 44.9	18 36.0	18 2.5	18 42.2
11 M	17 19 23.0	19 5.8	22 18.6	14 6.6	6 54.5	10 26.1	29 4.6	8 39.2	13 46.4	18 39.4	18 4.8	18 43.6
12 T	17 23 19.5	20 6.7	22 15.4	26 52.6	6 14.6	10 54.1	29 49.9	8 36.0	13 47.8	18 42.7	18 7.0	18 45.0
13 W	17 27 16.1	21 7.7	22 12.3	9♊28.2	5 45.8	11 23.7	0♑35.3	8 32.7	13 49.1	18 46.1	18 9.3	18 46.3
14 T	17 31 12.7	22 8.7	22 9.1	21 53.5	5 28.3	11 54.9	1 20.7	8 29.1	13 50.3	18 49.4	18 11.5	18 47.7
15 F	17 35 9.2	23 9.7	22 5.9	4♋ 8.8	5 21.4	12 27.6	2 6.1	8 25.4	13 51.4	18 52.6	18 13.8	18 48.9
16 S	17 39 5.8	24 10.8	22 2.7	16 14.5	5D24.8	13 1.9	2 51.6	8 21.5	13 52.4	18 55.9	18 16.1	18 50.2
17 S	17 43 2.3	25 11.8	21 59.6	28 11.9	5 37.5	13 37.5	3 37.2	8 17.4	13 53.3	18 59.1	18 18.3	18 51.4
18 M	17 46 58.9	26 12.8	21 56.4	10♌ 3.0	5 58.9	14 14.5	4 22.8	8 13.1	13 54.0	19 2.2	18 20.6	18 52.7
19 T	17 50 55.4	27 13.9	21 53.2	21 50.8	6 28.0	14 52.9	5 8.4	8 8.7	13 54.7	19 5.4	18 22.8	18 53.8
20 W	17 54 52.0	28 15.0	21 50.0	3♍39.3	7 4.2	15 32.5	5 54.1	8 4.1	13 55.3	19 8.6	18 25.1	18 55.0
21 T	17 58 48.6	29 16.1	21 46.9	15 33.0	7 46.6	16 13.3	6 39.9	7 59.3	13 55.7	19 11.7	18 27.3	18 56.1
22 F	18 2 45.1	0♑17.2	21 43.7	27 37.1	8 34.5	16 55.3	7 25.7	7 54.4	13 56.0	19 14.7	18 29.5	18 57.2
23 S	18 6 41.7	1 18.3	21 40.5	9♎57.3	9 27.2	17 38.4	8 11.5	7 49.2	13 56.2	19 17.8	18 31.8	18 58.2
24 S	18 10 38.2	2 19.5	21 37.3	22 38.8	10 24.3	18 22.6	8 57.4	7 44.0	13 56.3	19 20.8	18 34.0	18 59.3
25 M	18 14 34.8	3 20.6	21 34.1	5♏46.4	11 25.3	19 7.8	9 43.3	7 38.5	13 56.3	19 23.7	18 36.2	19 0.2
26 T	18 18 31.3	4 21.8	21 31.0	19 23.0	12 29.5	19 54.0	10 29.3	7 32.9	13R56.1	19 26.6	18 38.4	19 1.2
27 W	18 22 27.9	5 22.9	21 27.8	3♐29.4	13 36.8	20 41.2	11 15.3	7 27.2	13 55.9	19 29.5	18 40.6	19 2.1
28 T	18 26 24.5	6 24.1	21 24.6	18 2.9	14 46.6	21 29.2	12 1.3	7 21.3	13 55.5	19 32.4	18 42.8	19 3.0
29 F	18 30 21.0	7 25.2	21 21.4	2♑57.5	15 58.7	22 18.2	12 47.4	7 15.2	13 55.1	19 35.2	18 44.9	19 3.8
30 S	18 34 17.6	8 26.4	21 18.3	18 4.4	17 12.9	23 8.0	13 33.6	7 9.0	13 54.5	19 38.0	18 47.1	19 4.6
31 S	18 38 14.1	9 27.6	21 15.1	3♒13.0	18 28.9	23 58.5	14 19.7	7 2.7	13 53.8	19 40.8	18 49.3	19 5.4
					DECLINATION at NOON							
1 F	16 39 57.4	21S47.4	2N50.5	18S19.0	23S 4.5	13S13.7	23S54.0	18N28.5	8N 5.8	16S53.7	21S29.7	8N17.5
4 M	16 51 47.1	22 13.6	2 54.3	14 40.3	21 43.6	12 53.2	24 2.9	18 30.2	8 3.8	16 56.7	21 30.3	8 17.0
7 T	17 3 36.8	22 35.9	2 58.0	3 22.3	20 18.2	12 42.3	24 9.4	18 32.4	8 2.1	16 59.5	21 31.0	8 16.5
10 S	17 15 26.4	22 54.3	3 1.8	8N57.5	19 8.6	12 40.2	24 13.6	18 35.0	8 0.8	17 2.4	21 31.6	8 16.3
13 W	17 27 16.1	23 8.5	3 5.6	17 3.4	18 30.0	12 45.8	24 15.5	18 38.1	7 59.9	17 5.1	21 32.2	8 16.1
16 S	17 39 5.8	23 18.7	3 9.3	17 56.0	18 24.7	12 58.3	24 14.9	18 41.6	7 59.4	17 7.8	21 32.8	8 16.1
19 T	17 50 55.4	23 24.6	3 13.1	11 52.8	18 45.8	13 16.6	24 11.9	18 45.5	7 59.2	17 10.4	21 33.4	8 16.3
22 F	18 2 45.1	23 26.3	3 16.8	1 28.1	19 23.9	13 39.7	24 6.5	18 49.8	7 59.4	17 12.9	21 34.0	8 16.6
25 M	18 14 34.8	23 23.8	3 20.6	10S 5.6	20 10.6	14 6.8	23 58.7	18 54.4	8 0.1	17 15.4	21 34.5	8 17.0
28 T	18 26 24.5	23 17.0	3 24.4	17 54.0	20 59.6	14 36.9	23 48.4	18 59.4	8 1.1	17 17.7	21 35.1	8 17.6
31 S	18 38 14.1	23 6.1	3 28.1	15 50.9	21 46.6	15 9.2	23 35.7	19 4.6	8 2.5	17 19.9	21 35.6	8 18.3

JANUARY 1979

LONGITUDE at NOON

DAY	EPHEMERIS SIDEREAL TIME h m s	☉ ° ′	☊ ° ′	☽ ° ′	☿ ° ′	♀ ° ′	♂ ° ′	♃ ° ′	♄ ° ′	♅ ° ′	♆ ° ′	♇ ° ′
1 M	18 42 10.7	10♑28.8	21♍11.9	18♒13.2	19♐46.5	24♏49.9	15♑ 5.9	6♌56.3	13♍53.0	19♏43.5	18♐51.4	19♎ 6.1
2 T	18 46 7.2	11 29.9	21 8.7	2♓57.2	21 5.5	25 42.0	15 52.2	6R49.7	13R52.1	19 46.1	18 53.5	19 6.8
3 W	18 50 3.8	12 31.1	21 5.6	17 20.0	22 25.8	26 34.8	16 38.5	6 43.0	13 51.1	19 48.8	18 55.6	19 7.5
4 T	18 54 0.4	13 32.3	21 2.4	1♈19.4	23 47.3	27 28.2	17 24.8	6 36.2	13 50.0	19 51.4	18 57.8	19 8.1
5 F	18 57 56.9	14 33.4	20 59.2	14 56.1	25 9.8	28 22.4	18 11.2	6 29.2	13 48.7	19 53.9	18 59.8	19 8.7
6 S	19 1 53.5	15 34.6	20 56.0	28 11.9	26 33.3	29 17.2	18 57.6	6 22.2	13 47.4	19 56.4	19 1.9	19 9.3
7 S	19 5 50.0	16 35.7	20 52.9	11♉ 9.6	27 57.7	0♐12.5	19 44.0	6 15.1	13 45.9	19 58.9	19 4.0	19 9.8
8 M	19 9 46.6	17 36.9	20 49.7	23 52.2	29 22.8	1 8.5	20 30.5	6 7.8	13 44.4	20 1.3	19 6.0	19 10.3
9 T	19 13 43.1	18 38.0	20 46.5	6♊22.3	0♑48.8	2 5.1	21 17.0	6 0.5	13 42.7	20 3.7	19 8.1	19 10.7
10 W	19 17 39.7	19 39.2	20 43.3	18 42.0	2 15.5	3 2.2	22 3.5	5 53.1	13 41.0	20 6.1	19 10.1	19 11.2
11 T	19 21 36.3	20 40.3	20 40.1	0♋53.0	3 42.8	3 59.8	22 50.1	5 45.6	13 39.2	20 8.4	19 12.1	19 11.6
12 F	19 25 32.8	21 41.4	20 37.0	12 56.7	5 10.8	4 58.0	23 36.7	5 38.1	13 37.2	20 10.6	19 14.1	19 11.9
13 S	19 29 29.4	22 42.5	20 33.8	24 54.2	6 39.4	5 56.6	24 23.3	5 30.4	13 35.1	20 12.8	19 16.1	19 12.2
14 S	19 33 25.9	23 43.6	20 30.6	6♌46.8	8 8.5	6 55.7	25 10.0	5 22.7	13 33.0	20 15.0	19 18.0	19 12.5
15 M	19 37 22.5	24 44.7	20 27.4	18 36.0	9 38.3	7 55.3	25 56.7	5 14.9	13 30.7	20 17.1	19 20.0	19 12.7
16 T	19 41 19.0	25 45.8	20 24.3	0♍24.1	11 8.6	8 55.3	26 43.4	5 7.1	13 28.3	20 19.2	19 21.9	19 12.9
17 W	19 45 15.6	26 46.9	20 21.1	12 13.9	12 39.5	9 55.8	27 30.1	4 59.2	13 25.9	20 21.2	19 23.8	19 13.1
18 T	19 49 12.1	27 48.0	20 17.9	24 8.8	14 11.0	10 56.7	28 16.9	4 51.3	13 23.3	20 23.2	19 25.7	19 13.2
19 F	19 53 8.7	28 49.0	20 14.7	6♎13.0	15 43.0	11 57.9	29 3.7	4 43.4	13 20.7	20 25.1	19 27.5	19 13.3
20 S	19 57 5.3	29 50.1	20 11.6	18 31.2	17 15.6	12 59.6	29 50.6	4 35.4	13 17.9	20 27.0	19 29.4	19 13.4
21 S	20 1 1.8	0♒51.2	20 8.4	1♏ 8.4	18 48.7	14 1.6	0♒37.4	4 27.4	13 15.1	20 28.8	19 31.2	19 13.4
22 M	20 4 58.4	1 52.2	20 5.2	14 9.2	20 22.4	15 4.0	1 24.3	4 19.4	13 12.2	20 30.6	19 33.0	19 13.4
23 T	20 8 54.9	2 53.3	20 2.0	27 37.5	21 56.8	16 6.7	2 11.3	4 11.3	13 9.2	20 32.4	19 34.8	19 13.4
24 W	20 12 51.5	3 54.3	19 58.8	11♐35.2	23 31.6	17 9.7	2 58.2	4 3.3	13 6.1	20 34.0	19 36.5	19R13.3
25 T	20 16 48.0	4 55.3	19 55.7	26 1.8	25 7.1	18 13.1	3 45.2	3 55.2	13 2.9	20 35.7	19 38.2	19 13.2
26 F	20 20 44.6	5 56.3	19 52.5	10♑53.4	26 43.2	19 16.8	4 32.2	3 47.2	12 59.6	20 37.3	19 39.9	19 13.0
27 S	20 24 41.1	6 57.4	19 49.3	26 2.8	28 20.0	20 20.7	5 19.2	3 39.2	12 56.2	20 38.8	19 41.6	19 12.8
28 S	20 28 37.7	7 58.4	19 46.1	11♒20.1	29 57.3	21 25.0	6 6.3	3 31.2	12 52.8	20 40.3	19 43.3	19 12.6
29 M	20 32 34.3	8 59.3	19 43.0	26 34.5	1♒35.4	22 29.5	6 53.3	3 23.2	12 49.3	20 41.7	19 44.9	19 12.3
30 T	20 36 30.8	10 0.3	19 39.8	11♓35.8	3 14.1	23 34.2	7 40.4	3 15.2	12 45.7	20 43.1	19 46.5	19 12.0
31 W	20 40 27.4	11 1.3	19 36.6	26 16.5	4 53.5	24 39.3	8 27.6	3 7.3	12 42.1	20 44.4	19 48.2	19 11.7

DECLINATION at NOON

DAY	EPHEMERIS SIDEREAL TIME h m s	☉	☊	☽	☿	♀	♂	♃	♄	♅	♆	♇
1 M	18 42 10.7	23S 1.5	3N29.4	12S49.7	22S 1.2	15S20.3	23S31.0	19N 6.4	8N 3.0	17S20.7	21S35.7	8N18.5
4 T	18 54 0.4	22 45.0	3 33.1	0 23.7	22 40.9	15 54.5	23 15.1	19 12.0	8 4.9	17 22.8	21 36.2	8 19.4
7 S	19 5 50.0	22 24.5	3 36.9	11N24.4	23 12.8	16 29.1	22 56.8	19 17.8	8 7.1	17 24.8	21 36.7	8 20.4
10 W	19 17 39.7	21 60.0	3 40.6	17 54.7	23 35.6	17 3.7	22 36.2	19 23.7	8 9.7	17 26.7	21 37.1	8 21.5
13 S	19 29 29.4	21 31.6	3 44.4	17 5.9	23 48.2	17 37.5	22 13.3	19 29.8	8 12.7	17 28.5	21 37.6	8 22.8
16 T	19 41 19.0	20 59.5	3 48.1	9 49.9	23 50.0	18 10.1	21 48.1	19 35.9	8 16.0	17 30.1	21 38.0	8 24.1
19 F	19 53 8.7	20 23.8	3 51.9	1S 1.7	23 40.2	18 41.0	21 20.7	19 42.1	8 19.5	17 31.7	21 38.3	8 25.6
22 M	20 4 58.4	19 44.6	3 55.6	12 0.9	23 18.4	19 9.5	20 51.2	19 48.2	8 23.4	17 33.1	21 38.7	8 27.2
25 T	20 16 48.0	19 2.1	3 59.3	18 16.3	22 44.2	19 35.4	20 19.5	19 54.3	8 27.6	17 34.4	21 39.0	8 28.9
28 S	20 28 37.7	18 16.5	4 3.1	14 23.9	21 57.4	19 58.1	19 45.8	20 0.3	8 32.1	17 35.6	21 39.3	8 30.7
31 W	20 40 27.4	17 27.8	4 6.8	2 10.4	20 57.5	20 17.2	19 10.2	20 6.2	8 36.7	17 36.7	21 39.6	8 32.6

FEBRUARY 1979

LONGITUDE at NOON

DAY	EPHEMERIS SIDEREAL TIME h m s	☉ ° ′	☊ ° ′	☽ ° ′	☿ ° ′	♀ ° ′	♂ ° ′	♃ ° ′	♄ ° ′	♅ ° ′	♆ ° ′	♇ ° ′
1 T	20 44 23.9	12♒ 2.2	19♍33.4	10♈31.9	6♒33.5	25♐44.5	9♒14.7	2♌59.5	12♍38.3	20♏45.7	19♐49.7	19♎11.4
2 F	20 48 20.5	13 3.1	19 30.2	24 20.5	8 14.3	26 50.0	10 1.9	2R51.6	12R34.5	20 46.9	19 51.3	19R11.0
3 S	20 52 17.0	14 4.0	19 27.1	7♉43.1	9 55.8	27 55.7	10 49.0	2 43.9	12 30.7	20 48.1	19 52.8	19 10.5
4 S	20 56 13.6	15 4.8	19 23.9	20 42.5	11 38.0	29 1.7	11 36.2	2 36.2	12 26.7	20 49.2	19 54.3	19 10.1
5 M	21 0 10.1	16 5.7	19 20.7	3♊21.9	13 21.0	0♑ 7.8	12 23.4	2 28.5	12 22.7	20 50.3	19 55.7	19 9.6
6 T	21 4 6.7	17 6.5	19 17.5	15 45.2	15 4.7	1 14.2	13 10.6	2 20.9	12 18.6	20 51.3	19 57.2	19 9.0
7 W	21 8 3.2	18 7.3	19 14.4	27 56.0	16 49.2	2 20.7	13 57.8	2 13.4	12 14.5	20 52.2	19 58.6	19 8.5
8 T	21 11 59.8	19 8.0	19 11.2	9♋57.5	18 34.4	3 27.4	14 45.0	2 6.0	12 10.3	20 53.1	19 59.9	19 7.9
9 F	21 15 56.4	20 8.7	19 8.0	21 52.6	20 20.4	4 34.4	15 32.2	1 58.7	12 6.1	20 54.0	20 1.3	19 7.2
10 S	21 19 52.9	21 9.5	19 4.8	3♌43.9	22 7.2	5 41.5	16 19.5	1 51.5	12 1.8	20 54.7	20 2.6	19 6.6
11 S	21 23 49.5	22 10.1	19 1.6	15 33.3	23 54.7	6 48.8	17 6.7	1 44.3	11 57.5	20 55.5	20 3.9	19 5.9
12 M	21 27 46.0	23 10.8	18 58.5	27 22.9	25 42.8	7 56.3	17 54.0	1 37.3	11 53.1	20 56.2	20 5.2	19 5.1
13 T	21 31 42.6	24 11.4	18 55.3	9♍14.5	27 31.7	9 3.9	18 41.3	1 30.4	11 48.6	20 56.8	20 6.4	19 4.4
14 W	21 35 39.1	25 12.1	18 52.1	21 10.2	29 21.2	10 11.7	19 28.6	1 23.5	11 44.2	20 57.3	20 7.6	19 3.6
15 T	21 39 35.7	26 12.7	18 48.9	3♎12.5	1♓11.3	11 19.7	20 15.9	1 16.8	11 39.6	20 57.9	20 8.8	19 2.8
16 F	21 43 32.2	27 13.2	18 45.8	15 24.0	3 1.9	12 27.8	21 3.2	1 10.3	11 35.1	20 58.3	20 9.9	19 1.9
17 S	21 47 28.8	28 13.8	18 42.6	27 47.9	4 52.9	13 36.1	21 50.5	1 3.8	11 30.5	20 58.7	20 11.0	19 1.0
18 S	21 51 25.3	29 14.3	18 39.4	10♏27.7	6 44.1	14 44.5	22 37.8	0 57.5	11 25.9	20 59.1	20 12.1	19 0.1
19 M	21 55 21.9	0♓14.8	18 36.2	23 26.8	8 35.6	15 53.0	23 25.1	0 51.3	11 21.2	20 59.4	20 13.2	18 59.2
20 T	21 59 18.4	1 15.3	18 33.0	6♐48.3	10 27.0	17 1.7	24 12.5	0 45.2	11 16.5	20 59.6	20 14.2	18 58.2
21 W	22 3 15.0	2 15.8	18 29.9	20 34.5	12 18.3	18 10.6	24 59.9	0 39.3	11 11.9	20 59.8	20 15.2	18 57.3
22 T	22 7 11.6	3 16.3	18 26.7	4♑45.7	14 9.0	19 19.5	25 47.2	0 33.5	11 7.1	20 60.0	20 16.2	18 56.2
23 F	22 11 8.1	4 16.7	18 23.5	19 20.5	15 59.0	20 28.6	26 34.6	0 27.9	11 2.4	21 0.0	20 17.1	18 55.2
24 S	22 15 4.7	5 17.1	18 20.3	4♒14.3	17 48.0	21 37.8	27 21.9	0 22.4	10 57.6	21 0.1	20 18.0	18 54.1
25 S	22 19 1.2	6 17.5	18 17.2	19 20.2	19 35.6	22 47.0	28 9.3	0 17.1	10 52.8	21R 0.0	20 18.9	18 53.0
26 M	22 22 57.8	7 17.8	18 14.0	4♓29.3	21 21.4	23 56.4	28 56.6	0 12.0	10 48.0	20 59.9	20 19.7	18 51.9
27 T	22 26 54.3	8 18.1	18 10.8	19 32.2	23 4.9	25 5.9	29 44.0	0 7.0	10 43.2	20 59.8	20 20.5	18 50.7
28 W	22 30 50.9	9 18.4	18 7.6	4♈20.2	24 45.7	26 15.5	0♓31.3	0 2.1	10 38.4	20 59.6	20 21.3	18 49.5

DECLINATION at NOON

DAY	EPHEMERIS SIDEREAL TIME h m s	☉	☊	☽	☿	♀	♂	♃	♄	♅	♆	♇
1 T	20 44 23.9	17S11.0	4N 8.1	2N19.6	20S34.7	20S22.8	18S57.9	20N 8.1	8N38.4	17S37.0	21S39.7	8N33.2
4 S	20 56 13.6	16 18.7	4 11.8	13 27.3	19 17.3	20 36.8	18 19.8	20 13.7	8 43.3	17 37.9	21 40.0	8 35.2
7 W	21 8 3.2	15 23.9	4 15.6	18 17.4	17 46.6	20 46.5	17 39.9	20 19.1	8 48.5	17 38.7	21 40.2	8 37.3
10 S	21 19 52.9	14 26.8	4 19.3	15 47.3	16 2.6	20 51.8	16 58.3	20 24.3	8 53.8	17 39.3	21 40.4	8 39.4
13 T	21 31 42.6	13 27.5	4 23.0	7 24.3	14 5.7	20 52.4	16 15.1	20 29.2	8 59.3	17 39.8	21 40.5	8 41.6
16 F	21 43 32.2	12 26.2	4 26.7	3S46.9	11 56.4	20 48.2	15 30.4	20 33.8	9 4.8	17 40.2	21 40.7	8 43.9
19 M	21 55 21.9	11 23.1	4 30.5	13 57.8	9 36.0	20 39.0	14 44.3	20 38.1	9 10.5	17 40.5	21 40.8	8 46.2
22 T	22 7 11.6	10 18.4	4 34.2	18 18.8	7 6.5	20 24.9	13 56.7	20 42.1	9 16.2	17 40.6	21 40.9	8 48.5
25 S	22 19 1.2	9 12.2	4 37.9	12 38.9	4 31.6	20 5.7	13 8.0	20 45.7	9 21.9	17 40.6	21 41.0	8 50.9
28 W	22 30 50.9	8 4.8	4 41.7	0N18.5	1 56.6	19 41.4	12 18.1	20 49.0	9 27.6	17 40.4	21 41.1	8 53.3

MARCH 1979

DAY	EPHEMERIS SIDEREAL TIME	☉	☊	☽	☿	♀	♂	♃	♄	♅	♆	♇
	h m s	° ′	° ′	° ′	° ′	° ′	° ′	° ′	° ′	° ′	° ′	° ′
LONGITUDE at NOON												
1 T	22 34 47.4	10 ♓ 18.7	18 ♍ 4.4	18 ♈ 46.6	26 ♓ 23.2	27 ♑ 25.2	1 ♓ 18.7	29 ♋ 57.5	10 ♍ 33.6	20 ♏ 59.3	20 ♐ 22.0	18 ♎ 48.3
2 F	22 38 44.0	11 18.9	18 1.3	2 ♉ 47.2	27 57.0	28 35.0	2 6.0	29 R 53.0	10 R 28.8	20 R 59.0	20 22.7	18 R 47.1
3 S	22 42 40.5	12 19.1	17 58.1	16 20.8	29 26.3	29 44.9	2 53.4	29 48.6	10 24.0	20 58.7	20 23.4	18 45.9
4 S	22 46 37.1	13 19.3	17 54.9	29 28.3	0 ♈ 50.7	0 ♒ 54.8	3 40.7	29 44.5	10 19.2	20 58.2	20 24.1	18 44.6
5 M	22 50 33.6	14 19.4	17 51.7	12 ♊ 12.4	2 9.5	2 4.9	4 28.0	29 40.5	10 14.4	20 57.8	20 24.7	18 43.3
6 T	22 54 30.2	15 19.5	17 48.6	24 36.9	3 22.2	3 15.0	5 15.3	29 36.7	10 9.6	20 57.2	20 25.2	18 42.0
7 W	22 58 26.7	16 19.5	17 45.4	6 ♋ 45.9	4 28.2	4 25.2	6 2.6	29 33.1	10 4.8	20 56.7	20 25.8	18 40.6
8 T	23 2 23.3	17 19.5	17 42.2	18 44.0	5 27.1	5 35.4	6 49.9	29 29.7	10 0.1	20 56.0	20 26.3	18 39.3
9 F	23 6 19.8	18 19.5	17 39.0	0 ♌ 35.4	6 18.4	6 45.8	7 37.2	29 26.4	9 55.3	20 55.4	20 26.7	18 37.9
10 S	23 10 16.4	19 19.5	17 35.8	12 23.8	7 1.7	7 56.2	8 24.5	29 23.4	9 50.6	20 54.6	20 27.2	18 36.5
11 S	23 14 12.9	20 19.4	17 32.7	24 12.7	7 36.7	9 6.7	9 11.8	29 20.5	9 45.9	20 53.9	20 27.6	18 35.1
12 M	23 18 9.5	21 19.2	17 29.5	6 ♍ 5.0	8 3.1	10 17.3	9 59.0	29 17.8	9 41.3	20 53.0	20 28.0	18 33.6
13 T	23 22 6.0	22 19.1	17 26.3	18 3.0	8 20.9	11 27.9	10 46.3	29 15.3	9 36.6	20 52.1	20 28.3	18 32.2
14 W	23 26 2.6	23 18.9	17 23.1	0 ♎ 9.0	8 30.0	12 38.7	11 33.5	29 13.1	9 32.1	20 51.3	20 28.6	18 30.7
15 T	23 29 59.2	24 18.7	17 20.0	12 24.3	8 30.4	13 49.4	12 20.7	29 11.0	9 27.5	20 50.3	20 28.9	18 29.2
16 F	23 33 55.7	25 18.5	17 16.8	24 50.7	8 R 22.4	15 0.3	13 7.9	29 9.0	9 23.0	20 49.3	20 29.1	18 27.7
17 S	23 37 52.3	26 18.2	17 13.6	7 ♏ 29.6	8 6.4	16 11.2	13 55.1	29 7.3	9 18.5	20 48.2	20 29.3	18 26.2
18 S	23 41 48.8	27 17.9	17 10.4	20 22.2	7 42.7	17 22.2	14 42.3	29 5.7	9 14.0	20 47.1	20 29.5	18 24.7
19 M	23 45 45.4	28 17.5	17 7.2	3 ♐ 30.1	7 12.1	18 33.2	15 29.5	29 4.4	9 9.6	20 45.9	20 29.7	18 23.1
20 T	23 49 41.9	29 17.2	17 4.1	16 54.5	6 35.2	19 44.3	16 16.6	29 3.2	9 5.2	20 44.7	20 29.8	18 21.6
21 W	23 53 38.5	0 ♈ 16.7	17 0.9	0 ♑ 36.3	5 53.0	20 55.4	17 3.8	29 2.3	9 0.9	20 43.4	20 29.8	18 20.0
22 T	23 57 35.0	1 16.3	16 57.7	14 35.8	5 6.5	22 6.6	17 50.9	29 1.5	8 56.6	20 42.1	20 29.9	18 18.4
23 F	0 1 31.6	2 15.9	16 54.5	28 52.3	4 16.7	23 17.9	18 38.0	29 0.9	8 52.4	20 40.7	20 29.9	18 16.8
24 S	0 5 28.1	3 15.4	16 51.3	13 ♒ 23.6	3 24.7	24 29.2	19 25.1	29 0.5	8 48.2	20 39.3	20 R 29.8	18 15.2
25 S	0 9 24.7	4 14.9	16 48.2	28 5.9	2 31.7	25 40.5	20 12.1	29 0.3	8 44.1	20 37.9	20 29.8	18 13.6
26 M	0 13 21.2	5 14.3	16 45.0	12 ♓ 53.7	1 38.7	26 51.9	20 59.2	29 0.3	8 40.1	20 36.4	20 29.7	18 12.0
27 T	0 17 17.8	6 13.7	16 41.8	27 40.2	0 46.9	28 3.3	21 46.2	29 D 0.5	8 36.1	20 34.9	20 29.5	18 10.3
28 W	0 21 14.3	7 13.1	16 38.6	12 ♈ 18.2	29 ♓ 57.1	29 14.8	22 33.2	29 0.9	8 32.1	20 33.3	20 29.4	18 8.7
29 T	0 25 10.9	8 12.5	16 35.5	26 40.9	29 10.3	0 ♓ 26.3	23 20.1	29 1.5	8 28.3	20 31.7	20 29.2	18 7.0
30 F	0 29 7.4	9 11.8	16 32.3	10 ♉ 43.1	28 27.2	1 37.9	24 7.1	29 2.2	8 24.5	20 30.0	20 28.9	18 5.4
31 S	0 33 4.0	10 11.1	16 29.1	24 21.4	27 48.4	2 49.5	24 54.0	29 3.2	8 20.8	20 28.3	20 28.7	18 3.7
DECLINATION at NOON												
1 T	22 34 47.4	7 S 42.1	4 N 42.9	4 N 48.2	1 S 6.1	19 S 32.3	12 S 1.2	20 N 50.0	9 N 29.5	17 S 40.4	21 S 41.1	8 N 54.1
4 S	22 46 37.1	6 33.3	4 46.6	15 6.8	1 N 17.5	19 1.4	11 9.9	20 52.8	9 35.2	17 40.1	21 41.1	8 56.5
7 W	22 58 26.7	5 23.8	4 50.3	18 16.2	3 22.4	18 25.8	10 17.6	20 55.3	9 40.8	17 39.6	21 41.1	8 58.9
10 S	23 10 16.4	4 13.6	4 54.1	14 9.1	4 59.9	17 45.4	9 24.5	20 57.3	9 46.2	17 39.1	21 41.1	9 1.3
13 T	23 22 6.0	3 2.9	4 57.8	4 46.2	6 2.4	17 0.5	8 30.7	20 59.0	9 51.6	17 38.4	21 41.0	9 3.7
16 F	23 33 55.7	1 51.9	5 1.5	6 S 37.7	6 25.1	16 11.2	7 36.2	21 0.3	9 56.8	17 37.6	21 41.0	9 6.0
19 M	23 45 45.4	0 40.7	5 5.2	15 48.9	6 6.5	15 17.8	6 41.1	21 1.2	10 1.9	17 36.7	21 40.9	9 8.4
22 T	23 57 35.0	0 N 30.4	5 8.9	17 57.8	5 11.0	14 20.4	5 45.5	21 1.8	10 6.7	17 35.7	21 40.8	9 10.7
25 S	0 9 24.7	1 41.3	5 12.6	10 29.3	3 48.7	13 19.4	4 49.5	21 2.0	10 11.3	17 34.5	21 40.6	9 12.9
28 W	0 21 14.3	2 51.9	5 16.3	2 N 49.2	2 14.2	12 14.9	3 53.3	21 1.8	10 15.7	17 33.3	21 40.5	9 15.1
31 S	0 33 4.0	4 2.0	5 20.0	14 10.1	0 42.2	11 7.3	2 56.8	21 1.3	10 19.9	17 32.0	21 40.3	9 17.3

APRIL 1979

DAY	EPHEMERIS SIDEREAL TIME	☉	☊	☽	☿	♀	♂	♃	♄	♅	♆	♇
LONGITUDE at NOON												
1 S	0 37 0.5	11 ♈ 10.3	16 ♍ 25.9	7 ♊ 34.7	27 ♓ 14.4	4 ♓ 1.1	25 ♓ 40.9	29 ♋ 4.3	8 ♍ 17.1	20 ♏ 26.6	20 ♐ 28.4	18 ♎ 2.0
2 M	0 40 57.1	12 9.5	16 22.7	20 24.2	26 R 45.5	5 12.8	26 27.8	29 5.7	8 R 13.5	20 R 24.8	20 R 28.0	18 R 0.3
3 T	0 44 53.6	13 8.7	16 19.6	2 ♋ 52.6	26 22.0	6 24.5	27 14.6	29 7.2	8 10.0	20 23.0	20 27.7	17 58.7
4 W	0 48 50.2	14 7.8	16 16.4	15 3.9	26 4.2	7 36.2	28 1.5	29 9.0	8 6.7	20 21.2	20 27.3	17 57.0
5 T	0 52 46.7	15 6.9	16 13.2	27 2.5	25 51.9	8 48.0	28 48.2	29 10.9	8 3.3	20 19.3	20 26.9	17 55.3
6 F	0 56 43.3	16 6.0	16 10.0	8 ♌ 53.5	25 45.1	9 59.8	29 35.0	29 12.9	8 0.0	20 17.4	20 26.5	17 53.7
7 S	1 0 39.8	17 5.0	16 6.9	20 41.8	25 43.9	11 11.6	0 ♈ 21.7	29 15.2	7 56.9	20 15.5	20 26.0	17 52.0
8 S	1 4 36.4	18 4.0	16 3.7	2 ♍ 32.0	25 D 48.1	12 23.4	1 8.4	29 17.7	7 53.8	20 13.5	20 25.5	17 50.3
9 M	1 8 32.9	19 2.9	16 0.5	14 28.1	25 57.6	13 35.3	1 55.1	29 20.3	7 50.7	20 11.5	20 24.9	17 48.6
10 T	1 12 29.5	20 1.8	15 57.3	26 33.6	26 12.1	14 47.2	2 41.7	29 23.1	7 47.8	20 9.4	20 24.3	17 46.9
11 W	1 16 26.1	21 0.7	15 54.1	8 ♎ 51.1	26 31.4	15 59.1	3 28.3	29 26.1	7 45.0	20 7.3	20 23.7	17 45.2
12 T	1 20 22.6	21 59.5	15 51.0	21 22.3	26 55.5	17 11.1	4 14.8	29 29.3	7 42.2	20 5.2	20 23.1	17 43.5
13 F	1 24 19.2	22 58.3	15 47.8	4 ♏ 8.1	27 24.0	18 23.1	5 1.3	29 32.6	7 39.5	20 3.1	20 22.4	17 41.9
14 S	1 28 15.7	23 57.1	15 44.6	17 8.5	27 56.7	19 35.1	5 47.8	29 36.1	7 37.0	20 0.9	20 21.7	17 40.2
15 S	1 32 12.3	24 55.8	15 41.4	0 ♐ 22.9	28 33.5	20 47.1	6 34.3	29 39.8	7 34.5	19 58.7	20 21.0	17 38.5
16 M	1 36 8.8	25 54.5	15 38.3	13 50.1	29 14.2	21 59.2	7 20.7	29 43.6	7 32.1	19 56.5	20 20.2	17 36.8
17 T	1 40 5.4	26 53.2	15 35.1	27 28.9	29 58.6	23 11.3	8 7.1	29 47.7	7 29.8	19 54.3	20 19.5	17 35.2
18 W	1 44 1.9	27 51.8	15 31.9	11 ♑ 18.2	0 ♈ 46.5	24 23.4	8 53.5	29 51.9	7 27.6	19 52.0	20 18.7	17 33.5
19 T	1 47 58.5	28 50.5	15 28.7	25 16.8	1 37.7	25 35.6	9 39.8	29 56.2	7 25.5	19 49.7	20 17.8	17 31.9
20 F	1 51 55.0	29 49.0	15 25.5	9 ♒ 23.7	2 32.1	26 47.8	10 26.1	0 ♌ 0.8	7 23.4	19 47.4	20 17.0	17 30.2
21 S	1 55 51.6	0 ♉ 47.6	15 22.4	23 37.6	3 29.5	27 60.0	11 12.3	0 5.4	7 21.5	19 45.1	20 16.1	17 28.6
22 S	1 59 48.1	1 46.2	15 19.2	7 ♓ 56.7	4 29.9	29 12.2	11 58.6	0 10.3	7 19.7	19 42.7	20 15.1	17 27.0
23 M	2 3 44.7	2 44.7	15 16.0	22 18.3	5 33.0	0 ♈ 24.4	12 44.7	0 15.3	7 18.0	19 40.4	20 14.2	17 25.3
24 T	2 7 41.2	3 43.2	15 12.8	6 ♈ 38.9	6 38.8	1 36.7	13 30.9	0 20.5	7 16.4	19 38.0	20 13.2	17 23.7
25 W	2 11 37.8	4 41.7	15 9.7	20 54.1	7 47.2	2 49.0	14 17.0	0 25.9	7 14.9	19 35.6	20 12.3	17 22.2
26 T	2 15 34.3	5 40.1	15 6.5	4 ♉ 58.9	8 58.1	4 1.3	15 3.1	0 31.3	7 13.5	19 33.2	20 11.2	17 20.6
27 F	2 19 30.9	6 38.5	15 3.3	18 48.6	10 11.3	5 13.6	15 49.1	0 37.0	7 12.2	19 30.8	20 10.2	17 19.0
28 S	2 23 27.5	7 36.8	15 0.1	2 ♊ 19.7	11 26.9	6 26.0	16 35.1	0 42.8	7 10.9	19 28.3	20 9.1	17 17.5
29 S	2 27 24.0	8 35.2	14 56.9	15 30.0	12 44.7	7 38.3	17 21.0	0 48.7	7 9.8	19 25.9	20 8.0	17 15.9
30 M	2 31 20.6	9 33.5	14 53.8	28 19.0	14 4.7	8 50.7	18 6.9	0 54.8	7 8.8	19 23.4	20 6.9	17 14.4
DECLINATION at NOON												
1 S	0 37 0.5	4 N 25.2	5 N 21.3	16 N 28.1	0 N 14.2	10 S 44.1	2 S 37.9	21 N 1.0	10 N 21.2	17 S 31.5	21 S 40.3	9 N 18.0
4 W	0 48 50.2	5 34.4	5 25.0	17 58.5	0 S 57.4	9 32.7	1 41.3	21 0.0	10 24.9	17 30.1	21 40.1	9 20.0
7 S	1 0 39.8	6 42.6	5 28.7	12 22.0	1 47.3	8 18.9	0 44.7	20 58.6	10 28.4	17 28.5	21 39.9	9 21.9
10 T	1 12 29.5	7 49.8	5 32.4	2 8.5	2 13.9	7 2.8	0 N 11.8	20 56.9	10 31.5	17 26.9	21 39.6	9 23.8
13 F	1 24 19.2	8 55.9	5 36.1	9 S 19.1	2 18.0	5 44.8	1 8.2	20 54.8	10 34.4	17 25.2	21 39.4	9 25.6
16 M	1 36 8.8	10 0.6	5 39.8	17 19.8	2 1.3	4 25.2	2 4.3	20 52.4	10 36.9	17 23.5	21 39.1	9 27.3
19 T	1 47 58.5	11 3.8	5 43.5	17 5.9	1 25.7	3 4.2	3 0.1	20 49.7	10 39.1	17 21.7	21 38.8	9 28.8
22 S	1 59 48.1	12 5.3	5 47.1	7 51.6	0 33.5	1 42.2	3 55.5	20 46.6	10 40.9	17 19.8	21 38.6	9 30.3
25 W	2 11 37.8	13 5.2	5 50.8	5 N 28.1	0 N 33.7	0 19.5	4 50.5	20 43.2	10 42.3	17 17.9	21 38.3	9 31.6
28 S	2 23 27.5	14 3.0	5 54.5	15 45.4	1 54.1	1 N 3.7	5 44.8	20 39.4	10 43.4	17 15.9	21 37.9	9 32.9

MAY 1979

LONGITUDE at NOON

DAY	EPHEMERIS SIDEREAL TIME	☉	☊	☾	☿	♀	♂	♃	♄	♅	♆	♇
	h m s	° ′	° ′	° ′	° ′	° ′	° ′	° ′	° ′	° ′	° ′	° ′
1 T	2 35 17.1	10♉31.7	14♍50.6	10♋48.1	15♈26.8	10♈ 3.0	18♈52.7	1♌ 1.1	7♍ 7.9	19♏20.9	20♐ 5.8	17♎12.9
2 W	2 39 13.7	11 30.0	14 47.4	23 0.4	16 51.1	11 15.4	19 38.5	1 7.5	7R 7.1	19R18.4	20R 4.6	17R11.3
3 T	2 43 10.2	12 28.2	14 44.2	4♌59.9	18 17.4	12 27.8	20 24.3	1 14.0	7 6.5	19 15.9	20 3.4	17 9.9
4 F	2 47 6.8	13 26.3	14 41.1	16 51.4	19 45.8	13 40.2	21 10.0	1 20.7	7 5.9	19 13.4	20 2.2	17 8.4
5 S	2 51 3.3	14 24.5	14 37.9	28 40.1	21 16.2	14 52.6	21 55.7	1 27.5	7 5.4	19 10.9	20 1.0	17 6.9
6 S	2 54 59.9	15 22.6	14 34.7	10♍31.5	22 48.6	16 5.1	22 41.3	1 34.4	7 5.0	19 8.4	19 59.7	17 5.5
7 M	2 58 56.4	16 20.6	14 31.5	22 30.6	24 23.0	17 17.5	23 26.8	1 41.5	7 4.7	19 5.8	19 58.5	17 4.1
8 T	3 2 53.0	17 18.7	14 28.3	4♎41.8	25 59.3	18 30.0	24 12.3	1 48.8	7 4.6	19 3.3	19 57.2	17 2.7
9 W	3 6 49.5	18 16.7	14 25.2	17 8.9	27 37.7	19 42.5	24 57.8	1 56.1	7 4.5	19 0.8	19 55.9	17 1.3
10 T	3 10 46.1	19 14.7	14 22.0	29 54.2	29 18.0	20 54.9	25 43.2	2 3.6	7D 4.6	18 58.3	19 54.5	16 59.9
11 F	3 14 42.7	20 12.6	14 18.8	12♏58.8	1♉ 0.3	22 7.4	26 28.6	2 11.2	7 4.7	18 55.7	19 53.2	16 58.6
12 S	3 18 39.2	21 10.5	14 15.6	26 22.0	2 44.5	23 20.0	27 13.9	2 19.0	7 5.0	18 53.2	19 51.8	16 57.2
13 S	3 22 35.8	22 8.4	14 12.5	10♐ 1.7	4 30.7	24 32.5	27 59.2	2 26.8	7 5.3	18 50.7	19 50.5	16 55.9
14 M	3 26 32.3	23 6.3	14 9.3	23 54.6	6 19.0	25 45.0	28 44.4	2 34.8	7 5.8	18 48.2	19 49.1	16 54.7
15 T	3 30 28.9	24 4.2	14 6.1	7♑56.7	8 9.2	26 57.6	29 29.6	2 42.9	7 6.3	18 45.6	19 47.7	16 53.4
16 W	3 34 25.4	25 2.0	14 2.9	22 4.3	10 1.4	28 10.2	0♉14.8	2 51.2	7 7.1	18 43.2	19 46.3	16 52.2
17 T	3 38 22.0	25 59.8	13 59.7	6♒14.0	11 55.6	29 22.8	0 59.9	2 59.6	7 7.8	18 40.7	19 44.8	16 51.0
18 F	3 42 18.5	26 57.6	13 56.6	20 23.4	13 51.7	0♉35.4	1 44.9	3 8.0	7 8.7	18 38.2	19 43.4	16 49.8
19 S	3 46 15.1	27 55.4	13 53.4	4♓31.0	15 49.7	1 48.0	2 29.9	3 16.6	7 9.7	18 35.7	19 41.9	16 48.6
20 S	3 50 11.7	28 53.2	13 50.2	18 35.8	17 49.6	3 0.7	3 14.9	3 25.3	7 10.8	18 33.2	19 40.4	16 47.5
21 M	3 54 8.2	29 50.9	13 47.0	2♈36.9	19 51.3	4 13.3	3 59.7	3 34.1	7 12.0	18 30.7	19 38.9	16 46.3
22 T	3 58 4.8	0♊48.6	13 43.9	16 32.9	21 54.8	5 26.0	4 44.6	3 43.1	7 13.3	18 28.3	19 37.4	16 45.3
23 W	4 2 1.3	1 46.3	13 40.7	0♉22.3	23 60.0	6 38.7	5 29.4	3 52.1	7 14.7	18 25.9	19 35.9	16 44.2
24 T	4 5 57.9	2 44.0	13 37.5	14 2.4	26 6.6	7 51.4	6 14.1	4 1.2	7 16.2	18 23.4	19 34.4	16 43.1
25 F	4 9 54.4	3 41.7	13 34.3	27 30.7	28 14.7	9 4.1	6 58.8	4 10.5	7 17.8	18 21.0	19 32.8	16 42.1
26 S	4 13 51.0	4 39.3	13 31.2	10♊44.5	0♊24.0	10 16.8	7 43.4	4 19.8	7 19.5	18 18.6	19 31.3	16 41.1
27 S	4 17 47.5	5 36.9	13 28.0	23 42.1	2 34.3	11 29.5	8 28.0	4 29.3	7 21.3	18 16.2	19 29.7	16 40.2
28 M	4 21 44.1	6 34.5	13 24.8	6♋22.6	4 45.4	12 42.2	9 12.5	4 38.9	7 23.2	18 13.9	19 28.1	16 39.2
29 T	4 25 40.7	7 32.1	13 21.6	18 46.6	6 57.0	13 55.0	9 57.0	4 48.5	7 25.2	18 11.5	19 26.6	16 38.3
30 W	4 29 37.2	8 29.7	13 18.4	0♌55.9	9 9.0	15 7.7	10 41.4	4 58.3	7 27.3	18 9.2	19 25.0	16 37.4
31 T	4 33 33.8	9 27.2	13 15.3	12 53.8	11 21.0	16 20.5	11 25.7	5 8.1	7 29.5	18 6.9	19 23.4	16 36.6

DECLINATION at NOON

DAY	EPHEMERIS SIDEREAL TIME	☉	☊	☾	☿	♀	♂	♃	♄	♅	♆	♇
1 T	2 35 17.1	14N58.8	5N58.2	18N22.4	3N26.3	2N27.0	6N38.5	20N35.4	10N44.2	17S 13.9	21S 37.6	9N34.0
4 F	2 47 6.8	15 52.4	6 1.9	13 25.1	5 8.7	3 50.2	7 31.5	20 31.0	10 44.6	17 11.9	21 37.3	9 35.0
7 M	2 58 56.4	16 43.5	6 5.5	3 31.5	7 0.2	5 12.9	8 23.7	20 26.3	10 44.6	17 9.9	21 36.9	9 35.8
10 T	3 10 46.1	17 32.2	6 9.2	8S 6.9	8 59.2	6 34.8	9 15.0	20 21.3	10 44.3	17 7.8	21 36.6	9 36.5
13 S	3 22 35.8	18 18.2	6 12.9	16 58.7	11 4.2	7 55.7	10 5.4	20 16.0	10 43.6	17 5.8	21 36.2	9 37.1
16 W	3 34 25.4	19 1.5	6 16.6	17 39.7	13 13.0	9 15.2	10 54.8	20 10.4	10 42.6	17 3.7	21 35.8	9 37.5
19 S	3 46 15.1	19 41.8	6 20.2	9 1.8	15 23.3	10 33.0	11 43.2	20 4.4	10 41.2	17 1.7	21 35.5	9 37.8
22 T	3 58 4.8	20 19.2	6 23.9	4N 1.7	17 31.4	11 48.9	12 30.4	19 58.2	10 39.4	16 59.7	21 35.1	9 38.0
25 F	4 9 54.4	20 53.4	6 27.5	14 55.0	19 33.2	13 2.4	13 16.4	19 51.7	10 37.3	16 57.8	21 34.7	9 38.0
28 M	4 21 44.1	21 24.4	6 31.2	18 39.9	21 23.3	14 13.2	14 1.1	19 44.9	10 34.9	16 55.8	21 34.3	9 37.8
31 T	4 33 33.8	21 52.1	6 34.9	14 30.1	22 56.5	15 21.1	14 44.5	19 37.8	10 32.2	16 53.9	21 33.9	9 37.6

JUNE 1979

LONGITUDE at NOON

DAY	EPHEMERIS SIDEREAL TIME	☉	☊	☾	☿	♀	♂	♃	♄	♅	♆	♇
1 F	4 37 30.3	10♊24.7	13♍12.1	24♌44.5	13♊32.8	17♉33.3	12♉10.0	5♌18.1	7♍31.8	18♏ 4.6	19♐21.8	16♎35.7
2 S	4 41 26.9	11 22.2	13 8.9	6♍32.8	15 44.1	18 46.1	12 54.2	5 28.1	7 34.2	18R 2.4	19R20.2	16R34.9
3 S	4 45 23.4	12 19.7	13 5.7	18 24.1	17 54.5	19 58.9	13 38.4	5 38.2	7 36.7	18 0.1	19 18.6	16 34.2
4 M	4 49 20.0	13 17.1	13 2.6	0♎23.9	20 4.0	21 11.7	14 22.5	5 48.5	7 39.3	17 57.9	19 17.0	16 33.4
5 T	4 53 16.6	14 14.6	12 59.4	12 37.5	22 12.1	22 24.5	15 6.6	5 58.8	7 41.9	17 55.7	19 15.4	16 32.7
6 W	4 57 13.1	15 12.0	12 56.2	25 9.5	24 18.9	23 37.4	15 50.6	6 9.2	7 44.8	17 53.6	19 13.8	16 32.1
7 T	5 1 9.7	16 9.4	12 53.0	8♏ 3.3	26 23.9	24 50.2	16 34.6	6 19.7	7 47.6	17 51.5	19 12.2	16 31.5
8 F	5 5 6.2	17 6.8	12 49.9	21 20.8	28 27.0	26 3.1	17 18.4	6 30.2	7 50.6	17 49.4	19 10.6	16 30.8
9 S	5 9 2.8	18 4.2	12 46.7	5♐ 1.6	0♋28.2	27 15.9	18 2.3	6 40.9	7 53.7	17 47.3	19 8.9	16 30.3
10 S	5 12 59.3	19 1.5	12 43.5	19 3.4	2 27.3	28 28.8	18 46.0	6 51.6	7 56.8	17 45.3	19 7.3	16 29.7
11 M	5 16 55.9	19 58.9	12 40.3	3♑21.3	4 24.2	29 41.7	19 29.7	7 2.4	8 0.0	17 43.3	19 5.7	16 29.2
12 T	5 20 52.4	20 56.2	12 37.1	17 49.3	6 18.9	0♊54.6	20 13.4	7 13.3	8 3.4	17 41.3	19 4.1	16 28.7
13 W	5 24 49.0	21 53.5	12 34.0	2♒21.1	8 11.3	2 7.5	20 57.0	7 24.2	8 6.8	17 39.4	19 2.4	16 28.2
14 T	5 28 45.6	22 50.8	12 30.8	16 50.7	10 1.3	3 20.5	21 40.5	7 35.3	8 10.3	17 37.4	19 0.8	16 27.8
15 F	5 32 42.1	23 48.1	12 27.6	1♓13.5	11 48.9	4 33.4	22 24.0	7 46.4	8 13.9	17 35.6	18 59.2	16 27.4
16 S	5 36 38.7	24 45.4	12 24.4	15 26.8	13 34.1	5 46.4	23 7.4	7 57.5	8 17.6	17 33.7	18 57.6	16 27.0
17 S	5 40 35.2	25 42.7	12 21.3	29 29.2	15 16.8	6 59.4	23 50.8	8 8.8	8 21.3	17 31.9	18 56.0	16 26.7
18 M	5 44 31.8	26 39.9	12 18.1	13♈20.2	16 57.1	8 12.4	24 34.1	8 20.1	8 25.2	17 30.1	18 54.4	16 26.4
19 T	5 48 28.3	27 37.2	12 14.9	26 59.9	18 35.0	9 25.5	25 17.4	8 31.5	8 29.1	17 28.4	18 52.8	16 26.1
20 W	5 52 24.9	28 34.5	12 11.7	10♉28.5	20 10.4	10 38.5	26 0.6	8 42.9	8 33.1	17 26.7	18 51.2	16 25.9
21 T	5 56 21.5	29 31.8	12 8.6	23 45.7	21 43.3	11 51.6	26 43.7	8 54.4	8 37.2	17 25.0	18 49.6	16 25.7
22 F	6 0 18.0	0♋29.0	12 5.4	6♊51.1	23 13.7	13 4.7	27 26.8	9 6.0	8 41.4	17 23.4	18 48.0	16 25.5
23 S	6 4 14.6	1 26.3	12 2.2	19 44.0	24 41.5	14 17.8	28 9.8	9 17.6	8 45.7	17 21.8	18 46.4	16 25.4
24 S	6 8 11.1	2 23.6	11 59.0	2♋23.9	26 6.8	15 30.9	28 52.7	9 29.3	8 50.0	17 20.3	18 44.8	16 25.3
25 M	6 12 7.7	3 20.8	11 55.8	14 50.5	27 29.6	16 44.1	29 35.6	9 41.1	8 54.5	17 18.8	18 43.3	16 25.2
26 T	6 16 4.2	4 18.0	11 52.7	27 4.5	28 49.7	17 57.2	0♊18.4	9 52.9	8 59.0	17 17.3	18 41.7	16 25.2
27 W	6 20 0.8	5 15.3	11 49.5	9♌ 7.3	0♌ 7.2	19 10.4	1 1.2	10 4.9	9 3.6	17 15.9	18 40.2	16D25.3
28 T	6 23 57.4	6 12.6	11 46.3	21 1.2	1 21.9	20 23.6	1 43.9	10 16.8	9 8.3	17 14.6	18 38.7	16 25.3
29 F	6 27 53.9	7 9.8	11 43.1	2♍49.6	2 33.8	21 36.8	2 26.6	10 28.8	9 13.0	17 13.2	18 37.2	16 25.4
30 S	6 31 50.5	8 7.0	11 40.0	14 36.7	3 43.0	22 50.0	3 9.1	10 40.8	9 17.8	17 11.9	18 35.7	16 25.5

DECLINATION at NOON

DAY	EPHEMERIS SIDEREAL TIME	☉	☊	☾	☿	♀	♂	♃	♄	♅	♆	♇
1 F	4 37 30.3	22N 0.5	6N36.1	11N46.4	23N22.9	15N43.1	14N58.7	19N35.4	10N31.2	16S 53.3	21S 33.8	9N37.4
4 M	4 49 20.0	22 23.6	6 39.7	1 13.6	24 26.6	16 46.6	15 40.2	19 27.9	10 28.0	16 51.5	21 33.4	9 37.0
7 T	5 1 9.7	22 43.2	6 43.4	10S 16.8	25 5.6	17 46.4	16 20.4	19 20.1	10 24.5	16 49.8	21 33.1	9 36.4
10 S	5 12 59.3	22 59.1	6 47.0	18 1.4	25 20.1	18 42.1	16 59.0	19 12.1	10 20.7	16 48.1	21 32.7	9 35.6
13 W	5 24 49.0	23 11.5	6 50.7	16 30.6	25 12.3	19 33.6	17 36.0	19 3.8	10 16.5	16 46.5	21 32.3	9 34.7
16 S	5 36 38.7	23 20.1	6 54.3	6 2.3	24 45.1	20 20.5	18 11.5	18 55.3	10 12.1	16 45.0	21 31.9	9 33.7
19 T	5 48 28.3	23 25.0	6 58.0	7N 2.8	24 1.8	21 2.5	18 45.3	18 46.5	10 7.4	16 43.5	21 31.6	9 32.6
22 F	6 0 18.0	23 26.3	7 1.6	16 30.1	23 5.7	21 39.4	19 17.4	18 37.4	10 2.5	16 42.2	21 31.2	9 31.3
25 M	6 12 7.7	23 23.8	7 5.2	18 27.3	21 59.9	22 11.0	19 47.8	18 28.1	9 57.2	16 41.0	21 30.9	9 29.9
28 T	6 23 57.4	23 17.6	7 8.9	12 53.3	20 47.5	22 36.9	20 16.5	18 18.6	9 51.7	16 39.8	21 30.6	9 28.3

JULY 1979

DAY	EPHEMERIS SIDEREAL TIME	☉	☊	☽	☿	♀	♂	♃	♄	♅	♆	♇
	h m s	° ′	° ′	° ′	° ′	° ′	° ′	° ′	° ′	° ′	° ′	° ′
LONGITUDE at NOON												
1 S	6 35 47.0	9♋ 4.2	11♍36.8	26♍27.1	4♌49.2	24♊ 3.3	3♊51.6	10♌52.9	9♍22.7	17♏10.7	18♐34.2	16♎25.6
2 M	6 39 43.6	10 1.4	11 33.6	8♎26.1	5 52.4	25 16.5	4 34.1	11 5.0	9 27.6	17R 9.5	18R32.7	16 25.8
3 T	6 43 40.1	10 58.6	11 30.4	20 39.1	6 52.6	26 29.8	5 16.4	11 17.2	9 32.7	17 8.3	18 31.2	16 26.0
4 W	6 47 36.7	11 55.8	11 27.3	3♏11.2	7 49.6	27 43.1	5 58.7	11 29.5	9 37.8	17 7.2	18 29.7	16 26.2
5 T	6 51 33.3	12 53.0	11 24.1	16 6.5	8 43.3	28 56.4	6 41.0	11 41.7	9 42.9	17 6.2	18 28.3	16 26.5
6 F	6 55 29.8	13 50.2	11 20.9	29 28.0	9 33.6	0♋ 9.7	7 23.1	11 54.1	9 48.2	17 5.2	18 26.9	16 26.8
7 S	6 59 26.4	14 47.4	11 17.7	13♐16.6	10 20.4	1 23.0	8 5.3	12 6.4	9 53.5	17 4.2	18 25.4	16 27.1
8 S	7 3 22.9	15 44.6	11 14.5	27 30.6	11 3.6	2 36.4	8 47.3	12 18.9	9 58.8	17 3.3	18 24.0	16 27.5
9 M	7 7 19.5	16 41.7	11 11.4	12♑ 5.3	11 43.0	3 49.7	9 29.3	12 31.3	10 4.3	17 2.4	18 22.7	16 27.9
10 T	7 11 16.0	17 38.9	11 8.2	26 54.1	12 18.6	5 3.1	10 11.2	12 43.8	10 9.8	17 1.6	18 21.3	16 28.4
11 W	7 15 12.6	18 36.1	11 5.0	11♒48.6	12 50.1	6 16.5	10 53.1	12 56.3	10 15.3	17 0.8	18 19.9	16 28.8
12 T	7 19 9.2	19 33.3	11 1.8	26 40.7	13 17.4	7 30.0	11 34.8	13 8.9	10 20.9	17 0.1	18 18.6	16 29.3
13 F	7 23 5.7	20 30.5	10 58.7	11♓23.3	13 40.4	8 43.4	12 16.6	13 21.5	10 26.6	16 59.4	18 17.3	16 29.9
14 S	7 27 2.3	21 27.7	10 55.5	25 51.3	13 58.9	9 56.9	12 58.2	13 34.1	10 32.4	16 58.7	18 16.0	16 30.4
15 S	7 30 58.8	22 24.9	10 52.3	10♈ 1.9	14 12.9	11 10.4	13 39.8	13 46.8	10 38.2	16 58.2	18 14.7	16 31.0
16 M	7 34 55.4	23 22.2	10 49.1	23 54.0	14 22.3	12 23.9	14 21.4	13 59.5	10 44.0	16 57.6	18 13.5	16 31.7
17 T	7 38 51.9	24 19.4	10 46.0	7♉27.9	14 26.8	13 37.5	15 2.9	14 12.2	10 49.9	16 57.2	18 12.2	16 32.4
18 W	7 42 48.5	25 16.7	10 42.8	20 44.9	14R26.6	14 51.1	15 44.3	14 25.1	10 56.0	16 56.8	18 11.0	16 33.1
19 T	7 46 45.1	26 14.0	10 39.6	3♊46.2	14 21.4	16 4.7	16 25.7	14 37.9	11 2.0	16 56.4	18 9.8	16 33.8
20 F	7 50 41.6	27 11.2	10 36.4	16 33.3	14 11.4	17 18.3	17 6.9	14 50.7	11 8.1	16 56.1	18 8.7	16 34.6
21 S	7 54 38.2	28 8.5	10 33.2	29 7.5	13 56.6	18 32.0	17 48.1	15 3.6	11 14.2	16 55.8	18 7.5	16 35.4
22 S	7 58 34.7	29 5.8	10 30.1	11♋30.1	13 37.1	19 45.6	18 29.3	15 16.4	11 20.4	16 55.6	18 6.4	16 36.3
23 M	8 2 31.3	0♌ 3.1	10 26.9	23 42.1	13 13.0	20 59.3	19 10.4	15 29.4	11 26.7	16 55.4	18 5.3	16 37.1
24 T	8 6 27.8	1 0.4	10 23.7	5♌44.9	12 44.7	22 13.0	19 51.4	15 42.3	11 33.0	16 55.3	18 4.2	16 38.0
25 W	8 10 24.4	1 57.8	10 20.5	17 40.0	12 12.4	23 26.8	20 32.3	15 55.2	11 39.3	16 55.2	18 3.1	16 38.9
26 T	8 14 20.9	2 55.1	10 17.4	29 29.5	11 36.6	24 40.5	21 13.2	16 8.2	11 45.7	16 55.2	18 2.1	16 39.9
27 F	8 18 17.5	3 52.4	10 14.2	11♍16.0	10 57.8	25 54.3	21 54.0	16 21.2	11 52.2	16 55.2	18 1.1	16 40.9
28 S	8 22 14.1	4 49.8	10 11.0	23 2.8	10 16.5	27 8.1	22 34.7	16 34.2	11 58.7	16D55.3	18 0.1	16 41.9
29 S	8 26 10.6	5 47.2	10 7.8	4♎53.5	9 33.4	28 21.9	23 15.3	16 47.3	12 5.2	16 55.4	17 59.1	16 43.0
30 M	8 30 7.2	6 44.5	10 4.7	16 52.7	8 49.2	29 35.7	23 55.9	17 0.3	12 11.8	16 55.6	17 58.2	16 44.1
31 T	8 34 3.7	7 41.9	10 1.5	29 4.9	8 4.6	0♌49.5	24 36.4	17 13.4	12 18.4	16 55.8	17 57.3	16 45.2
DECLINATION at NOON												
1 S	6 35 47.0	23N 7.7	7N12.5	2N42.9	19N31.2	22N57.1	20N43.4	18N 8.8	9N46.0	16S38.8	21S30.3	9N26.7
4 W	6 47 36.7	22 54.2	7 16.1	8S44.3	18 13.7	23 11.3	21 8.4	17 58.8	9 40.0	16 37.9	21 30.0	9 24.9
7 S	6 59 26.4	22 37.1	7 19.7	17 20.1	16 57.8	23 19.5	21 31.7	17 48.6	9 33.8	16 37.1	21 29.7	9 23.0
10 T	7 11 16.0	22 16.5	7 23.3	17 21.7	15 46.4	23 21.5	21 53.1	17 38.1	9 27.4	16 36.4	21 29.4	9 21.0
13 F	7 23 5.7	21 52.4	7 27.0	7 27.1	14 42.5	23 17.4	22 12.6	17 27.5	9 20.7	16 35.9	21 29.2	9 18.9
16 M	7 34 55.4	21 25.0	7 30.6	5N54.7	13 49.1	23 7.1	22 30.2	17 16.7	9 13.9	16 35.5	21 28.9	9 16.7
19 T	7 46 45.1	20 54.2	7 34.2	15 51.7	13 9.4	22 50.7	22 46.0	17 5.6	9 6.8	16 35.2	21 28.7	9 14.4
22 S	7 58 34.7	20 20.3	7 37.8	18 35.7	12 46.3	22 28.2	22 59.8	16 54.4	8 59.6	16 35.0	21 28.5	9 12.0
25 W	8 10 24.4	19 43.4	7 41.4	13 45.0	12 41.9	21 59.8	23 11.8	16 43.0	8 52.2	16 35.0	21 28.4	9 9.5
28 S	8 22 14.1	19 3.4	7 45.0	3 56.8	12 56.3	21 25.6	23 21.9	16 31.5	8 44.7	16 35.1	21 28.2	9 6.9
31 T	8 34 3.7	18 20.7	7 48.6	7S22.5	13 28.0	20 45.7	23 30.2	16 19.8	8 37.0	16 35.3	21 28.1	9 4.3

AUGUST 1979

DAY	EPHEMERIS SIDEREAL TIME	☉	☊	☽	☿	♀	♂	♃	♄	♅	♆	♇
LONGITUDE at NOON												
1 W	8 38 0.3	8♌39.3	9♍58.3	11♏35.0	7♌20.5	2♌ 3.4	25♊16.9	17♌26.4	12♍25.1	16♏56.1	17♐56.4	16♎46.3
2 T	8 41 56.8	9 36.7	9 55.1	24 27.3	6R37.8	3 17.3	25 57.2	17 39.5	12 31.8	16 56.5	17R55.5	16 47.5
3 F	8 45 53.4	10 34.1	9 51.9	7♐45.4	5 57.1	4 31.2	26 37.5	17 52.6	12 38.6	16 56.9	17 54.7	16 48.7
4 S	8 49 49.9	11 31.5	9 48.8	21 31.3	5 19.3	5 45.1	27 17.8	18 5.7	12 45.3	16 57.3	17 53.9	16 50.0
5 S	8 53 46.5	12 29.0	9 45.6	5♑44.9	4 45.1	6 59.0	27 57.9	18 18.9	12 52.2	16 57.8	17 53.1	16 51.2
6 M	8 57 43.0	13 26.4	9 42.4	20 23.0	4 15.3	8 13.0	28 38.0	18 32.0	12 59.0	16 58.4	17 52.4	16 52.5
7 T	9 1 39.6	14 23.9	9 39.2	5♒19.9	3 50.4	9 26.9	29 18.0	18 45.1	13 5.9	16 59.0	17 51.6	16 53.9
8 W	9 5 36.2	15 21.4	9 36.1	20 27.6	3 31.0	10 41.0	29 58.0	18 58.3	13 12.9	16 59.7	17 51.0	16 55.3
9 T	9 9 32.7	16 18.9	9 32.9	5♓36.5	3 17.6	11 55.0	0♋37.8	19 11.5	13 19.9	17 0.4	17 50.3	16 56.6
10 F	9 13 29.3	17 16.4	9 29.7	20 37.6	3 10.6	13 9.0	1 17.6	19 24.6	13 26.9	17 1.2	17 49.7	16 58.0
11 S	9 17 25.8	18 14.0	9 26.5	5♈23.4	3 10.2	14 23.1	1 57.4	19 37.8	13 33.9	17 2.0	17 49.1	16 59.5
12 S	9 21 22.4	19 11.5	9 23.3	19 48.5	3D16.6	15 37.1	2 37.0	19 50.9	13 41.0	17 2.8	17 48.5	17 0.9
13 M	9 25 18.9	20 9.1	9 20.2	3♉50.1	3 30.2	16 51.2	3 16.6	20 4.1	13 48.1	17 3.7	17 48.0	17 2.4
14 T	9 29 15.5	21 6.7	9 17.0	17 27.7	3 50.8	18 5.4	3 56.1	20 17.2	13 55.2	17 4.7	17 47.4	17 3.9
15 W	9 33 12.0	22 4.3	9 13.8	0♊42.5	4 18.7	19 19.5	4 35.6	20 30.4	14 2.4	17 5.7	17 47.0	17 5.5
16 T	9 37 8.6	23 2.0	9 10.6	13 36.7	4 53.7	20 33.7	5 14.9	20 43.5	14 9.6	17 6.8	17 46.5	17 7.1
17 F	9 41 5.1	23 59.7	9 7.5	26 13.1	5 35.7	21 47.9	5 54.2	20 56.7	14 16.8	17 7.9	17 46.1	17 8.7
18 S	9 45 1.7	24 57.4	9 4.3	8♋34.6	6 24.7	23 2.1	6 33.5	21 9.8	14 24.0	17 9.1	17 45.7	17 10.3
19 S	9 48 58.2	25 55.1	9 1.1	20 44.3	7 20.5	24 16.3	7 12.6	21 23.0	14 31.3	17 10.3	17 45.3	17 11.9
20 M	9 52 54.8	26 52.9	8 57.9	2♌44.8	8 22.9	25 30.5	7 51.7	21 36.1	14 38.5	17 11.6	17 45.0	17 13.6
21 T	9 56 51.4	27 50.7	8 54.7	14 38.5	9 31.6	26 44.8	8 30.7	21 49.2	14 45.9	17 12.9	17 44.7	17 15.3
22 W	10 0 47.9	28 48.5	8 51.6	26 27.7	10 46.4	27 59.1	9 9.6	22 2.3	14 53.2	17 14.2	17 44.4	17 17.0
23 T	10 4 44.5	29 46.3	8 48.4	8♍14.8	12 6.8	29 13.4	9 48.4	22 15.4	15 0.5	17 15.7	17 44.2	17 18.8
24 F	10 8 41.0	0♍44.2	8 45.2	20 1.8	13 32.7	0♍27.7	10 27.2	22 28.5	15 7.9	17 17.1	17 44.0	17 20.5
25 S	10 12 37.6	1 42.1	8 42.0	1♎51.5	15 3.5	1 42.0	11 5.8	22 41.6	15 15.3	17 18.6	17 43.8	17 22.3
26 S	10 16 34.1	2 40.0	8 38.9	13 46.4	16 38.8	2 56.4	11 44.4	22 54.7	15 22.7	17 20.2	17 43.6	17 24.1
27 M	10 20 30.7	3 37.9	8 35.7	25 49.7	18 18.2	4 10.7	12 22.9	23 7.7	15 30.1	17 21.8	17 43.5	17 26.0
28 T	10 24 27.2	4 35.8	8 32.5	8♏ 4.8	20 1.2	5 25.1	13 1.3	23 20.7	15 37.5	17 23.5	17 43.4	17 27.8
29 W	10 28 23.8	5 33.9	8 29.3	20 35.4	21 47.4	6 39.5	13 39.7	23 33.8	15 45.0	17 25.2	17D43.5	17 29.8
30 T	10 32 20.3	6 31.8	8 26.1	3♐25.2	23 36.3	7 53.9	14 18.0	23 46.8	15 52.5	17 27.0	17R43.4	17 31.7
31 F	10 36 16.9	7 29.9	8 23.0	16 37.5	25 27.4	9 8.3	14 56.2	23 59.8	15 59.9	17 28.8	17D43.5	17 33.6
DECLINATION at NOON												
1 W	8 38 0.3	18N 5.8	7N49.8	10S52.3	13N41.6	20N31.2	23N32.5	16N15.9	8N34.4	16S35.5	21S28.1	9N 3.4
4 S	8 49 49.9	17 19.5	7 53.4	18 4.2	14 29.3	19 44.2	23 38.3	16 4.0	8 26.5	16 35.9	21 28.0	9 0.7
7 T	9 1 39.6	16 30.7	7 57.0	16 8.3	15 22.0	18 52.1	23 42.2	15 52.0	8 18.5	16 36.4	21 27.9	8 57.9
10 F	9 13 29.3	15 39.5	8 0.6	4 43.9	16 13.2	17 55.2	23 44.4	15 39.8	8 10.4	16 37.1	21 27.9	8 55.0
13 M	9 25 18.9	14 46.0	8 4.2	8N42.7	16 56.8	16 53.8	23 44.8	15 27.6	8 2.1	16 37.9	21 27.9	8 52.1
16 T	9 37 8.6	13 50.4	8 7.7	17 13.0	17 27.2	15 48.1	23 43.4	15 15.2	7 53.8	16 38.8	21 27.9	8 49.2
19 S	9 48 58.2	12 52.8	8 11.3	17 58.2	17 39.3	14 38.5	23 40.3	15 2.8	7 45.4	16 39.9	21 28.0	8 46.2
22 W	10 0 47.9	11 53.3	8 14.9	11 39.6	17 29.0	13 25.2	23 35.6	14 50.3	7 36.9	16 41.1	21 28.0	8 43.2
25 S	10 12 37.6	10 52.2	8 18.5	1 11.9	16 53.3	12 8.6	23 29.3	14 37.8	7 28.4	16 42.4	21 28.1	8 40.2
28 T	10 24 27.2	9 49.5	8 22.0	9S52.0	15 51.5	10 49.1	23 21.3	14 25.2	7 19.8	16 43.8	21 28.3	8 37.1
31 F	10 36 16.9	8 45.4	8 25.6	17 32.7	14 25.3	9 26.8	23 11.9	14 12.6	7 11.1	16 45.4	21 28.4	8 34.1

SEPTEMBER 1979

DAY	EPHEMERIS SIDEREAL TIME	☉	☊	☽	☿	♀	♂	♃	♄	♅	♆	♇
	h m s	° ′	° ′	° ′	° ′	° ′	° ′	° ′	° ′	° ′	° ′	° ′
						LONGITUDE at NOON						
1 S	10 40 13.4	8♍27.9	8♍19.8	0♑14.8	27♌20.2	10♍22.7	15♋34.3	24♌12.7	16♍ 7.4	17♏30.6	17♐43.5	17♎35.5
2 S	10 44 10.0	9 26.0	8 16.6	14 18.2	29 14.5	11 37.2	16 12.3	24 25.6	16 14.9	17 32.5	17 43.6	17 37.5
3 M	10 48 6.5	10 24.0	8 13.4	28 46.6	1♍ 9.8	12 51.6	16 50.2	24 38.5	16 22.4	17 34.5	17 43.7	17 39.5
4 T	10 52 3.1	11 22.1	8 10.3	13♒36.6	3 5.8	14 6.1	17 28.0	24 51.4	16 29.9	17 36.4	17 43.9	17 41.5
5 W	10 55 59.6	12 20.3	8 7.1	28 41.9	5 2.2	15 20.5	18 5.8	25 4.2	16 37.4	17 38.5	17 44.0	17 43.5
6 T	10 59 56.2	13 18.4	8 3.9	13♓54.1	6 58.7	16 35.0	18 43.5	25 17.0	16 44.9	17 40.5	17 44.3	17 45.5
7 F	11 3 52.7	14 16.6	8 0.7	29 3.7	8 55.0	17 49.5	19 21.0	25 29.8	16 52.5	17 42.6	17 44.5	17 47.6
8 S	11 7 49.3	15 14.8	7 57.5	14♈ 1.6	10 51.1	19 4.0	19 58.5	25 42.6	16 60.0	17 44.8	17 44.8	17 49.6
9 S	11 11 45.9	16 13.1	7 54.4	28 40.0	12 46.6	20 18.5	20 36.0	25 55.3	17 7.5	17 47.0	17 45.1	17 51.7
10 M	11 15 42.4	17 11.4	7 51.2	12♉53.8	14 41.6	21 33.0	21 13.3	26 8.0	17 15.0	17 49.2	17 45.5	17 53.8
11 T	11 19 39.0	18 9.7	7 48.0	26 40.5	16 35.8	22 47.6	21 50.5	26 20.6	17 22.5	17 51.5	17 45.8	17 55.9
12 W	11 23 35.5	19 8.0	7 44.8	10♊ 0.2	18 29.2	24 2.1	22 27.7	26 33.3	17 30.1	17 53.8	17 46.2	17 58.1
13 T	11 27 32.1	20 6.4	7 41.7	22 55.1	20 21.7	25 16.7	23 4.8	26 45.9	17 37.6	17 56.2	17 46.7	18 0.2
14 F	11 31 28.6	21 4.9	7 38.5	5♋28.4	22 13.3	26 31.3	23 41.8	26 58.4	17 45.1	17 58.6	17 47.2	18 2.4
15 S	11 35 25.2	22 3.3	7 35.3	17 44.3	24 3.9	27 45.9	24 18.6	27 10.9	17 52.6	18 1.1	17 47.7	18 4.6
16 S	11 39 21.7	23 1.8	7 32.1	29 47.0	25 53.5	29 0.5	24 55.4	27 23.4	18 0.1	18 3.6	17 48.2	18 6.8
17 M	11 43 18.3	24 0.3	7 28.9	11♌40.7	27 42.1	0♎15.1	25 32.1	27 35.8	18 7.7	18 6.1	17 48.8	18 9.0
18 T	11 47 14.8	24 58.9	7 25.8	23 29.2	29 29.6	1 29.7	26 8.7	27 48.2	18 15.2	18 8.6	17 49.4	18 11.2
19 W	11 51 11.4	25 57.5	7 22.6	5♍15.9	1♎16.2	2 44.4	26 45.3	28 0.6	18 22.7	18 11.3	17 50.1	18 13.5
20 T	11 55 7.9	26 56.2	7 19.4	17 3.6	3 1.7	3 59.0	27 21.7	28 12.9	18 30.2	18 13.9	17 50.8	18 15.7
21 F	11 59 4.5	27 54.8	7 16.2	28 54.8	4 46.2	5 13.7	27 58.0	28 25.1	18 37.6	18 16.6	17 51.5	18 18.0
22 S	12 3 1.0	28 53.5	7 13.0	10♎51.6	6 29.7	6 28.3	28 34.2	28 37.3	18 45.1	18 19.3	17 52.2	18 20.3
23 S	12 6 57.6	29 52.3	7 9.9	22 56.0	8 12.1	7 43.0	29 10.3	28 49.5	18 52.5	18 22.1	17 53.0	18 22.5
24 M	12 10 54.1	0♎51.0	7 6.7	5♏ 9.7	9 53.6	8 57.7	29 46.3	29 1.5	18 60.0	18 24.9	17 53.8	18 24.8
25 T	12 14 50.7	1 49.8	7 3.5	17 34.5	11 34.2	10 12.3	0♌22.2	29 13.6	19 7.4	18 27.7	17 54.6	18 27.1
26 W	12 18 47.2	2 48.6	7 0.3	0♐12.5	13 13.7	11 27.0	0 58.0	29 25.6	19 14.8	18 30.6	17 55.5	18 29.4
27 T	12 22 43.8	3 47.5	6 57.2	13 5.8	14 52.4	12 41.7	1 33.7	29 37.5	19 22.2	18 33.4	17 56.3	18 31.7
28 F	12 26 40.3	4 46.4	6 54.0	26 16.6	16 30.1	13 56.4	2 9.3	29 49.4	19 29.5	18 36.4	17 57.3	18 34.1
29 S	12 30 36.9	5 45.3	6 50.8	9♑46.9	18 6.9	15 11.1	2 44.7	0♍ 1.2	19 36.9	18 39.3	17 58.2	18 36.4
30 S	12 34 33.4	6 44.2	6 47.6	23 38.1	19 42.9	16 25.8	3 20.1	0 12.9	19 44.2	18 42.3	17 59.2	18 38.7
						DECLINATION at NOON						
1 S	10 40 13.4	8N23.8	8N26.8	18S30.8	13N51.8	8N58.9	23N 8.4	14N 8.4	7N 8.3	16S45.9	21S28.5	8N33.0
4 T	10 52 3.1	7 18.0	8 30.4	14 35.8	11 59.4	7 33.7	22 57.0	13 55.7	6 59.6	16 47.6	21 28.7	8 30.0
7 F	11 3 52.7	6 11.3	8 33.9	2 5.1	9 53.1	6 6.6	22 44.2	13 43.1	6 50.9	16 49.4	21 28.9	8 26.9
10 M	11 15 42.4	5 3.6	8 37.5	11N 9.0	7 37.8	4 37.9	22 30.1	13 30.5	6 42.2	16 51.4	21 29.1	8 23.8
13 T	11 27 32.1	3 55.1	8 41.0	18 7.9	5 17.3	3 8.0	22 14.6	13 17.9	6 33.6	16 53.4	21 29.4	8 20.8
16 S	11 39 21.7	2 46.0	8 44.6	16 57.5	2 54.8	1 37.1	21 58.0	13 5.3	6 24.9	16 55.5	21 29.7	8 17.7
19 W	11 51 11.4	1 36.4	8 48.1	9 18.1	0 32.4	0 5.7	21 40.2	12 52.8	6 16.3	16 57.7	21 30.0	8 14.7
22 S	12 3 1.0	0 26.4	8 51.7	1S42.1	1S48.2	1S26.0	21 21.3	12 40.5	6 7.7	16 60.0	21 30.4	8 11.7
25 T	12 14 50.7	0S43.7	8 55.2	12 21.7	4 5.8	2 57.6	21 1.4	12 28.2	5 59.2	17 2.3	21 30.8	8 8.8
28 F	12 26 40.3	1 53.8	8 58.7	18 24.4	6 19.3	4 28.8	20 40.5	12 16.0	5 50.8	17 4.8	21 31.2	8 5.9

OCTOBER 1979

DAY	EPHEMERIS SIDEREAL TIME	☉	☊	☽	☿	♀	♂	♃	♄	♅	♆	♇
						LONGITUDE at NOON						
1 M	12 38 30.0	7♎43.2	6♍44.4	7♒50.4	21♎18.0	17♎40.4	3♌55.3	0♍24.6	19♍51.5	18♏45.3	18♐ 0.2	18♎41.1
2 T	12 42 26.5	8 42.2	6 41.3	22 22.7	22 52.2	18 55.1	4 30.5	0 36.2	19 58.8	18 48.4	18 1.3	18 43.4
3 W	12 46 23.1	9 41.2	6 38.1	7♓11.3	24 25.6	20 9.8	5 5.5	0 47.8	20 6.0	18 51.5	18 2.3	18 45.8
4 T	12 50 19.6	10 40.3	6 34.9	22 10.6	25 58.1	21 24.5	5 40.4	0 59.2	20 13.2	18 54.6	18 3.5	18 48.1
5 F	12 54 16.2	11 39.3	6 31.7	7♈12.8	27 29.9	22 39.2	6 15.2	1 10.7	20 20.4	18 57.7	18 4.6	18 50.5
6 S	12 58 12.8	12 38.5	6 28.6	22 9.0	29 0.8	23 53.9	6 49.9	1 22.0	20 27.6	19 0.9	18 5.7	18 52.9
7 S	13 2 9.3	13 37.6	6 25.4	6♉50.7	0♏30.9	25 8.6	7 24.5	1 33.3	20 34.8	19 4.1	18 6.9	18 55.2
8 M	13 6 5.9	14 36.8	6 22.2	21 10.9	2 0.1	26 23.3	7 58.9	1 44.5	20 41.9	19 7.3	18 8.2	18 57.6
9 T	13 10 2.4	15 36.0	6 19.0	5♊ 5.0	3 28.6	27 38.0	8 33.3	1 55.6	20 49.0	19 10.5	18 9.4	18 60.0
10 W	13 13 59.0	16 35.4	6 15.8	18 31.4	4 56.3	28 52.8	9 7.5	2 6.7	20 56.1	19 13.9	18 10.7	19 2.4
11 T	13 17 55.5	17 34.7	6 12.7	1♋30.8	6 23.1	0♏ 7.5	9 41.6	2 17.7	21 3.1	19 17.2	18 12.0	19 4.8
12 F	13 21 52.1	18 34.0	6 9.5	14 6.4	7 49.1	1 22.2	10 15.6	2 28.6	21 10.1	19 20.5	18 13.4	19 7.2
13 S	13 25 48.6	19 33.4	6 6.3	26 22.2	9 14.3	2 37.0	10 49.4	2 39.5	21 17.0	19 23.8	18 14.7	19 9.6
14 S	13 29 45.2	20 32.8	6 3.1	8♌23.2	10 38.5	3 51.7	11 23.1	2 50.2	21 23.9	19 27.2	18 16.1	19 12.0
15 M	13 33 41.7	21 32.3	5 60.0	20 14.7	12 1.8	5 6.4	11 56.7	3 0.9	21 30.8	19 30.6	18 17.5	19 14.3
16 T	13 37 38.3	22 31.8	5 56.8	2♍ 1.6	13 24.2	6 21.2	12 30.2	3 11.4	21 37.6	19 34.0	18 19.0	19 16.7
17 W	13 41 34.8	23 31.3	5 53.6	13 48.4	14 45.6	7 35.9	13 3.5	3 21.9	21 44.4	19 37.4	18 20.4	19 19.1
18 T	13 45 31.4	24 30.9	5 50.4	25 39.2	16 5.9	8 50.6	13 36.6	3 32.3	21 51.2	19 40.9	18 21.9	19 21.5
19 F	13 49 27.9	25 30.5	5 47.2	7♎37.0	17 25.1	10 5.4	14 9.7	3 42.6	21 57.9	19 44.4	18 23.5	19 23.9
20 S	13 53 24.5	26 30.1	5 44.1	19 44.1	18 43.2	11 20.1	14 42.5	3 52.8	22 4.6	19 47.9	18 25.0	19 26.2
21 S	13 57 21.0	27 29.8	5 40.9	2♏ 2.3	19 59.9	12 34.9	15 15.3	4 2.9	22 11.2	19 51.4	18 26.6	19 28.6
22 M	14 1 17.6	28 29.5	5 37.7	14 32.3	21 15.4	13 49.6	15 47.9	4 13.0	22 17.8	19 54.9	18 28.2	19 31.0
23 T	14 5 14.1	29 29.2	5 34.5	27 14.4	22 29.3	15 4.4	16 20.3	4 22.9	22 24.3	19 58.5	18 29.8	19 33.3
24 W	14 9 10.7	0♏29.0	5 31.4	10♐ 8.8	23 41.6	16 19.1	16 52.6	4 32.7	22 30.8	20 2.0	18 31.4	19 35.7
25 T	14 13 7.3	1 28.8	5 28.2	23 15.4	24 52.2	17 33.9	17 24.7	4 42.4	22 37.2	20 5.6	18 33.1	19 38.0
26 F	14 17 3.8	2 28.6	5 25.0	6♑34.5	26 0.9	18 48.6	17 56.7	4 52.1	22 43.6	20 9.2	18 34.8	19 40.4
27 S	14 21 0.4	3 28.5	5 21.8	20 6.6	27 7.4	20 3.3	18 28.5	5 1.6	22 50.0	20 12.8	18 36.5	19 42.7
28 S	14 24 56.9	4 28.4	5 18.6	3♒52.3	28 11.6	21 18.1	19 0.1	5 11.0	22 56.2	20 16.4	18 38.2	19 45.0
29 M	14 28 53.5	5 28.3	5 15.5	17 51.9	29 13.3	22 32.8	19 31.6	5 20.3	23 2.5	20 20.1	18 40.0	19 47.3
30 T	14 32 50.0	6 28.2	5 12.3	2♓ 5.5	0♐12.0	23 47.5	20 2.9	5 29.5	23 8.6	20 23.7	18 41.8	19 49.6
31 W	14 36 46.6	7 28.2	5 9.1	16 31.7	1 7.6	25 2.3	20 34.0	5 38.6	23 14.8	20 27.4	18 43.6	19 52.0
						DECLINATION at NOON						
1 M	12 38 30.0	3S 3.8	9N 2.3	15S44.7	8S28.2	5S59.2	20N18.8	12N 4.0	5N42.4	17S 7.3	21S31.6	8N 3.0
4 T	12 50 19.6	4 13.4	9 5.8	4 15.8	10 31.7	7 28.5	19 56.2	11 52.1	5 34.2	17 9.9	21 32.0	8 0.2
7 S	13 2 9.3	5 22.7	9 9.3	9N35.6	12 29.2	8 56.4	19 32.9	11 40.4	5 26.0	17 12.5	21 32.5	7 57.5
10 W	13 13 59.0	6 31.3	9 12.8	17 51.8	14 20.3	10 22.6	19 8.9	11 28.9	5 18.0	17 15.2	21 32.9	7 54.8
13 S	13 25 48.6	7 39.1	9 16.3	17 30.3	16 4.2	11 46.6	18 44.4	11 17.5	5 10.1	17 18.0	21 33.4	7 52.2
16 T	13 37 38.3	8 46.0	9 19.8	10 16.2	17 40.4	13 8.1	18 19.3	11 6.5	5 2.3	17 20.8	21 33.9	7 49.7
19 F	13 49 27.9	9 51.8	9 23.4	0S39.6	19 8.1	14 26.8	17 53.8	10 55.7	4 54.7	17 23.6	21 34.4	7 47.3
22 M	14 1 17.6	10 56.3	9 26.9	11 41.6	20 26.4	15 42.3	17 27.9	10 45.1	4 47.3	17 26.5	21 35.0	7 44.9
25 T	14 13 7.3	11 59.3	9 30.4	18 22.7	21 34.2	16 54.3	17 1.7	10 34.9	4 40.0	17 29.4	21 35.5	7 42.7
28 S	14 24 56.9	13 0.7	9 33.8	16 35.3	22 30.5	18 2.3	16 35.4	10 24.9	4 33.0	17 32.3	21 36.0	7 40.5
31 W	14 36 46.6	14 0.2	9 37.3	6 7.3	23 13.4	19 6.1	16 8.9	10 15.3	4 26.1	17 35.3	21 36.6	7 38.4

NOVEMBER 1979

DAY	EPHEMERIS SIDEREAL TIME	☉	☊	☽	☿	♀	♂	♃	♄	♅	♆	♇
	h m s	° ′	° ′	° ′	° ′	° ′	° ′	° ′	° ′	° ′	° ′	° ′
LONGITUDE at NOON												
1 T	14 40 43.1	8♏28.2	5♍ 5.9	1♈ 7.4	1♐59.6	26♏17.0	21♌ 5.0	5♍47.6	23♍20.9	20♏31.1	18♐45.4	19♎54.3
2 F	14 44 39.7	9 28.3	5 2.8	15 47.8	2 47.6	27 31.7	21 35.8	5 56.4	23 26.9	20 34.8	18 47.3	19 56.6
3 S	14 48 36.2	10 28.3	4 59.6	0♉26.4	3 31.2	28 46.4	22 6.4	6 5.1	23 32.8	20 38.4	18 49.1	19 58.8
4 S	14 52 32.8	11 28.4	4 56.4	14 56.0	4 9.9	0♐ 1.1	22 36.9	6 13.8	23 38.7	20 42.1	18 51.0	20 1.1
5 M	14 56 29.3	12 28.5	4 53.2	29 9.5	4 43.1	1 15.8	23 7.1	6 22.2	23 44.5	20 45.8	18 52.9	20 3.3
6 T	15 0 25.9	13 28.6	4 50.0	13♊ 1.5	5 10.2	2 30.5	23 37.2	6 30.6	23 50.2	20 49.5	18 54.8	20 5.6
7 W	15 4 22.5	14 28.8	4 46.9	26 28.8	5 30.6	3 45.2	24 7.1	6 38.9	23 55.9	20 53.3	18 56.7	20 7.8
8 T	15 8 19.0	15 29.0	4 43.7	9♋30.8	5 43.6	4 59.9	24 36.7	6 47.0	24 1.6	20 57.0	18 58.7	20 10.0
9 F	15 12 15.6	16 29.3	4 40.5	22 8.9	5 48.6	6 14.6	25 6.2	6 55.0	24 7.1	21 0.7	19 0.7	20 12.2
10 S	15 16 12.1	17 29.5	4 37.3	4♌26.8	5R44.7	7 29.3	25 35.5	7 2.9	24 12.6	21 4.4	19 2.6	20 14.4
11 S	15 20 8.7	18 29.8	4 34.2	16 29.1	5 31.6	8 44.0	26 4.6	7 10.6	24 18.0	21 8.2	19 4.6	20 16.5
12 M	15 24 5.2	19 30.2	4 31.0	28 21.1	5 8.6	9 58.7	26 33.5	7 18.2	24 23.4	21 11.9	19 6.7	20 18.7
13 T	15 28 1.8	20 30.6	4 27.8	10♍ 8.4	4 35.5	11 13.4	27 2.1	7 25.7	24 28.7	21 15.6	19 8.7	20 20.8
14 W	15 31 58.3	21 31.0	4 24.6	21 56.5	3 52.3	12 28.1	27 30.6	7 33.0	24 33.9	21 19.4	19 10.7	20 23.0
15 T	15 35 54.9	22 31.4	4 21.4	3♎50.3	2 59.2	13 42.8	27 58.8	7 40.2	24 39.0	21 23.1	19 12.8	20 25.1
16 F	15 39 51.5	23 31.9	4 18.3	15 54.1	1 57.1	14 57.5	28 26.8	7 47.3	24 44.1	21 26.8	19 14.9	20 27.1
17 S	15 43 48.0	24 32.4	4 15.1	28 11.1	0 47.1	16 12.1	28 54.5	7 54.2	24 49.1	21 30.6	19 17.0	20 29.2
18 S	15 47 44.6	25 32.9	4 11.9	10♏43.3	29♏31.0	17 26.8	29 22.0	8 0.9	24 54.0	21 34.3	19 19.1	20 31.3
19 M	15 51 41.1	26 33.4	4 8.7	23 31.5	28 11.0	18 41.5	29 49.3	8 7.6	24 58.8	21 38.0	19 21.2	20 33.3
20 T	15 55 37.7	27 34.0	4 5.6	6♐35.1	26 49.6	19 56.2	0♍16.3	8 14.0	25 3.6	21 41.7	19 23.3	20 35.3
21 W	15 59 34.2	28 34.7	4 2.4	19 52.7	25 29.6	21 10.9	0 43.1	8 20.4	25 8.3	21 45.5	19 25.5	20 37.4
22 T	16 3 30.8	29 35.3	3 59.2	3♑22.1	24 13.5	22 25.6	1 9.6	8 26.6	25 12.9	21 49.2	19 27.6	20 39.3
23 F	16 7 27.3	0♐35.9	3 56.0	17 1.0	23 3.7	23 40.2	1 35.9	8 32.6	25 17.4	21 52.9	19 29.8	20 41.3
24 S	16 11 23.9	1 36.6	3 52.9	0♒47.6	22 2.4	24 54.9	2 1.8	8 38.4	25 21.8	21 56.6	19 32.0	20 43.2
25 S	16 15 20.5	2 37.3	3 49.7	14 40.7	21 11.2	26 9.5	2 27.5	8 44.1	25 26.1	22 0.3	19 34.2	20 45.1
26 M	16 19 17.0	3 38.0	3 46.5	28 39.4	20 31.0	27 24.1	2 53.0	8 49.7	25 30.4	22 4.0	19 36.4	20 47.0
27 T	16 23 13.6	4 38.7	3 43.3	12♓43.4	20 2.3	28 38.7	3 18.1	8 55.0	25 34.6	22 7.7	19 38.5	20 48.9
28 W	16 27 10.1	5 39.4	3 40.1	26 52.3	19 45.3	29 53.3	3 42.9	9 0.3	25 38.6	22 11.3	19 40.8	20 50.7
29 T	16 31 6.7	6 40.2	3 37.0	11♈ 4.8	19 39.5	1♑ 7.9	4 7.5	9 5.3	25 42.6	22 15.0	19 43.0	20 52.5
30 F	16 35 3.2	7 40.9	3 33.8	25 18.5	19D44.5	2 22.5	4 31.7	9 10.2	25 46.5	22 18.6	19 45.2	20 54.3
DECLINATION at NOON												
1 T	14 40 43.1	14S19.6	9N38.5	1S29.5	23S24.4	19S26.3	16N 0.1	10N12.2	4N23.9	17S36.3	21S36.8	7N37.7
4 S	14 52 32.8	15 16.4	9 42.0	11N48.5	23 46.2	20 23.9	15 33.5	10 3.1	4 17.4	17 39.2	21 37.4	7 35.8
7 W	15 4 22.5	16 11.0	9 45.5	18 39.9	23 48.6	21 16.3	15 7.1	9 54.4	4 11.1	17 42.2	21 37.9	7 34.0
10 S	15 16 12.1	17 3.1	9 49.0	16 36.2	23 27.4	22 3.4	14 40.8	9 46.1	4 5.0	17 45.2	21 38.5	7 32.3
13 T	15 28 1.8	17 52.6	9 52.4	8 8.9	22 37.5	22 44.9	14 14.8	9 38.2	3 59.2	17 48.1	21 39.1	7 30.8
16 F	15 39 51.5	18 39.3	9 55.9	3S13.6	21 16.1	23 20.4	13 49.0	9 30.8	3 53.7	17 51.1	21 39.6	7 29.3
19 M	15 51 41.1	19 23.1	9 59.4	13 53.7	19 29.0	23 49.7	13 23.8	9 23.9	3 48.5	17 54.0	21 40.2	7 28.0
22 T	16 3 30.8	20 3.7	10 2.8	19 1.2	17 36.6	24 12.6	12 59.0	9 17.4	3 43.5	17 56.9	21 40.8	7 26.8
25 S	16 15 20.5	20 41.1	10 6.3	14 50.6	16 7.0	24 29.0	12 34.9	9 11.5	3 38.9	17 59.8	21 41.4	7 25.7
28 W	16 27 10.1	21 14.9	10 9.7	3 3.4	15 18.8	24 38.7	12 11.5	9 6.1	3 34.6	18 2.7	21 41.9	7 24.8

DECEMBER 1979

DAY	EPHEMERIS SIDEREAL TIME	☉	☊	☽	☿	♀	♂	♃	♄	♅	♆	♇
LONGITUDE at NOON												
1 S	16 38 59.8	8♐41.7	3♍30.6	9♉30.1	19♏59.5	3♑37.1	4♍55.7	9♍14.9	25♍50.4	22♏22.3	19♐47.4	20♎56.1
2 S	16 42 56.3	9 42.5	3 27.4	23 34.8	20 23.7	4 51.7	5 19.3	9 19.5	25 54.1	22 25.9	19 49.6	20 57.8
3 M	16 46 52.9	10 43.3	3 24.3	7♊27.9	20 56.2	6 6.2	5 42.6	9 23.8	25 57.7	22 29.5	19 51.9	20 59.6
4 T	16 50 49.5	11 44.2	3 21.1	21 4.8	21 36.1	7 20.7	6 5.6	9 28.1	26 1.2	22 33.1	19 54.1	21 1.3
5 W	16 54 46.0	12 45.0	3 17.9	4♋22.3	22 22.5	8 35.3	6 28.3	9 32.1	26 4.7	22 36.6	19 56.4	21 2.9
6 T	16 58 42.6	13 45.9	3 14.7	17 18.9	23 14.8	9 49.8	6 50.6	9 36.0	26 8.0	22 40.2	19 58.6	21 4.6
7 F	17 2 39.1	14 46.8	3 11.6	29 55.0	24 12.2	11 4.3	7 12.6	9 39.7	26 11.3	22 43.7	20 0.9	21 6.2
8 S	17 6 35.7	15 47.7	3 8.4	12♌12.8	25 14.0	12 18.7	7 34.2	9 43.2	26 14.5	22 47.2	20 3.1	21 7.8
9 S	17 10 32.2	16 48.7	3 5.2	24 15.7	26 19.8	13 33.2	7 55.5	9 46.5	26 17.5	22 50.7	20 5.4	21 9.3
10 M	17 14 28.8	17 49.6	3 2.0	6♍ 8.5	27 28.9	14 47.7	8 16.4	9 49.7	26 20.5	22 54.2	20 7.7	21 10.9
11 T	17 18 25.4	18 50.6	2 58.8	17 56.5	28 40.9	16 2.1	8 36.9	9 52.6	26 23.4	22 57.7	20 9.9	21 12.4
12 W	17 22 21.9	19 51.6	2 55.7	29 45.3	29 55.5	17 16.6	8 57.1	9 55.5	26 26.2	23 1.2	20 12.2	21 13.9
13 T	17 26 18.5	20 52.7	2 52.5	11♎40.3	1♐12.2	18 31.0	9 16.8	9 58.1	26 28.8	23 4.6	20 14.5	21 15.3
14 F	17 30 15.0	21 53.7	2 49.3	23 46.7	2 30.9	19 45.5	9 36.1	10 0.5	26 31.4	23 8.0	20 16.8	21 16.8
15 S	17 34 11.6	22 54.7	2 46.1	6♏ 8.7	3 51.2	20 59.9	9 55.0	10 2.7	26 33.9	23 11.4	20 19.0	21 18.2
16 S	17 38 8.1	23 55.8	2 43.0	18 49.7	5 13.0	22 14.2	10 13.5	10 4.8	26 36.2	23 14.7	20 21.3	21 19.5
17 M	17 42 4.7	24 56.9	2 39.8	1♐51.3	6 36.0	23 28.6	10 31.6	10 6.6	26 38.5	23 18.1	20 23.6	21 20.8
18 T	17 46 1.3	25 58.0	2 36.6	15 13.2	8 0.1	24 43.0	10 49.2	10 8.3	26 40.6	23 21.4	20 25.8	21 22.1
19 W	17 49 57.8	26 59.1	2 33.4	28 53.6	9 25.1	25 57.3	11 6.3	10 9.8	26 42.7	23 24.6	20 28.1	21 23.4
20 T	17 53 54.4	28 0.2	2 30.3	12♑48.9	10 51.0	27 11.6	11 23.0	10 11.0	26 44.6	23 27.9	20 30.3	21 24.6
21 F	17 57 50.9	29 1.3	2 27.1	26 54.9	12 17.6	28 25.9	11 39.2	10 12.1	26 46.4	23 31.1	20 32.6	21 25.8
22 S	18 1 47.5	0♑ 2.4	2 23.9	11♒ 6.9	13 44.9	29 40.2	11 54.9	10 13.0	26 48.2	23 34.3	20 34.8	21 27.0
23 S	18 5 44.0	1 3.5	2 20.7	25 20.9	15 12.8	0♒54.4	12 10.1	10 13.7	26 49.8	23 37.5	20 37.0	21 28.2
24 M	18 9 40.6	2 4.7	2 17.5	9♓33.7	16 41.3	2 8.6	12 24.8	10 14.2	26 51.3	23 40.6	20 39.3	21 29.3
25 T	18 13 37.2	3 5.8	2 14.4	23 43.3	18 10.2	3 22.8	12 39.0	10 14.5	26 52.7	23 43.7	20 41.5	21 30.3
26 W	18 17 33.7	4 6.9	2 11.2	7♈48.3	19 39.5	4 37.0	12 52.7	10 14.6	26 54.0	23 46.8	20 43.7	21 31.4
27 T	18 21 30.3	5 8.1	2 8.0	21 48.1	21 9.3	5 51.1	13 5.9	10 14.6	26 55.2	23 49.8	20 45.9	21 32.4
28 F	18 25 26.8	6 9.2	2 4.8	5♉41.6	22 39.5	7 5.2	13 18.5	10R14.3	26 56.3	23 52.8	20 48.1	21 33.4
29 S	18 29 23.4	7 10.3	2 1.7	19 27.7	24 10.0	8 19.3	13 30.6	10 13.8	26 57.2	23 55.8	20 50.3	21 34.3
30 S	18 33 19.9	8 11.5	1 58.5	3♊ 4.8	25 41.0	9 33.3	13 42.1	10 13.2	26 58.1	23 58.8	20 52.5	21 35.2
31 M	18 37 16.5	9 12.6	1 55.3	16 30.8	27 12.2	10 47.3	13 53.0	10 12.3	26 58.9	24 1.7	20 54.7	21 36.1
DECLINATION at NOON												
1 S	16 38 59.8	21S45.1	10N13.2	10N18.5	15S13.6	24S41.7	11N48.9	9N 1.3	3N30.7	18S 5.5	21S42.5	7N24.0
4 T	16 50 49.5	22 11.6	10 16.6	18 23.2	15 42.1	24 37.8	11 27.3	8 57.0	3 27.0	18 8.2	21 43.0	7 23.3
7 F	17 2 39.1	22 34.2	10 20.1	17 30.7	16 32.8	24 27.2	11 6.7	8 53.4	3 23.7	18 11.0	21 43.6	7 22.8
10 M	17 14 28.8	22 52.9	10 23.5	9 34.3	17 35.8	24 9.9	10 47.2	8 50.3	3 20.8	18 13.6	21 44.1	7 22.4
13 T	17 26 18.5	23 7.5	10 26.9	1S39.1	18 43.7	23 46.0	10 28.9	8 47.9	3 18.2	18 16.2	21 44.6	7 22.1
16 S	17 38 8.1	23 18.0	10 30.4	12 41.4	19 51.5	23 15.7	10 12.1	8 46.1	3 16.0	18 18.8	21 45.1	7 22.0
19 W	17 49 57.8	23 24.3	10 33.8	18 56.9	20 55.6	22 39.2	9 56.7	8 45.0	3 14.2	18 21.3	21 45.6	7 22.0
22 S	18 1 47.5	23 26.3	10 37.2	15 46.0	21 53.6	21 56.6	9 43.0	8 44.5	3 12.8	18 23.7	21 46.1	7 22.2
25 T	18 13 37.2	23 24.2	10 40.6	4 18.6	22 43.8	21 8.3	9 31.0	8 44.7	3 11.8	18 26.0	21 46.5	7 22.5
28 F	18 25 26.8	23 17.8	10 44.0	9N 3.3	23 24.9	20 14.5	9 20.9	8 45.5	3 11.1	18 28.3	21 47.0	7 23.0
31 M	18 37 16.5	23 7.2	10 47.5	17 52.2	23 56.0	19 15.7	9 12.8	8 47.0	3 10.9	18 30.5	21 47.4	7 23.6

JANUARY 1980

DAY	EPHEMERIS SIDEREAL TIME	☉	☊	☽	☿	♀	♂	♃	♄	♅	♆	♇
	h m s	° ′	° ′	° ′	° ′	° ′	° ′	° ′	° ′	° ′	° ′	° ′
						LONGITUDE at NOON						
1 T	18 41 13.1	10♑13.7	1♍52.1	29♊43.7	28♐43.8	12♒ 1.3	14♍ 3.4	10♍11.2	26♍59.5	24♏ 4.5	20♐56.9	21♎36.9
2 W	18 45 9.6	11 14.9	1 49.0	12♋41.9	0♑15.9	13 15.3	14 13.2	10R10.1	27 0.1	24 7.4	20 59.1	21 37.8
3 T	18 49 6.2	12 16.0	1 45.8	25 24.4	1 48.2	14 29.2	14 22.3	10 8.6	27 0.5	24 10.2	21 1.2	21 38.5
4 F	18 53 2.7	13 17.2	1 42.6	7♌51.4	3 20.9	15 43.0	14 30.9	10 7.0	27 0.8	24 13.0	21 3.3	21 39.3
5 S	18 56 59.3	14 18.3	1 39.4	20 4.0	4 53.9	16 56.8	14 38.8	10 5.2	27 1.0	24 15.7	21 5.5	21 40.0
6 S	19 0 55.8	15 19.4	1 36.2	2♍ 4.8	6 27.3	18 10.6	14 46.0	10 3.2	27 1.1	24 18.4	21 7.6	21 40.6
7 M	19 4 52.4	16 20.6	1 33.1	13 57.1	8 1.1	19 24.3	14 52.7	10 1.0	27 1.1	24 21.1	21 9.7	21 41.3
8 T	19 8 49.0	17 21.7	1 29.9	25 45.1	9 35.3	20 38.0	14 58.6	9 58.6	27R 1.0	24 23.7	21 11.8	21 41.9
9 W	19 12 45.5	18 22.9	1 26.7	7♎33.7	11 9.9	21 51.7	15 3.9	9 56.0	27 0.8	24 26.3	21 13.8	21 42.4
10 T	19 16 42.1	19 24.0	1 23.5	19 28.1	12 44.9	23 5.3	15 8.4	9 53.2	27 0.4	24 28.8	21 15.9	21 42.9
11 F	19 20 38.6	20 25.1	1 20.4	1♏33.4	14 20.3	24 18.9	15 12.3	9 50.2	26 60.0	24 31.3	21 17.9	21 43.4
12 S	19 24 35.2	21 26.3	1 17.2	13 54.7	15 56.2	25 32.4	15 15.5	9 47.1	26 59.4	24 33.8	21 20.0	21 43.9
13 S	19 28 31.7	22 27.4	1 14.0	26 36.3	17 32.5	26 45.9	15 17.9	9 43.8	26 58.7	24 36.2	21 22.0	21 44.3
14 M	19 32 28.3	23 28.6	1 10.8	9♐41.2	19 9.3	27 59.3	15 19.6	9 40.3	26 58.0	24 38.5	21 24.0	21 44.7
15 T	19 36 24.9	24 29.7	1 7.7	23 10.7	20 46.6	29 12.7	15 20.5	9 36.6	26 57.1	24 40.9	21 25.9	21 45.0
16 W	19 40 21.4	25 30.8	1 4.5	7♑ 4.2	22 24.4	0♓26.1	15 20.7	9 32.7	26 56.1	24 43.1	21 27.9	21 45.3
17 T	19 44 18.0	26 32.0	1 1.3	21 18.5	24 2.7	1 39.4	15R20.1	9 28.7	26 55.0	24 45.4	21 29.8	21 45.6
18 F	19 48 14.5	27 33.1	0 58.1	5♒48.5	25 41.6	2 52.6	15 18.8	9 24.4	26 53.8	24 47.6	21 31.8	21 45.8
19 S	19 52 11.1	28 34.2	0 54.9	20 28.0	27 20.9	4 5.8	15 16.7	9 20.0	26 52.4	24 49.7	21 33.7	21 46.0
20 S	19 56 7.6	29 35.3	0 51.8	5♓ 9.8	29 0.9	5 18.9	15 13.8	9 15.5	26 51.0	24 51.8	21 35.6	21 46.2
21 M	20 0 4.2	0♒36.4	0 48.6	19 47.8	0♒41.4	6 32.0	15 10.1	9 10.7	26 49.5	24 53.9	21 37.4	21 46.3
22 T	20 4 0.7	1 37.5	0 45.4	4♈16.9	2 22.4	7 45.0	15 5.7	9 5.9	26 47.9	24 55.9	21 39.3	21 46.4
23 W	20 7 57.3	2 38.5	0 42.2	18 33.4	4 4.1	8 58.0	15 0.4	9 0.8	26 46.2	24 57.9	21 41.1	21 46.5
24 T	20 11 53.9	3 39.6	0 39.1	2♉35.4	5 46.2	10 10.8	14 54.3	8 55.6	26 44.3	24 59.8	21 42.9	21 46.5
25 F	20 15 50.4	4 40.6	0 35.9	16 22.1	7 29.0	11 23.6	14 47.5	8 50.3	26 42.4	25 1.6	21 44.7	21 46.5
26 S	20 19 47.0	5 41.6	0 32.7	29 53.5	9 12.3	12 36.3	14 39.8	8 44.8	26 40.4	25 3.5	21 46.5	21R46.4
27 S	20 23 43.5	6 42.5	0 29.5	13♊10.1	10 56.1	13 49.0	14 31.4	8 39.1	26 38.2	25 5.2	21 48.2	21 46.3
28 M	20 27 40.1	7 43.5	0 26.4	26 12.6	12 40.5	15 1.5	14 22.1	8 33.3	26 36.0	25 6.9	21 49.9	21 46.2
29 T	20 31 36.6	8 44.4	0 23.2	9♋ 1.6	14 25.3	16 14.0	14 12.1	8 27.4	26 33.7	25 8.6	21 51.6	21 46.0
30 W	20 35 33.2	9 45.4	0 20.0	21 37.9	16 10.6	17 26.4	14 1.3	8 21.3	26 31.3	25 10.2	21 53.3	21 45.8
31 T	20 39 29.7	10 46.3	0 16.8	4♌ 2.1	17 56.2	18 38.8	13 49.7	8 15.1	26 28.7	25 11.8	21 55.0	21 45.6
						DECLINATION at NOON						
1 T	18 41 13.1	23S 2.7	10N48.6	18N58.8	24S 4.0	18S54.9	9N10.5	8N47.7	3N10.9	18S31.2	21S47.6	7N23.8
4 F	18 53 2.7	22 46.6	10 52.0	16 25.3	24 20.6	17 49.7	9 5.2	8 50.1	3 11.1	18 33.3	21 48.0	7 24.5
7 M	19 4 52.4	22 26.4	10 55.4	7 28.1	24 25.5	16 40.2	9 2.1	8 53.1	3 11.8	18 35.2	21 48.4	7 25.4
10 T	19 16 42.1	22 2.2	10 58.8	3S57.7	24 18.2	15 26.6	9 1.4	8 56.7	3 12.9	18 37.1	21 48.7	7 26.4
13 S	19 28 31.7	21 34.1	11 2.2	14 21.2	23 58.2	14 9.3	9 3.2	9 1.0	3 14.3	18 38.9	21 49.1	7 27.6
16 W	19 40 21.4	21 2.3	11 5.6	19 7.4	23 25.2	12 48.8	9 7.5	9 5.9	3 16.1	18 40.6	21 49.4	7 28.8
19 S	19 52 11.1	20 26.8	11 8.9	13 53.3	22 38.8	11 25.3	9 14.5	9 11.4	3 18.3	18 42.2	21 49.7	7 30.2
22 T	20 4 0.7	19 47.9	11 12.3	1 2.8	21 38.8	9 59.2	9 24.0	9 17.4	3 20.8	18 43.6	21 50.0	7 31.7
25 F	20 15 50.4	19 5.7	11 15.7	11N50.0	20 25.0	8 30.9	9 36.2	9 23.9	3 23.7	18 45.0	21 50.3	7 33.3
28 M	20 27 40.1	18 20.3	11 19.0	18 42.0	18 57.3	7 0.8	9 50.9	9 30.9	3 27.0	18 46.3	21 50.5	7 35.0
31 T	20 39 29.7	17 32.0	11 22.4	17 3.6	17 16.1	5 29.1	10 8.0	9 38.3	3 30.5	18 47.4	21 50.8	7 36.8

FEBRUARY 1980

DAY	EPHEMERIS SIDEREAL TIME	☉	☊	☽	☿	♀	♂	♃	♄	♅	♆	♇
						LONGITUDE at NOON						
1 F	20 43 26.3	11♒47.2	0♍13.6	16♌15.5	19♒42.1	19♓51.0	13♍37.4	8♍ 8.8	26♍26.1	25♏13.3	21♐56.6	21♎45.3
2 S	20 47 22.9	12 48.0	0 10.5	28 19.2	21 28.3	21 3.1	13R24.2	8R 2.3	26R23.4	25 14.8	21 58.2	21R45.0
3 S	20 51 19.4	13 48.9	0 7.3	10♍15.0	23 14.6	22 15.2	13 10.4	7 55.8	26 20.6	25 16.2	21 59.8	21 44.7
4 M	20 55 16.0	14 49.7	0 4.1	22 5.5	25 0.8	23 27.2	12 55.8	7 49.1	26 17.8	25 17.5	22 1.3	21 44.3
5 T	20 59 12.5	15 50.5	0 0.9	3♎53.5	26 46.9	24 39.1	12 40.4	7 42.3	26 14.8	25 18.8	22 2.8	21 43.9
6 W	21 3 9.1	16 51.4	29♌57.8	15 42.5	28 32.5	25 50.9	12 24.4	7 35.4	26 11.7	25 20.1	22 4.3	21 43.5
7 T	21 7 5.6	17 52.1	29 54.6	27 36.8	0♓17.6	27 2.6	12 7.6	7 28.4	26 8.6	25 21.3	22 5.8	21 43.0
8 F	21 11 2.2	18 52.9	29 51.4	9♏40.7	2 1.8	28 14.2	11 50.2	7 21.3	26 5.4	25 22.4	22 7.2	21 42.5
9 S	21 14 58.7	19 53.7	29 48.2	21 58.8	3 44.8	29 25.7	11 32.1	7 14.1	26 2.1	25 23.5	22 8.7	21 42.0
10 S	21 18 55.3	20 54.4	29 45.0	4♐35.8	5 26.2	0♈37.1	11 13.4	7 6.8	25 58.7	25 24.6	22 10.0	21 41.4
11 M	21 22 51.8	21 55.1	29 41.9	17 35.5	7 5.7	1 48.4	10 54.1	6 59.5	25 55.2	25 25.6	22 11.4	21 40.8
12 T	21 26 48.4	22 55.9	29 38.7	1♑ 1.0	8 42.7	2 59.6	10 34.3	6 52.1	25 51.8	25 26.6	22 12.8	21 40.2
13 W	21 30 45.0	23 56.6	29 35.5	14 53.3	10 16.8	4 10.7	10 13.8	6 44.6	25 48.2	25 27.5	22 14.1	21 39.5
14 T	21 34 41.5	24 57.2	29 32.3	29 11.4	11 47.5	5 21.7	9 52.9	6 37.0	25 44.5	25 28.3	22 15.4	21 38.8
15 F	21 38 38.1	25 57.9	29 29.2	13♒51.8	13 13.9	6 32.6	9 31.5	6 29.4	25 40.7	25 29.1	22 16.6	21 38.1
16 S	21 42 34.6	26 58.5	29 26.0	28 48.1	14 35.7	7 43.3	9 9.6	6 21.7	25 36.9	25 29.8	22 17.8	21 37.3
17 S	21 46 31.2	27 59.1	29 22.8	13♓52.3	15 52.0	8 54.0	8 47.4	6 14.0	25 33.0	25 30.4	22 19.0	21 36.5
18 M	21 50 27.7	28 59.7	29 19.6	28 55.5	17 2.2	10 4.5	8 24.8	6 6.2	25 29.1	25 31.0	22 20.2	21 35.7
19 T	21 54 24.3	0♓ 0.2	29 16.4	13♈49.1	18 5.5	11 14.9	8 1.9	5 58.4	25 25.1	25 31.6	22 21.3	21 34.8
20 W	21 58 20.8	1 0.7	29 13.3	28 26.4	19 1.4	12 25.2	7 38.7	5 50.6	25 21.0	25 32.1	22 22.4	21 33.9
21 T	22 2 17.4	2 1.2	29 10.1	12♉42.7	19 49.1	13 35.3	7 15.3	5 42.7	25 16.9	25 32.5	22 23.5	21 33.0
22 F	22 6 13.9	3 1.6	29 6.9	26 36.0	20 28.1	14 45.3	6 51.7	5 34.9	25 12.7	25 32.9	22 24.5	21 32.1
23 S	22 10 10.5	4 2.1	29 3.7	10♊ 6.0	20 58.0	15 55.1	6 28.0	5 27.0	25 8.5	25 33.3	22 25.5	21 31.1
24 S	22 14 7.0	5 2.4	29 0.6	23 14.4	21 18.2	17 4.8	6 4.2	5 19.1	25 4.2	25 33.5	22 26.5	21 30.1
25 M	22 18 3.6	6 2.8	28 57.4	6♋ 3.5	21 28.7	18 14.4	5 40.3	5 11.2	24 59.8	25 33.8	22 27.4	21 29.1
26 T	22 22 0.1	7 3.1	28 54.2	18 36.2	21 29.3	19 23.8	5 16.5	5 3.3	24 55.5	25 33.9	22 28.3	21 28.0
27 W	22 25 56.7	8 3.4	28 51.0	0♌55.5	21R20.1	20 33.0	4 52.7	4 55.4	24 51.1	25 34.1	22 29.2	21 26.9
28 T	22 29 53.2	9 3.7	28 47.8	13 4.2	21 1.4	21 42.1	4 29.0	4 47.6	24 46.6	25 34.1	22 30.1	21 25.8
29 F	22 33 49.8	10 3.9	28 44.7	25 4.6	20 33.8	22 51.0	4 5.5	4 39.7	24 42.1	25 34.1	22 30.9	21 24.7
						DECLINATION at NOON						
1 F	20 43 26.3	17S15.2	11N23.5	14N49.8	16S39.5	4S58.2	10N14.2	9N40.8	3N31.8	18S47.8	21S50.8	7N37.4
4 M	20 55 16.0	16 23.2	11 26.9	5 1.6	14 41.4	3 25.0	10 34.3	9 48.7	3 35.8	18 48.8	21 51.0	7 39.3
7 T	21 7 5.6	15 28.6	11 30.2	6S24.8	12 32.6	1 51.1	10 56.4	9 56.9	3 40.0	18 49.6	21 51.2	7 41.3
10 S	21 18 55.3	14 31.6	11 33.6	15 52.3	10 16.0	0 16.7	11 20.2	10 5.4	3 44.6	18 50.4	21 51.4	7 43.3
13 W	21 30 45.0	13 32.4	11 36.9	18 55.2	7 56.3	1N17.9	11 45.2	10 14.1	3 49.3	18 51.1	21 51.5	7 45.5
16 S	21 42 34.6	12 31.3	11 40.3	11 51.0	5 40.8	2 52.1	12 11.1	10 23.0	3 54.3	18 51.6	21 51.6	7 47.6
19 T	21 54 24.3	11 28.3	11 43.6	2N 1.2	3 38.7	4 25.9	12 37.5	10 31.9	3 59.5	18 52.0	21 51.7	7 49.9
22 F	22 6 13.9	10 23.7	11 46.9	14 14.5	2 0.6	5 58.8	13 3.7	10 40.9	4 4.9	18 52.3	21 51.8	7 52.2
25 M	22 18 3.6	9 17.6	11 50.2	19 3.4	0 56.7	7 30.6	13 29.3	10 49.8	4 10.4	18 52.5	21 51.8	7 54.5
28 T	22 29 53.2	8 10.4	11 53.6	15 28.1	0 34.7	9 0.9	13 53.8	10 58.7	4 16.0	18 52.6	21 51.9	7 56.8

MARCH 1980

DAY	EPHEMERIS SIDEREAL TIME	☉	☊	☽	☿	♀	♂	♃	♄	♅	♆	♇
	h m s	° ′	° ′	° ′	° ′	° ′	° ′	° ′	° ′	° ′	° ′	° ′
					LONGITUDE at NOON							
1 S	22 37 46.4	11♓ 4.1	28♌41.5	6♍59.2	19♓57.8	23♈59.8	3♍42.1	4♍31.9	24♍37.6	25♏34.1	22♐31.7	21♎23.5
2 S	22 41 42.9	12 4.2	28 38.3	18 50.0	19R14.5	25 8.3	3R18.9	4R24.1	24R33.0	25R34.0	22 32.4	21R22.3
3 M	22 45 39.5	13 4.4	28 35.1	0♎39.0	18 25.0	26 16.7	2 56.0	4 16.4	24 28.4	25 33.8	22 33.1	21 21.1
4 T	22 49 36.0	14 4.5	28 32.0	12 28.4	17 30.6	27 25.0	2 33.5	4 8.8	24 23.9	25 33.7	22 33.9	21 19.9
5 W	22 53 32.6	15 4.6	28 28.8	24 20.4	16 32.5	28 33.0	2 11.2	4 1.1	24 19.2	25 33.4	22 34.5	21 18.7
6 T	22 57 29.1	16 4.7	28 25.6	6♏17.8	15 32.2	29 40.8	1 49.3	3 53.5	24 14.6	25 33.1	22 35.1	21 17.4
7 F	23 1 25.7	17 4.7	28 22.4	18 23.8	14 31.2	0♉48.5	1 27.9	3 46.0	24 9.9	25 32.7	22 35.7	21 16.1
8 S	23 5 22.2	18 4.7	28 19.2	0♐41.8	13 30.9	1 55.9	1 6.9	3 38.5	24 5.2	25 32.3	22 36.3	21 14.8
9 S	23 9 18.8	19 4.6	28 16.1	13 15.5	12 32.6	3 3.2	0 46.3	3 31.1	24 0.5	25 31.8	22 36.8	21 13.4
10 M	23 13 15.3	20 4.6	28 12.9	26 8.8	11 37.4	4 10.2	0 26.3	3 23.8	23 55.7	25 31.3	22 37.3	21 12.0
11 T	23 17 11.9	21 4.5	28 9.7	9♑25.2	10 46.3	5 17.1	0 6.9	3 16.6	23 51.0	25 30.7	22 37.7	21 10.7
12 W	23 21 8.4	22 4.4	28 6.5	23 7.2	10 0.0	6 23.7	29♌48.0	3 9.4	23 46.2	25 30.1	22 38.2	21 9.3
13 T	23 25 5.0	23 4.2	28 3.4	7♒15.9	9 19.3	7 30.1	29 29.7	3 2.3	23 41.5	25 29.4	22 38.6	21 7.8
14 F	23 29 1.5	24 4.1	28 0.2	21 50.1	8 44.4	8 36.3	29 12.1	2 55.4	23 36.7	25 28.7	22 38.9	21 6.4
15 S	23 32 58.1	25 3.9	27 57.0	6♓45.7	8 15.8	9 42.3	28 55.1	2 48.5	23 32.0	25 27.9	22 39.2	21 4.9
16 S	23 36 54.6	26 3.6	27 53.8	21 55.8	7 53.5	10 48.0	28 38.8	2 41.7	23 27.2	25 27.0	22 39.5	21 3.4
17 M	23 40 51.2	27 3.4	27 50.6	7♈11.1	7 37.6	11 53.5	28 23.2	2 35.1	23 22.5	25 26.2	22 39.8	21 1.9
18 T	23 44 47.7	28 3.1	27 47.5	22 21.4	7 27.9	12 58.7	28 8.3	2 28.5	23 17.7	25 25.2	22 40.0	21 0.4
19 W	23 48 44.3	29 2.7	27 44.3	7♉16.8	7 24.4	14 3.6	27 54.2	2 22.1	23 13.0	25 24.2	22 40.2	20 58.9
20 T	23 52 40.8	0♈ 2.3	27 41.1	21 49.9	7D26.9	15 8.3	27 40.8	2 15.8	23 8.3	25 23.2	22 40.3	20 57.4
21 F	23 56 37.4	1 1.9	27 37.9	5♊56.1	7 35.1	16 12.8	27 28.2	2 9.6	23 3.6	25 22.1	22 40.4	20 55.8
22 S	0 0 33.9	2 1.5	27 34.8	19 34.0	7 48.8	17 16.9	27 16.3	2 3.6	22 58.9	25 21.0	22 40.5	20 54.2
23 S	0 4 30.5	3 1.0	27 31.6	2♋44.6	8 7.7	18 20.8	27 5.2	1 57.7	22 54.3	25 19.8	22 40.6	20 52.7
24 M	0 8 27.1	4 0.5	27 28.4	15 31.1	8 31.5	19 24.3	26 55.0	1 51.9	22 49.7	25 18.6	22 40.6	20 51.1
25 T	0 12 23.6	4 59.9	27 25.2	27 57.6	9 0.0	20 27.6	26 45.5	1 46.3	22 45.1	25 17.4	22 40.6	20 49.5
26 W	0 16 20.2	5 59.3	27 22.0	10♌ 8.4	9 32.9	21 30.5	26 36.8	1 40.9	22 40.6	25 16.1	22 40.6	20 47.9
27 T	0 20 16.7	6 58.7	27 18.9	22 8.1	10 10.0	22 33.0	26 28.9	1 35.5	22 36.0	25 14.7	22R40.5	20 46.3
28 F	0 24 13.3	7 58.0	27 15.7	4♍ 0.5	10 51.0	23 35.3	26 21.7	1 30.3	22 31.5	25 13.3	22 40.4	20 44.7
29 S	0 28 9.8	8 57.3	27 12.5	15 49.4	11 35.7	24 37.1	26 15.4	1 25.3	22 27.1	25 11.9	22 40.2	20 43.0
30 S	0 32 6.4	9 56.6	27 9.3	27 37.5	12 23.9	25 38.7	26 9.8	1 20.4	22 22.6	25 10.4	22 40.0	20 41.4
31 M	0 36 2.9	10 55.8	27 6.1	9♎27.2	13 15.4	26 39.8	26 5.0	1 15.7	22 18.3	25 8.8	22 39.8	20 39.7
					DECLINATION at NOON							
1 S	22 37 46.4	7S24.9	11N55.8	9N36.1	0S44.4	10N 0.1	14N 9.3	11N 4.5	4N19.8	18S52.6	21S51.9	7N58.4
4 T	22 49 36.0	6 15.9	11 59.1	1S35.9	1 32.1	11 27.3	14 31.1	11 13.0	4 25.6	18 52.4	21 51.9	8 0.8
7 F	23 1 25.7	5 6.2	12 2.4	12 19.7	2 49.1	12 52.2	14 50.8	11 21.4	4 31.4	18 52.2	21 51.9	8 3.1
10 M	23 13 15.3	3 55.8	12 5.7	18 41.7	4 18.8	14 14.6	15 8.1	11 29.5	4 37.2	18 51.9	21 51.9	8 5.5
13 T	23 25 5.0	2 45.0	12 9.0	16 33.3	5 45.3	15 34.1	15 22.9	11 37.2	4 43.1	18 51.4	21 51.8	8 7.9
16 S	23 36 54.6	1 34.0	12 12.3	5 4.1	6 57.5	16 50.6	15 35.0	11 44.6	4 48.9	18 50.8	21 51.7	8 10.2
19 W	23 48 44.3	0 22.8	12 15.5	9N21.0	7 49.7	18 3.7	15 44.4	11 51.5	4 54.6	18 50.1	21 51.7	8 12.6
22 S	0 0 33.9	0N48.3	12 18.8	18 9.7	8 20.2	19 13.1	15 51.0	11 58.0	5 0.2	18 49.3	21 51.6	8 14.8
25 T	0 12 23.6	1 59.2	12 22.1	17 56.5	8 29.7	20 18.8	15 54.8	12 4.0	5 5.7	18 48.5	21 51.4	8 17.1
28 F	0 24 13.3	3 9.6	12 25.4	10 28.4	8 19.7	21 20.3	15 56.0	12 9.5	5 11.0	18 47.5	21 51.3	8 19.3
31 M	0 36 2.9	4 19.5	12 28.6	0S38.8	7 51.8	22 17.6	15 54.7	12 14.4	5 16.2	18 46.4	21 51.2	8 21.4

APRIL 1980

DAY	EPHEMERIS SIDEREAL TIME	☉	☊	☽	☿	♀	♂	♃	♄	♅	♆	♇
					LONGITUDE at NOON							
1 T	0 39 59.5	11♈54.9	27♌ 3.0	21♎20.6	14♓10.0	27♉40.6	26♌ 1.0	1♍11.2	22♍13.9	25♏ 7.3	22♐39.6	20♎38.0
2 W	0 43 56.0	12 54.1	26 59.8	3♏19.2	15 7.6	28 40.9	25R57.7	1R 6.8	22R 9.6	25R 5.7	22R39.3	20R36.4
3 T	0 47 52.6	13 53.2	26 56.6	15 24.6	16 8.0	29 40.9	25 55.2	1 2.5	22 5.4	25 4.0	22 39.0	20 34.7
4 F	0 51 49.1	14 52.3	26 53.4	27 38.5	17 11.1	0♊40.4	25 53.5	0 58.5	22 1.2	25 2.3	22 38.6	20 33.0
5 S	0 55 45.7	15 51.3	26 50.3	10♐ 2.9	18 16.7	1 39.5	25 52.5	0 54.6	21 57.0	25 0.6	22 38.2	20 31.3
6 S	0 59 42.2	16 50.4	26 47.1	22 40.2	19 24.8	2 38.2	25 52.2	0 50.9	21 52.9	24 58.8	22 37.8	20 29.7
7 M	1 3 38.8	17 49.3	26 43.9	5♑33.0	20 35.1	3 36.4	25D52.7	0 47.3	21 48.9	24 57.0	22 37.4	20 28.0
8 T	1 7 35.3	18 48.3	26 40.7	18 44.2	21 47.7	4 34.1	25 53.9	0 43.9	21 44.9	24 55.2	22 36.9	20 26.3
9 W	1 11 31.9	19 47.2	26 37.5	2♒16.7	23 2.5	5 31.4	25 55.8	0 40.7	21 41.0	24 53.3	22 36.4	20 24.6
10 T	1 15 28.4	20 46.1	26 34.4	16 12.3	24 19.3	6 28.1	25 58.4	0 37.7	21 37.2	24 51.4	22 35.9	20 22.9
11 F	1 19 25.0	21 45.0	26 31.2	0♓31.7	25 38.2	7 24.3	26 1.7	0 34.9	21 33.4	24 49.4	22 35.3	20 21.2
12 S	1 23 21.5	22 43.9	26 28.0	15 13.1	26 59.0	8 20.1	26 5.7	0 32.2	21 29.7	24 47.5	22 34.7	20 19.5
13 S	1 27 18.1	23 42.7	26 24.8	0♈12.0	28 21.7	9 15.2	26 10.4	0 29.7	21 26.0	24 45.5	22 34.1	20 17.8
14 M	1 31 14.6	24 41.5	26 21.7	15 21.0	29 46.3	10 9.8	26 15.8	0 27.4	21 22.4	24 43.4	22 33.5	20 16.1
15 T	1 35 11.2	25 40.3	26 18.5	0♉30.6	1♈12.7	11 3.8	26 21.8	0 25.4	21 19.0	24 41.4	22 32.8	20 14.5
16 W	1 39 7.8	26 39.0	26 15.3	15 30.3	2 40.8	11 57.2	26 28.5	0 23.4	21 15.5	24 39.3	22 32.1	20 12.8
17 T	1 43 4.3	27 37.7	26 12.1	0♊11.0	4 10.8	12 50.0	26 35.8	0 21.7	21 12.2	24 37.2	22 31.4	20 11.1
18 F	1 47 0.9	28 36.3	26 8.9	14 26.0	5 42.4	13 42.1	26 43.7	0 20.1	21 8.9	24 35.0	22 30.6	20 9.5
19 S	1 50 57.4	29 34.9	26 5.8	28 12.0	7 15.8	14 33.5	26 52.3	0 18.8	21 5.7	24 32.8	22 29.8	20 7.8
20 S	1 54 54.0	0♉33.5	26 2.6	11♋28.8	8 50.9	15 24.1	27 1.4	0 17.6	21 2.6	24 30.6	22 29.0	20 6.1
21 M	1 58 50.5	1 32.1	25 59.4	24 18.8	10 27.7	16 14.1	27 11.2	0 16.6	20 59.5	24 28.4	22 28.1	20 4.5
22 T	2 2 47.1	2 30.6	25 56.2	6♌46.1	12 6.2	17 3.3	27 21.5	0 15.8	20 56.6	24 26.1	22 27.3	20 2.8
23 W	2 6 43.6	3 29.0	25 53.1	18 55.8	13 46.4	17 51.6	27 32.4	0 15.2	20 53.7	24 23.8	22 26.3	20 1.2
24 T	2 10 40.2	4 27.5	25 49.9	0♍53.1	15 28.4	18 39.2	27 43.9	0 14.7	20 50.9	24 21.5	22 25.4	19 59.6
25 F	2 14 36.7	5 25.9	25 46.7	12 43.1	17 12.0	19 25.9	27 55.9	0 14.5	20 48.2	24 19.2	22 24.5	19 58.0
26 S	2 18 33.3	6 24.2	25 43.5	24 30.6	18 57.4	20 11.7	28 8.4	0 14.4	20 45.6	24 16.9	22 23.5	19 56.4
27 S	2 22 29.8	7 22.6	25 40.3	6♎19.3	20 44.5	20 56.5	28 21.5	0D14.5	20 43.1	24 14.5	22 22.5	19 54.8
28 M	2 26 26.4	8 20.9	25 37.2	18 12.4	22 33.3	21 40.4	28 35.1	0 14.9	20 40.7	24 12.1	22 21.4	19 53.2
29 T	2 30 22.9	9 19.1	25 34.0	0♏12.3	24 23.8	22 23.3	28 49.1	0 15.3	20 38.3	24 9.7	22 20.4	19 51.6
30 W	2 34 19.5	10 17.4	25 30.8	12 20.5	26 16.1	23 5.2	29 3.7	0 16.0	20 36.1	24 7.3	22 19.3	19 50.0
					DECLINATION at NOON							
1 T	0 39 59.5	4N42.7	12N29.7	4S31.2	7S38.8	22N35.7	15N53.7	12N15.9	5N17.9	18S46.0	21S51.1	8N22.1
4 F	0 51 49.1	5 51.6	12 33.0	14 37.9	6 49.6	23 27.0	15 49.2	12 20.2	5 22.7	18 44.8	21 50.9	8 24.1
7 M	1 3 38.8	6 59.6	12 36.2	19 15.2	5 46.0	24 13.7	15 42.4	12 23.8	5 27.4	18 43.6	21 50.8	8 26.1
10 T	1 15 28.4	8 6.5	12 39.5	14 58.9	4 29.3	24 55.6	15 33.5	12 26.8	5 31.8	18 42.2	21 50.6	8 28.0
13 S	1 27 18.1	9 12.3	12 42.7	2 25.8	3 0.5	25 32.8	15 22.6	12 29.3	5 36.0	18 40.8	21 50.4	8 29.8
16 W	1 39 7.8	10 16.7	12 46.0	11N43.4	1 20.6	26 5.1	15 9.7	12 31.1	5 39.8	18 39.3	21 50.2	8 31.4
19 S	1 50 57.4	11 19.5	12 49.2	19 4.2	0N29.5	26 32.6	14 55.0	12 32.3	5 43.4	18 37.7	21 49.9	8 33.0
22 T	2 2 47.1	12 20.7	12 52.4	16 52.3	2 28.9	26 55.3	14 38.5	12 33.0	5 46.7	18 36.1	21 49.7	8 34.5
25 F	2 14 36.7	13 20.0	12 55.6	8 3.6	4 36.7	27 13.2	14 20.4	12 33.0	5 49.6	18 34.4	21 49.4	8 35.9
28 M	2 26 26.4	14 17.3	12 58.8	3S29.3	6 51.6	27 26.6	14 0.8	12 32.4	5 52.2	18 32.7	21 49.2	8 37.2

MAY 1980

DAY	EPHEMERIS SIDEREAL TIME	☉	☊	☽	☿	♀	♂	♃	♄	♅	♆	♇
	h m s	° ′	° ′	° ′	° ′	° ′	° ′	° ′	° ′	° ′	° ′	° ′
LONGITUDE at NOON												
1 T	2 38 16.1	11♉15.6	25♌27.6	24♏38.1	28♈10.2	23♊45.9	29♌18.7	0♍16.9	20♍34.0	24♏ 4.9	22♐18.2	19♎48.5
2 F	2 42 12.6	12 13.8	25 24.5	7♐ 5.7	0♉ 6.0	24 25.6	29 34.2	0 17.9	20R31.9	24R 2.5	22R17.1	19R47.0
3 S	2 46 9.2	13 11.9	25 21.3	19 43.8	2 3.5	25 4.1	29 50.2	0 19.1	20 29.9	24 0.0	22 15.9	19 45.4
4 S	2 50 5.7	14 10.0	25 18.1	2♑33.2	4 2.7	25 41.4	0♍ 6.6	0 20.5	20 28.1	23 57.5	22 14.7	19 43.9
5 M	2 54 2.3	15 8.1	25 14.9	15 35.0	6 3.5	26 17.4	0 23.5	0 22.1	20 26.3	23 55.1	22 13.5	19 42.4
6 T	2 57 58.8	16 6.3	25 11.7	28 50.6	8 6.0	26 52.2	0 40.8	0 23.9	20 24.7	23 52.6	22 12.4	19 41.0
7 W	3 1 55.4	17 4.3	25 8.6	12♒21.8	10 10.0	27 25.6	0 58.5	0 25.8	20 23.1	23 50.2	22 11.1	19 39.6
8 T	3 5 51.9	18 2.3	25 5.4	26 10.1	12 15.5	27 57.7	1 16.6	0 27.9	20 21.6	23 47.7	22 9.9	19 38.1
9 F	3 9 48.5	19 0.4	25 2.2	10♓16.6	14 22.3	28 28.2	1 35.2	0 30.2	20 20.2	23 45.1	22 8.6	19 36.7
10 S	3 13 45.0	19 58.3	24 59.0	24 40.8	16 30.3	28 57.3	1 54.1	0 32.7	20 18.9	23 42.6	22 7.3	19 35.3
11 S	3 17 41.6	20 56.3	24 55.9	9♈20.2	18 39.4	29 24.9	2 13.5	0 35.3	20 17.8	23 40.1	22 6.0	19 33.9
12 M	3 21 38.2	21 54.3	24 52.7	24 9.7	20 49.3	29 50.8	2 33.2	0 38.2	20 16.7	23 37.6	22 4.6	19 32.5
13 T	3 25 34.7	22 52.2	24 49.5	9♉ 2.3	22 59.9	0♋15.1	2 53.3	0 41.1	20 15.7	23 35.1	22 3.3	19 31.2
14 W	3 29 31.3	23 50.1	24 46.3	23 49.2	25 10.9	0 37.7	3 13.7	0 44.3	20 14.8	23 32.6	22 1.9	19 29.9
15 T	3 33 27.8	24 47.9	24 43.1	8♊21.9	27 22.0	0 58.5	3 34.6	0 47.6	20 14.1	23 30.0	22 0.5	19 28.6
16 F	3 37 24.4	25 45.8	24 40.0	22 33.5	29 33.0	1 17.4	3 55.8	0 51.1	20 13.4	23 27.5	21 59.1	19 27.3
17 S	3 41 20.9	26 43.6	24 36.8	6♋19.4	1♊43.7	1 34.4	4 17.3	0 54.8	20 12.8	23 25.0	21 57.7	19 26.0
18 S	3 45 17.5	27 41.4	24 33.6	19 38.2	3 53.6	1 49.5	4 39.2	0 58.6	20 12.4	23 22.5	21 56.3	19 24.8
19 M	3 49 14.0	28 39.2	24 30.4	2♌30.9	6 2.6	2 2.5	5 1.4	1 2.6	20 12.0	23 20.0	21 54.8	19 23.6
20 T	3 53 10.6	29 36.9	24 27.3	15 0.9	8 10.3	2 13.4	5 24.0	1 6.8	20 11.8	23 17.5	21 53.4	19 22.4
21 W	3 57 7.2	0♊34.6	24 24.1	27 12.7	10 16.6	2 22.2	5 46.9	1 11.1	20 11.6	23 15.0	21 51.9	19 21.2
22 T	4 1 3.7	1 32.3	24 20.9	9♍11.4	12 21.2	2 28.7	6 10.1	1 15.6	20 11.6	23 12.5	21 50.4	19 20.1
23 F	4 5 0.3	2 30.0	24 17.7	21 2.6	14 23.8	2 33.0	6 33.6	1 20.2	20 11.6	23 10.0	21 48.9	19 18.9
24 S	4 8 56.8	3 27.6	24 14.6	2♎51.4	16 24.3	2 35.0	6 57.4	1 25.0	20D11.8	23 7.6	21 47.4	19 17.9
25 S	4 12 53.4	4 25.2	24 11.4	14 42.7	18 22.6	2R34.6	7 21.4	1 30.0	20 12.0	23 5.1	21 45.9	19 16.8
26 M	4 16 49.9	5 22.8	24 8.2	26 40.3	20 18.4	2 31.8	7 45.8	1 35.1	20 12.4	23 2.7	21 44.3	19 15.7
27 T	4 20 46.5	6 20.4	24 5.0	8♏47.5	22 11.8	2 26.7	8 10.5	1 40.4	20 12.9	23 0.3	21 42.8	19 14.8
28 W	4 24 43.0	7 18.0	24 1.8	21 6.2	24 2.5	2 19.1	8 35.5	1 45.8	20 13.5	22 57.9	21 41.3	19 13.8
29 T	4 28 39.6	8 15.5	23 58.7	3♐37.7	25 50.5	2 9.0	9 0.7	1 51.3	20 14.2	22 55.5	21 39.7	19 12.8
30 F	4 32 36.2	9 13.0	23 55.5	16 22.1	27 35.8	1 56.5	9 26.1	1 57.0	20 14.9	22 53.1	21 38.1	19 11.9
31 S	4 36 32.7	10 10.5	23 52.3	29 19.0	29 18.3	1 41.6	9 51.8	2 2.9	20 15.8	22 50.7	21 36.6	19 11.0
DECLINATION at NOON												
1 T	2 38 16.1	15N12.5	13N 2.1	14S 3.6	9N12.3	27N35.5	13N39.7	12N31.3	5N54.4	18S30.9	21S48.9	8N38.3
4 S	2 50 5.7	16 5.5	13 5.3	19 23.7	11 36.8	27 40.1	13 17.1	12 29.5	5 56.3	18 29.1	21 48.7	8 39.3
7 W	3 1 55.4	16 56.0	13 8.5	15 59.8	14 2.2	27 40.5	12 53.3	12 27.2	5 57.8	18 27.3	21 48.4	8 40.2
10 S	3 13 45.0	17 44.0	13 11.6	4 22.9	16 25.0	27 37.1	12 28.1	12 24.3	5 58.9	18 25.5	21 48.1	8 40.9
13 T	3 25 34.7	18 29.4	13 14.8	9N56.3	18 40.3	27 29.8	12 1.7	12 20.8	5 59.7	18 23.6	21 47.8	8 41.5
16 F	3 37 24.4	19 12.0	13 18.0	18 48.7	20 42.7	27 18.9	11 34.1	12 16.8	6 0.1	18 21.8	21 47.5	8 42.0
19 M	3 49 14.0	19 51.6	13 21.2	17 47.0	22 27.0	27 4.5	11 5.3	12 12.3	6 0.1	18 19.9	21 47.2	8 42.4
22 T	4 1 3.7	20 28.2	13 24.4	9 20.6	23 49.4	26 46.5	10 35.4	12 7.2	5 59.8	18 18.1	21 46.9	8 42.6
25 S	4 12 53.4	21 1.6	13 27.5	2S11.9	24 48.0	26 24.9	10 4.4	12 1.7	5 59.1	18 16.3	21 46.6	8 42.6
28 W	4 24 43.0	21 31.7	13 30.7	13 11.7	25 23.0	25 59.5	9 32.4	11 55.6	5 57.9	18 14.5	21 46.3	8 42.5
31 S	4 36 32.7	21 58.5	13 33.8	19 23.3	25 36.4	25 30.1	8 59.4	11 49.0	5 56.5	18 12.7	21 46.0	8 42.3

JUNE 1980

DAY	EPHEMERIS SIDEREAL TIME	☉	☊	☽	☿	♀	♂	♃	♄	♅	♆	♇
LONGITUDE at NOON												
1 S	4 40 29.3	11♊ 8.0	23♌49.1	12♑27.8	0♋58.0	1♋24.4	10♍17.8	2♍ 8.9	20♍16.8	22♏48.4	21♐35.0	19♎10.1
2 M	4 44 25.8	12 5.4	23 46.0	25 47.7	2 34.8	1R 4.8	10 44.0	2 15.0	20 17.9	22R46.0	21R33.4	19R 9.3
3 T	4 48 22.4	13 2.9	23 42.8	9♒18.2	4 8.7	0 43.0	11 10.5	2 21.3	20 19.1	22 43.7	21 31.8	19 8.4
4 W	4 52 18.9	14 0.3	23 39.6	22 59.4	5 39.7	0 19.0	11 37.2	2 27.7	20 20.3	22 41.4	21 30.2	19 7.6
5 T	4 56 15.5	14 57.7	23 36.4	6♓51.2	7 7.8	29♊52.9	12 4.2	2 34.2	20 21.7	22 39.2	21 28.6	19 6.9
6 F	5 0 12.1	15 55.1	23 33.3	20 53.8	8 32.9	29 24.9	12 31.4	2 40.9	20 23.2	22 36.9	21 27.0	19 6.1
7 S	5 4 8.6	16 52.5	23 30.1	5♈ 6.6	9 55.0	28 55.1	12 58.8	2 47.7	20 24.8	22 34.7	21 25.4	19 5.4
8 S	5 8 5.2	17 49.9	23 26.9	19 28.0	11 14.0	28 23.6	13 26.4	2 54.7	20 26.5	22 32.5	21 23.7	19 4.8
9 M	5 12 1.7	18 47.3	23 23.7	3♉54.8	12 30.0	27 50.7	13 54.3	3 1.8	20 28.3	22 30.3	21 22.1	19 4.1
10 T	5 15 58.3	19 44.7	23 20.5	18 22.5	13 42.8	27 16.4	14 22.4	3 9.0	20 30.1	22 28.2	21 20.5	19 3.5
11 W	5 19 54.8	20 42.1	23 17.4	2♊45.1	14 52.5	26 41.1	14 50.7	3 16.3	20 32.1	22 26.0	21 18.9	19 2.9
12 T	5 23 51.4	21 39.4	23 14.2	16 56.6	15 58.9	26 4.9	15 19.2	3 23.8	20 34.2	22 23.9	21 17.2	19 2.4
13 F	5 27 48.0	22 36.8	23 11.0	0♋51.5	17 2.0	25 28.0	15 48.0	3 31.4	20 36.4	22 21.9	21 15.6	19 1.8
14 S	5 31 44.5	23 34.1	23 7.8	14 26.0	18 1.7	24 50.6	16 16.9	3 39.1	20 38.6	22 19.8	21 14.0	19 1.4
15 S	5 35 41.1	24 31.4	23 4.7	27 37.9	18 57.9	24 13.1	16 46.1	3 46.9	20 41.0	22 17.8	21 12.4	19 0.9
16 M	5 39 37.6	25 28.7	23 1.5	10♌27.6	19 50.5	23 35.6	17 15.4	3 54.9	20 43.5	22 15.9	21 10.8	19 0.5
17 T	5 43 34.2	26 26.1	22 58.3	22 57.1	20 39.5	22 58.4	17 45.0	4 3.0	20 46.1	22 14.0	21 9.2	19 0.1
18 W	5 47 30.7	27 23.3	22 55.1	5♍ 9.7	21 24.7	22 21.6	18 14.8	4 11.2	20 48.7	22 12.1	21 7.6	18 59.8
19 T	5 51 27.3	28 20.6	22 52.0	17 9.9	22 6.1	21 45.7	18 44.7	4 19.5	20 51.5	22 10.2	21 6.0	18 59.5
20 F	5 55 23.9	29 17.9	22 48.8	29 2.7	22 43.4	21 10.6	19 14.8	4 28.0	20 54.3	22 8.4	21 4.4	18 59.2
21 S	5 59 20.4	0♋15.1	22 45.6	10♎53.4	23 16.7	20 36.8	19 45.1	4 36.5	20 57.3	22 6.6	21 2.8	18 58.9
22 S	6 3 17.0	1 12.3	22 42.4	22 46.9	23 45.8	20 4.3	20 15.6	4 45.2	21 0.3	22 4.8	21 1.2	18 58.7
23 M	6 7 13.5	2 9.6	22 39.2	4♏48.0	24 10.5	19 33.4	20 46.2	4 53.9	21 3.4	22 3.1	20 59.6	18 58.5
24 T	6 11 10.1	3 6.8	22 36.1	17 0.4	24 30.9	19 4.1	21 17.1	5 2.8	21 6.6	22 1.4	20 58.0	18 58.3
25 W	6 15 6.6	4 4.0	22 32.9	29 27.3	24 46.8	18 36.8	21 48.1	5 11.7	21 9.9	21 59.7	20 56.4	18 58.2
26 T	6 19 3.2	5 1.2	22 29.7	12♐10.4	24 58.2	18 11.4	22 19.2	5 20.8	21 13.3	21 58.1	20 54.9	18 58.1
27 F	6 22 59.8	5 58.4	22 26.5	25 10.5	25 4.9	17 48.1	22 50.5	5 30.0	21 16.7	21 56.5	20 53.3	18 58.0
28 S	6 26 56.3	6 55.6	22 23.4	8♑27.0	25 7.1	17 27.1	23 22.0	5 39.3	21 20.3	21 55.0	20 51.8	18 58.0
29 S	6 30 52.9	7 52.7	22 20.2	21 58.2	25R 4.6	17 8.3	23 53.7	5 48.6	21 23.9	21 53.5	20 50.2	18 58.0
30 M	6 34 49.4	8 49.9	22 17.0	5♒42.1	24 57.6	16 51.8	24 25.5	5 58.1	21 27.6	21 52.0	20 48.7	18 58.1
DECLINATION at NOON												
1 S	4 40 29.3	22N 6.7	13N34.9	19S36.4	25N36.5	25N19.4	8N48.3	11N46.8	5N55.9	18S12.1	21S45.9	8N42.2
4 W	4 52 18.9	22 28.9	13 38.0	13 53.3	25 25.1	24 44.4	8 14.1	11 39.6	5 54.0	18 10.4	21 45.6	8 41.8
7 S	5 4 8.6	22 47.5	13 41.2	1 7.4	24 58.8	24 5.4	7 39.0	11 32.0	5 51.7	18 8.7	21 45.3	8 41.2
10 T	5 15 58.3	23 2.6	13 44.3	12N26.4	24 20.5	23 22.8	7 3.0	11 23.9	5 49.1	18 7.1	21 45.0	8 40.5
13 F	5 27 48.0	23 14.0	13 47.4	19 29.4	23 33.3	22 37.4	6 26.2	11 1..4	5 46.1	18 5.6	21 44.7	8 39.7
16 M	5 39 37.6	23 21.7	13 50.5	16 39.9	22 39.9	21 50.7	5 48.7	11 6.5	5 42.7	18 4.1	21 44.4	8 38.7
19 T	5 51 27.3	23 25.8	13 53.7	7 6.8	21 43.2	21 4.4	5 10.3	10 57.2	5 39.1	18 2.7	21 44.1	8 37.6
22 S	6 3 17.0	23 26.1	13 56.8	4S40.7	20 45.9	20 20.3	4 31.3	10 47.5	5 35.1	18 1.3	21 43.8	8 36.4
25 W	6 15 6.6	23 22.6	13 59.9	15 4.5	19 50.8	19 40.3	3 51.5	10 37.4	5 30.8	18 0.1	21 43.6	8 35.0
28 S	6 26 56.3	23 15.5	14 3.0	19 42.0	19 0.5	19 5.8	3 11.2	10 27.0	5 26.2	17 58.9	21 43.3	8 33.5

JULY 1980

LONGITUDE at NOON

DAY	EPHEMERIS SIDEREAL TIME h m s	☉ ° ′	☊ ° ′	☽ ° ′	☿ ° ′	♀ ° ′	♂ ° ′	♃ ° ′	♄ ° ′	♅ ° ′	♆ ° ′	♇ ° ′
1 T	6 38 46.0	9♋47.1	22♌13.8	19♒35.9	24♋46.1	16♊37.8	24♍57.5	6♍ 7.7	21♍31.4	21♏50.6	20♐47.2	18≏58.1
2 W	6 42 42.5	10 44.3	22 10.7	3♓37.2	24R 30.2	16R 26.1	25 29.6	6 17.3	21 35.3	21R 49.2	20R 45.7	18D 58.3
3 T	6 46 39.1	11 41.5	22 7.5	17 43.9	24 10.3	16 16.8	26 1.8	6 27.1	21 39.3	21 47.9	20 44.2	18 58.4
4 F	6 50 35.7	12 38.7	22 4.3	1♈54.0	23 46.4	16 10.0	26 34.3	6 36.9	21 43.4	21 46.6	20 42.7	18 58.6
5 S	6 54 32.2	13 35.9	22 1.1	16 5.7	23 19.1	16 5.5	27 6.8	6 46.9	21 47.5	21 45.4	20 41.2	18 58.8
6 S	6 58 28.8	14 33.1	21 58.0	0♉17.1	22 48.5	16 3.5	27 39.5	6 56.9	21 51.7	21 44.2	20 39.8	18 59.0
7 M	7 2 25.3	15 30.3	21 54.8	14 26.1	22 15.2	16D 3.7	28 12.4	7 7.0	21 56.0	21 43.0	20 38.3	18 59.3
8 T	7 6 21.9	16 27.5	21 51.6	28 30.0	21 39.8	16 6.3	28 45.5	7 17.2	22 0.4	21 42.0	20 37.0	18 59.7
9 W	7 10 18.4	17 24.8	21 48.4	12♊25.8	21 2.6	16 11.2	29 18.6	7 27.5	22 4.9	21 40.9	20 35.6	19 0.0
10 T	7 14 15.0	18 22.0	21 45.2	26 10.4	20 24.4	16 18.2	29 51.9	7 37.9	22 9.4	21 39.9	20 34.2	19 0.4
11 F	7 18 11.6	19 19.2	21 42.1	9♋40.9	19 45.8	16 27.4	0≏25.4	7 48.4	22 14.0	21 38.9	20 32.8	19 0.8
12 S	7 22 8.1	20 16.5	21 38.9	22 55.2	19 7.4	16 38.6	0 59.0	7 58.9	22 18.7	21 38.0	20 31.4	19 1.2
13 S	7 26 4.7	21 13.7	21 35.7	5♌52.1	18 30.0	16 51.9	1 32.7	8 9.5	22 23.4	21 37.1	20 30.1	19 1.7
14 M	7 30 1.2	22 11.0	21 32.5	18 31.7	17 54.1	17 7.2	2 6.6	8 20.2	22 28.2	21 36.3	20 28.8	19 2.2
15 T	7 33 57.8	23 8.2	21 29.4	0♍55.2	17 20.5	17 24.4	2 40.6	8 31.0	22 33.1	21 35.5	20 27.4	19 2.8
16 W	7 37 54.3	24 5.5	21 26.2	13 5.1	16 49.7	17 43.4	3 14.7	8 41.8	22 38.1	21 34.8	20 26.2	19 3.4
17 T	7 41 50.9	25 2.7	21 23.0	25 4.5	16 22.3	18 4.2	3 49.0	8 52.7	22 43.2	21 34.1	20 24.9	19 4.0
18 F	7 45 47.4	25 60.0	21 19.8	6≏57.6	15 58.8	18 26.7	4 23.4	9 3.7	22 48.3	21 33.5	20 23.6	19 4.6
19 S	7 49 44.0	26 57.2	21 16.7	18 48.8	15 39.7	18 51.0	4 57.9	9 14.8	22 53.4	21 32.9	20 22.4	19 5.3
20 S	7 53 40.6	27 54.5	21 13.5	0♏42.8	15 25.4	19 16.8	5 32.6	9 25.9	22 58.7	21 32.4	20 21.2	19 6.0
21 M	7 57 37.1	28 51.8	21 10.3	12 44.6	15 16.1	19 44.2	6 7.3	9 37.1	23 4.0	21 31.9	20 20.0	19 6.8
22 T	8 1 33.7	29 49.0	21 7.1	24 58.5	15 12.3	20 13.1	6 42.2	9 48.3	23 9.4	21 31.5	20 18.9	19 7.6
23 W	8 5 30.2	0♌46.3	21 3.9	7♐28.5	15D 14.1	20 43.5	7 17.2	9 59.7	23 14.8	21 31.1	20 17.7	19 8.4
24 T	8 9 26.8	1 43.6	21 0.8	20 17.6	15 21.6	21 15.2	7 52.4	10 11.0	23 20.3	21 30.8	20 16.6	19 9.2
25 F	8 13 23.3	2 40.9	20 57.6	3♑27.5	15 35.1	21 48.3	8 27.6	10 22.5	23 25.9	21 30.5	20 15.5	19 10.1
26 S	8 17 19.9	3 38.2	20 54.4	16 58.5	15 54.5	22 22.8	9 3.0	10 34.0	23 31.5	21 30.3	20 14.4	19 11.0
27 S	8 21 16.5	4 35.5	20 51.2	0♒49.3	16 20.0	22 58.4	9 38.5	10 45.6	23 37.2	21 30.1	20 13.4	19 11.9
28 M	8 25 13.0	5 32.8	20 48.1	14 56.9	16 51.6	23 35.3	10 14.1	10 57.2	23 42.9	21 30.0	20 12.4	19 12.9
29 T	8 29 9.6	6 30.2	20 44.9	29 17.1	17 29.2	24 13.5	10 49.9	11 8.9	23 48.7	21 30.0	20 11.4	19 14.0
30 W	8 33 6.1	7 27.6	20 41.7	13♓44.8	18 12.8	24 52.7	11 25.7	11 20.6	23 54.6	21 29.9	20 10.4	19 15.0
31 T	8 37 2.7	8 25.0	20 38.5	28 15.0	19 2.4	25 33.0	12 1.6	11 32.4	24 0.5	21D 30.0	20 9.5	19 16.1

DECLINATION at NOON

DAY	SIDEREAL TIME	☉	☊	☽	☿	♀	♂	♃	♄	♅	♆	♇
1 T	6 38 46.0	23N 4.7	14N 6.1	14S 50.6	18N 17.7	18N 37.6	2N 30.3	10N 16.2	5N 21.3	17S 57.9	21S 43.1	8N 31.9
4 F	6 50 35.7	22 50.3	14 9.2	2 22.9	17 44.6	18 16.1	1 48.8	10 5.1	5 16.2	17 56.9	21 42.8	8 30.2
7 M	7 2 25.3	22 32.3	14 12.2	11N 14.2	17 23.1	18 1.3	1 6.8	9 53.7	5 10.7	17 56.0	21 42.6	8 28.4
10 T	7 14 15.0	22 10.8	14 15.3	19 9.6	17 14.2	17 52.8	0 24.3	9 41.9	5 5.0	17 55.3	21 42.4	8 26.4
13 S	7 26 4.7	21 45.9	14 18.4	17 32.3	17 18.0	17 49.7	0S 18.6	9 29.9	4 59.1	17 54.6	21 42.2	8 24.3
16 W	7 37 54.3	21 17.6	14 21.5	8 31.3	17 33.3	17 51.4	1 1.9	9 17.6	4 52.8	17 54.1	21 42.0	8 22.2
19 S	7 49 44.0	20 46.1	14 24.5	3S 13.6	17 58.2	17 56.8	1 45.5	9 5.0	4 46.4	17 53.7	21 41.9	8 19.9
22 T	8 1 33.7	20 11.4	14 27.6	13 55.6	18 29.7	18 5.3	2 29.5	8 52.1	4 39.7	17 53.4	21 41.7	8 17.6
25 F	8 13 23.3	19 33.7	14 30.6	19 33.5	19 4.5	18 15.9	3 13.7	8 39.0	4 32.9	17 53.2	21 41.6	8 15.1
28 M	8 25 13.0	18 53.0	14 33.6	15 53.4	19 38.5	18 27.8	3 58.1	8 25.7	4 25.8	17 53.1	21 41.5	8 12.6
31 T	8 37 2.7	18 9.6	14 36.7	3 41.1	20 7.2	18 40.3	4 42.7	8 12.1	4 18.5	17 53.2	21 41.4	8 10.0

AUGUST 1980

LONGITUDE at NOON

DAY	SIDEREAL TIME h m s	☉ ° ′	☊ ° ′	☽ ° ′	☿ ° ′	♀ ° ′	♂ ° ′	♃ ° ′	♄ ° ′	♅ ° ′	♆ ° ′	♇ ° ′
1 F	8 40 59.2	9♌22.4	20♌35.3	12♈42.8	19♋57.8	26♊14.3	12≏37.7	11♍44.3	24♍ 6.5	21♏30.1	20♐ 8.5	19≏17.2
2 S	8 44 55.8	10 19.8	20 32.2	27 4.2	20 58.9	26 56.7	13 13.8	11 56.2	24 12.5	21 30.2	20R 7.6	19 18.3
3 S	8 48 52.3	11 17.2	20 29.0	11♉16.2	22 5.8	27 40.0	13 50.1	12 8.1	24 18.6	21 30.4	20 6.8	19 19.4
4 M	8 52 48.9	12 14.6	20 25.8	25 16.7	23 18.1	28 24.2	14 26.5	12 20.1	24 24.7	21 30.6	20 5.9	19 20.6
5 T	8 56 45.4	13 12.1	20 22.6	9♊ 4.1	24 35.7	29 9.4	15 3.0	12 32.2	24 30.9	21 30.9	20 5.1	19 21.8
6 W	9 0 42.0	14 9.6	20 19.5	22 37.9	25 58.5	29 55.4	15 39.6	12 44.3	24 37.1	21 31.2	20 4.3	19 23.1
7 T	9 4 38.6	15 7.1	20 16.3	5♋57.6	27 26.2	0♋42.3	16 16.3	12 56.4	24 43.4	21 31.6	20 3.6	19 24.4
8 F	9 8 35.1	16 4.7	20 13.1	19 3.1	28 58.5	1 29.9	16 53.2	13 8.6	24 49.7	21 32.1	20 2.8	19 25.7
9 S	9 12 31.7	17 2.2	20 9.9	1♌54.7	0♌35.2	2 18.3	17 30.1	13 20.8	24 56.1	21 32.6	20 2.1	19 27.0
10 S	9 16 28.2	17 59.8	20 6.8	14 32.7	2 16.0	3 7.5	18 7.2	13 33.1	25 2.5	21 33.1	20 1.4	19 28.4
11 M	9 20 24.8	18 57.4	20 3.6	26 58.0	4 0.5	3 57.4	18 44.3	13 45.4	25 9.0	21 33.7	20 0.8	19 29.8
12 T	9 24 21.3	19 55.0	20 0.4	9♍11.7	5 48.3	4 47.9	19 21.6	13 57.8	25 15.5	21 34.4	20 0.2	19 31.2
13 W	9 28 17.9	20 52.6	19 57.2	21 15.6	7 39.1	5 39.1	19 59.0	14 10.2	25 22.1	21 35.1	19 59.6	19 32.6
14 T	9 32 14.4	21 50.3	19 54.0	3≏12.0	9 32.5	6 31.0	20 36.4	14 22.6	25 28.7	21 35.9	19 59.0	19 34.1
15 F	9 36 11.0	22 47.9	19 50.9	15 3.7	11 28.1	7 23.5	21 14.0	14 35.1	25 35.3	21 36.7	19 58.5	19 35.6
16 S	9 40 7.5	23 45.6	19 47.7	26 54.3	13 25.4	8 16.6	21 51.7	14 47.6	25 42.0	21 37.5	19 58.0	19 37.1
17 S	9 44 4.1	24 43.3	19 44.5	8♏47.6	15 24.1	9 10.2	22 29.5	15 0.1	25 48.7	21 38.4	19 57.5	19 38.7
18 M	9 48 0.7	25 41.0	19 41.3	20 48.0	17 23.9	10 4.4	23 7.3	15 12.7	25 55.5	21 39.4	19 57.1	19 40.3
19 T	9 51 57.2	26 38.8	19 38.2	3♐ 0.0	19 24.4	10 59.2	23 45.4	15 25.3	26 2.3	21 40.5	19 56.7	19 41.9
20 W	9 55 53.8	27 36.6	19 35.0	15 28.0	21 25.2	11 54.5	24 23.4	15 38.0	26 9.2	21 41.5	19 56.3	19 43.6
21 T	9 59 50.3	28 34.4	19 31.8	28 15.9	23 26.1	12 50.3	25 1.6	15 50.6	26 16.0	21 42.7	19 56.0	19 45.2
22 F	10 3 46.9	29 32.2	19 28.6	11♑27.0	25 26.9	13 46.6	25 39.9	16 3.3	26 22.9	21 43.8	19 55.7	19 46.9
23 S	10 7 43.4	0♍30.0	19 25.4	25 3.0	27 27.3	14 43.4	26 18.2	16 16.0	26 29.9	21 45.0	19 55.4	19 48.6
24 S	10 11 40.0	1 27.8	19 22.3	9♒ 4.0	29 27.1	15 40.6	26 56.7	16 28.7	26 36.8	21 46.3	19 55.1	19 50.3
25 M	10 15 36.5	2 25.7	19 19.1	23 27.6	1♍26.2	16 38.3	27 35.3	16 41.5	26 43.8	21 47.6	19 54.9	19 52.1
26 T	10 19 33.1	3 23.5	19 15.9	8♓ 9.1	3 24.4	17 36.5	28 13.9	16 54.3	26 50.8	21 49.0	19 54.7	19 53.9
27 W	10 23 29.6	4 21.5	19 12.7	23 2.0	5 21.7	18 35.1	28 52.6	17 7.1	26 57.9	21 50.4	19 54.5	19 55.7
28 T	10 27 26.2	5 19.4	19 9.6	7♈58.1	7 18.0	19 34.1	29 31.5	17 19.9	27 5.0	21 51.9	19 54.4	19 57.5
29 F	10 31 22.7	6 17.4	19 6.4	22 49.5	9 13.2	20 33.5	0♏10.4	17 32.7	27 12.1	21 53.4	19 54.3	19 59.3
30 S	10 35 19.3	7 15.4	19 3.2	7♉29.0	11 7.2	21 33.3	0 49.4	17 45.6	27 19.2	21 54.9	19 54.3	20 1.2
31 S	10 39 15.8	8 13.4	19 0.0	21 51.5	13 0.1	22 33.4	1 28.5	17 58.5	27 26.4	21 56.5	19 54.2	20 3.1

DECLINATION at NOON

DAY	SIDEREAL TIME	☉	☊	☽	☿	♀	♂	♃	♄	♅	♆	♇
1 F	8 40 59.2	17N 54.5	14N 37.7	1N 9.6	20N 14.8	18N 44.5	4S 57.6	8N 7.6	4N 16.0	17S 53.2	21S 41.4	8N 9.1
4 M	8 52 48.9	17 7.6	14 40.7	13 58.3	20 28.8	18 56.6	5 42.3	7 53.7	4 8.5	17 53.4	21 41.3	8 6.4
7 T	9 4 38.6	16 18.1	14 43.7	19 37.1	20 26.1	19 7.8	6 27.0	7 39.7	4 0.8	17 53.8	21 41.3	8 3.7
10 S	9 16 28.2	15 26.3	14 46.7	15 58.2	20 2.4	19 17.5	7 11.8	7 25.5	3 53.0	17 54.2	21 41.3	8 0.8
13 W	9 28 17.9	14 32.2	14 49.8	5 58.6	19 15.0	19 25.2	7 56.4	7 11.2	3 45.0	17 54.8	21 41.3	7 58.0
16 S	9 40 7.5	13 36.1	14 52.8	5S 50.1	18 3.8	19 30.3	8 41.0	6 56.7	3 36.9	17 55.5	21 41.3	7 55.1
19 T	9 51 57.2	12 38.0	14 55.7	15 41.9	16 31.0	19 32.6	9 25.4	6 42.0	3 28.7	17 56.3	21 41.4	7 52.1
22 F	10 3 46.9	11 38.1	14 58.7	19 38.7	14 40.4	19 31.7	10 9.6	6 27.3	3 20.3	17 57.3	21 41.4	7 49.1
25 M	10 15 36.5	10 36.6	15 1.7	13 58.9	12 36.7	19 27.2	10 53.4	6 12.4	3 11.9	17 58.3	21 41.5	7 46.1
28 T	10 27 26.2	9 33.6	15 4.7	0 25.6	10 24.0	19 18.9	11 36.9	5 57.4	3 3.3	17 59.5	21 41.7	7 43.1
31 S	10 39 15.8	8 29.2	15 7.7	13N 8.8	8 6.0	19 6.7	12 20.0	5 42.4	2 54.7	18 0.8	21 41.8	7 40.0

SEPTEMBER 1980

DAY	EPHEMERIS SIDEREAL TIME	☉	☊	☽	☿	♀	♂	♃	♄	♅	♆	♇
	h m s	° ′	° ′	° ′	° ′	° ′	° ′	° ′	° ′	° ′	° ′	° ′
						LONGITUDE at NOON						
1 M	10 43 12.4	9♍11.5	18♌56.8	5♊53.9	14♍51.7	23♋34.0	2♏ 7.7	18♍11.4	27♍33.6	21♏58.2	19♐54.2	20♎ 5.0
2 T	10 47 8.9	10 9.5	18 53.7	19 35.2	16 42.2	24 34.9	2 47.0	18 24.3	27 40.8	21 59.9	19D54.3	20 7.0
3 W	10 51 5.5	11 7.7	18 50.5	2♋56.2	18 31.4	25 36.2	3 26.4	18 37.2	27 48.0	22 1.6	19 54.3	20 8.9
4 T	10 55 2.1	12 5.8	18 47.3	15 58.6	20 19.4	26 37.8	4 5.9	18 50.1	27 55.3	22 3.4	19 54.4	20 10.9
5 F	10 58 58.6	13 4.0	18 44.1	28 44.7	22 6.2	27 39.8	4 45.5	19 3.1	28 2.5	22 5.3	19 54.6	20 12.9
6 S	11 2 55.2	14 2.3	18 40.9	11♌16.9	23 51.9	28 42.0	5 25.1	19 16.0	28 9.8	22 7.2	19 54.7	20 14.9
7 S	11 6 51.7	15 0.5	18 37.8	23 37.4	25 36.3	29 44.6	6 4.9	19 29.0	28 17.1	22 9.1	19 54.9	20 16.9
8 M	11 10 48.3	15 58.8	18 34.6	5♍48.3	27 19.5	0♌47.5	6 44.7	19 42.0	28 24.5	22 11.1	19 55.2	20 19.0
9 T	11 14 44.8	16 57.2	18 31.4	17 51.5	29 1.7	1 50.7	7 24.7	19 55.0	28 31.9	22 13.1	19 55.5	20 21.1
10 W	11 18 41.4	17 55.5	18 28.2	29 48.6	0♎42.6	2 54.2	8 4.8	20 8.0	28 39.2	22 15.2	19 55.8	20 23.2
11 T	11 22 37.9	18 53.9	18 25.1	11♎41.5	2 22.5	3 58.0	8 44.9	20 21.0	28 46.6	22 17.3	19 56.1	20 25.3
12 F	11 26 34.5	19 52.3	18 21.9	23 32.0	4 1.2	5 2.0	9 25.1	20 34.0	28 54.0	22 19.5	19 56.5	20 27.4
13 S	11 30 31.0	20 50.7	18 18.7	5♏22.5	5 38.8	6 6.2	10 5.4	20 47.0	29 1.4	22 21.7	19 56.9	20 29.5
14 S	11 34 27.6	21 49.2	18 15.5	17 15.9	7 15.3	7 10.8	10 45.8	20 60.0	29 8.8	22 23.9	19 57.3	20 31.7
15 M	11 38 24.1	22 47.7	18 12.3	29 15.5	8 50.8	8 15.6	11 26.3	21 13.0	29 16.2	22 26.2	19 57.8	20 33.8
16 T	11 42 20.7	23 46.2	18 9.2	11♐25.1	10 25.2	9 20.6	12 6.9	21 25.9	29 23.6	22 28.5	19 58.3	20 36.0
17 W	11 46 17.2	24 44.7	18 6.0	23 48.9	11 58.5	10 25.9	12 47.5	21 38.9	29 31.0	22 30.9	19 58.8	20 38.2
18 T	11 50 13.8	25 43.3	18 2.8	6♑31.3	13 30.9	11 31.4	13 28.2	21 51.9	29 38.5	22 33.3	19 59.4	20 40.4
19 F	11 54 10.3	26 41.9	17 59.6	19 36.4	15 2.1	12 37.1	14 9.1	22 4.9	29 45.9	22 35.7	19 60.0	20 42.6
20 S	11 58 6.9	27 40.5	17 56.5	3♒ 7.5	16 32.4	13 43.1	14 50.0	22 17.9	29 53.3	22 38.2	20 0.6	20 44.9
21 S	12 2 3.4	28 39.2	17 53.3	17 6.4	18 1.6	14 49.3	15 30.9	22 30.8	0♎ 0.8	22 40.7	20 1.2	20 47.1
22 M	12 5 60.0	29 37.9	17 50.1	1♓32.6	19 29.7	15 55.7	16 12.0	22 43.8	0 8.2	22 43.3	20 1.9	20 49.4
23 T	12 9 56.5	0♎36.6	17 46.9	16 22.7	20 56.8	17 2.3	16 53.1	22 56.7	0 15.7	22 45.9	20 2.7	20 51.6
24 W	12 13 53.1	1 35.4	17 43.7	1♈30.0	22 22.9	18 9.2	17 34.4	23 9.6	0 23.1	22 48.5	20 3.4	20 53.9
25 T	12 17 49.6	2 34.1	17 40.6	16 45.1	23 47.9	19 16.2	18 15.7	23 22.5	0 30.6	22 51.2	20 4.2	20 56.2
26 F	12 21 46.2	3 32.9	17 37.4	1♉57.5	25 11.7	20 23.5	18 57.1	23 35.4	0 38.0	22 53.9	20 5.0	20 58.5
27 S	12 25 42.7	4 31.8	17 34.2	16 56.9	26 34.5	21 30.9	19 38.5	23 48.3	0 45.4	22 56.7	20 5.9	21 0.8
28 S	12 29 39.3	5 30.7	17 31.0	1♊35.4	27 56.1	22 38.6	20 20.1	24 1.2	0 52.9	22 59.4	20 6.7	21 3.1
29 M	12 33 35.9	6 29.6	17 27.9	15 48.1	29 16.5	23 46.4	21 1.7	24 14.0	1 0.3	23 2.3	20 7.6	21 5.4
30 T	12 37 32.4	7 28.6	17 24.7	29 33.4	0♏35.7	24 54.5	21 43.5	24 26.9	1 7.8	23 5.2	20 8.6	21 7.8
						DECLINATION at NOON						
1 M	10 43 12.4	8N 7.4	15N 8.6	16N18.2	7N19.3	19N 1.7	12S34.2	5N37.3	2N51.9	18S 1.2	21S41.9	7N39.0
4 T	10 55 2.1	7 1.4	15 11.6	19 32.8	4 58.3	18 43.8	13 16.6	5 22.2	2 43.2	18 2.6	21 42.0	7 35.9
7 S	11 6 51.7	5 54.4	15 14.6	13 56.7	2 37.4	18 21.7	13 58.4	5 7.0	2 34.4	18 4.1	21 42.2	7 32.9
10 W	11 18 41.4	4 46.4	15 17.5	3 8.3	0 18.1	17 55.2	14 39.6	4 51.7	2 25.6	18 5.8	21 42.4	7 29.8
13 S	11 30 31.0	3 37.7	15 20.4	8S33.7	1S58.6	17 24.3	15 20.0	4 36.5	2 16.8	18 7.5	21 42.7	7 26.7
16 T	11 42 20.7	2 28.5	15 23.4	17 22.0	4 11.6	16 49.1	15 59.6	4 21.2	2 8.0	18 9.3	21 42.9	7 23.7
19 F	11 54 10.3	1 18.8	15 26.3	19 25.7	6 20.2	16 9.5	16 38.4	4 6.0	1 59.2	18 11.2	21 43.2	7 20.7
22 M	12 5 60.0	0 8.8	15 29.2	11 55.4	8 23.8	15 25.7	17 16.2	3 50.7	1 50.4	18 13.2	21 43.5	7 17.7
25 T	12 17 49.6	1S 1.3	15 32.1	2N34.7	10 21.6	14 37.8	17 52.9	3 35.5	1 41.6	18 15.2	21 43.8	7 14.7
28 S	12 29 39.3	2 11.4	15 35.1	15 33.5	12 13.0	13 45.9	18 28.6	3 20.4	1 32.9	18 17.3	21 44.2	7 11.8

OCTOBER 1980

DAY	EPHEMERIS SIDEREAL TIME	☉	☊	☽	☿	♀	♂	♃	♄	♅	♆	♇
						LONGITUDE at NOON						
1 W	12 41 29.0	8♎27.6	17♌21.5	12♋52.2	1♏53.6	26♌ 2.7	22♏25.3	24♍39.7	1♎15.2	23♏ 8.0	20♐ 9.6	21♎10.2
2 T	12 45 25.5	9 26.7	17 18.3	25 47.4	3 10.1	27 11.1	23 7.1	24 52.5	1 22.6	23 11.0	20 10.6	21 12.5
3 F	12 49 22.1	10 25.8	17 15.1	8♌23.0	4 25.2	28 19.7	23 49.1	25 5.3	1 30.0	23 13.9	20 11.6	21 14.9
4 S	12 53 18.6	11 24.9	17 12.0	20 42.9	5 38.8	29 28.5	24 31.1	25 18.0	1 37.3	23 16.9	20 12.7	21 17.2
5 S	12 57 15.2	12 24.0	17 8.8	2♍51.3	6 50.8	0♍37.4	25 13.2	25 30.8	1 44.7	23 19.9	20 13.8	21 19.6
6 M	13 1 11.7	13 23.2	17 5.6	14 51.5	8 1.0	1 46.4	25 55.5	25 43.4	1 52.1	23 23.0	20 14.9	21 22.0
7 T	13 5 8.3	14 22.4	17 2.4	26 46.4	9 9.4	2 55.7	26 37.7	25 56.1	1 59.4	23 26.0	20 16.1	21 24.4
8 W	13 9 4.8	15 21.7	16 59.3	8♎38.4	10 15.8	4 5.0	27 20.1	26 8.7	2 6.7	23 29.1	20 17.2	21 26.7
9 T	13 13 1.4	16 21.0	16 56.1	20 29.3	11 20.0	5 14.6	28 2.5	26 21.4	2 14.1	23 32.3	20 18.5	21 29.1
10 F	13 16 57.9	17 20.3	16 52.9	2♏20.6	12 21.9	6 24.3	28 45.1	26 33.9	2 21.3	23 35.4	20 19.7	21 31.5
11 S	13 20 54.5	18 19.7	16 49.7	14 13.9	13 21.3	7 34.1	29 27.7	26 46.5	2 28.6	23 38.6	20 21.0	21 33.9
12 S	13 24 51.0	19 19.1	16 46.5	26 10.8	14 17.8	8 44.0	0♐10.3	26 59.0	2 35.9	23 41.8	20 22.3	21 36.3
13 M	13 28 47.6	20 18.5	16 43.4	8♐13.5	15 11.3	9 54.1	0 53.1	27 11.4	2 43.1	23 45.1	20 23.6	21 38.7
14 T	13 32 44.1	21 18.0	16 40.2	20 24.7	16 1.5	11 4.4	1 35.9	27 23.8	2 50.3	23 48.4	20 24.9	21 41.1
15 W	13 36 40.7	22 17.5	16 37.0	2♑47.6	16 47.9	12 14.7	2 18.8	27 36.2	2 57.5	23 51.7	20 26.3	21 43.5
16 T	13 40 37.2	23 17.0	16 33.8	15 26.1	17 30.3	13 25.2	3 1.8	27 48.6	3 4.6	23 55.0	20 27.7	21 45.9
17 F	13 44 33.8	24 16.6	16 30.6	28 24.2	18 8.3	14 35.8	3 44.8	28 0.9	3 11.8	23 58.3	20 29.1	21 48.3
18 S	13 48 30.4	25 16.1	16 27.5	11♒45.9	18 41.3	15 46.6	4 28.0	28 13.1	3 18.9	24 1.7	20 30.6	21 50.7
19 S	13 52 26.9	26 15.7	16 24.3	25 34.2	19 8.9	16 57.4	5 11.1	28 25.3	3 26.0	24 5.1	20 32.1	21 53.0
20 M	13 56 23.5	27 15.4	16 21.1	9♓50.4	19 30.6	18 8.4	5 54.4	28 37.5	3 33.0	24 8.5	20 33.6	21 55.4
21 T	14 0 20.0	28 15.1	16 17.9	24 33.2	19 45.9	19 19.6	6 37.8	28 49.7	3 40.1	24 11.9	20 35.2	21 57.9
22 W	14 4 16.6	29 14.8	16 14.8	9♈37.7	19 54.1	20 30.8	7 21.2	29 1.7	3 47.0	24 15.4	20 36.7	22 0.2
23 T	14 8 13.1	0♏14.5	16 11.6	24 55.5	19 54.7	21 42.1	8 4.7	29 13.8	3 54.0	24 18.9	20 38.3	22 2.6
24 F	14 12 9.7	1 14.3	16 8.4	10♉15.7	19R47.1	22 53.6	8 48.2	29 25.7	4 0.9	24 22.4	20 39.9	22 5.0
25 S	14 16 6.2	2 14.1	16 5.2	25 26.7	19 31.0	24 5.1	9 31.8	29 37.6	4 7.8	24 25.9	20 41.6	22 7.4
26 S	14 20 2.8	3 13.9	16 2.0	10♊18.2	19 5.8	25 16.8	10 15.5	29 49.5	4 14.6	24 29.4	20 43.2	22 9.7
27 M	14 23 59.3	4 13.7	15 58.9	24 43.0	18 31.5	26 28.6	10 59.2	0♎ 1.3	4 21.4	24 32.9	20 44.9	22 12.1
28 T	14 27 55.9	5 13.6	15 55.7	8♋37.6	17 48.0	27 40.4	11 43.1	0 13.0	4 28.2	24 36.5	20 46.6	22 14.4
29 W	14 31 52.4	6 13.6	15 52.5	22 2.3	16 55.7	28 52.4	12 26.9	0 24.7	4 34.9	24 40.0	20 48.3	22 16.8
30 T	14 35 49.0	7 13.5	15 49.3	4♌59.6	15 55.1	0♎ 4.5	13 10.9	0 36.3	4 41.6	24 43.6	20 50.1	22 19.1
31 F	14 39 45.5	8 13.5	15 46.2	17 33.9	14 47.5	1 16.7	13 54.9	0 47.9	4 48.3	24 47.2	20 51.8	22 21.4
						DECLINATION at NOON						
1 W	12 41 29.0	3S21.3	15N38.0	19N47.3	13S57.1	12N50.2	19S 3.0	3N 5.3	1N24.2	18S19.6	21S44.5	7N 9.0
4 S	12 53 18.6	4 30.9	15 40.8	14 43.6	15 33.0	11 50.8	19 36.2	2 50.3	1 15.5	18 21.8	21 44.9	7 6.1
7 T	13 5 8.3	5 40.0	15 43.7	4 9.2	16 59.5	10 48.1	20 8.0	2 35.4	1 7.0	18 24.2	21 45.3	7 3.4
10 F	13 16 57.9	6 48.5	15 46.6	7S43.0	18 15.3	9 42.2	20 38.4	2 20.6	0 58.5	18 26.6	21 45.7	7 0.7
13 M	13 28 47.6	7 56.2	15 49.5	16 59.5	19 18.4	8 33.3	21 7.3	2 5.9	0 50.1	18 29.0	21 46.1	6 58.1
16 T	13 40 37.2	9 2.8	15 52.4	19 51.2	20 6.1	7 21.8	21 34.6	1 51.4	0 41.8	18 31.5	21 46.5	6 55.5
19 S	13 52 26.9	10 8.3	15 55.2	13 39.3	20 35.0	6 7.9	22 0.1	1 37.1	0 33.6	18 34.0	21 47.0	6 53.1
22 W	14 4 16.6	11 12.4	15 58.1	0N 9.3	20 40.1	4 51.8	22 23.9	1 22.9	0 25.6	18 36.6	21 47.4	6 50.7
25 S	14 16 6.2	12 15.0	16 0.9	14 17.8	20 15.1	3 34.0	22 45.9	1 8.9	0 17.7	18 39.2	21 47.9	6 48.4
28 T	14 27 55.9	13 15.9	16 3.7	20 3.7	19 13.9	2 14.5	23 5.9	0 55.2	0 10.0	18 41.8	21 48.4	6 46.2
31 F	14 39 45.5	14 14.9	16 6.6	15 39.4	17 34.7	0 53.9	23 24.0	0 41.7	0 2.4	18 44.5	21 48.8	6 44.1

NOVEMBER 1980

LONGITUDE at NOON

DAY	EPHEMERIS SIDEREAL TIME	☉	☊	☽	☿	♀	♂	♃	♄	♅	♆	♇
	h m s	° ′	° ′	° ′	° ′	° ′	° ′	° ′	° ′	° ′	° ′	° ′
1 S	14 43 42.1	9♏13.6	15♌43.0	29♌50.2	13♏34.3	2♎29.0	14♐39.0	0♎59.4	4♎54.9	24♏50.8	20♐53.6	22♎23.8
2 S	14 47 38.7	10 13.7	15 39.8	11♍53.4	12R17.4	3 41.4	15 23.2	1 10.8	5 1.4	24 54.5	20 55.4	22 26.1
3 M	14 51 35.2	11 13.8	15 36.6	23 48.4	10 59.0	4 53.9	16 7.4	1 22.2	5 7.9	24 58.1	20 57.3	22 28.4
4 T	14 55 31.8	12 13.9	15 33.5	5♎39.2	9 41.7	6 6.4	16 51.7	1 33.5	5 14.4	25 1.8	20 59.1	22 30.7
5 W	14 59 28.3	13 14.1	15 30.3	17 29.1	8 27.8	7 19.0	17 36.1	1 44.7	5 20.8	25 5.4	21 1.0	22 32.9
6 T	15 3 24.9	14 14.3	15 27.1	29 20.5	7 19.8	8 31.8	18 20.5	1 55.9	5 27.2	25 9.1	21 2.9	22 35.2
7 F	15 7 21.4	15 14.6	15 23.9	11♏15.2	6 19.7	9 44.6	19 5.1	2 7.0	5 33.5	25 12.8	21 4.8	22 37.5
8 S	15 11 18.0	16 14.8	15 20.7	23 14.7	5 29.1	10 57.5	19 49.6	2 18.0	5 39.8	25 16.5	21 6.7	22 39.7
9 S	15 15 14.5	17 15.1	15 17.6	5♐19.8	4 49.2	12 10.4	20 34.3	2 28.9	5 46.0	25 20.2	21 8.7	22 41.9
10 M	15 19 11.1	18 15.5	15 14.4	17 31.7	4 20.8	13 23.4	21 19.0	2 39.8	5 52.2	25 23.9	21 10.6	22 44.2
11 T	15 23 7.6	19 15.9	15 11.2	29 51.8	4 4.2	14 36.6	22 3.8	2 50.6	5 58.3	25 27.6	21 12.6	22 46.4
12 W	15 27 4.2	20 16.2	15 8.0	12♑21.8	3 59.1	15 49.8	22 48.6	3 1.3	6 4.4	25 31.3	21 14.6	22 48.6
13 T	15 31 0.8	21 16.6	15 4.9	25 4.3	4D 5.1	17 3.0	23 33.5	3 11.9	6 10.4	25 35.0	21 16.7	22 50.8
14 F	15 34 57.3	22 17.1	15 1.7	8♒ 2.3	4 21.6	18 16.3	24 18.4	3 22.4	6 16.3	25 38.8	21 18.7	22 52.9
15 S	15 38 53.9	23 17.5	14 58.5	21 18.9	4 47.8	19 29.7	25 3.4	3 32.8	6 22.2	25 42.5	21 20.7	22 55.1
16 S	15 42 50.4	24 18.0	14 55.3	4♓57.2	5 22.8	20 43.1	25 48.5	3 43.1	6 28.0	25 46.2	21 22.8	22 57.2
17 M	15 46 47.0	25 18.5	14 52.1	18 59.2	6 5.7	21 56.6	26 33.6	3 53.4	6 33.7	25 49.9	21 24.9	22 59.3
18 T	15 50 43.5	26 19.0	14 49.0	3♈25.0	6 55.7	23 10.1	27 18.8	4 3.5	6 39.4	25 53.6	21 26.9	23 1.4
19 W	15 54 40.1	27 19.5	14 45.8	18 11.9	7 51.8	24 23.7	28 4.0	4 13.6	6 45.0	25 57.4	21 29.0	23 3.5
20 T	15 58 36.6	28 20.1	14 42.6	3♉14.1	8 53.4	25 37.4	28 49.3	4 23.6	6 50.6	26 1.1	21 31.2	23 5.5
21 F	16 2 33.2	29 20.7	14 39.4	18 22.9	9 59.7	26 51.1	29 34.6	4 33.4	6 56.1	26 4.8	21 33.3	23 7.6
22 S	16 6 29.8	0♐21.3	14 36.3	3♊27.9	11 10.0	28 4.8	0♑20.0	4 43.2	7 1.5	26 8.5	21 35.4	23 9.6
23 S	16 10 26.3	1 21.9	14 33.1	18 18.7	12 23.8	29 18.7	1 5.4	4 52.9	7 6.9	26 12.2	21 37.6	23 11.6
24 M	16 14 22.9	2 22.5	14 29.9	2♋47.2	13 40.7	0♏32.6	1 50.9	5 2.5	7 12.2	26 15.9	21 39.7	23 13.5
25 T	16 18 19.4	3 23.2	14 26.7	16 48.2	15 0.0	1 46.5	2 36.5	5 11.9	7 17.4	26 19.7	21 41.9	23 15.5
26 W	16 22 16.0	4 23.9	14 23.6	0♌20.0	16 21.5	3 0.5	3 22.1	5 21.3	7 22.5	26 23.4	21 44.1	23 17.4
27 T	16 26 12.5	5 24.6	14 20.4	13 23.7	17 44.9	4 14.5	4 7.7	5 30.5	7 27.6	26 27.0	21 46.2	23 19.4
28 F	16 30 9.1	6 25.4	14 17.2	26 2.8	19 9.8	5 28.6	4 53.5	5 39.7	7 32.6	26 30.7	21 48.4	23 21.2
29 S	16 34 5.7	7 26.2	14 14.0	8♍22.0	20 36.0	6 42.7	5 39.2	5 48.7	7 37.5	26 34.4	21 50.6	23 23.1
30 S	16 38 2.2	8 27.0	14 10.8	20 26.4	22 3.4	7 56.9	6 25.0	5 57.6	7 42.4	26 38.1	21 52.9	23 25.0

DECLINATION at NOON

DAY	EPHEMERIS SIDEREAL TIME	☉	☊	☽	☿	♀	♂	♃	♄	♅	♆	♇
1 S	14 43 42.1	14S 34.2	16N 7.5	12N37.2	16S54.5	0N26.8	23S 29.5	0N37.2	0 0.0	18S45.4	21S49.0	6N43.4
4 T	14 55 31.8	15 30.5	16 10.3	1 14.9	14 44.3	0S55.0	23 44.8	0 24.0	0S 7.4	18 48.0	21 49.5	6 41.5
7 F	15 7 21.4	16 24.4	16 13.2	10S 28.5	12 44.1	2 17.4	23 58.0	0 11.1	0 14.5	18 50.7	21 49.9	6 39.6
10 M	15 19 11.1	17 16.0	16 16.0	18 39.4	11 22.2	3 39.8	24 8.9	0S 1.5	0 21.4	18 53.4	21 50.4	6 37.9
13 T	15 31 0.8	18 4.8	16 18.8	19 27.5	10 50.5	5 2.2	24 17.6	0 13.8	0 28.1	18 56.1	21 50.9	6 36.2
16 S	15 42 50.4	18 50.8	16 21.6	11 19.8	11 4.8	6 23.9	24 24.0	0 25.8	0 34.5	18 58.8	21 51.4	6 34.7
19 W	15 54 40.1	19 33.8	16 24.3	2N57.9	11 53.2	7 44.9	24 28.0	0 37.4	0 40.7	19 1.4	21 51.8	6 33.3
22 S	16 6 29.8	20 13.5	16 27.1	16 12.0	13 3.4	9 4.6	24 29.6	0 48.6	0 46.7	19 4.1	21 52.3	6 32.1
25 T	16 18 19.4	20 50.0	16 29.9	20 7.7	14 25.7	10 22.8	24 28.8	0 59.5	0 52.3	19 6.7	21 52.8	6 31.0
28 F	16 30 9.1	21 22.9	16 32.7	13 52.9	15 52.9	11 39.2	24 25.5	1 10.0	0 57.7	19 9.3	21 53.2	6 30.0

DECEMBER 1980

LONGITUDE at NOON

DAY	EPHEMERIS SIDEREAL TIME	☉	☊	☽	☿	♀	♂	♃	♄	♅	♆	♇
1 M	16 41 58.8	9♐27.8	14♌ 7.7	2♎21.4	23♏31.6	9♏11.2	7♑10.9	6♎ 6.5	7♎47.1	26♏41.7	21♐55.1	23♎26.8
2 T	16 45 55.3	10 28.7	14 4.5	14 12.0	25 0.7	10 25.5	7 56.9	6 15.2	7 51.9	26 45.4	21 57.3	23 28.6
3 W	16 49 51.9	11 29.6	14 1.3	26 2.2	26 30.4	11 39.8	8 42.9	6 23.8	7 56.5	26 49.1	21 59.6	23 30.4
4 T	16 53 48.4	12 30.5	13 58.1	7♏55.8	28 0.6	12 54.1	9 28.9	6 32.2	8 1.0	26 52.7	22 1.8	23 32.2
5 F	16 57 45.0	13 31.4	13 55.0	19 55.3	29 31.3	14 8.5	10 15.0	6 40.6	8 5.5	26 56.3	22 4.1	23 33.9
6 S	17 1 41.6	14 32.3	13 51.8	2♐ 2.8	1♐ 2.3	15 22.9	11 1.1	6 48.8	8 9.8	26 59.9	22 6.3	23 35.6
7 S	17 5 38.1	15 33.3	13 48.6	14 19.2	2 33.7	16 37.4	11 47.3	6 56.8	8 14.1	27 3.5	22 8.6	23 37.2
8 M	17 9 34.7	16 34.2	13 45.4	26 45.3	4 5.3	17 51.9	12 33.5	7 4.8	8 18.3	27 7.1	22 10.8	23 38.9
9 T	17 13 31.2	17 35.2	13 42.3	9♑21.5	5 37.2	19 6.4	13 19.7	7 12.6	8 22.4	27 10.7	22 13.1	23 40.5
10 W	17 17 27.8	18 36.2	13 39.1	22 8.0	7 9.3	20 20.9	14 6.0	7 20.3	8 26.4	27 14.2	22 15.3	23 42.1
11 T	17 21 24.3	19 37.2	13 35.9	5♒ 5.7	8 41.6	21 35.5	14 52.4	7 27.8	8 30.4	27 17.7	22 17.6	23 43.7
12 F	17 25 20.9	20 38.2	13 32.7	18 15.5	10 14.0	22 50.1	15 38.8	7 35.3	8 34.2	27 21.2	22 19.9	23 45.2
13 S	17 29 17.5	21 39.2	13 29.5	1♓38.9	11 46.5	24 4.7	16 25.2	7 42.5	8 38.0	27 24.7	22 22.1	23 46.7
14 S	17 33 14.0	22 40.3	13 26.4	15 17.3	13 19.3	25 19.4	17 11.7	7 49.7	8 41.6	27 28.2	22 24.4	23 48.2
15 M	17 37 10.6	23 41.3	13 23.2	29 11.9	14 52.1	26 34.0	17 58.2	7 56.7	8 45.2	27 31.6	22 26.7	23 49.6
16 T	17 41 7.1	24 42.4	13 20.0	13♈22.8	16 25.1	27 48.7	18 44.7	8 3.5	8 48.7	27 35.0	22 28.9	23 51.1
17 W	17 45 3.7	25 43.4	13 16.8	27 48.4	17 58.2	29 3.4	19 31.3	8 10.3	8 52.0	27 38.4	22 31.2	23 52.4
18 T	17 49 0.2	26 44.5	13 13.7	12♉25.4	19 31.5	0♐18.1	20 17.9	8 16.8	8 55.3	27 41.8	22 33.4	23 53.8
19 F	17 52 56.8	27 45.5	13 10.5	27 8.1	21 4.9	1 32.9	21 4.6	8 23.3	8 58.5	27 45.2	22 35.7	23 55.1
20 S	17 56 53.4	28 46.6	13 7.3	11♊49.5	22 38.4	2 47.7	21 51.3	8 29.5	9 1.6	27 48.5	22 38.0	23 56.4
21 S	18 0 49.9	29 47.7	13 4.1	26 21.9	24 12.2	4 2.4	22 38.0	8 35.7	9 4.6	27 51.8	22 40.2	23 57.7
22 M	18 4 46.5	0♑48.8	13 1.0	10♋38.3	25 46.1	5 17.3	23 24.7	8 41.6	9 7.5	27 55.1	22 42.5	23 58.9
23 T	18 8 43.0	1 49.9	12 57.8	24 33.5	27 20.3	6 32.1	24 11.6	8 47.5	9 10.4	27 58.4	22 44.8	24 0.2
24 W	18 12 39.6	2 51.0	12 54.6	8♌ 4.6	28 54.6	7 47.0	24 58.4	8 53.2	9 13.1	28 1.7	22 47.0	24 1.3
25 T	18 16 36.1	3 52.1	12 51.4	21 11.1	0♑29.2	9 1.9	25 45.2	8 58.7	9 15.7	28 4.9	22 49.2	24 2.5
26 F	18 20 32.7	4 53.3	12 48.3	3♍54.7	2 4.0	10 16.7	26 32.1	9 4.0	9 18.2	28 8.0	22 51.5	24 3.6
27 S	18 24 29.3	5 54.4	12 45.1	16 18.6	3 39.1	11 31.7	27 19.0	9 9.2	9 20.6	28 11.2	22 53.7	24 4.7
28 S	18 28 25.8	6 55.5	12 41.9	28 27.0	5 14.4	12 46.6	28 6.0	9 14.2	9 22.9	28 14.3	22 55.9	24 5.7
29 M	18 32 22.4	7 56.7	12 38.7	10♎24.9	6 50.1	14 1.5	28 53.0	9 19.1	9 25.2	28 17.4	22 58.1	24 6.7
30 T	18 36 18.9	8 57.8	12 35.5	22 17.2	8 26.0	15 16.5	29 40.0	9 23.8	9 27.3	28 20.4	23 0.3	24 7.7
31 W	18 40 15.5	9 59.0	12 32.4	4♏ 8.8	10 2.2	16 31.5	0♒27.0	9 28.3	9 29.3	28 23.5	23 2.5	24 8.6

DECLINATION at NOON

DAY	EPHEMERIS SIDEREAL TIME	☉	☊	☽	☿	♀	♂	♃	♄	♅	♆	♇
1 M	16 41 58.8	21S52.2	16N35.4	2N34.7	17S20.2	12S53.3	24S 19.8	1S 20.0	1S 2.8	19S 11.9	21S53.7	6N29.1
4 T	16 53 48.4	22 17.8	16 38.2	9S 22.8	18 44.2	14 4.8	24 11.6	1 29.7	1 7.6	19 14.4	21 54.1	6 28.4
7 S	17 5 38.1	22 39.4	16 40.9	18 14.4	20 2.6	15 13.3	24 1.0	1 38.8	1 12.1	19 16.9	21 54.6	6 27.8
10 W	17 17 27.8	22 57.1	16 43.6	19 54.0	21 13.7	16 18.4	23 47.9	1 47.5	1 16.3	19 19.4	21 55.0	6 27.4
13 S	17 29 17.5	23 10.6	16 46.4	12 30.2	22 16.3	17 19.9	23 32.3	1 55.6	1 20.1	19 21.8	21 55.4	6 27.0
16 T	17 41 7.1	23 20.0	16 49.1	1N 7.3	23 9.5	18 17.4	23 14.3	2 3.3	1 23.6	19 24.1	21 55.8	6 26.9
19 F	17 52 56.8	23 25.3	16 51.8	14 41.6	23 52.4	19 10.5	22 54.0	2 10.4	1 26.8	19 26.4	21 56.2	6 26.8
22 M	18 4 46.5	23 26.3	16 54.5	20 22.5	24 24.4	19 58.8	22 31.3	2 17.0	1 29.6	19 28.7	21 56.6	6 26.9
25 T	18 16 36.1	23 23.0	16 57.2	15 16.7	24 44.8	20 42.2	22 6.3	2 23.0	1 32.0	19 30.8	21 56.9	6 27.2
28 S	18 28 25.8	23 15.5	16 59.9	4 6.9	24 53.0	21 20.3	21 39.0	2 28.4	1 34.1	19 33.0	21 57.3	6 27.5
31 W	18 40 15.5	23 3.9	17 2.6	8S 2.2	24 48.6	21 52.9	21 9.5	2 33.2	1 35.8	19 35.0	21 57.6	6 28.1

JANUARY 1981

DAY	EPHEMERIS SIDEREAL TIME	☉	☊	☽	☿	♀	♂	♃	♄	♅	♆	♇
	h m s	° ′	° ′	° ′	° ′	° ′	° ′	° ′	° ′	° ′	° ′	° ′
						LONGITUDE at NOON						
1 T	18 44 12.0	11♑ 0.1	12♌29.2	16♏ 4.3	11♑38.8	17♐46.4	1♒14.1	9♎32.7	9♎31.2	28♏26.5	23♐ 4.7	24♎ 9.5
2 F	18 48 8.6	12 1.3	12 26.0	28 7.3	13 15.7	19 1.4	2 1.2	9 36.9	9 32.9	28 29.4	23 6.9	24 10.4
3 S	18 52 5.2	13 2.5	12 22.8	10♐21.1	14 53.0	20 16.5	2 48.3	9 40.9	9 34.6	28 32.4	23 9.0	24 11.2
4 S	18 56 1.7	14 3.7	12 19.7	22 47.6	16 30.7	21 31.5	3 35.5	9 44.7	9 36.2	28 35.3	23 11.2	24 12.0
5 M	18 59 58.3	15 4.8	12 16.5	5♑28.2	18 8.7	22 46.5	4 22.6	9 48.4	9 37.7	28 38.1	23 13.3	24 12.8
6 T	19 3 54.8	16 6.0	12 13.3	18 23.1	19 47.0	24 1.5	5 9.8	9 51.9	9 39.0	28 40.9	23 15.4	24 13.5
7 W	19 7 51.4	17 7.2	12 10.1	1♒32.0	21 25.8	25 16.6	5 57.0	9 55.2	9 40.3	28 43.7	23 17.6	24 14.2
8 T	19 11 47.9	18 8.3	12 7.0	14 53.8	23 4.9	26 31.6	6 44.3	9 58.3	9 41.4	28 46.5	23 19.7	24 14.9
9 F	19 15 44.5	19 9.5	12 3.8	28 27.3	24 44.4	27 46.7	7 31.5	10 1.2	9 42.5	28 49.2	23 21.8	24 15.5
10 S	19 19 41.1	20 10.7	12 0.6	12♓11.3	26 24.2	29 1.8	8 18.8	10 4.0	9 43.4	28 51.9	23 23.8	24 16.1
11 S	19 23 37.6	21 11.8	11 57.4	26 4.5	28 4.3	0♑16.8	9 6.1	10 6.6	9 44.2	28 54.5	23 25.9	24 16.6
12 M	19 27 34.2	22 12.9	11 54.2	10♈ 5.7	29 44.8	1 31.9	9 53.4	10 9.0	9 45.0	28 57.1	23 27.9	24 17.2
13 T	19 31 30.7	23 14.1	11 51.1	24 13.6	1♒25.5	2 47.0	10 40.8	10 11.3	9 45.6	28 59.7	23 30.0	24 17.7
14 W	19 35 27.3	24 15.2	11 47.9	8♉26.3	3 6.5	4 2.1	11 28.1	10 13.3	9 46.1	29 2.2	23 32.0	24 18.1
15 T	19 39 23.8	25 16.3	11 44.7	22 41.6	4 47.5	5 17.1	12 15.5	10 15.1	9 46.5	29 4.7	23 34.0	24 18.5
16 F	19 43 20.4	26 17.4	11 41.5	6♊56.4	6 28.7	6 32.2	13 2.8	10 16.8	9 46.8	29 7.1	23 36.0	24 18.9
17 S	19 47 17.0	27 18.5	11 38.4	21 7.2	8 9.9	7 47.3	13 50.2	10 18.3	9 47.0	29 9.5	23 38.0	24 19.3
18 S	19 51 13.5	28 19.5	11 35.2	5♋ 9.9	9 50.9	9 2.4	14 37.6	10 19.6	9 47.0	29 11.8	23 39.9	24 19.6
19 M	19 55 10.1	29 20.6	11 32.0	19 0.8	11 31.7	10 17.4	15 25.0	10 20.7	9 47.0	29 14.1	23 41.9	24 19.8
20 T	19 59 6.6	0♒21.6	11 28.8	2♌36.4	13 12.1	11 32.5	16 12.4	10 21.6	9R46.8	29 16.4	23 43.8	24 20.0
21 W	20 3 3.2	1 22.7	11 25.7	15 54.6	14 51.9	12 47.6	16 59.8	10 22.3	9 46.6	29 18.6	23 45.7	24 20.2
22 T	20 6 59.7	2 23.7	11 22.5	28 54.2	16 30.9	14 2.7	17 47.2	10 22.8	9 46.2	29 20.8	23 47.6	24 20.4
23 F	20 10 56.3	3 24.7	11 19.3	11♍35.6	18 8.8	15 17.8	18 34.7	10 23.2	9 45.7	29 22.9	23 49.4	24 20.5
24 S	20 14 52.8	4 25.7	11 16.1	24 0.2	19 45.3	16 32.9	19 22.1	10 23.3	9 45.2	29 25.0	23 51.2	24 20.6
25 S	20 18 49.4	5 26.7	11 12.9	6♎10.9	21 20.0	17 48.0	20 9.5	10 23.3	9 44.5	29 27.0	23 53.1	24 20.7
26 M	20 22 46.0	6 27.7	11 9.8	18 11.1	22 52.5	19 3.1	20 57.0	10R23.0	9 43.7	29 29.0	23 54.8	24 20.7
27 T	20 26 42.5	7 28.6	11 6.6	0♏ 5.2	24 22.4	20 18.2	21 44.4	10 22.6	9 42.8	29 30.9	23 56.6	24R20.6
28 W	20 30 39.1	8 29.6	11 3.4	11 57.7	25 49.2	21 33.3	22 31.9	10 22.0	9 41.8	29 32.8	23 58.4	24 20.6
29 T	20 34 35.6	9 30.5	11 0.2	23 53.3	27 12.1	22 48.4	23 19.4	10 21.2	9 40.7	29 34.7	24 0.1	24 20.5
30 F	20 38 32.2	10 31.5	10 57.1	5♐56.7	28 30.6	24 3.5	24 6.8	10 20.2	9 39.5	29 36.5	24 1.8	24 20.4
31 S	20 42 28.7	11 32.4	10 53.9	18 12.2	29 44.0	25 18.6	24 54.3	10 19.0	9 38.1	29 38.2	24 3.5	24 20.2
						DECLINATION at NOON						
1 T	18 44 12.0	22S59.0	17N 3.5	11S40.5	24S44.3	22S 2.5	20S59.2	2S34.7	1S36.3	19S35.7	21S57.7	6N28.3
4 S	18 56 1.7	22 41.9	17 6.2	19 21.1	24 22.3	22 27.3	20 26.9	2 38.7	1 37.5	19 37.6	21 58.0	6 29.0
7 W	19 7 51.4	22 20.6	17 8.8	18 59.0	23 46.6	22 46.1	19 52.5	2 42.1	1 38.3	19 39.5	21 58.3	6 29.8
10 S	19 19 41.1	21 55.4	17 11.5	9 30.7	22 56.9	22 58.6	19 16.1	2 44.8	1 38.7	19 41.2	21 58.6	6 30.7
13 T	19 31 30.7	21 26.4	17 14.1	4N42.3	21 53.2	23 4.9	18 37.9	2 46.9	1 38.8	19 42.9	21 58.9	6 31.8
16 F	19 43 20.4	20 53.7	17 16.8	16 48.1	20 35.6	23 4.9	17 57.8	2 48.3	1 38.5	19 44.6	21 59.1	6 33.0
19 M	19 55 10.1	20 17.3	17 19.4	20 8.6	19 4.7	22 58.4	17 16.0	2 49.1	1 37.8	19 46.1	21 59.4	6 34.3
22 T	20 6 59.7	19 37.6	17 22.1	13 23.5	17 21.7	22 45.7	16 32.6	2 49.2	1 36.7	19 47.5	21 59.6	6 35.7
25 S	20 18 49.4	18 54.5	17 24.7	1 32.4	15 29.2	22 26.6	15 47.6	2 48.6	1 35.2	19 48.8	21 59.8	6 37.2
28 W	20 30 39.1	18 8.4	17 27.3	10S23.3	13 31.2	22 1.4	15 1.2	2 47.4	1 33.4	19 50.1	21 59.9	6 38.9
31 S	20 42 28.7	17 19.3	17 29.9	18 43.3	11 34.4	21 30.2	14 13.4	2 45.5	1 31.2	19 51.2	22 0.1	6 40.6

FEBRUARY 1981

DAY	EPHEMERIS SIDEREAL TIME	☉	☊	☽	☿	♀	♂	♃	♄	♅	♆	♇
						LONGITUDE at NOON						
1 S	20 46 25.3	12♒33.3	10♌50.7	0♑43.3	0♓51.6	26♑33.7	25♒41.8	10♎17.6	9♎36.7	29♏39.9	24♐ 5.1	24♎20.0
2 M	20 50 21.8	13 34.2	10 47.5	13 32.7	1 52.4	27 48.8	26 29.3	10R16.0	9R35.2	29 41.6	24 6.8	24R19.7
3 T	20 54 18.4	14 35.1	10 44.3	26 41.9	2 45.8	29 3.9	27 16.8	10 14.3	9 33.6	29 43.2	24 8.4	24 19.5
4 W	20 58 15.0	15 36.0	10 41.2	10♒10.7	3 31.0	0♒19.0	28 4.3	10 12.3	9 31.9	29 44.8	24 10.0	24 19.2
5 T	21 2 11.5	16 36.8	10 38.0	23 57.7	4 7.1	1 34.1	28 51.7	10 10.2	9 30.0	29 46.3	24 11.6	24 18.9
6 F	21 6 8.1	17 37.6	10 34.8	7♓59.9	4 33.6	2 49.2	29 39.2	10 7.9	9 28.1	29 47.7	24 13.1	24 18.5
7 S	21 10 4.6	18 38.4	10 31.6	22 13.4	4 49.8	4 4.3	0♓26.7	10 5.3	9 26.1	29 49.1	24 14.6	24 18.1
8 S	21 14 1.2	19 39.2	10 28.5	6♈33.4	4 55.4	5 19.4	1 14.1	10 2.6	9 24.0	29 50.4	24 16.1	24 17.6
9 M	21 17 57.7	20 40.0	10 25.3	20 55.4	4R50.2	6 34.4	2 1.6	9 59.8	9 21.7	29 51.7	24 17.6	24 17.1
10 T	21 21 54.3	21 40.7	10 22.1	5♉15.1	4 34.1	7 49.5	2 49.0	9 56.7	9 19.4	29 53.0	24 19.0	24 16.6
11 W	21 25 50.8	22 41.4	10 18.9	19 29.3	4 7.6	9 4.5	3 36.5	9 53.5	9 17.0	29 54.2	24 20.4	24 16.1
12 T	21 29 47.4	23 42.1	10 15.8	3♊35.5	3 31.1	10 19.6	4 23.9	9 50.0	9 14.5	29 55.3	24 21.8	24 15.5
13 F	21 33 43.9	24 42.7	10 12.6	17 32.0	2 45.7	11 34.6	5 11.3	9 46.4	9 11.9	29 56.4	24 23.1	24 14.9
14 S	21 37 40.5	25 43.3	10 9.4	1♋17.8	1 52.6	12 49.7	5 58.7	9 42.7	9 9.2	29 57.4	24 24.4	24 14.2
15 S	21 41 37.0	26 43.9	10 6.2	14 52.2	0 53.1	14 4.7	6 46.1	9 38.7	9 6.4	29 58.4	24 25.7	24 13.6
16 M	21 45 33.6	27 44.5	10 3.0	28 14.5	29♒48.9	15 19.7	7 33.4	9 34.6	9 3.6	29 59.3	24 27.0	24 12.9
17 T	21 49 30.2	28 45.0	9 59.9	11♌24.5	28 41.8	16 34.7	8 20.8	9 30.3	9 0.6	0♐ 0.1	24 28.2	24 12.1
18 W	21 53 26.7	29 45.5	9 56.7	24 21.5	27 33.7	17 49.7	9 8.1	9 25.9	8 57.6	0 1.0	24 29.4	24 11.3
19 T	21 57 23.3	0♓46.0	9 53.5	7♍ 5.6	26 26.2	19 4.7	9 55.4	9 21.3	8 54.5	0 1.7	24 30.6	24 10.5
20 F	22 1 19.8	1 46.4	9 50.3	19 36.7	25 21.0	20 19.7	10 42.8	9 16.5	8 51.3	0 2.4	24 31.7	24 9.7
21 S	22 5 16.4	2 46.8	9 47.2	1♎55.7	24 19.4	21 34.6	11 30.1	9 11.6	8 48.1	0 3.1	24 32.8	24 8.8
22 S	22 9 12.9	3 47.2	9 44.0	14 4.0	23 22.8	22 49.6	12 17.3	9 6.6	8 44.7	0 3.7	24 33.9	24 7.9
23 M	22 13 9.5	4 47.6	9 40.8	26 3.8	22 32.0	24 4.6	13 4.6	9 1.3	8 41.3	0 4.2	24 35.0	24 7.0
24 T	22 17 6.0	5 48.0	9 37.6	7♏58.0	21 47.7	25 19.6	13 51.9	8 56.0	8 37.8	0 4.7	24 36.0	24 6.1
25 W	22 21 2.6	6 48.3	9 34.4	19 50.2	21 10.4	26 34.5	14 39.1	8 50.5	8 34.3	0 5.2	24 37.0	24 5.1
26 T	22 24 59.1	7 48.6	9 31.3	1♐44.6	20 40.2	27 49.5	15 26.3	8 44.9	8 30.6	0 5.5	24 38.0	24 4.1
27 F	22 28 55.7	8 48.9	9 28.1	13 45.9	20 17.3	29 4.4	16 13.5	8 39.1	8 26.9	0 5.9	24 38.9	24 3.1
28 S	22 32 52.2	9 49.2	9 24.9	25 58.9	20 1.6	0♓19.3	17 0.7	8 33.1	8 23.2	0 6.1	24 39.8	24 2.0
						DECLINATION at NOON						
1 S	20 46 25.3	17S 2.3	17N30.8	20S 1.3	10S57.2	21S18.5	13S57.1	2S44.7	1S30.4	19S51.6	22S 0.1	6N41.2
4 W	20 58 15.0	16 9.6	17 33.4	17 37.6	9 16.4	20 39.6	13 7.6	2 41.9	1 27.8	19 52.6	22 0.3	6 43.0
7 S	21 10 4.6	15 14.4	17 36.0	6 17.5	8 1.2	19 55.1	12 16.9	2 38.5	1 24.8	19 53.5	22 0.4	6 44.9
10 T	21 21 54.3	14 16.8	17 38.5	8N19.1	7 22.1	19 5.4	11 25.2	2 34.4	1 21.5	19 54.4	22 0.5	6 46.9
13 F	21 33 43.9	13 17.1	17 41.1	18 38.3	7 24.8	18 10.7	10 32.6	2 29.7	1 17.9	19 55.1	22 0.6	6 49.0
16 M	21 45 33.6	12 15.5	17 43.7	19 22.8	8 6.1	17 11.3	9 39.0	2 24.4	1 14.0	19 55.7	22 0.6	6 51.1
19 T	21 57 23.3	11 12.1	17 46.2	11 3.8	9 13.6	16 7.6	8 44.8	2 18.6	1 9.8	19 56.2	22 0.7	6 53.3
22 S	22 9 12.9	10 7.2	17 48.8	1S14.0	10 30.4	14 59.8	7 49.8	2 12.2	1 5.4	19 56.6	22 0.7	6 55.5
25 W	22 21 2.6	9 0.8	17 51.3	12 43.4	11 42.3	13 48.3	6 54.2	2 5.4	1 0.7	19 56.9	22 0.7	6 57.8
28 S	22 32 52.2	7 53.2	17 53.9	19 42.4	12 40.5	12 33.4	5 58.2	1 58.0	0 55.8	19 57.1	22 0.7	7 0.1

MARCH 1981

LONGITUDE at NOON

DAY	EPHEMERIS SIDEREAL TIME	☉	☊	☽	☿	♀	♂	♃	♄	♅	♆	♇
	h m s	° ′	° ′	° ′	° ′	° ′	° ′	° ′	° ′	° ′	° ′	° ′
1 S	22 36 48.8	10♓49.4	9♌21.7	8♑28.3	19♒52.9	1♓34.2	17♓47.8	8♎27.1	8♎19.3	0♐ 6.4	24♐40.7	24♎ 0.9
2 M	22 40 45.3	11 49.6	9 18.6	21 18.3	19R51.0	2 49.2	18 35.0	8R20.9	8R15.4	0 6.5	24 41.5	23R59.8
3 T	22 44 41.9	12 49.8	9 15.4	4♒32.0	19D55.5	4 4.1	19 22.1	8 14.6	8 11.5	0 6.6	24 42.3	23 58.7
4 W	22 48 38.5	13 49.9	9 12.2	18 11.0	20 6.2	5 18.9	20 9.2	8 8.2	8 7.4	0 6.7	24 43.0	23 57.5
5 T	22 52 35.0	14 50.0	9 9.0	2♓14.6	20 22.6	6 33.8	20 56.2	8 1.6	8 3.4	0 6.7	24 43.8	23 56.3
6 F	22 56 31.6	15 50.1	9 5.8	16 39.6	20 44.4	7 48.7	21 43.3	7 55.0	7 59.2	0R 6.6	24 44.5	23 55.1
7 S	23 0 28.1	16 50.2	9 2.7	1♈20.6	21 11.3	9 3.6	22 30.3	7 48.3	7 55.0	0 6.5	24 45.1	23 53.9
8 S	23 4 24.7	17 50.2	8 59.5	16 10.0	21 43.0	10 18.4	23 17.2	7 41.4	7 50.8	0 6.3	24 45.8	23 52.6
9 M	23 8 21.2	18 50.2	8 56.3	0♉59.6	22 19.1	11 33.3	24 4.2	7 34.5	7 46.5	0 6.1	24 46.4	23 51.3
10 T	23 12 17.8	19 50.2	8 53.1	15 41.7	22 59.3	12 48.1	24 51.1	7 27.4	7 42.2	0 5.8	24 46.9	23 50.0
11 W	23 16 14.3	20 50.1	8 49.9	0♊10.2	23 43.3	14 2.9	25 38.0	7 20.3	7 37.9	0 5.5	24 47.5	23 48.7
12 T	23 20 10.9	21 50.0	8 46.8	14 21.4	24 31.0	15 17.7	26 24.9	7 13.1	7 33.4	0 5.1	24 48.0	23 47.3
13 F	23 24 7.4	22 49.8	8 43.6	28 13.6	25 22.0	16 32.4	27 11.7	7 5.8	7 29.0	0 4.7	24 48.5	23 45.9
14 S	23 28 4.0	23 49.6	8 40.4	11♋47.2	26 16.2	17 47.2	27 58.5	6 58.5	7 24.5	0 4.2	24 48.9	23 44.5
15 S	23 32 0.5	24 49.4	8 37.2	25 3.6	27 13.3	19 1.9	28 45.3	6 51.1	7 20.0	0 3.7	24 49.3	23 43.1
16 M	23 35 57.1	25 49.1	8 34.1	8♌ 4.6	28 13.2	20 16.7	29 32.0	6 43.6	7 15.5	0 3.1	24 49.7	23 41.7
17 T	23 39 53.6	26 48.9	8 30.9	20 52.5	29 15.8	21 31.4	0♈18.8	6 36.2	7 11.0	0 2.5	24 50.0	23 40.3
18 W	23 43 50.2	27 48.5	8 27.7	3♍28.8	0♓20.7	22 46.1	1 5.4	6 28.6	7 6.4	0 1.8	24 50.3	23 38.8
19 T	23 47 46.7	28 48.2	8 24.5	15 55.1	1 28.1	24 0.8	1 52.1	6 21.0	7 1.8	0 1.1	24 50.6	23 37.4
20 F	23 51 43.3	29 47.8	8 21.3	28 12.4	2 37.6	25 15.5	2 38.7	6 13.4	6 57.2	0 0.3	24 50.8	23 35.9
21 S	23 55 39.8	0♈47.3	8 18.2	10♎21.8	3 49.3	26 30.1	3 25.2	6 5.7	6 52.5	29♏59.4	24 51.0	23 34.3
22 S	23 59 36.4	1 46.8	8 15.0	22 24.1	5 2.9	27 44.8	4 11.7	5 58.0	6 47.9	29 58.5	24 51.2	23 32.8
23 M	0 3 32.9	2 46.3	8 11.8	4♏20.9	6 18.5	28 59.4	4 58.2	5 50.3	6 43.2	29 57.6	24 51.3	23 31.3
24 T	0 7 29.5	3 45.8	8 8.6	16 13.8	7 36.0	0♈14.0	5 44.7	5 42.5	6 38.5	29 56.6	24 51.4	23 29.7
25 W	0 11 26.0	4 45.2	8 5.5	28 5.5	8 55.3	1 28.6	6 31.1	5 34.8	6 33.8	29 55.6	24 51.5	23 28.1
26 T	0 15 22.6	5 44.6	8 2.3	9♐59.0	10 16.3	2 43.2	7 17.5	5 27.0	6 29.2	29 54.5	24 51.5	23 26.6
27 F	0 19 19.2	6 44.0	7 59.1	21 58.4	11 39.0	3 57.8	8 3.8	5 19.3	6 24.5	29 53.4	24 51.5	23 25.0
28 S	0 23 15.7	7 43.3	7 55.9	4♑ 8.2	13 3.4	5 12.3	8 50.1	5 11.5	6 19.8	29 52.2	24 51.5	23 23.4
29 S	0 27 12.3	8 42.6	7 52.7	16 33.4	14 29.3	6 26.9	9 36.4	5 3.8	6 15.1	29 51.0	24R51.4	23 21.7
30 M	0 31 8.8	9 41.9	7 49.6	29 18.7	15 56.8	7 41.4	10 22.6	4 56.1	6 10.4	29 49.7	24 51.3	23 20.1
31 T	0 35 5.4	10 41.2	7 46.4	12♒28.8	17 25.9	8 55.9	11 8.8	4 48.4	6 5.7	29 48.4	24 51.2	23 18.5

DECLINATION at NOON

DAY	EPHEMERIS SIDEREAL TIME	☉	☊	☽	☿	♀	♂	♃	♄	♅	♆	♇
1 S	22 36 48.8	7S30.5	17N54.7	20S23.6	12S56.1	12S 7.7	5S39.4	1S55.5	0S54.2	19S57.1	22S 0.7	7N 0.9
4 W	22 48 38.5	6 21.6	17 57.2	16 2.0	13 30.9	10 48.8	4 42.9	1 47.6	0 49.0	19 57.2	22 0.7	7 3.2
7 S	23 0 28.1	5 11.9	17 59.8	3 9.3	13 47.8	9 27.3	3 46.0	1 39.3	0 43.8	19 57.2	22 0.7	7 5.5
10 T	23 12 17.8	4 1.5	18 2.3	11N36.7	13 47.6	8 3.5	2 49.0	1 30.8	0 38.3	19 57.0	22 0.7	7 7.9
13 F	23 24 7.4	2 50.8	18 4.8	19 58.4	13 31.3	6 37.8	1 51.9	1 21.9	0 32.8	19 56.8	22 0.6	7 10.2
16 M	23 35 57.1	1 39.7	18 7.3	18 4.1	13 0.2	5 10.5	0 54.8	1 12.9	0 27.2	19 56.4	22 0.5	7 12.5
19 T	23 47 46.7	0 28.6	18 9.7	8 19.5	12 14.9	3 42.0	0N 2.2	1 3.8	0 21.6	19 56.0	22 0.5	7 14.8
22 S	23 59 36.4	0N42.5	18 12.2	4S12.1	11 16.5	2 12.5	0 59.1	0 54.5	0 15.9	19 55.4	22 0.4	7 17.1
25 W	0 11 26.0	1 53.4	18 14.7	15 2.4	10 5.6	0 42.4	1 55.7	0 45.3	0 10.2	19 54.8	22 0.3	7 19.3
28 S	0 23 15.7	3 3.8	18 17.1	20 27.7	8 42.7	0N48.0	2 52.0	0 36.0	0 4.5	19 54.1	22 0.2	7 21.5
31 T	0 35 5.4	4 13.8	18 19.6	17 21.7	7 8.6	2 18.4	3 48.0	0 26.9	0N 1.1	19 53.3	22 0.0	7 23.7

APRIL 1981

LONGITUDE at NOON

DAY	EPHEMERIS SIDEREAL TIME	☉	☊	☽	☿	♀	♂	♃	♄	♅	♆	♇
1 W	0 39 1.9	11♈40.4	7♌43.2	26♒ 6.6	18♓56.5	10♈10.4	11♈55.0	4♎40.7	6♎ 1.0	29♏47.0	24♐51.0	23♎16.8
2 T	0 42 58.5	12 39.6	7 40.0	10♓13.4	20 28.6	11 24.9	12 41.1	4R33.1	5R56.4	29R45.6	24R50.8	23R15.2
3 F	0 46 55.0	13 38.8	7 36.9	24 47.4	22 2.2	12 39.4	13 27.2	4 25.4	5 51.8	29 44.2	24 50.6	23 13.5
4 S	0 50 51.6	14 37.9	7 33.7	9♈43.2	23 37.3	13 53.9	14 13.2	4 17.9	5 47.1	29 42.7	24 50.3	23 11.9
5 S	0 54 48.1	15 37.0	7 30.5	24 52.5	25 13.9	15 8.3	14 59.2	4 10.4	5 42.5	29 41.2	24 50.0	23 10.2
6 M	0 58 44.7	16 36.0	7 27.3	10♉ 4.8	26 52.0	16 22.7	15 45.2	4 2.9	5 38.0	29 39.6	24 49.7	23 8.5
7 T	1 2 41.2	17 35.1	7 24.1	25 9.4	28 31.6	17 37.2	16 31.1	3 55.6	5 33.5	29 38.0	24 49.4	23 6.9
8 W	1 6 37.8	18 34.1	7 21.0	9♊57.1	0♈12.6	18 51.6	17 17.0	3 48.2	5 28.9	29 36.4	24 49.0	23 5.2
9 T	1 10 34.3	19 33.0	7 17.8	24 22.1	1 55.1	20 6.0	18 2.8	3 41.0	5 24.5	29 34.7	24 48.6	23 3.5
10 F	1 14 30.9	20 32.0	7 14.6	8♋21.5	3 39.1	21 20.3	18 48.6	3 33.8	5 20.0	29 33.0	24 48.1	23 1.8
11 S	1 18 27.4	21 30.8	7 11.4	21 55.6	5 24.6	22 34.6	19 34.3	3 26.7	5 15.6	29 31.2	24 47.6	23 0.1
12 S	1 22 24.0	22 29.7	7 8.3	5♌ 6.5	7 11.7	23 49.0	20 20.0	3 19.7	5 11.2	29 29.4	24 47.1	22 58.4
13 M	1 26 20.5	23 28.5	7 5.1	17 57.7	9 0.2	25 3.3	21 5.6	3 12.8	5 6.9	29 27.5	24 46.6	22 56.7
14 T	1 30 17.1	24 27.2	7 1.9	0♍32.6	10 50.3	26 17.5	21 51.2	3 5.9	5 2.6	29 25.7	24 46.0	22 55.0
15 W	1 34 13.7	25 25.9	6 58.7	12 55.0	12 42.0	27 31.8	22 36.7	2 59.2	4 58.3	29 23.8	24 45.4	22 53.3
16 T	1 38 10.2	26 24.6	6 55.5	25 7.7	14 35.2	28 46.0	23 22.2	2 52.6	4 54.1	29 21.8	24 44.7	22 51.6
17 F	1 42 6.8	27 23.3	6 52.4	7♎13.2	16 29.9	0♉ 0.2	24 7.6	2 46.0	4 50.0	29 19.8	24 44.1	22 50.0
18 S	1 46 3.3	28 21.9	6 49.2	19 13.4	18 26.2	1 14.4	24 53.0	2 39.6	4 45.9	29 17.8	24 43.4	22 48.3
19 S	1 49 59.9	29 20.5	6 46.0	1♏ 9.6	20 24.0	2 28.6	25 38.4	2 33.3	4 41.8	29 15.8	24 42.7	22 46.6
20 M	1 53 56.4	0♉19.0	6 42.8	13 3.2	22 23.3	3 42.8	26 23.7	2 27.2	4 37.8	29 13.7	24 41.9	22 44.9
21 T	1 57 53.0	1 17.5	6 39.6	24 55.5	24 24.1	4 56.9	27 8.9	2 21.1	4 33.9	29 11.6	24 41.1	22 43.2
22 W	2 1 49.5	2 16.0	6 36.5	6♐48.2	26 26.3	6 11.1	27 54.1	2 15.2	4 30.0	29 9.5	24 40.3	22 41.6
23 T	2 5 46.1	3 14.5	6 33.3	18 43.5	28 29.8	7 25.2	28 39.3	2 9.4	4 26.2	29 7.4	24 39.5	22 39.9
24 F	2 9 42.6	4 12.9	6 30.1	0♑44.3	0♉34.7	8 39.3	29 24.4	2 3.7	4 22.4	29 5.2	24 38.6	22 38.3
25 S	2 13 39.2	5 11.3	6 26.9	12 54.4	2 40.7	9 53.4	0♉ 9.4	1 58.2	4 18.7	29 3.0	24 37.7	22 36.6
26 S	2 17 35.7	6 9.7	6 23.8	25 17.9	4 47.7	11 7.5	0 54.4	1 52.8	4 15.1	29 0.8	24 36.8	22 35.0
27 M	2 21 32.3	7 8.1	6 20.6	7♒59.6	6 55.6	12 21.5	1 39.4	1 47.5	4 11.5	28 58.5	24 35.9	22 33.4
28 T	2 25 28.8	8 6.4	6 17.4	21 4.1	9 4.2	13 35.6	2 24.3	1 42.4	4 8.1	28 56.3	24 34.9	22 31.8
29 W	2 29 25.4	9 4.8	6 14.2	4♓35.2	11 13.2	14 49.7	3 9.2	1 37.5	4 4.7	28 54.0	24 33.9	22 30.2
30 T	2 33 22.0	10 3.0	6 11.1	18 35.4	13 22.5	16 3.7	3 54.0	1 32.7	4 1.3	28 51.7	24 32.9	22 28.6

DECLINATION at NOON

DAY	EPHEMERIS SIDEREAL TIME	☉	☊	☽	☿	♀	♂	♃	♄	♅	♆	♇
1 W	0 39 1.9	4N37.0	18N20.4	14S13.8	6S34.8	2N48.4	4N 6.5	0S23.9	0N 2.9	19S53.0	21S60.0	7N24.4
4 S	0 50 51.6	5 46.0	18 22.8	0 12.9	4 46.4	4 18.2	5 1.7	0 14.9	0 8.4	19 52.1	21 59.9	7 26.4
7 T	1 2 41.2	6 54.2	18 25.3	14N22.3	2 47.9	5 47.3	5 56.4	0 6.2	0 13.7	19 51.1	21 59.7	7 28.4
10 F	1 14 30.9	8 1.2	18 27.7	20 41.0	0 40.0	7 15.1	6 50.4	0N 2.2	0 18.9	19 50.0	21 59.6	7 30.3
13 M	1 26 20.5	9 7.0	18 30.1	16 17.4	1N36.7	8 41.6	7 43.7	0 10.3	0 24.0	19 48.8	21 59.4	7 32.2
16 T	1 38 10.2	10 11.5	18 32.5	5 19.9	4 1.3	10 6.2	8 36.2	0 18.0	0 28.8	19 47.6	21 59.2	7 33.9
19 S	1 49 59.9	11 14.4	18 34.9	7S13.0	6 32.4	11 28.7	9 27.7	0 25.3	0 33.5	19 46.3	21 59.0	7 35.5
22 W	2 1 49.5	12 15.7	18 37.3	17 11.2	9 8.1	12 48.8	10 18.4	0 32.1	0 37.9	19 45.0	21 58.9	7 37.1
25 S	2 13 39.2	13 15.1	18 39.7	20 50.2	11 45.6	14 6.1	11 8.0	0 38.5	0 42.0	19 43.6	21 58.7	7 38.5
28 T	2 25 28.8	14 12.7	18 42.1	15 42.7	14 21.2	15 20.3	11 56.5	0 44.2	0 45.9	19 42.1	21 58.5	7 39.8

MAY 1981

DAY	EPHEMERIS SIDEREAL TIME	☉	☊	☽	☿	♀	♂	♃	♄	♅	♆	♇
	h m s	° ′	° ′	° ′	° ′	° ′	° ′	° ′	° ′	° ′	° ′	° ′
						LONGITUDE at NOON						
1 F	2 37 18.5	11♉ 1.3	6♌ 7.9	3♈ 4.5	15♉31.8	17♉17.7	4♉38.8	1♎28.0	3♎58.0	28♏49.4	24♐31.9	22♎27.0
2 S	2 41 15.1	11 59.5	6 4.7	17 58.8	17 40.8	18 31.7	5 23.5	1R23.5	3R54.8	28R47.0	24R30.8	22R25.4
3 S	2 45 11.6	12 57.7	6 1.5	3♉11.0	19 49.2	19 45.6	6 8.2	1 19.1	3 51.7	28 44.6	24 29.7	22 23.8
4 M	2 49 8.2	13 55.9	5 58.3	18 31.0	21 56.8	20 59.6	6 52.8	1 15.0	3 48.7	28 42.2	24 28.6	22 22.3
5 T	2 53 4.7	14 54.0	5 55.2	3♊46.8	24 3.1	22 13.5	7 37.3	1 10.9	3 45.7	28 39.8	24 27.4	22 20.8
6 W	2 57 1.3	15 52.1	5 52.0	18 47.9	26 8.0	23 27.5	8 21.9	1 7.1	3 42.9	28 37.4	24 26.3	22 19.2
7 T	3 0 57.8	16 50.2	5 48.8	3♋25.9	28 11.1	24 41.4	9 6.3	1 3.4	3 40.1	28 35.0	24 25.1	22 17.7
8 F	3 4 54.4	17 48.3	5 45.6	17 36.4	0♊12.2	25 55.3	9 50.7	0 59.9	3 37.4	28 32.5	24 23.9	22 16.2
9 S	3 8 50.9	18 46.3	5 42.5	1♌18.2	2 11.1	27 9.1	10 35.1	0 56.5	3 34.8	28 30.1	24 22.7	22 14.8
10 S	3 12 47.5	19 44.3	5 39.3	14 32.9	4 7.4	28 23.0	11 19.4	0 53.4	3 32.2	28 27.6	24 21.4	22 13.3
11 M	3 16 44.1	20 42.2	5 36.1	27 24.1	6 1.1	29 36.8	12 3.6	0 50.4	3 29.8	28 25.2	24 20.1	22 11.9
12 T	3 20 40.6	21 40.2	5 32.9	9♍55.8	7 52.0	0♊50.6	12 47.8	0 47.6	3 27.4	28 22.7	24 18.9	22 10.5
13 W	3 24 37.2	22 38.1	5 29.7	22 12.6	9 39.9	2 4.4	13 31.9	0 44.9	3 25.2	28 20.2	24 17.6	22 9.1
14 T	3 28 33.7	23 35.9	5 26.6	4♎18.6	11 24.7	3 18.2	14 16.0	0 42.4	3 23.0	28 17.7	24 16.2	22 7.7
15 F	3 32 30.3	24 33.8	5 23.4	16 17.4	13 6.3	4 32.0	15 0.0	0 40.1	3 20.9	28 15.2	24 14.9	22 6.3
16 S	3 36 26.8	25 31.6	5 20.2	28 11.9	14 44.6	5 45.7	15 44.0	0 38.0	3 18.9	28 12.7	24 13.5	22 5.0
17 S	3 40 23.4	26 29.4	5 17.0	10♏ 4.5	16 19.6	6 59.4	16 27.9	0 36.1	3 17.0	28 10.2	24 12.2	22 3.6
18 M	3 44 19.9	27 27.1	5 13.9	21 57.0	17 51.2	8 13.1	17 11.7	0 34.3	3 15.3	28 7.7	24 10.8	22 2.3
19 T	3 48 16.5	28 24.9	5 10.7	3♐50.9	19 19.4	9 26.9	17 55.6	0 32.8	3 13.6	28 5.2	24 9.4	22 1.1
20 W	3 52 13.1	29 22.6	5 7.5	15 47.6	20 44.1	10 40.5	18 39.4	0 31.4	3 12.0	28 2.7	24 8.0	21 59.8
21 T	3 56 9.6	0♊20.3	5 4.3	27 48.8	22 5.2	11 54.2	19 23.1	0 30.2	3 10.5	28 0.2	24 6.5	21 58.6
22 F	4 0 6.2	1 18.0	5 1.2	9♑56.4	23 22.7	13 7.8	20 6.7	0 29.1	3 9.1	27 57.7	24 5.1	21 57.4
23 S	4 4 2.7	2 15.7	4 58.0	22 13.0	24 36.5	14 21.5	20 50.3	0 28.3	3 7.8	27 55.2	24 3.6	21 56.2
24 S	4 7 59.3	3 13.3	4 54.8	4♒41.7	25 46.7	15 35.1	21 33.8	0 27.6	3 6.5	27 52.7	24 2.1	21 55.0
25 M	4 11 55.8	4 10.9	4 51.6	17 26.0	26 53.1	16 48.7	22 17.3	0 27.1	3 5.4	27 50.2	24 0.6	21 53.9
26 T	4 15 52.4	5 8.5	4 48.4	0♓29.7	27 55.6	18 2.3	23 0.8	0 26.8	3 4.4	27 47.7	23 59.1	21 52.8
27 W	4 19 48.9	6 6.1	4 45.3	13 56.2	28 54.4	19 15.9	23 44.2	0 26.7	3 3.5	27 45.3	23 57.6	21 51.7
28 T	4 23 45.5	7 3.7	4 42.1	27 47.9	29 49.1	20 29.4	24 27.5	0 26.7	3 2.7	27 42.8	23 56.1	21 50.6
29 F	4 27 42.1	8 1.3	4 38.9	12♈ 5.5	0♋39.9	21 43.0	25 10.8	0D26.9	3 1.9	27 40.3	23 54.6	21 49.6
30 S	4 31 38.6	8 58.8	4 35.7	26 46.9	1 26.5	22 56.5	25 54.0	0 27.3	3 1.3	27 37.9	23 53.0	21 48.6
31 S	4 35 35.2	9 56.4	4 32.6	11♉46.8	2 9.0	24 10.0	26 37.2	0 27.9	3 0.8	27 35.5	23 51.4	21 47.6
						DECLINATION at NOON						
1 F	2 37 18.5	15N 8.1	18N44.4	2S 39.0	16N49.9	16N31.0	12N43.9	0N49.5	0N49.5	19S 40.6	21S 58.3	7N41.0
4 M	2 49 8.2	16 1.2	18 46.8	12N38.6	19 6.1	17 38.0	13 30.1	0 54.1	0 52.7	19 39.1	21 58.1	7 42.1
7 T	3 0 57.8	16 52.0	18 49.1	20 45.4	21 4.9	18 40.9	14 15.0	0 58.1	0 55.7	19 37.5	21 57.8	7 43.1
10 S	3 12 47.5	17 40.3	18 51.5	17 16.7	22 42.6	19 39.3	14 58.6	1 1.5	0 58.3	19 35.9	21 57.6	7 43.9
13 W	3 24 37.2	18 25.8	18 53.8	6 30.1	23 57.5	20 33.0	15 40.8	1 4.3	1 0.6	19 34.3	21 57.4	7 44.6
16 S	3 36 26.8	19 8.6	18 56.1	6S 9.7	24 49.9	21 21.6	16 21.5	1 6.4	1 2.6	19 32.7	21 57.2	7 45.2
19 T	3 48 16.5	19 48.5	18 58.4	16 37.9	25 21.3	22 4.9	17 0.8	1 7.8	1 4.1	19 31.0	21 57.0	7 45.6
22 F	4 0 6.2	20 25.3	19 0.8	21 2.8	25 34.0	22 42.6	17 38.5	1 8.6	1 5.3	19 29.4	21 56.7	7 45.9
25 M	4 11 55.8	20 59.0	19 3.0	16 47.6	25 30.6	23 14.5	18 14.6	1 8.7	1 6.2	19 27.7	21 56.5	7 46.0
28 T	4 23 45.5	21 29.4	19 5.3	4 41.2	25 13.6	23 40.4	18 49.0	1 8.2	1 6.7	19 26.1	21 56.3	7 46.0
31 S	4 35 35.2	21 56.5	19 7.6	10N34.1	24 45.6	24 0.1	19 21.8	1 7.1	1 6.8	19 24.5	21 56.1	7 45.9

JUNE 1981

DAY	EPHEMERIS SIDEREAL TIME	☉	☊	☽	☿	♀	♂	♃	♄	♅	♆	♇
						LONGITUDE at NOON						
1 M	4 39 31.7	10♊53.9	4♌29.4	26♉56.9	2♋47.3	25♊23.6	27♉20.3	0♎28.7	3♎ 0.4	27♏33.0	23♐49.9	21♎46.6
2 T	4 43 28.3	11 51.4	4 26.2	12♊ 7.3	3 21.2	26 37.1	28 3.4	0 29.7	3R 0.1	27R30.6	23R48.3	21R45.7
3 W	4 47 24.8	12 48.9	4 23.0	27 7.4	3 50.7	27 50.5	28 46.4	0 30.8	2 59.8	27 28.2	23 46.7	21 44.8
4 T	4 51 21.4	13 46.3	4 19.9	11♋48.6	4 15.8	29 4.0	29 29.3	0 32.1	2 59.7	27 25.9	23 45.1	21 43.9
5 F	4 55 18.0	14 43.8	4 16.7	26 5.0	4 36.3	0♋17.5	0♊12.2	0 33.6	2 59.7	27 23.5	23 43.5	21 43.1
6 S	4 59 14.5	15 41.2	4 13.5	9♌53.6	4 52.2	1 30.9	0 55.1	0 35.2	2D59.8	27 21.2	23 41.9	21 42.2
7 S	5 3 11.1	16 38.6	4 10.3	23 14.8	5 3.6	2 44.3	1 37.9	0 37.1	3 0.0	27 18.8	23 40.3	21 41.4
8 M	5 7 7.6	17 36.0	4 7.1	6♍10.9	5 10.3	3 57.7	2 20.6	0 39.1	3 0.3	27 16.5	23 38.7	21 40.7
9 T	5 11 4.2	18 33.4	4 4.0	18 45.5	5 12.6	5 11.2	3 3.3	0 41.3	3 0.8	27 14.3	23 37.2	21 40.0
10 W	5 15 0.7	19 30.8	4 0.8	1♎ 3.1	5R10.2	6 24.5	3 46.0	0 43.7	3 1.3	27 12.0	23 35.5	21 39.3
11 T	5 18 57.3	20 28.2	3 57.6	13 8.1	5 3.5	7 37.9	4 28.5	0 46.2	3 1.9	27 9.8	23 33.9	21 38.6
12 F	5 22 53.9	21 25.5	3 54.4	25 5.1	4 52.5	8 51.2	5 11.0	0 48.9	3 2.6	27 7.6	23 32.3	21 38.0
13 S	5 26 50.4	22 22.8	3 51.3	6♏57.9	4 37.4	10 4.5	5 53.5	0 51.8	3 3.4	27 5.4	23 30.7	21 37.4
14 S	5 30 47.0	23 20.1	3 48.1	18 49.8	4 18.4	11 17.8	6 35.9	0 54.9	3 4.3	27 3.2	23 29.1	21 36.8
15 M	5 34 43.5	24 17.4	3 44.9	0♐43.6	3 55.9	12 31.1	7 18.2	0 58.1	3 5.3	27 1.1	23 27.4	21 36.3
16 T	5 38 40.1	25 14.6	3 41.7	12 41.5	3 30.3	13 44.4	8 0.5	1 1.4	3 6.4	26 59.0	23 25.8	21 35.7
17 W	5 42 36.6	26 11.9	3 38.6	24 45.3	3 1.8	14 57.6	8 42.8	1 5.0	3 7.6	26 56.9	23 24.2	21 35.3
18 T	5 46 33.2	27 9.2	3 35.4	6♑56.4	2 31.1	16 10.8	9 24.9	1 8.7	3 8.9	26 54.8	23 22.6	21 34.8
19 F	5 50 29.8	28 6.4	3 32.2	19 16.3	1 58.5	17 24.0	10 7.1	1 12.5	3 10.3	26 52.8	23 21.0	21 34.4
20 S	5 54 26.3	29 3.6	3 29.0	1♒46.5	1 24.6	18 37.2	10 49.1	1 16.6	3 11.8	26 50.8	23 19.3	21 34.0
21 S	5 58 22.9	0♋ 0.9	3 25.8	14 28.6	0 50.1	19 50.4	11 31.2	1 20.7	3 13.4	26 48.9	23 17.7	21 33.7
22 M	6 2 19.4	0 58.1	3 22.7	27 24.6	0 15.4	21 3.5	12 13.1	1 25.1	3 15.1	26 46.9	23 16.1	21 33.3
23 T	6 6 16.0	1 55.3	3 19.5	10♓36.5	29♊41.2	22 16.7	12 55.0	1 29.6	3 16.9	26 45.0	23 14.5	21 33.0
24 W	6 10 12.6	2 52.5	3 16.3	24 6.1	29 8.1	23 29.8	13 36.9	1 34.2	3 18.8	26 43.2	23 12.9	21 32.8
25 T	6 14 9.1	3 49.8	3 13.1	7♈54.8	28 36.7	24 42.9	14 18.7	1 39.0	3 20.8	26 41.3	23 11.3	21 32.6
26 F	6 18 5.7	4 47.0	3 10.0	22 2.8	28 7.4	25 56.0	15 0.5	1 44.0	3 22.9	26 39.5	23 9.8	21 32.4
27 S	6 22 2.2	5 44.2	3 6.8	6♉28.5	27 40.8	27 9.1	15 42.2	1 49.1	3 25.0	26 37.8	23 8.2	21 32.2
28 S	6 25 58.8	6 41.4	3 3.6	21 8.6	27 17.4	28 22.2	16 23.9	1 54.4	3 27.3	26 36.0	23 6.6	21 32.1
29 M	6 29 55.3	7 38.7	3 0.4	5♊57.3	26 57.5	29 35.2	17 5.5	1 59.8	3 29.7	26 34.4	23 5.0	21 32.0
30 T	6 33 51.9	8 35.9	2 57.3	20 47.7	26 41.6	0♌48.3	17 47.1	2 5.4	3 32.2	26 32.7	23 3.5	21 32.0
						DECLINATION at NOON						
1 M	4 39 31.7	22N 4.7	19N 8.4	14N56.1	24N34.2	24N 5.3	19N32.4	1N 6.5	1N 6.8	19S 23.9	21S 56.0	7N45.8
4 T	4 51 21.4	22 27.2	19 10.6	21 5.6	23 55.0	24 16.5	20 2.9	1 4.5	1 6.4	19 22.3	21 55.8	7 45.5
7 S	5 3 11.1	22 46.2	19 12.9	15 29.1	23 10.2	24 21.4	20 31.6	1 1.8	1 5.7	19 20.8	21 55.5	7 45.1
10 W	5 15 0.7	23 1.6	19 15.1	3 36.9	22 21.8	24 19.8	20 58.5	0 58.5	1 4.5	19 19.3	21 55.3	7 44.4
13 S	5 26 50.4	23 13.3	19 17.4	8S 58.7	21 32.3	24 11.7	21 23.6	0 54.6	1 3.0	19 17.8	21 55.1	7 43.7
16 T	5 38 40.1	23 21.3	19 19.6	18 25.3	20 44.3	23 57.2	21 46.8	0 50.1	1 1.2	19 16.4	21 54.9	7 42.8
19 F	5 50 29.8	23 25.6	19 21.8	20 55.5	20 0.7	23 36.4	22 8.1	0 45.0	0 59.0	19 15.0	21 54.7	7 41.8
22 M	6 2 19.4	23 26.2	19 24.1	14 29.0	19 24.5	23 9.4	22 27.5	0 39.4	0 56.5	19 13.7	21 54.5	7 40.7
25 T	6 14 9.1	23 23.1	19 26.3	1 14.9	18 58.6	22 36.3	22 45.1	0 33.2	0 53.6	19 12.5	21 54.3	7 39.4
28 S	6 25 58.8	23 16.3	19 28.5	13N16.7	18 45.3	21 57.5	23 0.7	0 26.5	0 50.4	19 11.3	21 54.1	7 38.1

JULY 1981

DAY	EPHEMERIS SIDEREAL TIME	☉	☊	☽	☿	♀	♂	♃	♄	♅	♆	♇
	h m s	° ′	° ′	° ′	° ′	° ′	° ′	° ′	° ′	° ′	° ′	° ′
					LONGITUDE at NOON							
1 W	6 37 48.5	9♋33.2	2♌54.1	5♋31.7	26♊29.8	2♌ 1.3	18♊28.6	2♎11.1	3♎34.7	26♏31.1	23♐ 2.0	21♎32.0
2 T	6 41 45.0	10 30.4	2 50.9	20 2.1	26R22.6	3 14.3	19 10.0	2 16.9	3 37.4	26R29.6	23R 0.5	21 32.0
3 F	6 45 41.6	11 27.6	2 47.7	4♌13.1	26 20.0	4 27.3	19 51.4	2 22.9	3 40.1	26 28.0	22 58.9	21 32.0
4 S	6 49 38.1	12 24.8	2 44.6	18 0.9	26D22.3	5 40.2	20 32.7	2 29.1	3 43.0	26 26.5	22 57.4	21D32.1
5 S	6 53 34.7	13 22.1	2 41.4	1♍24.3	26 29.5	6 53.2	21 14.0	2 35.4	3 45.9	26 25.1	22 55.9	21 32.2
6 M	6 57 31.2	14 19.3	2 38.2	14 23.9	26 41.7	8 6.1	21 55.2	2 41.8	3 48.9	26 23.7	22 54.5	21 32.4
7 T	7 1 27.8	15 16.5	2 35.0	27 2.2	26 59.1	9 19.0	22 36.4	2 48.3	3 52.0	26 22.3	22 53.0	21 32.6
8 W	7 5 24.4	16 13.7	2 31.8	9♎22.7	27 21.6	10 31.9	23 17.5	2 55.0	3 55.2	26 21.0	22 51.5	21 32.8
9 T	7 9 20.9	17 10.9	2 28.7	21 29.6	27 49.2	11 44.7	23 58.6	3 1.8	3 58.5	26 19.7	22 50.1	21 33.0
10 F	7 13 17.5	18 8.1	2 25.5	3♏27.4	28 21.9	12 57.5	24 39.6	3 8.8	4 1.9	26 18.5	22 48.6	21 33.3
11 S	7 17 14.0	19 5.3	2 22.3	15 20.6	28 59.7	14 10.3	25 20.5	3 15.9	4 5.3	26 17.3	22 47.2	21 33.6
12 S	7 21 10.6	20 2.5	2 19.1	27 13.4	29 42.5	15 23.1	26 1.4	3 23.1	4 8.9	26 16.1	22 45.8	21 34.0
13 M	7 25 7.1	20 59.7	2 16.0	9♐ 9.6	0♋30.4	16 35.8	26 42.3	3 30.4	4 12.5	26 15.0	22 44.4	21 34.4
14 T	7 29 3.7	21 56.9	2 12.8	21 12.4	1 23.2	17 48.5	27 23.1	3 37.9	4 16.2	26 14.0	22 43.1	21 34.8
15 W	7 33 0.3	22 54.1	2 9.6	3♑24.3	2 20.9	19 1.2	28 3.8	3 45.5	4 20.0	26 13.0	22 41.7	21 35.3
16 T	7 36 56.8	23 51.3	2 6.4	15 47.5	3 23.5	20 13.9	28 44.5	3 53.2	4 23.9	26 12.0	22 40.4	21 35.7
17 F	7 40 53.4	24 48.6	2 3.3	28 23.2	4 30.8	21 26.5	29 25.1	4 1.0	4 27.8	26 11.1	22 39.1	21 36.3
18 S	7 44 49.9	25 45.8	2 0.1	11♒12.3	5 42.8	22 39.1	0♋ 5.7	4 8.9	4 31.8	26 10.2	22 37.8	21 36.8
19 S	7 48 46.5	26 43.0	1 56.9	24 15.1	6 59.4	23 51.7	0 46.2	4 17.0	4 36.0	26 9.4	22 36.5	21 37.4
20 M	7 52 43.0	27 40.3	1 53.7	7♓31.6	8 20.6	25 4.3	1 26.7	4 25.2	4 40.1	26 8.6	22 35.2	21 38.0
21 T	7 56 39.6	28 37.6	1 50.5	21 1.7	9 46.2	26 16.9	2 7.2	4 33.5	4 44.5	26 8.0	22 34.1	21 38.7
22 W	8 0 36.1	29 34.8	1 47.4	4♈44.7	11 16.0	27 29.4	2 47.6	4 41.9	4 48.8	26 7.3	22 32.8	21 39.4
23 T	8 4 32.7	0♌32.1	1 44.2	18 39.8	12 50.1	28 41.8	3 27.9	4 50.5	4 53.2	26 6.7	22 31.6	21 40.1
24 F	8 8 29.3	1 29.4	1 41.0	2♉45.8	14 28.1	29 54.3	4 8.2	4 59.1	4 57.7	26 6.1	22 30.5	21 40.9
25 S	8 12 25.8	2 26.7	1 37.8	17 0.9	16 9.9	1♍ 6.7	4 48.4	5 7.8	5 2.3	26 5.6	22 29.3	21 41.7
26 S	8 16 22.4	3 24.1	1 34.7	1♊22.5	17 55.3	2 19.1	5 28.6	5 16.7	5 6.9	26 5.1	22 28.2	21 42.5
27 M	8 20 18.9	4 21.4	1 31.5	15 47.2	19 44.1	3 31.5	6 8.7	5 25.6	5 11.7	26 4.6	22 27.1	21 43.3
28 T	8 24 15.5	5 18.8	1 28.3	0♋11.0	21 35.9	4 43.9	6 48.8	5 34.7	5 16.5	26 4.3	22 26.0	21 44.2
29 W	8 28 12.0	6 16.2	1 25.1	14 29.3	23 30.5	5 56.2	7 28.8	5 43.9	5 21.3	26 3.9	22 24.9	21 45.1
30 T	8 32 8.6	7 13.5	1 22.0	28 37.6	25 27.6	7 8.5	8 8.8	5 53.1	5 26.3	26 3.7	22 23.9	21 46.1
31 F	8 36 5.1	8 11.0	1 18.8	12♌31.6	27 26.8	8 20.7	8 48.7	6 2.5	5 31.3	26 3.4	22 22.9	21 47.1
					DECLINATION at NOON							
1 W	6 37 48.5	23N 5.8	19N30.7	21N 0.4	18N45.3	21N13.1	23N14.3	0N19.2	0N46.8	19S10.2	21S53.9	7N36.5
4 S	6 49 38.1	22 51.6	19 32.8	16 50.3	18 58.1	20 23.3	23 26.1	0 11.4	0 42.9	19 9.2	21 53.7	7 34.9
7 T	7 1 27.8	22 33.9	19 35.0	5 9.0	19 22.0	19 28.5	23 35.9	0 3.2	0 38.8	19 8.3	21 53.6	7 33.1
10 F	7 13 17.5	22 12.7	19 37.2	7S42.8	19 54.1	18 28.9	23 43.8	0S 5.5	0 34.3	19 7.4	21 53.4	7 31.3
13 M	7 25 7.1	21 48.1	19 39.3	17 41.1	20 31.0	17 24.9	23 49.7	0 14.7	0 29.5	19 6.7	21 53.3	7 29.3
16 T	7 36 56.8	21 20.1	19 41.5	21 4.1	21 8.5	16 16.8	23 53.7	0 24.2	0 24.4	19 6.0	21 53.1	7 27.2
19 S	7 48 46.5	20 48.8	19 43.6	15 21.3	21 41.9	15 4.8	23 55.9	0 34.2	0 19.1	19 5.5	21 53.0	7 25.0
22 W	8 0 36.1	20 14.4	19 45.7	2 26.4	22 6.0	13 49.3	23 56.2	0 44.6	0 13.5	19 5.0	21 52.9	7 22.7
25 S	8 12 25.8	19 36.9	19 47.9	12N 1.5	22 15.6	12 30.6	23 54.6	0 55.4	0 7.6	19 4.7	21 52.8	7 20.4
28 T	8 24 15.5	18 56.5	19 50.0	20 40.4	22 6.0	11 9.1	23 51.2	1 6.5	0 1.5	19 4.4	21 52.8	7 17.9
31 F	8 36 5.1	18 13.3	19 52.1	18 0.0	21 33.6	9 45.1	23 46.0	1 18.0	0S 4.8	19 4.3	21 52.7	7 15.4

AUGUST 1981

DAY	EPHEMERIS SIDEREAL TIME	☉	☊	☽	☿	♀	♂	♃	♄	♅	♆	♇
					LONGITUDE at NOON							
1 S	8 40 1.7	9♌ 8.4	1♌15.6	26♌ 8.1	29♋27.7	9♍33.0	9♋28.6	6♎11.9	5♎36.3	26♏ 3.3	22♐21.9	21♎48.1
2 S	8 43 58.3	10 5.8	1 12.4	9♍25.2	1♌30.1	10 45.2	10 8.4	6 21.5	5 41.5	26R 3.1	22R20.9	21 49.1
3 M	8 47 54.8	11 3.3	1 9.2	22 22.5	3 33.6	11 57.3	10 48.1	6 31.2	5 46.7	26 3.1	22 20.0	21 50.2
4 T	8 51 51.4	12 0.7	1 6.1	5♎ 0.8	5 37.8	13 9.5	11 27.8	6 40.9	5 52.0	26 3.1	22 19.1	21 51.3
5 W	8 55 47.9	12 58.2	1 2.9	17 22.3	7 42.4	14 21.6	12 7.5	6 50.8	5 57.3	26 3.1	22 18.2	21 52.4
6 T	8 59 44.5	13 55.7	0 59.7	29 30.4	9 47.2	15 33.6	12 47.1	7 0.7	6 2.7	26D 3.2	22 17.3	21 53.6
7 F	9 3 41.0	14 53.2	0 56.5	11♏28.9	11 51.8	16 45.7	13 26.6	7 10.7	6 8.2	26 3.3	22 16.5	21 54.8
8 S	9 7 37.6	15 50.7	0 53.4	23 22.5	13 56.0	17 57.7	14 6.1	7 20.8	6 13.7	26 3.5	22 15.7	21 56.0
9 S	9 11 34.1	16 48.2	0 50.2	5♐15.6	15 59.7	19 9.6	14 45.6	7 31.0	6 19.3	26 3.7	22 14.9	21 57.3
10 M	9 15 30.7	17 45.8	0 47.0	17 12.9	18 2.5	20 21.5	15 24.9	7 41.3	6 24.9	26 4.0	22 14.2	21 58.6
11 T	9 19 27.3	18 43.4	0 43.8	29 18.8	20 4.6	21 33.4	16 4.3	7 51.7	6 30.7	26 4.4	22 13.5	21 59.9
12 W	9 23 23.8	19 40.9	0 40.6	11♑37.0	22 5.5	22 45.2	16 43.6	8 2.2	6 36.4	26 4.8	22 12.8	22 1.3
13 T	9 27 20.4	20 38.5	0 37.5	24 10.5	24 5.3	23 57.0	17 22.8	8 12.7	6 42.3	26 5.3	22 12.1	22 2.6
14 F	9 31 16.9	21 36.1	0 34.3	7♒ 1.4	26 3.8	25 8.8	18 2.0	8 23.3	6 48.1	26 5.8	22 11.5	22 4.1
15 S	9 35 13.5	22 33.7	0 31.1	20 10.4	28 1.1	26 20.5	18 41.1	8 34.0	6 54.0	26 6.3	22 10.9	22 5.5
16 S	9 39 10.0	23 31.4	0 27.9	3♓37.2	29 57.0	27 32.1	19 20.2	8 44.8	7 0.0	26 6.9	22 10.3	22 6.9
17 M	9 43 6.6	24 29.1	0 24.8	17 19.9	1♍51.6	28 43.7	19 59.2	8 55.6	7 6.1	26 7.6	22 9.8	22 8.4
18 T	9 47 3.1	25 26.7	0 21.6	1♈16.0	3 44.8	29 55.3	20 38.2	9 6.5	7 12.1	26 8.3	22 9.3	22 9.9
19 W	9 50 59.7	26 24.5	0 18.4	15 21.8	5 36.6	1♎ 6.8	21 17.1	9 17.5	7 18.3	26 9.0	22 8.8	22 11.5
20 T	9 54 56.2	27 22.2	0 15.2	29 33.7	7 27.0	2 18.3	21 56.0	9 28.6	7 24.5	26 9.9	22 8.3	22 13.0
21 F	9 58 52.8	28 20.0	0 12.0	13♉48.2	9 16.0	3 29.7	22 34.8	9 39.7	7 30.7	26 10.7	22 7.9	22 14.6
22 S	10 2 49.3	29 17.8	0 8.9	28 2.2	11 3.7	4 41.1	23 13.5	9 50.9	7 37.0	26 11.6	22 7.5	22 16.2
23 S	10 6 45.9	0♍15.6	0 5.7	12♊13.2	12 49.9	5 52.4	23 52.3	10 2.2	7 43.3	26 12.6	22 7.1	22 17.9
24 M	10 10 42.5	1 13.5	0 2.5	26 19.2	14 34.8	7 3.7	24 30.9	10 13.5	7 49.7	26 13.6	22 6.8	22 19.5
25 T	10 14 39.0	2 11.3	29♋59.3	10♋18.7	16 18.3	8 15.0	25 9.5	10 24.9	7 56.1	26 14.7	22 6.5	22 21.2
26 W	10 18 35.6	3 9.3	29 56.2	24 10.2	18 0.5	9 26.2	25 48.1	10 36.4	8 2.6	26 15.8	22 6.2	22 23.0
27 T	10 22 32.1	4 7.2	29 53.0	7♌51.9	19 41.4	10 37.4	26 26.6	10 47.9	8 9.1	26 16.9	22 6.0	22 24.7
28 F	10 26 28.7	5 5.2	29 49.8	21 22.2	21 21.0	11 48.5	27 5.1	10 59.5	8 15.6	26 18.1	22 5.8	22 26.5
29 S	10 30 25.2	6 3.2	29 46.6	4♍39.4	22 59.2	12 59.6	27 43.5	11 11.1	8 22.2	26 19.4	22 5.6	22 28.3
30 S	10 34 21.8	7 1.2	29 43.4	17 42.3	24 36.2	14 10.6	28 21.8	11 22.8	8 28.9	26 20.7	22 5.5	22 30.1
31 M	10 38 18.3	7 59.3	29 40.3	0♎29.9	26 11.9	15 21.6	29 0.1	11 34.6	8 35.5	26 22.1	22 5.4	22 31.9
					DECLINATION at NOON							
1 S	8 40 1.7	17N58.3	19N52.8	14N51.8	21N17.5	9N16.5	23N43.9	1S21.9	0S 7.0	19S 4.3	21S52.7	7N14.5
4 T	8 51 51.4	17 11.5	19 54.9	2 20.2	20 13.7	7 49.6	23 36.3	1 33.8	0 13.6	19 4.3	21 52.7	7 11.9
7 F	9 3 41.0	16 22.2	19 56.9	10S20.0	18 48.3	6 20.9	23 27.1	1 46.0	0 20.4	19 4.4	21 52.7	7 9.2
10 M	9 15 30.7	15 30.6	19 59.0	19 9.0	17 5.3	4 50.7	23 16.2	1 58.5	0 27.5	19 4.6	21 52.7	7 6.4
13 T	9 27 20.4	14 36.7	20 1.1	20 36.0	15 8.8	3 19.4	23 3.7	2 11.2	0 34.7	19 5.0	21 52.7	7 3.6
16 S	9 39 10.0	13 40.8	20 3.1	12 46.1	13 2.7	1 47.2	22 49.5	2 24.2	0 42.1	19 5.4	21 52.7	7 0.7
19 W	9 50 59.7	12 42.9	20 5.2	1N24.9	10 50.6	0 14.5	22 33.9	2 37.5	0 49.6	19 6.0	21 52.8	6 57.8
22 S	10 2 49.3	11 43.1	20 7.2	15 9.9	8 35.0	1S 18.4	22 16.7	2 50.9	0 57.3	19 6.7	21 52.8	6 54.9
25 T	10 14 39.0	10 41.7	20 9.2	21 9.5	6 18.1	2 51.3	21 58.2	3 4.6	1 5.2	19 7.4	21 52.9	6 51.9
28 F	10 26 28.7	9 38.8	20 11.2	16 3.5	4 1.6	4 23.8	21 38.2	3 18.4	1 13.1	19 8.3	21 53.0	6 48.9
31 M	10 38 18.3	8 34.5	20 13.2	3 52.9	1 46.6	5 55.7	21 16.9	3 32.4	1 21.2	19 9.3	21 53.2	6 45.9

SEPTEMBER 1981

DAY	EPHEMERIS SIDEREAL TIME	☉	☊	☽	☿	♀	♂	♃	♄	♅	♆	♇
	h m s	° ′	° ′	° ′	° ′	° ′	° ′	° ′	° ′	° ′	° ′	° ′
LONGITUDE at NOON												
1 T	10 42 14.9	8♍57.4	29♋37.1	13♎ 2.5	27♍46.4	16♎32.5	29♋38.4	11♎46.5	8♎42.3	26♏23.5	22♐ 5.3	22♎33.8
2 W	10 46 11.4	9 55.5	29 33.9	25 20.8	29 19.6	17 43.4	0♌16.6	11 58.3	8 49.0	26 25.0	22 5.3	22 35.7
3 T	10 50 8.0	10 53.6	29 30.7	7♏27.2	0♎51.5	18 54.2	0 54.7	12 10.3	8 55.8	26 26.5	22 5.3	22 37.6
4 F	10 54 4.5	11 51.8	29 27.6	19 24.6	2 22.2	20 4.9	1 32.8	12 22.2	9 2.6	26 28.1	22 5.3	22 39.5
5 S	10 58 1.1	12 50.0	29 24.4	1♐16.8	3 51.6	21 15.6	2 10.8	12 34.3	9 9.5	26 29.7	22 5.3	22 41.5
6 S	11 1 57.6	13 48.2	29 21.2	13 8.5	5 19.7	22 26.3	2 48.7	12 46.3	9 16.4	26 31.3	22D 5.4	22 43.4
7 M	11 5 54.2	14 46.4	29 18.0	25 4.6	6 46.5	23 36.8	3 26.6	12 58.5	9 23.3	26 33.0	22 5.6	22 45.4
8 T	11 9 50.7	15 44.6	29 14.8	7♑10.0	8 12.1	24 47.3	4 4.5	13 10.6	9 30.2	26 34.8	22 5.7	22 47.4
9 W	11 13 47.3	16 42.9	29 11.7	19 29.8	9 36.3	25 57.8	4 42.3	13 22.8	9 37.2	26 36.6	22 5.9	22 49.4
10 T	11 17 43.9	17 41.2	29 8.5	2♒ 8.1	10 59.2	27 8.1	5 20.0	13 35.1	9 44.2	26 38.4	22 6.1	22 51.5
11 F	11 21 40.4	18 39.6	29 5.3	15 8.4	12 20.7	28 18.4	5 57.7	13 47.4	9 51.2	26 40.3	22 6.4	22 53.5
12 S	11 25 37.0	19 37.9	29 2.1	28 32.2	13 40.8	29 28.7	6 35.3	13 59.7	9 58.3	26 42.2	22 6.6	22 55.6
13 S	11 29 33.5	20 36.3	28 59.0	12♓19.4	14 59.5	0♏38.8	7 12.9	14 12.1	10 5.3	26 44.2	22 7.0	22 57.7
14 M	11 33 30.1	21 34.7	28 55.8	26 27.4	16 16.7	1 48.9	7 50.4	14 24.5	10 12.4	26 46.2	22 7.3	22 59.8
15 T	11 37 26.6	22 33.2	28 52.6	10♈51.6	17 32.3	2 58.9	8 27.8	14 37.0	10 19.6	26 48.3	22 7.7	23 1.9
16 W	11 41 23.2	23 31.7	28 49.4	25 25.4	18 46.3	4 8.8	9 5.2	14 49.5	10 26.7	26 50.4	22 8.1	23 4.1
17 T	11 45 19.7	24 30.2	28 46.2	10♉ 2.1	19 58.6	5 18.7	9 42.6	15 2.0	10 33.9	26 52.6	22 8.6	23 6.2
18 F	11 49 16.3	25 28.7	28 43.1	24 34.9	21 9.1	6 28.5	10 19.8	15 14.6	10 41.1	26 54.7	22 9.0	23 8.4
19 S	11 53 12.8	26 27.3	28 39.9	8♊58.9	22 17.7	7 38.2	10 57.1	15 27.2	10 48.3	26 57.0	22 9.5	23 10.6
20 S	11 57 9.4	27 25.9	28 36.7	23 10.7	23 24.4	8 47.8	11 34.3	15 39.8	10 55.5	26 59.3	22 10.1	23 12.8
21 M	12 1 5.9	28 24.6	28 33.5	7♋ 8.7	24 28.9	9 57.4	12 11.4	15 52.5	11 2.7	27 1.6	22 10.7	23 15.0
22 T	12 5 2.5	29 23.4	28 30.4	20 52.9	25 31.2	11 6.9	12 48.5	16 5.2	11 10.1	27 4.0	22 11.3	23 17.3
23 W	12 8 59.0	0♎22.1	28 27.2	4♌23.7	26 31.0	12 16.3	13 25.5	16 18.0	11 17.3	27 6.4	22 12.0	23 19.6
24 T	12 12 55.6	1 20.9	28 24.0	17 42.2	27 28.2	13 25.7	14 2.4	16 30.7	11 24.6	27 8.8	22 12.6	23 21.8
25 F	12 16 52.1	2 19.7	28 20.8	0♍49.1	28 22.6	14 34.9	14 39.3	16 43.5	11 31.9	27 11.3	22 13.4	23 24.1
26 S	12 20 48.7	3 18.5	28 17.6	13 44.7	29 14.0	15 44.1	15 16.1	16 56.3	11 39.2	27 13.8	22 14.1	23 26.4
27 S	12 24 45.2	4 17.4	28 14.5	26 29.1	0♏ 2.1	16 53.1	15 52.9	17 9.1	11 46.6	27 16.4	22 14.9	23 28.6
28 M	12 28 41.8	5 16.4	28 11.3	9♎ 2.3	0 46.6	18 2.1	16 29.6	17 22.0	11 53.9	27 19.0	22 15.7	23 30.9
29 T	12 32 38.3	6 15.3	28 8.1	21 24.3	1 27.2	19 11.0	17 6.2	17 34.8	12 1.2	27 21.6	22 16.5	23 33.3
30 W	12 36 34.9	7 14.3	28 4.9	3♏35.5	2 3.7	20 19.8	17 42.8	17 47.7	12 8.6	27 24.3	22 17.4	23 35.6
DECLINATION at NOON												
1 T	10 42 14.9	8N12.7	20N13.9	0S37.4	1N 2.2	6S26.2	21N 9.5	3S37.2	1S23.9	19S 9.6	21S53.2	6N44.8
4 F	10 54 4.5	7 6.8	20 15.9	12 51.9	1S 9.0	7 56.7	20 46.5	3 51.4	1 32.1	19 10.7	21 53.4	6 41.8
7 M	11 5 54.2	5 59.8	20 17.9	20 19.8	3 16.1	9 25.9	20 22.3	4 5.7	1 40.5	19 12.0	21 53.5	6 38.8
10 T	11 17 43.9	4 52.0	20 19.9	19 47.9	5 18.3	10 53.4	19 57.0	4 20.2	1 48.8	19 13.3	21 53.7	6 35.7
13 S	11 29 33.5	3 43.4	20 21.8	10 4.8	7 14.8	12 18.9	19 30.5	4 34.7	1 57.3	19 14.7	21 53.9	6 32.7
16 W	11 41 23.2	2 34.2	20 23.8	5N 6.1	9 4.5	13 42.1	19 3.1	4 49.4	2 5.8	19 16.1	21 54.2	6 29.6
19 S	11 53 12.8	1 24.5	20 25.7	17 52.4	10 46.2	15 2.7	18 34.6	5 4.1	2 14.3	19 17.7	21 54.4	6 26.6
22 T	12 5 2.5	0 14.6	20 27.7	21 1.0	12 18.5	16 20.4	18 5.2	5 18.9	2 22.9	19 19.4	21 54.6	6 23.6
25 F	12 16 52.1	0S55.6	20 29.6	13 37.2	13 39.5	17 34.8	17 35.0	5 33.7	2 31.5	19 21.1	21 54.9	6 20.6
28 M	12 28 41.8	2 5.7	20 31.5	0 45.5	14 46.6	18 45.8	17 4.0	5 48.5	2 40.0	19 22.9	21 55.2	6 17.7

OCTOBER 1981

DAY	EPHEMERIS SIDEREAL TIME	☉	☊	☽	☿	♀	♂	♃	♄	♅	♆	♇
LONGITUDE at NOON												
1 T	12 40 31.4	8♎13.3	28♋ 1.7	15♏37.3	2♏35.5	21♏28.5	18♌19.3	18♎ 0.6	12♎15.9	27♏27.0	22♐18.3	23♎37.9
2 F	12 44 28.0	9 12.4	27 58.6	27 31.7	3 2.4	22 37.0	18 55.7	18 13.5	12 23.3	27 29.7	22 19.2	23 40.2
3 S	12 48 24.6	10 11.4	27 55.4	9♐21.5	3 23.9	23 45.5	19 32.1	18 26.5	12 30.7	27 32.5	22 20.1	23 42.6
4 S	12 52 21.1	11 10.5	27 52.2	21 10.8	3 39.6	24 53.9	20 8.4	18 39.4	12 38.0	27 35.3	22 21.1	23 44.9
5 M	12 56 17.7	12 9.7	27 49.0	3♑ 4.0	3 49.0	26 2.1	20 44.6	18 52.4	12 45.4	27 38.2	22 22.2	23 47.3
6 T	13 0 14.2	13 8.8	27 45.9	15 6.4	3 51.7	27 10.3	21 20.8	19 5.4	12 52.8	27 41.1	22 23.2	23 49.7
7 W	13 4 10.8	14 8.0	27 42.7	27 23.2	3R47.2	28 18.3	21 56.9	19 18.4	13 0.1	27 44.0	22 24.3	23 52.0
8 T	13 8 7.3	15 7.3	27 39.5	9♒59.7	3 35.1	29 26.2	22 32.9	19 31.4	13 7.5	27 46.9	22 25.4	23 54.4
9 F	13 12 3.9	16 6.5	27 36.3	23 0.6	3 15.1	0♐33.9	23 8.9	19 44.4	13 14.9	27 49.9	22 26.5	23 56.8
10 S	13 16 0.4	17 5.8	27 33.1	6♓29.0	2 46.9	1 41.6	23 44.8	19 57.4	13 22.2	27 52.9	22 27.7	23 59.2
11 S	13 19 57.0	18 5.1	27 30.0	20 25.9	2 10.5	2 49.0	24 20.6	20 10.4	13 29.6	27 56.0	22 28.9	24 1.6
12 M	13 23 53.5	19 4.5	27 26.8	4♈49.4	1 26.1	3 56.4	24 56.4	20 23.4	13 36.9	27 59.0	22 30.1	24 4.0
13 T	13 27 50.1	20 3.9	27 23.6	19 34.5	0 33.9	5 3.6	25 32.1	20 36.5	13 44.3	28 2.2	22 31.4	24 6.4
14 W	13 31 46.6	21 3.3	27 20.4	4♉32.9	29♎34.7	6 10.7	26 7.7	20 49.5	13 51.7	28 5.3	22 32.7	24 8.8
15 T	13 35 43.2	22 2.8	27 17.3	19 35.1	28 29.4	7 17.6	26 43.3	21 2.5	13 59.0	28 8.5	22 34.0	24 11.2
16 F	13 39 39.7	23 2.3	27 14.1	4♊31.6	27 19.5	8 24.3	27 18.7	21 15.6	14 6.3	28 11.7	22 35.4	24 13.6
17 S	13 43 36.3	24 1.8	27 10.9	19 14.3	26 6.5	9 30.9	27 54.2	21 28.6	14 13.6	28 14.9	22 36.7	24 16.0
18 S	13 47 32.8	25 1.3	27 7.7	3♋38.0	24 52.5	10 37.3	28 29.5	21 41.6	14 20.9	28 18.1	22 38.1	24 18.4
19 M	13 51 29.4	26 0.9	27 4.5	17 40.5	23 39.6	11 43.6	29 4.8	21 54.6	14 28.2	28 21.4	22 39.5	24 20.8
20 T	13 55 26.0	27 0.6	27 1.4	1♌21.7	22 30.0	12 49.6	29 39.9	22 7.6	14 35.4	28 24.7	22 41.0	24 23.2
21 W	13 59 22.5	28 0.3	26 58.2	14 43.3	21 25.7	13 55.5	0♍15.0	22 20.6	14 42.7	28 28.0	22 42.5	24 25.6
22 T	14 3 19.1	28 60.0	26 55.0	27 47.7	20 28.7	15 1.3	0 50.1	22 33.7	14 49.9	28 31.3	22 44.0	24 28.0
23 F	14 7 15.6	29 59.7	26 51.8	10♍37.7	19 40.6	16 6.8	1 25.0	22 46.6	14 57.1	28 34.7	22 45.5	24 30.4
24 S	14 11 12.2	0♏59.5	26 48.7	23 15.4	19 2.5	17 12.1	1 59.9	22 59.6	15 4.3	28 38.0	22 47.0	24 32.8
25 S	14 15 8.7	1 59.4	26 45.5	5♎42.6	18 35.4	18 17.3	2 34.7	23 12.6	15 11.5	28 41.4	22 48.6	24 35.2
26 M	14 19 5.3	2 59.2	26 42.3	18 0.7	18 19.7	19 22.2	3 9.4	23 25.6	15 18.7	28 44.9	22 50.2	24 37.6
27 T	14 23 1.8	3 59.1	26 39.1	0♏10.6	18 15.4	20 27.0	3 44.0	23 38.5	15 25.8	28 48.3	22 51.8	24 40.0
28 W	14 26 58.4	4 59.0	26 35.9	12 13.1	18D22.3	21 31.5	4 18.6	23 51.4	15 32.9	28 51.8	22 53.5	24 42.4
29 T	14 30 54.9	5 59.0	26 32.8	24 9.2	18 39.9	22 35.7	4 53.0	24 4.3	15 40.0	28 55.3	22 55.2	24 44.7
30 F	14 34 51.5	6 59.0	26 29.6	6♐ 0.3	19 7.6	23 39.8	5 27.4	24 17.2	15 47.0	28 58.8	22 56.8	24 47.1
31 S	14 38 48.0	7 59.0	26 26.4	17 48.6	19 44.4	24 43.6	6 1.6	24 30.1	15 54.1	29 2.3	22 58.6	24 49.5
DECLINATION at NOON												
1 T	12 40 31.4	3S15.7	20N33.4	11S54.0	15S36.5	19S53.0	16N32.2	6S 3.4	2S48.6	19S24.8	21S55.5	6N14.8
4 S	12 52 21.1	4 25.3	20 35.3	20 4.9	16 4.4	20 56.0	15 59.7	6 18.2	2 57.2	19 26.7	21 55.8	6 12.0
7 W	13 4 10.8	5 34.5	20 37.2	20 35.2	16 4.4	21 54.6	15 26.6	6 33.0	3 5.7	19 28.7	21 56.1	6 9.2
10 S	13 16 0.4	6 43.0	20 39.1	12 1.1	15 29.5	22 48.6	14 53.0	6 47.8	3 14.2	19 30.8	21 56.5	6 6.5
13 T	13 27 50.1	7 50.7	20 41.0	3N 4.2	14 14.7	23 37.6	14 18.8	7 2.6	3 22.7	19 32.9	21 56.8	6 3.8
16 F	13 39 39.7	8 57.4	20 42.8	17 6.5	12 22.0	24 21.5	13 44.1	7 17.2	3 31.0	19 35.0	21 57.2	6 1.2
19 M	13 51 29.4	10 2.9	20 44.7	21 26.4	10 7.1	25 0.0	13 9.1	7 31.8	3 39.3	19 37.2	21 57.5	5 58.7
22 T	14 3 19.1	11 7.2	20 46.5	14 38.6	7 58.9	25 33.0	12 33.7	7 46.3	3 47.5	19 39.5	21 57.9	5 56.3
25 S	14 15 8.7	12 9.9	20 48.3	2 1.0	6 26.1	26 0.4	11 58.0	8 0.7	3 55.6	19 41.7	21 58.3	5 53.9
28 W	14 26 58.4	13 11.0	20 50.2	10S55.6	5 44.0	26 22.0	11 22.1	8 15.0	4 3.6	19 44.0	21 58.6	5 51.7
31 S	14 38 48.0	14 10.3	20 52.0	19 48.5	5 52.1	26 37.8	10 46.0	8 29.1	4 11.5	19 46.4	21 59.0	5 49.5

NOVEMBER 1981

LONGITUDE at NOON

DAY	EPHEMERIS SIDEREAL TIME	☉	☊	☽	☿	♀	♂	♃	♄	♅	♆	♇
	h m s	° ′	° ′	° ′	° ′	° ′	° ′	° ′	° ′	° ′	° ′	° ′
1 S	14 42 44.6	8♏59.0	26♋23.2	29♐36.9	20♎29.7	25♐47.1	6♍35.8	24♎43.0	16♎ 1.1	29♏ 5.8	23♐ 0.3	24♎51.8
2 M	14 46 41.2	9 59.1	26 20.1	11♑28.9	21 22.4	26 50.4	7 9.9	24 55.8	16 8.0	29 9.4	23 2.1	24 54.2
3 T	14 50 37.7	10 59.3	26 16.9	23 29.1	22 21.9	27 53.4	7 43.9	25 8.6	16 15.0	29 13.0	23 3.9	24 56.5
4 W	14 54 34.3	11 59.4	26 13.7	5♒42.4	23 27.1	28 56.1	8 17.8	25 21.4	16 21.9	29 16.6	23 5.7	24 58.9
5 T	14 58 30.8	12 59.5	26 10.5	18 14.1	24 37.4	29 58.5	8 51.6	25 34.2	16 28.8	29 20.2	23 7.5	25 1.2
6 F	15 2 27.4	13 59.7	26 7.4	1♓ 9.4	25 52.0	1♑ 0.6	9 25.3	25 46.9	16 35.6	29 23.8	23 9.4	25 3.5
7 S	15 6 23.9	14 59.9	26 4.2	14 32.5	27 10.4	2 2.3	9 58.9	25 59.6	16 42.4	29 27.4	23 11.2	25 5.8
8 S	15 10 20.5	16 0.2	26 1.0	28 25.8	28 31.9	3 3.7	10 32.4	26 12.2	16 49.2	29 31.0	23 13.1	25 8.1
9 M	15 14 17.0	17 0.4	25 57.8	12♈49.2	29 56.1	4 4.8	11 5.8	26 24.9	16 55.9	29 34.6	23 15.0	25 10.3
10 T	15 18 13.6	18 0.7	25 54.6	27 38.9	1♏22.5	5 5.5	11 39.1	26 37.5	17 2.6	29 38.3	23 16.9	25 12.6
11 W	15 22 10.2	19 1.0	25 51.5	12♉47.6	2 50.7	6 5.8	12 12.4	26 50.0	17 9.3	29 42.0	23 18.9	25 14.9
12 T	15 26 6.7	20 1.3	25 48.3	28 5.2	4 20.5	7 5.8	12 45.5	27 2.5	17 15.9	29 45.6	23 20.8	25 17.1
13 F	15 30 3.3	21 1.7	25 45.1	13♊20.3	5 51.5	8 5.3	13 18.5	27 15.0	17 22.4	29 49.3	23 22.8	25 19.3
14 S	15 33 59.8	22 2.1	25 41.9	28 22.5	7 23.5	9 4.4	13 51.3	27 27.5	17 28.9	29 53.0	23 24.8	25 21.5
15 S	15 37 56.4	23 2.5	25 38.8	13♋ 4.1	8 56.3	10 3.0	14 24.1	27 39.9	17 35.4	29 56.7	23 26.8	25 23.7
16 M	15 41 52.9	24 3.0	25 35.6	27 20.4	10 29.7	11 1.3	14 56.8	27 52.2	17 41.9	0♐ 0.4	23 28.8	25 25.9
17 T	15 45 49.5	25 3.4	25 32.4	11♌10.3	12 3.6	11 59.0	15 29.4	28 4.6	17 48.2	0 4.1	23 30.9	25 28.1
18 W	15 49 46.0	26 4.0	25 29.2	24 35.0	13 37.8	12 56.3	16 1.8	28 16.8	17 54.6	0 7.8	23 32.9	25 30.2
19 T	15 53 42.6	27 4.5	25 26.0	7♍37.2	15 12.4	13 53.1	16 34.2	28 29.1	18 0.9	0 11.5	23 35.0	25 32.3
20 F	15 57 39.2	28 5.1	25 22.9	20 20.4	16 47.1	14 49.4	17 6.4	28 41.3	18 7.1	0 15.2	23 37.1	25 34.5
21 S	16 1 35.7	29 5.7	25 19.7	2♎48.3	18 21.9	15 45.1	17 38.5	28 53.4	18 13.3	0 18.9	23 39.1	25 36.6
22 S	16 5 32.3	0♐ 6.3	25 16.5	15 4.1	19 56.8	16 40.2	18 10.5	29 5.5	18 19.4	0 22.6	23 41.3	25 38.6
23 M	16 9 28.8	1 7.0	25 13.3	27 10.8	21 31.7	17 34.8	18 42.3	29 17.5	18 25.5	0 26.3	23 43.4	25 40.7
24 T	16 13 25.4	2 7.7	25 10.2	9♏10.7	23 6.7	18 28.9	19 14.1	29 29.6	18 31.6	0 30.1	23 45.6	25 42.8
25 W	16 17 21.9	3 8.4	25 7.0	21 5.5	24 41.5	19 22.2	19 45.7	29 41.5	18 37.5	0 33.8	23 47.7	25 44.8
26 T	16 21 18.5	4 9.2	25 3.8	2♐57.0	26 16.3	20 14.9	20 17.1	29 53.4	18 43.4	0 37.5	23 49.9	25 46.8
27 F	16 25 15.0	5 9.9	25 0.6	14 46.6	27 51.1	21 7.0	20 48.4	0♏ 5.2	18 49.3	0 41.2	23 52.0	25 48.8
28 S	16 29 11.6	6 10.7	24 57.5	26 36.1	29 25.8	21 58.3	21 19.6	0 16.9	18 55.1	0 44.9	23 54.2	25 50.8
29 S	16 33 8.2	7 11.5	24 54.3	8♑27.3	1♐ 0.4	22 48.8	21 50.6	0 28.6	19 0.8	0 48.6	23 56.4	25 52.7
30 M	16 37 4.7	8 12.3	24 51.1	20 23.1	2 34.9	23 38.6	22 21.5	0 40.2	19 6.5	0 52.3	23 58.6	25 54.6

DECLINATION at NOON

DAY	EPHEMERIS SIDEREAL TIME	☉	☊	☽	☿	♀	♂	♃	♄	♅	♆	♇
1 S	14 42 44.6	14S29.6	20N52.6	21S14.1	6S 4.3	26S41.8	10N33.9	8S33.8	4S14.1	19S47.1	21S59.1	5N48.8
4 W	14 54 34.3	15 26.0	20 54.4	19 43.4	7 3.4	26 49.9	9 57.7	8 47.7	4 21.8	19 49.5	21 59.5	5 46.8
7 S	15 6 23.9	16 20.2	20 56.2	9 37.2	8 26.5	26 52.2	9 21.4	9 1.5	4 29.3	19 51.9	21 59.9	5 44.9
10 T	15 18 13.6	17 11.9	20 57.9	5N55.6	10 3.7	26 48.9	8 45.2	9 15.0	4 36.6	19 54.2	22 0.3	5 43.0
13 F	15 30 3.3	18 0.9	20 59.7	19 5.3	11 47.6	26 40.0	8 9.0	9 28.4	4 43.8	19 56.6	22 0.7	5 41.3
16 M	15 41 52.9	18 47.1	21 1.5	20 57.2	13 33.0	26 25.9	7 32.9	9 41.5	4 50.8	19 59.0	22 1.1	5 39.8
19 T	15 53 42.6	19 30.3	21 3.2	11 57.6	15 16.3	26 6.7	6 57.0	9 54.5	4 57.6	20 1.4	22 1.4	5 38.3
22 S	16 5 32.3	20 10.4	21 5.0	1S17.6	16 55.2	25 42.7	6 21.4	10 7.2	5 4.2	20 3.7	22 1.8	5 36.9
25 W	16 17 21.9	20 47.2	21 6.7	13 39.5	18 28.0	25 14.4	5 46.0	10 19.7	5 10.6	20 6.1	22 2.2	5 35.7
28 S	16 29 11.6	21 20.4	21 8.4	21 5.5	19 53.4	24 41.9	5 10.9	10 31.9	5 16.7	20 8.4	22 2.5	5 34.6

DECEMBER 1981

LONGITUDE at NOON

DAY	EPHEMERIS SIDEREAL TIME	☉	☊	☽	☿	♀	♂	♃	♄	♅	♆	♇
1 T	16 41 1.3	9♐13.1	24♋47.9	2♒26.6	4♐ 9.3	24♑27.6	22♍52.2	0♏51.8	19♎12.1	0♐56.0	24♐ 0.8	25♎56.5
2 W	16 44 57.8	10 14.0	24 44.7	14 41.5	5 43.7	25 15.8	23 22.8	1 3.3	19 17.6	0 59.7	24 3.0	25 58.4
3 T	16 48 54.4	11 14.8	24 41.6	27 12.3	7 18.0	26 3.0	23 53.3	1 14.7	19 23.1	1 3.4	24 5.2	26 0.2
4 F	16 52 50.9	12 15.7	24 38.4	10♓ 3.2	8 52.3	26 49.4	24 23.5	1 26.0	19 28.5	1 7.0	24 7.4	26 2.0
5 S	16 56 47.5	13 16.6	24 35.2	23 18.3	10 26.5	27 34.7	24 53.7	1 37.3	19 33.8	1 10.7	24 9.7	26 3.8
6 S	17 0 44.1	14 17.5	24 32.0	7♈ 0.7	12 0.7	28 19.1	25 23.6	1 48.5	19 39.1	1 14.3	24 11.9	26 5.6
7 M	17 4 40.6	15 18.4	24 28.9	21 11.4	13 34.9	29 2.5	25 53.4	1 59.7	19 44.3	1 18.0	24 14.1	26 7.4
8 T	17 8 37.2	16 19.3	24 25.7	5♉49.0	15 9.1	29 44.7	26 23.1	2 10.7	19 49.4	1 21.6	24 16.4	26 9.1
9 W	17 12 33.7	17 20.3	24 22.5	20 48.5	16 43.4	0♒25.8	26 52.5	2 21.7	19 54.5	1 25.2	24 18.6	26 10.8
10 T	17 16 30.3	18 21.2	24 19.3	6♊ 2.0	18 17.6	1 5.7	27 21.8	2 32.6	19 59.5	1 28.8	24 20.9	26 12.5
11 F	17 20 26.9	19 22.2	24 16.2	21 19.3	19 51.9	1 44.4	27 51.0	2 43.4	20 4.4	1 32.4	24 23.1	26 14.1
12 S	17 24 23.4	20 23.2	24 13.0	6♋29.6	21 26.3	2 21.8	28 19.9	2 54.1	20 9.2	1 35.9	24 25.4	26 15.7
13 S	17 28 20.0	21 24.1	24 9.8	21 23.5	23 0.8	2 57.9	28 48.7	3 4.8	20 14.0	1 39.5	24 27.7	26 17.3
14 M	17 32 16.5	22 25.1	24 6.6	5♌54.0	24 35.3	3 32.6	29 17.3	3 15.4	20 18.6	1 43.0	24 29.9	26 18.9
15 T	17 36 13.1	23 26.2	24 3.5	19 57.6	26 10.0	4 5.9	29 45.8	3 25.9	20 23.3	1 46.6	24 32.2	26 20.5
16 W	17 40 9.6	24 27.3	24 0.3	3♍33.4	27 44.8	4 37.7	0♎14.0	3 36.3	20 27.8	1 50.1	24 34.5	26 22.0
17 T	17 44 6.2	25 28.3	23 57.1	16 42.8	29 19.8	5 8.0	0 42.0	3 46.6	20 32.2	1 53.6	24 36.8	26 23.5
18 F	17 48 2.8	26 29.4	23 53.9	29 29.2	0♑54.8	5 36.6	1 9.9	3 56.8	20 36.6	1 57.1	24 39.0	26 24.9
19 S	17 51 59.3	27 30.5	23 50.7	11♎56.3	2 30.1	6 3.5	1 37.5	4 6.9	20 40.9	2 0.5	24 41.3	26 26.3
20 S	17 55 55.9	28 31.6	23 47.6	24 8.4	4 5.5	6 28.8	2 4.9	4 16.9	20 45.1	2 4.0	24 43.6	26 27.7
21 M	17 59 52.4	29 32.7	23 44.4	6♏ 9.7	5 41.0	6 52.2	2 32.1	4 26.8	20 49.2	2 7.4	24 45.8	26 29.1
22 T	18 3 49.0	0♑33.8	23 41.2	18 3.8	7 16.8	7 13.8	2 59.1	4 36.7	20 53.2	2 10.8	24 48.1	26 30.4
23 W	18 7 45.5	1 34.9	23 38.0	29 54.1	8 52.7	7 33.5	3 25.9	4 46.4	20 57.1	2 14.1	24 50.4	26 31.7
24 T	18 11 42.1	2 36.1	23 34.9	11♐43.3	10 28.8	7 51.2	3 52.4	4 56.0	21 1.0	2 17.5	24 52.6	26 33.0
25 F	18 15 38.7	3 37.2	23 31.7	23 33.9	12 5.0	8 6.8	4 18.7	5 5.5	21 4.8	2 20.8	24 54.9	26 34.2
26 S	18 19 35.2	4 38.4	23 28.5	5♑27.7	13 41.3	8 20.3	4 44.7	5 14.9	21 8.4	2 24.1	24 57.1	26 35.4
27 S	18 23 31.8	5 39.5	23 25.3	17 26.6	15 17.8	8 31.6	5 10.6	5 24.2	21 12.0	2 27.3	24 59.3	26 36.6
28 M	18 27 28.3	6 40.7	23 22.2	29 32.4	16 54.3	8 40.7	5 36.1	5 33.4	21 15.5	2 30.6	25 1.6	26 37.7
29 T	18 31 24.9	7 41.9	23 19.0	11♒47.1	18 30.9	8 47.5	6 1.4	5 42.5	21 18.9	2 33.8	25 3.8	26 38.8
30 W	18 35 21.4	8 43.0	23 15.8	24 12.9	20 7.4	8 51.9	6 26.5	5 51.4	21 22.2	2 37.0	25 6.0	26 39.9
31 T	18 39 18.0	9 44.2	23 12.6	6♓52.2	21 43.9	8 53.9	6 51.3	6 0.3	21 25.4	2 40.1	25 8.2	26 40.9

DECLINATION at NOON

DAY	EPHEMERIS SIDEREAL TIME	☉	☊	☽	☿	♀	♂	♃	♄	♅	♆	♇
1 T	16 41 1.3	21S50.0	21N10.1	20S25.9	21S10.3	24S 5.9	4N36.3	10S43.8	5S22.6	20S10.7	22S 2.9	5N33.7
4 F	16 52 50.9	22 15.9	21 11.8	11 18.4	22 18.1	23 26.6	4 2.2	10 55.4	5 28.3	20 13.0	22 3.2	5 32.9
7 M	17 4 40.6	22 37.8	21 13.5	3N27.5	23 15.9	22 44.7	3 28.6	11 6.7	5 33.7	20 15.3	22 3.6	5 32.2
10 T	17 16 30.3	22 55.8	21 15.2	17 34.8	24 3.1	22 0.5	2 55.6	11 17.7	5 38.8	20 17.5	22 3.9	5 31.6
13 S	17 28 20.0	23 9.7	21 16.9	21 37.3	24 39.2	21 14.8	2 23.1	11 28.4	5 43.6	20 19.7	22 4.2	5 31.2
16 W	17 40 9.6	23 19.4	21 18.5	13 23.8	25 3.4	20 28.0	1 51.4	11 38.7	5 48.2	20 21.8	22 4.5	5 30.9
19 S	17 51 59.3	23 25.0	21 20.2	0 1.2	25 15.2	19 40.8	1 20.4	11 48.7	5 52.4	20 23.9	22 4.8	5 30.7
22 T	18 3 49.0	23 26.3	21 21.8	12S39.6	25 14.1	18 53.7	0 50.2	11 58.3	5 56.4	20 26.0	22 5.1	5 30.7
25 F	18 15 38.7	23 23.4	21 23.4	20 44.5	24 59.6	18 7.6	0 20.9	12 7.6	6 0.0	20 28.0	22 5.3	5 30.9
28 M	18 27 28.3	23 16.3	21 25.1	20 53.4	24 31.3	17 23.0	0S 7.4	12 16.4	6 3.3	20 29.9	22 5.6	5 31.1
31 T	18 39 18.0	23 5.0	21 26.7	12 25.8	23 49.1	16 40.7	0 34.7	12 24.9	6 6.3	20 31.8	22 5.8	5 31.5

JANUARY 1982

DAY	EPHEMERIS SIDEREAL TIME	☉	☊	☽	☿	♀	♂	♃	♄	♅	♆	♇
	h m s	° ′	° ′	° ′	° ′	° ′	° ′	° ′	° ′	° ′	° ′	° ′
LONGITUDE at NOON												
1 F	18 43 14.6	10♑45.3	23♋ 9.4	19♓47.6	23♑20.2	8♒53.5	7♎15.8	6♏ 9.0	21♎28.5	2♐43.3	25♐10.4	26♎41.9
2 S	18 47 11.1	11 46.5	23 6.3	3♈ 1.7	24 56.2	8R50.5	7 40.0	6 17.6	21 31.5	2 46.4	25 12.6	26 42.9
3 S	18 51 7.7	12 47.7	23 3.1	16 36.6	26 31.9	8 45.1	8 4.0	6 26.1	21 34.4	2 49.4	25 14.8	26 43.8
4 M	18 55 4.2	13 48.8	22 59.9	0♉33.5	28 7.1	8 37.1	8 27.6	6 34.4	21 37.2	2 52.5	25 17.0	26 44.7
5 T	18 59 0.8	14 50.0	22 56.7	14 52.0	29 41.7	8 26.6	8 51.1	6 42.7	21 40.0	2 55.5	25 19.2	26 45.6
6 W	19 2 57.3	15 51.1	22 53.6	29 29.6	1♒15.4	8 13.6	9 14.1	6 50.8	21 42.6	2 58.5	25 21.4	26 46.5
7 T	19 6 53.9	16 52.3	22 50.4	14♊21.7	2 48.0	7 58.0	9 36.9	6 58.8	21 45.2	3 1.4	25 23.5	26 47.3
8 F	19 10 50.5	17 53.4	22 47.2	29 21.3	4 19.2	7 40.0	9 59.4	7 6.7	21 47.6	3 4.3	25 25.6	26 48.0
9 S	19 14 47.0	18 54.5	22 44.0	14♋20.2	5 48.8	7 19.7	10 21.6	7 14.4	21 49.9	3 7.2	25 27.8	26 48.8
10 S	19 18 43.6	19 55.6	22 40.9	29 9.9	7 16.4	6 57.0	10 43.4	7 22.0	21 52.1	3 10.1	25 29.9	26 49.5
11 M	19 22 40.1	20 56.7	22 37.7	13♌42.9	8 41.5	6 32.1	11 4.9	7 29.4	21 54.3	3 12.9	25 32.0	26 50.1
12 T	19 26 36.7	21 57.8	22 34.5	27 53.5	10 3.7	6 5.2	11 26.1	7 36.7	21 56.3	3 15.6	25 34.1	26 50.7
13 W	19 30 33.2	22 58.9	22 31.3	11♍38.6	11 22.4	5 36.3	11 46.9	7 43.9	21 58.2	3 18.3	25 36.1	26 51.3
14 T	19 34 29.8	24 0.0	22 28.2	24 57.4	12 37.0	5 5.7	12 7.4	7 51.0	22 0.0	3 21.0	25 38.2	26 51.9
15 F	19 38 26.4	25 1.1	22 25.0	7♎51.5	13 46.9	4 33.5	12 27.5	7 57.9	22 1.8	3 23.7	25 40.2	26 52.4
16 S	19 42 22.9	26 2.2	22 21.8	20 23.8	14 51.3	3 59.9	12 47.3	8 4.6	22 3.4	3 26.3	25 42.2	26 52.9
17 S	19 46 19.5	27 3.3	22 18.6	2♏38.3	15 49.4	3 25.2	13 6.7	8 11.2	22 4.9	3 28.9	25 44.3	26 53.3
18 M	19 50 16.0	28 4.4	22 15.4	14 39.7	16 40.3	2 49.6	13 25.7	8 17.7	22 6.3	3 31.4	25 46.2	26 53.7
19 T	19 54 12.6	29 5.5	22 12.3	26 32.5	17 23.3	2 13.2	13 44.2	8 24.0	22 7.6	3 33.9	25 48.2	26 54.1
20 W	19 58 9.1	0♒ 6.6	22 9.1	8♐21.4	17 57.3	1 36.5	14 2.4	8 30.2	22 8.8	3 36.4	25 50.2	26 54.4
21 T	20 2 5.7	1 7.7	22 5.9	20 10.5	18 21.6	0 59.6	14 20.2	8 36.2	22 9.8	3 38.8	25 52.1	26 54.7
22 F	20 6 2.3	2 8.7	22 2.7	2♑ 3.4	18 35.4	0 22.7	14 37.5	8 42.0	22 10.8	3 41.1	25 54.0	26 55.0
23 S	20 9 58.8	3 9.8	21 59.6	14 3.2	18 38.2	29♑46.2	14 54.4	8 47.7	22 11.7	3 43.5	25 55.9	26 55.2
24 S	20 13 55.4	4 10.8	21 56.4	26 12.2	18R29.6	29 10.2	15 10.9	8 53.3	22 12.4	3 45.8	25 57.8	26 55.4
25 M	20 17 51.9	5 11.8	21 53.2	8♒32.3	18 9.4	28 35.1	15 26.9	8 58.7	22 13.1	3 48.0	25 59.7	26 55.5
26 T	20 21 48.5	6 12.9	21 50.0	21 4.6	17 38.0	28 1.1	15 42.5	9 3.9	22 13.7	3 50.2	26 1.6	26 55.7
27 W	20 25 45.0	7 13.9	21 46.9	3♓49.8	16 55.8	27 28.3	15 57.5	9 9.0	22 14.1	3 52.4	26 3.4	26 55.8
28 T	20 29 41.6	8 14.9	21 43.7	16 48.3	16 4.0	26 56.9	16 12.1	9 13.9	22 14.5	3 54.5	26 5.2	26 55.8
29 F	20 33 38.1	9 15.8	21 40.5	0♈ 0.4	15 3.8	26 27.2	16 26.2	9 18.6	22 14.7	3 56.5	26 7.0	26 55.8
30 S	20 37 34.7	10 16.8	21 37.3	13 26.0	13 57.1	25 59.3	16 39.8	9 23.2	22 14.8	3 58.6	26 8.8	26 55.8
31 S	20 41 31.3	11 17.7	21 34.1	27 5.3	12 45.8	25 33.4	16 52.8	9 27.6	22 14.8	4 0.5	26 10.5	26R55.7
DECLINATION at NOON												
1 F	18 43 14.6	23S 0.3	21N27.2	8S 8.3	23S32.0	16S27.3	0S43.6	12S27.6	6S 7.2	20S32.4	22S 5.9	5N31.7
4 M	18 55 4.2	22 43.4	21 28.8	6N45.4	22 31.5	15 49.2	1 9.5	12 35.6	6 9.7	20 34.2	22 6.1	5 32.3
7 T	19 6 53.9	22 22.5	21 30.4	19 16.5	21 18.3	15 15.0	1 34.2	12 43.1	6 11.9	20 35.9	22 6.3	5 33.0
10 S	19 18 43.6	21 57.7	21 32.0	20 56.1	19 54.1	14 45.3	1 57.8	12 50.1	6 13.8	20 37.6	22 6.5	5 33.8
13 W	19 30 33.2	21 29.0	21 33.5	10 54.4	18 22.4	14 20.5	2 20.0	12 56.7	6 15.3	20 39.2	22 6.7	5 34.8
16 S	19 42 22.9	20 56.5	21 35.1	3S 3.7	16 48.7	14 1.0	2 40.9	13 2.9	6 16.4	20 40.7	22 6.9	5 35.8
19 T	19 54 12.6	20 20.5	21 36.6	15 6.7	15 21.2	13 46.9	3 0.4	13 8.6	6 17.2	20 42.2	22 7.0	5 37.0
22 F	20 6 2.3	19 41.0	21 38.2	21 34.4	14 10.4	13 38.0	3 18.3	13 13.9	6 17.6	20 43.5	22 7.2	5 38.4
25 M	20 17 51.9	18 58.2	21 39.7	19 32.4	13 27.1	13 34.1	3 34.6	13 18.6	6 17.7	20 44.8	22 7.3	5 39.8
28 T	20 29 41.6	18 12.3	21 41.2	9 9.3	13 18.0	13 34.7	3 49.3	13 22.9	6 17.4	20 46.1	22 7.4	5 41.3
31 S	20 41 31.3	17 23.4	21 42.7	5N32.4	13 41.7	13 39.3	4 2.2	13 26.7	6 16.8	20 47.2	22 7.5	5 42.9

FEBRUARY 1982

DAY	EPHEMERIS SIDEREAL TIME	☉	☊	☽	☿	♀	♂	♃	♄	♅	♆	♇
LONGITUDE at NOON												
1 M	20 45 27.8	12♒18.6	21♋31.0	10♉57.9	11♒32.0	25♑ 9.6	17♎ 5.4	9♏31.8	22♎14.7	4♐ 2.4	26♐12.2	26♎55.6
2 T	20 49 24.4	13 19.5	21 27.8	25 3.2	10R17.9	24R48.0	17 17.4	9 35.9	22R14.5	4 4.3	26 13.9	26R55.5
3 W	20 53 20.9	14 20.3	21 24.6	9♊20.0	9 5.6	24 28.7	17 28.9	9 39.7	22 14.2	4 6.1	26 15.6	26 55.3
4 T	20 57 17.5	15 21.2	21 21.4	23 45.9	7 56.9	24 11.7	17 39.8	9 43.4	22 13.8	4 7.9	26 17.2	26 55.1
5 F	21 1 14.0	16 22.0	21 18.3	8♋17.6	6 53.3	23 57.2	17 50.2	9 47.0	22 13.3	4 9.6	26 18.8	26 54.9
6 S	21 5 10.6	17 22.8	21 15.1	22 50.4	5 56.1	23 45.1	17 60.0	9 50.3	22 12.7	4 11.3	26 20.4	26 54.6
7 S	21 9 7.1	18 23.5	21 11.9	7♌18.8	5 6.2	23 35.5	18 9.2	9 53.5	22 11.9	4 12.9	26 22.0	26 54.3
8 M	21 13 3.7	19 24.3	21 8.7	21 37.0	4 24.2	23 28.4	18 17.8	9 56.5	22 11.1	4 14.5	26 23.5	26 53.9
9 T	21 17 0.3	20 25.0	21 5.5	5♍39.7	3 50.3	23 23.9	18 25.8	9 59.4	22 10.2	4 16.0	26 25.0	26 53.5
10 W	21 20 56.8	21 25.7	21 2.4	19 22.6	3 24.7	23 21.7	18 33.2	10 2.0	22 9.1	4 17.5	26 26.5	26 53.1
11 T	21 24 53.4	22 26.3	20 59.2	2♎43.4	3 7.2	23D22.1	18 40.0	10 4.5	22 8.0	4 18.9	26 28.0	26 52.7
12 F	21 28 49.9	23 27.0	20 56.0	15 41.5	2 57.5	23 24.9	18 46.1	10 6.8	22 6.7	4 20.3	26 29.4	26 52.2
13 S	21 32 46.5	24 27.6	20 52.8	28 18.2	2 55.3	23 30.0	18 51.6	10 8.9	22 5.4	4 21.6	26 30.9	26 51.7
14 S	21 36 43.0	25 28.3	20 49.7	10♏36.4	3D 0.2	23 37.4	18 56.4	10 10.8	22 3.9	4 22.9	26 32.2	26 51.1
15 M	21 40 39.6	26 28.9	20 46.5	22 40.0	3 11.7	23 47.2	19 0.6	10 12.5	22 2.4	4 24.1	26 33.6	26 50.5
16 T	21 44 36.1	27 29.5	20 43.3	4♐34.0	3 29.5	23 59.1	19 4.1	10 14.1	22 0.8	4 25.3	26 35.0	26 50.0
17 W	21 48 32.7	28 30.1	20 40.1	16 23.2	3 53.1	24 13.2	19 6.8	10 15.5	21 59.0	4 26.5	26 36.3	26 49.3
18 T	21 52 29.2	29 30.6	20 36.9	28 12.8	4 21.9	24 29.3	19 8.8	10 16.7	21 57.2	4 27.5	26 37.6	26 48.6
19 F	21 56 25.8	0♓31.1	20 33.8	10♑ 7.8	4 55.7	24 47.5	19 10.2	10 17.6	21 55.2	4 28.5	26 38.8	26 47.9
20 S	22 0 22.3	1 31.6	20 30.6	22 12.4	5 34.0	25 7.6	19 10.7	10 18.4	21 53.2	4 29.5	26 40.0	26 47.2
21 S	22 4 18.9	2 32.1	20 27.4	4♒30.3	6 16.6	25 29.6	19R10.6	10 19.0	21 51.0	4 30.4	26 41.2	26 46.4
22 M	22 8 15.5	3 32.5	20 24.2	17 3.9	7 3.0	25 53.3	19 9.7	10 19.5	21 48.8	4 31.2	26 42.4	26 45.6
23 T	22 12 12.0	4 32.9	20 21.1	29 54.7	7 52.9	26 18.9	19 8.0	10 19.7	21 46.5	4 32.0	26 43.5	26 44.7
24 W	22 16 8.6	5 33.3	20 17.9	13♓ 2.7	8 46.2	26 46.0	19 5.6	10 19.7	21 44.1	4 32.8	26 44.6	26 43.9
25 T	22 20 5.1	6 33.7	20 14.7	26 26.6	9 42.5	27 14.9	19 2.4	10R19.6	21 41.6	4 33.5	26 45.6	26 43.0
26 F	22 24 1.7	7 34.0	20 11.5	10♈ 4.4	10 41.6	27 45.2	18 58.5	10 19.2	21 39.0	4 34.1	26 46.7	26 42.0
27 S	22 27 58.2	8 34.3	20 8.3	23 53.2	11 43.4	28 17.0	18 53.7	10 18.7	21 36.3	4 34.7	26 47.7	26 41.1
28 S	22 31 54.8	9 34.6	20 5.2	7♉50.1	12 47.7	28 50.3	18 48.2	10 18.0	21 33.5	4 35.2	26 48.6	26 40.1
DECLINATION at NOON												
1 M	20 45 27.8	17S 6.5	21N43.2	10N22.4	13S55.2	13S41.5	4S 6.1	13S27.8	6S16.5	20S47.5	22S 7.5	5N43.5
4 T	20 57 17.5	16 14.0	21 44.7	20 46.6	14 45.7	13 50.1	4 16.6	13 30.9	6 15.4	20 48.6	22 7.6	5 45.2
7 S	21 9 7.1	15 19.0	21 46.2	19 45.3	15 40.6	14 0.8	4 25.1	13 33.5	6 13.9	20 49.5	22 7.6	5 47.0
10 W	21 20 56.8	14 21.6	21 47.7	8 14.4	16 30.6	14 12.8	4 31.6	13 35.6	6 12.2	20 50.4	22 7.7	5 49.0
13 S	21 32 46.5	13 22.1	21 49.1	6S 1.6	17 10.8	14 25.2	4 36.1	13 37.2	6 10.0	20 51.1	22 7.7	5 50.9
16 T	21 44 36.1	12 20.7	21 50.6	17 16.8	17 39.0	14 37.1	4 38.4	13 38.2	6 7.6	20 51.8	22 7.7	5 53.0
19 F	21 56 25.8	11 17.4	21 52.0	21 59.2	17 54.5	14 48.1	4 38.5	13 38.8	6 4.9	20 52.4	22 7.7	5 55.1
22 M	22 8 15.5	10 12.5	21 53.5	17 49.0	17 57.1	14 57.3	4 36.2	13 38.8	6 1.8	20 52.9	22 7.7	5 57.2
25 T	22 20 5.1	9 6.3	21 54.9	5 40.8	17 47.1	15 4.2	4 31.7	13 38.2	5 58.5	20 53.3	22 7.7	5 59.4
28 S	22 31 54.8	7 58.8	21 56.3	9N27.8	17 24.4	15 8.4	4 24.7	13 37.2	5 54.9	20 53.6	22 7.7	6 1.7

MARCH 1982

DAY	EPHEMERIS SIDEREAL TIME (h m s)	☉ (° ′)	☊ (° ′)	☽ (° ′)	☿ (° ′)	♀ (° ′)	♂ (° ′)	♃ (° ′)	♄ (° ′)	♅ (° ′)	♆ (° ′)	♇ (° ′)
LONGITUDE at NOON												
1 M	22 35 51.3	10♓34.8	20♋ 2.0	21♉52.4	13♒54.2	29♑24.9	18♎42.0	10♏17.1	21♎30.6	4♐35.7	26♐49.6	26♎39.1
2 T	22 39 47.9	11 35.0	19 58.8	5♊58.1	15 3.0	0♒ 0.9	18R34.9	10R16.0	21R27.7	4 36.1	26 50.5	26R38.0
3 W	22 43 44.4	12 35.2	19 55.6	20 5.6	16 13.7	0 38.1	18 27.1	10 14.7	21 24.7	4 36.4	26 51.4	26 37.0
4 T	22 47 41.0	13 35.3	19 52.5	4♋13.6	17 26.4	1 16.6	18 18.5	10 13.2	21 21.6	4 36.7	26 52.2	26 35.9
5 F	22 51 37.5	14 35.4	19 49.3	18 20.9	18 40.9	1 56.2	18 9.1	10 11.6	21 18.4	4 37.0	26 53.0	26 34.7
6 S	22 55 34.1	15 35.5	19 46.1	2♌25.8	19 57.1	2 37.0	17 59.0	10 9.7	21 15.1	4 37.2	26 53.8	26 33.6
7 S	22 59 30.6	16 35.5	19 42.9	16 26.0	21 15.0	3 18.8	17 48.1	10 7.7	21 11.8	4 37.3	26 54.6	26 32.4
8 M	23 3 27.2	17 35.5	19 39.7	0♍18.6	22 34.5	4 1.7	17 36.4	10 5.5	21 8.4	4 37.4	26 55.3	26 31.2
9 T	23 7 23.8	18 35.5	19 36.6	14 0.3	23 55.6	4 45.7	17 24.1	10 3.2	21 5.0	4 37.5	26 56.0	26 30.1
10 W	23 11 20.3	19 35.5	19 33.4	27 27.9	25 18.2	5 30.6	17 11.0	10 0.6	21 1.4	4 37.5	26 56.6	26 28.8
11 T	23 15 16.9	20 35.4	19 30.2	10♎38.7	26 42.2	6 16.4	16 57.1	9 57.8	20 57.8	4R37.4	26 57.3	26 27.5
12 F	23 19 13.4	21 35.2	19 27.0	23 31.3	28 7.5	7 3.1	16 42.6	9 54.9	20 54.1	4 37.3	26 57.8	26 26.2
13 S	23 23 10.0	22 35.1	19 23.9	6♏ 5.9	29 34.3	7 50.7	16 27.3	9 51.8	20 50.4	4 37.1	26 58.4	26 24.9
14 S	23 27 6.5	23 34.9	19 20.7	18 23.8	1♓ 2.4	8 39.1	16 11.3	9 48.5	20 46.6	4 36.9	26 58.9	26 23.6
15 M	23 31 3.1	24 34.6	19 17.5	0♐27.9	2 31.8	9 28.3	15 54.7	9 45.1	20 42.7	4 36.6	26 59.4	26 22.2
16 T	23 34 59.6	25 34.4	19 14.3	12 22.3	4 2.6	10 18.2	15 37.4	9 41.5	20 38.8	4 36.3	26 59.8	26 20.9
17 W	23 38 56.2	26 34.1	19 11.1	24 11.6	5 34.6	11 8.9	15 19.5	9 37.7	20 34.8	4 35.9	27 0.3	26 19.5
18 T	23 42 52.7	27 33.8	19 8.0	6♑ 1.2	7 7.9	12 0.3	15 1.0	9 33.7	20 30.8	4 35.5	27 0.7	26 18.1
19 F	23 46 49.3	28 33.5	19 4.8	17 56.6	8 42.6	12 52.4	14 41.9	9 29.6	20 26.7	4 35.0	27 1.0	26 16.6
20 S	23 50 45.8	29 33.1	19 1.6	0♒ 3.1	10 18.4	13 45.1	14 22.3	9 25.3	20 22.5	4 34.4	27 1.3	26 15.2
21 S	23 54 42.4	0♈32.7	18 58.4	12 25.4	11 55.6	14 38.5	14 2.1	9 20.8	20 18.3	4 33.8	27 1.6	26 13.7
22 M	23 58 38.9	1 32.3	18 55.3	25 7.4	13 34.1	15 32.4	13 41.5	9 16.2	20 14.1	4 33.2	27 1.9	26 12.2
23 T	0 2 35.5	2 31.8	18 52.1	8♓11.4	15 13.8	16 26.9	13 20.4	9 11.4	20 9.8	4 32.5	27 2.1	26 10.7
24 W	0 6 32.0	3 31.3	18 48.9	21 37.9	16 54.8	17 22.0	12 58.9	9 6.5	20 5.5	4 31.7	27 2.2	26 9.2
25 T	0 10 28.6	4 30.8	18 45.7	5♈25.3	18 37.1	18 17.6	12 37.0	9 1.4	20 1.2	4 30.9	27 2.4	26 7.7
26 F	0 14 25.1	5 30.3	18 42.5	19 30.0	20 20.8	19 13.7	12 14.8	8 56.2	19 56.8	4 30.1	27 2.5	26 6.1
27 S	0 18 21.7	6 29.7	18 39.4	3♉46.7	22 5.7	20 10.3	11 52.4	8 50.8	19 52.3	4 29.2	27 2.6	26 4.5
28 S	0 22 18.2	7 29.1	18 36.2	18 9.5	23 52.0	21 7.3	11 29.6	8 45.3	19 47.9	4 28.2	27 2.6	26 3.0
29 M	0 26 14.8	8 28.4	18 33.0	2♊32.9	25 39.7	22 4.8	11 6.7	8 39.7	19 43.4	4 27.2	27 2.7	26 1.4
30 T	0 30 11.4	9 27.7	18 29.8	16 52.4	27 28.7	23 2.8	10 43.7	8 33.9	19 38.9	4 26.2	27 2.7	25 59.8
31 W	0 34 7.9	10 27.0	18 26.7	1♋ 5.0	29 19.1	24 1.1	10 20.5	8 28.0	19 34.4	4 25.2	27R 2.6	25 58.2

DAY	EPHEMERIS SIDEREAL TIME (h m s)	☉	☊	☽	☿	♀	♂	♃	♄	♅	♆	♇
DECLINATION at NOON												
1 M	22 35 51.3	7S36.0	21N56.8	13N57.9	17S14.1	15S 9.1	4S21.9	13S36.7	5S53.6	20S53.7	22S 7.7	6N 2.4
4 T	22 47 41.0	6 27.2	21 58.2	21 52.5	16 35.0	15 9.0	4 11.9	13 35.0	5 49.7	20 53.9	22 7.6	6 4.7
7 S	22 59 30.6	5 17.6	21 59.5	17 59.8	15 43.8	15 5.4	3 59.6	13 32.7	5 45.5	20 54.0	22 7.6	6 7.0
10 W	23 11 20.3	4 7.3	22 0.9	5 17.1	14 40.8	14 57.8	3 45.1	13 30.0	5 41.1	20 54.0	22 7.5	6 9.3
13 S	23 23 10.0	2 56.6	22 2.3	8S56.8	13 26.2	14 46.2	3 28.7	13 26.7	5 36.6	20 54.0	22 7.4	6 11.6
16 T	23 34 59.6	1 45.6	22 3.6	19 11.9	12 0.2	14 30.5	3 10.3	13 23.0	5 31.8	20 53.8	22 7.4	6 13.9
19 F	23 46 49.3	0 34.4	22 5.0	22 3.6	10 23.0	14 10.4	2 50.3	13 18.8	5 26.9	20 53.6	22 7.3	6 16.2
22 M	23 58 38.9	0N36.7	22 6.3	15 53.9	8 35.0	13 46.0	2 29.0	13 14.2	5 21.9	20 53.3	22 7.2	6 18.4
25 T	0 10 28.6	1 47.6	22 7.6	2 19.2	6 36.3	13 17.3	2 6.6	13 9.1	5 16.7	20 52.9	22 7.1	6 20.6
28 S	0 22 18.2	2 58.2	22 8.9	13N 1.4	4 27.4	12 44.4	1 43.7	13 3.7	5 11.5	20 52.4	22 7.0	6 22.8
31 W	0 34 7.9	4 8.3	22 10.2	21 54.7	2 8.8	12 7.3	1 20.7	12 57.9	5 6.2	20 51.8	22 6.9	6 25.0

APRIL 1982

DAY	EPHEMERIS SIDEREAL TIME (h m s)	☉	☊	☽	☿	♀	♂	♃	♄	♅	♆	♇
LONGITUDE at NOON												
1 T	0 38 4.5	11♈26.2	18♋23.5	15♋ 8.9	1♈10.8	24♒59.9	9♎57.3	8♏22.0	19♎29.8	4♐24.0	27♐ 2.5	25♎56.6
2 F	0 42 1.0	12 25.4	18 20.3	29 3.9	3 3.9	25 59.0	9R34.0	8R15.8	19R25.3	4R22.8	27R 2.4	25R55.0
3 S	0 45 57.6	13 24.5	18 17.1	12♌49.8	4 58.4	26 58.6	9 10.8	8 9.6	19 20.7	4 21.6	27 2.3	25 53.3
4 S	0 49 54.1	14 23.7	18 13.9	26 26.5	6 54.2	27 58.5	8 47.6	8 3.2	19 16.1	4 20.3	27 2.1	25 51.7
5 M	0 53 50.7	15 22.7	18 10.8	9♍53.8	8 51.4	28 58.7	8 24.6	7 56.7	19 11.5	4 19.0	27 1.9	25 50.0
6 T	0 57 47.2	16 21.7	18 7.6	23 10.8	10 49.9	29 59.3	8 1.7	7 50.1	19 6.8	4 17.7	27 1.6	25 48.4
7 W	1 1 43.8	17 20.7	18 4.4	6♎16.3	12 49.7	1♓ 0.3	7 39.0	7 43.4	19 2.2	4 16.3	27 1.3	25 46.7
8 T	1 5 40.3	18 19.7	18 1.2	19 8.9	14 50.8	2 1.5	7 16.6	7 36.6	18 57.6	4 14.8	27 1.0	25 45.0
9 F	1 9 36.9	19 18.6	17 58.1	1♏47.9	16 53.0	3 3.1	6 54.4	7 29.8	18 52.9	4 13.3	27 0.7	25 43.3
10 S	1 13 33.4	20 17.5	17 54.9	14 12.9	18 56.3	4 5.0	6 32.6	7 22.8	18 48.3	4 11.8	27 0.3	25 41.7
11 S	1 17 30.0	21 16.4	17 51.7	26 24.9	21 0.6	5 7.1	6 11.1	7 15.8	18 43.7	4 10.2	26 59.9	25 40.0
12 M	1 21 26.5	22 15.2	17 48.5	8♐25.8	23 5.7	6 9.6	5 50.0	7 8.6	18 39.1	4 8.6	26 59.5	25 38.3
13 T	1 25 23.1	23 14.0	17 45.3	20 18.4	25 11.5	7 12.3	5 29.3	7 1.4	18 34.4	4 7.0	26 59.0	25 36.6
14 W	1 29 19.6	24 12.8	17 42.2	2♑ 6.7	27 17.8	8 15.3	5 9.2	6 54.2	18 29.8	4 5.3	26 58.5	25 34.9
15 T	1 33 16.2	25 11.5	17 39.0	13 55.6	29 24.4	9 18.6	4 49.5	6 46.8	18 25.2	4 3.5	26 58.0	25 33.2
16 F	1 37 12.8	26 10.2	17 35.8	25 50.1	1♉31.1	10 22.1	4 30.3	6 39.5	18 20.7	4 1.8	26 57.4	25 31.5
17 S	1 41 9.3	27 8.9	17 32.6	7♒56.0	3 37.5	11 25.8	4 11.7	6 32.0	18 16.1	3 60.0	26 56.8	25 29.8
18 S	1 45 5.9	28 7.6	17 29.5	20 18.4	5 43.4	12 29.8	3 53.7	6 24.5	18 11.6	3 58.1	26 56.2	25 28.1
19 M	1 49 2.4	29 6.2	17 26.3	3♓ 2.2	7 48.5	13 34.0	3 36.4	6 17.0	18 7.1	3 56.3	26 55.5	25 26.4
20 T	1 52 59.0	0♉ 4.9	17 23.1	16 11.0	9 52.5	14 38.5	3 19.7	6 9.5	18 2.6	3 54.4	26 54.9	25 24.8
21 W	1 56 55.5	1 3.4	17 19.9	29 46.4	11 54.9	15 43.1	3 3.6	6 1.9	17 58.1	3 52.5	26 54.2	25 23.1
22 T	2 0 52.1	2 2.0	17 16.7	13♈47.6	13 55.6	16 47.9	2 48.2	5 54.3	17 53.7	3 50.5	26 53.4	25 21.4
23 F	2 4 48.6	3 0.5	17 13.6	28 11.1	15 54.2	17 52.9	2 33.6	5 46.6	17 49.3	3 48.5	26 52.7	25 19.7
24 S	2 8 45.2	3 59.0	17 10.4	12♉50.7	17 50.3	18 58.1	2 19.6	5 38.9	17 44.9	3 46.5	26 51.9	25 18.1
25 S	2 12 41.7	4 57.4	17 7.2	27 38.7	19 43.7	20 3.5	2 6.5	5 31.3	17 40.6	3 44.4	26 51.1	25 16.4
26 M	2 16 38.3	5 55.9	17 4.0	12♊26.7	21 34.2	21 9.0	1 54.1	5 23.6	17 36.3	3 42.3	26 50.2	25 14.7
27 T	2 20 34.8	6 54.2	17 0.9	27 7.5	23 21.5	22 14.7	1 42.4	5 15.9	17 32.1	3 40.2	26 49.3	25 13.1
28 W	2 24 31.4	7 52.6	16 57.7	11♋35.9	25 5.4	23 20.6	1 31.6	5 8.3	17 27.9	3 38.1	26 48.4	25 11.4
29 T	2 28 27.9	8 50.9	16 54.5	25 48.6	26 45.6	24 26.7	1 21.5	5 0.6	17 23.7	3 35.9	26 47.5	25 9.8
30 F	2 32 24.5	9 49.2	16 51.3	9♌44.5	28 22.2	25 32.8	1 12.2	4 53.0	17 19.6	3 33.7	26 46.5	25 8.2

DAY	EPHEMERIS SIDEREAL TIME (h m s)	☉	☊	☽	☿	♀	♂	♃	♄	♅	♆	♇
DECLINATION at NOON												
1 T	0 38 4.5	4N31.5	22N10.7	22N16.5	1S20.6	11S54.0	1S13.0	12S55.9	5S 4.4	20S51.6	22S 6.9	6N25.7
4 S	0 49 54.1	5 40.5	22 12.0	15 36.6	1N 9.9	11 11.6	0 50.5	12 49.6	4 59.1	20 50.9	22 6.7	6 27.7
7 W	1 1 43.8	6 48.7	22 13.2	2 0.4	3 47.7	10 25.4	0 28.9	12 43.0	4 53.8	20 50.2	22 6.6	6 29.7
10 S	1 13 33.4	7 55.8	22 14.5	11S49.8	6 31.1	9 35.6	0 8.5	12 36.2	4 48.5	20 49.4	22 6.5	6 31.7
13 T	1 25 23.1	9 1.7	22 15.8	20 49.3	9 17.0	8 42.3	0N10.1	12 29.2	4 43.3	20 48.5	22 6.4	6 33.5
16 F	1 37 12.8	10 6.3	22 17.0	21 44.8	12 1.4	7 45.8	0 26.8	12 22.0	4 38.2	20 47.5	22 6.2	6 35.3
19 M	1 49 2.4	11 9.4	22 18.2	13 47.2	14 39.1	6 46.3	0 41.2	12 14.6	4 33.1	20 46.5	22 6.1	6 37.0
22 T	2 0 52.1	12 10.8	22 19.5	0N48.6	17 4.5	5 44.0	0 53.2	12 7.2	4 28.2	20 45.5	22 6.0	6 38.6
25 S	2 12 41.7	13 10.5	22 20.7	15 57.7	19 12.5	4 39.3	1 2.5	11 59.7	4 23.5	20 44.3	22 5.8	6 40.0
28 W	2 24 31.4	14 8.2	22 21.9	22 34.1	20 59.7	3 32.5	1 9.0	11 52.2	4 18.9	20 43.2	22 5.7	6 41.4

MAY 1982

DAY	EPHEMERIS SIDEREAL TIME	☉	☊	☽	☿	♀	♂	♃	♄	♅	♆	♇
	h m s	° ′	° ′	° ′	° ′	° ′	° ′	° ′	° ′	° ′	° ′	° ′
						LONGITUDE at NOON						
1 S	2 36 21.1	10♉47.4	16♋48.1	23♌24.0	29♉54.8	26♓39.2	1♎ 3.8	4♏45.4	17♎15.5	3♐31.5	26♐45.5	25♎ 6.5
2 S	2 40 17.6	11 45.6	16 45.0	6♍48.1	1♊23.5	27 45.7	0R56.1	4R37.8	17R11.5	3R29.2	26R44.5	25R 4.9
3 M	2 44 14.2	12 43.8	16 41.8	19 58.1	2 48.0	28 52.3	0 49.2	4 30.3	17 7.6	3 27.0	26 43.5	25 3.3
4 T	2 48 10.7	13 42.0	16 38.6	2♎55.2	4 8.4	29 59.0	0 43.2	4 22.7	17 3.7	3 24.7	26 42.4	25 1.7
5 W	2 52 7.3	14 40.1	16 35.4	15 40.2	5 24.4	1♈ 5.9	0 37.9	4 15.3	16 59.8	3 22.4	26 41.4	25 0.2
6 T	2 56 3.8	15 38.2	16 32.3	28 13.7	6 36.2	2 13.0	0 33.4	4 7.9	16 56.1	3 20.0	26 40.3	24 58.6
7 F	3 0 0.4	16 36.2	16 29.1	10♏36.2	7 43.5	3 20.1	0 29.7	4 0.5	16 52.4	3 17.7	26 39.1	24 57.1
8 S	3 3 56.9	17 34.2	16 25.9	22 48.5	8 46.3	4 27.4	0 26.8	3 53.2	16 48.7	3 15.3	26 38.0	24 55.5
9 S	3 7 53.5	18 32.2	16 22.7	4♐51.4	9 44.5	5 34.8	0 24.7	3 46.0	16 45.1	3 12.9	26 36.8	24 54.0
10 M	3 11 50.1	19 30.2	16 19.5	16 46.5	10 38.1	6 42.4	0 23.3	3 38.8	16 41.6	3 10.6	26 35.6	24 52.5
11 T	3 15 46.6	20 28.2	16 16.4	28 36.2	11 27.1	7 50.1	0 22.8	3 31.8	16 38.2	3 8.2	26 34.5	24 51.1
12 W	3 19 43.2	21 26.1	16 13.2	10♑23.5	12 11.4	8 57.9	0D23.0	3 24.8	16 34.8	3 5.8	26 33.2	24 49.6
13 T	3 23 39.7	22 24.1	16 10.0	22 12.1	12 50.8	10 5.7	0 23.9	3 17.8	16 31.5	3 3.3	26 32.0	24 48.1
14 F	3 27 36.3	23 21.9	16 6.8	4♒ 6.6	13 25.4	11 13.7	0 25.5	3 11.0	16 28.2	3 0.9	26 30.7	24 46.7
15 S	3 31 32.8	24 19.8	16 3.7	16 11.7	13 55.0	12 21.9	0 27.9	3 4.2	16 25.1	2 58.4	26 29.4	24 45.3
16 S	3 35 29.4	25 17.6	16 0.5	28 32.7	14 19.8	13 30.1	0 31.1	2 57.5	16 22.0	2 56.0	26 28.1	24 43.9
17 M	3 39 25.9	26 15.5	15 57.3	11♓14.5	14 39.7	14 38.4	0 34.9	2 51.0	16 19.0	2 53.5	26 26.7	24 42.5
18 T	3 43 22.5	27 13.3	15 54.1	24 21.3	14 54.6	15 46.8	0 39.5	2 44.5	16 16.0	2 51.0	26 25.4	24 41.1
19 W	3 47 19.1	28 11.1	15 51.0	7♈55.8	15 4.6	16 55.3	0 44.7	2 38.2	16 13.2	2 48.5	26 24.0	24 39.8
20 T	3 51 15.6	29 8.8	15 47.8	21 58.6	15 9.8	18 3.9	0 50.7	2 31.9	16 10.4	2 46.1	26 22.6	24 38.4
21 F	3 55 12.2	0♊ 6.6	15 44.6	6♉27.5	15 10.2	19 12.6	0 57.3	2 25.8	16 7.7	2 43.6	26 21.2	24 37.1
22 S	3 59 8.7	1 4.3	15 41.4	21 17.3	15R 5.9	20 21.3	1 4.6	2 19.8	16 5.1	2 41.1	26 19.8	24 35.9
23 S	4 3 5.3	2 2.0	15 38.2	6♊20.0	14 57.2	21 30.2	1 12.6	2 13.9	16 2.6	2 38.6	26 18.4	24 34.6
24 M	4 7 1.8	2 59.7	15 35.1	21 26.4	14 44.2	22 39.1	1 21.3	2 8.2	16 0.1	2 36.1	26 16.9	24 33.4
25 T	4 10 58.4	3 57.3	15 31.9	6♋27.1	14 27.3	23 48.1	1 30.5	2 2.5	15 57.8	2 33.6	26 15.5	24 32.2
26 W	4 14 55.0	4 55.0	15 28.7	21 14.3	14 6.6	24 57.2	1 40.5	1 57.1	15 55.5	2 31.1	26 14.0	24 31.0
27 T	4 18 51.5	5 52.6	15 25.5	5♌42.6	13 42.6	26 6.3	1 51.0	1 51.7	15 53.4	2 28.6	26 12.5	24 29.8
28 F	4 22 48.1	6 50.2	15 22.4	19 49.1	13 15.8	27 15.6	2 2.2	1 46.5	15 51.3	2 26.1	26 11.0	24 28.7
29 S	4 26 44.6	7 47.7	15 19.2	3♍33.0	12 46.5	28 24.9	2 13.9	1 41.4	15 49.3	2 23.6	26 9.5	24 27.5
30 S	4 30 41.2	8 45.3	15 16.0	16 55.4	12 15.2	29 34.2	2 26.2	1 36.5	15 47.4	2 21.1	26 8.0	24 26.5
31 M	4 34 37.7	9 42.8	15 12.8	29 58.2	11 42.6	0♉43.7	2 39.2	1 31.8	15 45.6	2 18.6	26 6.5	24 25.4
						DECLINATION at NOON						
1 S	2 36 21.1	15N 3.8	22N23.1	16N39.2	22N24.6	2S 23.7	1N12.7	11S 44.8	4S 14.5	20S 41.9	22S 5.5	6N42.7
4 T	2 48 10.7	15 57.1	22 24.2	3 22.7	23 27.1	1 13.3	1 13.7	11 37.5	4 10.3	20 40.6	22 5.4	6 43.8
7 F	3 0 0.4	16 48.1	22 25.4	10S 39.2	24 8.4	0 1.5	1 11.9	11 30.3	4 6.4	20 39.3	22 5.2	6 44.9
10 M	3 11 50.1	17 36.5	22 26.6	20 24.5	24 29.9	1N11.4	1 7.4	11 23.4	4 2.7	20 38.0	22 5.1	6 45.8
13 T	3 23 39.7	18 22.3	22 27.7	22 17.6	24 33.4	2 25.0	1 0.4	11 16.7	3 59.3	20 36.6	22 4.9	6 46.5
16 S	3 35 29.4	19 5.3	22 28.9	15 20.4	24 20.3	3 39.2	0 50.9	11 10.2	3 56.1	20 35.2	22 4.8	6 47.2
19 W	3 47 19.1	19 45.4	22 30.0	1 33.3	23 52.3	4 53.6	0 39.0	11 4.1	3 53.3	20 33.8	22 4.6	6 47.7
22 S	3 59 8.7	20 22.5	22 31.1	14N 6.9	23 10.9	6 7.8	0 24.9	10 58.4	3 50.7	20 32.4	22 4.5	6 48.1
25 T	4 10 58.4	20 56.5	22 32.2	22 36.8	22 18.6	7 21.7	0 8.6	10 53.0	3 48.5	20 31.0	22 4.3	6 48.3
28 F	4 22 48.1	21 27.2	22 33.3	17 46.3	21 18.5	8 34.8	0S 9.7	10 48.1	3 46.6	20 29.5	22 4.2	6 48.4
31 M	4 34 37.7	21 54.5	22 34.4	4 38.6	20 15.1	9 46.9	0 30.0	10 43.6	3 45.1	20 28.1	22 4.0	6 48.4

JUNE 1982

DAY	EPHEMERIS SIDEREAL TIME	☉	☊	☽	☿	♀	♂	♃	♄	♅	♆	♇
						LONGITUDE at NOON						
1 T	4 38 34.3	10♊40.4	15♋ 9.7	12♎44.0	11♊ 9.2	1♉53.2	2♎52.7	1♏27.2	15♎44.0	2♐16.2	26♐ 5.0	24♎24.4
2 W	4 42 30.8	11 37.8	15 6.5	25 15.1	10R35.6	3 2.8	3 6.7	1R22.7	15R42.4	2R13.8	26R 3.4	24R23.4
3 T	4 46 27.4	12 35.3	15 3.3	7♏34.1	10 2.2	4 12.4	3 21.3	1 18.4	15 40.8	2 11.3	26 1.8	24 22.4
4 F	4 50 24.0	13 32.7	15 0.1	19 42.9	9 29.9	5 22.1	3 36.4	1 14.3	15 39.4	2 8.9	26 0.3	24 21.5
5 S	4 54 20.5	14 30.1	14 56.9	1♐43.6	8 58.9	6 31.9	3 52.0	1 10.3	15 38.1	2 6.5	25 58.7	24 20.5
6 S	4 58 17.1	15 27.5	14 53.8	13 38.1	8 30.0	7 41.7	4 8.1	1 6.5	15 36.9	2 4.1	25 57.1	24 19.6
7 M	5 2 13.6	16 24.9	14 50.6	25 28.2	8 3.5	8 51.6	4 24.7	1 2.8	15 35.7	2 1.7	25 55.5	24 18.7
8 T	5 6 10.2	17 22.3	14 47.4	7♑16.0	7 40.0	10 1.6	4 41.8	0 59.4	15 34.7	1 59.3	25 53.9	24 17.9
9 W	5 10 6.8	18 19.7	14 44.2	19 4.1	7 19.7	11 11.6	4 59.4	0 56.0	15 33.8	1 56.9	25 52.3	24 17.1
10 T	5 14 3.3	19 17.0	14 41.1	0♒55.2	7 3.1	12 21.7	5 17.5	0 52.9	15 32.9	1 54.6	25 50.7	24 16.3
11 F	5 17 59.9	20 14.4	14 37.9	12 52.7	6 50.4	13 31.8	5 36.0	0 49.9	15 32.2	1 52.2	25 49.1	24 15.5
12 S	5 21 56.4	21 11.7	14 34.7	25 0.6	6 41.8	14 42.0	5 55.0	0 47.1	15 31.6	1 49.9	25 47.5	24 14.8
13 S	5 25 53.0	22 9.0	14 31.5	7♓22.7	6 37.5	15 52.3	6 14.4	0 44.4	15 31.0	1 47.6	25 45.9	24 14.1
14 M	5 29 49.5	23 6.3	14 28.4	20 3.4	6D37.6	17 2.6	6 34.2	0 42.0	15 30.6	1 45.4	25 44.3	24 13.4
15 T	5 33 46.1	24 3.6	14 25.2	3♈ 6.5	6 42.3	18 13.0	6 54.5	0 39.7	15 30.2	1 43.1	25 42.6	24 12.8
16 W	5 37 42.7	25 0.9	14 22.0	16 35.2	6 51.5	19 23.4	7 15.2	0 37.5	15 30.0	1 40.9	25 41.0	24 12.2
17 T	5 41 39.2	25 58.2	14 18.8	0♉30.9	7 5.4	20 33.9	7 36.3	0 35.6	15 29.8	1 38.7	25 39.4	24 11.6
18 F	5 45 35.8	26 55.5	14 15.6	14 53.0	7 23.8	21 44.5	7 57.8	0 33.8	15 29.8	1 36.5	25 37.8	24 11.1
19 S	5 49 32.3	27 52.8	14 12.5	29 38.2	7 46.8	22 55.1	8 19.7	0 32.3	15D29.9	1 34.3	25 36.2	24 10.6
20 S	5 53 28.9	28 50.1	14 9.3	14♊40.5	8 14.4	24 5.8	8 42.0	0 30.9	15 30.0	1 32.2	25 34.5	24 10.1
21 M	5 57 25.4	29 47.4	14 6.1	29 51.5	8 46.5	25 16.5	9 4.7	0 29.6	15 30.3	1 30.1	25 32.9	24 9.6
22 T	6 1 22.0	0♋44.7	14 2.9	15♋ 1.6	9 23.0	26 27.3	9 27.8	0 28.6	15 30.7	1 28.1	25 31.3	24 9.3
23 W	6 5 18.6	1 42.0	13 59.8	0♌ 1.6	10 3.9	27 38.1	9 51.2	0 27.8	15 31.1	1 26.0	25 29.7	24 8.9
24 T	6 9 15.1	2 39.2	13 56.6	14 43.9	10 49.0	28 48.9	10 15.0	0 27.1	15 31.7	1 24.0	25 28.1	24 8.5
25 F	6 13 11.7	3 36.5	13 53.4	29 3.2	11 38.4	29 59.8	10 39.2	0 26.6	15 32.4	1 22.0	25 26.5	24 8.2
26 S	6 17 8.2	4 33.7	13 50.2	12♍56.9	12 32.0	1♊10.8	11 3.7	0 26.3	15 33.1	1 20.1	25 24.9	24 7.9
27 S	6·21 4.8	5 30.9	13 47.1	26 24.9	13 29.6	2 21.8	11 28.6	0 26.2	15 34.0	1 18.1	25 23.3	24 7.7
28 M	6 25 1.3	6 28.1	13 43.9	9♎28.7	14 31.4	3 32.8	11 53.8	0 26.2	15 35.0	1 16.2	25 21.7	24 7.5
29 T	6 28 57.9	7 25.4	13 40.7	22 11.3	15 37.1	4 43.9	12 19.3	0D26.4	15 36.0	1 14.4	25 20.2	24 7.3
30 W	6 32 54.5	8 22.6	13 37.5	4♏36.2	16 46.8	5 55.0	12 45.2	0 26.8	15 37.2	1 12.6	25 18.6	24 7.1
						DECLINATION at NOON						
1 T	4 38 34.3	22N 2.9	22N34.7	0S 14.3	19N54.2	10N10.7	0S 37.2	10S 42.3	3S 44.6	20S 27.6	22S 4.0	6N48.3
4 F	4 50 24.0	22 25.6	22 35.8	13 36.4	18 55.2	11 20.9	0 59.8	10 38.5	3 43.5	20 26.2	22 3.8	6 48.1
7 M	5 2 13.6	22 44.8	22 36.9	21 44.9	18 6.3	12 29.4	1 24.0	10 35.2	3 42.8	20 24.8	22 3.7	6 47.7
10 T	5 14 3.3	23 0.5	22 37.9	21 30.1	17 31.8	13 35.9	1 49.8	10 32.4	3 42.4	20 23.4	22 3.5	6 47.2
13 S	5 25 53.0	23 12.5	22 38.9	12 45.2	17 14.3	14 40.1	2 17.0	10 30.2	3 42.3	20 22.1	22 3.4	6 46.6
16 W	5 37 42.7	23 20.8	22 40.0	1N39.6	17 14.4	15 41.5	2 45.5	10 28.6	3 42.6	20 20.8	22 3.2	6 45.8
19 S	5 49 32.3	23 25.4	22 41.0	16 30.4	17 31.0	16 40.0	3 15.3	10 27.5	3 43.3	20 19.5	22 3.1	6 44.9
22 T	6 1 22.0	23 26.3	22 42.0	22 45.0	18 1.7	17 35.2	3 46.2	10 27.0	3 44.3	20 18.3	22 3.0	6 43.9
25 F	6 13 11.7	23 23.5	22 43.0	15 21.2	18 43.7	18 26.7	4 18.2	10 27.0	3 45.7	20 17.1	22 2.9	6 42.7
28 M	6 25 1.3	23 17.0	22 44.0	1 6.0	19 33.7	19 14.4	4 51.2	10 27.6	3 47.4	20 15.9	22 2.7	6 41.4

JULY 1982

DAY	EPHEMERIS SIDEREAL TIME	☉	☊	☽	☿	♀	♂	♃	♄	♅	♆	♇
	h m s	° ′	° ′	° ′	° ′	° ′	° ′	° ′	° ′	° ′	° ′	° ′
LONGITUDE at NOON												
1 T	6 36 51.0	9♋19.7	13♋34.4	16♏47.0	18♊ 0.3	7♊ 6.2	13♎11.3	0♏27.4	15♎38.4	1♐10.8	25♐17.0	24♎ 7.0
2 F	6 40 47.6	10 16.9	13 31.2	28 47.3	19 17.8	8 17.4	13 37.8	0 28.2	15 39.8	1R 9.0	25R15.5	24R 6.9
3 S	6 44 44.1	11 14.1	13 28.0	10♐40.6	20 39.0	9 28.6	14 4.6	0 29.1	15 41.2	1 7.3	25 13.9	24 6.9
4 S	6 48 40.7	12 11.3	13 24.8	22 29.8	22 4.0	10 39.9	14 31.6	0 30.3	15 42.8	1 5.6	25 12.4	24 6.9
5 M	6 52 37.3	13 8.5	13 21.6	4♑17.7	23 32.6	11 51.3	14 59.0	0 31.6	15 44.4	1 4.0	25 10.9	24 6.9
6 T	6 56 33.8	14 5.7	13 18.5	16 6.6	25 5.0	13 2.7	15 26.6	0 33.0	15 46.2	1 2.4	25 9.4	24 6.9
7 W	7 0 30.4	15 2.8	13 15.3	27 58.9	26 40.8	14 14.2	15 54.5	0 34.7	15 48.0	1 0.8	25 7.8	24D 7.0
8 T	7 4 26.9	16 0.0	13 12.1	9♒56.9	28 20.2	15 25.7	16 22.7	0 36.5	15 49.9	0 59.3	25 6.4	24 7.1
9 F	7 8 23.5	16 57.2	13 8.9	22 2.7	0♋ 3.0	16 37.2	16 51.2	0 38.5	15 52.0	0 57.8	25 4.9	24 7.3
10 S	7 12 20.0	17 54.4	13 5.8	4♓18.9	1 49.1	17 48.8	17 19.9	0 40.7	15 54.1	0 56.4	25 3.4	24 7.5
11 S	7 16 16.6	18 51.6	13 2.6	16 48.2	3 38.3	19 0.4	17 48.9	0 43.0	15 56.3	0 55.0	25 2.0	24 7.7
12 M	7 20 13.2	19 48.8	12 59.4	29 33.1	5 30.4	20 12.1	18 18.2	0 45.6	15 58.6	0 53.6	25 0.5	24 8.0
13 T	7 24 9.7	20 46.1	12 56.2	12♈36.6	7 25.5	21 23.9	18 47.7	0 48.3	16 1.1	0 52.3	24 59.1	24 8.3
14 W	7 28 6.3	21 43.3	12 53.1	26 0.9	9 23.0	22 35.7	19 17.5	0 51.2	16 3.6	0 51.1	24 57.7	24 8.6
15 T	7 32 2.8	22 40.5	12 49.9	9♉47.6	11 22.9	23 47.6	19 47.5	0 54.2	16 6.1	0 49.8	24 56.3	24 9.0
16 F	7 35 59.4	23 37.8	12 46.7	23 57.1	13 24.8	24 59.5	20 17.7	0 57.4	16 8.8	0 48.7	24 55.0	24 9.4
17 S	7 39 55.9	24 35.0	12 43.5	8♊28.0	15 28.5	26 11.4	20 48.2	1 0.8	16 11.6	0 47.5	24 53.6	24 9.8
18 S	7 43 52.5	25 32.3	12 40.3	23 16.6	17 33.6	27 23.4	21 19.0	1 4.3	16 14.5	0 46.4	24 52.3	24 10.3
19 M	7 47 49.1	26 29.6	12 37.2	8♋17.0	19 39.9	28 35.4	21 50.0	1 8.0	16 17.4	0 45.4	24 50.9	24 10.7
20 T	7 51 45.6	27 26.8	12 34.0	23 21.4	21 47.0	29 47.5	22 21.2	1 11.8	16 20.4	0 44.4	24 49.6	24 11.3
21 W	7 55 42.2	28 24.1	12 30.8	8♌21.1	23 54.7	0♋59.6	22 52.6	1 15.9	16 23.6	0 43.4	24 48.3	24 11.8
22 T	7 59 38.7	29 21.4	12 27.6	23 7.6	26 2.5	2 11.7	23 24.3	1 20.1	16 26.8	0 42.5	24 47.1	24 12.4
23 F	8 3 35.3	0♌18.7	12 24.5	7♍34.0	28 10.3	3 23.9	23 56.2	1 24.4	16 30.1	0 41.6	24 45.8	24 13.1
24 S	8 7 31.8	1 16.1	12 21.3	21 35.6	0♌17.8	4 36.2	24 28.3	1 28.9	16 33.5	0 40.8	24 44.6	24 13.7
25 S	8 11 28.4	2 13.4	12 18.1	5♎10.4	2 24.7	5 48.4	25 0.6	1 33.6	16 36.9	0 40.0	24 43.4	24 14.4
26 M	8 15 24.9	3 10.7	12 14.9	18 18.9	4 30.9	7 0.8	25 33.1	1 38.4	16 40.5	0 39.3	24 42.2	24 15.1
27 T	8 19 21.5	4 8.0	12 11.8	1♏ 3.5	6 36.1	8 13.1	26 5.9	1 43.4	16 44.1	0 38.6	24 41.0	24 15.9
28 W	8 23 18.1	5 5.4	12 8.6	13 27.6	8 40.2	9 25.5	26 38.8	1 48.5	16 47.9	0 38.0	24 39.9	24 16.7
29 T	8 27 14.6	6 2.7	12 5.4	25 35.8	10 43.1	10 38.0	27 11.9	1 53.8	16 51.7	0 37.5	24 38.8	24 17.5
30 F	8 31 11.2	7 0.1	12 2.2	7♐32.7	12 44.7	11 50.5	27 45.3	1 59.3	16 55.6	0 36.9	24 37.7	24 18.4
31 S	8 35 7.7	7 57.5	11 59.0	19 22.7	14 44.9	13 3.0	28 18.8	2 4.8	16 59.5	0 36.5	24 36.6	24 19.3
DECLINATION at NOON												
1 T	6 36 51.0	23N 6.8	22N44.9	12S36.6	20N27.8	19N57.8	5S25.1	10S28.8	3S49.4	20S14.9	22S 2.6	6N40.0
4 S	6 48 40.7	22 52.9	22 45.9	21 20.5	21 21.9	20 36.8	5 59.8	10 30.6	3 51.8	20 13.9	22 2.5	6 38.5
7 W	7 0 30.4	22 35.5	22 46.8	21 52.8	22 11.4	21 11.0	6 35.2	10 32.9	3 54.5	20 12.9	22 2.4	6 36.8
10 S	7 12 20.0	22 14.5	22 47.8	13 45.5	22 51.1	21 40.3	7 11.2	10 35.7	3 57.5	20 12.1	22 2.3	6 35.0
13 T	7 24 9.7	21 50.2	22 48.7	0N 6.5	23 15.7	22 4.4	7 47.8	10 39.1	4 0.9	20 11.3	22 2.3	6 33.1
16 F	7 35 59.4	21 22.4	22 49.6	14 51.9	23 20.4	22 23.1	8 24.9	10 43.0	4 4.5	20 10.6	22 2.2	6 31.1
19 M	7 47 49.1	20 51.4	22 50.5	22 42.9	23 1.7	22 36.3	9 2.5	10 47.4	4 8.5	20 9.9	22 2.1	6 29.0
22 T	7 59 38.7	20 17.2	22 51.4	17 0.0	22 18.8	22 43.8	9 40.3	10 52.4	4 12.7	20 9.4	22 2.1	6 26.8
25 S	8 11 28.4	19 39.9	22 52.3	2 43.8	21 13.0	22 45.5	10 18.5	10 57.8	4 17.3	20 8.9	22 2.0	6 24.6
28 W	8 23 18.1	18 59.8	22 53.2	11S32.2	19 47.5	22 41.4	10 56.9	11 3.6	4 22.0	20 8.6	22 2.0	6 22.2
31 S	8 35 7.7	18 16.8	22 54.0	20 53.5	18 6.5	22 31.4	11 35.4	11 9.9	4 27.1	20 8.3	22 2.0	6 19.7

AUGUST 1982

DAY	EPHEMERIS SIDEREAL TIME	☉	☊	☽	☿	♀	♂	♃	♄	♅	♆	♇
LONGITUDE at NOON												
1 S	8 39 4.3	8♌54.8	11♋55.9	1♑10.2	16♌43.6	14♋15.6	28♎52.5	2♏10.6	17♎ 3.6	0♐36.0	24♐35.6	24♎20.2
2 M	8 43 0.8	9 52.2	11 52.7	12 58.9	18 40.8	15 28.2	29 26.4	2 16.4	17 7.7	0R35.7	24R34.5	24 21.1
3 T	8 46 57.4	10 49.7	11 49.5	24 52.0	20 36.5	16 40.9	0♏ 0.6	2 22.5	17 12.0	0 35.4	24 33.6	24 22.2
4 W	8 50 53.9	11 47.1	11 46.3	6♒52.0	22 30.6	17 53.6	0 34.8	2 28.7	17 16.2	0 35.1	24 32.6	24 23.2
5 T	8 54 50.5	12 44.5	11 43.2	19 1.0	24 23.2	19 6.4	1 9.3	2 35.0	17 20.6	0 34.9	24 31.7	24 24.2
6 F	8 58 47.1	13 42.0	11 40.0	1♓20.5	26 14.1	20 19.2	1 43.9	2 41.4	17 25.0	0 34.7	24 30.7	24 25.3
7 S	9 2 43.6	14 39.4	11 36.8	13 51.6	28 3.5	21 32.0	2 18.7	2 48.0	17 29.5	0 34.6	24 29.8	24 26.4
8 S	9 6 40.2	15 36.9	11 33.6	26 35.4	29 51.3	22 44.9	2 53.7	2 54.7	17 34.1	0 34.5	24 29.0	24 27.6
9 M	9 10 36.7	16 34.4	11 30.5	9♈32.7	1♍37.6	23 57.8	3 28.8	3 1.6	17 38.7	0 34.5	24 28.1	24 28.8
10 T	9 14 33.3	17 32.0	11 27.3	22 44.4	3 22.3	25 10.8	4 4.1	3 8.6	17 43.5	0D34.6	24 27.3	24 30.0
11 W	9 18 29.8	18 29.5	11 24.1	6♉11.2	5 5.4	26 23.8	4 39.6	3 15.7	17 48.3	0 34.6	24 26.5	24 31.2
12 T	9 22 26.4	19 27.1	11 20.9	19 54.0	6 47.1	27 36.9	5 15.3	3 22.9	17 53.1	0 34.8	24 25.7	24 32.5
13 F	9 26 22.9	20 24.7	11 17.7	3♊53.0	8 27.2	28 50.0	5 51.1	3 30.3	17 58.0	0 35.0	24 25.0	24 33.7
14 S	9 30 19.5	21 22.3	11 14.6	18 7.9	10 5.8	0♌ 3.2	6 27.1	3 37.8	18 3.0	0 35.2	24 24.3	24 35.1
15 S	9 34 16.1	22 20.0	11 11.4	2♋37.0	11 43.0	1 16.4	7 3.2	3 45.5	18 8.1	0 35.5	24 23.6	24 36.4
16 M	9 38 12.6	23 17.7	11 8.2	17 16.9	13 18.6	2 29.6	7 39.5	3 53.2	18 13.3	0 35.8	24 23.0	24 37.8
17 T	9 42 9.2	24 15.4	11 5.0	2♌ 2.6	14 52.8	3 42.9	8 16.0	4 1.1	18 18.5	0 36.2	24 22.4	24 39.2
18 W	9 46 5.7	25 13.1	11 1.9	16 47.5	16 25.4	4 56.2	8 52.6	4 9.1	18 23.7	0 36.7	24 21.8	24 40.6
19 T	9 50 2.3	26 10.8	10 58.7	1♍24.3	17 56.6	6 9.6	9 29.4	4 17.3	18 29.1	0 37.2	24 21.2	24 42.1
20 F	9 53 58.8	27 8.6	10 55.5	15 46.0	19 26.3	7 23.0	10 6.3	4 25.5	18 34.4	0 37.7	24 20.7	24 43.6
21 S	9 57 55.4	28 6.4	10 52.3	29 46.9	20 54.5	8 36.5	10 43.4	4 33.9	18 39.9	0 38.3	24 20.2	24 45.1
22 S	10 1 51.9	29 4.2	10 49.1	13♎23.4	22 21.2	9 50.0	11 20.7	4 42.4	18 45.4	0 39.0	24 19.7	24 46.7
23 M	10 5 48.5	0♍ 2.0	10 46.0	26 34.5	23 46.3	11 3.5	11 58.1	4 51.0	18 51.0	0 39.7	24 19.3	24 48.2
24 T	10 9 45.0	0 59.9	10 42.8	9♏21.3	25 9.9	12 17.1	12 35.6	4 59.8	18 56.7	0 40.5	24 18.9	24 49.9
25 W	10 13 41.6	1 57.8	10 39.6	21 46.8	26 31.9	13 30.7	13 13.3	5 8.6	19 2.4	0 41.3	24 18.5	24 51.5
26 T	10 17 38.1	2 55.7	10 36.4	3♐55.2	27 52.2	14 44.3	13 51.2	5 17.5	19 8.1	0 42.2	24 18.2	24 53.2
27 F	10 21 34.7	3 53.6	10 33.3	15 51.6	29 10.9	15 58.0	14 29.1	5 26.6	19 13.9	0 43.1	24 17.9	24 54.9
28 S	10 25 31.3	4 51.6	10 30.1	27 41.2	0♎27.9	17 11.7	15 7.2	5 35.7	19 19.8	0 44.1	24 17.6	24 56.6
29 S	10 29 27.8	5 49.5	10 26.9	9♑29.0	1 43.1	18 25.5	15 45.5	5 45.0	19 25.7	0 45.1	24 17.3	24 58.3
30 M	10 33 24.4	6 47.5	10 23.7	21 20.0	2 56.5	19 39.3	16 23.8	5 54.4	19 31.7	0 46.2	24 17.1	25 0.0
31 T	10 37 20.9	7 45.5	10 20.5	3♒18.3	4 8.0	20 53.1	17 2.3	6 3.8	19 37.7	0 47.3	24 16.9	25 1.8
DECLINATION at NOON												
1 S	8 39 4.3	18N 1.8	22N54.3	22S20.0	17N30.0	22N26.8	11S48.2	11S12.1	4S28.9	20S 8.2	22S 2.0	6N18.9
4 W	8 50 53.9	17 15.3	22 55.2	20 35.3	15 34.2	22 9.0	12 26.7	11 19.0	4 34.3	20 8.1	22 2.0	6 16.3
7 S	9 2 43.6	16 26.2	22 56.0	10 32.5	13 31.2	21 45.5	13 5.1	11 26.3	4 39.9	20 8.0	22 2.0	6 13.7
10 T	9 14 33.3	15 34.8	22 56.8	4N 5.2	11 23.8	21 16.3	13 43.4	11 33.9	4 45.8	20 8.1	22 2.0	6 11.0
13 F	9 26 22.9	14 41.1	22 57.6	17 43.0	9 14.1	20 41.5	14 21.4	11 41.9	4 51.8	20 8.2	22 2.1	6 8.2
16 M	9 38 12.6	13 45.3	22 58.4	22 43.6	7 3.9	20 1.3	14 59.2	11 50.3	4 58.1	20 8.4	22 2.1	6 5.4
19 T	9 50 2.3	12 47.5	22 59.2	14 35.9	4 54.7	19 16.0	15 36.5	11 59.0	5 4.6	20 8.8	22 2.2	6 2.6
22 S	10 1 51.9	11 47.9	23 0.0	0S32.8	2 47.8	18 25.7	16 13.4	12 8.0	5 11.3	20 9.2	22 2.3	5 59.7
25 W	10 13 41.6	10 46.6	23 0.8	14 22.8	0 44.4	17 30.6	16 49.8	12 17.3	5 18.1	20 9.7	22 2.3	5 56.7
28 S	10 25 31.3	9 43.8	23 1.5	22 8.3	1S14.3	16 31.1	17 25.5	12 26.9	5 25.1	20 10.3	22 2.5	5 53.7
31 T	10 37 20.9	8 39.6	23 2.3	21 13.4	3 7.0	15 27.4	18 0.4	12 36.7	5 32.3	20 11.1	22 2.6	5 50.7

SEPTEMBER 1982

LONGITUDE at NOON

DAY	EPHEMERIS SIDEREAL TIME h m s	☉ ° ′	☊ ° ′	☽ ° ′	☿ ° ′	♀ ° ′	♂ ° ′	♃ ° ′	♄ ° ′	♅ ° ′	♆ ° ′	♇ ° ′
1 W	10 41 17.5	8♍43.5	10♋17.4	15♒27.1	5♎17.4	22♌ 7.0	17♏41.0	6♏13.4	19♎43.7	0♐48.4	24♐16.8	25♎ 3.6
2 T	10 45 14.0	9 41.6	10 14.2	27 48.9	6 24.8	23 20.9	18 19.7	6 23.1	19 49.9	0 49.7	24R16.6	25 5.4
3 F	10 49 10.6	10 39.7	10 11.0	10♓25.1	7 30.1	24 34.8	18 58.6	6 32.8	19 56.0	0 50.9	24 16.5	25 7.3
4 S	10 53 7.1	11 37.8	10 7.8	23 15.9	8 33.0	25 48.8	19 37.6	6 42.7	20 2.2	0 52.2	24 16.5	25 9.1
5 S	10 57 3.7	12 35.9	10 4.7	6♈20.7	9 33.5	27 2.8	20 16.8	6 52.6	20 8.5	0 53.6	24 16.5	25 11.0
6 M	11 1 0.2	13 34.1	10 1.5	19 38.4	10 31.4	28 16.8	20 56.0	7 2.7	20 14.8	0 55.0	24 16.5	25 12.9
7 T	11 4 56.8	14 32.3	9 58.3	3♉ 7.7	11 26.6	29 30.9	21 35.4	7 12.8	20 21.1	0 56.5	24 16.5	25 14.9
8 W	11 8 53.3	15 30.5	9 55.1	16 47.1	12 18.9	0♍45.0	22 14.9	7 23.1	20 27.5	0 58.0	24D16.6	25 16.8
9 T	11 12 49.9	16 28.8	9 51.9	0♊35.7	13 8.1	1 59.2	22 54.6	7 33.4	20 34.0	0 59.5	24 16.7	25 18.8
10 F	11 16 46.4	17 27.1	9 48.8	14 32.9	13 53.9	3 13.4	23 34.3	7 43.8	20 40.5	1 1.1	24 16.8	25 20.8
11 S	11 20 43.0	18 25.4	9 45.6	28 38.0	14 36.2	4 27.6	24 14.2	7 54.3	20 47.0	1 2.8	24 17.0	25 22.8
12 S	11 24 39.5	19 23.8	9 42.4	12♋50.4	15 14.7	5 41.9	24 54.2	8 4.9	20 53.5	1 4.5	24 17.2	25 24.8
13 M	11 28 36.1	20 22.2	9 39.2	27 8.6	15 49.0	6 56.2	25 34.3	8 15.6	21 0.1	1 6.2	24 17.4	25 26.9
14 T	11 32 32.7	21 20.7	9 36.1	11♌30.0	16 19.1	8 10.5	26 14.6	8 26.4	21 6.8	1 8.1	24 17.7	25 29.0
15 W	11 36 29.2	22 19.2	9 32.9	25 50.9	16 44.3	9 24.9	26 55.0	8 37.2	21 13.5	1 9.9	24 18.0	25 31.1
16 T	11 40 25.8	23 17.7	9 29.7	10♍ 6.2	17 4.5	10 39.3	27 35.4	8 48.1	21 20.2	1 11.8	24 18.4	25 33.2
17 F	11 44 22.3	24 16.3	9 26.5	24 10.5	17 19.3	11 53.7	28 16.0	8 59.1	21 27.0	1 13.7	24 18.7	25 35.3
18 S	11 48 18.9	25 14.8	9 23.3	7♎59.0	17 28.4	13 8.2	28 56.8	9 10.2	21 33.8	1 15.7	24 19.1	25 37.4
19 S	11 52 15.4	26 13.4	9 20.2	21 27.6	17 31.3	14 22.7	29 37.6	9 21.3	21 40.6	1 17.7	24 19.6	25 39.6
20 M	11 56 12.0	27 12.1	9 17.0	4♏34.3	17R27.7	15 37.2	0♐18.5	9 32.5	21 47.4	1 19.8	24 20.0	25 41.8
21 T	12 0 8.5	28 10.8	9 13.8	17 19.2	17 17.3	16 51.7	0 59.6	9 43.8	21 54.3	1 21.9	24 20.5	25 43.9
22 W	12 4 5.1	29 9.4	9 10.6	29 44.1	16 60.0	18 6.3	1 40.7	9 55.2	22 1.2	1 24.0	24 21.1	25 46.1
23 T	12 8 1.6	0♎ 8.2	9 7.5	11♐52.5	16 35.4	19 20.9	2 22.0	10 6.6	22 8.1	1 26.2	24 21.6	25 48.4
24 F	12 11 58.2	1 6.9	9 4.3	23 48.8	16 3.6	20 35.5	3 3.4	10 18.1	22 15.1	1 28.5	24 22.2	25 50.6
25 S	12 15 54.7	2 5.7	9 1.1	5♑38.3	15 24.6	21 50.1	3 44.9	10 29.7	22 22.1	1 30.7	24 22.9	25 52.8
26 S	12 19 51.3	3 4.5	8 57.9	17 26.6	14 38.7	23 4.8	4 26.4	10 41.3	22 29.1	1 33.1	24 23.5	25 55.1
27 M	12 23 47.8	4 3.4	8 54.7	29 19.0	13 46.3	24 19.5	5 8.1	10 53.0	22 36.1	1 35.4	24 24.2	25 57.3
28 T	12 27 44.4	5 2.2	8 51.6	11♒20.8	12 48.3	25 34.2	5 49.9	11 4.8	22 43.2	1 37.8	24 24.9	25 59.6
29 W	12 31 40.9	6 1.1	8 48.4	23 36.1	11 45.6	26 48.9	6 31.8	11 16.6	22 50.3	1 40.3	24 25.7	26 1.9
30 T	12 35 37.5	7 0.1	8 45.2	6♓ 8.3	10 39.4	28 3.7	7 13.8	11 28.5	22 57.4	1 42.7	24 26.5	26 4.2

DECLINATION at NOON

DAY	h m s	☉	☊	☽	☿	♀	♂	♃	♄	♅	♆	♇
1 W	10 41 17.5	8N17.9	23N 2.5	18S53.6	3S43.0	15N 5.3	18S11.9	12S40.0	5S34.7	20S11.3	22S 2.6	5N49.7
4 S	10 53 7.1	7 12.1	23 3.3	7 5.6	5 25.4	13 56.4	18 45.7	12 50.2	5 42.0	20 12.1	22 2.8	5 46.7
7 T	11 4 56.8	6 5.3	23 4.0	8N 8.1	6 57.9	12 44.0	19 18.6	13 0.5	5 49.5	20 13.1	22 2.9	5 43.7
10 F	11 16 46.4	4 57.5	23 4.7	20 18.0	8 18.1	11 28.4	19 50.5	13 11.0	5 57.0	20 14.1	22 3.1	5 40.7
13 M	11 28 36.1	3 48.9	23 5.4	22 7.5	9 22.9	10 9.9	20 21.2	13 21.7	6 4.7	20 15.2	22 3.2	5 37.6
16 T	11 40 25.8	2 39.7	23 6.1	11 47.8	10 8.2	8 48.8	20 50.7	13 32.6	6 12.4	20 16.4	22 3.4	5 34.6
19 S	11 52 15.4	1 30.1	23 6.8	3S47.7	10 28.7	7 25.4	21 19.0	13 43.6	6 20.3	20 17.6	22 3.6	5 31.6
22 W	12 4 5.1	0 20.1	23 7.4	16 55.6	10 18.2	6 0.1	21 45.9	13 54.7	6 28.2	20 18.9	22 3.9	5 28.6
25 S	12 15 54.7	0S50.0	23 8.1	22 58.5	9 30.9	4 33.2	22 11.2	14 5.9	6 36.1	20 20.3	22 4.1	5 25.6
28 T	12 27 44.4	2 0.1	23 8.7	19 56.2	8 4.9	3 5.1	22 35.1	14 17.2	6 44.1	20 21.8	22 4.3	5 22.7

OCTOBER 1982

LONGITUDE at NOON

DAY	h m s	☉	☊	☽	☿	♀	♂	♃	♄	♅	♆	♇
1 F	12 39 34.0	7♎59.0	8♋42.0	18♓59.2	9♎31.3	29♍18.4	7♐55.9	11♏40.5	23♎ 4.5	1♐45.3	24♐27.3	26♎ 6.5
2 S	12 43 30.6	8 58.0	8 38.9	2♈ 9.3	8R22.9	0♎33.2	8 38.0	11 52.4	23 11.6	1 47.8	24 28.2	26 8.8
3 S	12 47 27.2	9 57.1	8 35.7	15 37.1	7 16.0	1 48.0	9 20.3	12 4.5	23 18.8	1 50.4	24 29.0	26 11.2
4 M	12 51 23.7	10 56.1	8 32.5	29 19.9	6 12.5	3 2.9	10 2.7	12 16.6	23 26.0	1 53.0	24 30.0	26 13.5
5 T	12 55 20.3	11 55.3	8 29.3	13♉14.2	5 14.2	4 17.8	10 45.2	12 28.8	23 33.2	1 55.8	24 30.9	26 15.9
6 W	12 59 16.8	12 54.4	8 26.1	27 16.0	4 22.6	5 32.7	11 27.7	12 41.0	23 40.4	1 58.5	24 31.9	26 18.3
7 T	13 3 13.4	13 53.6	8 23.0	11♊21.8	3 39.2	6 47.6	12 10.3	12 53.3	23 47.6	2 1.2	24 32.9	26 20.6
8 F	13 7 9.9	14 52.8	8 19.8	25 29.2	3 5.1	8 2.5	12 53.1	13 5.6	23 54.9	2 4.0	24 34.0	26 23.0
9 S	13 11 6.5	15 52.0	8 16.6	9♋36.2	2 41.2	9 17.5	13 35.9	13 18.0	24 2.1	2 6.8	24 35.0	26 25.4
10 S	13 15 3.0	16 51.3	8 13.4	23 41.9	2 27.9	10 32.4	14 18.8	13 30.4	24 9.4	2 9.6	24 36.1	26 27.7
11 M	13 18 59.6	17 50.7	8 10.3	7♌45.5	2 25.5	11 47.4	15 1.8	13 42.9	24 16.6	2 12.5	24 37.3	26 30.1
12 T	13 22 56.1	18 50.0	8 7.1	21 46.0	2D33.9	13 2.4	15 44.9	13 55.4	24 23.9	2 15.4	24 38.4	26 32.5
13 W	13 26 52.7	19 49.4	8 3.9	5♍42.0	2 52.9	14 17.5	16 28.1	14 7.9	24 31.2	2 18.4	24 39.6	26 34.9
14 T	13 30 49.2	20 48.9	8 0.7	19 31.1	3 21.8	15 32.5	17 11.4	14 20.5	24 38.5	2 21.3	24 40.8	26 37.3
15 F	13 34 45.8	21 48.4	7 57.5	3♎10.5	4 0.1	16 47.6	17 54.8	14 33.2	24 45.8	2 24.4	24 42.1	26 39.7
16 S	13 38 42.3	22 47.9	7 54.4	16 37.1	4 47.1	18 2.6	18 38.2	14 45.8	24 53.1	2 27.4	24 43.3	26 42.1
17 S	13 42 38.9	23 47.4	7 51.2	29 48.4	5 41.9	19 17.7	19 21.8	14 58.5	25 0.4	2 30.5	24 44.6	26 44.5
18 M	13 46 35.4	24 47.0	7 48.0	12♏42.5	6 43.8	20 32.9	20 5.4	15 11.3	25 7.7	2 33.6	24 46.0	26 46.9
19 T	13 50 32.0	25 46.6	7 44.8	25 19.0	7 52.0	21 48.0	20 49.1	15 24.1	25 15.0	2 36.7	24 47.3	26 49.4
20 W	13 54 28.6	26 46.3	7 41.7	7♐38.9	9 5.7	23 3.1	21 32.9	15 36.9	25 22.3	2 39.8	24 48.7	26 51.8
21 T	13 58 25.1	27 46.0	7 38.5	19 44.5	10 24.1	24 18.3	22 16.8	15 49.8	25 29.6	2 43.0	24 50.1	26 54.2
22 F	14 2 21.7	28 45.7	7 35.3	1♑39.4	11 46.6	25 33.4	23 0.8	16 2.6	25 36.8	2 46.2	24 51.5	26 56.6
23 S	14 6 18.2	29 45.4	7 32.1	13 28.1	13 12.5	26 48.6	23 44.8	16 15.6	25 44.1	2 49.5	24 53.0	26 59.0
24 S	14 10 14.8	0♏45.2	7 28.9	25 15.7	14 41.3	28 3.7	24 28.9	16 28.5	25 51.4	2 52.7	24 54.5	27 1.4
25 M	14 14 11.3	1 45.0	7 25.8	7♒ 7.7	16 12.5	29 18.9	25 13.1	16 41.5	25 58.7	2 56.0	24 56.0	27 3.8
26 T	14 18 7.9	2 44.8	7 22.6	19 9.5	17 45.7	0♏34.2	25 57.4	16 54.5	26 6.0	2 59.4	24 57.6	27 6.3
27 W	14 22 4.4	3 44.7	7 19.4	1♓26.2	19 20.4	1 49.4	26 41.7	17 7.5	26 13.3	3 2.7	24 59.2	27 8.7
28 T	14 26 1.0	4 44.6	7 16.2	14 2.2	20 56.4	3 4.6	27 26.2	17 20.6	26 20.5	3 6.1	25 0.7	27 11.1
29 F	14 29 57.5	5 44.5	7 13.1	27 0.6	22 33.3	4 19.8	28 10.6	17 33.6	26 27.8	3 9.4	25 2.4	27 13.5
30 S	14 33 54.1	6 44.4	7 9.9	10♈22.6	24 10.9	5 35.0	28 55.2	17 46.7	26 35.0	3 12.8	25 4.0	27 15.8
31 S	14 37 50.7	7 44.4	7 6.7	24 7.5	25 49.1	6 50.2	29 39.8	17 59.8	26 42.2	3 16.2	25 5.7	27 18.2

DECLINATION at NOON

DAY	h m s	☉	☊	☽	☿	♀	♂	♃	♄	♅	♆	♇
1 F	12 39 34.0	3S10.1	23N 9.3	8S41.1	6S 7.1	1N35.9	22S57.2	14S28.6	6S52.1	20S23.4	22S 4.6	5N19.8
4 M	12 51 23.7	4 19.7	23 10.0	6N51.2	3 56.5	0 6.2	23 17.6	14 40.0	7 0.2	20 25.0	22 4.8	5 17.0
7 T	13 3 13.4	5 28.9	23 10.6	19 53.8	1 59.5	1S23.9	23 36.2	14 51.5	7 8.2	20 26.6	22 5.1	5 14.2
10 S	13 15 3.0	6 37.4	23 11.2	22 42.4	0 39.4	2 54.0	23 52.9	15 2.9	7 16.2	20 28.4	22 5.3	5 11.4
13 W	13 26 52.7	7 45.2	23 11.7	13 22.8	0 7.8	4 23.7	24 7.6	15 14.4	7 24.3	20 30.1	22 5.6	5 8.7
16 S	13 38 42.3	8 52.0	23 12.3	1S57.2	0 24.2	5 52.6	24 20.3	15 25.9	7 32.3	20 31.9	22 5.9	5 6.1
19 T	13 50 32.0	9 57.7	23 12.9	15 50.5	1 20.4	7 20.6	24 30.8	15 37.3	7 40.2	20 33.8	22 6.2	5 3.5
22 F	14 2 21.7	11 2.1	23 13.4	22 59.5	2 45.6	8 47.1	24 39.2	15 48.7	7 48.1	20 35.7	22 6.5	5 1.1
25 M	14 14 11.3	12 5.0	23 14.0	20 59.9	4 29.7	10 11.9	24 45.3	16 0.0	7 56.0	20 37.6	22 6.8	4 58.7
28 T	14 26 1.0	13 6.2	23 14.5	10 37.0	6 24.5	11 34.5	24 49.2	16 11.3	8 3.8	20 39.6	22 7.1	4 56.4
31 S	14 37 50.7	14 5.6	23 15.0	4N51.8	8 24.0	12 54.7	24 50.7	16 22.5	8 11.5	20 41.6	22 7.4	4 54.1

NOVEMBER 1982

LONGITUDE at NOON

DAY	EPHEMERIS SIDEREAL TIME h m s	☉ ° ′	☊ ° ′	☽ ° ′	☿ ° ′	♀ ° ′	♂ ° ′	♃ ° ′	♄ ° ′	♅ ° ′	♆ ° ′	♇ ° ′
1 M	14 41 47.2	8♏44.4	7♋ 3.5	8♉12.3	27♎27.7	8♏ 5.5	0♑24.5	18♏13.0	26♎49.4	3♐19.7	25♐ 7.3	27♎20.6
2 T	14 45 43.8	9 44.4	7 0.3	22 32.2	29 6.4	9 20.7	1 9.2	18 26.1	26 56.6	3 23.1	25 9.1	27 23.0
3 W	14 49 40.3	10 44.5	6 57.2	7♊ 1.0	0♏45.3	10 36.0	1 54.0	18 39.3	27 3.8	3 26.6	25 10.8	27 25.3
4 T	14 53 36.9	11 44.6	6 54.0	21 32.7	2 24.1	11 51.2	2 38.9	18 52.4	27 10.9	3 30.1	25 12.5	27 27.7
5 F	14 57 33.4	12 44.7	6 50.8	6♋ 1.7	4 2.9	13 6.5	3 23.9	19 5.6	27 18.1	3 33.6	25 14.3	27 30.1
6 S	15 1 30.0	13 44.8	6 47.6	20 23.9	5 41.6	14 21.8	4 8.9	19 18.8	27 25.2	3 37.1	25 16.1	27 32.4
7 S	15 5 26.5	14 45.0	6 44.5	4♌36.6	7 20.1	15 37.1	4 53.9	19 32.0	27 32.3	3 40.7	25 17.9	27 34.7
8 M	15 9 23.1	15 45.3	6 41.3	18 38.4	8 58.3	16 52.4	5 39.1	19 45.3	27 39.3	3 44.2	25 19.8	27 37.0
9 T	15 13 19.6	16 45.5	6 38.1	2♍28.7	10 36.3	18 7.7	6 24.3	19 58.5	27 46.4	3 47.8	25 21.6	27 39.4
10 W	15 17 16.2	17 45.8	6 34.9	16 7.3	12 14.1	19 23.0	7 9.6	20 11.7	27 53.4	3 51.4	25 23.5	27 41.7
11 T	15 21 12.8	18 46.2	6 31.7	29 34.1	13 51.5	20 38.3	7 54.9	20 25.0	28 0.4	3 55.0	25 25.4	27 44.0
12 F	15 25 9.3	19 46.5	6 28.6	12♎48.9	15 28.7	21 53.7	8 40.3	20 38.2	28 7.4	3 58.6	25 27.3	27 46.2
13 S	15 29 5.9	20 46.9	6 25.4	25 51.1	17 5.6	23 9.0	9 25.7	20 51.5	28 14.3	4 2.2	25 29.2	27 48.5
14 S	15 33 2.4	21 47.4	6 22.2	8♏40.4	18 42.2	24 24.3	10 11.3	21 4.8	28 21.3	4 5.9	25 31.2	27 50.8
15 M	15 36 59.0	22 47.8	6 19.0	21 16.3	20 18.5	25 39.7	10 56.8	21 18.0	28 28.1	4 9.5	25 33.1	27 53.0
16 T	15 40 55.5	23 48.3	6 15.9	3♐39.2	21 54.6	26 55.1	11 42.5	21 31.3	28 35.0	4 13.2	25 35.2	27 55.3
17 W	15 44 52.1	24 48.8	6 12.7	15 49.8	23 30.4	28 10.4	12 28.2	21 44.6	28 41.9	4 16.9	25 37.2	27 57.5
18 T	15 48 48.7	25 49.4	6 9.5	27 49.9	25 5.9	29 25.8	13 13.9	21 57.8	28 48.7	4 20.5	25 39.2	27 59.7
19 F	15 52 45.2	26 49.9	6 6.3	9♑41.9	26 41.2	0♐41.1	13 59.7	22 11.1	28 55.4	4 24.2	25 41.2	28 1.9
20 S	15 56 41.8	27 50.5	6 3.2	21 29.2	28 16.2	1 56.5	14 45.6	22 24.3	29 2.1	4 27.9	25 43.3	28 4.0
21 S	16 0 38.3	28 51.1	5 60.0	3♒15.9	29 51.0	3 11.9	15 31.5	22 37.6	29 8.8	4 31.6	25 45.3	28 6.2
22 M	16 4 34.9	29 51.7	5 56.8	15 6.6	1♐25.6	4 27.2	16 17.4	22 50.8	29 15.4	4 35.3	25 47.4	28 8.3
23 T	16 8 31.4	0♐52.4	5 53.6	27 6.4	3 0.0	5 42.6	17 3.4	23 4.0	29 22.0	4 39.0	25 49.5	28 10.5
24 W	16 12 28.0	1 53.0	5 50.4	9♓20.4	4 34.3	6 58.0	17 49.5	23 17.2	29 28.6	4 42.6	25 51.6	28 12.6
25 T	16 16 24.5	2 53.7	5 47.3	21 53.5	6 8.4	8 13.3	18 35.6	23 30.4	29 35.1	4 46.3	25 53.7	28 14.6
26 F	16 20 21.1	3 54.4	5 44.1	4♈49.8	7 42.3	9 28.7	19 21.7	23 43.6	29 41.6	4 50.0	25 55.9	28 16.7
27 S	16 24 17.7	4 55.1	5 40.9	18 12.0	9 16.1	10 44.0	20 7.9	23 56.7	29 48.0	4 53.7	25 58.0	28 18.7
28 S	16 28 14.2	5 55.8	5 37.7	2♉ 1.2	10 49.9	11 59.4	20 54.1	24 9.9	29 54.4	4 57.4	26 0.1	28 20.8
29 M	16 32 10.8	6 56.6	5 34.6	16 15.6	12 23.5	13 14.7	21 40.3	24 23.0	0♏ 0.7	5 1.1	26 2.3	28 22.8
30 T	16 36 7.3	7 57.3	5 31.4	0♊51.2	13 57.0	14 30.1	22 26.6	24 36.1	0 7.0	5 4.8	26 4.5	28 24.8

DECLINATION at NOON

DAY	EPHEMERIS SIDEREAL TIME h m s	☉ ° ′	☊ ° ′	☽ ° ′	☿ ° ′	♀ ° ′	♂ ° ′	♃ ° ′	♄ ° ′	♅ ° ′	♆ ° ′	♇ ° ′
1 M	14 41 47.2	14S24.9	23N15.2	10N10.2	9S 4.1	13S20.8	24S50.7	16S26.2	8S14.0	20S42.3	22S 7.5	4N53.4
4 T	14 53 36.9	15 21.5	23 15.7	21 56.1	11 3.5	14 37.2	24 49.1	16 37.3	8 21.6	20 44.3	22 7.8	4 51.3
7 S	15 5 26.5	16 15.8	23 16.2	21 32.5	12 59.8	15 50.2	24 45.1	16 48.2	8 29.0	20 46.3	22 8.0	4 49.3
10 W	15 17 16.2	17 7.7	23 16.7	9 56.5	14 51.1	16 59.6	24 38.6	16 59.0	8 36.3	20 48.4	22 8.3	4 47.5
13 S	15 29 5.9	17 57.0	23 17.1	5S30.3	16 36.1	18 4.9	24 29.8	17 9.7	8 43.5	20 50.4	22 8.6	4 45.7
16 T	15 40 55.5	18 43.5	23 17.6	18 15.4	18 13.9	19 5.9	24 18.4	17 20.3	8 50.6	20 52.5	22 8.9	4 44.0
19 F	15 52 45.2	19 27.0	23 18.0	23 32.6	19 43.7	20 2.2	24 4.7	17 30.7	8 57.5	20 54.5	22 9.2	4 42.5
22 M	16 4 34.9	20 7.4	23 18.5	19 32.5	21 4.7	20 53.4	23 48.6	17 40.9	9 4.3	20 56.6	22 9.5	4 41.0
25 T	16 16 24.5	20 44.4	23 18.9	7 53.7	22 16.4	21 39.2	23 30.0	17 50.9	9 10.9	20 58.6	22 9.7	4 39.7
28 S	16 28 14.2	21 17.9	23 19.3	7N49.1	23 18.1	22 19.3	23 9.1	18 0.7	9 17.3	21 0.7	22 10.0	4 38.6

DECEMBER 1982

LONGITUDE at NOON

DAY	EPHEMERIS SIDEREAL TIME h m s	☉ ° ′	☊ ° ′	☽ ° ′	☿ ° ′	♀ ° ′	♂ ° ′	♃ ° ′	♄ ° ′	♅ ° ′	♆ ° ′	♇ ° ′
1 W	16 40 3.9	8♐58.1	5♋28.2	15♊41.4	15♐30.5	15♐45.5	23♑12.9	24♏49.2	0♏13.3	5♐ 8.5	26♐ 6.7	28♎26.7
2 T	16 44 0.4	9 58.9	5 25.0	0♋38.4	17 3.9	17 0.8	23 59.3	25 2.2	0 19.5	5 12.2	26 8.8	28 28.7
3 F	16 47 57.0	10 59.8	5 21.9	15 33.7	18 37.2	18 16.2	24 45.7	25 15.3	0 25.6	5 15.9	26 11.0	28 30.6
4 S	16 51 53.6	12 0.6	5 18.7	0♌20.2	20 10.5	19 31.5	25 32.1	25 28.3	0 31.7	5 19.6	26 13.3	28 32.5
5 S	16 55 50.1	13 1.5	5 15.5	14 51.9	21 43.8	20 46.9	26 18.6	25 41.3	0 37.7	5 23.3	26 15.5	28 34.3
6 M	16 59 46.7	14 2.4	5 12.3	29 5.5	23 17.0	22 2.3	27 5.1	25 54.2	0 43.7	5 27.0	26 17.7	28 36.2
7 T	17 3 43.2	15 3.3	5 9.2	12♍59.3	24 50.2	23 17.7	27 51.7	26 7.2	0 49.7	5 30.7	26 20.0	28 38.1
8 W	17 7 39.8	16 4.3	5 6.0	26 33.2	26 23.3	24 33.0	28 38.3	26 20.1	0 55.5	5 34.3	26 22.2	28 39.9
9 T	17 11 36.4	17 5.2	5 2.8	9♎48.3	27 56.4	25 48.4	29 24.9	26 33.0	1 1.4	5 38.0	26 24.4	28 41.7
10 F	17 15 32.9	18 6.2	4 59.6	22 46.3	29 29.4	27 3.8	0♒11.6	26 45.8	1 7.1	5 41.6	26 26.7	28 43.4
11 S	17 19 29.5	19 7.2	4 56.4	5♏29.1	1♑ 2.3	28 19.1	0 58.3	26 58.6	1 12.8	5 45.3	26 28.9	28 45.1
12 S	17 23 26.0	20 8.2	4 53.3	17 58.6	2 35.1	29 34.5	1 45.0	27 11.4	1 18.4	5 48.9	26 31.2	28 46.8
13 M	17 27 22.6	21 9.2	4 50.1	0♐16.5	4 7.7	0♑49.9	2 31.8	27 24.1	1 24.0	5 52.5	26 33.5	28 48.5
14 T	17 31 19.1	22 10.3	4 46.9	12 24.5	5 40.1	2 5.2	3 18.5	27 36.8	1 29.5	5 56.1	26 35.7	28 50.2
15 W	17 35 15.7	23 11.4	4 43.7	24 24.3	7 12.2	3 20.6	4 5.3	27 49.4	1 34.9	5 59.7	26 38.0	28 51.8
16 T	17 39 12.3	24 12.4	4 40.6	6♑17.7	8 44.0	4 36.0	4 52.2	28 2.1	1 40.3	6 3.2	26 40.2	28 53.4
17 F	17 43 8.8	25 13.5	4 37.4	18 6.6	10 15.4	5 51.3	5 39.0	28 14.6	1 45.6	6 6.8	26 42.5	28 54.9
18 S	17 47 5.4	26 14.6	4 34.2	29 53.5	11 46.3	7 6.7	6 25.9	28 27.1	1 50.9	6 10.3	26 44.8	28 56.5
19 S	17 51 1.9	27 15.7	4 31.0	11♒41.2	13 16.5	8 22.0	7 12.8	28 39.6	1 56.0	6 13.9	26 47.1	28 58.0
20 M	17 54 58.5	28 16.8	4 27.9	23 33.0	14 45.9	9 37.4	7 59.8	28 52.0	2 1.1	6 17.4	26 49.3	28 59.5
21 T	17 58 55.0	29 17.9	4 24.7	5♓32.8	16 14.4	10 52.7	8 46.7	29 4.4	2 6.1	6 20.9	26 51.6	29 0.9
22 W	18 2 51.6	0♑19.0	4 21.5	17 44.7	17 41.7	12 8.1	9 33.7	29 16.7	2 11.1	6 24.3	26 53.9	29 2.3
23 T	18 6 48.2	1 20.1	4 18.3	0♈13.2	19 7.7	13 23.4	10 20.7	29 29.0	2 16.0	6 27.8	26 56.1	29 3.7
24 F	18 10 44.7	2 21.2	4 15.1	13 2.4	20 32.0	14 38.7	11 7.7	29 41.2	2 20.8	6 31.2	26 58.4	29 5.1
25 S	18 14 41.3	3 22.4	4 12.0	26 16.2	21 54.3	15 54.0	11 54.7	29 53.3	2 25.5	6 34.6	27 0.6	29 6.4
26 S	18 18 37.8	4 23.5	4 8.8	9♉56.8	23 14.3	17 9.3	12 41.7	0♐ 5.4	2 30.1	6 38.0	27 2.9	29 7.7
27 M	18 22 34.4	5 24.6	4 5.6	24 5.1	24 31.6	18 24.6	13 28.7	0 17.5	2 34.7	6 41.4	27 5.1	29 8.9
28 T	18 26 31.0	6 25.8	4 2.4	8♊39.2	25 45.6	19 39.9	14 15.8	0 29.5	2 39.2	6 44.8	27 7.4	29 10.2
29 W	18 30 27.5	7 26.9	3 59.3	23 34.4	26 55.8	20 55.2	15 2.9	0 41.4	2 43.7	6 48.1	27 9.7	29 11.4
30 T	18 34 24.1	8 28.0	3 56.1	8♋43.4	28 1.5	22 10.5	15 50.0	0 53.2	2 48.0	6 51.4	27 11.9	29 12.6
31 F	18 38 20.6	9 29.1	3 52.9	23 57.0	29 2.2	23 25.7	16 37.0	1 5.0	2 52.2	6 54.7	27 14.1	29 13.7

DECLINATION at NOON

DAY	EPHEMERIS SIDEREAL TIME h m s	☉ ° ′	☊ ° ′	☽ ° ′	☿ ° ′	♀ ° ′	♂ ° ′	♃ ° ′	♄ ° ′	♅ ° ′	♆ ° ′	♇ ° ′
1 W	16 40 3.9	21S47.8	23N19.7	20N60.0	24S 9.1	22S53.6	22S45.9	18S10.4	9S23.5	21S 2.7	22S10.3	4N37.5
4 S	16 51 53.6	22 13.9	23 20.1	22 20.2	24 48.9	23 21.6	22 20.4	18 19.8	9 29.5	21 4.7	22 10.5	4 36.6
7 T	17 3 43.2	22 36.2	23 20.4	11 12.7	25 16.9	23 43.3	21 52.6	18 29.1	9 35.3	21 6.7	22 10.7	4 35.8
10 F	17 15 32.9	22 54.5	23 20.8	4S12.6	25 32.5	23 58.5	21 22.7	18 38.1	9 40.9	21 8.6	22 11.0	4 35.1
13 M	17 27 22.6	23 8.7	23 21.2	17 19.2	25 35.1	24 7.0	20 50.6	18 46.8	9 46.2	21 10.6	22 11.2	4 34.6
16 T	17 39 12.3	23 18.8	23 21.5	23 29.1	25 24.5	24 8.9	20 16.5	18 55.4	9 51.3	21 12.5	22 11.4	4 34.2
19 S	17 51 1.9	23 24.8	23 21.8	20 22.9	25 0.3	24 4.0	19 40.4	19 3.7	9 56.2	21 14.3	22 11.6	4 34.0
22 W	18 2 51.6	23 26.4	23 22.2	9 31.3	24 23.0	23 52.3	19 2.4	19 11.7	10 0.8	21 16.1	22 11.7	4 33.9
25 S	18 14 41.3	23 23.9	23 22.5	5N33.2	23 33.3	23 34.1	18 22.6	19 19.5	10 5.2	21 17.9	22 11.9	4 33.9
28 T	18 26 31.0	23 17.1	23 22.8	19 28.7	22 33.1	23 9.3	17 41.1	19 27.1	10 9.3	21 19.6	22 12.1	4 34.0
31 F	18 38 20.6	23 6.1	23 23.1	23 4.8	21 26.1	22 38.2	16 57.9	19 34.4	10 13.1	21 21.3	22 12.2	4 34.3

JANUARY 1983

LONGITUDE at NOON

DAY	EPHEMERIS SIDEREAL TIME h m s	☉ ° ′	☊ ° ′	☽ ° ′	☿ ° ′	♀ ° ′	♂ ° ′	♃ ° ′	♄ ° ′	♅ ° ′	♆ ° ′	♇ ° ′
1 S	18 42 17.2	10♑30.3	3♋49.7	9♌ 5.2	29♑57.0	24♑41.0	17♒24.1	1♐16.8	2♏56.4	6♐57.9	27♐16.4	29♎14.8
2 S	18 46 13.7	11 31.4	3 46.6	23 59.3	0♒45.0	25 56.2	18 11.2	1 28.4	3 0.5	7 1.1	27 18.6	29 15.9
3 M	18 50 10.3	12 32.6	3 43.4	8♍32.4	1 25.5	27 11.5	18 58.3	1 40.0	3 4.5	7 4.3	27 20.8	29 16.9
4 T	18 54 6.9	13 33.7	3 40.2	22 40.2	1 57.5	28 26.7	19 45.4	1 51.5	3 8.4	7 7.5	27 23.0	29 17.9
5 W	18 58 3.4	14 34.8	3 37.0	6♎21.6	2 20.0	29 41.9	20 32.5	2 2.9	3 12.2	7 10.6	27 25.2	29 18.9
6 T	19 1 60.0	15 36.0	3 33.9	19 37.4	2 32.4	0♒57.1	21 19.7	2 14.3	3 16.0	7 13.7	27 27.4	29 19.8
7 F	19 5 56.5	16 37.2	3 30.7	2♏30.2	2 33.7	2 12.3	22 6.8	2 25.6	3 19.6	7 16.8	27 29.5	29 20.7
8 S	19 9 53.1	17 38.3	3 27.5	15 3.3	2R23.5	3 27.5	22 53.9	2 36.8	3 23.2	7 19.9	27 31.7	29 21.6
9 S	19 13 49.6	18 39.5	3 24.3	27 20.7	2 1.5	4 42.7	23 41.1	2 48.0	3 26.7	7 22.9	27 33.8	29 22.4
10 M	19 17 46.2	19 40.6	3 21.1	9♐26.0	1 27.7	5 57.9	24 28.2	2 59.0	3 30.0	7 25.9	27 36.0	29 23.2
11 T	19 21 42.8	20 41.8	3 18.0	21 22.7	0 42.6	7 13.1	25 15.3	3 10.0	3 33.3	7 28.8	27 38.1	29 24.0
12 W	19 25 39.3	21 42.9	3 14.8	3♑13.8	29♑47.2	8 28.2	26 2.5	3 20.9	3 36.5	7 31.7	27 40.2	29 24.7
13 T	19 29 35.9	22 44.1	3 11.6	15 2.1	28 42.9	9 43.4	26 49.6	3 31.7	3 39.6	7 34.6	27 42.3	29 25.4
14 F	19 33 32.4	23 45.2	3 8.4	26 49.6	27 31.5	10 58.5	27 36.8	3 42.4	3 42.6	7 37.5	27 44.4	29 26.1
15 S	19 37 29.0	24 46.4	3 5.3	8♒38.5	26 15.3	12 13.6	28 23.9	3 53.0	3 45.5	7 40.3	27 46.5	29 26.7
16 S	19 41 25.5	25 47.5	3 2.1	20 30.8	24 56.8	13 28.7	29 11.0	4 3.5	3 48.3	7 43.1	27 48.6	29 27.3
17 M	19 45 22.1	26 48.6	2 58.9	2♓28.4	23 38.3	14 43.8	29 58.2	4 14.0	3 51.1	7 45.8	27 50.6	29 27.8
18 T	19 49 18.7	27 49.8	2 55.7	14 33.9	22 22.3	15 58.9	0♓45.3	4 24.4	3 53.7	7 48.6	27 52.7	29 28.4
19 W	19 53 15.2	28 50.9	2 52.6	26 49.6	21 10.8	17 14.0	1 32.5	4 34.6	3 56.3	7 51.2	27 54.7	29 28.8
20 T	19 57 11.8	29 51.9	2 49.4	9♈18.6	20 5.6	18 29.0	2 19.6	4 44.8	3 58.7	7 53.9	27 56.7	29 29.3
21 F	20 1 8.3	0♒53.0	2 46.2	22 4.3	19 8.0	19 44.1	3 6.7	4 54.8	4 1.0	7 56.5	27 58.7	29 29.7
22 S	20 5 4.9	1 54.0	2 43.0	5♉ 9.9	18 18.9	20 59.0	3 53.8	5 4.7	4 3.2	7 59.0	28 0.7	29 30.0
23 S	20 9 1.4	2 55.1	2 39.8	18 38.5	17 38.8	22 14.0	4 40.8	5 14.6	4 5.3	8 1.5	28 2.6	29 30.4
24 M	20 12 58.0	3 56.1	2 36.7	2♊31.9	17 7.9	23 29.0	5 27.9	5 24.3	4 7.4	8 4.0	28 4.5	29 30.6
25 T	20 16 54.6	4 57.1	2 33.5	16 50.8	16 46.1	24 43.9	6 14.9	5 34.0	4 9.3	8 6.4	28 6.4	29 30.9
26 W	20 20 51.1	5 58.1	2 30.3	1♋33.3	16 33.2	25 58.8	7 2.0	5 43.5	4 11.1	8 8.8	28 8.3	29 31.1
27 T	20 24 47.7	6 59.0	2 27.1	16 34.7	16 28.7	27 13.7	7 49.0	5 52.9	4 12.8	8 11.1	28 10.2	29 31.3
28 F	20 28 44.2	7 60.0	2 24.0	1♌47.5	16D32.1	28 28.5	8 36.0	6 2.2	4 14.4	8 13.4	28 12.1	29 31.4
29 S	20 32 40.8	9 0.9	2 20.8	17 2.0	16 43.0	29 43.4	9 22.9	6 11.4	4 15.9	8 15.7	28 13.9	29 31.6
30 S	20 36 37.3	10 1.8	2 17.6	2♍ 7.8	17 0.7	0♓58.2	10 9.9	6 20.5	4 17.4	8 17.9	28 15.7	29 31.6
31 M	20 40 33.9	11 2.7	2 14.4	16 55.4	17 24.6	2 12.9	10 56.8	6 29.4	4 18.7	8 20.1	28 17.5	29 31.7

DECLINATION at NOON

DAY	SIDEREAL TIME	☉	☊	☽	☿	♀	♂	♃	♄	♅	♆	♇
1 S	18 42 17.2	23S 1.5	23N23.1	20N54.4	21S 3.1	22S26.4	16S43.1	19S36.7	10S14.3	21S21.9	22S12.3	4N34.4
4 T	18 54 6.9	22 45.0	23 23.4	7 40.3	19 55.8	21 47.1	15 57.9	19 43.7	10 17.7	21 23.5	22 12.4	4 34.9
7 F	19 5 56.5	22 24.4	23 23.7	7S57.5	18 57.7	21 2.0	15 11.2	19 50.3	10 20.9	21 25.0	22 12.5	4 35.5
10 M	19 17 46.2	21 59.9	23 23.9	19 39.9	18 17.2	20 11.3	14 23.1	19 56.7	10 23.7	21 26.5	22 12.6	4 36.2
13 T	19 29 35.9	21 31.5	23 24.2	23 34.3	17 59.2	19 15.3	13 33.8	20 2.9	10 26.3	21 28.0	22 12.7	4 37.1
16 S	19 41 25.5	20 59.3	23 24.4	18 15.3	18 2.5	18 14.3	12 43.3	20 8.7	10 28.5	21 29.4	22 12.8	4 38.0
19 W	19 53 15.2	20 23.5	23 24.6	6 1.8	18 21.0	17 8.7	11 51.8	20 14.3	10 30.5	21 30.7	22 12.8	4 39.1
22 S	20 5 4.9	19 44.3	23 24.8	9N 1.0	18 47.9	15 58.9	10 59.2	20 19.6	10 32.1	21 32.0	22 12.9	4 40.3
25 T	20 16 54.6	19 1.8	23 25.0	21 15.3	19 18.0	14 45.1	10 5.8	20 24.7	10 33.4	21 33.2	22 12.9	4 41.6
28 F	20 28 44.2	18 16.1	23 25.2	22 8.3	19 47.2	13 27.7	9 11.7	20 29.4	10 34.4	21 34.3	22 12.9	4 43.0
31 M	20 40 33.9	17 27.5	23 25.3	9 44.1	20 12.5	12 7.1	8 16.8	20 33.9	10 35.1	21 35.4	22 12.9	4 44.5

FEBRUARY 1983

LONGITUDE at NOON

DAY	SIDEREAL TIME	☉	☊	☽	☿	♀	♂	♃	♄	♅	♆	♇
1 T	20 44 30.4	12♒ 3.6	2♋11.3	1♎18.0	17♑54.4	3♓27.7	11♓43.8	6♐38.3	4♏19.9	8♐22.2	28♐19.3	29♎31.7
2 W	20 48 27.0	13 4.5	2 8.1	15 11.8	18 29.4	4 42.4	12 30.7	6 47.0	4 21.0	8 24.3	28 21.0	29R31.6
3 T	20 52 23.6	14 5.3	2 4.9	28 36.2	19 9.2	5 57.1	13 17.6	6 55.6	4 22.0	8 26.3	28 22.7	29 31.6
4 F	20 56 20.1	15 6.2	2 1.7	11♏33.1	19 53.4	7 11.8	14 4.4	7 4.1	4 22.8	8 28.3	28 24.4	29 31.5
5 S	21 0 16.7	16 7.0	1 58.5	24 6.4	20 41.6	8 26.5	14 51.3	7 12.4	4 23.6	8 30.3	28 26.1	29 31.3
6 S	21 4 13.2	17 7.8	1 55.4	6♐20.7	21 33.5	9 41.1	15 38.1	7 20.7	4 24.3	8 32.2	28 27.8	29 31.1
7 M	21 8 9.8	18 8.6	1 52.2	18 21.1	22 28.7	10 55.7	16 24.9	7 28.8	4 24.9	8 34.0	28 29.4	29 30.9
8 T	21 12 6.3	19 9.5	1 49.0	0♑12.6	23 26.9	12 10.4	17 11.8	7 36.8	4 25.4	8 35.9	28 31.1	29 30.7
9 W	21 16 2.9	20 10.2	1 45.8	11 59.5	24 27.9	13 24.9	17 58.5	7 44.6	4 25.8	8 37.6	28 32.6	29 30.4
10 T	21 19 59.4	21 11.0	1 42.7	23 45.8	25 31.5	14 39.4	18 45.3	7 52.3	4 26.0	8 39.3	28 34.2	29 30.1
11 F	21 23 56.0	22 11.7	1 39.5	5♒34.5	26 37.4	15 53.9	19 32.0	7 59.9	4 26.2	8 41.0	28 35.7	29 29.8
12 S	21 27 52.6	23 12.4	1 36.3	17 28.2	27 45.5	17 8.4	20 18.7	8 7.3	4 26.2	8 42.6	28 37.2	29 29.4
13 S	21 31 49.1	24 13.1	1 33.1	29 28.5	28 55.6	18 22.8	21 5.4	8 14.6	4R26.1	8 44.1	28 38.7	29 29.0
14 M	21 35 45.7	25 13.7	1 30.0	11♓36.9	0♒ 7.6	19 37.2	21 52.0	8 21.8	4 26.0	8 45.6	28 40.2	29 28.5
15 T	21 39 42.2	26 14.4	1 26.8	23 54.4	1 21.4	20 51.6	22 38.6	8 28.8	4 25.7	8 47.1	28 41.6	29 28.0
16 W	21 43 38.8	27 15.0	1 23.6	6♈22.0	2 36.9	22 5.9	23 25.2	8 35.6	4 25.3	8 48.5	28 43.0	29 27.5
17 T	21 47 35.3	28 15.6	1 20.4	19 0.9	3 53.9	23 20.2	24 11.8	8 42.3	4 24.8	8 49.9	28 44.3	29 26.9
18 F	21 51 31.9	29 16.1	1 17.2	1♉52.7	5 12.4	24 34.4	24 58.3	8 48.9	4 24.2	8 51.2	28 45.7	29 26.3
19 S	21 55 28.4	0♓16.6	1 14.1	14 59.1	6 32.3	25 48.6	25 44.8	8 55.3	4 23.5	8 52.4	28 47.0	29 25.7
20 S	21 59 25.0	1 17.1	1 10.9	28 22.5	7 53.5	27 2.8	26 31.2	9 1.6	4 22.7	8 53.6	28 48.3	29 25.1
21 M	22 3 21.5	2 17.6	1 7.7	12♊ 4.7	9 16.0	28 16.9	27 17.7	9 7.7	4 21.8	8 54.8	28 49.5	29 24.4
22 T	22 7 18.1	3 18.0	1 4.5	26 7.1	10 39.8	29 31.0	28 4.1	9 13.7	4 20.8	8 55.8	28 50.8	29 23.6
23 W	22 11 14.7	4 18.4	1 1.4	10♋29.9	12 4.8	0♈45.0	28 50.4	9 19.5	4 19.7	8 56.9	28 52.0	29 22.9
24 T	22 15 11.2	5 18.8	0 58.2	25 10.8	13 31.0	1 59.0	29 36.7	9 25.1	4 18.5	8 57.9	28 53.1	29 22.1
25 F	22 19 7.8	6 19.1	0 55.0	10♌ 5.3	14 58.3	3 12.9	0♈23.0	9 30.6	4 17.2	8 58.8	28 54.3	29 21.3
26 S	22 23 4.3	7 19.4	0 51.8	25 6.1	16 26.7	4 26.8	1 9.3	9 35.9	4 15.8	8 59.7	28 55.4	29 20.5
27 S	22 27 0.9	8 19.7	0 48.6	10♍ 4.2	17 56.3	5 40.7	1 55.5	9 41.1	4 14.3	9 0.5	28 56.5	29 19.6
28 M	22 30 57.4	9 19.9	0 45.5	24 50.2	19 26.9	6 54.5	2 41.7	9 46.1	4 12.7	9 1.3	28 57.5	29 18.7

DECLINATION at NOON

DAY	SIDEREAL TIME	☉	☊	☽	☿	♀	♂	♃	♄	♅	♆	♇
1 T	20 44 30.4	17S10.7	23N25.4	4N14.1	20S19.6	11S39.6	7S58.4	20S35.4	10S35.3	21S35.7	22S12.9	4N45.1
4 F	20 56 20.1	16 18.4	23 25.5	11S24.6	20 36.2	10 15.2	7 2.8	20 39.5	10 35.6	21 36.7	22 12.9	4 46.7
7 M	21 8 9.8	15 23.6	23 25.7	21 34.8	20 44.2	8 48.5	6 6.7	20 43.4	10 35.5	21 37.6	22 12.9	4 48.4
10 T	21 19 59.4	14 26.4	23 25.8	23 6.8	20 42.6	7 19.7	5 10.2	20 47.0	10 35.2	21 38.4	22 12.9	4 50.2
13 S	21 31 49.1	13 27.0	23 25.9	15 38.2	20 30.7	5 49.1	4 13.4	20 50.3	10 34.5	21 39.2	22 12.9	4 52.1
16 W	21 43 38.8	12 25.7	23 26.0	2 8.3	20 7.8	4 17.2	3 16.4	20 53.4	10 33.5	21 39.9	22 12.9	4 54.1
19 S	21 55 28.4	11 22.5	23 26.1	12N44.4	19 33.8	2 44.3	2 19.2	20 56.3	10 32.2	21 40.5	22 12.8	4 56.1
22 T	22 7 18.1	10 17.8	23 26.2	22 50.0	18 48.3	1 10.7	1 22.1	20 58.8	10 30.6	21 41.1	22 12.8	4 58.2
25 F	22 19 7.8	9 11.7	23 26.3	20 43.2	17 51.4	0N23.2	0 25.0	21 1.2	10 28.7	21 41.5	22 12.7	5 0.3
28 M	22 30 57.4	8 4.3	23 26.4	6 38.9	16 42.9	1 57.1	0N32.0	21 3.2	10 26.6	21 41.9	22 12.6	5 2.5

MARCH 1983

LONGITUDE at NOON

DAY	EPHEMERIS SIDEREAL TIME h m s	☉ ° ′	☊ ° ′	☽ ° ′	☿ ° ′	♀ ° ′	♂ ° ′	♃ ° ′	♄ ° ′	♅ ° ′	♆ ° ′	♇ ° ′
1 T	22 34 54.0	10♓20.2	0♋42.3	9♎15.9	20♒58.7	8♈ 8.3	3♈27.8	9♐51.0	4♏11.1	9♐ 2.1	28♐58.6	29♎17.8
2 W	22 38 50.5	11 20.4	0 39.1	23 15.6	22 31.6	9 22.0	4 13.9	9 55.7	4R 9.3	9 2.7	28 59.6	29R16.8
3 T	22 42 47.1	12 20.5	0 35.9	6♏46.8	24 5.5	10 35.6	5 0.0	10 0.2	4 7.4	9 3.3	29 0.5	29 15.8
4 F	22 46 43.6	13 20.6	0 32.8	19 50.0	25 40.4	11 49.2	5 46.0	10 4.6	4 5.4	9 3.9	29 1.4	29 14.8
5 S	22 50 40.2	14 20.8	0 29.6	2♐27.9	27 16.5	13 2.8	6 32.0	10 8.7	4 3.4	9 4.4	29 2.3	29 13.8
6 S	22 54 36.7	15 20.8	0 26.4	14 45.0	28 53.7	14 16.3	7 18.0	10 12.7	4 1.2	9 4.9	29 3.2	29 12.7
7 M	22 58 33.3	16 20.9	0 23.2	26 46.6	0♓31.9	15 29.7	8 3.9	10 16.6	3 58.9	9 5.3	29 4.0	29 11.6
8 T	23 2 29.8	17 20.9	0 20.0	8♑38.2	2 11.3	16 43.1	8 49.8	10 20.2	3 56.6	9 5.6	29 4.8	29 10.5
9 W	23 6 26.4	18 20.9	0 16.9	20 25.1	3 51.7	17 56.5	9 35.6	10 23.7	3 54.1	9 5.9	29 5.6	29 9.3
10 T	23 10 23.0	19 20.9	0 13.7	2♒12.4	5 33.3	19 9.8	10 21.4	10 27.0	3 51.6	9 6.2	29 6.3	29 8.1
11 F	23 14 19.5	20 20.8	0 10.5	14 4.3	7 16.0	20 23.0	11 7.2	10 30.1	3 49.0	9 6.3	29 7.0	29 6.9
12 S	23 18 16.1	21 20.8	0 7.3	26 4.0	8 59.9	21 36.2	11 52.9	10 33.1	3 46.3	9 6.5	29 7.7	29 5.7
13 S	23 22 12.6	22 20.6	0 4.2	8♓13.9	10 44.9	22 49.4	12 38.6	10 35.9	3 43.5	9 6.5	29 8.3	29 4.5
14 M	23 26 9.2	23 20.5	0 1.0	20 35.4	12 31.1	24 2.5	13 24.2	10 38.5	3 40.6	9 6.6	29 8.9	29 3.2
15 T	23 30 5.7	24 20.3	29♊57.8	3♈ 9.0	14 18.5	25 15.5	14 9.8	10 40.9	3 37.7	9R 6.5	29 9.5	29 1.9
16 W	23 34 2.3	25 20.1	29 54.6	15 54.6	16 7.1	26 28.4	14 55.4	10 43.1	3 34.6	9 6.4	29 10.0	29 0.6
17 T	23 37 58.8	26 19.9	29 51.4	28 51.8	17 56.9	27 41.3	15 40.9	10 45.1	3 31.5	9 6.3	29 10.5	28 59.2
18 F	23 41 55.4	27 19.6	29 48.3	12♉ 0.1	19 47.9	28 54.2	16 26.3	10 47.0	3 28.3	9 6.1	29 11.0	28 57.9
19 S	23 45 51.9	28 19.3	29 45.1	25 19.5	21 40.1	0♉ 7.0	17 11.8	10 48.7	3 25.1	9 5.9	29 11.4	28 56.5
20 S	23 49 48.5	29 18.9	29 41.9	8♊50.2	23 33.5	1 19.7	17 57.1	10 50.1	3 21.7	9 5.6	29 11.8	28 55.1
21 M	23 53 45.0	0♈18.5	29 38.7	22 32.9	25 28.1	2 32.3	18 42.5	10 51.4	3 18.3	9 5.2	29 12.1	28 53.7
22 T	23 57 41.6	1 18.1	29 35.6	6♋28.5	27 23.9	3 44.9	19 27.8	10 52.6	3 14.9	9 4.9	29 12.5	28 52.3
23 W	0 1 38.1	2 17.6	29 32.4	20 37.1	29 20.8	4 57.4	20 13.0	10 53.5	3 11.4	9 4.4	29 12.8	28 50.8
24 T	0 5 34.7	3 17.1	29 29.2	4♌57.9	1♈18.9	6 9.9	20 58.2	10 54.3	3 7.8	9 3.9	29 13.1	28 49.4
25 F	0 9 31.2	4 16.6	29 26.0	19 28.4	3 18.0	7 22.2	21 43.4	10 54.8	3 4.1	9 3.4	29 13.3	28 47.9
26 S	0 13 27.8	5 16.0	29 22.8	4♍ 4.2	5 18.0	8 34.5	22 28.4	10 55.2	3 0.4	9 2.8	29 13.5	28 46.4
27 S	0 17 24.3	6 15.4	29 19.7	18 39.1	7 19.0	9 46.7	23 13.5	10 55.4	2 56.6	9 2.1	29 13.7	28 44.8
28 M	0 21 20.9	7 14.7	29 16.5	3♎ 6.1	9 20.7	10 58.9	23 58.5	10 55.4	2 52.7	9 1.4	29 13.8	28 43.3
29 T	0 25 17.5	8 14.0	29 13.3	17 18.2	11 23.1	12 10.9	24 43.4	10R55.2	2 48.8	9 0.6	29 13.9	28 41.8
30 W	0 29 14.0	9 13.3	29 10.1	1♏ 9.8	13 25.9	13 22.9	25 28.3	10 54.8	2 44.8	8 59.8	29 14.0	28 40.2
31 T	0 33 10.6	10 12.5	29 6.9	14 37.7	15 29.0	14 34.8	26 13.2	10 54.2	2 40.8	8 59.0	29 14.0	28 38.6

DECLINATION at NOON

DAY	SID. TIME	☉	☊	☽	☿	♀	♂	♃	♄	♅	♆	♇
1 T	22 34 54.0	7S41.6	23N26.4	0N55.6	16S17.5	2N28.4	0N50.9	21S 3.9	10S25.8	21S42.0	22S12.6	5N 3.2
4 F	22 46 43.6	6 32.8	23 26.4	14S28.1	14 53.5	4 1.9	1 47.6	21 5.6	10 23.3	21 42.3	22 12.5	5 5.4
7 M	22 58 33.3	5 23.2	23 26.5	23 0.8	13 18.1	5 34.6	2 43.9	21 7.1	10 20.5	21 42.6	22 12.5	5 7.7
10 T	23 10 23.0	4 13.0	23 26.5	22 12.8	11 31.3	7 6.2	3 39.8	21 8.4	10 17.4	21 42.7	22 12.4	5 9.9
13 S	23 22 12.6	3 2.3	23 26.5	12 46.5	9 33.1	8 36.4	4 35.3	21 9.4	10 14.2	21 42.8	22 12.3	5 12.2
16 W	23 34 2.3	1 51.2	23 26.5	1N49.2	7 24.0	10 4.9	5 30.2	21 10.2	10 10.7	21 42.8	22 12.2	5 14.4
19 S	23 45 51.9	0 40.1	23 26.5	16 21.0	5 4.3	11 31.4	6 24.5	21 10.8	10 7.0	21 42.7	22 12.1	5 16.7
22 T	23 57 41.6	0N31.1	23 26.5	23 54.1	2 34.6	12 55.5	7 18.2	21 11.1	10 3.1	21 42.6	22 12.0	5 18.9
25 F	0 9 31.2	1 42.0	23 26.4	18 38.6	0N 3.9	14 16.8	8 11.0	21 11.2	9 59.0	21 42.3	22 11.9	5 21.1
28 M	0 21 20.9	2 52.6	23 26.4	3 21.0	2 49.4	15 35.1	9 3.0	21 11.0	9 54.8	21 42.1	22 11.8	5 23.3
31 T	0 33 10.6	4 2.6	23 26.3	12S54.3	5 38.9	16 50.0	9 54.1	21 10.7	9 50.4	21 41.7	22 11.7	5 25.4

APRIL 1983

LONGITUDE at NOON

DAY	SID. TIME	☉	☊	☽	☿	♀	♂	♃	♄	♅	♆	♇
1 F	0 37 7.1	11♈11.7	29♊ 3.8	27♏40.9	17♈32.2	15♉46.6	26♈58.0	10♐53.5	2♏36.8	8♐58.1	29♐14.0	28♎37.0
2 S	0 41 3.7	12 10.9	29 0.6	10♐20.8	19 35.2	16 58.3	27 42.7	10R52.5	2R32.7	8R57.1	29 14.0	28R35.4
3 S	0 45 0.2	13 10.1	28 57.4	22 40.6	21 37.7	18 10.0	28 27.4	10 51.4	2 28.5	8 56.1	29R13.9	28 33.8
4 M	0 48 56.8	14 9.2	28 54.2	4♑44.9	23 39.4	19 21.6	29 12.1	10 50.1	2 24.3	8 55.1	29 13.8	28 32.2
5 T	0 52 53.3	15 8.3	28 51.1	16 38.9	25 39.9	20 33.1	29 56.7	10 48.6	2 20.1	8 54.0	29 13.7	28 30.6
6 W	0 56 49.9	16 7.3	28 47.9	28 27.9	27 39.0	21 44.5	0♉41.3	10 46.9	2 15.8	8 52.8	29 13.5	28 28.9
7 T	1 0 46.4	17 6.4	28 44.7	10♒17.5	29 36.2	22 55.8	1 25.8	10 45.0	2 11.5	8 51.7	29 13.3	28 27.3
8 F	1 4 43.0	18 5.4	28 41.5	22 12.6	1♉31.2	24 7.1	2 10.3	10 43.0	2 7.1	8 50.4	29 13.1	28 25.6
9 S	1 8 39.5	19 4.3	28 38.3	4♓17.4	3 23.6	25 18.3	2 54.7	10 40.7	2 2.7	8 49.2	29 12.8	28 23.9
10 S	1 12 36.1	20 3.3	28 35.2	16 35.2	5 13.1	26 29.3	3 39.1	10 38.3	1 58.3	8 47.8	29 12.5	28 22.3
11 M	1 16 32.6	21 2.2	28 32.0	29 8.2	6 59.3	27 40.3	4 23.4	10 35.7	1 53.9	8 46.5	29 12.2	28 20.6
12 T	1 20 29.2	22 1.1	28 28.8	11♈57.3	8 41.9	28 51.3	5 7.8	10 33.0	1 49.4	8 45.1	29 11.9	28 19.0
13 W	1 24 25.7	22 60.0	28 25.6	25 2.1	10 20.5	0♊ 2.1	5 52.0	10 30.0	1 45.0	8 43.7	29 11.5	28 17.3
14 T	1 28 22.3	23 58.8	28 22.5	8♉21.3	11 55.0	1 12.8	6 36.2	10 26.9	1 40.4	8 42.2	29 11.0	28 15.6
15 F	1 32 18.9	24 57.6	28 19.3	21 52.9	13 25.1	2 23.4	7 20.3	10 23.6	1 35.9	8 40.6	29 10.6	28 13.9
16 S	1 36 15.4	25 56.3	28 16.1	5♊34.6	14 50.5	3 34.0	8 4.4	10 20.1	1 31.4	8 39.1	29 10.1	28 12.2
17 S	1 40 12.0	26 55.0	28 12.9	19 24.6	16 11.1	4 44.4	8 48.4	10 16.4	1 26.8	8 37.4	29 9.6	28 10.5
18 M	1 44 8.5	27 53.7	28 9.7	3♋21.2	17 26.8	5 54.7	9 32.4	10 12.6	1 22.2	8 35.8	29 9.0	28 8.8
19 T	1 48 5.1	28 52.3	28 6.6	17 23.3	18 37.3	7 4.9	10 16.4	10 8.6	1 17.7	8 34.1	29 8.5	28 7.1
20 W	1 52 1.6	29 50.9	28 3.4	1♌30.1	19 42.5	8 15.0	11 0.2	10 4.5	1 13.1	8 32.4	29 7.8	28 5.4
21 T	1 55 58.2	0♉49.5	28 0.2	15 40.4	20 42.4	9 25.0	11 44.1	10 0.1	1 8.5	8 30.6	29 7.2	28 3.7
22 F	1 59 54.7	1 48.0	27 57.0	29 52.6	21 36.8	10 34.9	12 27.8	9 55.7	1 3.9	8 28.8	29 6.5	28 2.0
23 S	2 3 51.3	2 46.5	27 53.9	14♍ 4.2	22 25.7	11 44.6	13 11.5	9 51.1	0 59.3	8 27.0	29 5.8	28 0.3
24 S	2 7 47.8	3 44.9	27 50.7	28 11.8	23 8.9	12 54.3	13 55.2	9 46.3	0 54.8	8 25.1	29 5.1	27 58.6
25 M	2 11 44.4	4 43.3	27 47.5	12♎11.3	23 46.6	14 3.8	14 38.8	9 41.3	0 50.2	8 23.2	29 4.4	27 57.0
26 T	2 15 40.9	5 41.7	27 44.3	25 58.6	24 18.5	15 13.2	15 22.4	9 36.3	0 45.6	8 21.3	29 3.6	27 55.3
27 W	2 19 37.5	6 40.1	27 41.2	9♏30.0	24 44.6	16 22.5	16 5.9	9 31.1	0 41.1	8 19.3	29 2.8	27 53.6
28 T	2 23 34.1	7 38.4	27 38.0	22 43.0	25 5.1	17 31.6	16 49.4	9 25.7	0 36.6	8 17.3	29 1.9	27 51.9
29 F	2 27 30.6	8 36.7	27 34.8	5♐36.6	25 19.9	18 40.6	17 32.8	9 20.2	0 32.0	8 15.3	29 1.1	27 50.3
30 S	2 31 27.2	9 34.9	27 31.6	18 11.3	25 29.1	19 49.5	18 16.1	9 14.6	0 27.5	8 13.2	29 0.2	27 48.6

DECLINATION at NOON

DAY	SID. TIME	☉	☊	☽	☿	♀	♂	♃	♄	♅	♆	♇
1 F	0 37 7.1	4N25.8	23N26.3	17S 8.8	6N35.6	17N14.2	10N10.9	21S10.5	9S48.9	21S41.6	22S11.7	5N26.1
4 M	0 48 56.8	5 34.9	23 26.2	23 56.6	9 24.0	18 24.1	11 0.6	21 9.8	9 44.4	21 41.1	22 11.6	5 28.2
7 T	1 0 46.4	6 43.2	23 26.1	20 56.5	12 5.1	19 29.9	11 49.4	21 9.0	9 39.8	21 40.6	22 11.5	5 30.2
10 S	1 12 36.1	7 50.4	23 26.0	9 51.1	14 32.9	20 31.4	12 37.0	21 7.9	9 35.1	21 40.0	22 11.4	5 32.1
13 W	1 24 25.7	8 56.5	23 25.9	5N31.9	16 42.5	21 28.1	13 23.4	21 6.5	9 30.4	21 39.4	22 11.3	5 34.0
16 S	1 36 15.4	10 1.2	23 25.8	19 25.4	18 30.1	22 20.0	14 8.6	21 5.0	9 25.7	21 38.7	22 11.2	5 35.8
19 T	1 48 5.1	11 4.5	23 25.7	24 6.1	19 53.8	23 6.6	14 52.5	21 3.2	9 20.9	21 37.9	22 11.1	5 37.5
22 F	1 59 54.7	12 6.0	23 25.5	15 46.7	20 53.0	23 47.8	15 35.1	21 1.3	9 16.2	21 37.1	22 11.0	5 39.1
25 M	2 11 44.4	13 5.8	23 25.4	0S17.8	21 27.6	24 23.3	16 16.2	20 59.1	9 11.5	21 36.3	22 10.9	5 40.6
28 T	2 23 34.1	14 3.6	23 25.2	15 43.7	21 38.0	24 53.1	16 55.9	20 56.8	9 6.9	21 35.4	22 10.8	5 42.1

MAY 1983

DAY	EPHEMERIS SIDEREAL TIME	☉	☊	☽	☿	♀	♂	♃	♄	♅	♆	♇
	h m s	° ′	° ′	° ′	° ′	° ′	° ′	° ′	° ′	° ′	° ′	° ′
						LONGITUDE at NOON						
1 S	2 35 23.7	10♉33.2	27♊28.4	0♑29.4	25♉32.9	20♊58.2	18♉59.4	9♐ 8.8	0♏23.1	8♐11.1	28♐59.3	27♎47.0
2 M	2 39 20.3	11 31.4	27 25.3	12 33.9	25R31.2	22 6.9	19 42.7	9R 2.9	0R18.6	8R 9.0	28R58.3	27R45.3
3 T	2 43 16.8	12 29.6	27 22.1	24 29.1	25 24.5	23 15.4	20 26.0	8 56.9	0 14.2	8 6.9	28 57.4	27 43.7
4 W	2 47 13.4	13 27.8	27 18.9	6♒19.8	25 12.7	24 23.7	21 9.1	8 50.8	0 9.8	8 4.8	28 56.4	27 42.1
5 T	2 51 9.9	14 25.9	27 15.7	18 11.0	24 56.4	25 31.9	21 52.3	8 44.5	0 5.4	8 2.6	28 55.4	27 40.5
6 F	2 55 6.5	15 24.0	27 12.6	0♓ 7.8	24 35.8	26 40.0	22 35.3	8 38.2	0 1.1	8 0.4	28 54.3	27 38.9
7 S	2 59 3.1	16 22.1	27 9.4	12 15.0	24 11.4	27 47.9	23 18.3	8 31.7	29♎56.8	7 58.1	28 53.3	27 37.3
8 S	3 2 59.6	17 20.2	27 6.2	24 36.7	23 43.6	28 55.7	24 1.3	8 25.1	29 52.5	7 55.9	28 52.2	27 35.8
9 M	3 6 56.2	18 18.3	27 3.0	7♈16.2	23 13.0	0♋ 3.3	24 44.2	8 18.4	29 48.3	7 53.6	28 51.1	27 34.2
10 T	3 10 52.7	19 16.3	26 59.8	20 15.3	22 40.1	1 10.8	25 27.1	8 11.6	29 44.1	7 51.3	28 49.9	27 32.6
11 W	3 14 49.3	20 14.3	26 56.7	3♉34.6	22 5.5	2 18.1	26 9.9	8 4.8	29 39.9	7 48.9	28 48.8	27 31.1
12 T	3 18 45.8	21 12.2	26 53.5	17 13.0	21 29.9	3 25.2	26 52.7	7 57.8	29 35.8	7 46.6	28 47.6	27 29.6
13 F	3 22 42.4	22 10.2	26 50.3	1♊ 7.7	20 53.9	4 32.2	27 35.4	7 50.8	29 31.8	7 44.3	28 46.4	27 28.1
14 S	3 26 38.9	23 8.1	26 47.1	15 15.1	20 18.0	5 39.0	28 18.1	7 43.7	29 27.8	7 41.9	28 45.2	27 26.6
15 S	3 30 35.5	24 6.0	26 44.0	29 31.0	19 43.0	6 45.6	29 0.7	7 36.5	29 23.8	7 39.5	28 43.9	27 25.1
16 M	3 34 32.1	25 3.9	26 40.8	13♋51.1	19 9.5	7 52.1	29 43.3	7 29.2	29 19.9	7 37.1	28 42.6	27 23.7
17 T	3 38 28.6	26 1.7	26 37.6	28 11.5	18 37.9	8 58.3	0♊25.8	7 21.9	29 16.1	7 34.7	28 41.4	27 22.2
18 W	3 42 25.2	26 59.5	26 34.4	12♌29.1	18 8.8	10 4.4	1 8.3	7 14.5	29 12.3	7 32.2	28 40.0	27 20.8
19 T	3 46 21.7	27 57.3	26 31.3	26 41.3	17 42.6	11 10.3	1 50.7	7 7.1	29 8.5	7 29.8	28 38.7	27 19.4
20 F	3 50 18.3	28 55.0	26 28.1	10♍46.2	17 19.8	12 15.9	2 33.1	6 59.7	29 4.9	7 27.4	28 37.4	27 18.0
21 S	3 54 14.8	29 52.8	26 24.9	24 42.1	17 0.6	13 21.4	3 15.4	6 52.2	29 1.3	7 24.9	28 36.0	27 16.7
22 S	3 58 11.4	0♊50.5	26 21.7	8♎27.6	16 45.3	14 26.6	3 57.7	6 44.6	28 57.7	7 22.4	28 34.6	27 15.3
23 M	4 2 8.0	1 48.1	26 18.5	22 1.3	16 34.2	15 31.6	4 39.9	6 37.0	28 54.2	7 20.0	28 33.3	27 14.0
24 T	4 6 4.5	2 45.8	26 15.4	5♏22.0	16 27.5	16 36.5	5 22.1	6 29.5	28 50.9	7 17.6	28 31.9	27 12.7
25 W	4 10 1.1	3 43.5	26 12.2	18 28.7	16 25.1	17 41.0	6 4.2	6 21.9	28 47.5	7 15.1	28 30.5	27 11.5
26 T	4 13 57.6	4 41.1	26 9.0	1♐20.7	16D27.2	18 45.3	6 46.3	6 14.3	28 44.3	7 12.6	28 29.0	27 10.2
27 F	4 17 54.2	5 38.6	26 5.8	13 58.1	16 33.8	19 49.4	7 28.3	6 6.6	28 41.1	7 10.1	28 27.6	27 9.0
28 S	4 21 50.7	6 36.2	26 2.7	26 21.7	16 45.0	20 53.2	8 10.3	5 59.0	28 38.0	7 7.6	28 26.1	27 7.8
29 S	4 25 47.3	7 33.7	25 59.5	8♑32.9	17 0.6	21 56.8	8 52.2	5 51.4	28 34.9	7 5.1	28 24.6	27 6.6
30 M	4 29 43.9	8 31.3	25 56.3	20 34.0	17 20.6	23 0.1	9 34.1	5 43.7	28 31.9	7 2.6	28 23.2	27 5.4
31 T	4 33 40.4	9 28.8	25 53.1	2♒28.1	17 45.0	24 3.1	10 15.9	5 36.1	28 29.0	7 0.2	28 21.6	27 4.3
						DECLINATION at NOON						
1 S	2 35 23.7	14N59.4	23N25.0	23S51.5	21N24.9	25N16.9	17N34.0	20S54.2	9S 2.4	21S34.4	22S10.7	5N43.4
4 W	2 47 13.4	15 52.9	23 24.9	21 56.8	20 49.4	25 34.7	18 10.7	20 51.5	8 58.0	21 33.4	22 10.6	5 44.6
7 S	2 59 3.1	16 44.1	23 24.7	11 36.7	19 54.2	25 46.5	18 45.7	20 48.6	8 53.7	21 32.4	22 10.5	5 45.7
10 T	3 10 52.7	17 32.7	23 24.4	3N33.2	18 44.1	25 52.2	19 19.0	20 45.6	8 49.5	21 31.3	22 10.4	5 46.6
13 F	3 22 42.4	18 18.8	23 24.2	18 17.7	17 26.2	25 51.9	19 50.7	20 42.4	8 45.6	21 30.2	22 10.3	5 47.5
16 M	3 34 32.1	19 2.0	23 24.0	24 22.6	16 8.8	25 45.6	20 20.7	20 39.1	8 41.8	21 29.0	22 10.2	5 48.2
19 T	3 46 21.7	19 42.4	23 23.7	16 55.9	15 0.3	25 33.4	20 48.9	20 35.6	8 38.2	21 27.9	22 10.1	5 48.8
22 S	3 58 11.4	20 19.7	23 23.5	1 19.7	14 7.3	25 15.6	21 15.3	20 32.1	8 34.9	21 26.7	22 10.0	5 49.3
25 W	4 10 1.1	20 53.9	23 23.2	14S18.8	13 33.7	24 52.3	21 39.8	20 28.5	8 31.8	21 25.5	22 10.0	5 49.6
28 S	4 21 50.7	21 24.8	23 22.9	23 30.6	13 20.9	24 23.7	22 2.6	20 24.9	8 28.9	21 24.3	22 9.9	5 49.8
31 T	4 33 40.4	21 52.4	23 22.6	22 43.8	13 28.3	23 50.2	22 23.4	20 21.3	8 26.3	21 23.1	22 9.8	5 49.8

JUNE 1983

DAY	EPHEMERIS SIDEREAL TIME	☉	☊	☽	☿	♀	♂	♃	♄	♅	♆	♇
						LONGITUDE at NOON						
1 W	4 37 37.0	10♊26.3	25♊50.0	14♒18.9	18♉13.6	25♋ 5.9	10♊57.7	5♐28.5	28♎26.2	6♐57.7	28♐20.1	27♎ 3.2
2 T	4 41 33.5	11 23.8	25 46.8	26 10.5	18 46.5	26 8.4	11 39.4	5R20.9	28R23.5	6R55.2	28R18.6	27R 2.1
3 F	4 45 30.1	12 21.2	25 43.6	8♓ 7.4	19 23.4	27 10.6	12 21.1	5 13.4	28 20.8	6 52.7	28 17.1	27 1.0
4 S	4 49 26.6	13 18.7	25 40.4	20 14.4	20 4.3	28 12.5	13 2.7	5 5.8	28 18.3	6 50.3	28 15.5	26 60.0
5 S	4 53 23.2	14 16.1	25 37.2	2♈35.8	20 49.0	29 14.0	13 44.3	4 58.4	28 15.8	6 47.8	28 14.0	26 59.0
6 M	4 57 19.8	15 13.6	25 34.1	15 15.8	21 37.6	0♌15.3	14 25.9	4 50.9	28 13.4	6 45.3	28 12.4	26 58.0
7 T	5 1 16.3	16 11.0	25 30.9	28 17.5	22 29.9	1 16.3	15 7.4	4 43.5	28 11.0	6 42.9	28 10.8	26 57.0
8 W	5 5 12.9	17 8.4	25 27.7	11♉42.7	23 25.8	2 16.9	15 48.9	4 36.2	28 8.8	6 40.4	28 9.2	26 56.1
9 T	5 9 9.4	18 5.8	25 24.5	25 31.6	24 25.2	3 17.2	16 30.3	4 28.9	28 6.7	6 38.0	28 7.7	26 55.2
10 F	5 13 6.0	19 3.2	25 21.4	9♊42.2	25 28.1	4 17.1	17 11.7	4 21.7	28 4.6	6 35.6	28 6.1	26 54.3
11 S	5 17 2.5	20 0.6	25 18.2	24 10.6	26 34.3	5 16.7	17 53.0	4 14.5	28 2.6	6 33.2	28 4.5	26 53.5
12 S	5 20 59.1	20 58.0	25 15.0	8♋51.2	27 43.9	6 15.9	18 34.3	4 7.4	28 0.8	6 30.8	28 2.9	26 52.7
13 M	5 24 55.7	21 55.3	25 11.8	23 37.2	28 56.8	7 14.7	19 15.5	4 0.4	27 59.0	6 28.4	28 1.3	26 51.9
14 T	5 28 52.2	22 52.7	25 8.7	8♌21.9	0♊12.9	8 13.1	19 56.8	3 53.6	27 57.3	6 26.1	27 59.7	26 51.2
15 W	5 32 48.8	23 50.0	25 5.5	22 58.8	1 32.2	9 11.1	20 37.9	3 46.8	27 55.8	6 23.8	27 58.1	26 50.4
16 T	5 36 45.3	24 47.4	25 2.3	7♍23.1	2 54.7	10 8.7	21 19.0	3 40.0	27 54.3	6 21.5	27 56.5	26 49.7
17 F	5 40 41.9	25 44.6	24 59.1	21 31.6	4 20.2	11 5.8	22 0.0	3 33.4	27 52.8	6 19.2	27 54.8	26 49.1
18 S	5 44 38.4	26 41.9	24 56.0	5♎22.6	5 48.9	12 2.4	22 41.1	3 26.9	27 51.5	6 16.9	27 53.2	26 48.4
19 S	5 48 35.0	27 39.2	24 52.8	18 55.6	7 20.6	12 58.5	23 22.0	3 20.4	27 50.3	6 14.6	27 51.6	26 47.8
20 M	5 52 31.6	28 36.4	24 49.6	2♏11.3	8 55.3	13 54.2	24 2.9	3 14.1	27 49.2	6 12.4	27 50.0	26 47.3
21 T	5 56 28.1	29 33.7	24 46.4	15 11.0	10 33.1	14 49.3	24 43.8	3 7.9	27 48.2	6 10.2	27 48.4	26 46.7
22 W	6 0 24.7	0♋30.9	24 43.2	27 55.9	12 13.8	15 43.9	25 24.6	3 1.8	27 47.3	6 8.0	27 46.7	26 46.2
23 T	6 4 21.2	1 28.1	24 40.1	10♐27.8	13 57.5	16 38.0	26 5.4	2 55.9	27 46.4	6 5.8	27 45.1	26 45.8
24 F	6 8 17.8	2 25.4	24 36.9	22 48.2	15 44.1	17 31.5	26 46.1	2 50.0	27 45.7	6 3.6	27 43.5	26 45.3
25 S	6 12 14.4	3 22.6	24 33.7	4♑58.6	17 33.5	18 24.4	27 26.8	2 44.3	27 45.1	6 1.5	27 41.9	26 44.9
26 S	6 16 10.9	4 19.8	24 30.5	17 0.9	19 25.6	19 16.7	28 7.4	2 38.7	27 44.5	5 59.4	27 40.3	26 44.5
27 M	6 20 7.5	5 17.0	24 27.4	28 56.8	21 20.4	20 8.3	28 48.0	2 33.3	27 44.1	5 57.4	27 38.7	26 44.2
28 T	6 24 4.0	6 14.2	24 24.2	10♒48.7	23 17.6	20 59.3	29 28.6	2 28.0	27 43.7	5 55.3	27 37.1	26 43.9
29 W	6 28 0.6	7 11.4	24 21.0	22 39.1	25 17.2	21 49.6	0♋ 9.1	2 22.8	27 43.5	5 53.3	27 35.5	26 43.6
30 T	6 31 57.1	8 8.5	24 17.8	4♓31.1	27 19.0	22 39.3	0 49.6	2 17.8	27 43.3	5 51.3	27 33.9	26 43.3
						DECLINATION at NOON						
1 W	4 37 37.0	22N 0.9	23N22.5	20S21.5	13N35.0	23N37.9	22N29.9	20S20.1	8S25.5	21S22.7	22S 9.8	5N49.8
4 S	4 49 26.6	22 23.9	23 22.2	8 41.9	14 6.4	22 58.2	22 48.3	20 16.4	8 23.3	21 21.5	22 9.7	5 49.7
7 T	5 1 16.3	22 43.5	23 21.9	6N44.0	14 52.9	22 14.1	23 4.7	20 12.8	8 21.4	21 20.3	22 9.6	5 49.4
10 F	5 13 6.0	22 59.4	23 21.6	20 31.1	15 51.6	21 26.1	23 19.2	20 9.3	8 19.8	21 19.1	22 9.6	5 49.0
13 M	5 24 55.7	23 11.7	23 21.3	23 52.2	16 59.6	20 34.4	23 31.8	20 5.9	8 18.4	21 17.9	22 9.5	5 48.5
16 T	5 36 45.3	23 20.3	23 20.9	13 28.3	18 13.8	19 39.5	23 42.5	20 2.5	8 17.4	21 16.7	22 9.5	5 47.8
19 S	5 48 35.0	23 25.2	23 20.5	2S56.0	19 30.6	18 41.8	23 51.2	19 59.4	8 16.7	21 15.6	22 9.4	5 47.0
22 W	6 0 24.7	23 26.4	23 20.2	17 20.5	20 46.5	17 41.6	23 57.9	19 56.4	8 16.4	21 14.5	22 9.3	5 46.1
25 S	6 12 14.4	23 23.9	23 19.8	24 15.2	21 56.8	16 39.3	24 2.8	19 53.6	8 16.3	21 13.4	22 9.3	5 45.0
28 T	6 24 4.0	23 17.7	23 19.4	21 9.4	22 56.6	15 35.4	24 5.7	19 51.0	8 16.6	21 12.4	22 9.3	5 43.8

JULY 1983

DAY	EPHEMERIS SIDEREAL TIME	☉	☊	☽	☿	♀	♂	♃	♄	♅	♆	♇
	h m s	° ′	° ′	° ′	° ′	° ′	° ′	° ′	° ′	° ′	° ′	° ′
LONGITUDE at NOON												
1 F	6 35 53.7	9♋ 5.7	24♊14.7	16♓28.2	29♊22.8	23♌28.2	1♋30.1	2♐12.9	27♎43.3	5♐49.4	27♐32.3	26♎43.1
2 S	6 39 50.3	10 2.9	24 11.5	28 34.3	1♋28.3	24 16.3	2 10.5	2R 8.2	27 43.3	5R47.5	27R30.7	26R42.9
3 S	6 43 46.8	11 0.1	24 8.3	10♈53.7	3 35.3	25 3.7	2 50.8	2 3.6	27D43.5	5 45.6	27 29.2	26 42.8
4 M	6 47 43.4	11 57.3	24 5.1	23 30.5	5 43.5	25 50.3	3 31.1	1 59.1	27 43.7	5 43.8	27 27.6	26 42.7
5 T	6 51 39.9	12 54.6	24 2.0	6♉28.7	7 52.6	26 36.1	4 11.5	1 54.9	27 44.1	5 42.0	27 26.1	26 42.6
6 W	6 55 36.5	13 51.8	23 58.8	19 51.3	10 2.4	27 21.0	4 51.7	1 50.8	27 44.6	5 40.2	27 24.6	26 42.6
7 T	6 59 33.1	14 49.0	23 55.6	3♊40.2	12 12.5	28 5.0	5 31.9	1 46.9	27 45.1	5 38.5	27 23.0	26 42.6
8 F	7 3 29.6	15 46.2	23 52.4	17 55.1	14 22.7	28 48.0	6 12.1	1 43.1	27 45.8	5 36.8	27 21.5	26 42.6
9 S	7 7 26.2	16 43.5	23 49.2	2♋33.2	16 32.6	29 30.1	6 52.2	1 39.4	27 46.5	5 35.1	27 20.0	26 42.6
10 S	7 11 22.7	17 40.7	23 46.1	17 29.0	18 42.0	0♍11.2	7 32.3	1 36.0	27 47.4	5 33.4	27 18.5	26D42.7
11 M	7 15 19.3	18 37.9	23 42.9	2♌34.7	20 50.8	0 51.3	8 12.3	1 32.7	27 48.3	5 31.8	27 17.0	26 42.9
12 T	7 19 15.8	19 35.2	23 39.7	17 41.1	22 58.6	1 30.3	8 52.3	1 29.6	27 49.4	5 30.3	27 15.5	26 43.0
13 W	7 23 12.4	20 32.4	23 36.5	2♍38.8	25 5.4	2 8.1	9 32.3	1 26.7	27 50.5	5 28.8	27 14.1	26 43.2
14 T	7 27 9.0	21 29.6	23 33.4	17 20.2	27 10.8	2 44.8	10 12.2	1 23.9	27 51.7	5 27.3	27 12.6	26 43.4
15 F	7 31 5.5	22 26.9	23 30.2	1♎39.7	29 14.9	3 20.3	10 52.1	1 21.3	27 53.1	5 25.9	27 11.2	26 43.7
16 S	7 35 2.1	23 24.1	23 27.0	15 34.8	1♌17.6	3 54.5	11 31.9	1 18.9	27 54.5	5 24.5	27 9.8	26 44.0
17 S	7 38 58.6	24 21.4	23 23.8	29 5.2	3 18.6	4 27.3	12 11.7	1 16.7	27 56.0	5 23.1	27 8.4	26 44.3
18 M	7 42 55.2	25 18.6	23 20.7	12♏12.6	5 18.0	4 58.8	12 51.5	1 14.6	27 57.7	5 21.8	27 7.0	26 44.7
19 T	7 46 51.7	26 15.8	23 17.5	24 59.9	7 15.7	5 28.8	13 31.2	1 12.8	27 59.4	5 20.5	27 5.6	26 45.1
20 W	7 50 48.3	27 13.1	23 14.3	7♐30.5	9 11.7	5 57.4	14 10.9	1 11.1	28 1.2	5 19.3	27 4.3	26 45.5
21 T	7 54 44.9	28 10.3	23 11.1	19 47.6	11 6.0	6 24.4	14 50.5	1 9.6	28 3.1	5 18.1	27 2.9	26 46.0
22 F	7 58 41.4	29 7.6	23 7.9	1♑54.7	12 58.4	6 49.8	15 30.1	1 8.3	28 5.1	5 17.0	27 1.6	26 46.5
23 S	8 2 38.0	0♌ 4.8	23 4.8	13 54.3	14 49.2	7 13.6	16 9.7	1 7.1	28 7.2	5 15.9	27 0.3	26 47.0
24 S	8 6 34.5	1 2.1	23 1.6	25 49.0	16 38.1	7 35.7	16 49.2	1 6.2	28 9.4	5 14.9	26 59.1	26 47.6
25 M	8 10 31.1	1 59.4	22 58.4	7♒40.7	18 25.3	7 55.9	17 28.7	1 5.4	28 11.7	5 13.9	26 57.8	26 48.2
26 T	8 14 27.6	2 56.7	22 55.2	19 31.5	20 10.8	8 14.5	18 8.2	1 4.8	28 14.1	5 13.0	26 56.6	26 48.8
27 W	8 18 24.2	3 54.0	22 52.1	1♓23.1	21 54.5	8 31.0	18 47.7	1 4.4	28 16.6	5 12.1	26 55.4	26 49.5
28 T	8 22 20.8	4 51.4	22 48.9	13 17.6	23 36.5	8 45.7	19 27.0	1 4.2	28 19.1	5 11.2	26 54.2	26 50.2
29 F	8 26 17.3	5 48.7	22 45.7	25 17.3	25 16.7	8 58.3	20 6.4	1 4.1	28 21.8	5 10.4	26 53.0	26 50.9
30 S	8 30 13.9	6 46.0	22 42.5	7♈25.2	26 55.2	9 8.9	20 45.7	1D 4.3	28 24.5	5 9.6	26 51.9	26 51.7
31 S	8 34 10.4	7 43.4	22 39.4	19 44.4	28 31.9	9 17.3	21 25.0	1 4.6	28 27.3	5 8.9	26 50.7	26 52.5
DECLINATION at NOON												
1 F	6 35 53.7	23N 7.7	23N19.0	10S 8.2	23N40.5	14N30.3	24N 6.8	19S48.6	8S17.2	21S11.4	22S 9.2	5N42.5
4 M	6 47 43.4	22 54.2	23 18.6	4N49.5	24 3.7	13 24.4	24 6.0	19 46.5	8 18.1	21 10.4	22 9.2	5 41.0
7 T	6 59 33.1	22 37.1	23 18.1	19 0.1	24 2.8	12 18.2	24 3.3	19 44.7	8 19.3	21 9.5	22 9.2	5 39.5
10 S	7 11 22.7	22 16.4	23 17.7	24 17.3	23 37.1	11 12.2	23 58.7	19 43.2	8 20.9	21 8.7	22 9.1	5 37.8
13 W	7 23 12.4	21 52.3	23 17.2	15 2.7	22 47.9	10 6.8	23 52.4	19 42.0	8 22.7	21 7.9	22 9.1	5 36.0
16 S	7 35 2.1	21 24.8	23 16.8	1S37.1	21 38.3	9 2.8	23 44.3	19 41.0	8 24.9	21 7.2	22 9.1	5 34.1
19 T	7 46 51.7	20 54.0	23 16.3	16 29.5	20 12.1	8 0.7	23 34.4	19 40.5	8 27.4	21 6.5	22 9.1	5 32.1
22 F	7 58 41.4	20 20.1	23 15.8	24 4.1	18 33.3	7 1.2	23 22.8	19 40.2	8 30.1	21 5.9	22 9.1	5 30.0
25 M	8 10 31.1	19 43.1	23 15.3	21 45.7	16 45.1	6 5.1	23 9.6	19 40.3	8 33.2	21 5.4	22 9.1	5 27.8
28 T	8 22 20.8	19 3.2	23 14.8	11 14.0	14 50.5	5 13.3	22 54.7	19 40.7	8 36.6	21 5.0	22 9.1	5 25.5
31 S	8 34 10.4	18 20.4	23 14.3	3N24.9	12 52.1	4 26.7	22 38.2	19 41.5	8 40.2	21 4.6	22 9.2	5 23.1

AUGUST 1983

DAY	EPHEMERIS SIDEREAL TIME	☉	☊	☽	☿	♀	♂	♃	♄	♅	♆	♇
LONGITUDE at NOON												
1 M	8 38 7.0	8♌40.8	22♊36.2	2♉18.7	0♍ 6.9	9♍23.6	22♋ 4.2	1♐ 5.1	28♎30.3	5♐ 8.3	26♐49.6	26♎53.3
2 T	8 42 3.5	9 38.2	22 33.0	15 12.0	1 40.2	9 27.8	22 43.4	1 5.8	28 33.3	5R 7.6	26R48.5	26 54.2
3 W	8 46 0.1	10 35.6	22 29.8	28 27.9	3 11.8	9 29.6	23 22.6	1 6.6	28 36.4	5 7.1	26 47.5	26 55.1
4 T	8 49 56.6	11 33.1	22 26.6	12♊ 9.4	4 41.7	9R29.2	24 1.8	1 7.7	28 39.5	5 6.6	26 46.4	26 56.0
5 F	8 53 53.2	12 30.5	22 23.5	26 17.9	6 9.7	9 26.5	24 40.9	1 8.9	28 42.8	5 6.1	26 45.4	26 57.0
6 S	8 57 49.8	13 28.0	22 20.3	10♋52.5	7 36.1	9 21.4	25 20.0	1 10.3	28 46.2	5 5.7	26 44.4	26 58.0
7 S	9 1 46.3	14 25.5	22 17.1	25 49.2	9 0.6	9 14.0	25 59.0	1 11.9	28 49.6	5 5.3	26 43.5	26 59.0
8 M	9 5 42.9	15 23.0	22 13.9	11♌ 0.9	10 23.3	9 4.2	26 38.0	1 13.7	28 53.1	5 5.0	26 42.5	27 0.0
9 T	9 9 39.4	16 20.6	22 10.8	26 17.8	11 44.2	8 52.0	27 17.0	1 15.6	28 56.7	5 4.7	26 41.6	27 1.1
10 W	9 13 36.0	17 18.1	22 7.6	11♍29.0	13 3.1	8 37.5	27 55.9	1 17.7	29 0.4	5 4.5	26 40.7	27 2.3
11 T	9 17 32.5	18 15.7	22 4.4	26 24.3	14 20.2	8 20.6	28 34.9	1 20.1	29 4.2	5 4.3	26 39.9	27 3.4
12 F	9 21 29.1	19 13.3	22 1.2	10♎56.1	15 35.2	8 1.4	29 13.7	1 22.5	29 8.0	5 4.2	26 39.0	27 4.6
13 S	9 25 25.6	20 10.9	21 58.1	24 59.8	16 48.2	7 40.0	29 52.6	1 25.2	29 11.9	5 4.1	26 38.2	27 5.8
14 S	9 29 22.2	21 8.5	21 54.9	8♏34.6	17 59.0	7 16.5	0♌31.4	1 28.1	29 16.0	5 4.1	26 37.5	27 7.0
15 M	9 33 18.8	22 6.2	21 51.7	21 42.0	19 7.6	6 50.8	1 10.1	1 31.1	29 20.0	5D 4.2	26 36.7	27 8.3
16 T	9 37 15.3	23 3.8	21 48.5	4♐25.7	20 14.0	6 23.3	1 48.9	1 34.3	29 24.3	5 4.3	26 36.0	27 9.7
17 W	9 41 11.9	24 1.5	21 45.3	16 50.0	21 18.0	5 53.8	2 27.6	1 37.7	29 28.5	5 4.5	26 35.4	27 11.0
18 T	9 45 8.4	24 59.2	21 42.2	28 59.6	22 19.4	5 22.7	3 6.2	1 41.2	29 32.8	5 4.7	26 34.7	27 12.3
19 F	9 49 5.0	25 56.9	21 39.0	10♑59.1	23 18.2	4 50.1	3 44.9	1 44.9	29 37.2	5 4.9	26 34.1	27 13.7
20 S	9 53 1.5	26 54.6	21 35.8	22 52.4	24 14.3	4 16.1	4 23.5	1 48.8	29 41.7	5 5.2	26 33.5	27 15.1
21 S	9 56 58.1	27 52.4	21 32.6	4♒42.9	25 7.4	3 41.0	5 2.0	1 52.8	29 46.2	5 5.5	26 32.9	27 16.6
22 M	10 0 54.6	28 50.1	21 29.5	16 33.2	25 57.5	3 5.0	5 40.5	1 57.0	29 50.8	5 5.9	26 32.3	27 18.1
23 T	10 4 51.2	29 47.9	21 26.3	28 25.5	26 44.3	2 28.3	6 19.0	2 1.4	29 55.5	5 6.4	26 31.8	27 19.6
24 W	10 8 47.7	0♍45.7	21 23.1	10♓21.3	27 27.7	1 51.1	6 57.5	2 5.9	0♏ 0.3	5 6.9	26 31.3	27 21.1
25 T	10 12 44.3	1 43.6	21 19.9	22 22.0	28 7.4	1 13.8	7 35.9	2 10.6	0 5.1	5 7.5	26 30.9	27 22.6
26 F	10 16 40.8	2 41.4	21 16.7	4♈28.9	28 43.2	0 36.5	8 14.3	2 15.4	0 10.0	5 8.1	26 30.5	27 24.2
27 S	10 20 37.4	3 39.3	21 13.6	16 43.8	29 15.0	29♌59.5	8 52.7	2 20.5	0 14.9	5 8.7	26 30.1	27 25.8
28 S	10 24 34.0	4 37.2	21 10.4	29 8.5	29 42.4	29 23.0	9 31.0	2 25.6	0 20.0	5 9.4	26 29.7	27 27.5
29 M	10 28 30.5	5 35.2	21 7.2	11♉45.7	0♎ 5.2	28 47.3	10 9.3	2 31.0	0 25.1	5 10.2	26 29.4	27 29.1
30 T	10 32 27.1	6 33.2	21 4.0	24 38.4	0 23.1	28 12.6	10 47.6	2 36.4	0 30.2	5 11.0	26 29.1	27 30.8
31 W	10 36 23.6	7 31.2	21 0.9	7♊49.9	0 35.8	27 39.1	11 25.9	2 42.1	0 35.4	5 11.9	26 28.8	27 32.5
DECLINATION at NOON												
1 M	8 38 7.0	18N 5.5	23N14.1	8N28.1	12N12.1	4N12.5	22N32.3	19S41.8	8S41.4	21S 4.5	22S 9.2	5N22.3
4 T	8 49 56.6	17 19.2	23 13.6	21 11.6	10 11.7	3 34.2	22 13.8	19 43.0	8 45.4	21 4.3	22 9.2	5 19.8
7 S	9 1 46.3	16 30.3	23 13.0	23 38.3	8 11.8	3 3.5	21 53.7	19 44.5	8 49.6	21 4.1	22 9.3	5 17.3
10 W	9 13 36.0	15 39.0	23 12.5	11 51.8	6 14.1	2 41.1	21 32.2	19 46.4	8 54.1	21 4.0	22 9.3	5 14.6
13 S	9 25 25.6	14 45.5	23 11.9	5S37.7	4 20.2	2 28.1	21 9.3	19 48.5	8 58.8	21 3.9	22 9.4	5 11.9
16 T	9 37 15.3	13 49.8	23 11.3	19 24.0	2 31.8	2 24.9	20 45.1	19 51.0	9 3.8	21 4.0	22 9.5	5 9.2
19 F	9 49 5.0	12 52.2	23 10.7	24 31.7	0 50.8	2 31.8	20 19.6	19 53.8	9 8.9	21 4.2	22 9.5	5 6.4
22 M	10 0 54.6	11 52.8	23 10.1	19 44.8	0S40.7	2 48.2	19 52.8	19 56.8	9 14.3	21 4.4	22 9.6	5 3.5
25 T	10 12 44.3	10 51.7	23 9.5	7 38.6	1 59.8	3 13.1	19 24.8	20 0.1	9 19.9	21 4.7	22 9.7	5 0.6
28 S	10 24 34.0	9 49.0	23 8.9	7N24.8	3 3.2	3 44.7	18 55.6	20 3.7	9 25.6	21 5.1	22 9.8	4 57.7
31 W	10 36 23.6	8 45.0	23 8.2	20 24.8	3 46.7	4 21.1	18 25.4	20 7.5	9 31.5	21 5.6	22 10.0	4 54.8

SEPTEMBER 1983

DAY	EPHEMERIS SIDEREAL TIME	☉	☊	☽	☿	♀	♂	♃	♄	♅	♆	♇
	h m s	° ′	° ′	° ′	° ′	° ′	° ′	° ′	° ′	° ′	° ′	° ′
LONGITUDE at NOON												
1 T	10 40 20.2	8♍29.2	20♊57.7	21♊23.2	0♎43.1	27♌ 6.9	12♌ 4.1	2♐47.9	0♏40.7	5♐12.8	26♐28.6	27♎34.2
2 F	10 44 16.7	9 27.3	20 54.5	5♋20.7	0 44.7	26R36.4	12 42.3	2 53.8	0 46.1	5 13.7	26R28.4	27 36.0
3 S	10 48 13.3	10 25.4	20 51.3	19 42.8	0R40.3	26 7.6	13 20.4	2 59.9	0 51.5	5 14.8	26 28.2	27 37.8
4 S	10 52 9.8	11 23.5	20 48.1	4♌27.5	0 29.9	25 40.6	13 58.6	3 6.1	0 56.9	5 15.8	26 28.0	27 39.6
5 M	10 56 6.4	12 21.7	20 45.0	19 29.5	0 13.1	25 15.7	14 36.7	3 12.5	1 2.5	5 16.9	26 27.9	27 41.4
6 T	11 0 2.9	13 20.0	20 41.8	4♍40.8	29♍50.0	24 52.9	15 14.8	3 19.1	1 8.1	5 18.2	26 27.9	27 43.3
7 W	11 3 59.5	14 18.2	20 38.6	19 50.7	29 20.4	24 32.3	15 52.8	3 25.8	1 13.8	5 19.4	26 27.9	27 45.2
8 T	11 7 56.0	15 16.5	20 35.4	4♎48.7	28 44.7	24 14.0	16 30.8	3 32.6	1 19.5	5 20.6	26 27.9	27 47.1
9 F	11 11 52.6	16 14.8	20 32.3	19 25.7	28 2.9	23 58.0	17 8.8	3 39.6	1 25.2	5 22.0	26 27.9	27 49.0
10 S	11 15 49.1	17 13.1	20 29.1	3♏35.7	27 15.6	23 44.3	17 46.7	3 46.7	1 31.1	5 23.3	26 27.9	27 50.9
11 S	11 19 45.7	18 11.4	20 25.9	17 16.2	26 23.3	23 33.0	18 24.6	3 53.9	1 36.9	5 24.7	26D28.0	27 52.9
12 M	11 23 42.3	19 9.8	20 22.7	0♐27.8	25 26.9	23 24.1	19 2.5	4 1.3	1 42.9	5 26.2	26 28.1	27 54.9
13 T	11 27 38.8	20 8.2	20 19.5	13 13.7	24 27.4	23 17.6	19 40.4	4 8.8	1 48.8	5 27.7	26 28.3	27 56.9
14 W	11 31 35.4	21 6.6	20 16.4	25 38.2	23 25.9	23 13.5	20 18.2	4 16.5	1 54.9	5 29.3	26 28.5	27 58.9
15 T	11 35 31.9	22 5.0	20 13.2	7♑46.5	22 23.7	23 11.8	20 55.9	4 24.3	2 0.9	5 30.9	26 28.7	28 0.9
16 F	11 39 28.5	23 3.5	20 10.0	19 44.0	21 22.4	23D12.5	21 33.7	4 32.2	2 7.1	5 32.5	26 29.0	28 3.0
17 S	11 43 25.0	24 2.0	20 6.8	1♒35.4	20 23.3	23 15.4	22 11.4	4 40.2	2 13.2	5 34.2	26 29.2	28 5.1
18 S	11 47 21.6	25 0.6	20 3.7	13 25.2	19 27.9	23 20.7	22 49.0	4 48.4	2 19.4	5 36.0	26 29.6	28 7.2
19 M	11 51 18.1	25 59.1	20 0.5	25 16.8	18 37.7	23 28.2	23 26.7	4 56.7	2 25.7	5 37.8	26 29.9	28 9.3
20 T	11 55 14.7	26 57.7	19 57.3	7♓13.0	17 54.0	23 37.9	24 4.3	5 5.1	2 32.0	5 39.6	26 30.3	28 11.4
21 W	11 59 11.2	27 56.3	19 54.1	19 15.6	17 18.0	23 49.7	24 41.9	5 13.6	2 38.4	5 41.5	26 30.7	28 13.6
22 T	12 3 7.8	28 55.0	19 50.9	1♈26.0	16 50.4	24 3.6	25 19.4	5 22.3	2 44.8	5 43.4	26 31.2	28 15.7
23 F	12 7 4.3	29 53.7	19 47.8	13 44.9	16 32.1	24 19.6	25 57.0	5 31.1	2 51.2	5 45.4	26 31.7	28 17.9
24 S	12 11 0.9	0♎52.4	19 44.6	26 13.0	16 23.5	24 37.5	26 34.4	5 40.0	2 57.7	5 47.4	26 32.2	28 20.1
25 S	12 14 57.4	1 51.1	19 41.4	8♉50.9	16D24.8	24 57.4	27 11.9	5 49.0	3 4.2	5 49.5	26 32.7	28 22.3
26 M	12 18 54.0	2 49.9	19 38.2	21 39.6	16 36.2	25 19.1	27 49.3	5 58.1	3 10.7	5 51.6	26 33.3	28 24.5
27 T	12 22 50.5	3 48.8	19 35.1	4♊40.8	16 57.5	25 42.7	28 26.8	6 7.4	3 17.4	5 53.8	26 34.0	28 26.8
28 W	12 26 47.1	4 47.7	19 31.9	17 56.2	17 28.4	26 7.9	29 4.2	6 16.8	3 24.0	5 56.0	26 34.6	28 29.0
29 T	12 30 43.7	5 46.6	19 28.7	1♋28.1	18 8.4	26 34.8	29 41.5	6 26.2	3 30.7	5 58.2	26 35.3	28 31.3
30 F	12 34 40.2	6 45.5	19 25.5	15 18.0	18 57.0	27 3.4	0♍18.8	6 35.8	3 37.4	6 0.5	26 36.0	28 33.6
DECLINATION at NOON												
1 T	10 40 20.2	8N23.3	23N 8.0	23N 7.6	3S55.9	4N33.8	18N15.1	20S 8.8	9S33.5	21S 5.8	22S10.0	4N53.8
4 S	10 52 9.8	7 17.6	23 7.4	22 28.0	4 4.9	5 13.0	17 43.4	20 12.9	9 39.7	21 6.3	22 10.1	4 50.8
7 W	11 3 59.5	6 10.7	23 6.7	8 37.4	3 42.2	5 51.8	17 10.8	20 17.2	9 46.0	21 7.0	22 10.3	4 47.8
10 S	11 15 49.1	5 3.0	23 6.0	9S14.9	2 44.8	6 28.6	16 37.3	20 21.7	9 52.4	21 7.8	22 10.4	4 44.8
13 T	11 27 38.8	3 54.5	23 5.3	21 44.8	1 15.0	7 2.1	16 2.8	20 26.4	9 58.9	21 8.6	22 10.6	4 41.8
16 F	11 39 28.5	2 45.3	23 4.6	24 25.4	0N36.5	7 31.3	15 27.6	20 31.2	10 5.6	21 9.5	22 10.8	4 38.8
19 M	11 51 18.1	1 35.8	23 3.9	17 22.1	2 31.1	7 55.3	14 51.6	20 36.2	10 12.4	21 10.4	22 10.9	4 35.8
22 T	12 3 7.8	0 25.9	23 3.2	3 55.0	4 8.0	8 13.8	14 14.8	20 41.3	10 19.2	21 11.5	22 11.1	4 32.8
25 S	12 14 57.4	0S44.2	23 2.5	11N22.5	5 10.5	8 26.4	13 37.4	20 46.5	10 26.2	21 12.6	22 11.3	4 29.9
28 W	12 26 47.1	1 54.3	23 1.7	22 48.9	5 30.6	8 32.9	12 59.3	20 51.8	10 33.2	21 13.7	22 11.5	4 26.9

OCTOBER 1983

DAY	EPHEMERIS SIDEREAL TIME	☉	☊	☽	☿	♀	♂	♃	♄	♅	♆	♇
LONGITUDE at NOON												
1 S	12 38 36.8	7♎44.5	19♊22.3	29♋27.0	19♍53.5	27♌33.5	0♍56.1	6♐45.5	3♏44.1	6♐ 2.8	26♐36.7	28♎35.9
2 S	12 42 33.3	8 43.5	19 19.2	13♌54.1	20 57.4	28 5.1	1 33.3	6 55.3	3 50.9	6 5.2	26 37.5	28 38.2
3 M	12 46 29.9	9 42.6	19 16.0	28 36.1	22 7.8	28 38.2	2 10.6	7 5.2	3 57.7	6 7.6	26 38.3	28 40.5
4 T	12 50 26.4	10 41.7	19 12.8	13♍27.2	23 24.1	29 12.7	2 47.7	7 15.2	4 4.5	6 10.0	26 39.2	28 42.8
5 W	12 54 23.0	11 40.8	19 9.6	28 19.6	24 45.5	29 48.5	3 24.9	7 25.3	4 11.3	6 12.5	26 40.0	28 45.1
6 T	12 58 19.5	12 40.0	19 6.5	13♎ 4.4	26 11.4	0♍25.5	4 2.0	7 35.5	4 18.2	6 15.0	26 40.9	28 47.4
7 F	13 2 16.1	13 39.2	19 3.3	27 33.2	27 41.1	1 3.9	4 39.1	7 45.7	4 25.1	6 17.6	26 41.9	28 49.8
8 S	13 6 12.6	14 38.4	19 0.1	11♏39.8	29 14.1	1 43.4	5 16.1	7 56.1	4 32.1	6 20.2	26 42.8	28 52.2
9 S	13 10 9.2	15 37.7	18 56.9	25 20.5	0♎49.7	2 24.1	5 53.2	8 6.6	4 39.0	6 22.8	26 43.8	28 54.5
10 M	13 14 5.7	16 37.0	18 53.7	8♐34.5	2 27.5	3 5.8	6 30.1	8 17.2	4 46.0	6 25.5	26 44.8	28 56.9
11 T	13 18 2.3	17 36.3	18 50.6	21 23.5	4 7.1	3 48.7	7 7.1	8 27.9	4 53.0	6 28.2	26 45.9	28 59.3
12 W	13 21 58.8	18 35.7	18 47.4	3♑51.0	5 48.0	4 32.5	7 44.0	8 38.7	5 0.1	6 30.9	26 47.0	29 1.6
13 T	13 25 55.4	19 35.1	18 44.2	16 1.6	7 30.0	5 17.4	8 20.8	8 49.5	5 7.1	6 33.7	26 48.1	29 4.0
14 F	13 29 52.0	20 34.5	18 41.0	28 0.5	9 12.7	6 3.2	8 57.7	9 0.5	5 14.2	6 36.5	26 49.2	29 6.4
15 S	13 33 48.5	21 33.9	18 37.9	9♒52.9	10 55.9	6 50.0	9 34.5	9 11.5	5 21.3	6 39.3	26 50.4	29 8.8
16 S	13 37 45.1	22 33.4	18 34.7	21 43.8	12 39.5	7 37.6	10 11.2	9 22.6	5 28.4	6 42.2	26 51.6	29 11.2
17 M	13 41 41.6	23 32.9	18 31.5	3♓37.6	14 23.1	8 26.1	10 48.0	9 33.8	5 35.5	6 45.1	26 52.8	29 13.6
18 T	13 45 38.2	24 32.5	18 28.3	15 37.9	16 6.8	9 15.4	11 24.7	9 45.1	5 42.7	6 48.1	26 54.2	29 16.1
19 W	13 49 34.7	25 32.1	18 25.1	27 47.5	17 50.2	10 5.6	12 1.3	9 56.5	5 49.9	6 51.1	26 55.4	29 18.5
20 T	13 53 31.3	26 31.7	18 22.0	10♈ 8.3	19 33.5	10 56.5	12 38.0	10 7.9	5 57.0	6 54.1	26 56.8	29 20.9
21 F	13 57 27.8	27 31.3	18 18.8	22 41.3	21 16.4	11 48.1	13 14.5	10 19.4	6 4.2	6 57.1	26 58.1	29 23.3
22 S	14 1 24.4	28 31.0	18 15.6	5♉26.7	22 59.0	12 40.5	13 51.1	10 31.0	6 11.4	7 0.2	26 59.5	29 25.8
23 S	14 5 20.9	29 30.7	18 12.4	18 24.1	24 41.2	13 33.6	14 27.6	10 42.7	6 18.6	7 3.3	27 0.9	29 28.2
24 M	14 9 17.5	0♏30.4	18 9.3	1♊33.3	26 22.9	14 27.3	15 4.1	10 54.4	6 25.8	7 6.4	27 2.3	29 30.6
25 T	14 13 14.0	1 30.2	18 6.1	14 53.5	28 4.1	15 21.8	15 40.5	11 6.2	6 33.0	7 9.6	27 3.7	29 33.0
26 W	14 17 10.6	2 30.0	18 2.9	28 24.8	29 44.9	16 16.8	16 16.9	11 18.1	6 40.2	7 12.7	27 5.2	29 35.4
27 T	14 21 7.2	3 29.8	17 59.7	12♋ 6.9	1♏25.1	17 12.5	16 53.3	11 30.0	6 47.4	7 15.9	27 6.7	29 37.8
28 F	14 25 3.7	4 29.7	17 56.5	26 0.1	3 4.9	18 8.7	17 29.6	11 42.0	6 54.7	7 19.2	27 8.3	29 40.2
29 S	14 29 0.3	5 29.6	17 53.4	10♌ 3.9	4 44.1	19 5.6	18 5.9	11 54.1	7 1.9	7 22.4	27 9.8	29 42.7
30 S	14 32 56.8	6 29.6	17 50.2	24 17.6	6 22.8	20 3.0	18 42.2	12 6.3	7 9.1	7 25.7	27 11.4	29 45.1
31 M	14 36 53.4	7 29.6	17 47.0	8♍38.9	8 1.1	21 0.9	19 18.4	12 18.5	7 16.4	7 29.0	27 13.0	29 47.5
DECLINATION at NOON												
1 S	12 38 36.8	3S 4.3	23N 1.0	23N29.4	5N 7.9	8N33.4	12N20.7	20S57.1	10S40.3	21S15.0	22S11.7	4N24.0
4 T	12 50 26.4	4 14.0	23 0.2	11 8.2	4 7.9	8 28.0	11 41.5	21 2.5	10 47.4	21 16.2	22 11.9	4 21.2
7 F	13 2 16.1	5 23.3	22 59.4	6S57.7	2 38.6	8 16.7	11 1.9	21 8.0	10 54.6	21 17.6	22 12.1	4 18.4
10 M	13 14 5.7	6 31.9	22 58.7	20 55.9	0 48.9	7 59.8	10 21.8	21 13.5	11 1.8	21 19.0	22 12.3	4 15.6
13 T	13 25 55.4	7 39.8	22 57.9	24 53.1	1S13.5	7 37.5	9 41.3	21 18.9	11 9.0	21 20.4	22 12.5	4 12.9
16 S	13 37 45.1	8 46.7	22 57.1	18 36.1	3 22.7	7 9.9	9 0.5	21 24.4	11 16.2	21 21.9	22 12.7	4 10.2
19 W	13 49 34.7	9 52.4	22 56.2	5 28.4	5 34.0	6 37.3	8 19.3	21 29.9	11 23.4	21 23.4	22 13.0	4 7.7
22 S	14 1 24.4	10 56.9	22 55.4	10N 8.5	7 44.5	6 0.0	7 38.0	21 35.3	11 30.6	21 25.0	22 13.2	4 5.1
25 T	14 13 14.0	11 59.9	22 54.6	22 25.7	9 51.9	5 18.2	6 56.4	21 40.6	11 37.8	21 26.6	22 13.4	4 2.7
28 F	14 25 3.7	13 1.2	22 53.7	24 10.3	11 54.7	4 32.3	6 14.6	21 45.9	11 44.9	21 28.2	22 13.6	4 0.4
31 M	14 36 53.4	14 0.7	22 52.8	13 4.1	13 51.8	3 42.4	5 32.8	21 51.1	11 52.0	21 29.8	22 13.8	3 58.1

NOVEMBER 1983

LONGITUDE at NOON

DAY	EPHEMERIS SIDEREAL TIME	☉	☊	☽	☿	♀	♂	♃	♄	♅	♆	♇
	h m s	° ′	° ′	° ′	° ′	° ′	° ′	° ′	° ′	° ′	° ′	° ′
1 T	14 40 49.9	8♏29.6	17♊43.8	23♍ 4.3	9♏38.9	21♍59.3	19♍54.6	12♐30.7	7♏23.6	7♐32.3	27♐14.6	29♎49.9
2 W	14 44 46.5	9 29.6	17 40.7	7♎29.1	11 16.2	22 58.2	20 30.7	12 43.1	7 30.9	7 35.7	27 16.3	29 52.3
3 T	14 48 43.0	10 29.7	17 37.5	21 47.8	12 53.0	23 57.6	21 6.8	12 55.5	7 38.1	7 39.0	27 18.0	29 54.7
4 F	14 52 39.6	11 29.9	17 34.3	5♏54.6	14 29.4	24 57.5	21 42.8	13 7.9	7 45.3	7 42.4	27 19.7	29 57.0
5 S	14 56 36.2	12 30.0	17 31.1	19 44.9	16 5.4	25 57.7	22 18.8	13 20.4	7 52.5	7 45.9	27 21.4	29 59.4
6 S	15 0 32.7	13 30.2	17 28.0	3♐15.2	17 40.9	26 58.5	22 54.8	13 33.0	7 59.8	7 49.3	27 23.1	0♏ 1.8
7 M	15 4 29.3	14 30.5	17 24.8	16 23.9	19 16.1	27 59.6	23 30.7	13 45.6	8 7.0	7 52.7	27 24.9	0 4.2
8 T	15 8 25.8	15 30.7	17 21.6	29 11.6	20 50.9	29 1.2	24 6.6	13 58.3	8 14.2	7 56.3	27 26.7	0 6.6
9 W	15 12 22.4	16 31.0	17 18.4	11♑40.1	22 25.3	0♎ 3.1	24 42.5	14 11.0	8 21.4	7 59.7	27 28.5	0 8.9
10 T	15 16 18.9	17 31.3	17 15.2	23 52.7	23 59.4	1 5.4	25 18.2	14 23.8	8 28.6	8 3.2	27 30.4	0 11.2
11 F	15 20 15.5	18 31.6	17 12.1	5♒53.6	25 33.2	2 8.1	25 54.0	14 36.6	8 35.8	8 6.8	27 32.2	0 13.6
12 S	15 24 12.0	19 32.0	17 8.9	17 47.6	27 6.6	3 11.1	26 29.6	14 49.5	8 42.9	8 10.3	27 34.1	0 15.9
13 S	15 28 8.6	20 32.4	17 5.7	29 39.4	28 39.7	4 14.5	27 5.3	15 2.4	8 50.1	8 13.9	27 36.0	0 18.2
14 M	15 32 5.2	21 32.8	17 2.5	11♓34.1	0♐12.5	5 18.2	27 40.8	15 15.3	8 57.2	8 17.4	27 37.9	0 20.5
15 T	15 36 1.7	22 33.2	16 59.4	23 36.1	1 45.1	6 22.2	28 16.4	15 28.3	9 4.3	8 21.0	27 39.8	0 22.8
16 W	15 39 58.3	23 33.6	16 56.2	5♈49.2	3 17.3	7 26.6	28 51.9	15 41.3	9 11.4	8 24.6	27 41.7	0 25.0
17 T	15 43 54.8	24 34.1	16 53.0	18 16.7	4 49.3	8 31.2	29 27.3	15 54.4	9 18.5	8 28.2	27 43.7	0 27.3
18 F	15 47 51.4	25 34.6	16 49.8	1♉ 0.5	6 21.1	9 36.2	0♎ 2.7	16 7.5	9 25.6	8 31.8	27 45.7	0 29.5
19 S	15 51 47.9	26 35.1	16 46.6	14 1.6	7 52.5	10 41.4	0 38.0	16 20.7	9 32.6	8 35.4	27 47.7	0 31.8
20 S	15 55 44.5	27 35.6	16 43.5	27 19.6	9 23.8	11 46.9	1 13.3	16 33.8	9 39.6	8 39.1	27 49.7	0 34.0
21 M	15 59 41.1	28 36.2	16 40.3	10♊53.3	10 54.7	12 52.7	1 48.5	16 47.0	9 46.6	8 42.7	27 51.7	0 36.2
22 T	16 3 37.6	29 36.8	16 37.1	24 40.3	12 25.4	13 58.8	2 23.7	17 0.3	9 53.6	8 46.3	27 53.8	0 38.4
23 W	16 7 34.2	0♐37.4	16 33.9	8♋38.0	13 55.9	15 5.2	2 58.8	17 13.6	10 0.5	8 50.0	27 55.8	0 40.6
24 T	16 11 30.7	1 38.0	16 30.8	22 43.4	15 26.0	16 11.7	3 33.9	17 26.9	10 7.4	8 53.7	27 57.9	0 42.7
25 F	16 15 27.3	2 38.7	16 27.6	6♌53.5	16 55.8	17 18.6	4 8.9	17 40.2	10 14.3	8 57.3	27 60.0	0 44.8
26 S	16 19 23.8	3 39.4	16 24.4	21 5.7	18 25.3	18 25.7	4 43.9	17 53.6	10 21.2	9 1.0	28 2.1	0 47.0
27 S	16 23 20.4	4 40.1	16 21.2	5♍17.7	19 54.4	19 33.0	5 18.8	18 6.9	10 28.0	9 4.7	28 4.2	0 49.1
28 M	16 27 17.0	5 40.8	16 18.1	19 27.2	21 23.1	20 40.5	5 53.7	18 20.4	10 34.8	9 8.4	28 6.3	0 51.2
29 T	16 31 13.5	6 41.7	16 14.9	3♎32.1	22 51.4	21 48.3	6 28.5	18 33.8	10 41.6	9 12.1	28 8.5	0 53.3
30 W	16 35 10.1	7 42.5	16 11.7	17 30.2	24 19.1	22 56.3	7 3.3	18 47.3	10 48.4	9 15.8	28 10.6	0 55.3

DECLINATION at NOON

DAY	EPHEMERIS SIDEREAL TIME	☉	☊	☽	☿	♀	♂	♃	♄	♅	♆	♇
1 T	14 40 49.9	14S20.1	22N52.5	7N27.9	14S29.4	3N25.0	5N18.8	21S52.8	11S54.4	21S30.4	22S13.9	3N57.4
4 F	14 52 39.6	15 17.0	22 51.7	10S19.2	16 17.7	2 30.5	4 36.8	21 57.9	12 1.4	21 32.1	22 14.1	3 55.2
7 M	15 4 29.3	16 11.6	22 50.8	22 46.2	17 58.4	1 32.8	3 54.9	22 2.8	12 8.3	21 33.8	22 14.3	3 53.2
10 T	15 16 18.9	17 3.7	22 49.9	24 29.1	19 31.1	0 32.4	3 12.9	22 7.7	12 15.2	21 35.5	22 14.5	3 51.2
13 S	15 28 8.6	17 53.2	22 48.9	16 17.2	20 55.1	0S30.4	2 31.1	22 12.4	12 21.9	21 37.2	22 14.7	3 49.4
16 W	15 39 58.3	18 39.9	22 48.0	2 12.9	22 9.8	1 35.2	1 49.3	22 17.0	12 28.6	21 38.9	22 14.9	3 47.7
19 S	15 51 47.9	19 23.6	22 47.1	13N23.6	23 14.6	2 41.8	1 7.8	22 21.4	12 35.1	21 40.7	22 15.1	3 46.0
22 T	16 3 37.6	20 4.2	22 46.1	24 8.3	24 8.9	3 49.8	0 26.4	22 25.6	12 41.6	21 42.4	22 15.3	3 44.5
25 F	16 15 27.3	20 41.4	22 45.2	22 30.9	24 52.2	4 58.9	0S14.8	22 29.7	12 47.9	21 44.1	22 15.4	3 43.2
28 M	16 27 17.0	21 15.3	22 44.2	9 0.9	25 23.7	6 8.6	0 55.7	22 33.6	12 54.0	21 45.8	22 15.6	3 41.9

DECEMBER 1983

LONGITUDE at NOON

DAY	EPHEMERIS SIDEREAL TIME	☉	☊	☽	☿	♀	♂	♃	♄	♅	♆	♇
1 T	16 39 6.6	8♐43.3	16♊ 8.5	1♏19.3	25♐46.1	24♎ 4.4	7♎37.9	19♐ 0.8	10♏55.1	9♐19.5	28♐12.8	0♏57.3
2 F	16 43 3.2	9 44.1	16 5.4	14 57.3	27 12.5	25 12.8	8 12.6	19 14.3	11 1.7	9 23.2	28 15.0	0 59.4
3 S	16 46 59.7	10 45.0	16 2.2	28 22.1	28 38.1	26 21.4	8 47.1	19 27.8	11 8.4	9 26.9	28 17.1	1 1.3
4 S	16 50 56.3	11 45.9	15 59.0	11♐32.2	0♑ 2.7	27 30.1	9 21.6	19 41.4	11 14.9	9 30.5	28 19.3	1 3.3
5 M	16 54 52.9	12 46.8	15 55.8	24 26.7	1 26.2	28 39.0	9 56.0	19 54.9	11 21.5	9 34.2	28 21.5	1 5.3
6 T	16 58 49.4	13 47.7	15 52.6	7♑ 5.5	2 48.5	29 48.1	10 30.4	20 8.5	11 28.0	9 37.9	28 23.7	1 7.2
7 W	17 2 46.0	14 48.7	15 49.5	19 29.6	4 9.3	0♏57.3	11 4.7	20 22.1	11 34.5	9 41.6	28 26.0	1 9.1
8 T	17 6 42.5	15 49.6	15 46.3	1♒40.8	5 28.3	2 6.7	11 38.9	20 35.7	11 40.9	9 45.3	28 28.2	1 10.9
9 F	17 10 39.1	16 50.6	15 43.1	13 41.8	6 45.4	3 16.3	12 13.0	20 49.3	11 47.3	9 49.0	28 30.4	1 12.8
10 S	17 14 35.6	17 51.6	15 39.9	25 36.1	8 0.1	4 26.0	12 47.1	21 2.9	11 53.6	9 52.6	28 32.6	1 14.6
11 S	17 18 32.2	18 52.6	15 36.8	7♓27.8	9 12.1	5 35.8	13 21.1	21 16.5	11 59.9	9 56.3	28 34.9	1 16.4
12 M	17 22 28.8	19 53.6	15 33.6	19 21.4	10 21.1	6 45.8	13 55.0	21 30.1	12 6.1	9 59.9	28 37.1	1 18.2
13 T	17 26 25.3	20 54.6	15 30.4	1♈21.7	11 26.4	7 55.9	14 28.8	21 43.7	12 12.3	10 3.6	28 39.4	1 20.0
14 W	17 30 21.9	21 55.6	15 27.2	13 33.4	12 27.5	9 6.2	15 2.6	21 57.4	12 18.5	10 7.2	28 41.6	1 21.7
15 T	17 34 18.4	22 56.6	15 24.1	26 0.7	13 23.8	10 16.6	15 36.3	22 11.0	12 24.5	10 10.8	28 43.9	1 23.4
16 F	17 38 15.0	23 57.7	15 20.9	8♉47.3	14 14.6	11 27.1	16 9.9	22 24.6	12 30.6	10 14.4	28 46.1	1 25.0
17 S	17 42 11.6	24 58.7	15 17.7	21 55.7	14 59.2	12 37.7	16 43.4	22 38.3	12 36.6	10 18.0	28 48.4	1 26.7
18 S	17 46 8.1	25 59.8	15 14.5	5♊27.0	15 36.6	13 48.5	17 16.8	22 51.9	12 42.5	10 21.6	28 50.7	1 28.3
19 M	17 50 4.7	27 0.8	15 11.4	19 20.3	16 6.1	14 59.4	17 50.2	23 5.5	12 48.4	10 25.2	28 52.9	1 29.9
20 T	17 54 1.2	28 1.9	15 8.2	3♋32.8	16 26.8	16 10.4	18 23.6	23 19.2	12 54.2	10 28.8	28 55.3	1 31.5
21 W	17 57 57.8	29 3.0	15 5.0	17 60.0	16 37.7	17 21.5	18 56.8	23 32.8	12 60.0	10 32.4	28 57.5	1 33.0
22 T	18 1 54.3	0♑ 4.1	15 1.8	2♌35.7	16 38.0	18 32.8	19 29.9	23 46.4	13 5.7	10 35.9	28 59.8	1 34.6
23 F	18 5 50.9	1 5.2	14 58.6	17 13.6	16R27.1	19 44.1	20 2.9	23 60.0	13 11.3	10 39.4	29 2.1	1 36.0
24 S	18 9 47.5	2 6.3	14 55.5	1♍47.4	16 4.6	20 55.5	20 35.9	24 13.6	13 16.9	10 42.9	29 4.3	1 37.5
25 S	18 13 44.0	3 7.4	14 52.3	16 12.1	15 30.2	22 7.1	21 8.7	24 27.1	13 22.4	10 46.4	29 6.6	1 38.9
26 M	18 17 40.6	4 8.6	14 49.1	0♎23.9	14 44.4	23 18.7	21 41.5	24 40.7	13 27.9	10 49.9	29 8.9	1 40.3
27 T	18 21 37.1	5 9.7	14 45.9	14 21.1	13 47.8	24 30.5	22 14.2	24 54.2	13 33.3	10 53.4	29 11.1	1 41.6
28 W	18 25 33.7	6 10.9	14 42.8	28 2.9	12 41.8	25 42.3	22 46.8	25 7.8	13 38.6	10 56.8	29 13.4	1 43.0
29 T	18 29 30.3	7 12.0	14 39.6	11♏29.6	11 28.3	26 54.2	23 19.2	25 21.3	13 43.8	11 0.2	29 15.6	1 44.3
30 F	18 33 26.8	8 13.2	14 36.4	24 42.1	10 9.5	28 6.2	23 51.6	25 34.8	13 49.0	11 3.6	29 17.9	1 45.5
31 S	18 37 23.4	9 14.4	14 33.2	7♐41.3	8 48.0	29 18.3	24 23.9	25 48.3	13 54.2	11 7.0	29 20.1	1 46.8

DECLINATION at NOON

DAY	EPHEMERIS SIDEREAL TIME	☉	☊	☽	☿	♀	♂	♃	♄	♅	♆	♇
1 T	16 39 6.6	21S45.5	22N43.2	8S27.2	25S43.0	7S18.6	1S36.3	22S37.3	13S 0.1	21S47.5	22S15.8	3N40.8
4 S	16 50 56.3	22 12.0	22 42.2	21 46.2	25 49.5	8 28.5	2 16.5	22 40.8	13 6.0	21 49.2	22 15.9	3 39.7
7 W	17 2 46.0	22 34.6	22 41.2	24 55.4	25 43.2	9 38.0	2 56.3	22 44.1	13 11.7	21 50.9	22 16.0	3 38.9
10 S	17 14 35.6	22 53.2	22 40.2	17 39.0	25 24.2	10 46.6	3 35.6	22 47.2	13 17.2	21 52.6	22 16.2	3 38.1
13 T	17 26 25.3	23 7.8	22 39.2	4 7.9	24 53.5	11 54.1	4 14.5	22 50.2	13 22.6	21 54.2	22 16.3	3 37.5
16 F	17 38 15.0	23 18.2	22 38.2	11N24.1	24 12.9	12 59.9	4 52.9	22 52.8	13 27.7	21 55.8	22 16.4	3 37.0
19 M	17 50 4.7	23 24.5	22 37.1	23 19.5	23 25.6	14 3.8	5 30.7	22 55.3	13 32.7	21 57.4	22 16.5	3 36.7
22 T	18 1 54.3	23 26.5	22 36.1	23 18.8	22 35.9	15 5.3	6 8.0	22 57.6	13 37.5	21 58.9	22 16.5	3 36.4
25 S	18 13 44.0	23 24.3	22 35.0	10 17.2	21 48.7	16 4.2	6 44.6	22 59.7	13 42.1	22 0.5	22 16.6	3 36.3
28 W	18 25 33.7	23 17.8	22 33.9	7S 8.2	21 7.7	17 0.0	7 20.6	23 1.5	13 46.5	22 1.9	22 16.7	3 36.4
31 S	18 37 23.4	23 7.2	22 32.9	20 51:2	20 35.8	17 52.4	7 55.9	23 3.1	13 50.6	22 3.4	22 16.7	3 36.5

JANUARY 1984

DAY	EPHEMERIS SIDEREAL TIME	☉	☊	☽	☿	♀	♂	♃	♄	♅	♆	♇
	h m s	° ′	° ′	° ′	° ′	° ′	° ′	° ′	° ′	° ′	° ′	° ′
						LONGITUDE at NOON						
1 S	18 41 19.9	10♑15.5	14♊30.1	20♐28.1	7♑26.5	0♐30.4	24♎56.1	26♐ 1.7	13♏59.2	11♐10.3	29♐22.4	1♏47.9
2 M	18 45 16.5	11 16.7	14 26.9	3♑ 3.5	6R 7.7	1 42.7	25 28.1	26 15.2	14 4.2	11 13.6	29 24.6	1 49.1
3 T	18 49 13.0	12 17.9	14 23.7	15 28.0	4 54.0	2 55.0	26 0.1	26 28.6	14 9.1	11 16.9	29 26.8	1 50.2
4 W	18 53 9.6	13 19.1	14 20.5	27 42.6	3 47.2	4 7.3	26 31.9	26 42.0	14 13.9	11 20.2	29 29.0	1 51.3
5 T	18 57 6.2	14 20.3	14 17.4	9♒48.3	2 48.8	5 19.8	27 3.6	26 55.3	14 18.7	11 23.5	29 31.3	1 52.4
6 F	19 1 2.7	15 21.5	14 14.2	21 46.7	1 59.9	6 32.3	27 35.2	27 8.7	14 23.4	11 26.7	29 33.5	1 53.4
7 S	19 4 59.3	16 22.6	14 11.0	3♓40.0	1 21.0	7 44.8	28 6.7	27 22.0	14 28.0	11 29.9	29 35.7	1 54.4
8 S	19 8 55.8	17 23.8	14 7.8	15 30.9	0 52.2	8 57.4	28 38.0	27 35.2	14 32.5	11 33.1	29 37.8	1 55.4
9 M	19 12 52.4	18 25.0	14 4.6	27 23.1	0 33.4	10 10.1	29 9.3	27 48.5	14 37.0	11 36.2	29 40.0	1 56.3
10 T	19 16 48.9	19 26.2	14 1.5	9♈20.6	0 24.2	11 22.9	29 40.4	28 1.7	14 41.4	11 39.4	29 42.2	1 57.3
11 W	19 20 45.5	20 27.3	13 58.3	21 28.0	0 24.0	12 35.7	0♏11.4	28 14.9	14 45.7	11 42.5	29 44.4	1 58.1
12 T	19 24 42.1	21 28.4	13 55.1	3♉50.2	0D32.2	13 48.5	0 42.3	28 28.0	14 49.9	11 45.5	29 46.5	1 59.0
13 F	19 28 38.6	22 29.6	13 51.9	16 31.8	0 48.1	15 1.4	1 13.0	28 41.1	14 54.0	11 48.5	29 48.7	1 59.8
14 S	19 32 35.2	23 30.7	13 48.8	29 37.1	1 11.2	16 14.3	1 43.6	28 54.2	14 58.0	11 51.5	29 50.8	2 0.5
15 S	19 36 31.7	24 31.8	13 45.6	13♊ 9.0	1 40.6	17 27.3	2 14.0	29 7.2	15 2.0	11 54.5	29 52.9	2 1.2
16 M	19 40 28.3	25 32.9	13 42.4	27 8.6	2 16.0	18 40.3	2 44.3	29 20.1	15 5.9	11 57.4	29 55.0	2 1.9
17 T	19 44 24.9	26 34.0	13 39.2	11♋34.3	2 56.5	19 53.4	3 14.5	29 33.1	15 9.7	12 0.3	29 57.1	2 2.6
18 W	19 48 21.4	27 35.0	13 36.1	26 21.6	3 41.9	21 6.5	3 44.5	29 45.9	15 13.4	12 3.2	29 59.1	2 3.2
19 T	19 52 18.0	28 36.1	13 32.9	11♌22.9	4 31.4	22 19.6	4 14.4	29 58.8	15 17.0	12 6.0	0♑ 1.2	2 3.7
20 F	19 56 14.5	29 37.2	13 29.7	26 28.9	5 24.9	23 32.8	4 44.1	0♑11.5	15 20.5	12 8.8	0 3.2	2 4.3
21 S	20 0 11.1	0♒38.2	13 26.5	11♍29.7	6 21.8	24 46.1	5 13.7	0 24.3	15 23.9	12 11.6	0 5.3	2 4.8
22 S	20 4 7.6	1 39.2	13 23.3	26 16.6	7 21.8	25 59.4	5 43.1	0 37.0	15 27.3	12 14.3	0 7.3	2 5.3
23 M	20 8 4.2	2 40.3	13 20.2	10♎43.5	8 24.6	27 12.7	6 12.4	0 49.6	15 30.5	12 17.0	0 9.3	2 5.7
24 T	20 12 0.8	3 41.3	13 17.0	24 47.1	9 30.1	28 26.1	6 41.5	1 2.2	15 33.7	12 19.6	0 11.3	2 6.1
25 W	20 15 57.3	4 42.3	13 13.8	8♏26.9	10 37.8	29 39.5	7 10.5	1 14.7	15 36.8	12 22.2	0 13.2	2 6.5
26 T	20 19 53.9	5 43.3	13 10.6	21 44.5	11 47.6	0♑52.9	7 39.2	1 27.2	15 39.8	12 24.8	0 15.1	2 6.8
27 F	20 23 50.4	6 44.3	13 7.5	4♐42.6	12 59.4	2 6.4	8 7.8	1 39.6	15 42.7	12 27.3	0 17.1	2 7.1
28 S	20 27 47.0	7 45.3	13 4.3	17 24.4	14 13.0	3 19.9	8 36.2	1 51.9	15 45.5	12 29.8	0 19.0	2 7.4
29 S	20 31 43.5	8 46.3	13 1.1	29 53.1	15 28.1	4 33.5	9 4.5	2 4.2	15 48.1	12 32.3	0 20.8	2 7.6
30 M	20 35 40.1	9 47.3	12 57.9	12♑11.4	16 44.9	5 47.0	9 32.5	2 16.4	15 50.7	12 34.7	0 22.7	2 7.7
31 T	20 39 36.6	10 48.2	12 54.8	24 21.6	18 3.0	7 0.6	10 0.3	2 28.6	15 53.2	12 37.0	0 24.6	2 7.9
						DECLINATION at NOON						
1 S	18 41 19.9	23S 2.7	22N32.5	23S 31.0	20S 27.6	18S 9.1	8S 7.5	23S 3.6	13S 51.9	22S 3.9	22S 16.7	3N36.6
4 W	18 53 9.6	22 46.5	22 31.4	24 2.4	20 12.1	18 56.4	8 41.8	23 4.9	13 55.8	22 5.3	22 16.7	3 37.0
7 S	19 4 59.3	22 26.2	22 30.3	14 54.0	20 11.4	19 39.4	9 15.4	23 6.1	13 59.4	22 6.6	22 16.8	3 37.5
10 T	19 16 48.9	22 2.0	22 29.1	0 39.8	20 24.3	20 18.0	9 48.1	23 7.0	14 2.8	22 7.9	22 16.8	3 38.1
13 F	19 28 38.6	21 33.9	22 28.0	14N22.6	20 46.4	20 51.7	10 20.1	23 7.7	14 5.9	22 9.2	22 16.8	3 38.8
16 M	19 40 28.3	21 2.0	22 26.9	24 28.0	21 12.7	21 20.4	10 51.1	23 8.2	14 8.8	22 10.4	22 16.7	3 39.7
19 T	19 52 18.0	20 26.5	22 25.7	21 28.4	21 38.6	21 43.7	11 21.4	23 8.5	14 11.4	22 11.5	22 16.7	3 40.6
22 S	20 4 7.6	19 47.6	22 24.5	6 5.8	22 0.7	22 1.5	11 50.7	23 8.6	14 13.8	22 12.7	22 16.7	3 41.7
25 W	20 15 57.3	19 5.4	22 23.4	11S 26.2	22 16.4	22 13.7	12 19.2	23 8.6	14 16.0	22 13.7	22 16.7	3 42.9
28 S	20 27 47.0	18 20.0	22 22.2	23 5.0	22 23.9	22 20.1	12 46.7	23 8.3	14 17.8	22 14.8	22 16.6	3 44.2
31 T	20 39 36.6	17 31.6	22 21.0	24 27.2	22 22.1	22 20.5	13 13.2	23 7.9	14 19.4	22 15.7	22 16.6	3 45.6

FEBRUARY 1984

DAY	EPHEMERIS SIDEREAL TIME	☉	☊	☽	☿	♀	♂	♃	♄	♅	♆	♇
						LONGITUDE at NOON						
1 W	20 43 33.2	11♒49.2	12♊51.6	6♒25.2	19♑22.4	8♑14.2	10♏28.0	2♑40.7	15♏55.6	12♐39.4	0♑26.4	2♏ 8.0
2 T	20 47 29.8	12 50.1	12 48.4	18 23.8	20 43.1	9 27.9	10 55.4	2 52.7	15 58.0	12 41.6	0 28.2	2 8.1
3 F	20 51 26.3	13 51.0	12 45.2	0♓18.4	22 4.9	10 41.5	11 22.6	3 4.7	16 0.2	12 43.9	0 30.0	2 8.1
4 S	20 55 22.9	14 51.8	12 42.0	12 10.5	23 27.9	11 55.2	11 49.7	3 16.5	16 2.3	12 46.1	0 31.7	2 8.1
5 S	20 59 19.4	15 52.7	12 38.9	24 1.7	24 51.9	13 8.9	12 16.5	3 28.4	16 4.3	12 48.2	0 33.4	2R 8.0
6 M	21 3 16.0	16 53.5	12 35.7	5♈54.4	26 17.0	14 22.7	12 43.1	3 40.1	16 6.2	12 50.3	0 35.2	2 8.0
7 T	21 7 12.5	17 54.4	12 32.5	17 51.5	27 43.0	15 36.4	13 9.4	3 51.7	16 8.0	12 52.4	0 36.8	2 7.9
8 W	21 11 9.1	18 55.1	12 29.3	29 56.8	29 9.9	16 50.1	13 35.6	4 3.3	16 9.7	12 54.4	0 38.5	2 7.7
9 T	21 15 5.6	19 55.9	12 26.2	12♉14.6	0♒37.8	18 3.9	14 1.5	4 14.8	16 11.3	12 56.3	0 40.2	2 7.5
10 F	21 19 2.2	20 56.7	12 23.0	24 49.8	2 6.7	19 17.8	14 27.2	4 26.3	16 12.8	12 58.3	0 41.8	2 7.4
11 S	21 22 58.8	21 57.4	12 19.8	7♊47.0	3 36.4	20 31.6	14 52.6	4 37.6	16 14.2	13 0.2	0 43.4	2 7.1
12 S	21 26 55.3	22 58.1	12 16.6	21 10.7	5 7.0	21 45.4	15 17.8	4 48.9	16 15.5	13 2.0	0 45.0	2 6.8
13 M	21 30 51.9	23 58.7	12 13.5	5♋ 3.5	6 38.5	22 59.2	15 42.7	5 0.0	16 16.7	13 3.8	0 46.5	2 6.5
14 T	21 34 48.4	24 59.4	12 10.3	19 26.1	8 10.8	24 13.0	16 7.3	5 11.1	16 17.8	13 5.5	0 48.0	2 6.1
15 W	21 38 45.0	25 60.0	12 7.1	4♌15.7	9 44.1	25 26.9	16 31.7	5 22.1	16 18.8	13 7.2	0 49.5	2 5.7
16 T	21 42 41.5	27 0.5	12 3.9	19 25.7	11 18.2	26 40.8	16 55.9	5 33.0	16 19.7	13 8.8	0 51.0	2 5.3
17 F	21 46 38.1	28 1.1	12 0.7	4♍46.3	12 53.2	27 54.6	17 19.8	5 43.8	16 20.4	13 10.4	0 52.4	2 4.8
18 S	21 50 34.6	29 1.6	11 57.6	20 5.8	14 29.0	29 8.5	17 43.4	5 54.6	16 21.1	13 11.9	0 53.8	2 4.4
19 S	21 54 31.2	0♓ 2.1	11 54.4	5♎12.7	16 5.8	0♒22.4	18 6.7	6 5.2	16 21.7	13 13.4	0 55.2	2 3.8
20 M	21 58 27.8	1 2.6	11 51.2	19 57.9	17 43.5	1 36.4	18 29.7	6 15.7	16 22.2	13 14.8	0 56.6	2 3.3
21 T	22 2 24.3	2 3.0	11 48.0	4♏15.9	19 22.1	2 50.3	18 52.4	6 26.1	16 22.5	13 16.2	0 57.9	2 2.7
22 W	22 6 20.9	3 3.5	11 44.9	18 4.9	21 1.7	4 4.3	19 14.8	6 36.5	16 22.8	13 17.6	0 59.2	2 2.0
23 T	22 10 17.4	4 3.9	11 41.7	1♐26.0	22 42.2	5 18.2	19 36.9	6 46.7	16 23.0	13 18.8	1 0.5	2 1.4
24 F	22 14 14.0	5 4.3	11 38.5	14 22.5	24 23.6	6 32.2	19 58.7	6 56.8	16 23.0	13 20.1	1 1.7	2 0.7
25 S	22 18 10.5	6 4.6	11 35.3	26 58.6	26 6.1	7 46.2	20 20.1	7 6.9	16 23.0	13 21.2	1 2.9	1 60.0
26 S	22 22 7.1	7 5.0	11 32.1	9♑18.8	27 49.5	9 0.2	20 41.2	7 16.8	16R22.8	13 22.4	1 4.1	1 59.2
27 M	22 26 3.6	8 5.3	11 29.0	21 27.4	29 33.9	10 14.2	21 1.9	7 26.6	16 22.5	13 23.4	1 5.2	1 58.4
28 T	22 30 0.2	9 5.6	11 25.8	3♒28.0	1♓19.3	11 28.2	21 22.3	7 36.3	16 22.2	13 24.5	1 6.4	1 57.6
29 W	22 33 56.7	10 5.8	11 22.6	15 23.7	3 5.8	12 42.2	21 42.3	7 45.9	16 21.7	13 25.4	1 7.5	1 56.7
						DECLINATION at NOON						
1 W	20 43 33.2	17S 14.8	22N20.6	22S 32.3	22S 19.2	22S 19.4	13S 21.8	23S 7.8	14S 19.9	22S 16.0	22S 16.5	3N46.1
4 S	20 55 22.9	16 22.7	22 19.4	11 39.3	22 3.5	22 11.9	13 47.0	23 7.2	14 21.2	22 16.9	22 16.5	3 47.6
7 T	21 7 12.5	15 28.0	22 18.2	3N 8.9	21 36.8	21 58.5	14 11.2	23 6.4	14 22.1	22 17.7	22 16.4	3 49.3
10 F	21 19 2.2	14 31.0	22 16.9	17 25.2	20 58.6	21 39.2	14 34.4	23 5.5	14 22.9	22 18.5	22 16.3	3 51.0
13 M	21 30 51.9	13 31.8	22 15.7	25 13.6	20 8.7	21 14.1	14 56.6	23 4.5	14 23.3	22 19.2	22 16.2	3 52.8
16 T	21 42 41.5	12 30.6	22 14.4	19 21.9	19 7.0	20 43.3	15 17.8	23 3.4	14 23.5	22 19.8	22 16.1	3 54.6
19 S	21 54 31.2	11 27.7	22 13.2	2 10.5	17 53.2	20 7.1	15 38.0	23 2.2	14 23.4	22 20.4	22 16.0	3 56.6
22 W	22 6 20.9	10 23.1	22 11.9	15S 14.7	16 27.3	19 25.6	15 57.1	23 0.9	14 23.1	22 21.0	22 15.9	3 58.6
25 S	22 18 10.5	9 17.0	22 10.6	24 42.3	14 49.3	18 38.9	16 15.2	22 59.5	14 22.5	22 21.5	22 15.8	4 0.6
28 T	22 30 0.2	8 9.7	22 9.3	23 11.9	12 59.2	17 47.4	16 32.3	22 58.1	14 21.6	22 21.9	22 15.7	4 2.7

MARCH 1984

LONGITUDE at NOON

DAY	EPHEMERIS SIDEREAL TIME h m s	☉ ° ′	☊ ° ′	☽ ° ′	☿ ° ′	♀ ° ′	♂ ° ′	♃ ° ′	♄ ° ′	♅ ° ′	♆ ° ′	♇ ° ′
1 T	22 37 53.3	11♓ 6.1	11♊19.4	27♒16.7	4♓53.3	13♒56.3	22♏ 2.0	7♑55.4	16♏21.1	13♐26.3	1♑ 8.5	1♏55.9
2 F	22 41 49.8	12 6.3	11 16.3	9♓ 8.7	6 41.9	15 10.3	22 21.3	8 4.8	16R20.5	13 27.3	1 9.6	1R55.0
3 S	22 45 46.4	13 6.5	11 13.1	21 1.0	8 31.5	16 24.4	22 40.2	8 14.0	16 19.8	13 28.1	1 10.6	1 54.1
4 S	22 49 43.0	14 6.6	11 9.9	2♈54.9	10 22.1	17 38.4	22 58.6	8 23.2	16 18.9	13 28.8	1 11.6	1 53.1
5 M	22 53 39.5	15 6.8	11 6.7	14 51.8	12 13.7	18 52.4	23 16.7	8 32.2	16 17.9	13 29.5	1 12.5	1 52.1
6 T	22 57 36.1	16 6.8	11 3.5	26 53.7	14 6.4	20 6.5	23 34.3	8 41.1	16 16.8	13 30.2	1 13.4	1 51.1
7 W	23 1 32.6	17 6.9	11 0.4	9♉ 3.0	16 0.1	21 20.5	23 51.6	8 49.8	16 15.7	13 30.8	1 14.3	1 50.0
8 T	23 5 29.2	18 6.9	10 57.2	21 22.9	17 54.7	22 34.6	24 8.3	8 58.5	16 14.4	13 31.3	1 15.1	1 48.9
9 F	23 9 25.7	19 6.9	10 54.0	3♊57.3	19 50.2	23 48.6	24 24.7	9 7.0	16 13.0	13 31.8	1 15.9	1 47.8
10 S	23 13 22.3	20 6.8	10 50.8	16 50.4	21 46.6	25 2.6	24 40.6	9 15.4	16 11.5	13 32.2	1 16.7	1 46.7
11 S	23 17 18.8	21 6.7	10 47.7	0♋ 6.3	23 43.8	26 16.7	24 56.0	9 23.6	16 10.0	13 32.6	1 17.4	1 45.6
12 M	23 21 15.4	22 6.6	10 44.5	13 48.5	25 41.6	27 30.7	25 11.0	9 31.7	16 8.3	13 32.9	1 18.2	1 44.4
13 T	23 25 11.9	23 6.4	10 41.3	27 58.6	27 40.0	28 44.7	25 25.4	9 39.7	16 6.5	13 33.2	1 18.8	1 43.2
14 W	23 29 8.5	24 6.2	10 38.1	12♌35.9	29 38.7	29 58.8	25 39.4	9 47.6	16 4.7	13 33.4	1 19.5	1 41.9
15 T	23 33 5.0	25 5.9	10 34.9	27 36.0	1♈37.7	1♓12.8	25 52.9	9 55.3	16 2.7	13 33.6	1 20.1	1 40.7
16 F	23 37 1.6	26 5.7	10 31.8	12♍51.0	3 36.7	2 26.8	26 5.9	10 2.9	16 0.7	13 33.7	1 20.7	1 39.4
17 S	23 40 58.1	27 5.3	10 28.6	28 10.2	5 35.5	3 40.8	26 18.4	10 10.3	15 58.6	13 33.8	1 21.2	1 38.1
18 S	23 44 54.7	28 5.0	10 25.4	13♎22.1	7 33.8	4 54.9	26 30.3	10 17.6	15 56.4	13 33.8	1 21.7	1 36.8
19 M	23 48 51.2	29 4.6	10 22.2	28 16.3	9 31.2	6 8.9	26 41.7	10 24.8	15 54.1	13R33.7	1 22.2	1 35.4
20 T	23 52 47.8	0♈ 4.2	10 19.1	12♏45.2	11 27.6	7 22.9	26 52.6	10 31.8	15 51.7	13 33.6	1 22.7	1 34.1
21 W	23 56 44.4	1 3.8	10 15.9	26 45.0	13 22.3	8 37.0	27 2.8	10 38.7	15 49.2	13 33.5	1 23.1	1 32.7
22 T	0 0 40.9	2 3.3	10 12.7	10♐15.2	15 15.2	9 51.0	27 12.5	10 45.4	15 46.6	13 33.3	1 23.5	1 31.3
23 F	0 4 37.5	3 2.8	10 9.5	23 18.2	17 5.7	11 5.1	27 21.7	10 52.0	15 44.0	13 33.1	1 23.9	1 29.9
24 S	0 8 34.0	4 2.3	10 6.3	5♑57.6	18 53.4	12 19.1	27 30.2	10 58.4	15 41.3	13 32.8	1 24.2	1 28.5
25 S	0 12 30.6	5 1.7	10 3.2	18 18.3	20 38.0	13 33.1	27 38.1	11 4.7	15 38.5	13 32.4	1 24.5	1 27.0
26 M	0 16 27.1	6 1.2	9 60.0	0♒25.2	22 18.8	14 47.2	27 45.3	11 10.8	15 35.6	13 32.0	1 24.7	1 25.6
27 T	0 20 23.7	7 0.5	9 56.8	12 22.9	23 55.6	16 1.2	27 51.9	11 16.8	15 32.6	13 31.5	1 24.9	1 24.1
28 W	0 24 20.2	7 59.9	9 53.6	24 15.4	25 28.0	17 15.2	27 57.9	11 22.6	15 29.5	13 31.0	1 25.1	1 22.5
29 T	0 28 16.8	8 59.2	9 50.5	6♓ 6.2	26 55.5	18 29.3	28 3.2	11 28.3	15 26.4	13 30.4	1 25.2	1 21.0
30 F	0 32 13.3	9 58.5	9 47.3	17 57.9	28 17.9	19 43.3	28 7.8	11 33.7	15 23.2	13 29.8	1 25.4	1 19.5
31 S	0 36 9.9	10 57.7	9 44.1	29 52.6	29 34.7	20 57.3	28 11.7	11 39.1	15 19.9	13 29.2	1 25.4	1 17.9

DECLINATION at NOON

DAY	EPHEMERIS SIDEREAL TIME h m s	☉ ° ′	☊ ° ′	☽ ° ′	☿ ° ′	♀ ° ′	♂ ° ′	♃ ° ′	♄ ° ′	♅ ° ′	♆ ° ′	♇ ° ′
1 T	22 37 53.3	7S 24.2	22N 8.4	16S 57.3	11S 39.1	17S 10.6	16S 43.1	22S 57.1	14S 20.9	22S 22.1	22S 15.6	4N 4.1
4 S	22 49 43.0	6 15.2	22 7.1	3 4.8	9 29.2	16 11.6	16 58.5	22 55.6	14 19.7	22 22.4	22 15.5	4 6.2
7 W	23 1 32.6	5 5.4	22 5.8	12N 2.7	7 8.0	15 8.6	17 12.8	22 54.0	14 18.1	22 22.7	22 15.4	4 8.4
10 S	23 13 22.3	3 55.0	22 4.4	23 22.7	4 36.4	14 1.7	17 26.1	22 52.5	14 16.4	22 22.9	22 15.2	4 10.6
13 T	23 25 11.9	2 44.2	22 3.1	24 13.8	1 56.0	12 51.4	17 38.3	22 50.9	14 14.4	22 23.0	22 15.1	4 12.8
16 F	23 37 1.6	1 33.2	22 1.7	11 21.7	0N 50.7	11 38.0	17 49.6	22 49.4	14 12.2	22 23.1	22 15.0	4 15.0
19 M	23 48 51.2	0 22.0	22 0.4	7S 46.4	3 39.8	10 21.6	17 59.9	22 47.9	14 9.8	22 23.2	22 14.9	4 17.2
22 T	0 0 40.9	0N 49.0	21 59.0	22 5.9	6 26.1	9 2.8	18 9.2	22 46.5	14 7.1	22 23.1	22 14.8	4 19.4
25 S	0 12 30.6	1 59.9	21 57.6	25 22.7	9 3.1	7 41.7	18 17.5	22 45.1	14 4.3	22 23.0	22 14.7	4 21.6
28 W	0 24 20.2	3 10.4	21 56.2	18 3.2	11 24.3	6 18.7	18 24.8	22 43.8	14 1.3	22 22.9	22 14.6	4 23.7
31 S	0 36 9.9	4 20.3	21 54.8	4 21.9	13 23.9	4 54.1	18 31.0	22 42.6	13 58.1	22 22.7	22 14.5	4 25.8

APRIL 1984

LONGITUDE at NOON

DAY	EPHEMERIS SIDEREAL TIME h m s	☉ ° ′	☊ ° ′	☽ ° ′	☿ ° ′	♀ ° ′	♂ ° ′	♃ ° ′	♄ ° ′	♅ ° ′	♆ ° ′	♇ ° ′
1 S	0 40 6.4	11♈57.0	9♊40.9	11♈51.8	0♉45.8	22♓11.3	28♏15.0	11♑44.2	15♏16.6	13♐28.4	1♑25.5	1♏16.4
2 M	0 44 3.0	12 56.1	9 37.7	23 56.8	1 50.8	23 25.3	28 17.5	11 49.2	15R13.2	13R27.7	1 25.5	1R14.8
3 T	0 47 59.5	13 55.3	9 34.6	6♉ 8.8	2 49.6	24 39.3	28 19.3	11 54.1	15 9.7	13 26.9	1 25.5	1 13.2
4 W	0 51 56.1	14 54.4	9 31.4	18 29.4	3 42.0	25 53.3	28 20.4	11 58.7	15 6.1	13 26.0	1R25.4	1 11.6
5 T	0 55 52.7	15 53.5	9 28.2	1♊ 0.2	4 27.8	27 7.3	28 20.8	12 3.2	15 2.5	13 25.1	1 25.3	1 10.0
6 F	0 59 49.2	16 52.5	9 25.0	13 43.6	5 7.0	28 21.3	28R20.4	12 7.5	14 58.8	13 24.1	1 25.2	1 8.3
7 S	1 3 45.8	17 51.5	9 21.9	26 42.4	5 39.4	29 35.3	28 19.3	12 11.7	14 55.1	13 23.1	1 25.1	1 6.7
8 S	1 7 42.3	18 50.5	9 18.7	9♋59.2	6 5.0	0♈49.2	28 17.5	12 15.7	14 51.3	13 22.1	1 24.9	1 5.1
9 M	1 11 38.9	19 49.4	9 15.5	23 36.7	6 23.8	2 3.2	28 14.9	12 19.5	14 47.4	13 21.0	1 24.7	1 3.4
10 T	1 15 35.4	20 48.3	9 12.3	7♌36.3	6 35.9	3 17.1	28 11.5	12 23.1	14 43.5	13 19.8	1 24.4	1 1.8
11 W	1 19 32.0	21 47.2	9 9.1	21 57.7	6 41.4	4 31.0	28 7.4	12 26.5	14 39.6	13 18.6	1 24.1	1 0.1
12 T	1 23 28.5	22 46.0	9 6.0	6♍38.5	6R40.4	5 45.0	28 2.6	12 29.8	14 35.6	13 17.4	1 23.8	0 58.4
13 F	1 27 25.1	23 44.8	9 2.8	21 33.3	6 33.3	6 58.9	27 57.0	12 33.0	14 31.6	13 16.1	1 23.5	0 56.8
14 S	1 31 21.6	24 43.6	8 59.6	6♎34.3	6 20.2	8 12.9	27 50.7	12 35.9	14 27.5	13 14.8	1 23.1	0 55.1
15 S	1 35 18.2	25 42.3	8 56.4	21 32.3	6 1.5	9 26.8	27 43.5	12 38.6	14 23.3	13 13.4	1 22.7	0 53.4
16 M	1 39 14.7	26 40.9	8 53.3	6♏18.3	5 37.8	10 40.7	27 35.6	12 41.2	14 19.2	13 12.0	1 22.3	0 51.7
17 T	1 43 11.3	27 39.6	8 50.1	20 44.8	5 9.4	11 54.6	27 27.0	12 43.6	14 15.0	13 10.6	1 21.8	0 50.0
18 W	1 47 7.9	28 38.2	8 46.9	4♐46.8	4 37.1	13 8.5	27 17.6	12 45.8	14 10.7	13 9.1	1 21.3	0 48.3
19 T	1 51 4.4	29 36.8	8 43.7	18 22.1	4 1.5	14 22.3	27 7.4	12 47.8	14 6.4	13 7.6	1 20.8	0 46.6
20 F	1 55 1.0	0♉35.3	8 40.5	1♑31.2	3 23.3	15 36.2	26 56.5	12 49.6	14 2.1	13 6.0	1 20.2	0 44.9
21 S	1 58 57.5	1 33.8	8 37.4	14 16.6	2 43.2	16 50.1	26 44.9	12 51.2	13 57.7	13 4.4	1 19.6	0 43.3
22 S	2 2 54.1	2 32.3	8 34.2	26 42.0	2 2.0	18 4.0	26 32.5	12 52.7	13 53.3	13 2.7	1 19.0	0 41.6
23 M	2 6 50.6	3 30.8	8 31.0	8♒52.0	1 20.5	19 17.8	26 19.4	12 54.0	13 48.9	13 1.0	1 18.4	0 39.9
24 T	2 10 47.2	4 29.2	8 27.8	20 51.3	0 39.5	20 31.7	26 5.6	12 55.1	13 44.5	12 59.3	1 17.7	0 38.2
25 W	2 14 43.7	5 27.7	8 24.7	2♓44.6	29♈59.5	21 45.6	25 51.1	12 56.0	13 40.1	12 57.5	1 17.0	0 36.5
26 T	2 18 40.3	6 26.0	8 21.5	14 36.0	29 21.4	22 59.4	25 36.0	12 56.7	13 35.6	12 55.7	1 16.2	0 34.8
27 F	2 22 36.8	7 24.4	8 18.3	26 29.4	28 45.8	24 13.3	25 20.2	12 57.2	13 31.1	12 53.9	1 15.5	0 33.1
28 S	2 26 33.4	8 22.7	8 15.1	8♈27.8	28 13.1	25 27.1	25 3.7	12 57.5	13 26.6	12 52.0	1 14.7	0 31.4
29 S	2 30 30.0	9 21.1	8 11.9	20 33.6	27 43.9	26 41.0	24 46.7	12 57.7	13 22.1	12 50.1	1 13.9	0 29.7
30 M	2 34 26.5	10 19.3	8 8.8	2♉48.6	27 18.5	27 54.8	24 29.1	12R57.6	13 17.5	12 48.2	1 13.0	0 28.1

DECLINATION at NOON

DAY	EPHEMERIS SIDEREAL TIME h m s	☉ ° ′	☊ ° ′	☽ ° ′	☿ ° ′	♀ ° ′	♂ ° ′	♃ ° ′	♄ ° ′	♅ ° ′	♆ ° ′	♇ ° ′
1 S	0 40 6.4	4N 43.5	21N 54.3	0N 48.6	13N 58.2	4S 25.6	18S 32.9	22S 42.2	13S 57.1	22S 22.6	22S 14.5	4N 26.5
4 W	0 51 56.1	5 52.4	21 52.9	15 42.9	15 22.5	2 59.4	18 37.7	22 41.2	13 53.7	22 22.3	22 14.4	4 28.6
7 S	1 3 45.8	7 0.5	21 51.5	25 4.9	16 17.2	1 32.4	18 41.5	22 40.2	13 50.2	22 22.0	22 14.3	4 30.5
10 T	1 15 35.4	8 7.4	21 50.0	22 40.3	16 40.8	0 4.9	18 44.2	22 39.4	13 46.5	22 21.6	22 14.2	4 32.5
13 F	1 27 25.1	9 13.1	21 48.6	7 55.6	16 32.8	1N 22.8	18 45.8	22 38.7	13 42.8	22 21.2	22 14.1	4 34.3
16 M	1 39 14.7	10 17.4	21 47.1	11S 7.4	15 54.6	2 50.4	18 46.2	22 38.2	13 39.0	22 20.7	22 14.0	4 36.1
19 T	1 51 4.4	11 20.2	21 45.6	23 56.9	14 50.7	4 17.6	18 45.6	22 37.8	13 35.1	22 20.2	22 14.0	4 37.8
22 S	2 2 54.1	12 21.3	21 44.1	24 42.3	13 28.7	5 44.1	18 43.7	22 37.6	13 31.1	22 19.6	22 13.9	4 39.4
25 W	2 14 43.7	13 20.6	21 42.6	15 19.6	11 59.3	7 9.6	18 40.6	22 37.5	13 27.1	22 19.0	22 13.8	4 41.0
28 S	2 26 33.4	14 18.0	21 41.1	0 43.1	10 33.7	8 33.6	18 36.2	22 37.6	13 23.1	22 18.3	22 13.8	4 42.4

MAY 1984

DAY	EPHEMERIS SIDEREAL TIME	☉	☊	☽	☿	♀	♂	♃	♄	♅	♆	♇
	h m s	° ′	° ′	° ′	° ′	° ′	° ′	° ′	° ′	° ′	° ′	° ′
LONGITUDE at NOON												
1 T	2 38 23.1	11♉17.6	8♊ 5.6	15♉14.2	26♈57.4	29♈ 8.7	24♏10.9	12♑57.4	13♏13.0	12♐46.2	1♑12.1	0♏26.4
2 W	2 42 19.6	12 15.8	8 2.4	27 51.3	26R40.6	0♉22.5	23R52.3	12R57.0	13R 8.5	12R44.2	1R11.2	0R24.8
3 T	2 46 16.2	13 14.0	7 59.2	10♊40.4	26 28.4	1 36.3	23 33.1	12 56.3	13 3.9	12 42.2	1 10.3	0 23.1
4 F	2 50 12.7	14 12.2	7 56.1	23 42.4	26 20.9	2 50.2	23 13.6	12 55.6	12 59.4	12 40.2	1 9.4	0 21.5
5 S	2 54 9.3	15 10.3	7 52.9	6♋57.8	26 18.1	4 4.0	22 53.6	12 54.6	12 54.9	12 38.1	1 8.4	0 19.9
6 S	2 58 5.8	16 8.4	7 49.7	20 27.2	26D20.1	5 17.7	22 33.3	12 53.4	12 50.4	12 36.0	1 7.4	0 18.3
7 M	3 2 2.4	17 6.5	7 46.5	4♌11.1	26 26.8	6 31.5	22 12.7	12 52.0	12 45.9	12 33.8	1 6.4	0 16.7
8 T	3 5 58.9	18 4.5	7 43.4	18 9.4	26 38.1	7 45.3	21 51.7	12 50.5	12 41.4	12 31.7	1 5.3	0 15.1
9 W	3 9 55.5	19 2.5	7 40.2	2♍21.2	26 54.0	8 59.1	21 30.6	12 48.7	12 36.9	12 29.5	1 4.2	0 13.5
10 T	3 13 52.1	20 0.5	7 37.0	16 44.5	27 14.4	10 12.8	21 9.2	12 46.8	12 32.4	12 27.3	1 3.1	0 11.9
11 F	3 17 48.6	20 58.4	7 33.8	1♎15.8	27 39.2	11 26.6	20 47.7	12 44.7	12 27.9	12 25.1	1 2.0	0 10.3
12 S	3 21 45.2	21 56.3	7 30.6	15 50.4	28 8.1	12 40.3	20 26.1	12 42.4	12 23.5	12 22.8	1 0.8	0 8.8
13 S	3 25 41.7	22 54.2	7 27.5	0♏22.5	28 41.2	13 54.1	20 4.5	12 40.0	12 19.0	12 20.5	0 59.7	0 7.3
14 M	3 29 38.3	23 52.1	7 24.3	14 46.0	29 18.3	15 7.8	19 42.8	12 37.3	12 14.6	12 18.2	0 58.5	0 5.7
15 T	3 33 34.8	24 49.9	7 21.1	28 55.4	29 59.1	16 21.5	19 21.1	12 34.5	12 10.3	12 15.9	0 57.3	0 4.2
16 W	3 37 31.4	25 47.7	7 17.9	12♐46.5	0♉43.7	17 35.3	18 59.5	12 31.5	12 5.9	12 13.6	0 56.0	0 2.7
17 T	3 41 28.0	26 45.5	7 14.8	26 16.6	1 31.9	18 49.0	18 38.0	12 28.3	12 1.6	12 11.2	0 54.8	0 1.3
18 F	3 45 24.5	27 43.2	7 11.6	9♑24.8	2 23.5	20 2.7	18 16.7	12 25.0	11 57.3	12 8.9	0 53.5	29♎59.8
19 S	3 49 21.1	28 41.0	7 8.4	22 12.0	3 18.4	21 16.4	17 55.6	12 21.4	11 53.1	12 6.5	0 52.2	29 58.4
20 S	3 53 17.6	29 38.7	7 5.2	4♒40.5	4 16.6	22 30.1	17 34.7	12 17.7	11 48.9	12 4.1	0 50.9	29 57.0
21 M	3 57 14.2	0♊36.4	7 2.1	16 53.6	5 18.0	23 43.9	17 14.1	12 13.9	11 44.7	12 1.7	0 49.6	29 55.6
22 T	4 1 10.7	1 34.1	6 58.9	28 55.5	6 22.4	24 57.6	16 53.8	12 9.8	11 40.6	11 59.3	0 48.2	29 54.2
23 W	4 5 7.3	2 31.7	6 55.7	10♓50.5	7 29.8	26 11.3	16 33.9	12 5.6	11 36.5	11 56.8	0 46.8	29 52.8
24 T	4 9 3.9	3 29.4	6 52.5	22 43.3	8 40.0	27 25.0	16 14.4	12 1.3	11 32.4	11 54.4	0 45.5	29 51.5
25 F	4 13 0.4	4 27.1	6 49.3	4♈38.4	9 53.2	28 38.8	15 55.4	11 56.8	11 28.5	11 52.0	0 44.1	29 50.2
26 S	4 16 57.0	5 24.7	6 46.2	16 39.8	11 9.0	29 52.5	15 36.8	11 52.1	11 24.5	11 49.6	0 42.7	29 48.9
27 S	4 20 53.5	6 22.3	6 43.0	28 51.1	12 27.6	1♊ 6.2	15 18.8	11 47.3	11 20.6	11 47.1	0 41.3	29 47.6
28 M	4 24 50.1	7 19.9	6 39.8	11♉15.2	13 48.9	2 19.9	15 1.3	11 42.3	11 16.8	11 44.6	0 39.8	29 46.4
29 T	4 28 46.6	8 17.4	6 36.6	23 54.1	15 12.9	3 33.6	14 44.4	11 37.2	11 13.0	11 42.2	0 38.4	29 45.1
30 W	4 32 43.2	9 15.0	6 33.5	6♊48.9	16 39.4	4 47.3	14 28.1	11 31.9	11 9.2	11 39.7	0 36.9	29 43.9
31 T	4 36 39.8	10 12.5	6 30.3	19 59.8	18 8.5	6 1.1	14 12.5	11 26.4	11 5.6	11 37.2	0 35.4	29 42.7
DECLINATION at NOON												
1 T	2 38 23.1	15N13.2	21N39.6	14N34.8	9N21.4	9N56.0	18S30.7	22S37.9	13S19.1	22S17.6	22S13.7	4N43.7
4 F	2 50 12.7	16 6.2	21 38.1	24 50.1	8 28.5	11 16.4	18 24.1	22 38.4	13 15.1	22 16.8	22 13.7	4 44.9
7 M	3 2 2.4	16 56.8	21 36.5	23 31.1	7 57.9	12 34.4	18 16.6	22 39.0	13 11.2	22 16.1	22 13.6	4 46.0
10 T	3 13 52.1	17 44.7	21 35.0	9 59.8	7 49.9	13 49.8	18 8.2	22 39.8	13 7.3	22 15.2	22 13.6	4 47.0
13 S	3 25 41.7	18 30.1	21 33.4	8S41.2	8 3.2	15 2.1	17 59.2	22 40.7	13 3.5	22 14.4	22 13.6	4 47.9
16 W	3 37 31.4	19 12.5	21 31.9	22 54.1	8 35.8	16 11.1	17 49.9	22 41.8	12 59.8	22 13.5	22 13.5	4 48.7
19 S	3 49 21.1	19 52.1	21 30.3	25 20.3	9 25.2	17 16.5	17 40.4	22 43.1	12 56.2	22 12.6	22 13.5	4 49.3
22 T	4 1 10.7	20 28.7	21 28.7	16 44.8	10 29.0	18 17.9	17 31.0	22 44.5	12 52.7	22 11.7	22 13.5	4 49.8
25 F	4 13 0.4	21 2.1	21 27.1	2 26.1	11 45.0	19 1..0	17 22.1	22 46.0	12 49.4	22 10.7	22 13.5	4 50.1
28 M	4 24 50.1	21 32.2	21 25.5	13N 3.2	13 10.6	20 7.5	17 13.9	22 47.6	12 46.2	22 9.8	22 13.5	4 50.4
31 T	4 36 39.8	21 59.0	21 23.9	24 17.3	14 43.6	20 55.2	17 6.7	22 49.3	12 43.3	22 8.8	22 13.5	4 50.5

JUNE 1984

DAY	EPHEMERIS SIDEREAL TIME	☉	☊	☽	☿	♀	♂	♃	♄	♅	♆	♇
LONGITUDE at NOON												
1 F	4 40 36.3	11♊10.0	6♊27.1	3♋26.1	19♉40.2	7♊14.8	13♏57.5	11♑20.9	11♏ 1.9	11♐34.7	0♑33.9	29♎41.6
2 S	4 44 32.9	12 7.5	6 23.9	17 6.2	21 14.5	8 28.5	13R43.3	11R15.2	10R58.4	11R32.2	0R32.4	29R40.4
3 S	4 48 29.4	13 5.0	6 20.8	0♌58.2	22 51.3	9 42.2	13 29.8	11 9.3	10 54.9	11 29.8	0 30.9	29 39.3
4 M	4 52 26.0	14 2.5	6 17.6	14 59.6	24 30.6	10 55.9	13 17.0	11 3.4	10 51.5	11 27.3	0 29.3	29 38.2
5 T	4 56 22.5	14 59.9	6 14.4	29 8.0	26 12.5	12 9.6	13 5.0	10 57.3	10 48.1	11 24.8	0 27.8	29 37.2
6 W	5 0 19.1	15 57.3	6 11.2	13♍20.7	27 56.9	13 23.3	12 53.8	10 51.1	10 44.8	11 22.3	0 26.2	29 36.1
7 T	5 4 15.7	16 54.7	6 8.1	27 35.2	29 43.7	14 37.0	12 43.4	10 44.8	10 41.6	11 19.9	0 24.7	29 35.1
8 F	5 8 12.2	17 52.1	6 4.9	11♎48.9	1♊33.0	15 50.7	12 33.7	10 38.3	10 38.5	11 17.4	0 23.1	29 34.1
9 S	5 12 8.8	18 49.5	6 1.7	25 59.4	3 24.8	17 4.3	12 24.9	10 31.8	10 35.4	11 14.9	0 21.5	29 33.2
10 S	5 16 5.3	19 46.8	5 58.5	10♏ 3.8	5 18.9	18 18.0	12 16.9	10 25.2	10 32.4	11 12.5	0 20.0	29 32.3
11 M	5 20 1.9	20 44.1	5 55.3	23 59.4	7 15.4	19 31.7	12 9.7	10 18.4	10 29.5	11 10.1	0 18.4	29 31.4
12 T	5 23 58.5	21 41.4	5 52.2	7♐43.7	9 14.1	20 45.4	12 3.4	10 11.6	10 26.6	11 7.6	0 16.8	29 30.5
13 W	5 27 55.0	22 38.7	5 49.0	21 14.3	11 14.9	21 59.1	11 57.8	10 4.7	10 23.9	11 5.2	0 15.2	29 29.7
14 T	5 31 51.6	23 36.0	5 45.8	4♑29.2	13 17.8	23 12.8	11 53.1	9 57.6	10 21.2	11 2.8	0 13.6	29 28.8
15 F	5 35 48.1	24 33.3	5 42.6	17 27.7	15 22.6	24 26.5	11 49.3	9 50.6	10 18.6	11 0.5	0 12.0	29 28.1
16 S	5 39 44.7	25 30.6	5 39.5	0♒ 9.5	17 29.0	25 40.2	11 46.2	9 43.4	10 16.1	10 58.1	0 10.4	29 27.4
17 S	5 43 41.2	26 27.9	5 36.3	12 35.8	19 36.9	26 53.9	11 44.0	9 36.2	10 13.7	10 55.7	0 8.8	29 26.6
18 M	5 47 37.8	27 25.1	5 33.1	24 48.5	21 46.1	28 7.6	11 42.5	9 28.9	10 11.3	10 53.4	0 7.2	29 25.9
19 T	5 51 34.4	28 22.4	5 29.9	6♓50.7	23 56.3	29 21.3	11 41.9	9 21.5	10 9.0	10 51.1	0 5.5	29 25.3
20 W	5 55 30.9	29 19.6	5 26.8	18 46.1	26 7.2	0♋35.0	11D42.1	9 14.1	10 6.8	10 48.8	0 3.9	29 24.6
21 T	5 59 27.5	0♋16.9	5 23.6	0♈39.1	28 18.6	1 48.7	11 43.1	9 6.6	10 4.7	10 46.5	0 2.3	29 24.0
22 F	6 3 24.0	1 14.1	5 20.4	12 34.2	0♋30.2	3 2.5	11 44.9	8 59.1	10 2.7	10 44.2	0 0.7	29 23.5
23 S	6 7 20.6	2 11.4	5 17.2	24 36.3	2 41.7	4 16.2	11 47.5	8 51.6	10 0.8	10 41.9	29♐59.1	29 22.9
24 S	6 11 17.2	3 8.6	5 14.1	6♉49.8	4 52.8	5 29.9	11 50.9	8 44.0	9 59.0	10 39.7	29 57.4	29 22.4
25 M	6 15 13.7	4 5.8	5 10.9	19 18.9	7 3.3	6 43.7	11 55.1	8 36.3	9 57.2	10 37.5	29 55.8	29 22.0
26 T	6 19 10.3	5 3.1	5 7.7	2♊ 6.8	9 13.0	7 57.4	12 0.0	8 28.7	9 55.6	10 35.3	29 54.2	29 21.5
27 W	6 23 6.8	6 0.3	5 4.5	15 15.6	11 21.6	9 11.1	12 5.7	8 21.0	9 54.0	10 33.1	29 52.6	29 21.1
28 T	6 27 3.4	6 57.5	5 1.3	28 45.8	13 29.0	10 24.9	12 12.2	8 13.3	9 52.5	10 31.0	29 51.0	29 20.7
29 F	6 30 59.9	7 54.8	4 58.2	12♋36.1	15 34.9	11 38.7	12 19.4	8 5.6	9 51.1	10 28.9	29 49.4	29 20.4
30 S	6 34 56.5	8 52.0	4 55.0	26 43.4	17 39.3	12 52.4	12 27.4	7 57.9	9 49.9	10 26.8	29 47.8	29 20.1
DECLINATION at NOON												
1 F	4 40 36.3	22N 7.1	21N23.3	25N47.1	15N15.8	21N 9.9	17S 4.6	22S49.9	12S42.3	22S 8.5	22S13.5	4N50.5
4 M	4 52 26.0	22 29.3	21 21.7	21 1.5	16 54.5	21 50.6	16 59.2	22 51.8	12 39.6	22 7.5	22 13.5	4 50.4
7 T	5 4 15.7	22 47.9	21 20.1	5 28.5	18 33.9	22 25.8	16 55.4	22 53.7	12 37.1	22 6.5	22 13.5	4 50.2
10 S	5 16 5.3	23 2.9	21 18.4	12S35.8	20 10.3	22 55.2	16 53.3	22 55.6	12 34.8	22 5.5	22 13.5	4 49.8
13 W	5 27 55.0	23 14.3	21 16.7	24 28.9	21 39.3	23 18.7	16 53.0	22 57.6	12 32.8	22 4.5	22 13.5	4 49.3
16 S	5 39 44.7	23 22.0	21 15.1	24 14.8	22 55.5	23 36.0	16 54.6	22 59.5	12 31.0	22 3.6	22 13.5	4 48.7
19 T	5 51 34.4	23 25.9	21 13.4	13 51.6	23 53.7	23 47.2	16 58.1	23 1.5	12 29.4	22 2.6	22 13.6	4 48.0
22 F	6 3 24.0	23 26.2	21 11.7	1N 4.2	24 29.5	23 52.0	17 3.4	23 3.5	12 28.1	22 1.7	22 13.6	4 47.1
25 M	6 15 13.7	23 22.7	21 10.0	16 4.5	24 40.3	23 50.5	17 10.6	23 5.4	12 27.1	22 0.8	22 13.6	4 46.1
28 T	6 27 3.4	23 15.6	21 8.3	25 25.3	24 26.1	23 42.6	17 19.6	23 7.3	12 26.3	21 59.9	22 13.7	4 44.9

JULY 1984

LONGITUDE at NOON

DAY	EPHEMERIS SIDEREAL TIME	☉	☊	☽	☿	♀	♂	♃	♄	♅	♆	♇
	h m s	° ′	° ′	° ′	° ′	° ′	° ′	° ′	° ′	° ′	° ′	° ′
1 S	6 38 53.1	9♋49.2	4♓51.8	11♌ 3.1	19♋42.1	14♋ 6.2	12♏36.1	7♑50.2	9♏48.7	10♐24.7	29♐46.2	29♎19.8
2 M	6 42 49.6	10 46.4	4 48.6	25 29.6	21 43.0	15 19.9	12 45.5	7R42.5	9R47.6	10R22.7	29R44.6	29R19.5
3 T	6 46 46.2	11 43.6	4 45.5	9♍57.4	23 42.2	16 33.7	12 55.6	7 34.9	9 46.6	10 20.7	29 43.0	29 19.3
4 W	6 50 42.7	12 40.8	4 42.3	24 21.4	25 39.5	17 47.5	13 6.5	7 27.2	9 45.7	10 18.8	29 41.5	29 19.1
5 T	6 54 39.3	13 38.0	4 39.1	8♎37.8	27 34.8	19 1.2	13 18.0	7 19.6	9 44.9	10 16.8	29 39.9	29 19.0
6 F	6 58 35.9	14 35.3	4 35.9	22 44.1	29 28.3	20 15.0	13 30.2	7 12.1	9 44.2	10 15.0	29 38.4	29 18.9
7 S	7 2 32.4	15 32.5	4 32.8	6♏39.1	1♌19.7	21 28.8	13 43.1	7 4.5	9 43.6	10 13.1	29 36.8	29 18.9
8 S	7 6 29.0	16 29.7	4 29.6	20 22.1	3 9.2	22 42.6	13 56.6	6 57.0	9 43.1	10 11.3	29 35.3	29 18.8
9 M	7 10 25.5	17 26.9	4 26.4	3♐53.2	4 56.7	23 56.4	14 10.7	6 49.5	9 42.7	10 9.4	29 33.8	29 18.8
10 T	7 14 22.1	18 24.1	4 23.2	17 12.4	6 42.2	25 10.1	14 25.5	6 42.1	9 42.4	10 7.7	29 32.3	29 18.8
11 W	7 18 18.6	19 21.2	4 20.1	0♑19.7	8 25.7	26 23.9	14 40.9	6 34.8	9 42.2	10 5.9	29 30.8	29D18.9
12 T	7 22 15.2	20 18.4	4 16.9	13 14.9	10 7.2	27 37.7	14 56.8	6 27.5	9 42.0	10 4.2	29 29.3	29 19.0
13 F	7 26 11.8	21 15.6	4 13.7	25 57.8	11 46.7	28 51.4	15 13.4	6 20.3	9 42.0	10 2.6	29 27.8	29 19.1
14 S	7 30 8.3	22 12.8	4 10.5	8♒28.4	13 24.3	0♌ 5.2	15 30.5	6 13.1	9D42.1	10 1.0	29 26.3	29 19.3
15 S	7 34 4.9	23 10.0	4 7.3	20 47.2	14 59.9	1 19.0	15 48.2	6 6.0	9 42.3	9 59.4	29 24.9	29 19.5
16 M	7 38 1.4	24 7.3	4 4.2	2♓55.5	16 33.5	2 32.8	16 6.4	5 59.0	9 42.5	9 57.8	29 23.4	29 19.7
17 T	7 41 58.0	25 4.5	4 1.0	14 55.1	18 5.0	3 46.6	16 25.2	5 52.1	9 42.9	9 56.3	29 22.0	29 20.0
18 W	7 45 54.5	26 1.7	3 57.8	26 48.9	19 34.6	5 0.4	16 44.5	5 45.3	9 43.4	9 54.9	29 20.6	29 20.3
19 T	7 49 51.1	26 59.0	3 54.6	8♈40.3	21 2.2	6 14.2	17 4.3	5 38.6	9 43.9	9 53.4	29 19.2	29 20.6
20 F	7 53 47.7	27 56.2	3 51.5	20 33.9	22 27.7	7 28.0	17 24.7	5 31.9	9 44.6	9 52.0	29 17.8	29 21.0
21 S	7 57 44.2	28 53.5	3 48.3	2♉34.2	23 51.1	8 41.8	17 45.6	5 25.4	9 45.3	9 50.7	29 16.5	29 21.4
22 S	8 1 40.8	29 50.8	3 45.1	14 46.4	25 12.4	9 55.6	18 6.9	5 19.0	9 46.2	9 49.4	29 15.1	29 21.8
23 M	8 5 37.3	0♌48.1	3 41.9	27 15.5	26 31.6	11 9.5	18 28.7	5 12.7	9 47.2	9 48.1	29 13.8	29 22.3
24 T	8 9 33.9	1 45.4	3 38.8	10♊ 6.0	27 48.6	12 23.3	18 51.1	5 6.5	9 48.2	9 46.9	29 12.5	29 22.8
25 W	8 13 30.4	2 42.7	3 35.6	23 21.2	29 3.3	13 37.1	19 13.9	5 0.4	9 49.4	9 45.7	29 11.2	29 23.3
26 T	8 17 27.0	3 40.0	3 32.4	7♋ 2.7	0♍15.7	14 50.9	19 37.1	4 54.5	9 50.6	9 44.6	29 9.9	29 23.9
27 F	8 21 23.6	4 37.5	3 29.2	21 9.8	1 25.8	16 4.8	20 0.9	4 48.7	9 52.0	9 43.6	29 8.7	29 24.5
28 S	8 25 20.1	5 34.8	3 26.0	5♌39.0	2 33.4	17 18.7	20 25.0	4 43.1	9 53.4	9 42.5	29 7.5	29 25.1
29 S	8 29 16.7	6 32.2	3 22.9	20 23.9	3 38.5	18 32.5	20 49.6	4 37.5	9 55.0	9 41.5	29 6.3	29 25.8
30 M	8 33 13.2	7 29.6	3 19.7	5♍16.5	4 40.9	19 46.4	21 14.7	4 32.1	9 56.6	9 40.6	29 5.1	29 26.5
31 T	8 37 9.8	8 27.0	3 16.5	20 8.0	5 40.6	21 0.2	21 40.2	4 26.9	9 58.3	9 39.7	29 3.9	29 27.3

DECLINATION at NOON

DAY	EPHEMERIS SIDEREAL TIME	☉	☊	☽	☿	♀	♂	♃	♄	♅	♆	♇
1 S	6 38 53.1	23N 4.7	21N 6.6	21N58.1	23N48.8	23N28.4	17S 30.3	23S 9.1	12S25.8	21S59.0	22S13.7	4N43.7
4 W	6 50 42.7	22 50.3	21 4.8	6 45.4	22 51.7	23 8.0	17 42.6	23 10.8	12 25.6	21 58.2	22 13.7	4 42.3
7 S	7 2 32.4	22 32.2	21 3.1	11S20.0	21 38.5	22 41.3	17 56.5	23 12.5	12 25.7	21 57.4	22 13.8	4 40.8
10 T	7 14 22.1	22 10.7	21 1.3	23 49.5	20 12.8	22 8.7	18 11.7	23 14.1	12 26.1	21 56.6	22 13.8	4 39.1
13 F	7 26 11.8	21 45.7	20 59.6	24 49.6	18 37.9	21 30.3	18 28.2	23 15.6	12 26.7	21 55.9	22 13.9	4 37.4
16 M	7 38 1.4	21 17.4	20 57.8	15 11.4	16 56.5	20 46.4	18 45.7	23 17.0	12 27.7	21 55.3	22 13.9	4 35.6
19 T	7 49 51.1	20 45.8	20 56.0	0 29.1	15 11.3	19 57.1	19 4.2	23 18.3	12 28.9	21 54.6	22 14.0	4 33.6
22 S	8 1 40.8	20 11.1	20 54.2	14N34.2	13 24.4	19 2.7	19 23.6	23 19.5	12 30.3	21 54.1	22 14.1	4 31.6
25 W	8 13 30.4	19 33.4	20 52.4	24 52.5	11 38.0	18 3.5	19 43.6	23 20.7	12 32.1	21 53.6	22 14.1	4 29.4
28 S	8 25 20.1	18 52.7	20 50.6	23 8.8	9 54.2	16 59.8	20 4.1	23 21.7	12 34.1	21 53.1	22 14.2	4 27.2
31 T	8 37 9.8	18 9.2	20 48.8	8 22.9	8 15.1	15 52.0	20 25.2	23 22.7	12 36.4	21 52.7	22 14.3	4 24.9

AUGUST 1984

LONGITUDE at NOON

DAY	EPHEMERIS SIDEREAL TIME	☉	☊	☽	☿	♀	♂	♃	♄	♅	♆	♇
1 W	8 41 6.3	9♌24.4	3♓13.3	4♎50.5	6♍37.4	22♌14.0	22♏ 6.0	4♑21.7	10♏ 0.1	9♐38.9	29♐ 2.8	29♎28.0
2 T	8 45 2.9	10 21.8	3 10.2	19 18.2	7 31.3	23 27.9	22 32.3	4R16.8	10 2.1	9R38.1	29R 1.7	29 28.8
3 F	8 48 59.5	11 19.3	3 7.0	3♏27.7	8 22.0	24 41.7	22 59.0	4 12.0	10 4.1	9 37.3	29 0.6	29 29.7
4 S	8 52 56.0	12 16.7	3 3.8	17 18.1	9 9.4	25 55.6	23 26.1	4 7.3	10 6.2	9 36.6	28 59.5	29 30.5
5 S	8 56 52.6	13 14.2	3 0.6	0♐49.9	9 53.4	27 9.4	23 53.5	4 2.8	10 8.4	9 35.9	28 58.5	29 31.4
6 M	9 0 49.1	14 11.6	2 57.5	14 5.1	10 33.8	28 23.2	24 21.3	3 58.5	10 10.7	9 35.3	28 57.4	29 32.4
7 T	9 4 45.7	15 9.1	2 54.3	27 5.5	11 10.4	29 37.0	24 49.5	3 54.4	10 13.0	9 34.8	28 56.4	29 33.3
8 W	9 8 42.2	16 6.6	2 51.1	9♑53.2	11 43.0	0♍50.9	25 18.1	3 50.4	10 15.5	9 34.3	28 55.5	29 34.3
9 T	9 12 38.8	17 4.1	2 47.9	22 29.8	12 11.4	2 4.7	25 47.0	3 46.5	10 18.1	9 33.8	28 54.5	29 35.4
10 F	9 16 35.3	18 1.7	2 44.7	4♒56.4	12 35.4	3 18.5	26 16.2	3 42.9	10 20.7	9 33.4	28 53.6	29 36.4
11 S	9 20 31.9	18 59.2	2 41.6	17 13.8	12 54.8	4 32.3	26 45.7	3 39.4	10 23.5	9 33.0	28 52.7	29 37.5
12 S	9 24 28.5	19 56.8	2 38.4	29 22.9	13 9.4	5 46.1	27 15.6	3 36.1	10 26.3	9 32.7	28 51.8	29 38.6
13 M	9 28 25.0	20 54.3	2 35.2	11♓24.6	13 18.9	6 59.9	27 45.8	3 32.9	10 29.2	9 32.4	28 51.0	29 39.8
14 T	9 32 21.6	21 52.0	2 32.0	23 20.1	13 23.3	8 13.7	28 16.4	3 30.0	10 32.2	9 32.2	28 50.1	29 41.0
15 W	9 36 18.1	22 49.6	2 28.9	5♈11.4	13R22.2	9 27.5	28 47.2	3 27.2	10 35.3	9 32.1	28 49.4	29 42.2
16 T	9 40 14.7	23 47.2	2 25.7	17 1.3	13 15.7	10 41.3	29 18.3	3 24.6	10 38.5	9 32.0	28 48.6	29 43.4
17 F	9 44 11.2	24 45.0	2 22.5	28 53.4	13 3.6	11 55.2	29 49.8	3 22.2	10 41.8	9 32.0	28 47.9	29 44.8
18 S	9 48 7.8	25 42.7	2 19.3	10♉51.9	12 45.7	13 9.0	0♐21.5	3 19.9	10 45.1	9 31.9	28 47.2	29 46.1
19 S	9 52 4.3	26 40.4	2 16.2	23 1.5	12 22.2	14 22.7	0 53.5	3 17.9	10 48.5	9D32.0	28 46.5	29 47.4
20 M	9 56 0.9	27 38.2	2 13.0	5♊27.7	11 53.1	15 36.5	1 25.8	3 16.0	10 52.1	9 32.1	28 45.9	29 48.8
21 T	9 59 57.5	28 35.9	2 9.8	18 15.3	11 18.8	16 50.3	1 58.4	3 14.3	10 55.7	9 32.2	28 45.2	29 50.1
22 W	10 3 54.0	29 33.8	2 6.6	1♋28.9	10 39.4	18 4.1	2 31.3	3 12.8	10 59.3	9 32.4	28 44.7	29 51.6
23 T	10 7 50.6	0♍31.6	2 3.4	15 11.4	9 55.4	19 17.9	3 4.4	3 11.5	11 3.1	9 32.7	28 44.1	29 53.0
24 F	10 11 47.1	1 29.5	2 0.3	29 23.3	9 7.5	20 31.7	3 37.8	3 10.3	11 6.9	9 33.0	28 43.6	29 54.5
25 S	10 15 43.7	2 27.4	1 57.1	14♌ 2.0	8 16.4	21 45.5	4 11.5	3 9.4	11 10.9	9 33.3	28 43.1	29 56.0
26 S	10 19 40.2	3 25.3	1 53.9	29 1.3	7 22.9	22 59.2	4 45.4	3 8.6	11 14.9	9 33.7	28 42.6	29 57.5
27 M	10 23 36.8	4 23.2	1 50.7	14♍12.1	6 27.9	24 13.0	5 19.6	3 8.1	11 18.9	9 34.2	28 42.1	29 59.1
28 T	10 27 33.3	5 21.2	1 47.6	29 23.6	5 32.7	25 26.8	5 54.1	3 7.7	11 23.1	9 34.7	28 41.7	0♏ 0.7
29 W	10 31 29.9	6 19.2	1 44.4	14♎25.4	4 38.2	26 40.5	6 28.8	3 7.5	11 27.3	9 35.3	28 41.4	0 2.3
30 T	10 35 26.4	7 17.2	1 41.2	29 9.2	3 45.8	27 54.3	7 3.7	3 7.5	11 31.6	9 35.9	28 41.0	0 3.9
31 F	10 39 23.0	8 15.3	1 38.0	13♏30.0	2 56.5	29 8.0	7 38.9	3D 7.8	11 36.0	9 36.5	28 40.7	0 5.6

DECLINATION at NOON

DAY	EPHEMERIS SIDEREAL TIME	☉	☊	☽	☿	♀	♂	♃	♄	♅	♆	♇
1 W	8 41 6.3	17N54.1	20N48.2	2N 4.6	7N43.5	15N28.5	20S 32.2	23S 23.0	12S 37.2	21S 52.6	22S 14.3	4N24.1
4 S	8 52 56.0	17 7.1	20 46.4	15S 35.3	6 14.4	14 15.5	20 53.6	23 23.8	12 39.9	21 52.3	22 14.4	4 21.6
7 T	9 4 45.7	16 17.6	20 44.5	25 23.2	4 56.0	12 59.2	21 15.1	23 24.6	12 42.7	21 52.1	22 14.5	4 19.1
10 F	9 16 35.3	15 25.8	20 42.7	23 17.9	3 51.8	11 39.7	21 36.5	23 25.4	12 45.8	21 51.9	22 14.6	4 16.6
13 M	9 28 25.0	14 31.7	20 40.8	11 51.8	3 5.5	10 17.5	21 57.7	23 26.0	12 49.2	21 51.8	22 14.7	4 13.9
16 T	9 40 14.7	13 35.6	20 39.0	3N22.0	2 41.5	8 52.9	22 18.6	23 26.6	12 52.8	21 51.8	22 14.8	4 11.2
19 S	9 52 4.3	12 37.5	20 37.1	17 43.6	2 43.8	7 26.1	22 39.1	23 27.1	12 56.6	21 51.8	22 14.9	4 8.5
22 W	10 3 54.0	11 37.6	20 35.2	25 52.8	3 15.2	5 57.5	22 59.0	23 27.6	13 0.6	21 51.9	22 15.0	4 5.7
25 S	10 15 43.7	10 36.1	20 33.3	21 10.3	4 15.0	4 27.4	23 18.2	23 28.1	13 4.8	21 52.1	22 15.1	4 2.8
28 T	10 27 33.3	9 33.0	20 31.4	4 18.4	5 37.4	2 56.2	23 36.7	23 28.5	13 9.2	21 52.3	22 15.3	3 60.0
31 F	10 39 23.0	8 28.5	20 29.5	14S 25.3	7 11.0	1 24.1	23 54.2	23 28.8	13 13.8	21 52.6	22 15.4	3 57.1

SEPTEMBER 1984

DAY	EPHEMERIS SIDEREAL TIME	☉	☊	☽	☿	♀	♂	♃	♄	♅	♆	♇
	h m s	° ′	° ′	° ′	° ′	° ′	° ′	° ′	° ′	° ′	° ′	° ′
LONGITUDE at NOON												
1 S	10 43 19.5	9 ♍ 13.4	1 ♊ 34.8	27 ♏ 25.8	2 ♍ 11.5	0 ♎ 21.7	8 ♐ 14.3	3 ♑ 8.1	11 ♏ 40.5	9 ♐ 37.3	28 ♐ 40.4	0 ♏ 7.3
2 S	10 47 16.1	10 11.4	1 31.7	10 ♐ 57.3	1 R 31.8	1 35.5	8 49.9	3 8.7	11 45.0	9 38.0	28 R 40.2	0 9.0
3 M	10 51 12.7	11 9.6	1 28.5	24 6.9	0 58.4	2 49.2	9 25.8	3 9.5	11 49.6	9 38.8	28 39.9	0 10.7
4 T	10 55 9.2	12 7.7	1 25.3	6 ♑ 57.8	0 32.2	4 2.9	10 1.9	3 10.5	11 54.3	9 39.7	28 39.8	0 12.5
5 W	10 59 5.8	13 5.9	1 22.1	19 33.4	0 13.8	5 16.5	10 38.2	3 11.6	11 59.0	9 40.6	28 39.6	0 14.3
6 T	11 3 2.3	14 4.0	1 19.0	1 ♒ 56.8	0 3.6	6 30.2	11 14.7	3 13.0	12 3.9	9 41.6	28 39.5	0 16.1
7 F	11 6 58.9	15 2.3	1 15.8	14 10.6	0 2.2	7 43.9	11 51.4	3 14.5	12 8.8	9 42.7	28 39.4	0 18.0
8 S	11 10 55.4	16 0.5	1 12.6	26 16.7	0 D 9.7	8 57.6	12 28.3	3 16.3	12 13.7	9 43.7	28 39.4	0 19.8
9 S	11 14 52.0	16 58.8	1 9.4	8 ♓ 16.9	0 26.1	10 11.2	13 5.4	3 18.2	12 18.7	9 44.9	28 39.4	0 21.7
10 M	11 18 48.5	17 57.1	1 6.2	20 12.5	0 51.5	11 24.8	13 42.7	3 20.2	12 23.8	9 46.0	28 39.4	0 23.6
11 T	11 22 45.1	18 55.4	1 3.1	2 ♈ 4.7	1 25.6	12 38.5	14 20.2	3 22.5	12 29.0	9 47.2	28 39.4	0 25.6
12 W	11 26 41.6	19 53.8	0 59.9	13 55.2	2 8.3	13 52.1	14 57.9	3 25.0	12 34.2	9 48.5	28 D 39.5	0 27.5
13 T	11 30 38.2	20 52.2	0 56.7	25 45.8	2 59.0	15 5.6	15 35.7	3 27.6	12 39.5	9 49.8	28 39.6	0 29.5
14 F	11 34 34.7	21 50.6	0 53.5	7 ♉ 39.4	3 57.4	16 19.2	16 13.8	3 30.4	12 44.8	9 51.2	28 39.7	0 31.4
15 S	11 38 31.3	22 49.1	0 50.4	19 39.1	5 3.0	17 32.8	16 52.0	3 33.4	12 50.2	9 52.6	28 39.9	0 33.5
16 S	11 42 27.8	23 47.6	0 47.2	1 ♊ 49.0	6 15.3	18 46.4	17 30.4	3 36.6	12 55.6	9 54.1	28 40.1	0 35.5
17 M	11 46 24.4	24 46.1	0 44.0	14 13.7	7 33.5	19 59.9	18 8.9	3 39.9	13 1.1	9 55.6	28 40.3	0 37.5
18 T	11 50 21.0	25 44.7	0 40.8	26 58.0	8 57.2	21 13.5	18 47.7	3 43.5	13 6.7	9 57.2	28 40.6	0 39.6
19 W	11 54 17.5	26 43.3	0 37.6	10 ♋ 6.3	10 25.7	22 27.0	19 26.6	3 47.2	13 12.4	9 58.8	28 40.9	0 41.7
20 T	11 58 14.1	27 41.9	0 34.5	23 42.3	11 58.4	23 40.5	20 5.7	3 51.1	13 18.0	10 0.4	28 41.2	0 43.8
21 F	12 2 10.6	28 40.6	0 31.3	7 ♌ 47.7	13 34.7	24 54.0	20 44.9	3 55.1	13 23.8	10 2.1	28 41.6	0 45.9
22 S	12 6 7.2	29 39.3	0 28.1	22 21.4	15 14.1	26 7.5	21 24.3	3 59.4	13 29.6	10 3.9	28 42.0	0 48.0
23 S	12 10 3.7	0 ♎ 38.1	0 24.9	7 ♍ 18.9	16 56.0	27 21.0	22 3.9	4 3.8	13 35.4	10 5.7	28 42.4	0 50.2
24 M	12 14 0.3	1 36.9	0 21.8	22 32.2	18 40.0	28 34.5	22 43.6	4 8.4	13 41.3	10 7.5	28 42.9	0 52.3
25 T	12 17 56.8	2 35.7	0 18.6	7 ♎ 50.8	20 25.6	29 48.0	23 23.5	4 13.2	13 47.3	10 9.4	28 43.4	0 54.5
26 W	12 21 53.4	3 34.5	0 15.4	23 3.5	22 12.4	1 ♏ 1.5	24 3.6	4 18.1	13 53.3	10 11.3	28 43.9	0 56.7
27 T	12 25 49.9	4 33.4	0 12.2	8 ♏ 0.2	24 0.1	2 14.9	24 43.8	4 23.2	13 59.4	10 13.3	28 44.5	0 58.9
28 F	12 29 46.5	5 32.4	0 9.0	22 33.9	25 48.4	3 28.4	25 24.2	4 28.5	14 5.5	10 15.4	28 45.2	1 1.2
29 S	12 33 43.0	6 31.3	0 5.9	6 ♐ 40.7	27 37.0	4 41.8	26 4.7	4 33.9	14 11.7	10 17.4	28 45.8	1 3.5
30 S	12 37 39.6	7 30.3	0 2.7	20 19.9	29 25.7	5 55.2	26 45.3	4 39.5	14 17.9	10 19.6	28 46.5	1 5.7
DECLINATION at NOON												
1 S	10 43 19.5	8N 6.8	20N28.8	19S 15.4	7N42.2	0N53.3	23S 59.8	23S 28.9	13S 15.3	21S 52.7	22S 15.4	3N56.1
4 T	10 55 9.2	7 0.8	20 26.9	26 12.0	9 7.9	0S 39.3	24 16.0	23 29.2	13 20.2	21 53.1	22 15.6	3 53.1
7 F	11 6 58.9	5 53.7	20 25.0	21 10.2	10 12.2	2 12.0	24 30.9	23 29.4	13 25.1	21 53.6	22 15.7	3 50.2
10 M	11 18 48.5	4 45.8	20 23.0	8 12.8	10 45.9	3 44.5	24 44.5	23 29.6	13 30.3	21 54.1	22 15.9	3 47.2
13 T	11 30 38.2	3 37.2	20 21.0	7N19.4	10 44.8	5 16.4	24 56.7	23 29.7	13 35.5	21 54.7	22 16.0	3 44.2
16 S	11 42 27.8	2 27.9	20 19.1	20 43.2	10 8.3	6 47.4	25 7.4	23 29.8	13 40.9	21 55.4	22 16.1	3 41.3
19 W	11 54 17.5	1 18.2	20 17.1	26 21.4	8 59.7	8 17.1	25 16.5	23 29.8	13 46.4	21 56.1	22 16.3	3 38.3
22 S	12 6 7.2	0 8.2	20 15.1	18 49.3	7 24.6	9 45.3	25 23.9	23 29.7	13 52.0	21 56.9	22 16.5	3 35.4
25 T	12 17 56.8	1S 1.9	20 13.1	0 31.7	5 30.0	11 11.7	25 29.6	23 29.6	13 57.8	21 57.7	22 16.6	3 32.4
28 F	12 29 46.5	2 12.1	20 11.1	17S 52.9	3 22.3	12 35.8	25 33.4	23 29.3	14 3.6	21 58.6	22 16.8	3 29.5

OCTOBER 1984

DAY	EPHEMERIS SIDEREAL TIME	☉	☊	☽	☿	♀	♂	♃	♄	♅	♆	♇
LONGITUDE at NOON												
1 M	12 41 36.1	8 ♎ 29.3	29 ♉ 59.5	3 ♑ 33.2	1 ♎ 14.4	7 ♏ 8.6	27 ♐ 26.1	4 ♑ 45.3	14 ♏ 24.1	10 ♐ 21.7	28 ♐ 47.2	1 ♏ 8.0
2 T	12 45 32.7	9 28.4	29 56.3	16 23.9	3 2.8	8 22.0	28 7.0	4 51.2	14 30.4	10 23.9	28 47.9	1 10.3
3 W	12 49 29.3	10 27.4	29 53.2	28 55.9	4 50.9	9 35.3	28 48.0	4 57.3	14 36.7	10 26.1	28 48.6	1 12.6
4 T	12 53 25.8	11 26.5	29 50.0	11 ♒ 13.3	6 38.6	10 48.7	29 29.2	5 3.5	14 43.1	10 28.4	28 49.4	1 14.9
5 F	12 57 22.4	12 25.6	29 46.8	23 19.8	8 25.7	12 2.0	0 ♑ 10.5	5 9.9	14 49.5	10 30.7	28 50.3	1 17.2
6 S	13 1 18.9	13 24.8	29 43.6	5 ♓ 18.8	10 12.3	13 15.3	0 51.9	5 16.4	14 56.0	10 33.1	28 51.1	1 19.5
7 S	13 5 15.5	14 24.0	29 40.4	17 13.0	11 58.2	14 28.6	1 33.5	5 23.1	15 2.5	10 35.5	28 52.0	1 21.8
8 M	13 9 12.0	15 23.2	29 37.3	29 4.9	13 43.5	15 41.8	2 15.1	5 30.0	15 9.0	10 37.9	28 52.9	1 24.2
9 T	13 13 8.6	16 22.4	29 34.1	10 ♈ 56.2	15 28.0	16 55.1	2 56.9	5 37.0	15 15.6	10 40.4	28 53.9	1 26.5
10 W	13 17 5.1	17 21.7	29 30.9	22 48.7	17 11.9	18 8.3	3 38.8	5 44.1	15 22.2	10 42.9	28 54.9	1 28.9
11 T	13 21 1.7	18 21.0	29 27.7	4 ♉ 44.1	18 55.0	19 21.5	4 20.8	5 51.4	15 28.8	10 45.5	28 55.9	1 31.2
12 F	13 24 58.2	19 20.4	29 24.6	16 44.2	20 37.5	20 34.6	5 2.9	5 58.8	15 35.5	10 48.1	28 56.9	1 33.6
13 S	13 28 54.8	20 19.8	29 21.4	28 51.5	22 19.2	21 47.8	5 45.1	6 6.4	15 42.2	10 50.7	28 58.0	1 36.0
14 S	13 32 51.3	21 19.2	29 18.2	11 ♊ 8.5	24 0.2	23 1.0	6 27.4	6 14.1	15 48.9	10 53.4	28 59.1	1 38.4
15 M	13 36 47.9	22 18.7	29 15.0	23 38.5	25 40.5	24 14.1	7 9.9	6 21.9	15 55.7	10 56.1	29 0.2	1 40.8
16 T	13 40 44.5	23 18.2	29 11.8	6 ♋ 25.0	27 20.1	25 27.2	7 52.4	6 29.9	16 2.5	10 58.8	29 1.4	1 43.2
17 W	13 44 41.0	24 17.7	29 8.7	19 31.4	28 59.1	26 40.3	8 35.0	6 38.1	16 9.3	11 1.6	29 2.6	1 45.6
18 T	13 48 37.6	25 17.3	29 5.5	3 ♌ 0.8	0 ♏ 37.4	27 53.3	9 17.8	6 46.3	16 16.1	11 4.4	29 3.8	1 48.0
19 F	13 52 34.1	26 17.0	29 2.3	16 55.2	2 15.1	29 6.5	10 0.7	6 54.8	16 23.1	11 7.3	29 5.1	1 50.5
20 S	13 56 30.7	27 16.6	28 59.1	1 ♍ 14.5	3 52.1	0 ♐ 19.5	10 43.6	7 3.3	16 30.0	11 10.2	29 6.3	1 52.9
21 S	14 0 27.2	28 16.3	28 56.0	15 56.2	5 28.6	1 32.5	11 26.7	7 12.0	16 36.9	11 13.1	29 7.6	1 55.3
22 M	14 4 23.8	29 16.1	28 52.8	0 ♎ 55.0	7 4.4	2 45.5	12 9.8	7 20.8	16 43.9	11 16.0	29 9.0	1 57.7
23 T	14 8 20.3	0 ♏ 15.8	28 49.6	16 2.8	8 39.7	3 58.5	12 53.0	7 29.7	16 50.8	11 19.0	29 10.3	2 0.1
24 W	14 12 16.9	1 15.6	28 46.4	1 ♏ 10.0	10 14.4	5 11.5	13 36.4	7 38.7	16 57.8	11 22.0	29 11.7	2 2.6
25 T	14 16 13.4	2 15.5	28 43.2	16 7.1	11 48.6	6 24.4	14 19.8	7 47.9	17 4.9	11 25.0	29 13.1	2 5.0
26 F	14 20 10.0	3 15.3	28 40.1	0 ♐ 46.0	13 22.2	7 37.3	15 3.3	7 57.2	17 11.9	11 28.1	29 14.6	2 7.4
27 S	14 24 6.6	4 15.2	28 36.9	15 0.9	14 55.4	8 50.2	15 46.9	8 6.6	17 19.0	11 31.2	29 16.1	2 9.8
28 S	14 28 3.1	5 15.1	28 33.7	28 49.1	16 28.0	10 3.1	16 30.6	8 16.1	17 26.0	11 34.3	29 17.5	2 12.2
29 M	14 31 59.7	6 15.1	28 30.5	12 ♑ 10.5	18 0.1	11 15.9	17 14.4	8 25.8	17 33.1	11 37.5	29 19.1	2 14.7
30 T	14 35 56.2	7 15.1	28 27.4	25 7.1	19 31.8	12 28.7	17 58.2	8 35.6	17 40.2	11 40.6	29 20.6	2 17.1
31 W	14 39 52.8	8 15.1	28 24.2	7 ♒ 42.2	21 2.9	13 41.5	18 42.1	8 45.4	17 47.3	11 43.8	29 22.2	2 19.5
DECLINATION at NOON												
1 M	12 41 36.1	3S 22.0	20N 9.1	26S 19.7	1N 7.2	13S 57.4	25S 35.3	23S 29.0	14S 9.5	21S 59.6	22S 16.9	3N 26.6
4 T	12 53 25.8	4 31.6	20 7.1	22 6.9	1S 11.1	15 16.0	25 35.2	23 28.6	14 15.4	22 0.6	22 17.1	3 23.8
7 S	13 5 15.5	5 40.7	20 5.0	9 31.2	3 29.6	16 31.3	25 33.1	23 28.1	14 21.4	22 1.6	22 17.2	3 21.0
10 W	13 17 5.1	6 49.1	20 3.0	6N 6.6	5 46.1	17 43.0	25 28.8	23 27.5	14 27.5	22 2.7	22 17.4	3 18.2
13 S	13 28 54.8	7 56.7	20 0.9	20 0.1	7 59.0	18 50.8	25 22.5	23 26.8	14 33.5	22 3.8	22 17.6	3 15.5
16 T	13 40 44.5	9 3.3	19 58.9	26 32.2	10 7.1	19 54.3	25 14.0	23 25.9	14 39.6	22 5.0	22 17.7	3 12.9
19 F	13 52 34.1	10 8.8	19 56.8	20 38.5	12 9.8	20 53.1	25 3.3	23 24.9	14 45.8	22 6.2	22 17.9	3 10.3
22 M	14 4 23.8	11 12.9	19 54.7	3 38.5	14 6.3	21 47.0	24 50.4	23 23.7	14 51.9	22 7.4	22 18.0	3 7.8
25 T	14 16 13.4	12 15.6	19 52.6	15S 40.1	15 55.9	22 35.7	24 35.3	23 22.4	14 58.1	22 8.7	22 18.2	3 5.4
28 S	14 28 3.1	13 16.5	19 50.5	26 10.2	17 38.1	23 18.8	24 17.9	23 21.0	15 4.2	22 10.0	22 18.3	3 3.0
31 W	14 39 52.8	14 15.5	19 48.4	23 7.3	19 12.4	23 56.0	23 58.4	23 19.3	15 10.3	22 11.3	22 18.4	3 0.7

NOVEMBER 1984

DAY	EPHEMERIS SIDEREAL TIME h m s	☉ ° ′	☊ ° ′	☽ ° ′	☿ ° ′	♀ ° ′	♂ ° ′	♃ ° ′	♄ ° ′	♅ ° ′	♆ ° ′	♇ ° ′
					LONGITUDE at NOON							
1 T	14 43 49.3	9♏15.1	28♉21.0	20♒ 0.0	22♏33.6	14♐54.3	19♑26.1	8♑55.4	17♏54.4	11♐47.1	29♐23.8	2♏21.9
2 F	14 47 45.9	10 15.2	28 17.8	2♓ 4.8	24 3.9	16 7.0	20 10.2	9 5.5	18 1.6	11 50.3	29 25.4	2 24.3
3 S	14 51 42.4	11 15.3	28 14.7	14 1.0	25 33.6	17 19.7	20 54.3	9 15.7	18 8.7	11 53.6	29 27.0	2 26.7
4 S	14 55 39.0	12 15.4	28 11.5	25 52.7	27 2.9	18 32.3	21 38.5	9 26.1	18 15.9	11 56.9	29 28.7	2 29.1
5 M	14 59 35.6	13 15.5	28 8.3	7♈43.2	28 31.7	19 44.9	22 22.8	9 36.5	18 23.0	12 0.2	29 30.4	2 31.5
6 T	15 3 32.1	14 15.7	28 5.1	19 35.8	0♐ 0.0	20 57.5	23 7.1	9 47.0	18 30.2	12 3.6	29 32.1	2 33.9
7 W	15 7 28.7	15 15.9	28 1.9	1♉32.8	1 27.8	22 10.1	23 51.5	9 57.6	18 37.4	12 6.9	29 33.8	2 36.3
8 T	15 11 25.2	16 16.1	27 58.8	13 36.4	2 55.0	23 22.6	24 36.0	10 8.4	18 44.6	12 10.3	29 35.6	2 38.7
9 F	15 15 21.8	17 16.4	27 55.6	25 48.3	4 21.8	24 35.1	25 20.5	10 19.2	18 51.8	12 13.8	29 37.4	2 41.1
10 S	15 19 18.3	18 16.7	27 52.4	8♊ 9.8	5 47.9	25 47.5	26 5.1	10 30.1	18 59.0	12 17.2	29 39.2	2 43.4
11 S	15 23 14.9	19 17.0	27 49.2	20 42.4	7 13.3	26 59.9	26 49.8	10 41.2	19 6.1	12 20.6	29 41.0	2 45.8
12 M	15 27 11.4	20 17.4	27 46.1	3♋27.4	8 38.1	28 12.3	27 34.4	10 52.3	19 13.3	12 24.1	29 42.9	2 48.1
13 T	15 31 8.0	21 17.8	27 42.9	16 26.4	10 2.1	29 24.6	28 19.2	11 3.5	19 20.5	12 27.6	29 44.7	2 50.4
14 W	15 35 4.6	22 18.2	27 39.7	29 40.8	11 25.3	0♑36.8	29 4.0	11 14.8	19 27.7	12 31.1	29 46.6	2 52.8
15 T	15 39 1.1	23 18.6	27 36.5	13♌11.8	12 47.5	1 49.1	29 48.8	11 26.2	19 34.9	12 34.6	29 48.5	2 55.1
16 F	15 42 57.7	24 19.1	27 33.4	27 0.2	14 8.8	3 1.2	0♒33.7	11 37.6	19 42.0	12 38.1	29 50.4	2 57.4
17 S	15 46 54.2	25 19.6	27 30.2	11♍ 5.9	15 28.9	4 13.4	1 18.7	11 49.2	19 49.2	12 41.6	29 52.4	2 59.7
18 S	15 50 50.8	26 20.1	27 27.0	25 27.7	16 47.7	5 25.5	2 3.7	12 0.8	19 56.4	12 45.2	29 54.3	3 1.9
19 M	15 54 47.3	27 20.7	27 23.8	10♎ 2.4	18 5.1	6 37.5	2 48.7	12 12.6	20 3.5	12 48.8	29 56.3	3 4.2
20 T	15 58 43.9	28 21.3	27 20.6	24 45.5	19 20.9	7 49.5	3 33.8	12 24.4	20 10.7	12 52.4	29 58.3	3 6.5
21 W	16 2 40.5	29 21.9	27 17.5	9♏30.8	20 34.8	9 1.5	4 19.0	12 36.3	20 17.8	12 56.0	0♑ 0.3	3 8.7
22 T	16 6 37.0	0♐22.6	27 14.3	24 11.3	21 46.7	10 13.4	5 4.2	12 48.3	20 24.9	12 59.6	0 2.3	3 10.9
23 F	16 10 33.6	1 23.2	27 11.1	8♐40.3	22 56.2	11 25.3	5 49.4	13 0.3	20 32.0	13 3.2	0 4.4	3 13.1
24 S	16 14 30.1	2 23.9	27 7.9	22 51.7	24 2.9	12 37.1	6 34.7	13 12.4	20 39.1	13 6.8	0 6.4	3 15.3
25 S	16 18 26.7	3 24.7	27 4.8	6♑41.5	25 6.5	13 48.8	7 20.0	13 24.7	20 46.2	13 10.4	0 8.5	3 17.5
26 M	16 22 23.2	4 25.4	27 1.6	20 7.5	26 6.6	15 0.5	8 5.4	13 36.9	20 53.3	13 14.1	0 10.6	3 19.6
27 T	16 26 19.8	5 26.1	26 58.4	3♒ 9.7	27 2.7	16 12.1	8 50.8	13 49.3	21 0.3	13 17.7	0 12.7	3 21.8
28 W	16 30 16.4	6 26.9	26 55.2	15 49.8	27 54.2	17 23.7	9 36.2	14 1.7	21 7.3	13 21.4	0 14.8	3 23.9
29 T	16 34 12.9	7 27.7	26 52.1	28 11.1	28 40.5	18 35.2	10 21.7	14 14.2	21 14.3	13 25.0	0 16.9	3 26.0
30 F	16 38 9.5	8 28.6	26 48.9	10♓17.7	29 20.9	19 46.6	11 7.2	14 26.8	21 21.4	13 28.7	0 19.1	3 28.1
					DECLINATION at NOON							
1 T	14 43 49.3	14S34.8	19N47.7	19S45.4	19S42.0	24S 7.1	23S51.4	23S18.7	15S12.3	22S11.8	22S18.5	2N60.0
4 S	14 55 39.0	15 31.0	19 45.6	5 53.4	21 4.8	24 36.3	23 29.0	23 16.9	15 18.4	22 13.1	22 18.6	2 57.8
7 W	15 7 28.7	16 25.0	19 43.5	9N51.0	22 18.3	24 59.1	23 4.4	23 14.8	15 24.4	22 14.5	22 18.7	2 55.8
10 S	15 19 18.3	17 16.4	19 41.3	22 38.9	23 21.8	25 15.4	22 37.7	23 12.5	15 30.3	22 15.8	22 18.9	2 53.8
13 T	15 31 8.0	18 5.2	19 39.2	26 23.9	24 14.8	25 25.2	22 9.0	23 10.1	15 36.2	22 17.2	22 19.0	2 52.0
16 F	15 42 57.7	18 51.2	19 37.0	17 28.6	24 56.4	25 28.3	21 38.2	23 7.4	15 42.0	22 18.6	22 19.1	2 50.2
19 M	15 54 47.3	19 34.2	19 34.9	0S23.4	25 26.1	25 24.8	21 5.5	23 4.5	15 47.8	22 20.0	22 19.2	2 48.6
22 T	16 6 37.0	20 14.0	19 32.7	18 31.8	25 43.2	25 14.7	20 30.8	23 1.4	15 53.4	22 21.4	22 19.2	2 47.0
25 S	16 18 26.7	20 50.4	19 30.5	26 37.2	25 47.4	24 58.0	19 54.3	22 58.1	15 59.0	22 22.8	22 19.3	2 45.6
28 W	16 30 16.4	21 23.3	19 28.3	21 1.7	25 38.4	24 34.8	19 16.0	22 54.5	16 4.5	22 24.1	22 19.4	2 44.3

DECEMBER 1984

DAY	EPHEMERIS SIDEREAL TIME h m s	☉ ° ′	☊ ° ′	☽ ° ′	☿ ° ′	♀ ° ′	♂ ° ′	♃ ° ′	♄ ° ′	♅ ° ′	♆ ° ′	♇ ° ′
					LONGITUDE at NOON							
1 S	16 42 6.0	9♐29.4	26♉45.7	22♓14.1	29♐54.6	20♑57.9	11♒52.7	14♑39.4	21♏28.3	13♐32.4	0♑21.2	3♏30.2
2 S	16 46 2.6	10 30.2	26 42.5	4♈ 5.2	0♑20.9	22 9.2	12 38.3	14 52.1	21 35.3	13 36.1	0 23.4	3 32.2
3 M	16 49 59.1	11 31.1	26 39.3	15 55.6	0 38.9	23 20.4	13 23.9	15 4.8	21 42.2	13 39.8	0 25.5	3 34.3
4 T	16 53 55.7	12 31.9	26 36.2	27 49.7	0 47.8	24 31.5	14 9.5	15 17.6	21 49.1	13 43.4	0 27.7	3 36.3
5 W	16 57 52.3	13 32.8	26 33.0	9♉51.2	0R46.7	25 42.4	14 55.1	15 30.5	21 55.9	13 47.1	0 29.9	3 38.3
6 T	17 1 48.8	14 33.7	26 29.8	22 3.3	0 35.1	26 53.4	15 40.7	15 43.4	22 2.8	13 50.8	0 32.1	3 40.2
7 F	17 5 45.4	15 34.6	26 26.6	4♊28.2	0 12.4	28 4.2	16 26.4	15 56.4	22 9.6	13 54.5	0 34.3	3 42.2
8 S	17 9 41.9	16 35.6	26 23.5	17 7.4	29♐38.2	29 14.9	17 12.0	16 9.4	22 16.4	13 58.1	0 36.5	3 44.1
9 S	17 13 38.5	17 36.5	26 20.3	0♋ 1.4	28 52.8	0♒25.5	17 57.7	16 22.5	22 23.1	14 1.8	0 38.7	3 46.0
10 M	17 17 35.1	18 37.5	26 17.1	13 10.0	27 56.7	1 36.0	18 43.4	16 35.6	22 29.8	14 5.5	0 41.0	3 47.9
11 T	17 21 31.6	19 38.4	26 13.9	26 32.2	26 51.1	2 46.5	19 29.2	16 48.8	22 36.5	14 9.1	0 43.2	3 49.7
12 W	17 25 28.2	20 39.4	26 10.8	10♌ 6.8	25 37.5	3 56.8	20 14.9	17 2.0	22 43.1	14 12.8	0 45.4	3 51.5
13 T	17 29 24.7	21 40.4	26 7.6	23 52.3	24 18.2	5 7.0	21 0.7	17 15.3	22 49.7	14 16.5	0 47.7	3 53.3
14 F	17 33 21.3	22 41.5	26 4.4	7♍47.1	22 55.7	6 17.1	21 46.4	17 28.6	22 56.3	14 20.1	0 49.9	3 55.1
15 S	17 37 17.8	23 42.5	26 1.2	21 49.7	21 32.8	7 27.0	22 32.2	17 42.0	23 2.8	14 23.7	0 52.2	3 56.9
16 S	17 41 14.4	24 43.6	25 58.1	5♎58.7	20 12.3	8 36.9	23 18.0	17 55.4	23 9.3	14 27.4	0 54.4	3 58.6
17 M	17 45 11.0	25 44.6	25 54.9	20 12.5	18 56.9	9 46.6	24 3.8	18 8.8	23 15.8	14 31.0	0 56.7	4 0.3
18 T	17 49 7.5	26 45.7	25 51.7	4♏28.8	17 48.6	10 56.3	24 49.6	18 22.3	23 22.2	14 34.6	0 58.9	4 2.0
19 W	17 53 4.1	27 46.8	25 48.5	18 45.0	16 49.3	12 5.7	25 35.5	18 35.9	23 28.6	14 38.2	1 1.2	4 3.6
20 T	17 57 0.6	28 48.0	25 45.3	2♐57.7	16 0.1	13 15.1	26 21.3	18 49.5	23 34.9	14 41.8	1 3.5	4 5.2
21 F	18 0 57.2	29 49.1	25 42.2	17 2.9	15 21.6	14 24.4	27 7.2	19 3.1	23 41.2	14 45.5	1 5.8	4 6.9
22 S	18 4 53.8	0♑50.3	25 39.0	0♑56.6	14 53.9	15 33.5	27 53.1	19 16.8	23 47.5	14 49.1	1 8.1	4 8.4
23 S	18 8 50.3	1 51.4	25 35.8	14 34.9	14 37.0	16 42.4	28 38.9	19 30.4	23 53.7	14 52.6	1 10.3	4 10.0
24 M	18 12 46.9	2 52.6	25 32.6	27 55.1	14 30.4	17 51.2	29 24.8	19 44.2	23 59.8	14 56.2	1 12.6	4 11.5
25 T	18 16 43.4	3 53.7	25 29.5	10♒55.6	14D33.5	18 59.8	0♓10.6	19 57.9	24 5.9	14 59.7	1 14.9	4 12.9
26 W	18 20 40.0	4 54.9	25 26.3	23 36.6	14 45.6	20 8.2	0 56.5	20 11.7	24 11.9	15 3.2	1 17.1	4 14.4
27 T	18 24 36.6	5 56.0	25 23.1	5♓59.6	15 5.8	21 16.5	1 42.4	20 25.5	24 17.9	15 6.7	1 19.4	4 15.8
28 F	18 28 33.1	6 57.2	25 19.9	18 7.7	15 33.5	22 24.6	2 28.3	20 39.3	24 23.8	15 10.2	1 21.7	4 17.2
29 S	18 32 29.7	7 58.4	25 16.8	0♈ 4.7	16 7.9	23 32.6	3 14.1	20 53.2	24 29.7	15 13.7	1 23.9	4 18.5
30 S	18 36 26.2	8 59.5	25 13.6	11 55.6	16 48.2	24 40.3	3 60.0	21 7.0	24 35.5	15 17.1	1 26.2	4 19.9
31 M	18 40 22.8	10 0.7	25 10.4	23 45.4	17 34.0	25 47.8	4 45.8	21 20.9	24 41.3	15 20.6	1 28.4	4 21.1
					DECLINATION at NOON							
1 S	16 42 6.0	21S52.6	19N26.1	7S29.0	25S16.5	24S 5.4	18S35.9	22S50.7	16S 9.8	22S25.5	22S19.4	2N43.1
4 T	16 53 55.7	22 18.1	19 23.9	8N15.8	24 41.9	23 29.9	17 54.3	22 46.7	16 15.1	22 26.9	22 19.5	2 42.1
7 F	17 5 45.4	22 39.7	19 21.7	21 40.2	23 55.0	22 48.7	17 11.1	22 42.4	16 20.2	22 28.2	22 19.5	2 41.2
10 M	17 17 35.1	22 57.3	19 19.5	26 32.1	22 56.8	22 1.8	16 26.5	22 37.9	16 25.2	22 29.6	22 19.5	2 40.4
13 T	17 29 24.7	23 10.9	19 17.2	18 29.4	21 50.6	21 9.8	15 40.4	22 33.2	16 30.0	22 30.9	22 19.5	2 39.7
16 S	17 41 14.4	23 20.3	19 15.0	1 22.5	20 46.4	20 12.8	14 53.1	22 28.2	16 34.7	22 32.2	22 19.5	2 39.1
19 W	17 53 4.1	23 25.4	19 12.7	16S39.7	19 58.3	19 11.2	14 4.6	22 23.0	16 39.3	22 33.5	22 19.5	2 38.7
22 S	18 4 53.8	23 26.4	19 10.5	26 20.0	19 36.1	18 5.4	13 14.9	22 17.5	16 43.7	22 34.7	22 19.5	2 38.4
25 T	18 16 43.4	23 23.1	19 8.2	22 16.4	19 39.6	16 55.6	12 24.1	22 11.8	16 47.9	22 35.9	22 19.4	2 38.3
28 F	18 28 33.1	23 15.6	19 5.9	9 7.4	20 2.3	15 42.4	11 32.4	22 5.9	16 52.0	22 37.1	22 19.4	2 38.3
31 M	18 40 22.8	23 3.9	19 3.7	6N36.6	20 36.3	14 26.0	10 39.9	21 59.8	16 55.9	22 38.3	22 19.3	2 38.4

JANUARY 1985

DAY	EPHEMERIS SIDEREAL TIME	☉	☊	☽	☿	♀	♂	♃	♄	♅	♆	♇
	h m s	° ′	° ′	° ′	° ′	° ′	° ′	° ′	° ′	° ′	° ′	° ′
						LONGITUDE at NOON						
1 T	18 44 19.3	11♑ 1.8	25♉ 7.2	5♉39.4	18♐24.4	26♒55.1	5♓31.7	21♑34.8	24♏47.0	15♐24.0	1♑30.7	4♏22.4
2 W	18 48 15.9	12 3.0	25 4.1	17 42.6	19 19.1	28 2.3	6 17.5	21 48.8	24 52.6	15 27.4	1 32.9	4 23.6
3 T	18 52 12.5	13 4.1	25 0.9	29 59.4	20 17.6	29 9.1	7 3.3	22 2.7	24 58.2	15 30.7	1 35.2	4 24.8
4 F	18 56 9.0	14 5.3	24 57.7	12♊33.6	21 19.4	0♓15.8	7 49.1	22 16.7	25 3.7	15 34.1	1 37.4	4 26.0
5 S	19 0 5.6	15 6.4	24 54.5	25 27.3	22 24.2	1 22.2	8 34.9	22 30.7	25 9.2	15 37.4	1 39.6	4 27.1
6 S	19 4 2.1	16 7.5	24 51.4	8♋41.5	23 31.6	2 28.4	9 20.7	22 44.7	25 14.6	15 40.7	1 41.8	4 28.2
7 M	19 7 58.7	17 8.7	24 48.2	22 15.2	24 41.3	3 34.3	10 6.5	22 58.7	25 19.9	15 44.0	1 44.0	4 29.3
8 T	19 11 55.3	18 9.8	24 45.0	6♌ 5.7	25 53.2	4 40.0	10 52.3	23 12.7	25 25.2	15 47.2	1 46.2	4 30.3
9 W	19 15 51.8	19 10.9	24 41.8	20 9.0	27 7.0	5 45.4	11 38.0	23 26.7	25 30.4	15 50.5	1 48.4	4 31.3
10 T	19 19 48.4	20 12.1	24 38.6	4♍20.4	28 22.5	6 50.5	12 23.8	23 40.8	25 35.5	15 53.7	1 50.6	4 32.3
11 F	19 23 44.9	21 13.2	24 35.5	18 35.2	29 39.6	7 55.4	13 9.5	23 54.9	25 40.6	15 56.9	1 52.8	4 33.2
12 S	19 27 41.5	22 14.4	24 32.3	2♎49.3	0♑58.1	8 60.0	13 55.2	24 8.9	25 45.6	16 0.0	1 55.0	4 34.1
13 S	19 31 38.0	23 15.5	24 29.1	16 59.9	2 17.8	10 4.2	14 40.9	24 23.0	25 50.5	16 3.2	1 57.1	4 35.0
14 M	19 35 34.6	24 16.6	24 25.9	1♏ 5.3	3 38.8	11 8.2	15 26.6	24 37.0	25 55.4	16 6.3	1 59.3	4 35.8
15 T	19 39 31.2	25 17.7	24 22.8	15 4.6	5 0.8	12 11.8	16 12.2	24 51.1	26 0.2	16 9.3	2 1.4	4 36.6
16 W	19 43 27.7	26 18.9	24 19.6	28 57.2	6 23.8	13 15.1	16 57.9	25 5.2	26 4.9	16 12.4	2 3.5	4 37.3
17 T	19 47 24.3	27 20.0	24 16.4	12♐42.8	7 47.7	14 18.1	17 43.5	25 19.2	26 9.5	16 15.4	2 5.6	4 38.1
18 F	19 51 20.8	28 21.1	24 13.2	26 20.3	9 12.6	15 20.7	18 29.1	25 33.3	26 14.1	16 18.3	2 7.7	4 38.7
19 S	19 55 17.4	29 22.2	24 10.1	9♑48.3	10 38.3	16 23.0	19 14.7	25 47.4	26 18.6	16 21.3	2 9.8	4 39.4
20 S	19 59 13.9	0♒23.3	24 6.9	23 5.1	12 4.7	17 24.9	20 0.2	26 1.4	26 23.0	16 24.2	2 11.9	4 40.0
21 M	20 3 10.5	1 24.4	24 3.7	6♒ 8.8	13 32.0	18 26.4	20 45.8	26 15.5	26 27.3	16 27.0	2 13.9	4 40.6
22 T	20 7 7.1	2 25.4	24 0.5	18 58.0	14 59.9	19 27.5	21 31.3	26 29.5	26 31.5	16 29.9	2 15.9	4 41.1
23 W	20 11 3.6	3 26.5	23 57.3	1♓31.9	16 28.6	20 28.2	22 16.8	26 43.6	26 35.7	16 32.7	2 17.9	4 41.6
24 T	20 15 0.2	4 27.5	23 54.2	13 51.1	17 58.0	21 28.4	23 2.3	26 57.6	26 39.8	16 35.5	2 19.9	4 42.1
25 F	20 18 56.7	5 28.6	23 51.0	25 57.3	19 28.1	22 28.2	23 47.8	27 11.6	26 43.8	16 38.2	2 21.9	4 42.5
26 S	20 22 53.3	6 29.6	23 47.8	7♈53.4	20 58.9	23 27.6	24 33.2	27 25.6	26 47.7	16 40.9	2 23.9	4 42.9
27 S	20 26 49.8	7 30.6	23 44.6	19 43.2	22 30.3	24 26.4	25 18.6	27 39.6	26 51.5	16 43.5	2 25.8	4 43.2
28 M	20 30 46.4	8 31.5	23 41.5	1♉31.5	24 2.4	25 24.7	26 4.0	27 53.6	26 55.2	16 46.2	2 27.8	4 43.6
29 T	20 34 43.0	9 32.5	23 38.3	13 23.6	25 35.2	26 22.6	26 49.3	28 7.5	26 58.9	16 48.7	2 29.7	4 43.8
30 W	20 38 39.5	10 33.4	23 35.1	25 25.1	27 8.6	27 19.8	27 34.6	28 21.4	27 2.5	16 51.3	2 31.6	4 44.1
31 T	20 42 36.1	11 34.3	23 31.9	7♊41.5	28 42.8	28 16.6	28 19.9	28 35.4	27 5.9	16 53.8	2 33.4	4 44.3
						DECLINATION at NOON						
1 T	18 44 19.3	22S59.1	19N 2.9	11N39.7	20S48.9	13S59.9	10S22.2	21S57.7	16S57.2	22S38.7	22S19.3	2N38.5
4 F	18 56 9.0	22 41.9	19 0.6	23 42.6	21 27.8	12 39.8	9 28.6	21 51.2	17 0.8	22 39.8	22 19.2	2 38.7
7 M	19 7 58.7	22 20.6	18 58.3	25 46.7	22 5.0	11 17.5	8 34.4	21 44.6	17 4.3	22 40.9	22 19.1	2 39.2
10 T	19 19 48.4	21 55.4	18 56.0	14 36.4	22 37.1	9 53.3	7 39.6	21 37.7	17 7.6	22 41.9	22 19.0	2 39.7
13 S	19 31 38.0	21 26.3	18 53.6	3S43.7	23 2.2	8 27.5	6 44.3	21 30.6	17 10.8	22 43.0	22 18.9	2 40.3
16 W	19 43 27.7	20 53.5	18 51.3	20 12.7	23 18.5	7 0.5	5 48.7	21 23.4	17 13.7	22 43.9	22 18.8	2 41.1
19 S	19 55 17.4	20 17.2	18 49.0	26 36.4	23 25.0	5 32.7	4 52.7	21 15.9	17 16.4	22 44.9	22 18.7	2 42.0
22 T	20 7 7.1	19 37.3	18 46.6	19 53.5	23 20.9	4 4.3	3 56.4	21 8.3	17 19.0	22 45.8	22 18.6	2 43.0
25 F	20 18 56.7	18 54.2	18 44.3	5 33.1	23 5.5	2 35.9	3 0.0	21 0.5	17 21.3	22 46.6	22 18.4	2 44.2
28 M	20 30 46.4	18 8.0	18 41.9	10N10.3	22 38.3	1 7.6	2 3.5	20 52.5	17 23.5	22 47.5	22 18.3	2 45.4
31 T	20 42 36.1	17 18.9	18 39.5	22 45.8	21 59.1	0N20.0	1 7.1	20 44.4	17 25.4	22 48.2	22 18.1	2 46.7

FEBRUARY 1985

DAY	EPHEMERIS SIDEREAL TIME	☉	☊	☽	☿	♀	♂	♃	♄	♅	♆	♇
						LONGITUDE at NOON						
1 F	20 46 32.6	12♒35.3	23♉28.8	20♊17.6	0♒17.6	29♓12.7	29♓ 5.2	28♑49.3	27♏ 9.4	16♐56.3	2♑35.3	4♏44.5
2 S	20 50 29.2	13 36.1	23 25.6	3♋17.4	1 53.2	0♈ 8.2	29 50.4	29 3.2	27 12.7	16 58.7	2 37.2	4 44.6
3 S	20 54 25.7	14 37.0	23 22.4	16 42.7	3 29.4	1 3.1	0♈35.6	29 17.0	27 15.9	17 1.1	2 39.0	4 44.7
4 M	20 58 22.3	15 37.8	23 19.2	0♌33.5	5 6.3	1 57.4	1 20.8	29 30.8	27 19.0	17 3.4	2 40.8	4 44.8
5 T	21 2 18.9	16 38.6	23 16.0	14 46.9	6 44.0	2 50.9	2 5.9	29 44.6	27 22.0	17 5.7	2 42.5	4 44.8
6 W	21 6 15.4	17 39.4	23 12.9	29 17.3	8 22.5	3 43.8	2 51.0	29 58.4	27 25.0	17 8.0	2 44.3	4 44.8
7 T	21 10 12.0	18 40.1	23 9.7	13♍57.6	10 1.7	4 35.9	3 36.0	0♒12.1	27 27.8	17 10.2	2 46.0	4 44.8
8 F	21 14 8.5	19 40.9	23 6.5	28 39.7	11 41.7	5 27.2	4 21.0	0 25.8	27 30.6	17 12.3	2 47.7	4R44.7
9 S	21 18 5.1	20 41.6	23 3.3	13♎16.7	13 22.5	6 17.8	5 6.0	0 39.5	27 33.2	17 14.5	2 49.4	4 44.6
10 S	21 22 1.6	21 42.3	23 0.2	27 43.0	15 4.1	7 7.6	5 51.0	0 53.1	27 35.8	17 16.5	2 51.0	4 44.4
11 M	21 25 58.2	22 43.0	22 57.0	11♏55.5	16 46.6	7 56.5	6 35.9	1 6.7	27 38.2	17 18.6	2 52.6	4 44.2
12 T	21 29 54.7	23 43.7	22 53.8	25 53.0	18 29.9	8 44.6	7 20.8	1 20.3	27 40.6	17 20.6	2 54.2	4 44.0
13 W	21 33 51.3	24 44.3	22 50.6	9♐35.8	20 14.0	9 31.8	8 5.6	1 33.9	27 42.9	17 22.5	2 55.8	4 43.8
14 T	21 37 47.8	25 45.0	22 47.5	23 4.8	21 59.0	10 18.0	8 50.4	1 47.4	27 45.1	17 24.4	2 57.4	4 43.5
15 F	21 41 44.4	26 45.6	22 44.3	6♑21.4	23 44.8	11 3.3	9 35.2	2 0.8	27 47.1	17 26.2	2 58.9	4 43.1
16 S	21 45 41.0	27 46.2	22 41.1	19 26.4	25 31.6	11 47.5	10 19.9	2 14.2	27 49.1	17 28.0	3 0.4	4 42.8
17 S	21 49 37.5	28 46.8	22 37.9	2♒20.5	27 19.2	12 30.8	11 4.7	2 27.6	27 51.0	17 29.8	3 1.9	4 42.4
18 M	21 53 34.1	29 47.3	22 34.7	15 3.6	29 7.6	13 12.9	11 49.3	2 40.9	27 52.8	17 31.5	3 3.3	4 41.9
19 T	21 57 30.6	0♓47.8	22 31.6	27 35.7	0♓56.9	13 53.9	12 34.0	2 54.2	27 54.5	17 33.2	3 4.7	4 41.5
20 W	22 1 27.2	1 48.3	22 28.4	9♓56.6	2 47.0	14 33.7	13 18.6	3 7.5	27 56.0	17 34.8	3 6.1	4 41.0
21 T	22 5 23.7	2 48.8	22 25.2	22 6.9	4 37.9	15 12.2	14 3.1	3 20.7	27 57.5	17 36.3	3 7.5	4 40.4
22 F	22 9 20.3	3 49.3	22 22.0	4♈ 7.5	6 29.7	15 49.6	14 47.7	3 33.9	27 58.9	17 37.9	3 8.9	4 39.9
23 S	22 13 16.8	4 49.7	22 18.9	16 0.3	8 22.0	16 25.5	15 32.2	3 46.9	28 0.2	17 39.3	3 10.2	4 39.3
24 S	22 17 13.4	5 50.1	22 15.7	27 48.3	10 15.0	17 0.1	16 16.6	3 60.0	28 1.4	17 40.7	3 11.5	4 38.7
25 M	22 21 10.0	6 50.5	22 12.5	9♉35.3	12 8.5	17 33.3	17 1.0	4 13.0	28 2.4	17 42.1	3 12.7	4 38.0
26 T	22 25 6.5	7 50.8	22 9.3	21 25.8	14 2.5	18 4.9	17 45.4	4 25.9	28 3.4	17 43.4	3 14.0	4 37.3
27 W	22 29 3.1	8 51.1	22 6.1	3♊24.9	15 56.7	18 35.0	18 29.7	4 38.7	28 4.3	17 44.7	3 15.2	4 36.6
28 T	22 32 59.6	9 51.3	22 3.0	15 38.3	17 51.0	19 3.4	19 14.0	4 51.6	28 5.0	17 45.9	3 16.3	4 35.8
						DECLINATION at NOON						
1 F	20 46 32.6	17S 1.9	18N38.7	25N18.5	21S43.3	0N49.0	0S48.3	20S41.6	17S26.0	22S48.5	22S18.1	2N47.2
4 M	20 58 22.3	16 9.2	18 36.4	24 31.7	20 47.5	2 15.2	0N 8.1	20 33.3	17 27.7	22 49.2	22 17.9	2 48.7
7 T	21 10 12.0	15 13.9	18 34.0	10 37.7	19 39.1	3 39.8	1 4.2	20 24.9	17 29.1	22 49.9	22 17.8	2 50.2
10 S	21 22 1.6	14 16.4	18 31.6	8S39.9	18 17.9	5 2.5	2 0.1	20 16.4	17 30.4	22 50.5	22 17.6	2 51.8
13 W	21 33 51.3	13 16.7	18 29.1	23 20.1	16 43.7	6 22.8	2 55.6	20 7.8	17 31.5	22 51.1	22 17.4	2 53.6
16 S	21 45 41.0	12 15.0	18 26.7	26 11.3	14 56.7	7 40.4	3 50.7	19 59.1	17 32.3	22 51.7	22 17.3	2 55.4
19 T	21 57 30.6	11 11.6	18 24.3	16 58.4	12 57.1	8 54.7	4 45.4	19 50.3	17 32.9	22 52.2	22 17.1	2 57.2
22 F	22 9 20.3	10 6.5	18 21.9	1 44.7	10 45.2	10 5.3	5 39.5	19 41.5	17 33.4	22 52.7	22 16.9	2 59.1
25 M	22 21 10.0	9 0.1	18 19.4	13N43.8	8 22.0	11 11.4	6 33.1	19 32.6	17 33.6	22 53.1	22 16.8	3 1.1
28 T	22 32 59.6	7 52.5	18 17.0	24 46.3	5 49.1	12 12.3	7 25.9	19 23.8	17 33.6	22 53.5	22 16.6	3 3.1

MARCH 1985

DAY	EPHEMERIS SIDEREAL TIME	☉	☊	☽	☿	♀	♂	♃	♄	♅	♆	♇
	h m s	° ′	° ′	° ′	° ′	° ′	° ′	° ′	° ′	° ′	° ′	° ′
LONGITUDE at NOON												
1 F	22 36 56.2	10♓51.5	21♉59.8	28♊11.2	19♓45.3	19♈30.2	19♈58.3	5♒ 4.3	28♏ 5.7	17♐47.0	3♑17.5	4♏35.0
2 S	22 40 52.7	11 51.7	21 56.6	11♋ 8.6	21 39.2	19 55.2	20 42.4	5 17.0	28 6.3	17 48.1	3 18.6	4R34.2
3 S	22 44 49.3	12 51.9	21 53.4	24 33.8	23 32.6	20 18.5	21 26.6	5 29.6	28 6.7	17 49.2	3 19.6	4 33.4
4 M	22 48 45.8	13 52.0	21 50.3	8♌28.1	25 25.1	20 39.8	22 10.7	5 42.2	28 7.1	17 50.2	3 20.7	4 32.5
5 T	22 52 42.4	14 52.1	21 47.1	22 50.1	27 16.4	20 59.2	22 54.8	5 54.7	28 7.3	17 51.1	3 21.7	4 31.6
6 W	22 56 38.9	15 52.1	21 43.9	7♍34.9	29 6.0	21 16.6	23 38.8	6 7.1	28 7.5	17 52.0	3 22.7	4 30.6
7 T	23 0 35.5	16 52.1	21 40.7	22 34.8	0♈53.6	21 32.0	24 22.8	6 19.4	28 7.5	17 52.8	3 23.6	4 29.7
8 F	23 4 32.0	17 52.1	21 37.5	7♎40.1	2 38.7	21 45.2	25 6.7	6 31.7	28 7.5	17 53.6	3 24.5	4 28.7
9 S	23 8 28.6	18 52.1	21 34.4	22 41.2	4 20.9	21 56.3	25 50.6	6 43.9	28R 7.3	17 54.4	3 25.4	4 27.6
10 S	23 12 25.2	19 52.0	21 31.2	7♏29.7	5 59.5	22 5.1	26 34.4	6 56.1	28 7.0	17 55.0	3 26.3	4 26.6
11 M	23 16 21.7	20 51.9	21 28.0	21 59.9	7 34.2	22 11.6	27 18.2	7 8.2	28 6.7	17 55.7	3 27.1	4 25.5
12 T	23 20 18.3	21 51.8	21 24.8	6♐ 8.8	9 4.3	22 15.8	28 2.0	7 20.2	28 6.2	17 56.2	3 27.9	4 24.4
13 W	23 24 14.8	22 51.6	21 21.7	19 55.9	10 29.5	22 17.6	28 45.7	7 32.1	28 5.7	17 56.8	3 28.7	4 23.3
14 T	23 28 11.4	23 51.4	21 18.5	3♑22.3	11 49.0	22R17.0	29 29.3	7 43.9	28 5.0	17 57.2	3 29.4	4 22.1
15 F	23 32 7.9	24 51.3	21 15.3	16 30.2	13 2.7	22 14.1	0♉13.0	7 55.7	28 4.3	17 57.7	3 30.1	4 21.0
16 S	23 36 4.5	25 51.0	21 12.1	29 21.9	14 9.8	22 8.6	0 56.6	8 7.4	28 3.4	17 58.1	3 30.8	4 19.8
17 S	23 40 1.0	26 50.8	21 8.9	11♒59.8	15 10.1	22 0.6	1 40.2	8 19.0	28 2.5	17 58.4	3 31.4	4 18.5
18 M	23 43 57.6	27 50.5	21 5.8	24 26.0	16 3.2	21 50.1	2 23.7	8 30.5	28 1.4	17 58.6	3 32.0	4 17.3
19 T	23 47 54.1	28 50.1	21 2.6	6♓42.1	16 48.8	21 37.2	3 7.1	8 42.0	28 0.2	17 58.8	3 32.6	4 16.0
20 W	23 51 50.7	29 49.8	20 59.4	18 49.4	17 26.8	21 21.8	3 50.5	8 53.3	27 59.0	17 59.0	3 33.1	4 14.7
21 T	23 55 47.2	0♈49.4	20 56.2	0♈49.2	17 56.8	21 4.0	4 33.9	9 4.5	27 57.6	17 59.1	3 33.6	4 13.4
22 F	23 59 43.8	1 48.9	20 53.1	12 42.9	18 18.9	20 43.8	5 17.2	9 15.7	27 56.2	17 59.1	3 34.1	4 12.0
23 S	0 3 40.3	2 48.5	20 49.9	24 32.2	18 33.0	20 21.4	6 0.5	9 26.8	27 54.6	17 59.1	3 34.5	4 10.6
24 S	0 7 36.9	3 48.0	20 46.7	6♉19.2	18 39.2	19 56.7	6 43.8	9 37.7	27 53.0	17R59.0	3 34.9	4 9.3
25 M	0 11 33.5	4 47.4	20 43.5	18 6.9	18R37.5	19 29.9	7 27.0	9 48.6	27 51.2	17 58.9	3 35.3	4 7.8
26 T	0 15 30.0	5 46.9	20 40.3	29 58.6	18 28.4	19 1.1	8 10.1	9 59.4	27 49.4	17 58.8	3 35.6	4 6.4
27 W	0 19 26.6	6 46.3	20 37.2	11♊58.5	18 12.1	18 30.5	8 53.2	10 10.0	27 47.5	17 58.5	3 35.9	4 5.0
28 T	0 23 23.1	7 45.6	20 34.0	24 11.2	17 49.1	17 58.2	9 36.3	10 20.6	27 45.5	17 58.3	3 36.2	4 3.5
29 F	0 27 19.7	8 44.9	20 30.8	6♋41.5	17 20.0	17 24.5	10 19.3	10 31.1	27 43.4	17 57.9	3 36.4	4 2.0
30 S	0 31 16.2	9 44.2	20 27.6	19 34.1	16 45.5	16 49.4	11 2.3	10 41.5	27 41.2	17 57.6	3 36.6	4 0.5
31 S	0 35 12.8	10 43.4	20 24.5	2♌53.0	16 6.3	16 13.3	11 45.2	10 51.7	27 38.9	17 57.1	3 36.7	3 59.0
DECLINATION at NOON												
1 F	22 36 56.2	7S29.7	18N16.2	26N29.8	4S56.4	12N31.3	7N43.3	19S20.8	17S33.6	22S53.6	22S16.6	3N 3.8
4 M	22 48 45.8	6 20.8	18 13.7	22 54.6	2 15.3	13 24.1	8 35.2	19 12.0	17 33.3	22 53.9	22 16.4	3 5.9
7 T	23 0 35.5	5 11.1	18 11.2	6 52.4	0N26.7	14 9.6	9 26.1	19 3.1	17 32.9	22 54.2	22 16.2	3 8.0
10 S	23 12 25.2	4 0.8	18 8.7	12S58.3	3 3.1	14 46.8	10 16.2	18 54.3	17 32.2	22 54.4	22 16.1	3 10.1
13 W	23 24 14.8	2 50.1	18 6.3	25 36.6	5 26.1	15 14.6	11 5.3	18 45.6	17 31.4	22 54.6	22 15.9	3 12.3
16 S	23 36 4.5	1 39.0	18 3.8	24 57.6	7 27.9	15 31.6	11 53.4	18 36.9	17 30.4	22 54.7	22 15.8	3 14.4
19 T	23 47 54.1	0 27.8	18 1.3	13 34.5	9 1.5	15 36.8	12 40.5	18 28.3	17 29.2	22 54.8	22 15.7	3 16.6
22 F	23 59 43.8	0N43.3	17 58.7	2N13.4	10 1.3	15 29.0	13 26.4	18 19.8	17 27.8	22 54.9	22 15.5	3 18.7
25 M	0 11 33.5	1 54.2	17 56.2	17 10.0	10 23.8	15 7.7	14 11.1	18 11.5	17 26.2	22 54.9	22 15.4	3 20.8
28 T	0 23 23.1	3 4.8	17 53.7	26 19.0	10 8.0	14 32.8	14 54.6	18 3.3	17 24.5	22 54.9	22 15.3	3 22.9
31 S	0 35 12.8	4 14.7	17 51.2	24 22.3	9 17.1	13 45.4	15 36.8	17 55.3	17 22.6	22 54.8	22 15.2	3 25.0

APRIL 1985

DAY	EPHEMERIS SIDEREAL TIME	☉	☊	☽	☿	♀	♂	♃	♄	♅	♆	♇
LONGITUDE at NOON												
1 M	0 39 9.3	11♈42.6	20♉21.3	16♌40.5	15♈23.4	15♈36.4	12♉28.1	11♒ 1.9	27♏36.5	17♐56.7	3♑36.9	3♏57.5
2 T	0 43 5.9	12 41.8	20 18.1	0♍56.8	14R37.5	14R58.9	13 10.9	11 11.9	27R34.1	17R56.1	3 37.0	3R56.0
3 W	0 47 2.4	13 40.9	20 14.9	15 39.1	13 49.8	14 21.0	13 53.7	11 21.9	27 31.5	17 55.5	3 37.0	3 54.4
4 T	0 50 59.0	14 40.0	20 11.7	0♎41.3	13 1.2	13 43.1	14 36.4	11 31.7	27 28.9	17 54.9	3 37.1	3 52.8
5 F	0 54 55.5	15 39.1	20 8.6	15 54.6	12 12.6	13 5.4	15 19.1	11 41.4	27 26.3	17 54.3	3 37.1	3 51.3
6 S	0 58 52.1	16 38.1	20 5.4	1♏ 8.9	11 25.0	12 28.0	16 1.8	11 51.0	27 23.5	17 53.6	3 37.1	3 49.7
7 S	1 2 48.6	17 37.1	20 2.2	16 14.0	10 39.2	11 51.4	16 44.3	12 0.5	27 20.6	17 52.8	3R37.0	3 48.1
8 M	1 6 45.2	18 36.0	19 59.0	1♐ 2.0	9 56.0	11 15.7	17 26.9	12 9.9	27 17.7	17 52.0	3 36.9	3 46.5
9 T	1 10 41.8	19 35.0	19 55.9	15 27.1	9 16.2	10 41.2	18 9.4	12 19.1	27 14.7	17 51.1	3 36.8	3 44.9
10 W	1 14 38.3	20 33.8	19 52.7	29 26.8	8 40.2	10 8.0	18 51.8	12 28.3	27 11.6	17 50.2	3 36.6	3 43.2
11 T	1 18 34.9	21 32.7	19 49.5	13♑ 0.9	8 8.5	9 36.4	19 34.3	12 37.3	27 8.4	17 49.2	3 36.4	3 41.6
12 F	1 22 31.4	22 31.5	19 46.3	26 11.1	7 41.6	9 6.5	20 16.6	12 46.1	27 5.2	17 48.2	3 36.2	3 39.9
13 S	1 26 28.0	23 30.4	19 43.1	9♒ 0.1	7 19.6	8 38.5	20 59.0	12 54.9	27 1.9	17 47.1	3 35.9	3 38.3
14 S	1 30 24.5	24 29.1	19 40.0	21 31.3	7 2.7	8 12.6	21 41.2	13 3.5	26 58.5	17 46.0	3 35.6	3 36.6
15 M	1 34 21.1	25 27.9	19 36.8	3♓48.2	6 51.1	7 48.7	22 23.5	13 12.0	26 55.1	17 44.8	3 35.3	3 34.9
16 T	1 38 17.6	26 26.6	19 33.6	15 53.9	6 44.7	7 27.1	23 5.7	13 20.4	26 51.6	17 43.6	3 34.9	3 33.3
17 W	1 42 14.2	27 25.3	19 30.4	27 51.5	6 43.6	7 7.9	23 47.8	13 28.6	26 48.0	17 42.4	3 34.5	3 31.6
18 T	1 46 10.7	28 23.9	19 27.3	9♈43.5	6D47.6	6 51.0	24 30.0	13 36.7	26 44.4	17 41.1	3 34.1	3 29.9
19 F	1 50 7.3	29 22.6	19 24.1	21 32.2	6 56.6	6 36.4	25 12.0	13 44.7	26 40.7	17 39.8	3 33.6	3 28.2
20 S	1 54 3.8	0♉21.2	19 20.9	3♉19.9	7 10.5	6 24.4	25 54.1	13 52.5	26 36.9	17 38.4	3 33.1	3 26.5
21 S	1 58 0.4	1 19.7	19 17.7	15 8.5	7 29.2	6 14.7	26 36.0	14 0.2	26 33.1	17 37.0	3 32.6	3 24.8
22 M	2 1 57.0	2 18.3	19 14.6	27 0.5	7 52.4	6 7.5	27 18.0	14 7.7	26 29.3	17 35.5	3 32.1	3 23.1
23 T	2 5 53.5	3 16.8	19 11.4	8♊58.2	8 20.0	6 2.7	27 59.9	14 15.1	26 25.4	17 34.0	3 31.5	3 21.4
24 W	2 9 50.1	4 15.2	19 8.2	21 4.6	8 51.9	6 0.3	28 41.7	14 22.4	26 21.4	17 32.5	3 30.9	3 19.7
25 T	2 13 46.6	5 13.7	19 5.0	3♋22.8	9 27.7	6 0.3	29 23.6	14 29.5	26 17.4	17 30.9	3 30.2	3 18.0
26 F	2 17 43.2	6 12.1	19 1.8	15 56.4	10 7.5	6D 2.7	0♊ 5.4	14 36.5	26 13.4	17 29.3	3 29.6	3 16.4
27 S	2 21 39.7	7 10.5	18 58.7	28 48.7	10 51.0	6 7.3	0 47.1	14 43.3	26 9.3	17 27.7	3 28.9	3 14.7
28 S	2 25 36.3	8 8.8	18 55.5	12♌ 3.0	11 37.9	6 14.1	1 28.8	14 49.9	26 5.2	17 26.0	3 28.2	3 13.0
29 M	2 29 32.8	9 7.1	18 52.3	25 41.8	12 28.3	6 23.2	2 10.4	14 56.5	26 1.0	17 24.2	3 27.5	3 11.3
30 T	2 33 29.4	10 5.3	18 49.1	9♍46.0	13 21.9	6 34.3	2 52.0	15 2.8	25 56.8	17 22.5	3 26.7	3 9.6
DECLINATION at NOON												
1 M	0 39 9.3	4N37.9	17N50.3	20N46.8	8N53.5	13N27.1	15N50.5	17S52.7	17S21.9	22S54.8	22S15.2	3N25.7
4 T	0 50 59.0	5 46.9	17 47.8	3 16.0	7 29.0	12 26.2	16 30.9	17 45.0	17 19.8	22 54.7	22 15.1	3 27.7
7 S	1 2 48.6	6 55.0	17 45.2	16S30.3	5 54.4	11 18.7	17 9.8	17 37.4	17 17.6	22 54.5	22 15.0	3 29.7
10 W	1 14 38.3	8 2.0	17 42.7	26 52.9	4 23.3	10 8.5	17 47.3	17 30.2	17 15.2	22 54.3	22 14.9	3 31.6
13 S	1 26 28.0	9 7.8	17 40.1	22 59.3	3 6.4	8 59.3	18 23.3	17 23.1	17 12.7	22 54.0	22 14.8	3 33.5
16 T	1 38 17.6	10 12.3	17 37.5	9 50.7	2 10.2	7 54.2	18 57.7	17 16.4	17 10.1	22 53.8	22 14.8	3 35.3
19 F	1 50 7.3	11 15.2	17 34.9	6N12.3	1 37.2	6 55.8	19 30.6	17 10.0	17 7.4	22 53.4	22 14.7	3 37.0
22 M	2 1 57.0	12 16.5	17 32.3	20 17.1	1 27.5	6 5.7	20 1.8	17 3.9	17 4.6	22 53.1	22 14.7	3 38.6
25 T	2 13 46.6	13 16.0	17 29.7	27 9.2	1 39.4	5 25.0	20 31.3	16 58.1	17 1.7	22 52.7	22 14.6	3 40.2
28 S	2 25 36.3	14 13.5	17 27.1	22 13.5	2 11.0	4 54.1	20 59.2	16 52.7	16 58.7	22 52.2	22 14.6	3 41.6

MAY 1985

DAY	EPHEMERIS SIDEREAL TIME	☉	☊	☽	☿	♀	♂	♃	♄	♅	♆	♇
	h m s	° ′	° ′	° ′	° ′	° ′	° ′	° ′	° ′	° ′	° ′	° ′
						LONGITUDE at NOON						
1 W	2 37 26.0	11♉ 3.6	18♉46.0	24♍14.6	14♈18.7	6♈47.6	3♊33.5	15♒ 9.0	25♏52.5	17♐20.7	3♑25.9	3♏ 7.9
2 T	2 41 22.5	12 1.7	18 42.8	9♎ 3.8	15 18.4	7 2.8	4 15.0	15 15.0	25R48.3	17R18.8	3R25.0	3R 6.2
3 F	2 45 19.1	12 59.9	18 39.6	24 7.6	16 21.1	7 20.0	4 56.5	15 20.9	25 44.0	17 17.0	3 24.2	3 4.6
4 S	2 49 15.6	13 58.0	18 36.4	9♏17.7	17 26.5	7 39.2	5 37.9	15 26.6	25 39.6	17 15.1	3 23.3	3 2.9
5 S	2 53 12.2	14 56.1	18 33.2	24 24.6	18 34.6	8 0.1	6 19.3	15 32.2	25 35.3	17 13.1	3 22.4	3 1.3
6 M	2 57 8.7	15 54.2	18 30.1	9♐19.5	19 45.3	8 22.9	7 0.6	15 37.6	25 30.9	17 11.2	3 21.4	2 59.6
7 T	3 1 5.3	16 52.2	18 26.9	23 55.0	20 58.5	8 47.3	7 41.9	15 42.9	25 26.5	17 9.2	3 20.4	2 58.0
8 W	3 5 1.8	17 50.3	18 23.7	8♑ 6.0	22 14.2	9 13.4	8 23.1	15 47.9	25 22.1	17 7.1	3 19.4	2 56.4
9 T	3 8 58.4	18 48.3	18 20.5	21 50.2	23 32.3	9 41.2	9 4.3	15 52.8	25 17.6	17 5.1	3 18.4	2 54.7
10 F	3 12 55.0	19 46.2	18 17.4	5♒ 7.8	24 52.8	10 10.4	9 45.5	15 57.6	25 13.2	17 3.0	3 17.4	2 53.1
11 S	3 16 51.5	20 44.2	18 14.2	18 0.8	26 15.6	10 41.2	10 26.6	16 2.1	25 8.7	17 0.9	3 16.3	2 51.5
12 S	3 20 48.1	21 42.1	18 11.0	0♓32.7	27 40.6	11 13.3	11 7.7	16 6.5	25 4.2	16 58.8	3 15.2	2 49.9
13 M	3 24 44.6	22 40.0	18 7.8	12 47.3	29 7.9	11 46.9	11 48.7	16 10.8	24 59.7	16 56.6	3 14.1	2 48.4
14 T	3 28 41.2	23 37.9	18 4.7	24 49.0	0♉37.3	12 21.7	12 29.7	16 14.8	24 55.2	16 54.4	3 13.0	2 46.8
15 W	3 32 37.7	24 35.8	18 1.5	6♈42.0	2 9.0	12 57.8	13 10.7	16 18.7	24 50.7	16 52.2	3 11.8	2 45.3
16 T	3 36 34.3	25 33.6	17 58.3	18 30.4	3 42.9	13 35.1	13 51.6	16 22.4	24 46.2	16 50.0	3 10.6	2 43.7
17 F	3 40 30.9	26 31.5	17 55.1	0♉17.5	5 18.9	14 13.6	14 32.6	16 26.0	24 41.8	16 47.8	3 9.5	2 42.2
18 S	3 44 27.4	27 29.3	17 51.9	12 6.5	6 57.1	14 53.1	15 13.4	16 29.3	24 37.3	16 45.5	3 8.3	2 40.7
19 S	3 48 24.0	28 27.1	17 48.8	23 60.0	8 37.4	15 33.8	15 54.3	16 32.5	24 32.8	16 43.2	3 7.0	2 39.3
20 M	3 52 20.5	29 24.9	17 45.6	6♊ 0.1	10 19.9	16 15.4	16 35.1	16 35.4	24 28.3	16 40.9	3 5.7	2 37.8
21 T	3 56 17.1	0♊22.6	17 42.4	18 9.0	12 4.5	16 58.1	17 15.8	16 38.2	24 23.8	16 38.6	3 4.5	2 36.3
22 W	4 0 13.6	1 20.3	17 39.2	0♋28.2	13 51.3	17 41.6	17 56.5	16 40.8	24 19.4	16 36.2	3 3.2	2 34.9
23 T	4 4 10.2	2 18.0	17 36.1	12 59.4	15 40.2	18 26.1	18 37.2	16 43.3	24 15.0	16 33.9	3 1.8	2 33.5
24 F	4 8 6.8	3 15.7	17 32.9	25 44.5	17 31.3	19 11.5	19 17.8	16 45.5	24 10.5	16 31.5	3 0.5	2 32.1
25 S	4 12 3.3	4 13.3	17 29.7	8♌44.9	19 24.4	19 57.7	19 58.4	16 47.6	24 6.1	16 29.1	2 59.1	2 30.7
26 S	4 15 59.9	5 10.9	17 26.5	22 2.3	21 19.7	20 44.7	20 38.9	16 49.4	24 1.8	16 26.7	2 57.8	2 29.3
27 M	4 19 56.4	6 8.5	17 23.4	5♍38.0	23 17.0	21 32.4	21 19.4	16 51.1	23 57.4	16 24.3	2 56.4	2 28.0
28 T	4 23 53.0	7 6.1	17 20.2	19 32.7	25 16.3	22 21.0	21 59.9	16 52.6	23 53.1	16 21.9	2 55.0	2 26.7
29 W	4 27 49.5	8 3.6	17 17.0	3♎46.0	27 17.6	23 10.2	22 40.3	16 53.9	23 48.8	16 19.4	2 53.5	2 25.4
30 T	4 31 46.1	9 1.2	17 13.8	18 16.3	29 20.7	24 0.1	23 20.7	16 55.0	23 44.5	16 17.0	2 52.1	2 24.1
31 F	4 35 42.7	9 58.7	17 10.7	2♏60.0	1♊25.6	24 50.7	24 1.1	16 55.9	23 40.3	16 14.6	2 50.6	2 22.8
						DECLINATION at NOON						
1 W	2 37 26.0	15N 8.9	17N24.5	6N13.0	2N59.9	4N32.8	21N25.3	16S47.7	16S55.7	22S51.8	22S14.6	3N43.0
4 S	2 49 15.6	16 2.0	17 21.9	13S48.9	4 4.3	4 20.8	21 49.6	16 43.0	16 52.6	22 51.3	22 14.6	3 44.3
7 T	3 1 5.3	16 52.7	17 19.3	26 23.9	5 22.0	4 17.6	22 12.2	16 38.8	16 49.5	22 50.7	22 14.6	3 45.4
10 F	3 12 55.0	17 40.9	17 16.6	23 59.3	6 51.4	4 22.6	22 32.9	16 35.1	16 46.4	22 50.2	22 14.6	3 46.5
13 M	3 24 44.6	18 26.5	17 14.0	11 12.4	8 30.7	4 35.1	22 51.8	16 31.7	16 43.3	22 49.6	22 14.7	3 47.4
16 T	3 36 34.3	19 9.2	17 11.3	4N49.3	10 18.2	4 54.2	23 8.8	16 28.9	16 40.1	22 49.0	22 14.7	3 48.2
19 S	3 48 24.0	19 49.1	17 8.7	19 17.4	12 12.2	5 19.2	23 24.0	16 26.5	16 37.1	22 48.3	22 14.7	3 48.9
22 W	4 0 13.6	20 25.9	17 6.0	26 59.7	14 10.4	5 49.5	23 37.3	16 24.6	16 34.0	22 47.7	22 14.8	3 49.5
25 S	4 12 3.3	20 59.6	17 3.3	23 5.1	16 10.2	6 24.3	23 48.7	16 23.2	16 31.1	22 47.0	22 14.8	3 49.9
28 T	4 23 53.0	21 29.9	17 0.6	8 16.3	18 8.5	7 3.0	23 58.3	16 22.4	16 28.2	22 46.3	22 14.9	3 50.2
31 F	4 35 42.7	21 57.0	16 57.9	11S13.2	20 0.9	7 45.0	24 5.9	16 22.0	16 25.4	22 45.6	22 15.0	3 50.4

JUNE 1985

DAY	EPHEMERIS SIDEREAL TIME	☉	☊	☽	☿	♀	♂	♃	♄	♅	♆	♇
						LONGITUDE at NOON						
1 S	4 39 39.2	10♊56.1	17♉ 7.5	17♏51.6	3♊32.1	25♈42.0	24♊41.4	16♒56.7	23♏36.1	16♐12.1	2♑49.2	2♏21.6
2 S	4 43 35.8	11 53.6	17 4.3	2♐44.5	5 40.1	26 33.8	25 21.7	16 57.2	23R32.0	16R 9.6	2R47.7	2R20.4
3 M	4 47 32.3	12 51.0	17 1.1	17 30.8	7 49.3	27 26.3	26 1.9	16 57.6	23 27.8	16 7.2	2 46.2	2 19.2
4 T	4 51 28.9	13 48.5	16 57.9	2♑ 3.3	9 59.6	28 19.4	26 42.2	16 57.7	23 23.8	16 4.7	2 44.7	2 18.1
5 W	4 55 25.4	14 45.9	16 54.8	16 15.7	12 10.8	29 13.0	27 22.3	16 57.7	23 19.7	16 2.2	2 43.2	2 16.9
6 T	4 59 22.0	15 43.3	16 51.6	0♒ 4.1	14 22.5	0♉ 7.2	28 2.5	16R57.5	23 15.7	15 59.8	2 41.7	2 15.8
7 F	5 3 18.6	16 40.7	16 48.4	13 26.8	16 34.6	1 1.9	28 42.6	16 57.2	23 11.9	15 57.3	2 40.2	2 14.8
8 S	5 7 15.1	17 38.1	16 45.2	26 24.3	18 46.7	1 57.1	29 22.7	16 56.6	23 8.0	15 54.9	2 38.6	2 13.7
9 S	5 11 11.7	18 35.5	16 42.1	8♓59.2	20 58.6	2 52.8	0♋ 2.7	16 55.8	23 4.1	15 52.4	2 37.1	2 12.7
10 M	5 15 8.2	19 32.8	16 38.9	21 15.1	23 10.0	3 49.0	0 42.8	16 54.8	23 0.3	15 49.9	2 35.5	2 11.7
11 T	5 19 4.8	20 30.2	16 35.7	3♈16.9	25 20.6	4 45.6	1 22.7	16 53.6	22 56.6	15 47.5	2 34.0	2 10.7
12 W	5 23 1.4	21 27.5	16 32.5	15 9.2	27 30.2	5 42.6	2 2.7	16 52.3	22 52.9	15 45.0	2 32.4	2 9.7
13 T	5 26 57.9	22 24.9	16 29.4	26 57.1	29 38.6	6 40.1	2 42.6	16 50.7	22 49.3	15 42.6	2 30.8	2 8.8
14 F	5 30 54.5	23 22.2	16 26.2	8♉45.2	1♋45.6	7 37.9	3 22.5	16 49.0	22 45.8	15 40.1	2 29.2	2 7.9
15 S	5 34 51.0	24 19.5	16 23.0	20 37.6	3 51.0	8 36.2	4 2.4	16 47.0	22 42.3	15 37.7	2 27.6	2 7.0
16 S	5 38 47.6	25 16.8	16 19.8	2♊37.8	5 54.6	9 34.8	4 42.2	16 44.9	22 38.8	15 35.3	2 26.0	2 6.2
17 M	5 42 44.2	26 14.1	16 16.7	14 48.5	7 56.4	10 33.9	5 22.0	16 42.6	22 35.5	15 32.8	2 24.4	2 5.4
18 T	5 46 40.7	27 11.4	16 13.5	27 11.7	9 56.2	11 33.2	6 1.7	16 40.1	22 32.2	15 30.4	2 22.8	2 4.6
19 W	5 50 37.3	28 8.7	16 10.3	9♋48.3	11 54.0	12 32.9	6 41.5	16 37.5	22 28.9	15 28.0	2 21.2	2 3.9
20 T	5 54 33.8	29 6.0	16 7.1	22 38.9	13 49.7	13 32.9	7 21.2	16 34.6	22 25.8	15 25.7	2 19.5	2 3.1
21 F	5 58 30.4	0♋ 3.3	16 3.9	5♌43.2	15 43.2	14 33.3	8 0.9	16 31.6	22 22.7	15 23.3	2 17.9	2 2.4
22 S	6 2 26.9	1 0.5	16 0.8	19 0.7	17 34.5	15 33.9	8 40.5	16 28.3	22 19.7	15 20.9	2 16.3	2 1.8
23 S	6 6 23.5	1 57.8	15 57.6	2♍30.9	19 23.6	16 34.8	9 20.1	16 24.9	22 16.7	15 18.6	2 14.7	2 1.2
24 M	6 10 20.1	2 55.0	15 54.4	16 13.1	21 10.5	17 36.1	9 59.7	16 21.4	22 13.9	15 16.3	2 13.1	2 0.6
25 T	6 14 16.6	3 52.2	15 51.2	0♎ 6.7	22 55.1	18 37.6	10 39.2	16 17.6	22 11.1	15 14.0	2 11.4	1 60.0
26 W	6 18 13.2	4 49.5	15 48.1	14 11.2	24 37.4	19 39.4	11 18.7	16 13.7	22 8.4	15 11.7	2 9.8	1 59.5
27 T	6 22 9.7	5 46.7	15 44.9	28 25.7	26 17.5	20 41.4	11 58.2	16 9.6	22 5.7	15 9.4	2 8.2	1 59.0
28 F	6 26 6.3	6 43.9	15 41.7	12♏48.3	27 55.3	21 43.8	12 37.7	16 5.4	22 3.2	15 7.2	2 6.6	1 58.5
29 S	6 30 2.9	7 41.1	15 38.5	27 16.3	29 30.9	22 46.3	13 17.2	16 1.0	22 0.8	15 5.0	2 5.0	1 58.1
30 S	6 33 59.4	8 38.3	15 35.4	11♐45.6	1♌ 4.1	23 49.1	13 56.5	15 56.4	21 58.4	15 2.8	2 3.4	1 57.7
						DECLINATION at NOON						
1 S	4 39 39.2	22N 5.2	16N57.0	17S 8.0	20N36.2	7N59.6	24N 8.0	16S22.0	16S24.5	22S45.3	22S15.0	3N50.4
4 T	4 51 28.9	22 27.6	16 54.3	27 4.1	22 13.0	8 45.3	24 13.1	16 22.4	16 21.8	22 44.6	22 15.1	3 50.4
7 F	5 3 18.6	22 46.6	16 51.6	21 46.5	23 31.9	9 33.0	24 16.3	16 23.2	16 19.2	22 43.9	22 15.1	3 50.3
10 M	5 15 8.2	23 1.9	16 48.9	7 28.6	24 28.4	10 22.4	24 17.7	16 24.6	16 16.8	22 43.1	22 15.2	3 50.1
13 T	5 26 57.9	23 13.5	16 46.2	8N38.9	25 0.1	11 12.8	24 17.2	16 26.5	16 14.5	22 42.4	22 15.3	3 49.7
16 S	5 38 47.6	23 21.5	16 43.5	21 59.5	25 6.9	12 3.9	24 14.9	16 29.0	16 12.4	22 41.6	22 15.4	3 49.1
19 W	5 50 37.3	23 25.8	16 40.7	27 8.9	24 50.6	12 55.2	24 10.7	16 31.9	16 10.5	22 40.9	22 15.5	3 48.5
22 S	6 2 26.9	23 26.4	16 38.0	20 0.6	24 14.2	13 46.2	24 4.7	16 35.3	16 8.7	22 40.1	22 15.6	3 47.7
25 T	6 14 16.6	23 23.2	16 35.2	3 25.1	23 21.1	14 36.5	23 57.0	16 39.2	16 7.1	22 39.4	22 15.7	3 46.8
28 F	6 26 6.3	23 16.3	16 32.5	15S18.6	22 14.8	15 25.8	23 47.5	16 43.5	16 5.7	22 38.7	22 15.8	3 45.7

JULY 1985

DAY	EPHEMERIS SIDEREAL TIME	☉	☊	☽	☿	♀	♂	♃	♄	♅	♆	♇
	h m s	° ′	° ′	° ′	° ′	° ′	° ′	° ′	° ′	° ′	° ′	° ′
LONGITUDE at NOON												
1 M	6 37 56.0	9♋35.5	15♉32.2	26♐11.2	2♌35.0	24♉52.2	14♋35.9	15♒51.7	21♏56.1	15♐ 0.6	2♑ 1.8	1♏57.3
2 T	6 41 52.5	10 32.7	15 29.0	10♑27.3	4 3.6	25 55.5	15 15.3	15R46.8	21R53.9	14R58.5	2R 0.2	1R57.0
3 W	6 45 49.1	11 29.8	15 25.8	24 28.4	5 29.8	26 59.0	15 54.6	15 41.7	21 51.7	14 56.4	1 58.6	1 56.7
4 T	6 49 45.6	12 27.0	15 22.7	8♒10.1	6 53.7	28 2.7	16 33.8	15 36.5	21 49.7	14 54.3	1 57.0	1 56.4
5 F	6 53 42.2	13 24.2	15 19.5	21 29.8	8 15.1	29 6.7	17 13.1	15 31.1	21 47.7	14 52.2	1 55.4	1 56.1
6 S	6 57 38.8	14 21.4	15 16.3	4♓26.7	9 34.1	0♊10.9	17 52.3	15 25.6	21 45.9	14 50.1	1 53.9	1 55.9
7 S	7 1 35.3	15 18.6	15 13.1	17 2.0	10 50.6	1 15.3	18 31.5	15 20.0	21 44.1	14 48.1	1 52.3	1 55.7
8 M	7 5 31.9	16 15.8	15 9.9	29 18.8	12 4.6	2 19.9	19 10.7	15 14.2	21 42.4	14 46.1	1 50.7	1 55.6
9 T	7 9 28.4	17 13.0	15 6.8	11♈21.1	13 16.0	3 24.7	19 49.9	15 8.3	21 40.8	14 44.2	1 49.2	1 55.5
10 W	7 13 25.0	18 10.2	15 3.6	23 13.9	14 24.7	4 29.7	20 29.0	15 2.3	21 39.3	14 42.2	1 47.6	1 55.4
11 T	7 17 21.6	19 7.4	15 0.4	5♉ 2.4	15 30.6	5 34.9	21 8.1	14 56.1	21 37.9	14 40.4	1 46.1	1 55.4
12 F	7 21 18.1	20 4.6	14 57.2	16 52.0	16 33.8	6 40.2	21 47.2	14 49.8	21 36.5	14 38.5	1 44.6	1 55.4
13 S	7 25 14.7	21 1.9	14 54.1	28 47.8	17 34.0	7 45.8	22 26.3	14 43.4	21 35.3	14 36.7	1 43.1	1 55.4
14 S	7 29 11.2	21 59.1	14 50.9	10♊54.1	18 31.2	8 51.5	23 5.3	14 36.8	21 34.2	14 34.9	1 41.6	1D55.5
15 M	7 33 7.8	22 56.3	14 47.7	23 14.6	19 25.2	9 57.4	23 44.4	14 30.2	21 33.1	14 33.1	1 40.1	1 55.5
16 T	7 37 4.3	23 53.6	14 44.5	5♋51.7	20 16.0	11 3.4	24 23.4	14 23.4	21 32.2	14 31.4	1 38.6	1 55.7
17 W	7 41 0.9	24 50.9	14 41.4	18 46.6	21 3.4	12 9.7	25 2.3	14 16.6	21 31.3	14 29.7	1 37.1	1 55.8
18 T	7 44 57.5	25 48.1	14 38.2	1♌58.8	21 47.3	13 16.0	25 41.3	14 9.6	21 30.6	14 28.0	1 35.7	1 56.0
19 F	7 48 54.0	26 45.5	14 35.0	15 26.9	22 27.6	14 22.6	26 20.3	14 2.6	21 29.9	14 26.5	1 34.3	1 56.3
20 S	7 52 50.6	27 42.7	14 31.8	29 8.2	23 4.0	15 29.3	26 59.2	13 55.5	21 29.4	14 24.9	1 32.9	1 56.6
21 S	7 56 47.1	28 40.0	14 28.7	12♍59.7	23 36.4	16 36.1	27 38.1	13 48.2	21 28.9	14 23.3	1 31.5	1 56.9
22 M	8 0 43.7	29 37.3	14 25.5	26 58.3	24 4.6	17 43.0	28 16.9	13 40.9	21 28.5	14 21.8	1 30.1	1 57.2
23 T	8 4 40.3	0♌34.6	14 22.3	11♎ 1.5	24 28.6	18 50.1	28 55.8	13 33.6	21 28.3	14 20.4	1 28.7	1 57.6
24 W	8 8 36.8	1 31.9	14 19.1	25 7.6	24 48.1	19 57.4	29 34.6	13 26.1	21 28.1	14 19.0	1 27.4	1 58.0
25 T	8 12 33.4	2 29.3	14 15.9	9♏15.3	25 3.0	21 4.7	0♌13.4	13 18.6	21 28.0	14 17.6	1 26.0	1 58.4
26 F	8 16 29.9	3 26.6	14 12.8	23 23.5	25 13.0	22 12.2	0 52.1	13 11.1	21 28.0	14 16.3	1 24.7	1 58.9
27 S	8 20 26.5	4 23.9	14 9.6	7♐31.1	25 18.2	23 19.9	1 30.9	13 3.5	21D28.2	14 15.0	1 23.4	1 59.4
28 S	8 24 23.0	5 21.2	14 6.4	21 36.3	25 18.4	24 27.7	2 9.6	12 55.9	21 28.4	14 13.7	1 22.2	1 59.9
29 M	8 28 19.6	6 18.6	14 3.2	5♑36.6	25R13.4	25 35.5	2 48.3	12 48.2	21 28.7	14 12.5	1 20.9	2 0.5
30 T	8 32 16.1	7 15.9	14 0.1	19 28.6	25 3.4	26 43.6	3 27.0	12 40.5	21 29.1	14 11.4	1 19.7	2 1.1
31 W	8 36 12.7	8 13.3	13 56.9	3♒ 8.9	24 48.2	27 51.7	4 5.6	12 32.7	21 29.6	14 10.2	1 18.4	2 1.8
DECLINATION at NOON												
1 M	6 37 56.0	23N 5.8	16N29.7	26S37.1	20N58.6	16N13.6	23N36.3	16S48.3	16S 4.6	22S38.0	22S16.0	3N44.6
4 T	6 49 45.6	22 51.6	16 26.9	23 5.2	19 35.4	16 59.6	23 23.4	16 53.4	16 3.6	22 37.3	22 16.1	3 43.3
7 S	7 1 35.3	22 33.8	16 24.2	9 9.4	18 7.9	17 43.4	23 8.8	16 58.9	16 2.8	22 36.6	22 16.2	3 41.9
10 W	7 13 25.0	22 12.6	16 21.4	7N10.4	16 38.7	18 24.6	22 52.7	17 4.8	16 2.3	22 36.0	22 16.3	3 40.4
13 S	7 25 14.7	21 47.9	16 18.6	20 58.7	15 10.3	19 3.0	22 34.9	17 10.9	16 2.0	22 35.4	22 16.4	3 38.7
16 T	7 37 4.3	21 19.8	16 15.8	27 10.6	13 45.3	19 38.1	22 15.6	17 17.3	16 1.9	22 34.8	22 16.6	3 37.0
19 F	7 48 54.0	20 48.5	16 13.0	21 0.5	12 26.5	20 9.7	21 54.9	17 23.9	16 2.0	22 34.2	22 16.7	3 35.1
22 M	8 0 43.7	20 14.0	16 10.1	4 38.9	11 16.8	20 37.4	21 32.6	17 30.6	16 2.4	22 33.7	22 16.8	3 33.2
25 T	8 12 33.4	19 36.5	16 7.3	14S 6.4	10 19.6	21 1.0	21 8.9	17 37.5	16 3.0	22 33.3	22 17.0	3 31.1
28 S	8 24 23.0	18 56.0	16 4.5	26 11.4	9 38.4	21 20.2	20 43.9	17 44.5	16 3.9	22 32.8	22 17.1	3 29.0
31 W	8 36 12.7	18 12.8	16 1.7	24 14.0	9 16.6	21 34.9	20 17.6	17 51.4	16 4.9	22 32.5	22 17.2	3 26.8

AUGUST 1985

DAY	EPHEMERIS SIDEREAL TIME	☉	☊	☽	☿	♀	♂	♃	♄	♅	♆	♇
LONGITUDE at NOON												
1 T	8 40 9.3	9♌10.7	13♉53.7	16♒33.9	24♌28.0	29♊ 0.0	4♌44.3	12♒24.9	21♏30.2	14♐ 9.2	1♑17.2	2♏ 2.4
2 F	8 44 5.8	10 8.0	13 50.5	29 41.5	24R 2.9	0♋ 8.4	5 22.9	12R17.2	21 30.9	14R 8.1	1R16.1	2 3.1
3 S	8 48 2.4	11 5.5	13 47.4	12♓30.2	23 33.1	1 16.9	6 1.5	12 9.4	21 31.7	14 7.2	1 14.9	2 3.9
4 S	8 51 58.9	12 2.9	13 44.2	25 0.7	22 58.9	2 25.6	6 40.1	12 1.6	21 32.6	14 6.2	1 13.8	2 4.7
5 M	8 55 55.5	13 0.3	13 41.0	7♈14.8	22 20.8	3 34.4	7 18.7	11 53.8	21 33.6	14 5.3	1 12.7	2 5.5
6 T	8 59 52.0	13 57.8	13 37.8	19 15.7	21 39.3	4 43.3	7 57.2	11 46.0	21 34.7	14 4.5	1 11.6	2 6.3
7 W	9 3 48.6	14 55.3	13 34.6	1♉ 7.9	20 54.9	5 52.3	8 35.8	11 38.2	21 35.9	14 3.7	1 10.5	2 7.2
8 T	9 7 45.2	15 52.8	13 31.5	12 56.3	20 8.3	7 1.4	9 14.3	11 30.4	21 37.2	14 2.9	1 9.5	2 8.1
9 F	9 11 41.7	16 50.4	13 28.3	24 46.3	19 20.5	8 10.7	9 52.8	11 22.7	21 38.6	14 2.3	1 8.5	2 9.1
10 S	9 15 38.3	17 47.9	13 25.1	6♊43.4	18 32.1	9 20.0	10 31.3	11 14.9	21 40.1	14 1.6	1 7.5	2 10.0
11 S	9 19 34.8	18 45.5	13 21.9	18 52.8	17 44.2	10 29.5	11 9.8	11 7.2	21 41.6	14 1.0	1 6.6	2 11.0
12 M	9 23 31.4	19 43.1	13 18.8	1♋19.1	16 57.5	11 39.0	11 48.3	10 59.6	21 43.3	14 0.5	1 5.6	2 12.1
13 T	9 27 27.9	20 40.7	13 15.6	14 5.5	16 13.1	12 48.7	12 26.7	10 52.0	21 45.0	13 60.0	1 4.7	2 13.1
14 W	9 31 24.5	21 38.4	13 12.4	27 14.1	15 31.9	13 58.5	13 5.1	10 44.4	21 46.9	13 59.5	1 3.8	2 14.2
15 T	9 35 21.0	22 36.0	13 9.2	10♌44.6	14 54.6	15 8.3	13 43.5	10 36.9	21 48.8	13 59.1	1 3.0	2 15.3
16 F	9 39 17.6	23 33.7	13 6.1	24 35.0	14 22.2	16 18.3	14 21.9	10 29.5	21 50.9	13 58.8	1 2.1	2 16.5
17 S	9 43 14.2	24 31.4	13 2.9	8♍41.3	13 55.4	17 28.4	15 0.3	10 22.1	21 53.0	13 58.4	1 1.3	2 17.7
18 S	9 47 10.7	25 29.2	12 59.7	22 58.4	13 34.6	18 38.5	15 38.7	10 14.8	21 55.2	13 58.2	1 0.5	2 18.9
19 M	9 51 7.3	26 26.9	12 56.5	7♎20.7	13 20.5	19 48.8	16 17.0	10 7.5	21 57.6	13 58.0	0 59.8	2 20.2
20 T	9 55 3.8	27 24.7	12 53.3	21 43.2	13 13.5	20 59.1	16 55.4	10 0.4	21 60.0	13 57.8	0 59.1	2 21.4
21 W	9 59 0.4	28 22.5	12 50.2	6♏ 1.9	13D14.0	22 9.6	17 33.7	9 53.3	22 2.5	13 57.7	0 58.4	2 22.8
22 T	10 2 56.9	29 20.3	12 47.0	20 14.3	13 22.0	23 20.1	18 12.0	9 46.4	22 5.1	13 57.7	0 57.7	2 24.1
23 F	10 6 53.5	0♍18.1	12 43.8	4♐19.0	13 37.8	24 30.7	18 50.3	9 39.5	22 7.7	13 57.7	0 57.1	2 25.5
24 S	10 10 50.0	1 15.9	12 40.6	18 15.3	14 1.5	25 41.4	19 28.5	9 32.7	22 10.5	13 57.7	0 56.5	2 26.9
25 S	10 14 46.6	2 13.8	12 37.5	2♑ 2.8	14 32.9	26 52.2	20 6.8	9 26.1	22 13.4	13D57.8	0 55.9	2 28.3
26 M	10 18 43.1	3 11.7	12 34.3	15 40.9	15 12.1	28 3.1	20 45.0	9 19.5	22 16.3	13 58.0	0 55.4	2 29.7
27 T	10 22 39.7	4 9.6	12 31.1	29 8.7	15 58.8	29 14.1	21 23.2	9 13.1	22 19.3	13 58.2	0 54.8	2 31.2
28 W	10 26 36.3	5 7.5	12 27.9	12♒24.9	16 52.8	0♌25.2	22 1.4	9 6.8	22 22.5	13 58.5	0 54.3	2 32.7
29 T	10 30 32.8	6 5.5	12 24.7	25 28.2	17 53.8	1 36.3	22 39.6	9 0.6	22 25.7	13 58.8	0 53.9	2 34.3
30 F	10 34 29.4	7 3.5	12 21.6	8♓17.6	19 1.7	2 47.6	23 17.9	8 54.6	22 29.0	13 59.2	0 53.5	2 35.9
31 S	10 38 25.9	8 1.5	12 18.4	20 52.3	20 15.8	3 58.9	23 56.0	8 48.7	22 32.4	13 59.6	0 53.1	2 37.5
DECLINATION at NOON												
1 T	8 40 9.3	17N57.8	16N 0.7	20S38.4	9N14.1	21N38.7	20N 8.5	17S53.8	16S 5.3	22S32.3	22S17.3	3N26.0
4 S	8 51 58.9	17 11.0	15 57.9	5 26.9	9 22.1	21 46.9	19 40.5	18 0.7	16 6.7	22 32.0	22 17.4	3 23.7
7 W	9 3 48.6	16 21.7	15 55.0	10N51.4	9 52.8	21 50.1	19 11.2	18 7.6	16 8.3	22 31.7	22 17.5	3 21.2
10 S	9 15 38.3	15 30.0	15 52.2	23 24.4	10 43.1	21 48.2	18 40.8	18 14.3	16 10.1	22 31.5	22 17.7	3 18.7
13 T	9 27 27.9	14 36.1	15 49.3	27 4.0	11 46.6	21 41.0	18 9.2	18 20.9	16 12.1	22 31.4	22 17.8	3 16.2
16 F	9 39 17.6	13 40.1	15 46.4	17 57.1	12 54.6	21 28.5	17 36.6	18 27.3	16 14.3	22 31.2	22 18.0	3 13.6
19 M	9 51 7.3	12 42.1	15 43.5	0S15.9	13 58.0	21 10.8	17 2.9	18 33.5	16 16.7	22 31.2	22 18.1	3 10.9
22 T	10 2 56.9	11 42.4	15 40.7	18 30.1	14 48.5	20 47.7	16 28.2	18 39.4	16 19.4	22 31.2	22 18.2	3 8.2
25 S	10 14 46.6	10 40.9	15 37.8	27 18.4	15 19.4	20 19.5	15 52.6	18 44.9	16 22.2	22 31.2	22 18.4	3 5.4
28 W	10 26 36.3	9 38.0	15 34.9	21 55.0	15 25.8	19 46.1	15 16.2	18 50.2	16 25.2	22 31.3	22 18.5	3 2.6
31 S	10 38 25.9	8 33.7	15 32.0	7 11.9	15 4.5	19 7.6	14 38.8	18 55.0	16 28.4	22 31.5	22 18.7	2 59.7

SEPTEMBER 1985

DAY	EPHEMERIS SIDEREAL TIME	☉	☊	☽	☿	♀	♂	♃	♄	♅	♆	♇
	h m s	° ′	° ′	° ′	° ′	° ′	° ′	° ′	° ′	° ′	° ′	° ′
LONGITUDE at NOON												
1 S	10 42 22.5	8♍59.6	12♉15.2	3♈12.8	21♌35.7	5♌10.3	24♌34.2	8♒42.9	22♏35.8	14♐ 0.1	0♑52.8	2♏39.1
2 M	10 46 19.0	9 57.6	12 12.0	15 20.4	23 1.2	6 21.8	25 12.3	8R37.3	22 39.4	14 0.6	0R52.4	2 40.7
3 T	10 50 15.6	10 55.7	12 8.9	27 17.5	24 31.6	7 33.4	25 50.5	8 31.8	22 43.0	14 1.1	0 52.1	2 42.4
4 W	10 54 12.1	11 53.8	12 5.7	9♉ 7.6	26 6.4	8 45.1	26 28.6	8 26.4	22 46.7	14 1.8	0 51.9	2 44.1
5 T	10 58 8.7	12 52.0	12 2.5	20 54.8	27 45.2	9 56.8	27 6.7	8 21.2	22 50.5	14 2.4	0 51.6	2 45.8
6 F	11 2 5.2	13 50.2	11 59.3	2♊44.0	29 27.4	11 8.7	27 44.8	8 16.2	22 54.3	14 3.1	0 51.4	2 47.6
7 S	11 6 1.8	14 48.4	11 56.1	14 40.4	1♍12.5	12 20.6	28 22.9	8 11.3	22 58.3	14 3.9	0 51.3	2 49.3
8 S	11 9 58.4	15 46.7	11 53.0	26 49.4	3 0.0	13 32.6	29 1.0	8 6.6	23 2.3	14 4.7	0 51.1	2 51.1
9 M	11 13 54.9	16 45.0	11 49.8	9♋16.1	4 49.5	14 44.7	29 39.1	8 2.0	23 6.4	14 5.6	0 51.0	2 52.9
10 T	11 17 51.5	17 43.3	11 46.6	22 4.6	6 40.6	15 56.8	0♍17.1	7 57.6	23 10.6	14 6.5	0 50.9	2 54.8
11 W	11 21 48.0	18 41.6	11 43.4	5♌18.1	8 32.8	17 9.0	0 55.2	7 53.4	23 14.8	14 7.5	0 50.9	2 56.6
12 T	11 25 44.6	19 40.0	11 40.3	18 57.5	10 25.8	18 21.4	1 33.2	7 49.3	23 19.2	14 8.5	0 50.9	2 58.5
13 F	11 29 41.1	20 38.5	11 37.1	3♍ 1.6	12 19.3	19 33.7	2 11.2	7 45.4	23 23.6	14 9.6	0 50.9	3 0.4
14 S	11 33 37.7	21 36.9	11 33.9	17 26.5	14 13.1	20 46.2	2 49.3	7 41.7	23 28.0	14 10.7	0D51.0	3 2.4
15 S	11 37 34.2	22 35.4	11 30.7	2♎ 6.1	16 6.8	21 58.7	3 27.3	7 38.2	23 32.6	14 11.9	0 51.0	3 4.3
16 M	11 41 30.8	23 33.9	11 27.5	16 52.9	18 0.3	23 11.3	4 5.3	7 34.8	23 37.2	14 13.1	0 51.2	3 6.3
17 T	11 45 27.3	24 32.5	11 24.4	1♏39.5	19 53.5	24 24.0	4 43.3	7 31.7	23 41.9	14 14.4	0 51.3	3 8.3
18 W	11 49 23.9	25 31.1	11 21.2	16 19.2	21 46.1	25 36.7	5 21.3	7 28.7	23 46.7	14 15.7	0 51.5	3 10.3
19 T	11 53 20.4	26 29.7	11 18.0	0♐47.1	23 38.1	26 49.5	5 59.2	7 25.9	23 51.5	14 17.1	0 51.7	3 12.3
20 F	11 57 17.0	27 28.4	11 14.8	15 0.1	25 29.5	28 2.4	6 37.2	7 23.4	23 56.4	14 18.6	0 52.0	3 14.4
21 S	12 1 13.5	28 27.0	11 11.7	28 56.7	27 20.1	29 15.3	7 15.2	7 21.0	24 1.4	14 20.1	0 52.3	3 16.5
22 S	12 5 10.1	29 25.7	11 8.5	12♑37.0	29 9.8	0♍28.3	7 53.1	7 18.7	24 6.4	14 21.6	0 52.7	3 18.6
23 M	12 9 6.7	0♎24.4	11 5.3	26 1.4	0♎58.6	1 41.3	8 31.0	7 16.7	24 11.5	14 23.1	0 53.0	3 20.7
24 T	12 13 3.2	1 23.2	11 2.1	9♒11.0	2 46.6	2 54.4	9 8.9	7 14.9	24 16.7	14 24.8	0 53.4	3 22.8
25 W	12 16 59.8	2 22.0	10 58.9	22 6.5	4 33.6	4 7.6	9 46.8	7 13.3	24 21.9	14 26.4	0 53.8	3 24.9
26 T	12 20 56.3	3 20.8	10 55.8	4♓49.0	6 19.8	5 20.8	10 24.7	7 11.8	24 27.2	14 28.1	0 54.3	3 27.1
27 F	12 24 52.9	4 19.6	10 52.6	17 19.2	8 5.0	6 34.1	11 2.6	7 10.6	24 32.6	14 29.9	0 54.8	3 29.3
28 S	12 28 49.4	5 18.5	10 49.4	29 37.9	9 49.3	7 47.4	11 40.5	7 9.5	24 38.0	14 31.7	0 55.3	3 31.5
29 S	12 32 46.0	6 17.4	10 46.2	11♈46.2	11 32.6	9 0.8	12 18.3	7 8.7	24 43.4	14 33.5	0 55.8	3 33.7
30 M	12 36 42.5	7 16.3	10 43.1	23 45.5	13 15.1	10 14.3	12 56.2	7 8.0	24 49.0	14 35.4	0 56.4	3 35.9
DECLINATION at NOON												
1 S	10 42 22.5	8N12.0	15N31.0	1S34.7	14N51.0	18N53.7	14N26.2	18S56.6	16S29.5	22S31.5	22S18.7	2N58.8
4 W	10 54 12.1	7 6.1	15 28.1	14N23.9	13 51.6	18 8.8	13 47.8	19 1.0	16 32.9	22 31.7	22 18.8	2 55.9
7 S	11 6 1.8	5 59.1	15 25.1	25 24.3	12 26.2	17 19.2	13 8.7	19 4.9	16 36.4	22 32.0	22 19.0	2 53.0
10 T	11 17 51.5	4 51.2	15 22.2	26 25.3	10 39.4	16 25.1	12 28.9	19 8.5	16 40.1	22 32.4	22 19.1	2 50.0
13 F	11 29 41.1	3 42.6	15 19.3	14 48.0	8 36.6	15 26.9	11 48.4	19 11.6	16 43.9	22 32.7	22 19.3	2 47.1
16 M	11 41 30.8	2 33.3	15 16.3	4S45.7	6 23.2	14 24.6	11 7.3	19 14.2	16 47.9	22 33.2	22 19.4	2 44.2
19 T	11 53 20.4	1 23.6	15 13.4	22 7.1	4 3.8	13 18.6	10 25.7	19 16.4	16 52.0	22 33.7	22 19.5	2 41.3
22 S	12 5 10.1	0 13.6	15 10.4	27 25.4	1 41.8	12 9.1	9 43.5	19 18.2	16 56.2	22 34.2	22 19.7	2 38.3
25 W	12 16 59.8	0S56.5	15 7.5	18 55.3	0S40.3	10 56.5	9 0.9	19 19.4	17 0.5	22 34.8	22 19.8	2 35.4
28 S	12 28 49.4	2 6.6	15 4.5	3 12.3	3 0.4	9 41.1	8 17.9	19 20.2	17 4.9	22 35.4	22 19.9	2 32.5

OCTOBER 1985

DAY	EPHEMERIS SIDEREAL TIME	☉	☊	☽	☿	♀	♂	♃	♄	♅	♆	♇
LONGITUDE at NOON												
1 T	12 40 39.1	8♎15.3	10♉39.9	5♉37.8	14♎56.7	11♍27.8	13♍34.0	7♒ 7.6	24♏54.6	14♐37.4	0♑57.0	3♏38.1
2 W	12 44 35.6	9 14.3	10 36.7	17 25.6	16 37.4	12 41.4	14 11.9	7R 7.3	25 0.2	14 39.3	0 57.7	3 40.4
3 T	12 48 32.2	10 13.3	10 33.5	29 12.2	18 17.3	13 55.1	14 49.7	7 7.2	25 5.9	14 41.4	0 58.4	3 42.6
4 F	12 52 28.7	11 12.4	10 30.3	11♊ 1.3	19 56.3	15 8.8	15 27.5	7D 7.4	25 11.6	14 43.4	0 59.1	3 44.9
5 S	12 56 25.3	12 11.5	10 27.2	22 57.3	21 34.5	16 22.5	16 5.3	7 7.7	25 17.4	14 45.5	0 59.8	3 47.2
6 S	13 0 21.8	13 10.7	10 24.0	5♋ 4.9	23 11.9	17 36.3	16 43.2	7 8.2	25 23.3	14 47.7	1 0.6	3 49.5
7 M	13 4 18.4	14 9.9	10 20.8	17 28.8	24 48.6	18 50.2	17 21.0	7 8.9	25 29.2	14 49.9	1 1.4	3 51.8
8 T	13 8 15.0	15 9.1	10 17.6	0♌13.8	26 24.4	20 4.1	17 58.8	7 9.9	25 35.2	14 52.1	1 2.2	3 54.1
9 W	13 12 11.5	16 8.4	10 14.5	13 23.4	27 59.5	21 18.1	18 36.6	7 11.0	25 41.2	14 54.4	1 3.1	3 56.4
10 T	13 16 8.1	17 7.7	10 11.3	27 0.3	29 33.9	22 32.1	19 14.3	7 12.3	25 47.2	14 56.7	1 4.0	3 58.8
11 F	13 20 4.6	18 7.1	10 8.1	11♍ 4.6	1♏ 7.6	23 46.2	19 52.2	7 13.9	25 53.4	14 59.1	1 5.0	4 1.2
12 S	13 24 1.2	19 6.5	10 4.9	25 34.3	2 40.5	25 0.4	20 29.9	7 15.6	25 59.6	15 1.5	1 6.0	4 3.5
13 S	13 27 57.7	20 5.9	10 1.8	10♎24.2	4 12.7	26 14.5	21 7.7	7 17.5	26 5.8	15 4.0	1 7.0	4 5.9
14 M	13 31 54.3	21 5.3	9 58.6	25 26.9	5 44.2	27 28.7	21 45.5	7 19.6	26 12.0	15 6.5	1 8.0	4 8.2
15 T	13 35 50.8	22 4.8	9 55.4	10♏33.6	7 15.1	28 43.0	22 23.2	7 21.9	26 18.3	15 9.0	1 9.0	4 10.6
16 W	13 39 47.4	23 4.4	9 52.2	25 35.2	8 45.2	29 57.3	23 0.9	7 24.4	26 24.6	15 11.6	1 10.1	4 13.0
17 T	13 43 43.9	24 3.9	9 49.0	10♐23.8	10 14.7	1♎11.6	23 38.7	7 27.1	26 31.0	15 14.2	1 11.3	4 15.4
18 F	13 47 40.5	25 3.5	9 45.9	24 53.7	11 43.5	2 26.0	24 16.4	7 29.9	26 37.4	15 16.8	1 12.4	4 17.8
19 S	13 51 37.1	26 3.1	9 42.7	9♑ 1.3	13 11.6	3 40.4	24 54.1	7 33.0	26 43.9	15 19.5	1 13.6	4 20.2
20 S	13 55 33.6	27 2.7	9 39.5	22 45.6	14 39.0	4 54.9	25 31.8	7 36.3	26 50.4	15 22.2	1 14.8	4 22.6
21 M	13 59 30.2	28 2.4	9 36.3	6♒ 7.3	16 5.6	6 9.4	26 9.4	7 39.7	26 56.9	15 24.9	1 16.0	4 25.0
22 T	14 3 26.7	29 2.1	9 33.2	19 8.3	17 31.5	7 23.9	26 47.1	7 43.3	27 3.5	15 27.7	1 17.3	4 27.5
23 W	14 7 23.3	0♏ 1.8	9 30.0	1♓51.1	18 56.7	8 38.4	27 24.8	7 47.2	27 10.1	15 30.5	1 18.6	4 29.9
24 T	14 11 19.8	1 1.6	9 26.8	14 18.6	20 21.1	9 53.0	28 2.4	7 51.2	27 16.7	15 33.3	1 19.9	4 32.3
25 F	14 15 16.4	2 1.4	9 23.6	26 33.6	21 44.6	11 7.6	28 40.1	7 55.3	27 23.4	15 36.2	1 21.3	4 34.7
26 S	14 19 12.9	3 1.2	9 20.4	8♈38.6	23 7.3	12 22.3	29 17.7	7 59.7	27 30.1	15 39.1	1 22.6	4 37.1
27 S	14 23 9.5	4 1.0	9 17.3	20 35.9	24 29.0	13 37.0	29 55.3	8 4.3	27 36.8	15 42.1	1 24.0	4 39.6
28 M	14 27 6.0	5 0.9	9 14.1	2♉27.9	25 49.8	14 51.7	0♎33.0	8 9.0	27 43.5	15 45.0	1 25.5	4 42.0
29 T	14 31 2.6	6 0.8	9 10.9	14 16.5	27 9.5	16 6.5	1 10.6	8 13.9	27 50.3	15 48.0	1 26.9	4 44.4
30 W	14 34 59.2	7 0.8	9 7.7	26 4.0	28 28.0	17 21.3	1 48.2	8 19.0	27 57.1	15 51.1	1 28.4	4 46.8
31 T	14 38 55.7	8 0.7	9 4.6	7♊52.7	29 45.3	18 36.1	2 25.8	8 24.2	28 4.0	15 54.1	1 29.9	4 49.3
DECLINATION at NOON												
1 T	12 40 39.1	3S16.5	15N 1.5	13N 4.8	5S17.4	8N23.0	7N34.4	19S20.6	17S 9.4	22S36.1	22S20.1	2N29.7
4 F	12 52 28.7	4 26.1	14 58.5	24 49.7	7 30.3	7 2.6	6 50.7	19 20.5	17 14.0	22 36.8	22 20.2	2 26.8
7 M	13 4 18.4	5 35.2	14 55.5	27 7.9	9 38.2	5 40.2	6 6.6	19 19.9	17 18.6	22 37.5	22 20.3	2 24.1
10 T	13 16 8.1	6 43.7	14 52.6	17 12.7	11 40.5	4 16.2	5 22.2	19 18.9	17 23.3	22 38.3	22 20.4	2 21.3
13 S	13 27 57.7	7 51.4	14 49.6	1S46.8	13 36.6	2 50.8	4 37.6	19 17.4	17 28.0	22 39.2	22 20.5	2 18.6
16 W	13 39 47.4	8 58.2	14 46.5	20 36.6	15 26.1	1 24.3	3 52.9	19 15.4	17 32.8	22 40.0	22 20.6	2 15.9
19 S	13 51 37.1	10 3.8	14 43.5	27 41.7	17 8.2	0S 2.8	3 8.0	19 13.0	17 37.6	22 40.9	22 20.7	2 13.4
22 T	14 3 26.7	11 8.0	14 40.5	20 1.7	18 42.5	1 30.3	2 23.1	19 10.2	17 42.5	22 41.8	22 20.8	2 10.8
25 F	14 15 16.4	12 10.7	14 37.5	4 39.6	20 8.2	2 57.8	1 38.1	19 6.9	17 47.3	22 42.8	22 20.9	2 8.4
28 M	14 27 6.0	13 11.7	14 34.5	11N44.9	21 24.7	4 25.1	0 53.1	19 3.1	17 52.1	22 43.7	22 20.9	2 6.0
31 T	14 38 55.7	14 10.9	14 31.4	24 8.5	22 31.2	5 51.7	0 8.1	18 59.0	17 57.0	22 44.7	22 21.0	2 3.7

NOVEMBER 1985

DAY	EPHEMERIS SIDEREAL TIME	☉	☊	☽	☿	♀	♂	♃	♄	♅	♆	♇
	h m s	° ′	° ′	° ′	° ′	° ′	° ′	° ′	° ′	° ′	° ′	° ′
LONGITUDE at NOON												
1 F	14 42 52.3	9♏ 0.8	9♉ 1.4	19♓45.2	1♐ 1.3	19♎51.0	3♎ 3.4	8♒29.7	28♏10.9	15♐57.3	1♑31.5	4♏51.7
2 S	14 46 48.8	10 0.8	8 58.2	1♋44.6	2 15.8	21 5.9	3 41.0	8 35.3	28 17.8	16 0.4	1 33.1	4 54.2
3 S	14 50 45.4	11 0.9	8 55.0	13 54.1	3 28.6	22 20.8	4 18.6	8 41.1	28 24.7	16 3.5	1 34.6	4 56.6
4 M	14 54 41.9	12 1.0	8 51.9	26 17.6	4 39.7	23 35.7	4 56.1	8 47.0	28 31.6	16 6.7	1 36.2	4 59.0
5 T	14 58 38.5	13 1.2	8 48.7	8♌58.8	5 48.7	24 50.7	5 33.7	8 53.1	28 38.6	16 9.9	1 37.9	5 1.4
6 W	15 2 35.0	14 1.3	8 45.5	22 1.5	6 55.4	26 5.7	6 11.2	8 59.4	28 45.6	16 13.1	1 39.5	5 3.8
7 T	15 6 31.6	15 1.5	8 42.3	5♍28.6	7 59.7	27 20.7	6 48.8	9 5.8	28 52.6	16 16.4	1 41.2	5 6.2
8 F	15 10 28.2	16 1.8	8 39.1	19 22.0	9 1.1	28 35.8	7 26.3	9 12.4	28 59.6	16 19.6	1 42.9	5 8.6
9 S	15 14 24.7	17 2.1	8 36.0	3♎41.7	9 59.4	29 50.8	8 3.9	9 19.2	29 6.6	16 22.9	1 44.6	5 11.0
10 S	15 18 21.3	18 2.4	8 32.8	18 25.1	10 54.1	1♏ 5.9	8 41.4	9 26.1	29 13.6	16 26.2	1 46.4	5 13.4
11 M	15 22 17.8	19 2.7	8 29.6	3♏26.8	11 44.8	2 21.0	9 18.9	9 33.2	29 20.7	16 29.6	1 48.2	5 15.8
12 T	15 26 14.4	20 3.1	8 26.4	18 39.0	12 31.1	3 36.2	9 56.4	9 40.4	29 27.8	16 32.9	1 50.0	5 18.1
13 W	15 30 10.9	21 3.5	8 23.3	3♐52.2	13 12.3	4 51.4	10 33.9	9 47.8	29 34.9	16 36.3	1 51.8	5 20.5
14 T	15 34 7.5	22 4.0	8 20.1	18 56.5	13 47.9	6 6.5	11 11.3	9 55.3	29 42.0	16 39.7	1 53.6	5 22.8
15 F	15 38 4.1	23 4.4	8 16.9	3♑43.3	14 17.1	7 21.7	11 48.8	10 3.0	29 49.1	16 43.2	1 55.5	5 25.2
16 S	15 42 0.6	24 4.9	8 13.7	18 6.3	14 39.4	8 36.9	12 26.2	10 10.9	29 56.2	16 46.6	1 57.3	5 27.5
17 S	15 45 57.2	25 5.4	8 10.6	2♒ 2.3	14 54.0	9 52.2	13 3.7	10 18.8	0♐ 3.3	16 50.1	1 59.2	5 29.8
18 M	15 49 53.7	26 5.9	8 7.4	15 30.5	15 0.0	11 7.4	13 41.1	10 27.0	0 10.4	16 53.5	2 1.1	5 32.2
19 T	15 53 50.3	27 6.5	8 4.2	28 32.8	14R56.9	12 22.7	14 18.5	10 35.3	0 17.6	16 57.0	2 3.1	5 34.5
20 W	15 57 46.8	28 7.0	8 1.0	11♓12.4	14 43.9	13 37.9	14 55.9	10 43.7	0 24.7	17 0.5	2 5.0	5 36.7
21 T	16 1 43.4	29 7.6	7 57.8	23 33.3	14 20.5	14 53.2	15 33.3	10 52.2	0 31.8	17 4.1	2 7.0	5 39.0
22 F	16 5 40.0	0♐ 8.3	7 54.7	5♈39.9	13 46.5	16 8.5	16 10.7	11 1.0	0 39.0	17 7.6	2 9.0	5 41.3
23 S	16 9 36.5	1 8.9	7 51.5	17 36.4	13 1.9	17 23.8	16 48.0	11 9.8	0 46.2	17 11.2	2 11.0	5 43.6
24 S	16 13 33.1	2 9.5	7 48.3	29 26.7	12 7.0	18 39.2	17 25.4	11 18.8	0 53.3	17 14.7	2 13.0	5 45.8
25 M	16 17 29.6	3 10.2	7 45.1	11♉14.2	11 2.8	19 54.5	18 2.7	11 27.9	1 0.5	17 18.3	2 15.1	5 48.0
26 T	16 21 26.2	4 10.9	7 42.0	23 1.8	9 50.7	21 9.8	18 40.0	11 37.1	1 7.6	17 21.9	2 17.1	5 50.2
27 W	16 25 22.7	5 11.6	7 38.8	4♊52.0	8 32.7	22 25.2	19 17.4	11 46.5	1 14.7	17 25.5	2 19.2	5 52.4
28 T	16 29 19.3	6 12.3	7 35.6	16 46.6	7 11.1	23 40.5	19 54.6	11 56.0	1 21.9	17 29.1	2 21.2	5 54.6
29 F	16 33 15.9	7 13.1	7 32.4	28 47.5	5 48.6	24 55.9	20 31.9	12 5.6	1 29.0	17 32.7	2 23.3	5 56.7
30 S	16 37 12.4	8 13.8	7 29.3	10♋56.4	4 28.0	26 11.3	21 9.2	12 15.3	1 36.1	17 36.3	2 25.4	5 58.9
DECLINATION at NOON												
1 F	14 42 52.3	14S30.2	14N30.4	26N29.3	22S51.0	6S20.4	0S 6.9	18S57.5	17S58.6	22S45.1	22S21.0	2N 2.9
4 M	14 54 41.9	15 26.6	14 27.4	25 57.9	23 42.6	7 45.6	0 51.8	18 52.7	18 3.4	22 46.1	22 21.1	2 0.8
7 T	15 6 31.6	16 20.8	14 24.3	13 55.2	24 21.8	9 9.4	1 36.6	18 47.6	18 8.2	22 47.1	22 21.1	1 58.7
10 S	15 18 21.3	17 12.5	14 21.2	5S28.7	24 47.3	10 31.5	2 21.2	18 42.0	18 13.0	22 48.1	22 21.2	1 56.7
13 W	15 30 10.9	18 1.5	14 18.2	23 5.9	24 57.5	11 51.4	3 5.6	18 36.0	18 17.7	22 49.1	22 21.2	1 54.7
16 S	15 42 0.6	18 47.7	14 15.1	27 6.0	24 50.2	13 8.8	3 49.8	18 29.6	18 22.4	22 50.2	22 21.2	1 52.9
19 T	15 53 50.3	19 30.9	14 12.0	16 38.5	24 22.5	14 23.3	4 33.6	18 22.8	18 27.0	22 51.2	22 21.2	1 51.2
22 F	16 5 40.0	20 11.0	14 8.9	0 25.4	23 31.1	15 34.6	5 17.2	18 15.6	18 31.6	22 52.3	22 21.2	1 49.6
25 M	16 17 29.6	20 47.6	14 5.9	15N23.0	22 14.5	16 42.3	6 0.3	18 8.0	18 36.1	22 53.3	22 21.2	1 48.2
28 T	16 29 19.3	21 20.8	14 2.8	25 58.2	20 38.8	17 46.1	6 43.1	18 0.1	18 40.5	22 54.4	22 21.1	1 46.8

DECEMBER 1985

DAY	EPHEMERIS SIDEREAL TIME	☉	☊	☽	☿	♀	♂	♃	♄	♅	♆	♇
LONGITUDE at NOON												
1 S	16 41 9.0	9♐14.6	7♉26.1	23♋15.0	3♐12.0	27♏26.7	21♎46.5	12♒25.2	1♐43.2	17♐40.0	2♑27.5	6♏ 1.0
2 M	16 45 5.5	10 15.4	7 22.9	5♌45.4	2R 2.9	28 42.1	22 23.7	12 35.1	1 50.3	17 43.6	2 29.7	6 3.1
3 T	16 49 2.1	11 16.3	7 19.7	18 29.7	1 2.8	29 57.5	23 0.9	12 45.2	1 57.4	17 47.2	2 31.8	6 5.2
4 W	16 52 58.7	12 17.1	7 16.5	1♍30.4	0 12.9	1♐12.9	23 38.2	12 55.5	2 4.5	17 50.9	2 34.0	6 7.3
5 T	16 56 55.2	13 18.0	7 13.4	14 50.0	29♏34.2	2 28.4	24 15.4	13 5.8	2 11.5	17 54.5	2 36.1	6 9.3
6 F	17 0 51.8	14 18.9	7 10.2	28 30.8	29 6.8	3 43.8	24 52.6	13 16.2	2 18.6	17 58.2	2 38.3	6 11.3
7 S	17 4 48.3	15 19.9	7 7.0	12♎33.8	28 50.9	4 59.3	25 29.8	13 26.8	2 25.6	18 1.9	2 40.5	6 13.3
8 S	17 8 44.9	16 20.8	7 3.8	26 58.8	28 45.9	6 14.7	26 6.9	13 37.4	2 32.6	18 5.5	2 42.7	6 15.3
9 M	17 12 41.4	17 21.8	7 0.7	11♏43.4	28D51.3	7 30.2	26 44.1	13 48.2	2 39.6	18 9.2	2 44.9	6 17.3
10 T	17 16 38.0	18 22.8	6 57.5	26 42.6	29 6.2	8 45.7	27 21.2	13 59.1	2 46.6	18 12.8	2 47.1	6 19.2
11 W	17 20 34.6	19 23.8	6 54.3	11♐48.8	29 29.9	10 1.2	27 58.3	14 10.1	2 53.6	18 16.5	2 49.3	6 21.2
12 T	17 24 31.1	20 24.8	6 51.1	26 52.6	0♐ 1.4	11 16.7	28 35.4	14 21.2	3 0.5	18 20.2	2 51.5	6 23.1
13 F	17 28 27.7	21 25.9	6 48.0	11♑44.7	0 40.1	12 32.2	29 12.5	14 32.4	3 7.5	18 23.9	2 53.8	6 25.0
14 S	17 32 24.2	22 27.0	6 44.8	26 16.6	1 25.0	13 47.7	29 49.6	14 43.7	3 14.4	18 27.5	2 56.0	6 26.8
15 S	17 36 20.8	23 28.0	6 41.6	10♒22.6	2 15.4	15 3.2	0♏26.6	14 55.1	3 21.2	18 31.2	2 58.3	6 28.6
16 M	17 40 17.4	24 29.1	6 38.4	23 60.0	3 10.8	16 18.7	1 3.6	15 6.6	3 28.1	18 34.9	3 0.5	6 30.4
17 T	17 44 13.9	25 30.1	6 35.3	7♓ 9.0	4 10.4	17 34.2	1 40.6	15 18.2	3 34.9	18 38.5	3 2.8	6 32.2
18 W	17 48 10.5	26 31.2	6 32.1	19 52.2	5 13.7	18 49.7	2 17.6	15 29.8	3 41.7	18 42.1	3 5.0	6 34.0
19 T	17 52 7.0	27 32.3	6 28.9	2♈13.8	6 20.4	20 5.2	2 54.6	15 41.6	3 48.4	18 45.8	3 7.3	6 35.7
20 F	17 56 3.6	28 33.4	6 25.7	14 18.9	7 29.9	21 20.7	3 31.5	15 53.5	3 55.2	18 49.4	3 9.6	6 37.4
21 S	18 0 0.2	29 34.5	6 22.6	26 12.7	8 42.0	22 36.2	4 8.4	16 5.4	4 1.9	18 53.0	3 11.8	6 39.1
22 S	18 3 56.7	0♑35.6	6 19.4	8♉ 0.5	9 56.3	23 51.7	4 45.3	16 17.4	4 8.5	18 56.6	3 14.1	6 40.7
23 M	18 7 53.3	1 36.7	6 16.2	19 46.8	11 12.5	25 7.2	5 22.1	16 29.5	4 15.1	19 0.2	3 16.4	6 42.3
24 T	18 11 49.8	2 37.8	6 13.0	1♊35.8	12 30.5	26 22.7	5 59.0	16 41.7	4 21.7	19 3.8	3 18.6	6 43.9
25 W	18 15 46.4	3 38.9	6 9.8	13 30.7	13 49.9	27 38.2	6 35.8	16 54.0	4 28.3	19 7.4	3 20.9	6 45.5
26 T	18 19 42.9	4 40.0	6 6.7	25 33.9	15 10.7	28 53.7	7 12.6	17 6.4	4 34.8	19 11.0	3 23.2	6 47.0
27 F	18 23 39.5	5 41.1	6 3.5	7♋47.0	16 32.7	0♑ 9.2	7 49.4	17 18.8	4 41.3	19 14.5	3 25.4	6 48.5
28 S	18 27 36.1	6 42.2	6 0.3	20 10.9	17 55.7	1 24.7	8 26.1	17 31.3	4 47.7	19 18.1	3 27.7	6 50.0
29 S	18 31 32.6	7 43.4	5 57.1	2♌46.0	19 19.7	2 40.2	9 2.8	17 43.9	4 54.1	19 21.6	3 30.0	6 51.4
30 M	18 35 29.2	8 44.5	5 54.0	15 32.4	20 44.6	3 55.7	9 39.5	17 56.5	5 0.5	19 25.1	3 32.2	6 52.8
31 T	18 39 25.7	9 45.6	5 50.8	28 30.4	22 10.2	5 11.2	10 16.2	18 9.2	5 6.8	19 28.6	3 34.5	6 54.2
DECLINATION at NOON												
1 S	16 41 9.0	21S50.4	13N59.7	26N23.0	19S 2.9	18S45.5	7S25.4	17S51.7	18S44.8	22S55.4	22S21.1	1N45.5
4 W	16 52 58.7	22 16.2	13 56.6	15 25.3	17 50.7	19 40.4	8 7.2	17 43.0	18 49.1	22 56.4	22 21.0	1 44.4
7 S	17 4 48.3	22 38.1	13 53.4	2S51.0	17 15.9	20 30.3	8 48.5	17 34.0	18 53.3	22 57.5	22 21.0	1 43.4
10 T	17 16 38.0	22 56.1	13 50.3	20 59.2	17 17.6	21 14.9	9 29.3	17 24.6	18 57.3	22 58.5	22 20.9	1 42.5
13 F	17 28 27.7	23 10.0	13 47.2	27 30.8	17 46.8	21 53.9	10 9.4	17 14.8	19 1.3	22 59.5	22 20.8	1 41.8
16 M	17 40 17.4	23 19.7	13 44.1	18 11.5	18 33.0	22 27.2	10 48.9	17 4.7	19 5.2	23 0.4	22 20.7	1 41.1
19 T	17 52 7.0	23 25.2	13 40.9	1 52.9	19 27.7	22 54.3	11 27.7	16 54.2	19 8.9	23 1.4	22 20.6	1 40.6
22 S	18 3 56.7	23 26.5	13 37.8	14N10.6	20 24.6	23 15.3	12 5.8	16 43.4	19 12.5	23 2.3	22 20.4	1 40.3
25 W	18 15 46.4	23 23.6	13 34.7	25 22.5	21 19.5	23 29.8	12 43.1	16 32.4	19 16.0	23 3.2	22 20.3	1 40.0
28 S	18 27 36.1	23 16.4	13 31.5	26 42.5	22 9.3	23 37.8	13 19.6	16 21.0	19 19.4	23 4.1	22 20.1	1 39.9
31 T	18 39 25.7	23 5.0	13 28.4	16 24.4	22 51.9	23 39.2	13 55.3	16 9.3	19 22.7	23 5.0	22 20.0	1 39.9

JANUARY 1986

DAY	EPHEMERIS SIDEREAL TIME	☉	☊	☽	☿	♀	♂	♃	♄	♅	♆	♇
	h m s	° ′	° ′	° ′	° ′	° ′	° ′	° ′	° ′	° ′	° ′	° ′
						LONGITUDE at NOON						
1 W	18 43 22.3	10♑46.8	5♉47.6	11♍40.4	23♐36.6	6♑26.7	10♏52.9	18♒22.0	5♐13.1	19♐32.1	3♑36.8	6♏55.5
2 T	18 47 18.9	11 47.9	5 44.4	25 3.2	25 3.6	7 42.1	11 29.5	18 34.9	5 19.3	19 35.5	3 39.0	6 56.8
3 F	18 51 15.4	12 49.1	5 41.3	8♎40.0	26 31.3	8 57.7	12 6.2	18 47.9	5 25.5	19 39.0	3 41.3	6 58.2
4 S	18 55 12.0	13 50.3	5 38.1	22 31.8	27 59.5	10 13.2	12 42.8	19 0.9	5 31.6	19 42.5	3 43.6	6 59.4
5 S	18 59 8.5	14 51.4	5 34.9	6♏39.2	29 28.3	11 28.7	13 19.3	19 13.9	5 37.7	19 45.9	3 45.8	7 0.7
6 M	19 3 5.1	15 52.6	5 31.7	21 1.7	0♑57.6	12 44.2	13 55.9	19 27.0	5 43.7	19 49.3	3 48.0	7 1.9
7 T	19 7 1.7	16 53.8	5 28.6	5♐36.9	2 27.4	13 59.7	14 32.4	19 40.2	5 49.7	19 52.7	3 50.3	7 3.0
8 W	19 10 58.2	17 55.0	5 25.4	20 20.3	3 57.7	15 15.2	15 8.8	19 53.5	5 55.7	19 56.0	3 52.5	7 4.1
9 T	19 14 54.8	18 56.1	5 22.2	5♑ 5.4	5 28.4	16 30.7	15 45.3	20 6.8	6 1.5	19 59.3	3 54.7	7 5.2
10 F	19 18 51.3	19 57.3	5 19.0	19 44.2	6 59.7	17 46.2	16 21.7	20 20.1	6 7.4	20 2.6	3 56.9	7 6.3
11 S	19 22 47.9	20 58.5	5 15.8	4♒ 9.0	8 31.4	19 1.7	16 58.0	20 33.5	6 13.1	20 5.9	3 59.1	7 7.3
12 S	19 26 44.4	21 59.6	5 12.7	18 13.1	10 3.6	20 17.2	17 34.4	20 47.0	6 18.8	20 9.2	4 1.3	7 8.3
13 M	19 30 41.0	23 0.8	5 9.5	1♓52.3	11 36.2	21 32.6	18 10.7	21 0.5	6 24.5	20 12.4	4 3.5	7 9.3
14 T	19 34 37.6	24 1.9	5 6.3	15 5.0	13 9.3	22 48.1	18 46.9	21 14.1	6 30.1	20 15.6	4 5.6	7 10.2
15 W	19 38 34.1	25 3.0	5 3.1	27 52.3	14 42.9	24 3.6	19 23.1	21 27.7	6 35.6	20 18.8	4 7.8	7 11.1
16 T	19 42 30.7	26 4.1	4 60.0	10♈17.4	16 17.0	25 19.0	19 59.3	21 41.3	6 41.1	20 21.9	4 9.9	7 11.9
17 F	19 46 27.2	27 5.2	4 56.8	22 24.8	17 51.6	26 34.5	20 35.5	21 55.1	6 46.5	20 25.1	4 12.1	7 12.7
18 S	19 50 23.8	28 6.3	4 53.6	4♉19.9	19 26.7	27 49.9	21 11.6	22 8.8	6 51.8	20 28.2	4 14.2	7 13.5
19 S	19 54 20.3	29 7.4	4 50.4	16 8.3	21 2.4	29 5.4	21 47.7	22 22.6	6 57.1	20 31.2	4 16.3	7 14.3
20 M	19 58 16.9	0♒ 8.5	4 47.3	27 55.5	22 38.5	0♒20.8	22 23.7	22 36.4	7 2.3	20 34.3	4 18.4	7 15.0
21 T	20 2 13.5	1 9.5	4 44.1	9♊46.7	24 15.3	1 36.2	22 59.7	22 50.3	7 7.4	20 37.3	4 20.5	7 15.6
22 W	20 6 10.0	2 10.5	4 40.9	21 46.1	25 52.5	2 51.6	23 35.6	23 4.2	7 12.5	20 40.2	4 22.5	7 16.3
23 T	20 10 6.6	3 11.6	4 37.7	3♋57.2	27 30.4	4 7.0	24 11.6	23 18.1	7 17.5	20 43.2	4 24.6	7 16.9
24 F	20 14 3.1	4 12.6	4 34.6	16 22.3	29 9.0	5 22.4	24 47.5	23 32.2	7 22.5	20 46.1	4 26.7	7 17.5
25 S	20 17 59.7	5 13.6	4 31.4	29 2.3	0♒48.1	6 37.8	25 23.3	23 46.2	7 27.4	20 49.0	4 28.7	7 18.0
26 S	20 21 56.2	6 14.6	4 28.2	11♌57.1	2 27.8	7 53.2	25 59.1	24 0.2	7 32.1	20 51.9	4 30.7	7 18.5
27 M	20 25 52.8	7 15.5	4 25.0	25 5.6	4 8.1	9 8.5	26 34.9	24 14.3	7 36.9	20 54.7	4 32.7	7 19.0
28 T	20 29 49.4	8 16.5	4 21.8	8♍26.1	5 49.2	10 23.9	27 10.6	24 28.4	7 41.5	20 57.5	4 34.6	7 19.4
29 W	20 33 45.9	9 17.4	4 18.7	21 56.8	7 30.9	11 39.2	27 46.2	24 42.5	7 46.1	21 0.2	4 36.6	7 19.8
30 T	20 37 42.5	10 18.3	4 15.5	5♎36.2	9 13.2	12 54.6	28 21.9	24 56.7	7 50.6	21 2.9	4 38.5	7 20.1
31 F	20 41 39.0	11 19.2	4 12.3	19 23.3	10 56.3	14 9.9	28 57.4	25 10.9	7 55.0	21 5.6	4 40.4	7 20.5
						DECLINATION at NOON						
1 W	18 43 22.3	23S 0.3	13N27.3	11N 1.8	23S 4.3	23S38.2	14S 7.0	16S 5.3	19S23.7	23S 5.3	22S19.9	1N39.9
4 S	18 55 12.0	22 43.4	13 24.1	7S36.8	23 35.1	23 30.9	14 41.6	15 53.2	19 26.8	23 6.1	22 19.7	1 40.1
7 T	19 7 1.7	22 22.5	13 21.0	23 39.5	23 55.9	23 16.9	15 15.2	15 40.9	19 29.8	23 6.9	22 19.5	1 40.4
10 F	19 18 51.3	21 57.6	13 17.8	26 45.4	24 5.8	22 56.5	15 47.9	15 28.3	19 32.6	23 7.7	22 19.4	1 40.8
13 M	19 30 41.0	21 28.8	13 14.6	15 1.2	24 4.2	22 29.8	16 19.7	15 15.4	19 35.3	23 8.5	22 19.2	1 41.4
16 T	19 42 30.7	20 56.3	13 11.4	2N 6.1	23 50.5	21 56.8	16 50.4	15 2.3	19 37.8	23 9.2	22 18.9	1 42.1
19 S	19 54 20.3	20 20.2	13 8.2	17 34.6	23 24.5	21 17.9	17 20.0	14 49.0	19 40.2	23 9.9	22 18.7	1 42.8
22 W	20 6 10.0	19 40.7	13 5.0	26 50.0	22 45.6	20 33.3	17 48.7	14 35.4	19 42.5	23 10.6	22 18.5	1 43.7
25 S	20 17 59.7	18 57.9	13 1.8	25 13.0	21 53.6	19 43.2	18 16.2	14 21.6	19 44.6	23 11.2	22 18.3	1 44.7
28 T	20 29 49.4	18 12.0	12 58.6	12 14.1	20 48.3	18 47.9	18 42.6	14 7.7	19 46.6	23 11.8	22 18.0	1 45.9
31 F	20 41 39.0	17 23.1	12 55.4	6S26.3	19 29.5	17 47.8	19 8.0	13 53.5	19 48.4	23 12.4	22 17.8	1 47.1

FEBRUARY 1986

DAY	EPHEMERIS SIDEREAL TIME	☉	☊	☽	☿	♀	♂	♃	♄	♅	♆	♇
						LONGITUDE at NOON						
1 S	20 45 35.6	12♒20.1	4♉ 9.1	3♏17.6	12♒40.0	15♒25.2	29♏33.0	25♒25.1	7♐59.4	21♐ 8.2	4♑42.3	7♏20.7
2 S	20 49 32.1	13 21.0	4 6.0	17 19.0	14 24.4	16 40.5	0♐ 8.5	25 39.3	8 3.6	21 10.8	4 44.2	7 21.0
3 M	20 53 28.7	14 21.9	4 2.8	1♐27.2	16 9.5	17 55.8	0 43.9	25 53.6	8 7.8	21 13.3	4 46.1	7 21.2
4 T	20 57 25.3	15 22.8	3 59.6	15 41.1	17 55.3	19 11.1	1 19.3	26 7.9	8 11.9	21 15.9	4 47.9	7 21.3
5 W	21 1 21.8	16 23.6	3 56.4	29 58.5	19 41.7	20 26.4	1 54.6	26 22.2	8 16.0	21 18.3	4 49.7	7 21.5
6 T	21 5 18.4	17 24.4	3 53.3	14♑15.8	21 28.7	21 41.7	2 29.9	26 36.5	8 19.9	21 20.8	4 51.5	7 21.6
7 F	21 9 14.9	18 25.2	3 50.1	28 28.3	23 16.2	22 56.9	3 5.1	26 50.8	8 23.8	21 23.2	4 53.3	7 21.6
8 S	21 13 11.5	19 26.0	3 46.9	12♒30.5	25 4.3	24 12.2	3 40.3	27 5.1	8 27.5	21 25.5	4 55.1	7 21.7
9 S	21 17 8.0	20 26.8	3 43.7	26 17.5	26 52.9	25 27.4	4 15.4	27 19.5	8 31.2	21 27.8	4 56.8	7R21.6
10 M	21 21 4.6	21 27.6	3 40.5	9♓45.2	28 41.8	26 42.7	4 50.4	27 33.9	8 34.8	21 30.1	4 58.5	7 21.6
11 T	21 25 1.2	22 28.3	3 37.4	22 51.6	0♓30.9	27 57.9	5 25.4	27 48.3	8 38.4	21 32.3	5 0.2	7 21.5
12 W	21 28 57.7	23 29.0	3 34.2	5♈36.5	2 20.2	29 13.1	6 0.3	28 2.7	8 41.8	21 34.5	5 1.9	7 21.4
13 T	21 32 54.3	24 29.7	3 31.0	18 1.7	4 9.4	0♓28.3	6 35.1	28 17.1	8 45.1	21 36.6	5 3.5	7 21.2
14 F	21 36 50.8	25 30.3	3 27.8	0♉10.5	5 58.5	1 43.5	7 9.9	28 31.5	8 48.4	21 38.8	5 5.2	7 21.1
15 S	21 40 47.4	26 31.0	3 24.7	12 7.3	7 47.1	2 58.6	7 44.6	28 45.9	8 51.6	21 40.8	5 6.7	7 20.8
16 S	21 44 43.9	27 31.6	3 21.5	23 57.2	9 35.0	4 13.7	8 19.3	29 0.3	8 54.7	21 42.8	5 8.3	7 20.6
17 M	21 48 40.5	28 32.1	3 18.3	5♊45.6	11 21.9	5 28.9	8 53.9	29 14.8	8 57.6	21 44.8	5 9.8	7 20.3
18 T	21 52 37.0	29 32.6	3 15.1	17 38.2	13 7.4	6 43.9	9 28.4	29 29.2	9 0.5	21 46.7	5 11.4	7 19.9
19 W	21 56 33.6	0♓33.1	3 11.9	29 39.8	14 51.2	7 59.0	10 2.8	29 43.6	9 3.3	21 48.6	5 12.8	7 19.6
20 T	22 0 30.1	1 33.6	3 8.8	11♋55.1	16 32.8	9 14.1	10 37.2	29 58.0	9 6.0	21 50.4	5 14.3	7 19.2
21 F	22 4 26.7	2 34.1	3 5.6	24 27.3	18 11.7	10 29.1	11 11.4	0♓12.4	9 8.6	21 52.2	5 15.7	7 18.7
22 S	22 8 23.3	3 34.5	3 2.4	7♌18.6	19 47.5	11 44.1	11 45.7	0 26.8	9 11.2	21 53.9	5 17.1	7 18.3
23 S	22 12 19.8	4 34.8	2 59.2	20 29.3	21 19.5	12 59.1	12 19.8	0 41.2	9 13.6	21 55.6	5 18.5	7 17.8
24 M	22 16 16.4	5 35.2	2 56.1	3♍58.4	22 47.1	14 14.1	12 53.9	0 55.6	9 15.9	21 57.2	5 19.9	7 17.2
25 T	22 20 12.9	6 35.5	2 52.9	17 43.4	24 9.8	15 29.0	13 27.9	1 10.0	9 18.1	21 58.8	5 21.2	7 16.6
26 W	22 24 9.5	7 35.8	2 49.7	1♎40.5	25 26.8	16 44.0	14 1.8	1 24.4	9 20.3	22 0.3	5 22.5	7 16.0
27 T	22 28 6.0	8 36.1	2 46.5	15 45.9	26 37.7	17 58.9	14 35.6	1 38.7	9 22.3	22 1.8	5 23.8	7 15.4
28 F	22 32 2.6	9 36.3	2 43.4	29 56.0	27 41.7	19 13.8	15 9.3	1 53.1	9 24.3	22 3.2	5 25.0	7 14.7
						DECLINATION at NOON						
1 S	20 45 35.6	17S 6.2	12N54.3	12S35.2	19S 0.3	17S26.8	19S16.2	13S48.8	19S49.0	23S12.6	22S17.7	1N47.5
4 T	20 57 25.3	16 13.6	12 51.1	26 2.1	17 23.4	16 20.7	19 40.0	13 34.4	19 50.6	23 13.2	22 17.5	1 48.9
7 F	21 9 14.9	15 18.6	12 47.9	25 21.9	15 33.3	15 10.4	20 2.6	13 19.9	19 52.1	23 13.7	22 17.2	1 50.3
10 M	21 21 4.6	14 21.1	12 44.7	11 37.7	13 30.5	13 56.5	20 24.1	13 5.3	19 53.5	23 14.2	22 17.0	1 51.9
13 T	21 32 54.3	13 21.6	12 41.4	5N55.0	11 16.3	12 39.1	20 44.3	12 50.5	19 54.7	23 14.6	22 16.8	1 53.5
16 S	21 44 43.9	12 20.0	12 38.2	20 35.4	8 52.9	11 18.7	21 3.4	12 35.6	19 55.7	23 15.0	22 16.5	1 55.2
19 W	21 56 33.6	11 16.7	12 34.9	27 44.0	6 24.1	9 55.6	21 21.3	12 20.6	19 56.7	23 15.4	22 16.3	1 56.9
22 S	22 8 23.3	10 11.9	12 31.7	23 19.6	3 55.4	8 30.1	21 38.0	12 5.5	19 57.4	23 15.8	22 16.1	1 58.7
25 T	22 20 12.9	9 5.6	12 28.4	8 5.2	1 34.5	7 2.7	21 53.6	11 50.4	19 58.1	23 16.1	22 15.8	2 0.6
28 F	22 32 2.6	7 58.1	12 25.2	11S21.2	0N29.4	5 33.6	22 7.9	11 35.2	19 58.6	23 16.4	22 15.6	2 2.6

MARCH 1986

DAY	EPHEMERIS SIDEREAL TIME	☉	☊	☾	☿	♀	♂	♃	♄	♅	♆	♇
	h m s	° ′	° ′	° ′	° ′	° ′	° ′	° ′	° ′	° ′	° ′	° ′
LONGITUDE at NOON												
1 S	22 35 59.1	10♓36.6	2♉40.2	14♏ 7.5	28♓38.2	20♓28.7	15♐43.0	2♓ 7.5	9♐26.1	22♐ 4.6	5♑26.2	7♏14.0
2 S	22 39 55.7	11 36.8	2 37.0	28 18.3	29 26.9	21 43.5	16 16.6	2 21.8	9 27.8	22 5.9	5 27.4	7R13.3
3 M	22 43 52.2	12 36.9	2 33.8	12♐26.7	0♈ 7.2	22 58.3	16 50.1	2 36.1	9 29.5	22 7.2	5 28.5	7 12.5
4 T	22 47 48.8	13 37.1	2 30.6	26 31.4	0 38.8	24 13.2	17 23.5	2 50.4	9 31.0	22 8.4	5 29.6	7 11.7
5 W	22 51 45.4	14 37.2	2 27.5	10♑31.3	1 1.3	25 28.0	17 56.8	3 4.7	9 32.5	22 9.6	5 30.7	7 10.9
6 T	22 55 41.9	15 37.3	2 24.3	24 24.6	1 14.6	26 42.8	18 30.0	3 19.0	9 33.8	22 10.8	5 31.8	7 10.1
7 F	22 59 38.5	16 37.4	2 21.1	8♒ 9.6	1 18.8	27 57.6	19 3.1	3 33.3	9 35.1	22 11.9	5 32.9	7 9.2
8 S	23 3 35.0	17 37.4	2 17.9	21 43.7	1R13.9	29 12.3	19 36.1	3 47.5	9 36.3	22 12.9	5 33.9	7 8.3
9 S	23 7 31.6	18 37.4	2 14.8	5♓ 4.9	1 0.1	0♈27.0	20 9.0	4 1.7	9 37.3	22 13.9	5 34.8	7 7.4
10 M	23 11 28.1	19 37.4	2 11.6	18 11.2	0 37.9	1 41.7	20 41.8	4 15.9	9 38.3	22 14.8	5 35.8	7 6.4
11 T	23 15 24.7	20 37.4	2 8.4	1♈ 1.4	0 7.9	2 56.4	21 14.5	4 30.0	9 39.1	22 15.7	5 36.7	7 5.4
12 W	23 19 21.2	21 37.3	2 5.2	13 35.4	29♓30.9	4 11.0	21 47.0	4 44.1	9 39.8	22 16.5	5 37.5	7 4.3
13 T	23 23 17.8	22 37.2	2 2.0	25 54.3	28 47.7	5 25.6	22 19.5	4 58.2	9 40.5	22 17.2	5 38.4	7 3.3
14 F	23 27 14.3	23 37.0	1 58.9	8♉ 0.2	27 59.5	6 40.2	22 51.8	5 12.3	9 41.0	22 18.0	5 39.2	7 2.2
15 S	23 31 10.9	24 36.8	1 55.7	19 56.3	27 7.4	7 54.8	23 24.0	5 26.3	9 41.5	22 18.6	5 39.9	7 1.1
16 S	23 35 7.4	25 36.6	1 52.5	1♊46.5	26 12.6	9 9.3	23 56.1	5 40.3	9 41.8	22 19.2	5 40.7	6 59.9
17 M	23 39 4.0	26 36.3	1 49.3	13 35.4	25 16.3	10 23.9	24 28.0	5 54.3	9 42.0	22 19.8	5 41.4	6 58.8
18 T	23 43 0.6	27 36.0	1 46.2	25 28.1	24 19.9	11 38.3	24 59.8	6 8.2	9 42.2	22 20.3	5 42.1	6 57.6
19 W	23 46 57.1	28 35.7	1 43.0	7♋29.5	23 24.5	12 52.8	25 31.5	6 22.1	9 42.2	22 20.7	5 42.7	6 56.4
20 T	23 50 53.7	29 35.3	1 39.8	19 44.7	22 31.1	14 7.2	26 3.1	6 36.0	9R42.1	22 21.1	5 43.3	6 55.1
21 F	23 54 50.2	0♈34.9	1 36.6	2♌17.7	21 40.8	15 21.6	26 34.5	6 49.8	9 41.9	22 21.4	5 43.9	6 53.9
22 S	23 58 46.8	1 34.4	1 33.4	15 12.1	20 54.4	16 36.0	27 5.8	7 3.6	9 41.7	22 21.7	5 44.4	6 52.6
23 S	0 2 43.3	2 33.9	1 30.3	28 29.7	20 12.5	17 50.3	27 36.9	7 17.3	9 41.3	22 22.0	5 45.0	6 51.3
24 M	0 6 39.9	3 33.4	1 27.1	12♍10.5	19 35.8	19 4.6	28 7.9	7 31.0	9 40.8	22 22.1	5 45.4	6 50.0
25 T	0 10 36.4	4 32.9	1 23.9	26 12.6	19 4.5	20 18.9	28 38.8	7 44.7	9 40.3	22 22.3	5 45.9	6 48.6
26 W	0 14 33.0	5 32.3	1 20.7	10♎32.3	18 39.0	21 33.1	29 9.5	7 58.3	9 39.6	22 22.3	5 46.3	6 47.3
27 T	0 18 29.5	6 31.6	1 17.6	25 4.0	18 19.3	22 47.3	29 40.1	8 11.9	9 38.8	22 22.4	5 46.7	6 45.9
28 F	0 22 26.1	7 31.0	1 14.4	9♏41.8	18 5.6	24 1.5	0♑10.6	8 25.4	9 38.0	22 22.4	5 47.1	6 44.5
29 S	0 26 22.6	8 30.3	1 11.2	24 19.3	17 57.8	25 15.7	0 40.8	8 38.9	9 37.0	22R22.3	5 47.4	6 43.1
30 S	0 30 19.2	9 29.6	1 8.0	8♐51.3	17 55.7	26 29.8	1 10.9	8 52.3	9 36.0	22 22.2	5 47.7	6 41.6
31 M	0 34 15.7	10 28.8	1 4.8	23 13.5	17D59.3	27 43.9	1 40.8	9 5.7	9 34.8	22 22.0	5 47.9	6 40.2
DECLINATION at NOON												
1 S	22 35 59.1	7S35.4	12N24.1	17S11.3	1N 5.2	5S 3.5	22S12.4	11S30.2	19S58.7	23S16.5	22S15.5	2N 3.2
4 T	22 47 48.8	6 26.6	12 20.8	27 38.0	2 31.4	3 32.7	22 25.3	11 14.9	19 59.0	23 16.8	22 15.3	2 5.2
7 F	22 59 38.5	5 16.9	12 17.5	23 8.8	3 19.9	2 1.0	22 37.0	10 59.7	19 59.2	23 17.0	22 15.1	2 7.2
10 M	23 11 28.1	4 6.6	12 14.2	7 52.3	3 25.9	0 28.7	22 47.5	10 44.5	19 59.2	23 17.3	22 14.9	2 9.3
13 T	23 23 17.8	2 55.8	12 10.9	9N38.0	2 50.4	1N 3.8	22 57.0	10 29.2	19 59.1	23 17.4	22 14.7	2 11.4
16 S	23 35 7.4	1 44.7	12 7.7	23 11.0	1 40.9	2 36.2	23 5.4	10 14.1	19 58.9	23 17.6	22 14.5	2 13.4
19 W	23 46 57.1	0 33.5	12 4.4	28 1.9	0 11.3	4 8.1	23 12.8	9 58.9	19 58.5	23 17.7	22 14.4	2 15.5
22 S	23 58 46.8	0N37.6	12 1.1	21 5.6	1S22.4	5 39.2	23 19.2	9 43.9	19 58.0	23 17.8	22 14.2	2 17.6
25 T	0 10 36.4	1 48.5	11 57.7	4 11.3	2 46.5	7 9.2	23 24.8	9 28.9	19 57.4	23 17.9	22 14.1	2 19.7
28 F	0 22 26.1	2 59.0	11 54.4	15S33.5	3 52.3	8 37.8	23 29.4	9 14.1	19 56.7	23 17.9	22 13.9	2 21.8
31 M	0 34 15.7	4 9.0	11 51.1	27 28.7	4 35.9	10 4.6	23 33.2	8 59.3	19 55.8	23 18.0	22 13.8	2 23.8

APRIL 1986

DAY	EPHEMERIS SIDEREAL TIME	☉	☊	☾	☿	♀	♂	♃	♄	♅	♆	♇
LONGITUDE at NOON												
1 T	0 38 12.3	11♈28.1	1♉ 1.7	7♑23.1	18♓ 8.3	28♈57.9	2♑10.6	9♓19.0	9♐33.6	22♐21.8	5♑48.1	6♏38.7
2 W	0 42 8.9	12 27.2	0 58.5	21 18.6	18 22.6	0♉12.0	2 40.1	9 32.2	9R32.2	22R21.5	5 48.3	6R37.2
3 T	0 46 5.4	13 26.4	0 55.3	4♒59.1	18 41.9	1 26.0	3 9.5	9 45.4	9 30.8	22 21.1	5 48.4	6 35.7
4 F	0 50 2.0	14 25.5	0 52.1	18 24.7	19 5.9	2 39.9	3 38.7	9 58.6	9 29.2	22 20.7	5 48.6	6 34.2
5 S	0 53 58.5	15 24.6	0 49.0	1♓35.7	19 34.5	3 53.9	4 7.7	10 11.7	9 27.6	22 20.3	5 48.6	6 32.6
6 S	0 57 55.1	16 23.7	0 45.8	14 32.5	20 7.4	5 7.8	4 36.5	10 24.7	9 25.9	22 19.8	5 48.7	6 31.1
7 M	1 1 51.6	17 22.7	0 42.6	27 15.8	20 44.5	6 21.7	5 5.1	10 37.7	9 24.1	22 19.3	5 48.7	6 29.5
8 T	1 5 48.2	18 21.7	0 39.4	9♈46.3	21 25.3	7 35.5	5 33.5	10 50.6	9 22.2	22 18.7	5 48.7	6 27.9
9 W	1 9 44.7	19 20.7	0 36.2	22 5.0	22 9.9	8 49.3	6 1.7	11 3.4	9 20.2	22 18.0	5R48.6	6 26.3
10 T	1 13 41.3	20 19.6	0 33.1	4♉13.2	22 58.0	10 3.1	6 29.7	11 16.2	9 18.1	22 17.3	5 48.5	6 24.7
11 F	1 17 37.8	21 18.6	0 29.9	16 12.7	23 49.3	11 16.9	6 57.4	11 28.9	9 15.9	22 16.6	5 48.4	6 23.1
12 S	1 21 34.4	22 17.4	0 26.7	28 5.7	24 43.8	12 30.6	7 24.9	11 41.6	9 13.6	22 15.8	5 48.3	6 21.5
13 S	1 25 30.9	23 16.3	0 23.5	9♊55.1	25 41.4	13 44.3	7 52.1	11 54.1	9 11.3	22 15.0	5 48.1	6 19.8
14 M	1 29 27.5	24 15.0	0 20.4	21 44.2	26 41.7	14 57.9	8 19.1	12 6.6	9 8.8	22 14.1	5 47.8	6 18.2
15 T	1 33 24.1	25 13.8	0 17.2	3♋37.0	27 44.8	16 11.5	8 45.9	12 19.1	9 6.3	22 13.1	5 47.6	6 16.5
16 W	1 37 20.6	26 12.5	0 14.0	15 37.7	28 50.5	17 25.1	9 12.4	12 31.4	9 3.7	22 12.1	5 47.3	6 14.9
17 T	1 41 17.2	27 11.2	0 10.8	27 50.8	29 58.7	18 38.6	9 38.7	12 43.7	9 1.0	22 11.1	5 47.0	6 13.2
18 F	1 45 13.7	28 9.9	0 7.6	10♌20.9	1♈ 9.3	19 52.2	10 4.8	12 56.0	8 58.3	22 10.1	5 46.7	6 11.6
19 S	1 49 10.3	29 8.5	0 4.5	23 11.8	2 22.2	21 5.6	10 30.5	13 8.1	8 55.5	22 9.0	5 46.3	6 9.9
20 S	1 53 6.8	0♉ 7.1	0 1.3	6♍27.0	3 37.4	22 19.1	10 56.0	13 20.1	8 52.6	22 7.8	5 45.9	6 8.2
21 M	1 57 3.4	1 5.6	29♈58.1	20 8.0	4 54.7	23 32.4	11 21.2	13 32.1	8 49.6	22 6.6	5 45.5	6 6.5
22 T	2 0 59.9	2 4.1	29 54.9	4♎14.9	6 14.2	24 45.8	11 46.1	13 44.0	8 46.5	22 5.3	5 45.0	6 4.8
23 W	2 4 56.5	3 2.6	29 51.8	18 45.0	7 35.7	25 59.1	12 10.7	13 55.8	8 43.4	22 4.0	5 44.5	6 3.1
24 T	2 8 53.1	4 1.0	29 48.6	3♏33.3	8 59.2	27 12.3	12 35.0	14 7.5	8 40.2	22 2.7	5 44.0	6 1.4
25 F	2 12 49.6	4 59.5	29 45.4	18 32.6	10 24.7	28 25.5	12 59.1	14 19.1	8 36.9	22 1.3	5 43.4	5 59.7
26 S	2 16 46.2	5 57.8	29 42.2	3♐34.6	11 52.1	29 38.7	13 22.8	14 30.6	8 33.6	21 59.9	5 42.8	5 58.1
27 S	2 20 42.7	6 56.2	29 39.1	18 30.8	13 21.5	0♊51.9	13 46.2	14 42.1	8 30.2	21 58.4	5 42.2	5 56.4
28 M	2 24 39.3	7 54.5	29 35.9	3♑13.7	14 52.8	2 5.0	14 9.2	14 53.5	8 26.7	21 56.9	5 41.5	5 54.7
29 T	2 28 35.8	8 52.8	29 32.7	17 37.9	16 25.9	3 18.0	14 32.0	15 4.7	8 23.2	21 55.4	5 40.9	5 53.0
30 W	2 32 32.4	9 51.1	29 29.5	1♒40.2	18 0.9	4 31.0	14 54.3	15 15.9	8 19.6	21 53.8	5 40.1	5 51.3
DECLINATION at NOON												
1 T	0 38 12.3	4N32.2	11N50.0	28S 5.2	4S45.4	10N33.1	23S34.3	8S54.4	19S55.5	23S18.0	22S13.8	2N24.5
4 F	0 50 2.0	5 41.3	11 46.7	20 3.5	4 58.9	11 57.0	23 37.2	8 39.9	19 54.5	23 17.9	22 13.7	2 26.5
7 M	1 1 51.6	6 49.5	11 43.4	3 42.4	4 51.3	13 18.4	23 39.3	8 25.5	19 53.4	23 17.9	22 13.6	2 28.4
10 T	1 13 41.3	7 56.6	11 40.0	13N18.1	4 24.5	14 36.9	23 40.9	8 11.2	19 52.2	23 17.8	22 13.5	2 30.4
13 S	1 25 30.9	9 2.6	11 36.7	25 18.4	3 40.6	15 52.1	23 42.0	7 57.2	19 50.8	23 17.7	22 13.4	2 32.2
16 W	1 37 20.6	10 7.2	11 33.4	27 37.1	2 41.2	17 3.8	23 42.7	7 43.4	19 49.4	23 17.6	22 13.4	2 34.0
19 S	1 49 10.3	11 10.3	11 30.0	18 22.7	1 27.8	18 11.6	23 43.1	7 29.8	19 47.9	23 17.5	22 13.4	2 35.7
22 T	2 0 59.9	12 11.7	11 26.7	0 25.5	0 2.0	19 15.2	23 43.3	7 16.5	19 46.3	23 17.3	22 13.3	2 37.4
25 F	2 12 49.6	13 11.3	11 23.3	18S58.1	1N35.1	20 14.2	23 43.3	7 3.5	19 44.6	23 17.1	22 13.3	2 38.9
28 M	2 24 39.3	14 8.9	11 19.9	28 7.5	3 22.4	21 8.3	23 43.4	6 50.7	19 42.9	23 16.8	22 13.3	2 40.4

MAY 1986

LONGITUDE at NOON

DAY	EPHEMERIS SIDEREAL TIME	☉	☊	☽	☿	♀	♂	♃	♄	♅	♆	♇
	h m s	° ′	° ′	° ′	° ′	° ′	° ′	° ′	° ′	° ′	° ′	° ′
1 T	2 36 28.9	10♉49.3	29♈26.3	15♒19.8	19♈37.8	5♊44.0	15♑16.3	15♓27.0	8♐15.9	21♐52.2	5♑39.4	5♏49.6
2 F	2 40 25.5	11 47.5	29 23.2	28 37.5	21 16.5	6 57.0	15 38.0	15 38.0	8R12.2	21R50.5	5R38.6	5R47.9
3 S	2 44 22.0	12 45.7	29 20.0	11♓35.2	22 57.1	8 9.9	15 59.3	15 48.9	8 8.4	21 48.8	5 37.8	5 46.2
4 S	2 48 18.6	13 43.9	29 16.8	24 15.6	24 39.6	9 22.8	16 20.1	15 59.6	8 4.6	21 47.1	5 37.0	5 44.5
5 M	2 52 15.2	14 42.0	29 13.6	6♈41.4	26 23.9	10 35.6	16 40.6	16 10.3	8 0.7	21 45.3	5 36.2	5 42.8
6 T	2 56 11.7	15 40.2	29 10.5	18 55.5	28 10.1	11 48.4	17 0.7	16 20.9	7 56.8	21 43.5	5 35.3	5 41.2
7 W	3 0 8.3	16 38.3	29 7.3	1♉ 0.2	29 58.1	13 1.2	17 20.3	16 31.4	7 52.8	21 41.7	5 34.4	5 39.5
8 T	3 4 4.8	17 36.3	29 4.1	12 57.9	1♉48.0	14 13.9	17 39.5	16 41.8	7 48.8	21 39.8	5 33.5	5 37.9
9 F	3 8 1.4	18 34.4	29 0.9	24 50.8	3 39.8	15 26.6	17 58.3	16 52.1	7 44.8	21 37.9	5 32.5	5 36.3
10 S	3 11 57.9	19 32.4	28 57.7	6♊40.7	5 33.5	16 39.3	18 16.7	17 2.2	7 40.7	21 36.0	5 31.6	5 34.6
11 S	3 15 54.5	20 30.4	28 54.6	18 29.8	7 29.0	17 51.8	18 34.5	17 12.3	7 36.6	21 34.0	5 30.6	5 33.0
12 M	3 19 51.1	21 28.4	28 51.4	0♋20.4	9 26.3	19 4.4	18 51.9	17 22.2	7 32.4	21 32.0	5 29.5	5 31.4
13 T	3 23 47.6	22 26.3	28 48.2	12 15.3	11 25.5	20 16.9	19 8.9	17 32.0	7 28.2	21 30.0	5 28.5	5 29.8
14 W	3 27 44.2	23 24.2	28 45.0	24 17.5	13 26.4	21 29.4	19 25.3	17 41.7	7 23.9	21 28.0	5 27.4	5 28.2
15 T	3 31 40.7	24 22.1	28 41.9	6♌30.5	15 29.0	22 41.8	19 41.2	17 51.3	7 19.7	21 25.9	5 26.3	5 26.6
16 F	3 35 37.3	25 19.9	28 38.7	18 58.2	17 33.3	23 54.1	19 56.6	18 0.7	7 15.4	21 23.8	5 25.2	5 25.0
17 S	3 39 33.8	26 17.8	28 35.5	1♍44.4	19 39.1	25 6.4	20 11.6	18 10.1	7 11.0	21 21.6	5 24.0	5 23.5
18 S	3 43 30.4	27 15.6	28 32.3	14 53.0	21 46.2	26 18.7	20 25.9	18 19.3	7 6.7	21 19.5	5 22.8	5 21.9
19 M	3 47 27.0	28 13.3	28 29.2	28 26.8	23 54.7	27 30.9	20 39.8	18 28.4	7 2.3	21 17.3	5 21.6	5 20.4
20 T	3 51 23.5	29 11.0	28 26.0	12♎27.4	26 4.3	28 43.1	20 53.1	18 37.3	6 57.9	21 15.1	5 20.4	5 18.9
21 W	3 55 20.1	0♊ 8.8	28 22.8	26 54.4	28 14.7	29 55.2	21 5.9	18 46.2	6 53.5	21 12.9	5 19.2	5 17.4
22 T	3 59 16.6	1 6.4	28 19.6	11♏44.4	0♊25.8	1♋ 7.2	21 18.0	18 54.9	6 49.1	21 10.6	5 17.9	5 15.9
23 F	4 3 13.2	2 4.1	28 16.5	26 51.3	2 37.4	2 19.2	21 29.7	19 3.4	6 44.6	21 8.3	5 16.7	5 14.4
24 S	4 7 9.7	3 1.7	28 13.3	12♐ 6.2	4 49.1	3 31.2	21 40.7	19 11.9	6 40.2	21 6.0	5 15.4	5 13.0
25 S	4 11 6.3	3 59.3	28 10.1	27 18.9	7 0.8	4 43.1	21 51.1	19 20.2	6 35.7	21 3.7	5 14.1	5 11.5
26 M	4 15 2.9	4 56.9	28 6.9	12♑19.3	9 12.0	5 54.9	22 0.9	19 28.4	6 31.3	21 1.4	5 12.7	5 10.1
27 T	4 18 59.4	5 54.5	28 3.7	26 59.4	11 22.6	7 6.7	22 10.1	19 36.4	6 26.8	20 59.1	5 11.4	5 8.7
28 W	4 22 56.0	6 52.1	28 0.6	11♒13.6	13 32.3	8 18.5	22 18.6	19 44.3	6 22.4	20 56.7	5 10.0	5 7.3
29 T	4 26 52.5	7 49.6	27 57.4	24 59.9	15 40.8	9 30.2	22 26.4	19 52.1	6 17.9	20 54.4	5 8.6	5 6.0
30 F	4 30 49.1	8 47.2	27 54.2	8♓18.9	17 48.0	10 41.8	22 33.7	19 59.8	6 13.5	20 52.0	5 7.3	5 4.7
31 S	4 34 45.6	9 44.7	27 51.0	21 13.1	19 53.5	11 53.4	22 40.2	20 7.3	6 9.0	20 49.6	5 5.9	5 3.4

DECLINATION at NOON

DAY	EPHEMERIS SIDEREAL TIME	☉	☊	☽	☿	♀	♂	♃	♄	♅	♆	♇
1 T	2 36 28.9	15N 4.5	11N16.6	21S 6.3	5N18.7	21N57.3	23S43.6	6S38.3	19S41.0	23S16.6	22S13.4	2N41.8
4 S	2 48 18.6	15 57.8	11 13.2	5 6.9	7 22.7	22 40.9	23 44.0	6 26.2	19 39.1	23 16.3	22 13.4	2 43.1
7 W	3 0 8.3	16 48.8	11 9.8	11N54.6	9 33.1	23 18.9	23 44.8	6 14.4	19 37.2	23 16.0	22 13.4	2 44.3
10 S	3 11 57.9	17 37.2	11 6.4	24 31.6	11 47.9	23 51.0	23 46.1	6 3.0	19 35.2	23 15.7	22 13.5	2 45.4
13 T	3 23 47.6	18 23.0	11 3.1	27 51.1	14 4.9	24 17.0	23 48.0	5 52.0	19 33.1	23 15.4	22 13.6	2 46.4
16 F	3 35 37.3	19 6.0	10 59.7	19 49.9	16 20.7	24 36.8	23 50.7	5 41.4	19 31.1	23 15.0	22 13.7	2 47.2
19 M	3 47 27.0	19 46.0	10 56.3	3 6.9	18 31.3	24 50.2	23 54.3	5 31.2	19 29.0	23 14.6	22 13.8	2 48.0
22 T	3 59 16.6	20 23.1	10 52.9	16S23.6	20 31.6	24 57.3	23 58.9	5 21.4	19 26.9	23 14.2	22 13.9	2 48.6
25 S	4 11 6.3	20 57.0	10 49.5	27 48.6	22 16.0	24 57.9	24 4.6	5 12.2	19 24.8	23 13.8	22 14.0	2 49.1
28 W	4 22 56.0	21 27.6	10 46.1	22 17.2	23 39.9	24 52.1	24 11.5	5 3.4	19 22.7	23 13.3	22 14.1	2 49.5
31 S	4 34 45.6	21 54.9	10 42.7	6 25.7	24 40.2	24 39.9	24 19.7	4 55.1	19 20.6	23 12.9	22 14.2	2 49.8

JUNE 1986

LONGITUDE at NOON

DAY	EPHEMERIS SIDEREAL TIME	☉	☊	☽	☿	♀	♂	♃	♄	♅	♆	♇
1 S	4 38 42.2	10♊42.3	27♈47.9	3♈46.3	21♊57.1	13♋ 5.0	22♑46.0	20♓14.6	6♐ 4.6	20♐47.2	5♑ 4.4	5♏ 2.1
2 M	4 42 38.8	11 39.8	27 44.7	16 2.9	23 58.8	14 16.4	22 51.1	20 21.8	6R 0.1	20R44.8	5R 3.0	5R 0.8
3 T	4 46 35.3	12 37.2	27 41.5	28 7.2	25 58.4	15 27.9	22 55.5	20 28.8	5 55.7	20 42.4	5 1.5	4 59.5
4 W	4 50 31.9	13 34.7	27 38.3	10♉ 3.0	27 55.7	16 39.2	22 59.2	20 35.7	5 51.3	20 39.9	5 0.1	4 58.3
5 T	4 54 28.4	14 32.2	27 35.2	21 53.9	29 50.7	17 50.5	23 2.2	20 42.4	5 46.9	20 37.5	4 58.6	4 57.1
6 F	4 58 25.0	15 29.6	27 32.0	3♊42.7	1♋43.3	19 1.8	23 4.4	20 49.0	5 42.5	20 35.1	4 57.1	4 55.9
7 S	5 2 21.6	16 27.0	27 28.8	15 31.7	3 33.5	20 13.0	23 5.9	20 55.4	5 38.2	20 32.6	4 55.6	4 54.7
8 S	5 6 18.1	17 24.5	27 25.6	27 23.0	5 21.1	21 24.1	23 6.6	21 1.7	5 33.8	20 30.1	4 54.1	4 53.6
9 M	5 10 14.7	18 21.9	27 22.5	9♋18.1	7 6.1	22 35.2	23 6.6	21 7.8	5 29.5	20 27.7	4 52.5	4 52.5
10 T	5 14 11.2	19 19.2	27 19.3	21 18.9	8 48.6	23 46.2	23R 5.8	21 13.8	5 25.2	20 25.2	4 51.0	4 51.4
11 W	5 18 7.8	20 16.6	27 16.1	3♌27.1	10 28.5	24 57.1	23 4.3	21 19.6	5 21.0	20 22.7	4 49.4	4 50.4
12 T	5 22 4.3	21 14.0	27 12.9	15 45.0	12 5.7	26 8.0	23 2.0	21 25.2	5 16.8	20 20.3	4 47.9	4 49.3
13 F	5 26 0.9	22 11.3	27 9.7	28 15.3	13 40.3	27 18.8	22 59.0	21 30.6	5 12.6	20 17.8	4 46.3	4 48.3
14 S	5 29 57.5	23 8.6	27 6.6	11♍ 0.9	15 12.3	28 29.5	22 55.2	21 35.9	5 8.4	20 15.4	4 44.7	4 47.3
15 S	5 33 54.0	24 5.9	27 3.4	24 5.3	16 41.5	29 40.2	22 50.7	21 41.0	5 4.3	20 12.9	4 43.1	4 46.4
16 M	5 37 50.6	25 3.2	27 0.2	7♎31.4	18 8.1	0♌50.8	22 45.4	21 46.0	5 0.3	20 10.4	4 41.6	4 45.5
17 T	5 41 47.1	26 0.5	26 57.0	21 21.8	19 31.9	2 1.3	22 39.4	21 50.8	4 56.3	20 8.0	4 40.0	4 44.6
18 W	5 45 43.7	26 57.8	26 53.9	5♏37.4	20 52.9	3 11.7	22 32.7	21 55.4	4 52.3	20 5.6	4 38.4	4 43.7
19 T	5 49 40.3	27 55.0	26 50.7	20 16.9	22 11.1	4 22.1	22 25.3	21 59.8	4 48.4	20 3.1	4 36.8	4 42.9
20 F	5 53 36.8	28 52.3	26 47.5	5♐16.2	23 26.5	5 32.4	22 17.2	22 4.1	4 44.5	20 0.7	4 35.2	4 42.1
21 S	5 57 33.4	29 49.5	26 44.3	20 27.9	24 38.9	6 42.6	22 8.3	22 8.2	4 40.7	19 58.3	4 33.6	4 41.3
22 S	6 1 29.9	0♋46.8	26 41.2	5♑42.0	25 48.4	7 52.7	21 58.8	22 12.1	4 36.9	19 55.9	4 32.0	4 40.6
23 M	6 5 26.5	1 44.0	26 38.0	20 48.0	26 54.8	9 2.8	21 48.7	22 15.9	4 33.2	19 53.5	4 30.3	4 39.9
24 T	6 9 23.1	2 41.2	26 34.8	5♒36.0	27 58.1	10 12.7	21 37.8	22 19.4	4 29.5	19 51.1	4 28.7	4 39.2
25 W	6 13 19.6	3 38.4	26 31.6	19 58.7	28 58.2	11 22.6	21 26.3	22 22.8	4 25.9	19 48.8	4 27.1	4 38.5
26 T	6 17 16.2	4 35.6	26 28.5	3♓52.3	29 55.0	12 32.3	21 14.2	22 26.0	4 22.3	19 46.4	4 25.5	4 37.9
27 F	6 21 12.7	5 32.8	26 25.3	17 16.4	0♌48.5	13 42.0	21 1.5	22 29.0	4 18.9	19 44.1	4 23.9	4 37.3
28 S	6 25 9.3	6 30.0	26 22.1	0♈13.0	1 38.5	14 51.6	20 48.2	22 31.8	4 15.4	19 41.7	4 22.2	4 36.7
29 S	6 29 5.9	7 27.2	26 18.9	12 46.1	2 24.9	16 1.1	20 34.4	22 34.5	4 12.1	19 39.4	4 20.6	4 36.2
30 M	6 33 2.4	8 24.4	26 15.7	25 0.6	3 7.5	17 10.6	20 20.1	22 36.9	4 8.8	19 37.1	4 19.0	4 35.7

DECLINATION at NOON

DAY	EPHEMERIS SIDEREAL TIME	☉	☊	☽	☿	♀	♂	♃	♄	♅	♆	♇
1 S	4 38 42.2	22N 3.3	10N41.5	0S33.5	24N54.8	24N34.4	24S22.8	4S52.4	19S19.9	23S12.7	22S14.3	2N49.8
4 W	4 50 31.9	22 26.0	10 38.1	15N44.6	25 22.7	24 13.9	24 32.9	4 44.8	19 17.9	23 12.2	22 14.4	2 49.9
7 S	5 2 21.6	22 45.2	10 34.7	26 21.0	25 27.9	23 47.3	24 44.4	4 37.8	19 15.9	23 11.8	22 14.6	2 49.9
10 T	5 14 11.2	23 0.8	10 31.3	26 45.1	25 13.3	23 14.8	24 57.3	4 31.3	19 14.0	23 11.3	22 14.7	2 49.7
13 F	5 26 0.9	23 12.8	10 27.8	16 14.1	24 41.9	22 36.6	25 11.6	4 25.5	19 12.1	23 10.8	22 14.9	2 49.4
16 M	5 37 50.6	23 21.0	10 24.4	1S19.0	23 57.1	21 52.9	25 27.0	4 20.2	19 10.3	23 10.2	22 15.1	2 49.0
19 T	5 49 40.3	23 25.6	10 21.0	19 39.7	23 1.9	21 4.1	25 43.6	4 15.5	19 8.6	23 9.7	22 15.3	2 48.4
22 S	6 1 29.9	23 26.4	10 17.5	28 0.1	21 59.4	20 10.4	26 0.9	4 11.5	19 6.9	23 9.2	22 15.4	2 47.7
25 W	6 13 19.6	23 23.6	10 14.1	19 15.5	20 52.4	19 12.1	26 18.9	4 8.1	19 5.4	23 8.7	22 15.6	2 46.9
28 S	6 25 9.3	23 17.0	10 10.6	2 2.4	19 43.8	18 9.5	26 37.1	4 5.3	19 4.0	23 8.2	22 15.8	2 46.0

JULY 1986

DAY	EPHEMERIS SIDEREAL TIME	☉	☊	☽	☿	♀	♂	♃	♄	♅	♆	♇
	h m s	° ′	° ′	° ′	° ′	° ′	° ′	° ′	° ′	° ′	° ′	° ′
						LONGITUDE at NOON						
1 T	6 36 59.0	9♋21.7	26♈12.6	7♉ 1.7	3♌46.4	18♌19.9	20♑ 5.2	22♓39.2	4♐ 5.5	19♐34.9	4♑17.4	4♏35.2
2 W	6 40 55.5	10 18.9	26 9.4	18 54.3	4 21.3	19 29.2	19R49.9	22 41.3	4R 2.3	19R32.6	4R15.8	4R34.8
3 T	6 44 52.1	11 16.1	26 6.2	0♊42.8	4 52.2	20 38.3	19 34.2	22 43.1	3 59.2	19 30.4	4 14.2	4 34.4
4 F	6 48 48.6	12 13.3	26 3.0	12 31.2	5 18.8	21 47.4	19 18.1	22 44.8	3 56.2	19 28.2	4 12.6	4 34.0
5 S	6 52 45.2	13 10.5	25 59.9	24 22.4	5 41.1	22 56.3	19 1.7	22 46.3	3 53.3	19 26.0	4 11.0	4 33.6
6 S	6 56 41.8	14 7.8	25 56.7	6♋18.6	5 59.0	24 5.2	18 44.9	22 47.6	3 50.4	19 23.8	4 9.4	4 33.3
7 M	7 0 38.3	15 5.0	25 53.5	18 21.6	6 12.3	25 13.9	18 28.0	22 48.7	3 47.6	19 21.7	4 7.8	4 33.1
8 T	7 4 34.9	16 2.2	25 50.3	0♌32.4	6 21.0	26 22.6	18 10.8	22 49.6	3 44.9	19 19.5	4 6.2	4 32.8
9 W	7 8 31.4	16 59.4	25 47.2	12 51.9	6 25.1	27 31.1	17 53.4	22 50.4	3 42.2	19 17.4	4 4.6	4 32.6
10 T	7 12 28.0	17 56.7	25 44.0	25 21.2	6R24.3	28 39.5	17 36.0	22 50.9	3 39.6	19 15.4	4 3.1	4 32.4
11 F	7 16 24.6	18 53.9	25 40.8	8♍ 1.5	6 18.9	29 47.9	17 18.5	22 51.3	3 37.2	19 13.4	4 1.5	4 32.3
12 S	7 20 21.1	19 51.2	25 37.6	20 54.3	6 8.8	0♍56.1	17 1.0	22 51.4	3 34.8	19 11.4	3 60.0	4 32.2
13 S	7 24 17.7	20 48.4	25 34.5	4♎ 1.8	5 54.0	2 4.2	16 43.5	22R51.3	3 32.5	19 9.4	3 58.5	4 32.2
14 M	7 28 14.2	21 45.6	25 31.3	17 26.3	5 34.7	3 12.1	16 26.1	22 51.1	3 30.3	19 7.5	3 56.9	4 32.1
15 T	7 32 10.8	22 42.8	25 28.1	1♏ 9.9	5 11.2	4 19.9	16 8.8	22 50.6	3 28.1	19 5.5	3 55.4	4 32.1
16 W	7 36 7.3	23 40.1	25 24.9	15 14.1	4 43.6	5 27.6	15 51.7	22 50.0	3 26.0	19 3.7	3 53.9	4D32.2
17 T	7 40 3.9	24 37.3	25 21.8	29 38.5	4 12.4	6 35.2	15 34.8	22 49.1	3 24.1	19 1.8	3 52.4	4 32.2
18 F	7 44 0.5	25 34.5	25 18.6	14♐20.9	3 38.0	7 42.6	15 18.2	22 48.1	3 22.2	18 60.0	3 50.9	4 32.3
19 S	7 47 57.0	26 31.7	25 15.4	29 15.9	3 0.8	8 49.8	15 1.9	22 46.9	3 20.4	18 58.2	3 49.5	4 32.4
20 S	7 51 53.6	27 29.0	25 12.2	14♑15.9	2 21.4	9 57.0	14 45.9	22 45.5	3 18.7	18 56.5	3 48.0	4 32.6
21 M	7 55 50.1	28 26.2	25 9.0	29 11.6	1 40.5	11 3.9	14 30.4	22 43.8	3 17.0	18 54.7	3 46.6	4 32.8
22 T	7 59 46.7	29 23.5	25 5.9	13♒53.6	0 58.8	12 10.8	14 15.2	22 42.0	3 15.5	18 53.1	3 45.1	4 33.0
23 W	8 3 43.2	0♌20.8	25 2.7	28 14.4	0 16.9	13 17.4	14 0.5	22 40.0	3 14.1	18 51.4	3 43.7	4 33.3
24 T	8 7 39.8	1 18.0	24 59.5	12♓ 9.0	29♋35.6	14 23.9	13 46.3	22 37.8	3 12.7	18 49.8	3 42.3	4 33.6
25 F	8 11 36.4	2 15.3	24 56.3	25 35.5	28 55.6	15 30.3	13 32.6	22 35.5	3 11.5	18 48.2	3 41.0	4 33.9
26 S	8 15 32.9	3 12.6	24 53.2	8♈35.1	28 17.8	16 36.5	13 19.4	22 32.9	3 10.3	18 46.7	3 39.6	4 34.3
27 S	8 19 29.5	4 9.9	24 50.0	21 10.7	27 42.7	17 42.5	13 6.9	22 30.1	3 9.2	18 45.2	3 38.3	4 34.7
28 M	8 23 26.0	5 7.3	24 46.8	3♉26.9	27 11.2	18 48.4	12 54.9	22 27.2	3 8.2	18 43.8	3 36.9	4 35.2
29 T	8 27 22.6	6 4.6	24 43.6	15 28.9	26 43.7	19 54.1	12 43.6	22 24.0	3 7.4	18 42.4	3 35.6	4 35.6
30 W	8 31 19.1	7 2.0	24 40.5	27 22.1	26 20.8	20 59.6	12 33.0	22 20.7	3 6.6	18 41.0	3 34.3	4 36.1
31 T	8 35 15.7	7 59.4	24 37.3	9♊11.6	26 3.1	22 4.9	12 23.0	22 17.2	3 5.9	18 39.7	3 33.1	4 36.7
						DECLINATION at NOON						
1 T	6 36 59.0	23N 6.8	10N 7.2	14N40.1	18N36.3	17N 3.0	26S55.3	4S 3.2	19S 2.7	23S 7.7	22S16.0	2N44.9
4 F	6 48 48.6	22 52.9	10 3.7	25 51.3	17 32.7	15 52.8	27 12.9	4 1.8	19 1.5	23 7.2	22 16.2	2 43.7
7 M	7 0 38.3	22 35.4	10 0.3	27 5.4	16 36.2	14 39.2	27 29.8	4 1.1	19 0.5	23 6.7	22 16.4	2 42.4
10 T	7 12 28.0	22 14.4	9 56.8	17 10.9	15 49.6	13 22.6	27 45.5	4 1.1	18 59.6	23 6.2	22 16.6	2 41.0
13 S	7 24 17.7	21 50.0	9 53.3	0 6.4	15 15.6	12 3.4	27 59.6	4 1.8	18 58.9	23 5.7	22 16.8	2 39.5
16 W	7 36 7.3	21 22.2	9 49.9	18S 1.3	14 56.6	10 41.7	28 11.9	4 3.1	18 58.3	23 5.3	22 17.0	2 37.8
19 S	7 47 57.0	20 51.1	9 46.4	27 56.4	14 53.8	9 18.0	28 22.2	4 5.2	18 57.9	23 4.9	22 17.2	2 36.1
22 T	7 59 46.7	20 16.9	9 42.9	21 11.4	15 6.7	7 52.6	28 30.5	4 7.9	18 57.6	23 4.5	22 17.4	2 34.2
25 F	8 11 36.4	19 39.6	9 39.4	3 59.5	15 33.3	6 25.8	28 36.6	4 11.3	18 57.5	23 4.1	22 17.6	2 32.3
28 M	8 23 26.0	18 59.4	9 35.9	13N24.6	16 9.9	4 57.8	28 40.7	4 15.4	18 57.6	23 3.7	22 17.8	2 30.2
31 T	8 35 15.7	18 16.4	9 32.4	25 20.8	16 52.2	3 28.9	28 42.7	4 20.1	18 57.8	23 3.4	22 18.0	2 28.1

AUGUST 1986

DAY	EPHEMERIS SIDEREAL TIME	☉	☊	☽	☿	♀	♂	♃	♄	♅	♆	♇
						LONGITUDE at NOON						
1 F	8 39 12.3	8♌56.9	24♈34.1	21♊ 2.0	25♋50.9	23♍10.1	12♑13.9	22♓13.6	3♐ 5.3	18♐38.4	3♑31.9	4♏37.3
2 S	8 43 8.8	9 54.3	24 30.9	2♋57.0	25R44.6	24 15.1	12R 5.4	22R 9.7	3R 4.8	18R37.2	3R30.6	4 37.9
3 S	8 47 5.4	10 51.7	24 27.7	14 59.6	25 44.4	25 19.9	11 57.7	22 5.7	3 4.4	18 36.0	3 29.4	4 38.6
4 M	8 51 1.9	11 49.2	24 24.6	27 12.0	25D50.6	26 24.5	11 50.8	22 1.5	3 4.1	18 34.9	3 28.2	4 39.2
5 T	8 54 58.5	12 46.7	24 21.4	9♌35.4	26 3.3	27 28.8	11 44.6	21 57.1	3 3.9	18 33.7	3 27.1	4 39.9
6 W	8 58 55.0	13 44.2	24 18.2	22 10.2	26 22.6	28 33.0	11 39.3	21 52.5	3 3.8	18 32.7	3 25.9	4 40.7
7 T	9 2 51.6	14 41.7	24 15.0	4♍56.5	26 48.5	29 36.9	11 34.8	21 47.8	3 3.8	18 31.7	3 24.8	4 41.5
8 F	9 6 48.2	15 39.2	24 11.9	17 54.2	27 21.2	0♎40.7	11 31.2	21 42.9	3D 3.9	18 30.7	3 23.7	4 42.3
9 S	9 10 44.7	16 36.7	24 8.7	1♎ 3.2	28 0.5	1 44.2	11 28.4	21 37.8	3 4.0	18 29.8	3 22.6	4 43.1
10 S	9 14 41.3	17 34.3	24 5.5	14 23.8	28 46.3	2 47.4	11 26.4	21 32.6	3 4.3	18 28.9	3 21.6	4 44.0
11 M	9 18 37.8	18 31.9	24 2.3	27 56.6	29 38.6	3 50.4	11 25.3	21 27.2	3 4.7	18 28.1	3 20.5	4 44.9
12 T	9 22 34.4	19 29.4	23 59.2	11♏42.5	0♌37.3	4 53.2	11 25.0	21 21.7	3 5.2	18 27.3	3 19.5	4 45.8
13 W	9 26 30.9	20 27.0	23 56.0	25 42.0	1 42.1	5 55.7	11D25.6	21 16.0	3 5.7	18 26.5	3 18.6	4 46.8
14 T	9 30 27.5	21 24.6	23 52.8	9♐54.8	2 52.8	6 57.9	11 27.0	21 10.2	3 6.4	18 25.8	3 17.6	4 47.8
15 F	9 34 24.0	22 22.3	23 49.6	24 19.3	4 9.3	7 59.8	11 29.2	21 4.2	3 7.2	18 25.2	3 16.7	4 48.8
16 S	9 38 20.6	23 19.9	23 46.4	8♑52.2	5 31.3	9 1.5	11 32.3	20 58.1	3 8.0	18 24.6	3 15.8	4 49.9
17 S	9 42 17.2	24 17.6	23 43.3	23 28.3	6 58.4	10 2.8	11 36.2	20 51.9	3 9.0	18 24.1	3 14.9	4 51.0
18 M	9 46 13.7	25 15.3	23 40.1	8♒ 1.0	8 30.3	11 3.9	11 41.0	20 45.5	3 10.0	18 23.6	3 14.1	4 52.1
19 T	9 50 10.3	26 13.0	23 36.9	22 23.5	10 6.7	12 4.6	11 46.5	20 39.1	3 11.2	18 23.1	3 13.2	4 53.3
20 W	9 54 6.8	27 10.7	23 33.7	6♓29.5	11 47.1	13 5.0	11 52.9	20 32.5	3 12.4	18 22.7	3 12.4	4 54.5
21 T	9 58 3.4	28 8.4	23 30.6	20 14.3	13 31.2	14 5.1	11 60.0	20 25.7	3 13.8	18 22.4	3 11.7	4 55.7
22 F	10 1 59.9	29 6.3	23 27.4	3♈35.8	15 18.6	15 4.8	12 8.0	20 19.0	3 15.3	18 22.1	3 11.0	4 57.0
23 S	10 5 56.5	0♍ 4.1	23 24.2	16 33.6	17 8.7	16 4.2	12 16.6	20 12.0	3 16.8	18 21.9	3 10.3	4 58.3
24 S	10 9 53.0	1 1.9	23 21.0	29 9.7	19 1.1	17 3.2	12 26.1	20 5.0	3 18.4	18 21.7	3 9.6	4 59.6
25 M	10 13 49.6	1 59.7	23 17.8	11♉27.5	20 55.5	18 1.9	12 36.3	19 57.8	3 20.1	18 21.6	3 9.0	5 1.0
26 T	10 17 46.2	2 57.6	23 14.7	23 31.4	22 51.4	19 0.1	12 47.2	19 50.6	3 22.0	18 21.5	3 8.3	5 2.3
27 W	10 21 42.7	3 55.5	23 11.5	5♊26.4	24 48.4	19 57.9	12 58.9	19 43.3	3 23.9	18 21.4	3 7.7	5 3.7
28 T	10 25 39.3	4 53.5	23 8.3	17 17.6	26 46.2	20 55.4	13 11.2	19 35.9	3 25.9	18 21.4	3 7.2	5 5.2
29 F	10 29 35.8	5 51.5	23 5.1	29 10.1	28 44.4	21 52.4	13 24.3	19 28.4	3 28.0	18D21.5	3 6.6	5 6.6
30 S	10 33 32.4	6 49.5	23 2.0	11♋ 8.2	0♍42.9	22 49.0	13 38.2	19 20.8	3 30.2	18 21.6	3 6.1	5 8.1
31 S	10 37 28.9	7 47.5	22 58.8	23 15.9	2 41.3	23 45.1	13 52.6	19 13.2	3 32.4	18 21.8	3 5.7	5 9.6
						DECLINATION at NOON						
1 F	8 39 12.3	18N 1.4	9N31.3	27N20.5	17N 6.6	2N59.1	28S42.9	4S21.8	18S57.9	23S 3.3	22S18.0	2N27.3
4 M	8 51 1.9	17 14.8	9 27.8	25 38.0	17 48.7	1 29.4	28 42.4	4 27.3	18 58.4	23 3.0	22 18.2	2 25.1
7 T	9 2 51.6	16 25.7	9 24.3	13 12.0	18 24.9	0S 0.4	28 40.1	4 33.4	18 59.0	23 2.7	22 18.4	2 22.8
10 S	9 14 41.3	15 34.2	9 20.8	4S58.8	18 50.2	1 30.3	28 36.3	4 40.1	18 59.8	23 2.5	22 18.6	2 20.4
13 W	9 26 30.9	14 40.5	9 17.3	21 51.8	18 59.8	2 59.7	28 30.9	4 47.3	19 0.8	23 2.3	22 18.8	2 17.9
16 S	9 38 20.6	13 44.6	9 13.8	28 3.8	18 49.3	4 28.5	28 24.3	4 54.9	19 1.9	23 2.2	22 19.0	2 15.4
19 T	9 50 10.3	12 46.9	9 10.2	18 12.6	18 15.2	5 56.4	28 16.4	5 3.0	19 3.2	23 2.1	22 19.1	2 12.8
22 F	10 1 59.9	11 47.2	9 6.7	0 3.6	17 16.1	7 23.2	28 7.3	5 11.5	19 4.7	23 2.0	22 19.3	2 10.1
25 M	10 13 49.6	10 46.0	9 3.2	16N54.0	15 53.1	8 48.4	27 57.2	5 20.3	19 6.3	23 2.0	22 19.5	2 7.4
28 T	10 25 39.3	9 43.2	8 59.7	27 2.8	14 9.6	10 12.0	27 46.0	5 29.3	19 8.0	23 2.0	22 19.7	2 4.7
31 S	10 37 28.9	8 38.9	8 56.1	26 29.9	12 10.1	11 33.7	27 33.8	5 38.6	19 10.0	23 2.0	22 19.8	2 1.9

SEPTEMBER 1986

DAY	EPHEMERIS SIDEREAL TIME	☉	☊	☾	☿	♀	♂	♃	♄	♅	♆	♇
	h m s	° ′	° ′	° ′	° ′	° ′	° ′	° ′	° ′	° ′	° ′	° ′
						LONGITUDE at NOON						
1 M	10 41 25.5	8 ♍ 45.6	22 ♈ 55.6	5 ♌ 36.2	4 ♍ 39.4	24 ♎ 40.8	14 ♑ 7.8	19 ♓ 5.5	3 ♐ 34.8	18 ♐ 22.0	3 ♑ 5.2	5 ♏ 11.1
2 T	10 45 22.0	9 43.7	22 52.4	18 11.0	6 37.0	25 35.9	14 23.7	18 R 57.8	3 37.3	18 22.2	3 R 4.8	5 12.7
3 W	10 49 18.6	10 41.8	22 49.3	1 ♍ 1.2	8 34.0	26 30.6	14 40.2	18 50.0	3 39.8	18 22.6	3 4.4	5 14.3
4 T	10 53 15.1	11 39.9	22 46.1	14 6.6	10 30.2	27 24.8	14 57.3	18 42.1	3 42.5	18 22.9	3 4.1	5 15.9
5 F	10 57 11.7	12 38.1	22 42.9	27 26.2	12 25.6	28 18.4	15 15.1	18 34.3	3 45.2	18 23.3	3 3.8	5 17.6
6 S	11 1 8.3	13 36.3	22 39.7	10 ♎ 58.5	14 20.1	29 11.4	15 33.6	18 26.4	3 48.0	18 23.8	3 3.5	5 19.3
7 S	11 5 4.8	14 34.6	22 36.5	24 41.6	16 13.6	0 ♏ 3.9	15 52.6	18 18.4	3 50.9	18 24.3	3 3.2	5 21.0
8 M	11 9 1.4	15 32.8	22 33.4	8 ♏ 33.8	18 6.0	0 55.8	16 12.3	18 10.5	3 53.9	18 24.9	3 3.0	5 22.7
9 T	11 12 57.9	16 31.1	22 30.2	22 33.5	19 57.3	1 47.0	16 32.5	18 2.5	3 57.0	18 25.5	3 2.8	5 24.4
10 W	11 16 54.5	17 29.4	22 27.0	6 ♐ 39.4	21 47.6	2 37.5	16 53.3	17 54.5	4 0.2	18 26.2	3 2.7	5 26.2
11 T	11 20 51.0	18 27.8	22 23.8	20 49.8	23 36.7	3 27.4	17 14.7	17 46.6	4 3.5	18 27.0	3 2.6	5 28.0
12 F	11 24 47.6	19 26.2	22 20.7	5 ♑ 3.0	25 24.8	4 16.6	17 36.7	17 38.6	4 6.9	18 27.8	3 2.5	5 29.9
13 S	11 28 44.1	20 24.6	22 17.5	19 16.7	27 11.7	5 5.1	17 59.2	17 30.7	4 10.3	18 28.6	3 2.5	5 31.7
14 S	11 32 40.7	21 23.0	22 14.3	3 ♒ 27.7	28 57.5	5 52.7	18 22.2	17 22.7	4 13.8	18 29.5	3 2.4	5 33.6
15 M	11 36 37.2	22 21.4	22 11.1	17 32.7	0 ♎ 42.2	6 39.6	18 45.7	17 14.8	4 17.4	18 30.4	3 2.4	5 35.5
16 T	11 40 33.8	23 19.9	22 7.9	1 ♓ 27.8	2 25.8	7 25.6	19 9.7	17 6.9	4 21.1	18 31.4	3 D 2.5	5 37.4
17 W	11 44 30.3	24 18.4	22 4.8	15 9.4	4 8.4	8 10.7	19 34.1	16 59.1	4 24.8	18 32.5	3 2.6	5 39.3
18 T	11 48 26.9	25 16.9	22 1.6	28 34.8	5 49.9	8 54.9	19 59.1	16 51.3	4 28.6	18 33.5	3 2.7	5 41.3
19 F	11 52 23.4	26 15.5	21 58.4	11 ♈ 42.1	7 30.3	9 38.2	20 24.5	16 43.5	4 32.6	18 34.7	3 2.8	5 43.2
20 S	11 56 20.0	27 14.1	21 55.2	24 31.1	9 9.7	10 20.6	20 50.3	16 35.8	4 36.6	18 35.9	3 3.0	5 45.2
21 S	12 0 16.6	28 12.7	21 52.1	7 ♉ 2.6	10 48.2	11 1.9	21 16.6	16 28.1	4 40.6	18 37.1	3 3.2	5 47.2
22 M	12 4 13.1	29 11.4	21 48.9	19 18.8	12 25.6	11 42.2	21 43.3	16 20.5	4 44.8	18 38.4	3 3.4	5 49.3
23 T	12 8 9.7	0 ♎ 10.1	21 45.7	1 ♊ 22.8	14 2.1	12 21.3	22 10.5	16 13.0	4 49.0	18 39.7	3 3.7	5 51.3
24 W	12 12 6.2	1 8.8	21 42.5	13 18.5	15 37.6	12 59.4	22 38.0	16 5.6	4 53.3	18 41.1	3 4.0	5 53.4
25 T	12 16 2.8	2 7.6	21 39.3	25 10.5	17 12.2	13 36.3	23 6.0	15 58.2	4 57.7	18 42.5	3 4.3	5 55.5
26 F	12 19 59.3	3 6.4	21 36.2	7 ♋ 3.5	18 45.9	14 11.9	23 34.3	15 50.9	5 2.1	18 44.0	3 4.7	5 57.6
27 S	12 23 55.9	4 5.3	21 33.0	19 2.3	20 18.6	14 46.3	24 3.0	15 43.7	5 6.6	18 45.5	3 5.1	5 59.7
28 S	12 27 52.4	5 4.2	21 29.8	1 ♌ 11.3	21 50.5	15 19.4	24 32.1	15 36.6	5 11.2	18 47.1	3 5.5	6 1.9
29 M	12 31 49.0	6 3.1	21 26.6	13 34.6	23 21.4	15 51.1	25 1.6	15 29.6	5 15.9	18 48.7	3 6.0	6 4.0
30 T	12 35 45.5	7 2.1	21 23.5	26 15.3	24 51.4	16 21.4	25 31.4	15 22.7	5 20.6	18 50.4	3 6.5	6 6.2
						DECLINATION at NOON						
1 M	10 41 25.5	8 N 17.2	8 N 54.9	23 N 42.4	11 N 27.6	12 S 0.4	27 S 29.5	5 S 41.7	19 S 10.6	23 S 2.0	22 S 19.9	2 N 0.9
4 T	10 53 15.1	7 11.4	8 51.4	9 8.4	9 14.1	13 19.0	27 15.9	5 51.2	19 12.7	23 2.1	22 20.0	1 58.1
7 S	11 5 4.8	6 4.4	8 47.9	9 S 51.4	6 54.9	14 35.0	27 1.2	6 0.7	19 14.9	23 2.3	22 20.2	1 55.3
10 W	11 16 54.5	4 56.6	8 44.3	25 4.6	4 32.9	15 48.2	26 45.4	6 10.3	19 17.3	23 2.4	22 20.3	1 52.4
13 S	11 28 44.1	3 48.0	8 40.8	27 12.3	2 10.5	16 58.1	26 28.4	6 19.7	19 19.8	23 2.7	22 20.5	1 49.5
16 T	11 40 33.8	2 38.9	8 37.2	14 40.0	0 S 10.5	18 4.6	26 10.3	6 29.1	19 22.4	23 2.9	22 20.6	1 46.6
19 F	11 52 23.4	1 29.3	8 33.7	3 N 51.2	2 29.0	19 7.2	25 51.0	6 38.2	19 25.1	23 3.2	22 20.7	1 43.7
22 M	12 4 13.1	0 19.3	8 30.1	19 57.7	4 44.0	20 5.7	25 30.5	6 47.1	19 27.9	23 3.5	22 20.8	1 40.9
25 T	12 16 2.8	0 S 50.7	8 26.6	28 5.3	6 54.6	20 59.6	25 8.7	6 55.7	19 30.8	23 3.9	22 21.0	1 38.0
28 S	12 27 52.4	2 0.9	8 23.0	24 56.7	9 0.3	21 48.7	24 45.6	7 3.9	19 33.7	23 4.3	22 21.1	1 35.1

OCTOBER 1986

DAY	EPHEMERIS SIDEREAL TIME	☉	☊	☾	☿	♀	♂	♃	♄	♅	♆	♇
						LONGITUDE at NOON						
1 W	12 39 42.1	8 ♎ 1.1	21 ♈ 20.3	9 ♍ 15.6	26 ♎ 20.6	16 ♏ 50.2	26 ♑ 1.6	15 ♓ 15.9	5 ♐ 25.4	18 ♐ 52.1	3 ♑ 7.1	6 ♏ 8.4
2 T	12 43 38.6	9 0.1	21 17.1	22 36.1	27 48.8	17 17.4	26 32.2	15 R 9.3	5 30.3	18 53.8	3 7.6	6 10.6
3 F	12 47 35.2	9 59.2	21 13.9	6 ♎ 16.0	29 16.1	17 43.2	27 3.1	15 2.8	5 35.3	18 55.7	3 8.3	6 12.9
4 S	12 51 31.8	10 58.3	21 10.7	20 12.9	0 ♏ 42.5	18 7.2	27 34.3	14 56.3	5 40.3	18 57.5	3 8.9	6 15.1
5 S	12 55 28.3	11 57.5	21 7.6	4 ♏ 23.4	2 7.9	18 29.5	28 5.8	14 50.1	5 45.4	18 59.4	3 9.6	6 17.4
6 M	12 59 24.9	12 56.6	21 4.4	18 43.0	3 32.4	18 50.0	28 37.7	14 43.9	5 50.5	19 1.4	3 10.3	6 19.6
7 T	13 3 21.4	13 55.8	21 1.2	3 ♐ 7.1	4 55.9	19 8.7	29 9.9	14 37.9	5 55.7	19 3.4	3 11.0	6 21.9
8 W	13 7 18.0	14 55.1	20 58.0	17 31.1	6 18.3	19 25.4	29 42.3	14 32.0	6 1.0	19 5.4	3 11.8	6 24.2
9 T	13 11 14.5	15 54.3	20 54.9	1 ♑ 51.2	7 39.7	19 40.2	0 ♒ 15.1	14 26.3	6 6.3	19 7.5	3 12.6	6 26.5
10 F	13 15 11.1	16 53.6	20 51.7	16 4.4	9 0.0	19 52.9	0 48.2	14 20.8	6 11.7	19 9.6	3 13.4	6 28.8
11 S	13 19 7.6	17 52.9	20 48.5	0 ♒ 8.2	10 19.1	20 3.5	1 21.5	14 15.4	6 17.1	19 11.8	3 14.3	6 31.1
12 S	13 23 4.2	18 52.3	20 45.3	14 1.1	11 37.0	20 12.0	1 55.1	14 10.1	6 22.7	19 14.0	3 15.1	6 33.5
13 M	13 27 0.7	19 51.7	20 42.1	27 42.1	12 53.6	20 18.2	2 28.9	14 5.0	6 28.2	19 16.2	3 16.1	6 35.8
14 T	13 30 57.3	20 51.1	20 39.0	11 ♓ 10.3	14 8.8	20 22.1	3 3.0	14 0.1	6 33.8	19 18.5	3 17.0	6 38.2
15 W	13 34 53.8	21 50.5	20 35.8	24 25.2	15 22.5	20 23.7	3 37.4	13 55.4	6 39.5	19 20.8	3 18.0	6 40.5
16 T	13 38 50.4	22 50.0	20 32.6	7 ♈ 26.5	16 34.7	20 R 23.0	4 12.0	13 50.8	6 45.2	19 23.2	3 19.0	6 42.9
17 F	13 42 47.0	23 49.5	20 29.4	20 14.2	17 45.1	20 19.9	4 46.8	13 46.4	6 51.0	19 25.6	3 20.1	6 45.3
18 S	13 46 43.5	24 49.0	20 26.3	2 ♉ 48.6	18 53.6	20 14.3	5 21.8	13 42.2	6 56.9	19 28.0	3 21.1	6 47.6
19 S	13 50 40.1	25 48.6	20 23.1	15 10.3	20 0.1	20 6.3	5 57.1	13 38.1	7 2.8	19 30.5	3 22.2	6 50.0
20 M	13 54 36.6	26 48.2	20 19.9	27 20.9	21 4.3	19 56.0	6 32.5	13 34.3	7 8.7	19 33.0	3 23.4	6 52.4
21 T	13 58 33.2	27 47.8	20 16.7	9 ♊ 22.3	22 6.1	19 43.1	7 8.2	13 30.6	7 14.7	19 35.6	3 24.5	6 54.8
22 W	14 2 29.7	28 47.5	20 13.5	21 17.0	23 5.2	19 28.0	7 44.1	13 27.1	7 20.7	19 38.2	3 25.7	6 57.2
23 T	14 6 26.3	29 47.2	20 10.4	3 ♋ 8.6	24 1.4	19 10.4	8 20.1	13 23.8	7 26.8	19 40.8	3 27.0	6 59.6
24 F	14 10 22.8	0 ♏ 47.0	20 7.2	15 0.8	24 54.3	18 50.7	8 56.5	13 20.8	7 33.0	19 43.6	3 28.3	7 2.1
25 S	14 14 19.4	1 46.8	20 4.0	26 57.8	25 43.5	18 28.6	9 32.9	13 17.8	7 39.2	19 46.3	3 29.5	7 4.5
26 S	14 18 16.0	2 46.6	20 0.8	9 ♌ 4.4	26 28.6	18 4.5	10 9.6	13 15.1	7 45.4	19 49.0	3 30.8	7 6.9
27 M	14 22 12.5	3 46.5	19 57.7	21 25.1	27 9.3	17 38.3	10 46.4	13 12.6	7 51.7	19 51.8	3 32.2	7 9.4
28 T	14 26 9.1	4 46.4	19 54.5	4 ♍ 4.3	27 45.0	17 10.3	11 23.4	13 10.3	7 58.0	19 54.6	3 33.5	7 11.8
29 W	14 30 5.6	5 46.3	19 51.3	17 5.4	28 15.3	16 40.5	12 0.6	13 8.1	8 4.3	19 57.4	3 34.9	7 14.2
30 T	14 34 2.2	6 46.3	19 48.1	0 ♎ 31.0	28 39.5	16 9.2	12 37.9	13 6.2	8 10.7	20 0.3	3 36.4	7 16.7
31 F	14 37 58.7	7 46.3	19 45.0	14 21.6	28 57.0	15 36.5	13 15.4	13 4.5	8 17.1	20 3.2	3 37.8	7 19.1
						DECLINATION at NOON						
1 W	12 39 42.1	3 S 10.9	8 N 19.4	11 N 20.6	11 S 0.3	22 S 32.5	24 S 21.1	7 S 11.7	19 S 36.8	23 S 4.7	22 S 21.2	1 N 32.3
4 S	12 51 31.8	4 20.6	8 15.8	7 S 50.8	12 54.1	23 10.3	23 55.3	7 19.1	19 39.9	23 5.2	22 21.2	1 29.5
7 T	13 3 21.4	5 29.8	8 12.3	24 16.3	14 41.1	23 41.7	23 28.1	7 25.9	19 43.1	23 5.7	22 21.3	1 26.7
10 F	13 15 11.1	6 38.3	8 8.7	27 42.0	16 20.4	24 5.7	22 59.5	7 32.2	19 46.4	23 6.2	22 21.4	1 24.0
13 M	13 27 0.7	7 46.1	8 5.1	16 14.7	17 51.4	24 21.5	22 29.4	7 37.8	19 49.6	23 6.8	22 21.5	1 21.3
16 T	13 38 50.4	8 52.9	8 1.5	1 N 49.3	19 12.9	24 28.1	21 58.0	7 42.9	19 53.0	23 7.3	22 21.5	1 18.6
19 S	13 50 40.1	9 58.5	7 57.9	18 28.1	20 23.9	24 24.5	21 25.2	7 47.3	19 56.3	23 7.9	22 21.6	1 16.1
22 W	14 2 29.7	11 2.8	7 54.3	27 44.3	21 22.7	24 9.6	20 51.0	7 51.0	19 59.7	23 8.5	22 21.6	1 13.5
25 S	14 14 19.4	12 5.7	7 50.8	25 54.6	22 7.3	23 42.9	20 15.5	7 54.1	20 3.1	23 9.2	22 21.6	1 11.1
28 T	14 26 9.1	13 6.9	7 47.2	13 35.9	22 35.0	23 4.0	19 38.6	7 56.4	20 6.5	23 9.8	22 21.6	1 8.7
31 F	14 37 58.7	14 6.2	7 43.5	5 S 6.6	22 42.0	22 13.4	19 0.4	7 58.1	20 9.9	23 10.5	22 21.6	1 6.3

NOVEMBER 1986

LONGITUDE at NOON

DAY	EPHEMERIS SIDEREAL TIME	☉	☊	☽	☿	♀	♂	♃	♄	♅	♆	♇
	h m s	° ′	° ′	° ′	° ′	° ′	° ′	° ′	° ′	° ′	° ′	° ′
1 S	14 41 55.3	8♏46.3	19♈41.8	28♎35.7	29♏ 7.2	15♏ 2.6	13♒53.1	13♓ 2.9	8♐23.6	20♐ 6.2	3♑39.3	7♏21.5
2 S	14 45 51.8	9 46.4	19 38.6	13♏ 9.2	29 9.5	14R27.7	14 31.0	13R 1.6	8 30.1	20 9.1	3 40.8	7 23.9
3 M	14 49 48.4	10 46.5	19 35.4	27 56.2	29R 3.3	13 52.1	15 8.9	13 0.5	8 36.7	20 12.1	3 42.3	7 26.4
4 T	14 53 45.0	11 46.6	19 32.2	12♐48.8	28 47.9	13 15.9	15 47.1	12 59.6	8 43.3	20 15.2	3 43.8	7 28.8
5 W	14 57 41.5	12 46.8	19 29.1	27 38.9	28 23.1	12 39.5	16 25.4	12 58.9	8 49.9	20 18.2	3 45.4	7 31.2
6 T	15 1 38.1	13 47.0	19 25.9	12♑19.4	27 48.5	12 3.0	17 3.8	12 58.4	8 56.5	20 21.3	3 47.0	7 33.6
7 F	15 5 34.6	14 47.2	19 22.7	26 44.6	27 4.2	11 26.7	17 42.4	12 58.1	9 3.2	20 24.4	3 48.6	7 36.1
8 S	15 9 31.2	15 47.4	19 19.5	10♒51.2	26 10.5	10 50.9	18 21.1	12 58.0	9 9.9	20 27.6	3 50.3	7 38.5
9 S	15 13 27.7	16 47.7	19 16.4	24 37.9	25 8.1	10 15.8	18 60.0	12D58.2	9 16.6	20 30.8	3 52.0	7 40.9
10 M	15 17 24.3	17 47.9	19 13.2	8♓ 5.2	23 58.3	9 41.6	19 38.9	12 58.5	9 23.4	20 34.0	3 53.7	7 43.3
11 T	15 21 20.9	18 48.2	19 10.0	21 14.5	22 42.8	9 8.6	20 18.0	12 59.0	9 30.2	20 37.2	3 55.4	7 45.7
12 W	15 25 17.4	19 48.6	19 6.8	4♈ 8.0	21 23.7	8 37.0	20 57.2	12 59.8	9 37.0	20 40.4	3 57.1	7 48.1
13 T	15 29 14.0	20 48.9	19 3.7	16 47.9	20 3.3	8 6.9	21 36.5	13 0.7	9 43.9	20 43.7	3 58.9	7 50.4
14 F	15 33 10.5	21 49.4	19 0.5	29 16.1	18 44.5	7 38.6	22 16.0	13 1.9	9 50.8	20 47.0	4 0.7	7 52.9
15 S	15 37 7.1	22 49.8	18 57.3	11♉34.3	17 29.6	7 12.1	22 55.5	13 3.3	9 57.7	20 50.3	4 2.5	7 55.2
16 S	15 41 3.6	23 50.2	18 54.1	23 44.1	16 21.1	6 47.7	23 35.1	13 4.9	10 4.6	20 53.7	4 4.3	7 57.6
17 M	15 45 0.2	24 50.7	18 50.9	5♊46.8	15 21.1	6 25.5	24 14.8	13 6.6	10 11.5	20 57.0	4 6.2	7 59.9
18 T	15 48 56.7	25 51.1	18 47.8	17 43.9	14 31.1	6 5.6	24 54.6	13 8.6	10 18.5	21 0.4	4 8.1	8 2.3
19 W	15 52 53.3	26 51.6	18 44.6	29 37.0	13 52.2	5 48.0	25 34.5	13 10.8	10 25.4	21 3.8	4 9.9	8 4.6
20 T	15 56 49.9	27 52.2	18 41.4	11♋28.1	13 24.9	5 32.8	26 14.5	13 13.1	10 32.4	21 7.2	4 11.8	8 6.9
21 F	16 0 46.4	28 52.8	18 38.2	23 20.0	13 9.3	5 20.0	26 54.5	13 15.7	10 39.4	21 10.7	4 13.8	8 9.3
22 S	16 4 43.0	29 53.4	18 35.1	5♌15.9	13 5.2	5 9.8	27 34.7	13 18.4	10 46.5	21 14.1	4 15.7	8 11.6
23 S	16 8 39.5	0♐54.0	18 31.9	17 19.7	13D11.9	5 2.0	28 14.9	13 21.4	10 53.5	21 17.6	4 17.7	8 13.8
24 M	16 12 36.1	1 54.6	18 28.7	29 35.8	13 28.8	4 56.8	28 55.2	13 24.6	11 0.5	21 21.1	4 19.6	8 16.1
25 T	16 16 32.7	2 55.3	18 25.5	12♍ 8.8	13 54.9	4 54.1	29 35.6	13 27.9	11 7.6	21 24.6	4 21.6	8 18.4
26 W	16 20 29.2	3 56.0	18 22.4	25 3.2	14 29.6	4 53.8	0♓16.1	13 31.5	11 14.7	21 28.1	4 23.6	8 20.6
27 T	16 24 25.8	4 56.7	18 19.2	8♎23.1	15 11.7	4D55.9	0 56.6	13 35.2	11 21.8	21 31.6	4 25.7	8 22.9
28 F	16 28 22.3	5 57.5	18 16.0	22 11.1	16 0.5	5 0.5	1 37.2	13 39.1	11 28.8	21 35.1	4 27.7	8 25.1
29 S	16 32 18.9	6 58.3	18 12.8	6♏27.5	16 55.2	5 7.4	2 17.9	13 43.2	11 35.9	21 38.7	4 29.8	8 27.3
30 S	16 36 15.4	7 59.1	18 9.7	21 9.9	17 55.0	5 16.5	2 58.7	13 47.6	11 43.0	21 42.3	4 31.8	8 29.5

DECLINATION at NOON

DAY	EPHEMERIS SIDEREAL TIME	☉	☊	☽	☿	♀	♂	♃	♄	♅	♆	♇
1 S	14 41 55.3	14S25.6	7N42.4	11S38.2	22S38.9	21S54.2	18S47.4	7S58.4	20S11.0	23S10.7	22S21.6	1N 5.6
4 T	14 53 45.0	15 22.2	7 38.7	26 26.3	22 10.1	20 50.4	18 7.6	7 59.1	20 14.4	23 11.4	22 21.6	1 3.4
7 F	15 5 34.6	16 16.6	7 35.1	25 55.1	21 7.9	19 39.8	17 26.4	7 59.1	20 17.8	23 12.1	22 21.6	1 1.2
10 M	15 17 24.3	17 8.4	7 31.5	11 49.6	19 31.3	18 25.8	16 44.1	7 58.3	20 21.2	23 12.8	22 21.5	0 59.2
13 T	15 29 14.0	17 57.7	7 27.9	6N16.2	17 31.5	17 12.1	16 0.7	7 56.8	20 24.5	23 13.5	22 21.5	0 57.3
16 S	15 41 3.6	18 44.1	7 24.3	21 27.4	15 34.7	16 2.3	15 16.2	7 54.6	20 27.8	23 14.2	22 21.4	0 55.4
19 W	15 52 53.3	19 27.5	7 20.7	28 16.5	14 9.8	14 59.3	14 30.6	7 51.7	20 31.1	23 14.9	22 21.3	0 53.6
22 S	16 4 43.0	20 7.8	7 17.1	23 47.0	13 31.4	14 5.4	13 44.2	7 48.1	20 34.3	23 15.6	22 21.2	0 52.0
25 T	16 16 32.7	20 44.8	7 13.4	9 56.2	13 37.3	13 21.5	12 56.8	7 43.8	20 37.4	23 16.3	22 21.1	0 50.5
28 F	16 28 22.3	21 18.3	7 9.8	8S49.2	14 16.4	12 48.3	12 8.5	7 38.8	20 40.5	23 17.0	22 21.0	0 49.0

DECEMBER 1986

LONGITUDE at NOON

DAY	EPHEMERIS SIDEREAL TIME	☉	☊	☽	☿	♀	♂	♃	♄	♅	♆	♇
1 M	16 40 12.0	8♐59.9	18♈ 6.5	6♐12.3	18♏59.3	5♏27.9	3♓39.5	13♓52.1	11♐50.2	21♐45.8	4♑33.9	8♏31.7
2 T	16 44 8.6	10 0.8	18 3.3	21 25.8	20 7.5	5 41.5	4 20.4	13 56.7	11 57.3	21 49.4	4 36.0	8 33.8
3 W	16 48 5.1	11 1.6	18 0.1	6♑39.8	21 19.0	5 57.2	5 1.3	14 1.6	12 4.4	21 53.0	4 38.1	8 35.9
4 T	16 52 1.7	12 2.5	17 56.9	21 43.4	22 33.4	6 14.9	5 42.3	14 6.7	12 11.5	21 56.6	4 40.3	8 38.1
5 F	16 55 58.2	13 3.5	17 53.8	6♒28.0	23 50.3	6 34.7	6 23.5	14 12.0	12 18.7	22 0.3	4 42.4	8 40.2
6 S	16 59 54.8	14 4.4	17 50.6	20 47.9	25 9.3	6 56.3	7 4.6	14 17.4	12 25.8	22 3.9	4 44.6	8 42.3
7 S	17 3 51.4	15 5.3	17 47.4	4♓40.8	26 30.1	7 19.8	7 45.8	14 23.0	12 32.9	22 7.5	4 46.7	8 44.4
8 M	17 7 47.9	16 6.3	17 44.2	18 7.2	27 52.5	7 45.1	8 27.0	14 28.8	12 40.0	22 11.2	4 48.9	8 46.4
9 T	17 11 44.5	17 7.2	17 41.1	1♈ 9.9	29 16.2	8 12.1	9 8.3	14 34.7	12 47.1	22 14.8	4 51.1	8 48.4
10 W	17 15 41.0	18 8.2	17 37.9	13 52.4	0♐41.1	8 40.8	9 49.6	14 40.8	12 54.2	22 18.5	4 53.3	8 50.4
11 T	17 19 37.6	19 9.1	17 34.7	26 19.0	2 7.0	9 11.1	10 31.0	14 47.1	13 1.3	22 22.1	4 55.5	8 52.4
12 F	17 23 34.1	20 10.1	17 31.5	8♉33.3	3 33.8	9 43.0	11 12.4	14 53.6	13 8.4	22 25.7	4 57.7	8 54.4
13 S	17 27 30.7	21 11.1	17 28.4	20 38.8	5 1.2	10 16.3	11 53.8	15 0.2	13 15.4	22 29.4	4 59.9	8 56.3
14 S	17 31 27.3	22 12.1	17 25.2	2♊38.3	6 29.4	10 51.2	12 35.3	15 7.0	13 22.5	22 33.0	5 2.1	8 58.2
15 M	17 35 23.8	23 13.1	17 22.0	14 33.9	7 58.1	11 27.4	13 16.8	15 14.0	13 29.6	22 36.7	5 4.4	9 0.1
16 T	17 39 20.4	24 14.1	17 18.8	26 27.2	9 27.3	12 4.9	13 58.3	15 21.1	13 36.6	22 40.3	5 6.6	9 2.0
17 W	17 43 16.9	25 15.2	17 15.7	8♋19.5	10 56.9	12 43.8	14 39.8	15 28.4	13 43.6	22 44.0	5 8.8	9 3.8
18 T	17 47 13.5	26 16.2	17 12.5	20 12.2	12 27.0	13 23.9	15 21.4	15 35.8	13 50.6	22 47.6	5 11.1	9 5.7
19 F	17 51 10.1	27 17.3	17 9.3	2♌ 6.9	13 57.4	14 5.2	16 3.0	15 43.4	13 57.6	22 51.3	5 13.3	9 7.5
20 S	17 55 6.6	28 18.3	17 6.1	14 5.5	15 28.1	14 47.6	16 44.7	15 51.2	14 4.6	22 54.9	5 15.6	9 9.2
21 S	17 59 3.2	29 19.4	17 2.9	26 10.8	16 59.1	15 31.2	17 26.4	15 59.1	14 11.6	22 58.5	5 17.8	9 11.0
22 M	18 2 59.7	0♑20.5	16 59.8	8♍26.1	18 30.4	16 15.8	18 8.0	16 7.1	14 18.5	23 2.2	5 20.1	9 12.7
23 T	18 6 56.3	1 21.6	16 56.6	20 55.3	20 2.0	17 1.4	18 49.8	16 15.3	14 25.4	23 5.8	5 22.4	9 14.4
24 W	18 10 52.9	2 22.8	16 53.4	3♎43.0	21 33.9	17 48.1	19 31.5	16 23.7	14 32.3	23 9.4	5 24.6	9 16.0
25 T	18 14 49.4	3 23.9	16 50.2	16 53.4	23 6.0	18 35.6	20 13.2	16 32.1	14 39.2	23 13.0	5 26.9	9 17.7
26 F	18 18 46.0	4 25.1	16 47.1	0♏30.5	24 38.5	19 24.1	20 55.1	16 40.8	14 46.1	23 16.7	5 29.2	9 19.3
27 S	18 22 42.5	5 26.2	16 43.9	14 36.2	26 11.1	20 13.5	21 36.9	16 49.6	14 52.9	23 20.3	5 31.5	9 20.9
28 S	18 26 39.1	6 27.4	16 40.7	29 10.3	27 44.1	21 3.6	22 18.7	16 58.5	14 59.7	23 23.9	5 33.8	9 22.5
29 M	18 30 35.6	7 28.5	16 37.5	14♐ 9.1	29 17.3	21 54.6	23 0.5	17 7.6	15 6.5	23 27.4	5 36.0	9 24.0
30 T	18 34 32.2	8 29.7	16 34.4	29 24.9	0♑50.7	22 46.3	23 42.4	17 16.8	15 13.3	23 31.0	5 38.3	9 25.5
31 W	18 38 28.8	9 30.9	16 31.2	14♑47.0	2 24.5	23 38.8	24 24.3	17 26.1	15 20.0	23 34.5	5 40.6	9 27.0

DECLINATION at NOON

DAY	EPHEMERIS SIDEREAL TIME	☉	☊	☽	☿	♀	♂	♃	♄	♅	♆	♇
1 M	16 40 12.0	21S48.2	7N 6.2	24S59.7	15S16.8	12S25.4	11S19.5	7S33.2	20S43.6	23S17.7	22S20.8	0N47.7
4 T	16 52 1.7	22 14.3	7 2.5	26 43.2	16 28.7	12 12.3	10 29.7	7 27.0	20 46.5	23 18.4	22 20.7	0 46.5
7 S	17 3 51.4	22 36.6	6 58.9	13 8.0	17 45.0	12 8.3	9 39.2	7 20.1	20 49.4	23 19.1	22 20.5	0 45.4
10 W	17 15 41.0	22 54.8	6 55.3	5N 2.0	19 0.9	12 12.3	8 48.2	7 12.6	20 52.2	23 19.7	22 20.3	0 44.5
13 S	17 27 30.7	23 9.0	6 51.6	20 28.4	20 12.9	12 23.5	7 56.6	7 4.5	20 55.0	23 20.4	22 20.1	0 43.6
16 T	17 39 20.4	23 19.0	6 48.0	28 3.1	21 19.0	12 40.8	7 4.6	6 55.8	20 57.7	23 21.0	22 19.9	0 42.9
19 F	17 51 10.1	23 24.9	6 44.3	24 26.1	22 17.3	13 3.4	6 12.1	6 46.6	21 0.2	23 21.6	22 19.7	0 42.3
22 M	18 2 59.7	23 26.6	6 40.7	11 21.9	23 6.6	13 30.3	5 19.4	6 36.8	21 2.7	23 22.3	22 19.5	0 41.9
25 T	18 14 49.4	23 24.0	6 37.0	6S35.0	23 46.1	14 0.6	4 26.3	6 26.6	21 5.1	23 22.8	22 19.2	0 41.5
28 S	18 26 39.1	23 17.1	6 33.4	23 14.5	24 14.9	14 33.5	3 33.1	6 15.8	21 7.4	23 23.4	22 19.0	0 41.3
31 W	18 38 28.8	23 6.1	6 29.7	27 35.3	24 32.4	15 8.1	2 39.7	6 4.5	21 9.6	23 24.0	22 18.7	0 41.2

JANUARY 1987

LONGITUDE at NOON

DAY	EPHEMERIS SIDEREAL TIME h m s	☉ ° ′	☊ ° ′	☽ ° ′	☿ ° ′	♀ ° ′	♂ ° ′	♃ ° ′	♄ ° ′	♅ ° ′	♆ ° ′	♇ ° ′
1 T	18 42 25.3	10♑32.1	16♈28.0	0♒ 3.6	3♑58.6	24♏31.9	25♓ 6.2	17♓35.6	15♐26.7	23♐38.1	5♑42.8	9♏28.4
2 F	18 46 21.9	11 33.3	16 24.8	15 3.3	5 33.0	25 25.7	25 48.1	17 45.2	15 33.3	23 41.6	5 45.1	9 29.8
3 S	18 50 18.4	12 34.4	16 21.7	29 38.1	7 7.7	26 20.2	26 30.0	17 54.9	15 39.9	23 45.1	5 47.4	9 31.2
4 S	18 54 15.0	13 35.6	16 18.5	13♓43.4	8 42.8	27 15.3	27 11.9	18 4.7	15 46.5	23 48.6	5 49.6	9 32.5
5 M	18 58 11.6	14 36.8	16 15.3	27 18.4	10 18.2	28 11.0	27 53.8	18 14.7	15 53.1	23 52.1	5 51.9	9 33.8
6 T	19 2 8.1	15 37.9	16 12.1	10♈25.3	11 54.0	29 7.3	28 35.8	18 24.8	15 59.6	23 55.5	5 54.1	9 35.1
7 W	19 6 4.7	16 39.1	16 9.0	23 8.1	13 30.1	0♐ 4.1	29 17.7	18 35.0	16 6.0	23 59.0	5 56.4	9 36.4
8 T	19 10 1.2	17 40.2	16 5.8	5♉31.5	15 6.7	1 1.4	29 59.7	18 45.4	16 12.5	24 2.4	5 58.6	9 37.6
9 F	19 13 57.8	18 41.4	16 2.6	17 40.6	16 43.7	1 59.3	0♈41.6	18 55.8	16 18.9	24 5.8	6 0.8	9 38.8
10 S	19 17 54.4	19 42.5	15 59.4	29 40.0	18 21.1	2 57.7	1 23.6	19 6.4	16 25.2	24 9.2	6 3.0	9 39.9
11 S	19 21 50.9	20 43.6	15 56.2	11♊33.7	19 58.9	3 56.6	2 5.5	19 17.0	16 31.5	24 12.6	6 5.3	9 41.0
12 M	19 25 47.5	21 44.7	15 53.1	23 25.1	21 37.2	4 55.9	2 47.5	19 27.8	16 37.8	24 15.9	6 7.5	9 42.1
13 T	19 29 44.0	22 45.9	15 49.9	5♋16.7	23 16.0	5 55.7	3 29.4	19 38.7	16 44.0	24 19.2	6 9.7	9 43.2
14 W	19 33 40.6	23 47.0	15 46.7	17 10.3	24 55.3	6 55.9	4 11.3	19 49.7	16 50.2	24 22.6	6 11.9	9 44.2
15 T	19 37 37.1	24 48.1	15 43.5	29 7.2	26 35.0	7 56.6	4 53.3	20 0.8	16 56.3	24 25.8	6 14.0	9 45.2
16 F	19 41 33.7	25 49.2	15 40.4	11♌ 8.6	28 15.3	8 57.7	5 35.2	20 12.1	17 2.4	24 29.1	6 16.3	9 46.2
17 S	19 45 30.3	26 50.3	15 37.2	23 15.4	29 56.0	9 59.1	6 17.2	20 23.4	17 8.5	24 32.4	6 18.4	9 47.1
18 S	19 49 26.8	27 51.3	15 34.0	5♍29.3	1♒37.1	11 0.9	6 59.1	20 34.8	17 14.4	24 35.6	6 20.6	9 48.0
19 M	19 53 23.4	28 52.4	15 30.8	17 52.1	3 18.8	12 3.1	7 41.0	20 46.3	17 20.4	24 38.8	6 22.7	9 48.8
20 T	19 57 19.9	29 53.5	15 27.7	0♎26.4	5 0.9	13 5.7	8 22.9	20 57.9	17 26.2	24 41.9	6 24.8	9 49.6
21 W	20 1 16.5	0♒54.5	15 24.5	13 15.4	6 43.5	14 8.6	9 4.8	21 9.6	17 32.1	24 45.0	6 26.9	9 50.4
22 T	20 5 13.0	1 55.6	15 21.3	26 22.5	8 26.5	15 11.8	9 46.7	21 21.4	17 37.8	24 48.1	6 29.0	9 51.2
23 F	20 9 9.6	2 56.6	15 18.1	9♏51.2	10 9.8	16 15.3	10 28.5	21 33.3	17 43.5	24 51.2	6 31.1	9 51.9
24 S	20 13 6.2	3 57.7	15 15.0	23 44.0	11 53.4	17 19.2	11 10.4	21 45.3	17 49.2	24 54.2	6 33.2	9 52.5
25 S	20 17 2.7	4 58.7	15 11.8	8♐ 1.8	13 37.3	18 23.3	11 52.3	21 57.3	17 54.8	24 57.3	6 35.3	9 53.2
26 M	20 20 59.3	5 59.7	15 8.6	22 42.7	15 21.4	19 27.7	12 34.1	22 9.5	18 0.3	25 0.2	6 37.3	9 53.8
27 T	20 24 55.8	7 0.7	15 5.4	7♑41.9	17 5.5	20 32.4	13 16.0	22 21.7	18 5.8	25 3.2	6 39.3	9 54.3
28 W	20 28 52.4	8 1.7	15 2.2	22 51.3	18 49.5	21 37.3	13 57.8	22 34.0	18 11.2	25 6.1	6 41.3	9 54.8
29 T	20 32 48.9	9 2.7	14 59.1	8♒ 0.6	20 33.3	22 42.5	14 39.6	22 46.5	18 16.6	25 9.0	6 43.3	9 55.3
30 F	20 36 45.5	10 3.7	14 55.9	22 59.0	22 16.7	23 48.0	15 21.5	22 58.9	18 21.9	25 11.8	6 45.3	9 55.8
31 S	20 40 42.1	11 4.6	14 52.7	7♓37.6	23 59.5	24 53.6	16 3.3	23 11.5	18 27.1	25 14.7	6 47.3	9 56.2

DECLINATION at NOON

DAY	EPHEMERIS SIDEREAL TIME h m s	☉	☊	☽	☿	♀	♂	♃	♄	♅	♆	♇
1 T	18 42 25.3	23S 1.5	6N28.5	24S53.7	24S35.6	15S19.9	2S21.9	6S 0.7	21S10.4	23S24.2	22S18.6	0N41.2
4 S	18 54 15.0	22 44.9	6 24.9	8 54.4	24 37.0	15 55.9	1 28.4	5 48.8	21 12.4	23 24.7	22 18.3	0 41.3
7 W	19 6 4.7	22 24.3	6 21.2	9N33.0	24 25.8	16 32.0	0 34.9	5 36.5	21 14.4	23 25.2	22 18.1	0 41.5
10 S	19 17 54.4	21 59.7	6 17.5	23 27.3	24 1.6	17 7.8	0N18.6	5 23.7	21 16.3	23 25.7	22 17.8	0 41.8
13 T	19 29 44.0	21 31.3	6 13.9	28 14.5	23 24.0	17 42.6	1 11.8	5 10.6	21 18.1	23 26.2	22 17.5	0 42.3
16 F	19 41 33.7	20 59.1	6 10.2	21 44.4	22 32.7	18 15.9	2 4.9	4 57.1	21 19.8	23 26.6	22 17.1	0 42.8
19 M	19 53 23.4	20 23.3	6 6.5	6 52.4	21 27.4	18 47.3	2 57.7	4 43.2	21 21.4	23 27.1	22 16.8	0 43.5
22 T	20 5 13.0	19 44.1	6 2.8	11S 9.6	20 8.2	19 16.1	3 50.2	4 29.0	21 22.9	23 27.5	22 16.5	0 44.3
25 S	20 17 2.7	19 1.5	5 59.2	25 40.1	18 35.3	19 42.1	4 42.3	4 14.5	21 24.3	23 27.9	22 16.2	0 45.2
28 W	20 28 52.4	18 15.8	5 55.5	26 24.7	16 49.4	20 4.7	5 33.9	3 59.6	21 25.6	23 28.2	22 15.9	0 46.2
31 S	20 40 42.1	17 27.1	5 51.8	11 27.7	14 51.9	20 23.6	6 25.1	3 44.5	21 26.8	23 28.6	22 15.5	0 47.3

FEBRUARY 1987

LONGITUDE at NOON

DAY	EPHEMERIS SIDEREAL TIME h m s	☉ ° ′	☊ ° ′	☽ ° ′	☿ ° ′	♀ ° ′	♂ ° ′	♃ ° ′	♄ ° ′	♅ ° ′	♆ ° ′	♇ ° ′
1 S	20 44 38.6	12♒ 5.5	14♈49.5	21♓50.1	25♒41.5	25♐59.5	16♈45.1	23♓24.1	18♐32.3	25♐17.4	6♑49.2	9♏56.6
2 M	20 48 35.2	13 6.4	14 46.4	5♈33.7	27 22.2	27 5.6	17 26.8	23 36.8	18 37.3	25 20.2	6 51.2	9 56.9
3 T	20 52 31.7	14 7.3	14 43.2	18 48.8	29 1.4	28 11.9	18 8.6	23 49.6	18 42.4	25 22.9	6 53.1	9 57.2
4 W	20 56 28.3	15 8.2	14 40.0	1♉38.1	0♓38.7	29 18.4	18 50.4	24 2.5	18 47.3	25 25.6	6 54.9	9 57.5
5 T	21 0 24.8	16 9.0	14 36.8	14 5.8	2 13.6	0♑25.1	19 32.1	24 15.4	18 52.2	25 28.2	6 56.8	9 57.7
6 F	21 4 21.4	17 9.9	14 33.7	26 17.0	3 45.7	1 32.0	20 13.9	24 28.4	18 57.1	25 30.9	6 58.7	9 58.0
7 S	21 8 18.0	18 10.7	14 30.5	8♊16.7	5 14.4	2 39.1	20 55.6	24 41.5	19 1.8	25 33.4	7 0.5	9 58.1
8 S	21 12 14.5	19 11.5	14 27.3	20 9.7	6 38.9	3 46.4	21 37.2	24 54.6	19 6.5	25 36.0	7 2.3	9 58.3
9 M	21 16 11.1	20 12.2	14 24.1	2♋ 0.4	7 58.8	4 53.8	22 18.9	25 7.8	19 11.1	25 38.4	7 4.1	9 58.4
10 T	21 20 7.6	21 12.9	14 20.9	13 52.5	9 13.2	6 1.4	23 0.5	25 21.0	19 15.6	25 40.9	7 5.9	9 58.4
11 W	21 24 4.2	22 13.6	14 17.8	25 48.8	10 21.6	7 9.1	23 42.1	25 34.3	19 20.0	25 43.3	7 7.6	9 58.4
12 T	21 28 0.7	23 14.3	14 14.6	7♌51.4	11 23.0	8 17.1	24 23.7	25 47.7	19 24.4	25 45.7	7 9.3	9 58.4
13 F	21 31 57.3	24 14.9	14 11.4	20 1.8	12 16.8	9 25.1	25 5.3	26 1.1	19 28.7	25 48.0	7 11.0	9 58.4
14 S	21 35 53.8	25 15.6	14 8.2	2♍20.9	13 2.3	10 33.3	25 46.8	26 14.6	19 32.9	25 50.3	7 12.7	9R58.3
15 S	21 39 50.4	26 16.2	14 5.1	14 49.5	13 38.9	11 41.7	26 28.4	26 28.1	19 37.0	25 52.5	7 14.4	9 58.1
16 M	21 43 47.0	27 16.7	14 1.9	27 28.4	14 5.9	12 50.2	27 9.9	26 41.7	19 41.1	25 54.7	7 16.0	9 58.0
17 T	21 47 43.5	28 17.3	13 58.7	10♎18.4	14 23.0	13 58.9	27 51.3	26 55.3	19 45.1	25 56.9	7 17.6	9 57.8
18 W	21 51 40.1	29 17.8	13 55.5	23 20.7	14 29.9	15 7.7	28 32.8	27 9.0	19 49.0	25 59.0	7 19.2	9 57.5
19 T	21 55 36.6	0♓18.3	13 52.3	6♏37.1	14R26.5	16 16.6	29 14.2	27 22.7	19 52.8	26 1.0	7 20.7	9 57.3
20 F	21 59 33.2	1 18.8	13 49.2	20 9.0	14 12.9	17 25.6	29 55.6	27 36.5	19 56.5	26 3.1	7 22.2	9 57.0
21 S	22 3 29.7	2 19.3	13 46.0	3♐57.7	13 49.4	18 34.8	0♉37.0	27 50.3	20 0.1	26 5.0	7 23.7	9 56.6
22 S	22 7 26.3	3 19.7	13 42.8	18 3.7	13 16.6	19 44.1	1 18.4	28 4.2	20 3.7	26 7.0	7 25.2	9 56.3
23 M	22 11 22.8	4 20.2	13 39.6	2♑25.9	12 35.4	20 53.5	1 59.7	28 18.1	20 7.2	26 8.8	7 26.6	9 55.8
24 T	22 15 19.4	5 20.6	13 36.5	17 1.3	11 46.8	22 3.0	2 41.1	28 32.0	20 10.5	26 10.7	7 28.1	9 55.4
25 W	22 19 16.0	6 20.9	13 33.3	1♒44.9	10 52.1	23 12.6	3 22.4	28 46.0	20 13.8	26 12.5	7 29.4	9 54.9
26 T	22 23 12.5	7 21.3	13 30.1	16 29.7	9 52.8	24 22.3	4 3.6	29 0.0	20 17.0	26 14.2	7 30.8	9 54.4
27 F	22 27 9.1	8 21.7	13 26.9	1♓ 8.2	8 50.4	25 32.2	4 44.9	29 14.1	20 20.2	26 16.0	7 32.2	9 53.9
28 S	22 31 5.6	9 22.0	13 23.8	15 33.0	7 46.5	26 42.1	5 26.2	29 28.2	20 23.2	26 17.6	7 33.5	9 53.3

DECLINATION at NOON

DAY	EPHEMERIS SIDEREAL TIME h m s	☉	☊	☽	☿	♀	♂	♃	♄	♅	♆	♇
1 S	20 44 38.6	17S10.3	5N50.6	4S57.2	14S10.5	20S29.1	6N42.1	3S39.4	21S27.2	23S28.7	22S15.4	0N47.7
4 W	20 56 28.3	16 17.9	5 46.9	13N33.0	12 2.0	20 42.7	7 32.5	3 23.9	21 28.3	23 29.0	22 15.1	0 49.0
7 S	21 8 18.0	15 23.0	5 43.2	25 48.9	9 50.7	20 51.9	8 22.3	3 8.2	21 29.3	23 29.3	22 14.8	0 50.3
10 T	21 20 7.6	14 25.8	5 39.5	27 46.9	7 44.3	20 56.6	9 11.4	2 52.2	21 30.2	23 29.6	22 14.4	0 51.7
13 F	21 31 57.3	13 26.5	5 35.8	18 38.9	5 52.5	20 56.5	9 59.7	2 36.1	21 31.0	23 29.9	22 14.1	0 53.2
16 M	21 43 47.0	12 25.1	5 32.1	2 12.4	4 26.7	20 51.5	10 47.2	2 19.7	21 31.8	23 30.2	22 13.8	0 54.8
19 T	21 55 36.6	11 22.0	5 28.4	15S45.0	3 37.1	20 41.5	11 33.9	2 3.2	21 32.4	23 30.4	22 13.5	0 56.5
22 S	22 7 26.3	10 17.2	5 24.7	27 36.7	3 30.5	20 26.5	12 19.6	1 46.6	21 33.0	23 30.6	22 13.2	0 58.2
25 W	22 19 16.0	9 11.0	5 21.0	24 31.2	4 6.0	20 6.4	13 4.4	1 29.8	21 33.5	23 30.8	22 12.9	0 60.0
28 S	22 31 5.6	8 3.6	5 17.3	7 49.0	5 13.7	19 41.2	13 48.2	1 12.8	21 33.9	23 31.0	22 12.6	1 1.8

MARCH 1987

DAY	EPHEMERIS SIDEREAL TIME	☉	☊	☽	☿	♀	♂	♃	♄	♅	♆	♇
	h m s	° ′	° ′	° ′	° ′	° ′	° ′	° ′	° ′	° ′	° ′	° ′
LONGITUDE at NOON												
1 S	22 35 2.2	10♓22.2	13♈20.6	29♓38.2	6♓42.7	27♑52.1	6♉ 7.4	29♓42.3	20♐26.2	26♐19.2	7♑34.8	9♏52.7
2 M	22 38 58.7	11 22.5	13 17.4	13♈20.2	5R40.4	29 2.1	6 48.6	29 56.5	20 29.0	26 20.8	7 36.0	9R52.1
3 T	22 42 55.3	12 22.7	13 14.2	26 37.7	4 40.9	0♒12.3	7 29.7	0♈10.7	20 31.8	26 22.3	7 37.2	9 51.4
4 W	22 46 51.8	13 22.8	13 11.0	9♉31.6	3 45.5	1 22.5	8 10.9	0 24.9	20 34.4	26 23.7	7 38.4	9 50.7
5 T	22 50 48.4	14 23.0	13 7.9	22 4.5	2 55.0	2 32.8	8 52.0	0 39.2	20 37.0	26 25.1	7 39.6	9 50.0
6 F	22 54 44.9	15 23.1	13 4.7	4♊20.2	2 10.1	3 43.2	9 33.1	0 53.4	20 39.5	26 26.5	7 40.7	9 49.2
7 S	22 58 41.5	16 23.1	13 1.5	16 23.3	1 31.5	4 53.6	10 14.1	1 7.7	20 41.9	26 27.8	7 41.8	9 48.4
8 S	23 2 38.1	17 23.2	12 58.3	28 18.4	0 59.3	6 4.2	10 55.2	1 22.0	20 44.1	26 29.0	7 42.9	9 47.6
9 M	23 6 34.6	18 23.2	12 55.2	10♋10.5	0 33.8	7 14.8	11 36.2	1 36.4	20 46.3	26 30.2	7 43.9	9 46.7
10 T	23 10 31.2	19 23.1	12 52.0	22 4.0	0 15.1	8 25.4	12 17.2	1 50.7	20 48.4	26 31.4	7 44.9	9 45.8
11 W	23 14 27.7	20 23.0	12 48.8	4♌ 2.8	0 3.0	9 36.2	12 58.1	2 5.1	20 50.4	26 32.5	7 45.9	9 44.9
12 T	23 18 24.3	21 22.9	12 45.6	16 10.2	29♒57.4	10 46.9	13 39.0	2 19.5	20 52.3	26 33.5	7 46.9	9 43.9
13 F	23 22 20.8	22 22.8	12 42.4	28 28.8	29D58.1	11 57.8	14 19.9	2 33.9	20 54.1	26 34.5	7 47.8	9 43.0
14 S	23 26 17.4	23 22.6	12 39.3	11♍ 0.3	0♓ 4.8	13 8.7	15 0.8	2 48.4	20 55.8	26 35.5	7 48.7	9 42.0
15 S	23 30 13.9	24 22.4	12 36.1	23 45.6	0 17.2	14 19.7	15 41.6	3 2.8	20 57.4	26 36.4	7 49.5	9 40.9
16 M	23 34 10.5	25 22.1	12 32.9	6♎44.9	0 35.1	15 30.7	16 22.4	3 17.3	20 58.9	26 37.2	7 50.3	9 39.9
17 T	23 38 7.0	26 21.9	12 29.7	19 57.9	0 58.1	16 41.8	17 3.2	3 31.7	21 0.4	26 38.0	7 51.1	9 38.8
18 W	23 42 3.6	27 21.5	12 26.6	3♏23.8	1 26.0	17 53.0	17 43.9	3 46.2	21 1.7	26 38.7	7 51.9	9 37.7
19 T	23 46 0.1	28 21.2	12 23.4	17 1.7	1 58.4	19 4.2	18 24.6	4 0.7	21 2.9	26 39.4	7 52.6	9 36.5
20 F	23 49 56.7	29 20.9	12 20.2	0♐50.4	2 35.1	20 15.5	19 5.3	4 15.3	21 4.1	26 40.1	7 53.4	9 35.4
21 S	23 53 53.3	0♈20.5	12 17.0	14 48.8	3 15.8	21 26.9	19 46.0	4 29.8	21 5.1	26 40.7	7 54.0	9 34.2
22 S	23 57 49.8	1 20.1	12 13.8	28 55.5	4 0.2	22 38.2	20 26.6	4 44.3	21 6.0	26 41.2	7 54.6	9 33.0
23 M	0 1 46.4	2 19.6	12 10.7	13♑ 8.5	4 48.2	23 49.7	21 7.2	4 58.8	21 6.8	26 41.7	7 55.2	9 31.8
24 T	0 5 42.9	3 19.1	12 7.5	27 25.6	5 39.5	25 1.1	21 47.8	5 13.3	21 7.5	26 42.1	7 55.8	9 30.5
25 W	0 9 39.5	4 18.6	12 4.3	11♒43.8	6 34.0	26 12.7	22 28.3	5 27.9	21 8.1	26 42.5	7 56.3	9 29.2
26 T	0 13 36.0	5 18.0	12 1.1	25 59.5	7 31.4	27 24.2	23 8.9	5 42.4	21 8.7	26 42.8	7 56.8	9 27.9
27 F	0 17 32.6	6 17.5	11 58.0	10♓ 8.6	8 31.6	28 35.8	23 49.4	5 56.9	21 9.1	26 43.1	7 57.3	9 26.6
28 S	0 21 29.1	7 16.9	11 54.8	24 7.1	9 34.4	29 47.5	24 29.8	6 11.5	21 9.4	26 43.3	7 57.7	9 25.2
29 S	0 25 25.7	8 16.2	11 51.6	7♈51.5	10 39.8	0♓59.2	25 10.3	6 26.0	21 9.6	26 43.5	7 58.1	9 23.9
30 M	0 29 22.2	9 15.6	11 48.4	21 19.0	11 47.5	2 10.9	25 50.7	6 40.5	21 9.7	26 43.6	7 58.5	9 22.5
31 T	0 33 18.8	10 14.8	11 45.2	4♉28.0	12 57.5	3 22.6	26 31.1	6 55.0	21 9.7	26 43.6	7 58.8	9 21.1
DECLINATION at NOON												
1 S	22 35 2.2	7S40.8	5N16.1	1S 8.8	5S40.8	19S31.7	14N 2.5	1S 7.1	21S34.0	23S31.1	22S12.5	1N 2.4
4 W	22 46 51.8	6 32.0	5 12.4	16N58.8	7 6.4	18 59.9	14 44.9	0 50.1	21 34.3	23 31.3	22 12.2	1 4.3
7 S	22 58 41.5	5 22.4	5 8.7	27 27.0	8 27.0	18 23.2	15 26.1	0 33.0	21 34.6	23 31.4	22 12.0	1 6.3
10 T	23 10 31.2	4 12.1	5 5.0	26 42.8	9 32.8	17 41.9	16 6.1	0 15.8	21 34.7	23 31.6	22 11.7	1 8.3
13 F	23 22 20.8	3 1.4	5 1.2	15 21.9	10 19.1	16 56.0	16 44.9	0N 1.5	21 34.8	23 31.7	22 11.5	1 10.3
16 M	23 34 10.5	1 50.4	4 57.5	2S16.8	10 45.1	16 5.8	17 22.3	0 18.8	21 34.9	23 31.8	22 11.3	1 12.3
19 T	23 46 0.1	0 39.3	4 53.8	19 51.7	10 51.4	15 11.5	17 58.5	0 36.0	21 34.8	23 31.9	22 11.1	1 14.3
22 S	23 57 49.8	0N31.8	4 50.1	28 35.1	10 39.5	14 13.2	18 33.3	0 53.3	21 34.8	23 32.0	22 10.9	1 16.3
25 W	0 9 39.5	1 42.8	4 46.4	21 39.0	10 10.7	13 11.3	19 6.6	1 10.6	21 34.6	23 32.1	22 10.7	1 18.4
28 S	0 21 29.1	2 53.4	4 42.6	3 47.3	9 26.6	12 6.0	19 38.6	1 27.9	21 34.4	23 32.2	22 10.5	1 20.4
31 T	0 33 18.8	4 3.5	4 38.9	14N57.3	8 28.3	10 57.7	20 9.0	1 45.0	21 34.2	23 32.2	22 10.4	1 22.4

APRIL 1987

DAY	EPHEMERIS SIDEREAL TIME	☉	☊	☽	☿	♀	♂	♃	♄	♅	♆	♇
LONGITUDE at NOON												
1 W	0 37 15.3	11♈14.1	11♈42.1	17♉18.4	14♓ 9.6	4♓34.4	27♉11.5	7♈ 9.5	21♐ 9.6	26♐43.6	7♑59.1	9♏19.6
2 T	0 41 11.9	12 13.3	11 38.9	29 51.1	15 23.9	5 46.2	27 51.8	7 24.0	21R 9.5	26 43.6	7 59.3	9R18.2
3 F	0 45 8.4	13 12.5	11 35.7	12♊ 8.4	16 40.2	6 58.0	28 32.1	7 38.5	21 9.2	26R43.5	7 59.6	9 16.7
4 S	0 49 5.0	14 11.6	11 32.5	24 13.5	17 58.4	8 9.9	29 12.4	7 53.0	21 8.8	26 43.3	7 59.8	9 15.2
5 S	0 53 1.6	15 10.7	11 29.4	6♋10.5	19 18.4	9 21.8	29 52.7	8 7.5	21 8.3	26 43.1	7 59.9	9 13.7
6 M	0 56 58.1	16 9.8	11 26.2	18 3.6	20 40.4	10 33.7	0♊32.9	8 21.9	21 7.7	26 42.8	8 0.0	9 12.2
7 T	1 0 54.7	17 8.8	11 23.0	29 57.6	22 4.0	11 45.7	1 13.1	8 36.4	21 7.0	26 42.5	8 0.1	9 10.7
8 W	1 4 51.2	18 7.8	11 19.8	11♌57.1	23 29.5	12 57.7	1 53.2	8 50.8	21 6.3	26 42.2	8 0.2	9 9.2
9 T	1 8 47.8	19 6.8	11 16.6	24 6.4	24 56.6	14 9.7	2 33.4	9 5.2	21 5.4	26 41.8	8 0.2	9 7.6
10 F	1 12 44.3	20 5.7	11 13.5	6♍29.5	26 25.4	15 21.7	3 13.5	9 19.6	21 4.5	26 41.4	8 0.3	9 6.1
11 S	1 16 40.9	21 4.6	11 10.3	19 9.2	27 55.9	16 33.8	3 53.6	9 34.0	21 3.4	26 40.8	8R 0.2	9 4.5
12 S	1 20 37.4	22 3.5	11 7.1	2♎ 7.5	29 28.0	17 45.9	4 33.6	9 48.4	21 2.2	26 40.3	8 0.1	9 2.9
13 M	1 24 34.0	23 2.3	11 3.9	15 25.3	1♈ 1.7	18 58.0	5 13.7	10 2.7	21 1.0	26 39.7	8 0.0	9 1.3
14 T	1 28 30.5	24 1.0	11 0.8	29 1.8	2 37.0	20 10.1	5 53.6	10 17.0	20 59.6	26 39.0	7 59.9	8 59.7
15 W	1 32 27.1	24 59.8	10 57.6	12♏54.8	4 14.0	21 22.3	6 33.6	10 31.3	20 58.2	26 38.3	7 59.7	8 58.1
16 T	1 36 23.7	25 58.5	10 54.4	27 1.0	5 52.6	22 34.4	7 13.5	10 45.5	20 56.6	26 37.6	7 59.5	8 56.4
17 F	1 40 20.2	26 57.2	10 51.2	11♐16.2	7 32.7	23 46.7	7 53.4	10 59.8	20 55.0	26 36.8	7 59.3	8 54.8
18 S	1 44 16.8	27 55.8	10 48.0	25 36.0	9 14.5	24 58.9	8 33.3	11 14.0	20 53.3	26 35.9	7 59.0	8 53.1
19 S	1 48 13.3	28 54.4	10 44.9	9♑56.2	10 57.9	26 11.1	9 13.1	11 28.2	20 51.5	26 35.0	7 58.7	8 51.5
20 M	1 52 9.9	29 53.0	10 41.7	24 12.9	12 43.0	27 23.4	9 53.0	11 42.3	20 49.6	26 34.1	7 58.4	8 49.8
21 T	1 56 6.4	0♉51.6	10 38.5	8♒23.6	14 29.6	28 35.7	10 32.8	11 56.4	20 47.6	26 33.1	7 58.0	8 48.1
22 W	2 0 3.0	1 50.1	10 35.3	22 26.0	16 18.0	29 48.0	11 12.5	12 10.5	20 45.5	26 32.0	7 57.6	8 46.5
23 T	2 3 59.5	2 48.7	10 32.2	6♓18.9	18 7.9	1♈ 0.4	11 52.3	12 24.6	20 43.3	26 30.9	7 57.2	8 44.8
24 F	2 7 56.1	3 47.1	10 29.0	20 1.1	19 59.6	2 12.7	12 32.0	12 38.6	20 41.1	26 29.8	7 56.8	8 43.1
25 S	2 11 52.6	4 45.6	10 25.8	3♈31.9	21 52.8	3 25.1	13 11.7	12 52.6	20 38.7	26 28.6	7 56.3	8 41.4
26 S	2 15 49.2	5 44.0	10 22.6	16 50.5	23 47.8	4 37.5	13 51.4	13 6.6	20 36.3	26 27.4	7 55.8	8 39.7
27 M	2 19 45.8	6 42.4	10 19.5	29 56.2	25 44.4	5 49.9	14 31.0	13 20.5	20 33.8	26 26.1	7 55.2	8 38.0
28 T	2 23 42.3	7 40.8	10 16.3	12♉48.5	27 42.6	7 2.4	15 10.6	13 34.4	20 31.2	26 24.8	7 54.6	8 36.3
29 W	2 27 38.9	8 39.1	10 13.1	25 27.2	29 42.4	8 14.8	15 50.2	13 48.2	20 28.5	26 23.5	7 54.0	8 34.6
30 T	2 31 35.4	9 37.4	10 9.9	7♊52.8	1♉43.8	9 27.3	16 29.8	14 2.0	20 25.8	26 22.1	7 53.4	8 32.9
DECLINATION at NOON												
1 W	0 37 15.3	4N26.7	4N37.7	19N58.1	8S 5.9	10S34.2	20N18.8	1N50.8	21S34.1	23S32.2	22S10.3	1N23.0
4 S	0 49 5.0	5 35.9	4 34.0	28 21.3	6 50.4	9 22.1	20 47.2	2 7.9	21 33.8	23 32.3	22 10.2	1 25.0
7 T	1 0 54.7	6 44.2	4 30.2	25 3.2	5 22.9	8 7.6	21 14.0	2 24.9	21 33.4	23 32.3	22 10.1	1 26.9
10 F	1 12 44.3	7 51.4	4 26.5	11 57.0	3 44.2	6 51.0	21 39.2	2 41.8	21 33.0	23 32.3	22 10.0	1 28.8
13 M	1 24 34.0	8 57.4	4 22.8	6S24.1	1 55.2	5 32.4	22 2.8	2 58.6	21 32.5	23 32.3	22 10.0	1 30.6
16 T	1 36 23.7	10 2.1	4 19.0	23 8.9	0N 3.6	4 12.3	22 24.6	3 15.3	21 32.0	23 32.3	22 9.9	1 32.4
19 S	1 48 13.3	11 5.3	4 15.3	28 18.4	2 11.3	2 51.0	22 44.8	3 31.8	21 31.4	23 32.3	22 9.9	1 34.1
22 W	2 0 3.0	12 6.8	4 11.6	17 47.1	4 27.0	1 28.6	23 3.3	3 48.2	21 30.8	23 32.3	22 9.9	1 35.8
25 S	2 11 52.6	13 6.6	4 7.8	0N44.3	6 49.6	0 5.5	23 20.1	4 4.4	21 30.1	23 32.2	22 9.9	1 37.4
28 T	2 23 42.3	14 4.5	4 4.1	18 16.7	9 17.3	1N17.9	23 35.0	4 20.4	21 29.4	23 32.2	22 9.9	1 38.9

MAY 1987

DAY	EPHEMERIS SIDEREAL TIME	☉	☊	☽	☿	♀	♂	♃	♄	♅	♆	♇
	h m s	° ′	° ′	° ′	° ′	° ′	° ′	° ′	° ′	° ′	° ′	° ′
						LONGITUDE at NOON						
1 F	2 35 32.0	10♉35.8	10♈ 6.7	20♊ 6.5	3♉46.7	10♈39.8	17♊ 9.4	14♈15.8	20♐23.0	26♐20.7	7♑52.8	8♏31.3
2 S	2 39 28.5	11 34.0	10 3.6	2♋10.0	5 51.0	11 52.2	17 48.9	14 29.5	20R20.1	26R19.2	7R52.1	8R29.6
3 S	2 43 25.1	12 32.2	10 0.4	14 6.3	7 56.7	13 4.7	18 28.4	14 43.2	20 17.1	26 17.7	7 51.3	8 27.9
4 M	2 47 21.6	13 30.4	9 57.2	25 58.9	10 3.6	14 17.2	19 7.9	14 56.8	20 14.1	26 16.2	7 50.6	8 26.2
5 T	2 51 18.2	14 28.6	9 54.0	7♌52.0	12 11.6	15 29.7	19 47.4	15 10.3	20 11.0	26 14.6	7 49.8	8 24.5
6 W	2 55 14.8	15 26.7	9 50.9	19 50.1	14 20.5	16 42.3	20 26.8	15 23.8	20 7.8	26 12.9	7 49.0	8 22.8
7 T	2 59 11.3	16 24.8	9 47.7	1♍58.1	16 30.1	17 54.8	21 6.2	15 37.3	20 4.5	26 11.3	7 48.2	8 21.1
8 F	3 3 7.9	17 22.8	9 44.5	14 20.8	18 40.3	19 7.3	21 45.5	15 50.7	20 1.2	26 9.6	7 47.3	8 19.5
9 S	3 7 4.4	18 20.8	9 41.3	27 2.5	20 50.7	20 19.9	22 24.9	16 4.1	19 57.8	26 7.8	7 46.4	8 17.8
10 S	3 11 1.0	19 18.8	9 38.2	10♎ 6.6	23 1.1	21 32.4	23 4.2	16 17.4	19 54.3	26 6.1	7 45.5	8 16.1
11 M	3 14 57.5	20 16.8	9 35.0	23 35.2	25 11.3	22 45.0	23 43.5	16 30.6	19 50.8	26 4.2	7 44.5	8 14.5
12 T	3 18 54.1	21 14.7	9 31.8	7♏28.3	27 20.9	23 57.6	24 22.7	16 43.8	19 47.3	26 2.4	7 43.6	8 12.8
13 W	3 22 50.7	22 12.6	9 28.6	21 43.6	29 29.7	25 10.2	25 2.0	16 56.9	19 43.6	26 0.5	7 42.6	8 11.2
14 T	3 26 47.2	23 10.5	9 25.4	6♐16.3	1♊37.4	26 22.8	25 41.2	17 10.0	19 39.9	25 58.6	7 41.6	8 9.6
15 F	3 30 43.8	24 8.3	9 22.3	20 59.7	3 43.6	27 35.4	26 20.4	17 23.0	19 36.2	25 56.7	7 40.5	8 8.0
16 S	3 34 40.3	25 6.2	9 19.1	5♑46.1	5 48.2	28 48.1	26 59.5	17 36.0	19 32.4	25 54.7	7 39.4	8 6.4
17 S	3 38 36.9	26 4.0	9 15.9	20 27.9	7 51.0	0♉ 0.7	27 38.7	17 48.9	19 28.6	25 52.7	7 38.4	8 4.8
18 M	3 42 33.4	27 1.8	9 12.7	4♒58.8	9 51.6	1 13.4	28 17.8	18 1.7	19 24.7	25 50.7	7 37.2	8 3.2
19 T	3 46 30.0	27 59.5	9 9.6	19 14.8	11 49.9	2 26.1	28 56.9	18 14.4	19 20.7	25 48.6	7 36.1	8 1.6
20 W	3 50 26.6	28 57.3	9 6.4	3♓13.6	13 45.8	3 38.8	29 36.0	18 27.1	19 16.7	25 46.6	7 34.9	8 0.0
21 T	3 54 23.1	29 55.0	9 3.2	16 55.0	15 39.0	4 51.5	0♋15.1	18 39.8	19 12.7	25 44.4	7 33.8	7 58.5
22 F	3 58 19.7	0♊52.8	9 0.0	0♈20.0	17 29.6	6 4.3	0 54.2	18 52.4	19 8.7	25 42.4	7 32.6	7 57.0
23 S	4 2 16.2	1 50.5	8 56.9	13 29.9	19 17.4	7 17.0	1 33.2	19 4.9	19 4.5	25 40.2	7 31.4	7 55.5
24 S	4 6 12.8	2 48.2	8 53.7	26 26.6	21 2.2	8 29.8	2 12.2	19 17.3	19 0.4	25 38.0	7 30.1	7 54.0
25 M	4 10 9.3	3 45.8	8 50.5	9♉11.2	22 44.1	9 42.5	2 51.2	19 29.6	18 56.2	25 35.8	7 28.9	7 52.5
26 T	4 14 5.9	4 43.5	8 47.3	21 45.1	24 23.0	10 55.3	3 30.1	19 41.9	18 52.0	25 33.6	7 27.6	7 51.0
27 W	4 18 2.5	5 41.1	8 44.1	4♊ 8.9	25 58.8	12 8.1	4 9.1	19 54.1	18 47.7	25 31.3	7 26.3	7 49.6
28 T	4 21 59.0	6 38.7	8 41.0	16 23.5	27 31.6	13 20.9	4 48.0	20 6.2	18 43.5	25 29.1	7 25.0	7 48.2
29 F	4 25 55.6	7 36.3	8 37.8	28 29.7	29 1.2	14 33.7	5 26.9	20 18.2	18 39.1	25 26.8	7 23.6	7 46.7
30 S	4 29 52.1	8 33.9	8 34.6	10♋28.7	0♋27.6	15 46.5	6 5.8	20 30.1	18 34.8	25 24.5	7 22.3	7 45.3
31 S	4 33 48.7	9 31.4	8 31.4	22 22.5	1 50.8	16 59.3	6 44.7	20 42.0	18 30.5	25 22.1	7 20.9	7 44.0
						DECLINATION at NOON						
1 F	2 35 32.0	15N 0.2	4N 0.3	27N54.9	11N48.0	2N41.5	23N48.3	4N36.2	21S28.7	23S32.1	22S10.0	1N40.3
4 M	2 47 21.6	15 53.8	3 56.6	25 53.2	14 18.3	4 4.8	23 59.7	4 51.8	21 28.0	23 32.0	22 10.0	1 41.6
7 T	2 59 11.3	16 44.9	3 52.8	13 50.1	16 44.1	5 27.5	24 9.4	5 7.2	21 27.1	23 31.9	22 10.1	1 42.8
10 S	3 11 1.0	17 33.5	3 49.1	3S55.6	19 0.1	6 49.4	24 17.2	5 22.3	21 26.3	23 31.8	22 10.2	1 43.9
13 W	3 22 50.7	18 19.5	3 45.4	21 27.2	21 0.8	8 10.2	24 23.3	5 37.2	21 25.5	23 31.7	22 10.3	1 45.0
16 S	3 34 40.3	19 2.7	3 41.6	28 25.8	22 41.7	9 29.6	24 27.5	5 51.8	21 24.6	23 31.6	22 10.5	1 45.9
19 T	3 46 30.0	19 43.0	3 37.9	18 51.5	23 60.0	10 47.2	24 30.0	6 6.2	21 23.6	23 31.4	22 10.6	1 46.7
22 F	3 58 19.7	20 20.3	3 34.1	0 41.8	24 54.8	12 2.8	24 30.6	6 20.2	21 22.7	23 31.3	22 10.8	1 47.4
25 M	4 10 9.3	20 54.4	3 30.4	16N53.5	25 27.2	13 16.0	24 29.5	6 33.9	21 21.7	23 31.1	22 10.9	1 47.9
28 T	4 21 59.0	21 25.4	3 26.6	27 22.2	25 39.4	14 26.5	24 26.7	6 47.4	21 20.8	23 30.9	22 11.1	1 48.4
31 S	4 33 48.7	21 52.9	3 22.8	26 27.2	25 34.1	15 33.9	24 22.0	7 0.4	21 19.8	23 30.7	22 11.3	1 48.7

JUNE 1987

DAY	EPHEMERIS SIDEREAL TIME	☉	☊	☽	☿	♀	♂	♃	♄	♅	♆	♇
						LONGITUDE at NOON						
1 M	4 37 45.3	10♊28.9	8♈28.3	4♌13.5	3♋10.8	18♉12.2	7♋23.5	20♈53.8	18♐26.1	25♐19.8	7♑19.5	7♏42.6
2 T	4 41 41.8	11 26.4	8 25.1	16 5.1	4 27.5	19 25.0	8 2.4	21 5.5	18R21.7	25R17.5	7R18.1	7R41.3
3 W	4 45 38.4	12 23.9	8 21.9	28 1.3	5 40.9	20 37.9	8 41.2	21 17.1	18 17.3	25 15.1	7 16.7	7 40.0
4 T	4 49 34.9	13 21.4	8 18.7	10♍ 6.8	6 50.8	21 50.7	9 20.0	21 28.6	18 12.9	25 12.7	7 15.2	7 38.7
5 F	4 53 31.5	14 18.8	8 15.6	22 26.5	7 57.4	23 3.6	9 58.7	21 40.0	18 8.5	25 10.3	7 13.8	7 37.4
6 S	4 57 28.0	15 16.2	8 12.4	5♎ 5.6	9 0.4	24 16.5	10 37.5	21 51.3	18 4.0	25 7.9	7 12.3	7 36.1
7 S	5 1 24.6	16 13.6	8 9.2	18 8.5	9 59.8	25 29.4	11 16.2	22 2.6	17 59.6	25 5.5	7 10.8	7 34.9
8 M	5 5 21.2	17 11.0	8 6.0	1♏38.6	10 55.6	26 42.3	11 54.9	22 13.7	17 55.1	25 3.1	7 9.3	7 33.7
9 T	5 9 17.7	18 8.4	8 2.9	15 37.5	11 47.6	27 55.2	12 33.6	22 24.8	17 50.7	25 0.7	7 7.8	7 32.5
10 W	5 13 14.3	19 5.7	7 59.7	0♐ 3.7	12 35.8	29 8.1	13 12.3	22 35.7	17 46.2	24 58.2	7 6.3	7 31.4
11 T	5 17 10.8	20 3.1	7 56.5	14 52.6	13 20.0	0♊21.1	13 50.9	22 46.6	17 41.8	24 55.8	7 4.8	7 30.2
12 F	5 21 7.4	21 0.4	7 53.3	29 56.5	14 0.3	1 34.1	14 29.6	22 57.4	17 37.4	24 53.4	7 3.3	7 29.2
13 S	5 25 4.0	21 57.7	7 50.1	15♑ 5.4	14 36.5	2 47.0	15 8.2	23 8.0	17 33.0	24 50.9	7 1.8	7 28.1
14 S	5 29 0.5	22 55.0	7 47.0	0♒ 9.0	15 8.4	4 0.0	15 46.8	23 18.6	17 28.6	24 48.5	7 0.2	7 27.0
15 M	5 32 57.1	23 52.3	7 43.8	14 58.4	15 36.1	5 13.0	16 25.4	23 29.0	17 24.2	24 46.0	6 58.6	7 26.0
16 T	5 36 53.6	24 49.6	7 40.6	29 27.2	15 59.4	6 26.1	17 4.0	23 39.3	17 19.8	24 43.6	6 57.1	7 25.0
17 W	5 40 50.2	25 46.9	7 37.4	13♓32.3	16 18.2	7 39.1	17 42.6	23 49.6	17 15.4	24 41.1	6 55.5	7 24.0
18 T	5 44 46.7	26 44.2	7 34.3	27 13.4	16 32.6	8 52.2	18 21.1	23 59.7	17 11.0	24 38.7	6 53.9	7 23.1
19 F	5 48 43.3	27 41.4	7 31.1	10♈32.2	16 42.4	10 5.2	18 59.6	24 9.7	17 6.7	24 36.2	6 52.3	7 22.2
20 S	5 52 39.9	28 38.7	7 27.9	23 31.5	16 47.7	11 18.3	19 38.2	24 19.6	17 2.4	24 33.8	6 50.7	7 21.3
21 S	5 56 36.4	29 36.0	7 24.7	6♉14.5	16 48.3	12 31.4	20 16.7	24 29.4	16 58.1	24 31.3	6 49.1	7 20.4
22 M	6 0 33.0	0♋33.2	7 21.6	18 44.3	16R44.5	13 44.6	20 55.2	24 39.1	16 53.8	24 28.9	6 47.5	7 19.6
23 T	6 4 29.5	1 30.5	7 18.4	1♊ 3.6	16 36.3	14 57.7	21 33.7	24 48.6	16 49.6	24 26.4	6 45.9	7 18.8
24 W	6 8 26.1	2 27.7	7 15.2	13 14.4	16 23.7	16 10.9	22 12.1	24 58.0	16 45.4	24 24.0	6 44.3	7 18.0
25 T	6 12 22.7	3 25.0	7 12.0	25 18.5	16 7.1	17 24.0	22 50.6	25 7.3	16 41.2	24 21.6	6 42.7	7 17.2
26 F	6 16 19.2	4 22.2	7 8.9	7♋17.0	15 46.5	18 37.2	23 29.0	25 16.5	16 37.1	24 19.2	6 41.0	7 16.5
27 S	6 20 15.8	5 19.5	7 5.7	19 11.2	15 22.3	19 50.4	24 7.5	25 25.6	16 33.0	24 16.8	6 39.4	7 15.8
28 S	6 24 12.3	6 16.7	7 2.5	1♌ 2.6	14 54.9	21 3.7	24 45.9	25 34.5	16 28.9	24 14.4	6 37.8	7 15.2
29 M	6 28 8.9	7 13.9	6 59.3	12 53.0	14 24.7	22 16.9	25 24.3	25 43.3	16 24.9	24 12.0	6 36.2	7 14.5
30 T	6 32 5.5	8 11.2	6 56.2	24 44.8	13 52.0	23 30.2	26 2.7	25 52.0	16 20.9	24 9.6	6 34.5	7 13.9
						DECLINATION at NOON						
1 M	4 37 45.3	22N 1.4	3N21.6	23N40.2	25N29.0	15N55.7	24N20.1	7N 4.7	21S19.5	23S30.6	22S11.4	1N48.8
4 T	4 49 34.9	22 24.4	3 17.8	10 3.9	25 4.9	16 58.6	24 13.2	7 17.3	21 18.5	23 30.4	22 11.6	1 49.0
7 S	5 1 24.6	22 43.8	3 14.1	7S50.8	24 30.0	17 57.8	24 4.5	7 29.5	21 17.5	23 30.2	22 11.8	1 49.0
10 W	5 13 14.3	22 59.7	3 10.3	23 59.9	23 47.2	18 52.9	23 54.2	7 41.4	21 16.5	23 29.9	22 12.1	1 48.9
13 S	5 25 4.0	23 11.9	3 6.6	27 32.8	22 59.1	19 43.6	23 42.2	7 52.9	21 15.5	23 29.7	22 12.3	1 48.7
16 T	5 36 53.6	23 20.5	3 2.8	14 37.1	22 8.3	20 29.7	23 28.6	8 4.0	21 14.5	23 29.4	22 12.5	1 48.4
19 F	5 48 43.3	23 25.4	2 59.0	4N22.1	21 17.2	21 10.8	23 13.4	8 14.6	21 13.6	23 29.1	22 12.8	1 47.9
22 M	6 0 33.0	23 26.5	2 55.3	20 33.2	20 28.5	21 46.8	22 56.6	8 24.9	21 12.7	23 28.9	22 13.1	1 47.3
25 T	6 12 22.7	23 23.9	2 51.5	28 14.2	19 44.5	22 17.3	22 38.2	8 34.7	21 11.8	23 28.6	22 13.3	1 46.6
28 S	6 24 12.3	23 17.7	2 47.7	24 22.4	19 7.5	22 42.2	22 18.4	8 44.0	21 11.0	23 28.3	22 13.6	1 45.7

JULY 1987

DAY	EPHEMERIS SIDEREAL TIME	☉	☊	☽	☿	♀	♂	♃	♄	♅	♆	♇
	h m s	° ′	° ′	° ′	° ′	° ′	° ′	° ′	° ′	° ′	° ′	° ′
LONGITUDE at NOON												
1 W	6 36 2.0	9♋ 8.4	6♈53.0	6♍41.3	13♋17.5	24♊43.4	26♋41.1	26♈ 0.5	16♐17.0	24♐ 7.3	6♑32.9	7♏13.4
2 T	6 39 58.6	10 5.6	6 49.8	18 46.3	12R41.7	25 56.7	27 19.5	26 8.9	16R13.1	24R 5.0	6R31.3	7R12.8
3 F	6 43 55.1	11 2.8	6 46.6	1♎ 4.4	12 5.2	27 10.1	27 57.9	26 17.2	16 9.3	24 2.7	6 29.7	7 12.4
4 S	6 47 51.7	12 0.0	6 43.4	13 40.4	11 28.6	28 23.4	28 36.2	26 25.4	16 5.6	24 0.4	6 28.1	7 11.9
5 S	6 51 48.3	12 57.2	6 40.3	26 39.1	10 52.5	29 36.7	29 14.6	26 33.4	16 1.8	23 58.1	6 26.5	7 11.5
6 M	6 55 44.8	13 54.4	6 37.1	10♏ 4.7	10 17.6	0♋50.1	29 52.9	26 41.2	15 58.2	23 55.8	6 24.9	7 11.1
7 T	6 59 41.4	14 51.6	6 33.9	23 59.7	9 44.4	2 3.4	0♌31.2	26 48.9	15 54.6	23 53.6	6 23.3	7 10.7
8 W	7 3 37.9	15 48.8	6 30.7	8♐24.1	9 13.7	3 16.8	1 9.5	26 56.5	15 51.0	23 51.4	6 21.7	7 10.4
9 T	7 7 34.5	16 46.0	6 27.6	23 14.7	8 45.8	4 30.2	1 47.8	27 3.9	15 47.5	23 49.2	6 20.1	7 10.1
10 F	7 11 31.0	17 43.1	6 24.4	8♑24.5	8 21.3	5 43.6	2 26.1	27 11.2	15 44.1	23 47.0	6 18.5	7 9.8
11 S	7 15 27.6	18 40.3	6 21.2	23 43.4	8 0.7	6 57.1	3 4.4	27 18.3	15 40.7	23 44.8	6 16.9	7 9.6
12 S	7 19 24.2	19 37.5	6 18.0	9♒ 0.1	7 44.4	8 10.5	3 42.6	27 25.3	15 37.4	23 42.7	6 15.4	7 9.4
13 M	7 23 20.7	20 34.7	6 14.9	24 3.7	7 32.7	9 24.0	4 20.9	27 32.1	15 34.2	23 40.6	6 13.8	7 9.2
14 T	7 27 17.3	21 31.9	6 11.7	8♓45.8	7 25.9	10 37.5	4 59.1	27 38.8	15 31.0	23 38.5	6 12.3	7 9.0
15 W	7 31 13.8	22 29.1	6 8.5	23 1.7	7 24.2	11 51.0	5 37.4	27 45.3	15 27.9	23 36.5	6 10.7	7 8.9
16 T	7 35 10.4	23 26.3	6 5.3	6♈49.9	7D27.8	13 4.6	6 15.6	27 51.7	15 24.9	23 34.4	6 9.2	7 8.9
17 F	7 39 7.0	24 23.5	6 2.2	20 11.6	7 36.9	14 18.2	6 53.9	27 57.9	15 21.9	23 32.5	6 7.7	7 8.8
18 S	7 43 3.5	25 20.8	5 59.0	3♉ 9.7	7 51.4	15 31.7	7 32.1	28 4.0	15 19.0	23 30.5	6 6.1	7 8.8
19 S	7 47 0.1	26 18.0	5 55.8	15 48.1	8 11.6	16 45.4	8 10.3	28 9.8	15 16.2	23 28.5	6 4.6	7D 8.9
20 M	7 50 56.6	27 15.3	5 52.6	28 10.9	8 37.4	17 59.0	8 48.5	28 15.6	15 13.5	23 26.6	6 3.2	7 8.9
21 T	7 54 53.2	28 12.6	5 49.4	10♊21.9	9 8.8	19 12.7	9 26.7	28 21.1	15 10.8	23 24.8	6 1.7	7 9.0
22 W	7 58 49.7	29 9.9	5 46.3	22 24.5	9 45.9	20 26.3	10 4.9	28 26.5	15 8.3	23 22.9	6 0.2	7 9.2
23 T	8 2 46.3	0♌ 7.2	5 43.1	4♋21.3	10 28.5	21 40.0	10 43.1	28 31.7	15 5.8	23 21.1	5 58.8	7 9.3
24 F	8 6 42.9	1 4.5	5 39.9	16 14.6	11 16.7	22 53.8	11 21.4	28 36.8	15 3.4	23 19.4	5 57.4	7 9.6
25 S	8 10 39.4	2 1.8	5 36.7	28 6.1	12 10.3	24 7.6	11 59.6	28 41.7	15 1.1	23 17.6	5 56.0	7 9.8
26 S	8 14 36.0	2 59.2	5 33.6	9♌57.4	13 9.3	25 21.3	12 37.8	28 46.4	14 58.8	23 15.9	5 54.6	7 10.1
27 M	8 18 32.5	3 56.5	5 30.4	21 50.0	14 13.6	26 35.1	13 16.0	28 50.9	14 56.7	23 14.3	5 53.2	7 10.4
28 T	8 22 29.1	4 53.9	5 27.2	3♍45.9	15 23.2	27 48.9	13 54.2	28 55.3	14 54.6	23 12.6	5 51.8	7 10.7
29 W	8 26 25.6	5 51.2	5 24.0	15 47.3	16 37.8	29 2.7	14 32.3	28 59.4	14 52.6	23 11.0	5 50.4	7 11.1
30 T	8 30 22.2	6 48.6	5 20.9	27 57.1	17 57.4	0♌16.6	15 10.5	29 3.4	14 50.7	23 9.5	5 49.1	7 11.5
31 F	8 34 18.8	7 46.0	5 17.7	10♎18.8	19 21.9	1 30.5	15 48.7	29 7.2	14 48.9	23 8.0	5 47.8	7 11.9
DECLINATION at NOON												
1 W	6 36 2.0	23N 7.7	2N44.0	11N22.5	18N39.6	23N 1.3	21N57.1	8N52.8	21S 10.2	23S 28.0	22S 13.9	1N44.8
4 S	6 47 51.7	22 54.1	2 40.2	5S59.4	18 22.3	23 14.4	21 34.4	9 1.2	21 9.4	23 27.7	22 14.1	1 43.7
7 T	6 59 41.4	22 36.9	2 36.4	22 22.9	18 16.8	23 21.5	21 10.2	9 9.1	21 8.7	23 27.4	22 14.4	1 42.5
10 F	7 11 31.0	22 16.2	2 32.7	28 10.5	18 23.0	23 22.4	20 44.8	9 16.5	21 8.1	23 27.1	22 14.7	1 41.2
13 M	7 23 20.7	21 52.0	2 28.9	16 38.3	18 40.0	23 17.1	20 18.0	9 23.4	21 7.5	23 26.9	22 14.9	1 39.7
16 T	7 35 10.4	21 24.5	2 25.1	2N50.5	19 5.7	23 5.6	19 50.0	9 29.7	21 7.0	23 26.6	22 15.2	1 38.2
19 S	7 47 0.1	20 53.7	2 21.3	19 43.4	19 37.2	22 48.0	19 20.7	9 35.5	21 6.6	23 26.3	22 15.5	1 36.5
22 W	7 58 49.7	20 19.7	2 17.6	28 8.4	20 10.9	22 24.4	18 50.2	9 40.8	21 6.3	23 26.0	22 15.8	1 34.8
25 S	8 10 39.4	19 42.7	2 13.8	25 4.1	20 42.4	21 54.8	18 18.6	9 45.5	21 6.1	23 25.8	22 16.0	1 32.9
28 T	8 22 29.1	19 2.7	2 10.0	12 30.5	21 7.2	21 19.5	17 45.9	9 49.6	21 5.9	23 25.6	22 16.3	1 31.0
31 F	8 34 18.8	18 19.8	2 6.2	4S37.2	21 20.0	20 38.6	17 12.1	9 53.2	21 5.9	23 25.3	22 16.5	1 28.9

AUGUST 1987

DAY	EPHEMERIS SIDEREAL TIME	☉	☊	☽	☿	♀	♂	♃	♄	♅	♆	♇
LONGITUDE at NOON												
1 S	8 38 15.3	8♌43.4	5♈14.5	22♎56.2	20♋50.9	2♌44.3	16♌26.8	29♈10.9	14♐47.1	23♐ 6.5	5♑46.5	7♏12.4
2 S	8 42 11.9	9 40.8	5 11.3	5♏53.5	22 24.4	3 58.2	17 5.0	29 14.3	14R45.5	23R 5.1	5R45.2	7 12.9
3 M	8 46 8.4	10 38.2	5 8.2	19 14.3	24 2.1	5 12.1	17 43.2	29 17.6	14 44.0	23 3.7	5 43.9	7 13.5
4 T	8 50 5.0	11 35.6	5 5.0	3♐ 1.5	25 43.7	6 26.1	18 21.3	29 20.6	14 42.5	23 2.3	5 42.7	7 14.0
5 W	8 54 1.5	12 33.0	5 1.8	17 16.0	27 29.0	7 40.0	18 59.5	29 23.5	14 41.1	23 1.0	5 41.5	7 14.7
6 T	8 57 58.1	13 30.5	4 58.6	1♑55.9	29 17.6	8 54.0	19 37.6	29 26.2	14 39.9	22 59.7	5 40.3	7 15.3
7 F	9 1 54.7	14 27.9	4 55.4	16 56.1	1♌ 9.2	10 8.0	20 15.8	29 28.7	14 38.7	22 58.5	5 39.1	7 16.0
8 S	9 5 51.2	15 25.4	4 52.3	2♒ 8.6	3 3.5	11 22.0	20 53.9	29 31.0	14 37.6	22 57.3	5 37.9	7 16.7
9 S	9 9 47.8	16 22.9	4 49.1	17 23.0	5 0.0	12 36.0	21 32.0	29 33.2	14 36.6	22 56.2	5 36.8	7 17.4
10 M	9 13 44.3	17 20.4	4 45.9	2♓28.8	6 58.4	13 50.0	22 10.2	29 35.1	14 35.7	22 55.1	5 35.7	7 18.2
11 T	9 17 40.9	18 17.9	4 42.7	17 16.7	8 58.4	15 4.1	22 48.3	29 36.9	14 34.9	22 54.0	5 34.6	7 19.0
12 W	9 21 37.4	19 15.5	4 39.6	1♈40.5	10 59.5	16 18.2	23 26.4	29 38.4	14 34.2	22 53.0	5 33.6	7 19.9
13 T	9 25 34.0	20 13.1	4 36.4	15 36.7	13 1.4	17 32.3	24 4.6	29 39.8	14 33.6	22 52.1	5 32.5	7 20.8
14 F	9 29 30.5	21 10.7	4 33.2	29 5.4	15 3.9	18 46.4	24 42.8	29 41.0	14 33.1	22 51.2	5 31.5	7 21.7
15 S	9 33 27.1	22 8.3	4 30.0	12♉ 8.3	17 6.5	20 0.6	25 20.9	29 41.9	14 32.7	22 50.3	5 30.6	7 22.6
16 S	9 37 23.7	23 6.0	4 26.9	24 48.9	19 9.1	21 14.8	25 59.1	29 42.7	14 32.4	22 49.5	5 29.6	7 23.6
17 M	9 41 20.2	24 3.6	4 23.7	7♊11.4	21 11.3	22 28.9	26 37.2	29 43.3	14 32.2	22 48.7	5 28.6	7 24.6
18 T	9 45 16.8	25 1.3	4 20.5	19 20.3	23 13.0	23 43.1	27 15.4	29 43.6	14 32.0	22 48.0	5 27.7	7 25.7
19 W	9 49 13.3	25 59.1	4 17.3	1♋19.6	25 14.0	24 57.4	27 53.5	29 43.8	14 32.0	22 47.3	5 26.8	7 26.7
20 T	9 53 9.9	26 56.8	4 14.1	13 13.2	27 14.2	26 11.6	28 31.7	29 43.8	14D32.1	22 46.7	5 26.0	7 27.8
21 F	9 57 6.4	27 54.6	4 11.0	25 4.3	29 13.5	27 25.9	29 9.9	29R43.5	14 32.2	22 46.1	5 25.1	7 29.0
22 S	10 1 3.0	28 52.4	4 7.8	6♌55.8	1♍11.6	28 40.2	29 48.0	29 43.1	14 32.5	22 45.6	5 24.3	7 30.1
23 S	10 4 59.5	29 50.2	4 4.6	18 49.7	3 8.7	29 54.4	0♍26.2	29 42.5	14 32.8	22 45.1	5 23.6	7 31.3
24 M	10 8 56.1	0♍48.1	4 1.4	0♍48.0	5 4.5	1♍ 8.8	1 4.4	29 41.6	14 33.3	22 44.7	5 22.8	7 32.6
25 T	10 12 52.7	1 45.9	3 58.3	12 52.3	6 59.1	2 23.1	1 42.6	29 40.6	14 33.8	22 44.3	5 22.1	7 33.8
26 W	10 16 49.2	2 43.9	3 55.1	25 4.4	8 52.5	3 37.4	2 20.7	29 39.4	14 34.5	22 43.9	5 21.4	7 35.1
27 T	10 20 45.8	3 41.8	3 51.9	7♎26.0	10 44.5	4 51.8	2 58.9	29 37.9	14 35.2	22 43.7	5 20.7	7 36.4
28 F	10 24 42.3	4 39.7	3 48.7	19 59.2	12 35.3	6 6.2	3 37.1	29 36.3	14 36.1	22 43.4	5 20.1	7 37.8
29 S	10 28 38.9	5 37.7	3 45.5	2♏46.3	14 24.7	7 20.6	4 15.3	29 34.5	14 37.0	22 43.2	5 19.5	7 39.1
30 S	10 32 35.4	6 35.7	3 42.4	15 49.8	16 12.9	8 34.9	4 53.5	29 32.4	14 38.1	22 43.1	5 18.9	7 40.5
31 M	10 36 32.0	7 33.7	3 39.2	29 12.1	17 59.8	9 49.4	5 31.7	29 30.2	14 39.2	22 43.0	5 18.3	7 42.0
DECLINATION at NOON												
1 S	8 38 15.3	18N 4.9	2N 5.0	10S 28.9	21N20.7	20N23.7	17N 0.6	9N54.2	21S 5.9	23S 25.3	22S 16.6	1N28.2
4 T	8 50 5.0	17 18.6	2 1.2	25 5.1	21 9.9	19 35.7	16 25.5	9 57.0	21 5.9	23 2/.0	22 16.9	1 26.1
7 F	9 1 54.7	16 29.7	1 57.4	27 18.4	20 36.9	18 42.7	15 49.4	9 59.1	21 6.1	23 24.9	22 17.1	1 23.8
10 M	9 13 44.3	15 38.4	1 53.6	13 2.7	19 40.1	17 44.8	15 12.4	10 0.6	21 6.4	23 24.7	22 17.4	1 21.5
13 T	9 25 34.0	14 44.9	1 49.9	7N10.7	18 20.5	16 42.5	14 34.6	10 1.6	21 6.7	23 24.5	22 17.6	1 19.2
16 S	9 37 23.7	13 49.2	1 46.1	22 54.7	16 41.1	15 36.0	13 55.9	10 1.9	21 7.2	23 24.4	22 17.8	1 16.7
19 W	9 49 13.3	12 51.6	1 42.3	28 36.4	14 46.2	14 25.7	13 16.4	10 1.6	21 7.8	23 24.3	22 18.1	1 14.2
22 S	10 1 3.0	11 52.1	1 38.5	22 41.4	12 40.1	13 11.7	12 36.1	10 0.6	21 8.5	23 24.2	22 18.3	1 11.6
25 T	10 12 52.7	10 50.9	1 34.7	8 21.0	10 26.6	11 54.5	11 55.2	9 59.1	21 9.2	23 24.1	22 18.5	1 9.0
28 F	10 24 42.3	9 48.2	1 30.9	9S16.4	8 8.9	10 34.3	11 13.5	9 56.9	21 10.1	23 24.1	22 18.7	1 6.3
31 M	10 36 32.0	8 44.0	1 27.2	24 15.4	5 49.4	9 11.6	10 31.3	9 54.1	21 11.1	23 24.1	22 18.9	1 3.6

SEPTEMBER 1987

DAY	EPHEMERIS SIDEREAL TIME	☉	☊	☾	☿	♀	♂	♃	♄	♅	♆	♇
	h m s	° ′	° ′	° ′	° ′	° ′	° ′	° ′	° ′	° ′	° ′	° ′
						LONGITUDE at NOON						
1 T	10 40 28.5	8♍31.7	3♈36.0	12♐54.8	19♍45.4	11♍ 3.8	6♍ 9.9	29♈27.8	14♐40.4	22♐43.0	5♑17.8	7♏43.4
2 W	10 44 25.1	9 29.8	3 32.8	26 58.7	21 29.8	12 18.2	6 48.1	29R25.1	14 41.8	22 43.0	5R17.3	7 44.9
3 T	10 48 21.6	10 27.9	3 29.7	11♑22.7	23 12.9	13 32.6	7 26.3	29 22.3	14 43.2	22D43.1	5 16.9	7 46.4
4 F	10 52 18.2	11 26.0	3 26.5	26 3.8	24 54.8	14 47.1	8 4.5	29 19.4	14 44.8	22 43.3	5 16.5	7 48.0
5 S	10 56 14.8	12 24.2	3 23.3	10♒56.3	26 35.4	16 1.6	8 42.7	29 16.2	14 46.4	22 43.4	5 16.1	7 49.6
6 S	11 0 11.3	13 22.3	3 20.1	25 52.9	28 14.8	17 16.1	9 21.0	29 12.8	14 48.1	22 43.7	5 15.8	7 51.2
7 M	11 4 7.9	14 20.5	3 16.9	10♓45.3	29 53.1	18 30.5	9 59.2	29 9.3	14 49.9	22 44.0	5 15.4	7 52.8
8 T	11 8 4.4	15 18.7	3 13.8	25 25.6	1♎30.1	19 45.0	10 37.4	29 5.5	14 51.8	22 44.3	5 15.1	7 54.5
9 W	11 12 1.0	16 16.9	3 10.6	9♈47.1	3 6.1	20 59.5	11 15.7	29 1.6	14 53.8	22 44.7	5 14.9	7 56.1
10 T	11 15 57.5	17 15.2	3 7.4	23 45.3	4 40.8	22 14.1	11 53.9	28 57.5	14 55.9	22 45.1	5 14.6	7 57.8
11 F	11 19 54.1	18 13.5	3 4.2	7♉18.4	6 14.5	23 28.6	12 32.1	28 53.2	14 58.0	22 45.6	5 14.4	7 59.6
12 S	11 23 50.6	19 11.9	3 1.1	20 26.5	7 46.9	24 43.1	13 10.4	28 48.7	15 0.3	22 46.1	5 14.2	8 1.3
13 S	11 27 47.2	20 10.2	2 57.9	3♊11.7	9 18.3	25 57.7	13 48.7	28 44.1	15 2.7	22 46.7	5 14.1	8 3.1
14 M	11 31 43.7	21 8.7	2 54.7	15 37.5	10 48.6	27 12.2	14 27.0	28 39.2	15 5.1	22 47.3	5 14.0	8 4.9
15 T	11 35 40.3	22 7.1	2 51.5	27 47.9	12 17.7	28 26.8	15 5.2	28 34.2	15 7.7	22 48.0	5 13.9	8 6.7
16 W	11 39 36.8	23 5.6	2 48.3	9♋47.5	13 45.7	29 41.4	15 43.5	28 29.1	15 10.3	22 48.7	5 13.9	8 8.6
17 T	11 43 33.4	24 4.1	2 45.2	21 40.7	15 12.5	0♎56.0	16 21.9	28 23.8	15 13.0	22 49.5	5 13.9	8 10.4
18 F	11 47 30.0	25 2.7	2 42.0	3♌31.8	16 38.2	2 10.6	17 0.2	28 18.3	15 15.8	22 50.4	5 13.9	8 12.3
19 S	11 51 26.5	26 1.2	2 38.8	15 24.6	18 2.7	3 25.2	17 38.5	28 12.6	15 18.7	22 51.3	5D14.0	8 14.2
20 S	11 55 23.1	26 59.9	2 35.6	27 22.5	19 26.0	4 39.8	18 16.8	28 6.9	15 21.7	22 52.2	5 14.0	8 16.2
21 M	11 59 19.6	27 58.5	2 32.5	9♍28.2	20 48.1	5 54.4	18 55.2	28 0.9	15 24.8	22 53.2	5 14.2	8 18.1
22 T	12 3 16.2	28 57.2	2 29.3	21 43.7	22 8.9	7 9.1	19 33.5	27 54.8	15 28.0	22 54.2	5 14.3	8 20.1
23 W	12 7 12.7	29 55.9	2 26.1	4♎10.8	23 28.4	8 23.7	20 11.9	27 48.6	15 31.2	22 55.3	5 14.5	8 22.1
24 T	12 11 9.3	0♎54.7	2 22.9	16 50.4	24 46.6	9 38.4	20 50.3	27 42.2	15 34.5	22 56.5	5 14.7	8 24.1
25 F	12 15 5.8	1 53.5	2 19.7	29 43.2	26 3.4	10 53.1	21 28.7	27 35.8	15 38.0	22 57.7	5 15.0	8 26.2
26 S	12 19 2.4	2 52.4	2 16.6	12♏49.6	27 18.7	12 7.7	22 7.1	27 29.1	15 41.5	22 59.0	5 15.3	8 28.3
27 S	12 22 58.9	3 51.2	2 13.4	26 9.8	28 32.5	13 22.4	22 45.5	27 22.4	15 45.1	23 0.3	5 15.7	8 30.3
28 M	12 26 55.5	4 50.1	2 10.2	9♐43.7	29 44.6	14 37.1	23 23.9	27 15.5	15 48.8	23 1.6	5 16.0	8 32.4
29 T	12 30 52.0	5 49.0	2 7.0	23 31.1	0♏54.9	15 51.8	24 2.4	27 8.5	15 52.5	23 3.0	5 16.4	8 34.5
30 W	12 34 48.6	6 48.0	2 3.9	7♑31.4	2 3.4	17 6.4	24 40.8	27 1.4	15 56.4	23 4.4	5 16.8	8 36.7
						DECLINATION at NOON						
1 T	10 40 28.5	8N22.4	1N25.9	27S 14.9	5N 2.8	8N43.5	10N17.1	9N53.1	21S 11.4	23S 24.1	22S 18.9	1N 2.7
4 F	10 52 18.2	7 16.6	1 22.1	25 39.6	2 43.6	7 17.9	9 34.1	9 49.5	21 12.5	23 24.1	22 19.1	0 59.9
7 M	11 4 7.9	6 9.8	1 18.3	9 19.9	0 26.3	5 50.4	8 50.6	9 45.3	21 13.7	23 24.1	22 19.3	0 57.2
10 T	11 15 57.5	5 2.1	1 14.5	11N 0.6	1S 48.1	4 21.4	8 6.6	9 40.6	21 14.9	23 24.2	22 19.4	0 54.4
13 S	11 27 47.2	3 53.7	1 10.7	25 19.0	3 58.8	2 51.3	7 22.1	9 35.4	21 16.3	23 24.3	22 19.6	0 51.5
16 W	11 39 36.8	2 44.5	1 7.0	28 17.9	6 4.9	1 20.2	6 37.3	9 29.6	21 17.7	23 24.4	22 19.7	0 48.7
19 S	11 51 26.5	1 34.9	1 3.2	19 54.4	8 5.8	0S 11.3	5 52.1	9 23.3	21 19.2	23 24.5	22 19.8	0 45.9
22 T	12 3 16.2	0 25.0	0 59.4	4 10.7	10 0.5	1 43.0	5 6.5	9 16.5	21 20.8	23 24.7	22 19.9	0 43.1
25 F	12 15 5.8	0S45.2	0 55.6	13S 39.1	11 48.4	3 14.7	4 20.7	9 9.4	21 22.4	23 24.9	22 20.0	0 40.2
28 M	12 26 55.5	1 55.3	0 51.8	26 44.1	13 28.3	4 45.8	3 34.6	9 1.8	21 24.1	23 25.1	22 20.1	0 37.4

OCTOBER 1987

DAY	EPHEMERIS SIDEREAL TIME	☉	☊	☾	☿	♀	♂	♃	♄	♅	♆	♇
						LONGITUDE at NOON						
1 T	12 38 45.1	7♎46.9	2♈ 0.7	21♑43.2	3♏ 9.9	18♎21.1	25♍19.2	26♈54.2	16♐ 0.3	23♐ 5.9	5♑17.3	8♏38.8
2 F	12 42 41.7	8 45.9	1 57.5	6♒ 4.5	4 14.3	19 35.8	25 57.7	26R46.9	16 4.3	23 7.5	5 17.8	8 41.0
3 S	12 46 38.3	9 44.9	1 54.3	20 32.1	5 16.4	20 50.4	26 36.1	26 39.5	16 8.3	23 9.0	5 18.3	8 43.2
4 S	12 50 34.8	10 44.0	1 51.2	5♓ 1.9	6 16.0	22 5.1	27 14.6	26 32.0	16 12.5	23 10.7	5 18.8	8 45.4
5 M	12 54 31.4	11 43.1	1 48.0	19 29.1	7 12.9	23 19.8	27 53.1	26 24.4	16 16.7	23 12.3	5 19.4	8 47.6
6 T	12 58 27.9	12 42.2	1 44.8	3♈48.2	8 6.9	24 34.5	28 31.5	26 16.8	16 21.0	23 14.1	5 20.0	8 49.8
7 W	13 2 24.5	13 41.4	1 41.6	17 54.5	8 57.7	25 49.2	29 10.0	26 9.1	16 25.4	23 15.8	5 20.7	8 52.0
8 T	13 6 21.0	14 40.5	1 38.4	1♉43.6	9 45.0	27 3.8	29 48.6	26 1.3	16 29.8	23 17.6	5 21.4	8 54.3
9 F	13 10 17.6	15 39.8	1 35.3	15 12.7	10 28.5	28 18.5	0♎27.1	25 53.5	16 34.3	23 19.5	5 22.1	8 56.5
10 S	13 14 14.1	16 39.0	1 32.1	28 20.6	11 7.9	29 33.2	1 5.6	25 45.6	16 38.9	23 21.4	5 22.8	8 58.8
11 S	13 18 10.7	17 38.3	1 28.9	11♊ 7.7	11 42.7	0♏47.9	1 44.2	25 37.6	16 43.6	23 23.4	5 23.6	9 1.1
12 M	13 22 7.2	18 37.6	1 25.7	23 36.0	12 12.5	2 2.6	2 22.7	25 29.6	16 48.3	23 25.3	5 24.4	9 3.4
13 T	13 26 3.8	19 37.0	1 22.6	5♋48.4	12 36.9	3 17.3	3 1.3	25 21.6	16 53.1	23 27.4	5 25.3	9 5.7
14 W	13 30 0.4	20 36.4	1 19.4	17 49.1	12 55.4	4 32.0	3 39.9	25 13.5	16 58.0	23 29.5	5 26.2	9 8.0
15 T	13 33 56.9	21 35.9	1 16.2	29 42.7	13 7.5	5 46.7	4 18.5	25 5.4	17 2.9	23 31.6	5 27.1	9 10.4
16 F	13 37 53.5	22 35.4	1 13.0	11♌33.9	13 12.6	7 1.4	4 57.2	24 57.4	17 8.0	23 33.8	5 28.1	9 12.8
17 S	13 41 50.0	23 34.9	1 9.8	23 27.4	13R10.3	8 16.1	5 35.8	24 49.3	17 13.0	23 36.0	5 29.0	9 15.1
18 S	13 45 46.6	24 34.5	1 6.7	5♍27.9	12 60.0	9 30.9	6 14.5	24 41.1	17 18.2	23 38.3	5 30.0	9 17.5
19 M	13 49 43.1	25 34.1	1 3.5	17 39.3	12 41.4	10 45.6	6 53.1	24 33.0	17 23.4	23 40.5	5 31.1	9 19.9
20 T	13 53 39.7	26 33.7	1 0.3	0♎ 4.8	12 14.1	12 0.3	7 31.8	24 24.9	17 28.6	23 42.9	5 32.1	9 22.2
21 W	13 57 36.2	27 33.4	0 57.1	12 46.7	11 38.0	13 15.0	8 10.5	24 16.8	17 34.0	23 45.3	5 33.2	9 24.6
22 T	14 1 32.8	28 33.1	0 54.0	25 46.0	10 53.3	14 29.7	8 49.2	24 8.7	17 39.4	23 47.7	5 34.3	9 27.0
23 F	14 5 29.3	29 32.8	0 50.8	9♏ 2.7	10 0.2	15 44.4	9 28.0	24 0.6	17 44.8	23 50.1	5 35.5	9 29.4
24 S	14 9 25.9	0♏32.6	0 47.6	22 35.2	8 59.5	16 59.1	10 6.7	23 52.6	17 50.3	23 52.6	5 36.7	9 31.8
25 S	14 13 22.5	1 32.4	0 44.4	6♐21.4	7 52.2	18 13.9	10 45.4	23 44.6	17 55.9	23 55.1	5 37.9	9 34.2
26 M	14 17 19.0	2 32.3	0 41.2	20 18.1	6 39.9	19 28.6	11 24.2	23 36.7	18 1.5	23 57.7	5 39.1	9 36.6
27 T	14 21 15.6	3 32.1	0 38.1	4♑22.2	5 24.4	20 43.3	12 3.0	23 28.8	18 7.2	24 0.3	5 40.4	9 39.1
28 W	14 25 12.1	4 32.0	0 34.9	18 30.6	4 7.8	21 58.0	12 41.8	23 21.0	18 12.9	24 3.0	5 41.7	9 41.5
29 T	14 29 8.7	5 31.9	0 31.7	2♒40.8	2 52.4	23 12.7	13 20.5	23 13.2	18 18.7	24 5.6	5 43.0	9 43.9
30 F	14 33 5.2	6 31.9	0 28.5	16 50.7	1 40.6	24 27.4	13 59.4	23 5.5	18 24.5	24 8.3	5 44.4	9 46.3
31 S	14 37 1.8	7 31.8	0 25.4	0♓58.5	0 34.6	25 42.1	14 38.2	22 57.9	18 30.4	24 11.1	5 45.7	9 48.7
						DECLINATION at NOON						
1 T	12 38 45.1	3S 5.3	0N48.0	26S36.7	14S58.9	6S 16.1	2N48.3	8N53.9	21S25.8	23S 25.3	22S 20.2	0N34.6
4 S	12 50 34.8	4 15.0	0 44.2	11 55.8	16 18.8	7 45.2	2 1.9	8 45.8	21 27.6	23 25.6	22 20.3	0 31.8
7 W	13 2 24.5	5 24.1	0 40.4	8N20.0	17 25.9	9 12.8	1 15.4	8 37.4	21 29.4	23 25.8	22 20.3	0 29.1
10 S	13 14 14.1	6 32.7	0 36.6	24 3.0	18 17.1	10 38.6	0 28.8	8 28.8	21 31.3	23 26.1	22 20.4	0 26.4
13 T	13 26 3.8	7 40.5	0 32.8	28 33.6	18 48.7	12 2.2	0S 17.8	8 20.1	21 33.1	23 26.4	22 20.4	0 23.7
16 F	13 37 53.5	8 47.4	0 29.1	21 13.7	18 55.4	13 23.3	1 4.5	8 11.3	21 35.0	23 26.8	22 20.4	0 21.1
19 M	13 49 43.1	9 53.2	0 25.3	6 6.3	18 30.5	14 41.5	1 51.1	8 2.6	21 37.0	23 27.1	22 20.4	0 18.5
22 T	14 1 32.8	10 57.7	0 21.5	11S54.0	17 27.7	15 56.5	2 37.6	7 53.8	21 38.9	23 27.4	22 20.4	0 15.9
25 S	14 13 22.5	12 0.7	0 17.7	25 59.5	15 45.8	17 7.8	3 23.9	7 45.2	21 40.8	23 27.8	22 20.4	0 13.5
28 W	14 25 12.1	13 2.1	0 13.9	27 6.1	13 36.0	18 15.1	4 10.1	7 36.8	21 42.8	23 28.1	22 20.3	0 11.1
31 S	14 37 1.8	14 1.6	0 10.1	13 38.0	11 25.0	19 18.1	4 56.0	7 28.7	21 44.7	23 28.5	22 20.2	0 8.8

NOVEMBER 1987

LONGITUDE at NOON

DAY	EPHEMERIS SIDEREAL TIME h m s	☉ ° ′	☊ ° ′	☽ ° ′	☿ ° ′	♀ ° ′	♂ ° ′	♃ ° ′	♄ ° ′	♅ ° ′	♆ ° ′	♇ ° ′
1 S	14 40 58.3	8♏31.8	0♈22.2	15♓ 2.7	29♎36.4	26♏56.8	15♎17.0	22♈50.3	18♐36.4	24♐13.9	5♑47.1	9♏51.2
2 M	14 44 54.9	9 31.9	0 19.0	29 1.6	28R47.7	28 11.5	15 55.9	22R42.9	18 42.4	24 16.7	5 48.6	9 53.6
3 T	14 48 51.5	10 31.9	0 15.8	12♈53.0	28 9.6	29 26.1	16 34.7	22 35.5	18 48.4	24 19.5	5 50.0	9 56.0
4 W	14 52 48.0	11 32.0	0 12.7	26 34.7	27 42.8	0♐40.8	17 13.6	22 28.3	18 54.5	24 22.4	5 51.5	9 58.5
5 T	14 56 44.6	12 32.1	0 9.5	10♉ 4.2	27 27.7	1 55.5	17 52.5	22 21.1	19 0.6	24 25.3	5 53.0	10 0.9
6 F	15 0 41.1	13 32.3	0 6.3	23 19.3	27 24.2	3 10.2	18 31.4	22 14.1	19 6.9	24 28.3	5 54.6	10 3.4
7 S	15 4 37.7	14 32.5	0 3.1	6♊18.3	27D31.7	4 24.9	19 10.4	22 7.2	19 13.1	24 31.3	5 56.2	10 5.8
8 S	15 8 34.2	15 32.7	29♓59.9	19 0.6	27 49.9	5 39.5	19 49.3	22 0.4	19 19.4	24 34.3	5 57.8	10 8.2
9 M	15 12 30.8	16 32.9	29 56.8	1♋26.8	28 17.8	6 54.2	20 28.3	21 53.7	19 25.7	24 37.3	5 59.4	10 10.6
10 T	15 16 27.4	17 33.2	29 53.6	13 38.6	28 54.6	8 8.8	21 7.2	21 47.1	19 32.0	24 40.4	6 1.0	10 13.0
11 W	15 20 23.9	18 33.5	29 50.4	25 39.0	29 39.5	9 23.5	21 46.2	21 40.7	19 38.4	24 43.5	6 2.7	10 15.5
12 T	15 24 20.5	19 33.8	29 47.2	7♌31.9	0♏31.5	10 38.1	22 25.2	21 34.4	19 44.8	24 46.6	6 4.4	10 17.9
13 F	15 28 17.0	20 34.2	29 44.1	19 22.0	1 29.8	11 52.8	23 4.3	21 28.2	19 51.3	24 49.7	6 6.1	10 20.3
14 S	15 32 13.6	21 34.6	29 40.9	1♍14.3	2 33.7	13 7.4	23 43.3	21 22.2	19 57.8	24 52.9	6 7.8	10 22.7
15 S	15 36 10.1	22 35.0	29 37.7	13 14.1	3 42.2	14 22.1	24 22.4	21 16.3	20 4.4	24 56.1	6 9.6	10 25.1
16 M	15 40 6.7	23 35.4	29 34.5	25 26.7	4 54.9	15 36.7	25 1.5	21 10.6	20 10.9	24 59.3	6 11.3	10 27.4
17 T	15 44 3.3	24 35.9	29 31.4	7♎56.4	6 11.1	16 51.4	25 40.5	21 5.1	20 17.5	25 2.5	6 13.1	10 29.8
18 W	15 47 59.8	25 36.5	29 28.2	20 47.1	7 30.3	18 6.0	26 19.7	20 59.7	20 24.2	25 5.8	6 15.0	10 32.2
19 T	15 51 56.4	26 37.0	29 25.0	4♏ 0.8	8 52.1	19 20.6	26 58.8	20 54.5	20 30.9	25 9.1	6 16.8	10 34.5
20 F	15 55 52.9	27 37.6	29 21.8	17 37.6	10 15.9	20 35.3	27 37.9	20 49.4	20 37.6	25 12.4	6 18.7	10 36.9
21 S	15 59 49.5	28 38.2	29 18.6	1♐35.6	11 41.6	21 49.9	28 17.1	20 44.6	20 44.3	25 15.8	6 20.5	10 39.2
22 S	16 3 46.0	29 38.8	29 15.5	15 50.5	13 8.7	23 4.5	28 56.3	20 39.9	20 51.1	25 19.1	6 22.4	10 41.6
23 M	16 7 42.6	0♐39.5	29 12.3	0♑16.5	14 37.1	24 19.1	29 35.4	20 35.4	20 57.9	25 22.5	6 24.3	10 43.9
24 T	16 11 39.2	1 40.1	29 9.1	14 47.0	16 6.4	25 33.7	0♏14.6	20 31.0	21 4.7	25 25.9	6 26.3	10 46.2
25 W	16 15 35.7	2 40.8	29 5.9	29 15.8	17 36.7	26 48.3	0 53.9	20 26.9	21 11.5	25 29.3	6 28.2	10 48.5
26 T	16 19 32.3	3 41.5	29 2.8	13♒37.8	19 7.6	28 2.9	1 33.1	20 22.9	21 18.4	25 32.7	6 30.2	10 50.8
27 F	16 23 28.8	4 42.3	28 59.6	27 50.0	20 39.1	29 17.5	2 12.4	20 19.2	21 25.3	25 36.2	6 32.2	10 53.1
28 S	16 27 25.4	5 43.0	28 56.4	11♓50.6	22 11.0	0♑32.1	2 51.6	20 15.6	21 32.2	25 39.7	6 34.2	10 55.4
29 S	16 31 21.9	6 43.8	28 53.2	25 39.5	23 43.3	1 46.7	3 30.9	20 12.3	21 39.2	25 43.2	6 36.3	10 57.6
30 M	16 35 18.5	7 44.6	28 50.1	9♈17.0	25 15.8	3 1.2	4 10.2	20 9.1	21 46.1	25 46.7	6 38.3	10 59.8

DECLINATION at NOON

DAY	EPHEMERIS SIDEREAL TIME h m s	☉	☊	☽	☿	♀	♂	♃	♄	♅	♆	♇
1 S	14 40 58.3	14S20.9	0N 8.8	7S17.3	10S46.7	19S38.1	5S11.3	7N26.0	21S45.3	23S28.6	22S20.2	0N 8.0
4 W	14 52 48.0	15 17.7	0 5.0	12N16.0	9 20.8	20 34.7	5 56.9	7 18.3	21 47.2	23 29.0	22 20.1	0 5.8
7 S	15 4 37.7	16 12.2	0 1.2	25 56.4	8 46.2	21 26.3	6 42.1	7 11.0	21 49.1	23 29.4	22 20.0	0 3.6
10 T	15 16 27.4	17 4.3	0S 2.6	27 43.9	8 59.7	22 12.5	7 27.0	7 4.1	21 51.0	23 29.8	22 19.9	0 1.5
13 F	15 28 17.0	17 53.7	0 6.3	18 16.0	9 49.7	22 52.9	8 11.5	6 57.6	21 52.8	23 30.2	22 19.8	0S 0.4
16 M	15 40 6.7	18 40.4	0 10.1	2 16.7	11 3.9	23 27.3	8 55.5	6 51.7	21 54.6	23 30.5	22 19.6	0 2.3
19 T	15 51 56.4	19 24.1	0 13.9	15S28.2	12 31.9	23 55.5	9 39.0	6 46.3	21 56.3	23 30.9	22 19.5	0 4.1
22 S	16 3 46.0	20 4.7	0 17.7	27 33.6	14 6.1	24 17.3	10 22.0	6 41.6	21 58.1	23 31.3	22 19.3	0 5.8
25 W	16 15 35.7	20 42.0	0 21.5	24 38.4	15 41.5	24 32.6	11 4.3	6 37.4	21 59.7	23 31.7	22 19.1	0 7.4
28 S	16 27 25.4	21 15.7	0 25.3	8 35.6	17 14.4	24 41.1	11 46.0	6 34.0	22 1.3	23 32.0	22 18.9	0 8.9

DECEMBER 1987

LONGITUDE at NOON

DAY	EPHEMERIS SIDEREAL TIME h m s	☉ ° ′	☊ ° ′	☽ ° ′	☿ ° ′	♀ ° ′	♂ ° ′	♃ ° ′	♄ ° ′	♅ ° ′	♆ ° ′	♇ ° ′
1 T	16 39 15.1	8♐45.4	28♓46.9	22♈43.8	26♏48.6	4♑15.7	4♏49.5	20♈ 6.1	21♐53.1	25♐50.2	6♑40.4	11♏ 2.1
2 W	16 43 11.6	9 46.2	28 43.7	6♉ 0.1	28 21.6	5 30.2	5 28.8	20R 3.3	22 0.1	25 53.7	6 42.4	11 4.3
3 T	16 47 8.2	10 47.0	28 40.5	19 5.9	29 54.6	6 44.7	6 8.1	20 0.7	22 7.1	25 57.2	6 44.5	11 6.5
4 F	16 51 4.7	11 47.8	28 37.4	2♊ 0.6	1♐27.8	7 59.2	6 47.5	19 58.4	22 14.1	26 0.8	6 46.6	11 8.6
5 S	16 55 1.3	12 48.7	28 34.2	14 43.6	3 1.1	9 13.7	7 26.8	19 56.2	22 21.1	26 4.3	6 48.7	11 10.8
6 S	16 58 57.9	13 49.6	28 31.0	27 14.4	4 34.5	10 28.2	8 6.2	19 54.2	22 28.1	26 7.9	6 50.8	11 12.9
7 M	17 2 54.4	14 50.4	28 27.8	9♋32.9	6 7.9	11 42.6	8 45.6	19 52.4	22 35.2	26 11.5	6 52.9	11 15.0
8 T	17 6 51.0	15 51.4	28 24.6	21 40.2	7 41.4	12 57.0	9 25.0	19 50.9	22 42.2	26 15.1	6 55.1	11 17.1
9 W	17 10 47.5	16 52.3	28 21.5	3♌37.9	9 14.9	14 11.5	10 4.4	19 49.5	22 49.3	26 18.7	6 57.2	11 19.2
10 T	17 14 44.1	17 53.2	28 18.3	15 28.9	10 48.4	15 25.9	10 43.9	19 48.4	22 56.4	26 22.3	6 59.4	11 21.3
11 F	17 18 40.6	18 54.2	28 15.1	27 17.1	12 22.1	16 40.3	11 23.4	19 47.4	23 3.5	26 25.9	7 1.6	11 23.3
12 S	17 22 37.2	19 55.2	28 11.9	9♍ 7.1	13 55.7	17 54.6	12 2.8	19 46.7	23 10.6	26 29.5	7 3.8	11 25.3
13 S	17 26 33.8	20 56.2	28 8.8	21 4.1	15 29.5	19 9.0	12 42.3	19 46.2	23 17.7	26 33.1	7 6.0	11 27.3
14 M	17 30 30.3	21 57.2	28 5.6	3♎13.6	17 3.3	20 23.4	13 21.9	19 45.9	23 24.8	26 36.7	7 8.2	11 29.3
15 T	17 34 26.9	22 58.3	28 2.4	15 41.1	18 37.2	21 37.7	14 1.4	19 45.8	23 31.9	26 40.4	7 10.4	11 31.3
16 W	17 38 23.4	23 59.3	27 59.2	28 31.6	20 11.2	22 52.0	14 41.0	19D45.9	23 39.0	26 44.0	7 12.6	11 33.2
17 T	17 42 20.0	25 0.4	27 56.1	11♏48.7	21 45.4	24 6.3	15 20.5	19 46.2	23 46.1	26 47.6	7 14.8	11 35.1
18 F	17 46 16.6	26 1.5	27 52.9	25 34.1	23 19.7	25 20.6	16 0.2	19 46.8	23 53.2	26 51.3	7 17.1	11 37.0
19 S	17 50 13.1	27 2.6	27 49.7	9♐46.6	24 54.1	26 34.9	16 39.8	19 47.5	24 0.3	26 54.9	7 19.3	11 38.9
20 S	17 54 9.7	28 3.7	27 46.5	24 22.0	26 28.6	27 49.2	17 19.4	19 48.5	24 7.4	26 58.6	7 21.6	11 40.8
21 M	17 58 6.2	29 4.8	27 43.4	9♑13.1	28 3.4	29 3.4	17 59.0	19 49.6	24 14.5	27 2.2	7 23.8	11 42.6
22 T	18 2 2.8	0♑ 6.0	27 40.2	24 10.7	29 38.3	0♒17.6	18 38.6	19 51.0	24 21.6	27 5.8	7 26.1	11 44.4
23 W	18 5 59.4	1 7.1	27 37.0	9♒ 5.6	1♑13.4	1 31.8	19 18.3	19 52.5	24 28.6	27 9.5	7 28.4	11 46.1
24 T	18 9 55.9	2 8.2	27 33.8	23 49.7	2 48.7	2 45.9	19 58.0	19 54.3	24 35.7	27 13.1	7 30.6	11 47.9
25 F	18 13 52.5	3 9.4	27 30.7	8♓17.2	4 24.3	4 0.0	20 37.7	19 56.3	24 42.8	27 16.7	7 32.9	11 49.6
26 S	18 17 49.0	4 10.5	27 27.5	22 25.4	6 0.1	5 14.1	21 17.4	19 58.5	24 49.8	27 20.4	7 35.2	11 51.3
27 S	18 21 45.6	5 11.7	27 24.3	6♈13.7	7 36.1	6 28.2	21 57.1	20 0.9	24 56.8	27 24.0	7 37.4	11 52.9
28 M	18 25 42.1	6 12.8	27 21.1	19 43.3	9 12.4	7 42.2	22 36.8	20 3.5	25 3.8	27 27.6	7 39.7	11 54.6
29 T	18 29 38.7	7 13.9	27 17.9	2♉56.3	10 49.0	8 56.2	23 16.5	20 6.3	25 10.8	27 31.2	7 42.0	11 56.2
30 W	18 33 35.3	8 15.1	27 14.8	15 54.9	12 25.9	10 10.2	23 56.3	20 9.3	25 17.8	27 34.8	7 44.2	11 57.7
31 T	18 37 31.8	9 16.2	27 11.6	28 41.0	14 3.0	11 24.1	24 36.0	20 12.4	25 24.8	27 38.3	7 46.5	11 59.3

DECLINATION at NOON

DAY	EPHEMERIS SIDEREAL TIME h m s	☉	☊	☽	☿	♀	♂	♃	♄	♅	♆	♇
1 T	16 39 15.1	21S45.9	0S29.1	10N39.3	18S42.3	24S42.8	12S27.0	6N31.2	22S 2.9	23S32.4	22S18.6	0S10.2
4 F	16 51 4.7	22 12.3	0 32.9	24 55.3	20 3.5	24 37.8	13 7.2	6 29.1	22 4.4	23 32.7	22 18.4	0 11.5
7 M	17 2 54.4	22 34.9	0 36.7	28 0.7	21 16.8	24 26.0	13 46.6	6 27.7	22 5.8	23 33.1	22 18.1	0 12.6
10 T	17 14 44.1	22 53.5	0 40.5	19 28.7	22 21.2	24 7.6	14 25.2	6 27.1	22 7.2	23 33.4	22 17.9	0 13.7
13 S	17 26 33.8	23 8.0	0 44.2	4 8.2	23 15.8	23 42.6	15 2.8	6 27.1	22 8.5	23 33.7	22 17.6	0 14.6
16 W	17 38 23.4	23 18.4	0 48.0	13S19.1	23 60.0	23 11.1	15 39.6	6 27.8	22 9.7	23 34.0	22 17.3	0 15.4
19 S	17 50 13.1	23 24.6	0 51.8	26 37.2	24 33.0	22 33.5	16 15.3	6 29.3	22 10.8	23 34.3	22 16.9	0 16.0
22 T	18 2 2.8	23 26.6	0 55.6	25 40.7	24 54.3	21 49.9	16 50.0	6 31.5	22 11.9	23 34.6	22 16.6	0 16.6
25 F	18 13 52.5	23 24.3	0 59.4	9 58.2	25 3.2	21 0.6	17 23.6	6 34.4	22 12.9	23 34.8	22 16.3	0 17.0
28 M	18 25 42.1	23 17.8	1 3.2	9N31.0	24 59.3	20 6.0	17 56.0	6 37.9	22 13.9	23 35.1	22 15.9	0 17.3
31 T	18 37 31.8	23 7.1	1 7.0	24 11.1	24 42.2	19 6.2	18 27.2	6 42.2	22 14.7	23 35.3	22 15.5	0 17.5

JANUARY 1988

DAY	EPHEMERIS SIDEREAL TIME	☉	☊	☽	☿	♀	♂	♃	♄	♅	♆	♇
	h m s	° ′	° ′	° ′	° ′	° ′	° ′	° ′	° ′	° ′	° ′	° ′
						LONGITUDE at NOON						
1 F	18 41 28.4	10♑17.3	27♓ 8.4	11♊16.3	15♑40.4	12♒38.0	25♏15.8	20♈15.8	25♐31.8	27♐41.9	7♑48.8	12♏ 0.8
2 S	18 45 24.9	11 18.5	27 5.2	23 41.8	17 18.1	13 51.8	25 55.6	20 19.4	25 38.7	27 45.5	7 51.0	12 2.3
3 S	18 49 21.5	12 19.6	27 2.1	5♋58.1	18 56.1	15 5.7	26 35.4	20 23.2	25 45.6	27 49.0	7 53.3	12 3.8
4 M	18 53 18.1	13 20.7	26 58.9	18 5.8	20 34.3	16 19.4	27 15.3	20 27.2	25 52.5	27 52.6	7 55.6	12 5.2
5 T	18 57 14.6	14 21.9	26 55.7	0♌ 5.9	22 12.8	17 33.1	27 55.1	20 31.3	25 59.4	27 56.1	7 57.8	12 6.6
6 W	19 1 11.2	15 23.0	26 52.5	11 59.5	23 51.5	18 46.8	28 35.0	20 35.7	26 6.2	27 59.6	8 0.1	12 8.0
7 T	19 5 7.7	16 24.2	26 49.4	23 48.6	25 30.4	20 0.5	29 14.8	20 40.2	26 13.0	28 3.1	8 2.3	12 9.3
8 F	19 9 4.3	17 25.3	26 46.2	5♍36.0	27 9.4	21 14.1	29 54.8	20 45.0	26 19.9	28 6.7	8 4.6	12 10.7
9 S	19 13 0.9	18 26.5	26 43.0	17 25.3	28 48.5	22 27.7	0♐34.7	20 49.9	26 26.6	28 10.1	8 6.9	12 11.9
10 S	19 16 57.4	19 27.6	26 39.8	29 20.9	0♒27.6	23 41.2	1 14.6	20 55.0	26 33.4	28 13.6	8 9.1	12 13.2
11 M	19 20 54.0	20 28.7	26 36.7	11♎27.7	2 6.7	24 54.7	1 54.5	21 0.2	26 40.1	28 17.0	8 11.4	12 14.4
12 T	19 24 50.5	21 29.9	26 33.5	23 51.0	3 45.6	26 8.1	2 34.5	21 5.7	26 46.8	28 20.4	8 13.6	12 15.6
13 W	19 28 47.1	22 31.0	26 30.3	6♏36.2	5 24.1	27 21.5	3 14.5	21 11.3	26 53.4	28 23.9	8 15.8	12 16.7
14 T	19 32 43.6	23 32.1	26 27.1	19 47.7	7 2.3	28 34.8	3 54.5	21 17.1	27 0.0	28 27.2	8 18.0	12 17.8
15 F	19 36 40.2	24 33.3	26 23.9	3♐28.6	8 39.7	29 48.1	4 34.5	21 23.1	27 6.6	28 30.6	8 20.2	12 18.9
16 S	19 40 36.8	25 34.4	26 20.8	17 39.5	10 16.4	1♓ 1.3	5 14.5	21 29.2	27 13.2	28 33.9	8 22.4	12 20.0
17 S	19 44 33.3	26 35.5	26 17.6	2♑18.1	11 51.9	2 14.4	5 54.5	21 35.5	27 19.7	28 37.3	8 24.6	12 21.0
18 M	19 48 29.9	27 36.7	26 14.4	17 18.2	13 26.0	3 27.6	6 34.6	21 42.0	27 26.2	28 40.6	8 26.8	12 21.9
19 T	19 52 26.4	28 37.8	26 11.2	2♒30.7	14 58.4	4 40.6	7 14.6	21 48.7	27 32.6	28 43.9	8 28.9	12 22.9
20 W	19 56 23.0	29 38.9	26 8.1	17 44.9	16 28.7	5 53.6	7 54.7	21 55.5	27 39.0	28 47.1	8 31.1	12 23.8
21 T	20 0 19.6	0♒39.9	26 4.9	2♓50.2	17 56.3	7 6.6	8 34.8	22 2.5	27 45.4	28 50.3	8 33.2	12 24.7
22 F	20 4 16.1	1 41.0	26 1.7	17 38.3	19 20.8	8 19.4	9 14.8	22 9.6	27 51.7	28 53.6	8 35.4	12 25.5
23 S	20 8 12.7	2 42.1	25 58.5	2♈ 3.6	20 41.6	9 32.2	9 54.9	22 16.9	27 58.0	28 56.7	8 37.5	12 26.3
24 S	20 12 9.2	3 43.1	25 55.4	16 3.8	21 58.1	10 45.0	10 35.1	22 24.4	28 4.2	28 59.9	8 39.6	12 27.1
25 M	20 16 5.8	4 44.1	25 52.2	29 39.2	23 9.5	11 57.6	11 15.2	22 32.0	28 10.4	29 3.0	8 41.7	12 27.8
26 T	20 20 2.3	5 45.1	25 49.0	12♉51.8	24 15.0	13 10.2	11 55.3	22 39.8	28 16.5	29 6.1	8 43.8	12 28.5
27 W	20 23 58.9	6 46.1	25 45.8	25 44.6	25 14.0	14 22.7	12 35.4	22 47.7	28 22.6	29 9.2	8 45.8	12 29.2
28 T	20 27 55.5	7 47.1	25 42.7	8♊20.8	26 5.4	15 35.1	13 15.6	22 55.8	28 28.6	29 12.2	8 47.9	12 29.8
29 F	20 31 52.0	8 48.1	25 39.5	20 43.7	26 48.7	16 47.5	13 55.8	23 4.1	28 34.6	29 15.3	8 50.0	12 30.4
30 S	20 35 48.6	9 49.0	25 36.3	2♋56.0	27 22.7	17 59.8	14 36.0	23 12.4	28 40.6	29 18.3	8 52.0	12 31.0
31 S	20 39 45.1	10 49.9	25 33.1	15 0.1	27 47.0	19 11.9	15 16.2	23 20.9	28 46.5	29 21.2	8 54.0	12 31.5
						DECLINATION at NOON						
1 F	18 41 28.4	23S 2.6	1S 8.2	26N55.1	24S33.4	18S45.2	18S37.4	6N43.7	22S15.0	23S35.4	22S15.4	0S17.5
4 M	18 53 18.1	22 46.4	1 12.0	26 49.3	23 57.9	17 39.2	19 6.9	6 48.8	22 15.8	23 35.6	22 15.0	0 17.5
7 T	19 5 7.7	22 26.1	1 15.8	16 5.3	23 8.4	16 28.9	19 35.2	6 54.5	22 16.5	23 35.8	22 14.6	0 17.4
10 S	19 16 57.4	22 1.9	1 19.6	0S 4.2	22 4.9	15 14.7	20 2.1	7 0.9	22 17.1	23 36.0	22 14.2	0 17.2
13 W	19 28 47.1	21 33.7	1 23.4	16 53.8	20 47.8	13 56.8	20 27.6	7 7.8	22 17.7	23 36.1	22 13.8	0 16.9
16 S	19 40 36.8	21 1.8	1 27.2	27 53.1	19 18.1	12 35.8	20 51.7	7 15.3	22 18.2	23 36.3	22 13.4	0 16.4
19 T	19 52 26.4	20 26.3	1 31.0	23 30.8	17 38.0	11 11.8	21 14.3	7 23.3	22 18.6	23 36.4	22 13.0	0 15.9
22 F	20 4 16.1	19 47.3	1 34.7	5 26.4	15 51.0	9 45.3	21 35.3	7 31.9	22 18.9	23 36.6	22 12.6	0 15.2
25 M	20 16 5.8	19 5.0	1 38.5	14N 7.9	14 3.1	8 16.7	21 54.8	7 40.9	22 19.2	23 36.7	22 12.2	0 14.4
28 T	20 27 55.5	18 19.5	1 42.3	26 34.5	12 22.8	6 46.2	22 12.7	7 50.5	22 19.4	23 36.8	22 11.8	0 13.5
31 S	20 39 45.1	17 31.1	1 46.1	27 21.8	11 1.2	5 14.3	22 29.0	8 0.4	22 19.6	23 36.9	22 11.3	0 12.5

FEBRUARY 1988

DAY	EPHEMERIS SIDEREAL TIME	☉	☊	☽	☿	♀	♂	♃	♄	♅	♆	♇
						LONGITUDE at NOON						
1 M	20 43 41.7	11♒50.8	25♓29.9	26♋57.9	28♒ 0.7	20♓24.0	15♐56.4	23♈29.6	28♐52.3	29♐24.1	8♑56.0	12♏32.0
2 T	20 47 38.2	12 51.7	25 26.8	8♌51.0	28 3.6	21 36.0	16 36.6	23 38.4	28 58.1	29 27.0	8 57.9	12 32.4
3 W	20 51 34.8	13 52.6	25 23.6	20 41.2	27R55.3	22 47.9	17 16.8	23 47.3	29 3.8	29 29.9	8 59.9	12 32.9
4 T	20 55 31.4	14 53.4	25 20.4	2♍30.0	27 35.9	23 59.7	17 57.0	23 56.3	29 9.5	29 32.7	9 1.8	12 33.2
5 F	20 59 27.9	15 54.2	25 17.2	14 19.6	27 5.6	25 11.4	18 37.3	24 5.5	29 15.1	29 35.5	9 3.7	12 33.6
6 S	21 3 24.5	16 55.0	25 14.1	26 12.6	26 25.2	26 23.0	19 17.6	24 14.8	29 20.6	29 38.3	9 5.6	12 33.9
7 S	21 7 21.0	17 55.8	25 10.9	8♎12.0	25 35.7	27 34.5	19 57.8	24 24.3	29 26.1	29 41.0	9 7.5	12 34.1
8 M	21 11 17.6	18 56.6	25 7.7	20 21.5	24 38.3	28 45.9	20 38.1	24 33.8	29 31.5	29 43.7	9 9.4	12 34.4
9 T	21 15 14.1	19 57.3	25 4.5	2♏45.4	23 34.7	29 57.2	21 18.4	24 43.5	29 36.9	29 46.3	9 11.2	12 34.6
10 W	21 19 10.7	20 58.1	25 1.4	15 27.9	22 26.8	1♈ 8.4	21 58.7	24 53.4	29 42.2	29 48.9	9 13.0	12 34.7
11 T	21 23 7.2	21 58.8	24 58.2	28 33.1	21 16.5	2 19.5	22 39.1	25 3.3	29 47.5	29 51.5	9 14.8	12 34.8
12 F	21 27 3.8	22 59.5	24 55.0	12♐ 4.4	20 5.7	3 30.5	23 19.4	25 13.4	29 52.6	29 54.0	9 16.6	12 34.9
13 S	21 31 0.4	24 0.2	24 51.8	26 3.6	18 56.3	4 41.3	23 59.8	25 23.6	29 57.8	29 56.5	9 18.3	12 35.0
14 S	21 34 56.9	25 0.8	24 48.6	10♑30.1	17 49.9	5 52.1	24 40.1	25 33.8	0♑ 2.8	29 59.0	9 20.1	12 35.0
15 M	21 38 53.5	26 1.5	24 45.5	25 20.3	16 48.1	7 2.7	25 20.5	25 44.3	0 7.8	0♑ 1.4	9 21.8	12 35.0
16 T	21 42 50.0	27 2.1	24 42.3	10♒27.6	15 52.0	8 13.3	26 0.9	25 54.8	0 12.7	0 3.8	9 23.4	12R34.9
17 W	21 46 46.6	28 2.7	24 39.1	25 42.8	15 2.4	9 23.6	26 41.3	26 5.4	0 17.5	0 6.1	9 25.1	12 34.8
18 T	21 50 43.1	29 3.3	24 35.9	10♓55.4	14 20.0	10 33.9	27 21.6	26 16.2	0 22.3	0 8.4	9 26.7	12 34.7
19 F	21 54 39.7	0♓ 3.9	24 32.8	25 55.8	13 45.1	11 44.1	28 2.1	26 27.1	0 27.0	0 10.7	9 28.4	12 34.5
20 S	21 58 36.2	1 4.4	24 29.6	10♈36.1	13 17.9	12 54.1	28 42.5	26 38.0	0 31.7	0 12.9	9 30.0	12 34.3
21 S	22 2 32.8	2 4.9	24 26.4	24 51.3	12 58.2	14 4.0	29 22.9	26 49.1	0 36.2	0 15.1	9 31.5	12 34.1
22 M	22 6 29.4	3 5.3	24 23.2	8♉39.4	12 46.0	15 13.7	0♑ 3.3	27 0.2	0 40.7	0 17.2	9 33.1	12 33.8
23 T	22 10 25.9	4 5.7	24 20.0	22 0.8	12 41.0	16 23.3	0 43.7	27 11.5	0 45.1	0 19.3	9 34.6	12 33.5
24 W	22 14 22.5	5 6.1	24 16.9	4♊57.9	12D42.8	17 32.7	1 24.1	27 22.8	0 49.4	0 21.3	9 36.1	12 33.2
25 T	22 18 19.0	6 6.5	24 13.7	17 34.2	12 51.1	18 41.9	2 4.6	27 34.3	0 53.7	0 23.3	9 37.5	12 32.8
26 F	22 22 15.6	7 6.8	24 10.5	29 53.5	13 5.6	19 51.0	2 45.0	27 45.8	0 57.8	0 25.3	9 38.9	12 32.4
27 S	22 26 12.1	8 7.1	24 7.3	11♋59.9	13 25.7	20 60.0	3 25.4	27 57.5	1 1.9	0 27.2	9 40.3	12 31.9
28 S	22 30 8.7	9 7.4	24 4.2	23 57.2	13 51.2	22 8.7	4 5.9	28 9.2	1 5.9	0 29.0	9 41.7	12 31.4
29 M	22 34 5.2	10 7.6	24 1.0	5♌48.9	14 21.7	23 17.3	4 46.3	28 21.0	1 9.8	0 30.8	9 43.1	12 30.9
						DECLINATION at NOON						
1 M	20 43 41.7	17S14.3	1S47.4	24N59.6	10S40.2	4S43.4	22S34.1	8N 3.9	22S19.7	23S36.9	22S11.2	0S12.1
4 T	20 55 31.4	16 22.2	1 51.1	12 19.1	10 0.9	3 10.0	22 48.2	8 14.4	22 19.8	23 37.0	22 10.8	0 11.0
7 S	21 7 21.0	15 27.6	1 54.9	4S28.6	10 1.0	1 36.0	23 0.5	8 25.3	22 19.8	23 37.1	22 10.4	0 9.8
10 W	21 19 10.7	14 30.6	1 58.7	20 24.6	10 37.5	0 1.6	23 11.2	8 36.6	22 19.8	23 37.1	22 9.9	0 8.5
13 S	21 31 0.4	13 31.4	2 2.5	28 36.0	11 38.0	1N32.9	23 20.1	8 48.2	22 19.8	23 37.2	22 9.5	0 7.1
16 T	21 42 50.0	12 30.1	2 6.3	21 2.6	12 46.6	3 7.1	23 27.3	9 0.1	22 19.7	23 37.2	22 9.1	0 5.6
19 F	21 54 39.7	11 27.1	2 10.0	1 23.1	13 50.3	4 40.7	23 32.7	9 12.4	22 19.6	23 37.3	22 8.8	0 4.0
22 M	22 6 29.4	10 22.4	2 13.8	17N56.6	14 41.8	6 13.5	23 36.3	9 24.9	22 19.5	23 37.3	22 8.4	0 2.4
25 T	22 18 19.0	9 16.3	2 17.6	28 4.7	15 18.0	7 45.0	23 38.2	9 37.7	22 19.3	23 37.3	22 8.0	0 0.7
28 S	22 30 8.7	8 9.0	2 21.4	25 46.7	15 38.4	9 15.0	23 38.2	9 50.6	22 19.1	23 37.4	22 7.6	0N 1.0

MARCH 1988

LONGITUDE at NOON

DAY	EPHEMERIS SIDEREAL TIME h m s	☉ ° ′	☊ ° ′	☽ ° ′	☿ ° ′	♀ ° ′	♂ ° ′	♃ ° ′	♄ ° ′	♅ ° ′	♆ ° ′	♇ ° ′
1 T	22 38 1.8	11♓ 7.8	23♓57.8	17♌37.9	14♒56.8	24♈25.7	5♑26.8	28♈32.9	1♑13.7	0♑32.6	9♑44.4	12♏30.4
2 W	22 41 58.3	12 8.0	23 54.6	29 26.8	15 36.1	25 33.9	6 7.2	28 44.9	1 17.5	0 34.3	9 45.7	12R29.8
3 T	22 45 54.9	13 8.1	23 51.5	11♍18.0	16 19.5	26 42.0	6 47.7	28 56.9	1 21.1	0 36.0	9 46.9	12 29.2
4 F	22 49 51.5	14 8.2	23 48.3	23 13.5	17 6.6	27 49.8	7 28.2	29 9.1	1 24.7	0 37.6	9 48.2	12 28.5
5 S	22 53 48.0	15 8.3	23 45.1	5♎15.1	17 57.1	28 57.5	8 8.7	29 21.3	1 28.2	0 39.1	9 49.4	12 27.9
6 S	22 57 44.6	16 8.4	23 41.9	17 25.1	18 50.8	0♉ 4.9	8 49.2	29 33.6	1 31.7	0 40.7	9 50.5	12 27.2
7 M	23 1 41.1	17 8.4	23 38.7	29 45.5	19 47.5	1 12.1	9 29.6	29 46.0	1 35.0	0 42.1	9 51.7	12 26.4
8 T	23 5 37.7	18 8.4	23 35.6	12♏18.7	20 47.0	2 19.2	10 10.2	29 58.4	1 38.3	0 43.6	9 52.8	12 25.6
9 W	23 9 34.2	19 8.3	23 32.4	25 7.4	21 49.2	3 26.0	10 50.7	0♉10.9	1 41.4	0 44.9	9 53.9	12 24.8
10 T	23 13 30.8	20 8.3	23 29.2	8♐14.0	22 53.8	4 32.6	11 31.2	0 23.5	1 44.5	0 46.3	9 54.9	12 24.0
11 F	23 17 27.3	21 8.2	23 26.0	21 40.9	24 0.8	5 39.0	12 11.7	0 36.2	1 47.6	0 47.6	9 56.0	12 23.2
12 S	23 21 23.9	22 8.1	23 22.9	5♑29.5	25 9.9	6 45.2	12 52.3	0 49.0	1 50.5	0 48.8	9 57.0	12 22.3
13 S	23 25 20.4	23 8.0	23 19.7	19 39.9	26 21.2	7 51.1	13 32.8	1 1.7	1 53.3	0 50.0	9 58.0	12 21.4
14 M	23 29 17.0	24 7.8	23 16.5	4♒10.6	27 34.4	8 56.8	14 13.3	1 14.6	1 56.0	0 51.1	9 58.9	12 20.4
15 T	23 33 13.5	25 7.6	23 13.3	18 57.9	28 49.5	10 2.2	14 53.8	1 27.5	1 58.6	0 52.2	9 59.8	12 19.4
16 W	23 37 10.1	26 7.4	23 10.1	3♓55.7	0♓ 6.4	11 7.4	15 34.3	1 40.5	2 1.1	0 53.2	10 0.7	12 18.4
17 T	23 41 6.7	27 7.1	23 7.0	18 56.4	1 25.0	12 12.4	16 14.8	1 53.6	2 3.6	0 54.2	10 1.5	12 17.4
18 F	23 45 3.2	28 6.8	23 3.8	3♈51.5	2 45.3	13 17.0	16 55.4	2 6.7	2 5.9	0 55.1	10 2.3	12 16.3
19 S	23 48 59.8	29 6.5	23 0.6	18 32.8	4 7.2	14 21.4	17 35.9	2 19.9	2 8.2	0 56.0	10 3.1	12 15.2
20 S	23 52 56.3	0♈ 6.1	22 57.4	2♉54.0	5 30.7	15 25.5	18 16.4	2 33.1	2 10.3	0 56.8	10 3.8	12 14.1
21 M	23 56 52.9	1 5.7	22 54.3	16 50.7	6 55.8	16 29.4	18 56.9	2 46.4	2 12.4	0 57.6	10 4.5	12 13.0
22 T	0 0 49.4	2 5.3	22 51.1	0♊21.1	8 22.3	17 32.9	19 37.3	2 59.7	2 14.4	0 58.3	10 5.2	12 11.8
23 W	0 4 46.0	3 4.8	22 47.9	13 25.8	9 50.3	18 36.1	20 17.8	3 13.1	2 16.2	0 58.9	10 5.8	12 10.6
24 T	0 8 42.5	4 4.3	22 44.7	26 7.2	11 19.7	19 39.0	20 58.3	3 26.5	2 18.0	0 59.5	10 6.4	12 9.4
25 F	0 12 39.1	5 3.7	22 41.5	8♋28.9	12 50.6	20 41.5	21 38.8	3 40.0	2 19.7	1 0.1	10 7.0	12 8.2
26 S	0 16 35.6	6 3.2	22 38.4	20 35.3	14 22.9	21 43.7	22 19.2	3 53.5	2 21.2	1 0.6	10 7.5	12 6.9
27 S	0 20 32.2	7 2.5	22 35.2	2♌31.1	15 56.5	22 45.6	22 59.7	4 7.1	2 22.7	1 1.0	10 8.1	12 5.6
28 M	0 24 28.7	8 1.9	22 32.0	14 20.8	17 31.6	23 47.0	23 40.1	4 20.7	2 24.1	1 1.4	10 8.5	12 4.3
29 T	0 28 25.3	9 1.1	22 28.8	26 8.8	19 8.1	24 48.1	24 20.6	4 34.3	2 25.4	1 1.8	10 9.0	12 3.0
30 W	0 32 21.8	10 0.4	22 25.7	7♍59.0	20 45.9	25 48.9	25 1.0	4 48.0	2 26.6	1 2.1	10 9.4	12 1.6
31 T	0 36 18.4	10 59.6	22 22.5	19 54.5	22 25.2	26 49.2	25 41.4	5 1.8	2 27.7	1 2.3	10 9.8	12 0.3

DECLINATION at NOON

DAY	EPHEMERIS SIDEREAL TIME h m s	☉ ° ′	☊ ° ′	☽ ° ′	☿ ° ′	♀ ° ′	♂ ° ′	♃ ° ′	♄ ° ′	♅ ° ′	♆ ° ′	♇ ° ′
1 T	22 38 1.8	7S 23.5	2S 23.9	18N 28.1	15S 43.2	10N 14.0	23S 37.3	9N 59.4	22S 19.0	23S 37.4	22S 7.4	0N 2.2
4 F	22 49 51.5	6 14.6	2 27.7	2 40.5	15 37.9	11 40.8	23 34.4	10 12.7	22 18.8	23 37.4	22 7.1	0 4.0
7 M	23 1 41.1	5 4.8	2 31.4	14S 21.1	15 18.3	13 5.3	23 29.8	10 26.2	22 18.5	23 37.5	22 6.8	0 5.9
10 T	23 13 30.8	3 54.4	2 35.2	26 44.1	14 44.8	14 27.2	23 23.4	10 39.8	22 18.3	23 37.5	22 6.5	0 7.8
13 S	23 25 20.4	2 43.6	2 39.0	26 41.3	13 58.3	15 46.3	23 15.2	10 53.5	22 18.1	23 37.5	22 6.2	0 9.7
16 W	23 37 10.1	1 32.5	2 42.7	11 41.6	12 59.2	17 2.2	23 5.3	11 7.4	22 17.8	23 37.6	22 5.9	0 11.7
19 S	23 48 59.8	0 21.3	2 46.5	9N 22.6	11 48.0	18 14.8	22 53.8	11 21.3	22 17.6	23 37.6	22 5.7	0 13.6
22 T	0 0 49.4	0N 49.8	2 50.3	24 59.7	10 25.2	19 23.7	22 40.6	11 35.3	22 17.4	23 37.6	22 5.4	0 15.6
25 F	0 12 39.1	2 0.7	2 54.0	28 15.4	8 51.2	20 28.8	22 25.8	11 49.4	22 17.1	23 37.7	22 5.2	0 17.5
28 M	0 24 28.7	3 11.2	2 57.8	19 41.6	7 6.4	21 29.7	22 9.3	12 3.4	22 16.9	23 37.7	22 5.0	0 19.5
31 T	0 36 18.4	4 21.1	3 1.6	4 16.2	5 11.2	22 26.4	21 51.4	12 17.5	22 16.7	23 37.8	22 4.9	0 21.4

APRIL 1988

LONGITUDE at NOON

DAY	EPHEMERIS SIDEREAL TIME h m s	☉ ° ′	☊ ° ′	☽ ° ′	☿ ° ′	♀ ° ′	♂ ° ′	♃ ° ′	♄ ° ′	♅ ° ′	♆ ° ′	♇ ° ′
1 F	0 40 15.0	11♈58.9	22♓19.3	1♎58.3	24♓ 5.9	27♉49.1	26♑21.9	5♉15.6	2♑28.7	1♑ 2.6	10♑10.1	11♏58.9
2 S	0 44 11.5	12 58.0	22 16.1	14 12.2	25 47.9	28 48.6	27 2.3	5 29.4	2 29.6	1 2.7	10 10.5	11R57.5
3 S	0 48 8.1	13 57.1	22 12.9	26 37.7	27 31.4	29 47.6	27 42.7	5 43.2	2 30.4	1 2.8	10 10.7	11 56.1
4 M	0 52 4.6	14 56.2	22 9.8	9♏15.9	29 16.3	0♊46.2	28 23.1	5 57.1	2 31.1	1 2.8	10 11.0	11 54.6
5 T	0 56 1.2	15 55.3	22 6.6	22 7.4	1♈ 2.6	1 44.3	29 3.5	6 11.0	2 31.7	1 2.8	10 11.2	11 53.2
6 W	0 59 57.7	16 54.3	22 3.4	5♐12.6	2 50.4	2 42.0	29 43.9	6 24.9	2 32.2	1R 2.7	10 11.4	11 51.7
7 T	1 3 54.3	17 53.3	22 0.2	18 31.7	4 39.7	3 39.1	0♒24.2	6 38.9	2 32.6	1 2.6	10 11.5	11 50.2
8 F	1 7 50.8	18 52.2	21 57.1	2♑ 5.0	6 30.4	4 35.8	1 4.6	6 52.9	2 32.9	1 2.4	10 11.6	11 48.7
9 S	1 11 47.4	19 51.2	21 53.9	15 52.3	8 22.6	5 31.9	1 44.9	7 6.9	2 33.1	1 2.2	10 11.7	11 47.1
10 S	1 15 43.9	20 50.1	21 50.7	29 53.4	10 16.2	6 27.4	2 25.3	7 21.0	2 33.2	1 1.9	10 11.7	11 45.6
11 M	1 19 40.5	21 49.0	21 47.5	14♒ 7.3	12 11.4	7 22.5	3 5.6	7 35.1	2 33.2	1 1.6	10 11.7	11 44.0
12 T	1 23 37.1	22 47.8	21 44.3	28 32.3	14 8.0	8 16.9	3 45.9	7 49.2	2R33.1	1 1.2	10 11.7	11 42.5
13 W	1 27 33.6	23 46.6	21 41.2	13♓ 5.2	16 6.1	9 10.7	4 26.1	8 3.3	2 32.9	1 0.8	10 11.7	11 40.9
14 T	1 31 30.2	24 45.4	21 38.0	27 41.5	18 5.5	10 3.9	5 6.4	8 17.5	2 32.6	1 0.3	10R11.6	11 39.3
15 F	1 35 26.7	25 44.2	21 34.8	12♈15.9	20 6.4	10 56.5	5 46.6	8 31.7	2 32.2	0 59.8	10 11.4	11 37.7
16 S	1 39 23.3	26 42.9	21 31.6	26 42.1	22 8.6	11 48.5	6 26.8	8 45.8	2 31.7	0 59.2	10 11.3	11 36.1
17 S	1 43 19.8	27 41.6	21 28.5	10♉54.1	24 12.0	12 39.7	7 7.0	9 0.1	2 31.1	0 58.6	10 11.1	11 34.5
18 M	1 47 16.4	28 40.3	21 25.3	24 47.1	26 16.6	13 30.2	7 47.1	9 14.3	2 30.4	0 57.9	10 10.9	11 32.8
19 T	1 51 12.9	29 38.9	21 22.1	8♊17.8	28 22.3	14 20.0	8 27.2	9 28.5	2 29.6	0 57.2	10 10.6	11 31.2
20 W	1 55 9.5	0♉37.5	21 18.9	21 25.0	0♉28.9	15 9.0	9 7.3	9 42.8	2 28.7	0 56.4	10 10.3	11 29.5
21 T	1 59 6.0	1 36.0	21 15.7	4♋ 9.6	2 36.2	15 57.2	9 47.3	9 57.1	2 27.7	0 55.6	10 10.0	11 27.9
22 F	2 3 2.6	2 34.6	21 12.6	16 34.2	4 44.1	16 44.6	10 27.4	10 11.4	2 26.7	0 54.8	10 9.7	11 26.2
23 S	2 6 59.2	3 33.1	21 9.4	28 42.4	6 52.3	17 31.1	11 7.4	10 25.7	2 25.5	0 53.9	10 9.3	11 24.6
24 S	2 10 55.7	4 31.5	21 6.2	10♌39.0	9 0.6	18 16.6	11 47.3	10 40.0	2 24.3	0 52.9	10 8.9	11 22.9
25 M	2 14 52.3	5 29.9	21 3.0	22 29.0	11 8.7	19 1.3	12 27.2	10 54.3	2 22.9	0 51.9	10 8.5	11 21.2
26 T	2 18 48.8	6 28.3	20 59.9	4♍17.6	13 16.4	19 45.0	13 7.1	11 8.6	2 21.5	0 50.8	10 8.0	11 19.5
27 W	2 22 45.4	7 26.7	20 56.7	16 9.8	15 23.3	20 27.6	13 47.0	11 22.9	2 19.9	0 49.7	10 7.5	11 17.8
28 T	2 26 41.9	8 25.0	20 53.5	28 9.9	17 29.1	21 9.2	14 26.8	11 37.2	2 18.3	0 48.6	10 7.0	11 16.1
29 F	2 30 38.5	9 23.3	20 50.3	10♎21.7	19 33.6	21 49.7	15 6.5	11 51.5	2 16.6	0 47.4	10 6.4	11 14.5
30 S	2 34 35.0	10 21.5	20 47.2	22 47.9	21 36.3	22 29.1	15 46.3	12 5.9	2 14.7	0 46.2	10 5.8	11 12.8

DECLINATION at NOON

DAY	EPHEMERIS SIDEREAL TIME h m s	☉ ° ′	☊ ° ′	☽ ° ′	☿ ° ′	♀ ° ′	♂ ° ′	♃ ° ′	♄ ° ′	♅ ° ′	♆ ° ′	♇ ° ′
1 F	0 40 15.0	4N 44.2	3S 2.8	1S 31.8	4S 30.5	22N 44.3	21S 45.1	12N 22.2	22S 16.7	23S 37.8	22S 4.8	0N 22.1
4 M	0 52 4.6	5 53.1	3 6.6	18 10.5	2 22.1	23 35.0	21 25.1	12 36.3	22 16.5	23 37.9	22 4.7	0 24.0
7 T	1 3 54.3	7 1.1	3 10.4	28 8.9	0 4.5	24 21.1	21 3.7	12 50.3	22 16.3	23 37.9	22 4.6	0 25.8
10 S	1 15 43.9	8 8.1	3 14.1	24 15.6	2N 21.4	25 2.5	20 40.9	13 4.3	22 16.2	23 38.0	22 4.5	0 27.7
13 W	1 27 33.6	9 13.8	3 17.9	7 28.0	4 54.6	25 39.1	20 16.7	13 18.3	22 16.1	23 38.0	22 4.4	0 29.5
16 S	1 39 23.3	10 18.2	3 21.6	13N 0.3	7 33.2	26 10.9	19 51.3	13 32.2	22 16.0	23 38.1	22 4.4	0 31.2
19 T	1 51 12.9	11 21.0	3 25.4	26 39.1	10 14.6	26 37.9	19 24.6	13 46.0	22 15.9	23 38.2	22 4.3	0 32.9
22 F	2 3 2.6	12 22.2	3 29.1	27 6.3	12 55.1	27 0.2	18 56.8	13 59.7	22 15.9	23 38.3	22 4.3	0 34.5
25 M	2 14 52.3	13 21.4	3 32.9	16 27.6	15 29.8	27 17.8	18 28.0	14 13.2	22 15.9	23 38.3	22 4.4	0 36.1
28 T	2 26 41.9	14 18.7	3 36.7	0 14.9	17 53.3	27 30.9	17 58.1	14 26.7	22 15.9	23 38.4	22 4.4	0 37.5

MAY 1988

DAY	EPHEMERIS SIDEREAL TIME	☉	☊	☽	☿	♀	♂	♃	♄	♅	♆	♇
	h m s	° ′	° ′	° ′	° ′	° ′	° ′	° ′	° ′	° ′	° ′	° ′
						LONGITUDE at NOON						
1 S	2 38 31.6	11♉19.7	20♓44.0	5♏30.2	23♉37.1	23♊ 7.3	16♒26.0	12♉20.2	2♑12.8	0♑44.9	10♑ 5.2	11♏11.1
2 M	2 42 28.2	12 17.9	20 40.8	18 29.2	25 35.6	23 44.3	17 5.6	12 34.5	2R10.9	0R43.6	10R 4.5	11R 9.4
3 T	2 46 24.7	13 16.1	20 37.6	1♐44.0	27 31.7	24 20.0	17 45.3	12 48.8	2 8.8	0 42.2	10 3.9	11 7.7
4 W	2 50 21.3	14 14.2	20 34.4	15 13.0	29 25.0	24 54.4	18 24.8	13 3.1	2 6.6	0 40.8	10 3.2	11 6.0
5 T	2 54 17.8	15 12.3	20 31.3	28 54.1	1♊15.4	25 27.4	19 4.4	13 17.5	2 4.4	0 39.4	10 2.4	11 4.3
6 F	2 58 14.4	16 10.4	20 28.1	12♑44.7	3 2.7	25 59.0	19 43.8	13 31.8	2 2.0	0 37.9	10 1.6	11 2.6
7 S	3 2 10.9	17 8.4	20 24.9	26 42.6	4 46.8	26 29.2	20 23.3	13 46.1	1 59.6	0 36.4	10 0.9	11 0.9
8 S	3 6 7.5	18 6.5	20 21.7	10♒46.0	6 27.5	26 57.8	21 2.7	14 0.4	1 57.1	0 34.8	10 0.0	10 59.2
9 M	3 10 4.0	19 4.5	20 18.6	24 53.4	8 4.7	27 24.8	21 42.0	14 14.7	1 54.5	0 33.2	9 59.2	10 57.6
10 T	3 14 0.6	20 2.5	20 15.4	9♓ 3.6	9 38.4	27 50.3	22 21.3	14 28.9	1 51.9	0 31.6	9 58.3	10 55.9
11 W	3 17 57.2	21 0.4	20 12.2	23 15.3	11 8.4	28 14.0	23 0.5	14 43.2	1 49.1	0 29.9	9 57.4	10 54.2
12 T	3 21 53.7	21 58.4	20 9.0	7♈26.5	12 34.7	28 36.0	23 39.6	14 57.5	1 46.3	0 28.2	9 56.5	10 52.6
13 F	3 25 50.3	22 56.3	20 5.9	21 34.7	13 57.2	28 56.3	24 18.8	15 11.8	1 43.5	0 26.5	9 55.6	10 51.0
14 S	3 29 46.8	23 54.2	20 2.7	5♉36.3	15 15.9	29 14.7	24 57.8	15 26.0	1 40.5	0 24.7	9 54.6	10 49.3
15 S	3 33 43.4	24 52.1	19 59.5	19 27.5	16 30.6	29 31.1	25 36.7	15 40.2	1 37.5	0 22.9	9 53.6	10 47.7
16 M	3 37 39.9	25 50.0	19 56.3	3♊ 4.5	17 41.5	29 45.5	26 15.6	15 54.4	1 34.4	0 21.1	9 52.5	10 46.1
17 T	3 41 36.5	26 47.8	19 53.1	16 24.1	18 48.2	29 57.9	26 54.3	16 8.6	1 31.2	0 19.2	9 51.5	10 44.5
18 W	3 45 33.1	27 45.6	19 50.0	29 24.6	19 51.0	0♋ 8.2	27 33.0	16 22.8	1 27.9	0 17.3	9 50.4	10 42.8
19 T	3 49 29.6	28 43.4	19 46.8	12♋ 5.6	20 49.5	0 16.3	28 11.7	16 36.9	1 24.6	0 15.3	9 49.3	10 41.3
20 F	3 53 26.2	29 41.1	19 43.6	24 28.6	21 43.9	0 22.2	28 50.2	16 51.1	1 21.2	0 13.3	9 48.2	10 39.7
21 S	3 57 22.7	0♊38.9	19 40.4	6♌36.4	22 34.0	0 25.9	29 28.7	17 5.2	1 17.8	0 11.3	9 47.0	10 38.1
22 S	4 1 19.3	1 36.6	19 37.3	18 32.9	23 19.8	0 27.2	0♓ 7.0	17 19.2	1 14.3	0 9.3	9 45.8	10 36.6
23 M	4 5 15.8	2 34.3	19 34.1	0♍22.9	24 1.1	0R26.1	0 45.3	17 33.3	1 10.7	0 7.2	9 44.7	10 35.0
24 T	4 9 12.4	3 31.9	19 30.9	12 11.9	24 38.0	0 22.7	1 23.5	17 47.3	1 7.1	0 5.2	9 43.4	10 33.5
25 W	4 13 9.0	4 29.5	19 27.7	24 5.1	25 10.3	0 16.8	2 1.6	18 1.3	1 3.4	0 3.0	9 42.2	10 32.0
26 T	4 17 5.5	5 27.1	19 24.6	6♎ 7.8	25 38.0	0 8.5	2 39.6	18 15.3	0 59.7	0 0.9	9 40.9	10 30.5
27 F	4 21 2.1	6 24.7	19 21.4	18 24.8	26 1.1	29♊57.8	3 17.5	18 29.2	0 55.9	29♐58.8	9 39.7	10 29.0
28 S	4 24 58.6	7 22.3	19 18.2	0♏59.9	26 19.5	29 44.6	3 55.3	18 43.1	0 52.1	29 56.6	9 38.4	10 27.5
29 S	4 28 55.2	8 19.8	19 15.0	13 55.5	26 33.2	29 29.0	4 33.0	18 57.0	0 48.2	29 54.4	9 37.1	10 26.1
30 M	4 32 51.8	9 17.3	19 11.8	27 12.4	26 42.2	29 11.1	5 10.6	19 10.8	0 44.3	29 52.1	9 35.7	10 24.7
31 T	4 36 48.3	10 14.8	19 8.7	10♐49.5	26 46.5	28 50.8	5 48.0	19 24.7	0 40.3	29 49.9	9 34.4	10 23.2
						DECLINATION at NOON						
1 S	2 38 31.6	15N13.9	3S40.4	16S40.5	20N 0.3	27N39.5	17S27.2	14N40.0	22S15.9	23S38.5	22S 4.5	0N38.9
4 W	2 50 21.3	16 6.8	3 44.2	27 39.6	21 46.9	27 43.8	16 55.5	14 53.1	22 15.9	23 38.6	22 4.6	0 40.2
7 S	3 2 10.9	16 57.3	3 47.9	24 54.6	23 11.3	27 44.0	16 22.9	15 6.1	22 16.0	23 38.6	22 4.7	0 41.5
10 T	3 14 0.6	17 45.3	3 51.6	9 11.3	24 13.2	27 40.2	15 49.6	15 18.9	22 16.1	23 38.7	22 4.8	0 42.6
13 F	3 25 50.3	18 30.6	3 55.4	10N47.3	24 54.0	27 32.5	15 15.6	15 31.6	22 16.2	23 38.8	22 5.0	0 43.6
16 M	3 37 39.9	19 13.1	3 59.1	25 29.5	25 15.5	27 21.0	14 41.0	15 44.0	22 16.3	23 38.8	22 5.2	0 44.5
19 T	3 49 29.6	19 52.7	4 2.9	27 34.2	25 20.0	27 5.6	14 6.0	15 56.3	22 16.4	23 38.9	22 5.4	0 45.3
22 S	4 1 19.3	20 29.2	4 6.6	17 48.0	25 9.7	26 46.2	13 30.6	16 8.3	22 16.5	23 38.9	22 5.6	0 46.0
25 W	4 13 9.0	21 2.5	4 10.4	2 1.8	24 46.7	26 22.8	12 54.8	16 20.1	22 16.7	23 39.0	22 5.8	0 46.6
28 S	4 24 58.6	21 32.6	4 14.1	14S55.3	24 13.0	25 54.9	12 18.8	16 31.7	22 16.8	23 39.0	22 6.1	0 47.1
31 T	4 36 48.3	21 59.3	4 17.8	26 58.5	23 30.6	25 22.5	11 42.7	16 43.0	22 17.0	23 39.1	22 6.3	0 47.4

JUNE 1988

DAY	EPHEMERIS SIDEREAL TIME	☉	☊	☽	☿	♀	♂	♃	♄	♅	♆	♇
						LONGITUDE at NOON						
1 W	4 40 44.9	11♊12.3	19♓ 5.5	24♐43.8	26♊46.3	28♊28.3	6♓25.4	19♉38.4	0♑36.3	29♐47.6	9♑33.0	10♏21.8
2 T	4 44 41.4	12 9.7	19 2.3	8♑51.1	26R41.5	28R 3.6	7 2.7	19 52.2	0R32.2	29R45.3	9R31.6	10R20.5
3 F	4 48 38.0	13 7.2	18 59.1	23 6.2	26 32.5	27 36.9	7 39.9	20 5.9	0 28.2	29 43.1	9 30.3	10 19.2
4 S	4 52 34.5	14 4.6	18 56.0	7♒24.2	26 19.2	27 8.3	8 16.9	20 19.6	0 24.0	29 40.8	9 28.9	10 17.8
5 S	4 56 31.1	15 2.1	18 52.8	21 41.1	26 2.1	26 37.8	8 53.8	20 33.2	0 19.9	29 38.4	9 27.4	10 16.5
6 M	5 0 27.7	15 59.5	18 49.6	5♓54.0	25 41.3	26 5.8	9 30.6	20 46.8	0 15.7	29 36.1	9 26.0	10 15.2
7 T	5 4 24.2	16 56.9	18 46.4	20 1.1	25 17.3	25 32.3	10 7.2	21 0.3	0 11.4	29 33.7	9 24.5	10 14.0
8 W	5 8 20.8	17 54.3	18 43.3	4♈ 1.7	24 50.4	24 57.7	10 43.7	21 13.9	0 7.2	29 31.4	9 23.1	10 12.7
9 T	5 12 17.3	18 51.7	18 40.1	17 55.2	24 21.1	24 21.9	11 20.0	21 27.3	0 2.9	29 29.0	9 21.6	10 11.5
10 F	5 16 13.9	19 49.0	18 36.9	1♉41.0	23 49.9	23 45.4	11 56.2	21 40.7	29♐58.6	29 26.6	9 20.1	10 10.3
11 S	5 20 10.5	20 46.4	18 33.7	15 18.0	23 17.3	23 8.3	12 32.3	21 54.1	29 54.2	29 24.2	9 18.6	10 9.1
12 S	5 24 7.0	21 43.7	18 30.6	28 44.8	22 43.8	22 30.9	13 8.1	22 7.4	29 49.9	29 21.7	9 17.1	10 7.9
13 M	5 28 3.6	22 41.1	18 27.4	11♊59.5	22 10.0	21 53.3	13 43.8	22 20.7	29 45.5	29 19.3	9 15.5	10 6.8
14 T	5 32 0.1	23 38.4	18 24.2	25 0.4	21 36.5	21 15.9	14 19.3	22 33.9	29 41.1	29 16.9	9 14.0	10 5.7
15 W	5 35 56.7	24 35.8	18 21.0	7♋46.4	21 3.9	20 38.8	14 54.7	22 47.1	29 36.7	29 14.4	9 12.4	10 4.6
16 T	5 39 53.3	25 33.1	18 17.9	20 17.0	20 32.8	20 2.3	15 29.8	23 0.2	29 32.3	29 12.0	9 10.9	10 3.6
17 F	5 43 49.8	26 30.4	18 14.7	2♌33.1	20 3.5	19 26.7	16 4.8	23 13.2	29 27.8	29 9.6	9 9.3	10 2.5
18 S	5 47 46.4	27 27.7	18 11.5	14 36.7	19 36.8	18 52.0	16 39.6	23 26.2	29 23.4	29 7.1	9 7.7	10 1.5
19 S	5 51 42.9	28 24.9	18 8.3	26 30.8	19 12.9	18 18.6	17 14.2	23 39.2	29 19.0	29 4.7	9 6.1	10 0.6
20 M	5 55 39.5	29 22.2	18 5.1	8♍19.5	18 52.3	17 46.7	17 48.6	23 52.1	29 14.5	29 2.2	9 4.5	9 59.6
21 T	5 59 36.0	0♋19.5	18 2.0	20 7.6	18 35.4	17 16.3	18 22.7	24 4.9	29 10.1	28 59.8	9 2.9	9 58.7
22 W	6 3 32.6	1 16.7	17 58.8	2♎ 0.3	18 22.5	16 47.7	18 56.7	24 17.6	29 5.7	28 57.3	9 1.3	9 57.8
23 T	6 7 29.2	2 13.9	17 55.6	14 3.2	18 13.8	16 21.0	19 30.5	24 30.3	29 1.2	28 54.9	8 59.7	9 56.9
24 F	6 11 25.7	3 11.2	17 52.4	26 21.5	18 9.5	15 56.4	20 4.1	24 43.0	28 56.9	28 52.5	8 58.2	9 56.2
25 S	6 15 22.3	4 8.4	17 49.3	8♏59.8	18D 9.8	15 33.8	20 37.4	24 55.6	28 52.5	28 50.0	8 56.6	9 55.4
26 S	6 19 18.8	5 5.6	17 46.1	22 1.7	18 14.8	15 13.5	21 10.4	25 8.1	28 48.1	28 47.6	8 54.9	9 54.6
27 M	6 23 15.4	6 2.8	17 42.9	5♐28.9	18 24.5	14 55.4	21 43.3	25 20.5	28 43.7	28 45.2	8 53.3	9 53.8
28 T	6 27 12.0	7 0.0	17 39.7	19 21.0	18 39.1	14 39.7	22 15.9	25 32.9	28 39.3	28 42.8	8 51.7	9 53.1
29 W	6 31 8.5	7 57.2	17 36.6	3♑34.8	18 58.5	14 26.3	22 48.3	25 45.2	28 34.9	28 40.3	8 50.1	9 52.4
30 T	6 35 5.1	8 54.4	17 33.4	18 5.2	19 22.8	14 15.3	23 20.4	25 57.4	28 30.6	28 37.9	8 48.5	9 51.8
						DECLINATION at NOON						
1 W	4 40 44.9	22N 7.5	4S19.1	28S19.4	23N14.9	25N10.7	11S30.6	16N46.7	22S17.1	23S39.1	22S 6.4	0N47.5
4 S	4 52 34.5	22 29.6	4 22.8	21 38.8	22 24.3	24 32.1	10 54.3	16 57.8	22 17.2	23 39.1	22 6.7	0 47.7
7 T	5 4 24.2	22 48.2	4 26.5	3 51.4	21 30.6	23 49.2	10 18.1	17 8.5	22 17.4	23 39.1	22 7.0	0 47.8
10 F	5 16 13.9	23 3.1	4 30.3	15N16.5	20 37.3	23 2.9	9 42.0	17 19.0	22 17.5	23 39.1	22 7.3	0 47.7
13 M	5 28 3.6	23 14.5	4 34.0	27 9.6	19 48.3	22 14.5	9 6.2	17 29.2	22 17.7	23 39.1	22 7.6	0 47.6
16 T	5 39 53.3	23 22.1	4 37.7	26 5.4	19 8.0	21 25.7	8 30.7	17 39.2	22 17.9	23 39.1	22 7.9	0 47.3
19 S	5 51 42.9	23 26.0	4 41.4	14 22.1	18 39.8	20 38.7	7 55.7	17 48.9	22 18.0	23 39.1	22 8.2	0 46.8
22 W	6 3 32.6	23 26.2	4 45.2	1S58.9	18 26.0	19 55.2	7 21.2	17 58.3	22 18.2	23 39.1	22 8.6	0 46.3
25 S	6 15 22.3	23 22.7	4 48.9	18 15.8	18 27.5	19 17.1	6 47.4	18 7.4	22 18.4	23 39.0	22 8.9	0 45.6
28 T	6 27 12.0	23 15.5	4 52.6	28 2.1	18 43.1	18 45.3	6 14.2	18 16.2	22 18.5	23 39.0	22 9.3	0 44.8

JULY 1988

DAY	EPHEMERIS SIDEREAL TIME h m s	☉ ° ′	☊ ° ′	☽ ° ′	☿ ° ′	♀ ° ′	♂ ° ′	♃ ° ′	♄ ° ′	♅ ° ′	♆ ° ′	♇ ° ′
LONGITUDE at NOON												
1 F	6 39 1.6	9♋51.6	17♓30.2	2♒45.1	19♊51.9	14♊ 6.8	23♓52.2	26♉ 9.6	28♐26.3	28♐35.6	8♑46.8	9♏51.2
2 S	6 42 58.2	10 48.7	17 27.0	17 27.2	20 25.8	14R 0.6	24 23.8	26 21.6	28R22.0	28R33.2	8R45.2	9R50.6
3 S	6 46 54.8	11 45.9	17 23.9	2♓ 4.9	21 4.5	13 56.9	24 55.1	26 33.6	28 17.8	28 30.8	8 43.6	9 50.0
4 M	6 50 51.3	12 43.1	17 20.7	16 33.0	21 47.9	13 55.5	25 26.1	26 45.6	28 13.5	28 28.5	8 42.0	9 49.5
5 T	6 54 47.9	13 40.3	17 17.5	0♈48.4	22 36.0	13D56.5	25 56.8	26 57.4	28 9.3	28 26.1	8 40.4	9 49.0
6 W	6 58 44.4	14 37.5	17 14.3	14 49.5	23 28.6	13 59.7	26 27.3	27 9.2	28 5.2	28 23.8	8 38.7	9 48.5
7 T	7 2 41.0	15 34.7	17 11.2	28 36.0	24 25.9	14 5.2	26 57.4	27 20.9	28 1.0	28 21.5	8 37.1	9 48.1
8 F	7 6 37.5	16 31.9	17 8.0	12♉ 8.4	25 27.6	14 12.9	27 27.1	27 32.5	27 56.9	28 19.2	8 35.5	9 47.7
9 S	7 10 34.1	17 29.1	17 4.8	25 27.3	26 33.7	14 22.8	27 56.6	27 44.0	27 52.9	28 16.9	8 33.9	9 47.3
10 S	7 14 30.7	18 26.3	17 1.6	8♊33.2	27 44.3	14 34.7	28 25.7	27 55.5	27 48.9	28 14.7	8 32.3	9 47.0
11 M	7 18 27.2	19 23.6	16 58.4	21 26.5	28 59.1	14 48.6	28 54.4	28 6.8	27 44.9	28 12.4	8 30.7	9 46.7
12 T	7 22 23.8	20 20.8	16 55.3	4♋ 7.4	0♋18.2	15 4.5	29 22.8	28 18.1	27 41.0	28 10.2	8 29.2	9 46.4
13 W	7 26 20.3	21 18.1	16 52.1	16 36.0	1 41.4	15 22.3	29 50.8	28 29.2	27 37.1	28 8.0	8 27.6	9 46.1
14 T	7 30 16.9	22 15.3	16 48.9	28 52.9	3 8.8	15 42.0	0♈18.4	28 40.3	27 33.3	28 5.9	8 26.0	9 45.9
15 F	7 34 13.5	23 12.6	16 45.7	10♌59.1	4 40.2	16 3.4	0 45.7	28 51.3	27 29.5	28 3.8	8 24.5	9 45.8
16 S	7 38 10.0	24 9.8	16 42.6	22 56.1	6 15.4	16 26.6	1 12.5	29 2.2	27 25.8	28 1.6	8 22.9	9 45.7
17 S	7 42 6.6	25 7.1	16 39.4	4♍46.3	7 54.4	16 51.4	1 38.9	29 13.0	27 22.1	27 59.5	8 21.4	9 45.6
18 M	7 46 3.1	26 4.4	16 36.2	16 33.1	9 37.1	17 17.7	2 4.9	29 23.7	27 18.5	27 57.5	8 19.9	9 45.5
19 T	7 49 59.7	27 1.6	16 33.0	28 20.2	11 23.2	17 45.6	2 30.5	29 34.3	27 15.0	27 55.4	8 18.4	9 45.5
20 W	7 53 56.2	27 58.9	16 29.9	10♎12.3	13 12.5	18 15.0	2 55.6	29 44.8	27 11.5	27 53.4	8 16.8	9 45.5
21 T	7 57 52.8	28 56.2	16 26.7	22 14.3	15 4.8	18 45.9	3 20.3	29 55.1	27 8.0	27 51.4	8 15.4	9 45.5
22 F	8 1 49.4	29 53.5	16 23.5	4♏31.3	16 60.0	19 18.1	3 44.5	0♊ 5.4	27 4.7	27 49.5	8 13.9	9D45.6
23 S	8 5 45.9	0♌50.7	16 20.3	17 8.3	18 57.6	19 51.6	4 8.2	0 15.6	27 1.3	27 47.6	8 12.4	9 45.7
24 S	8 9 42.5	1 48.0	16 17.2	0♐ 9.4	20 57.4	20 26.4	4 31.5	0 25.6	26 58.1	27 45.7	8 10.9	9 45.8
25 M	8 13 39.0	2 45.3	16 14.0	13 37.5	22 59.1	21 2.5	4 54.3	0 35.6	26 54.9	27 43.8	8 9.5	9 46.0
26 T	8 17 35.6	3 42.6	16 10.8	27 33.4	25 2.3	21 39.7	5 16.6	0 45.4	26 51.8	27 42.0	8 8.1	9 46.2
27 W	8 21 32.1	4 40.0	16 7.6	11♑55.1	27 6.7	22 18.1	5 38.3	0 55.2	26 48.8	27 40.2	8 6.7	9 46.4
28 T	8 25 28.7	5 37.3	16 4.4	26 38.0	29 12.0	22 57.6	5 59.6	1 4.8	26 45.8	27 38.4	8 5.3	9 46.7
29 F	8 29 25.3	6 34.6	16 1.3	11♒35.0	1♌17.9	23 38.2	6 20.3	1 14.3	26 43.0	27 36.7	8 3.9	9 47.0
30 S	8 33 21.8	7 32.0	15 58.1	26 37.4	3 24.0	24 19.8	6 40.5	1 23.7	26 40.1	27 35.0	8 2.5	9 47.3
31 S	8 37 18.4	8 29.3	15 54.9	11♓36.3	5 30.1	25 2.4	7 0.1	1 32.9	26 37.4	27 33.4	8 1.2	9 47.7

DAY	EPHEMERIS SIDEREAL TIME h m s	☉ ° ′	☊ ° ′	☽ ° ′	☿ ° ′	♀ ° ′	♂ ° ′	♃ ° ′	♄ ° ′	♅ ° ′	♆ ° ′	♇ ° ′
DECLINATION at NOON												
1 F	6 39 1.6	23N 4.6	4S56.3	22S56.5	19N10.9	18N20.5	5S41.9	18N24.8	22S18.7	23S38.9	22S 9.6	0N43.9
4 M	6 50 51.3	22 50.1	5 0.0	5 16.4	19 47.7	18 2.6	5 10.5	18 33.0	22 18.8	23 38.9	22 10.0	0 42.9
7 T	7 2 41.0	22 32.0	5 3.7	14N11.7	20 30.0	17 51.5	4 40.1	18 40.9	22 19.0	23 38.8	22 10.3	0 41.8
10 S	7 14 30.7	22 10.4	5 7.4	26 42.7	21 13.6	17 46.3	4 10.9	18 48.6	22 19.2	23 38.8	22 10.7	0 40.5
13 W	7 26 20.3	21 45.4	5 11.2	26 44.2	21 53.9	17 46.3	3 42.9	18 55.9	22 19.3	23 38.7	22 11.0	0 39.1
16 S	7 38 10.0	21 17.0	5 14.9	15 42.1	22 25.9	17 50.7	3 16.3	19 2.9	22 19.5	23 38.6	22 11.4	0 37.7
19 T	7 49 59.7	20 45.3	5 18.6	0S25.9	22 44.1	17 58.5	2 51.2	19 9.7	22 19.7	23 38.5	22 11.7	0 36.1
22 F	8 1 49.4	20 10.6	5 22.3	16 43.8	22 43.7	18 8.9	2 27.7	19 16.1	22 19.9	23 38.4	22 12.0	0 34.4
25 M	8 13 39.0	19 32.8	5 26.0	27 33.8	22 20.9	18 21.1	2 5.8	19 22.2	22 20.1	23 38.3	22 12.4	0 32.6
28 T	8 25 28.7	18 52.1	5 29.7	24 36.5	21 34.2	18 34.2	1 45.6	19 28.0	22 20.4	23 38.3	22 12.7	0 30.7
31 S	8 37 18.4	18 8.6	5 33.4	7 27.2	20 24.5	18 47.7	1 27.3	19 33.4	22 20.6	23 38.2	22 13.0	0 28.8

AUGUST 1988

DAY	EPHEMERIS SIDEREAL TIME h m s	☉ ° ′	☊ ° ′	☽ ° ′	☿ ° ′	♀ ° ′	♂ ° ′	♃ ° ′	♄ ° ′	♅ ° ′	♆ ° ′	♇ ° ′
LONGITUDE at NOON												
1 M	8 41 14.9	9♌26.7	15♓51.7	26♓24.1	7♌35.9	25♊46.0	7♈19.2	1♊42.1	26♐34.8	27♐31.7	7♑59.8	9♏48.1
2 T	8 45 11.5	10 24.1	15 48.6	10♈55.3	9 41.2	26 30.5	7 37.6	1 51.1	26R32.2	27R30.2	7R58.5	9 48.6
3 W	8 49 8.0	11 21.5	15 45.4	25 6.5	11 45.8	27 15.9	7 55.5	1 60.0	26 29.7	27 28.6	7 57.2	9 49.0
4 T	8 53 4.6	12 19.0	15 42.2	8♉56.5	13 49.6	28 2.1	8 12.7	2 8.7	26 27.2	27 27.1	7 56.0	9 49.6
5 F	8 57 1.2	13 16.5	15 39.0	22 25.9	15 52.3	28 49.3	8 29.3	2 17.4	26 25.0	27 25.7	7 54.8	9 50.2
6 S	9 0 57.7	14 13.9	15 35.9	5♊35.9	17 53.9	29 37.1	8 45.2	2 25.9	26 22.7	27 24.3	7 53.5	9 50.7
7 S	9 4 54.3	15 11.5	15 32.7	18 28.6	19 54.2	0♋25.8	9 0.5	2 34.3	26 20.5	27 22.9	7 52.3	9 51.3
8 M	9 8 50.8	16 9.0	15 29.5	1♋ 6.2	21 53.2	1 15.1	9 15.1	2 42.6	26 18.4	27 21.5	7 51.1	9 52.0
9 T	9 12 47.4	17 6.5	15 26.3	13 30.7	23 50.8	2 5.2	9 28.9	2 50.7	26 16.4	27 20.2	7 50.0	9 52.7
10 W	9 16 43.9	18 4.1	15 23.1	25 44.0	25 47.0	2 56.0	9 42.1	2 58.7	26 14.5	27 19.0	7 48.8	9 53.4
11 T	9 20 40.5	19 1.7	15 20.0	7♌48.0	27 41.8	3 47.4	9 54.5	3 6.5	26 12.7	27 17.8	7 47.7	9 54.1
12 F	9 24 37.1	19 59.3	15 16.8	19 44.4	29 35.1	4 39.4	10 6.3	3 14.2	26 11.0	27 16.6	7 46.6	9 54.9
13 S	9 28 33.6	20 56.9	15 13.6	1♍35.2	1♍26.9	5 32.1	10 17.2	3 21.7	26 9.3	27 15.5	7 45.5	9 55.7
14 S	9 32 30.2	21 54.6	15 10.4	13 22.6	3 17.3	6 25.3	10 27.4	3 29.1	26 7.8	27 14.4	7 44.5	9 56.6
15 M	9 36 26.7	22 52.2	15 7.3	25 8.9	5 6.2	7 19.2	10 36.9	3 36.4	26 6.3	27 13.3	7 43.4	9 57.4
16 T	9 40 23.3	23 49.9	15 4.1	6♎57.3	6 53.6	8 13.5	10 45.5	3 43.5	26 4.9	27 12.3	7 42.4	9 58.4
17 W	9 44 19.8	24 47.6	15 0.9	18 51.1	8 39.6	9 8.4	10 53.4	3 50.4	26 3.6	27 11.4	7 41.4	9 59.3
18 T	9 48 16.4	25 45.3	14 57.7	0♏54.3	10 24.2	10 3.9	11 0.5	3 57.3	26 2.5	27 10.5	7 40.5	10 0.3
19 F	9 52 12.9	26 43.1	14 54.5	13 11.2	12 7.3	10 59.8	11 6.8	4 3.9	26 1.4	27 9.6	7 39.6	10 1.3
20 S	9 56 9.5	27 40.8	14 51.4	25 46.0	13 48.9	11 56.2	11 12.2	4 10.4	26 0.4	27 8.8	7 38.7	10 2.3
21 S	10 0 6.0	28 38.6	14 48.2	8♐43.0	15 29.2	12 53.1	11 16.9	4 16.7	25 59.5	27 8.1	7 37.8	10 3.4
22 M	10 4 2.6	29 36.4	14 45.0	22 5.3	17 8.1	13 50.4	11 20.7	4 22.9	25 58.7	27 7.4	7 36.9	10 4.5
23 T	10 7 59.2	0♍34.2	14 41.8	5♑54.8	18 45.6	14 48.2	11 23.7	4 28.9	25 58.0	27 6.7	7 36.1	10 5.6
24 W	10 11 55.7	1 32.0	14 38.7	20 11.5	20 21.7	15 46.4	11 25.9	4 34.8	25 57.3	27 6.1	7 35.3	10 6.8
25 T	10 15 52.3	2 29.9	14 35.5	4♒52.6	21 56.5	16 45.1	11 27.2	4 40.5	25 56.8	27 5.5	7 34.5	10 8.0
26 F	10 19 48.8	3 27.8	14 32.3	19 52.4	23 30.0	17 44.2	11 27.8	4 46.1	25 56.5	27 5.0	7 33.9	10 9.3
27 S	10 23 45.4	4 25.7	14 29.1	5♓ 3.0	25 2.0	18 43.6	11R27.5	4 51.4	25 56.1	27 4.6	7 33.1	10 10.5
28 S	10 27 41.9	5 23.7	14 26.0	20 14.8	26 32.7	19 43.5	11 26.3	4 56.6	25 55.9	27 4.2	7 32.5	10 11.8
29 M	10 31 38.5	6 21.6	14 22.8	5♈18.7	28 2.0	20 43.7	11 24.3	5 1.7	25 55.8	27 3.8	7 31.8	10 13.1
30 T	10 35 35.0	7 19.6	14 19.6	20 6.3	29 30.0	21 44.3	11 21.4	5 6.5	25 55.7	27 3.5	7 31.2	10 14.5
31 W	10 39 31.6	8 17.6	14 16.4	4♉32.0	0♎56.6	22 45.2	11 17.7	5 11.2	25D55.8	27 3.2	7 30.6	10 15.9

DAY	EPHEMERIS SIDEREAL TIME h m s	☉ ° ′	☊ ° ′	☽ ° ′	☿ ° ′	♀ ° ′	♂ ° ′	♃ ° ′	♄ ° ′	♅ ° ′	♆ ° ′	♇ ° ′
DECLINATION at NOON												
1 M	8 41 14.9	17N53.5	5S34.6	0S26.4	19N56.6	18N52.1	1S21.6	19N35.2	22S20.7	23S38.1	22S13.1	0N28.1
4 T	8 53 4.6	17 6.5	5 38.3	18N30.1	18 21.2	19 4.8	1 5.9	19 40.3	22 21.0	23 38.1	22 13.5	0 26.0
7 S	9 4 54.3	16 17.0	5 42.0	28 7.7	16 31.1	19 16.3	0 52.3	19 45.1	22 21.3	23 38.0	22 13.8	0 23.8
10 W	9 16 43.9	15 25.1	5 45.7	24 51.1	14 30.5	19 26.1	0 40.9	19 49.5	22 21.6	23 37.9	22 14.1	0 21.6
13 S	9 28 33.6	14 30.9	5 49.4	11 58.6	12 22.7	19 33.6	0 31.8	19 53.7	22 21.9	23 37.8	22 14.4	0 19.3
16 T	9 40 23.3	13 34.7	5 53.0	4S38.7	10 10.7	19 38.5	0 24.9	19 57.5	22 22.3	23 37.8	22 14.6	0 16.9
19 F	9 52 12.9	12 36.6	5 56.7	20 6.7	7 56.6	19 40.3	0 20.4	20 1.0	22 22.7	23 37.7	22 14.9	0 14.5
22 M	10 4 2.6	11 36.7	6 0.4	28 25.5	5 42.1	19 38.8	0 18.2	20 4.3	22 23.1	23 37.7	22 15.2	0 12.0
25 T	10 15 52.3	10 35.1	6 4.1	22 17.7	3 28.9	19 33.7	0 18.2	20 7.2	22 23.6	23 37.6	22 15.4	0 9.4
28 S	10 27 41.9	9 32.1	6 7.8	3 20.3	1 17.9	19 24.7	0 20.5	20 9.8	22 24.1	23 37.6	22 15.6	0 6.8
31 W	10 39 31.6	8 27.7	6 11.4	16N52.7	0S49.7	19 11.6	0 24.9	20 12.1	22 24.6	23 37.6	22 15.9	0 4.2

SEPTEMBER 1988

LONGITUDE at NOON

DAY	EPHEMERIS SIDEREAL TIME h m s	☉ ° ′	☊ ° ′	☽ ° ′	☿ ° ′	♀ ° ′	♂ ° ′	♃ ° ′	♄ ° ′	♅ ° ′	♆ ° ′	♇ ° ′
1 T	10 43 28.1	9♍15.7	14♓13.2	18♉32.5	2♎21.8	23♋46.5	11♈13.1	5♊15.7	25♐55.9	27♐ 3.0	7♑30.0	10♏17.3
2 F	10 47 24.7	10 13.7	14 10.1	2♊ 7.2	3 45.5	24 48.2	11R 7.7	5 20.0	25 56.2	27R 2.8	7R29.5	10 18.7
3 S	10 51 21.3	11 11.9	14 6.9	15 17.4	5 7.9	25 50.2	11 1.5	5 24.2	25 56.6	27 2.7	7 29.0	10 20.2
4 S	10 55 17.8	12 10.0	14 3.7	28 5.5	6 28.7	26 52.5	10 54.4	5 28.2	25 57.0	27 2.6	7 28.5	10 21.6
5 M	10 59 14.4	13 8.2	14 0.5	10♋35.0	7 48.1	27 55.1	10 46.5	5 32.0	25 57.6	27 2.6	7 28.1	10 23.2
6 T	11 3 10.9	14 6.4	13 57.4	22 49.5	9 5.8	28 58.0	10 37.8	5 35.6	25 58.2	27 2.6	7 27.7	10 24.7
7 W	11 7 7.5	15 4.6	13 54.2	4♌52.5	10 22.0	0♌ 1.2	10 28.4	5 39.0	25 58.9	27D 2.7	7 27.3	10 26.3
8 T	11 11 4.0	16 2.9	13 51.0	16 47.3	11 36.5	1 4.7	10 18.2	5 42.2	25 59.8	27 2.8	7 26.9	10 27.9
9 F	11 15 0.6	17 1.2	13 47.8	28 37.1	12 49.3	2 8.5	10 7.2	5 45.3	26 0.7	27 3.0	7 26.6	10 29.5
10 S	11 18 57.1	17 59.6	13 44.6	10♍24.3	14 0.2	3 12.5	9 55.6	5 48.1	26 1.8	27 3.3	7 26.3	10 31.2
11 S	11 22 53.7	18 57.9	13 41.5	22 11.4	15 9.2	4 16.8	9 43.2	5 50.8	26 2.9	27 3.6	7 26.1	10 32.8
12 M	11 26 50.2	19 56.3	13 38.3	4♎ 0.8	16 16.3	5 21.4	9 30.2	5 53.3	26 4.1	27 3.9	7 25.9	10 34.5
13 T	11 30 46.8	20 54.8	13 35.1	15 54.5	17 21.1	6 26.2	9 16.6	5 55.6	26 5.5	27 4.3	7 25.7	10 36.3
14 W	11 34 43.3	21 53.2	13 31.9	27 55.0	18 23.7	7 31.3	9 2.4	5 57.7	26 6.9	27 4.7	7 25.5	10 38.0
15 T	11 38 39.9	22 51.7	13 28.8	10♏ 4.8	19 23.9	8 36.6	8 47.7	5 59.6	26 8.4	27 5.2	7 25.4	10 39.8
16 F	11 42 36.5	23 50.3	13 25.6	22 26.7	20 21.6	9 42.2	8 32.5	6 1.3	26 10.1	27 5.8	7 25.4	10 41.7
17 S	11 46 33.0	24 48.8	13 22.4	5♐ 3.7	21 16.5	10 47.9	8 16.9	6 2.8	26 11.8	27 6.4	7 25.3	10 43.5
18 S	11 50 29.6	25 47.4	13 19.2	17 58.9	22 8.4	11 53.9	8 0.8	6 4.1	26 13.6	27 7.1	7 25.3	10 45.3
19 M	11 54 26.1	26 46.0	13 16.0	1♑15.1	22 57.1	13 0.1	7 44.3	6 5.2	26 15.5	27 7.8	7 25.3	10 47.2
20 T	11 58 22.7	27 44.6	13 12.9	14 54.5	23 42.4	14 6.5	7 27.6	6 6.1	26 17.5	27 8.5	7 25.3	10 49.1
21 W	12 2 19.2	28 43.3	13 9.7	28 58.2	24 23.9	15 13.1	7 10.5	6 6.8	26 19.6	27 9.3	7D25.4	10 51.0
22 T	12 6 15.8	29 42.0	13 6.5	13♒25.4	25 1.5	16 19.9	6 53.2	6 7.3	26 21.8	27 10.2	7 25.5	10 52.9
23 F	12 10 12.3	0♎40.7	13 3.3	28 13.1	25 34.7	17 27.0	6 35.8	6 7.7	26 24.1	27 11.1	7 25.7	10 54.9
24 S	12 14 8.9	1 39.4	13 0.2	13♓15.6	26 3.3	18 34.2	6 18.2	6 7.8	26 26.4	27 12.1	7 25.8	10 56.9
25 S	12 18 5.4	2 38.2	12 57.0	28 25.0	26 26.8	19 41.6	6 0.5	6R 7.7	26 28.9	27 13.1	7 26.0	10 58.9
26 M	12 22 2.0	3 37.0	12 53.8	13♈32.3	26 44.8	20 49.2	5 42.7	6 7.4	26 31.5	27 14.1	7 26.3	11 0.9
27 T	12 25 58.5	4 35.8	12 50.6	28 28.0	26 57.0	21 57.0	5 25.0	6 6.9	26 34.1	27 15.2	7 26.6	11 2.9
28 W	12 29 55.1	5 34.7	12 47.4	13♉ 4.2	27 3.0	23 5.0	5 7.3	6 6.2	26 36.8	27 16.4	7 26.9	11 5.0
29 T	12 33 51.7	6 33.6	12 44.3	27 15.5	27R 2.2	24 13.2	4 49.7	6 5.3	26 39.7	27 17.6	7 27.2	11 7.1
30 F	12 37 48.2	7 32.6	12 41.1	10♊59.1	26 54.5	25 21.6	4 32.3	6 4.2	26 42.6	27 18.8	7 27.6	11 9.2

DECLINATION at NOON

DAY	EPHEMERIS SIDEREAL TIME h m s	☉ ° ′	☊ ° ′	☽ ° ′	☿ ° ′	♀ ° ′	♂ ° ′	♃ ° ′	♄ ° ′	♅ ° ′	♆ ° ′	♇ ° ′
1 T	10 43 28.1	8N 5.9	6S 12.6	21N56.2	1S 31.3	19N 6.3	0S 26.8	20N12.8	22S 24.7	23S 37.5	22S 15.9	0N 3.3
4 S	10 55 17.8	6 59.9	6 16.3	28 34.1	3 32.8	18 47.5	0 34.0	20 14.7	22 25.3	23 37.5	22 16.1	0 0.6
7 W	11 7 7.5	5 52.8	6 20.0	22 18.2	5 28.6	18 24.4	0 43.0	20 16.3	22 25.9	23 37.5	22 16.3	0S 2.1
10 S	11 18 57.1	4 44.8	6 23.7	7 59.1	7 17.5	17 56.8	0 53.5	20 17.6	22 26.4	23 37.5	22 16.5	0 4.9
13 T	11 30 46.8	3 36.1	6 27.3	8S 50.2	8 58.1	17 24.9	1 5.3	20 18.6	22 27.1	23 37.6	22 16.6	0 7.6
16 F	11 42 36.5	2 26.8	6 31.0	23 7.9	10 28.7	16 48.5	1 17.9	20 19.3	22 27.7	23 37.6	22 16.8	0 10.4
19 M	11 54 26.1	1 17.1	6 34.6	28 29.0	11 47.0	16 7.9	1 30.9	20 19.7	22 28.3	23 37.6	22 16.9	0 13.2
22 T	12 6 15.8	0 7.2	6 38.3	19 22.6	12 50.0	15 23.1	1 43.8	20 19.7	22 29.0	23 37.7	22 17.0	0 16.0
25 S	12 18 5.4	1S 2.9	6 41.9	0N34.3	13 33.7	14 34.1	1 56.3	20 19.5	22 29.7	23 37.7	22 17.1	0 18.7
28 W	12 29 55.1	2 13.0	6 45.6	20 3.6	13 52.9	13 41.2	2 7.9	20 19.0	22 30.4	23 37.8	22 17.2	0 21.5

OCTOBER 1988

LONGITUDE at NOON

DAY	EPHEMERIS SIDEREAL TIME h m s	☉ ° ′	☊ ° ′	☽ ° ′	☿ ° ′	♀ ° ′	♂ ° ′	♃ ° ′	♄ ° ′	♅ ° ′	♆ ° ′	♇ ° ′
1 S	12 41 44.8	8♎31.6	12♓37.9	24♊14.9	26♎39.3	26♌30.1	4♈15.0	6♊ 2.9	26♐45.6	27♐20.1	7♑28.0	11♏11.3
2 S	12 45 41.3	9 30.6	12 34.7	7♋ 5.3	26R16.5	27 38.8	3R57.9	6R 1.4	26 48.6	27 21.5	7 28.4	11 13.4
3 M	12 49 37.9	10 29.7	12 31.6	19 33.7	25 46.0	28 47.7	3 41.2	5 59.7	26 51.8	27 22.9	7 28.9	11 15.6
4 T	12 53 34.4	11 28.8	12 28.4	1♌44.8	25 7.7	29 56.7	3 24.7	5 57.8	26 55.1	27 24.3	7 29.4	11 17.7
5 W	12 57 31.0	12 27.9	12 25.2	13 43.2	24 21.8	1♍ 5.9	3 8.6	5 55.7	26 58.4	27 25.8	7 29.9	11 19.9
6 T	13 1 27.5	13 27.1	12 22.0	25 33.7	23 28.9	2 15.3	2 53.0	5 53.4	27 1.9	27 27.4	7 30.5	11 22.1
7 F	13 5 24.1	14 26.4	12 18.8	7♍20.4	22 29.6	3 24.8	2 37.8	5 51.0	27 5.4	27 29.0	7 31.2	11 24.4
8 S	13 9 20.6	15 25.6	12 15.7	19 7.2	21 24.9	4 34.5	2 23.1	5 48.3	27 9.0	27 30.6	7 31.8	11 26.6
9 S	13 13 17.2	16 24.9	12 12.5	0♎57.2	20 16.2	5 44.3	2 8.9	5 45.4	27 12.7	27 32.3	7 32.5	11 28.8
10 M	13 17 13.7	17 24.2	12 9.3	12 53.0	19 5.1	6 54.2	1 55.3	5 42.3	27 16.5	27 34.1	7 33.2	11 31.1
11 T	13 21 10.3	18 23.6	12 6.1	24 56.5	17 53.4	8 4.3	1 42.2	5 39.0	27 20.3	27 35.8	7 33.9	11 33.3
12 W	13 25 6.9	19 23.0	12 3.0	7♏ 9.3	16 43.2	9 14.5	1 29.8	5 35.5	27 24.2	27 37.7	7 34.7	11 35.6
13 T	13 29 3.4	20 22.4	11 59.8	19 32.5	15 36.5	10 24.9	1 18.1	5 31.9	27 28.2	27 39.5	7 35.5	11 37.9
14 F	13 32 60.0	21 21.9	11 56.6	2♐ 7.3	14 35.2	11 35.4	1 7.0	5 28.0	27 32.3	27 41.4	7 36.3	11 40.2
15 S	13 36 56.5	22 21.4	11 53.4	14 54.8	13 41.1	12 45.9	0 56.7	5 24.0	27 36.5	27 43.4	7 37.2	11 42.5
16 S	13 40 53.1	23 20.9	11 50.2	27 56.3	12 55.7	13 56.7	0 47.1	5 19.7	27 40.7	27 45.4	7 38.1	11 44.9
17 M	13 44 49.6	24 20.4	11 47.1	11♑13.2	12 20.2	15 7.5	0 38.2	5 15.3	27 45.1	27 47.5	7 39.0	11 47.2
18 T	13 48 46.2	25 20.0	11 43.9	24 46.9	11 55.4	16 18.5	0 30.1	5 10.7	27 49.4	27 49.6	7 39.9	11 49.5
19 W	13 52 42.7	26 19.6	11 40.7	8♒38.6	11 41.7	17 29.5	0 22.8	5 6.0	27 53.9	27 51.7	7 40.9	11 51.9
20 T	13 56 39.3	27 19.3	11 37.5	22 48.7	11 39.2	18 40.7	0 16.3	5 1.1	27 58.5	27 53.9	7 41.9	11 54.3
21 F	14 0 35.8	28 18.9	11 34.4	7♓16.1	11D47.8	19 52.0	0 10.5	4 56.0	28 3.1	27 56.1	7 43.0	11 56.6
22 S	14 4 32.4	29 18.6	11 31.2	21 58.0	12 7.0	21 3.4	0 5.6	4 50.7	28 7.7	27 58.3	7 44.1	11 59.0
23 S	14 8 29.0	0♏18.3	11 28.0	6♈49.4	12 36.2	22 15.0	0 1.4	4 45.3	28 12.5	28 0.6	7 45.2	12 1.4
24 M	14 12 25.5	1 18.1	11 24.8	21 43.4	13 14.6	23 26.6	29♓58.1	4 39.7	28 17.3	28 3.0	7 46.3	12 3.8
25 T	14 16 22.1	2 17.9	11 21.7	6♉31.6	14 1.5	24 38.3	29 55.5	4 33.9	28 22.2	28 5.4	7 47.5	12 6.2
26 W	14 20 18.6	3 17.7	11 18.5	21 5.9	14 56.0	25 50.2	29 53.8	4 28.0	28 27.2	28 7.8	7 48.7	12 8.6
27 T	14 24 15.2	4 17.5	11 15.3	5♊19.4	15 57.2	27 2.1	29 52.8	4 22.0	28 32.2	28 10.2	7 49.9	12 11.0
28 F	14 28 11.7	5 17.5	11 12.1	19 7.6	17 4.5	28 14.2	29 52.7	4 15.8	28 37.3	28 12.8	7 51.2	12 13.4
29 S	14 32 8.3	6 17.4	11 8.9	2♋28.6	18 16.8	29 26.4	29D53.3	4 9.5	28 42.5	28 15.3	7 52.5	12 15.9
30 S	14 36 4.8	7 17.4	11 5.8	15 23.3	19 33.6	0♎38.6	29 54.7	4 3.0	28 47.7	28 17.9	7 53.8	12 18.3
31 M	14 40 1.4	8 17.4	11 2.6	27 54.6	20 54.2	1 50.9	29 56.9	3 56.4	28 53.0	28 20.5	7 55.2	12 20.7

DECLINATION at NOON

DAY	EPHEMERIS SIDEREAL TIME h m s	☉ ° ′	☊ ° ′	☽ ° ′	☿ ° ′	♀ ° ′	♂ ° ′	♃ ° ′	♄ ° ′	♅ ° ′	♆ ° ′	♇ ° ′
1 S	12 41 44.8	3S 22.9	6S 49.2	28N28.6	13S 41.1	12N44.5	2S 18.2	20N18.2	22S 31.1	23S 37.8	22S 17.3	0S 24.2
4 T	12 53 34.4	4 32.5	6 52.9	23 12.5	12 52.0	11 44.2	2 27.0	20 17.3	22 31.7	23 37.9	22 17.3	0 27.0
7 F	13 5 24.1	5 41.6	6 56.5	9 22.5	11 22.9	10 40.5	2 33.8	20 15.7	22 32.4	23 38.0	22 17.3	0 29.7
10 M	13 17 13.7	6 50.1	7 0.2	7S 25.0	9 20.6	9 33.7	2 38.3	20 13.9	22 33.1	23 38.1	22 17.3	0 32.3
13 T	13 29 3.4	7 57.7	7 3.8	22 10.0	7 5.7	8 24.1	2 40.4	20 11.9	22 33.8	23 38.2	22 17.3	0 35.0
16 S	13 40 53.1	9 4.3	7 7.4	28 25.8	5 7.2	7 11.8	2 39.9	20 9.7	22 34.5	23 38.3	22 17.3	0 37.6
19 W	13 52 42.7	10 9.7	7 11.1	20 56.4	3 49.9	5 57.2	2 36.6	20 7.1	22 35.1	23 38.4	22 17.2	0 40.1
22 S	14 4 32.4	11 13.8	7 14.7	2 28.1	3 23.7	4 40.5	2 30.7	20 4.3	22 35.7	23 38.5	22 17.2	0 42.6
25 T	14 16 22.1	12 16.4	7 18.3	17N35.1	3 45.6	3 22.1	2 22.1	20 1.2	22 36.3	23 38.6	22 17.1	0 45.0
28 F	14 28 11.7	13 17.3	7 21.9	28 3.6	4 45.2	2 2.2	2 11.0	19 57.8	22 36.9	23 38.7	22 17.0	0 47.4
31 M	14 40 1.4	14 16.3	7 25.5	24 6.2	6 10.7	0 41.1	1 57.4	19 54.3	22 37.4	23 38.8	22 16.9	0 49.7

NOVEMBER 1988

DAY	EPHEMERIS SIDEREAL TIME (h m s)	☉ (° ′)	☊ (° ′)	☽ (° ′)	☿ (° ′)	♀ (° ′)	♂ (° ′)	♃ (° ′)	♄ (° ′)	♅ (° ′)	♆ (° ′)	♇ (° ′)
					LONGITUDE at NOON							
1 T	14 43 58.0	9♏17.4	10♓59.4	10♌ 6.7	22♎18.0	3♎ 3.4	29♓59.8	3♊49.7	28♐58.3	28♐23.1	7♑56.5	12♏23.1
2 W	14 47 54.5	10 17.5	10 56.2	22 5.0	23 44.5	4 15.9	0♈ 3.6	3R42.8	29 3.7	28 25.8	7 57.9	12 25.6
3 T	14 51 51.1	11 17.6	10 53.1	3♍54.7	25 13.2	5 28.5	0 8.0	3 35.8	29 9.2	28 28.5	7 59.3	12 28.0
4 F	14 55 47.6	12 17.7	10 49.9	15 41.2	26 43.8	6 41.2	0 13.3	3 28.7	29 14.7	28 31.3	8 0.8	12 30.4
5 S	14 59 44.2	13 17.9	10 46.7	27 29.5	28 15.8	7 54.0	0 19.3	3 21.5	29 20.3	28 34.1	8 2.3	12 32.8
6 S	15 3 40.7	14 18.1	10 43.5	9♎23.6	29 49.1	9 6.8	0 26.0	3 14.2	29 26.0	28 36.9	8 3.8	12 35.3
7 M	15 7 37.3	15 18.3	10 40.4	21 27.1	1♏23.3	10 19.8	0 33.4	3 6.8	29 31.7	28 39.7	8 5.3	12 37.7
8 T	15 11 33.9	16 18.6	10 37.2	3♏42.3	2 58.2	11 32.8	0 41.6	2 59.3	29 37.4	28 42.6	8 6.8	12 40.1
9 W	15 15 30.4	17 18.9	10 34.0	16 10.6	4 33.7	12 45.9	0 50.5	2 51.7	29 43.2	28 45.5	8 8.4	12 42.5
10 T	15 19 27.0	18 19.2	10 30.8	28 52.4	6 9.5	13 59.0	1 0.1	2 44.0	29 49.1	28 48.5	8 10.0	12 45.0
11 F	15 23 23.5	19 19.6	10 27.6	11♐47.3	7 45.7	15 12.3	1 10.3	2 36.3	29 55.0	28 51.5	8 11.7	12 47.4
12 S	15 27 20.1	20 19.9	10 24.5	24 54.5	9 22.1	16 25.6	1 21.3	2 28.4	0♑ 1.0	28 54.5	8 13.3	12 49.8
13 S	15 31 16.6	21 20.3	10 21.3	8♑13.0	10 58.5	17 38.9	1 32.9	2 20.6	0 7.0	28 57.5	8 15.0	12 52.2
14 M	15 35 13.2	22 20.8	10 18.1	21 42.1	12 34.9	18 52.3	1 45.2	2 12.6	0 13.0	29 0.6	8 16.7	12 54.6
15 T	15 39 9.7	23 21.2	10 14.9	5♒21.3	14 11.4	20 5.8	1 58.1	2 4.6	0 19.2	29 3.7	8 18.4	12 57.0
16 W	15 43 6.3	24 21.7	10 11.8	19 10.8	15 47.7	21 19.3	2 11.6	1 56.6	0 25.3	29 6.8	8 20.2	12 59.4
17 T	15 47 2.9	25 22.2	10 8.6	3♓10.6	17 23.9	22 32.9	2 25.8	1 48.5	0 31.5	29 9.9	8 21.9	13 1.8
18 F	15 50 59.4	26 22.8	10 5.4	17 20.7	19 0.1	23 46.6	2 40.6	1 40.4	0 37.8	29 13.1	8 23.8	13 4.2
19 S	15 54 56.0	27 23.3	10 2.2	1♈39.9	20 36.1	25 0.3	2 55.9	1 32.3	0 44.1	29 16.3	8 25.6	13 6.6
20 S	15 58 52.5	28 23.9	9 59.1	16 5.8	22 11.8	26 14.1	3 11.8	1 24.1	0 50.4	29 19.6	8 27.4	13 9.0
21 M	16 2 49.1	29 24.4	9 55.9	0♉34.5	23 47.5	27 27.9	3 28.2	1 15.9	0 56.8	29 22.8	8 29.3	13 11.3
22 T	16 6 45.7	0♐25.0	9 52.7	15 0.4	25 22.9	28 41.8	3 45.2	1 7.7	1 3.2	29 26.1	8 31.1	13 13.7
23 W	16 10 42.2	1 25.7	9 49.5	29 17.2	26 58.2	29 55.7	4 2.7	0 59.6	1 9.7	29 29.3	8 33.0	13 16.0
24 T	16 14 38.8	2 26.3	9 46.3	13♊18.8	28 33.3	1♏ 9.7	4 20.7	0 51.4	1 16.1	29 32.7	8 34.9	13 18.3
25 F	16 18 35.3	3 27.0	9 43.2	27 0.3	0♐ 8.3	2 23.7	4 39.3	0 43.2	1 22.7	29 36.0	8 36.8	13 20.7
26 S	16 22 31.9	4 27.7	9 40.0	10♋18.7	1 43.2	3 37.7	4 58.3	0 35.1	1 29.2	29 39.3	8 38.8	13 23.0
27 S	16 26 28.4	5 28.4	9 36.8	23 13.5	3 17.9	4 51.9	5 17.8	0 26.9	1 35.8	29 42.7	8 40.8	13 25.3
28 M	16 30 25.0	6 29.1	9 33.6	5♌46.2	4 52.4	6 6.0	5 37.7	0 18.8	1 42.4	29 46.1	8 42.7	13 27.5
29 T	16 34 21.6	7 29.9	9 30.5	18 0.1	6 26.9	7 20.2	5 58.1	0 10.8	1 49.1	29 49.5	8 44.7	13 29.8
30 W	16 38 18.1	8 30.7	9 27.3	29 59.8	8 1.3	8 34.5	6 18.9	0 2.7	1 55.8	29 52.9	8 46.7	13 32.1
					DECLINATION at NOON							
1 T	14 43 58.0	14S35.5	7S26.8	20N21.1	6S43.2	0N13.8	1S52.4	19N53.0	22S37.6	23S38.8	22S16.8	0S50.5
4 F	14 55 47.6	15 31.7	7 30.4	5 22.6	8 28.0	1S 8.3	1 35.7	19 49.2	22 38.1	23 38.9	22 16.7	0 52.7
7 M	15 7 37.3	16 25.7	7 34.0	11S20.3	10 18.8	2 31.0	1 16.9	19 45.1	22 38.5	23 39.0	22 16.5	0 54.8
10 T	15 19 27.0	17 17.1	7 37.6	24 42.0	12 10.8	3 53.7	0 56.0	19 40.9	22 38.9	23 39.1	22 16.3	0 56.9
13 S	15 31 16.6	18 5.9	7 41.2	27 40.3	14 0.6	5 16.1	0 33.1	19 36.5	22 39.3	23 39.2	22 16.1	0 58.8
16 W	15 43 6.3	18 51.8	7 44.8	16 51.7	15 46.0	6 38.0	0 8.3	19 32.0	22 39.6	23 39.3	22 15.9	1 0.7
19 S	15 54 56.0	19 34.8	7 48.4	2N18.1	17 25.5	7 58.9	0N18.1	19 27.4	22 39.8	23 39.3	22 15.6	1 2.5
22 T	16 6 45.7	20 14.5	7 52.0	20 39.6	18 57.7	9 18.6	0 46.1	19 22.8	22 40.0	23 39.4	22 15.3	1 4.2
25 F	16 18 35.3	20 50.8	7 55.6	28 12.0	20 21.8	10 36.7	1 15.4	19 18.1	22 40.1	23 39.4	22 15.1	1 5.8
28 M	16 30 25.0	21 23.7	7 59.2	21 33.2	21 37.0	11 52.8	1 46.0	19 13.5	22 40.2	23 39.5	22 14.8	1 7.3

DECEMBER 1988

DAY	EPHEMERIS SIDEREAL TIME (h m s)	☉ (° ′)	☊ (° ′)	☽ (° ′)	☿ (° ′)	♀ (° ′)	♂ (° ′)	♃ (° ′)	♄ (° ′)	♅ (° ′)	♆ (° ′)	♇ (° ′)
					LONGITUDE at NOON							
1 T	16 42 14.7	9♐31.5	9♓24.1	11♍50.4	9♐35.6	9♏48.8	6♈40.2	29♉54.8	2♑ 2.5	29♐56.4	8♑48.8	13♏34.3
2 F	16 46 11.2	10 32.4	9 20.9	23 37.8	11 9.8	11 3.1	7 1.9	29R46.8	2 9.3	29 59.8	8 50.8	13 36.5
3 S	16 50 7.8	11 33.2	9 17.8	5♎27.4	12 44.0	12 17.5	7 24.1	29 39.0	2 16.0	0♑ 3.3	8 52.9	13 38.8
4 S	16 54 4.3	12 34.1	9 14.6	17 24.4	14 18.2	13 31.9	7 46.6	29 31.2	2 22.8	0 6.8	8 55.0	13 41.0
5 M	16 58 0.9	13 35.0	9 11.4	29 33.3	15 52.3	14 46.4	8 9.5	29 23.4	2 29.7	0 10.3	8 57.0	13 43.1
6 T	17 1 57.5	14 35.9	9 8.2	11♏57.5	17 26.5	16 0.9	8 32.8	29 15.8	2 36.5	0 13.8	8 59.1	13 45.3
7 W	17 5 54.0	15 36.9	9 5.1	24 39.2	19 0.6	17 15.4	8 56.5	29 8.2	2 43.4	0 17.3	9 1.3	13 47.5
8 T	17 9 50.6	16 37.9	9 1.9	7♐39.0	20 34.8	18 29.9	9 20.6	29 0.8	2 50.3	0 20.9	9 3.4	13 49.6
9 F	17 13 47.1	17 38.9	8 58.7	20 55.9	22 9.1	19 44.6	9 45.1	28 53.4	2 57.3	0 24.5	9 5.6	13 51.8
10 S	17 17 43.7	18 39.9	8 55.5	4♑27.8	23 43.4	20 59.2	10 9.9	28 46.1	3 4.2	0 28.0	9 7.7	13 53.8
11 S	17 21 40.3	19 40.9	8 52.3	18 11.5	25 17.7	22 13.8	10 35.0	28 39.0	3 11.2	0 31.6	9 9.9	13 55.9
12 M	17 25 36.8	20 41.9	8 49.2	2♒ 4.0	26 52.1	23 28.5	11 0.5	28 31.9	3 18.2	0 35.2	9 12.1	13 58.0
13 T	17 29 33.4	21 43.0	8 46.0	16 2.1	28 26.6	24 43.1	11 26.3	28 25.0	3 25.1	0 38.8	9 14.3	14 0.0
14 W	17 33 29.9	22 44.0	8 42.8	0♓ 3.6	0♑ 1.1	25 57.9	11 52.4	28 18.2	3 32.2	0 42.4	9 16.4	14 2.0
15 T	17 37 26.5	23 45.0	8 39.6	14 7.2	1 35.7	27 12.6	12 18.8	28 11.5	3 39.2	0 46.0	9 18.6	14 4.0
16 F	17 41 23.1	24 46.1	8 36.5	28 12.0	3 10.4	28 27.3	12 45.5	28 5.0	3 46.2	0 49.6	9 20.9	14 6.0
17 S	17 45 19.6	25 47.2	8 33.3	12♈17.3	4 45.2	29 42.1	13 12.6	27 58.5	3 53.3	0 53.2	9 23.1	14 8.0
18 S	17 49 16.2	26 48.2	8 30.1	26 22.2	6 20.0	0♐56.9	13 39.9	27 52.3	4 0.3	0 56.8	9 25.3	14 9.9
19 M	17 53 12.7	27 49.3	8 26.9	10♉24.8	7 54.8	2 11.7	14 7.4	27 46.2	4 7.4	1 0.4	9 27.5	14 11.8
20 T	17 57 9.3	28 50.4	8 23.8	24 22.6	9 29.7	3 26.5	14 35.3	27 40.2	4 14.4	1 4.0	9 29.8	14 13.7
21 W	18 1 5.8	29 51.4	8 20.6	8♊12.2	11 4.5	4 41.3	15 3.4	27 34.4	4 21.5	1 7.7	9 32.0	14 15.5
22 T	18 5 2.4	0♑52.5	8 17.4	21 50.0	12 39.3	5 56.2	15 31.7	27 28.7	4 28.6	1 11.3	9 34.3	14 17.4
23 F	18 8 59.0	1 53.6	8 14.2	5♋12.6	14 14.0	7 11.1	16 0.3	27 23.2	4 35.7	1 14.9	9 36.5	14 19.2
24 S	18 12 55.5	2 54.7	8 11.1	18 17.6	15 48.5	8 26.0	16 29.1	27 17.9	4 42.8	1 18.5	9 38.8	14 21.0
25 S	18 16 52.1	3 55.8	8 7.9	1♌ 4.0	17 22.8	9 40.9	16 58.2	27 12.7	4 49.9	1 22.1	9 41.0	14 22.7
26 M	18 20 48.6	4 57.0	8 4.7	13 32.4	18 56.8	10 55.8	17 27.5	27 7.7	4 57.0	1 25.8	9 43.3	14 24.5
27 T	18 24 45.2	5 58.1	8 1.5	25 44.8	20 30.3	12 10.8	17 57.0	27 2.9	5 4.1	1 29.4	9 45.6	14 26.2
28 W	18 28 41.8	6 59.2	7 58.4	7♍44.3	22 3.2	13 25.7	18 26.7	26 58.3	5 11.2	1 33.0	9 47.8	14 27.8
29 T	18 32 38.3	8 0.3	7 55.2	19 35.5	23 35.5	14 40.7	18 56.6	26 53.8	5 18.3	1 36.6	9 50.1	14 29.5
30 F	18 36 34.9	9 1.5	7 52.0	1♎23.4	25 6.8	15 55.7	19 26.8	26 49.6	5 25.4	1 40.2	9 52.4	14 31.2
31 S	18 40 31.4	10 2.7	7 48.8	13 13.2	26 37.0	17 10.7	19 57.1	26 45.5	5 32.5	1 43.8	9 54.7	14 32.8
					DECLINATION at NOON							
1 T	16 42 14.7	21S52.9	8S 2.8	6N56.0	22S42.7	13S 6.6	2N17.8	19N 8.9	22S40.2	23S39.5	22S14.4	1S 8.6
4 S	16 54 4.3	22 18.4	8 6.3	9S41.9	23 38.1	14 17.7	2 50.6	19 4.3	22 40.1	23 39.5	22 14.1	1 9.9
7 W	17 5 54.0	22 40.0	8 9.9	23 38.2	24 22.6	15 25.8	3 24.4	18 59.9	22 40.0	23 39.5	22 13.7	1 11.1
10 S	17 17 43.7	22 57.5	8 13.5	27 51.9	24 55.6	16 30.4	3 59.0	18 55.7	22 39.8	23 39.5	22 13.4	1 12.1
13 T	17 29 33.4	23 11.0	8 17.1	17 49.9	25 16.6	17 31.3	4 34.5	18 51.7	22 39.6	23 39.5	22 13.0	1 13.1
16 F	17 41 23.1	23 20.3	8 20.6	0N53.8	25 24.9	18 28.1	5 10.6	18 47.9	22 39.2	23 39.4	22 12.6	1 13.9
19 M	17 53 12.7	23 25.5	8 24.2	19 11.9	25 20.1	19 20.4	5 47.3	18 44.3	22 38.8	23 39.4	22 12.1	1 14.6
22 T	18 5 2.4	23 26.4	8 27.8	28 3.5	25 1.7	20 8.0	6 24.4	18 41.1	22 38.4	23 39.3	22 11.7	1 15.2
25 S	18 16 52.1	23 23.0	8 31.3	22 48.7	24 29.6	20 50.6	7 1.9	18 38.2	22 37.8	23 39.2	22 11.2	1 15.7
28 W	18 28 41.8	23 15.5	8 34.9	8 34.4	23 43.8	21 27.7	7 39.7	18 35.6	22 37.2	23 39.1	22 10.8	1 16.0
31 S	18 40 31.4	23 3.7	8 38.4	8S 2.2	22 45.0	21 59.3	8 17.8	18 33.4	22 36.6	23 39.0	22 10.3	1 16.2

JANUARY 1989

DAY	EPHEMERIS SIDEREAL TIME	☉	☊	☽	☿	♀	♂	♃	♄	♅	♆	♇
	h m s	° ′	° ′	° ′	° ′	° ′	° ′	° ′	° ′	° ′	° ′	° ′
						LONGITUDE at NOON						
1 S	18 44 28.0	11♑ 3.8	7♓45.6	25♎10.5	28♑ 5.9	18♐25.8	20♈27.6	26♉41.6	5♑39.6	1♑47.4	9♑57.0	14♏34.3
2 M	18 48 24.6	12 5.0	7 42.5	7♏20.4	29 33.0	19 40.8	20 58.3	26R37.9	5 46.6	1 51.0	9 59.2	14 35.9
3 T	18 52 21.1	13 6.2	7 39.3	19 47.4	0♒58.1	20 55.8	21 29.2	26 34.3	5 53.7	1 54.6	10 1.5	14 37.4
4 W	18 56 17.7	14 7.4	7 36.1	2♐35.0	2 20.8	22 10.9	22 0.3	26 31.0	6 0.8	1 58.1	10 3.8	14 38.9
5 T	19 0 14.2	15 8.5	7 32.9	15 44.9	3 40.6	23 26.0	22 31.5	26 27.9	6 7.8	2 1.7	10 6.0	14 40.3
6 F	19 4 10.8	16 9.7	7 29.8	29 17.2	4 57.0	24 41.0	23 3.0	26 24.9	6 14.9	2 5.3	10 8.3	14 41.8
7 S	19 8 7.3	17 10.9	7 26.6	13♑ 9.7	6 9.3	25 56.1	23 34.6	26 22.2	6 21.9	2 8.8	10 10.6	14 43.2
8 S	19 12 3.9	18 12.0	7 23.4	27 18.5	7 17.0	27 11.2	24 6.3	26 19.7	6 28.9	2 12.3	10 12.8	14 44.5
9 M	19 16 0.5	19 13.2	7 20.2	11♒38.6	8 19.3	28 26.3	24 38.3	26 17.4	6 35.9	2 15.8	10 15.1	14 45.9
10 T	19 19 57.0	20 14.4	7 17.1	26 4.2	9 15.4	29 41.4	25 10.3	26 15.2	6 42.9	2 19.3	10 17.3	14 47.2
11 W	19 23 53.6	21 15.5	7 13.9	10♓30.2	10 4.3	0♑56.5	25 42.6	26 13.3	6 49.8	2 22.8	10 19.6	14 48.4
12 T	19 27 50.1	22 16.7	7 10.7	24 52.3	10 45.4	2 11.6	26 15.0	26 11.6	6 56.8	2 26.3	10 21.8	14 49.7
13 F	19 31 46.7	23 17.8	7 7.5	9♈ 7.5	11 17.5	3 26.7	26 47.5	26 10.1	7 3.7	2 29.7	10 24.0	14 50.9
14 S	19 35 43.3	24 18.9	7 4.4	23 14.0	11 39.9	4 41.8	27 20.2	26 8.8	7 10.6	2 33.1	10 26.2	14 52.0
15 S	19 39 39.8	25 20.0	7 1.2	7♉10.6	11 51.9	5 56.9	27 53.0	26 7.7	7 17.5	2 36.6	10 28.5	14 53.2
16 M	19 43 36.4	26 21.1	6 58.0	20 56.7	11 52.6	7 12.0	28 25.9	26 6.8	7 24.3	2 40.0	10 30.7	14 54.3
17 T	19 47 32.9	27 22.2	6 54.8	4♊31.8	11R41.8	8 27.1	28 59.0	26 6.2	7 31.1	2 43.3	10 32.9	14 55.3
18 W	19 51 29.5	28 23.3	6 51.6	17 55.4	11 19.3	9 42.2	29 32.1	26 5.7	7 37.9	2 46.7	10 35.1	14 56.4
19 T	19 55 26.0	29 24.3	6 48.5	1♋ 6.6	10 45.2	10 57.4	0♉ 5.4	26 5.5	7 44.7	2 50.0	10 37.2	14 57.4
20 F	19 59 22.6	0♒25.4	6 45.3	14 4.8	10 0.3	12 12.5	0 38.9	26 5.4	7 51.5	2 53.4	10 39.4	14 58.4
21 S	20 3 19.2	1 26.5	6 42.1	26 49.3	9 5.5	13 27.6	1 12.4	26D 5.6	7 58.2	2 56.7	10 41.6	14 59.3
22 S	20 7 15.7	2 27.5	6 38.9	9♌20.2	8 2.3	14 42.7	1 46.0	26 6.0	8 4.9	2 60.0	10 43.8	15 0.2
23 M	20 11 12.3	3 28.5	6 35.8	21 38.0	6 52.5	15 57.8	2 19.8	26 6.5	8 11.6	3 3.2	10 45.9	15 1.1
24 T	20 15 8.8	4 29.5	6 32.6	3♍44.1	5 38.4	17 13.0	2 53.6	26 7.3	8 18.2	3 6.5	10 48.0	15 1.9
25 W	20 19 5.4	5 30.5	6 29.4	15 40.9	4 22.2	18 28.1	3 27.5	26 8.3	8 24.8	3 9.7	10 50.1	15 2.7
26 T	20 23 1.9	6 31.4	6 26.2	27 31.3	3 6.2	19 43.2	4 1.5	26 9.4	8 31.4	3 12.8	10 52.2	15 3.5
27 F	20 26 58.5	7 32.4	6 23.1	9♎19.1	1 52.5	20 58.3	4 35.6	26 10.8	8 37.9	3 16.0	10 54.3	15 4.2
28 S	20 30 55.1	8 33.4	6 19.9	21 8.8	0 43.1	22 13.4	5 9.8	26 12.4	8 44.4	3 19.1	10 56.4	15 4.9
29 S	20 34 51.6	9 34.3	6 16.7	3♏ 5.2	29♑39.6	23 28.6	5 44.1	26 14.2	8 50.8	3 22.2	10 58.4	15 5.6
30 M	20 38 48.2	10 35.2	6 13.5	15 13.2	28 43.1	24 43.7	6 18.5	26 16.2	8 57.2	3 25.3	11 0.5	15 6.2
31 T	20 42 44.7	11 36.1	6 10.3	27 37.7	27 54.6	25 58.8	6 53.0	26 18.4	9 3.6	3 28.3	11 2.5	15 6.8
						DECLINATION at NOON						
1 S	18 44 28.0	22S 58.9	8S 39.6	13S 19.0	22S 22.7	22S 8.6	8N 30.5	18N 32.8	22S 36.3	23S 39.0	22S 10.2	1S 16.3
4 W	18 56 17.7	22 41.6	8 43.1	25 40.6	21 9.1	22 32.3	9 8.7	18 31.1	22 35.6	23 38.9	22 9.7	1 16.4
7 S	19 8 7.3	22 20.3	8 46.7	26 51.0	19 48.0	22 50.0	9 47.0	18 29.8	22 34.8	23 38.7	22 9.2	1 16.3
10 T	19 19 57.0	21 55.0	8 50.2	13 38.3	18 25.0	23 1.4	10 25.3	18 29.0	22 33.9	23 38.6	22 8.7	1 16.2
13 F	19 31 46.7	21 25.9	8 53.8	6N 14.7	17 8.3	23 6.6	11 3.6	18 28.5	22 33.0	23 38.4	22 8.2	1 15.9
16 M	19 43 36.4	20 53.1	8 57.3	22 49.2	16 7.8	23 5.4	11 41.6	18 28.5	22 32.0	23 38.3	22 7.7	1 15.5
19 T	19 55 26.0	20 16.7	9 0.8	28 6.3	15 33.2	22 57.8	12 19.4	18 29.0	22 31.0	23 38.1	22 7.1	1 15.0
22 S	20 7 15.7	19 36.8	9 4.4	20 6.3	15 28.8	22 43.8	12 57.0	18 29.9	22 29.9	23 37.9	22 6.6	1 14.4
25 W	20 19 5.4	18 53.7	9 7.9	4 45.2	15 51.1	22 23.6	13 34.1	18 31.2	22 28.8	23 37.7	22 6.1	1 13.7
28 S	20 30 55.1	18 7.5	9 11.4	11S 45.3	16 29.6	21 57.3	14 10.8	18 32.9	22 27.7	23 37.6	22 5.6	1 12.8
31 T	20 42 44.7	17 18.4	9 14.9	24 42.0	17 13.5	21 25.0	14 47.0	18 35.1	22 26.5	23 37.4	22 5.1	1 11.9

FEBRUARY 1989

DAY	EPHEMERIS SIDEREAL TIME	☉	☊	☽	☿	♀	♂	♃	♄	♅	♆	♇
						LONGITUDE at NOON						
1 W	20 46 41.3	12♒37.0	6♓ 7.2	10♐22.9	27♑14.5	27♑13.9	7♉27.6	26♉20.7	9♑ 9.9	3♑31.4	11♑ 4.5	15♏ 7.3
2 T	20 50 37.8	13 37.9	6 4.0	23 32.3	26R43.0	28 29.1	8 2.2	26 23.3	9 16.2	3 34.4	11 6.5	15 7.9
3 F	20 54 34.4	14 38.8	6 0.8	7♑ 7.4	26 20.2	29 44.2	8 36.9	26 26.1	9 22.5	3 37.3	11 8.5	15 8.3
4 S	20 58 31.0	15 39.7	5 57.6	21 7.9	26 5.7	0♒59.3	9 11.7	26 29.1	9 28.7	3 40.2	11 10.4	15 8.8
5 S	21 2 27.5	16 40.5	5 54.5	5♒30.9	25 59.3	2 14.4	9 46.6	26 32.2	9 34.8	3 43.1	11 12.4	15 9.2
6 M	21 6 24.1	17 41.3	5 51.3	20 11.2	26D 0.5	3 29.5	10 21.6	26 35.6	9 40.9	3 46.0	11 14.3	15 9.5
7 T	21 10 20.6	18 42.2	5 48.1	5♓ 1.9	26 8.8	4 44.6	10 56.6	26 39.2	9 47.0	3 48.8	11 16.2	15 9.9
8 W	21 14 17.2	19 42.9	5 44.9	19 55.3	26 23.9	5 59.7	11 31.7	26 42.9	9 53.0	3 51.6	11 18.1	15 10.2
9 T	21 18 13.7	20 43.7	5 41.8	4♈43.7	26 45.1	7 14.8	12 6.9	26 46.8	9 59.0	3 54.4	11 19.9	15 10.4
10 F	21 22 10.3	21 44.5	5 38.6	19 20.9	27 12.0	8 30.0	12 42.2	26 51.0	10 4.9	3 57.1	11 21.8	15 10.7
11 S	21 26 6.8	22 45.2	5 35.4	3♉42.2	27 44.1	9 45.0	13 17.5	26 55.3	10 10.8	3 59.8	11 23.7	15 10.9
12 S	21 30 3.4	23 45.9	5 32.2	17 45.1	28 21.1	11 0.1	13 52.9	26 59.8	10 16.6	4 2.5	11 25.5	15 11.0
13 M	21 33 60.0	24 46.5	5 29.0	1♊28.8	29 2.4	12 15.2	14 28.3	27 4.5	10 22.3	4 5.1	11 27.2	15 11.1
14 T	21 37 56.5	25 47.1	5 25.9	14 53.6	29 47.9	13 30.2	15 3.8	27 9.3	10 28.0	4 7.7	11 29.0	15 11.2
15 W	21 41 53.1	26 47.7	5 22.7	28 0.7	0♒37.0	14 45.2	15 39.3	27 14.3	10 33.7	4 10.2	11 30.7	15 11.3
16 T	21 45 49.6	27 48.3	5 19.5	10♋51.8	1 29.6	16 0.3	16 14.9	27 19.5	10 39.2	4 12.7	11 32.5	15 11.3
17 F	21 49 46.2	28 48.8	5 16.3	23 28.8	2 25.3	17 15.3	16 50.5	27 24.9	10 44.7	4 15.2	11 34.1	15R11.2
18 S	21 53 42.7	29 49.3	5 13.2	5♌53.5	3 23.9	18 30.3	17 26.2	27 30.5	10 50.2	4 17.6	11 35.8	15 11.2
19 S	21 57 39.3	0♓49.8	5 10.0	18 7.4	4 25.3	19 45.3	18 2.0	27 36.2	10 55.6	4 20.0	11 37.5	15 11.1
20 M	22 1 35.8	1 50.3	5 6.8	0♍12.4	5 29.1	21 0.3	18 37.8	27 42.1	11 0.9	4 22.3	11 39.1	15 10.9
21 T	22 5 32.4	2 50.7	5 3.6	12 10.1	6 35.3	22 15.3	19 13.6	27 48.1	11 6.2	4 24.6	11 40.7	15 10.8
22 W	22 9 29.0	3 51.1	5 0.5	24 2.4	7 43.6	23 30.3	19 49.4	27 54.3	11 11.4	4 26.9	11 42.2	15 10.5
23 T	22 13 25.5	4 51.4	4 57.3	5♎51.5	8 53.9	24 45.3	20 25.4	28 0.7	11 16.6	4 29.1	11 43.8	15 10.3
24 F	22 17 22.1	5 51.8	4 54.1	17 40.2	10 6.2	26 0.2	21 1.3	28 7.2	11 21.6	4 31.3	11 45.3	15 10.0
25 S	22 21 18.6	6 52.1	4 50.9	29 31.3	11 20.3	27 15.2	21 37.3	28 13.9	11 26.7	4 33.4	11 46.8	15 9.7
26 S	22 25 15.2	7 52.4	4 47.7	11♏28.5	12 36.1	28 30.1	22 13.3	28 20.8	11 31.6	4 35.5	11 48.3	15 9.4
27 M	22 29 11.7	8 52.7	4 44.6	23 35.8	13 53.5	29 45.1	22 49.4	28 27.8	11 36.5	4 37.6	11 49.7	15 9.0
28 T	22 33 8.3	9 52.9	4 41.4	5♐57.3	15 12.5	1♓ 0.0	23 25.5	28 35.0	11 41.3	4 39.6	11 51.1	15 8.6
						DECLINATION at NOON						
1 W	20 46 41.3	17S 1.4	9S 16.1	27S 10.8	17S 27.9	21S 12.9	14N 58.9	18N 35.9	22S 26.1	23S 37.3	22S 4.9	1S 11.6
4 S	20 58 31.0	16 8.6	9 19.6	25 23.0	18 7.6	20 32.9	15 34.4	18 38.6	22 24.9	23 37.1	22 4.4	1 10.5
7 T	21 10 20.6	15 13.3	9 23.1	9 39.3	18 39.8	19 47.4	16 9.2	18 41.6	22 23.7	23 36.9	22 3.9	1 9.4
10 F	21 22 10.3	14 15.7	9 26.6	10N 60.0	19 2.7	18 56.7	16 43.4	18 45.1	22 22.4	23 36.7	22 3.4	1 8.1
13 M	21 33 60.0	13 15.9	9 30.1	25 37.3	19 15.1	18 1.0	17 16.8	18 48.9	22 21.2	23 36.5	22 2.9	1 6.8
16 T	21 45 49.6	12 14.2	9 33.6	27 16.0	19 16.5	17 0.8	17 49.4	18 53.0	22 19.9	23 36.4	22 2.4	1 5.4
19 S	21 57 39.3	11 10.8	9 37.1	16 51.3	19 6.4	15 56.2	18 21.1	18 57.5	22 18.7	23 36.2	22 1.9	1 3.9
22 W	22 9 29.0	10 5.9	9 40.6	0 46.0	18 44.7	14 47.6	18 51.9	19 2.3	22 17.4	23 36.0	22 1.5	1 2.4
25 S	22 21 18.6	8 59.5	9 44.1	15S 20.7	18 11.3	13 35.4	19 21.7	19 7.3	22 16.2	23 35.8	22 1.0	1 0.8
28 T	22 33 8.3	7 51.9	9 47.6	26 30.7	17 26.2	12 19.8	19 50.4	19 12.6	22 15.0	23 35.7	22 0.6	0 59.1

MARCH 1989

LONGITUDE at NOON

DAY	EPHEMERIS SIDEREAL TIME h m s	☉ ° ′	☊ ° ′	☽ ° ′	☿ ° ′	♀ ° ′	♂ ° ′	♃ ° ′	♄ ° ′	♅ ° ′	♆ ° ′	♇ ° ′
1 W	22 37 4.8	10♓53.2	4♓38.2	18♐37.4	16♒32.9	2♓14.9	24♉ 1.6	28♉42.3	11♑46.0	4♑41.6	11♑52.5	15♏ 8.1
2 T	22 41 1.4	11 53.4	4 35.0	1♑39.8	17 54.8	3 29.9	24 37.8	28 49.7	11 50.7	4 43.5	11 53.9	15R 7.6
3 F	22 44 57.9	12 53.6	4 31.9	15 7.7	19 18.1	4 44.8	25 14.1	28 57.4	11 55.3	4 45.4	11 55.2	15 7.2
4 S	22 48 54.5	13 53.7	4 28.7	29 2.6	20 42.7	5 59.7	25 50.3	29 5.1	11 59.8	4 47.2	11 56.5	15 6.6
5 S	22 52 51.1	14 53.8	4 25.5	13♒23.9	22 8.7	7 14.6	26 26.6	29 13.0	12 4.3	4 49.0	11 57.8	15 6.0
6 M	22 56 47.6	15 53.9	4 22.3	28 8.3	23 35.8	8 29.5	27 3.0	29 21.1	12 8.7	4 50.7	11 59.1	15 5.4
7 T	23 0 44.2	16 54.0	4 19.1	13♓10.0	25 4.3	9 44.4	27 39.3	29 29.3	12 13.0	4 52.4	12 0.3	15 4.8
8 W	23 4 40.7	17 54.0	4 16.0	28 20.5	26 33.9	10 59.2	28 15.7	29 37.6	12 17.2	4 54.0	12 1.5	15 4.1
9 T	23 8 37.3	18 54.0	4 12.8	13♈30.2	28 4.8	12 14.1	28 52.1	29 46.0	12 21.3	4 55.6	12 2.6	15 3.4
10 F	23 12 33.8	19 54.0	4 9.6	28 29.8	29 36.9	13 28.9	29 28.6	29 54.6	12 25.4	4 57.2	12 3.8	15 2.6
11 S	23 16 30.4	20 53.9	4 6.4	13♉11.3	1♓10.1	14 43.7	0♊ 5.1	0♊ 3.4	12 29.3	4 58.7	12 4.8	15 1.8
12 S	23 20 26.9	21 53.8	4 3.3	27 29.5	2 44.6	15 58.5	0 41.6	0 12.2	12 33.2	5 0.1	12 5.9	15 1.0
13 M	23 24 23.5	22 53.7	4 0.1	11♊21.9	4 20.2	17 13.3	1 18.1	0 21.2	12 37.0	5 1.5	12 7.0	15 0.2
14 T	23 28 20.0	23 53.5	3 56.9	24 48.4	5 57.1	18 28.1	1 54.7	0 30.3	12 40.8	5 2.8	12 8.0	14 59.3
15 W	23 32 16.6	24 53.3	3 53.7	7♋51.1	7 35.1	19 42.9	2 31.2	0 39.5	12 44.4	5 4.1	12 8.9	14 58.4
16 T	23 36 13.1	25 53.0	3 50.5	20 33.0	9 14.3	20 57.6	3 7.8	0 48.9	12 48.0	5 5.4	12 9.9	14 57.5
17 F	23 40 9.7	26 52.7	3 47.4	2♌57.7	10 54.8	22 12.3	3 44.5	0 58.4	12 51.5	5 6.6	12 10.8	14 56.5
18 S	23 44 6.3	27 52.4	3 44.2	15 9.0	12 36.4	23 27.0	4 21.1	1 7.9	12 54.9	5 7.7	12 11.7	14 55.6
19 S	23 48 2.8	28 52.0	3 41.0	27 10.5	14 19.3	24 41.7	4 57.8	1 17.6	12 58.2	5 8.8	12 12.5	14 54.5
20 M	23 51 59.4	29 51.6	3 37.8	9♍ 5.3	16 3.4	25 56.4	5 34.4	1 27.5	13 1.4	5 9.9	12 13.3	14 53.5
21 T	23 55 55.9	0♈51.2	3 34.7	20 56.0	17 48.8	27 11.0	6 11.1	1 37.4	13 4.5	5 10.9	12 14.1	14 52.4
22 W	23 59 52.5	1 50.7	3 31.5	2♎45.0	19 35.5	28 25.7	6 47.8	1 47.4	13 7.6	5 11.8	12 14.9	14 51.4
23 T	0 3 49.0	2 50.2	3 28.3	14 34.4	21 23.4	29 40.3	7 24.6	1 57.6	13 10.5	5 12.7	12 15.6	14 50.2
24 F	0 7 45.6	3 49.7	3 25.1	26 26.1	23 12.7	0♈55.0	8 1.3	2 7.9	13 13.5	5 13.6	12 16.3	14 49.1
25 S	0 11 42.1	4 49.2	3 21.9	8♏22.1	25 3.2	2 9.6	8 38.1	2 18.2	13 16.2	5 14.4	12 17.0	14 48.0
26 S	0 15 38.7	5 48.6	3 18.8	20 24.5	26 55.0	3 24.2	9 14.9	2 28.7	13 18.9	5 15.1	12 17.6	14 46.8
27 M	0 19 35.2	6 47.9	3 15.6	2♐35.9	28 48.2	4 38.7	9 51.6	2 39.3	13 21.5	5 15.8	12 18.2	14 45.6
28 T	0 23 31.8	7 47.3	3 12.4	14 59.2	0♈42.6	5 53.3	10 28.4	2 49.9	13 24.0	5 16.4	12 18.7	14 44.3
29 W	0 27 28.3	8 46.6	3 9.2	27 37.7	2 38.4	7 7.8	11 5.2	3 0.7	13 26.4	5 17.0	12 19.3	14 43.1
30 T	0 31 24.9	9 45.8	3 6.1	10♑34.8	4 35.4	8 22.4	11 42.1	3 11.5	13 28.8	5 17.5	12 19.8	14 41.8
31 F	0 35 21.5	10 45.1	3 2.9	23 53.8	6 33.6	9 36.9	12 18.9	3 22.5	13 31.0	5 18.0	12 20.2	14 40.5

DECLINATION at NOON

DAY	EPHEMERIS SIDEREAL TIME h m s	☉ ° ′	☊ ° ′	☽ ° ′	☿ ° ′	♀ ° ′	♂ ° ′	♃ ° ′	♄ ° ′	♅ ° ′	♆ ° ′	♇ ° ′
1 W	22 37 4.8	7S29.1	9S48.7	28S 4.7	17S 8.6	11S53.9	19N59.8	19N14.4	22S14.6	23S35.6	22S 0.5	0S58.6
4 S	22 48 54.5	6 20.1	9 52.2	23 23.4	16 7.9	10 34.4	20 27.1	19 20.0	22 13.4	23 35.5	22 0.1	0 56.9
7 T	23 0 44.2	5 10.4	9 55.7	5 54.8	14 55.7	9 12.4	20 53.3	19 25.8	22 12.3	23 35.4	21 59.7	0 55.1
10 F	23 12 33.8	4 0.0	9 59.1	14N54.6	13 32.1	7 48.2	21 18.4	19 31.8	22 11.2	23 35.2	21 59.3	0 53.3
13 M	23 24 23.5	2 49.2	10 2.6	27 19.8	11 57.3	6 22.0	21 42.2	19 38.0	22 10.1	23 35.1	21 59.0	0 51.4
16 T	23 36 13.1	1 38.2	10 6.1	25 30.5	10 11.4	4 54.4	22 4.7	19 44.3	22 9.1	23 35.1	21 58.6	0 49.6
19 S	23 48 2.8	0 27.0	10 9.5	13 6.9	8 14.6	3 25.6	22 25.9	19 50.8	22 8.2	23 35.0	21 58.3	0 47.7
22 W	23 59 52.5	0N44.0	10 13.0	3S20.8	6 7.2	1 55.9	22 45.8	19 57.3	22 7.3	23 34.9	21 58.1	0 45.8
25 S	0 11 42.1	1 54.9	10 16.4	18 42.9	3 49.6	0 25.6	23 4.3	20 4.0	22 6.5	23 34.9	21 57.8	0 43.9
28 T	0 23 31.8	3 5.4	10 19.9	27 40.6	1 22.4	1N 4.8	23 21.3	20 10.7	22 5.7	23 34.9	21 57.6	0 42.0
31 F	0 35 21.5	4 15.4	10 23.3	24 39.2	1N13.3	2 35.2	23 36.9	20 17.4	22 5.1	23 34.9	21 57.4	0 40.2

APRIL 1989

LONGITUDE at NOON

DAY	EPHEMERIS SIDEREAL TIME h m s	☉ ° ′	☊ ° ′	☽ ° ′	☿ ° ′	♀ ° ′	♂ ° ′	♃ ° ′	♄ ° ′	♅ ° ′	♆ ° ′	♇ ° ′
1 S	0 39 18.0	11♈44.3	2♓59.7	7♒37.3	8♈33.1	10♈51.4	12♊55.8	3♊33.5	13♑33.1	5♑18.4	12♑20.6	14♏39.1
2 S	0 43 14.6	12 43.5	2 56.5	21 46.5	10 33.7	12 5.9	13 32.6	3 44.7	13 35.2	5 18.8	12 21.0	14R 37.8
3 M	0 47 11.1	13 42.7	2 53.3	6♓20.5	12 35.4	13 20.4	14 9.5	3 55.9	13 37.1	5 19.1	12 21.4	14 36.4
4 T	0 51 7.7	14 41.8	2 50.2	21 15.8	14 38.1	14 34.8	14 46.4	4 7.2	13 39.0	5 19.4	12 21.7	14 35.0
5 W	0 55 4.2	15 40.9	2 47.0	6♈25.5	16 41.6	15 49.3	15 23.3	4 18.6	13 40.7	5 19.6	12 22.0	14 33.6
6 T	0 59 0.8	16 40.0	2 43.8	21 40.6	18 45.9	17 3.7	16 0.3	4 30.1	13 42.4	5 19.8	12 22.3	14 32.2
7 F	1 2 57.3	17 39.0	2 40.6	6♉50.6	20 50.7	18 18.1	16 37.2	4 41.7	13 43.9	5 19.9	12 22.5	14 30.7
8 S	1 6 53.9	18 38.0	2 37.5	21 45.3	22 55.8	19 32.5	17 14.2	4 53.3	13 45.4	5 20.0	12 22.7	14 29.3
9 S	1 10 50.4	19 36.9	2 34.3	6♊17.0	25 1.1	20 46.9	17 51.1	5 5.1	13 46.8	5 20.0	12 22.8	14 27.8
10 M	1 14 47.0	20 35.9	2 31.1	20 20.8	27 6.3	22 1.3	18 28.1	5 16.9	13 48.0	5R 19.9	12 23.0	14 26.3
11 T	1 18 43.5	21 34.7	2 27.9	3♋55.2	29 11.1	23 15.6	19 5.1	5 28.8	13 49.2	5 19.8	12 23.1	14 24.8
12 W	1 22 40.1	22 33.6	2 24.7	17 1.6	1♉15.1	24 29.9	19 42.1	5 40.7	13 50.3	5 19.7	12 23.1	14 23.3
13 T	1 26 36.7	23 32.4	2 21.6	29 43.3	3 18.1	25 44.2	20 19.1	5 52.7	13 51.2	5 19.5	12 23.1	14 21.7
14 F	1 30 33.2	24 31.2	2 18.4	12♌ 4.8	5 19.8	26 58.5	20 56.1	6 4.9	13 52.2	5 19.3	12 23.2	14 20.2
15 S	1 34 29.8	25 30.0	2 15.2	24 11.0	7 19.7	28 12.8	21 33.1	6 17.1	13 52.9	5 19.0	12R 23.1	14 18.6
16 S	1 38 26.3	26 28.7	2 12.0	6♍ 6.7	9 17.6	29 27.0	22 10.1	6 29.3	13 53.6	5 18.7	12 23.1	14 17.1
17 M	1 42 22.9	27 27.3	2 8.9	17 56.5	11 13.0	0♉41.3	22 47.2	6 41.6	13 54.2	5 18.3	12 23.0	14 15.5
18 T	1 46 19.4	28 25.9	2 5.7	29 44.1	13 5.8	1 55.5	23 24.2	6 54.0	13 54.7	5 17.8	12 22.8	14 13.9
19 W	1 50 16.0	29 24.5	2 2.5	11♎32.8	14 55.5	3 9.6	24 1.2	7 6.4	13 55.1	5 17.3	12 22.6	14 12.3
20 T	1 54 12.5	0♉23.1	1 59.3	23 25.0	16 42.0	4 23.8	24 38.2	7 18.9	13 55.3	5 16.8	12 22.4	14 10.6
21 F	1 58 9.1	1 21.6	1 56.2	5♏22.7	18 24.9	5 38.0	25 15.3	7 31.4	13 55.5	5 16.2	12 22.2	14 9.0
22 S	2 2 5.6	2 20.1	1 53.0	17 27.3	20 4.0	6 52.1	25 52.3	7 44.0	13 55.6	5 15.5	12 21.9	14 7.4
23 S	2 6 2.2	3 18.6	1 49.8	29 39.9	21 39.2	8 6.2	26 29.4	7 56.7	13 55.6	5 14.8	12 21.6	14 5.7
24 M	2 9 58.8	4 17.0	1 46.6	12♐ 1.8	23 10.2	9 20.3	27 6.4	8 9.4	13R 55.5	5 14.1	12 21.3	14 4.1
25 T	2 13 55.3	5 15.4	1 43.4	24 34.4	24 37.0	10 34.4	27 43.5	8 22.2	13 55.3	5 13.3	12 20.9	14 2.4
26 W	2 17 51.9	6 13.8	1 40.3	7♑19.3	25 59.3	11 48.4	28 20.5	8 35.0	13 55.0	5 12.5	12 20.5	14 0.7
27 T	2 21 48.4	7 12.1	1 37.1	20 18.9	27 17.1	13 2.5	28 57.6	8 47.9	13 54.6	5 11.6	12 20.1	13 59.0
28 F	2 25 45.0	8 10.5	1 33.9	3♒35.3	28 30.3	14 16.5	29 34.7	9 0.9	13 54.1	5 10.7	12 19.7	13 57.4
29 S	2 29 41.5	9 8.8	1 30.7	17 11.2	29 38.8	15 30.6	0♋11.8	9 13.8	13 53.5	5 9.7	12 19.2	13 55.7
30 S	2 33 38.1	10 7.0	1 27.6	1♓ 8.1	0♊42.4	16 44.6	0 48.8	9 26.9	13 52.8	5 8.7	12 18.7	13 54.0

DECLINATION at NOON

DAY	EPHEMERIS SIDEREAL TIME h m s	☉ ° ′	☊ ° ′	☽ ° ′	☿ ° ′	♀ ° ′	♂ ° ′	♃ ° ′	♄ ° ′	♅ ° ′	♆ ° ′	♇ ° ′
1 S	0 39 18.0	4N38.5	10S24.4	20S37.7	2N 6.9	3N 5.3	23N41.8	20N19.7	22S 4.8	23S34.9	21S57.3	0S39.5
4 T	0 51 7.7	5 47.6	10 27.9	2 4.5	4 51.4	4 35.0	23 55.5	20 26.5	22 4.3	23 34.9	21 57.1	0 37.7
7 F	1 2 57.3	6 55.7	10 31.3	18N 7.4	7 39.4	6 3.9	24 7.6	20 33.3	22 3.8	23 35.0	21 57.0	0 35.9
10 M	1 14 47.0	8 2.7	10 34.7	28 0.8	10 26.8	7 31.6	24 18.2	20 40.1	22 3.4	23 35.0	21 56.9	0 34.1
13 T	1 26 36.7	9 8.6	10 38.1	23 1.8	13 8.3	8 57.8	24 27.2	20 46.8	22 3.1	23 35.1	21 56.8	0 32.3
16 S	1 38 26.3	10 13.0	10 41.6	9 4.4	15 38.5	10 22.2	24 34.7	20 53.5	22 2.9	23 35.2	21 56.8	0 30.6
19 W	1 50 16.0	11 15.9	10 45.0	7S27.3	17 51.9	11 44.3	24 40.6	21 0.2	22 2.8	23 35.3	21 56.7	0 28.9
22 S	2 2 5.6	12 17.1	10 48.4	21 43.1	19 44.8	13 4.0	24 44.9	21 6.8	22 2.8	23 35.5	21 56.7	0 27.3
25 T	2 13 55.3	13 16.6	10 51.8	28 1.6	21 15.2	14 20.8	24 47.6	21 13.3	22 2.8	23 35.6	21 56.8	0 25.8
28 F	2 25 45.0	14 14.0	10 55.2	21 44.3	22 22.7	15 34.4	24 48.7	21 19.7	22 3.0	23 35.8	21 56.8	0 24.3

MAY 1989

LONGITUDE at NOON

DAY	EPHEMERIS SIDEREAL TIME	☉	☊	☽	☿	♀	♂	♃	♄	♅	♆	♇
	h m s	° ′	° ′	° ′	° ′	° ′	° ′	° ′	° ′	° ′	° ′	° ′
1 M	2 37 34.6	11♉ 5.3	1♓24.4	15♓26.7	1♊41.2	17♉58.6	1♋25.9	9♊40.0	13♑52.0	5♑ 7.6	12♑18.1	13♏52.3
2 T	2 41 31.2	12 3.5	1 21.2	0♈ 5.2	2 35.0	19 12.5	2 3.0	9 53.1	13R51.1	5R 6.5	12R17.5	13R50.6
3 W	2 45 27.8	13 1.7	1 18.0	14 59.6	3 23.8	20 26.5	2 40.2	10 6.3	13 50.1	5 5.3	12 16.9	13 48.9
4 T	2 49 24.3	13 59.9	1 14.8	0♉ 2.6	4 7.6	21 40.4	3 17.3	10 19.5	13 49.1	5 4.1	12 16.3	13 47.2
5 F	2 53 20.9	14 58.1	1 11.7	15 5.2	4 46.2	22 54.4	3 54.4	10 32.8	13 47.9	5 2.9	12 15.7	13 45.6
6 S	2 57 17.4	15 56.2	1 8.5	29 57.6	5 19.7	24 8.3	4 31.6	10 46.1	13 46.7	5 1.6	12 15.0	13 43.9
7 S	3 1 14.0	16 54.3	1 5.3	14♊30.9	5 47.9	25 22.2	5 8.7	10 59.4	13 45.3	5 0.3	12 14.2	13 42.2
8 M	3 5 10.5	17 52.4	1 2.1	28 38.9	6 10.9	26 36.1	5 45.8	11 12.8	13 43.9	4 58.9	12 13.5	13 40.5
9 T	3 9 7.1	18 50.4	0 59.0	12♋18.5	6 28.7	27 50.0	6 23.0	11 26.2	13 42.3	4 57.5	12 12.7	13 38.8
10 W	3 13 3.6	19 48.4	0 55.8	25 29.6	6 41.4	29 3.8	7 0.1	11 39.6	13 40.7	4 56.1	12 11.9	13 37.1
11 T	3 17 0.2	20 46.4	0 52.6	8♌14.8	6 48.8	0♊17.7	7 37.3	11 53.1	13 39.0	4 54.6	12 11.0	13 35.5
12 F	3 20 56.8	21 44.3	0 49.4	20 38.1	6 51.3	1 31.5	8 14.4	12 6.6	13 37.1	4 53.0	12 10.2	13 33.8
13 S	3 24 53.3	22 42.3	0 46.3	2♍44.8	6R48.8	2 45.2	8 51.6	12 20.1	13 35.2	4 51.5	12 9.3	13 32.1
14 S	3 28 49.9	23 40.1	0 43.1	14 40.2	6 41.6	3 59.0	9 28.7	12 33.7	13 33.2	4 49.9	12 8.4	13 30.5
15 M	3 32 46.4	24 38.0	0 39.9	26 29.5	6 29.8	5 12.8	10 5.9	12 47.3	13 31.2	4 48.2	12 7.4	13 28.8
16 T	3 36 43.0	25 35.8	0 36.7	8♎17.7	6 13.8	6 26.5	10 43.1	13 0.9	13 29.0	4 46.5	12 6.5	13 27.2
17 W	3 40 39.5	26 33.6	0 33.5	20 8.6	5 53.9	7 40.2	11 20.2	13 14.5	13 26.8	4 44.8	12 5.5	13 25.5
18 T	3 44 36.1	27 31.1	0 30.4	2♏ 5.8	5 30.4	8 53.9	11 57.4	13 28.2	13 24.4	4 43.1	12 4.4	13 23.9
19 F	3 48 32.7	28 29.1	0 27.2	14 11.4	5 3.8	10 7.6	12 34.5	13 41.9	13 22.0	4 41.3	12 3.4	13 22.3
20 S	3 52 29.2	29 26.8	0 24.0	26 27.2	4 34.5	11 21.2	13 11.7	13 55.6	13 19.5	4 39.5	12 2.3	13 20.7
21 S	3 56 25.8	0♊24.5	0 20.8	8♐53.7	4 3.1	12 34.9	13 48.9	14 9.3	13 16.9	4 37.6	12 1.2	13 19.1
22 M	4 0 22.3	1 22.2	0 17.7	21 31.4	3 30.2	13 48.5	14 26.0	14 23.1	13 14.3	4 35.7	12 0.1	13 17.5
23 T	4 4 18.9	2 19.9	0 14.5	4♑20.2	2 56.2	15 2.1	15 3.2	14 36.9	13 11.6	4 33.8	11 59.0	13 15.9
24 W	4 8 15.4	3 17.5	0 11.3	17 20.3	2 21.9	16 15.7	15 40.4	14 50.6	13 8.8	4 31.9	11 57.8	13 14.3
25 T	4 12 12.0	4 15.1	0 8.1	0♒32.1	1 47.8	17 29.3	16 17.6	15 4.5	13 5.9	4 29.9	11 56.6	13 12.8
26 F	4 16 8.6	5 12.8	0 5.0	13 56.4	1 14.6	18 42.9	16 54.8	15 18.3	13 3.0	4 27.9	11 55.5	13 11.3
27 S	4 20 5.1	6 10.4	0 1.8	27 34.3	0 42.7	19 56.5	17 32.0	15 32.2	12 59.9	4 25.9	11 54.3	13 9.8
28 S	4 24 1.7	7 8.0	29♒58.6	11♓26.7	0 12.7	21 10.0	18 9.2	15 46.0	12 56.8	4 23.8	11 53.0	13 8.3
29 M	4 27 58.2	8 5.5	29 55.4	25 34.3	29♉45.1	22 23.5	18 46.4	15 59.9	12 53.7	4 21.8	11 51.8	13 6.8
30 T	4 31 54.8	9 3.1	29 52.3	9♈56.3	29 20.4	23 37.1	19 23.6	16 13.7	12 50.4	4 19.6	11 50.5	13 5.3
31 W	4 35 51.4	10 0.6	29 49.1	24 30.0	28 58.9	24 50.6	20 0.8	16 27.6	12 47.1	4 17.5	11 49.2	13 3.8

DECLINATION at NOON

DAY	EPHEMERIS SIDEREAL TIME	☉	☊	☽	☿	♀	♂	♃	♄	♅	♆	♇
1 M	2 37 34.6	15N 9.4	10S58.6	4S40.9	23N 7.9	16N44.5	24N48.1	21N26.0	22S 3.3	23S35.9	21S56.9	0S22.9
4 T	2 49 24.3	16 2.6	11 2.0	15N28.9	23 31.7	17 50.8	24 46.0	21 32.1	22 3.6	23 36.1	21 57.0	0 21.6
7 S	3 1 14.0	16 53.3	11 5.3	27 24.7	23 35.4	18 52.9	24 42.3	21 38.1	22 4.1	23 36.3	21 57.2	0 20.4
10 W	3 13 3.6	17 41.5	11 8.7	23 57.0	23 20.1	19 50.5	24 36.9	21 44.0	22 4.6	23 36.6	21 57.3	0 19.3
13 S	3 24 53.3	18 27.0	11 12.1	10 22.4	22 46.9	20 43.3	24 29.9	21 49.7	22 5.2	23 36.8	21 57.5	0 18.2
16 T	3 36 43.0	19 9.7	11 15.5	6S 5.1	21 58.1	21 31.0	24 21.4	21 55.3	22 5.9	23 37.0	21 57.7	0 17.3
19 F	3 48 32.7	19 49.5	11 18.8	20 40.4	20 56.7	22 13.3	24 11.3	22 0.6	22 6.7	23 37.3	21 57.9	0 16.4
22 M	4 0 22.3	20 26.3	11 22.2	27 48.9	19 47.8	22 49.9	23 59.7	22 5.8	22 7.6	23 37.5	21 58.2	0 15.7
25 T	4 12 12.0	20 59.9	11 25.6	22 25.8	18 37.9	23 20.8	23 46.5	22 10.8	22 8.5	23 37.8	21 58.5	0 15.0
28 S	4 24 1.7	21 30.2	11 28.9	6 18.6	17 33.9	23 45.5	23 31.8	22 15.6	22 9.5	23 38.0	21 58.8	0 14.5
31 W	4 35 51.4	21 57.2	11 32.3	13N19.7	16 42.3	24 4.1	23 15.6	22 20.2	22 10.5	23 38.3	21 59.1	0 14.1

JUNE 1989

LONGITUDE at NOON

DAY	EPHEMERIS SIDEREAL TIME	☉	☊	☽	☿	♀	♂	♃	♄	♅	♆	♇
1 T	4 39 47.9	10♊58.1	29♒45.9	9♉10.9	28♉40.9	26♊ 4.0	20♋38.1	16♊41.5	12♑43.7	4♑15.3	11♑47.8	13♏ 2.4
2 F	4 43 44.5	11 55.6	29 42.7	23 52.4	28R26.8	27 17.5	21 15.3	16 55.4	12R40.3	4R13.2	11R46.5	13R 1.0
3 S	4 47 41.0	12 53.1	29 39.5	8♊26.9	28 16.7	28 31.0	21 52.5	17 9.3	12 36.8	4 11.0	11 45.1	12 59.5
4 S	4 51 37.6	13 50.6	29 36.4	22 46.9	28 10.9	29 44.4	22 29.8	17 23.2	12 33.3	4 8.7	11 43.8	12 58.2
5 M	4 55 34.1	14 48.1	29 33.2	6♋46.5	28 9.4	0♋57.9	23 7.0	17 37.1	12 29.6	4 6.5	11 42.4	12 56.8
6 T	4 59 30.7	15 45.5	29 30.0	20 21.9	28D12.3	2 11.3	23 44.3	17 51.0	12 26.0	4 4.2	11 41.0	12 55.4
7 W	5 3 27.3	16 42.9	29 26.8	3♌32.0	28 19.8	3 24.7	24 21.5	18 5.0	12 22.2	4 1.9	11 39.5	12 54.1
8 T	5 7 23.8	17 40.4	29 23.7	16 18.1	28 31.7	4 38.0	24 58.8	18 18.9	12 18.5	3 59.6	11 38.1	12 52.8
9 F	5 11 20.4	18 37.7	29 20.5	28 43.3	28 48.2	5 51.4	25 36.1	18 32.8	12 14.6	3 57.3	11 36.7	12 51.5
10 S	5 15 16.9	19 35.1	29 17.3	10♍51.9	29 9.1	7 4.7	26 13.3	18 46.7	12 10.7	3 55.0	11 35.2	12 50.2
11 S	5 19 13.5	20 32.5	29 14.1	22 49.0	29 34.4	8 18.1	26 50.6	19 0.6	12 6.8	3 52.6	11 33.7	12 49.0
12 M	5 23 10.1	21 29.8	29 11.0	4♎40.1	0♊ 4.1	9 31.4	27 27.9	19 14.5	12 2.8	3 50.3	11 32.2	12 47.8
13 T	5 27 6.6	22 27.1	29 7.8	16 30.2	0 38.0	10 44.7	28 5.2	19 28.4	11 58.8	3 47.9	11 30.7	12 46.6
14 W	5 31 3.2	23 24.4	29 4.6	28 24.2	1 16.2	11 57.9	28 42.5	19 42.3	11 54.8	3 45.5	11 29.2	12 45.4
15 T	5 34 59.7	24 21.7	29 1.4	10♏26.2	1 58.6	13 11.2	29 19.8	19 56.2	11 50.7	3 43.1	11 27.7	12 44.2
16 F	5 38 56.3	25 19.1	28 58.3	22 39.4	2 45.0	14 24.4	29 57.1	20 10.1	11 46.6	3 40.8	11 26.2	12 43.2
17 S	5 42 52.8	26 16.3	28 55.1	5♐ 5.9	3 35.4	15 37.6	0♌34.4	20 23.9	11 42.4	3 38.3	11 24.6	12 42.1
18 S	5 46 49.4	27 13.6	28 51.9	17 46.8	4 29.6	16 50.8	1 11.7	20 37.8	11 38.2	3 35.9	11 23.1	12 41.0
19 M	5 50 46.0	28 10.8	28 48.7	0♑42.2	5 27.8	18 4.0	1 49.0	20 51.6	11 34.0	3 33.5	11 21.5	12 39.9
20 T	5 54 42.5	29 8.1	28 45.5	13 51.3	6 29.7	19 17.1	2 26.3	21 5.4	11 29.8	3 31.1	11 19.9	12 38.9
21 W	5 58 39.1	0♋ 5.3	28 42.4	27 12.9	7 35.4	20 30.3	3 3.7	21 19.2	11 25.5	3 28.6	11 18.4	12 37.9
22 T	6 2 35.6	1 2.5	28 39.2	10♒45.5	8 44.7	21 43.4	3 41.0	21 33.0	11 21.2	3 26.2	11 16.8	12 36.9
23 F	6 6 32.2	1 59.8	28 36.0	24 27.9	9 57.6	22 56.5	4 18.3	21 46.8	11 16.8	3 23.8	11 15.2	12 36.0
24 S	6 10 28.8	2 57.0	28 32.8	8♓19.1	11 14.1	24 9.6	4 55.7	22 0.6	11 12.5	3 21.3	11 13.6	12 35.1
25 S	6 14 25.3	3 54.2	28 29.7	22 18.3	12 34.2	25 22.6	5 33.0	22 14.3	11 8.1	3 18.9	11 12.0	12 34.2
26 M	6 18 21.9	4 51.4	28 26.5	6♈24.8	13 57.8	26 35.7	6 10.4	22 28.0	11 3.7	3 16.4	11 10.4	12 33.3
27 T	6 22 18.4	5 48.7	28 23.3	20 37.4	15 24.8	27 48.7	6 47.8	22 41.7	10 59.3	3 14.0	11 8.8	12 32.5
28 W	6 26 15.0	6 45.9	28 20.1	4♉54.3	16 55.2	29 1.7	7 25.1	22 55.4	10 54.9	3 11.5	11 7.1	12 31.7
29 T	6 30 11.6	7 43.1	28 17.0	19 12.5	18 29.0	0♌14.7	8 2.5	23 9.1	10 50.5	3 9.1	11 5.5	12 30.9
30 F	6 34 8.1	8 40.3	28 13.8	3♊28.0	20 6.1	1 27.7	8 39.9	23 22.7	10 46.1	3 6.7	11 3.9	12 30.2

DECLINATION at NOON

DAY	EPHEMERIS SIDEREAL TIME	☉	☊	☽	☿	♀	♂	♃	♄	♅	♆	♇
1 T	4 39 47.9	22N 5.5	11S33.4	19N 1.3	16N28.6	24N 8.9	23N 9.9	22N21.7	22S10.9	23S38.4	21S59.2	0S14.0
4 S	4 51 37.6	22 27.9	11 36.7	27 49.7	15 59.9	24 19.0	22 51.7	22 26.0	22 12.0	23 38.6	21 59.5	0 13.7
7 W	5 3 27.3	22 46.8	11 40.0	21 26.2	15 50.2	24 22.6	22 32.1	22 30.1	22 13.2	23 38.9	21 59.9	0 13.6
10 S	5 15 16.9	23 2.0	11 43.4	6 28.5	15 59.0	24 19.8	22 11.1	22 34.0	22 14.4	23 39.1	22 0.2	0 13.6
13 T	5 27 6.6	23 13.6	11 46.7	9S58.8	16 24.5	24 10.5	21 48.8	22 37.6	22 15.7	23 39.4	22 0.6	0 13.7
16 F	5 38 56.3	23 21.6	11 50.0	23 18.2	17 4.2	23 54.8	21 25.0	22 41.1	22 16.9	23 39.6	22 1.0	0 13.9
19 M	5 50 46.0	23 25.8	11 53.3	27 40.9	17 55.1	23 32.8	21 0.0	22 44.3	22 18.2	23 39.8	22 1.4	0 14.3
22 T	6 2 35.6	23 26.3	11 56.7	18 55.5	18 53.8	23 4.7	20 33.7	22 47.3	22 19.5	23 40.0	22 1.8	0 14.7
25 S	6 14 25.3	23 23.1	11 60.0	1 2.8	19 56.9	22 30.6	20 6.2	22 50.0	22 20.9	23 40.3	22 2.2	0 15.3
28 W	6 26 15.0	23 16.2	12 3.3	17N37.3	21 0.2	21 50.7	19 37.4	22 52.6	22 22.2	23 40.5	22 2.7	0 16.0

DAY	EPHEMERIS SIDEREAL TIME	☉	☊	☽	☿	♀	♂	♃	♄	♅	♆	♇
	h m s	° ′	° ′	° ′	° ′	° ′	° ′	° ′	° ′	° ′	° ′	° ′
LONGITUDE at NOON												
1 S	6 38 4.7	9♋37.6	28♒10.6	17♊36.2	21♊46.5	2♌40.6	9♌17.3	23♊36.3	10♑41.6	3♑ 4.3	11♑ 2.3	12♏29.5
2 S	6 42 1.2	10 34.8	28 7.4	1♋32.4	23 30.1	3 53.6	9 54.8	23 49.9	10R37.2	3R 1.8	11R 0.6	12R28.8
3 M	6 45 57.8	11 32.0	28 4.3	15 12.3	25 16.8	5 6.5	10 32.2	24 3.4	10 32.7	2 59.4	10 59.0	12 28.1
4 T	6 49 54.3	12 29.2	28 1.1	28 33.2	27 6.4	6 19.4	11 9.6	24 17.0	10 28.3	2 57.0	10 57.4	12 27.5
5 W	6 53 50.9	13 26.5	27 57.9	11♌33.9	28 59.0	7 32.3	11 47.1	24 30.5	10 23.9	2 54.6	10 55.8	12 26.9
6 T	6 57 47.5	14 23.7	27 54.7	24 14.7	0♋54.2	8 45.1	12 24.6	24 43.9	10 19.4	2 52.2	10 54.1	12 26.4
7 F	7 1 44.0	15 21.0	27 51.6	6♍37.7	2 52.1	9 58.0	13 2.1	24 57.4	10 15.1	2 49.9	10 52.6	12 25.9
8 S	7 5 40.6	16 18.2	27 48.4	18 46.1	4 52.2	11 10.8	13 39.6	25 10.8	10 10.7	2 47.6	10 51.0	12 25.4
9 S	7 9 37.1	17 15.4	27 45.2	0♎44.1	6 54.4	12 23.6	14 17.1	25 24.1	10 6.3	2 45.2	10 49.3	12 24.9
10 M	7 13 33.7	18 12.6	27 42.0	12 36.3	8 58.4	13 36.4	14 54.6	25 37.5	10 1.9	2 42.9	10 47.7	12 24.5
11 T	7 17 30.3	19 9.8	27 38.8	24 27.8	11 4.0	14 49.1	15 32.1	25 50.7	9 57.6	2 40.6	10 46.1	12 24.1
12 W	7 21 26.8	20 7.0	27 35.7	6♏23.6	13 10.9	16 1.8	16 9.6	26 4.0	9 53.2	2 38.3	10 44.5	12 23.7
13 T	7 25 23.4	21 4.3	27 32.5	18 28.1	15 18.7	17 14.5	16 47.1	26 17.2	9 48.9	2 36.0	10 42.9	12 23.4
14 F	7 29 19.9	22 1.5	27 29.3	0♐45.5	17 27.2	18 27.2	17 24.6	26 30.3	9 44.6	2 33.7	10 41.4	12 23.1
15 S	7 33 16.5	22 58.7	27 26.1	13 18.9	19 36.1	19 39.8	18 2.2	26 43.5	9 40.4	2 31.5	10 39.8	12 22.8
16 S	7 37 13.0	23 55.9	27 23.0	26 10.3	21 45.0	20 52.4	18 39.7	26 56.5	9 36.1	2 29.3	10 38.2	12 22.6
17 M	7 41 9.6	24 53.1	27 19.8	9♑20.6	23 53.7	22 4.9	19 17.3	27 9.6	9 31.9	2 27.1	10 36.6	12 22.4
18 T	7 45 6.2	25 50.4	27 16.6	22 48.9	26 2.0	23 17.5	19 54.9	27 22.5	9 27.8	2 24.9	10 35.1	12 22.2
19 W	7 49 2.7	26 47.6	27 13.4	6♒33.4	28 9.5	24 30.0	20 32.5	27 35.5	9 23.6	2 22.7	10 33.5	12 22.1
20 T	7 52 59.3	27 44.8	27 10.3	20 31.2	0♌16.2	25 42.5	21 10.1	27 48.3	9 19.5	2 20.6	10 32.0	12 22.0
21 F	7 56 55.8	28 42.1	27 7.1	4♓38.9	2 21.9	26 54.9	21 47.7	28 1.2	9 15.5	2 18.5	10 30.5	12 21.9
22 S	8 0 52.4	29 39.3	27 3.9	18 52.8	4 26.4	28 7.3	22 25.3	28 14.0	9 11.4	2 16.4	10 29.0	12 21.9
23 S	8 4 49.0	0♌36.6	27 0.7	3♈ 9.6	6 29.5	29 19.7	23 2.9	28 26.7	9 7.5	2 14.4	10 27.5	12 21.9
24 M	8 8 45.5	1 33.9	26 57.6	17 26.2	8 31.2	0♍32.1	23 40.6	28 39.4	9 3.5	2 12.3	10 26.0	12 21.9
25 T	8 12 42.1	2 31.2	26 54.4	1♉40.1	10 31.5	1 44.4	24 18.2	28 52.0	8 59.7	2 10.3	10 24.5	12D22.0
26 W	8 16 38.6	3 28.6	26 51.2	15 49.0	12 30.2	2 56.7	24 55.9	29 4.6	8 55.8	2 8.4	10 23.0	12 22.1
27 T	8 20 35.2	4 25.9	26 48.0	29 50.9	14 27.3	4 9.0	25 33.6	29 17.1	8 52.0	2 6.4	10 21.6	12 22.2
28 F	8 24 31.7	5 23.3	26 44.8	13♊43.8	16 22.9	5 21.3	26 11.4	29 29.6	8 48.3	2 4.6	10 20.2	12 22.4
29 S	8 28 28.3	6 20.7	26 41.7	27 25.8	18 16.8	6 33.5	26 49.1	29 42.0	8 44.7	2 2.7	10 18.8	12 22.6
30 S	8 32 24.9	7 18.1	26 38.5	10♋55.1	20 9.0	7 45.7	27 26.9	29 54.3	8 41.0	2 0.8	10 17.4	12 22.9
31 M	8 36 21.4	8 15.5	26 35.3	24 10.3	21 59.5	8 57.9	28 4.6	0♋ 6.6	8 37.5	1 59.0	10 16.0	12 23.2
DECLINATION at NOON												
1 S	6 38 4.7	23N 5.6	12S 6.6	27N37.9	21N59.5	21N 5.3	19N 7.5	22N54.9	22S23.5	23S40.7	22S 3.1	0S16.8
4 T	6 49 54.3	22 51.4	12 9.8	22 48.9	22 49.5	20 14.6	18 36.4	22 56.9	22 24.8	23 40.9	22 3.5	0 17.7
7 F	7 1 44.0	22 33.5	12 13.1	8 13.4	23 25.2	19 18.8	18 4.2	22 58.8	22 26.1	23 41.0	22 3.9	0 18.8
10 M	7 13 33.7	22 12.2	12 16.4	8S25.8	23 41.4	18 18.4	17 30.9	23 0.5	22 27.4	23 41.2	22 4.4	0 19.9
13 T	7 25 23.4	21 47.5	12 19.7	22 15.6	23 34.4	17 13.6	16 56.6	23 1.9	22 28.6	23 41.3	22 4.8	0 21.2
16 S	7 37 13.0	21 19.4	12 23.0	27 53.1	23 2.8	16 4.7	16 21.3	23 3.1	22 29.9	23 41.5	22 5.2	0 22.6
19 W	7 49 2.7	20 48.0	12 26.2	20 19.0	22 7.8	14 52.1	15 45.1	23 4.1	22 31.1	23 41.6	22 5.6	0 24.1
22 S	8 0 52.4	20 13.5	12 29.5	2 31.1	20 52.0	13 36.0	15 8.0	23 4.9	22 32.2	23 41.7	22 6.1	0 25.6
25 T	8 12 42.1	19 36.0	12 32.8	16N31.9	19 19.5	12 16.8	14 30.0	23 5.5	22 33.3	23 41.8	22 6.5	0 27.3
28 F	8 24 31.7	18 55.5	12 36.0	27 24.4	17 34.2	10 54.8	13 51.1	23 6.0	22 34.4	23 41.9	22 6.9	0 29.1
31 M	8 36 21.4	18 12.2	12 39.2	23 59.9	15 39.5	9 30.4	13 11.5	23 6.2	22 35.5	23 42.0	22 7.3	0 31.0

AUGUST 1989

DAY	EPHEMERIS SIDEREAL TIME	☉	☊	☽	☿	♀	♂	♃	♄	♅	♆	♇
LONGITUDE at NOON												
1 T	8 40 18.0	9♌12.9	26♒32.1	7♌10.4	23♌48.5	10♍10.0	28♌42.4	0♋18.8	8♑34.0	1♑57.2	10♑14.6	12♏23.5
2 W	8 44 14.5	10 10.3	26 29.0	19 55.1	25 35.7	11 22.1	29 20.2	0 30.9	8R30.5	1R55.5	10R13.2	12 23.8
3 T	8 48 11.1	11 7.8	26 25.8	2♍24.8	27 21.4	12 34.2	29 58.0	0 43.0	8 27.1	1 53.8	10 11.9	12 24.2
4 F	8 52 7.6	12 5.2	26 22.6	14 41.0	29 5.4	13 46.2	0♍35.8	0 55.0	8 23.8	1 52.1	10 10.6	12 24.6
5 S	8 56 4.2	13 2.7	26 19.4	26 45.8	0♍47.8	14 58.2	1 13.7	1 6.9	8 20.6	1 50.4	10 9.3	12 25.0
6 S	9 0 0.7	14 0.2	26 16.3	8♎42.3	2 28.5	16 10.1	1 51.5	1 18.8	8 17.4	1 48.8	10 8.0	12 25.5
7 M	9 3 57.3	14 57.7	26 13.1	20 34.2	4 7.7	17 22.1	2 29.4	1 30.6	8 14.3	1 47.3	10 6.7	12 26.0
8 T	9 7 53.9	15 55.2	26 9.9	2♏25.5	5 45.3	18 33.9	3 7.3	1 42.3	8 11.2	1 45.7	10 5.5	12 26.6
9 W	9 11 50.4	16 52.8	26 6.7	14 20.9	7 21.2	19 45.8	3 45.2	1 53.9	8 8.3	1 44.3	10 4.3	12 27.2
10 T	9 15 47.0	17 50.3	26 3.5	26 24.9	8 55.6	20 57.6	4 23.1	2 5.5	8 5.4	1 42.8	10 3.1	12 27.8
11 F	9 19 43.5	18 47.9	26 0.4	8♐42.1	10 28.4	22 9.3	5 1.0	2 16.9	8 2.5	1 41.4	10 1.9	12 28.4
12 S	9 23 40.1	19 45.4	25 57.2	21 16.5	11 59.6	23 21.0	5 39.0	2 28.3	7 59.8	1 40.0	10 0.7	12 29.1
13 S	9 27 36.6	20 43.0	25 54.0	4♑11.4	13 29.2	24 32.7	6 17.0	2 39.7	7 57.1	1 38.7	9 59.6	12 29.8
14 M	9 31 33.2	21 40.6	25 50.8	17 28.9	14 57.2	25 44.3	6 54.9	2 50.9	7 54.6	1 37.4	9 58.5	12 30.6
15 T	9 35 29.7	22 38.3	25 47.7	1♒ 9.3	16 23.5	26 55.9	7 32.9	3 2.0	7 52.0	1 36.2	9 57.4	12 31.4
16 W	9 39 26.3	23 35.9	25 44.5	15 11.5	17 48.2	28 7.4	8 10.9	3 13.1	7 49.6	1 35.0	9 56.3	12 32.2
17 T	9 43 22.9	24 33.6	25 41.3	29 31.9	19 11.2	29 18.8	8 49.0	3 24.1	7 47.3	1 33.8	9 55.3	12 33.0
18 F	9 47 19.4	25 31.3	25 38.1	14♓ 5.8	20 32.6	0♎30.3	9 27.1	3 35.0	7 45.1	1 32.8	9 54.3	12 34.0
19 S	9 51 16.0	26 29.0	25 34.9	28 46.7	21 52.2	1 41.7	10 5.1	3 45.8	7 42.9	1 31.7	9 53.3	12 34.9
20 S	9 55 12.5	27 26.7	25 31.8	13♈28.2	23 9.9	2 53.0	10 43.2	3 56.5	7 40.8	1 30.7	9 52.3	12 35.8
21 M	9 59 9.1	28 24.5	25 28.6	28 4.3	24 25.9	4 4.3	11 21.3	4 7.1	7 38.8	1 29.7	9 51.4	12 36.8
22 T	10 3 5.6	29 22.3	25 25.4	12♉29.9	25 40.0	5 15.6	11 59.5	4 17.6	7 36.9	1 28.8	9 50.5	12 37.8
23 W	10 7 2.2	0♍20.1	25 22.2	26 41.5	26 52.1	6 26.7	12 37.6	4 28.0	7 35.0	1 27.9	9 49.6	12 38.8
24 T	10 10 58.7	1 18.0	25 19.1	10♊37.1	28 2.2	7 37.9	13 15.8	4 38.3	7 33.3	1 27.0	9 48.7	12 39.9
25 F	10 14 55.3	2 15.8	25 15.9	24 15.9	29 10.1	8 49.0	13 54.0	4 48.5	7 31.7	1 26.2	9 47.9	12 41.0
26 S	10 18 51.9	3 13.7	25 12.7	7♋38.2	0♎15.9	10 0.0	14 32.2	4 58.6	7 30.1	1 25.5	9 47.1	12 42.1
27 S	10 22 48.4	4 11.7	25 9.5	20 44.9	1 19.3	11 11.0	15 10.5	5 8.7	7 28.6	1 24.8	9 46.3	12 43.3
28 M	10 26 45.0	5 9.6	25 6.4	3♌37.1	2 20.3	12 22.0	15 48.7	5 18.6	7 27.3	1 24.1	9 45.5	12 44.5
29 T	10 30 41.5	6 7.6	25 3.2	16 15.9	3 18.7	13 32.9	16 27.0	5 28.3	7 26.0	1 23.5	9 44.8	12 45.7
30 W	10 34 38.1	7 5.7	24 60.0	28 42.7	4 14.4	14 43.7	17 5.3	5 38.0	7 24.8	1 23.0	9 44.1	12 47.0
31 T	10 38 34.6	8 3.7	24 56.8	10♍58.8	5 7.2	15 54.5	17 43.7	5 47.6	7 23.7	1 22.5	9 43.4	12 48.3
DECLINATION at NOON												
1 T	8 40 18.0	17N57.1	12S40.3	20N 6.5	14N59.8	9N 1.7	12N58.1	23N 6.3	22S35.8	23S42.1	22S 7.4	0S31.6
4 F	8 52 7.6	17 10.3	12 43.6	4 27.2	12 57.4	7 34.5	12 17.4	23 6.3	22 36.8	23 42.1	22 7.8	0 33.6
7 M	9 3 57.3	16 20.9	12 46.8	12S 1.7	10 52.0	6 5.5	11 36.0	23 6.2	22 37.8	23 42.2	22 8.2	0 35.7
10 T	9 15 47.0	15 29.2	12 50.0	24 29.0	8 45.4	4 35.1	10 54.0	23 5.9	22 38.7	23 42.3	22 8.5	0 37.8
13 S	9 27 36.6	14 35.3	12 53.3	27 31.2	6 39.4	3 3.6	10 11.3	23 5.4	22 39.5	23 42.3	22 8.9	0 40.0
16 W	9 39 26.3	13 39.3	12 56.5	17 12.9	4 35.3	1 31.4	9 28.0	23 4.9	22 40.4	23 42.3	22 9.2	0 42.3
19 S	9 51 16.0	12 41.4	12 59.7	2N 9.5	2 34.6	0S 1.4	8 44.2	23 4.2	22 41.1	23 42.4	22 9.5	0 44.7
22 T	10 3 5.6	11 41.6	13 2.9	20 28.9	0 38.5	1 34.3	7 59.9	23 3.4	22 41.8	23 42.4	22 9.8	0 47.1
25 F	10 14 55.3	10 40.2	13 6.1	27 57.7	1S11.4	3 7.1	7 15.0	23 2.5	22 42.5	23 42.4	22 10.1	0 49.5
28 M	10 26 45.0	9 37.2	13 9.3	21 17.5	2 53.5	4 39.6	6 29.8	23 1.6	22 43.2	23 42.4	22 10.4	0 52.0
31 T	10 38 34.6	8 32.8	13 12.5	6 10.4	4 25.8	6 11.3	5 44.1	23 0.5	22 43.7	23 42.4	22 10.7	0 54.6

SEPTEMBER 1989

DAY	EPHEMERIS SIDEREAL TIME	☉	☊	☽	☿	♀	♂	♃	♄	♅	♆	♇
	h m s	° ′	° ′	° ′	° ′	° ′	° ′	° ′	° ′	° ′	° ′	° ′
						LONGITUDE at NOON						
1 F	10 42 31.2	9♍ 1.8	24♒53.6	23♍ 5.5	5♎56.9	17♎ 5.3	18♍22.0	5♋57.1	7♑22.7	1♑22.0	9♑42.8	12♏49.6
2 S	10 46 27.7	9 59.9	24 50.5	5♎ 4.7	6 43.4	18 15.9	19 0.4	6 6.4	7R21.8	1R21.6	9R42.2	12 51.0
3 S	10 50 24.3	10 58.0	24 47.3	16 58.3	7 26.4	19 26.6	19 38.8	6 15.6	7 21.0	1 21.3	9 41.6	12 52.3
4 M	10 54 20.8	11 56.2	24 44.1	28 49.0	8 5.7	20 37.1	20 17.2	6 24.7	7 20.3	1 21.0	9 41.1	12 53.7
5 T	10 58 17.4	12 54.3	24 40.9	10♏39.7	8 41.0	21 47.6	20 55.7	6 33.7	7 19.6	1 20.7	9 40.6	12 55.2
6 W	11 2 13.9	13 52.6	24 37.8	22 34.1	9 12.0	22 58.1	21 34.1	6 42.6	7 19.1	1 20.5	9 40.1	12 56.6
7 T	11 6 10.5	14 50.8	24 34.6	4♐36.2	9 38.6	24 8.4	22 12.6	6 51.3	7 18.7	1 20.3	9 39.6	12 58.1
8 F	11 10 7.1	15 49.1	24 31.4	16 50.3	10 0.3	25 18.8	22 51.2	6 60.0	7 18.4	1 20.3	9 39.2	12 59.7
9 S	11 14 3.6	16 47.4	24 28.2	29 20.9	10 16.9	26 29.0	23 29.7	7 8.5	7 18.2	1 20.2	9 38.8	13 1.2
10 S	11 18 0.2	17 45.7	24 25.0	12♑12.2	10 27.9	27 39.2	24 8.2	7 16.8	7 18.1	1 20.2	9 38.5	13 2.8
11 M	11 21 56.7	18 44.0	24 21.9	25 27.6	10 33.2	28 49.3	24 46.8	7 25.1	7 18.1	1D20.3	9 38.1	13 4.4
12 T	11 25 53.3	19 42.4	24 18.7	9♒ 9.3	10R32.4	29 59.3	25 25.4	7 33.2	7 18.1	1 20.4	9 37.8	13 6.0
13 W	11 29 49.8	20 40.7	24 15.5	23 17.7	10 25.2	1♏ 9.2	26 4.0	7 41.1	7D18.3	1 20.5	9 37.6	13 7.7
14 T	11 33 46.4	21 39.2	24 12.3	7♓50.3	10 11.3	2 19.1	26 42.7	7 49.0	7 18.6	1 20.7	9 37.3	13 9.4
15 F	11 37 42.9	22 37.6	24 9.2	22 42.2	9 50.7	3 28.9	27 21.4	7 56.6	7 18.9	1 21.0	9 37.1	13 11.1
16 S	11 41 39.5	23 36.1	24 6.0	7♈45.9	9 23.2	4 38.6	28 0.0	8 4.2	7 19.4	1 21.3	9 37.0	13 12.8
17 S	11 45 36.0	24 34.6	24 2.8	22 52.0	8 48.9	5 48.2	28 38.8	8 11.6	7 20.0	1 21.7	9 36.8	13 14.6
18 M	11 49 32.6	25 33.1	23 59.6	7♉51.2	8 7.9	6 57.7	29 17.5	8 18.9	7 20.6	1 22.1	9 36.7	13 16.3
19 T	11 53 29.1	26 31.7	23 56.4	22 35.4	7 20.6	8 7.2	29 56.3	8 26.0	7 21.4	1 22.5	9 36.7	13 18.1
20 W	11 57 25.7	27 30.3	23 53.3	6♊58.9	6 27.6	9 16.5	0♎35.1	8 33.0	7 22.2	1 23.0	9 36.6	13 20.0
21 T	12 1 22.3	28 29.0	23 50.1	20 58.6	5 29.6	10 25.8	1 13.9	8 39.8	7 23.2	1 23.6	9 36.6	13 21.8
22 F	12 5 18.8	29 27.6	23 46.9	4♋34.2	4 27.8	11 35.0	1 52.8	8 46.5	7 24.2	1 24.2	9 36.6	13 23.7
23 S	12 9 15.4	0♎26.4	23 43.7	17 47.0	3 23.2	12 44.2	2 31.7	8 53.0	7 25.4	1 24.9	9D36.7	13 25.6
24 S	12 13 11.9	1 25.1	23 40.6	0♌39.8	2 17.5	13 53.2	3 10.6	8 59.4	7 26.6	1 25.6	9 36.8	13 27.5
25 M	12 17 8.5	2 23.9	23 37.4	13 15.7	1 12.0	15 2.1	3 49.5	9 5.6	7 28.0	1 26.3	9 36.9	13 29.4
26 T	12 21 5.0	3 22.8	23 34.2	25 38.1	0 8.6	16 11.0	4 28.5	9 11.7	7 29.4	1 27.2	9 37.1	13 31.4
27 W	12 25 1.6	4 21.6	23 31.0	7♍49.9	29♍ 8.9	17 19.8	5 7.5	9 17.6	7 30.9	1 28.0	9 37.2	13 33.4
28 T	12 28 58.1	5 20.6	23 27.8	19 53.6	28 14.5	18 28.4	5 46.5	9 23.3	7 32.6	1 28.9	9 37.5	13 35.4
29 F	12 32 54.7	6 19.5	23 24.7	1♎51.5	27 26.9	19 37.0	6 25.6	9 28.9	7 34.3	1 30.0	9 37.8	13 37.4
30 S	12 36 51.2	7 18.5	23 21.5	13 45.3	26 47.3	20 45.5	7 4.7	9 34.4	7 36.2	1 31.0	9 38.1	13 39.5
						DECLINATION at NOON						
1 F	10 42 31.2	8N11.1	13S13.6	0N31.3	4S53.9	6S41.7	5N28.8	23N 0.2	22S43.9	23S42.4	22S10.8	0S55.4
4 M	10 54 20.8	7 5.1	13 16.7	15S25.9	6 8.9	8 12.0	4 42.6	22 59.1	22 44.4	23 42.4	22 11.0	0 58.0
7 T	11 6 10.5	5 58.1	13 19.9	26 9.6	7 6.9	9 40.9	3 56.2	22 57.9	22 44.9	23 42.4	22 11.2	1 0.7
10 S	11 18 0.2	4 50.3	13 23.1	26 29.0	7 43.2	11 8.1	3 9.5	22 56.7	22 45.3	23 42.4	22 11.4	1 3.4
13 W	11 29 49.8	3 41.7	13 26.3	13 57.9	7 52.3	12 33.2	2 22.5	22 55.6	22 45.7	23 42.4	22 11.6	1 6.0
16 S	11 41 39.5	2 32.5	13 29.4	6N18.0	7 28.4	13 56.0	1 35.4	22 54.4	22 46.0	23 42.4	22 11.7	1 8.7
19 T	11 53 29.1	1 22.8	13 32.6	23 26.7	6 27.5	15 16.1	0 48.2	22 53.2	22 46.3	23 42.3	22 11.9	1 11.4
22 F	12 5 18.8	0 12.9	13 35.7	27 24.0	4 51.1	16 33.3	0 0.8	22 52.1	22 46.5	23 42.3	22 12.0	1 14.1
25 M	12 17 8.5	0S57.3	13 38.9	17 53.5	2 50.6	17 47.3	0S46.7	22 51.0	22 46.7	23 42.3	22 12.1	1 16.9
28 T	12 28 58.1	2 7.4	13 42.0	2 1.6	0 47.0	18 57.7	1 34.1	22 49.9	22 46.8	23 42.2	22 12.2	1 19.6

OCTOBER 1989

DAY	EPHEMERIS SIDEREAL TIME	☉	☊	☽	☿	♀	♂	♃	♄	♅	♆	♇
						LONGITUDE at NOON						
1 S	12 40 47.8	8♎17.5	23♒18.3	25♎36.7	26♍16.8	21♏53.8	7♎43.8	9♋39.6	7♑38.1	1♑32.0	9♑38.4	13♏41.5
2 M	12 44 44.3	9 16.6	23 15.1	7♏27.3	25R56.1	23 2.1	8 23.0	9 44.7	7 40.1	1 33.2	9 38.8	13 43.6
3 T	12 48 40.9	10 15.7	23 12.0	19 19.2	25 45.7	24 10.2	9 2.1	9 49.6	7 42.2	1 34.3	9 39.1	13 45.7
4 W	12 52 37.4	11 14.8	23 8.8	1♐14.7	25D45.8	25 18.2	9 41.3	9 54.3	7 44.4	1 35.6	9 39.6	13 47.8
5 T	12 56 34.0	12 13.9	23 5.6	13 16.9	25 56.4	26 26.1	10 20.5	9 58.8	7 46.7	1 36.8	9 40.0	13 50.0
6 F	13 0 30.6	13 13.1	23 2.4	25 29.2	26 17.3	27 33.9	10 59.8	10 3.2	7 49.1	1 38.1	9 40.5	13 52.1
7 S	13 4 27.1	14 12.3	22 59.2	7♑55.6	26 48.0	28 41.5	11 39.1	10 7.4	7 51.6	1 39.5	9 41.0	13 54.3
8 S	13 8 23.7	15 11.5	22 56.1	20 40.6	27 27.9	29 49.1	12 18.4	10 11.4	7 54.2	1 40.9	9 41.6	13 56.5
9 M	13 12 20.2	16 10.7	22 52.9	3♒48.2	28 16.4	0♐56.4	12 57.7	10 15.3	7 56.9	1 42.4	9 42.2	13 58.7
10 T	13 16 16.8	17 10.0	22 49.7	17 22.0	29 12.8	2 3.6	13 37.1	10 19.0	7 59.6	1 43.9	9 42.8	14 0.9
11 W	13 20 13.3	18 9.3	22 46.5	1♓24.0	0♎16.3	3 10.7	14 16.5	10 22.4	8 2.5	1 45.5	9 43.5	14 3.1
12 T	13 24 9.9	19 8.7	22 43.4	15 54.1	1 26.1	4 17.6	14 55.9	10 25.7	8 5.4	1 47.1	9 44.2	14 5.3
13 F	13 28 6.4	20 8.1	22 40.2	0♈48.7	2 41.5	5 24.4	15 35.3	10 28.8	8 8.5	1 48.7	9 44.9	14 7.6
14 S	13 32 3.0	21 7.5	22 37.0	16 1.0	4 1.8	6 31.0	16 14.8	10 31.8	8 11.6	1 50.4	9 45.6	14 9.9
15 S	13 35 59.5	22 6.9	22 33.8	1♉21.0	5 26.2	7 37.4	16 54.3	10 34.5	8 14.8	1 52.1	9 46.4	14 12.1
16 M	13 39 56.1	23 6.4	22 30.6	16 37.4	6 54.2	8 43.7	17 33.9	10 37.1	8 18.1	1 53.9	9 47.2	14 14.4
17 T	13 43 52.7	24 5.9	22 27.5	1♊39.2	8 25.1	9 49.8	18 13.4	10 39.4	8 21.4	1 55.8	9 48.1	14 16.7
18 W	13 47 49.2	25 5.4	22 24.3	16 18.0	9 58.5	10 55.7	18 53.0	10 41.6	8 24.9	1 57.7	9 49.0	14 19.0
19 T	13 51 45.8	26 5.0	22 21.1	0♋28.9	11 33.9	12 1.4	19 32.7	10 43.6	8 28.4	1 59.6	9 49.9	14 21.4
20 F	13 55 42.3	27 4.7	22 17.9	14 10.5	13 10.9	13 7.0	20 12.4	10 45.4	8 32.1	2 1.6	9 50.9	14 23.7
21 S	13 59 38.9	28 4.4	22 14.8	27 24.2	14 49.1	14 12.4	20 52.1	10 47.0	8 35.8	2 3.6	9 51.8	14 26.1
22 S	14 3 35.4	29 4.1	22 11.6	10♌13.3	16 28.3	15 17.5	21 31.8	10 48.4	8 39.6	2 5.7	9 52.8	14 28.4
23 M	14 7 32.0	0♏ 3.8	22 8.4	22 42.4	18 8.2	16 22.5	22 11.6	10 49.6	8 43.5	2 7.8	9 53.9	14 30.8
24 T	14 11 28.5	1 3.6	22 5.2	4♍56.1	19 48.6	17 27.2	22 51.4	10 50.6	8 47.5	2 9.9	9 54.9	14 33.2
25 W	14 15 25.1	2 3.4	22 2.0	16 58.9	21 29.3	18 31.7	23 31.2	10 51.4	8 51.5	2 12.1	9 56.0	14 35.5
26 T	14 19 21.6	3 3.2	21 58.9	28 54.6	23 10.1	19 36.0	24 11.1	10 52.0	8 55.6	2 14.3	9 57.2	14 37.9
27 F	14 23 18.2	4 3.1	21 55.7	10♎46.6	24 51.0	20 40.1	24 51.0	10 52.4	8 59.8	2 16.6	9 58.3	14 40.3
28 S	14 27 14.8	5 3.0	21 52.5	22 37.2	26 31.8	21 43.9	25 31.0	10 52.6	9 4.1	2 18.9	9 59.5	14 42.7
29 S	14 31 11.3	6 3.0	21 49.3	4♏28.5	28 12.4	22 47.5	26 10.9	10 52.6	9 8.4	2 21.2	10 0.7	14 45.1
30 M	14 35 7.9	7 3.0	21 46.2	16 21.7	29 52.8	23 50.8	26 50.9	10R52.4	9 12.8	2 23.6	10 2.0	14 47.5
31 T	14 39 4.4	8 3.0	21 43.0	28 18.4	1♏33.0	24 53.9	27 31.0	10 51.9	9 17.3	2 26.1	10 3.2	14 49.9
						DECLINATION at NOON						
1 S	12 40 47.8	3S17.4	13S45.1	14S 3.8	0N55.4	20S 4.3	2S21.6	22N49.0	22S46.8	23S42.2	22S12.2	1S22.3
4 W	12 52 37.4	4 27.0	13 48.3	25 23.5	1 58.1	21 6.7	3 9.0	22 48.1	22 46.8	23 42.1	22 12.3	1 25.0
7 S	13 4 27.1	5 36.1	13 51.4	26 55.5	2 13.9	22 4.7	3 56.2	22 47.3	22 46.8	23 42.0	22 12.3	1 27.6
10 T	13 16 16.8	6 44.6	13 54.5	16 14.2	1 44.9	22 58.0	4 43.3	22 46.6	22 46.6	23 42.0	22 12.3	1 30.2
13 F	13 28 6.4	7 52.3	13 57.6	3N 6.1	0 38.9	23 46.4	5 30.2	22 46.0	22 46.5	23 41.9	22 12.2	1 32.8
16 M	13 39 56.1	8 58.9	14 0.7	21 37.3	0S53.9	24 29.6	6 16.8	22 45.6	22 46.2	23 41.8	22 12.2	1 35.4
19 T	13 51 45.8	10 4.4	14 3.8	27 30.5	2 44.4	25 7.5	7 3.2	22 45.3	22 45.9	23 41.7	22 12.1	1 37.9
22 S	14 3 35.4	11 8.7	14 6.9	18 49.0	4 44.8	25 39.9	7 49.2	22 45.2	22 45.5	23 41.6	22 12.0	1 40.4
25 W	14 15 25.1	12 11.4	14 10.0	3 17.0	6 49.6	26 6.7	8 34.8	22 45.1	22 45.1	23 41.5	22 11.9	1 42.8
28 S	14 27 14.8	13 12.4	14 13.1	12S48.8	8 54.8	26 27.7	9 19.9	22 45.3	22 44.5	23 41.3	22 11.7	1 45.2
31 T	14 39 4.4	14 11.6	14 16.2	24 38.0	10 57.5	26 43.0	10 4.6	22 45.6	22 43.9	23 41.2	22 11.5	1 47.5

NOVEMBER 1989

LONGITUDE at NOON

DAY	EPHEMERIS SIDEREAL TIME	☉	☊	☾	☿	♀	♂	♃	♄	♅	♆	♇
	h m s	° ′	° ′	° ′	° ′	° ′	° ′	° ′	° ′	° ′	° ′	° ′
1 W	14 43 1.0	9♏ 3.0	21♒39.8	10♐19.7	3♏12.8	25♐56.6	28♎11.0	10♋51.3	9♑21.9	2♑28.5	10♑ 4.5	14♏52.4
2 T	14 46 57.5	10 3.1	21 36.6	22 27.4	4 52.3	26 59.1	28 51.1	10R50.5	9 26.6	2 31.0	10 5.9	14 54.8
3 F	14 50 54.1	11 3.2	21 33.5	4♑43.7	6 31.4	28 1.3	29 31.3	10 49.5	9. 31.3	2 33.6	10 7.2	14 57.2
4 S	14 54 50.6	12 3.3	21 30.3	17 11.6	8 10.2	29 3.2	0♏11.4	10 48.3	9 36.1	2 36.2	10 8.6	14 59.6
5 S	14 58 47.2	13 3.5	21 27.1	29 54.5	9 48.5	0♑ 4.7	0 51.6	10 46.9	9 40.9	2 38.8	10 10.0	15 2.0
6 M	15 2 43.8	14 3.7	21 23.9	12♒56.2	11 26.5	1 5.9	1 31.8	10 45.3	9 45.9	2 41.4	10 11.5	15 4.5
7 T	15 6 40.3	15 3.9	21 20.7	26 20.4	13 4.1	2 6.8	2 12.1	10 43.4	9 50.9	2 44.1	10 12.9	15 6.9
8 W	15 10 36.9	16 4.1	21 17.6	10♓10.1	14 41.3	3 7.2	2 52.4	10 41.4	9 55.9	2 46.8	10 14.4	15 9.3
9 T	15 14 33.4	17 4.3	21 14.4	24 26.6	16 18.2	4 7.3	3 32.7	10 39.2	10 1.1	2 49.6	10 15.9	15 11.7
10 F	15 18 30.0	18 4.7	21 11.2	9♈ 8.6	17 54.7	5 7.1	4 13.1	10 36.9	10 6.3	2 52.4	10 17.5	15 14.2
11 S	15 22 26.5	19 5.0	21 8.0	24 11.3	19 30.9	6 6.4	4 53.5	10 34.3	10 11.6	2 55.3	10 19.1	15 16.6
12 S	15 26 23.1	20 5.3	21 4.9	9♉26.5	21 6.7	7 5.2	5 33.9	10 31.5	10 16.9	2 58.1	10 20.7	15 19.1
13 M	15 30 19.7	21 5.7	21 1.7	24 43.6	22 42.1	8 3.6	6 14.4	10 28.5	10 22.3	3 1.0	10 22.3	15 21.5
14 T	15 34 16.2	22 6.0	20 58.5	9♊51.0	24 17.3	9 1.6	6 54.9	10 25.3	10 27.7	3 3.9	10 23.9	15 23.9
15 W	15 38 12.8	23 6.5	20 55.3	24 38.6	25 52.2	9 59.0	7 35.4	10 21.9	10 33.2	3 6.9	10 25.6	15 26.3
16 T	15 42 9.3	24 6.9	20 52.2	8♋59.4	27 26.8	10 56.0	8 15.9	10 18.4	10 38.8	3 9.8	10 27.3	15 28.7
17 F	15 46 5.9	25 7.4	20 49.0	22 50.2	29 1.2	11 52.5	8 56.5	10 14.6	10 44.4	3 12.9	10 29.0	15 31.1
18 S	15 50 2.4	26 7.9	20 45.8	6♌11.0	0♐35.3	12 48.4	9 37.2	10 10.7	10 50.1	3 15.9	10 30.8	15 33.5
19 S	15 53 59.0	27 8.4	20 42.6	19 4.5	2 9.2	13 43.8	10 17.9	10 6.6	10 55.8	3 19.0	10 32.5	15 35.9
20 M	15 57 55.6	28 9.0	20 39.4	1♍35.2	3 42.9	14 38.6	10 58.6	10 2.3	11 1.6	3 22.0	10 34.3	15 38.3
21 T	16 1 52.1	29 9.6	20 36.3	13 48.2	5 16.4	15 32.8	11 39.3	9 57.8	11 7.4	3 25.2	10 36.1	15 40.7
22 W	16 5 48.7	0♐10.2	20 33.1	25 48.8	6 49.7	16 26.4	12 20.1	9 53.1	11 13.3	3 28.3	10 37.9	15 43.0
23 T	16 9 45.2	1 10.8	20 29.9	7♎41.8	8 22.9	17 19.4	13 0.9	9 48.3	11 19.3	3 31.5	10 39.8	15 45.4
24 F	16 13 41.8	2 11.5	20 26.7	19 31.7	9 55.9	18 11.7	13 41.8	9 43.3	11 25.3	3 34.7	10 41.6	15 47.8
25 S	16 17 38.3	3 12.2	20 23.6	1♏21.9	11 28.7	19 3.3	14 22.6	9 38.1	11 31.3	3 37.9	10 43.5	15 50.1
26 S	16 21 34.9	4 12.9	20 20.4	13 15.3	13 1.5	19 54.2	15 3.6	9 32.8	11 37.4	3 41.1	10 45.4	15 52.4
27 M	16 25 31.5	5 13.7	20 17.2	25 13.6	14 34.0	20 44.3	15 44.5	9 27.3	11 43.6	3 44.4	10 47.3	15 54.8
28 T	16 29 28.0	6 14.5	20 14.0	7♐18.2	16 6.5	21 33.7	16 25.5	9 21.6	11 49.8	3 47.7	10 49.3	15 57.1
29 W	16 33 24.6	7 15.2	20 10.9	19 30.1	17 38.8	22 22.2	17 6.6	9 15.8	11 56.0	3 51.0	10 51.2	15 59.4
30 T	16 37 21.1	8 16.1	20 7.7	1♑49.9	19 11.0	23 9.9	17 47.6	9 9.8	12 2.3	3 54.3	10 53.2	16 1.7

DECLINATION at NOON

DAY	EPHEMERIS SIDEREAL TIME	☉	☊	☾	☿	♀	♂	♃	♄	♅	♆	♇
1 W	14 43 1.0	14S30.9	14S17.2	26S42.5	11S37.6	26S46.9	10S19.4	22N45.7	22S43.7	23S41.2	22S11.5	1S48.2
4 S	14 54 50.6	15 27.3	14 20.2	25 10.6	13 34.3	26 54.5	11 3.3	22 46.2	22 43.0	23 41.0	22 11.3	1 50.4
7 T	15 6 40.3	16 21.4	14 23.3	12 21.7	15 25.0	26 56.5	11 46.5	22 46.9	22 42.3	23 40.8	22 11.0	1 52.5
10 F	15 18 30.0	17 13.1	14 26.4	7N 1.5	17 8.8	26 52.9	12 29.1	22 47.7	22 41.4	23 40.7	22 10.8	1 54.6
13 M	15 30 19.7	18 2.0	14 29.4	23 47.2	18 44.9	26 43.9	13 11.0	22 48.6	22 40.5	23 40.5	22 10.5	1 56.6
16 T	15 42 9.3	18 48.2	14 32.4	26 28.2	20 12.6	26 29.7	13 52.0	22 49.7	22 39.5	23 40.3	22 10.2	1 58.5
19 S	15 53 59.0	19 31.3	14 35.5	15 13.7	21 31.4	26 10.6	14 32.2	22 50.9	22 38.4	23 40.0	22 9.9	2 0.3
22 W	16 5 48.7	20 11.3	14 38.5	1S 0.6	22 40.6	25 46.9	15 11.5	22 52.3	22 37.2	23 39.8	22 9.5	2 2.0
25 S	16 17 38.3	20 48.0	14 41.5	16 23.6	23 39.5	25 19.0	15 49.9	22 53.7	22 36.0	23 39.5	22 9.2	2 3.6
28 T	16 29 28.0	21 21.2	14 44.5	26 13.8	24 27.7	24 47.1	16 27.2	22 55.2	22 34.6	23 39.3	22 8.8	2 5.1

DECEMBER 1989

LONGITUDE at NOON

DAY	EPHEMERIS SIDEREAL TIME	☉	☊	☾	☿	♀	♂	♃	♄	♅	♆	♇
1 F	16 41 17.7	9♐16.9	20♒ 4.5	14♑18.7	20♐43.1	23♑56.7	18♏28.8	9♋ 3.8	12♑ 8.7	3♑57.7	10♑55.2	16♏ 4.0
2 S	16 45 14.2	10 17.8	20 1.3	26 57.6	22 14.9	24 42.6	19 9.9	8R57.5	12 15.0	4 1.1	10 57.2	16 6.3
3 S	16 49 10.8	11 18.6	19 58.2	9♒48.6	23 46.6	25 27.5	19 51.1	8 51.1	12 21.4	4 4.5	10 59.3	16 8.5
4 M	16 53 7.4	12 19.5	19 55.0	22 54.0	25 18.2	26 11.4	20 32.3	8 44.6	12 27.9	4 7.9	11 1.3	16 10.8
5 T	16 57 3.9	13 20.4	19 51.8	6♓16.4	26 49.4	26 54.2	21 13.5	8 37.9	12 34.4	4 11.3	11 3.4	16 13.0
6 W	17 1 0.5	14 21.3	19 48.6	19 58.1	28 20.5	27 35.9	21 54.8	8 31.1	12 40.9	4 14.8	11 5.4	16 15.2
7 T	17 4 57.0	15 22.2	19 45.4	4♈ 0.7	29 51.2	28 16.5	22 36.1	8 24.2	12 47.5	4 18.2	11 7.5	16 17.4
8 F	17 8 53.6	16 23.2	19 42.3	18 23.8	1♑21.5	28 55.9	23 17.4	8 17.2	12 54.0	4 21.7	11 9.6	16 19.6
9 S	17 12 50.2	17 24.1	19 39.1	3♉ 5.0	2 51.5	29 34.0	23 58.8	8 10.1	13 0.7	4 25.2	11 11.7	16 21.7
10 S	17 16 46.7	18 25.1	19 35.9	17 58.8	4 20.9	0♒10.8	24 40.2	8 2.9	13 7.3	4 28.7	11 13.8	16 23.9
11 M	17 20 43.3	19 26.0	19 32.7	2♊57.3	5 49.7	0 46.2	25 21.6	7 55.5	13 14.0	4 32.2	11 16.0	16 26.0
12 T	17 24 39.8	20 27.0	19 29.6	17 51.3	7 17.7	1 20.3	26 3.1	7 48.1	13 20.7	4 35.7	11 18.1	16 28.1
13 W	17 28 36.4	21 28.0	19 26.4	2♋31.6	8 44.9	1 52.9	26 44.6	7 40.6	13 27.5	4 39.2	11 20.3	16 30.2
14 T	17 32 32.9	22 29.0	19 23.2	16 50.8	10 11.1	2 23.9	27 26.2	7 33.0	13 34.3	4 42.8	11 22.5	16 32.2
15 F	17 36 29.5	23 30.0	19 20.0	0♌44.3	11 36.1	2 53.4	28 7.8	7 25.4	13 41.1	4 46.3	11 24.6	16 34.3
16 S	17 40 26.1	24 31.0	19 16.9	14 10.3	12 59.6	3 21.2	28 49.4	7 17.6	13 47.9	4 49.9	11 26.8	16 36.3
17 S	17 44 22.6	25 32.1	19 13.7	27 9.9	14 21.4	3 47.3	29 31.1	7 9.8	13 54.7	4 53.4	11 29.0	16 38.3
18 M	17 48 19.2	26 33.1	19 10.5	9♍46.2	15 41.2	4 11.7	0♐12.8	7 1.9	14 1.6	4 57.0	11 31.2	16 40.3
19 T	17 52 15.7	27 34.2	19 7.3	22 3.4	16 58.7	4 34.2	0 54.5	6 54.0	14 8.5	5 0.6	11 33.4	16 42.3
20 W	17 56 12.3	28 35.3	19 4.2	4♎ 6.7	18 13.4	4 54.8	1 36.3	6 46.0	14 15.5	5 4.2	11 35.7	16 44.2
21 T	18 0 8.9	29 36.4	19 1.0	16 1.3	19 24.8	5 13.5	2 18.1	6 38.0	14 22.4	5 7.8	11 37.9	16 46.2
22 F	18 4 5.4	0♑37.6	18 57.8	27 52.1	20 32.6	5 30.3	2 60.0	6 30.0	14 29.4	5 11.4	11 40.2	16 48.1
23 S	18 8 2.0	1 38.7	18 54.6	9♏43.5	21 35.9	5 44.9	3 41.9	6 21.9	14 36.4	5 15.0	11 42.4	16 50.0
24 S	18 11 58.5	2 39.8	18 51.4	21 39.5	22 34.2	5 57.3	4 23.8	6 13.8	14 43.4	5 18.6	11 44.7	16 51.8
25 M	18 15 55.1	3 41.0	18 48.3	3♐43.0	23 26.7	6 7.6	5 5.8	6 5.6	14 50.4	5 22.3	11 46.9	16 53.7
26 T	18 19 51.7	4 42.1	18 45.1	15 56.2	24 12.6	6 15.6	5 47.8	5 57.5	14 57.4	5 25.9	11 49.2	16 55.5
27 W	18 23 48.2	5 43.3	18 41.9	28 20.3	24 51.0	6 21.2	6 29.8	5 49.3	15 4.5	5 29.5	11 51.4	16 57.3
28 T	18 27 44.8	6 44.4	18 38.7	10♑56.0	25 21.0	6 24.6	7 11.9	5 41.2	15 11.5	5 33.1	11 53.7	16 59.0
29 F	18 31 41.3	7 45.6	18 35.6	23 43.5	25 41.8	6 25.4	7 54.0	5 33.0	15 18.6	5 36.7	11 56.0	17 0.7
30 S	18 35 37.9	8 46.8	18 32.4	6♒42.6	25 52.4	6R23.9	8 36.1	5 24.9	15 25.7	5 40.3	11 58.2	17 2.4
31 S	18 39 34.4	9 48.0	18 29.2	19 53.2	25R52.1	6 19.8	9 18.3	5 16.8	15 32.8	5 43.9	12 0.5	17 4.1

DECLINATION at NOON

DAY	EPHEMERIS SIDEREAL TIME	☉	☊	☾	☿	♀	♂	♃	♄	♅	♆	♇
1 F	16 41 17.7	21S50.7	14S47.6	25S31.2	25S 4.5	24S11.7	17S 3.4	22N56.8	22S33.2	23S39.0	22S 8.4	2S 6.6
4 M	16 53 7.4	22 16.5	14 50.6	13 32.2	25 29.2	23 33.4	17 38.5	22 58.4	22 31.7	23 38.7	22 8.0	2 7.9
7 T	17 4 57.0	22 38.3	14 53.5	4N54.4	25 41.3	22 52.5	18 12.3	23 0.1	22 30.1	23 38.3	22 7.5	2 9.1
10 S	17 16 46.7	22 56.2	14 56.5	22 2.8	25 40.4	22 9.7	18 44.9	23 1.8	22 28.5	23 38.0	22 7.0	2 10.2
13 W	17 28 36.4	23 10.0	14 59.5	27 2.5	25 26.4	21 25.5	19 16.1	23 3.5	22 26.7	23 37.7	22 6.6	2 11.2
16 S	17 40 26.1	23 19.7	15 2.5	16 53.3	24 59.3	20 40.5	19 46.0	23 5.2	22 24.9	23 37.3	22 6.1	2 12.1
19 T	17 52 15.7	23 25.2	15 5.5	0 29.5	24 20.0	19 55.3	20 14.4	23 6.9	22 23.0	23 36.9	22 5.5	2 12.8
22 F	18 4 5.4	23 26.4	15 8.4	15S13.1	23 30.3	19 10.5	20 41.2	23 8.5	22 21.0	23 36.5	22 5.0	2 13.5
25 M	18 15 55.1	23 23.4	15 11.4	25 43.7	22 33.3	18 26.8	21 6.6	23 10.1	22 18.9	23 36.1	22 4.5	2 14.1
28 T	18 27 44.8	23 16.2	15 14.4	26 1.2	21 34.1	17 44.8	21 30.2	23 11.6	22 16.8	23 35.7	22 3.9	2 14.5
31 S	18 39 34.4	23 4.8	15 17.3	14 35.4	20 39.4	17 5.2	21 52.2	23 13.0	22 14.6	23 35.2	22 3.3	2 14.8

JANUARY 1990

LONGITUDE at NOON

DAY	EPHEMERIS SIDEREAL TIME	☉	☊	☾	☿	♀	♂	♃	♄	♅	♆	♇
	h m s	° ′	° ′	° ′	° ′	° ′	° ′	° ′	° ′	° ′	° ′	° ′
1 M	18 43 31.0	10♑49.1	18♒26.0	3♓15.5	25♑40.3	6♒13.3	10♐ 0.5	5♋ 8.7	15♑39.9	5♑47.5	12♑ 2.8	17♏ 5.8
2 T	18 47 27.6	11 50.3	18 22.9	16 49.7	25R16.6	6R 4.2	10 42.7	5R 0.6	15 47.0	5 51.1	12 5.1	17 7.4
3 W	18 51 24.1	12 51.4	18 19.7	0♈36.3	24 41.1	5 52.6	11 25.0	4 52.6	15 54.1	5 54.7	12 7.3	17 9.0
4 T	18 55 20.7	13 52.6	18 16.5	14 35.1	23 54.2	5 38.5	12 7.3	4 44.7	16 1.2	5 58.3	12 9.6	17 10.5
5 F	18 59 17.2	14 53.8	18 13.3	28 45.7	22 57.0	5 21.9	12 49.7	4 36.8	16 8.3	6 1.9	12 11.9	17 12.1
6 S	19 3 13.8	15 54.9	18 10.2	13♉ 6.3	21 50.7	5 2.9	13 32.1	4 28.9	16 15.4	6 5.4	12 14.2	17 13.6
7 S	19 7 10.4	16 56.1	18 7.0	27 33.6	20 37.4	4 41.5	14 14.5	4 21.1	16 22.5	6 9.0	12 16.4	17 15.1
8 M	19 11 6.9	17 57.2	18 3.8	12♊ 3.0	19 19.3	4 17.9	14 56.9	4 13.4	16 29.6	6 12.6	12 18.7	17 16.5
9 T	19 15 3.5	18 58.3	18 0.6	26 29.0	17 59.1	3 52.1	15 39.4	4 5.8	16 36.7	6 16.1	12 21.0	17 17.9
10 W	19 19 0.0	19 59.4	17 57.5	10♋45.6	16 39.3	3 24.3	16 21.9	3 58.2	16 43.8	6 19.6	12 23.2	17 19.3
11 T	19 22 56.6	21 0.5	17 54.3	24 47.3	15 22.3	2 54.6	17 4.4	3 50.7	16 50.9	6 23.2	12 25.5	17 20.7
12 F	19 26 53.1	22 1.7	17 51.1	8♌29.9	14 10.4	2 23.3	17 47.0	3 43.3	16 58.0	6 26.7	12 27.7	17 22.0
13 S	19 30 49.7	23 2.8	17 47.9	21 51.2	13 5.3	1 50.4	18 29.7	3 36.0	17 5.1	6 30.2	12 30.0	17 23.3
14 S	19 34 46.3	24 3.9	17 44.7	4♍50.7	12 8.4	1 16.3	19 12.3	3 28.8	17 12.2	6 33.7	12 32.2	17 24.6
15 M	19 38 42.8	25 5.0	17 41.6	17 29.5	11 20.5	0 41.1	19 55.0	3 21.7	17 19.3	6 37.1	12 34.4	17 25.8
16 T	19 42 39.4	26 6.0	17 38.4	29 50.6	10 42.1	0 5.0	20 37.7	3 14.8	17 26.3	6 40.6	12 36.6	17 27.0
17 W	19 46 35.9	27 7.1	17 35.2	11♎57.6	10 13.3	29♑28.5	21 20.5	3 7.9	17 33.4	6 44.0	12 38.9	17 28.1
18 T	19 50 32.5	28 8.2	17 32.0	23 55.0	9 53.9	28 51.6	22 3.3	3 1.2	17 40.4	6 47.5	12 41.1	17 29.3
19 F	19 54 29.1	29 9.3	17 28.9	5♏47.6	9 43.7	28 14.6	22 46.2	2 54.5	17 47.4	6 50.9	12 43.3	17 30.4
20 S	19 58 25.6	0♒10.4	17 25.7	17 40.3	9 42.2	27 37.9	23 29.0	2 48.1	17 54.5	6 54.3	12 45.5	17 31.4
21 S	20 2 22.2	1 11.4	17 22.5	29 37.6	9D48.7	27 1.6	24 12.0	2 41.7	18 1.5	6 57.7	12 47.7	17 32.5
22 M	20 6 18.7	2 12.5	17 19.3	11♐43.7	10 2.7	26 26.0	24 55.0	2 35.5	18 8.5	7 1.1	12 49.9	17 33.5
23 T	20 10 15.3	3 13.6	17 16.2	24 2.0	10 23.6	25 51.4	25 37.9	2 29.5	18 15.4	7 4.4	12 52.0	17 34.5
24 W	20 14 11.8	4 14.6	17 13.0	6♑35.1	10 50.7	25 17.9	26 21.0	2 23.6	18 22.4	7 7.7	12 54.2	17 35.4
25 T	20 18 8.4	5 15.7	17 9.8	19 24.6	11 23.6	24 45.9	27 4.0	2 17.8	18 29.3	7 11.0	12 56.3	17 36.3
26 F	20 22 5.0	6 16.7	17 6.6	2♒30.9	12 1.7	24 15.3	27 47.1	2 12.2	18 36.2	7 14.3	12 58.5	17 37.2
27 S	20 26 1.5	7 17.7	17 3.4	15 53.4	12 44.4	23 46.6	28 30.2	2 6.7	18 43.1	7 17.5	13 0.6	17 38.0
28 S	20 29 58.1	8 18.7	17 0.3	29 30.5	13 31.5	23 19.7	29 13.4	2 1.4	18 49.9	7 20.8	13 2.7	17 38.8
29 M	20 33 54.6	9 19.6	16 57.1	13♓19.9	14 22.4	22 54.9	29 56.6	1 56.3	18 56.8	7 24.0	13 4.8	17 39.5
30 T	20 37 51.2	10 20.6	16 53.9	27 18.9	15 16.8	22 32.2	0♑39.8	1 51.4	19 3.6	7 27.1	13 6.9	17 40.3
31 W	20 41 47.7	11 21.5	16 50.7	11♈24.9	16 14.4	22 11.8	1 23.0	1 46.6	19 10.4	7 30.3	13 8.9	17 40.9

DECLINATION at NOON

DAY	EPHEMERIS SIDEREAL TIME	☉	☊	☾	☿	♀	♂	♃	♄	♅	♆	♇
1 M	18 43 31.0	23S 0.1	15S 18.3	8S 56.4	20S 23.4	16S 52.6	21S 59.1	23N 13.5	22S 13.9	23S 35.1	22S 3.1	2S 14.9
4 T	18 55 20.7	22 43.1	15 21.2	9N 48.3	19 45.4	16 17.2	22 18.8	23 14.8	22 11.6	23 34.7	22 2.5	2 15.0
7 S	19 7 10.4	22 22.2	15 24.1	24 35.7	19 24.1	15 45.7	22 36.7	23 16.1	22 9.3	23 34.2	22 2.0	2 15.1
10 W	19 19 0.0	21 57.2	15 27.1	26 3.5	19 18.5	15 18.4	22 52.7	23 17.3	22 6.9	23 33.8	22 1.4	2 15.0
13 S	19 30 49.7	21 28.4	15 30.0	13 45.8	19 25.8	14 55.8	23 6.8	23 18.4	22 4.4	23 33.3	22 0.8	2 14.9
16 T	19 42 39.4	20 55.9	15 32.9	3S 14.7	19 42.6	14 38.1	23 18.9	23 19.4	22 1.9	23 32.8	22 0.2	2 14.6
19 F	19 54 29.1	20 19.8	15 35.8	18 19.2	20 5.7	14 25.2	23 29.1	23 20.3	21 59.4	23 32.3	21 59.6	2 14.2
22 M	20 6 18.7	19 40.2	15 38.7	26 54.8	20 31.1	14 17.2	23 37.2	23 21.1	21 56.8	23 31.8	21 58.9	2 13.6
25 T	20 18 8.4	18 57.4	15 41.6	24 24.9	20 55.3	14 13.6	23 43.3	23 21.9	21 54.2	23 31.3	21 58.3	2 13.0
28 S	20 29 58.1	18 11.4	15 44.5	10 31.6	21 15.0	14 14.1	23 47.3	23 22.6	21 51.5	23 30.9	21 57.7	2 12.3
31 W	20 41 47.7	17 22.4	15 47.4	8N 29.8	21 28.2	14 18.2	23 49.3	23 23.2	21 48.9	23 30.4	21 57.1	2 11.5

FEBRUARY 1990

LONGITUDE at NOON

DAY	EPHEMERIS SIDEREAL TIME	☉	☊	☾	☿	♀	♂	♃	♄	♅	♆	♇
1 T	20 45 44.3	12♒22.4	16♒47.6	25♈35.0	17♑14.9	21♑53.6	2♑ 6.3	1♋42.0	19♑17.1	7♑63.4	13♑11.0	17♏41.6
2 F	20 49 40.8	13 23.3	16 44.4	9♉46.9	18 18.0	21R37.9	2 49.6	1R37.5	19 23.8	7 36.5	13 13.0	17 42.2
3 S	20 53 37.4	14 24.2	16 41.2	23 58.2	19 23.6	21 24.6	3 32.9	1 33.3	19 30.5	7 39.6	13 15.0	17 42.8
4 S	20 57 34.0	15 25.0	16 38.0	8♊ 6.6	20 31.4	21 13.8	4 16.3	1 29.2	19 37.2	7 42.6	13 17.0	17 43.3
5 M	21 1 30.5	16 25.8	16 34.9	22 10.0	21 41.3	21 5.4	4 59.7	1 25.4	19 43.8	7 45.7	13 19.0	17 43.8
6 T	21 5 27.1	17 26.6	16 31.7	6♋ 6.0	22 53.0	20 59.6	5 43.1	1 21.7	19 50.4	7 48.6	13 21.0	17 44.3
7 W	21 9 23.6	18 27.4	16 28.5	19 52.3	24 6.6	20 56.2	6 26.6	1 18.2	19 56.9	7 51.6	13 22.9	17 44.7
8 T	21 13 20.2	19 28.1	16 25.3	3♌26.7	25 21.7	20 55.2	7 10.1	1 14.8	20 3.4	7 54.5	13 24.8	17 45.1
9 F	21 17 16.7	20 28.9	16 22.1	16 47.2	26 38.5	20D56.7	7 53.6	1 11.7	20 9.9	7 57.4	13 26.7	17 45.5
10 S	21 21 13.3	21 29.6	16 19.0	29 52.4	27 56.6	21 0.6	8 37.1	1 8.8	20 16.4	8 0.3	13 28.6	17 45.8
11 S	21 25 9.9	22 30.2	16 15.8	12♍41.9	29 16.2	21 6.8	9 20.7	1 6.0	20 22.8	8 3.1	13 30.5	17 46.1
12 M	21 29 6.4	23 30.9	16 12.6	25 15.8	0♒37.1	21 15.4	10 4.4	1 3.5	20 29.2	8 6.0	13 32.4	17 46.4
13 T	21 33 3.0	24 31.6	16 9.4	7♎35.5	1 59.1	21 26.1	10 48.1	1 1.2	20 35.5	8 8.7	13 34.2	17 46.6
14 W	21 36 59.5	25 32.2	16 6.3	19 43.1	3 22.4	21 39.1	11 31.7	0 59.0	20 41.8	8 11.4	13 36.1	17 46.8
15 T	21 40 56.1	26 32.8	16 3.1	1♏41.8	4 46.9	21 54.1	12 15.5	0 57.1	20 48.0	8 14.1	13 37.8	17 46.9
16 F	21 44 52.6	27 33.4	15 59.9	13 35.3	6 12.4	22 11.2	12 59.2	0 55.3	20 54.2	8 16.8	13 39.6	17 47.0
17 S	21 48 49.2	28 33.9	15 56.7	25 28.1	7 39.0	22 30.3	13 43.0	0 53.8	21 0.3	8 19.4	13 41.4	17 47.1
18 S	21 52 45.7	29 34.5	15 53.6	7♐24.6	9 6.7	22 51.3	14 26.8	0 52.4	21 6.4	8 22.0	13 43.1	17 47.2
19 M	21 56 42.3	0♓35.0	15 50.4	19 29.8	10 35.5	23 14.2	15 10.7	0 51.2	21 12.5	8 24.6	13 44.8	17R47.1
20 T	22 0 38.8	1 35.5	15 47.2	1♑48.1	12 5.2	23 38.9	15 54.6	0 50.3	21 18.5	8 27.1	13 46.5	17 47.1
21 W	22 4 35.4	2 35.9	15 44.0	14 23.6	13 36.0	24 5.3	16 38.5	0 49.5	21 24.4	8 29.6	13 48.1	17 47.0
22 T	22 8 32.0	3 36.4	15 40.8	27 19.3	15 7.7	24 33.3	17 22.4	0 49.0	21 30.3	8 32.0	13 49.7	17 46.9
23 F	22 12 28.5	4 36.8	15 37.7	10♒37.3	16 40.5	25 2.9	18 6.4	0 48.6	21 36.1	8 34.4	13 51.4	17 46.8
24 S	22 16 25.1	5 37.2	15 34.5	24 17.6	18 14.2	25 34.1	18 50.4	0 48.4	21 41.9	8 36.7	13 52.9	17 46.6
25 S	22 20 21.6	6 37.6	15 31.3	8♓18.4	19 49.0	26 6.7	19 34.4	0D48.5	21 47.7	8 39.1	13 54.5	17 46.4
26 M	22 24 18.2	7 37.9	15 28.1	22 36.1	21 24.7	26 40.7	20 18.4	0 48.7	21 53.3	8 41.3	13 56.0	17 46.1
27 T	22 28 14.7	8 38.2	15 25.0	7♈ 5.3	23 1.4	27 16.1	21 2.5	0 49.2	21 59.0	8 43.6	13 57.5	17 45.9
28 W	22 32 11.3	9 38.5	15 21.8	21 39.8	24 39.2	27 52.7	21 46.6	0 49.8	22 4.5	8 45.7	13 59.0	17 45.5

DECLINATION at NOON

DAY	EPHEMERIS SIDEREAL TIME	☉	☊	☾	☿	♀	♂	♃	♄	♅	♆	♇
1 T	20 45 44.3	17S 5.5	15S 48.3	14N 29.1	21S 30.8	14S 20.2	23S 49.5	23N 23.4	21S 48.0	23S 30.2	21S 56.9	2S 11.2
4 S	20 57 34.0	16 12.9	15 51.2	26 30.7	21 32.5	14 28.0	23 48.6	23 24.0	21 45.3	23 29.7	21 56.3	2 10.2
7 W	21 9 23.6	15 17.9	15 54.1	24 19.1	21 24.5	14 37.6	23 45.6	23 24.5	21 42.6	23 29.2	21 55.7	2 9.2
10 S	21 21 13.3	14 20.5	15 56.9	10 22.2	21 6.0	14 48.3	23 40.5	23 25.0	21 40.0	23 28.8	21 55.1	2 8.1
13 T	21 33 3.0	13 20.9	15 59.8	6S 47.3	20 36.5	14 59.3	23 33.2	23 25.5	21 37.3	23 28.3	21 54.5	2 6.9
16 F	21 44 52.6	12 19.4	16 2.6	20 56.2	19 55.7	15 9.7	23 23.8	23 25.9	21 34.6	23 27.9	21 53.9	2 5.6
19 M	21 56 42.3	11 16.1	16 5.4	27 26.0	19 3.3	15 19.0	23 12.3	23 26.4	21 32.0	23 27.5	21 53.4	2 4.2
22 T	22 8 32.0	10 11.2	16 8.3	22 23.7	17 59.3	15 26.4	22 58.8	23 26.8	21 29.4	23 27.0	21 52.8	2 2.8
25 S	22 20 21.6	9 4.9	16 11.1	6 38.5	16 43.6	15 31.5	22 43.1	23 27.1	21 26.8	23 26.6	21 52.3	2 1.3
28 W	22 32 11.3	7 57.3	16 13.9	12N 51.1	15 16.2	15 33.8	22 25.4	23 27.5	21 24.3	23 26.3	21 51.8	1 59.7

NOVEMBER 1989

LONGITUDE at NOON

DAY	EPHEMERIS SIDEREAL TIME	☉	☊	☽	☿	♀	♂	♃	♄	♅	♆	♇
	h m s	° ′	° ′	° ′	° ′	° ′	° ′	° ′	° ′	° ′	° ′	° ′
1 W	14 43 1.0	9♏ 3.0	21♒39.8	10♐19.7	3♏12.8	25♐56.6	28♎11.0	10♋51.3	9♑21.9	2♑28.5	10♑ 4.5	14♏52.4
2 T	14 46 57.5	10 3.1	21 36.6	22 27.4	4 52.3	26 59.1	28 51.1	10R50.5	9 26.6	2 31.0	10 5.9	14 54.8
3 F	14 50 54.1	11 3.2	21 33.5	4♑43.7	6 31.4	28 1.3	29 31.3	10 49.5	9 31.3	2 33.6	10 7.2	14 57.2
4 S	14 54 50.6	12 3.3	21 30.3	17 11.6	8 10.2	29 3.2	0♏11.4	10 48.3	9 36.1	2 36.2	10 8.6	14 59.6
5 S	14 58 47.2	13 3.5	21 27.1	29 54.5	9 48.5	0♑ 4.7	0 51.6	10 46.9	9 40.9	2 38.8	10 10.0	15 2.0
6 M	15 2 43.8	14 3.7	21 23.9	12♒56.2	11 26.5	1 5.9	1 31.8	10 45.3	9 45.9	2 41.4	10 11.5	15 4.5
7 T	15 6 40.3	15 3.9	21 20.7	26 20.4	13 4.1	2 6.8	2 12.1	10 43.4	9 50.9	2 44.1	10 12.9	15 6.9
8 W	15 10 36.9	16 4.1	21 17.6	10♓10.1	14 41.3	3 7.2	2 52.4	10 41.4	9 55.9	2 46.8	10 14.4	15 9.3
9 T	15 14 33.4	17 4.3	21 14.4	24 26.6	16 18.2	4 7.3	3 32.7	10 39.2	10 1.1	2 49.6	10 15.9	15 11.7
10 F	15 18 30.0	18 4.7	21 11.2	9♈ 8.6	17 54.7	5 7.1	4 13.1	10 36.9	10 6.3	2 52.4	10 17.5	15 14.2
11 S	15 22 26.5	19 5.0	21 8.0	24 11.3	19 30.9	6 6.4	4 53.5	10 34.3	10 11.6	2 55.3	10 19.1	15 16.6
12 S	15 26 23.1	20 5.3	21 4.9	9♉26.5	21 6.7	7 5.2	5 33.9	10 31.5	10 16.9	2 58.1	10 20.7	15 19.1
13 M	15 30 19.7	21 5.7	21 1.7	24 43.6	22 42.1	8 3.6	6 14.4	10 28.5	10 22.3	3 1.0	10 22.3	15 21.5
14 T	15 34 16.2	22 6.0	20 58.5	9♊51.0	24 17.3	9 1.6	6 54.9	10 25.3	10 27.7	3 3.9	10 23.9	15 23.9
15 W	15 38 12.8	23 6.5	20 55.3	24 38.6	25 52.2	9 59.0	7 35.4	10 21.9	10 33.2	3 6.9	10 25.6	15 26.3
16 T	15 42 9.3	24 6.9	20 52.2	8♋59.4	27 26.8	10 56.0	8 15.9	10 18.4	10 38.8	3 9.8	10 27.3	15 28.7
17 F	15 46 5.9	25 7.4	20 49.0	22 50.2	29 1.2	11 52.5	8 56.5	10 14.6	10 44.4	3 12.9	10 29.0	15 31.1
18 S	15 50 2.4	26 7.9	20 45.8	6♌11.0	0♐35.3	12 48.4	9 37.2	10 10.7	10 50.1	3 15.9	10 30.8	15 33.5
19 S	15 53 59.0	27 8.4	20 42.6	19 4.5	2 9.2	13 43.8	10 17.9	10 6.6	10 55.8	3 19.0	10 32.5	15 35.9
20 M	15 57 55.6	28 9.0	20 39.4	1♍35.2	3 42.9	14 38.6	10 58.6	10 2.3	11 1.6	3 22.0	10 34.3	15 38.3
21 T	16 1 52.1	29 9.6	20 36.3	13 48.2	5 16.4	15 32.8	11 39.3	9 57.8	11 7.4	3 25.2	10 36.1	15 40.7
22 W	16 5 48.7	0♐10.2	20 33.1	25 48.8	6 49.7	16 26.4	12 20.1	9 53.1	11 13.3	3 28.3	10 37.9	15 43.0
23 T	16 9 45.2	1 10.8	20 29.9	7♎41.8	8 22.9	17 19.4	13 0.9	9 48.3	11 19.3	3 31.5	10 39.8	15 45.4
24 F	16 13 41.8	2 11.5	20 26.7	19 31.7	9 55.9	18 11.7	13 41.8	9 43.3	11 25.3	3 34.7	10 41.6	15 47.8
25 S	16 17 38.3	3 12.2	20 23.6	1♏21.9	11 28.7	19 3.3	14 22.6	9 38.1	11 31.3	3 37.9	10 43.5	15 50.1
26 S	16 21 34.9	4 12.9	20 20.4	13 15.3	13 1.5	19 54.2	15 3.6	9 32.8	11 37.4	3 41.1	10 45.4	15 52.4
27 M	16 25 31.5	5 13.7	20 17.2	25 13.6	14 34.0	20 44.3	15 44.5	9 27.3	11 43.6	3 44.4	10 47.3	15 54.8
28 T	16 29 28.0	6 14.5	20 14.0	7♐18.2	16 6.5	21 33.7	16 25.5	9 21.6	11 49.8	3 47.7	10 49.3	15 57.1
29 W	16 33 24.6	7 15.2	20 10.9	19 30.1	17 38.8	22 22.2	17 6.6	9 15.8	11 56.0	3 51.0	10 51.2	15 59.4
30 T	16 37 21.1	8 16.1	20 7.7	1♑49.9	19 11.0	23 9.9	17 47.6	9 9.8	12 2.3	3 54.3	10 53.2	16 1.7

DECLINATION at NOON

DAY	EPHEMERIS SIDEREAL TIME	☉	☊	☽	☿	♀	♂	♃	♄	♅	♆	♇
1 W	14 43 1.0	14S30.9	14S17.2	26S42.5	11S37.6	26S46.9	10S19.4	22N45.7	22S43.7	23S41.2	22S11.5	1S48.2
4 S	14 54 50.6	15 27.3	14 20.2	25 10.6	13 34.3	26 54.5	11 3.3	22 46.2	22 43.0	23 41.0	22 11.3	1 50.4
7 T	15 6 40.3	16 21.4	14 23.3	12 21.7	15 25.0	26 56.5	11 46.5	22 46.9	22 42.3	23 40.8	22 11.0	1 52.5
10 F	15 18 30.0	17 13.1	14 26.4	7N 1.5	17 8.8	26 52.9	12 29.1	22 47.7	22 41.4	23 40.7	22 10.8	1 54.6
13 M	15 30 19.7	18 2.0	14 29.4	23 47.2	18 44.9	26 43.9	13 11.0	22 48.6	22 40.5	23 40.5	22 10.5	1 56.6
16 T	15 42 9.3	18 48.2	14 32.4	26 28.2	20 12.6	26 29.7	13 52.0	22 49.7	22 39.5	23 40.3	22 10.2	1 58.5
19 S	15 53 59.0	19 31.3	14 35.5	15 13.7	21 31.4	26 10.6	14 32.2	22 50.9	22 38.4	23 40.0	22 9.9	2 0.3
22 W	16 5 48.7	20 11.3	14 38.5	1S 0.6	22 40.6	25 46.9	15 11.5	22 52.3	22 37.2	23 39.8	22 9.5	2 2.0
25 S	16 17 38.3	20 48.0	14 41.5	16 23.6	23 39.5	25 19.0	15 49.9	22 53.7	22 36.0	23 39.5	22 9.2	2 3.6
28 T	16 29 28.0	21 21.2	14 44.5	26 13.8	24 27.7	24 47.1	16 27.2	22 55.2	22 34.6	23 39.3	22 8.8	2 5.1

DECEMBER 1989

LONGITUDE at NOON

DAY	EPHEMERIS SIDEREAL TIME	☉	☊	☽	☿	♀	♂	♃	♄	♅	♆	♇
1 F	16 41 17.7	9♐16.9	20♒ 4.5	14♑18.7	20♐43.1	23♑56.7	18♏28.8	9♋ 3.8	12♑ 8.7	3♑57.7	10♑55.2	16♏ 4.0
2 S	16 45 14.2	10 17.8	20 1.3	26 57.6	22 14.9	24 42.6	19 9.9	8R57.5	12 15.0	4 1.1	10 57.2	16 6.3
3 S	16 49 10.8	11 18.6	19 58.2	9♒48.6	23 46.6	25 27.5	19 51.1	8 51.1	12 21.4	4 4.5	10 59.3	16 8.5
4 M	16 53 7.4	12 19.5	19 55.0	22 54.0	25 18.2	26 11.4	20 32.3	8 44.6	12 27.9	4 7.9	11 1.3	16 10.8
5 T	16 57 3.9	13 20.4	19 51.8	6♓16.4	26 49.4	26 54.2	21 13.5	8 37.9	12 34.4	4 11.3	11 3.4	16 13.0
6 W	17 1 0.5	14 21.3	19 48.6	19 58.1	28 20.5	27 35.9	21 54.8	8 31.1	12 40.9	4 14.8	11 5.4	16 15.2
7 T	17 4 57.0	15 22.2	19 45.4	4♈ 0.7	29 51.2	28 16.5	22 36.1	8 24.2	12 47.5	4 18.2	11 7.5	16 17.4
8 F	17 8 53.6	16 23.2	19 42.3	18 23.8	1♑21.5	28 55.9	23 17.4	8 17.2	12 54.0	4 21.7	11 9.6	16 19.6
9 S	17 12 50.2	17 24.1	19 39.1	3♉ 5.0	2 51.5	29 34.0	23 58.8	8 10.1	13 0.7	4 25.2	11 11.7	16 21.7
10 S	17 16 46.7	18 25.1	19 35.9	17 58.8	4 20.9	0♒10.8	24 40.2	8 2.9	13 7.3	4 28.7	11 13.8	16 23.9
11 M	17 20 43.3	19 26.0	19 32.7	2♊57.3	5 49.7	0 46.2	25 21.6	7 55.5	13 14.0	4 32.2	11 16.0	16 26.0
12 T	17 24 39.8	20 27.0	19 29.6	17 51.3	7 17.7	1 20.3	26 3.1	7 48.1	13 20.7	4 35.7	11 18.1	16 28.1
13 W	17 28 36.4	21 28.0	19 26.4	2♋31.6	8 44.9	1 52.9	26 44.6	7 40.6	13 27.5	4 39.2	11 20.3	16 30.2
14 T	17 32 32.9	22 29.0	19 23.2	16 50.8	10 11.1	2 23.9	27 26.2	7 33.0	13 34.3	4 42.8	11 22.5	16 32.2
15 F	17 36 29.5	23 30.0	19 20.0	0♌44.3	11 36.1	2 53.4	28 7.8	7 25.4	13 41.1	4 46.3	11 24.6	16 34.3
16 S	17 40 26.1	24 31.0	19 16.9	14 10.3	12 59.6	3 21.2	28 49.4	7 17.6	13 47.9	4 49.9	11 26.8	16 36.3
17 S	17 44 22.6	25 32.1	19 13.7	27 9.9	14 21.4	3 47.3	29 31.1	7 9.8	13 54.7	4 53.4	11 29.0	16 38.3
18 M	17 48 19.2	26 33.1	19 10.5	9♍46.2	15 41.2	4 11.7	0♐12.8	7 1.9	14 1.6	4 57.0	11 31.2	16 40.3
19 T	17 52 15.7	27 34.2	19 7.3	22 3.4	16 58.7	4 34.2	0 54.5	6 54.0	14 8.5	5 0.6	11 33.4	16 42.3
20 W	17 56 12.3	28 35.3	19 4.2	4♎ 6.7	18 13.4	4 54.8	1 36.3	6 46.0	14 15.5	5 4.2	11 35.7	16 44.2
21 T	18 0 8.9	29 36.4	19 1.0	16 1.3	19 24.8	5 13.5	2 18.1	6 38.0	14 22.4	5 7.8	11 37.9	16 46.2
22 F	18 4 5.4	0♑37.6	18 57.8	27 52.1	20 32.6	5 30.3	2 60.0	6 30.0	14 29.4	5 11.4	11 40.2	16 48.1
23 S	18 8 2.0	1 38.7	18 54.6	9♏43.5	21 35.9	5 44.9	3 41.9	6 21.9	14 36.4	5 15.0	11 42.4	16 50.0
24 S	18 11 58.5	2 39.8	18 51.4	21 39.5	22 34.2	5 57.3	4 23.8	6 13.8	14 43.4	5 18.6	11 44.7	16 51.8
25 M	18 15 55.1	3 41.0	18 48.3	3♐43.0	23 26.7	6 7.6	5 5.8	6 5.6	14 50.4	5 22.3	11 46.9	16 53.7
26 T	18 19 51.7	4 42.1	18 45.1	15 56.2	24 12.6	6 15.6	5 47.8	5 57.5	14 57.4	5 25.9	11 49.2	16 55.5
27 W	18 23 48.2	5 43.3	18 41.9	28 20.3	24 51.0	6 21.2	6 29.8	5 49.3	15 4.5	5 29.5	11 51.4	16 57.3
28 T	18 27 44.8	6 44.4	18 38.7	10♑56.0	25 21.0	6 24.6	7 11.9	5 41.2	15 11.5	5 33.1	11 53.7	16 59.0
29 F	18 31 41.3	7 45.6	18 35.6	23 43.5	25 41.8	6 25.4	7 54.0	5 33.0	15 18.6	5 36.7	11 56.0	17 0.7
30 S	18 35 37.9	8 46.8	18 32.4	6♒42.6	25 52.4	6R23.9	8 36.1	5 24.9	15 25.7	5 40.3	11 58.2	17 2.4
31 S	18 39 34.4	9 48.0	18 29.2	19 53.2	25R52.1	6 19.8	9 18.3	5 16.8	15 32.8	5 43.9	12 0.5	17 4.1

DECLINATION at NOON

DAY	EPHEMERIS SIDEREAL TIME	☉	☊	☽	☿	♀	♂	♃	♄	♅	♆	♇
1 F	16 41 17.7	21S50.7	14S47.6	25S31.2	25S 4.5	24S11.7	17S 3.4	22N56.8	22S33.2	23S39.0	22S 8.4	2S 6.6
4 M	16 53 7.4	22 16.5	14 50.6	13 32.2	25 29.2	23 33.4	17 38.5	22 58.4	22 31.7	23 38.7	22 8.0	2 7.9
7 T	17 4 57.0	22 38.3	14 53.5	4N54.4	25 41.3	22 52.5	18 12.3	23 0.1	22 30.1	23 38.3	22 7.5	2 9.1
10 S	17 16 46.7	22 56.2	14 56.5	22 2.8	25 40.4	22 9.7	18 44.9	23 1.8	22 28.5	23 38.0	22 7.0	2 10.2
13 W	17 28 36.4	23 10.0	14 59.5	27 2.5	25 26.4	21 25.5	19 16.1	23 3.5	22 26.7	23 37.7	22 6.6	2 11.2
16 S	17 40 26.1	23 19.7	15 2.5	16 53.3	24 59.3	20 40.5	19 46.0	23 5.2	22 24.9	23 37.3	22 6.1	2 12.1
19 T	17 52 15.7	23 25.2	15 5.5	0 29.5	24 20.0	19 55.3	20 14.4	23 6.9	22 23.0	23 36.9	22 5.5	2 12.8
22 F	18 4 5.4	23 26.4	15 8.4	15S13.1	23 30.3	19 10.5	20 41.2	23 8.5	22 21.0	23 36.5	22 5.0	2 13.5
25 M	18 15 55.1	23 23.4	15 11.4	25 43.7	22 33.3	18 26.8	21 6.6	23 10.1	22 18.9	23 36.1	22 4.5	2 14.1
28 T	18 27 44.8	23 16.2	15 14.4	26 1.2	21 34.1	17 44.8	21 30.2	23 11.6	22 16.8	23 35.7	22 3.9	2 14.5
31 S	18 39 34.4	23 4.8	15 17.3	14 35.4	20 39.4	17 5.2	21 52.2	23 13.0	22 14.6	23 35.2	22 3.3	2 14.8

JANUARY 1990

DAY	EPHEMERIS SIDEREAL TIME h m s	☉ ° '	☊ ° '	☽ ° '	☿ ° '	♀ ° '	♂ ° '	♃ ° '	♄ ° '	♅ ° '	♆ ° '	♇ ° '
						LONGITUDE at NOON						
1 M	18 43 31.0	10♑49.1	18♒26.0	3♓15.5	25♑40.3	6♒13.3	10♐ 0.5	5♋ 8.7	15♑39.9	5♑47.5	12♑ 2.8	17♏ 5.8
2 T	18 47 27.6	11 50.3	18 22.9	16 49.7	25R16.6	6R 4.2	10 42.7	5R 0.6	15 47.0	5 51.1	12 5.1	17 7.4
3 W	18 51 24.1	12 51.4	18 19.7	0♈36.3	24 41.1	5 52.6	11 25.0	4 52.6	15 54.1	5 54.7	12 7.3	17 9.0
4 T	18 55 20.7	13 52.6	18 16.5	14 35.1	23 54.2	5 38.5	12 7.3	4 44.7	16 1.2	5 58.3	12 9.6	17 10.5
5 F	18 59 17.2	14 53.8	18 13.3	28 45.7	22 57.0	5 21.9	12 49.7	4 36.8	16 8.3	6 1.9	12 11.9	17 12.1
6 S	19 3 13.8	15 54.9	18 10.2	13♉ 6.3	21 50.7	5 2.9	13 32.1	4 28.9	16 15.4	6 5.4	12 14.2	17 13.6
7 S	19 7 10.4	16 56.1	18 7.0	27 33.6	20 37.4	4 41.5	14 14.5	4 21.1	16 22.5	6 9.0	12 16.4	17 15.1
8 M	19 11 6.9	17 57.2	18 3.8	12♊ 3.0	19 19.3	4 17.9	14 56.9	4 13.4	16 29.6	6 12.6	12 18.7	17 16.5
9 T	19 15 3.5	18 58.3	18 0.6	26 29.0	17 59.1	3 52.1	15 39.4	4 5.8	16 36.7	6 16.1	12 21.0	17 17.9
10 W	19 19 0.0	19 59.4	17 57.5	10♋45.6	16 39.3	3 24.3	16 21.9	3 58.2	16 43.8	6 19.6	12 23.2	17 19.3
11 T	19 22 56.6	21 0.5	17 54.3	24 47.3	15 22.3	2 54.6	17 4.4	3 50.7	16 50.9	6 23.2	12 25.5	17 20.7
12 F	19 26 53.1	22 1.7	17 51.1	8♌29.9	14 10.4	2 23.3	17 47.0	3 43.3	16 58.0	6 26.7	12 27.7	17 22.0
13 S	19 30 49.7	23 2.8	17 47.9	21 51.2	13 5.3	1 50.4	18 29.7	3 36.0	17 5.1	6 30.2	12 30.0	17 23.3
14 S	19 34 46.3	24 3.9	17 44.7	4♍50.7	12 8.4	1 16.3	19 12.3	3 28.8	17 12.2	6 33.7	12 32.2	17 24.6
15 M	19 38 42.8	25 5.0	17 41.6	17 29.5	11 20.5	0 41.1	19 55.0	3 21.7	17 19.3	6 37.1	12 34.4	17 25.8
16 T	19 42 39.4	26 6.0	17 38.4	29 50.6	10 42.1	0 5.0	20 37.7	3 14.8	17 26.3	6 40.6	12 36.6	17 27.0
17 W	19 46 35.9	27 7.1	17 35.2	11♎57.6	10 13.3	29♑28.5	21 20.5	3 7.9	17 33.4	6 44.0	12 38.9	17 28.1
18 T	19 50 32.5	28 8.2	17 32.0	23 55.0	9 53.9	28 51.6	22 3.3	3 1.2	17 40.4	6 47.5	12 41.1	17 29.3
19 F	19 54 29.1	29 9.3	17 28.9	5♏47.6	9 43.7	28 14.6	22 46.2	2 54.5	17 47.4	6 50.9	12 43.3	17 30.4
20 S	19 58 25.6	0♒10.4	17 25.7	17 40.3	9 42.2	27 37.9	23 29.0	2 48.1	17 54.5	6 54.3	12 45.5	17 31.4
21 S	20 2 22.2	1 11.4	17 22.5	29 37.6	9D48.7	27 1.6	24 12.0	2 41.7	18 1.5	6 57.7	12 47.7	17 32.5
22 M	20 6 18.7	2 12.5	17 19.3	11♐43.7	10 2.7	26 26.0	24 55.0	2 35.5	18 8.5	7 1.1	12 49.9	17 33.5
23 T	20 10 15.3	3 13.6	17 16.2	24 2.0	10 23.6	25 51.4	25 37.9	2 29.5	18 15.4	7 4.4	12 52.0	17 34.5
24 W	20 14 11.8	4 14.6	17 13.0	6♑35.1	10 50.7	25 17.9	26 21.0	2 23.6	18 22.4	7 7.7	12 54.2	17 35.4
25 T	20 18 8.4	5 15.7	17 9.8	19 24.6	11 23.6	24 45.9	27 4.0	2 17.8	18 29.3	7 11.0	12 56.3	17 36.3
26 F	20 22 5.0	6 16.7	17 6.6	2♒30.9	12 1.7	24 15.3	27 47.1	2 12.2	18 36.2	7 14.3	12 58.5	17 37.2
27 S	20 26 1.5	7 17.7	17 3.4	15 53.4	12 44.4	23 46.6	28 30.2	2 6.7	18 43.1	7 17.5	13 0.6	17 38.0
28 S	20 29 58.1	8 18.7	17 0.3	29 30.5	13 31.5	23 19.7	29 13.4	2 1.4	18 49.9	7 20.8	13 2.7	17 38.8
29 M	20 33 54.6	9 19.6	16 57.1	13♓19.9	14 22.4	22 54.9	29 56.6	1 56.3	18 56.8	7 24.0	13 4.8	17 39.5
30 T	20 37 51.2	10 20.6	16 53.9	27 18.9	15 16.8	22 32.2	0♑39.8	1 51.4	19 3.6	7 27.1	13 6.9	17 40.3
31 W	20 41 47.7	11 21.5	16 50.7	11♈24.9	16 14.4	22 11.8	1 23.0	1 46.6	19 10.4	7 30.3	13 8.9	17 40.9
						DECLINATION at NOON						
1 M	18 43 31.0	23S 0.1	15S 18.3	8S 56.4	20S 23.4	16S 52.6	21S 59.1	23N 13.5	22S 13.9	23S 35.1	22S 3.1	2S 14.9
4 T	18 55 20.7	22 43.1	15 21.2	9N 48.3	19 45.4	16 17.2	22 18.8	23 14.8	22 11.6	23 34.7	22 2.5	2 15.0
7 S	19 7 10.4	22 22.2	15 24.1	24 35.7	19 24.1	15 45.7	22 36.7	23 16.1	22 9.3	23 34.2	22 2.0	2 15.1
10 W	19 19 0.0	21 57.2	15 27.1	26 3.5	19 18.5	15 18.4	22 52.7	23 17.3	22 6.9	23 33.8	22 1.4	2 15.0
13 S	19 30 49.7	21 28.4	15 30.0	13 45.8	19 25.8	14 55.8	23 6.8	23 18.4	22 4.4	23 33.3	22 0.8	2 14.9
16 T	19 42 39.4	20 55.9	15 32.9	3S 14.7	19 42.6	14 38.1	23 18.9	23 19.4	22 1.9	23 32.8	22 0.2	2 14.6
19 F	19 54 29.1	20 19.8	15 35.8	18 19.2	20 5.7	14 25.2	23 29.1	23 20.3	21 59.4	23 32.3	21 59.6	2 14.2
22 M	20 6 18.7	19 40.2	15 38.7	26 54.8	20 31.1	14 17.2	23 37.2	23 21.1	21 56.8	23 31.8	21 58.9	2 13.6
25 T	20 18 8.4	18 57.4	15 41.6	24 24.9	20 55.3	14 13.6	23 43.3	23 21.9	21 54.2	23 31.3	21 58.3	2 13.0
28 S	20 29 58.1	18 11.4	15 44.5	10 31.6	21 15.0	14 14.1	23 47.3	23 22.6	21 51.5	23 30.9	21 57.7	2 12.3
31 W	20 41 47.7	17 22.4	15 47.4	8N 29.8	21 28.2	14 18.2	23 49.3	23 23.2	21 48.9	23 30.4	21 57.1	2 11.5

FEBRUARY 1990

DAY	EPHEMERIS SIDEREAL TIME h m s	☉ ° '	☊ ° '	☽ ° '	☿ ° '	♀ ° '	♂ ° '	♃ ° '	♄ ° '	♅ ° '	♆ ° '	♇ ° '
						LONGITUDE at NOON						
1 T	20 45 44.3	12♒22.4	16♒47.6	25♈35.0	17♑14.9	21♑53.6	2♑ 6.3	1♋42.0	19♑17.1	7♑63.4	13♑11.0	17♏41.6
2 F	20 49 40.8	13 23.3	16 44.4	9♉46.9	18 18.0	21R37.9	2 49.6	1R37.5	19 23.8	7 36.5	13 13.0	17 42.2
3 S	20 53 37.4	14 24.2	16 41.2	23 58.2	19 23.6	21 24.6	3 32.9	1 33.3	19 30.5	7 39.6	13 15.0	17 42.8
4 S	20 57 34.0	15 25.0	16 38.0	8♊ 6.6	20 31.4	21 13.8	4 16.3	1 29.2	19 37.2	7 42.6	13 17.0	17 43.3
5 M	21 1 30.5	16 25.8	16 34.9	22 10.0	21 41.3	21 5.4	4 59.7	1 25.4	19 43.8	7 45.7	13 19.0	17 43.8
6 T	21 5 27.1	17 26.6	16 31.7	6♋ 6.0	22 53.0	20 59.6	5 43.1	1 21.7	19 50.4	7 48.6	13 21.0	17 44.3
7 W	21 9 23.6	18 27.4	16 28.5	19 52.3	24 6.6	20 56.2	6 26.6	1 18.2	19 56.9	7 51.6	13 22.9	17 44.7
8 T	21 13 20.2	19 28.1	16 25.3	3♌26.7	25 21.7	20 55.2	7 10.1	1 14.8	20 3.4	7 54.5	13 24.8	17 45.1
9 F	21 17 16.7	20 28.9	16 22.1	16 47.2	26 38.5	20D56.7	7 53.6	1 11.7	20 9.9	7 57.4	13 26.7	17 45.5
10 S	21 21 13.3	21 29.6	16 19.0	29 52.4	27 56.6	21 0.6	8 37.1	1 8.8	20 16.4	8 0.3	13 28.6	17 45.8
11 S	21 25 9.9	22 30.2	16 15.8	12♍41.9	29 16.2	21 6.8	9 20.7	1 6.0	20 22.8	8 3.1	13 30.5	17 46.1
12 M	21 29 6.4	23 30.9	16 12.6	25 15.8	0♒37.1	21 15.4	10 4.4	1 3.5	20 29.2	8 6.0	13 32.4	17 46.4
13 T	21 33 3.0	24 31.6	16 9.4	7♎35.5	1 59.1	21 26.1	10 48.1	1 1.2	20 35.5	8 8.7	13 34.2	17 46.6
14 W	21 36 59.5	25 32.2	16 6.3	19 43.1	3 22.4	21 39.1	11 31.7	0 59.0	20 41.8	8 11.4	13 36.1	17 46.8
15 T	21 40 56.1	26 32.8	16 3.1	1♏41.8	4 46.9	21 54.1	12 15.5	0 57.1	20 48.0	8 14.1	13 37.8	17 46.9
16 F	21 44 52.6	27 33.4	15 59.9	13 35.3	6 12.4	22 11.2	12 59.2	0 55.3	20 54.2	8 16.8	13 39.6	17 47.0
17 S	21 48 49.2	28 33.9	15 56.7	25 28.1	7 39.0	22 30.3	13 43.0	0 53.8	21 0.3	8 19.4	13 41.4	17 47.1
18 S	21 52 45.7	29 34.5	15 53.6	7♐24.6	9 6.7	22 51.3	14 26.8	0 52.4	21 6.4	8 22.0	13 43.1	17 47.2
19 M	21 56 42.3	0♓35.0	15 50.4	19 29.8	10 35.5	23 14.2	15 10.7	0 51.2	21 12.5	8 24.6	13 44.8	17R47.1
20 T	22 0 38.8	1 35.5	15 47.2	1♑48.1	12 5.2	23 38.9	15 54.6	0 50.3	21 18.5	8 27.1	13 46.5	17 47.1
21 W	22 4 35.4	2 35.9	15 44.0	14 23.6	13 36.0	24 5.3	16 38.5	0 49.5	21 24.4	8 29.6	13 48.1	17 47.0
22 T	22 8 32.0	3 36.4	15 40.8	27 19.3	15 7.7	24 33.3	17 22.4	0 49.0	21 30.3	8 32.0	13 49.7	17 46.9
23 F	22 12 28.5	4 36.8	15 37.7	10♒37.3	16 40.5	25 2.9	18 6.4	0 48.6	21 36.1	8 34.4	13 51.4	17 46.8
24 S	22 16 25.1	5 37.2	15 34.5	24 17.6	18 14.2	25 34.1	18 50.4	0 48.4	21 41.9	8 36.7	13 52.9	17 46.6
25 S	22 20 21.6	6 37.6	15 31.3	8♓18.4	19 49.0	26 6.7	19 34.4	0D48.5	21 47.7	8 39.1	13 54.5	17 46.4
26 M	22 24 18.2	7 37.9	15 28.1	22 36.1	21 24.7	26 40.7	20 18.4	0 48.7	21 53.3	8 41.3	13 56.0	17 46.1
27 T	22 28 14.7	8 38.2	15 25.0	7♈ 5.3	23 1.4	27 16.1	21 2.5	0 49.2	21 59.0	8 43.6	13 57.5	17 45.9
28 W	22 32 11.3	9 38.5	15 21.8	21 39.8	24 39.2	27 52.7	21 46.6	0 49.8	22 4.5	8 45.7	13 59.0	17 45.5
						DECLINATION at NOON						
1 T	20 45 44.3	17S 5.5	15S 48.3	14N 29.1	21S 30.8	14S 20.2	23S 49.5	23N 23.4	21S 48.0	23S 30.2	21S 56.9	2S 11.2
4 S	20 57 34.0	16 12.9	15 51.2	26 30.7	21 32.5	14 28.0	23 48.6	23 24.0	21 45.3	23 29.7	21 56.3	2 10.2
7 W	21 9 23.6	15 17.9	15 54.1	24 19.1	21 24.5	14 37.6	23 45.6	23 24.5	21 42.6	23 29.2	21 55.7	2 9.2
10 S	21 21 13.3	14 20.5	15 56.9	10 22.2	21 6.0	14 48.3	23 40.5	23 25.0	21 40.0	23 28.8	21 55.1	2 8.1
13 T	21 33 3.0	13 20.9	15 59.8	6S 47.3	20 36.5	14 59.3	23 33.2	23 25.5	21 37.3	23 28.3	21 54.5	2 6.9
16 F	21 44 52.6	12 19.4	16 2.6	20 56.2	19 55.7	15 9.7	23 23.8	23 25.9	21 34.6	23 27.9	21 53.9	2 5.6
19 M	21 56 42.3	11 16.1	16 5.4	27 26.0	19 3.3	15 19.0	23 12.3	23 26.4	21 32.0	23 27.5	21 53.4	2 4.2
22 T	22 8 32.0	10 11.2	16 8.3	22 23.7	17 59.3	15 26.4	22 58.8	23 26.8	21 29.4	23 27.0	21 52.8	2 2.8
25 S	22 20 21.6	9 4.9	16 11.1	6 38.5	16 43.6	15 31.5	22 43.1	23 27.1	21 26.8	23 26.6	21 52.3	2 1.3
28 W	22 32 11.3	7 57.3	16 13.9	12N 51.1	15 16.2	15 33.8	22 25.4	23 27.5	21 24.3	23 26.3	21 51.8	1 59.7

MARCH 1990

DAY	EPHEMERIS SIDEREAL TIME	☉	☊	☽	☿	♀	♂	♃	♄	♅	♆	♇
	h m s	° ′	° ′	° ′	° ′	° ′	° ′	° ′	° ′	° ′	° ′	° ′
LONGITUDE at NOON												
1 T	22 36 7.8	10♓38.8	15♒18.6	6♉13.3	26♒17.9	28♑30.7	22♑30.7	0♋50.7	22♑10.0	8♑47.9	14♑ 0.5	17♏45.2
2 F	22 40 4.4	11 39.0	15 15.4	20 40.4	27 57.7	29 9.8	23 14.8	0 51.7	22 15.5	8 50.0	14 1.9	17R44.8
3 S	22 44 0.9	12 39.2	15 12.2	4♊57.0	29 38.5	29 50.0	23 59.0	0 53.0	22 20.9	8 52.1	14 3.3	17 44.4
4 S	22 47 57.5	13 39.3	15 9.1	19 0.4	1♓20.4	0♒31.4	24 43.2	0 54.4	22 26.2	8 54.1	14 4.6	17 43.9
5 M	22 51 54.1	14 39.5	15 5.9	2♋49.7	3 3.4	1 13.9	25 27.4	0 56.1	22 31.5	8 56.1	14 6.0	17 43.5
6 T	22 55 50.6	15 39.5	15 2.7	16 24.7	4 47.4	1 57.3	26 11.7	0 57.9	22 36.7	8 58.0	14 7.4	17 43.0
7 W	22 59 47.2	16 39.6	14 59.5	29 46.0	6 32.5	2 41.7	26 55.9	0 59.9	22 41.8	8 59.9	14 8.6	17 42.4
8 T	23 3 43.7	17 39.6	14 56.4	12♌54.3	8 18.7	3 27.1	27 40.2	1 2.1	22 46.9	9 1.7	14 9.9	17 41.8
9 F	23 7 40.3	18 39.5	14 53.2	25 50.4	10 6.0	4 13.4	28 24.5	1 4.5	22 51.9	9 3.5	14 11.1	17 41.2
10 S	23 11 36.8	19 39.5	14 50.0	8♍34.8	11 54.5	5 0.5	29 8.9	1 7.1	22 56.8	9 5.3	14 12.3	17 40.5
11 S	23 15 33.4	20 39.4	14 46.8	21 8.0	13 44.1	5 48.5	29 53.2	1 9.9	23 1.6	9 7.0	14 13.5	17 39.9
12 M	23 19 29.9	21 39.2	14 43.6	3♎30.5	15 34.8	6 37.3	0♒37.6	1 12.8	23 6.4	9 8.6	14 14.6	17 39.1
13 T	23 23 26.5	22 39.1	14 40.5	15 43.2	17 26.7	7 26.9	1 22.0	1 16.0	23 11.2	9 10.2	14 15.7	17 38.4
14 W	23 27 23.0	23 38.9	14 37.3	27 47.1	19 19.7	8 17.3	2 6.4	1 19.3	23 15.8	9 11.8	14 16.8	17 37.6
15 T	23 31 19.6	24 38.7	14 34.1	9♏44.3	21 13.9	9 8.3	2 50.9	1 22.8	23 20.4	9 13.3	14 17.9	17 36.8
16 F	23 35 16.1	25 38.4	14 30.9	21 37.3	23 9.1	10 0.1	3 35.4	1 26.5	23 24.9	9 14.8	14 18.9	17 36.0
17 S	23 39 12.7	26 38.1	14 27.8	3♐29.3	25 5.4	10 52.5	4 19.9	1 30.4	23 29.3	9 16.2	14 19.9	17 35.1
18 S	23 43 9.2	27 37.8	14 24.6	15 24.3	27 2.7	11 45.6	5 4.4	1 34.4	23 33.7	9 17.5	14 20.8	17 34.2
19 M	23 47 5.8	28 37.5	14 21.4	27 26.8	29 1.0	12 39.2	5 48.9	1 38.6	23 37.9	9 18.9	14 21.8	17 33.3
20 T	23 51 2.4	29 37.1	14 18.2	9♑41.8	1♈ 0.1	13 33.5	6 33.5	1 43.0	23 42.1	9 20.1	14 22.7	17 32.3
21 W	23 54 58.9	0♈36.7	14 15.0	22 14.1	3 0.0	14 28.4	7 18.1	1 47.6	23 46.3	9 21.3	14 23.5	17 31.3
22 T	23 58 55.5	1 36.3	14 11.9	5♒ 8.1	5 0.6	15 23.7	8 2.7	1 52.3	23 50.3	9 22.5	14 24.4	17 30.3
23 F	0 2 52.0	2 35.8	14 8.7	18 27.5	7 1.7	16 19.7	8 47.3	1 57.3	23 54.3	9 23.6	14 25.2	17 29.3
24 S	0 6 48.6	3 35.3	14 5.5	2♓14.1	9 3.1	17 16.1	9 32.0	2 2.3	23 58.2	9 24.7	14 25.9	17 28.2
25 S	0 10 45.1	4 34.8	14 2.3	16 27.3	11 4.6	18 13.0	10 16.6	2 7.6	24 2.0	9 25.7	14 26.7	17 27.1
26 M	0 14 41.7	5 34.3	13 59.2	1♈ 3.8	13 6.0	19 10.4	11 1.3	2 13.0	24 5.7	9 26.7	14 27.4	17 26.1
27 T	0 18 38.2	6 33.7	13 56.0	15 56.9	15 7.0	20 8.2	11 46.0	2 18.6	24 9.4	9 27.6	14 28.1	17 24.9
28 W	0 22 34.8	7 33.1	13 52.8	0♉58.2	17 7.4	21 6.4	12 30.7	2 24.4	24 12.9	9 28.5	14 28.7	17 23.7
29 T	0 26 31.3	8 32.5	13 49.6	15 57.9	19 6.6	22 5.0	13 15.4	2 30.2	24 16.4	9 29.3	14 29.3	17 22.5
30 F	0 30 27.9	9 31.8	13 46.4	0♊47.3	21 4.5	23 4.1	14 0.1	2 36.3	24 19.8	9 30.1	14 29.9	17 21.3
31 S	0 34 24.4	10 31.0	13 43.3	15 19.5	23 0.6	24 3.5	14 44.9	2 42.5	24 23.1	9 30.8	14 30.4	17 20.1
DECLINATION at NOON												
1 T	22 36 7.8	7S34.6	16S14.8	18N27.1	14S44.4	15S33.8	22S19.0	23N27.6	21S23.5	23S26.1	21S51.6	1S59.2
4 S	22 47 57.5	6 25.7	16 17.6	27 22.3	13 1.4	15 31.8	21 58.6	23 28.0	21 21.0	23 25.8	21 51.1	1 57.6
7 W	22 59 47.2	5 16.0	16 20.4	21 39.4	11 6.7	15 26.3	21 36.3	23 28.3	21 18.6	23 25.5	21 50.7	1 55.9
10 S	23 11 36.8	4 5.7	16 23.2	6 31.2	9 0.7	15 16.8	21 12.0	23 28.6	21 16.3	23 25.2	21 50.2	1 54.2
13 T	23 23 26.5	2 55.0	16 26.0	10S18.2	6 43.6	15 3.3	20 45.8	23 28.8	21 14.1	23 24.9	21 49.8	1 52.4
16 F	23 35 16.1	1 44.0	16 28.8	23 7.2	4 16.0	14 45.6	20 17.8	23 29.0	21 11.9	23 24.7	21 49.4	1 50.7
19 M	23 47 5.8	0 32.8	16 31.6	27 15.8	1 39.0	14 23.7	19 48.0	23 29.2	21 9.9	23 24.4	21 49.1	1 48.9
22 T	23 58 55.5	0N38.3	16 34.3	19 53.6	1N 5.6	13 57.4	19 16.4	23 29.4	21 7.9	23 24.2	21 48.8	1 47.1
25 S	0 10 45.1	1 49.2	16 37.1	2 54.8	3 54.9	13 26.9	18 43.2	23 29.4	21 6.1	23 24.1	21 48.5	1 45.3
28 W	0 22 34.8	2 59.8	16 39.8	16N26.4	6 45.0	12 52.2	18 8.4	23 29.5	21 4.3	23 24.0	21 48.2	1 43.5
31 S	0 34 24.4	4 9.9	16 42.6	27 0.3	9 30.3	12 13.5	17 32.1	23 29.4	21 2.7	23 23.9	21 47.9	1 41.6

APRIL 1990

DAY	EPHEMERIS SIDEREAL TIME	☉	☊	☽	☿	♀	♂	♃	♄	♅	♆	♇
LONGITUDE at NOON												
1 S	0 38 21.0	11♈30.3	13♒40.1	29♊30.6	24♈54.6	25♒ 3.3	15♒29.6	2♋48.9	24♑26.3	9♑31.4	14♑30.9	17♏18.8
2 M	0 42 17.6	12 29.5	13 36.9	13♋19.3	26 46.0	26 3.4	16 14.4	2 55.4	24 29.4	9 32.0	14 31.4	17R17.5
3 T	0 46 14.1	13 28.6	13 33.7	26 46.4	28 34.5	27 3.9	16 59.1	3 2.1	24 32.4	9 32.6	14 31.8	17 16.2
4 W	0 50 10.7	14 27.7	13 30.6	9♌54.3	0♉19.6	28 4.7	17 43.9	3 8.9	24 35.4	9 33.1	14 32.3	17 14.9
5 T	0 54 7.2	15 26.8	13 27.4	22 45.7	2 1.1	29 5.8	18 28.7	3 15.8	24 38.2	9 33.5	14 32.6	17 13.5
6 F	0 58 3.8	16 25.8	13 24.2	5♍23.4	3 38.5	0♓ 7.3	19 13.4	3 22.9	24 41.0	9 33.9	14 33.0	17 12.2
7 S	1 2 0.3	17 24.8	13 21.0	17 50.0	5 11.5	1 9.1	19 58.2	3 30.2	24 43.7	9 34.3	14 33.3	17 10.8
8 S	1 5 56.9	18 23.8	13 17.8	0♎ 7.5	6 39.9	2 11.1	20 43.1	3 37.6	24 46.3	9 34.6	14 33.5	17 9.4
9 M	1 9 53.4	19 22.7	13 14.7	12 17.4	8 3.4	3 13.5	21 27.9	3 45.1	24 48.8	9 34.8	14 33.8	17 7.9
10 T	1 13 50.0	20 21.6	13 11.5	24 20.9	9 21.7	4 16.1	22 12.7	3 52.7	24 51.2	9 35.0	14 34.0	17 6.5
11 W	1 17 46.5	21 20.5	13 8.3	6♏19.2	10 34.7	5 19.0	22 57.5	4 0.5	24 53.5	9 35.2	14 34.2	17 5.0
12 T	1 21 43.1	22 19.3	13 5.1	18 13.6	11 42.1	6 22.2	23 42.4	4 8.4	24 55.7	9 35.2	14 34.3	17 3.6
13 F	1 25 39.6	23 18.1	13 2.0	0♐ 5.6	12 43.9	7 25.6	24 27.2	4 16.5	24 57.8	9 35.3	14 34.4	17 2.1
14 S	1 29 36.2	24 16.9	12 58.8	11 57.6	13 39.8	8 29.2	25 12.1	4 24.7	24 59.9	9 35.3	14 34.5	17 0.6
15 S	1 33 32.8	25 15.6	12 55.6	23 52.5	14 29.8	9 33.1	25 57.0	4 33.0	25 1.8	9R35.2	14 34.5	16 59.0
16 M	1 37 29.3	26 14.4	12 52.4	5♑54.1	15 13.9	10 37.3	26 41.9	4 41.5	25 3.7	9 35.1	14 34.6	16 57.5
17 T	1 41 25.9	27 13.1	12 49.2	18 6.6	15 51.8	11 41.7	27 26.7	4 50.0	25 5.4	9 35.0	14 34.6	16 56.0
18 W	1 45 22.4	28 11.7	12 46.1	0♒35.0	16 23.6	12 46.2	28 11.6	4 58.7	25 7.1	9 34.8	14R34.5	16 54.4
19 T	1 49 19.0	29 10.4	12 42.9	13 24.1	16 49.3	13 51.0	28 56.5	5 7.5	25 8.7	9 34.5	14 34.4	16 52.8
20 F	1 53 15.5	0♉ 9.0	12 39.7	26 38.4	17 8.8	14 56.0	29 41.4	5 16.4	25 10.1	9 34.2	14 34.3	16 51.3
21 S	1 57 12.1	1 7.5	12 36.5	10♓21.1	17 22.3	16 1.1	0♓26.3	5 25.5	25 11.5	9 33.8	14 34.1	16 49.7
22 S	2 1 8.6	2 6.1	12 33.4	24 33.5	17 29.8	17 6.5	1 11.1	5 34.6	25 12.7	9 33.4	14 33.9	16 48.0
23 M	2 5 5.2	3 4.6	12 30.2	9♈13.5	17 31.4	18 12.0	1 56.0	5 43.9	25 13.9	9 32.9	14 33.7	16 46.4
24 T	2 9 1.7	4 3.1	12 27.0	24 15.5	17R27.4	19 17.7	2 40.9	5 53.3	25 15.0	9 32.4	14 33.5	16 44.8
25 W	2 12 58.3	5 1.5	12 23.8	9♉30.6	17 17.9	20 23.6	3 25.7	6 2.7	25 16.0	9 31.8	14 33.2	16 43.1
26 T	2 16 54.9	5 60.0	12 20.7	24 47.7	17 3.3	21 29.6	4 10.6	6 12.3	25 16.8	9 31.2	14 32.9	16 41.5
27 F	2 20 51.4	6 58.4	12 17.5	9♊55.6	16 44.0	22 35.8	4 55.4	6 22.0	25 17.6	9 30.6	14 32.5	16 39.8
28 S	2 24 48.0	7 56.7	12 14.3	24 44.8	16 20.2	23 42.1	5 40.3	6 31.8	25 18.3	9 29.8	14 32.1	16 38.2
29 S	2 28 44.5	8 55.0	12 11.1	9♋ 9.2	15 52.6	24 48.6	6 25.1	6 41.8	25 18.9	9 29.1	14 31.7	16 36.5
30 M	2 32 41.1	9 53.3	12 7.9	23 6.4	15 21.7	25 55.2	7 9.9	6 51.8	25 19.3	9 28.3	14 31.3	16 34.8
DECLINATION at NOON												
1 S	0 38 21.0	4N33.1	16S43.5	27N 4.3	10N23.3	11S59.7	17S19.6	23N29.4	21S 2.2	23S23.9	21S47.9	1S41.0
4 W	0 50 10.7	5 42.1	16 46.2	18 11.3	12 52.8	11 15.7	16 41.4	23 29.2	21 0.8	23 23.8	21 47.7	1 39.2
7 S	1 2 0.3	6 50.3	16 48.9	2 15.3	15 3.8	10 28.0	16 1.7	23 29.0	20 59.5	23 23.8	21 47.5	1 37.5
10 T	1 13 50.0	7 57.4	16 51.6	13S50.2	16 58.2	9 36.7	15 20.8	23 28.6	20 58.3	23 23.8	21 47.4	1 35.7
13 F	1 25 39.6	9 3.3	16 54.3	24 53.0	18 15.4	8 42.0	14 38.6	23 28.2	20 57.3	23 23.9	21 47.3	1 34.0
16 M	1 37 29.3	10 7.8	16 57.0	26 22.5	19 12.2	7 44.2	13 55.2	23 27.6	20 56.4	23 23.9	21 47.2	1 32.4
19 T	1 49 19.0	11 10.9	16 59.7	16 47.1	19 41.8	6 43.4	13 10.8	23 26.9	20 55.7	23 24.1	21 47.1	1 30.7
22 S	2 1 8.6	12 12.3	17 2.4	0N53.9	19 44.3	5 40.0	12 25.3	23 26.1	20 55.1	23 24.2	21 47.1	1 29.2
25 W	2 12 58.3	13 11.9	17 5.1	19 23.7	19 20.2	4 34.3	11 38.9	23 25.1	20 54.7	23 24.4	21 47.2	1 27.6
28 S	2 24 48.0	14 9.6	17 7.8	27 2.1	18 31.8	3 26.4	10 51.7	23 24.0	20 54.5	23 24.6	21 47.2	1 26.2

MAY 1990

LONGITUDE at NOON

DAY	EPHEMERIS SIDEREAL TIME h m s	☉ ° ′	☊ ° ′	☽ ° ′	☿ ° ′	♀ ° ′	♂ ° ′	♃ ° ′	♄ ° ′	♅ ° ′	♆ ° ′	♇ ° ′
1 T	2 36 37.6	10♉51.6	12♒ 4.8	6♌36.6	14♉48.0	27♓ 2.0	7♓54.7	7♋ 1.9	25♑19.7	9♑27.4	14♑30.8	16♏33.2
2 W	2 40 34.2	11 49.8	12 1.6	19 42.6	14R12.2	28 8.9	8 39.5	7 12.1	25 20.0	9R26.5	14R30.3	16R31.5
3 T	2 44 30.7	12 48.0	11 58.4	2♍28.0	13 34.9	29 15.9	9 24.2	7 22.4	25 20.2	9 25.6	14 29.8	16 29.8
4 F	2 48 27.3	13 46.2	11 55.2	14 56.8	12 56.9	0♈23.0	10 9.0	7 32.8	25 20.3	9 24.6	14 29.2	16 28.1
5 S	2 52 23.8	14 44.3	11 52.1	27 13.0	12 18.8	1 30.3	10 53.7	7 43.3	25 20.3	9 23.5	14 28.6	16 26.4
6 S	2 56 20.4	15 42.4	11 48.9	9♎20.1	11 41.4	2 37.7	11 38.5	7 53.8	25R20.1	9 22.5	14 28.0	16 24.7
7 M	3 0 17.0	16 40.5	11 45.7	21 20.7	11 5.2	3 45.3	12 23.2	8 4.5	25 20.0	9 21.4	14 27.4	16 23.1
8 T	3 4 13.5	17 38.5	11 42.5	3♏17.0	10 30.8	4 52.9	13 7.9	8 15.3	25 19.7	9 20.2	14 26.7	16 21.4
9 W	3 8 10.1	18 36.5	11 39.3	15 10.8	9 58.9	6 0.6	13 52.6	8 26.1	25 19.3	9 19.0	14 26.0	16 19.7
10 T	3 12 6.6	19 34.5	11 36.2	27 3.4	9 29.8	7 8.5	14 37.3	8 37.1	25 18.8	9 17.7	14 25.2	16 18.0
11 F	3 16 3.2	20 32.5	11 33.0	8♐56.1	9 4.1	8 16.5	15 21.9	8 48.1	25 18.2	9 16.4	14 24.5	16 16.4
12 S	3 19 59.7	21 30.4	11 29.8	20 50.7	8 42.0	9 24.6	16 6.6	8 59.1	25 17.5	9 15.1	14 23.7	16 14.7
13 S	3 23 56.3	22 28.3	11 26.6	2♑49.2	8 24.0	10 32.7	16 51.2	9 10.3	25 16.7	9 13.7	14 22.9	16 13.0
14 M	3 27 52.9	23 26.2	11 23.5	14 54.2	8 10.1	11 41.0	17 35.8	9 21.5	25 15.8	9 12.3	14 22.0	16 11.3
15 T	3 31 49.4	24 24.0	11 20.3	27 9.2	8 0.7	12 49.4	18 20.3	9 32.8	25 14.9	9 10.8	14 21.1	16 9.7
16 W	3 35 46.0	25 21.9	11 17.1	9♒38.1	7 55.7	13 57.9	19 4.9	9 44.2	25 13.8	9 9.3	14 20.2	16 8.0
17 T	3 39 42.5	26 19.7	11 13.9	22 25.3	7 55.4	15 6.5	19 49.4	9 55.7	25 12.6	9 7.8	14 19.3	16 6.3
18 F	3 43 39.1	27 17.5	11 10.8	5♓34.9	7D59.6	16 15.2	20 33.9	10 7.2	25 11.4	9 6.2	14 18.3	16 4.7
19 S	3 47 35.6	28 15.3	11 7.6	19 10.6	8 8.4	17 23.9	21 18.4	10 18.8	25 10.0	9 4.6	14 17.4	16 3.1
20 S	3 51 32.2	29 13.0	11 4.4	3♈14.5	8 21.7	18 32.8	22 2.8	10 30.5	25 8.6	9 2.9	14 16.3	16 1.4
21 M	3 55 28.8	0♊10.8	11 1.2	17 45.9	8 39.5	19 41.7	22 47.2	10 42.3	25 7.1	9 1.2	14 15.3	15 59.8
22 T	3 59 25.3	1 8.5	10 58.0	2♉41.1	9 1.7	20 50.7	23 31.6	10 54.1	25 5.4	8 59.5	14 14.3	15 58.2
23 W	4 3 21.9	2 6.2	10 54.9	17 52.8	9 28.1	21 59.8	24 15.9	11 5.9	25 3.7	8 57.8	14 13.2	15 56.6
24 T	4 7 18.4	3 3.9	10 51.7	3♊10.7	9 58.8	23 9.0	25 0.2	11 17.9	25 1.9	8 56.0	14 12.1	15 55.0
25 F	4 11 15.0	4 1.6	10 48.5	18 23.6	10 33.5	24 18.3	25 44.5	11 29.9	24 60.0	8 54.1	14 10.9	15 53.4
26 S	4 15 11.5	4 59.2	10 45.3	3♋21.0	11 12.1	25 27.6	26 28.7	11 42.0	24 58.0	8 52.3	14 9.8	15 51.8
27 S	4 19 8.1	5 56.8	10 42.2	17 55.1	11 54.6	26 37.0	27 12.8	11 54.1	24 55.9	8 50.4	14 8.6	15 50.3
28 M	4 23 4.7	6 54.5	10 39.0	2♌ 1.7	12 40.9	27 46.4	27 57.0	12 6.3	24 53.8	8 48.5	14 7.5	15 48.8
29 T	4 27 1.2	7 52.1	10 35.8	15 39.6	13 30.7	28 56.0	28 41.1	12 18.5	24 51.6	8 46.6	14 6.3	15 47.2
30 W	4 30 57.8	8 49.6	10 32.6	28 50.6	14 24.1	0♉ 5.5	29 25.1	12 30.8	24 49.3	8 44.6	14 5.0	15 45.7
31 T	4 34 54.3	9 47.2	10 29.5	11♍38.0	15 20.9	1 15.2	0♈ 9.1	12 43.2	24 46.8	8 42.6	14 3.8	15 44.2

DECLINATION at NOON

DAY	EPHEMERIS SIDEREAL TIME h m s	☉	☊	☽	☿	♀	♂	♃	♄	♅	♆	♇
1 T	2 36 37.6	15N 5.1	17S 10.4	19N 5.1	17N23.6	2S 16.7	10S 3.8	23N22.7	20S54.4	23S24.8	21S47.3	1S24.8
4 F	2 48 27.3	15 58.4	17 13.1	3 24.2	16 2.9	1 5.5	9 15.2	23 21.3	20 54.5	23 25.1	21 47.4	1 23.5
7 M	3 0 17.0	16 49.3	17 15.7	12S40.2	14 39.1	0N 7.1	8 25.9	23 19.6	20 54.8	23 25.4	21 47.6	1 22.3
10 T	3 12 6.6	17 37.7	17 18.4	24 10.2	13 21.8	1 20.6	7 36.2	23 17.9	20 55.2	23 25.7	21 47.7	1 21.1
13 S	3 23 56.3	18 23.4	17 21.0	26 28.8	12 18.9	2 34.9	6 45.9	23 15.9	20 55.7	23 26.1	21 48.0	1 20.1
16 W	3 35 46.0	19 6.4	17 23.6	17 53.6	11 35.6	3 49.5	5 55.4	23 13.7	20 56.5	23 26.4	21 48.2	1 19.1
19 S	3 47 35.6	19 46.4	17 26.3	1 21.4	11 13.9	5 4.3	5 4.5	23 11.4	20 57.4	23 26.8	21 48.5	1 18.2
22 T	3 59 25.3	20 23.5	17 28.9	17N 5.7	11 13.8	6 18.9	4 13.4	23 8.8	20 58.4	23 27.2	21 48.8	1 17.4
25 F	4 11 15.0	20 57.3	17 31.5	26 51.1	11 33.5	7 33.1	3 22.2	23 6.0	20 59.6	23 27.6	21 49.1	1 16.8
28 M	4 23 4.7	21 28.0	17 34.1	20 20.1	12 11.0	8 46.4	2 31.0	23 3.1	21 0.9	23 28.1	21 49.4	1 16.2
31 T	4 34 54.3	21 55.2	17 36.6	4 40.4	13 3.5	9 58.6	1 39.9	22 59.9	21 2.4	23 28.5	21 49.8	1 15.7

JUNE 1990

LONGITUDE at NOON

DAY	EPHEMERIS SIDEREAL TIME h m s	☉ ° ′	☊ ° ′	☽ ° ′	☿ ° ′	♀ ° ′	♂ ° ′	♃ ° ′	♄ ° ′	♅ ° ′	♆ ° ′	♇ ° ′
1 F	4 38 50.9	10♊44.7	10♒26.3	24♍ 6.1	16♉21.0	2♉24.9	0♈53.1	12♋55.6	24♑44.4	8♑40.5	14♑ 2.5	15♏42.7
2 S	4 42 47.4	11 42.2	10 23.1	6♎19.5	17 24.4	3 34.6	1 36.9	13 8.0	24R41.8	8R38.5	14R 1.2	15R41.2
3 S	4 46 44.0	12 39.6	10 19.9	18 22.4	18 31.0	4 44.5	2 20.8	13 20.5	24 39.1	8 36.4	13 59.9	15 39.8
4 M	4 50 40.6	13 37.1	10 16.8	0♏18.6	19 40.7	5 54.4	3 4.6	13 33.0	24 36.4	8 34.3	13 58.6	15 38.3
5 T	4 54 37.1	14 34.5	10 13.6	12 11.4	20 53.5	7 4.3	3 48.3	13 45.6	24 33.6	8 32.1	13 57.2	15 36.9
6 W	4 58 33.7	15 31.9	10 10.4	24 3.4	22 9.3	8 14.3	4 32.0	13 58.3	24 30.7	8 30.0	13 55.8	15 35.5
7 T	5 2 30.2	16 29.3	10 7.2	5♐56.7	23 28.1	9 24.4	5 15.7	14 10.9	24 27.8	8 27.8	13 54.5	15 34.1
8 F	5 6 26.8	17 26.7	10 4.0	17 52.9	24 49.8	10 34.5	5 59.2	14 23.7	24 24.8	8 25.6	13 53.1	15 32.8
9 S	5 10 23.4	18 24.0	10 0.9	29 53.7	26 14.4	11 44.7	6 42.8	14 36.4	24 21.7	8 23.3	13 51.6	15 31.4
10 S	5 14 19.9	19 21.4	9 57.7	12♑ 0.4	27 41.9	12 55.0	7 26.2	14 49.2	24 18.5	8 21.1	13 50.2	15 30.1
11 M	5 18 16.5	20 18.7	9 54.5	24 14.9	29 12.3	14 5.3	8 9.7	15 2.0	24 15.3	8 18.8	13 48.8	15 28.8
12 T	5 22 13.0	21 16.1	9 51.3	6♒39.5	0♊45.5	15 15.6	8 53.0	15 14.9	24 12.0	8 16.5	13 47.3	15 27.5
13 W	5 26 9.6	22 13.4	9 48.2	19 16.7	2 21.5	16 26.0	9 36.3	15 27.8	24 8.6	8 14.2	13 45.8	15 26.2
14 T	5 30 6.1	23 10.7	9 45.0	2♓ 9.5	4 0.4	17 36.5	10 19.5	15 40.8	24 5.2	8 11.9	13 44.4	15 25.0
15 F	5 34 2.7	24 8.0	9 41.8	15 20.9	5 42.0	18 47.1	11 2.7	15 53.8	24 1.7	8 9.6	13 42.9	15 23.8
16 S	5 37 59.3	25 5.3	9 38.6	28 53.7	7 26.3	19 57.7	11 45.8	16 6.8	23 58.1	8 7.3	13 41.3	15 22.6
17 S	5 41 55.8	26 2.6	9 35.5	12♈49.4	9 13.4	21 8.3	12 28.8	16 19.8	23 54.5	8 4.9	13 39.8	15 21.4
18 M	5 45 52.4	26 60.0	9 32.3	27 8.3	11 3.2	22 19.0	13 11.8	16 33.0	23 50.9	8 2.6	13 38.3	15 20.3
19 T	5 49 48.9	27 57.2	9 29.1	11♉47.7	12 55.5	23 29.8	13 54.7	16 46.1	23 47.2	8 0.2	13 36.8	15 19.2
20 W	5 53 45.5	28 54.5	9 25.9	26 42.6	14 50.4	24 40.6	14 37.5	16 59.2	23 43.4	7 57.8	13 35.2	15 18.1
21 T	5 57 42.1	29 51.8	9 22.8	11♊45.4	16 47.7	25 51.4	15 20.3	17 12.4	23 39.6	7 55.4	13 33.7	15 17.0
22 F	6 1 38.6	0♋49.1	9 19.6	26 46.8	18 47.2	27 2.3	16 2.9	17 25.6	23 35.7	7 53.0	13 32.1	15 16.0
23 S	6 5 35.2	1 46.4	9 16.4	11♋37.6	20 49.0	28 13.3	16 45.5	17 38.8	23 31.8	7 50.6	13 30.5	15 14.9
24 S	6 9 31.7	2 43.6	9 13.2	26 10.1	22 52.7	29 24.3	17 27.9	17 52.0	23 27.8	7 48.2	13 28.9	15 13.9
25 M	6 13 28.3	3 40.9	9 10.1	10♌18.9	24 58.2	0♊35.3	18 10.3	18 5.3	23 23.8	7 45.7	13 27.4	15 13.0
26 T	6 17 24.9	4 38.1	9 6.9	24 1.4	27 5.3	1 46.4	18 52.6	18 18.6	23 19.7	7 43.3	13 25.8	15 12.0
27 W	6 21 21.4	5 35.4	9 3.7	7♍17.7	29 13.7	2 57.5	19 34.8	18 31.9	23 15.6	7 40.9	13 24.2	15 11.1
28 T	6 25 18.0	6 32.6	9 0.5	20 9.8	1♋23.1	4 8.6	20 16.9	18 45.2	23 11.5	7 38.4	13 22.5	15 10.2
29 F	6 29 14.5	7 29.8	8 57.3	2♎41.3	3 33.3	5 19.8	20 58.9	18 58.5	23 7.3	7 36.0	13 20.9	15 9.4
30 S	6 33 11.1	8 27.0	8 54.2	14 56.4	5 44.0	6 31.1	21 40.8	19 11.9	23 3.1	7 33.5	13 19.3	15 8.5

DECLINATION at NOON

DAY	EPHEMERIS SIDEREAL TIME h m s	☉	☊	☽	☿	♀	♂	♃	♄	♅	♆	♇
1 F	4 38 50.9	22N 3.6	17S37.5	0S57.6	13N23.9	10N22.4	1S22.9	22N58.8	21S 2.9	23S28.7	21S49.9	1S15.6
4 M	4 50 40.6	22 26.2	17 40.1	16 16.9	14 32.5	11 32.7	0 31.9	22 55.3	21 4.5	23 29.1	21 50.3	1 15.3
7 T	5 2 30.2	22 45.4	17 42.6	25 45.0	15 49.9	12 41.1	0N18.9	22 51.6	21 6.3	23 29.6	21 50.7	1 15.1
10 S	5 14 19.9	23 0.9	17 45.2	25 9.1	17 13.4	13 47.5	1 9.3	22 47.8	21 8.2	23 30.1	21 51.1	1 15.0
13 W	5 26 9.6	23 12.8	17 47.8	14 5.3	18 39.8	14 51.4	1 59.5	22 43.7	21 10.1	23 30.5	21 51.6	1 15.0
16 S	5 37 59.3	23 21.1	17 50.3	3N14.0	20 5.6	15 52.5	2 49.1	22 39.3	21 12.2	23 31.0	21 52.0	1 15.2
19 T	5 49 48.9	23 25.6	17 52.8	20 16.1	21 26.5	16 50.6	3 38.3	22 34.8	21 14.3	23 31.5	21 52.5	1 15.5
22 F	6 1 38.6	23 26.4	17 55.4	26 47.8	22 37.6	17 45.4	4 26.9	22 30.0	21 16.5	23 31.9	21 52.9	1 15.8
25 M	6 13 28.3	23 23.5	17 57.9	17 25.3	23 33.6	18 36.4	5 14.8	22 25.1	21 18.8	23 32.4	21 53.4	1 16.3
28 T	6 25 18.0	23 16.8	18 0.4	0 39.1	24 9.4	19 23.4	6 2.0	22 19.9	21 21.1	23 32.9	21 53.9	1 16.9

JULY 1990

DAY	EPHEMERIS SIDEREAL TIME	☉	☊	☽	☿	♀	♂	♃	♄	♅	♆	♇
	h m s	° ′	° ′	° ′	° ′	° ′	° ′	° ′	° ′	° ′	° ′	° ′
LONGITUDE at NOON												
1 S	6 37 7.6	9♋24.2	8♒51.0	26♎59.6	7♋54.9	7♊42.4	22♈22.6	19♋25.3	22♑58.9	7♑31.1	13♑17.7	15♏ 7.8
2 M	6 41 4.2	10 21.4	8 47.8	8♏55.3	10 5.7	8 53.7	23 4.3	19 38.6	22R54.6	7R28.7	13R16.1	15R 7.0
3 T	6 45 0.8	11 18.6	8 44.6	20 47.7	12 16.1	10 5.1	23 45.9	19 52.0	22 50.3	7 26.2	13 14.5	15 6.2
4 W	6 48 57.3	12 15.8	8 41.5	2♐40.3	14 25.9	11 16.5	24 27.4	20 5.4	22 46.0	7 23.8	13 12.8	15 5.5
5 T	6 52 53.9	13 13.0	8 38.3	14 36.2	16 34.9	12 28.0	25 8.8	20 18.9	22 41.7	7 21.4	13 11.2	15 4.9
6 F	6 56 50.4	14 10.2	8 35.1	26 38.0	18 42.9	13 39.5	25 50.1	20 32.3	22 37.3	7 19.0	13 9.6	15 4.2
7 S	7 0 47.0	15 7.4	8 31.9	8♑47.5	20 49.6	14 51.0	26 31.3	20 45.7	22 32.9	7 16.6	13 8.0	15 3.6
8 S	7 4 43.6	16 4.6	8 28.8	21 6.3	22 55.1	16 2.6	27 12.4	20 59.2	22 28.5	7 14.2	13 6.3	15 3.0
9 M	7 8 40.1	17 1.8	8 25.6	3♒35.9	24 59.0	17 14.3	27 53.4	21 12.7	22 24.2	7 11.8	13 4.8	15 2.5
10 T	7 12 36.7	17 59.0	8 22.4	16 17.1	27 1.4	18 26.0	28 34.2	21 26.1	22 19.8	7 9.5	13 3.2	15 2.0
11 W	7 16 33.2	18 56.2	8 19.2	29 11.1	29 2.0	19 37.8	29 15.0	21 39.6	22 15.3	7 7.1	13 1.5	15 1.5
12 T	7 20 29.8	19 53.4	8 16.1	12♓19.0	1♌ 1.0	20 49.6	29 55.6	21 53.0	22 10.9	7 4.7	12 59.9	15 1.0
13 F	7 24 26.3	20 50.6	8 12.9	25 41.8	2 58.2	22 1.4	0♉36.1	22 6.5	22 6.5	7 2.4	12 58.3	15 0.6
14 S	7 28 22.9	21 47.8	8 9.7	9♈20.4	4 53.6	23 13.3	1 16.5	22 19.9	22 2.0	7 0.0	12 56.7	15 0.2
15 S	7 32 19.5	22 45.0	8 6.5	23 14.9	6 47.1	24 25.2	1 56.7	22 33.4	21 57.6	6 57.7	12 55.1	14 59.8
16 M	7 36 16.0	23 42.3	8 3.3	7♉24.7	8 38.8	25 37.2	2 36.9	22 46.9	21 53.1	6 55.4	12 53.5	14 59.5
17 T	7 40 12.6	24 39.5	8 0.2	21 48.1	10 28.7	26 49.2	3 16.8	23 0.3	21 48.7	6 53.1	12 51.9	14 59.2
18 W	7 44 9.1	25 36.8	7 57.0	6♊21.5	12 16.7	28 1.3	3 56.7	23 13.8	21 44.2	6 50.9	12 50.4	14 58.9
19 T	7 48 5.7	26 34.1	7 53.8	21 0.2	14 2.9	29 13.4	4 36.4	23 27.2	21 39.8	6 48.6	12 48.8	14 58.7
20 F	7 52 2.2	27 31.4	7 50.6	5♋38.1	15 47.2	0♋25.5	5 15.9	23 40.7	21 35.4	6 46.4	12 47.2	14 58.5
21 S	7 55 58.8	28 28.7	7 47.5	20 8.9	17 29.7	1 37.7	5 55.3	23 54.1	21 31.0	6 44.2	12 45.7	14 58.3
22 S	7 59 55.4	29 26.0	7 44.3	4♌26.5	19 10.3	2 50.0	6 34.6	24 7.6	21 26.6	6 42.0	12 44.1	14 58.2
23 M	8 3 51.9	0♌23.3	7 41.1	18 26.1	20 49.2	4 2.3	7 13.7	24 21.0	21 22.2	6 39.8	12 42.6	14 58.1
24 T	8 7 48.5	1 20.6	7 37.9	2♍ 4.5	22 26.1	5 14.6	7 52.6	24 34.4	21 17.9	6 37.7	12 41.1	14 58.0
25 W	8 11 45.0	2 17.9	7 34.8	15 20.4	24 1.3	6 27.0	8 31.4	24 47.8	21 13.6	6 35.6	12 39.6	14 58.0
26 T	8 15 41.6	3 15.3	7 31.6	28 14.4	25 34.6	7 39.4	9 10.0	25 1.2	21 9.2	6 33.5	12 38.1	14 58.0
27 F	8 19 38.1	4 12.6	7 28.4	10♎48.5	27 6.1	8 51.8	9 48.4	25 14.6	21 5.0	6 31.4	12 36.6	14 58.0
28 S	8 23 34.7	5 10.0	7 25.2	23 5.9	28 35.7	10 4.3	10 26.7	25 27.9	21 0.7	6 29.3	12 35.1	14D58.1
29 S	8 27 31.3	6 7.3	7 22.0	5♏10.7	0♍ 3.4	11 16.8	11 4.8	25 41.3	20 56.5	6 27.3	12 33.7	14 58.2
30 M	8 31 27.8	7 4.7	7 18.9	17 7.4	1 29.3	12 29.4	11 42.8	25 54.6	20 52.4	6 25.4	12 32.3	14 58.4
31 T	8 35 24.4	8 2.1	7 15.7	29 0.3	2 53.3	13 42.0	12 20.5	26 7.9	20 48.2	6 23.4	12 30.8	14 58.6

DAY	EPHEMERIS SIDEREAL TIME	☉	☊	☽	☿	♀	♂	♃	♄	♅	♆	♇
DECLINATION at NOON												
1 S	6 37 7.6	23N 6.5	18S 2.9	15S 10.7	24N21.5	20N 6.2	6N48.3	22N14.5	21S 23.5	23S 33.3	21S54.4	1S 17.7
4 W	6 48 57.3	22 52.6	18 5.4	25 19.7	24 8.5	20 44.4	7 33.9	22 9.0	21 25.9	23 33.7	21 54.9	1 18.5
7 S	7 0 47.0	22 35.1	18 7.9	25 39.0	23 31.3	21 17.9	8 18.5	22 3.2	21 28.3	23 34.2	21 55.4	1 19.5
10 T	7 12 36.7	22 14.0	18 10.4	15 10.2	22 32.9	21 46.3	9 2.2	21 57.2	21 30.7	23 34.6	21 55.9	1 20.5
13 F	7 24 26.3	21 49.6	18 12.8	1N54.3	21 16.8	22 9.5	9 44.9	21 51.1	21 33.1	23 35.0	21 56.5	1 21.7
16 M	7 36 16.0	21 21.7	18 15.3	18 57.5	19 46.8	22 27.3	10 26.5	21 44.7	21 35.5	23 35.3	21 57.0	1 23.0
19 T	7 48 5.7	20 50.6	18 17.8	26 56.5	18 6.5	22 39.4	11 7.0	21 38.2	21 37.9	23 35.7	21 57.5	1 24.3
22 S	7 59 55.4	20 16.3	18 20.2	19 24.3	16 18.9	22 45.9	11 46.3	21 31.5	21 40.2	23 36.0	21 58.0	1 25.8
25 W	8 11 45.0	19 39.0	18 22.7	2 46.2	14 26.5	22 46.5	12 24.4	21 24.7	21 42.5	23 36.4	21 58.4	1 27.4
28 S	8 23 34.7	18 58.7	18 25.1	13S 43.8	12 31.7	22 41.3	13 1.2	21 17.7	21 44.8	23 36.7	21 58.9	1 29.1
31 T	8 35 24.4	18 15.6	18 27.5	24 43.6	10 36.4	22 30.2	13 36.9	21 10.6	21 46.9	23 37.0	21 59.4	1 30.9

AUGUST 1990

DAY	EPHEMERIS SIDEREAL TIME	☉	☊	☽	☿	♀	♂	♃	♄	♅	♆	♇
LONGITUDE at NOON												
1 W	8 39 20.9	8♌59.5	7♒12.5	10♐53.9	4♍15.3	14♋54.7	12♉58.1	26♋21.2	20♑44.1	6♑21.5	12♑29.4	14♏58.8
2 T	8 43 17.5	9 56.9	7 9.3	22 52.4	5 35.3	16 7.4	13 35.5	26 34.5	20R40.0	6R19.6	12R28.0	14 59.0
3 F	8 47 14.0	10 54.3	7 6.2	4♑59.3	6 53.2	17 20.1	14 12.7	26 47.7	20 36.0	6 17.7	12 26.6	14 59.3
4 S	8 51 10.6	11 51.7	7 3.0	17 17.6	8 9.1	18 32.9	14 49.7	27 0.9	20 32.0	6 15.9	12 25.3	14 59.6
5 S	8 55 7.2	12 49.2	6 59.8	29 49.5	9 22.9	19 45.7	15 26.5	27 14.1	20 28.1	6 14.1	12 23.9	14 60.0
6 M	8 59 3.7	13 46.6	6 56.6	12♒36.3	10 34.4	20 58.6	16 3.1	27 27.2	20 24.2	6 12.3	12 22.6	15 0.3
7 T	9 3 0.3	14 44.1	6 53.5	25 38.5	11 43.7	22 11.5	16 39.5	27 40.4	20 20.3	6 10.6	12 21.3	15 0.8
8 W	9 6 56.8	15 41.6	6 50.3	8♓55.9	12 50.7	23 24.4	17 15.8	27 53.5	20 16.5	6 8.9	12 20.0	15 1.2
9 T	9 10 53.4	16 39.1	6 47.1	22 27.3	13 55.1	24 37.4	17 51.8	28 6.6	20 12.8	6 7.3	12 18.7	15 1.7
10 F	9 14 49.9	17 36.6	6 43.9	6♈11.3	14 57.1	25 50.4	18 27.6	28 19.6	20 9.1	6 5.6	12 17.5	15 2.2
11 S	9 18 46.5	18 34.1	6 40.7	20 6.0	15 56.3	27 3.5	19 3.2	28 32.6	20 5.4	6 4.0	12 16.2	15 2.7
12 S	9 22 43.0	19 31.7	6 37.6	4♉ 9.3	16 52.8	28 16.7	19 38.5	28 45.6	20 1.9	6 2.5	12 15.0	15 3.3
13 M	9 26 39.6	20 29.3	6 34.4	18 19.1	17 46.4	29 29.8	20 13.7	28 58.6	19 58.3	6 1.0	12 13.8	15 3.9
14 T	9 30 36.2	21 26.9	6 31.2	2♊33.0	18 36.9	0♌43.0	20 48.6	29 11.5	19 54.9	5 59.5	12 12.6	15 4.6
15 W	9 34 32.7	22 24.6	6 28.0	16 48.6	19 24.2	1 56.3	21 23.2	29 24.4	19 51.5	5 58.1	12 11.5	15 5.3
16 T	9 38 29.3	23 22.2	6 24.9	1♋ 3.3	20 8.0	3 9.6	21 57.6	29 37.2	19 48.1	5 56.7	12 10.4	15 6.0
17 F	9 42 25.8	24 19.9	6 21.7	15 14.2	20 48.3	4 22.9	22 31.8	29 50.0	19 44.9	5 55.3	12 9.3	15 6.7
18 S	9 46 22.4	25 17.7	6 18.5	29 18.0	21 24.7	5 36.3	23 5.7	0♌ 2.8	19 41.7	5 54.0	12 8.2	15 7.5
19 S	9 50 18.9	26 15.4	6 15.3	13♌11.6	21 57.1	6 49.8	23 39.4	0 15.5	19 38.5	5 52.7	12 7.1	15 8.3
20 M	9 54 15.5	27 13.2	6 12.2	26 52.0	22 25.4	8 3.3	24 12.8	0 28.2	19 35.5	5 51.6	12 6.1	15 9.2
21 T	9 58 12.0	28 11.0	6 9.0	10♍16.5	22 49.1	9 16.8	24 45.9	0 40.9	19 32.6	5 50.4	12 5.1	15 10.1
22 W	10 2 8.6	29 8.8	6 5.8	23 23.8	23 8.0	10 30.3	25 18.7	0 53.4	19 29.6	5 49.2	12 4.2	15 11.0
23 T	10 6 5.2	0♍ 6.7	6 2.6	6♎13.1	23 22.0	11 43.9	25 51.2	1 6.0	19 26.8	5 48.1	12 3.2	15 12.0
24 F	10 10 1.7	1 4.5	5 59.4	18 45.4	23 30.7	12 57.5	26 23.5	1 18.5	19 24.1	5 47.1	12 2.3	15 13.0
25 S	10 13 58.3	2 2.4	5 56.3	1♏ 2.4	23 34.0	14 11.2	26 55.4	1 30.9	19 21.4	5 46.1	12 1.4	15 14.0
26 S	10 17 54.8	3 0.3	5 53.1	13 7.3	23R31.6	15 24.9	27 27.0	1 43.3	19 18.8	5 45.1	12 0.5	15 15.0
27 M	10 21 51.4	3 58.2	5 49.9	25 3.7	23 23.4	16 38.6	27 58.4	1 55.6	19 16.3	5 44.2	11 59.6	15 16.1
28 T	10 25 47.9	4 56.2	5 46.7	6♐56.2	23 9.2	17 52.4	28 29.4	2 7.9	19 13.8	5 43.3	11 58.8	15 17.2
29 W	10 29 44.5	5 54.1	5 43.6	18 49.4	22 48.8	19 6.2	29 0.1	2 20.1	19 11.5	5 42.5	11 58.0	15 18.3
30 T	10 33 41.0	6 52.1	5 40.4	0♑48.3	22 22.5	20 20.0	29 30.5	2 32.3	19 9.2	5 41.7	11 57.3	15 19.5
31 F	10 37 37.6	7 50.1	5 37.2	12 57.4	21 50.1	21 33.8	0♊ 0.5	2 44.4	19 7.0	5 41.0	11 56.5	15 20.7

DAY	EPHEMERIS SIDEREAL TIME	☉	☊	☽	☿	♀	♂	♃	♄	♅	♆	♇
DECLINATION at NOON												
1 W	8 39 20.9	18N 0.7	18S 28.3	26S 26.4	9N58.2	22N25.2	13N48.4	21N 8.2	21S 47.6	23S 37.1	21S59.5	1S 31.5
4 S	8 51 10.6	17 14.1	18 30.7	24 7.2	8 5.2	22 6.3	14 22.3	21 0.9	21 49.7	23 37.3	22 0.0	1 33.3
7 T	9 3 0.3	16 24.9	18 33.1	11 24.5	6 15.9	21 41.7	14 54.9	20 53.5	21 51.7	23 37.6	22 0.4	1 35.3
10 F	9 14 49.9	15 33.4	18 35.5	6N36.2	4 32.3	21 11.3	15 26.1	20 45.9	21 53.7	23 37.8	22 0.9	1 37.3
13 M	9 26 39.6	14 39.7	18 37.9	22 14.7	2 56.5	20 35.5	15 56.0	20 38.3	21 55.5	23 38.0	22 1.3	1 39.4
16 T	9 38 29.3	13 43.8	18 40.3	26 33.2	1 31.1	19 54.3	16 24.6	20 30.6	21 57.3	23 38.2	22 1.7	1 41.6
19 S	9 50 18.9	12 46.0	18 42.7	16 20.4	0 19.0	19 8.0	16 51.8	20 22.8	21 58.9	23 38.3	22 2.1	1 43.9
22 W	10 2 8.6	11 46.3	18 45.0	0S51.1	0S 36.0	18 16.7	17 17.6	20 14.9	22 0.5	23 38.5	22 2.4	1 46.2
25 S	10 13 58.3	10 45.3	18 47.4	16 42.2	1 9.4	17 20.7	17 42.2	20 7.1	22 1.9	23 38.6	22 2.8	1 48.6
28 T	10 25 47.9	9 42.1	18 49.7	25 56.1	1 16.4	16 20.3	18 5.4	19 59.1	22 3.2	23 38.7	22 3.1	1 51.0
31 F	10 37 37.6	8 37.9	18 52.1	24 56.0	0 52.6	15 15.7	18 27.3	19 51.2	22 4.4	23 38.8	22 3.4	1 53.4

SEPTEMBER 1990

DAY	EPHEMERIS SIDEREAL TIME	☉	☊	☾	☿	♀	♂	♃	♄	♅	♆	♇
	h m s	° ′	° ′	° ′	° ′	° ′	° ′	° ′	° ′	° ′	° ′	° ′
LONGITUDE at NOON												
1 S	10 41 34.1	8♍48.2	5♒34.0	25♑21.0	21♍12.0	22♌47.7	0♊30.2	2♌56.5	19♑ 4.9	5♑40.3	11♑55.8	15♏21.9
2 S	10 45 30.7	9 46.2	5 30.8	8♒ 2.4	20R28.6	24 1.7	0 59.6	3 8.5	19R 2.9	5R39.7	11R55.1	15 23.2
3 M	10 49 27.2	10 44.3	5 27.7	21 3.8	19 40.3	25 15.7	1 28.6	3 20.4	19 1.0	5 39.1	11 54.5	15 24.5
4 T	10 53 23.8	11 42.4	5 24.5	4♓26.0	18 47.8	26 29.7	1 57.3	3 32.3	18 59.2	5 38.6	11 53.9	15 25.8
5 W	10 57 20.4	12 40.5	5 21.3	18 7.9	17 52.0	27 43.7	2 25.6	3 44.1	18 57.4	5 38.1	11 53.3	15 27.1
6 T	11 1 16.9	13 38.7	5 18.1	2♈ 6.7	16 53.9	28 57.8	2 53.5	3 55.8	18 55.8	5 37.7	11 52.7	15 28.5
7 F	11 5 13.5	14 36.9	5 15.0	16 18.5	15 54.7	0♍11.9	3 21.1	4 7.5	18 54.2	5 37.3	11 52.2	15 29.9
8 S	11 9 10.0	15 35.1	5 11.8	0♉38.1	14 55.6	1 26.0	3 48.2	4 19.1	18 52.7	5 36.9	11 51.7	15 31.4
9 S	11 13 6.6	16 33.4	5 8.6	15 0.5	13 58.0	2 40.2	4 15.0	4 30.6	18 51.4	5 36.6	11 51.2	15 32.8
10 M	11 17 3.1	17 31.7	5 5.4	29 21.0	13 3.2	3 54.5	4 41.4	4 42.1	18 50.1	5 36.5	11 50.8	15 34.4
11 T	11 20 59.7	18 30.1	5 2.2	13♊36.1	12 12.5	5 8.7	5 7.4	4 53.5	18 48.9	5 36.3	11 50.4	15 35.9
12 W	11 24 56.2	19 28.4	4 59.1	27 43.4	11 27.2	6 23.0	5 32.9	5 4.8	18 47.8	5 36.1	11 50.0	15 37.4
13 T	11 28 52.8	20 26.8	4 55.9	11♋41.6	10 48.4	7 37.4	5 57.9	5 16.0	18 46.8	5 36.0	11 49.7	15 39.0
14 F	11 32 49.3	21 25.3	4 52.7	25 30.1	10 17.2	8 51.7	6 22.5	5 27.2	18 45.9	5 36.0	11 49.3	15 40.6
15 S	11 36 45.9	22 23.7	4 49.5	9♌ 8.5	9 54.2	10 6.1	6 46.7	5 38.3	18 45.1	5 36.0	11 49.1	15 42.2
16 S	11 40 42.4	23 22.2	4 46.4	22 36.3	9 40.1	11 20.5	7 10.4	5 49.3	18 44.4	5D36.1	11 48.8	15 43.9
17 M	11 44 39.0	24 20.8	4 43.2	5♍52.9	9 35.4	12 35.0	7 33.6	6 0.2	18 43.8	5 36.2	11 48.6	15 45.6
18 T	11 48 35.5	25 19.3	4 40.0	18 57.4	9D40.2	13 49.5	7 56.3	6 11.0	18 43.3	5 36.4	11 48.4	15 47.3
19 W	11 52 32.1	26 18.0	4 36.8	1♎49.1	9 54.6	15 4.0	8 18.5	6 21.7	18 42.9	5 36.6	11 48.2	15 49.0
20 T	11 56 28.7	27 16.6	4 33.6	14 27.4	10 18.4	16 18.5	8 40.1	6 32.4	18 42.6	5 36.9	11 48.1	15 50.8
21 F	12 0 25.2	28 15.3	4 30.5	26 52.4	10 51.5	17 33.1	9 1.3	6 42.9	18 42.4	5 37.2	11 48.0	15 52.5
22 S	12 4 21.8	29 14.0	4 27.3	9♏ 5.0	11 33.4	18 47.7	9 21.9	6 53.4	18 42.2	5 37.5	11 48.0	15 54.3
23 S	12 8 18.3	0♎12.7	4 24.1	21 7.1	12 23.8	20 2.3	9 41.9	7 3.8	18 42.2	5 38.0	11 48.0	15 56.2
24 M	12 12 14.9	1 11.4	4 20.9	3♐ 1.5	13 21.9	21 16.9	10 1.5	7 14.1	18D42.3	5 38.5	11 48.0	15 58.0
25 T	12 16 11.4	2 10.2	4 17.8	14 52.0	14 27.2	22 31.6	10 20.4	7 24.2	18 42.5	5 39.0	11 48.0	15 59.9
26 W	12 20 8.0	3 9.0	4 14.6	26 43.0	15 39.1	23 46.2	10 38.7	7 34.3	18 42.8	5 39.6	11D48.1	16 1.8
27 T	12 24 4.5	4 7.9	4 11.4	8♑39.6	16 56.9	25 0.9	10 56.5	7 44.3	18 43.1	5 40.2	11 48.2	16 3.7
28 F	12 28 1.1	5 6.8	4 8.2	20 47.0	18 19.9	26 15.7	11 13.7	7 54.2	18 43.6	5 40.9	11 48.3	16 5.6
29 S	12 31 57.6	6 5.7	4 5.0	3♒10.3	19 47.4	27 30.4	11 30.2	8 4.0	18 44.2	5 41.6	11 48.5	16 7.6
30 S	12 35 54.2	7 4.6	4 1.9	15 54.3	21 18.9	28 45.2	11 46.2	8 13.7	18 44.9	5 42.4	11 48.7	16 9.6
DECLINATION at NOON												
1 S	10 41 34.1	8N16.2	18S52.9	22S 6.7	0S37.3	14N53.4	18N34.3	19N48.6	22S 4.8	23S38.8	22S 3.5	1S54.3
4 T	10 53 23.8	7 10.4	18 55.2	7 39.3	0N29.6	13 43.7	18 54.6	19 40.6	22 5.9	23 38.9	22 3.8	1 56.8
7 F	11 5 13.5	6 3.5	18 57.5	10N52.8	2 3.1	12 30.7	19 13.7	19 32.7	22 6.8	23 38.9	22 4.0	1 59.3
10 M	11 17 3.1	4 55.7	18 59.8	24 39.6	3 50.0	11 14.4	19 31.7	19 24.9	22 7.6	23 38.9	22 4.3	2 1.9
13 T	11 28 52.8	3 47.1	19 2.1	25 5.4	5 32.3	9 55.3	19 48.5	19 17.0	22 8.3	23 38.9	22 4.5	2 4.5
16 S	11 40 42.4	2 37.9	19 4.4	12 37.9	6 52.6	8 33.7	20 4.3	19 9.3	22 8.9	23 38.9	22 4.7	2 7.1
19 W	11 52 32.1	1 28.3	19 6.7	4S35.3	7 38.7	7 9.9	20 19.0	19 1.6	22 9.4	23 38.8	22 4.8	2 9.8
22 S	12 4 21.8	0 18.3	19 9.0	19 20.2	7 45.0	5 44.2	20 32.9	18 54.1	22 9.7	23 38.8	22 5.0	2 12.4
25 T	12 16 11.4	0S51.8	19 11.2	26 30.2	7 12.0	4 17.0	20 45.9	18 46.7	22 9.9	23 38.7	22 5.1	2 15.1
28 F	12 28 1.1	2 1.9	19 13.5	23 6.9	6 4.6	2 48.5	20 58.0	18 39.4	22 10.0	23 38.6	22 5.2	2 17.7

OCTOBER 1990

DAY	EPHEMERIS SIDEREAL TIME	☉	☊	☾	☿	♀	♂	♃	♄	♅	♆	♇
LONGITUDE at NOON												
1 M	12 39 50.7	8♎ 3.6	3♒58.7	29♒ 2.5	22♍53.7	0♎ 0.0	12♊ 1.5	8♌23.3	18♑45.7	5♑43.3	11♑49.0	16♏11.6
2 T	12 43 47.3	9 2.6	3 55.5	12♓36.8	24 31.3	1 14.8	12 16.1	8 32.7	18 46.6	5 44.2	11 49.3	16 13.6
3 W	12 47 43.8	10 1.6	3 52.3	26 36.6	26 11.1	2 29.6	12 30.1	8 42.1	18 47.6	5 45.1	11 49.6	16 15.7
4 T	12 51 40.4	11 0.7	3 49.2	10♈58.8	27 52.8	3 44.5	12 43.5	8 51.3	18 48.6	5 46.1	11 49.9	16 17.7
5 F	12 55 37.0	11 59.8	3 46.0	25 37.5	29 35.9	4 59.3	12 56.1	9 0.4	18 49.8	5 47.1	11 50.3	16 19.8
6 S	12 59 33.5	12 58.9	3 42.8	10♉24.9	1♎20.0	6 14.2	13 8.0	9 9.5	18 51.1	5 48.2	11 50.7	16 21.9
7 S	13 3 30.1	13 58.0	3 39.6	25 12.7	3 4.9	7 29.1	13 19.2	9 18.4	18 52.4	5 49.3	11 51.2	16 24.0
8 M	13 7 26.6	14 57.2	3 36.4	9♊53.3	4 50.3	8 44.1	13 29.7	9 27.1	18 53.9	5 50.5	11 51.6	16 26.2
9 T	13 11 23.2	15 56.5	3 33.3	24 20.8	6 36.0	9 59.0	13 39.5	9 35.8	18 55.5	5 51.7	11 52.2	16 28.3
10 W	13 15 19.7	16 55.8	3 30.1	8♋32.0	8 21.8	11 14.0	13 48.5	9 44.3	18 57.1	5 53.0	11 52.7	16 30.5
11 T	13 19 16.3	17 55.1	3 26.9	22 25.8	10 7.6	12 29.0	13 56.7	9 52.7	18 58.9	5 54.4	11 53.3	16 32.6
12 F	13 23 12.8	18 54.4	3 23.7	6♌ 2.5	11 53.1	13 44.0	14 4.1	10 1.0	19 0.7	5 55.7	11 53.9	16 34.8
13 S	13 27 9.4	19 53.8	3 20.6	19 23.8	13 38.4	14 59.0	14 10.7	10 9.2	19 2.7	5 57.2	11 54.5	16 37.1
14 S	13 31 5.9	20 53.2	3 17.4	2♍31.3	15 23.2	16 14.1	14 16.5	10 17.2	19 4.7	5 58.6	11 55.2	16 39.3
15 M	13 35 2.5	21 52.7	3 14.2	15 26.6	17 7.7	17 29.1	14 21.5	10 25.1	19 6.9	6 0.2	11 55.9	16 41.5
16 T	13 38 59.0	22 52.2	3 11.0	28 10.8	18 51.6	18 44.2	14 25.7	10 32.9	19 9.1	6 1.7	11 56.6	16 43.8
17 W	13 42 55.6	23 51.8	3 7.8	10♎44.6	20 35.0	19 59.3	14 29.0	10 40.5	19 11.4	6 3.4	11 57.4	16 46.0
18 T	13 46 52.2	24 51.3	3 4.7	23 8.4	22 17.9	21 14.4	14 31.4	10 48.0	19 13.9	6 5.0	11 58.2	16 48.3
19 F	13 50 48.7	25 50.9	3 1.5	5♏22.7	24 0.1	22 29.5	14 33.0	10 55.3	19 16.4	6 6.7	11 59.0	16 50.6
20 S	13 54 45.3	26 50.6	2 58.3	17 27.8	25 41.8	23 44.6	14 33.7	11 2.6	19 19.0	6 8.5	11 59.9	16 52.9
21 S	13 58 41.8	27 50.3	2 55.1	29 25.2	27 22.9	24 59.8	14R33.5	11 9.6	19 21.7	6 10.3	12 0.8	16 55.2
22 M	14 2 38.4	28 50.0	2 52.0	11♐16.7	29 3.4	26 15.0	14 32.5	11 16.6	19 24.5	6 12.2	12 1.8	16 57.6
23 T	14 6 34.9	29 49.8	2 48.8	23 5.0	0♏43.3	27 30.2	14 30.6	11 23.4	19 27.4	6 14.1	12 2.7	16 59.9
24 W	14 10 31.5	0♏49.5	2 45.6	4♑53.8	2 22.6	28 45.3	14 27.7	11 30.0	19 30.4	6 16.0	12 3.7	17 2.3
25 T	14 14 28.0	1 49.3	2 42.4	16 47.6	4 1.3	0♏ 0.5	14 24.0	11 36.5	19 33.5	6 18.0	12 4.8	17 4.6
26 F	14 18 24.6	2 49.1	2 39.2	28 51.5	5 39.4	1 15.7	14 19.4	11 42.8	19 36.6	6 20.0	12 5.8	17 7.0
27 S	14 22 21.1	3 49.0	2 36.1	11♒10.8	7 17.0	2 30.9	14 13.9	11 48.9	19 39.9	6 22.1	12 6.9	17 9.3
28 S	14 26 17.7	4 48.9	2 32.9	23 50.9	8 54.1	3 46.1	14 7.5	11 55.0	19 43.2	6 24.2	12 8.0	17 11.7
29 M	14 30 14.3	5 48.8	2 29.7	6♓56.6	10 30.6	5 1.3	14 0.3	12 0.8	19 46.6	6 26.4	12 9.1	17 14.1
30 T	14 34 10.8	6 48.7	2 26.5	20 31.2	12 6.7	6 16.5	13 52.2	12 6.5	19 50.1	6 28.6	12 10.3	17 16.5
31 W	14 38 7.4	7 48.7	2 23.4	4♈35.7	13 42.2	7 31.7	13 43.1	12 12.0	19 53.7	6 30.8	12 11.5	17 18.9
DECLINATION at NOON												
1 M	12 39 50.7	3S11.9	19S15.7	9S53.8	4N29.9	1N19.2	21N 9.5	18N32.3	22S 9.9	23S38.4	22S 5.2	2S20.3
4 T	12 51 40.4	4 21.5	19 18.0	8N34.8	2 36.0	0S10.7	21 20.3	18 25.4	22 9.7	23 38.3	22 5.2	2 23.0
7 S	13 3 30.1	5 30.6	19 20.2	23 38.7	0 29.8	1 40.9	21 30.4	18 18.8	22 9.4	23 38.1	22 5.2	2 25.6
10 W	13 15 19.7	6 39.1	19 22.4	25 22.1	1S42.8	3 10.9	21 40.0	18 12.3	22 9.0	23 37.9	22 5.2	2 28.1
13 S	13 27 9.4	7 46.9	19 24.6	13 45.5	3 57.7	4 40.5	21 49.0	18 6.1	22 8.4	23 37.7	22 5.2	2 30.7
16 T	13 38 59.0	8 53.7	19 26.9	3S 0.2	6 11.9	6 9.4	21 57.5	18 0.2	22 7.8	23 37.5	22 5.1	2 33.2
19 F	13 50 48.7	9 59.3	19 29.1	18 0.9	8 23.3	7 37.1	22 5.5	17 54.5	22 6.9	23 37.2	22 5.0	2 35.7
22 M	14 2 38.4	11 3.7	19 31.2	26 1.4	10 30.3	9 3.4	22 13.0	17 49.2	22 6.0	23 37.0	22 4.9	2 38.1
25 T	14 14 28.0	12 6.5	19 33.4	23 45.0	12 32.0	10 27.9	22 19.9	17 44.2	22 4.9	23 36.7	22 4.7	2 40.5
28 S	14 26 17.7	13 7.7	19 35.6	11 50.5	14 27.4	11 50.1	22 26.3	17 39.6	22 3.7	23 36.3	22 4.5	2 42.9
31 W	14 38 7.4	14 7.0	19 37.7	5N54.1	16 15.9	13 9.8	22 31.9	17 35.4	22 2.4	23 36.0	22 4.3	2 45.1

NOVEMBER 1990

DAY	EPHEMERIS SIDEREAL TIME	☉	☊	☽	☿	♀	♂	♃	♄	♅	♆	♇
	h m s	° ′	° ′	° ′	° ′	° ′	° ′	° ′	° ′	° ′	° ′	° ′
LONGITUDE at NOON												
1 T	14 42 3.9	8♏48.6	2♒20.2	19♈ 8.0	15♏17.3	8♏47.0	13♊33.3	12♌17.4	19♑57.4	6♑33.1	12♑12.8	17♏21.3
2 F	14 46 0.5	9 48.7	2 17.0	4♉ 2.5	16 51.9	10 2.2	13R22.6	12 22.6	20 1.2	6 35.4	12 14.0	17 23.7
3 S	14 49 57.0	10 48.7	2 13.8	19 10.4	18 26.1	11 17.5	13 11.0	12 27.7	20 5.0	6 37.8	12 15.3	17 26.1
4 S	14 53 53.6	11 48.8	2 10.7	4♊21.1	19 59.9	12 32.7	12 58.6	12 32.5	20 8.9	6 40.2	12 16.6	17 28.5
5 M	14 57 50.1	12 48.9	2 7.5	19 24.4	21 33.3	13 48.0	12 45.4	12 37.3	20 12.9	6 42.6	12 18.0	17 30.9
6 T	15 1 46.7	13 49.1	2 4.3	4♋11.6	23 6.3	15 3.2	12 31.4	12 41.8	20 17.0	6 45.1	12 19.3	17 33.3
7 W	15 5 43.3	14 49.2	2 1.1	18 37.2	24 38.9	16 18.5	12 16.6	12 46.2	20 21.2	6 47.6	12 20.7	17 35.7
8 T	15 9 39.8	15 49.4	1 57.9	2♌38.9	26 11.1	17 33.8	12 1.1	12 50.4	20 25.4	6 50.2	12 22.2	17 38.2
9 F	15 13 36.4	16 49.7	1 54.8	16 16.9	27 43.0	18 49.1	11 44.8	12 54.4	20 29.7	6 52.7	12 23.6	17 40.6
10 S	15 17 32.9	17 50.0	1 51.6	29 33.2	29 14.6	20 4.4	11 27.8	12 58.2	20 34.1	6 55.4	12 25.1	17 43.0
11 S	15 21 29.5	18 50.3	1 48.4	12♍30.8	0♐45.8	21 19.7	11 10.1	13 1.9	20 38.6	6 58.0	12 26.6	17 45.4
12 M	15 25 26.0	19 50.7	1 45.2	25 12.8	2 16.7	22 35.0	10 51.8	13 5.4	20 43.2	7 0.8	12 28.2	17 47.9
13 T	15 29 22.6	20 51.1	1 42.1	7♎42.0	3 47.2	23 50.4	10 32.9	13 8.7	20 47.8	7 3.5	12 29.8	17 50.3
14 W	15 33 19.2	21 51.5	1 38.9	20 0.9	5 17.3	25 5.7	10 13.3	13 11.8	20 52.5	7 6.3	12 31.3	17 52.7
15 T	15 37 15.7	22 51.9	1 35.7	2♏11.3	6 47.1	26 21.0	9 53.3	13 14.7	20 57.3	7 9.1	12 32.9	17 55.2
16 F	15 41 12.3	23 52.4	1 32.5	14 14.5	8 16.6	27 36.4	9 32.7	13 17.5	21 2.1	7 11.9	12 34.6	17 57.6
17 S	15 45 8.8	24 52.9	1 29.4	26 11.9	9 45.6	28 51.7	9 11.8	13 20.0	21 7.0	7 14.8	12 36.2	17 60.0
18 S	15 49 5.4	25 53.4	1 26.2	8♐ 4.5	11 14.3	0♐ 7.0	8 50.4	13 22.4	21 12.0	7 17.6	12 37.9	18 2.4
19 M	15 53 1.9	26 54.0	1 23.0	19 53.9	12 42.5	1 22.4	8 28.6	13 24.6	21 17.0	7 20.6	12 39.6	18 4.8
20 T	15 56 58.5	27 54.6	1 19.8	1♑42.1	14 10.2	2 37.7	8 6.6	13 26.6	21 22.2	7 23.5	12 41.4	18 7.2
21 W	16 0 55.0	28 55.1	1 16.6	13 31.7	15 37.4	3 53.1	7 44.3	13 28.3	21 27.3	7 26.5	12 43.1	18 9.6
22 T	16 4 51.6	29 55.8	1 13.5	25 26.1	17 4.0	5 8.4	7 21.9	13 29.9	21 32.6	7 29.5	12 44.9	18 12.0
23 F	16 8 48.2	0♐56.4	1 10.3	7♒29.4	18 30.0	6 23.8	6 59.3	13 31.3	21 37.9	7 32.6	12 46.7	18 14.4
24 S	16 12 44.7	1 57.1	1 7.1	19 46.3	19 55.3	7 39.1	6 36.6	13 32.6	21 43.3	7 35.6	12 48.5	18 16.7
25 S	16 16 41.3	2 57.7	1 3.9	2♓21.9	21 19.8	8 54.5	6 13.8	13 33.6	21 48.7	7 38.7	12 50.3	18 19.1
26 M	16 20 37.8	3 58.4	1 0.8	15 20.9	22 43.4	10 9.8	5 51.1	13 34.4	21 54.2	7 41.9	12 52.2	18 21.5
27 T	16 24 34.4	4 59.1	0 57.6	28 47.3	24 5.9	11 25.2	5 28.5	13 35.0	21 59.8	7 45.0	12 54.1	18 23.8
28 W	16 28 31.0	5 59.9	0 54.4	12♈43.6	25 27.2	12 40.5	5 5.9	13 35.4	22 5.4	7 48.2	12 55.9	18 26.2
29 T	16 32 27.5	7 0.6	0 51.2	27 9.6	26 47.2	13 55.9	4 43.6	13 35.7	22 11.0	7 51.4	12 57.9	18 28.5
30 F	16 36 24.1	8 1.4	0 48.1	12♉ 1.4	28 5.6	15 11.2	4 21.5	13 35.7	22 16.8	7 54.6	12 59.8	18 30.8
DECLINATION at NOON												
1 T	14 42 3.9	14S26.3	19S38.5	12N 0.3	16S50.4	13S35.8	22N33.7	17N34.1	22S 1.9	23S35.9	22S 4.2	2S45.9
4 S	14 53 53.6	15 22.8	19 40.6	25 9.7	18 28.8	14 51.6	22 38.3	17 30.3	22 0.5	23 35.5	22 4.0	2 48.1
7 W	15 5 43.3	16 17.1	19 42.7	23 15.0	19 58.9	16 4.0	22 42.0	17 27.1	21 58.8	23 35.1	22 3.7	2 50.2
10 S	15 17 32.9	17 9.0	19 44.9	9 23.1	21 20.2	17 12.7	22 44.7	17 24.2	21 57.1	23 34.7	22 3.4	2 52.2
13 T	15 29 22.6	17 58.2	19 47.0	7S18.1	22 32.1	18 17.3	22 46.3	17 21.8	21 55.2	23 34.3	22 3.0	2 54.2
16 F	15 41 12.3	18 44.6	19 49.1	20 46.5	23 34.0	19 17.4	22 46.7	17 19.9	21 53.2	23 33.8	22 2.7	2 56.1
19 M	15 53 1.9	19 28.0	19 51.2	26 18.3	24 25.2	20 12.8	22 45.9	17 18.5	21 51.1	23 33.3	22 2.3	2 58.0
22 T	16 4 51.6	20 8.3	19 53.3	21 25.7	25 5.0	21 3.0	22 43.9	17 17.5	21 48.9	23 32.8	22 1.9	2 59.7
25 S	16 16 41.3	20 45.2	19 55.4	8 3.0	25 33.0	21 47.9	22 40.9	17 17.1	21 46.5	23 32.3	22 1.4	3 1.3
28 W	16 28 31.0	21 18.6	19 57.5	9N31.9	25 48.6	22 26.9	22 36.9	17 17.2	21 44.1	23 31.7	22 1.0	3 2.9

DECEMBER 1990

DAY	EPHEMERIS SIDEREAL TIME	☉	☊	☽	☿	♀	♂	♃	♄	♅	♆	♇
LONGITUDE at NOON												
1 S	16 40 20.6	9♐ 2.1	0♒44.9	27♉12.1	29♐22.2	16♐26.6	3♊59.6	13♌35.5	22♑22.6	7♑57.8	13♑ 1.7	18♏33.1
2 S	16 44 17.2	10 2.9	0 41.7	12♊31.5	0♑36.7	17 41.9	3R38.0	13R35.2	22 28.4	8 1.1	13 3.7	18 35.4
3 M	16 48 13.7	11 3.8	0 38.5	27 48.3	1 48.9	18 57.3	3 16.8	13 34.7	22 34.3	8 4.4	13 5.7	18 37.7
4 T	16 52 10.3	12 4.7	0 35.3	12♋52.1	2 58.3	20 12.6	2 56.0	13 33.9	22 40.3	8 7.8	13 7.7	18 40.0
5 W	16 56 6.9	13 5.5	0 32.2	27 34.8	4 4.6	21 28.0	2 35.6	13 33.0	22 46.3	8 11.1	13 9.8	18 42.3
6 T	17 0 3.4	14 6.4	0 29.0	11♌51.6	5 7.2	22 43.3	2 15.7	13 31.8	22 52.3	8 14.4	13 11.8	18 44.5
7 F	17 3 60.0	15 7.3	0 25.8	25 40.9	6 5.7	23 58.6	1 56.3	13 30.5	22 58.4	8 17.8	13 13.8	18 46.7
8 S	17 7 56.5	16 8.2	0 22.6	9♍ 3.8	6 59.4	25 14.0	1 37.4	13 28.9	23 4.6	8 21.2	13 15.9	18 49.0
9 S	17 11 53.1	17 9.2	0 19.5	22 3.0	7 47.6	26 29.3	1 19.1	13 27.2	23 10.8	8 24.6	13 18.0	18 51.2
10 M	17 15 49.6	18 10.1	0 16.3	4♎42.0	8 29.7	27 44.7	1 1.4	13 25.2	23 17.0	8 28.0	13 20.1	18 53.3
11 T	17 19 46.2	19 11.1	0 13.1	17 4.9	9 4.8	29 0.0	0 44.4	13 23.1	23 23.3	8 31.4	13 22.2	18 55.5
12 W	17 23 42.8	20 12.1	0 9.9	29 15.4	9 32.1	0♑15.4	0 28.0	13 20.8	23 29.6	8 34.9	13 24.3	18 57.7
13 T	17 27 39.3	21 13.1	0 6.8	11♏16.8	9 50.7	1 30.7	0 12.3	13 18.3	23 36.0	8 38.4	13 26.4	18 59.8
14 F	17 31 35.9	22 14.2	0 3.6	23 12.1	9 59.8	2 46.1	29♉57.3	13 15.5	23 42.4	8 41.8	13 28.6	19 1.9
15 S	17 35 32.4	23 15.2	0 0.4	5♐ 3.6	9R58.4	4 1.4	29 43.1	13 12.6	23 48.8	8 45.3	13 30.7	19 4.0
16 S	17 39 29.0	24 16.3	29♑57.2	16 53.4	9 46.0	5 16.8	29 29.7	13 9.5	23 55.3	8 48.8	13 32.9	19 6.1
17 M	17 43 25.6	25 17.4	29 54.1	28 43.2	9 22.1	6 32.1	29 17.0	13 6.2	24 1.9	8 52.3	13 35.1	19 8.2
18 T	17 47 22.1	26 18.4	29 50.9	10♑34.7	8 46.6	7 47.5	29 5.1	13 2.8	24 8.4	8 55.9	13 37.3	19 10.2
19 W	17 51 18.7	27 19.5	29 47.7	22 30.0	7 59.6	9 2.8	28 54.0	12 59.1	24 15.0	8 59.4	13 39.5	19 12.2
20 T	17 55 15.2	28 20.6	29 44.5	4♒31.3	7 2.0	10 18.1	28 43.7	12 55.2	24 21.7	9 2.9	13 41.7	19 14.2
21 F	17 59 11.8	29 21.8	29 41.4	16 41.4	5 55.0	11 33.4	28 34.3	12 51.2	24 28.4	9 6.5	13 43.9	19 16.2
22 S	18 3 8.4	0♑22.9	29 38.2	29 3.4	4 40.5	12 48.8	28 25.7	12 47.0	24 35.1	9 10.1	13 46.1	19 18.2
23 S	18 7 4.9	1 24.0	29 35.0	11♓40.9	3 20.8	14 4.1	28 17.9	12 42.6	24 41.8	9 13.6	13 48.3	19 20.1
24 M	18 11 1.5	2 25.2	29 31.8	24 37.7	1 58.5	15 19.4	28 11.0	12 38.1	24 48.6	9 17.3	13 50.6	19 22.1
25 T	18 14 58.0	3 26.3	29 28.6	7♈57.0	0 36.4	16 34.7	28 4.9	12 33.4	24 55.4	9 20.8	13 52.8	19 24.0
26 W	18 18 54.6	4 27.4	29 25.5	21 41.3	29♐17.2	17 50.0	27 59.7	12 28.5	25 2.2	9 24.4	13 55.1	19 25.8
27 T	18 22 51.1	5 28.5	29 22.3	5♉51.5	28 3.2	19 5.3	27 55.2	12 23.5	25 9.1	9 28.0	13 57.3	19 27.7
28 F	18 26 47.7	6 29.6	29 19.1	20 26.2	26 56.6	20 20.6	27 51.6	12 18.2	25 15.9	9 31.6	13 59.6	19 29.5
29 S	18 30 44.3	7 30.8	29 15.9	5♊20.8	25 58.9	21 35.8	27 48.8	12 12.9	25 22.8	9 35.2	14 1.9	19 31.3
30 S	18 34 40.8	8 31.9	29 12.8	20 28.3	25 11.0	22 51.1	27 46.8	12 7.3	25 29.8	9 38.8	14 4.1	19 33.1
31 M	18 38 37.4	9 33.0	29 9.6	5♋39.5	24 33.4	24 6.3	27 45.6	12 1.7	25 36.7	9 42.4	14 6.4	19 34.8
DECLINATION at NOON												
1 S	16 40 20.6	21S48.4	19S59.5	23N55.9	25S51.4	23S 0.1	22N32.2	17N17.8	21S41.5	23S31.1	22S 0.5	3S 4.3
4 T	16 52 10.3	22 14.5	20 1.6	24 14.4	25 41.7	23 27.0	22 26.9	17 18.8	21 38.8	23 30.5	21 60.0	3 5.7
7 F	17 3 60.0	22 36.7	20 3.6	10 45.9	25 19.8	23 47.5	22 21.4	17 20.4	21 36.0	23 29.9	21 59.4	3 6.9
10 M	17 15 49.6	22 54.9	20 5.7	6S11.8	24 47.1	24 1.5	22 15.8	17 22.6	21 33.0	23 29.3	21 58.9	3 8.1
13 T	17 27 39.3	23 9.1	20 7.7	20 0.4	24 5.8	24 8.8	22 10.5	17 25.2	21 30.0	23 28.6	21 58.3	3 9.1
16 S	17 39 29.0	23 19.1	20 9.7	26 13.1	23 18.8	24 9.4	22 5.8	17 28.3	21 26.9	23 27.9	21 57.7	3 10.1
19 W	17 51 18.7	23 24.9	20 11.7	22 4.5	22 29.0	24 3.2	22 1.7	17 31.9	21 23.6	23 27.2	21 57.1	3 10.9
22 S	18 3 8.4	23 26.5	20 13.7	9 16.6	21 39.5	23 50.4	21 58.7	17 35.9	21 20.3	23 26.5	21 56.5	3 11.6
25 T	18 14 58.0	23 23.8	20 15.7	7N40.6	20 55.1	23 30.9	21 56.6	17 40.4	21 16.9	23 25.8	21 55.8	3 12.2
28 F	18 26 47.7	23 16.9	20 17.7	22 32.4	20 23.5	23 5.0	21 55.8	17 45.2	21 13.3	23 25.0	21 55.2	3 12.7
31 M	18 38 37.4	23 5.9	20 19.7	25 19.7	20 10.8	22 32.7	21 56.1	17 50.5	21 9.7	23 24.3	21 54.5	3 13.1

JANUARY 1991

DAY	EPHEMERIS SIDEREAL TIME	☉	☊	☽	☿	♀	♂	♃	♄	♅	♆	♇
	h m s	° ′	° ′	° ′	° ′	° ′	° ′	° ′	° ′	° ′	° ′	° ′
						LONGITUDE at NOON						
1 T	18 42 33.9	10♑34.1	29♑ 6.4	20♋44.6	24♐ 6.4	25♑21.5	27♉45.2	11♌55.8	25♑43.7	9♑46.0	14♑ 8.6	19♏36.5
2 W	18 46 30.5	11 35.3	29 3.2	5♌34.5	23R49.6	26 36.8	27D45.5	11R49.9	25 50.6	9 49.6	14 10.9	19 38.2
3 T	18 50 27.1	12 36.4	29 0.1	20 2.3	23 42.6	27 52.0	27 46.6	11 43.7	25 57.6	9 53.1	14 13.2	19 39.9
4 F	18 54 23.6	13 37.5	28 56.9	4♍ 4.0	23D45.0	29 7.2	27 48.5	11 37.5	26 4.6	9 56.7	14 15.5	19 41.5
5 S	18 58 20.2	14 38.7	28 53.7	17 38.3	23 55.8	0♒22.4	27 51.1	11 31.1	26 11.7	10 0.3	14 17.7	19 43.1
6 S	19 2 16.7	15 39.8	28 50.5	0♎46.3	24 14.6	1 37.6	27 54.5	11 24.6	26 18.7	10 3.9	14 20.0	19 44.7
7 M	19 6 13.3	16 41.0	28 47.4	13 30.7	24 40.5	2 52.7	27 58.6	11 18.0	26 25.8	10 7.5	14 22.3	19 46.3
8 T	19 10 9.8	17 42.1	28 44.2	25 55.4	25 12.9	4 7.9	28 3.4	11 11.2	26 32.9	10 11.1	14 24.5	19 47.8
9 W	19 14 6.4	18 43.3	28 41.0	8♏ 4.7	25 51.1	5 23.1	28 8.9	11 4.3	26 39.9	10 14.6	14 26.8	19 49.3
10 T	19 18 3.0	19 44.4	28 37.8	20 3.1	26 34.5	6 38.2	28 15.1	10 57.4	26 47.0	10 18.2	14 29.1	19 50.8
11 F	19 21 59.5	20 45.6	28 34.6	1♐54.8	27 22.6	7 53.4	28 22.0	10 50.3	26 54.2	10 21.7	14 31.3	19 52.2
12 S	19 25 56.1	21 46.7	28 31.5	13 43.5	28 14.9	9 8.5	28 29.6	10 43.1	27 1.3	10 25.3	14 33.6	19 53.6
13 S	19 29 52.6	22 47.9	28 28.3	25 32.7	29 10.9	10 23.6	28 37.8	10 35.8	27 8.4	10 28.8	14 35.9	19 55.0
14 M	19 33 49.2	23 49.1	28 25.1	7♑25.2	0♑10.3	11 38.8	28 46.7	10 28.5	27 15.6	10 32.4	14 38.2	19 56.4
15 T	19 37 45.7	24 50.2	28 21.9	19 23.1	1 12.7	12 53.9	28 56.2	10 21.0	27 22.7	10 35.9	14 40.4	19 57.7
16 W	19 41 42.3	25 51.3	28 18.8	1♒28.5	2 17.8	14 9.0	29 6.4	10 13.5	27 29.8	10 39.4	14 42.7	19 59.0
17 T	19 45 38.9	26 52.4	28 15.6	13 42.9	3 25.4	15 24.0	29 17.1	10 5.9	27 37.0	10 42.9	14 44.9	20 0.2
18 F	19 49 35.4	27 53.5	28 12.4	26 7.9	4 35.1	16 39.1	29 28.4	9 58.2	27 44.1	10 46.4	14 47.1	20 1.5
19 S	19 53 32.0	28 54.6	28 9.2	8♓44.8	5 46.8	17 54.1	29 40.4	9 50.5	27 51.3	10 49.9	14 49.3	20 2.7
20 S	19 57 28.5	29 55.7	28 6.1	21 35.3	7 0.4	19 9.1	29 52.9	9 42.7	27 58.4	10 53.3	14 51.6	20 3.8
21 M	20 1 25.1	0♒56.8	28 2.9	4♈40.8	8 15.6	20 24.1	0♊ 5.9	9 34.8	28 5.5	10 56.8	14 53.8	20 4.9
22 T	20 5 21.6	1 57.9	27 59.7	18 2.9	9 32.3	21 39.1	0 19.6	9 26.9	28 12.7	11 0.2	14 56.0	20 6.0
23 W	20 9 18.2	2 58.9	27 56.5	1♉42.5	10 50.4	22 54.0	0 33.7	9 19.0	28 19.8	11 3.6	14 58.2	20 7.1
24 T	20 13 14.8	3 59.9	27 53.3	15 40.3	12 9.8	24 8.9	0 48.4	9 11.1	28 26.9	11 7.0	15 0.3	20 8.1
25 F	20 17 11.3	5 0.9	27 50.2	29 55.6	13 30.4	25 23.8	1 3.5	9 3.1	28 34.0	11 10.3	15 2.5	20 9.1
26 S	20 21 7.9	6 1.9	27 47.0	14♊26.2	14 52.1	26 38.7	1 19.2	8 55.1	28 41.1	11 13.7	15 4.7	20 10.0
27 S	20 25 4.4	7 2.9	27 43.8	29 8.3	16 14.9	27 53.6	1 35.4	8 47.1	28 48.2	11 17.0	15 6.8	20 11.0
28 M	20 29 1.0	8 3.8	27 40.6	13♋56.4	17 38.7	29 8.4	1 52.0	8 39.1	28 55.3	11 20.3	15 8.9	20 11.8
29 T	20 32 57.5	9 4.8	27 37.5	28 43.6	19 3.5	0♓23.2	2 9.1	8 31.0	29 2.4	11 23.6	15 11.1	20 12.7
30 W	20 36 54.1	10 5.7	27 34.3	13♌22.7	20 29.2	1 38.0	2 26.6	8 23.0	29 9.4	11 26.9	15 13.2	20 13.5
31 T	20 40 50.7	11 6.6	27 31.1	27 46.8	21 55.8	2 52.7	2 44.5	8 15.0	29 16.5	11 30.1	15 15.3	20 14.3
						DECLINATION at NOON						
1 T	18 42 33.9	23S 1.3	20S 20.3	22N 30.2	20S 10.9	22S 20.6	21N 56.5	17N 52.3	21S 8.5	23S 24.0	21S 54.3	3S 13.2
4 F	18 54 23.6	22 44.7	20 22.3	7 7.2	20 22.5	21 40.2	21 58.5	17 57.9	21 4.8	23 23.3	21 53.6	3 13.4
7 M	19 6 13.3	22 24.0	20 24.3	10S 2.5	20 46.2	20 54.0	22 1.7	18 3.9	21 1.0	23 22.5	21 52.9	3 13.6
10 T	19 18 3.0	21 59.4	20 26.2	22 28.5	21 15.9	20 2.3	22 5.9	18 10.1	20 57.2	23 21.7	21 52.2	3 13.6
13 S	19 29 52.6	21 30.9	20 28.1	26 12.7	21 46.3	19 5.3	22 11.3	18 16.5	20 53.3	23 20.9	21 51.5	3 13.5
16 W	19 41 42.3	20 58.6	20 30.1	19 31.3	22 13.5	18 3.4	22 17.7	18 23.0	20 49.3	23 20.1	21 50.8	3 13.3
19 S	19 53 32.0	20 22.8	20 32.0	5 4.9	22 34.9	16 57.0	22 25.0	18 29.7	20 45.3	23 19.3	21 50.1	3 13.0
22 T	20 5 21.6	19 43.5	20 33.9	11N 53.7	22 48.5	15 46.4	22 33.1	18 36.4	20 41.2	23 18.5	21 49.3	3 12.5
25 F	20 17 11.3	19 0.9	20 35.8	24 31.7	22 52.9	14 31.9	22 41.8	18 43.1	20 37.1	23 17.7	21 48.6	3 12.0
28 M	20 29 1.0	18 15.2	20 37.7	23 59.9	22 47.2	13 13.8	22 51.2	18 49.8	20 33.0	23 16.9	21 47.9	3 11.4
31 T	20 40 50.7	17 26.5	20 39.5	9 46.9	22 30.6	11 52.7	23 0.9	18 56.4	20 28.8	23 16.1	21 47.2	3 10.7

FEBRUARY 1991

DAY	EPHEMERIS SIDEREAL TIME	☉	☊	☽	☿	♀	♂	♃	♄	♅	♆	♇
						LONGITUDE at NOON						
1 F	20 44 47.2	12♒ 7.5	27♑27.9	11♍50.5	23♑23.2	4♓ 7.4	3♊ 2.9	8♌ 7.0	29♑23.5	11♑33.4	15♑17.3	20♏15.0
2 S	20 48 43.8	13 8.3	27 24.8	25 30.5	24 51.5	5 22.1	3 21.7	7R59.1	29 30.5	11 36.6	15 19.4	20 15.7
3 S	20 52 40.3	14 9.2	27 21.6	8♎45.6	26 20.6	6 36.8	3 40.9	7 51.1	29 37.5	11 39.7	15 21.5	20 16.4
4 M	20 56 36.9	15 10.1	27 18.4	21 36.8	27 50.6	7 51.5	4 0.5	7 43.2	29 44.5	11 42.9	15 23.5	20 17.1
5 T	21 0 33.4	16 10.9	27 15.2	4♏ 6.7	29 21.3	9 6.1	4 20.5	7 35.4	29 51.5	11 46.1	15 25.6	20 17.7
6 W	21 4 30.0	17 11.7	27 12.0	16 19.2	0♒52.8	10 20.7	4 40.8	7 27.5	29 58.4	11 49.2	15 27.6	20 18.3
7 T	21 8 26.5	18 12.5	27 8.9	28 18.8	2 25.1	11 35.2	5 1.5	7 19.8	0♒ 5.4	11 52.2	15 29.6	20 18.8
8 F	21 12 23.1	19 13.3	27 5.7	10♐10.4	3 58.2	12 49.8	5 22.6	7 12.0	0 12.2	11 55.3	15 31.5	20 19.3
9 S	21 16 19.7	20 14.0	27 2.5	21 58.9	5 32.1	14 4.3	5 44.0	7 4.4	0 19.1	11 58.3	15 33.5	20 19.8
10 S	21 20 16.2	21 14.8	26 59.3	3♑48.9	7 6.9	15 18.7	6 5.8	6 56.8	0 26.0	12 1.3	15 35.4	20 20.2
11 M	21 24 12.8	22 15.5	26 56.2	15 44.5	8 42.4	16 33.2	6 27.9	6 49.3	0 32.8	12 4.3	15 37.4	20 20.6
12 T	21 28 9.3	23 16.2	26 53.0	27 49.3	10 18.7	17 47.6	6 50.3	6 41.8	0 39.6	12 7.2	15 39.3	20 21.0
13 W	21 32 5.9	24 16.9	26 49.8	10♒ 5.8	11 55.9	19 2.0	7 13.1	6 34.5	0 46.3	12 10.1	15 41.1	20 21.3
14 T	21 36 2.4	25 17.6	26 46.6	22 35.9	13 33.9	20 16.3	7 36.1	6 27.2	0 53.1	12 12.9	15 43.0	20 21.6
15 F	21 39 59.0	26 18.2	26 43.5	5♓20.5	15 12.7	21 30.6	7 59.5	6 20.0	0 59.8	12 15.8	15 44.8	20 21.8
16 S	21 43 55.5	27 18.8	26 40.3	18 19.8	16 52.4	22 44.9	8 23.2	6 12.9	1 6.4	12 18.6	15 46.7	20 22.0
17 S	21 47 52.1	28 19.4	26 37.1	1♈33.0	18 33.0	23 59.1	8 47.2	6 6.0	1 13.1	12 21.3	15 48.5	20 22.2
18 M	21 51 48.7	29 20.0	26 33.9	14 59.2	20 14.5	25 13.3	9 11.4	5 59.1	1 19.7	12 24.1	15 50.2	20 22.3
19 T	21 55 45.2	0♓20.5	26 30.7	28 37.0	21 56.9	26 27.5	9 35.9	5 52.4	1 26.2	12 26.8	15 52.0	20 22.4
20 W	21 59 41.8	1 21.0	26 27.6	12♉25.2	23 40.2	27 41.6	10 0.7	5 45.7	1 32.8	12 29.4	15 53.7	20 22.5
21 T	22 3 38.3	2 21.5	26 24.4	26 22.7	25 24.4	28 55.6	10 25.8	5 39.2	1 39.2	12 32.1	15 55.4	20 22.5
22 F	22 7 34.9	3 21.9	26 21.2	10♊28.2	27 9.6	0♈ 9.7	10 51.1	5 32.9	1 45.7	12 34.7	15 57.1	20 22.5
23 S	22 11 31.4	4 22.3	26 18.0	24 40.5	28 55.7	1 23.6	11 16.7	5 26.6	1 52.1	12 37.2	15 58.8	20 22.5
24 S	22 15 28.0	5 22.7	26 14.9	8♋57.9	0♓42.8	2 37.6	11 42.5	5 20.5	1 58.5	12 39.7	16 0.4	20R22.4
25 M	22 19 24.5	6 23.1	26 11.7	23 17.8	2 30.9	3 51.5	12 8.6	5 14.6	2 4.8	12 42.3	16 2.1	20 22.3
26 T	22 23 21.1	7 23.4	26 8.5	7♌37.0	4 20.0	5 5.3	12 34.8	5 8.8	2 11.1	12 44.7	16 3.7	20 22.2
27 W	22 27 17.6	8 23.7	26 5.3	21 51.2	6 10.0	6 19.1	13 1.3	5 3.1	2 17.4	12 47.1	16 5.2	20 22.0
28 T	22 31 14.2	9 23.9	26 2.1	5♍55.8	8 0.9	7 32.8	13 28.0	4 57.6	2 23.6	12 49.5	16 6.8	20 21.8
						DECLINATION at NOON						
1 F	20 44 47.2	17S 9.7	20S 40.2	3N 44.3	22S 22.6	11S 25.0	23N 4.3	18N 58.6	20S 27.4	23S 15.8	21S 46.9	3S 10.4
4 M	20 56 36.9	16 17.3	20 42.0	13S 16.6	21 50.9	10 0.1	23 14.5	19 5.1	20 23.2	23 15.0	21 46.2	3 9.6
7 T	21 8 26.5	15 22.4	20 43.9	24 12.9	21 7.4	8 32.9	23 24.9	19 11.4	20 19.1	23 14.2	21 45.5	3 8.7
10 S	21 20 16.2	14 25.2	20 45.7	25 32.5	20 11.8	7 3.8	23 35.4	19 17.4	20 14.9	23 13.5	21 44.8	3 7.6
13 W	21 32 5.9	13 25.8	20 47.6	16 39.3	19 3.9	5 32.9	23 45.9	19 23.3	20 10.7	23 12.8	21 44.2	3 6.5
16 S	21 43 55.5	12 24.3	20 49.4	0 54.5	17 43.8	4 0.8	23 56.2	19 28.8	20 6.6	23 12.0	21 43.5	3 5.4
19 T	21 55 45.2	11 21.2	20 51.2	15N 50.3	16 11.2	2 27.7	24 6.4	19 34.1	20 2.5	23 11.3	21 42.9	3 4.1
22 F	22 7 34.9	10 16.4	20 53.0	25 47.5	14 26.1	0 54.0	24 16.2	19 39.0	19 58.4	23 10.7	21 42.2	3 2.8
25 M	22 19 24.5	9 10.2	20 54.8	21 48.7	12 28.8	0N 40.1	24 25.7	19 43.6	19 54.3	23 10.0	21 41.6	3 1.4
28 T	22 31 14.2	8 2.8	20 56.6	6 20.7	10 19.4	2 14.0	24 34.6	19 47.8	19 50.4	23 9.4	21 41.0	2 59.9

MARCH 1991

LONGITUDE at NOON

DAY	EPHEMERIS SIDEREAL TIME	☉	☊	☾	☿	♀	♂	♃	♄	♅	♆	♇
	h m s	° ′	° ′	° ′	° ′	° ′	° ′	° ′	° ′	° ′	° ′	° ′
1 F	22 35 10.8	10♓24.1	25♑59.0	19♍46.3	9♓52.8	8♈46.5	13♊54.9	4♌52.2	2♒29.7	12♑51.8	16♑ 8.3	20♏21.5
2 S	22 39 7.3	11 24.3	25 55.8	3♎19.1	11 45.5	10 0.1	14 22.0	4R47.0	2 35.8	12 54.1	16 9.8	20R21.2
3 S	22 43 3.9	12 24.5	25 52.6	16 31.7	13 39.2	11 13.7	14 49.3	4 41.9	2 41.8	12 56.3	16 11.3	20 20.9
4 M	22 47 0.4	13 24.6	25 49.4	29 23.4	15 33.6	12 27.2	15 16.8	4 37.0	2 47.8	12 58.5	16 12.7	20 20.5
5 T	22 50 57.0	14 24.7	25 46.3	11♏55.4	17 28.8	13 40.7	15 44.5	4 32.3	2 53.8	13 0.7	16 14.1	20 20.1
6 W	22 54 53.5	15 24.8	25 43.1	24 10.1	19 24.7	14 54.1	16 12.4	4 27.7	2 59.7	13 2.8	16 15.5	20 19.7
7 T	22 58 50.1	16 24.8	25 39.9	6♐11.3	21 21.1	16 7.5	16 40.5	4 23.3	3 5.6	13 4.9	16 16.8	20 19.3
8 F	23 2 46.6	17 24.9	25 36.7	18 3.9	23 17.9	17 20.8	17 8.7	4 19.1	3 11.3	13 6.9	16 18.2	20 18.8
9 S	23 6 43.2	18 24.9	25 33.5	29 52.8	25 14.9	18 34.1	17 37.1	4 15.1	3 17.1	13 8.9	16 19.5	20 18.2
10 S	23 10 39.7	19 24.8	25 30.4	11♑43.4	27 12.0	19 47.3	18 5.7	4 11.2	3 22.8	13 10.8	16 20.7	20 17.7
11 M	23 14 36.3	20 24.8	25 27.2	23 41.0	29 8.9	21 0.5	18 34.5	4 7.5	3 28.4	13 12.7	16 22.0	20 17.1
12 T	23 18 32.8	21 24.7	25 24.0	5♒50.2	1♈ 5.4	22 13.6	19 3.4	4 4.0	3 34.0	13 14.6	16 23.2	20 16.5
13 W	23 22 29.4	22 24.6	25 20.8	18 15.0	3 1.1	23 26.6	19 32.5	4 0.6	3 39.5	13 16.4	16 24.4	20 15.8
14 T	23 26 25.9	23 24.4	25 17.7	0♓58.0	4 55.8	24 39.6	20 1.8	3 57.5	3 44.9	13 18.1	16 25.5	20 15.1
15 F	23 30 22.5	24 24.3	25 14.5	14 0.7	6 49.1	25 52.5	20 31.2	3 54.5	3 50.3	13 19.8	16 26.7	20 14.4
16 S	23 34 19.1	25 24.1	25 11.3	27 22.8	8 40.5	27 5.4	21 0.8	3 51.7	3 55.6	13 21.5	16 27.8	20 13.6
17 S	23 38 15.6	26 23.8	25 8.1	11♈ 2.2	10 29.6	28 18.2	21 30.5	3 49.1	4 0.9	13 23.1	16 28.8	20 12.9
18 M	23 42 12.2	27 23.6	25 4.9	24 55.6	12 16.1	29 31.0	22 0.4	3 46.8	4 6.2	13 24.8	16 29.9	20 12.1
19 T	23 46 8.7	28 23.3	25 1.8	8♉58.9	13 59.3	0♉43.6	22 30.4	3 44.6	4 11.3	13 26.3	16 30.9	20 11.3
20 W	23 50 5.3	29 22.9	24 58.6	23 7.9	15 38.9	1 56.3	23 0.5	3 42.5	4 16.4	13 27.8	16 31.9	20 10.4
21 T	23 54 1.8	0♈22.6	24 55.4	7♊18.7	17 14.4	3 8.8	23 30.8	3 40.7	4 21.4	13 29.2	16 32.8	20 9.5
22 F	23 57 58.4	1 22.1	24 52.2	21 28.7	18 45.3	4 21.3	24 1.2	3 39.1	4 26.3	13 30.6	16 33.7	20 8.6
23 S	0 1 54.9	2 21.7	24 49.1	5♋35.9	20 11.2	5 33.7	24 31.7	3 37.6	4 31.2	13 31.9	16 34.6	20 7.6
24 S	0 5 51.5	3 21.2	24 45.9	19 39.4	21 31.7	6 46.0	25 2.4	3 36.4	4 36.0	13 33.2	16 35.4	20 6.6
25 M	0 9 48.0	4 20.6	24 42.7	3♌38.4	22 46.4	7 58.2	25 33.1	3 35.3	4 40.7	13 34.4	16 36.3	20 5.6
26 T	0 13 44.6	5 20.1	24 39.5	17 32.1	23 55.0	9 10.4	26 4.0	3 34.4	4 45.3	13 35.6	16 37.0	20 4.6
27 W	0 17 41.1	6 19.4	24 36.3	1♍19.1	24 57.1	10 22.5	26 35.0	3 33.8	4 49.9	13 36.7	16 37.8	20 3.5
28 T	0 21 37.7	7 18.8	24 33.2	14 57.6	25 52.5	11 34.5	27 6.2	3 33.3	4 54.4	13 37.8	16 38.5	20 2.4
29 F	0 25 34.2	8 18.1	24 30.0	28 25.3	26 41.0	12 46.4	27 37.4	3 33.0	4 58.9	13 38.8	16 39.2	20 1.3
30 S	0 29 30.8	9 17.4	24 26.8	11♎39.7	27 22.5	13 58.2	28 8.7	3 32.9	5 3.2	13 39.8	16 39.8	20 0.1
31 S	0 33 27.4	10 16.6	24 23.6	24 39.0	27 56.7	15 10.0	28 40.1	3D33.0	5 7.5	13 40.8	16 40.5	19 59.0

DECLINATION at NOON

DAY	EPHEMERIS SIDEREAL TIME	☉	☊	☾	☿	♀	♂	♃	♄	♅	♆	♇
1 F	22 35 10.8	7S40.1	20S57.2	0N17.5	9S33.7	2N45.2	24N37.5	19N49.1	19S49.1	23S 9.2	21S40.8	2S59.4
4 M	22 47 0.4	6 31.3	20 59.0	16S 3.2	7 9.2	4 18.6	24 45.7	19 52.8	19 45.2	23 8.6	21 40.3	2 57.9
7 T	22 58 50.1	5 21.7	21 0.7	25 15.5	4 34.7	5 51.2	24 53.2	19 56.1	19 41.4	23 8.0	21 39.7	2 56.3
10 S	23 10 39.7	4 11.5	21 2.5	24 15.3	1 52.5	7 22.6	25 0.0	19 58.9	19 37.6	23 7.5	21 39.2	2 54.7
13 W	23 22 29.4	3 0.7	21 4.2	13 34.3	0N54.1	8 52.6	25 6.0	20 1.4	19 34.0	23 7.1	21 38.7	2 53.1
16 S	23 34 19.1	1 49.7	21 6.0	3N 1.9	3 40.1	10 20.8	25 11.2	20 3.5	19 30.5	23 6.6	21 38.3	2 51.4
19 T	23 46 8.7	0 38.5	21 7.7	19 9.7	6 19.1	11 46.9	25 15.5	20 5.1	19 27.0	23 6.2	21 37.9	2 49.7
22 F	23 57 58.4	0N32.7	21 9.4	26 1.0	8 44.0	13 10.6	25 18.7	20 6.3	19 23.7	23 5.9	21 37.5	2 48.0
25 M	0 9 48.0	1 43.6	21 11.1	18 39.2	10 48.1	14 31.4	25 21.0	20 7.1	19 20.6	23 5.5	21 37.1	2 46.3
28 T	0 21 37.7	2 54.2	21 12.8	2 23.1	12 25.8	15 49.2	25 22.2	20 7.4	19 17.6	23 5.3	21 36.8	2 44.5
31 S	0 33 27.4	4 4.2	21 14.5	14S12.8	13 32.8	17 3.5	25 22.3	20 7.4	19 14.7	23 5.0	21 36.5	2 42.8

APRIL 1991

LONGITUDE at NOON

DAY	EPHEMERIS SIDEREAL TIME	☉	☊	☾	☿	♀	♂	♃	♄	♅	♆	♇
1 M	0 37 23.9	11♈15.8	24♑20.5	7♏22.1	28♈23.7	16♉21.7	29♊11.7	3♌33.3	5♒11.7	13♑41.7	16♑41.0	19♏57.8
2 T	0 41 20.5	12 15.0	24 17.3	19 49.0	28 43.4	17 33.3	29 43.3	3 33.7	5 15.8	13 42.5	16 41.6	19R56.6
3 W	0 45 17.0	13 14.2	24 14.1	2♐ 1.2	28 55.8	18 44.8	0♋15.0	3 34.4	5 19.9	13 43.3	16 42.1	19 55.3
4 T	0 49 13.6	14 13.3	24 10.9	14 1.5	29 1.1	19 56.2	0 46.8	3 35.2	5 23.8	13 44.0	16 42.6	19 54.1
5 F	0 53 10.1	15 12.4	24 7.7	25 53.6	28R59.4	21 7.6	1 18.8	3 36.3	5 27.7	13 44.7	16 43.1	19 52.8
6 S	0 57 6.7	16 11.4	24 4.6	7♑42.1	28 51.0	22 18.8	1 50.8	3 37.5	5 31.6	13 45.3	16 43.5	19 51.5
7 S	1 1 3.2	17 10.4	24 1.4	19 32.4	28 36.2	23 30.0	2 22.9	3 38.9	5 35.3	13 45.9	16 43.9	19 50.1
8 M	1 4 59.8	18 9.5	23 58.2	1♒30.0	28 15.5	24 41.1	2 55.1	3 40.6	5 39.0	13 46.5	16 44.3	19 48.8
9 T	1 8 56.3	19 8.5	23 55.0	13 40.2	27 49.3	25 52.1	3 27.4	3 42.3	5 42.5	13 46.9	16 44.6	19 47.5
10 W	1 12 52.9	20 7.4	23 51.9	26 8.1	27 18.2	27 3.0	3 59.8	3 44.3	5 46.0	13 47.4	16 44.9	19 46.1
11 T	1 16 49.4	21 6.3	23 48.7	8♓57.6	26 43.0	28 13.8	4 32.2	3 46.5	5 49.4	13 47.7	16 45.2	19 44.7
12 F	1 20 46.0	22 5.2	23 45.5	22 11.2	26 4.3	29 24.6	5 4.8	3 48.8	5 52.7	13 48.1	16 45.4	19 43.2
13 S	1 24 42.5	23 4.0	23 42.3	5♈49.2	25 22.9	0♊35.2	5 37.4	3 51.3	5 56.0	13 48.3	16 45.6	19 41.8
14 S	1 28 39.1	24 2.8	23 39.1	19 49.6	24 39.7	1 45.7	6 10.1	3 54.0	5 59.1	13 48.5	16 45.7	19 40.3
15 M	1 32 35.7	25 1.6	23 36.0	4♉ 8.0	23 55.5	2 56.2	6 42.9	3 56.9	6 2.1	13 48.7	16 45.8	19 38.9
16 T	1 36 32.2	26 0.4	23 32.8	18 38.2	23 11.2	4 6.5	7 15.8	3 59.9	6 5.1	13 48.8	16 45.9	19 37.4
17 W	1 40 28.8	26 59.1	23 29.6	3♊13.3	22 27.5	5 16.7	7 48.7	4 3.1	6 8.0	13 48.9	16 46.0	19 35.9
18 T	1 44 25.3	27 57.8	23 26.4	17 46.6	21 45.3	6 26.8	8 21.7	4 6.6	6 10.7	13 48.9	16 46.0	19 34.3
19 F	1 48 21.9	28 56.4	23 23.3	2♋12.7	21 5.2	7 36.8	8 54.8	4 10.1	6 13.4	13 48.9	16 46.0	19 32.8
20 S	1 52 18.4	29 55.0	23 20.1	16 28.4	20 28.0	8 46.7	9 28.0	4 13.9	6 16.0	13R48.8	16 46.0	19 31.2
21 S	1 56 15.0	0♉53.6	23 16.9	0♌31.9	19 54.0	9 56.5	10 1.2	4 17.8	6 18.5	13 48.6	16R45.9	19 29.7
22 M	2 0 11.5	1 52.1	23 13.7	14 22.7	19 23.9	11 6.1	10 34.5	4 21.9	6 21.0	13 48.4	16 45.8	19 28.1
23 T	2 4 8.1	2 50.6	23 10.5	28 1.4	18 58.0	12 15.7	11 7.9	4 26.2	6 23.3	13 48.2	16 45.6	19 26.5
24 W	2 8 4.6	3 49.1	23 7.4	11♍28.5	18 36.6	13 25.1	11 41.3	4 30.6	6 25.5	13 47.9	16 45.5	19 24.9
25 T	2 12 1.2	4 47.5	23 4.2	24 44.3	18 19.8	14 34.4	12 14.8	4 35.2	6 27.7	13 47.6	16 45.3	19 23.3
26 F	2 15 57.8	5 45.9	23 1.0	7♎48.7	18 7.9	15 43.5	12 48.4	4 39.9	6 29.7	13 47.2	16 45.0	19 21.7
27 S	2 19 54.3	6 44.3	22 57.8	20 41.6	18 1.0	16 52.5	13 22.0	4 44.8	6 31.6	13 46.7	16 44.7	19 20.1
28 S	2 23 50.9	7 42.6	22 54.7	3♏22.3	17 59.0	18 1.4	13 55.6	4 49.9	6 33.5	13 46.3	16 44.4	19 18.4
29 M	2 27 47.4	8 40.9	22 51.5	15 50.7	18D 1.9	19 10.2	14 29.4	4 55.2	6 35.3	13 45.8	16 44.2	19 16.8
30 T	2 31 44.0	9 39.2	22 48.3	28 7.0	18 9.7	20 18.8	15 3.2	5 0.5	6 37.0	13 45.2	16 43.8	19 15.2

DECLINATION at NOON

DAY	EPHEMERIS SIDEREAL TIME	☉	☊	☾	☿	♀	♂	♃	♄	♅	♆	♇
1 M	0 37 23.9	4N27.4	21S15.1	18S35.7	13N47.8	17N27.5	25N22.1	20N 7.3	19S13.8	23S 5.0	21S36.4	2S42.2
4 T	0 49 13.6	5 36.5	21 16.7	25 43.2	14 9.9	18 36.8	25 20.7	20 6.7	19 11.1	23 4.8	21 36.2	2 40.5
7 S	1 1 3.2	6 44.8	21 18.4	22 25.1	13 57.5	19 41.9	25 18.1	20 5.7	19 8.6	23 4.7	21 36.0	2 38.8
10 W	1 12 52.9	7 52.0	21 20.0	10 17.1	13 12.7	20 42.6	25 14.4	20 4.3	19 6.3	23 4.6	21 35.8	2 37.1
13 S	1 24 42.5	8 58.0	21 21.7	6N41.4	12 1.4	21 38.6	25 9.4	20 2.5	19 4.1	23 4.6	21 35.6	2 35.4
16 T	1 36 32.2	10 2.7	21 23.3	21 42.9	10 33.5	22 29.6	25 3.1	20 0.4	19 2.2	23 4.6	21 35.5	2 33.8
19 F	1 48 21.9	11 5.9	21 24.9	25 11.7	9 1.2	23 15.4	24 55.6	19 57.8	19 0.4	23 4.7	21 35.5	2 32.2
22 M	2 0 11.5	12 7.5	21 26.5	14 44.0	7 36.2	23 55.7	24 46.8	19 54.9	18 58.8	23 4.8	21 35.5	2 30.7
25 T	2 12 1.2	13 7.2	21 28.1	1S59.6	6 27.5	24 30.4	24 36.7	19 51.5	18 57.5	23 5.0	21 35.5	2 29.2
28 S	2 23 50.9	14 5.0	21 29.7	17 15.5	5 40.1	24 59.2	24 25.3	19 47.9	18 56.3	23 5.2	21 35.5	2 27.8

MAY 1991

DAY	EPHEMERIS SIDEREAL TIME	☉	☊	☾	☿	♀	♂	♃	♄	♅	♆	♇
	h m s	° ′	° ′	° ′	° ′	° ′	° ′	° ′	° ′	° ′	° ′	° ′
						LONGITUDE at NOON						
1 W	2 35 40.5	10♉37.4	22♑45.1	10♐12.3	18♈22.3	21♊27.3	15♋37.0	5♌ 6.1	6♒38.5	13♑44.5	16♑43.4	19♏13.5
2 T	2 39 37.1	11 35.6	22 42.0	22 8.5	18 39.4	22 35.6	16 10.9	5 11.8	6 40.0	13R43.9	16R43.0	19R11.9
3 F	2 43 33.6	12 33.8	22 38.8	3♑58.4	19 1.2	23 43.8	16 44.9	5 17.6	6 41.4	13 43.1	16 42.5	19 10.2
4 S	2 47 30.2	13 32.0	22 35.6	15 45.9	19 27.2	24 51.9	17 18.9	5 23.6	6 42.7	13 42.4	16 42.0	19 8.5
5 S	2 51 26.7	14 30.1	22 32.4	27 35.5	19 57.5	25 59.8	17 53.0	5 29.7	6 43.9	13 41.5	16 41.5	19 6.9
6 M	2 55 23.3	15 28.2	22 29.2	9♒32.3	20 31.9	27 7.5	18 27.1	5 36.0	6 45.0	13 40.7	16 41.0	19 5.2
7 T	2 59 19.9	16 26.3	22 26.1	21 41.5	21 10.2	28 15.1	19 1.2	5 42.4	6 46.0	13 39.7	16 40.4	19 3.5
8 W	3 3 16.4	17 24.4	22 22.9	4♓ 8.6	21 52.3	29 22.5	19 35.5	5 49.0	6 46.8	13 38.8	16 39.8	19 1.8
9 T	3 7 13.0	18 22.4	22 19.7	16 58.1	22 38.0	0♋29.8	20 9.7	5 55.7	6 47.6	13 37.8	16 39.1	19 0.1
10 F	3 11 9.5	19 20.4	22 16.5	0♈13.7	23 27.2	1 36.9	20 44.1	6 2.5	6 48.3	13 36.7	16 38.5	18 58.4
11 S	3 15 6.1	20 18.4	22 13.4	13 57.0	24 19.8	2 43.8	21 18.5	6 9.5	6 48.9	13 35.6	16 37.8	18 56.8
12 S	3 19 2.6	21 16.4	22 10.2	28 7.0	25 15.6	3 50.6	21 52.9	6 16.6	6 49.4	13 34.5	16 37.0	18 55.1
13 M	3 22 59.2	22 14.4	22 7.0	12♉39.9	26 14.5	4 57.2	22 27.4	6 23.8	6 49.8	13 33.3	16 36.3	18 53.4
14 T	3 26 55.8	23 12.3	22 3.8	27 29.1	27 16.5	6 3.6	23 1.9	6 31.2	6 50.1	13 32.1	16 35.5	18 51.7
15 W	3 30 52.3	24 10.2	22 0.6	12♊26.1	28 21.3	7 9.8	23 36.5	6 38.7	6 50.3	13 30.8	16 34.7	18 50.0
16 T	3 34 48.9	25 8.1	21 57.5	27 22.2	29 29.0	8 15.9	24 11.1	6 46.4	6 50.5	13 29.5	16 33.9	18 48.4
17 F	3 38 45.4	26 5.9	21 54.3	12♋ 9.5	0♉39.5	9 21.7	24 45.8	6 54.2	6 50.5	13 28.1	16 33.0	18 46.7
18 S	3 42 42.0	27 3.7	21 51.1	26 42.0	1 52.6	10 27.3	25 20.5	7 2.1	6R50.4	13 26.7	16 32.1	18 45.0
19 S	3 46 38.5	28 1.5	21 47.9	10♌56.3	3 8.3	11 32.8	25 55.3	7 10.1	6 50.2	13 25.3	16 31.2	18 43.4
20 M	3 50 35.1	28 59.3	21 44.8	24 51.3	4 26.7	12 38.0	26 30.2	7 18.3	6 49.9	13 23.9	16 30.3	18 41.8
21 T	3 54 31.6	29 57.1	21 41.6	8♍27.0	5 47.5	13 43.0	27 5.0	7 26.5	6 49.6	13 22.3	16 29.3	18 40.1
22 W	3 58 28.2	0♊54.8	21 38.4	21 44.9	7 10.8	14 47.8	27 39.9	7 34.9	6 49.1	13 20.8	16 28.3	18 38.5
23 T	4 2 24.8	1 52.4	21 35.2	4♎46.8	8 36.6	15 52.3	28 14.8	7 43.4	6 48.5	13 19.2	16 27.3	18 36.9
24 F	4 6 21.3	2 50.1	21 32.1	17 34.4	10 4.8	16 56.6	28 49.8	7 52.0	6 47.8	13 17.6	16 26.3	18 35.2
25 S	4 10 17.9	3 47.7	21 28.9	0♏ 9.2	11 35.4	18 0.6	29 24.8	8 0.7	6 47.1	13 15.9	16 25.2	18 33.6
26 S	4 14 14.4	4 45.3	21 25.7	12 32.7	13 8.3	19 4.4	29 59.9	8 9.6	6 46.2	13 14.2	16 24.1	18 32.0
27 M	4 18 11.0	5 42.9	21 22.5	24 46.1	14 43.7	20 7.9	0♌35.0	8 18.5	6 45.2	13 12.5	16 23.0	18 30.4
28 T	4 22 7.5	6 40.5	21 19.4	6♐50.5	16 21.4	21 11.2	1 10.1	8 27.6	6 44.2	13 10.7	16 21.8	18 28.9
29 W	4 26 4.1	7 38.0	21 16.2	18 47.5	18 1.5	22 14.1	1 45.3	8 36.7	6 43.0	13 8.9	16 20.7	18 27.3
30 T	4 30 0.7	8 35.6	21 13.0	0♑38.7	19 44.0	23 16.8	2 20.5	8 46.0	6 41.8	13 7.1	16 19.5	18 25.7
31 F	4 33 57.2	9 33.1	21 9.8	12 26.6	21 28.8	24 19.2	2 55.7	8 55.3	6 40.5	13 5.2	16 18.3	18 24.2
						DECLINATION at NOON						
1 W	2 35 40.5	15N 0.7	21S31.3	25S16.4	5N16.0	25N22.2	24N12.6	19N43.8	18S55.4	23S 5.5	21S35.6	2S26.4
4 S	2 47 30.2	15 54.2	21 32.9	22 59.4	5 14.6	25 39.1	23 58.7	19 39.4	18 54.7	23 5.8	21 35.7	2 25.1
7 T	2 59 19.9	16 45.3	21 34.4	11 49.5	5 34.1	25 50.0	23 43.4	19 34.7	18 54.2	23 6.1	21 35.9	2 23.9
10 F	3 11 9.5	17 33.9	21 36.0	4N27.0	6 12.5	25 54.9	23 26.8	19 29.6	18 53.9	23 6.5	21 36.1	2 22.7
13 M	3 22 59.2	18 19.9	21 37.5	20 7.5	7 7.3	25 53.8	23 9.0	19 24.1	18 53.9	23 6.9	21 36.3	2 21.7
16 T	3 34 48.9	19 3.0	21 39.1	25 24.5	8 16.3	25 46.7	22 49.9	19 18.3	18 54.0	23 7.4	21 36.6	2 20.7
19 S	3 46 38.5	19 43.3	21 40.6	15 44.4	9 37.4	25 33.9	22 29.5	19 12.2	18 54.5	23 7.8	21 36.9	2 19.8
22 W	3 58 28.2	20 20.6	21 42.1	0S52.6	11 8.4	25 15.4	22 7.8	19 5.8	18 55.1	23 8.4	21 37.2	2 19.0
25 S	4 10 17.9	20 54.7	21 43.6	16 15.0	12 47.4	24 51.5	21 44.9	18 59.0	18 55.9	23 8.9	21 37.5	2 18.3
28 T	4 22 7.5	21 25.6	21 45.1	24 54.1	14 32.1	24 22.5	21 20.9	18 52.0	18 57.0	23 9.5	21 37.9	2 17.7
31 F	4 33 57.2	21 53.1	21 46.6	23 29.0	16 20.0	23 48.6	20 55.6	18 44.6	18 58.3	23 10.1	21 38.3	2 17.2

JUNE 1991

DAY	EPHEMERIS SIDEREAL TIME	☉	☊	☾	☿	♀	♂	♃	♄	♅	♆	♇
						LONGITUDE at NOON						
1 S	4 37 53.8	10♊30.6	21♑ 6.6	24♑14.0	23♉15.9	25♋21.4	3♌31.0	9♌ 4.8	6♒39.0	13♑ 3.3	16♑17.1	18♏22.7
2 S	4 41 50.3	11 28.1	21 3.5	6♒ 4.5	25 5.4	26 23.2	4 6.3	9 14.3	6R37.5	13R 1.4	16R15.8	18R21.1
3 M	4 45 46.9	12 25.5	21 0.3	18 2.2	26 57.2	27 24.7	4 41.7	9 24.0	6 35.9	12 59.4	16 14.6	18 19.6
4 T	4 49 43.5	13 23.0	20 57.1	0♓11.6	28 51.2	28 25.8	5 17.1	9 33.8	6 34.2	12 57.4	16 13.3	18 18.2
5 W	4 53 40.0	14 20.4	20 53.9	12 37.6	0♊47.5	29 26.7	5 52.5	9 43.6	6 32.4	12 55.4	16 12.0	18 16.7
6 T	4 57 36.6	15 17.9	20 50.8	25 24.6	2 45.9	0♌27.2	6 28.0	9 53.6	6 30.5	12 53.4	16 10.7	18 15.2
7 F	5 1 33.1	16 15.3	20 47.6	8♈36.7	4 46.5	1 27.3	7 3.5	10 3.6	6 28.6	12 51.3	16 9.3	18 13.8
8 S	5 5 29.7	17 12.7	20 44.4	22 16.3	6 49.0	2 27.2	7 39.1	10 13.7	6 26.5	12 49.2	16 8.0	18 12.4
9 S	5 9 26.2	18 10.1	20 41.2	6♉23.9	8 53.4	3 26.6	8 14.7	10 24.0	6 24.4	12 47.1	16 6.6	18 11.0
10 M	5 13 22.8	19 7.5	20 38.1	20 57.3	10 59.5	4 25.7	8 50.4	10 34.3	6 22.2	12 45.0	16 5.2	18 9.6
11 T	5 17 19.4	20 4.9	20 34.9	5♊51.2	13 7.1	5 24.4	9 26.0	10 44.7	6 19.9	12 42.9	16 3.8	18 8.3
12 W	5 21 15.9	21 2.3	20 31.7	20 57.9	15 16.1	6 22.6	10 1.8	10 55.2	6 17.5	12 40.7	16 2.4	18 6.9
13 T	5 25 12.5	21 59.7	20 28.5	6♋ 7.9	17 26.2	7 20.5	10 37.5	11 5.8	6 15.0	12 38.5	16 1.0	18 5.6
14 F	5 29 9.0	22 57.0	20 25.3	21 11.9	19 37.1	8 17.9	11 13.3	11 16.4	6 12.4	12 36.2	15 59.5	18 4.3
15 S	5 33 5.6	23 54.3	20 22.2	6♌ 1.5	21 48.7	9 14.9	11 49.1	11 27.1	6 9.8	12 34.0	15 58.1	18 3.0
16 S	5 37 2.1	24 51.7	20 19.0	20 31.0	24 0.6	10 11.4	12 25.0	11 37.9	6 7.1	12 31.7	15 56.6	18 1.8
17 M	5 40 58.7	25 49.0	20 15.8	4♍37.1	26 12.5	11 7.4	13 0.9	11 48.8	6 4.3	12 29.4	15 55.1	18 0.5
18 T	5 44 55.3	26 46.3	20 12.6	18 18.9	28 24.2	12 2.9	13 36.8	11 59.8	6 1.4	12 27.1	15 53.6	17 59.3
19 W	5 48 51.8	27 43.5	20 9.5	1♎37.4	0♋35.4	12 57.9	14 12.8	12 10.8	5 58.5	12 24.8	15 52.1	17 58.1
20 T	5 52 48.4	28 40.8	20 6.3	14 34.8	2 45.9	13 52.4	14 48.8	12 21.9	5 55.5	12 22.5	15 50.5	17 57.0
21 F	5 56 44.9	29 38.0	20 3.1	27 13.8	4 55.4	14 46.3	15 24.8	12 33.1	5 52.4	12 20.1	15 49.0	17 55.8
22 S	6 0 41.5	0♋35.3	19 59.9	9♏37.6	7 3.7	15 39.6	16 0.8	12 44.3	5 49.2	12 17.8	15 47.5	17 54.7
23 S	6 4 38.1	1 32.5	19 56.8	21 49.2	9 10.6	16 32.3	16 36.9	12 55.6	5 46.0	12 15.4	15 45.9	17 53.6
24 M	6 8 34.6	2 29.7	19 53.6	3♐51.3	11 16.0	17 24.4	17 13.1	13 7.0	5 42.7	12 13.0	15 44.3	17 52.5
25 T	6 12 31.2	3 26.9	19 50.4	15 46.5	13 19.8	18 15.9	17 49.2	13 18.4	5 39.3	12 10.7	15 42.8	17 51.5
26 W	6 16 27.7	4 24.2	19 47.2	27 37.1	15 21.7	19 6.7	18 25.4	13 29.9	5 35.9	12 8.3	15 41.2	17 50.5
27 T	6 20 24.3	5 21.4	19 44.1	9♑25.3	17 21.9	19 56.8	19 1.6	13 41.5	5 32.4	12 5.9	15 39.6	17 49.5
28 F	6 24 20.8	6 18.5	19 40.9	21 13.4	19 20.0	20 46.2	19 37.9	13 53.1	5 28.9	12 3.4	15 38.0	17 48.5
29 S	6 28 17.4	7 15.7	19 37.7	3♒ 3.7	21 16.2	21 34.9	20 14.2	14 4.8	5 25.3	12 1.0	15 36.4	17 47.6
30 S	6 32 14.0	8 12.9	19 34.5	14 58.8	23 10.4	22 22.8	20 50.5	14 16.6	5 21.6	11 58.6	15 34.8	17 46.7
						DECLINATION at NOON						
1 S	4 37 53.8	22N 1.5	21S47.0	20S50.1	16N56.2	23N36.2	20N46.9	18N42.1	18S58.7	23S10.3	21S38.4	2S17.1
4 T	4 49 43.5	22 24.5	21 48.5	8 12.7	18 43.5	22 56.2	20 20.1	18 34.3	19 0.3	23 10.9	21 38.9	2 16.7
7 F	5 1 33.1	22 43.9	21 50.0	8N 7.1	20 25.7	22 12.0	19 52.1	18 26.2	19 2.0	23 11.6	21 39.3	2 16.4
10 M	5 13 22.8	22 59.8	21 51.4	22 16.6	21 58.0	21 23.9	19 23.0	18 17.9	19 4.0	23 12.2	21 39.8	2 16.3
13 T	5 25 12.5	23 12.0	21 52.8	24 28.4	23 15.0	20 32.4	18 52.8	18 9.2	19 6.1	23 12.9	21 40.3	2 16.3
16 S	5 37 2.1	23 20.5	21 54.3	12 2.9	24 11.6	19 37.7	18 21.6	18 0.3	19 8.4	23 13.6	21 40.8	2 16.4
19 W	5 48 51.8	23 25.3	21 55.7	5S14.7	24 44.3	18 40.2	17 49.3	17 51.1	19 10.9	23 14.3	21 41.4	2 16.6
22 S	6 0 41.5	23 26.4	21 57.1	19 21.7	24 51.7	17 40.5	17 16.0	17 41.6	19 13.5	23 15.0	21 41.9	2 16.9
25 T	6 12 31.2	23 23.8	21 58.5	25 33.1	24 34.8	16 38.9	16 41.7	17 31.9	19 16.2	23 15.6	21 42.5	2 17.3
28 F	6 24 20.8	23 17.5	21 59.8	21 33.2	23 56.2	15 35.9	16 6.5	17 21.9	19 19.1	23 16.3	21 43.0	2 17.8

JULY 1991

DAY	EPHEMERIS SIDEREAL TIME	☉	☊	☽	☿	♀	♂	♃	♄	♅	♆	♇
	h m s	° ′	° ′	° ′	° ′	° ′	° ′	° ′	° ′	° ′	° ′	° ′
						LONGITUDE at NOON						
1 M	6 36 10.5	9♋10.2	19♑31.4	27♒ 1.8	25♋ 2.6	23♌ 9.9	21♌26.9	14♌28.4	5♒17.9	11♑56.2	15♑33.2	17♏45.9
2 T	6 40 7.1	10 7.4	19 28.2	9♓15.9	26 52.6	23 56.2	22 3.3	14 40.3	5R14.1	11R53.8	15R31.6	17R45.0
3 W	6 44 3.6	11 4.6	19 25.0	21 44.6	28 40.6	24 41.7	22 39.7	14 52.2	5 10.3	11 51.4	15 30.0	17 44.2
4 T	6 48 0.2	12 1.8	19 21.8	4♈31.6	0♌26.5	25 26.2	23 16.1	15 4.2	5 6.4	11 48.9	15 28.4	17 43.4
5 F	6 51 56.8	12 59.0	19 18.6	17 40.1	2 10.3	26 9.9	23 52.6	15 16.2	5 2.5	11 46.5	15 26.8	17 42.6
6 S	6 55 53.3	13 56.2	19 15.5	1♉12.8	3 52.1	26 52.6	24 29.2	15 28.3	4 58.5	11 44.1	15 25.1	17 41.9
7 S	6 59 49.9	14 53.4	19 12.3	15 11.0	5 31.7	27 34.3	25 5.7	15 40.4	4 54.5	11 41.7	15 23.5	17 41.2
8 M	7 3 46.4	15 50.6	19 9.1	29 34.1	7 9.2	28 15.0	25 42.3	15 52.6	4 50.5	11 39.2	15 21.9	17 40.5
9 T	7 7 43.0	16 47.8	19 5.9	14♊18.9	8 44.6	28 54.7	26 18.9	16 4.8	4 46.4	11 36.8	15 20.3	17 39.9
10 W	7 11 39.5	17 45.1	19 2.8	29 19.9	10 17.9	29 33.2	26 55.6	16 17.1	4 42.2	11 34.4	15 18.6	17 39.2
11 T	7 15 36.1	18 42.3	18 59.6	14♋29.1	11 49.1	0♍10.7	27 32.3	16 29.4	4 38.0	11 32.0	15 17.0	17 38.7
12 F	7 19 32.7	19 39.6	18 56.4	29 37.4	13 18.2	0 46.9	28 9.1	16 41.7	4 33.8	11 29.6	15 15.4	17 38.1
13 S	7 23 29.2	20 36.8	18 53.2	14♌35.7	14 45.1	1 21.9	28 45.8	16 54.1	4 29.6	11 27.2	15 13.8	17 37.6
14 S	7 27 25.8	21 34.0	18 50.1	29 16.2	16 9.8	1 55.7	29 22.7	17 6.6	4 25.3	11 24.8	15 12.2	17 37.1
15 M	7 31 22.3	22 31.3	18 46.9	13♍33.4	17 32.3	2 28.1	29 59.5	17 19.1	4 21.0	11 22.4	15 10.5	17 36.6
16 T	7 35 18.9	23 28.5	18 43.7	27 24.4	18 52.6	2 59.1	0♍36.4	17 31.6	4 16.7	11 20.1	15 8.9	17 36.2
17 W	7 39 15.5	24 25.8	18 40.5	10♎48.8	20 10.6	3 28.6	1 13.3	17 44.2	4 12.3	11 17.7	15 7.3	17 35.8
18 T	7 43 12.0	25 23.0	18 37.3	23 48.3	21 26.2	3 56.7	1 50.2	17 56.7	4 7.9	11 15.4	15 5.7	17 35.4
19 F	7 47 8.6	26 20.3	18 34.2	6♏25.9	22 39.4	4 23.2	2 27.2	18 9.4	4 3.5	11 13.1	15 4.2	17 35.1
20 S	7 51 5.1	27 17.5	18 31.0	18 45.5	23 50.1	4 48.1	3 4.2	18 22.0	3 59.1	11 10.8	15 2.6	17 34.8
21 S	7 55 1.7	28 14.8	18 27.8	0♐51.3	24 58.3	5 11.3	3 41.3	18 34.7	3 54.7	11 8.5	15 1.0	17 34.6
22 M	7 58 58.2	29 12.1	18 24.6	12 47.3	26 3.9	5 32.8	4 18.4	18 47.5	3 50.3	11 6.3	14 59.5	17 34.4
23 T	8 2 54.8	0♌ 9.4	18 21.5	24 37.4	27 6.8	5 52.5	4 55.5	19 0.2	3 45.9	11 4.0	14 57.9	17 34.2
24 W	8 6 51.4	1 6.7	18 18.3	6♑25.1	28 6.8	6 10.3	5 32.6	19 13.0	3 41.4	11 1.8	14 56.4	17 34.0
25 T	8 10 47.9	2 3.9	18 15.1	18 13.4	29 3.9	6 26.2	6 9.8	19 25.8	3 37.0	10 59.5	14 54.8	17 33.9
26 F	8 14 44.5	3 1.2	18 11.9	0♒ 5.0	29 58.0	6 40.2	6 47.0	19 38.7	3 32.5	10 57.3	14 53.3	17 33.8
27 S	8 18 41.0	3 58.5	18 8.8	12 2.1	0♍48.9	6 52.1	7 24.2	19 51.5	3 28.0	10 55.2	14 51.8	17 33.7
28 S	8 22 37.6	4 55.9	18 5.6	24 6.7	1 36.5	7 1.9	8 1.5	20 4.4	3 23.6	10 53.0	14 50.3	17 33.7
29 M	8 26 34.1	5 53.2	18 2.4	6♓20.7	2 20.6	7 9.6	8 38.8	20 17.3	3 19.1	10 50.9	14 48.8	17 33.7
30 T	8 30 30.7	6 50.5	17 59.2	18 46.0	3 1.2	7 15.1	9 16.1	20 30.2	3 14.7	10 48.8	14 47.3	17D33.8
31 W	8 34 27.2	7 47.9	17 56.1	1♈24.4	3 37.9	7 18.4	9 53.5	20 43.2	3 10.2	10 46.7	14 45.9	17 33.8
						DECLINATION at NOON						
1 M	6 36 10.5	23N 7.5	22S 1.2	9S25.6	22N59.2	14N31.8	15N30.4	17N11.7	19S22.1	23S17.0	21S43.6	2S18.5
4 T	6 48 0.2	22 53.8	22 2.6	6N30.2	21 47.6	13 27.1	14 53.4	17 1.2	19 25.2	23 17.7	21 44.2	2 19.2
7 S	6 59 49.9	22 36.6	22 3.9	20 55.8	20 24.8	12 22.4	14 15.5	16 50.6	19 28.4	23 18.4	21 44.7	2 20.1
10 W	7 11 39.5	22 15.8	22 5.3	25 13.3	18 53.7	11 18.0	13 36.8	16 39.6	19 31.6	23 19.0	21 45.3	2 21.0
13 S	7 23 29.2	21 51.6	22 6.6	14 15.4	17 17.3	10 14.7	12 57.3	16 28.5	19 35.0	23 19.6	21 45.9	2 22.1
16 T	7 35 18.9	21 24.0	22 7.9	3S29.4	15 37.9	9 12.9	12 17.1	16 17.2	19 38.3	23 20.3	21 46.5	2 23.3
19 F	7 47 8.6	20 53.2	22 9.2	18 25.6	13 57.9	8 13.5	11 36.1	16 5.7	19 41.7	23 20.9	21 47.1	2 24.6
22 M	7 58 58.2	20 19.1	22 10.5	25 26.1	12 19.6	7 17.1	10 54.5	15 53.9	19 45.1	23 21.5	21 47.6	2 25.9
25 T	8 10 47.9	19 42.1	22 11.8	22 16.2	10 45.4	6 24.6	10 12.2	15 42.1	19 48.5	23 22.0	21 48.2	2 27.4
28 S	8 22 37.6	19 2.1	22 13.1	10 37.0	9 17.7	5 36.9	9 29.3	15 30.0	19 51.9	23 22.6	21 48.8	2 29.0
31 W	8 34 27.2	18 19.3	22 14.4	5N 9.7	7 59.3	4 54.9	8 45.8	15 17.8	19 55.2	23 23.1	21 49.3	2 30.6

AUGUST 1991

DAY	EPHEMERIS SIDEREAL TIME	☉	☊	☽	☿	♀	♂	♃	♄	♅	♆	♇
						LONGITUDE at NOON						
1 T	8 38 23.8	8♌45.3	17♑52.9	14♈17.9	4♍10.7	7♍19.4	10♍30.9	20♌56.2	3♒ 5.8	10♑44.6	14♑44.4	17♏33.9
2 F	8 42 20.4	9 42.7	17 49.7	27 28.3	4 39.3	7R18.1	11 8.4	21 9.2	3R 1.4	10R42.6	14R43.0	17 34.1
3 S	8 46 16.9	10 40.1	17 46.5	10♉57.5	5 3.6	7 14.5	11 45.9	21 22.2	2 57.0	10 40.6	14 41.5	17 34.2
4 S	8 50 13.5	11 37.6	17 43.3	24 46.7	5 23.4	7 8.5	12 23.4	21 35.2	2 52.6	10 38.6	14 40.1	17 34.5
5 M	8 54 10.0	12 35.0	17 40.2	8♊55.9	5 38.5	7 0.1	13 0.9	21 48.2	2 48.2	10 36.7	14 38.7	17 34.7
6 T	8 58 6.6	13 32.5	17 37.0	23 24.0	5 48.7	6 49.4	13 38.5	22 1.3	2 43.8	10 34.8	14 37.4	17 35.0
7 W	9 2 3.1	14 30.0	17 33.8	8♋ 7.8	5 53.8	6 36.4	14 16.2	22 14.4	2 39.5	10 32.9	14 36.0	17 35.3
8 T	9 5 59.7	15 27.5	17 30.6	23 2.1	5 53.8	6 21.0	14 53.9	22 27.4	2 35.2	10 31.1	14 34.7	17 35.6
9 F	9 9 56.2	16 25.1	17 27.5	7♌59.7	5R48.4	6 3.2	15 31.6	22 40.5	2 30.9	10 29.2	14 33.3	17 36.0
10 S	9 13 52.8	17 22.6	17 24.3	22 52.7	5 37.7	5 43.3	16 9.3	22 53.6	2 26.7	10 27.4	14 32.0	17 36.4
11 S	9 17 49.4	18 20.2	17 21.1	7♍32.8	5 21.6	5 21.1	16 47.1	23 6.7	2 22.5	10 25.7	14 30.8	17 36.9
12 M	9 21 45.9	19 17.8	17 17.9	21 53.3	5 0.1	4 56.8	17 25.0	23 19.9	2 18.3	10 24.0	14 29.5	17 37.4
13 T	9 25 42.5	20 15.5	17 14.7	5♎49.4	4 33.3	4 30.5	18 2.8	23 33.0	2 14.2	10 22.3	14 28.3	17 37.9
14 W	9 29 39.0	21 13.1	17 11.6	19 19.1	4 1.4	4 2.3	18 40.7	23 46.2	2 10.1	10 20.7	14 27.1	17 38.5
15 T	9 33 35.6	22 10.7	17 8.4	2♏22.6	3 24.7	3 32.3	19 18.7	23 59.3	2 6.0	10 19.1	14 25.9	17 39.1
16 F	9 37 32.1	23 8.4	17 5.2	15 2.3	2 43.7	3 0.7	19 56.6	24 12.4	2 2.0	10 17.5	14 24.7	17 39.7
17 S	9 41 28.7	24 6.1	17 2.0	27 22.1	1 58.9	2 27.6	20 34.6	24 25.5	1 58.0	10 16.0	14 23.5	17 40.3
18 S	9 45 25.2	25 3.8	16 58.9	9♐26.5	1 10.9	1 53.2	21 12.7	24 38.7	1 54.1	10 14.5	14 22.4	17 41.0
19 M	9 49 21.8	26 1.5	16 55.7	21 20.5	0 20.6	1 17.8	21 50.7	24 51.8	1 50.2	10 13.0	14 21.3	17 41.7
20 T	9 53 18.4	26 59.2	16 52.5	3♑ 9.1	29♌28.7	0 41.6	22 28.9	25 4.9	1 46.4	10 11.6	14 20.2	17 42.5
21 W	9 57 14.9	27 57.0	16 49.3	14 56.7	28 36.3	0 4.7	23 7.0	25 18.1	1 42.6	10 10.2	14 19.1	17 43.3
22 T	10 1 11.5	28 54.7	16 46.2	26 47.6	27 44.4	29♌27.5	23 45.2	25 31.2	1 38.9	10 8.9	14 18.1	17 44.1
23 F	10 5 8.0	29 52.5	16 43.0	8♒45.1	26 54.1	28 50.1	24 23.4	25 44.3	1 35.2	10 7.6	14 17.1	17 44.9
24 S	10 9 4.6	0♍50.3	16 39.8	20 51.8	26 6.4	28 12.9	25 1.7	25 57.4	1 31.6	10 6.4	14 16.1	17 45.8
25 S	10 13 1.1	1 48.2	16 36.6	3♓ 9.6	25 22.3	27 36.0	25 40.0	26 10.5	1 28.1	10 5.2	14 15.1	17 46.7
26 M	10 16 57.7	2 46.0	16 33.4	15 39.8	24 42.9	26 59.7	26 18.3	26 23.6	1 24.6	10 4.0	14 14.1	17 47.7
27 T	10 20 54.2	3 43.9	16 30.3	28 22.7	24 9.0	26 24.2	26 56.7	26 36.6	1 21.2	10 2.9	14 13.2	17 48.7
28 W	10 24 50.8	4 41.8	16 27.1	11♈18.6	23 41.5	25 49.8	27 35.1	26 49.7	1 17.8	10 1.8	14 12.3	17 49.7
29 T	10 28 47.3	5 39.8	16 23.9	24 27.3	23 21.0	25 16.6	28 13.5	27 2.8	1 14.6	10 0.8	14 11.5	17 50.7
30 F	10 32 43.9	6 37.8	16 20.7	7♉48.7	23 8.1	24 45.0	28 52.0	27 15.8	1 11.3	9 59.8	14 10.6	17 51.8
31 S	10 36 40.4	7 35.8	16 17.6	21 22.8	23 3.1	24 14.9	29 30.5	27 28.8	1 8.2	9 58.8	14 9.8	17 52.9
						DECLINATION at NOON						
1 T	8 38 23.8	18N 4.4	22S14.8	10N27.9	7N35.9	4N42.3	8N31.2	15N13.7	19S56.3	23S23.2	21S49.5	2S31.2
4 S	8 50 13.5	17 18.0	22 16.0	23 5.3	6 35.0	4 9.4	7 47.0	15 1.3	19 59.6	23 23.7	21 50.0	2 33.0
7 W	9 2 3.1	16 29.0	22 17.3	24 9.9	5 51.7	3 44.5	7 2.2	14 48.7	20 2.8	23 24.2	21 50.5	2 34.8
10 S	9 13 52.8	15 37.7	22 18.5	11 6.9	5 29.8	3 28.4	6 17.1	14 36.1	20 6.0	23 24.6	21 51.0	2 36.8
13 T	9 25 42.5	14 44.0	22 19.7	6S58.8	5 32.8	3 21.7	5 31.4	14 23.3	20 9.0	23 25.0	21 51.5	2 38.8
16 F	9 37 32.1	13 48.3	22 20.9	20 48.1	6 2.5	3 24.7	4 45.4	14 10.4	20 12.0	23 25.3	21 52.0	2 40.9
19 M	9 49 21.8	12 50.7	22 22.1	25 31.9	6 57.5	3 37.1	3 59.1	13 57.4	20 14.8	23 25.7	21 52.4	2 43.0
22 T	10 1 11.5	11 51.2	22 23.3	20 3.7	8 11.8	3 58.1	3 12.4	13 44.4	20 17.5	23 26.0	21 52.9	2 45.2
25 S	10 13 1.1	10 50.1	22 24.5	6 57.1	9 35.0	4 26.1	2 25.5	13 31.3	20 20.1	23 26.2	21 53.3	2 47.5
28 W	10 24 50.8	9 47.4	22 25.7	9N 9.7	10 54.7	4 59.2	1 38.4	13 18.1	20 22.5	23 26.4	21 53.7	2 49.8
31 S	10 36 40.4	8 43.3	22 26.8	22 13.7	11 59.5	5 35.4	0 51.0	13 4.9	20 24.8	23 26.6	21 54.0	2 52.2

SEPTEMBER 1991

DAY	EPHEMERIS SIDEREAL TIME	☉	☊	☽	☿	♀	♂	♃	♄	♅	♆	♇
	h m s	° ′	° ′	° ′	° ′	° ′	° ′	° ′	° ′	° ′	° ′	° ′
LONGITUDE at NOON												
1 S	10 40 37.0	8♍33.8	16♑14.4	5♊ 9.8	23♌ 6.4	23♌46.7	0♎ 9.1	27♌41.8	1♒ 5.1	9♑57.9	14♑ 9.0	17♏54.0
2 M	10 44 33.6	9 31.9	16 11.2	19 9.8	23D18.2	23R20.4	0 47.8	27 54.9	1R 2.2	9R57.1	14R 8.3	17 55.2
3 T	10 48 30.1	10 30.0	16 8.0	3♋22.1	23 38.5	22 56.1	1 26.4	28 7.9	0 59.2	9 56.3	14 7.6	17 56.4
4 W	10 52 26.7	11 28.1	16 4.8	17 45.5	24 7.2	22 34.0	2 5.1	28 20.8	0 56.4	9 55.6	14 6.9	17 57.7
5 T	10 56 23.2	12 26.3	16 1.7	2♌17.2	24 44.2	22 14.2	2 43.9	28 33.7	0 53.6	9 54.8	14 6.2	17 58.9
6 F	11 0 19.8	13 24.5	15 58.5	16 53.0	25 29.4	21 56.6	3 22.6	28 46.7	0 50.9	9 54.2	14 5.6	18 0.2
7 S	11 4 16.3	14 22.7	15 55.3	1♍27.2	26 22.2	21 41.4	4 1.5	28 59.6	0 48.3	9 53.6	14 5.0	18 1.5
8 S	11 8 12.9	15 21.0	15 52.1	15 53.1	27 22.5	21 28.6	4 40.3	29 12.4	0 45.7	9 53.0	14 4.4	18 2.9
9 M	11 12 9.4	16 19.3	15 49.0	0♎ 4.4	28 29.8	21 18.2	5 19.2	29 25.3	0 43.3	9 52.5	14 3.9	18 4.3
10 T	11 16 6.0	17 17.6	15 45.8	13 55.8	29 43.5	21 10.1	5 58.2	29 38.1	0 40.9	9 52.0	14 3.4	18 5.7
11 W	11 20 2.5	18 16.0	15 42.6	27 24.0	1♍ 3.2	21 4.5	6 37.2	29 50.9	0 38.6	9 51.6	14 2.9	18 7.1
12 T	11 23 59.1	19 14.3	15 39.4	10♏27.9	2 28.2	21 1.3	7 16.2	0♍ 3.6	0 36.4	9 51.2	14 2.4	18 8.6
13 F	11 27 55.6	20 12.7	15 36.2	23 8.7	3 58.1	21 0.4	7 55.3	0 16.3	0 34.3	9 50.9	14 2.0	18 10.1
14 S	11 31 52.2	21 11.2	15 33.1	5♐29.4	5 32.3	21D 1.9	8 34.4	0 29.0	0 32.3	9 50.7	14 1.6	18 11.6
15 S	11 35 48.7	22 9.6	15 29.9	17 34.1	7 10.1	21 5.6	9 13.5	0 41.7	0 30.3	9 50.4	14 1.2	18 13.1
16 M	11 39 45.3	23 8.1	15 26.7	29 28.1	8 51.1	21 11.6	9 52.7	0 54.3	0 28.5	9 50.3	14 0.9	18 14.7
17 T	11 43 41.9	24 6.6	15 23.5	11♑16.7	10 34.8	21 19.9	10 31.9	1 6.8	0 26.7	9 50.2	14 0.6	18 16.3
18 W	11 47 38.4	25 5.2	15 20.4	23 5.3	12 20.5	21 30.3	11 11.2	1 19.4	0 25.1	9 50.1	14 0.3	18 17.9
19 T	11 51 35.0	26 3.7	15 17.2	4♒58.9	14 8.0	21 42.8	11 50.5	1 31.9	0 23.5	9 50.1	14 0.1	18 19.6
20 F	11 55 31.5	27 2.3	15 14.0	17 2.0	15 56.8	21 57.3	12 29.9	1 44.3	0 22.0	9 50.1	13 59.9	18 21.3
21 S	11 59 28.1	28 0.9	15 10.8	29 18.0	17 46.6	22 13.9	13 9.3	1 56.8	0 20.7	9D50.2	13 59.7	18 23.0
22 S	12 3 24.6	28 59.6	15 7.6	11♓49.3	19 37.0	22 32.4	13 48.7	2 9.1	0 19.4	9 50.3	13 59.6	18 24.7
23 M	12 7 21.2	29 58.3	15 4.5	24 37.1	21 27.8	22 52.9	14 28.2	2 21.5	0 18.2	9 50.6	13 59.5	18 26.5
24 T	12 11 17.7	0♎57.0	15 1.3	7♈41.1	23 18.6	23 15.1	15 7.7	2 33.8	0 17.1	9 50.8	13 59.5	18 28.3
25 W	12 15 14.3	1 55.8	14 58.1	21 0.0	25 9.4	23 39.1	15 47.3	2 46.0	0 16.1	9 51.1	13 59.4	18 30.1
26 T	12 19 10.8	2 54.6	14 54.9	4♉31.7	26 60.0	24 4.9	16 26.9	2 58.2	0 15.2	9 51.4	13 59.4	18 31.9
27 F	12 23 7.4	3 53.4	14 51.8	18 13.7	28 50.1	24 32.3	17 6.5	3 10.4	0 14.4	9 51.8	13 59.4	18 33.8
28 S	12 27 3.9	4 52.3	14 48.6	2♊ 3.6	0♎39.8	25 1.3	17 46.2	3 22.5	0 13.7	9 52.3	13D59.5	18 35.6
29 S	12 31 0.5	5 51.1	14 45.4	15 59.6	2 29.0	25 31.8	18 26.0	3 34.5	0 13.1	9 52.8	13 59.6	18 37.5
30 M	12 34 57.0	6 50.1	14 42.2	0♋ 0.5	4 17.4	26 3.8	19 5.8	3 46.5	0 12.6	9 53.3	13 59.7	18 39.4
DECLINATION at NOON												
1 S	10 40 37.0	8N21.6	22S27.2	24N34.6	12N16.1	5N47.8	0N35.2	13N 0.5	20S25.5	23S26.7	21S54.1	2S53.0
4 W	10 52 26.7	7 15.8	22 28.4	22 15.2	12 47.6	6 24.8	0S12.4	12 47.3	20 27.6	23 26.9	21 54.5	2 55.4
7 S	11 4 16.3	6 8.9	22 29.5	7 38.9	12 48.2	7 0.4	1 0.0	12 34.1	20 29.5	23 27.0	21 54.8	2 57.9
10 T	11 16 6.0	5 1.2	22 30.6	10S 9.8	12 16.5	7 33.3	1 47.7	12 20.8	20 31.2	23 27.1	21 55.0	3 0.4
13 F	11 27 55.6	3 52.7	22 31.7	22 31.1	11 13.8	8 2.2	2 35.5	12 7.7	20 32.7	23 27.1	21 55.3	3 2.9
16 M	11 39 45.3	2 43.5	22 32.8	24 56.6	9 44.3	8 26.6	3 23.1	11 54.5	20 34.1	23 27.1	21 55.5	3 5.4
19 T	11 51 35.0	1 33.9	22 33.9	17 27.8	7 53.8	8 45.9	4 10.7	11 41.4	20 35.3	23 27.1	21 55.7	3 8.0
22 S	12 3 24.6	0 24.0	22 35.0	3 17.1	5 48.4	8 59.6	4 58.2	11 28.4	20 36.3	23 27.0	21 55.8	3 10.5
25 W	12 15 14.3	0S46.0	22 36.0	12N49.4	3 33.8	9 7.6	5 45.5	11 15.5	20 37.1	23 27.0	21 56.0	3 13.1
28 S	12 27 3.9	1 56.1	22 37.1	23 57.2	1 14.5	9 9.8	6 32.6	11 2.7	20 37.7	23 26.8	21 56.1	3 15.7

OCTOBER 1991

DAY	EPHEMERIS SIDEREAL TIME	☉	☊	☽	☿	♀	♂	♃	♄	♅	♆	♇
LONGITUDE at NOON												
1 T	12 38 53.6	7♎49.1	14♑39.0	14♋ 5.6	6♎ 5.2	26♌37.3	19♎45.6	3♍58.4	0♒12.2	9♑53.9	13♑59.9	18♏41.4
2 W	12 42 50.1	8 48.1	14 35.9	28 14.1	7 52.2	27 12.2	20 25.5	4 10.3	0R11.9	9 54.6	14 0.1	18 43.3
3 T	12 46 46.7	9 47.1	14 32.7	12♌24.9	9 38.5	27 48.3	21 5.4	4 22.1	0 11.7	9 55.3	14 0.3	18 45.3
4 F	12 50 43.3	10 46.2	14 29.5	26 36.0	11 24.0	28 25.8	21 45.4	4 33.8	0 11.6	9 56.0	14 0.6	18 47.3
5 S	12 54 39.8	11 45.3	14 26.3	10♍44.4	13 8.7	29 4.5	22 25.4	4 45.5	0 11.6	9 56.8	14 0.9	18 49.3
6 S	12 58 36.4	12 44.5	14 23.2	24 46.2	14 52.6	29 44.4	23 5.4	4 57.2	0 11.6	9 57.7	14 1.2	18 51.4
7 M	13 2 32.9	13 43.7	14 20.0	8♎36.9	16 35.6	0♍25.4	23 45.6	5 8.7	0D11.8	9 58.6	14 1.5	18 53.4
8 T	13 6 29.5	14 42.9	14 16.8	22 12.3	18 17.9	1 7.5	24 25.7	5 20.2	0 12.1	9 59.5	14 1.9	18 55.5
9 W	13 10 26.0	15 42.2	14 13.6	5♏29.2	19 59.4	1 50.6	25 5.9	5 31.7	0 12.5	10 0.5	14 2.4	18 57.6
10 T	13 14 22.6	16 41.5	14 10.4	18 26.1	21 40.1	2 34.8	25 46.1	5 43.0	0 13.0	10 1.6	14 2.8	18 59.7
11 F	13 18 19.1	17 40.8	14 7.3	1♐ 3.0	23 20.1	3 19.9	26 26.4	5 54.3	0 13.6	10 2.7	14 3.3	19 1.8
12 S	13 22 15.7	18 40.2	14 4.1	13 21.8	24 59.3	4 6.0	27 6.8	6 5.5	0 14.3	10 3.8	14 3.8	19 4.0
13 S	13 26 12.2	19 39.6	14 0.9	25 25.8	26 37.7	4 53.0	27 47.1	6 16.7	0 15.1	10 5.0	14 4.4	19 6.2
14 M	13 30 8.8	20 39.0	13 57.7	7♑19.5	28 15.5	5 40.9	28 27.6	6 27.8	0 16.0	10 6.3	14 5.1	19 8.4
15 T	13 34 5.3	21 38.5	13 54.6	19 7.9	29 52.6	6 29.7	29 8.1	6 38.8	0 17.0	10 7.6	14 5.7	19 10.6
16 W	13 38 1.9	22 38.0	13 51.4	0♒56.6	1♏28.9	7 19.2	29 48.6	6 49.7	0 18.1	10 9.0	14 6.3	19 12.8
17 T	13 41 58.4	23 37.5	13 48.2	12 51.0	3 4.7	8 9.5	0♏29.2	7 0.5	0 19.3	10 10.4	14 7.0	19 15.0
18 F	13 45 55.0	24 37.0	13 45.0	24 56.5	4 39.7	9 0.6	1 9.8	7 11.3	0 20.6	10 11.8	14 7.8	19 17.2
19 S	13 49 51.6	25 36.6	13 41.8	7♓17.6	6 14.1	9 52.4	1 50.4	7 21.9	0 22.0	10 13.3	14 8.5	19 19.5
20 S	13 53 48.1	26 36.2	13 38.7	19 57.7	7 47.9	10 44.9	2 31.1	7 32.5	0 23.5	10 14.9	14 9.3	19 21.8
21 M	13 57 44.7	27 35.8	13 35.5	2♈58.7	9 21.1	11 38.1	3 11.8	7 43.0	0 25.1	10 16.5	14 10.1	19 24.0
22 T	14 1 41.2	28 35.5	13 32.3	16 20.7	10 53.7	12 32.0	3 52.6	7 53.4	0 26.8	10 18.1	14 11.0	19 26.3
23 W	14 5 37.8	29 35.2	13 29.1	0♉ 2.1	12 25.7	13 26.5	4 33.4	8 3.7	0 28.6	10 19.8	14 11.9	19 28.6
24 T	14 9 34.3	0♏34.9	13 26.0	13 59.2	13 57.2	14 21.7	5 14.3	8 13.9	0 30.5	10 21.5	14 12.8	19 30.9
25 F	14 13 30.9	1 34.7	13 22.8	28 7.7	15 28.1	15 17.5	5 55.2	8 24.1	0 32.5	10 23.3	14 13.7	19 33.2
26 S	14 17 27.4	2 34.5	13 19.6	12♊22.5	16 58.4	16 13.8	6 36.2	8 34.1	0 34.6	10 25.1	14 14.7	19 35.6
27 S	14 21 24.0	3 34.3	13 16.4	26 39.1	18 28.2	17 10.7	7 17.2	8 44.0	0 36.7	10 27.0	14 15.7	19 37.9
28 M	14 25 20.5	4 34.2	13 13.2	10♋54.1	19 57.4	18 8.2	7 58.3	8 53.9	0 39.0	10 28.9	14 16.7	19 40.2
29 T	14 29 17.1	5 34.1	13 10.1	25 5.1	21 26.0	19 6.2	8 39.4	9 3.6	0 41.4	10 30.8	14 17.8	19 42.6
30 W	14 33 13.7	6 34.0	13 6.9	9♌10.6	22 54.1	20 4.7	9 20.5	9 13.3	0 43.8	10 32.8	14 18.9	19 45.0
31 T	14 37 10.2	7 34.0	13 3.7	23 10.0	24 21.5	21 3.7	10 1.7	9 22.8	0 46.4	10 34.9	14 20.0	19 47.3
DECLINATION at NOON												
1 T	12 38 53.6	3S 6.1	22S38.1	22N47.3	1S 6.1	9N 6.2	7S19.4	10N50.0	20S38.1	23S26.7	21S56.1	3S18.2
4 F	12 50 43.3	4 15.8	22 39.2	9 30.4	3 25.8	8 56.8	8 5.9	10 37.5	20 38.3	23 26.5	21 56.2	3 20.8
7 M	13 2 32.9	5 25.0	22 40.2	7S59.3	5 42.7	8 41.9	8 52.0	10 25.1	20 38.3	23 26.3	21 56.2	3 23.3
10 T	13 14 22.6	6 33.7	22 41.2	21 17.4	7 55.6	8 21.6	9 37.7	10 12.9	20 38.2	23 26.0	21 56.1	3 25.8
13 S	13 26 12.2	7 41.5	22 42.2	24 56.7	10 3.6	7 56.1	10 22.9	10 0.9	20 37.8	23 25.7	21 56.1	3 28.3
16 W	13 38 1.9	8 48.3	22 43.2	18 28.7	12 6.0	7 25.5	11 7.6	9 49.2	20 37.2	23 25.4	21 56.0	3 30.8
19 S	13 49 51.6	9 54.1	22 44.2	5 3.1	14 2.1	6 50.2	11 51.6	9 37.6	20 36.4	23 25.0	21 55.9	3 33.2
22 T	14 1 41.2	10 58.5	22 45.1	11N 3.3	15 51.3	6 10.4	12 35.0	9 26.4	20 35.5	23 24.6	21 55.7	3 35.6
25 F	14 13 30.9	12 1.4	22 46.1	23 10.8	17 33.3	5 26.2	13 17.6	9 15.4	20 34.3	23 24.2	21 55.5	3 38.0
28 M	14 25 20.5	13 2.7	22 47.0	23 6.7	19 7.3	4 38.1	13 59.5	9 4.7	20 33.0	23 23.7	21 55.3	3 40.3
31 T	14 37 10.2	14 2.2	22 48.0	10 38.7	20 32.8	3 46.2	14 40.6	8 54.4	20 31.4	23 23.2	21 55.0	3 42.5

NOVEMBER 1991

LONGITUDE at NOON

DAY	EPHEMERIS SIDEREAL TIME (h m s)	☉ (° ′)	☊ (° ′)	☽ (° ′)	☿ (° ′)	♀ (° ′)	♂ (° ′)	♃ (° ′)	♄ (° ′)	♅ (° ′)	♆ (° ′)	♇ (° ′)
1 F	14 41 6.8	8 ♏ 34.0	13 ♑ 0.5	7 ♍ 2.6	25 ♏ 48.4	22 ♍ 3.2	10 ♏ 43.0	9 ♍ 32.2	0 ♒ 49.0	10 ♑ 36.9	14 ♑ 21.2	19 ♏ 49.7
2 S	14 45 3.3	9 34.0	12 57.4	20 47.4	27 14.7	23 3.1	11 24.3	9 41.5	0 51.8	10 39.1	14 22.4	19 52.1
3 S	14 48 59.9	10 34.1	12 54.2	4 ♎ 23.2	28 40.3	24 3.5	12 5.7	9 50.8	0 54.6	10 41.2	14 23.6	19 54.5
4 M	14 52 56.4	11 34.3	12 51.0	17 48.1	0 ♐ 5.2	25 4.3	12 47.1	9 59.9	0 57.6	10 43.5	14 24.9	19 56.9
5 T	14 56 53.0	12 34.5	12 47.8	1 ♏ 0.3	1 29.3	26 5.6	13 28.6	10 8.9	1 0.6	10 45.7	14 26.2	19 59.3
6 W	15 0 49.5	13 34.6	12 44.6	13 58.0	2 52.7	27 7.2	14 10.1	10 17.8	1 3.7	10 48.0	14 27.5	20 1.7
7 T	15 4 46.1	14 34.9	12 41.5	26 40.4	4 15.2	28 9.2	14 51.7	10 26.5	1 6.9	10 50.4	14 28.8	20 4.2
8 F	15 8 42.7	15 35.1	12 38.3	9 ♐ 7.3	5 36.8	29 11.6	15 33.3	10 35.2	1 10.2	10 52.7	14 30.2	20 6.6
9 S	15 12 39.2	16 35.4	12 35.1	21 19.9	6 57.3	0 ♎ 14.3	16 14.9	10 43.7	1 13.6	10 55.2	14 31.6	20 9.0
10 S	15 16 35.8	17 35.7	12 31.9	3 ♑ 20.6	8 16.8	1 17.4	16 56.6	10 52.1	1 17.1	10 57.6	14 33.0	20 11.4
11 M	15 20 32.3	18 36.0	12 28.8	15 12.4	9 34.9	2 20.9	17 38.3	11 0.3	1 20.6	11 0.1	14 34.4	20 13.8
12 T	15 24 28.9	19 36.3	12 25.6	26 59.8	10 51.7	3 24.6	18 20.1	11 8.5	1 24.3	11 2.6	14 35.9	20 16.2
13 W	15 28 25.4	20 36.7	12 22.4	8 ♒ 47.5	12 7.0	4 28.7	19 2.0	11 16.5	1 28.0	11 5.2	14 37.4	20 18.6
14 T	15 32 22.0	21 37.1	12 19.2	20 40.8	13 20.5	5 33.1	19 43.8	11 24.4	1 31.8	11 7.8	14 38.9	20 21.1
15 F	15 36 18.5	22 37.5	12 16.1	2 ♓ 45.1	14 32.1	6 37.8	20 25.8	11 32.1	1 35.7	11 10.4	14 40.5	20 23.5
16 S	15 40 15.1	23 38.0	12 12.9	15 5.4	15 41.5	7 42.8	21 7.7	11 39.8	1 39.7	11 13.1	14 42.1	20 25.9
17 S	15 44 11.7	24 38.4	12 9.7	27 46.3	16 48.4	8 48.1	21 49.8	11 47.2	1 43.7	11 15.8	14 43.7	20 28.3
18 M	15 48 8.2	25 38.9	12 6.5	10 ♈ 51.0	17 52.6	9 53.6	22 31.8	11 54.6	1 47.9	11 18.5	14 45.3	20 30.7
19 T	15 52 4.8	26 39.4	12 3.3	24 20.9	18 53.5	10 59.5	23 13.9	12 1.8	1 52.1	11 21.3	14 46.9	20 33.1
20 W	15 56 1.3	27 39.9	12 0.2	8 ♉ 15.4	19 50.9	12 5.6	23 56.1	12 8.9	1 56.4	11 24.1	14 48.6	20 35.5
21 T	15 59 57.9	28 40.5	11 57.0	22 31.4	20 44.2	13 11.9	24 38.3	12 15.8	2 0.7	11 26.9	14 50.3	20 37.9
22 F	16 3 54.4	29 41.1	11 53.8	7 ♊ 3.5	21 32.9	14 18.5	25 20.6	12 22.6	2 5.2	11 29.8	14 52.0	20 40.3
23 S	16 7 51.0	0 ♐ 41.7	11 50.6	21 45.0	22 16.4	15 25.4	26 2.9	12 29.2	2 9.7	11 32.7	14 53.8	20 42.7
24 S	16 11 47.6	1 42.3	11 47.5	6 ♋ 28.7	22 54.0	16 32.4	26 45.2	12 35.7	2 14.3	11 35.6	14 55.5	20 45.1
25 M	16 15 44.1	2 43.0	11 44.3	21 8.1	23 25.2	17 39.8	27 27.7	12 42.1	2 19.0	11 38.7	14 57.4	20 47.5
26 T	16 19 40.7	3 43.7	11 41.1	5 ♌ 37.9	23 48.9	18 47.4	28 10.1	12 48.3	2 23.8	11 41.6	14 59.2	20 49.9
27 W	16 23 37.2	4 44.4	11 37.9	19 54.6	24 4.6	19 55.1	28 52.6	12 54.4	2 28.6	11 44.7	15 1.0	20 52.3
28 T	16 27 33.8	5 45.1	11 34.8	3 ♍ 56.5	24 11.3	21 3.1	29 35.2	13 0.3	2 33.5	11 47.7	15 2.8	20 54.6
29 F	16 31 30.3	6 45.9	11 31.6	17 42.8	24 R 8.3	22 11.3	0 ♐ 17.8	13 6.0	2 38.5	11 50.8	15 4.7	20 57.0
30 S	16 35 26.9	7 46.7	11 28.4	1 ♎ 13.9	23 55.0	23 19.7	1 0.4	13 11.6	2 43.5	11 53.9	15 6.6	20 59.3

DECLINATION at NOON

DAY	SIDEREAL TIME	☉	☊	☽	☿	♀	♂	♃	♄	♅	♆	♇
1 F	14 41 6.8	14S21.6	22S48.3	5N 3.9	20S59.3	3N28.1	14S54.1	8N51.0	20S30.9	23S23.0	21S55.0	3S43.3
4 M	14 52 56.4	15 18.3	22 49.2	11S38.3	22 12.5	2 31.7	15 33.9	8 41.1	20 29.1	23 22.5	21 54.7	3 45.5
7 T	15 4 46.1	16 12.8	22 50.1	22 53.5	23 15.7	1 32.5	16 12.7	8 31.6	20 27.1	23 21.9	21 54.3	3 47.6
10 S	15 16 35.8	17 4.9	22 51.0	24 5.2	24 8.0	0 30.6	16 50.5	8 22.5	20 24.9	23 21.3	21 54.0	3 49.6
13 W	15 28 25.4	17 54.3	22 51.9	15 44.5	24 48.9	0S33.6	17 27.1	8 13.8	20 22.6	23 20.6	21 53.6	3 51.6
16 S	15 40 15.1	18 40.9	22 52.8	1 35.8	25 17.3	1 39.7	18 2.6	8 5.5	20 20.1	23 19.9	21 53.2	3 53.5
19 T	15 52 4.8	19 24.6	22 53.6	14N 5.4	25 32.7	2 47.4	18 36.7	7 57.8	20 17.4	23 19.2	21 52.7	3 55.3
22 F	16 3 54.4	20 5.1	22 54.5	24 17.8	25 34.1	3 56.4	19 9.5	7 50.4	20 14.5	23 18.5	21 52.2	3 57.0
25 M	16 15 44.1	20 42.3	22 55.3	20 48.8	25 20.8	5 6.3	19 41.0	7 43.6	20 11.4	23 17.7	21 51.7	3 58.7
28 T	16 27 33.8	21 16.0	22 56.2	6 9.0	24 51.7	6 16.8	20 10.9	7 37.3	20 8.2	23 16.9	21 51.2	4 0.2

DECEMBER 1991

LONGITUDE at NOON

DAY	SIDEREAL TIME	☉	☊	☽	☿	♀	♂	♃	♄	♅	♆	♇
1 S	16 39 23.5	8 ♐ 47.5	11 ♑ 25.2	14 ♎ 30.2	23 ♐ 30.9	24 ♎ 28.2	1 ♐ 43.1	13 ♍ 17.0	2 ♒ 48.6	11 ♑ 57.0	15 ♑ 8.5	21 ♏ 1.7
2 M	16 43 20.0	9 48.3	11 22.0	27 32.7	22 R 55.6	25 37.0	2 25.9	13 22.3	2 53.8	12 0.2	15 10.4	21 4.0
3 T	16 47 16.6	10 49.2	11 18.9	10 ♏ 21.7	22 9.4	26 45.9	3 8.7	13 27.3	2 59.0	12 3.3	15 12.4	21 6.3
4 W	16 51 13.1	11 50.1	11 15.7	22 58.1	21 12.7	27 55.1	3 51.5	13 32.3	3 4.3	12 6.5	15 14.3	21 8.6
5 T	16 55 9.7	12 51.0	11 12.5	5 ♐ 22.5	20 6.6	29 4.3	4 34.4	13 37.0	3 9.7	12 9.8	15 16.3	21 10.9
6 F	16 59 6.2	13 51.9	11 9.3	17 35.8	18 52.8	0 ♏ 13.8	5 17.4	13 41.6	3 15.1	12 13.0	15 18.3	21 13.2
7 S	17 3 2.8	14 52.8	11 6.2	29 39.1	17 33.4	1 23.4	6 0.3	13 46.0	3 20.6	12 16.3	15 20.3	21 15.4
8 S	17 6 59.4	15 53.8	11 3.0	11 ♑ 34.2	16 10.9	2 33.1	6 43.4	13 50.3	3 26.2	12 19.6	15 22.4	21 17.7
9 M	17 10 55.9	16 54.7	10 59.8	23 23.6	14 48.2	3 43.0	7 26.5	13 54.3	3 31.8	12 22.9	15 24.4	21 19.9
10 T	17 14 52.5	17 55.7	10 56.6	5 ♒ 10.2	13 27.9	4 53.0	8 9.6	13 58.2	3 37.5	12 26.2	15 26.5	21 22.2
11 W	17 18 49.0	18 56.7	10 53.5	16 57.7	12 12.8	6 3.2	8 52.8	14 2.0	3 43.2	12 29.6	15 28.5	21 24.4
12 T	17 22 45.6	19 57.7	10 50.3	28 50.2	11 5.0	7 13.5	9 36.0	14 5.5	3 49.0	12 32.9	15 30.6	21 26.6
13 F	17 26 42.2	20 58.7	10 47.1	10 ♓ 52.5	10 6.3	8 23.9	10 19.3	14 8.9	3 54.8	12 36.3	15 32.7	21 28.7
14 S	17 30 38.7	21 59.7	10 43.9	23 9.2	9 18.0	9 34.4	11 2.6	14 12.0	4 0.7	12 39.7	15 34.8	21 30.9
15 S	17 34 35.3	23 0.7	10 40.8	5 ♈ 45.2	8 40.6	10 45.1	11 45.9	14 15.0	4 6.7	12 43.1	15 37.0	21 33.0
16 M	17 38 31.8	24 1.8	10 37.6	18 44.6	8 14.4	11 56.0	12 29.4	14 17.9	4 12.8	12 46.6	15 39.2	21 35.2
17 T	17 42 28.4	25 2.9	10 34.4	2 ♉ 10.2	7 59.2	13 6.9	13 12.8	14 20.5	4 18.8	12 50.0	15 41.3	21 37.3
18 W	17 46 24.9	26 3.9	10 31.2	16 3.3	7 54.5	14 17.9	13 56.3	14 23.0	4 24.9	12 53.5	15 43.5	21 39.4
19 T	17 50 21.5	27 5.0	10 28.0	0 ♊ 22.8	7 D 59.7	15 29.0	14 39.8	14 25.3	4 31.1	12 57.0	15 45.6	21 41.5
20 F	17 54 18.1	28 6.0	10 24.9	15 4.8	8 14.0	16 40.3	15 23.4	14 27.3	4 37.3	13 0.5	15 47.8	21 43.5
21 S	17 58 14.6	29 7.1	10 21.7	0 ♋ 2.8	8 36.7	17 51.6	16 7.0	14 29.2	4 43.5	13 4.0	15 50.0	21 45.6
22 S	18 2 11.2	0 ♑ 8.2	10 18.5	15 8.6	9 6.9	19 3.1	16 50.7	14 30.9	4 49.8	13 7.5	15 52.2	21 47.6
23 M	18 6 7.7	1 9.3	10 15.3	0 ♌ 12.9	9 43.9	20 14.6	17 34.4	14 32.5	4 56.2	13 11.0	15 54.4	21 49.6
24 T	18 10 4.3	2 10.4	10 12.2	15 7.4	10 26.9	21 26.3	18 18.2	14 33.8	5 2.5	13 14.5	15 56.6	21 51.6
25 W	18 14 0.9	3 11.5	10 9.0	29 45.3	11 15.2	22 38.0	19 2.0	14 34.9	5 9.0	13 18.0	15 58.9	21 53.5
26 T	18 17 57.4	4 12.6	10 5.8	14 ♍ 2.0	12 8.3	23 49.9	19 45.9	14 35.9	5 15.4	13 21.6	16 1.1	21 55.4
27 F	18 21 54.0	5 13.7	10 2.6	27 55.6	13 5.6	25 1.8	20 29.8	14 36.6	5 21.9	13 25.1	16 3.3	21 57.3
28 S	18 25 50.5	6 14.9	9 59.5	11 ♎ 26.1	14 6.5	26 13.8	21 13.7	14 37.2	5 28.5	13 28.7	16 5.6	21 59.2
29 S	18 29 47.1	7 16.0	9 56.3	24 34.9	15 10.8	27 25.9	21 57.7	14 37.5	5 35.1	13 32.3	16 7.8	22 1.1
30 M	18 33 43.6	8 17.2	9 53.1	7 ♏ 24.5	16 17.9	28 38.1	22 41.8	14 37.7	5 41.7	13 35.8	16 10.1	22 2.9
31 T	18 37 40.2	9 18.3	9 49.9	19 57.7	17 27.6	29 50.4	23 25.8	14 37.7	5 48.3	13 39.4	16 12.3	22 4.7

DECLINATION at NOON

DAY	SIDEREAL TIME	☉	☊	☽	☿	♀	♂	♃	♄	♅	♆	♇
1 S	16 39 23.5	21S46.1	22S57.0	10S30.3	24S 5.7	7S27.4	20S39.3	7N31.6	20S 4.9	23S16.0	21S50.6	4S 1.7
4 W	16 51 13.1	22 12.5	22 57.8	22 12.9	23 2.0	8 37.9	21 6.1	7 26.4	20 1.3	23 15.2	21 50.1	4 3.1
7 S	17 3 2.8	22 35.0	22 58.6	24 22.4	21 44.2	9 47.7	21 31.2	7 21.9	19 57.7	23 14.3	21 49.5	4 4.4
10 T	17 14 52.5	22 53.5	22 59.4	16 47.3	20 24.8	10 56.7	21 54.5	7 17.9	19 53.8	23 13.4	21 48.8	4 5.5
13 F	17 26 42.2	23 8.0	23 0.2	3 12.9	19 22.6	12 4.3	22 16.1	7 14.5	19 49.8	23 12.4	21 48.2	4 6.6
16 M	17 38 31.8	23 18.4	23 0.9	12N 9.9	18 50.6	13 10.2	22 35.7	7 11.8	19 45.7	23 11.4	21 47.5	4 7.6
19 T	17 50 21.5	23 24.5	23 1.7	23 31.2	18 49.5	14 14.1	22 53.5	7 9.7	19 41.4	23 10.4	21 46.8	4 8.5
22 S	18 2 11.2	23 26.4	23 2.4	22 5.5	19 12.4	15 15.5	23 9.2	7 8.3	19 37.0	23 9.4	21 46.1	4 9.2
25 W	18 14 0.9	23 24.1	23 3.1	7 45.3	19 50.0	16 14.2	23 22.9	7 7.5	19 32.5	23 8.4	21 45.3	4 9.9
28 S	18 25 50.5	23 17.6	23 3.9	9S23.7	20 34.7	17 9.7	23 34.6	7 7.4	19 27.9	23 7.3	21 44.6	4 10.5
31 T	18 37 40.2	23 6.9	23 4.6	21 38.3	21 20.6	18 1.7	23 44.1	7 8.0	19 23.2	23 6.3	21 43.8	4 10.9

JANUARY 1992

DAY	EPHEMERIS SIDEREAL TIME	☉	☊	☽	☿	♀	♂	♃	♄	♅	♆	♇
	h m s	° ′	° ′	° ′	° ′	° ′	° ′	° ′	° ′	° ′	° ′	° ′
						LONGITUDE at NOON						
1 W	18 41 36.8	10♑19.5	9♑46.8	2♐17.2	18♐39.5	1♐ 2.7	24♐10.0	14♍37.4	5♒55.0	13♑43.0	16♑14.6	22♏ 6.5
2 T	18 45 33.3	11 20.7	9 43.6	14 25.9	19 53.5	2 15.1	24 54.2	14R37.0	6 1.8	13 46.6	16 16.9	22 8.3
3 F	18 49 29.9	12 21.8	9 40.4	26 26.2	21 9.3	3 27.6	25 38.4	14 36.4	6 8.5	13 50.1	16 19.1	22 10.0
4 S	18 53 26.4	13 23.0	9 37.2	8♑20.2	22 26.6	4 40.1	26 22.7	14 35.6	6 15.3	13 53.7	16 21.4	22 11.7
5 S	18 57 23.0	14 24.2	9 34.0	20 10.1	23 45.4	5 52.7	27 7.0	14 34.6	6 22.1	13 57.3	16 23.7	22 13.4
6 M	19 1 19.5	15 25.4	9 30.9	1♒57.9	25 5.5	7 5.4	27 51.4	14 33.4	6 29.0	14 0.9	16 26.0	22 15.1
7 T	19 5 16.1	16 26.6	9 27.7	13 45.7	26 26.8	8 18.1	28 35.8	14 32.0	6 35.9	14 4.5	16 28.3	22 16.7
8 W	19 9 12.7	17 27.8	9 24.5	25 35.9	27 49.1	9 30.9	29 20.2	14 30.5	6 42.8	14 8.1	16 30.5	22 18.4
9 T	19 13 9.2	18 28.9	9 21.3	7♓31.5	29 12.3	10 43.7	0♑ 4.7	14 28.7	6 49.7	14 11.7	16 32.8	22 19.9
10 F	19 17 5.8	19 30.1	9 18.2	19 35.5	0♑36.5	11 56.6	0 49.2	14 26.7	6 56.7	14 15.3	16 35.1	22 21.5
11 S	19 21 2.3	20 31.2	9 15.0	1♈51.6	2 1.5	13 9.5	1 33.7	14 24.5	7 3.7	14 18.8	16 37.4	22 23.0
12 S	19 24 58.9	21 32.4	9 11.8	14 23.7	3 27.3	14 22.5	2 18.3	14 22.2	7 10.6	14 22.4	16 39.6	22 24.5
13 M	19 28 55.5	22 33.5	9 8.6	27 15.7	4 53.9	15 35.5	3 3.0	14 19.6	7 17.7	14 25.9	16 41.9	22 25.9
14 T	19 32 52.0	23 34.6	9 5.5	10♉31.0	6 21.1	16 48.6	3 47.7	14 16.9	7 24.7	14 29.5	16 44.2	22 27.4
15 W	19 36 48.6	24 35.7	9 2.3	24 12.4	7 49.0	18 1.7	4 32.4	14 14.0	7 31.7	14 33.0	16 46.4	22 28.8
16 T	19 40 45.1	25 36.8	8 59.1	8♊20.8	9 17.5	19 14.9	5 17.1	14 10.9	7 38.8	14 36.6	16 48.7	22 30.1
17 F	19 44 41.7	26 37.9	8 55.9	22 54.9	10 46.7	20 28.0	6 1.9	14 7.6	7 45.9	14 40.1	16 50.9	22 31.5
18 S	19 48 38.2	27 39.0	8 52.8	7♋50.9	12 16.4	21 41.3	6 46.7	14 4.2	7 53.0	14 43.6	16 53.2	22 32.8
19 S	19 52 34.8	28 40.0	8 49.6	23 1.6	13 46.8	22 54.5	7 31.6	14 0.5	8 0.1	14 47.1	16 55.4	22 34.0
20 M	19 56 31.4	29 41.1	8 46.4	8♌17.9	15 17.7	24 7.9	8 16.5	13 56.7	8 7.2	14 50.6	16 57.6	22 35.3
21 T	20 0 27.9	0♒42.1	8 43.2	23 29.6	16 49.3	25 21.2	9 1.5	13 52.7	8 14.3	14 54.1	16 59.9	22 36.5
22 W	20 4 24.5	1 43.1	8 40.0	8♍26.9	18 21.4	26 34.6	9 46.5	13 48.6	8 21.5	14 57.6	17 2.1	22 37.7
23 T	20 8 21.0	2 44.2	8 36.9	23 2.1	19 54.1	27 48.0	10 31.5	13 44.2	8 28.6	15 1.0	17 4.3	22 38.8
24 F	20 12 17.6	3 45.2	8 33.7	7♎10.6	21 27.4	29 1.5	11 16.5	13 39.7	8 35.8	15 4.5	17 6.5	22 39.9
25 S	20 16 14.1	4 46.2	8 30.5	20 50.7	23 1.4	0♑15.0	12 1.7	13 35.1	8 42.9	15 7.9	17 8.7	22 41.0
26 S	20 20 10.7	5 47.2	8 27.3	4♏ 3.3	24 35.9	1 28.6	12 46.8	13 30.2	8 50.1	15 11.3	17 10.9	22 42.0
27 M	20 24 7.3	6 48.2	8 24.2	16 51.3	26 11.1	2 42.2	13 32.0	13 25.3	8 57.3	15 14.8	17 13.1	22 43.1
28 T	20 28 3.8	7 49.2	8 21.0	29 18.7	27 46.9	3 55.8	14 17.3	13 20.1	9 4.5	15 18.1	17 15.2	22 44.1
29 W	20 32 0.4	8 50.2	8 17.8	11♐30.0	29 23.4	5 9.4	15 2.5	13 14.8	9 11.7	15 21.5	17 17.4	22 45.0
30 T	20 35 56.9	9 51.1	8 14.6	23 29.5	1♒ 0.5	6 23.1	15 47.8	13 9.4	9 18.9	15 24.9	17 19.5	22 45.9
31 F	20 39 53.5	10 52.1	8 11.5	5♑21.5	2 38.2	7 36.8	16 33.2	13 3.7	9 26.1	15 28.2	17 21.7	22 46.8

DAY	EPHEMERIS SIDEREAL TIME	☉	☊	☽	☿	♀	♂	♃	♄	♅	♆	♇
						DECLINATION at NOON						
1 W	18 41 36.8	23S 2.3	23S 4.8	23S47.5	21S35.5	18S18.2	23S46.7	7N 8.3	19S21.5	23S 5.9	21S43.5	4S11.0
4 S	18 53 26.4	22 46.1	23 5.5	23 19.2	22 17.0	19 5.0	23 53.3	7 9.8	19 16.7	23 4.8	21 42.8	4 11.4
7 T	19 5 16.1	22 25.7	23 6.2	13 51.6	22 52.0	19 47.5	23 57.7	7 11.9	19 11.6	23 3.7	21 42.0	4 11.6
10 F	19 17 5.8	22 1.4	23 6.9	0N26.8	23 19.0	20 25.4	23 59.8	7 14.7	19 6.6	23 2.6	21 41.2	4 11.7
13 M	19 28 55.5	21 33.2	23 7.5	15 11.9	23 36.5	20 58.4	23 59.7	7 18.2	19 1.4	23 1.5	21 40.3	4 11.6
16 T	19 40 45.1	21 1.2	23 8.2	24 25.6	23 43.6	21 26.2	23 57.2	7 22.3	18 56.2	23 0.4	21 39.5	4 11.5
19 S	19 52 34.8	20 25.7	23 8.8	20 17.2	23 39.8	21 48.7	23 52.5	7 27.0	18 50.8	22 59.3	21 38.7	4 11.3
22 W	20 4 24.5	19 46.7	23 9.4	4 13.8	23 24.3	22 5.6	23 45.5	7 32.3	18 45.5	22 58.1	21 37.9	4 11.0
25 S	20 16 14.1	19 4.4	23 10.0	12S54.4	22 56.7	22 16.8	23 36.1	7 38.2	18 40.0	22 57.0	21 37.1	4 10.5
28 T	20 28 3.8	18 18.9	23 10.7	23 19.4	22 16.8	22 22.2	23 24.5	7 44.6	18 34.5	22 55.9	21 36.2	4 10.0
31 F	20 39 53.5	17 30.4	23 11.2	23 43.6	21 24.1	22 21.6	23 10.6	7 51.5	18 29.0	22 54.8	21 35.4	4 9.4

FEBRUARY 1992

DAY	EPHEMERIS SIDEREAL TIME	☉	☊	☽	☿	♀	♂	♃	♄	♅	♆	♇
						LONGITUDE at NOON						
1 S	20 43 50.0	11♒53.0	8♑ 8.3	17♑ 9.4	4♒16.7	8♑50.5	17♑18.5	12♍58.0	9♒33.2	15♑31.5	17♑23.8	22♏47.7
2 S	20 47 46.6	12 53.9	8 5.1	28 56.3	5 55.9	10 4.2	18 3.9	12R52.1	9 40.4	15 34.8	17 25.9	22 48.5
3 M	20 51 43.1	13 54.8	8 1.9	10♒44.8	7 35.7	11 18.0	18 49.4	12 46.1	9 47.6	15 38.0	17 28.0	22 49.2
4 T	20 55 39.7	14 55.7	7 58.7	22 36.7	9 16.3	12 31.7	19 34.8	12 39.9	9 54.7	15 41.3	17 30.0	22 50.0
5 W	20 59 36.3	15 56.5	7 55.6	4♓33.8	10 57.7	13 45.5	20 20.4	12 33.6	10 1.9	15 44.5	17 32.1	22 50.7
6 T	21 3 32.8	16 57.4	7 52.4	16 37.8	12 39.8	14 59.3	21 5.9	12 27.2	10 9.1	15 47.7	17 34.2	22 51.4
7 F	21 7 29.4	17 58.2	7 49.2	28 50.3	14 22.7	16 13.2	21 51.5	12 20.7	10 16.2	15 50.9	17 36.2	22 52.0
8 S	21 11 25.9	18 59.0	7 46.0	11♈13.3	16 6.3	17 27.0	22 37.0	12 14.0	10 23.3	15 54.0	17 38.2	22 52.6
9 S	21 15 22.5	19 59.8	7 42.9	23 49.0	17 50.7	18 40.8	23 22.7	12 7.3	10 30.5	15 57.2	17 40.2	22 53.1
10 M	21 19 19.0	21 0.5	7 39.7	6♉40.1	19 36.0	19 54.7	24 8.3	12 0.4	10 37.6	16 0.2	17 42.2	22 53.7
11 T	21 23 15.6	22 1.2	7 36.5	19 49.4	21 22.0	21 8.6	24 54.0	11 53.4	10 44.7	16 3.3	17 44.1	22 54.1
12 W	21 27 12.1	23 1.9	7 33.3	3♊19.6	23 8.7	22 22.5	25 39.7	11 46.4	10 51.7	16 6.4	17 46.1	22 54.6
13 T	21 31 8.7	24 2.6	7 30.1	17 12.6	24 56.3	23 36.4	26 25.5	11 39.2	10 58.8	16 9.4	17 48.0	22 55.0
14 F	21 35 5.2	25 3.2	7 27.0	1♋29.3	26 44.6	24 50.3	27 11.2	11 32.0	11 5.8	16 12.4	17 49.9	22 55.4
15 S	21 39 1.8	26 3.8	7 23.8	16 8.1	28 33.6	26 4.2	27 57.0	11 24.7	11 12.9	16 15.3	17 51.8	22 55.7
16 S	21 42 58.4	27 4.4	7 20.6	1♌ 5.1	0♓23.3	27 18.2	28 42.8	11 17.3	11 19.9	16 18.2	17 53.7	22 56.1
17 M	21 46 54.9	28 5.0	7 17.4	16 13.4	2 13.7	28 32.2	29 28.7	11 9.9	11 26.9	16 21.2	17 55.6	22 56.4
18 T	21 50 51.5	29 5.5	7 14.3	1♍23.5	4 4.7	29 46.1	0♒14.6	11 2.4	11 33.9	16 24.1	17 57.4	22 56.6
19 W	21 54 48.0	0♓ 6.0	7 11.1	16 25.4	5 56.1	1♒ 0.1	1 0.5	10 54.8	11 40.8	16 26.9	17 59.2	22 56.8
20 T	21 58 44.6	1 6.5	7 7.9	1♎ 9.5	7 47.9	2 14.1	1 46.5	10 47.1	11 47.8	16 29.7	18 1.0	22 57.0
21 F	22 2 41.1	2 6.9	7 4.7	15 28.8	9 40.0	3 28.1	2 32.4	10 39.5	11 54.7	16 32.5	18 2.8	22 57.1
22 S	22 6 37.7	3 7.4	7 1.6	29 19.2	11 32.2	4 42.1	3 18.4	10 31.7	12 1.5	16 35.2	18 4.5	22 57.2
23 S	22 10 34.2	4 7.8	6 58.4	12♏40.1	13 24.3	5 56.1	4 4.4	10 24.0	12 8.4	16 37.9	18 6.2	22 57.3
24 M	22 14 30.8	5 8.1	6 55.2	25 33.5	15 16.1	7 10.2	4 50.5	10 16.2	12 15.2	16 40.6	18 7.9	22 57.3
25 T	22 18 27.3	6 8.5	6 52.0	8♐ 3.2	17 7.5	8 24.2	5 36.6	10 8.3	12 22.0	16 43.2	18 9.6	22 57.3
26 W	22 22 23.9	7 8.8	6 48.8	20 14.1	18 58.0	9 38.3	6 22.6	10 0.5	12 28.8	16 45.8	18 11.2	22R57.2
27 T	22 26 20.5	8 9.2	6 45.7	2♑11.7	20 47.3	10 52.3	7 8.8	9 52.6	12 35.5	16 48.4	18 12.9	22 57.1
28 F	22 30 17.0	9 9.4	6 42.5	14 1.2	22 35.1	12 6.4	7 54.9	9 44.7	12 42.2	16 50.9	18 14.5	22 57.0
29 S	22 34 13.6	10 9.7	6 39.3	25 47.4	24 21.0	13 20.5	8 41.1	9 36.9	12 48.8	16 53.4	18 16.1	22 56.9

DAY	EPHEMERIS SIDEREAL TIME	☉	☊	☽	☿	♀	♂	♃	♄	♅	♆	♇
						DECLINATION at NOON						
1 S	20 43 50.0	17S13.6	23S11.4	21S39.8	21S 3.7	22S20.0	23S 5.4	7N53.9	18S27.2	22S54.4	21S35.2	4S 9.2
4 T	20 55 39.7	16 21.5	23 12.0	10 37.1	19 53.7	22 11.5	22 48.5	8 1.4	18 21.6	22 53.3	21 34.4	4 8.4
7 F	21 7 29.4	15 26.8	23 12.6	4N12.2	18 30.7	21 57.0	22 29.4	8 9.3	18 16.1	22 52.3	21 33.6	4 7.6
10 M	21 19 19.0	14 29.7	23 13.1	18 3.7	16 54.4	21 36.7	22 8.0	8 17.6	18 10.5	22 51.2	21 32.8	4 6.7
13 T	21 31 8.7	13 30.5	23 13.7	24 43.9	15 5.1	21 10.5	21 44.5	8 26.1	18 4.9	22 50.2	21 32.0	4 5.7
16 S	21 42 58.4	12 29.3	23 14.2	18 1.1	13 3.1	20 38.7	21 18.9	8 34.9	17 59.4	22 49.2	21 31.2	4 4.6
19 W	21 54 48.0	11 26.3	23 14.7	0 59.4	10 49.0	20 1.5	20 51.3	8 43.8	17 53.8	22 48.2	21 30.5	4 3.5
22 S	22 6 37.7	10 21.6	23 15.3	15S41.4	8 24.3	19 18.9	20 21.6	8 52.9	17 48.3	22 47.2	21 29.8	4 2.3
25 T	22 18 27.3	9 15.6	23 15.8	24 11.2	5 51.4	18 31.3	19 50.0	9 2.1	17 42.8	22 46.3	21 29.1	4 1.0
28 F	22 30 17.0	8 8.2	23 16.2	22 10.7	3 14.0	17 38.9	19 16.5	9 11.2	17 37.4	22 45.4	21 28.4	3 59.6

MARCH 1992

LONGITUDE at NOON

DAY	EPHEMERIS SIDEREAL TIME	☉	☊	☽	☿	♀	♂	♃	♄	♅	♆	♇
	h m s	° ′	° ′	° ′	° ′	° ′	° ′	° ′	° ′	° ′	° ′	° ′
1 S	22 38 10.1	11♓ 9.9	6♑36.1	7♒34.5	26♓ 4.4	14♒34.6	9♒27.3	9♍29.0	12♒55.5	16♑55.8	18♑17.6	22♏56.7
2 M	22 42 6.7	12 10.1	6 33.0	19 26.0	27 45.0	15 48.6	10 13.5	9R21.1	13 2.1	16 58.2	18 19.1	22R56.4
3 T	22 46 3.2	13 10.3	6 29.8	1♓24.3	29 22.1	17 2.7	10 59.7	9 13.3	13 8.6	17 0.6	18 20.6	22 56.2
4 W	22 49 59.8	14 10.5	6 26.6	13 31.4	0♈55.3	18 16.8	11 45.9	9 5.4	13 15.1	17 2.9	18 22.1	22 55.9
5 T	22 53 56.3	15 10.6	6 23.4	25 48.2	2 23.9	19 30.9	12 32.2	8 57.6	13 21.6	17 5.2	18 23.6	22 55.6
6 F	22 57 52.9	16 10.7	6 20.2	8♈15.3	3 47.4	20 45.0	13 18.5	8 49.8	13 28.1	17 7.5	18 25.0	22 55.2
7 S	23 1 49.4	17 10.7	6 17.1	20 53.2	5 5.3	21 59.1	14 4.8	8 42.1	13 34.5	17 9.7	18 26.4	22 54.8
8 S	23 5 46.0	18 10.8	6 13.9	3♉42.3	6 16.9	23 13.2	14 51.1	8 34.4	13 40.8	17 11.8	18 27.8	22 54.4
9 M	23 9 42.5	19 10.8	6 10.7	16 43.4	7 21.9	24 27.3	15 37.4	8 26.8	13 47.2	17 14.0	18 29.1	22 53.9
10 T	23 13 39.1	20 10.7	6 7.5	29 57.6	8 19.7	25 41.4	16 23.8	8 19.2	13 53.5	17 16.1	18 30.4	22 53.5
11 W	23 17 35.6	21 10.6	6 4.4	13♊26.4	9 9.9	26 55.5	17 10.1	8 11.7	13 59.7	17 18.1	18 31.7	22 52.9
12 T	23 21 32.2	22 10.5	6 1.2	27 11.5	9 52.2	28 9.6	17 56.5	8 4.2	14 5.8	17 20.1	18 33.0	22 52.4
13 F	23 25 28.8	23 10.4	5 58.0	11♋13.8	10 26.2	29 23.7	18 42.9	7 56.8	14 12.0	17 22.1	18 34.2	22 51.8
14 S	23 29 25.3	24 10.2	5 54.8	25 33.3	10 51.8	0♓37.8	19 29.2	7 49.5	14 18.1	17 24.0	18 35.4	22 51.1
15 S	23 33 21.9	25 9.9	5 51.6	10♌ 8.3	11 8.9	1 51.9	20 15.6	7 42.2	14 24.1	17 25.9	18 36.6	22 50.5
16 M	23 37 18.4	26 9.6	5 48.5	24 54.4	11 17.5	3 5.9	21 2.0	7 35.1	14 30.1	17 27.7	18 37.7	22 49.8
17 T	23 41 15.0	27 9.3	5 45.3	9♍45.2	11 17.7	4 20.0	21 48.5	7 28.0	14 36.0	17 29.4	18 38.8	22 49.1
18 W	23 45 11.5	28 9.0	5 42.1	24 32.6	11R 9.7	5 34.1	22 34.9	7 21.0	14 41.9	17 31.2	18 39.9	22 48.3
19 T	23 49 8.1	29 8.6	5 38.9	9♎ 8.0	10 53.8	6 48.1	23 21.3	7 14.2	14 47.7	17 32.9	18 40.9	22 47.5
20 F	23 53 4.6	0♈ 8.2	5 35.7	23 23.8	10 30.5	8 2.2	24 7.8	7 7.4	14 53.4	17 34.5	18 42.0	22 46.7
21 S	23 57 1.2	1 7.8	5 32.6	7♏15.0	10 0.5	9 16.3	24 54.2	7 0.7	14 59.2	17 36.1	18 42.9	22 45.9
22 S	0 0 57.7	2 7.3	5 29.4	20 39.1	9 24.4	10 30.4	25 40.7	6 54.1	15 4.8	17 37.6	18 43.9	22 45.0
23 M	0 4 54.3	3 6.8	5 26.2	3♐36.7	8 43.1	11 44.4	26 27.2	6 47.7	15 10.4	17 39.1	18 44.8	22 44.1
24 T	0 8 50.8	4 6.2	5 23.0	16 10.4	7 57.7	12 58.5	27 13.7	6 41.4	15 15.9	17 40.6	18 45.7	22 43.2
25 W	0 12 47.4	5 5.7	5 19.9	28 24.6	7 9.0	14 12.6	28 0.2	6 35.2	15 21.4	17 42.0	18 46.6	22 42.2
26 T	0 16 43.9	6 5.1	5 16.7	10♑24.4	6 18.1	15 26.6	28 46.7	6 29.1	15 26.8	17 43.3	18 47.4	22 41.2
27 F	0 20 40.5	7 4.5	5 13.5	22 15.4	5 26.3	16 40.7	29 33.2	6 23.2	15 32.2	17 44.6	18 48.2	22 40.2
28 S	0 24 37.0	8 3.8	5 10.3	4♒ 3.0	4 34.4	17 54.8	0♓19.7	6 17.4	15 37.5	17 45.9	18 49.0	22 39.2
29 S	0 28 33.6	9 3.1	5 7.1	15 52.3	3 43.6	19 8.8	1 6.2	6 11.7	15 42.7	17 47.1	18 49.7	22 38.1
30 M	0 32 30.1	10 2.5	5 4.0	27 47.8	2 54.9	20 22.9	1 52.8	6 6.2	15 47.9	17 48.3	18 50.4	22 37.0
31 T	0 36 26.7	11 1.7	5 0.8	9♓52.9	2 8.9	21 37.0	2 39.3	6 0.8	15 53.0	17 49.4	18 51.1	22 35.9

DECLINATION at NOON

DAY	EPHEMERIS SIDEREAL TIME	☉	☊	☽	☿	♀	♂	♃	♄	♅	♆	♇
1 S	22 38 10.1	7S 22.7	23S 16.6	15S 57.0	1S 29.3	17S 1.4	18S 53.1	9N 17.3	17S 33.8	22S 44.8	21S 28.0	3S 58.7
4 W	22 49 59.8	6 13.7	23 17.0	2 13.4	1N 2.0	16 1.6	18 16.6	9 26.3	17 28.5	22 44.0	21 27.3	3 57.3
7 S	23 1 49.4	5 3.9	23 17.5	12N 40.6	3 19.1	14 57.8	17 38.4	9 35.2	17 23.3	22 43.2	21 26.7	3 55.8
10 T	23 13 39.1	3 53.4	23 17.9	23 5.4	5 13.4	13 50.2	16 58.6	9 43.8	17 18.1	22 42.5	21 26.1	3 54.3
13 F	23 25 28.8	2 42.6	23 18.4	22 33.2	6 36.8	12 39.2	16 17.2	9 52.2	17 13.0	22 41.8	21 25.6	3 52.7
16 M	23 37 18.4	1 31.6	23 18.8	9 39.9	7 23.3	11 25.1	15 34.4	10 0.3	17 8.1	22 41.1	21 25.1	3 51.1
19 T	23 49 8.1	0 20.5	23 19.2	8S 12.9	7 29.5	10 8.1	14 50.1	10 8.0	17 3.3	22 40.5	21 24.6	3 49.5
22 S	0 0 57.7	0N 50.6	23 19.6	21 19.7	6 56.1	8 48.8	14 4.6	10 15.3	16 58.6	22 40.0	21 24.1	3 47.8
25 W	0 12 47.4	2 1.5	23 20.0	24 1.9	5 49.3	7 27.2	13 17.8	10 22.1	16 54.0	22 39.5	21 23.7	3 46.2
28 S	0 24 37.0	3 11.9	23 20.4	16 52.5	4 20.8	6 3.8	12 29.9	10 28.5	16 49.6	22 39.1	21 23.4	3 44.5
31 T	0 36 26.7	4 21.9	23 20.7	3 39.1	2 45.5	4 38.8	11 40.9	10 34.4	16 45.3	22 38.7	21 23.0	3 42.9

APRIL 1992

LONGITUDE at NOON

DAY	EPHEMERIS SIDEREAL TIME	☉	☊	☽	☿	♀	♂	♃	♄	♅	♆	♇
1 W	0 40 23.3	12♈ 0.9	4♑57.6	22♓10.0	1♈26.5	22♓51.0	3♓25.8	5♍55.6	15♒58.1	17♑50.4	18♑51.8	22♏34.8
2 T	0 44 19.8	13 0.1	4 54.4	4♈40.6	0R48.2	24 5.1	4 12.3	5R50.5	16 3.0	17 51.4	18 52.4	22R33.6
3 F	0 48 16.4	13 59.3	4 51.3	17 24.9	0 14.7	25 19.1	4 58.9	5 45.6	16 7.9	17 52.4	18 52.9	22 32.4
4 S	0 52 12.9	14 58.4	4 48.1	0♉22.4	29♓46.1	26 33.2	5 45.4	5 40.8	16 12.8	17 53.3	18 53.5	22 31.2
5 S	0 56 9.5	15 57.5	4 44.9	13 32.2	29 22.8	27 47.2	6 31.9	5 36.2	16 17.5	17 54.1	18 54.0	22 30.0
6 M	1 0 6.0	16 56.6	4 41.7	26 53.0	29 4.9	29 1.2	7 18.4	5 31.7	16 22.2	17 55.0	18 54.4	22 28.7
7 T	1 4 2.6	17 55.6	4 38.5	10♊23.8	28 52.6	0♈15.2	8 4.9	5 27.5	16 26.8	17 55.7	18 54.9	22 27.4
8 W	1 7 59.1	18 54.6	4 35.4	24 4.3	28 45.7	1 29.2	8 51.4	5 23.4	16 31.4	17 56.4	18 55.3	22 26.1
9 T	1 11 55.7	19 53.5	4 32.2	7♋54.3	28 44.3	2 43.2	9 37.9	5 19.4	16 35.8	17 57.1	18 55.6	22 24.8
10 F	1 15 52.2	20 52.4	4 29.0	21 53.7	28D48.2	3 57.2	10 24.3	5 15.6	16 40.2	17 57.7	18 56.0	22 23.4
11 S	1 19 48.8	21 51.3	4 25.8	6♌ 2.4	28 57.3	5 11.2	11 10.8	5 12.0	16 44.5	17 58.2	18 56.3	22 22.0
12 S	1 23 45.3	22 50.1	4 22.7	20 19.3	29 11.4	6 25.1	11 57.2	5 8.6	16 48.8	17 58.7	18 56.6	22 20.7
13 M	1 27 41.9	23 48.9	4 19.5	4♍42.1	29 30.3	7 39.1	12 43.7	5 5.4	16 52.9	17 59.1	18 56.8	22 19.3
14 T	1 31 38.4	24 47.6	4 16.3	19 6.7	29 53.9	8 53.0	13 30.1	5 2.3	16 57.0	17 59.5	18 57.0	22 17.8
15 W	1 35 35.0	25 46.3	4 13.1	3♎28.0	0♈21.9	10 7.0	14 16.5	4 59.4	17 1.0	17 59.9	18 57.2	22 16.4
16 T	1 39 31.6	26 45.0	4 9.9	17 40.2	0 54.3	11 20.9	15 3.0	4 56.7	17 4.9	18 0.2	18 57.3	22 14.9
17 F	1 43 28.1	27 43.6	4 6.8	1♏37.6	1 30.6	12 34.8	15 49.4	4 54.2	17 8.8	18 0.4	18 57.4	22 13.5
18 S	1 47 24.7	28 42.3	4 3.6	15 15.8	2 10.9	13 48.7	16 35.8	4 51.8	17 12.5	18 0.6	18 57.5	22 12.0
19 S	1 51 21.2	29 40.8	4 0.4	28 32.3	2 54.8	15 2.6	17 22.1	4 49.6	17 16.2	18 0.8	18 57.5	22 10.5
20 M	1 55 17.8	0♉39.4	3 57.2	11♐26.5	3 42.3	16 16.6	18 8.6	4 47.7	17 19.9	18 0.9	18 57.6	22 9.0
21 T	1 59 14.3	1 38.0	3 54.1	23 59.7	4 33.1	17 30.5	18 54.9	4 45.9	17 23.4	18 0.9	18 57.6	22 7.5
22 W	2 3 10.9	2 36.5	3 50.9	6♑15.2	5 27.2	18 44.4	19 41.3	4 44.2	17 26.8	18 0.9	18R57.5	22 5.9
23 T	2 7 7.4	3 34.9	3 47.7	18 17.0	6 24.3	19 58.3	20 27.6	4 42.8	17 30.2	18 0.9	18 57.4	22 4.4
24 F	2 11 4.0	4 33.4	3 44.5	0♒10.2	7 24.3	21 12.2	21 13.9	4 41.5	17 33.4	18R 0.7	18 57.3	22 2.8
25 S	2 15 0.5	5 31.8	3 41.3	11 59.9	8 27.2	22 26.1	22 0.2	4 40.5	17 36.6	18 0.6	18 57.1	22 1.2
26 S	2 18 57.1	6 30.2	3 38.2	23 51.6	9 32.8	23 39.9	22 46.5	4 39.6	17 39.7	18 0.4	18 56.9	21 59.6
27 M	2 22 53.7	7 28.5	3 35.0	5♓50.0	10 40.9	24 53.8	23 32.7	4 38.9	17 42.7	18 0.1	18 56.7	21 58.0
28 T	2 26 50.2	8 26.9	3 31.8	17 59.6	11 51.6	26 7.7	24 19.0	4 38.4	17 45.6	17 59.8	18 56.5	21 56.4
29 W	2 30 46.8	9 25.2	3 28.6	0♈23.8	13 4.7	27 21.6	25 5.2	4 38.0	17 48.4	17 59.4	18 56.2	21 54.8
30 T	2 34 43.3	10 23.4	3 25.5	13 4.9	14 20.2	28 35.4	25 51.4	4 37.9	17 51.1	17 59.0	18 55.9	21 53.1

DECLINATION at NOON

DAY	EPHEMERIS SIDEREAL TIME	☉	☊	☽	☿	♀	♂	♃	♄	♅	♆	♇
1 W	0 40 23.3	4N45.0	23S 20.9	1N23.1	2N14.7	4S 10.3	11S 24.4	10N36.2	16S 44.0	22S 38.6	21S 22.9	3S 42.4
4 S	0 52 12.9	5 54.0	23 21.2	15 48.3	0 50.9	2 43.8	10 34.1	10 41.4	16 39.9	22 38.3	21 22.6	3 40.7
7 T	1 4 2.6	7 2.0	23 21.5	23 58.7	0S 14.0	1 16.6	9 43.0	10 45.9	16 36.1	22 38.1	21 22.4	3 39.1
10 F	1 15 52.2	8 8.9	23 21.9	20 5.2	0 56.3	0N 11.1	8 51.2	10 49.9	16 32.5	22 37.9	21 22.2	3 37.5
13 M	1 27 41.9	9 14.6	23 22.2	5 39.6	1 15.2	1 38.9	7 58.7	10 53.3	16 29.0	22 37.8	21 22.0	3 35.9
16 T	1 39 31.6	10 18.8	23 22.5	11S 26.4	1 12.0	3 6.6	7 5.6	10 56.1	16 25.8	22 37.7	21 21.9	3 34.3
19 S	1 51 21.2	11 21.6	23 22.8	22 36.2	0 48.5	4 33.8	6 12.0	10 58.2	16 22.7	22 37.7	21 21.8	3 32.8
22 W	2 3 10.9	12 22.7	23 23.1	22 57.0	0 6.8	6 0.2	5 17.9	10 59.8	16 19.9	22 37.8	21 21.8	3 31.3
25 S	2 15 0.5	13 22.0	23 23.3	14 3.6	0N 51.0	7 25.5	4 23.5	11 0.7	16 17.4	22 37.9	21 21.8	3 29.9
28 T	2 26 50.2	14 19.2	23 23.6	0 11.3	2 3.1	8 49.3	3 28.9	11 1.0	16 15.0	22 38.1	21 21.9	3 28.5

MAY 1992

DAY	EPHEMERIS SIDEREAL TIME	☉	☊	☽	☿	♀	♂	♃	♄	♅	♆	♇
	h m s	° ′	° ′	° ′	° ′	° ′	° ′	° ′	° ′	° ′	° ′	° ′
						LONGITUDE at NOON						
1 F	2 38 39.9	11♉21.7	3♑22.3	26♈ 3.8	15♈38.0	29♈49.3	26♓37.6	4♍37.9	17♒53.8	17♑58.6	18♑55.5	21♏51.5
2 S	2 42 36.4	12 19.9	3 19.1	9♉20.1	16 58.0	1♉ 3.1	27 23.7	4D38.1	17 56.3	17R58.0	18R55.1	21R49.8
3 S	2 46 33.0	13 18.1	3 15.9	22 52.2	18 20.2	2 17.0	28 9.8	4 38.5	17 58.8	17 57.5	18 54.7	21 48.2
4 M	2 50 29.5	14 16.3	3 12.8	6♊37.4	19 44.6	3 30.8	28 55.9	4 39.1	18 1.1	17 56.9	18 54.3	21 46.5
5 T	2 54 26.1	15 14.4	3 9.6	20 32.8	21 11.0	4 44.6	29 42.0	4 39.9	18 3.4	17 56.2	18 53.8	21 44.9
6 W	2 58 22.6	16 12.5	3 6.4	4♋35.4	22 39.6	5 58.4	0♈28.0	4 40.9	18 5.6	17 55.5	18 53.3	21 43.2
7 T	3 2 19.2	17 10.6	3 3.2	18 42.6	24 10.2	7 12.3	1 14.0	4 42.0	18 7.7	17 54.8	18 52.8	21 41.5
8 F	3 6 15.8	18 8.7	3 0.0	2♌52.4	25 42.8	8 26.1	2 0.0	4 43.3	18 9.7	17 54.0	18 52.2	21 39.9
9 S	3 10 12.3	19 6.7	2 56.9	17 2.8	27 17.5	9 39.8	2 45.9	4 44.8	18 11.6	17 53.1	18 51.6	21 38.2
10 S	3 14 8.9	20 4.6	2 53.7	1♍12.5	28 54.2	10 53.6	3 31.9	4 46.5	18 13.4	17 52.2	18 51.0	21 36.5
11 M	3 18 5.4	21 2.6	2 50.5	15 19.5	0♉33.0	12 7.5	4 17.8	4 48.4	18 15.1	17 51.3	18 50.4	21 34.9
12 T	3 22 2.0	22 0.6	2 47.3	29 21.6	2 13.7	13 21.2	5 3.6	4 50.5	18 16.7	17 50.4	18 49.7	21 33.2
13 W	3 25 58.5	22 58.4	2 44.2	13♎16.3	3 56.4	14 35.0	5 49.4	4 52.7	18 18.2	17 49.3	18 49.0	21 31.5
14 T	3 29 55.1	23 56.3	2 41.0	27 0.8	5 41.2	15 48.7	6 35.2	4 55.1	18 19.6	17 48.3	18 48.2	21 29.8
15 F	3 33 51.6	24 54.1	2 37.8	10♏32.2	7 28.0	17 2.5	7 20.9	4 57.7	18 21.0	17 47.2	18 47.5	21 28.2
16 S	3 37 48.2	25 51.9	2 34.6	23 48.4	9 16.8	18 16.2	8 6.6	5 0.4	18 22.2	17 46.0	18 46.7	21 26.5
17 S	3 41 44.8	26 49.7	2 31.5	6♐47.8	11 7.6	19 30.0	8 52.3	5 3.3	18 23.3	17 44.8	18 45.9	21 24.8
18 M	3 45 41.3	27 47.5	2 28.3	19 30.2	13 0.4	20 43.7	9 37.9	5 6.4	18 24.4	17 43.6	18 45.0	21 23.1
19 T	3 49 37.9	28 45.2	2 25.1	1♑56.3	14 55.3	21 57.4	10 23.5	5 9.6	18 25.3	17 42.3	18 44.1	21 21.5
20 W	3 53 34.4	29 42.9	2 21.9	14 8.3	16 52.1	23 11.2	11 9.1	5 13.0	18 26.1	17 40.9	18 43.2	21 19.8
21 T	3 57 31.0	0♊40.6	2 18.7	26 9.2	18 50.8	24 24.9	11 54.6	5 16.6	18 26.9	17 39.6	18 42.3	21 18.2
22 F	4 1 27.5	1 38.3	2 15.6	8♒ 2.8	20 51.5	25 38.6	12 40.1	5 20.4	18 27.5	17 38.2	18 41.3	21 16.5
23 S	4 5 24.1	2 36.0	2 12.4	19 53.5	22 53.9	26 52.3	13 25.6	5 24.3	18 28.0	17 36.7	18 40.4	21 14.9
24 S	4 9 20.7	3 33.6	2 9.2	1♓46.2	24 58.1	28 6.1	14 11.0	5 28.3	18 28.5	17 35.2	18 39.4	21 13.3
25 M	4 13 17.2	4 31.3	2 6.0	13 45.6	27 3.9	29 19.8	14 56.3	5 32.6	18 28.8	17 33.7	18 38.3	21 11.6
26 T	4 17 13.8	5 28.9	2 2.9	25 56.4	29 11.3	0♊33.5	15 41.7	5 37.0	18 29.1	17 32.1	18 37.3	21 10.0
27 W	4 21 10.3	6 26.5	1 59.7	8♈23.0	1♊19.9	1 47.2	16 26.9	5 41.5	18 29.2	17 30.5	18 36.2	21 8.4
28 T	4 25 6.9	7 24.0	1 56.5	21 8.5	3 29.7	3 1.0	17 12.2	5 46.2	18 29.3	17 28.9	18 35.1	21 6.8
29 F	4 29 3.4	8 21.6	1 53.3	4♉15.3	5 40.5	4 14.7	17 57.4	5 51.1	18R29.2	17 27.2	18 34.0	21 5.2
30 S	4 32 60.0	9 19.2	1 50.2	17 43.9	7 51.9	5 28.4	18 42.5	5 56.1	18 29.1	17 25.5	18 32.8	21 3.7
31 S	4 36 56.6	10 16.7	1 47.0	1♊33.1	10 3.8	6 42.1	19 27.6	6 1.3	18 28.8	17 23.8	18 31.6	21 2.1
						DECLINATION at NOON						
1 F	2 38 39.9	15N14.4	23S23.8	14N24.2	3N27.9	10N11.4	2S34.1	11N 0.7	16S12.9	22S38.4	21S22.0	3S27.2
4 M	2 50 29.5	16 7.3	23 24.1	23 32.9	5 3.7	11 31.4	1 39.2	10 59.7	16 11.1	22 38.7	21 22.1	3 25.9
7 T	3 2 19.2	16 57.8	23 24.3	20 36.7	6 49.2	12 49.0	0 44.3	10 58.2	16 9.6	22 39.0	21 22.3	3 24.7
10 S	3 14 8.9	17 45.7	23 24.5	6 51.9	8 42.8	14 3.9	0N10.4	10 56.0	16 8.2	22 39.4	21 22.5	3 23.6
13 W	3 25 58.5	18 31.0	23 24.7	9S53.6	10 43.1	15 15.7	1 5.0	10 53.3	16 7.2	22 39.9	21 22.7	3 22.6
16 S	3 37 48.2	19 13.4	23 24.9	21 45.9	12 48.0	16 24.1	1 59.4	10 49.9	16 6.4	22 40.4	21 23.0	3 21.7
19 T	3 49 37.9	19 52.9	23 25.1	23 19.9	14 55.2	17 28.8	2 53.4	10 46.1	16 5.9	22 41.0	21 23.3	3 20.8
22 F	4 1 27.5	20 29.4	23 25.3	15 12.0	17 1.7	18 29.5	3 47.0	10 41.6	16 5.7	22 41.6	21 23.7	3 20.0
25 M	4 13 17.2	21 2.7	23 25.4	1 46.0	19 3.4	19 25.8	4 40.1	10 36.6	16 5.8	22 42.2	21 24.0	3 19.3
28 T	4 25 6.9	21 32.8	23 25.6	12N48.0	20 55.6	20 17.5	5 32.7	10 31.1	16 6.1	22 42.9	21 24.5	3 18.7
31 S	4 36 56.6	21 59.5	23 25.7	22 58.9	22 32.6	21 4.2	6 24.7	10 25.1	16 6.7	22 43.7	21 24.9	3 18.2

JUNE 1992

DAY	EPHEMERIS SIDEREAL TIME	☉	☊	☽	☿	♀	♂	♃	♄	♅	♆	♇
						LONGITUDE at NOON						
1 M	4 40 53.1	11♊14.3	1♑43.8	15♊40.2	12♊15.9	7♊55.9	20♈12.7	6♍ 6.7	18♒28.5	17♑22.1	18♑30.5	21♏ 0.6
2 T	4 44 49.7	12 11.8	1 40.6	0♋ 0.9	14 27.9	9 9.6	20 57.7	6 12.1	18R28.1	17R20.2	18R29.3	20R59.1
3 W	4 48 46.2	13 9.3	1 37.4	14 30.0	16 39.6	10 23.3	21 42.6	6 17.8	18 27.5	17 18.4	18 28.1	20 57.5
4 T	4 52 42.8	14 6.7	1 34.3	29 2.0	18 50.6	11 37.0	22 27.5	6 23.5	18 26.9	17 16.5	18 26.8	20 56.0
5 F	4 56 39.3	15 4.2	1 31.1	13♌32.0	21 0.7	12 50.8	23 12.3	6 29.5	18 26.2	17 14.6	18 25.5	20 54.5
6 S	5 0 35.9	16 1.6	1 27.9	27 55.6	23 9.7	14 4.5	23 57.1	6 35.5	18 25.3	17 12.7	18 24.2	20 53.0
7 S	5 4 32.5	16 59.0	1 24.7	12♍ 9.6	25 17.3	15 18.2	24 41.8	6 41.7	18 24.4	17 10.7	18 22.9	20 51.6
8 M	5 8 29.0	17 56.4	1 21.6	26 11.8	27 23.4	16 31.9	25 26.4	6 48.1	18 23.4	17 8.7	18 21.6	20 50.1
9 T	5 12 25.6	18 53.7	1 18.4	10♎ 0.8	29 27.7	17 45.6	26 11.0	6 54.5	18 22.3	17 6.7	18 20.2	20 48.7
10 W	5 16 22.1	19 51.1	1 15.2	23 35.8	1♋30.2	18 59.3	26 55.6	7 1.2	18 21.1	17 4.7	18 18.9	20 47.3
11 T	5 20 18.7	20 48.4	1 12.0	6♏56.7	3 30.6	20 13.0	27 40.0	7 7.9	18 19.8	17 2.6	18 17.5	20 45.9
12 F	5 24 15.2	21 45.7	1 8.9	20 3.3	5 29.0	21 26.7	28 24.4	7 14.8	18 18.4	17 0.5	18 16.1	20 44.5
13 S	5 28 11.8	22 43.0	1 5.7	2♐56.0	7 25.1	22 40.4	29 8.8	7 21.8	18 16.9	16 58.4	18 14.7	20 43.2
14 S	5 32 8.4	23 40.3	1 2.5	15 35.1	9 19.0	23 54.1	29 53.1	7 28.9	18 15.3	16 56.2	18 13.2	20 41.8
15 M	5 36 4.9	24 37.6	0 59.3	28 1.5	11 10.7	25 7.7	0♉37.4	7 36.2	18 13.6	16 54.1	18 11.8	20 40.5
16 T	5 40 1.5	25 34.9	0 56.1	10♑16.3	12 60.0	26 21.4	1 21.5	7 43.6	18 11.9	16 51.9	18 10.3	20 39.2
17 W	5 43 58.0	26 32.1	0 53.0	22 21.2	14 46.9	27 35.1	2 5.7	7 51.1	18 10.0	16 49.7	18 8.9	20 37.9
18 T	5 47 54.6	27 29.4	0 49.8	4♒18.3	16 31.5	28 48.8	2 49.7	7 58.8	18 8.1	16 47.4	18 7.4	20 36.7
19 F	5 51 51.2	28 26.6	0 46.6	16 10.6	18 13.7	0♋ 2.6	3 33.7	8 6.5	18 6.1	16 45.2	18 5.9	20 35.5
20 S	5 55 47.7	29 23.9	0 43.4	28 1.1	19 53.5	1 16.3	4 17.7	8 14.4	18 4.0	16 42.9	18 4.4	20 34.3
21 S	5 59 44.3	0♋21.1	0 40.3	9♓53.8	21 30.8	2 30.0	5 1.6	8 22.4	18 1.8	16 40.6	18 2.9	20 33.1
22 M	6 3 40.8	1 18.4	0 37.1	21 52.9	23 5.8	3 43.7	5 45.4	8 30.6	17 59.5	16 38.4	18 1.4	20 32.0
23 T	6 7 37.4	2 15.7	0 33.9	4♈ 2.7	24 38.3	4 57.5	6 29.2	8 38.8	17 57.1	16 36.1	17 59.8	20 30.8
24 W	6 11 33.9	3 12.9	0 30.7	16 27.6	26 8.4	6 11.2	7 12.8	8 47.2	17 54.7	16 33.7	17 58.3	20 29.7
25 T	6 15 30.5	4 10.1	0 27.6	29 11.8	27 36.0	7 24.9	7 56.4	8 55.7	17 52.2	16 31.4	17 56.7	20 28.6
26 F	6 19 27.1	5 7.3	0 24.4	12♉18.6	29 1.0	8 38.7	8 40.0	9 4.2	17 49.5	16 29.1	17 55.2	20 27.5
27 S	6 23 23.6	6 4.6	0 21.2	25 50.0	0♌23.6	9 52.4	9 23.4	9 12.9	17 46.8	16 26.7	17 53.6	20 26.5
28 S	6 27 20.2	7 1.8	0 18.0	9♊46.5	1 43.6	11 6.1	10 6.8	9 21.7	17 44.1	16 24.3	17 52.0	20 25.5
29 M	6 31 16.7	7 59.0	0 14.9	24 6.2	3 0.9	12 19.9	10 50.2	9 30.6	17 41.2	16 21.9	17 50.4	20 24.5
30 T	6 35 13.3	8 56.3	0 11.7	8♋45.0	4 15.6	13 33.7	11 33.4	9 39.6	17 38.3	16 19.5	17 48.8	20 23.5
						DECLINATION at NOON						
1 M	4 40 53.1	22N 7.6	23S25.7	24N 1.7	23N 0.7	21N18.6	6N41.9	10N23.0	16S 6.9	22S43.9	21S25.1	3S18.1
4 T	4 52 42.8	22 29.7	23 25.8	17 54.0	24 10.1	21 58.3	7 32.8	10 16.3	16 7.9	22 44.7	21 25.5	3 17.7
7 S	5 4 32.5	22 48.2	23 26.0	2 22.5	24 55.2	22 32.4	8 23.0	10 9.1	16 9.1	22 45.5	21 26.1	3 17.5
10 W	5 16 22.1	23 3.1	23 26.1	13S40.5	25 15.5	23 0.7	9 12.3	10 1.4	16 10.6	22 46.3	21 26.6	3 17.3
13 S	5 28 11.8	23 14.4	23 26.1	23 9.6	25 12.3	23 23.1	10 0.6	9 53.3	16 12.4	22 47.1	21 27.1	3 17.2
16 T	5 40 1.5	23 22.0	23 26.2	22 9.6	24 48.5	23 39.3	10 48.0	9 44.8	16 14.4	22 48.0	21 27.7	3 17.3
19 F	5 51 51.2	23 25.9	23 26.3	12 22.8	24 7.4	23 49.3	11 34.3	9 35.8	16 16.6	22 48.9	21 28.3	3 17.5
22 M	6 3 40.8	23 26.0	23 26.3	1N35.0	23 12.3	23 52.9	12 19.4	9 26.4	16 19.1	22 49.8	21 28.9	3 17.8
25 T	6 15 30.5	23 22.5	23 26.4	15 32.0	22 6.4	23 50.2	13 3.4	9 16.6	16 21.8	22 50.7	21 29.5	3 18.1
28 S	6 27 20.2	23 15.2	23 26.4	23 47.3	20 52.8	23 41.1	13 46.2	9 6.5	16 24.7	22 51.6	21 30.2	3 18.6

JULY 1992

DAY	EPHEMERIS SIDEREAL TIME h m s	☉ ° ′	☊ ° ′	☽ ° ′	☿ ° ′	♀ ° ′	♂ ° ′	♃ ° ′	♄ ° ′	♅ ° ′	♆ ° ′	♇ ° ′
					LONGITUDE at NOON							
1 W	6 39 9.9	9♋53.5	0♑8.5	23♋36.6	5♌27.6	14♋47.4	12♉16.6	9♍48.8	17♒35.3	16♑17.1	17♑47.2	20♏22.6
2 T	6 43 6.4	10 50.7	0 5.3	8♌33.3	6 36.8	16 1.2	12 59.7	9 58.0	17R32.2	16R14.7	17R45.6	20R21.7
3 F	6 47 3.0	11 47.9	0 2.1	23 26.9	7 43.2	17 14.9	13 42.7	10 7.3	17 29.1	16 12.3	17 44.0	20 20.8
4 S	6 50 59.5	12 45.2	29♐59.0	8♍10.0	8 46.6	18 28.7	14 25.6	10 16.7	17 25.8	16 9.9	17 42.4	20 20.0
5 S	6 54 56.1	13 42.4	29 55.8	22 37.1	9 47.0	19 42.5	15 8.4	10 26.2	17 22.5	16 7.5	17 40.7	20 19.2
6 M	6 58 52.6	14 39.6	29 52.6	6♎44.4	10 44.3	20 56.2	15 51.2	10 35.8	17 19.2	16 5.1	17 39.1	20 18.4
7 T	7 2 49.2	15 36.8	29 49.4	20 30.6	11 38.3	22 10.0	16 33.9	10 45.5	17 15.8	16 2.6	17 37.5	20 17.6
8 W	7 6 45.8	16 34.0	29 46.3	3♏55.9	12 29.0	23 23.8	17 16.5	10 55.3	17 12.3	16 0.2	17 35.9	20 16.9
9 T	7 10 42.3	17 31.2	29 43.1	17 1.7	13 16.2	24 37.5	17 59.0	11 5.2	17 8.7	15 57.8	17 34.2	20 16.2
10 F	7 14 38.9	18 28.4	29 39.9	29 50.4	13 59.9	25 51.3	18 41.4	11 15.2	17 5.1	15 55.4	17 32.6	20 15.5
11 S	7 18 35.4	19 25.6	29 36.7	12♐24.2	14 39.8	27 5.1	19 23.7	11 25.3	17 1.5	15 52.9	17 31.0	20 14.9
12 S	7 22 32.0	20 22.8	29 33.6	24 45.7	15 15.8	28 18.8	20 6.0	11 35.4	16 57.8	15 50.5	17 29.4	20 14.3
13 M	7 26 28.5	21 20.0	29 30.4	6♑57.2	15 47.9	29 32.6	20 48.2	11 45.7	16 54.0	15 48.2	17 27.8	20 13.7
14 T	7 30 25.1	22 17.2	29 27.2	19 0.5	16 15.7	0♌46.4	21 30.3	11 56.0	16 50.2	15 45.8	17 26.2	20 13.2
15 W	7 34 21.7	23 14.4	29 24.0	0♒57.7	16 39.3	2 0.2	22 12.3	12 6.4	16 46.3	15 43.4	17 24.6	20 12.7
16 T	7 38 18.2	24 11.6	29 20.9	12 50.8	16 58.4	3 14.0	22 54.2	12 16.9	16 42.4	15 41.0	17 23.0	20 12.2
17 F	7 42 14.8	25 8.9	29 17.7	24 41.6	17 12.9	4 27.7	23 36.1	12 27.4	16 38.4	15 38.6	17 21.4	20 11.7
18 S	7 46 11.3	26 6.1	29 14.5	6♓32.6	17 22.8	5 41.5	24 17.8	12 38.1	16 34.4	15 36.2	17 19.8	20 11.3
19 S	7 50 7.9	27 3.3	29 11.3	18 26.3	17 27.8	6 55.3	24 59.5	12 48.8	16 30.3	15 33.9	17 18.2	20 10.9
20 M	7 54 4.4	28 0.6	29 8.1	0♈26.0	17 28.0	8 9.1	25 41.0	12 59.6	16 26.2	15 31.5	17 16.6	20 10.5
21 T	7 58 1.0	28 57.9	29 5.0	12 35.2	17R23.2	9 22.9	26 22.5	13 10.4	16 22.1	15 29.2	17 15.0	20 10.2
22 W	8 1 57.6	29 55.1	29 1.8	24 57.8	17 13.5	10 36.7	27 3.9	13 21.4	16 17.9	15 26.8	17 13.4	20 9.9
23 T	8 5 54.1	0♌52.4	28 58.6	7♉38.0	16 58.9	11 50.5	27 45.1	13 32.4	16 13.7	15 24.5	17 11.8	20 9.7
24 F	8 9 50.7	1 49.7	28 55.4	20 39.7	16 39.6	13 4.3	28 26.3	13 43.4	16 9.4	15 22.2	17 10.3	20 9.4
25 S	8 13 47.2	2 47.1	28 52.3	4♊6.2	16 15.6	14 18.1	29 7.4	13 54.6	16 5.1	15 20.0	17 8.7	20 9.2
26 S	8 17 43.8	3 44.4	28 49.1	17 59.5	15 47.2	15 31.9	29 48.4	14 5.8	16 0.8	15 17.7	17 7.2	20 9.1
27 M	8 21 40.3	4 41.8	28 45.9	2♋19.6	15 14.8	16 45.7	0♊29.3	14 17.1	15 56.5	15 15.4	17 5.6	20 8.9
28 T	8 25 36.9	5 39.1	28 42.7	17 3.6	14 38.7	17 59.6	1 10.0	14 28.4	15 52.1	15 13.2	17 4.1	20 8.9
29 W	8 29 33.4	6 36.5	28 39.6	2♌6.0	13 59.4	19 13.4	1 50.7	14 39.8	15 47.7	15 11.0	17 2.6	20 8.8
30 T	8 33 30.0	7 33.9	28 36.4	17 18.3	13 17.5	20 27.2	2 31.3	14 51.3	15 43.3	15 8.8	17 1.1	20 8.8
31 F	8 37 26.6	8 31.3	28 33.2	2♍30.2	12 33.6	21 41.0	3 11.7	15 2.8	15 38.8	15 6.7	16 59.6	20 8.8
					DECLINATION at NOON							
1 W	6 39 9.9	23N 4.3	23S26.4	19N20.8	19N34.3	23N25.7	14N27.6	8N55.9	16S27.8	22S52.5	21S30.8	3S19.2
4 S	6 50 59.5	22 49.7	23 26.4	3 58.9	18 13.6	23 4.0	15 7.7	8 45.0	16 31.1	22 53.4	21 31.5	3 19.9
7 T	7 2 49.2	22 31.6	23 26.4	12S36.1	16 53.5	22 36.2	15 46.4	8 33.8	16 34.6	22 54.3	21 32.1	3 20.7
10 F	7 14 38.9	22 10.0	23 26.4	22 45.5	15 36.6	22 2.5	16 23.6	8 22.2	16 38.2	22 55.2	21 32.8	3 21.6
13 M	7 26 28.5	21 44.9	23 26.3	22 41.1	14 25.9	21 23.1	16 59.4	8 10.3	16 41.9	22 56.0	21 33.5	3 22.7
16 T	7 38 18.2	21 16.5	23 26.3	13 34.5	13 24.4	20 38.0	17 33.7	7 58.1	16 45.8	22 56.9	21 34.1	3 23.8
19 S	7 50 7.9	20 44.9	23 26.3	0N 7.8	12 35.4	19 47.7	18 6.4	7 45.7	16 49.8	22 57.7	21 34.8	3 25.0
22 W	8 1 57.6	20 10.1	23 26.2	14 4.6	12 2.2	18 52.4	18 37.5	7 32.9	16 53.9	22 58.6	21 35.4	3 26.3
25 S	8 13 47.2	19 32.3	23 26.1	23 14.2	11 47.3	17 52.4	19 7.1	7 19.9	16 58.1	22 59.4	21 36.1	3 27.7
28 T	8 25 36.9	18 51.5	23 26.0	20 51.8	11 52.4	16 47.9	19 35.0	7 6.6	17 2.3	23 0.1	21 36.7	3 29.2
31 F	8 37 26.6	18 8.0	23 25.9	6 18.0	12 17.2	15 39.2	20 1.3	6 53.2	17 6.5	23 0.9	21 37.3	3 30.8

AUGUST 1992

DAY	EPHEMERIS SIDEREAL TIME h m s	☉ ° ′	☊ ° ′	☽ ° ′	☿ ° ′	♀ ° ′	♂ ° ′	♃ ° ′	♄ ° ′	♅ ° ′	♆ ° ′	♇ ° ′
					LONGITUDE at NOON							
1 S	8 41 23.1	9♌28.7	28♐30.0	17♍31.9	11♌48.6	22♌54.8	3♊52.1	15♍14.4	15♒34.4	15♑4.5	16♑58.1	20♏8.8
2 S	8 45 19.7	10 26.2	28 26.8	2♎14.7	11R 3.1	24 8.7	4 32.3	15 26.1	15R29.9	15R 2.4	16R56.7	20D 8.9
3 M	8 49 16.2	11 23.7	28 23.7	16 33.1	10 18.0	25 22.5	5 12.4	15 37.8	15 25.5	15 0.4	16 55.3	20 9.1
4 T	8 53 12.8	12 21.1	28 20.5	0♏24.5	9 34.1	26 36.3	5 52.4	15 49.6	15 21.0	14 58.3	16 53.8	20 9.2
5 W	8 57 9.3	13 18.6	28 17.3	13 49.1	8 52.3	27 50.2	6 32.3	16 1.4	15 16.5	14 56.3	16 52.4	20 9.4
6 T	9 1 5.9	14 16.1	28 14.1	26 49.4	8 13.4	29 4.0	7 12.1	16 13.3	15 12.0	14 54.2	16 51.0	20 9.6
7 F	9 5 2.5	15 13.6	28 11.0	9♐28.9	7 38.1	0♍17.8	7 51.8	16 25.2	15 7.5	14 52.3	16 49.6	20 9.8
8 S	9 8 59.0	16 11.1	28 7.8	21 51.6	7 7.2	1 31.6	8 31.3	16 37.2	15 3.1	14 50.3	16 48.3	20 10.1
9 S	9 12 55.6	17 8.6	28 4.6	4♑1.5	6 41.3	2 45.4	9 10.7	16 49.2	14 58.6	14 48.4	16 46.9	20 10.4
10 M	9 16 52.1	18 6.1	28 1.4	16 2.4	6 21.1	3 59.1	9 50.0	17 1.3	14 54.1	14 46.5	16 45.6	20 10.8
11 T	9 20 48.7	19 3.7	27 58.2	27 57.5	6 7.0	5 12.9	10 29.2	17 13.4	14 49.6	14 44.6	16 44.3	20 11.2
12 W	9 24 45.2	20 1.2	27 55.1	9♒49.4	5 59.3	6 26.7	11 8.2	17 25.5	14 45.1	14 42.8	16 43.0	20 11.6
13 T	9 28 41.8	20 58.8	27 51.9	21 40.2	5 58.5	7 40.5	11 47.2	17 37.7	14 40.7	14 41.0	16 41.7	20 12.0
14 F	9 32 38.3	21 56.4	27 48.7	3♓31.7	6D 4.8	8 54.3	12 26.0	17 50.0	14 36.2	14 39.2	16 40.5	20 12.5
15 S	9 36 34.9	22 54.0	27 45.5	15 25.6	6 18.3	10 8.0	13 4.7	18 2.2	14 31.8	14 37.5	16 39.2	20 13.0
16 S	9 40 31.4	23 51.7	27 42.4	27 23.5	6 39.1	11 21.8	13 43.3	18 14.6	14 27.4	14 35.8	16 38.0	20 13.6
17 M	9 44 28.0	24 49.4	27 39.2	9♈27.6	7 7.2	12 35.5	14 21.7	18 26.9	14 23.0	14 34.1	16 36.8	20 14.2
18 T	9 48 24.6	25 47.1	27 36.0	21 40.0	7 42.6	13 49.3	14 60.0	18 39.3	14 18.7	14 32.5	16 35.6	20 14.8
19 W	9 52 21.1	26 44.8	27 32.8	4♉3.9	8 25.3	15 3.1	15 38.2	18 51.8	14 14.3	14 30.9	16 34.5	20 15.4
20 T	9 56 17.7	27 42.6	27 29.7	16 42.5	9 15.0	16 16.8	16 16.2	19 4.2	14 10.0	14 29.3	16 33.4	20 16.1
21 F	10 0 14.2	28 40.3	27 26.5	29 39.7	10 11.7	17 30.6	16 54.1	19 16.7	14 5.7	14 27.8	16 32.3	20 16.8
22 S	10 4 10.8	29 38.1	27 23.3	12♊58.8	11 15.0	18 44.3	17 31.9	19 29.3	14 1.5	14 26.3	16 31.2	20 17.6
23 S	10 8 7.3	0♍36.0	27 20.1	26 43.0	12 24.7	19 58.0	18 9.5	19 41.8	13 57.2	14 24.9	16 30.1	20 18.4
24 M	10 12 3.9	1 33.9	27 16.9	10♋53.8	13 40.5	21 11.8	18 47.0	19 54.5	13 53.1	14 23.6	16 29.1	20 19.2
25 T	10 16 0.4	2 31.8	27 13.8	25 30.1	15 1.9	22 25.6	19 24.4	20 7.1	13 49.0	14 22.2	16 28.1	20 20.1
26 W	10 19 57.0	3 29.7	27 10.6	10♌28.1	16 28.7	23 39.3	20 1.6	20 19.8	13 44.9	14 20.9	16 27.1	20 21.0
27 T	10 23 53.5	4 27.7	27 7.4	25 40.6	18 0.4	24 53.0	20 38.6	20 32.5	13 40.8	14 19.6	16 26.2	20 21.9
28 F	10 27 50.1	5 25.7	27 4.2	10♍57.5	19 36.4	26 6.7	21 15.5	20 45.2	13 36.8	14 18.4	16 25.3	20 22.8
29 S	10 31 46.6	6 23.7	27 1.1	26 7.6	21 16.5	27 20.4	21 52.2	20 58.0	13 32.8	14 17.2	16 24.4	20 23.8
30 S	10 35 43.2	7 21.7	26 57.9	11♎0.7	22 60.0	28 34.2	22 28.8	21 10.7	13 28.9	14 16.0	16 23.5	20 24.8
31 M	10 39 39.8	8 19.7	26 54.7	25 29.0	24 46.5	29 47.8	23 5.2	21 23.5	13 25.0	14 14.9	16 22.6	20 25.9
					DECLINATION at NOON							
1 S	8 41 23.1	17N52.8	23S25.9	0N16.6	12N29.3	15N15.5	20N 9.7	6N48.6	17S 7.9	23S 1.1	21S37.5	3S31.3
4 T	8 53 12.8	17 5.8	23 25.8	15S47.0	13 15.0	14 1.9	20 33.8	6 34.8	17 12.1	23 1.8	21 38.1	3 33.0
7 F	9 5 2.5	16 16.2	23 25.7	23 39.4	14 9.7	12 44.9	20 56.2	6 20.8	17 16.4	23 2.5	21 38.7	3 34.8
10 M	9 16 52.1	15 24.3	23 25.5	21 3.1	15 6.4	11 24.9	21 17.0	6 6.6	17 20.6	23 3.1	21 39.3	3 36.7
13 T	9 28 41.8	14 30.2	23 25.4	10 27.9	15 57.9	10 2.2	21 36.1	5 52.3	17 24.7	23 3.7	21 39.8	3 38.6
16 S	9 40 31.4	13 34.1	23 25.2	3N37.6	16 37.9	8 37.1	21 53.6	5 37.8	17 28.8	23 4.2	21 40.4	3 40.6
19 W	9 52 21.1	12 35.9	23 25.0	16 47.0	17 0.9	7 10.0	22 9.5	5 23.1	17 32.8	23 4.7	21 40.9	3 42.7
22 S	10 4 10.8	11 36.0	23 24.9	23 43.7	17 2.2	5 41.1	22 23.8	5 8.3	17 36.7	23 5.2	21 41.4	3 44.8
25 T	10 16 0.4	10 34.4	23 24.7	18 47.1	16 38.3	4 10.7	22 36.6	4 53.4	17 40.4	23 5.6	21 41.8	3 47.0
28 F	10 27 50.1	9 31.3	23 24.5	2 59.8	15 47.8	2 39.3	22 47.8	4 38.4	17 44.0	23 6.0	21 42.2	3 49.2
31 M	10 39 39.8	8 26.8	23 24.2	14S 1.0	14 31.4	1 7.1	22 57.5	4 23.2	17 47.5	23 6.3	21 42.7	3 51.5

SEPTEMBER 1992

LONGITUDE at NOON

DAY	EPHEMERIS SIDEREAL TIME h m s	☉ ° ′	☊ ° ′	☽ ° ′	☿ ° ′	♀ ° ′	♂ ° ′	♃ ° ′	♄ ° ′	♅ ° ′	♆ ° ′	♇ ° ′
1 T	10 43 36.3	9♍17.8	26♐51.5	9♏28.4	26♌35.5	1♎ 1.5	23♊41.4	21♍36.3	13♒21.2	14♑13.9	16♑21.8	20♏26.9
2 W	10 47 32.9	10 15.9	26 48.3	22 58.1	28 26.6	2 15.2	24 17.5	21 49.2	13R17.5	14R12.9	16R21.0	20 28.1
3 T	10 51 29.4	11 14.0	26 45.2	6♐ 0.1	0♍19.4	3 28.9	24 53.4	22 2.0	13 13.8	14 11.9	16 20.2	20 29.2
4 F	10 55 26.0	12 12.2	26 42.0	18 38.3	2 13.4	4 42.5	25 29.1	22 14.9	13 10.1	14 11.0	16 19.5	20 30.4
5 S	10 59 22.5	13 10.4	26 38.8	0♑57.4	4 8.3	5 56.2	26 4.6	22 27.8	13 6.5	14 10.1	16 18.8	20 31.6
6 S	11 3 19.1	14 8.6	26 35.6	13 2.7	6 3.7	7 9.8	26 40.0	22 40.7	13 3.0	14 9.3	16 18.1	20 32.8
7 M	11 7 15.6	15 6.8	26 32.5	24 58.7	7 59.5	8 23.4	27 15.2	22 53.6	12 59.6	14 8.5	16 17.5	20 34.1
8 T	11 11 12.2	16 5.0	26 29.3	6♒49.9	9 55.2	9 37.0	27 50.3	23 6.5	12 56.2	14 7.7	16 16.8	20 35.3
9 W	11 15 8.7	17 3.3	26 26.1	18 39.8	11 50.8	10 50.6	28 25.1	23 19.4	12 52.8	14 7.1	16 16.2	20 36.7
10 T	11 19 5.3	18 1.6	26 22.9	0♓31.2	13 46.0	12 4.2	28 59.8	23 32.4	12 49.6	14 6.4	16 15.7	20 38.0
11 F	11 23 1.8	18 59.9	26 19.7	12 26.2	15 40.7	13 17.7	29 34.3	23 45.3	12 46.4	14 5.8	16 15.1	20 39.4
12 S	11 26 58.4	19 58.3	26 16.6	24 26.3	17 34.8	14 31.3	0♋ 8.6	23 58.3	12 43.3	14 5.3	16 14.6	20 40.8
13 S	11 30 54.9	20 56.7	26 13.4	6♈32.7	19 28.1	15 44.8	0 42.7	24 11.2	12 40.3	14 4.8	16 14.2	20 42.2
14 M	11 34 51.5	21 55.2	26 10.2	18 46.4	21 20.6	16 58.4	1 16.7	24 24.2	12 37.3	14 4.4	16 13.8	20 43.7
15 T	11 38 48.0	22 53.6	26 7.0	1♉ 8.5	23 12.2	18 11.9	1 50.4	24 37.2	12 34.5	14 4.0	16 13.4	20 45.2
16 W	11 42 44.6	23 52.1	26 3.9	13 40.6	25 2.9	19 25.4	2 23.9	24 50.2	12 31.6	14 3.6	16 13.0	20 46.7
17 T	11 46 41.1	24 50.6	26 0.7	26 24.9	26 52.6	20 38.9	2 57.3	25 3.2	12 28.9	14 3.3	16 12.6	20 48.3
18 F	11 50 37.7	25 49.2	25 57.5	9♊23.8	28 41.3	21 52.4	3 30.4	25 16.2	12 26.3	14 3.1	16 12.3	20 49.9
19 S	11 54 34.3	26 47.8	25 54.3	22 40.3	0♎29.0	23 5.8	4 3.3	25 29.2	12 23.7	14 2.9	16 12.0	20 51.5
20 S	11 58 30.8	27 46.4	25 51.1	6♋17.1	2 15.8	24 19.3	4 36.0	25 42.1	12 21.2	14 2.8	16 11.8	20 53.1
21 M	12 2 27.4	28 45.1	25 48.0	20 16.1	4 1.5	25 32.8	5 8.4	25 55.1	12 18.8	14 2.7	16 11.6	20 54.7
22 T	12 6 23.9	29 43.8	25 44.8	4♌37.8	5 46.2	26 46.2	5 40.7	26 8.1	12 16.5	14 2.6	16 11.4	20 56.4
23 W	12 10 20.5	0♎42.6	25 41.6	19 19.8	7 30.0	27 59.6	6 12.7	26 21.1	12 14.3	14 2.6	16 11.2	20 58.1
24 T	12 14 17.0	1 41.4	25 38.4	4♍17.3	9 12.8	29 13.0	6 44.5	26 34.0	12 12.1	14D 2.7	16 11.1	20 59.9
25 F	12 18 13.6	2 40.2	25 35.2	19 22.2	10 54.6	0♏26.4	7 16.0	26 47.0	12 10.1	14 2.8	16 11.0	21 1.6
26 S	12 22 10.1	3 39.0	25 32.1	4♎24.7	12 35.5	1 39.8	7 47.3	26 60.0	12 8.1	14 2.9	16 11.0	21 3.4
27 S	12 26 6.7	4 37.9	25 28.9	19 14.8	14 15.4	2 53.2	8 18.3	27 12.9	12 6.3	14 3.1	16 10.9	21 5.2
28 M	12 30 3.2	5 36.9	25 25.7	3♏44.0	15 54.5	4 6.6	8 49.1	27 25.8	12 4.5	14 3.4	16D11.0	21 7.0
29 T	12 33 59.8	6 35.8	25 22.5	17 46.9	17 32.6	5 19.9	9 19.6	27 38.8	12 2.8	14 3.7	16 11.0	21 8.9
30 W	12 37 56.3	7 34.8	25 19.4	1♐21.0	19 9.9	6 33.3	9 49.9	27 51.7	12 1.2	14 4.1	16 11.1	21 10.7

DECLINATION at NOON

DAY	SIDEREAL TIME	☉	☊	☽	☿	♀	♂	♃	♄	♅	♆	♇
1 T	10 43 36.3	8N 5.0	23S24.2	18S13.5	14N 0.7	0N36.3	23N 0.4	4N18.2	17S48.7	23S 6.4	21S42.8	3S52.3
4 F	10 55 26.0	6 59.0	23 23.9	23 44.9	12 15.3	0S56.4	23 8.2	4 2.9	17 51.9	23 6.7	21 43.1	3 54.6
7 M	11 7 15.6	5 52.0	23 23.7	18 51.2	10 13.8	2 29.1	23 14.6	3 47.7	17 55.0	23 6.9	21 43.5	3 57.0
10 T	11 19 5.3	4 44.0	23 23.4	7 6.0	8 1.4	4 1.4	23 19.7	3 32.3	17 57.9	23 7.1	21 43.8	3 59.4
13 S	11 30 54.9	3 35.4	23 23.2	7N 6.9	5 42.4	5 33.2	23 23.5	3 17.0	18 0.6	23 7.3	21 44.1	4 1.8
16 W	11 42 44.6	2 26.1	23 22.9	19 10.4	3 20.3	7 4.0	23 26.1	3 1.6	18 3.0	23 7.3	21 44.3	4 4.2
19 S	11 54 34.3	1 16.4	23 22.6	23 31.3	0 57.6	8 33.5	23 27.6	2 46.2	18 5.3	23 7.4	21 44.5	4 6.7
22 T	12 6 23.9	0 6.4	23 22.3	16 2.6	1S23.7	10 1.4	23 28.1	2 30.8	18 7.3	23 7.4	21 44.7	4 9.2
25 F	12 18 13.6	1S 3.7	23 22.0	0S22.5	3 42.4	11 27.4	23 27.6	2 15.5	18 9.1	23 7.3	21 44.8	4 11.7
28 M	12 30 3.2	2 13.8	23 21.7	16 26.5	5 57.2	12 51.1	23 26.3	2 0.2	18 10.6	23 7.2	21 45.0	4 14.2

OCTOBER 1992

LONGITUDE at NOON

DAY	SIDEREAL TIME h m s	☉ ° ′	☊ ° ′	☽ ° ′	☿ ° ′	♀ ° ′	♂ ° ′	♃ ° ′	♄ ° ′	♅ ° ′	♆ ° ′	♇ ° ′
1 T	12 41 52.9	8♎33.8	25♐16.2	14♐27.2	20♎46.3	7♏46.6	10♋19.9	28♍ 4.6	11♒59.7	14♑ 4.5	16♑11.2	21♏12.6
2 F	12 45 49.4	9 32.8	25 13.0	27 8.6	22 21.8	8 59.9	10 49.6	28 17.4	11R58.3	14 5.0	16 11.3	21 14.5
3 S	12 49 46.0	10 31.9	25 9.8	9♑29.5	23 56.5	10 13.2	11 19.0	28 30.3	11 57.0	14 5.5	16 11.5	21 16.5
4 S	12 53 42.5	11 31.0	25 6.6	21 35.3	25 30.4	11 26.4	11 48.2	28 43.1	11 55.8	14 6.0	16 11.7	21 18.4
5 M	12 57 39.1	12 30.2	25 3.5	3♒31.1	27 3.6	12 39.7	12 17.1	28 56.0	11 54.8	14 6.7	16 12.0	21 20.5
6 T	13 1 35.7	13 29.4	25 0.3	15 22.1	28 35.9	13 52.9	12 45.7	29 8.8	11 53.8	14 7.4	16 12.3	21 22.4
7 W	13 5 32.2	14 28.6	24 57.1	27 12.6	0♏ 7.4	15 6.1	13 14.0	29 21.5	11 52.9	14 8.1	16 12.6	21 24.5
8 T	13 9 28.8	15 27.8	24 53.9	9♓ 6.4	1 38.1	16 19.3	13 42.0	29 34.3	11 52.0	14 8.9	16 13.0	21 26.5
9 F	13 13 25.3	16 27.0	24 50.8	21 6.4	3 8.1	17 32.5	14 9.7	29 47.0	11 51.3	14 9.7	16 13.3	21 28.6
10 S	13 17 21.9	17 26.3	24 47.6	3♈14.6	4 37.2	18 45.6	14 37.1	29 59.7	11 50.7	14 10.6	16 13.8	21 30.6
11 S	13 21 18.4	18 25.6	24 44.4	15 32.3	6 5.6	19 58.7	15 4.1	0♎12.3	11 50.2	14 11.5	16 14.2	21 32.7
12 M	13 25 15.0	19 25.0	24 41.2	27 60.0	7 33.2	21 11.8	15 30.9	0 25.0	11 49.8	14 12.5	16 14.7	21 34.8
13 T	13 29 11.5	20 24.4	24 38.0	10♉38.1	8 60.0	22 24.9	15 57.3	0 37.6	11 49.5	14 13.5	16 15.2	21 37.0
14 W	13 33 8.1	21 23.8	24 34.9	23 26.7	10 25.9	23 37.9	16 23.3	0 50.1	11 49.3	14 14.6	16 15.7	21 39.1
15 T	13 37 4.6	22 23.2	24 31.7	6♊26.2	11 51.1	24 51.0	16 49.1	1 2.7	11 49.2	14 15.7	16 16.3	21 41.3
16 F	13 41 1.2	23 22.7	24 28.5	19 37.6	13 15.4	26 4.0	17 14.5	1 15.2	11 49.2	14 16.9	16 16.9	21 43.4
17 S	13 44 57.7	24 22.3	24 25.3	3♋ 1.8	14 38.8	27 17.0	17 39.5	1 27.6	11D49.3	14 18.1	16 17.6	21 45.6
18 S	13 48 54.3	25 21.9	24 22.2	16 40.2	16 1.2	28 29.9	18 4.1	1 40.1	11 49.5	14 19.3	16 18.2	21 47.8
19 M	13 52 50.8	26 21.5	24 19.0	0♌33.9	17 22.7	29 42.9	18 28.4	1 52.5	11 49.8	14 20.7	16 19.0	21 50.0
20 T	13 56 47.4	27 21.1	24 15.8	14 43.1	18 43.2	0♐55.8	18 52.3	2 4.8	11 50.2	14 22.0	16 19.7	21 52.3
21 W	14 0 44.0	28 20.8	24 12.6	29 6.5	20 2.6	2 8.7	19 15.8	2 17.1	11 50.7	14 23.4	16 20.5	21 54.5
22 T	14 4 40.5	29 20.5	24 9.4	13♍41.2	21 20.8	3 21.6	19 38.8	2 29.4	11 51.3	14 24.9	16 21.3	21 56.8
23 F	14 8 37.1	0♏20.3	24 6.3	28 21.8	22 37.8	4 34.5	20 1.5	2 41.6	11 52.0	14 26.4	16 22.1	21 59.0
24 S	14 12 33.6	1 20.1	24 3.1	13♎ 1.6	23 53.4	5 47.4	20 23.8	2 53.8	11 52.8	14 28.0	16 23.0	22 1.3
25 S	14 16 30.2	2 19.9	23 59.9	27 32.9	25 7.5	7 0.2	20 45.6	3 5.9	11 53.7	14 29.6	16 23.9	22 3.6
26 M	14 20 26.7	3 19.8	23 56.7	11♏48.9	26 20.2	8 13.0	21 7.0	3 18.1	11 54.7	14 31.3	16 24.9	22 6.0
27 T	14 24 23.3	4 19.7	23 53.6	25 44.0	27 31.0	9 25.8	21 27.9	3 30.1	11 55.9	14 33.0	16 25.8	22 8.3
28 W	14 28 19.8	5 19.7	23 50.4	9♐15.3	28 39.8	10 38.6	21 48.3	3 42.1	11 57.1	14 34.7	16 26.8	22 10.6
29 T	14 32 16.4	6 19.6	23 47.2	22 21.9	29 46.6	11 51.3	22 8.3	3 54.0	11 58.4	14 36.5	16 27.9	22 13.0
30 F	14 36 12.9	7 19.6	23 44.0	5♑ 5.6	0♐51.0	13 4.0	22 27.8	4 5.9	11 59.8	14 38.4	16 28.9	22 15.3
31 S	14 40 9.5	8 19.6	23 40.9	17 29.5	1 52.8	14 16.7	22 46.8	4 17.7	12 1.3	14 40.3	16 30.0	22 17.7

DECLINATION at NOON

DAY	SIDEREAL TIME	☉	☊	☽	☿	♀	♂	♃	♄	♅	♆	♇
1 T	12 41 52.9	3S23.7	23S21.3	23S25.7	8S 7.5	14S12.2	23N24.3	1N44.9	18S11.9	23S 7.0	21S45.0	4S16.7
4 S	12 53 42.5	4 33.3	23 21.0	19 26.6	10 12.6	15 30.2	23 21.5	1 29.7	18 12.9	23 6.8	21 45.1	4 19.1
7 W	13 5 32.2	5 42.4	23 20.6	8 13.5	12 11.8	16 45.0	23 18.2	1 14.6	18 13.7	23 6.6	21 45.1	4 21.6
10 S	13 17 21.9	6 50.8	23 20.3	5N50.8	14 4.7	17 56.1	23 14.5	0 59.6	18 14.3	23 6.3	21 45.0	4 24.1
13 T	13 29 11.5	7 58.3	23 19.9	18 16.5	15 50.6	19 3.1	23 10.4	0 44.8	18 14.5	23 5.9	21 45.0	4 26.5
16 F	13 41 1.2	9 4.9	23 19.5	23 20.9	17 28.9	20 5.8	23 6.1	0 30.0	18 14.5	23 5.5	21 44.8	4 28.9
19 M	13 52 50.8	10 10.3	23 19.1	16 59.8	18 59.0	21 3.9	23 1.7	0 15.4	18 14.3	23 5.1	21 44.7	4 31.2
22 T	14 4 40.5	11 14.4	23 18.7	1 46.0	20 20.0	21 56.9	22 57.4	0 1.0	18 13.8	23 4.6	21 44.5	4 33.6
25 S	14 16 30.2	12 17.0	23 18.2	14S30.6	21 31.2	22 44.6	22 53.2	0S13.2	18 13.0	23 4.0	21 44.3	4 35.9
28 W	14 28 19.8	13 17.9	23 17.8	22 59.6	22 31.3	23 26.8	22 49.4	0 27.3	18 12.0	23 3.4	21 44.0	4 38.1
31 S	14 40 9.5	14 16.9	23 17.3	20 6.9	23 19.1	24 3.1	22 46.1	0 41.1	18 10.7	23 2.8	21 43.8	4 40.3

NOVEMBER 1992

DAY	EPHEMERIS SIDEREAL TIME	☉	☊	☽	☿	♀	♂	♃	♄	♅	♆	♇
	h m s	° ′	° ′	° ′	° ′	° ′	° ′	° ′	° ′	° ′	° ′	° ′
LONGITUDE at NOON												
1 S	14 44 6.1	9♏19.7	23♐37.7	29♑37.9	2♐51.6	15♐29.3	23♋ 5.4	4♎29.4	12♒ 3.0	14♑42.2	16♑31.1	22♏20.0
2 M	14 48 2.6	10 19.7	23 34.5	11♒35.7	3 47.2	16 41.9	23 23.4	4 41.1	12 4.7	14 44.2	16 32.3	22 22.4
3 T	14 51 59.2	11 19.8	23 31.3	23 28.0	4 39.2	17 54.5	23 40.9	4 52.8	12 6.5	14 46.2	16 33.5	22 24.8
4 W	14 55 55.7	12 19.9	23 28.1	5♓19.8	5 27.1	19 7.0	23 57.8	5 4.3	12 8.4	14 48.2	16 34.7	22 27.1
5 T	14 59 52.3	13 20.1	23 25.0	17 15.6	6 10.5	20 19.5	24 14.3	5 15.8	12 10.4	14 50.3	16 35.9	22 29.5
6 F	15 3 48.8	14 20.3	23 21.8	29 19.4	6 48.8	21 32.0	24 30.2	5 27.3	12 12.6	14 52.5	16 37.2	22 31.9
7 S	15 7 45.4	15 20.5	23 18.6	11♈34.1	7 21.5	22 44.4	24 45.5	5 38.7	12 14.8	14 54.7	16 38.5	22 34.3
8 S	15 11 41.9	16 20.7	23 15.4	24 2.0	7 47.9	23 56.7	25 0.3	5 50.0	12 17.1	14 56.9	16 39.8	22 36.7
9 M	15 15 38.5	17 20.9	23 12.3	6♉44.1	8 7.3	25 9.1	25 14.5	6 1.2	12 19.5	14 59.1	16 41.1	22 39.1
10 T	15 19 35.0	18 21.2	23 9.1	19 40.6	8 19.2	26 21.4	25 28.1	6 12.4	12 22.0	15 1.4	16 42.5	22 41.5
11 W	15 23 31.6	19 21.5	23 5.9	2♊51.0	8 22.7	27 33.6	25 41.1	6 23.4	12 24.6	15 3.8	16 43.9	22 43.9
12 T	15 27 28.2	20 21.9	23 2.7	16 14.1	8R17.3	28 45.8	25 53.4	6 34.5	12 27.3	15 6.2	16 45.4	22 46.3
13 F	15 31 24.7	21 22.2	22 59.5	29 48.6	8 2.2	29 58.0	26 5.2	6 45.4	12 30.1	15 8.6	16 46.8	22 48.7
14 S	15 35 21.3	22 22.6	22 56.4	13♋33.1	7 37.2	1♑10.1	26 16.3	6 56.3	12 32.9	15 11.1	16 48.3	22 51.1
15 S	15 39 17.8	23 23.1	22 53.2	27 26.4	7 1.8	2 22.1	26 26.8	7 7.0	12 35.9	15 13.6	16 49.8	22 53.6
16 M	15 43 14.4	24 23.6	22 50.0	11♌27.4	6 16.2	3 34.2	26 36.6	7 17.8	12 39.0	15 16.1	16 51.4	22 56.0
17 T	15 47 10.9	25 24.1	22 46.8	25 34.7	5 20.8	4 46.2	26 45.7	7 28.4	12 42.2	15 18.7	16 53.0	22 58.4
18 W	15 51 7.5	26 24.6	22 43.7	9♍46.9	4 16.5	5 58.1	26 54.1	7 39.0	12 45.4	15 21.3	16 54.6	23 0.8
19 T	15 55 4.1	27 25.1	22 40.5	24 1.6	3 4.5	7 10.0	27 1.8	7 49.4	12 48.7	15 24.0	16 56.2	23 3.2
20 F	15 59 0.6	28 25.7	22 37.3	8♎16.1	1 47.0	8 21.8	27 8.8	7 59.8	12 52.2	15 26.7	16 57.8	23 5.7
21 S	16 2 57.2	29 26.3	22 34.1	22 26.6	0 26.1	9 33.6	27 15.0	8 10.0	12 55.7	15 29.4	16 59.5	23 8.1
22 S	16 6 53.7	0♐27.0	22 31.0	6♏29.2	29♏ 4.4	10 45.3	27 20.5	8 20.2	12 59.3	15 32.1	17 1.2	23 10.5
23 M	16 10 50.3	1 27.7	22 27.8	20 19.8	27 44.7	11 57.0	27 25.3	8 30.3	13 3.0	15 34.9	17 2.9	23 12.9
24 T	16 14 46.8	2 28.3	22 24.6	3♐55.0	26 29.7	13 8.6	27 29.2	8 40.3	13 6.7	15 37.7	17 4.6	23 15.2
25 W	16 18 43.4	3 29.1	22 21.4	17 12.5	25 21.7	14 20.1	27 32.4	8 50.2	13 10.6	15 40.6	17 6.4	23 17.6
26 T	16 22 40.0	4 29.8	22 18.2	0♑11.2	24 22.6	15 31.6	27 34.8	8 60.0	13 14.5	15 43.4	17 8.1	23 20.0
27 F	16 26 36.5	5 30.5	22 15.1	12 51.4	23 33.8	16 43.0	27 36.4	9 9.7	13 18.6	15 46.3	17 9.9	23 22.4
28 S	16 30 33.1	6 31.3	22 11.9	25 14.9	22 56.2	17 54.4	27 37.2	9 19.2	13 22.7	15 49.3	17 11.8	23 24.8
29 S	16 34 29.6	7 32.1	22 8.7	7♒24.4	22 30.3	19 5.6	27 37.2	9 28.7	13 26.9	15 52.3	17 13.6	23 27.1
30 M	16 38 26.2	8 32.9	22 5.5	19 23.6	22 15.8	20 16.8	27R36.3	9 38.1	13 31.2	15 55.3	17 15.5	23 29.5
DECLINATION at NOON												
1 S	14 44 6.1	14S 36.1	23S 17.2	17S 9.7	23S 32.0	24S 13.8	22N 45.1	0S 45.6	18S 10.2	23S 2.6	21S 43.6	4S 41.0
4 W	14 55 55.7	15 32.3	23 16.7	4 57.2	24 0.7	24 41.9	22 42.5	0 59.1	18 8.6	23 1.8	21 43.3	4 43.1
7 S	15 7 45.4	16 26.2	23 16.3	9N 3.6	24 12.4	25 3.7	22 40.8	1 12.4	18 6.7	23 1.1	21 42.9	4 45.2
10 T	15 19 35.0	17 17.5	23 15.8	20 18.8	24 3.7	25 19.0	22 39.9	1 25.3	18 4.6	23 0.3	21 42.5	4 47.2
13 F	15 31 24.7	18 6.3	23 15.3	22 42.0	23 30.4	25 27.8	22 40.1	1 38.0	18 2.2	22 59.5	21 42.1	4 49.1
16 M	15 43 14.4	18 52.2	23 14.8	13 30.0	22 28.2	25 29.9	22 41.5	1 50.4	17 59.6	22 58.6	21 41.6	4 51.0
19 T	15 55 4.1	19 35.0	23 14.2	2S 25.8	20 56.9	25 25.3	22 44.2	2 2.4	17 56.8	22 57.7	21 41.1	4 52.8
22 S	16 6 53.7	20 14.7	23 13.7	17 11.3	19 7.9	25 14.2	22 48.4	2 14.1	17 53.7	22 56.7	21 40.5	4 54.5
25 W	16 18 43.4	20 51.1	23 13.2	23 13.0	17 25.8	24 56.5	22 54.1	2 25.4	17 50.4	22 55.7	21 40.0	4 56.1
28 S	16 30 33.1	21 23.9	23 12.6	18 12.1	16 15.7	24 32.4	23 1.3	2 36.4	17 46.9	22 54.7	21 39.4	4 57.6

DECEMBER 1992

DAY	EPHEMERIS SIDEREAL TIME	☉	☊	☽	☿	♀	♂	♃	♄	♅	♆	♇
LONGITUDE at NOON												
1 T	16 42 22.7	9♐33.7	22♐ 2.4	1♓17.0	22♏12.4	21♑27.9	27♋34.7	9♎47.4	13♒35.5	15♑58.3	17♑17.3	23♏31.8
2 W	16 46 19.3	10 34.6	21 59.2	13 9.1	22D19.6	22 39.0	27R32.2	9 56.5	13 39.9	16 1.3	17 19.2	23 34.1
3 T	16 50 15.9	11 35.4	21 56.0	25 4.8	22 36.5	23 49.9	27 28.8	10 5.6	13 44.4	16 4.4	17 21.2	23 36.5
4 F	16 54 12.4	12 36.3	21 52.8	7♈ 8.8	23 2.2	25 0.8	27 24.7	10 14.5	13 49.0	16 7.5	17 23.1	23 38.8
5 S	16 58 9.0	13 37.2	21 49.7	19 25.1	23 36.0	26 11.5	27 19.6	10 23.3	13 53.7	16 10.6	17 25.0	23 41.1
6 S	17 2 5.5	14 38.1	21 46.5	1♉57.5	24 16.9	27 22.2	27 13.8	10 32.0	13 58.4	16 13.8	17 27.0	23 43.4
7 M	17 6 2.1	15 39.0	21 43.3	14 48.3	25 4.3	28 32.8	27 7.1	10 40.7	14 3.3	16 17.0	17 29.1	23 45.7
8 T	17 9 58.6	16 40.0	21 40.1	27 58.8	25 57.1	29 43.3	26 59.6	10 49.1	14 8.2	16 20.2	17 31.1	23 48.0
9 W	17 13 55.2	17 40.9	21 36.9	11♊28.9	26 54.9	0♒53.6	26 51.2	10 57.5	14 13.1	16 23.5	17 33.1	23 50.2
10 T	17 17 51.8	18 41.8	21 33.8	25 16.9	27 57.0	2 3.9	26 41.9	11 5.7	14 18.2	16 26.7	17 35.1	23 52.5
11 F	17 21 48.3	19 42.8	21 30.6	9♋19.7	29 2.8	3 14.0	26 31.9	11 13.8	14 23.3	16 30.0	17 37.2	23 54.7
12 S	17 25 44.9	20 43.8	21 27.4	23 33.5	0♐11.8	4 24.0	26 21.0	11 21.8	14 28.4	16 33.3	17 39.2	23 56.9
13 S	17 29 41.4	21 44.8	21 24.2	7♌53.6	1 23.7	5 33.9	26 9.2	11 29.6	14 33.6	16 36.6	17 41.3	23 59.1
14 M	17 33 38.0	22 45.8	21 21.1	22 15.6	2 38.1	6 43.7	25 56.7	11 37.3	14 38.9	16 39.9	17 43.4	24 1.3
15 T	17 37 34.5	23 46.8	21 17.9	6♍35.5	3 54.6	7 53.4	25 43.3	11 44.9	14 44.3	16 43.2	17 45.5	24 3.5
16 W	17 41 31.1	24 47.9	21 14.7	20 49.9	5 12.9	9 2.9	25 29.1	11 52.3	14 49.7	16 46.6	17 47.7	24 5.6
17 T	17 45 27.7	25 48.9	21 11.5	4♎56.4	6 32.9	10 12.3	25 14.2	11 59.7	14 55.2	16 50.0	17 49.8	24 7.8
18 F	17 49 24.2	26 50.0	21 8.4	18 53.3	7 54.4	11 21.6	24 58.4	12 6.8	15 0.8	16 53.4	17 51.9	24 9.9
19 S	17 53 20.8	27 51.1	21 5.2	2♏39.4	9 17.0	12 30.7	24 42.0	12 13.9	15 6.4	16 56.8	17 54.1	24 12.0
20 S	17 57 17.3	28 52.2	21 2.0	16 13.8	10 40.8	13 39.7	24 24.8	12 20.7	15 12.1	17 0.2	17 56.3	24 14.1
21 M	18 1 13.9	29 53.3	20 58.8	29 36.0	12 5.5	14 48.5	24 6.9	12 27.5	15 17.8	17 3.7	17 58.4	24 16.1
22 T	18 5 10.4	0♑54.5	20 55.7	12♐45.3	13 31.0	15 57.2	23 48.3	12 34.1	15 23.6	17 7.1	18 0.6	24 18.2
23 W	18 9 7.0	1 55.6	20 52.5	25 41.4	14 57.3	17 5.7	23 29.1	12 40.5	15 29.5	17 10.6	18 2.8	24 20.2
24 T	18 13 3.6	2 56.7	20 49.3	8♑24.2	16 24.3	18 14.1	23 9.3	12 46.8	15 35.4	17 14.1	18 5.0	24 22.2
25 F	18 17 0.1	3 57.9	20 46.1	20 53.9	17 51.9	19 22.3	22 48.9	12 53.0	15 41.3	17 17.6	18 7.3	24 24.2
26 S	18 20 56.7	4 59.0	20 42.9	3♒11.4	19 20.1	20 30.4	22 27.9	12 59.0	15 47.4	17 21.1	18 9.5	24 26.1
27 S	18 24 53.2	6 0.2	20 39.8	15 18.3	20 48.8	21 38.2	22 6.5	13 4.8	15 53.4	17 24.6	18 11.7	24 28.1
28 M	18 28 49.8	7 1.4	20 36.6	27 16.8	22 18.0	22 45.9	21 44.6	13 10.6	15 59.6	17 28.2	18 14.0	24 30.0
29 T	18 32 46.4	8 2.6	20 33.4	9♓ 9.8	23 47.6	23 53.4	21 22.3	13 16.1	16 5.8	17 31.7	18 16.2	24 31.9
30 W	18 36 42.9	9 3.7	20 30.2	21 1.2	25 17.6	25 0.6	20 59.6	13 21.5	16 12.0	17 35.2	18 18.5	24 33.8
31 T	18 40 39.5	10 4.9	20 27.1	2♈55.2	26 48.0	26 7.7	20 36.6	13 26.7	16 18.3	17 38.8	18 20.7	24 35.7
DECLINATION at NOON												
1 T	16 42 22.7	21S 53.1	23S 12.0	6S 23.1	15S 48.3	24S 2.1	23N 10.1	2S 46.9	17S 43.1	22S 53.6	21S 38.7	4S 59.1
4 F	16 54 12.4	22 18.5	23 11.5	7N 30.3	15 59.1	23 25.8	23 20.6	2 57.0	17 39.2	22 52.5	21 38.0	5 0.4
7 M	17 6 2.1	22 40.0	23 10.9	19 18.0	16 37.4	22 43.7	23 32.5	3 6.7	17 35.0	22 51.3	21 37.3	5 1.7
10 T	17 17 51.8	22 57.5	23 10.3	23 0.4	17 32.4	21 56.2	23 45.8	3 15.9	17 30.6	22 50.1	21 36.6	5 2.9
13 S	17 29 41.4	23 11.0	23 9.7	14 35.3	18 35.6	21 3.5	24 0.5	3 24.7	17 26.1	22 48.9	21 35.9	5 4.0
16 W	17 41 31.1	23 20.2	23 9.0	1S 13.7	19 40.7	20 6.0	24 16.2	3 33.0	17 21.3	22 47.7	21 35.1	5 4.9
19 S	17 53 20.8	23 25.3	23 8.4	16 8.1	20 43.6	19 3.9	24 32.8	3 40.7	17 16.4	22 46.4	21 34.3	5 5.8
22 T	18 5 10.4	23 26.2	23 7.8	23 7.8	21 41.4	17 57.7	24 49.9	3 48.0	17 11.3	22 45.1	21 33.5	5 6.6
25 F	18 17 0.1	23 22.8	23 7.1	19 15.3	22 32.1	16 47.6	25 7.1	3 54.7	17 6.1	22 43.8	21 32.7	5 7.3
28 M	18 28 49.8	23 15.2	23 6.4	7 54.1	23 14.2	15 34.1	25 24.1	4 0.8	17 0.6	22 42.4	21 31.8	5 7.9
31 T	18 40 39.5	23 3.4	23 5.7	5N 53.1	23 46.6	14 17.5	25 40.5	4 6.4	16 55.1	22 41.0	21 31.0	5 8.3

JANUARY 1993

DAY	EPHEMERIS SIDEREAL TIME	☉	☊	☽	☿	♀	♂	♃	♄	♅	♆	♇
	h m s	° ′	° ′	° ′	° ′	° ′	° ′	° ′	° ′	° ′	° ′	° ′
LONGITUDE at NOON												
1 F	18 44 36.0	11♑ 6.0	20♐23.9	14♈56.3	28♐18.8	27♒14.5	20♋13.3	13♎31.7	16♒24.6	17♑42.3	18♑23.0	24♏37.5
2 S	18 48 32.6	12 7.2	20 20.7	27 9.3	29 50.0	28 21.1	19R49.8	13 36.6	16 30.9	17 45.9	18 25.3	24 39.3
3 S	18 52 29.1	13 8.3	20 17.5	9♉39.0	1♑21.6	29 27.4	19 26.1	13 41.3	16 37.3	17 49.4	18 27.5	24 41.1
4 M	18 56 25.7	14 9.5	20 14.4	22 29.3	2 53.5	0♓33.5	19 2.3	13 45.9	16 43.8	17 53.0	18 29.8	24 42.8
5 T	19 0 22.3	15 10.6	20 11.2	5♊43.3	4 25.9	1 39.4	18 38.4	13 50.2	16 50.3	17 56.6	18 32.1	24 44.5
6 W	19 4 18.8	16 11.7	20 8.0	19 22.6	5 58.6	2 45.0	18 14.4	13 54.4	16 56.8	18 0.1	18 34.3	24 46.2
7 T	19 8 15.4	17 12.9	20 4.8	3♋26.5	7 31.7	3 50.3	17 50.4	13 58.5	17 3.4	18 3.7	18 36.6	24 47.9
8 F	19 12 11.9	18 14.0	20 1.7	17 52.1	9 5.2	4 55.4	17 26.5	14 2.4	17 10.0	18 7.3	18 38.9	24 49.5
9 S	19 16 8.5	19 15.1	19 58.5	2♌33.7	10 39.2	6 0.1	17 2.7	14 6.1	17 16.6	18 10.8	18 41.2	24 51.2
10 S	19 20 5.0	20 16.2	19 55.3	17 24.1	12 13.5	7 4.6	16 39.1	14 9.6	17 23.3	18 14.4	18 43.4	24 52.8
11 M	19 24 1.6	21 17.3	19 52.1	2♍15.1	13 48.3	8 8.8	16 15.6	14 12.9	17 30.0	18 18.0	18 45.7	24 54.3
12 T	19 27 58.2	22 18.4	19 48.9	16 58.9	15 23.5	9 12.6	15 52.3	14 16.1	17 36.8	18 21.5	18 48.0	24 55.8
13 W	19 31 54.7	23 19.6	19 45.8	1♎29.2	16 59.2	10 16.1	15 29.4	14 19.1	17 43.6	18 25.1	18 50.2	24 57.4
14 T	19 35 51.3	24 20.7	19 42.6	15 42.0	18 35.4	11 19.3	15 6.7	14 21.9	17 50.4	18 28.6	18 52.5	24 58.8
15 F	19 39 47.8	25 21.8	19 39.4	29 35.6	20 12.0	12 22.2	14 44.5	14 24.5	17 57.2	18 32.2	18 54.8	25 0.3
16 S	19 43 44.4	26 22.9	19 36.2	13♏ 9.9	21 49.2	13 24.6	14 22.6	14 27.0	18 4.1	18 35.7	18 57.0	25 1.7
17 S	19 47 40.9	27 24.0	19 33.1	26 26.3	23 26.9	14 26.8	14 1.1	14 29.2	18 11.0	18 39.3	18 59.3	25 3.1
18 M	19 51 37.5	28 25.1	19 29.9	9♐26.9	25 5.1	15 28.6	13 40.3	14 31.3	18 18.0	18 42.9	19 1.6	25 4.5
19 T	19 55 34.1	29 26.2	19 26.7	22 13.6	26 43.9	16 29.9	13 19.8	14 33.2	18 24.9	18 46.4	19 3.8	25 5.8
20 W	19 59 30.6	0♒27.3	19 23.5	4♑48.5	28 23.3	17 30.9	12 60.0	14 34.9	18 31.9	18 49.9	19 6.1	25 7.1
21 T	20 3 27.2	1 28.4	19 20.4	17 13.1	0♒ 3.2	18 31.4	12 40.7	14 36.4	18 38.9	18 53.4	19 8.3	25 8.4
22 F	20 7 23.7	2 29.4	19 17.2	29 28.8	1 43.7	19 31.5	12 22.0	14 37.8	18 46.0	18 56.9	19 10.5	25 9.6
23 S	20 11 20.3	3 30.5	19 14.0	11♒36.6	3 24.7	20 31.2	12 4.0	14 38.9	18 53.0	19 0.4	19 12.8	25 10.8
24 S	20 15 16.8	4 31.5	19 10.8	23 37.7	5 6.4	21 30.4	11 46.7	14 39.8	19 0.1	19 3.9	19 15.0	25 12.0
25 M	20 19 13.4	5 32.6	19 7.6	5♓33.3	6 48.7	22 29.1	11 30.1	14 40.6	19 7.2	19 7.3	19 17.2	25 13.1
26 T	20 23 10.0	6 33.6	19 4.5	17 25.4	8 31.6	23 27.2	11 14.1	14 41.1	19 14.3	19 10.8	19 19.4	25 14.2
27 W	20 27 6.5	7 34.6	19 1.3	29 16.2	10 15.0	24 24.9	10 59.0	14 41.5	19 21.4	19 14.2	19 21.6	25 15.3
28 T	20 31 3.1	8 35.5	18 58.1	11♈ 9.0	11 59.1	25 22.0	10 44.5	14 41.7	19 28.6	19 17.7	19 23.8	25 16.3
29 F	20 34 59.6	9 36.5	18 54.9	23 7.6	13 43.7	26 18.6	10 30.9	14 41.7	19 35.7	19 21.1	19 25.9	25 17.3
30 S	20 38 56.2	10 37.4	18 51.8	5♉16.4	15 28.8	27 14.6	10 18.0	14R41.5	19 42.9	19 24.5	19 28.1	25 18.3
31 S	20 42 52.7	11 38.3	18 48.6	17 40.2	17 14.4	28 9.9	10 6.0	14 41.1	19 50.1	19 27.8	19 30.2	25 19.2
DECLINATION at NOON												
1 F	18 44 36.0	22S58.5	23S 5.5	10N19.6	23S55.2	13S51.3	25N45.7	4S 8.1	16S53.2	22S40.6	21S30.7	5S 8.5
4 M	18 56 25.7	22 41.2	23 4.8	20 51.0	24 13.4	12 31.2	26 0.7	4 12.9	16 47.4	22 39.2	21 29.8	5 8.8
7 T	19 8 15.4	22 19.9	23 4.1	22 18.1	24 20.2	11 9.0	26 14.3	4 17.1	16 41.5	22 37.8	21 28.9	5 9.0
10 S	19 20 5.0	21 54.6	23 3.4	11 29.4	24 15.0	9 44.9	26 26.3	4 20.7	16 35.5	22 36.4	21 28.0	5 9.2
13 W	19 31 54.7	21 25.5	23 2.7	5S17.3	23 57.4	8 19.3	26 36.6	4 23.7	16 29.4	22 34.9	21 27.1	5 9.2
16 S	19 43 44.4	20 52.6	23 1.9	18 50.5	23 27.0	6 52.6	26 45.0	4 26.0	16 23.1	22 33.5	21 26.2	5 9.1
19 T	19 55 34.1	20 16.1	23 1.2	23 6.6	22 43.3	5 25.1	26 51.6	4 27.7	16 16.8	22 32.1	21 25.2	5 9.0
22 F	20 7 23.7	19 36.2	23 0.4	17 7.0	21 46.1	3 57.3	26 56.4	4 28.7	16 10.4	22 30.6	21 24.3	5 8.7
25 M	20 19 13.4	18 53.1	22 59.7	4 51.9	20 35.2	2 29.4	26 59.5	4 29.0	16 3.9	22 29.2	21 23.4	5 8.3
28 T	20 31 3.1	18 6.8	22 58.9	8N48.8	19 10.6	1 2.0	27 1.0	4 28.7	15 57.3	22 27.8	21 22.5	5 7.8
31 S	20 42 52.7	17 17.7	22 58.1	19 44.6	17 32.5	0N24.8	27 1.2	4 27.7	15 50.6	22 26.4	21 21.6	5 7.3

FEBRUARY 1993

DAY	EPHEMERIS SIDEREAL TIME	☉	☊	☽	☿	♀	♂	♃	♄	♅	♆	♇
LONGITUDE at NOON												
1 M	20 46 49.3	12♒39.2	18♐45.4	0♊23.9	19♒ 0.5	29♓ 4.6	9♋54.7	14♎40.5	19♒57.2	19♑31.2	19♑32.4	25♏20.1
2 T	20 50 45.8	13 40.1	18 42.2	13 32.0	20 46.9	29 58.7	9R44.2	14R39.7	20 4.4	19 34.5	19 34.5	25 21.0
3 W	20 54 42.4	14 40.9	18 39.1	27 7.8	22 33.7	0♈52.1	9 34.5	14 38.7	20 11.6	19 37.8	19 36.6	25 21.8
4 T	20 58 39.0	15 41.8	18 35.9	11♋12.9	24 20.7	1 44.7	9 25.7	14 37.6	20 18.9	19 41.1	19 38.7	25 22.6
5 F	21 2 35.5	16 42.6	18 32.7	25 45.7	26 7.7	2 36.7	9 17.6	14 36.2	20 26.1	19 44.4	19 40.8	25 23.4
6 S	21 6 32.1	17 43.3	18 29.5	10♌41.4	27 54.7	3 27.8	9 10.3	14 34.7	20 33.3	19 47.7	19 42.8	25 24.1
7 S	21 10 28.6	18 44.1	18 26.3	25 52.1	29 41.4	4 18.2	9 3.9	14 33.0	20 40.5	19 50.9	19 44.9	25 24.8
8 M	21 14 25.2	19 44.9	18 23.2	11♍ 7.2	1♓27.8	5 7.7	8 58.3	14 31.1	20 47.8	19 54.2	19 47.0	25 25.5
9 T	21 18 21.7	20 45.6	18 20.0	26 15.6	3 13.4	5 56.4	8 53.4	14 29.0	20 55.0	19 57.4	19 49.0	25 26.1
10 W	21 22 18.3	21 46.3	18 16.8	11♎ 7.8	4 58.1	6 44.2	8 49.3	14 26.8	21 2.3	20 0.6	19 51.0	25 26.7
11 T	21 26 14.8	22 47.0	18 13.6	25 37.0	6 41.5	7 31.1	8 46.0	14 24.3	21 9.5	20 3.7	19 53.0	25 27.2
12 F	21 30 11.4	23 47.6	18 10.5	9♏39.9	8 23.1	8 17.0	8 43.5	14 21.7	21 16.7	20 6.8	19 54.9	25 27.8
13 S	21 34 7.9	24 48.3	18 7.3	23 16.4	10 2.7	9 1.9	8 41.7	14 18.8	21 23.9	20 9.9	19 56.9	25 28.2
14 S	21 38 4.5	25 48.9	18 4.1	6♐28.5	11 39.7	9 45.8	8 40.7	14 15.8	21 31.2	20 13.0	19 58.8	25 28.7
15 M	21 42 1.1	26 49.5	18 0.9	19 19.6	13 13.6	10 28.6	8 40.5	14 12.6	21 38.4	20 16.0	20 0.7	25 29.1
16 T	21 45 57.6	27 50.1	17 57.7	1♑53.6	14 43.8	11 10.3	8D41.0	14 9.3	21 45.6	20 19.0	20 2.6	25 29.5
17 W	21 49 54.2	28 50.7	17 54.6	14 14.4	16 9.7	11 50.9	8 42.2	14 5.7	21 52.8	20 22.0	20 4.5	25 29.8
18 T	21 53 50.7	29 51.2	17 51.4	26 25.2	17 30.7	12 30.3	8 44.2	14 2.0	21 60.0	20 25.0	20 6.4	25 30.1
19 F	21 57 47.3	0♓51.7	17 48.2	8♒28.8	18 46.0	13 8.4	8 46.9	13 58.1	22 7.2	20 27.9	20 8.2	25 30.4
20 S	22 1 43.8	1 52.2	17 45.0	20 27.4	19 55.1	13 45.3	8 50.3	13 54.0	22 14.3	20 30.8	20 10.0	25 30.6
21 S	22 5 40.4	2 52.7	17 41.9	2♓22.4	20 57.1	14 20.8	8 54.4	13 49.8	22 21.5	20 33.7	20 11.8	25 30.8
22 M	22 9 36.9	3 53.1	17 38.7	14 15.2	21 51.6	14 54.9	8 59.2	13 45.4	22 28.7	20 36.5	20 13.6	25 31.0
23 T	22 13 33.5	4 53.6	17 35.5	26 7.0	22 37.9	15 27.5	9 4.7	13 40.8	22 35.8	20 39.3	20 15.4	25 31.1
24 W	22 17 30.0	5 53.9	17 32.3	7♈59.3	23 15.4	15 58.6	9 10.8	13 36.1	22 42.9	20 42.1	20 17.1	25 31.2
25 T	22 21 26.6	6 54.3	17 29.1	19 54.2	23 43.8	16 28.2	9 17.6	13 31.2	22 50.0	20 44.8	20 18.8	25 31.2
26 F	22 25 23.1	7 54.6	17 26.0	1♉54.3	24 2.7	16 56.1	9 25.0	13 26.2	22 57.1	20 47.5	20 20.5	25 31.2
27 S	22 29 19.7	8 54.9	17 22.8	14 3.0	24 11.9	17 22.3	9 33.1	13 21.0	23 4.2	20 50.2	20 22.1	25 31.2
28 S	22 33 16.3	9 55.2	17 19.6	26 24.3	24R11.4	17 46.8	9 41.7	13 15.7	23 11.2	20 52.9	20 23.8	25R31.1
DECLINATION at NOON												
1 M	20 46 49.3	17S 0.7	22S57.8	21N55.6	16S56.8	0N53.5	27N 1.0	4S27.3	15S48.4	22S25.9	21S21.3	5S 7.1
4 T	20 58 39.0	16 7.9	22 57.0	21 7.7	15 1.3	2 18.6	26 59.6	4 25.4	15 41.7	22 24.5	21 20.4	5 6.4
7 S	21 10 28.6	15 12.6	22 56.2	8 31.6	12 54.2	3 42.0	26 57.2	4 23.0	15 35.0	22 23.2	21 19.5	5 5.6
10 W	21 22 18.3	14 15.0	22 55.4	8S43.9	10 37.8	5 3.3	26 54.0	4 19.9	15 28.2	22 21.8	21 18.6	5 4.8
13 S	21 34 7.9	13 15.2	22 54.5	20 44.4	8 16.0	6 22.0	26 50.1	4 16.1	15 21.4	22 20.5	21 17.7	5 3.9
16 T	21 45 57.6	12 13.5	22 53.7	22 18.4	5 54.7	7 37.7	26 45.6	4 11.8	15 14.6	22 19.2	21 16.9	5 2.9
19 F	21 57 47.3	11 10.1	22 52.8	14 26.5	3 41.9	8 49.8	26 40.5	4 6.8	15 7.9	22 17.9	21 16.0	5 1.8
22 M	22 9 36.9	10 5.0	22 51.9	1 35.4	1 47.7	9 57.7	26 34.9	4 1.3	15 1.1	22 16.7	21 15.2	5 0.7
25 T	22 21 26.6	8 58.6	22 51.0	11N42.3	0 22.4	11 0.8	26 28.8	3 55.2	14 54.3	22 15.5	21 14.4	4 59.5
28 S	22 33 16.3	7 51.0	22 50.2	21 6.2	0N24.8	11 58.1	26 22.2	3 48.7	14 47.6	22 14.3	21 13.7	4 58.2

MARCH 1993

DAY	EPHEMERIS SIDEREAL TIME	☉	☊	☽	☿	♀	♂	♃	♄	♅	♆	♇
	h m s	° ′	° ′	° ′	° ′	° ′	° ′	° ′	° ′	° ′	° ′	° ′
						LONGITUDE at NOON						
1 M	22 37 12.8	10♓55.4	17♐16.4	9♊ 2.9	24♓ 1.4	18♈ 9.5	9♋51.1	13♎10.2	23♒18.3	20♑55.5	20♑25.4	25♏31.1
2 T	22 41 9.4	11 55.6	17 13.3	22 3.3	23R42.1	18 30.2	10 0.9	13R 4.6	23 25.3	20 58.1	20 27.0	25R31.0
3 W	22 45 5.9	12 55.8	17 10.1	5♋29.8	23 14.1	18 49.0	10 11.4	12 58.9	23 32.2	21 0.6	20 28.6	25 30.8
4 T	22 49 2.5	13 55.9	17 6.9	19 25.3	22 38.1	19 5.8	10 22.4	12 53.0	23 39.2	21 3.1	20 30.1	25 30.6
5 F	22 52 59.0	14 56.0	17 3.7	3♌50.2	21 55.1	19 20.4	10 33.9	12 47.0	23 46.1	21 5.5	20 31.6	25 30.4
6 S	22 56 55.6	15 56.0	17 0.5	18 41.8	21 6.0	19 33.0	10 46.0	12 40.8	23 53.0	21 7.9	20 33.1	25 30.1
7 S	23 0 52.1	16 56.1	16 57.4	3♍53.6	20 12.2	19 43.3	10 58.6	12 34.6	23 59.9	21 10.3	20 34.6	25 29.8
8 M	23 4 48.7	17 56.0	16 54.2	19 15.5	19 15.0	19 51.3	11 11.7	12 28.2	24 6.7	21 12.7	20 36.0	25 29.5
9 T	23 8 45.2	18 56.0	16 51.0	4♎35.7	18 15.7	19 57.0	11 25.3	12 21.7	24 13.5	21 15.0	20 37.4	25 29.1
10 W	23 12 41.8	19 55.9	16 47.8	19 42.7	17 15.9	20 0.4	11 39.4	12 15.1	24 20.3	21 17.2	20 38.8	25 28.7
11 T	23 16 38.3	20 55.8	16 44.7	4♏27.1	16 16.8	20 1.3	11 54.0	12 8.4	24 27.0	21 19.4	20 40.2	25 28.3
12 F	23 20 34.9	21 55.7	16 41.5	18 43.6	15 19.6	19R59.8	12 9.1	12 1.6	24 33.7	21 21.6	20 41.5	25 27.8
13 S	23 24 31.4	22 55.5	16 38.3	2♐30.3	14 25.5	19 55.9	12 24.6	11 54.7	24 40.4	21 23.7	20 42.8	25 27.3
14 S	23 28 28.0	23 55.3	16 35.1	15 48.4	13 35.3	19 49.5	12 40.6	11 47.7	24 47.1	21 25.8	20 44.1	25 26.8
15 M	23 32 24.5	24 55.1	16 31.9	28 41.3	12 50.0	19 40.5	12 56.9	11 40.7	24 53.7	21 27.9	20 45.3	25 26.2
16 T	23 36 21.1	25 54.9	16 28.8	11♑13.5	12 10.0	19 29.1	13 13.8	11 33.5	25 0.2	21 29.9	20 46.5	25 25.6
17 W	23 40 17.6	26 54.6	16 25.6	23 29.7	11 35.9	19 15.3	13 31.0	11 26.3	25 6.8	21 31.9	20 47.7	25 25.0
18 T	23 44 14.2	27 54.3	16 22.4	5♒34.3	11 7.8	18 59.0	13 48.7	11 19.0	25 13.3	21 33.8	20 48.8	25 24.3
19 F	23 48 10.8	28 53.9	16 19.2	17 31.5	10 45.9	18 40.2	14 6.7	11 11.6	25 19.7	21 35.7	20 50.0	25 23.6
20 S	23 52 7.3	29 53.6	16 16.1	29 24.6	10 30.3	18 19.2	14 25.2	11 4.1	25 26.1	21 37.5	20 51.1	25 22.9
21 S	23 56 3.9	0♈53.2	16 12.9	11♓16.0	10 20.8	17 55.9	14 44.0	10 56.6	25 32.5	21 39.3	20 52.1	25 22.1
22 M	0 0 0.4	1 52.8	16 9.7	23 7.9	10 17.5	17 30.5	15 3.3	10 49.2	25 38.8	21 41.1	20 53.2	25 21.4
23 T	0 3 57.0	2 52.3	16 6.5	5♈ 1.5	10D20.0	17 2.9	15 22.9	10 41.6	25 45.1	21 42.8	20 54.2	25 20.6
24 W	0 7 53.5	3 51.8	16 3.3	16 58.3	10 28.2	16 33.5	15 42.9	10 33.9	25 51.4	21 44.4	20 55.2	25 19.7
25 T	0 11 50.1	4 51.3	16 0.2	28 59.6	10 41.7	16 2.3	16 3.2	10 26.3	25 57.5	21 46.0	20 56.1	25 18.9
26 F	0 15 46.6	5 50.8	15 57.0	11♉ 7.1	11 0.5	15 29.5	16 23.8	10 18.6	26 3.7	21 47.6	20 57.0	25 17.9
27 S	0 19 43.2	6 50.2	15 53.8	23 22.8	11 24.1	14 55.3	16 44.8	10 10.9	26 9.7	21 49.1	20 57.9	25 17.0
28 S	0 23 39.7	7 49.5	15 50.6	5♊49.7	11 52.4	14 20.0	17 6.2	10 3.2	26 15.8	21 50.5	20 58.7	25 16.0
29 M	0 27 36.3	8 48.8	15 47.5	18 31.0	12 25.1	13 43.6	17 27.8	9 55.4	26 21.8	21 51.9	20 59.5	25 15.1
30 T	0 31 32.8	9 48.1	15 44.3	1♋30.3	13 2.0	13 6.5	17 49.8	9 47.7	26 27.7	21 53.3	21 0.3	25 14.0
31 W	0 35 29.4	10 47.4	15 41.1	14 51.4	13 42.8	12 28.9	18 12.0	9 39.9	26 33.6	21 54.6	21 1.1	25 13.0
						DECLINATION at NOON						
1 M	22 37 12.8	7S28.2	22S49.8	22N31.5	0N31.1	12N15.9	26N20.0	3S46.4	14S45.4	22S13.9	21S13.4	4S57.8
4 T	22 49 2.5	6 19.3	22 48.9	19 22.9	0 20.4	13 4.2	26 12.8	3 39.2	14 38.8	22 12.8	21 12.7	4 56.5
7 S	23 0 52.1	5 9.6	22 48.0	5 32.1	0S30.2	13 44.5	26 5.2	3 31.6	14 32.2	22 11.8	21 12.0	4 55.1
10 W	23 12 41.8	3 59.3	22 47.1	11S35.0	1 49.3	14 15.7	25 57.0	3 23.6	14 25.7	22 10.8	21 11.3	4 53.7
13 S	23 24 31.4	2 48.5	22 46.1	21 49.5	3 20.5	14 36.4	25 48.4	3 15.3	14 19.3	22 9.8	21 10.7	4 52.2
16 T	23 36 21.1	1 37.4	22 45.2	20 49.7	4 48.0	14 45.4	25 39.1	3 6.8	14 12.9	22 9.0	21 10.1	4 50.7
19 F	23 48 10.8	0 26.3	22 44.2	11 22.1	6 0.7	14 41.7	25 29.3	2 58.0	14 6.7	22 8.1	21 9.6	4 49.2
22 M	0 0 0.4	0N44.9	22 43.2	1N49.7	6 53.1	14 24.6	25 18.8	2 49.0	14 0.6	22 7.4	21 9.1	4 47.6
25 T	0 11 50.1	1 55.8	22 42.2	14 28.7	7 23.5	13 53.8	25 7.6	2 39.9	13 54.6	22 6.7	21 8.6	4 46.1
28 S	0 23 39.7	3 6.3	22 41.2	22 1.2	7 32.5	13 10.2	24 55.7	2 30.8	13 48.8	22 6.0	21 8.1	4 44.5
31 W	0 35 29.4	4 16.2	22 40.2	20 2.5	7 21.6	12 15.5	24 43.1	2 21.6	13 43.1	22 5.5	21 7.7	4 43.0

APRIL 1993

DAY	EPHEMERIS SIDEREAL TIME	☉	☊	☽	☿	♀	♂	♃	♄	♅	♆	♇
						LONGITUDE at NOON						
1 T	0 39 25.9	11♈46.6	15♐37.9	28♋37.1	14♓27.2	11♈51.1	18♋34.6	9♎32.2	26♒39.4	21♑55.9	21♑ 1.8	25♏11.9
2 F	0 43 22.5	12 45.7	15 34.7	12♌48.6	15 15.2	11R13.2	18 57.4	9R24.5	26 45.1	21 57.1	21 2.5	25R10.8
3 S	0 47 19.0	13 44.9	15 31.6	27 24.8	16 6.5	10 35.6	19 20.6	9 16.8	26 50.8	21 58.3	21 3.1	25 9.7
4 S	0 51 15.6	14 44.0	15 28.4	12♍21.4	17 0.9	9 58.5	19 44.0	9 9.1	26 56.5	21 59.4	21 3.7	25 8.6
5 M	0 55 12.1	15 43.0	15 25.2	27 30.8	17 58.3	9 22.2	20 7.7	9 1.4	27 2.1	22 0.5	21 4.3	25 7.4
6 T	0 59 8.7	16 42.0	15 22.0	12♎43.1	18 58.5	8 46.9	20 31.6	8 53.8	27 7.6	22 1.5	21 4.9	25 6.2
7 W	1 3 5.3	17 41.0	15 18.9	27 47.6	20 1.5	8 12.8	20 55.8	8 46.2	27 13.1	22 2.5	21 5.4	25 5.0
8 T	1 7 1.8	18 40.0	15 15.7	12♏34.7	21 6.9	7 40.2	21 20.2	8 38.6	27 18.5	22 3.4	21 5.9	25 3.8
9 F	1 10 58.4	19 38.9	15 12.5	26 57.5	22 14.9	7 9.1	21 44.9	8 31.1	27 23.8	22 4.3	21 6.3	25 2.5
10 S	1 14 54.9	20 37.8	15 9.3	10♐52.2	23 25.2	6 39.9	22 9.9	8 23.7	27 29.1	22 5.1	21 6.7	25 1.2
11 S	1 18 51.5	21 36.6	15 6.1	24 18.5	24 37.7	6 12.6	22 35.0	8 16.3	27 34.4	22 5.9	21 7.1	24 59.9
12 M	1 22 48.0	22 35.5	15 3.0	7♑18.3	25 52.5	5 47.4	23 0.5	8 9.0	27 39.6	22 6.6	21 7.5	24 58.6
13 T	1 26 44.6	23 34.3	14 59.8	19 55.2	27 9.4	5 24.4	23 26.1	8 1.8	27 44.7	22 7.3	21 7.9	24 57.3
14 W	1 30 41.1	24 33.1	14 56.6	2♒13.9	28 28.3	5 3.7	23 51.9	7 54.6	27 49.7	22 7.9	21 8.2	24 55.9
15 T	1 34 37.7	25 31.8	14 53.4	14 19.1	29 49.1	4 45.3	24 18.0	7 47.5	27 54.6	22 8.5	21 8.4	24 54.5
16 F	1 38 34.2	26 30.5	14 50.2	26 15.5	1♈11.9	4 29.3	24 44.3	7 40.4	27 59.5	22 9.0	21 8.6	24 53.1
17 S	1 42 30.8	27 29.2	14 47.1	8♓ 7.4	2 36.6	4 15.7	25 10.7	7 33.5	28 4.3	22 9.5	21 8.8	24 51.7
18 S	1 46 27.3	28 27.9	14 43.9	19 58.4	4 3.2	4 4.5	25 37.4	7 26.6	28 9.1	22 9.9	21 9.0	24 50.3
19 M	1 50 23.9	29 26.5	14 40.7	1♈51.5	5 31.5	3 55.9	26 4.3	7 19.9	28 13.8	22 10.3	21 9.1	24 48.8
20 T	1 54 20.4	0♉25.1	14 37.5	13 49.0	7 1.7	3 49.6	26 31.4	7 13.2	28 18.4	22 10.6	21 9.2	24 47.3
21 W	1 58 17.0	1 23.7	14 34.4	25 52.7	8 33.7	3 45.8	26 58.7	7 6.6	28 22.9	22 10.9	21 9.2	24 45.8
22 T	2 2 13.6	2 22.2	14 31.2	8♉ 4.0	10 7.4	3 44.4	27 26.2	7 0.2	28 27.3	22 11.1	21 9.3	24 44.3
23 F	2 6 10.1	3 20.7	14 28.0	20 24.0	11 42.8	3D45.4	27 53.8	6 53.9	28 31.7	22 11.2	21 9.3	24 42.8
24 S	2 10 6.7	4 19.2	14 24.8	2♊54.0	13 20.0	3 48.7	28 21.7	6 47.7	28 36.0	22 11.4	21R 9.2	24 41.3
25 S	2 14 3.2	5 17.6	14 21.7	15 35.3	14 59.0	3 54.2	28 49.7	6 41.6	28 40.2	22 11.4	21 9.1	24 39.7
26 M	2 17 59.8	6 16.0	14 18.5	28 29.6	16 39.7	4 2.0	29 17.9	6 35.6	28 44.4	22 11.4	21 9.0	24 38.2
27 T	2 21 56.3	7 14.4	14 15.3	11♋38.7	18 22.1	4 11.9	29 46.3	6 29.8	28 48.5	22 11.4	21 8.9	24 36.6
28 W	2 25 52.9	8 12.8	14 12.1	25 4.4	20 6.3	4 23.9	0♌14.8	6 24.1	28 52.4	22R11.3	21 8.7	24 35.0
29 T	2 29 49.4	9 11.1	14 8.9	8♌48.4	21 52.2	4 38.0	0 43.5	6 18.5	28 56.4	22 11.2	21 8.5	24 33.4
30 F	2 33 46.0	10 9.3	14 5.8	22 51.2	23 39.9	4 54.1	1 12.4	6 13.1	29 0.2	22 11.0	21 8.3	24 31.8
						DECLINATION at NOON						
1 T	0 39 25.9	4N39.4	22S39.9	16N57.4	7S13.9	11N55.3	24N38.7	2S18.6	13S41.3	22S 5.3	21S 7.6	4S42.4
4 S	0 51 15.6	5 48.3	22 38.9	2 14.2	6 39.3	10 50.1	24 24.9	2 9.6	13 35.8	22 4.8	21 7.3	4 40.9
7 W	1 3 5.3	6 56.4	22 37.8	14S 5.8	5 48.8	9 41.2	24 10.3	2 0.7	13 30.5	22 4.4	21 7.0	4 39.3
10 S	1 14 54.9	8 3.4	22 36.8	22 18.2	4 43.9	8 32.2	23 54.9	1 52.0	13 25.4	22 4.1	21 6.7	4 37.8
13 T	1 26 44.6	9 9.2	22 35.7	18 56.4	3 25.8	7 26.6	23 38.6	1 43.5	13 20.5	22 3.8	21 6.5	4 36.2
16 F	1 38 34.2	10 13.6	22 34.7	8 8.8	1 55.8	6 27.1	23 21.3	1 35.4	13 15.8	22 3.6	21 6.4	4 34.7
19 M	1 50 23.9	11 16.5	22 33.6	5N11.7	0 14.8	5 35.5	23 3.1	1 27.6	13 11.3	22 3.5	21 6.3	4 33.3
22 T	2 2 13.6	12 17.8	22 32.5	16 58.2	1N36.2	4 52.9	22 44.0	1 20.2	13 7.1	22 3.5	21 6.2	4 31.9
25 S	2 14 3.2	13 17.2	22 31.4	22 23.1	3 36.2	4 19.9	22 23.8	1 13.2	13 3.1	22 3.5	21 6.2	4 30.5
28 W	2 25 52.9	14 14.6	22 30.3	17 39.3	5 44.3	3 56.5	22 2.7	1 6.8	12 59.3	22 3.6	21 6.2	4 29.1

MAY 1993

DAY	EPHEMERIS SIDEREAL TIME	☉	☊	☽	☿	♀	♂	♃	♄	♅	♆	♇
	h m s	° ′	° ′	° ′	° ′	° ′	° ′	° ′	° ′	° ′	° ′	° ′
LONGITUDE at NOON												
1 S	2 37 42.5	11♉ 7.6	14♐ 2.6	7♍12.0	25♈29.4	5♈12.1	1♌41.4	6♎ 7.8	29♒ 3.9	22♑10.7	21♑ 8.0	24♏30.2
2 S	2 41 39.1	12 5.8	13 59.4	21 47.9	27 20.6	5 32.0	2 10.6	6R 2.7	29 7.6	22R10.4	21R 7.7	24R28.6
3 M	2 45 35.6	13 4.0	13 56.2	6♎34.1	29 13.6	5 53.7	2 40.0	5 57.7	29 11.2	22 10.2	21 7.4	24 27.0
4 T	2 49 32.2	14 2.1	13 53.1	21 23.7	1♉ 8.4	6 17.1	3 9.4	5 52.9	29 14.7	22 9.8	21 7.0	24 25.4
5 W	2 53 28.8	15 0.2	13 49.9	6♏ 8.9	3 4.9	6 42.2	3 39.0	5 48.2	29 18.1	22 9.3	21 6.7	24 23.8
6 T	2 57 25.3	15 58.3	13 46.7	20 42.2	5 3.2	7 9.0	4 8.8	5 43.6	29 21.4	22 8.9	21 6.2	24 22.1
7 F	3 1 21.9	16 56.3	13 43.5	4♐57.2	7 3.2	7 37.3	4 38.7	5 39.3	29 24.7	22 8.3	21 5.8	24 20.5
8 S	3 5 18.4	17 54.3	13 40.3	18 49.6	9 4.8	8 7.1	5 8.7	5 35.0	29 27.8	22 7.7	21 5.3	24 18.8
9 S	3 9 15.0	18 52.3	13 37.2	2♑17.5	11 8.1	8 38.4	5 38.8	5 31.0	29 30.9	22 7.1	21 4.8	24 17.1
10 M	3 13 11.5	19 50.3	13 34.0	15 21.2	13 12.9	9 11.1	6 9.1	5 27.1	29 33.9	22 6.4	21 4.2	24 15.5
11 T	3 17 8.1	20 48.3	13 30.8	28 2.8	15 19.1	9 45.1	6 39.5	5 23.3	29 36.8	22 5.7	21 3.6	24 13.8
12 W	3 21 4.6	21 46.2	13 27.6	10♒25.8	17 26.6	10 20.5	7 10.0	5 19.8	29 39.6	22 4.9	21 3.0	24 12.1
13 T	3 25 1.2	22 44.1	13 24.5	22 34.2	19 35.2	10 57.1	7 40.7	5 16.4	29 42.3	22 4.1	21 2.4	24 10.5
14 F	3 28 57.8	23 42.0	13 21.3	4♓32.8	21 44.9	11 34.8	8 11.5	5 13.1	29 44.9	22 3.3	21 1.7	24 8.8
15 S	3 32 54.3	24 39.9	13 18.1	16 26.0	23 55.3	12 13.8	8 42.4	5 10.1	29 47.4	22 2.4	21 1.0	24 7.1
16 S	3 36 50.9	25 37.7	13 14.9	28 18.3	26 6.3	12 53.8	9 13.4	5 7.2	29 49.8	22 1.4	21 0.3	24 5.4
17 M	3 40 47.4	26 35.5	13 11.7	10♈13.7	28 17.5	13 34.9	9 44.6	5 4.5	29 52.2	22 0.4	20 59.6	24 3.8
18 T	3 44 44.0	27 33.3	13 8.6	22 15.5	0♊28.8	14 17.0	10 15.9	5 2.0	29 54.4	21 59.4	20 58.8	24 2.1
19 W	3 48 40.5	28 31.1	13 5.4	4♉26.6	2 39.9	15 0.0	10 47.2	4 59.6	29 56.6	21 58.3	20 58.0	24 0.4
20 T	3 52 37.1	29 28.9	13 2.2	16 48.9	4 50.5	15 44.1	11 18.7	4 57.4	29 58.6	21 57.1	20 57.1	23 58.8
21 F	3 56 33.6	0♊26.6	12 59.0	29 23.9	7 0.2	16 28.9	11 50.4	4 55.4	0♓ 0.6	21 56.0	20 56.3	23 57.1
22 S	4 0 30.2	1 24.4	12 55.9	12♊12.4	9 8.9	17 14.7	12 22.1	4 53.6	0 2.5	21 54.8	20 55.4	23 55.4
23 S	4 4 26.8	2 22.1	12 52.7	25 14.7	11 16.3	18 1.3	12 53.9	4 52.0	0 4.3	21 53.5	20 54.5	23 53.8
24 M	4 8 23.3	3 19.8	12 49.5	8♋30.7	13 22.1	18 48.7	13 25.9	4 50.6	0 6.0	21 52.2	20 53.6	23 52.2
25 T	4 12 19.9	4 17.4	12 46.3	21 59.8	15 26.1	19 36.8	13 58.0	4 49.3	0 7.6	21 50.9	20 52.6	23 50.6
26 W	4 16 16.4	5 15.1	12 43.2	5♌41.6	17 28.2	20 25.7	14 30.1	4 48.2	0 9.0	21 49.5	20 51.6	23 48.9
27 T	4 20 13.0	6 12.7	12 40.0	19 35.2	19 28.0	21 15.3	15 2.4	4 47.3	0 10.4	21 48.1	20 50.6	23 47.3
28 F	4 24 9.5	7 10.2	12 36.8	3♍39.5	21 25.6	22 5.5	15 34.7	4 46.5	0 11.7	21 46.6	20 49.5	23 45.7
29 S	4 28 6.1	8 7.8	12 33.6	17 52.6	23 20.8	22 56.4	16 7.2	4 46.0	0 12.9	21 45.1	20 48.5	23 44.1
30 S	4 32 2.7	9 5.3	12 30.4	2♎12.2	25 13.4	23 47.9	16 39.7	4 45.6	0 14.0	21 43.6	20 47.4	23 42.5
31 M	4 35 59.2	10 2.8	12 27.3	16 35.3	27 3.5	24 40.1	17 12.3	4 45.4	0 15.0	21 42.0	20 46.3	23 40.9
DECLINATION at NOON												
1 S	2 37 42.5	15N10.0	22S29.1	4N 3.1	7N59.0	3N42.5	21N40.6	1S 0.8	12S55.8	22S 3.8	21S 6.3	4S27.9
4 T	2 49 32.2	16 3.1	22 28.0	12S 6.0	10 18.9	3 37.3	21 17.5	0 55.4	12 52.5	22 4.0	21 6.4	4 26.6
7 F	3 1 21.9	16 53.7	22 26.9	21 46.8	12 41.7	3 40.4	20 53.4	0 50.6	12 49.6	22 4.3	21 6.6	4 25.5
10 M	3 13 11.5	17 41.9	22 25.7	19 42.4	15 4.4	3 51.0	20 28.3	0 46.4	12 46.9	22 4.7	21 6.8	4 24.4
13 T	3 25 1.2	18 27.3	22 24.5	9 18.6	17 23.0	4 8.6	20 2.2	0 42.7	12 44.4	22 5.2	21 7.0	4 23.3
16 S	3 36 50.9	19 10.0	22 23.4	3N57.6	19 32.5	4 32.2	19 35.1	0 39.7	12 42.3	22 5.7	21 7.3	4 22.4
19 W	3 48 40.5	19 49.8	22 22.2	16 2.2	21 27.5	5 1.4	19 7.0	0 37.4	12 40.5	22 6.3	21 7.6	4 21.5
22 S	4 0 30.2	20 26.5	22 21.0	22 15.0	23 3.1	5 35.2	18 38.0	0 35.6	12 39.0	22 6.9	21 8.0	4 20.7
25 T	4 12 19.9	21 0.1	22 19.8	18 17.9	24 15.8	6 13.3	18 7.9	0 34.6	12 37.7	22 7.6	21 8.4	4 20.0
28 F	4 24 9.5	21 30.4	22 18.5	5 17.6	25 4.4	6 54.9	17 36.9	0 34.2	12 36.8	22 8.4	21 8.8	4 19.4
31 M	4 35 59.2	21 57.4	22 17.3	10S32.7	25 29.8	7 39.4	17 5.0	0 34.5	12 36.2	22 9.2	21 9.3	4 18.9

JUNE 1993

DAY	EPHEMERIS SIDEREAL TIME	☉	☊	☽	☿	♀	♂	♃	♄	♅	♆	♇
LONGITUDE at NOON												
1 T	4 39 55.8	11♊ 0.3	12♐24.1	0♏57.8	28♊50.9	25♈32.8	17♌45.1	4♎45.4	0♓15.9	21♑40.4	20♑45.1	23♏39.3
2 W	4 43 52.3	11 57.8	12 20.9	15 15.4	0♋35.6	26 26.1	18 17.9	4D45.6	0 16.7	21R38.7	20R44.0	23R37.7
3 T	4 47 48.9	12 55.2	12 17.7	29 23.7	2 17.6	27 20.0	18 50.8	4 46.0	0 17.4	21 37.1	20 42.8	23 36.2
4 F	4 51 45.4	13 52.7	12 14.6	13♐18.6	3 56.8	28 14.3	19 23.8	4 46.5	0 18.0	21 35.3	20 41.6	23 34.6
5 S	4 55 42.0	14 50.1	12 11.4	26 56.7	5 33.2	29 9.2	19 56.8	4 47.2	0 18.5	21 33.6	20 40.4	23 33.1
6 S	4 59 38.6	15 47.5	12 8.2	10♑16.1	7 6.7	0♉ 4.6	20 30.0	4 48.1	0 18.9	21 31.8	20 39.1	23 31.6
7 M	5 3 35.1	16 44.9	12 5.0	23 15.9	8 37.4	1 0.5	21 3.3	4 49.2	0 19.3	21 30.0	20 37.9	23 30.1
8 T	5 7 31.7	17 42.2	12 1.9	5♒56.9	10 5.3	1 56.9	21 36.6	4 50.4	0 19.5	21 28.1	20 36.6	23 28.6
9 W	5 11 28.2	18 39.6	11 58.7	18 21.0	11 30.2	2 53.7	22 10.0	4 51.8	0 19.6	21 26.3	20 35.3	23 27.1
10 T	5 15 24.8	19 37.0	11 55.5	0♓31.3	12 52.2	3 50.9	22 43.5	4 53.4	0 19.6	21 24.4	20 34.0	23 25.7
11 F	5 19 21.3	20 34.3	11 52.3	12 31.5	14 11.2	4 48.5	23 17.1	4 55.2	0R19.5	21 22.4	20 32.6	23 24.2
12 S	5 23 17.9	21 31.6	11 49.2	24 25.9	15 27.1	5 46.6	23 50.8	4 57.1	0 19.3	21 20.4	20 31.3	23 22.8
13 S	5 27 14.5	22 29.0	11 46.0	6♈19.1	16 40.1	6 45.0	24 24.5	4 59.3	0 19.1	21 18.4	20 29.9	23 21.4
14 M	5 31 11.0	23 26.3	11 42.8	18 15.7	17 49.9	7 43.9	24 58.4	5 1.6	0 18.7	21 16.5	20 28.5	23 20.1
15 T	5 35 7.6	24 23.7	11 39.6	0♉20.1	18 56.5	8 43.0	25 32.3	5 4.1	0 18.2	21 14.4	20 27.1	23 18.7
16 W	5 39 4.1	25 21.0	11 36.4	12 36.2	19 59.9	9 42.6	26 6.3	5 6.7	0 17.7	21 12.3	20 25.7	23 17.3
17 T	5 43 0.7	26 18.3	11 33.3	25 7.2	20 59.9	10 42.4	26 40.4	5 9.5	0 17.0	21 10.2	20 24.3	23 16.0
18 F	5 46 57.2	27 15.6	11 30.1	7♊55.5	21 56.5	11 42.6	27 14.6	5 12.5	0 16.2	21 8.1	20 22.8	23 14.7
19 S	5 50 53.8	28 12.9	11 26.9	21 2.1	22 49.6	12 43.1	27 48.8	5 15.6	0 15.4	21 6.0	20 21.4	23 13.4
20 S	5 54 50.4	29 10.2	11 23.7	4♋26.9	23 39.2	13 43.9	28 23.1	5 18.9	0 14.4	21 3.8	20 19.9	23 12.1
21 M	5 58 46.9	0♋ 7.4	11 20.6	18 8.5	24 25.0	14 45.0	28 57.5	5 22.4	0 13.3	21 1.6	20 18.4	23 10.9
22 T	6 2 43.5	1 4.7	11 17.4	2♌ 4.3	25 6.9	15 46.4	29 32.0	5 26.1	0 12.2	20 59.4	20 16.9	23 9.6
23 W	6 6 40.0	2 2.0	11 14.2	16 10.8	25 45.0	16 48.1	0♍ 6.5	5 29.9	0 10.9	20 57.1	20 15.4	23 8.4
24 T	6 10 36.6	2 59.2	11 11.0	0♍24.3	26 19.0	17 50.0	0 41.1	5 33.8	0 9.6	20 54.9	20 13.8	23 7.3
25 F	6 14 33.2	3 56.4	11 7.9	14 40.7	26 48.9	18 52.2	1 15.8	5 38.0	0 8.1	20 52.6	20 12.3	23 6.1
26 S	6 18 29.7	4 53.7	11 4.7	28 56.8	27 14.5	19 54.6	1 50.6	5 42.3	0 6.6	20 50.3	20 10.8	23 5.0
27 S	6 22 26.3	5 50.9	11 1.5	13♎ 9.6	27 35.7	20 57.3	2 25.4	5 46.7	0 5.0	20 48.0	20 9.2	23 3.9
28 M	6 26 22.8	6 48.1	10 58.3	27 17.0	27 52.5	22 0.2	3 0.3	5 51.3	0 3.3	20 45.7	20 7.6	23 2.8
29 T	6 30 19.4	7 45.3	10 55.2	11♏17.1	28 4.7	23 3.4	3 35.3	5 56.1	0 1.5	20 43.4	20 6.1	23 1.7
30 W	6 34 15.9	8 42.5	10 52.0	25 8.5	28 12.4	24 6.8	4 10.3	6 1.0	29♒59.6	20 41.1	20 4.5	23 0.7
DECLINATION at NOON												
1 T	4 39 55.8	22N 5.6	22S16.9	15S 4.4	25N33.4	7N54.9	16N54.2	0S34.7	12S36.1	22S 9.5	21S 9.5	4S18.8
4 F	4 51 45.4	22 27.9	22 15.7	22 17.6	25 31.3	8 42.7	16 21.1	0 35.8	12 35.9	22 10.4	21 10.0	4 18.4
7 M	5 3 35.1	22 46.7	22 14.4	18 0.4	25 11.9	9 32.3	15 47.1	0 37.6	12 36.1	22 11.3	21 10.6	4 18.1
10 T	5 15 24.8	23 2.0	22 13.1	6 26.8	24 38.4	10 23.2	15 12.2	0 40.0	12 36.5	22 12.2	21 11.1	4 17.9
13 S	5 27 14.5	23 13.5	22 11.9	6N55.8	23 53.9	11 15.1	14 36.4	0 43.0	12 37.3	22 13.2	21 11.7	4 17.8
16 W	5 39 4.1	23 21.4	22 10.6	18 6.2	23 1.4	12 7.4	13 59.9	0 46.6	12 38.4	22 14.2	21 12.4	4 17.8
19 S	5 50 53.8	23 25.6	22 9.3	22 19.7	22 3.7	12 59.6	13 22.5	0 50.9	12 39.7	22 15.3	21 13.0	4 17.9
22 T	6 2 43.5	23 26.1	22 8.0	15 46.7	21 3.6	13 51.4	12 44.3	0 55.7	12 41.4	22 16.3	21 13.7	4 18.1
25 F	6 14 33.2	23 22.8	22 6.6	1 12.0	20 3.8	14 42.4	12 5.3	1 1.1	12 43.4	22 17.4	21 14.4	4 18.4
28 M	6 26 22.8	23 15.8	22 5.3	13S56.9	19 7.3	15 32.2	11 25.7	1 7.0	12 45.7	22 18.5	21 15.1	4 18.8

JULY 1993

DAY	EPHEMERIS SIDEREAL TIME	☉	☊	☽	☿	♀	♂	♃	♄	♅	♆	♇
	h m s	° ′	° ′	° ′	° ′	° ′	° ′	° ′	° ′	° ′	° ′	° ′
					LONGITUDE at NOON							
1 T	6 38 12.5	9♋39.7	10♐48.8	8♐49.7	28♋15.3	25♉10.4	4♍45.4	6♎ 6.1	29♒57.6	20♑38.7	20♑ 2.9	22♏59.7
2 F	6 42 9.1	10 36.9	10 45.6	22 19.3	28R13.7	26 14.2	5 20.6	6 11.3	29R55.5	20R36.3	20R 1.3	22R58.7
3 S	6 46 5.6	11 34.0	10 42.4	5♑36.1	28 7.4	27 18.2	5 55.8	6 16.6	29 53.3	20 34.0	19 59.7	22 57.8
4 S	6 50 2.2	12 31.2	10 39.3	18 38.9	27 56.6	28 22.5	6 31.1	6 22.1	29 51.1	20 31.6	19 58.1	22 56.8
5 M	6 53 58.7	13 28.5	10 36.1	1♒27.3	27 41.4	29 27.0	7 6.5	6 27.8	29 48.8	20 29.3	19 56.5	22 56.0
6 T	6 57 55.3	14 25.6	10 32.9	14 1.0	27 21.9	0♊31.7	7 41.9	6 33.6	29 46.4	20 26.9	19 54.9	22 55.1
7 W	7 1 51.8	15 22.8	10 29.7	26 21.1	26 58.4	1 36.5	8 17.4	6 39.6	29 43.9	20 24.5	19 53.3	22 54.3
8 T	7 5 48.4	16 20.0	10 26.6	8♓29.5	26 31.2	2 41.6	8 53.0	6 45.7	29 41.3	20 22.1	19 51.7	22 53.4
9 F	7 9 45.0	17 17.2	10 23.4	20 28.7	26 0.7	3 46.8	9 28.6	6 51.9	29 38.7	20 19.6	19 50.1	22 52.7
10 S	7 13 41.5	18 14.4	10 20.2	2♈22.5	25 27.3	4 52.2	10 4.3	6 58.2	29 35.9	20 17.2	19 48.4	22 51.9
11 S	7 17 38.1	19 11.6	10 17.0	14 14.9	24 51.6	5 57.8	10 40.0	7 4.7	29 33.1	20 14.8	19 46.8	22 51.2
12 M	7 21 34.6	20 8.8	10 13.9	26 10.7	24 14.0	7 3.6	11 15.9	7 11.4	29 30.2	20 12.4	19 45.2	22 50.5
13 T	7 25 31.2	21 6.1	10 10.7	8♉14.8	23 35.2	8 9.6	11 51.8	7 18.1	29 27.2	20 10.0	19 43.6	22 49.8
14 W	7 29 27.7	22 3.3	10 7.5	20 31.9	22 55.8	9 15.7	12 27.7	7 25.0	29 24.2	20 7.6	19 41.9	22 49.2
15 T	7 33 24.3	23 0.5	10 4.3	3♊ 6.5	22 16.5	10 21.9	13 3.7	7 32.1	29 21.0	20 5.1	19 40.3	22 48.6
16 F	7 37 20.9	23 57.8	10 1.1	16 2.2	21 38.0	11 28.4	13 39.8	7 39.2	29 17.8	20 2.7	19 38.7	22 48.0
17 S	7 41 17.4	24 55.1	9 58.0	29 21.3	21 1.0	12 35.0	14 16.0	7 46.5	29 14.6	20 0.3	19 37.1	22 47.4
18 S	7 45 14.0	25 52.3	9 54.8	13♋ 4.0	20 26.1	13 41.7	14 52.2	7 53.9	29 11.2	19 57.9	19 35.5	22 46.9
19 M	7 49 10.5	26 49.6	9 51.6	27 8.7	19 54.0	14 48.6	15 28.5	8 1.5	29 7.8	19 55.5	19 33.9	22 46.4
20 T	7 53 7.1	27 46.9	9 48.4	11♌31.1	19 25.3	15 55.6	16 4.8	8 9.1	29 4.4	19 53.1	19 32.2	22 46.0
21 W	7 57 3.6	28 44.2	9 45.3	26 5.3	19 0.5	17 2.7	16 41.2	8 16.9	29 0.8	19 50.7	19 30.6	22 45.6
22 T	8 1 0.2	29 41.5	9 42.1	10♍44.2	18 40.1	18 10.0	17 17.7	8 24.8	28 57.2	19 48.4	19 29.0	22 45.2
23 F	8 4 56.8	0♌38.8	9 38.9	25 21.1	18 24.5	19 17.5	17 54.2	8 32.9	28 53.6	19 46.0	19 27.5	22 44.8
24 S	8 8 53.3	1 36.1	9 35.7	9♎49.9	18 14.1	20 25.0	18 30.8	8 41.0	28 49.8	19 43.7	19 25.9	22 44.5
25 S	8 12 49.9	2 33.4	9 32.6	24 6.6	18 9.2	21 32.7	19 7.5	8 49.3	28 46.1	19 41.3	19 24.3	22 44.2
26 M	8 16 46.4	3 30.8	9 29.4	8♏ 9.0	18D10.0	22 40.5	19 44.3	8 57.7	28 42.3	19 39.0	19 22.8	22 44.0
27 T	8 20 43.0	4 28.1	9 26.2	21 56.4	18 16.7	23 48.5	20 21.0	9 6.2	28 38.4	19 36.7	19 21.2	22 43.8
28 W	8 24 39.5	5 25.5	9 23.0	5♐29.3	18 29.5	24 56.5	20 57.9	9 14.8	28 34.5	19 34.4	19 19.7	22 43.6
29 T	8 28 36.1	6 22.8	9 19.8	18 48.6	18 48.4	26 4.7	21 34.8	9 23.5	28 30.5	19 32.1	19 18.1	22 43.4
30 F	8 32 32.6	7 20.2	9 16.7	1♑55.3	19 13.4	27 13.0	22 11.7	9 32.3	28 26.5	19 29.9	19 16.6	22 43.3
31 S	8 36 29.2	8 17.5	9 13.5	14 50.3	19 44.7	28 21.4	22 48.7	9 41.2	28 22.4	19 27.6	19 15.1	22 43.2
					DECLINATION at NOON							
1 T	6 38 12.5	23N 5.2	22S 4.0	22S 3.9	18N16.8	16N20.4	10N45.3	1S13.5	12S48.2	22S19.6	21S15.8	4S19.3
4 S	6 50 2.2	22 51.0	22 2.6	19 3.5	17 34.9	17 6.6	10 4.3	1 20.5	12 51.1	22 20.7	21 16.5	4 20.0
7 W	7 1 51.8	22 33.1	22 1.3	8 1.4	17 4.0	17 50.5	9 22.6	1 28.0	12 54.1	22 21.8	21 17.2	4 20.7
10 S	7 13 41.5	22 11.8	21 59.9	5N23.5	16 45.8	18 31.7	8 40.4	1 36.0	12 57.4	22 22.9	21 18.0	4 21.5
13 T	7 25 31.2	21 47.0	21 58.5	16 57.0	16 41.1	19 9.9	7 57.5	1 44.5	13 1.0	22 24.0	21 18.7	4 22.5
16 F	7 37 20.9	21 18.9	21 57.1	22 18.3	16 49.4	19 44.8	7 14.1	1 53.4	13 4.8	22 25.1	21 19.4	4 23.5
19 M	7 49 10.5	20 47.5	21 55.7	17 7.0	17 9.4	20 16.0	6 30.1	2 2.7	13 8.7	22 26.2	21 20.2	4 24.6
22 T	8 1 0.2	20 12.9	21 54.3	2 47.9	17 38.3	20 43.2	5 45.7	2 12.5	13 12.9	22 27.3	21 20.9	4 25.8
25 S	8 12 49.9	19 35.3	21 52.9	12S49.4	18 12.9	21 6.3	5 0.8	2 22.7	13 17.2	22 28.3	21 21.6	4 27.1
28 W	8 24 39.5	18 54.8	21 51.5	21 41.6	18 49.3	21 24.9	4 15.5	2 33.2	13 21.7	22 29.3	21 22.3	4 28.5
31 S	8 36 29.2	18 11.5	21 50.0	19 46.6	19 23.3	21 38.8	3 29.8	2 44.1	13 26.3	22 30.3	21 23.0	4 30.0

AUGUST 1993

DAY	EPHEMERIS SIDEREAL TIME	☉	☊	☽	☿	♀	♂	♃	♄	♅	♆	♇
					LONGITUDE at NOON							
1 S	8 40 25.8	9♌14.9	9♐10.3	27♑34.1	20♋22.2	29♊29.9	23♍25.8	9♎50.3	28♒18.3	19♑25.4	19♑13.6	22♏43.2
2 M	8 44 22.3	10 12.3	9 7.1	10♒ 6.9	21 5.8	0♋38.6	24 2.9	9 59.4	28R14.1	19R23.2	19R12.1	22R43.1
3 T	8 48 18.9	11 9.7	9 4.0	22 29.1	21 55.5	1 47.4	24 40.1	10 8.6	28 9.9	19 21.0	19 10.6	22 43.1
4 W	8 52 15.4	12 7.2	9 0.8	4♓41.3	22 51.3	2 56.2	25 17.3	10 18.0	28 5.7	19 18.8	19 9.1	22D43.2
5 T	8 56 12.0	13 4.6	8 57.6	16 44.5	23 52.9	4 5.2	25 54.6	10 27.4	28 1.4	19 16.7	19 7.7	22 43.3
6 F	9 0 8.5	14 2.1	8 54.4	28 40.7	25 0.3	5 14.4	26 32.0	10 36.9	27 57.1	19 14.5	19 6.3	22 43.4
7 S	9 4 5.1	14 59.5	8 51.3	10♈32.3	26 13.2	6 23.6	27 9.4	10 46.5	27 52.8	19 12.4	19 4.8	22 43.5
8 S	9 8 1.6	15 57.0	8 48.1	22 22.9	27 31.6	7 32.9	27 46.9	10 56.2	27 48.4	19 10.4	19 3.4	22 43.7
9 M	9 11 58.2	16 54.6	8 44.9	4♉16.7	28 55.1	8 42.4	28 24.4	11 6.1	27 44.0	19 8.3	19 2.0	22 43.9
10 T	9 15 54.8	17 52.1	8 41.7	16 18.4	0♌23.6	9 51.9	29 2.0	11 16.0	27 39.6	19 6.3	19 0.7	22 44.2
11 W	9 19 51.3	18 49.7	8 38.5	28 33.3	1 56.7	11 1.6	29 39.7	11 26.0	27 35.2	19 4.3	18 59.3	22 44.4
12 T	9 23 47.9	19 47.3	8 35.4	11♊ 6.5	3 34.2	12 11.4	0♎17.4	11 36.0	27 30.7	19 2.3	18 57.9	22 44.8
13 F	9 27 44.4	20 44.9	8 32.2	24 2.6	5 15.6	13 21.2	0 55.2	11 46.2	27 26.2	19 0.4	18 56.6	22 45.1
14 S	9 31 41.0	21 42.5	8 29.0	7♋25.2	7 0.7	14 31.2	1 33.1	11 56.5	27 21.7	18 58.5	18 55.3	22 45.5
15 S	9 35 37.5	22 40.2	8 25.8	21 16.1	8 49.1	15 41.3	2 11.0	12 6.8	27 17.2	18 56.6	18 54.0	22 45.9
16 M	9 39 34.1	23 37.9	8 22.7	5♌34.0	10 40.3	16 51.5	2 49.0	12 17.3	27 12.8	18 54.8	18 52.8	22 46.4
17 T	9 43 30.6	24 35.6	8 19.5	20 14.9	12 34.0	18 1.7	3 27.0	12 27.8	27 8.2	18 53.0	18 51.6	22 46.9
18 W	9 47 27.2	25 33.4	8 16.3	5♍11.4	14 29.7	19 12.1	4 5.1	12 38.4	27 3.7	18 51.2	18 50.3	22 47.4
19 T	9 51 23.7	26 31.1	8 13.1	20 14.4	16 27.0	20 22.5	4 43.3	12 49.1	26 59.2	18 49.4	18 49.1	22 48.0
20 F	9 55 20.3	27 28.9	8 9.9	5♎13.8	18 25.5	21 33.0	5 21.5	12 59.8	26 54.6	18 47.7	18 47.9	22 48.5
21 S	9 59 16.8	28 26.7	8 6.8	20 1.2	20 25.0	22 43.7	5 59.7	13 10.7	26 50.1	18 46.0	18 46.8	22 49.2
22 S	10 3 13.4	29 24.5	8 3.6	4♏30.4	22 25.0	23 54.4	6 38.1	13 21.6	26 45.6	18 44.4	18 45.6	22 49.8
23 M	10 7 10.0	0♍22.3	8 0.4	18 38.2	24 25.3	25 5.1	7 16.5	13 32.5	26 41.1	18 42.8	18 44.5	22 50.5
24 T	10 11 6.5	1 20.2	7 57.2	2♐23.9	26 25.6	26 16.0	7 54.9	13 43.6	26 36.5	18 41.2	18 43.4	22 51.2
25 W	10 15 3.1	2 18.1	7 54.1	15 49.0	28 25.6	27 27.0	8 33.4	13 54.7	26 32.0	18 39.7	18 42.4	22 52.0
26 T	10 18 59.6	3 16.0	7 50.9	28 55.8	0♍25.2	28 38.0	9 12.0	14 5.9	26 27.6	18 38.2	18 41.3	22 52.8
27 F	10 22 56.2	4 13.9	7 47.7	11♑47.0	2 24.1	29 49.2	9 50.6	14 17.1	26 23.1	18 36.7	18 40.3	22 53.6
28 S	10 26 52.7	5 11.8	7 44.5	24 25.3	4 22.3	1♌ 0.4	10 29.3	14 28.5	26 18.6	18 35.3	18 39.3	22 54.4
29 S	10 30 49.3	6 9.8	7 41.3	6♒52.6	6 19.7	2 11.7	11 8.0	14 39.8	26 14.2	18 33.9	18 38.3	22 55.3
30 M	10 34 45.8	7 7.8	7 38.2	19 10.8	8 16.0	3 23.0	11 46.8	14 51.3	26 9.8	18 32.6	18 37.4	22 56.2
31 T	10 38 42.4	8 5.8	7 35.0	1♓21.0	10 11.4	4 34.5	12 25.6	15 2.8	26 5.4	18 31.3	18 36.5	22 57.2
					DECLINATION at NOON							
1 S	8 40 25.8	17N56.5	21S49.5	17S 0.5	19N33.3	21N42.4	3N14.5	2S47.8	13S27.8	22S30.6	21S23.2	4S30.5
4 W	8 52 15.4	17 9.6	21 48.1	5 6.3	19 56.9	21 49.8	2 28.4	2 59.2	13 32.6	22 31.5	21 23.9	4 32.1
7 S	9 4 5.1	16 20.3	21 46.6	8N10.1	20 6.8	21 52.1	1 42.0	3 10.8	13 37.4	22 32.4	21 24.6	4 33.8
10 T	9 15 54.8	15 28.6	21 45.1	18 38.1	19 58.4	21 49.3	0 55.4	3 22.8	13 42.2	22 33.3	21 25.2	4 35.5
13 F	9 27 44.4	14 34.6	21 43.6	22 2.2	19 27.8	21 41.2	0 8.5	3 35.0	13 47.1	22 34.1	21 25.9	4 37.4
16 M	9 39 34.1	13 38.6	21 42.1	14 49.0	18 33.1	21 27.8	0S38.6	3 47.6	13 52.0	22 34.9	21 26.5	4 39.3
19 T	9 51 23.7	12 40.5	21 40.6	0S39.5	17 14.7	21 9.0	1 25.8	4 0.3	13 56.9	22 35.6	21 27.0	4 41.2
22 S	10 3 13.4	11 40.7	21 39.1	15 40.3	15 35.6	20 45.0	2 13.2	4 13.3	14 1.8	22 36.2	21 27.6	4 43.2
25 W	10 15 3.1	10 39.3	21 37.6	22 2.1	13 40.0	20 15.7	3 0.5	4 26.5	14 6.6	22 36.9	21 28.1	4 45.3
28 S	10 26 52.7	9 36.3	21 36.0	17 40.0	11 32.5	19 41.3	3 47.9	4 39.9	14 11.3	22 37.4	21 28.6	4 47.4
31 T	10 38 42.4	8 32.0	21 34.5	6 21.1	9 17.2	19 1.9	4 35.2	4 53.5	14 16.0	22 38.0	21 29.1	4 49.6

SEPTEMBER 1993

LONGITUDE at NOON

DAY	EPHEMERIS SIDEREAL TIME	☉	☊	☽	☿	♀	♂	♃	♄	♅	♆	♇
	h m s	° ′	° ′	° ′	° ′	° ′	° ′	° ′	° ′	° ′	° ′	° ′
1 W	10 42 38.9	9♍ 3.8	7♐31.8	13♓24.2	12♍ 5.6	5♌46.1	13♎ 4.5	15♎14.4	26♒ 1.0	18♑30.0	18♑35.6	22♏58.2
2 T	10 46 35.5	10 1.9	7 28.6	25 21.5	13 58.7	6 57.7	13 43.5	15 26.0	25R56.7	18R28.8	18R34.7	22 59.2
3 F	10 50 32.0	10 60.0	7 25.5	7♈14.2	15 50.6	8 9.4	14 22.5	15 37.7	25 52.4	18 27.6	18 33.9	23 0.2
4 S	10 54 28.6	11 58.1	7 22.3	19 4.2	17 41.4	9 21.2	15 1.6	15 49.4	25 48.1	18 26.5	18 33.1	23 1.3
5 S	10 58 25.1	12 56.2	7 19.1	0♉54.1	19 30.9	10 33.1	15 40.7	16 1.3	25 43.9	18 25.4	18 32.3	23 2.4
6 M	11 2 21.7	13 54.5	7 15.9	12 47.4	21 19.4	11 45.1	16 19.9	16 13.2	25 39.8	18 24.5	18 31.6	23 3.6
7 T	11 6 18.3	14 52.7	7 12.7	24 47.9	23 6.5	12 57.1	16 59.2	16 25.1	25 35.6	18 23.5	18 30.9	23 4.8
8 W	11 10 14.8	15 50.9	7 9.6	7♊ 0.6	24 52.6	14 9.2	17 38.5	16 37.0	25 31.5	18 22.5	18 30.2	23 6.0
9 T	11 14 11.4	16 49.2	7 6.4	19 30.4	26 37.4	15 21.4	18 17.9	16 49.1	25 27.4	18 21.6	18 29.5	23 7.2
10 F	11 18 7.9	17 47.5	7 3.2	2♋22.5	28 21.1	16 33.7	18 57.3	17 1.1	25 23.4	18 20.8	18 28.9	23 8.4
11 S	11 22 4.5	18 45.9	7 0.0	15 41.2	0♎ 3.7	17 46.0	19 36.8	17 13.3	25 19.4	18 19.9	18 28.3	23 9.7
12 S	11 26 1.0	19 44.3	6 56.9	29 29.3	1 45.1	18 58.4	20 16.4	17 25.4	25 15.5	18 19.2	18 27.7	23 11.1
13 M	11 29 57.6	20 42.7	6 53.7	13♌47.2	3 25.4	20 10.9	20 56.0	17 37.6	25 11.6	18 18.5	18 27.1	23 12.4
14 T	11 33 54.1	21 41.2	6 50.5	28 32.1	5 4.7	21 23.5	21 35.7	17 49.9	25 7.8	18 17.8	18 26.6	23 13.8
15 W	11 37 50.7	22 39.7	6 47.3	13♍37.3	6 42.8	22 36.1	22 15.4	18 2.2	25 4.1	18 17.2	18 26.1	23 15.2
16 T	11 41 47.2	23 38.2	6 44.1	28 53.3	8 19.9	23 48.8	22 55.2	18 14.5	25 0.4	18 16.6	18 25.7	23 16.6
17 F	11 45 43.8	24 36.7	6 41.0	14♎ 8.8	9 56.0	25 1.6	23 35.1	18 26.9	24 56.7	18 16.1	18 25.2	23 18.1
18 S	11 49 40.3	25 35.3	6 37.8	29 13.1	11 31.0	26 14.4	24 15.0	18 39.4	24 53.1	18 15.6	18 24.8	23 19.6
19 S	11 53 36.9	26 33.9	6 34.6	13♏57.8	13 5.0	27 27.3	24 55.0	18 51.8	24 49.6	18 15.2	18 24.5	23 21.1
20 M	11 57 33.4	27 32.6	6 31.4	28 17.8	14 38.0	28 40.3	25 35.0	19 4.3	24 46.2	18 14.8	18 24.2	23 22.6
21 T	12 1 30.0	28 31.3	6 28.2	12♐11.2	16 10.0	29 53.3	26 15.1	19 16.9	24 42.8	18 14.5	18 23.9	23 24.2
22 W	12 5 26.5	29 30.0	6 25.1	25 38.9	17 41.0	1♍ 6.4	26 55.3	19 29.5	24 39.5	18 14.2	18 23.6	23 25.8
23 T	12 9 23.1	0♎28.7	6 21.9	8♑43.6	19 11.0	2 19.5	27 35.5	19 42.1	24 36.3	18 14.0	18 23.4	23 27.4
24 F	12 13 19.6	1 27.4	6 18.7	21 28.7	20 40.0	3 32.7	28 15.7	19 54.7	24 33.1	18 13.8	18 23.2	23 29.1
25 S	12 17 16.2	2 26.2	6 15.5	3♒58.0	22 7.9	4 45.9	28 56.1	20 7.4	24 30.0	18 13.7	18 23.0	23 30.8
26 S	12 21 12.7	3 25.0	6 12.4	16 14.9	23 34.9	5 59.2	29 36.5	20 20.1	24 27.0	18 13.6	18 22.9	23 32.5
27 M	12 25 9.3	4 23.9	6 9.2	28 22.7	25 0.8	7 12.7	0♏16.9	20 32.8	24 24.1	18 13.6	18 22.8	23 34.2
28 T	12 29 5.9	5 22.8	6 6.0	10♓23.5	26 25.7	8 26.1	0 57.4	20 45.6	24 21.3	18D13.7	18 22.7	23 36.0
29 W	12 33 2.4	6 21.7	6 2.8	22 19.5	27 49.5	9 39.6	1 38.0	20 58.4	24 18.5	18 13.8	18 22.7	23 37.8
30 T	12 36 59.0	7 20.6	5 59.6	4♈12.4	29 12.2	10 53.1	2 18.6	21 11.2	24 15.8	18 13.9	18 22.7	23 39.6

DECLINATION at NOON

DAY	EPHEMERIS SIDEREAL TIME	☉	☊	☽	☿	♀	♂	♃	♄	♅	♆	♇
1 W	10 42 38.9	8N10.3	21S34.0	1S56.1	8N31.0	18N47.7	4S50.9	4S58.1	14S17.5	22S38.1	21S29.2	4S50.4
4 S	10 54 28.6	7 4.4	21 32.4	10N54.3	6 10.5	18 1.8	5 38.1	5 11.9	14 22.0	22 38.6	21 29.7	4 52.6
7 T	11 6 18.3	5 57.4	21 30.8	19 58.4	3 48.8	17 11.3	6 25.1	5 25.9	14 26.3	22 38.9	21 30.1	4 54.9
10 F	11 18 7.9	4 49.5	21 29.3	21 13.1	1 27.9	16 16.3	7 11.9	5 39.9	14 30.4	22 39.3	21 30.4	4 57.2
13 M	11 29 57.6	3 40.8	21 27.7	12 14.0	0S51.0	15 17.2	7 58.5	5 54.1	14 34.4	22 39.5	21 30.7	4 59.5
16 T	11 41 47.2	2 31.6	21 26.1	3S48.5	3 6.7	14 14.1	8 44.8	6 8.4	14 38.2	22 39.7	21 31.0	5 1.9
19 S	11 53 36.9	1 21.9	21 24.4	17 48.5	5 18.6	13 7.3	9 30.6	6 22.8	14 41.8	22 39.9	21 31.3	5 4.2
22 W	12 5 26.5	0 12.0	21 22.8	21 37.0	7 25.8	11 57.2	10 16.1	6 37.2	14 45.1	22 40.0	21 31.5	5 6.6
25 S	12 17 16.2	0S58.1	21 21.2	15 3.2	9 27.6	10 43.9	11 1.1	6 51.7	14 48.2	22 40.0	21 31.7	5 9.0
28 T	12 29 5.9	2 8.2	21 19.5	3 0.1	11 23.4	9 27.8	11 45.5	7 6.2	14 51.0	22 39.9	21 31.8	5 11.4

OCTOBER 1993

LONGITUDE at NOON

DAY	EPHEMERIS SIDEREAL TIME	☉	☊	☽	☿	♀	♂	♃	♄	♅	♆	♇
1 F	12 40 55.5	8♎19.6	5♐56.5	16♈ 3.4	0♏33.8	12♍ 6.7	2♏59.3	21♎24.0	24♒13.2	18♑14.1	18♑22.7	23♏41.4
2 S	12 44 52.1	9 18.6	5 53.3	27 54.4	1 54.2	13 20.4	3 40.0	21 36.9	24R10.7	18 14.3	18D22.8	23 43.2
3 S	12 48 48.6	10 17.7	5 50.1	9♉47.2	3 13.4	14 34.1	4 20.8	21 49.7	24 8.2	18 14.6	18 22.9	23 45.1
4 M	12 52 45.2	11 16.7	5 46.9	21 44.2	4 31.3	15 47.9	5 1.7	22 2.6	24 5.9	18 14.9	18 23.0	23 47.0
5 T	12 56 41.7	12 15.9	5 43.8	3♊48.4	5 47.9	17 1.7	5 42.6	22 15.5	24 3.6	18 15.3	18 23.2	23 48.9
6 W	13 0 38.3	13 15.0	5 40.6	16 3.6	7 3.1	18 15.6	6 23.6	22 28.5	24 1.5	18 15.7	18 23.4	23 50.8
7 T	13 4 34.8	14 14.2	5 37.4	28 33.8	8 16.8	19 29.5	7 4.6	22 41.4	23 59.4	18 16.2	18 23.6	23 52.8
8 F	13 8 31.4	15 13.4	5 34.2	11♋23.3	9 28.8	20 43.5	7 45.7	22 54.4	23 57.4	18 16.8	18 23.9	23 54.8
9 S	13 12 27.9	16 12.7	5 31.0	24 36.3	10 39.2	21 57.5	8 26.8	23 7.3	23 55.5	18 17.4	18 24.2	23 56.7
10 S	13 16 24.5	17 12.0	5 27.9	8♌15.9	11 47.7	23 11.6	9 8.1	23 20.3	23 53.7	18 18.0	18 24.5	23 58.8
11 M	13 20 21.0	18 11.3	5 24.7	22 23.5	12 54.3	24 25.7	9 49.3	23 33.3	23 51.9	18 18.7	18 24.8	24 0.8
12 T	13 24 17.6	19 10.7	5 21.5	6♍58.0	13 58.6	25 39.9	10 30.7	23 46.3	23 50.3	18 19.4	18 25.2	24 2.8
13 W	13 28 14.1	20 10.1	5 18.3	21 54.9	15 0.7	26 54.1	11 12.1	23 59.4	23 48.8	18 20.2	18 25.7	24 4.9
14 T	13 32 10.7	21 9.6	5 15.2	7♎ 6.4	16 0.1	28 8.4	11 53.6	24 12.4	23 47.4	18 21.1	18 26.1	24 7.0
15 F	13 36 7.2	22 9.1	5 12.0	22 22.5	16 56.8	29 22.7	12 35.1	24 25.4	23 46.0	18 22.0	18 26.6	24 9.1
16 S	13 40 3.8	23 8.6	5 8.8	7♏32.4	17 50.3	0♎37.1	13 16.7	24 38.5	23 44.8	18 22.9	18 27.2	24 11.2
17 S	13 44 0.4	24 8.2	5 5.6	22 26.5	18 40.5	1 51.5	13 58.3	24 51.5	23 43.7	18 23.9	18 27.7	24 13.4
18 M	13 47 56.9	25 7.8	5 2.4	6♐57.8	19 27.0	3 5.9	14 40.1	25 4.6	23 42.7	18 25.0	18 28.4	24 15.6
19 T	13 51 53.5	26 7.4	4 59.3	21 2.2	20 9.3	4 20.4	15 21.8	25 17.7	23 41.8	18 26.1	18 29.0	24 17.8
20 W	13 55 50.0	27 7.1	4 56.1	4♑38.9	20 47.0	5 34.9	16 3.6	25 30.7	23 40.9	18 27.2	18 29.7	24 19.9
21 T	13 59 46.6	28 6.8	4 52.9	17 49.4	21 19.7	6 49.4	16 45.5	25 43.8	23 40.2	18 28.4	18 30.4	24 22.1
22 F	14 3 43.1	29 6.5	4 49.7	0♒36.9	21 46.9	8 4.0	17 27.5	25 56.8	23 39.6	18 29.7	18 31.1	24 24.4
23 S	14 7 39.7	0♏ 6.2	4 46.6	13 5.2	22 8.1	9 18.6	18 9.4	26 9.8	23 39.1	18 31.0	18 31.9	24 26.6
24 S	14 11 36.2	1 6.0	4 43.4	25 18.7	22 22.6	10 33.2	18 51.5	26 22.9	23 38.6	18 32.3	18 32.7	24 28.8
25 M	14 15 32.8	2 5.7	4 40.2	7♓21.5	22 29.9	11 47.9	19 33.6	26 35.9	23 38.3	18 33.7	18 33.5	24 31.1
26 T	14 19 29.3	3 5.6	4 37.0	19 17.2	22R29.4	13 2.6	20 15.8	26 48.9	23 38.1	18 35.1	18 34.3	24 33.3
27 W	14 23 25.9	4 5.4	4 33.8	1♈ 9.1	22 20.5	14 17.3	20 58.0	27 1.9	23 38.0	18 36.6	18 35.2	24 35.6
28 T	14 27 22.4	5 5.3	4 30.7	12 60.0	22 2.9	15 32.1	21 40.3	27 14.9	23 38.0	18 38.2	18 36.1	24 37.9
29 F	14 31 19.0	6 5.2	4 27.5	24 52.0	21 36.0	16 46.9	22 22.6	27 27.9	23D38.1	18 39.7	18 37.1	24 40.2
30 S	14 35 15.6	7 5.1	4 24.3	6♉47.2	20 59.8	18 1.7	23 5.0	27 40.9	23 38.3	18 41.4	18 38.1	24 42.5
31 S	14 39 12.1	8 5.1	4 21.1	18 47.3	20 14.3	19 16.6	23 47.5	27 53.8	23 38.6	18 43.0	18 39.1	24 44.8

DECLINATION at NOON

DAY	EPHEMERIS SIDEREAL TIME	☉	☊	☽	☿	♀	♂	♃	♄	♅	♆	♇
1 F	12 40 55.5	3S18.1	21S17.9	9N49.5	13S12.6	8N 9.2	12S29.4	7S20.7	14S53.6	22S39.8	21S31.9	5S13.8
4 M	12 52 45.2	4 27.7	21 16.2	19 15.9	14 54.2	6 48.3	13 12.5	7 35.3	14 55.9	22 39.7	21 32.0	5 16.2
7 T	13 4 34.8	5 36.8	21 14.5	21 17.9	16 27.5	5 25.5	13 55.0	7 49.8	14 57.9	22 39.4	21 32.0	5 18.6
10 S	13 16 24.5	6 45.3	21 12.9	13 43.1	17 51.3	4 1.1	14 36.6	8 4.3	14 59.6	22 39.1	21 32.0	5 21.0
13 W	13 28 14.1	7 53.0	21 11.2	1S17.6	19 4.1	2 35.4	15 17.4	8 18.7	15 1.1	22 38.8	21 31.9	5 23.3
16 S	13 40 3.8	8 59.7	21 9.5	16 10.6	20 4.0	1 8.7	15 57.2	8 33.1	15 2.2	22 38.4	21 31.8	5 25.7
19 T	13 51 53.5	10 5.2	21 7.7	21 34.5	20 48.5	0S18.6	16 36.1	8 47.5	15 3.0	22 37.9	21 31.6	5 28.0
22 F	14 3 43.1	11 9.4	21 6.0	15 45.0	21 14.1	1 46.2	17 13.8	9 1.7	15 3.5	22 37.3	21 31.4	5 30.3
25 M	14 15 32.8	12 12.1	21 4.3	3 59.0	21 16.0	3 13.8	17 50.4	9 15.9	15 3.7	22 36.7	21 31.2	5 32.5
28 T	14 27 22.4	13 13.1	21 2.5	8N49.6	20 47.9	4 41.0	18 25.8	9 29.9	15 3.6	22 36.1	21 30.9	5 34.7
31 S	14 39 12.1	14 12.2	21 0.8	18 39.4	19 43.9	6 7.6	18 59.9	9 43.8	15 3.2	22 35.4	21 30.6	5 36.8

NOVEMBER 1993

DAY	EPHEMERIS SIDEREAL TIME	☉	☊	☽	☿	♀	♂	♃	♄	♅	♆	♇
	h m s	° ′	° ′	° ′	° ′	° ′	° ′	° ′	° ′	° ′	° ′	° ′
					LONGITUDE at NOON							
1 M	14 43 8.7	9♏ 5.1	4♐18.0	0♊53.9	19♏19.8	20♎31.5	24♏30.0	28♎ 6.8	23♒39.0	18♑44.8	18♑40.1	24♏47.2
2 T	14 47 5.2	10 5.2	4 14.8	13 9.2	18R 17.3	21 46.4	25 12.5	28 19.7	23 39.5	18 46.5	18 41.2	24 49.5
3 W	14 51 1.8	11 5.2	4 11.6	25 35.1	17 7.8	23 1.3	25 55.2	28 32.6	23 40.1	18 48.3	18 42.3	24 51.9
4 T	14 54 58.3	12 5.3	4 8.4	8♋14.2	15 53.1	24 16.3	26 37.8	28 45.5	23 40.8	18 50.2	18 43.5	24 54.2
5 F	14 58 54.9	13 5.5	4 5.2	21 9.1	14 35.1	25 31.3	27 20.6	28 58.4	23 41.6	18 52.1	18 44.6	24 56.6
6 S	15 2 51.4	14 5.6	4 2.1	4♌22.5	13 16.2	26 46.3	28 3.4	29 11.2	23 42.5	18 54.0	18 45.8	24 58.9
7 S	15 6 48.0	15 5.9	3 58.9	17 56.6	11 58.9	28 1.4	28 46.3	29 24.0	23 43.5	18 56.0	18 47.0	25 1.3
8 M	15 10 44.5	16 6.1	3 55.7	1♍52.7	10 45.7	29 16.5	29 29.2	29 36.9	23 44.7	18 58.1	18 48.3	25 3.7
9 T	15 14 41.1	17 6.4	3 52.5	16 10.3	9 38.9	0♏31.6	0♐12.2	29 49.7	23 45.9	19 0.2	18 49.6	25 6.1
10 W	15 18 37.7	18 6.7	3 49.4	0♎47.1	8 40.6	1 46.7	0 55.3	0♏ 2.4	23 47.3	19 2.3	18 50.9	25 8.5
11 T	15 22 34.2	19 7.1	3 46.2	15 38.4	7 52.2	3 1.8	1 38.4	0 15.1	23 48.7	19 4.4	18 52.3	25 10.9
12 F	15 26 30.8	20 7.5	3 43.0	0♏37.1	7 14.8	4 17.0	2 21.5	0 27.8	23 50.2	19 6.6	18 53.6	25 13.3
13 S	15 30 27.3	21 7.9	3 39.8	15 35.1	6 49.0	5 32.2	3 4.8	0 40.5	23 51.9	19 8.9	18 55.0	25 15.7
14 S	15 34 23.9	22 8.3	3 36.7	0♐23.7	6 34.9	6 47.4	3 48.1	0 53.1	23 53.6	19 11.2	18 56.5	25 18.1
15 M	15 38 20.4	23 8.7	3 33.5	14 55.4	6 32.3	8 2.6	4 31.4	1 5.7	23 55.4	19 13.5	18 57.9	25 20.5
16 T	15 42 17.0	24 9.2	3 30.3	29 4.8	6D40.6	9 17.9	5 14.8	1 18.3	23 57.4	19 15.9	18 59.4	25 22.9
17 W	15 46 13.5	25 9.7	3 27.1	12♑48.9	6 59.2	10 33.1	5 58.2	1 30.8	23 59.4	19 18.3	19 0.9	25 25.3
18 T	15 50 10.1	26 10.3	3 23.9	26 7.1	7 27.2	11 48.4	6 41.7	1 43.3	24 1.6	19 20.7	19 2.4	25 27.7
19 F	15 54 6.7	27 10.8	3 20.8	9♒ 1.0	8 3.8	13 3.7	7 25.3	1 55.7	24 3.8	19 23.2	19 4.0	25 30.1
20 S	15 58 3.2	28 11.4	3 17.6	21 33.7	8 48.0	14 18.9	8 8.9	2 8.1	24 6.1	19 25.7	19 5.6	25 32.5
21 S	16 1 59.8	29 12.0	3 14.4	3♓49.0	9 38.9	15 34.2	8 52.6	2 20.4	24 8.6	19 28.2	19 7.2	25 34.9
22 M	16 5 56.3	0♐12.6	3 11.2	15 51.5	10 35.9	16 49.6	9 36.3	2 32.7	24 11.1	19 30.8	19 8.8	25 37.3
23 T	16 9 52.9	1 13.2	3 8.1	27 45.9	11 38.0	18 4.9	10 20.1	2 45.0	24 13.7	19 33.4	19 10.4	25 39.7
24 W	16 13 49.4	2 13.9	3 4.9	9♈36.4	12 44.6	19 20.2	11 3.9	2 57.2	24 16.5	19 36.1	19 12.1	25 42.1
25 T	16 17 46.0	3 14.5	3 1.7	21 27.0	13 55.1	20 35.5	11 47.8	3 9.3	24 19.3	19 38.8	19 13.8	25 44.5
26 F	16 21 42.6	4 15.2	2 58.5	3♉21.4	15 8.9	21 50.9	12 31.7	3 21.4	24 22.2	19 41.5	19 15.5	25 46.9
27 S	16 25 39.1	5 15.9	2 55.4	15 22.5	16 25.6	23 6.3	13 15.7	3 33.5	24 25.2	19 44.3	19 17.3	25 49.3
28 S	16 29 35.7	6 16.7	2 52.2	27 32.4	17 44.8	24 21.6	13 59.7	3 45.5	24 28.3	19 47.1	19 19.1	25 51.7
29 M	16 33 32.2	7 17.5	2 49.0	9♊53.1	19 6.0	25 37.1	14 43.9	3 57.5	24 31.6	19 49.9	19 20.9	25 54.1
30 T	16 37 28.8	8 18.2	2 45.8	22 25.6	20 29.1	26 52.5	15 28.0	4 9.4	24 34.8	19 52.8	19 22.7	25 56.4
					DECLINATION at NOON							
1 M	14 43 8.7	14S31.4	21S 0.2	20N31.9	19S14.2	6S36.2	19S10.9	9S48.4	15S 2.9	22S35.1	21S30.5	5S37.5
4 T	14 54 58.3	15 27.8	20 58.4	20 9.1	17 22.8	8 1.3	19 43.2	10 2.1	15 2.1	22 34.3	21 30.1	5 39.6
7 S	15 6 48.0	16 21.9	20 56.7	10 36.4	15 14.1	9 24.9	20 13.9	10 15.7	15 0.9	22 33.5	21 29.7	5 41.6
10 W	15 18 37.7	17 13.5	20 54.9	4S35.8	13 18.4	10 46.6	20 43.1	10 29.1	14 59.5	22 32.5	21 29.3	5 43.6
13 S	15 30 27.3	18 2.4	20 53.1	18 1.4	12 2.6	12 6.1	21 10.7	10 42.3	14 57.7	22 31.6	21 28.8	5 45.5
16 T	15 42 17.0	18 48.6	20 51.3	21 6.4	11 36.5	13 23.1	21 36.6	10 55.3	14 55.6	22 30.5	21 28.3	5 47.3
19 F	15 54 6.7	19 31.7	20 49.4	13 19.9	11 54.4	14 37.1	22 0.7	11 8.1	14 53.2	22 29.5	21 27.7	5 49.1
22 M	16 5 56.3	20 11.6	20 47.6	0 49.0	12 44.3	15 47.8	22 22.9	11 20.7	14 50.5	22 28.3	21 27.1	5 50.8
25 T	16 17 46.0	20 48.2	20 45.8	11N37.5	13 54.3	16 54.8	22 43.3	11 33.0	14 47.6	22 27.1	21 26.5	5 52.4
28 S	16 29 35.7	21 21.3	20 43.9	20 6.4	15 14.8	17 57.8	23 1.6	11 45.1	14 44.3	22 25.9	21 25.8	5 53.9

DECEMBER 1993

DAY	EPHEMERIS SIDEREAL TIME	☉	☊	☽	☿	♀	♂	♃	♄	♅	♆	♇
					LONGITUDE at NOON							
1 W	16 41 25.3	9♐19.0	2♐42.6	5♋10.8	21♏53.6	28♏ 7.9	16♐12.2	4♏21.2	24♒38.2	19♑55.7	19♑24.5	25♏58.8
2 T	16 45 21.9	10 19.8	2 39.5	18 9.2	23 19.4	29 23.3	16 56.5	4 33.0	24 41.7	19 58.6	19 26.4	26 1.1
3 F	16 49 18.5	11 20.7	2 36.3	1♌21.0	24 46.2	0♐38.7	17 40.8	4 44.7	24 45.2	20 1.5	19 28.3	26 3.5
4 S	16 53 15.0	12 21.5	2 33.1	14 46.6	26 14.0	1 54.1	18 25.2	4 56.3	24 48.9	20 4.5	19 30.2	26 5.8
5 S	16 57 11.6	13 22.4	2 29.9	28 25.8	27 42.6	3 9.6	19 9.6	5 7.9	24 52.6	20 7.5	19 32.1	26 8.1
6 M	17 1 8.1	14 23.3	2 26.8	12♍18.6	29 11.8	4 25.0	19 54.0	5 19.5	24 56.4	20 10.6	19 34.0	26 10.5
7 T	17 5 4.7	15 24.2	2 23.6	26 24.1	0♐41.5	5 40.5	20 38.6	5 30.9	25 0.3	20 13.6	19 36.0	26 12.8
8 W	17 9 1.2	16 25.2	2 20.4	10♎41.0	2 11.8	6 56.0	21 23.2	5 42.3	25 4.3	20 16.7	19 37.9	26 15.1
9 T	17 12 57.8	17 26.1	2 17.2	25 6.9	3 42.4	8 11.4	22 7.8	5 53.6	25 8.4	20 19.8	19 39.9	26 17.3
10 F	17 16 54.4	18 27.1	2 14.1	9♏38.0	5 13.4	9 26.9	22 52.5	6 4.8	25 12.6	20 22.9	19 41.9	26 19.6
11 S	17 20 50.9	19 28.1	2 10.9	24 9.8	6 44.6	10 42.4	23 37.2	6 16.0	25 16.8	20 26.1	19 43.9	26 21.9
12 S	17 24 47.5	20 29.1	2 7.7	8♐36.7	8 16.2	11 57.9	24 22.0	6 27.1	25 21.1	20 29.3	19 46.0	26 24.1
13 M	17 28 44.0	21 30.2	2 4.5	22 53.2	9 47.9	13 13.4	25 6.8	6 38.1	25 25.5	20 32.5	19 48.0	26 26.3
14 T	17 32 40.6	22 31.2	2 1.3	6♑54.1	11 19.9	14 28.9	25 51.7	6 49.1	25 30.0	20 35.7	19 50.1	26 28.6
15 W	17 36 37.1	23 32.3	1 58.2	20 35.5	12 52.1	15 44.4	26 36.7	6 59.9	25 34.6	20 39.0	19 52.1	26 30.8
16 T	17 40 33.7	24 33.3	1 55.0	3♒55.1	14 24.4	16 59.9	27 21.6	7 10.7	25 39.2	20 42.3	19 54.2	26 33.0
17 F	17 44 30.3	25 34.4	1 51.8	16 52.5	15 56.9	18 15.4	28 6.7	7 21.4	25 43.9	20 45.5	19 56.3	26 35.1
18 S	17 48 26.8	26 35.5	1 48.6	29 29.0	17 29.6	19 30.9	28 51.8	7 32.0	25 48.7	20 48.9	19 58.5	26 37.3
19 S	17 52 23.4	27 36.6	1 45.5	11♓47.5	19 2.4	20 46.4	29 36.9	7 42.5	25 53.6	20 52.2	20 0.6	26 39.4
20 M	17 56 19.9	28 37.7	1 42.3	23 51.9	20 35.5	22 2.0	0♑22.1	7 52.9	25 58.6	20 55.6	20 2.8	26 41.6
21 T	18 0 16.5	29 38.8	1 39.1	5♈46.7	22 8.7	23 17.5	1 7.3	8 3.3	26 3.6	20 58.9	20 4.9	26 43.7
22 W	18 4 13.0	0♑39.9	1 35.9	17 36.9	23 42.1	24 33.0	1 52.6	8 13.5	26 8.7	21 2.3	20 7.1	26 45.8
23 T	18 8 9.6	1 41.0	1 32.8	29 27.6	25 15.6	25 48.5	2 37.9	8 23.6	26 13.8	21 5.7	20 9.3	26 47.9
24 F	18 12 6.2	2 42.1	1 29.6	11♉23.4	26 49.4	27 4.0	3 23.2	8 33.7	26 19.1	21 9.1	20 11.5	26 49.9
25 S	18 16 2.7	3 43.2	1 26.4	23 28.7	28 23.4	28 19.5	4 8.6	8 43.6	26 24.4	21 12.6	20 13.7	26 52.0
26 S	18 19 59.3	4 44.3	1 23.2	5♊47.0	29 57.6	29 35.0	4 54.1	8 53.5	26 29.7	21 16.0	20 15.9	26 54.0
27 M	18 23 55.8	5 45.5	1 20.1	18 21.0	1♑32.1	0♑50.5	5 39.6	9 3.2	26 35.1	21 19.4	20 18.1	26 56.0
28 T	18 27 52.4	6 46.6	1 16.9	1♋11.9	3 6.8	2 6.0	6 25.1	9 12.9	26 40.6	21 22.9	20 20.3	26 57.9
29 W	18 31 48.9	7 47.7	1 13.7	14 20.1	4 41.8	3 21.5	7 10.7	9 22.4	26 46.2	21 26.4	20 22.5	26 59.9
30 T	18 35 45.5	8 48.8	1 10.5	27 44.4	6 17.1	4 37.0	7 56.3	9 31.8	26 51.8	21 29.9	20 24.8	27 1.8
31 F	18 39 42.1	9 49.9	1 7.3	11♌22.7	7 52.7	5 52.5	8 41.9	9 41.2	26 57.5	21 33.4	20 27.0	27 3.7
					DECLINATION at NOON							
1 W	16 41 25.3	21S50.8	20S42.1	20N31.3	16S39.3	18S56.5	23S18.0	11S56.9	14S40.8	22S24.6	21S25.1	5S55.4
4 S	16 53 15.0	22 16.5	20 40.2	11 35.7	18 3.1	19 50.5	23 32.2	12 8.4	14 37.0	22 23.3	21 24.4	5 56.8
7 T	17 5 4.7	22 38.4	20 38.3	3S 1.2	19 23.0	20 39.4	23 44.3	12 19.7	14 32.9	22 21.9	21 23.6	5 58.0
10 F	17 16 54.4	22 56.2	20 36.5	16 41.3	20 36.9	21 23.1	23 54.2	12 30.7	14 28.6	22 20.5	21 22.8	5 59.2
13 M	17 28 44.0	23 10.0	20 34.6	21 27.5	21 43.2	22 1.1	24 1.8	12 41.3	14 24.0	22 19.1	21 22.0	6 0.3
16 T	17 40 33.7	23 19.6	20 32.7	14 48.4	22 40.6	22 33.2	24 7.1	12 51.7	14 19.2	22 17.6	21 21.1	6 1.3
19 S	17 52 23.4	23 25.0	20 30.8	2 20.9	23 28.4	22 59.2	24 10.1	13 1.7	14 14.2	22 16.1	21 20.3	6 2.2
22 W	18 4 13.0	23 26.2	20 28.8	10N21.0	24 5.7	23 19.0	24 10.8	13 11.4	14 8.9	22 14.5	21 19.4	6 3.1
25 S	18 16 2.7	23 23.2	20 26.9	19 28.0	24 31.8	23 32.3	24 9.0	13 20.7	14 3.4	22 12.9	21 18.5	6 3.8
28 T	18 27 52.4	23 15.9	20 25.0	20 57.3	24 46.1	23 39.1	24 4.9	13 29.6	13 57.7	22 11.3	21 17.5	6 4.4
31 F	18 39 42.1	23 4.4	20 23.0	12 43.2	24 48.1	23 39.3	23 58.4	13 38.2	13 51.8	22 9.7	21 16.6	6 4.9

JANUARY 1994

DAY	EPHEMERIS SIDEREAL TIME	☉	☊	☾	☿	♀	♂	♃	♄	♅	♆	♇
	h m s	° ′	° ′	° ′	° ′	° ′	° ′	° ′	° ′	° ′	° ′	° ′
						LONGITUDE at NOON						
1 S	18 43 38.6	10♑51.1	1♐ 4.2	25♌12.3	9♑28.6	7♑ 8.0	9♑27.6	9♏50.4	27♒ 3.2	21♑36.9	20♑29.2	27♏ 5.6
2 S	18 47 35.2	11 52.2	1 1.0	9♍10.2	11 4.8	8 23.5	10 13.4	9 59.5	27 9.0	21 40.4	20 31.5	27 7.5
3 M	18 51 31.7	12 53.4	0 57.8	23 13.6	12 41.4	9 39.0	10 59.2	10 8.5	27 14.9	21 43.9	20 33.8	27 9.3
4 T	18 55 28.3	13 54.5	0 54.6	7♎20.1	14 18.3	10 54.5	11 45.0	10 17.4	27 20.8	21 47.4	20 36.0	27 11.1
5 W	18 59 24.8	14 55.7	0 51.5	21 27.9	15 55.7	12 10.0	12 30.9	10 26.1	27 26.7	21 51.0	20 38.3	27 12.9
6 T	19 3 21.4	15 56.8	0 48.3	5♏35.6	17 33.4	13 25.5	13 16.8	10 34.8	27 32.8	21 54.5	20 40.5	27 14.7
7 F	19 7 18.0	16 58.0	0 45.1	19 41.9	19 11.5	14 41.0	14 2.7	10 43.3	27 38.8	21 58.1	20 42.8	27 16.4
8 S	19 11 14.5	17 59.1	0 41.9	3♐45.1	20 50.0	15 56.4	14 48.7	10 51.7	27 45.0	22 1.6	20 45.1	27 18.1
9 S	19 15 11.1	19 0.3	0 38.8	17 43.2	22 28.9	17 11.9	15 34.8	10 60.0	27 51.2	22 5.2	20 47.4	27 19.8
10 M	19 19 7.6	20 1.5	0 35.6	1♑33.6	24 8.3	18 27.5	16 20.9	11 8.2	27 57.4	22 8.8	20 49.7	27 21.5
11 T	19 23 4.2	21 2.7	0 32.4	15 13.3	25 48.0	19 43.0	17 7.0	11 16.2	28 3.7	22 12.3	20 52.0	27 23.1
12 W	19 27 0.7	22 3.8	0 29.2	28 39.1	27 28.1	20 58.4	17 53.1	11 24.1	28 10.1	22 15.9	20 54.2	27 24.7
13 T	19 30 57.3	23 4.9	0 26.0	11♒48.9	29 8.6	22 13.9	18 39.3	11 31.9	28 16.4	22 19.4	20 56.5	27 26.3
14 F	19 34 53.9	24 6.1	0 22.9	24 41.1	0♒49.4	23 29.4	19 25.5	11 39.5	28 22.9	22 23.0	20 58.8	27 27.9
15 S	19 38 50.4	25 7.2	0 19.7	7♓15.6	2 30.6	24 44.9	20 11.8	11 47.0	28 29.3	22 26.5	21 1.1	27 29.4
16 S	19 42 47.0	26 8.3	0 16.5	19 33.9	4 12.0	26 0.3	20 58.1	11 54.3	28 35.9	22 30.1	21 3.3	27 30.9
17 M	19 46 43.5	27 9.4	0 13.3	1♈38.5	5 53.7	27 15.8	21 44.4	12 1.5	28 42.4	22 33.6	21 5.6	27 32.3
18 T	19 50 40.1	28 10.5	0 10.2	13 33.3	7 35.5	28 31.2	22 30.8	12 8.6	28 49.0	22 37.2	21 7.9	27 33.8
19 W	19 54 36.6	29 11.6	0 7.0	25 22.9	9 17.4	29 46.6	23 17.1	12 15.6	28 55.6	22 40.7	21 10.1	27 35.2
20 T	19 58 33.2	0♒12.7	0 3.8	7♉12.5	10 59.4	1♒ 2.1	24 3.6	12 22.3	29 2.3	22 44.3	21 12.4	27 36.6
21 F	20 2 29.8	1 13.7	0 0.6	19 7.6	12 41.1	2 17.5	24 50.0	12 29.0	29 9.0	22 47.8	21 14.6	27 37.9
22 S	20 6 26.3	2 14.7	29♏57.5	1♊13.4	14 22.7	3 32.9	25 36.5	12 35.5	29 15.8	22 51.3	21 16.9	27 39.2
23 S	20 10 22.9	3 15.8	29 54.3	13 34.9	16 3.7	4 48.3	26 23.0	12 41.8	29 22.6	22 54.8	21 19.1	27 40.5
24 M	20 14 19.4	4 16.8	29 51.1	26 16.1	17 44.2	6 3.6	27 9.5	12 48.0	29 29.4	22 58.3	21 21.3	27 41.7
25 T	20 18 16.0	5 17.7	29 47.9	9♋19.5	19 23.7	7 19.0	27 56.1	12 54.1	29 36.2	23 1.8	21 23.6	27 43.0
26 W	20 22 12.5	6 18.7	29 44.7	22 45.9	21 2.1	8 34.4	28 42.7	12 60.0	29 43.1	23 5.3	21 25.8	27 44.1
27 T	20 26 9.1	7 19.7	29 41.6	6♌34.1	22 38.9	9 49.7	29 29.3	13 5.7	29 50.0	23 8.8	21 28.0	27 45.3
28 F	20 30 5.6	8 20.6	29 38.4	20 40.3	24 13.9	11 5.1	0♒15.9	13 11.3	29 57.0	23 12.3	21 30.2	27 46.4
29 S	20 34 2.2	9 21.5	29 35.2	4♍59.4	25 46.6	12 20.4	1 2.6	13 16.7	0♓ 3.9	23 15.7	21 32.4	27 47.5
30 S	20 37 58.8	10 22.4	29 32.0	19 25.2	27 16.5	13 35.7	1 49.3	13 22.0	0 10.9	23 19.2	21 34.6	27 48.6
31 M	20 41 55.3	11 23.4	29 28.9	3♎51.6	28 43.0	14 51.1	2 36.1	13 27.2	0 18.0	23 22.6	21 36.8	27 49.6
						DECLINATION at NOON						
1 S	18 43 38.6	22S59.7	20S22.4	8N16.9	24S45.9	23S37.9	23S55.7	13S41.0	13S49.8	22S 9.1	21S16.2	6S 5.1
4 T	18 55 28.3	22 42.7	20 20.4	6S48.0	24 30.8	23 29.3	23 46.0	13 49.0	13 43.7	22 7.4	21 15.3	6 5.5
7 F	19 7 18.0	22 21.7	20 18.4	18 44.5	24 2.2	23 14.2	23 33.9	13 56.7	13 37.3	22 5.8	21 14.3	6 5.8
10 M	19 19 7.6	21 56.7	20 16.5	20 54.4	23 19.9	22 52.6	23 19.3	14 4.0	13 30.8	22 4.0	21 13.3	6 6.0
13 T	19 30 57.3	21 27.8	20 14.5	12 37.8	22 23.6	22 24.6	23 2.5	14 10.9	13 24.2	22 2.3	21 12.3	6 6.0
16 S	19 42 47.0	20 55.3	20 12.5	0N19.8	21 13.3	21 50.6	22 43.3	14 17.3	13 17.4	22 0.6	21 11.2	6 6.0
19 W	19 54 36.6	20 19.1	20 10.5	12 36.2	19 49.2	21 10.6	22 21.8	14 23.3	13 10.4	21 58.9	21 10.2	6 5.9
22 S	20 6 26.3	19 39.5	20 8.4	20 24.1	18 12.1	20 24.9	21 58.0	14 28.9	13 3.4	21 57.2	21 9.2	6 5.7
25 T	20 18 16.0	18 56.7	20 6.4	19 58.5	16 23.4	19 33.8	21 32.1	14 34.0	12 56.2	21 55.4	21 8.2	6 5.5
28 F	20 30 5.6	18 10.7	20 4.4	9 53.4	14 25.8	18 37.6	21 3.9	14 38.7	12 48.9	21 53.7	21 7.2	6 5.1
31 M	20 41 55.3	17 21.7	20 2.3	5S23.1	12 23.9	17 36.6	20 33.7	14 42.9	12 41.5	21 52.0	21 6.1	6 4.6

FEBRUARY 1994

DAY	EPHEMERIS SIDEREAL TIME	☉	☊	☾	☿	♀	♂	♃	♄	♅	♆	♇
						LONGITUDE at NOON						
1 T	20 45 51.9	12♒24.3	29♏25.7	18♎13.5	0♓ 5.6	16♒ 6.4	3♒22.8	13♏32.1	0♓25.0	23♑26.1	21♑38.9	27♏50.6
2 W	20 49 48.4	13 25.1	29 22.5	2♏27.4	1 23.5	17 21.7	4 9.6	13 36.9	0 32.1	23 29.5	21 41.1	27 51.6
3 T	20 53 45.0	14 26.0	29 19.3	16 31.7	2 36.0	18 37.0	4 56.4	13 41.5	0 39.2	23 32.8	21 43.2	27 52.5
4 F	20 57 41.5	15 26.9	29 16.2	0♐25.7	3 42.5	19 52.3	5 43.2	13 45.9	0 46.3	23 36.2	21 45.4	27 53.4
5 S	21 1 38.1	16 27.7	29 13.0	14 9.6	4 42.1	21 7.5	6 30.1	13 50.2	0 53.4	23 39.6	21 47.5	27 54.3
6 S	21 5 34.6	17 28.5	29 9.8	27 43.8	5 34.0	22 22.8	7 16.9	13 54.3	1 0.6	23 42.9	21 49.6	27 55.1
7 M	21 9 31.2	18 29.3	29 6.6	11♑ 8.3	6 17.5	23 38.1	8 3.8	13 58.3	1 7.8	23 46.2	21 51.7	27 55.9
8 T	21 13 27.8	19 30.1	29 3.4	24 22.7	6 51.8	24 53.3	8 50.8	14 2.0	1 15.0	23 49.5	21 53.7	27 56.6
9 W	21 17 24.3	20 30.8	29 0.3	7♒26.1	7 16.4	26 8.5	9 37.7	14 5.6	1 22.2	23 52.8	21 55.8	27 57.3
10 T	21 21 20.9	21 31.6	28 57.1	20 17.5	7 30.7	27 23.7	10 24.7	14 9.0	1 29.4	23 56.0	21 57.8	27 58.0
11 F	21 25 17.4	22 32.3	28 53.9	2♓56.0	7 34.5	28 39.0	11 11.6	14 12.3	1 36.6	23 59.3	21 59.9	27 58.7
12 S	21 29 14.0	23 33.0	28 50.7	15 21.3	7R27.5	29 54.1	11 58.6	14 15.3	1 43.9	24 2.5	22 1.9	27 59.3
13 S	21 33 10.5	24 33.7	28 47.6	27 33.8	7 9.9	1♓ 9.3	12 45.6	14 18.2	1 51.1	24 5.7	22 3.9	27 59.8
14 M	21 37 7.1	25 34.3	28 44.4	9♈35.1	6 42.1	2 24.5	13 32.7	14 20.9	1 58.4	24 8.9	22 5.8	28 0.4
15 T	21 41 3.6	26 34.9	28 41.2	21 28.0	6 4.7	3 39.6	14 19.7	14 23.4	2 5.6	24 12.0	22 7.8	28 0.9
16 W	21 45 0.2	27 35.5	28 38.0	3♉16.2	5 18.7	4 54.7	15 6.8	14 25.7	2 12.9	24 15.1	22 9.8	28 1.4
17 T	21 48 56.7	28 36.1	28 34.8	15 4.1	4 25.3	6 9.8	15 53.8	14 27.9	2 20.2	24 18.2	22 11.7	28 1.8
18 F	21 52 53.3	29 36.6	28 31.7	26 57.1	3 25.9	7 24.9	16 40.9	14 29.9	2 27.5	24 21.3	22 13.6	28 2.2
19 S	21 56 49.8	0♓37.1	28 28.5	9♊ 0.7	2 22.2	8 40.0	17 28.0	14 31.6	2 34.8	24 24.3	22 15.5	28 2.6
20 S	22 0 46.4	1 37.6	28 25.3	21 20.3	1 16.0	9 55.0	18 15.1	14 33.2	2 42.1	24 27.3	22 17.3	28 2.9
21 M	22 4 43.0	2 38.1	28 22.1	4♋ 1.3	0 8.9	11 10.1	19 2.2	14 34.7	2 49.4	24 30.4	22 19.2	28 3.2
22 T	22 8 39.5	3 38.5	28 19.0	17 7.4	29♒ 2.6	12 25.1	19 49.3	14 35.9	2 56.7	24 33.3	22 21.1	28 3.5
23 W	22 12 36.1	4 38.9	28 15.8	0♌41.0	27 58.6	13 40.1	20 36.5	14 36.9	3 4.0	24 36.2	22 22.9	28 3.7
24 T	22 16 32.6	5 39.2	28 12.6	14 41.7	26 58.4	14 55.0	21 23.6	14 37.8	3 11.3	24 39.1	22 24.6	28 3.9
25 F	22 20 29.2	6 39.6	28 9.4	29 6.4	26 3.1	16 10.0	22 10.7	14 38.5	3 18.6	24 42.0	22 26.4	28 4.0
26 S	22 24 25.7	7 39.9	28 6.2	13♍49.0	25 13.5	17 24.9	22 57.9	14 38.9	3 25.9	24 44.8	22 28.1	28 4.1
27 S	22 28 22.3	8 40.1	28 3.1	28 41.2	24 30.4	18 39.8	23 45.0	14 39.2	3 33.1	24 47.6	22 29.9	28 4.2
28 M	22 32 18.8	9 40.4	27 59.9	13♎34.2	23 54.0	19 54.7	24 32.2	14 39.3	3 40.4	24 50.4	22 31.6	28 4.3
						DECLINATION at NOON						
1 T	20 45 51.9	17S 4.8	20S 1.7	10S15.6	11S43.4	17S15.3	20S23.2	14S44.2	12S39.0	21S51.4	21S 5.8	6S 4.4
4 F	20 57 41.5	16 12.2	19 59.6	20 11.9	9 47.0	16 8.3	19 50.2	14 47.8	12 31.5	21 49.7	21 4.8	6 3.9
7 M	21 9 31.2	15 17.1	19 57.5	19 39.5	8 6.4	14 57.4	19 15.3	14 51.0	12 23.9	21 48.1	21 3.8	6 3.2
10 T	21 21 20.9	14 19.7	19 55.5	10 1.8	6 53.3	13 42.7	18 38.5	14 53.6	12 16.3	21 46.4	21 2.8	6 2.4
13 S	21 33 10.5	13 20.1	19 53.4	3N 3.3	6 17.9	12 24.8	17 60.0	14 55.8	12 8.6	21 44.8	21 1.9	6 1.6
16 W	21 45 0.2	12 18.5	19 51.3	14 36.4	6 25.0	11 3.8	17 19.7	14 57.5	12 0.9	21 43.2	21 0.9	6 0.7
19 S	21 56 49.8	11 15.2	19 49.2	20 51.7	7 10.7	9 40.2	16 37.7	14 58.6	11 53.2	21 41.6	20 60.0	5 59.7
22 T	22 8 39.5	10 10.3	19 47.1	18 34.1	8 21.8	8 14.3	15 54.2	14 59.4	11 45.4	21 40.1	20 59.1	5 58.7
25 F	22 20 29.2	9 4.0	19 45.0	7 5.0	9 41.5	6 46.5	15 9.3	14 59.6	11 37.7	21 38.6	20 58.2	5 57.6
28 M	22 32 18.8	7 56.5	19 42.8	8S32.8	10 55.2	5 17.1	14 22.9	14 59.3	11 29.9	21 37.2	20 57.4	5 56.5

MARCH 1994

LONGITUDE at NOON

DAY	EPHEMERIS SIDEREAL TIME h m s	☉ ° ′	☊ ° ′	☽ ° ′	☿ ° ′	♀ ° ′	♂ ° ′	♃ ° ′	♄ ° ′	♅ ° ′	♆ ° ′	♇ ° ′
1 T	22 36 15.4	10♓40.6	27♏56.7	28♎19.9	23♒24.7	21♓ 9.5	25♒19.3	14♏39.2	3♓47.7	24♑53.2	22♑33.2	28♏ 4.3
2 W	22 40 11.9	11 40.7	27 53.5	12♏52.1	23R 2.6	22 24.3	26 6.5	14R39.0	3 54.9	24 55.9	22 34.9	28R 4.2
3 T	22 44 8.5	12 40.9	27 50.4	27 7.3	22 47.5	23 39.2	26 53.7	14 38.5	4 2.2	24 58.5	22 36.5	28 4.2
4 F	22 48 5.0	13 41.0	27 47.2	11♐ 4.2	22 39.3	24 54.0	27 40.9	14 37.9	4 9.4	25 1.2	22 38.1	28 4.1
5 S	22 52 1.6	14 41.1	27 44.0	24 43.2	22 37.7	26 8.7	28 28.1	14 37.0	4 16.6	25 3.8	22 39.7	28 3.9
6 S	22 55 58.1	15 41.2	27 40.8	8♑ 5.7	22D42.5	27 23.5	29 15.3	14 36.0	4 23.9	25 6.4	22 41.2	28 3.8
7 M	22 59 54.7	16 41.3	27 37.6	21 13.5	22 53.3	28 38.2	0♓ 2.5	14 34.8	4 31.1	25 8.9	22 42.8	28 3.6
8 T	23 3 51.2	17 41.3	27 34.5	4♒ 8.3	23 9.9	29 52.9	0 49.7	14 33.4	4 38.2	25 11.4	22 44.3	28 3.3
9 W	23 7 47.8	18 41.3	27 31.3	16 51.4	23 31.8	1♈ 7.6	1 36.8	14 31.8	4 45.4	25 13.8	22 45.7	28 3.1
10 T	23 11 44.4	19 41.3	27 28.1	29 23.5	23 58.7	2 22.3	2 24.0	14 30.0	4 52.6	25 16.3	22 47.2	28 2.7
11 F	23 15 40.9	20 41.2	27 24.9	11♓45.4	24 30.3	3 37.0	3 11.2	14 28.0	4 59.7	25 18.7	22 48.6	28 2.4
12 S	23 19 37.5	21 41.1	27 21.8	23 57.5	25 6.3	4 51.6	3 58.4	14 25.9	5 6.8	25 21.0	22 50.0	28 2.0
13 S	23 23 34.0	22 41.0	27 18.6	6♈ 0.7	25 46.5	6 6.2	4 45.6	14 23.5	5 13.9	25 23.3	22 51.4	28 1.6
14 M	23 27 30.6	23 40.9	27 15.4	17 56.3	26 30.5	7 20.8	5 32.8	14 21.1	5 21.0	25 25.6	22 52.7	28 1.2
15 T	23 31 27.1	24 40.7	27 12.2	29 46.1	27 18.1	8 35.3	6 20.0	14 18.4	5 28.0	25 27.8	22 54.1	28 0.8
16 W	23 35 23.7	25 40.5	27 9.0	11♉32.9	28 9.0	9 49.9	7 7.2	14 15.5	5 35.1	25 30.0	22 55.3	28 0.2
17 T	23 39 20.2	26 40.2	27 5.9	23 20.3	29 3.1	11 4.3	7 54.3	14 12.4	5 42.0	25 32.2	22 56.6	27 59.7
18 F	23 43 16.8	27 39.9	27 2.7	5♊12.6	0♓ 0.1	12 18.8	8 41.5	14 9.2	5 49.0	25 34.3	22 57.8	27 59.1
19 S	23 47 13.3	28 39.6	26 59.5	17 14.6	0 59.9	13 33.2	9 28.6	14 5.8	5 55.9	25 36.3	22 59.0	27 58.5
20 S	23 51 9.9	29 39.2	26 56.3	29 31.6	2 2.4	14 47.6	10 15.7	14 2.2	6 2.9	25 38.3	23 0.2	27 57.9
21 M	23 55 6.4	0♈38.8	26 53.1	12♋ 8.8	3 7.3	16 2.0	11 2.8	13 58.5	6 9.7	25 40.3	23 1.3	27 57.2
22 T	23 59 3.0	1 38.4	26 50.0	25 10.8	4 14.6	17 16.3	11 49.9	13 54.6	6 16.6	25 42.2	23 2.4	27 56.5
23 W	0 2 59.5	2 37.9	26 46.8	8♌40.9	5 24.1	18 30.6	12 37.0	13 50.5	6 23.4	25 44.1	23 3.5	27 55.8
24 T	0 6 56.1	3 37.4	26 43.6	22 40.6	6 35.7	19 44.9	13 24.1	13 46.2	6 30.2	25 46.0	23 4.5	27 55.0
25 F	0 10 52.6	4 36.8	26 40.4	7♍ 8.1	7 49.4	20 59.2	14 11.2	13 41.8	6 36.9	25 47.8	23 5.5	27 54.2
26 S	0 14 49.2	5 36.2	26 37.3	21 58.7	9 5.1	22 13.4	14 58.2	13 37.3	6 43.6	25 49.5	23 6.5	27 53.4
27 S	0 18 45.7	6 35.6	26 34.1	7♎ 4.5	10 22.6	23 27.5	15 45.2	13 32.6	6 50.3	25 51.2	23 7.5	27 52.6
28 M	0 22 42.3	7 34.9	26 30.9	22 15.6	11 42.0	24 41.7	16 32.3	13 27.7	6 56.9	25 52.9	23 8.4	27 51.7
29 T	0 26 38.8	8 34.2	26 27.7	7♏22.1	13 3.1	25 55.8	17 19.3	13 22.7	7 3.5	25 54.5	23 9.3	27 50.8
30 W	0 30 35.4	9 33.5	26 24.5	22 15.1	14 25.9	27 9.9	18 6.2	13 17.5	7 10.1	25 56.1	23 10.1	27 49.9
31 T	0 34 31.9	10 32.7	26 21.4	6♐48.4	15 50.4	28 23.9	18 53.2	13 12.2	7 16.6	25 57.6	23 11.0	27 48.9

DECLINATION at NOON

DAY	EPHEMERIS SIDEREAL TIME h m s	☉ ° ′	☊ ° ′	☽ ° ′	☿ ° ′	♀ ° ′	♂ ° ′	♃ ° ′	♄ ° ′	♅ ° ′	♆ ° ′	♇ ° ′
1 T	22 36 15.4	7S33.8	19S42.1	13S 8.3	11S16.8	4S47.0	14S 7.2	14S59.1	11S27.3	21S36.7	20S57.1	5S56.1
4 F	22 48 5.0	6 25.0	19 40.0	20 52.2	12 10.1	3 15.9	13 19.1	14 58.2	11 19.6	21 35.3	20 56.3	5 54.8
7 M	22 59 54.7	5 15.3	19 37.8	17 42.0	12 44.7	1 44.0	12 29.8	14 56.8	11 11.9	21 34.0	20 55.5	5 53.6
10 T	23 11 44.4	4 5.0	19 35.7	6 58.0	13 0.8	0 11.7	11 39.5	14 54.9	11 4.3	21 32.7	20 54.7	5 52.2
13 S	23 23 34.0	2 54.2	19 33.5	5N55.9	12 59.3	1N20.9	10 48.1	14 52.5	10 56.7	21 31.5	20 54.0	5 50.9
16 W	23 35 23.7	1 43.1	19 31.3	16 27.6	12 41.3	2 53.2	9 55.9	14 49.7	10 49.2	21 30.4	20 53.3	5 49.5
19 S	23 47 13.3	0 32.0	19 29.1	20 55.4	12 8.1	4 25.0	9 2.9	14 46.4	10 41.8	21 29.3	20 52.7	5 48.1
22 T	23 59 3.0	0N39.1	19 26.9	16 44.2	11 20.7	5 56.0	8 9.1	14 42.6	10 34.5	21 28.3	20 52.1	5 46.6
25 F	0 10 52.6	1 50.0	19 24.7	4 14.2	10 20.1	7 25.8	7 14.7	14 38.5	10 27.3	21 27.3	20 51.6	5 45.2
28 M	0 22 42.3	3 0.5	19 22.5	11S13.7	9 6.8	8 54.1	6 19.8	14 33.9	10 20.2	21 26.5	20 51.1	5 43.7
31 T	0 34 31.9	4 10.5	19 20.3	20 22.0	7 41.8	10 20.6	5 24.4	14 29.0	10 13.2	21 25.7	20 50.6	5 42.2

APRIL 1994

LONGITUDE at NOON

DAY	EPHEMERIS SIDEREAL TIME h m s	☉ ° ′	☊ ° ′	☽ ° ′	☿ ° ′	♀ ° ′	♂ ° ′	♃ ° ′	♄ ° ′	♅ ° ′	♆ ° ′	♇ ° ′
1 F	0 38 28.5	11♈31.9	26♏18.2	20♐58.7	17♓16.6	29♈37.9	19♓40.2	13♏ 6.8	7♓23.1	25♑59.1	23♑11.8	27♏47.9
2 S	0 42 25.1	12 31.1	26 15.0	4♑45.1	18 44.3	0♉51.9	20 27.1	13R 1.2	7 29.5	26 0.5	23 12.5	27R46.9
3 S	0 46 21.6	13 30.2	26 11.8	18 8.7	20 13.6	2 5.9	21 14.0	12 55.5	7 35.9	26 1.9	23 13.3	27 45.8
4 M	0 50 18.2	14 29.4	26 8.7	1♒11.9	21 44.6	3 19.9	22 1.0	12 49.7	7 42.3	26 3.3	23 14.0	27 44.8
5 T	0 54 14.7	15 28.5	26 5.5	13 57.2	23 17.0	4 33.8	22 47.9	12 43.7	7 48.6	26 4.5	23 14.7	27 43.7
6 W	0 58 11.3	16 27.6	26 2.3	26 27.7	24 51.0	5 47.6	23 34.7	12 37.6	7 54.9	26 5.8	23 15.3	27 42.6
7 T	1 2 7.8	17 26.6	25 59.1	8♓45.9	26 26.5	7 1.5	24 21.6	12 31.4	8 1.1	26 7.0	23 15.9	27 41.5
8 F	1 6 4.4	18 25.6	25 55.9	20 54.2	28 3.4	8 15.3	25 8.4	12 25.0	8 7.3	26 8.1	23 16.5	27 40.3
9 S	1 10 0.9	19 24.6	25 52.8	2♈54.7	29 42.0	9 29.1	25 55.2	12 18.6	8 13.4	26 9.2	23 17.0	27 39.1
10 S	1 13 57.5	20 23.5	25 49.6	14 49.0	1♈22.0	10 42.8	26 42.0	12 12.0	8 19.4	26 10.2	23 17.5	27 37.9
11 M	1 17 54.0	21 22.4	25 46.4	26 39.1	3 3.5	11 56.5	27 28.7	12 5.4	8 25.4	26 11.2	23 18.0	27 36.6
12 T	1 21 50.6	22 21.3	25 43.2	8♉26.7	4 46.6	13 10.2	28 15.5	11 58.6	8 31.4	26 12.2	23 18.4	27 35.4
13 W	1 25 47.1	23 20.1	25 40.1	20 14.2	6 31.2	14 23.8	29 2.1	11 51.8	8 37.3	26 13.1	23 18.8	27 34.1
14 T	1 29 43.7	24 18.9	25 36.9	2♊ 4.2	8 17.3	15 37.4	29 48.8	11 44.8	8 43.1	26 13.9	23 19.2	27 32.8
15 F	1 33 40.2	25 17.7	25 33.7	13 59.8	10 5.0	16 51.0	0♈35.4	11 37.8	8 48.9	26 14.7	23 19.5	27 31.5
16 S	1 37 36.8	26 16.4	25 30.5	26 4.8	11 54.3	18 4.5	1 22.0	11 30.7	8 54.7	26 15.4	23 19.8	27 30.1
17 S	1 41 33.3	27 15.1	25 27.3	8♋23.1	13 45.1	19 18.0	2 8.6	11 23.5	9 0.3	26 16.1	23 20.1	27 28.7
18 M	1 45 29.9	28 13.8	25 24.2	20 59.1	15 37.5	20 31.5	2 55.2	11 16.3	9 6.0	26 16.8	23 20.4	27 27.4
19 T	1 49 26.4	29 12.4	25 21.0	3♌57.0	17 31.4	21 44.9	3 41.7	11 9.0	9 11.5	26 17.4	23 20.6	27 26.0
20 W	1 53 23.0	0♉11.0	25 17.8	17 20.2	19 27.0	22 58.2	4 28.1	11 1.6	9 17.0	26 17.9	23 20.7	27 24.5
21 T	1 57 19.6	1 9.5	25 14.6	1♍10.9	21 24.1	24 11.6	5 14.6	10 54.2	9 22.4	26 18.4	23 20.9	27 23.1
22 F	2 1 16.1	2 8.0	25 11.5	15 28.9	23 22.7	25 24.9	6 1.0	10 46.7	9 27.8	26 18.8	23 21.0	27 21.7
23 S	2 5 12.7	3 6.5	25 8.3	0♎11.7	25 22.8	26 38.1	6 47.4	10 39.2	9 33.1	26 19.2	23 21.0	27 20.2
24 S	2 9 9.2	4 4.9	25 5.1	15 13.4	27 24.5	27 51.3	7 33.7	10 31.7	9 38.3	26 19.6	23 21.1	27 18.7
25 M	2 13 5.8	5 3.4	25 1.9	0♏26.0	29 27.5	29 4.5	8 20.1	10 24.2	9 43.6	26 19.9	23 21.1	27 17.2
26 T	2 17 2.3	6 1.8	24 58.7	15 39.5	1♉31.9	0♊17.6	9 6.3	10 16.6	9 48.7	26 20.1	23 21.1	27 15.7
27 W	2 20 58.9	7 0.1	24 55.6	0♐44.2	3 37.5	1 30.7	9 52.6	10 9.0	9 53.7	26 20.3	23 21.1	27 14.2
28 T	2 24 55.4	7 58.4	24 52.4	15 31.9	5 44.2	2 43.8	10 38.8	10 1.3	9 58.7	26 20.5	23R21.0	27 12.7
29 F	2 28 52.0	8 56.7	24 49.2	29 56.6	7 52.0	3 56.8	11 24.9	9 53.7	10 3.6	26 20.5	23 20.8	27 11.1
30 S	2 32 48.5	9 55.0	24 46.0	13♑55.4	10 0.5	5 9.7	12 11.1	9 46.0	10 8.4	26 20.6	23 20.7	27 9.6

DECLINATION at NOON

DAY	EPHEMERIS SIDEREAL TIME h m s	☉ ° ′	☊ ° ′	☽ ° ′	☿ ° ′	♀ ° ′	♂ ° ′	♃ ° ′	♄ ° ′	♅ ° ′	♆ ° ′	♇ ° ′
1 F	0 38 28.5	4N33.7	19S19.5	20S50.1	7S10.9	10N49.0	5S 5.9	14S27.2	10S10.9	21S25.4	20S50.5	5S41.7
4 M	0 50 18.2	5 42.7	19 17.3	15 15.1	5 31.0	12 12.5	4 10.0	14 21.8	10 4.1	21 24.7	20 50.0	5 40.2
7 T	1 2 7.8	6 50.9	19 15.1	3 37.7	3 40.6	13 33.4	3 13.9	14 16.1	9 57.5	21 24.1	20 49.7	5 38.8
10 S	1 13 57.5	7 58.0	19 12.8	8N52.5	1 40.4	14 51.3	2 17.7	14 10.0	9 51.1	21 23.6	20 49.4	5 37.3
13 W	1 25 47.1	9 3.9	19 10.5	18 7.8	0N29.0	16 6.0	1 21.4	14 3.7	9 44.8	21 23.2	20 49.1	5 35.8
16 S	1 37 36.8	10 8.5	19 8.3	20 35.3	2 46.8	17 17.0	0 25.1	13 57.2	9 38.7	21 22.8	20 48.9	5 34.4
19 T	1 49 26.4	11 11.5	19 6.0	14 27.9	5 12.0	18 24.1	0N31.0	13 50.5	9 32.8	21 22.5	20 48.8	5 33.0
22 F	2 1 16.1	12 12.8	19 3.7	1 12.7	7 43.1	19 26.8	1 27.0	13 43.6	9 27.2	21 22.4	20 48.7	5 31.6
25 M	2 13 5.8	13 12.4	19 1.4	13S35.1	10 17.9	20 25.0	2 22.7	13 36.6	9 21.7	21 22.3	20 48.6	5 30.3
28 T	2 24 55.4	14 10.0	18 59.1	20 42.4	12 53.5	21 18.3	3 18.1	13 29.6	9 16.5	21 22.2	20 48.6	5 29.0

MAY 1994

DAY	EPHEMERIS SIDEREAL TIME	☉	☊	☽	☿	♀	♂	♃	♄	♅	♆	♇
	h m s	° ′	° ′	° ′	° ′	° ′	° ′	° ′	° ′	° ′	° ′	° ′
						LONGITUDE at NOON						
1 S	2 36 45.1	10♉53.2	24♏42.9	27♑27.6	12♉ 9.6	6♊22.6	12♈57.2	9♏38.4	10♓13.2	26♑20.6	23♑20.5	27♏ 8.0
2 M	2 40 41.6	11 51.5	24 39.7	10♒34.8	14 19.1	7 35.5	13 43.2	9R30.7	10 17.9	26R20.5	23R20.3	27R 6.4
3 T	2 44 38.2	12 49.6	24 36.5	23 19.9	16 28.7	8 48.4	14 29.3	9 23.1	10 22.5	26 20.4	23 20.0	27 4.8
4 W	2 48 34.8	13 47.8	24 33.3	5♓46.4	18 38.3	10 1.2	15 15.2	9 15.4	10 27.1	26 20.2	23 19.7	27 3.2
5 T	2 52 31.3	14 46.0	24 30.1	17 58.1	20 47.4	11 13.9	16 1.2	9 7.8	10 31.5	26 20.0	23 19.4	27 1.6
6 F	2 56 27.9	15 44.1	24 27.0	29 58.9	22 55.8	12 26.7	16 47.1	9 0.2	10 35.9	26 19.8	23 19.1	26 59.9
7 S	3 0 24.4	16 42.2	24 23.8	11♈52.2	25 3.2	13 39.3	17 33.0	8 52.7	10 40.3	26 19.4	23 18.7	26 58.3
8 S	3 4 21.0	17 40.2	24 20.6	23 41.1	27 9.3	14 52.0	18 18.8	8 45.1	10 44.5	26 19.1	23 18.3	26 56.7
9 M	3 8 17.5	18 38.3	24 17.4	5♉28.5	29 13.8	16 4.6	19 4.6	8 37.7	10 48.7	26 18.7	23 17.8	26 55.0
10 T	3 12 14.1	19 36.3	24 14.3	17 16.8	1♊16.5	17 17.1	19 50.3	8 30.2	10 52.7	26 18.2	23 17.4	26 53.4
11 W	3 16 10.6	20 34.3	24 11.1	29 8.2	3 17.1	18 29.6	20 36.0	8 22.9	10 56.7	26 17.7	23 16.9	26 51.7
12 T	3 20 7.2	21 32.3	24 7.9	11♊ 5.0	5 15.3	19 42.1	21 21.6	8 15.5	11 0.7	26 17.2	23 16.3	26 50.1
13 F	3 24 3.8	22 30.2	24 4.7	23 9.3	7 11.1	20 54.5	22 7.2	8 8.3	11 4.5	26 16.5	23 15.8	26 48.4
14 S	3 28 0.3	23 28.1	24 1.5	5♋23.6	9 4.2	22 6.9	22 52.8	8 1.1	11 8.3	26 15.9	23 15.2	26 46.7
15 S	3 31 56.9	24 26.0	23 58.4	17 50.4	10 54.4	23 19.2	23 38.3	7 54.0	11 11.9	26 15.2	23 14.6	26 45.1
16 M	3 35 53.4	25 23.9	23 55.2	0♌32.5	12 41.8	24 31.6	24 23.8	7 47.0	11 15.6	26 14.5	23 13.9	26 43.5
17 T	3 39 50.0	26 21.7	23 52.0	13 32.3	14 26.0	25 43.8	25 9.2	7 40.0	11 19.1	26 13.7	23 13.3	26 41.8
18 W	3 43 46.5	27 19.5	23 48.8	26 52.6	16 7.1	26 56.0	25 54.5	7 33.1	11 22.5	26 12.9	23 12.6	26 40.1
19 T	3 47 43.1	28 17.3	23 45.7	10♍35.0	17 45.0	28 8.1	26 39.9	7 26.3	11 25.8	26 12.0	23 11.8	26 38.5
20 F	3 51 39.6	29 15.0	23 42.5	24 40.1	19 19.6	29 20.2	27 25.1	7 19.7	11 29.1	26 11.1	23 11.1	26 36.8
21 S	3 55 36.2	0♊12.7	23 39.3	9♎ 6.9	20 50.8	0♋32.2	28 10.3	7 13.1	11 32.3	26 10.1	23 10.3	26 35.1
22 S	3 59 32.8	1 10.4	23 36.1	23 52.1	22 18.7	1 44.1	28 55.5	7 6.6	11 35.3	26 9.1	23 9.4	26 33.5
23 M	4 3 29.3	2 8.1	23 33.0	8♏50.3	23 43.2	2 56.0	29 40.6	7 0.2	11 38.3	26 8.0	23 8.6	26 31.8
24 T	4 7 25.9	3 5.7	23 29.8	23 54.0	25 4.2	4 7.9	0♉25.6	6 53.9	11 41.2	26 6.9	23 7.7	26 30.2
25 W	4 11 22.4	4 3.4	23 26.6	8♐54.7	26 21.6	5 19.7	1 10.6	6 47.8	11 44.0	26 5.7	23 6.8	26 28.5
26 T	4 15 19.0	5 1.0	23 23.4	23 43.9	27 35.6	6 31.4	1 55.6	6 41.7	11 46.7	26 4.6	23 5.9	26 26.9
27 F	4 19 15.5	5 58.5	23 20.2	8♑14.4	28 45.9	7 43.1	2 40.5	6 35.8	11 49.4	26 3.3	23 4.9	26 25.2
28 S	4 23 12.1	6 56.1	23 17.1	22 21.0	29 52.5	8 54.7	3 25.3	6 30.0	11 51.9	26 2.0	23 3.9	26 23.6
29 S	4 27 8.6	7 53.6	23 13.9	6♒ 1.3	0♋55.4	10 6.3	4 10.1	6 24.4	11 54.3	26 0.7	23 2.9	26 22.0
30 M	4 31 5.2	8 51.2	23 10.7	19 15.1	1 54.5	11 17.8	4 54.9	6 18.9	11 56.7	25 59.4	23 1.9	26 20.3
31 T	4 35 1.8	9 48.7	23 7.5	2♓ 4.3	2 49.8	12 29.3	5 39.6	6 13.5	11 58.9	25 58.0	23 0.9	26 18.7
						DECLINATION at NOON						
1 S	2 36 45.1	15N 5.5	18S56.8	16S 1.2	15N25.7	22N 6.3	4N13.0	13S22.6	9S11.5	21S22.3	20S48.7	5S27.8
4 W	2 48 34.8	15 58.8	18 54.5	4 34.8	17 49.3	22 49.0	5 7.5	13 15.5	9 6.8	21 22.5	20 48.8	5 26.6
7 S	3 0 24.4	16 49.7	18 52.2	7N57.0	19 59.0	23 25.9	6 1.3	13 8.6	9 2.3	21 22.7	20 48.9	5 25.5
10 T	3 12 14.1	17 38.0	18 49.8	17 34.1	21 49.9	23 56.9	6 54.5	13 1.7	8 58.2	21 23.0	20 49.1	5 24.4
13 F	3 24 3.8	18 23.7	18 47.5	20 39.7	23 18.9	24 21.8	7 46.9	12 55.0	8 54.3	21 23.4	20 49.4	5 23.4
16 M	3 35 53.4	19 6.7	18 45.1	15 16.5	24 24.9	24 40.5	8 38.6	12 48.6	8 50.6	21 23.9	20 49.6	5 22.5
19 T	3 47 43.1	19 46.7	18 42.7	2 54.0	25 8.6	24 52.9	9 29.3	12 42.4	8 47.3	21 24.5	20 50.0	5 21.6
22 S	3 59 32.8	20 23.6	18 40.4	11S43.4	25 31.8	24 58.8	10 19.1	12 36.4	8 44.3	21 25.1	20 50.4	5 20.8
25 W	4 11 22.4	20 57.4	18 38.0	20 25.2	25 37.1	24 58.3	11 7.8	12 30.8	8 41.6	21 25.8	20 50.8	5 20.1
28 S	4 23 12.1	21 28.0	18 35.6	17 8.0	25 27.1	24 51.4	11 55.5	12 25.6	8 39.2	21 26.6	20 51.2	5 19.5
31 T	4 35 1.8	21 55.2	18 33.2	5 51.3	25 4.6	24 38.2	12 42.0	12 20.7	8 37.2	21 27.4	20 51.7	5 19.0

JUNE 1994

DAY	EPHEMERIS SIDEREAL TIME	☉	☊	☽	☿	♀	♂	♃	♄	♅	♆	♇
						LONGITUDE at NOON						
1 W	4 38 58.3	10♊46.2	23♏ 4.4	14♓32.3	3♋41.1	13♋40.7	6♉24.2	6♏ 8.2	12♓ 1.1	25♑56.5	22♑59.8	26♏17.1
2 T	4 42 54.9	11 43.7	23 1.2	26 43.3	4 28.4	14 52.0	7 8.8	6R 3.1	12 3.2	25R55.1	22R58.7	26R15.5
3 F	4 46 51.4	12 41.2	22 58.0	8♈41.8	5 11.7	16 3.3	7 53.4	5 58.1	12 5.2	25 53.6	22 57.6	26 13.9
4 S	4 50 48.0	13 38.6	22 54.8	20 32.6	5 50.7	17 14.6	8 37.8	5 53.3	12 7.0	25 52.0	22 56.4	26 12.4
5 S	4 54 44.5	14 36.1	22 51.7	2♉19.9	6 25.5	18 25.7	9 22.3	5 48.6	12 8.8	25 50.4	22 55.2	26 10.8
6 M	4 58 41.1	15 33.6	22 48.5	14 7.7	6 56.0	19 36.9	10 6.7	5 44.2	12 10.5	25 48.8	22 54.1	26 9.3
7 T	5 2 37.7	16 31.0	22 45.3	25 59.4	7 22.1	20 47.9	10 51.0	5 39.8	12 12.1	25 47.2	22 52.9	26 7.8
8 W	5 6 34.2	17 28.4	22 42.1	7♊57.7	7 43.7	21 58.9	11 35.3	5 35.6	12 13.6	25 45.5	22 51.7	26 6.2
9 T	5 10 30.8	18 25.8	22 38.9	20 5.0	8 0.7	23 9.8	12 19.5	5 31.5	12 15.0	25 43.8	22 50.4	26 4.7
10 F	5 14 27.3	19 23.2	22 35.8	2♋23.0	8 13.2	24 20.7	13 3.6	5 27.7	12 16.3	25 42.0	22 49.1	26 3.2
11 S	5 18 23.9	20 20.6	22 32.6	14 52.9	8 21.2	25 31.5	13 47.7	5 23.9	12 17.5	25 40.2	22 47.8	26 1.8
12 S	5 22 20.4	21 18.0	22 29.4	27 35.7	8 24.5	26 42.2	14 31.7	5 20.4	12 18.6	25 38.4	22 46.5	26 0.3
13 M	5 26 17.0	22 15.3	22 26.2	10♌32.1	8R23.3	27 52.9	15 15.7	5 17.0	12 19.6	25 36.5	22 45.2	25 58.8
14 T	5 30 13.6	23 12.7	22 23.1	23 43.0	8 17.7	29 3.4	15 59.6	5 13.8	12 20.5	25 34.6	22 43.8	25 57.4
15 W	5 34 10.1	24 10.0	22 19.9	7♍ 8.8	8 7.8	0♌14.0	16 43.4	5 10.7	12 21.3	25 32.7	22 42.5	25 56.0
16 T	5 38 6.7	25 7.3	22 16.7	20 50.1	7 53.7	1 24.4	17 27.2	5 7.9	12 22.0	25 30.7	22 41.1	25 54.6
17 F	5 42 3.2	26 4.6	22 13.5	4♎47.1	7 35.6	2 34.7	18 10.9	5 5.2	12 22.6	25 28.8	22 39.7	25 53.2
18 S	5 45 59.8	27 1.8	22 10.4	18 59.3	7 14.0	3 45.0	18 54.5	5 2.7	12 23.1	25 26.7	22 38.3	25 51.8
19 S	5 49 56.3	27 59.1	22 7.2	3♏25.0	6 48.9	4 55.2	19 38.1	5 0.3	12 23.5	25 24.7	22 36.9	25 50.5
20 M	5 53 52.9	28 56.3	22 4.0	18 1.3	6 21.0	6 5.3	20 21.6	4 58.1	12 23.8	25 22.7	22 35.4	25 49.2
21 T	5 57 49.5	29 53.6	22 0.8	2♐43.8	5 50.5	7 15.3	21 5.1	4 56.2	12 24.0	25 20.6	22 34.0	25 47.9
22 W	6 1 46.0	0♋50.8	21 57.7	17 26.4	5 18.1	8 25.2	21 48.5	4 54.3	12 24.1	25 18.5	22 32.5	25 46.6
23 T	6 5 42.6	1 48.0	21 54.5	2♑ 2.4	4 44.1	9 35.0	22 31.8	4 52.7	12 24.1	25 16.3	22 31.0	25 45.3
24 F	6 9 39.1	2 45.2	21 51.3	16 25.0	4 9.3	10 44.8	23 15.1	4 51.2	12R24.0	25 14.2	22 29.5	25 44.1
25 S	6 13 35.7	3 42.4	21 48.1	0♒28.6	3 34.2	11 54.5	23 58.3	4 50.0	12 23.8	25 12.0	22 28.0	25 42.9
26 S	6 17 32.2	4 39.6	21 44.9	14 9.2	2 59.3	13 4.0	24 41.5	4 48.9	12 23.5	25 9.8	22 26.5	25 41.7
27 M	6 21 28.8	5 36.9	21 41.8	27 25.2	2 25.4	14 13.5	25 24.6	4 48.0	12 23.2	25 7.7	22 25.0	25 40.5
28 T	6 25 25.4	6 34.1	21 38.6	10♓17.1	1 53.0	15 22.9	26 7.6	4 47.2	12 22.7	25 5.4	22 23.5	25 39.4
29 W	6 29 21.9	7 31.3	21 35.4	22 47.2	1 22.6	16 32.2	26 50.6	4 46.7	12 22.1	25 3.2	22 21.9	25 38.3
30 T	6 33 18.5	8 28.5	21 32.2	4♈59.4	0 54.7	17 41.4	27 33.5	4 46.3	12 21.4	25 0.9	22 20.3	25 37.2
						DECLINATION at NOON						
1 W	4 38 58.3	22N 3.6	18S32.4	1S31.8	24N54.7	24N32.3	12N57.3	12S19.2	8S36.6	21S27.7	20S51.9	5S18.8
4 S	4 50 48.0	22 26.2	18 30.0	10N42.2	24 19.3	24 10.8	13 42.2	12 14.9	8 34.9	21 28.7	20 52.5	5 18.4
7 T	5 2 37.7	22 45.3	18 27.6	19 3.3	23 37.1	23 43.2	14 25.8	12 11.1	8 33.6	21 29.6	20 53.0	5 18.1
10 F	5 14 27.3	23 0.8	18 25.2	20 8.4	22 50.5	23 9.7	15 8.0	12 7.8	8 32.7	21 30.7	20 53.6	5 17.8
13 M	5 26 17.0	23 12.7	18 22.7	12 41.6	22 1.7	22 30.6	15 48.9	12 5.0	8 32.1	21 31.8	20 54.3	5 17.7
16 T	5 38 6.7	23 20.9	18 20.3	0S37.8	21 13.2	21 46.1	16 28.2	12 2.7	8 31.9	21 32.9	20 55.0	5 17.6
19 S	5 49 56.3	23 25.3	18 17.8	14 20.0	20 27.3	20 56.5	17 6.1	12 0.9	8 31.9	21 34.1	20 55.7	5 17.7
22 W	6 1 46.0	23 26.1	18 15.4	20 44.1	19 46.9	20 2.1	17 42.4	11 59.6	8 32.4	21 35.3	20 56.4	5 17.9
25 S	6 13 35.7	23 23.2	18 12.9	15 23.1	19 14.5	19 3.2	18 17.1	11 58.9	8 33.1	21 36.5	20 57.1	5 18.1
28 T	6 25 25.4	23 16.5	18 10.5	3 8.5	18 52.7	18 0.0	18 50.1	11 58.7	8 34.2	21 37.7	20 57.9	5 18.5

JULY 1994

DAY	EPHEMERIS SIDEREAL TIME	☉	☊	☽	☿	♀	♂	♃	♄	♅	♆	♇
	h m s	° ′	° ′	° ′	° ′	° ′	° ′	° ′	° ′	° ′	° ′	° ′
LONGITUDE at NOON												
1 F	6 37 15.0	9♋25.7	21♏29.1	16♈58.3	0♋29.9	18♌50.5	28♉16.3	4♏46.1	12♓20.7	24♑58.6	22♑18.8	25♏36.1
2 S	6 41 11.6	10 22.9	21 25.9	28 49.1	0R 8.6	19 59.5	28 59.1	4 46.1	12R19.8	24R56.3	22R17.2	25R35.0
3 S	6 45 8.2	11 20.1	21 22.7	10♉37.0	29♊51.2	21 8.4	29 41.8	4D46.2	12 18.8	24 54.0	22 15.6	25 34.0
4 M	6 49 4.7	12 17.4	21 19.5	22 26.7	29 38.0	22 17.2	0♊24.4	4 46.6	12 17.7	24 51.7	22 14.0	25 33.0
5 T	6 53 1.3	13 14.6	21 16.4	4♊22.9	29 29.3	23 25.9	1 7.0	4 47.1	12 16.6	24 49.3	22 12.4	25 32.0
6 W	6 56 57.8	14 11.8	21 13.2	16 29.1	29 25.3	24 34.5	1 49.5	4 47.8	12 15.3	24 47.0	22 10.8	25 31.1
7 T	7 0 54.4	15 9.0	21 10.0	28 48.2	29D26.2	25 43.0	2 31.9	4 48.7	12 13.9	24 44.6	22 9.2	25 30.1
8 F	7 4 50.9	16 6.2	21 6.8	11♋21.9	29 32.1	26 51.3	3 14.3	4 49.7	12 12.5	24 42.2	22 7.6	25 29.2
9 S	7 8 47.5	17 3.5	21 3.6	24 11.0	29 43.2	27 59.6	3 56.6	4 50.9	12 10.9	24 39.9	22 6.0	25 28.4
10 S	7 12 44.1	18 0.7	21 0.5	7♌15.1	29 59.5	29 7.7	4 38.8	4 52.4	12 9.3	24 37.5	22 4.4	25 27.5
11 M	7 16 40.6	18 57.9	20 57.3	20 33.2	0♋21.0	0♍15.7	5 20.9	4 54.0	12 7.5	24 35.1	22 2.7	25 26.7
12 T	7 20 37.2	19 55.2	20 54.1	4♍ 3.7	0 47.7	1 23.6	6 3.0	4 55.7	12 5.7	24 32.7	22 1.1	25 25.9
13 W	7 24 33.7	20 52.4	20 50.9	17 44.8	1 19.7	2 31.4	6 45.0	4 57.7	12 3.8	24 30.3	21 59.5	25 25.2
14 T	7 28 30.3	21 49.6	20 47.8	1♎35.2	1 56.8	3 39.0	7 26.9	4 59.8	12 1.8	24 27.9	21 57.9	25 24.5
15 F	7 32 26.8	22 46.9	20 44.6	15 33.6	2 39.2	4 46.5	8 8.8	5 2.1	11 59.7	24 25.5	21 56.2	25 23.8
16 S	7 36 23.4	23 44.1	20 41.4	29 39.0	3 26.7	5 53.9	8 50.6	5 4.6	11 57.5	24 23.0	21 54.6	25 23.1
17 S	7 40 19.9	24 41.3	20 38.2	13♏50.4	4 19.3	7 1.1	9 32.3	5 7.2	11 55.2	24 20.6	21 53.0	25 22.5
18 M	7 44 16.5	25 38.6	20 35.1	28 6.7	5 16.9	8 8.2	10 14.0	5 10.1	11 52.9	24 18.3	21 51.4	25 21.9
19 T	7 48 13.1	26 35.9	20 31.9	12♐25.3	6 19.5	9 15.2	10 55.5	5 13.1	11 50.4	24 15.9	21 49.8	25 21.4
20 W	7 52 9.6	27 33.1	20 28.7	26 43.2	7 27.0	10 21.9	11 37.0	5 16.2	11 47.9	24 13.5	21 48.2	25 20.8
21 T	7 56 6.2	28 30.4	20 25.5	10♑56.1	8 39.3	11 28.5	12 18.4	5 19.5	11 45.3	24 11.1	21 46.6	25 20.3
22 F	8 0 2.7	29 27.6	20 22.3	24 59.3	9 56.3	12 35.0	12 59.8	5 23.0	11 42.6	24 8.7	21 45.0	25 19.8
23 S	8 3 59.3	0♌24.9	20 19.2	8♒47.9	11 17.9	13 41.3	13 41.0	5 26.7	11 39.8	24 6.3	21 43.4	25 19.4
24 S	8 7 55.8	1 22.2	20 16.0	22 18.3	12 44.0	14 47.4	14 22.2	5 30.5	11 36.9	24 3.9	21 41.8	25 19.0
25 M	8 11 52.4	2 19.4	20 12.8	5♓28.1	14 14.4	15 53.3	15 3.4	5 34.5	11 34.0	24 1.5	21 40.2	25 18.6
26 T	8 15 49.0	3 16.7	20 9.6	18 16.7	15 49.1	16 59.1	15 44.4	5 38.6	11 31.0	23 59.1	21 38.6	25 18.2
27 W	8 19 45.5	4 14.1	20 6.5	0♈45.5	17 27.8	18 4.7	16 25.4	5 42.9	11 27.9	23 56.8	21 37.0	25 17.9
28 T	8 23 42.1	5 11.4	20 3.3	12 57.3	19 10.3	19 10.1	17 6.3	5 47.4	11 24.7	23 54.4	21 35.4	25 17.6
29 F	8 27 38.6	6 8.7	20 0.1	24 56.2	20 56.4	20 15.3	17 47.1	5 52.0	11 21.5	23 52.1	21 33.9	25 17.4
30 S	8 31 35.2	7 6.1	19 56.9	6♉47.2	22 45.7	21 20.4	18 27.9	5 56.7	11 18.2	23 49.7	21 32.3	25 17.1
31 S	8 35 31.7	8 3.5	19 53.8	18 35.6	24 38.1	22 25.2	19 8.6	6 1.7	11 14.8	23 47.4	21 30.8	25 17.0
DECLINATION at NOON												
1 F	6 37 15.0	23N 6.2	18S 8.0	9N28.0	18N43.1	16N52.9	19N21.5	11S59.1	8S35.7	21S39.0	20S58.7	5S18.9
4 M	6 49 4.7	22 52.2	18 5.5	18 25.0	18 46.2	15 42.3	19 51.1	12 0.0	8 37.4	21 40.3	20 59.4	5 19.5
7 T	7 0 54.4	22 34.6	18 3.0	20 24.8	19 1.3	14 28.3	20 19.0	12 1.5	8 39.5	21 41.6	21 0.2	5 20.1
10 S	7 12 44.1	22 13.6	18 0.5	13 41.9	19 26.4	13 11.5	20 45.2	12 3.5	8 41.9	21 42.9	21 1.0	5 20.9
13 W	7 24 33.7	21 49.0	17 58.0	0 37.1	19 58.7	11 52.0	21 9.5	12 6.0	8 44.7	21 44.2	21 1.8	5 21.7
16 S	7 36 23.4	21 21.2	17 55.5	13S 9.0	20 34.4	10 30.2	21 32.0	12 9.1	8 47.7	21 45.5	21 2.7	5 22.7
19 T	7 48 13.1	20 50.0	17 52.9	20 30.3	21 9.4	9 6.3	21 52.7	12 12.7	8 51.0	21 46.8	21 3.5	5 23.7
22 F	8 0 2.7	20 15.8	17 50.4	16 41.0	21 38.8	7 40.9	22 11.5	12 16.7	8 54.5	21 48.1	21 4.3	5 24.8
25 M	8 11 52.4	19 38.4	17 47.8	4 57.5	21 57.5	6 14.0	22 28.5	12 21.2	8 58.4	21 49.4	21 5.1	5 26.0
28 T	8 23 42.1	18 58.2	17 45.3	7N58.0	22 0.2	4 46.1	22 43.7	12 26.2	9 2.4	21 50.6	21 5.9	5 27.3
31 S	8 35 31.7	18 15.1	17 42.7	17 31.5	21 42.6	3 17.3	22 57.0	12 31.6	9 6.7	21 51.8	21 6.6	5 28.7

AUGUST 1994

DAY	EPHEMERIS SIDEREAL TIME	☉	☊	☽	☿	♀	♂	♃	♄	♅	♆	♇
LONGITUDE at NOON												
1 M	8 39 28.3	9♌ 0.9	19♏50.6	0♊26.9	26♋33.1	23♍29.9	19♊49.2	6♏ 6.8	11♓11.4	23♑45.1	21♑29.2	25♏16.8
2 T	8 43 24.8	9 58.3	19 47.4	12 26.2	28 30.6	24 34.3	20 29.7	6 12.0	11R 7.9	23R42.8	21R27.7	25R16.7
3 W	8 47 21.4	10 55.7	19 44.2	24 38.2	0♌30.0	25 38.5	21 10.2	6 17.4	11 4.3	23 40.5	21 26.2	25 16.6
4 T	8 51 18.0	11 53.2	19 41.0	7♋ 6.7	2 31.0	26 42.6	21 50.5	6 22.9	11 0.7	23 38.3	21 24.7	25 16.5
5 F	8 55 14.5	12 50.7	19 37.9	19 54.0	4 33.3	27 46.4	22 30.8	6 28.6	10 57.0	23 36.0	21 23.2	25 16.5
6 S	8 59 11.1	13 48.2	19 34.7	3♌ 1.1	6 36.6	28 50.0	23 11.0	6 34.4	10 53.2	23 33.8	21 21.7	25 16.5
7 S	9 3 7.6	14 45.7	19 31.5	16 27.2	8 40.5	29 53.3	23 51.2	6 40.4	10 49.4	23 31.6	21 20.3	25D16.6
8 M	9 7 4.2	15 43.2	19 28.3	0♍ 9.8	10 44.8	0♎56.5	24 31.2	6 46.6	10 45.5	23 29.5	21 18.9	25 16.7
9 T	9 11 0.7	16 40.8	19 25.2	14 5.3	12 49.0	1 59.4	25 11.2	6 52.9	10 41.6	23 27.3	21 17.4	25 16.8
10 W	9 14 57.3	17 38.3	19 22.0	28 9.6	14 53.0	3 2.0	25 51.1	6 59.3	10 37.6	23 25.2	21 16.0	25 17.0
11 T	9 18 53.8	18 35.9	19 18.8	12♎18.7	16 56.5	4 4.3	26 30.9	7 5.8	10 33.6	23 23.1	21 14.6	25 17.1
12 F	9 22 50.4	19 33.5	19 15.6	26 29.3	18 59.3	5 6.4	27 10.6	7 12.5	10 29.5	23 21.0	21 13.2	25 17.4
13 S	9 26 46.9	20 31.1	19 12.4	10♏39.1	21 1.4	6 8.2	27 50.2	7 19.4	10 25.4	23 18.9	21 11.9	25 17.6
14 S	9 30 43.5	21 28.7	19 9.3	24 46.5	23 2.5	7 9.7	28 29.7	7 26.3	10 21.2	23 16.9	21 10.5	25 17.9
15 M	9 34 40.0	22 26.4	19 6.1	8♐50.7	25 2.5	8 10.9	29 9.1	7 33.4	10 17.0	23 14.9	21 9.2	25 18.2
16 T	9 38 36.6	23 24.0	19 2.9	22 50.9	27 1.3	9 11.8	29 48.5	7 40.7	10 12.8	23 12.9	21 7.9	25 18.6
17 W	9 42 33.2	24 21.7	18 59.7	6♑45.7	28 58.9	10 12.4	0♋27.7	7 48.0	10 8.5	23 11.0	21 6.6	25 19.0
18 T	9 46 29.7	25 19.4	18 56.6	20 33.5	0♍55.2	11 12.6	1 6.9	7 55.5	10 4.2	23 9.0	21 5.3	25 19.4
19 F	9 50 26.3	26 17.1	18 53.4	4♒11.9	2 50.2	12 12.5	1 46.0	8 3.1	9 59.8	23 7.2	21 4.0	25 19.8
20 S	9 54 22.8	27 14.8	18 50.2	17 38.2	4 43.9	13 12.1	2 25.0	8 10.9	9 55.4	23 5.3	21 2.8	25 20.3
21 S	9 58 19.4	28 12.6	18 47.0	0♓50.0	6 36.2	14 11.2	3 3.9	8 18.7	9 51.0	23 3.5	21 1.6	25 20.8
22 M	10 2 15.9	29 10.3	18 43.8	13 45.5	8 27.1	15 10.1	3 42.8	8 26.7	9 46.6	23 1.7	21 0.4	25 21.4
23 T	10 6 12.5	0♍ 8.1	18 40.7	26 24.1	10 16.6	16 8.5	4 21.5	8 34.8	9 42.1	22 59.9	20 59.2	25 22.0
24 W	10 10 9.0	1 5.9	18 37.5	8♈46.4	12 4.8	17 6.5	5 0.2	8 43.1	9 37.6	22 58.2	20 58.1	25 22.6
25 T	10 14 5.6	2 3.8	18 34.3	20 54.4	13 51.6	18 4.1	5 38.7	8 51.4	9 33.1	22 56.5	20 56.9	25 23.2
26 F	10 18 2.1	3 1.7	18 31.1	2♉51.3	15 37.1	19 1.3	6 17.2	8 59.9	9 28.6	22 54.8	20 55.8	25 23.9
27 S	10 21 58.7	3 59.6	18 28.0	14 41.2	17 21.2	19 58.1	6 55.6	9 8.5	9 24.1	22 53.2	20 54.8	25 24.7
28 S	10 25 55.2	4 57.5	18 24.8	26 29.0	19 4.1	20 54.4	7 33.9	9 17.2	9 19.5	22 51.6	20 53.7	25 25.4
29 M	10 29 51.8	5 55.5	18 21.6	8♊20.1	20 45.6	21 50.3	8 12.1	9 26.0	9 15.0	22 50.1	20 52.7	25 26.2
30 T	10 33 48.3	6 53.5	18 18.4	20 20.0	22 25.9	22 45.6	8 50.2	9 34.9	9 10.4	22 48.6	20 51.7	25 27.1
31 W	10 37 44.9	7 51.5	18 15.2	2♋33.8	24 4.8	23 40.5	9 28.2	9 44.0	9 5.9	22 47.1	20 50.7	25 27.9
DECLINATION at NOON												
1 M	8 39 28.3	18N 0.1	17S41.9	19N23.5	21N31.6	2N47.6	23N 1.0	12S33.6	9S 8.2	21S52.2	21S 6.9	5S29.2
4 T	8 51 18.0	17 13.5	17 39.3	19 35.0	20 42.7	1 18.2	23 11.9	12 39.6	9 12.8	21 53.4	21 7.6	5 30.7
7 S	9 3 7.6	16 24.3	17 36.7	11 7.6	19 30.7	0S11.4	23 20.9	12 46.0	9 17.5	21 54.5	21 8.4	5 32.3
10 W	9 14 57.3	15 32.7	17 34.2	2S51.7	17 58.2	1 40.8	23 28.1	12 52.8	9 22.4	21 55.6	21 9.1	5 33.9
13 S	9 26 46.9	14 39.0	17 31.6	15 43.6	16 9.3	3 9.9	23 33.6	12 60.0	9 27.5	21 56.7	21 9.8	5 35.6
16 T	9 38 36.6	13 43.1	17 29.0	20 26.7	14 8.2	4 38.2	23 37.3	13 7.5	9 32.6	21 57.7	21 10.5	5 37.4
19 F	9 50 26.3	12 45.3	17 26.3	14 29.1	11 58.8	6 5.6	23 39.3	13 15.4	9 37.9	21 58.6	21 11.1	5 39.3
22 M	10 2 15.9	11 45.7	17 23.7	2 12.2	9 44.2	7 31.7	23 39.6	13 23.6	9 43.2	21 59.5	21 11.8	5 41.2
25 T	10 14 5.6	10 44.4	17 21.1	10N16.6	7 27.1	8 56.4	23 38.2	13 32.1	9 48.6	22 0.4	21 12.4	5 43.1
28 S	10 25 55.2	9 41.5	17 18.5	18 36.5	5 9.2	10 19.2	23 35.2	13 40.8	9 53.9	22 1.1	21 12.9	5 45.2
31 W	10 37 44.9	8 37.3	17 15.8	19 49.5	2 52.3	11 40.0	23 30.7	13 49.8	9 59.3	22 1.8	21 13.5	5 47.2

SEPTEMBER 1994

LONGITUDE at NOON

DAY	EPHEMERIS SIDEREAL TIME h m s	☉ ° ′	☊ ° ′	☽ ° ′	☿ ° ′	♀ ° ′	♂ ° ′	♃ ° ′	♄ ° ′	♅ ° ′	♆ ° ′	♇ ° ′
1 T	10 41 41.5	8♍49.6	18♏12.1	15♋ 6.2	25♍42.5	24♎34.8	10♋ 6.1	9♏53.1	9♓ 1.3	22♑45.6	20♑49.8	25♏28.8
2 F	10 45 38.0	9 47.7	18 8.9	28 0.7	27 19.0	25 28.7	10 43.9	10 2.4	8R56.7	22R44.2	20R48.8	25 29.7
3 S	10 49 34.6	10 45.8	18 5.7	11♌19.0	28 54.2	26 22.0	11 21.6	10 11.7	8 52.1	22 42.9	20 47.9	25 30.7
4 S	10 53 31.1	11 44.0	18 2.5	25 1.0	0♎28.2	27 14.7	11 59.3	10 21.2	8 47.5	22 41.6	20 47.0	25 31.6
5 M	10 57 27.7	12 42.2	17 59.4	9♍ 4.1	2 0.9	28 6.8	12 36.8	10 30.7	8 43.0	22 40.3	20 46.2	25 32.7
6 T	11 1 24.2	13 40.4	17 56.2	23 23.7	3 32.5	28 58.3	13 14.2	10 40.4	8 38.4	22 39.1	20 45.4	25 33.7
7 W	11 5 20.8	14 38.6	17 53.0	7♎53.6	5 2.8	29 49.2	13 51.5	10 50.1	8 33.9	22 37.9	20 44.6	25 34.8
8 T	11 9 17.3	15 36.9	17 49.8	22 27.4	6 31.9	0♏39.4	14 28.6	11 0.0	8 29.3	22 36.7	20 43.8	25 35.9
9 F	11 13 13.9	16 35.2	17 46.6	6♏59.2	7 59.7	1 28.9	15 5.7	11 10.0	8 24.8	22 35.6	20 43.1	25 37.0
10 S	11 17 10.4	17 33.5	17 43.5	21 24.3	9 26.3	2 17.7	15 42.7	11 20.0	8 20.3	22 34.6	20 42.3	25 38.2
11 S	11 21 7.0	18 31.8	17 40.3	5♐39.6	10 51.6	3 5.7	16 19.5	11 30.2	8 15.9	22 33.5	20 41.7	25 39.4
12 M	11 25 3.5	19 30.2	17 37.1	19 43.4	12 15.7	3 52.9	16 56.3	11 40.4	8 11.4	22 32.6	20 41.0	25 40.6
13 T	11 29 0.1	20 28.6	17 33.9	3♑35.3	13 38.4	4 39.4	17 32.9	11 50.7	8 7.0	22 31.6	20 40.4	25 41.9
14 W	11 32 56.6	21 27.0	17 30.8	17 15.0	14 59.8	5 25.0	18 9.5	12 1.1	8 2.6	22 30.8	20 39.8	25 43.2
15 T	11 36 53.2	22 25.5	17 27.6	0♒42.7	16 19.9	6 9.7	18 45.9	12 11.6	7 58.2	22 29.9	20 39.2	25 44.5
16 F	11 40 49.7	23 23.9	17 24.4	13 58.2	17 38.5	6 53.5	19 22.2	12 22.2	7 53.9	22 29.2	20 38.7	25 45.8
17 S	11 44 46.3	24 22.4	17 21.2	27 1.2	18 55.6	7 36.3	19 58.4	12 32.9	7 49.6	22 28.4	20 38.2	25 47.2
18 S	11 48 42.8	25 21.0	17 18.0	9♓51.4	20 11.2	8 18.1	20 34.4	12 43.7	7 45.3	22 27.7	20 37.7	25 48.6
19 M	11 52 39.4	26 19.6	17 14.9	22 28.6	21 25.2	8 59.0	21 10.4	12 54.5	7 41.2	22 27.1	20 37.3	25 50.1
20 T	11 56 35.9	27 18.2	17 11.7	4♈52.8	22 37.6	9 38.7	21 46.3	13 5.5	7 37.0	22 26.5	20 36.9	25 51.6
21 W	12 0 32.5	28 16.8	17 8.5	17 4.8	23 48.1	10 17.3	22 22.0	13 16.5	7 32.9	22 26.0	20 36.6	25 53.0
22 T	12 4 29.1	29 15.5	17 5.3	29 6.1	24 56.8	10 54.7	22 57.6	13 27.5	7 28.8	22 25.5	20 36.2	25 54.6
23 F	12 8 25.6	0♎14.2	17 2.2	10♉59.1	26 3.5	11 31.0	23 33.1	13 38.7	7 24.7	22 25.0	20 35.9	25 56.1
24 S	12 12 22.2	1 12.9	16 59.0	22 47.1	27 8.1	12 6.0	24 8.4	13 49.9	7 20.7	22 24.6	20 35.6	25 57.7
25 S	12 16 18.7	2 11.7	16 55.8	4♊33.9	28 10.4	12 39.7	24 43.7	14 1.2	7 16.8	22 24.3	20 35.4	25 59.3
26 M	12 20 15.3	3 10.5	16 52.6	16 24.2	29 10.3	13 12.0	25 18.8	14 12.6	7 12.9	22 24.0	20 35.1	26 0.9
27 T	12 24 11.8	4 9.3	16 49.4	28 22.9	0♏ 7.6	13 43.0	25 53.8	14 24.0	7 9.1	22 23.7	20 35.0	26 2.5
28 W	12 28 8.4	5 8.2	16 46.3	10♋35.2	1 2.1	14 12.5	26 28.6	14 35.5	7 5.3	22 23.5	20 34.8	26 4.2
29 T	12 32 4.9	6 7.1	16 43.1	23 6.0	1 53.5	14 40.5	27 3.3	14 47.1	7 1.6	22 23.4	20 34.7	26 5.9
30 F	12 36 1.5	7 6.1	16 39.9	5♌59.7	2 41.6	15 6.9	27 37.9	14 58.7	6 58.0	22 23.3	20 34.6	26 7.6

DECLINATION at NOON

DAY	EPHEMERIS SIDEREAL TIME h m s	☉	☊	☽	☿	♀	♂	♃	♄	♅	♆	♇
1 T	10 41 41.5	8N15.6	17S15.0	18N19.8	2N 7.0	12S 6.5	23N28.9	13S52.9	10S 1.1	22S 2.1	21S13.6	5S47.9
4 S	10 53 31.1	7 9.7	17 12.3	8 27.4	0S 6.9	13 24.1	23 22.3	14 2.2	10 6.4	22 2.7	21 14.1	5 50.1
7 W	11 5 20.8	6 2.8	17 9.6	6S 3.3	2 17.5	14 39.1	23 14.4	14 11.8	10 11.7	22 3.3	21 14.6	5 52.2
10 S	11 17 10.4	4 55.0	17 7.0	17 41.4	4 23.7	15 51.1	23 5.1	14 21.5	10 16.9	22 3.8	21 15.0	5 54.4
13 T	11 29 0.1	3 46.4	17 4.3	19 38.4	6 24.9	16 59.8	22 54.4	14 31.5	10 21.9	22 4.2	21 15.4	5 56.7
16 F	11 40 49.7	2 37.3	17 1.6	11 44.6	8 20.0	18 4.9	22 42.5	14 41.6	10 26.8	22 4.6	21 15.7	5 58.9
19 M	11 52 39.4	1 27.6	16 58.9	0N47.6	10 8.1	19 5.9	22 29.5	14 51.8	10 31.6	22 4.8	21 16.0	6 1.2
22 T	12 4 29.1	0 17.7	16 56.2	12 31.3	11 48.1	20 2.6	22 15.3	15 2.2	10 36.2	22 5.1	21 16.3	6 3.5
25 S	12 16 18.7	0S52.4	16 53.5	19 23.0	13 18.5	20 54.6	22 0.0	15 12.6	10 40.6	22 5.2	21 16.5	6 5.8
28 W	12 28 8.4	2 2.5	16 50.8	18 46.1	14 37.4	21 41.2	21 43.8	15 23.2	10 44.7	22 5.3	21 16.7	6 8.1

OCTOBER 1994

LONGITUDE at NOON

DAY	EPHEMERIS SIDEREAL TIME h m s	☉	☊	☽	☿	♀	♂	♃	♄	♅	♆	♇
1 S	12 39 58.0	8♎ 5.1	16♏36.7	19♌19.2	3♏26.1	15♏31.7	28♋12.4	15♏10.5	6♓54.4	22♑23.2	20♑34.6	26♏ 9.4
2 S	12 43 54.6	9 4.1	16 33.5	3♍ 5.8	4 6.7	15 54.8	28 46.7	15 22.2	6R50.9	22 23.2	20R34.5	26 11.1
3 M	12 47 51.1	10 3.2	16 30.4	17 18.0	4 43.1	16 16.2	29 20.8	15 34.1	6 47.4	22D23.3	20 34.5	26 12.9
4 T	12 51 47.7	11 2.3	16 27.2	1♎52.0	5 14.8	16 35.8	29 54.9	15 46.0	6 44.1	22 23.4	20D34.6	26 14.8
5 W	12 55 44.2	12 1.4	16 24.0	16 41.3	5 41.5	16 53.5	0♌28.7	15 57.9	6 40.7	22 23.5	20 34.7	26 16.6
6 T	12 59 40.8	13 0.6	16 20.8	1♏38.0	6 2.6	17 9.3	1 2.4	16 10.0	6 37.5	22 23.7	20 34.8	26 18.5
7 F	13 3 37.3	13 59.8	16 17.7	16 33.7	6 17.9	17 23.1	1 36.0	16 22.0	6 34.4	22 24.0	20 34.9	26 20.4
8 S	13 7 33.9	14 59.0	16 14.5	1♐20.9	6 26.7	17 34.8	2 9.4	16 34.2	6 31.3	22 24.3	20 35.1	26 22.3
9 S	13 11 30.4	15 58.3	16 11.3	15 53.8	6 28.7	17 44.4	2 42.7	16 46.4	6 28.3	22 24.7	20 35.3	26 24.2
10 M	13 15 27.0	16 57.7	16 8.1	0♑ 8.9	6R23.4	17 51.9	3 15.8	16 58.7	6 25.4	22 25.1	20 35.6	26 26.2
11 T	13 19 23.5	17 57.0	16 4.9	14 4.4	6 10.3	17 57.1	3 48.8	17 10.9	6 22.6	22 25.6	20 35.9	26 28.2
12 W	13 23 20.1	18 56.3	16 1.8	27 40.2	5 49.0	17 60.0	4 21.5	17 23.3	6 19.8	22 26.1	20 36.2	26 30.2
13 T	13 27 16.6	19 55.7	15 58.6	10♒57.3	5 19.5	18 0.5	4 54.1	17 35.7	6 17.1	22 26.7	20 36.6	26 32.2
14 F	13 31 13.2	20 55.1	15 55.4	23 57.5	4 41.6	17R58.7	5 26.6	17 48.1	6 14.6	22 27.3	20 37.0	26 34.2
15 S	13 35 9.8	21 54.6	15 52.2	6♓42.3	3 55.5	17 54.5	5 58.9	18 0.6	6 12.1	22 28.0	20 37.4	26 36.2
16 S	13 39 6.3	22 54.1	15 49.1	19 13.7	3 1.6	17 47.8	6 31.0	18 13.1	6 9.7	22 28.7	20 37.8	26 38.3
17 M	13 43 2.9	23 53.6	15 45.9	1♈33.4	2 0.7	17 38.7	7 2.9	18 25.7	6 7.3	22 29.4	20 38.3	26 40.4
18 T	13 46 59.4	24 53.1	15 42.7	13 42.8	0 53.9	17 27.2	7 34.7	18 38.3	6 5.1	22 30.3	20 38.8	26 42.5
19 W	13 50 56.0	25 52.7	15 39.5	25 43.8	29♎42.6	17 13.3	8 6.2	18 51.0	6 3.0	22 31.1	20 39.4	26 44.6
20 T	13 54 52.5	26 52.3	15 36.3	7♉37.9	28 28.5	16 57.0	8 37.6	19 3.7	6 0.9	22 32.0	20 40.0	26 46.7
21 F	13 58 49.1	27 51.9	15 33.2	19 27.3	27 13.8	16 38.4	9 8.9	19 16.4	5 59.0	22 33.0	20 40.6	26 48.9
22 S	14 2 45.6	28 51.6	15 30.0	1♊14.3	26 0.7	16 17.5	9 39.9	19 29.2	5 57.1	22 34.0	20 41.2	26 51.1
23 S	14 6 42.2	29 51.3	15 26.8	13 1.9	24 51.3	15 54.4	10 10.7	19 42.0	5 55.3	22 35.1	20 41.9	26 53.2
24 M	14 10 38.7	0♏51.0	15 23.6	24 53.3	23 47.8	15 29.2	10 41.4	19 54.8	5 53.7	22 36.2	20 42.6	26 55.4
25 T	14 14 35.3	1 50.8	15 20.5	6♋52.6	22 52.0	15 2.1	11 11.8	20 7.7	5 52.1	22 37.4	20 43.4	26 57.6
26 W	14 18 31.8	2 50.6	15 17.3	19 3.9	22 5.6	14 33.1	11 42.1	20 20.6	5 50.6	22 38.6	20 44.1	26 59.9
27 T	14 22 28.4	3 50.5	15 14.1	1♌31.6	21 29.6	14 2.5	12 12.1	20 33.6	5 49.3	22 39.9	20 44.9	27 2.1
28 F	14 26 24.9	4 50.4	15 10.9	14 20.0	21 4.7	13 30.5	12 42.0	20 46.5	5 48.0	22 41.2	20 45.8	27 4.4
29 S	14 30 21.5	5 50.3	15 7.7	27 32.8	20 51.4	12 57.1	13 11.6	20 59.5	5 46.8	22 42.5	20 46.7	27 6.6
30 S	14 34 18.1	6 50.3	15 4.6	11♍12.4	20 49.5	12 22.7	13 41.0	21 12.6	5 45.7	22 44.0	20 47.6	27 8.9
31 M	14 38 14.6	7 50.3	15 1.4	25 19.5	20D58.7	11 47.4	14 10.2	21 25.7	5 44.8	22 45.5	20 48.6	27 11.2

DECLINATION at NOON

DAY	EPHEMERIS SIDEREAL TIME h m s	☉	☊	☽	☿	♀	♂	♃	♄	♅	♆	♇
1 S	12 39 58.0	3S12.4	16S48.1	10N 6.0	15S42.3	22S22.1	21N26.7	15S33.8	10S48.7	22S 5.3	21S16.8	6S10.4
4 T	12 51 47.7	4 22.1	16 45.4	4S 1.2	16 29.7	22 56.6	21 8.7	15 44.5	10 52.4	22 5.2	21 16.9	6 12.7
7 F	13 3 37.3	5 31.2	16 42.6	16 39.2	16 55.1	23 23.8	20 50.1	15 55.2	10 55.8	22 5.0	21 16.9	6 15.0
10 M	13 15 27.0	6 39.8	16 39.9	19 43.3	16 52.3	23 43.0	20 30.8	16 5.9	10 58.9	22 4.8	21 16.9	6 17.4
13 T	13 27 16.6	7 47.5	16 37.2	12 26.7	16 14.5	23 53.2	20 10.9	16 16.7	11 1.7	22 4.5	21 16.8	6 19.6
16 S	13 39 6.3	8 54.2	16 34.4	0 16.1	14 56.7	23 53.1	19 50.5	16 27.4	11 4.2	22 4.1	21 16.7	6 21.9
19 W	13 50 56.0	9 59.8	16 31.6	11N32.9	13 1.6	23 41.8	19 29.8	16 38.1	11 6.4	22 3.6	21 16.6	6 24.1
22 S	14 2 45.6	11 4.1	16 28.9	18 56.2	10 46.3	23 18.4	19 8.7	16 48.8	11 8.3	22 3.1	21 16.4	6 26.3
25 T	14 14 35.3	12 6.9	16 26.1	19 5.2	8 40.3	22 42.6	18 47.4	16 59.4	11 9.8	22 2.5	21 16.2	6 28.5
28 F	14 26 24.9	13 8.0	16 23.3	11 27.4	7 12.1	21 54.7	18 26.0	17 10.0	11 11.0	22 1.8	21 15.9	6 30.6
31 M	14 38 14.6	14 7.4	16 20.5	1S50.7	6 35.4	20 56.0	18 4.5	17 20.5	11 11.8	22 1.0	21 15.6	6 32.7

NOVEMBER 1994

DAY	EPHEMERIS SIDEREAL TIME	☉	☊	☽	☿	♀	♂	♃	♄	♅	♆	♇
	h m s	° ′	° ′	° ′	° ′	° ′	° ′	° ′	° ′	° ′	° ′	° ′
LONGITUDE at NOON												
1 T	14 42 11.2	8♏50.4	14♏58.2	9♎52.2	21♎18.5	11♏11.5	14♌39.1	21♏38.7	5♓43.9	22♑47.0	20♑49.5	27♏13.5
2 W	14 46 7.7	9 50.4	14 55.0	24 45.9	21 48.1	10R35.1	15 7.9	21 51.8	5R43.2	22 48.5	20 50.5	27 15.8
3 T	14 50 4.3	10 50.5	14 51.9	9♏53.2	22 26.7	9 58.7	15 36.3	22 5.0	5 42.5	22 50.1	20 51.6	27 18.1
4 F	14 54 0.8	11 50.7	14 48.7	25 5.0	23 13.4	9 22.3	16 4.6	22 18.1	5 41.9	22 51.8	20 52.6	27 20.5
5 S	14 57 57.4	12 50.8	14 45.5	10♐11.9	24 7.4	8 46.3	16 32.5	22 31.3	5 41.5	22 53.5	20 53.7	27 22.8
6 S	15 1 53.9	13 51.0	14 42.3	25 5.0	25 7.7	8 10.8	17 0.3	22 44.5	5 41.1	22 55.2	20 54.8	27 25.1
7 M	15 5 50.5	14 51.2	14 39.1	9♑37.7	26 13.7	7 36.1	17 27.7	22 57.7	5 40.9	22 57.0	20 56.0	27 27.5
8 T	15 9 47.0	15 51.5	14 36.0	23 46.1	27 24.4	7 2.5	17 54.9	23 10.9	5 40.7	22 58.8	20 57.2	27 29.8
9 W	15 13 43.6	16 51.8	14 32.8	7♒28.6	28 39.4	6 30.1	18 21.9	23 24.1	5 40.7	23 0.7	20 58.4	27 32.2
10 T	15 17 40.2	17 52.0	14 29.6	20 46.3	29 57.8	5 59.2	18 48.5	23 37.4	5D40.8	23 2.6	20 59.6	27 34.6
11 F	15 21 36.7	18 52.4	14 26.4	3♓41.2	1♏19.3	5 29.9	19 14.9	23 50.6	5 41.0	23 4.6	21 0.9	27 36.9
12 S	15 25 33.3	19 52.7	14 23.3	16 16.7	2 43.3	5 2.4	19 41.0	24 3.9	5 41.2	23 6.6	21 2.2	27 39.3
13 S	15 29 29.8	20 53.1	14 20.1	28 36.2	4 9.4	4 36.8	20 6.9	24 17.1	5 41.6	23 8.6	21 3.5	27 41.7
14 M	15 33 26.4	21 53.4	14 16.9	10♈43.5	5 37.3	4 13.4	20 32.4	24 30.4	5 42.1	23 10.7	21 4.9	27 44.1
15 T	15 37 22.9	22 53.9	14 13.7	22 41.8	7 6.6	3 52.1	20 57.6	24 43.7	5 42.7	23 12.9	21 6.3	27 46.5
16 W	15 41 19.5	23 54.3	14 10.6	4♉34.0	8 37.1	3 33.1	21 22.6	24 57.0	5 43.4	23 15.1	21 7.7	27 48.8
17 T	15 45 16.0	24 54.8	14 7.4	16 22.9	10 8.6	3 16.5	21 47.2	25 10.3	5 44.2	23 17.3	21 9.1	27 51.2
18 F	15 49 12.6	25 55.2	14 4.2	28 10.7	11 40.8	3 2.4	22 11.5	25 23.6	5 45.1	23 19.5	21 10.6	27 53.6
19 S	15 53 9.2	26 55.8	14 1.0	9♊59.5	13 13.7	2 50.7	22 35.5	25 36.9	5 46.1	23 21.8	21 12.1	27 56.0
20 S	15 57 5.7	27 56.3	13 57.8	21 51.5	14 47.0	2 41.4	22 59.2	25 50.2	5 47.3	23 24.2	21 13.6	27 58.4
21 M	16 1 2.3	28 56.9	13 54.7	3♋48.9	16 20.7	2 34.8	23 22.6	26 3.5	5 48.5	23 26.6	21 15.2	28 0.9
22 T	16 4 58.8	29 57.5	13 51.5	15 54.0	17 54.7	2 30.6	23 45.6	26 16.8	5 49.9	23 29.0	21 16.8	28 3.3
23 W	16 8 55.4	0♐58.1	13 48.3	28 9.6	19 28.9	2 28.8	24 8.2	26 30.1	5 51.3	23 31.5	21 18.4	28 5.7
24 T	16 12 51.9	1 58.8	13 45.1	10♌38.7	21 3.1	2D29.5	24 30.5	26 43.3	5 52.8	23 33.9	21 20.0	28 8.1
25 F	16 16 48.5	2 59.4	13 42.0	23 24.6	22 37.5	2 32.7	24 52.4	26 56.6	5 54.5	23 36.5	21 21.6	28 10.4
26 S	16 20 45.0	4 0.1	13 38.8	6♍30.3	24 11.9	2 38.2	25 14.0	27 9.9	5 56.2	23 39.0	21 23.3	28 12.8
27 S	16 24 41.6	5 0.9	13 35.6	19 58.9	25 46.4	2 46.0	25 35.2	27 23.1	5 58.1	23 41.6	21 25.0	28 15.2
28 M	16 28 38.2	6 1.6	13 32.4	3♎52.1	27 20.8	2 56.2	25 55.9	27 36.4	5 60.0	23 44.3	21 26.7	28 17.6
29 T	16 32 34.7	7 2.4	13 29.3	18 10.3	28 55.2	3 8.5	26 16.3	27 49.6	6 2.0	23 46.9	21 28.4	28 20.0
30 W	16 36 31.3	8 3.2	13 26.1	2♏51.4	0♐29.6	3 23.0	26 36.3	28 2.8	6 4.2	23 49.6	21 30.2	28 22.3
DECLINATION at NOON												
1 T	14 42 11.2	14S 26.7	16S 19.6	6S 42.3	6S 34.5	20S 34.4	17N 57.4	17S 24.0	11S 12.0	22S 0.7	21S 15.4	6S 33.4
4 F	14 54 0.8	15 23.2	16 16.8	18 6.8	7 1.2	19 25.0	17 36.1	17 34.3	11 12.4	21 59.9	21 15.1	6 35.4
7 M	15 5 50.5	16 17.5	16 14.0	18 45.6	8 2.3	18 11.3	17 15.0	17 44.6	11 12.4	21 59.0	21 14.6	6 37.4
10 T	15 17 40.2	17 9.3	16 11.2	9 33.8	9 25.8	16 57.1	16 54.2	17 54.7	11 12.0	21 58.0	21 14.1	6 39.3
13 S	15 29 29.8	17 58.5	16 8.4	2N 57.7	11 2.0	15 46.0	16 33.9	18 4.7	11 11.3	21 56.9	21 13.6	6 41.2
16 W	15 41 19.5	18 44.8	16 5.5	13 56.1	12 43.8	14 41.1	16 14.1	18 14.6	11 10.3	21 55.8	21 13.1	6 43.0
19 S	15 53 9.2	19 28.2	16 2.7	19 43.2	14 26.3	13 44.7	15 54.9	18 24.2	11 8.9	21 54.6	21 12.5	6 44.7
22 T	16 4 58.8	20 8.4	15 59.8	17 54.0	16 6.2	12 58.2	15 36.5	18 33.8	11 7.1	21 53.3	21 11.8	6 46.4
25 F	16 16 48.5	20 45.3	15 57.0	8 47.4	17 41.3	12 22.2	15 18.9	18 43.1	11 5.0	21 52.0	21 11.1	6 48.0
28 M	16 28 38.2	21 18.7	15 54.1	4S 42.1	19 9.7	11 56.8	15 2.4	18 52.3	11 2.6	21 50.6	21 10.4	6 49.5

DECEMBER 1994

DAY	EPHEMERIS SIDEREAL TIME	☉	☊	☽	☿	♀	♂	♃	♄	♅	♆	♇
LONGITUDE at NOON												
1 T	16 40 27.8	9♐ 4.1	13♏22.9	17♏50.9	2♐ 3.9	3♏39.6	26♌55.8	28♏16.1	6♓ 6.4	23♑52.4	21♑32.0	28♏24.7
2 F	16 44 24.4	10 4.9	13 19.7	3♐ 1.4	3 38.2	3 58.3	27 14.9	28 29.2	6 8.8	23 55.2	21 33.8	28 27.1
3 S	16 48 20.9	11 5.8	13 16.5	18 13.6	5 12.5	4 18.9	27 33.6	28 42.4	6 11.2	23 58.0	21 35.6	28 29.4
4 S	16 52 17.5	12 6.7	13 13.4	3♑17.5	6 46.7	4 41.3	27 51.8	28 55.6	6 13.8	24 0.8	21 37.4	28 31.8
5 M	16 56 14.1	13 7.6	13 10.2	18 4.0	8 20.9	5 5.7	28 9.6	29 8.7	6 16.4	24 3.7	21 39.3	28 34.1
6 T	17 0 10.6	14 8.5	13 7.0	2♒26.3	9 55.1	5 31.7	28 26.8	29 21.8	6 19.2	24 6.6	21 41.2	28 36.4
7 W	17 4 7.2	15 9.4	13 3.8	16 20.6	11 29.2	5 59.5	28 43.7	29 34.9	6 22.0	24 9.5	21 43.1	28 38.8
8 T	17 8 3.7	16 10.4	13 0.7	29 46.1	13 3.3	6 28.9	28 60.0	29 48.0	6 25.0	24 12.4	21 45.0	28 41.1
9 F	17 12 0.3	17 11.3	12 57.5	12♓44.7	14 37.5	6 59.9	29 15.8	0♐ 1.0	6 28.0	24 15.4	21 47.0	28 43.4
10 S	17 15 56.8	18 12.3	12 54.3	25 19.7	16 11.6	7 32.5	29 31.2	0 14.0	6 31.1	24 18.4	21 48.9	28 45.7
11 S	17 19 53.4	19 13.3	12 51.1	7♈35.8	17 45.9	8 6.5	29 46.0	0 27.0	6 34.3	24 21.5	21 50.9	28 48.0
12 M	17 23 50.0	20 14.3	12 48.0	19 37.7	19 20.2	8 41.9	0♍ 0.3	0 40.0	6 37.7	24 24.6	21 53.0	28 50.3
13 T	17 27 46.5	21 15.3	12 44.8	1♉30.3	20 54.5	9 18.7	0 14.1	0 52.9	6 41.1	24 27.7	21 55.0	28 52.5
14 W	17 31 43.1	22 16.3	12 41.6	13 18.0	22 28.9	9 56.8	0 27.3	1 5.8	6 44.6	24 30.8	21 57.0	28 54.8
15 T	17 35 39.6	23 17.3	12 38.4	25 4.7	24 3.4	10 36.2	0 40.0	1 18.6	6 48.2	24 33.9	21 59.0	28 57.0
16 F	17 39 36.2	24 18.4	12 35.2	6♊53.5	25 38.1	11 16.8	0 52.1	1 31.4	6 51.9	24 37.1	22 1.1	28 59.2
17 S	17 43 32.7	25 19.4	12 32.1	18 47.2	27 12.8	11 58.5	1 3.6	1 44.2	6 55.6	24 40.3	22 3.2	29 1.4
18 S	17 47 29.3	26 20.5	12 28.9	0♋47.4	28 47.7	12 41.4	1 14.6	1 56.9	6 59.5	24 43.5	22 5.3	29 3.6
19 M	17 51 25.9	27 21.5	12 25.7	12 55.9	0♑22.8	13 25.4	1 24.9	2 9.6	7 3.4	24 46.7	22 7.4	29 5.8
20 T	17 55 22.4	28 22.6	12 22.5	25 13.6	1 58.0	14 10.4	1 34.7	2 22.2	7 7.5	24 50.0	22 9.5	29 8.0
21 W	17 59 19.0	29 23.7	12 19.4	7♌41.6	3 33.4	14 56.5	1 43.8	2 34.8	7 11.6	24 53.3	22 11.6	29 10.1
22 T	18 3 15.5	0♑24.7	12 16.2	20 21.1	5 9.0	15 43.5	1 52.2	2 47.4	7 15.8	24 56.6	22 13.7	29 12.2
23 F	18 7 12.1	1 25.9	12 13.0	3♍13.5	6 44.8	16 31.4	2 0.1	2 59.9	7 20.1	24 59.9	22 15.9	29 14.4
24 S	18 11 8.6	2 27.0	12 9.8	16 20.5	8 20.8	17 20.2	2 7.2	3 12.4	7 24.4	25 3.2	22 18.0	29 16.5
25 S	18 15 5.2	3 28.1	12 6.7	29 44.0	9 57.0	18 9.9	2 13.7	3 24.8	7 28.9	25 6.5	22 20.2	29 18.5
26 M	18 19 1.8	4 29.2	12 3.5	13♎25.8	11 33.4	19 0.4	2 19.6	3 37.2	7 33.4	25 9.9	22 22.4	29 20.6
27 T	18 22 58.3	5 30.4	12 0.3	27 27.1	13 9.9	19 51.7	2 24.7	3 49.5	7 38.0	25 13.3	22 24.6	29 22.6
28 W	18 26 54.9	6 31.5	11 57.1	11♏47.9	14 46.7	20 43.8	2 29.1	4 1.8	7 42.7	25 16.7	22 26.8	29 24.6
29 T	18 30 51.4	7 32.7	11 53.9	26 26.4	16 23.6	21 36.6	2 32.7	4 14.0	7 47.4	25 20.1	22 29.0	29 26.6
30 F	18 34 48.0	8 33.9	11 50.8	11♐18.1	18 0.7	22 30.0	2 35.7	4 26.1	7 52.3	25 23.5	22 31.2	29 28.6
31 S	18 38 44.5	9 35.0	11 47.6	26 16.3	19 37.8	23 24.2	2 37.9	4 38.2	7 57.2	25 27.0	22 33.4	29 30.6
DECLINATION at NOON												
1 T	16 40 27.8	21S 48.5	15S 51.3	16S 52.5	20S 30.5	11S 41.5	14N 47.1	19S 1.3	10S 59.8	21S 49.2	21S 9.7	6S 51.0
4 S	16 52 17.5	22 14.5	15 48.4	19 27.7	21 42.6	11 35.5	14 33.0	19 10.1	10 56.7	21 47.7	21 8.9	6 52.3
7 W	17 4 7.2	22 36.7	15 45.5	10 56.9	22 45.1	11 37.8	14 20.3	19 18.6	10 53.3	21 46.1	21 8.0	6 53.6
10 S	17 15 56.8	22 54.8	15 42.7	1N 46.2	23 37.5	11 47.6	14 9.1	19 27.0	10 49.5	21 44.5	21 7.2	6 54.8
13 T	17 27 46.5	23 8.9	15 39.8	13 5.5	24 19.0	12 3.9	13 59.6	19 35.1	10 45.5	21 42.9	21 6.3	6 55.9
16 F	17 39 36.2	23 18.9	15 36.9	19 30.0	24 49.1	12 25.7	13 51.9	19 43.0	10 41.1	21 41.2	21 5.4	6 56.9
19 M	17 51 25.9	23 24.7	15 34.0	18 25.3	25 7.1	12 52.2	13 46.2	19 50.7	10 36.5	21 39.4	21 4.4	6 57.9
22 T	18 3 15.5	23 26.2	15 31.1	9 51.5	25 12.5	13 22.4	13 42.4	19 58.2	10 31.6	21 37.7	21 3.4	6 58.7
25 S	18 15 5.2	23 23.5	15 28.2	3S 9.6	25 4.8	13 55.6	13 40.9	20 5.3	10 26.4	21 35.8	21 2.4	6 59.5
28 W	18 26 54.9	23 16.6	15 25.2	15 31.1	24 43.6	14 30.9	13 41.7	20 12.3	10 20.9	21 34.0	21 1.4	7 0.1
31 S	18 38 44.5	23 5.5	15 22.3	19 54.6	24 8.5	15 7.7	13 44.8	20 19.0	10 15.2	21 32.1	21 0.4	7 0.7

JANUARY 1995

LONGITUDE at NOON

DAY	EPHEMERIS SIDEREAL TIME h m s	☉ ° ′	☊ ° ′	☾ ° ′	☿ ° ′	♀ ° ′	♂ ° ′	♃ ° ′	♄ ° ′	♅ ° ′	♆ ° ′	♇ ° ′
1 S	18 42 41.1	10♑36.2	11♏44.4	11♑12.5	21♑15.0	24♏19.0	2♍39.3	4♐50.3	8♓ 2.2	25♑30.4	22♑35.7	29♏32.5
2 M	18 46 37.7	11 37.4	11 41.2	25 57.5	22 52.2	25 14.4	2 40.1	5 2.3	8 7.3	25 33.9	22 38.0	29 35.5
3 T	18 50 34.2	12 38.6	11 38.1	10♒23.1	24 29.4	26 10.4	2R40.0	5 14.2	8 12.4	25 37.4	22 40.3	29 37.4
4 W	18 54 30.8	13 39.8	11 34.9	24 23.7	26 6.4	27 7.0	2 39.1	5 26.0	8 17.6	25 40.8	22 42.5	29 39.2
5 T	18 58 27.3	14 41.0	11 31.7	7♓56.2	27 43.1	28 4.1	2 37.5	5 37.8	8 22.9	25 44.3	22 44.8	29 41.1
6 F	19 2 23.9	15 42.1	11 28.5	21 1.0	29 19.5	29 1.7	2 35.0	5 49.5	8 28.2	25 47.8	22 47.0	29 42.9
7 S	19 6 20.4	16 43.3	11 25.4	3♈40.4	0♒55.3	29 59.9	2 31.8	6 1.2	8 33.6	25 51.3	22 49.3	29 44.7
8 S	19 10 17.0	17 44.5	11 22.2	15 58.8	2 30.5	0♐58.5	2 27.8	6 12.7	8 39.1	25 54.9	22 51.6	29 46.5
9 M	19 14 13.6	18 45.6	11 19.0	28 1.2	4 4.7	1 57.6	2 22.9	6 24.2	8 44.7	25 58.4	22 53.8	29 48.2
10 T	19 18 10.1	19 46.8	11 15.8	9♉53.1	5 37.9	2 57.2	2 17.3	6 35.6	8 50.3	26 1.9	22 56.1	29 50.0
11 W	19 22 6.7	20 47.9	11 12.7	21 40.2	7 9.6	3 57.2	2 10.9	6 47.0	8 55.9	26 5.4	22 58.4	29 51.7
12 T	19 26 3.2	21 49.0	11 9.5	3♊27.3	8 39.5	4 57.6	2 3.6	6 58.3	9 1.7	26 9.0	23 0.7	29 53.3
13 F	19 29 59.8	22 50.1	11 6.3	15 18.8	10 7.3	5 58.4	1 55.6	7 9.4	9 7.5	26 12.5	23 2.9	29 55.0
14 S	19 33 56.3	23 51.2	11 3.1	27 18.2	11 32.6	6 59.7	1 46.8	7 20.5	9 13.3	26 16.0	23 5.2	29 56.6
15 S	19 37 52.9	24 52.3	10 59.9	9♋28.2	12 54.7	8 1.3	1 37.1	7 31.6	9 19.2	26 19.6	23 7.5	29 58.2
16 M	19 41 49.5	25 53.4	10 56.8	21 50.2	14 13.3	9 3.3	1 26.7	7 42.5	9 25.2	26 23.1	23 9.8	29 59.7
17 T	19 45 46.0	26 54.5	10 53.6	4♌24.8	15 27.5	10 5.6	1 15.4	7 53.4	9 31.2	26 26.7	23 12.0	0♐ 1.3
18 W	19 49 42.6	27 55.6	10 50.4	17 11.8	16 36.8	11 8.3	1 3.4	8 4.1	9 37.3	26 30.2	23 14.3	0 2.8
19 T	19 53 39.1	28 56.6	10 47.2	0♍10.6	17 40.3	12 11.4	0 50.6	8 14.8	9 43.4	26 33.8	23 16.6	0 4.3
20 F	19 57 35.7	29 57.7	10 44.1	13 20.6	18 37.3	13 14.8	0 37.0	8 25.4	9 49.6	26 37.3	23 18.8	0 5.7
21 S	20 1 32.2	0♒58.7	10 40.9	26 41.2	19 26.8	14 18.4	0 22.7	8 35.9	9 55.9	26 40.8	23 21.1	0 7.1
22 S	20 5 28.8	1 59.8	10 37.7	10♎12.5	20 8.1	15 22.5	0 7.6	8 46.3	10 2.2	26 44.4	23 23.4	0 8.6
23 M	20 9 25.3	3 0.8	10 34.5	23 54.8	20 40.3	16 26.7	29♌51.8	8 56.7	10 8.6	26 47.9	23 25.7	0 9.9
24 T	20 13 21.9	4 1.9	10 31.4	7♏48.7	21 2.5	17 31.3	29 35.3	9 6.9	10 14.9	26 51.5	23 27.9	0 11.3
25 W	20 17 18.5	5 2.9	10 28.2	21 54.6	21 14.2	18 36.1	29 18.0	9 17.0	10 21.4	26 55.0	23 30.1	0 12.6
26 T	20 21 15.0	6 3.9	10 25.0	6♐11.9	21 14.7	19 41.2	29 0.1	9 27.0	10 27.9	26 58.5	23 32.4	0 13.8
27 F	20 25 11.6	7 4.9	10 21.8	20 38.6	21R 3.8	20 46.6	28 41.6	9 36.9	10 34.4	27 2.0	23 34.6	0 15.1
28 S	20 29 8.1	8 5.9	10 18.6	5♑11.0	20 41.6	21 52.2	28 22.4	9 46.7	10 41.0	27 5.5	23 36.8	0 16.3
29 S	20 33 4.7	9 6.9	10 15.5	19 43.4	20 8.2	22 58.0	28 2.6	9 56.4	10 47.6	27 9.0	23 39.0	0 17.5
30 M	20 37 1.2	10 7.8	10 12.3	4♒ 9.0	19 24.4	24 4.0	27 42.3	10 6.0	10 54.2	27 12.5	23 41.2	0 18.6
31 T	20 40 57.8	11 8.8	10 9.1	18 21.1	18 31.4	25 10.3	27 21.4	10 15.5	11 0.9	27 15.9	23 43.4	0 19.7

DECLINATION at NOON

DAY	EPHEMERIS SIDEREAL TIME h m s	☉	☊	☾	☿	♀	♂	♃	♄	♅	♆	♇
1 S	18 42 41.1	23S 0.8	15S 21.3	18S 39.7	23S 53.7	15S 20.1	13N 46.4	20S 21.2	10S 13.2	21S 31.5	21S 0.0	7S 0.8
4 W	18 54 30.8	22 44.2	15 18.4	8 41.5	23 0.0	15 57.7	13 52.9	20 27.6	10 7.2	21 29.6	20 59.0	7 1.7
7 S	19 6 20.4	22 23.5	15 15.5	4N 23.6	21 52.8	16 35.2	14 1.9	20 33.7	10 0.9	21 27.6	20 57.9	7 2.0
10 T	19 18 10.1	21 58.8	15 12.5	14 59.7	20 33.1	17 12.1	14 13.5	20 39.6	9 54.4	21 25.7	20 56.8	7 2.3
13 F	19 29 59.8	21 30.3	15 9.5	19 53.4	19 3.1	17 47.7	14 27.4	20 45.2	9 47.7	21 23.7	20 55.7	7 2.4
16 M	19 41 49.5	20 58.1	15 6.6	17 0.5	17 26.4	18 21.6	14 43.8	20 50.5	9 40.8	21 21.7	20 54.6	7 2.5
19 T	19 53 39.1	20 22.2	15 3.6	6 57.8	15 49.2	18 53.2	15 2.3	20 55.6	9 33.8	21 19.7	20 53.5	7 2.5
22 S	20 5 28.8	19 42.9	15 0.6	6S 24.5	14 20.2	19 22.3	15 22.9	21 0.5	9 26.5	21 17.7	20 52.3	7 2.3
25 W	20 17 18.5	19 0.2	14 57.7	17 18.2	13 10.3	19 48.2	15 45.2	21 5.0	9 19.1	21 15.7	20 51.2	7 2.1
28 S	20 29 8.1	18 14.5	14 54.7	19 14.9	12 30.2	20 10.7	16 9.0	21 9.4	9 11.5	21 13.7	20 50.1	7 1.8
31 T	20 40 57.8	17 25.7	14 51.7	10 36.7	12 26.2	20 29.3	16 33.8	21 13.5	9 3.8	21 11.7	20 49.0	7 1.4

FEBRUARY 1995

LONGITUDE at NOON

DAY	EPHEMERIS SIDEREAL TIME h m s	☉ ° ′	☊ ° ′	☾ ° ′	☿ ° ′	♀ ° ′	♂ ° ′	♃ ° ′	♄ ° ′	♅ ° ′	♆ ° ′	♇ ° ′
1 W	20 44 54.3	12♒ 9.7	10♏ 5.9	2♓13.8	17♒30.5	26♐16.8	27♌ 0.1	10♐24.9	11♓ 7.7	27♑19.4	23♑45.6	0♐20.8
2 T	20 48 50.9	13 10.6	10 2.8	15 43.4	16R23.4	27 23.4	26R38.3	10 34.1	11 14.5	27 22.9	23 47.8	0 21.8
3 F	20 52 47.5	14 11.5	9 59.6	28 48.5	15 12.3	28 30.3	26 16.0	10 43.3	11 21.3	27 26.3	23 50.0	0 22.9
4 S	20 56 44.0	15 12.4	9 56.4	11♈30.1	13 59.2	29 37.3	25 53.5	10 52.3	11 28.1	27 29.7	23 52.1	0 23.8
5 S	21 0 40.6	16 13.2	9 53.2	23 51.1	12 46.1	0♑44.5	25 30.5	11 1.2	11 35.0	27 33.1	23 54.3	0 24.8
6 M	21 4 37.1	17 14.1	9 50.0	5♉55.9	11 35.1	1 51.9	25 7.3	11 10.0	11 41.9	27 36.5	23 56.4	0 25.7
7 T	21 8 33.7	18 14.9	9 46.9	17 49.7	10 27.8	2 59.5	24 43.9	11 18.7	11 48.9	27 39.9	23 58.5	0 26.6
8 W	21 12 30.2	19 15.6	9 43.7	29 38.1	9 25.9	4 7.2	24 20.3	11 27.2	11 55.8	27 43.3	24 0.6	0 27.4
9 T	21 16 26.8	20 16.4	9 40.5	11♊26.6	8 30.3	5 15.1	23 56.5	11 35.6	12 2.8	27 46.6	24 2.7	0 28.2
10 F	21 20 23.3	21 17.1	9 37.3	23 20.4	7 42.0	6 23.1	23 32.6	11 43.9	12 9.9	27 49.9	24 4.8	0 29.0
11 S	21 24 19.9	22 17.8	9 34.2	5♋24.2	7 1.4	7 31.3	23 8.6	11 52.1	12 16.9	27 53.2	24 6.9	0 29.7
12 S	21 28 16.4	23 18.5	9 31.0	17 41.5	6 28.9	8 39.6	22 44.7	12 0.2	12 24.1	27 56.6	24 9.0	0 30.5
13 M	21 32 13.0	24 19.2	9 27.8	0♌14.7	6 4.4	9 48.1	22 20.8	12 8.1	12 31.2	27 59.8	24 11.0	0 31.1
14 T	21 36 9.6	25 19.8	9 24.6	13 4.9	5 47.9	10 56.7	21 56.9	12 15.8	12 38.3	28 3.1	24 13.0	0 31.8
15 W	21 40 6.1	26 20.4	9 21.4	26 11.7	5 39.0	12 5.5	21 33.2	12 23.5	12 45.5	28 6.3	24 15.0	0 32.4
16 T	21 44 2.7	27 20.9	9 18.3	9♍33.5	5 37.5	13 14.4	21 9.6	12 31.0	12 52.7	28 9.5	24 17.0	0 32.9
17 F	21 47 59.2	28 21.5	9 15.1	23 8.1	5D43.0	14 23.4	20 46.3	12 38.3	12 59.9	28 12.7	24 19.0	0 33.5
18 S	21 51 55.8	29 22.0	9 11.9	6♎52.6	5 55.0	15 32.5	20 23.1	12 45.6	13 7.1	28 15.9	24 20.9	0 34.0
19 S	21 55 52.3	0♓22.5	9 8.7	20 44.6	6 13.0	16 41.7	20 0.3	12 52.7	13 14.3	28 19.0	24 22.9	0 34.4
20 M	21 59 48.9	1 23.0	9 5.6	4♏42.0	6 36.8	17 51.1	19 37.8	12 59.6	13 21.6	28 22.1	24 24.8	0 34.9
21 T	22 3 45.4	2 23.4	9 2.4	18 43.5	7 5.8	19 0.6	19 15.7	13 6.4	13 28.8	28 25.2	24 26.7	0 35.2
22 W	22 7 42.0	3 23.9	8 59.2	2♐48.2	7 39.7	20 10.2	18 53.9	13 13.0	13 36.1	28 28.3	24 28.5	0 35.6
23 T	22 11 38.5	4 24.3	8 56.0	16 55.4	8 18.1	21 19.9	18 32.6	13 19.5	13 43.4	28 31.3	24 30.4	0 35.9
24 F	22 15 35.1	5 24.7	8 52.8	1♑ 3.9	9 0.6	22 29.7	18 11.8	13 25.9	13 50.7	28 34.3	24 32.2	0 36.2
25 S	22 19 31.6	6 25.0	8 49.7	15 11.8	9 47.0	23 39.6	17 51.5	13 32.1	13 58.0	28 37.3	24 34.1	0 36.4
26 S	22 23 28.2	7 25.4	8 46.5	29 16.2	10 36.9	24 49.6	17 31.8	13 38.2	14 5.4	28 40.3	24 35.8	0 36.7
27 M	22 27 24.7	8 25.7	8 43.3	13♒13.7	11 30.1	25 59.7	17 12.6	13 44.0	14 12.7	28 43.2	24 37.6	0 36.8
28 T	22 31 21.3	9 26.0	8 40.1	27 0.1	12 26.3	27 9.9	16 54.1	13 49.8	14 20.1	28 46.1	24 39.4	0 37.0

DECLINATION at NOON

DAY	EPHEMERIS SIDEREAL TIME h m s	☉	☊	☾	☿	♀	♂	♃	♄	♅	♆	♇
1 W	20 44 54.3	17S 8.9	14S 50.7	6S 21.0	12S 32.7	20S 34.7	16N 42.2	21S 14.8	9S 1.2	21S 11.0	20S 48.6	7S 1.3
4 S	20 56 44.0	16 16.5	14 47.7	6N 43.4	13 10.9	20 47.8	17 7.6	21 18.6	8 53.3	21 9.0	20 47.5	7 0.8
7 T	21 8 33.7	15 21.6	14 44.7	16 25.7	14 6.4	20 56.5	17 32.8	21 22.1	8 45.3	21 7.0	20 46.4	7 0.2
10 F	21 20 23.3	14 24.3	14 41.6	19 45.7	15 5.1	21 0.5	17 57.5	21 25.4	8 37.3	21 5.1	20 45.3	6 59.6
13 M	21 32 13.0	13 24.9	14 38.6	15 14.4	15 57.4	20 59.7	18 21.1	21 28.4	8 29.1	21 3.2	20 44.3	6 58.8
16 T	21 44 2.7	12 23.5	14 35.6	3 59.9	16 38.4	20 53.9	18 43.2	21 31.3	8 20.8	21 1.3	20 43.2	6 58.0
19 S	21 55 52.3	11 20.4	14 32.6	9S 28.9	17 6.3	20 43.1	19 3.6	21 33.9	8 12.5	20 59.4	20 42.2	6 57.2
22 W	22 7 42.0	10 15.6	14 29.5	18 36.5	17 20.6	20 27.1	19 21.8	21 36.3	8 4.2	20 57.6	20 41.2	6 56.2
25 S	22 19 31.6	9 9.4	14 26.5	17 54.6	17 21.3	20 6.1	19 37.6	21 38.4	7 55.8	20 55.8	20 40.2	6 55.2
28 T	22 31 21.3	8 1.9	14 23.4	8 0.9	17 8.7	19 39.9	19 51.0	21 40.4	7 47.3	20 54.1	20 39.3	6 54.2

MARCH 1995

DAY	EPHEMERIS SIDEREAL TIME	☉	☊	☽	☿	♀	♂	♃	♄	♅	♆	♇
	h m s	° ′	° ′	° ′	° ′	° ′	° ′	° ′	° ′	° ′	° ′	° ′
LONGITUDE at NOON												
1 W	22 35 17.9	10 ♓ 26.3	8 ♏ 37.0	10 ♓ 31.7	13 ♒ 25.4	28 ♑ 20.1	16 ♌ 36.1	13 ♐ 55.4	14 ♓ 27.4	28 ♑ 49.0	24 ♑ 41.1	0 ♐ 37.1
2 T	22 39 14.4	11 26.5	8 33.8	23 45.8	14 27.2	29 30.5	16 R 18.9	14 0.8	14 34.8	28 51.8	24 42.8	0 37.1
3 F	22 43 11.0	12 26.7	8 30.6	6 ♈ 40.8	15 31.4	0 ♒ 40.9	16 2.3	14 6.0	14 42.2	28 54.6	24 44.5	0 37.2
4 S	22 47 7.5	13 26.9	8 27.4	19 17.0	16 37.9	1 51.4	15 46.4	14 11.1	14 49.5	28 57.4	24 46.2	0 37.2
5 S	22 51 4.1	14 27.1	8 24.2	1 ♉ 36.0	17 46.6	3 2.0	15 31.3	14 16.1	14 56.9	29 0.2	24 47.8	0 37.2
6 M	22 55 0.6	15 27.2	8 21.1	13 40.8	18 57.4	4 12.6	15 16.9	14 20.9	15 4.3	29 2.9	24 49.4	0 R 37.1
7 T	22 58 57.2	16 27.2	8 17.9	25 35.6	20 10.1	5 23.3	15 3.2	14 25.5	15 11.7	29 5.6	24 51.0	0 37.0
8 W	23 2 53.7	17 27.3	8 14.7	7 ♊ 25.1	21 24.6	6 34.0	14 50.3	14 29.9	15 19.0	29 8.2	24 52.6	0 36.9
9 T	23 6 50.3	18 27.3	8 11.5	19 14.6	22 40.9	7 44.9	14 38.2	14 34.1	15 26.4	29 10.8	24 54.1	0 36.7
10 F	23 10 46.8	19 27.2	8 8.4	1 ♋ 9.3	23 58.9	8 55.7	14 26.8	14 38.2	15 33.8	29 13.4	24 55.6	0 36.5
11 S	23 14 43.4	20 27.1	8 5.2	13 14.3	25 18.5	10 6.7	14 16.3	14 42.1	15 41.1	29 15.9	24 57.1	0 36.2
12 S	23 18 39.9	21 27.0	8 2.0	25 34.2	26 39.7	11 17.7	14 6.5	14 45.9	15 48.5	29 18.4	24 58.6	0 35.9
13 M	23 22 36.5	22 26.9	7 58.8	8 ♌ 12.4	28 2.3	12 28.7	13 57.5	14 49.5	15 55.8	29 20.9	25 0.0	0 35.6
14 T	23 26 33.0	23 26.7	7 55.6	21 11.4	29 26.5	13 39.8	13 49.3	14 52.8	16 3.1	29 23.3	25 1.4	0 35.3
15 W	23 30 29.6	24 26.5	7 52.5	4 ♍ 31.6	0 ♓ 52.0	14 51.0	13 41.9	14 56.1	16 10.5	29 25.7	25 2.8	0 34.9
16 T	23 34 26.1	25 26.2	7 49.3	18 12.0	2 19.0	16 2.2	13 35.2	14 59.1	16 17.8	29 28.1	25 4.1	0 34.5
17 F	23 38 22.7	26 25.9	7 46.1	2 ♎ 9.7	3 47.3	17 13.5	13 29.4	15 2.0	16 25.1	29 30.4	25 5.5	0 34.0
18 S	23 42 19.2	27 25.6	7 42.9	16 20.6	5 17.0	18 24.8	13 24.3	15 4.7	16 32.4	29 32.6	25 6.8	0 33.6
19 S	23 46 15.8	28 25.3	7 39.8	0 ♏ 40.0	6 48.0	19 36.2	13 20.0	15 7.2	16 39.6	29 34.9	25 8.0	0 33.0
20 M	23 50 12.3	29 24.9	7 36.6	15 2.9	8 20.4	20 47.7	13 16.5	15 9.5	16 46.9	29 37.1	25 9.3	0 32.5
21 T	23 54 8.9	0 ♈ 24.5	7 33.4	29 25.1	9 54.1	21 59.1	13 13.7	15 11.6	16 54.1	29 39.2	25 10.5	0 31.9
22 W	23 58 5.4	1 24.0	7 30.2	13 ♐ 43.3	11 29.0	23 10.7	13 11.7	15 13.6	17 1.4	29 41.3	25 11.7	0 31.3
23 T	0 2 2.0	2 23.6	7 27.0	27 55.0	13 5.3	24 22.3	13 10.4	15 15.4	17 8.6	29 43.4	25 12.8	0 30.7
24 F	0 5 58.5	3 23.1	7 23.9	11 ♑ 58.5	14 42.9	25 33.9	13 9.9	15 17.0	17 15.8	29 45.4	25 13.9	0 30.0
25 S	0 9 55.1	4 22.6	7 20.7	25 52.5	16 21.9	26 45.6	13 D 10.1	15 18.4	17 22.9	29 47.4	25 15.0	0 29.3
26 S	0 13 51.7	5 22.0	7 17.5	9 ♒ 36.1	18 2.1	27 57.3	13 11.0	15 19.6	17 30.1	29 49.4	25 16.1	0 28.6
27 M	0 17 48.2	6 21.5	7 14.3	23 8.1	19 43.7	29 9.1	13 12.7	15 20.7	17 37.2	29 51.3	25 17.1	0 27.9
28 T	0 21 44.8	7 20.8	7 11.1	6 ♓ 27.6	21 26.6	0 ♓ 20.9	13 15.1	15 21.5	17 44.3	29 53.1	25 18.1	0 27.1
29 W	0 25 41.3	8 20.2	7 8.0	19 33.6	23 10.8	1 32.7	13 18.1	15 22.2	17 51.4	29 54.9	25 19.1	0 26.2
30 T	0 29 37.9	9 19.5	7 4.8	2 ♈ 25.5	24 56.4	2 44.5	13 21.9	15 22.6	17 58.5	29 56.7	25 20.1	0 25.4
31 F	0 33 34.4	10 18.8	7 1.6	15 3.1	26 43.4	3 56.4	13 26.3	15 22.9	18 5.5	29 58.4	25 21.0	0 24.5
DECLINATION at NOON												
1 W	22 35 17.9	7 S 39.2	14 S 22.4	3 S 41.3	17 S 1.6	19 S 30.1	19 N 54.9	21 S 41.0	7 S 44.5	20 S 53.5	20 S 39.0	6 S 53.8
4 S	22 47 7.5	6 30.4	14 19.3	8 N 58.4	16 31.9	18 57.3	20 4.8	21 42.7	7 36.1	20 51.9	20 38.1	6 52.7
7 T	22 58 57.2	5 20.8	14 16.3	17 32.2	15 49.7	18 19.7	20 12.0	21 44.2	7 27.6	20 50.2	20 37.2	6 51.5
10 F	23 10 46.8	4 10.5	14 13.2	19 14.3	14 55.3	17 37.4	20 16.8	21 45.5	7 19.2	20 48.7	20 36.3	6 50.3
13 M	23 22 36.5	2 59.8	14 10.1	13 14.2	13 49.1	16 50.6	20 19.1	21 46.6	7 10.8	20 47.2	20 35.5	6 49.0
16 T	23 34 26.1	1 48.8	14 7.0	1 7.8	12 31.3	15 59.5	20 19.0	21 47.5	7 2.4	20 45.8	20 34.8	6 47.7
19 S	23 46 15.8	0 37.7	14 3.9	12 S 9.5	11 2.1	15 4.3	20 16.7	21 48.2	6 54.1	20 44.5	20 34.1	6 46.4
22 W	23 58 5.4	0 N 33.4	14 0.8	19 16.7	9 22.0	14 5.2	20 12.4	21 48.7	6 45.9	20 43.2	20 33.4	6 45.1
25 S	0 9 55.1	1 44.4	13 57.7	15 55.6	7 31.1	13 2.5	20 6.1	21 49.1	6 37.7	20 42.0	20 32.8	6 43.7
28 T	0 21 44.8	2 55.0	13 54.6	4 57.8	5 29.8	11 56.5	19 58.0	21 49.2	6 29.6	20 40.9	20 32.2	6 42.3
31 F	0 33 34.4	4 5.0	13 51.5	7 N 37.9	3 18.5	10 47.4	19 48.1	21 49.2	6 21.6	20 39.8	20 31.6	6 40.9

APRIL 1995

DAY	EPHEMERIS SIDEREAL TIME	☉	☊	☽	☿	♀	♂	♃	♄	♅	♆	♇
LONGITUDE at NOON												
1 S	0 37 31.0	11 ♈ 18.1	6 ♏ 58.4	27 ♈ 26.9	28 ♓ 31.7	5 ♓ 8.3	13 ♌ 31.4	15 ♐ 23.0	18 ♓ 12.5	0 ♒ 0.1	25 ♑ 21.8	0 ♐ 23.6
2 S	0 41 27.5	12 17.3	6 55.3	9 ♉ 38.2	0 ♈ 21.5	6 20.3	13 37.2	15 R 22.9	18 19.5	0 1.7	25 22.7	0 R 22.7
3 M	0 45 24.1	13 16.5	6 52.1	21 39.1	2 12.6	7 32.3	13 43.6	15 22.6	18 26.4	0 3.3	25 23.5	0 21.7
4 T	0 49 20.6	14 15.6	6 48.9	3 ♊ 32.4	4 5.1	8 44.3	13 50.7	15 22.1	18 33.3	0 4.8	25 24.3	0 20.7
5 W	0 53 17.2	15 14.7	6 45.7	15 21.8	5 59.0	9 56.3	13 58.4	15 21.5	18 40.2	0 6.3	25 25.0	0 19.7
6 T	0 57 13.7	16 13.8	6 42.5	27 11.5	7 54.3	11 8.3	14 6.7	15 20.6	18 47.0	0 7.8	25 25.7	0 18.6
7 F	1 1 10.3	17 12.8	6 39.4	9 ♋ 6.0	9 51.0	12 20.4	14 15.6	15 19.6	18 53.8	0 9.2	25 26.4	0 17.6
8 S	1 5 6.8	18 11.8	6 36.2	21 10.1	11 49.1	13 32.5	14 25.1	15 18.3	19 0.6	0 10.5	25 27.1	0 16.5
9 S	1 9 3.4	19 10.8	6 33.0	3 ♌ 28.6	13 48.4	14 44.6	14 35.1	15 16.9	19 7.3	0 11.8	25 27.7	0 15.3
10 M	1 12 59.9	20 9.7	6 29.8	16 5.7	15 49.1	15 56.8	14 45.8	15 15.3	19 14.0	0 13.1	25 28.3	0 14.2
11 T	1 16 56.5	21 8.6	6 26.7	29 5.0	17 51.0	17 8.9	14 57.0	15 13.5	19 20.7	0 14.3	25 28.8	0 13.0
12 W	1 20 53.0	22 7.4	6 23.5	12 ♍ 28.6	19 54.1	18 21.1	15 8.7	15 11.6	19 27.3	0 15.4	25 29.3	0 11.8
13 T	1 24 49.6	23 6.2	6 20.3	26 16.8	21 58.2	19 33.3	15 21.0	15 9.4	19 33.8	0 16.5	25 29.8	0 10.6
14 F	1 28 46.1	24 5.0	6 17.1	10 ♎ 28.0	24 3.3	20 45.6	15 33.8	15 7.1	19 40.4	0 17.6	25 30.3	0 9.4
15 S	1 32 42.7	25 3.7	6 13.9	24 58.1	26 9.1	21 57.8	15 47.1	15 4.6	19 46.9	0 18.6	25 30.7	0 8.1
16 S	1 36 39.3	26 2.5	6 10.8	9 ♏ 41.5	28 15.7	23 10.1	16 0.9	15 2.0	19 53.4	0 19.6	25 31.1	0 6.9
17 M	1 40 35.8	27 1.1	6 7.6	24 31.0	0 ♉ 22.5	24 22.4	16 15.1	14 59.1	19 59.8	0 20.5	25 31.5	0 5.6
18 T	1 44 32.4	27 59.8	6 4.4	9 ♐ 19.4	2 29.6	25 34.8	16 29.9	14 56.1	20 6.1	0 21.4	25 31.8	0 4.3
19 W	1 48 28.9	28 58.4	6 1.2	23 60.0	4 36.7	26 47.1	16 45.1	14 52.9	20 12.4	0 22.2	25 32.1	0 2.9
20 T	1 52 25.5	29 57.0	5 58.1	8 ♑ 27.6	6 43.3	27 59.5	17 0.8	14 49.5	20 18.7	0 22.9	25 32.3	0 1.5
21 F	1 56 22.0	0 ♉ 55.5	5 54.9	22 38.7	8 49.4	29 11.9	17 16.9	14 45.9	20 24.9	0 23.7	25 32.6	0 0.2
22 S	2 0 18.6	1 54.1	5 51.7	6 ♒ 31.6	10 54.5	0 ♈ 24.3	17 33.4	14 42.2	20 31.1	0 24.3	25 32.7	29 ♏ 58.8
23 S	2 4 15.1	2 52.6	5 48.5	20 5.8	12 58.3	1 36.7	17 50.4	14 38.3	20 37.2	0 24.9	25 32.9	29 57.3
24 M	2 8 11.7	3 51.0	5 45.3	3 ♓ 22.1	15 0.6	2 49.1	18 7.8	14 34.3	20 43.2	0 25.5	25 33.0	29 55.9
25 T	2 12 8.2	4 49.5	5 42.2	16 21.7	17 0.9	4 1.6	18 25.6	14 30.0	20 49.2	0 26.0	25 33.1	29 54.5
26 W	2 16 4.8	5 47.9	5 39.0	29 6.3	18 59.1	5 14.1	18 43.8	14 25.7	20 55.2	0 26.5	25 33.2	29 53.0
27 T	2 20 1.3	6 46.3	5 35.8	11 ♈ 37.6	20 54.7	6 26.6	19 2.4	14 21.1	21 1.1	0 26.9	25 33.2	29 51.5
28 F	2 23 57.9	7 44.7	5 32.6	23 57.1	22 47.6	7 39.1	19 21.4	14 16.4	21 6.9	0 27.2	25 33.2	29 50.0
29 S	2 27 54.4	8 43.0	5 29.5	6 ♉ 6.7	24 37.4	8 51.6	19 40.8	14 11.6	21 12.7	0 27.5	25 R 33.1	29 48.5
30 S	2 31 51.0	9 41.3	5 26.3	18 8.0	26 24.1	10 4.1	20 0.6	14 6.6	21 18.5	0 27.8	25 33.1	29 47.0
DECLINATION at NOON												
1 S	0 37 31.0	4 N 28.2	13 S 50.5	11 N 15.7	2 S 32.6	10 S 23.7	19 N 44.4	21 S 49.2	6 S 19.0	20 S 39.5	20 S 31.5	6 S 40.5
4 T	0 49 20.6	5 37.4	13 47.3	18 26.2	0 9.0	9 11.0	19 32.3	21 49.0	6 11.2	20 38.6	20 31.0	6 39.1
7 F	1 1 10.3	6 45.6	13 44.2	18 25.2	2 N 22.9	7 55.9	19 18.6	21 48.5	6 3.5	20 37.8	20 30.6	6 37.7
10 M	1 12 59.9	7 52.8	13 41.1	11 3.3	5 1.6	6 38.7	19 3.5	21 48.0	5 55.9	20 37.0	20 30.2	6 36.3
13 T	1 24 49.6	8 58.8	13 37.9	1 S 35.8	7 44.9	5 19.7	18 47.0	21 47.2	5 48.5	20 36.4	20 29.9	6 34.9
16 S	1 36 39.3	10 3.4	13 34.8	14 21.3	10 29.6	3 59.2	18 29.2	21 46.3	5 41.2	20 35.8	20 29.7	6 33.6
19 W	1 48 28.9	11 6.5	13 31.6	19 20.6	13 11.4	2 37.4	18 10.1	21 45.2	5 34.1	20 35.4	20 29.5	6 32.2
22 S	2 0 18.6	12 8.0	13 28.5	13 30.7	15 44.9	1 14.7	17 49.8	21 44.0	5 27.2	20 35.0	20 29.3	6 30.9
25 T	2 12 8.2	13 7.8	13 25.3	1 40.8	18 4.6	0 N 8.6	17 28.2	21 42.5	5 20.5	20 34.7	20 29.2	6 29.7
28 F	2 23 57.9	14 5.5	13 22.2	10 N 17.4	20 5.9	1 32.2	17 5.5	21 41.0	5 14.0	20 34.6	20 29.2	6 28.4

MAY 1995

DAY	EPHEMERIS SIDEREAL TIME	☉	☊	☽	☿	♀	♂	♃	♄	♅	♆	♇
	h m s	° ′	° ′	° ′	° ′	° ′	° ′	° ′	° ′	° ′	° ′	° ′
LONGITUDE at NOON												
1 M	2 35 47.6	10♉39.6	5♏23.1	0♊ 2.9	28♉ 7.4	11♈16.7	20♌20.7	14♐ 1.4	21♓24.1	0♒28.0	25♑33.0	29♏45.4
2 T	2 39 44.1	11 37.8	5 19.9	11 53.6	29 47.1	12 29.2	20 41.2	13R56.1	21 29.7	0 28.2	25R32.8	29R43.9
3 W	2 43 40.7	12 36.1	5 16.7	23 42.6	1♊23.1	13 41.8	21 2.1	13 50.7	21 35.3	0 28.3	25 32.7	29 42.3
4 T	2 47 37.2	13 34.2	5 13.6	5♋32.9	2 55.2	14 54.4	21 23.2	13 45.1	21 40.8	0 28.3	25 32.4	29 40.7
5 F	2 51 33.8	14 32.4	5 10.4	17 28.0	4 23.5	16 7.0	21 44.8	13 39.4	21 46.2	0 28.3	25 32.2	29 39.2
6 S	2 55 30.3	15 30.5	5 7.2	29 31.7	5 47.7	17 19.6	22 6.6	13 33.6	21 51.5	0 28.3	25 31.9	29 37.6
7 S	2 59 26.9	16 28.6	5 4.0	11♌48.2	7 7.9	18 32.2	22 28.8	13 27.6	21 56.9	0 28.3	25 31.7	29 36.0
8 M	3 3 23.4	17 26.7	5 0.9	24 21.6	8 23.8	19 44.8	22 51.3	13 21.6	22 2.1	0R28.1	25 31.4	29 34.4
9 T	3 7 20.0	18 24.7	4 57.7	7♍16.1	9 35.5	20 57.5	23 14.1	13 15.4	22 7.3	0 27.9	25 31.0	29 32.8
10 W	3 11 16.5	19 22.7	4 54.5	20 34.9	10 42.9	22 10.1	23 37.2	13 9.1	22 12.3	0 27.7	25 30.6	29 31.2
11 T	3 15 13.1	20 20.7	4 51.3	4♎20.1	11 45.9	23 22.7	24 0.6	13 2.6	22 17.4	0 27.4	25 30.2	29 29.5
12 F	3 19 9.7	21 18.6	4 48.1	18 31.9	12 44.5	24 35.4	24 24.3	12 56.1	22 22.3	0 27.1	25 29.7	29 27.9
13 S	3 23 6.2	22 16.5	4 45.0	3♏ 7.8	13 38.5	25 48.0	24 48.2	12 49.5	22 27.2	0 26.7	25 29.2	29 26.3
14 S	3 27 2.8	23 14.4	4 41.8	18 3.0	14 28.0	27 0.7	25 12.4	12 42.8	22 32.0	0 26.2	25 28.7	29 24.6
15 M	3 30 59.3	24 12.2	4 38.6	3♐ 9.8	15 12.9	28 13.4	25 36.9	12 35.9	22 36.8	0 25.8	25 28.2	29 23.0
16 T	3 34 55.9	25 10.1	4 35.4	18 19.2	15 53.1	29 26.1	26 1.7	12 29.0	22 41.4	0 25.2	25 27.6	29 21.3
17 W	3 38 52.4	26 7.9	4 32.3	3♑21.6	16 28.5	0♉38.8	26 26.7	12 22.1	22 46.0	0 24.6	25 27.0	29 19.6
18 T	3 42 49.0	27 5.6	4 29.1	18 8.6	16 59.2	1 51.5	26 51.9	12 15.0	22 50.5	0 24.0	25 26.3	29 18.0
19 F	3 46 45.5	28 3.4	4 25.9	2♒34.3	17 25.0	3 4.3	27 17.4	12 7.9	22 55.0	0 23.3	25 25.7	29 16.3
20 S	3 50 42.1	29 1.2	4 22.7	16 35.2	17 46.0	4 17.0	27 43.2	12 0.6	22 59.3	0 22.6	25 25.0	29 14.7
21 S	3 54 38.7	29 58.9	4 19.6	0♓10.6	18 2.1	5 29.8	28 9.2	11 53.4	23 3.6	0 21.9	25 24.3	29 13.0
22 M	3 58 35.2	0♊56.6	4 16.4	13 21.9	18 13.4	6 42.6	28 35.4	11 46.0	23 7.9	0 21.1	25 23.5	29 11.3
23 T	4 2 31.8	1 54.3	4 13.2	26 11.7	18 19.9	7 55.4	29 1.9	11 38.6	23 12.0	0 20.2	25 22.7	29 9.7
24 W	4 6 28.3	2 52.0	4 10.0	8♈43.4	18 21.6	9 8.2	29 28.5	11 31.2	23 16.0	0 19.3	25 21.9	29 8.0
25 T	4 10 24.9	3 49.6	4 6.8	21 0.7	18R18.8	10 21.0	29 55.5	11 23.7	23 20.0	0 18.3	25 21.1	29 6.4
26 F	4 14 21.4	4 47.3	4 3.7	3♉ 7.0	18 11.4	11 33.8	0♍22.6	11 16.2	23 23.9	0 17.3	25 20.2	29 4.7
27 S	4 18 18.0	5 44.9	4 0.5	15 5.3	17 59.7	12 46.7	0 49.9	11 8.6	23 27.7	0 16.3	25 19.3	29 3.1
28 S	4 22 14.5	6 42.5	3 57.3	26 58.4	17 44.1	13 59.6	1 17.6	11 1.1	23 31.5	0 15.3	25 18.5	29 1.5
29 M	4 26 11.1	7 40.1	3 54.1	8♊48.5	17 24.7	15 12.4	1 45.3	10 53.5	23 35.1	0 14.2	25 17.5	28 59.8
30 T	4 30 7.7	8 37.7	3 51.0	20 37.8	17 1.8	16 25.3	2 13.3	10 45.8	23 38.7	0 13.0	25 16.6	28 58.2
31 W	4 34 4.2	9 35.2	3 47.8	2♋28.0	16 35.9	17 38.2	2 41.5	10 38.2	23 42.1	0 11.8	25 15.6	28 56.6

DAY	EPHEMERIS SIDEREAL TIME	☉	☊	☽	☿	♀	♂	♃	♄	♅	♆	♇
DECLINATION at NOON												
1 M	2 35 47.6	15N 1.2	13S19.0	18N 0.9	21N45.7	2N55.9	16N41.6	21S39.2	5S 7.7	20S34.5	20S29.2	6S27.2
4 T	2 47 37.2	15 54.7	13 15.8	18 44.8	23 3.1	4 19.2	16 16.7	21 37.3	5 1.7	20 34.5	20 29.3	6 26.1
7 S	2 59 26.9	16 45.8	13 12.6	12 11.8	23 58.5	5 42.0	15 50.6	21 35.3	4 55.8	20 34.7	20 29.4	6 25.0
10 W	3 11 16.5	17 34.3	13 9.4	0 17.6	24 33.2	7 3.9	15 23.5	21 33.1	4 50.2	20 34.9	20 29.6	6 24.0
13 S	3 23 6.2	18 20.2	13 6.2	12S46.1	24 49.1	8 24.6	14 55.3	21 30.8	4 44.9	20 35.2	20 29.8	6 23.0
16 T	3 34 55.9	19 3.4	13 3.0	19 21.6	24 48.0	9 43.8	14 26.2	21 28.3	4 39.9	20 35.6	20 30.1	6 22.1
19 F	3 46 45.5	19 43.6	12 59.8	14 28.3	24 31.5	11 1.1	13 56.1	21 25.8	4 35.1	20 36.1	20 30.4	6 21.2
22 M	3 58 35.2	20 20.8	12 56.6	2 42.6	24 1.4	12 16.4	13 25.0	21 23.1	4 30.6	20 36.7	20 30.8	6 20.5
25 T	4 10 24.9	20 54.9	12 53.4	9N24.8	23 19.4	13 29.2	12 53.0	21 20.3	4 26.5	20 37.3	20 31.2	6 19.8
28 S	4 22 14.5	21 25.7	12 50.2	17 36.7	22 27.7	14 39.2	12 20.0	21 17.5	4 22.6	20 38.1	20 31.7	6 19.2
31 W	4 34 4.2	21 53.2	12 46.9	19 2.9	21 29.4	15 46.2	11 46.2	21 14.6	4 19.0	20 38.9	20 32.2	6 18.6

JUNE 1995

DAY	EPHEMERIS SIDEREAL TIME	☉	☊	☽	☿	♀	♂	♃	♄	♅	♆	♇
LONGITUDE at NOON												
1 T	4 38 0.8	10♊32.8	3♏44.6	14♋21.3	16♊ 7.5	18♉51.1	3♍ 9.9	10♐30.5	23♓45.5	0♒10.5	25♑14.6	28♏54.9
2 F	4 41 57.3	11 30.3	3 41.4	26 20.0	15R36.9	20 4.0	3 38.5	10R22.9	23 48.8	0R 9.2	25R13.5	28R53.3
3 S	4 45 53.9	12 27.8	3 38.3	8♌26.6	15 4.8	21 16.9	4 7.3	10 15.2	23 52.0	0 7.9	25 12.4	28 51.7
4 S	4 49 50.4	13 25.2	3 35.1	20 44.2	14 31.7	22 29.8	4 36.2	10 7.6	23 55.2	0 6.5	25 11.4	28 50.1
5 M	4 53 47.0	14 22.7	3 31.9	3♍16.4	13 58.2	23 42.7	5 5.4	9 60.0	23 58.2	0 5.1	25 10.2	28 48.5
6 T	4 57 43.6	15 20.1	3 28.7	16 6.6	13 24.8	24 55.6	5 34.7	9 52.4	24 1.1	0 3.6	25 9.1	28 46.9
7 W	5 1 40.1	16 17.5	3 25.5	29 18.6	12 52.1	26 8.6	6 4.2	9 44.8	24 4.0	0 2.2	25 7.9	28 45.4
8 T	5 5 36.7	17 14.9	3 22.4	12♎55.3	12 20.7	27 21.5	6 33.9	9 37.3	24 6.7	0 0.6	25 6.8	28 43.8
9 F	5 9 33.2	18 12.3	3 19.2	26 58.4	11 51.0	28 34.5	7 3.7	9 29.8	24 9.4	29♑59.1	25 5.6	28 42.3
10 S	5 13 29.8	19 9.6	3 16.0	11♏27.6	11 23.7	29 47.5	7 33.7	9 22.3	24 12.0	29 57.5	25 4.3	28 40.8
11 S	5 17 26.3	20 7.0	3 12.8	26 19.7	10 59.2	1♊ 0.5	8 3.9	9 14.9	24 14.4	29 55.8	25 3.1	28 39.2
12 M	5 21 22.9	21 4.3	3 9.7	11♐28.6	10 37.8	2 13.5	8 34.3	9 7.5	24 16.8	29 54.1	25 1.8	28 37.7
13 T	5 25 19.5	22 1.6	3 6.5	26 45.2	10 19.9	3 26.5	9 4.7	9 0.2	24 19.1	29 52.4	25 0.6	28 36.2
14 W	5 29 16.0	22 58.9	3 3.3	11♑58.9	10 5.8	4 39.5	9 35.4	8 53.0	24 21.3	29 50.7	24 59.3	28 34.8
15 T	5 33 12.6	23 56.2	3 0.1	26 59.3	9 55.8	5 52.5	10 6.2	8 45.8	24 23.4	29 48.9	24 57.9	28 33.3
16 F	5 37 9.1	24 53.5	2 57.0	11♒37.8	9 50.1	7 5.6	10 37.2	8 38.7	24 25.4	29 47.1	24 56.6	28 31.9
17 S	5 41 5.7	25 50.7	2 53.8	25 49.1	9 48.8	8 18.7	11 8.3	8 31.7	24 27.4	29 45.3	24 55.3	28 30.4
18 S	5 45 2.2	26 48.0	2 50.6	9♓31.2	9D52.1	9 31.8	11 39.6	8 24.8	24 29.2	29 43.5	24 53.9	28 29.1
19 M	5 48 58.8	27 45.3	2 47.4	22 44.9	9 60.0	10 44.9	12 11.0	8 17.9	24 31.0	29 41.6	24 52.5	28 27.7
20 T	5 52 55.4	28 42.6	2 44.2	5♈33.3	10 12.4	11 58.1	12 42.5	8 11.1	24 32.6	29 39.6	24 51.1	28 26.3
21 W	5 56 51.9	29 39.8	2 41.1	18 0.7	10 29.6	13 11.2	13 14.2	8 4.4	24 34.1	29 37.7	24 49.7	28 24.9
22 T	6 0 48.5	0♋37.1	2 37.9	0♉11.9	10 51.4	14 24.4	13 46.0	7 57.8	24 35.5	29 35.7	24 48.3	28 23.6
23 F	6 4 45.0	1 34.3	2 34.7	12 11.4	11 17.8	15 37.6	14 18.0	7 51.3	24 36.9	29 33.7	24 46.8	28 22.3
24 S	6 8 41.6	2 31.6	2 31.5	24 3.8	11 48.8	16 50.7	14 50.1	7 44.9	24 38.1	29 31.6	24 45.4	28 21.0
25 S	6 12 38.1	3 28.8	2 28.4	5♊52.7	12 24.3	18 4.0	15 22.4	7 38.7	24 39.2	29 29.6	24 43.9	28 19.7
26 M	6 16 34.7	4 26.1	2 25.2	17 41.2	13 4.3	19 17.2	15 54.8	7 32.5	24 40.3	29 27.5	24 42.4	28 18.4
27 T	6 20 31.3	5 23.3	2 22.0	29 31.7	13 48.7	20 30.4	16 27.3	7 26.5	24 41.2	29 25.4	24 40.9	28 17.2
28 W	6 24 27.8	6 20.5	2 18.8	11♋26.1	14 37.4	21 43.7	16 60.0	7 20.5	24 42.0	29 23.2	24 39.4	28 16.0
29 T	6 28 24.4	7 17.8	2 15.7	23 26.0	15 30.4	22 57.0	17 32.8	7 14.8	24 42.8	29 21.1	24 37.8	28 14.8
30 F	6 32 20.9	8 15.0	2 12.5	5♌32.6	16 27.7	24 10.3	18 5.7	7 9.1	24 43.4	29 18.9	24 36.3	28 13.6

DAY	EPHEMERIS SIDEREAL TIME	☉	☊	☽	☿	♀	♂	♃	♄	♅	♆	♇
DECLINATION at NOON												
1 T	4 38 0.8	22N 1.6	12S45.9	17N50.6	21N 9.2	16N 7.8	11N34.7	21S13.6	4S17.9	20S39.2	20S32.4	6S18.5
4 S	4 49 50.4	22 24.5	12 42.6	9 51.1	20 8.7	17 10.1	10 59.7	21 10.7	4 14.7	20 40.2	20 32.9	6 18.0
7 W	5 1 40.1	22 43.9	12 39.4	2S29.4	19 12.8	18 8.6	10 23.9	21 7.7	4 11.9	20 41.2	20 33.6	6 17.7
10 S	5 13 29.8	22 59.7	12 36.1	14 42.0	18 26.6	19 3.0	9 47.2	21 4.8	4 9.4	20 42.3	20 34.2	6 17.4
13 T	5 25 19.5	23 11.9	12 32.9	19 20.6	17 54.5	19 52.9	9 9.9	21 1.9	4 7.3	20 43.4	20 34.9	6 17.3
16 F	5 37 9.1	23 20.4	12 29.6	12 24.3	17 38.7	20 38.1	8 31.7	20 59.0	4 5.5	20 44.6	20 35.6	6 17.2
19 M	5 48 58.8	23 25.1	12 26.4	0N14.7	17 39.9	21 18.4	7 52.9	20 56.2	4 4.0	20 45.8	20 36.3	6 17.2
22 T	6 0 48.5	23 26.2	12 23.1	11 52.4	17 56.8	21 53.4	7 13.3	20 53.6	4 2.9	20 47.1	20 37.1	6 17.3
25 S	6 12 38.1	23 23.5	12 19.8	18 38.3	18 27.2	22 22.9	6 33.1	20 51.0	4 2.2	20 48.5	20 37.9	6 17.5
28 W	6 24 27.8	23 17.1	12 16.6	18 16.8	19 8.1	22 46.8	5 52.3	20 48.6	4 1.8	20 49.9	20 38.7	6 17.8

JULY 1995

DAY	EPHEMERIS SIDEREAL TIME	☉	☊	☽	☿	♀	♂	♃	♄	♅	♆	♇
	h m s	° ′	° ′	° ′	° ′	° ′	° ′	° ′	° ′	° ′	° ′	° ′
LONGITUDE at NOON												
1 S	6 36 17.5	9♋12.2	2♏ 9.3	17♌47.5	17♊29.1	25♊23.6	18♍38.8	7♐ 3.6	24♓43.9	29♑16.7	24♑34.8	28♏12.5
2 S	6 40 14.0	10 9.4	2 6.1	0♍12.3	18 34.6	26 36.9	19 11.9	6R58.2	24 44.3	29R14.5	24R33.2	28R11.4
3 M	6 44 10.6	11 6.6	2 2.9	12 49.3	19 44.1	27 50.2	19 45.3	6 52.9	24 44.7	29 12.2	24 31.6	28 10.3
4 T	6 48 7.2	12 3.9	1 59.8	25 41.0	20 57.7	29 3.6	20 18.7	6 47.8	24 44.9	29 10.0	24 30.1	28 9.2
5 W	6 52 3.7	13 1.1	1 56.6	8♎50.5	22 15.2	0♋17.0	20 52.2	6 42.9	24 45.0	29 7.7	24 28.5	28 8.1
6 T	6 56 0.3	13 58.3	1 53.4	22 20.4	23 36.6	1 30.4	21 25.9	6 38.1	24 45.1	29 5.4	24 26.9	28 7.1
7 F	6 59 56.8	14 55.4	1 50.2	6♏13.1	25 1.9	2 43.8	21 59.7	6 33.4	24R45.0	29 3.1	24 25.3	28 6.1
8 S	7 3 53.4	15 52.6	1 47.1	20 29.6	26 30.9	3 57.2	22 33.6	6 28.9	24 44.8	29 0.8	24 23.7	28 5.2
9 S	7 7 49.9	16 49.9	1 43.9	5♐ 8.4	28 3.8	5 10.7	23 7.6	6 24.6	24 44.6	28 58.5	24 22.2	28 4.3
10 M	7 11 46.5	17 47.0	1 40.7	20 5.3	29 40.2	6 24.1	23 41.8	6 20.4	24 44.2	28 56.2	24 20.5	28 3.3
11 T	7 15 43.0	18 44.2	1 37.5	5♑13.1	1♋20.1	7 37.6	24 16.0	6 16.4	24 43.7	28 53.8	24 18.9	28 2.5
12 W	7 19 39.6	19 41.4	1 34.4	20 22.2	3 3.5	8 51.1	24 50.3	6 12.6	24 43.2	28 51.5	24 17.3	28 1.6
13 T	7 23 36.2	20 38.6	1 31.2	5♒22.2	4 50.2	10 4.6	25 24.8	6 8.9	24 42.5	28 49.1	24 15.7	28 0.8
14 F	7 27 32.7	21 35.8	1 28.0	20 3.7	6 40.0	11 18.1	25 59.3	6 5.3	24 41.7	28 46.7	24 14.1	27 60.0
15 S	7 31 29.3	22 33.0	1 24.8	4♓19.9	8 32.8	12 31.6	26 34.0	6 2.0	24 40.9	28 44.3	24 12.4	27 59.2
16 S	7 35 25.8	23 30.2	1 21.6	18 7.1	10 28.3	13 45.2	27 8.8	5 58.8	24 39.9	28 41.9	24 10.8	27 58.4
17 M	7 39 22.4	24 27.4	1 18.5	1♈25.2	12 26.4	14 58.8	27 43.6	5 55.8	24 38.8	28 39.6	24 9.2	27 57.7
18 T	7 43 18.9	25 24.7	1 15.3	14 16.4	14 26.7	16 12.4	28 18.6	5 52.9	24 37.7	28 37.2	24 7.6	27 57.0
19 W	7 47 15.5	26 21.9	1 12.1	26 45.0	16 28.9	17 26.1	28 53.7	5 50.2	24 36.4	28 34.7	24 5.9	27 56.4
20 T	7 51 12.1	27 19.2	1 8.9	8♉55.8	18 32.8	18 39.7	29 28.9	5 47.7	24 35.0	28 32.3	24 4.3	27 55.7
21 F	7 55 8.6	28 16.4	1 5.8	20 54.2	20 38.1	19 53.4	0♎ 4.2	5 45.4	24 33.6	28 29.9	24 2.7	27 55.1
22 S	7 59 5.2	29 13.7	1 2.6	2♊45.4	22 44.3	21 7.1	0 39.6	5 43.3	24 32.0	28 27.5	24 1.1	27 54.6
23 S	8 3 1.7	0♌11.0	0 59.4	14 34.0	24 51.3	22 20.8	1 15.1	5 41.3	24 30.4	28 25.1	23 59.5	27 54.0
24 M	8 6 58.3	1 8.3	0 56.2	26 23.9	26 58.6	23 34.6	1 50.7	5 39.5	24 28.7	28 22.7	23 57.9	27 53.5
25 T	8 10 54.8	2 5.6	0 53.1	8♋18.2	29 6.1	24 48.3	2 26.5	5 37.9	24 26.8	28 20.3	23 56.2	27 53.0
26 W	8 14 51.4	3 3.0	0 49.9	20 19.3	1♌13.4	26 2.1	3 2.3	5 36.5	24 24.9	28 17.9	23 54.6	27 52.6
27 T	8 18 47.9	4 0.3	0 46.7	2♌28.8	3 20.2	27 15.9	3 38.2	5 35.3	24 22.9	28 15.5	23 53.0	27 52.2
28 F	8 22 44.5	4 57.7	0 43.5	14 47.5	5 26.4	28 29.8	4 14.2	5 34.2	24 20.8	28 13.1	23 51.5	27 51.8
29 S	8 26 41.1	5 55.0	0 40.3	27 16.0	7 31.8	29 43.6	4 50.3	5 33.4	24 18.6	28 10.7	23 49.9	27 51.5
30 S	8 30 37.6	6 52.5	0 37.2	9♍54.9	9 36.3	0♌57.5	5 26.6	5 32.7	24 16.3	28 8.4	23 48.3	27 51.2
31 M	8 34 34.2	7 49.8	0 34.0	22 44.7	11 39.5	2 11.4	6 2.9	5 32.2	24 14.0	28 6.1	23 46.8	27 50.9
DECLINATION at NOON												
1 S	6 36 17.5	23N 7.1	12S13.3	10N50.6	19N56.1	23N 4.8	5N10.8	20S46.4	4S 1.8	20S51.3	20S39.5	6S18.2
4 T	6 48 7.2	22 53.4	12 10.0	1S 5.5	20 47.3	23 16.8	4 28.8	20 44.4	4 2.1	20 52.7	20 40.4	6 18.7
7 F	6 59 56.8	22 36.1	12 6.7	13 18.2	21 37.4	23 22.7	3 46.3	20 42.5	4 2.8	20 54.2	20 41.2	6 19.3
10 M	7 11 46.5	22 15.4	12 3.4	19 21.6	22 21.5	23 22.4	3 3.2	20 40.9	4 3.9	20 55.7	20 42.1	6 20.0
13 T	7 23 36.2	21 51.1	12 0.1	14 3.6	22 54.4	23 16.0	2 19.8	20 39.6	4 5.2	20 57.1	20 43.0	6 20.7
16 S	7 35 25.8	21 23.5	11 56.8	1 29.7	23 10.9	23 3.4	1 35.9	20 38.5	4 7.0	20 58.6	20 43.9	6 21.6
19 W	7 47 15.5	20 52.7	11 53.5	10N42.8	23 6.4	22 44.6	0 51.6	20 37.6	4 9.1	21 0.1	20 44.7	6 22.5
22 S	7 59 5.2	20 18.6	11 50.2	18 8.7	22 38.2	22 19.8	0 7.0	20 37.0	4 11.5	21 1.6	20 45.6	6 23.6
25 T	8 10 54.8	19 41.5	11 46.8	18 34.3	21 46.0	21 49.2	0S38.0	20 36.7	4 14.2	21 3.1	20 46.5	6 24.7
28 F	8 22 44.5	19 1.5	11 43.5	11 45.4	20 31.8	21 12.7	1 23.2	20 36.7	4 17.3	21 4.6	20 47.4	6 25.9
31 M	8 34 34.2	18 18.6	11 40.2	0 4.7	18 59.2	20 30.8	2 8.6	20 37.0	4 20.6	21 6.0	20 48.2	6 27.2

AUGUST 1995

DAY	EPHEMERIS SIDEREAL TIME	☉	☊	☽	☿	♀	♂	♃	♄	♅	♆	♇
LONGITUDE at NOON												
1 T	8 38 30.7	8♌47.2	0♏30.8	5♎46.7	13♌41.5	3♌25.3	6♎39.3	5♐31.9	24♓11.5	28♑ 3.7	23♑45.2	27♏50.7
2 W	8 42 27.3	9 44.7	0 27.6	19 2.3	15 42.2	4 39.2	7 15.8	5R31.8	24R 9.0	28R 1.4	23R43.7	27R50.4
3 T	8 46 23.8	10 42.1	0 24.5	2♏33.2	17 41.4	5 53.1	7 52.4	5D31.9	24 6.3	27 59.0	23 42.1	27 50.3
4 F	8 50 20.4	11 39.5	0 21.3	16 21.0	19 39.2	7 7.1	8 29.1	5 32.1	24 3.6	27 56.7	23 40.6	27 50.1
5 S	8 54 16.9	12 36.9	0 18.1	0♐26.7	21 35.5	8 21.1	9 5.9	5 32.5	24 0.8	27 54.4	23 39.1	27 50.0
6 S	8 58 13.5	13 34.4	0 14.9	14 49.7	23 30.3	9 35.0	9 42.8	5 33.2	23 57.9	27 52.1	23 37.6	27 49.9
7 M	9 2 10.1	14 31.9	0 11.8	29 27.5	25 23.5	10 49.0	10 19.7	5 33.9	23 55.0	27 49.8	23 36.1	27 49.9
8 T	9 6 6.6	15 29.3	0 8.6	14♑15.1	27 15.1	12 3.1	10 56.8	5 34.9	23 51.9	27 47.6	23 34.6	27 49.8
9 W	9 10 3.2	16 26.8	0 5.4	29 5.3	29 5.2	13 17.1	11 33.9	5 36.1	23 48.8	27 45.3	23 33.1	27D49.9
10 T	9 13 59.7	17 24.3	0 2.2	13♒49.8	0♍53.8	14 31.1	12 11.1	5 37.4	23 45.6	27 43.1	23 31.7	27 49.9
11 F	9 17 56.3	18 21.9	29♎59.0	28 20.2	2 40.8	15 45.2	12 48.4	5 38.9	23 42.4	27 40.9	23 30.2	27 50.0
12 S	9 21 52.8	19 19.4	29 55.9	12♓29.9	4 26.3	16 59.3	13 25.8	5 40.7	23 39.0	27 38.7	23 28.8	27 50.1
13 S	9 25 49.4	20 17.0	29 52.7	26 14.7	6 10.3	18 13.4	14 3.3	5 42.5	23 35.6	27 36.6	23 27.4	27 50.3
14 M	9 29 45.9	21 14.6	29 49.5	9♈33.0	7 52.8	19 27.5	14 40.9	5 44.6	23 32.2	27 34.4	23 26.0	27 50.4
15 T	9 33 42.5	22 12.2	29 46.3	22 26.0	9 33.8	20 41.7	15 18.6	5 46.8	23 28.6	27 32.3	23 24.6	27 50.7
16 W	9 37 39.0	23 9.8	29 43.2	4♉56.8	11 13.3	21 55.9	15 56.3	5 49.2	23 25.0	27 30.2	23 23.3	27 50.9
17 T	9 41 35.6	24 7.5	29 40.0	17 9.7	12 51.3	23 10.0	16 34.1	5 51.8	23 21.3	27 28.1	23 21.9	27 51.2
18 F	9 45 32.1	25 5.2	29 36.8	29 9.8	14 27.9	24 24.2	17 12.1	5 54.6	23 17.6	27 26.1	23 20.6	27 51.5
19 S	9 49 28.7	26 2.9	29 33.6	11♊ 2.5	16 3.0	25 38.5	17 50.1	5 57.5	23 13.8	27 24.1	23 19.3	27 51.9
20 S	9 53 25.3	27 0.7	29 30.4	22 52.7	17 36.7	26 52.8	18 28.2	6 0.7	23 10.0	27 22.1	23 18.0	27 52.3
21 M	9 57 21.8	27 58.4	29 27.3	4♋45.2	19 8.9	28 7.0	19 6.4	6 4.0	23 6.1	27 20.1	23 16.8	27 52.7
22 T	10 1 18.4	28 56.2	29 24.1	16 43.9	20 39.7	29 21.3	19 44.7	6 7.5	23 2.1	27 18.2	23 15.5	27 53.2
23 W	10 5 14.9	29 54.1	29 20.9	28 51.9	22 9.0	0♍35.6	20 23.1	6 11.1	22 58.1	27 16.3	23 14.3	27 53.7
24 T	10 9 11.5	0♍51.9	29 17.7	11♌11.4	23 36.8	1 49.9	21 1.5	6 14.9	22 54.0	27 14.4	23 13.1	27 54.2
25 F	10 13 8.0	1 49.8	29 14.6	23 43.6	25 3.2	3 4.2	21 40.1	6 18.9	22 49.9	27 12.6	23 11.9	27 54.7
26 S	10 17 4.6	2 47.7	29 11.4	6♍28.8	26 28.0	4 18.6	22 18.7	6 23.0	22 45.7	27 10.8	23 10.7	27 55.3
27 S	10 21 1.1	3 45.6	29 8.2	19 26.8	27 51.3	5 32.9	22 57.4	6 27.3	22 41.5	27 9.0	23 9.6	27 55.9
28 M	10 24 57.7	4 43.6	29 5.0	2♎36.8	29 13.1	6 47.3	23 36.2	6 31.8	22 37.3	27 7.2	23 8.5	27 56.6
29 T	10 28 54.2	5 41.5	29 1.8	15 58.1	0♎33.3	8 1.7	24 15.1	6 36.5	22 33.0	27 5.5	23 7.4	27 57.3
30 W	10 32 50.8	6 39.5	28 58.7	29 30.4	1 51.8	9 16.1	24 54.0	6 41.3	22 28.6	27 3.8	23 6.3	27 58.0
31 T	10 36 47.3	7 37.5	28 55.5	13♏13.1	3 8.7	10 30.5	25 33.1	6 46.2	22 24.3	27 2.2	23 5.3	27 58.8
DECLINATION at NOON												
1 T	8 38 30.7	18N 3.7	11S39.1	4S11.5	18N24.9	20N15.6	2S23.8	20S37.2	4S21.8	21S 6.5	20S48.5	6S27.6
4 F	8 50 20.4	17 17.3	11 35.7	15 21.1	16 34.1	19 26.6	3 9.5	20 37.8	4 25.6	21 7.9	20 49.3	6 29.0
7 M	9 2 10.1	16 28.3	11 32.4	19 5.1	14 34.1	18 32.6	3 55.3	20 38.8	4 29.6	21 9.2	20 50.2	6 30.5
10 T	9 13 59.7	15 37.0	11 29.0	12 0.4	12 27.9	17 33.9	4 41.1	20 40.0	4 33.8	21 10.6	20 51.0	6 32.1
13 S	9 25 49.4	14 43.4	11 25.7	1N 0.8	10 18.1	16 30.7	5 27.0	20 41.6	4 38.3	21 11.9	20 51.7	6 33.7
16 W	9 37 39.0	13 47.8	11 22.3	12 39.2	8 6.8	15 23.5	6 12.8	20 43.4	4 43.1	21 13.1	20 52.5	6 35.3
19 S	9 49 28.7	12 50.1	11 19.0	18 42.1	5 55.5	14 12.4	6 58.6	20 45.4	4 48.0	21 14.3	20 53.2	6 37.1
22 T	10 1 18.4	11 50.6	11 15.6	17 27.5	3 45.7	12 57.7	7 44.2	20 47.7	4 53.1	21 15.4	20 53.9	6 38.9
25 F	10 13 8.0	10 49.4	11 12.2	9 17.1	1 38.6	11 39.9	8 29.7	20 50.3	4 58.3	21 16.5	20 54.6	6 40.8
28 M	10 24 57.7	9 46.6	11 8.9	3S 1.6	0S24.7	10 19.3	9 14.9	20 53.1	5 3.7	21 17.5	20 55.2	6 42.7
31 T	10 36 47.3	8 42.5	11 5.5	14 28.8	2 22.9	8 56.1	9 59.8	20 56.1	5 9.2	21 18.4	20 55.9	6 44.6

SEPTEMBER 1995

DAY	EPHEMERIS SIDEREAL TIME	☉	☊	☽	☿	♀	♂	♃	♄	♅	♆	♇
	h m s	° ′	° ′	° ′	° ′	° ′	° ′	° ′	° ′	° ′	° ′	° ′
						LONGITUDE at NOON						
1 F	10 40 43.9	8♍35.6	28♎52.3	27♏ 6.4	4♎23.8	11♍44.9	26♎12.2	6♐51.4	22♓19.9	27♑ 0.6	23♑ 4.3	27♏59.5
2 S	10 44 40.4	9 33.7	28 49.1	11♐ 9.7	5 37.1	12 59.3	26 51.4	6 56.7	22R 15.4	26R 59.0	23R 3.3	28 0.4
3 S	10 48 37.0	10 31.7	28 45.9	25 22.4	6 48.6	14 13.8	27 30.7	7 2.1	22 11.0	26 57.5	23 2.3	28 1.2
4 M	10 52 33.5	11 29.8	28 42.8	9♑42.5	7 58.0	15 28.2	28 10.1	7 7.7	22 6.5	26 56.0	23 1.3	28 2.1
5 T	10 56 30.1	12 28.0	28 39.6	24 6.8	9 5.5	16 42.7	28 49.5	7 13.5	22 2.0	26 54.5	23 0.4	28 3.0
6 W	11 0 26.6	13 26.1	28 36.4	8♒30.9	10 10.7	17 57.1	29 29.0	7 19.4	21 57.4	26 53.1	22 59.5	28 4.0
7 T	11 4 23.2	14 24.3	28 33.2	22 49.4	11 13.7	19 11.6	0♏ 8.6	7 25.4	21 52.9	26 51.7	22 58.7	28 5.0
8 F	11 8 19.8	15 22.5	28 30.1	6♓56.7	12 14.2	20 26.1	0 48.3	7 31.6	21 48.3	26 50.4	22 57.8	28 6.0
9 S	11 12 16.3	16 20.8	28 26.9	20 48.1	13 12.2	21 40.6	1 28.1	7 38.0	21 43.7	26 49.1	22 57.0	28 7.0
10 S	11 16 12.9	17 19.1	28 23.7	4♈19.9	14 7.5	22 55.1	2 8.0	7 44.5	21 39.2	26 47.9	22 56.3	28 8.1
11 M	11 20 9.4	18 17.4	28 20.5	17 30.5	14 59.9	24 9.7	2 47.9	7 51.2	21 34.5	26 46.7	22 55.5	28 9.2
12 T	11 24 6.0	19 15.7	28 17.3	0♉19.8	15 49.1	25 24.2	3 27.9	7 58.0	21 29.9	26 45.5	22 54.8	28 10.4
13 W	11 28 2.5	20 14.1	28 14.2	12 49.8	16 35.1	26 38.7	4 7.9	8 4.9	21 25.3	26 44.4	22 54.1	28 11.5
14 T	11 31 59.1	21 12.5	28 11.0	25 3.6	17 17.4	27 53.3	4 48.1	8 12.0	21 20.7	26 43.3	22 53.4	28 12.7
15 F	11 35 55.6	22 10.9	28 7.8	7♊ 5.2	17 55.9	29 7.8	5 28.3	8 19.2	21 16.0	26 42.3	22 52.8	28 14.0
16 S	11 39 52.2	23 9.4	28 4.6	18 59.4	18 30.2	0♎22.4	6 8.6	8 26.5	21 11.4	26 41.3	22 52.2	28 15.2
17 S	11 43 48.7	24 7.9	28 1.5	0♋51.1	19 0.2	1 36.9	6 49.0	8 34.0	21 6.8	26 40.3	22 51.6	28 16.5
18 M	11 47 45.3	25 6.5	27 58.3	12 45.1	19 25.3	2 51.5	7 29.5	8 41.6	21 2.2	26 39.4	22 51.1	28 17.8
19 T	11 51 41.8	26 5.0	27 55.1	24 46.1	19 45.3	4 6.1	8 10.0	8 49.4	20 57.6	26 38.6	22 50.6	28 19.2
20 W	11 55 38.4	27 3.7	27 51.9	6♌58.2	19 59.9	5 20.7	8 50.6	8 57.3	20 53.0	26 37.8	22 50.1	28 20.5
21 T	11 59 34.9	28 2.3	27 48.7	19 24.4	20 8.6	6 35.3	9 31.3	9 5.3	20 48.4	26 37.0	22 49.6	28 21.9
22 F	12 3 31.5	29 1.0	27 45.6	2♍ 7.1	20 11.0	7 49.9	10 12.1	9 13.4	20 43.8	26 36.3	22 49.2	28 23.4
23 S	12 7 28.0	29 59.7	27 42.4	15 7.2	20R 6.9	9 4.6	10 53.0	9 21.7	20 39.3	26 35.6	22 48.8	28 24.8
24 S	12 11 24.6	0♎58.5	27 39.2	28 24.5	19 55.9	10 19.2	11 33.9	9 30.1	20 34.8	26 35.0	22 48.4	28 26.3
25 M	12 15 21.1	1 57.3	27 36.0	11♎57.6	19 37.7	11 33.8	12 15.0	9 38.6	20 30.3	26 34.4	22 48.1	28 27.8
26 T	12 19 17.7	2 56.1	27 32.9	25 44.4	19 12.2	12 48.5	12 56.1	9 47.3	20 25.8	26 33.9	22 47.8	28 29.4
27 W	12 23 14.2	3 54.9	27 29.7	9♏42.0	18 39.3	14 3.1	13 37.2	9 56.1	20 21.3	26 33.4	22 47.5	28 30.9
28 T	12 27 10.8	4 53.8	27 26.5	23 47.6	17 59.1	15 17.8	14 18.5	10 5.0	20 16.9	26 33.0	22 47.3	28 32.5
29 F	12 31 7.3	5 52.7	27 23.3	7♐58.1	17 11.9	16 32.4	14 59.8	10 14.0	20 12.6	26 32.6	22 47.1	28 34.2
30 S	12 35 3.9	6 51.7	27 20.1	22 11.1	16 18.2	17 47.1	15 41.2	10 23.1	20 8.2	26 32.3	22 46.9	28 35.8
						DECLINATION at NOON						
1 F	10 40 43.9	8N20.8	11S 4.4	17S 2.2	3S 1.0	8N27.9	10S 14.7	20S 57.1	5S 11.0	21S 18.7	20S 56.0	6S 45.3
4 M	10 52 33.5	7 15.1	11 1.0	18 11.9	4 50.7	7 1.8	10 59.1	21 0.4	5 16.6	21 19.6	20 56.6	6 47.3
7 T	11 4 23.2	6 8.3	10 57.6	9 30.8	6 32.1	5 34.0	11 43.1	21 3.9	5 22.2	21 20.3	20 57.1	6 49.4
10 S	11 16 12.9	5 0.6	10 54.2	3N33.2	8 3.5	4 4.8	12 26.6	21 7.5	5 27.8	21 21.0	20 57.6	6 51.5
13 W	11 28 2.5	3 52.1	10 50.8	14 19.7	9 22.4	2 34.4	13 9.5	21 11.3	5 33.5	21 21.7	20 58.0	6 53.6
16 S	11 39 52.2	2 43.0	10 47.4	18 53.1	10 25.7	1 3.3	13 51.8	21 15.3	5 39.1	21 22.2	20 58.4	6 55.8
19 T	11 51 41.8	1 33.4	10 44.0	16 2.8	11 9.2	0S 28.3	14 33.4	21 19.4	5 44.6	21 22.7	20 58.8	6 57.9
22 F	12 3 31.5	0 23.5	10 40.6	6 44.5	11 27.6	2 0.1	15 14.2	21 23.5	5 50.1	21 23.0	20 59.1	7 0.1
25 M	12 15 21.1	0S 46.6	10 37.1	5S 56.8	11 14.5	3 31.6	15 54.1	21 27.8	5 55.4	21 23.3	20 59.4	7 2.3
28 T	12 27 10.8	1 56.8	10 33.7	16 23.1	10 24.2	5 2.6	16 33.2	21 32.2	6 0.7	21 23.5	20 59.6	7 4.5

OCTOBER 1995

DAY	EPHEMERIS SIDEREAL TIME	☉	☊	☽	☿	♀	♂	♃	♄	♅	♆	♇
						LONGITUDE at NOON						
1 S	12 39 0.4	7♎50.7	27♎17.0	6♑24.1	15♎18.9	19♎ 1.8	16♏22.7	10♐32.4	20♓ 4.0	26♑32.1	22♑46.9	28♏37.5
2 M	12 42 57.0	8 49.7	27 13.8	20 34.9	14R 14.9	20 16.4	17 4.3	10 41.7	19R 59.7	26R 31.9	22R 46.8	28 39.2
3 T	12 46 53.5	9 48.7	27 10.6	4♒41.2	13 7.5	21 31.1	17 45.9	10 51.2	19 55.5	26 31.7	22 46.7	28 41.0
4 W	12 50 50.1	10 47.8	27 7.4	18 40.9	11 58.4	22 45.7	18 27.6	11 0.8	19 51.3	26 31.6	22 46.6	28 42.7
5 T	12 54 46.7	11 46.9	27 4.2	2♓31.5	10 49.2	24 0.4	19 9.3	11 10.5	19 47.2	26 31.5	22 46.6	28 44.5
6 F	12 58 43.2	12 46.0	27 1.1	16 10.7	9 41.9	25 15.1	19 51.1	11 20.3	19 43.1	26 31.5	22D 46.7	28 46.3
7 S	13 2 39.8	13 45.2	26 57.9	29 36.4	8 38.4	26 29.7	20 33.0	11 30.1	19 39.1	26 31.5	22 46.7	28 48.1
8 S	13 6 36.3	14 44.3	26 54.7	12♈47.2	7 40.4	27 44.4	21 15.0	11 40.1	19 35.1	26D 31.6	22 46.8	28 49.9
9 M	13 10 32.9	15 43.6	26 51.5	25 42.1	6 49.6	28 59.0	21 57.1	11 50.2	19 31.2	26 31.7	22 47.0	28 51.8
10 T	13 14 29.4	16 42.8	26 48.4	8♉21.1	6 7.3	0♏13.7	22 39.2	12 0.4	19 27.4	26 31.9	22 47.1	28 53.7
11 W	13 18 26.0	17 42.1	26 45.2	20 45.2	5 34.7	1 28.3	23 21.4	12 10.7	19 23.6	26 32.1	22 47.3	28 55.6
12 T	13 22 22.5	18 41.4	26 42.0	2♊56.4	5 12.6	2 43.0	24 3.6	12 21.1	19 19.9	26 32.4	22 47.6	28 57.5
13 F	13 26 19.1	19 40.8	26 38.8	14 57.3	5 1.3	3 57.7	24 46.0	12 31.6	19 16.2	26 32.7	22 47.8	28 59.4
14 S	13 30 15.6	20 40.2	26 35.6	26 51.6	5 0.9	5 12.3	25 28.4	12 42.2	19 12.6	26 33.1	22 48.1	29 1.4
15 S	13 34 12.2	21 39.6	26 32.5	8♋43.3	5D 11.4	6 27.0	26 10.8	12 52.9	19 9.1	26 33.6	22 48.5	29 3.4
16 M	13 38 8.7	22 39.1	26 29.3	20 37.0	5 32.4	7 41.7	26 53.4	13 3.7	19 5.6	26 34.0	22 48.8	29 5.4
17 T	13 42 5.3	23 38.6	26 26.1	2♌37.2	6 3.3	8 56.3	27 36.0	13 14.5	19 2.2	26 34.6	22 49.2	29 7.4
18 W	13 46 1.8	24 38.2	26 22.9	14 48.6	6 43.4	10 11.0	28 18.7	13 25.5	18 58.9	26 35.2	22 49.7	29 9.5
19 T	13 49 58.4	25 37.8	26 19.8	27 15.5	7 32.0	11 25.7	29 1.5	13 36.5	18 55.6	26 35.8	22 50.1	29 11.5
20 F	13 53 54.9	26 37.4	26 16.6	10♍ 1.4	8 28.2	12 40.4	29 44.3	13 47.6	18 52.5	26 36.5	22 50.6	29 13.6
21 S	13 57 51.5	27 37.1	26 13.4	23 8.8	9 31.3	13 55.1	0♐27.2	13 58.8	18 49.4	26 37.2	22 51.2	29 15.7
22 S	14 1 48.0	28 36.8	26 10.2	6♎38.7	10 40.4	15 9.8	1 10.2	14 10.2	18 46.4	26 38.1	22 51.8	29 17.9
23 M	14 5 44.6	29 36.6	26 7.0	20 30.3	11 54.7	16 24.5	1 53.3	14 21.6	18 43.5	26 38.9	22 52.4	29 20.0
24 T	14 9 41.2	0♏36.3	26 3.9	4♏41.0	13 13.6	17 39.2	2 36.4	14 33.0	18 40.7	26 39.8	22 53.0	29 22.1
25 W	14 13 37.7	1 36.1	26 0.7	19 6.4	14 36.4	18 53.8	3 19.6	14 44.6	18 37.9	26 40.8	22 53.7	29 24.3
26 T	14 17 34.3	2 36.0	25 57.5	3♐40.9	16 2.4	20 8.5	4 2.9	14 56.2	18 35.2	26 41.8	22 54.4	29 26.5
27 F	14 21 30.8	3 35.8	25 54.3	18 18.1	17 31.1	21 23.2	4 46.2	15 7.9	18 32.7	26 42.8	22 55.1	29 28.7
28 S	14 25 27.4	4 35.7	25 51.2	2♑52.1	19 2.1	22 37.9	5 29.6	15 19.6	18 30.2	26 43.9	22 55.9	29 30.9
29 S	14 29 23.9	5 35.7	25 48.0	17 17.9	20 34.9	23 52.6	6 13.1	15 31.5	18 27.8	26 45.0	22 56.7	29 33.1
30 M	14 33 20.5	6 35.6	25 44.8	1♒31.6	22 9.2	25 7.2	6 56.6	15 43.4	18 25.4	26 46.2	22 57.5	29 35.3
31 T	14 37 17.0	7 35.6	25 41.6	15 31.2	23 44.7	26 21.9	7 40.2	15 55.3	18 23.2	26 47.5	22 58.4	29 37.6
						DECLINATION at NOON						
1 S	12 39 0.4	3S 6.7	10S 30.3	18S 21.0	8S 54.9	6S 32.7	17S 11.2	21S 36.6	6S 5.7	21S 23.7	20S 59.7	7S 6.8
4 W	12 50 50.1	4 16.4	10 26.9	10 35.0	6 54.2	8 1.6	17 48.2	21 41.1	6 10.5	21 23.7	20 59.8	7 9.0
7 S	13 2 39.8	5 25.6	10 23.4	2N 2.1	4 42.2	9 29.0	18 24.0	21 45.5	6 15.2	21 23.6	20 59.9	7 11.2
10 T	13 14 29.4	6 34.1	10 20.0	13 15.3	2 46.4	10 54.4	18 58.6	21 50.1	6 19.6	21 23.5	20 59.9	7 13.4
13 F	13 26 19.1	7 41.9	10 16.6	18 39.1	1 29.8	12 17.6	19 31.8	21 54.6	6 23.8	21 23.3	20 59.9	7 15.6
16 M	13 38 8.7	8 48.7	10 13.1	16 39.2	1 2.8	13 38.2	20 3.7	21 59.0	6 27.7	21 23.0	20 59.8	7 17.8
19 T	13 49 58.4	9 54.4	10 9.7	8 8.7	1 23.5	14 55.8	20 34.1	22 3.5	6 31.3	21 22.5	20 59.7	7 19.9
22 S	14 1 48.0	10 58.9	10 6.2	4S 17.6	2 23.0	16 10.1	21 3.0	22 7.9	6 34.6	21 22.0	20 59.5	7 22.1
25 W	14 13 37.7	12 1.8	10 2.7	15 32.4	3 49.9	17 20.7	21 30.2	22 12.3	6 37.6	21 21.5	20 59.3	7 24.2
28 S	14 25 27.4	13 3.1	9 59.3	18 34.0	5 34.4	18 27.3	21 55.7	22 16.5	6 40.2	21 20.8	20 59.0	7 26.2
31 T	14 37 17.0	14 2.6	9 55.8	11 24.4	7 28.3	19 29.5	22 19.4	22 20.7	6 42.5	21 20.0	20 58.6	7 28.3

NOVEMBER 1995

LONGITUDE at NOON

DAY	EPHEMERIS SIDEREAL TIME	☉	☊	☽	☿	♀	♂	♃	♄	♅	♆	♇
	h m s	° ′	° ′	° ′	° ′	° ′	° ′	° ′	° ′	° ′	° ′	° ′
1 W	14 41 13.6	8♏35.6	25♎38.4	29♒15.5	25♎21.0	27♏36.6	8♐23.8	16♐ 7.4	18♓21.1	26♑48.8	22♑59.3	29♏39.8
2 T	14 45 10.1	9 35.6	25 35.3	12♓44.7	26 58.1	28 51.2	9 7.6	16 19.5	18R 19.1	26 50.1	23 0.2	29 42.1
3 F	14 49 6.7	10 35.7	25 32.1	25 59.2	28 35.6	0♐ 5.9	9 51.3	16 31.7	18 17.2	26 51.5	23 1.1	29 44.4
4 S	14 53 3.2	11 35.8	25 28.9	8♈59.8	0♏13.5	1 20.5	10 35.2	16 43.9	18 15.3	26 52.9	23 2.1	29 46.6
5 S	14 56 59.8	12 35.9	25 25.7	21 47.5	1 51.6	2 35.1	11 19.1	16 56.2	18 13.6	26 54.4	23 3.1	29 48.9
6 M	15 0 56.4	13 36.0	25 22.6	4♉23.0	3 29.8	3 49.8	12 3.1	17 8.6	18 11.9	26 56.0	23 4.2	29 51.3
7 T	15 4 52.9	14 36.2	25 19.4	16 47.4	5 8.0	5 4.4	12 47.1	17 21.0	18 10.4	26 57.5	23 5.3	29 53.6
8 W	15 8 49.5	15 36.4	25 16.2	29 1.5	6 46.2	6 19.0	13 31.2	17 33.5	18 9.0	26 59.2	23 6.4	29 55.9
9 T	15 12 46.0	16 36.6	25 13.0	11♊ 6.7	8 24.2	7 33.6	14 15.3	17 46.0	18 7.6	27 0.8	23 7.5	29 58.2
10 F	15 16 42.6	17 36.9	25 9.8	23 4.8	10 2.0	8 48.3	14 59.6	17 58.6	18 6.4	27 2.5	23 8.7	0♐ 0.6
11 S	15 20 39.1	18 37.2	25 6.7	4♋57.9	11 39.7	10 2.9	15 43.9	18 11.2	18 5.2	27 4.3	23 9.9	0 2.9
12 S	15 24 35.7	19 37.6	25 3.5	16 49.0	13 17.2	11 17.5	16 28.2	18 24.0	18 4.3	27 6.2	23 11.2	0 5.3
13 M	15 28 32.2	20 37.9	25 0.3	28 41.5	14 54.4	12 32.1	17 12.7	18 36.7	18 3.3	27 8.0	23 12.4	0 7.7
14 T	15 32 28.8	21 38.3	24 57.1	10♌39.5	16 31.4	13 46.7	17 57.1	18 49.5	18 2.5	27 9.9	23 13.7	0 10.0
15 W	15 36 25.4	22 38.7	24 54.0	22 47.4	18 8.1	15 1.3	18 41.7	19 2.3	18 1.8	27 11.8	23 15.0	0 12.4
16 T	15 40 21.9	23 39.2	24 50.8	5♍ 9.8	19 44.5	16 15.9	19 26.3	19 15.2	18 1.2	27 13.8	23 16.4	0 14.8
17 F	15 44 18.5	24 39.7	24 47.6	17 51.4	21 20.7	17 30.5	20 10.9	19 28.2	18 0.7	27 15.8	23 17.8	0 17.1
18 S	15 48 15.0	25 40.2	24 44.4	0♎56.0	22 56.6	18 45.1	20 55.6	19 41.2	18 0.2	27 17.9	23 19.2	0 19.5
19 S	15 52 11.6	26 40.7	24 41.3	14 26.7	24 32.3	19 59.7	21 40.4	19 54.2	17 60.0	27 20.0	23 20.6	0 21.9
20 M	15 56 8.1	27 41.3	24 38.1	28 24.4	26 7.8	21 14.3	22 25.3	20 7.3	17 59.8	27 22.2	23 22.0	0 24.3
21 T	16 0 4.7	28 41.9	24 34.9	12♏47.8	27 43.1	22 28.9	23 10.2	20 20.4	17 59.7	27 24.4	23 23.5	0 26.7
22 W	16 4 1.2	29 42.5	24 31.7	27 32.6	29 18.1	23 43.5	23 55.1	20 33.5	17 59.7	27 26.6	23 25.0	0 29.1
23 T	16 7 57.8	0♐43.2	24 28.5	12♐31.7	0♐52.9	24 58.0	24 40.1	20 46.7	17D 59.8	27 28.9	23 26.6	0 31.5
24 F	16 11 54.4	1 43.8	24 25.4	27 36.2	2 27.6	26 12.6	25 25.2	20 59.9	18 0.1	27 31.2	23 28.1	0 33.8
25 S	16 15 50.9	2 44.5	24 22.2	12♑36.5	4 2.1	27 27.1	26 10.3	21 13.2	18 0.4	27 33.6	23 29.7	0 36.2
26 S	16 19 47.5	3 45.3	24 19.0	27 24.0	5 36.4	28 41.7	26 55.5	21 26.5	18 0.9	27 36.0	23 31.3	0 38.6
27 M	16 23 44.0	4 46.0	24 15.8	11♒52.3	7 10.6	29 56.2	27 40.8	21 39.8	18 1.4	27 38.4	23 33.0	0 41.0
28 T	16 27 40.6	5 46.7	24 12.7	25 57.9	8 44.7	1♑10.8	28 26.1	21 53.2	18 2.1	27 40.9	23 34.6	0 43.4
29 W	16 31 37.1	6 47.5	24 9.5	9♓40.0	10 18.7	2 25.3	29 11.4	22 6.6	18 2.9	27 43.4	23 36.3	0 45.8
30 T	16 35 33.7	7 48.3	24 6.3	22 59.6	11 52.5	3 39.8	29 56.8	22 20.0	18 3.7	27 45.9	23 38.0	0 48.1

DECLINATION at NOON

DAY	EPHEMERIS SIDEREAL TIME	☉	☊	☽	☿	♀	♂	♃	♄	♅	♆	♇
1 W	14 41 13.6	14S 21.9	9S 54.7	7S 33.8	8S 7.4	19S 49.2	22S 26.9	22S 22.1	6S 43.2	21S 19.8	20S 58.5	7S 28.9
4 S	14 53 3.2	15 18.7	9 51.2	5N 1.8	10 5.4	20 45.0	22 48.2	22 26.2	6 45.0	21 18.9	20 58.1	7 30.9
7 T	15 4 52.9	16 13.1	9 47.7	15 6.1	12 2.2	21 35.6	23 7.4	22 30.1	6 46.5	21 18.0	20 57.7	7 32.8
10 F	15 16 42.6	17 5.1	9 44.2	18 52.8	13 55.3	22 20.8	23 24.6	22 33.9	6 47.6	21 16.9	20 57.2	7 34.7
13 M	15 28 32.2	17 54.5	9 40.7	15 17.8	15 43.0	23 0.2	23 39.8	22 37.6	6 48.3	21 15.8	20 56.6	7 36.5
16 T	15 40 21.9	18 41.1	9 37.3	5 49.4	17 24.2	23 33.5	23 52.8	22 41.1	6 48.7	21 14.6	20 56.0	7 38.3
19 S	15 52 11.6	19 24.7	9 33.8	6S 40.9	18 57.8	24 0.6	24 3.5	22 44.5	6 48.6	21 13.3	20 55.4	7 40.0
22 W	16 4 1.2	20 5.2	9 30.3	16 58.3	20 23.1	24 21.3	24 12.0	22 47.7	6 48.2	21 12.0	20 54.7	7 41.6
25 S	16 15 50.9	20 42.4	9 26.8	17 49.3	21 39.3	24 35.3	24 18.2	22 50.7	6 47.4	21 10.6	20 54.0	7 43.2
28 T	16 27 40.6	21 16.1	9 23.3	8 38.6	22 45.9	24 42.7	24 22.0	22 53.5	6 46.2	21 9.1	20 53.2	7 44.7

DECEMBER 1995

LONGITUDE at NOON

DAY	EPHEMERIS SIDEREAL TIME	☉	☊	☽	☿	♀	♂	♃	♄	♅	♆	♇
1 F	16 39 30.2	8♐49.1	24♎ 3.1	5♈59.5	13♐26.3	4♑54.3	0♑42.3	22♐33.4	18♓ 4.7	27♑48.5	23♑39.7	0♐50.5
2 S	16 43 26.8	9 49.9	23 60.0	18 42.5	15 0.1	6 8.7	1 27.8	22 46.9	18 5.8	27 51.1	23 41.5	0 52.9
3 S	16 47 23.4	10 50.8	23 56.8	1♉11.9	16 33.8	7 23.2	2 13.3	23 0.4	18 7.1	27 53.8	23 43.3	0 55.3
4 M	16 51 19.9	11 51.6	23 53.6	13 30.4	18 7.4	8 37.7	2 58.9	23 13.9	18 8.4	27 56.5	23 45.1	0 57.6
5 T	16 55 16.5	12 52.5	23 50.4	25 40.3	19 41.1	9 52.1	3 44.6	23 27.4	18 9.8	27 59.2	23 46.9	0 60.0
6 W	16 59 13.0	13 53.4	23 47.2	7♊43.7	21 14.6	11 6.5	4 30.3	23 41.0	18 11.3	28 2.0	23 48.8	1 2.3
7 T	17 3 9.6	14 54.3	23 44.1	19 41.9	22 48.2	12 20.9	5 16.0	23 54.5	18 12.9	28 4.8	23 50.6	1 4.7
8 F	17 7 6.1	15 55.2	23 40.9	1♋36.5	24 21.8	13 35.3	6 1.8	24 8.1	18 14.7	28 7.6	23 52.5	1 7.0
9 S	17 11 2.7	16 56.1	23 37.7	13 28.7	25 55.3	14 49.7	6 47.7	24 21.7	18 16.5	28 10.4	23 54.4	1 9.3
10 S	17 14 59.3	17 57.0	23 34.5	25 20.3	27 28.9	16 4.0	7 33.5	24 35.3	18 18.4	28 13.3	23 56.3	1 11.6
11 M	17 18 55.8	18 58.0	23 31.4	7♌13.6	29 2.4	17 18.3	8 19.5	24 49.0	18 20.4	28 16.2	23 58.2	1 13.9
12 T	17 22 52.4	19 59.0	23 28.2	19 11.5	0♑35.9	18 32.7	9 5.5	25 2.6	18 22.6	28 19.1	24 0.2	1 16.2
13 W	17 26 48.9	20 60.0	23 25.0	1♍17.4	2 9.3	19 47.0	9 51.5	25 16.3	18 24.8	28 22.1	24 2.2	1 18.5
14 T	17 30 45.5	22 1.0	23 21.8	13 35.6	3 42.7	21 1.3	10 37.6	25 29.9	18 27.2	28 25.1	24 4.2	1 20.8
15 F	17 34 42.0	23 2.0	23 18.7	26 10.6	5 15.9	22 15.5	11 23.7	25 43.6	18 29.6	28 28.1	24 6.2	1 23.0
16 S	17 38 38.6	24 3.1	23 15.5	9♎ 7.0	6 49.1	23 29.8	12 9.9	25 57.3	18 32.1	28 31.2	24 8.2	1 25.3
17 S	17 42 35.2	25 4.2	23 12.3	22 29.1	8 22.0	24 44.0	12 56.1	26 10.9	18 34.8	28 34.2	24 10.2	1 27.5
18 M	17 46 31.7	26 5.3	23 9.1	6♏19.8	9 54.7	25 58.2	13 42.3	26 24.6	18 37.5	28 37.3	24 12.3	1 29.7
19 T	17 50 28.3	27 6.3	23 5.9	20 39.7	11 27.0	27 12.4	14 28.6	26 38.3	18 40.4	28 40.4	24 14.3	1 31.9
20 W	17 54 24.8	28 7.5	23 2.8	5♐26.6	12 59.0	28 26.6	15 15.0	26 52.0	18 43.3	28 43.6	24 16.4	1 34.1
21 T	17 58 21.4	29 8.6	22 59.6	20 34.4	14 30.4	29 40.8	16 1.4	27 5.7	18 46.3	28 46.8	24 18.5	1 36.3
22 F	18 2 17.9	0♑ 9.7	22 56.4	5♑53.7	16 1.2	0♒54.9	16 47.8	27 19.4	18 49.5	28 50.0	24 20.6	1 38.5
23 S	18 6 14.5	1 10.9	22 53.2	21 12.9	17 31.2	2 9.0	17 34.3	27 33.1	18 52.7	28 53.2	24 22.7	1 40.6
24 S	18 10 11.1	2 12.0	22 50.1	6♒20.7	19 0.3	3 23.1	18 20.8	27 46.8	18 56.1	28 56.5	24 24.9	1 42.8
25 M	18 14 7.6	3 13.2	22 46.9	21 7.6	20 28.1	4 37.2	19 7.4	28 0.5	18 59.5	28 59.7	24 27.1	1 44.9
26 T	18 18 4.2	4 14.3	22 43.7	5♓27.6	21 54.5	5 51.2	19 54.0	28 14.2	19 3.0	29 3.0	24 29.2	1 47.0
27 W	18 22 0.7	5 15.5	22 40.5	19 18.5	23 19.2	7 5.2	20 40.6	28 27.8	19 6.6	29 6.3	24 31.4	1 49.1
28 T	18 25 57.3	6 16.6	22 37.4	2♈41.2	24 41.9	8 19.2	21 27.2	28 41.5	19 10.3	29 9.6	24 33.6	1 51.2
29 F	18 29 53.8	7 17.8	22 34.2	15 38.7	26 2.1	9 33.1	22 13.9	28 55.1	19 14.1	29 12.9	24 35.8	1 53.2
30 S	18 33 50.4	8 18.9	22 31.0	28 15.3	27 19.4	10 47.0	23 0.6	29 8.7	19 17.9	29 16.3	24 38.0	1 55.2
31 S	18 37 47.0	9 20.1	22 27.8	10♉35.6	28 33.3	12 0.8	23 47.4	29 22.3	19 21.9	29 19.7	24 40.2	1 57.2

DECLINATION at NOON

DAY	EPHEMERIS SIDEREAL TIME	☉	☊	☽	☿	♀	♂	♃	♄	♅	♆	♇
1 F	16 39 30.2	21S 46.2	9S 19.8	3N 59.6	23S 42.2	24S 43.3	24S 23.4	22S 56.2	6S 44.7	21S 7.5	20S 52.4	7S 46.1
4 M	16 51 19.9	22 12.5	9 16.2	14 23.7	24 27.6	24 37.0	24 22.5	22 58.7	6 42.7	21 5.9	20 51.6	7 47.5
7 T	17 3 9.6	22 35.0	9 12.7	18 54.2	25 1.5	24 24.1	24 19.0	23 0.9	6 40.4	21 4.2	20 50.7	7 48.7
10 S	17 14 59.3	22 53.5	9 9.2	16 3.7	25 23.3	24 4.5	24 13.2	23 3.0	6 37.7	21 2.5	20 49.8	7 49.9
13 W	17 26 48.9	23 7.9	9 5.7	7 11.1	25 32.4	23 38.4	24 4.8	23 4.8	6 34.7	21 0.6	20 48.8	7 51.0
16 S	17 38 38.6	23 18.2	9 2.2	4S 52.0	25 28.4	23 5.8	23 54.1	23 6.4	6 31.3	20 58.8	20 47.8	7 52.1
19 T	17 50 28.3	23 24.3	8 58.6	15 45.4	25 10.9	22 27.2	23 40.8	23 7.9	6 27.6	20 56.9	20 46.8	7 53.0
22 F	18 2 17.9	23 26.2	8 55.1	18 31.2	24 39.9	21 42.6	23 25.1	23 9.1	6 23.5	20 54.9	20 45.7	7 53.9
25 M	18 14 7.6	23 23.9	8 51.6	10 12.3	23 55.8	20 52.4	23 7.1	23 10.0	6 19.1	20 52.9	20 44.7	7 54.6
28 T	18 25 57.3	23 17.3	8 48.0	2N 43.4	22 59.6	19 56.8	22 46.6	23 10.8	6 14.4	20 50.8	20 43.6	7 55.3
31 S	18 37 47.0	23 6.5	8 44.5	13 35.2	21 53.6	18 56.2	22 23.8	23 11.4	6 9.4	20 48.7	20 42.4	7 55.9

JANUARY 1996

DAY	EPHEMERIS SIDEREAL TIME h m s	☉ ° ′	☊ ° ′	☽ ° ′	☿ ° ′	♀ ° ′	♂ ° ′	♃ ° ′	♄ ° ′	♅ ° ′	♆ ° ′	♇ ° ′
					LONGITUDE at NOON							
1 M	18 41 43.5	10♑21.2	22♎24.6	22♉44.0	29♑43.2	13♒14.6	24♑34.2	29♐35.9	19♓25.9	29♑23.0	24♑42.4	1♐59.2
2 T	18 45 40.1	11 22.4	22 21.5	4♊44.3	0♒48.6	14 28.4	25 21.0	29 49.5	19 30.1	29 26.4	24 44.6	2 1.2
3 W	18 49 36.6	12 23.5	22 18.3	16 39.6	1 48.6	15 42.1	26 7.8	0♑ 3.1	19 34.3	29 29.8	24 46.9	2 3.1
4 T	18 53 33.2	13 24.7	22 15.1	28 32.6	2 42.4	16 55.8	26 54.7	0 16.6	19 38.6	29 33.3	24 49.1	2 5.1
5 F	18 57 29.7	14 25.8	22 11.9	10♋24.8	3 29.3	18 9.5	27 41.6	0 30.1	19 43.0	29 36.7	24 51.3	2 7.0
6 S	19 1 26.3	15 26.9	22 8.8	22 17.8	4 8.3	19 23.0	28 28.5	0 43.6	19 47.4	29 40.1	24 53.6	2 8.8
7 S	19 5 22.9	16 28.1	22 5.6	4♌12.7	4 38.5	20 36.6	29 15.5	0 57.1	19 52.0	29 43.6	24 55.8	2 10.7
8 M	19 9 19.4	17 29.2	22 2.4	16 10.8	4 59.1	21 50.1	0♒ 2.5	1 10.5	19 56.6	29 47.1	24 58.1	2 12.5
9 T	19 13 16.0	18 30.3	21 59.2	28 13.8	5 9.2	23 3.6	0 49.5	1 23.9	20 1.3	29 50.5	25 0.4	2 14.3
10 W	19 17 12.5	19 31.5	21 56.1	10♍24.0	5R 8.1	24 17.0	1 36.5	1 37.3	20 6.1	29 54.0	25 2.6	2 16.1
11 T	19 21 9.1	20 32.6	21 52.9	22 44.2	4 55.3	25 30.3	2 23.6	1 50.7	20 11.0	29 57.5	25 4.9	2 17.9
12 F	19 25 5.6	21 33.7	21 49.7	5♎18.1	4 30.8	26 43.6	3 10.7	2 4.0	20 15.9	0♒ 1.0	25 7.2	2 19.6
13 S	19 29 2.2	22 34.9	21 46.5	18 9.7	3 54.6	27 56.9	3 57.8	2 17.3	20 20.9	0 4.5	25 9.4	2 21.3
14 S	19 32 58.7	23 36.1	21 43.3	1♏23.3	3 7.4	29 10.1	4 45.0	2 30.7	20 26.1	0 8.1	25 11.8	2 23.1
15 M	19 36 55.3	24 37.2	21 40.2	15 2.2	2 10.1	0♓23.3	5 32.1	2 43.9	20 31.2	0 11.6	25 14.0	2 24.7
16 T	19 40 51.9	25 38.3	21 37.0	29 8.6	1 4.5	1 36.4	6 19.3	2 57.1	20 36.5	0 15.1	25 16.3	2 26.4
17 W	19 44 48.4	26 39.4	21 33.8	13♐42.2	29♑52.3	2 49.4	7 6.5	3 10.3	20 41.8	0 18.6	25 18.6	2 28.0
18 T	19 48 45.0	27 40.5	21 30.6	28 39.3	28 36.0	4 2.4	7 53.8	3 23.4	20 47.2	0 22.2	25 20.9	2 29.5
19 F	19 52 41.5	28 41.7	21 27.5	13♑52.7	27 17.8	5 15.3	8 41.0	3 36.5	20 52.6	0 25.7	25 23.1	2 31.1
20 S	19 56 38.1	29 42.8	21 24.3	29 11.8	26 0.3	6 28.2	9 28.3	3 49.5	20 58.1	0 29.2	25 25.4	2 32.6
21 S	20 0 34.6	0♒43.9	21 21.1	14♒25.0	24 45.6	7 41.0	10 15.6	4 2.5	21 3.7	0 32.8	25 27.7	2 34.1
22 M	20 4 31.2	1 44.9	21 17.9	29 21.5	23 35.8	8 53.7	11 2.9	4 15.5	21 9.4	0 36.3	25 29.9	2 35.6
23 T	20 8 27.8	2 46.0	21 14.8	13♓53.1	22 32.4	10 6.4	11 50.2	4 28.4	21 15.1	0 39.8	25 32.2	2 37.0
24 W	20 12 24.3	3 47.1	21 11.6	27 55.4	21 36.7	11 19.0	12 37.6	4 41.2	21 20.8	0 43.4	25 34.5	2 38.4
25 T	20 16 20.9	4 48.1	21 8.4	11♈27.5	20 49.6	12 31.5	13 24.9	4 54.0	21 26.7	0 46.9	25 36.7	2 39.8
26 F	20 20 17.4	5 49.1	21 5.2	24 31.5	20 11.3	13 43.9	14 12.3	5 6.8	21 32.6	0 50.4	25 39.0	2 41.1
27 S	20 24 14.0	6 50.1	21 2.0	7♉11.4	19 42.1	14 56.3	14 59.6	5 19.5	21 38.5	0 53.9	25 41.2	2 42.5
28 S	20 28 10.5	7 51.1	20 58.9	19 32.0	19 21.8	16 8.6	15 47.0	5 32.2	21 44.6	0 57.4	25 43.5	2 43.7
29 M	20 32 7.1	8 52.0	20 55.7	1♊38.4	19 10.2	17 20.8	16 34.4	5 44.8	21 50.6	1 1.0	25 45.7	2 45.0
30 T	20 36 3.6	9 53.0	20 52.5	13 35.6	19 6.8	18 32.8	17 21.8	5 57.3	21 56.8	1 4.5	25 47.9	2 46.2
31 W	20 40 0.2	10 53.9	20 49.3	25 27.7	19D11.2	19 44.9	18 9.2	6 9.8	22 2.9	1 8.0	25 50.1	2 47.4

DAY	EPHEMERIS SIDEREAL TIME h m s	☉	☊	☽	☿	♀	♂	♃	♄	♅	♆	♇
					DECLINATION at NOON							
1 M	18 41 43.5	23S 2.0	8S 43.3	16N 3.9	21S 30.1	18S 35.0	22S 15.7	23S 11.5	6S 7.6	20S 48.0	20S 42.1	7S 56.1
4 T	18 53 33.2	22 45.7	8 39.8	18 52.6	20 17.6	17 28.2	21 49.9	23 11.8	6 2.2	20 45.8	20 40.9	7 56.6
7 S	19 5 22.9	22 25.4	8 36.2	14 27.3	19 8.0	16 17.2	21 21.8	23 11.8	5 56.5	20 43.7	20 39.7	7 56.9
10 W	19 17 12.5	22 1.0	8 32.7	4 35.8	18 10.2	15 2.4	20 51.6	23 11.7	5 50.6	20 41.5	20 38.6	7 57.2
13 S	19 29 2.2	21 32.8	8 29.1	7S 24.0	17 32.7	13 44.0	20 19.3	23 11.3	5 44.3	20 39.2	20 37.4	7 57.4
16 T	19 40 51.9	21 0.8	8 25.5	16 57.8	17 20.2	12 22.4	19 44.9	23 10.8	5 37.8	20 37.0	20 36.1	7 57.6
19 F	19 52 41.5	20 25.2	8 22.0	17 46.4	17 30.1	10 58.0	19 8.5	23 10.1	5 31.1	20 34.7	20 34.9	7 57.6
22 M	20 4 31.2	19 46.1	8 18.4	8 1.5	17 55.1	9 31.2	18 30.3	23 9.1	5 24.2	20 32.5	20 33.7	7 57.5
25 T	20 16 20.9	19 3.8	8 14.8	5N 15.0	18 27.1	8 2.3	17 50.3	23 8.0	5 17.0	20 30.2	20 32.5	7 57.4
28 S	20 28 10.5	18 18.3	8 11.3	15 14.0	19 0.3	6 31.6	17 8.5	23 6.8	5 9.7	20 27.9	20 31.3	7 57.1
31 W	20 40 0.2	17 29.8	8 7.7	18 46.9	19 30.8	4 59.5	16 25.2	23 5.3	5 2.1	20 25.6	20 30.1	7 56.8

FEBRUARY 1996

DAY	EPHEMERIS SIDEREAL TIME h m s	☉ ° ′	☊ ° ′	☽ ° ′	☿ ° ′	♀ ° ′	♂ ° ′	♃ ° ′	♄ ° ′	♅ ° ′	♆ ° ′	♇ ° ′
					LONGITUDE at NOON							
1 T	20 43 56.7	11♒54.8	20♎46.2	7♋18.5	19♑22.8	20♓56.8	18♒56.6	6♑22.2	22♓ 9.2	1♒11.4	25♑52.3	2♐48.6
2 F	20 47 53.3	12 55.7	20 43.0	19 10.7	19 41.0	22 8.6	19 44.1	6 34.5	22 15.5	1 14.9	25 54.5	2 49.7
3 S	20 51 49.9	13 56.5	20 39.8	1♌ 6.4	20 5.5	23 20.3	20 31.5	6 46.8	22 21.8	1 18.4	25 56.7	2 50.8
4 S	20 55 46.4	14 57.4	20 36.6	13 7.2	20 35.6	24 32.0	21 19.0	6 59.1	22 28.2	1 21.9	25 59.0	2 51.9
5 M	20 59 43.0	15 58.2	20 33.5	25 13.9	21 10.9	25 43.5	22 6.4	7 11.3	22 34.7	1 25.3	26 1.1	2 52.9
6 T	21 3 39.5	16 59.0	20 30.3	7♍27.8	21 50.9	26 54.9	22 53.8	7 23.4	22 41.2	1 28.8	26 3.3	2 53.9
7 W	21 7 36.1	17 59.8	20 27.1	19 49.7	22 35.2	28 6.2	23 41.3	7 35.4	22 47.7	1 32.2	26 5.4	2 54.9
8 T	21 11 32.6	19 0.6	20 23.9	2♎21.4	23 23.4	29 17.4	24 28.7	7 47.4	22 54.3	1 35.6	26 7.6	2 55.8
9 F	21 15 29.2	20 1.3	20 20.7	15 4.6	24 15.2	0♈28.5	25 16.2	7 59.3	23 0.9	1 39.0	26 9.7	2 56.7
10 S	21 19 25.7	21 2.1	20 17.6	28 2.0	25 10.4	1 39.4	26 3.6	8 11.1	23 7.6	1 42.4	26 11.8	2 57.6
11 S	21 23 22.3	22 2.8	20 14.4	11♏16.2	26 8.5	2 50.3	26 51.1	8 22.8	23 14.3	1 45.8	26 13.9	2 58.4
12 M	21 27 18.8	23 3.5	20 11.2	24 50.0	27 9.4	4 1.0	27 38.5	8 34.5	23 21.0	1 49.1	26 16.0	2 59.2
13 T	21 31 15.4	24 4.1	20 8.0	8♐45.1	28 12.9	5 11.7	28 26.0	8 46.1	23 27.8	1 52.5	26 18.1	2 60.0
14 W	21 35 12.0	25 4.8	20 4.9	23 1.9	29 18.8	6 22.2	29 13.5	8 57.6	23 34.6	1 55.8	26 20.1	3 0.7
15 T	21 39 8.5	26 5.4	20 1.7	7♑38.5	0♒26.8	7 32.6	0♓ 0.9	9 9.1	23 41.5	1 59.1	26 22.2	3 1.4
16 F	21 43 5.1	27 6.1	19 58.5	22 30.2	1 36.9	8 42.8	0 48.4	9 20.4	23 48.4	2 2.4	26 24.2	3 2.0
17 S	21 47 1.6	28 6.7	19 55.3	7♒29.8	2 48.9	9 52.9	1 35.8	9 31.7	23 55.4	2 5.7	26 26.2	3 2.7
18 S	21 50 58.2	29 7.2	19 52.1	22 28.1	4 2.6	11 2.9	2 23.3	9 42.9	24 2.3	2 8.9	26 28.2	3 3.3
19 M	21 54 54.7	0♓ 7.8	19 49.0	7♓15.7	5 18.1	12 12.8	3 10.7	9 53.9	24 9.3	2 12.1	26 30.2	3 3.8
20 T	21 58 51.3	1 8.3	19 45.8	21 44.6	6 35.1	13 22.5	3 58.1	10 5.0	24 16.4	2 15.3	26 32.1	3 4.3
21 W	22 2 47.8	2 8.8	19 42.6	5♈49.1	7 53.6	14 32.1	4 45.6	10 15.9	24 23.4	2 18.5	26 34.1	3 4.8
22 T	22 6 44.4	3 9.3	19 39.4	19 26.7	9 13.5	15 41.5	5 33.0	10 26.7	24 30.5	2 21.7	26 36.0	3 5.3
23 F	22 10 40.9	4 9.7	19 36.3	2♉37.6	10 34.9	16 50.8	6 20.4	10 37.4	24 37.7	2 24.8	26 37.9	3 5.7
24 S	22 14 37.5	5 10.1	19 33.1	15 24.0	11 57.5	17 59.9	7 7.8	10 48.0	24 44.8	2 27.9	26 39.8	3 6.0
25 S	22 18 34.0	6 10.5	19 29.9	27 49.8	13 21.4	19 8.9	7 55.2	10 58.6	24 52.0	2 31.1	26 41.7	3 6.4
26 M	22 22 30.6	7 10.9	19 26.7	9♊59.7	14 46.6	20 17.6	8 42.6	11 9.0	24 59.2	2 34.1	26 43.6	3 6.7
27 T	22 26 27.1	8 11.2	19 23.5	21 58.7	16 12.9	21 26.2	9 29.9	11 19.4	25 6.5	2 37.2	26 45.4	3 7.0
28 W	22 30 23.7	9 11.4	19 20.4	3♋51.7	17 40.4	22 34.6	10 17.3	11 29.6	25 13.7	2 40.2	26 47.2	3 7.2
29 T	22 34 20.2	10 11.7	19 17.2	15 43.0	19 9.1	23 42.9	11 4.6	11 39.7	25 21.0	2 43.2	26 49.0	3 7.4

DAY	EPHEMERIS SIDEREAL TIME h m s	☉	☊	☽	☿	♀	♂	♃	♄	♅	♆	♇
					DECLINATION at NOON							
1 T	20 43 56.7	17S 13.0	8S 6.5	18N 19.9	19S 39.8	4S 28.5	16S 10.4	23S 4.8	4S 59.6	20S 24.9	20S 29.7	7S 56.7
4 S	20 55 46.4	16 20.9	8 2.9	12 27.3	20 2.5	2 55.1	15 25.0	23 3.2	4 51.8	20 22.6	20 28.5	7 56.3
7 W	21 7 36.1	15 26.2	7 59.3	1 45.8	20 17.1	1 21.0	14 38.1	23 1.5	4 43.9	20 20.4	20 27.3	7 55.8
10 S	21 19 25.7	14 29.1	7 55.7	9S 60.0	20 22.5	0N 13.4	13 50.0	22 59.6	4 35.8	20 18.1	20 26.1	7 55.2
13 T	21 31 15.4	13 29.8	7 52.1	17 53.0	20 17.6	1 47.8	13 0.6	22 57.6	4 27.6	20 15.9	20 24.9	7 54.6
16 F	21 43 5.1	12 28.6	7 48.5	16 32.0	20 2.0	3 21.9	12 10.0	22 55.5	4 19.3	20 13.8	20 23.8	7 53.9
19 M	21 54 54.7	11 25.5	7 45.0	5 43.7	19 35.3	4 55.3	11 18.4	22 53.3	4 10.8	20 11.6	20 22.6	7 53.1
22 T	22 6 44.4	10 20.8	7 41.3	7N 29.0	18 57.3	6 27.8	10 25.9	22 51.0	4 2.3	20 9.5	20 21.5	7 52.2
25 S	22 18 34.0	9 14.7	7 37.7	16 26.3	18 7.7	7 59.1	9 32.4	22 48.7	3 53.7	20 7.4	20 20.5	7 51.4
28 W	22 30 23.7	8 7.4	7 34.1	18 22.0	17 6.6	9 28.8	8 38.3	22 46.3	3 45.0	20 5.4	20 19.4	7 50.4

MARCH 1996

DAY	EPHEMERIS SIDEREAL TIME	☉	☊	☾	☿	♀	♂	♃	♄	♅	♆	♇
	h m s	° ′	° ′	° ′	° ′	° ′	° ′	° ′	° ′	° ′	° ′	° ′
						LONGITUDE at NOON						
1 F	22 38 16.8	11♓11.9	19♎14.0	27♋36.6	20♒38.9	24♈50.9	11♓51.9	11♑49.7	25♓28.3	2♒46.1	26♑50.7	3♐ 7.6
2 S	22 42 13.4	12 12.1	19 10.8	9♌35.8	22 9.8	25 58.8	12 39.2	11 59.6	25 35.6	2 49.0	26 52.5	3 7.7
3 S	22 46 9.9	13 12.2	19 7.7	21 42.9	23 41.8	27 6.4	13 26.4	12 9.4	25 42.9	2 51.9	26 54.2	3 7.8
4 M	22 50 6.5	14 12.3	19 4.5	3♍59.7	25 15.0	28 13.9	14 13.7	12 19.1	25 50.2	2 54.8	26 55.9	3 7.9
5 T	22 54 3.0	15 12.4	19 1.3	16 27.2	26 49.2	29 21.1	15 0.9	12 28.7	25 57.6	2 57.6	26 57.5	3 7.9
6 W	22 57 59.6	16 12.4	18 58.1	29 6.2	28 24.6	0♉28.1	15 48.2	12 38.2	26 4.9	3 0.5	26 59.2	3 7.9
7 T	23 1 56.1	17 12.4	18 54.9	11♎56.9	0♓ 1.1	1 34.9	16 35.3	12 47.5	26 12.3	3 3.2	27 0.8	3R 7.8
8 F	23 5 52.7	18 12.4	18 51.8	24 59.7	1 38.7	2 41.5	17 22.5	12 56.8	26 19.7	3 6.0	27 2.4	3 7.8
9 S	23 9 49.2	19 12.4	18 48.6	8♏15.0	3 17.4	3 47.9	18 9.7	13 5.9	26 27.1	3 8.7	27 4.0	3 7.6
10 S	23 13 45.8	20 12.3	18 45.4	21 43.2	4 57.2	4 54.0	18 56.8	13 14.9	26 34.5	3 11.4	27 5.5	3 7.5
11 M	23 17 42.3	21 12.2	18 42.2	5♐24.8	6 38.2	5 59.9	19 43.9	13 23.8	26 41.9	3 14.0	27 7.1	3 7.3
12 T	23 21 38.9	22 12.1	18 39.0	19 19.9	8 20.4	7 5.5	20 31.0	13 32.6	26 49.3	3 16.6	27 8.6	3 7.1
13 W	23 25 35.4	23 11.9	18 35.9	3♑28.0	10 3.7	8 10.9	21 18.1	13 41.2	26 56.8	3 19.2	27 10.0	3 6.8
14 T	23 29 32.0	24 11.8	18 32.7	17 47.4	11 48.2	9 16.1	22 5.2	13 49.7	27 4.2	3 21.7	27 11.5	3 6.6
15 F	23 33 28.5	25 11.5	18 29.5	2♒15.3	13 33.9	10 21.0	22 52.2	13 58.1	27 11.7	3 24.2	27 12.9	3 6.2
16 S	23 37 25.1	26 11.3	18 26.3	16 47.2	15 20.8	11 25.6	23 39.2	14 6.3	27 19.1	3 26.7	27 14.3	3 5.9
17 S	23 41 21.6	27 11.1	18 23.2	1♓17.6	17 8.9	12 30.0	24 26.2	14 14.5	27 26.6	3 29.2	27 15.7	3 5.5
18 M	23 45 18.2	28 10.8	18 20.0	15 40.6	18 58.3	13 34.0	25 13.2	14 22.5	27 34.0	3 31.6	27 17.0	3 5.1
19 T	23 49 14.7	29 10.5	18 16.8	29 50.5	20 48.8	14 37.8	26 0.1	14 30.3	27 41.5	3 33.9	27 18.3	3 4.7
20 W	23 53 11.3	0♈10.1	18 13.6	13♈42.6	22 40.6	15 41.3	26 47.0	14 38.0	27 48.9	3 36.3	27 19.6	3 4.2
21 T	23 57 7.8	1 9.7	18 10.4	27 13.9	24 33.7	16 44.4	27 33.9	14 45.6	27 56.4	3 38.5	27 20.9	3 3.7
22 F	0 1 4.4	2 9.3	18 7.3	10♉23.4	26 27.9	17 47.2	28 20.8	14 53.0	28 3.8	3 40.8	27 22.1	3 3.1
23 S	0 5 0.9	3 8.8	18 4.1	23 11.7	28 23.4	18 49.7	29 7.6	15 0.3	28 11.2	3 43.0	27 23.3	3 2.5
24 S	0 8 57.5	4 8.3	18 0.9	5♊41.0	0♈20.1	19 51.9	29 54.3	15 7.5	28 18.7	3 45.1	27 24.4	3 1.9
25 M	0 12 54.0	5 7.7	17 57.7	17 54.6	2 17.9	20 53.7	0♈41.1	15 14.4	28 26.1	3 47.2	27 25.6	3 1.3
26 T	0 16 50.6	6 7.1	17 54.6	29 56.6	4 16.8	21 55.1	1 27.8	15 21.3	28 33.5	3 49.3	27 26.7	3 0.6
27 W	0 20 47.2	7 6.5	17 51.4	11♋51.6	6 16.8	22 56.2	2 14.5	15 28.0	28 40.9	3 51.3	27 27.7	2 59.9
28 T	0 24 43.7	8 5.9	17 48.2	23 44.3	8 17.7	23 56.9	3 1.1	15 34.5	28 48.3	3 53.3	27 28.8	2 59.1
29 F	0 28 40.3	9 5.2	17 45.0	5♌39.2	10 19.5	24 57.1	3 47.7	15 40.9	28 55.7	3 55.3	27 29.8	2 58.4
30 S	0 32 36.8	10 4.4	17 41.8	17 40.5	12 22.1	25 57.0	4 34.3	15 47.2	29 3.0	3 57.2	27 30.8	2 57.6
31 S	0 36 33.4	11 3.6	17 38.7	29 52.0	14 25.2	26 56.4	5 20.8	15 53.3	29 10.4	3 59.0	27 31.7	2 56.7
						DECLINATION at NOON						
1 F	22 38 16.8	7S 21.9	7S 31.7	15N 38.4	16S 19.5	10N 27.5	8S 1.8	22S 44.7	3S 39.2	20S 4.1	20S 18.7	7S 49.7
4 M	22 50 6.5	6 12.9	7 28.1	6 42.8	14 59.3	11 53.9	7 6.6	22 42.3	3 30.5	20 2.2	20 17.8	7 48.7
7 T	23 1 56.1	5 3.2	7 24.5	5S 10.3	13 27.6	13 18.0	6 10.8	22 39.9	3 21.7	20 0.3	20 16.8	7 47.6
10 S	23 13 45.8	3 52.8	7 20.9	15 19.8	11 44.6	14 39.4	5 14.6	22 37.4	3 12.9	19 58.5	20 15.9	7 46.4
13 W	23 25 35.4	2 42.0	7 17.3	18 18.4	9 50.4	15 58.0	4 18.1	22 35.0	3 4.0	19 56.8	20 15.0	7 45.3
16 S	23 37 25.1	1 30.9	7 13.6	11 26.9	7 45.2	17 13.3	3 21.4	22 32.7	2 55.2	19 55.1	20 14.2	7 44.1
19 T	23 49 14.7	0 19.7	7 10.0	1N 22.4	5 29.4	18 25.3	2 24.4	22 30.4	2 46.4	19 53.5	20 13.4	7 42.8
22 F	0 1 4.4	0N 51.4	7 6.4	12 57.3	3 3.5	19 33.6	1 27.5	22 28.2	2 37.7	19 52.0	20 12.6	7 41.6
25 M	0 12 54.0	2 2.3	7 2.7	18 18.1	0 28.5	20 38.0	0 30.5	22 26.0	2 28.9	19 50.5	20 11.9	7 40.3
28 T	0 24 43.7	3 12.7	6 59.1	16 11.1	2N 14.2	21 38.4	0N 26.3	22 24.0	2 20.3	19 49.2	20 11.3	7 39.0
31 S	0 36 33.4	4 22.6	6 55.5	7 52.7	5 2.1	22 34.4	1 23.0	22 22.0	2 11.7	19 47.9	20 10.7	7 37.7

APRIL 1996

DAY	EPHEMERIS SIDEREAL TIME	☉	☊	☾	☿	♀	♂	♃	♄	♅	♆	♇
						LONGITUDE at NOON						
1 M	0 40 29.9	12♈ 2.8	17♎35.5	12♍16.6	16♈28.7	27♉55.3	6♈ 7.3	15♑59.2	29♓17.7	4♒ 0.9	27♑32.7	2♐55.9
2 T	0 44 26.5	13 2.0	17 32.3	24 56.2	18 32.4	28 53.9	6 53.8	16 5.0	29 25.0	4 2.6	27 33.5	2R 55.0
3 W	0 48 23.0	14 1.1	17 29.1	7♎52.2	20 36.1	29 51.9	7 40.2	16 10.6	29 32.3	4 4.4	27 34.4	2 54.1
4 T	0 52 19.6	15 0.2	17 25.9	21 4.4	22 39.5	0♊49.4	8 26.6	16 16.1	29 39.6	4 6.1	27 35.2	2 53.1
5 F	0 56 16.1	15 59.2	17 22.8	4♏32.0	24 42.3	1 46.5	9 12.9	16 21.4	29 46.9	4 7.7	27 36.0	2 52.2
6 S	1 0 12.7	16 58.2	17 19.6	18 13.5	26 44.2	2 43.0	9 59.3	16 26.5	29 54.1	4 9.3	27 36.8	2 51.2
7 S	1 4 9.2	17 57.3	17 16.4	2♐ 6.5	28 44.8	3 39.0	10 45.6	16 31.6	0♈ 1.4	4 10.9	27 37.6	2 50.2
8 M	1 8 5.8	18 56.2	17 13.2	16 8.6	0♉43.8	4 34.5	11 31.8	16 36.4	0 8.6	4 12.4	27 38.3	2 49.2
9 T	1 12 2.3	19 55.1	17 10.1	0♑17.0	2 40.8	5 29.3	12 18.0	16 41.0	0 15.7	4 13.8	27 38.9	2 48.1
10 W	1 15 58.9	20 54.0	17 6.9	14 29.2	4 35.4	6 23.6	13 4.2	16 45.5	0 22.9	4 15.3	27 39.6	2 47.0
11 T	1 19 55.4	21 52.9	17 3.7	28 42.7	6 27.4	7 17.3	13 50.3	16 49.8	0 30.0	4 16.6	27 40.2	2 45.9
12 F	1 23 52.0	22 51.7	17 0.5	12♒54.9	8 16.3	8 10.3	14 36.4	16 53.9	0 37.1	4 17.9	27 40.7	2 44.7
13 S	1 27 48.5	23 50.5	16 57.3	27 3.4	10 1.9	9 2.7	15 22.4	16 57.9	0 44.2	4 19.2	27 41.3	2 43.6
14 S	1 31 45.1	24 49.3	16 54.2	11♓ 5.8	11 43.8	9 54.4	16 8.4	17 1.7	0 51.2	4 20.4	27 41.8	2 42.4
15 M	1 35 41.6	25 48.1	16 51.0	24 59.5	13 21.8	10 45.4	16 54.4	17 5.3	0 58.2	4 21.6	27 42.2	2 41.1
16 T	1 39 38.2	26 46.8	16 47.8	8♈42.1	14 55.6	11 35.8	17 40.3	17 8.7	1 5.2	4 22.7	27 42.7	2 39.9
17 W	1 43 34.7	27 45.5	16 44.6	22 11.3	16 25.0	12 25.3	18 26.2	17 12.0	1 12.2	4 23.8	27 43.1	2 38.6
18 T	1 47 31.3	28 44.1	16 41.5	5♉25.5	17 49.9	13 14.1	19 12.0	17 15.1	1 19.1	4 24.8	27 43.5	2 37.4
19 F	1 51 27.9	29 42.8	16 38.3	18 23.5	19 10.0	14 2.1	19 57.8	17 18.0	1 26.0	4 25.8	27 43.8	2 36.1
20 S	1 55 24.4	0♉41.4	16 35.1	1♊ 5.4	20 25.3	14 49.2	20 43.6	17 20.7	1 32.8	4 26.7	27 44.1	2 34.7
21 S	1 59 21.0	1 39.9	16 31.9	13 32.0	21 35.5	15 35.4	21 29.3	17 23.2	1 39.6	4 27.6	27 44.4	2 33.4
22 M	2 3 17.5	2 38.4	16 28.7	25 45.2	22 40.5	16 20.8	22 14.9	17 25.5	1 46.4	4 28.4	27 44.6	2 32.0
23 T	2 7 14.1	3 36.9	16 25.6	7♋47.8	23 40.4	17 5.2	23 0.5	17 27.7	1 53.1	4 29.2	27 44.8	2 30.6
24 W	2 11 10.6	4 35.4	16 22.4	19 43.4	24 34.9	17 48.6	23 46.1	17 29.7	1 59.8	4 29.9	27 45.0	2 29.2
25 T	2 15 7.2	5 33.8	16 19.2	1♌36.3	25 24.0	18 31.0	24 31.6	17 31.5	2 6.4	4 30.6	27 45.1	2 27.8
26 F	2 19 3.7	6 32.2	16 16.0	13 31.0	26 7.6	19 12.4	25 17.0	17 33.1	2 13.0	4 31.2	27 45.2	2 26.4
27 S	2 23 0.3	7 30.5	16 12.9	25 32.1	26 45.8	19 52.6	26 2.4	17 34.5	2 19.6	4 31.8	27 45.3	2 25.0
28 S	2 26 56.8	8 28.9	16 9.7	7♍44.5	27 18.4	20 31.7	26 47.8	17 35.8	2 26.2	4 32.4	27 45.4	2 23.5
29 M	2 30 53.4	9 27.2	16 6.5	20 12.1	27 45.4	21 9.6	27 33.2	17 36.8	2 32.7	4 32.9	27 45.4	2 22.1
30 T	2 34 49.9	10 25.4	16 3.3	2♎58.4	28 6.8	21 46.3	28 18.4	17 37.7	2 39.1	4 33.3	27 45.4	2 20.6
						DECLINATION at NOON						
1 M	0 40 29.9	4N 45.7	6S 54.3	4N 9.5	5N 58.7	22N 52.1	1N 41.8	22S 21.4	2S 8.8	19S 47.5	20S 10.5	7S 37.3
4 T	0 52 19.6	5 54.6	6 50.6	7S 53.1	8 47.9	23 42.2	2 38.1	22 19.7	2 0.3	19 46.4	20 10.0	7 36.0
7 S	1 4 9.2	7 2.6	6 47.0	16 54.9	11 32.2	24 27.7	3 34.0	22 18.1	1 51.9	19 45.4	20 9.5	7 34.7
10 W	1 15 58.9	8 9.5	6 43.3	17 24.1	14 5.7	25 8.5	4 29.4	22 16.6	1 43.6	19 44.4	20 9.1	7 33.4
13 S	1 27 48.5	9 15.1	6 39.7	8 40.6	16 22.9	25 44.6	5 24.3	22 15.4	1 35.4	19 43.6	20 8.8	7 32.1
16 T	1 39 38.2	10 19.4	6 36.0	4N 10.0	18 19.7	26 15.9	6 18.6	22 14.3	1 27.4	19 42.8	20 8.5	7 30.8
19 F	1 51 27.9	11 22.2	6 32.4	14 40.1	19 53.6	26 42.4	7 12.2	22 13.4	1 19.4	19 42.2	20 8.2	7 29.6
22 M	2 3 17.5	12 23.3	6 28.7	18 28.2	21 3.6	27 4.2	8 5.1	22 12.8	1 11.7	19 41.7	20 8.0	7 28.4
25 T	2 15 7.2	13 22.5	6 25.0	14 50.1	21 49.7	27 21.5	8 57.1	22 12.3	1 4.1	19 41.3	20 7.9	7 27.2
28 S	2 26 56.8	14 19.8	6 21.4	5 34.3	22 12.4	27 34.2	9 48.2	22 12.1	0 56.6	19 40.9	20 7.9	7 26.0

MAY 1996

DAY	EPHEMERIS SIDEREAL TIME h m s	☉ ° ′	☊ ° ′	☽ ° ′	☿ ° ′	♀ ° ′	♂ ° ′	♃ ° ′	♄ ° ′	♅ ° ′	♆ ° ′	♇ ° ′
					LONGITUDE at NOON							
1 W	2 38 46.5	11♉23.6	16♎ 0.1	16♎ 5.9	28♉22.7	22♊21.6	29♈ 3.6	17♑38.4	2♈45.5	4♒33.7	27♑45.3	2♐19.1
2 T	2 42 43.0	12 21.8	15 57.0	29 35.2	28 33.1	22 55.6	29 48.8	17 38.9	2 51.8	4 34.0	27R45.2	2R17.5
3 F	2 46 39.6	13 20.0	15 53.8	13♏25.5	28 38.1	23 28.3	0♉33.9	17 39.2	2 58.1	4 34.3	27 45.1	2 16.0
4 S	2 50 36.2	14 18.1	15 50.6	27 33.8	28R37.8	23 59.5	1 19.0	17 39.3	3 4.3	4 34.5	27 44.9	2 14.5
5 S	2 54 32.7	15 16.2	15 47.4	11♐55.6	28 32.4	24 29.2	2 4.0	17R39.2	3 10.5	4 34.7	27 44.8	2 12.9
6 M	2 58 29.3	16 14.2	15 44.3	26 25.2	28 22.1	24 57.3	2 48.9	17 39.0	3 16.6	4 34.8	27 44.5	2 11.3
7 T	3 2 25.8	17 12.3	15 41.1	10♑56.7	28 7.2	25 23.9	3 33.9	17 38.5	3 22.7	4 34.9	27 44.3	2 9.8
8 W	3 6 22.4	18 10.3	15 37.9	25 24.4	27 48.1	25 48.8	4 18.7	17 37.9	3 28.8	4 34.9	27 44.0	2 8.2
9 T	3 10 18.9	19 8.3	15 34.7	9♒44.1	27 25.0	26 12.0	5 3.5	17 37.0	3 34.7	4 34.9	27 43.7	2 6.6
10 F	3 14 15.5	20 6.3	15 31.5	23 52.7	26 58.6	26 33.4	5 48.3	17 36.0	3 40.7	4 34.9	27 43.3	2 5.0
11 S	3 18 12.0	21 4.2	15 28.4	7♓48.7	26 29.2	26 53.0	6 33.0	17 34.8	3 46.5	4R34.7	27 43.0	2 3.3
12 S	3 22 8.6	22 2.2	15 25.2	21 31.6	25 57.4	27 10.8	7 17.7	17 33.4	3 52.3	4 34.6	27 42.6	2 1.7
13 M	3 26 5.1	23 0.1	15 22.0	5♈ 1.4	25 23.8	27 26.5	8 2.3	17 31.8	3 58.1	4 34.4	27 42.1	2 0.1
14 T	3 30 1.7	23 58.0	15 18.8	18 18.7	24 48.9	27 40.3	8 46.9	17 30.1	4 3.8	4 34.1	27 41.6	1 58.5
15 W	3 33 58.3	24 55.9	15 15.7	1♉23.6	24 13.5	27 52.0	9 31.4	17 28.1	4 9.4	4 33.8	27 41.1	1 56.8
16 T	3 37 54.8	25 53.7	15 12.5	14 16.4	23 38.1	28 1.6	10 15.9	17 26.0	4 15.0	4 33.4	27 40.6	1 55.2
17 F	3 41 51.4	26 51.5	15 9.3	26 57.4	23 3.4	28 9.1	11 0.3	17 23.7	4 20.5	4 33.0	27 40.0	1 53.5
18 S	3 45 47.9	27 49.3	15 6.1	9♊26.7	22 29.9	28 14.3	11 44.6	17 21.2	4 25.9	4 32.5	27 39.5	1 51.9
19 S	3 49 44.5	28 47.2	15 3.0	21 45.0	21 58.2	28 17.2	12 29.0	17 18.5	4 31.3	4 32.1	27 38.9	1 50.3
20 M	3 53 41.0	29 44.9	14 59.8	3♋53.1	21 28.8	28 17.8	13 13.2	17 15.6	4 36.6	4 31.5	27 38.2	1 48.6
21 T	3 57 37.6	0♊42.7	14 56.6	15 53.0	21 2.1	28R16.1	13 57.4	17 12.6	4 41.9	4 30.9	27 37.5	1 47.0
22 W	4 1 34.1	1 40.4	14 53.4	27 47.1	20 38.7	28 11.9	14 41.6	17 9.4	4 47.0	4 30.3	27 36.8	1 45.3
23 T	4 5 30.7	2 38.0	14 50.2	9♌38.7	20 18.7	28 5.3	15 25.7	17 6.0	4 52.1	4 29.6	27 36.1	1 43.7
24 F	4 9 27.3	3 35.7	14 47.1	21 31.8	20 2.6	27 56.3	16 9.7	17 2.4	4 57.2	4 28.8	27 35.3	1 42.0
25 S	4 13 23.8	4 33.3	14 43.9	3♍30.9	19 50.5	27 44.8	16 53.7	16 58.7	5 2.1	4 28.0	27 34.5	1 40.3
26 S	4 17 20.4	5 30.9	14 40.7	15 41.1	19 42.6	27 30.9	17 37.6	16 54.8	5 7.0	4 27.2	27 33.7	1 38.7
27 M	4 21 16.9	6 28.5	14 37.5	28 7.2	19 39.1	27 14.7	18 21.4	16 50.7	5 11.8	4 26.3	27 32.9	1 37.0
28 T	4 25 13.5	7 26.1	14 34.4	10♎53.9	19D40.1	26 56.0	19 5.2	16 46.5	5 16.6	4 25.4	27 32.0	1 35.4
29 W	4 29 10.0	8 23.6	14 31.2	24 4.8	19 45.5	26 35.0	19 49.0	16 42.1	5 21.3	4 24.4	27 31.1	1 33.8
30 T	4 33 6.6	9 21.1	14 28.0	7♏42.3	19 55.4	26 11.8	20 32.7	16 37.5	5 25.9	4 23.4	27 30.2	1 32.1
31 F	4 37 3.2	10 18.6	14 24.8	21 46.2	20 9.8	25 46.5	21 16.3	16 32.8	5 30.4	4 22.4	27 29.2	1 30.5
					DECLINATION at NOON							
1 W	2 38 46.5	15N14.9	6S17.7	6S24.9	22N12.3	27N42.4	10N38.3	22S12.0	0S49.4	19S40.7	20S 7.9	7S24.9
4 S	2 50 36.2	16 7.7	6 14.0	16 18.1	21 50.2	27 46.4	11 27.3	22 12.3	0 42.3	19 40.6	20 7.9	7 23.8
7 T	3 2 25.8	16 58.2	6 10.4	17 49.4	21 7.7	27 46.2	12 15.3	22 12.7	0 35.5	19 40.6	20 8.0	7 22.8
10 F	3 14 15.5	17 46.1	6 6.7	9 38.1	20 8.1	27 41.8	13 2.1	22 13.4	0 28.9	19 40.7	20 8.2	7 21.8
13 M	3 26 5.1	18 31.3	6 3.0	2N58.2	18 56.3	27 33.3	13 47.6	22 14.3	0 22.5	19 41.0	20 8.4	7 20.9
16 T	3 37 54.8	19 13.7	5 59.3	13 49.9	17 39.7	27 20.7	14 31.8	22 15.4	0 16.3	19 41.3	20 8.7	7 20.0
19 S	3 49 44.5	19 53.2	5 55.7	18 30.8	16 26.4	27 3.9	15 14.7	22 16.7	0 10.4	19 41.7	20 9.0	7 19.3
22 W	4 1 34.1	20 29.7	5 52.0	15 40.1	15 24.0	26 42.6	15 56.2	22 18.2	0 4.7	19 42.2	20 9.4	7 18.5
25 S	4 13 23.8	21 2.9	5 48.3	6 58.7	14 38.2	26 16.6	16 36.2	22 20.0	0N 0.7	19 42.9	20 9.9	7 17.9
28 T	4 25 13.5	21 32.9	5 44.6	4S43.7	14 12.0	25 45.6	17 14.7	22 21.9	0 5.8	19 43.6	20 10.4	7 17.3
31 F	4 37 3.2	21 59.6	5 40.9	15 18.6	14 6.1	25 9.5	17 51.6	22 24.0	0 10.7	19 44.4	20 10.9	7 16.8

JUNE 1996

DAY	EPHEMERIS SIDEREAL TIME h m s	☉ ° ′	☊ ° ′	☽ ° ′	☿ ° ′	♀ ° ′	♂ ° ′	♃ ° ′	♄ ° ′	♅ ° ′	♆ ° ′	♇ ° ′
					LONGITUDE at NOON							
1 S	4 40 59.7	11♊16.1	14♎21.7	6♐13.8	20♉28.6	25♊19.2	21♉59.9	16♑27.9	5♈34.8	4♒21.3	27♑28.2	1♐28.9
2 S	4 44 56.3	12 13.5	14 18.5	20 59.5	20 51.8	24R49.9	22 43.4	16R22.9	5 39.2	4R20.1	27R27.2	1R27.2
3 M	4 48 52.8	13 11.0	14 15.3	5♑55.2	21 19.4	24 18.9	23 26.9	16 17.8	5 43.5	4 18.9	27 26.2	1 25.6
4 T	4 52 49.4	14 8.4	14 12.1	20 51.9	21 51.1	23 46.3	24 10.3	16 12.4	5 47.7	4 17.7	27 25.2	1 24.0
5 W	4 56 45.9	15 5.8	14 8.9	5♒40.9	22 27.0	23 12.4	24 53.6	16 7.0	5 51.8	4 16.4	27 24.1	1 22.4
6 T	5 0 42.5	16 3.2	14 5.8	20 15.4	23 6.9	22 37.3	25 36.9	16 1.4	5 55.9	4 15.1	27 23.0	1 20.8
7 F	5 4 39.0	17 0.6	14 2.6	4♓31.1	23 50.8	22 1.2	26 20.2	15 55.7	5 59.9	4 13.8	27 21.9	1 19.3
8 S	5 8 35.6	17 58.0	13 59.4	18 26.2	24 38.6	21 24.4	27 3.4	15 49.8	6 3.7	4 12.4	27 20.7	1 17.7
9 S	5 12 32.2	18 55.4	13 56.2	2♈ 1.0	25 30.2	20 47.1	27 46.6	15 43.9	6 7.6	4 11.0	27 19.6	1 16.2
10 M	5 16 28.7	19 52.8	13 53.1	15 17.3	26 25.4	20 9.5	28 29.7	15 37.8	6 11.3	4 9.5	27 18.4	1 14.6
11 T	5 20 25.3	20 50.1	13 49.9	28 17.3	27 24.3	19 31.9	29 12.7	15 31.5	6 15.0	4 8.0	27 17.2	1 13.1
12 W	5 24 21.8	21 47.5	13 46.7	11♉ 3.5	28 26.7	18 54.5	29 55.7	15 25.2	6 18.5	4 6.5	27 16.0	1 11.6
13 T	5 28 18.4	22 44.8	13 43.5	23 37.9	29 32.6	18 17.6	0♊38.6	15 18.7	6 22.0	4 4.9	27 14.7	1 10.0
14 F	5 32 14.9	23 42.1	13 40.4	6♊ 2.3	0♊41.8	17 41.4	1 21.5	15 12.2	6 25.4	4 3.3	27 13.4	1 8.6
15 S	5 36 11.5	24 39.5	13 37.2	18 17.9	1 54.5	17 6.0	2 4.3	15 5.5	6 28.6	4 1.6	27 12.1	1 7.1
16 S	5 40 8.1	25 36.8	13 34.0	0♋25.7	3 10.5	16 31.8	2 47.1	14 58.7	6 31.8	3 59.9	27 10.8	1 5.6
17 M	5 44 4.6	26 34.1	13 30.8	12 26.7	4 29.7	15 58.9	3 29.7	14 51.8	6 35.0	3 58.2	27 9.5	1 4.1
18 T	5 48 1.2	27 31.4	13 27.6	24 22.2	5 52.2	15 27.5	4 12.4	14 44.9	6 38.0	3 56.5	27 8.2	1 2.7
19 W	5 51 57.7	28 28.6	13 24.5	6♌13.9	7 17.9	14 57.7	4 55.0	14 37.8	6 40.9	3 54.7	27 6.8	1 1.3
20 T	5 55 54.3	29 25.9	13 21.3	18 4.2	8 46.7	14 29.8	5 37.5	14 30.7	6 43.7	3 52.9	27 5.4	0 59.9
21 F	5 59 50.8	0♋23.2	13 18.1	29 56.2	10 18.7	14 3.8	6 19.9	14 23.5	6 46.5	3 51.0	27 4.0	0 58.5
22 S	6 3 47.4	1 20.4	13 14.9	11♍53.9	11 53.8	13 39.8	7 2.4	14 16.2	6 49.1	3 49.1	27 2.6	0 57.1
23 S	6 7 44.0	2 17.7	13 11.8	24 1.8	13 32.1	13 18.0	7 44.7	14 8.9	6 51.7	3 47.2	27 1.2	0 55.8
24 M	6 11 40.5	3 14.9	13 8.6	6♎24.8	15 13.3	12 58.5	8 27.0	14 1.5	6 54.1	3 45.3	26 59.7	0 54.4
25 T	6 15 37.1	4 12.1	13 5.4	19 8.1	16 57.5	12 41.2	9 9.2	13 54.1	6 56.5	3 43.3	26 58.3	0 53.1
26 W	6 19 33.6	5 9.3	13 2.2	2♏16.3	18 44.7	12 26.2	9 51.4	13 46.6	6 58.8	3 41.3	26 56.8	0 51.8
27 T	6 23 30.2	6 6.5	12 59.1	15 52.7	20 34.7	12 13.6	10 33.5	13 39.0	7 1.0	3 39.3	26 55.3	0 50.6
28 F	6 27 26.7	7 3.7	12 55.9	29 58.7	22 27.4	12 3.5	11 15.5	13 31.4	7 3.1	3 37.2	26 53.8	0 49.3
29 S	6 31 23.3	8 0.9	12 52.7	14♐32.8	24 22.8	11 55.7	11 57.5	13 23.8	7 5.0	3 35.2	26 52.3	0 48.1
30 S	6 35 19.9	8 58.1	12 49.5	29 29.8	26 20.8	11 50.3	12 39.5	13 16.2	7 7.0	3 33.1	26 50.8	0 46.9
					DECLINATION at NOON							
1 S	4 40 59.7	22N 7.7	5S39.7	17S28.3	14N 8.5	24N56.3	18N 3.5	22S24.7	0N12.2	19S44.7	20S11.1	7S16.6
4 T	4 52 49.4	22 29.7	5 36.0	16 49.3	14 28.1	24 13.4	18 38.3	22 27.0	0 16.6	19 45.6	20 11.7	7 16.2
7 F	5 4 39.0	22 48.2	5 32.3	6 45.9	15 4.0	23 26.4	19 11.3	22 29.4	0 20.8	19 46.7	20 12.3	7 15.9
10 M	5 16 28.7	23 3.1	5 28.6	6N 0.2	15 53.7	22 36.5	19 42.7	22 31.9	0 24.7	19 47.8	20 13.0	7 15.6
13 T	5 28 18.4	23 14.3	5 24.9	15 37.0	16 54.1	21 45.6	20 12.3	22 34.5	0 28.2	19 48.9	20 13.7	7 15.5
16 S	5 40 8.1	23 21.9	5 21.2	18 33.9	18 2.2	20 55.8	20 40.1	22 37.1	0 31.4	19 50.2	20 14.5	7 15.4
19 W	5 51 57.7	23 25.7	5 17.5	14 12.5	19 14.5	20 9.1	21 6.1	22 39.9	0 34.2	19 51.5	20 15.3	7 15.4
22 S	6 3 47.4	23 25.8	5 13.8	4 38.9	20 27.5	19 27.5	21 30.2	22 42.6	0 36.7	19 52.9	20 16.1	7 15.5
25 T	6 15 37.1	23 22.2	5 10.1	7S 1.9	21 36.9	18 52.2	21 52.5	22 45.4	0 38.9	19 54.3	20 16.9	7 15.7
28 F	6 27 26.7	23 14.9	5 6.4	16 34.1	22 37.8	18 23.9	22 12.9	22 48.1	0 40.8	19 55.8	20 17.8	7 16.0

JULY 1996

DAY	EPHEMERIS SIDEREAL TIME	☉	☊	☽	☿	♀	♂	♃	♄	♅	♆	♇
	h m s	° ′	° ′	° ′	° ′	° ′	° ′	° ′	° ′	° ′	° ′	° ′
LONGITUDE at NOON												
1 M	6 39 16.4	9♋55.3	12♎46.3	14♑41.2	28♊21.0	11♊47.3	13♊21.4	13♑ 8.6	7♈ 8.8	3♒31.0	26♑49.3	0♐45.7
2 T	6 43 13.0	10 52.5	12 43.2	29 56.2	0♋23.3	11R46.6	14 3.2	13R 0.9	7 10.5	3R28.8	26R47.8	0R44.6
3 W	6 47 9.5	11 49.7	12 40.0	15♒ 4.1	2 27.5	11D48.3	14 45.0	12 53.2	7 12.1	3 26.7	26 46.2	0 43.4
4 T	6 51 6.1	12 46.8	12 36.8	29 55.3	4 33.3	11 52.2	15 26.7	12 45.5	7 13.6	3 24.5	26 44.7	0 42.3
5 F	6 55 2.6	13 44.0	12 33.6	14♓23.8	6 40.6	11 58.4	16 8.3	12 37.8	7 15.0	3 22.3	26 43.1	0 41.2
6 S	6 58 59.2	14 41.2	12 30.5	28 26.4	8 48.9	12 6.7	16 49.9	12 30.1	7 16.3	3 20.1	26 41.5	0 40.2
7 S	7 2 55.8	15 38.4	12 27.3	12♈ 3.3	10 58.1	12 17.2	17 31.5	12 22.4	7 17.5	3 17.8	26 39.9	0 39.1
8 M	7 6 52.3	16 35.6	12 24.1	25 16.4	13 7.7	12 29.8	18 13.0	12 14.8	7 18.6	3 15.6	26 38.3	0 38.1
9 T	7 10 48.9	17 32.8	12 20.9	8♉ 9.2	15 17.6	12 44.4	18 54.4	12 7.1	7 19.6	3 13.3	26 36.7	0 37.1
10 W	7 14 45.4	18 30.0	12 17.8	20 45.2	17 27.4	13 0.9	19 35.8	11 59.5	7 20.4	3 11.0	26 35.1	0 36.2
11 T	7 18 42.0	19 27.3	12 14.6	3♊ 8.0	19 36.8	13 19.3	20 17.1	11 51.9	7 21.2	3 8.7	26 33.5	0 35.2
12 F	7 22 38.5	20 24.5	12 11.4	15 20.5	21 45.7	13 39.6	20 58.4	11 44.3	7 21.9	3 6.4	26 31.9	0 34.3
13 S	7 26 35.1	21 21.7	12 8.2	27 25.4	23 53.8	14 1.6	21 39.6	11 36.8	7 22.5	3 4.1	26 30.3	0 33.4
14 S	7 30 31.7	22 19.0	12 5.0	9♋24.5	26 0.9	14 25.3	22 20.7	11 29.3	7 23.0	3 1.7	26 28.7	0 32.6
15 M	7 34 28.2	23 16.2	12 1.9	21 19.4	28 6.8	14 50.6	23 1.8	11 21.9	7 23.4	2 59.4	26 27.1	0 31.7
16 T	7 38 24.8	24 13.5	11 58.7	3♌11.4	0♌11.5	15 17.5	23 42.8	11 14.5	7 23.7	2 57.0	26 25.4	0 30.9
17 W	7 42 21.3	25 10.7	11 55.5	15 2.1	2 14.7	15 46.0	24 23.8	11 7.2	7 23.9	2 54.6	26 23.8	0 30.2
18 T	7 46 17.9	26 8.0	11 52.3	26 53.3	4 16.4	16 15.9	25 4.7	10 60.0	7 24.0	2 52.2	26 22.2	0 29.4
19 F	7 50 14.4	27 5.3	11 49.2	8♍47.2	6 16.6	16 47.2	25 45.6	10 52.8	7R23.9	2 49.9	26 20.6	0 28.7
20 S	7 54 11.0	28 2.5	11 46.0	20 46.8	8 15.1	17 19.9	26 26.4	10 45.8	7 23.8	2 47.5	26 18.9	0 28.0
21 S	7 58 7.5	28 59.9	11 42.8	2♎55.9	10 12.0	17 53.9	27 7.1	10 38.8	7 23.6	2 45.1	26 17.4	0 27.4
22 M	8 2 4.1	29 57.2	11 39.6	15 18.7	12 7.1	18 29.2	27 47.8	10 31.9	7 23.3	2 42.7	26 15.7	0 26.8
23 T	8 6 0.7	0♌54.4	11 36.5	27 59.8	14 0.5	19 5.6	28 28.4	10 25.1	7 22.9	2 40.3	26 14.1	0 26.2
24 W	8 9 57.2	1 51.7	11 33.3	11♏ 3.7	15 52.1	19 43.3	29 9.0	10 18.4	7 22.3	2 37.9	26 12.5	0 25.6
25 T	8 13 53.8	2 49.0	11 30.1	24 34.3	17 42.1	20 22.0	29 49.5	10 11.8	7 21.7	2 35.5	26 10.9	0 25.1
26 F	8 17 50.3	3 46.4	11 26.9	8♐33.8	19 30.3	21 1.9	0♋29.9	10 5.3	7 21.0	2 33.1	26 9.3	0 24.6
27 S	8 21 46.9	4 43.7	11 23.7	23 2.0	21 16.7	21 42.7	1 10.3	9 58.9	7 20.2	2 30.7	26 7.7	0 24.1
28 S	8 25 43.4	5 41.0	11 20.6	7♑55.3	23 1.4	22 24.7	1 50.6	9 52.6	7 19.2	2 28.3	26 6.1	0 23.7
29 M	8 29 40.0	6 38.3	11 17.4	23 6.5	24 44.5	23 7.5	2 30.9	9 46.4	7 18.2	2 25.9	26 4.5	0 23.3
30 T	8 33 36.5	7 35.7	11 14.2	8♒25.5	26 25.8	23 51.4	3 11.0	9 40.4	7 17.1	2 23.5	26 2.9	0 22.9
31 W	8 37 33.1	8 33.0	11 11.0	23 41.1	28 5.4	24 36.1	3 51.2	9 34.5	7 15.8	2 21.1	26 1.3	0 22.6
DECLINATION at NOON												
1 M	6 39 16.4	23N 4.0	5S 2.7	17S39.1	23N24.9	18N 2.8	22N31.4	22S50.8	0N42.3	19S57.3	20S18.7	7S16.4
4 T	6 51 6.1	22 49.4	4 59.0	8 18.8	23 53.2	17 48.8	22 48.0	22 53.4	0 43.4	19 58.9	20 19.6	7 16.8
7 S	7 2 55.8	22 31.2	4 55.3	4N47.2	23 58.5	17 41.4	23 2.6	22 56.0	0 44.2	20 0.5	20 20.5	7 17.4
10 W	7 14 45.4	22 9.6	4 51.5	14 54.9	23 39.1	17 39.6	23 15.4	22 58.5	0 44.6	20 2.1	20 21.4	7 18.0
13 S	7 26 35.1	21 44.5	4 47.8	18 33.8	22 55.6	17 42.7	23 26.2	23 1.0	0 44.6	20 3.8	20 22.4	7 18.7
16 T	7 38 24.8	21 16.0	4 44.1	14 55.1	21 50.4	17 49.7	23 35.1	23 3.3	0 44.3	20 5.4	20 23.3	7 19.6
19 F	7 50 14.4	20 44.4	4 40.4	5 47.8	20 27.3	17 59.8	23 42.0	23 5.5	0 43.6	20 7.1	20 24.3	7 20.5
22 M	8 2 4.1	20 9.5	4 36.7	5S38.7	18 50.3	18 12.1	23 47.1	23 7.6	0 42.6	20 8.8	20 25.2	7 21.4
25 T	8 13 53.8	19 31.7	4 32.9	15 29.4	17 2.9	18 25.8	23 50.3	23 9.5	0 41.3	20 10.4	20 26.2	7 22.5
28 S	8 25 43.4	18 50.9	4 29.2	18 9.3	15 8.3	18 40.1	23 51.7	23 11.3	0 39.5	20 12.1	20 27.1	7 23.7
31 W	8 37 33.1	18 7.4	4 25.5	10 9.8	13 9.0	18 54.4	23 51.1	23 13.0	0 37.5	20 13.7	20 28.0	7 24.9

AUGUST 1996

DAY	EPHEMERIS SIDEREAL TIME	☉	☊	☽	☿	♀	♂	♃	♄	♅	♆	♇
LONGITUDE at NOON												
1 T	8 41 29.7	9♌30.4	11♎ 7.9	8♓42.7	29♌43.3	25♊21.7	4♋31.3	9♑28.7	7♈14.5	2♒18.8	25♑59.7	0♐22.3
2 F	8 45 26.2	10 27.8	11 4.7	23 22.3	1♍19.5	26 8.2	5 11.3	9R23.1	7R13.1	2R16.4	25R58.2	0R22.0
3 S	8 49 22.8	11 25.2	11 1.5	7♈35.0	2 54.0	26 55.5	5 51.3	9 17.6	7 11.6	2 14.0	25 56.6	0 21.7
4 S	8 53 19.3	12 22.7	10 58.3	21 19.6	4 26.8	27 43.6	6 31.2	9 12.2	7 10.0	2 11.7	25 55.1	0 21.5
5 M	8 57 15.9	13 20.1	10 55.1	4♉37.3	5 58.0	28 32.4	7 11.0	9 7.0	7 8.3	2 9.3	25 53.5	0 21.3
6 T	9 1 12.4	14 17.6	10 52.0	17 31.2	7 27.4	29 22.0	7 50.8	9 1.9	7 6.4	2 7.0	25 52.0	0 21.2
7 W	9 5 9.0	15 15.1	10 48.8	0♊ 5.3	8 55.1	0♋12.2	8 30.6	8 57.0	7 4.5	2 4.7	25 50.5	0 21.1
8 T	9 9 5.5	16 12.6	10 45.6	12 23.7	10 21.1	1 3.2	9 10.3	8 52.2	7 2.6	2 2.4	25 49.0	0 21.0
9 F	9 13 2.1	17 10.1	10 42.4	24 30.5	11 45.3	1 54.8	9 49.9	8 47.6	7 0.5	2 0.1	25 47.5	0 21.0
10 S	9 16 58.6	18 7.7	10 39.3	6♋29.4	13 7.8	2 47.0	10 29.5	8 43.1	6 58.3	1 57.8	25 46.0	0 20.9
11 S	9 20 55.2	19 5.3	10 36.1	18 23.4	14 28.4	3 39.9	11 9.0	8 38.9	6 56.1	1 55.6	25 44.6	0D21.0
12 M	9 24 51.8	20 2.9	10 32.9	0♌14.9	15 47.2	4 33.3	11 48.5	8 34.7	6 53.7	1 53.3	25 43.2	0 21.1
13 T	9 28 48.3	21 0.6	10 29.7	12 6.1	17 4.1	5 27.3	12 27.9	8 30.8	6 51.2	1 51.1	25 41.7	0 21.1
14 W	9 32 44.9	21 58.2	10 26.6	23 58.6	18 19.0	6 21.9	13 7.2	8 27.0	6 48.7	1 48.9	25 40.3	0 21.3
15 T	9 36 41.4	22 55.9	10 23.4	5♍54.3	19 31.8	7 16.9	13 46.5	8 23.3	6 46.1	1 46.7	25 38.9	0 21.4
16 F	9 40 38.0	23 53.5	10 20.2	17 54.7	20 42.6	8 12.5	14 25.7	8 19.9	6 43.4	1 44.5	25 37.5	0 21.6
17 S	9 44 34.5	24 51.3	10 17.0	0♎ 2.0	21 51.2	9 8.6	15 4.8	8 16.6	6 40.6	1 42.3	25 36.1	0 21.8
18 S	9 48 31.1	25 49.0	10 13.8	12 18.8	22 57.6	10 5.1	15 43.9	8 13.5	6 37.7	1 40.2	25 34.8	0 22.1
19 M	9 52 27.6	26 46.7	10 10.7	24 48.0	24 1.5	11 2.1	16 22.9	8 10.6	6 34.7	1 38.1	25 33.4	0 22.4
20 T	9 56 24.2	27 44.5	10 7.5	7♏33.0	25 3.0	11 59.6	17 1.8	8 7.9	6 31.7	1 36.0	25 32.1	0 22.7
21 W	10 0 20.7	28 42.3	10 4.3	20 37.2	26 1.9	12 57.5	17 40.7	8 5.3	6 28.6	1 34.0	25 30.8	0 23.0
22 T	10 4 17.3	29 40.1	10 1.1	4♐ 3.7	26 58.1	13 55.8	18 19.6	8 3.0	6 25.4	1 31.9	25 29.6	0 23.4
23 F	10 8 13.8	0♍37.9	9 58.0	17 54.8	27 51.3	14 54.5	18 58.3	8 0.8	6 22.1	1 29.9	25 28.3	0 23.9
24 S	10 12 10.4	1 35.7	9 54.8	2♑10.6	28 41.5	15 53.7	19 37.0	7 58.8	6 18.7	1 28.0	25 27.1	0 24.3
25 S	10 16 6.9	2 33.6	9 51.6	16 49.2	29 28.5	16 53.2	20 15.7	7 57.0	6 15.3	1 26.0	25 25.8	0 24.8
26 M	10 20 3.5	3 31.5	9 48.4	1♒45.6	0♎12.0	17 53.1	20 54.2	7 55.3	6 11.8	1 24.1	25 24.6	0 25.3
27 T	10 24 0.1	4 29.4	9 45.2	16 52.3	0 51.8	18 53.4	21 32.7	7 53.9	6 8.3	1 22.2	25 23.5	0 25.9
28 W	10 27 56.6	5 27.3	9 42.1	1♓59.6	1 27.8	19 54.0	22 11.2	7 52.7	6 4.6	1 20.3	25 22.3	0 26.5
29 T	10 31 53.2	6 25.3	9 38.9	16 58.1	1 59.7	20 55.0	22 49.6	7 51.6	6 1.0	1 18.5	25 21.2	0 27.1
30 F	10 35 49.7	7 23.2	9 35.7	1♈39.2	2 27.1	21 56.4	23 27.9	7 50.7	5 57.2	1 16.7	25 20.1	0 27.7
31 S	10 39 46.3	8 21.2	9 32.5	15 57.0	2 50.0	22 58.0	24 6.2	7 50.0	5 53.4	1 15.0	25 19.0	0 28.4
DECLINATION at NOON												
1 T	8 41 29.7	17N52.3	4S24.2	5S52.0	12N28.6	18N59.0	23N50.6	23S13.6	0N36.7	20S14.3	20S28.4	7S25.3
4 S	8 53 19.3	17 5.2	4 20.5	7N21.5	10 26.6	19 12.2	23 47.7	23 15.1	0 34.2	20 15.9	20 29.3	7 26.6
7 W	9 5 9.0	16 15.6	4 16.8	16 18.6	8 24.5	19 24.0	23 43.0	23 16.5	0 31.4	20 17.5	20 30.2	7 28.0
10 S	9 16 58.6	15 23.7	4 13.0	18 11.2	6 24.0	19 33.8	23 36.6	23 17.8	0 28.2	20 19.0	20 31.0	7 29.5
13 T	9 28 48.3	14 29.6	4 9.3	13 2.6	4 26.7	19 41.2	23 28.5	23 18.9	0 24.8	20 20.5	20 31.9	7 31.0
16 F	9 40 38.0	13 33.3	4 5.6	3 5.7	2 34.1	19 45.8	23 18.7	23 19.9	0 21.0	20 22.0	20 32.7	7 32.6
19 M	9 52 27.6	12 35.2	4 1.8	8S15.4	0 47.8	19 47.2	23 7.3	23 20.8	0 17.0	20 23.4	20 33.5	7 34.3
22 T	10 4 17.3	11 35.3	3 58.1	16 45.3	0S50.1	19 45.1	22 54.4	23 21.6	0 12.7	20 24.7	20 34.3	7 36.0
25 S	10 16 6.9	10 33.7	3 54.3	17 17.0	2 17.3	19 39.3	22 40.0	23 22.3	0 8.2	20 26.0	20 35.0	7 37.8
28 W	10 27 56.6	9 30.6	3 50.6	7 52.9	3 30.9	19 29.5	22 24.1	23 22.8	0 3.5	20 27.2	20 35.7	7 39.6
31 S	10 39 46.3	8 26.2	3 46.8	5N37.5	4 27.1	19 15.6	22 6.7	23 23.3	0S 1.4	20 28.4	20 36.4	7 41.5

SEPTEMBER 1996

LONGITUDE at NOON

DAY	EPHEMERIS SIDEREAL TIME h m s	☉ ° ′	☊ ° ′	☽ ° ′	☿ ° ′	♀ ° ′	♂ ° ′	♃ ° ′	♄ ° ′	♅ ° ′	♆ ° ′	♇ ° ′
1 S	10 43 42.8	9♍19.3	9♎29.3	29♈48.4	3♎ 7.9	24♋ 0.1	24♋44.4	7♑49.6	5♈49.5	1♒13.3	25♑18.0	0♐29.2
2 M	10 47 39.4	10 17.4	9 26.2	13♉12.9	3 20.6	25 2.4	25 22.6	7R49.3	5R45.6	1R11.6	25R17.0	0 30.0
3 T	10 51 35.9	11 15.5	9 23.0	26 12.2	3 27.7	26 5.1	26 0.6	7 49.2	5 41.6	1 9.9	25 15.9	0 30.7
4 W	10 55 32.5	12 13.7	9 19.8	8♊49.6	3 29.1	27 8.0	26 38.7	7D49.3	5 37.6	1 8.3	25 15.0	0 31.6
5 T	10 59 29.0	13 11.8	9 16.6	21 9.2	3R24.5	28 11.2	27 16.6	7 49.5	5 33.5	1 6.7	25 14.0	0 32.4
6 F	11 3 25.6	14 10.0	9 13.5	3♋15.4	3 13.6	29 14.8	27 54.5	7 50.0	5 29.3	1 5.2	25 13.1	0 33.3
7 S	11 7 22.1	15 8.3	9 10.3	15 12.6	2 56.4	0♌18.6	28 32.3	7 50.6	5 25.1	1 3.7	25 12.2	0 34.2
8 S	11 11 18.7	16 6.5	9 7.1	27 4.8	2 32.6	1 22.6	29 10.1	7 51.5	5 20.9	1 2.2	25 11.3	0 35.2
9 M	11 15 15.2	17 4.8	9 3.9	8♌55.6	2 2.3	2 27.0	29 47.8	7 52.5	5 16.6	1 0.7	25 10.4	0 36.1
10 T	11 19 11.8	18 3.2	9 0.7	20 48.2	1 25.7	3 31.6	0♌25.4	7 53.7	5 12.2	0 59.3	25 9.6	0 37.2
11 W	11 23 8.3	19 1.5	8 57.6	2♍45.1	0 43.0	4 36.4	1 3.0	7 55.1	5 7.8	0 58.0	25 8.8	0 38.2
12 T	11 27 4.9	19 59.9	8 54.4	14 48.4	29♍54.6	5 41.5	1 40.5	7 56.7	5 3.4	0 56.7	25 8.0	0 39.3
13 F	11 31 1.4	20 58.4	8 51.2	26 59.8	29 1.3	6 46.8	2 17.9	7 58.5	4 59.0	0 55.4	25 7.3	0 40.4
14 S	11 34 58.0	21 56.8	8 48.0	9♎20.8	28 3.7	7 52.4	2 55.2	8 0.5	4 54.5	0 54.2	25 6.6	0 41.5
15 S	11 38 54.5	22 55.3	8 44.9	21 52.7	27 3.1	8 58.2	3 32.5	8 2.7	4 50.0	0 53.0	25 5.9	0 42.7
16 M	11 42 51.1	23 53.8	8 41.7	4♏37.1	26 0.5	10 4.1	4 9.7	8 5.0	4 45.4	0 51.8	25 5.2	0 43.9
17 T	11 46 47.6	24 52.4	8 38.5	17 35.5	24 57.4	11 10.4	4 46.8	8 7.6	4 40.9	0 50.7	25 4.6	0 45.1
18 W	11 50 44.2	25 51.0	8 35.3	0♐49.2	23 55.3	12 16.8	5 23.9	8 10.3	4 36.3	0 49.7	25 4.0	0 46.4
19 T	11 54 40.7	26 49.6	8 32.1	14 19.6	22 55.7	13 23.4	6 0.9	8 13.2	4 31.7	0 48.7	25 3.5	0 47.7
20 F	11 58 37.3	27 48.2	8 29.0	28 7.5	22 0.0	14 30.2	6 37.8	8 16.3	4 27.0	0 47.7	25 2.9	0 49.0
21 S	12 2 33.9	28 46.9	8 25.8	12♑12.8	21 9.9	15 37.3	7 14.6	8 19.5	4 22.4	0 46.8	25 2.4	0 50.3
22 S	12 6 30.4	29 45.6	8 22.6	26 34.3	20 26.5	16 44.5	7 51.4	8 23.0	4 17.8	0 46.0	25 2.0	0 51.7
23 M	12 10 27.0	0♎44.3	8 19.4	11♒ 8.8	19 51.1	17 51.9	8 28.1	8 26.7	4 13.1	0 45.1	25 1.6	0 53.1
24 T	12 14 23.5	1 43.1	8 16.3	25 51.7	19 24.4	18 59.5	9 4.8	8 30.5	4 8.5	0 44.3	25 1.2	0 54.6
25 W	12 18 20.1	2 41.8	8 13.1	10♓36.7	19 7.3	20 7.3	9 41.3	8 34.5	4 3.8	0 43.6	25 0.8	0 56.0
26 T	12 22 16.6	3 40.6	8 9.9	25 17.0	19 0.1	21 15.3	10 17.8	8 38.6	3 59.1	0 42.9	25 0.4	0 57.5
27 F	12 26 13.2	4 39.5	8 6.7	9♈45.7	19D 3.0	22 23.4	10 54.2	8 43.0	3 54.4	0 42.3	25 0.1	0 59.0
28 S	12 30 9.7	5 38.3	8 3.5	23 57.2	19 16.1	23 31.8	11 30.5	8 47.5	3 49.7	0 41.7	24 59.8	1 0.6
29 S	12 34 6.3	6 37.3	8 0.4	7♉47.3	19 39.2	24 40.3	12 6.7	8 52.2	3 45.1	0 41.1	24 59.6	1 2.1
30 M	12 38 2.8	7 36.2	7 57.2	21 14.0	20 11.8	25 48.9	12 42.9	8 57.0	3 40.4	0 40.6	24 59.4	1 3.7

DECLINATION at NOON

DAY	EPHEMERIS SIDEREAL TIME h m s	☉ ° ′	☊ ° ′	☽ ° ′	☿ ° ′	♀ ° ′	♂ ° ′	♃ ° ′	♄ ° ′	♅ ° ′	♆ ° ′	♇ ° ′
1 S	10 43 42.8	8N 4.4	3S45.6	9N35.9	4S41.3	19N 9.9	22N 0.7	23S23.4	0S 3.1	20S28.7	20S36.6	7S42.1
4 W	10 55 32.5	6 58.4	3 41.8	17 15.7	5 7.2	18 50.2	21 41.6	23 23.7	0 8.3	20 29.8	20 37.2	7 44.0
7 S	11 7 22.1	5 51.3	3 38.1	17 24.1	5 4.0	18 26.1	21 21.2	23 23.9	0 13.6	20 30.7	20 37.8	7 46.0
10 T	11 19 11.8	4 43.4	3 34.3	10 53.8	4 27.0	17 57.6	20 59.5	23 24.0	0 19.0	20 31.6	20 38.3	7 48.0
13 F	11 31 1.4	3 34.7	3 30.6	0 16.3	3 14.6	17 24.7	20 36.8	23 24.0	0 24.6	20 32.4	20 38.8	7 50.0
16 M	11 42 51.1	2 25.4	3 26.8	10S49.5	1 32.2	16 47.3	20 12.9	23 23.8	0 30.2	20 33.2	20 39.3	7 52.1
19 T	11 54 40.7	1 15.7	3 23.1	17 42.6	0N25.8	16 5.7	19 48.0	23 23.5	0 35.9	20 33.8	20 39.7	7 54.2
22 S	12 6 30.4	0 5.7	3 19.3	15 55.0	2 18.1	15 19.8	19 22.1	23 23.2	0 41.5	20 34.3	20 40.0	7 56.3
25 W	12 18 20.1	1S 4.3	3 15.5	5 19.9	3 44.0	14 29.8	18 55.2	23 22.7	0 47.2	20 34.8	20 40.3	7 58.4
28 S	12 30 9.7	2 14.4	3 11.8	7N56.2	4 29.8	13 35.9	18 27.6	23 22.0	0 52.9	20 35.1	20 40.5	8 0.5

OCTOBER 1996

LONGITUDE at NOON

DAY	EPHEMERIS SIDEREAL TIME h m s	☉ ° ′	☊ ° ′	☽ ° ′	☿ ° ′	♀ ° ′	♂ ° ′	♃ ° ′	♄ ° ′	♅ ° ′	♆ ° ′	♇ ° ′
1 T	12 41 59.4	8♎35.2	7♎54.0	4♊17.2	20♍53.4	26♌57.8	13♌19.0	9♑ 2.0	3♈35.7	0♒40.2	24♑59.2	1♐ 5.3
2 W	12 45 55.9	9 34.2	7 50.8	16 58.7	21 43.6	28 6.8	13 55.0	9 7.2	3R31.1	0R39.8	24R59.0	1 7.0
3 T	12 49 52.5	10 33.2	7 47.6	29 21.6	22 41.6	29 16.0	14 30.9	9 12.5	3 26.4	0 39.5	24 58.9	1 8.7
4 F	12 53 49.0	11 32.3	7 44.5	11♋29.7	23 46.7	0♍25.3	15 6.8	9 18.1	3 21.8	0 39.2	24 58.8	1 10.3
5 S	12 57 45.6	12 31.5	7 41.3	23 27.5	24 58.2	1 34.8	15 42.5	9 23.7	3 17.2	0 38.9	24 58.8	1 12.1
6 S	13 1 42.1	13 30.6	7 38.1	5♌19.8	26 15.4	2 44.4	16 18.2	9 29.6	3 12.6	0 38.7	24 58.8	1 13.8
7 M	13 5 38.7	14 29.9	7 34.9	17 11.0	27 37.4	3 54.2	16 53.9	9 35.6	3 8.1	0 38.6	24 58.8	1 15.6
8 T	13 9 35.2	15 29.1	7 31.8	29 5.4	29 3.8	5 4.1	17 29.4	9 41.7	3 3.6	0 38.5	24 58.8	1 17.4
9 W	13 13 31.8	16 28.4	7 28.6	11♍ 6.7	0♎33.7	6 14.2	18 4.8	9 48.1	2 59.1	0 38.4	24D58.9	1 19.2
10 T	13 17 28.3	17 27.7	7 25.4	23 18.1	2 6.8	7 24.4	18 40.2	9 54.5	2 54.6	0 38.4	24 59.0	1 21.0
11 F	13 21 24.9	18 27.1	7 22.2	5♎41.9	3 42.3	8 34.7	19 15.4	10 1.2	2 50.2	0D38.5	24 59.2	1 22.9
12 S	13 25 21.4	19 26.5	7 19.0	18 19.7	5 19.9	9 45.1	19 50.6	10 8.0	2 45.8	0 38.6	24 59.4	1 24.7
13 S	13 29 18.0	20 25.9	7 15.9	1♏12.2	6 59.2	10 55.8	20 25.7	10 15.0	2 41.5	0 38.8	24 59.6	1 26.7
14 M	13 33 14.5	21 25.4	7 12.7	14 19.4	8 39.6	12 6.5	21 0.7	10 22.0	2 37.1	0 39.0	24 59.9	1 28.6
15 T	13 37 11.1	22 24.9	7 9.5	27 40.6	10 21.1	13 17.3	21 35.6	10 29.3	2 32.9	0 39.2	25 0.2	1 30.6
16 W	13 41 7.7	23 24.4	7 6.3	11♐14.7	12 3.2	14 28.3	22 10.4	10 36.7	2 28.6	0 39.6	25 0.5	1 32.5
17 T	13 45 4.2	24 24.0	7 3.2	25 0.3	13 45.7	15 39.3	22 45.1	10 44.2	2 24.5	0 39.9	25 0.8	1 34.5
18 F	13 49 0.8	25 23.5	6 60.0	8♑56.0	15 28.6	16 50.5	23 19.7	10 51.9	2 20.4	0 40.3	25 1.2	1 36.5
19 S	13 52 57.3	26 23.2	6 56.8	23 0.1	17 11.5	18 1.8	23 54.2	10 59.7	2 16.3	0 40.8	25 1.6	1 38.5
20 S	13 56 53.9	27 22.8	6 53.6	7♒10.8	18 54.3	19 13.2	24 28.6	11 7.7	2 12.3	0 41.3	25 2.1	1 40.6
21 M	14 0 50.4	28 22.5	6 50.4	21 26.1	20 37.1	20 24.7	25 2.9	11 15.8	2 8.3	0 41.9	25 2.6	1 42.6
22 T	14 4 47.0	29 22.2	6 47.3	5♓43.7	22 19.6	21 36.3	25 37.1	11 24.0	2 4.4	0 42.5	25 3.1	1 44.7
23 W	14 8 43.5	0♏21.9	6 44.1	20 0.6	24 1.8	22 48.0	26 11.2	11 32.4	2 0.6	0 43.2	25 3.6	1 46.8
24 T	14 12 40.1	1 21.6	6 40.9	4♈13.3	25 43.6	23 59.8	26 45.2	11 40.9	1 56.8	0 43.9	25 4.2	1 48.9
25 F	14 16 36.6	2 21.4	6 37.7	18 17.9	27 25.1	25 11.7	27 19.0	11 49.5	1 53.1	0 44.7	25 4.9	1 51.0
26 S	14 20 33.2	3 21.2	6 34.6	2♉10.7	29 6.1	26 23.7	27 52.8	11 58.3	1 49.5	0 45.5	25 5.5	1 53.2
27 S	14 24 29.7	4 21.1	6 31.4	15 48.1	0♏46.7	27 35.8	28 26.5	12 7.1	1 45.9	0 46.3	25 6.2	1 55.3
28 M	14 28 26.3	5 21.0	6 28.2	29 7.6	2 26.8	28 48.0	29 0.1	12 16.2	1 42.4	0 47.3	25 6.9	1 57.5
29 T	14 32 22.8	6 20.9	6 25.0	12♊ 8.0	4 6.4	0♎ 0.3	29 33.5	12 25.3	1 39.0	0 48.2	25 7.7	1 59.7
30 W	14 36 19.4	7 20.8	6 21.8	24 49.4	5 45.6	1 12.7	0♍ 6.9	12 34.6	1 35.6	0 49.3	25 8.4	2 1.9
31 T	14 40 16.0	8 20.8	6 18.7	7♋13.3	7 24.3	2 25.2	0 40.1	12 43.9	1 32.4	0 50.3	25 9.3	2 4.1

DECLINATION at NOON

DAY	EPHEMERIS SIDEREAL TIME h m s	☉ ° ′	☊ ° ′	☽ ° ′	☿ ° ′	♀ ° ′	♂ ° ′	♃ ° ′	♄ ° ′	♅ ° ′	♆ ° ′	♇ ° ′
1 T	12 41 59.4	3S24.3	3S 8.0	16N40.1	4N31.1	12N38.3	17N59.1	23S21.3	0S58.4	20S35.4	20S40.7	8S 2.6
4 F	12 53 49.0	4 33.8	3 4.3	17 40.7	3 50.9	11 37.1	17 29.9	23 20.4	1 3.9	20 35.5	20 40.9	8 4.7
7 M	13 5 38.7	5 42.9	3 0.5	11 46.1	2 36.5	10 32.6	16 60.0	23 19.4	1 9.3	20 35.6	20 41.0	8 6.9
10 T	13 17 28.3	6 51.3	2 56.7	1 25.2	0 57.1	9 25.0	16 29.5	23 18.2	1 14.6	20 35.5	20 41.0	8 9.0
13 S	13 29 18.0	7 58.9	2 53.0	9S56.5	0S58.7	8 14.5	15 58.4	23 16.8	1 19.6	20 35.4	20 41.0	8 11.1
16 W	13 41 7.7	9 5.5	2 49.2	17 27.8	3 3.9	7 1.5	15 26.9	23 15.3	1 24.5	20 35.1	20 40.9	8 13.2
19 S	13 52 57.3	10 10.9	2 45.4	16 27.9	5 13.1	5 46.3	14 55.0	23 13.7	1 29.2	20 34.8	20 40.8	8 15.2
22 T	14 4 47.0	11 14.9	2 41.7	6 47.9	7 22.8	4 29.0	14 22.7	23 11.8	1 33.6	20 34.4	20 40.6	8 17.3
25 F	14 16 36.6	12 17.4	2 37.9	6N18.1	9 30.1	3 10.1	13 50.1	23 9.8	1 37.7	20 33.8	20 40.3	8 19.3
28 M	14 28 26.3	13 18.3	2 34.1	15 58.7	11 33.4	1 49.7	13 17.3	23 7.6	1 41.6	20 33.2	20 40.0	8 21.2
31 T	14 40 16.0	14 17.2	2 30.4	18 2.2	13 31.3	0 28.2	12 44.3	23 5.2	1 45.2	20 32.4	20 39.7	8 23.2

NOVEMBER 1996

DAY	EPHEMERIS SIDEREAL TIME	☉	☊	☽	☿	♀	♂	♃	♄	♅	♆	♇
	h m s	° ′	° ′	° ′	° ′	° ′	° ′	° ′	° ′	° ′	° ′	° ′
						LONGITUDE at NOON						
1 F	14 44 12.5	9♏20.8	6♎15.5	19♋22.5	9♏ 2.5	3♎37.8	1♍13.3	12♑53.4	1♈29.2	0♒51.4	25♑10.1	2♐ 6.3
2 S	14 48 9.1	10 20.9	6 12.3	1♌21.0	10 40.3	4 50.4	1 46.3	13 3.1	1R26.1	0 52.6	25 11.0	2 8.5
3 S	14 52 5.6	11 21.0	6 9.1	13 13.2	12 17.6	6 3.2	2 19.2	13 12.9	1 23.1	0 53.9	25 11.9	2 10.8
4 M	14 56 2.2	12 21.2	6 6.0	25 3.9	13 54.5	7 16.1	2 52.0	13 22.7	1 20.1	0 55.1	25 12.9	2 13.1
5 T	14 59 58.7	13 21.3	6 2.8	6♍58.4	15 31.0	8 29.0	3 24.6	13 32.7	1 17.3	0 56.5	25 13.8	2 15.3
6 W	15 3 55.3	14 21.5	5 59.6	19 1.5	17 7.0	9 42.0	3 57.2	13 42.8	1 14.5	0 57.8	25 14.9	2 17.6
7 T	15 7 51.8	15 21.8	5 56.4	1♎17.6	18 42.7	10 55.0	4 29.6	13 53.0	1 11.8	0 59.2	25 15.9	2 19.9
8 F	15 11 48.4	16 22.0	5 53.2	13 50.4	20 18.0	12 8.2	5 1.8	14 3.3	1 9.2	1 0.7	25 17.0	2 22.2
9 S	15 15 44.9	17 22.3	5 50.1	26 42.3	21 52.9	13 21.4	5 34.0	14 13.7	1 6.7	1 2.2	25 18.1	2 24.5
10 S	15 19 41.5	18 22.6	5 46.9	9♏54.5	23 27.5	14 34.7	6 5.9	14 24.2	1 4.3	1 3.8	25 19.2	2 26.8
11 M	15 23 38.1	19 23.0	5 43.7	23 26.2	25 1.8	15 48.0	6 37.8	14 34.8	1 2.0	1 5.4	25 20.3	2 29.2
12 T	15 27 34.6	20 23.4	5 40.5	7♐15.1	26 35.8	17 1.4	7 9.5	14 45.5	0 59.7	1 7.0	25 21.5	2 31.5
13 W	15 31 31.2	21 23.8	5 37.4	21 17.6	28 9.4	18 14.9	7 41.1	14 56.4	0 57.6	1 8.7	25 22.7	2 33.8
14 T	15 35 27.7	22 24.2	5 34.2	5♑29.1	29 42.8	19 28.4	8 12.5	15 7.3	0 55.6	1 10.4	25 24.0	2 36.2
15 F	15 39 24.3	23 24.7	5 31.0	19 44.8	1♐15.9	20 42.0	8 43.8	15 18.3	0 53.6	1 12.2	25 25.3	2 38.5
16 S	15 43 20.8	24 25.2	5 27.8	4♒ 0.5	2 48.7	21 55.7	9 14.9	15 29.4	0 51.8	1 14.1	25 26.6	2 40.9
17 S	15 47 17.4	25 25.7	5 24.6	18 13.0	4 21.3	23 9.3	9 45.9	15 40.6	0 50.1	1 15.9	25 27.9	2 43.2
18 M	15 51 13.9	26 26.2	5 21.5	2♓20.3	5 53.7	24 23.1	10 16.7	15 52.0	0 48.4	1 17.9	25 29.3	2 45.6
19 T	15 55 10.5	27 26.7	5 18.3	16 21.0	7 25.8	25 36.9	10 47.3	16 3.3	0 46.9	1 19.8	25 30.7	2 48.0
20 W	15 59 7.0	28 27.3	5 15.1	0♈14.6	8 57.7	26 50.8	11 17.8	16 14.8	0 45.5	1 21.8	25 32.1	2 50.3
21 T	16 3 3.6	29 27.9	5 11.9	14 0.3	10 29.4	28 4.7	11 48.1	16 26.4	0 44.1	1 23.9	25 33.5	2 52.7
22 F	16 7 0.2	0♐28.5	5 8.8	27 37.4	12 0.8	29 18.6	12 18.3	16 38.1	0 42.9	1 26.0	25 35.0	2 55.1
23 S	16 10 56.7	1 29.1	5 5.6	11♉ 4.8	13 32.0	0♏32.6	12 48.3	16 49.8	0 41.8	1 28.1	25 36.5	2 57.5
24 S	16 14 53.3	2 29.8	5 2.4	24 20.8	15 3.1	1 46.7	13 18.2	17 1.7	0 40.8	1 30.3	25 38.1	2 59.9
25 M	16 18 49.8	3 30.5	4 59.2	7♊24.0	16 33.8	3 0.8	13 47.9	17 13.6	0 39.9	1 32.5	25 39.6	3 2.3
26 T	16 22 46.4	4 31.1	4 56.1	20 12.9	18 4.2	4 15.0	14 17.3	17 25.6	0 39.1	1 34.8	25 41.2	3 4.6
27 W	16 26 42.9	5 31.9	4 52.9	2♋47.2	19 34.4	5 29.2	14 46.7	17 37.6	0 38.4	1 37.1	25 42.8	3 7.0
28 T	16 30 39.5	6 32.6	4 49.7	15 7.2	21 4.3	6 43.4	15 15.8	17 49.7	0 37.8	1 39.4	25 44.4	3 9.4
29 F	16 34 36.1	7 33.4	4 46.5	27 14.4	22 33.8	7 57.7	15 44.7	18 2.0	0 37.3	1 41.8	25 46.1	3 11.8
30 S	16 38 32.6	8 34.1	4 43.3	9♌11.7	24 2.9	9 12.0	16 13.5	18 14.2	0 37.0	1 44.2	25 47.7	3 14.1
						DECLINATION at NOON						
1 F	14 44 12.5	14S 36.4	2S 29.1	16N 59.2	14S 9.3	0N 0.8	12N 33.3	23S 4.4	1S 46.4	20S 32.2	20S 39.6	8S 23.8
4 M	14 56 2.2	15 32.6	2 25.3	9 50.7	15 58.6	1S 21.7	12 0.2	23 1.7	1 49.5	20 31.3	20 39.1	8 25.7
7 T	15 7 51.8	16 26.4	2 21.5	1S 2.2	17 40.6	2 44.5	11 27.1	22 58.8	1 52.3	20 30.3	20 38.7	8 27.6
10 S	15 19 41.5	17 17.8	2 17.8	12 9.1	19 14.6	4 7.4	10 54.0	22 55.7	1 54.8	20 29.3	20 38.1	8 29.4
13 W	15 31 31.2	18 6.5	2 14.0	18 13.1	20 40.0	5 29.9	10 21.1	22 52.4	1 57.0	20 28.1	20 37.5	8 31.1
16 S	15 43 20.8	18 52.4	2 10.2	14 48.1	21 56.3	6 51.8	9 48.4	22 48.8	1 58.7	20 26.9	20 36.9	8 32.8
19 T	15 55 10.5	19 35.3	2 6.4	3 43.4	23 2.8	8 12.7	9 15.9	22 45.0	2 0.1	20 25.5	20 36.2	8 34.4
22 F	16 7 0.2	20 14.9	2 2.7	8N 55.7	23 58.9	9 32.3	8 43.7	22 41.0	2 1.1	20 24.1	20 35.5	8 36.0
25 M	16 18 49.8	20 51.2	1 58.9	17 9.8	24 44.0	10 50.2	8 11.9	22 36.7	2 1.7	20 22.6	20 34.7	8 37.5
28 T	16 30 39.5	21 24.0	1 55.1	17 36.5	25 17.5	12 6.0	7 40.6	22 32.3	2 1.9	20 21.0	20 33.9	8 39.0

DECEMBER 1996

DAY	EPHEMERIS SIDEREAL TIME	☉	☊	☽	☿	♀	♂	♃	♄	♅	♆	♇
						LONGITUDE at NOON						
1 S	16 42 29.2	9♐35.0	4♎40.2	21♌ 2.5	25♐31.5	10♏26.4	16♍42.0	18♑26.6	0♈36.7	1♒46.7	25♑49.4	3♐16.5
2 M	16 46 25.7	10 35.8	4 37.0	2♍51.6	26 59.7	11 40.8	17 10.4	18 39.0	0R36.5	1 49.1	25 51.1	3 18.9
3 T	16 50 22.3	11 36.6	4 33.8	14 44.0	28 27.2	12 55.2	17 38.5	18 51.5	0 36.5	1 51.7	25 52.9	3 21.2
4 W	16 54 18.8	12 37.5	4 30.6	26 45.3	29 54.0	14 9.7	18 6.5	19 4.1	0 36.5	1 54.2	25 54.7	3 23.6
5 T	16 58 15.4	13 38.4	4 27.5	9♎ 0.7	1♑20.0	15 24.2	18 34.2	19 16.7	0D36.7	1 56.8	25 56.4	3 25.9
6 F	17 2 11.9	14 39.4	4 24.3	21 35.3	2 45.1	16 38.8	19 1.8	19 29.4	0 37.0	1 59.4	25 58.3	3 28.3
7 S	17 6 8.5	15 40.3	4 21.1	4♏33.1	4 9.1	17 53.3	19 29.1	19 42.2	0 37.4	2 2.1	26 0.1	3 30.6
8 S	17 10 5.1	16 41.3	4 17.9	17 56.3	5 31.7	19 8.0	19 56.1	19 55.0	0 37.9	2 4.8	26 1.9	3 32.9
9 M	17 14 1.6	17 42.2	4 14.8	1♐45.2	6 52.9	20 22.6	20 23.0	20 7.9	0 38.5	2 7.5	26 3.8	3 35.3
10 T	17 17 58.2	18 43.2	4 11.6	15 57.2	8 12.3	21 37.3	20 49.6	20 20.9	0 39.2	2 10.3	26 5.7	3 37.6
11 W	17 21 54.7	19 44.3	4 8.4	0♑27.0	9 29.7	22 52.0	21 15.9	20 33.9	0 40.0	2 13.1	26 7.6	3 39.9
12 T	17 25 51.3	20 45.3	4 5.2	15 7.6	10 44.6	24 6.7	21 42.0	20 46.9	0 40.9	2 15.9	26 9.5	3 42.2
13 F	17 29 47.8	21 46.3	4 2.0	29 50.9	11 56.8	25 21.4	22 7.9	21 0.0	0 42.0	2 18.8	26 11.5	3 44.5
14 S	17 33 44.4	22 47.4	3 58.9	14♒29.4	13 5.7	26 36.2	22 33.5	21 13.2	0 43.1	2 21.7	26 13.4	3 46.7
15 S	17 37 41.0	23 48.5	3 55.7	28 57.4	14 10.9	27 51.0	22 58.9	21 26.5	0 44.4	2 24.7	26 15.5	3 49.1
16 M	17 41 37.5	24 49.5	3 52.5	13♓11.2	15 11.7	29 5.8	23 23.9	21 39.7	0 45.8	2 27.6	26 17.5	3 51.3
17 T	17 45 34.1	25 50.6	3 49.3	27 9.5	16 7.5	0♐20.6	23 48.7	21 53.0	0 47.2	2 30.6	26 19.5	3 53.6
18 W	17 49 30.6	26 51.7	3 46.2	10♈52.4	16 57.6	1 35.5	24 13.3	22 6.4	0 48.8	2 33.6	26 21.5	3 55.8
19 T	17 53 27.2	27 52.8	3 43.0	24 21.1	17 41.2	2 50.3	24 37.5	22 19.8	0 50.5	2 36.6	26 23.6	3 58.0
20 F	17 57 23.7	28 53.8	3 39.8	7♉37.0	18 17.4	4 5.2	25 1.4	22 33.3	0 52.3	2 39.7	26 25.6	4 0.2
21 S	18 1 20.3	29 54.9	3 36.6	20 41.3	18 45.4	5 20.1	25 25.1	22 46.8	0 54.2	2 42.8	26 27.7	4 2.4
22 S	18 5 16.9	0♑56.0	3 33.5	3♊34.7	19 4.2	6 35.0	25 48.5	23 0.3	0 56.2	2 45.9	26 29.8	4 4.6
23 M	18 9 13.4	1 57.1	3 30.3	16 17.6	19 13.0	7 49.9	26 11.5	23 13.9	0 58.3	2 49.0	26 31.9	4 6.8
24 T	18 13 10.0	2 58.2	3 27.1	28 50.0	19R10.9	9 4.8	26 34.3	23 27.5	1 0.5	2 52.1	26 34.0	4 8.9
25 W	18 17 6.5	3 59.3	3 23.9	11♋11.7	18 57.5	10 19.8	26 56.7	23 41.1	1 2.8	2 55.3	26 36.1	4 11.0
26 T	18 21 3.1	5 0.5	3 20.7	23 23.0	18 32.2	11 34.8	27 18.8	23 54.8	1 5.2	2 58.5	26 38.3	4 13.2
27 F	18 24 59.6	6 1.6	3 17.6	5♌24.9	17 55.2	12 49.7	27 40.6	24 8.5	1 7.7	3 1.7	26 40.4	4 15.3
28 S	18 28 56.2	7 2.7	3 14.4	17 19.0	17 6.8	14 4.7	28 2.0	24 22.2	1 10.3	3 5.0	26 42.6	4 17.3
29 S	18 32 52.8	8 3.8	3 11.2	29 8.0	16 8.0	15 19.7	28 23.1	24 36.0	1 13.0	3 8.2	26 44.8	4 19.4
30 M	18 36 49.3	9 5.0	3 8.0	10♍55.5	15 0.2	16 34.8	28 43.9	24 49.8	1 15.8	3 11.5	26 47.0	4 21.5
31 T	18 40 45.9	10 6.1	3 4.9	22 45.9	13 45.4	17 49.8	29 4.2	25 3.7	1 18.7	3 14.8	26 49.2	4 23.5
						DECLINATION at NOON						
1 S	16 42 29.2	21S 53.1	1S 51.3	11N 5.8	25S 38.9	13S 19.5	7N 9.8	22S 27.5	2S 1.7	20S 19.4	20S 33.0	8S 40.3
4 W	16 54 18.8	22 18.5	1 47.5	0 34.4	25 47.6	14 30.2	6 39.5	22 22.5	2 1.1	20 17.6	20 32.1	8 41.6
7 S	17 6 8.5	22 40.0	1 43.8	10S 43.2	25 43.3	15 37.8	6 10.0	22 17.3	2 0.1	20 15.8	20 31.2	8 42.9
10 T	17 17 58.2	22 57.5	1 40.0	17 58.5	25 26.3	16 41.9	5 41.2	22 11.8	1 58.8	20 13.9	20 30.2	8 44.0
13 F	17 29 47.8	23 10.9	1 36.2	15 44.2	24 57.0	17 42.1	5 13.2	22 6.1	1 57.0	20 12.0	20 29.2	8 45.1
16 M	17 41 37.5	23 20.2	1 32.4	4 55.5	24 17.0	18 38.3	4 46.2	22 0.1	1 54.9	20 9.9	20 28.1	8 46.1
19 T	17 53 27.2	23 25.2	1 28.6	7N 49.5	23 29.2	19 29.8	4 20.1	21 53.9	1 52.3	20 7.8	20 27.0	8 47.0
22 S	18 5 16.9	23 26.0	1 24.9	16 37.3	22 37.7	20 16.6	3 55.0	21 47.4	1 49.4	20 5.7	20 25.9	8 47.9
25 W	18 17 6.5	23 22.6	1 21.1	18 2.2	21 47.9	20 58.2	3 31.1	21 40.7	1 46.2	20 3.5	20 24.7	8 48.6
28 S	18 28 56.2	23 15.0	1 17.3	12 14.1	21 4.9	21 34.5	3 8.5	21 33.8	1 42.6	20 1.2	20 23.5	8 49.3
31 T	18 40 45.9	23 3.2	1 13.5	2 5.4	20 32.0	22 5.0	2 47.1	21 26.6	1 38.6	19 58.9	20 22.3	8 49.9

JANUARY 1997

LONGITUDE at NOON

DAY	EPHEMERIS SIDEREAL TIME	☉	☊	☽	☿	♀	♂	♃	♄	♅	♆	♇
	h m s	° ′	° ′	° ′	° ′	° ′	° ′	° ′	° ′	° ′	° ′	° ′
1 W	18 44 42.4	11♑ 7.3	3♎ 1.7	4♎44.2	12♑26.0	19♐ 4.9	29♍24.3	25♑17.5	1♈21.7	3♒18.1	26♑51.4	4♐25.5
2 T	18 48 39.0	12 8.4	2 58.5	16 56.0	11R 4.6	20 19.9	29 43.9	25 31.4	1 24.9	3 21.5	26 53.6	4 27.5
3 F	18 52 35.5	13 9.6	2 55.3	29 26.8	9 43.8	21 35.0	0♎ 3.1	25 45.3	1 28.1	3 24.8	26 55.8	4 29.5
4 S	18 56 32.1	14 10.8	2 52.2	12♏21.5	8 26.3	22 50.1	0 21.9	25 59.3	1 31.4	3 28.2	26 58.0	4 31.4
5 S	19 0 28.7	15 12.0	2 49.0	25 44.1	7 14.3	24 5.2	0 40.4	26 13.3	1 34.8	3 31.6	27 0.3	4 33.4
6 M	19 4 25.2	16 13.2	2 45.8	9♐36.2	6 9.5	25 20.4	0 58.4	26 27.3	1 38.3	3 35.0	27 2.6	4 35.3
7 T	19 8 21.8	17 14.3	2 42.6	23 56.7	5 13.4	26 35.5	1 16.0	26 41.3	1 41.9	3 38.4	27 4.8	4 37.2
8 W	19 12 18.3	18 15.5	2 39.5	8♑41.1	4 26.7	27 50.6	1 33.1	26 55.3	1 45.6	3 41.8	27 7.1	4 39.0
9 T	19 16 14.9	19 16.7	2 36.3	23 41.8	3 50.0	29 5.7	1 49.8	27 9.4	1 49.3	3 45.2	27 9.3	4 40.9
10 F	19 20 11.4	20 17.9	2 33.1	8♒48.9	3 23.2	0♑20.9	2 6.0	27 23.4	1 53.2	3 48.7	27 11.6	4 42.7
11 S	19 24 8.0	21 19.0	2 29.9	23 52.1	3 6.2	1 36.0	2 21.8	27 37.5	1 57.1	3 52.1	27 13.8	4 44.5
12 S	19 28 4.6	22 20.2	2 26.7	8♓42.7	2 58.6	2 51.1	2 37.1	27 51.6	2 1.2	3 55.6	27 16.1	4 46.3
13 M	19 32 1.1	23 21.3	2 23.6	23 14.4	2D59.8	4 6.3	2 51.9	28 5.6	2 5.3	3 59.1	27 18.4	4 48.0
14 T	19 35 57.7	24 22.5	2 20.4	7♈24.1	3 9.2	5 21.4	3 6.2	28 19.7	2 9.5	4 2.6	27 20.7	4 49.7
15 W	19 39 54.2	25 23.6	2 17.2	21 11.2	3 26.1	6 36.5	3 20.0	28 33.8	2 13.8	4 6.1	27 22.9	4 51.4
16 T	19 43 50.8	26 24.7	2 14.0	4♉37.0	3 49.9	7 51.7	3 33.3	28 48.0	2 18.2	4 9.5	27 25.2	4 53.1
17 F	19 47 47.3	27 25.8	2 10.9	17 44.0	4 20.0	9 6.8	3 46.1	29 2.1	2 22.7	4 13.0	27 27.5	4 54.7
18 S	19 51 43.9	28 26.9	2 7.7	0♊34.9	4 55.8	10 21.9	3 58.3	29 16.2	2 27.2	4 16.5	27 29.8	4 56.3
19 S	19 55 40.4	29 27.9	2 4.5	13 12.2	5 36.7	11 37.1	4 10.0	29 30.3	2 31.9	4 20.1	27 32.0	4 57.9
20 M	19 59 37.0	0♒29.0	2 1.3	25 38.3	6 22.3	12 52.2	4 21.2	29 44.4	2 36.6	4 23.6	27 34.3	4 59.5
21 T	20 3 33.6	1 30.0	1 58.1	7♋54.8	7 12.0	14 7.4	4 31.7	29 58.5	2 41.4	4 27.1	27 36.6	5 1.0
22 W	20 7 30.1	2 31.0	1 55.0	20 3.1	8 5.5	15 22.5	4 41.8	0♒12.7	2 46.2	4 30.6	27 38.9	5 2.5
23 T	20 11 26.7	3 32.1	1 51.8	2♌ 4.3	9 2.3	16 37.6	4 51.2	0 26.8	2 51.2	4 34.1	27 41.1	5 4.0
24 F	20 15 23.2	4 33.1	1 48.6	13 59.5	10 2.3	17 52.8	5 0.0	0 40.9	2 56.2	4 37.6	27 43.4	5 5.4
25 S	20 19 19.8	5 34.0	1 45.4	25 50.3	11 5.1	19 7.9	5 8.2	0 55.0	3 1.3	4 41.2	27 45.7	5 6.9
26 S	20 23 16.3	6 35.1	1 42.3	7♍38.5	12 10.4	20 23.1	5 15.9	1 9.2	3 6.5	4 44.7	27 48.0	5 8.3
27 M	20 27 12.9	7 36.0	1 39.1	19 26.7	13 18.0	21 38.2	5 22.9	1 23.2	3 11.8	4 48.2	27 50.2	5 9.7
28 T	20 31 9.4	8 37.0	1 35.9	1♎18.2	14 27.7	22 53.4	5 29.2	1 37.3	3 17.1	4 51.8	27 52.5	5 11.0
29 W	20 35 6.0	9 37.9	1 32.7	13 17.0	15 39.3	24 8.5	5 34.9	1 51.4	3 22.5	4 55.3	27 54.7	5 12.3
30 T	20 39 2.6	10 38.8	1 29.6	25 27.7	16 52.8	25 23.7	5 39.9	2 5.5	3 28.0	4 58.8	27 56.9	5 13.6
31 F	20 42 59.1	11 39.8	1 26.4	7♏55.1	18 7.8	26 38.8	5 44.2	2 19.5	3 33.5	5 2.3	27 59.2	5 14.8

DECLINATION at NOON

DAY	EPHEMERIS SIDEREAL TIME	☉	☊	☽	☿	♀	♂	♃	♄	♅	♆	♇
1 W	18 44 42.4	22S 58.3	1S 12.2	1S 41.7	20S 23.5	22S 13.9	2N 40.3	21S 24.2	1S 37.2	19S 58.2	20S 21.9	8S 50.0
4 S	18 56 32.1	22 40.9	1 8.4	12 27.0	20 6.4	22 36.6	2 20.8	21 16.7	1 32.8	19 55.8	20 20.7	8 50.5
7 T	19 8 21.8	22 19.5	1 4.7	18 19.5	20 2.6	22 53.2	2 2.8	21 9.0	1 28.0	19 53.4	20 19.4	8 50.9
10 F	19 20 11.4	21 54.2	1 0.9	14 11.0	20 11.8	23 3.6	1 46.6	21 1.1	1 22.9	19 51.0	20 18.1	8 51.2
13 M	19 32 1.1	21 25.0	0 57.1	2 2.2	20 31.0	23 7.6	1 32.0	20 53.0	1 17.5	19 48.5	20 16.9	8 51.4
16 T	19 43 50.8	20 52.1	0 53.3	10N25.0	20 55.6	23 5.2	1 19.3	20 44.7	1 11.9	19 46.1	20 15.6	8 51.5
19 S	19 55 40.4	20 15.7	0 49.5	17 35.4	21 21.0	22 56.4	1 8.5	20 36.1	1 5.9	19 43.6	20 14.3	8 51.6
22 W	20 7 30.1	19 35.8	0 45.7	17 12.8	21 43.6	22 41.4	0 59.7	20 27.5	0 59.7	19 41.1	20 12.9	8 51.6
25 S	20 19 19.8	18 52.6	0 41.9	10 12.4	22 0.5	22 20.0	0 53.0	20 18.6	0 53.2	19 38.6	20 11.6	8 51.4
28 T	20 31 9.4	18 6.3	0 38.1	0S 23.6	22 9.8	21 52.5	0 48.5	20 9.6	0 46.5	19 36.0	20 10.3	8 51.3
31 F	20 42 59.1	17 17.2	0 34.4	11 7.8	22 10.0	21 19.1	0 46.3	20 0.4	0 39.6	19 33.5	20 9.0	8 51.0

FEBRUARY 1997

LONGITUDE at NOON

DAY	EPHEMERIS SIDEREAL TIME	☉	☊	☽	☿	♀	♂	♃	♄	♅	♆	♇
1 S	20 46 55.7	12♒40.7	1♎23.2	20♏44.3	19♑24.4	27♑53.9	5♎47.8	2♒33.5	3♈39.1	5♒ 5.8	28♑ 1.4	5♐16.0
2 S	20 50 52.2	13 41.6	1 20.0	3♐59.4	20 42.5	29 9.1	5 50.8	2 47.6	3 44.7	5 9.3	28 3.6	5 17.2
3 M	20 54 48.8	14 42.4	1 16.8	17 43.4	22 1.8	0♒24.2	5 53.0	3 1.6	3 50.5	5 12.8	28 5.8	5 18.3
4 T	20 58 45.3	15 43.3	1 13.7	1♑57.0	23 22.5	1 39.4	5 54.5	3 15.6	3 56.3	5 16.2	28 8.0	5 19.4
5 W	21 2 41.9	16 44.1	1 10.5	16 37.6	24 44.3	2 54.5	5 55.2	3 29.5	4 2.1	5 19.7	28 10.2	5 20.5
6 T	21 6 38.4	17 45.0	1 7.3	1♒39.6	26 7.3	4 9.6	5 55.2	3 43.5	4 8.0	5 23.2	28 12.4	5 21.6
7 F	21 10 35.0	18 45.8	1 4.1	16 54.1	27 31.3	5 24.8	5R54.5	3 57.4	4 14.0	5 26.6	28 14.5	5 22.6
8 S	21 14 31.5	19 46.6	1 1.0	2♓10.4	28 56.4	6 39.9	5 53.0	4 11.3	4 20.1	5 30.1	28 16.7	5 23.6
9 S	21 18 28.1	20 47.3	0 57.8	17 18.0	0♒22.5	7 55.0	5 50.7	4 25.2	4 26.2	5 33.5	28 18.8	5 24.5
10 M	21 22 24.7	21 48.1	0 54.6	2♈ 8.3	1 49.6	9 10.1	5 47.7	4 39.0	4 32.3	5 36.9	28 21.0	5 25.4
11 T	21 26 21.2	22 48.8	0 51.4	16 35.3	3 17.6	10 25.2	5 43.9	4 52.8	4 38.5	5 40.3	28 23.1	5 26.3
12 W	21 30 17.8	23 49.5	0 48.2	0♉36.1	4 46.6	11 40.3	5 39.3	5 6.6	4 44.8	5 43.7	28 25.2	5 27.2
13 T	21 34 14.3	24 50.2	0 45.1	14 10.8	6 16.5	12 55.4	5 34.0	5 20.4	4 51.1	5 47.1	28 27.3	5 28.0
14 F	21 38 10.9	25 50.8	0 41.9	27 21.2	7 47.3	14 10.4	5 27.8	5 34.1	4 57.5	5 50.5	28 29.3	5 28.8
15 S	21 42 7.4	26 51.4	0 38.7	10♊10.2	9 19.0	15 25.5	5 20.9	5 47.8	5 3.9	5 53.8	28 31.4	5 29.5
16 S	21 46 4.0	27 52.0	0 35.5	22 41.6	10 51.7	16 40.6	5 13.3	6 1.5	5 10.4	5 57.2	28 33.5	5 30.3
17 M	21 50 0.5	28 52.6	0 32.4	4♋58.7	12 25.2	17 55.7	5 4.8	6 15.1	5 17.0	6 0.5	28 35.5	5 30.9
18 T	21 53 57.1	29 53.1	0 29.2	17 5.1	13 59.7	19 10.7	4 55.5	6 28.7	5 23.5	6 3.8	28 37.6	5 31.6
19 W	21 57 53.6	0♓53.6	0 26.0	29 3.6	15 35.0	20 25.7	4 45.5	6 42.2	5 30.2	6 7.1	28 39.6	5 32.2
20 T	22 1 50.2	1 54.0	0 22.8	10♌56.9	17 11.3	21 40.7	4 34.7	6 55.7	5 36.8	6 10.4	28 41.5	5 32.8
21 F	22 5 46.7	2 54.5	0 19.6	22 47.1	18 48.5	22 55.7	4 23.1	7 9.1	5 43.5	6 13.6	28 43.5	5 33.3
22 S	22 9 43.3	3 54.9	0 16.5	4♍36.1	20 26.6	24 10.7	4 10.8	7 22.5	5 50.3	6 16.8	28 45.5	5 33.8
23 S	22 13 39.8	4 55.2	0 13.3	16 26.0	22 5.7	25 25.7	3 57.8	7 35.9	5 57.1	6 20.0	28 47.4	5 34.3
24 M	22 17 36.4	5 55.6	0 10.1	28 18.7	23 45.8	26 40.7	3 44.0	7 49.2	6 3.9	6 23.2	28 49.3	5 34.7
25 T	22 21 33.0	6 55.9	0 6.9	10♎16.5	25 26.8	27 55.7	3 29.4	8 2.5	6 10.8	6 26.3	28 51.2	5 35.1
26 W	22 25 29.5	7 56.2	0 3.8	22 22.3	27 8.8	29 10.6	3 14.2	8 15.7	6 17.7	6 29.5	28 53.1	5 35.5
27 T	22 29 26.1	8 56.5	0 0.6	4♏38.9	28 51.9	0♓25.6	2 58.2	8 28.9	6 24.6	6 32.6	28 54.9	5 35.8
28 F	22 33 22.6	9 56.7	29♍57.4	17 10.0	0♓35.9	1 40.5	2 41.6	8 42.0	6 31.6	6 35.7	28 56.8	5 36.1

DECLINATION at NOON

DAY	EPHEMERIS SIDEREAL TIME	☉	☊	☽	☿	♀	♂	♃	♄	♅	♆	♇
1 S	20 46 55.7	17S 0.1	0S 33.1	14S 4.0	22S 7.9	21S 6.7	0N 46.1	19S 57.3	0S 37.2	19S 32.7	20S 8.6	8S 50.9
4 T	20 58 45.3	16 7.3	0 29.3	18 16.3	21 54.7	20 25.6	0 47.1	19 48.0	0 30.0	19 30.1	20 7.3	8 50.5
7 F	21 10 35.0	15 12.0	0 25.5	12 26.2	21 30.6	19 39.1	0 50.7	19 38.5	0 22.5	19 27.6	20 6.0	8 50.1
10 M	21 22 24.7	14 14.3	0 21.7	0N36.3	20 55.2	18 47.5	0 56.8	19 28.9	0 14.9	19 25.2	20 4.7	8 49.5
13 T	21 34 14.3	13 14.5	0 17.9	12 34.2	20 8.3	17 50.9	1 5.4	19 19.2	0 7.1	19 22.7	20 3.4	8 49.0
16 S	21 46 4.0	12 12.8	0 14.1	18 3.8	19 9.7	16 49.8	1 16.5	19 9.5	0N 0.9	19 20.2	20 2.2	8 48.3
19 W	21 57 53.6	11 9.4	0 10.3	15 55.2	17 59.1	15 44.4	1 30.1	18 59.7	0 9.0	19 17.8	20 1.0	8 47.6
22 S	22 9 43.3	10 4.4	0 6.5	7 49.1	16 36.6	14 35.1	1 46.1	18 49.8	0 17.2	19 15.5	19 59.8	8 46.8
25 T	22 21 33.0	8 58.0	0 2.8	3S 5.8	15 2.2	13 22.2	2 4.3	18 39.9	0 25.6	19 13.1	19 58.6	8 46.0
28 F	22 33 22.6	7 50.3	0N 1.0	13 10.1	13 15.7	12 6.0	2 24.5	18 29.9	0 34.0	19 10.9	19 57.5	8 45.1

MARCH 1997

DAY	EPHEMERIS SIDEREAL TIME	☉	☊	☽	☿	♀	♂	♃	♄	♅	♆	♇
	h m s	° ′	° ′	° ′	° ′	° ′	° ′	° ′	° ′	° ′	° ′	° ′
LONGITUDE at NOON												
1 S	22 37 19.2	10♓56.9	29♍54.2	29♏59.1	2♓21.0	2♓55.5	2♎24.3	8♒55.1	6♈38.6	6♒38.7	28♑58.6	5♐36.3
2 S	22 41 15.7	11 57.1	29 51.0	13♐ 9.6	4 7.1	4 10.4	2R 6.4	9 8.1	6 45.7	6 41.8	29 0.4	5 36.6
3 M	22 45 12.3	12 57.3	29 47.9	26 44.2	5 54.3	5 25.3	1 47.9	9 21.1	6 52.7	6 44.8	29 2.1	5 36.8
4 T	22 49 8.8	13 57.5	29 44.7	10♑44.3	7 42.6	6 40.2	1 28.7	9 34.0	6 59.8	6 47.8	29 3.9	5 36.9
5 W	22 53 5.4	14 57.6	29 41.5	25 9.3	9 31.9	7 55.1	1 9.0	9 46.9	7 7.0	6 50.7	29 5.6	5 37.0
6 T	22 57 1.9	15 57.7	29 38.3	9♒56.0	11 22.3	9 10.0	0 48.8	9 59.6	7 14.2	6 53.7	29 7.3	5 37.1
7 F	23 0 58.5	16 57.7	29 35.2	24 58.4	13 13.7	10 24.9	0 28.1	10 12.4	7 21.4	6 56.5	29 9.0	5 37.2
8 S	23 4 55.0	17 57.8	29 32.0	10♓ 8.2	15 6.2	11 39.8	0 6.9	10 25.0	7 28.6	6 59.4	29 10.7	5 37.2
9 S	23 8 51.6	18 57.8	29 28.8	25 16.0	16 59.8	12 54.7	29♍45.3	10 37.7	7 35.9	7 2.3	29 12.3	5 37.2
10 M	23 12 48.1	19 57.8	29 25.6	10♈12.5	18 54.4	14 9.5	29 23.3	10 50.2	7 43.2	7 5.1	29 13.9	5R37.1
11 T	23 16 44.7	20 57.7	29 22.4	24 49.9	20 49.9	15 24.4	29 0.9	11 2.7	7 50.5	7 7.9	29 15.5	5 37.0
12 W	23 20 41.2	21 57.6	29 19.3	9♉ 3.1	22 46.3	16 39.2	28 38.3	11 15.1	7 57.8	7 10.6	29 17.1	5 36.9
13 T	23 24 37.8	22 57.5	29 16.1	22 49.5	24 43.6	17 54.0	28 15.4	11 27.4	8 5.2	7 13.4	29 18.6	5 36.8
14 F	23 28 34.3	23 57.3	29 12.9	6♊ 9.1	26 41.6	19 8.8	27 52.3	11 39.7	8 12.5	7 16.0	29 20.1	5 36.6
15 S	23 32 30.9	24 57.1	29 9.7	19 4.0	28 40.3	20 23.5	27 29.0	11 51.8	8 19.9	7 18.7	29 21.6	5 36.3
16 S	23 36 27.4	25 56.9	29 6.6	1♋37.4	0♈39.5	21 38.3	27 5.5	12 4.0	8 27.3	7 21.3	29 23.1	5 36.1
17 M	23 40 24.0	26 56.6	29 3.4	13 53.5	2 39.0	22 53.0	26 42.0	12 16.0	8 34.7	7 23.9	29 24.5	5 35.8
18 T	23 44 20.5	27 56.3	29 0.2	25 56.5	4 38.7	24 7.7	26 18.5	12 27.9	8 42.2	7 26.4	29 25.9	5 35.4
19 W	23 48 17.1	28 55.9	28 57.0	7♌50.8	6 38.3	25 22.4	25 55.0	12 39.8	8 49.6	7 28.9	29 27.3	5 35.1
20 T	23 52 13.6	29 55.5	28 53.8	19 40.2	8 37.6	26 37.1	25 31.5	12 51.6	8 57.1	7 31.4	29 28.6	5 34.7
21 F	23 56 10.2	0♈55.1	28 50.7	1♍28.3	10 36.3	27 51.8	25 8.1	13 3.3	9 4.5	7 33.8	29 29.9	5 34.3
22 S	0 0 6.8	1 54.6	28 47.5	13 18.2	12 34.1	29 6.4	24 44.9	13 14.9	9 12.0	7 36.2	29 31.2	5 33.8
23 S	0 4 3.3	2 54.1	28 44.3	25 12.5	14 30.5	0♈21.1	24 21.8	13 26.5	9 19.5	7 38.6	29 32.5	5 33.3
24 M	0 7 59.9	3 53.6	28 41.1	7♎13.3	16 25.3	1 35.7	23 59.0	13 37.9	9 27.0	7 40.9	29 33.7	5 32.8
25 T	0 11 56.4	4 53.0	28 37.9	19 22.5	18 18.0	2 50.3	23 36.4	13 49.3	9 34.5	7 43.2	29 34.9	5 32.2
26 W	0 15 53.0	5 52.4	28 34.8	1♏41.8	20 8.3	4 4.9	23 14.1	14 0.6	9 42.0	7 45.4	29 36.1	5 31.6
27 T	0 19 49.5	6 51.8	28 31.6	14 12.8	21 55.6	5 19.4	22 52.2	14 11.8	9 49.5	7 47.6	29 37.3	5 31.0
28 F	0 23 46.1	7 51.1	28 28.4	26 57.0	23 39.6	6 34.0	22 30.6	14 22.8	9 57.0	7 49.8	29 38.4	5 30.4
29 S	0 27 42.6	8 50.4	28 25.2	9♐56.0	25 19.8	7 48.5	22 9.5	14 33.8	10 4.5	7 51.9	29 39.5	5 29.7
30 S	0 31 39.2	9 49.7	28 22.1	23 11.4	26 56.0	9 3.1	21 48.9	14 44.8	10 12.1	7 54.0	29 40.6	5 29.0
31 M	0 35 35.7	10 49.0	28 18.9	6♑44.4	28 27.6	10 17.6	21 28.7	14 55.6	10 19.6	7 56.1	29 41.6	5 28.3
DECLINATION at NOON												
1 S	22 37 19.2	7S27.6	0N 2.3	15S37.2	12S37.6	11S39.9	2N31.6	18S26.6	0N36.9	19S10.1	19S57.1	8S44.8
4 T	22 49 8.8	6 18.6	0 6.1	17 51.2	10 35.3	10 19.9	2 54.1	18 16.7	0 45.4	19 7.9	19 56.0	8 43.9
7 F	23 0 58.5	5 8.9	0 9.9	10 25.3	8 21.5	8 57.4	3 18.0	18 6.8	0 54.1	19 5.8	19 55.0	8 42.9
10 M	23 12 48.1	3 58.5	0 13.7	3N 4.1	5 56.8	7 32.7	3 42.8	17 56.9	1 2.8	19 3.7	19 54.0	8 41.8
13 T	23 24 37.8	2 47.7	0 17.5	14 19.1	3 22.2	6 6.2	4 8.1	17 47.1	1 11.6	19 1.6	19 53.0	8 40.8
16 S	23 36 27.4	1 36.6	0 21.3	18 8.1	0 39.4	4 38.3	4 33.4	17 37.3	1 20.4	18 59.7	19 52.1	8 39.6
19 W	23 48 17.1	0 25.5	0 25.1	14 19.5	2N 8.8	3 9.2	4 58.2	17 27.7	1 29.3	18 57.8	19 51.2	8 38.5
22 S	0 0 6.8	0N45.6	0 28.8	5 15.3	4 58.2	1 39.4	5 22.1	17 18.2	1 38.1	18 56.0	19 50.4	8 37.3
25 T	0 11 56.4	1 56.4	0 32.6	5S51.1	7 43.3	0 9.0	5 44.7	17 8.7	1 46.9	18 54.3	19 49.6	8 36.2
28 F	0 23 46.1	3 6.9	0 36.4	15 5.6	10 17.8	1N21.5	6 5.5	16 59.5	1 55.8	18 52.7	19 48.9	8 35.0
31 M	0 35 35.7	4 16.8	0 40.2	18 2.3	12 35.3	2 51.9	6 24.2	16 50.4	2 4.6	18 51.2	19 48.2	8 33.8

APRIL 1997

DAY	EPHEMERIS SIDEREAL TIME	☉	☊	☽	☿	♀	♂	♃	♄	♅	♆	♇
LONGITUDE at NOON												
1 T	0 39 32.3	11♈48.2	28♍15.7	20♑35.7	29♈54.3	11♈32.1	21♍ 9.0	15♒ 6.3	10♈27.2	7♒58.1	29♑42.6	5♐27.5
2 W	0 43 28.8	12 47.4	28 12.5	4♒45.3	1♉15.9	12 46.6	20R49.9	15 16.9	10 34.7	8 0.0	29 43.6	5R26.7
3 T	0 47 25.4	13 46.5	28 9.3	19 11.6	2 32.0	14 1.1	20 31.3	15 27.5	10 42.2	8 2.0	29 44.5	5 25.9
4 F	0 51 21.9	14 45.7	28 6.2	3♓51.3	3 42.3	15 15.6	20 13.4	15 37.9	10 49.7	8 3.8	29 45.4	5 25.0
5 S	0 55 18.5	15 44.7	28 3.0	18 39.7	4 46.8	16 30.0	19 56.1	15 48.2	10 57.2	8 5.7	29 46.3	5 24.1
6 S	0 59 15.0	16 43.8	27 59.8	3♈30.0	5 45.1	17 44.4	19 39.4	15 58.4	11 4.7	8 7.5	29 47.1	5 23.2
7 M	1 3 11.6	17 42.8	27 56.6	18 15.1	6 37.1	18 58.8	19 23.4	16 8.4	11 12.2	8 9.2	29 47.9	5 22.3
8 T	1 7 8.1	18 41.8	27 53.5	2♉47.5	7 22.7	20 13.2	19 8.2	16 18.4	11 19.7	8 10.9	29 48.7	5 21.3
9 W	1 11 4.7	19 40.8	27 50.3	17 1.2	8 1.8	21 27.6	18 53.6	16 28.3	11 27.2	8 12.5	29 49.5	5 20.3
10 T	1 15 1.2	20 39.7	27 47.1	0♊51.8	8 34.3	22 42.0	18 39.8	16 38.0	11 34.7	8 14.1	29 50.2	5 19.3
11 F	1 18 57.8	21 38.6	27 43.9	14 17.4	9 0.2	23 56.3	18 26.8	16 47.7	11 42.1	8 15.7	29 50.9	5 18.2
12 S	1 22 54.3	22 37.5	27 40.7	27 18.0	9 19.5	25 10.6	18 14.5	16 57.2	11 49.6	8 17.2	29 51.5	5 17.1
13 S	1 26 50.9	23 36.3	27 37.6	9♋56.0	9 32.2	26 24.9	18 3.0	17 6.6	11 57.0	8 18.7	29 52.1	5 16.0
14 M	1 30 47.4	24 35.1	27 34.4	22 14.7	9 38.5	27 39.2	17 52.3	17 15.9	12 4.4	8 20.1	29 52.7	5 14.9
15 T	1 34 44.0	25 33.8	27 31.2	4♌18.6	9 38.5	28 53.5	17 42.3	17 25.0	12 11.8	8 21.5	29 53.3	5 13.8
16 W	1 38 40.6	26 32.5	27 28.0	16 12.5	9R32.4	0♉ 7.7	17 33.2	17 34.0	12 19.2	8 22.8	29 53.8	5 12.6
17 T	1 42 37.1	27 31.2	27 24.9	28 1.4	9 20.5	1 21.9	17 24.8	17 42.9	12 26.6	8 24.1	29 54.3	5 11.4
18 F	1 46 33.7	28 29.8	27 21.7	9♍49.9	9 3.2	2 36.1	17 17.2	17 51.7	12 33.9	8 25.3	29 54.7	5 10.2
19 S	1 50 30.2	29 28.4	27 18.5	21 42.3	8 40.8	3 50.3	17 10.4	18 0.4	12 41.2	8 26.5	29 55.1	5 8.9
20 S	1 54 26.8	0♉27.0	27 15.3	3♎42.3	8 14.0	5 4.5	17 4.5	18 9.0	12 48.6	8 27.7	29 55.6	5 7.7
21 M	1 58 23.3	1 25.5	27 12.1	15 52.7	7 43.1	6 18.7	16 59.3	18 17.3	12 55.9	8 28.8	29 55.9	5 6.4
22 T	2 2 19.9	2 24.0	27 9.0	28 15.8	7 8.8	7 32.8	16 54.9	18 25.6	13 3.1	8 29.8	29 56.2	5 5.1
23 W	2 6 16.4	3 22.5	27 5.8	10♏52.7	6 31.9	8 46.9	16 51.2	18 33.7	13 10.4	8 30.8	29 56.5	5 3.8
24 T	2 10 13.0	4 20.9	27 2.6	23 43.8	5 53.0	10 1.0	16 48.4	18 41.7	13 17.6	8 31.8	29 56.8	5 2.5
25 F	2 14 9.5	5 19.3	26 59.4	6♐49.1	5 12.9	11 15.0	16 46.2	18 49.6	13 24.8	8 32.7	29 57.0	5 1.1
26 S	2 18 .1	6 17.7	26 56.2	20 7.8	4 32.3	12 29.1	16 44.9	18 57.3	13 31.9	8 33.5	29 57.2	4 59.7
27 S	2 22 2.6	7 16.0	26 53.1	3♑38.9	3 52.0	13 43.1	16 44.3	19 4.9	13 39.0	8 34.3	29 57.4	4 58.3
28 M	2 25 59.2	8 14.4	26 49.9	17 21.6	3 12.6	14 57.1	16D44.4	19 12.3	13 46.1	8 35.0	29 57.5	4 56.9
29 T	2 29 55.7	9 12.7	26 46.7	1♒14.9	2 34.9	16 11.1	16 45.3	19 19.6	13 53.2	8 35.7	29 57.6	4 55.5
30 W	2 33 52.3	10 10.9	26 43.5	15 17.9	1 59.5	17 25.1	16 47.0	19 26.8	14 0.2	8 36.4	29 57.6	4 54.1
DECLINATION at NOON												
1 T	0 39 32.3	4N40.0	0N41.5	17S 0.5	13N16.4	3N22.0	6N29.9	16S47.4	2N 7.5	18S50.7	19S48.0	8S33.4
4 F	0 51 21.9	5 49.0	0 45.3	8 1.2	15 3.3	4 51.6	6 45.5	16 38.6	2 16.3	18 49.3	19 47.4	8 32.2
7 M	1 3 11.6	6 57.1	0 49.1	5N31.4	16 23.3	6 20.4	6 58.4	16 30.0	2 25.0	18 48.0	19 46.8	8 30.9
10 T	1 15 1.2	8 4.1	0 52.9	15 46.5	17 14.3	7 47.9	7 8.5	16 21.6	2 33.6	18 46.8	19 46.4	8 29.7
13 S	1 26 50.9	9 9.9	0 56.6	17 56.0	17 35.2	9 13.8	7 15.7	16 13.5	2 42.2	18 45.7	19 45.9	8 28.5
16 W	1 38 40.6	10 14.3	1 0.4	12 36.1	17 25.8	10 37.8	7 20.1	16 5.6	2 50.6	18 44.8	19 45.6	8 27.3
19 S	1 50 30.2	11 17.1	1 4.2	2 42.9	16 47.4	11 59.5	7 21.7	15 58.1	2 59.0	18 43.9	19 45.3	8 26.2
22 T	2 2 19.9	12 18.3	1 8.0	8S26.1	15 44.2	13 18.7	7 20.5	15 50.9	3 7.3	18 43.1	19 45.0	8 25.0
25 F	2 14 9.5	13 17.7	1 11.8	16 41.3	14 23.6	14 35.0	7 16.7	15 44.0	3 15.4	18 42.5	19 44.9	8 23.9
28 M	2 25 59.2	14 15.1	1 15.6	17 27.8	12 55.5	15 48.0	7 10.3	15 37.5	3 23.4	18 42.0	19 44.8	8 22.8

MAY 1997

DAY	EPHEMERIS SIDEREAL TIME	☉	☊	☽	☿	♀	♂	♃	♄	♅	♆	♇
	h m s	° ′	° ′	° ′	° ′	° ′	° ′	° ′	° ′	° ′	° ′	° ′
LONGITUDE at NOON												
1 T	2 37 48.9	11♉ 9.2	26♍40.4	29♒29.6	1♉26.9	18♉39.1	16♍49.3	19♒33.8	14♈ 7.2	8♒37.0	29♑57.7	4♐52.6
2 F	2 41 45.4	12 7.4	26 37.2	13♓48.4	0R57.6	19 53.1	16 52.3	19 40.6	14 14.2	8 37.5	29R57.6	4R51.1
3 S	2 45 42.0	13 5.6	26 34.0	28 11.8	0 32.0	21 7.0	16 56.1	19 47.3	14 21.1	8 38.0	29 57.6	4 49.6
4 S	2 49 38.5	14 3.8	26 30.8	12♈36.6	0 10.4	22 20.9	17 0.6	19 53.9	14 28.0	8 38.5	29 57.5	4 48.1
5 M	2 53 35.1	15 1.9	26 27.7	26 58.1	29♈53.1	23 34.9	17 5.7	20 0.3	14 34.9	8 38.9	29 57.4	4 46.6
6 T	2 57 31.6	16 0.0	26 24.5	11♉11.4	29 40.3	24 48.8	17 11.5	20 6.5	14 41.7	8 39.2	29 57.3	4 45.1
7 W	3 1 28.2	16 58.1	26 21.3	25 11.4	29 32.1	26 2.6	17 18.0	20 12.6	14 48.5	8 39.5	29 57.1	4 43.5
8 T	3 5 24.7	17 56.2	26 18.1	8♊53.6	29 28.6	27 16.5	17 25.2	20 18.5	14 55.3	8 39.8	29 56.9	4 42.0
9 F	3 9 21.3	18 54.2	26 14.9	22 15.1	29D29.7	28 30.4	17 33.0	20 24.2	15 2.0	8 40.0	29 56.7	4 40.4
10 S	3 13 17.8	19 52.2	26 11.8	5♋14.8	29 35.6	29 44.2	17 41.5	20 29.8	15 8.6	8 40.1	29 56.4	4 38.8
11 S	3 17 14.4	20 50.2	26 8.6	17 53.4	29 46.1	0♊58.0	17 50.6	20 35.3	15 15.3	8 40.3	29 56.2	4 37.3
12 M	3 21 11.0	21 48.2	26 5.4	0♌13.3	0♉ 1.2	2 11.8	18 0.3	20 40.6	15 21.9	8 40.3	29 55.8	4 35.7
13 T	3 25 7.5	22 46.1	26 2.2	12 18.2	0 20.7	3 25.6	18 10.6	20 45.7	15 28.4	8 40.3	29 55.5	4 34.1
14 W	3 29 4.1	23 44.0	25 59.1	24 12.7	0 44.6	4 39.4	18 21.5	20 50.6	15 34.9	8 40.3	29 55.1	4 32.5
15 T	3 33 0.6	24 41.8	25 55.9	6♍ 2.0	1 12.7	5 53.1	18 33.0	20 55.4	15 41.3	8R40.2	29 54.6	4 30.9
16 F	3 36 57.2	25 39.7	25 52.7	17 51.4	1 44.9	7 6.8	18 45.0	20 60.0	15 47.7	8 40.0	29 54.2	4 29.2
17 S	3 40 53.7	26 37.5	25 49.5	29 46.1	2 21.2	8 20.5	18 57.6	21 4.4	15 54.0	8 39.8	29 53.7	4 27.6
18 S	3 44 50.3	27 35.2	25 46.3	11♎50.8	3 1.3	9 34.2	19 10.8	21 8.7	16 0.3	8 39.6	29 53.2	4 26.0
19 M	3 48 46.8	28 33.0	25 43.2	24 9.4	3 45.1	10 47.8	19 24.4	21 12.7	16 6.5	8 39.3	29 52.6	4 24.4
20 T	3 52 43.4	29 30.7	25 40.0	6♏44.9	4 32.6	12 1.5	19 38.6	21 16.6	16 12.7	8 39.0	29 52.1	4 22.7
21 W	3 56 39.9	0♊28.4	25 36.8	19 38.8	5 23.5	13 15.1	19 53.4	21 20.4	16 18.8	8 38.6	29 51.5	4 21.1
22 T	4 0 36.5	1 26.1	25 33.6	2♐51.1	6 17.9	14 28.7	20 8.6	21 23.9	16 24.9	8 38.1	29 50.8	4 19.4
23 F	4 4 33.1	2 23.7	25 30.5	16 20.6	7 15.5	15 42.3	20 24.3	21 27.3	16 30.9	8 37.7	29 50.2	4 17.8
24 S	4 8 29.6	3 21.4	25 27.3	0♑ 4.5	8 16.4	16 55.8	20 40.5	21 30.5	16 36.9	8 37.1	29 49.5	4 16.1
25 S	4 12 26.2	4 19.0	25 24.1	13 59.5	9 20.3	18 9.4	20 57.1	21 33.5	16 42.8	8 36.5	29 48.7	4 14.5
26 M	4 16 22.7	5 16.6	25 20.9	28 1.9	10 27.3	19 22.9	21 14.2	21 36.3	16 48.6	8 35.9	29 48.0	4 12.8
27 T	4 20 19.3	6 14.1	25 17.8	12♒ 8.4	11 37.3	20 36.5	21 31.8	21 39.0	16 54.4	8 35.2	29 47.2	4 11.2
28 W	4 24 15.8	7 11.7	25 14.6	26 16.7	12 50.1	21 50.0	21 49.8	21 41.5	17 0.2	8 34.5	29 46.4	4 9.5
29 T	4 28 12.4	8 9.3	25 11.4	10♓24.9	14 5.8	23 3.5	22 8.3	21 43.7	17 5.8	8 33.8	29 45.6	4 7.9
30 F	4 32 9.0	9 6.8	25 8.2	24 31.9	15 24.2	24 16.9	22 27.1	21 45.8	17 11.4	8 32.9	29 44.7	4 6.2
31 S	4 36 5.5	10 4.3	25 5.0	8♈36.7	16 45.5	25 30.4	22 46.4	21 47.7	17 17.0	8 32.1	29 43.8	4 4.6
DECLINATION at NOON												
1 T	2 37 48.9	15N10.4	1N19.4	9S 19.9	11N31.0	16N57.5	7N 1.4	15S 31.4	3N31.3	18S 41.6	19S 44.7	8S 21.8
4 S	2 49 38.5	16 3.5	1 23.2	3N46.6	10 19.2	18 3.0	6 50.2	15 25.7	3 39.0	18 41.3	19 44.7	8 20.7
7 W	3 1 28.2	16 54.1	1 26.9	14 51.5	9 26.5	19 4.3	6 36.8	15 20.4	3 46.5	18 41.1	19 44.8	8 19.8
10 S	3 13 17.8	17 42.3	1 30.7	18 16.1	8 55.8	20 1.1	6 21.2	15 15.5	3 53.9	18 41.1	19 44.9	8 18.8
13 T	3 25 7.5	18 27.7	1 34.5	13 38.1	8 47.6	20 53.0	6 3.6	15 11.1	4 1.1	18 41.1	19 45.1	8 18.0
16 F	3 36 57.2	19 10.4	1 38.3	4 2.5	9 0.5	21 39.7	5 44.2	15 7.2	4 8.1	18 41.3	19 45.4	8 17.2
19 M	3 48 46.8	19 50.1	1 42.1	7S 12.2	9 32.5	22 21.0	5 22.9	15 3.8	4 14.9	18 41.6	19 45.7	8 16.4
22 T	4 0 36.5	20 26.8	1 45.8	16 11.0	10 21.1	22 56.6	4 60.0	15 0.9	4 21.4	18 42.0	19 46.1	8 15.7
25 S	4 12 26.2	21 0.3	1 49.6	17 55.0	11 24.0	23 26.4	4 35.5	14 58.5	4 27.8	18 42.5	19 46.5	8 15.1
28 W	4 24 15.8	21 30.6	1 53.4	10 23.7	12 38.7	23 50.0	4 9.5	14 56.6	4 33.9	18 43.2	19 47.0	8 14.5
31 S	4 36 5.5	21 57.5	1 57.2	2N23.2	14 2.7	24 7.4	3 42.1	14 55.2	4 39.8	18 43.9	19 47.5	8 14.0

JUNE 1997

DAY	EPHEMERIS SIDEREAL TIME	☉	☊	☽	☿	♀	♂	♃	♄	♅	♆	♇
LONGITUDE at NOON												
1 S	4 40 2.1	11♊ 1.9	25♍ 1.9	22♈38.1	18♉ 9.4	26♊43.9	23♍ 6.2	21♒49.5	17♈22.5	8♒31.2	29♑43.0	4♐ 3.0
2 M	4 43 58.6	11 59.4	24 58.7	6♉34.1	19 36.1	27 57.3	23 26.3	21 51.0	17 27.9	8R30.3	29R42.0	4R 1.4
3 T	4 47 55.2	12 56.9	24 55.5	20 22.2	21 5.3	29 10.8	23 46.9	21 52.4	17 33.3	8 29.3	29 41.1	3 59.8
4 W	4 51 51.7	13 54.3	24 52.3	3♊59.6	22 37.2	0♋24.2	24 7.8	21 53.5	17 38.6	8 28.3	29 40.1	3 58.1
5 T	4 55 48.3	14 51.8	24 49.2	17 23.3	24 11.8	1 37.6	24 29.1	21 54.5	17 43.8	8 27.2	29 39.1	3 56.5
6 F	4 59 44.8	15 49.2	24 46.0	0♋30.9	25 48.9	2 50.9	24 50.8	21 55.3	17 48.9	8 26.1	29 38.0	3 54.9
7 S	5 3 41.4	16 46.7	24 42.8	13 20.9	27 28.7	4 4.3	25 12.8	21 55.8	17 54.0	8 24.9	29 37.0	3 53.3
8 S	5 7 38.0	17 44.1	24 39.6	25 53.4	29 11.0	5 17.7	25 35.3	21 56.2	17 59.0	8 23.7	29 35.9	3 51.7
9 M	5 11 34.5	18 41.5	24 36.5	8♌ 9.8	0♊55.9	6 31.0	25 58.0	21 56.4	18 3.9	8 22.4	29 34.8	3 50.1
10 T	5 15 31.1	19 38.8	24 33.3	20 12.8	2 43.3	7 44.3	26 21.2	21 56.4	18 8.8	8 21.1	29 33.6	3 48.6
11 W	5 19 27.6	20 36.2	24 30.1	2♍ 6.4	4 33.2	8 57.6	26 44.7	21R56.2	18 13.6	8 19.8	29 32.5	3 47.0
12 T	5 23 24.2	21 33.5	24 26.9	13 55.2	6 25.6	10 10.8	27 8.5	21 55.8	18 18.3	8 18.4	29 31.3	3 45.5
13 F	5 27 20.7	22 30.9	24 23.7	25 44.5	8 20.4	11 24.1	27 32.6	21 55.2	18 22.9	8 17.0	29 30.1	3 43.9
14 S	5 31 17.3	23 28.2	24 20.6	7♎39.8	10 17.6	12 37.3	27 57.1	21 54.5	18 27.5	8 15.6	29 28.9	3 42.4
15 S	5 35 13.9	24 25.5	24 17.4	19 46.4	12 17.0	13 50.5	28 21.8	21 53.5	18 31.9	8 14.1	29 27.6	3 40.9
16 M	5 39 10.4	25 22.8	24 14.2	2♏ 9.3	14 18.5	15 3.7	28 46.9	21 52.3	18 36.3	8 12.6	29 26.4	3 39.4
17 T	5 43 7.0	26 20.0	24 11.0	14 52.3	16 22.0	16 16.9	29 12.3	21 51.0	18 40.7	8 11.0	29 25.1	3 37.9
18 W	5 47 3.5	27 17.3	24 7.9	27 57.9	18 27.3	17 30.0	29 38.0	21 49.5	18 44.9	8 9.4	29 23.8	3 36.4
19 T	5 51 0.1	28 14.5	24 4.7	11♐26.6	20 34.2	18 43.1	0♎ 3.9	21 47.8	18 49.1	8 7.8	29 22.5	3 34.9
20 F	5 54 56.6	29 11.8	24 1.5	25 17.0	22 42.5	19 56.2	0 30.2	21 45.9	18 53.1	8 6.1	29 21.1	3 33.5
21 S	5 58 53.2	0♋ 9.0	23 58.3	9♑25.2	24 52.0	21 9.3	0 56.7	21 43.8	18 57.1	8 4.4	29 19.8	3 32.1
22 S	6 2 49.8	1 6.3	23 55.2	23 46.1	27 2.4	22 22.4	1 23.5	21 41.5	19 1.1	8 2.7	29 18.4	3 30.7
23 M	6 6 46.3	2 3.5	23 52.0	8♒13.5	29 13.4	23 35.5	1 50.6	21 39.1	19 4.9	8 1.0	29 17.1	3 29.3
24 T	6 10 42.9	3 0.7	23 48.8	22 41.4	1♋24.8	24 48.5	2 17.9	21 36.4	19 8.7	7 59.2	29 15.7	3 27.9
25 W	6 14 39.4	3 57.9	23 45.6	7♓ 5.2	3 36.2	26 1.5	2 45.5	21 33.6	19 12.3	7 57.3	29 14.2	3 26.6
26 T	6 18 36.0	4 55.1	23 42.4	21 21.5	5 47.4	27 14.5	3 13.3	21 30.6	19 15.9	7 55.5	29 12.8	3 25.2
27 F	6 22 32.5	5 52.3	23 39.3	5♈28.5	7 58.1	28 27.5	3 41.4	21 27.4	19 19.4	7 53.6	29 11.3	3 23.9
28 S	6 26 29.1	6 49.5	23 36.1	19 25.3	10 8.1	29 40.4	4 9.8	21 24.0	19 22.8	7 51.6	29 9.9	3 22.6
29 S	6 30 25.7	7 46.8	23 32.9	3♉11.8	12 17.2	0♌53.4	4 38.3	21 20.5	19 26.1	7 49.7	29 8.4	3 21.3
30 M	6 34 22.2	8 44.0	23 29.7	16 47.8	14 25.1	2 6.3	5 7.2	21 16.7	19 29.4	7 47.7	29 6.9	3 20.0
DECLINATION at NOON												
1 S	4 40 2.1	22N 5.7	1N58.5	6N41.2	14N32.4	24N11.8	3N32.7	14S 54.9	4N41.7	18S 44.2	19S 47.7	8S 13.8
4 W	4 51 51.7	22 28.0	2 2.2	16 21.0	16 4.9	24 20.7	3 3.5	14 54.3	4 47.3	18 45.0	19 48.3	8 13.4
7 S	5 3 41.4	22 46.8	2 6.0	18 1.7	17 40.5	24 23.2	2 33.1	14 54.3	4 52.5	18 46.0	19 49.0	8 13.1
10 T	5 15 31.1	23 2.0	2 9.8	12 2.7	19 16.0	24 19.2	2 1.5	14 54.8	4 57.6	18 47.1	19 49.7	8 12.9
13 F	5 27 20.7	23 13.5	2 13.6	1 48.0	20 47.2	24 8.7	1 28.9	14 55.9	5 2.3	18 48.2	19 50.4	8 12.7
16 M	5 39 10.4	23 21.4	2 17.3	9S 18.8	22 9.5	23 51.9	0 55.2	14 57.6	5 6.7	18 49.5	19 51.2	8 12.6
19 T	5 51 0.1	23 25.5	2 21.1	17 17.9	23 17.6	23 28.8	0 20.6	14 59.8	5 10.9	18 50.8	19 52.0	8 12.6
22 S	6 2 49.8	23 26.0	2 24.9	17 4.5	24 6.3	22 59.6	0S 14.9	15 2.5	5 14.8	18 52.2	19 52.9	8 12.7
25 W	6 14 39.4	23 22.7	2 28.7	7 36.7	24 31.6	22 24.4	0 51.2	15 5.7	5 18.3	18 53.6	19 53.8	8 12.8
28 S	6 26 29.1	23 15.7	2 32.4	5N31.1	24 31.8	21 43.5	1 28.3	15 9.5	5 21.6	18 55.2	19 54.7	8 13.1

JULY 1997

DAY	EPHEMERIS SIDEREAL TIME	☉	☊	☽	☿	♀	♂	♃	♄	♅	♆	♇
	h m s	° ′	° ′	° ′	° ′	° ′	° ′	° ′	° ′	° ′	° ′	° ′
LONGITUDE a NOON												
1 T	6 38 18.8	9♋41.2	23♍26.6	0♓13.1	16♋31.7	3♌19.2	5♎36.2	21♒12.8	19♈32.5	7♒45.7	29♑ 5.4	3♐18.8
2 W	6 42 15.3	10 38.4	23 23.4	13 27.1	18 36.9	4 32.0	6 5.5	21R 8.7	19 35.5	7R43.7	29R 3.9	3R17.6
3 T	6 46 11.9	11 35.6	23 20.2	26 28.6	20 40.4	5 44.9	6 35.1	21 4.5	19 38.5	7 41.6	29 2.4	3 16.4
4 F	6 50 8.4	12 32.9	23 17.0	9♋17.0	22 42.3	6 57.7	7 4.9	21 0.1	19 41.3	7 39.5	29 0.8	3 15.2
5 S	6 54 5.0	13 30.1	23 13.9	21 51.7	24 42.4	8 10.6	7 34.8	20 55.5	19 44.1	7 37.4	28 59.3	3 14.0
6 S	6 58 1.6	14 27.3	23 10.7	4♌12.8	26 40.7	9 23.3	8 5.1	20 50.8	19 46.8	7 35.3	28 57.7	3 12.9
7 M	7 1 58.1	15 24.5	23 7.5	16 21.4	28 37.2	10 36.1	8 35.5	20 45.9	19 49.3	7 33.1	28 56.2	3 11.8
8 T	7 5 54.7	16 21.7	23 4.3	28 19.6	0♌31.7	11 48.9	9 6.1	20 40.8	19 51.8	7 31.0	28 54.6	3 10.7
9 W	7 9 51.2	17 19.0	23 1.1	10♍10.3	2 24.3	13 1.6	9 37.0	20 35.6	19 54.2	7 28.8	28 53.0	3 9.7
10 T	7 13 47.8	18 16.2	22 58.0	21 57.5	4 15.0	14 14.3	10 8.1	20 30.2	19 56.5	7 26.6	28 51.4	3 8.6
11 F	7 17 44.3	19 13.4	22 54.8	3♎45.9	6 3.7	15 26.9	10 39.4	20 24.7	19 58.7	7 24.3	28 49.8	3 7.6
12 S	7 21 40.9	20 10.6	22 51.6	15 40.4	7 50.5	16 39.6	11 10.8	20 19.1	20 0.8	7 22.1	28 48.2	3 6.6
13 S	7 25 37.5	21 7.9	22 48.4	27 46.6	9 35.4	17 52.2	11 42.5	20 13.3	20 2.8	7 19.9	28 46.7	3 5.7
14 M	7 29 34.0	22 5.1	22 45.3	10♏ 9.5	11 18.2	19 4.8	12 14.4	20 7.4	20 4.7	7 17.6	28 45.1	3 4.8
15 T	7 33 30.6	23 2.3	22 42.1	22 53.8	12 59.2	20 17.4	12 46.4	20 1.4	20 6.5	7 15.3	28 43.4	3 3.9
16 W	7 37 27.1	23 59.5	22 38.9	6♐ 3.1	14 38.2	21 29.9	13 18.7	19 55.2	20 8.2	7 13.0	28 41.8	3 3.0
17 T	7 41 23.7	24 56.7	22 35.7	19 39.0	16 15.2	22 42.4	13 51.1	19 48.9	20 9.8	7 10.7	28 40.2	3 2.2
18 F	7 45 20.2	25 54.0	22 32.6	3♑40.8	17 50.3	23 54.8	14 23.7	19 42.4	20 11.3	7 8.3	28 38.6	3 1.3
19 S	7 49 16.8	26 51.2	22 29.4	18 5.2	19 23.4	25 7.3	14 56.5	19 35.9	20 12.7	7 6.0	28 37.0	3 0.6
20 S	7 53 13.3	27 48.4	22 26.2	2♒46.3	20 54.6	26 19.7	15 29.4	19 29.3	20 14.0	7 3.6	28 35.3	2 59.8
21 M	7 57 9.9	28 45.7	22 23.0	17 36.6	22 23.8	27 32.0	16 2.5	19 22.5	20 15.2	7 1.3	28 33.7	2 59.0
22 T	8 1 6.5	29 42.9	22 19.8	2♓28.0	23 51.0	28 44.4	16 35.8	19 15.7	20 16.3	6 58.9	28 32.1	2 58.3
23 W	8 5 3.0	0♌40.2	22 16.7	17 13.0	25 16.2	29 56.7	17 9.3	19 8.7	20 17.3	6 56.5	28 30.5	2 57.7
24 T	8 8 59.6	1 37.5	22 13.5	1♈46.0	26 39.4	1♍ 8.9	17 42.9	19 1.6	20 18.1	6 54.2	28 28.8	2 57.0
25 F	8 12 56.1	2 34.8	22 10.3	16 3.3	28 0.5	2 21.2	18 16.7	18 54.5	20 18.9	6 51.8	28 27.2	2 56.4
26 S	8 16 52.7	3 32.1	22 7.1	0♉ 3.3	29 19.4	3 33.4	18 50.7	18 47.3	20 19.6	6 49.4	28 25.6	2 55.8
27 S	8 20 49.2	4 29.4	22 4.0	13 45.7	0♍36.2	4 45.6	19 24.8	18 40.0	20 20.2	6 47.0	28 24.0	2 55.3
28 M	8 24 45.8	5 26.8	22 0.8	27 11.3	1 50.9	5 57.7	19 59.1	18 32.6	20 20.7	6 44.6	28 22.4	2 54.7
29 T	8 28 42.3	6 24.2	21 57.6	10♊21.2	3 3.2	7 9.8	20 33.5	18 25.2	20 21.1	6 42.2	28 20.7	2 54.2
30 W	8 32 38.9	7 21.5	21 54.4	23 16.6	4 13.2	8 21.9	21 8.1	18 17.6	20 21.3	6 39.8	28 19.1	2 53.8
31 T	8 36 35.5	8 18.9	21 51.3	5♋58.7	5 20.8	9 34.0	21 42.9	18 10.1	20 21.5	6 37.4	28 17.5	2 53.3
DECLINATION at NOON												
1 T	6 38 18.8	23N 5.0	2N36.2	15N38.6	24N 7.4	20N57.1	2S 6.1	15S13.8	5N24.5	18S56.8	19S55.6	8S13.4
4 F	6 50 8.4	22 50.7	2 40.0	18 18.3	23 20.8	20 5.5	2 44.5	15 18.6	5 27.1	18 58.4	19 56.6	8 13.8
7 M	7 1 58.1	22 32.8	2 43.7	13 7.2	22 15.6	19 8.9	3 23.6	15 23.8	5 29.4	19 0.1	19 57.5	8 14.3
10 T	7 13 47.8	22 11.4	2 47.5	3 12.7	20 55.4	18 7.7	4 3.1	15 29.4	5 31.3	19 1.9	19 58.5	8 14.9
13 S	7 25 37.5	21 46.6	2 51.3	7S51.9	19 23.8	17 2.1	4 43.2	15 35.4	5 32.9	19 3.6	19 59.5	8 15.5
16 W	7 37 27.1	21 18.5	2 55.0	16 28.1	17 44.0	15 52.6	5 23.7	15 41.8	5 34.2	19 5.4	20 0.6	8 16.3
19 S	7 49 16.8	20 47.1	2 58.8	17 42.1	15 58.7	14 39.3	6 4.5	15 48.5	5 35.1	19 7.2	20 1.6	8 17.1
22 T	8 1 6.5	20 12.5	3 2.6	9 4.9	14 10.3	13 22.7	6 45.5	15 55.4	5 35.7	19 9.1	20 2.6	8 18.0
25 F	8 12 56.1	19 34.9	3 6.3	4N16.9	12 20.9	12 3.0	7 26.9	16 2.5	5 35.9	19 10.9	20 3.6	8 19.0
28 M	8 24 45.8	18 54.4	3 10.1	14 55.5	10 32.6	10 40.6	8 8.3	16 9.8	5 35.8	19 12.7	20 4.6	8 20.0
31 T	8 36 35.5	18 11.0	3 13.8	18 20.2	8 47.4	9 15.8	8 49.9	16 17.3	5 35.3	19 14.6	20 5.6	8 21.2

AUGUST 1997

DAY	EPHEMERIS SIDEREAL TIME	☉	☊	☽	☿	♀	♂	♃	♄	♅	♆	♇
LONGITUDE at NOON												
1 F	8 40 32.0	9♌16.4	21♍48.1	18♋28.5	6♍25.9	10♍46.0	22♎17.8	18♒ 2.5	20♈21.6	6♒35.0	28♑15.9	2♐52.9
2 S	8 44 28.6	10 13.8	21 44.9	0♌46.9	7 28.3	11 58.0	22 52.9	17R54.8	20R21.5	6R32.6	28R14.4	2R52.6
3 S	8 48 25.1	11 11.3	21 41.7	12 55.2	8 28.1	13 10.0	23 28.2	17 47.1	20 21.4	6 30.2	28 12.8	2 52.3
4 M	8 52 21.7	12 8.7	21 38.5	24 54.5	9 25.1	14 21.9	24 3.6	17 39.4	20 21.2	6 27.8	28 11.3	2 52.0
5 T	8 56 18.2	13 6.2	21 35.4	6♍46.8	10 19.0	15 33.8	24 39.1	17 31.6	20 20.8	6 25.5	28 9.7	2 51.7
6 W	9 0 14.8	14 3.7	21 32.2	18 34.5	11 9.9	16 45.6	25 14.8	17 23.8	20 20.4	6 23.1	28 8.1	2 51.4
7 T	9 4 11.3	15 1.2	21 29.0	0♎20.7	11 57.6	17 57.4	25 50.6	17 16.0	20 19.8	6 20.7	28 6.6	2 51.2
8 F	9 8 7.9	15 58.7	21 25.8	12 8.9	12 41.8	19 9.2	26 26.6	17 8.2	20 19.2	6 18.4	28 5.1	2 51.1
9 S	9 12 4.4	16 56.3	21 22.7	24 3.4	13 22.4	20 20.9	27 2.7	17 0.3	20 18.4	6 16.0	28 3.5	2 50.9
10 S	9 16 1.0	17 53.8	21 19.5	6♏ 8.9	13 59.2	21 32.6	27 39.0	16 52.5	20 17.5	6 13.7	28 2.0	2 50.8
11 M	9 19 57.6	18 51.4	21 16.3	18 30.1	14 32.1	22 44.2	28 15.4	16 44.7	20 16.6	6 11.4	28 0.5	2 50.7
12 T	9 23 54.1	19 49.0	21 13.1	1♐11.9	15 0.7	23 55.8	28 51.9	16 36.9	20 15.5	6 9.0	27 59.1	2 50.7
13 W	9 27 50.7	20 46.6	21 9.9	14 18.0	15 25.0	25 7.3	29 28.5	16 29.1	20 14.3	6 6.7	27 57.6	2 50.7
14 T	9 31 47.2	21 44.2	21 6.8	27 51.4	15 44.6	26 18.8	0♏ 5.3	16 21.3	20 13.1	6 4.5	27 56.1	2 50.7
15 F	9 35 43.8	22 41.8	21 3.6	11♑52.7	15 59.4	27 30.2	0 42.3	16 13.5	20 11.7	6 2.2	27 54.7	2D50.8
16 S	9 39 40.3	23 39.4	21 0.4	26 20.1	16 9.1	28 41.6	1 19.3	16 5.8	20 10.2	5 59.9	27 53.3	2 50.8
17 S	9 43 36.9	24 37.1	20 57.2	11♒ 8.9	16 13.6	29 52.9	1 56.5	15 58.2	20 8.7	5 57.7	27 51.8	2 51.0
18 M	9 47 33.4	25 34.8	20 54.1	26 11.9	16R12.6	1♎ 4.2	2 33.8	15 50.5	20 7.0	5 55.5	27 50.4	2 51.1
19 T	9 51 30.0	26 32.5	20 50.9	11♓20.2	16 6.0	2 15.5	3 11.2	15 43.0	20 5.3	5 53.3	27 49.1	2 51.3
20 W	9 55 26.5	27 30.2	20 47.7	26 24.5	15 53.7	3 26.7	3 48.8	15 35.4	20 3.4	5 51.1	27 47.7	2 51.5
21 T	9 59 23.1	28 28.0	20 44.5	11♈16.6	15 35.6	4 37.8	4 26.4	15 28.0	20 1.5	5 48.9	27 46.4	2 51.8
22 F	10 3 19.6	29 25.8	20 41.3	25 50.3	15 11.8	5 48.9	5 4.2	15 20.6	19 59.4	5 46.8	27 45.0	2 52.1
23 S	10 7 16.2	0♍23.6	20 38.2	10♉ 1.8	14 42.3	6 59.9	5 42.2	15 13.3	19 57.3	5 44.7	27 43.7	2 52.4
24 S	10 11 12.7	1 21.5	20 35.0	23 49.9	14 7.4	8 10.9	6 20.2	15 6.0	19 55.1	5 42.6	27 42.5	2 52.8
25 M	10 15 9.3	2 19.3	20 31.8	7♊14.9	13 27.3	9 21.9	6 58.4	14 58.9	19 52.8	5 40.6	27 41.2	2 53.2
26 T	10 19 5.9	3 17.2	20 28.6	20 18.6	12 42.6	10 32.7	7 36.7	14 51.8	19 50.4	5 38.5	27 40.0	2 53.6
27 W	10 23 2.4	4 15.1	20 25.5	3♋ 3.6	11 53.8	11 43.6	8 15.1	14 44.8	19 47.9	5 36.5	27 38.7	2 54.1
28 T	10 26 59.0	5 13.1	20 22.3	15 32.6	11 1.7	12 54.3	8 53.6	14 37.9	19 45.3	5 34.5	27 37.5	2 54.6
29 F	10 30 55.5	6 11.1	20 19.1	27 48.5	10 7.1	14 5.0	9 32.3	14 31.1	19 42.6	5 32.6	27 36.3	2 55.1
30 S	10 34 52.1	7 9.1	20 15.9	9♌53.9	9 11.1	15 15.7	10 11.1	14 24.4	19 39.8	5 30.6	27 35.2	2 55.7
31 S	10 38 48.6	8 7.2	20 12.7	21 51.3	8 14.8	16 26.3	10 49.9	14 17.9	19 36.9	5 28.7	27 34.0	2 56.2
DECLINATION at NOON												
1 F	8 40 32.0	17N56.0	3N15.1	17N38.9	8N13.3	8N47.1	9S 3.8	16S19.8	5N35.1	19S15.2	20S 6.0	8S21.6
4 M	8 52 21.7	17 9.1	3 18.9	11 7.8	6 35.4	7 19.5	9 45.4	16 27.3	5 34.1	19 17.0	20 7.0	8 22.8
7 T	9 4 11.3	16 19.7	3 22.6	0 43.3	5 5.8	5 50.3	10 27.0	16 34.8	5 32.9	19 18.7	20 7.9	8 24.1
10 S	9 16 1.0	15 28.0	3 26.4	10S 0.4	3 47.3	4 19.8	11 8.5	16 42.3	5 31.3	19 20.5	20 8.9	8 25.5
13 W	9 27 50.7	14 34.0	3 30.1	17 20.4	2 43.4	2 48.2	11 49.9	16 49.7	5 29.3	19 22.2	20 9.8	8 26.9
16 S	9 39 40.3	13 38.0	3 33.9	16 44.2	1 57.9	1 15.8	12 30.9	16 56.9	5 27.1	19 23.9	20 10.7	8 28.4
19 T	9 51 30.0	12 40.0	3 37.6	6 35.6	1 35.2	0S16.9	13 11.7	17 4.0	5 24.5	19 25.5	20 11.6	8 30.0
22 F	10 3 19.6	11 40.3	3 41.4	7N 5.4	1 39.7	1 49.8	13 52.0	17 10.8	5 21.6	19 27.1	20 12.5	8 31.6
25 M	10 15 9.3	10 38.8	3 45.1	16 26.4	2 14.2	3 22.6	14 31.9	17 17.4	5 18.5	19 28.6	20 13.3	8 33.3
28 T	10 26 59.0	9 35.8	3 48.9	17 48.5	3 17.9	4 54.8	15 11.2	17 23.7	5 15.0	19 30.1	20 14.1	8 35.0
31 S	10 38 48.6	8 31.5	3 52.6	11 52.6	4 44.6	6 26.4	15 49.9	17 29.6	5 11.3	19 31.5	20 14.8	8 36.7

SEPTEMBER 1997

LONGITUDE at NOON

DAY	EPHEMERIS SIDEREAL TIME	☉	☊	☽	☿	♀	♂	♃	♄	♅	♆	♇
	h m s	° ′	° ′	° ′	° ′	° ′	° ′	° ′	° ′	° ′	° ′	° ′
1 M	10 42 45.2	9♍ 5.2	20♍ 9.6	3♍43.0	7♍19.4	17♎36.9	11♏28.9	14♒11.4	19♈34.0	5♒26.9	27♑32.9	2♐56.9
2 T	10 46 41.7	10 3.3	20 6.4	15 31.0	6R26.1	18 47.4	12 8.1	14R 5.1	19R31.0	5R25.0	27R31.8	2 57.5
3 W	10 50 38.3	11 1.5	20 3.2	27 17.7	5 36.1	19 57.8	12 47.3	13 58.9	19 27.9	5 23.2	27 30.7	2 58.2
4 T	10 54 34.8	11 59.6	20 0.0	9♎ 5.4	4 50.5	21 8.1	13 26.7	13 52.8	19 24.7	5 21.4	27 29.7	2 58.9
5 F	10 58 31.4	12 57.8	19 56.9	20 56.9	4 10.6	22 18.5	14 6.1	13 46.9	19 21.4	5 19.7	27 28.7	2 59.7
6 S	11 2 27.9	13 56.0	19 53.7	2♏55.1	3 37.1	23 28.7	14 45.7	13 41.1	19 18.1	5 18.0	27 27.7	3 0.5
7 S	11 6 24.5	14 54.2	19 50.5	15 3.4	3 11.0	24 38.9	15 25.4	13 35.4	19 14.7	5 16.3	27 26.7	3 1.3
8 M	11 10 21.0	15 52.5	19 47.3	27 25.7	2 53.0	25 48.9	16 5.2	13 29.9	19 11.2	5 14.7	27 25.7	3 2.2
9 T	11 14 17.6	16 50.8	19 44.1	10♐ 5.6	2 43.5	26 59.0	16 45.1	13 24.5	19 7.6	5 13.1	27 24.8	3 3.1
10 W	11 18 14.1	17 49.1	19 41.0	23 6.8	2 42.9	28 8.9	17 25.1	13 19.3	19 4.0	5 11.5	27 23.9	3 4.0
11 T	11 22 10.7	18 47.4	19 37.8	6♑32.4	2D51.3	29 18.8	18 5.2	13 14.3	19 0.3	5 10.0	27 23.1	3 4.9
12 F	11 26 7.2	19 45.8	19 34.6	20 24.2	3 9.0	0♏28.6	18 45.4	13 9.4	18 56.5	5 8.5	27 22.2	3 5.9
13 S	11 30 3.8	20 44.2	19 31.4	4♒42.1	3 35.6	1 38.3	19 25.7	13 4.6	18 52.7	5 7.0	27 21.4	3 6.9
14 S	11 34 0.3	21 42.6	19 28.2	19 23.8	4 11.2	2 48.0	20 6.2	13 0.1	18 48.8	5 5.7	27 20.7	3 8.0
15 M	11 37 56.9	22 41.1	19 25.1	4♓23.9	4 55.2	3 57.5	20 46.7	12 55.7	18 44.9	5 4.3	27 19.9	3 9.1
16 T	11 41 53.4	23 39.6	19 21.9	19 34.9	5 47.4	5 7.0	21 27.3	12 51.5	18 40.9	5 3.0	27 19.2	3 10.2
17 W	11 45 50.0	24 38.1	19 18.7	4♈47.5	6 47.2	6 16.3	22 8.0	12 47.5	18 36.8	5 1.7	27 18.5	3 11.3
18 T	11 49 46.6	25 36.6	19 15.5	19 52.1	7 54.0	7 25.6	22 48.8	12 43.6	18 32.7	5 0.4	27 17.8	3 12.5
19 F	11 53 43.1	26 35.2	19 12.4	4♉40.2	9 7.4	8 34.8	23 29.7	12 39.9	18 28.5	4 59.2	27 17.2	3 13.7
20 S	11 57 39.7	27 33.8	19 9.2	19 5.4	10 26.7	9 43.9	24 10.7	12 36.4	18 24.3	4 58.0	27 16.6	3 14.9
21 S	12 1 36.2	28 32.4	19 6.0	3♊ 4.4	11 51.2	10 52.9	24 51.8	12 33.0	18 20.0	4 56.9	27 16.0	3 16.2
22 M	12 5 32.8	29 31.1	19 2.8	16 36.0	13 20.3	12 1.9	25 33.0	12 29.9	18 15.7	4 55.8	27 15.5	3 17.5
23 T	12 9 29.3	0♎29.8	18 59.6	29 41.8	14 53.5	13 10.7	26 14.3	12 26.9	18 11.3	4 54.8	27 14.9	3 18.8
24 W	12 13 25.9	1 28.6	18 56.5	12♋24.5	16 30.1	14 19.4	26 55.7	12 24.1	18 6.9	4 53.8	27 14.4	3 20.1
25 T	12 17 22.4	2 27.3	18 53.3	24 48.1	18 9.5	15 28.1	27 37.2	12 21.5	18 2.5	4 52.9	27 14.0	3 21.5
26 F	12 21 19.0	3 26.2	18 50.1	6♌56.6	19 51.4	16 36.6	28 18.8	12 19.1	17 58.0	4 52.0	27 13.6	3 22.9
27 S	12 25 15.5	4 25.0	18 46.9	18 54.3	21 35.1	17 45.0	29 0.5	12 16.9	17 53.4	4 51.1	27 13.2	3 24.3
28 S	12 29 12.1	5 23.9	18 43.8	0♍45.0	23 20.3	18 53.4	29 42.3	12 14.9	17 48.9	4 50.3	27 12.8	3 25.8
29 M	12 33 8.6	6 22.9	18 40.6	12 32.3	25 6.7	20 1.6	0♐24.2	12 13.0	17 44.3	4 49.6	27 12.5	3 27.2
30 T	12 37 5.2	7 21.9	18 37.4	24 19.1	26 53.8	21 9.7	1 6.1	12 11.4	17 39.7	4 48.9	27 12.2	3 28.8

DECLINATION at NOON

DAY	EPHEMERIS SIDEREAL TIME	☉	☊	☽	☿	♀	♂	♃	♄	♅	♆	♇
1 M	10 42 45.2	8N 9.7	3N53.9	8N47.0	5N16.7	6S56.7	16S 2.7	17S31.5	5N10.0	19S31.9	20S15.0	8S37.3
4 T	10 54 34.8	7 3.8	3 57.6	1S58.9	6 54.4	8 26.7	16 40.5	17 36.9	5 5.9	19 33.2	20 15.7	8 39.2
7 S	11 6 24.5	5 56.8	4 1.4	12 10.5	8 22.0	9 55.3	17 17.5	17 42.0	5 1.6	19 34.4	20 16.4	8 41.0
10 W	11 18 14.1	4 48.9	4 5.1	17 58.3	9 26.0	11 22.1	17 53.6	17 46.5	4 57.1	19 35.5	20 17.0	8 42.9
13 S	11 30 3.8	3 40.3	4 8.8	15 26.2	9 57.4	12 46.9	18 28.7	17 50.7	4 52.4	19 36.5	20 17.5	8 44.8
16 T	11 41 53.4	2 31.1	4 12.6	4 6.6	9 52.2	14 9.3	19 2.8	17 54.3	4 47.5	19 37.5	20 18.0	8 46.8
19 F	11 53 43.1	1 21.4	4 16.3	9N32.7	9 11.0	15 29.0	19 35.7	17 57.5	4 42.4	19 38.3	20 18.5	8 48.8
22 M	12 5 32.8	0 11.5	4 20.0	17 30.1	7 57.9	16 45.7	20 7.4	18 0.2	4 37.2	19 39.1	20 18.9	8 50.7
25 T	12 17 22.4	0S58.6	4 23.8	16 53.9	6 19.2	17 59.1	20 37.8	18 2.4	4 32.0	19 39.7	20 19.3	8 52.7
28 S	12 29 12.1	2 8.7	4 27.5	9 35.5	4 22.1	19 8.9	21 6.8	18 4.1	4 26.6	19 40.3	20 19.6	8 54.8

OCTOBER 1997

LONGITUDE at NOON

DAY	EPHEMERIS SIDEREAL TIME	☉	☊	☽	☿	♀	♂	♃	♄	♅	♆	♇
1 W	12 41 1.7	8♎20.9	18♍34.2	6♎ 8.0	28♍41.4	22♏17.7	1♐48.2	12♒10.0	17♈35.1	4♒48.2	27♑11.9	3♐30.3
2 T	12 44 58.3	9 19.9	18 31.0	18 1.3	0♎29.3	23 25.6	2 30.4	12R 8.7	17R30.4	4R47.6	27R11.7	3 31.9
3 F	12 48 54.8	10 19.0	18 27.9	0♏ 0.8	2 17.3	24 33.4	3 12.6	12 7.7	17 25.7	4 47.0	27 11.5	3 33.5
4 S	12 52 51.4	11 18.1	18 24.7	12 8.5	4 5.2	25 41.0	3 55.0	12 6.8	17 21.0	4 46.5	27 11.3	3 35.1
5 S	12 56 47.9	12 17.3	18 21.5	24 26.4	5 52.9	26 48.6	4 37.4	12 6.3	17 16.4	4 46.1	27 11.2	3 36.8
6 M	13 0 44.5	13 16.4	18 18.3	6♐56.3	7 40.2	27 55.9	5 20.0	12 5.8	17 11.6	4 45.7	27 11.1	3 38.4
7 T	13 4 41.0	14 15.6	18 15.1	19 40.6	9 27.0	29 3.2	6 2.6	12 5.6	17 6.9	4 45.3	27 11.1	3 40.1
8 W	13 8 37.6	15 14.9	18 12.0	2♑41.7	11 13.3	0♐10.3	6 45.2	12 5.5	17 2.2	4 45.0	27 11.0	3 41.8
9 T	13 12 34.1	16 14.1	18 8.8	16 1.8	12 59.1	1 17.2	7 28.0	12D 5.7	16 57.4	4 44.7	27 11.0	3 43.6
10 F	13 16 30.7	17 13.4	18 5.6	29 42.8	14 44.2	2 24.0	8 10.9	12 6.1	16 52.7	4 44.5	27D11.1	3 45.3
11 S	13 20 27.2	18 12.7	18 2.4	13♒45.8	16 28.7	3 30.7	8 53.8	12 6.6	16 47.9	4 44.3	27 11.1	3 47.1
12 S	13 24 23.8	19 12.1	17 59.3	28 10.3	18 12.5	4 37.1	9 36.9	12 7.4	16 43.2	4 44.2	27 11.2	3 48.9
13 M	13 28 20.4	20 11.5	17 56.1	12♓53.6	19 55.6	5 43.4	10 20.0	12 8.4	16 38.5	4 44.1	27 11.4	3 50.8
14 T	13 32 16.9	21 10.9	17 52.9	27 51.0	21 38.1	6 49.6	11 3.1	12 9.5	16 33.8	4 44.1	27 11.5	3 52.6
15 W	13 36 13.5	22 10.3	17 49.7	12♈55.1	23 19.8	7 55.5	11 46.4	12 10.9	16 29.1	4 44.1	27 11.7	3 54.5
16 T	13 40 10.0	23 9.8	17 46.5	27 57.4	25 0.9	9 1.3	12 29.7	12 12.4	16 24.4	4D44.2	27 12.0	3 56.4
17 F	13 44 6.6	24 9.3	17 43.4	12♉48.6	26 41.3	10 6.8	13 13.2	12 14.2	16 19.7	4 44.4	27 12.2	3 58.3
18 S	13 48 3.1	25 8.8	17 40.2	27 20.7	28 21.0	11 12.2	13 56.7	12 16.1	16 15.0	4 44.5	27 12.5	4 0.2
19 S	13 51 59.7	26 8.4	17 37.0	11♊28.0	0♏ 0.1	12 17.4	14 40.2	12 18.2	16 10.4	4 44.8	27 12.9	4 2.2
20 M	13 55 56.2	27 8.0	17 33.8	25 7.5	1 38.6	13 22.4	15 23.9	12 20.6	16 5.8	4 45.1	27 13.2	4 4.2
21 T	13 59 52.8	28 7.7	17 30.7	8♋19.2	3 16.4	14 27.1	16 7.6	12 23.1	16 1.2	4 45.4	27 13.6	4 6.2
22 W	14 3 49.3	29 7.4	17 27.5	21 5.3	4 53.6	15 31.7	16 51.4	12 25.8	15 56.6	4 45.8	27 14.1	4 8.2
23 T	14 7 45.9	0♏ 7.1	17 24.3	3♌29.5	6 30.3	16 36.0	17 35.3	12 28.7	15 52.1	4 46.2	27 14.5	4 10.2
24 F	14 11 42.4	1 6.9	17 21.1	15 36.6	8 6.3	17 40.1	18 19.3	12 31.8	15 47.6	4 46.7	27 15.0	4 12.3
25 S	14 15 39.0	2 6.7	17 17.9	27 31.8	9 41.8	18 43.9	19 3.3	12 35.1	15 43.1	4 47.3	27 15.6	4 14.3
26 S	14 19 35.5	3 6.6	17 14.8	9♍20.2	11 16.9	19 47.6	19 47.5	12 38.7	15 38.8	4 47.9	27 16.2	4 16.5
27 M	14 23 32.1	4 6.4	17 11.6	21 6.4	12 51.3	20 50.9	20 31.7	12 42.3	15 34.4	4 48.5	27 16.8	4 18.6
28 T	14 27 28.6	5 6.3	17 8.4	2♎54.5	14 25.3	21 54.0	21 15.9	12 46.2	15 30.0	4 49.2	27 17.4	4 20.7
29 W	14 31 25.2	6 6.3	17 5.2	14 48.1	15 58.8	22 56.9	22 0.3	12 50.2	15 25.8	4 50.0	27 18.1	4 22.8
30 T	14 35 21.8	7 6.3	17 2.1	26 49.8	17 31.7	23 59.4	22 44.7	12 54.4	15 21.5	4 50.8	27 18.8	4 25.0
31 F	14 39 18.3	8 6.3	16 58.9	9♏ 1.3	19 4.3	25 1.7	23 29.2	12 58.9	15 17.3	4 51.6	27 19.5	4 27.1

DECLINATION at NOON

DAY	EPHEMERIS SIDEREAL TIME	☉	☊	☽	☿	♀	♂	♃	♄	♅	♆	♇
1 W	12 41 1.7	3S18.6	4N31.2	1S 4.1	2N13.2	20S14.9	21S34.3	18S 5.3	4N21.1	19S40.7	20S19.8	8S56.8
4 S	12 52 51.4	4 28.2	4 35.0	11 30.3	0S 2.1	21 16.7	22 0.2	18 5.9	4 15.7	19 41.0	20 20.0	8 58.8
7 T	13 4 41.0	5 37.4	4 38.7	17 48.5	2 19.9	22 14.1	22 24.5	18 6.1	4 10.2	19 41.3	20 20.1	9 0.8
10 F	13 16 30.7	6 45.8	4 42.4	16 17.5	4 37.1	23 6.8	22 47.1	18 5.7	4 4.7	19 41.4	20 20.2	9 2.8
13 M	13 28 20.4	7 53.4	4 46.1	6 9.7	6 51.7	23 54.5	23 7.8	18 4.8	3 59.3	19 41.4	20 20.2	9 4.9
16 T	13 40 10.0	9 0.1	4 49.9	7N42.6	9 2.4	24 37.1	23 26.7	18 3.4	3 54.0	19 41.3	20 20.1	9 6.8
19 S	13 51 59.7	10 5.5	4 53.6	17 3.3	11 8.0	25 14.4	23 43.5	18 1.5	3 48.8	19 41.1	20 20.0	9 8.8
22 W	14 3 49.3	11 9.7	4 57.3	17 25.9	13 7.8	25 46.2	23 58.3	17 59.1	3 43.7	19 40.8	20 19.9	9 10.8
25 S	14 15 39.0	12 12.4	5 1.0	10 32.4	15 1.0	26 12.4	24 11.0	17 56.2	3 38.7	19 40.3	20 19.6	9 12.7
28 T	14 27 28.6	13 13.4	5 4.7	0S 1.1	16 47.2	26 33.0	24 21.6	17 52.8	3 34.0	19 39.8	20 19.4	9 14.6
31 F	14 39 18.3	14 12.5	5 8.4	10 45.9	18 25.7	26 47.8	24 29.9	17 49.0	3 29.4	19 39.1	20 19.0	9 16.5

NOVEMBER 1997

DAY	EPHEMERIS SIDEREAL TIME	☉	☊	☽	☿	♀	♂	♃	♄	♅	♆	♇
	h m s	° ′	° ′	° ′	° ′	° ′	° ′	° ′	° ′	° ′	° ′	° ′
LONGITUDE at NOON												
1 S	14 43 14.9	9♏ 6.3	16♍55.7	21♏24.0	20♏36.3	26♐ 3.6	24♐13.7	13♒ 3.5	15♈13.2	4♒52.5	27♑20.3	4♐29.3
2 S	14 47 11.4	10 6.4	16 52.5	3♐58.2	22 7.9	27 5.2	24 58.3	13 8.2	15R 9.1	4 53.5	27 21.1	4 31.5
3 M	14 51 8.0	11 6.5	16 49.3	16 44.4	23 39.1	28 6.6	25 43.0	13 13.2	15 5.1	4 54.5	27 22.0	4 33.7
4 T	14 55 4.5	12 6.6	16 46.2	29 42.7	25 9.8	29 7.5	26 27.8	13 18.3	15 1.1	4 55.5	27 22.8	4 35.9
5 W	14 59 1.1	13 6.8	16 43.0	12♑53.5	26 40.1	0♑ 8.1	27 12.6	13 23.6	14 57.3	4 56.6	27 23.7	4 38.1
6 T	15 2 57.6	14 7.0	16 39.8	26 17.4	28 10.0	1 8.4	27 57.5	13 29.1	14 53.4	4 57.8	27 24.6	4 40.4
7 F	15 6 54.2	15 7.2	16 36.6	9♒55.2	29 39.4	2 8.2	28 42.5	13 34.8	14 49.7	4 59.0	27 25.6	4 42.6
8 S	15 10 50.7	16 7.4	16 33.5	23 47.7	1♐ 8.4	3 7.7	29 27.5	13 40.6	14 46.0	5 0.2	27 26.6	4 44.9
9 S	15 14 47.3	17 7.7	16 30.3	7♓55.3	2 36.8	4 6.7	0♑12.6	13 46.6	14 42.4	5 1.5	27 27.6	4 47.2
10 M	15 18 43.9	18 7.9	16 27.1	22 17.2	4 4.8	5 5.3	0 57.7	13 52.8	14 38.8	5 2.9	27 28.7	4 49.4
11 T	15 22 40.4	19 8.2	16 23.9	6♈51.2	5 32.3	6 3.5	1 42.9	13 59.1	14 35.3	5 4.3	27 29.8	4 51.7
12 W	15 26 37.0	20 8.6	16 20.8	21 33.0	6 59.3	7 1.2	2 28.2	14 5.6	14 31.9	5 5.7	27 30.9	4 54.0
13 T	15 30 33.5	21 8.9	16 17.6	6♉16.5	8 25.6	7 58.3	3 13.5	14 12.2	14 28.6	5 7.2	27 32.0	4 56.3
14 F	15 34 30.1	22 9.3	16 14.4	20 54.2	9 51.4	8 55.0	3 58.8	14 19.1	14 25.4	5 8.7	27 33.2	4 58.6
15 S	15 38 26.6	23 9.7	16 11.2	5♊18.7	11 16.5	9 51.2	4 44.3	14 26.0	14 22.2	5 10.3	27 34.4	5 1.0
16 S	15 42 23.2	24 10.2	16 8.0	19 23.5	12 40.9	10 46.8	5 29.8	14 33.2	14 19.2	5 12.0	27 35.7	5 3.3
17 M	15 46 19.7	25 10.7	16 4.9	3♋ 4.1	14 4.4	11 41.9	6 15.3	14 40.5	14 16.2	5 13.6	27 36.9	5 5.7
18 T	15 50 16.3	26 11.2	16 1.7	16 18.7	15 27.0	12 36.4	7 0.9	14 47.9	14 13.3	5 15.4	27 38.2	5 8.0
19 W	15 54 12.8	27 11.7	15 58.5	29 8.1	16 48.6	13 30.2	7 46.6	14 55.5	14 10.5	5 17.1	27 39.6	5 10.4
20 T	15 58 9.4	28 12.2	15 55.3	11♌35.1	18 9.1	14 23.4	8 32.3	15 3.3	14 7.8	5 18.9	27 40.9	5 12.7
21 F	16 2 6.0	29 12.8	15 52.2	23 44.0	19 28.3	15 16.0	9 18.0	15 11.2	14 5.1	5 20.8	27 42.3	5 15.1
22 S	16 6 2.5	0♐13.4	15 49.0	5♍40.0	20 46.0	16 7.9	10 3.9	15 19.2	14 2.6	5 22.7	27 43.7	5 17.4
23 S	16 9 59.1	1 14.1	15 45.8	17 28.7	22 2.1	16 59.1	10 49.7	15 27.4	14 0.1	5 24.6	27 45.1	5 19.8
24 M	16 13 55.6	2 14.7	15 42.6	29 15.6	23 16.3	17 49.5	11 35.7	15 35.7	13 57.8	5 26.6	27 46.6	5 22.1
25 T	16 17 52.2	3 15.4	15 39.4	11♎ 5.8	24 28.4	18 39.2	12 21.6	15 44.2	13 55.5	5 28.6	27 48.1	5 24.5
26 W	16 21 48.7	4 16.1	15 36.3	23 4.0	25 38.0	19 28.1	13 7.7	15 52.8	13 53.3	5 30.7	27 49.6	5 26.9
27 T	16 25 45.3	5 16.9	15 33.1	5♏13.7	26 44.9	20 16.2	13 53.7	16 1.6	13 51.3	5 32.8	27 51.1	5 29.2
28 F	16 29 41.9	6 17.7	15 29.9	17 37.4	27 48.5	21 3.4	14 39.9	16 10.5	13 49.3	5 35.0	27 52.7	5 31.6
29 S	16 33 38.4	7 18.4	15 26.7	0♐16.3	28 48.5	21 49.7	15 26.0	16 19.5	13 47.5	5 37.2	27 54.3	5 34.0
30 S	16 37 35.0	8 19.3	15 23.6	13 10.5	29 44.4	22 35.0	16 12.3	16 28.7	13 45.7	5 39.4	27 55.9	5 36.3
DECLINATION at NOON												
1 S	14 43 14.9	14S31.8	5N 9.7	13S43.0	18S56.7	26S51.5	24S32.1	17S47.6	3N27.9	19S38.9	20S18.9	9S17.1
4 T	14 55 4.5	15 28.1	5 13.4	18 26.2	20 24.1	26 58.8	24 37.4	17 43.1	3 23.7	19 38.1	20 18.5	9 18.9
7 F	15 6 54.2	16 22.2	5 17.1	14 43.2	21 42.5	27 0.4	24 40.3	17 38.1	3 19.7	19 37.1	20 18.0	9 20.7
10 M	15 18 43.9	17 13.8	5 20.8	3 24.9	22 51.4	26 56.7	24 40.8	17 32.6	3 15.9	19 36.1	20 17.5	9 22.4
13 T	15 30 33.5	18 2.7	5 24.5	10N 1.2	23 49.9	26 47.6	24 39.0	17 26.7	3 12.5	19 35.0	20 16.9	9 24.1
16 S	15 42 23.2	18 48.8	5 28.2	17 58.8	24 37.6	26 33.5	24 34.6	17 20.4	3 9.4	19 33.8	20 16.2	9 25.7
19 W	15 54 12.8	19 31.8	5 31.9	16 39.4	25 13.7	26 14.6	24 27.9	17 13.6	3 6.6	19 32.4	20 15.5	9 27.3
22 S	16 6 2.5	20 11.7	5 35.6	8 31.3	25 37.6	25 51.2	24 18.6	17 6.4	3 4.1	19 31.0	20 14.8	9 28.8
25 T	16 17 52.2	20 48.3	5 39.3	2S28.0	25 48.9	25 23.7	24 7.0	16 58.7	3 2.0	19 29.5	20 14.0	9 30.3
28 F	16 29 41.9	21 21.4	5 42.9	12 51.4	25 47.4	24 52.5	23 52.8	16 50.7	3 0.3	19 27.9	20 13.1	9 31.7

DECEMBER 1997

DAY	EPHEMERIS SIDEREAL TIME	☉	☊	☽	☿	♀	♂	♃	♄	♅	♆	♇
LONGITUDE at NOON												
1 M	16 41 31.5	9♐20.1	15♍20.4	26♐19.0	0♑35.5	23♑19.4	16♑58.5	16♒38.0	13♈44.0	5♒41.7	27♑57.5	5♐38.7
2 T	16 45 28.1	10 20.9	15 17.2	9♑40.0	1 21.2	24 2.7	17 44.8	16 47.4	13R42.5	5 44.0	27 59.2	5 41.0
3 W	16 49 24.6	11 21.8	15 14.0	23 11.6	2 0.7	24 45.0	18 31.2	16 56.9	13 41.0	5 46.4	28 0.9	5 43.4
4 T	16 53 21.2	12 22.7	15 10.9	6♒51.8	2 33.4	25 26.2	19 17.6	17 6.6	13 39.7	5 48.8	28 2.6	5 45.7
5 F	16 57 17.7	13 23.6	15 7.7	20 39.6	2 58.4	26 6.2	20 4.1	17 16.4	13 38.5	5 51.2	28 4.3	5 48.1
6 S	17 1 14.3	14 24.5	15 4.5	4♓34.1	3 14.9	26 45.0	20 50.5	17 26.3	13 37.3	5 53.7	28 6.1	5 50.4
7 S	17 5 10.9	15 25.5	15 1.3	18 35.1	3 22.0	27 22.6	21 37.1	17 36.4	13 36.3	5 56.2	28 7.9	5 52.8
8 M	17 9 7.4	16 26.4	14 58.1	2♈42.4	3R18.8	27 58.8	22 23.7	17 46.6	13 35.4	5 58.7	28 9.7	5 55.2
9 T	17 13 4.0	17 27.3	14 55.0	16 54.9	3 4.8	28 33.6	23 10.2	17 56.9	13 34.6	6 1.3	28 11.5	5 57.5
10 W	17 17 0.5	18 28.3	14 51.8	1♉10.9	2 39.5	29 7.0	23 56.9	18 7.3	13 33.9	6 3.9	28 13.4	5 59.8
11 T	17 20 57.1	19 29.3	14 48.6	15 27.0	2 2.7	29 38.8	24 43.5	18 17.8	13 33.3	6 6.6	28 15.2	6 2.1
12 F	17 24 53.6	20 30.2	14 45.4	29 38.8	1 14.7	0♒ 9.2	25 30.2	18 28.4	13 32.8	6 9.3	28 17.1	6 4.4
13 S	17 28 50.2	21 31.2	14 42.3	13♊41.2	0 16.2	0 37.9	26 16.9	18 39.1	13 32.5	6 12.0	28 19.0	6 6.7
14 S	17 32 46.8	22 32.2	14 39.1	27 29.1	29♐ 8.4	1 4.9	27 3.7	18 50.0	13 32.2	6 14.7	28 20.9	6 9.0
15 M	17 36 43.3	23 33.2	14 35.9	10♋58.4	27 53.2	1 30.2	27 50.5	19 0.9	13 32.1	6 17.5	28 22.9	6 11.3
16 T	17 40 39.9	24 34.3	14 32.7	24 6.7	26 32.9	1 53.7	28 37.3	19 11.9	13 32.0	6 20.3	28 24.8	6 13.6
17 W	17 44 36.4	25 35.3	14 29.6	6♌53.5	25 10.0	2 15.3	29 24.1	19 23.1	13D32.1	6 23.2	28 26.8	6 15.9
18 T	17 48 33.0	26 36.3	14 26.4	19 20.3	23 47.6	2 35.1	0♒11.0	19 34.3	13 32.2	6 26.0	28 28.8	6 18.1
19 F	17 52 29.5	27 37.4	14 23.2	1♍30.1	22 28.2	2 52.8	0 57.9	19 45.7	13 32.5	6 28.9	28 30.8	6 20.3
20 S	17 56 26.1	28 38.5	14 20.0	13 27.4	21 14.3	3 8.4	1 44.9	19 57.1	13 32.9	6 31.9	28 32.8	6 22.6
21 S	18 0 22.7	29 39.6	14 16.8	25 17.1	20 8.1	3 22.0	2 31.8	20 8.6	13 33.4	6 34.8	28 34.9	6 24.8
22 M	18 4 19.2	0♑40.7	14 13.7	7♎ 4.8	19 11.1	3 33.4	3 18.8	20 20.3	13 34.0	6 37.8	28 36.9	6 27.0
23 T	18 8 15.8	1 41.8	14 10.5	18 56.1	18 24.3	3 42.5	4 5.8	20 32.0	13 34.8	6 40.8	28 39.0	6 29.2
24 W	18 12 12.3	2 42.9	14 7.3	0♏56.3	17 48.2	3 49.4	4 52.9	20 43.8	13 35.6	6 43.8	28 41.1	6 31.4
25 T	18 16 8.9	3 44.1	14 4.1	13 10.0	17 22.9	3 53.9	5 40.0	20 55.7	13 36.5	6 46.9	28 43.2	6 33.5
26 F	18 20 5.4	4 45.2	14 1.0	25 41.0	17 8.2	3 56.1	6 27.0	21 7.7	13 37.6	6 50.0	28 45.3	6 35.7
27 S	18 24 2.0	5 46.4	13 57.8	8♐31.4	17 3.5	3R55.8	7 14.2	21 19.8	13 38.8	6 53.1	28 47.4	6 37.8
28 S	18 27 58.6	6 47.6	13 54.6	21 42.1	17D 8.3	3 53.1	8 1.4	21 32.0	13 40.1	6 56.3	28 49.6	6 40.0
29 M	18 31 55.1	7 48.8	13 51.4	5♑11.6	17 21.8	3 47.9	8 48.5	21 44.3	13 41.5	6 59.5	28 51.8	6 42.1
30 T	18 35 51.7	8 49.9	13 48.3	18 57.5	17 43.2	3 40.2	9 35.7	21 56.6	13 43.0	7 2.7	28 53.9	6 44.2
31 W	18 39 48.2	9 51.1	13 45.1	2♒55.8	18 11.9	3 30.0	10 22.9	22 9.0	13 44.6	7 5.9	28 56.1	6 46.2
DECLINATION at NOON												
1 M	16 41 31.5	21S50.9	5N46.6	18S28.1	25S33.1	24S18.0	23S36.3	16S42.2	2N58.9	19S26.2	20S12.2	9S33.0
4 T	16 53 21.2	22 16.6	5 50.3	15 31.9	25 6.6	23 40.7	23 17.3	16 33.3	2 57.9	19 24.4	20 11.3	9 34.3
7 S	17 5 10.9	22 38.4	5 54.0	4 47.8	24 28.9	23 1.1	22 56.0	16 24.1	2 57.3	19 22.5	20 10.2	9 35.5
10 W	17 17 0.5	22 56.2	5 57.7	8N28.6	23 41.0	22 19.7	22 32.3	16 14.4	2 57.1	19 20.5	20 9.2	9 36.7
13 S	17 28 50.2	23 10.0	6 1.4	17 28.1	22 44.3	21 37.1	22 6.3	16 4.4	2 57.2	19 18.5	20 8.1	9 37.7
16 T	17 40 39.9	23 19.5	6 5.0	17 30.2	21 42.6	20 54.0	21 38.1	15 54.0	2 57.8	19 16.3	20 7.0	9 38.7
19 F	17 52 29.5	23 24.9	6 8.7	9 56.6	20 45.3	20 10.8	21 7.8	15 43.3	2 58.7	19 14.1	20 5.9	9 39.6
22 M	18 4 19.2	23 26.1	6 12.4	0S57.0	20 4.7	19 28.2	20 35.3	15 32.2	3 0.1	19 11.9	20 4.7	9 40.4
25 T	18 16 8.9	23 23.0	6 16.0	11 37.2	19 48.6	18 46.8	20 0.7	15 20.8	3 1.8	19 9.5	20 3.4	9 41.2
28 S	18 27 58.6	23 15.8	6 19.7	18 11.9	19 55.6	18 7.2	19 24.2	15 9.0	3 3.9	19 7.1	20 2.2	9 41.9
31 W	18 39 48.2	23 4.3	6 23.4	16 21.5	20 19.5	17 30.0	18 45.8	14 56.9	3 6.4	19 4.7	20 0.9	9 42.5

JANUARY 1998

DAY	EPHEMERIS SIDEREAL TIME	☉	☊	☾	☿	♀	♂	♃	♄	♅	♆	♇
	h m s	° ′	° ′	° ′	° ′	° ′	° ′	° ′	° ′	° ′	° ′	° ′
						LONGITUDE at NOON						
1 T	18 43 44.8	10♑52.3	13♍41.9	17♒ 2.3	18♐47.0	3♒17.2	11♒10.1	22♒21.5	13♈46.3	7♒ 9.1	28♑58.3	6♐48.3
2 F	18 47 41.3	11 53.5	13 38.7	1♓12.8	19 27.9	3R 2.1	11 57.3	22 34.1	13 48.1	7 12.3	29 0.5	6 50.3
3 S	18 51 37.9	12 54.6	13 35.6	15 24.2	20 14.1	2 44.4	12 44.6	22 46.7	13 50.0	7 15.6	29 2.7	6 52.3
4 S	18 55 34.5	13 55.8	13 32.4	29 34.0	21 4.8	2 24.4	13 31.8	22 59.4	13 52.0	7 18.9	29 4.9	6 54.3
5 M	18 59 31.0	14 56.9	13 29.2	13♈40.9	21 59.7	2 2.1	14 19.1	23 12.2	13 54.2	7 22.2	29 7.1	6 56.3
6 T	19 3 27.6	15 58.1	13 26.0	27 43.8	22 58.2	1 37.5	15 6.4	23 25.1	13 56.4	7 25.5	29 9.3	6 58.2
7 W	19 7 24.1	16 59.2	13 22.8	11♉41.9	23 60.0	1 10.9	15 53.7	23 38.0	13 58.8	7 28.8	29 11.6	7 0.2
8 T	19 11 20.7	18 0.4	13 19.7	25 34.0	25 4.7	0 42.3	16 41.0	23 51.0	14 1.2	7 32.2	29 13.8	7 2.1
9 F	19 15 17.2	19 1.5	13 16.5	9♊18.3	26 12.0	0 11.9	17 28.3	24 4.0	14 3.8	7 35.5	29 16.0	7 4.0
10 S	19 19 13.8	20 2.6	13 13.3	22 52.7	27 21.6	29♑39.9	18 15.6	24 17.1	14 6.4	7 38.9	29 18.3	7 5.8
11 S	19 23 10.4	21 3.8	13 10.1	6♋14.9	28 33.3	29 6.4	19 2.9	24 30.3	14 9.2	7 42.3	29 20.5	7 7.7
12 M	19 27 6.9	22 4.9	13 7.0	19 22.8	29 46.9	28 31.8	19 50.2	24 43.5	14 12.0	7 45.7	29 22.8	7 9.5
13 T	19 31 3.5	23 6.0	13 3.8	2♌14.9	1♑ 2.2	27 56.2	20 37.5	24 56.8	14 15.0	7 49.1	29 25.1	7 11.3
14 W	19 35 0.0	24 7.1	13 0.6	14 50.8	2 19.0	27 19.9	21 24.9	25 10.2	14 18.0	7 52.6	29 27.3	7 13.1
15 T	19 38 56.6	25 8.2	12 57.4	27 11.2	3 37.3	26 43.1	22 12.2	25 23.6	14 21.2	7 56.0	29 29.6	7 14.8
16 F	19 42 53.1	26 9.2	12 54.3	9♍18.1	4 56.8	26 6.1	22 59.5	25 37.0	14 24.4	7 59.5	29 31.9	7 16.6
17 S	19 46 49.7	27 10.3	12 51.1	21 14.5	6 17.5	25 29.2	23 46.9	25 50.5	14 27.8	8 2.9	29 34.2	7 18.3
18 S	19 50 46.2	28 11.5	12 47.9	3♎ 4.5	7 39.4	24 52.6	24 34.2	26 4.1	14 31.2	8 6.4	29 36.5	7 20.0
19 M	19 54 42.8	29 12.5	12 44.7	14 52.4	9 2.3	24 16.6	25 21.6	26 17.8	14 34.8	8 9.9	29 38.8	7 21.6
20 T	19 58 39.4	0♒13.6	12 41.5	26 43.5	10 26.1	23 41.4	26 8.9	26 31.4	14 38.4	8 13.4	29 41.0	7 23.3
21 W	20 2 35.9	1 14.7	12 38.4	8♏43.1	11 50.8	23 7.3	26 56.3	26 45.1	14 42.1	8 16.9	29 43.3	7 24.9
22 T	20 6 32.5	2 15.7	12 35.2	20 56.3	13 16.4	22 34.4	27 43.6	26 58.9	14 45.9	8 20.4	29 45.6	7 26.4
23 F	20 10 29.0	3 16.8	12 32.0	3♐27.5	14 42.9	22 3.1	28 30.9	27 12.7	14 49.8	8 23.9	29 47.9	7 28.0
24 S	20 14 25.6	4 17.8	12 28.8	16 20.5	16 10.1	21 33.4	29 18.3	27 26.5	14 53.8	8 27.4	29 50.1	7 29.5
25 S	20 18 22.1	5 18.8	12 25.7	29 37.3	17 38.1	21 5.5	0♓ 5.6	27 40.4	14 57.9	8 30.9	29 52.4	7 31.0
26 M	20 22 18.7	6 19.8	12 22.5	13♑18.1	19 6.8	20 39.7	0 52.9	27 54.3	15 2.1	8 34.4	29 54.7	7 32.4
27 T	20 26 15.2	7 20.9	12 19.3	27 21.0	20 36.3	20 15.9	1 40.2	28 8.3	15 6.4	8 37.9	29 56.9	7 33.9
28 W	20 30 11.8	8 21.8	12 16.1	11♒41.8	22 6.4	19 54.3	2 27.6	28 22.3	15 10.7	8 41.4	29 59.2	7 35.3
29 T	20 34 8.4	9 22.8	12 12.9	26 14.8	23 37.3	19 35.1	3 14.9	28 36.3	15 15.2	8 44.9	0♒ 1.4	7 36.6
30 F	20 38 4.9	10 23.8	12 9.8	10♓53.6	25 8.9	19 18.2	4 2.2	28 50.3	15 19.7	8 48.4	0 3.7	7 38.0
31 S	20 42 1.5	11 24.7	12 6.6	25 31.6	26 41.2	19 3.7	4 49.4	29 4.4	15 24.3	8 51.9	0 5.9	7 39.3
						DECLINATION at NOON						
1 T	18 43 44.8	22S59.5	6N24.6	13S39.2	20S29.8	17S18.2	18S32.6	14S52.8	3N 7.3	19S 3.9	20S 0.5	9S42.7
4 S	18 55 34.5	22 42.5	6 28.3	1 34.2	21 4.7	16 45.1	17 51.8	14 40.4	3 10.3	19 1.3	19 59.1	9 43.1
7 W	19 7 24.1	22 21.5	6 31.9	11N 8.9	21 40.9	16 15.6	17 9.3	14 27.6	3 13.6	18 58.8	19 57.8	9 43.6
10 S	19 19 13.8	21 56.5	6 35.6	18 14.5	22 14.5	15 50.1	16 25.2	14 14.6	3 17.3	18 56.2	19 56.5	9 43.9
13 T	19 31 3.5	21 27.6	6 39.2	16 29.6	22 42.5	15 28.8	15 39.5	14 1.3	3 21.3	18 53.5	19 55.1	9 44.1
16 F	19 42 53.1	20 55.0	6 42.9	7 55.1	23 2.9	15 12.1	14 52.5	13 47.7	3 25.6	18 50.9	19 53.7	9 44.3
19 M	19 54 42.8	20 18.8	6 46.5	3S 12.4	23 14.3	14 59.8	14 4.1	13 33.9	3 30.3	18 48.2	19 52.3	9 44.4
22 T	20 6 32.5	19 39.2	6 50.2	13 17.3	23 15.6	14 52.1	13 14.4	13 19.9	3 35.3	18 45.5	19 50.9	9 44.4
25 S	20 18 22.1	18 56.3	6 53.8	18 30.9	23 6.1	14 48.6	12 23.6	13 5.6	3 40.5	18 42.7	19 49.5	9 44.4
28 W	20 30 11.8	18 10.3	6 57.4	14 50.1	22 45.3	14 48.9	11 31.8	12 51.1	3 46.1	18 40.0	19 48.1	9 44.2
31 S	20 42 1.5	17 21.3	7 1.1	3 0.4	22 12.7	14 52.6	10 39.0	12 36.5	3 51.9	18 37.2	19 46.7	9 44.0

FEBRUARY 1998

DAY	EPHEMERIS SIDEREAL TIME	☉	☊	☾	☿	♀	♂	♃	♄	♅	♆	♇
						LONGITUDE at NOON						
1 S	20 45 58.0	12♒25.6	12♍ 3.4	10♈ 3.4	28♑14.2	18♑51.7	5♓36.7	29♒18.6	15♈29.0	8♒55.4	0♒ 8.2	7♐40.6
2 M	20 49 54.6	13 26.5	12 0.2	24 25.0	29 47.9	18R42.1	6 24.0	29 32.7	15 33.8	8 58.9	0 10.4	7 41.8
3 T	20 53 51.1	14 27.4	11 57.1	8♉33.7	1♒22.3	18 35.0	7 11.2	29 46.9	15 38.6	9 2.4	0 12.6	7 43.0
4 W	20 57 47.7	15 28.3	11 53.9	22 28.2	2 57.5	18 30.4	7 58.5	0♓ 1.1	15 43.5	9 5.9	0 14.9	7 44.2
5 T	21 1 44.2	16 29.1	11 50.7	6♊ 8.0	4 33.3	18 28.2	8 45.7	0 15.3	15 48.5	9 9.4	0 17.1	7 45.4
6 F	21 5 40.8	17 29.9	11 47.5	19 33.3	6 9.9	18D28.5	9 32.9	0 29.6	15 53.6	9 12.9	0 19.3	7 46.5
7 S	21 9 37.3	18 30.7	11 44.4	2♋44.5	7 47.3	18 31.1	10 20.1	0 43.9	15 58.8	9 16.4	0 21.5	7 47.6
8 S	21 13 33.9	19 31.5	11 41.2	15 42.1	9 25.5	18 36.2	11 7.3	0 58.2	16 4.1	9 19.9	0 23.7	7 48.7
9 M	21 17 30.5	20 32.2	11 38.0	28 26.5	11 4.4	18 43.5	11 54.4	1 12.5	16 9.4	9 23.4	0 25.8	7 49.8
10 T	21 21 27.0	21 32.9	11 34.8	10♌58.3	12 44.1	18 53.1	12 41.5	1 26.9	16 14.7	9 26.8	0 28.0	7 50.8
11 W	21 25 23.6	22 33.6	11 31.6	23 18.4	14 24.6	19 4.9	13 28.6	1 41.2	16 20.2	9 30.2	0 30.2	7 51.7
12 T	21 29 20.1	23 34.3	11 28.5	5♍27.7	16 6.0	19 18.8	14 15.7	1 55.6	16 25.7	9 33.7	0 32.3	7 52.6
13 F	21 33 16.7	24 34.9	11 25.3	17 28.0	17 48.2	19 34.9	15 2.8	2 10.0	16 31.3	9 37.1	0 34.4	7 53.5
14 S	21 37 13.2	25 35.5	11 22.1	29 21.4	19 31.3	19 52.9	15 49.8	2 24.4	16 36.9	9 40.5	0 36.5	7 54.4
15 S	21 41 9.8	26 36.1	11 18.9	11♎10.5	21 15.2	20 12.9	16 36.8	2 38.8	16 42.7	9 43.9	0 38.6	7 55.2
16 M	21 45 6.3	27 36.7	11 15.8	22 58.8	22 60.0	20 34.8	17 23.8	2 53.2	16 48.5	9 47.3	0 40.7	7 56.0
17 T	21 49 2.9	28 37.3	11 12.6	4♏50.2	24 45.7	20 58.6	18 10.8	3 7.6	16 54.3	9 50.7	0 42.8	7 56.8
18 W	21 52 59.4	29 37.8	11 9.4	16 49.1	26 32.3	21 24.1	18 57.7	3 22.0	17 0.2	9 54.0	0 44.8	7 57.5
19 T	21 56 56.0	0♓38.3	11 6.2	28 59.9	28 19.8	21 51.3	19 44.6	3 36.5	17 6.2	9 57.4	0 46.9	7 58.2
20 F	22 0 52.5	1 38.8	11 3.0	11♐27.5	0♓ 8.1	22 20.1	20 31.5	3 50.9	17 12.2	10 0.7	0 48.9	7 58.9
21 S	22 4 49.1	2 39.3	10 59.9	24 16.0	1 57.4	22 50.5	21 18.4	4 5.4	17 18.3	10 4.0	0 50.9	7 59.5
22 S	22 8 45.7	3 39.7	10 56.7	7♑28.8	3 47.5	23 22.4	22 5.3	4 19.8	17 24.5	10 7.3	0 52.9	8 0.1
23 M	22 12 42.2	4 40.1	10 53.5	21 8.0	5 38.5	23 55.8	22 52.1	4 34.3	17 30.7	10 10.6	0 54.9	8 0.7
24 T	22 16 38.8	5 40.5	10 50.3	5♒13.5	7 30.3	24 30.5	23 38.9	4 48.7	17 37.0	10 13.8	0 56.8	8 1.2
25 W	22 20 35.3	6 40.9	10 47.2	19 42.8	9 22.8	25 6.6	24 25.7	5 3.2	17 43.3	10 17.1	0 58.8	8 1.7
26 T	22 24 31.9	7 41.3	10 44.0	4♓31.0	11 16.1	25 44.0	25 12.4	5 17.7	17 49.7	10 20.3	1 0.7	8 2.1
27 F	22 28 28.4	8 41.6	10 40.8	19 30.9	13 9.9	26 22.6	25 59.1	5 32.1	17 56.1	10 23.5	1 2.6	8 2.6
28 S	22 32 25.0	9 41.9	10 37.6	4♈33.8	15 4.3	27 2.3	26 45.8	5 46.5	18 2.6	10 26.7	1 4.5	8 2.9
						DECLINATION at NOON						
1 S	20 45 58.0	17S 4.4	7N 2.3	1N37.1	21S59.2	14S54.5	10S21.2	12S31.6	3N53.9	18S36.3	19S46.2	9S43.9
4 W	20 57 47.7	16 11.8	7 5.9	13 34.0	21 10.4	15 1.5	9 27.3	12 16.7	4 0.1	18 33.6	19 44.8	9 43.6
7 S	21 9 37.3	15 16.7	7 9.6	18 32.7	20 9.2	15 10.3	8 32.7	12 1.6	4 6.5	18 30.8	19 43.4	9 43.2
10 T	21 21 27.0	14 19.2	7 13.2	14 58.4	18 55.4	15 19.9	7 37.4	11 46.4	4 13.2	18 28.1	19 42.1	9 42.8
13 F	21 33 16.7	13 19.6	7 16.8	5 32.6	17 28.9	15 29.6	6 41.5	11 31.1	4 20.0	18 25.4	19 40.7	9 42.3
16 M	21 45 6.3	12 18.1	7 20.4	5S 36.6	15 49.6	15 38.7	5 45.3	11 15.7	4 27.1	18 22.7	19 39.4	9 41.7
19 T	21 56 56.0	11 14.8	7 24.1	14 52.1	13 57.7	15 46.5	4 48.6	11 0.2	4 34.3	18 20.0	19 38.1	9 41.1
22 S	22 8 45.7	10 9.8	7 27.7	18 30.6	11 53.3	15 52.4	3 51.7	10 44.5	4 41.7	18 17.4	19 36.8	9 40.4
25 W	22 20 35.3	9 3.5	7 31.3	13 6.6	9 37.1	15 55.9	2 54.6	10 28.8	4 49.3	18 14.8	19 35.5	9 39.6
28 S	22 32 25.0	7 56.0	7 34.9	0 10.4	7 9.9	15 56.6	1 57.4	10 13.1	4 57.1	18 12.2	19 34.3	9 38.9

MARCH 1998

DAY	EPHEMERIS SIDEREAL TIME	☉	☊	☽	☿	♀	♂	♃	♄	♅	♆	♇
	h m s	° ′	° ′	° ′	° ′	° ′	° ′	° ′	° ′	° ′	° ′	° ′
LONGITUDE at NOON												
1 S	22 36 21.5	10♓42.2	10♍34.4	19♈31.1	16♓59.1	27♑43.3	27♓32.5	6♓ 1.0	18♈ 9.2	10♒29.9	1♒ 6.4	8♐ 3.3
2 M	22 40 18.1	11 42.4	10 31.3	4♉15.4	18 54.1	28 25.2	28 19.1	6 15.5	18 15.8	10 33.0	1 8.2	8 3.7
3 T	22 44 14.6	12 42.6	10 28.1	18 41.0	20 49.2	29 8.2	29 5.7	6 29.9	18 22.4	10 36.1	1 10.1	8 3.9
4 W	22 48 11.2	13 42.7	10 24.9	2♊44.8	22 44.1	29 52.2	29 52.2	6 44.3	18 29.1	10 39.2	1 11.9	8 4.2
5 T	22 52 7.7	14 42.9	10 21.7	16 25.9	24 38.7	0♒37.2	0♈38.8	6 58.7	18 35.8	10 42.2	1 13.6	8 4.4
6 F	22 56 4.3	15 43.0	10 18.5	29 44.9	26 32.6	1 23.0	1 25.2	7 13.1	18 42.6	10 45.3	1 15.4	8 4.6
7 S	23 0 0.8	16 43.0	10 15.4	12♋43.9	28 25.4	2 9.8	2 11.7	7 27.4	18 49.4	10 48.3	1 17.1	8 4.7
8 S	23 3 57.4	17 43.0	10 12.2	25 25.3	0♈16.9	2 57.4	2 58.1	7 41.8	18 56.2	10 51.3	1 18.9	8 4.8
9 M	23 7 53.9	18 43.0	10 9.0	7♌52.1	2 6.7	3 45.9	3 44.4	7 56.1	19 3.1	10 54.2	1 20.5	8 4.9
10 T	23 11 50.5	19 42.9	10 5.8	20 6.9	3 54.3	4 35.1	4 30.8	8 10.4	19 10.1	10 57.1	1 22.2	8 4.9
11 W	23 15 47.0	20 42.8	10 2.7	2♍12.3	5 39.2	5 25.1	5 17.0	8 24.7	19 17.0	11 0.0	1 23.9	8 4.9
12 T	23 19 43.6	21 42.7	9 59.5	14 10.5	7 21.0	6 15.8	6 3.3	8 39.0	19 24.1	11 2.9	1 25.5	8 4.9
13 F	23 23 40.1	22 42.6	9 56.3	26 3.6	8 59.2	7 7.2	6 49.5	8 53.3	19 31.1	11 5.7	1 27.1	8R 4.8
14 S	23 27 36.7	23 42.4	9 53.1	7♎53.7	10 33.2	7 59.3	7 35.7	9 7.5	19 38.2	11 8.5	1 28.6	8 4.7
15 S	23 31 33.3	24 42.2	9 49.9	19 42.7	12 2.6	8 52.1	8 21.8	9 21.7	19 45.3	11 11.3	1 30.2	8 4.6
16 M	23 35 29.8	25 41.9	9 46.8	1♏33.1	13 26.8	9 45.5	9 7.9	9 35.9	19 52.4	11 14.1	1 31.7	8 4.4
17 T	23 39 26.4	26 41.6	9 43.6	13 27.3	14 45.4	10 39.5	9 53.9	9 50.0	19 59.6	11 16.8	1 33.2	8 4.2
18 W	23 43 22.9	27 41.3	9 40.4	25 28.5	15 58.0	11 34.1	10 39.9	10 4.2	20 6.8	11 19.5	1 34.7	8 4.0
19 T	23 47 19.5	28 41.0	9 37.2	7♐39.9	17 4.2	12 29.2	11 25.9	10 18.3	20 14.1	11 22.1	1 36.1	8 3.7
20 F	23 51 16.0	29 40.6	9 34.1	20 5.5	18 3.5	13 24.9	12 11.8	10 32.3	20 21.3	11 24.7	1 37.5	8 3.4
21 S	23 55 12.6	0♈40.2	9 30.9	2♑49.0	18 55.7	14 21.1	12 57.7	10 46.4	20 28.6	11 27.3	1 38.9	8 3.0
22 S	23 59 9.1	1 39.8	9 27.7	15 54.2	19 40.6	15 17.9	13 43.6	11 0.4	20 36.0	11 29.9	1 40.3	8 2.7
23 M	0 3 5.7	2 39.4	9 24.5	29 24.2	20 17.9	16 15.1	14 29.4	11 14.4	20 43.3	11 32.4	1 41.7	8 2.3
24 T	0 7 2.2	3 38.9	9 21.3	13♒20.8	20 47.4	17 12.7	15 15.2	11 28.3	20 50.7	11 34.9	1 43.0	8 1.9
25 W	0 10 58.8	4 38.4	9 18.2	27 43.7	21 9.1	18 10.8	16 0.9	11 42.2	20 58.1	11 37.3	1 44.2	8 1.4
26 T	0 14 55.3	5 37.8	9 15.0	12♓30.2	21 23.1	19 9.3	16 46.6	11 56.1	21 5.5	11 39.7	1 45.5	8 0.9
27 F	0 18 51.9	6 37.2	9 11.8	27 34.6	21 29.3	20 8.2	17 32.3	12 9.9	21 12.9	11 42.1	1 46.7	8 0.4
28 S	0 22 48.4	7 36.6	9 8.6	12♈48.5	21R27.9	21 7.5	18 17.9	12 23.7	21 20.4	11 44.4	1 47.9	7 59.8
29 S	0 26 45.0	8 36.0	9 5.5	28 1.9	21 19.3	22 7.2	19 3.4	12 37.4	21 27.9	11 46.7	1 49.1	7 59.2
30 M	0 30 41.5	9 35.3	9 2.3	13♉ 4.6	21 3.6	23 7.3	19 48.9	12 51.1	21 35.3	11 49.0	1 50.2	7 58.6
31 T	0 34 38.1	10 34.6	8 59.1	27 48.1	20 41.5	24 7.7	20 34.4	13 4.8	21 42.8	11 51.2	1 51.3	7 57.9
DECLINATION at NOON												
1 S	22 36 21.5	7S33.2	7N36.1	4N32.6	6S18.7	15S56.1	1S38.3	10S 7.8	4N59.7	18S11.4	19S33.9	9S38.6
4 W	22 48 11.2	6 24.3	7 39.7	15 33.2	3 40.1	15 52.3	0 41.2	9 52.0	5 7.6	18 8.9	19 32.7	9 37.7
7 S	23 0 0.8	5 14.6	7 43.3	18 21.6	0 56.9	15 45.0	0N15.9	9 36.2	5 15.6	18 6.5	19 31.5	9 36.8
10 T	23 11 50.5	4 4.3	7 46.9	13 0.9	1N45.9	15 33.7	1 12.8	9 20.3	5 23.8	18 4.1	19 30.4	9 35.9
13 F	23 23 40.1	2 53.6	7 50.5	2 51.8	4 21.6	15 18.5	2 9.4	9 4.5	5 32.0	18 1.8	19 29.4	9 34.9
16 M	23 35 29.8	1 42.6	7 54.1	8S 9.6	6 42.5	14 59.0	3 5.7	8 48.7	5 40.3	17 59.6	19 28.3	9 33.9
19 T	23 47 19.5	0 31.4	7 57.7	16 23.7	8 41.3	14 35.3	4 1.5	8 33.0	5 48.6	17 57.5	19 27.4	9 32.8
22 S	23 59 9.1	0N39.7	8 1.3	18 13.8	10 11.4	14 7.4	4 56.9	8 17.3	5 57.0	17 55.4	19 26.4	9 31.8
25 W	0 10 58.8	1 50.6	8 4.9	11 10.4	11 8.0	13 35.2	5 51.7	8 1.7	6 5.5	17 53.4	19 25.6	9 30.7
28 S	0 22 48.4	3 1.2	8 8.4	2N28.1	11 27.9	12 58.9	6 45.8	7 46.2	6 14.0	17 51.5	19 24.8	9 29.6
31 T	0 34 38.1	4 11.2	8 12.0	14 41.7	11 10.5	12 18.6	7 39.2	7 30.7	6 22.5	17 49.7	19 24.0	9 28.5

APRIL 1998

DAY	EPHEMERIS SIDEREAL TIME	☉	☊	☽	☿	♀	♂	♃	♄	♅	♆	♇
LONGITUDE at NOON												
1 W	0 38 34.6	11♈33.8	8♍55.9	12♊ 6.5	20♈13.4	25♒ 8.4	21♈19.8	13♓18.4	21♈50.4	11♒53.4	1♒52.4	7♐57.2
2 T	0 42 31.2	12 33.0	8 52.7	25 57.1	19R40.0	26 9.4	22 5.2	13 31.9	21 57.9	11 55.5	1 53.4	7R56.5
3 F	0 46 27.7	13 32.2	8 49.6	9♋20.0	19 2.0	27 10.8	22 50.5	13 45.4	22 5.4	11 57.6	1 54.4	7 55.8
4 S	0 50 24.3	14 31.3	8 46.4	22 17.5	18 20.3	28 12.5	23 35.8	13 58.9	22 13.0	11 59.6	1 55.4	7 55.0
5 S	0 54 20.8	15 30.4	8 43.2	4♌53.3	17 35.8	29 14.5	24 21.0	14 12.3	22 20.5	12 1.6	1 56.4	7 54.2
6 M	0 58 17.4	16 29.5	8 40.0	17 11.6	16 49.3	0♓16.7	25 6.1	14 25.6	22 28.1	12 3.6	1 57.3	7 53.3
7 T	1 2 13.9	17 28.5	8 36.8	29 16.8	16 1.9	1 19.3	25 51.3	14 38.9	22 35.7	12 5.5	1 58.2	7 52.5
8 W	1 6 10.5	18 27.5	8 33.7	11♍13.0	15 14.4	2 22.1	26 36.3	14 52.1	22 43.3	12 7.4	1 59.0	7 51.6
9 T	1 10 7.0	19 26.4	8 30.5	23 3.8	14 27.7	3 25.1	27 21.4	15 5.3	22 50.9	12 9.2	1 59.8	7 50.7
10 F	1 14 3.6	20 25.3	8 27.3	4♎52.4	13 42.8	4 28.5	28 6.3	15 18.4	22 58.4	12 11.0	2 0.6	7 49.7
11 S	1 18 0.2	21 24.2	8 24.1	16 41.3	13 0.3	5 32.0	28 51.2	15 31.5	23 6.0	12 12.8	2 1.4	7 48.7
12 S	1 21 56.7	22 23.0	8 21.0	28 32.6	12 21.0	6 35.9	29 36.2	15 44.5	23 13.7	12 14.5	2 2.2	7 47.8
13 M	1 25 53.3	23 21.8	8 17.8	10♏27.9	11 45.3	7 39.9	0♉21.0	15 57.5	23 21.3	12 16.2	2 2.9	7 46.8
14 T	1 29 49.8	24 20.6	8 14.6	22 29.0	11 13.9	8 44.2	1 5.8	16 10.4	23 28.9	12 17.8	2 3.5	7 45.7
15 W	1 33 46.4	25 19.4	8 11.4	4♐37.6	10 47.0	9 48.7	1 50.5	16 23.2	23 36.5	12 19.4	2 4.2	7 44.6
16 T	1 37 42.9	26 18.1	8 8.2	16 55.6	10 24.9	10 53.4	2 35.2	16 35.9	23 44.1	12 20.9	2 4.8	7 43.5
17 F	1 41 39.5	27 16.7	8 5.1	29 25.3	10 7.8	11 58.3	3 19.8	16 48.6	23 51.7	12 22.4	2 5.3	7 42.4
18 S	1 45 36.0	28 15.4	8 1.9	12♑ 9.6	9 55.9	13 3.4	4 4.4	17 1.2	23 59.3	12 23.8	2 5.9	7 41.3
19 S	1 49 32.6	29 14.0	7 58.7	25 11.4	9 49.1	14 8.7	4 48.9	17 13.8	24 6.8	12 25.2	2 6.4	7 40.1
20 M	1 53 29.1	0♉12.6	7 55.5	8♒33.7	9 47.5	15 14.2	5 33.4	17 26.2	24 14.4	12 26.6	2 6.9	7 38.9
21 T	1 57 25.7	1 11.2	7 52.4	22 18.9	9D51.0	16 19.9	6 17.8	17 38.6	24 22.0	12 27.9	2 7.3	7 37.7
22 W	2 1 22.2	2 9.7	7 49.2	6♓28.4	9 59.5	17 25.7	7 2.2	17 51.0	24 29.6	12 29.1	2 7.7	7 36.4
23 T	2 5 18.8	3 8.2	7 46.0	21 1.5	10 12.9	18 31.7	7 46.5	18 3.2	24 37.1	12 30.3	2 8.1	7 35.2
24 F	2 9 15.3	4 6.7	7 42.8	5♈54.7	10 31.0	19 37.9	8 30.8	18 15.4	24 44.6	12 31.5	2 8.4	7 33.9
25 S	2 13 11.9	5 5.2	7 39.6	21 1.8	10 53.7	20 44.3	9 15.1	18 27.5	24 52.2	12 32.6	2 8.7	7 32.6
26 S	2 17 8.4	6 3.6	7 36.5	6♉13.7	11 20.7	21 50.7	9 59.3	18 39.5	24 59.7	12 33.6	2 9.0	7 31.3
27 M	2 21 5.0	7 2.0	7 33.3	21 20.1	11 52.0	22 57.3	10 43.4	18 51.4	25 7.2	12 34.6	2 9.2	7 29.9
28 T	2 25 1.6	8 0.4	7 30.1	6♊11.0	12 27.3	24 4.1	11 27.5	19 3.3	25 14.7	12 35.6	2 9.4	7 28.6
29 W	2 28 58.1	8 58.7	7 26.9	20 38.5	13 6.5	25 11.0	12 11.5	19 15.0	25 22.2	12 36.5	2 9.6	7 27.2
30 T	2 32 54.7	9 57.0	7 23.8	4♋37.8	13 49.5	26 18.0	12 55.5	19 26.7	25 29.6	12 37.3	2 9.7	7 25.8
DECLINATION at NOON												
1 W	0 38 34.6	4N34.4	8N13.2	17N 4.1	10N56.8	12S 4.3	7N56.8	7S25.6	6N25.3	17S49.2	19S23.8	9S28.1
4 S	0 50 24.3	5 43.4	8 16.8	17 46.3	9 55.4	11 18.8	8 49.1	7 10.4	6 33.8	17 47.5	19 23.1	9 27.0
7 T	1 2 13.9	6 51.6	8 20.4	10 48.1	8 31.2	10 29.6	9 40.5	6 55.3	6 42.3	17 45.9	19 22.5	9 25.9
10 F	1 14 3.6	7 58.6	8 23.9	0 3.6	6 57.1	9 37.0	10 30.9	6 40.4	6 50.7	17 44.5	19 21.9	9 24.8
13 M	1 25 53.3	9 4.5	8 27.5	10S41.6	5 26.3	8 41.0	11 20.4	6 25.7	6 59.1	17 43.1	19 21.4	9 23.7
16 T	1 37 42.9	10 9.0	8 31.1	17 43.6	4 9.5	7 41.9	12 8.7	6 11.2	7 7.5	17 41.9	19 21.0	9 22.5
19 S	1 49 32.6	11 12.0	8 34.6	17 34.6	3 13.2	6 40.0	12 55.9	5 56.9	7 15.8	17 40.8	19 20.6	9 21.5
22 W	2 1 22.2	12 13.4	8 38.2	8 54.3	2 40.1	5 35.6	13 41.8	5 42.8	7 24.1	17 39.8	19 20.3	9 20.4
25 S	2 13 11.9	13 13.0	8 41.7	5N 2.4	2 30.1	4 28.8	14 26.5	5 29.0	7 32.2	17 39.0	19 20.1	9 19.3
28 T	2 25 1.6	14 10.6	8 45.3	16 20.0	2 42.0	3 20.0	15 9.9	5 15.4	7 40.3	17 38.2	19 19.9	9 18.3

MAY 1998

DAY	EPHEMERIS SIDEREAL TIME	☉	☊	☽	☿	♀	♂	♃	♄	♅	♆	♇
	h m s	° ′	° ′	° ′	° ′	° ′	° ′	° ′	° ′	° ′	° ′	° ′
						LONGITUDE at NOON						
1 F	2 36 51.2	10♉55.3	7♍20.6	18♋ 7.6	14♈36.0	27♓25.2	13♉39.4	19♓38.3	25♈37.1	12♒38.2	2♒ 9.8	7♐24.4
2 S	2 40 47.8	11 53.5	7 17.4	1♌ 9.3	15 25.9	28 32.4	14 23.3	19 49.8	25 44.5	12 38.9	2 9.9	7R22.9
3 S	2 44 44.3	12 51.8	7 14.2	13 46.6	16 19.1	29 39.9	15 7.2	20 1.2	25 51.9	12 39.7	2 10.0	7 21.5
4 M	2 48 40.9	13 49.9	7 11.0	26 3.9	17 15.5	0♈47.4	15 50.9	20 12.5	25 59.3	12 40.3	2 10.0	7 20.1
5 T	2 52 37.4	14 48.0	7 7.9	8♍ 6.6	18 14.9	1 55.0	16 34.6	20 23.7	26 6.6	12 41.0	2 10.0	7 18.6
6 W	2 56 34.0	15 46.2	7 4.7	19 59.8	19 17.2	3 2.8	17 18.3	20 34.9	26 14.0	12 41.5	2R 9.9	7 17.1
7 T	3 0 30.5	16 44.2	7 1.5	1♎48.2	20 22.3	4 10.6	18 1.9	20 45.9	26 21.3	12 42.0	2 9.8	7 15.6
8 F	3 4 27.1	17 42.3	6 58.3	13 36.1	21 30.1	5 18.6	18 45.5	20 56.8	26 28.5	12 42.5	2 9.7	7 14.1
9 S	3 8 23.6	18 40.3	6 55.2	25 26.7	22 40.6	6 26.6	19 29.0	21 7.6	26 35.8	12 42.9	2 9.6	7 12.6
10 S	3 12 20.2	19 38.2	6 52.0	7♏22.7	23 53.7	7 34.8	20 12.4	21 18.4	26 43.0	12 43.3	2 9.4	7 11.0
11 M	3 16 16.8	20 36.2	6 48.8	19 25.9	25 9.3	8 43.0	20 55.8	21 29.0	26 50.2	12 43.6	2 9.1	7 9.5
12 T	3 20 13.3	21 34.1	6 45.6	1♐37.6	26 27.3	9 51.4	21 39.1	21 39.5	26 57.4	12 43.9	2 8.9	7 7.9
13 W	3 24 9.9	22 32.0	6 42.4	13 58.6	27 47.7	10 59.9	22 22.4	21 49.9	27 4.5	12 44.1	2 8.6	7 6.4
14 T	3 28 6.4	23 29.9	6 39.3	26 29.6	29 10.5	12 8.4	23 5.7	22 0.2	27 11.6	12 44.3	2 8.3	7 4.8
15 F	3 32 3.0	24 27.8	6 36.1	9♑11.5	0♉35.5	13 17.1	23 48.9	22 10.4	27 18.7	12 44.4	2 8.0	7 3.2
16 S	3 35 59.5	25 25.6	6 32.9	22 5.3	2 2.9	14 25.8	24 32.0	22 20.5	27 25.7	12 44.5	2 7.6	7 1.6
17 S	3 39 56.1	26 23.4	6 29.7	5♒12.6	3 32.5	15 34.7	25 15.1	22 30.5	27 32.7	12 44.5	2 7.2	6 60.0
18 M	3 43 52.6	27 21.2	6 26.6	18 35.4	5 4.4	16 43.6	25 58.1	22 40.4	27 39.7	12 44.5	2 6.7	6 58.4
19 T	3 47 49.2	28 19.0	6 23.4	2♓15.4	6 38.5	17 52.6	26 41.1	22 50.1	27 46.6	12R44.4	2 6.3	6 56.8
20 W	3 51 45.8	29 16.7	6 20.2	16 14.2	8 14.8	19 1.7	27 24.0	22 59.8	27 53.5	12 44.3	2 5.8	6 55.1
21 T	3 55 42.3	0♊14.5	6 17.0	0♈32.0	9 53.3	20 10.9	28 6.9	23 9.3	28 0.3	12 44.1	2 5.2	6 53.5
22 F	3 59 38.9	1 12.2	6 13.9	15 7.2	11 34.0	21 20.1	28 49.8	23 18.7	28 7.1	12 43.9	2 4.7	6 51.9
23 S	4 3 35.4	2 9.9	6 10.7	29 55.6	13 17.0	22 29.4	29 32.6	23 28.0	28 13.9	12 43.6	2 4.1	6 50.2
24 S	4 7 32.0	3 7.6	6 7.5	14♉50.6	15 2.2	23 38.9	0♊15.4	23 37.2	28 20.7	12 43.3	2 3.5	6 48.7
25 M	4 11 28.5	4 5.3	6 4.3	29 43.8	16 49.5	24 48.4	0 58.0	23 46.2	28 27.4	12 42.9	2 2.9	6 47.0
26 T	4 15 25.1	5 2.9	6 1.1	14♊26.1	18 39.0	25 57.9	1 40.7	23 55.1	28 34.0	12 42.5	2 2.2	6 45.4
27 W	4 19 21.6	6 0.6	5 58.0	28 49.5	20 30.7	27 7.5	2 23.3	24 3.8	28 40.6	12 42.1	2 1.5	6 43.7
28 T	4 23 18.2	6 58.2	5 54.8	12♋48.4	22 24.5	28 17.1	3 5.8	24 12.5	28 47.2	12 41.5	2 0.7	6 42.1
29 F	4 27 14.8	7 55.7	5 51.6	26 20.1	24 20.5	29 26.9	3 48.3	24 21.0	28 53.7	12 41.0	1 60.0	6 40.4
30 S	4 31 11.3	8 53.3	5 48.4	9♌24.6	26 18.5	0♉36.6	4 30.7	24 29.4	29 0.1	12 40.4	1 59.2	6 38.8
31 S	4 35 7.9	9 50.8	5 45.3	22 4.6	28 18.6	1 46.5	5 13.1	24 37.6	29 6.5	12 39.7	1 58.4	6 37.2
						DECLINATION at NOON						
1 F	2 36 51.2	15N 6.1	8N48.8	18N19.6	3N13.5	2S 9.5	15N51.8	5S 2.2	7N48.2	17S37.6	19S19.8	9S17.3
4 M	2 48 40.9	15 59.3	8 52.3	11 48.5	4 2.4	0 57.4	16 32.4	4 49.3	7 56.1	17 37.1	19 19.8	9 16.4
7 T	3 0 30.5	16 50.2	8 55.9	1 8.6	5 6.6	0N15.8	17 11.4	4 36.7	8 3.8	17 36.7	19 19.8	9 15.5
10 S	3 12 20.2	17 38.5	8 59.4	9S52.1	6 24.1	1 29.9	17 48.9	4 24.4	8 11.4	17 36.5	19 19.9	9 14.6
13 W	3 24 9.9	18 24.2	9 2.9	17 31.5	7 53.0	2 44.7	18 24.7	4 12.6	8 18.9	17 36.3	19 20.1	9 13.8
16 S	3 35 59.5	19 7.0	9 6.5	18 7.4	9 31.6	3 59.8	18 59.0	4 1.1	8 26.2	17 36.3	19 20.3	9 13.0
19 T	3 47 49.2	19 47.0	9 10.0	10 18.1	11 18.0	5 15.0	19 31.5	3 50.0	8 33.4	17 36.5	19 20.6	9 12.3
22 F	3 59 38.9	20 23.9	9 13.5	3N 3.7	13 10.2	6 29.9	20 2.4	3 39.3	8 40.3	17 36.7	19 21.0	9 11.6
25 M	4 11 28.5	20 57.7	9 17.0	15 13.5	15 6.1	7 44.3	20 31.5	3 29.1	8 47.2	17 37.1	19 21.4	9 11.0
28 T	4 23 18.2	21 28.3	9 20.5	18 49.8	17 2.7	8 57.7	20 58.8	3 19.3	8 53.8	17 37.6	19 21.8	9 10.5
31 S	4 35 7.9	21 55.5	9 24.0	13 2.4	18 56.5	10 10.0	21 24.3	3 10.0	9 0.2	17 38.2	19 22.4	9 10.0

JUNE 1998

DAY	EPHEMERIS SIDEREAL TIME	☉	☊	☽	☿	♀	♂	♃	♄	♅	♆	♇
						LONGITUDE at NOON						
1 M	4 39 4.4	10♊48.4	5♍42.1	4♍24.1	0♊20.6	2♉56.4	5♊55.4	24♓45.7	29♈12.9	12♒39.0	1♒57.5	6♐35.5
2 T	4 43 1.0	11 45.8	5 38.9	16 28.2	2 24.4	4 6.3	6 37.7	24 53.6	29 19.2	12R38.3	1R56.6	6R33.9
3 W	4 46 57.5	12 43.3	5 35.7	28 22.3	4 30.0	5 16.3	7 19.9	25 1.5	29 25.4	12 37.5	1 55.7	6 32.2
4 T	4 50 54.1	13 40.8	5 32.6	10♎11.7	6 37.1	6 26.4	8 2.1	25 9.1	29 31.6	12 36.6	1 54.8	6 30.6
5 F	4 54 50.7	14 38.2	5 29.4	22 1.4	8 45.6	7 36.5	8 44.2	25 16.7	29 37.7	12 35.8	1 53.9	6 29.0
6 S	4 58 47.2	15 35.6	5 26.2	3♏55.5	10 55.4	8 46.7	9 26.2	25 24.1	29 43.8	12 34.8	1 52.9	6 27.4
7 S	5 2 43.8	16 33.0	5 23.0	15 57.3	13 6.1	9 56.9	10 8.2	25 31.3	29 49.8	12 33.9	1 51.9	6 25.8
8 M	5 6 40.3	17 30.4	5 19.8	28 9.5	15 17.5	11 7.2	10 50.2	25 38.4	29 55.8	12 32.8	1 50.8	6 24.2
9 T	5 10 36.9	18 27.7	5 16.7	10♐33.4	17 29.4	12 17.6	11 32.1	25 45.3	0♉ 1.7	12 31.8	1 49.8	6 22.6
10 W	5 14 33.4	19 25.1	5 13.5	23 9.7	19 41.4	13 28.0	12 14.0	25 52.1	0 7.6	12 30.7	1 48.7	6 21.0
11 T	5 18 30.0	20 22.4	5 10.3	5♑58.3	21 53.4	14 38.4	12 55.8	25 58.8	0 13.4	12 29.5	1 47.6	6 19.4
12 F	5 22 26.6	21 19.7	5 7.1	18 58.7	24 5.1	15 48.9	13 37.5	26 5.3	0 19.1	12 28.4	1 46.5	6 17.8
13 S	5 26 23.1	22 17.1	5 4.0	2♒10.5	26 16.1	16 59.5	14 19.2	26 11.6	0 24.8	12 27.1	1 45.4	6 16.3
14 S	5 30 19.7	23 14.4	5 0.8	15 33.4	28 26.4	18 10.1	15 1.0	26 17.8	0 30.4	12 25.9	1 44.2	6 14.7
15 M	5 34 16.2	24 11.7	4 57.6	29 7.4	0♋35.4	19 20.8	15 42.6	26 23.8	0 36.0	12 24.6	1 43.1	6 13.2
16 T	5 38 12.8	25 9.0	4 54.4	12♓52.8	2 43.2	20 31.5	16 24.1	26 29.7	0 41.4	12 23.2	1 41.8	6 11.7
17 W	5 42 9.3	26 6.3	4 51.3	26 50.1	4 49.5	21 42.3	17 5.7	26 35.4	0 46.8	12 21.9	1 40.6	6 10.2
18 T	5 46 5.9	27 3.6	4 48.1	10♈59.0	6 54.2	22 53.1	17 47.1	26 40.9	0 52.2	12 20.4	1 39.4	6 8.6
19 F	5 50 2.5	28 0.9	4 44.9	25 18.5	8 57.0	24 4.0	18 28.6	26 46.3	0 57.5	12 19.0	1 38.1	6 7.1
20 S	5 53 59.0	28 58.1	4 41.7	9♉45.9	10 58.0	25 14.9	19 10.0	26 51.5	1 2.7	12 17.5	1 36.8	6 5.7
21 S	5 57 55.6	29 55.4	4 38.5	24 17.1	12 57.1	26 25.9	19 51.3	26 56.5	1 7.8	12 15.9	1 35.5	6 4.2
22 M	6 1 52.1	0♋52.7	4 35.4	8♊46.1	14 54.0	27 36.9	20 32.6	27 1.4	1 12.9	12 14.3	1 34.2	6 2.7
23 T	6 5 48.7	1 49.9	4 32.2	23 6.6	16 48.9	28 48.0	21 13.8	27 6.0	1 17.9	12 12.7	1 32.8	6 1.3
24 W	6 9 45.2	2 47.2	4 29.0	7♋12.5	18 41.7	29 59.1	21 55.0	27 10.5	1 22.8	12 11.1	1 31.5	5 59.9
25 T	6 13 41.8	3 44.4	4 25.8	20 58.8	20 32.2	1♊10.3	22 36.2	27 14.9	1 27.6	12 9.4	1 30.1	5 58.5
26 F	6 17 38.4	4 41.7	4 22.7	4♌22.7	22 20.6	2 21.4	23 17.3	27 19.0	1 32.4	12 7.7	1 28.7	5 57.1
27 S	6 21 34.9	5 38.9	4 19.5	17 23.5	24 6.8	3 32.7	23 58.3	27 23.0	1 37.1	12 5.9	1 27.3	5 55.7
28 S	6 25 31.5	6 36.2	4 16.3	0♍ 2.4	25 50.8	4 44.0	24 39.3	27 26.8	1 41.7	12 4.1	1 25.8	5 54.4
29 M	6 29 28.0	7 33.4	4 13.1	12 22.6	27 32.6	5 55.3	25 20.3	27 30.4	1 46.2	12 2.3	1 24.4	5 53.0
30 T	6 33 24.6	8 30.6	4 10.0	24 28.1	29 12.1	7 6.6	26 1.2	27 33.8	1 50.7	12 0.5	1 22.9	5 51.7
						DECLINATION at NOON						
1 M	4 39 4.4	22N 3.8	9N25.2	9N48.4	19N33.1	10N33.8	21N32.4	3S 7.0	9N 2.3	17S38.4	19S22.6	9S 9.8
4 T	4 50 54.1	22 26.4	9 28.7	1S23.2	21 16.1	11 44.1	21 55.4	2 58.4	9 8.5	17 39.2	19 23.2	9 9.5
7 S	5 2 43.8	22 45.5	9 32.2	12 3.9	22 45.0	12 52.4	22 16.5	2 50.4	9 14.4	17 40.1	19 23.8	9 9.1
10 W	5 14 33.4	23 0.9	9 35.7	18 30.7	23 54.4	13 58.6	22 35.8	2 42.8	9 20.1	17 41.1	19 24.5	9 8.9
13 S	5 26 23.1	23 12.7	9 39.2	17 4.4	24 40.5	15 2.2	22 53.1	2 35.8	9 25.6	17 42.2	19 25.3	9 8.7
16 T	5 38 12.8	23 20.9	9 42.7	7 27.3	25 1.5	16 3.1	23 8.5	2 29.4	9 30.9	17 43.4	19 26.1	9 8.6
19 F	5 50 2.5	23 25.3	9 46.1	6N 5.6	24 57.9	17 0.8	23 22.0	2 23.6	9 35.9	17 44.7	19 26.9	9 8.6
22 M	6 1 52.1	23 26.0	9 49.6	16 46.9	24 32.0	17 55.0	23 33.5	2 18.4	9 40.7	17 46.0	19 27.8	9 8.6
25 T	6 13 41.8	23 23.0	9 53.1	18 25.8	23 47.0	18 45.5	23 43.1	2 13.8	9 45.2	17 47.5	19 28.7	9 8.8
28 S	6 25 31.5	23 16.3	9 56.6	11 13.0	22 46.4	19 31.9	23 50.7	2 9.9	9 49.4	17 49.1	19 29.7	9 9.0

JULY 1998

DAY	EPHEMERIS SIDEREAL TIME h m s	☉ ° ′	☊ ° ′	☾ ° ′	☿ ° ′	♀ ° ′	♂ ° ′	♃ ° ′	♄ ° ′	♅ ° ′	♆ ° ′	♇ ° ′
LONGITUDE at NOON												
1 W	6 37 21.1	9♋27.8	4♍ 6.8	6♎23.9	0♌49.5	8♊18.0	26♊42.0	27♓37.1	1♉55.1	11♒58.6	1♒21.5	5♐50.4
2 T	6 41 17.7	10 25.0	4 3.6	18 15.1	2 24.5	9 29.5	27 22.8	27 40.2	1 59.4	11R56.7	1R20.0	5R49.1
3 F	6 45 14.3	11 22.2	4 0.4	0♏ 6.7	3 57.4	10 41.0	28 3.6	27 43.0	2 3.6	11 54.7	1 18.5	5 47.9
4 S	6 49 10.8	12 19.4	3 57.3	12 3.7	5 27.9	11 52.5	28 44.3	27 45.7	2 7.7	11 52.8	1 17.0	5 46.6
5 S	6 53 7.4	13 16.6	3 54.1	24 10.2	6 56.3	13 4.1	29 25.0	27 48.3	2 11.8	11 50.8	1 15.5	5 45.5
6 M	6 57 3.9	14 13.8	3 50.9	6♐29.5	8 22.2	14 15.7	0♋ 5.6	27 50.6	2 15.8	11 48.8	1 14.0	5 44.3
7 T	7 1 0.5	15 11.0	3 47.7	19 3.8	9 45.9	15 27.3	0 46.2	27 52.7	2 19.7	11 46.8	1 12.4	5 43.1
8 W	7 4 57.0	16 8.2	3 44.5	1♑54.3	11 7.2	16 39.0	1 26.7	27 54.7	2 23.5	11 44.7	1 10.9	5 42.0
9 T	7 8 53.6	17 5.4	3 41.4	15 1.0	12 26.1	17 50.8	2 7.2	27 56.4	2 27.2	11 42.6	1 9.3	5 40.9
10 F	7 12 50.2	18 2.5	3 38.2	28 22.7	13 42.5	19 2.6	2 47.6	27 58.0	2 30.8	11 40.5	1 7.7	5 39.8
11 S	7 16 46.7	18 59.7	3 35.0	11♒57.7	14 56.4	20 14.4	3 28.0	27 59.4	2 34.4	11 38.4	1 6.2	5 38.7
12 S	7 20 43.3	19 56.9	3 31.8	25 43.8	16 7.8	21 26.3	4 8.4	28 0.6	2 37.8	11 36.2	1 4.6	5 37.6
13 M	7 24 39.8	20 54.1	3 28.7	9♓38.8	17 16.5	22 38.2	4 48.7	28 1.5	2 41.2	11 34.0	1 3.0	5 36.6
14 T	7 28 36.4	21 51.3	3 25.5	23 40.7	18 22.5	23 50.1	5 28.9	28 2.3	2 44.4	11 31.8	1 1.4	5 35.6
15 W	7 32 32.9	22 48.5	3 22.3	7♈47.7	19 25.8	25 2.1	6 9.1	28 2.9	2 47.6	11 29.6	0 59.8	5 34.6
16 T	7 36 29.5	23 45.8	3 19.1	21 58.1	20 26.1	26 14.2	6 49.3	28 3.3	2 50.7	11 27.4	0 58.2	5 33.7
17 F	7 40 26.0	24 43.0	3 16.0	6♉10.4	21 23.5	27 26.3	7 29.5	28 3.5	2 53.7	11 25.1	0 56.6	5 32.8
18 S	7 44 22.6	25 40.3	3 12.8	20 22.3	22 17.7	28 38.4	8 9.5	28 3.5	2 56.6	11 22.9	0 54.9	5 31.9
19 S	7 48 19.2	26 37.5	3 9.6	4♊31.2	23 8.8	29 50.6	8 49.6	28R 3.3	2 59.4	11 20.6	0 53.3	5 31.0
20 M	7 52 15.7	27 34.8	3 6.4	18 34.1	23 56.5	1♋ 2.9	9 29.6	28 3.0	3 2.1	11 18.3	0 51.7	5 30.1
21 T	7 56 12.3	28 32.1	3 3.2	2♋27.4	24 40.7	2 15.1	10 9.6	28 2.4	3 4.8	11 16.0	0 50.1	5 29.3
22 W	8 0 8.8	29 29.4	3 0.1	16 7.8	25 21.2	3 27.5	10 49.5	28 1.6	3 7.3	11 13.6	0 48.4	5 28.5
23 T	8 4 5.4	0♌26.7	2 56.9	29 32.6	25 58.0	4 39.8	11 29.4	28 0.6	3 9.7	11 11.3	0 46.8	5 27.8
24 F	8 8 1.9	1 24.0	2 53.7	12♌40.0	26 30.8	5 52.2	12 9.2	27 59.4	3 12.0	11 8.9	0 45.2	5 27.1
25 S	8 11 58.5	2 21.3	2 50.5	25 29.3	26 59.5	7 4.7	12 49.0	27 58.1	3 14.2	11 6.6	0 43.6	5 26.4
26 S	8 15 55.0	3 18.7	2 47.4	8♍ 1.4	27 23.9	8 17.2	13 28.8	27 56.5	3 16.4	11 4.3	0 42.0	5 25.7
27 M	8 19 51.6	4 16.1	2 44.2	20 18.1	27 43.8	9 29.7	14 8.5	27 54.8	3 18.5	11 1.9	0 40.4	5 25.1
28 T	8 23 48.2	5 13.4	2 41.0	2♎22.5	27 59.1	10 42.3	14 48.1	27 52.8	3 20.4	10 59.5	0 38.7	5 24.5
29 W	8 27 44.7	6 10.8	2 37.8	14 18.3	28 9.6	11 54.9	15 27.8	27 50.7	3 22.2	10 57.1	0 37.1	5 23.9
30 T	8 31 41.3	7 8.2	2 34.6	26 10.0	28 15.1	13 7.5	16 7.3	27 48.3	3 23.9	10 54.7	0 35.5	5 23.3
31 F	8 35 37.8	8 5.5	2 31.5	8♏ 2.4	28 15.6	14 20.2	16 46.9	27 45.8	3 25.6	10 52.3	0 33.9	5 22.8
DECLINATION at NOON												
1 W	6 37 21.1	23N 6.0	10N 0.0	0N 3.8	21N33.7	20N14.0	23N56.5	2S 6.6	9N53.4	17S50.7	19S30.7	9S 9.3
4 S	6 49 10.8	22 52.0	10 3.5	10S53.1	20 12.0	20 51.5	24 0.3	2 4.0	9 57.1	17 52.4	19 31.7	9 9.6
7 T	7 1 0.5	22 34.4	10 6.9	18 5.4	18 44.1	21 24.1	24 2.2	2 2.0	10 0.5	17 54.1	19 32.7	9 10.1
10 F	7 12 50.2	22 13.3	10 10.4	17 40.6	17 12.8	21 51.7	24 2.2	2 0.8	10 3.7	17 55.9	19 33.7	9 10.6
13 M	7 24 39.8	21 48.7	10 13.8	8 35.3	15 40.5	22 14.0	24 0.3	2 0.2	10 6.5	17 57.8	19 34.8	9 11.2
16 T	7 36 29.5	21 20.8	10 17.3	4N52.2	14 9.7	22 30.7	23 56.6	2 0.3	10 9.1	17 59.7	19 35.9	9 11.9
19 S	7 48 19.2	20 49.7	10 20.7	15 56.7	12 42.8	22 41.9	23 51.1	2 1.2	10 11.3	18 1.6	19 37.0	9 12.6
22 W	8 0 8.8	20 15.3	10 24.2	18 46.2	11 22.8	22 47.3	23 43.8	2 2.7	10 13.2	18 3.5	19 38.0	9 13.5
25 S	8 11 58.5	19 38.0	10 27.6	12 29.9	10 12.4	22 46.9	23 34.7	2 4.9	10 14.9	18 5.5	19 39.1	9 14.4
28 T	8 23 48.2	18 57.6	10 31.0	1 31.1	9 15.2	22 40.6	23 23.9	2 7.8	10 16.2	18 7.5	19 40.2	9 15.4
31 F	8 35 37.8	18 14.5	10 34.4	9S37.8	8 34.7	22 28.5	23 11.4	2 11.4	10 17.2	18 9.5	19 41.3	9 16.4

AUGUST 1998

DAY	EPHEMERIS SIDEREAL TIME h m s	☉ ° ′	☊ ° ′	☾ ° ′	☿ ° ′	♀ ° ′	♂ ° ′	♃ ° ′	♄ ° ′	♅ ° ′	♆ ° ′	♇ ° ′
LONGITUDE at NOON												
1 S	8 39 34.4	9♌ 2.9	2♍28.3	20♏ 0.1	28♌11.0	15♋32.9	17♋26.3	27♓43.1	3♉27.1	10♒50.0	0♒32.3	5♐22.3
2 S	8 43 30.9	10 0.3	2 25.1	2♐ 7.9	28R 1.2	16 45.7	18 5.8	27R40.2	3 28.5	10R47.6	0R30.7	5R21.9
3 M	8 47 27.5	10 57.7	2 21.9	14 29.8	27 46.1	17 58.5	18 45.2	27 37.1	3 29.8	10 45.2	0 29.1	5 21.5
4 T	8 51 24.0	11 55.2	2 18.8	27 9.2	27 26.0	19 11.3	19 24.5	27 33.8	3 31.1	10 42.8	0 27.5	5 21.1
5 W	8 55 20.6	12 52.6	2 15.6	10♑ 8.4	27 0.8	20 24.2	20 3.8	27 30.3	3 32.2	10 40.4	0 25.9	5 20.7
6 T	8 59 17.2	13 50.0	2 12.4	23 28.3	26 30.8	21 37.1	20 43.1	27 26.7	3 33.2	10 38.0	0 24.3	5 20.4
7 F	9 3 13.7	14 47.5	2 9.2	7♒ 8.2	25 56.3	22 50.1	21 22.3	27 22.9	3 34.1	10 35.6	0 22.8	5 20.1
8 S	9 7 10.3	15 45.0	2 6.1	21 5.9	25 17.7	24 3.1	22 1.5	27 18.9	3 34.9	10 33.2	0 21.2	5 19.8
9 S	9 11 6.8	16 42.5	2 2.9	5♓17.8	24 35.6	25 16.1	22 40.7	27 14.7	3 35.6	10 30.8	0 19.7	5 19.6
10 M	9 15 3.4	17 40.0	1 59.7	19 39.5	23 50.4	26 29.2	23 19.8	27 10.3	3 36.2	10 28.4	0 18.1	5 19.4
11 T	9 18 59.9	18 37.5	1 56.5	4♈ 6.2	23 3.1	27 42.3	23 58.8	27 5.8	3 36.7	10 26.1	0 16.6	5 19.2
12 W	9 22 56.5	19 35.1	1 53.3	18 33.0	22 14.2	28 55.5	24 37.9	27 1.1	3 37.1	10 23.7	0 15.1	5 19.0
13 T	9 26 53.0	20 32.7	1 50.2	2♉56.0	21 24.8	0♌ 8.7	25 16.9	26 56.3	3 37.4	10 21.4	0 13.6	5 18.9
14 F	9 30 49.6	21 30.3	1 47.0	17 11.7	20 35.7	1 22.0	25 55.8	26 51.3	3 37.6	10 19.0	0 12.1	5 18.9
15 S	9 34 46.1	22 27.9	1 43.8	1♊17.7	19 47.9	2 35.3	26 34.7	26 46.1	3 37.6	10 16.7	0 10.6	5 18.8
16 S	9 38 42.7	23 25.6	1 40.6	15 12.3	19 2.5	3 48.7	27 13.7	26 40.8	3 37.6	10 14.4	0 9.2	5D18.9
17 M	9 42 39.2	24 23.3	1 37.5	28 54.2	18 20.2	5 2.1	27 52.5	26 35.3	3R37.5	10 12.1	0 7.7	5 18.9
18 T	9 46 35.8	25 21.0	1 34.3	12♋22.7	17 42.0	6 15.5	28 31.3	26 29.6	3 37.3	10 9.8	0 6.3	5 19.0
19 W	9 50 32.4	26 18.8	1 31.1	25 37.4	17 8.8	7 29.0	29 10.1	26 23.8	3 36.9	10 7.5	0 4.9	5 19.0
20 T	9 54 28.9	27 16.5	1 27.9	8♌38.0	16 41.2	8 42.5	29 48.8	26 17.9	3 36.5	10 5.3	0 3.4	5 19.2
21 F	9 58 25.5	28 14.3	1 24.7	21 24.7	16 20.0	9 56.1	0♌27.5	26 11.8	3 35.9	10 3.0	0 2.1	5 19.3
22 S	10 2 22.0	29 12.1	1 21.6	3♍58.0	16 5.6	11 9.6	1 6.1	26 5.6	3 35.3	10 0.8	0 0.7	5 19.5
23 S	10 6 18.6	0♍10.0	1 18.4	16 18.6	15 58.4	12 23.3	1 44.7	25 59.2	3 34.5	9 58.6	29♑59.3	5 19.8
24 M	10 10 15.1	1 7.8	1 15.2	28 28.1	15D58.9	13 36.9	2 23.3	25 52.8	3 33.6	9 56.4	29 58.0	5 20.0
25 T	10 14 11.7	2 5.7	1 12.0	10♎28.5	16 7.2	14 50.6	3 1.8	25 46.2	3 32.6	9 54.2	29 56.7	5 20.3
26 W	10 18 8.2	3 3.6	1 8.9	22 22.5	16 23.5	16 4.4	3 40.3	25 39.4	3 31.6	9 52.1	29 55.4	5 20.6
27 T	10 22 4.8	4 1.5	1 5.7	4♏13.5	16 47.8	17 18.1	4 18.7	25 32.6	3 30.4	9 50.0	29 54.1	5 21.0
28 F	10 26 1.3	4 59.5	1 2.5	16 5.1	17 20.1	18 31.9	4 57.1	25 25.7	3 29.1	9 47.9	29 52.8	5 21.4
29 S	10 29 57.9	5 57.4	0 59.3	28 1.7	18 0.1	19 45.8	5 35.4	25 18.6	3 27.7	9 45.8	29 51.6	5 21.8
30 S	10 33 54.4	6 55.4	0 56.1	10♐ 7.7	18 47.8	20 59.7	6 13.7	25 11.5	3 26.2	9 43.7	29 50.4	5 22.3
31 M	10 37 51.0	7 53.4	0 53.0	22 27.6	19 43.0	22 13.6	6 52.0	25 4.2	3 24.6	9 41.7	29 49.2	5 22.8
DECLINATION at NOON												
1 S	8 39 34.4	17N59.6	10N35.6	12S47.0	8N25.5	22N23.1	23N 6.9	2S12.7	10N17.5	18S10.1	19S41.7	9S16.8
4 T	8 51 24.0	17 12.9	10 39.0	18 40.1	8 12.7	22 3.1	22 52.3	2 17.2	10 18.1	18 12.1	19 42.7	9 18.0
7 F	9 3 13.7	16 23.7	10 42.4	16 23.0	8 23.6	21 37.4	22 36.1	2 22.3	10 18.4	18 14.1	19 43.8	9 19.2
10 M	9 15 3.4	15 32.2	10 45.8	5 36.8	8 58.1	21 6.1	22 18.3	2 28.0	10 18.3	18 16.0	19 44.8	9 20.5
13 T	9 26 53.0	14 38.4	10 49.2	8N 7.4	9 53.0	20 29.2	21 59.1	2 34.3	10 18.0	18 18.0	19 45.8	9 21.8
16 S	9 38 42.7	13 42.5	10 52.6	17 30.9	11 1.3	19 47.0	21 38.4	2 41.1	10 17.3	18 19.8	19 46.8	9 23.2
19 W	9 50 32.4	12 44.7	10 56.0	17 58.1	12 13.4	18 59.7	21 16.3	2 48.4	10 16.4	18 21.7	19 47.8	9 24.7
22 S	10 2 22.0	11 45.0	10 59.4	10 16.2	13 19.4	18 7.5	20 52.8	2 56.3	10 15.1	18 23.5	19 48.7	9 26.2
25 T	10 14 11.7	10 43.7	11 2.8	1S 4.7	14 10.5	17 10.6	20 28.1	3 4.5	10 13.5	18 25.2	19 49.6	9 27.7
28 F	10 26 1.3	9 40.8	11 6.2	11 45.7	14 40.0	16 9.4	20 2.2	3 13.1	10 11.6	18 26.9	19 50.5	9 29.3
31 M	10 37 51.0	8 36.6	11 9.6	18 17.6	14 42.9	15 4.1	19 35.0	3 22.1	10 9.4	18 28.5	19 51.3	9 31.0

SEPTEMBER 1998

DAY	EPHEMERIS SIDEREAL TIME	☉	☊	☽	☿	♀	♂	♃	♄	♅	♆	♇
	h m s	° ′	° ′	° ′	° ′	° ′	° ′	° ′	° ′	° ′	° ′	° ′
						LONGITUDE at NOON						
1 T	10 41 47.5	8♍51.5	0♍49.8	5♑ 5.7	20♌45.1	23♌27.5	7♌30.2	24♓56.9	3♉23.0	9♒39.7	29♑48.0	5♐23.3
2 W	10 45 44.1	9 49.5	0 46.6	18 5.5	21 54.0	24 41.5	8 8.4	24R49.5	3R21.2	9R37.7	29R46.8	5 23.9
3 T	10 49 40.6	10 47.6	0 43.4	1♒29.5	23 9.2	25 55.5	8 46.6	24 42.0	3 19.3	9 35.8	29 45.7	5 24.5
4 F	10 53 37.2	11 45.7	0 40.3	15 18.3	24 30.2	27 9.5	9 24.7	24 34.5	3 17.3	9 33.9	29 44.6	5 25.1
5 S	10 57 33.8	12 43.8	0 37.1	29 30.8	25 56.5	28 23.6	10 2.7	24 26.8	3 15.2	9 32.0	29 43.5	5 25.8
6 S	11 1 30.3	13 42.0	0 33.9	14♓ 3.2	27 27.8	29 37.8	10 40.8	24 19.2	3 13.1	9 30.2	29 42.5	5 26.5
7 M	11 5 26.9	14 40.2	0 30.7	28 49.7	29 3.2	0♍51.9	11 18.8	24 11.4	3 10.9	9 28.4	29 41.5	5 27.2
8 T	11 9 23.4	15 38.5	0 27.5	13♈43.1	0♍42.5	2 6.1	11 56.7	24 3.7	3 8.5	9 26.6	29 40.4	5 28.0
9 W	11 13 20.0	16 36.7	0 24.4	28 35.3	2 25.0	3 20.3	12 34.7	23 55.8	3 6.1	9 24.8	29 39.5	5 28.8
10 T	11 17 16.5	17 35.0	0 21.2	13♉18.9	4 10.3	4 34.5	13 12.5	23 47.9	3 3.5	9 23.1	29 38.5	5 29.6
11 F	11 21 13.1	18 33.3	0 18.0	27 48.1	5 57.8	5 48.8	13 50.4	23 40.0	3 0.9	9 21.4	29 37.6	5 30.4
12 S	11 25 9.6	19 31.7	0 14.8	11♊58.9	7 47.1	7 3.1	14 28.2	23 32.1	2 58.2	9 19.8	29 36.7	5 31.3
13 S	11 29 6.2	20 30.1	0 11.6	25 49.6	9 37.8	8 17.5	15 5.9	23 24.1	2 55.4	9 18.1	29 35.8	5 32.3
14 M	11 33 2.7	21 28.5	0 8.5	9♋20.3	11 29.6	9 31.8	15 43.6	23 16.1	2 52.5	9 16.6	29 34.9	5 33.2
15 T	11 36 59.3	22 26.9	0 5.3	22 32.0	13 22.1	10 46.3	16 21.3	23 8.1	2 49.5	9 15.0	29 34.1	5 34.2
16 W	11 40 55.8	23 25.4	0 2.1	5♌26.9	15 14.9	12 0.7	16 59.0	23 0.1	2 46.4	9 13.5	29 33.3	5 35.2
17 T	11 44 52.4	24 24.0	29♌58.9	18 7.0	17 7.9	13 15.2	17 36.6	22 52.1	2 43.3	9 12.0	29 32.5	5 36.2
18 F	11 48 48.9	25 22.5	29 55.8	0♍34.6	19 0.9	14 29.7	18 14.1	22 44.1	2 40.0	9 10.6	29 31.8	5 37.3
19 S	11 52 45.5	26 21.1	29 52.6	12 51.6	20 53.6	15 44.2	18 51.7	22 36.2	2 36.7	9 9.2	29 31.1	5 38.4
20 S	11 56 42.0	27 19.8	29 49.4	24 59.8	22 45.9	16 58.8	19 29.1	22 28.2	2 33.3	9 7.9	29 30.4	5 39.6
21 M	12 0 38.6	28 18.4	29 46.2	7♎ 0.7	24 37.7	18 13.3	20 6.6	22 20.3	2 29.8	9 6.6	29 29.7	5 40.7
22 T	12 4 35.1	29 17.1	29 43.0	18 56.2	26 28.8	19 28.0	20 44.0	22 12.4	2 26.3	9 5.3	29 29.1	5 41.9
23 W	12 8 31.7	0♎15.9	29 39.9	0♏48.0	28 19.2	20 42.6	21 21.3	22 4.5	2 22.7	9 4.1	29 28.5	5 43.1
24 T	12 12 28.2	1 14.6	29 36.7	12 38.3	0♎ 8.9	21 57.2	21 58.6	21 56.7	2 19.0	9 2.9	29 27.9	5 44.4
25 F	12 16 24.8	2 13.4	29 33.5	24 29.8	1 57.8	23 11.9	22 35.9	21 49.0	2 15.2	9 1.7	29 27.4	5 45.7
26 S	12 20 21.3	3 12.2	29 30.3	6♐25.7	3 45.8	24 26.6	23 13.1	21 41.3	2 11.4	9 0.6	29 26.9	5 47.0
27 S	12 24 17.9	4 11.1	29 27.2	18 29.7	5 32.9	25 41.4	23 50.3	21 33.7	2 7.6	8 59.6	29 26.5	5 48.4
28 M	12 28 14.4	5 10.0	29 24.0	0♑45.9	7 19.2	26 56.1	24 27.5	21 26.1	2 3.6	8 58.6	29 26.0	5 49.8
29 T	12 32 11.0	6 8.9	29 20.8	13 18.8	9 4.5	28 10.9	25 4.6	21 18.6	1 59.6	8 57.7	29 25.6	5 51.2
30 W	12 36 7.6	7 7.9	29 17.6	26 12.8	10 49.0	29 25.7	25 41.6	21 11.2	1 55.5	8 56.8	29 25.3	5 52.6
						DECLINATION at NOON						
1 T	10 41 47.5	8N14.9	11N10.7	18S56.3	14N37.5	14N41.4	19N25.7	3S25.1	10N 8.6	18S29.0	19S51.6	9S31.6
4 F	10 53 37.2	7 9.1	11 14.1	14 50.1	14 1.4	13 31.1	18 57.1	3 34.4	10 6.1	18 30.6	19 52.3	9 33.3
7 M	11 5 26.9	6 2.1	11 17.4	2 41.5	12 56.5	12 17.4	18 27.3	3 43.8	10 3.3	18 32.0	19 53.0	9 35.0
10 T	11 17 16.5	4 54.4	11 20.8	11N 3.4	11 26.0	11 0.5	17 56.6	3 53.4	10 0.2	18 33.3	19 53.7	9 36.8
13 S	11 29 6.2	3 45.8	11 24.2	18 34.9	9 35.1	9 40.9	17 24.9	4 3.1	9 56.8	18 34.6	19 54.3	9 38.6
16 W	11 40 55.8	2 36.6	11 27.5	16 40.1	7 29.4	8 18.8	16 52.3	4 12.7	9 53.3	18 35.8	19 54.9	9 40.5
19 S	11 52 45.5	1 27.0	11 30.9	7 41.5	5 14.4	6 54.6	16 18.8	4 22.2	9 49.5	18 36.9	19 55.4	9 42.3
22 T	12 4 35.1	0 17.1	11 34.2	3S50.7	2 54.2	5 28.6	15 44.6	4 31.7	9 45.5	18 37.8	19 55.9	9 44.2
25 F	12 16 24.8	0S53.0	11 37.6	13 52.7	0 32.3	4 1.0	15 9.6	4 40.9	9 41.3	18 38.7	19 56.3	9 46.1
28 M	12 28 14.4	2 3.2	11 40.9	18 55.3	1S49.0	2 32.3	14 33.9	4 49.8	9 36.9	18 39.5	19 56.7	9 48.0

OCTOBER 1998

DAY	EPHEMERIS SIDEREAL TIME	☉	☊	☽	☿	♀	♂	♃	♄	♅	♆	♇
						LONGITUDE at NOON						
1 T	12 40 4.1	8♎ 6.8	29♌14.4	9♒31.6	12♎32.6	0♎40.5	26♌18.6	21♓ 3.9	1♉51.4	8♒55.9	29♑24.9	5♐54.0
2 F	12 44 0.7	9 5.8	29 11.3	23 17.7	14 15.3	1 55.3	26 55.6	20R56.7	1R47.2	8R55.1	29R24.6	5 55.5
3 S	12 47 57.2	10 4.8	29 8.1	7♓31.7	15 57.1	3 10.1	27 32.5	20 49.5	1 43.0	8 54.3	29 24.3	5 57.0
4 S	12 51 53.8	11 3.9	29 4.9	22 11.4	17 38.1	4 25.0	28 9.3	20 42.5	1 38.7	8 53.6	29 24.1	5 58.6
5 M	12 55 50.3	12 3.0	29 1.7	7♈11.5	19 18.2	5 39.9	28 46.2	20 35.6	1 34.3	8 52.9	29 23.9	6 0.1
6 T	12 59 46.9	13 2.1	28 58.5	22 23.7	20 57.5	6 54.8	29 23.0	20 28.8	1 30.0	8 52.3	29 23.7	6 1.7
7 W	13 3 43.4	14 1.2	28 55.4	7♉37.7	22 36.0	8 9.7	29 59.7	20 22.1	1 25.5	8 51.7	29 23.5	6 3.3
8 T	13 7 40.0	15 0.4	28 52.2	22 43.0	24 13.7	9 24.6	0♍36.4	20 15.5	1 21.1	8 51.1	29 23.4	6 5.0
9 F	13 11 36.5	15 59.7	28 49.0	7♊30.7	25 50.7	10 39.6	1 13.0	20 9.1	1 16.5	8 50.6	29 23.3	6 6.6
10 S	13 15 33.1	16 58.9	28 45.8	21 54.5	27 26.9	11 54.5	1 49.7	20 2.7	1 12.0	8 50.2	29 23.3	6 8.3
11 S	13 19 29.6	17 58.2	28 42.7	5♋51.6	29 2.4	13 9.5	2 26.2	19 56.5	1 7.4	8 49.8	29 23.2	6 10.0
12 M	13 23 26.2	18 57.6	28 39.5	19 21.9	0♏37.1	14 24.5	3 2.7	19 50.5	1 2.8	8 49.5	29D23.3	6 11.8
13 T	13 27 22.7	19 57.0	28 36.3	2♌27.7	2 11.2	15 39.6	3 39.2	19 44.6	0 58.2	8 49.2	29 23.3	6 13.5
14 W	13 31 19.3	20 56.4	28 33.1	15 12.3	3 44.5	16 54.6	4 15.7	19 38.8	0 53.5	8 48.9	29 23.4	6 15.3
15 T	13 35 15.8	21 55.9	28 29.9	27 39.9	5 17.2	18 9.7	4 52.0	19 33.2	0 48.8	8 48.7	29 23.5	6 17.1
16 F	13 39 12.4	22 55.3	28 26.8	9♍54.3	6 49.2	19 24.7	5 28.4	19 27.8	0 44.1	8 48.6	29 23.7	6 18.9
17 S	13 43 8.9	23 54.9	28 23.6	21 59.0	8 20.6	20 39.8	6 4.7	19 22.5	0 39.3	8 48.5	29 23.8	6 20.8
18 S	13 47 5.5	24 54.5	28 20.4	3♎57.3	9 51.3	21 55.0	6 41.0	19 17.4	0 34.6	8 48.5	29 24.1	6 22.7
19 M	13 51 2.0	25 54.1	28 17.2	15 51.3	11 21.4	23 10.1	7 17.1	19 12.4	0 29.8	8 48.5	29 24.4	6 24.6
20 T	13 54 58.6	26 53.8	28 14.1	27 43.0	12 50.8	24 25.2	7 53.3	19 7.6	0 25.1	8D48.6	29 24.6	6 26.5
21 W	13 58 55.2	27 53.4	28 10.9	9♏34.1	14 19.5	25 40.4	8 29.4	19 3.0	0 20.3	8 48.7	29 25.0	6 28.4
22 T	14 2 51.7	28 53.1	28 7.7	21 25.9	15 47.6	26 55.5	9 5.4	18 58.6	0 15.5	8 48.9	29 25.3	6 30.4
23 F	14 6 48.3	29 52.9	28 4.5	3♐20.3	17 15.0	28 10.7	9 41.4	18 54.3	0 10.7	8 49.1	29 25.7	6 32.4
24 S	14 10 44.8	0♏52.6	28 1.3	15 19.0	18 41.8	29 25.9	10 17.3	18 50.2	0 5.9	8 49.4	29 26.1	6 34.4
25 S	14 14 41.4	1 52.4	27 58.2	27 24.7	20 7.8	0♏41.1	10 53.2	18 46.3	0 1.1	8 49.7	29 26.6	6 36.4
26 M	14 18 37.9	2 52.3	27 55.0	9♑40.6	21 33.1	1 56.3	11 29.0	18 42.6	29♈56.3	8 50.0	29 27.1	6 38.4
27 T	14 22 34.5	3 52.1	27 51.8	22 10.3	22 57.6	3 11.5	12 4.8	18 39.1	29 51.5	8 50.5	29 27.6	6 40.4
28 W	14 26 31.0	4 52.0	27 48.6	4♒58.1	24 21.3	4 26.7	12 40.5	18 35.8	29 46.7	8 50.9	29 28.2	6 42.5
29 T	14 30 27.6	5 51.9	27 45.5	18 8.1	25 44.2	5 41.9	13 16.1	18 32.6	29 42.0	8 51.5	29 28.7	6 44.6
30 F	14 34 24.1	6 51.8	27 42.3	1♓43.9	27 6.1	6 57.1	13 51.7	18 29.7	29 37.2	8 52.0	29 29.4	6 46.7
31 S	14 38 20.7	7 51.8	27 39.1	15 47.7	28 27.1	8 12.3	14 27.2	18 27.0	29 32.5	8 52.7	29 30.0	6 48.8
						DECLINATION at NOON						
1 T	12 40 4.1	3S13.1	11N44.2	16S 2.0	4S 8.0	1N 2.8	13N57.6	4S58.4	9N32.4	18S40.1	19S57.0	9S49.9
4 S	12 51 53.8	4 22.7	11 47.5	4 49.5	6 23.4	0S27.2	13 20.6	5 6.6	9 27.7	18 40.6	19 57.2	9 51.9
7 W	13 3 43.4	5 31.8	11 50.9	9N34.1	8 34.2	1 57.4	12 43.2	5 14.3	9 22.9	18 41.1	19 57.4	9 53.8
10 S	13 15 33.1	6 40.3	11 54.2	18 24.6	10 39.8	3 27.4	12 5.2	5 21.6	9 18.1	18 41.4	19 57.5	9 55.7
13 T	13 27 22.7	7 48.0	11 57.5	17 15.5	12 39.5	4 56.9	11 26.8	5 28.4	9 13.1	18 41.6	19 57.6	9 57.6
16 F	13 39 12.4	8 54.7	12 0.8	8 38.5	14 32.8	6 25.6	10 48.0	5 34.6	9 8.2	18 41.6	19 57.6	9 59.5
19 M	13 51 2.0	10 0.3	12 4.1	2S52.4	16 19.1	7 53.2	10 8.9	5 40.1	9 3.2	18 41.6	19 57.5	10 1.4
22 T	14 2 51.7	11 4.6	12 7.4	13 16.8	17 57.9	9 19.2	9 29.5	5 45.1	8 58.2	18 41.4	19 57.3	10 3.2
25 S	14 14 41.4	12 7.4	12 10.7	18 57.1	19 28.5	10 43.3	8 49.8	5 49.3	8 53.2	18 41.1	19 57.1	10 5.1
28 W	14 26 31.0	13 8.6	12 14.0	17 0.9	20 50.3	12 5.1	8 10.0	5 52.9	8 48.3	18 40.7	19 56.9	10 6.9
31 S	14 38 20.7	14 7.8	12 17.3	6 57.4	22 2.7	13 24.4	7 30.0	5 55.8	8 43.5	18 40.1	19 56.5	10 8.7

NOVEMBER 1998

DAY	EPHEMERIS SIDEREAL TIME	☉	☊	☽	☿	♀	♂	♃	♄	♅	♆	♇
	h m s	° ′	° ′	° ′	° ′	° ′	° ′	° ′	° ′	° ′	° ′	° ′
LONGITUDE at NOON												
1 S	14 42 17.2	8♏51.8	27♌35.9	0♈19.6	29♏47.1	9♏27.5	15♍ 2.7	18♓24.4	29♈27.8	8♒53.3	29♑30.7	6♐50.9
2 M	14 46 13.8	9 51.8	27 32.7	15 16.0	1♐ 5.9	10 42.8	15 38.1	18R22.1	29R23.1	8 54.1	29 31.4	6 53.0
3 T	14 50 10.4	10 51.9	27 29.6	0♉30.0	2 23.5	11 58.0	16 13.5	18 19.9	29 18.4	8 54.8	29 32.2	6 55.2
4 W	14 54 6.9	11 51.9	27 26.4	15 51.4	3 39.7	13 13.2	16 48.8	18 18.0	29 13.8	8 55.7	29 33.0	6 57.4
5 T	14 58 3.5	12 52.1	27 23.2	1♊ 8.6	4 54.5	14 28.5	17 24.0	18 16.2	29 9.2	8 56.5	29 33.8	6 59.5
6 F	15 2 0.0	13 52.2	27 20.0	16 10.3	6 7.6	15 43.7	17 59.2	18 14.7	29 4.7	8 57.5	29 34.6	7 1.7
7 S	15 5 56.6	14 52.4	27 16.9	0♋47.8	7 18.8	16 59.0	18 34.4	18 13.4	29 0.1	8 58.4	29 35.5	7 3.9
8 S	15 9 53.1	15 52.6	27 13.7	14 56.3	8 28.1	18 14.3	19 9.5	18 12.3	28 55.7	8 59.5	29 36.5	7 6.2
9 M	15 13 49.7	16 52.9	27 10.5	28 34.4	9 35.0	19 29.6	19 44.5	18 11.3	28 51.2	9 0.6	29 37.4	7 8.4
10 T	15 17 46.2	17 53.1	27 7.3	11♌43.7	10 39.4	20 44.9	20 19.5	18 10.6	28 46.8	9 1.7	29 38.4	7 10.7
11 W	15 21 42.8	18 53.4	27 4.2	24 28.1	11 40.9	22 0.2	20 54.3	18 10.1	28 42.5	9 2.9	29 39.4	7 12.9
12 T	15 25 39.3	19 53.8	27 1.0	6♍52.4	12 39.2	23 15.5	21 29.2	18 9.8	28 38.2	9 4.1	29 40.4	7 15.2
13 F	15 29 35.9	20 54.2	26 57.8	19 1.5	13 33.9	24 30.8	22 3.9	18 9.7	28 33.9	9 5.4	29 41.5	7 17.5
14 S	15 33 32.5	21 54.6	26 54.6	1♎ 0.3	14 24.4	25 46.1	22 38.6	18D 9.8	28 29.7	9 6.7	29 42.6	7 19.8
15 S	15 37 29.0	22 55.0	26 51.4	12 53.1	15 10.3	27 1.4	23 13.2	18 10.1	28 25.6	9 8.1	29 43.8	7 22.0
16 M	15 41 25.6	23 55.5	26 48.3	24 43.4	15 51.1	28 16.7	23 47.8	18 10.6	28 21.5	9 9.5	29 44.9	7 24.3
17 T	15 45 22.1	24 56.0	26 45.1	6♏34.0	16 26.0	29 32.1	24 22.3	18 11.3	28 17.4	9 11.0	29 46.1	7 26.6
18 W	15 49 18.7	25 56.5	26 41.9	18 26.7	16 54.4	0♐47.4	24 56.7	18 12.2	28 13.5	9 12.5	29 47.3	7 29.0
19 T	15 53 15.2	26 57.0	26 38.7	0♐23.1	17 15.6	2 2.7	25 31.0	18 13.4	28 9.6	9 14.0	29 48.6	7 31.3
20 F	15 57 11.8	27 57.6	26 35.6	12 24.3	17 28.9	3 18.1	26 5.3	18 14.7	28 5.7	9 15.6	29 49.9	7 33.6
21 S	16 1 8.3	28 58.2	26 32.4	24 31.4	17 33.4	4 33.4	26 39.4	18 16.2	28 2.0	9 17.3	29 51.2	7 35.9
22 S	16 5 4.9	29 58.8	26 29.2	6♑45.6	17R28.4	5 48.8	27 13.5	18 18.0	27 58.3	9 19.0	29 52.5	7 38.3
23 M	16 9 1.5	0♐59.5	26 26.0	19 8.8	17 13.3	7 4.1	27 47.6	18 20.0	27 54.6	9 20.8	29 53.9	7 40.6
24 T	16 12 58.0	2 0.1	26 22.8	1♒43.2	16 47.7	8 19.4	28 21.5	18 22.1	27 51.1	9 22.5	29 55.3	7 42.9
25 W	16 16 54.6	3 0.8	26 19.7	14 32.0	16 11.2	9 34.8	28 55.4	18 24.5	27 47.6	9 24.4	29 56.7	7 45.3
26 T	16 20 51.1	4 1.5	26 16.5	27 38.4	15 24.1	10 50.1	29 29.2	18 27.0	27 44.2	9 26.3	29 58.1	7 47.6
27 F	16 24 47.7	5 2.2	26 13.3	11♓ 5.8	14 26.8	12 5.5	0♎ 2.8	18 29.8	27 40.9	9 28.2	29 59.6	7 50.0
28 S	16 28 44.2	6 2.9	26 10.1	24 56.8	13 20.5	13 20.8	0 36.5	18 32.8	27 37.7	9 30.2	0♒ 1.1	7 52.3
29 S	16 32 40.8	7 3.7	26 7.0	9♈12.6	12 6.6	14 36.2	1 10.0	18 36.0	27 34.6	9 32.2	0 2.7	7 54.7
30 M	16 36 37.4	8 4.5	26 3.8	23 51.8	10 47.3	15 51.5	1 43.5	18 39.3	27 31.6	9 34.3	0 4.2	7 57.1
DECLINATION at NOON												
1 S	14 42 17.2	14S27.1	12N18.3	2S17.5	22S24.6	13S50.2	7N16.6	5S56.6	8N41.9	18S39.9	19S56.4	10S 9.3
4 W	14 54 6.9	15 23.6	12 21.6	11N53.2	23 23.0	15 5.4	6 36.5	5 58.5	8 37.3	18 39.2	19 56.0	10 11.0
7 S	15 5 56.6	16 17.8	12 24.9	19 12.2	24 9.9	16 17.2	5 56.3	5 59.6	8 32.7	18 38.4	19 55.5	10 12.7
10 T	15 17 46.2	17 9.6	12 28.2	15 55.2	24 44.3	17 25.1	5 16.2	6 0.1	8 28.4	18 37.5	19 55.0	10 14.4
13 F	15 29 35.9	17 58.8	12 31.4	6 1.5	25 5.0	18 29.0	4 36.1	5 59.8	8 24.2	18 36.4	19 54.4	10 16.0
16 M	15 41 25.6	18 45.1	12 34.7	5S39.3	25 10.6	19 28.3	3 56.1	5 58.7	8 20.2	18 35.3	19 53.8	10 17.6
19 T	15 53 15.2	19 28.5	12 37.9	15 21.6	24 59.2	20 22.8	3 16.2	5 56.9	8 16.5	18 34.0	19 53.0	10 19.1
22 S	16 5 4.9	20 8.6	12 41.2	19 28.0	24 28.3	21 12.1	2 36.6	5 54.4	8 13.0	18 32.6	19 52.3	10 20.5
25 W	16 16 54.6	20 45.5	12 44.4	15 31.2	23 35.2	21 55.9	1 57.2	5 51.2	8 9.8	18 31.1	19 51.5	10 22.0
28 S	16 28 44.2	21 18.9	12 47.6	4 15.6	22 19.0	22 33.9	1 18.1	5 47.3	8 6.8	18 29.5	19 50.6	10 23.3

DECEMBER 1998

DAY	EPHEMERIS SIDEREAL TIME	☉	☊	☽	☿	♀	♂	♃	♄	♅	♆	♇
LONGITUDE at NOON												
1 T	16 40 33.9	9♐ 5.3	26♌ 0.6	8♉49.8	9♐25.0	17♐ 6.8	2♎16.8	18♓42.9	27♈28.6	9♒36.4	0♒ 5.8	7♐59.4
2 W	16 44 30.5	10 6.1	25 57.4	23 58.9	8R 2.5	18 22.2	2 50.1	18 46.6	27R25.7	9 38.5	0 7.4	8 1.8
3 T	16 48 27.0	11 6.9	25 54.3	9♊ 9.0	6 42.6	19 37.5	3 23.3	18 50.5	27 22.9	9 40.7	0 9.1	8 4.1
4 F	16 52 23.6	12 7.7	25 51.1	24 9.4	5 28.0	20 52.8	3 56.3	18 54.7	27 20.2	9 42.9	0 10.7	8 6.5
5 S	16 56 20.1	13 8.6	25 47.9	8♋50.4	4 20.9	22 8.1	4 29.3	18 59.0	27 17.6	9 45.1	0 12.4	8 8.8
6 S	17 0 16.7	14 9.5	25 44.7	23 5.4	3 23.0	23 23.5	5 2.2	19 3.5	27 15.1	9 47.4	0 14.1	8 11.2
7 M	17 4 13.2	15 10.3	25 41.5	6♌51.3	2 35.7	24 38.8	5 35.1	19 8.2	27 12.7	9 49.8	0 15.8	8 13.5
8 T	17 8 9.8	16 11.3	25 38.4	20 8.1	1 59.5	25 54.1	6 7.8	19 13.0	27 10.4	9 52.2	0 17.6	8 15.8
9 W	17 12 6.4	17 12.2	25 35.2	2♍58.4	1 34.8	27 9.4	6 40.4	19 18.1	27 8.2	9 54.6	0 19.3	8 18.2
10 T	17 16 2.9	18 13.2	25 32.0	15 26.5	1 21.2	28 24.7	7 12.9	19 23.3	27 6.1	9 57.0	0 21.1	8 20.5
11 F	17 19 59.5	19 14.1	25 28.8	27 37.4	1 18.4	29 40.1	7 45.3	19 28.7	27 4.1	9 59.5	0 22.9	8 22.8
12 S	17 23 56.0	20 15.1	25 25.7	9♎36.4	1D25.7	0♑55.4	8 17.6	19 34.3	27 2.2	10 2.0	0 24.8	8 25.1
13 S	17 27 52.6	21 16.1	25 22.5	21 28.6	1 42.3	2 10.7	8 49.8	19 40.1	27 0.3	10 4.6	0 26.6	8 27.4
14 M	17 31 49.1	22 17.2	25 19.3	3♏18.4	2 7.4	3 26.1	9 21.9	19 46.0	26 58.6	10 7.2	0 28.5	8 29.7
15 T	17 35 45.7	23 18.2	25 16.1	15 9.9	2 40.1	4 41.4	9 53.9	19 52.1	26 57.0	10 9.8	0 30.4	8 32.0
16 W	17 39 42.3	24 19.3	25 13.0	27 5.8	3 19.6	5 56.7	10 25.8	19 58.4	26 55.5	10 12.5	0 32.3	8 34.3
17 T	17 43 38.8	25 20.3	25 9.8	9♐ 8.4	4 5.2	7 12.0	10 57.5	20 4.9	26 54.1	10 15.2	0 34.2	8 36.6
18 F	17 47 35.4	26 21.4	25 6.6	21 19.1	4 56.1	8 27.3	11 29.1	20 11.5	26 52.9	10 17.9	0 36.2	8 38.9
19 S	17 51 31.9	27 22.5	25 3.4	3♑38.7	5 51.8	9 42.7	12 0.6	20 18.3	26 51.7	10 20.7	0 38.1	8 41.1
20 S	17 55 28.5	28 23.7	25 0.3	16 7.8	6 51.6	10 58.0	12 32.0	20 25.3	26 50.7	10 23.5	0 40.2	8 43.4
21 M	17 59 25.0	29 24.8	24 57.1	28 46.9	7 55.1	12 13.3	13 3.3	20 32.5	26 49.7	10 26.3	0 42.2	8 45.6
22 T	18 3 21.6	0♑25.9	24 53.9	11♒36.7	9 1.7	13 28.6	13 34.4	20 39.8	26 48.9	10 29.2	0 44.2	8 47.9
23 W	18 7 18.2	1 27.0	24 50.7	24 38.2	10 11.2	14 43.9	14 5.4	20 47.2	26 48.1	10 32.1	0 46.2	8 50.1
24 T	18 11 14.7	2 28.1	24 47.5	7♓53.1	11 23.1	15 59.2	14 36.3	20 54.8	26 47.5	10 35.0	0 48.3	8 52.3
25 F	18 15 11.3	3 29.3	24 44.4	21 22.9	12 37.2	17 14.5	15 7.0	21 2.6	26 47.0	10 37.9	0 50.4	8 54.5
26 S	18 19 7.8	4 30.4	24 41.2	5♈ 9.3	13 53.2	18 29.8	15 37.5	21 10.5	26 46.6	10 40.9	0 52.4	8 56.6
27 S	18 23 4.4	5 31.5	24 38.0	19 12.8	15 10.8	19 45.0	16 8.0	21 18.6	26 46.3	10 43.9	0 54.5	8 58.8
28 M	18 27 0.9	6 32.7	24 34.8	3♉33.0	16 30.0	21 0.3	16 38.3	21 26.8	26 46.1	10 46.9	0 56.6	9 1.0
29 T	18 30 57.5	7 33.8	24 31.7	18 7.1	17 50.5	22 15.5	17 8.4	21 35.1	26 46.0	10 50.0	0 58.8	9 3.1
30 W	18 34 54.1	8 34.9	24 28.5	2♊50.4	19 12.2	23 30.8	17 38.4	21 43.6	26D46.1	10 53.1	1 0.9	9 5.2
31 T	18 38 50.6	9 36.0	24 25.3	17 36.1	20 34.9	24 46.0	18 8.3	21 52.3	26 46.2	10 56.1	1 3.0	9 7.3
DECLINATION at NOON												
1 T	16 40 33.9	21S48.7	12N50.8	9N52.9	20S46.7	23S 6.0	0N39.2	5S42.6	8N 4.2	18S27.7	19S49.6	10S24.6
4 F	16 52 23.6	22 14.6	12 54.1	18 55.2	19 16.9	23 31.8	0 0.8	5 37.3	8 1.9	18 25.9	19 48.6	10 25.8
7 M	17 4 13.2	22 36.8	12 57.3	17 3.2	18 11.8	23 51.1	0S37.2	5 31.4	7 59.9	18 24.0	19 47.6	10 27.0
10 T	17 16 2.9	22 54.9	13 0.5	7 24.0	17 43.1	24 3.9	1 14.8	5 24.8	7 58.2	18 22.0	19 46.5	10 28.1
13 S	17 27 52.6	23 9.0	13 3.7	4S25.8	17 48.5	24 10.0	1 51.9	5 17.5	7 56.9	18 19.9	19 45.4	10 29.1
16 W	17 39 42.3	23 18.9	13 6.9	14 35.3	18 18.9	24 9.4	2 28.4	5 9.7	7 55.9	18 17.7	19 44.2	10 30.1
19 S	17 51 31.9	23 24.7	13 10.1	19 30.0	19 4.4	24 2.1	3 4.4	5 1.2	7 55.3	18 15.4	19 43.0	10 31.0
22 T	18 3 21.6	23 26.2	13 13.3	16 18.3	19 56.9	23 48.0	3 39.7	4 52.2	7 55.1	18 13.1	19 41.8	10 31.8
25 F	18 15 11.3	23 23.5	13 16.5	5 38.8	20 50.6	23 27.4	4 14.4	4 42.6	7 55.2	18 10.7	19 40.5	10 32.6
28 M	18 27 0.9	23 16.5	13 19.6	8N 8.5	21 41.4	23 0.3	4 48.3	4 32.5	7 55.7	18 8.2	19 39.2	10 33.3
31 T	18 38 50.6	23 5.4	13 22.8	18 12.3	22 26.7	22 26.9	5 21.5	4 21.8	7 56.6	18 5.6	19 37.8	10 33.9

JANUARY 1999

LONGITUDE at NOON

DAY	EPHEMERIS SIDEREAL TIME (h m s)	☉ (° ′)	☊ (° ′)	☽ (° ′)	☿ (° ′)	♀ (° ′)	♂ (° ′)	♃ (° ′)	♄ (° ′)	♅ (° ′)	♆ (° ′)	♇ (° ′)
1 F	18 42 47.2	10♑37.2	24♌22.1	2♋16.4	21♐58.7	26♑ 1.2	18♎38.0	22♓ 1.1	26♈46.5	10♒59.3	1♒ 5.2	9♐ 9.4
2 S	18 46 43.7	11 38.3	24 19.0	16 43.5	23 23.3	27 16.4	19 7.5	22 10.0	26 46.9	11 2.4	1 7.4	9 11.4
3 S	18 50 40.3	12 39.4	24 15.8	0♌51.2	24 48.6	28 31.6	19 36.9	22 19.1	26 47.3	11 5.6	1 9.5	9 13.5
4 M	18 54 36.8	13 40.6	24 12.6	14 35.4	26 14.8	29 46.7	20 6.1	22 28.3	26 47.9	11 8.8	1 11.7	9 15.5
5 T	18 58 33.4	14 41.7	24 9.4	27 54.6	27 41.6	1♒ 1.9	20 35.2	22 37.6	26 48.6	11 12.0	1 13.9	9 17.5
6 W	19 2 30.0	15 42.8	24 6.2	10♍49.5	29 9.0	2 17.1	21 4.1	22 47.0	26 49.5	11 15.2	1 16.1	9 19.5
7 T	19 6 26.5	16 44.0	24 3.1	23 22.8	0♑37.1	3 32.2	21 32.8	22 56.6	26 50.4	11 18.5	1 18.3	9 21.5
8 F	19 10 23.1	17 45.1	23 59.9	5♎38.4	2 5.7	4 47.4	22 1.4	23 6.4	26 51.4	11 21.7	1 20.6	9 23.5
9 S	19 14 19.6	18 46.2	23 56.7	17 40.9	3 34.9	6 2.5	22 29.8	23 16.2	26 52.6	11 25.0	1 22.8	9 25.4
10 S	19 18 16.2	19 47.4	23 53.5	29 35.4	5 4.7	7 17.7	22 58.0	23 26.2	26 53.9	11 28.4	1 25.1	9 27.4
11 M	19 22 12.7	20 48.6	23 50.4	11♏26.8	6 34.9	8 32.8	23 26.0	23 36.3	26 55.3	11 31.7	1 27.3	9 29.3
12 T	19 26 9.3	21 49.7	23 47.2	23 19.7	8 5.6	9 47.9	23 53.8	23 46.5	26 56.7	11 35.0	1 29.6	9 31.1
13 W	19 30 5.9	22 50.9	23 44.0	5♐18.2	9 36.9	11 3.0	24 21.4	23 56.9	26 58.3	11 38.4	1 31.8	9 33.0
14 T	19 34 2.4	23 52.0	23 40.8	17 25.7	11 8.6	12 18.0	24 48.8	24 7.3	27 0.0	11 41.7	1 34.1	9 34.8
15 F	19 37 59.0	24 53.1	23 37.7	29 44.7	12 40.9	13 33.1	25 16.0	24 17.9	27 1.8	11 45.1	1 36.4	9 36.6
16 S	19 41 55.5	25 54.2	23 34.5	12♑16.8	14 13.6	14 48.2	25 43.0	24 28.6	27 3.8	11 48.5	1 38.6	9 38.4
17 S	19 45 52.1	26 55.4	23 31.3	25 2.6	15 46.9	16 3.2	26 9.8	24 39.4	27 5.8	11 51.9	1 40.9	9 40.1
18 M	19 49 48.6	27 56.5	23 28.1	8♒ 2.3	17 20.7	17 18.2	26 36.3	24 50.3	27 7.9	11 55.3	1 43.2	9 41.9
19 T	19 53 45.2	28 57.6	23 24.9	21 15.2	18 55.0	18 33.2	27 2.6	25 1.3	27 10.1	11 58.8	1 45.4	9 43.6
20 W	19 57 41.8	29 58.7	23 21.8	4♓40.4	20 29.8	19 48.2	27 28.7	25 12.4	27 12.5	12 2.2	1 47.7	9 45.3
21 T	20 1 38.3	0♒59.8	23 18.6	18 16.9	22 5.2	21 3.1	27 54.6	25 23.6	27 14.9	12 5.6	1 50.0	9 46.9
22 F	20 5 34.9	2 0.8	23 15.4	2♈ 3.6	23 41.2	22 18.1	28 20.2	25 34.9	27 17.5	12 9.1	1 52.3	9 48.5
23 S	20 9 31.4	3 1.9	23 12.2	15 59.7	25 17.7	23 33.0	28 45.6	25 46.4	27 20.1	12 12.6	1 54.5	9 50.2
24 S	20 13 28.0	4 2.9	23 9.1	0♉ 3.9	26 54.8	24 47.9	29 10.7	25 57.9	27 22.9	12 16.0	1 56.8	9 51.7
25 M	20 17 24.5	5 3.9	23 5.9	14 14.9	28 32.5	26 2.8	29 35.5	26 9.5	27 25.8	12 19.5	1 59.1	9 53.3
26 T	20 21 21.1	6 4.9	23 2.7	28 30.4	0♒10.8	27 17.6	0♏ 0.1	26 21.2	27 28.7	12 23.0	2 1.4	9 54.8
27 W	20 25 17.6	7 5.9	22 59.5	12♊47.9	1 49.8	28 32.4	0 24.5	26 33.0	27 31.8	12 26.5	2 3.6	9 56.3
28 T	20 29 14.2	8 6.8	22 56.4	27 3.6	3 29.4	29 47.2	0 48.5	26 44.9	27 34.9	12 30.0	2 5.9	9 57.8
29 F	20 33 10.8	9 7.8	22 53.2	11♋13.5	5 9.6	1♓ 2.0	1 12.3	26 56.9	27 38.2	12 33.5	2 8.2	9 59.2
30 S	20 37 7.3	10 8.7	22 50.0	25 13.4	6 50.6	2 16.7	1 35.8	27 9.0	27 41.6	12 37.0	2 10.4	10 0.6
31 S	20 41 3.9	11 9.6	22 46.8	8♌59.4	8 32.2	3 31.5	1 59.1	27 21.2	27 45.1	12 40.5	2 12.7	10 2.0

DECLINATION at NOON

DAY	EPHEMERIS SIDEREAL TIME (h m s)	☉ (° ′)	☊ (° ′)	☽ (° ′)	☿ (° ′)	♀ (° ′)	♂ (° ′)	♃ (° ′)	♄ (° ′)	♅ (° ′)	♆ (° ′)	♇ (° ′)
1 F	18 42 47.2	23S 0.7	13N23.9	19N26.4	22S40.2	22S14.4	5S32.4	4S18.2	7N56.9	18S 4.7	19S37.4	10S34.0
4 M	18 54 36.8	22 44.1	13 27.0	15 45.7	23 15.0	21 32.9	6 4.6	4 6.9	7 58.3	18 2.1	19 36.0	10 34.5
7 T	19 6 26.5	22 23.4	13 30.2	5 4.4	23 40.5	20 45.7	6 36.0	3 55.1	7 60.0	17 59.4	19 34.6	10 35.0
10 S	19 18 16.2	21 58.7	13 33.3	6S50.4	23 55.8	19 53.0	7 6.5	3 42.9	8 2.0	17 56.6	19 33.1	10 35.3
13 W	19 30 5.9	21 30.1	13 36.5	16 11.1	23 60.0	18 55.2	7 36.1	3 30.3	8 4.4	17 53.8	19 31.7	10 35.6
16 S	19 41 55.5	20 57.8	13 39.6	19 31.5	23 52.6	17 52.5	8 4.7	3 17.3	8 7.2	17 51.0	19 30.2	10 35.8
19 T	19 53 45.2	20 21.9	13 42.8	14 20.1	23 33.1	16 45.3	8 32.3	3 3.8	8 10.3	17 48.1	19 28.7	10 35.9
22 F	20 5 34.9	19 42.6	13 45.9	2 16.7	23 1.1	15 33.9	8 58.9	2 50.0	8 13.7	17 45.2	19 27.2	10 36.0
25 M	20 17 24.5	18 60.0	13 49.0	11N 7.9	22 16.2	14 18.7	9 24.5	2 35.9	8 17.4	17 42.3	19 25.8	10 36.0
28 T	20 29 14.2	18 14.2	13 52.2	19 5.0	21 18.3	13 0.1	9 49.0	2 21.4	8 21.5	17 39.4	19 24.3	10 35.9
31 S	20 41 3.9	17 25.5	13 55.3	16 51.0	20 7.1	11 38.4	10 12.4	2 6.7	8 25.8	17 36.4	19 22.8	10 35.7

FEBRUARY 1999

LONGITUDE at NOON

DAY	EPHEMERIS SIDEREAL TIME (h m s)	☉ (° ′)	☊ (° ′)	☽ (° ′)	☿ (° ′)	♀ (° ′)	♂ (° ′)	♃ (° ′)	♄ (° ′)	♅ (° ′)	♆ (° ′)	♇ (° ′)
1 M	20 45 0.4	12♒10.5	22♌43.6	22♌28.5	10♒14.5	4♓46.2	2♏22.1	27♓33.4	27♈48.6	12♒44.0	2♒15.0	10♐ 3.4
2 T	20 48 57.0	13 11.4	22 40.5	5♍39.0	11 57.6	6 0.8	2 44.7	27 45.7	27 52.2	12 47.5	2 17.2	10 4.7
3 W	20 52 53.5	14 12.2	22 37.3	18 30.5	13 41.3	7 15.4	3 7.0	27 58.1	27 56.0	12 51.0	2 19.5	10 6.0
4 T	20 56 50.1	15 13.1	22 34.1	1♎ 3.9	15 25.7	8 30.0	3 29.1	28 10.6	27 59.8	12 54.5	2 21.7	10 7.3
5 F	21 0 46.6	16 13.9	22 30.9	13 21.7	17 10.9	9 44.6	3 50.8	28 23.2	28 3.7	12 58.0	2 23.9	10 8.5
6 S	21 4 43.2	17 14.7	22 27.8	25 26.9	18 56.7	10 59.1	4 12.1	28 35.8	28 7.7	13 1.5	2 26.2	10 9.7
7 S	21 8 39.7	18 15.5	22 24.6	7♏23.7	20 43.2	12 13.7	4 33.2	28 48.5	28 11.8	13 5.0	2 28.4	10 10.9
8 M	21 12 36.3	19 16.3	22 21.4	19 16.5	22 30.4	13 28.1	4 53.9	29 1.3	28 16.0	13 8.4	2 30.6	10 12.0
9 T	21 16 32.9	20 17.0	22 18.2	1♐10.0	24 18.2	14 42.6	5 14.2	29 14.1	28 20.3	13 11.9	2 32.8	10 13.1
10 W	21 20 29.4	21 17.8	22 15.0	13 8.9	26 6.6	15 57.0	5 34.2	29 27.0	28 24.7	13 15.4	2 35.0	10 14.2
11 T	21 24 26.0	22 18.5	22 11.9	25 17.7	27 55.6	17 11.4	5 53.8	29 40.0	28 29.1	13 18.9	2 37.1	10 15.3
12 F	21 28 22.5	23 19.2	22 8.7	7♑40.2	29 44.9	18 25.7	6 13.0	29 53.1	28 33.7	13 22.3	2 39.3	10 16.3
13 S	21 32 19.1	24 19.9	22 5.5	20 19.5	1♓34.6	19 40.1	6 31.8	0♈ 6.2	28 38.3	13 25.8	2 41.4	10 17.3
14 S	21 36 15.6	25 20.5	22 2.3	3♒17.5	3 24.6	20 54.4	6 50.3	0 19.4	28 43.0	13 29.2	2 43.6	10 18.2
15 M	21 40 12.2	26 21.2	21 59.2	16 34.9	5 14.6	22 8.6	7 8.3	0 32.6	28 47.8	13 32.7	2 45.7	10 19.1
16 T	21 44 8.7	27 21.8	21 56.0	0♓11.0	7 4.6	23 22.8	7 25.9	0 45.9	28 52.6	13 36.1	2 47.8	10 20.0
17 W	21 48 5.3	28 22.4	21 52.8	14 3.5	8 54.3	24 37.0	7 43.1	0 59.3	28 57.6	13 39.5	2 49.9	10 20.8
18 T	21 52 1.8	29 23.0	21 49.6	28 9.2	10 43.5	25 51.1	7 59.8	1 12.7	29 2.6	13 42.9	2 52.0	10 21.7
19 F	21 55 58.4	0♓23.5	21 46.4	12♈23.8	12 31.9	27 5.2	8 16.1	1 26.2	29 7.7	13 46.3	2 54.1	10 22.4
20 S	21 59 54.9	1 24.0	21 43.3	26 43.0	14 19.2	28 19.3	8 32.0	1 39.7	29 12.9	13 49.7	2 56.2	10 23.2
21 S	22 3 51.5	2 24.5	21 40.1	11♉ 2.6	16 5.1	29 33.3	8 47.4	1 53.4	29 18.2	13 53.1	2 58.3	10 23.9
22 M	22 7 48.1	3 25.0	21 36.9	25 19.0	17 49.1	0♈47.3	9 2.3	2 7.0	29 23.6	13 56.5	3 0.3	10 24.6
23 T	22 11 44.6	4 25.4	21 33.7	9♊29.3	19 30.7	2 1.2	9 16.7	2 20.7	29 29.0	13 59.8	3 2.3	10 25.3
24 W	22 15 41.2	5 25.8	21 30.6	23 31.5	21 9.5	3 15.1	9 30.7	2 34.4	29 34.4	14 3.1	3 4.3	10 25.9
25 T	22 19 37.7	6 26.1	21 27.4	7♋24.3	22 45.0	4 28.9	9 44.1	2 48.2	29 40.0	14 6.4	3 6.3	10 26.5
26 F	22 23 34.3	7 26.5	21 24.2	21 6.5	24 16.5	5 42.7	9 57.1	3 2.0	29 45.6	14 9.7	3 8.3	10 27.0
27 S	22 27 30.8	8 26.7	21 21.0	4♌37.3	25 43.4	6 56.4	10 9.5	3 15.8	29 51.3	14 13.0	3 10.2	10 27.5
28 S	22 31 27.4	9 27.0	21 17.8	17 56.1	27 5.2	8 10.1	10 21.4	3 29.7	29 57.0	14 16.2	3 12.1	10 28.0

DECLINATION at NOON

DAY	EPHEMERIS SIDEREAL TIME (h m s)	☉ (° ′)	☊ (° ′)	☽ (° ′)	☿ (° ′)	♀ (° ′)	♂ (° ′)	♃ (° ′)	♄ (° ′)	♅ (° ′)	♆ (° ′)	♇ (° ′)
1 M	20 45 0.4	17S 8.6	13N56.3	14N 3.2	19S40.4	11S10.5	10S19.9	2S 1.7	8N27.3	17S35.4	19S22.3	10S35.6
4 T	20 56 50.1	16 16.2	13 59.4	2 37.7	18 11.3	9 45.2	10 41.8	1 46.5	8 32.0	17 32.5	19 20.8	10 35.4
7 S	21 8 39.7	15 21.3	14 2.5	9S 8.3	16 28.9	8 17.6	11 2.4	1 31.1	8 37.0	17 29.5	19 19.3	10 35.1
10 W	21 20 29.4	14 24.1	14 5.6	17 28.5	14 33.3	6 48.1	11 21.9	1 15.5	8 42.3	17 26.5	19 17.8	10 34.7
13 S	21 32 19.1	13 24.6	14 8.7	19 8.2	12 25.5	5 17.0	11 40.1	0 59.6	8 47.7	17 23.6	19 16.4	10 34.3
16 T	21 44 8.7	12 23.2	14 11.8	12 5.9	10 6.8	3 44.7	11 56.9	0 43.5	8 53.5	17 20.7	19 14.9	10 33.8
19 F	21 55 58.4	11 20.0	14 14.9	1N 9.3	7 39.5	2 11.4	12 12.5	0 27.2	8 59.4	17 17.8	19 13.5	10 33.2
22 M	22 7 48.1	10 15.2	14 17.9	13 58.3	5 7.8	0 37.6	12 26.7	0 10.8	9 5.6	17 14.9	19 12.1	10 32.6
25 T	22 19 37.7	9 9.0	14 21.0	19 31.2	2 37.6	0N56.5	12 39.5	0N 5.8	9 11.9	17 12.0	19 10.8	10 31.9
28 S	22 31 27.4	8 1.6	14 24.0	15 5.1	0 16.8	2 30.4	12 50.8	0 22.5	9 18.5	17 9.3	19 9.4	10 31.2

MARCH 1999

DAY	EPHEMERIS SIDEREAL TIME	☉	☊	☽	☿	♀	♂	♃	♄	♅	♆	♇
	h m s	° ′	° ′	° ′	° ′	° ′	° ′	° ′	° ′	° ′	° ′	° ′
	LONGITUDE at NOON											
1 M	22 35 23.9	10♓27.2	21♌14.7	1♍ 2.0	28♓21.3	9♈23.7	10♏32.8	3♈43.7	0♉ 2.8	14♒19.5	3♒14.0	10♐28.4
2 T	22 39 20.5	11 27.4	21 11.5	13 54.6	29 31.0	10 37.2	10 43.6	3 57.7	0 8.7	14 22.7	3 15.9	10 28.8
3 W	22 43 17.0	12 27.6	21 8.3	26 33.9	0♈33.8	11 50.7	10 53.8	4 11.7	0 14.7	14 25.9	3 17.8	10 29.2
4 T	22 47 13.6	13 27.7	21 5.1	9♎ 0.1	1 29.1	13 4.2	11 3.5	4 25.7	0 20.7	14 29.0	3 19.7	10 29.5
5 F	22 51 10.1	14 27.8	21 2.0	21 14.5	2 16.5	14 17.6	11 12.6	4 39.8	0 26.7	14 32.2	3 21.5	10 29.8
6 S	22 55 6.7	15 27.9	20 58.8	3♏18.7	2 55.5	15 30.9	11 21.1	4 53.9	0 32.9	14 35.3	3 23.3	10 30.1
7 S	22 59 3.2	16 27.9	20 55.6	15 15.6	3 25.9	16 44.2	11 29.0	5 8.1	0 39.1	14 38.4	3 25.1	10 30.3
8 M	23 2 59.8	17 28.0	20 52.4	27 8.5	3 47.3	17 57.4	11 36.3	5 22.3	0 45.3	14 41.5	3 26.9	10 30.5
9 T	23 6 56.3	18 28.0	20 49.2	9♐ 1.3	3 59.8	19 10.6	11 42.9	5 36.5	0 51.6	14 44.5	3 28.6	10 30.7
10 W	23 10 52.9	19 27.9	20 46.1	20 58.8	4 3.1	20 23.7	11 48.9	5 50.7	0 58.0	14 47.6	3 30.3	10 30.8
11 T	23 14 49.4	20 27.9	20 42.9	3♑ 5.5	3R57.7	21 36.8	11 54.2	6 5.0	1 4.4	14 50.6	3 32.0	10 30.9
12 F	23 18 46.0	21 27.8	20 39.7	15 26.4	3 43.6	22 49.8	11 58.9	6 19.3	1 10.8	14 53.6	3 33.7	10 31.0
13 S	23 22 42.5	22 27.7	20 36.5	28 5.9	3 21.4	24 2.7	12 2.8	6 33.6	1 17.4	14 56.5	3 35.4	10 31.0
14 S	23 26 39.1	23 27.6	20 33.4	11♒ 7.5	2 51.6	25 15.7	12 6.2	6 48.0	1 24.0	14 59.5	3 37.1	10 31.0
15 M	23 30 35.7	24 27.4	20 30.2	24 33.4	2 15.1	26 28.5	12 8.7	7 2.3	1 30.6	15 2.4	3 38.7	10 31.0
16 T	23 34 32.2	25 27.2	20 27.0	8♓24.1	1 32.6	27 41.2	12 10.6	7 16.7	1 37.3	15 5.3	3 40.2	10R30.9
17 W	23 38 28.8	26 27.0	20 23.8	22 37.6	0 45.2	28 53.9	12 11.8	7 31.1	1 44.0	15 8.1	3 41.8	10 30.8
18 T	23 42 25.3	27 26.7	20 20.6	7♈ 9.5	29♓54.1	0♉ 6.6	12 12.2	7 45.5	1 50.7	15 10.9	3 43.3	10 30.6
19 F	23 46 21.9	28 26.4	20 17.5	21 53.2	29 0.4	1 19.1	12R11.8	7 60.0	1 57.5	15 13.7	3 44.8	10 30.4
20 S	23 50 18.4	29 26.1	20 14.3	6♉41.0	28 5.4	2 31.6	12 10.8	8 14.4	2 4.4	15 16.4	3 46.3	10 30.2
21 S	23 54 15.0	0♈25.7	20 11.1	21 25.0	27 10.1	3 44.1	12 9.0	8 28.9	2 11.3	15 19.1	3 47.8	10 30.0
22 M	23 58 11.5	1 25.3	20 7.9	5♊58.7	26 15.9	4 56.4	12 6.4	8 43.4	2 18.2	15 21.8	3 49.2	10 29.7
23 T	0 2 8.1	2 24.9	20 4.7	20 17.3	25 23.6	6 8.7	12 3.1	8 57.8	2 25.2	15 24.5	3 50.6	10 29.4
24 W	0 6 4.6	3 24.4	20 1.6	4♋18.3	24 34.3	7 20.9	11 59.0	9 12.3	2 32.2	15 27.1	3 52.0	10 29.0
25 T	0 10 1.2	4 23.8	19 58.4	18 1.2	23 48.7	8 33.0	11 54.2	9 26.8	2 39.3	15 29.7	3 53.3	10 28.6
26 F	0 13 57.7	5 23.3	19 55.2	1♌26.9	23 7.6	9 45.1	11 48.6	9 41.3	2 46.4	15 32.2	3 54.6	10 28.2
27 S	0 17 54.3	6 22.7	19 52.0	14 36.8	22 31.5	10 57.0	11 42.2	9 55.9	2 53.5	15 34.7	3 55.9	10 27.8
28 S	0 21 50.8	7 22.0	19 48.9	27 33.0	22 0.6	12 8.9	11 35.1	10 10.4	3 0.6	15 37.2	3 57.2	10 27.3
29 M	0 25 47.4	8 21.4	19 45.7	10♍16.9	21 35.4	13 20.7	11 27.2	10 24.9	3 7.8	15 39.7	3 58.4	10 26.8
30 T	0 29 43.9	9 20.6	19 42.5	22 50.1	21 16.0	14 32.4	11 18.5	10 39.4	3 15.1	15 42.1	3 59.6	10 26.2
31 W	0 33 40.5	10 19.9	19 39.3	5♎13.6	21 2.3	15 44.1	11 9.1	10 53.9	3 22.3	15 44.4	4 0.8	10 25.7

DAY	EPHEMERIS SIDEREAL TIME	☉	☊	☽	☿	♀	♂	♃	♄	♅	♆	♇
	DECLINATION at NOON											
1 M	22 35 23.9	7S38.8	14N25.1	11N52.0	0N26.5	3N 1.6	12S54.3	0N28.1	9N20.7	17S 8.3	19S 9.0	10S31.0
4 T	22 47 13.6	6 30.1	14 28.1	0S 2.6	2 20.6	4 34.9	13 3.7	0 45.0	9 27.4	17 5.6	19 7.7	10 30.2
7 S	22 59 3.2	5 20.5	14 31.2	11 26.2	3 43.9	6 7.3	13 11.6	1 1.9	9 34.3	17 2.9	19 6.5	10 29.4
10 W	23 10 52.9	4 10.2	14 34.2	18 34.3	4 29.0	7 38.6	13 18.0	1 18.9	9 41.4	17 0.3	19 5.3	10 28.5
13 S	23 22 42.5	2 59.5	14 37.2	18 28.5	4 32.1	9 8.3	13 22.8	1 36.0	9 48.5	16 57.7	19 4.1	10 27.6
16 T	23 34 32.2	1 48.4	14 40.3	9 47.7	3 54.4	10 36.2	13 25.9	1 53.2	9 55.8	16 55.2	19 3.0	10 26.7
19 F	23 46 21.9	0 37.2	14 43.3	4N21.2	2 43.4	12 1.9	13 27.3	2 10.3	10 3.2	16 52.8	19 1.9	10 25.8
22 M	23 58 11.5	0N33.9	14 46.3	16 22.3	1 13.0	13 25.1	13 27.0	2 27.5	10 10.7	16 50.5	19 0.9	10 24.8
25 T	0 10 1.2	1 44.8	14 49.3	19 24.1	0S21.2	14 45.5	13 25.0	2 44.6	10 18.2	16 48.2	18 59.9	10 23.8
28 S	0 21 50.8	2 55.4	14 52.3	12 50.5	1 45.7	16 2.7	13 21.3	3 1.7	10 25.8	16 46.1	18 59.0	10 22.8
31 W	0 33 40.5	4 5.4	14 55.3	1 11.4	2 51.7	17 16.5	13 15.9	3 18.8	10 33.4	16 44.0	18 58.2	10 21.8

APRIL 1999

DAY	EPHEMERIS SIDEREAL TIME	☉	☊	☽	☿	♀	♂	♃	♄	♅	♆	♇
	LONGITUDE at NOON											
1 T	0 37 37.0	11♈19.1	19♌36.1	17♎28.3	20♓54.5	16♉55.6	10♏58.9	11♈ 8.4	3♉29.6	15♒46.8	4♒ 2.0	10♐25.1
2 F	0 41 33.6	12 18.3	19 33.0	29 35.1	20R52.3	18 7.0	10R48.0	11 23.0	3 36.9	15 49.1	4 3.1	10R24.4
3 S	0 45 30.1	13 17.4	19 29.8	11♏35.1	20D55.7	19 18.4	10 36.3	11 37.5	3 44.2	15 51.3	4 4.2	10 23.8
4 S	0 49 26.7	14 16.6	19 26.6	23 30.0	21 4.5	20 29.7	10 24.0	11 52.0	3 51.7	15 53.6	4 5.3	10 23.1
5 M	0 53 23.2	15 15.7	19 23.4	5♐22.0	21 18.5	21 40.9	10 10.8	12 6.5	3 59.0	15 55.8	4 6.3	10 22.4
6 T	0 57 19.8	16 14.8	19 20.3	17 14.1	21 37.4	22 52.0	9 57.0	12 21.0	4 6.5	15 57.9	4 7.3	10 21.6
7 W	1 1 16.3	17 13.8	19 17.1	29 10.1	22 1.1	24 3.0	9 42.4	12 35.5	4 13.9	15 60.0	4 8.2	10 20.9
8 T	1 5 12.9	18 12.8	19 13.9	11♑14.3	22 29.4	25 13.9	9 27.2	12 50.0	4 21.4	16 2.1	4 9.2	10 20.0
9 F	1 9 9.5	19 11.7	19 10.7	23 31.6	23 2.0	26 24.7	9 11.2	13 4.5	4 28.8	16 4.1	4 10.1	10 19.2
10 S	1 13 6.0	20 10.7	19 7.5	6♒ 7.0	23 38.6	27 35.5	8 54.7	13 19.0	4 36.3	16 6.0	4 11.0	10 18.3
11 S	1 17 2.6	21 9.6	19 4.4	19 5.1	24 19.2	28 46.1	8 37.5	13 33.4	4 43.9	16 8.0	4 11.8	10 17.4
12 M	1 20 59.1	22 8.5	19 1.2	2♓29.7	25 3.4	29 56.6	8 19.7	13 47.9	4 51.4	16 9.9	4 12.6	10 16.5
13 T	1 24 55.7	23 7.3	18 58.0	16 23.0	25 51.2	1♊ 7.1	8 1.3	14 2.3	4 59.0	16 11.7	4 13.4	10 15.6
14 W	1 28 52.2	24 6.1	18 54.8	0♈44.3	26 42.3	2 17.4	7 42.4	14 16.7	5 6.5	16 13.5	4 14.1	10 14.6
15 T	1 32 48.8	25 4.9	18 51.7	15 29.8	27 36.5	3 27.6	7 22.9	14 31.1	5 14.1	16 15.3	4 14.8	10 13.6
16 F	1 36 45.3	26 3.7	18 48.5	0♉32.6	28 33.8	4 37.7	7 3.0	14 45.5	5 21.7	16 17.0	4 15.5	10 12.5
17 S	1 40 41.9	27 2.4	18 45.3	15 43.0	29 34.0	5 47.7	6 42.6	14 59.8	5 29.3	16 18.7	4 16.2	10 11.5
18 S	1 44 38.4	28 1.1	18 42.1	0♊50.2	0♈36.9	6 57.6	6 21.9	15 14.2	5 37.0	16 20.3	4 16.8	10 10.4
19 M	1 48 35.0	28 59.8	18 38.9	15 44.7	1 42.4	8 7.4	6 0.7	15 28.5	5 44.6	16 21.9	4 17.4	10 9.3
20 T	1 52 31.5	29 58.4	18 35.8	0♋19.1	2 50.5	9 17.1	5 39.3	15 42.8	5 52.2	16 23.4	4 17.9	10 8.2
21 W	1 56 28.1	0♉57.0	18 32.6	14 29.4	4 1.0	10 26.6	5 17.5	15 57.1	5 59.9	16 24.9	4 18.4	10 7.0
22 T	2 0 24.6	1 55.5	18 29.4	28 14.7	5 13.8	11 36.1	4 55.6	16 11.3	6 7.5	16 26.3	4 18.9	10 5.8
23 F	2 4 21.2	2 54.0	18 26.2	11♌36.4	6 29.0	12 45.4	4 33.4	16 25.5	6 15.2	16 27.7	4 19.4	10 4.6
24 S	2 8 17.7	3 52.5	18 23.1	24 37.3	7 46.3	13 54.5	4 11.1	16 39.7	6 22.9	16 29.1	4 19.8	10 3.4
25 S	2 12 14.3	4 51.0	18 19.9	7♍20.8	9 5.8	15 3.6	3 48.7	16 53.9	6 30.6	16 30.5	4 20.2	10 2.2
26 M	2 16 10.9	5 49.4	18 16.7	19 50.3	10 27.4	16 12.5	3 26.2	17 8.0	6 38.2	16 31.7	4 20.6	10 1.0
27 T	2 20 7.4	6 47.7	18 13.5	2♎ 9.0	11 51.0	17 21.3	3 3.7	17 22.1	6 45.9	16 32.9	4 20.9	9 59.7
28 W	2 24 4.0	7 46.1	18 10.3	14 19.3	13 16.6	18 29.9	2 41.2	17 36.2	6 53.6	16 34.1	4 21.2	9 58.4
29 T	2 28 0.5	8 44.4	18 7.2	26 23.1	14 44.2	19 38.4	2 18.8	17 50.2	7 1.2	16 35.2	4 21.4	9 57.1
30 F	2 31 57.1	9 42.7	18 4.0	8♏22.0	16 13.8	20 46.7	1 56.5	18 4.2	7 8.9	16 36.3	4 21.7	9 55.7

DAY	EPHEMERIS SIDEREAL TIME	☉	☊	☽	☿	♀	♂	♃	♄	♅	♆	♇
	DECLINATION at NOON											
1 T	0 37 37.0	4N28.6	14N56.3	2S55.5	3S 8.9	17N40.2	13S13.7	3N24.5	10N36.0	16S43.4	18S57.9	10S21.5
4 S	0 49 26.7	5 37.7	14 59.3	13 43.2	3 44.9	18 48.9	13 5.9	3 41.5	10 43.7	16 41.4	18 57.2	10 20.4
7 W	1 1 16.3	6 46.0	15 2.3	19 27.8	3 58.2	19 53.3	12 56.6	3 58.5	10 51.4	16 39.6	18 56.5	10 19.4
10 S	1 13 6.0	7 53.1	15 5.2	17 32.1	3 50.2	20 53.3	12 45.6	4 15.3	10 59.1	16 37.9	18 55.8	10 18.4
13 T	1 24 55.7	8 59.1	15 8.2	7 26.5	3 22.9	21 48.5	12 33.1	4 32.1	11 6.8	16 36.3	18 55.2	10 17.4
16 F	1 36 45.3	10 3.8	15 11.2	7N11.7	2 38.2	22 38.7	12 19.4	4 48.7	11 14.6	16 34.8	18 54.7	10 16.3
19 M	1 48 35.0	11 7.0	15 14.1	18 10.6	1 38.0	23 23.6	12 4.6	5 5.2	11 22.2	16 33.4	18 54.3	10 15.3
22 T	2 0 24.6	12 8.5	15 17.1	18 44.1	0 23.9	24 3.1	11 49.1	5 21.5	11 29.9	16 32.2	18 53.9	10 14.3
25 S	2 12 14.3	13 8.2	15 20.0	10 16.5	1N 2.6	24 36.9	11 33.1	5 37.7	11 37.5	16 31.1	18 53.6	10 13.4
28 W	2 24 4.0	14 6.0	15 22.9	1S50.2	2 40.3	25 4.9	11 16.9	5 53.7	11 45.1	16 30.1	18 53.4	10 12.4

MAY 1999

LONGITUDE at NOON

DAY	EPHEMERIS SIDEREAL TIME	☉	☊	☽	☿	♀	♂	♃	♄	♅	♆	♇
	h m s	° ′	° ′	° ′	° ′	° ′	° ′	° ′	° ′	° ′	° ′	° ′
1 S	2 35 53.6	10♉40.9	18♌ 0.8	20♏17.2	17♈45.3	21♊54.9	1♏34.4	18♈18.1	7♉16.6	16♒37.3	4♒21.9	9♐54.4
2 S	2 39 50.2	11 39.1	17 57.6	2♐10.0	19 18.7	23 2.9	1R12.4	18 32.0	7 24.2	16 38.3	4 22.0	9R53.0
3 M	2 43 46.7	12 37.3	17 54.5	14 2.0	20 54.0	24 10.8	0 50.7	18 45.9	7 31.9	16 39.2	4 22.1	9 51.6
4 T	2 47 43.3	13 35.5	17 51.3	25 55.1	22 31.3	25 18.5	0 29.3	18 59.7	7 39.5	16 40.1	4 22.2	9 50.2
5 W	2 51 39.8	14 33.6	17 48.1	7♑52.3	24 10.4	26 26.1	0 8.2	19 13.5	7 47.1	16 40.9	4 22.3	9 48.8
6 T	2 55 36.4	15 31.7	17 44.9	19 57.0	25 51.4	27 33.5	29♎47.5	19 27.3	7 54.8	16 41.7	4 22.3	9 47.3
7 F	2 59 33.0	16 29.8	17 41.7	2♒13.3	27 34.3	28 40.7	29 27.1	19 41.0	8 2.4	16 42.4	4 22.3	9 45.9
8 S	3 3 29.5	17 27.8	17 38.6	14 45.8	29 19.1	29 47.8	29 7.2	19 54.7	8 10.0	16 43.1	4 22.3	9 44.4
9 S	3 7 26.1	18 25.9	17 35.4	27 39.3	1♉ 5.9	0♋54.7	28 47.8	20 8.3	8 17.6	16 43.7	4R22.2	9 42.9
10 M	3 11 22.6	19 23.9	17 32.2	10♓58.2	2 54.5	2 1.4	28 28.8	20 21.9	8 25.2	16 44.3	4 22.1	9 41.4
11 T	3 15 19.2	20 21.9	17 29.0	24 45.6	4 45.1	3 8.0	28 10.5	20 35.4	8 32.8	16 44.8	4 22.0	9 39.9
12 W	3 19 15.7	21 19.9	17 25.9	9♈ 2.4	6 37.5	4 14.3	27 52.7	20 48.9	8 40.3	16 45.3	4 21.8	9 38.4
13 T	3 23 12.3	22 17.8	17 22.7	23 46.5	8 31.9	5 20.5	27 35.5	21 2.3	8 47.9	16 45.8	4 21.6	9 36.8
14 F	3 27 8.8	23 15.8	17 19.5	8♉52.0	10 28.1	6 26.5	27 18.9	21 15.7	8 55.4	16 46.2	4 21.3	9 35.3
15 S	3 31 5.4	24 13.7	17 16.3	24 9.7	12 26.2	7 32.3	27 3.0	21 29.0	9 2.9	16 46.5	4 21.1	9 33.7
16 S	3 35 1.9	25 11.6	17 13.1	9♊28.3	14 26.2	8 37.9	26 47.8	21 42.3	9 10.4	16 46.8	4 20.8	9 32.2
17 M	3 38 58.5	26 9.4	17 10.0	24 36.3	16 27.9	9 43.3	26 33.3	21 55.5	9 17.9	16 47.1	4 20.5	9 30.6
18 T	3 42 55.1	27 7.3	17 6.8	9♋24.6	18 31.3	10 48.5	26 19.6	22 8.7	9 25.3	16 47.2	4 20.1	9 29.1
19 W	3 46 51.6	28 5.1	17 3.6	23 47.0	20 36.3	11 53.4	26 6.5	22 21.8	9 32.8	16 47.4	4 19.7	9 27.5
20 T	3 50 48.2	29 2.8	17 0.4	7♌41.1	22 42.8	12 58.2	25 54.3	22 34.8	9 40.2	16 47.5	4 19.3	9 25.9
21 F	3 54 44.7	0♊ 0.6	16 57.3	21 7.6	24 50.7	14 2.7	25 42.8	22 47.7	9 47.5	16 47.5	4 18.9	9 24.3
22 S	3 58 41.3	0 58.3	16 54.1	4♍ 9.3	26 59.8	15 6.9	25 32.2	23 0.6	9 54.9	16 47.5	4 18.4	9 22.6
23 S	4 2 37.8	1 56.0	16 50.9	16 49.9	29 9.9	16 10.9	25 22.3	23 13.5	10 2.2	16R47.4	4 17.9	9 21.0
24 M	4 6 34.4	2 53.7	16 47.7	29 13.9	1♊20.8	17 14.6	25 13.2	23 26.3	10 9.5	16 47.3	4 17.3	9 19.4
25 T	4 10 30.9	3 51.3	16 44.6	11♎25.4	3 32.2	18 18.1	25 4.9	23 39.0	10 16.8	16 47.2	4 16.7	9 17.8
26 W	4 14 27.5	4 48.9	16 41.4	23 28.1	5 44.0	19 21.3	24 57.5	23 51.6	10 24.0	16 47.0	4 16.1	9 16.2
27 T	4 18 24.1	5 46.5	16 38.2	5♏25.1	7 55.9	20 24.3	24 50.8	24 4.2	10 31.2	16 46.7	4 15.5	9 14.5
28 F	4 22 20.6	6 44.1	16 35.0	17 18.9	10 7.5	21 26.9	24 45.0	24 16.7	10 38.4	16 46.4	4 14.8	9 12.9
29 S	4 26 17.2	7 41.6	16 31.8	29 11.4	12 18.6	22 29.2	24 40.0	24 29.1	10 45.5	16 46.1	4 14.1	9 11.3
30 S	4 30 13.7	8 39.1	16 28.7	11♐ 4.1	14 29.0	23 31.3	24 35.8	24 41.4	10 52.6	16 45.7	4 13.4	9 9.6
31 M	4 34 10.3	9 36.7	16 25.5	22 58.5	16 38.3	24 33.0	24 32.4	24 53.7	10 59.7	16 45.2	4 12.7	9 8.0

DECLINATION at NOON

DAY	EPHEMERIS SIDEREAL TIME	☉	☊	☽	☿	♀	♂	♃	♄	♅	♆	♇
1 S	2 35 53.6	15N 1.6	15N25.9	13S 0.1	4N27.8	25N27.0	11S 1.1	6N 9.5	11N52.6	16S29.2	18S53.3	10S11.5
4 T	2 47 43.3	15 55.0	15 28.8	19 26.3	6 24.1	25 43.1	10 45.8	6 25.1	11 60.0	16 28.5	18 53.2	10 10.6
7 F	2 59 33.0	16 46.1	15 31.7	18 22.4	8 27.7	25 53.2	10 31.4	6 40.5	12 7.3	16 27.9	18 53.2	10 9.8
10 M	3 11 22.6	17 34.6	15 34.6	9 19.1	10 37.1	25 57.3	10 18.2	6 55.7	12 14.6	16 27.4	18 53.2	10 9.0
13 T	3 23 12.3	18 20.5	15 37.5	4N56.6	12 50.2	25 55.4	10 6.7	7 10.6	12 21.7	16 27.1	18 53.3	10 8.2
16 S	3 35 1.9	19 3.7	15 40.4	17 18.0	15 4.6	25 47.6	9 57.0	7 25.3	12 28.8	16 26.9	18 53.5	10 7.5
19 W	3 46 51.6	19 43.9	15 43.3	19 26.4	17 16.7	25 34.2	9 49.3	7 39.8	12 35.7	16 26.8	18 53.8	10 6.8
22 S	3 58 41.3	20 21.1	15 46.2	11 26.1	19 22.0	25 15.1	9 43.9	7 53.9	12 42.5	16 26.9	18 54.1	10 6.2
25 T	4 10 30.9	20 55.1	15 49.0	0S42.1	21 15.3	24 50.8	9 40.8	8 7.7	12 49.1	16 27.1	18 54.5	10 5.6
28 F	4 22 20.6	21 25.9	15 51.9	12 10.6	22 51.3	24 21.3	9 40.2	8 21.3	12 55.6	16 27.5	18 55.0	10 5.1
31 M	4 34 10.3	21 53.4	15 54.7	19 16.5	24 5.5	23 47.1	9 41.9	8 34.5	13 2.0	16 27.9	18 55.5	10 4.7

JUNE 1999

LONGITUDE at NOON

DAY	EPHEMERIS SIDEREAL TIME	☉	☊	☽	☿	♀	♂	♃	♄	♅	♆	♇
1 T	4 38 6.8	10♊34.2	16♌22.3	4♑56.3	18♊46.4	25♋34.4	24♎29.8	25♈ 5.9	11♉ 6.7	16♒44.7	4♒11.9	9♐ 6.3
2 W	4 42 3.4	11 31.6	16 19.1	16 59.3	20 52.9	26 35.5	24R28.0	25 18.0	11 13.7	16R44.2	4R11.1	9R 4.7
3 T	4 45 60.0	12 29.1	16 16.0	29 10.0	22 57.8	27 36.3	24 27.0	25 30.1	11 20.7	16 43.6	4 10.3	9 3.1
4 F	4 49 56.5	13 26.5	16 12.8	11♒31.4	25 0.8	28 36.7	24 26.8	25 42.0	11 27.6	16 43.0	4 9.4	9 1.5
5 S	4 53 53.1	14 24.0	16 9.6	24 7.0	27 1.8	29 36.7	24D27.4	25 53.9	11 34.5	16 42.3	4 8.5	8 59.8
6 S	4 57 49.6	15 21.5	16 6.4	7♓ 0.8	29 0.6	0♌36.4	24 28.8	26 5.8	11 41.4	16 41.6	4 7.6	8 58.2
7 M	5 1 46.2	16 18.9	16 3.3	20 16.4	0♋57.2	1 35.7	24 31.0	26 17.5	11 48.2	16 40.8	4 6.7	8 56.6
8 T	5 5 42.7	17 16.3	16 0.1	3♈57.0	2 51.5	2 34.7	24 33.9	26 29.1	11 55.0	16 40.0	4 5.7	8 55.0
9 W	5 9 39.3	18 13.7	15 56.9	18 4.0	4 43.4	3 33.2	24 37.5	26 40.7	12 1.7	16 39.2	4 4.7	8 53.4
10 T	5 13 35.9	19 11.1	15 53.7	2♉36.5	6 32.8	4 31.3	24 41.9	26 52.1	12 8.3	16 38.3	4 3.7	8 51.8
11 F	5 17 32.4	20 8.5	15 50.5	17 30.5	8 19.8	5 29.0	24 47.1	27 3.5	12 15.0	16 37.3	4 2.7	8 50.2
12 S	5 21 29.0	21 5.8	15 47.4	2♊38.8	10 4.3	6 26.3	24 52.9	27 14.8	12 21.5	16 36.3	4 1.6	8 48.6
13 S	5 25 25.5	22 3.2	15 44.2	17 51.7	11 46.2	7 23.1	24 59.6	27 26.0	12 28.1	16 35.3	4 0.5	8 47.0
14 M	5 29 22.1	23 0.5	15 41.0	2♋58.6	13 25.6	8 19.4	25 6.9	27 37.0	12 34.6	16 34.2	3 59.4	8 45.4
15 T	5 33 18.6	23 57.9	15 37.8	17 49.8	15 2.4	9 15.3	25 14.9	27 48.0	12 41.0	16 33.1	3 58.3	8 43.9
16 W	5 37 15.2	24 55.2	15 34.7	2♌18.1	16 36.6	10 10.6	25 23.7	27 58.9	12 47.4	16 31.9	3 57.1	8 42.3
17 T	5 41 11.8	25 52.5	15 31.5	16 19.4	18 8.2	11 5.5	25 33.1	28 9.7	12 53.7	16 30.7	3 56.0	8 40.8
18 F	5 45 8.3	26 49.8	15 28.3	29 52.8	19 37.2	11 59.8	25 43.2	28 20.4	12 60.0	16 29.4	3 54.8	8 39.2
19 S	5 49 4.9	27 47.1	15 25.1	12♍59.9	21 3.5	12 53.5	25 54.0	28 30.9	13 6.2	16 28.1	3 53.5	8 37.7
20 S	5 53 1.4	28 44.3	15 22.0	25 43.8	22 27.2	13 46.6	26 5.4	28 41.4	13 12.3	16 26.8	3 52.3	8 36.2
21 M	5 56 58.0	29 41.6	15 18.8	8♎ 8.8	23 48.1	14 39.2	26 17.4	28 51.8	13 18.4	16 25.4	3 51.0	8 34.7
22 T	6 0 54.5	0♋38.8	15 15.6	20 19.4	25 6.3	15 31.1	26 30.1	29 2.0	13 24.5	16 24.0	3 49.8	8 33.2
23 W	6 4 51.1	1 36.1	15 12.4	2♏20.0	26 21.7	16 22.4	26 43.4	29 12.2	13 30.5	16 22.6	3 48.5	8 31.7
24 T	6 8 47.7	2 33.3	15 9.3	14 14.5	27 34.2	17 13.0	26 57.3	29 22.2	13 36.4	16 21.1	3 47.1	8 30.3
25 F	6 12 44.2	3 30.5	15 6.1	26 6.6	28 43.8	18 2.9	27 11.8	29 32.1	13 42.3	16 19.5	3 45.8	8 28.8
26 S	6 16 40.8	4 27.7	15 2.9	7♐59.0	29 50.4	18 52.1	27 26.9	29 42.0	13 48.1	16 18.0	3 44.4	8 27.4
27 S	6 20 37.3	5 25.0	14 59.7	19 54.2	0♌54.0	19 40.5	27 42.6	29 51.7	13 53.9	16 16.4	3 43.1	8 26.1
28 M	6 24 33.9	6 22.2	14 56.5	1♑54.0	1 54.4	20 28.2	27 58.7	0♉ 1.3	13 59.6	16 14.8	3 41.7	8 24.7
29 T	6 28 30.4	7 19.4	14 53.4	14 0.0	2 51.5	21 15.0	28 15.5	0 10.7	14 5.2	16 13.1	3 40.3	8 23.3
30 W	6 32 27.0	8 16.5	14 50.2	26 13.8	3 45.4	22 1.0	28 32.7	0 20.1	14 10.7	16 11.4	3 38.9	8 21.9

DECLINATION at NOON

DAY	EPHEMERIS SIDEREAL TIME	☉	☊	☽	☿	♀	♂	♃	♄	♅	♆	♇
1 T	4 38 6.8	22N 1.8	15N55.7	20S 5.8	24N24.9	23N34.6	9S43.0	8N38.8	13N 4.1	16S28.1	18S55.7	10S 4.5
4 F	4 49 56.5	22 24.7	15 58.5	17 3.2	25 6.7	22 54.4	9 47.9	8 51.6	13 10.3	16 28.8	18 56.3	10 4.2
7 M	5 1 46.2	22 44.0	16 1.4	6 35.2	25 24.4	22 10.1	9 55.2	9 4.1	13 16.3	16 29.5	18 56.9	10 3.9
10 T	5 13 35.9	22 59.8	16 4.2	7N41.2	25 20.1	21 22.1	10 4.6	9 16.2	13 22.1	16 30.4	18 57.6	10 3.6
13 S	5 25 25.5	23 11.9	16 7.1	18 39.0	24 56.8	20 30.8	10 16.3	9 27.9	13 27.7	16 31.4	18 58.4	10 3.4
16 W	5 37 15.2	23 20.4	16 9.9	18 37.9	24 17.7	19 36.4	10 29.9	9 39.2	13 33.2	16 32.5	18 59.2	10 3.3
19 S	5 49 4.9	23 25.1	16 12.7	8 59.6	23 26.1	18 39.5	10 45.6	9 50.2	13 38.5	16 33.7	19 0.1	10 3.3
22 T	6 0 54.5	23 26.1	16 15.5	3S33.7	22 25.1	17 40.4	11 3.1	10 0.8	13 43.5	16 35.0	19 1.0	10 3.4
25 F	6 12 44.2	23 23.4	16 18.3	14 23.0	21 17.6	16 39.5	11 22.3	10 10.9	13 48.4	16 36.5	19 1.9	10 3.5
28 M	6 24 33.9	23 17.0	16 21.1	19 59.8	20 6.5	15 37.4	11 43.0	10 20.6	13 53.1	16 38.0	19 2.9	10 3.7

JULY 1999

LONGITUDE at NOON

DAY	EPHEMERIS SIDEREAL TIME	☉	☊	☽	☿	♀	♂	♃	♄	♅	♆	♇
	h m s	° ′	° ′	° ′	° ′	° ′	° ′	° ′	° ′	° ′	° ′	° ′
1 T	6 36 23.6	9♋13.7	14♌47.0	8♒36.9	4♌35.8	22♌46.2	28♎50.5	0♉29.3	14♉16.2	16♒ 9.7	3♒37.5	8♐20.6
2 F	6 40 20.1	10 10.9	14 43.8	21 11.1	5 22.6	23 30.4	29 8.8	0 38.4	14 21.6	16R 7.9	3R36.0	8R19.2
3 S	6 44 16.7	11 8.1	14 40.7	3♓58.4	6 5.8	24 13.7	29 27.6	0 47.4	14 27.0	16 6.1	3 34.6	8 17.9
4 S	6 48 13.2	12 5.3	14 37.5	17 1.0	6 45.2	24 56.1	29 46.9	0 56.2	14 32.3	16 4.3	3 33.1	8 16.7
5 M	6 52 9.8	13 2.5	14 34.3	0♈21.1	7 20.7	25 37.4	0♏ 6.7	1 4.9	14 37.5	16 2.4	3 31.6	8 15.4
6 T	6 56 6.3	13 59.7	14 31.1	14 0.5	7 52.1	26 17.7	0 27.0	1 13.5	14 42.6	16 0.6	3 30.1	8 14.1
7 W	7 0 2.9	14 56.9	14 28.0	28 0.1	8 19.4	26 57.0	0 47.7	1 22.0	14 47.7	15 58.6	3 28.6	8 12.9
8 T	7 3 59.5	15 54.1	14 24.8	12♉19.2	8 42.3	27 35.1	1 8.9	1 30.3	14 52.7	15 56.7	3 27.0	8 11.7
9 F	7 7 56.0	16 51.3	14 21.6	26 55.2	9 0.8	28 12.0	1 30.6	1 38.5	14 57.6	15 54.7	3 25.5	8 10.5
10 S	7 11 52.6	17 48.5	14 18.4	11♊43.3	9 14.8	28 47.8	1 52.6	1 46.5	15 2.5	15 52.7	3 24.0	8 9.4
11 S	7 15 49.1	18 45.8	14 15.2	26 36.5	9 24.2	29 22.3	2 15.2	1 54.4	15 7.3	15 50.7	3 22.4	8 8.2
12 M	7 19 45.7	19 43.0	14 12.1	11♋26.9	9 28.9	29 55.6	2 38.2	2 2.2	15 12.0	15 48.6	3 20.8	8 7.1
13 T	7 23 42.2	20 40.2	14 8.9	26 6.6	9R28.8	0♍27.5	3 1.6	2 9.8	15 16.6	15 46.5	3 19.3	8 6.0
14 W	7 27 38.8	21 37.5	14 5.7	10♌28.8	9 23.9	0 57.9	3 25.4	2 17.3	15 21.1	15 44.4	3 17.7	8 5.0
15 T	7 31 35.4	22 34.7	14 2.5	24 28.7	9 14.2	1 27.0	3 49.6	2 24.6	15 25.6	15 42.3	3 16.1	8 3.9
16 F	7 35 31.9	23 32.0	13 59.4	8♍ 4.1	8 59.9	1 54.5	4 14.2	2 31.8	15 29.9	15 40.1	3 14.5	8 2.9
17 S	7 39 28.5	24 29.2	13 56.2	21 14.9	8 40.9	2 20.4	4 39.3	2 38.8	15 34.2	15 38.0	3 12.9	8 1.9
18 S	7 43 25.0	25 26.5	13 53.0	4♎ 2.9	8 17.7	2 44.8	5 4.7	2 45.7	15 38.5	15 35.8	3 11.3	8 1.0
19 M	7 47 21.6	26 23.8	13 49.8	16 31.2	7 50.2	3 7.4	5 30.5	2 52.4	15 42.6	15 33.6	3 9.7	8 0.0
20 T	7 51 18.1	27 21.0	13 46.7	28 43.9	7 19.0	3 28.3	5 56.6	2 59.0	15 46.7	15 31.4	3 8.1	7 59.1
21 W	7 55 14.7	28 18.3	13 43.5	10♏45.4	6 44.4	3 47.4	6 23.2	3 5.4	15 50.6	15 29.2	3 6.5	7 58.2
22 T	7 59 11.3	29 15.6	13 40.3	22 40.1	6 6.9	4 4.5	6 50.0	3 11.6	15 54.5	15 26.9	3 4.8	7 57.4
23 F	8 3 7.8	0♌12.8	13 37.1	4♐32.5	5 27.1	4 19.8	7 17.2	3 17.7	15 58.3	15 24.6	3 3.2	7 56.5
24 S	8 7 4.4	1 10.1	13 33.9	16 26.3	4 45.5	4 33.0	7 44.8	3 23.7	16 2.0	15 22.3	3 1.6	7 55.7
25 S	8 11 0.9	2 7.4	13 30.8	28 25.0	4 3.0	4 44.2	8 12.7	3 29.4	16 5.6	15 20.0	2 60.0	7 55.0
26 M	8 14 57.5	3 4.7	13 27.6	10♑31.4	3 20.1	4 53.3	8 40.9	3 35.0	16 9.1	15 17.7	2 58.3	7 54.2
27 T	8 18 54.0	4 2.0	13 24.4	22 47.7	2 37.8	5 0.2	9 9.4	3 40.5	16 12.5	15 15.4	2 56.7	7 53.5
28 W	8 22 50.6	4 59.3	13 21.2	5♒15.5	1 56.7	5 5.0	9 38.3	3 45.7	16 15.9	15 13.0	2 55.1	7 52.8
29 T	8 26 47.1	5 56.6	13 18.1	17 56.0	1 17.6	5 7.4	10 7.4	3 50.8	16 19.1	15 10.7	2 53.4	7 52.1
30 F	8 30 43.7	6 54.0	13 14.9	0♓49.7	0 41.3	5 7.6	10 36.9	3 55.7	16 22.3	15 8.3	2 51.8	7 51.5
31 S	8 34 40.3	7 51.3	13 11.7	13 57.1	0 8.4	5R 5.4	11 6.6	4 0.5	16 25.4	15 6.0	2 50.2	7 50.9

DECLINATION at NOON

DAY	EPHEMERIS SIDEREAL TIME	☉	☊	☽	☿	♀	♂	♃	♄	♅	♆	♇
1 T	6 36 23.6	23N 7.0	16N23.9	17S42.2	18N54.6	14N34.5	12S 5.2	10N29.9	13N57.5	16S39.6	19S 3.9	10S 3.9
4 S	6 48 13.2	22 53.3	16 26.7	7 48.3	17 44.7	13 31.2	12 28.6	10 38.8	14 1.7	16 41.3	19 4.9	10 4.2
7 W	7 0 2.9	22 36.0	16 29.4	6N 3.0	16 39.6	12 28.1	12 53.3	10 47.1	14 5.7	16 43.0	19 6.0	10 4.7
10 S	7 11 52.6	22 15.1	16 32.2	17 38.3	15 42.4	11 25.7	13 19.0	10 55.1	14 9.5	16 44.9	19 7.1	10 5.1
13 T	7 23 42.2	21 50.9	16 35.0	19 25.5	14 56.0	10 24.6	13 45.6	11 2.5	14 13.1	16 46.8	19 8.2	10 5.7
16 F	7 35 31.9	21 23.2	16 37.7	10 36.8	14 23.5	9 25.4	14 13.1	11 9.4	14 16.4	16 48.7	19 9.4	10 6.3
19 M	7 47 21.6	20 52.3	16 40.5	2S 8.4	14 7.0	8 28.9	14 41.3	11 15.9	14 19.4	16 50.7	19 10.5	10 7.0
22 T	7 59 11.3	20 18.2	16 43.2	13 24.7	14 7.7	7 35.9	15 10.1	11 21.8	14 22.2	16 52.8	19 11.6	10 7.8
25 S	8 11 0.9	19 41.1	16 45.9	19 43.6	14 25.0	6 47.3	15 39.3	11 27.2	14 24.8	16 54.8	19 12.8	10 8.6
28 W	8 22 50.6	19 1.1	16 48.7	18 16.0	14 56.5	6 3.9	16 9.0	11 32.1	14 27.1	16 56.9	19 13.9	10 9.6
31 S	8 34 40.3	18 18.2	16 51.4	8 49.8	15 37.8	5 26.8	16 38.8	11 36.5	14 29.2	16 59.0	19 15.1	10 10.5

AUGUST 1999

LONGITUDE at NOON

DAY	EPHEMERIS SIDEREAL TIME	☉	☊	☽	☿	♀	♂	♃	♄	♅	♆	♇
1 S	8 38 36.8	8♌48.7	13♌ 8.5	27♓18.2	29♋39.7	5♍ 0.9	11♏36.6	4♉ 5.1	16♉28.3	15♒ 3.6	2♒48.6	7♐50.3
2 M	8 42 33.4	9 46.1	13 5.4	10♈52.8	29R15.6	4R54.0	12 7.0	4 9.5	16 31.2	15R 1.2	2R47.0	7R49.8
3 T	8 46 29.9	10 43.5	13 2.2	24 40.7	28 56.7	4 44.7	12 37.6	4 13.7	16 34.0	14 58.8	2 45.4	7 49.3
4 W	8 50 26.5	11 40.9	12 59.0	8♉40.9	28 43.5	4 33.1	13 8.4	4 17.8	16 36.7	14 56.4	2 43.7	7 48.8
5 T	8 54 23.0	12 38.4	12 55.8	22 52.1	28 36.3	4 19.1	13 39.6	4 21.6	16 39.2	14 54.0	2 42.1	7 48.3
6 F	8 58 19.6	13 35.8	12 52.6	7♊12.1	28 35.4	4 2.8	14 11.0	4 25.3	16 41.7	14 51.6	2 40.5	7 47.9
7 S	9 2 16.1	14 33.3	12 49.5	21 37.8	28D41.1	3 44.1	14 42.7	4 28.8	16 44.1	14 49.2	2 39.0	7 47.5
8 S	9 6 12.7	15 30.9	12 46.3	6♋ 5.3	28 53.4	3 23.4	15 14.8	4 32.2	16 46.5	14 46.9	2 37.4	7 47.2
9 M	9 10 9.2	16 28.4	12 43.1	20 29.8	29 12.5	3 0.4	15 47.0	4 35.3	16 48.7	14 44.5	2 35.9	7 46.9
10 T	9 14 5.8	17 26.0	12 39.9	4♌46.5	29 38.5	2 35.3	16 19.5	4 38.3	16 50.7	14 42.1	2 34.3	7 46.6
11 W	9 18 2.4	18 23.5	12 36.8	18 50.5	0♌11.2	2 8.3	16 52.2	4 41.0	16 52.7	14 39.7	2 32.7	7 46.3
12 T	9 21 58.9	19 21.1	12 33.6	2♍38.0	0 50.8	1 39.4	17 25.2	4 43.6	16 54.6	14 37.3	2 31.2	7 46.1
13 F	9 25 55.5	20 18.7	12 30.4	16 6.3	1 37.1	1 8.8	17 58.4	4 46.0	16 56.4	14 34.9	2 29.6	7 45.9
14 S	9 29 52.0	21 16.4	12 27.2	29 14.2	2 30.0	0 36.6	18 31.9	4 48.1	16 58.1	14 32.6	2 28.1	7 45.7
15 S	9 33 48.6	22 14.0	12 24.0	12♎ 2.0	3 29.3	0 3.1	19 5.6	4 50.1	16 59.7	14 30.2	2 26.6	7 45.6
16 M	9 37 45.1	23 11.7	12 20.9	24 31.5	4 34.9	29♌28.4	19 39.6	4 51.9	17 1.1	14 27.8	2 25.1	7 45.5
17 T	9 41 41.7	24 9.3	12 17.7	6♏45.6	5 46.5	28 52.7	20 13.8	4 53.5	17 2.5	14 25.5	2 23.6	7 45.4
18 W	9 45 38.2	25 7.0	12 14.5	18 48.1	7 3.9	28 16.3	20 48.2	4 54.9	17 3.8	14 23.1	2 22.1	7 45.4
19 T	9 49 34.8	26 4.8	12 11.3	0♐43.3	8 26.8	27 39.3	21 22.8	4 56.1	17 4.9	14 20.8	2 20.7	7 45.4
20 F	9 53 31.3	27 2.5	12 8.2	12 35.9	9 54.7	27 2.0	21 57.6	4 57.1	17 6.0	14 18.5	2 19.2	7 45.4
21 S	9 57 27.9	28 0.2	12 5.0	24 30.4	11 27.5	26 24.7	22 32.7	4 57.9	17 6.9	14 16.2	2 17.8	7D45.5
22 S	10 1 24.4	28 58.0	12 1.8	6♑31.4	13 4.6	25 47.6	23 7.9	4 58.5	17 7.8	14 13.9	2 16.4	7 45.6
23 M	10 5 21.0	29 55.8	11 58.6	18 42.7	14 45.7	25 10.9	23 43.4	4 58.9	17 8.5	14 11.6	2 15.0	7 45.7
24 T	10 9 17.6	0♍53.6	11 55.4	1♒ 7.8	16 30.3	24 34.8	24 19.1	4 59.1	17 9.2	14 9.3	2 13.6	7 45.9
25 W	10 13 14.1	1 51.4	11 52.3	13 49.0	18 18.0	23 59.7	24 54.9	4 59.1	17 9.7	14 7.1	2 12.2	7 46.1
26 T	10 17 10.7	2 49.3	11 49.1	26 47.7	20 8.4	23 25.7	25 31.0	4R59.0	17 10.1	14 4.8	2 10.9	7 46.3
27 F	10 21 7.2	3 47.2	11 45.9	10♓ 3.9	22 0.9	22 52.9	26 7.2	4 58.6	17 10.4	14 2.6	2 9.6	7 46.6
28 S	10 25 3.8	4 45.1	11 42.7	23 36.6	23 55.2	22 21.7	26 43.6	4 58.0	17 10.7	14 0.4	2 8.3	7 46.9
29 S	10 29 0.3	5 43.1	11 39.6	7♈23.8	25 50.9	21 52.3	27 20.3	4 57.3	17 10.8	13 58.3	2 7.0	7 47.3
30 M	10 32 56.9	6 41.0	11 36.4	21 22.4	27 47.5	21 24.6	27 57.1	4 56.3	17 10.8	13 56.1	2 5.7	7 47.6
31 T	10 36 53.4	7 39.0	11 33.2	5♉29.0	29 44.8	20 58.9	28 34.0	4 55.1	17R10.7	13 54.0	2 4.5	7 48.0

DECLINATION at NOON

DAY	EPHEMERIS SIDEREAL TIME	☉	☊	☽	☿	♀	♂	♃	♄	♅	♆	♇
1 S	8 38 36.8	18N 3.3	16N52.3	4S28.0	15N52.9	5N16.0	16S48.8	11N37.8	14N29.8	16S59.8	19S15.5	10S10.9
4 W	8 50 26.5	17 16.8	16 55.0	9N23.8	16 39.4	4 48.7	17 18.7	11 41.4	14 31.5	17 1.9	19 16.6	10 11.9
7 S	9 2 16.1	16 27.9	16 57.7	19 3.0	17 23.5	4 29.8	17 48.7	11 44.5	14 33.0	17 4.0	19 17.7	10 13.1
10 T	9 14 5.8	15 36.5	17 0.4	18 20.2	17 59.8	4 19.8	18 18.5	11 47.0	14 34.2	17 6.1	19 18.8	10 14.3
13 F	9 25 55.5	14 42.9	17 3.1	8 8.7	18 23.3	4 19.2	18 48.2	11 48.9	14 35.1	17 8.2	19 19.9	10 15.5
16 M	9 37 45.1	13 47.2	17 5.7	4S50.6	18 29.3	4 27.7	19 17.4	11 50.2	14 35.8	17 10.3	19 21.0	10 16.8
19 T	9 49 34.8	12 49.5	17 8.4	15 23.1	18 13.5	4 44.6	19 46.3	11 50.9	14 36.2	17 12.3	19 22.1	10 18.2
22 S	10 1 24.4	11 50.0	17 11.1	20 8.9	17 33.0	5 8.8	20 14.6	11 51.1	14 36.3	17 14.3	19 23.1	10 19.6
25 W	10 13 14.1	10 48.8	17 13.7	16 45.2	16 27.3	5 38.6	20 42.2	11 50.6	14 36.2	17 16.3	19 24.0	10 21.1
28 S	10 25 3.8	9 46.1	17 16.4	5 40.7	14 58.2	6 11.9	21 9.0	11 49.6	14 35.8	17 18.2	19 25.0	10 22.6
31 T	10 36 53.4	8 41.9	17 19.0	8N27.1	13 9.4	6 46.8	21 35.0	11 48.0	14 35.1	17 20.0	19 25.9	10 24.2

SEPTEMBER 1999

LONGITUDE at NOON

DAY	EPHEMERIS SIDEREAL TIME	☉	☊	☽	☿	♀	♂	♃	♄	♅	♆	♇
	h m s	° ′	° ′	° ′	° ′	° ′	° ′	° ′	° ′	° ′	° ′	° ′
1 W	10 40 50.0	8♍37.0	11♌30.0	19♉40.4	1♍42.5	20♌35.3	29♏11.2	4♉53.7	17♉10.5	13♒51.9	2♒ 3.2	7♐48.5
2 T	10 44 46.5	9 35.1	11 26.8	3♊53.5	3 40.3	20R13.9	29 48.5	4R52.1	17R10.2	13R49.8	2R 2.0	7 48.9
3 F	10 48 43.1	10 33.2	11 23.7	18 5.8	5 37.9	19 54.8	0♐26.0	4 50.4	17 9.7	13 47.8	2 0.8	7 49.4
4 S	10 52 39.6	11 31.3	11 20.5	2♋15.0	7 35.1	19 38.0	1 3.7	4 48.4	17 9.2	13 45.7	1 59.7	7 50.0
5 S	10 56 36.2	12 29.5	11 17.3	16 19.5	9 31.9	19 23.6	1 41.6	4 46.2	17 8.6	13 43.7	1 58.5	7 50.5
6 M	11 0 32.7	13 27.7	11 14.1	0♌17.4	11 28.0	19 11.5	2 19.6	4 43.8	17 7.8	13 41.7	1 57.4	7 51.1
7 T	11 4 29.3	14 25.9	11 11.0	14 6.9	13 23.3	19 1.9	2 57.8	4 41.2	17 7.0	13 39.8	1 56.3	7 51.8
8 W	11 8 25.8	15 24.1	11 7.8	27 46.0	15 17.8	18 54.8	3 36.2	4 38.5	17 6.0	13 37.8	1 55.2	7 52.4
9 T	11 12 22.4	16 22.4	11 4.6	11♍12.7	17 11.3	18 50.0	4 14.7	4 35.5	17 5.0	13 35.9	1 54.2	7 53.1
10 F	11 16 18.9	17 20.7	11 1.4	24 25.2	19 3.8	18 47.6	4 53.4	4 32.4	17 3.8	13 34.1	1 53.2	7 53.8
11 S	11 20 15.5	18 19.1	10 58.2	7♎22.3	20 55.4	18 47.5	5 32.2	4 29.0	17 2.5	13 32.2	1 52.1	7 54.6
12 S	11 24 12.1	19 17.4	10 55.1	20 3.5	22 45.8	18D49.8	6 11.2	4 25.5	17 1.1	13 30.4	1 51.2	7 55.4
13 M	11 28 8.6	20 15.9	10 51.9	2♏29.4	24 35.2	18 54.4	6 50.4	4 21.7	16 59.7	13 28.7	1 50.2	7 56.2
14 T	11 32 5.2	21 14.3	10 48.7	14 41.7	26 23.5	19 1.2	7 29.7	4 17.8	16 58.1	13 26.9	1 49.3	7 57.1
15 W	11 36 1.7	22 12.7	10 45.5	26 43.1	28 10.7	19 10.2	8 9.2	4 13.7	16 56.4	13 25.2	1 48.4	7 58.0
16 T	11 39 58.3	23 11.2	10 42.3	8♐37.3	29 56.8	19 21.3	8 48.8	4 9.5	16 54.6	13 23.5	1 47.5	7 58.9
17 F	11 43 54.8	24 9.7	10 39.2	20 28.6	1♎41.9	19 34.5	9 28.6	4 5.0	16 52.7	13 21.9	1 46.7	7 59.8
18 S	11 47 51.4	25 8.3	10 36.0	2♑21.8	3 25.8	19 49.8	10 8.5	4 0.4	16 50.7	13 20.3	1 45.9	8 0.8
19 S	11 51 47.9	26 6.9	10 32.8	14 22.0	5 8.8	20 7.0	10 48.6	3 55.6	16 48.7	13 18.8	1 45.1	8 1.9
20 M	11 55 44.5	27 5.5	10 29.6	26 34.3	6 50.7	20 26.2	11 28.7	3 50.7	16 46.5	13 17.3	1 44.4	8 2.9
21 T	11 59 41.0	28 4.1	10 26.5	9♒ 3.1	8 31.6	20 47.1	12 9.1	3 45.5	16 44.2	13 15.8	1 43.7	8 4.0
22 W	12 3 37.6	29 2.8	10 23.3	21 52.2	10 11.5	21 9.9	12 49.5	3 40.2	16 41.9	13 14.4	1 43.0	8 5.1
23 T	12 7 34.1	0♎ 1.4	10 20.1	5♓ 3.9	11 50.4	21 34.5	13 30.1	3 34.8	16 39.4	13 12.9	1 42.3	8 6.3
24 F	12 11 30.7	1 0.1	10 16.9	18 38.9	13 28.3	22 0.7	14 10.8	3 29.2	16 36.8	13 11.6	1 41.7	8 7.4
25 S	12 15 27.2	1 58.9	10 13.7	2♈35.7	15 5.2	22 28.5	14 51.6	3 23.4	16 34.2	13 10.3	1 41.0	8 8.6
26 S	12 19 23.8	2 57.7	10 10.6	16 50.4	16 41.3	22 58.0	15 32.5	3 17.5	16 31.4	13 9.0	1 40.5	8 9.8
27 M	12 23 20.3	3 56.5	10 7.4	1♉17.6	18 16.4	23 28.9	16 13.6	3 11.4	16 28.6	13 7.7	1 39.9	8 11.1
28 T	12 27 16.9	4 55.3	10 4.2	15 50.7	19 50.6	24 1.3	16 54.8	3 5.2	16 25.7	13 6.5	1 39.4	8 12.4
29 W	12 31 13.4	5 54.2	10 1.0	0♊23.1	21 23.9	24 35.2	17 36.1	2 58.9	16 22.7	13 5.4	1 38.9	8 13.7
30 T	12 35 10.0	6 53.1	9 57.9	14 49.3	22 56.3	25 10.4	18 17.5	2 52.4	16 19.6	13 4.3	1 38.4	8 15.0

DECLINATION at NOON

DAY	EPHEMERIS SIDEREAL TIME	☉	☊	☽	☿	♀	♂	♃	♄	♅	♆	♇
1 W	10 40 50.0	8N20.3	17N19.9	12N39.0	12N29.7	6N58.5	21S43.4	11N47.3	14N34.8	17S20.6	19S26.2	10S24.7
4 S	10 52 39.6	7 14.5	17 22.5	20 1.3	10 22.5	7 32.7	22 8.0	11 44.9	14 33.8	17 22.4	19 27.0	10 26.3
7 T	11 4 29.3	6 7.7	17 25.1	16 42.7	8 6.7	8 4.7	22 31.5	11 42.0	14 32.6	17 24.0	19 27.8	10 27.9
10 F	11 16 18.9	4 59.9	17 27.7	5 23.5	5 46.1	8 33.3	22 53.8	11 38.4	14 31.1	17 25.6	19 28.6	10 29.6
13 M	11 28 8.6	3 51.4	17 30.3	7S32.9	3 23.6	8 57.8	23 14.7	11 34.3	14 29.3	17 27.1	19 29.3	10 31.3
16 T	11 39 58.3	2 42.3	17 32.9	17 10.0	1 1.3	9 17.6	23 34.3	11 29.7	14 27.3	17 28.5	19 29.9	10 33.0
19 S	11 51 47.9	1 32.7	17 35.5	20 16.0	1S19.2	9 32.2	23 52.3	11 24.6	14 25.1	17 29.8	19 30.5	10 34.8
22 W	12 3 37.6	0 22.8	17 38.1	15 2.6	3 36.7	9 41.5	24 8.7	11 19.0	14 22.6	17 31.0	19 31.1	10 36.6
25 S	12 15 27.2	0S47.3	17 40.7	2 36.0	5 50.3	9 45.2	24 23.4	11 12.9	14 19.9	17 32.1	19 31.6	10 38.4
28 T	12 27 16.9	1 57.3	17 43.3	11N42.5	7 59.2	9 43.4	24 36.4	11 6.4	14 17.0	17 33.1	19 32.0	10 40.2

OCTOBER 1999

LONGITUDE at NOON

DAY	EPHEMERIS SIDEREAL TIME	☉	☊	☽	☿	♀	♂	♃	♄	♅	♆	♇
1 F	12 39 6.5	7♎52.1	9♌54.7	29♊ 5.4	24♎27.9	25♌46.9	18♐59.1	2♉45.8	16♉16.4	13♒ 3.2	1♒38.0	8♐16.4
2 S	12 43 3.1	8 51.1	9 51.5	13♋ 9.3	25 58.6	26 24.7	19 40.8	2R39.1	16R13.2	13R 2.2	1R37.6	8 17.8
3 S	12 46 59.6	9 50.1	9 48.3	27 0.3	27 28.4	27 3.8	20 22.5	2 32.2	16 9.8	13 1.2	1 37.3	8 19.2
4 M	12 50 56.2	10 49.2	9 45.1	10♌38.6	28 57.3	27 44.0	21 4.4	2 25.2	16 6.4	13 0.3	1 36.9	8 20.7
5 T	12 54 52.8	11 48.3	9 42.0	24 4.9	0♏25.4	28 25.3	21 46.5	2 18.1	16 2.9	12 59.4	1 36.6	8 22.2
6 W	12 58 49.3	12 47.5	9 38.8	7♍19.7	1 52.6	29 7.7	22 28.6	2 10.9	15 59.3	12 58.5	1 36.4	8 23.7
7 T	13 2 45.9	13 46.7	9 35.6	20 23.4	3 18.9	29 51.2	23 10.8	2 3.6	15 55.7	12 57.7	1 36.1	8 25.2
8 F	13 6 42.4	14 45.9	9 32.4	3♎15.8	4 44.2	0♍35.6	23 53.2	1 56.2	15 51.9	12 57.0	1 35.9	8 26.8
9 S	13 10 39.0	15 45.2	9 29.3	15 56.7	6 8.7	1 21.0	24 35.6	1 48.7	15 48.1	12 56.3	1 35.8	8 28.3
10 S	13 14 35.5	16 44.5	9 26.1	28 25.9	7 32.2	2 7.5	25 18.3	1 41.2	15 44.3	12 55.7	1 35.7	8 30.0
11 M	13 18 32.1	17 43.8	9 22.9	10♏43.6	8 54.7	2 54.7	26 0.9	1 33.5	15 40.4	12 55.1	1 35.6	8 31.6
12 T	13 22 28.6	18 43.2	9 19.7	22 50.5	10 16.2	3 42.8	26 43.7	1 25.8	15 36.4	12 54.5	1 35.5	8 33.3
13 W	13 26 25.2	19 42.6	9 16.5	4♐48.5	11 36.5	4 31.8	27 26.6	1 18.0	15 32.3	12 54.0	1 35.5	8 35.0
14 T	13 30 21.7	20 42.0	9 13.4	16 40.2	12 55.8	5 21.5	28 9.6	1 10.2	15 28.2	12 53.5	1 35.5	8 36.7
15 F	13 34 18.3	21 41.5	9 10.2	28 29.1	14 13.8	6 12.0	28 52.7	1 2.2	15 24.0	12 53.1	1 35.5	8 38.4
16 S	13 38 14.8	22 41.0	9 7.0	10♑19.7	15 30.6	7 3.3	29 35.8	0 54.3	15 19.8	12 52.8	1D35.6	8 40.2
17 S	13 42 11.4	23 40.5	9 3.8	22 16.9	16 46.0	7 55.3	0♑19.1	0 46.3	15 15.5	12 52.5	1 35.7	8 42.0
18 M	13 46 7.9	24 40.0	9 0.7	4♒26.1	17 59.9	8 48.0	1 2.4	0 38.2	15 11.1	12 52.2	1 35.8	8 43.8
19 T	13 50 4.5	25 39.6	8 57.5	16 52.7	19 12.2	9 41.4	1 45.9	0 30.2	15 6.7	12 52.0	1 36.0	8 45.6
20 W	13 54 1.0	26 39.2	8 54.3	29 41.6	20 22.8	10 35.4	2 29.4	0 22.1	15 2.3	12 51.8	1 36.2	8 47.4
21 T	13 57 57.6	27 38.8	8 51.1	12♓56.7	21 31.6	11 30.1	3 13.0	0 14.0	14 57.8	12 51.7	1 36.4	8 49.3
22 F	14 1 54.1	28 38.5	8 47.9	26 40.0	22 38.2	12 25.3	3 56.7	0 5.8	14 53.3	12 51.7	1 36.7	8 51.2
23 S	14 5 50.7	29 38.2	8 44.8	10♈50.8	23 42.7	13 21.2	4 40.5	29♈57.7	14 48.7	12 51.7	1 37.0	8 53.1
24 S	14 9 47.3	0♏37.9	8 41.6	25 25.3	24 44.6	14 17.6	5 24.4	29 49.6	14 44.1	12 51.7	1 37.3	8 55.0
25 M	14 13 43.8	1 37.7	8 38.4	10♉16.7	25 43.9	15 14.6	6 8.3	29 41.4	14 39.5	12D51.8	1 37.7	8 57.0
26 T	14 17 40.4	2 37.5	8 35.2	25 16.1	26 40.1	16 12.2	6 52.3	29 33.3	14 34.8	12 51.9	1 38.1	8 58.9
27 W	14 21 36.9	3 37.3	8 32.1	10♊13.9	27 32.9	17 10.2	7 36.4	29 25.2	14 30.1	12 52.1	1 38.6	9 0.9
28 T	14 25 33.5	4 37.1	8 28.9	25 1.4	28 22.1	18 8.8	8 20.6	29 17.2	14 25.4	12 52.4	1 39.0	9 2.9
29 F	14 29 30.0	5 37.0	8 25.7	9♋32.5	29 7.1	19 7.9	9 4.9	29 9.1	14 20.6	12 52.7	1 39.5	9 4.9
30 S	14 33 26.6	6 37.0	8 22.5	23 43.7	29 47.5	20 7.4	9 49.2	29 1.1	14 15.9	12 53.0	1 40.1	9 7.0
31 S	14 37 23.1	7 37.0	8 19.3	7♌34.2	0♐22.9	21 7.5	10 33.6	28 53.2	14 11.1	12 53.5	1 40.7	9 9.1

DECLINATION at NOON

DAY	EPHEMERIS SIDEREAL TIME	☉	☊	☽	☿	♀	♂	♃	♄	♅	♆	♇
1 F	12 39 6.5	3S 7.3	17N45.8	19N60.0	10S 2.8	9N36.0	24S47.4	10N59.5	14N13.9	17S34.0	19S32.3	10S42.0
4 M	12 50 56.2	4 16.9	17 48.4	17 30.5	12 0.6	9 23.1	24 56.6	10 52.2	14 10.7	17 34.8	19 32.6	10 43.8
7 T	13 2 45.9	5 26.1	17 50.9	6 45.3	13 52.0	9 4.9	25 3.7	10 44.6	14 7.2	17 35.4	19 32.9	10 45.6
10 S	13 14 35.5	6 34.7	17 53.4	6S18.8	15 36.2	8 41.4	25 8.7	10 36.8	14 3.7	17 35.9	19 33.0	10 47.4
13 W	13 26 25.2	7 42.5	17 56.0	16 35.4	17 12.6	8 12.9	25 11.7	10 28.7	13 59.9	17 36.3	19 33.1	10 49.2
16 S	13 38 14.8	8 49.4	17 58.5	20 32.9	18 40.4	7 39.6	25 12.4	10 20.5	13 56.1	17 36.6	19 33.2	10 51.0
19 T	13 50 4.5	9 55.1	18 1.0	16 22.2	19 58.6	7 1.8	25 10.9	10 12.1	13 52.1	17 36.7	19 33.1	10 52.8
22 F	14 1 54.1	10 59.5	18 3.5	4 42.2	21 6.1	6 19.5	25 7.1	10 3.8	13 48.0	17 36.7	19 33.0	10 54.6
25 M	14 13 43.8	12 2.3	18 6.0	10N 8.6	22 1.2	5 33.2	25 1.1	9 55.4	13 43.9	17 36.6	19 32.9	10 56.3
28 T	14 25 33.5	13 3.6	18 8.5	19 52.6	22 42.0	4 43.0	24 52.7	9 47.1	13 39.7	17 36.3	19 32.6	10 58.0
31 S	14 37 23.1	14 3.0	18 11.0	18 17.6	23 5.9	3 49.3	24 42.0	9 38.9	13 35.5	17 35.9	19 32.3	10 59.7

NOVEMBER 1999

LONGITUDE at NOON

DAY	EPHEMERIS SIDEREAL TIME	☉	☊	☽	☿	♀	♂	♃	♄	♅	♆	♇
	h m s	° ′	° ′	° ′	° ′	° ′	° ′	° ′	° ′	° ′	° ′	° ′
1 M	14 41 19.7	8 ♏ 37.0	8 ♌ 16.2	21 ♌ 5.0	0 ♐ 52.6	22 ♍ 8.0	11 ♑ 18.1	28 ♈ 45.3	14 ♉ 6.3	12 ♒ 53.9	1 ♒ 41.3	9 ♐ 11.1
2 T	14 45 16.2	9 37.0	8 13.0	4 ♍ 18.1	1 16.1	23 8.8	12 2.7	28 R 37.4	14 R 1.5	12 54.4	1 41.9	9 13.2
3 W	14 49 12.8	10 37.1	8 9.8	17 16.1	1 32.8	24 10.1	12 47.3	28 29.6	13 56.7	12 55.0	1 42.6	9 15.3
4 T	14 53 9.4	11 37.2	8 6.6	0 ♎ 1.2	1 41.9	25 11.8	13 32.0	28 21.9	13 51.8	12 55.6	1 43.3	9 17.5
5 F	14 57 5.9	12 37.4	8 3.5	12 35.2	1 42.9	26 13.9	14 16.7	28 14.2	13 47.0	12 56.2	1 44.1	9 19.6
6 S	15 1 2.5	13 37.6	8 0.3	24 59.4	1 R 35.2	27 16.4	15 1.5	28 6.7	13 42.1	12 56.9	1 44.8	9 21.7
7 S	15 4 59.0	14 37.8	7 57.1	7 ♏ 14.7	1 18.1	28 19.2	15 46.4	27 59.2	13 37.3	12 57.7	1 45.6	9 23.9
8 M	15 8 55.6	15 38.0	7 53.9	19 21.9	0 51.3	29 22.4	16 31.4	27 51.8	13 32.4	12 58.5	1 46.5	9 26.1
9 T	15 12 52.1	16 38.3	7 50.7	1 ♐ 21.7	0 14.7	0 ♎ 25.9	17 16.4	27 44.5	13 27.6	12 59.4	1 47.3	9 28.3
10 W	15 16 48.7	17 38.6	7 47.6	13 15.3	29 ♏ 28.1	1 29.7	18 1.5	27 37.3	13 22.7	13 0.3	1 48.2	9 30.5
11 T	15 20 45.2	18 38.9	7 44.4	25 4.6	28 32.2	2 33.9	18 46.7	27 30.2	13 17.9	13 1.2	1 49.2	9 32.7
12 F	15 24 41.8	19 39.3	7 41.2	6 ♑ 52.2	27 27.8	3 38.3	19 31.9	27 23.2	13 13.1	13 2.2	1 50.1	9 34.9
13 S	15 28 38.3	20 39.6	7 38.0	18 41.4	26 16.2	4 43.1	20 17.1	27 16.3	13 8.3	13 3.3	1 51.1	9 37.1
14 S	15 32 34.9	21 40.0	7 34.9	0 ♒ 36.7	24 59.3	5 48.1	21 2.5	27 9.6	13 3.5	13 4.4	1 52.2	9 39.4
15 M	15 36 31.5	22 40.5	7 31.7	12 42.7	23 39.2	6 53.5	21 47.8	27 3.0	12 58.8	13 5.6	1 53.2	9 41.6
16 T	15 40 28.0	23 40.9	7 28.5	25 4.9	22 18.6	7 59.1	22 33.3	26 56.5	12 54.0	13 6.8	1 54.3	9 43.9
17 W	15 44 24.6	24 41.4	7 25.3	7 ♓ 48.5	21 0.0	9 4.9	23 18.7	26 50.2	12 49.3	13 8.0	1 55.4	9 46.2
18 T	15 48 21.1	25 41.9	7 22.2	20 58.2	19 46.2	10 11.1	24 4.3	26 44.0	12 44.7	13 9.3	1 56.6	9 48.4
19 F	15 52 17.7	26 42.4	7 19.0	4 ♈ 37.4	18 39.3	11 17.4	24 49.8	26 38.0	12 40.0	13 10.7	1 57.8	9 50.7
20 S	15 56 14.2	27 42.9	7 15.8	18 47.1	17 41.3	12 24.1	25 35.5	26 32.1	12 35.4	13 12.1	1 59.0	9 53.0
21 S	16 0 10.8	28 43.5	7 12.6	3 ♉ 25.3	16 53.8	13 31.0	26 21.2	26 26.4	12 30.9	13 13.6	2 0.2	9 55.4
22 M	16 4 7.3	29 44.1	7 9.4	18 25.9	16 17.4	14 38.1	27 6.9	26 20.9	12 26.4	13 15,1	2 1.5	9 57.7
23 T	16 8 3.9	0 ♐ 44.7	7 6.3	3 ♊ 40.0	15 52.8	15 45.4	27 52.6	26 15.5	12 21.9	13 16.6	2 2.8	9 60.0
24 W	16 12 0.5	1 45.3	7 3.1	18 56.5	15 39.7	16 53.0	28 38.4	26 10.2	12 17.5	13 18.2	2 4.1	10 2.3
25 T	16 15 57.0	2 46.0	6 59.9	4 ♋ 4.6	15 37.9	18 0.8	29 24.2	26 5.1	12 13.1	13 19.8	2 5.5	10 4.6
26 F	16 19 53.6	3 46.6	6 56.7	18 55.3	15 D 46.8	19 8.8	0 ♒ 10.1	26 0.2	12 8.7	13 21.5	2 6.9	10 6.9
27 S	16 23 50.1	4 47.3	6 53.6	3 ♌ 22.7	16 5.6	20 17.0	0 56.0	25 55.5	12 4.5	13 23.2	2 8.3	10 9.3
28 S	16 27 46.7	5 48.1	6 50.4	17 24.4	16 33.4	21 25.3	1 41.9	25 51.0	12 0.2	13 25.0	2 9.7	10 11.6
29 M	16 31 43.2	6 48.8	6 47.2	1 ♍ 0.4	17 9.4	22 33.9	2 27.9	25 46.6	11 56.0	13 26.8	2 11.2	10 13.9
30 T	16 35 39.8	7 49.6	6 44.0	14 13.0	17 52.6	23 42.7	3 13.9	25 42.4	11 51.9	13 28.7	2 12.7	10 16.3

DECLINATION at NOON

DAY	EPHEMERIS SIDEREAL TIME	☉	☊	☽	☿	♀	♂	♃	♄	♅	♆	♇
1 M	14 41 19.7	14 S 22.4	18 N 11.8	15 N 30.5	23 S 9.6	3 N 30.6	24 S 37.9	9 N 36.2	13 N 34.1	17 S 35.8	19 S 32.2	11 S 0.3
4 T	14 53 9.4	15 19.1	18 14.3	3 36.2	23 5.0	2 32.6	24 24.1	9 28.3	13 29.9	17 35.2	19 31.8	11 2.0
7 S	15 4 59.0	16 13.5	18 16.7	9 S 12.2	22 33.1	1 31.8	24 8.0	9 20.7	13 25.7	17 34.5	19 31.3	11 3.6
10 W	15 16 48.7	17 5.6	18 19.2	18 22.2	21 28.7	0 28.4	23 49.5	9 13.4	13 21.6	17 33.7	19 30.8	11 5.2
13 S	15 28 38.3	17 54.9	18 21.6	20 34.9	19 51.4	0 S 37.0	23 28.7	9 6.4	13 17.5	17 32.7	19 30.2	11 6.7
16 T	15 40 28.0	18 41.5	18 24.0	14 40.1	17 53.6	1 44.3	23 5.7	8 59.9	13 13.5	17 31.7	19 29.6	11 8.2
19 F	15 52 17.7	19 25.1	18 26.5	2 6.2	16 1.7	2 53.1	22 40.5	8 53.9	13 9.6	17 30.5	19 28.9	11 9.7
22 M	16 4 7.3	20 5.5	18 28.9	12 N 34.1	14 43.4	4 3.0	22 13.1	8 48.4	13 5.9	17 29.1	19 28.1	11 11.1
25 T	16 15 57.0	20 42.7	18 31.3	20 42.7	14 10.9	5 13.7	21 43.5	8 43.4	13 2.3	17 27.7	19 27.2	11 12.4
28 S	16 27 46.7	21 16.3	18 33.7	16 36.7	14 20.6	6 24.8	21 11.9	8 39.0	12 58.8	17 26.1	19 26.3	11 13.7

DECEMBER 1999

LONGITUDE at NOON

DAY	EPHEMERIS SIDEREAL TIME	☉	☊	☽	☿	♀	♂	♃	♄	♅	♆	♇
1 W	16 39 36.4	8 ♐ 50.4	6 ♌ 40.9	27 ♍ 5.3	18 ♏ 42.2	24 ♎ 51.7	3 ♒ 59.9	25 ♈ 38.4	11 ♉ 47.9	13 ♒ 30.6	2 ♒ 14.2	10 ♐ 18.6
2 T	16 43 32.9	9 51.2	6 37.7	9 ♎ 40.9	19 37.5	26 0.8	4 46.0	25 R 34.6	11 R 43.9	13 32.6	2 15.7	10 20.9
3 F	16 47 29.5	10 52.1	6 34.5	22 3.1	20 37.7	27 10.1	5 32.1	25 31.0	11 40.0	13 34.5	2 17.3	10 23.3
4 S	16 51 26.0	11 53.0	6 31.3	4 ♏ 14.9	21 42.3	28 19.6	6 18.3	25 27.6	11 36.1	13 36.6	2 18.9	10 25.6
5 S	16 55 22.6	12 53.9	6 28.1	16 18.7	22 50.5	29 29.2	7 4.4	25 24.3	11 32.3	13 38.7	2 20.5	10 28.0
6 M	16 59 19.1	13 54.8	6 25.0	28 16.5	24 2.0	0 ♏ 39.0	7 50.6	25 21.3	11 28.6	13 40.8	2 22.2	10 30.3
7 T	17 3 15.7	14 55.7	6 21.8	10 ♐ 9.8	25 16.3	1 48.9	8 36.9	25 18.5	11 25.0	13 42.9	2 23.8	10 32.6
8 W	17 7 12.3	15 56.7	6 18.6	22 0.1	26 33.0	2 59.0	9 23.2	25 15.9	11 21.4	13 45.1	2 25.5	10 35.0
9 T	17 11 8.8	16 57.6	6 15.4	3 ♑ 49.1	27 51.7	4 9.2	10 9.4	25 13.4	11 18.0	13 47.4	2 27.2	10 37.3
10 F	17 15 5.4	17 58.6	6 12.3	15 38.5	29 12.2	5 19.6	10 55.8	25 11.2	11 14.6	13 49.7	2 29.0	10 39.6
11 S	17 19 1.9	18 59.6	6 9.1	27 31.0	0 ♐ 34.3	6 30.0	11 42.1	25 9.2	11 11.3	13 52.0	2 30.7	10 41.9
12 S	17 22 58.5	20 0.6	6 5.9	9 ♒ 29.4	1 57.7	7 40.7	12 28.5	25 7.5	11 8.1	13 54.4	2 32.6	10 44.3
13 M	17 26 55.0	21 1.7	6 2.7	21 37.5	3 22.2	8 51.4	13 14.9	25 5.9	11 5.0	13 56.8	2 34.4	10 46.6
14 T	17 30 51.6	22 2.7	5 59.6	3 ♓ 59.5	4 47.7	10 2.2	14 1.3	25 4.5	11 1.9	13 59.2	2 36.2	10 48.9
15 W	17 34 48.2	23 3.7	5 56.4	16 39.8	6 14.1	11 13.2	14 47.7	25 3.3	10 58.9	14 1.7	2 38.0	10 51.2
16 T	17 38 44.7	24 4.8	5 53.2	29 42.8	7 41.2	12 24.2	15 34.2	25 2.3	10 56.1	14 4.2	2 39.9	10 53.5
17 F	17 42 41.3	25 5.8	5 50.0	13 ♈ 12.1	9 9.0	13 35.4	16 20.6	25 1.6	10 53.3	14 6.8	2 41.8	10 55.8
18 S	17 46 37.8	26 6.9	5 46.8	27 10.0	10 37.3	14 46.7	17 7.1	25 1.0	10 50.6	14 9.3	2 43.7	10 58.1
19 S	17 50 34.4	27 7.9	5 43.7	11 ♉ 36.0	12 6.2	15 58.0	17 53.5	25 0.7	10 48.0	14 11.9	2 45.6	11 0.3
20 M	17 54 30.9	28 9.0	5 40.5	26 26.8	13 35.5	17 9.5	18 40.0	25 0.6	10 45.5	14 14.6	2 47.6	11 2.6
21 T	17 58 27.5	29 10.1	5 37.3	11 ♊ 35.7	15 5.3	18 21.1	19 26.5	25 0.6	10 43.2	14 17.3	2 49.5	11 4.8
22 W	18 2 24.1	0 ♑ 11.1	5 34.1	26 53.1	16 35.4	19 32.8	20 13.0	25 D 0.9	10 40.9	14 20.0	2 51.5	11 7.1
23 T	18 6 20.6	1 12.2	5 31.0	12 ♋ 8.3	18 5.8	20 44.5	20 59.5	25 1.4	10 38.7	14 22.7	2 53.5	11 9.3
24 F	18 10 17.2	2 13.3	5 27.8	27 11.1	19 36.6	21 56.4	21 46.0	25 2.1	10 36.6	14 25.5	2 55.5	11 11.5
25 S	18 14 13.7	3 14.4	5 24.6	11 ♌ 53.3	21 7.8	23 8.3	22 32.5	25 3.1	10 34.6	14 28.3	2 57.5	11 13.7
26 S	18 18 10.3	4 15.5	5 21.4	26 9.8	22 39.2	24 20.4	23 19.0	25 4.2	10 32.7	14 31.2	2 59.6	11 15.9
27 M	18 22 6.8	6 16.6	5 18.3	9 ♍ 58.6	24 10.9	25 32.5	24 5.5	25 5.5	10 30.9	14 34.0	3 1.6	11 18.1
28 T	18 26 3.4	6 17.8	5 15.1	23 20.2	25 42.9	26 44.7	24 52.1	25 7.0	10 29.2	14 36.9	3 3.7	11 20.3
29 W	18 29 60.0	7 18.9	5 11.9	6 ♎ 17.3	27 15.2	27 57.0	25 38.6	25 8.8	10 27.7	14 39.9	3 5.8	11 22.4
30 T	18 33 56.5	8 20.1	5 8.7	18 53.4	28 47.8	29 9.4	26 25.1	25 10.7	10 26.2	14 42.8	3 7.9	11 24.6
31 F	18 37 53.1	9 21.2	5 5.5	1 ♏ 12.5	0 ♑ 20.8	0 ♐ 21.8	27 11.7	25 12.9	10 24.9	14 45.8	3 10.0	11 26.7

DECLINATION at NOON

DAY	EPHEMERIS SIDEREAL TIME	☉	☊	☽	☿	♀	♂	♃	♄	♅	♆	♇
1 W	16 39 36.4	21 S 46.4	18 N 36.1	4 N 49.4	15 S 1.2	7 S 36.0	20 S 38.2	8 N 35.3	12 N 55.6	17 S 24.4	19 S 25.4	11 S 15.0
4 S	16 51 26.0	22 12.7	18 38.5	8 S 8.2	16 1.1	8 46.9	20 2.7	8 32.1	12 52.5	17 22.6	19 24.4	11 16.1
7 T	17 3 15.7	22 35.1	18 40.9	17 50.8	17 11.1	9 57.2	19 25.2	8 29.6	12 49.7	17 20.7	19 23.3	11 17.3
10 F	17 15 5.4	22 53.6	18 43.2	20 52.2	18 24.4	11 6.4	18 45.9	8 27.8	12 47.2	17 18.7	19 22.2	11 18.3
13 M	17 26 55.0	23 8.0	18 45.6	15 45.0	19 36.6	12 14.2	18 4.9	8 26.7	12 44.9	17 16.6	19 21.0	11 19.3
16 T	17 38 44.7	23 18.3	18 47.9	4 1.8	20 44.4	13 20.2	17 22.3	8 26.3	12 42.8	17 14.4	19 19.8	11 20.3
19 S	17 50 34.4	23 24.4	18 50.3	10 N 24.8	21 45.8	14 24.1	16 38.1	8 26.6	12 41.0	17 12.1	19 18.6	11 21.1
22 W	18 2 24.1	23 26.2	18 52.6	20 15.3	22 39.0	15 25.4	15 52.4	8 27.6	12 39.6	17 9.7	19 17.3	11 21.9
25 S	18 14 13.7	23 23.9	18 54.9	17 55.1	23 23.1	16 23.8	15 5.4	8 29.2	12 38.4	17 7.2	19 15.9	11 22.7
28 T	18 26 3.4	23 17.2	18 57.3	6 17.8	23 57.0	17 19.0	14 17.1	8 31.5	12 37.5	17 4.7	19 14.5	11 23.3
31 F	18 37 53.1	23 6.4	18 59.6	6 S 58.9	24 20.0	18 10.7	13 27.5	8 34.5	12 37.0	17 2.0	19 13.1	11 23.9

LUNAR PHASES

1950

Month	Day	Phase	Time	A/P
JAN	4	F	7:48	A
	11	¾	10:32	A
	18	N	8:00	A
	26	¼	4:40	A
FEB	2	F	10:17	P
	9	¾	6:33	P
	16	N	10:53	P
	25	¼	1:53	P
MAR	4	F	10:34	A
	11	¾	2:39	A
	18	N	3:21	P
	26	¼	8:10	P
APR	2	F	8:49	P
	9	¾	11:43	A
	17	N	8:26	A
	25	¼	10:40	A
MAY	2	F	5:20	A
	8	¾	10:32	P
	17	N	0:55	A
	24	¼	9:29	P
	31	F	0:44	P
JUN	7	¾	11:36	A
	15	N	3:53	P
	23	¼	5:13	A
	29	F	7:59	P
JUL	7	¾	2:54	A
	15	N	5:06	A
	22	¼	10:51	A
	29	F	4:18	A
AUG	5	¾	7:56	P
	13	N	4:49	P
	20	¼	3:36	P
	27	F	2:52	P
SEP	4	¾	1:54	P
	12	N	3:29	A
	18	¼	8:55	P
	26	F	4:22	A
OCT	4	¾	7:54	A
	11	N	1:34	P
	18	¼	4:18	A
	25	F	8:47	P
NOV	3	¾	1:01	A
	9	N	11:26	P
	16	¼	3:07	P
	24	F	3:15	P
DEC	2	¾	4:22	P
	9	N	9:29	P
	16	¼	5:57	A
	24	F	10:24	A

1951

Month	Day	Phase	Time	A/P
JAN	1	¾	5:12	A
	7	N	8:11	P
	15	¼	0:23	A
	23	F	4:48	A
	30	¾	3:14	P
FEB	6	N	7:54	P
	13	¼	8:56	P
	21	F	9:13	P
	28	¾	11:00	P
MAR	7	N	8:51	P
	15	¼	5:40	P
	23	F	10:50	A
	30	¾	5:35	A
APR	6	N	10:52	A
	14	¼	0:56	P
	21	F	9:31	P
	28	¾	0:18	P
MAY	6	N	1:36	A
	14	¼	5:32	A
	21	F	5:45	A
	27	¾	8:17	P
JUN	4	N	4:41	P
	12	¼	6:52	P
	19	F	0:37	P
	26	¾	6:22	A
JUL	4	N	7:49	A
	12	¼	4:57	A
	18	F	7:18	A
	25	¾	7:00	P
AUG	2	N	10:40	P
	10	¼	0:23	P
	17	F	3:00	A
	24	¾	10:21	A
SEP	1	N	0:50	P
	8	¼	6:17	P
	15	F	0:39	P
	23	¾	4:14	A
OCT	1	N	1:57	A
	8	¼	0:01	A
	15	F	0:52	P
	22	¼	11:56	P
	30	N	1:55	P
NOV	6	¼	6:59	A
	13	F	3:53	P
	21	¾	8:02	P
	29	N	1:01	A
DEC	5	¼	4:21	P
	13	F	9:31	A
	21	¾	2:38	P
	28	N	11:44	A

1952

Month	Day	Phase	Time	A/P
JAN	4	¼	4:43	A
	12	F	4:56	A
	20	¾	6:10	A
	26	N	10:27	P
FEB	2	¼	8:02	P
	11	F	0:29	A
	18	¾	6:02	P
	25	N	9:16	A
MAR	3	¼	1:44	P
	11	F	6:15	P
	19	¾	2:40	A
	25	N	8:13	P
APR	2	¼	8:49	A
	10	F	8:54	A
	17	¾	9:08	A
	24	N	7:28	A
MAY	2	¼	3:58	A
	9	F	8:16	P
	16	¾	2:40	P
	23	N	7:28	P
	31	¼	9:47	P
JUN	8	F	5:07	A
	14	¾	8:28	P
	22	N	8:46	P
	30	¼	1:12	P
JUL	7	F	0:34	P
	14	¾	3:43	A
	21	N	11:31	P
	30	¼	1:52	A
AUG	5	F	7:41	P
	12	¾	1:28	P
	20	N	3:21	P
	28	¼	0:04	P
SEP	4	F	3:20	A
	11	¾	2:37	A
	19	N	7:22	A
	26	¼	8:31	P
OCT	3	F	0:16	P
	10	¾	7:33	P
	18	N	10:43	P
	26	¼	4:05	A
NOV	1	F	11:10	P
	9	¾	3:44	P
	17	N	0:56	P
	24	¼	11:35	A
DEC	1	F	0:42	P
	9	¾	1:22	P
	17	N	2:03	A
	23	¼	7:52	P
	31	F	5:06	A

1953

Month	Day	Phase	Time	A/P
JAN	8	¾	10:10	A
	15	N	2:09	P
	22	¼	5:43	A
	29	F	11:45	P
FEB	7	¾	4:10	A
	14	N	1:11	A
	20	¼	5:45	A
	28	F	6:59	P
MAR	8	¾	6:27	P
	15	N	11:05	A
	22	¼	8:11	A
	30	F	0:55	P
APR	7	¾	4:59	A
	13	N	8:10	P
	21	¼	0:41	A
	29	F	4:21	A
MAY	6	¾	0:21	P
	13	N	5:06	A
	20	¼	6:21	P
	28	F	5:04	P
JUN	4	¾	5:36	P
	11	N	2:55	P
	19	¼	0:02	P
	27	F	3:30	A
JUL	3	¾	10:04	A
	11	N	2:29	A
	19	¼	4:48	A
	26	F	0:21	P
AUG	2	¾	3:17	A
	9	N	4:11	P
	17	¼	8:09	P
	24	F	8:21	P
	31	¾	10:47	A
SEP	8	N	7:49	A
	16	¼	9:50	A
	23	F	4:16	A
	29	¾	9:52	P
OCT	8	N	0:41	A
	15	¼	9:45	P
	22	F	0:56	P
	29	¾	1:10	P
NOV	6	N	5:58	P
	14	¼	7:53	A
	20	F	11:13	P
	28	¾	8:17	A
DEC	6	N	10:49	A
	13	¼	4:31	P
	20	F	11:44	A
	28	¾	5:44	A

1954

Month	Day	Phase	Time	A/P
JAN	5	N	2:22	A
	12	¼	0:22	A
	19	F	2:37	A
	27	¾	3:29	A
FEB	3	N	3:56	P
	10	¼	8:30	A
	17	F	7:18	P
	25	¾	11:30	P
MAR	5	N	3:12	A
	11	¼	5:52	P
	19	F	0:43	P
	27	¾	4:14	P
APR	3	N	0:25	P
	10	¼	5:06	A
	18	F	5:49	A
	26	¾	4:58	A
MAY	2	N	8:23	P
	9	¼	6:18	P
	17	F	9:48	P
	25	¾	1:50	P
JUN	1	N	4:03	A
	8	¼	9:14	A
	16	F	0:06	P
	23	¾	7:46	P
	30	N	0:26	P
JUL	8	¼	1:34	A
	16	F	0:30	A
	23	¾	0:14	A
	29	N	10:20	P
AUG	6	¼	6:51	P
	14	F	11:04	P
	23	¾	4:52	A
	28	N	10:21	A
SEP	5	¼	0:29	P
	12	F	8:20	P
	19	¾	11:12	A
	27	N	0:51	A
OCT	5	¼	5:32	A
	12	F	5:10	A
	18	¾	8:31	A
	26	N	5:48	P
NOV	3	¼	8:55	P
	10	F	2:30	P
	17	¾	9:33	A
	25	N	0:31	P
DEC	3	¼	9:57	A
	10	F	0:57	A
	17	¾	2:22	A
	25	N	7:34	A

1955

Month	Day	Phase	Time	A/P
JAN	1	¼	8:29	P
	8	F	0:45	P
	15	¾	10:14	P
	24	N	1:07	A
	31	¼	5:06	A
FEB	7	F	1:43	A
	14	¾	7:40	P
	22	N	3:55	P
MAR	1	¼	0:41	P
	8	F	3:42	P
	16	¾	4:37	P
	24	N	3:43	A
	30	¼	8:10	P
APR	7	F	6:36	A
	15	¾	11:01	A
	22	N	1:07	P
	29	¼	4:24	A
MAY	6	F	10:15	P
	15	¾	1:43	A
	21	N	8:59	P
	28	¼	2:02	P
JUN	5	F	2:09	P
	13	¾	0:38	P
	20	N	4:12	A
	27	¼	1:45	A
JUL	5	F	5:29	A
	12	¾	8:31	P
	19	N	11:35	A
	26	¼	4:00	P
AUG	3	F	7:31	P
	11	¾	2:33	A
	17	N	7:59	P
	25	¼	8:52	A
SEP	2	F	8:00	A
	9	¾	8:00	A
	16	N	6:20	A
	24	¼	3:41	A
OCT	1	F	7:18	P
	8	¾	2:04	P
	15	N	7:33	P
	23	¼	11:05	P
	31	F	6:04	A
NOV	6	¾	9:57	P
	14	N	0:02	P
	22	¼	5:30	P
	29	F	4:51	P
DEC	6	¾	8:36	A
	14	N	7:08	A
	22	¼	9:40	A
	29	F	3:44	A

1956

Month	Day	Phase	Time	A/P
J^N	4	¾	10:42	P
	13	N	3:02	A
	20	¼	10:59	P
	27	F	2:41	P
FEB	3	¾	4:09	P
	11	N	9:38	P
	19	¼	9:22	A
	26	F	1:42	A
MAR	4	¾	11:54	A
	12	N	1:37	P
	19	¼	5:14	P
	26	F	1:12	P
APR	3	¾	8:07	A
	11	N	2:39	A
	17	¼	11:29	P
	25	F	1:41	A
MAY	3	¾	2:56	A
	10	N	1:05	P
	17	¼	5:16	A
	24	F	3:27	P
JUN	1	¾	7:14	P
	8	N	9:30	P
	15	¼	11:57	A
	23	F	6:14	A
JUL	1	¾	8:41	A
	8	N	4:38	A
	14	¼	8:47	P
	22	F	9:30	P
	30	¾	7:32	P
AUG	6	N	11:25	A
	13	¼	8:46	A
	21	F	0:38	P
	29	¾	4:13	A
SEP	4	N	6:58	P
	12	¼	0:14	A
	20	F	3:20	A
	27	¾	11:26	A
OCT	4	N	4:25	A
	11	¼	6:45	P
	19	F	5:25	P
	26	¾	6:03	P
NOV	2	N	4:44	P
	10	¼	3:10	P
	18	F	6:45	A
	25	¾	1:13	A
DEC	2	N	8:13	A
	10	¼	11:52	A
	17	F	7:07	P
	24	¾	10:10	A

1957

Month	Day	Phase	Time	A/P
JAN	1	N	2:14	A
	9	¼	7:07	A
	16	F	6:22	A
	22	¾	9:48	P
	30	N	9:26	P
FEB	7	¼	11:24	P
	14	F	4:39	P
	21	¾	0:19	P
MAR	1	N	4:13	P
	9	¼	11:51	A
	16	F	2:22	A
	23	¾	5:05	A
	31	N	9:20	A
APR	7	¼	8:33	P
	14	F	0:10	P
	21	¾	11:01	P
	29	N	11:54	P
MAY	7	¼	2:30	A
	13	F	10:35	P
	21	¾	5:04	P
	29	N	11:40	A
JUN	5	¼	7:10	A
	12	F	10:03	A
	20	¾	10:23	A
	27	N	8:54	P
JUL	4	¼	0:10	P
	11	F	10:50	P
	20	¾	2:18	A
	27	N	4:29	A
AUG	2	¼	6:56	P
	10	F	1:09	P
	18	¾	4:17	P
	25	N	11:33	A
SEP	1	¼	4:35	A
	9	F	4:56	A
	17	¾	4:03	A
	23	N	7:19	P
	30	¼	5:50	P
OCT	8	F	9:43	P
	16	¾	1:45	P
	23	N	4:44	A
	30	¼	10:49	A
NOV	7	F	2:33	P
	14	¾	10:00	P
	21	N	4:20	P
	29	¼	6:58	A
DEC	7	F	6:16	A
	14	¾	5:46	A
	21	N	6:12	A
	29	¼	4:53	A

1958

Month	Day	Phase	Time	A/P
JAN	5	F	8:09	P
	12	¾	2:02	P
	19	N	10:09	P
	28	¼	2:17	A
FEB	4	F	8:06	A
	10	¾	11:34	P
	18	N	3:39	P
	26	¼	8:52	P
MAR	5	F	6:29	P
	12	¾	10:48	A
	20	N	9:51	A
	28	¼	11:19	A
APR	4	F	3:45	A
	10	¾	11:51	P
	19	N	3:24	A
	26	¼	9:36	P
MAY	3	F	0:24	P
	10	¾	2:38	P
	18	N	7:01	P
	26	¼	4:39	A
JUN	1	F	8:56	P
	9	¾	7:00	A
	17	N	8:00	A
	24	¼	9:45	A
JUL	1	F	6:05	A
	9	¾	0:22	A
	16	N	6:34	P
	23	¼	2:20	P
	30	F	4:48	P
AUG	7	¾	5:50	P
	15	N	3:34	A
	21	¼	7:45	P
	29	F	5:54	A
SEP	6	¾	10:25	A
	13	N	0:03	P
	20	¼	3:18	A
	27	F	9:45	P
OCT	6	¾	1:21	A
	12	N	8:53	P
	19	¼	2:08	P
	27	F	3:41	P
NOV	4	¾	2:20	P
	11	N	6:34	A
	18	¼	5:00	A
	26	F	10:18	A
DEC	4	¾	1:25	A
	10	N	5:24	P
	17	¼	11:53	P
	26	F	3:55	A

1959

Month	Day	Phase	Time	A/P
JAN	2	¾	10:51	A
	9	N	5:34	A
	16	¼	9:27	P
	24	F	7:33	P
	31	¾	7:07	P
FEB	7	N	7:23	P
	15	¼	7:21	P
	23	F	8:54	A
MAR	2	¾	2:55	A
	9	N	10:52	A
	17	¼	3:11	P
	24	F	8:03	P
	31	¾	11:07	A
APR	8	N	3:30	A
	16	¼	7:33	A
	23	F	5:14	A
	29	¾	8:39	P
MAY	7	N	8:12	P
	15	¼	8:10	P
	22	F	0:57	P
	29	¾	8:14	A
JUN	6	N	11:54	A
	14	¼	5:23	A
	20	F	8:00	P
	27	¾	10:13	P
JUL	6	N	2:01	A
	13	¼	0:02	P
	20	F	3:34	A
	27	¾	2:23	P
AUG	4	N	2:34	P
	11	¼	5:10	P
	18	F	0:51	P
	26	¾	8:04	A
SEP	3	N	1:56	A
	9	¼	10:08	P
	17	F	0:52	A
	25	¾	2:23	A
OCT	2	N	0:31	P
	9	¼	4:23	A
	16	F	3:59	P
	24	¾	8:22	P
	31	N	10:42	P
NOV	7	¼	1:24	P
	15	F	9:42	A
	23	¾	1:04	P
	30	N	8:46	A
DEC	7	¼	2:12	A
	15	F	4:50	A
	23	¾	3:29	A
	29	N	7:10	P

1960

Month	Day	Phase	Time	
JAN	5	¼	6:54	P
	13	F	11:51	P
	21	¾	3:01	P
	28	N	6:16	A
FEB	4	¼	2:27	P
	12	F	5:25	P
	19	¾	11:48	P
	26	N	6:24	P
MAR	5	¼	11:06	A
	13	F	8:26	A
	20	¾	6:41	A
	27	N	7:38	A
APR	4	¼	7:05	A
	11	F	8:28	A
	18	¾	0:57	P
	25	N	9:45	P
MAY	4	¼	1:01	A
	11	F	5:43	A
	17	¾	7:55	P
	25	N	0:27	P
JUN	2	¼	4:02	P
	9	F	1:02	P
	16	¾	4:36	A
	24	N	3:28	A
JUL	2	¼	3:49	A
	8	F	7:37	P
	15	¾	3:43	P
	23	N	6:31	P
	31	¼	0:39	P
AUG	7	F	2:41	A
	14	¾	5:37	A
	22	N	9:16	A
	29	¼	7:23	P
SEP	5	F	11:19	A
	12	¾	10:20	P
	20	N	11:13	P
	28	¼	1:13	A
OCT	4	F	10:17	P
	12	¾	5:26	P
	20	N	0:03	P
	27	¼	7:34	A
NOV	3	F	11:58	A
	11	¾	1:48	P
	18	N	11:47	P
	25	¼	3:42	P
DEC	3	F	4:25	A
	11	¾	9:39	A
	18	N	10:47	A
	25	¼	2:30	A

1961

Month	Day	Phase	Time	
JAN	1	F	11:07	P
	10	¾	3:03	A
	16	N	9:31	P
	23	¼	4:14	P
	31	F	6:47	P
FEB	8	¾	4:50	P
	15	N	8:11	A
	22	¼	8:35	A
MAR	2	F	1:35	P
	10	¾	2:58	A
	16	N	6:51	P
	24	¼	2:49	A
APR	1	F	5:48	A
	8	¾	10:16	A
	15	N	5:38	A
	22	¼	9:50	P
	30	F	6:41	P
MAY	7	¾	3:58	P
	14	N	4:55	P
	22	¼	4:19	P
	30	F	4:38	A
JUN	5	¾	9:19	P
	13	N	5:17	A
	21	¼	9:02	A
	28	F	0:38	P
JUL	5	¾	3:33	A
	12	N	7:12	P
	20	¼	11:14	P
	27	F	7:51	P
AUG	3	¾	11:48	A
	11	N	10:37	A
	19	¼	10:52	A
	26	F	3:14	A
SEP	1	¾	11:06	P
	10	N	2:50	A
	17	¼	8:24	P
	24	F	11:34	A
OCT	1	¾	2:11	P
	9	N	6:53	P
	17	¼	4:35	A
	23	F	9:31	P
	31	¾	8:59	A
NOV	8	N	9:59	A
	15	¼	0:13	P
	22	F	9:44	A
	30	¾	6:19	A
DEC	7	N	11:52	P
	14	¼	8:06	P
	22	F	0:43	A
	30	¾	3:58	A

1962

Month	Day	Phase	Time	
JAN	6	N	0:36	P
	13	¼	5:02	A
	20	F	6:17	P
	28	¾	11:37	P
FEB	5	N	0:11	A
	11	¼	3:43	P
	19	F	1:19	P
	27	¾	3:50	P
MAR	6	N	10:31	A
	13	¼	4:39	A
	21	F	7:56	A
	29	¾	4:12	A
APR	4	N	7:46	P
	11	¼	7:51	P
	20	F	0:34	A
	27	¾	1:00	P
MAY	4	N	4:25	A
	11	¼	0:45	P
	19	F	2:33	P
	26	¾	7:06	P
JUN	2	N	1:27	P
	10	¼	6:22	A
	18	F	2:03	A
	24	¾	11:43	P
JUL	1	N	11:53	P
	9	¼	11:40	P
	17	F	11:41	A
	24	¾	4:19	A
	31	N	0:24	P
AUG	8	¼	3:56	P
	15	F	8:10	P
	22	¾	10:27	A
	30	N	3:10	A
SEP	7	¼	6:45	A
	14	F	4:12	A
	20	¾	7:36	P
	28	N	7:40	P
OCT	6	¼	7:55	P
	13	F	0:34	P
	20	¾	8:48	A
	28	N	1:06	P
NOV	5	¼	7:15	A
	11	F	10:04	P
	19	¾	2:10	A
	27	N	6:30	A
DEC	4	¼	4:49	P
	11	F	9:28	A
	18	¾	10:43	P
	26	N	11:00	P

1963

Month	Day	Phase	Time	
JAN	3	¼	1:02	A
	9	F	11:09	P
	17	¾	8:35	P
	25	N	1:43	P
FEB	1	¼	8:51	A
	8	F	2:52	P
	16	¾	5:39	P
	24	N	2:06	A
MAR	2	¼	5:18	P
	10	F	7:49	A
	18	¾	0:08	P
	25	N	0:10	P
APR	1	¼	3:15	A
	9	F	0:58	A
	17	¾	2:53	A
	23	N	8:29	P
	30	¼	3:08	P
MAY	8	F	5:24	P
	16	¾	1:37	P
	23	N	4:00	A
	30	¼	4:56	A
JUN	7	F	8:31	A
	14	¾	8:54	P
	21	N	11:46	A
	28	¼	8:24	P
JUL	6	F	9:56	P
	14	¾	1:58	A
	20	N	8:43	P
	28	¼	1:14	P
AUG	5	F	9:31	A
	12	¾	6:22	A
	19	N	7:35	A
	27	¼	6:55	A
SEP	3	F	7:34	P
	10	¾	11:43	A
	17	N	8:51	P
	26	¼	0:39	A
OCT	3	F	4:44	A
	9	¾	7:28	P
	17	N	0:43	P
	25	¼	5:21	P
NOV	1	F	1:56	P
	8	¾	6:37	A
	16	N	6:51	A
	24	¼	7:56	A
	30	F	11:55	P
DEC	7	¾	9:35	P
	16	N	2:07	A
	23	¼	7:55	P
	30	F	11:04	A

1964

Month	Day	Phase	Time	
JAN	6	¾	3:59	P
	14	N	8:44	P
	22	¼	5:29	A
	28	F	11:23	P
FEB	5	¾	0:43	P
	13	N	1:02	P
	20	¼	1:25	P
	27	F	0:40	P
MAR	6	¾	10:01	A
	14	N	2:14	A
	20	¼	8:40	P
	28	F	2:49	A
APR	5	¾	5:46	A
	12	N	0:38	P
	19	¼	4:10	A
	26	F	5:50	P
MAY	4	¾	10:20	P
	11	N	9:02	P
	18	¼	0:43	P
	26	F	9:30	A
JUN	3	¾	11:08	A
	10	N	4:23	A
	16	¼	11:02	P
	25	F	1:09	A
JUL	2	¾	8:31	P
	9	N	11:31	A
	16	¼	11:48	A
	24	F	3:59	P
AUG	1	¾	3:30	A
	7	N	7:17	P
	15	¼	3:20	A
	23	F	5:26	A
	30	¾	9:16	A
SEP	6	N	4:34	A
	13	¼	9:24	P
	21	F	5:31	P
	28	¾	3:02	P
OCT	5	N	4:20	P
	13	¼	4:57	P
	21	F	4:46	A
	27	¾	9:59	P
NOV	4	N	7:17	A
	12	¼	0:21	P
	19	F	3:44	P
	26	¾	7:11	A
DEC	4	N	1:19	A
	12	¼	6:02	A
	19	F	2:42	A
	25	¾	7:28	P

1965

Month	Day	Phase	Time	
JAN	2	N	9:07	P
	10	¼	9:00	P
	17	F	1:38	P
	24	¾	11:08	A
FEB	9	N	4:36	P
	9	¼	8:53	A
	16	F	0:27	A
	23	¾	5:40	A
MAR	3	N	9:56	A
	10	¼	5:53	P
	17	F	11:24	A
	25	¾	1:37	A
APR	2	N	0:21	A
	9	¼	0:40	A
	15	F	11:03	P
	23	¾	9:07	P
MAY	1	N	11:56	A
	8	¼	6:20	A
	15	F	11:53	A
	23	¾	2:41	P
	30	N	9:13	P
JUN	6	¼	0:12	P
	14	F	2:00	A
	22	¾	5:37	A
	29	N	4:53	A
JUL	5	¼	7:37	P
	13	F	5:03	P
	21	¾	5:54	P
	28	N	11:45	A
AUG	4	¼	5:48	A
	12	F	8:23	A
	20	¾	3:51	A
	26	N	6:51	P
SEP	2	¼	7:28	P
	10	F	11:33	P
	18	¾	11:59	A
	25	N	3:18	A
OCT	2	¼	0:38	P
	10	F	2:14	P
	17	¾	7:00	P
	24	N	2:12	P
NOV	1	¼	8:27	A
	9	F	4:16	A
	16	¾	1:54	A
	23	N	4:11	A
DEC	1	¼	5:25	A
	8	F	5:22	P
	15	¾	9:52	A
	22	N	9:04	P
	31	¼	1:47	A

1966

Month	Day	Phase	Time	
JAN	7	F	5:17	A
	13	¾	8:00	P
	21	N	3:47	P
	29	¼	7:49	P
FEB	5	F	3:59	P
	12	¾	8:53	A
	20	N	10:49	A
	28	¼	10:16	A
MAR	7	F	1:46	A
	14	¾	0:20	A
	22	N	4:47	A
	29	¼	8:44	P
APR	5	F	11:14	A
	12	¾	5:29	P
	20	N	8:36	P
	28	¼	3:50	A
MAY	4	F	9:01	P
	12	¾	11:20	A
	20	N	9:43	A
	27	¼	8:51	A
JUN	3	F	7:41	A
	11	¾	4:59	A
	18	N	8:09	P
	25	¼	1:23	P
JUL	2	F	7:37	P
	10	¾	9:43	P
	18	N	4:31	A
	24	¼	7:00	P
AUG	1	F	9:06	A
	9	¾	0:56	P
	16	N	11:48	A
	23	¼	3:02	A
	31	F	0:15	A
SEP	8	¾	2:08	A
	14	N	7:14	P
	21	¼	2:25	P
	29	F	4:48	P
OCT	7	¾	1:09	P
	14	N	3:52	A
	21	¼	5:35	A
	29	F	10:01	A
NOV	5	¾	10:19	P
	12	N	2:27	P
	20	¼	0:21	A
	28	F	2:41	A
DEC	5	¾	6:23	A
	12	N	3:14	A
	19	¼	9:42	P
	27	F	5:44	P

1967

Month	Day	Phase	Time	
JAN	3	¾	2:20	P
	10	N	6:07	P
	18	¼	7:42	P
	26	F	6:41	A
FEB	1	¾	11:04	P
	9	N	10:45	A
	17	¼	3:57	P
	24	F	5:44	P
MAR	3	¾	9:11	A
	11	N	4:30	A
	19	¼	8:32	A
	26	F	3:21	A
APR	1	¾	8:59	P
	9	N	10:21	P
	17	¼	8:48	P
	24	F	0:04	P
MAY	1	¾	10:33	A
	9	N	2:56	P
	17	¼	5:18	A
	23	F	8:23	P
	31	¾	1:53	A
JUN	8	N	5:14	A
	15	¼	11:12	A
	22	F	4:58	A
	29	¾	6:40	P
JUL	7	N	5:01	P
	14	¼	3:54	P
	21	F	2:40	P
	29	¾	0:15	P
AUG	6	N	2:49	A
	12	¼	8:45	P
	20	F	2:27	A
	28	¾	5:36	A
SEP	4	N	11:38	A
	11	¼	3:06	A
	18	F	5:00	P
	26	¾	9:44	P
OCT	3	N	8:25	P
	10	¼	0:12	P
	18	F	10:12	A
	26	¾	0:04	P
NOV	2	N	5:49	A
	9	¼	1:00	A
	17	F	4:53	A
	25	¾	0:24	A
DEC	1	N	4:10	P
	8	¼	5:58	P
	16	F	11:22	P
	24	¾	10:49	A
	31	N	3:39	A

1968

Month	Day	Phase	Time	
JAN	7	¼	2:23	P
	15	F	4:12	P
	22	¾	7:39	P
	29	N	4:30	P
FEB	6	¼	0:21	P
	14	F	6:44	A
	21	¾	3:28	A
	28	N	6:56	A
MAR	7	¼	9:21	A
	14	F	6:53	P
	21	¾	11:08	A
	28	N	10:49	P
APR	6	¼	3:28	A
	13	F	4:52	A
	19	¾	7:36	P
	27	N	3:22	P
MAY	5	¼	5:55	P
	12	F	1:05	P
	19	¾	5:45	A
	27	N	7:30	A
JUN	4	¼	4:47	A
	10	F	8:14	P
	17	¾	6:14	P
	25	N	10:25	P
JUL	3	¼	0:42	P
	10	F	3:18	A
	17	¾	9:12	A
	25	N	11:50	A
AUG	1	¼	6:35	P
	8	F	11:33	A
	16	¾	2:14	A
	23	N	11:57	P
	30	¼	11:35	P
SEP	6	F	10:08	P
	14	¾	8:32	P
	22	N	11:09	A
	29	¼	5:07	A
OCT	6	F	11:47	A
	14	¾	3:06	P
	21	N	9:45	P
	28	¼	0:40	P
NOV	5	F	4:26	A
	13	¾	8:54	A
	20	N	8:02	A
	26	¼	11:31	P
DEC	4	F	11:08	P
	13	¾	0:50	A
	19	N	6:19	P
	26	¼	2:15	P

1969

Month	Day	Phase	Time	
JAN	3	F	6:28	P
	11	¾	2:01	P
	18	N	4:59	A
	25	¼	8:24	A
FEB	2	F	0:57	P
	10	¾	0:09	P
	16	N	4:26	A
	24	¼	4:31	A
MAR	4	F	5:18	A
	11	¾	7:45	A
	18	N	4:52	A
	26	¼	0:49	A
APR	2	F	6:46	P
	9	¾	1:59	P
	16	N	6:17	P
	24	¼	7:45	P
MAY	2	F	5:14	A
	8	¾	8:12	P
	16	N	8:27	A
	24	¼	0:16	P
	31	F	1:19	P
JUN	7	¾	3:40	A
	14	N	11:09	P
	23	¼	1:45	A
	29	F	8:04	P
JUL	6	¾	1:18	P
	14	N	2:12	P
	22	¼	0:10	P
	29	F	2:46	A
AUG	5	¾	1:39	A
	13	N	5:17	A
	20	¼	8:04	P
	27	F	10:33	A
SEP	3	¾	4:59	P
	11	N	7:57	P
	19	¼	2:25	A
	25	F	8:22	P
OCT	3	¾	11:06	A
	11	N	9:40	A
	18	¼	8:32	A
	25	F	8:45	A
NOV	2	¾	7:15	A
	9	N	10:12	P
	16	¼	3:46	P
	23	F	11:55	P
DEC	2	¾	3:51	A
	9	N	9:43	A
	16	¼	1:10	A
	23	F	5:36	P
	31	¾	10:53	P

LUNAR PHASES

1970

Month	Day	Phase	Time	A/P
JAN	7	N	8:36	P
	14	¼	1:19	P
	22	F	0:57	P
	30	¾	2:39	P
FEB	6	N	7:13	A
	13	¼	4:11	A
	21	F	8:20	A
MAR	1	¾	2:34	A
	7	N	5:43	P
	14	¼	9:16	P
	23	F	1:53	A
	30	¾	11:05	A
APR	6	N	4:10	A
	13	¼	3:44	P
	21	F	4:22	P
	28	¾	5:19	P
MAY	5	N	2:52	P
	13	¼	10:26	A
	21	F	3:38	A
	27	¾	10:32	P
JUN	4	N	2:22	A
	12	¼	4:07	A
	19	F	0:28	P
	26	¾	4:02	A
JUL	3	N	3:19	P
	11	¼	7:44	P
	18	F	7:59	P
	25	¾	11:00	A
AUG	2	N	5:59	A
	10	¼	8:51	A
	17	F	3:16	A
	23	¾	8:35	P
	31	N	10:02	P
SEP	8	¼	7:39	P
	15	F	11:10	A
	22	¾	9:43	A
	30	N	2:32	P
OCT	8	¼	4:44	A
	14	F	8:22	P
	22	¾	2:48	A
	30	N	6:29	A
NOV	6	¼	0:48	P
	13	F	7:29	A
	20	¾	11:14	P
	28	N	9:15	P
DEC	5	¼	8:36	P
	12	F	9:04	P
	20	¾	9:10	P
	28	N	10:43	A

1971

Month	Day	Phase	Time	A/P
JAN	4	¼	4:56	A
	11	F	1:21	P
	19	¾	6:09	P
	26	N	10:56	P
FEB	2	¼	2:31	P
	10	F	7:42	A
	18	¾	0:14	P
	25	N	9:49	A
MAR	4	¼	2:02	A
	12	F	2:34	A
	20	¾	2:31	A
	26	N	7:24	P
APR	2	¼	3:47	P
	10	F	8:11	P
	18	¾	0:59	P
	25	N	4:02	A
MAY	2	¼	7:35	A
	10	F	11:24	A
	17	¾	8:16	P
	24	N	0:33	P
JUN	1	¼	0:43	A
	9	F	0:04	A
	16	¾	1:25	A
	22	N	9:58	P
	30	¼	6:11	P
JUL	8	F	10:37	A
	15	¾	5:47	A
	22	N	9:16	A
	30	¼	11:08	A
AUG	6	F	7:43	P
	13	¾	10:56	A
	20	N	10:54	P
	29	¼	2:57	A
SEP	5	F	4:03	A
	11	¾	6:24	P
	19	N	2:43	P
	27	¼	5:18	P
OCT	4	F	0:20	P
	11	¾	5:30	A
	19	N	8:00	A
	27	¼	5:55	A
NOV	2	F	9:20	P
	9	¾	8:52	P
	18	N	1:47	A
	25	¼	4:38	P
DEC	2	F	7:49	A
	9	¾	4:03	P
	17	N	7:04	P
	25	¼	1:36	A
	31	F	8:20	P

1972

Month	Day	Phase	Time	A/P
JAN	8	¾	1:32	P
	16	N	10:53	A
	23	¼	9:30	A
	30	F	10:59	A
FEB	7	¾	11:12	A
	15	N	0:30	A
	21	¼	5:21	P
	29	F	3:13	A
MAR	8	¾	7:06	A
	15	N	11:35	A
	22	¼	2:13	A
	29	F	8:06	P
APR	6	¾	11:45	P
	13	N	8:32	P
	20	¼	0:46	P
	28	F	0:45	P
MAY	6	¾	0:27	P
	13	N	4:09	A
	20	¼	1:17	A
	28	F	4:28	A
JUN	4	¾	9:22	P
	11	N	11:31	A
	18	¼	3:42	P
	26	F	6:47	P
JUL	4	¾	3:26	A
	10	N	7:40	P
	18	¼	7:47	A
	26	F	7:24	A
AUG	2	¾	8:03	A
	9	N	5:27	A
	17	¼	1:10	A
	24	F	6:23	P
	31	¾	0:49	P
SEP	7	N	5:29	P
	15	¼	7:14	P
	23	F	4:08	A
	29	¾	7:17	P
OCT	7	N	8:09	A
	15	¼	0:56	P
	22	F	1:26	P
	29	¾	4:42	A
NOV	6	N	1:22	A
	14	¼	5:02	A
	20	F	11:07	P
	27	¾	5:45	P
DEC	5	N	8:25	P
	13	¼	6:36	P
	20	F	9:46	A
	27	¾	10:28	A

1973

Month	Day	Phase	Time	A/P
JAN	4	N	3:43	P
	12	¼	5:28	A
	18	F	9:29	P
	26	¾	6:06	A
FEB	3	N	9:24	A
	10	¼	2:06	P
	17	F	10:08	A
	25	¾	3:12	A
MAR	5	N	0:08	A
	11	¼	9:26	P
	18	F	11:34	P
	26	¾	11:47	P
APR	3	N	11:46	A
	10	¼	4:29	A
	17	F	1:52	P
	25	¾	6:00	P
MAY	2	N	8:56	P
	9	¼	0:07	P
	17	F	4:59	A
	25	¾	8:41	A
JUN	1	N	4:35	A
	7	¼	9:12	P
	15	F	8:36	P
	23	¾	7:46	P
	30	N	11:39	A
JUL	7	¼	8:27	A
	15	F	11:57	A
	23	¾	3:58	A
	29	N	7:00	P
AUG	5	¼	10:28	P
	14	F	2:17	A
	21	¾	10:23	A
	28	N	3:26	A
SEP	4	¼	3:23	P
	12	F	3:17	P
	19	¾	4:11	P
	26	N	1:55	P
OCT	4	¼	10:33	A
	12	F	3:10	A
	18	¾	10:33	P
	26	N	3:17	A
NOV	3	¼	6:30	A
	10	F	2:28	P
	17	¾	6:35	A
	24	N	7:56	P
DEC	3	¼	1:30	A
	10	F	1:35	A
	16	¾	5:13	P
	24	N	3:08	P

1974

Month	Day	Phase	Time	A/P
JAN	1	¼	6:07	P
	8	F	0:37	P
	15	¾	7:05	A
	23	N	11:03	A
	31	¼	7:40	A
FEB	6	F	11:25	P
	14	¾	0:05	A
	22	N	5:35	A
MAR	1	¼	6:03	P
	8	F	10:04	A
	15	¾	7:16	P
	23	N	9:25	P
	31	¼	1:45	A
APR	6	F	9:01	P
	14	¾	2:59	P
	22	N	10:17	A
	29	¼	7:40	A
MAY	6	F	8:55	A
	14	¾	9:30	A
	21	N	8:35	P
	28	¼	1:04	P
JUN	4	F	10:11	P
	13	¾	1:46	A
	20	N	4:56	A
	26	¼	7:21	P
JUL	4	F	0:41	P
	12	¾	3:29	P
	19	N	0:07	P
	26	¼	3:52	A
AUG	3	F	3:58	A
	11	¾	2:47	A
	17	N	7:02	P
	24	¼	3:39	P
SEP	1	F	7:26	A
	9	¾	0:02	P
	16	N	2:46	A
	23	¼	7:09	A
OCT	1	F	10:39	A
	8	¾	7:46	P
	15	N	0:26	P
	23	¼	1:54	A
	31	F	1:20	A
NOV	7	¾	2:48	A
	14	N	0:54	A
	21	¼	10:40	P
	29	F	3:11	P
DEC	6	¾	10:11	A
	13	N	4:26	P
	21	¼	7:44	P
	29	F	3:52	A

1975

Month	Day	Phase	Time	A/P
JAN	4	¾	7:05	P
	12	N	10:21	A
	20	¼	3:15	P
	27	F	3:10	P
FEB	3	¾	6:24	A
	11	N	5:18	A
	19	¼	7:40	A
	26	F	1:15	A
MAR	4	¾	8:21	P
	12	N	11:48	P
	20	¼	8:05	P
	27	F	10:37	A
APR	3	¾	0:26	P
	11	N	4:40	P
	19	¼	4:42	A
	25	F	7:56	P
MAY	3	¾	5:45	A
	11	N	7:06	A
	18	¼	10:30	A
	25	F	5:51	A
JUN	1	¾	11:24	P
	9	N	6:50	P
	16	¼	2:59	P
	23	F	4:55	P
JUL	1	¾	4:38	P
	9	N	4:11	A
	15	¼	7:48	P
	23	F	5:29	A
	31	¾	8:49	A
AUG	7	N	11:58	A
	14	¼	2:24	A
	21	F	7:49	P
	29	¾	11:20	P
SEP	5	N	7:20	P
	12	¼	0:00	P
	20	F	11:51	A
	28	¾	11:47	A
OCT	5	N	3:24	A
	12	¼	1:16	A
	20	F	5:07	A
	27	¾	10:08	P
NOV	3	N	1:06	P
	10	¼	6:22	P
	18	F	10:29	P
	26	¾	6:53	A
DEC	3	N	0:51	A
	10	¼	2:40	P
	18	F	2:40	P
	25	¾	2:53	P

1976

Month	Day	Phase	Time	A/P
JAN	1	N	2:41	P
	9	¼	0:40	P
	17	F	4:48	A
	23	¾	11:05	P
	31	N	6:21	A
FEB	8	¼	10:06	A
	15	F	4:44	P
	22	¾	8:17	A
	29	N	11:26	P
MAR	9	¼	4:39	A
	16	F	2:53	A
	22	¾	6:55	P
	30	N	5:09	P
APR	7	¼	7:03	P
	14	F	11:50	A
	21	¾	7:15	A
	29	N	10:20	A
MAY	7	¼	5:18	A
	13	F	8:05	P
	20	¾	9:23	P
	29	N	1:48	A
JUN	5	¼	0:21	P
	12	F	4:16	A
	19	¾	1:16	P
	27	N	2:51	P
JUL	4	¼	5:29	P
	11	F	1:10	P
	19	¾	6:30	A
	27	N	1:39	A
AUG	2	¼	10:07	P
	9	F	11:44	P
	18	¾	0:14	A
	25	N	11:01	A
SEP	1	¼	3:36	A
	8	F	0:53	P
	16	¾	5:21	P
	23	N	7:56	P
	30	¼	11:13	A
OCT	8	F	4:56	A
	16	¾	9:00	A
	23	N	5:10	A
	29	¼	10:06	P
NOV	6	F	11:16	P
	14	¾	10:40	P
	21	N	3:12	P
	28	¼	1:00	P
DEC	6	F	6:16	P
	14	¾	10:15	A
	21	N	2:09	A
	28	¼	7:49	A

1977

Month	Day	Phase	Time	A/P
JAN	5	F	0:11	P
	12	¾	7:56	P
	19	N	2:12	P
	27	¼	5:13	A
FEB	4	F	3:57	A
	11	¾	4:08	A
	18	N	3:38	A
	26	¼	2:51	A
MAR	5	F	5:14	P
	12	¾	11:36	A
	19	N	6:34	P
	27	¼	10:27	P
APR	4	F	4:10	A
	10	¾	7:15	P
	18	N	10:36	A
	26	¼	2:43	P
MAY	3	F	1:04	P
	10	¾	4:09	A
	18	N	2:52	A
	26	¼	3:21	A
JUN	1	F	8:32	P
	8	¾	3:08	P
	16	N	6:24	P
	24	¼	0:45	P
JUL	1	F	3:25	A
	8	¾	4:40	A
	16	N	8:37	A
	23	¼	7:39	P
	30	F	10:53	A
AUG	6	¾	8:41	P
	14	N	9:32	P
	22	¼	1:05	A
	28	F	8:11	P
SEP	5	¾	2:34	P
	13	N	9:24	A
	20	¼	6:19	A
	27	F	8:18	A
OCT	5	¾	9:22	A
	12	N	8:32	P
	19	¼	0:47	P
	26	F	11:36	P
NOV	4	¾	3:59	A
	11	N	7:10	A
	17	¼	9:53	P
	25	F	5:32	P
DEC	3	¾	9:17	P
	10	N	5:34	P
	17	¼	10:38	A
	25	F	0:50	P

1978

Month	Day	Phase	Time	A/P
JAN	2	¾	0:08	P
	9	N	4:00	A
	16	¼	3:04	A
	24	F	7:57	A
	31	¾	11:52	P
FEB	7	N	2:55	P
	14	¼	10:12	P
	23	F	1:27	A
MAR	2	¾	8:35	A
	9	N	2:37	A
	16	¼	6:22	P
	24	F	4:21	P
	31	¾	3:12	P
APR	7	N	3:16	P
	15	¼	1:57	P
	23	F	4:12	A
	29	¾	9:03	P
MAY	7	N	4:48	A
	15	¼	7:41	A
	22	F	1:18	P
	29	¾	3:31	A
JUN	5	N	7:02	P
	13	¼	10:45	P
	20	F	8:32	P
	27	¾	11:45	A
JUL	5	N	9:52	A
	13	¼	10:50	A
	20	F	3:06	A
	26	¾	10:32	P
AUG	4	N	1:02	A
	11	¼	8:07	P
	18	F	10:15	A
	25	¾	0:19	P
SEP	2	N	4:10	P
	10	¼	3:21	A
	16	F	7:02	P
	24	¾	5:09	A
OCT	2	N	6:42	A
	9	¼	9:39	A
	16	F	6:10	A
	24	¾	0:35	A
	31	N	8:07	P
NOV	7	¼	4:19	P
	14	F	8:01	P
	22	¾	9:25	P
	30	N	8:20	A
DEC	7	¼	0:35	A
	14	F	0:32	P
	22	¾	5:42	P
	29	N	7:37	P

1979

Month	Day	Phase	Time	A/P
JAN	5	¼	11:16	A
	13	F	7:10	A
	21	¾	11:24	A
	28	N	6:20	A
FEB	4	¼	0:37	A
	12	F	2:40	A
	20	¾	1:18	A
	26	N	4:46	P
MAR	5	¼	4:24	P
	13	F	9:15	P
	21	¾	11:23	A
	28	N	3:00	A
APR	4	¼	9:58	A
	12	F	1:16	P
	19	¾	6:31	P
	26	N	1:16	P
MAY	4	¼	4:27	P
	12	F	2:02	A
	18	¾	11:58	P
	26	N	0:01	A
JUN	2	¼	10:38	P
	10	F	11:56	A
	17	¾	5:02	A
	24	N	11:59	A
JUL	2	¼	3:25	P
	9	F	8:00	P
	16	¾	11:00	A
	24	N	1:42	A
AUG	1	¼	5:58	A
	8	F	3:22	A
	14	¾	7:03	P
	22	N	5:11	P
	30	¼	6:10	P
SEP	6	F	10:59	A
	13	¾	6:16	A
	21	N	9:48	A
	29	¼	4:21	A
OCT	5	F	7:36	P
	12	¾	9:25	P
	21	N	2:24	A
	28	¼	1:07	P
NOV	4	F	5:48	A
	11	¾	4:25	P
	19	N	6:05	P
	26	¼	9:09	P
DEC	3	F	6:09	P
	11	¾	2:00	P
	19	N	8:24	A
	26	¼	5:12	A

LUNAR PHASES

1980

JAN	2	F	9:03	A
	10	¾	11:51	A
	17	N	9:20	P
	24	¼	1:59	P
FEB	1	F	2:22	P
	9	¾	7:36	A
	16	N	8:52	A
	23	¼	0:15	A
MAR	1	F	9:01	P
	9	¾	11:50	P
	16	N	6:57	P
	23	¼	0:32	P
	31	F	3:15	P
APR	8	¾	0:07	P
	15	N	3:47	A
	22	¼	3:00	A
	30	F	7:36	A
MAY	7	¾	8:51	P
	14	N	0:01	P
	21	¼	7:17	P
	29	F	9:29	P
JUN	6	¾	2:54	A
	12	N	8:39	P
	20	¼	0:33	P
	28	F	9:03	A
JUL	5	¾	7:28	A
	12	N	6:47	A
	20	¼	5:52	A
	27	F	6:55	P
AUG	3	¾	0:01	P
	10	N	7:10	P
	18	¼	10:29	P
	26	F	3:43	A
SEP	1	¾	6:08	P
	9	N	10:01	A
	17	¼	1:55	P
	24	F	0:09	P
OCT	1	¾	3:19	A
	9	N	2:51	A
	17	¼	3:48	A
	23	F	8:53	P
	30	¾	4:34	P
NOV	7	N	8:44	P
	15	¼	3:48	P
	22	F	6:40	A
	29	¾	10:00	A
DEC	7	N	2:36	P
	15	¼	1:48	A
	21	F	6:09	P
	29	¾	6:33	A

1981

JAN	6	N	7:25	A
	13	¼	10:11	A
	20	F	7:40	A
	28	¾	4:20	A
FEB	4	N	10:15	P
	11	¼	5:50	P
	18	F	10:59	P
	27	¾	1:15	A
MAR	6	N	10:32	A
	13	¼	1:51	A
	20	F	3:23	P
	28	¾	7:35	P
APR	4	N	8:20	P
	11	¼	11:11	A
	19	F	8:00	A
	27	¾	10:16	A
MAY	4	N	4:20	A
	10	¼	10:23	P
	19	F	0:05	A
	26	¾	9:01	P
JUN	2	N	11:32	A
	9	¼	11:34	A
	17	F	3:05	P
	25	¾	4:26	A
JUL	1	N	7:04	P
	9	¼	2:40	A
	17	F	4:40	A
	24	¾	9:41	A
	31	N	3:53	A
AUG	7	¼	7:27	P
	15	F	4:38	P
	22	¾	2:17	P
	29	N	2:45	P
SEP	6	¼	1:27	P
	14	F	3:10	A
	20	¾	7:48	P
	28	N	4:08	A
OCT	6	¼	7:46	A
	13	F	0:50	P
	20	¾	3:42	A
	27	N	8:15	P
NOV	5	¼	1:10	A
	11	F	10:28	P
	18	¾	2:55	P
	26	N	2:40	P
DEC	4	¼	4:23	P
	11	F	8:42	A
	18	¾	5:48	A
	26	N	10:11	A

1982

JAN	3	¼	4:47	A
	9	F	7:54	P
	16	¾	11:59	P
	25	N	4:57	A
FEB	1	¼	2:29	P
	8	F	7:58	P
	15	¾	8:22	P
	23	N	9:14	P
MAR	2	¼	10:16	P
	9	F	8:46	P
	17	¾	5:16	P
	25	N	10:19	A
APR	1	¼	5:09	A
	8	F	10:19	A
	16	¾	0:43	P
	23	N	8:30	P
	30	¼	0:08	P
MAY	8	F	0:46	A
	16	¾	5:12	A
	23	N	4:41	A
	29	¼	8:07	P
JUN	6	F	4:00	P
	14	¾	6:07	P
	21	N	11:53	A
	28	¼	5:57	A
JUL	6	F	7:33	A
	14	¾	3:48	A
	20	N	6:58	P
	27	¼	6:23	P
AUG	4	F	10:35	P
	12	¾	11:09	A
	19	N	2:46	A
	26	¼	9:51	A
SEP	3	F	0:29	P
	10	¾	5:20	P
	17	N	0:10	P
	25	¼	4:08	A
OCT	3	F	1:09	A
	9	¾	11:27	P
	17	N	0:05	A
	25	¼	0:09	A
NOV	1	F	0:58	P
	8	¾	6:39	A
	15	N	3:11	P
	23	¼	8:07	P
DEC	1	F	0:22	A
	7	¾	3:54	P
	15	N	9:19	A
	23	¼	2:18	P
	30	F	11:34	A

1983

JAN	6	¾	4:01	A
	14	N	5:09	A
	22	¼	5:35	A
	28	F	10:27	P
FEB	4	¾	7:18	P
	13	N	0:33	A
	20	¼	5:33	P
	27	F	8:59	A
MAR	6	¾	1:17	P
	14	N	5:44	P
	22	¼	2:26	A
	28	F	7:28	P
APR	5	¾	8:39	A
	13	N	7:59	A
	20	¼	8:59	A
	27	F	6:32	A
MAY	5	¾	3:44	A
	12	N	7:26	P
	19	¼	2:18	P
	26	F	6:49	P
JUN	3	¾	9:08	P
	11	N	4:38	P
	17	¼	7:47	P
	25	F	8:33	A
JUL	3	¾	0:13	P
	10	N	0:19	P
	17	¼	2:51	A
	24	F	11:28	P
AUG	2	¾	0:53	A
	8	N	7:19	P
	15	¼	0:48	P
	23	F	3:00	P
	31	¾	11:23	A
SEP	7	N	2:36	A
	14	¼	2:25	A
	22	F	6:37	A
	29	¾	8:06	P
OCT	6	N	11:17	A
	13	¼	7:43	P
	21	F	9:54	P
	29	¾	3:38	P
NOV	4	N	10:22	P
	12	¼	3:50	P
	20	F	0:30	P
	27	¾	10:51	A
DEC	4	N	0:27	P
	12	¼	1:10	P
	20	F	2:01	A
	26	¾	6:53	P

1984

JAN	3	N	5:17	A
	11	¼	9:49	A
	18	F	2:06	P
	25	¾	4:49	A
FEB	1	N	11:47	P
	10	¼	4:01	A
	17	F	0:42	A
	23	¾	5:13	P
MAR	2	N	6:32	P
	10	¼	6:28	P
	17	F	10:11	A
	24	¾	7:59	A
APR	1	N	0:11	P
	9	¼	4:52	A
	15	F	7:12	P
	23	¾	0:27	A
MAY	1	N	3:47	A
	8	¼	11:51	A
	15	F	4:30	A
	22	¾	5:46	P
	30	N	4:49	P
JUN	6	¼	4:42	P
	13	F	2:43	P
	21	¾	11:11	A
	29	N	3:19	A
JUL	5	¼	9:05	P
	13	F	2:21	A
	21	¾	4:02	A
	28	N	11:52	A
AUG	4	¼	2:34	A
	11	F	3:44	P
	19	¾	7:42	P
	26	N	7:27	P
SEP	2	¼	10:31	A
	10	F	7:02	A
	18	¾	9:32	A
	25	N	3:12	A
OCT	1	¼	9:53	P
	9	F	11:59	P
	17	¾	9:15	P
	24	N	0:09	P
	31	¼	1:09	P
NOV	8	F	5:44	P
	16	¾	7:00	A
	22	N	10:58	P
	30	¼	8:02	A
DEC	8	F	10:54	A
	15	¾	3:26	P
	22	N	11:48	A
	30	¼	5:29	A

1985

JAN	7	F	2:17	A
	13	¾	11:28	P
	21	N	2:29	A
	29	¼	3:30	A
FEB	5	F	3:20	P
	12	¾	7:58	A
	19	N	6:44	P
	27	¼	11:42	P
MAR	7	F	2:14	A
	13	¾	5:35	P
	21	N	0:00	P
	29	¼	4:12	P
APR	5	F	11:33	A
	12	¾	4:43	A
	20	N	5:23	A
	28	¼	4:26	A
MAY	4	F	7:54	P
	11	¾	5:35	P
	19	N	9:42	P
	27	¼	0:57	P
JUN	3	F	3:51	A
	10	¾	8:20	A
	18	N	11:59	A
	25	¼	6:54	P
JUL	2	F	0:09	P
	10	¾	0:51	A
	17	N	11:57	P
	24	¼	11:40	P
	31	F	9:42	P
AUG	8	¾	6:29	P
	16	N	10:07	A
	23	¼	4:37	A
	30	F	9:28	A
SEP	7	¾	0:17	P
	14	N	7:21	P
	21	¼	11:04	A
	29	F	0:10	A
OCT	7	¾	5:05	A
	14	N	4:34	A
	20	¼	8:14	P
	28	F	5:39	P
NOV	5	¾	8:07	P
	12	N	2:21	P
	19	¼	9:05	A
	27	F	0:43	P
DEC	5	¾	9:02	A
	12	N	0:55	A
	19	¼	1:59	A
	27	F	7:31	A

1986

JAN	3	¾	7:48	P
	10	N	0:23	P
	17	¼	10:14	P
	26	F	0:32	A
FEB	2	¾	4:42	A
	9	N	0:56	A
	16	¼	7:56	P
	24	F	3:03	P
MAR	3	¾	0:18	P
	10	N	2:53	P
	18	¼	4:40	P
	26	F	3:03	A
APR	1	¾	7:31	P
	9	N	6:09	A
	17	¼	10:36	A
	24	F	0:47	P
MAY	1	¾	3:23	A
	8	N	10:11	P
	17	¼	1:01	A
	23	F	8:46	P
	30	¾	0:56	P
JUN	7	N	2:01	P
	15	¼	0:01	P
	22	F	3:43	A
	29	¾	0:54	A
JUL	7	N	4:56	A
	14	¼	8:11	P
	21	F	10:41	P
	28	¾	3:35	P
AUG	5	N	6:37	P
	13	¼	2:22	A
	19	F	6:55	A
	27	¾	8:40	A
SEP	4	N	7:11	A
	11	¼	7:42	A
	18	F	5:35	A
	26	¾	3:19	A
OCT	3	N	6:56	P
	10	¼	1:29	P
	17	F	7:23	P
	25	¾	10:27	P
NOV	2	N	6:03	A
	8	¼	9:12	P
	16	F	0:13	P
	24	¾	4:51	P
DEC	1	N	4:44	P
	8	¼	8:03	A
	16	F	7:06	A
	24	¾	9:18	A
	31	N	3:11	A

1987

JAN	6	¼	10:36	P
	15	F	2:32	A
	22	¾	10:46	P
	29	N	1:46	P
FEB	5	¼	4:22	P
	13	F	8:59	P
	21	¾	8:57	A
	28	N	0:52	A
MAR	7	¼	11:59	A
	15	F	1:14	P
	22	¾	4:23	P
	29	N	0:47	P
APR	6	¼	7:49	A
	14	F	2:32	A
	20	¾	10:16	P
	28	N	1:35	A
MAY	6	¼	2:27	A
	13	F	0:51	P
	20	¾	4:03	A
	27	N	3:15	P
JUN	4	¼	6:54	P
	11	F	8:50	P
	18	¾	11:04	A
	26	N	5:38	A
JUL	4	¼	8:35	A
	11	F	3:34	A
	17	¾	8:18	P
	25	N	8:39	P
AUG	2	¼	7:25	P
	9	F	10:18	A
	16	¾	8:26	A
	24	N	0:00	P
SEP	1	¼	3:49	A
	7	F	6:14	P
	14	¾	11:46	P
	23	N	3:09	A
	30	¼	10:40	A
OCT	7	F	4:13	A
	14	¾	6:07	P
	22	N	5:29	P
	29	¼	5:11	P
NOV	5	F	4:47	P
	13	¾	2:39	P
	21	N	6:34	A
	28	¼	0:38	A
DEC	5	F	8:02	A
	13	¾	11:42	A
	20	N	6:26	A
	27	¼	10:02	A

1988

JAN	4	F	1:42	A
	12	¾	7:05	A
	19	N	5:26	A
	25	¼	9:54	P
FEB	2	F	8:53	P
	10	¾	11:02	P
	17	N	3:55	P
	24	¼	0:16	P
MAR	3	F	4:02	P
	11	¾	10:57	A
	18	N	2:03	A
	25	¼	4:43	A
APR	2	F	9:22	A
	9	¾	7:22	P
	16	N	0:01	P
	23	¼	10:33	P
MAY	1	F	11:42	P
	9	¾	1:24	A
	15	N	10:12	P
	23	¼	4:50	P
	31	F	10:54	A
JUN	7	¾	6:23	A
	14	N	9:15	A
	22	¼	10:24	A
	29	F	7:47	P
JUL	6	¾	11:37	A
	13	N	9:54	P
	22	¼	2:15	A
	29	F	3:26	A
AUG	4	¾	6:23	P
	12	N	0:32	P
	20	¼	3:53	P
	27	F	10:57	A
SEP	3	¾	3:51	A
	11	N	4:50	A
	19	¼	3:19	A
	25	F	7:08	A
OCT	2	¾	4:59	P
	10	N	9:50	P
	18	¼	1:02	P
	25	F	4:36	A
NOV	1	¾	10:13	A
	9	N	2:21	P
	16	¼	9:36	P
	23	F	3:54	P
DEC	1	¾	6:51	A
	9	N	5:37	A
	16	¼	5:41	A
	23	F	5:30	A
	31	¾	4:58	A

1989

JAN	7	N	7:23	P
	14	¼	1:59	P
	21	F	9:35	P
	30	¾	2:03	A
FEB	6	N	7:38	A
	12	¼	11:16	P
	20	F	3:33	P
	28	¾	8:09	P
MAR	7	N	6:20	P
	14	¼	10:12	A
	22	F	9:59	A
	30	¾	10:23	A
APR	6	N	3:33	A
	12	¼	11:14	P
	21	F	3:14	A
	28	¾	8:47	P
MAY	5	N	11:47	A
	12	¼	2:21	P
	20	F	6:17	P
	28	¾	4:02	A
JUN	3	N	7:54	P
	11	¼	7:00	A
	19	F	6:58	A
	26	¾	9:10	A
JUL	3	N	5:00	A
	11	¼	0:20	A
	18	F	5:43	P
	25	¾	1:32	P
AUG	1	N	4:07	P
	9	¼	5:30	P
	17	F	3:08	A
	23	¾	6:41	P
	31	N	5:46	A
SEP	8	¼	9:50	A
	15	F	11:52	A
	22	¾	2:11	A
	29	N	9:48	P
OCT	8	¼	0:53	A
	14	F	8:33	P
	21	¾	1:20	P
	29	N	3:28	P
NOV	6	¼	2:12	P
	13	F	5:52	A
	20	¾	4:45	A
	28	N	9:42	A
DEC	6	¼	1:27	A
	12	F	4:31	P
	19	¾	11:56	P
	28	N	3:21	A

LUNAR PHASES

1990

Month	Day	Phase	Time	A/P
JAN	4	¼	10:41	A
	11	F	4:58	A
	18	¾	9:18	P
	26	N	7:21	P
FEB	2	¼	6:33	P
	9	F	7:17	P
	17	¾	6:49	P
	25	N	8:55	A
MAR	4	¼	2:06	A
	11	F	11:00	A
	19	¾	2:32	P
	26	N	7:49	P
APR	2	¼	10:25	A
	10	F	3:20	A
	18	¾	7:04	A
	25	N	4:28	A
MAY	1	¼	8:19	P
	9	F	7:32	P
	17	¾	7:46	P
	24	N	11:48	A
	31	¼	8:12	A
JUN	8	F	11:02	A
	16	¾	4:49	A
	22	N	6:56	P
	29	¼	10:09	P
JUL	8	F	1:25	A
	15	¾	11:05	A
	22	N	2:55	A
	29	¼	2:03	P
AUG	6	F	2:21	P
	13	¾	3:55	P
	20	N	0:40	P
	28	¼	7:35	A
SEP	5	F	1:47	A
	11	¾	8:54	P
	19	N	0:47	A
	27	¼	2:07	A
OCT	4	F	0:03	P
	11	¾	3:32	A
	18	N	3:38	P
	26	¼	8:28	P
NOV	2	F	9:49	P
	9	¾	1:03	P
	17	N	9:06	A
	25	¼	1:13	P
DEC	2	F	7:50	A
	9	¾	2:05	A
	17	N	4:23	A
	25	¼	3:17	A
	31	F	6:36	P

1991

Month	Day	Phase	Time	A/P
JAN	7	¾	6:36	P
	15	N	11:51	P
	23	¼	2:23	P
	30	F	6:11	A
FEB	6	¾	1:53	P
	14	N	5:33	P
	21	¼	10:59	P
	28	F	6:26	P
MAR	8	¾	10:33	A
	16	N	8:12	A
	23	¼	6:04	A
	30	F	7:18	A
APR	7	¾	6:47	A
	14	N	7:39	P
	21	¼	0:40	P
	28	F	9:00	P
MAY	7	¾	0:47	A
	14	N	4:37	A
	20	¼	7:47	P
	28	F	11:38	A
JUN	5	¾	3:31	P
	12	N	0:07	P
	19	¼	4:20	A
	27	F	3:00	A
JUL	5	¾	2:51	A
	11	N	7:07	P
	18	¼	3:12	P
	26	F	6:26	P
AUG	3	¾	11:27	A
	10	N	2:29	A
	17	¼	5:02	A
	25	F	9:08	A
SEP	1	¾	6:18	P
	8	N	11:02	A
	15	¼	10:03	P
	23	F	10:41	P
OCT	1	¾	0:31	A
	7	N	9:40	P
	15	¼	5:34	P
	23	F	11:09	A
	30	¾	7:12	A
NOV	6	N	11:12	A
	14	¼	2:03	P
	21	F	10:57	P
	28	¾	3:22	P
DEC	6	N	3:57	A
	14	¼	9:33	A
	21	F	10:24	A
	28	¾	1:56	A

1992

Month	Day	Phase	Time	A/P
JAN	4	N	11:11	P
	13	¼	2:33	A
	19	F	9:29	P
	26	¾	3:28	P
FEB	3	N	7:01	P
	11	¼	4:16	P
	18	F	8:05	A
	25	¾	7:57	A
MAR	4	N	1:23	P
	12	¼	2:37	A
	18	F	6:19	P
	26	¾	2:31	A
APR	3	N	5:02	A
	10	¼	10:07	A
	17	F	4:43	A
	24	¾	9:41	P
MAY	2	N	5:46	P
	9	¼	3:45	P
	16	F	4:04	P
	24	¾	3:54	P
JUN	1	N	3:58	A
	7	¼	8:48	P
	15	F	4:51	A
	23	¾	8:12	A
	30	N	0:19	P
JUL	7	¼	2:45	A
	14	F	7:07	P
	22	¾	10:13	P
	29	N	7:36	P
AUG	5	¼	11:00	A
	13	F	10:28	A
	21	¾	10:02	A
	28	N	2:43	A
SEP	3	¼	10:40	P
	12	F	2:18	A
	19	¾	7:54	A
	26	N	10:41	A
OCT	3	¼	2:13	P
	11	F	6:04	P
	19	¾	4:13	A
	25	N	8:35	P
NOV	2	¼	9:12	A
	10	F	9:21	A
	17	¾	11:40	A
	24	N	9:12	A
DEC	2	¼	6:18	A
	9	F	11:42	P
	16	¾	7:14	P
	24	N	0:44	A

1993

Month	Day	Phase	Time	A/P
JAN	1	¼	3:40	A
	8	F	0:38	P
	15	¾	4:02	A
	22	N	6:28	P
	30	¼	11:21	P
FEB	6	F	11:56	P
	13	¾	2:58	P
	21	N	1:06	P
MAR	1	¼	3:47	P
	8	F	9:47	A
	15	¾	4:18	A
	23	N	7:16	A
	31	¼	4:11	A
APR	6	F	6:44	P
	13	¾	7:40	P
	21	N	11:50	P
	29	¼	0:42	P
MAY	6	F	3:35	A
	13	¾	0:21	P
	21	N	2:08	P
	28	¼	6:22	P
JUN	4	F	1:03	P
	12	¾	5:37	A
	20	N	1:54	A
	26	¼	10:44	P
JUL	3	F	11:46	P
	11	¾	10:50	P
	19	N	11:25	A
	26	¼	3:26	A
AUG	2	F	0:11	P
	10	¾	3:21	P
	17	N	7:29	P
	24	¼	9:59	A
SEP	1	F	2:34	A
	9	¾	6:28	A
	16	N	3:11	A
	22	¼	7:33	P
	30	F	6:55	P
OCT	8	¾	7:36	P
	15	N	11:37	A
	22	¼	8:53	A
	30	F	0:39	P
NOV	7	¾	6:37	A
	13	N	9:35	P
	21	¼	2:05	A
	29	F	6:32	A
DEC	6	¾	3:50	P
	13	N	9:28	A
	20	¼	10:27	P
	28	F	11:06	P

1994

Month	Day	Phase	Time	A/P
JAN	5	¾	0:02	A
	11	N	11:11	P
	19	¼	8:28	P
	27	F	1:24	P
FEB	3	¾	8:07	A
	10	N	2:31	P
	18	¼	5:48	P
	26	F	1:16	A
MAR	4	¾	4:54	P
	12	N	7:06	A
	20	¼	0:15	P
	27	F	11:10	A
APR	3	¾	2:56	A
	11	N	0:18	A
	19	¼	2:35	A
	25	F	7:46	P
MAY	2	¾	2:34	P
	10	N	5:08	P
	18	¼	0:51	P
	25	F	3:40	P
JUN	1	¾	4:04	A
	9	N	8:28	A
	16	¼	7:58	P
	23	F	11:34	A
	30	¾	7:32	P
JUL	8	N	9:39	P
	16	¼	1:13	A
	22	F	8:17	P
	30	¾	0:41	P
AUG	7	N	8:46	A
	14	¼	5:58	A
	21	F	6:48	A
	29	¾	6:42	A
SEP	5	N	6:34	P
	12	¼	11:35	A
	19	F	8:02	P
	28	¾	0:25	A
OCT	5	N	3:56	A
	11	¼	7:18	P
	19	F	0:19	P
	27	¾	4:45	P
NOV	3	N	1:37	P
	10	¼	6:15	A
	18	F	6:58	A
	26	¾	7:05	A
DEC	2	N	11:55	P
	9	¼	9:07	P
	18	F	2:18	A
	25	¾	7:07	P

1995

Month	Day	Phase	Time	A/P
JAN	1	N	10:57	A
	8	¼	3:47	P
	16	F	8:28	P
	24	¾	4:59	A
	30	N	10:49	P
FEB	7	¼	0:55	P
	15	F	0:17	P
	22	¾	1:05	P
MAR	1	N	11:49	A
	9	¼	10:15	A
	17	F	1:27	A
	23	¾	8:11	P
	31	N	2:10	A
APR	8	¼	5:36	A
	15	F	0:09	P
	22	¾	3:19	A
	29	N	5:38	P
MAY	7	¼	9:45	P
	14	F	8:49	P
	21	¾	11:37	A
	29	N	9:29	A
JUN	6	¼	10:27	A
	13	F	4:04	A
	19	¾	10:02	P
	28	N	0:51	A
JUL	5	¼	8:04	P
	12	F	10:50	A
	19	¾	11:11	A
	27	N	3:14	P
AUG	4	¼	3:17	A
	10	F	6:17	P
	18	¾	3:05	A
	26	N	4:32	A
SEP	2	¼	9:04	A
	9	F	3:38	A
	16	¾	9:11	P
	24	N	4:56	P
OCT	1	¼	2:37	P
	8	F	3:53	P
	16	¾	4:27	P
	24	N	4:37	A
	30	¼	9:18	P
NOV	7	F	7:22	A
	15	¾	11:41	A
	22	N	3:44	P
	29	¼	6:29	A
DEC	7	F	1:28	A
	15	¾	5:32	A
	22	N	2:23	A
	28	¼	7:08	P

1996

Month	Day	Phase	Time	A/P
JAN	5	F	8:52	P
	13	¾	8:46	P
	20	N	0:52	P
	27	¼	11:15	A
FEB	4	F	3:59	P
	12	¾	8:38	A
	18	N	11:31	P
	26	¼	5:54	A
MAR	5	F	9:24	A
	12	¾	5:16	P
	19	N	10:46	A
	27	¼	1:32	A
APR	4	F	0:08	A
	10	¾	11:37	P
	17	N	10:50	P
	25	¼	8:41	P
MAY	3	F	11:49	A
	10	¾	5:05	A
	17	N	11:47	A
	25	¼	2:14	P
JUN	1	F	8:48	P
	8	¾	11:07	A
	16	N	1:37	A
	24	¼	5:25	A
JUL	1	F	3:59	A
	7	¾	6:56	P
	15	N	4:16	P
	23	¼	5:50	P
	30	F	10:36	A
AUG	6	¾	5:26	A
	14	N	7:35	A
	22	¼	3:38	A
	28	F	5:53	P
SEP	4	¾	7:07	P
	12	N	11:08	P
	20	¼	11:24	A
	27	F	2:52	A
OCT	4	¾	0:05	P
	12	N	2:16	P
	19	¼	6:10	P
	26	F	2:12	P
NOV	3	¾	7:52	A
	11	N	4:17	A
	18	¼	1:10	A
	25	F	4:11	A
DEC	3	¾	5:07	A
	10	N	4:57	P
	17	¼	9:32	A
	24	F	8:42	P

1997

Month	Day	Phase	Time	A/P
JAN	2	¾	1:46	A
	9	N	4:27	A
	15	¼	8:03	P
	23	F	3:12	P
	31	¾	7:41	P
FEB	7	N	3:07	P
	14	¼	8:59	A
	22	F	10:28	A
MAR	2	¾	9:39	A
	9	N	1:16	A
	16	¼	0:07	A
	24	F	4:47	A
	31	¾	7:39	P
APR	7	N	11:03	A
	14	¼	5:01	P
	22	F	8:35	P
	30	¾	2:38	A
MAY	6	N	8:48	P
	14	¼	10:56	A
	22	F	9:15	A
	29	¾	7:53	A
JUN	5	N	7:05	A
	13	¼	4:53	A
	20	F	7:10	P
	27	¾	0:43	P
JUL	4	N	6:41	P
	12	¼	9:45	P
	20	F	3:21	A
	26	¾	6:29	P
AUG	3	N	8:15	A
	11	¼	0:44	P
	18	F	10:56	A
	25	¾	2:25	A
SEP	1	N	11:53	P
	10	¼	1:32	A
	16	F	6:51	P
	23	¾	1:36	P
OCT	1	N	4:53	P
	9	¼	0:23	P
	16	F	3:47	A
	23	¾	4:50	A
	31	N	10:02	A
NOV	7	¼	9:45	P
	14	F	2:13	P
	21	¾	11:59	P
	30	N	2:15	A
DEC	7	¼	6:10	A
	14	F	2:38	A
	21	¾	9:44	P
	29	N	4:58	P

1998

Month	Day	Phase	Time	A/P
JAN	5	¼	2:19	P
	12	F	5:25	P
	20	¾	7:41	P
	28	N	6:02	A
FEB	3	¼	10:55	P
	11	F	10:24	A
	19	¾	3:28	P
	26	N	5:27	P
MAR	5	¼	8:42	A
	13	F	4:36	A
	21	¾	7:39	A
	28	N	3:15	A
APR	3	¼	8:20	P
	11	F	10:25	P
	19	¾	7:54	P
	26	N	11:42	A
MAY	3	¼	10:05	A
	11	F	2:31	P
	19	¾	4:37	A
	25	N	7:33	P
JUN	2	¼	1:46	A
	10	F	4:20	A
	17	¾	10:39	A
	24	N	3:51	A
JUL	1	¼	6:44	P
	9	F	4:02	P
	16	¾	3:15	P
	23	N	1:45	P
	31	¼	0:06	P
AUG	8	F	2:11	A
	14	¾	7:50	P
	22	N	2:04	A
	30	¼	5:08	A
SEP	6	F	11:22	A
	13	¾	1:59	A
	20	N	5:03	P
	28	¼	9:12	P
OCT	5	F	8:13	P
	12	¾	11:12	A
	20	N	10:11	A
	28	¼	11:47	A
NOV	4	F	5:19	A
	11	¾	0:29	A
	19	N	4:28	A
	27	¼	0:24	A
DEC	3	F	3:20	P
	10	¾	5:55	P
	18	N	10:44	P
	26	¼	10:47	A

1999

Month	Day	Phase	Time	A/P
JAN	2	F	2:51	A
	9	¾	2:23	P
	17	N	3:47	P
	24	¼	7:16	P
	31	F	4:08	P
FEB	8	¾	11:59	A
	16	N	6:40	A
	23	¼	2:44	A
MAR	2	F	7:00	A
	10	¾	8:42	A
	17	N	6:49	P
	24	¼	10:19	A
	31	F	10:50	P
APR	9	¾	2:52	A
	16	N	4:23	A
	22	¼	7:03	P
	30	F	2:56	P
MAY	8	¾	5:30	P
	15	N	0:06	P
	22	¼	5:35	A
	30	F	6:41	A
JUN	7	¾	4:21	A
	13	N	7:04	P
	20	¼	6:14	P
	28	F	9:39	P
JUL	6	¾	11:58	A
	13	N	2:25	A
	20	¼	9:01	A
	28	F	11:26	A
AUG	4	¾	5:28	P
	11	N	11:10	A
	19	¼	1:48	A
	26	F	11:49	P
SEP	2	¾	10:18	P
	9	N	10:04	P
	17	¼	8:07	P
	25	F	10:52	A
OCT	2	¾	4:03	A
	9	N	11:36	A
	17	¼	3:01	P
	24	F	9:04	P
	31	¾	0:05	P
NOV	8	N	3:54	A
	16	¼	9:04	A
	23	F	7:05	A
	29	¾	11:20	P
DEC	7	N	10:33	P
	16	¼	0:51	A
	22	F	5:33	P
	29	¾	2:06	P

DIURNAL PROPORTIONAL LOGARITHMS

	0	1	2	3	4	5	6	7	8	9	10	11
0	∞	1.3802	1.0792	.90309	.77815	.68124	.60206	.53511	.47712	.42597	.38021	.33882
1	3.1584	1.3730	1.0756	.90068	.77635	.67980	.60086	.53408	.47622	.42517	.37949	.33816
2	2.8573	1.3660	1.0720	.89829	.77455	.67836	.59965	.53305	.47532	.42436	.37877	.33750
3	2.6812	1.3590	1.0685	.89591	.77276	.67692	.59846	.53202	.47442	.42356	.37805	.33685
4	2.5563	1.3522	1.0649	.89354	.77097	.67549	.59726	.53100	.47352	.42276	.37733	.33620
5	2.4594	1.3454	1.0615	.89119	.76920	.67406	.59607	.52997	.47262	.42197	.37661	.33554
6	2.3802	1.3388	1.0580	.88885	.76743	.67264	.59488	.52895	.47173	.42117	.37589	.33489
7	2.3133	1.3323	1.0546	.88652	.76567	.67122	.59370	.52793	.47083	.42038	.37517	.33424
8	2.2553	1.3259	1.0512	.88420	.76391	.66981	.59251	.52692	.46994	.41958	.37446	.33359
9	2.2041	1.3195	1.0478	.88190	.76216	.66840	.59134	.52591	.46905	.41879	.37375	.33294
10	2.1584	1.3133	1.0444	.87961	.76042	.66700	.59016	.52489	.46817	.41800	.37303	.33229
11	2.1170	1.3071	1.0411	.87733	.75869	.66560	.58899	.52389	.46728	.41721	.37232	.33164
12	2.0792	1.3010	1.0378	.87506	.75696	.66421	.58782	.52288	.46640	.41642	.37161	.33099
13	2.0444	1.2950	1.0345	.87281	.75524	.66282	.58665	.52187	.46552	.41564	.37090	.33035
14	2.0122	1.2891	1.0313	.87056	.75353	.66143	.58549	.52087	.46464	.41485	.37019	.32970
15	1.9823	1.2833	1.0280	.86833	.75182	.66005	.58433	.51987	.46376	.41407	.36949	.32906
16	1.9542	1.2775	1.0248	.86611	.75012	.65868	.58317	.51888	.46288	.41329	.36878	.32842
17	1.9279	1.2719	1.0216	.86390	.74843	.65730	.58202	.51788	.46201	.41251	.36808	.32777
18	1.9031	1.2663	1.0185	.86170	.74674	.65594	.58087	.51689	.46113	.41173	.36737	.32713
19	1.8796	1.2607	1.0153	.85951	.74506	.65457	.57972	.51590	.46026	.41095	.36667	.32649
20	1.8573	1.2553	1.0122	.85733	.74339	.65321	.57858	.51491	.45939	.41017	.36597	.32585
21	1.8361	1.2499	1.0091	.85517	.74172	.65186	.57744	.51392	.45852	.40940	.36527	.32522
22	1.8159	1.2445	1.0061	.85301	.74006	.65051	.57630	.51294	.45766	.40863	.36457	.32458
23	1.7966	1.2393	1.0030	.85087	.73841	.64916	.57516	.51196	.45679	.40785	.36387	.32394
24	1.7782	1.2341	1.0000	.84873	.73676	.64782	.57403	.51098	.45593	.40708	.36318	.32331
25	1.7604	1.2289	0.9970	.84661	.73512	.64648	.57290	.51000	.45507	.40631	.36248	.32267
26	1.7434	1.2239	0.9940	.84450	.73348	.64514	.57178	.50903	.45421	.40555	.36179	.32204
27	1.7270	1.2188	0.9910	.84239	.73185	.64382	.57065	.50805	.45335	.40478	.36110	.32141
28	1.7112	1.2139	0.9881	.84030	.73023	.64249	.56953	.50708	.45250	.40401	.36040	.32077
29	1.6960	1.2090	0.9852	.83822	.72861	.64117	.56841	.50612	.45165	.40325	.35971	.32014
30	1.6812	1.2041	0.9823	.83614	.72700	.63985	.56730	.50515	.45079	.40249	.35902	.31951
31	1.6670	1.1993	0.9794	.83408	.72539	.63853	.56619	.50419	.44994	.40173	.35833	.31889
32	1.6532	1.1946	0.9765	.83203	.72379	.63722	.56508	.50322	.44909	.40097	.35765	.31826
33	1.6398	1.1899	0.9737	.82998	.72220	.63592	.56397	.50226	.44825	.40021	.35696	.31763
34	1.6269	1.1852	0.9708	.82795	.72061	.63462	.56287	.50131	.44740	.39945	.35627	.31700
35	1.6143	1.1806	0.9680	.82592	.71903	.63332	.56177	.50035	.44656	.39869	.35559	.31638
36	1.6021	1.1761	0.9652	.82391	.71745	.63202	.56067	.49940	.44571	.39794	.35491	.31575
37	1.5902	1.1716	0.9625	.83190	.71588	.63073	.55957	.49845	.44487	.39719	.35422	.31513
38	1.5786	1.1671	0.9597	.81991	.71432	.62945	.55848	.49750	.44403	.39643	.35354	.31451
39	1.5673	1.1627	0.9570	.81792	.71276	.62816	.55739	.49655	.44320	.39568	.35286	.31389
40	1.5563	1.1584	0.9542	.81594	.71120	.62688	.55630	.45960	.44236	.39493	.35218	.31327
41	1.5456	1.1540	0.9515	.81397	.70966	.62561	.55522	.49466	.44153	.39419	.35150	.31265
42	1.5351	1.1498	0.9488	.81201	.70811	.62434	.55414	.49372	.44069	.39344	.35083	.31203
43	1.5249	1.1455	0.9462	.81006	.70658	.62307	.55306	.49278	.43986	.39269	.35015	.31141
44	1.5149	1.1413	0.9435	.80811	.70504	.62180	.55198	.49184	.43903	.39195	.34948	.31079
45	1.5051	1.1372	0.9409	.80618	.70352	.62054	.55091	.49091	.43820	.39121	.34880	.31017
46	1.4956	1.1331	0.9383	.80425	.70200	.61929	.54984	.48998	.43738	.39047	.34813	.30956
47	1.4863	1.1290	0.9356	.80234	.70048	.61803	.54877	.48905	.43655	.38972	.34746	.30894
48	1.4771	1.1249	0.9331	.80043	.69897	.61678	.54770	.48812	.43573	.38899	.34679	.30833
49	1.4682	1.1209	0.9305	.79853	.69746	.61554	.54664	.48719	.43491	.38825	.34612	.30772
50	1.4594	1.1170	0.9279	.79663	.69596	.61429	.54558	.48626	.43409	.38751	.34545	.30710
51	1.4508	1.1130	0.9254	.79475	.69447	.61306	.54452	.48534	.43327	.38678	.34478	.30649
52	1.4424	1.1091	0.9228	.79287	.69298	.61182	.54347	.48442	.43245	.38604	.34412	.30588
53	1.4341	1.1053	0.9203	.79101	.69149	.61059	.54241	.48350	.43164	.38531	.34345	.30527
54	1.4260	1.1015	0.9178	.78915	.69002	.60936	.54136	.48258	.43082	.38458	.34279	.30466
55	1.4180	1.0977	0.9153	.78729	.68854	.60813	.54031	.48167	.43001	.38385	.34212	.30406
56	1.4102	1.0939	0.9129	.78545	.68707	.60691	.53927	.48076	.42920	.38312	.34146	.30345
57	1.4025	1.0902	0.9104	.78361	.68561	.60569	.53823	.47984	.42839	.38239	.34080	.30284
58	1.3949	1.0865	0.9079	.78179	.68415	.60448	.53719	.47893	.42758	.38166	.34014	.30224
59	1.3875	1.0828	0.9055	.77996	.68269	.60327	.53615	.47803	.42677	.38094	.33948	.30163

DIURNAL PROPORTIONAL LOGARITHMS

	12	13	14	15	16	17	18	19	20	21	22	23
0	.30103	.26627	.23408	.20412	.17609	.14976	.12494	.10146	.07918	.05799	.03779	.01848
1	.30043	.26571	.23357	.20364	.17564	.14934	.12454	.10108	.07882	.05765	.03746	.01817
2	.29983	.26516	.23305	.20316	.17519	.14891	.12414	.10070	.07846	.05730	.03713	.01786
3	.29923	.26460	.23254	.20268	.17474	.14849	.12373	.10032	.07810	.05696	.03680	.01754
4	.29862	.26405	.23202	.20219	.17429	.14806	.12333	.09994	.07774	.05662	.03648	.01723
5	.29802	.26349	.23151	.20171	.17384	.14764	.12293	.09956	.07738	.05627	.03615	.01691
6	.29743	.26294	.23099	.20124	.17339	.14722	.12253	.09918	.07702	.05593	.03582	.01660
7	.29683	.26239	.23048	.20076	.17294	.14679	.12213	.09880	.07666	.05559	.03549	.01629
8	.29623	.26184	.22997	.20028	.17249	.14637	.12173	.09842	.07630	.05524	.03517	.01597
9	.29564	.26129	.22946	.19980	.17204	.14595	.12134	.09804	.07594	.05490	.03484	.01566
10	.29504	.26074	.22894	.19932	.17159	.14553	.12094	.09767	.07558	.05456	.03451	.01535
11	.29445	.26019	.22843	.19884	.17114	.14510	.12054	.09729	.07522	.05422	.03418	.01504
12	.29385	.25964	.22792	.19837	.17070	.14468	.12014	.09691	.07486	.05388	.03386	.01472
13	.29326	.25909	.22741	.19789	.17025	.14426	.11974	.09653	.07450	.05353	.03353	.01441
14	.29267	.25854	.22691	.19742	.16980	.14384	.11935	.09616	.07414	.05319	.03321	.01410
15	.29208	.25800	.22640	.19694	.16936	.14342	.11895	.09578	.07379	.05285	.03288	.01379
16	.29149	.25745	.22589	.19647	.16891	.14300	.11855	.09540	.07343	.05251	.03256	.01348
17	.29090	.25690	.22538	.19599	.16847	.14258	.11816	.09503	.07307	.05217	.03223	.01317
18	.29031	.25636	.22488	.19552	.16802	.14217	.11776	.09465	.07272	.05183	.03191	.01286
19	.28972	.25582	.22437	.19505	.16758	.14175	.11737	.09428	.07236	.05149	.03158	.01254
20	.28913	.25527	.22386	.19457	.16714	.14133	.11697	.09390	.07200	.05115	.03126	.01224
21	.28855	.25473	.22336	.19410	.16669	.14091	.11658	.09353	.07165	.05081	.03093	.01193
22	.28796	.25419	.22286	.19363	.16625	.14050	.11618	.09316	.07129	.05048	.03061	.01162
23	.28737	.25365	.22235	.19316	.16581	.14008	.11579	.09278	.07094	.05014	.03029	.01131
24	.28679	.25311	.22185	.19269	.16537	.13966	.11539	.09241	.07058	.04980	.02996	.01100
25	.28621	.25257	.22135	.19222	.16493	.13925	.11500	.09204	.07023	.04946	.02964	.01069
26	.28562	.25203	.22084	.19175	.16449	.13883	.11461	.09166	.06987	.04912	.02932	.01038
27	.28504	.25149	.22034	.19128	.16405	.13842	.11422	.09129	.06952	.04878	.02900	.01007
28	.28446	.25095	.21984	.19082	.16361	.13800	.11382	.09092	.06916	.04845	.02867	.00976
29	.28388	.25041	.21934	.19035	.16317	.13759	.11343	.09055	.06881	.04811	.02835	.00945
30	.28330	.24988	.21884	.18988	.16273	.13717	.11304	.09018	.06846	.04777	.02803	.00914
31	.28272	.24934	.21835	.18941	.16229	.13676	.11265	.08981	.06811	.04744	.02771	.00884
32	.28214	.24881	.21785	.18895	.16185	.13635	.11226	.08943	.06775	.04710	.02739	.00853
33	.28157	.24827	.21735	.18848	.16141	.13594	.11187	.08906	.06740	.04676	.02707	.00822
34	.28099	.24774	.21685	.18802	.16098	.13552	.11148	.08869	.06705	.04643	.02674	.00791
35	.28042	.24721	.21635	.18755	.16054	.13511	.11109	.08832	.06670	.04609	.02642	.00761
36	.27984	.24667	.21586	.18709	.16010	.13470	.11070	.08796	.06634	.04576	.02610	.00730
37	.27927	.24614	.21536	.18662	.15967	.13429	.11031	.08759	.06599	.04542	.02578	.00699
38	.27869	.24561	.21487	.18616	.15923	.13388	.10992	.08722	.06564	.04509	.02546	.00669
39	.27812	.24508	.21437	.18570	.15880	.13347	.10953	.08685	.06529	.04475	.02514	.00638
40	.27755	.24455	.21388	.18524	.15836	.13306	.10915	.08648	.06494	.04442	.02482	.00607
41	.27698	.24402	.21339	.18477	.15793	.13265	.10876	.08611	.06459	.04409	.02451	.00577
42	.27641	.24349	.21289	.18431	.15749	.13224	.10837	.08575	.06424	.04375	.02419	.00546
43	.27584	.24296	.21240	.18385	.15706	.13183	.10798	.08538	.06389	.04342	.02387	.00516
44	.27527	.24244	.21191	.18339	.15663	.13142	.10760	.08501	.06354	.04309	.02355	.00485
45	.27470	.24191	.21142	.18293	.15620	.13101	.10721	.08464	.06319	.04275	.02323	.00455
46	.27413	.24138	.21093	.18247	.15576	.13061	.10683	.08428	.06284	.04242	.02291	.00424
47	.27357	.24086	.21044	.18201	.15533	.13020	.10644	.08391	.06250	.04209	.02259	.00394
48	.27300	.24033	.20995	.18155	.15490	.12979	.10605	.08355	.06215	.04176	.02228	.00363
49	.27244	.23981	.20946	.18110	.15447	.12939	.10567	.08318	.06180	.04142	.02196	.00333
50	.27187	.23928	.20897	.18064	.15404	.12898	.10529	.08282	.06145	.04109	.02164	.00303
51	.27131	.23876	.20849	.18018	.15361	.12857	.10490	.08245	.06111	.04076	.02133	.00272
52	.27075	.23824	.20800	.17973	.15318	.12817	.10452	.08209	.06076	.04043	.02101	.00242
53	.27018	.23772	.20751	.17927	.15275	.12776	.10413	.08172	.06041	.04010	.02069	.00212
54	.26962	.23720	.20703	.17881	.15233	.12736	.10375	.08136	.06007	.03977	.02038	.00181
55	.26906	.23668	.20654	.17836	.15190	.12695	.10337	.08099	.05972	.03944	.02006	.00151
56	.26850	.23616	.20606	.17791	.15147	.12655	.10298	.08063	.05937	.03911	.01975	.00121
57	.26794	.23564	.20557	.17745	.15104	.12615	.10260	.08027	.05903	.03878	.01943	.00091
58	.26738	.23512	.20509	.17700	.15062	.12574	.10222	.07991	.05868	.03845	.01911	.00060
59	.26683	.23460	.20460	.17654	.15019	.12534	.10184	.07954	.05834	.03812	.01880	.00030